Merriam-Webster's Crossword Puzzle Dictionary

Third Edition

Merriam-Webster, Incorporated
Springfield, Massachusetts, U.S.A.

A GENUINE MERRIAM-WEBSTER

The name Webster alone is no guarantee of excellence. It is used by a number of publishers and may serve mainly to mislead an unwary buyer.

Merriam-Webster™ is the name you should look for when you consider the purchase of dictionaries or other fine reference books. It carries the reputation of a company that has been publishing since 1831 and is your assurance of quality and authority.

ISBN-13: 978-0-87779-639-8
ISBN-10: 0-87779-639-4

Library of Congress Cataloging-in-Publication Data

Merriam-Webster's crossword puzzle dictionary. – 3rd. ed.
p. cm.
Includes bibliographical references and index.
ISBN-13: 978-0-87779-639-8 (alk. paper)
ISBN-10: 0-87779-639-4 (alk. paper)
1. Crossword puzzles – Glossaries, vocabularies, etc. 2. Large type books.
I. Merriam-Webster, Inc. II. Title: Crossword puzzle dictionary.
GV1507.C7M45 2007
793.73′2—dc22

2007030784

Printed and bound in the United States of America
2345QW/M11100908

Preface

This new edition of MERRIAM-WEBSTER'S CROSSWORD PUZZLE DICTIONARY is designed to meet the needs of the many crossword puzzlers who have found that most crossword dictionaries are set in type too small for comfortable use. Although even the print here will not be adequate for the seriously vision-impaired, we believe that, by improving significantly on the legibility of newspapers and most reference books, the dictionary will prove usable by all but a small number of active puzzle solvers.

Note that, despite its enlarged type, the dictionary you are holding is an *unabridged* edition, containing several thousand more words than any crossword dictionary previously published by Merriam-Webster. Not a word has been sacrificed for the sake of readability. The text has been thoroughly updated to include many terms and names that have only recently entered the general English vocabulary: recent slang *(plotz, himbo, crunk, bubkes),* sports stars *(A-Rod, Zidane),* computer languages *(SQL, JADE),* automobiles *(Mini, Prius),* Nobel Prize winners *(Pamuk, Yunus),* national currencies *(kroon, som, manat),* actors and actresses *(Alba, Falco)*—not to mention all the familiar words and names that show up with enough frequency in contemporary puzzle grids to have earned the name of "crosswordese": *asea, Oreo, aloe, A-one, espy, ciao, ta-ta, e'er, erose, amah, etui, Odie, tec, Tey, olio, ern, ASAP, Opie, ad-in, ecru, luau,* and a legion of others.

As crossword constructors continue to aim for ever fresher and cleverer clues and answers, we hope this updated reference will prove to be the indispensable tool for filling in those final few elusive letters in crosswords of all kinds for puzzlers of every ability and age.

The previous editions of *Merriam-Webster's Crossword Dictionary* appeared in 1981 and 1997; their principal editors were, respectively, James G. Lowe and Michael G. Belanger. The present edition was edited by C. Roger Davis and Mark Stevens. The volume was typeset by Dedicated Business Services of New Market, Iowa. Special thanks are due to J. Robert Ramsay, Patricia H. Green, and Eileen M. Haraty for their many excellent contributions to the word lists in this new volume.

Explanatory Notes

This dictionary is organized to make it easy to find answer words with a specific number of letters. Every answer word follows a numeral indicating the number of letters it contains. The answer words generally run up to 13 letters; an exception to this limit is made for multiword titles of works, to allow for those clues that omit one or two words from a title, perhaps enough for a five-or ten-letter answer.

As in any crossword dictionary, a single list of answer words will often include words representing various parts of speech. Thus, the entry for **fast** includes synonyms for the adjective *(rapid),* the noun *(diet),* and the verb *(abstain),* all in a continuous list. Since puzzle clues are often intentionally ambiguous as to which meaning is intended, listing all possible synonyms together represents the ideal format for the puzzle solver.

Since puzzle creators rarely provide a clue whose answer word shares the clue's root, such root-related words have generally been omitted from the answer lists. Thus, *singular* does not appear at **single**, *basal* does not appear at **basic**, and *papa* does not appear at **pop**. However, since clues do occasionally share a standard prefix (such as *re-* or *un-*) with an answer word, we have retained a number of clue/answer-word pairs of this kind (**redo**/*remodel*, **unsettle**/*unnerve,* etc.).

When one entry word simply adds a suffix to another entry word, as when **shared** follows **share**, the answer list for the suffixed entry word will usually omit any words that merely add the same suffix to a word in the stem word's list. For example, since **share** includes such answer words as *divide* and *prorate,* the list at **shared** omits *divided* and *prorated*. Therefore, the user who encounters a clue with a familiar suffix will occasionally want to look at a neighboring entry to be sure of finding all the possible synonyms.

When a personal name is entered as an answer term, the first name generally appears in parentheses and is ignored in the letter count. In cases where the first name is the one normally encountered—e.g., for historical figures such as *Napoleon* and *Galileo,* or fictional characters such as *Atticus* and *Scout Finch*—the last name is generally parenthesized instead. When a title begins with an article *(A, An,* or *The),* the article is parenthesized and omitted from the letter count. In a list of geographic entities (**river**, **bay**, **peak**, **mountain**, etc.), any generic term that forms part of a proper name (*River, Bay, Peak, Mount,* etc.) is similarly omitted from the letter count. If none of the answers as listed fits the blanks for a given clue, you should naturally check to see if adding a parenthesized or omitted element might produce the desired answer.

In the many entries that are broken into subentries, the subheadings often consist of a single word, which should usually be read as either preceding or following the main entry word. Thus, at **liquor**, the subheadings include **inferior** (which should be read as "inferior liquor") and **measure** (which should be read as "liquor measure"). The subentry **combining form** lists the kinds of word fragments, usually Greek or Latin in origin, that are commonly called roots (*omni, derm, geo,* etc.).

The dictionary is best used somewhat imaginatively. If you fail to find a clue word at its own entry, look up a synonym; only rarely will you fail to find one. If a clue takes a form such as *Basque game, white wine,* or *Italian tenor* and the dictionary provides no such entry, check at the entry for the generic term—**game**, **wine**, **tenor**, etc.

A

A1
4 best, tops **5** prime **6** tip-top **7** optimal, perfect **8** splendid, superior, top-notch **9** excellent, first-rate, front-rank, matchless, top-drawer **10** blue-ribbon, first-class

Aaron
brother: 5 Moses
father: 5 Amram
sister: 6 Miriam

aback
7 unaware **8** suddenly, unawares **10** by surprise **12** unexpectedly

abaft
4 back **5** after **6** astern, behind **8** rearward **9** sternward

abalone
7 mollusc, mollusk **9** gastropod

abandon
4 cede, drop, dump, ease, jilt, junk, play, quit **5** cease, chuck, ditch, leave, let go, scrap, yield **6** desert, disown, give up, laxity, maroon, reject, resign, strand, vacate **7** back out, bail out, cast off, discard, drop out, forsake, freedom, liberty, license, pull out, retreat **8** abdicate, give over, hand over, renounce, wildness, withdraw **9** looseness, repudiate, surrender, throw over **10** enthusiasm, exuberance, relinquish, wantonness **11** discontinue, leave behind, spontaneity, unrestraint **12** carelessness, heedlessness, intemperance, recklessness, unconstraint **13** impulsiveness

abandoned
4 free, lewd, lorn, wild **5** loose **6** gave up, jilted, vacant, wanton **7** cast off, corrupt, given up, outcast, uncouth **8** cast away, depraved, derelict, desolate, forsaken **9** cast aside, debauched, destitute, dissolute, lecherous, neglected, reprobate, shameless **10** degenerate, dissipated, friendless, lascivious, left behind, licentious, profligate, unoccupied **11** uninhibited **12** incorrigible, uncontrolled, unrestrained

abase
5 lower, shame **6** defame, demean, demote, grovel, humble, lessen, reduce **7** cheapen, degrade, devalue, put down **8** belittle **9** denigrate, discredit, disparage, downgrade, humiliate **10** depreciate, undervalue

abash
4 faze **5** mix up, shame, upset **6** dismay, puzzle, rattle **7** confuse, mortify, mystify **8** confound **9** discomfit, embarrass **10** discompose, disconcert

abashment
6 unease **7** chagrin **8** disquiet **9** confusion **12** discomfiture, discomposure

abate
3 ebb, end **4** ease, fade, fall, omit, slow, void, stem, wane **5** allay, annul, close, let up, quash, taper **6** deduct, lessen, negate, recede, reduce, relent, weaken **7** abolish, decline, deprive, die down, dwindle, ease off, nullify, slacken, subside **8** decrease, diminish, mitigate, moderate **9** alleviate, eradicate **10** invalidate

abatement
6 ebbing, rebate, waning **8** decrease, discount **9** declining, deduction, dwindling, exemption, lessening, reduction, shrinkage **10** diminution, subsidence **11** subtraction

abattoir
8 shambles

Abba ___
4 Eban

abbey
6 friary **7** convent **8** cloister **9** monastery

abbot
female: 6 abbess

abbreviate
3 cut **4** clip, trim **5** prune **6** cut out, reduce **7** abridge, curtail, cut back, shorten **8** compress, condense, contract, cut short, truncate

abbreviation
5 brief **6** digest, précis, sketch **7** acronym, cutting, outline **8** abstract, clipping, synopsis, trimming **10** abridgment, shortening **11** curtailment **12** condensation

ABC island
5 Aruba **7** Baranof, Bonaire, Curaçao **9** Admiralty, Chichagof

abdicate
4 cede, drop, quit **5** evade, forgo, leave, waive, yield **6** abjure, give up, reject, resign **7** abandon, cast off, discard **8** abnegate, disclaim, hand over, renounce, withdraw **9** repudiate, surrender **10** relinquish

abdomen
3 gut, pot **5** belly, tummy **6** middle, paunch **7** midriff, stomach **8** potbelly **9** bay window **10** midsection **11** breadbasket
depression: 5 navel

abduct
4 grab, take **5** seize **6** kidnap, remove, snatch **8** carry off, draw away, take away **9** carry away, steal away **10** spirit away **11** make off with

Abduction from the Seraglio
character: 5 Osmin, Selim **8** Belmonte, Pedrillo **9** Konstanze
composer: 6 Mozart (Wolfgang Amadeus)

abecedarian
4 tyro **6** novice **7** amateur, dabbler, learner **8** beginner, initiate, neophyte **9** beginning, smatterer **10** apprentice, dilettante, elementary **11** rudimentary **12** alphabetical

Abel
brother: 4 Cain, Seth
father: 4 Adam
mother: 3 Eve
slayer: 4 Cain

Abelard
son: 9 Astrolabe
wife: 7 Heloise

abele
6 poplar

aberrant
3 odd **7** deviant, strange, unusual **8** abnormal, atypical, peculiar, straying **9** anomalous, deviating, different, eccentric, irregular, unnatural, untypical **11** exceptional, nonstandard

aberration
4 slip **5** quirk **6** change, oddity **7** anomaly, mistake **8** mutation, straying **9** curiosity, deviation, exception, wandering **10** deflection, difference, distortion, divergence **11** abnormality, peculiarity **12** eccentricity, irregularity

abet
3 aid, egg **4** ally, back, help, prod, spur, urge **5** boost, egg on **6** assist, exhort, foment, incite, second, stir up **7** condone, endorse, forward, promote, support **8** advocate **9** encourage, instigate **11** countenance

abettor
4 aide, ally **6** backup, cohort, helper **7** inciter, partner **8** fomenter **9** accessory, supporter **10** accomplice, instigator **11** confederate, conspirator **12** collaborator

abeyance
4 lull, rest **5** break, lapse, pause **6** recess **7** respite, time-out, waiting **8** breather, interval **10** inactivity, quiescence, suspension **12** intermission, interruption

abeyant
7 dormant **8** deferred, inactive, recessed **9** postponed, quiescent, suspended **11** interrupted

abhor
4 hate **5** scorn **6** detest, loathe, reject, revile, vilify **7** contemn, despise, disdain, dislike **8** execrate **9** abominate, excoriate, repudiate

abhorrence
4 evil, hate **6** hatred, horror **7** disgust **8** aversion, distaste, loathing **9** repulsion, revulsion **10** repugnance **11** abomination, detestation

abhorrent
4 base, foul, vile **5** awful **6** horrid, odious **7** beastly, hateful, heinous **8** damnable, horrible, horrific **9** atrocious, execrable, invidious, loathsome, monstrous, obnoxious, repellent, repugnant, repulsive, revolting **10** abominable, deplorable, despicable, detestable, disgusting **12** contemptible **13** reprehensible

abide
4 bear, last, live, stay, wait **5** await, brook, dwell, exist, stand, tarry **6** accede, accept, comply, endure, keep on, linger, remain, reside, stay on, suffer **7** consent, hang out, inhabit, persist, sojourn, stomach, subsist, swallow, wait for **8** continue, live with, stand for, tolerate **9** put up with, withstand

abiding
4 fast, firm, sure **6** steady **7** durable, eternal, lasting, staying **8** constant, enduring, timeless **9** complying, perpetual, steadfast **10** continuing, persistent, persisting, unchanging **11** everlasting, unfaltering

abigail
4 maid

Abigail
brother: 5 David
husband: 5 David, Nabal
mother: 5 Amasa
son: 7 Chileah

ability
4 bent, gift **5** craft, flair, knack, might, savvy, skill **6** talent **7** aptness, command, faculty, know-how, mastery, prowess **8** aptitude, capacity, facility **9** adeptness, dexterity, expertise, handiness, ingenuity, potential **10** adroitness, capability, cleverness, competence, efficiency **11** proficiency **12** skillfulness **13** qualification

abject
3 low **4** base, mean, poor, vile **5** lowly, sorry **6** dismal, humble, shabby, sordid **7** debased, fawning, forlorn, ignoble, pitiful, servile **8** cast down, degraded, dejected, downcast, hopeless, pathetic, pitiable, rejected, resigned, wretched **9** afflicted, destitute, groveling, miserable, worthless **10** deplorable, obsequious, spiritless,

submissive **11** deferential, downtrodden, subservient **12** contemptible, dishonorable, ingratiating

abjure
4 cede, deny **5** avoid, spurn **6** desert, disown, recall, recant, reject, refuse, revoke **7** abandon, disavow, decline, forsake, retract **8** disclaim, forswear, renounce, take back, withdraw **9** repudiate, surrender **10** relinquish **11** abstain from

ablaze
5 afire, aglow, fiery **6** aflame, alight, on fire **7** burning, flaming, excited, flaring, ignited, radiant

able
3 apt, fit **4** keen **5** adept, alert, sharp, smart **6** adroit, clever, expert, facile, suited **7** capable, skilled **8** skillful, talented **9** competent, effective, effectual, efficient, qualified **10** proficient **11** intelligent, resourceful **12** accomplished, enterprising

able-bodied
3 fit **4** hale **5** hardy, lusty, sound, stout **6** brawny, hearty, robust, strong, sturdy **7** capable **8** stalwart, vigorous **9** strapping

ablution
4 bath **6** laving **7** bathing, washing **8** lavation **9** cleansing, immersion **12** purification

abnegate
4 cede, deny, drop **5** forgo, waive, yield **6** abjure, give up, recant, revoke, vacate **7** disavow, gainsay **8** disallow, disclaim, forswear, renounce, withdraw **9** repudiate, surrender **10** contradict, contravene, relinquish

abnegation
6 denial **9** surrender **10** abstinence, self-denial **12** renouncement, renunciation

Abner
cousin: **4** Saul
father: **3** Ner
slayer: **4** Joab

abnormal
3 odd **5** freak, outré, undue, weird **6** off-key **7** bizarre, deviant, strange, unusual **8** aberrant, atypical, freakish, peculiar **9** anomalous, divergent, eccentric, irregular, unnatural **11** heteroclite **13** preternatural

abnormality
4 flaw **6** oddity **7** anomaly **8** deviance **9** deviation, exception **10** aberration, difference **12** irregularity

abode
3 hut **4** home, nest, tent **5** house **7** address, lodging, sojourn **8** domicile, dwelling **9** residence **10** habitation
conical: **5** tepee **6** teepee

abolish
3 end **4** undo, kill, void **5** abate, annul, erase, quash **6** cancel, negate, recall, repeal, revoke, vacate **7** destroy, nullify, rescind, retract, reverse, wipe out **8** abrogate, disallow, dissolve, overturn, prohibit **9** eliminate, eradicate, terminate **10** do away with, extinguish, invalidate

abolitionist
4 Mott (Lucretia), Weld (Theodore) **5** Brown (John), Child (Lydia), Lundy (Benjamin), Smith (Gerrit), Stowe (Harriet Beecher) **6** Birney (James), Lowell (James Russell), Parker (Theodore), Tappan (Arthur), Tubman (Harriet) **7** Lincoln (Abraham) **8** Douglass (Frederick), Garrison (William Lloyd), Phillips (Wendell), Whittier (John Greenleaf)

abominable
5 awful, nasty **6** cursed, horrid, odious **7** hateful, heinous **8** horrible, shocking, terrible, wretched **9** abhorrent, loathsome, offensive, repellent, repugnant, repulsive, revolting **10** deplorable, despicable, detestable, disgusting **12** contemptible

abominable snowman
4 yeti

abominate
4 damn, hate **5** abhor, curse, scorn **6** detest, loathe, revile **7** despise **8** execrate **9** repudiate

abomination
4 evil, hate **5** scorn **6** hatred, horror, plague **7** disdain, disgust, dislike **8** anathema, aversion, contempt, distaste, loathing **9** repulsion, revulsion **10** abhorrence, repugnance, repugnancy **11** detestation

aboriginal
5 first **6** native **7** ancient, endemic, primary **8** earliest, original, primeval **9** primitive **10** indigenous, primordial **13** autochthonous

aborigine
6 native **7** ancient **8** indigene **10** autochthon

abort
4 drop, halt, stop **5** check, expel, scrap, scrub **6** arrest, cancel **7** abandon, call off **8** cut short **9** interrupt, terminate

abortive
4 vain **5** empty **6** futile, unripe **7** failing, useless **9** fruitless, worthless **10** unavailing, unfruitful **11** ineffective, ineffectual **12** unproductive, unsuccessful

abound
4 flow, teem **5** burst, crawl, crowd, flood, swarm, swell **6** throng **8** overflow

abounding
4 full, rife **5** laden **6** filled, full of, jammed, packed **7** copious, profuse, replete, stuffed, teeming

8 abundant, swarming, thronged **9** alive with, bristling, plenteous, plentiful **11** overflowing

about
4 as to, back, in re, near, nigh, over, some **5** again, anent, circa, round **6** almost, around, nearby, nearly **7** apropos, close to, roughly **8** backward **9** as regards, in general, in reverse, regarding **10** as concerns, concerning, in regard to, more or less, relating to, relative to, respecting **11** dealing with, practically, referring to **12** with regard to **13** approximately, concerned with, in reference to, with respect to

about-face
4 turn **7** reverse **8** reversal **9** turnabout

above
3 o'er **4** atop, over, past **5** aloft, supra **6** beyond **8** overhead **9** exceeding
prefix: **4** over **5** hyper, super, supra

above all
7 chiefly **9** primarily **10** especially **11** principally **12** particularly

aboveboard
4 free, open **5** frank **6** candid, honest, openly **7** frankly, up front **8** candidly, honestly, straight, truthful **10** truthfully, forthright, scrupulous

abracadabra
5 charm, magic **6** babble, jargon **9** gibberish **10** double talk, mumbo jumbo **11** incantation **12** gobbledygook **13** mystification

abrade
3 bug, irk, rub **4** burn, fret, gall, rasp, wear **5** annoy, chafe, erode, grate, graze, upset, weary **6** bother, ruffle, scrape **7** corrode, eat away, perturb, provoke, roughen **8** irritate, wear away, wear down **9** aggravate, grind down

Abraham
brother: **5** Haran, Nahor
concubine: **5** Hagar
father: **5** Terah
grandfather: **5** Nahor
grandson: **4** Esau
nephew: **3** Lot
son: **5** Isaac, Medan, Shuah **6** Midian, Zimran **7** Ishmael
well: **9** Beer-Sheba
wife: **5** Sarah **7** Keturah

abrasion
5 chafe, scuff **6** scrape **7** chafing, erosion, grating, rubbing, scratch **8** friction, grinding, scraping, scuffing **10** irritation, scratching

abrasive
5 emery, rough, sharp **6** biting, pumice **7** wearing **8** annoying **9** smoothing, polishing **10** irritating **11** Carborundum, garnet paper

abreast
6 beside, next to, versed, with-it **7** versant **8** familiar, informed, up-to-date **9** au courant **10** acquainted, conversant

abridge
3 cut **4** pare, trim **5** limit, prune **6** lessen, narrow, reduce **7** curtail, cut back, shorten **8** boil down, compress, condense, cut short, diminish, restrict, truncate **9** summarize **10** abbreviate

abridgment
5 brief **6** digest **7** capsule, cutting, summary **8** abstract, synopsis **9** lessening, reduction, short form **10** diminution, shortening **11** compression, contraction, curtailment, restriction **12** abbreviation, condensation

abroad
4 afar, away **5** about **6** afield, astray, widely **7** touring **8** overseas **9** elsewhere, traveling

abrogate
3 end **4** undo, void **5** abate, annul, quash **6** cancel, negate, repeal, revoke, vacate **7** abolish, blot out, nullify, rescind, reverse **8** dissolve **9** discharge **10** extinguish, invalidate, obliterate

abrupt
4 curt **5** bluff, blunt, brief, brisk, gruff, hasty, sharp, sheer, short, steep **6** cut off, snippy, sudden **7** brusque, hurried **8** headlong **9** broken off, impetuous **10** unexpected **11** precipitate, precipitous **13** unceremonious

abruptness
10 brusquerie **12** precipitance

Absalom
commander: **5** Amasa
father: **5** David
mother: **7** Maachah
sister: **5** Tamar
slayer: **4** Joab

abscess
4 boil, sore **5** botch, ulcer **6** lesion, pimple, trauma **7** blister, pustule **8** furuncle **9** carbuncle

abscond
4 bolt, flee, quit, skip **5** break, leave **6** decamp, escape, run off **7** run away, take off **8** slip away, sneak off **9** disappear, sneak away, steal away

absence
4 AWOL, lack, need, void, want **6** dearth, defect, vacuum **7** default, drought, failure, sick-out, vacancy **9** privation **10** deficiency, inadequacy **11** absenteeism, inattention **13** insufficiency

absent
4 away, AWOL, gone, lost **6** no-show **7** bemused, faraway, lacking, missing, omitted, wanting, without **8** distrait, heedless **9** elsewhere, forgetful **10** abstracted, distracted **11** inattentive, preoccupied

absentminded
4 lost **7** bemused, faraway **8** distrait, dreaming, heedless, unseeing **9** forgetful, oblivious, unheeding, unmindful **10** abstracted, distracted, unnoticing **11** inattentive, inconscient, preoccupied, unconscious, unobserving

absolute
4 full, pure, real, true **5** ideal, sheer, total, utter **6** actual, entire, simple, strict **7** eternal, factual, genuine, perfect, supreme, unmixed **8** autarkic, complete, despotic, flawless, infinite, outright, positive, ultimate, simplest, thorough, unflawed **9** arbitrary, autarchic, boundless, downright, embodying, imperious, masterful, sovereign, unalloyed, undiluted, unlimited **10** autocratic, autonomous, consummate, impeccable, monocratic, tyrannical **11** categorical, dictatorial, domineering, fundamental, independent, unequivocal, unmitigated, unqualified **12** indisputable, totalitarian, unrestrained, unrestricted **13** authoritarian, unconditional

absolutely
5 fully **6** wholly **7** utterly **8** entirely **9** doubtless, perfectly **10** completely, definitely, positively, thoroughly **11** doubtlessly **13** unequivocally

absolution
6 pardon **7** amnesty, freeing, release **9** releasing, remission **10** letting off **11** exculpation, exoneration, forgiveness **12** dispensation

absolutism
9 Caesarism, despotism **12** dictatorship

absolve
4 free **5** clear, let go, remit, spare **6** acquit, excuse, exempt, let off, pardon **7** forgive, release, relieve, set free **8** dispense **9** discharge, exculpate, exonerate, vindicate

absorb
4 bear, blot **5** imbue, learn, sop up, use up **6** assume, embody, endure, engage, imbibe, infuse, ingest, soak up, sponge, suck up, take in, take up **7** acquire, consume, drink in, engross, immerse, involve, receive, sustain **8** permeate **9** preoccupy, transform **10** assimilate **11** incorporate

absorbed
4 deep, into, lost, rapt **6** intent **7** engaged, wrapped **8** caught up, immersed, involved **9** engrossed, wrapped up **10** captivated, fascinated **11** preoccupied

absorbing
9 arresting, consuming **10** engrossing, intriguing **11** captivating, fascinating, interesting **12** monopolizing, preoccupying

abstain
4 curb, deny, diet, fast, keep, pass, stop **5** avoid, forgo, spurn **6** abjure, eschew, give up, pass up, refuse, reject **7** decline, forbear, refrain **8** abnegate, forswear, hold back, keep from, renounce, swear off, teetotal, withhold **9** constrain, do without **11** deny oneself

abstemious
5 sober **6** chaste, strict **7** ascetic, austere, sparing **9** abstinent, continent, temperate **10** restrained **11** self-denying

abstinence
6 denial **7** fasting **8** chastity, sobriety **9** soberness **10** continence, self-denial, temperance **12** renunciation **13** self-restraint

abstract
5 brief, ideal **6** detach, digest, précis **7** epitome, neutral, outline, shorten, summary, utopian **8** academic, breviary, condense, detached, notional, separate, synopsis **9** disengage, summarize **10** abridgment, conceptual, conspectus, disconnect, dissociate, impersonal **11** appropriate, impractical, speculative, theoretical **12** condensation, hypothetical, transcendent **13** disinterested

abstracted
4 lost, rapt **6** absent, intent **7** bemused, faraway **8** absorbed, distrait, heedless **9** engrossed, oblivious, unheeding, unmindful, unminding, withdrawn **11** inattentive, inconscient, preoccupied, unconscious **12** absentminded

abstruse
4 deep **5** heavy **6** knotty, occult **7** complex **8** esoteric, hermetic, involved, profound **9** difficult, intricate, recondite **11** complicated

absurd
5 balmy, comic, crazy, droll, inane, loony, potty, silly, wacky **6** insane **7** asinine, fatuous, foolish, idiotic **8** farcical **9** illogical, laughable, ludicrous **10** irrational, ridiculous **11** harebrained **12** preposterous, unreasonable

absurdity
5 farce, folly **7** inanity **8** nonsense **9** craziness, dottiness, silliness **11** foolishness, incongruity, witlessness **13** ludicrousness, senselessness

abundance
6 bounty, excess, plenty, riches, wealth **9** affluence, profusion **10** lavishness, prosperity **11** prodigality
Scottish: 5 routh

abundant
4 full, lush, rich, rife **5** ample **6** filled, galore, lavish, plenty **7** aplenty, copious, crammed, crowded, liberal, profuse, replete **8** fruitful, prolific **9** abounding, bounteous, bountiful, extensive, luxuriant, plenteous, plentiful

abuse
3 mar **4** harm, hurt, rail **5** anger, decry, shame, spoil, wrong **6** damage, debase, deride, impair, injure, misuse, revile, vilify **7** calumny, corrupt, cursing, exploit, obloquy, oppress, profane **8** belittle, berating, derision, derogate, disgrace, ill-treat, maltreat, mistreat, swearing **9** blaspheme, contumely, desecrate, disparage, harshness, invective, manhandle, mishandle, persecute, profanity **10** defamation, depreciate, malignment, revilement, scurrility **11** disapproval **12** billingsgate, denunciation, vilification, vituperation

abusive
5 dirty, harsh **6** odious **7** corrupt **8** scurrile **9** injurious, insulting, invective, offending, offensive, truculent **10** calumnious, defamatory, scurrilous **11** blasphemous, castigating, opprobrious **12** calumniating, contumelious, sharp-tongued, vituperative, vituperatory

abut
4 join, link **5** flank, touch, verge **6** adjoin, border, butt on **8** border on, neighbor **9** lie beside **11** butt against, communicate

abutting
4 next **6** beside, joined, next to **7** joining, verging **8** adjacent, next door, touching **9** adjoining, bordering, impinging **10** connecting, contiguous, juxtaposed **11** bordering on, coextensive, coterminous, neighboring **12** conterminous

abysmal
4 deep, vast **7** endless **8** infinite, profound, unending, wretched **9** boundless, cavernous, plumbless, soundless, unplumbed **10** bottomless, fathomless, unmeasured **11** illimitable, measureless **12** immeasurable, unfathomable

abyss
3 pit **4** gulf, hell, hole, void **5** abysm, chasm, depth, gorge, hades, Sheol **6** Tophet **7** fissure, Gehenna, inferno **8** crevasse, deepness **9** perdition **10** underworld

academia
10 university **12** professoriat

academic
3 don **5** pupil, tutor **6** closet, fellow, master **7** bookish, learned, scholar, student **8** abstract, gownsman, lecturer, pedantic **9** professor, scholarly **10** scholastic **11** book-learned, conjectural, impractical, speculative, theoretical **12** conventional, hypothetical

academic period
4 term **7** quarter **8** semester **9** trimester

academy
5 lycée **6** lyceum **7** college, society **9** institute **10** prep school **12** conservatory

Academy Award winner
picture:
1927-28: 5 Wings
1928-29: 14 Broadway Melody
1929-30: 25 All Quiet on the Western Front
1930-31: 8 Cimarron
1931-32: 10 Grand Hotel
1932-33: 9 Cavalcade
1934: 18 It Happened One Night
1935: 17 Mutiny on the Bounty
1936: 16 The Great Ziegfeld
1937: 15 Life of Emile Zola
1938: 20 You Can't Take It with You
1939: 15 Gone with the Wind
1940: 7 Rebecca
1941: 19 How Green Was My Valley
1942: 10 Mrs. Miniver
1943: 10 Casablanca
1944: 10 Going My Way
1945: 11 Lost Weekend (The)
1946: 19 Best Years of Our Lives (The)
1947: 19 Gentleman's Agreement
1948: 6 Hamlet
1949: 14 All the King's Men
1950: 11 All About Eve
1951: 15 American in Paris (An)
1952: 19 Greatest Show on Earth (The)
1953: 18 From Here to Eternity
1954: 15 On the Waterfront
1955: 5 Marty
1956: 26 Around the World in Eighty Days
1957: 20 Bridge on the River Kwai (The)
1958: 4 Gigi
1959: 6 Ben-Hur
1960: 9 Apartment (The)
1961: 13 West Side Story
1962: 16 Lawrence of Arabia
1963: 8 Tom Jones
1964: 10 My Fair Lady
1965: 12 Sound of Music (The)
1966: 16 Man for All Seasons (A)
1967: 19 In the Heat of the Night
1968: 6 Oliver
1969: 14 Midnight Cowboy
1970: 6 Patton
1971: 16 French Connection (The)
1972: 9 Godfather (The)
1973: 5 Sting (The)
1974: 9 Godfather (Part Two, The)
1975: 25 One Flew over the Cuckoo's Nest
1976: 5 Rocky
1977: 9 Annie Hall
1978: 10 Deer Hunter (The)
1979: 14 Kramer vs. Kramer
1980: 14 Ordinary People
1981: 14 Chariots of Fire
1982: 6 Gandhi

1983: **17** Terms of Endearment
1984: **7** Amadeus
1985: **11** Out of Africa
1986: **7** Platoon
1987: **11** Last Emperor (The)
1988: **7** Rain Man
1989: **16** Driving Miss Daisy
1990: **16** Dances with Wolves
1991: **17** Silence of the Lambs (The)
1992: **10** Unforgiven
1993: **14** Schindler's List
1994: **11** Forrest Gump
1995: **10** Braveheart
1996: **14** English Patient (The)
1997: **7** Titanic
1998: **17** Shakespeare in Love
1999: **14** American Beauty
2000: **9** Gladiator
2001: **13** Beautiful Mind (A)
2002: **7** Chicago
2003: **14** Lord of the Rings (The)
2004: **17** Million Dollar Baby
2005: **5** Crash
2006: **8** Departed (The)

actor:

1927-28: **8** Jannings (Emil)
1928-29: **6** Baxter (Warner)
1929-30: **6** Arliss (George)
1930-31: **9** Barrymore (Lionel)
1931-32: **5** Beery (Wallace), March (Fredric)
1932-33: **8** Laughton (Charles)
1934: **5** Gable (Clark)
1935: **8** McLaglen (Victor)
1936: **4** Muni (Paul)
1937: **5** Tracy (Spencer)
1938: **5** Tracy (Spencer)
1939: **5** Donat (Robert)
1940: **7** Stewart (James)
1941: **6** Cooper (Gary)
1942: **6** Cagney (James)
1943: **5** Lukas (Paul)
1944: **6** Crosby (Bing)
1945: **7** Milland (Ray)
1946: **5** March (Fredric)
1947: **6** Colman (Ronald)
1948: **7** Olivier (Laurence)
1949: **8** Crawford (Broderick)
1950: **6** Ferrer (José)
1951: **6** Bogart (Humphrey)
1952: **6** Cooper (Gary)
1953: **6** Holden (William)
1954: **6** Brando (Marlon)
1955: **8** Borgnine (Ernest)
1956: **7** Brynner (Yul)
1957: **8** Guinness (Alec)
1958: **5** Niven (David)
1959: **6** Heston (Charlton)
1960: **9** Lancaster (Burt)
1961: **6** Schell (Maximilian)
1962: **4** Peck (Gregory)
1963: **7** Poitier (Sidney)
1964: **8** Harrison (Rex)
1965: **6** Marvin (Lee)
1966: **8** Scofield (Paul)
1967: **7** Steiger (Rod)
1968: **9** Robertson (Cliff)
1969: **5** Wayne (John)
1970: **5** Scott (George C.)
1971: **7** Hackman (Gene)
1972: **6** Brando (Marlon)
1973: **6** Lemmon (Jack)
1974: **6** Carney (Art)
1975: **9** Nicholson (Jack)
1976: **5** Finch (Peter)
1977: **8** Dreyfuss (Richard)
1978: **6** Voight (Jon)
1979: **7** Hoffman (Dustin)
1980: **6** De Niro (Robert)
1981: **5** Fonda (Henry)
1982: **8** Kingsley (Ben)
1983: **6** Duvall (Robert)
1984: **7** Abraham (F. Murray)
1985: **4** Hurt (William)
1986: **6** Newman (Paul)
1987: **7** Douglas (Michael)
1988: **7** Hoffman (Dustin)
1989: **8** Day-Lewis (Daniel)
1990: **5** Irons (Jeremy)
1991: **7** Hopkins (Anthony)
1992: **6** Pacino (Al)
1993: **5** Hanks (Tom)
1994: **5** Hanks (Tom)
1995: **4** Cage (Nicholas)
1996: **4** Rush (Geoffrey)
1997: **9** Nicholson (Jack)
1998: **7** Benigni (Roberto)
1999: **6** Spacey (Kevin)
2000: **5** Crowe (Russell)
2001: **10** Washington (Denzel)
2002: **5** Brody (Adrien)
2003: **4** Penn (Sean)
2004: **4** Foxx (Jamie)
2005: **7** Hoffman (Philip Seymour)
2006: **8** Whitaker (Forest)

actress:

1927-28: **6** Gaynor (Janet)
1928-29: **8** Pickford (Mary)
1929-30: **7** Shearer (Norma)
1930-31: **8** Dressler (Marie)
1931-32: **5** Hayes (Helen)
1932-33: **7** Hepburn (Katharine)
1934: **7** Colbert (Claudette)
1935: **5** Davis (Bette)
1936: **6** Rainer (Luise)

1937: **6** Rainer (Luise)
1938: **5** Davis (Bette)
1939: **5** Leigh (Vivien)
1940: **6** Rogers (Ginger)
1941: **8** Fontaine (Joan)
1942: **6** Garson (Greer)
1943: **5** Jones (Jennifer)
1944: **7** Bergman (Ingrid)
1945: **8** Crawford (Joan)
1946: **11** de Havilland (Olivia)
1947: **5** Young (Loretta)
1948: **5** Wyman (Jane)
1949: **11** de Havilland (Olivia)
1950: **8** Holliday (Judy)
1951: **5** Leigh (Vivien)
1952: **5** Booth (Shirley)
1953: **7** Hepburn (Audrey)
1954: **5** Kelly (Grace)
1955: **7** Magnani (Anna)
1956: **7** Bergman (Ingrid)
1957: **8** Woodward (Joanne)
1958: **7** Hayward (Susan)
1959: **8** Signoret (Simone)
1960: **6** Taylor (Elizabeth)
1961: **5** Loren (Sophia)
1962: **8** Bancroft (Anne)
1963: **4** Neal (Patricia)
1964: **7** Andrews (Julie)
1965: **8** Christie (Julie)
1966: **6** Taylor (Elizabeth)
1967: **7** Hepburn (Katharine)
1968: **7** Hepburn (Katharine) **9** Streisand (Barbra)
1969: **5** Smith (Maggie)
1970: **7** Jackson (Glenda)
1971: **5** Fonda (Jane)
1972: **8** Minnelli (Liza)
1973: **7** Jackson (Glenda)
1974: **7** Burstyn (Ellen)
1975: **8** Fletcher (Louise)
1976: **7** Dunaway (Faye)
1977: **6** Keaton (Diane)
1978: **5** Fonda (Jane)
1979: **5** Field (Sally)
1980: **6** Spacek (Sissy)
1981: **7** Hepburn (Katharine)
1982: **6** Streep (Meryl)
1983: **8** MacLaine (Shirley)
1984: **5** Field (Sally)
1985: **4** Page (Geraldine)
1986: **6** Matlin (Marlee)
1987: **4** Cher
1988: **6** Foster (Jodie)
1989: **5** Tandy (Jessica)
1990: **5** Bates (Kathy)
1991: **6** Foster (Jodie)
1992: **8** Thompson (Emma)
1993: **6** Hunter (Holly)
1994: **5** Lange (Jessica)
1995: **8** Sarandon (Susan)
1996: **9** McDormand (Frances)
1997: **4** Hunt (Helen)
1998: **7** Paltrow (Gwyneth)
1999: **5** Swank (Hilary)
2000: **7** Roberts (Julia)
2001: **5** Berry (Halle)
2002: **6** Kidman (Nicole)
2003: **6** Theron (Charlize)
2004: **5** Swank (Hilary)
2005: **11** Witherspoon (Reese)
2006: **6** Mirren (Helen)

accede
3 let **5** admit, agree, allow, grant, yield **6** accept, assent, comply, concur, give in, permit **7** agree to, approve, concede, consent **9** acquiesce, cooperate, subscribe

accelerando
6 faster **7** speed up **10** speeding up

accelerate
3 gun, rev **4** grow, roll **5** hurry, impel, rev up, speed **6** hasten, open up, step up **7** quicken, speed up **8** expedite, increase **9** fast-track **10** peel rubber

acceleration
7 speedup **8** hurrying, spurring **9** hastening, revving up **10** increasing, quickening, speeding up, stepping up

accent
4 beat, lilt, tone **5** acute, grave, meter, pulse, throb **6** rhythm, stress, weight **7** cadence **8** emphasis **9** diacritic, pulsation **10** inflection, intonation
Irish: **6** brogue
Scottish: **4** burr
Southern: **5** drawl

accept
3 bow, buy, see **4** bear, gain, okay, take **5** admit, adopt, agree, catch, favor, go for, grasp, yield **6** accede, admire, affirm, assent, endure, follow, take in, take on **7** agree to, approve, believe, receive, respect, swallow, welcome **8** assent to, bear with, hold with, live with, stand for, tolerate **9** acquiesce, agree with, undertake **10** capitulate, comprehend, concur with, understand **11** acknowledge, countenance, subscribe to

acceptable
4 good, okay **6** decent, worthy **7** average, welcome **8** adequate, all right, bearable, ordinary, passable, pleasing, standard, suitable **9** endurable, tolerable **10** sufficient **11** commonplace, respectable, supportable **12** satisfactory **13** unexceptional, unimpeachable

acceptably
4 well **5** amply **7** capably **8** properly, suitably

9 fittingly, tolerably **10** becomingly **11** competently **13** appropriately

acceptant
4 open **8** amenable, friendly, swayable **9** favorable, receptive, recipient, welcoming **10** open-minded, responsive **11** persuadable, persuasible, susceptible

acceptation
4 gist **5** point, sense **6** import **7** meaning, message, purport **9** intention **10** intendment **12** significance, significancy **13** signification, understanding

accepted
5 usual **6** common, normal, proper **7** correct, regular, routine **8** approved, everyday, expected, habitual, ordinary, orthodox, received **9** customary **10** accustomed, recognized, sanctioned **11** established, traditional **12** conventional

access
3 fit, way **4** adit, door, gust, pang, path, road, turn **5** burst, entry, get at, onset, route, sally, spell, throe **6** attack, avenue, entrée **7** contact, flare-up, ingress, passage, seizure **8** approach, entrance, eruption, increase, outburst **9** admission, explosion **10** admittance

accessible
4 near, open **5** handy **6** public, usable **8** possible **9** available, operative, reachable **10** attainable, employable, obtainable **11** practicable **12** approachable, unrestricted

accession
4 rise **5** raise **8** addition, approach, increase, outburst, taking on **9** accretion, adherence, increment, induction **10** admittance, assumption, attainment, succession **11** acquisition **12** augmentation, inauguration

accessory
3 aid **4** aide, prop, trim **5** extra, frill **6** helper **7** abettor, adjunct, fitting, insider, partner **8** addition, adjuvant, appendix **9** accretion, adornment, ancillary, appendage, assistant, associate, auxiliary, increment, secondary, tributary **10** accomplice, coincident, collateral, concurrent, decoration, incidental, subsidiary **11** appurtenant, concomitant, confederate, conspirator, subordinate, subservient **12** appurtenance, contributory **13** accompaniment, coconspirator, supplementary

accident
3 hap, lot **4** fate, luck, odds **5** fluke **6** chance, gamble, hazard, kismet, mishap **7** bad luck, destiny **8** calamity, casualty, fortuity, incident **9** mischance **10** misfortune **12** misadventure

accidental
3 odd **4** flat **5** fluky, sharp **6** casual, chance, flukey, random **7** unmeant **8** by chance, careless **9** chromatic, dependent, extempore, impromptu, unplanned, unwitting **10** coincident, contingent, fortuitous, unexpected, unforeseen, unintended **11** conditional, inadvertent **12** coincidental, uncalculated **13** unintentional

acclaim
4 hail, clap, laud **5** cheer, éclat, exalt, extol, glory, honor, kudos, roose **6** homage, praise, salute **7** applaud, approve, commend, glorify, magnify, ovation, root for **8** applause, plaudits **10** compliment

acclimate
5 adapt **6** adjust, change, harden, season **7** toughen **9** condition, habituate

accolade
4 bays, fame **5** award, badge, honor, kudos **6** praise **7** laurels, tribute **8** approval **10** decoration **11** distinction

accommodate
3 fit **4** hold, rent, suit **5** adapt, alter, board, defer, favor, house, humor, lodge, put up, yield **6** adjust, attune, bestow, billet, change, encase, harbor, modify, oblige, please, submit, tailor, take in **7** cater to, conform, contain, enclose, furnish, indulge, quarter, receive, shelter **8** accustom, allow for, domicile **9** entertain, harmonize, integrate, reconcile **11** domiciliate, make room for

accommodating
7 amiable, helpful, willing **8** gracious, obliging **9** adaptable **10** hospitable, solicitous, thoughtful **11** considerate, cooperative

accommodations
3 inn **4** digs, keep, room **5** hotel, lodge, motel **6** hostel **7** housing, lodging, shelter **8** hostelry, lodgment, quarters **9** residence **12** room and board

accompaniment
6 backup **7** adjunct **8** addition **9** accessory, associate, attendant, corollary **10** supplement **11** concomitant, enhancement **12** augmentation

accompany
4 join **5** bring, guide, pilot **6** attend, convoy, escort, go with **7** combine, conduct, consort **8** chaperon, come with **9** associate **10** appear with, go together **11** perform with

accompanying
8 incident **9** accessory, ancillary, attendant, attending, secondary **10** associated, coincident, collateral **11** concomitant

accomplice
4 aide, ally **5** aider **6** flunky, helper, stooge **7** abettor, partner **9** accessory, assistant, associate **11** confederate, conspirator, subordinate **13** coconspirator

accomplish
3 win **4** gain **5** reach, score **6** attain, effect, fulfil, rack up **7** achieve, execute, fulfill, perfect, pull off, realize, succeed **8** bring off, carry out, complete **9** discharge **10** bring about

accomplished
4 able **5** adept **6** expert **7** skilled **8** finished, masterly, skillful, talented **9** practiced **10** proficient

accomplishment
3 act, art **4** deed, feat **5** craft, doing, skill **7** ability **9** adeptness, expertise **10** attainment, capability, completion **11** achievement, acquirement, proficiency

accord
4 deal, fuse, give, jibe, pact **5** agree, award, blend, chime, fit in, grant, match, merge, tally, union **6** affirm, assent, concur, confer, treaty **7** compact, concert, conform, empathy, entente, harmony, rapport **8** affinity, coincide, dovetail, sympathy **9** agreement, harmonize, reconcile **10** attraction, conformity, consonance, correspond, solidarity **11** concordance **13** understanding

accordant
8 agreeing **9** congruous, consonant **10** conforming, harmonious **13** correspondent

accordingly
2 so **4** duly, ergo, then, thus **5** hence **9** therefore, thereupon **12** consequently

accost
3 dog **4** call, dare, face, hail **5** annoy, beard, cross, front, hound, worry **6** bother, call to **7** affront, outface, outrage **8** approach, confront **9** challenge **10** buttonhole

accouchement
7 lying-in **8** childbed, delivery **10** childbirth **11** confinement, parturition

account
3 tab, use **4** bill, deem, note, rate, view **5** avail, basis, favor, score, story, track, value, worth **6** assess, client, esteem, reason, reckon, record, regard, report, repute **7** analyze, explain, expound, justify, recital, version **8** appraise, consider, customer, estimate **9** chronicle, narrative, rationale, reckoning, statement **11** explanation **13** consideration
book: **6** ledger

accountable
6 liable **8** amenable **10** answerable **11** explainable, responsible

accounting
11 bookkeeping
method: **4** FIFO, FILO, LIFO

accoutre
3 arm, rig **4** deck, gear **5** adorn, dress, equip, fix up, ready **6** attire, fit out, outfit, supply **7** appoint, furnish, prepare, provide, turn out **9** provision

accoutrement
3 kit **4** gear **6** outfit, tackle **7** regalia **8** tackling **9** accessory, apparatus, equipment, machinery, trappings **10** provisions **11** furnishings, habiliments **12** appointments **13** paraphernalia

accredit
2 OK **3** lay **4** okay **5** refer **6** assign, attest, charge, credit, enable **7** approve, ascribe, certify, commend, empower, endorse, license, warrant **8** sanction, validate, vouch for **9** attribute, authorize, recognize, recommend **10** commission, credential

accretion
4 rise **5** raise **6** growth **7** buildup **8** addition, increase **9** accession, appendage, increment **10** attachment **11** enlargement **12** accumulation, augmentation

accrue
4 grow **5** amass **6** gather, pile up **7** build up, collect, compile **8** increase **10** accumulate, amalgamate **11** agglomerate

accumulate
4 heap, grow, mass, pile **5** add to, amass, hoard, lay by, lay in, lay up, stock, store **6** accrue, garner, gather, pile up, rack up, roll up **7** acquire, backlog, collect, compile, lay down, stack up, store up **8** assemble, increase **9** stockpile

accumulation
4 bank, heap, mass, pile **5** hoard, stock, store, trove **6** growth **7** backlog, buildup, reserve **8** increase **9** accretion, amassment **10** collection **11** aggregation, enlargement

accumulative
6 heaped **7** growing **8** additive, additory **9** summative **10** collective, increasing **11** aggregative **12** augmentative

accuracy
8 veracity **9** certainty, exactness, precision **10** definition, exactitude **11** correctness, preciseness **12** definiteness

accurate
4 just, nice, true **5** exact, right **6** actual, dead on, proper, spot on **7** certain, correct, factual, precise **8** definite, reliable, rigorous **9** authentic, error-free, errorless **10** dependable

accursed
4 vile **6** odious **7** hateful **8** damnable **9** abhorrent, execrable, loathsome, offensive, repugnant, revolting **10** abominable, despicable, detestable

accusation
3 rap **6** charge **9** complaint **10** allegation, indictment **12** denunciation
false: 7 calumny

accuse
3 tax **5** blame, brand **6** allege, charge, delate, finger, impute, indict **7** arraign, ascribe, censure, impeach **8** admonish, denounce, reproach **9** criminate, criticize, inculpate, reprobate **10** denunciate **11** incriminate

accustom
3 use **4** wont **5** adapt, inure **6** adjust, harden, season **7** conform **9** habituate **11** acclimatize, familiarize

accustomed
3 set **5** usual **6** normal **7** chronic, regular, routine **8** accepted, everyday, familiar, habitual, ordinary, standard **9** customary **10** habituated **11** commonplace, established, traditional **12** conventional

ace
3 bit, jot, pip, top **4** atom, hair, iota, mite, star **5** crumb, minim, pilot, point, score, speck **6** Bishop (Billy), bullet, defeat, master, winner **7** whisker **8** molecule, particle, Red Baron **9** first rate, hole in one **10** Richthofen (Manfred von) **11** hairbreadth, tennis score **12** Rickenbacker (Eddie)

ace and face card
7 natural **9** blackjack

acedia
5 ennui **6** apathy **7** boredom, languor **8** lethargy

acerbate
3 vex **5** anger, annoy, peeve **6** madden **7** incense, inflame **8** embitter, irritate **9** aggravate **10** exasperate

acerbic
4 acid, sour, tart **5** acrid, harsh, rough, sharp **7** caustic, cutting, satiric **8** stinging **9** acidulous, corrosive, sarcastic **10** astringent

acerbity
7 acidity, sarcasm **8** acrimony, asperity, sourness, tartness **9** harshness, roughness, surliness **10** bitterness, causticity

Achates' companion
6 Aeneas

ache
3 yen **4** hurt, long, pain, pang, pine, pity, sigh **5** crave, smart, throb, yearn **6** hanker, hunger, stitch, suffer, thirst, twinge **8** yearning **11** commiserate
Scottish: 6 stound

Achebe novel
15 Things Fall Apart

Acheron
5 Hades, river

achieve
2 do **3** get, win **4** gain **5** reach, score **6** attain, effect, finish, obtain, rack up, secure **7** acquire, execute, fulfill, get done, perform, realize, succeed **8** carry out, complete, conclude **9** actualize **10** accomplish

achievement
4 deed, feat **6** finish **7** exploit, success **10** attainment, completion **11** acquisition, tour de force

Achilles
adviser: 6 Nestor
companion: 9 Patroclus
father: 6 Peleus
horse: 7 Xanthus
lover: 7 Briseis
mother: 6 Thetis
slayer: 5 Paris
victim: 6 Hector
vulnerable part: 4 heel

aching
4 hurt, sore **6** in pain **7** hurtful, hurting, painful **8** yearning **9** disturbed **10** afflictive, distressed **13** compassionate

acicular
5 acute, peaky, piked, sharp **6** peaked, pointy, spiked **7** pointed

acid
4 sour, tart **5** acerb **7** acerbic, acetose, caustic **8** stinging **9** corrosive, sarcastic, vitriolic
bleaching: 6 oxalic
fatty: 6 capric **7** caproic, stearic **8** caprylic
found in apples: 5 malic
found in cranberries: 7 benzoic
found in grapes: 8 tartaric
found in lemons: 6 citric
found in rhubarb: 6 oxalic
found in sour milk: 6 lactic
indicator: 6 litmus
kind: 5 amino, boric, iodic, malic, oleic **6** acetic, bromic, formic, nitric, oxalic, tannic **7** nitrous, silicic **8** carbolic, carbonic, muriatic, sulfuric **9** aqua regia **12** hydrochloric
neutralizer: 4 base **6** alkali
tanning: 6 tannic **8** catechin
vinegar: 6 acetic

acidulous
3 dry **4** sour, tart **5** acerb, harsh, sharp **6** biting **7** acerbic, acetose, cutting, piquant, pungent **9** sarcastic

Acis
lover: 7 Galatea
slayer: 10 Polyphemus

acknowledge
3 own **4** avow, deem, tell, view **5** admit, agree, allow, grant, let on, own up **6** accede, accept, fess up, reveal **7** concede, confess, declare, divulge, profess **8** announce, consider, disclose, proclaim **9** recognize

acknowledgment
6 assent, avowal, credit, notice **9** admission **10** confession **11** affirmation, declaration, recognition

acme
3 cap, top **4** apex, peak **6** apogee, climax, summit, tiptop, vertex, zenith **8** capstone, pinnacle, ultimate **9** high point **10** perfection **11** culmination

acorn tree
3 oak

acoustic
5 aural **6** audile **8** auditory **9** unplugged

acquaint
4 clue, tell, warn **6** advise, fill in, inform, notify, orient, reveal **7** apprise, present **8** accustom, disclose **9** enlighten, introduce **11** familiarize

acquaintance
4 mate **5** amigo, crony, grasp **6** friend **7** comrade, contact **9** associate, colleague, companion **10** cognizance, experience **11** familiarity

acquainted
6 versed **7** abreast, in touch **8** familiar, informed, up-to-date **9** au courant **10** conversant

acquiesce
3 bow, yes **5** agree, allow, bow to, yield **6** accede, accept, assent, comply, concur, give in, submit **7** consent, go along **9** reconcile, subscribe

acquiescence
6 assent **7** consent **8** giving in, yielding **9** deference **10** acceptance, compliance, conformity, submission **11** resignation

acquiescent
6 docile **7** passive **8** resigned, yielding **10** submissive **11** unresistant, unresisting **12** nonresistant, nonresisting

acquire
3 add, buy, get, win **4** earn, form, gain, land **5** amass, annex **6** garner, obtain, pick up, secure, take on **7** bring in, collect, develop, procure **10** accumulate

acquirement
8 addition **9** accretion **11** acquisition

acquisition
4 gain **5** prize **7** winning **8** addition, learning, property, purchase **9** accretion

acquisitive
5 eager, itchy **6** grabby, greedy **8** covetous, desirous, grasping **10** avaricious

acquit
3 act **4** bear, free **5** carry, clear, let go **6** behave, deport, let off **7** absolve, comport, conduct, perform, release, set free **8** liberate **9** discharge, exculpate, exonerate, vindicate

acres
4 area, land **5** lands **6** estate **7** demesne, expanse, holding **8** property

acrid
4 acid, sour **5** harsh, nasty, sharp **6** biting, bitter **7** austere, burning, caustic, cutting, pungent **8** stinging **9** trenchant **10** astringent, irritating **11** acrimonious

acrimonious
3 mad **5** angry, cross, irate, sharp, testy **6** biting, bitter, cranky, ireful **7** acerbic, caustic, cutting **9** indignant, irascible, rancorous **11** belligerent, contentious, quarrelsome

acrimony
5 anger, spite **6** animus, malice, rancor **7** ill will **8** acerbity, asperity, mordancy **9** animosity, antipathy, harshness, virulence **10** bitterness **11** malevolence

Acrisius
daughter: **5** Danaë
slayer: **7** Perseus

acrobat
7 gymnast **9** aerialist, trapezist **11** funambulist

across
4 over **6** beyond **7** athwart **12** transversely
prefix: **5** trans

act
3 law, run **4** bear, bill, deed, fake, feat, mime, play, pose, sham, work **5** bluff, feign, front, put-on, serve, stunt **6** affect, appear, behave, shtick **7** exploit, operate, perform, portray, pretend, routine, statute **8** function, pretense, simulate **9** officiate **10** masquerade **11** counterfeit, impersonate
wrongful: **3** sin **4** tort **5** crime, error, fault **7** default, misdeed, offense

acting
6 pro tem **7** interim, playing **9** ad interim, dramatics, imitating, portrayal, temporary **10** pro tempore **12** entertaining

actinium symbol
2 Ac

action
4 case, deed, move, step, stir, suit, work **5** cause, doing **6** battle, bustle, combat **7** lawsuit, process, service **8** activity, behavior, conflict, fighting, function **9** execution, operation, procedure **10** engagement, proceeding **11** performance

action painter
5 Kline (Franz) **7** Pollock (Jackson) **9** de Kooning (Willem)

action painting
7 tachism

activate
4 stir, wake **5** rally, rouse, set up, waken **6** arouse, awaken, call up, turn on **8** energize, mobilize, motivate, vitalize **9** stimulate

active
4 busy, live, spry **5** agile, alert, alive, brisk, going **6** at work, in play, lively, moving **7** driving, dynamic, flowing, on the go, running, working **8** animated, bustling, emitting, erupting, spirited, vigorous **9** effective, energetic, operating, operative, sprightly **11** functioning, industrious **12** enterprising

activity
6 action, bustle, motion **7** process, pursuit, venture **8** exercise, exertion **10** exercising, liveliness **11** undertaking

actor
4 mime, star **5** mimic **6** mummer, player **7** artiste, trouper **8** thespian **9** performer **11** participant **12** impersonator
name: **3** Cox (Wally), Fox (James, Michael J.), Lee (Bruce), Lom (Herbert), Mix (Tom), Ray (Aldo) **4** Alda (Alan, Robert), Bean (Orson), Blue (Ben), Bond (Ward), Caan (James), Cage (Nicholas), Cobb (Lee J.), Coco (James), Culp (Robert), Dean (James), Depp (Johnny), Dern (Bruce), Duff (Howard), Egan (Richard), Falk (Peter), Ford (Glenn, Harrison), Foxx (Redd), Geer (Will), Gere (Richard), Grey (Joel), Hill (Arthur), Hope (Bob), Hurt (John, William), Ives (Burl), Kaye (Danny), Kean (Edmund), Keel (Howard), Ladd (Alan), Lahr (Bert), Lord (Jack), Lowe (Rob), Lunt (Alfred), Marx (Chico, Groucho, Harpo, Zeppo), Muni (Paul), Ngor (Haing S.), Peck (Gregory), Penn (Sean), Pitt (Brad), Raft (George), Reid (Wallace), Roth (Tim), Ryan (Robert), Shaw (Robert), Tati (Jacques), Tone (Franchot), Torn (Rip), Tune (Tommy), Wahl (Ken), Webb (Clifton, Jack), Wynn (Ed, Keenan), York (Michael) **5** Adler (Luther), Allen (Fred, Tim, Woody), Arkin (Adam, Alan), Asner (Ed), Autry (Gene), Ayres (Lew), Bacon (Kevin), Barry (Gene), Bates (Alan), Beery (Wallace), Benny (Jack), Berle (Milton), Boone (Richard), Booth (Edwin), Boyer (Charles), Brand (Neville), Burns (George), Caine (Michael), Candy (John), Chase (Chevy), Clift (Montgomery), Cosby (Bill), Dafoe (Willem), Davis (Clifton, Ossie, Sammy Jr.), Delon (Alain), Donat (Robert), Evans (Maurice), Ewell (Tom), Finch (Peter), Firth (Colin, Peter), Flynn (Errol), Fonda (Henry, Peter), Franz (Dennis), Gabin (Jean), Gable (Clark), Gould (Elliot), Grant (Cary, Hugh), Gwenn (Edmund), Hanks (Tom), Hardy (Oliver), Hauer (Rutger), Hawke (Ethan), Hayes (Gabby), Hogan (Paul), Irons (Jeremy), Jaffe (Sam), Jones (Dean, James Earl, Tommy Lee), Kazan (Elia), Keach (Stacy), Keith (Brian, David), Kelly (Gene), Kiley (Richard), Kline (Kevin), Kotto (Yaphet), Lamas (Fernando, Lorenzo), Lanza (Mario), Lewis (Jerry, Richard), Lloyd (Harold), Lorre (Peter), Lukas (Paul), Lynde (Paul), March (Fredric), Mason (James), McCoy (Tim), Mills (John), Mineo (Sal), Moore (Dudley, Roger, Victor), Neill (Sam), Nimoy (Leonard), Niven (David), Nolte (Nick), Olmos (Edward James), O'Neal (Patrick, Ryan), O'Shea (Milo), Payne (John), Perry (Luke Matthew), Pesci (Joe), Power (Tyrone), Price (Vincent), Pryce (Jonathan), Quaid (Dennis, Randy), Quinn (Aidan, Anthony), Rains (Claude), Reeve (Christopher), Scott (Campbell, George C., Randolph), Segal (George), Sheen (Charlie, Martin), Smits (Jimmy), Stack (Robert), Stamp (Terence), Sydow (Max von), Tracy (Spencer), Wayne (John), Wilde (Cornel), Wills (Chill), Woods (James), Young (Gig, Robert) **6** Abbott (Bud), Albert (Eddie), Ameche (Don), Arness (James), Backus (Jim), Balsam (Martin), Barker (Lex), Baxter (Warner), Beatty (Ned, Warren), Begley (Ed), Blades (Ruben), Bogart (Humphrey), Bolger (Ray), Brando (Marlon), Brooks (Albert, Mel), Burton (Richard), Caesar (Sid), Cagney (James), Cantor (Eddie), Cariou (Len), Carney (Art), Carrey (Jim), Carvey (Dana), Chaney (Lon), Cleese (John), Coburn (Charles, James), Colman (Ronald), Conrad (Robert, William), Conway (Tim, Tom), Coogan (Jackie), Cooper (Gary), Cotten (Joseph), Coward (Noël), Crabbe (Buster), Crenna (Richard), Cronyn (Hume), Crosby (Bing), Cruise (Tom), Culkin (Macaulay), Curtis (Tony), Dailey (Dan), Dalton (Timothy), Danson (Ted), Danton (Ray), Darren (James), De Niro (Robert), de Sica (Vittorio), De Vito (Danny), Dillon (Matt), Downey (Robert), Dullea (Keir), Duryea (Dan), Duvall (Robert), Ferrer (José, Mel), Fields (W.C.), Finney (Albert), Garcia (Andy), Garner (James), Gibson (Hoot, Mel), Glover (Danny), Graves (Peter), Greene (Lorne), Grodin (Charles), Harris (Ed, Richard), Harvey (Laurence), Hayden (Sterling), Heflin (Van), Heston (Charlton), Hingle (Pat), Holden (Bill), Hopper (Dennis, William), Howard (Leslie, Ron, Trevor), Hudson (Rock), Hunter (Jeffrey, Tab), Huston (John, Walter), Hutton (Jim, Timothy), Irving (Henry), Jacobi (Derek, Lou), Jagger (Dean), Keaton (Buster, Michael), Keitel (Harvey), Kilmer (Val), Knotts (Don), Landau (Martin), Landon (Michael), Laurel (Stan), Lemmon (Jack), Liotta (Ray), Lugosi (Bela), MacRae (Gordon), Malden (Karl), Martin (Dean, Steve), Marvin (Lee), Massey (Raymond), Mature (Victor), McCrea (Joel), Meeker (Ralph), Menjou (Adolphe), Mifune (Toshiro), Modine (Matthew), Morley (Robert),

Mostel (Zero), Murphy (Audie, Eddie), Murray (Bill, Don), Neeson (Liam), Nelson (Ozzie), Newley (Anthony), Newman (Paul), O'Brian (Hugh), O'Brien (Edmund, Pat), Oldman (Gary), O'Toole (Peter), Pacino (Al), Parker (Fess), Poston (Tom), Powell (Dick), Quayle (Anthony), Reeves (Keanu, Steve), Reiner (Carl, Rob), Reiser (Paul), Rennie (Michael), Ritter (John, Tex), Rogers (Roy, Wayne, Will), Romero (Cesar), Rooney (Mickey), Rourke (Mickey), Schell (Maximilian), Seagal (Steven), Sharif (Omar), Slezak (Walter), Snipes (Wesley), Spacey (Kevin), Spader (James), Swayze (Patrick), Taylor (Robert, Rod), Thomas (Danny, Richard), Turpin (Ben), Vallee (Rudy), Vaughn (Robert), Voight (Jon), Wagner (Robert), Walker (Robert), Warden (Jack), Wayans (Damon, Keenen Ivory), Weaver (Dennis, Fritz), Welles (Orson), Werner (Oskar), Wilder (Gene), Willis (Bruce) **7** Abraham (F. Murray), Andrews (Dana), Astaire (Fred), Aykroyd (Dan), Baldwin (Alec, Daniel, Stephen, William), Bellamy (Ralph), Bogarde (Dirk), Branagh (Kenneth), Bridges (Beau, Jeff, Lloyd), Bronson (Charles), Brosnan (Pierce), Brynner (Yul), Burbage (Richard), Bushman (Francis X.), Buttons (Red), Calhern (Louis), Calhoun (Rory), Cameron (Rod), Carroll (Leo G.), Chaplin (Charlie), Clooney (George), Connery (Sean), Connors (Chuck), Conried (Hans), Costner (Kevin), Crystal (Billy), Daniels (Jeff), da Silva (Howard), DeLuise (Dom), Dennehy (Brian), Donahue (Troy), Donlevy (Brian), Douglas (Kirk, Melvyn, Michael, Paul), Durante (Jimmy), Edwards (Vince), Feldman (Marty), Fiennes (Ralph), Freeman (Morgan), Garrick (David), Gazzara (Ben), Gielgud (John), Gleason (Jackie), Goodman (John), Gosling (Ryan), Gossett (Lou), Grammer (Kelsey), Granger (Farley, Stewart), Gulager (Clu), Hackman (Gene), Henreid (Paul), Hoffman (Dustin), Homolka (Oscar), Hopkins (Anthony), Hoskins (Bob), Janssen (David), Johnson (Ben, Don, Van), Jourdan (Louis), Jurgens (Curt), Karloff (Boris), Kennedy (Arthur, George), Klugman (Jack), Lawford (Peter), Leonard (Robert Sean, Sheldon), Lithgow (John), MacLane (Barton), Maharis (George), Mathers (Jerry), Matthau (Walter), McCarey (Leo), McGavin (Darren), McQueen (Steve), Milland (Ray), Mitchum (Robert), Montand (Yves), Morales (Esai), Navarro (Ramon), Newhart (Bob), O'Connor (Carroll, Donald), Olivier (Laurence), Palance (Jack), Paulsen (Pat), Peppard (George), Perkins (Anthony), Pickens (Slim), Pidgeon (Walter), Poitier (Sidney), Preston (Robert), Randall (Tony), Redford (Robert), Rickman (Alan), Robards (Jason), Robbins (Tim), Robeson (Paul), Roberts (Pernell, Tony), Sanders (George), Savalas (Telly), Scourby (Alexander), Selleck (Tom), Sellers (Peter), Shatner (William), Shepard (Sam), Silvers (Phil), Sinatra (Frank), Skelton (Red), Skinner (Otis), Steiger (Rod), Stewart (James, Patrick), Stooges (Three), Tamblyn (Russ), Ustinov (Peter), Van Dyke (Dick, Jerry), Wallach (Eli), Widmark (Richard), Wilding (Michael), Winters (Jonathan), Woolley (Monty) **8** Banderas (Antonio), Barrault (Jean-Louis), Basehart (Richard), Belmondo (Jean-Paul), Berenger (Tom), Blackmer (Sidney), Borgnine (Ernest), Buchanan (Edgar), Buchholz (Horst), Chandler (Jeff), Costello (Lou), Crawford (Broderick, Michael), Cummings (Robert), Day-Lewis (Daniel), DiCaprio (Leonardo), Dreyfuss (Richard), Eastwood (Clint), Forsythe (John), Garfield (John), Goldblum (Jeff), Griffith (Andy), Guinness (Alec), Harrison (Noel, Rex), Hemmings (David), Holbrook (Hal), Holloway (Stanley), Houseman (John), Jannings (Emil), Kingsley (Ben), Langella (Frank), Laughton (Charles), Marshall (E.G., Herbert), McDowall (Roddy), McDowell (Malcolm), McGregor (Ewan), McLaglen (Victor), Meredith (Burgess), Rathbone (Basil), Redgrave (Michael), Reynolds (Burt), Ritchard (Cyril), Robinson (Edward G.), Sarrazin (Michael), Scofield (Paul), Seinfeld (Jerry), Stallone (Sylvester), Stroheim (Erich von), Sullivan (Barry), Travolta (John), Turturro (John), Van Damme (Jean-Claude), Von Sydow (Max), Whitaker (Forest), Whitmore (James), Williams (Robin) **9** Amsterdam (Morey), Barrymore (John, Lionel), Brandauer (Klaus Maria), Broderick (Matthew), Carnovsky (Morris), Carradine (David, John, Keith, Robert), Courtenay (Tom), Depardieu (Gérard), Fairbanks (Douglas), Fishburne (Larry), Franciosa (Anthony), Hardwicke (Cedric), Harrelson (Woody), Hyde-White (Wilfrid), Lancaster (Burt), MacMurray (Fred), Malkovich (John), Montalban (Ricardo), Nicholson (Jack), Pleasance (Donald), Robertson (Cliff, Dale), Strasberg (Lee), Tarantino (Quentin), Valentino (Rudolph), Zimbalist (Efrem) **10** Fitzgerald (Barry), Hasselhoff (David), Montgomery (Robert), Richardson (Ralph), Sutherland (Donald, Kiefer), Washington (Denzel) **11** Chamberlain (Richard), Greenstreet (Sydney), Mastroianni (Marcello), Trintignant (Jean-Louis) **13** Kristofferson (Kris)

actor's
quest: 4 part, role
signal: 3 cue

actress
3 Bow (Clara), Cox (Courtney), Day (Doris), Dee (Ruby, Sandra), Dru (Joanne), Gam (Rita), Loy (Myrna), May (Elaine), Rae (Charlotte) **4** Alba (Jessica), Ball (Lucille), Bara (Theda), Barr (Roseanne), Cass (Peggy), Cher, Coca (Imogene), Cruz (Penelope), Dahl (Arlene), Daly

(Tyne), Dern (Laura), Diaz (Cameron), Dors (Diana), Down (Lesley-Ann), Duke (Patty), Duse (Eleonora), Eden (Barbara), Foch (Nina), Garr (Teri), Gish (Dorothy, Lillian), Grey (Jennifer), Gwyn (Nell), Hawn (Goldie), Holm (Celeste), Hunt (Helen, Linda, Marsha), Hurt (Mary Beth), Hyer (Martha), Ivey (Judith), Kahn (Madeline), Kerr (Deborah), Lake (Veronica), Lisi (Virna), Long (Nia, Shelley), Main (Marjorie), Mayo (Virginia), Neal (Patricia), Olin (Lena), Page (Geraldine), Raye (Martha), Rigg (Diana), Ross (Diana, Katharine), Rush (Barbara), Ryan (Meg, Peggy), Shue (Elisabeth), Weld (Tuesday), West (Mae), Wood (Natalie, Peggy), Wray (Fay), York (Susannah) **5** Adams (Maude), Aimee (Anouk), Allen (Joan, Gracie, Karen, Nancy), Alley (Kirstie), Arden (Eve), Astor (Mary), Bates (Kathy), Berry (Halle), Black (Karen), Bloom (Claire), Blyth (Ann), Booth (Shirley), Brice (Fanny), Britt (May), Bruce (Virginia), Buzzi (Ruth), Caron (Leslie), Close (Glenn), Crain (Jeanne), Danes (Claire), Davis (Bette, Geena, Judy), Dench (Judi), Derek (Bo), Dunne (Irene), Eggar (Samantha), Evans (Edith), Falco (Edie), Field (Sally), Fonda (Bridget, Jane), Gabor (Eva, Zsa Zsa), Garbo (Greta), Gless (Sharon), Grant (Lee), Greer (Jane), Grier (Pam), Hagen (Uta), Hasso (Signe), Hayek (Salma), Hayes (Helen), Heche (Anne), Henie (Sonja), Howes (Sally Ann), Jones (Cherry, Jennifer, Shirley), Kazan (Lainie), Kelly (Grace, Patsy), Kurtz (Swoosie), Lahti (Christine), Lange (Hope, Jessica), Leigh (Janet, Jennifer Jason, Vivien), Lenya (Lotte), Lewis (Juliette), Loren (Sophia), Mason (Marsha, Pamela), Meara (Anne), Miles (Sarah, Vera), Moore (Demi, Julianne, Mary Tyler, Terry), Naldi (Nita), North (Sheree), Novak (Kim), O'Hara (Maureen), Olson (Nancy), O'Neal (Tatum), Perez (Rosie), Picon (Molly), Pitts (Zasu), Reese (Della), Ricci (Christina), Roman (Ruth), Ruehl (Mercedes), Ryder (Winona), Saint (Eva Marie), Scott (Lizbeth, Martha), Shire (Talia), Smith (Alexis, Maggie), Stone (Sharon), Storm (Gale), Swank (Hilary), Tandy (Jessica), Terry (Ellen), Tomei (Marisa), Tyler (Liv), Tyson (Cicely), Watts (Naomi), Welch (Raquel), Wiest (Dianne), Wyatt (Jane), Wyman (Jane), Young (Sean, Loretta) **6** Adjani (Isabelle), Angeli (Pier), Arthur (Beatrice, Jean), Ashley (Elizabeth), Bacall (Lauren), Bardot (Brigitte), Barkin (Ellen), Barrie (Wendy), Baxter (Anne), Bening (Annette), Bergen (Candice, Polly), Bisset (Jacqueline), Blaine (Vivian), Brooks (Louise), Bujold (Genevieve), Butler (Brett), Cannon (Dyan), Carter (Dixie, Lynda, Nell), Cooper (Gladys), Crouse (Lindsay), Curtin (Jane), Curtis (Jamie Lee), Danner (Blythe), Davies (Marion), Del Rio (Dolores), Dennis (Sandy), Diller (Phyllis), Draper (Ruth), Driver (Minnie), Dumont (Margaret), Duncan (Sandy), Durbin (Deanna), Duvall (Shelley), Ekberg (Anita), Ekland (Britt), Fabray (Nanette), Farmer (Frances), Farrow (Mia), Feldon (Barbara), Fisher (Carrie), Foster (Jodie), Garner (Peggy Ann), Garson (Greer), Gaynor (Mitzi), Gordon (Ruth), Grable (Betty), Grimes (Tammy), Hannah (Daryl), Harlow (Jean), Harper (Jessica, Tess, Valerie), Harris (Barbara, Julie, Rosemary), Hedren (Tippi), Hiller (Wendy), Hunter (Holly, Kim), Hussey (Ruth), Huston (Anjelica), Hutton (Betty), Irving (Amy), Keaton (Diane), Keeler (Ruby), Kidman (Nicole), Kinski (Nastassja), Knight (Shirley), Lamarr (Hedy), Lamour (Dorothy), Lasser (Louise), Laurie (Piper), Lillie (Beatrice), Louise (Tina), Lupino (Ida), MacRae (Sheila), Malone (Dorothy), Martin (Mary), Matlin (Marlee), McGraw (Ali), Merkel (Una), Merman (Ethel), Midler (Bette), Miller (Ann), Mirren (Helen), Monroe (Marilyn), Moreau (Jeanne), Moreno (Rita), Oberon (Merle), O'Brien (Margaret), Oliver (Edna May), Palmer (Lili), Paquin (Anna), Parker (Eleanor, Mary-Louise, Sarah Jessica, Suzy), Peters (Bernadette), Powers (Stephanie), Prowse (Juliet), Rainer (Luise), Rashad (Phylicia), Remick (Lee), Ritter (Thelma), Rivera (Chita), Rogers (Ginger), Scales (Prunella), Seberg (Jean), Sidney (Sylvia), Somers (Suzanne), Sommer (Elke), Spacek (Sissy), Streep (Meryl), Taylor (Elizabeth), Temple (Shirley), Theron (Charlize), Thomas (Marlo), Tiffin (Pamela), Tomlin (Lily), Turner (Kathleen, Lana), Walker (Nancy), Warren (Lesley Ann), Watson (Emily), Weaver (Sigourney), Wilson (Marie), Winger (Debra), Wright (Teresa), Wynter (Dana) **7** Allyson (June), Andress (Ursula), Andrews (Julie), Aniston (Jennifer), Bassett (Angela), Bennett (Constance, Joan), Bergman (Ingrid), Binoche (Juliette), Blethyn (Brenda), Buckley (Betty), Bullock (Sandra), Burnett (Carol), Burstyn (Ellen), Colbert (Claudette), Collins (Joan, Pauline), Cornell (Katherine), Cushman (Charlotte), Darnell (Linda), DeCarlo (Yvonne), Delaney (Dana), Deneuve (Catherine), Dukakis (Olympia), Dunaway (Faye), Dunnock (Mildred), Fawcett (Farrah), Fleming (Rhonda), Fricker (Brenda), Gardner (Ava), Garland (Judy), Gershon (Gina), Gingold (Hermione), Goddard (Paulette), Grahame (Gloria), Grayson (Kathryn), Hayward (Susan), Heckart (Eileen), Hepburn (Audrey, Katharine), Hershey (Barbara), Jackson (Anne, Glenda, Kate), Langtry (Lillie), Learned (Michael), Lombard (Carole), MacGraw (Ali), Madonna, Magnani (Anna), Mangano (Silvana), McGuire (Dorothy), McKenna (Siobhan), McQueen (Butterfly), Meadows (Audrey, Jayne), Mimieux (Yvette), Miranda (Carmen), Mulgrew (Kate), Natwick (Mildred), Parsons (Estelle), Perlman (Rhea), Perrine (Valerie), Plummer

(Amanda), Podesta (Rosanna), Portman (Natalie), Roberts (Julia), Russell (Jane, Rosalind, Theresa), Scacchi (Greta), Sevigny (Chloë), Shearer (Norma), Shields (Brooke), Siddons (Sarah), Simmons (Jean), Sorvino (Mira), Sothern (Ann), Stevens (Connie, Stella), Stritch (Elaine), Swanson (Gloria), Swinton (Tilda), Thaxter (Phyllis), Thurman (Uma), Tierney (Gene), Ullmann (Liv), Verdugo (Elena), Winfrey (Oprah), Winslet (Kate), Winters (Shelley), Withers (Jane), Woodard (Alfre) **8** Anderson (Judith, Loni, Melissa Sue), Arquette (Patricia, Rosanna), Ashcroft (Peggy), Bancroft (Anne), Bankhead (Tallulah), Basinger (Kim), Blondell (Joan), Byington (Spring), Caldwell (Zoe), Campbell (Mrs. Patrick), Channing (Carol, Stockard), Charisse (Cyd), Christie (Julie), Crawford (Joan), DeMornay (Rebecca), Dewhurst (Colleen), Dietrich (Marlene), Dressler (Marie), Fletcher (Louise), Fontaine (Joan), Fontanne (Lynn), Goldberg (Whoopi), Griffith (Melanie), Hayworth (Rita), Holliday (Judy), Lansbury (Angela), Lawrence (Gertrude), Leachman (Cloris), Leighton (Margaret), Lindfors (Viveca), Lockhart (June), Lovelace (Linda), MacLaine (Shirley), McDaniel (Hattie), Mercouri (Melina), Minnelli (Liza), Nelligan (Kate), Neuwirth (Bebe), O'Donnell (Rosie), Pfeiffer (Michelle), Pickford (Mary), Prentiss (Paula), Redgrave (Lynn, Vanessa), Reynolds (Debbie), Roseanne, Rowlands (Gena), Sarandon (Susan), Shepherd (Cybill), Signoret (Simone), Spelling (Tori), Stanwyck (Barbara), Straight (Beatrice), Sullavan (Margaret), Talmadge (Norma), Thompson (Emma, Sada), Van Doren (Mamie), Vardalos (Nia), Williams (Esther), Woodward (Joanne) **9** Alexander (Jane), Barrymore (Drew, Ethel), Bernhardt (Sarah), Blanchett (Cate), Cardinale (Claudia), Christian (Linda), Clayburgh (Jill), Dandridge (Dorothy), DeGeneres (Ellen), Dickinson (Angie), Fairchild (Morgan), Henderson (Florence), Kellerman (Sally), Mansfield (Jayne), McDonnell (Mary), Moorehead (Agnes), O'Sullivan (Maureen), Pleshette (Suzanne), Plowright (Joan), Schneider (Romy), Singleton (Penny), Stapleton (Jean, Maureen), Strasberg (Susan), Streisand (Barbra), Struthers (Sally), Thorndike (Sybil), Vera-Ellen, Zellweger (Renée) **10** Ann-Margret, Lanchester (Elsa), Montgomery (Elizabeth), Richardson (Miranda, Natasha), Rossellini (Isabella), Rutherford (Margaret), Tushingham (Rita) **11** de Havilland (Olivia), McCambridge (Mercedes), Riefenstahl (Leni), Silverstone (Alicia), Steenburgen (Mary) **12** Bonham-Carter (Helena), Lollabrigida (Gina), Mastrantonio (Mary Elizabeth)

actual
4 echt, hard, live, real, true **5** exact **6** extant, living **7** certain, current, de facto, factual, genuine **8** absolute, bona fide, concrete, definite, existent, existing, material, physical, positive, tangible **9** authentic, objective, veritable **10** legitimate, phenomenal **12** indisputable

actuality
4 fact **5** being, truth **7** reality **9** existence, substance **10** embodiment **11** incarnation, materiality

actually
4 very **5** truly **6** indeed, in fact, really **7** de facto, no doubt **9** genuinely, in reality, veritably **10** absolutely

actuate
4 move, spur, stir **5** drive, impel, rouse **6** arouse, excite, propel, set off, turn on **7** provoke, trigger **8** activate, energize, mobilize, motivate, vitalize

act up
5 cut up **7** show off **9** misbehave **11** misfunction

acumen
3 wit **6** acuity, vision, wisdom **7** insight **8** keenness **9** acuteness, sharpness **10** astuteness, perception, shrewdness **11** discernment, penetration, percipience **12** perspicacity

acute
4 dire, keen **5** sharp **6** urgent **7** crucial, exigent, intense, pointed **8** critical, incisive, piercing, shooting, stabbing **9** knifelike, observant, trenchant **10** perceptive **11** penetrating, quick-witted, sharp-witted

ad ___
3 hoc, lib, rem **7** hominem, interim, nauseam **9** infinitum

adage
3 saw **4** rule **5** axiom, maxim, motto **6** byword, saying, truism **7** proverb **8** aphorism, apothegm

adagio
4 slow **5** tempo

Adah
husband: **4** Esau **6** Lamech
son: **5** Jabal, Jubal **7** Eliphaz

Adam
grandson: **4** Enos **5** Enoch
rib: **3** Eve
son: **4** Abel, Cain, Seth
wife: **3** Eve **6** Lilith

Adam ___
4 Bede **5** Smith

adamant
3 set **4** firm, hard **5** rigid, stiff, stone, tough

6 flinty 8 immobile, obdurate, resolute 9 immovable, unbending, unswaying 10 determined, inflexible, unbendable, unyielding 11 unbreakable

adapt
3 fit 4 suit 5 alter, shape, yield 6 adjust, change, modify, revise, square, tailor 7 arrange, conform, remodel 9 acclimate, habituate, reconcile 11 acclimatize, accommodate

adaptable
6 mobile, pliant, supple 7 ductile, plastic, pliable 8 flexible, moldable 9 malleable, versatile

adaptation
6 change 8 revision 9 reworking 10 adjustment, alteration 12 modification

ad astra per ____
6 aspera

add
3 sum, tot 4 cast, foot, join, tote 5 affix, annex, count, tally, total, unite 6 append, attach, figure, reckon, tack on, take on 7 augment, compute, count up, enlarge, improve, include 8 compound, increase, totalize 9 build onto, calculate 10 supplement

Addams family
5 Gomez 7 Pugsley 8 Morticia 9 Grandmama, Wednesday 11 Uncle Fester
servants: 5 Lurch, Thing

added
3 new 4 else, more 5 extra, fresh, other 7 another, farther, further 9 accessory 10 additional 13 supplementary

addendum
5 extra, rider 8 addition 10 supplement

adder
5 snake, viper 10 calculator 12 hognose snake

addict
3 fan, nut 4 bias, buff 5 hound, lover 6 abuser, devote, junkie, zealot 7 booster, devotee, fanatic, groupie, habitué 9 habituate, surrender 10 aficionado, enthusiast

addition
4 plus, rise 5 annex, extra, raise, rider 7 accrual, adjunct 8 addendum, appendix, increase 9 accession, accessory, accretion, extension, increment 10 supplement 11 enlargement 12 appurtenance, augmentation

additional
see **added**

additionally
3 too 4 also, more, then 5 again 6 as well 7 besides, further 8 likewise, moreover 11 furthermore

additive
5 extra 8 extender 9 summative, substance

addle
5 mix up, spoil 6 muddle, puzzle 7 confuse, fluster, nonplus, perplex 8 befuddle, bewilder, confound, distract, throw off 9 dumbfound

add-on
3 ell 7 adjunct 9 accessory 11 enhancement

address
3 aim, air, set, URL 4 hail, send, tact, talk 5 apply, court, grace, greet, level, place, point, poise, remit, route, skill, speak, treat 6 call to, devote, direct, pursue, relate, salute, speech 7 bearing, consign, deliver, forward, know-how, lecture, oration, speak to, write to 8 appeal to, approach, converse, deal with, deftness, delivery, demeanor, dispatch, identify, location, petition, position, presence, transmit 9 attention, dexterity, diplomacy, expertise 10 adroitness, competence, directions, efficiency 11 comportment, designation, proficiency, savoir faire

adduce
3 lay 4 cite 5 claim, offer 6 allege, submit, tender 7 advance, present, proffer, propose, refer to, suggest 8 document 9 exemplify 10 illustrate

add up
3 sum 5 count, tally, total 6 amount, reckon 7 compute 9 make sense

add up to
4 mean 5 spell 6 amount, denote, import, intend 7 compute, connote, express, signify

adept
3 pro 4 able, deft, whiz 5 crack, savvy 6 adroit, expert, master, wizard 7 skilled 8 masterly, skillful, virtuoso 9 dexterous, masterful 10 proficient 11 crackerjack 12 professional

adequacy
5 might 6 enough 7 ability 8 capacity 10 capability, competence, sufficient 11 sufficiency 13 qualification

adequate
6 common, decent, enough 8 all right, passable, pleasing, standard, suitable 9 competent, sufficing 10 acceptable, sufficient 11 comfortable 12 satisfactory 13 unexceptional, unimpeachable

adequately
4 well 5 amply, right 6 enough 8 all right, passably, properly, suitably 9 fittingly, tolerably 12 sufficiently 13 appropriately

adhere
4 bond, glue 5 cling, paste, stick 6 attach, bind to, cement, cleave, cohere, fasten 7 stick to 8 hold fast

adherence
4 bond **5** cling **7** loyalty **8** adhesion, clinging, cohesion, fidelity, sticking **9** constancy **10** attachment **12** faithfulness

adherent
3 fan, ist **6** cohort, votary **7** devotee, sectary **8** disciple, follower, henchman, partisan, stalwart **9** satellite, supporter **10** aficionado

adhering
6 clingy, sticky **7** binding

adhesive
4 glue **5** epoxy, gluey, gooey, gummy, stamp, tacky **6** cement, clingy, gummed, sticky **7** holding, stickum **8** adhering, fastener, mucilage, sticking **9** attaching

adieu
3 bye **4** ciao, ta-ta **5** congé **6** bye-bye, so long **7** cheerio, good-bye, parting, toodles **8** farewell, toodle-oo **11** leave-taking

ad interim
6 acting, pro tem **9** temporary **10** pro tempore **11** temporarily

adios
4 by-by, ciao, ta-ta **5** adieu, later **6** bye-bye, so long **7** cheerio, goodbye, toodles **8** farewell, toodle-oo **10** hasta luego

adipose
3 fat **4** oily **5** fatty **6** greasy **7** fatlike

adit
3 way **4** door **5** entry **6** access, entrée, tunnel **7** ingress, passage **8** entrance **9** mine entry **10** passageway **12** mine entrance

adjacent
4 near **5** close **6** beside, nearby, next to **8** abutting, next door, touching **9** adjoining, alongside, bordering **10** contiguous, juxtaposed, near-at-hand **11** close-at-hand, neighboring **12** conterminous

adjoin
3 add **4** abut, link, line, meet **5** annex, touch, verge **6** append, attach, border, butt on, couple **7** connect, impinge **8** neighbor **11** communicate

adjourn
4 move, rise, stay **5** defer, delay **6** hold up, put off, recess, shelve **7** hold off, suspend **8** dissolve, hold over, postpone, prorogue **9** prorogate

adjudge
4 deem, rule **5** award, grant **6** decide, settle, umpire **7** mediate, referee **9** arbitrate

adjunct
5 added, affix **6** joined **8** addendum, addition, appanage, appendix, attached **9** accessory, accretion, appendage, assistant, associate, auxiliary **10** attachment **12** appurtenance

adjure
3 beg, bid **4** urge **6** exhort **7** beseech, entreat, command, implore, require **9** importune **10** supplicate

adjust
3 fit, fix, rig **4** suit, tune **5** adapt, order, right **6** accord, attune, modify, orient, settle, square, tailor, tune up **7** arrange, conform, correct, rectify, resolve **8** modulate, regulate **9** habituate, harmonize, reconcile **11** accommodate

adjutant
4 aide **6** deputy

adjuvant
4 aide **6** aiding, helper **8** enhancer, modifier **9** accessory, ancillary, assisting, auxiliary **10** collateral, subsidiary **11** appurtenant **12** contributory

ad-lib
9 extempore, improvise, impromptu **10** improvised, off-the-cuff, unprepared **11** extemporize, spontaneous, unrehearsed

Admetus
father: **6** Pheres
wife: **8** Alcestis

administer
3 run **4** boss, deal, give, head **5** issue **6** direct, govern, head up, manage **7** conduct, control, deal out, deliver, dole out, execute, give out, mete out, oversee, perform, provide **8** carry out, dispense, share out **9** apportion, supervise **10** distribute, portion out

administration
6 regime **7** control **9** direction **10** governance, presidency
system of: **11** bureaucracy

administrator
4 boss, exec, head **5** chief **7** manager, officer **8** director, official, overseer **9** executive **10** supervisor

admirable
6 august, worthy **8** laudable **9** deserving, estimable, excellent, meritable **11** commendable, meritorious, outstanding **12** praiseworthy

admiral
American: **4** Byrd (Richard), Sims (William) **5** Dewey (George), Stark (Harold) **6** Halsey (Bull), Nimitz (Chester) **7** Zumwalt (Elmo) **8** Farragut (David), Rickover (Hyman), Spruance (Raymond)
Chinese: **7** Zheng He
Confederate: **6** Semmes (Raphael)
Dutch: **5** Tromp (Maarten)
English: **5** Drake (Francis) **6** Nelson (Horatio), Rodney (George), Vernon (Edward) **7** Hawkins (John) **8** Beaufort (Francis), Jellicoe (John), Villiers (George) **11** Mountbatten (Louis)

fictional: **10** Hornblower (Horatio)
French: **10** Villeneuve (Pierre-Charles)
German: **4** Spee (Graf Maximilian von) **6** Dönitz (Karl), Raeder (Erich) **7** Doenitz (Karl), Tirpitz (Alfred von)
Japanese: **4** Togo (Hideki) **5** Yonai (Mitsumasa) **8** Yamamoto (Isoroku)
Spanish: **8** Menéndez (Pedro)

admiration
5 favor **6** esteem, praise, regard **7** account, delight, respect **8** applause, approval, pleasure **9** affection **10** estimation **11** approbation **12** appreciation

admire
5 adore, honor, prize, value **6** esteem, praise, regard, relish, revere **7** adulate, applaud, approve, cherish, commend, respect **8** consider, treasure **9** delight in **10** appreciate

admirer
3 fan **4** beau, buff **7** booster, devotee, fancier **8** believer, follower, partisan **9** supporter **10** enthusiast

admission
3 way **4** door, gate **5** entry **6** access, assent, entrée **7** ingress **8** entrance **10** admittance, concession, confession **11** affirmation

admit
3 own **4** avow, take **5** agree, allow, enter, grant, let in, let on, lodge, own up **6** accept, fess up, harbor, permit, suffer, take in **7** concede, confess, receive, shelter, welcome **9** entertain, introduce, recognize **11** acknowledge

admix
5 blend, merge **6** mingle **7** combine **8** commingle, compound, immingle **9** commingle **11** intermingle

admixture
5 alloy, blend, combo **6** fusion **7** amalgam **8** compound **9** aggregate, composite **12** amalgamation

admonish
4 warn **5** alert, chide **6** lesson, monish, rebuke, talk to **7** caution, counsel, reprove, speak to **8** call down, forewarn, reproach **9** criticize, reprimand

admonition
3 tip **6** caveat, rebuke **7** caution, chiding, reproof, warning **8** reproach **9** criticism, reprimand **11** disapproval, forewarning

ado
4 fuss, stir **5** tizzy, whirl, worry **6** bother, bustle, flurry, hubbub, pother **7** concern, problem, trouble, turmoil **9** commotion, confusion **10** difficulty

adolescence
5 youth **7** puberty **8** minority **9** greenness **10** juvenility, pubescence **12** youthfulness

adolescent
4 teen **5** minor **6** teener **7** teenage **8** immature, preadult, teenager, youthful **9** pubescent

Adonai
3 God **4** YHWH **6** Elohim, Yahweh

Adonijah
brother: **5** Amnon **7** Absalom, Chileab
father: **5** David
mother: **7** Haggith
slayer: **7** Benaiah

Adonis
lover: **5** Venus **9** Aphrodite
mother: **5** Myrrh **6** Myrrha
slayer: **4** boar

adopt
4 pick, take **5** raise **6** accept, affect, assume, choose, select, take on, take up **7** care for, embrace, endorse, espouse

adoption
6 choice **7** raising, support **8** espousal, taking in **9** embracing, selection **11** embracement

adorable
4 cute, dear **7** darling, lovable, winsome **8** charming, pleasing, precious **9** appealing **10** attractive, delightful

adoration
4 love **5** ardor, honor **6** esteem, praise **7** passion, worship **8** devotion, idolatry **9** adulation, affection, reverence **10** admiration **11** idolization

adore
4 love **5** honor, prize **6** admire, dote on, esteem, revere **7** cherish, idolize, respect, worship **8** dote upon, treasure, venerate **9** affection, delight in, reverence

adorn
4 deck, trim **5** fix up, grace **6** bedeck, enrich, pretty **7** dress up, enhance, enliven, furbish, garnish, smarten **8** beautify, decorate, ornament, prettify **9** embellish

adornment
5 decor, frill **6** finery **7** garnish **8** ornament, trimming **9** accessory, caparison **10** decoration **13** embellishment

ad rem
3 apt **7** apropos, fitting, germane **8** apposite, material, relevant **9** pertinent **10** applicable, relevantly, to the point **11** applicative, applicatory

adrift
4 asea, lost **5** at sea, loose **6** afloat **7** aimless, mixed up **8** confused, floating, unmoored **10** anchorless, bewildered **11** disoriented, purposeless

adroit
3 apt **4** able, deft **5** adept, canny, handy, savvy,

smart **6** astute, clever, expert, nimble, shrewd **7** cunning, skilled **8** skillful, talented **9** dexterous, ingenious **11** intelligent, quick-witted, resourceful **13** perspicacious

adroitness
3 art **4** gift **5** craft, flair, knack, savvy, skill **7** address, cunning, know-how, prowess **8** deftness **9** adeptness, dexterity, expertise, ingenuity, readiness **10** cleverness, expertness **12** intelligence

adulation
7 acclaim, baloney, blarney, fawning, tribute, worship **8** applause, flattery, soft soap **10** overpraise **11** hero-worship **12** blandishment

adulatory
7 buttery, fawning **8** unctuous **9** kowtowing **10** flattering, obsequious, oleaginous **11** bootlicking, sycophantic

adult
4 aged, ripe **5** grown **6** mature **7** grown-up, matured, ripened **9** full-blown, full-grown **11** full-fledged

adulterate
3 cut **4** thin **5** alloy, dirty, taint, water **6** debase, defile, dilute, doctor, dope up, impair, weaken **7** cheapen, corrupt, defiled, degrade, devalue, diluted, falsify, pollute, tainted, thinned **8** degraded, denature, impurify, polluted, spurious **9** water down **10** tamper with **11** contaminate

adumbrate
3 dim, fog **4** bode, call, hint, mist, veil **5** augur, cloud **6** darken, shadow, sketch **7** becloud, bespeak, betoken, obscure, outline, portend, predict, presage, suggest **8** block out, disclose, forebode, forecast, foretell, indicate, intimate, prophesy **9** obfuscate, prefigure **10** foreshadow, overshadow **11** prefigurate **12** characterize

adumbration
4 hint, sign **5** shade, umbra **6** shadow **7** outline **8** penumbra **10** indication, intimation, suggestion

advance
3 aid **4** cite, help, lend, loan, move, rise **5** get on, march, money, raise, serve **6** assist, course, foster, mature, prefer, supply, uplift **7** deposit, develop, elevate, forward, furnish, further, headway, ongoing, present, proceed, promote, propose, upgrade **8** approach, get along, heighten, increase, progress **9** encourage, evolution, provision **10** accelerate, bring about **11** development, furtherance, improvement, progression **12** breakthrough

advanced
3 old **5** first **6** far out **7** forward, in front, leading, liberal, radical **8** far ahead, foremost **9** developed **10** precocious **11** broad-minded, progressive

advancement
4 gain, rise **5** boost **6** growth **7** headway **8** progress **9** elevation, promotion **10** betterment, preference **11** improvement, progression

advantage
4 boon, edge, gain, good, help, lead, odds **5** asset, avail, serve **6** better, profit **7** account, benefit, mastery **8** blessing, interest, leverage **9** allowance, head start, upper hand **10** ascendancy, domination, leadership, prosperity **11** superiority **12** running start

advantageous
4 good **6** timely, toward, useful **7** benefic, gainful, helpful **8** favoring, salutary **9** conducive, desirable, expedient, favorable, fortunate, promising **10** beneficial, profitable, propitious, worthwhile

advent
5 onset **6** coming **7** arrival **8** approach **9** beginning

adventitious
5 fluky **6** casual, chance, flukey **8** by chance **9** unplanned **10** accidental, contingent, fortuitous, incidental, unexpected

adventure
3 try **4** feat, risk, trip **5** quest, wager **6** chance, gamble, hazard **7** exploit **8** escapade **9** undertake **10** enterprise, experience

adventurous
4 bold, rash **5** brash, risky **6** daring **8** intrepid, reckless **9** audacious, dangerous, daredevil, foolhardy, hazardous, impetuous, imprudent **10** innovative **12** enterprising

adversary
3 con, foe **4** anti **5** enemy, rival **7** opposer **8** opponent, opposing **10** antagonist, competitor

adverse
3 bad **4** anti **7** counter, harmful, hostile, hurtful, opposed **8** contrary, damaging, negative, opposing, opposite **9** injurious **11** deleterious, detrimental, obstructive, unfavorable **12** antagonistic, antipathetic

adversity
4 dole **5** trial **6** misery, mishap **7** bad luck, bad news, trouble **8** bad break, distress, hard time, hardship **9** mischance, suffering **10** difficulty, ill fortune, misfortune

advert
4 cite, note **5** refer **6** allude, notice, remark **7** bring up, mention, observe **8** indicate, point out

advertent
5 aware **7** heedful, mindful **9** attentive, intentive, observant, regardful

advertise
4 drum, hype, plug, puff, push, tout **5** boost, pitch **6** blazon, herald, inform, notify, report **7** advance, apprise, build up, declare, promote, publish, sponsor **8** announce, ballyhoo, proclaim **9** broadcast, publicize **10** annunciate, promulgate

advertisement
4 bill, plug, sign **5** blurb, flyer, promo **6** notice, poster, want ad **7** affiche **8** circular **9** billboard, broadcast, promotion, publicity **10** commercial **11** declaration, publication **12** announcement, proclamation

advertising award
4 Clio

advice
3 aid, tip **4** help, news, view, word **5** input **6** notice **7** caution, counsel, opinion, tidings, warning **8** guidance, teaching **10** admonition, suggestion **11** information, instruction **12** intelligence

advisable
4 wise **5** sound **6** seemly **7** politic, prudent **8** sensible, suitable, tactical **9** desirable, expedient, practical **10** worthwhile **11** recommended **12** advantageous

advise
3 tip **4** tell, tout, urge, warn **5** guide **6** clue in, confer, enjoin, fill in, inform, notify, tip off, wise up **7** apprise, caution, consult, counsel, suggest **8** acquaint, forewarn, instruct, point out **9** encourage, prescribe, recommend

advised
7 studied, weighed **8** designed, intended **10** calculated, considered, deliberate, thought out **11** intentional **12** premeditated

adviser
5 coach, guide **6** mentor **7** counsel, tipster **9** counselor **10** consultant, instructor

advisory
7 guiding, helping **9** educative **10** counseling **12** consultative **13** informational

advocacy
3 aid **6** urging **7** backing, defense, support **9** promotion

advocate
4 back, push, tout, urge **5** favor **6** backer, defend, preach, uphold **7** promote, propose, support **8** argue for, backstop, champion, exponent, plump for, side with **9** encourage, expounder, proponent, recommend, spokesman, supporter **11** countenance

Aeacus
father: **4** Zeus
mother: **6** Aegina
son: **6** Peleus **7** Telamon

Aedon
brother: **7** Amphion
sister-in-law: **5** Niobe
son (victim): **6** Itylus

Aeëtes
daughter: **5** Medea
father: **6** Helios

aegis
4 care, ward **5** armor, guard **6** charge, shield **7** backing, control, defense, support **8** auspices, guidance, security **9** influence, patronage, safeguard **10** protection **11** sponsorship

Aegisthus
father: **8** Thyestes
lover: **12** Clytemnestra
mother: **7** Pelopia
slayer: **7** Orestes
victim: **6** Atreus **9** Agamemnon

Aeneas
companion: **7** Achates
father: **8** Anchises
lover: **4** Dido
mother: **5** Venus **9** Aphrodite
son: **5** Iulus **8** Ascanius
wife: **6** Creusa **7** Lavinia

Aeneid
author: **6** Vergil, Virgil
first words: **16** arma virumque cano
hero: **6** Aeneas

Aeolus
daughter: **7** Alcyone **8** Halcyone
father: **8** Poseidon

aeon
3 age **4** time **6** period **8** blue moon, duration

aerate
7 lighten, freshen, refresh **9** oxygenate, ventilate

aerlal
4 high **5** lofty **6** flying, vapory **7** antenna, soaring **8** birdlike, elevated, ethereal, fanciful, towering, vaporous **9** pneumatic **10** impalpable **11** atmospheric, forward pass

aerie
4 nest **7** citadel, lookout **9** penthouse
resident: **5** eagle **6** eaglet

aeroembolism
5 bends

aeronaut
4 Fogg (Phileas) **5** pilot **7** aviator **8** Zeppelin (Ferdinand, Graf von) **10** balloonist

Aerope
husband: **6** Atreus
lover: **8** Thyestes
son: **8** Menelaus **9** Agamemnon

aery
see **aerial**
Aesculapius
daughter: **6** Hygeia **7** Panacea
father: **6** Apollo
slayer: **4** Zeus **7** Jupiter
teacher: **6** Chiron
wife: **6** Epione
Aeson
brother: **6** Pelias
son: **5** Jason
aesthete
4 buff **6** expert **7** devotee **9** authority **10** dilettante **11** appreciator, cognoscente, connoisseur
aesthetic
6 artful **8** artistic, creative, pleasing **9** beautiful, sensitive **10** attractive, harmonious
afar
5 apart **6** remote **7** distant
affable
4 kind, open, warm **6** at ease, genial, gentle, kindly, polite **7** amiable, cordial **8** friendly, gracious, obliging, pleasant, sociable **9** congenial, courteous
affair
4 case, love **5** amour, fling, worry **6** action, matter **7** concern, liaison, palaver, romance **8** business, function, interest, intrigue, occasion **9** dalliance, happening, procedure **10** proceeding **12** relationship
affect
3 act **4** fake, move, sham, stir, sway **5** act on, adopt, alter, bluff, fancy, feign, haunt, put on, touch **6** assume, change, strike **7** act upon, disturb, impress, inspire, pretend **8** frequent, simulate **9** cultivate, influence
affectation
3 air **4** airs, pose, sham, show **6** facade **8** pretense **9** mannerism **10** pretension **13** artificiality
affected
5 apish, false, moved, phony, put-on **6** phoney **7** altered, assumed, changed, feigned, stilted **8** disposed, inclined, involved, mannered, precious, spurious **9** concerned, conscious, contrived, insincere, pretended, unnatural **10** artificial **11** overrefined, pretentious **13** self-conscious
affecting
3 sad **6** lively, moving **7** pitiful **8** exciting, poignant, touching **9** thrilling **10** disturbing, impressive **11** distressing, influential
affection
4 bias, love **5** trait **6** doting, liking, malady, virtue, warmth **7** ailment, concern, disease, emotion, feature, feeling, illness, leaning, passion, quality **8** devotion, disorder, fondness, interest, penchant, property, sickness, sympathy **9** attention, attribute, character, complaint, condition, sentiment **10** attachment, propensity, tenderness **12** predilection
affectionate
4 dear, fond, warm **6** caring, doting, loving, tender **7** devoted **8** friendly **11** sympathetic
affective
6 moving **7** emotive **8** stirring, touching **9** emotional
affectivity
7 emotion, feeling, passion **9** sentiment
affianced
7 engaged, pledged **8** intended, plighted, promised **9** betrothed, committed **10** contracted
affiche
4 bill, list **6** notice, poster **7** placard **8** handbill
affidavit
4 oath **9** testimony **11** affirmation, declaration
affiliate
4 ally, join **5** annex, unite **6** branch **7** combine, connect, partner **9** associate
affiliated
4 akin **5** bound **6** allied, joined, linked **7** kindred, related **9** connected, dependent **10** associated
affiliation
4 club **5** tie-in, union **6** hookup, league **7** cahoots, company, joining **8** alliance **10** connection, fellowship **11** association, combination, conjunction, partnership
affinity
6 simile **7** analogy, kinship, rapport **8** likeness, relation, sympathy **9** alikeness **10** attraction, similarity, similitude **11** resemblance **13** compatibility
affirm
3 say, yes **4** aver, avow, okay **5** state, swear, vouch **6** assent, assert, attest, depose, ratify, uphold **7** certify, confirm, declare, profess, protest, testify, witness **8** dedicate, validate **9** guarantee
affirmative
3 A-OK, aye, yea, yes **4** yeah **5** roger **6** assent, aye-aye, yessir **7** right on **8** approval, positive **9** affirming, approving, asserting, assertion, endorsing, favorable, ratifying **10** confirming, supporting **11** affirmation
affix
3 add, tag **4** bind, glue, join, nail, tack **5** annex, paste, put on, rivet, stick, tag on **6** append, attach, fasten, tack on **7** impress, stick on, subjoin **8** addition **9** appendage **10** attachment
afflict
3 try, vex **4** pain, rack **5** annoy, beset, harry, press, smite, worry, wound, wring **6** bother,

burden, harass, harrow, injure, martyr, pester, plague, strike, suffer **7** agonize, anguish, torment, torture, trouble **8** distress

afflicted
6 pained, rueful, woeful **7** doleful, injured, unhappy, worried **8** dolorous, stricken, troubled, wretched **9** disturbed, miserable, sorrowful, tormented **10** distressed

affliction
3 woe **4** care **5** cross, grief, trial **6** ordeal, plague, sorrow **7** anguish, illness, scourge, torment, trouble **8** distress, hardship, sickness **9** adversity, heartache, infirmity **10** misfortune **11** tribulation

afflictive
3 sad **4** dire, sore **6** aching, bitter, woeful **7** galling, hurtful, hurting, painful **8** grievous, mournful **9** sorrowful **10** calamitous, deplorable, lamentable **11** distasteful, distressing, regrettable, troublesome, unfortunate, unpalatable **13** heartbreaking

affluence
5 means, worth **6** bounty, influx, plenty, riches, wealth **8** opulence, property, richness **9** abundance, plenitude, profusion, resources **10** prosperity

affluent
4 full, rich **5** flush **6** loaded **7** copious, flowing, moneyed, opulent, upscale, wealthy, well-off **8** abundant, well-to-do **9** bountiful, plentiful, tributary, well-fixed **10** prosperous, well-heeled

afford
4 able, bear, give **5** allow, grant, incur, offer, spare, stand **6** bestow, confer, donate, impart, manage, supply **7** furnish, present, support, sustain

affordable
5 cheap **6** modest **7** low-cost **8** bearable **10** manageable, reasonable **11** inexpensive

affray
3 row **5** clash, fight, melee, scrap **6** fracas, rumpus **7** dispute, quarrel, ruction, scuffle **8** disorder, skirmish

affront
3 vex **4** face, meet, slap, slur **5** abuse, anger, annoy, wrong **6** injury, insult, offend, slight **7** offense, outrage, put down **8** contempt, rudeness **9** aspersion, criticize, encounter, indignity

Afghanistan
capital: **5** Kabul
city: **5** Herat **8** Kandahar **12** Mazar-i-Sharif
ethnic group: **7** Pashtun
language: **4** Dari **6** Pashto
monetary unit: **7** Afghani
neighbor: **4** Iran **5** China **8** Pakistan **10** Tajikistan, Uzbekistan **12** Turkmenistan

aficionado
3 fan **4** buff **5** hound, lover **6** expert **7** admirer, devotee, habitué **10** enthusiast **11** appreciator

afield
4 afar, away, awry **5** amiss, badly, wrong **6** abroad, astray **8** straying **9** elsewhere, off course

afire
3 hot **5** aglow, fiery **6** ablaze, aflame, alight, red-hot **7** blazing, burning, excited, flaming, flaring, ignited, kindled **8** inflamed, in flames **9** energized, excitable **10** passionate **11** conflagrant

afloat
4 asea **5** at sea **6** adrift, buoyed **9** supported, sustained

afraid
4 wary **5** chary, jumpy, loath, scary, sorry, timid **6** averse, scared, trepid **7** anxious, fearful, uneager, worried **8** cautious, hesitant, skittish, timorous **9** concerned, regretful, reluctant, unwilling **10** frightened **11** disinclined **12** apprehensive

afresh
3 new **4** anew, over **5** again, newly **6** de novo, encore **8** once more, repeated **9** once again

Africa
country: **4** Chad, Mali, Togo **5** Benin, Congo, Egypt, Gabon, Ghana, Kenya, Libya, Niger, Sudan, Zaire **6** Angola, Gambia, Guinea, Malawi, Rwanda, Uganda, Zambia **7** Algeria, Burundi, Comoros, Eritrea, Lesotho, Liberia, Morocco, Namibia, Nigeria, Senegal, Somalia, Tunisia **8** Botswana, Cameroon, Djibouti, Ethiopia, Tanzania, Zimbabwe **9** Cape Verde, Mauritius, Swaziland **10** Ivory Coast, Madagascar, Mauritania, Mozambique, Seychelles **11** Burkina Faso, Côte d'Ivoire, Sierra Leone, South Africa **12** Guinea-Bissau
ethnic group: **3** Ibo **4** Akan, Arab, Baya, Boer, Copt, Fula, Issa, Jebu, Moor, Zulu **5** Bantu, Fulah, Galla, Hausa, Kongo, Mande, Pygmy, Swazi, Wolof, Xhosa **6** Berber, Fulani, Hamite, Herero, Kikuyu, Nubian, Somali, Tuareg, Ubangi, Yoruba **7** Ashanti, Bedouin, Bushman, Malinke, Swahili, Touareg **8** Egyptian, Mandingo **9** Hottentot
language: **3** Ibo **4** Taal **5** Bantu, Galla, Hausa, Xhosa **6** Arabic, Berber, Somali, Yoruba **7** Amharic, Bambara, Swahili **8** Malagasy **9** Afrikaans

aft
6 astern **8** rearmost, rearward **9** sternward

after
4 back, hind, next, past, rear **5** below, later, since **6** astern, back of, behind, beyond, hinder

7 ensuing 8 hindmost 9 following, posterior, sternward 10 subsequent

after all
3 yet 5 still 6 at last, though 7 finally, however 8 in the end 11 nonetheless 12 nevertheless

aftereffect
5 issue 6 result, upshot 7 fallout, outcome 11 consequence, eventuality

afterlife
6 beyond 8 eternity 9 hereafter

aftermath
4 wake 6 effect, result, upshot 12 consequences, repercussion

afterward
4 next, soon, then 5 later 6 behind 7 by and by, thereon 8 latterly 9 hereafter 10 thereafter 12 subsequently

afterword
5 envoi 6 epilog 8 epilogue

Agag
kingdom: 6 Amalek
slayer: 6 Samuel

again
3 bis 4 also, anew, back, over 6 afresh, de novo, encore 8 once more

again and again
3 oft 4 much 5 often 8 ofttimes 10 frequently, oftentimes, repeatedly 11 continually

against
3 con 4 anti 6 contra, facing, versus 7 vis-à-vis 8 fronting, opposite, touching
prefix: 4 anti 6 contra 7 counter

Agamemnon
avenger: 7 Orestes
brother: 8 Menelaus
daughter: 7 Electra 9 Iphigenia
father: 6 Atreus
slayer: 9 Aegisthus
son: 7 Orestes
wife: 12 Clytemnestra

agape
4 love, open 6 amazed 7 yawning 8 wide open 9 astounded, love feast 10 astonished, confounded 11 dumbfounded, overwhelmed 13 thunderstruck

agate
3 taw 4 type 6 marble, quartz 7 shooter 8 type size

agave
4 aloe 5 yucca
drink: 6 mescal, pulque
product: 4 hemp 5 sisal

Agave
father: 6 Cadmus
husband: 6 Echion
mother: 8 Harmonia
sister: 3 Ino 6 Semele 7 Autonoë
son: 8 Pentheus

age
3 eon, era 4 aeon, grow, span, time 5 epoch, ripen, stage 6 grow up, mature, mellow, period 7 develop 8 blue moon, division, interval, lifetime, majority, maturate 10 generation

aged
3 old 4 ripe, worn 5 cured, hoary, olden 6 mellow, senior 7 ancient, antique, elderly, matured, ripened 8 grown old, timeworn 9 developed, senescent, venerable 11 patriarchal 12 antediluvian

ageless
7 endless, eternal, lasting 8 dateless, enduring, immortal, timeless 9 immutable 11 everlasting

agency
4 firm 5 cause, force, means, organ, power 6 action, bureau, medium, office 7 company, channel, vehicle 8 activity, auspices, business, division, function, ministry 9 mechanism, operation 10 department, instrument 12 organization 13 establishment

agenda
5 slate 6 docket, lineup 7 program 8 calendar, schedule, to-do list 9 timetable
entry: 4 item

Agenor
brother: 5 Belus
daughter: 6 Europa
father: 7 Antenor, Neptune 8 Poseidon
mother: 5 Libya
son: 6 Cadmus

agent
3 fed, spy 4 G-man, narc, T-man, tool 5 actor, means, organ, proxy, spook 6 broker, deputy, factor, medium 7 channel, proctor, steward, vehicle 8 assignee, attorney, executor, minister, ministry 9 activator, go-between, middleman, operative 10 instrument, procurator

age-old
7 ancient, antique 9 venerable 10 immemorial 11 traditional

agglomerate
4 heap, mass, pile, rock 6 gather 7 cluster, collect 9 aggregate 10 collection 11 aggregation

agglomeration
4 heap 5 hoard, trove 7 cluster 9 aggregate, amassment, gathering 10 collection, cumulation 11 aggregation

aggrandize
4 hype 5 boost 6 beef up, expand, extend, praise 7 augment, build up, enhance, enlarge, ennoble, glorify, inflate, magnify 8 heighten, increase, multiply 11 distinguish

aggravate
3 vex **4** gall **5** anger, annoy, grate, mount, peeve, pique, rouse, upset **6** burn up, deepen, nettle, worsen **7** bedevil, disturb, enhance, inflame, magnify, perturb, provoke **8** heighten, increase, irritate **9** intensify **10** exacerbate

aggravation
4 pain **5** worry **6** bother **9** annoyance, worsening **11** provocation

aggregate
3 all, sum **4** body, bulk, floc **5** add up, gross, total, whole **6** amount, gather **7** collect **8** entirety, quantity, totality **9** composite **10** cumulative **11** agglomerate **12** conglomerate **13** agglomeration

aggregation
4 body, mass **5** crowd, group, hoard, total, trove **7** cluster, company **8** assembly **9** amassment, gathering **10** assemblage, collection, cumulation **11** agglomerate **12** accumulation

aggression
4 push, raid **5** fight, onset **6** attack **7** assault, offense **8** invasion **9** hostility, incursion, offensive, onslaught, pugnacity **10** assailment **12** belligerence **13** combativeness

aggressive
5 pushy **6** fierce, severe **7** hostile, scrappy, vicious, warlike **8** emphatic, forceful, militant **9** assertive, attacking, combative, energetic, intrusive, offensive **11** belligerent, contentious, domineering, hard-hitting **12** enterprising

aggrieve
4 hurt, pain **5** annoy, harry, upset, worry, wrong **6** harass, injure, plague **7** afflict, oppress, torment, trouble **8** distress **9** constrain, persecute

aghast
4 agog, awed **6** afraid, amazed, scared **7** anxious, fearful, shocked, stunned **8** appalled, dismayed, startled **9** awestruck, horrified, terrified **10** astonished, confounded, frightened **11** dumbfounded, overwhelmed **13** thunderstruck

agile
4 deft, spry **5** alert, brisk, catty, lithe, quick, zippy **6** active, adroit, limber, lively, nimble, supple **7** lissome **9** adaptable, dexterous, sprightly

agitate
4 move, rile, roil, rock, stir, toss **5** argue, churn, peeve, shake, upset **6** arouse, bother, excite, flurry, joggle, ruffle, stir up **7** discuss, dispute, disturb, fluster, perturb, provoke, tempest, trouble, unhinge **8** disquiet, irritate, unsettle **9** thrash out **10** discompose

agitation
4 flap, fuss, stir, to-do **5** clash **6** bustle, clamor, debate, flurry, lather, tumult **7** dispute, ferment, tempest, turmoil **9** commotion, confusion **10** turbulence **11** disturbance

agitator
5 rebel **6** shaker **7** inciter, stirrer **8** fomenter, inflamer **9** disrupter **10** instigator **11** provocateur

Aglaia
see **Graces**

Aglauros
father: **7** Cecrops
sister: **5** Herse **9** Pandrosos

aglow
4 warm **5** afire **6** bright, aflame, alight **7** excited, radiant, shining **8** gleaming, luminous

agnate
4 akin, like **5** alike **6** allied, joined, linked **7** cognate, connate, kindred, kinsman, related, similar **8** relation, relative **9** analogous **10** affiliated **11** consanguine **13** corresponding

agnostic
7 doubter, skeptic **8** doubting **10** questioner, undogmatic **11** uncommitted **12** noncommittal

Agnus ___
3 Dei

ago
4 back, gone, past, yore **5** since **6** before

agog
4 avid, keen **5** eager **6** roused **7** excited, fervent **8** desirous **9** expectant, impatient **12** enthusiastic

agon
5 clash **6** battle, strife **7** contest **8** conflict, struggle

agonize
4 fret, gall, hurt, pain, rack **5** chafe **6** harrow, squirm, suffer, writhe **7** afflict, torment, torture, trouble **8** distress, stew over, struggle **10** excruciate

agonizing
6 fierce **7** extreme, intense, painful, racking, tearing **9** harrowing, suffering, torturing, torturous **10** tormenting **12** excruciating

agony
4 pain **5** dolor, pangs **6** misery **7** anguish, passion, torment, torture **8** distress, outburst, struggle **9** suffering **10** affliction

agora
6 market **11** marketplace **12** meeting place

agrarian
5 rural **6** rustic **8** pastoral **10** campestral **12** agricultural

agree
3 buy, set, yes **4** jibe, okay, suit **5** admit, check, equal, fit in, match, tally **6** accede, accept, accord, assent, concur, settle, square **7** comport, concede, concert, concord, conform, consent

8 check out, coincide, dovetail **9** acquiesce, harmonize, recognize, subscribe **10** correspond **11** acknowledge

agreeable
4 nice, open **5** ready **7** affable, welcome, willing **8** amenable, in accord, pleasant, pleasing **9** approving, congenial, congruous, consonant, favorable, receptive **10** acceptable, compatible, concurring, consenting, consistent **11** pleasurable, sympathetic

agreed
3 aye, yea, yep, yes **4** okay **8** all right, of course **9** certainly **10** definitely, positively

agreement
4 bond, deal, pact **6** accord, assent, treaty **7** bargain, compact, concord, consent, entente, harmony **8** contract, covenant **9** concordat **10** acceptance, consonance **11** arrangement, concordance, concurrence

agree with
3 fit **4** suit **5** befit **6** assist, become **7** support **10** go together

agricultural
5 rural **7** bucolic **8** agrarian, pastoral

agriculture
7 farming, tillage **8** agronomy, ranching **9** husbandry **11** cultivation, soil culture

Agrippina
brother: 8 Caligula
husband: 8 Claudius
son: 4 Nero

aground
5 stuck **6** ashore **7** beached **8** disabled, stranded
run: 3 sew

ague
3 flu **5** chill, fever **7** malaria, shivers **9** influenza, shivering **10** blackwater

Ahab
daughter: 8 Athaliah
father: 4 Omri
prey: 8 Moby-Dick
ship: 6 Pequod
wife: 7 Jezebel

Ahasuerus
kingdom: 6 Persia
wife: 6 Esther, Vashti

Ahaz
kingdom: 5 Judah
son: 8 Hezekiah
wife: 3 Abi

Ahaziah
father: 4 Ahab **5** Joram **7** Jehoram
kingdom: 5 Judah **6** Israel
mother: 7 Jezebel **8** Athaliah
sister: 9 Jehosheba **11** Jehosobeath

ahead
4 ante, fore,on top **6** before, dormie, onward **7** earlier, forward, in front, leading, onwards **8** foremost, forwards, previous **9** in advance **10** beforehand

Ahinoam
father: 7 Ahimaaz
husband: 4 Saul **5** David
son: 5 Amnon

Ah, Wilderness! author
6 O'Neill (Eugene)

aid
4 abet, care, hand, help, lift **6** assist, helper, relief, rescue, succor **7** backing, comfort, help out, support, sustain **8** befriend **9** assistant, attendant, subsidize **10** assistance, benefactor, mitigation **11** alleviation

Aida
composer: 5 Verdi (Giuseppe)
father: 8 Amonasro
lover: 7 Radames
rival: 7 Amneris

aide
4 ass't **6** deputy, helper, second **7** orderly **8** adjutant, sidekick **9** assistant, attendant, coadjutor **10** coadjutant, lieutenant

aikido
10 martial art

ail
4 ache, hurt, pain **5** upset, worry **6** bother **7** afflict, disturb, trouble **8** distress

ailing
3 ill, low **4** down, sick, weak **6** in pain, poorly, sickly, unwell **8** below par, diseased **9** enfeebled **10** indisposed **11** debilitated

ailment
6 malady, unrest **7** disease, ferment, illness, turmoil **8** disorder, disquiet, sickness, syndrome **9** affection, complaint, condition, infirmity **10** inquietude, uneasiness **11** disquietude, restiveness **12** restlessness

aim
3 end, try **4** cast, goal, head, mark, mean, plan, want, wish **5** angle, essay, focus, level, point, slant, train **6** aspire, design, desire, direct, intend, intent, object, strive, target, zero in **7** address, attempt, propose, purpose **8** ambition, endeavor **9** objective **11** contemplate

aimless
6 random **7** wayward **8** goalless **9** desultory, haphazard, hit-or-miss, irregular, pointless, unplanned **10** designless **11** purposeless

air
3 sky **4** aura, mien, mood, song, tune, vent **5** style **6** manner, melody, reveal, strain **7** bear-

ing, divulge, express, feeling, quality **8** demeanor **9** broadcast, character, ventilate **10** atmosphere, deportment

aircraft
5 blimp, drone, plane **6** glider **7** airship, balloon, chopper **8** aerodyne, aerostat, airplane, jetliner, zeppelin **9** dirigible **10** helicopter
carrier: **7** flattop
designer: **6** Fokker (Anthony), Martin (Glenn) **7** Junkers (Hugo), Tupolev (Andrei) **8** Northrop (Jack), Sikorsky (Igor), Yakovlev (Alexander) **13** Messerschmitt (Willy)

airless
5 close **6** stuffy, sultry **8** stagnant, stifling **11** suffocating

airline
3 JAL, KLM, LOT, TWA **4** BOAC, El Al **5** Delta, Pan Am, USAir, Varig **6** Iberia, Qantas, Sabena, United, Virgin **7** Eastern, JetBlue, Olympic **8** Aeroflot, Alitalia, American, Swissair **9** Aer Lingus, Air France, Lufthansa, Northwest, Southwest, U.S. Airways **11** Continental, Pan American

airman
3 ace **5** flier, flyer, pilot **6** flyboy **7** aviator **8** aeronaut

air movement
4 gust, wind **5** draft **6** breath, breeze **7** updraft **9** downdraft

air navigation system
5 loran, navar, radar

airplane
3 jet **5** avion **6** bomber **7** fighter **8** autogiro, autogyro **9** transport
A-bomb-dropper: **8** Enola Gay
battle: **8** dogfight
body: **8** fuselage
engine: **3** jet **6** fanjet **7** propjet **8** turbofan, turbojet **9** turboprop
engine casing: **7** nacelle
engineless: **6** glider
instrument: **5** radar, radio **7** compass **9** altimeter, gyroscope **10** tachometer **11** transponder
maneuver: **4** buzz, dive, loop, roll **8** nosedive **9** chandelle **10** barrel roll
movement: **3** yaw **4** bank, spin **5** pitch **8** tailspin
part: **3** fin **4** flap, nose, prop, tail, wing **5** cabin, wheel **6** engine, rudder **7** aileron **8** airscrew, elevator **9** empennage, propeller **10** stabilizer
pilotless: **5** drone
safety machine: **6** deicer
shelter: **6** hangar
supersonic: **3** SST
target: **6** drogue
vapor: **8** contrail

air plant
6 orchid **8** epiphyte **9** bromeliad, kalanchoe **11** Spanish moss **12** strangler fig

airport
5 field **7** helipad **8** heliport **9** aerodrome
abbreviation: **3** ETA, ETD
building: **8** terminal
flag: **8** windsock
name:
Atlanta: **10** Hartsfield
Boston: **5** Logan
Chicago: **5** O'Hare **6** Midway
Dublin: **7** Shannon
London: **7** Gatwick **8** Heathrow
Los Angeles: **3** LAX
New York: **3** JFK **7** Kennedy **9** La Guardia
Paris: **4** Orly **8** DeGaulle **9** Le Bourget
Rome: **7** Da Vinci
Washington: **6** Dulles, Reagan **8** National
part: **5** apron, tower **6** runway **7** taxiway

Airport author
6 Hailey (Arthur)

airs
4 pose, show **5** front **6** vanity **7** hauteur **8** pretense **9** loftiness, mannerism, vainglory **10** pretension **11** affectation, insincerity, ostentation **13** artificiality

airship
3 jet **5** blimp, plane **8** zeppelin **9** dirigible

airtight
4 shut **6** closed, sealed **7** certain **8** hermetic, ironclad **10** impervious **11** impermeable, irrefutable **12** indisputable, invulnerable **13** incontestable

airy
4 open, rare, thin **5** blowy, fresh, gusty, light, lofty, proud, windy **6** aerial, bouncy, breezy, dainty, unreal **7** buoyant, gaseous, soaring, tenuous **8** affected, animated, delicate, ethereal, graceful, illusory, rarefied, spirited, towering, vaporous, volatile **9** expansive, frivolous, pneumatic, resilient, sprightly, vivacious **10** diaphanous, ventilated **11** atmospheric, skyscraping **12** effervescent, high-spirited

Ajax
4 hero **5** Greek **7** warrior
father: **6** Oileus **7** Telamon
opponent: **6** Hector
participant: **9** Trojan War

akin
4 like, same **5** alike **6** allied **7** kindred, related, similar, uniform **8** parallel **9** analogous, consonant **10** affiliated, comparable, compatible **11** consanguine **13** corresponding

Alabama
capital: **10** Montgomery

city: **5** Selma **6** Mobile **10** Birmingham, Huntsville, Tuscaloosa **12** Muscle Shoals
college, university: **6** Auburn **8** Tuskegee
mountain: **6** Cheaha
nickname: **6** Cotton (State) **12** Heart of Dixie
river: **6** Mobile **7** Alabama **9** Tombigbee
state bird: **12** yellowhammer
state flower: **8** camellia
state tree: **12** longleaf pine

alacrity
8 dispatch **9** briskness, eagerness, quickness, readiness **10** enthusiasm, expedition, liveliness, promptness **11** promptitude, willingness **12** cheerfulness

Alamo
city: **10** San Antonio
hero: **5** Bowie (Jim) **6** Travis (William) **8** Crockett (Davy)

alamo
6 poplar **10** cottonwood

à la mode
4 chic, tony **6** trendy **7** dashing, stylish **8** up-to-date **9** exclusive **11** fashionable **12** with ice cream

alarm
3 SOS **4** bell, fear, horn **5** alert, dread, panic, scare, siren, spook, upset **6** dismay, excite, fright, signal, terror, tocsin **7** anxiety, disturb, red flag, startle, terrify, unnerve, warning **8** distress, frighten **9** terrorize **11** forewarning, trepidation **12** apprehension **13** consternation

alas
3 heu, woe **4** darn, drat **5** alack, oy vey **7** woe is me

Alaska
capital: **6** Juneau
city: **4** Nome **5** Sitka **6** Barrow **9** Anchorage, Fairbanks **10** Prudhoe Bay
island group: **6** Kodiak **8** Aleutian, Pribilof
mountain, range: **6** Brooks, Denali **8** McKinley, Wrangell
nickname: **12** Last Frontier
park: **6** Denali, Katmai
river: **5** Yukon
state bird: **9** ptarmigan
state flower: **11** forget-me-not
state tree: **11** sitka spruce

alb
4 gown **8** vestment

Albania
capital: **6** Tirana, Tiranë
city: **5** Korçë, Vlorë **6** Durrës **7** Shkodër
ethnic group: **4** Gheg, Tosk
monetary unit: **3** lek
neighbor: **6** Greece **9** Macedonia **10** Montenegro
part of: **7** Balkans
peninsula: **6** Balkan
sea: **8** Adriatic

albatross
5 check, goony, worry **6** burden, gooney **7** anxiety, seabird **9** hindrance, millstone, restraint **11** encumbrance

Albee play
7 Sandbox (The) **8** Seascape, Zoo Story (The) **9** Tiny Alice **13** American Dream (The) **14** Three Tall Women **16** A Delicate Balance **25** Who's Afraid of Virginia Woolf?

albeit
5 still, while **6** even if, much as, though **7** despite, whereas **8** although **10** even though

Alberta
capital: **8** Edmonton
city: **5** Banff **7** Calgary
lake: **6** Claire, Louise **9** Athabasca
mountain, range: **7** Rockies **8** Columbia
provincial flower: **8** wild rose
river: **4** Milk **5** Peace **9** Athabasca

Albion
7 England

album
3 ana **4** book **6** jacket, record **7** garland, omnibus **8** notebook, pictures, register **9** anthology, portfolio, scrapbook **10** collection, miscellany

Alcestis
father: **6** Pelias
husband: **7** Admetus
rescuer: **8** Heracles, Hercules

alchemist
5 Faust **10** Paracelsus

alchemy
5 charm, magic **7** panacea, sorcery **8** wizardry **9** conjuring **10** necromancy

Alcina
sister: **7** Morgana **10** Logistilla
victim: **6** Rogero **8** Astolpho, Ruggiero

Alcinous
daughter: **8** Nausicaa
wife: **5** Arete

Alcmaeon
father: **10** Amphiaraus
mother: **8** Eriphyle
wife: **10** Callirrhoe

Alcmene
husband: **10** Amphitryon
son: **8** Heracles, Hercules

alcohol
4 grog **5** booze, hooch, juice, sauce **6** hootch, liquor, red-eye, rotgut, tipple **7** spirits **8** home brew **9** aqua vitae, firewater, moonshine

name: **4** amyl **5** butyl, cetyl, ethyl **6** glycol, methyl, sterol **7** butanol, ethanol, mannite, menthol **8** glycerin, glycerol, inositol, mannitol, methanol **9** isopropyl **11** cholesterol
used in perfumes: **5** nerol **7** borneol **8** geraniol, linalool

alcoholic
4 hard **5** dipso, drunk **6** brewed **8** drunkard **9** distilled, fermented, inebriant, inebriate, spiritous **10** spirituous **11** dipsomaniac, inebriating **12** intoxicating

alcoholic drink
see under **beverage**

Alcott novel
7 Jo's Boys **9** Little Men **11** Little Women

alcove
4 nook **5** niche **6** gazebo, recess **9** belvedere **11** summerhouse
Japanese: **8** tokonoma

Alcyone
father: **5** Atlas **6** Aeolus
husband: **4** Ceyx
mother: **7** Pleione
sisters: **8** Pleiades

ale
3 nog **4** beer, brew, nogg

aleatory
4 iffy **5** dicey, risky, shaky **6** chancy **9** hazardous, uncertain **10** contingent, precarious, vulnerable **11** problematic, speculative **13** unpredictable

alehouse
3 bar, pub **6** bistro, saloon, tavern **7** taproom **8** beer hall **10** beer garden **11** rathskeller

alembic
5 still **6** filter **9** distiller

alert
3 SOS **4** keen, warn **5** alarm, quick, ready, sharp, smart **6** brainy, bright, clever, lively, notify, tip off, tocsin **7** heedful, mindful, on guard, red flag, wakeful **8** animated, forewarn, open-eyed, vigilant, watchful **9** attentive, mercurial, sprightly, wide-awake **10** perceptive **11** intelligent, quick-witted
Scottish: **4** gleg **8** wakerife

Aleutian island
3 Fox **4** Adak, Atka, Attu, Near **5** Amlia, Kiska **6** Unimak **8** Unalaska **9** Andreanof
town: **11** Dutch Harbor

alewife
4 fish **7** herring **8** menhaden

Alexander
birthplace: **5** Pella
conquest: **4** Tyre **5** Egypt, Issus **6** Greece, Persia **7** Parthia **8** Granicus
father: **6** Philip
general: **9** Antipater
horse: **10** Bucephalus
kingdom: **9** Macedonia
mother: **8** Olympias
teacher: **9** Aristotle
wife: **6** Roxana

alfalfa
3 hay **6** forage, legume **7** lucerne

alfresco
7 open-air, outdoor, outside **8** outdoors **9** out-of-door **10** out-of-doors

alga
6 desmid, diatom **7** seaweed
blue-green: **6** nostoc
brown: **4** kelp **5** fucus **8** rockweed
green: **9** chlorella
red: **4** nori

algebra term
4 root **6** factor **8** binomial, equation, monomial, variable **9** quadratic **10** polynomial

Algeria
capital: **7** Algiers
city: **4** Bône, Oran **6** Annaba **11** Constantine
coast: **7** Barbary
desert: **6** Sahara
ethnic group: **4** Arab **6** Berber
language: **6** Arabic, Berber
monetary unit: **5** dinar
mountain range: **5** Atlas **12** Saharan Atlas
neighbor: **4** Mali **5** Libya, Niger **7** Morocco, Tunisia **10** Mauritania

Algren novel
17 Walk on the Wild Side (A) **19** Man with the Golden Arm (The)

Ali
son: **5** Hasan **6** Husayn
wife: **6** Fatima

alias
3 AKA **6** anonym, handle **7** moniker, pen name **8** nickname **9** false name, pseudonym, stage name **10** also called, nom de plume **11** nom de guerre

Ali Baba's spell
10 Open Sesame

alibi
4 plea **5** clear, cover, proof **6** answer, excuse **7** account, cover up, defense, pretext **9** assertion, exonerate **11** explanation

alien
6 exotic **7** foreign, opposed, strange **8** estrange, outsider, stranger, transfer **9** estranged, extrinsic, foreigner, outlander **10** extraneous, outlandish **12** incompatible

alienate
4 part **5** repel **6** assign, convey, divide, offend,

oppose **7** break up, turn off **8** disunify, disunite, estrange, separate, sign over, transfer **9** disaffect

alienation
5 break **6** breach **7** discord, divorce, rupture **8** division **10** conveyance, separation **12** disaffection, estrangement

alight
4 land **5** fiery **6** arrive, bright, on fire, settle **7** blazing, burning, deplane, descend, detrain, flaming, flaring, get down, glowing, ignited, shining **8** dismount **9** touch down **11** conflagrant

align
4 ally, join, line, true **5** agree, array, order, range **6** adjust, follow, line up **8** regulate **9** affiliate, associate **10** straighten

alike
4 akin, same **7** similar **8** parallel **9** analogous, consonant **10** comparable **13** corresponding

alikeness
6 simile **7** analogy **8** affinity, alliance, relation **9** closeness, semblance **10** comparison, connection, similarity, similitude **11** resemblance

aliment
4 eats, fare, feed, food, grub **7** nourish, nurture, sustain **9** nutriment **10** sustenance **11** nourishment

alimentary
9 nutritive **10** nourishing, sustaining **11** nutritional
canal: **7** enteron

alimony
4 keep **5** bread **6** living, upkeep **7** support **9** allowance, provision **10** livelihood, sustenance **11** maintenance, subsistence

alive
4 rife, spry **5** alert, awake, aware, brisk, fresh, quick, ready, vital **6** active, extant, living, moving, viable **7** animate, dynamic, knowing, replete, running, teeming, working, zestful **8** animated, existent, existing, sensible, sentient, swarming, thronged **9** abounding, breathing, cognizant, conscious, energetic, operative, sensitive, wide-awake **11** functioning, overflowing

alkali
4 base, salt **9** substance **11** soluble salt
metal: **6** cesium, sodium **7** lithium **8** francium, rubidium **9** potassium **10** monovalent
opposite: **4** acid

alkaline
5 acrid, basic, salty **6** bitter **7** antacid, caustic, soluble **8** chemical
substance: **3** lye **4** lime, soda **5** borax **6** potash **7** ammonia, antacid **8** pearl ash, saltwort **11** caustic soda

alkaloid
4 base
medicinal: **5** ergot **7** codeine, emetine, eserine, quinine **8** atropine, caffeine, lobeline, morphine **9** ephedrine, quinidine, reserpine **11** scopolamine
narcotic: **6** heroin **7** cocaine, codeine **8** morphine
poisonous: **8** atropine, nicotine, solanine **11** scopolamine

all
3 sum **4** each **5** every, gross, total, whole **6** entire, in toto, purely, wholly **7** exactly, totally, utterly **8** complete, entirety, everyone, outright, totality **9** aggregate, everybody **10** altogether, everything
combining form: **3** pan **4** omni, pant

all-around
7 general, overall, skilled **8** complete, sweeping, synoptic **9** adaptable, competent, many-sided, panoramic, universal, versatile **10** consummate, proficient **11** wide-ranging **12** encompassing **13** comprehensive

allay
4 balm, calm, ease, lull **5** abate, quell, quiet, still **6** lessen, reduce, settle, soothe, subdue **7** assuage, compose, lighten, mollify, quieten, relieve **8** decrease, diminish, mitigate, moderate **9** alleviate **11** tranquilize

all but
4 most, much, nigh **5** about **6** almost, nearly **8** as much as, in effect **9** just about, virtually **11** essentially, practically

All Creatures Great and Small author
7 Herriot (James)

allegation
5 claim **6** charge, report **9** assertion, statement **10** contention, profession **11** declaration

allege
3 say **4** avow, cite **5** claim, offer, state **6** adduce, assert, attest, charge, submit **7** advance, contend, declare, present, profess **8** maintain **10** put forward

alleged
7 accused, dubious, reputed, suspect **8** doubtful, so-called, supposed **9** described, pretended, purported, soi-disant **10** ostensible, self-styled **12** questionable

allegiance
4 duty **5** ardor, piety **6** fealty, homage **7** loyalty **8** devotion, fidelity **9** adherence, constancy, obedience **10** dedication, obligation **11** devotedness **12** faithfulness

allegiant
4 firm, true **5** liege, loyal **6** ardent, steady **7** devoted, dutiful, staunch **8** constant, faithful, resolute **9** steadfast **10** dependable

allegorical
5 moral **6** fabled **8** mythical, symbolic **9** legendary, spiritual **10** emblematic, exegetical, fictitious, figurative **12** iconographic, illustrative, metaphorical

allegory
4 myth, tale **5** fable, story **6** emblem, symbol **7** parable **8** apologue **9** symbolism **10** figuration **12** typification

allegro
4 fast **5** brisk **6** bouncy, lively **8** animated, spirited **9** sprightly

Allende novel
17 House of the Spirits (The)

allergy
5 dread **6** hatred **7** disgust, dislike **8** aversion, distaste, hay fever **9** antipathy, disliking, rejection, repulsion

alleviate
4 cure, ease **5** allay **6** lessen, reduce, remedy **7** assuage, lighten, mollify, relieve **8** decrease, diminish, mitigate

alleviation
4 ease **6** relief **7** decline **8** decrease, easement **9** lessening, reduction **10** diminution, mitigation

alley
4 lane, walk **6** marble, street **7** passage **10** backstreet

all-fired
7 totally, utterly **9** extremely **10** absolutely, completely **11** excessively

alliance
3 tie **4** axis, bloc, bond, pact **5** union **6** accord, league, treaty **7** compact, concord **8** affinity, relation **9** coalition **10** connection, federation **11** affiliation, association, combination, confederacy, conjunction, partnership, unification **12** relationship **13** confederation
international: **3** CIS, OAS **4** APEC, EFTA, NATO, OECD, OPEC **5** ASEAN, CENTO, NORAD, SEATO **7** CARICOM **8** Interpol **10** Warsaw Pact

allied
4 akin **5** bound **6** agnate, joined, linked, united **7** cognate, connate, kindred, related, unified **8** in league **9** connected **10** affiliated, associated, connatural **11** consanguine

alligator
11 crocodilian
relative: **4** croc **6** caiman, cayman **9** crocodile

alligator pear
7 avocado

all in
4 dead, used, worn **5** spent, tired **6** bushed, done in, used up **7** drained, far-gone, worn-out **8** depleted **9** dead tired, exhausted, washed-out

all in all
5 in all **6** mainly **7** en masse, largely **9** generally **10** altogether, by and large, on the whole

All in the Family
character: **5** Edith (Bunker) **6** Archie (Bunker), Gloria **7** Michael
creator: **4** Lear (Norman)
nickname: **7** Dingbat **8** Meathead
setting: **6** Queens **7** Astoria
star: **6** Reiner (Rob) **7** O'Connor (Carroll) **9** Stapleton (Jean), Struthers (Sally)
theme song: **16** Those Were the Days

allocate
4 give **5** allot, slice **6** assign, divide **7** dish out, divvy up, dole out, earmark, mete out, prorate **8** set apart **9** admeasure, apportion, designate **10** distribute

allocution
4 talk **5** spiel **6** sermon, speech **7** address, lecture, oration, oratory, pep talk **11** exhortation

allot
4 give **5** grant, share **6** accord, assign **7** deal out, divvy up, dole out, mete out **8** allocate, dispense, set aside **9** admeasure, apportion **10** distribute

allotment
3 cut, lot **4** bite, part **5** chunk, piece, quota, share, slice **6** ration **7** measure, portion **9** allowance, provision **13** apportionment

all-out
4 full **5** total **6** entire, utmost **7** maximum **8** absolute, complete, thorough **9** full-blown, full-scale, unlimited **12** totalitarian **13** thorough-going

all over
8 wherever **9** all around **10** everyplace, everywhere, far and near, far and wide, high and low, thoroughly, throughout

allow
3 let, lot, own **4** avow, give **5** admit, allot, brook, grant, leave, let on, stand **6** assign, endure, permit, suffer **7** concede, confess, consent, entitle, forbear, mete out **8** allocate, tolerate **9** apportion **11** acknowledge

allowance
3 aid, cut, lot, pay, sum **4** bite, edge, help, part, tare, tret **5** grant, leave, piece, quota, share, slice **6** amount, permit, ration **7** consent, measure, partage, portion, quantum, subsidy, vantage **8** handicap, pittance, quantity, sanction **9** advantage, allotment, head start, reduction **10** adjustment, allocation, assistance, concession, permission, sufferance, toleration **13** accommodation, apportionment, authorization

alloy
5 blend **6** fusion **7** amalgam, mixture **8** compound **9** admixture, composite **10** adulterant **11** interfusion **12** amalgamation, intermixture
brass-like: 6 latten
copper-sulfur: 6 niello
copper-tin: 6 bronze
copper-zinc: 5 brass **6** tombac
enamel-like: 6 niello
gold-like: 6 ormolu
gold-silver: 8 electrum
iron-carbon: 5 steel
iron-nickel: 5 invar
mercury: 7 amalgam
tin-lead: 5 terne **6** pewter, solder
used in jewelry: 6 tombac

all-powerful
6 mighty **7** supreme **8** absolute, almighty **10** invincible, omnipotent **11** controlling

all right
3 A-OK, aye, yea, yep, yes **4** good, okay, safe, well **5** A-okay **6** agreed, decent, proper, surely **7** average **8** adequate, of course, passable, passably, pleasing, standard, very well **9** agreeable, certainly, tolerable, tolerably **10** acceptably, adequately, definitely, positively, sufficient, well enough **12** satisfactory

all round
see **all-around**

All the King's Men author
6 Warren (Robert Penn)

allude
4 hint **5** imply, point, refer **7** bring up, suggest **8** indicate, intimate

allure
4 draw, pull **5** charm, tempt **6** appeal, entice, lead on, seduce **7** attract, beguile, enchant, glamour, win over **8** charisma, inveigle, persuade **9** captivate, fascinate, magnetism, magnetize **10** attraction **11** enchantment, fascination

alluring
4 sexy **6** lovely **7** winning, winsome **8** charming, inviting, pleasing **9** appealing, beguiling, glamorous, seductive **10** appetizing, attractive, bewitching, enchanting **11** captivating, fascinating

ally
4 join **5** unite **6** friend, helper **7** comrade, partner **8** federate **9** accessory, affiliate, associate, auxiliary, bedfellow, colleague, supporter **10** accomplice **11** confederate **12** collaborator

almighty
4 very **6** hugely, mighty **7** awfully, godlike, supreme **8** absolute **9** extremely **10** invincible, omnipotent **11** all-powerful, exceedingly

almost
4 nigh **5** about **6** all but, nearly **8** as good as, as much as, not quite, well-nigh **9** just about, virtually **11** essentially, practically **13** approximately
Scottish: 6 feckly

alms
4 gift **6** relief **7** present **8** donation, offering **10** assistance **11** benefaction, beneficence **12** contribution

aloe
9 emollient, succulent

Aloeus
father: 7 Neptune **8** Poseidon
mother: 6 Canace
son: 4 Otus **9** Ephialtes
wife: 9 Iphimedia

aloft
4 high, over **5** above **6** on high, upward **7** skyward **8** in flight, overhead

aloha
4 by-by, ciao, hail **5** hello, howdy **6** bye-bye, good-by, so long **7** good-bye, welcome **8** farewell, greeting **9** greetings
State: 6 Hawaii

alone
4 only, sole, solo, stag **5** apart **6** singly, solely, unique, wholly **7** isolate, removed **8** detached, entirely, isolated, peerless, singular, solitary **9** matchless, unequaled, unmatched, unrivaled **10** nothing but, unequalled, unexampled, unexcelled **11** exclusively, unsurpassed **12** incomparable, unparalleled, unrepeatable **13** unaccompanied

aloneness
8 solitude **9** isolation, seclusion **10** uniqueness

along
3 too, yet **4** also, near, with **5** forth, there **6** as well, at hand, on hand, onward **7** besides, forward **8** likewise, moreover **11** furthermore **12** accompanying, additionally

alongside
6 beside, next to **8** touching **9** adjoining, bordering

aloof
3 shy **4** cold, cool **5** apart, proud **6** casual, chilly, frigid, offish, remote **7** distant, haughty, removed, stuck up **8** arrogant, detached, reserved, reticent, solitary **9** incurious, unbending, uncurious, withdrawn **10** disdainful, restrained, unfriendly, unsociable **11** constrained, indifferent, standoffish, unconcerned **12** uninterested **13** disinterested

alopecia
8 baldness

alp
4 peak **5** mount **8** mountain

alpaca
4 wool **5** cloth **6** mammal
habitat: 4 Peru **5** Andes **7** Bolivia

alpha
4 dawn **5** first, start **6** outset **7** dawning, genesis, opening **9** beginning **12** commencement

alphabet
4 ABC's **7** letters
Arabic: 2 ba, fa, ha, ra, ta, ya, za **3** ayn, dad, dal, gaf, jim, kaf, kha, lam, mim, nun, qaf, sad, sin, tha, waw, zay **4** alif, dhal, shin **5** ghayn
Greek: 2 mu, nu, pi, xi **3** chi, eta, phi, psi, rho, tau **4** beta, iota, zeta **5** alpha, delta, gamma, kappa, omega, sigma, theta **6** lambda **7** epsilon, omicron, upsilon
Hebrew: 2 he, pe **3** mem, nun, sin, taw, tet, vav, waw, yod **4** alef, ayin, beth, heth, kaph, koph, qoph, resh, shin, teth **5** aleph, gimel, lamed, sadhe, tsade, zayin **6** daleth, samekh
Old Irish: 4 ogam **5** ogham
runic: 7 futhark

Alpheus
beloved: 8 Arethusa
father: 7 Oceanus
form: 5 river
mother: 6 Tethys

Alpine
animal: 4 ibex **7** chamois
dress: 6 dirndl
house: 6 chalet
lake: 4 Como, Iseo **5** Garda **6** Geneva **7** Lucerne **8** Bodensee, Maggiore **9** Constance, Neuchâtel
pass: 3 col **5** Cenis **7** Brenner, Simplon **9** St. Bernard
peak: 5 Blanc, Eiger **7** Bernina **8** Jungfrau **10** Matterhorn
plant: 9 edelweiss
primrose: 8 auricula
resort: 5 Davos **7** Bolzano, Zermatt **8** Chamonix, Grenoble, St. Moritz **9** Innsbruck **10** Interlaken **11** Saint Moritz
river: 5 Rhine, Rhône
snowfield: 4 firn, névé
staff: 10 alpenstock
state: 5 Tirol, Tyrol
tunnel: 5 Blanc, Cenis **7** Arlberg, Simplon **10** St. Gotthard
wind: 4 bora, föhn **5** foehn

already
4 even, once **5** by now, prior **6** before, by then **7** earlier, just now **8** formerly **9** before now **10** by this time, heretofore, previously

also
3 and, too **4** more, plus **5** again, along **6** as well **7** besides, further **8** likewise, moreover **9** along with, including, similarly **10** in addition **11** furthermore **12** additionally

also-ran
3 dud **5** loser **7** failure, wannabe, washout **8** defeated, runner-up

altar
6 shrine
boy: 6 server **7** acolyte
cloth: 4 pall **7** frontal
constellation: 3 Ara
hanging: 6 dorsal, dossal
platform: 8 predella
screen: 7 reredos
shelf: 7 retable
site: 4 apse, bema
vessel: 5 cruet, paten **7** chalice **8** ciborium **10** monstrance

alter
3 fix **4** geld, spay, turn, vary **5** adapt **6** adjust, change, doctor, modify, mutate, neuter, revamp **7** remodel **8** castrate, moderate, modulate **9** refashion

alteration
4 turn **5** shift **6** change **8** mutation, revision **9** variation **10** adaptation, adjustment, changeover, conversion, remodeling, transition **12** modification

altercate
4 spat, tiff **5** argue, scrap **6** bicker, hassle **7** dispute, quarrel, wrangle **8** squabble **9** caterwaul

altercation
3 row **4** beef, flap, spat, tiff **5** brawl **6** blowup, combat, fracas, hassle **7** contest, dispute, quarrel, rhubarb, wrangle **8** argument, squabble **9** bickering **10** falling-out **11** controversy, embroilment

alternate
3 sub **5** proxy **6** backup, by turn, change, fill-in, rotate, second **7** another, relieve, stand-in **8** periodic, rotating **9** change off, fluctuate, recurrent, recurring, replacing, surrogate **10** equivalent, every other, periodical, substitute **11** every second, pinch hitter, replacement **12** intermittent

alternately
6 in lieu, rather **7** instead **10** preferably

alternative
5 other, proxy **6** backup, choice, option, second **7** another **8** atypical, druthers, election **9** different, selection, surrogate **10** preference, substitute **11** contingency, nonstandard, possibility

Althaea
father: **8** Thestius
husband: **6** Oeneus
son (victim): **8** Meleager

although
4 when **5** still, while **6** albeit, even if, much as **7** despite, howbeit, whereas

altitude
6 height **8** eminence **9** elevation, high level

altitudinous
4 high, tall **7** eminent **8** elevated

alto
3 Day (Doris), Lee (Peggy) **4** Cher, Kitt (Eartha), Piaf (Édith) **5** Baker (Janet), Lenya (Lotte) **6** London (Julie), Merman (Ethel) **7** Clooney (Rosemary), Ferrier (Kathleen), Vaughan (Sarah) **8** Anderson (Marian), Dietrich (Marlene) **9** Forrester (Maureen) **10** Chookasian (Lili) **13** Schumann-Heink (Ernestine)

altogether
4 nude, well **5** fully, in all, quite **6** in toto, wholly **7** all told, en masse, exactly, totally, utterly **8** all in all, entirely **9** generally, perfectly **10** absolutely, by and large, completely, on the whole, thoroughly

altruism
7 charity **8** sympathy **10** compassion, generosity **11** benevolence **12** philanthropy, selflessness **13** unselfishness

altruistic
3 big **6** humane **8** generous **9** unselfish **10** benevolent, bighearted, charitable, openhanded **11** considerate, magnanimous, noble-minded **12** humanitarian **13** philanthropic

alum
4 grad **6** emetic **7** styptic **8** graduate **10** astringent

aluminum
source: **7** bauxite
symbol: **2** Al

always
3 e'er **4** ever **7** forever **8** evermore, for keeps **9** at any rate, endlessly, eternally **10** at all times, constantly, in any event, invariably **11** continually, forevermore, in perpetuum, perpetually, unceasingly **12** consistently, continuously

Amahl and the Night Visitors composer
7 Menotti (Gian Carlo)

amalgamate
3 mix **4** ally, fuse, meld, pool **5** admix, alloy, merge, unify, unite **6** mingle **7** combine **8** coalesce, compound, intermix **9** commingle, integrate **11** consolidate, intermingle

amalgamation
5 alloy, blend, union **6** fusion, merger **7** joining, melding, merging, mixture, uniting **8** alliance, compound **9** admixture, coalition, composite **10** commixture **12** intermixture **13** consolidation

Amalthea
form: **4** goat
horn: **10** cornucopia
nursling: **4** Zeus

amanita
8 death cap, mushroom **9** fly agaric **10** death angel

amanuensis
6 scribe **7** copyist **9** scrivener, secretary **11** transcriber **12** stenographer

amass
4 bulk, heap, make, pile **5** hoard, lay up, store, uplay **6** accrue, garner, gather, pile up, roll up **7** acquire, collect, compile, round up, store up **8** assemble, cumulate **9** aggregate, stockpile **10** accumulate **12** come together

amassment
4 pile **5** clump, group, hoard, stack, stock, store, trove **7** cluster **8** assembly, quantity **9** gathering, stockpile **10** assemblage, collection, cumulation **11** aggregation **12** accumulation **13** agglomeration

amateur
4 tyro **6** layman, novice, tinker, votary **7** admirer, dabbler, devotee, learner **8** aspirant, beginner, neophyte, putterer **9** greenhorn, smatterer **10** apprentice, dilettante, enthusiast, uninitiate **11** abecedarian

amateurish
3 raw **5** green **6** simple **7** artless **8** dabbling, inexpert **9** deficient, unskilled, untutored **10** dilettante, unfinished, unpolished, unskillful **12** dilettantist, unproficient **13** inexperienced

amative
see **amorous**

amatory
6 ardent, erotic, loving, tender **7** sensual **8** romantic **9** erogenous, seductive **10** passionate **11** aphrodisiac

amaze
4 daze **5** floor **6** wonder **7** astound, nonplus, perplex, startle **8** astonish, bewilder, blow away, bowl over, confound, surprise **9** dumbfound **10** admiration **11** flabbergast

amazement
3 awe **6** marvel, wonder **8** surprise **9** marveling **10** admiration, perplexity, wonderment **12** astonishment, bewilderment, confoundment

amazing
7 awesome **8** striking, stunning, wondrous **9** marvelous, startling, wonderful **10** astounding, impressive, miraculous, stupendous, surprising **11** astonishing, bewildering, spectacular **12** breathtaking

Amazon
6 parrot **8** giantess **12** woman warrior
tributary: 5 Negro (Rio)

ambassador
5 agent, envoy **6** legate **8** diplomat, emissary **9** messenger
papal: 6 nuncio

amber
5 ocher, ochre, resin, rosin **6** orange, yellow **7** saffron

ambience
4 aura, mood, tone **6** flavor, medium, milieu **7** climate **10** atmosphere **11** environment **12** surroundings

ambient
5 music **6** milieu **7** general, setting **8** everyday **9** prevalent **10** atmosphere, prevailing **11** atmospheric, environment, mise-en-scène **12** encompassing, surroundings **13** environmental

ambiguity
5 doubt **6** enigma, puzzle **7** evasion **9** equivoque, obscurity, vagueness **11** incertitude, uncertainty **12** doubtfulness, equivocality, equivocation **13** double meaning

ambiguous
5 vague **6** opaque, unsure **7** cryptic, dubious, inexact, obscure, unclear **8** doubtful, puzzling, two-edged **9** enigmatic, equivocal, tenebrous, uncertain, unsettled **10** indefinite, inexplicit **11** problematic **12** inconclusive, questionable

ambit
4 area, room **5** field, limit, orbit, range, reach, scope, space, sweep **6** border, bounds, extent, limits, radius, sphere **7** breadth, circuit, compass, expanse, purview **8** boundary, confines **9** extension, perimeter, periphery **13** circumference

ambition
3 aim **4** goal, hope, itch, push, wish, zeal **5** ardor, dream, drive, vigor **6** desire, energy, hunger, spirit, target, thirst **7** avidity, craving, purpose **8** appetite, striving, yearning **9** eagerness, intention, objective **10** aspiration, enterprise, enthusiasm, get-up-and-go, initiative, pretension

ambitious
4 avid, bold, keen **5** eager, pushy **6** driven, hungry, intent **7** driving, zealous **8** aspiring, desirous, striving **9** energetic **10** aggressive **11** hard-working **12** enterprising, enthusiastic

ambivalent
5 mixed **6** unsure **7** warring **8** clashing, wavering **9** equivocal, uncertain, undecided **10** unresolved **11** fluctuating, vacillating **13** contradictory

amble
4 gait, walk **5** dally, drift, mosey **6** dawdle, linger, stroll, wander **7** meander, saunter

ambrosia
6 dainty, regale **7** dessert, perfume **8** delicacy, ointment

ambrosial
5 balmy, spicy, sweet **6** savory **7** scented **8** aromatic, fragrant, heavenly, luscious, perfumed, pleasing, redolent **9** delicious **10** delectable, delightful **11** scrumptious

ambulate
4 hoof, move, pace, step, walk **5** tread, troop **6** foot it, hoof it **7** traipse

ambulatory
6 moving, on foot, roving **7** nomadic, roaming, walking **8** vagabond **9** itinerant **11** peripatetic

ambush
4 jump, lurk, trap **5** snare **6** assail, attack, entrap, lay for, waylay **7** assault, ensnare **8** surprise **9** ambuscade **11** concealment

ameliorate
3 fix **4** help, lift, mend **5** amend, raise **6** better, perk up, remedy, reform **7** elevate, enhance, improve, lighten, relieve, upgrade **8** mitigate **9** alleviate **10** convalesce, recuperate

amenable
4 open, tame **6** docile, liable, pliant, suited **7** plastic, pliable, subdued, subject, willing **8** biddable, in accord, obedient, yielding **9** adaptable, agreeable, complying, malleable, receptive, tractable **10** answerable, consenting, responsive, submissive **11** accountable, acquiescent, cooperative, responsible

amend
3 fix **4** help **5** alter, right **6** better, change, modify, reform, remedy, repair, revise, square **7** correct, improve, rectify **8** put right **9** meliorate **10** ameliorate

amendment
5 rider **6** change **7** codicil **8** addendum, revision **10** alteration, attachment, correction **11** enhancement, improvement **12** modification

amends
7 redress **8** reprisal **9** indemnity, quittance **10** recompense, reparation **11** restitution **12** compensation

amenities
5 mores **6** polish **7** decorum, manners **8** civility, courtesy **9** etiquette, propriety **12** social graces

amenity
5 charm, frill **6** luxury **7** comfort, quality **8** civility, courtesy, facility **9** advantage, etiquette, geniality, pleasance **10** affability, amiability, betterment, cordiality, enrichment, pleasantry, politeness **11** convenience, enhancement, improvement, sociability **12** agreeability, graciousness, pleasantness

ament
6 catkin

amerce
3 tax **4** dock, fine, levy **5** exact, mulct **6** punish **7** hit with, make pay **8** penalize

amercement
4 fine **5** mulct **7** damages, forfeit, penalty **10** assessment, punishment, reparation

American League
Baltimore: 7 Orioles
Boston: 6 Red Sox
Anaheim: 6 Angels
Chicago: 8 White Sox
Cleveland: 7 Indians
Detroit: 6 Tigers
Kansas City: 6 Royals
Minnesota: 5 Twins
New York: 7 Yankees
Oakland: 9 Athletics
Seattle: 8 Mariners
Tampa Bay: 9 Devil Rays
Texas: 7 Rangers
Toronto: 8 Blue Jays

American Samoa
capital: 8 Pago Pago
island, island group: 4 Rose **5** Aunuu, Manua **6** Swains **7** Tutuila
language: 6 Samoan

America's Cup winner
6 Ranger **7** Alinghi, Freedom **8** Columbia, Intrepid **9** Weatherly **10** Black Magic, Courageous

America, the Beautiful
music: 4 Ward (Samuel Augustus)
words: 5 Bates (Katherine Lee)

americium symbol
2 Am

Amfortas
father: 7 Titurel
opera: 8 Parsifal

amiability
7 amenity **9** geniality, pleasance **10** cordiality **11** sociability **12** complaisance, congeniality, friendliness, pleasantness, sociableness **13** agreeableness, enjoyableness

amiable
4 kind, warm **6** genial, gentle, kindly **7** affable, cordial, likable **8** cheerful, friendly, gracious, likeable, obliging, sociable **9** agreeable, congenial, courteous **10** responsive **11** complaisant, good-humored, good-natured, warm-hearted

amicable
7 cordial, pacific **8** empathic, friendly, peaceful, sociable **9** congenial, peaceable **10** harmonious, like-minded, neighborly **11** sympathetic **13** understanding

amid
4 over **5** among, midst **6** during **7** amongst, between **10** throughout

amigo
3 pal **4** chum, mate, pard **6** friend **7** comrade, partner **8** sidekick **9** companion, confidant **12** acquaintance

amino acid
4 dopa **6** leucin, lysine, serine, toluid, valine **7** cystein, cystine, glycine, leucine, proline, toluide **8** cysteine, dopamine, histidin, thyroxin, toluidin, tyrosine

Amis, Kingsley
novel: 8 Lucky Jim
son: 6 Martin

Amis, Martin
father: 8 Kingsley
novel: 5 Money **10** Time's Arrow **11** Information (The) **12** London Fields

amiss
3 bad **4** awry, poor **5** badly, wrong **6** afield, astray, faulty, flawed **7** wrongly **8** erringly, faultily **9** defective, imperfect **10** improperly, mistakenly, out of place **11** erroneously, imperfectly, incorrectly, unfavorably **12** inaccurately **13** inappropriate

amity
5 union **6** accord, comity, unison **7** concert, concord, harmony **8** alliance, goodwill **9** agreement **10** cordiality, friendship, kindliness **11** concurrence **12** friendliness

Ammonite
6 Semite
god: 6 Molech, Moloch

ammunition
4 ammo, shot **5** bombs **6** rounds, shells **7** charges **8** armament, grenades, missiles, ordnance **10** cartridges **11** projectiles

Amneris's rival
4 Aïda

amnesty
6 pardon **7** freeing, release **8** immunity, reprieve **9** discharge **10** absolution **11** forgiveness **12** dispensation

Amnon
father: 5 David
half sister: 5 Tamar
mother: 7 Ahinoam

amoeba
4 blob **8** rhizopod **9** protozoan

Amon
father: 8 Manasseh
son: 6 Josiah

Amonasro's daughter
4 Aïda

among
3 mid **4** amid **5** midst **6** amidst, within **7** between
other things: **9** inter alia
prefix: **5** inter

amorist
4 rake, wolf **5** lover, Romeo **7** Don Juan, gallant, playboy **8** Casanova, lothario, paramour **9** womanizer **12** heartbreaker

amorous
6 ardent, erotic, in love **7** amative, amatory, lustful **8** enamored, romantic **10** infatuated, passionate **11** aphrodisiac, impassioned

amorousness
4 love, lust **5** amour, ardor **6** desire **7** passion **9** eroticism

amorphous
7 unclear **8** formless, inchoate, nebulous, unformed, unshaped **9** shapeless, undefined **10** indistinct **11** nondescript **12** disorganized **13** characterless
mass: **4** blob

amortize
5 repay **6** pay off, reduce **7** pay down **8** write off

amount
4 bulk, dose **5** add up, equal, price, total **6** dosage, matter, number, upshot **7** purport, quantum **8** quantity **9** aggregate, substance
owed: **4** debt
small: **3** bit, jot **4** atom, drop, iota, mite, whit **5** minim, spark, speck, trace **7** modicum, smidgen **8** molecule, particle **9** scintilla

amour
4 love **5** fling, lover **6** affair **7** liaison, passion, romance **8** intimacy, intrigue **9** dalliance **10** love affair **12** entanglement, relationship

amour propre
5 pride **6** egoism, vanity **7** conceit, egotism **8** self-love, vainness **9** vainglory **10** narcissism, self-esteem, self-regard **11** self-conceit, self-respect **12** pridefulness **13** conceitedness

amphetamines
5 speed **6** dexies, hearts, uppers **7** bennies, Dexoxyn **8** greenies, pep pills, Preludin **9** Dexedrine **10** Benzedrine, Methedrine

amphibian
burrowing: **9** caecilian
genus: **4** Hyla, Rana
legless: **9** caecilian
tailed: **3** eft **4** newt **10** salamander
tailless: **4** frog, toad **8** bullfrog, tree toad **10** batrachian
wormlike: **9** caecilian
young: **7** tadpole **8** polliwog

Amphion
brother: **6** Zethus
conquest: **6** Thebes
father: **4** Zeus
mother: **7** Antiope
sister: **5** Aedon
wife: **5** Niobe

amphitheater
4 bowl **5** arena **7** stadium **8** coliseum **10** auditorium, hippodrome

Amphitrite
father: **6** Nereus
husband: **7** Neptune **8** Poseidon
mother: **5** Doris
son: **6** Triton

Amphitryon's wife
7 Alcmene

amphora
3 jar, jug, urn **4** ewer, vase **5** crock, flask **6** carafe, flagon, vessel

ample
4 wide **5** buxom, great, large, roomy **6** lavish, plenty, portly **7** copious, liberal, profuse **8** abundant, generous, handsome, spacious **9** bounteous, bountiful, capacious, expansive, extensive, plenteous, plentiful **10** commodious, sufficient **11** substantial

amplify
5 boost, raise, swell **6** dilate, expand, extend, jack up **7** augment, develop, distend, enhance, enlarge, inflate, magnify **8** increase **9** elaborate, intensify **10** supplement

amplitude
4 size **5** range, scale, scope, space **6** amount, extent, spread **7** bigness, breadth, expanse, stretch **8** distance, fullness, wideness **9** abundance, expansion, greatness, largeness, magnitude, roominess **12** spaciousness **13** capaciousness

amulet
4 juju, luck **5** charm **6** fetish, grigri, mascot **7** periapt **8** gris-gris, talisman **10** lucky piece, phylactery **11** rabbit's-foot

amuse
4 wile **5** charm, cheer **6** appeal, divert, engage, occupy, please, regale, tickle **7** animate, beguile, delight, enchant, enliven, gladden **8** distract, interest, recreate **9** entertain, fascinate

amusement
3 fun **4** play **7** delight, pastime **8** pleasure **9** diversion, enjoyment **10** recreation **11** distraction

amusing
3 fun **5** droll, funny **7** comical, risible **8** engaging, humorous, pleasing **9** diverting, enjoyable **9** laughable **12** entertaining

Amycus
father: 7 Neptune 8 Poseidon
friend: 8 Heracles, Hercules
mother: 5 Melia

ana
5 album, varia 7 sayings 9 anecdotes, anthology 10 collection, miscellany 11 memorabilia, miscellanea

anabasis
5 march 7 advance, headway, retreat 8 progress 11 advancement, progression

anagogic
6 arcane, hidden, mystic, occult, secret 7 obscure 8 esoteric, mystical, telestic 9 spiritual 10 symbolical 11 allegorical

analects
5 album 6 digest 7 garland, omnibus 8 treasury 9 anthology, selection 10 compendium, miscellany 11 compilation, florilegium

analgesic
6 opiate 7 anodyne 10 anesthetic, painkiller

analogous
4 akin, like 5 alike 7 kindred, similar, related, uniform 8 parallel 9 consonant 10 comparable, equivalent, resembling

analogue
5 match 7 cognate 8 parallel 9 correlate 10 similarity 11 correlation, counterpart, equivalence 13 correspondent

analogy
6 simile 8 affinity, likeness, metaphor, parallel, relation 9 agreement, alikeness, semblance 10 comparison, similarity, similitude 11 correlation, equivalence, resemblance

analysis
5 assay, audit, proof, study 6 method, review, report, survey 7 finding, inquiry 8 division 9 breakdown, partition, statement 10 dissection, inspection, resolution, separation 11 examination 13 clarification

analytic
6 cogent, subtle 7 logical, testing 8 studious 9 organized 10 diagnostic, scientific, systematic 11 proposition, questioning 13 investigative, ratiocinative

analyze
4 part, test 5 assay, parse, study 6 divide 7 dissect, examine, inspect, resolve 8 classify, consider, separate 9 anatomize, break down, decompose, interpret 10 decompound, scrutinize 11 deconstruct, distinguish, investigate

Ananias
4 liar 9 falsifier 12 prevaricator
father: 9 Nedebaeus
wife (coconspirator): 8 Sapphira

anarchism
4 riot 6 theory 7 misrule 8 disorder 9 distemper, rebellion 11 lawlessness

anarchist
5 rebel 6 rioter 8 agitator, mutineer, provoker, revolter 9 dissident, insurgent 10 malcontent 11 provocateur 13 revolutionary
famous: 6 Tucker (Benjamin), Zerzan (John) 7 Bakunin (Mikhail), Chomsky (Noam), Goldman (Emma), Stirner (Max) 8 Christie (Stuart), Proudhon (Pierre-Joseph) 9 Kropotkin (Peter)

anarchy
4 riot 5 chaos 7 misrule, mob rule, turmoil 8 disarray, disorder 9 confusion, distemper, mobocracy, rebellion 10 ochlocracy, revolution 11 lawlessness 13 nongovernment

anathema
3 ban 4 bane 5 curse, enemy, odium, taboo 6 pariah 7 bugbear, censure, malison, outcast, reproof 8 loathing 9 damnation, bête noire 10 black beast, execration 11 abomination, commination, detestation, imprecation, malediction 12 condemnation, denunciation

anathematize
3 ban 4 damn, oust 5 curse, expel 6 banish 7 condemn 8 denounce, execrate 9 objurgate, proscribe 13 excommunicate

anatomical depression
5 fossa, fovea

anatomical tube
3 vas 4 duct 5 canal

anatomist
5 Wolff (Kaspar) 6 Harvey (William) 8 Vesalius (Andreas)

anatomize
5 cut up 7 analyze, dissect 8 separate 9 break down, decompose

anatomy
5 frame, mummy 6 makeup 8 analysis, division, skeleton 9 framework, histology, structure 10 dissection, morphology, physiology 11 examination

Anaxo
brother: 10 Amphitryon
daughter: 7 Alcmene
father: 7 Alcaeus
husband: 9 Electryon

ancestor
8 forebear, foregoer 9 ascendant, precursor, prototype 10 antecedent, antecessor, forefather, forerunner, progenitor 11 predecessor 12 primogenitor

ancestral
6 family, inborn, inbred, lineal 7 genetic 8 familial

9 inherited 10 bequeathed, hereditary 11 consanguine, patrimonial
sequence: 8 pedigree 9 bloodline, genealogy

ancestry
4 line, race 5 blood, breed, stock 6 family, origin, source 7 descent, history, kindred, lineage 8 heritage, pedigree 9 parentage 10 derivation, extraction

Anchises' son
6 Aeneas

anchor
4 moor 5 kedge 6 secure 7 grapnel, mooring 8 mainstay
network news: 4 Daly (John), Hume (Brit) 5 Chung (Connie) 6 Brokaw (Tom), Couric (Katie), Gibson (Charles), Koppel (Ted), Lehrer (Jim), Murrow (Edward R.), Rather (Dan), Swayze (John Cameron) 7 Edwards (Douglas), Huntley (Chet), Walters (Barbara) 8 Brinkley (David), Cronkite (Walter), Jennings (Peter), Reasoner (Harry), Reynolds (Frank), Williams (Brian) 10 Chancellor (John)
part: 3 arm 4 bill, ring 5 crown, fluke, shank, stock

anchorage
4 port 5 haven, roads 6 harbor, refuge, riding 7 mooring, shelter 9 harborage, roadstead

anchorite
5 loner 6 hermit 7 recluse 8 solitary

anchors ___
6 aweigh

ancient
3 old 4 aged 5 hoary, olden 6 age-old, primal 7 antique, archaic, elderly 8 Noachian, old-timer, primeval, timeworn 9 venerable 10 primordial 12 antediluvian

ancient capital
4 Susa 5 Aksum, Balkh, Calah, Isker, Kalhu, Ninus, Pella, Petra, Sibir 6 Angkor, Bactra, Nimrud, Sardis 7 Babylon, Knossos, Memphis, Nineveh, Samaria, Shushan 10 Persepolis

ancient city
Asia Minor: 4 Nice, Teos 5 Tyana 6 Edessa, Nicaea 7 Antioch 13 Halicarnassus
Babylonia: 4 Sura 5 Agade, Akkad, Eridu, Larsa 7 Ellasar
Bengal: 4 Gaur 9 Lakhnauti
Canaan: 5 Gezer
Cyprus: 7 Salamis
Egypt: 5 Tanis 6 Thebes 7 Memphis 10 Heliopolis
Etruria: 4 Veii
Euphrates River: 7 Babylon
Greece: 5 Crisa 6 Athens, Sparta 7 Calydon 10 Lacedaemon
Ionia: 4 Myus, Teos 5 Chios, Samos 6 Priene 7 Ephesus, Lebedos, Miletus, Phocaea 8 Colophon, Erythrae 10 Clazomenae
Italy: 5 Locri 7 Pompeii 8 Siracusa, Syracuse 11 Herculaneum
Latium: 5 Gabii 9 Alba Longa
Mayan: 4 Cobá 5 Tikal, Tulum, Uxmal 8 Palenque 11 Chichén Itzá
Nile River: 5 Meroë
North Africa: 5 Utica 8 Carthage
Palestine: 4 Gaza 5 Ekron, Endor, Sodom 6 Beroea, Bethel, Gilead, Hebron 7 Jericho, Samaria 8 Ashkelon 9 Capernaum, Jerusalem
Peloponnesus: 5 Tegea 6 Sparta 7 Corinth
Sumeria: 4 Kish, Uruk 5 Erech, Larsa 6 Lagash
Turkey: 5 Assos, Assus 9 Byzantium

ancient country
Adriatic coast: 7 Illyria
Africa: 10 Mauretania
Arabian Peninsula: 5 Sheba
Asia: 4 Aram 5 Media, Minni, Syria 7 Armenia, Ash Sham, Bactria
Asia Minor: 5 Lydia, Mysia 6 Aeolis, Pontus 7 Cilicia, Phrygia 8 Bithynia
Balkan: 7 Macedon 9 Macedonia
Black Sea: 7 Colchis
Dead Sea: 4 Edom
Euphrates River: 9 Babylonia
Europe: 4 Gaul 5 Dacia 6 Gallia
gold-rich: 5 Ophir
Italy: 6 Latium 7 Etruria
Nile valley: 4 Cush
Peloponnesus: 4 Elis 7 Arcadia
Syria: 9 Phoenicia

ancient empire
6 Median 7 Hittite, Persian 8 Assyrian, Athenian, Chaldean, Seleucid 9 Ptolemaic 10 Babylonian

ancient kingdom
Anglo-Saxon: 6 Wessex
Asia: 4 Ghor, Ghur
Celtic: 7 Cumbria
China: 3 Shu
Euphrates valley: 4 Hira 7 Al-Hirah
Greece: 8 Pergamon, Pergamum
North Of Assyria: 3 Van 6 Ararat, Urartu
Palestine: 5 Judah 6 Israel
Persian Gulf: 4 Elam
Portugal: 7 Algarve
Spain: 4 Leon 6 Aragon 7 Castile, Galicia, Granada, Navarre
Syria: 4 Moab
Welsh: 5 Powys
West Sahara: 4 Gana 5 Ghana

ancient monument
6 sphinx 7 obelisk, pyramid

ancient royal forest
4 Dean 8 Sherwood

ancient town
Africa: **4** Zama
Armenia: **4** Dwin, Tvin
Asia Minor: **4** Soli **5** Derbe, Issus, Soloi
Attica: **6** Icaria
Black Sea: **5** Olbia **9** Apollonia
Greece: **4** Abae, Opus **8** Marathon
Italy: **4** Elea, Luna **5** Cumae, Velia
Latium: **5** Ardea, Cures
Macedonia: **5** Pydna, Stobi **9** Apollonia
Peloponnesus: **5** Asine
Persia: **6** Hormuz **8** Harmozia
Sicily: **5** Hybla
Spain: **5** Munda
Tatar: **5** Isker, Sibir
Wendish: **5** Julin

ancilla
3 aid **4** aide, ally, hand, help **6** helper **9** assistant, attendant, supporter

ancillary
5 extra **8** adjuvant, incident **9** accessory, attendant, attending, auxiliary, satellite, secondary **10** additional, coincident, collateral, subsidiary, supporting **11** appurtenant, concomitant, subordinate, subservient **12** accompanying, contributory **13** supplementary

andante
4 slow **5** tempo **7** relaxed, walking **8** moderate

Anderson play
7 High Tor **8** Key Largo **9** Winterset **11** Valley Forge **14** What Price Glory

Anderson book
9 Poor White **12** Dark Laughter **13** Winesburg Ohio

Andes
grazer: **5** llama **6** alpaca, guemal, huemal, vicuña **7** camelid, guanaco
native: **4** Inca
peak: **9** Aconcagua, Huascarán

andiron
7 firedog

Andorra
capital: **7** Andorra
language: **7** Catalan
liberator: **11** Charlemagne
monetary unit: **4** euro
monetary unit, former: **6** peseta **11** French franc
mountain range: **8** Pyrenees
neighbor: **5** Spain **6** France
river: **6** Valira

Andrea ____
5 Doria **8** del Sarto

androgynous
7 epicene **8** bisexual **9** unisexual

android
5 robot **9** automaton

Andromache
husband: **6** Hector
son: **8** Astyanax, Molossus

Andromeda
father: **7** Cepheus
husband: **7** Perseus
mother: **10** Cassiopeia
rescuer: **7** Perseus

Andy Griffith Show
actor: **6** Bavier (Francis), Howard (Ron), Knotts (Don), Nabors (Jim)
character: **4** Opie (Taylor) **5** Gomer (Pyle) **6** Barney (Fife) **7** Aunt Bee

anecdote
4 tale, yarn **5** story **7** account, episode, recital **8** relation **9** narration, narrative **12** recollection, reminiscence

anemic
3 wan **4** pale, thin, weak **5** pasty **6** feeble, pallid, sickly, watery **7** insipid **8** ischemic **9** bloodless, colorless **10** spiritless

anemone
9 buttercup **10** windflower

anent
4 as to, in re **5** about, as for **7** apropos **8** touching **9** as regards **10** concerning **13** with respect to

anesthetic
6 opiate **7** anodyne **9** analgesic **10** painkiller, palliative
medical: **5** ether **6** spinal **8** morphine, procaine **9** halothane, novocaine **10** benzocaine, chloroform, tetracaine **11** scopolamine
suffix: **5** caine

anesthetize
4 numb, stun **6** benumb, deaden **8** etherize, knock out **9** narcotize **11** desensitize

anesthetized
4 dead, numb **5** inert **6** asleep, torpid **10** insensible **11** insensitive, unconscious

anew
4 over **5** again **6** afresh, de novo, lately, of late **8** once more, recently

angel
6 backer, cherub, patron, seraph, surety **7** sponsor **8** backer-up, guardian **9** celestial, guarantor, supporter **10** benefactor **11** underwriter
biblical: **5** Uriel **7** Gabriel, Michael, Raphael
fallen: **7** Lucifer
hierarchy: **6** powers **7** thrones, virtues **8** cherubim, seraphim **9** dominions
Mormon: **6** Moroni
of death: **6** Azrael

Angel Clare's bride
4 Tess

angelic
4 holy, pure **5** godly **6** divine **7** saintly **8** cherubic, ethereal, heavenly **9** celestial **11** beneficient

Angelica
father: **9** Galaphron
husband: **6** Medoro
lover: **7** Orlando

Angelou work
13 Heart of a Woman (The) **25** I Know Why the Caged Bird Sings

anger
3 ire, vex **4** bile, boil, burn, fume, fury, gall, huff, rage, rant, rave, rile **5** storm, upset, wrath **6** choler, dander, enrage, madden, nettle, offend, seethe **7** affront, bristle, dudgeon, incense, outrage, provoke, steam up, umbrage **8** acrimony **9** animosity, infuriate **10** antagonism, antagonize, exasperate

angle
3 aim, bow **4** axil, bend, bias, fish, hand, skew, turn **5** facet, slant **6** aspect, corner, crotch, dogleg **7** flexure, outlook, turning **9** direction, viewpoint **10** standpoint

angler
6 fisher **8** monkfish **9** fisherman, goosefish

Anglo-Saxon
assembly: **4** moot **5** gemot **6** gemote
council: **9** heptarchy
county: **5** shire
court: **4** moot **5** gemot **6** gemote
crown tax: **4** geld
epic: **7** Beowulf
free servant: **5** thane, thegn
god: **3** Ing
goddess of fate: **4** Wyrd
historian: **4** Bede
king: **3** Ine, Ini **4** Edwy **5** Edgar, Edred **6** Alfred, Edmund, Edward, Egbert **8** Ethelred
kingdom: **4** Kent **5** Essex **6** Mercia, Sussex, Wessex **10** East Anglia **11** Northumbria
king's council: **5** witan
letter: **3** edh, eth, wen, wyn **4** rune, wynn **5** thorn
nobleman: **4** earl
poet: **4** scop
prince: **8** atheling
sheriff: **5** reeve
slave: **4** esne
warrior: **5** thane, thegn

Angola
capital: **6** Luanda
city: **6** Huambo **7** Lubango **8** Benguela
exclave: **7** Cabinda
language: **10** Portuguese
monetary unit: **6** kwanza
neighbor: **5** Congo **6** Zambia **7** Namibia **11** South Africa
river: **5** Congo

angora
3 cat **4** goat, hair, wool, yarn **6** mohair, rabbit

angry
3 hot, mad **4** sore **5** irate, riled, riley, upset, vexed, wroth **6** fuming, heated, ireful, wrathy **7** enraged, furious, riled up, teed off **8** choleric, incensed, inflamed, maddened, wrathful **9** indignant, irritated **10** aggravated, infuriated **11** acrimonious, exasperated

angst
4 fear **5** agita, worry **6** unease **7** anxiety, concern **8** disquiet, distress **10** insecurity **11** disquietude, fretfulness **12** apprehension

Anguilla
island, island group: **3** Dog **4** Seal **5** Scrub **7** Leeward
location: **10** West Indies
territory of: **7** Britain

anguish
3 rue, woe **4** ache, care, dole, hurt, pain, pang **5** agony, dread, grief, throe, worry **6** misery, regret, sorrow, throes **7** anxiety, torment, torture **8** distress, hardship **9** heartache, suffering **10** affliction, heartbreak **12** wretchedness

angular
4 bony, edgy, lank, lean, thin **5** gaunt, lanky, spare, stiff **6** forked, skinny, zigzag **7** pointed, scraggy, scrawny **8** cornered, rawboned, ungainly **9** roughhewn **10** unfinished, ungraceful, unpolished

ani
6 cuckoo

anima
4 soul **6** psyche, spirit

animadversion
4 slam, slur **7** censure, obloquy **9** aspersion, criticism **10** accusation, imputation, reflection **11** insinuation **12** reprehension

animadvert
6 notice **7** observe **9** criticize

animal
5 beast, brute, feral **6** brutal, carnal, ferine **7** beastly, bestial, brutish, critter, fleshly, sensual, swinish, wilding **8** creature, wildling
antlered: **3** elk **4** axis, deer **5** moose **7** caribou **8** reindeer
aquatic: **3** eel **4** fish, frog, seal **5** otter, whale **6** dugong, sea cow, walrus **7** dolphin, manatee, octopus **8** bryozoan, porpoise **9** alligator, crocodile

arboreal: **2** ai **4** bird **5** chimp, coati, koala, lemur, sloth **6** gibbon, monkey **7** opossum, tarsier **8** kinkajou, marmoset, squirrel **9** orangutan
burrowing: **4** mole **5** brock, ratel **6** badger, gopher, marmot, rabbit **7** echidna **9** armadillo, groundhog, woodchuck
castrated: **2** ox **5** capon, steer **6** barrow, wether **7** gelding
coat: **3** fur **4** hair, hide **6** pelage
draft: **2** ox **3** yak **4** mule, oxen (plural) **5** horse **6** donkey **8** elephant
exhibit: **3** zoo
extinct: **3** moa **4** dodo, urus **6** quagga **7** mammoth **8** dinosaur, eohippus, mastodon **9** trilobite
female: **3** cow, dam, doe, ewe, hen, pen, roe, sow **4** mare, puss **5** bitch, goose, jenny, nanny, vixen **6** jennet **7** lioness
four-footed: **9** quadruped
four-limbed: **8** tetrapod
free-swimming: **6** nekton
hibernating: **4** bear, frog, toad **5** skunk, snake **7** polecat **8** chipmunk **9** groundhog, woodchuck
horned: **2** ox **3** ram, yak **4** bull, goat, ibex, kudu **5** addax, bison, eland, rhino **6** cattle, koodoo **7** buffalo, gazelle, giraffe, unicorn **8** antelope
humped: **2** ox **3** elk, yak **4** zebu **5** bison, camel, moose
imaginary: **5** snark **6** Harvey **10** hippogriff
male: **3** cob, ram, tom **4** boar, buck, bull, cock, stag, stud **5** billy, steer **6** gander **7** gobbler, rooster **8** bachelor, stallion
many-celled: **8** metazoan
many-footed: **9** centipede, millipede
meat-eating: **9** carnivore
mythical: **5** Hydra **6** dragon, kraken, sphinx **7** centaur, griffin, mermaid, Pegasus, unicorn **8** basilisk, Cerberus, Minotaur
one-celled: **9** protozoan
Peruvian: **5** llama **6** alpaca, vicuña
plant-eating: **9** herbivore
skin disease: **5** mange
spotted: **4** axis, paca **6** calico, jaguar, ocelot **7** cheetah, leopard, piebald **8** skewbald **9** dalmatian
striped: **4** kudu **5** tiger, zebra **6** koodoo, quagga
tender: **8** herdsman
trail: **3** pug **4** foil, slot **5** spoor
tusked: **6** walrus **7** warthog **8** elephant
two-footed: **5** biped
web-footed: **4** duck, frog, toad **5** goose, otter **6** beaver **8** duckbill, platypus
young: **3** cub, kid, kit, pup **4** calf, colt, fawn, foal, joey, lamb **5** bunny, chick, kitty, poult, shoat, stirk, whelp **6** cygnet, farrow, heifer, kitten, piglet **7** bullock, gosling, lambkin **8** suckling, yeanling, yearling **9** fledgling

animal behavior
study of: **8** ethology

animal fat
4 suet **6** tallow

animalism
4 lust **7** abandon **8** vitality **9** carnality **10** sensualism, sensuality **11** lustfulness, physicality, unrestraint

animalize
4 warp **6** debase **7** corrupt, deprave, pervert, vitiate **9** brutalize **10** bestialize, demoralize

animal life
5 fauna

animal sound
3 arf, baa, bay, caw, coo, low, mew, moo **4** bark, bray, buzz, crow, hiss, hoot, howl, meow, purr, roar, yelp **5** bleat, chirp, croak, drone, growl, grunt, miaow, neigh, quack **6** bellow, gibber, gobble, warble **7** screech, twitter

animate
4 fire, live, move, spur, stir, urge **5** alert, alive, cheer, drive, exalt, impel, liven, nerve, spark, steel, vital **6** active, arouse, excite, inform, kindle, lively, living, moving, viable, vivify **7** actuate, chirk up, dynamic, enliven, hearten, inspire, quicken, refresh **8** activate, embolden, energize, inspirit, motivate, spirited, vitalize **9** breathing, encourage, energized, enhearten, make alive, stimulate **10** invigorate

animated
3 gay **4** keen **5** alert, alive, peppy, quick, vivid, vital **6** lively, living **7** dynamic, excited, vibrant, zestful **8** spirited, vigorous **9** activated, energetic, energized, exuberant, sprightly, vitalized, vivacious **12** high-spirited

animation
3 pep, vim, zip **4** brio, dash, élan, life, toon, zing **5** oomph, verve **6** energy, esprit, gaiety, spirit **7** cartoon, dynamic **8** dynamism, vitality, vivacity **10** liveliness
unit: **3** cel **4** cell

animato
5 brisk, tempo **6** lively **8** spirited **9** energetic, sprightly

animosity
4 hate **5** venom **6** animus, enmity, hatred, rancor **7** dislike, ill will **8** acrimony **9** antipathy, hostility **10** antagonism, resentment

animus
4 plan, soul **6** design, enmity, intent, pneuma, psyche, rancor, spirit **7** dislike, ill will, meaning, purpose **9** antipathy, élan vital, hostility, intention **10** antagonism, intendment, opposition, vital force **11** disposition, malevolence

Anjou
4 pear
capital: **6** Angers
native: **7** Angevin

ankle
5 talus **6** tarsus

Anna Karenina
author: **7** Tolstoy (Leo)
character: **5** Dolly, Kitty, Levin (Konstantin), Stiva **6** Andrei (Karenin) **7** Vronsky (Count Alexei) **8** Ivanovna (Countess Lidia), Seriozha
film star: **4** Bean (Sean) **5** Bloom (Claire), Garbo (Greta), Leigh (Vivien), March (Fredric), Reeve (Christopher) **6** Bisset (Jacqueline) **7** Connery (Sean), Marceau (Sophie) **10** Richardson (Ralph)
radio star: **4** Peck (Gregory) **7** Bergman (Ingrid)

annals
6 record **7** account, history **8** archives, register **9** chronicle

annelid
4 worm **5** leech **9** earthworm

annex
3 add, arm, cop, ell, win **4** gain, hook, join, land, take, wing **5** add on, affix, seize, tag on **6** adjoin, append, attach, fasten, obtain, pick up, secure, tack on, take on **7** acquire, connect, preempt, procure, subjoin **8** accroach, addition, appendix, arrogate, superadd, take over **9** extension **10** attachment, commandeer, subsidiary, supplement **11** appropriate, expropriate, incorporate

Annie Oakley
4 comp, pass **10** free ticket, markswoman

annihilate
4 do in, kill, raze, rout, ruin, undo **5** abate, annul, crush, erase, quash, quell, wrack, wreck **6** murder, negate, quench, rub out, squash, uproot, vanish **7** abolish, blot out, destroy, expunge, nullify, put down, root out, vitiate, wipe out **8** abrogate, demolish, massacre, suppress, vanquish **9** eradicate, extirpate, liquidate, slaughter **10** extinguish, invalidate, obliterate **11** exterminate

annihilation
7 killing **8** massacre **9** abolition **11** destruction, elimination, liquidation, termination **12** obliteration **13** extermination

anniversary
hundredth: **9** centenary **10** centennial
tenth: **9** decennial
thousandth: **10** millennial

Anno ____
6 Domini

annotate
5 gloss **6** remark **7** comment, explain **8** footnote **9** elucidate, interpret **10** commentate

announce
4 call, tell **5** augur, issue, sound, state **6** attest, blazon, herald, impart, report, reveal, signal **7** bespeak, declare, divulge, forerun, give out, portend, predict, presage, present, publish, release, signify, trumpet **8** disclose, forecast, foreshow, foretell, indicate, proclaim **9** advertise, broadcast, harbinger, make known, publicize **10** give notice, make public, promulgate **11** preindicate

announcement
4 news **5** promo **6** notice, report **7** message, release **8** briefing, bulletin **9** broadcast, statement **10** communiqué, disclosure **11** declaration, publication **12** proclamation, promulgation **13** advertisement, communication

announcer
2 DJ **5** emcee **6** deejay, herald, veejay **9** anchorman, voice-over **10** disc jockey, disk jockey, newscaster **11** anchorwoman, broadcaster, commentator **12** anchorperson, sportscaster

annoy
3 bug, irk, vex **4** bait, fret, gall, miff **5** chafe, chivy, harry, peeve, tease, upset, worry **6** badger, bother, harass, heckle, hector, molest, needle, nettle, pester, plague, ruffle **7** agitate, bedevil, disturb, hagride, perturb, provoke, tick off **8** distress, irritate **9** beleaguer
Scottish: **4** fash

annoyance
4 drag, to-do **5** trial, upset, worry **6** bother, nettle, plague, strain **7** problem, trouble **8** distress, headache, irritant, nuisance, vexation **10** affliction, harassment, irritation **11** aggravation, botheration, disturbance, indignation, provocation **12** exasperation

annoying
5 pesky **8** tiresome **9** troubling, vexatious **10** disturbing, irritating **11** aggravating, distressing, troublesome **12** exasperating

annual
5 plant **6** flower, yearly **7** almanac **8** each year, yearbook, yearlong **9** every year

annul
4 undo, void **5** abate, erase, quash **6** cancel, delete, efface, negate, revoke, vacate **7** abolish, blot out, expunge, nullify, redress, rescind, retract, reverse, vitiate, wipe out **8** abrogate, dissolve **9** cancel out, discharge, frustrate **10** annihilate, counteract, extinguish, invalidate, neutralize, obliterate **11** countermand

annunciate
see **announce**

anodyne
4 balm **5** bland **6** opiate, relief, remedy **7** soother **8** narcotic, nepenthe, painless,

sedative **9** analgesic, calmative, innocuous, soporific **10** anesthetic, depressant, pain-killer, palliative **11** inoffensive, unoffending **12** tranquilizer

anoint
3 rub **4** daub, laud, name **5** anele, apply, bless, honor, smear **6** choose, hallow, ordain **7** confirm, massage **8** dedicate, sanctify, set apart, venerate **9** designate **10** consecrate

anomalous
3 odd **6** off-key **7** deviant, strange, unusual **8** aberrant, abnormal, atypical, peculiar **9** deviating, deviatory, divergent, irregular, unnatural, untypical **10** unexpected **11** heteroclite, incongruous, paradoxical **12** inconsistent **13** nonconforming, preternatural

anomaly
5 freak, quirk **6** oddity **7** paradox **9** departure, deviation, exception **10** aberration, divergence **11** abnormality, incongruity, peculiarity **12** idiosyncrasy, irregularity **13** inconsistency

anomie
4 flux **6** unrest **7** anxiety, inertia **10** alienation, insecurity **11** disquietude, instability, uncertainty **12** disaffection, estrangement, indifference, restlessness

anon
4 soon **5** later **7** by and by, shortly **8** directly, in a while **9** presently **10** before long **11** after a while

anonym
5 alias **6** handle **7** pen name **8** nickname **10** nom de plume **11** assumed name, nom de guerre

anonymous
7 unknown, unnamed **8** nameless, not named, unsigned **9** incognito **11** unspecified **12** unidentified, unrecognized

anorak
5 parka

another
3 new **4** else, more **5** added, fresh **7** farther, further, one more **9** different **10** additional **11** alternative, someone else **13** something else

anschluss
5 union **6** league **8** alliance **9** coalition **10** federation **11** confederacy **13** confederation

answer
4 fill, meet, plea, RSVP **5** atone, plead, rebut, reply, serve, solve **6** come in, refute, rejoin, result, retort, return **7** conform, defense, explain, fulfill, respond, satisfy **8** antiphon, rebuttal, response, solution **9** rejoinder **10** refutation **11** recriminate **13** countercharge

answerable
5 bound **6** liable **7** obliged, subject **8** amenable **9** compelled, duty-bound, obligated **11** accountable, constrained, responsible

ant
5 emmet **9** carpenter
relating to: **6** formic

Antaean
4 huge **5** giant **6** heroic **7** mammoth, titanic **8** colossal, enormous, gigantic **9** cyclopean **10** gargantuan

Antaeus
father: **7** Neptune **8** Poseidon
mother: **4** Gaea
slayer: **8** Heracles, Hercules

antagonism
3 con **6** animus, enmity, hatred, rancor **7** discord **8** conflict, friction **9** animosity, antipathy, hostility **10** antithesis, contention, dissension, opposition, resistance **11** contrariety **12** disagreement

antagonist
3 con, foe **4** anti **5** enemy, match **6** muscle **7** opposer **8** chemical, opponent **9** adversary, contender

antagonistic
4 anti **6** averse **7** adverse, hostile, opposed **8** clashing, contrary, inimical, opposing **9** bellicose, combative, rancorous, truculent **11** belligerent, conflicting, contentious **12** antipathetic

Antarctica sea
4 Ross **7** Weddell **8** Amundsen

ante
3 bet, pay, pot **4** cost, risk **5** level, pay up, price, put up, stake, wager **6** stakes **7** produce

anteater
8 aardvark, pangolin, tamandua

antecede
7 forerun, precede, predate **8** foredate, go before

antecedence
8 priority **10** precedence, precession, preference

antecedent
4 fore, line **5** cause, prior **6** former, reason **7** earlier **8** ancestor, anterior, forebear, foregoer, occasion, previous **9** condition, foregoing, precedent, preceding, precursor, prototype **10** forerunner, progenitor **11** determinant, predecessor

antedate
7 forerun, precede **11** anachronize

antediluvian
3 old **4** aged, fogy **5** hoary, passé **6** age-old, fogram, fossil, square **7** ancient, antique, archaic **8** mossback, Noachian, obsolete, outdated, outmoded, primeval, timeworn **9** out-

of-date, primitive **10** antiquated, fuddy-duddy **12** old-fashioned **13** stick-in-the-mud

antelope
3 gnu, kob **4** guib, kudu, oryx, poku, puku, topi, tora **5** addax, bongo, eland, nyala, oribi, serow **6** dik-dik, duiker, impala, koodoo, lechwe, nilgai **7** blesbok, chamois, gazelle, gemsbok, gerenuk, sassaby **8** bushbuck, reedbuck, steinbok **9** springbok, waterbuck **10** hartebeest
female: 3 doe
genus: 4 Oryx
male: 4 buck
young: 3 kid
(see also **gazelle**)

antenna
4 wire **6** aerial, device, dipole, sensor **8** monopole, receiver

antennae
4 ears **11** sensitivity **13** receptiveness

anterior
4 past **5** prior **6** former **8** previous **9** foregoing, precedent, preceding **10** antecedent

anteroom
5 entry, foyer, lobby **6** alcove **9** vestibule

Anteros
brother: 4 Eros
father: 4 Ares, Mars
mother: 5 Venus **9** Aphrodite
opposite: 4 Eros

anthem
4 hymn, song **5** chant, paean, psalm **8** canticle

anthology
3 ana **5** album **6** digest, reader **7** garland, omnibus **8** analects, treasury **9** selection **10** assortment, collection, compendium, miscellany **11** compilation, florilegium

anthropoid
3 ape **4** saki, titi **5** biped **6** bonobo, gibbon, monkey, uakari **7** bipedal, gorilla, macaque, manlike, primate, tamarin, tarsier **8** capuchin, hominoid, humanoid, marmoset **9** orangutan **10** chimpanzee

anthropologist
4 Boas (Franz), Dart (Raymond), Mead (Margaret) **5** Sapir (Edward), Tylor (Edward Burnett) **6** Frazer (James George), Geertz (Clifford), Leakey (Louis), Morgan (Lewis Henry) **7** Bateson (Gregory), Kroeber (Alfred Louis) **8** Benedict (Ruth) **10** Malinowski (Bronisław) **11** Lévi-Strauss (Claude)

anti
3 con **6** averse **7** adverse, against, counter, opposed, opposer **8** contrary, opponent, opposing **9** adversary, opposed to **10** antagonist **12** antagonistic, antipathetic, in opposition

antiaircraft fire
4 flak

antibiotic
7 colicin **8** neomycin, viomycin **9** polymyxin **10** bacitracin, novobiocin, penicillin **11** bacteriocin, tyrothricin **12** streptomycin, tetracycline

antic
3 gag **4** dido, joke, lark, romp **5** caper, comic, prank, trick **6** frisky, frolic, lively **7** comical, foolish, playful **8** escapade, farcical, prankish, spirited **9** high jinks, laughable, ludicrous, sprightly **10** frolicsome, rollicking, shenanigan, tomfollery **11** mischievous, monkeyshine **12** monkeyshines **13** practical joke

anticipate
3 see **4** wait **5** await, check **6** divine, expect **7** counter, count on, foresee, prepare, presage, prevent, wait for **8** forecast, foreknow, foretell **9** apprehend, forestall, prevision, visualize **10** prepare for

anticipation
7 inkling, outlook, promise **8** awaiting, forecast, prospect **9** awareness, foresight, foretaste **10** expectancy **11** expectation, realization **12** apprehension **13** visualization

Anticlea
father: 9 Autolycus
husband: 7 Laertes
son: 7 Ulysses **8** Odysseus

antidote
4 cure, drug **6** remedy **7** negator **8** medicine **9** nullifier **10** corrective, counteract, preventive **11** counterstep, neutralizer **12** counteragent **13** counteractant, counteractive

Antigone
brother: 9 Polynices **10** Polyneices
father: 7 Oedipus
mother: 7 Jocasta
sister: 6 Ismene
uncle: 5 Creon

Antigua and Barbuda
capital: 7 St. Johns
island: 7 Antigua, Barbuda, Redonda

Antilochus
father: 6 Nestor
friend: 8 Achilles
slayer: 6 Memnon

antimony symbol
2 Sb

Antiope
father: 6 Asopus
husband: 5 Lycus **7** Theseus
queen of: 7 Amazons
son: 6 Zethus **7** Amphion **10** Hippolytus

antipasto
9 appetizer **11** hors d'oeuvre **12** hors d'oeuvres

antipathetic
5 loath **6** averse, loathe **7** adverse, hostile, opposed **8** aversive, clashing, contrary, inimical, opposing, opposite **9** abhorrent, loathsome, repellent, repugnant, repulsive **10** discordant, unfriendly **11** conflicting, distasteful, ill-disposed, uncongenial **12** antagonistic **13** contradictory

antipathy
4 hate **6** animus, enmity, hatred, rancor **7** allergy, dislike, ill will **8** aversion, distaste, loathing **9** animosity, hostility **10** abhorrence, antagonism, opposition, repellency

antiphon
5 psalm, reply, verse **6** answer, anthem, return **7** respond **8** response

antipodal
5 polar **7** adverse, counter, opposed, reverse **8** contrary, converse, opposite **9** diametric **11** conflicting, contrasting, diametrical **12** antithetical **13** contradictory

antipode
6 contra **7** counter, reverse **8** contrary, converse, flip side, opposite **9** other side **11** counterpole

antiquate
7 outdate, outmode **8** obsolete **9** obsolesce **12** superannuate

antiquated
3 old **4** aged **5** dated, fusty, hoary, moldy, passé **6** bygone, old hat **7** ancient, antique, archaic **8** obsolete, old-timey, outmoded **9** out-of-date **10** oldfangled, out-of-style **11** discredited, obsolescent **12** antediluvian, old-fashioned **13** inappropriate, superannuated

antique
3 old **4** aged **5** dated, hoary, olden, passé, relic **6** age-old, bygone, rarity **7** ancient, archaic, vintage **8** artifact, heirloom, old-timey, outdated, outmoded, timeworn **9** ancestral, objet d'art, out-of-date, venerable **10** antiquated, oldfangled **12** antediluvian, old-fashioned

antiseptic
6 iodine **7** alcohol, sterile **8** hygienic, peroxide, sanitary **9** boric acid, carvacrol, germicide, merbromin **10** gramicidin, sterilized **12** carbolic acid, disinfectant
pioneer: **6** Lister (Joseph)

antisocial
7 ascetic, austere, hostile **8** eremitic, solitary **9** alienated, reclusive, withdrawn **10** unfriendly **11** standoffish **12** antagonistic, misanthropic

antithesis
3 con **6** contra **7** counter, reverse **8** antipode, antipole, contrary, contrast, converse, opposite **10** antagonism, opposition **11** counterpole

antithetical
5 polar **6** contra **7** counter, reverse **8** contrary, converse, opposite **9** antipodal, diametric **10** antipodean **11** diametrical **13** contradictory

antitoxin
4 sera (plural) **5** serum **11** neutralizer

antiwar
6 irenic **8** pacifist **10** nonviolent, pacifistic

Antony, Mark
defeat: **6** Actium
friend: **6** Caesar
lover: **9** Cleopatra
wife: **7** Octavia

anxiety
4 care, fear **5** agita, doubt, dread, panic, worry **6** unease **7** concern **8** distress, mistrust, suspense **9** self-doubt, suffering **10** uneasiness **11** disquietude, uncertainty **12** apprehension

anxious
4 avid, keen **5** eager **6** afraid, ardent, scared, uneasy **7** alarmed, fearful, worried **8** agitated, desirous, troubled, worrying **9** impatient, perturbed, terrified **10** breathless, disquieted, frightened **12** apprehensive

any
3 all **4** a bit, some **5** every **7** a little, several **8** whatever

anyhow
6 random **7** however **8** at random, randomly **9** hit-or-miss **10** carelessly, regardless **11** haphazardly **13** helter-skelter

anymore
3 now **5** today **8** nowadays **9** presently, these days

anyone
3 all **9** everybody

anything
5 aught

anytime
4 ever **8** whenever

anyway
4 ever, once **5** at all **7** however **12** nevertheless

anywise
5 at all

apace
4 fast **6** versed **7** abreast, flat-out, hastily, quickly, rapidly, swiftly **8** informed, up-to-date, speedily **9** posthaste **12** lickety-split **13** expeditiously

Apache
chief: **7** Cochise **8** Geronimo
subgroups: **7** Cibecue **9** Jicarilla, Mescalero **10** Chiricahua

apart
5 alone, aside **6** singly **7** asunder, removed **8** detached, isolated, one by one **9** severally **10** separately **12** individually **13** independently, unaccompanied
prefix: 3 dis

apart from
3 bar, but **4** save **6** except, saving **7** barring, besides **9** except for, excepting, excluding, other than, outside of **11** exclusive of

apartheid
8 division **9** partition **10** separation, separatism **11** segregation **12** separateness

apartment
4 flat, room **5** rooms, suite **6** rental **7** chamber, housing, lodging **8** building, dwelling **9** residence **10** maisonette **13** accommodation

apathetic
4 dull, flat, limp **5** inert **6** stolid, torpid **7** languid, passive, unmoved **8** sluggish **9** impassive, untouched **10** anesthetic, insensible, phlegmatic, spiritless **11** emotionless, indifferent, insensitive **12** unresponsive **13** disinterested

apathy
6 torpor **8** coldness, dullness, lethargy, obduracy, stoicism **9** aloofness, disregard, inertness, lassitude, passivity, stolidity, torpidity, unconcern **10** detachment, dispassion **11** callousness, disinterest, impassivity **12** heedlessness, indifference, listlessness **13** insensibility, insensitivity

ape
4 copy, mime, mock **5** mimic **6** bonobo, gibbon, parody, pongid, simian **7** copycat, emulate, gorilla, imitate, siamang, take off **8** simulate, travesty **9** burlesque, orangutan **10** anthropoid, caricature, chimpanzee **11** impersonate

aperçu
5 brief **6** digest, précis, sketch, survey **7** insight, outline **8** syllabus **10** compendium, impression

aperitif
3 kir **4** whet **5** drink **6** Pastis, Pernod, sherry **7** Campari, Cinzano **8** cocktail **9** appetizer

aperture
3 gap **4** hole, vent **5** chink **6** outlet **7** opening, orifice, pinhole

apery
7 mimicry **9** imitation

apex
3 cap, tip, top **4** acme, cusp, peak, roof **5** crest, crown, limit, point **6** apogee, climax, summit, vertex, zenith **8** capstone, pinnacle, ultimate **9** crescendo, sublimity **11** culmination, ne plus ultra **12** quintessence

aphorism
3 saw **4** rule **5** adage, axiom, maxim, moral **6** dictum, saying, truism **7** precept, proverb **8** apothegm

aphrodisiac
6 erotic **7** amative, amatory, amorous, lustful **8** excitant **10** passionate

Aphrodite
Roman counterpart: 5 Venus
consort: 4 Ares **6** Vulcan **10** Hephaestus
father: 4 Zeus **7** Jupiter
goddess of: 4 love
mother: 5 Dione
sister: 6 Athena **7** Artemis
son: 4 Eros **6** Aeneas **7** Priapus

apiarist
9 beekeeper

apical
3 top **7** highest, topmost **8** loftiest **9** uppermost

apiculture
10 beekeeping

apiece
3 per **4** a pop, each **6** singly, to each **7** for each **8** one by one **9** per capita, severally **10** separately **12** individually, respectively

apish
5 phony, silly **6** phoney **7** slavish **8** affected **9** emulative, imitative **10** artificial

aplenty
4 full **5** ample **6** galore, indeed **7** copious, greatly **8** abundant, very much **9** extremely

aplomb
4 ease **5** poise **6** polish **8** coolness, easiness **9** assurance, certainty, certitude, composure **10** confidence, equanimity **11** nonchalance, savoir faire **12** self-reliance **13** self-assurance

apocalypse
6 augury, oracle, vision **8** disaster, prophecy **10** Armageddon, prediction, revelation

apocalyptic
4 dire **5** awful **7** baleful, baneful, fateful, fearful, ominous **8** Delphian, dreadful, oracular, terrible **9** appalling, climactic, grandiose, prophetic **10** foreboding, predicting **11** foretelling, prophetical, threatening **12** inauspicious
book: 10 Revelation **11** Revelations

apocryphal
5 false, wrong **6** untrue **7** dubious **8** doubtful, spurious **9** incorrect, ungenuine **10** fictitious, inaccurate, unverified **11** unauthentic **12** questionable

apogee
4 acme, apex, peak **6** climax, summit, zenith **8** capstone, meridian, pinnacle **9** high point **11** culmination

Apollo
6 Helios **7** Phoebus

beloved: **6** Cyrene, Daphne **8** Calliope
birthplace: **5** Delos
father: **4** Zeus **7** Jupiter
mother: **4** Leto **6** Latona
oracle: **6** Delphi
sister: **5** Diana **7** Artemis
son: **3** Ion **7** Orpheus
temple: **6** Delphi

apologetic
5 sorry **6** rueful **8** contrite, penitent **9** regretful, repentant **10** remorseful **11** penitential **12** compunctious

apologia
4 plea **6** excuse, reason **7** defense **8** argument **11** elucidation, explanation **13** clarification, justification

apologize
5 atone **6** lament, regret, repent **7** confess **9** beg pardon **10** make amends

apologue
4 myth, tale **5** fable, story **7** parable **8** allegory

apology
4 plea **6** amends, excuse **7** redress, regrets **8** mea culpa **9** admission, makeshift **10** concession, confession

apoplexy
4 esca **6** stroke

apostasy
7 perfidy **9** defection, desertion, disavowal, falseness, rejection **11** abandonment, repudiation **12** disaffection, renunciation

apostate
7 heretic, traitor **8** defector, deserter, recreant, renegade, turncoat **9** turnabout

apostatize
4 turn **6** defect, desert **7** abandon, forsake, sell out **8** renounce **9** repudiate

a posteriori
9 inductive

apostle
4 John, Jude, Paul **5** James, Judas, Peter, Silas, Simon **6** Andrew, Philip, Thomas **7** Matthew **8** Barnabas, disciple, follower, Matthias, preacher **9** missioner **10** colporteur, evangelist, missionary **11** Bartholomew **12** propagandist
of Germany: **8** Boniface
of Ireland: **7** Patrick
of the English: **9** Augustine
of the French: **5** Denis
of the Gauls: **8** Irenaeus
of the Gentiles: **4** Paul
of the Goths: **7** Ulfilas
to the Indians: **9** John Eliot

apothecary
7 chemist **8** druggist, pharmacy **9** drugstore **10** pharmacist

apothegm
see **aphorism**

apotheosis
6 height **7** epitome **8** exemplar, ultimate **9** archetype, elevation **10** embodiment, exaltation **11** deification, ennoblement, idolization, lionization **12** enshrinement, quintessence **13** glorification

appall
3 awe **4** faze **5** alarm, shake, shock **6** dismay **7** horrify, outrage, overawe, perturb **8** confound, distress **10** disconcert **11** consternate

appalled
6 aghast **11** dumbfounded

appalling
5 awful **6** horrid **7** fearful **8** daunting, dreadful, horrible, horrific, shocking, terrible **9** atrocious, dismaying, frightful, loathsome **10** disgusting, formidable, horrifying

appanage
5 grant, right **7** adjunct **8** property **9** endowment, privilege **10** birthright, perquisite **11** prerogative

apparatus
4 gear, tool **5** gismo, gizmo **6** device, gadget, outfit, tackle, widget **7** utensil **8** matériel, tackling **9** equipment, implement, machinery **10** instrument **11** contraption **13** accouterments, accoutrements, paraphernalia

apparel
4 clad, duds, garb, gear, robe, suit, togs **5** adorn, array, dress, getup, habit **6** attire, clothe, livery, outfit **7** clothes, costume, garment, raiment, threads, vesture **8** clothing, enclothe, glad rags, vestment **9** embellish **11** habiliments

apparent
5 clear, overt, plain **6** patent **7** evident, obvious, seeming, visible **8** distinct, manifest, palpable **9** succedent **10** noticeable, observable **11** discernible, perceivable, perceptible

apparition
5 ghost, shade, umbra **6** shadow, spirit, vision, wraith **7** fantasm, phantom, specter **8** illusion, phantasm **10** appearance, phenomenon **13** hallucination

appeal
3 ask, beg, bid **4** call, lure, plea, pray, pull, suit, urge **5** apply, brace, charm, crave, plead **6** accuse, allure, charge, excite, invoke, sue for **7** attract, beseech, entreat, glamour, implore, request **8** call upon, charisma, entreaty, interest, intrigue, petition **9** fascinate, importune, magnetism, seduction **10** allurement, attraction, supplicate **11** application, fascination, imploration **12** drawing power, solicitation, supplication

appealing
8 alluring, charming, pleading, pleasant, pleasing **9** agreeable **10** attractive, bewitching, enchanting **11** captivating, fascinating

appear
4 look, loom, rise, seem, show **5** arise, issue, occur **6** arrive, emerge, show up, turn up **7** emanate **8** resemble **9** come forth **11** materialize

appearance
3 air **4** face, form, look, mien, pose, show **5** debut, dress, front, guise, image **6** advent, aspect, facade, manner **7** arrival, bearing, display, seeming **8** attitude, demeanor, illusion **9** semblance **10** impression, occurrence, simulacrum **11** countenance **13** manifestation

appease
4 calm, ease **5** allay, quiet **6** buy off, pacify, soothe **7** assuage, concede, content, gratify, mollify, placate, relieve, satisfy, sweeten **10** conciliate, propitiate

appellation
4 name **5** brand, label, nomen, style, title **7** moniker **8** cognomen **10** identifier **11** designation **12** denomination

append
3 add **5** add on, affix, annex, tag on **6** adjoin, attach, tack on **7** subjoin **10** supplement

appendage
3 arm, fin, leg, tab, tag **4** barb, flap, horn, limb, seta, tail, wing **5** extra **6** cercus, member **7** adjunct, antenna, elytron, stipule **8** pedipalp, pendicle, tentacle **9** accessory, auxiliary, extremity **10** attachment, collateral, incidental, projection, supplement **12** appurtenance, nonessential, protuberance

appendix
5 notes, rider **7** adjunct, codicil **8** addendum, addition **9** accessory, appendage **10** attachment, supplement **12** appurtenance

apperception
5 grasp **9** awareness **10** cognizance **11** realization, recognition **12** apprehension, assimilation **13** comprehension, introspection, understanding

appertain
4 bear **5** apply, refer **6** bear on, belong, relate **8** bear upon **10** be relevant **11** be connected, be pertinent

appetence
3 yen **5** taste **6** desire, hunger, relish, thirst **7** craving, longing, stomach **8** fondness

appetent
4 agog, avid, keen **5** eager **6** ardent **7** anxious, craving, lusting, thirsty **8** desirous, yearning **9** impatient **10** breathless

appetite
3 yen **4** bent, itch, lust, urge **5** taste **6** desire, hunger, liking, relish **7** craving, leaning, longing, passion, stomach **8** cupidity, fondness, gluttony, penchant, soft spot, voracity, weakness, yearning **9** hankering **10** preference, proclivity, propensity **11** inclination

appetizer
4 whet **5** snack **6** canapé, savory, tidbit **7** starter **8** aperitif, cocktail, stimulus **9** antipasto **11** amuse-bouche, hors d'oeuvre

appetizing
5 tasty **6** savory **8** saporous, tempting **9** agreeable, appealing, aperitive, flavorful, palatable, relishing, toothsome **10** delectable, flavorsome **11** scrumptious, tantalizing **13** mouth-watering

applaud
4 clap, hail, laud, root **5** bravo, cheer, extol **6** praise, rise to **7** acclaim, approve, commend **9** recommend **10** compliment

applause
4 hand **5** round **6** bravos, cheers, praise **7** acclaim, hurrahs, ovation, rooting **8** accolade, approval, cheering, clapping, plaudits **11** acclamation **12** commendation

apple
4 crab, Fuji, Gala, pome **6** Empire, Macoun, pippin, russet **7** Baldwin, costard, Duchess, Winesap **8** Braeburn, Cortland, greening, Jonagold, Jonathan, McIntosh **9** Delicious **10** Rome Beauty **11** Granny Smith, Gravenstein, Northern Spy, Transparent
dessert: **5** crisp
juice: **5** cider
sugar: **4** ates **8** sweetsop

applejack
5 cider **6** brandy, liquor **8** calvados **9** hard cider

apple knocker
see **rustic**

apple-polish
4 fawn **5** toady **6** kowtow **7** cater to, flatter, honey up, truckle **8** butter up **10** curry favor, ingratiate

apple-polisher
5 toady **6** yes-man **8** bootlick, groveler, lickspit **9** flatterer, sycophant **11** lickspittle

applesauce
5 hooey **6** bunkum **7** baloney, rubbish, twaddle **8** malarkey, nonsense **9** poppycock

appliance
6 device **7** utensil **9** implement **10** instrument **11** application
kitchen: **4** oven **5** mixer, range, stove **6** fridge **7** blender, toaster **9** can opener, microwave **10** dishwasher **12** refrigerator

applicability
3 use **7** account, fitness, utility **9** advantage, relevance **10** usefulness

applicable
3 apt, fit **4** just, meet **5** ad rem **6** seemly, suited, useful **7** apropos, fitting, germane **8** apposite, material, relevant, suitable **9** befitting, pertinent **10** felicitous **11** appropriate

applicant
6 seeker **7** hopeful **8** aspirant, inquirer **9** candidate, job-hunter, job-seeker

application
3 use **4** form, heed, plea, suit **5** study **6** appeal, debate, effort, letter **7** request **8** entreaty, exercise, exertion, industry, petition **9** assiduity, attention, diligence, operation, treatment **10** dedication **11** requisition, utilization

appliqué
5 decal

apply
3 dab, use **4** bend, give, turn, urge **5** press, put on, refer **6** accost, affect, appeal, assign, bear on, bestow, devote, direct, employ, engage, handle, relate, resort, take on **7** address, beseech, concern, entreat, execute, implore, involve, pertain, utilize **8** approach, bear upon, exercise, petition, set about **9** appertain, implement, importune, undertake **10** administer, buckle down

appoint
3 arm, fix, rig, set, tap **4** gear, name **5** equip **6** assign, decide, fit out, outfit, supply **7** dress up, furbish, furnish, provide, turn out **8** accouter, accoutre, accredit, delegate, nominate **9** authorize, designate, determine, embellish, provision **10** commission

appointment
3 job **4** date, meet, post, spot **5** berth, place, tryst **6** billet, choice, office **7** meeting **8** election, position **9** equipment, selection, situation **10** assignment, connection, engagement, rendezvous **11** arrangement, assignation, designation

appointments
7 fitting **8** equipage **9** equipment, trappings **11** furnishings **13** accouterments, accoutrements

apportion
3 cut, lot **4** give, mete, part **5** allot, allow, cut up, divvy, quota, serve, share, slice, split **6** assign, bestow, divide, parcel, ration **7** deal out, dish out, divvy up, dole out, measure, mete out, prorate, split up **8** allocate, dispense, separate, share out **9** admeasure, partition **10** administer, distribute

apportionment
3 cut, lot **4** part **5** piece, quota, share, slice, split **6** ration **7** measure, quantum **9** allotment, allowance **10** allocation, assignment

apposite
3 apt **4** just **5** ad rem **6** proper, suited, timely **7** apropos, fitting, germane, right on **8** material, on target, relevant, suitable **9** pertinent **10** applicable **11** appropriate

appositeness
7 aptness, fitness **9** relevance **10** pertinence, timeliness **11** suitability

appraisal
5 stock **6** rating, survey **7** pricing **8** estimate, judgment **9** valuation **10** assessment, estimation, evaluation

appraise
3 eye, fix, set **4** rate, size **5** assay, audit, gauge, judge, price, set at, value **6** assess, figure, size up, survey **7** adjudge, examine, inspect, measure, valuate **8** estimate, evaluate, look over **9** calculate, figure out

appreciable
5 clear, plain **6** marked **7** evident, obvious **8** apparent, clear-cut, concrete, manifest, material, palpable, sensible, tangible **10** detectable, measurable, noticeable, observable **11** discernible, perceptible, substantial **12** considerable

appreciate
4 gain, go up, grow, know, like, love, rise **5** enjoy, grasp, judge, prize, savor, value **6** admire, esteem, fathom, regard, relish **7** apprize, cherish, cognize, enhance, improve, inflate, realize, respect **8** evaluate, increase, treasure **9** apprehend, delight in, recognize **10** comprehend, understand

appreciation
4 gain, rise **6** growth, regard, thanks **7** tribute **8** increase, judgment **9** awareness, gratitude, inflation **10** evaluation, perception **11** recognition, sensitivity, testimonial **12** gratefulness

apprehend
3 nab **4** bust, fear, grab, know, nail, read, twig **5** catch, grasp, run in, seize, sense **6** absorb, accept, arrest, collar, detain, divine, fathom, pick up, take in **7** capture, catch on, cognize, compass, foresee, make out, preknow, realize **8** conceive **9** recognize, visualize **10** anticipate, appreciate, understand

apprehensible
5 clear, lucid, plain **7** evident, obvious **8** distinct, explicit, knowable, luminous **9** graspable **10** fathomable

apprehension
3 ken **4** care, fear, idea **5** alarm, angst, dread, grasp, pinch, worry **6** arrest, notion, pickup, unease **7** anxiety, capture, concern, seizure,

thought **8** disquiet, judgment **9** agitation, awareness, detention, knowledge, misgiving, suspicion **10** conception, foreboding, perception, solicitude, uneasiness **11** disquietude, premonition **13** understanding

apprehensive
5 alive, awake, aware, sharp **6** afraid, astute, scared, uneasy **7** anxious, fearful, knowing, worried **8** sensible, sentient, troubled **9** cognizant, conscious, observant, sensitive **10** discerning, disquieted, insightful, perceptive

apprentice
4 bind, tiro, tyro **5** pupil **6** novice, rookie **7** learner, starter, student, trainee **8** beginner, freshman, neophyte, newcomer **9** novitiate **10** tenderfoot

apprenticed
5 bound **7** obliged, pledged **8** articled **9** obligated **10** indentured

apprise
4 clue, post, tell, warn **6** advise, clue in, fill in, impart, inform, notify, reveal, wise up **7** let know **8** acquaint, announce, describe, disclose **9** make known **11** communicate

apprize
5 value **6** admire, esteem, regard, relish **7** cherish **8** hold dear, treasure **10** appreciate, rate highly

approach
4 near, nigh **5** reach, rival, verge **6** avenue, border, gain on **7** address, advance, apply to, attempt, descent **8** draw near, overture **11** approximate

approachable
7 affable **8** friendly, sociable **9** agreeable, congenial, reachable, receptive **10** accessible, attainable

approaching
6 coming **7** nearing **8** expected, imminent, oncoming, upcoming **11** forthcoming

approbate
4 back, like **5** favor **6** accept, assent, praise **7** applaud, approve, commend, consent, endorse, support **8** sanction **9** recommend **11** countenance

approbation
2 OK **3** nod **4** euge, okay **5** bravo, favor **6** esteem, praise **7** acclaim, consent, support **8** applause, approval, sanction **10** admiration, permission **11** endorsement, recognition **12** commendation

appropriate
3 apt, cop, due, fit **4** grab, just, lift, meet, take, true **5** allot, annex, claim, exact, filch, grasp, pinch, right, seize, steal, swipe, usurp **6** assign, assume, budget, devote, pilfer, proper, snatch, snitch, suited, timely, useful, worthy **7** apropos, desired, earmark, fitting, germane, merited, preempt, purloin **8** accroach, apposite, arrogate, deserved, eligible, entitled, relevant, rightful, set apart, set aside, suitable **9** befitting, opportune, pertinent, requisite **10** acceptable, admissible, applicable, commandeer, compatible, confiscate, convenient, felicitous, seasonable

appropriately
4 well **5** amply, aptly, right **8** properly, suitably **9** fittingly **10** acceptably, adequately, becomingly

appropriateness
3 use **5** order **7** account, aptness, fitness, service, utility **8** meetness **9** advantage, propriety, relevance, rightness **10** expediency, usefulness **13** applicability

appropriation
5 grant **7** funding, stipend, subsidy **9** allotment, allowance **10** allocation, assignment, earmarking, subvention

approval
2 OK **3** nod **4** okay **5** favor, leave, say-so **6** assent **7** consent, go-ahead, license, support **8** applause, blessing, sanction, suffrage **10** acceptance, compliment, green light, permission **11** approbation, benediction, concurrence, endorsement **12** commendation, confirmation, ratification **13** authorization

approve
2 OK **4** okay **5** clear, favor, go for **6** accept, back up, praise, ratify, uphold **7** applaud, certify, commend, condone, confirm, endorse, initial, mandate, stand by, support, sustain **8** accredit, hold with, sanction **9** approbate, authorize, encourage **10** compliment **11** countenance

approximate
4 near **5** close, rough, touch **6** almost **7** similar, verge on **8** approach, ballpark, come near **10** resembling

approximately
4 most, nigh, or so **5** about, circa **6** all but, almost, nearly **7** close to **8** well-nigh **9** just about **10** more or less **11** practically

approximation
8 likeness, nearness **9** closeness **10** similarity **11** resemblance

appurtenance
7 adjunct **8** addition, appendix, ornament **9** accessory, apparatus, appendage **10** attachment **11** furnishings **13** accompaniment

appurtenant
5 extra **8** adjuvant **9** accessory, ancillary, auxiliary **10** additional, collateral, subsidiary **11** subordinate, subservient **12** accompanying, contributory

apricot
3 ume **4** ansu

a priori
8 provable, reasoned **9** deducible, deductive, derivable, inferable **11** inferential, presumptive

apron
5 stage **6** shield **7** garment **8** pinafore **9** extension

apropos
3 apt **4** as to, in re, meet **5** about, ad rem, anent, aptly, as for **6** proper, timely **7** fitting, germane, related **8** apposite, material, relevant, suitable, suitably, touching **9** as regards, opportune, pertinent, regarding **10** applicable, concerning, respecting **11** applicative, in respect to

apt
3 fit **4** just **5** alert, given, prone, quick, ready, savvy, smart **6** bright, clever, liable, likely, prompt, proper **7** apropos, fitting, germane, tending **8** apposite, disposed, inclined, relevant, suitable **9** befitting, pertinent, qualified **10** felicitous, responsive **11** appropriate, intelligent

aptitude
4 bent, gift **5** flair, knack, savvy **6** genius, liking, talent **7** ability, faculty, fitness **8** capacity, tendency **10** capability, cleverness, proclivity, propensity **11** disposition, inclination, suitability **12** predilection

aptness
4 bent, gift **5** flair, knack, skill **6** genius, talent **7** ability, faculty, fitness **8** tendency **9** propriety, readiness **10** capability, cleverness, expediency, likelihood **11** inclination, suitability **12** intelligence

aquanaut
5 diver **10** scuba diver

aquarium
4 tank **8** fish tank

aqua vitae
4 grog **5** booze, drink, hooch **6** brandy, cognac, liquor, tipple **7** alcohol, spirits **8** schnapps

aqueduct
5 canal **6** course **7** channel, conduit, passage **8** waterway **11** watercourse

aqueous
5 fluid **6** liquid, watery **9** liquefied

Aquila
5 eagle **13** constellation
star: **6** Altair

Aquitaine
7 Guienne
queen: **7** Eleanor

aquiver
5 shaky **7** quaking, shaking, trembly **9** shivering, trembling, tremulant, tremulous

Arab
chief: **4** emir **5** sheik **6** sheikh, sultan
country: **4** Iraq, Oman **5** Egypt, Libya, Qatar, Sudan, Syria, Yemen **6** Jordan, Kuwait **7** Algeria, Bahrain, Lebanon, Morocco, Tunisia **11** Saudi Arabia

arable
7 fertile **8** fruitful, tillable **10** cultivable, productive

Arachne
father: **5** Idmon
form: **6** spider
mother: **6** Cyrene
rival: **6** Athena **7** Minerva

arachnid
4 mite, tick **6** acarus, spider **8** scorpion **9** arthropod, phalangid, tarantula **10** harvestman **13** daddy longlegs

arbiter
3 ump **5** judge **6** expert, umpire **7** referee **8** mediator **9** authority, moderator **11** adjudicator

arbitrary
4 rash **6** chance, random **7** erratic, offhand, wayward, willful **8** fanciful, heedless **9** frivolous, impetuous, whimsical **10** capricious, subjective **10** irrational **12** unreasonable **13** discretionary

arbitrate
5 judge **6** settle, umpire **7** adjudge, mediate, referee **9** intervene **10** adjudicate **12** intermediate

arbitrator
5 judge **6** umpire **7** referee, settler **8** mediator **9** moderator **11** adjudicator

arbor
4 axle, beam **5** bower, frame, shaft **7** pergola, shelter, spindle

arc
3 bow, lob **4** arch, bend, path **5** curve, round **7** rainbow **9** curvation, curvature **11** measurement, progression

arcade
6 arches, loggia **7** gallery **10** passageway
game: **8** Skee-Ball
pioneer: **5** Atari

arcadia
4 Eden, Zion **6** heaven, utopia **7** Elysium, nirvana **8** paradise **9** fairyland, Shangri-la **10** wonderland

arcane
6 hidden, mystic, occult, opaque, secret **7** obscure, unknown **8** abstruse, esoteric **9** recondite **10** cabalistic, mysterious, unknowable **11** inscrutable **12** impenetrable **13** unaccountable

Arcas
father: **4** Zeus **7** Jupiter
mother: **8** Callisto

arch
3 bow, coy, sly **4** bend, hump, pert **5** curve, fresh, saucy, vault **6** camber, cheeky, impish **7** playful, roguish, waggish **8** flippant, malapert **9** curvature **10** coquettish **11** mischievous
inner curve: **6** soffit **8** intrados
kind: **4** ogee **5** ogive, round, Tudor **6** lancet **7** rampart, trefoil **9** horseshoe, primitive, segmental **10** shouldered **11** equilateral **12** basket-handle
outer curve: **8** extrados
part: **6** impost **8** keystone, springer, voussoir

archaeological site
Africa: **8** Zimbabwe **13** Great Zimbabwe
Britain: **7** Avebury **9** Skara Brae, Sutton Hoo **10** Stonehenge
Cambodia: **6** Angkor **9** Angkor Wat
Crete: **7** Knossos
Egypt: **4** Giza **5** Luxor **6** Abydos, Karnak, Naqada, Thebes **7** Memphis **9** El-Bahnasa **11** Oxyrhynchus
Greece: **6** Delphi **7** Mycenae, Olympia
Guatemala: **5** Tikal
Honduras: **5** Copán
Indonesia: **9** Borobudur
Iran: **10** Persepolis
Iraq: **4** Isin, Nuzi **6** Nimrud **7** Babylon, Nineveh, Samarra
Israel: **7** Jericho
Italy: **7** Pompeii **11** Herculaneum
Lebanon: **6** Byblos **7** Baalbek
Mexico: **5** Mitla, Tulum, Uxmal **8** Palenque **10** Monte Albán **11** Chichén Itzá
Peru: **11** Machu Picchu
Syria: **7** Palmyra
Tunisia: **8** Carthage, Kairouan
Turkey: **4** Troy **6** Knidos **8** Hisarlik, Pergamon **9** Hissarlik
Uzbekistan: **9** Samarkand

archaeologist
4 Bell (Gertrude), Dart (Raymond) **5** Evans (Arthur) **6** Carter (Howard), Childe (V. Gordon), Kidder (Alfred), Petrie (Flinders) **7** Thomsen (Christian), Woolley (Leonard), Worsaae (Jens) **8** Breasted (James Henry), Goodyear (William) **10** Schliemann (Heinrich) **11** Champollion (Jean-François), Winckelmann (Johann)

archaic
3 old **5** dated, olden, passé **6** bygone **7** ancient, antique **8** obsolete, outdated **9** out-of-date, primitive, unevolved **10** antiquated **11** undeveloped **12** old-fashioned

archangel
5 Uriel **7** Gabriel, Michael, Raphael

arched
4 bent **5** bowed, round **6** curved **7** curving, rounded

archer
4 Tell (William) **5** Cupid **6** bowman **9** Robin Hood **11** Sagittarius

archery
9 toxophily

archetypal
5 ideal, model **7** classic, perfect, typical **9** classical, exemplary **10** consummate **12** paradigmatic, prototypical

archetype
4 idea **5** ideal, model **6** mirror **7** epitome, essence, example, pattern **8** exemplar, original, paradigm, standard **9** beau ideal, prototype **10** apotheosis, embodiment, protoplast **12** quintessence

archfiend
5 demon, devil, Satan **6** diablo **7** Lucifer

Archie
character: **5** Betty, Lodge (Hiram) **6** Archie, Reggie **7** Andrews (Fred, Mary), Jughead **8** Veronica
creator: **7** Montana (Bob)
Jughead's pet: **6** Hot Dog
school: **9** Riverdale
school staff: **6** Grundy (Geraldine), Kleats (Coach) **7** Beazley (Miss), Clayton (Coach), Svenson (Mr.) **10** Flutesnoot (Prof.), Weatherbee (Mr. Waldo)
shop owner: **7** Pop Tate

Archimedes
5 Greek **8** inventor
cry: **6** eureka
discovery: **5** screw **8** buoyancy **9** principle **11** water raiser

archipelago
Asian: **5** Malay
Canada: **6** Arctic
Japan: **4** Goto **9** Gotoretto
Norway: **11** Spitsbergen
Papua New Guinea: **8** Bismarck **9** Louisiade
Philippines: **4** Sulu
off Scotland: **7** Orcades, Orkneys
United States: **9** Alexander

architect
5 maker **7** creator **8** designer, inventor **9** generator **10** originator
American: **3** Pei (I. M.) **4** Hood (Raymond), Kahn (Louis) **5** Gehry (Frank), McKim (Charles), Meier (Richard), Roche (Kevin), Stone (Edward Durell), Weese (Harry), White (Stanford) **6** Breuer (Marcel), Fuller (Buckminster), Graves (Michael), Morgan (Julia), Neutra (Richard), Rogers (Isaiah), Soleri (Paolo), Upjohn (Richard), Walter (Thomas), Warren (William), Wright (Frank Lloyd) **7** Burnham (Daniel), Gilbert (Cass), Johnson (Philip), Latrobe (Benjamin), Olmsted

(Frederick Law), Renwick (James), Sturgis (John Hubbard), Venturi (Robert) **8** Bulfinch (Charles), Saarinen (Eero, Eliel), Sullivan (Louis), Thornton (William), Yamasaki (Minoru) **10** Richardson (Henry Hobson)
Austrian: **4** Loos (Adolf) **6** Wagner (Otto)
Brazilian: **8** Niemeyer (Oscar)
Canadian: **6** Safdie (Moshe)
Dutch: **8** Koolhaas (Rem), Rietveld (Gerrit)
English: **4** Nash (John), Shaw (Richard), Wood (John), Wren (Christopher) **5** Jones (Inigo), Scott (George Gilbert), Wyatt (James) **6** Foster (Norman), Rogers (Richard), Street (George Edmund), Voysey (Charles) **7** Lutyens (Edwin) **8** Vanbrugh (John)
Finnish: **5** Aalto (Alvar) **8** Saarinen (Eero, Eliel)
French: **6** Perret (Auguste) **7** Garnier (Tony), L'Enfant (Pierre-Charles) **11** Le Corbusier **12** Viollet-le-Duc (Eugène)
German: **7** Gropius (Walter) **8** Schinkel (Karl) **10** Mendelsohn (Erich)
Israeli: **6** Safdie (Moshe)
Italian: **5** Nervi (Pier Luigi), Piano (Renzo) **6** Romano (Giulio), Soleri (Paolo) **7** Alberti (Leon Battista), Bernini (Gian Lorenzo), da Vinci (Leonardo), Orcagna, Peruzzi (Baldassare), Raphael, Vignola (Giacomo da) **8** Bramante (Donato), Leonardo (da Vinci), Palladio (Andrea), Sangallo (Giuliano da), Terragni (Giuseppe) **9** Borromini (Francesco), Sansovino (Jacopo) **12** Michelangelo
Japanese: **5** Tange (Kenzo) **8** Yamasaki (Minoru)
Roman: **9** Vitruvius
Scottish: **10** Mackintosh (Charles Rennie)
Spanish: **5** Gaudí (Antonio)
Swedish: **7** Asplund (Erik Gunnar)

architecture
6 design, makeup **9** formation **11** composition **12** constitution, construction
ornament: **4** boss, fret **5** gutta **6** finial, volute **7** cabling, console, crocket, diglyph **8** triglyph, vignette **9** arabesque, modillion
style: **5** Doric, Ionic, Tudor **6** Gothic, Norman, Rococo **7** Baroque **8** Colonial, Georgian **9** Byzantine, Victorian **10** Corinthian, Romanesque

archive
4 file **6** record **7** collect, history, library, records **8** document, register **9** chronicle **10** collection, repository

archon
10 magistrate

arctic
3 icy **4** cold **5** chill, gelid **6** chilly, frigid, frosty, wintry **7** glacial, numbing **8** freezing, hibernal **11** hyperborean
animal: **3** auk, fox **4** bear, hare, seal, vole **5** sable, whale **6** ermine, marten **7** caribou, lemming **8** reindeer **9** polar bear, ptarmigan
base: **4** Etah **5** Thule **6** Barrow **11** Point Barrow
bird: **3** auk
cetacean: **7** narwhal
current: **8** Labrador
dog: **5** husky **7** Samoyed **8** malamute
explorer: **4** Byrd (Richard), Cook (Frederick) **5** Bylot (Robert), Davis (John), Peary (Robert) **6** Baffin (William), Bering (Vitus), Henson (Matthew), Hudson (Henry), Nansen (Fridtjof), Nobile (Umberto) **7** Barents (Willem), Bennett (Floyd), Wilkins (George), Wrangel (Ferdinand) **8** Amundsen (Roald) **9** Ellsworth (Lincoln), Mackenzie (Alexander), MacMillan (Donald) **10** Stefansson (Vilhjalmus)
forest: **5** taiga
jacket: **5** parka **6** anorak
people: **4** Lapp **5** Aleut, Inuit, Yakut **6** Eskimo, Tungus **7** Chukchi, Samoyed
sea: **4** Kara **6** Laptev **7** Barents, Chukchi **8** Beaufort
transport: **7** dogsled
treeless plains: **6** tundra

ardent
3 hot **4** agog, avid, keen, true **5** eager, fiery, loyal **6** fervid, fierce, heated, intent, red-hot, strong, torrid **7** blazing, burning, devoted, earnest, fervent, flaming, glowing, intense, shining, staunch, zealous **8** constant, desirous, faithful, powerful, resolute, sizzling, vehement, white-hot **9** allegiant, impatient, impetuous, impulsive, perfervid, scorching, steadfast **10** breathless, hot-blooded, passionate **11** impassioned **12** enthusiastic

ardor
4 élan, fire, heat, zeal, zest, zing **5** gusto, verve, vigor **6** energy, fealty, fervor, spirit, warmth **7** avidity, loyalty, passion **8** devotion, fidelity **9** eagerness, intensity, vehemence **10** allegiance, enthusiasm, excitement **12** faithfulness

arduous
4 hard **5** harsh, rough, sheer, steep, tight, tough **6** severe, taxing, tiring, trying, uphill **7** labored **8** grueling, rigorous, toilsome **9** difficult, effortful, gruelling, laborious, punishing, strenuous **10** formidable **11** precipitate, precipitous

area
4 belt, turf, zone **5** field, place, range, realm, scene, space, tract **6** domain, locale, region, sector, sphere **7** expanse, stretch **8** district, locality, province, vicinity **9** bailiwick, territory **12** neighborhood
unit: **3** ure **4** acre **7** hectare

arena
5 field, scene, stage **6** sphere **7** stadium, theater **8** activity, building, coliseum, province **10** hippodrome **12** amphitheater
level: **4** tier

Ares
Roman counterpart: **4** Mars
consort: **9** Aphrodite
father: **4** Zeus
mother: **4** Enyo, Hera
sister: **4** Eris
son: **5** Remus **7** Romulus

arête
5 crest, ridge

Arethusa
5 nymph **6** spring **9** wood nymph
pursuer: **7** Alpheus

argent
6 silver **7** silvern, silvery **9** whiteness

Argentina
capital: **11** Buenos Aires
city: **6** Paraná **7** Córdoba, La Plata, Rosario, Santa Fe **11** Mar del Plata
desert: **9** Patagonia
language: **7** Spanish
leader: **5** Perón (Juan)
monetary unit: **4** peso
mountain, range: **5** Andes **9** Aconcagua
neighbor: **5** Chile **6** Brazil **7** Bolivia, Uruguay **8** Paraguay
plain: **6** Pampas
river: **5** Plata (Río de la) **6** Paraná **8** Colorado **12** Río de la Plata
volcano: **5** Maipo **9** Tupungato

Arges
7 Cyclops
brother: **7** Brontes **8** Steropes
father: **6** Uranus
mother: **4** Gaea

argon symbol
2 Ar

Argonaut
4 hero **10** adventurer **13** paper nautilus
leader: **5** Jason

argosy
4 ship **5** fleet **6** armada, supply **8** flotilla

argot
4 cant **5** idiom, lingo, slang **6** jargon, patois, patter **7** dialect **10** vernacular

arguable
4 moot **7** dubious **8** doubtful **9** debatable, in dispute, uncertain **10** disputable **11** contestable, problematic **12** questionable

argue
5 claim, clash, prove **6** assert, attest, bicker, debate, differ, induce, object, reason **7** agitate, canvass, contend, discuss, dispute, dissent, justify, protest, quarrel, quibble, stickle, testify, witness, wrangle **8** announce, conflict, consider, disagree, indicate, maintain, persuade, polemize, squabble **9** thrash out **10** polemicize **11** expostulate, remonstrate

argument
3 row **4** case, feud, flap, fuss **5** claim, proof, set-to, theme, topic **6** debate, dustup, hassle, motive, reason, rumpus, thesis **7** defense, dispute, polemic, sorites, subject, summary, wrangle **8** abstract, evidence, rebuttal **9** amplitude, assertion, discourse **10** contention, discussion, dissension, squabbling **11** controversy, disputation, embroilment **12** disagreement

argumentation
6 debate **7** dispute, oratory **8** forensic, rhetoric **9** dialectic, reasoning **10** discussion **11** controversy, disputation

argumentative
4 moot **9** in dispute, litigious, polemical **11** contentious, quarrelsome **12** disputatious, questionable **13** controversial

Argus
father: **4** Zeus
mother: **5** Niobe
slayer: **6** Hermes

Argus-eyed
5 alert **8** watchful **9** all-seeing

argyle
4 sock **6** design **7** diamond, pattern **8** Campbell

aria
3 air, lay **4** hymn, lied, solo, song, tune **5** ditty **6** melody **7** descant

Ariadne
father: **5** Minos
husband: **7** Theseus
island home: **5** Naxos
mother: **8** Pasiphaë

arid
3 dry **4** drab, dull, sere **5** dusty, vapid **6** barren, boring, desert, dreary, jejune **7** bone-dry, insipid, parched, sterile, tedious, thirsty **8** droughty, lifeless, weariful **9** dryasdust, infertile, unwatered, waterless, wearisome **10** lackluster, spiritless, unfruitful **12** moistureless **13** uninteresting

Ariel
6 spirit
master: **8** Prospero

Aries
3 ram **13** constellation

aright
4 well **5** fitly **6** justly, nicely **8** decently, properly **9** correctly, fittingly, precisely **10** accurately, decorously

Ariosto epic
14 Orlando Furioso

arise
4 go up, lift, soar, wake **5** awake, begin, get up, issue, mount, occur, start **6** appear, ascend, aspire, come up, crop up, emerge, spring, uprear, wake up **7** emanate, proceed **8** commence **9** originate

Aristaeus
father: **6** Apollo
mother: **6** Cyrene
son: **7** Actaeon
wife: **7** Autonoë

aristocracy
5 elite, state **6** gentry, jet set **7** who's who **8** nobility, noblesse **9** beau monde, blue blood, gentility, haut monde **10** government, patricians, patriciate, upper class, upper crust

aristocrat
9 blue blood, gentleman, patrician
ancient Greek: **8** eupatrid
Russian: **5** boyar **6** boyard

aristocratic
5 aloof, elite, noble **6** lordly **7** courtly, elegant, genteel, haughty, refined, stately **8** highborn, well-born, well-bred **9** dignified, exclusive, patrician **10** privileged, upper-class, upper-crust **11** blue-blooded

Aristophanes play
5 Birds (The), Frogs (The), Wasps (The) **6** Clouds (The), Plutus **10** Lysistrata

arithmetic
4 math **8** addition, counting, figuring **9** ciphering, reckoning **10** estimation **11** calculation, computation, mathematics

Arizona
capital: **7** Phoenix
city: **4** Mesa, Yuma **5** Tempe **6** Bisbee, Sedona, Tucson **8** Glendale, Prescott **9** Flagstaff **10** Scottsdale
mountain: **9** Humphreys (Peak)
nickname: **11** Grand Canyon (State)
park: **15** Petrified Forest
river: **4** Gila, Salt **8** Colorado
state bird: **10** cactus wren
state flower: **7** saguaro (cactus)
state tree: **9** palo verde

ark
3 den **4** ship **5** chest, haven **6** adytum, asylum, refuge **7** convent, retreat, shelter **8** hideaway **9** safe house, sanctuary **10** repository, Torah chest
landfall: **6** Ararat
wood: **6** gopher **7** cypress

Arkansas
capital: **10** Little Rock
city: **4** Hope **9** Fort Smith, Pine Bluff **10** Hot Springs **11** Bentonville **12** Fayetteville
mountain, range: **5** Ozark **8** Magazine
nickname: **17** Land of Opportunity
river: **3** Red
state bird: **11** mockingbird
state flower: **12** apple blossom
state tree: **12** loblolly pine

arm
3 bay, ell, gun, rig **4** cove, gear, gulf, limb, wing **5** annex, bayou, equip, firth, force, inlet, power **6** fit out, harbor, muscle, outfit, slough, weapon **7** appoint, furnish, turn out **8** accouter, strength **9** extension
bone: **4** ulna **6** radius **7** humerus
combining form: **6** brachi **7** brachio
muscle: **6** biceps **7** triceps

armada
4 navy **5** boats, fleet, force, group, ships **7** vessels **8** flotilla, warships

armadillo
4 apar, peba, tatu
relative: **5** sloth **8** anteater, tamandua

armament
4 arms **5** armor **6** weapon **7** defense **8** ordnance, security, weaponry **9** munitions, safeguard **10** ammunition, protection

armamentarium
4 fund **5** stock, store **6** supply **9** inventory

armchair
6 remote **8** fauteuil **9** vicarious **11** theoretical

armed forces
4 army, navy **6** troops **7** marines **8** air force, military **10** servicemen

Armenia
capital: **7** Yerevan
city: **6** Gyumri **8** Vanadzor
lake: **5** Sevan
monetary unit: **4** dram
mountain, range: **7** Aragats **8** Caucasus
neighbor: **4** Iran **6** Turkey **7** Georgia **10** Azerbaijan
river: **5** Araks

armistice
5 truce **9** agreement, cease-fire **10** suspension

armor
4 mail **5** aegis, cover, guard **6** shield **7** buckler **8** security **9** safeguard **10** protection

arm: **8** brassard
body: **7** cuirass
armpit: **8** pallette
buttocks: **5** culet
coat: **7** hauberk **10** brigandine
face: **5** visor **6** beaver
flexible: **4** mail
foot: **8** solleret
hand: **7** gantlet **8** gauntlet
head: **6** helmet
horse: **4** bard **5** barde **8** chamfron
leg: **6** greave **7** jambeau
mail: **4** coif **7** hauberk
suit: **7** panoply
thigh: **4** tace **5** tasse **6** cuisse, tuille
throat: **6** gorget

armory
4 dump **5** depot, plant, range, store **7** arsenal, factory **8** magazine **10** collection, storehouse

armpit
6 axilla **8** underarm
Scottish: **5** oxter

arms
7 ensigns, warfare **8** weaponry

army
4 host **5** flock, horde **6** legion **7** militia **9** multitude
combat arm: **5** armor **8** infantry **9** artillery
commission: **6** brevet **7** reserve
Fort: **3** Dix, Lee, Ord **4** Drum, Hood, Knox, Myer, Polk, Sill **5** Bliss, Bragg, Irwin, Lewis, McCoy, Meade, Riley, Story **6** Carson, Eustis, Gillem, Gordon, Greely, McNair, Monroe, Rucker **7** Belvoir, Benning, Detrick, Jackson, Ritchie, Shafter, Stewart **8** Buchanan, Campbell, Hamilton, Holabird, Huachuca, Monmouth **9** McClellan, McPherson **10** Richardson, Sam Houston, Wainwright **11** Leavenworth
law enforcer: **2** MP
mascot: **4** mule
meal: **3** MRE **4** chow, mess
mine layer: **6** sapper
NCO: **8** corporal, sergeant
officer: **5** major **7** captain, colonel, general, warrant **10** lieutenant
post: **4** base, camp, fort
postal abbreviation: **3** APO
ration: **3** MRE
relating to: **7** martial **8** military
school: **3** OCS, OTS **7** academy **9** West Point
signaler: **6** bugler
store: **2** PX **10** commissary **12** post exchange
unit: **5** corps, squad, troop **7** brigade, cavalry, company, platoon **8** division, regiment **9** battalion
vehicle: **4** jeep, tank **6** Abrams, Humvee **7** Bradley **9** half-track

Arnaz, Desi
character: **5** Ricky (Ricardo)
company: **6** Desilu
mentor: **6** Cougat (Xavier)
signature song: **6** Babalu
star of: **9** I Love Lucy
wife: **4** Ball (Lucille), Lucy

aroma
4 balm, odor **5** scent, smell, spice **6** flavor **7** bouquet, incense, perfume **9** fragrance, redolence

aromatic
5 balmy, spicy, sweet **6** savory **7** odorous, perfumy, pungent, scented **8** fragrant, perfumed, redolent **9** ambrosial

around
4 near, nigh **5** about, circa **6** nearby **7** through
prefix: **4** ambi, peri **5** amphi **6** circum

around-the-clock
8 constant, unending **9** ceaseless, continual, incessant, perpetual, unceasing **10** continuous **11** unremitting **13** uninterrupted

arouse
4 fire, stir, wake, whet **5** alert, awake, pique, rally, waken **6** awaken, bestir, excite, fire up, foment, incite, kindle, work up **7** agitate, inflame **9** challenge, stimulate

arraign
3 tax, try **5** blame **6** accuse, charge, indict, summon **9** criminate, inculpate **11** incriminate

arrange
4 plan, sort **5** adapt, array, chart, order, score, unify **6** assort, codify, deploy, design, devise, lay out, line up, map out, scheme, set out, settle **7** dispose, marshal, prepare, work out **8** organize, sequence **9** blueprint, harmonize, integrate, methodize **10** bring about, categorize, instrument, symphonize, synthesize **11** choreograph, orchestrate, systematize

arrangement
5 array, order, setup **6** format, layout, lineup, series **8** grouping, ordering, sequence **9** structure **10** adaptation, deployment **11** disposition **12** distribution
floral: **4** posy **7** bouquet, garland

arrant
4 rank **5** gross, total, utter **6** brassy, brazen **7** blatant, extreme, flat-out **8** absolute, complete, impudent, infernal, overbold **9** barefaced, downright, egregious, out-and-out, shameless, unabashed **10** immoderate, unblushing

arras
6 screen **7** drapery **8** curtains, tapestry

array
3 lot **4** clad, garb, pomp, show **5** adorn, batch,

bunch, clump, dress, group, order **6** attire, bundle, clothe, draw up, finery, lineup, parade **7** apparel, arrange, cluster, display, dispose, garment, marshal, militia, panoply, raiment, variety **8** clothing, decorate, enclothe, organize, spectrum **9** formation **10** assortment **11** systematize

arrears
3 due **4** debt **5** claim, debit **7** deficit **9** liability **10** balance due, obligation **12** indebtedness

arrest
3 nab, tab, tag **4** bust, grab, halt, hold, jail, slow, snag, stay, stem, stop **5** block, catch, check, pinch, run in, seize, stall **6** collar, detain, haul in, lock up, pick up, pull in, retard, take in **7** capture, contain, seizure **8** imprison, obstruct, restrain **9** apprehend, detention, interrupt **11** incarcerate **12** apprehension

arresting
6 marked, signal **7** salient **8** striking **9** affective, appealing, prominent **10** attractive, compelling, enchanting, impressive, noticeable, remarkable **11** conspicuous, eye-catching, outstanding

arrival
6 advent, coming **7** landing, success **8** entrance, incoming **9** emergence **10** appearance

arrive
4 come, land, show **5** get in, get to, reach **6** appear, show up, thrive, turn up **7** prosper, succeed **8** flourish

arriviste
7 parvenu, upstart **8** roturier **12** nouveau riche

arrogance
3 ego **4** airs, gall **5** brass, cheek, pride **6** hubris **7** conceit, disdain, hauteur **8** self-love **9** loftiness **11** haughtiness

arrogant
5 cocky, proud **6** lordly, snooty **7** haughty, pompous **8** cavalier, fastuous, insolent, superior **9** egotistic **10** disdainful, high-handed, peremptory **11** domineering, magisterial, overbearing **12** supercilious **13** high-and-mighty, self-important

arrogate
4 grab, take **5** annex, claim, seize, usurp **6** assume, demand **7** ascribe, preempt **8** accroach, take over **9** sequester **10** commandeer, confiscate **11** appropriate, expropriate

arrow
4 dart **5** shaft
poison: **4** inée, upas **6** curare

arrowroot
5 plant, tuber **6** starch **7** coontie

Arrowsmith's wife
5 Leora

arroyo
3 gap **4** draw **5** brook, chasm, cleft, clove, creek, gorge, gulch, gully **6** coulee, ravine **7** channel **11** watercourse

Ars Amatoria poet
4 Ovid

arsenal
4 dump **5** depot, stock, store **6** armory, supply **7** factory, weapons **8** magazine, ordnance **9** stockpile **10** depository, repertoire, repository, storehouse

arsenic symbol
2 As

arson
6 firing **8** torching **9** pyromania **12** incendiarism

arsonist
5 firer, torch **7** firebug **10** incendiary

art
5 craft, skill **6** métier **7** finesse, know-how **8** artifice, painting, vocation **9** dexterity, expertise, sculpture **10** handicraft
botanical: **6** bonsai
faddish: **6** kitsch
style: **2** op **3** pop **4** dada **6** cubist, rococo **7** fauvist, realist, surreal **8** abstract, futurist **9** classical **10** naturalist, surrealist **12** naturalistic, surrealistic **13** expressionist, impressionist

art deco
5 style **6** design
designer: **4** Erté

Artemis
Roman counterpart: **5** Diana
birthplace: **5** Delos
brother: **6** Apollo
father: **4** Zeus
mother: **4** Leto
priestess: **9** Iphigenia

artery
3 way **4** duct, line, path, road, tube **5** aorta, track **6** avenue, course, street, vessel **7** carotid, channel, conduit, highway, passage, pathway **8** coronary **9** boulevard **12** thoroughfare

artful
3 sly **4** foxy, wily **5** adept, sharp, slick, smart, suave **6** adroit, astute, clever, crafty, shrewd, smooth, tricky **7** cunning **8** guileful, skillful **9** dexterous, ingenious **10** artificial, diplomatic

arthropod
3 bee, fly **4** crab, mite, moth, tick **6** beetle, insect, shrimp, spider **7** lobster **8** arachnid, barnacle, diplopod, myriapod, scorpion **9** butterfly, centipede, cockroach, millipede, trilobite **10** crustacean
body segment: **6** somite, telson **8** metamere

Arthur
see **King Arthur**

article
2 an **3** the **4** bind, item, part **5** essay, paper, piece, point, theme, thing **6** matter, object **7** element, feature, passage, section **10** particular **11** composition, stipulation
French: 3 les, une
German: 3 das, dem, den, der, des, die, ein **4** eine
Spanish: 2 un **3** las, los, una

articled
5 bound **10** indentured

articulate
3 say **4** join, link, oral, talk **5** clear, hinge, joint, lucid, shape, speak, state, utter, vocal, voice **6** couple, fluent, prolix, relate, spoken, voiced **7** connect, express, jointed **8** coherent, definite, distinct, eloquent, vocalize **9** effective, enunciate, harmonize, integrate, pronounce, verbalize **10** coordinate, expressive **11** concatenate **12** intelligible, smooth-spoken

artifact
5 curio, relic **6** legacy, rarity, trophy **7** remnant, spin-off, vestige **8** creation, heirloom **9** by-product, handcraft, handiwork **10** handicraft **11** contrivance, fabrication

artifice
4 play, ploy, ruse, wile **5** craft, feint, guile, skill, trick **6** deceit, device, gambit **7** cunning, slyness **8** facility, foxiness, trickery, wiliness **9** adeptness, canniness, chicanery, duplicity, ingenuity, stratagem **10** adroitness, artfulness, cleverness, craftiness

artificial
4 fake, faux, mock, sham **5** bogus, dummy, faked, false, phony, put-on **6** ersatz, forced, hollow, unreal **7** assumed, feigned, in vitro, labored, man-made, plastic, pretend **8** affected, mannered, spurious **9** contrived, imitation, insincere, simulated, synthetic, unnatural **10** fabricated, factitious, fictitious, substitute

artillery
4 arms **5** canon, force **6** rocket **7** battery, bazooka, gunnery, weapons **8** cannonry, howitzer, ordnance, weaponry **9** munitions

artisan
6 worker **7** builder, workman **8** producer **9** carpenter, craftsman **12** craftsperson

artist
7 painter **8** sculptor, virtuoso
garb: 5 smock
knife: 7 spatula
medium: 3 oil **5** paint **6** pastel **7** tempera **8** charcoal **10** watercolor
pigment board: 7 palette
stand: 5 easel
workshop: 6 studio **7** atelier
(see also **painter**)

artless
4 free, open, pure, true **5** crude, naive, plain **6** direct, honest, simple **7** genuine, natural, sincere, unaware **8** trusting **9** childlike, guileless, ingenuous, unstudied **10** aboveboard, forthright, unaffected, uncultured, unschooled **12** unartificial, unsuspicious

Art of Love poet
4 Ovid

arty
5 showy **6** pseudo **8** affected, imposing **9** overblown **11** pretentious **12** high-sounding

Aruba
capital: 10 Oranjestad
language: 5 Dutch **10** Papiamento
monetary unit: 6 florin
part of: 11 Netherlands

as
3 for, who **4** coin, like, that, when **5** being, since, which, while **6** though **7** because **11** considering, for instance

ASAP
4 stat **6** at once **11** immediately

as a rule
6 mainly, mostly **7** usually **8** commonly **9** generally **10** frequently, ordinarily

Ascanius
5 Iulus
father: 6 Aeneas

ascend
4 go up, lift, rise, soar **5** arise, climb, crest, mount, scale **6** aspire, move up, occupy **7** lift off, take off **8** escalade, escalate, surmount

ascendancy
4 rule **5** power, reign **7** command, control, mastery **8** dominion **9** authority, dominance, influence, supremacy **10** domination, prepotency **11** preeminence, sovereignty **13** preponderance

ascendant
6 master, rising **7** regnant **8** ancestor, dominant, forebear, relative, superior **9** paramount, precursor, prevalent, sovereign **10** commanding, forefather, forerunner, prevailing, progenitor **11** controlling, overbearing, predecessor, predominant, predominate **12** preponderant, primogenitor

ascension
4 rise **6** rising **7** going up, scaling **8** climbing, mounting

ascent
4 ramp, rise **5** climb, grade, slope **6** rising **7** advance, incline **8** gradient, progress **9** acclivity, elevation, uplifting

ascertain
5 learn **7** catch on, find out, unearth **8** discover, make sure **9** determine, establish, figure out

ascetic
5 stoic **6** hermit, severe **7** austere, eremite, recluse **9** abstinent, anchoress, anchorite, mortified **10** abstemious, astringent, forbearing, restrained **11** disciplined, self-denying
ancient Hebrew: **6** Essene
Buddhist: **5** bonze
early Christian: **7** stylite
Hindu: **4** yogi **5** fakir, sadhu, Yogin
Muslim: **4** Sufi

Asclepius
see **Aesculapius**

ascribe
3 lay **4** cite **5** infer, refer **6** assign, charge, credit, impute **7** chalk up **8** accredit **9** attribute, reference **10** conjecture

Asenath
husband: **6** Joseph
son: **7** Ephraim **8** Manasseh

aseptic
4 cool, flat **5** clean **7** sterile **8** germ-free, hygienic, sanitary **9** unfeeling **10** restrained, sterilized **11** emotionless, unemotional

asexual
6 agamic

as for
4 in re **5** about, anent **7** apropos **9** regarding **10** concerning, respecting **12** with regard to

as good as
4 nigh **6** all but, almost, nearly **8** in effect, well-nigh **9** basically, in essence, just about, virtually **11** essentially, practically

ash
4 soot, tree, wood **7** cinders, residue **8** clinkers

ashamed
6 abased, abject, guilty **7** abashed, humbled **8** contrite, penitent **9** chagrined, mortified, repentant **10** humiliated **11** discomfited, embarrassed

ashen
3 wan **4** gray, pale **5** faded, pasty, waxen **6** doughy, pallid, sallow, sickly **7** ghostly **8** blanched, bleached **9** bloodless, colorless **10** corpselike

Asher
daughter: **5** Serah
father: **5** Jacob
mother: **6** Zilpah
son: **4** Isui **6** Beriah, Ishuah, Jimnah

ashes
5 ruins **6** pallor **7** remains

ashy
3 wan **4** drab, pale **5** livid, waxen **6** doughy, leaden, pallid **7** ghastly, greyish **8** blanched **9** bloodless, colorless, washed-out **10** cadaverous

Asia
country: **4** Laos **5** Burma, China, India, Japan, Korea, Nepal **6** Bhutan, Russia, Taiwan **7** Armenia, Georgia, Myanmar, Vietnam **8** Cambodia, Malaysia, Mongolia, Pakistan, Sri Lanka, Thailand **9** Indonesia, Kampuchea, Kazakstan, Singapore **10** Azerbaijan, Bangladesh, Kazakhstan, Kyrgyzstan, North Korea, South Korea, Tajikistan, Uzbekistan **11** Afghanistan, Philippines **12** Turkmenistan
ethnic group: **3** Han, Lao, Tai **4** Arab, Kurd, Moor, Shan **5** Karen, Khmer, Malay, Tajik, Tamil, Uzbek **6** Burman, Lepcha, Manchu, Mongol, Sindhi **7** Baluchi, Bengali, Persian, Punjabi, Tibetan **8** Armenian, Assyrian, Javanese **9** Dravidian, Indo-Aryan, Sinhalese **10** Circassian, Montagnard, Singhalese
language: **3** Lao **4** Ainu, Urdu **5** Hindi, Malay, Tamil, Uzbek **6** Arabic, Bahasa, Korean, Nepali **7** Bengali, Burmese, Khalkha, Kurdish, Persian, Tibetan, Turkish **8** Armenian, Japanese, Javanese, Mandarin **9** Cambodian **10** Vietnamese

Asia Minor
8 Anatolia
country: **6** Turkey
region: **5** Ionia

Asian inland sea
4 Aral

Asian Sasquatch
4 yeti

aside
4 away **5** apart **7** tangent **8** away from **9** in reserve, privately **10** digression, discursion **11** parenthesis

aside from
3 bar, but **4** save **6** bating, except **7** barring, besides **9** excepting, excluding, other than, outside of

Asimov, Isaac
forte: **5** sci-fi
work: **6** I Robot **9** Nightfall **10** Foundation (Trilogy)

asinine
5 crazy, daffy, silly **6** absurd, simple **7** fatuous, foolish, idiotic, puerile, witless **8** mindless **9** brainless **10** irrational, ridiculous **11** nonsensical

ask
3 beg, bid **4** pray, quiz, seek **5** crave, exact, grill, plead, query **6** appeal, demand, desire, invite **7** beseech, call for, canvass, consult, enquire, entreat, examine, implore, inquire, request, require, solicit **8** petition, question **9** catechize, importune **10** supplicate **11** interrogate
Scottish: **5** speer, speir

askance
8 sidelong, sideways **9** cynically, obliquely **10** critically, doubtfully, doubtingly, scornfully **11** skeptically **12** suspiciously **13** distrustfully, mistrustfully

asker
6 beggar, prayer, suitor **7** speaker **9** suppliant **10** petitioner, questioner, supplicant **11** supplicator

askew
4 awry **6** turned **8** cockeyed **9** crookedly

aslant
4 awry **5** askew **7** crooked **8** cockeyed, sideways, sidewise **9** obliquely

asleep
4 dead, idle, numb **5** inert **6** dozing, numbed **7** defunct, dormant, napping **8** benumbed, deadened, inactive, in repose, not alert, sluggish **9** senseless, unfeeling **10** insensible, slumbering, unanimated **11** indifferent, unconscious **12** anesthetized

as long as
3 for **5** since **6** seeing **7** because, whereas **8** provided **11** considering **12** provided that

as much as
6 all but, almost **8** well-nigh **11** essentially, practically

aspect
3 air **4** look, mien, side **5** angle, facet, phase, scene, slant **6** regard, status **7** bearing, seeming **8** exposure, position **9** direction **10** appearance **11** perspective

aspen
4 tree **6** poplar

asperity
5 rigor **8** acerbity, acrimony, grimness, hardness, hardship, mordancy, severity, tartness **9** harshness, roughness, sharpness **10** bitterness, difficulty, unevenness **12** irregularity, irritability

asperse
4 slur **5** libel, smear, sully **6** attack, defame, insult, malign, vilify **7** baptize, slander, tarnish, traduce **8** bad mouth, dishonor, sprinkle **9** denigrate, insinuate **10** calumniate

aspersion
4 muck, slam, slur **5** abuse **7** calumny, obloquy, slander **9** invective, stricture **10** defamation, detraction **11** denigration **12** vilification, vituperation **13** animadversion

asphalt
4 pave **7** bitumen, surface **8** blacktop, pavement

asphyxiate
4 kill **5** choke, drown **6** stifle **7** smother **8** strangle, throttle **9** suffocate

aspirant
6 seeker **7** hopeful, seeking **9** applicant, candidate, contender

aspiration
3 aim **4** goal, urge, wish **5** dream **6** desire, intent, object **7** craving, longing, passion, pursuit **8** ambition, striving, yearning **9** breathing, objective **10** pretension **13** ambitiousness

aspire
3 aim, try **4** long, pant, rise, seek, soar, want, wish **5** arise, mount, yearn **6** ascend, desire, hunger, strive, thirst

aspiring
7 longing, seeking, wanting, wishful **8** striving, vaulting, yearning **9** ambitious

as regards
4 in re **7** apropos **8** touching **10** concerning, respecting

ass
4 dolt, fool, jerk, moke, mule **5** burro, dunce, idiot **6** donkey, nitwit **8** bonehead, imbecile **10** nincompoop
female: **5** jenny
male: **4** jack
wild Asian: **5** kiang **6** onager

assai
4 very

assail
4 bash, beat **5** abuse, beset, blast, pound, storm **6** attack, berate, buffet, charge, fall on, malign, oppugn, pummel, revile, strike, vilify **7** assault, bombard **8** fall upon, lambaste **9** break down

assassin
3 gun **5** bravo **6** gunman, hit man, killer **7** torpedo **8** murderer **9** cutthroat **10** hatchet man, triggerman
of Caesar: **6** Brutus **7** Cassius
of Garfield: **7** Guiteau (Charles Julius)
of J. F. Kennedy: **6** Oswald (Lee Harvey)
of M. L. King: **3** Ray (James Earl)
of Lincoln: **5** Booth (John Wilkes)
of Marat: **6** Corday (Charlotte)
of McKinley: **8** Czolgosz (Leon)
of R. F. Kennedy: **6** Sirhan (Sirhan)

assassinate
4 do in, kill, slay **6** finish, murder, rub out

7 bump off, execute, gun down, put away, take out **8** dispatch, knock off **9** eliminate, liquidate

assault
3 mug, war **4** raid **5** beset, fight, onset, set-to, storm **6** assail, attack, charge, fall on, strike, threat **7** aggress, besiege, mugging, offense **8** fall upon, invasion, storming **9** incursion, offensive, onslaught, violation **10** aggression

assay
3 try **4** rate, seek, test **5** judge, offer, prove, trial, value, weigh **6** assess, result, rating, strive, survey **7** analyze, attempt, examine, inspect, measure, valuate, venture **8** analysis, appraise, endeavor, estimate, evaluate, struggle **9** appraisal, undertake, valuation **10** assessment, evaluation, inspection **11** examination, measurement

assemblage
5 crowd, group **6** muster **7** company, turnout **8** audience **9** gathering **10** collection **11** aggregation, composition, convergence **12** congregation

assemble
4 call, form, make, mass, meet, mold **5** amass, build, clump, group, shape, unite **6** gather, muster, summon **7** cluster, collect, convene, convoke, fashion, marshal, produce, round up **8** congress, contrive **9** aggregate, forgather **10** accumulate, congregate **11** fit together, manufacture, put together **12** call together, come together **13** bring together

assembly
4 bevy **5** bunch, covey, crowd, flock, group, party, plena (plural), rally, set-up **6** muster, plenum, troupe **7** cluster, meeting **8** conclave **9** congeries, gathering **10** collection **11** association, fabrication, get-together, manufacture **12** congregation, construction
American Indian: **6** powwow
ancient Greek: **8** ecclesia
ancient Roman: **7** comitia
Anglo-Saxon: **4** moot **5** gemot **6** gemote **8** folkmoot, folkmote
ecclesiastical: **5** synod **10** consistory
legislative: **4** diet **6** senate **8** congress **10** parliament
place: **4** hall, room **5** agora **10** auditorium
Russian: **4** duma
witches': **6** sabbat **7** sabbath

assent
2 OK **3** nod, yes, yup **4** okay, yeah **5** agree, uh-huh **6** accede, accord, concur, say yes **7** approve, consent, embrace **8** approval, sanction, thumbs-up **9** accession, acquiesce, admission, agreement, subscribe **10** acceptance, permission **11** affirmation, concurrence **12** acquiescence

assert
3 say **4** aver, avow **5** argue, claim, posit, state, utter, voice **6** adduce, affirm, allege, attest, avouch, defend, depose, insist, submit **7** advance, contend, declare, express, justify, profess, protest, publish, warrant **8** announce, maintain, proclaim **9** broadcast, postulate, predicate **10** promulgate

assertion
6 avowal **8** averment **9** affidavit, statement **10** allegation, avouchment, contention, deposition, disclosure, insistence, profession **11** affirmation, attestation, declaration **12** asseveration **13** pronouncement

assertive
4 firm, sure **5** pushy **6** strong **7** assured, certain, decided, pushing **8** cocksure, emphatic, forceful, positive **9** confident, energetic, insistent **10** aggressive, resounding **11** affirmative, distinctive, self-assured **13** self-confident

assess
3 fix, tax **4** deem, levy, rate **5** assay, exact, judge, put on, set at, value, weigh **6** charge, figure, impose, reckon, survey **7** account, compute, subject, valuate **8** appraise, consider, estimate, evaluate **9** determine

assessment
3 fee, tax **4** duty, levy, toll **6** charge, impost, rating, tariff **8** estimate, judgment **9** appraisal, valuation **10** estimation, evaluation **12** appraisement

asset
4 boon, good, plus **5** merit **6** credit **7** benefit **8** blessing, resource **9** advantage **11** distinction
opposite: **9** liability

assets
5 items, means, money **6** wealth **7** capital **8** bankroll, holdings, property **9** resources, valuables **11** possessions

asseverate
4 aver, avow **5** state **6** affirm, assert, attest, avouch, depose, insist **7** certify, contend, declare, profess **8** maintain, proclaim **9** pronounce

assiduous
4 busy **5** eager **6** active **7** moiling, zealous **8** diligent, sedulous, tireless **9** attentive, laborious **10** persistent, unflagging **11** hard-working, industrious **13** indefatigable

assiduously
4 hard **6** busily **9** earnestly, intensely **10** diligently, thoroughly **11** intensively **12** exhaustively, meticulously, persistently **13** painstakingly, unremittingly

assign
3 fix, lay, set **4** cede, deed, give, name **5** allot, allow, refer **6** charge, convey, credit, define, impute, remise, settle **7** appoint, ascribe, chalk

up, earmark, lay down, mete out, specify, station **8** accredit, allocate, delegate, make over, relegate, sign over, transfer **9** admeasure, apportion, attribute, designate, establish, prescribe **10** pigeonhole

assignation
4 date **5** tryst **7** meeting **9** allotment **10** engagement, rendezvous **11** appointment, get-together

assignee
5 agent, proxy **6** deputy, factor **7** officer **8** attorney, delegate

assignment
3 job **4** beat, duty, post, task, work **5** chore, stint **6** office **8** homework, position, transfer **9** allotment **10** allocation, delegation, obligation **11** designation

assimilate
5 adapt, adopt, grasp, learn, liken, match **6** absorb, adjust, digest, equate, imbibe, soak up, take in, take up **7** blend in, compare, conform **8** parallel **10** comprehend, understand **11** incorporate

assimilation
8 taking in **9** awareness **10** absorption, conversion **11** mindfulness, recognition **12** apperception **13** consciousness, incorporation

assist
3 aid **4** abet, back, help, lift **5** boost, do for, serve, stead **6** relief, succor **7** backing, benefit, comfort, help out, secours, service, support, work for **8** benefact, work with **9** accompany, cooperate, open doors

assistance
3 aid **4** hand, help, lift **5** boost **6** relief, succor **7** backing, benefit, comfort, secours, service, subsidy, support **8** abetment **9** upholding **10** subvention, supporting **11** cooperation

assistant
3 aid **4** aide, ally, help **5** aider **6** backer, backup, deputy, flunky, helper, second **7** acolyte, ancilla, orderly **8** adjutant, henchman **9** attendant, auxiliary, coadjutor **10** accomplice, aide-de-camp, coadjutant, lieutenant **12** right-hand man

assistive
6 aiding, useful **7** helpful **10** beneficial **11** serviceable

assize
3 law **4** rule, writ **5** canon, edict **6** decree **7** finding, inquest, precept, statute, verdict **8** standard **9** ordinance, prescript **10** regulation

associate
3 pal **4** ally, chum, join, link, mate, pair, yoke **5** blend, buddy, crony, group, match, merge, unite **6** cohort, comate, couple, fellow, friend, hobnob, relate, worker **7** bracket, combine, compeer, comrade, conjoin, connect, consort, partner **8** confrere, coworker, employee, familiar, federate, identify, intimate **9** affiliate, bedfellow, colleague, companion, confidant, copartner, secondary **10** accomplice, amalgamate, compatriot, complement, confidante **11** concomitant, confederate, correlative **12** acquaintance **13** accompaniment

association
3 tie **4** band, bloc, bond, clan, club, crew, hint, tong **5** group, guild, order, tie-up, union **6** hookup, league **7** circuit, concert, linkage, linking, society **8** alliance, congress, overtone, relation, sodality, teamwork **9** coalition, undertone **10** conference, connection, federation, fellowship, fraternity, mental link, suggestion **11** affiliation, brotherhood, combination, conjunction, connotation, cooperation, implication, partnership **12** conjointment, organization, relationship, togetherness **13** collaboration

assort
5 class, group, order **6** codify, divide **7** arrange **8** classify, stratify **9** associate, designate, harmonize, methodize **10** categorize, distribute, pigeonhole **11** systematize

assorted
4 like **5** mixed **6** fitted, motley, suited, sundry, varied **7** adapted, diverse, matched, similar, various **9** different **11** diversified, conformable **12** conglomerate, multifarious **13** heterogeneous, miscellaneous

assortment
4 olio **5** array, group **6** choice, jumble, medley **7** mélange, mixture, variety **8** mishmash, mixed bag, pastiche **9** diversity, potpourri, selection **10** collection, hodgepodge, miscellany **11** gallimaufry

assuage
4 calm, cool, ease **5** allay, quiet **6** lessen, pacify, quench, reduce, soften, soothe, temper **7** appease, lighten, mollify, placate, relieve, sweeten **8** decrease, mitigate, moderate **9** alleviate **10** conciliate, propitiate

as such
5 per se **8** by itself **9** in essence, virtually **11** essentially **13** fundamentally, intrinsically

assumably
6 likely, surely **7** no doubt **8** probably **9** doubtless **10** most likely, presumably

assume
3 act, don **4** fake, sham, take **5** adopt, bluff, feign, posit, put on, seize, usurp **6** affect, draw on, expect, reckon, slip on, take in, take on, take up **7** believe, imagine, preempt, premise, presume, pretend, receive, suppose, suspect **8** accroach, arrogate, shoulder, simulate, take over **9** postulate, undertake **10** commandeer, presuppose, understand **11** appropriate, counterfeit

assumed
4 fake, sham **5** bogus, false, given, put on, tacit **6** made-up, phoney **7** feigned **8** affected, delusory, putative, spurious, supposed **9** deceptive, pretended, simulated **10** artificial, fictitious

assumption
5 posit **6** belief, thesis **7** conceit, premise, seizure, surmise **8** takeover **9** arrogance, postulate **10** acceptance, arrogation, conjecture, pretension, usurpation **11** expectation, supposition, undertaking **13** appropriation

assurance
3 say **4** oath, word **5** nerve, say-so, troth **6** aplomb, parole, pledge, safety, surety **7** promise, support, warrant **8** audacity, boldness, safeness, security, sureness, temerity, warranty **9** assertion, brashness, certainty, certitude, cockiness, composure, guarantee, hardiness, self-trust **10** brazenness, confidence, conviction, equanimity, profession **11** affirmation, presumption

assure
4 aver **5** bet on, cinch, swear **6** affirm, attest, ensure, insure, pledge, secure, soothe **7** certify, comfort, confirm, promise, satisfy **8** convince, persuade **9** guarantee **11** make certain

assured
3 set **4** cool **5** fixed **6** secure **7** certain, decided, settled **8** clear-cut, composed, definite, positive, sanguine **9** assertive, collected, confident, undoubted, unruffled **10** guaranteed, pronounced **11** beyond doubt, made certain, unflappable **13** imperturbable, self-confident, self-satisfied

assuredly
9 certainly, doubtless **10** positively **11** confidently, undoubtedly, without fail

assuredness
6 surety **9** certainty, certitude **10** confidence, conviction

Assyria
capital: **5** Calah **7** Nineveh
city: **5** Ashur, Assur
god: **3** Sin **4** Asur, Nabu **5** Ashur, Nusku **6** Tammuz **7** Ninurta
goddess: **6** Ishtar
king: **3** Pul **6** Sargon **11** Sennacherib, Shalmaneser **12** Ashurbanipal
language: **7** Aramaic
queen: **9** Semiramis
river: **6** Tigris
writing: **9** cuneiform

astatine symbol
2 At

asterisk
4 star **6** symbol **9** character

astern
3 aft **4** baft, rear, tail **5** abaft **6** back of, behind **8** backward, rearmost, rearward

asteroid
5 Ceres

Asterope
father: **5** Atlas
mother: **7** Pleione
sisters: **8** Pleiades

asthma
7 allergy **8** disorder

as to
4 in re **5** about, anent **7** apropos **9** regarding **10** concerning, respecting **11** according to

astonish
4 daze, stun **5** amaze, floor, shock **7** astound, stagger, startle, stupefy **8** blow away, bowl over, confound, dumfound, surprise **9** dumbfound, take aback **11** flabbergast

astonishing
7 amazing **8** stunning, wondrous **9** marvelous, startling, wonderful **10** astounding, miraculous, prodigious, staggering, stupendous, surprising **11** spectacular **12** breathtaking

astonishment
3 awe **5** shock **6** wonder **8** surprise **9** amazement, confusion **10** perplexity, wonderment **12** bewilderment, stupefaction **13** consternation

astound
4 daze, stun **5** amaze, shock **7** confuse **8** astonish, bewilder, confound, dumfound, surprise **9** dumbfound, overwhelm, take aback **11** flabbergast

Astraea
father: **4** Zeus **7** Jupiter
mother: **6** Themis

astral
6 dreamy, starry **7** exalted, highest, stellar **8** elevated, sidereal **9** celestial, top-drawer, unworldly, visionary **10** top-ranking **11** high-ranking **12** otherworldly

astray
4 awry **5** amiss, badly, wrong **6** adrift, afield **7** in error **9** off course
lead: **6** seduce

astride
8 bridging, spanning **10** on each side, straddling

astringent
4 acid, keen **5** acerb, acrid, harsh, sharp, stern **6** biting, bitter, severe, strict **7** acerbic, ascetic, austere, caustic, cutting, puckery, pungent, styptic **8** incisive, stinging **10** irritating **11** contracting **12** constrictive

astrolabe successor
7 sextant

astrologer
5 Dixon (Jeane), Faust **9** stargazer, Zoroaster **11** horoscopist, Nostradamus

astrological aspect
5 trine **7** sextile **8** quartile **10** opposition **11** conjunction

astronaut
4 Ride (Sally) **5** Glenn (John), White (Edward), Young (John) **6** Aldrin (Buzz), Cooper (Gordon), Lovell (James), Worden (Alfred) **7** Bluford (Guion), Collins (Michael), Gagarin (Yuri), Grissom (Gus), Jemison (Mae), Schirra (Walter), Shepard (Alan), Yegorov (Boris) **8** Stafford (Thomas) **9** Armstrong (Neil), Carpenter (Scott), McAuliffe (Christa) **10** Tereshkova (Valentina)

astronomer
American: **3** See (Thomas Jefferson) **5** Sagan (Carl) **6** Hubble (Edwin), Lowell (Percival) **7** Langley (Samuel), Newcomb (Simon), Shapley (Harlow) **8** Bowditch (Nathaniel), Mitchell (Maria), Tombaugh (Clyde) **9** Pickering (Edward) **11** Schlesinger (Frank)
Austrian: **13** Schwarzschild (Karl)
Danish: **5** Brahe (Tycho)
Dutch: **4** Oort (Jan Hendrik) **6** Sitter (Willem de) **7** Huygens (Christiaan)
English: **4** Ryle (Martin), Wren (Christopher) **6** Halley (Edmond), Lovell (Bernard) **7** Lockyer (Joseph), Parsons (William) **8** Herschel (Caroline, John, William)
French: **6** Picard (Jean) **7** Laplace (Pierre-Simon de), Messier (Charles)
German: **4** Wolf (Maximilian) **5** Vogel (Hermann) **6** Bessel (Friedrich), Kepler (Johannes), Müller (Johann), Struve (Otto)
Greek: **12** Eratosthenes
Italian: **7** Galileo (Galilei) **12** Schiaparelli (Giovanni)
Persian: **11** Omar Khayyám
Polish: **10** Copernicus (Nicolaus)
Swedish: **7** Celsius (Anders)
Swiss: **6** Zwicky (Fritz)

astute
3 sly **4** cagy, deep, foxy, keen, wily **5** cagey, canny, heady, quick, savvy, sharp **6** artful, clever, crafty, shrewd, tricky **7** cunning, knowing **8** guileful **9** insidious, sagacious **11** calculating **13** perspicacious

astuteness
3 wit **6** acumen **8** wiliness **9** canniness **10** craftiness **11** discernment, percipience **12** perspicacity

Astyanax
father: **6** Hector
mother: **10** Andromache

asunder
4 torn **5** apart, split **7** divided **9** into parts, separated

as usual
8 normally, wontedly **9** routinely **10** habitually, ordinarily **11** customarily **12** consistently

as well
3 and, too, yet **4** also, even, just, more, plus **7** besides, further **8** likewise, moreover **9** along with, including, similarly **10** in addition **11** furthermore **12** additionally

as well as
3 and **4** plus **7** besides **9** along with **11** not counting **12** in addition to, together with

as yet
5 so far, to now **7** earlier, thus far **8** hitherto, until now **10** to this time **12** to the present

asylum
4 home, port **5** cover, haven **6** covert, harbor, refuge **7** retreat, shelter **8** hospital, security **9** harborage, safe house, sanctuary **10** protection, sanatorium **11** institution

asymmetric
6 uneven **7** not even, unequal **8** lopsided **9** irregular **10** unbalanced **12** overbalanced

Atalanta
husband: **8** Melanion
suitor: **10** Hippomenes

at all
4 ever, once **6** anyway **7** anytime **10** whatsoever

atavism
9 reversion, throwback **10** recurrence

ataxia
5 chaos, snarl **6** huddle, muddle **7** clutter **8** disarray, disorder **9** confusion

atelier
6 studio **8** workroom, workshop

Athamas
daughter: **5** Helle
father: **6** Aeolus
son: **7** Phrixos, Phrixus **8** Learchus
wife: **3** Ino **7** Nephele

Athena
Roman counterpart: **7** Minerva
attribute: **3** owl **5** Aegis **7** serpent
city: **6** Athens
father: **4** Zeus
names: **4** Nike **6** Pallas **9** Parthenos
shield: **5** Aegis
statue: **9** Palladium
temple: **9** Parthenon

athenaeum
6 museum **7** library **8** archives **10** repository

Athens
citadel: **9** Acropolis
founder: **7** Cecrops
last king: **6** Codrus
lawgiver: **5** Solon
marketplace: **5** agora
rival: **6** Sparta
senate: **5** boule
temple: **9** Parthenon

athirst
4 avid, keen **5** eager **6** ardent **7** anxious **8** desiring, desirous, yearning **9** impatient

athlete
4 jock **5** sport **6** player **7** acrobat, gymnast, tumbler **9** sportsman **10** competitor **11** sportswoman

athlete's foot
8 ringworm **10** tinea pedis

athletic
6 brawny, robust, sinewy **8** sporting, vigorous **9** strapping, strenuous
contest: **4** agon, game **5** match
field: **4** oval, ring, rink **5** arena, court **7** diamond, stadium **8** gridiron
prize: **3** cup **5** medal **6** trophy, wreath

athletics
5 games, races **6** events, sports **7** contest **8** exercise **9** exercises **10** gymnastics, recreation **12** calisthenics

athwart
4 over **5** cross **6** across, beyond **9** crossways, crosswise, opposed to **12** transversely

Atlanta's civic center
4 Omni

Atlas
brother: **10** Prometheus
daughter: **5** Hyads **6** Hyades **8** Pleiades **10** Atlantides
father: **7** Iapetus
mother: **7** Clymene
race: **5** Titan
wife: **7** Pleione

at last
7 finally

Atli
wife (slayer): **6** Gudrun

atmosphere
3 air **4** aura, mood, tone **6** medium, milieu **7** ambient, climate, feeling, quality **8** ambiance, ambience **11** environment, mise-en-scène **12** surroundings
stratum: **9** exosphere **10** ionosphere, mesosphere **11** chemosphere, ozonosphere, troposphere **12** stratosphere, thermosphere
sun's: **12** chromosphere

atmospheric
4 airy **6** aerial **8** ethereal

atoll
6 island
equatorial area: **5** Baker
Indian Ocean: **4** Male
Kiribati: **4** Beru
Marshall Islands: **6** Bikini **8** Eniwetok
Tuamotu: **4** Anaa **5** Chain
Tuvalu: **8** Funafuti

atom
3 bit, jot **4** iota, mite, whit **5** minim, speck, touch, trace **6** tittle **7** modicum, smidgen **8** particle **9** scintilla
charged: **3** ion **5** anion
group: **7** radical

atomic particle
3 ion **4** beta, muon, pion **5** alpha, boson, meson **6** baryon, hadron, lepton, proton **7** fermion, hyperon, neutron, nucleon **8** electron, mesotron, neutrino, positron, thermion
hypothetical: **5** quark **6** parton

atomic weapon
5 A-bomb, H-bomb **6** Fat Man **9** Little Boy

atomize
4 nuke, ruin **5** smash, wreck **6** divide, rub out **7** break up, destroy, shatter **8** demolish, destruct, disperse, dynamite, fragment, nebulize **9** break down, devastate, pulverize **10** disconnect

at once
3 now, PDQ **4** ASAP, away, both, stat **6** pronto **8** directly, first off, right now, together **9** forthwith, instanter, instantly, right away **11** immediately, straightway **12** concurrently, straightaway

atone
3 pay **6** redeem, repair, repent **7** correct, expiate, rectify, redress, satisfy **10** compensate, make amends, recompense

atoner
8 penitent

atop
4 upon

Atossa
father: **5** Cyrus
husband: **6** Darius **7** Smerdes **8** Cambyses
son: **6** Xerxes

at random
5 about **6** anyhow **7** anywise **8** by chance **9** aimlessly, haphazard **10** carelessly **11** any which way, haphazardly **12** accidentally **13** helter-skelter

at rest
4 dead **5** still **8** inactive, lifeless, reposing, sleeping, tranquil, unmoving **9** quiescent

10 motionless, stationary, untroubled **11** trouble-free

Atreus
brother: **8** Thyestes
father: **6** Pelops
mother: **10** Hippodamia
slayer: **9** Aegisthus
son: **8** Menelaus **9** Agamemnon **11** Pleisthenes
victim: **11** Pleisthenes
wife: **6** Aerope

atrium
5 court, patio

atrocious
4 foul, vile **5** awful, cruel **6** brutal, horrid, odious, savage, wicked **7** heinous, noisome, obscene **8** barbaric, horrible, shocking, terrible **9** appalling, desperate, execrable, loathsome, monstrous, offensive, repulsive, revolting, sickening **10** abominable, despicable, detestable, disgusting, horrifying, outrageous, scandalous **12** contemptible

atrocity
4 evil **5** crime **6** horror, infamy **7** cruelty, outrage **8** enormity, savagery **9** barbarity, brutality **11** abomination, heinousness **13** monstrousness

atrophy
7 decline, wasting **9** decadence, waste away **10** devolution **11** declination **12** degeneration **13** deterioration

attach
3 fix, tie **4** bind, hook, link **5** affix, annex, latch, rivet, stick, unite **6** adhere, append, assign, fasten, secure **7** ascribe, connect **8** make fast **9** associate, attribute

attached
5 bound, fixed **7** sessile

attachment
3 tag, tie **4** bond, link, love **6** fealty **7** loyalty, seizure **8** addition, adhesion, devotion, fastener, fidelity, fondness **9** accessory, adherence, affection, connector, constancy **10** allegiance, connection **12** faithfulness

attack
4 bout, jump, raid, rush **5** beset, blitz, drive, fight, foray, onset, sally, siege, spasm, spell, storm, throe **6** access, ambush, assail, banzai, battle, charge, fall on, harass, have at, invade, irrupt, onrush, sortie, strike, tackle **7** aggress, assault, barrage, besiege, bombard, lay into, offense, seizure **8** fall upon, invasion, outbreak, paroxysm **9** beleaguer, incursion, offensive, onslaught, pugnacity **10** aggression, blitzkrieg

attain
3 get, win **4** gain **5** reach, score **6** arrive, come to, effect, make it, obtain, rack up **7** achieve, fulfill, pull off, realize, succeed **8** bring off, complete **10** accomplish

attainment
4 feat **6** finish **7** arrival **10** completion **11** achievement, acquirement, acquisition, fulfillment, realization

attempt
3 bid, try **4** seek, shot, stab **5** assay, crack, essay, offer, trial **6** attack, effort, strive, tackle **7** assault, venture **8** endeavor, striving, struggle **9** undertake **11** undertaking **12** make an effort

attend
3 aid, see **4** be at, go to, hear, heed, help, mark, mind, note **5** apply, catch, nurse, see to, serve, visit, watch **6** assist, convoy, doctor, drop in, escort, go with, harken, listen, notice, show up, turn up, wait on **7** be there, care for, conduct, hearken, oversee, pay heed, work for **8** chaperon, stay with, wait upon **9** accompany, chaperone, companion, look after, supervise **11** concentrate

attendant
4 aide, page **5** valet **6** escort, helper, lackey **7** orderly, servant **9** ancillary, assistant **10** bridesmaid, coincident **11** chamberlain, concomitant **12** accompanying
ancient Roman: **6** lictor
in court: **7** bailiff **8** tipstaff

attendants
5 suite, train **7** cortege, retinue **9** entourage

attendee
4 goer

attention
4 care, heed, mark, note **5** study **6** notice, regard, remark **7** amenity, command, concern, respect, service, thought **8** civility, courtesy, industry, scrutiny **9** assiduity, awareness, deference, diligence, gallantry, spotlight, treatment **10** absorption, cognizance, observance, politeness **11** application, mindfulness, observation, sensibility **12** deliberation **13** concentration, consciousness, consideration

attention getter
4 ahem **5** gavel

attentive
4 kind **5** alert, awake, aware, civil **6** intent, polite **7** all ears, devoted, gallant, heedful, mindful **8** gracious, obliging, open-eyed **9** advertent, courteous, observant, regardful **10** interested, respectful, solicitous, thoughtful **11** considerate **13** concentrating

attenuate
3 sap **4** rare, slim, thin **5** abate, blunt, reedy **6** lessen, rarefy, shrink, slight, stalky, subtle, twiggy, weaken **7** cripple, deflate, disable,

reduced, slender, squinny, subtile, tenuous, unbrace **8** contract, enfeeble, mitigate, rarefied, tapering, wiredraw **9** constrict, dissipate, undermine **10** become thin, become fine, become less, debilitate

attest
4 aver, show **5** argue, prove, swear, vouch **6** adjure, affirm, assert, verify **7** certify, confirm, declare, display, exhibit, point to, support, sustain, swear to, testify, warrant, witness **8** announce, indicate, manifest **9** establish **10** asseverate **11** bear witness, demonstrate **12** authenticate

attestation
5 proof **7** witness **8** evidence **9** testament, testimony **10** validation **11** declaration, testimonial **12** confirmation

attic
4 loft, room **6** garret **7** storage **8** cockloft

Attica
6 Greece
division: 4 deme

at times
9 sometimes **10** now and then, on occasion **11** now and again **12** occasionally

attire
4 clad, duds, garb, gear, togs, wear **5** array, drape, dress, getup, habit, tog up **6** clothe, enrobe, fit out, outfit **7** apparel, clothes, costume, garment, raiment, threads **8** clothing, garments, glad rags **11** habiliments

attitude
4 pose, view **5** angle, stand **6** manner, stance **7** bearing, mind-set, outlook, posture **8** carriage, demeanor, position, pretense **10** standpoint **11** inclination, perspective, point of view

attitudinize
4 mask, pose, sham **6** affect **7** pass for, pass off, posture, pretend, show off **10** masquerade

attorney
5 agent, proxy **6** deputy, factor, lawyer **7** counsel **8** advocate, assignee **9** barrister, counselor, solicitor **10** counsellor, legal eagle, mouthpiece

attract
4 draw, lure, wile **5** charm, court, tempt **6** allure, appeal, beckon, draw in, entice, invite, seduce **7** beguile, bewitch, enchant, solicit **8** appeal to, interest, intrigue, inveigle **9** captivate, fascinate, influence, magnetize

attraction
4 bait, call, draw, lure, pull **5** charm **6** allure, appeal, liking **8** affinity, cynosure, sympathy **9** affection, chemistry, magnetism, seduction **10** allurement **12** drawing power

attractive
4 cute, fair, sexy **5** bonny, dishy **6** comely, lovely, luring, pretty **7** Circean, likable, winsome **8** alluring, charming, engaging, enticing, fetching, handsome, inviting, magnetic, mesmeric, tempting **9** appealing, beauteous, beautiful, beckoning, glamorous, seductive **10** bewitching, enchanting **11** captivating, fascinating, good-looking, tantalizing **13** prepossessing

attractiveness
5 charm **6** appeal, beauty, glamor **7** glamour

attribute
3 lay **4** mark, sign **5** apply, facet, pin on, point, refer, trait **6** aspect, assign, charge, credit, emblem, impute, symbol, virtue **7** ascribe, connect, earmark, explain, feature, quality **8** accredit, classify, property **9** adjective, character, designate

attrition
3 rue **4** ruth, wear **6** sorrow **7** erosion, penance, remorse, rubbing, wearing **8** abrasion, friction, grinding **9** penitence, penitency, reduction, weakening **10** repentance **12** contriteness

attritional
5 sorry **6** rueful **8** contrite, penitent **9** regretful, repentant **10** apologetic, remorseful **11** penitential

attune
6 accord, adjust **7** balance, conform **9** harmonize, integrate, reconcile **10** coordinate, proportion **11** accommodate

Atwood novel
7 Cat's Eye **12** Oryx and Crake **13** Handmaid's Tale (The)

atypical
3 odd **5** queer **7** deviant, strange, unusual **8** aberrant, abnormal, peculiar **9** anomalous, deviative, different, divergent, irregular, unnatural **11** exceptional, heteroclite, nonstandard **13** preternatural

auberge
3 inn **5** hotel, lodge **6** hostel, tavern **7** hospice **8** hostelry **9** roadhouse **11** caravansary, public house

Auber opera
10 Fra Diavolo

auburn
4 rust **5** henna **6** russet **8** chestnut **11** burnt sienna **12** reddish-brown

Auchincloss novel
9 Embezzler (The) **13** East Side Story **14** Rector of Justin (The)

au courant
3 mod **4** up on **5** awake, aware, hep to, hip to,

savvy **6** modern, modish, versed **7** abreast, current, in touch, knowing, stylish, versant, witting **8** familiar, informed, sentient, up-to-date **9** cognizant, conscious, plugged in **10** acquainted, conversant **11** fashionable **12** contemporary **13** up-to-the-minute

auction
4 sale, sell

audacious
4 bold, rash **5** brash, brave, cocky, risky, saucy **6** brazen, cheeky, daring **7** valiant **8** arrogant, fearless, impudent, insolent, intrepid, reckless, unafraid, uncurbed **9** daredevil, dauntless, foolhardy, shameless, undaunted, venturous **10** courageous, ungoverned, unhampered **11** adventurous, impertinent, temerarious, uninhibited, untrammeled, venturesome **12** unrestrained **13** adventuresome

audacity
4 gall **5** brass, cheek, moxie, nerve, spunk **6** mettle, spirit **7** courage **8** boldness, chutzpah, rashness, temerity **9** assurance, arrogance, brashness, cockiness, disregard, hardihood, hardiness, impudence, insolence **10** brazenness, effrontery **12** recklessness

audible
5 aural, clear, heard **8** distinct **9** auricular

audibly
5 aloud **7** aurally, clearly, out loud

audience
5 crowd, group, house **6** public **7** hearing, gallery, hearers, meeting **8** admirers, assembly, audition, devotees **9** clientele, following, gathering, interview, listeners **10** assemblage, spectators

audile
see **auditory**

audio
5 sound

audit
4 scan **5** check, probe **6** go over, report, review, survey, verify **7** analyze, balance, checkup, examine, inspect **8** analysis, scrutiny **10** inspection, scrutinize **11** examination **13** investigation

audition
4 test **5** trial **6** tryout **7** hearing, reading

auditor
8 examiner, listener **9** inspector **10** accountant, controller **11** comptroller

auditory
5 aural **8** acoustic

Auel, Jean
novel: 17 Clan of the Cave Bear (The)
series: 14 Earth's Children

au fait
4 able **5** right **6** decent, proper, versed **7** abreast, capable, correct, versant **8** becoming, decorous, familiar, informed, relevant **9** befitting, competent, qualified **10** acquainted, conforming, conversant, to the point

au fond
8 at bottom **9** basically, in essence **11** essentially **13** fundamentally

Augean
9 difficult **10** formidable **11** distasteful
stable: 3 sty **4** sink **5** filth, Sodom **7** cesspit **8** cesspool

auger
3 bit **5** borer, drill, screw **6** gimlet, trepan, wimble **9** corkscrew

Auge's son
8 Telephus

aught
3 all, nil, nix, zip **4** nada, zero **5** zilch **6** cipher **7** nothing **8** anything, goose egg **10** everything

augment
3 wax **4** grow, hike, rise **5** add to, boost, build, exalt, mount, raise **6** beef up, expand, extend **7** amplify, build up, develop, enhance, enlarge, magnify **9** intensify, reinforce **8** compound, heighten, increase, multiply **10** aggrandize, supplement **11** make greater

augmentation
4 rise **5** annex, extra, raise **7** adjunct, buildup **8** addition, increase **9** accession, accretion, increment **10** complement, enrichment **11** enhancement, enlargement

augur
4 bode, seer **6** herald, oracle **7** betoken, diviner, portend, predict, presage, promise, prophet, suggest **8** forebode, forecast, foreshow, foretell, indicate, prophesy, soothsay **9** adumbrate, foretoken, harbinger, predictor, prefigure **10** forecaster, foreshadow, foreteller, prophesier, soothsayer, vaticinate **11** Nostradamus **13** prognosticate

augury
4 omen, sign **5** token **6** herald **7** auspice, portent, presage, warning **8** bodement, forecast, prophecy **9** foretoken, harbinger **10** divination, forerunner, prediction, prognostic **11** forewarning

august
5 grand, noble, regal **6** lordly **7** eminent, stately **8** baronial, imposing, majestic, princely, splendid **9** dignified, grandiose **11** magnificent

auk
5 alcid **7** seabird
genus: 4 Alca

au naturel
3 raw **4** nude **5** naked, plain **6** unclad **8** stripped **9** unclothed, undressed **10** stark naked

aunt
French: **5** tante
German: **5** Tante
Italian: **3** zia
Japanese: **6** obasan
Spanish: **3** tía

aura
3 air **4** feel, glow, halo, mood, tone, vibe **5** aroma, vibes **6** nimbus **7** aureole, feeling, quality **8** ambience, mystique, radiance, stimulus **9** emanation, semblance, sensation **10** atmosphere

aural
6 audile **7** audible **8** acoustic, auditory **9** auricular

aureate
6 florid, golden **7** flowery, orotund **8** sonorous **9** bombastic, grandiose, overblown **10** euphuistic, rhetorical **11** declamatory **13** grandiloquent

aureole
4 aura, halo, ring **5** crown, light **6** circle, corona, nimbus **8** radiance

au revoir
4 by-by, ciao, ta-ta **5** adieu, adios **6** bye-bye, so long **7** good-bye **8** farewell **11** arrivederci

auricular
see **aural**

Auriga star
7 Capella

aurora
4 dawn, morn **7** dawning, morning, sunrise **8** cockcrow, daybreak

Aurora
Roman counterpart: **3** Eos
goddess of: **4** dawn
husband: **8** Tithonus
son: **6** Memnon

auslander
5 alien **7** inconnu **8** outsider, stranger **9** foreigner

auspice
4 omen, sign **10** divination

auspices
5 aegis **6** charge **7** backing, support **8** guidance **9** influence, patronage **11** sponsorship, supervision

auspicious
5 lucky **6** bright, timely **7** hopeful **9** favorable, fortunate, opportune, promising, well-timed **10** propitious, prosperous **11** encouraging

Austen, Jane
novel: **4** Emma **10** Persuasion **13** Mansfield Park **15** Northanger Abbey **17** Pride and Prejudice **19** Sense and Sensibility

Auster
see **Notus**

austere
4 bare, cold, dour, firm, grim, hard **5** acrid, bleak, grave, harsh, plain, rigid, sharp, spare, stern **6** bitter, severe, simple, somber, strict **7** ascetic, serious, spartan **8** exacting **9** stringent, unadorned, unfeeling **10** astringent, restrained **11** self-denying

austerity
5 rigor **6** thrift **7** economy **8** acerbity, asperity, coldness, grimness, hardness, rigidity, severity **9** harshness, parsimony, privation, solemnity, spareness, sternness, stiffness **10** self-denial, simplicity, strictness, stringency **11** unadornment **13** self-restraint

Australia
capital: **8** Canberra
city: **5** Perth **6** Darwin, Sydney **8** Adelaide, Brisbane **9** Melbourne, Newcastle
desert: **10** Great Sandy **13** Great Victoria
ethnic group: **9** Aborigine
island: **6** Fraser **8** Kangaroo, Melville, Tasmania
lake: **4** Eyre
monetary unit: **6** dollar
mountain, range: **9** Ayers Rock **9** Kosciusko **13** Great Dividing
reef: **12** Great Barrier
river: **4** Swan **6** Murray **7** Darling **8** Flinders **11** Cooper Creek **12** Coopers Creek
strait: **4** Bass **6** Torres

Austria
capital: **6** Vienna
city: **4** Graz, Linz **8** Salzburg **9** Innsbruck **10** Klagenfurt
lake: **10** Neusiedler
monetary unit: **4** euro
monetary unit, former: **9** schilling
mountain: **13** Grossglockner
mountain range: **4** Alps
neighbor: **5** Italy **7** Croatia, Germany, Hungary **8** Slovakia, Slovenia **11** Switzerland **13** Czech Republic, Liechtenstein
river: **3** Ems **6** Danube

autarchy
see **autocracy**

autarkic
4 free **8** separate **9** sovereign **10** autonomous, self-ruling **11** independent, self-reliant **13** self-governing

autarky
7 freedom **8** autonomy **12** independence, self-reliance

authentic
4 real, true **5** legit, pukka, right, solid, sound,

valid **6** actual, trusty **7** certain, factual, for real, genuine **8** accurate, bona fide, credible, faithful, reliable **9** undoubted, veritable **10** convincing, dependable, legitimate, sure-enough **11** indubitable, trustworthy **12** questionless

authenticate
5 prove, vouch **6** adduce, attest, verify **7** bear out, certify, confirm, justify, voucher, warrant **8** accredit, notarize, validate **11** corroborate **12** substantiate

author
5 maker **6** penman, scribe, writer **7** creator **8** inventor, novelist, prosaist **9** generator **10** originator
American: 3 Bly (Robert), Fox (Paula), Nin (Anaïs), Poe (Edgar Allan), Tan (Amy) **4** Agee (James), Baum (L. Frank), Buck (Pearl S.), Cain (James M.), Cook (Robin), Dana (Richard Henry), Fast (Howard), Ford (Richard), Grey (Zane), Jong (Erica), Mann (Thomas), Puzo (Mario), Rand (Ayn), Rice (Anne), Roth (Philip), Shaw (Irwin), Uris (Leon), West (Nathanael), Wouk (Herman) **5** Aiken (Conrad), Alger (Horatio), Banks (Russell), Barth (John), Benét (Stephen Vincent), Blume (Judy), Boyle (T. Coraghessan), Brown (Rita Mae), Clark (Mary Higgins), Crane (Hart, Stephen), Dunne (Dominick, John Gregory), Elkin (Stanley), Ellis (Bret Easton), Foote (Horton), Haley (Alex), Harte (Bret), Henry (O.), Jaffe (Rona), Jakes (John), James (Henry), Levin (Ira), Lewis (Sinclair), Lurie (Alison), Mason (Bobbie Ann), Oates (Joyce Carol), O'Hara (John), Ozick (Cynthia), Paine (Thomas), Paley (Grace), Potok (Chaim), Price (Reynolds, Richard), Steel (Danielle), Stein (Gertrude), Stone (Irving), Stout (Rex), Stowe (Harriet Beecher), Turow (Scott), Twain (Mark), Tyler (Anne), Vidal (Gore), Welty (Eudora), White (Edmund, E. B., T. H.), Wolfe (Thomas, Tom), Wylie (Elinor) **6** Alcott (Louisa May), Asimov (Isaac), Auster (Paul), Bellow (Saul), Berger (Thomas), Bierce (Ambrose), Bowles (Paul), Cabell (James Branch), Capote (Truman), Cather (Willa), Chopin (Kate), Clancy (Tom), Conroy (Pat), Cooper (James Fenimore), Dickey (James), Didion (Joan), Ellroy (James), Ferber (Edna), French (Marilyn), Gaddis (William), Gaines (Ernest J.), Gilroy (Frank), Godwin (Gail), Hailey (Arthur), Harris (Frank, Joel Chandler), Hawkes (John), Heller (Joseph), Hersey (John), Hinton (S. E.), Holmes (Oliver Wendell), Hughes (Langston), Hunter (Evan), Irving (John, Washington), Jewett (Sarah Orne), Kidder (Tracy), Koontz (Dean), Krantz (Judith), L'Amour (Louis), L'Engle (Madeleine), Le Guin (Ursula K.), London (Jack), Mailer (Norman), McBain (Ed), Miller (Arthur, Henry, Joaquin, May), Morley (Christopher), Morris (Wright), Mosley (Walter), Norris (Frank), Parker (Dorothy), Piercy (Marge), Porter (Katherine Anne, William Sydney), Proulx (E. Annie), Runyon (Damon), Sarton (May), Sheehy (Gail), Singer (Isaac Bashevis), Smiley (Jane), Styron (William), Taylor (Peter), Updike (John), Walker (Alice), Waller (Robert James), Warren (Robert Penn), Wilder (Laura Ingalls, Thornton), Wilson (August, Edmund, Harriet, Lanford), Wister (Owen), Wright (James, Richard) **7** Baldwin (Faith, James), Beattie (Ann), Cheever (John), Clavell (James), Clemens (Samuel Langhorne), Collins (Jackie), Connell (Evan), Cozzens (James Gould), DeLillo (Don), Dreiser (Theodore), Ellison (Ralph), Erdrich (Louise), Farrell (James T.), Francis (Dick), Franzen (Jonathan), Gardner (Erle Stanley), Garland (Hamlin), Glasgow (Ellen), Goldman (William), Grafton (Sue), Grisham (John), Hammett (Dashiell), Heyward (DuBose), Howells (William Dean), Hurston (Zora Neale), Jackson (Shirley), Jarrell (Randall), Johnson (Diane, James), Keillor (Garrison), Kennedy (William), Kerouac (Jack), Kincaid (Jamaica), Lardner (Ring), Leonard (Elmore), Malamud (Bernard), Marquis (Don), Masters (Edgar Lee), McCourt (Frank), Mumford (Lewis), Nabokov (Vladimir), O'Connor (Flannery), Pynchon (Thomas), Rexroth (Kenneth), Richter (Conrad), Roberts (Elizabeth Madox, Kenneth, Nora), Saroyan (William), Sheehan (Neil), Sheldon (Sidney), Theroux (Paul), Thoreau (Henry David), Thurber (James), Wallace (Lew), Wharton (Edith) **8** Anderson (Maxwell, Poul, Regina, Sherwood), Benchley (Peter), Bradbury (Ray), Bradford (Barbara Taylor), Caldwell (Erskine), Chandler (Raymond), Cornwell (Patricia), Crichton (Michael), Doctorow (E. L.), Faulkner (William), Kingston (Maxine Hong), Marquand (John P.), McCarthy (Cormac, Mary), McMillan (Terry), McMurtry (Larry), Melville (Herman), Michener (James), Mitchell (Donald Grant, Margaret, S. Weir), Morrison (Toni), Remarque (Erich Maria), Rinehart (Mary Roberts), Salinger (J. D.), Sandburg (Carl), Sinclair (Upton), Spillane (Mickey), Stockton (Frank R.), Vonnegut (Kurt), Wambaugh (Joseph) **9** Burroughs (Edgar Rice, John, William S.), Dos Passos (John), Hawthorne (Nathaniel), Hemingway (Ernest), Hillerman (Tony), Isherwood (Christopher), McCullers (Carson), Steinbeck (John), Wodehouse (P. G.), Woollcott (Alexander) **10** Cunningham (Michael), Fitzgerald (F. Scott), Kingsolver (Barbara), Tarkington (Booth) **11** Auchincloss (Louis), Matthiessen (Peter)
Argentinian: 6 Borges (Jorge Luis)
Australian: 4 West (Morris L.) **5** Stead (Christina), White (Patrick) **7** Clavell (James), Idriess (Ion) **8** Keneally (Thomas) **10** McCullough (Colleen), Richardson (Henry Handel)

Austrian: **5** Kafka (Franz) **6** Handke (Peter) **7** Jelinek (Elfriede), Suttner (Bertha) **8** Bernhard (Thomas) **10** Schnitzler (Arthur)
Brazilian: **6** Coelho (Paulo)
Canadian: **3** Roy (Camille, Gabrielle) **5** Kirby (William), Moore (Brian), Munro (Alice) **6** Atwood (Margaret), Davies (Robertson) **7** Leacock (Stephen), Raddall (Thomas), Richler (Mordecai), Service (Robert), Shields (Carol) **8** Woodcock (George) **9** de la Roche (Mazo), MacLennan (Hugh)
Chilean: **6** Donoso (José) **7** Allende (Isabel)
Chinese: **5** Han Yu
Colombian: **7** Márquez (Gabriel García)
Czech: **5** Capek (Karel), Hasek (Jaroslav) **7** Kundera (Milan)
Danish: **4** Rode (Helge), Wied (Gustav) **6** Jensen (Johannes Vilhelm) **7** Dinesen (Isak), Holberg (Ludwig)
Dutch: **6** Vondel (Joost van den)
Egyptian: **7** Mahfouz (Naguib)
English: **4** Amis (Kingsley, Martin), Dahl (Roald), Ford (Ford Madox, John), Lyly (John), Saki, Snow (C. P.), Ward (Mrs. Humphry), West (Rebecca) **5** Byatt (A. S.), Defoe (Daniel), Doyle (Authur Conan), Eliot (George, Thomas Stearns), Evans (Mary Ann), Frayn (Michael), Hardy (Thomas), James (Henry, P. D.), Lewis (C. S., Monk, Wyndham), Lowry (Malcolm), Milne (A. A.), Munro (H. H.), Powys (John Cowper, Llewelyn, Theodore Francis), Reade (Charles), Spark (Muriel), Waugh (Alec, Evelyn), Wells (Charles Jeremiah, H. G.), White (T. H.), Wilde (Oscar), Woolf (Leonard, Virginia), Young (Arthur, Edward, Francis Brett) **6** Ambler (Eric), Archer (Jeffrey), Austen (Jane), Belloc (Hilaire), Brontë (Anne, Charlotte, Emily), Bunyan (John), Butler (Samuel), Clarke (Arthur C.), Conrad (Joseph), Fowles (John), Graves (Robert), Greene (Graham, Robert), Hilton (James), Hudson (W. H.), Huxley (Aldous), Malory (Thomas), McEwan (Ian), O'Brian (Patrick), Orwell (George), Potter (Beatrix), Powell (Anthony), Sayers (Dorothy L.), Sterne (Laurence), Stoker (Bram), Storey (David), Walton (Izaak) **7** Ballard (J. G.), Burgess (Anthony), Burnett (Frances Hodgson), Carroll (Lewis), Clavell (James), Collins (Wilkie), Dickens (Charles), Dodgson (Charles), Durrell (Lawrence), Fleming (Ian), Follett (Ken), Forster (E. M.), Forsyth (Frederick), Golding (Louis, William), Kipling (Rudyard), Le Carré (John), Lessing (Doris), Lofting (Hugh), Maugham (Robin, W. Somerset), Murdoch (Iris), Naipaul (V. S.), Rendell (Ruth), Rowling (J. K.), Sassoon (Siegfried), Shelley (Mary Wollstonecraft, Percy Bysshe), Sitwell (Edith, Osbert, Sacheverell), Southey (Robert), Stewart (Mary), Surtees (Robert Smith), Tolkien (J. R. R.), Walpole (Horace, Hugh), Wyndham (John) **8** Christie (Agatha), Fielding (Henry), Forester (C. S.), Koestler (Arthur), Lawrence (D. H., T. E.), Macaulay (Rose, Thomas Babington), Meredith (George), Sillitoe (Alan), Smollett (Tobias), Strachey (Lytton), Trollope (Anthony), Zangwill (Israel) **9** De Quincey (Thomas), Du Maurier (Daphne, George), Goldsmith (Oliver), Isherwood (Christopher), Mansfield (Katherine), Masefield (John), Priestley (J. B.), Radcliffe (Ann), Stevenson (Robert Louis), Thackeray (William Makepeace), Wodehouse (P. D.) **10** Chesterton (Gilbert Keith), Galsworthy (John), Richardson (Dorothy, Samuel) **12** Quiller-Couch (Arthur Thomas)
Finnish: **7** Waltari (Mika) **9** Sillanpää (Frans Eemil)
French: **3** Nin (Anaïs) **4** Gide (André), Hugo (Victor), Kock (Charles-Paul de), Sade (Marquis de), Sand (George), Zola (Emile) **5** Beyle (Marie Henri), Camus (Albert), Dumas (Alexandre), Genet (Jean), Sagan (Françoise), Staël (Germaine de), Verne (Jules), Vigny (Alfred-Victor) **6** Balzac (Honoré de), Daudet (Alphonse), France (Anatole), Lesage (Alain-René, Proust (Marcel), Sartre (Jean-Paul) **7** Cocteau (Jean), Colette, Gautier (Léon, Théophile), Malraux (André), Mauriac (Claude, François), Maurois (André), Merimée (Prosper), Rolland (Romain), Romains (Jules), Simenon (Georges) **8** Beauvoir (Simone de), Flaubert (Gustave), Marivaux (Pierre), Rabelais (François), Stendhal, Voltaire **9** Giraudoux (Jean) **10** Maupassant (Guy de), Saint-Simon (Duke de) **12** Robbe-Grillet (Alain), Saint-Exupéry (Antoine de)
German: **4** Böll (Heinrich), Mann (Thomas) **5** Grass (Gunter), Hesse (Hermann), Kafka (Franz), Storm (Theodor), Tieck (Ludwig), Zweig (Stefan) **6** Goethe (Johann Wolfgang von), Toller (Ernst) **7** Fontane (Theodor), Richter (Jean Paul), Wieland (Christoph Martin) **8** Hoffmann (E. T. A., Heinrich), Remarque (Erich Maria), Schlegel (August Wilhelm von, Friedrich von, Johann Elias) **9** Hauptmann (Gerhart), Sudermann (Hermann) **10** Wassermann (Jakob)
Greek: **5** Homer **6** Hesiod, Lucian, Pindar, Sappho **7** Plautus, Terence **8** Xenophon **9** Aeschylus, Euripedes, Herodotus, Sophocles **10** Thucydides **11** Kazantzakis (Nikos)
Hungarian: **5** Jókai (Mór)
Icelandic: **7** Laxness (Halldór)
Indian: **7** Rushdie (Salman)
Irish: **5** Behan (Brendan), Doyle (Roddy), Joyce (James), Moore (Brian), Synge (J. M.), Wilde (Oscar) **6** O'Brien (Edna), Stoker (Bram) **7** Beckett (Samuel), O'Connor (Frank), Russell (George William) **8** O'Faolain (Julia, Sean), Stephens (James) **9** O'Flaherty (Liam)
Italian: **3** Eco (Umberto) **5** Verga (Giovanni) **6** Silone (Ignazio) **7** Calvino (Italo), Manzoni (Alessandro), Moravia (Alberto) **9** Boccaccio

(Giovanni), Vittorini (Elio) **10** Pirandello (Luigi), Straparola (Gianfrancesco)
Japanese: **7** Mishima (Yukio) **8** Kawabata (Yasunari), Murakami (Haruki), Murasaki (Shikibu) **9** Yokomitsu (Riichi), Yoshikawa (Eiji)
Lebanese: **6** Gibran (Khalil)
Mexican: **7** Fuentes (Carlos)
Nigerian: **6** Achebe (Chinua) **7** Soyinka (Wole), Tutuola (Amos)
Norwegian: **3** Lie (Jonas) **6** Hamsun (Knut), Undset (Sigrid) **7** Rolvaag (Ole) **8** Bjornson (Bjornstjerne), Kielland (Alexander)
Peruvian: **11** Vargas Llosa (Mario)
Polish: **3** Lem (Stanislaw) **7** Reymont (Wladyslaw) **8** Zeromski (Stefan) **10** Gombrowicz (Witold) **11** Sienkiewicz (Henryk)
Portuguese: **6** Pessoa (Fernando) **8** Saramago (José)
Roman: **4** Livy **5** Pliny, Varro (Marcus Terentius) **7** Tacitus **8** Apuleius **9** Petronius
Russian: **5** Gogol (Nikolai), Gorki (Maxim), Gorky (Maxim) **7** Chekhov (Anton), Pushkin (Alexander), Tolstoy (Leo) **8** Andreyev (Leonid), Turgenev (Ivan), Zamyatin (Yevgeny) **9** Ehrenburg (Ilya), Lermontov (Mikhail), Pasternak (Boris), Sholokhov (Mikhail) **10** Dostoevsky (Fyodor) **11** Dostoyevsky (Fyodor), Yevtushenko (Yevgeny) **12** Solzhenitsyn (Alexander)
Scottish: **3** Tey (Josephine) **4** Lang (Andrew) **5** Scott (Alexander, Walter) **6** Barrie (James M.), Buchan (John) **8** Urquhart (Thomas) **9** Stevenson (Robert Louis)
South African: **5** Paton (Alan) **6** Fugard (Athol) **7** Coetzee (J. M.) **8** Gordimer (Nadine)
Spanish: **6** Baroja (Pio) **7** Alarcón (Pedro Antonio de) **9** Cervantes (Miguel de)
Swedish: **7** Johnson (Eyvind), Rydberg (Viktor) **8** Lagerlöf (Selma) **10** Lagerkvist (Pär), Strindberg (August)
Swiss: **4** Wyss (Johann Rudolf) **5** Spyri (Johanna) **6** Frisch (Max) **9** Spitteler (Carl)
Trinidadian: **7** Naipaul (V. S.)
Welsh: **4** Owen (Alun, Daniel, Goronwy, John) **5** Evans (David, Evan), Wynne (Ellis)
Yiddish: **4** Asch (Sholem) **6** Singer (Isaac Bashevis) **8** Aleichem (Sholem)

authoritarian
5 harsh, rigid **6** despot, severe, strict, tyrant **8** absolute, autocrat, despotic, dictator, dogmatic **9** imperious, stringent **10** absolutist, autocratic, oppressive, totalistic, tyrannical **11** dictatorial, doctrinaire, domineering, magisterial **12** totalitarian

authoritative
4 sure, true **5** legal, legit, sound **6** lawful, proven **7** factual **8** accepted, accurate, approved, attested, dogmatic, official, orthodox, reliable, verified **9** canonical, cathedral, confirmed, imperious, trustable, validated **10** autocratic, commanding, definitive, dependable, documented, dominating, ex cathedra, legitimate, sanctioned **11** dictatorial, doctrinaire, domineering, irrefutable, magisterial, overbearing, trustworthy **12** indisputable

authority
4 rule, sway **5** clout, force, power, right, say-so **6** agency, charge, credit, expert, master, weight **7** command, control, grounds, license, mastery, warrant **8** citation, decision, dominion, prestige **9** influence, testimony **10** domination, governance, government, management **12** jurisdiction

authorization
4 okay, word **5** leave **6** permit **7** consent, go-ahead, license, mandate **8** approval, sanction **9** agreement, allowance, clearance **10** green light, permission, sufferance **11** approbation

authorize
3 let **4** okay, vest **5** allow **6** affirm, enable, invest, permit **7** approve, confirm, empower, endorse, entitle, license, qualify, warrant **8** accredit, sanction, vouch for **9** give leave, recognize **10** commission **11** countenance

auto
see **automobile**

autobahn
7 highway **8** turnpike **10** expressway **12** superhighway

autobiography
4 life, vita **5** diary **6** memoir **7** account, journal **9** life story **11** confessions **13** reminiscences

autochthonous
6 native **7** endemic **8** original **10** aboriginal, indigenous

autocracy
7 czarism, tyranny **8** monarchy **9** despotism, monocracy **12** absolute rule, dictatorship

autocrat
4 czar, duce, emir, lord, raja, shah, tsar, tzar **5** mogul, rajah, ruler **6** caliph, despot, sultan, tyrant **7** magnate, monarch **8** dictator, oligarch, overlord **9** potentate, sovereign **10** absolutist

autocratic
7 haughty **8** absolute, arrogant, despotic **9** arbitrary, imperious, tyrannous **10** monocratic, tyrannical **11** dictatorial, domineering, overbearing

autodidactic
10 self-taught **12** self-educated

autograph
3 ink, pen **4** sign **5** write **7** endorse **8** original **9** signature, subscribe **11** endorsement, John Hancock

Autolycus
daughter: **8** Anticlea
father: **6** Hermes **7** Mercury

automated
7 robotic **9** by machine, motorized **10** electrical, electronic, mechanical, mechanized, programmed **12** computerized

automatic
6 reflex **8** habitual **9** impulsive, reflexive **10** mechanical, self-acting, unprompted **11** instinctive, involuntary, perfunctory, spontaneous, unmeditated
prefix: **4** self

automaton
5 droid, golem, robot **7** android, machine **9** mechanism

automobile
3 bus, car **5** buggy, coupe, racer, sedan **6** beater, jalopy, tourer, wheels **7** clunker, flivver, hardtop, machine **8** dragster, motorcar, roadster, runabout **9** hatchback, limousine **10** rust bucket **11** convertible
American: **3** Geo, Reo **4** Cord, Dart, Ford, Fury, Jeep, Nash, Neon, Olds, Vega **5** Buick, Dodge, Eagle, Edsel, Essex, Pinto, T-bird **6** Cougar, DeSoto, Duster, Fraser, Hudson, Kaiser, Model A, Model T, Saturn, Tucker, Willys **7** Charger, LaSalle, LeBaron, LeSabre, Lincoln, Maxwell, Mercury, Mustang, Packard, Pontiac, Rambler, Seville **8** Cadillac, Chrysler, Corvette, Eldorado, Franklin, Plymouth **9** Barracuda, Chevrolet, Hupmobile **10** Duesenberg, Oldsmobile, Studebaker **11** Continental, Pierce-Arrow, Thunderbird
British: **2** MG **3** Jag **4** Mini **5** Lotus **6** Anglia, Arnage, Austin, Cooper, DeSoto, Jaguar, Morris **7** Bentley, Daimler, Hillman, Phantom, Sunbeam, Triumph **8** Vauxhall **9** Land Rover **10** Range Rover, Rolls-Royce **11** Aston Martin, Silver Ghost **12** Austin-Healey
French: **5** Simca **7** Citroën, Peugeot, Renault
German: **3** BMW **4** Audi, Benz, Opel **7** Daimler, Maybach, Porsche, Quattro **8** Mercedes **10** Volkswagen **12** Mercedes-Benz
Italian: **4** Fiat **6** Lancia **7** Bugatti, Ferrari **8** Maserati **9** Alfa-Romeo **11** Lamborghini
Japanese: **5** Acura, Honda, Isuzu, Lexus, Mazda **6** Datsun, Altima, Maxima, Nissan, Subaru, Toyota **8** Infiniti **10** Mitsubishi
Korean: **3** Kia **6** Daewoo **7** Hyundai
Serbian: **4** Yugo
Swedish: **4** Saab **5** Volvo

automobile safety device
3 ABS **6** air bag **8** seat belt

automotive pioneer
4 Benz (Carl Friedrich), Ford (Henry), Olds (Ransom), Otto (Nikolaus), Pope (Albert) **5** Evans (Oliver), Rolls (Charles), Roper (Sylvester) **6** Cugnot (Nicholas Joseph), Duryea (Charles E., J. Frank), Lenoir (Etienne), Winton (Alexander) **7** Bugatti (Ettore), Citroën (André-Gustave), Daimler (Gottlieb), Peugeot (Armand), Stanley (Francis, Freelan) **8** Morrison (William) **10** Lanchester (Frederick William)

Autonoë
father: **6** Cadmus
husband: **9** Aristaeus
mother: **8** Harmonia
sister: **5** Agave
son: **7** Actaeon

autonomous
4 free **8** autarkic, separate **9** sovereign **10** self-ruling **11** independent, self-reliant **12** self-governed, uncontrolled **13** self-contained, self-governing

autonomy
7 autarky, freedom **8** home rule, self-rule **11** sovereignty **12** independence

autopsy
6 assess **7** examine **8** evaluate, necropsy **10** assessment, dissection, evaluation, postmortem **11** examination

auto racer
4 Foyt (A. J.), Hill (Graham) **5** Clark (Jim), Mears (Rick), Petty (Richard), Unser (Al, Bobby) **6** Carter (Pancho), Fangio (Juan), Vogler (Rich) **7** Brabham (Jack), Stewart (Jackie) **8** Andretti (Mario, Michael), Johncock (Gordon) **9** Earnhardt (Dale) **10** Rutherford (Johnny)

autumn
4 fall **6** season **8** maturity

auxiliary
4 aide **5** spare **6** backup, helper **7** reserve **8** adjutant, adjuvant **9** accessory, ancillary, assistant, coadjutor, secondary **10** accomplice, additional, collateral, subsidiary **11** appurtenant, subservient **12** contributory **13** complementary, supplementary
verb: **3** are, can, did, had, has, may, was **4** been, does, have, must, were, will **5** could, might, ought, shall, would **6** should

avail
3 aid, use **4** gain, good, help **5** asset, serve **6** profit **7** account, benefit, fitness, satisfy, service **9** advantage, relevance **10** usefulness **13** applicability

available
5 handy, on tap, ready, valid **6** at hand, on hand, usable **7** present, willing **8** prepared **9** qualified **10** accessible, attainable, convenient, obtainable, procurable **11** purchasable

avalanche
4 mass, rush **5** drown, flood, slide **6** deluge **7** overrun, smother **8** inundate, mudslide, overflow, rockfall **9** landslide, overwhelm, rockslide, snowslide **10** inundation **12** accumulation

Avalon
8 paradise

avant-garde
7 radical 8 advanced, contempo 10 innovative, pioneering 11 cutting-edge, leading-edge, progressive 12 experimental 13 up-to-the-minute

avarice
5 greed 7 avidity 8 cupidity, rapacity, voracity 10 greediness 12 covetousness

avaricious
6 grabby, greedy, stingy 7 miserly 8 covetous, esurient, grasping, ravenous 9 mercenary, rapacious 11 acquisitive

avatar
4 type 5 image 7 epitome 8 exemplar 9 archetype 10 apotheosis, embodiment, expression 11 incarnation, reification 13 manifestation
of Vishnu: 4 Rama

avaunt
4 away 5 hence, leave, scram 6 beat it, depart, get out

ave
4 hail 8 farewell, greeting

avenge
5 repay, right 6 punish 7 get even, pay back, redress, requite 9 fight back, retaliate, vindicate

avenue
3 way 4 path, road 5 drive, means, route, track 6 access, artery, course, street 7 channel, parkway, pathway 8 approach 9 boulevard 10 passageway 12 thoroughfare

aver
4 avow 5 prove, state, swear 6 affirm, allege, assert, attest, avouch, depose, insist, verify 7 declare, profess, protest, testify, warrant 8 maintain 9 guarantee, predicate

average
3 par 4 fair, mean, norm, so-so 5 usual 6 common, divide, equate, figure, median, medium, middle, normal 7 balance, even out, typical 8 everyday, midpoint, moderate, ordinary 12 intermediate

averagely
4 so-so 6 enough, fairly, rather 8 passably 9 tolerably 10 moderately

averse
5 balky, loath 6 afraid 7 hostile, opposed, uneager 8 allergic, hesitant 9 reluctant, resistant, unwilling 10 indisposed 11 disinclined 12 antipathetic

aversion
4 fear, hate 5 dread 6 hatred, horror 7 allergy, disgust, dislike 8 disfavor, distaste, loathing 9 antipathy, disliking, repulsion, revulsion 10 abhorrence, antagonism, repugnance 11 abomination, detestation, displeasure 13 indisposition

aversive
8 ungenial 9 repellent, repugnant 11 uncongenial 12 antipathetic 13 unsympathetic

avert
4 foil, halt, turn, veer, ward 5 avoid, check, deter 6 thwart 7 deflect, fend off, forfend, obviate, prevent, rule out, ward off 8 go around, stave off, turn away 9 forestall, turn aside

avian
6 flying, winged 8 birdlike, ornithic

aviary
4 cage 8 birdcage, dovecote 9 birdhouse, enclosure

aviator
3 ace 4 Post (Wiley) 5 flier, pilot 6 airman, Cessna (Clyde), flyboy, Wright (Orville, Wilbur), Yeager (Chuck) 7 birdman, Earhart (Amelia) 8 aeronaut 9 bush pilot, Lindbergh (Charles) 10 Richthofen (Manfred von) 12 Rickenbacker (Eddie)

avid
4 agog, keen 5 eager 6 ardent, greedy, hungry 7 anxious, athirst, craving, fervent, thirsty, zealous 8 appetent, covetous, desirous, grasping 9 impatient 10 breathless, insatiable 12 enthusiastic

avidity
4 zeal 5 greed 6 fervor, thirst 7 avarice, craving 8 cupidity, keenness, rapacity 9 eagerness 10 greediness

Avis competitor
5 Hertz

___ avis
4 rara

avocation
5 hobby 7 pastime, pursuit 8 sideline 9 amusement, diversion 10 recreation

avoid
4 bilk, duck, miss, shun, snub 5 annul, avert, dodge, elude, evade, shirk, skirt 6 bypass, divert, escape, eschew, pass up 7 abstain, prevent, refrain 8 preclude, sidestep, stay away, withdraw 9 keep clear 11 refrain from 12 keep away from

avoidance
5 dodge 6 escape 7 dodging, elusion, evasion 8 escaping, escapism, eschewal, shirking, shunning 9 runaround 10 abstinence

avouch
3 own 4 aver, avow 5 admit, claim, state, swear 6 affirm, assert, depose, insist 7 certify, confess, confirm, declare, profess, testify 9 predicate, pronounce 11 acknowledge, corroborate

avow
3 own **4** aver **5** admit, allow, grant, let on, own up, state, swear **6** affirm, assert, avouch, depose **7** concede, confess, declare, profess, protest **8** disclose, maintain, proclaim **9** predicate **11** acknowledge

avowal
6 assent **9** admission, assertion, statement **10** profession **11** affirmation, attestation, declaration

avowedly
6 openly **7** frankly **8** candidly **9** allegedly **10** apparently, ostensibly, supposedly

await
4 bide, hope, stay **5** abide **6** expect **7** count on, look for **8** watch for **10** anticipate, hang around

awake
4 stir **5** alert, alive, aware, rouse **6** active, arouse, bestir, excite, revive, roused, stir up **7** animate, aroused, excited, on guard **8** activate, sensible, sentient, vigilant, watchful **9** attentive, cognizant, conscious, observant, stimulate, stirred up

award
4 gift, give, kudo **5** allot, badge, endow, grant, honor, kudos, medal, prize **6** accord, bestow, confer, donate, ribbon, trophy **7** concede, laurels, tribute **8** accolade, citation, donation **9** vouchsafe **10** blue ribbon, decoration, distribute **11** distinction
advertising: **4** Addy, Andy, Clio
broadcasting: **7** Peabody
cable: **5** Telly
cartooning: **6** Ignatz, Reuben
comic books: **6** Eisner, Harvey
computing: **6** Turing
horror writing: **10** Bram Stoker
Internet: **5** Webby
motion picture: **5** Annie, Oscar **6** Razzie, Saturn **7** Academy **11** Golden Globe
mystery novel: **5** Edgar **6** Agatha
record: **6** Grammy
remodeling: **9** Chrysalis
romance novel: **4** Rita
science & technology: **11** Enrico Fermi
science-fiction: **4** Hugo **6** Nebula
software: **5** Codie
television: **4** Emmy
theater: **4** Obie, Tony

aware
4 onto **5** alert, alive, awake **7** heedful, knowing, mindful, tuned in, witting **8** informed, sensible, sentient, vigilant **9** attentive, au courant, cognizant, conscious, observant **10** conversant, perceptive **12** apprehensive **13** knowledgeable

awash
4 full **6** afloat, filled, jammed, loaded, packed **7** brimful, covered, crammed, crowded, flooded, run-over, stuffed **8** brimming, chockful **9** chockfull **11** overflowing

away
3 far, fro, now, off, out **4** afar, gone **5** along, apart, aside, forth, hence **6** abroad, absent, afield, far off **7** distant, lacking, missing, not here **9** elsewhere **11** incessantly **12** continuously

away from
6 beyond

awe
5 alarm, amaze, scare **6** wonder **7** inspire, startle **8** astonish **9** amazement, reverence **10** veneration, wonderment **11** flabbergast **12** astonishment

aweless
4 bold **5** brave **7** valiant **8** fearless, intrepid, unafraid **9** dauntless, undaunted **10** courageous

awesome
3 rad **6** august **7** amazing, sublime **8** imposing, terrific, wondrous **10** formidable, impressive **11** astonishing **12** breathtaking **13** extraordinary

awful
3 bad **4** dire, very **5** nasty **6** odious **7** hateful, heinous **8** dreadful, horrible, horrific, shocking, terrible, terrific **9** appalling, atrocious, extremely, frightful, loathsome, offensive **10** deplorable, disgusting, formidable

awfully
4 much, very **6** hugely, vastly **7** greatly **8** terribly, whopping **9** extremely, immensely **10** dreadfully, enormously **11** exceedingly

awhile
7 briefly **8** for a time **11** temporarily

awkward
5 gawky, inept, messy, nerdy, splay **6** clumsy, gauche, klutzy, wooden **7** artless, gawkish, halting, lumpish, unhandy, unhappy **8** bumbling, bungling, tactless, ungainly **9** graceless, ham-handed, ill-chosen, inelegant, lumbering, maladroit **10** blundering, ungraceful, unskillful **11** heavy-handed, unfortunate **12** embarrassing, incommodious, inconvenient, infelicitous

awl
4 tool **7** piercer

awning
6 canopy **7** marquee **8** sunshade
ancient Roman: **8** velarium

awry
5 amiss, askew, atilt, wrong **6** astray **7** askance, crooked **8** cockeyed **9** cock-a-hoop, crookedly
Scottish: **5** agley

ax, axe
3 adz, can, hew **4** adze, boot, chop, fire, sack **6** bounce **7** boot out, chopper, cleaver, dismiss, hatchet, kick out **8** tomahawk **9** discharge, terminate
blade: 3 bit
handle: 5 helve

axillary
4 alar

axiom
3 law **4** rule **5** adage, maxim, moral, truth **6** dictum, truism **7** precept, theorem **8** aphorism, apothegm **9** postulate, principle **10** principium **11** fundamental

axiomatic
5 given **7** assumed, certain, obvious **8** accepted, absolute, manifest, provable **10** aphoristic, understood **11** fundamental, indubitable, self-evident **12** unquestioned

axis
4 line, pole, stem **5** point, pivot **8** alliance **9** continuum, plant stem **11** partnership **12** straight line, turning point

axle
3 bar, pin, rod **4** beam **5** bogie, shaft **7** spindle, support

aye
3 yea, yep, yes **4** amen, okay, ever, vote **6** agreed, always **8** all right **11** affirmative, continually

Azerbaijan
capital: 4 Baku
city: 5 Gäncä **8** Sumqayit
exclave: 8 Naxçivan **11** Nakhichevan
monetary unit: 5 manat
neighbor: 4 Iran **6** Russia **7** Armenia, Georgia
river: 4 Kura **5** Araks
sea: 7 Caspian

Azores
capital: 12 Ponta Delgada
city: 5 Horta
island: 4 Pico **5** Corvo, Faial, Lajes **6** Flores **8** São Jorge, Terceura **9** São Miguel **10** Santa Maria
part of: 8 Portugal

Aztec
capital: 12 Tenochtitlán
conqueror: 6 Cortés, Cortéz
emperor: 9 Moctezuma, Montezuma
god: 4 Xipe **6** Tlaloc **9** Xipetotec **12** Quetzalcoatl
hero: 4 Nata
language: 7 Nahuatl
temple: 8 teocalli

azure
3 sky **4** blue **5** color **7** sky blue

B

baa
5 bleat

Babbitt
10 conformist, middlebrow, philistine
author: 5 Lewis (Sinclair)

babble
3 gab, jaw, yak, yap **4** blab, chat, go on, gush, rant, rave **5** clack, prate, run on **6** burble, drivel, gibber, gossip, jabber, murmur, patter, piffle, rattle, yammer **7** blabber, blather, chatter, maunder, palaver, prattle, twaddle **8** nonsense, idle talk **9** gibberish **11** jabberwocky

babe
3 cub, tot **4** doll, girl **5** bairn, child, chick, cutie, toots, woman **6** infant, hottie **7** bambino, papoose, neonate, newborn **8** bantling, nursling

babel
3 ado, din, row **4** to-do **5** hoo-ha **6** bedlam, clamor, hubbub, jangle, outcry, racket, ruckus, tumult, uproar **7** clangor, discord, ferment, turmoil **8** brouhaha, clangour, foofaraw **9** cacophony, commotion, confusion **10** dissonance, hullabaloo, hurly-burly, turbulence **11** pandemonium **12** vociferation

baboon
3 oaf **4** clod, dolt, goon, lout **6** chacma, galoot, simian **7** palooka **8** lunkhead, mandrill, meathead **9** hamadryas

babushka
6 granny **7** bandana **8** bandanna, kerchief

baby
3 pet, tot **4** tiny **5** bairn, sissy, spoil **6** cocker, coddle, cosset, dote on, infant, pamper **7** bambino, cater to, indulge, neonate, newborn, papoose, toddler **8** bantling, dote upon, nursling, suckling, weanling **11** mollycoddle
ailment: 5 colic, croup
bed: 4 crib **6** cradle **8** bassinet
bedroom: 7 nursery
breechcloth: 6 diaper
cap: 6 biggin, bonnet
carriage: 4 pram **5** buggy **8** stroller **12** perambulator
doctor: 12 pediatrician
food: 3 pap **4** milk **6** pablum **7** pabulum
garment: 7 rompers
Italian: 7 bambino
napkin: 3 bib
outfit: 7 layette
powder: 4 talc
shoe: 6 bootee
Spanish: 4 bebé, nene

baby grand
5 piano

babyhood
7 infancy **10** diaper days, immaturity

babyish
5 petty **7** foolish, puerile, spoiled **8** childish, immature, juvenile **9** infantile, infantine

Babylonian
6 lavish **9** luxurious
abode of the dead: 5 Aralu
capital: 7 Babylon
chaos: 4 Apsu
city: 5 Akkad **6** Cunaxa
crown prince: 10 Belshazzar
division: 5 Akkad, Sumer
first ruler: 6 Nimrod
god: 3 Bel **4** Adad, Addu, Enki, Enzu, Irra, Nabu, Nebo **6** Marduk, Tammuz **7** Shamash
goddess: 4 Erua, Gula **5** Belit **6** Ishtar
hero: 9 Gilgamesh
king: 6 Sargon **9** Hammurabi **12** Ashurbanipal
priest: 2 en
river: 6 Tigris **9** Euphrates
tower: 5 Babel **8** ziggurat
waters: 4 Apsu **6** Tiamat
winged dragon: 6 Tiamat

baccalaureate
6 degree **9** bachelor's **10** graduation

bacchanal
6 maenad
see also **bacchanalia**

bacchanalia
4 bash, orgy **5** binge, revel, spree **6** bender, excess **7** blowout, carouse, debauch, revelry, wassail **8** carnival, festival, wingding **11** celebration, dissipation, merrymaking

bacchanalian
4 wild **7** drunken, riotous **8** frenzied **9** debauched, orgiastic **12** intoxicating
cry 4 evoe **5** evohe

Bacchus
8 Dionysus
attendant: **6** maenad **9** bacchante
father: **4** Zeus **7** Jupiter
lover: **5** Venus **9** Aphrodite
mother: **6** Semele
son: **7** Priapus
staff: **7** thyrsus

Bach, Johann Sebastian
birthplace: **8** Eisenach
genre: **5** fugue, motet, suite **6** sonata **7** cantata, chorale, partita, prelude, toccata **8** concerto, fantasia, oratorio, sinfonia
home: **7** Leipzig
instrument: **5** organ **11** harpsichord
musical style: **7** baroque
religion: **8** Lutheran

back
3 aft, aid **4** abet, fund, help, hind, rear **5** abaft, about, bet on, dorsa (plural), spine, stake, stern **6** assist, astern, dorsum, hinder, recede, uphold **7** endorse, finance, promote, retract, retreat, reverse, sponsor, support **8** advocate, bankroll, champion, rearward, side with **9** in reverse, posterior, retrocede, subsidize **10** retrograde
ailment: **7** lumbago **10** rheumatism
muscle: **3** lat **4** trap **8** rhomboid **9** trapezius
of an arthropod: **6** tergum
of an insect: **5** notum
of the neck: **4** nape **6** scruff
prefix: **4** post **5** retro
relating to: **6** dorsal

back answer
3 lip **6** retort **7** riposte **8** comeback, repartee **9** rejoinder, wisecrack **10** return shot **11** parting shot

backbite
4 slam, slur **5** abuse, decry, knock, libel, smear, sully, taint **6** defame, defile, malign, vilify **7** asperse, put down, run down, slander, traduce **8** bad-mouth, belittle, besmirch, derogate, diminish **9** denigrate, discredit

backbiter
6 gossip **7** defamer, traitor **9** detractor, slanderer **10** talebearer

backbiting
5 abuse, smear, spite **6** gossip **7** abusing, calumny, obloquy, scandal, slander **8** libelous, smearing **9** aspersion, cattiness, gossiping, invective, maligning, traducing, vilifying **10** calumnious, defamation, defamatory, scandalous, slandering, slanderous **11** denigration **12** belittlement, depreciation, spitefulness, vituperation **13** disparagement

backbone
4 base, grit, guts, will **5** basis, moxie, nerve, spine, spunk **6** mettle, pillar, rachis **7** resolve, support **8** mainstay, tenacity **9** character, fortitude, framework, toughness, vertebrae **10** foundation, moral fiber, resolution **12** spinal column **13** determination, steadfastness

backbreaking
6 taxing, tiring **7** arduous, onerous **8** grueling, toilsome **9** fatiguing, gruelling, laborious, punishing, strenuous, torturous, wearisome **10** burdensome, exhausting

backchat
6 banter, gossip **10** persiflage

backcomb
5 tease

backcountry
4 bush **6** sticks **7** boonies, outback **8** frontier, interior **9** boondocks **10** hinterland

backcourtman
5 guard

back down
4 balk **5** admit, demur, welsh, yield **6** beg off, bow out, cry off, give in, give up, recall, recant, renege **7** concede, disavow, retract, retreat **8** take back, withdraw **9** surrender, weasel out **10** chicken out

backdrop
6 milieu **7** climate, context, scenery, setting **8** stage set **10** atmosphere, background **11** environment, mise-en-scène **12** surroundings

backer
4 ally **5** angel **6** patron, surety **7** sponsor **8** advocate, defender, exponent, follower, investor, promoter **9** auxiliary, guarantor, proponent, supporter **10** bankroller, benefactor, meal ticket

backfire
4 fail **5** blast **6** fizzle, go awry **7** go amiss, go wrong **8** miscarry, ricochet **9** boomerang, discharge, explosion **10** disappoint, spring back **11** fall through **13** counteraction

backgammon
board section: **5** table
piece: **5** stone
wedge: **5** point

background
4 base, tone **6** milieu **7** history, scenery, setting **8** heritage, training **9** education **10** experience, supporting **13** circumstances, qualification

backhanded
7 devious, oblique **8** indirect, derisive, sneering **9** insulting, sarcastic **10** roundabout **12** disingenuous **13** condescending
compliment: **6** insult, slight **7** put-down **9** aspersion

backing
3 aid **4** help **5** aegis, funds **7** harmony, support

8 auspices 9 patronage, promotion 10 assistance 11 endorsement, sponsorship 13 accompaniment, encouragement

backland
see **backcountry**

backlash
5 slack 6 recoil 8 kickback, reaction, response, ricochet 11 retaliation 12 repercussion

backlog
4 pile 5 hoard, stock, store 6 pile up, supply 7 nest egg, reserve 9 inventory, reservoir, stockpile 12 accumulation

back of
5 abaft 6 behind 9 following

back off
see **back down**

back out
4 quit 5 leave, welsh, yield 6 beg off, desert, give up, renege 7 forsake 8 withdraw 9 surrender

backpack
4 gear, hike 5 tramp 6 duffel, ramble 8 knapsack, rucksack 9 haversack

backpedal
see **back down**

backset
see **setback**

backside
3 bum 4 butt, rear, rump, seat, tail, tush 5 fanny, hiney, stern 6 behind, bottom, breech, far end, heinie 8 buttocks, derriere, haunches 9 fundament, posterior 12 hindquarters

backslide
4 fall, sink, slip 5 lapse 6 return, revert 7 go wrong, regress, relapse 9 retrovert 10 degenerate, go downhill, recidivate 11 deteriorate

backstabbing
4 slur 5 smear 6 malice 7 calumny, scandal, slander 8 betrayal 9 treachery 10 defamation, detraction, traitorous 11 treacherous 12 belittlement, depreciation, vilification 13 disparagement

backstairs
6 covert, secret, sneaky, sordid 7 furtive 8 hush-hush 9 secretive 10 scandalous 11 clandestine, underhanded 13 surreptitious

backstop
5 fence 6 screen, uphold 7 bolster, support 8 advocate, champion, side with

back talk
3 lip 4 guff, sass 5 cheek, mouth, sauce 9 freshness, impudence, insolence 12 impertinence

backtrack
7 regress, retrace, retreat, reverse 8 turn tail

backward
4 dull, slow, rear 5 abaft, dense 6 averse, astern, behind, stupid 7 awkward, delayed, moronic 8 ignorant, inverted, rearward, retarded, reversed, stagnant 9 benighted, dimwitted, in reverse 10 half-witted, retrograde, slow-witted, uncultured 11 thickheaded, undeveloped 12 feebleminded, simpleminded, uncultivated 13 unprogressive

backwoods
see **backcountry**

backwoodsman
4 hick, rube 5 swain, yokel 6 rustic 7 bumpkin, hayseed 9 hillbilly 10 clodhopper, country boy, provincial 11 mountaineer

bacon
side: 6 flitch, gammon
slice: 6 rasher

Bacon, Francis
work: 12 Novum Organum

bacteria
5 cocci 6 coccus 7 bacilli, vibrios 8 bacillus, spirilla 9 spirillum
culture medium: 4 agar
destroyer: 10 antibiotic
pathogenic: 5 E. coli

bacterial disease
6 plague, typhus 7 anthrax, leprosy, tetanus, typhoid 8 botulism, syphilis 9 gonorrhea, infection, pneumonia 10 diphtheria, meningitis 11 shigellosis

bacteriologist
American: 6 Enders (John Franklin) 7 Noguchi (Hideyo), Theiler (Max)
British: 7 Fleming (Alexander)
French: 5 Widal (Fernand) 7 Nicolle (Charles-Jean-Henri), Pasteur (Louis)
German: 4 Cohn (Ferdinand Julius), Koch (Robert) 5 Klebs (Edwin) 7 Behring (Emil von), Ehrlich (Paul), Löffler (Friedrich) 10 Wassermann (August von)
Japanese: 8 Kitasato (Shibasaburo)
Russian: 11 Metchnikoff (Elie)
Swiss: 6 Yersin (Alexandre-Emile-John)

bad
3 ill, low 4 evil, foul, sour 5 amiss, awful, lousy, wrong 6 crummy, putrid, rancid, rotten, sinful, wicked 7 harmful, hateful, hurtful, immoral, naughty, noisome, noxious, spoiled, tainted, vicious 8 damaging, dreadful, inferior, perverse, terrible, wretched 9 abhorrent, defective, execrable, injurious, loathsome, obnoxious, offensive, putrefied, reprobate, repulsive, sickening 10 disgusting, iniquitous 11 deleterious, detrimental, distasteful, intolerable 12 unacceptable 13 objectionable
comparative: 5 worse
prefix: 3 dys, mis
superlative: 5 worst

bad blood
7 ill will 10 bitterness, ill feeling

Badebec
husband: 9 Gargantua
son: 10 Pantagruel

Baden
3 spa 6 resort 9 hot spring

badge
3 pin 4 arms, logo, mark, seal, sign 5 award, honor, kudos, medal, token 6 button, emblem, ensign 7 laurels 8 accolade, hallmark, insignia 10 coat of arms, decoration 11 distinction, purple heart

badger
3 bug, nag 4 bait, goad, ride 5 annoy, brock, chivy, harry, hound, ratel 6 chivvy, harass, hassle, heckle, hector, needle, pester, plague 7 torment 8 bullyrag 9 importune

Badger State
9 Wisconsin

badinage
4 play 6 banter, joking 7 jesting, joshing, kidding, ribbing, teasing 8 backchat, chitchat, repartee 9 cross talk 10 persiflage

badland
4 wild 5 waste, wilds 6 barren, desert 7 outback 8 wildness 10 wilderness 11 hill country

bad mark
3 gig 7 demerit

bad-tempered
4 dour, sour 5 cross, sulky, surly, testy 6 crabby, cranky, crusty, grumpy, ornery, sullen, touchy 7 grouchy, peevish 8 choleric, petulant 9 crotchety, dyspeptic, irascible, irritable, splenetic 10 ill-humored, ill-natured, unpleasant 11 quarrelsome 12 cantankerous, curmudgeonly, disagreeable, misanthropic

Baedeker
5 guide 6 manual 8 handbook 9 guidebook, vade mecum 10 compendium 11 enchiridion, travel guide

baffle
4 balk, foil 5 addle, block, floor, mix up, stump 6 bemuse, hinder, impede, muddle, puzzle, thwart 7 barrier, confuse, flummox, mystify, nonplus, perplex 8 befuddle, bewilder, confound 9 deflector, dumbfound, frustrate 10 circumvent, disappoint, disconcert

bafflement
9 confusion 10 bemusement, perplexity 12 bewilderment

bag
3 cop, nab, kit, net, sag, win 4 flop, grip, hook, kill, land, nail, poke, sack, tote, trap 5 biddy, bulge, catch, crone, forgo, pouch, purse, seize, shoot, snare, steal, udder 6 beldam, collar, duffel, duffle, give up, secure, valise 7 abandon, acquire, capture, satchel 8 backpack, knapsack, reticule, suitcase 9 apprehend, haversack 12 protuberance

bagatelle
6 trifle, whimsy 9 plaything

baggage
4 gear 5 hussy, stuff, tramp, trull, wench 6 burden, things, wanton 7 carry-on, effects, jezebel, luggage, parcels, trollop 8 obstacle, matériel, slattern, strumpet 9 equipment, hindrance 10 impediment, prostitute 11 impedimenta 13 paraphernalia

baggy
5 loose

Baghdad
founder: 6 Mansur
river: 6 Tigris

bagnio
4 crib, stew 7 brothel, lupanar 8 bordello, cathouse 10 bawdy house, whorehouse

bagpipe
part: 5 drone 7 bourdon, chanter
sound: 5 skirl

Bahamas
capital: 6 Nassau
island: 3 Cat 5 Abaco 6 Andros, Inagua 7 Watling 9 Eleuthera, Mayaguana 11 Grand Bahama, San Salvador 13 New Providence
neighbor: 4 Cuba

Bahrain
capital: 6 Manama
island: 6 Sitrah 7 Bahrain 10 Al Muharraq
language: 6 Arabic
monetary unit: 5 dinar
ruler: 4 amir, emir 5 ameer, hakim

bail
3 bar, dip 4 bond, flee, lade 5 ladle, scoop 6 handle, pledge, surety 7 release 8 guaranty, security, warranty 9 guarantee 10 collateral 12 recognizance

bailiwick
4 area, turf, zone 5 field, realm 6 domain, sphere 7 demesne, purview, terrain 8 district, dominion, province 9 champaign, specialty, territory 10 discipline 12 jurisdiction

bailout
3 aid 6 relief, rescue 7 subsidy 11 benefaction, deliverance

bairn
3 kid, tot 4 babe, baby, tyke 5 child 6 infant

bait
3 nag, try, vex 4 lure, ride, trap 5 abuse, chase, chivy, decoy, harry, hound, leger, snare, taunt, tease, tempt, worry 6 allure, badger, come-on, entice, entrap, harass, heckle, hector, lead on,

molest, pester, seduce **7** beguile, torment, torture **8** bullyrag, inveigle, ridicule **9** persecute, seduction, sweetener **10** attraction, allurement, enticement, temptation
and switch: **4** lure **5** trick **8** inveigle **10** substitute

bake
4 burn, char, cook, fire, kiln **5** broil, roast, toast **6** scorch **7** scallop, scollop, swelter

baked clay
7 ceramic

baker's dozen
8 thirteen

bakers' yeast
6 leaven **9** leavening

baking
3 hot **5** fiery **6** red-hot, torrid **7** burning **8** broiling, scalding, sizzling, white-hot **9** scorching
chamber: **4** kiln, oven

baksheesh
3 tip **4** alms **5** bribe, favor **6** grease, reward **7** payment **8** gratuity **9** emolument **12** compensation

Balaam
beast: **3** ass **6** donkey
father: **4** Beor

balance
4 rest **5** level, poise, scale, weigh **6** adjust, excess, make up, offset, set off, square, stasis **7** harmony, remains, remnant, residue **8** atone for, equalize, outweigh, residual, residuum, symmetry **9** composure, congruity, equipoise, harmonize, remainder, stability **10** compensate, counteract, difference, equanimity, neutralize, proportion, steadiness **11** consistency, countervail, equilibrium, self-control **12** counterpoise

balanced
4 fair **5** equal **6** offset, stable, steady **7** equable, weighed **9** equitable, impartial **10** evenhanded, harmonized, stabilized

balcony
6 piazza **7** catwalk, gallery **8** platform **9** mezzanine
section: **4** loge

bald
4 bare, nude **5** blunt, naked, plain, stark **6** barren, severe, shaven, smooth **8** glabrous, hairless, palpable, treeless **9** depilated, unadorned, uncovered **10** deforested, forthright **11** undisguised, unvarnished

baldachin
4 silk **6** canopy, fabric

Balder, Baldur
father: **4** Odin
mother: **5** Frigg **6** Frigga
slayer: **3** Höd **4** Hoth, Loke, Loki **5** Hoder, Hothr
wife: **5** Nanna

balderdash
3 rot **4** bosh, bull, bunk **5** bilge, crock, hooey **6** blague, bunkum, drivel **7** baloney, eyewash, garbage, hogwash, palaver, rubbish, twaddle **8** buncombe, claptrap, malarkey, nonsense, tommyrot **9** poppycock **10** tomfoolery **11** foolishness **13** horsefeathers

bald-faced
4 bold **6** arrant, brazen **7** blatant, defiant **8** impudent, insolent **9** audacious, shameless, unabashed **11** impertinent

baldness
8 alopecia **12** hairlessness

baldpate
7 widgeon **8** skinhead

Baldwin, James
essay: **17** Nobody Knows My Name, Notes of a Native Son
novel: **12** Fire Next Time (The) **13** Giovanni's Room **14** Another Country **21** Go Tell It on the Mountain
play: **21** Blues for Mister Charlie

balefire
6 beacon

baleful
4 dire, evil **6** deadly, malign **7** direful, fateful, harmful, hostile, malefic, ominous **8** menacing, sinister **9** ill-boding, ill-omened, malignant **10** maleficent, malevolent, pernicious **11** apocalyptic, threatening **12** unpropitious

balk
3 bar, gag, jib, shy **4** beam, dash, foil, ruin **5** block, check, demur, plank, stall **6** baffle, boggle, desist, flinch, hinder, rafter, refuse, thwart **7** prevent, scruple, stumble **8** hang back, hesitate, obstruct **9** frustrate, hindrance **10** circumvent, disappoint

balky
5 loath **6** averse, ornery, mulish, unruly **7** froward, restive, wayward, willful **8** contrary, hesitant, perverse, stubborn **9** immovable, obstinate, reluctant **10** unreliable **11** intractable, wrongheaded **12** cross-grained, recalcitrant **13** uncooperative, unpredictable

ball
3 orb, wad **4** prom **5** dance, globe, round **6** sphere **8** spheroid
batted high: **3** fly
batted straight: **5** liner
high-arching: **3** lob
of thread or yarn: **4** clew
ornamental: **6** pom-pom, pompon
tiny: **7** globule

ballad
3 lay **4** poem, song
singer: 8 minstrel **10** troubadour

ballast
4 load **5** poise **6** steady **7** balance, freight **8** balancer **9** stabilize, weigh down **10** dead weight, stabilizer **12** counterpoise **13** counterweight

ballerina
6 dancer **8** coryphée, danseuse **9** toe dancer **11** dancing girl
skirt: 4 tutu
see also **dancer**

ballet
4 Agon **6** Apollo, Jewels, Sylvia **7** Giselle, Orpheus **8** Bayadère (La), Coppélia, Firebird (The), Raimonda, Raymonda, Swan Lake, Sylphide (La) **9** Fancy Free, Petrushka, Sylphides (Les) **10** Don Quixote, Nutcracker (The), Petrouchka **12** Rite of Spring (The)
company: 5 Kirov **7** Joffrey **8** Imperial
costume: 4 tutu **6** tights **7** leotard
dancer: 7 danseur **8** coryphée, danseuse **9** ballerina
for two: 9 pas de deux
handrail: 5 barre
jump: 4 jeté **9** entrechat
knee bend: 4 plié
position: 6 pointe **8** attitude **9** arabesque
step: 3 pas **8** glissade
turn: 6 chaîné **9** pirouette

Ballets ____
6 Russes

ball game
see at **game**

Ballo in Maschera composer
5 Verdi (Giuseppe)

balloon sail
9 spinnaker

ball-shaped
7 globoid, globose **8** globular, spheroid **9** globulous, spherical

ball up
4 clew, daze **5** addle **6** fuddle, jumble, muddle, puzzle, tangle **7** confuse, fluster **8** befuddle, bewilder, bollix up, confound, distract, throw off **9** disorient

ballyhoo
4 hype, tout **6** blazon, herald, hoopla, hubbub, tumult **7** promote, trumpet **8** brouhaha **9** commotion, publicity **12** extravaganza

balm
4 lull **5** aroma, cream, quiet, salve, scent, spice **6** chrism, relief, remedy, solace **7** anodyne, bouquet, comfort, incense, perfume, soother, unction, unguent **8** easement, ointment **9** emollient, fragrance, redolence **10** palliative **11** consolation, restorative

balmacaan
8 overcoat

balm of Gilead
6 poplar **7** soother **8** restorer **9** balsam fir **11** restorative **12** balsam poplar

balmy
4 calm, daft, mild, nuts, soft **5** crazy, loony, nutty, potty, silly, sweet, wacky **6** gentle, insane, smooth **7** cracked, foolish, lenient, summery **8** aromatic, deranged, fragrant, perfumed, peaceful, pleasant, pleasing, redolent, soothing, tropical **9** agreeable, ambrosial, temperate

baloney
3 rot **4** bosh, bull, bunk **5** bilge, hokum, hooey **6** bunkum, humbug **7** hogwash, rubbish **8** buncombe, claptrap, nonsense **9** poppycock **10** balderdash **11** foolishness

balsam poplar
9 tacamahac **12** balm of Gilead

Balthazar's gift
5 myrrh

Baltic
city: 4 Riga **7** Tallinn **8** Helsinki **9** Stockholm
native: 4 Lett, Sorb, Wend **7** Latvian **8** Estonian, Prussian **10** Lithuanian
state: 6 Latvia **7** Estonia **9** Lithuania

Baltimore team
5 Blast, Colts **6** Ravens **7** Orioles

balustrade
4 rail **5** fence **7** railing **8** banister, handrail

Balzac character
4 Pons (Cousin) **5** Bette (Cousin) **6** Goriot (Père), Vidocq **7** Chabert (Colonel), Eugénie (Grandet), Grandet, Vautrin **8** Rubempré (Lucien de) **9** Birotteau, Rastignac (Eugène de) **13** Henri de Marsay

Bambi author
6 Salten (Felix)

bambino
3 kid, tot **4** babe, baby, tyke **5** bairn, child **6** cherub, Christ, infant, moppet, nipper **7** toddler

bamboozle
3 con **4** bilk, dupe, fool, gull, hoax, hose, scam **5** stump, trick **6** baffle, befool, diddle, puzzle **7** chicane, confuse, deceive, defraud, mislead, perplex, swindle **8** befuddle, confound, flimflam, hoodwink, throw off **9** frustrate **11** hornswoggle

ban
3 bar **5** curse, taboo **6** enjoin, forbid, outlaw **7** censure, exclude **8** anathema, prohibit, suppress **9** damnation, interdict, proscribe

10 injunction **11** forbiddance, malediction, prohibition, suppression **12** denunciation, interdiction, proscription

Ban
ally: **6** Arthur
son: **8** Lancelot

banal
4 blah, dull, flat **5** bland, corny, ho-hum, tired, trite, usual, vapid **6** common, jejune, stupid **7** clichéd, humdrum, insipid, prosaic, sapless, trivial **8** ordinary **9** hackneyed, quotidian, wearisome **10** namby-pamby, pedestrian, uninspired, wishy-washy **11** commonplace

banality
5 ennui **6** cliché, old saw, truism **7** bromide, inanity, old song **8** chestnut, monotony, prosaism **9** platitude **10** dreariness, shibboleth, triviality **11** commonplace, old chestnut, tediousness

banana
3 fei

banana-like fruit
8 plantain

banausic
4 blah, drab, dull, poky **6** dreary, earthy, stodgy **7** humdrum, mundane, routine, secular, sensual, tedious, worldly **8** everyday, material, plodding, temporal, workaday **9** practical, pragmatic **10** monotonous, pedestrian **11** acquisitive, utilitarian **13** materialistic, uninteresting

band
4 belt, bevy, club, crew, gang, gird, sash, tape **5** bunch, corps, covey, group, horde, party, strap, strip, troop, unite **6** concur, fillet, girdle, league, outfit, ribbon, team up, troupe **7** cluster, combine, company, coterie **8** cincture, engirdle, ensemble, symphony **9** cooperate, orchestra **10** federation
horizontal: **4** fess
Mexican: **8** mariachi
neck: **6** torque
small: **5** combo

bandage
4 bind **5** cover, dress, gauze, truss **6** swathe **7** plaster, swaddle **8** compress, dressing

bandanna
8 babushka, kerchief **9** headscarf **11** neckerchief

bandeau
3 bra **5** strip **6** fillet, ribbon, stripe **7** tube top **8** swimwear **9** brassiere

banderilla
4 dart

banderole
4 flag, jack **6** banner, burgee, colors, ensign, pennon, scroll **7** pennant **8** bannerol, standard, streamer

bandicoot
3 rat

bandit
6 outlaw, raider, robber, sacker **7** brigand, cateran, forager, ravager **8** marauder, pillager **9** cutthroat, desperado, holdup man, plunderer **10** freebooter, highwayman **11** bushwhacker

bandleader
7 maestro **9** conductor
famous: **3** Rey (Alvino) **4** Shaw (Artie), Ward (Hedley), Welk (Lawrence) **5** Basie (Count), Brown (Les), Cugat (Xavier), Faith (Percy), Heath (Ted), James (Harry), Jones (Spike), Kyser (Kay), Lewis (Ted), Lopez (Vincent), Owens (Buck), Prado (Pérez), Sousa (John Philip) **6** Cotton (Billy), Dorsey (Jimmy, Tommy), Duchin (Eddie, Peter), Herman (Woody), Hylton (Jack), Kenton (Stan), Miller (Glenn), Mingus (Charles), Waring (Fred) **7** Goodman (Benny), Trotter (John Scott) **8** Calloway (Cab), Giordano (Vince), Lombardo (Guy), Whiteman (Paul) **9** Ellington (Duke), Henderson (Fletcher), Mantovani

bandolier
4 belt, sash

bandwagon
3 fad **4** chic, mode, rage **5** craze, style, trend, vogue **7** fashion

bandy
3 bat **4** flip, swap, toss **5** argue, bowed **6** banter **7** discuss, shuffle **8** exchange **9** bowlegged, pass about **11** interchange

bane
3 woe **4** pest, ruin **5** curse, death, venom, virus **6** blight, burden, plague, poison **7** bugaboo, bugbear, scourge, torment, undoing **8** anathema, calamity, downfall, nuisance **9** bête noire, contagion, destroyer, ruination **10** affliction, pestilence **11** destruction

baneful
4 dire, evil **5** fatal **6** deadly **7** fateful, harmful, hurtful, malefic, noxious, ominous **9** ill-boding, ill-omened, injurious, malignant, pestilent, unhealthy **10** disastrous, pernicious **11** apocalyptic, deleterious, pestiferous, threatening **12** pestilential, unpropitious

bang
3 bat, box, hit, pop, rap **4** bash, beat, belt, blow, boom, bump, clap, peal, push, rape, shot, slam, sock, wham, whop **5** blast, burst, crack, crash, noise, pound, punch, smack, smash, sound, vigor, whack **6** fringe, report, strike, thrill, wallop **7** collide, exactly, resound **8** smack-dab, squarely **9** explosion **10** detonation

banger
7 athlete, sausage

Bangkok native
4 Thai

Bangladesh
capital: **5** Dacca, Dhaka
city: **6** Khulna **10** Chittagong
former name: **6** Bengal
language: **7** Bengali
monetary unit: **4** taka
neighbor: **5** Burma, India **7** Myanmar
river: **5** Padma **6** Ganges, Jamuna **11** Brahmaputra

bangle
4 disk **5** charm **6** anklet, bauble **7** pendant, trinket **8** bracelet, wristlet

bang-up
3 ace **4** fine **5** dandy, primo, super **6** far-out, superb **7** capital **8** champion, fabulous, five-star, splendid, top-notch **9** excellent, first-rate **10** first-class **11** spectacular

banish
3 ban **4** oust **5** debar, eject, evict, exile, expel **6** deport, dispel, put out, run out **7** cast out, dismiss, exclude, shut out, turn out **8** drive out, relegate, send away **9** discharge, ostracize, rusticate, transport **10** expatriate **13** excommunicate

banishment
5 exile **7** banning **8** eviction **9** discharge, expulsion, ostracism **10** dispelling, relegation **11** deportation, dissolution **12** displacement

banister
3 bar **4** rail **7** railing **10** balustrade

bank
3 row **4** edge, heap, hill, mass, pile, rank, save, tier, tilt **5** amass, array, beach, coast, group, hoard, levee, marge, mound, pitch, shoal, shore, slope, stack, stash **6** coffer, dealer, invest, margin, rivage, strand **7** deposit, incline, lay away, pyramid **8** lakeside, lay aside, salt away, seafront, set aside, sock away, squirrel, treasury **9** riverside **10** repository, storehouse **11** credit union **12** squirrel away
machine: **3** ATM

bank on
5 trust **7** believe

bankroll
4 back, fund **5** endow, funds, stake **6** pay for **7** capital, finance, sponsor, support **9** grubstake, subsidize **10** capitalize, underwrite

bankrupt
4 bare, bust, do in, ruin **5** break, drain, empty, strip, spent, use up, wreck **6** broken, divest, failed, fold up **7** deplete, deprive, exhaust, lacking, sterile **8** depleted, indebted **9** destitute, exhausted, pauperize, penniless **10** impoverish **12** impoverished

bankruptcy
4 lack, ruin **6** penury **7** failure **9** depletion, ruination, sterility, total loss **10** barrenness, exhaustion, insolvency **11** destitution, liquidation

banned
5 taboo **6** barred **7** illegal, illicit, tabooed **8** enjoined, verboten **9** forbidden **10** contraband, disallowed, prohibited, proscribed **11** interdicted

banner
4 flag, jack **6** burgee, ensign, pennon **7** pendant, pennant **8** banderol, gonfalon, standard, streamer **9** banderole
Roman: **7** labarum **8** vexillum

bannerol
see **banderole**

banquet
4 feed **5** feast, roast **6** dinner, regale, repast, spread

banquette
4 seat, sofa **5** bench, shelf **8** platform, sidewalk

Banquo
5 ghost
murderer: **7** Macbeth

banshee
6 keener, wailer

bantam
3 wee **4** arch, fowl, mini, pert, runt, tiny **5** dwarf, saucy, small **6** cheeky, little, petite **8** insolent, malapert **9** combative, undersize **10** diminutive, undersized

banter
3 fun, kid, rag, rib, wit **4** fool, jest, jive, joke, josh, razz **5** chaff, dally, jolly, tease **7** jesting, joshing, kidding, mockery, ragging, razzing, ribbing, teasing **8** backchat, back talk, badinage, chitchat, drollery, exchange, repartee **9** challenge, small talk **10** persiflage, pleasantry **11** give-and-take

bantling
4 babe, baby **5** bairn **6** infant **7** bambino, newborn, papoose

baptize
3 dip, dub **4** call, name, soak **5** douse, title **6** anoint, drench, purify **7** asperse, cleanse, entitle, immerse **8** christen, dedicate, initiate, sprinkle **9** designate **10** consecrate, denominate, regenerate

bar
3 ban, dam, pub, rod, tap **4** curb, dive, fess, halt, save, stop **5** block, court, estop, ingot, limit, stick, strip **6** bistro, except, impede, lounge, saloon, tavern **7** barrier, cantina, delimit, exclude, gin mill, rule out, taproom **8** alehouse, blockade, count out, obstacle, obstruct, restrict, tribunal **9** barricade, eliminate, honky-tonk, nightclub, roadhouse **11** obstruction, rathskeller **12** circumscribe, watering hole
type: **3** raw **4** cash, fern, open, roll, tiki **6** sports

barb
3 dig **4** dart, hook **5** quill, shaft, thorn **6** zinger

Barbados
capital: **10** Bridgetown
location: **10** West Indies

barbarian
3 Hun **4** Goth, lout, rude, wild **5** beast, crude, brute **6** savage, Vandal **7** lowbrow, uncouth **8** Visigoth **9** foreigner, Ostrogoth, primitive **10** uncultured **11** uncivilized **12** uncultivated

barbaric
4 wild **5** crude, rough **6** brutal, coarse, savage **7** beastly, boorish, brutish, loutish, uncouth **8** churlish **9** atrocious, monstrous, primitive, unrefined **11** uncivilized

barbarism
8 malaprop, rudeness, solecism **9** vulgarism, vulgarity **10** coarseness, corruption **11** impropriety, malapropism **12** backwardness, unseemliness

barbarity
7 cruelty **8** atrocity, savagery **9** brutality, depravity **10** inhumanity, savageness **11** viciousness **12** ruthlessness **13** monstrousness

barbarous
4 base, fell, grim, rude, vile, wild **5** cruel, harsh **6** brutal, fierce, Gothic, savage, unholy, vulgar, wicked **7** brutish, Hunnish, inhuman, lowbrow, uncivil, ungodly, vicious, wolfish **8** backward, fiendish, inhumane, ruthless, sadistic **9** benighted, ferocious, graceless, heartless, merciless, monstrous, primitive, tasteless, truculent **10** abominable, outlandish, outrageous, philistine, unmerciful **11** unchristian, uncivilized **12** uncultivated

Barbary state
5 Tunis **7** Algiers, Morocco, Tripoli

barbecue
5 grill, roast **7** cookout, roaster

barber
3 bob, cut **4** clip, crop, trim **5** shave, shear **6** shaver, tonsor **7** clipper, cropper **8** coiffeur **9** coiffeuse **10** beautician, haircutter **11** hairdresser, hair stylist

Barber of Seville
author: **12** Beaumarchais (Pierre-Augustin de)
character: **6** Figaro, Rosina, Rosine **7** Bartolo, Basilio **8** Almaviva, Bartholo
composer: **7** Rossini (Gioacchino) **9** Paisiello (Giovanni)

bard
4 muse, poet, scop **5** skald **8** jongleur, minstrel **9** balladist **10** Parnassian, troubadour
fictitious: **6** Ossian

Bard of Avon
11 Shakespeare (William)

bare
4 bald, mere, nude, void **5** empty, naked, shorn, stark, strip **6** barren, denude, devoid, expose, peeled, reveal, unclad, unveil, vacant **7** denuded, disrobe, emptied, exposed, uncover **8** bankrupt, disclose, stripped **9** unclothed, uncovered, undressed

barefaced
4 bald, bold, open **5** blunt, naked **6** arrant, brassy, brazen **7** blatant, glaring, obvious **8** flagrant, impudent, overbold **9** audacious, beardless, shameless, unabashed **10** unblushing **11** temerarious, unconcealed

barefoot
6 unshod **8** shoeless **9** discalced

bareheaded
7 hatless

barely
4 just **6** hardly, scarce **7** faintly **8** meagerly, scarcely

bargain
3 buy **4** bond, deal, pact, swap **5** agree, steal, trade, truck, value **6** barter, confer, dicker, haggle, higgle, palter, pledge **7** chaffer, compact, savings, traffic **8** closeout, contract, covenant, exchange, giveaway, good deal, huckster, markdown, transact **9** agreement, good value, negotiate, reduction **10** compromise, convention, loss leader, pennyworth **11** arrangement, transaction **13** understanding

barge
3 hoy **4** scow **5** clump, stump **6** lumber **7** galumph, stumble

baritone
4 Prey (Hermann) **5** Gobbi (Tito) **6** Bailey (Norman), London (George), Milnes (Sherrill), Terfel (Bryn), Warren (Leonard) **7** Hampson (Thomas), MacNeil (Cornell), Merrill (Robert), Tibbett (Lawrence) **8** Raimondi (Ruggero), Warfield (William)

barium symbol
2 Ba

bark
3 arf, bay, yap, yip **4** snap, woof, yelp **5** snarl **6** bellow
mulberry: **4** tapa

barkeeper
see **bartender**

barker
4 tout **5** shill **6** hawker **8** pitchman

Barlow epic
9 Columbiad

barman
see **bartender**

Barmecidal
5 empty, false **6** unreal **7** fictive **8** apparent, illusive, illusory **9** imaginary **10** chimerical, ostensible **13** insubstantial

barn
6 stable
area of: **4** loft **7** hayloft

barnacle
5 leech **7** sponger **8** hanger-on, nuisance, parasite **9** dependent, free rider **10** crustacean, freeloader

barnstorm
8 campaign

Barnum
elephant: **5** Jumbo
midget: **8** Tom Thumb
partner: **6** Bailey

barnyard
4 foul, rude **5** crass, crude, dirty, nasty **6** coarse, earthy, filthy, ribald, smutty, vulgar **7** obscene, raunchy, uncouth **8** indecent **9** tasteless **10** indelicate **12** scatological

baron
4 lord, peer **5** mogul, noble **6** tycoon **7** kingpin, magnate **8** overlord **13** industrialist

baronial
5 ample, grand, noble **6** august, lordly **7** stately **8** imposing, majestic, princely **9** grandiose **10** commanding, impressive **11** magnificent, resplendent

baroque
6 florid, ornate, rococo **7** complex **8** dramatic **9** excessive, grotesque, irregular **10** flamboyant, ornamented **11** embellished, extravagant **12** ostentatious **13** overdecorated

Baroque
architect: **4** Wren (Christopher) **7** Bernini (Gian Lorenzo), Guarini (Guarino), Maderno (Carlo) **9** Borromini (Francesco)
composer: **4** Bach (Johann Sebastian) **5** Lully (Jean-Baptiste) **6** Handel (George Frideric), Rameau (Jean-Philippe), Schütz (Heinrich) **7** Corelli (Arcangelo), Purcell (Henry), Vivaldi (Antonio) **8** Albinoni (Tommaso), Couperin (François), Telemann (Georg Philipp) **9** Pachelbel (Johann), Scarlatti (Alessandro, Domenico) **10** Monteverdi (Claudio)
painter: **4** Hals (Frans) **5** Steen (Jan) **6** Claude (Lorrain), Rubens (Peter Paul) **7** El Greco, Holbein (Hans), Poussin (Nicolas), Van Dyck (Anthony), Vermeer (Jan) **8** Carracci (Agostino, Annibale, Lodovico), Ter Borch (Gerard) **9** Rembrandt (van Rijn), Velázquez (Diego) **10** Caravaggio
sculptor: **5** Puget (Pierre) **7** Bernini (Gian Lorenzo), Coustou (Guillaume, Nicholas), Pigalle (Jean-Baptiste) **8** Coysevox (Antoine), Girardon (François)

barrack
4 jeer, root **5** cheer, scoff, taunt **6** billet, casern, deride, hector **7** caserne **8** quarters

barrage
3 dam **4** fire, hail, mass **5** blitz, burst, salvo, storm, surge **6** deluge, shower, stream, volley **7** gunfire, torrent **8** drumfire, shelling **9** broadside, cannonade, crossfire, fusillade, onslaught **11** bombardment

barranca
4 bank **5** bluff, gully **6** arroyo

barrel
3 keg, tun, vat **4** butt, cask, drum, peck, race, rush, tear **5** hurry **6** firkin, hasten **8** hogshead
maker: **6** cooper
part: **4** hoop **5** stave
stopper: **4** bung
support: **6** gantry

barrelhouse
4 dive **5** hurry, joint **7** hangout **9** honky-tonk

barren
3 dry **4** arid, bare, poor **5** bleak, empty, stark, stony, waste **6** desert, devoid, effete, futile, fallow **7** badland, lacking, parched, sterile, wanting **8** desolate, heirless, impotent **9** childless, fruitless, infertile, unbearing, unfertile, wasteland **10** unfruitful, untillable **11** unrewarding **12** hardscrabble, unproductive, unprofitable

barricade
5 block, fence **7** barrier **8** blockade **9** roadblock
of trees: **6** abatis

Barrie character
4 Hook (Capt.), John, Nana, Smee **5** Peter, Tommy, Wendy **7** Michael **8** Crichton **9** Tiger Lily **10** Tinker Bell **11** Captain Hook

barrier
see **barricade**

barring
3 but **4** save **6** bating, except, saving **7** besides, without **9** aside from, excluding, excepting, outside of **11** exclusive of

barrio
4 slum, turf, ward **6** ghetto **7** quarter, section **8** district, precinct **12** neighborhood

barrister
6 lawyer **7** counsel **8** advocate, attorney **9** counselor

barroom
3 pub **6** lounge, saloon, tavern **7** gin mill, rum room, taproom **8** alehouse, beer hall, dramshop, drinkery, groggery, grogshop **9** beer joint, roadhouse **12** watering hole

bartender
7 tapster **8** boniface **10** mixologist **12** saloonkeeper

barter
4 swap **5** trade, truck **7** bargain, traffic **8** exchange

Bartered Bride composer
7 Smetana (Bedrich)

Barth novel
7 Chimera **12** Giles Goat-Boy **13** Sot-Weed Factor (The)

Baruch
father: **6** Neriah, Zabbai
occupation: **6** scribe

basal
5 basic, vital **6** bottom, lowest **7** minimal, primary, radical **8** simplest **9** beginning, essential, undermost **10** bottommost, elementary, primordial, underlying **11** fundamental, preliminary, rudimentary **12** foundational
layer: **4** sima

base
3 bad, bed, fix, key, low **4** camp, evil, foot, fort, foul, home, mean, poor, post, prop, rest, root, seat, site, ugly, vile **5** build, cheap, dirty, found, hinge, lousy, lowly, nadir, plant, set up, sorry, stand **6** bottom, coarse, common, depend, derive, filthy, ground, humble, menial, origin, paltry, scurvy, shoddy, sleazy, sordid, source, trashy, wicked **7** bedrock, caitiff, essence, footing, ignoble, lowborn, low-down, pitiful, servile, squalid, support **8** beggarly, buttress, cowardly, garrison, inferior, pedestal, plebeian, recreant, unwashed, unworthy, wretched **9** construct, dastardly, degrading, establish, framework, loathsome, low-minded, predicate, principle **10** abominable, despicable, foundation, groundwork, substratum, unennobled **11** disgraceful, humiliating, ignominious **12** contemptible, meanspirited, substructure, underpinning

baseball
abbreviation: **2** AB, AL, BA, BB, BI, CF, DH, DP, ER, FA, HR, IP, LF, LP, NL, RF, SB, SO, SS, WP **3** ERA, LOB, MVP, RBI
reputed founder: **9** Doubleday (Abner)
glove: **4** mitt
official: **3** ump **6** umpire
pitch: **4** drop, heat **5** curve, smoke **6** change, heater, sinker, slider, slurve **7** spitter **8** change-up, fadeaway, fastball, fork ball, knuckler, palm ball, spitball **9** brushback, screwball **11** knuckleball **12** change of pace, knuckle curve
player: **6** batter **7** baseman, catcher, fielder, pitcher **9** infielder, shortstop **10** base runner, outfielder **11** left fielder **12** right fielder **13** center fielder
term: **3** bag, bat, box, fan, fly, out, run, tag, tap, tip **4** balk, ball, base, bean, bunt, cage, deck, foul, hook, line, mitt, no-no, pill, pole, save, walk **5** alley, apple, bench, bloop, clout, count, drive, error, flare, fungo, glove, homer, liner, mound, pop-up, slide, swing **6** assist, clutch, double, dugout, groove, ground, inning, inside, pop fly, pop-out, powder, putout, relief, rubber, runner, single, strike, triple, windup **7** battery, blooper, bullpen, cleanup, diamond, floater, fly ball, home run, infield, manager, outside, pickoff, rhubarb, sidearm, squeeze, stretch **8** baseline, beanball, delivery, foul ball, grounder, keystone, no-hitter, outfield, pinch-hit, rosin bag, southpaw **9** full count, home plate, hot corner, line drive, sacrifice, strikeout, two-bagger **10** double play, frozen rope, ground ball, scratch hit, strike zone **11** knuckleball, pinch hitter, squeeze play, three-bagger
(see also **American League, National League**)

baseballer
3 Ott (Mel) **4** Alou (Felipe, Jesús, Matty, Moises), A-Rod, Bell (George), Cobb (Ty), Cone (David), Dean (Dizzy), Fisk (Carlton), Ford (Whitey), Foxx (Jimmy), Kaat (Jim), Mays (Willie), Rice (Jim), Rose (Pete), Ruth (Babe), Ryan (Nolan), Sosa (Sammy) **5** Aaron (Henry), Anson (Cap), Banks (Ernie), Belle (Albert), Bench (Johnny), Berra (Yogi), Boggs (Wade), Bonds (Barry), Brett (George), Brock (Lou), Brown (Kevin), Carew (Rod), Clark (Will), Damon (Johnny), Davis (Mark), Green (Shawn), Grove (Lefty), Gwynn (Tony), Henke (Tom), Jeter (Derek), Kiner (Ralph), Maris (Roger), Mauer (Joe), Paige (Satchel), Perez (Tony), Perry (Gaylord), Smith (Lee), Spahn (Warren), Staub (Rusty), Tiant (Luis), Viola (Frank), Weeks (Rickie), Young (Cy), Yount (Robin) **6** Dawson (Andre), Feller (Bob), Foster (George), Franco (John), Garvey (Steve), Gehrig (Lou), Gibson (Bob, Josh, Kirk), Gooden (Dwight), Herzog (Whitey), Hunter (Catfish), Koufax (Sandy), Lajoie (Nap), Maddux (Greg), Mantle (Mickey), Morgan (Joe), Murphy (Dale), Murray (Eddie), Musial (Stan), Palmer (Jim), Piazza (Mike), Raines (Tim), Ripken (Cal), Seaver (Tom), Sisler (George), Sutter (Bruce), Sutton (Don), Thomas (Frank), Vaughn (Mo), Wagner (Honus), Walker (Larry) **7** Bagwell (Jeff), Canseco (José), Carlton (Steve), Clemens (Roger), Coleman (Vince), Collins (Eddie), Delgado (Carlos), Fingers (Rollie), Griffey (Ken), Hornsby (Roger), Hubbell (Carl), Jackson (Joe, Reggie), Johnson (Randy, Walter), Justice (David), Leonard (Buck), McGwire (Mark), Mondesi (Raul), Puckett (Kirby), Ramirez (Manny), Reardon (Jeff), Schmidt (Mike), Simmons (Al), Speaker (Tris) **8** Anderson (Sparky), Blyleven (Bert), Clemente (Roberto), DiMaggio (Joe), Guerrero (Vladimir), Martinez (Pedro), Mitchell (Kevin), Righetti (Dave), Robinson (Brooks, Frank, Jackie), Williams (Bernie, Ted), Winfield (Dave) **9** Alexander (Grover), Eckersley (Dennis), Gehringer (Charlie), Greenberg (Hank), Henderson (Rickey), Hernandez (Willie), Hershiser (Orel), Killebrew (Harmon), Mathewson

(Christy), Mattingly (Don), Rodriguez (Alex), Sheffield (Gary) **10** Campanella (Roy), Conigliaro (Tony), Strawberry (Darryl), Valenzuela (Fernando) **11** Garciaparra (Nomar), Yastrzemski (Carl)

baseball team
see **American League; National League**

baseboard
7 molding **8** skirting

baseless
4 idle, thin, vain **5** empty, false, wrong **6** feeble, flimsy **9** frivolous, pointless, senseless, unfounded, untenable **10** fallacious, gratuitous, groundless, inadequate, incredible, ungrounded **11** uncalled-for, unconfirmed, unnecessary, unsupported, unsustained, unwarranted **12** indefensible, contemptible, unpersuasive **13** unjustifiable

basement
6 bottom, cellar, ground **7** bedrock **10** foundation, groundwork, substratum **12** substructure

base on balls
4 walk

bash
3 bat, hit **4** belt, blow, fete, gala, slam, whop **5** blast, crack, crash, party, pound, smack, smash, thump, whack **6** attack, pummel, soiree, strike, wallop **7** blowout, shindig **8** wingding

Bashemath
father: **7** Ishmael
husband: **4** Esau
sister: **8** Nebaioth

bashful
3 coy, shy **5** chary, mousy, timid **6** demure, modest **7** abashed, nervous **8** blushing, reserved, retiring, timorous **9** diffident, reluctant, shrinking, unassured **11** unassertive

basic
3 key **4** main **5** chief **6** bottom, innate, simple **7** capital, central, element, minimum, primary, radical **8** cardinal, inherent, rudiment **9** beginning, elemental, essential, intrinsic, primitive, principal, unadorned **10** elementary, underlying **11** fundamental **12** foundational

basically
6 au fond, mainly, mostly **7** at heart, chiefly, firstly, overall **8** in effect **9** generally, in essence, primarily

basic point
4 crux, gist, pith **5** heart **6** kernel **7** essence

basilica
6 church **7** minster **9** cathedral

basics
4 ABCs

basin
3 dip, pan, sag **4** bowl, sink **6** cirque, hollow **7** sinkage **8** sinkhole, washbowl **9** concavity **10** depression
liturgical: **5** stoup **7** piscina

basis
3 bed **4** crux, root, seat, seed **5** heart, nexus **6** bottom, ground, reason **7** bedrock, essence, footing, grounds, nucleus, premise, support, warrant **9** authority, postulate, principle **10** assumption, foundation, groundwork, substratum **11** fundamental, presumption **12** substructure, underpinning **13** justification

bask
3 sun **4** loll **5** glory, revel, relax **6** lounge, wallow, welter **7** indulge **8** sunbathe **9** luxuriate

basket
6 bushel, gabion **7** pannier
angler's: **5** creel
material: **5** osier **6** raffia

basketball
inventor: **8** Naismith (James)
official: **6** umpire **7** referee
player: **5** cager, guard **6** center **7** forward **8** hoopster, swingman **10** point guard
team: **4** five **7** quintet
term: **3** gun, jam, key **4** cage, dunk, pass **5** board, hoops, lay-up, press, shoot, tip-in **6** freeze, screen, tap-off, tip-off, travel **7** dribble, keyhole, rebound, throw-in, time-out **8** alley-oop, jump ball, slam dunk **9** backboard, backcourt, field goal, free throw **11** ball control
(see also **National Basketball Association**)

basketballer
3 Bol (Manute) **4** Bird (Larry), Ming (Yao), Nash (Steve), Redd (Michael), Reed (Willis), West (Jerry, Mark) **5** Allen (Ray), Barry (Rick), Brand (Elton), Cousy (Bob), Davis (Baron), Ewing (Patrick), Mikan (George), O'Neal (Shaq, Shaquille), Price (Mark) **6** Baylor (Elgin), Blount (Mark), Boozer (Carlos), Bryant (Kobe), Carter (Vince), Cowens (Dave), Duncan (Tim), Erving (Julius), Gervin (George), Jordan (Michael), Malone (Jeff, Karl, Moses), McAdoo (Bob), McHale (Kevin), Miller (Brad, Reggie), Parish (Robert), Pierce (Paul, Ricky), Pippin (Scottie), Rodman (Dennis), Skiles (Scott), Thomas (Kenny), Thorpe (Otis), Walton (Bill), Worthy (James) **7** Barkley (Charles), Billups (Chauncey), Dampier (Erick), Dawkins (Darryl), Edwards (James), Frazier (Walt), Garnett (Kevin), Hilario (Nene), Houston (Allan), Iverson (Allen), Jackson (Lauren), Jamison (Antawn), Johnson (Magic), McGrady (Tracy), Russell (Bill), Rollins (Tree), Taurasi (Diana), Wallace (Ben), Wilkins (Dominique) **8** Auerbach (Red), Cardinal (Brian), Havlicek (John), Magloire (Jamaal), Nowitzki (Dirk),

Olajuwon (Akeem), Randolph (Zach), Robinson (David), Stockton (John), Thompson (Tina), Williams (Buck) **9** Donaldson (James), Ferdinand (Marie), Holdsclaw (Chamique), Robertson (Oscar) **10** Stojakovic (Predrag), Williamson (Corliss) **11** Abdul-Jabbar (Kareem), Chamberlain (Wilt)

Basmath's father
7 Solomon

Basque
6 bodice
cap: 5 beret
game: 6 pelota **7** jai alai
mountains: 8 Pyrenees
province: 5 Alava **7** Vizcaya **9** Guipúzcoa

bass
3 low **4** deep **6** singer **8** cabrilla
famous: 5 Hines (Jerome), Pinza (Ezio), Ramey (Samuel), Siepi (Cesare), Tozzi (Giorgio) **6** Hotter (Hans), London (George), Morris (James) **7** Plishka (Paul), Robeson (Paul), Talvela (Martti) **8** Flagello (Ezio), Ghiaurov (Nicolai), Raimondi (Ruggero) **9** Chaliapin (Fyodor), Christoff (Boris)

Bassanio's beloved
6 Portia

bassinet
6 cradle, basket

bastard
5 cross **6** by-blow, hybrid **7** mongrel **9** love child **12** natural child
combining form: 4 noth **5** notho

bastardize
4 warp **5** taint **6** debase, defile **7** corrupt, debauch, degrade, deprave, pervert, pollute, vitiate **9** brutalize **10** adulterate, bestialize, demoralize, depreciate **11** contaminate

baste
3 sew **4** beat, drub, lash, mill, pelt, rail, tack, whip **5** paste, scold **6** batter, berate, larrup, pummel, revile, stitch, thrash, wallop **7** bawl out, belabor, chew out, clobber, moisten, tell off, trounce, upbraid **8** bless out, chastise **9** dress down **10** tongue-lash

bastille
4 jail **6** prison **9** bridewell

bastinado
3 bat, rod **4** bash, beat, blow, cane, club **5** birch, crack, pound, smack, smash, stick, whack **6** cudgel, paddle, strike, switch, thwack, wallop **8** bludgeon **9** truncheon

bastion
5 tower **7** bulwark, citadel, parapet, rampart, redoubt **8** fastness, fortress **10** breastwork, stronghold **13** fortification

bat
3 bag, bop, hag **4** belt, biff, blow, bust, club, slam, sock, swat, whop, wink **5** biddy, blink, crone, smack **6** cudgel, thwack **7** meander **8** bludgeon **9** flying fox, truncheon **10** knobkerrie, shillelagh **11** pipistrelle

batch
3 lot, set **5** array, bunch, clump, crowd, group **6** bundle, clutch, parcel **7** cluster **8** quantity, shipment **10** assemblage, assortment, collection **11** aggregation **12** accumulation

bate
3 bar **4** omit **5** check **6** deduct, except, reduce **7** cut back, exclude, suspend **8** diminish, moderate, restrain, subtract

bateau
4 boat, dory **5** craft, skiff **6** dinghy, launch **7** shallop

bath
3 spa, tub **4** soak, wash **5** hydro, wells **6** shower **7** springs **8** ablution **13** watering place

bathe
3 dip, lap, lip, sop, tub, wet **4** bask, lave, soak, soap, swim, wash **5** clean, douse, flood, rinse, flush, souse, steep **6** shower **7** cleanse, immerse, pervade, suffuse **8** irrigate

bathetic
5 mushy, soppy, stale, tired, trite **6** drippy **7** clichéd, cloying, gushing, maudlin, mawkish **9** emotional, hackneyed, schmaltzy **10** lachrymose **11** commonplace, sentimental, stereotyped, tear-jerking **13** anticlimactic, overemotional, stereotypical

bathhouse
5 sauna **6** cabana

bathing suit
6 bikini, trunks **7** bandeau, maillot

bathos
7 letdown **8** banality, comedown **9** triteness **10** anticlimax

bathroom
3 lav, loo **4** john **5** privy **6** toilet **8** lavatory, outhouse

Bathsheba
father: 5 Eliam
husband: 5 David, Uriah
son: 7 Solomon

bathtub gin
5 hooch **6** rotgut **7** bootleg **8** homebrew **9** moonshine **11** mountain dew

Batman
alias: 13 Matches Malone
bat-signal: 11 searchlight
butler: 6 Alfred
creator: 4 Kane (Bob)
film director: 5 Nolan (Christopher) **6** Burton (Tim)

film star: **4** Bale (Christian), West (Adam) **6** Carrey (Jim), DeVito (Danny), Keaton (Michael), Kilmer (Val) **7** Clooney (George), Thurman (Uma) **8** Meredith (Burgess), Pfeiffer (Michelle) **9** Nicholson (Jack)
secret identity: **10** Bruce Wayne
setting: **6** Gotham
sidekick: **5** Robin
TV star: **4** Ward (Burt), West (Adam) **8** McDowall (Roddy)
villain: **5** Chill (Joe), Joker **7** Penguin, Riddler, Two-Face **8** Catwoman, Clayface, Deadshot, Mr. Freeze **9** Mad Hatter, Poison Ivy, Scarecrow

baton
3 rod **4** club, mace, wand **5** billy, staff, stick **6** cudgel **7** war club **8** bludgeon **9** billy club, truncheon **10** nightstick

____ Bator
4 Ulan

batrachian
4 frog, toad **9** amphibian

battalion
4 army, host, unit **5** force, horde **6** legion, throng, troops **8** squadron **10** contingent, detachment

batter
4 bash, beat, drub, hurt, maul, mush **5** baste, break, dough, paste, pound, wreck **6** bruise, buffet, bung up, hitter, mangle, pommel, pummel, thrash, wallop **7** assault, belabor, bombard, clobber, coating, contuse, cripple, lambast **8** demolish, lambaste

battery
3 lot, set **4** body, guns **5** abuse, array, batch, bunch, clump, group, suite **6** bundle, cannon, series **7** assault, beating, cluster **8** thumping **9** artillery, onslaught **10** energy cell **11** gunnery unit
terminal: **5** anode **7** cathode

battle
4 fray **5** brush, clash, fight **6** action, assail, attack, combat, sortie **7** assault, contend, contest **8** conflict, skirmish, struggle **9** encounter, onslaught, scrimmage **10** engagement **11** hostilities

battle-ax
5 harpy, scold, shrew **6** virago **8** harridan **9** termagant, Xanthippe

Battle Born State
6 Nevada

battle cry
6 banzai

battlement
4 wall **7** barrier, bastion, bulwark, parapet, rampart **10** protection

battling
5 at war

batty
3 mad **4** daft, nuts, zany **5** barmy, crazy, kooky, loony, nutty, potty, wacky **6** crazed, cuckoo, insane, maniac, screwy, whacko **7** bananas, bonkers, cracked, idiotic, lunatic **8** deranged **9** bedlamite

bauble
3 toy **5** curio **6** gewgaw, trifle **7** bibelot, novelty, trinket, whatnot **8** gimcrack, ornament **9** objet d'art, plaything **10** knickknack

Baucis's husband
8 Philemon

Bavaria
6 Bayern
capital: **6** Munich
city: **8** Augsburg, Bayreuth, Würzburg **9** Nuremberg
king: **6** Ludwig
patron saint: **6** Rupert

bawd
4 drab, moll, tart **5** madam, tramp, whore **6** floozy, harlot, hooker **7** trollop **8** strumpet **10** prostitute **11** nightwalker **12** streetwalker

bawdy
4 blue, lewd **5** crude, dirty **6** coarse, erotic, ribald, risqué, smutty, vulgar **7** obscene **8** indecent, prurient **9** lecherous, offensive, salacious **10** lascivious, libidinous, licentious, suggestive

bawdy house
4 crib, stew **6** bagnio **7** brothel, lupanar **8** bordello

bawl
3 cry, sob **4** howl, roar, rout, wail, weep, yell, yowl **5** shout **6** bellow, berate, boohoo, clamor, holler, outcry, scream, shriek, squall **7** blubber, bluster

bawl out
3 wig **4** lash **5** baste, scold **6** berate, rebuke **7** censure, chew out, condemn, tell off, upbraid **8** bless out, denounce, tear into **9** castigate, dress down, reprimand **10** tongue-lash

bay
3 arm **4** cove, gulf, howl, loch, nook, wail **5** award, bight, crown, firth, honor, inlet, niche **6** harbor, laurel, recess **7** garland, laurels **8** accolade **10** decoration
Aegean Sea: **5** Anzac
Africa: **6** Walvis
Alaska: **7** Glacier
Antarctica: **3** Ice **8** Amundsen
Argentina: **6** Blanca
Atlantic Ocean: **6** Baffin
Australia: **5** Anson, Shark **6** Botany, Sharks **7** Repulse **9** Discovery

Baltic: **4** Hano, Kiel **6** Danzig, Kieler **9** Pomerania **10** Pomeranian, Pommersche
Beaufort Sea: **7** Prudhoe **9** Mackenzie
Brazil: **9** Guanabara
Bristol Channel: **10** Carmarthen
California: **5** Morro **8** Monterey, San Diego
Canada: **5** Fundy **6** Hudson **7** Repulse
Capetown: **5** Table
Caribbean Sea: **5** Limón **8** Chetumal
Central America: **7** Fonseca
Cuba: **10** Guantánamo
East River: **8** Flushing
Egypt: **6** Abu Qir
Eire: **4** Clew **7** Brandon
English Channel: **3** Tor **4** Lyme
Europe: **6** Biscay
Florida: **8** Biscayne
Greenland: **6** Baffin **8** Melville
Gulf of Alaska: **12** Resurrection
Gulf of California: **5** Adair
Gulf of Guinea: **5** Benin **6** Biafra
Gulf of Mexico: **5** Tampa **6** Mobile **7** Aransas **8** Campeche, Sarasota **9** Matagorda, Pensacola **10** San Antonio, Terrebonne **11** Atchafalaya, Ponce de Leon **12** Apalachicola **13** Corpus Christi
Gulf of St. Lawrence: **5** Bonne, Gaspé
Hawaii: **5** Koloa, Lawai
Hong Kong: **4** Deep
Honshu: **3** Ise **5** Mutsu, Osaka, Owari, Tokyo **6** Atsuta, Sagami
Indian Ocean: **6** Bengal
Indonesia: **8** Humboldt
Irish Sea: **4** Luce **7** Dundalk
Jamaica: **4** Long
Japan: **4** Tosa
Java Sea: **7** Batavia **8** Djakarta
Lake Erie: **8** Sandusky
Lake Huron: **7** Saginaw, Thunder
Lake Michigan: **5** Green **13** Grand Traverse
Lake Ontario: **11** Irondequoit
Lake Superior: **5** Huron **8** Keweenaw **9** Whitefish
Long Island Sound: **6** Oyster
Maine: **5** Casco **7** Machias **9** Penobscot
Maryland-Virginia: **10** Chesapeake **12** Chincoteague
Massachusetts: **6** Boston **7** Cape Cod **8** Buzzards, Plymouth
New Brunswick: **13** Passamaquoddy
Newfoundland: **4** Hare **5** White **7** Fortune
New Jersey: **5** Great **6** Newark **7** Raritan **8** Barnegat
New York: **7** Jamaica
North Carolina: **6** Onslow
Northwest Territories: **5** Wager **7** Repulse **8** Franklin **9** Frobisher
Oregon: **4** Coos
Puerto Rico: **5** Sucia
Quebec: **6** Ungava
Rhode Island: **12** Narragansett
Sea of Japan: **13** Peter the Great
South Carolina: **4** Bull, Long
South China Sea: **5** Subic, Subig **7** Camranh
Spain: **5** Cadiz
Strait of Gibraltar: **7** Tangier
Sydney: **6** Botany
Tasmania: **5** Storm
Texas: **7** Trinity
Tyrrhenian Sea: **6** Naples **7** Paestum
Wales: **10** Caernarfon, Caernarvon
Washington: **5** Dabob **6** Skagit
West Indies: **5** Coral

bayou
5 creek, marsh **6** slough **9** everglade, tributary
Louisiana: **5** Macon **9** Barataria, Lafourche **10** Terrebonne
Mississippi: **9** Chickasaw

Bay State
13 Massachusetts

bay window
3 gut, pot **5** oriel, tummy **6** paunch **8** potbelly **9** beer belly, spare tire **11** corporation, breadbasket

bazaar
4 fair, mall, mart, souk **6** market **7** benefit **8** emporium, exchange **11** marketplace

bazooka's target
4 tank

be
4 live **5** exist

beach
4 bank **5** Cocoa, coast, Omaha, shore **6** Malibu, Pebble, strand, Venice **7** seaside, shingle, Waikiki **8** cast away, lakeside, littoral, seashore **9** lakeshore **10** Clearwater, Copacabana, oceanfront, run aground
resort: **4** lido

____ Beach
3 Amy **4** Long, Palm, Vero **5** Dover, Miami, Omaha **6** Delray, Myrtle, Ormond **7** Daytona, Riviera, Waikiki **8** Imperial, Virginia

beached
6 ashore **7** aground **8** grounded, marooned, stranded **9** abandoned

beachhead
8 foothold

beachwear
see **bathing suit**

beacon
4 buoy, sign **5** flare, guide **6** pharos, signal

7 bonfire, lantern 8 balefire 9 watchfire 10 lighthouse, signal fire 11 inspiration, transmitter 12 guiding light

bead
3 dab, dot, pea 4 blob, drop 6 bubble 7 driblet, globule 8 spherule

beak
3 neb, nib 4 bill, nose 5 snoot, snout, spout 6 pecker, schnoz 7 schnozz 8 mandible 9 proboscis, schnozzle

beaker
3 cup 6 carafe, goblet, vessel 8 decanter

beaklike part
7 rostrum

be-all and end-all
3 sum 4 pith, root, soul 5 total, whole 6 bottom 7 essence 8 entirety, sum total, totality 9 aggregate, substance 10 prime cause 12 quintessence

beam
3 bar, ray 4 balk, boom, burn, glow, grin, I-bar, spar 5 flare, flash, gleam, joist, plank, shaft, shine, shoot, smile, strut 6 girder, lintel, rafter, signal, streak, stream, timber 7 radiate 8 transmit 9 broadcast

beaming
6 bright, joyful, lucent 7 fulgent, lambent, radiant 8 animated, cheerful, luminous 9 brilliant, effulgent, refulgent 12 incandescent

bean
3 soy, wax 4 bush, conk, dome, fava, head, lima, mung, navy, pate, pole, poll, snap, soya 5 baked, brain, broad, horse, jelly, pinto 6 belfry, coffee, frijol, kidney, legume, noddle, noggin, noodle, string 7 jumping 9 headpiece 10 stringless
curd: 4 tofu
of India: 3 urd

beanery
4 café 5 diner, grill 9 hash house 10 coffee shop, restaurant 11 greasy spoon 12 luncheonette

beano
5 bingo

Bean Town
6 Boston

bear
3 lug 4 tote 5 abide, allow, beget, bring, brook, bruin, carry, stand, touch 6 accept, behave, convey, deport, endure, permit, suffer 7 comport, condone, conduct, deliver, stomach, support, sustain, swallow, undergo 8 engender, generate, shoulder, tolerate 9 procreate, propagate, reproduce, transport 10 bring forth 11 countenance
Alaskan: 5 polar 6 Kodiak
Australian: 5 koala
constellation: 4 Ursa 9 Ursa Major, Ursa Minor
genus: 5 Ursus
kind: 3 sun 5 black, brown, honey, koala, polar, sloth 6 Kodiak 7 grizzly 10 spectacled
Kipling: 5 Baloo 7 Adam-zad
relating to: 6 ursine
young: 3 cub

bearable
7 livable, tenable 8 adequate, passable 9 allowable, endurable, tolerable 10 acceptable, admissible, good enough, manageable, sufferable 11 supportable, sustainable

bearcat
5 panda

beard
4 dare, defy, face, fuzz 5 brave, front 6 goatee 7 outface, stubble, Vandyke 8 confront, imperial, whiskers 9 challenge, soul patch
on grain: 3 awn

bearded
5 bushy, fuzzy, hairy 6 shaggy, tufted 7 bristly, goateed, hirsute, stubbly 8 unshaven 9 whiskered 11 bewhiskered

bear down
4 rout 5 crush, quell 6 burden, defeat, reduce, subdue 7 conquer, overrun, trample 8 overcome, vanquish 9 emphasize, overpower, overwhelm, subjugate

bearer
4 mule 5 envoy 6 coolie, porter, runner 7 carrier, courier 8 conveyor, emissary 9 go-between, messenger 11 internuncio

bear hug
6 clinch

bearing
3 air, set 4 look, mien, pose 5 poise 6 aspect, manner, stance 7 address, conduct, display, posture 8 attitude, behavior, carriage, delivery, demeanor, presence, relation 9 demeanour, direction 10 connection, deportment 11 comportment

bearish
4 curt 5 gruff, rough, terse, surly 6 cranky, ornery 7 anxious, dubious, prickly, uncouth 8 cautious, vinegary 9 crotchety, irascible 10 ill-humored 11 pessimistic 12 cantankerous

bearlike
6 ursine

bear out
4 show 5 prove 6 attest, uphold, verify 7 certify, confirm, justify 8 validate, vouch for 9 vindicate 11 corroborate, demonstrate 12 authenticate, substantiate

bear up
4 cope, fare, prop **5** brace, get by **6** endure, uphold **7** bolster, support, sustain **8** buttress, get along, maintain, underpin

beast
5 brute **6** animal **7** critter, monster, varmint **8** behemoth, creature, gargoyle

beastly
4 foul, mean, vile **5** awful, brute, feral, nasty **6** animal, brutal, odious **7** bestial, brutish, inhuman, ogreish, swinish **8** horrible, terrible **9** barbarous, revolting **10** abominable, detestable

beat
3 box, get, gyp, hit, lam, rap, tan, top **4** balk, belt, best, cane, dash, drub, drum, dump, flap, flog, foil, lash, lick, maul, pelt, rout, ruin, stir, tick, trim, whip, whop **5** baste, cheat, cozen, excel, forge, lay on, meter, outdo, paste, pound, pulse, punch, rhyme, route, scoop, scour, smear, spent, stick, stump, swing, throb, tread, tromp, whack, whisk **6** baffle, batter, better, buffet, cudgel, defeat, diddle, exceed, forage, hammer, larrup, muss up, patrol, pummel, rhythm, rounds, strike, thrash, thresh, thwart, wallop **7** belabor, clobber, circuit, conquer, exhaust, fashion, fatigue, lambast, lay down, prevail, pulsate, ransack, rough up, shellac, surpass, swindle, triumph, trounce **8** bewilder, bludgeon, Bohemian, lambaste, outshine, outsmart, outstrip, overcome, precinct **9** exhausted, frustrate, palpitate, pulsation, shattered, transcend, vibration **10** circumvent, pistolwhip **11** oscillation

beating
4 rout **5** lumps **6** defeat, hiding, mayhem **7** assault, setback **9** hammering, pulsation, throbbing **11** palpitation, shellacking

beatitude
3 joy **5** bliss **7** delight, ecstasy, rapture **8** euphoria, gladness, rhapsody **9** happiness, transport **10** exaltation, joyfulness **11** blessedness **12** blissfulness

Beatles
4 John (Lennon), Paul (McCartney) **5** Ringo (Starr) **6** George (Harrison) **7** Fab Four
album: **8** Revolver **9** Abbey Road, Sgt. Pepper **10** Rubber Soul
early: **4** Best (Pete) **9** Quarrymen (The), Sutcliffe (Stuart)
manager: **5** Klein (Allen) **7** Epstein (Brian)
producer: **6** Martin (George)
wife: **5** Linda **7** Yoko Ono

beatnik
5 rebel **6** hippie **7** radical **8** Bohemian **9** dissident **11** flower child **13** nonconformist

beat-up
6 shabby **7** rickety, worn-out **8** decrepit, tattered **9** crumbling **10** broken-down, ramshackle, tumble-down **11** dilapidated

beau
5 dandy, flame, lover, swain, wooer **6** steady, suitor **7** admirer, beloved **8** paramour, truelove, young man **9** boyfriend **10** sweetheart

Beau Brummell
3 fop **5** dandy, swell **7** coxcomb, gallant **8** macaroni **11** petit-maître **12** lounge lizard

beau ideal
5 guide, model **6** mirror **7** epitome, example, paragon, pattern **8** exemplar, paradigm, standard **9** archetype **12** quintessence

Beaumarchais hero
6 Figaro

beau monde
5 elite **6** gentry, jet set **7** society **8** smart set **10** glitterati, upper crust

beauteous
see **beautiful**

beautiful
4 fair **5** bonny **6** comely, lovely, pretty **7** radiant **8** glorious, gorgeous, handsome, splendid, stunning **9** exquisite **10** attractive **11** good-looking, resplendent, well-favored

beautiful people
6 jet set **8** smart set **9** haut monde **10** glitterati **11** high society

beautify
4 deck, gild, trim **5** adorn, array, fix up, grace, prank, primp **6** bedeck, doll up **7** dress up, festoon, garland, garnish, gussy up, enhance, improve **8** decorate, ornament, prettify, spruce up **9** embellish, glamorize

beauty
5 asset, belle, dream, merit, peach **6** appeal, eyeful, looker, lovely **7** charmer, dazzler, stunner **8** knockout **9** eye-opener, good looks **10** good-looker, loveliness
mark: **4** mole

beaver
6 castor, rodent
home: **5** lodge
project: **3** dam
skin: **4** plew
young: **3** kit, pup

Beaver State
6 Oregon

becalm
4 hush, lull, stop **5** allay, quiet, stall, still **6** arrest, pacify, sedate, settle, soothe, steady, subdue **7** assuage, compose, quieten **11** tranquilize

because
3 for, now **4** that **5** since **7** being as, whereas

8 being how, as long as, seeing as **10** inasmuch as

because of
4 over **5** due to **7** owing to, through **8** thanks to **10** by reason of **11** on account of

Beckett work
4 Not I, Play, Watt **6** Molloy, Murphy **7** Endgame **9** Happy Days, Unnamable (The) **10** Eleutheria, Malone Dies **14** Krapp's Last Tape **15** Waiting for Godot

beckon
3 bid, nod **4** lure, wave **6** allure, entice, invite, motion, signal, summon **7** attract

becloud
3 dim, fog **4** blur, hide, veil **5** addle, bedim, befog, cloak, muddy **6** impair, darken, muddle, puzzle, shroud **7** confuse, eclipse, obscure, perplex **8** befuddle **9** obfuscate **10** overshadow

become
3 fit, get, wax **4** grow, suit **5** befit **6** go with **7** enhance, flatter **8** turn into

becoming
3 apt **5** right **6** decent, proper, seemly **7** correct, fitting **8** decorous, suitable, tasteful **9** befitting **10** attractive, flattering, well-chosen **11** appropriate, comme il faut

bed
3 cot **4** base, bunk, crib, doss, sack, twin **5** basis, berth, layer **6** bottom, cradle, double, ground, Murphy, pallet **7** bedrock, stratum, trundle **8** rollaway **10** foundation, substratum
of India: **7** charpoy

bedaub
4 coat **5** cover, smear **6** smudge **7** overlay, plaster

bedazzle
4 daze **5** blind

bedcover
5 duvet, quilt **6** afghan, spread **7** blanket **8** coverlet **9** comforter **11** counterpane

bedeck
4 trim **5** adorn, array, prank **6** attire, bedaub, jazz up **7** appoint, bedizen, dress up, festoon, furbish, garland, garnish, gussy up **8** accouter, accoutre, beautify, decorate, ornament, prettify **9** embellish

bedevil
5 annoy, harry, spoil, tease, worry **6** harass, needle, nettle, pester, plague **7** hagride, provoke, torment, trouble **8** bewilder **10** exasperate

bedevilment
6 bother **7** torment, trouble **8** disorder, vexation **9** annoyance, confusion **10** irritation **11** aggravation **12** bewilderment

bedfellow
4 ally **5** crony **7** comrade **9** associate, colleague **10** compatriot **11** confederate **12** collaborator

bedim
3 fog **4** blur, mask, veil **5** befog, blear, cloud, gloom, shade **6** darken, muddle, shadow, shroud **7** becloud, confuse, eclipse, obscure **9** obfuscate

bedizen
4 deck, garb, gild **5** adorn, array, endue **6** doll up, dude up, invest, outfit, rig out **7** costume, dandify, dress up, garnish, gussy up, turn out **8** beautify, ornament **9** caparison, embellish

bedlam
3 ado **5** chaos, furor **6** asylum, clamor, furore, hubbub, tumult, uproar, welter **7** turmoil **8** foofaraw, madhouse, upheaval **9** commotion, maelstrom **10** hurly-burly **11** pandemonium

bedlamite
3 mad, nut **4** loon, nuts **5** batty, crazy, loony **6** insane, madman, maniac **7** cracked, lunatic **8** demented, deranged

bedouin
4 Arab **5** nomad

bedraggled
5 faded, seedy **6** shabby, ragtag, untidy **7** muddied, rundown, unkempt **8** decrepit, dripping, slovenly, tattered **10** disheveled, disarrayed, disordered, down-at-heel, ramshackle, threadbare **11** dilapidated

bedridden
6 laid up, shut-in **8** confined **12** hospitalized

bedrock
4 base, core, foot, root **5** axiom, basic, basis, floor, nadir **6** bottom, depths, ground **7** footing, support **10** foundation, groundwork, substratum **11** fundamental **12** substructure, underpinning

bedroom
7 boudoir, chamber

bedspread
8 coverlet **11** counterpane

bed-wetting
8 enuresis

bee
food: **6** nectar
genus: **4** Apis
glue: **8** propolis
group: **5** swarm **6** colony
house: **4** hive **6** apiary
kind: **5** drone, mason, queen **6** mining, sewing, worker **8** quilting, spelling **9** carpenter
nest: **4** hive, skep
product: **3** wax **5** honey
relating to: **8** apiarian
wax cells: **9** honeycomb

beechnuts
4 mast

beef
4 crab, fuss, meat, veal 5 bitch, brawn, gripe 6 grouse, muscle 7 grumble 9 bellyache, complaint, grievance
cut: 3 rib 4 loin, rump, side 5 chuck, flank, plate, round, shank 7 brisket, sirloin 10 tenderloin 11 porterhouse
grade: 5 prime 6 choice 7 utility 8 standard 10 commercial
order: 4 rare 6 medium 8 well-done

beefcake
4 hunk, stud 5 himbo

beefeater
5 guard 6 sentry, warder, yeoman

beefy
5 bulky, burly, hefty, husky, meaty 6 brawny, fleshy, robust, stocky, sturdy 7 massive 8 muscular, thickset 9 strapping 11 substantial

Beehive State
4 Utah

beekeeper
8 apiarist 12 apiculturist

beekeeping
10 apiculture

beeline
3 fly, nip, zip 4 race, whiz 5 hurry, speed 6 bullet, hasten, hustle, rocket 7 hotfoot 8 expedite, highball 10 make tracks 12 shortest path

Beelzebub
5 devil, fiend, Satan 6 diablo 7 Evil One, Lucifer, Old Nick, serpent 8 Apollyon 9 adversary, archfiend

beer
3 ale, IPA 4 bock, brew, suds 5 draft, lager, stout, weiss 6 porter 7 brewski, cerveza, pilsner 8 pilsener
vessel: 3 mug 4 toby 5 stein 6 flagon, seidel 7 tankard 8 schooner 9 blackjack
drinking place: 3 bar, inn, pub 6 saloon, tavern 7 taproom 8 alehouse 11 public house, rathskeller
ingredient: 4 hops, malt 5 yeast 6 barley
maker: 6 brewer
mythical inventor: 9 Gambrinus
plant: 7 brewery
Russian: 5 kvass
Scottish: 10 barley-bree

Beeri
daughter: 6 Judith
son: 5 Hosea

beet
5 chard 6 mangel, wurzel 10 Swiss chard
family: 9 goosefoot

Beethoven, Ludwig van
birthplace: 4 Bonn
opera: 7 Fidelio
overture: 6 Egmont 7 Leonore 10 Coriolanus
sonata: 7 Tempest 8 Kreutzer 9 Moonlight, Waldstein 10 Pathétique 12 Appassionata
symphony: 6 Choral, Eroica 8 Pastoral

beetle
3 bug, jut 5 bulge 6 insect, scarab, scurry 7 project 8 overhang, protrude, stand out, stick out
click: 6 elater 7 firefly
dung: 6 scarab 9 tumblebug
front wing: 6 elytra (plural) 7 elytron
fruit-eating: 8 curculio
insect-eating: 7 ladybug 8 ladybird
kind: 4 bean, dung, fire, June, stag 5 click, flour, grain, tiger, water 6 carpet, chafer, ground, May bug, museum 7 blister, cadelle, carabid, firefly, goldbug, goliath, June bug, vedalia 8 ambrosia, Japanese 9 longicorn, potato bug 10 cockchafer, rhinoceros
order: 10 Coleoptera
ornament: 6 scarab
snouted: 6 weevil 7 billbug 8 curculio 9 wood borer
young: 4 grub 5 larva 6 larvae (plural) 8 wireworm

beet soup
6 borsch 7 borscht

befall
3 hap 5 ensue, occur 6 betide, chance, follow, happen 7 come off, develop, fall out 8 happen to 9 come about, eventuate, transpire

befit
4 meet, suit 6 become, go with 9 agree with, chime with 10 accord with, be right for 11 be proper for

befitting
3 apt 4 just, meet 5 happy, right 6 decent, proper, seemly 7 correct 8 becoming, decorous, suitable 10 conforming, felicitous 11 appropriate, comme il faut

befog
3 dim 4 blur, hide, veil 5 bedim, blear, cloak, cloud, muddy 6 darken, puzzle 7 becloud, confuse, eclipse, envelop, obscure, perplex 8 bewilder, confound 9 obfuscate, overcloud 10 overshadow

befool
4 dupe, gull, hoax, play 5 cozen, trick 6 delude 7 chicane, deceive, mislead 8 hoodwink 9 bamboozle, victimize 11 hornswoggle

before
3 ere 4 ante, once, till, up to 5 ahead, until 6 facing, sooner, up till 7 ahead of, already,

earlier, prior to **8** formerly **9** in advance, in front of, preceding **10** previously **11** in advance of
prefix: **3** pre, pro **4** ante, fore

befoul
3 mar, tar **4** slur, soil **5** dirty, smear, spoil, sully, taint **6** defame, defile, malign, smudge **7** blacken, pollute, profane, spatter, tarnish, traduce **8** besmirch **9** bespatter, denigrate **10** adulterate **11** contaminate

befuddle
4 daze **5** addle, mix up **6** ball up, baffle, bemuse, muddle **7** confuse, fluster, perplex, stupefy **8** bewilder, confound, distract, throw off **9** disorient

befuddlement
3 fog **4** daze, haze, maze **5** mix-up **6** muddle, stupor **9** confusion **10** perplexity, puzzlement **11** distraction

beg
3 ask, bum, dun, nag, sue **4** pray, urge **5** apply, brace, cadge, crave, evade, hit on, mooch, plead, press, worry **6** adjure, appeal, call on, demand, invoke, pester **7** beseech, besiege, conjure, entreat, implore, request, solicit **8** petition, sidestep **9** importune, panhandle **10** supplicate

beget
4 bear, sire **5** breed, bring, cause, forge, hatch, spawn, yield **6** create, effect, father **7** produce **8** engender, generate, multiply, result in **9** procreate, propagate, reproduce **10** bring about

beggar
4 hobo, defy, ruin **5** tramp **6** bummer, cadger, fellow, pauper, prayer, sponge, suitor **7** moocher, sponger **8** bankrupt, deadbeat, vagabond **9** overwhelm, pauperize, schnorrer, suppliant **10** down-and-out, freeloader, impoverish, panhandler, petitioner, supplicant **11** bindle stiff, supplicator **12** street person

beggared
4 flat, poor **5** broke, needy **6** ruined **7** drained **8** bankrupt, dirt poor, indigent, strapped, wiped out **9** destitute, insolvent, penniless, penurious, tapped out **10** pauperized **11** impecunious, overwhelmed **12** dispossessed, impoverished

beggarly
3 low **4** base, mean, poor **5** cheap, lowly, nasty, petty, sorry **6** cheesy, meager, measly, paltry, scanty, scurvy, shabby, shoddy, trashy **7** ignoble, miserly, pitiful, squalid **8** pitiable, inferior, wretched **9** miserable, niggardly **10** despicable, despisable **11** ignominious **12** contemptible, parsimonious

Beggar's Opera
music: **7** Pepusch (John)
painting: **7** Hogarth (William)
text: **3** Gay (John)

beggarweed
6 dodder **9** knotgrass **11** tick trefoil

beggary
4 need, want **6** penury **7** bumming, cadging, poverty **8** mooching, pleading **9** indigence, neediness, pauperism, privation **10** meagerness, mendicancy **11** destitution, panhandling

begin
4 dawn, open, rise **5** arise, cause, dig in, enter, found, mount, set to, start **6** appear, attack, be born, broach, create, effect, emerge, get off, induce, invent, launch, spring, sprout, tackle, take up, tee off **7** break in, emanate, jump off, kick off, lead off, prepare, usher in **8** activate, commence, embark on, engender, initiate **9** establish, instigate, institute, introduce, originate **10** embark upon, inaugurate, issue forth **11** break ground

beginner
4 colt, tiro, tyro **6** newbie, new kid, novice, rookie **7** recruit, starter, student, trainee **8** freshman, neophyte, newcomer **9** fledgling, greenhorn, novitiate **10** apprentice, catechumen, tenderfoot **11** abecedarian

beginning
4 dawn, font, rise, root **5** alpha, basal, birth, fount, get-go, onset, start **6** day one, origin, outset, primal, source, spring **7** dawning, genesis, infancy, initial, kickoff, nascent, opening **8** creation, exordium, outstart, prologue, rudiment, simplest **9** elemental, emergence, inception, incipient **10** appearance, elementary, incipiency, initiative, initiatory, opening gun, rudimental **11** origination, rudimentary **12** commencement, inauguration, introductory

begird
3 hem **4** belt, bind, ring **5** beset, fence, hem in, round **6** circle, corral, girdle, immure **7** confine, enclose, wreathe **8** encircle, engirdle, surround **9** encompass **12** circumscribe

beg off
5 demur, welsh **6** bow out, cop out, opt out, pass up, refuse, renege **7** back out, bail out, decline, drop out, pull out **8** back down, withdraw

begone
5 leave, scram, split **6** beat it, decamp, depart, get out **7** buzz off, get lost, skiddoo, take off, vamoose **8** clear out, hightail, shove off **9** skedaddle **10** make tracks

begrime
3 tar **4** foul, soil, spot **5** dirty, muddy, smear, spoil, sully, taint **6** defile, mess up, muck up, smirch, smooch, smudge, smutch **7** blacken, corrupt, pollute, tarnish **8** besmirch **11** contaminate

begrudge
4 envy **6** resent

beguile
3 con **4** draw, dupe, fool, hoax, lure, play, snow, wile **5** bluff, charm, fleet, trick **6** allure, beckon, betray, delude, divert, entice, humbug, lead on, seduce, take in **7** attract, bewitch, deceive, enchant, engross, exploit, finesse, mislead **8** distract, hoodwink, intrigue, maneuver **9** captivate, fascinate, while away **10** manipulate **11** double-cross

beguiling
4 wily **5** false **6** artful, subtle **8** alluring, deluding, delusive, delusory **9** deceitful, deceiving, deceptive, insidious, seductive **10** bewitching, chimerical, enchanting, fallacious, misleading **11** enthralling

Behan's autobiography
10 Borstal Boy

behave
3 act, run **5** carry, react **6** acquit, be good, deport, direct, manage **7** comport, conduct, disport, perform **8** function

behavior
3 act, air, way **4** mien, tone, ways **6** action, aspect, custom, habits, manner **7** bearing, conduct **8** demeanor, presence, response **10** deportment **11** comportment

behead
4 head, kill **7** execute **9** decollate **10** decapitate, guillotine

beheaded noblewoman
8 Jane Grey (Lady) **9** Catherine (Howard) **10** Anne Boleyn

behemoth
5 giant, jumbo, whale **7** goliath, mammoth, monster **8** colossus **9** leviathan **11** monstrosity

behemothic
4 huge **5** jumbo **7** mammoth, massive, titanic **8** colossal, gigantic, towering **9** Herculean, monstrous **10** gargantuan **11** elephantine

behest
3 say **4** will, wish, word, writ **5** edict, order **6** charge, demand, urging **7** bidding, command, dictate, mandate, precept, request **9** direction, enjoinder, ordinance, prescript, prompting **10** injunction **11** commandment, exhortation, instruction **12** solicitation

behind
3 can **4** late, next, rump **5** after, fanny **6** back of, bottom, heinie **7** backing **8** backside, buttocks, derriere, trailing **9** following, posterior **10** supporting **12** subsequent to
prefix: **4** post **5** retro

behindhand
3 lax **4** late, slow **5** slack, tardy **6** in debt, remiss **7** belated, delayed, laggard, overdue **8** backward, careless, derelict **9** in arrears, negligent, unmindful **10** delinquent, neglectful, unpunctual **11** undeveloped

behold
3 see **4** espy, note, view **6** descry, notice **7** discern, observe, witness
French: **5** voilà
Latin: **4** ecce

beholden
5 bound **7** obliged **8** grateful, indebted **9** duty-bound, obligated

beholder
4 seer **6** gawker, viewer **7** watcher, witness **8** observer, onlooker, passerby **9** bystander, spectator **10** eyewitness **12** rubbernecker

beige
3 tan **4** buff, ecru **7** vanilla

being
3 ens, man **4** body, esse, life, self, soul **5** human, stuff, thing **6** entity, matter, mortal, nature, object, person, spirit **7** essence **8** creature, existent, material **9** actuality, character, existence, personage, something, substance **10** individual **11** personality **12** essentiality **13** individuality
celestial: **6** cherub, seraph

bejeweled
7 studded **8** sequined, spangled **9** encrusted **10** bespangled, gem-studded, ornamented

Bel
Sumerian counterpart: **5** Enlil
wife: **5** Belit **6** Beltis

Bel ___
3 Air **5** Paese

bel ___
5 canto **6** esprit

Bela
father: **4** Beor **8** Benjamin
son: **3** Ard

belabor
4 beat, drub, flog **5** baste, pound, scold **6** batter, berate, buffet, pummel, thrash, wallop **7** lambast, scourge, tell off, upbraid **8** chastise, lambaste, tear into **9** criticize, fulminate, overstate **10** flagellate **11** overexplain

Belarus
capital: **5** Minsk
city: **6** Homyel **7** Vitebsk **8** Mahilyow **9** Vitsyebsk
language: **7** Russian **10** Belarusian **11** Belarussian
monetary unit: **5** rubel, ruble **7** kapeyka

neighbor: **6** Latvia, Poland, Russia **7** Ukraine **9** Lithuania
river: **3** Bug **5** Neman **7** Dnieper, Pripyat

belated
4 late, slow **5** tardy **6** remiss **7** delayed, laggard, overdue **10** behindhand, behind time, unpunctual

Belau
see **Palau**

belch
4 burp, emit, gush, spew, vent, void **5** eject, eruct, erupt, expel, issue, spout, spurt, vomit **6** hiccup, irrupt **7** explode, extrude **8** disgorge **10** eructation **11** expectorate

beldam
3 hag **5** crone **8** old woman

beleaguer
3 bug, dog, hem, nag, vex **4** gnaw **5** annoy, beset, harry, hound, siege, storm, tease, worry **6** assail, attack, badger, bother, fall on, harass, invest, pester, plague **7** bedevil, besiege, hagride, put upon, set upon, trouble **8** blockade, fall upon

belfry
7 steeple **8** carillon **9** bell tower, campanile
dweller: **3** bat

Belgium
capital: **8** Brussels
city: **4** Gent **5** Ghent, Liège **7** Antwerp **9** Charleroi
ethnic group: **7** Fleming, Flemish, Walloon
language: **5** Dutch **7** Flemish
monetary unit: **4** euro
monetary unit, former: **5** franc
neighbor: **6** France **7** Germany **10** Luxembourg **11** Netherlands
plain: **8** Flanders
port: **7** Antwerp **8** Oostende
river: **4** Yser **5** Meuse **7** Schlede
sea: **5** North
sleuth: **6** Poirot (Hercule), Suchet (David)

belie
4 deny, hide, warp **5** color, twist **6** expose, doctor, garble **7** conceal, confute, distort, falsify, gainsay, pervert, trump up **8** confront, denounce, disagree, disguise, disprove, miscolor, misstate, negative **9** disaffirm, gloss over, repudiate **10** contradict, contravene, controvert **11** dissimulate **12** misrepresent

belief
3 ism **4** idea, mind, view **5** axiom, credo, creed, dogma, faith, hunch, tenet, trust **6** assent, avowal, credit, surety, theory, thesis **7** concept, feeling, opinion, precept, surmise, theorem **8** credence, doctrine, firmness, religion, sureness **9** assurance, certainty, certitude, intuition, postulate, principle, sentiment **10** acceptance, assumption, confidence, contention, conviction, hypothesis, impression, persuasion **11** supposition

believable
5 solid, sound, valid **6** cogent, likely **7** logical, tenable **8** credible, possible, probable, reliable **9** authentic, colorable, plausible **10** convincing, creditable, persuasive, reasonable **11** conceivable, trustworthy

believe
3 buy **4** deem, hold, know **5** lap up, think, trust **6** accept, affirm, assume, credit, expect, reckon **7** fall for, imagine, profess, suppose, suspect, swallow **8** conceive, consider **10** conjecture, presuppose, understand

belittle
3 cut, pan **5** abuse, decry, knock, scorn **6** deride, insult, jeer at, revile **7** cut down, put down, run down, sneer at **8** bad-mouth, derogate, diminish, discount, minimize, write off **9** criticize, discredit, disparage, dispraise, downgrade, underrate **10** depreciate, undervalue **13** underestimate

belittlement
5 abuse, scorn **7** calumny, jeering, scandal, slander **8** derision, ridicule **9** aspersion **10** backbiting, defamation, detraction **11** denigration **12** backstabbing, depreciation

Belize
capital: **8** Belmopan
city: **10** Belize City
ethnic group: **4** Maya **5** Mayan
mountain: **8** Victoria
neighbor: **6** Mexico **9** Guatemala
river: **5** Hondo
sea: **9** Caribbean

bell
4 peal **5** chime, knell **6** tocsin

belle
5 siren **6** beauty, eyeful **7** charmer **8** knockout, ornament **11** enchantress, femme fatale

Bellerophon
father: **7** Glaucus **8** Poseidon
grandfather: **8** Sisyphus
horse: **7** Pegasus
victim: **7** Chimera

belles lettres
10 literature

belletrist
8 novelist **4** poet **6** author, writer **9** dramatist **10** playwright

bellflower
9 campanula

___ belli
5 casus

bellicose
6 ornery 7 hawkish, hostile, martial, scrappy, warlike 8 factious, fighting, militant 9 assertive, combative, truculent 10 aggressive, pugnacious, rebellious 11 belligerent, contentious, hot-tempered, quarrelsome 12 disputatious, gladiatorial

belligerence
5 fight 6 attack, enmity, rancor, spleen 7 ill will 9 hostility, militancy, petulance, pugnacity 10 aggression, antagonism, truculence 11 bellicosity 12 churlishness 13 combativeness

belligerent
6 ardent, fierce 7 fighter, hostile, scrappy, soldier, warlike, warring, warrior 8 battling, churlish, fighting, invading, militant, opponent, petulant 9 aggressor, attacking, bellicose, combatant, combative, disputant, splenetic, truculent 10 aggressive, antagonist, pugnacious 11 contentious, hot-tempered, quarrelsome 12 antagonistic, disputatious

Bellini
opera: 5 Norma 6 Pirata (Il) 8 Puritani (I) 10 Sonnambula (La)
sleepwalker: 5 Amina

Bell Jar author
5 Plath (Sylvia)

bell metal
6 bronze

bellow
3 bay, cry, moo 4 bark, bawl, bray, howl, roar, rout, yowl 5 shout 6 clamor, holler 7 bluster

Bellow character
4 Rose (Billy) 5 Chick 6 Herzog (Moses E.) 7 Citrine (Charlie), Sammler (Arthur) 8 Humboldt, Fonstein (Harry) 9 Henderson 10 Ravelstein (Abe), Augie March

bell ringer
6 toller 9 Quasimodo 12 carillonneur 13 campanologist

bell ringing
11 campanology

bell-shaped
11 campanulate

bell sound
4 bong, boom, ding, dong, peal, ring, ting, toll 5 chime, clang, knell 6 tinkle

bell tower
6 belfry 7 clocher 8 carillon 9 campanile

___ bellum
4 ante, post

bellwether
4 dean, lead 5 doyen, guide, pilot 6 leader 7 pioneer 8 lodestar 9 harbinger 10 forerunner 11 trend setter

belly
3 gut, pot 5 tummy 6 paunch, venter 7 abdomen, midriff, stomach 9 bay window 10 front porch, midsection 11 breadbasket
Scottish: 4 wame

bellyache
4 beef, carp, crab, fret, fuss, moan, yawp 5 bitch, bleat, colic, gripe, whine 6 grouse, snivel, squawk, yammer 7 grumble 8 complain 11 let off steam 12 collywobbles

bellyacher
4 crab 5 crank 6 griper, grouch, whiner 7 grouser 8 grumbler, sourpuss 10 complainer, crosspatch, malcontent 11 faultfinder

belly button
5 navel

belong
3 fit, set 4 suit, vest 5 agree, apply, befit, chime, fit in, match, tally 6 accord, attach, become, reside 7 pertain 9 correlate, harmonize 10 correspond

belongings
3 kit 4 gear 5 goods, stuff 6 assets, estate, legacy, things 7 baggage, effects 8 chattels, movables, property 9 patrimony 11 attachments, impedimenta, inheritance, possessions 13 appurtenances

beloved
3 gra, pet 4 baby, beau, dear, idol, love 5 flame, honey, lover, swain, sweet 6 adored, steady 7 darling, dearest, dear one, doted on, sweetie 8 favorite, idolized, ladylove, old flame, precious, truelove 9 boyfriend, cherished, inamorata, treasured 10 girlfriend, heartthrob, sweetheart, sweetie pie

below
5 infra, 'neath, under 7 beneath 10 underneath
prefix: 3 sub 5 infra

belt
3 bat, bop 4 area, band, bash, biff, blow, gird, loop, ring, sash, slam, slug, sock, whap, whop, zone 5 smack, smash, strap, strip 6 begird, cestus, circle, engird, girdle, region, wallop 7 baldric, clobber, stretch 8 begirdle, ceinture, cincture, encircle, engirdle 9 bandoleer, bandolier, territory, waistband 10 cummerbund
celestial: 6 zodiac

beltway
8 ring road

Belus
brother: 6 Agenor
daughter: 4 Dido
father: 7 Neptune 8 Poseidon

mother: **5** Libya
son: **6** Danaus **7** Cepheus, Phineus **8** Aegyptus

belvedere
6 alcove, cupola, gazebo, pagoda **7** balcony, terrace **10** widow's walk **11** garden house, summerhouse, observatory

bemedaled
9 decorated **10** beribboned

bemired
4 miry, oozy **5** boggy, dirty, grimy, gummy, gunky, muddy, stuck **6** filthy, soiled, swampy **7** swamped

bemoan
3 rue **4** wail, weep **6** bewail, grieve, lament, oppose, regret **7** deplore **8** complain, object to **10** sorrow over **12** disapprove of

bemuse
4 daze **5** addle **6** absorb, muddle, puzzle **7** confuse, mystify, nonplus, perplex **8** bewilder, distract **10** disconcert

bemused
3 wry **4** lost **6** absent, remote **7** faraway **8** distrait **9** distraite **10** abstracted, distracted **11** preoccupied **12** absentminded **13** lost in thought

bench
5 court **6** settee, settle, thwart **7** counter **8** platform **9** worktable
church: **3** pew
outdoor: **6** exedra
upholstered: **9** banquette

benchmark
4 norm **5** basis, gauge, guide, model, scale **7** measure **8** exemplar, paradigm, standard **9** criterion, guideline, milestone, yardstick **10** touchstone

benchwarmer
5 scrub

bend
3 arc, bow, sag **4** arch, bank, cave, curl, flex, hang, hook, lean, mold, sway, tend, tilt, turn, veer, warp **5** angle, crook, curve, round, shape, shift, stoop, twist, yield **6** compel, corner, buckle, direct, double, fasten, kowtow, subdue, submit, zigzag **7** deflect, dispose, distort, flexure, turning **8** lean over **9** curvature, deviation, genuflect **10** compromise, predispose

bendable
5 lithe **6** limber, pliant, supple **7** elastic, plastic, pliable **8** flexible, moldable **9** malleable, tractable **11** manipulable

bender
see **binge**

____ bene
4 nota

beneath
5 below, under
prefix: **3** hyp, sub **4** hypo **5** infra

____ Benedict
4 eggs

benediction
4 boon, okay **5** favor, grace **6** orison, thanks **7** benefit, benison, godsend **8** approval, blessing **9** advantage **11** approbation **12** consecration, thanksgiving

benefaction
4 alms, care, fund, gift, help **5** favor, grant **6** relief **7** charity, comfort, handout, largess, service, subsidy **8** donation, largesse, oblation, offering, windfall **9** endowment, patronage **10** assistance **12** contribution, ministration

benefactor
5 angel, donor **6** backer, patron **7** grantor, sponsor **9** supporter, sustainer **11** contributor, underwriter

beneficence
see **benefaction**

beneficent
4 kind **6** benign, caring, giving **8** generous **10** altruistic, bighearted, charitable, ungrudging **11** kindhearted, magnanimous **13** compassionate, philanthropic

beneficial
4 good **5** brave, tonic **6** benign, toward, useful **7** helpful **8** favoring, salutary, valuable **9** favorable, healthful, nurturing, wholesome **10** profitable, propitious, salubrious **12** advantageous, constructive

beneficiary
4 heir **5** donee, payee **7** grantee, heiress, legatee **8** assignee **9** inheritor, recipient

beneficiate
5 treat **6** reduce **7** prepare, process

benefit
3 aid **4** boon, gain, good, help, perk, sake **5** avail, extra, favor, serve **6** assist, behalf, better, profit, relief, succor **7** account, advance, charity, further, godsend, improve, promote, relieve, welfare **8** blessing, interest **9** advantage, well-being **10** ameliorate, fund-raiser, prosperity **11** good fortune **12** contribute to

benevolence
4 boon, gift, help **5** amity, favor, grant **6** comity, relief **7** caritas, charity **8** altruism, clemency, goodness, goodwill, humanity, kindness **10** compassion, compliment, kindliness **11** magnanimity

benevolent
4 good, kind, warm **6** caring, do-good, humane, kindly **7** helpful, liberal **8** generous, tolerant **10** altruistic, beneficent, bighearted, charitable,

openhanded **11** considerate, magnanimous, warmhearted **12** eleemosynary, humanitarian **13** compassionate, philanthropic, tenderhearted

Ben Hur author
7 Wallace (Lew)

benighted
6 obtuse, unread **8** backward, ignorant, untaught **9** untutored, unwitting **10** illiterate, uneducated, uninformed, unlettered, unschooled **11** know-nothing **12** uncultivated **13** unenlightened, unprogressive

benign
4 kind, mild **6** genial, gentle, humane, kindly, mellow **7** amiable, clement **8** gracious, harmless, merciful, pleasant **9** favorable, fortunate, healthful, temperate, wholesome **10** auspicious, benevolent, charitable, forbearing, propitious, remediable **11** good-hearted **12** noncancerous

Benin
capital: **9** Porto-Novo
city: **7** Cotonou
coast: **5** Slave
ethnic group: **3** Fon **6** Fulani, Yoruba
former name: **7** Dahomey
language: **3** Fon **6** French
monetary unit: **5** franc
neighbor: **4** Togo **5** Niger **7** Nigeria **11** Burkina Faso
river: **5** Ouémé

benison
5 grace **8** blessing **11** benediction **12** consecration

Benjamin
brother: **6** Joseph
father: **5** Jacob
mother: **6** Rachel

bent
3 set **4** bias, gift **5** arced, bowed, flair, knack **6** arched, curved, intent, talent **7** decided, faculty, leaning **8** aptitude, capacity, penchant, resolute, resolved, tendency **10** determined, proclivity, propensity **11** disposition, inclination **12** predilection

benumb
4 daze, dull, stun **5** blunt, chill **6** deaden, freeze **7** petrify, stupefy **8** etherize, paralyze **10** immobilize **11** desensitize

benumbed
4 cold **6** frozen **9** unfeeling **10** insensible **11** insensitive **12** anesthetized

Beowulf
drink: **4** mead
monster: **7** Grendel

bequeath
4 gift, will **5** endow, grant, leave **6** bestow, commit, confer, devise, hand on, impart, legate, pass on **7** furnish, present **8** hand down, make over, transmit

bequest
3 lot **4** gift **5** share, trust **6** devise, estate, legacy **7** portion **8** heritage **10** settlement **11** inheritance

berate
3 jaw **4** rail, rate **5** chide, scold **6** rail at, rebuke, revile **7** bawl out, blister, chew out, condemn, reprove, tell off, upbraid **8** admonish, chastise, reproach **9** castigate, criticize, reprimand **10** tongue-lash, vituperate

berceuse
7 lullaby **10** cradlesong

bereave
3 rob **4** lose **5** seize, strip **6** divest, remove **7** deprive **8** take away **10** confiscate, disinherit, dispossess **11** appropriate, requisition

bereaved
8 mourning **9** sorrowful, sorrowing **10** distressed **11** heartbroken **13** grief-stricken

bereavement
3 rue, woe **4** loss **5** dolor, grief **6** misery, pining, regret, sorrow **7** anguish, despair, remorse, sadness **8** grieving, mourning **9** dejection, heartache **10** affliction, depression, desolation **11** deprivation, despondency, lamentation, tribulation

bereft
4 lorn **5** shorn **6** devoid, robbed **7** fleeced, forlorn, wanting **8** beggared, deprived, desolate, divested, stricken, stripped **9** destitute **10** despondent **12** disconsolate, dispossessed, impoverished

Bergen's dummy
7 Charlie (McCarthy) **8** Mortimer (Snerd)

Berger novel
12 Little Big Man

Bergman role
4 Ilsa

berkelium symbol
2 Bk

berm
4 path **5** ledge, mound, shelf **8** shoulder

Bermuda
capital: **8** Hamilton
territory of: **7** Britain

Bernice
brother: **7** Agrippa
father: **5** Herod
husband: **6** Polemo
lover: **5** Titus **9** Vespasian

berry
3 haw **5** cubeb, fruit, grape **7** currant, madrona, madrone **8** allspice **9** saskatoon

berserk
3 ape **4** amok **5** amuck, crazy **6** crazed, insane **7** bonkers, lunatic **8** demented, deranged, frenzied

berth
3 bed, cot **4** dock, moor, pier, port, post, quay, slip, spot **5** cabin, jetty, levee, place, wharf **6** billet, office **8** position **9** anchorage, situation **10** connection **11** appointment, compartment **13** accommodation

beryllium symbol
2 Be

beseech
see **beg**

beset
3 dog, hem, try, vex **4** gird, ring **5** harry, hem in, storm, worry **6** assail, attack, badger, circle, fall on, harass, infest, pester, plague, strike **7** assault, besiege, overrun, trouble, torture **8** blockade, encircle, fall upon, surround **9** beleaguer, encompass, overswarm

besetment
3 nag **4** bane, pain, pest **5** curse, trial **6** blight, bother, gadfly, pester, plague **7** torment **8** irritant, nuisance, vexation **9** annoyance **10** affliction, botherment, holy terror **11** aggravation, botheration

besetting
6 urgent **7** driving **8** dominant **9** obsessive **10** compelling, persistent **11** omnipresent **12** overwhelming

beside
4 near, nigh **6** next to

besides
3 too **4** also, else, plus, save **5** added, extra **6** and all, as well, beyond, except, to boot **7** barring, farther, further, without **8** as well as, likewise, moreover, more than **9** aside from, along with, exceeding, excluding, other than, otherwise, outside of **10** in addition **11** exclusive of, furthermore, not counting **12** additionally, together with

besiege
3 nag **4** ring, trap **5** beset, hem in, hound **6** assail, attack, circle, girdle, harass, pester, plague **7** assault, confine, environ, trouble **8** blockade, encircle, surround **9** beleaguer, encompass

besmear
see **smear**

besmirch
4 blot, foul, slur, soil **5** dirty, libel, stain, sully, taint **6** defile, damage, impugn, malign **7** asperse, slander, tarnish **8** disgrace, dishonor

besom
5 broom

besotted
5 dotty, drunk **7** charmed, muddled, smitten **8** enamored **9** enchanted **10** captivated, fascinated, infatuated, spellbound **11** intoxicated

bespatter
see **spatter**

bespeak
3 ask **4** book, hire, show **5** imply **6** accost, attest, desire, evince, reveal **7** address, apply to, betoken, connote, lecture, portend, request, reserve, signify, solicit, suggest, testify, witness **8** announce, approach, foretell, indicate, intimate, petition **9** preengage **10** prearrange

bespoke
8 tailored **10** custom-made

best
3 gem, top **4** beat, pick, tops **5** cream, elite, excel, model, one-up, outdo, pride, prime, prize **6** choice, defeat, exceed, finest **7** conquer, leading, optimal, optimum, paragon, premium, supreme, surpass **8** exemplar, foremost, greatest, nonesuch, outshine, outstrip, overcome **9** matchless, nonpareil, number-one, paramount, transcend, unequaled **11** outstanding **12** incomparable
combining form: **6** aristo

bestial
4 vile, wild **5** brute, cruel, feral **6** animal, brutal, carnal, fierce, malign, savage **7** beastly, brutish, inhuman, swinish, vicious **8** depraved, inhumane **9** ferocious **10** degenerate

bestialize
4 ruin, warp **5** abase **6** debase, defile **7** corrupt, debauch, degrade, deprave, pervert, pollute, subvert, vitiate, violate **9** brutalize **10** bastardize, demoralize

bestir
3 fly, rip **4** dash, flit, goad, race, rush, spur, stir, tear, urge, wake, whet **5** rally, rouse, scoot, waken, whirl **6** arouse, awaken, hasten, hustle, kindle **8** get going, scramble **9** challenge

bestow
4 give **5** apply, award, grant **6** confer, devote, donate, lavish **7** hand out, present **8** bequeath, give away
Scottish: **7** propine

bestower
5 donor, giver **6** patron **7** donator **8** altruist **9** conferrer, patroness, presenter **10** benefactor **12** benefactress **13** good Samaritan

bestrew
3 dot, sow **6** pepper, shower **7** diffuse, disject, scatter, speckle, stipple **8** disperse, sprinkle **9** broadcast, interlard **10** distribute **11** disseminate

bestride
5 mount, tower **8** dominate, loom over, straddle **9** stand over

bet
3 pot **4** ante, game, play, risk, shot **5** put on, stake, wager **6** gamble, hazard, parlay, pledge **7** lay odds, venture
racing: **6** exacta **8** perfecta, quinella, quiniela
taker: **6** bookie

Betelgeuse
4 star
constellation: **5** Orion

betel palm
5 areca

bête noire
4 bane, hate, ruin **5** trial **6** animus, horror **7** bugbear, nemesis, scourge, torment, undoing **8** anathema, aversion, downfall **9** ruination **10** black beast

bethink
4 cite, mind **6** call up, recall, remind, retain, review, revive **7** flash on **8** hark back, look back, remember, summon up **9** conjure up, recollect, reminisce **10** call to mind, retrospect

Bethuel
daughter: **7** Rebekah
father: **5** Nahor
mother: **6** Milcah
son: **5** Laban
uncle: **7** Abraham

betide
4 fall **5** break, ensue, occur **6** befall, chance, happen **7** come off, develop, fall out **8** commence **9** come about, transpire

betimes
4 anon, soon **5** early **6** pronto, seldom, timely **7** too soon **8** directly, far ahead, fitfully, promptly **9** presently **10** before long, now and then, on occasion, seasonably **11** prematurely **12** occasionally, sporadically

betoken
4 bode, omen, show, warn **5** argue, augur **6** attest, denote, hint at **7** bespeak, point to, portend, presage, promise, signify, suggest, testify, witness **8** announce, forebode, evidence, foreshow, foretell, indicate, intimate, prophesy **9** prefigure **10** foreshadow **13** prognosticate

betray
4 dupe, jilt, trap **5** rat on, snare, spill, split **6** desert, entrap, evince, finger, inform, reveal, seduce, take in, tattle, tell on, turn in, unveil **7** abandon, beguile, deceive, divulge, forsake, let down, let slip, sell out, traduce **8** blurt out, denounce, disclose, discover, evidence, give away, manifest **10** apostatize, break faith **11** double-cross

betrayal
4 leak **7** perfidy, sellout, treason **8** exposure **9** duplicity, falseness, Judas kiss, treachery **10** disclosure, infidelity, revelation **13** faithlessness

betrayer
3 rat **4** fink, nark **5** Judas **6** snitch **7** stoolie, tattler, traitor **8** apostate, defector, informer, quisling, renegade, squealer, turncoat **10** talebearer, tattletale **11** backstabber, stool pigeon

betroth
3 wed **5** marry **6** pledge **7** espouse **8** affiance

betrothal
6 pledge **8** espousal **10** engagement

betrothed
6 fiancé **7** engaged, fiancée, pledged **8** intended, plighted, promised, wife-to-be **9** affianced, bride-to-be, spoken for **10** contracted **11** husband-to-be

better
3 fix, top, win **4** beat, help, mend, more, well **5** amend, cured, elder, excel, finer, outdo **6** exceed, fitter, repair **7** advance, correct, enhance, further, greater, improve, largest, mending, rectify, success, surpass, triumph, victory **8** greatest, improved, outshine, outstrip, stronger, superior, whip hand, worthier **9** advantage, desirable, excellent, healthier, improving, meliorate, preferred, transcend, upper hand **10** ameliorate, preferable, preferably, recovering, surpassing

bettor
7 gambler, wagerer

between
4 amid **5** among, twixt **6** within **7** betwixt
prefix: **5** inter, intra

betweentimes
11 at intervals

bevel
4 bias, cant **5** angle, grade, slant, slope **7** chamfer, incline, oblique **8** diagonal

beverage
3 ade, nog, pop, tea **4** chai, cola, kava, maté, milk, soda **5** cider, cocoa, drink, juice, mocha, shake **6** coffee, eggnog, frappe, malted, nectar **7** potable, soda pop **8** lemonade, libation, potation **9** drinkable, milk shake
alcoholic: **3** ale, gin, rum **4** beer, grog, mead, nipa, wine **5** cider, julep, negus, punch, stout, toddy, vodka **6** bishop, brandy, caudle, cooler, liquor, rickey, shandy, sherry, whisky **7** liqueur, martini, sangria, tequila, whiskey **8** cocktail, highball, sillabub, syllabub, vermouth
Arab: **4** arak **6** arrack
Australasian: **4** kava
Balkan: **9** slivovitz
British: **5** perry, stout **6** porter

carbonated: **4** cola, soda **5** tonic **6** rickey **7** Perrier, seltzer, soda pop **8** club soda, root beer **9** ginger ale
central Asian: **6** kumiss **7** koumiss
Dutch: **7** schnaps **8** schnapps
from milk: **5** kefir **6** kumiss **7** koumiss
Greek: **4** ouzo **7** retsina
Hawaiian: **3** ‘ava
Irish: **6** poteen **10** usquebaugh
Japanese: **4** sake
medicinal: **6** elixir, tisane
Mexican: **6** pulque **7** tequila
of the gods: **6** nectar
Oriental: **4** arak, sake, saki **6** arrack
Russian: **5** kefir, kvass, vodka
Scottish: **6** scotch
South American: **4** maté **5** yerba **9** yerba maté
Swedish: **5** glogg
Turkish: **4** raki
West Indies: **3** rum
see also **cocktail**

bevy
3 mob **4** band, club, crew, gang, herd, knot, pack **5** bunch, covey, crowd, drove, flock, group, horde, party, swarm **6** clutch, gaggle, troupe **7** cluster, company, coterie **8** assembly **9** menagerie, multitude **10** assemblage, collection

bewail
3 rue **4** keen, moan, weep **5** mourn **6** bemoan, grieve, lament, regret **7** deplore

beware
4 heed, mark, mind, note, shun **5** avoid, watch **6** attend, notice **7** look out **8** take heed, watch out

bewhiskered
5 bushy **7** bearded, goateed, hirsute, stubbly **8** unshaven

bewilder
3 fog **4** daze, stun **5** addle, amaze, befog, mix up, stump **6** baffle, ball up, bemuse, fuddle, muddle, puzzle, rattle **7** confuse, fluster, mystify, nonplus, perplex, stumble **8** befuddle, confound, distract **9** disorient, dumbfound **10** disconcert

bewilderment
3 awe **4** daze **6** wonder **8** surprise **9** amazement, confusion **10** perplexity, puzzlement **11** distraction **12** astonishment, discomfiture, stupefaction **13** consternation

bewitch
3 hex **4** draw, pull, snow, take, wile **5** charm, spell, trick **6** allure, dazzle, seduce, voodoo **7** attract, bedevil, beguile, control, delight, enchant, possess **8** demonize, ensorcel, enthrall, entrance, intrigue, overlook **9** captivate, enrapture, ensorcell, fascinate, hypnotize, magnetize, mesmerize, spellbind

Bewitched
character: **6** Darrin, Endora **7** Maurice, Tabitha **8** Samantha **9** Aunt Clara
creator: **4** Saks (Sol)
film director: **6** Ephron (Nora)
film star: **5** Caine (Michael) **6** Kidman (Nicole) **7** Ferrell (Will) **8** MacLaine (Shirley)
TV star: **4** York (Dick) **7** Sargent (Dick) **9** Moorehead (Agnes) **10** Montgomery (Elizabeth)

bewitching
4 foxy **5** siren **7** magical **8** alluring, charming, engaging, enticing, magnetic, mesmeric **9** seductive **10** attractive **12** irresistible

bewitchment
3 hex **4** jinx **5** charm, magic, spell **6** trance **7** evil eye, sorcery **8** black art, wizardry **9** conjuring **10** necromancy **11** conjuration, enchantment, incantation, thaumaturgy

beyond
4 over, past **5** above, after **6** across, beside, yonder **7** besides, further, outside **8** as well as **9** afterlife, hereafter, otherwise **10** afterworld **12** over and above
prefix: **4** meta, over, para **5** extra, hyper, super, trans, ultra **6** preter

Bhutan
capital: **7** Thimphu
ethnic group: **6** Bhutia **8** Assamese, Nepalese **9** Mongolian, Sharcrops
language: **8** Dzongkha
monetary unit: **8** ngultrum
mountain range: **8** Himalaya **13** Great Himalaya
neighbor: **5** China, India, Tibet
plain: **5** Duars

bias
4 bend, bent, skew, sway, tilt, turn **5** angle, bevel, slant **7** beveled, bigotry, dispose, distort, incline, leaning, oblique, slanted **8** diagonal, penchant, slanting, tendency **9** crosswise, inclining, influence, prejudice, proneness, viewpoint **10** diagonally, favoritism, partiality, propensity, predispose, prepossess, proclivity, standpoint, transverse **11** disposition, inclination **12** one-sidedness, predilection **13** preconception

biased
6 racist, swayed, unfair, warped **7** bigoted, colored, partial, slanted **8** disposed, inclined, one-sided, partisan, slanting **9** jaundiced, sectarian, unneutral **10** influenced, interested, prejudiced **11** opinionated, predisposed, tendentious

bibelot
5 curio **6** bauble, gewgaw, trifle **7** memento, novelty, trinket, whatnot **8** gimcrack, ornament **9** objet d'art **10** knickknack

Bible

abbreviation: **3** Col, Cor, Dan, Eph, Gal, Gen, Hab, Heb, Hos, Jas, Jer, Jon, Lam, Lev, Mal, Mic, Neh, Num, Pet, Rev, Rom, Sam, Tim, Tit **4** Deut, Ezek, Josh, Judg, Obad, Phil, Prov, Zech, Zeph **5** Chron, Thess **6** Eccles, Philem
Apocrypha book: **5** Tobit **6** Baruch, Esdras, Esther, Judith **7** Susanna **8** Manasseh, Manasses **9** Maccabees
New Testament book: **4** Acts, John, Jude, Luke, Mark **5** James, Peter, Titus **6** Romans **7** Hebrews, Matthew, Timothy **8** Philemon **9** Ephesians, Galatians **10** Colossians, Revelation **11** Corinthians, Philippians **13** Thessalonians
Old Testament book: **3** Job **4** Amos, Ezra, Joel, Ruth **5** Hosea, Jonah, Kings, Micah, Nahum **6** Daniel, Esther, Exodus, Haggai, Isaiah, Joshua, Judges, Psalms, Samuel **7** Ezekiel, Genesis, Malachi, Numbers, Obadiah **8** Habakkuk, Jeremiah, Nehemiah, Proverbs **9** Leviticus, Zechariah, Zephaniah **10** Chronicles **11** Deuteronomy **12** Ecclesiastes, Lamentations **13** Song of Solomon
part: **4** book **5** verse **7** chapter **9** testament
translator: **4** Knox (Ronald Arbuthnott) **5** Eliot (John) **6** Jerome, Luther (Martin) **7** Erasmus (Desiderius), Tyndale (William), Zwingli (Huldrych) **8** Andrewes (Lancelot), Wycliffe (John) **9** Coverdale (Miles)
version: **5** Douay **6** Coptic, Gothic, Syriac **7** Vulgate **9** Jerusalem, King James, Masoretic **10** New English, Septuagint

Biblical

animal: **8** behemoth
ascetic order: **6** Essene
battle: **7** Jericho
battle site: **10** Armageddon
charioteer: **4** Jehu
city, town: **4** Cana, Gaza, Tyre, Zoar **5** Endor, Golan, Haifa, Joppa, Sidon, Sodom **6** Asshur, Bethel, Emmaus, Gilgal, Hebron, Mizpah, Shiloh, Smyrna, Tarsus **7** Antioch, Baalbec, Bethany, Corinth, Ephesus, Ephraim, Jericho, Magdala, Nineveh, Samaria **8** Caesarea, Damascus, Gomorrah, Nazareth, Philippi, Tiberias **9** Beersheba, Bethlehem, Capernaum, Jerusalem
coin:
(see at **Hebrew**)
desert: **5** Sinai
garden: **4** Eden **8** Paradise
giant: **7** Goliath
giant slayer: **5** David
hill: **4** Zion **7** Calvary
hunter: **6** Nimrod
judge: **3** Eli **4** Ehud **6** Gideon, Samson, Samuel **7** Deborah, Jephtha **8** Jephthah
king: **3** Asa **4** Ahab, Amon, Elah, Jehu, Saul **5** David, Herod, Hiram **6** Josiah **7** Azariah, Menahem, Solomon **8** Hezekiah, Jeroboam, Manasseh, Rehoboam, Zedekiah **9** Zechariah **11** Jehoshaphat
land: **3** Nod **4** Aram, Elam, Moab, Seba **5** Judah, Judea, Magog **6** Canaan, Goshen, Israel, Judaea **7** Chaldea, Galilee, Samaria **9** Palestine
land of plenty: **6** Goshen
measure:
(see at **Hebrew**)
mountain: **4** Nebo **5** Horeb, Sinai, Tabor **6** Ararat, Carmel, Gilboa, Gilead, Hermon, Moriah, Olivet, Pisgah **7** Lebanon
name: **3** Asa, Bel, Dan, Eli, Eve, Gad, Ham, Ira, Job, Lot, Uri **4** Abel, Adam, Ahab, Amon, Boaz, Cain, Elam, Enos, Esau, Jael, Jehu, Joel, John, Lael, Leah, Levi, Mark, Mary, Mica, Moab, Noah, Omar, Onan, Paul, Reba, Ruth, Sara, Saul, Seth, Shem **5** Aaron, Abner, Amram, Asher, Caleb, David, Dinah, Elias, Enoch, Ethan, Hagar, Heman, Herod, Hosea, Isaac, Jacob, James, Jared, Jesse, Jonah, Jubal, Judah, Judas, Laban, Micah, Moses, Naomi, Peter, Rufus, Sarah, Sheba, Simon, Tamar, Tubal, Uriah, Uriel, Zadok **6** Ashhur, Balaam, Baruch, Canaan, Daniel, Elijah, Elisha, Esther, Gideon, Gilead, Hannah, Hebron, Isaiah, Israel, Jeshua, Jethro, Joanna, Joseph, Joshua, Josiah, Judith, Martha, Miriam, Nathan, Nimrod, Pasach, Philip, Pilate, Rachel, Reuben, Salome, Samson, Samuel, Simeon, Thomas, Tobias
patriarch:
(see at **Hebrew**)
people: **6** Kenite, Levite **7** Amorite, Edomite, Elamite, Moabite **9** Israelite
plains: **6** Sharon **7** Jericho
plotter: **5** Haman
poem: **5** psalm
pool: **8** Bethesda
priest: **3** Eli **4** Levi **5** Aaron, Annas **8** Caiaphas
Promised Land: **6** Canaan
pronoun: **2** ye **3** thy **4** thee, thou **5** thine
prophet:
(see **prophet**)
Psalmist: **5** David
punishment: **7** stoning
queen: **5** Sheba **6** Esther **7** Jezebel
quotation: **4** text
river: **4** Nile **6** Jordan
sacred object: **4** urim **7** thummin
scribe: **6** Baruch
sea: **3** Red **4** Dead **7** Galilee
sea monster: **9** Leviathan
spice: **5** aloes, myrrh **6** cassia **7** calamus **8** cinnamon **12** frankincense
spy: **5** Caleb
strongman: **6** Samson

temptress: **3** Eve **7** Delilah
text set to music: **8** oratorio
thief: **8** Barabbas
tree: **5** cedar
twin: **4** Esau **5** Jacob
valley: **4** Baca, Elah **6** Hinnon, Kidron, Shaveh, Siddim
weed: **4** tare
witch's home: **5** Endor

bibliography
4 list **7** catalog, history **8** book list **13** reference list

bibliopole
7 bookman **10** book dealer, bookseller

bibulous
6 spongy **7** thirsty **8** drinking **9** absorbent **10** absorptive

bicker
3 row **4** spar, spat, tiff **5** argue, clack, fight, scrap **6** gurgle, hassle **7** brabble, clatter, contend, dispute, fall out, flicker, quarrel, quibble, wrangle **8** squabble

bickering
3 row **4** at it, spat **5** brawl, run-in **6** blowup, fracas, hassle, ruckus, rumpus, strife **7** discord, dispute, quarrel, rhubarb, wrangle **8** squabble **11** altercation, embroilment

bicycle
4 bike
brake: **7** caliper, coaster
for two: **6** tandem
gear shift: **10** derailleur
rider: **6** cycler **7** cyclist
track: **9** velodrome

bid
3 ask, say, try **4** call, tell, warn, wish **5** essay, greet, offer, order **6** amount, charge, direct, effort, enjoin, invite, render, summon, tender **7** attempt, command, proffer, request, require, venture **8** endeavor, instruct, proposal **10** invitation, submission **11** proposition

biddable
4 mild **6** docile, pliant **7** amiable, pliable, willing **8** amenable, obedient, obliging **9** malleable, tractable **10** governable, manageable **11** acquiescent, cooperative, good-natured **13** accommodating

bidding
4 call, word **5** offer, order **6** behest, charge, demand, notice, tender **7** auction, command, dictate, mandate, request, summons **9** ordinance, summoning **10** injunction, invitation **11** commandment, instruction **12** proclamation

biddy
3 bag, bat, hag, hen **4** drab, trot **5** crone, witch **6** beldam **7** chicken

bide
4 live, stay, wait **5** await, dwell, tarry **6** hang in, linger, remain, reside **7** hang out, sojourn **8** continue, sit tight, tolerate **10** hang around **11** stick around

bier
10 catafalque

biff
3 bop, box, hit, jab, zap **4** bash, belt, blow, clip, ding, nail, slam, slug, sock, swat, whop **5** blast, catch, clout, pound, slosh, smack, thump, whack **6** strike, thwack, wallop

bifurcate
3 cut **4** fork **5** halve, split **6** bisect, branch, cleave, divide **8** separate **9** branch out **11** dichotomize, dichotomous

bifurcation
4 fork **6** branch **8** division **9** dichotomy, partition, radiation **10** separation

big
3 fat **4** full, hard, huge, main, mega, tall, vast **5** adult, ample, chief, great, grown, heavy, hefty, husky, large, lofty, major, proud, roomy **6** bumper, hugely **7** capital, copious, crammed, crowded, eminent, grown-up, hulking, leading, liberal, mammoth, massive, monster, notable, popular, replete, sizable, stuffed, swollen, weighty **8** colossal, enormous, generous, gracious, imposing, inflated, material, oversize, princely, spacious, swelling **9** capacious, chock-full, distended, extensive, heavy duty, humongous, important, momentous, overblown, paramount, ponderous, principal, prominent, unselfish **10** commodious, large-scale, preeminent, prodigious, voluminous **11** heavyweight, magnanimous, major-league, overflowing, significant, substantial **12** considerable **13** comprehensive, consequential
prefix: **4** mega

big bang theorist
5 Gamow (George)

Big Bertha
6 cannon **8** howitzer
birthplace: **5** Essen
manufacturer: **5** Krupp

Big ___, Cal.
3 Sur

Big Dipper
constellation: **9** Ursa Major
star: **5** Alcor, Dubhe, Merak, Mizar

bigfoot
9 Sasquatch

biggety
4 bold, vain, wise **5** fresh, nervy, sassy **6** cheeky, snippy, snooty, uppity **7** forward,

stuck-up **8** impudent, insolent, puffed up, snobbish **9** conceited **11** smart-alecky **13** self-important

bighearted
6 giving **7** liberal **8** generous **9** forgiving **10** altruistic, benevolent, charitable, munificent, openhanded **11** magnanimous **13** compassionate

big house
3 can, jug, pen **4** coop, jail **5** clink, joint **6** cooler, lockup, prison **7** slammer **8** bastille, hoosegow, stockade **9** bridewell **11** reformatory **12** penitentiary

bight
3 arm, bay **4** cove, gulf **6** harbor

bigmouthed
4 loud, rude **8** boastful **10** boisterous

bigness
4 size **5** scale, scope **6** extent, volume **9** amplitude, immensity, magnitude **10** dimensions, importance

bigot
6 racist **8** jingoist **9** extremist, racialist **10** chauvinist **11** supremacist

bigoted
6 biased, narrow, unfair **9** hidebound, illiberal, sectarian **10** brassbound, intolerant, prejudiced **11** small-minded **12** narrow-minded

bigotry
4 bias **6** racism **9** apartheid, prejudice **10** xenophobia **11** intolerance

big shot
3 VIP **4** czar **5** celeb, mogul, nabob **6** fat cat, tycoon **7** kingpin, notable, pooh-bah **8** higher-up, luminary, top brass **9** celebrity, dignitary, personage **13** high-muck-a-muck

Big Ten team
4 Iowa (Hawkeyes) **6** Purdue (Boilermakers) **7** Indiana (Hoosiers) **8** Illinois (Fighting Illini), Michigan (Wolverines) **9** Minnesota (Golden Gophers), Ohio State (Buckeyes), Penn State (Nittany Lions), Wisconsin (Badgers) **12** Northwestern (Wildcats) **13** Michigan State (Spartans)

big-time
5 major **7** eminent, greatly, leading **8** renowned **9** high-level, important, paramount, prominent **10** large-scale **11** influential, major-league

big top
4 tent **6** circus

bigwig
3 VIP **5** heavy, mogul, nabob **6** honcho, kahuna **7** kingpin, magnate, notable **8** luminary, somebody **9** dignitary, personage **11** heavy hitter, muckety-muck **13** high-muck-a-muck

bijou
3 gem **5** jewel **8** gemstone

bijouterie
6 jewels **7** jewelry **8** trinkets **10** decoration

bike
5 cycle **7** scooter **10** motorcycle **12** motor-scooter

bilge
3 rot **4** bull, bunk, guff **5** hooey, trash **6** bunkum **7** baloney, garbage, hogwash, malarky, rubbish, twaddle **8** claptrap, nonsense **9** poppycock, silliness **10** balderdash **11** foolishness

bilk
3 con, gyp **4** balk, beat, dash, duck, dupe, foil, fool, hoax, hose, kite, milk, rook, ruin, scam, take **5** avoid, cheat, cozen, dodge, elude, evade, shake, shaft, skirt, stiff, trick **6** baffle, chisel, chouse, diddle, double, escape, eschew, fleece, rip off, sucker, thwart **7** deceive, defraud, prevent, swindle **8** flimflam, hoodwink, sidestep, stave off **9** frustrate **10** circumvent

bill
3 dun, fin, neb, nib, one, tab, ten **4** beak, bone, buck, chit, list, note, skin **5** check, fiver, score, visor **6** charge, damage, dollar, notice, poster, roster, tenner **7** account, charges, invoice, placard, program, sawbuck, smacker, ten-spot **8** Hamilton, mandible **9** greenback, reckoning, smackeroo, statement
part: **4** cere

billet
3 bar, bed, gig, hut, job, rod **4** post, slab, spar, spot **5** berth, board, house, ingot, lodge, place, put up, stick, strip **6** bestow, canton, harbor, office **7** quarter **8** domicile, position, quarters, vocation **9** entertain, situation **10** assignment, connection, employment, encampment, livelihood, profession, occupation **11** appointment

billet-doux
8 mash note **10** love letter

billfold
6 wallet

billiards term
3 cue **4** foot, head, jaws, kiss, long, peas, pool, race, rack, spot **5** break, carom, chalk, count, masse **6** bridge, cannon, corner, crotch, inning, miscue, nurses, pocket, stance, string **7** bricole, cue ball, cushion, ferrule, kitchen, pyramid, scratch, shooter, snooker **8** apex ball, balkline, bank shot, cue stick, dead ball, jump shot, rotation, triangle **9** clean bank, eight ball **10** chuck nurse, head string, object ball **12** balance point

billingsgate
5 abuse **6** tirade **7** obloquy **9** contumely, invective **10** revilement, scurrility **12** vilification, vituperation

billion
British: **8** milliard
combining form: **4** giga

billionth
combining form: **4** nano
bill of fare
4 menu **7** program **11** carte du jour
billow
4 mass, wave **5** bulge, cloud, surge, swell **6** puff up, roller **7** balloon, upsurge
Billy Budd
author: **8** Melville (Herman)
character: **4** Vere (Captain) **8** Claggert (John)
billy club
4 cane **5** baton **6** cudgel, paddle **8** bludgeon **9** bastinado, truncheon **10** knobkerrie, nightstick
bin
4 crib **5** frame, stall **6** bunker, hamper, trough **9** container **10** receptacle
binary
4 twin, dual **5** duple **6** double, duplex, paired **7** coupled, matched, twofold **9** dualistic
bind
3 tie **4** frap, gird, tape, wrap **5** chain, cinch, strap, tie up, truss **6** cement, commit, fasten, fetter, ligate, pinion **7** bandage, confine, enchain, shackle, trammel **8** enfetter, restrain **9** constrain, constrict, indenture
binder
4 file **5** cover **6** folder, jacket **7** wrapper **9** harvester
binding
8 required **9** mandatory, requisite **10** obligatory
bindlestiff
4 hobo
binge
3 jag **4** orgy, riot, soak, tear, time, toot **5** blast, booze, fling, party, revel, souse, spree, stint **6** bender **7** blowoff, blowout, carouse, debauch, rampage, revelry, shindig, splurge, surfeit, wassail **8** carousal, gluttony **9** bacchanal, brannigan **10** debauchery, indulgence **11** bacchanalia, celebration **12** intemperance
bingo
3 yes **5** beano **7** correct
biographer
American: **5** Weems (Parson) **6** Parton (James) **7** Freeman (Douglas) **8** Bradford (Gamaliel), Sandburg (Carl) **10** McCullough (David)
English: **6** Aubrey (John), Morley (John), Walton (Izaak) **8** Strachey (Lytton)
French: **7** Maurois (André)
German: **6** Ludwig (Emil)
Greek: **8** Plutarch
Italian: **6** Vasari (Giorgio)
Roman: **9** Suetonius
Scottish **7** Boswell (James)
biography
3 bio **4** life, obit, vita **5** diary, story **6** memoir **7** history, profile **8** obituary **11** confessions
biological category
5 class, genus, order **6** family, phylum **7** kingdom, species, variety **10** subspecies
bionomics
7 ecology
Bip's creator
7 Marceau (Marcel)
bird
2 io **3** ani, auk, daw, eme, emu, ern, iwa, jay, kea, mew, moa, owl, poe, tit, tui **4** Alca, Anas, chat, Chen, coot, crow, dove, duck, erne, guan, gull, hawk, ibis, iiwi, kite, kiwi, knot, koko, lark, loon, loro, lory, mina, moho, myna, Olor, Pavo, Pica, rail, rhea, rook, ruff, shag, skua, smew, sora, Sula, swan, teal, tern, Uria, wren, Xema **5** booby, brant, buteo, cahow, crake, crane, eagle, egret, finch, galah, goose, grebe, heron, junco, macaw, merle, murre, mynah, noddy, ousel, ouzel, owlet, pewee, pewit, pipit, quail, raven, robin, stilt, snipe, stork, swift, veery, vireo **6** avocet, barbet, bulbul, canary, chough, chukar, condor, corbie, cuckoo, curlew, drongo, dunlin, falcon, fulmar, gannet, godwit, grouse, hoopoe, jabiru, jacana, jaeger, kakapo, linnet, magpie, martin, merlin, mud hen, oriole, osprey, parrot, peahen, peewit, petrel, phoebe, plover, puffin, raptor, ratite, redleg, scoter, shrike, takahe, thrush, tomtit, toucan, towhee, trogon, turaco, turkey, verdin, wigeon, willet **7** anhinga, apteryx, bittern, blue jay, bunting, bustard, buzzard, catbird, chicken, courser, creeper, dovekie, flicker, goshawk, grackle, harrier, jacamar, jackdaw, kestrel, kinglet, lapwing, limpkin, mallard, marabou, moorhen, oilbird, ostrich, peacock, pelican, penguin, pintail, quetzal, redwing, sawbill, skimmer, skylark, sparrow, swallow, tanager, tattler, titlark, touraco, vulture, wagtail, warbler, waxbill, waxwing, widgeon **8** baldpate, bellbird, blackcap, bobolink, bobwhite, brantail, caracara, cardinal, cockatoo, curassow, dabchick, dotterel, flamingo, guacharo, hornbill, killdeer, lorikeet, lyrebird, marsh hen, moorfowl, murrelet, nightjar, nuthatch, oxpecker, parakeet, pheasant, Philomel, redshank, redstart, screamer, shoebill, shoveler, starling, thrasher, throstle, titmouse, tragopan, troupial, wheatear, whimbrel, wildfowl, woodcock, woodlark **9** accipiter, albatross, broadbill, cassowary, chaffinch, chickadee, cormorant, crossbill, francolin, gallinule, guillemot, gyrfalcon, kittiwake, merganser, nighthawk, owl parrot, partridge, phalarope, ptarmigan, razorbill, sandpiper, snakebird, spoonbill, stonechat, trumpeter, turnstone **10** bufflehead, chiffchaff, flycatcher, goatsucker, kingfisher, shearwater, sheathbill **11** lammergeier, nightingale **12** whippoorwill

class: **4** Aves
colony: **5** roost **7** rookery
combining form: **5** ornis **6** ornith **7** ornitho **8** ornithes (plural)
extinct: **3** moa **4** dodo **9** aepyornis, solitaire
mythical: **3** roc **7** phoenix
relating to: **5** avian **8** ornithic
sound: **3** caw, coo **4** chip, crow, honk, hoot, peep **5** cheep, chirp, cluck, croak, quack, trill, tweet **6** squawk **7** screech, twitter
unfledged: **4** eyas **5** chick **8** nestling

birdbrain
4 clod, dodo, dolt, goof, loon **5** dummy, dunce, idiot, moron, ninny **6** nitwit **7** airhead, dullard, halfwit **8** dumbbell, imbecile, meathead, numskull **9** dumb bunny, ignoramus, numbskull, simpleton **10** nincompoop **11** featherhead

birdcage
6 aviary

birdlife
8 avifauna

bird pepper
9 chiltepin

birds' eggs
study of: **6** oology

birth
4 dawn, stem **5** arise, issue, onset, start **6** create, outset, spring **7** emanate, genesis, lineage, opening **8** delivery, generate, geniture, nascence, nascency, nativity, pedigree **9** beginning, originate **10** extraction **11** parturition **12** commencement

birth-control leader
6 Sanger (Margaret)

birth flower
April: **5** daisy
August: **9** gladiolus
December: **10** poinsettia
February: **8** primrose
January: **9** carnation
July: **8** sweet pea
June: **4** rose
March: **6** violet
May: **15** lily of the valley
November: **13** chrysanthemum
October: **6** dahlia
September: **5** aster

birthmark
4 mole **5** nevus, point, trait **7** feature **13** discoloration

Birth of a Nation director
8 Griffith (D. W.)

birthright
3 due, lot **6** legacy **7** bequest, portion **8** appanage, heirloom, heritage **9** patrimony **11** entitlement, inheritance

birthroot
8 trillium

birthstone
April: **7** diamond **8** sapphire
August: **7** peridot **8** sardonyx
December: **6** zircon **9** turquoise
February: **8** amethyst
January: **6** garnet
July: **4** ruby
June: **5** agate, pearl **11** alexandrite
March: **6** jasper **10** aquamarine, bloodstone
May: **7** emerald
November: **5** topaz
October: **4** opal **10** tourmaline
September: **8** sapphire **10** chrysolite

biscotti flavor
5 anise

biscuit
4 rusk, snap **6** cookie **7** cracker **8** cracknel, hardtack

bishop
district: **7** diocese
headdress: **5** miter, mitre
seat of office: **3** see
skullcap: **9** zucchetto
staff: **7** crosier, crozier
throne: **8** cathedra

bishopric
3 see **7** diocese

bismuth symbol
2 Bi

bison
European: **6** wisent **7** aurochs
family: **7** Bovidae
North American: **7** buffalo

bistered
4 dark **5** brown, dusky, swart, tawny **6** brunet, tanned **7** swarthy **8** brunette **11** dark-skinned

bistro
3 bar, pub **4** café **5** joint **6** nitery, tavern **7** barroom, cabaret, hot spot, niterie, taproom **8** snack bar **9** coffee bar, nightclub, night spot **10** coffee shop **11** rathskeller **13** watering place

bit
3 dab, dot, end, jot, tad **4** atom, dash, drop, iota, lump, mite, part, rein, tick, time, whet **5** borer, flake, grain, minim, pinch, scrap, shard, shred, slice, space, speck, spell, trace, while **6** minute, moment, morsel, rather, second **7** portion, segment, smidgen, stretch, trickle **8** fraction, fragment, molecule, mouthful, particle, somewhat

bit by bit
6 evenly **9** by degrees, gradually, piecemeal **12** continuously **13** slow and steady

bitch goddess
7 success

bite
3 cut, eat, lot, nip **4** chaw, chew, edge, etch, food, gnaw, kick, meal, nosh, pain, part, rust, snap, tang, tapa, zest **5** champ, chomp, erode, munch, piece, quota, share, slice, snack, stink, taste, tooth **6** crunch, morsel, nibble **7** corrode, eat away, eat into, engrave, portion **8** mouthful **9** masticate, occlusion

biting
3 raw **4** cold **5** bleak, crisp, harsh, nippy, sharp **6** bitter, severe **7** acerbic, caustic, cutting, mordant, satiric **8** freezing, incisive, piercing, scathing **9** sarcastic, trenchant **11** penetrating

bitter
4 acid, tart **5** acerb, acrid, harsh, sharp **6** severe **7** acerbic, caustic, galling, hostile, painful **8** grievous, virulent **9** rancorous, vitriolic **11** acrimonious

bitterness
4 gall **6** rancor **7** ill will **8** acridity, acrimony, asperity, coldness **9** animosity, antipathy **10** resentment

bittersweet
4 vine **8** poignant **10** nightshade

bitumen
3 tar **5** pitch **7** asphalt **8** blacktop

bivalve
4 clam, spat **6** cockle, mussel, oyster **7** geoduck, mollusc, mollusk, piddock, scallop **9** lampshell **10** brachiopod

bivouac
4 camp, tent **6** billet, encamp, laager, maroon **7** shelter, sojourn **10** encampment

bizarre
3 odd **5** antic, outré, queer, weird **7** curious, oddball, strange, uncanny, unusual **8** abnormal, atypical, freakish, peculiar, quixotic, singular **9** anomalous, eccentric, fantastic, grotesque, unearthly, unnatural **10** outlandish, outrageous **11** extravagant

bizarrerie
5 freak **6** oddity **7** anomaly, caprice, oddness **9** curiosity, weirdness **10** aberration

Bizet opera
6 Carmen

blab
3 gab, gas, jaw, yak **4** chat, leak, sing, talk, tell **5** run on, spill **6** babble, betray, burble, gabble, gossip, inform, jabber, reveal, snitch, squeal, tattle, tell on, yammer **7** blather, chatter, divulge, let slip, palaver, prattle **8** blurt out, disclose, give away, go public

blabber
3 gab, rat **4** chat, fink **5** clack, drool, prate **6** babble, canary, drivel, gabber, gabble, gossip, jabber, magpie, prater, ramble **7** blather, chatter, palaver, prattle, twaddle **8** idle talk, jabberer, prattler **9** chatterer **10** chatterbox, tattletale

blabbermouth
3 rat **4** fink **5** yenta **6** canary, gabber, gossip, magpie, prater, snitch **7** windbag **8** busybody, jabberer, prattler **10** chatterbox, talebearer, tattletale **11** stool pigeon

black
3 jet **4** ebon, inky, noir, onyx **5** ebony, raven, sable **6** pitchy **8** charcoal, funereal **9** pitch-dark
combining form: **3** mel **4** atro, mela, melo **5** melam, melan **6** melano

blackball
3 bar **4** veto, shun, snub **5** block, spurn **6** ice out, refuse, reject, strike **7** boycott, exclude, keep out, rule out **9** interdict, ostracize **11** vote against

black bass
7 sunfish

black beast
see **bête noire**

Black Beauty author
6 Sewell (Anna)

black cohosh
7 bugbane

black crappie
7 sunfish **10** calico bass

black death
6 plague **13** bubonic plague

black diamond
4 coal **8** hematite **9** carbonado

blacken
3 dim, fog, ink **4** blot, burn, char, sear, slur, soil, soot **5** cloud, libel, shade, singe, smear, sully, taint **6** bruise, darken, defame, defile, malign, scorch, vilify **7** asperse, cloud up, eclipse, slander, traduce **8** besmirch, dishonor **10** calumniate

black eye
4 blot, onus, slur **5** stain **6** bruise, defeat, shiner, stigma **7** setback

blackfish
5 whale **6** tautog **10** pilot whale

Black Forest
11 Schwarzwald
city: **10** Baden-Baden
peak: **8** Feldberg
product: **11** cuckoo clock
river: **5** Rhein, Rhine **6** Danube, Neckar

black gold
3 oil **9** petroleum

blackguard
4 heel, punk **5** abuse, cheat, knave, rogue **6** rascal **7** hoodlum, lowlife, ruffian, villain **8** hooligan, scalawag **9** charlatan, miscreant, reprobate, scoundrel **10** delinquent, mountebank **11** rapscallion

blackhead
3 zit **4** spot **5** sebum **6** pimple **10** larval clam

blackjack
3 oak, sap **4** bash, club, cosh **6** coerce **7** pontoon, tankard **8** bludgeon **9** twenty-one, vingt-et-un **10** sphalerite

black lead
8 graphite

black letter
6 Gothic **7** Fraktur **10** Old English

blacklist
3 bar **4** oust **5** expel, purge, smear **6** banish, impugn **7** boycott, condemn, exclude, shut out **8** denounce **9** ostracize, proscribe **10** stigmatize

blackmail
5 bleed **6** extort, payoff **7** milking, squeeze **8** chantage, coercion **9** extortion, hush money, shake down

Blackmore novel
10 Lorna Doone

black out
4 edit, wipe **5** annul, erase, faint, swoon **6** cancel, censor, cut off, darken, delete, efface, excise **7** conceal, eclipse, expunge **8** collapse, make dark, sanitize, suppress **9** eradicate, expurgate **10** blue-pencil, obliterate

blackpoll
7 warbler

Black Prince
6 Edward

Black Sea
arm: **4** Azov
city: **5** Yalta **6** Odessa **9** Constanta
peninsula: **6** Crimea **7** Crimean

Blackshirt
7 fascist

blacksmith
6 forger **7** farrier, striker **10** horseshoer

blacktail
8 mule deer

blackthorn
4 plum, sloe

black widow
6 spider

bladder
3 sac **4** cyst **5** pouch **7** blister, vacuole **7** vesicle
gall: **9** cholecyst

blade
4 beau, buck, dude, edge, leaf, shiv **5** knife, sword **6** runner **9** swordsman

blah
4 bosh, dull, flat, tame **5** ho-hum, hooey, tired, vapid **6** boring, bunkum, dreary, humbug, stodgy **7** humdrum **8** banausic, lifeless, mediocre, nonsense, plodding **10** balderdash, lackluster, monotonous, pedestrian **11** indifferent, uninspiring **13** uninteresting

Blake work
5 Tiger (The), Tyger (The) **10** Book of Thel (The) **16** Songs of Innocence **17** Songs of Experience

blamable
see **blameworthy**

blame
3 rap **4** onus **5** fault, guilt, knock **6** accuse, charge, finger, indict **7** censure, condemn **8** denounce, reproach **9** criticize, liability, reprehend, reprobate **10** accusation, imputation **11** culpability **12** condemnation, denunciation, reprehension
Scottish: **4** wite, wyte **6** dirdum

blameless
4 good, pure **5** clean, moral **7** perfect, upright **8** innocent, unguilty, virtuous **9** crimeless, exemplary, faultless, guiltless, honorable, lily-white, righteous, unsullied **10** immaculate, impeccable, inculpable **13** unimpeachable

blameworthy
3 lax **5** amiss **6** guilty, liable, sinful **7** at fault **8** criminal, culpable, derelict **9** negligent **10** answerable, censurable, delinquent, indictable, punishable **11** disgraceful, inexcusable, responsible **12** dishonorable **13** reprehensible, objectionable

blanch
4 fade, pale **5** quail, scald, start **6** bleach, shrink, whiten **7** decolor, lighten, parboil **8** etiolate

blanched
3 wan **4** ashy, pale **5** ashen, faded, livid, peaky, waxen, white **6** anemic, doughy, pallid, peaked **7** ghostly **9** bloodless, colorless, washed out **10** cadaverous

Blancheflor's beloved
6 Flores, Floris

bland
4 dull, flat, blah, mild, soft **5** balmy, banal, vapid **6** boring, gentle, pablum **7** insipid, restful, sapless **8** soothing **9** calmative **10** complacent, flavorless, monotonous, namby-pamby, wishy-washy **12** ingratiating **13** nonirritating

blandish
3 con, woo **4** coax, fawn, urge **5** cozen **6** cajole, stroke **7** blarney, flatter, wheedle **8** butter up, inveigle, soft-soap **9** importune, sweet-talk **10** curry favor

blandishment
3 oil **5** honey **7** blarney, eyewash, incense, promise **8** flattery, soft soap **9** adulation,

seduction, sweet talk **10** allurement, compliment, inducement, sycophancy, temptation

blank
3 gap **4** bare, dull, seal, skip, void **5** chasm, dazed, empty, space **6** stupid, vacant, virgin **7** deadpan, obscure, vacuous **8** complete, omission, outright, spotless, unfilled **9** impassive **10** empty space, interstice, obliterate **11** featureless **12** inexpressive, unexpressive

blanket
4 bury, hide **5** cover, quilt, throw **6** afghan, stroud **7** overlay **8** coverlet, mackinaw, sweeping **9** comforter **10** overspread

blankness
6 vacuum **7** nullity, vacancy, vacuity **9** emptiness **10** desolation

blare
4 roar **5** blast, shout **6** clamor, jangle **7** trumpet

blaring
4 loud **5** sharp **6** brassy, shrill **7** clarion, jarring, roaring **8** blinding, piercing, strident **9** deafening, dissonant **10** stentorian **11** ear-piercing, penetrating, stentorious **12** earsplitting

blarney
3 con, oil **4** coax, bunk **5** charm, honey, hooey **6** bunkum, cajole, humbug **7** baloney, incense, wheedle **8** blandish, buncombe, cajolery, flattery, inveigle, nonsense, soft soap **9** adulation, sweet-talk **11** compliments **12** blandishment, inveiglement

blasé
4 cool **5** bored, jaded, sated **6** breezy **7** knowing, offhand, unmoved, worldly **9** apathetic, incurious, surfeited, unexcited **10** world-weary **11** indifferent, unconcerned, worldly-wise **12** disenchanted, uninterested **13** disillusioned, sophisticated

blaspheme
4 cuss **5** abuse, curse, swear **6** revile **7** pollute, profane **8** denounce, execrate **9** castigate, excoriate

blasphemous
6 coarse, sinful **7** godless, impious, obscene, profane, ungodly **10** irreverent **12** sacrilegious **13** disrespectful

blasphemy
3 sin **5** abuse, error **6** heresy **7** cursing, cussing, impiety, mockery **8** swearing **9** profanity, sacrilege, violation **10** execration, heterodoxy, iconoclasm **11** desecration, imprecation, irreverence, malediction, profanation

blast
3 din **4** bang, beat, blow, boom, clap, dash, gale, gust, kill, peal, ruin, slam, toot **5** blare, burst, crack, crash, salvo, shoot, smash, wreck **6** attack, blight, blow up, damage, squall, wallop **7** destroy, lambast, shatter, shrivel, trumpet **8** dynamite, lambaste, outburst **9** explosion, castigate, discharge, overwhelm, shock wave **10** annihilate, detonation

blat
4 bray **5** blurt **6** cry out **7** exclaim **8** blurt out

blatant
4 bald, loud **5** brash, clear, gaudy, naked, noisy, overt, saucy **6** arrant, brassy, brazen, crying, flashy, garish, patent, tawdry, vulgar **7** glaring, jarring, obvious **8** flagrant, immodest, impudent, insolent, manifest, overbold, strident **9** barefaced, clamorous, obtrusive, shameless, unabashed **10** boisterous, outrageous, scurrilous, unblushing, vociferous **11** conspicuous, loudmouthed, transparent **12** ear-splitting, obstreperous

blather
3 gab, gas, jaw, rot, yak **4** bosh, gush, rave, stir **5** bleat, drool, hokum, prate **6** babble, bunkum, drivel, effuse, gabble, jabber, natter, yammer **7** blabber, chatter, enthuse, palaver, prattle, rubbish, twaddle **8** chitchat, claptrap, idle talk, nonsense **9** commotion **10** balderdash, doubletalk, flapdoodle **12** gobbledygook

blaze
4 burn, fire **5** burst, flame, flare, glare, shine **7** flare up **8** eruption, outburst **10** incandesce **13** conflagration
Scottish: 3 low **4** lowe

blazer
6 marker, reefer **9** sport coat **10** sports coat **12** sports jacket

blazes
4 hell **5** abyss, Hades, Sheol **6** Tophet **7** Gehenna, inferno **9** perdition **11** netherworld

blazing
4 keen **5** afire, fiery **6** aflame, alight, ardent, fervid, on fire, red-hot **7** burning, fervent, flaming, flaring, furious, glowing, ignited, intense, lighted **8** dazzling, feverish, powerful, speeding, white-hot **9** brilliant, perfervid **11** conflagrant, impassioned **12** incandescent **13** scintillating

blazon
4 deck **5** adorn, sound **7** declare, display, publish, trumpet **8** announce, proclaim **9** advertise, broadcast **10** coat of arms, promulgate **11** ostentation

bleach
3 dim **4** fade, pale **5** white **6** blanch, blench, purify, whiten **7** decolor, launder, wash out **8** etiolate, peroxide, sanitize **9** whitewash

bleak
3 raw, sad **4** bare, cold, dour, drab, grim, wild **5** chill, drear, empty, harsh, stark **6** barren, chilly,

dismal, dreary, gloomy, lonely, severe, somber, wintry **7** austere, exposed, joyless **8** blighted, desolate, funereal, hopeless **9** cheerless, windswept, woebegone **10** depressing, despondent, oppressive, melancholy

blear
3 dim, fog **4** blur, dull, mist, murk, veil **5** bedim, faint, vague **6** hidden, shroud **7** becloud, obscure, shadowy, unclear **10** indistinct

bleary
3 dim **5** all in, faint, filmy, fuzzy, milky, spent, tired, vague **6** pooped, sapped, used-up, wasted **7** blurred, drained, obscure, shadowy, unclear, worn-out **8** depleted **9** enervated, exhausted, washed-out **10** indistinct

bleat
3 baa **4** blat, carp, crab, fuss, yawp **5** gripe, whine **6** bellow, grouse, squawk, yammer **7** blather, grumble, whimper **8** complain **9** bellyache

bleed
3 sap, run **4** milk, ooze, pity, seep **5** drain, exude, leech, mulct **6** extort, fleece **7** diffuse, extract **9** blackmail **10** hemorrhage

blemish
3 mar **4** blot, flaw, harm, mark, maim, mole, scar, spot, vice, wart **5** fault, nevus, spoil, stain **6** blotch, damage, deface, defect, impair, injure, pimple, stigma **7** blacken, distort, freckle, pervert, tarnish, vitiate **8** impurity, mutilate, pockmark **9** birthmark **12** imperfection **13** disfigurement

blench
3 shy **4** balk, duck, fade **5** blink, cower, quail, quake, start, wince **6** flinch, purify, recoil, shrink, whiten **7** launder, shy away, squinch, tremble **8** draw back, etiolate **9** whitewash

blend
3 fit, mix **4** brew, fuse, meld, weld **5** admix, alloy, merge, unify, union, unite **6** commix, fusion, go with, hybrid, mingle **7** amalgam, combine, mélange, mixture **8** beverage, coalesce, compound, conflate, immingle, infusion, intermix, mishmash **9** admixture, commingle, composite, harmonize, integrate **10** amalgamate, commixture, concoction, synthesize **12** adulteration, amalgamation, intermixture

blender setting
3 mix **4** chop, whip **5** grate, mince, puree **7** liquefy

blesbok
8 antelope

bless
4 laud **5** exalt, extol, endow, favor, grace **6** anoint, bestow, hallow, praise, uphold **7** approve, beatify, glorify, magnify **8** enshrine, eulogize, make holy, sanctify **10** consecrate

blessed
4 holy **5** happy, lucky **6** joyous, sacred **7** saintly **8** beatific, hallowed **9** beatified, fortunate, venerated **10** inviolable, sacrosanct, sanctified **11** consecrated

blessedness
5 bliss **8** felicity, sanctity **9** beatitude, godliness, happiness **12** blissfulness

blessing
4 boon, good, okay **5** asset, favor, grace **6** assent, bounty, thanks **7** benefit, benison, consent, fortune, godsend, support **8** approval, good luck, windfall **9** advantage **10** invocation, permission **11** approbation, benediction, endorsement, good fortune, valediction **12** commendation, consecration, thanksgiving **13** encouragement

"____ bleu!"
5 Sacré

blight
3 mar, nip **4** bane, dash, ruin **5** blast, decay, spoil, wreck **6** canker, wither **7** disease, scourge, shrivel **9** withering **10** pestilence **13** deterioration

blimp
7 airship **8** zeppelin **9** dirigible

blind
4 boma, daze, dull **5** decoy, front, shade, shill **6** dazzle **7** eyeless, muddled, shutter **8** bedazzle, jalousie, unseeing **9** enclosure, sightless **10** visionless

blind alley
6 pocket **7** dead end, impasse **8** cul-de-sac, deadlock **9** stone wall **10** standstill **11** obstruction

blind god
4 Eros, Hodr, Hoth **5** Cupid, Hoder, Hodur, Hothr

blindworm
8 slowworm

blink
3 bat **4** wink **5** flash, yield **6** give in, squint **7** flicker, flutter, nictate, twinkle **9** nictitate **11** scintillate

blink at
4 omit **5** clear, let go **6** bypass, excuse, forget, ignore, slight **7** condone, connive, let pass, neglect **8** discount, overlook, pass over **9** disregard, exonerate, whitewash

blip
6 censor, screen **9** deviation, expurgate, radar spot **10** bowdlerize

bliss
3 joy **4** Zion **6** Canaan, heaven **7** ecstasy, elation, elysium, nirvana, rapture **8** empyrean, euphoria, paradise **9** beatitude, cloud nine, happiness **10** exaltation **11** blessedness

blissful
5 happy **6** divine, elated, joyful, joyous **8** beatific, ecstatic, euphoric **9** ambrosial, delighted, entranced, rapturous **10** delightful, entrancing

blissfulness
3 joy **7** ecstasy **8** euphoria **9** beatitude, happiness **10** exaltation **11** contentment

blister
4 bleb, flay, lash **5** blain, bulla, slash **6** assail, canker, scathe, scorch **7** lambast, scarify, scourge, vesicle **8** lambaste **9** castigate, excoriate

blithe
3 gay **4** boon **5** happy, jolly, merry, sunny **6** bouncy, casual, cheery, chirpy, jaunty, jocund, jovial **7** gleeful **8** carefree, careless, cheerful, chirrupy, gladsome, heedless, mirthful **9** lightsome, sprightly, unworried, vivacious **10** untroubled **11** thoughtless **12** lighthearted

blitz
4 raid, rush **6** attack **7** air raid, bombard, bombing **8** shelling **9** offensive, onslaught **10** mass attack **11** bombardment

blitzkrieg
6 attack **7** assault, bombing **9** offensive, onslaught **11** bombardment

blizzard
4 gale **6** squall **8** whiteout **9** snowstorm

bloat
5 bulge, swell **6** billow, expand, fatten, puff up **7** balloon, distend, enlarge, inflate **10** distension

bloated
5 puffy, tumid **6** puffed **7** pompous, swollen **8** arrogant, enlarged, inflated **9** distended, overblown, overlarge **11** pretentious **13** self-important

bloc
4 band, ring **5** cabal, party, union **6** clique, league **7** combine, faction **8** alliance **9** coalition **10** consortium, contingent, federation **11** association, combination **13** confederation

block
3 bar **4** clog, fill, hunk, Lego, plug, slab, stop, wall, wing **5** brick, choke, chunk, close, ingot **6** cut off, hinder, impede **7** barrier, congest, occlude, stopper **8** obstacle, obstruct **9** barricade, hindrance, intercept

blockade
3 bar **4** stop, wall **5** beset, hem in, siege **6** shut in **7** barrier, besiege **8** close off, encircle, obstruct, stoppage **9** barricade, beleaguer, blank wall, hindrance, roadblock **10** impediment **11** obstruction

blockage
3 bar **4** clog, halt **7** barrier **8** obstacle, stoppage **10** impediment **11** obstruction

blockbuster
4 bomb **11** spectacular

blockhead
3 oaf **4** clod, dolt, dope, fool **5** clunk, dummy, dunce, idiot, moron, ninny **6** nitwit **7** halfwit, jackass **8** clodpole, clodpoll, dumbbell, imbecile, numskull **9** ignoramus, lamebrain, numbskull, simpleton **10** nincompoop **12** featherbrain

blockheaded
4 dull, dumb **5** dense, thick **6** obtuse, stupid **7** doltish **9** brainless, dim-witted **10** slow-witted

block out
4 mark **5** chart, close, draft, frame **6** hinder, screen, sketch **7** obscure, outline, prepare, repress, shut off **8** indicate, obstruct **9** adumbrate, formulate

block up
3 dam **4** clog, fill, plug, stop **5** choke **7** congest

bloke
3 guy, man **4** chap, gent **6** fellow **9** gentleman

blond
4 fair, gold, pale **5** light, sandy, straw, tawny **6** flaxen, golden **7** towhead **8** platinum **9** champagne, towheaded **10** fair-haired **11** sandy-haired **12** honey-colored

blood
4 gore **7** descent, kindred, kinship, lineage **8** ancestry **10** extraction
cancer of: **8** leukemia
cell: **3** red **5** white **8** hemocyte, monocyte, platelet **9** corpuscle, leukocyte **10** lymphocyte **11** erythrocyte, granulocyte
clot: **8** thrombus
coloring matter: **10** hemoglobin
combining form: **3** hem **4** hemo
disease: **6** anemia **8** leukemia **10** hemophilia
factor: **2** Rh
fluid part: **5** serum **6** plasma
of the gods: **5** ichor
particle in: **7** embolus
poisoning: **6** pyemia **7** toxemia **10** septicemia
pressure: **8** systolic **9** diastolic
relating to: **5** hemic
serum: **6** plasma
study of: **10** hematology
sugar: **7** glucose

bloodbath
7 carnage, slaying **8** butchery, massacre **9** slaughter **10** decimation **12** annihilation **13** extermination

bloodless
3 wan **4** ashy, dull, pale, weak **5** ashen, waxen **6** anemic, feeble, pallid, sallow, torpid **8** listless **9** insensate, unfeeling **10** insensible, nonviolent **11** coldhearted, passionless, unemotional

bloodletting
4 gore **7** carnage, killing **8** butchery, shambles, violence **9** slaughter **10** phlebotomy **11** venesection

bloodline
6 family, strain **7** descent, lineage **8** ancestry, pedigree **10** family tree

bloodroot
7 puccoon

bloodshed
4 gore **7** carnage, killing **8** butchery **9** slaughter

bloodstained
4 gory **6** grisly **7** imbrued, wounded **8** sanguine **10** sanguinary **11** ensanguined, sanguineous

bloodstone
10 chalcedony

bloodsucker
3 ked **4** tick **5** lamia, leech **6** lizard, sponge **7** sponger, vampire **8** hanger-on, parasite, sheep ked **10** freeloader **12** lounge lizard

bloodthirsty
5 rabid **8** ravening, sanguine **9** cutthroat, homicidal, murdering, murderous, predatory, voracious **10** sanguinary **11** sanguineous

blood vessel
4 vein **5** aorta **6** artery **7** jugular **9** capillary
combining form: 3 vas **4** angi, vasi, vaso **5** angio

bloody
4 gory, grim, very **5** cruel **6** damage, damned, deadly, grisly **7** blasted, hateful, imbrued, wounded **8** accursed, infernal, sanguine **9** cutthroat, homicidal, murdering, murderous **10** detestable, sanguinary **11** ensanguined, sanguineous **12** death-dealing, slaughtering

bloom
4 blow, glow, open, posy **5** blush **6** floret, flower, thrive, unfold **7** blossom, burgeon, coating, develop, dusting, prosper **8** flourish, rosiness **10** cloudiness, effloresce **13** discoloration

blooper
4 goof, slip, trip **5** boner, break, error, fluff, gaffe, lapse **6** boo-boo, bungle, howler, slipup **7** blunder, faux pas, fly ball, misstep, mistake, offense **8** solecism **9** indecorum, false step **11** impropriety **12** indiscretion

blossom
3 bud, wax **4** blow, glow, grow, open, posy **5** bloom, blush, flush **6** expand, flower, mature, thrive, unfold **7** burgeon, develop, prosper **8** flourish, floweret, progress **10** effloresce, peak period **13** efflorescence

blot
4 blur, mark, onus, slur, smut, soil, spot **5** brand, odium, smear, speck, stain, sully **6** absorb, smudge, stigma **7** bestain, blemish, spatter, tarnish **8** black eye, discolor, disgrace **9** bespatter, moral flaw

blotch
4 mark, spot **5** stain **6** macula, macule, mottle, smudge **7** blemish, splotch **12** imperfection

blot out
4 raze, void **5** annul, crush, erase, quash, quell, scrub **6** cancel, delete, efface, squash **7** abolish, destroy, expunge **9** eliminate, eradicate, extirpate **10** annihilate, extinguish, obliterate **11** exterminate

blotto
see **drunk**

blouse
5 middy, shell, shirt, smock, tunic **6** guimpe

bloviate
4 rail, rant, rave **5** mouth, orate, spout **7** bluster, carry on, declaim, inveigh, soapbox, talk big **8** harangue, perorate, sound off, splutter **9** hold forth **10** vociferate

blow
3 bop, fan, hit, jar **4** bang, bash, belt, biff, bump, cuff, damn, fail, gasp, gust, huff, pipe, puff, slam, slug, swat, toot, whop, wind **5** boast, botch, crack, drive, erupt, leave, pound, punch, shock, slosh, smack, smash, sound, spend, waste, whack **6** buffet, depart, impact, mishap, thwack, wallop **7** assault, breathe, chagrin, consume, debacle, explode, flutter, fritter, trumpet **8** calamity, disaster, flounder, knockout, squander **9** bombshell, collision, dissipate, throw away **10** concussion, misfortune, trifle away **11** catastrophe

blow-by-blow
4 full **5** fussy **6** minute **7** careful, precise **8** detailed, itemized, thorough **10** exhaustive, meticulous, scrupulous **13** thoroughgoing

blowhard
see **boaster**

blow in
4 land **5** pop by **6** appear, arrive, drop by, show up, turn up **7** hit town **11** materialize

blowout
4 bash, fete, gala, riot, tear **5** binge, blast, break, party, split, spree **6** frolic, shindy **7** shindig, victory **8** carousal, flat tire **9** festivity

blowsy
5 dingy, ruddy **6** florid, frowsy, sloppy, untidy **7** flushed, healthy, unkempt **8** blooming, blushing **10** bedraggled

blow up
4 bomb, burn, fume, rage **5** bloat, burst, erupt, flare, go off, storm, swell **6** expand, lose it, seethe **7** bristle, distend, enlarge, explode, inflate,

magnify, rupture, shatter **8** boil over, demolish, detonate, dynamite, heighten, mushroom **9** discredit, fulminate, overstate **10** aggrandize

blowy
4 airy, wild **5** fresh, gusty, windy **6** breezy, stormy **7** squally **8** blustery **9** windswept **11** tempestuous

blubber
3 cry, fat, sob **4** bawl, flab, keen, lard, pipe, wail, weep **5** flesh **6** snivel **7** carry on **8** whale fat

bludgeon
3 bat **4** club **5** baton, billy, bully **6** attack, cudgel, hector **7** bluster, war club **8** browbeat, bulldoze, bullyrag **9** bastinado, billy club, blackjack, strong-arm, truncheon **10** intimidate, nightstick
British: **4** cosh

blue
3 low, sad, sea **4** cyan, down, glum, lewd, navy, racy **5** bawdy, ocean, royal, salty, spicy **6** cobalt, gloomy, risqué **7** naughty, profane, unhappy **8** dejected, downcast, indecent, off-color **9** depressed, woebegone **10** despondent, dispirited, melancholy, suggestive **11** downhearted
combining form: **4** cyan **5** cyano
dark: **4** anil **5** perse **6** indigo
dye: **4** woad
grayish: **5** merle, slate
greenish: **4** aqua, cyan, teal **5** beryl **6** cobalt **7** azurite **9** turquoise
reddish: **5** smalt **6** marine, purple, violet **7** cyanine, gentian, lobelia
sky: **5** azure **8** cerulean

____ Blue
3 Ben **9** Little Boy

blue blood
4 lady, lord, peer **5** elite, noble **6** aristo **7** royalty **8** nobleman **9** gentility, gentleman, patrician **10** aristocrat, noblewoman **11** gentle birth, gentlewoman

bluebonnet
4 Scot **11** Texas lupine

Blue Boy painter
12 Gainsborough (Thomas)

bluecoat
3 cop, law **4** fuzz **5** bobby **6** copper **9** constable, patrolman, policeman

Bluegrass State
8 Kentucky

Blue Grotto site
5 Capri

bluejacket
4 mate, salt, swab **5** limey **6** sailor, seaman **7** swabbie **9** sailorman

blue jeans
5 Levis **6** denims

blue moon
3 age, eon, era **4** aeon **5** epoch **7** dog's age **8** eternity, lifetime **10** generation

bluenose
4 prig, snob **5** prude **7** puritan **9** Mrs. Grundy, nice Nelly **10** goody-goody

bluenosed
4 prim **5** rigid **6** prissy, proper, square, stuffy **7** prudish **8** overnice, priggish **9** Victorian **10** scrupulous, tight-laced **11** puritanical, strait-laced

blue-pencil
3 cut **4** edit, trim **5** emend **6** cut out, delete, excise, remove, revise **7** clean up **8** boil down, cross out **9** strike out, tighten up

bluepoint
6 oyster

blueprint
3 map **4** cast, plan, plot **5** chart, draft, frame, model, trace **6** design, devise, rubric, scheme, set out, sketch **7** arrange, diagram, outline, picture, project **8** game plan, strategy **9** delineate **10** conception, rough draft **11** description

blue-ribbon
3 top **4** A-one **5** prime, prize **6** Grade A, tiptop **7** capital, premier, stellar **8** five-star, topnotch, superior **9** excellent, first-rate, top-drawer **10** first-class, top-quality, world-class **11** outstanding **12** prize-winning

blues
4 funk **5** dumps, gloom, grief **6** lament **7** sadness, trouble **8** doldrums, glumness **9** dejection, pessimism **10** depression, desolation, low spirits, melancholy, woefulness **11** despondency, melancholia, unhappiness **12** hopelessness, mournfulness

blues musician
3 Guy (Buddy) **4** Cray (Robert), King (Albert, B. B.), Wolf (Howlin') **5** Bland (Bobby "Blue"), Brown (Clarence "Gatemouth"), Dixon (Willie), Foley (Sue), Handy (W. C.), James (Elmore), Myers (Sam), Smith (Bessie), Wells (Junior) **6** Hooker (John Lee), Rainey (Gertrude "Ma"), Taylor (Koko), Turner (Joe), Walker (T-Bone), Waters (Ethel, Muddy) **7** Broonzy (Big Bill), Diddley (Bo), Collins (Albert), Hammond (John), Hopkins (Sam "Lightnin'"), Johnson (Robert), Rushing (Jimmy) **8** Burnside (R. L.), Copeland (Johnny) **9** Jefferson (Blind Lemon), Leadbelly, Ledbetter (Huddie) **10** Williamson (John Lee, Sonny Boy)

bluff
3 act, con **4** curt, fake, fool, jive, ruse, sham, show **5** blunt, cliff, feign, frank, gruff, rough, trick **6** abrupt, betray, candid, crusty, delude, direct, hearty, humbug **7** beguile, brusque,

deceive, fake out, mislead, playact, pretend **8** headland, pretense **9** deception, outspoken, precipice, steep bank **10** escarpment, forthright, no-nonsense, promontory, subterfuge **11** counterfeit, double-cross, plainspoken, short-spoken **13** unceremonious

blunder
3 err **4** bull, gaff, goof, mess, muff, slip, trip **5** boner, botch, error, fluff, gaffe, gum up, lapse, lurch, misdo, snafu **6** bobble, bollix, bumble, bungle, foul up, fumble, goof up, howler, mess up, wander **7** balls-up, blooper, failure, faux pas, louse up, misstep, mistake, screw up, stumble **8** disaster, flounder **12** indiscretion, misadventure

blunderbuss
3 gun **4** dolt **5** klutz **6** galoot, lummox **7** bungler, firearm **8** bonehead, numskull **9** blockhead, numbskull **10** stumblebum **13** butterfingers

blunt
4 bald, calm, curt **5** allay, bluff, brief, frank, gruff, plain, rough, terse **6** abrupt, benumb, candid, crusty, deaden, direct, lessen, obtuse **7** brusque, rounded, uncivil **8** enfeeble, not sharp, snippety **10** forthright **11** desensitize, insensitive, plainspoken, unvarnished **12** discourteous **13** unceremonious

blur
3 dim, fog **4** blot, dull, mist **5** befog, blear, cloud, muddy, smear, stain, taint **6** smudge, stigma **7** becloud, besmear, confuse, obscure, tarnish **8** besmirch, discolor
in printing: **6** mackle

blurb
2 ad **4** hype, plug, puff **5** press, promo **6** notice **7** write-up **8** good word **9** promotion **12** commendation

blurry
4 hazy **5** vague **6** cloudy **7** clouded, unclear **9** undefined, unfocused **10** indistinct

blurt
4 blab, blat, bolt **5** spill **6** cry out, let out **7** divulge, exclaim, let slip, spit out **8** disclose, give away **9** ejaculate

blush
4 burn, glow, rose, view **5** bloom, color, flame, flush, rouge **6** mantle, pinken, redden, ruddle **7** blossom, crimson, redness, turn red **8** mantling, rosiness

bluster
4 bawl, crow, gust, huff, rage, roar, rout **5** blast, bully, prate, storm, strut, vaunt **6** bellow, clamor, hector, lean on **7** bombast, bravado, dragoon, roister, swagger, talk big **8** boasting, browbeat, bulldoze, bullyrag, domineer **9** gasconade **10** grandstand, intimidate **11** braggadocio

blustery
4 wild **5** blowy, gusty, rough **6** drafty, raging, raving, stormy **7** furious, squally, violent **9** truculent, turbulent **10** boisterous, tumultuous **11** tempestuous

boa
5 scarf, snake

Boadicea clan
5 Iceni

boar
3 pig **4** male **5** swine

board
4 fare, feed, food, lath, slab, slat **5** catch, get on, hop on, house, lodge, meals, panel, plank, put up, table **6** billet, embark **7** emplane, entrain, quarter **9** directors **11** directorate
artist's: **7** palette
mystic: **5** Ouija

boarder
5 guest **6** lodger, renter, roomer, tenant

board game
see at **game**

boarding house
6 hostel **7** hospice, lodging, pension **8** pensione

boardwalk
7 gangway **9** esplanade, promenade

boast
3 own **4** blow, brag, crow, have, puff **5** exalt, exult, glory, mouth, prate, preen, strut, vaunt **6** parade **7** bluster, bombast, bravado, contain, enlarge, exhibit, inflate, possess, show off, swagger, talk big **9** gasconade **10** exaggerate, grandstand **11** rodomontade **12** exaggeration

boaster
6 gascon **7** egotist, peacock, show-off **8** big mouth, blowhard, braggart **11** braggadocio, rodomontade

boastful
4 vain **5** cocky **6** braggy **8** arrogant, braggart, puffed-up, vaunting **9** bigheaded, conceited, egotistic **11** egotistical, pretentious, swellheaded **12** vainglorious **13** swelled-headed
Scottish: **6** vaunty

boat
3 ark, hoy, tug **4** dhow, dory, junk, pram, prau, proa, punt, scow, ship, yawl **5** balsa, barge, canoe, coble, ferry, kayak, ketch, scull, shell, skiff, sloop, smack, umiak, yacht **6** bateau, bugeye, caïque, cutter, dinghy, hooker, lateen, lugger, packet, sampan, vessel, wherry **7** caravel, coracle, cruiser, currach, curragh, gondola, inboard, lighter, pinnace, pirogue, pontoon, shallop, steamer, trawler, vedette, vidette **8** outboard, runabout, schooner, trimaran **9** catamaran, hydrofoil

bottom projection: 4 keel
captain: 5 pilot 6 master 7 skipper
dock, basin: 6 marina
front end of: 3 bow 4 fore, prow
on a ship: 3 gig 6 launch 7 pinnace
race: 7 regatta
rear end of: 3 aft 5 stern
song: 6 chanty, shanty 7 chantey 9 barcarole 10 barcarolle

boatman
3 tar 4 mate, swab 5 limey 6 Charon, sailor 7 mariner, oarsman, paddler 8 deckhand, water dog 9 gondolier, navigator

boat-shaped
8 scaphoid 9 navicular

Boaz's wife
4 Ruth

bob
3 jig, nod, rap, tap 4 buff, clip, crop, dock, trim 5 bunch, float 6 bounce, curtsy, jiggle, jounce, polish, trifle, wobble 7 cluster, curtsey, nosegay 8 shilling 9 genuflect

bobbery
3 ado, din, row 4 fray, riot 5 babel, noise 6 bedlam, hubbub, racket, ruckus, rumpus 7 ferment, ruction 9 commotion, confusion 10 hullabaloo, hurly-burly 11 disturbance, pandemonium

bobbin
4 pirn 5 quill, spool, wheel 7 spindle 8 cylinder

bobble
3 bob, dud 4 flub, goof, mess, muff 5 botch, error, fluff, gum up 6 ball up, bollix, bumble, bungle, flub up, fumble, goof up, muff up 7 blooper, failure, louse up, mistake

bobby
3 law 6 copper, peeler 7 officer 9 constable, patrolman, policeman

bobwhite
5 quail 9 partridge

Boccaccio
beloved: 9 Fiammetta
tales: 9 Decameron

bode
4 hint 5 augur 6 signal, warn of 7 betoken, portend, presage, promise, signify, suggest 8 foreshow, indicate 9 foretoken, prefigure 10 foreshadow

bodega
3 bar, pub 6 saloon 7 barroom, grocery 8 wineshop 12 general store

bodement
4 omen, sign 5 hunch 6 augury 7 portent, presage 8 prophecy 9 foretoken, harbinger 10 foreboding, intimation, prediction, prognostic 11 premonition 12 presentiment

bodiless
7 ghostly 8 ethereal, spectral 9 unfleshly 10 discarnate, immaterial, unphysical 11 disembodied, incorporeal, nonmaterial 12 apparitional 13 insubstantial

bodily
6 carnal 7 en masse, earthly, fleshly, sensual, somatic, totally 8 corporal, entirely, physical, visceral 9 corporeal 10 altogether, completely 11 unspiritual

bodkin
4 shiv 5 blade, knife, shank 6 dagger, lancet, needle 7 poniard 8 stiletto

____ bodkins
4 odds

body
4 bulk, core, form, hull, mass, soma 5 frame, stiff, stock, torso 6 corpse, corpus 7 anatomy, cadaver, carcass, chassis, corpora (plural), remains 8 physique 9 aggregate, substance
combining form: 4 dema, soma, some, somi (plural) 5 somat, somia, somus 6 somata (plural), somato
human: 4 clay

body cavity
5 cecum, sinus 6 coelom 7 abdomen 8 hemocoel

body check
5 block

bodyguard
7 retinue 9 attendant, protector

body of water
3 bay, sea 4 cove, gulf, lake, pond, pool 5 bight, brook, creek, fiord, firth, fjord, inlet, ocean, river 6 harbor, lagoon, puddle, stream 7 channel, estuary 9 reservoir

body passage
4 duct, vein 5 canal 6 artery, meatus, ureter, vagina, venule, vessel 7 trachea, urethra 8 bronchus 9 arteriole, capillary, esophagus, intestine 10 bronchiole 13 bronchial tube, fallopian tube

body politic
5 state 6 nation 11 nation-state

boffo
3 gag, gas, hit 4 wild 5 laugh 6 scream 7 sold-out 8 smash-hit, smashing 10 successful 11 sensational

bog
3 fen 4 mire, quag 5 delay, marsh, swamp 6 impede, morass, muskeg, slough, slow up 8 quagmire 9 swampland

boggy
4 miry 5 mucky 6 marshy, quaggy, swampy 7 sloughy

Bogart, Humphrey
film: **6** Sahara **7** Dead End, Sabrina **8** Big Sleep (The), Key Largo **10** Casablanca, High Sierra **11** Caine Mutiny (The) **12** African Queen (The) **13** Maltese Falcon (The) **15** Petrified Forest (The) **16** To Have and Have Not **24** Treasure of the Sierra Madre (The)
wife: **6** Bacall (Lauren)

bog down
4 flag, mire **5** choke, delay, stall **6** detain, falter, hang up, hinder, impede, retard, slow up **7** embroil, set back, slacken **8** encumber, keep back, obstruct, slow down **9** lose steam **10** decelerate

bogey
5 ghost, haunt, shade, spook **6** scarer, shadow, spirit, wraith **7** phantom, specter **8** phantasm, revenant **10** apparition

bogeyman
5 spook **7** bugbear, chimera, monster, phantom, specter, spectre **10** apparition

boggle
4 balk, mess, muff, stun **5** amaze, botch, fudge, gum up, shock, wreck **6** bollix, bungle, cobble, goof up, mess up, strain **7** astound, louse up, nonplus, stagger, stumble, stupefy **8** astonish, bewilder, bowl over, confound **9** dumbfound, mishandle, mismanage, overwhelm, take aback **11** flabbergast

boggy
4 miry **5** mucky **6** marshy, quaggy, swampy **7** sloughy

bogus
4 fake, mock, sham **5** false, phony, pseud, snide **6** ersatz, forged, pseudo **7** fictive, pretend **8** invented, specious, spurious **9** brummagem, concocted, imitation, pinchbeck, simulated, trumped up **10** artificial, fabricated, fraudulent, mendacious **11** counterfeit

Bohème, La
character: **4** Mimi **7** Rodolfo
composer: **7** Puccini (Giacomo)
setting: **5** Paris

bohemian
4 arty, boho **5** artsy, gypsy, hippy **6** hippie **7** beatnik, dropout, oddball, offbeat **8** maverick, vagabond, wanderer **9** eccentric **10** avant-garde, free spirit, iconoclast, unorthodox **13** nonconformist

boil
3 jet **4** bolt, brew, burn, cook, dash, foam, fume, gush, moil, race, rage, rush, spew, spot, stew, vent **5** anger, churn, erupt, fling, froth, poach, shoot, storm, swirl **6** blow up, bubble, charge, canker, coddle, decoct, pimple, seethe, simmer **7** abscess, agitate, bristle, ferment, flare up, pustule, smolder **8** furuncle **9** carbuncle, discharge **10** effervesce **11** excrescence

boil down
4 pare, trim **6** amount, decoct, reduce **7** distill **8** compress, condense, simplify, truncate **9** summarize, synopsize **10** streamline **11** concentrate, encapsulate

boiler suit
8 coverall

boiling
3 hot **5** fiery **6** baking, red-hot, sultry, torrid **7** burning, febrile **8** agitated, roasting, scalding, sizzling, tropical **9** scorching **10** blistering

boil over
4 burn, fume, rage **5** erupt **6** blow up, bridle, see red, seethe **7** bristle, flare up

boisterous
4 loud, wild **5** noisy, rowdy **6** lively, stormy, unruly **7** blatant, raucous, riotous **8** strident **9** clamorous, convivial, turbulent **10** disorderly, disruptive, rollicking, tumultuous, uproarious, vociferous **11** loudmouthed, tempestuous **12** high-spirited, obstreperous, rambunctious, ungovernable, unrestrained

Boito opera
11 Mefistofele

bold
4 edgy, free, pert, rude **5** bluff, brave, fresh, gutsy, nervy, sassy, saucy, sheer, showy, steep **6** arrant, brassy, brazen, bright, cheeky, daring, heroic **7** doughty, forward, glaring, obvious, valiant **8** cocksure, fearless, impudent, insolent, intrepid, resolute, unafraid, valorous **9** audacious, dauntless, intrusive, prominent, shameless, undaunted **10** courageous, pronounced **11** adventurous, impertinent, smart-alecky, venturesome **12** enterprising, presumptuous

boldness
4 gall, grit **5** drive, nerve, valor **6** aplomb, mettle, spirit **8** audacity, backbone, chutzpah, temerity **9** arrogance, challenge, hardihood, impudence, insolence **10** brazenness, disrespect, effrontery **11** discourtesy **12** impertinence

Bolero composer
5 Ravel (Maurice)

Bolivia
ancient culture: **4** Inca **10** Tiahuanaco
capital: **5** La Paz, Sucre
city: **6** El Alto **9** Santa Cruz **10** Cochabamba
conqueror: **7** Pizarro (Hernando)
Indian people: **6** Aymara **7** Quechua
lake: **5** Poopó **8** Titicaca
language: **6** Aymara **7** Quechua, Spanish
monetary unit: **9** boliviano
mountain, range: **5** Andes **6** Sajama
neighbor: **4** Peru **5** Chile **6** Brazil **8** Paraguay **9** Argentina
river: **4** Beni **5** Abuna **6** Mamoré **7** Guaporé **9** Pilcomayo

bollix
4 flub, mess, muff, ruin **5** botch, gum up, mix-up, snafu, spoil, upset **6** bobble, bumble, bungle, foul up, fumble, goof up, jumble, mess up, muck up, muddle, muff up **7** balls-up, confuse, louse up, screw up **8** dishevel, disorder, scramble, unsettle **9** mishandle, mismanage

bolo
5 knife **7** machete

Bolshevik
3 Red **6** commie **7** comrade **8** Leninist, tovarich, tovarish **9** communist

bolshevism
7 Marxism **8** Leninism **9** communism

bolster
3 aid **4** buoy, gird, help, husk, prop **5** boost, brace, carry, cheer **6** assist, bear up, buoy up, pillow, upbear, uphold **7** bulwark, cushion, fortify, hearten, shore up, support, sustain **8** backstop, buttress, maintain **9** encourage, reinforce **10** strengthen **12** underpinning **13** reinforcement

bolt
3 bar, fly, rod, run **4** cram, dash, dart, flee, gulp, jump, lock, race, rush, tear, wolf **5** arrow, blurt, bound, chase, dowel, flush, rivet, scarf, scoot, shoot, skirr, slosh, start **6** charge, decamp, devour, gobble, guzzle, secure, spring **7** abscond, exclaim, hotfoot, make off, missile, rigidly, scamper, startle, take off **8** blurt out, hightail **9** skedaddle **10** make tracks, take flight **11** ingurgitate **13** thunderstroke

bomb
3 dud, hit **4** bust, dull, fail, flop, sink, zero **5** blast, blitz, lemon, loser, pound, shell **6** blow up **7** debacle, destroy, failure, home run, success, washout, wipe out **8** detonate, disaster, fall flat, long pass, long shot, spray can

bombard
4 pelt **5** blast, blitz, shell, storm **6** attack, assail, cannon, hammer, pepper, shower, strafe, strike **7** assault, barrage **8** catapult **9** cannonade

bombardment
4 hail **5** burst, salvo **6** attack, shower, volley **7** barrage, battery **8** drumfire **9** broadside, cannonade, fusillade, onslaught

bombardon
4 bass **8** bass tuba

bombast
4 rant **6** hot air **7** bluster, fustian, oration **8** rhapsody, tumidity **9** fancy talk, pomposity, turgidity **10** pretension **11** rodomontade

bombastic
5 wordy **6** prolix, turgid **7** aureate, flowery, orotund, pompous, swollen **8** inflated, puffed-up **9** overblown **10** euphuistic, rhetorical **11** declamatory, overwrought **12** magniloquent **13** grandiloquent

____ Bombeck
4 Erma

bombed
4 high **5** drunk, fried, stiff, tight **6** blotto, stoned, wasted **8** comatose, tanked up **9** plastered **10** inebriated **11** intoxicated

bombinate
3 hum **4** buzz, purr, whir **5** drone, strum, thrum **6** bumble, rumble **7** grumble

bombshell
4 blow, jolt **5** shock **6** marvel **8** surprise **9** curveball, sensation **10** revelation **11** thunderbolt

Bonaduce role
5 Danny

bona fide
4 real, sure, true **5** valid **6** actual **7** earnest, genuine, sincere **8** sterling **9** authentic, undoubted, veritable **10** legitimate, sure-enough **11** indubitable, in good faith **13** authenticated

bona fides
6 candor **7** probity **8** goodwill **9** good faith, sincerity **10** reputation **11** reliability, sincereness

bonanza
4 mine **5** catch, hoard **7** pay dirt **8** Golconda, gold mine, treasure, treasury, windfall **12** extravaganza **13** treasure trove

bonbon
5 candy, sweet **7** fondant **9** sweetmeat, sugarplum **10** confection

bond
3 tie **4** bail, fuse, knot, link, pact, yoke **5** nexus **6** cement, fetter, pledge, surety **7** bargain, compact, linkage, promise, shackle, warrant **8** adhesive, affinity, cohesion, contract, covenant, guaranty, ligament, ligature, security, vinculum, warranty **9** adherence, agreement, coherence, guarantee **10** attachment, connection, connective, obligation

bondage
4 yoke **6** chains, thrall **7** durance, fetters, helotry, peonage, serfage, serfdom, slavery **9** captivity, detention, servitude, thralldom, vassalage, villenage **10** subjection **11** enslavement, subjugation **12** imprisonment

bondman
4 peon, serf **5** helot, slave **6** vassal

bondsman
4 peon, serf **5** helot, slave **6** surety **7** chattel

bone
ankle: **4** tali (plural) **5** talus, tarsi (plural) **6** tarsus
arm: **4** ulna **5** radii (plural), ulnae (plural) **6** radius **7** humerus
back: **5** spine **8** vertebra **9** vertebrae (plural)
breast: **7** sternum

calf: **6** fibula
cavity: **5** fossa
change into: **6** ossify
cheek: **5** malar **6** zygoma
chest: **3** rib
collar: **8** clavicle
combining form: **4** oste **5** osteo
face: **5** malar, nasal **7** frontal
finger: **7** phalanx **8** phalange
foot: **5** tarsi (plural) **6** tarsus **9** calcaneum, calcaneus **10** astragalus, metatarsus
hand: **10** metacarpus
head: **5** skull, vomer **7** cranium **8** parietal, sphenoid **9** occipital
heel: **9** calcaneum, calcaneus
hip: **5** ilium, pubis **6** pelvis **7** ischium
jaw: **7** maxilla **8** mandible
kneecap: **7** patella
leg: **5** femur, tibia **6** fibula **7** patella
lower back: **6** coccyx, sacrum
middle ear: **5** anvil, incus **6** hammer, stapes **7** malleus, stirrup
pelvis: **5** ilium
projection: **7** mastoid
relating to: **6** osteal
shin: **5** tibia **6** tibiae (plural)
shoulder blade: **7** scapula **8** scapulae (plural)
small: **7** ossicle
substance: **6** ossein
temporal process: **7** mastoid
thigh: **5** femur
toe: **7** phalanx **8** phalange
U-shaped: **5** hyoid
wrist: **5** carpi (plural) **6** carpus

bonehead
4 clod **5** dunce, moron **6** cretin, dimwit, nitwit **7** halfwit **8** clodpole, clodpoll, lunkhead, numskull **9** ignoramus, lamebrain, numbskull **12** featherbrain

bonelike
7 osseous, osteoid

boner
see **blooper**

bone up
4 cram **5** study **6** review, revise **8** pore over

bong
4 bell, dong, peal, ring, toll **5** chime, knell, sound **6** hookah, strike **7** resound **9** water pipe **11** reverberate

boniface
7 barkeep **8** publican, taverner **9** barkeeper, innkeeper **12** saloonkeeper

Bonjour Tristesse author
5 Sagan (Françoise)

bonkers
3 ape, mad, off **4** daft, loco, nuts, wild **5** batty, crazy, dotty, giddy, loony, potty **6** cuckoo, insane **7** bananas, haywire **8** demented, deranged, unhinged

bon mot
4 jest, quip **5** crack, sally **6** zinger **7** epigram, riposte **8** one-liner, repartee **9** witticism

bonny
4 fair, fine **6** comely, lovely, pretty **7** winsome **8** pleasing **9** beauteous, beautiful, excellent **10** attractive, delightful **11** good-looking

bon ton
4 élan **5** flair, style **6** gentry, jet set **7** fashion, society **8** elegance, smart set **9** haut monde, propriety **11** high society

bonus
4 gift, plus **6** reward **7** benefit, payment, premium **8** dividend **12** compensation **13** fringe benefit

bon vivant
7 epicure, flaneur, gourmet, trifler **8** aesthete, gourmand **10** aficionado, dilettante, gastronome **11** cognoscente, connoisseur **12** boulevardier, gastronomist, man-about-town

bony
4 lank, lean, thin **5** gaunt, lanky, spare **6** barren, skinny, twiggy **7** angular, osseous, scraggy, scrawny, starved **8** rawboned, skeletal, underfed **9** emaciated **10** cadaverous

boo
4 hiss, hoot, jeer, razz **6** bellow, deride, heckle, revile **7** catcall **9** raspberry, shout down

boob
3 oaf **4** dolt, dope, goof, goon, boor **5** chump, dunce, goose, ninny **6** breast, dumb ox **7** blunder, fathead, mistake, tomfool **8** lunkhead **9** simpleton **10** dunderhead, philistine

boo-boo
see **blooper**

booby hatch
6 asylum, bedlam **8** bughouse, loony bin, madhouse, nuthouse **9** funny farm **11** institution

booby trap
4 mine **5** snare **6** hazard **7** pitfall, springe **8** deadfall, land mine

boodle
3 wad **4** bilk, haul, heap, loot, mint, perk, take **5** booty, prize, spoil **6** bundle, packet, payola, spoils **7** fortune, plunder, present **8** kickback **9** incentive **10** bribe money, inducement

book
4 list, text, tome **5** album, bible, codex, enter, folio, novel, tract **6** charge, engage, enroll, folder, line up, manual, octavo, quarto, record, script, volume **7** catalog, edition, reserve **8** hardback, inscribe, register, schedule, softback, treatise **9** hardcover, monograph, paperback, preengage **10** compendium **11** publication

binding: **4** case, sewn, tape, Yapp **5** cloth **7** leather, perfect **9** hardcover
combining form: **6** biblio
of hours: **5** Horae
of Mass: **6** missal
of psalms: **7** psalter
part: **4** head, mull, tail **5** board, cover, crash, envoy, hinge, joint, spine **6** gutter, lining **7** chapter, flyleaf, preface **8** appendix, fore edge, foreword **9** text block **10** dedication

bookie
see **bookmaker**

bookish
5 nerdy **6** formal **7** erudite, learned **8** academic, cerebral, literary, pedantic, studious, well-read **9** scholarly **10** longhaired **12** intellectual, professorial

bookkeeping term
4 loss **5** asset, audit, check, debit, entry, yield **6** budget, credit, equity, income, ledger, margin, profit, return **7** account, accrual, balance, expense, invoice, revenue, voucher **8** discount, dividend, interest, write off **9** inventory, liability **10** appreciate, depreciate, fiscal year **11** double entry **12** amortization, appreciation, balance sheet, depreciation, variable cost

booklet
8 brochure, opuscule, pamphlet

bookmaker
6 binder, bookie, editor **7** printer **9** bet holder, oddsmaker, publisher

book of account
6 ledger, record **7** journal **8** register

bookplate
5 label **8** ex libris

bookstall
5 booth, kiosk **9** newsstand

boom
3 wax **4** bang, clap, grow, rise, slam, spar, wham **5** blast, boost, burst, crack, crash, sound, smash, swell **6** do well, expand, growth, rumble, thrive **7** explode, prosper, resound, thunder **8** flourish, kick hard, long beam **9** expansion **10** bull market, detonation, prosperity **11** reverberate
opposite: **4** bust

boomerang
6 recoil **7** rebound **8** backfire, backlash, come back, kick back, ricochet **10** bounce back

booming
4 bass, deep **6** robust **7** roaring **8** affluent, resonant, sonorous, thriving **9** deafening **10** prospering, prosperous, successful **11** flourishing

boon
3 aid, gay **4** gift, good, help **5** asset, grant, favor, jolly, merry, token **6** blithe, bounty, jocund, jovial **7** benefit, festive, gleeful, godsend, largess, present **8** blessing, largesse, mirthful, windfall **9** advantage, convivial, privilege **10** indulgence **11** benediction, benefaction

boondocks
5 wilds **6** sticks **7** outback **8** backland, frontier **9** backwater, backwoods, provinces, rural area **10** hinterland **11** backcountry, countryside **12** back of beyond

boondoggle
4 cord, hoax, scam **5** fraud, hokum **6** hustle **7** fast one, hatband, lanyard, swindle **8** flimflam **10** fool around, mess around **11** horse around

boor
3 cad, oaf **4** lout, hick, rube **5** brute, chuff, churl, clown, yahoo, yokel **6** lummox, rustic **7** buffoon, bumpkin, hayseed, peasant **9** ignoramus, vulgarian **10** clodhopper, philistine, provincial

boorish
4 rude **5** crass, crude, rough **6** coarse, common, rugged, vulgar **7** apelike, ill-bred, loutish, lowbred, lumpish, uncivil, uncouth **8** churlish, cloddish, clownish, impolite, insolent, lubberly, swainish **9** graceless, offensive, tasteless, unrefined **10** philistine, provincial, robustious, uncultured, ungracious, unmannerly, unpolished, unsociable **11** bad-mannered, clodhopping, ill-mannered, uncivilized **12** discourteous, uncultivated **13** disrespectful

boost
3 aid **4** hike, lift, jump, plug, push, rise **5** raise, steal **6** assist, beef up, expand, extend, foster, jack up **7** advance, amplify, augment, elevate, magnify, promote, support **8** heighten, increase, shoplift **9** advertise, encourage, expansion, promotion **10** assistance **11** helping hand **13** encouragement

booster
3 fan **4** hypo, shot **6** backer, Jaycee, patron, rocket, rooter **7** vaccine **8** champion, defender, promoter, upholder **9** amplifier, expositor, injection, proponent, supporter **10** shoplifter **11** inoculation

boot
2 ax **3** axe, can **4** bang, fire, kick, sack **5** chuck, eject, evict, expel, start **6** bounce, thrill **7** dismiss, kick out, start up **8** throw out **9** discharge, dismissal, terminate
kind: **5** wader **6** arctic, chukka, gaiter, galosh, mukluk **7** jodhpur, shoepac **8** balmoral, cothurni (plural), overshoe, shoepack **9** cothurnus **10** Wellington

Boötes star
8 Arcturus

booth
4 nook **5** berth, bower, kiosk, stall, stand **6** carrel **9** enclosure **11** compartment

bootleg
3 hot, run **5** hooch **6** pirate **7** illicit, smuggle **9** irregular, moonshine **10** bathtub gin, contraband **11** black market, mountain dew **12** unauthorized

bootless
4 vain **5** empty **6** futile, hollow **7** useless **8** abortive, impotent, nugatory **9** fruitless, valueless, worthless **10** profitless, unavailing **11** ineffective, ineffectual **12** unproductive, unprofitable, unsuccessful

bootlick
4 fawn **5** cower, crawl, creep, toady **6** cringe, grovel, kowtow, stroke **7** cater to, flatter, truckle **8** blandish **9** brownnose, importune, seek favor **10** curry favor **11** apple-polish **12** bow and scrape

bootlicker
4 toad **5** toady **6** lackey, lapdog, minion, yes-man **7** doormat, spaniel **8** hanger-on **9** sycophant **11** lickspittle

booty
4 haul, lift, loot, pelf, swag, take **5** prize, spoil, yield **6** spoils **7** pillage, plunder, rear end, seizure, takings **8** buttocks

booze
4 brew, grog, swig **5** binge, drink, hooch, juice, quaff, sauce, souse, swill **6** guzzle, imbibe, liquor, rotgut, tank up, tipple **7** alcohol, carouse, put away, spirits, swizzle **8** cocktail, liquor up **9** aqua vitae, firewater, knock back, moonshine

boozehound
3 sot **4** lush, wino **5** drunk, hoser, souse **7** guzzler **8** drunkard **9** alcoholic, inebriate **11** dipsomaniac

bop
3 bat, box, hit, jab, pop, rap **4** bash, bean, belt, biff, boff, blow, clip, cuff, jive, slug, sock, swat, whop **5** clock, pound, smack, thump, whack **8** plant one

borax
4 junk

Bordeaux wine
district: **5** Médoc **6** Graves
grape: **6** Malbec, Merlot **8** Cabernet
name: **5** Arsac, Ludon, Macau **6** Moulis **7** Labarde, Margaux, Pomerol **8** Cantenac, St. Julien, Pauillac **9** St. Emilion, St. Estèphe, St. Laurent
red: **6** claret

bordello
see **brothel**

border
3 hem, lip, rim **4** abut, brim, edge, join, line, pale, trim **5** bound, brink, flank, frame, limit, march, skirt, touch, verge **6** adjoin, bounds, butt on, define, fringe, limbus, margin, trench **7** contour, outline, selvage **8** approach, boundary, frontier, neighbor, sideline, surround **9** marchland, perimeter, periphery **11** butt against, communicate
heraldry: **4** orle
inlaid: **8** purfling
raised: **7** coaming

bordereau
4 note **6** record **7** account **10** memorandum

bordering
4 nigh **5** close **6** almost, next to **7** meeting, verging **8** abutting, adjacent, touching **9** adjoining, alongside, close upon, impinging **10** approximal, contiguous, juxtaposed **11** coterminous, neighboring, practically

borderland
5 march **6** fringe, margin **8** frontier **9** marchland

borderline
4 pale **6** almost, nearly **7** dubious, unclear **8** boundary, doubtful, marginal, unstable **9** ambiguous, debatable, dubitable, equivocal, perimeter, uncertain, undecided, unsettled **11** demarcation, problematic **12** intermediate **13** indeterminate

border state
8 Delaware, Kentucky, Maryland, Missouri, Virginia

bore
3 irk **4** drag, drip, mine, peer, pill, ream, sink, tire, yawn **5** auger, drill, drone, gouge, prick, punch **6** burrow, pierce, tunnel **7** bromide, caliber, fatigue **8** diameter, puncture **9** penetrate, perforate, soporific **10** dullsville

boreal
3 icy **4** cold, cool **5** chill, gelid, polar **6** arctic, bitter, chilly, frosty, frigid, tundra **7** glacial, wintery **8** freezing, northern **9** northerly

Boreas
beloved: **8** Orithyia
brother: **5** Notus **8** Hesperus, Zephyrus
father: **8** Astraeus
mother: **3** Eos
son: **5** Zetes **6** Calais

boredom
5 blahs, ennui **6** apathy, stupor, tedium, torpor **7** fatigue **8** doldrums, dullness, flatness, monotony **9** lassitude, weariness **11** incuriosity, tediousness **12** indifference

Borges work
5 Aleph (The) **10** Labyrinths

Borgia
4 Juan **6** Alonso, Cesare **7** Alfonso, Rodrigo **8** Lucrezia

boring
3 dry **4** arid, drab, dull, flat, zero **5** ho-hum,

vapid **6** dreary, stodgy, tiring **7** humdrum, tedious **8** bromidic, drudging, lifeless, tiresome **9** wearisome **10** lackluster, lacklustre, monotonous, pedestrian, unexciting **13** uninteresting

boring tool
5 drill, auger **6** trepan

Boris Godunov composer
10 Mussorgsky (Modest) **11** Moussorgsky (Modest)

born
3 née **6** innate, native **8** destined, inherent **9** intrinsic **10** congenital, deep-seated
combining form: **3** gen **4** gene **6** genous **7** genetic

borne by the wind
6 aeolic, eolian **7** aeolian

Borneo
ethnic group: **4** Dyak **5** Dayak
mountain: **8** Kinabalu
nation: **6** Brunei
river: **6** Rabang

Born Free
author: **7** Adamson (Joy)
lion: **4** Elsa

Borodin opera
10 Prince Igor

borough
4 town **5** burgh **7** village **8** township

bosh
see **bunkum**

Bosnia-Herzegovina
capital: **8** Sarajevo
language: **7** Serbian **8** Croatian **13** Serbo-Croatian
monetary unit: **4** mark **5** dinar
neighbor: **6** Serbia **7** Croatia
part of: **7** Balkans
sea: **8** Adriatic

bosom
4 bust, core, soul, teat **5** chest, close, heart **6** breast **7** embrace **8** feelings, intimate **10** affections, conscience

bosomy
5 built, busty, buxom, curvy **6** chesty, zaftig **7** shapely, stacked **9** Junoesque **11** full-figured

boss
4 capo, head, stud **5** chief, neato **6** direct, honcho, leader, manage, master, survey, worthy **7** command, foreman, headman, oversee **8** director, employer, overlook, overseer, superior **9** chieftain, excellent, first-rate, supervise **10** supervisor, taskmaster **11** superintend
African: **5** bwana

bossy
3 cow **4** calf **7** studded **8** despotic, imperial **9** arbitrary, assertive, imperious, masterful **10** autocratic, high-handed, imperative, oppressive, peremptory, tyrannical **11** controlling, dictatorial, domineering, magisterial, overbearing

botanist
American: **4** Gray (Asa) **5** Sears (Paul B.) **6** Bailey (Liberty), Bessey (Charles), Carver (George Washington) **7** Bartram (John, William), Burbank (Luther) **9** Fairchild (David)
Austrian: **6** Mendel (Gregor)
British: **6** Sloane (Sir Hans)
Danish: **7** Warming (Johannes)
Dutch: **7** De Vries (Hugo)
French: **7** Lamarck (Chevalier de)
German: **4** Cohn (Ferdinand), Mohl (Hugo von) **5** Sachs (Julius von)
Irish: **6** Harvey (William)
Scottish: **5** Brown (Robert)
Swedish: **8** Linnaeus (Carolus)
Swiss: **6** Nägeli (Karl) **8** Candolle (Augustin)

botany branch
7 ecology **8** algology, bryology, mycology **9** phycology **10** morphology, palynology, physiology **11** hydroponics, paleobotany, pteridology, systematics **12** bacteriology

botch
4 blow, flop, flub, foul, goof, mess, muck, muff, ruin **5** fluff, gum up, misdo, mix-up, snafu, snarl, spoil **6** bobble, boggle, bollix, bumble, bungle, fiasco, fumble, goof up, mess up, muddle **7** balls-up, blunder, confuse, louse up, washout **8** bugger up, disaster, disorder, dishevel, mishmash, shambles **9** mishandle, mismanage, patchwork **10** discompose, hodgepodge, misconduct

botchy
5 messy **6** blowsy, blowzy, frowsy, frowzy, sloppy, untidy **7** chaotic **8** careless, confused, slapdash, slipshod, slovenly

both
combining form: **3** bis
prefix: **4** ambi, amph **5** amphi

bother
3 ado, bug, irk, nag, vex **4** drag, fret, fuss, gall, pest, pain **5** annoy, eat at, harry, trial, upset **6** badger, flurry, harass, needle, pester, plague, ruffle **7** afflict, agitate, anxiety, bedevil, concern, disturb, fluster, perturb, provoke, torment, trouble **8** disquiet, headache, irritant, nuisance, vexation **9** aggravate, annoyance **10** discompose, exasperate, irritation **11** aggravation, intrude upon **12** exasperation **13** inconvenience

botheration
4 damn, pain, pest **5** trial **6** plague **7** torment **8** headache, irritant, nuisance, vexation **9** annoyance **10** difficulty, irritation **11** aggravation, provocation **12** exasperation **13** inconvenience

Botswana
capital: **8** Gaborone
city: **11** Francistown
desert: **8** Kalahari
former name: **12** Bechuanaland
language: **6** Tswana
monetary unit: **4** pula
neighbor: **7** Namibia **8** Zimbabwe **11** South Africa
river: **5** Chobe **6** Molopo **7** Limpopo **8** Okavango

bottle
4 vial **5** cruet, cruse, flask, phial **6** ampule, carafe, fiasco, flacon, magnum, vessel **7** ampoule **8** decanter, jeroboam **9** container

bottle gourd
8 calabash

bottleneck
5 choke **6** hinder, impede, narrow **7** impasse **8** obstacle, obstruct, paralyze, slowdown, throttle **9** hindrance **10** choke point, congestion, traffic jam **11** obstruction

bottom
3 bum **4** base, boat, core, foot, root, pith, rump, seat, ship, sole, soul, tail, tush **5** basal, basic, basis, fanny, found, nadir **6** behind, breech, heinie, lowest, source **7** bedrock, essence, footing, primary, rear end **8** backside, buttocks, derriere, pedestal, pediment **9** establish, fundament, lowermost, posterior, predicate, principle, underbody, undermost, underside **10** foundation, nethermost, underbelly, underlying, underneath **11** fundamental, lowest point **12** undersurface

bottomless
4 deep, vast **7** abysmal, endless **8** baseless, enduring, profound, unending **9** boundless, unlimited **10** groundless, unfillable, ungrounded **11** everlasting, inestimable, never-ending **12** immeasurable, incalculable, unfathomable **13** inexhaustible

bottommost
4 last **5** least **6** lowest **7** deepest

bough
3 arm **4** limb **5** shoot **6** branch **8** offshoot

boulder
4 rock

boulevard
4 road **6** artery, avenue, street **7** terrace **8** main drag **9** esplanade, promenade **10** high street **12** thoroughfare

boulevardier
7 flaneur, trifler **9** bon vivant **10** aficionado, dilettante **11** cognoscente, connoisseur **12** man-about-town

bounce
2 ax **3** axe, can, hop, pep, vim, zip **4** fire, jump, leap, oust, sack, zest **5** expel, vault, verve, vigor **6** energy, hurdle, spirit, spring **7** bluster, boot out, dismiss, kick out, rebound, saltate, sparkle **8** buoyancy, ricochet, vitality **9** animation, discharge, eliminate, terminate **10** ebullience, elasticity, liveliness

bounce back
5 rally **6** perk up, pick up, recoil, return, revive **7** cheer up, improve, rebound, recover **8** backfire **9** boomerang **10** recuperate, turn around

bounce off
5 carom **7** rebound **8** ricochet

bouncer
4 goon **5** guard **8** houseman, sentinel, watchman **9** muscleman

bouncing ball game
5 jacks

bouncy
3 gay **4** airy **5** peppy, perky **6** blithe, cheery, jaunty, jocund, lively **7** buoyant, elastic **8** animated, volatile **9** ebullient, energetic, expansive, exuberant, resilient, sprightly **10** unsinkable **12** effervescent, high-spirited **13** irrepressible

bound
3 end, hem, hop, rim **4** bolt, edge, jump, leap, term, skip **5** caper, frisk, hem in, limit, skirt, vault, verge **6** border, bounce, define, demark, driven, finite, fringe, gambol, hurdle, margin, spring, sprint **7** confine, delimit, enclose, hotfoot, limited, mark out, obliged, pledged, rebound, saltate **8** articled, beholden, confined, confines, enslaved, resolved, restrain, surround **9** compelled, demarcate, obligated **10** determined, indentured, limitation **11** apprenticed, responsible **12** circumscribe

boundary
3 hem **4** mete, pale **5** ambit, limit **6** limits, margin **7** compass, outline **8** confines, environs, purlieus **9** perimeter, precincts **10** borderline **11** demarcation **13** circumference

bounder
3 cad, cur, dog **4** boor, worm **5** knave, louse, rogue **6** rascal, rotter

boundless
4 vast **5** great **7** endless **8** infinite **9** excessive, limitless, unbounded, unlimited **10** indefinite, unconfined, unmeasured **11** illimitable, measureless **12** immeasurable, unrestricted **13** inexhaustible, unsurpassable

bounteous
5 ample **6** benign, lavish **7** copious, liberal, profuse **8** abundant, generous, handsome, prodigal **9** bountiful, capacious, expansive, extensive, plenteous, plentiful, unsparing **10** beneficent,

big-hearted, freehanded, munificent, openhanded, voluminous **11** magnanimous, overflowing

bountiful
see **bounteous**

bounty
5 grant, prize, yield **6** deluge, plenty, reward, wealth **7** payment, premium **8** plethora, richness **9** abundance, affluence, plenitude, profusion **10** cornucopia, generosity, inducement, liberality, luxuriance, prosperity **11** benevolence, copiousness **12** compensation

Bounty
captain: **5** Bligh (William)
event: **6** mutiny
first mate: **9** Christian (Fletcher)
letters: **3** HMS

bouquet
4 balm, kudo, odor, posy **5** aroma, kudos, scent, spice, spray **6** eulogy, medley **7** acclaim, corsage, essence, garland, incense, nosegay, perfume **8** accolade, encomium **9** fragrance, redolence **10** compliment **11** arrangement, boutonniere **12** commendation

bourgeois
7 burgher **8** ordinary **10** conformist, philistine **11** middle-class **12** conventional

bourgeoisie
11 middle class, third estate

Bourne Identity author
6 Ludlum (Robert)

bout
3 jag, run **4** game, meet, term, tour, turn **5** match, round, shift, siege, spell, spasm, spree, stint, throe, trick **6** attack **7** contest, session **8** outbreak **9** smackdown **10** engagement

boutique
4 shop **8** emporium

bovine
2 ox **3** cow, yak **4** anoa, bull, calf, gaur, neat, zebu **5** bison, steer, stirk **6** heifer, placid, torpid, wisent **7** aurochs, banteng, buffalo, bullock, cowlike **8** longhorn
genus: **3** Bos
sound: **3** low, moo

bow
3 arc, bob, dip, nod **4** arch, bend, knot, lout, prow, turn **5** angle, crook, curve, debut, defer, hunch, round, stoop, yield **6** archer, congee, curtsy, give in, kowtow, relent, salaam, salute, submit **7** concede, curtsey, flexure, incline, rainbow, succumb, turning **9** curvation, curvature, genuflect, obeisance, surrender **10** capitulate **11** buckle under **12** knuckle under
ornament: **10** figurehead

Bow, Clara
6 It girl

bowdlerize
4 blip, edit **6** censor, excise, purify, screen **7** abridge, cleanse, distort, launder **8** sanitize **9** expurgate **10** adulterate, blue-pencil

bowed
4 bent **5** arced, bandy **6** arched, curved **11** bandy-legged, curvilinear

bowel
3 gut **6** paunch **9** intestine

bower
5 arbor **6** anchor **7** enclose, pergola, retreat **9** apartment

bowery
7 skid row

bowfin
4 amia **7** mudfish

bowl
5 arena, basin, jorum, mazer, stade, tazza **6** tureen, vessel **7** stadium **8** coliseum **12** amphitheater

bowlegged
5 bandy

bowler
3 hat **5** derby **6** kegler

Bowl game
5 Super
Abilene: **5** Pecan
Anaheim: **7** Freedom
Atlanta: **5** Peach
Dallas: **6** Cotton
El Paso: **3** Sun
Fresno: **10** California
Honolulu: **5** Aloha
Houston: **10** Bluebonnet
Jacksonville: **5** Gator
Memphis: **7** Liberty
Miami: **6** Orange **8** Carquest
Mobile: **6** Senior
New Orleans: **5** Sugar
Orlando: **13** Florida Citrus
Pasadena: **4** Rose
San Diego: **7** Holiday
Shreveport: **12** Independence
Tampa: **10** Hall of Fame
Tempe: **6** Fiesta
Tucson: **6** Copper

bowling
7 kegling
British: **8** skittles
Italian: **5** bocce, bocci **6** boccie
term: **3** pin **4** hook, lane, spot **5** curve, frame, spare, split **6** gutter, strike, string, turkey **7** duckpin **9** candlepin

bowl over
3 awe, wow **4** daze, fell, stun **5** floor, shock, throw **6** boggle, dismay **7** astound, flatten, impress, stupefy **8** blow away, surprise **9** bring down, dumbfound, knock down, overwhelm **10** disconcert

bow out
4 exit, fold, quit **5** leave, welsh **6** beg off, give up, retire **8** withdraw **9** surrender

box
3 bin **4** case, cell, chop, cuff, duke, inro, loge, slap, sock, spar **5** booth, chest, clout, crate, fight, punch, smack, stall, trunk **6** buffet, carton, casket, coffer, coffin, encase, hopper, packet **7** confine, enclose, package **9** container, enclosure, rectangle **10** pigeonhole, receptacle **11** compartment

boxer
7 fighter, palooka **8** pugilist **9** flyweight **11** heavyweight, lightweight **12** bantamweight, middleweight, welterweight **13** featherweight
champ: **3** Ali (Muhammad) **4** Bowe (Riddick) **5** Bruno (Frank), Jones (Roy), Lewis (Lennox), Louis (Joe), Moore (Archie), Tyson (Mike) **6** Hagler (Marvin), Hearns (Thomas), Holmes (Larry), McCall (Oliver), Moorer (Michael), Seldon (Bruce), Spinks (Leon, Michael), Tunney (Gene), Walker (Mickey) **7** Charles (Ezzard), Corbett (James), Dempsey (Jack), Douglas (Buster), Foreman (George), Frazier (Joe), Johnson (Jack), LaMotta (Jake), Leonard (Sugar Ray), Sharkey (Jack), Walcott (Joe), Willard (Jess) **8** de la Hoya (Oscar), Marciano (Rocky), Robinson (Sugar Ray), Sullivan (John L.) **9** Armstrong (Henry), Holyfield (Evander), Patterson (Floyd), Schmeling (Max)

boxing
8 pugilism **10** fisticuffs **13** prizefighting
term: **2** KO **3** jab, TKO **4** blow, bout, duck, foul, hook, kayo, ring, rope, spar **5** break, count, feint, glove, match, parry, punch, round, swing **6** bucket, canvas, corner **7** low blow, referee **8** heavy bag, knockout, uppercut **9** knockdown **11** punching bag

boy
3 lad, son, tad **5** gamin, puppy, sonny **6** laddie, nipper, shaver **9** shaveling, stripling, youngster
combining form: **3** ped **4** paed, paid, pedo **5** paedo, paido
errand: **5** gofer **8** lobbygow
French: **6** garçon
Italian: **7** ragazzo
Latin: **4** puer
mischievous: **6** urchin
Spanish: **4** niño **8** muchacho

boyfriend
4 beau **5** swain **6** fiancé, old man, suitor **7** main man **9** inamorato

Boy Scout
founder: **11** Baden-Powell (Robert)
gathering: **8** jamboree
motto: **10** be prepared
rank: **4** Life (Scout), Star (Scout) **5** Eagle (Scout) **10** Tenderfoot
unit: **5** troop **6** patrol

Boys Town
founder: **8** Flanagan (Edward)
star: **6** Crosby (Bing)
state: **8** Nebraska

bozo
3 oaf **4** boob, clod, dodo, dolt, dope, fool, goof, jerk, mutt, simp, yo-yo **5** chump, dummy, dunce, idiot, moron, ninny, noddy, stupe **6** dimwit, donkey, dum-dum, nitwit, noodle **7** airhead, dullard, pinhead **8** bonehead, clodpoll, dumbbell, dumbhead, imbecile, lunkhead, meathead, numskull **9** birdbrain, blockhead, ignoramus, lamebrain, numbskull, simpleton, thickhead **10** dunderhead, hammerhead, nincompoop **11** chowderhead, chucklehead, knucklehead

B.P.O.E. member
3 Elk

Brabantio's daughter
9 Desdemona

brabble
3 row **4** beef, feud, flap, riot, spat, tiff **5** argue, scrap, set to **6** bicker, blowup, fracas, grouse **7** dispute, fall out, palaver, quarrel, rhubarb, scuffle, wrangle **8** argument, squabble **9** altercate, bickering, brannigan, caterwaul, wrangling **10** falling-out **11** altercation, disputation, embroilment

brace
3 arm, bar, duo, tie **4** dyad, gird, pair, prop, stay **5** clamp, ready, shore, steel, strut, truss **6** accost, bear up, column, couple, demand, splint, steady, uphold **7** bolster, bracket, enliven, fortify, freshen, prepare, refresh, shore up, support, sustain, tighten, twosome **8** buttress **9** reinforce **10** cantilever, exhilarate, invigorate, strengthen **12** underpinning **13** underpropping

bracelet
6 bangle **7** manacle **8** wristlet

bracing
4 keen **5** brisk, crisp, fresh, nippy, sharp, tonic **6** biting, chilly **7** rousing **8** stirring **9** animating **10** energizing, quickening **11** restorative, stimulating, stimulative **12** exhilarating, invigorating

bracken
4 fern **5** brake, brush, scrub **11** undergrowth

bracket
3 arm **4** join, link, omit **5** brace **6** couple, relate, remove **7** combine, compare, conjoin, connect, embrace, enclose, include, support **8** buttress, encircle, leave out, put aside, set aside **9** associate, encompass **11** parenthesis **12** strengthener

brackish
4 sour **5** acrid, briny, salty **6** saline, salted **9** repulsive, sickening **10** nauseating

bract
4 leaf **5** glume **6** paleat, spathe **8** phyllary

brad
4 nail

Bradamant
brother: **7** Rinaldo
husband: **6** Rogero **8** Ruggiero

Bradbury, Ray
forte: **5** sci-fi **7** fantasy
work: **13** Dandelion Wine **14** Illustrated Man (The) **17** Martian Chronicles (The)

Brady Bunch
actor: **4** Reed (Robert) **5** Davis (Ann B.), Olsen (Susan), Plumb (Eve) **6** Knight (Christopher) **8** Williams (Barry) **9** Henderson (Florence), McCormick (Maureen) **10** Lookinland (Mike)
character: **3** Jan **4** Greg **5** Alice, Bobby, Cindy, Peter, Tiger **6** Marcia **9** Mike Brady
creator: **8** Schwartz (Sherwood)

brae
4 bank, hill **5** slope **8** hillside

brag
3 gas **4** blow, crow, puff **5** boast, mouth, prate, vaunt **7** show off, swagger, talk big **9** cockiness, gasconade **10** grandstand **11** rodomontade

braggadocio
6 hot air **7** boaster, bombast, bravado, conceit, puffery, swagger, windbag **8** blowhard, boasting, braggart, bragging **9** arrogance, cockiness, pomposity **10** cockalorum, pretension, swaggering **11** fanfaronade

braggart
6 blower **7** boaster, egotist, vaunter, windbag **8** big mouth, blowhard **9** big talker, know-it-all, swaggerer, vulgarian **11** braggadocio

Brahmin
8 highbrow **9** blueblood, patrician **10** aristocrat

braid
4 plat **5** plait, queue **7** galloon, pigtail **8** soutache **9** interlace **10** intertwine, interweave

brain
3 wit **4** bean, conk, mind **7** concuss **9** intellect **10** gray matter **12** intelligence
bone: **5** skull **7** cranium
channel: **4** iter
clot: **10** thrombosis
gland: **6** pineal **9** pituitary
layer: **6** cortex
lobe: **6** limbic, vermis **7** frontal **8** parietal, temporal **9** occipital
membrane: **3** pia **4** dura **6** meninx **8** pia mater **9** arachnoid, dura mater
part: **4** lobe **6** fornix **7** medulla **8** cerebrum, thalamus **9** sensorium, ventricle **10** cerebellum, hemisphere **12** diencephalon
relating to: **8** cerebral **10** encephalic
ridge: **4** gyri (plural) **5** gyrus
scan: **3** EEG, MEG, MRI, PET
vertebrate: **10** encephalon
wave record: **3** EEG

brainchild
4 idea, opus, work **6** animus, scheme, theory **7** coinage **9** handiwork, invention **10** hypothesis, innovation **11** achievement, chef-d'oeuvre, contrivance

brainiac
3 wiz **4** whiz **6** genius **7** prodigy

brainless
3 dim **5** dense, silly, thick **6** simple, stupid **7** asinine, foolish, idiotic, moronic, vacuous, witless **9** dim-witted, nitwitted **10** acephalous **12** feebleminded

brainpower
3 wit **5** sense **6** smarts **8** aptitude, capacity, sagacity **9** intellect, mentality, mother wit **10** perception **11** discernment, penetration **12** intelligence **13** comprehension

brains
4 mind **6** smarts **9** intellect **12** intelligence

brainsick
3 mad **4** daft **5** batty, crazy, manic, potty **6** crazed, insane, mental **7** cracked, haywire, lunatic **8** aberrant, demented, deranged, maniacal, unhinged **9** bedlamite, delirious, disturbed **10** disordered, incoherent, irrational, unbalanced

brainstorm
3 rap, jaw **4** idea **6** confer, huddle **7** discuss, dream up, think up **8** cogitate, mull over **9** mental fit **10** groupthink, kick around, toss around **11** inspiration, put together

brainteaser
5 poser, rebus **6** puzzle, riddle **7** stumper **9** conundrum **10** cryptogram

brainwashing
10 propaganda **11** mind control, reeducation

brainy
4 keen **5** quick, savvy, sharp, smart **6** adroit, astute, bright, clever **9** eggheaded, brilliant,

sagacious **10** discerning, precocious **11** intelligent, quick-witted, ready-witted **13** knowledgeable, perspicacious

brake
4 curb, slow, stop **5** block **6** damper, hinder, impede, retard, slough **7** barrier, bracken, slacken **8** blockade, obstacle, obstruct, slow down **9** deterrent, hindrance **10** constraint, decelerate **11** bracken fern

bramble
4 burr **5** brier, furze, gorse, hedge, shrub, thorn **6** nettle **7** thistle

branch
3 arm, leg **4** fork, limb, rami (plural), spur, wing **5** bough, ramus **6** office, ramify **7** chapter, diverge, outpost **8** division **9** tributary **10** subsidiary

branched
6 ramate, ramose

brand
4 blot, blur, logo, make, mark, onus, sear, slur, sort, spot, type **5** badge, class, odium, stain, stamp, sword, taint, torch **6** accuse, charge, impute, stigma, stripe **7** species, variety **8** black eye, disgrace, insignia, logotype **9** trademark **10** stigmatize

brandish
4 wave **5** flash, shake, sport, swing, wield **6** flaunt, parade **7** display, exhibit, show off **8** flourish

brand-new
4 mint **5** fresh **6** latest, unused, virgin **8** up-to-date **9** untouched **11** cutting-edge **13** inexperienced

brandy
4 marc, ouzo, raki **5** Pisco **6** cognac, grappa, kirsch, Metaxa **7** liqueur **8** Armagnac, calvados, digestif, eau-de-vie **9** applejack, framboise, slivovitz
cocktail: **7** sidecar, stinger **9** Alexander

brannigan
3 row **4** bust, flap, spat, tiff **5** binge, fight, set-to, spree **6** bender, blowup, hassle, ruckus **7** brabble, discord, dispute, quarrel, wassail, wrangle **8** squabble **10** falling-out **11** altercation

brash
4 bold, flip, pert **5** cocky, gutsy, hasty, nervy, saucy **6** brassy, brazen, cheeky, madcap, uppish, uppity **7** brittle, forward **8** arrogant, cocksure, flippant, impudent, insolent, reckless, tactless **9** audacious, bumptious, ebullient, energetic, exuberant, hot-headed, impetuous, impolitic, maladroit, unabashed, untactful **10** ill-advised, incautious **11** overweening, thoughtless **12** high-spirited, presumptuous, undiplomatic, unrestrained **13** disrespectful, inconsiderate, irrepressible, self-assertive

brashness
4 gall, grit, guts **5** brass, cheek, crust, nerve, pluck **6** aplomb, daring, mettle, spirit **8** audacity, chutzpah, temerity **9** assurance **10** confidence, effrontery **11** presumption

brass
4 gall **5** cheek, nerve **8** audacity, chutzpah **9** brashness, impudence, insolence **10** confidence, effrontery **11** presumption **12** impertinence

brassbound
3 set **5** brash, rigid **6** brazen, narrow **7** adamant, bigoted, forward **8** obdurate **9** illiberal, presuming, obstinate, unbending **10** implacable, inflexible, intolerant, relentless, unswayable, unyielding **11** opinionated, small-minded, unrelenting **12** narrow-minded, presumptuous, single-minded **13** dyed-in-the-wool, self-asserting, self-assertive

brasserie
10 restaurant

brass hat
3 VIP **4** boss **5** elder **6** better, senior **7** big shot **8** big whell, higher-up, superior

brassica
4 kale, rape **5** colza **6** turnip **7** cabbage, mustard **8** broccoli, collards, kohlrabi, rutabaga **11** cauliflower

brass tacks
5 facts **7** details **11** nitty-gritty, particulars

brass worker
7 brazier

brassy
see **brazen**

brat
3 imp **4** punk **6** urchin **10** holy terror

bravado
5 bluff **6** hot air **7** bluster, bombast **8** audacity, boasting, boldness, bragging, defiance, vaunting **9** gasconade **10** blustering, pretension, swaggering **11** braggadocio, grandiosity **12** boastfulness

brave
4 bold, dare, defy, face, game, meet, risk **5** beard, gutsy, hardy, manly, nervy, noble, stout **6** daring, heroic, manful, plucky, spunky, take on **7** defiant, doughty, gallant, valiant, venture **8** confront, face down, fearless, intrepid, reckless, resolute, spirited, splendid, stalwart, unafraid, valorous **9** audacious, challenge, dauntless, excellent,

steadfast, undaunted, withstand **10** courageous **11** boldhearted, indomitable, lionhearted, undauntable, unflinching, venturesome **12** stouthearted **13** adventuresome

Brave New World author
6 Huxley (Aldous)

bravery
4 grit, guts **5** nerve, pluck, valor **6** daring, mettle, spirit **7** courage, heroism **8** audacity, boldness, temerity **9** derring-do, fortitude, gallantry **11** intrepidity **12** fearlessness, intrepidness
false: **7** bravado

bravo
3 olé **4** euge, rave, thug **5** cheer **6** encore, gunman, hit man, killer **7** ovation, plaudit, villain **8** applause, assassin **9** desperado

bravura
4 bold **5** showy **6** daring, florid, ornate **8** dazzling, skillful, virtuoso **9** brilliant

brawl
3 row **4** feud, flap, fray, fuss, maul, riot, spar, spat, tiff **5** clash, broil, fight, melee, scrap, set-to **6** affray, battle, bicker, dustup, fracas, rumble, tussle **7** bobbery, brabble, contend, quarrel, rhubarb, ruction, scuffle, wrangle **8** dogfight, skirmish, slugfest **9** fistfight, imbroglio, scrimmage **10** donnybrook, fisticuffs, free-for-all **11** altercation, disturbance

brawn
4 beef, meat, thew **5** clout, flesh, might, power, sinew **6** muscle **8** strength **9** puissance **10** headcheese

brawny
5 beefy, burly, husky, lusty, tough **6** robust, sinewy, stocky, strong, sturdy **8** athletic, muscular, powerful, thickset, vigorous **9** strapping, well-built **10** able-bodied

bray
4 mill **5** crush, grind, pound **6** bellow, hee-haw, pestle, powder **7** atomize, trumpet **9** pulverize

brazen
4 bold, loud **5** brash, gaudy, noisy, showy **6** arrant, brassy, cheeky **7** blatant, defiant, forward, glaring, jarring **8** flagrant, impudent, insolent **9** audacious, barefaced, obtrusive, shameless, unabashed **10** outrageous, procacious, unblushing **11** conspicuous, impertinent **12** contumelious, presumptuous **13** disrespectful

Brazil
capital: **8** Brasília
city: **5** Belém **6** Recife **8** Salvador, São Paulo **12** Rio de Janeiro **13** Belo Horizonte
discoverer: **6** Cabral (Pedro)
island: **6** Marajó **7** Caviana
language: **10** Portuguese
monetary unit: **4** real
neighbor: **4** Peru **6** Guyana **7** Bolivia, Uruguay **8** Colombia, Paraguay, Suriname **9** Argentina, Venezuela **12** French Guiana
river: **4** Pará **6** Amazon **8** Parnaíba **10** Alto Paraná **12** São Francisco
state: **4** Acre, Pará **5** Amapá, Bahia, Ceará, Goiás, Piauí **6** Paraná

breach
3 gap **4** gash, hole, leap, open, rent, rift, slit **5** break, chasm, cleft, crack, split **6** hiatus, lacuna, schism **7** break in, discord, disrupt, fissure, infract, interim, opening, rupture, violate **8** aperture, disunity, division, fracture, infringe, interval, trespass **9** disregard, severance, violation **10** alienation, contravene, infraction, separation, transgress **11** delinquency, dereliction **12** disaffection, disobedience, estrangement, infringement, interruption **13** contravention, discontinuity, noncompliance, nonobservance, transgression

bread
3 bun **4** food, pita, rusk, wrap **5** bagel, money, scone, toast **6** living, muffin, sippet **7** biscuit, crouton, edibles, stollen **8** victuals, zwieback **9** provender **10** livelihood, provisions, sustenance **11** comestibles, maintenance, subsistence
communion: **4** host **5** wafer **9** Eucharist
from heaven: **5** manna
ingredient: **4** meal **5** flour, yeast **6** leaven
Jewish: **5** matzo **6** hallah, matzoh **7** challah
maker: **5** baker
Scottish: **7** bannock
spread: **3** jam **4** oleo **5** jelly **6** butter **9** margarine
unleavened: **5** matzo **6** matzoh

bread and butter
4 keep, work **6** basics, living **7** support **8** mainstay, victuals **10** employment, livelihood, occupation, sustenance **9** nutriment **11** maintenance, necessities, subsistence **12** alimentation

breadbasket
3 gut **5** belly, tummy **6** paunch **7** abdomen, stomach **8** potbelly **9** bay window, beer belly

breadth
4 area, size, span **5** range, reach, scope, space, sweep, width **6** extent, spread **7** compass, expanse, stretch **8** distance, fullness, latitude, vastness, wideness **9** amplitude, expansion, magnitude **10** liberality

break
3 gap **4** bust, dash, halt, knap, leak, luck, rest, rift, ruin, tame **5** burst, clear, crack, inure, sever,

solve, spell **6** breach, chance, decode, divide, escape, exceed, hiatus, impair, lacuna, refute, relief, reveal **7** destroy, divulge, fall out, interim, lighten, opening, respite, rupture, shatter, surpass, suspend, take ten, time-out, violate **8** accustom, bankrupt, breather, decipher, disclose, division, downtime, fracture, good luck, interval, moderate, take five **9** interlude, interrupt **10** annihilate, controvert, impoverish **11** discontinue, disjunction, dislocation, opportunity, suspensions **12** intermission, interruption **13** discontinuity

breakable
4 weak **5** frail **6** flimsy **7** brittle, fragile, friable **8** delicate **9** frangible

breakaway
4 prop **7** escapee **8** offshoot, renegade, seceding

break down
4 fail, fold, sort, wilt **5** class, decay, index **6** cave in, digest, give in **7** analyze, crumble, crumple, give out, give way, go crazy, succumb **8** classify, collapse, dissolve **9** anatomize, decompose, fall apart **12** disintegrate

breakdown
5 crash, decay, smash, study, wreck **6** mishap **7** crack-up, debacle, failure, smashup **8** analysis, collapse, taxonomy **9** cataclysm, partition **10** disruption, dissection, resolution **11** dysfunction, examination, prostration

breaker
4 wave **6** billow, comber, roller

Breakfast at Tiffany's author
6 Capote (Truman)

breakfront
7 cabinet **8** bookcase

break in
4 tame **5** train **6** breach, burgle, gentle, invade **7** intrude **8** initiate **9** condition, habituate, interfere, interpose, interrupt

breakneck
4 fast **5** fleet, hasty, quick, rapid, swift **6** racing, speedy, unsafe **8** meteoric **10** harefooted **11** precipitous

break off
3 end **4** drop, halt, kill, stop **5** abort, cease, scrub, sever **6** cancel, detach **7** curtail, scratch, suspend **8** cut short **9** terminate **11** discontinue

break out
4 bolt, flee **5** arise, erupt, flare **6** emerge, escape **7** explode **8** mushroom, separate

break through
5 burst **6** breach, emerge, pierce **7** rupture, surface **8** overcome **9** penetrate

breakthrough
4 find, gain, hike, leap, rise **5** boost **7** advance, radical, upgrade **8** advanced, increase, landmark **9** invention, milestone **10** avant-garde, innovation **11** cutting-edge, development, exceptional, progressive, quantum leap

break up
3 end **4** halt, knap, part **6** divide, sunder **7** destroy, disband, disjoin, disrupt, rupture, scatter, shatter **8** disperse, dissever, dissolve, disunite, separate **9** decompose, dismantle, pulverize, terminate **12** disintegrate

breakup
4 rift **5** split **7** divorce, parting **8** analysis **9** dispersal **10** dissection, separation **11** dissolution

breakwater
5 groin, jetty **7** seawall

breast
5 bosom, chest, heart
animal: **7** brisket
combining form: **3** maz **4** mast, mazo **5** masto, stern, steth **6** mastia (plural), sterno, stetho

breastbone
7 sternum

breast-feed
5 nurse **6** suckle **7** nourish

breastwork
7 barrier, bastion, bulwark, defense, parapet, rampart **9** barricade, earthwork **10** embankment **13** fortification, reinforcement

breath
4 gasp, gust, hint, puff **5** let-up, pause, trace, whiff **6** breeze **7** respite **10** exhalation, inhalation, suggestion

breathe
4 emit, sigh **5** exude, utter, voice **6** endure, exhale, expire, inhale, murmur **7** confide, express, give off, inspire, persist, radiate, respire, subsist, survive, whisper

breather
4 lull, rest, stay, vent **5** break, let-up, pause, spell **6** hiatus, recess **7** caesura, respite **8** downtime **9** remission **12** interruption

breathing
labored: **7** dyspnea
normal: **6** eupnea
rapid: **8** polypnea

breathing apparatus
10 respirator
underwater: **5** scuba

breathing orifice
4 nose **5** mouth **8** blowhole, spiracle

breathless
4 agog, avid, keen **5** eager **6** ardent **7** anxious, gasping, intense **8** gripping **9** expectant, impatient **11** short-winded **13** on tenterhooks

breathtaking
6 moving **7** awesome **8** dramatic, exciting, imposing, stunning, wondrous **9** panoramic, thrilling **10** impressive, staggering **11** astonishing, magnificent, spectacular **12** awe-inspiring, overwhelming **13** heart-stirring

Brecht play
4 Baal **13** Life of Galileo (The), Mother Courage **15** Seven Deadly Sins (The), Threepenny Opera (The) **20** Caucasian Chalk Circle (The)

breech
3 bum **4** duff, rear, rump, seat, tail **5** fanny **6** behind, bottom, heinie **7** keester, keister, rear end **8** backside, buttocks, derriere, haunches **9** fundament, posterior **12** hindquarters

breechclout
5 dhoti **9** loincloth

breed
3 ilk **4** bear, grow, kind, make, mate, race, rear, sire, sort, type **5** beget, brand, cause, class, cross, genus, hatch, likes, raise, stock, yield **6** couple, create, father, induce, nature, strain, stripe **7** bring up, develop, educate, lineage, nurture, produce, species, variety **8** copulate, engender, generate, mate with, multiply **9** cultivate, procreate, propagate, reproduce **10** discipline, extraction, give rise to, impregnate, inseminate

breeding
4 line **5** grace, taste **6** polish **7** culture, decorum, lineage, manners **8** ancestry, civility, courtesy, pedigree **9** genealogy, gentility, propriety **10** refinement, upbringing **11** cultivation

breeding ground
6 hotbed, origin **8** hothouse **10** forcing bed, mating spot **12** forcing house

breeze
3 zip **4** flit, sail, snap, waft **5** cinch, draft, waltz **6** zephyr **8** duck soup, kid stuff **10** child's play

breezy
4 airy, cool **5** fresh, gusty, windy **6** blithe, casual, drafty **7** offhand, relaxed **8** carefree, careless, detached, informal **9** easygoing **10** insouciant, nonchalant **11** unconcerned **12** devil-may-care, lighthearted

Breton
4 Celt

____ breve
4 alla

breviary
5 brief **6** digest, précis **7** epitome, essence, outline, rundown, summary **8** abstract, boil-down, synopsis **9** reduction **10** abridgment, conspectus, prayer book **11** abridgement **12** condensation, divine office

brevity
7 economy **8** laconism **9** briefness, concision, crispness, pithiness, shortness, terseness **10** transience

brew
3 ale, tea **4** beer, loom, mull, plan, plot, suds **5** drink, lager, stout **6** cook up, foment, gather, impend, infuse, porter, scheme, stir up **7** concoct, ferment **8** contrive

briar
4 burr, pipe **5** furze, gorse, shrub, thorn **6** nettle **7** bramble, thistle

Briareus
7 Aegaeon
father: **6** Uranus
mother: **4** Gaea

bribe
3 buy, fix, sop **6** buy off, payoff, payola, square, suborn **7** corrupt **9** incentive **10** enticement, inducement, tamper with

bric-a-brac
6 curios **8** trinkets **9** ornaments **10** objets d'art **11** gingerbread, knickknacks **13** embellishment

brick
5 block, gaffe **7** blunder
layer: **5** mason
laying: **7** masonry
material: **4** clay, marl
oven: **4** kiln
row: **6** course
sun-dried: **5** adobe
toy: **4** Lego
trough for carrying: **3** hod

bridal
7 nuptial, spousal **8** conjugal **9** connubial **11** matrimonial
path: **5** aisle

bridal wreath
6 spirea

bridewell
3 can, jug, pen **4** coop, jail **5** clink, joint **6** lock-up, prison **7** slammer **8** bastille **12** penitentiary

bridge
4 join, link, span **5** unite **7** connect **8** overpass, traverse
great: **8** Brooklyn **10** Golden Gate
kind: **4** arch, draw, rope **5** swing, truss **7** bascule, covered, natural, pontoon, trestle, viaduct **10** cantilever, suspension
term: **3** bid **4** book, east, pass, ruff, slam, suit, void, west **5** bonus, dummy, north, raise, south, trick, trump **6** double, renege, rubber **7** auction, finesse, no-trump, overbid **8** contract, jump call, redouble **9** grand slam, overtrick, singleton **10** little slam, undertrick, vulnerable

bridgelike game
5 whist **6** hearts

bridle
3 bit **4** curb, fume, rein, rule **5** check, flare, quell **6** govern, halter, hold in, manage, master, rein in, ruffle, seethe, subdue **7** bristle, control, flare up, inhibit, repress **8** hold back, moderate, restrain, suppress, withhold **9** constrain, deterrent, hackamore, restraint

brief
4 curt **5** pithy, short, terse **6** abrupt, digest, inform **7** brusque, concise, epitome, laconic, outline, passing, summary **8** abstract, breviary, fleeting, succinct, synopsis **9** momentary, transient **10** abridgment, conspectus **11** abridgement, compendious **12** condensation **13** short and sweet

briefs alternative
6 boxers

brig
3 can, jug, pen **4** coop, jail **5** clink **6** cooler, lockup, prison **7** slammer **8** stockade **9** guardroom **10** guardhouse

brigade
4 army, unit **5** force, group **6** troops **10** contingent, detachment

brigand
6 bandit, bummer, looter, pirate, raider **7** cateran, corsair, forager, rustler **8** marauder, pillager **9** buccaneer, plunderer **10** freebooter, highwayman

brigandage
7 pillage, sacking **10** despoiling, ransacking **11** depredation

bright
4 fair, keen **5** aglow, alert, clear, light, lucid, quick, shiny, smart, sunny, vivid **6** brainy, cheery, clever, lively, lucent **7** beaming, blazing, flaming, fulgent, glowing, lambent, lighted, radiant, shining **8** cheerful, dazzling, gleaming, luminous, lustrous, sunshiny **9** brilliant, effulgent, favorable, refulgent, sparkling **10** auspicious, glittering, precocious, propitious, shimmering **11** illuminated, intelligent, quick-witted **12** incandescent **13** scintillating

brighten
4 buoy **5** cheer, clear, shine **6** look up, perk up, polish, revive, solace **7** burnish, cheer up, clear up, enhance, enliven, furbish, gladden, hearten, improve **8** illumine **10** illuminate

brightness
5 éclat, shine **6** luster, lustre **8** radiance, splendor **10** brilliance, effulgence, luminosity
measure of: **3** lux **5** lumen **6** candle **7** candela **10** foot-candle

brilliance
see **brightness**

brilliant
6 ablaze, brainy, genius, lucent, superb **7** beaming, fulgent, lambent, radiant, shining, stellar **8** dazzling, luminous, masterly, striking **9** effulgent, ingenious, refulgent, sparkling **10** glittering **11** exceptional **12** incandescent

brilliantine
6 pomade **9** hair cream

brim
3 hem, lip, rim **4** edge, fill, well **5** brink, skirt, verge, visor **6** border, fill up, fringe, margin **7** run over **8** overflow, well over **9** perimeter, periphery **13** circumference

brimming
4 full **5** awash, flush **6** filled, jammed, loaded, packed **7** crammed, crowded, replete, stuffed, teeming, welling **8** bursting, overfull, suffused, swarming, swelling **9** chock-full, jam-packed **11** chockablock, running over

brimstone
6 sulfur

brine
3 sea **4** deep, main **5** ocean **8** seawater **9** salt water

bring
3 lug **4** lead, pack, tote **5** carry, fetch, gross, yield **6** convey **7** attract, produce **9** transport

bring about
3 win **5** beget, cause **6** create, draw on, effect, secure **7** procure, produce, trigger **8** engender, generate, result in **10** accomplish, effectuate, give rise to

bring around
4 hook, sway, turn **7** convert, win over **8** convince, persuade, talk into **9** argue into, prevail on, sweet-talk **11** prevail upon

bring back
5 renew **6** recall, recoup, return, revive **7** recover, reprise, restore, salvage **8** retrieve, revivify **9** reinstate **10** repatriate **11** reestablish

bring down
3 bag, hew **4** drop, fell, raze **5** floor, level, shoot **6** defeat, depose, ground, humble, lay low, reduce **7** depress, flatten **8** demolish, overturn **9** humiliate, overthrow, prostrate, undermine

bring forth
4 bear **5** beget, yield **6** create, elicit, invent **7** deliver, produce **8** generate **9** propagate, reproduce **10** give rise to

bring forward
6 adduce, submit, tender, unveil **7** advance, present, produce, proffer **9** introduce

bring in
3 pay, net, win **4** draw, earn, gain, make, sell **5** fetch, gross, yield **6** garner, return, secure **7** acquire, be worth, realize **9** introduce

bring off
6 effect, finish, rescue **7** achieve, execute, realize, succeed **8** carry out **9** discharge, implement **10** accomplish, consummate, effectuate **12** carry through

bring out
4 cull **5** educe, utter, voice **6** elicit, reveal **7** declare, enhance, explain, extract **8** disclose, showcase **9** elucidate, highlight, introduce

bring together
3 mix, wed **4** herd, join, link, yoke **5** amass, batch, blend, group, marry, merge, rally, unify, unite **6** corral, muster **7** collect, compact, compile, convene, round up **8** assemble **9** aggregate, integrate, reconcile, stockpile **10** synthesize **11** consolidate

bring up
4 moot, rear **5** breed, raise, refer, teach, train, vomit **6** advert, allude, broach, foster, school **7** advance, educate, mention, nurture, propose, suggest, touch on **8** point out, instruct **9** cultivate, introduce **10** put forward **11** regurgitate

brink
3 hem, rim **4** bank, brim, edge **5** point, skirt, verge **6** border, fringe, margin **9** extremity, perimeter, periphery, threshold

briny
5 salty **6** saline

brio
3 pep, vim, zip **4** dash, élan, fire, life, zest, zing **5** ardor, flair, gusto, oomph, style, verve, vigor **6** bounce, esprit, fervor, spirit **7** panache, passion, sparkle **8** dynamism, vivacity **9** animation

brioche
4 roll

Briseis' lover
8 Achilles

brisk
4 busy, fast, keen, spry, yare **5** agile, fresh, nippy, quick, sharp, zippy **6** lively, nimble, snappy, speedy **7** bracing **8** animated, bustling, vigorous **9** energetic, sprightly **10** refreshing **11** stimulating **12** invigorating

bristle
4 boil, burn, fume, seta **5** anger, quill, setae (plural), spine **6** arista, chaeta, seethe **7** chaetae (plural)
Scottish: **5** birse

bristle-like appendage
3 awn **4** seta **6** arista

British
air force: **3** RAF
cathedral city: **3** Ely **4** York **5** Ripon, Truro, Wells **6** Durham, Exeter **7** Chester, Lincoln **8** Coventry, Hereford, St. David's **9** Lichfield, Salisbury, Wakefield, Worcester **10** Canterbury, Gloucester
Channel Island: **4** Sark **6** Jersey **8** Alderney, Guernsey
coin, current: **5** pence (plural), penny, pound
coin, old: **3** bob **5** crown, groat, noble **6** bawbee, florin, George, guinea, tanner, teston **8** farthing, shilling **9** halfcrown, halfpenny, sovereign **10** threepence
colony, former: **4** Aden, Cape **5** Adana, Kenya, Malta, Natal **6** Ceylon, Cyprus, Gambia **7** Jamaica, Sarawak **9** Gold Coast, Singapore, Transvaal **10** Basutoland, New Zealand **11** Orange River, Sierra Leone **12** Bechuanaland
county: **4** Avon, Kent, York **5** Derby, Devon, Essex, Gwent **6** Dorset, Durham, Oxford, Surrey, Sussex **7** Bedford, Cumbria, Norfolk, Rutland, Suffolk, Warwick **8** Cheshire, Cornwall, Hereford, Hertford, Somerset, Stafford **9** Berkshire, Cleveland, Hampshire, Lancaster, Leicester, Wiltshire, Worcester **10** Cumberland, Gloucester, Humberside, Lancashire, Merseyside, Shropshire **11** Westmorland **12** Lincolnshire
court, local: **8** hustings
court, medieval: **4** eyre
era: **9** Edwardian, Victorian **11** Elizabethan
forest: **5** Arden, weald **8** Sherwood
king, legendary: **3** Lud **4** Beli, Bran **6** Arthur **7** Artegal, Belinus, Elidure **8** Brannius
language, ancient: **6** Celtic, Cymric **9** Brythonic
legislature: **10** Parliament
medical system: **3** NHS
news agency: **7** Reuters
nobleman: **4** duke, earl, peer **5** baron **6** prince **8** marquess, viscount
order: **6** Garter
people, early: **5** Celts, Iceni, Jutes, Picts **6** Angles, Saxons
political party: **4** Tory, Whig **6** Labour **12** Conservative
pope: **8** Adrian IV
prince: **5** Harry **6** Andrew, Edward **7** Charles, William
princess: **4** Anne **5** Diana **8** Margaret
prison: **5** Tower (of London) **7** Newgate **8** Dartmoor
queen, ancient: **8** Boadicea, Boudicca
resort: **4** Bath **7** Margate **8** Brighton **9** Blackpool
royal house: **4** York **5** Tudor **6** Stuart **7** Hanover, Windsor **9** Lancaster **11** Plantagenet

royal residence: **7** Windsor **8** Balmoral **10** Buckingham
school: **4** Eton **5** Rugby **6** Harrow **10** Winchester
school, military: **9** Sandhurst
spa: **4** Bath **5** Epsom **6** Buxton **7** Malvern, Matlock **8** Brighton **9** Harrogate **10** Cheltenham

British Columbia
capital: **8** Victoria
city: **6** Surrey **7** Burnaby **8** Richmond **9** Vancouver
mountain: **11** Fairweather
provincial flower: **7** dogwood (Pacific)

British Honduras
6 Belize

brittle
4 curt **5** crisp, frail, stiff **6** infirm **7** crumbly, fragile, friable **9** breakable, frangible, inelastic, irritable, sensitive **10** perishable, transitory

broach
3 tap **4** moot **6** open up **7** bring up, mention, propose, suggest **8** initiate **9** introduce **10** put forward

broad
4 wide **7** general, liberal **8** extended, generous, spacious, sweeping, tolerant **9** expansive, extensive
combining form: **4** eury, lati, plat **5** platy

broadcast
3 air, sow **4** beam, show **5** radio, strew **6** blazon, report, spread **7** bestrew, declare, publish, scatter **8** announce, proclaim, televise, transmit **9** advertise, publicize **10** bruit about, promulgate **11** communicate, declaration, disseminate, publication **12** announcement, proclamation, promulgation, transmission

broaden
4 open **5** swell, widen **6** dilate, expand, extend, fatten, spread **7** amplify, augment, distend, enlarge, thicken **8** increase **10** supplement

broadloom
6 carpet

broad-minded
4 open **7** liberal **8** catholic, eclectic, flexible, tolerant, unbiased **9** accepting, indulgent, unbigoted **10** forbearing, undogmatic **11** progressive **12** unjudgmental, unprejudiced

broadsheet
7 tabloid **9** newspaper

broadside
4 hail **5** burst, salvo, sheet, storm **6** shower, volley **7** barrage, torrent **8** at random **9** cannonade, fusillade, laterally, obliquely **11** bombardment

broadtail
4 hawk **5** sheep **7** karakul **8** lambskin

Broadway backer
5 angel

Brobdingnagian
4 huge **5** giant, jumbo **7** hulking, immense, mammoth, massive, titanic **8** colossal, gigantic, towering **9** cyclopean, humongous, monstrous **10** gargantuan, prodigious **11** elephantine

brochette
4 spit **6** skewer

brochure
5 flier, flyer **7** booklet **8** pamphlet

brogue
4 lilt, shoe **6** accent, oxford **7** dialect

broil
3 row **4** bake, burn, char, cook, fray, riot, sear **5** brawl, clash, fight, grill, melee, roast, run-in, toast **6** affray, fracas, scorch, tumult **7** bobbery, rhubarb, ruction, swelter, wrangle **8** disorder, squabble **10** donnybrook, free-for-all **11** disturbance

broiling
3 hot **5** fiery **6** baking, red-hot, torrid **7** blazing, burning **8** ovenlike, scalding, sizzling, white-hot **9** scorching **10** blistering, oppressive, sweltering

broke
4 poor **5** needy, spent **6** busted, ruined **7** drained **8** bankrupt, beggared, dirt poor, indigent, strapped, wiped out **9** destitute, insolvent, out of cash, penniless, penurious, played out **10** cleaned out **11** impecunious

broke-in
4 tame **5** tamed **6** docile

broken
4 shot **5** tamed **6** beaten, busted, cut off, faulty **7** crushed, haywire, humbled, subdued **8** bankrupt, defeated, violated, weakened **9** depressed, disrupted, fractured, heartsick, shattered, sorrowful **11** discouraged, demoralized, interrupted **12** disconnected, disheartened **13** discontinuous

broken-down
7 rickety **8** battered, decaying, decrepit **9** crumbling, neglected **10** threadbare, ramshackle **11** debilitated, dilapidated **12** deteriorated

brokenhearted
7 crushed, unhappy **8** dejected, dolorous, hopeless, wretched **9** depressed, heartsick, sorrowful **10** despairing, despondent **12** inconsolable **13** grief-stricken

broker
5 agent **6** factor **8** diplomat, mediator **9** financier, go-between, middleman **10** interagent, interceder, matchmaker, negotiator **11** intercessor **12** intermediary **13** intermediator

brolly
8 umbrella 11 bumbershoot

bromide
4 bore, drip, lump, pill, yawn 5 drone, grind 6 cliché, old saw, truism 7 proverb 8 banality, chestnut, prosaism, sedative 9 platitude, soporific 10 shibboleth, triviality 11 commonplace, rubber stamp

bromidic
3 dry 4 arid, dull 5 banal, bland, dusty, stale, trite 6 boring 7 humdrum, insipid, tedious 8 shopworn, tiresome 9 dryasdust, moth-eaten, wearisome 10 monotonous, pedestrian, unoriginal 11 commonplace 13 unimaginative, uninteresting

bromine symbol
2 Br

bronco
5 horse 6 cayuse 7 mustang
Australian: 6 brumby

Brontë
character: 9 Catherine, Rochester 10 Heathcliff
novel: 7 Shirley 8 Jane Eyre, Villette 16 Wuthering Heights
sisters: 4 Anne 5 Emily 9 Charlotte

Bronx cheer
3 boo 4 hoot, jeer, razz 5 taunt 7 catcall 9 raspberry

brooch
3 pin 4 clip 5 clasp 8 fastener

brood
3 set, sit 4 fret, mope, muse, stew, sulk 5 cover, flock, gloom, hatch, worry 6 litter, ponder, repine 7 despond, progeny 8 children, meditate, ruminate 9 offspring

brook
4 bear, burn, gill, race, rill 5 abide, creek, stand 6 arroyo, endure, rillet, runnel, stream, suffer 7 rivulet, stomach, swallow 8 stand for, tolerate
Scottish: 6 burnie

Brookner novel
10 Hotel du Lac

broom
5 besom, brush, shrub, sweep, whisk 7 heather

broth
5 stock 8 bouillon, consommé

brothel
4 crib, stew 6 bagnio 7 lupanar 8 bordello, cathouse 9 call house 10 bawdy house, whorehouse

brother
3 kin 4 monk 5 friar 7 comrade, sibling
French: 5 frère
Italian: 3 fra 5 frate 8 fratello
Latin: 6 frater
relating to: 9 fraternal
Spanish: 7 hermano

brotherhood
4 club, gang 5 amity, guild, order, union 6 league 7 kinship, society 8 alliance, sodality 10 fellowship, fraternity, friendship 11 association, camaraderie, comradeship, confederacy 12 togetherness 13 consanguinity, secret society

brotherly
9 fraternal

Brothers Karamazov
4 Ivan 5 Mitya 6 Alexei, Alexey, Dmitri, Dmitry 7 Alyosha 10 Smerdyakov

brought up
4 bred 6 raised, reared

brouhaha
3 din 4 coil, flap, fuss, riot, to-do 5 babel, broil, hoo-ha, whirl 6 bedlam, clamor, fracas, furore, hubbub, hurrah, jangle, pother, racket, ruckus, rumpus, shindy, tumult, uproar 7 ferment 8 foofaraw 9 agitation, commotion 10 excitement, hullabaloo, hurly-burly 11 pandemonium

brow
3 top 4 mien 5 front, crest, crown 8 forehead 9 gangplank 10 expression 11 countenance

browbeat
3 cow 5 beset, bully, harry, press 6 badger, carp at, coerce, harass, hector, lean on 7 bluster, dragoon 8 bludgeon, bulldoze, bullyrag, domineer, overbear, pressure 9 tyrannize 10 intimidate

brown
4 sear 5 dusky, toast 6 scorch, tanned 7 swarthy
dark: 5 mocha, sepia, umber 9 chocolate
grayish: 3 dun 6 bister, bistre
light: 3 tan 4 ecru, fawn 5 beige, hazel, khaki, tawny
moderate: 4 teak 6 sienna
reddish: 3 bay 4 roan 5 henna 6 auburn, russet, sorrel, titian 8 chestnut
yellowish: 6 bronze 12 butterscotch

Brown Bomber
5 Louis (Joe)

brown coal
7 lignite

brownie
3 elf, fay 5 fairy, pixie 6 sprite

Browning poem
8 Prospice, Sordello 11 Aurora Leigh, Pippa Passes 12 Rabbi Ben Ezra 13 Fra Lippo Lippi, My Last Duchess 14 How Do I Love Thee?

brown recluse
6 spider

brownshirt
4 Nazi **12** storm trooper

browse
4 crop, feed, scan, shop, skim **5** graze, munch **6** forage, nibble, peruse **7** dip into, pasture **8** glance at, look over **10** glance over **11** flip through, leaf through, look through, skim through **12** thumb through

Broz, Josip
4 Tito

bruin
4 bear

bruise
5 pound, wound **6** batter, damage, injure, injury **7** contuse **8** abrasion, discolor **9** contusion **13** discoloration

bruit about
6 blazon, gossip, report, spread **7** declare, publish **8** announce, proclaim **9** advertise, broadcast, circulate **10** annunciate, pass around, promulgate **11** blaze abroad

brume
3 fog **4** film, haze, mist, murk **5** vapor **6** miasma **8** haziness **11** obscuration

brummagem
4 fake, sham **5** bogus, false, gaudy, phony, showy **6** ersatz, pseudo, shoddy, tinsel, tawdry **7** chintzy **8** spurious **9** imitation, pinchbeck, tasteless **10** fabricated, fictitious **11** counterfeit, make-believe

brunch cocktail
5 shrub **6** mimosa **7** bellini **10** Bloody Mary **11** screwdriver

Brunei
capital: 17 Bandar Seri Begawan
island: 6 Borneo
language: 5 Malay
neighbor: 8 Malaysia
sea: 10 South China

brunet
3 jet **4** dark, onyx **5** dusky, ebony, raven, sable, sooty, swart **6** swarth **7** swarthy **8** bistered, obsidian **10** dark-haired **11** brown-haired

Brunhild
5 queen **7** heroine **8** Valkyrie
husband: 6 Gunnar **7** Gunther
lover: 9 Siegfried

brunt
4 jolt **5** shock **6** burden, impact

brush
4 clip, kiss, skim **5** broom, clash, graze, run-in, scrap, scrub, shave, sweep, whisk **6** glance, scrape, tussle **7** contact, thicket **8** skirmish **9** encounter, shrubbery, sideswipe **11** undergrowth

brusque
4 curt, tart **5** bluff, blunt, brief, gruff, rough, short, surly, terse **6** abrupt, crusty, snippy **7** uncivil **8** impolite, snippety, succinct **10** peremptory, ungracious **11** ill-mannered **12** discourteous

brutal
4 hard **5** cruel, feral, harsh **6** rugged, savage, severe **7** beastly, bestial, callous, inhuman, swinish, vicious **8** barbaric, pitiless, ruthless, sadistic **9** barbarous, ferocious, merciless **10** relentless **11** cold-blooded, remorseless **12** bloodthirsty

brutalize
5 abuse **6** debase, harden **7** corrupt, debauch, deprave, pervert, roughen, subvert, vitiate **8** maltreat, mistreat **9** manhandle **10** bestialize

brute
4 ogre **5** beast, cruel, feral **6** animal, savage **7** beastly, bestial, inhuman, piggish, swinish, varmint **8** creature **10** troglodyte **11** instinctive

brutish
3 low **4** base, vile **5** crude, feral, gross, rough, stony **6** animal, carnal, coarse, scurvy, strong **7** beastly, bestial, boorish, inhuman, obscene, piggish, swinish, uncivil, uncouth **8** barbaric, degraded, depraved, inhumane, physical, sadistic **9** primitive, truculent, unrefined **11** animalistic, uncivilized

bryophyte
4 moss **8** hornwort **9** liverwort

Brythonic
see **Cymric**

bubble
3 sac **4** blob, boil, dome, fizz, foam, moil **5** churn, froth, slosh, spume, swash **6** burble, gurgle, seethe, simmer **7** ferment, globule, vesicle **10** effervesce

bubbly
5 alive, fizzy, foamy, jolly, perky, sudsy **6** cheery, frothy, lively **7** buoyant, excited **8** animated, effusive **9** champagne, ebullient, exuberant, sparkling **10** carbonated

buccaneer
5 rover **6** cowboy, pirate, sea dog **7** corsair, sea wolf **8** picaroon, sea rover **9** sea robber **10** freebooter

buck
3 fop, guy, lad, lug **4** balk, bear, bill, chap, clam, dude, jerk, load, male, move, note, oner, pack, stag, tote, trip **5** cadet, carry, dandy, ferry, fight, money, pitch, repel, stark, throw, token **6** combat, dollar, fellow, oppose, resist, unseat **7** coxcomb, trestle **8** antelope, bank note, sawhorse, traverse **9** greenback, withstand, workhorse **10** completely **11** Beau Brummel

bucket
3 fly, run **4** pail, rush, whiz **5** hurry, speed **6** barrel, basket, hasten, hustle, vessel **9** clamshell **10** receptacle

Buckeye State
4 Ohio

buckle
4 bend, clip, fold, hasp, kink, warp **5** catch, clamp, clasp, heave, yield **6** cave in, fasten **7** contort, crumple, harness **8** collapse **9** fastening **10** coffee cake

buckle under
3 bow **4** cave, fold, give **5** defer, yield **6** cave in, submit **7** concede, succumb **8** collapse **9** surrender **10** capitulate **11** admit defeat

Buck novel
9 Good Earth (The)

buckram
4 taut **5** stiff **6** wooden **8** starched **9** cardboard, unbending **10** inflexible **11** interlining

bucks
4 kale **5** bread, dough, money, moola **6** dinero, do-re-mi, moolah **7** lettuce **10** greenbacks

buck up
4 buoy, lift **5** cheer, rally **6** solace **7** comfort, console, gladden, improve, refresh, smarten **8** brighten **9** encourage **10** strengthen

____ buco
4 osso

bucolic
5 rural **6** rustic **7** georgic, halcyon, idyllic **8** agrarian, arcadian, pastoral **10** campestral, provincial **11** countrified, picturesque

bud
4 germ, seed **5** gemma, spark **6** sprout **7** burgeon **9** pullulate **10** primordium
combining form: **5** blast **6** blasto

Buddha
7 Gautama **10** Siddhartha
dialogues: **5** sutra
disciple: **6** Ananda
enemy: **4** Mara
Japanese: **5** Amida, Amita
mother: **4** Maya
son: **6** Rahula
teachings: **6** dharma
wife: **9** Yasodhara

Buddhist
chant: **6** mantra
dialogues: **5** sutra
enlightenment: **6** satori
evil spirit: **4** Mara
fate: **5** karma
language: **4** Pali **8** Sanskrit
monk: **4** lama **5** arhat, bonze
sacred city: **5** Lhasa
saint: **5** arhat
scripture: **5** sutra **6** sutras **9** Pali canon
sect, tradition: **3** Son, Zen **4** Chan **5** Kegon **6** Huayan, Tendai **7** Tiantai **8** Hinayana, Mahayana, Nichiren, Pure Land **9** Theravada, Vajrayana
shrine: **4** tope **5** stupa **7** chorten
spell: **6** mantra
spiritual leader: **4** guru **9** Dalai Lama
state of happiness: **7** nirvana
temple: **6** pagoda
title: **7** mahatma
tree of enlightenment: **2** bo **5** bodhi, pipal

buddy
3 mac, pal **4** chum, mate **5** crony **6** comate, fellow, friend **7** compeer, comrade, partner **8** coworker, playmate, sidekick **9** associate, companion **10** accomplice **11** confederate

buddy-buddy
5 close, pally, thick, tight **6** chummy **8** intimate **10** palsy-walsy **11** inseparable

budge
4 move **5** shift, yield **7** give way

budgerigar
6 parrot **8** parakeet

budget
5 funds, means **6** amount, ration, supply **8** allocate, estimate **9** allowance, apportion, resources

buff
3 fan, fit, nut, rub, tan **4** ecru, fawn, sand, wipe **5** beige, brush, fiend, freak, glaze, gloss, lover, shine, toned **6** addict, expert, polish, votary **7** admirer, burnish, devotee, fanatic, fancier, furbish, groupie, habitué **8** follower **9** yellowish **10** aficionado, altogether, enthusiast **11** connoisseur, yellow-brown

buffalo
4 anoa, arna, bilk, faze **5** bison, bovid, stump **6** baffle, muddle, rattle **7** carabao, confuse, defraud, flummox, fluster, nonplus, perplex, swindle **8** befuddle, bewilder, confound, hoodwink **9** bamboozle, dumbfound

buffalo grass
5 grama

buffer
6 screen, shield **7** buckler, bulwark, cushion **8** absorber, mediator, polisher **9** safeguard **10** protection **12** intermediary

buffet
3 box, hit, rap **4** beat, blip, blow, bump, chop, cuff, drub, jolt, move, poke, slap, sock **5** clout, drive, force, pound, punch, smack, spank **6** batter, hammer, pummel, thrash, wallop **7** belabor, clobber, counter, lambast **8** lambaste, salad bar **9** sideboard

buffoon
3 wag **4** dolt, fool, goof, lout, zany **5** antic, clown, comic, droll, dunce, joker, yokel **6** jester **7** bumpkin, dullard **8** bonehead **9** blockhead, harlequin **10** clodhopper **11** merry-andrew

bug
3 fad, fan, irk, nag, nut, spy, tap, vex **4** buff, flaw, fret, gall, germ, rage **5** annoy, bulge, craze, fiend, freak, mania, peeve **6** badger, bother, defect, insect, malady, needle, nettle, pester, plague, zealot **7** disease, fanatic, microbe, provoke, wiretap **8** irritate, listen in, protrude, sickness **9** eavesdrop, infection, obsession **10** enthusiast **12** imperfection **13** microorganism

bugaboo
see **bugbear**

bugbear
4 bane, bogy, fear, ogre **5** bogey, bogie, poser **6** goblin, teaser **7** bugaboo, problem, specter, spectre **8** anathema, bogeyman, phantasm **9** bête noire, boogerman, boogeyman, hobgoblin **10** black beast **11** abomination

buggy
4 cart, tram **6** go-cart, jalopy **8** carriage

bugle
call: **4** mess, taps **5** drill **6** sennet, tattoo **7** fanfare, retreat, tantara **8** assembly, reveille
relative: **6** cornet **7** trumpet **10** flugelhorn
sound: **5** blare

build
3 wax **4** body, form, make, mode, mold, rise **5** boost, erect, forge, frame, habit, mount, put up, raise, set up, shape, swell **6** expand, figure **7** amplify, augment, compose, enlarge, fashion, magnify, produce, upsurge **8** assemble, compound, engineer, escalate, heighten, increase, multiply, physique **9** construct, establish, fabricate, institute, intensify, originate **10** accelerate, inaugurate, strengthen **11** fit together, manufacture **12** conformation, constitution

builder
5 mason **9** carpenter **10** bricklayer, contractor

builder's knot
10 clove hitch

building
3 hut **5** house **7** edifice **8** dwelling **9** structure
addition: **3** ell **4** wing **5** annex
block: **4** Lego **5** brick
compartment: **3** bay **4** room **6** office
connector: **9** breezeway
farm: **4** barn, crib, shed, silo
for apartments: **8** tenement
for arms: **7** arsenal
for gambling: **6** casino
for grain: **4** silo **7** granary **8** elevator
for horses: **6** stable
for manufacture: **4** shop **5** plant **7** factory
for music: **10** auditorium
for sports: **3** gym **4** bowl **5** arena **7** stadium **8** coliseum **9** gymnasium **10** hippodrome
material: **4** iron, wood **5** adobe, brick, glass, steel, stone **6** cement **8** concrete
projection: **3** bay, ell **4** wing **5** annex **6** dormer **7** cornice
round: **7** rotunda

building kit
5 Legos **10** Erector set **11** Lincoln Logs

build up
4 hype, plug, puff **5** boost, brace, erect **6** accrue, expand, extend, praise **7** collect, develop, enhance, fortify, improve, promote **8** buttress, heighten, increase **9** advertise, construct, establish, intensify, publicize **10** accumulate, aggrandize, strengthen

buildup
4 hype, puff, to-do **6** growth, hoopla **8** increase, ballyhoo **9** accretion, expansion, promotion, publicity **10** escalation **11** development, enhancement, enlargement **12** accumulation, augmentation **13** strengthening

built-in
6 inborn, inbred, innate **8** included, inherent **9** essential, ingrained, intrinsic **10** congenital, deep-seated, indwelling **11** established, fundamental **12** constitutive, incorporated

bulb
4 leek, lily, sego **5** onion, tulip **6** allium, dahlia, garlic, squill **8** daffodil, hyacinth **9** amaryllis, narcissus
segment: **5** clove

bulb-like bud
4 corm **5** tuber **7** rhizome

Bulgaria
capital: **5** Sofia
city: **4** Ruse **5** Stara, Varna **6** Burgas, Pleven, Zagora **7** Plovdiv
monetary unit: **3** lev
mountain, range: **6** Balkan, Musala **7** Rhodope
neighbor: **6** Greece, Serbia, Turkey **7** Romania **9** Macedonia
part of: **7** Balkans
river: **6** Danube **7** Maritsa
sea: **5** Black

bulge
3 bag, jut, sac, sag **4** blob, bump, edge, lump, poke **5** bloat, pouch, swell **6** beetle, billow, bubble, bug out, dilate, excess, expand **7** balloon, distend, inflate, project, puff out **8** overhang, protrude, stand out, stick out, swelling **9** allowance, head start **10** distension, projection, promontory, protrusion **11** excrescence, protuberate **12** protuberance

bulk
4 body, core, heft, loom, mass **5** fiber, swell, total **6** amount, corpus, expand, volume **7** bigness, quantum **8** majority, quantity, stand out **9** aggregate, magnitude, substance

bulky
3 fat **5** beefy, hefty, husky, large, obese, stout **7** massive **8** cumbrous, unwieldy **9** corpulent, ponderous **10** cumbersome, overweight **11** substantial

bull
4 bunk, male, slip, toro, trip **5** boner, edict, error, fluff, force, hooey, lapse **6** bovine, bungle, decree, el toro **7** baloney, blooper, blunder, hogwash, mistake **8** nonsense **9** detective
combining form: **4** taur **5** tauri, tauro

bulldoze
3 cow **4** move, push, raze **5** abash, bully, clear, cream, elbow, force, level, press, scare, shove **6** coerce, hector, hustle, jostle, lean on, menace, propel, thrust **7** bluster, clobber, dragoon, flatten, oppress, trounce **8** bludgeon, browbeat, bullyrag, demolish, domineer, restrain, shoulder **9** terrorize, tyrannize **10** intimidate, obliterate

bullet
3 ace **4** slug **6** dumdum, tracer **9** cartridge **10** projectile
size: **7** caliber, calibre

bulletin
4 news **5** flash, scoop **6** notice, report **7** account, catalog, gazette, message, missive, release **8** briefing, calendar, dispatch, magazine, register **9** catalogue, statement **10** communiqué, periodical **12** announcement

bull fiddle
10 contrabass, double bass

bullfighter
6 torero **7** matador, picador **8** toreador **11** cuadrillero **12** banderillero
famous: **6** Arruza **7** Ordóñez **8** Belmonte, Joselito, Manolete **9** Dominguin **10** El Cordobés

bullfighting
arena: **5** plaza
cheer: **3** olé
hero: **6** torero **7** matador **8** toreador
lancer: **7** picador
red cloth: **6** muleta
Spanish: **7** corrida
team: **9** cuadrilla

bullheaded
6 mulish **7** adamant, willful **8** contrary, obdurate, perverse, stubborn **9** insistent, obstinate, pigheaded **10** headstrong, refractory, self-willed, unyielding **11** intractable, stiff-necked **12** intransigent, pertinacious, strong-willed

bullish
4 rosy **6** brawny, rising, upbeat **7** booming **9** advancing, expanding, favorable **10** optimistic

bully
3 cow **4** goon, pimp, punk, thug **5** abuse, heavy, meany, tease, tough **6** harass, hector, meanie, menace, pander, pick on, rascal **7** bluster, buffalo, dragoon, harrier, oppress, ruffian, torment, torture **8** bludgeon, browbeat, bulldoze, bullyrag, harasser, threaten **9** bulldozer, persecute, victimize, tormenter, tyrannize **10** browbeater, corned beef, intimidate, persecutor **11** intimidator

bullyrag
see **bulldoze**

bulrush
4 reed, tule **5** sedge **7** cattail, papyrus

bulwark
4 wall **6** screen, shield **7** barrier, bastion, parapet, rampart, seawall **8** buttress, fortress, palisade **9** earthwork, safeguard **10** breakwater, breastwork, embankment, stronghold **13** fortification

bum
3 beg, vag **4** bust, hobo, idle, laze, lazy, loaf, loll, slug, wino **5** binge, cadge, drunk, hit up, idler, mooch, tramp **6** bottom, dawdle, loafer, loiter, lounge, slouch, unfair **7** depress, drifter, feel low, goof off, rear end, vagrant, wheedle **8** buttocks, derelict, fainéant, slugabed, sluggard, vagabond **9** do-nothing, goldbrick, importune, lazybones, panhandle, transient

bumbershoot
6 brolly **8** umbrella

bumble
3 mar **4** blow, flub, muff **5** botch, fluff, gum up, lurch **6** bobble, bollix, bungle, falter, fumble, mess up, muck up, rumble, slip up, teeter, totter **7** blunder, screw up, stagger, stumble **8** flounder

bumbling
5 inept, gawky **6** clumsy, gauche, klutzy **7** awkward, halting, unhandy **8** ungainly **9** all thumbs, graceless, ham-handed, incapable, maladroit, unskilled **11** heavy-handed, incompetent **13** butterfingers, uncoordinated

bummer
3 dud **4** drag, flop, hobo **5** tramp **6** beggar, cadger, downer, sponge, too bad **7** failure, forager, moocher, sponger **8** deadbeat, vagabond **9** tough luck **10** freebooter, panhandler, rotten luck, wet blanket

bump
3 bop, hit, jar, ram, rap, wen **4** bang, bash, bust, jolt, knot, lump, oust, slam **5** break, carom, clash, crack, crash, gnarl, knock, prang, shift, shock, shove, wound **6** demote, growth, impact, injury, jostle, jounce, nodule, remove, strike,

wallop **7** collide, degrade, demerit, pothole, run into **8** demotion, dislodge, displace, swelling **9** carbuncle, collision, contusion, convexity **10** concussion, projection, protrusion **12** protuberance

bumpkin
3 oaf **4** boor, hick, lout, rube **5** clown, swain, yokel **6** rustic **7** hayseed, peasant **9** chawbacon, hillbilly, simpleton **10** clodhopper, country boy, countryman, provincial

bump off
3 ice **4** do in, kill, slay **5** erase, snuff **6** murder, rub out **7** butcher, execute, take out **8** knock off **9** eliminate, liquidate **11** assassinate

Bumppo, Natty
alias: 7 Hawkeye **10** Deerslayer, Pathfinder
creator: 6 Cooper (James Fenimore)

bumptious
5 cocky, pushy **8** arrogant, impudent **9** audacious, obnoxious, obtrusive, officious **13** self-assertive

bumpy
5 jerky, nubby, ridgy, rough **6** bouncy, jouncy, knobby, knotty, patchy, pimply, uneven **7** jolting, nodular **9** difficult, irregular

bun
4 load, roll **6** pastry

bunch
3 lot, set, wen **4** band, bevy, bump, clot, crew, knot, lump, mass, push, slew **5** batch, clump, covey, crowd, flock, group, party, spray, stack, swell **6** bundle, circle, clutch, gather, huddle, parcel, throng **7** bouquet, collect, cluster **8** assembly, protrude, swelling **9** gathering **10** assemblage, assortment, collection, congregate **11** aggregation **12** accumulation

bunco steerer
3 gyp **6** con man **7** cheater, diddler, grifter, sharper **8** swindler **9** defrauder, trickster **12** double-dealer **13** confidence man

bundle
3 lot, pot, set, wad **4** bale, body, heap, mint, pack, pile, wrap **5** array, batch, bunch, clump, group, sheaf, truss **6** fardel, packet, parcel **7** cluster, fortune **8** fascicle **10** assortment

bung
4 plug **5** cecum, spile **7** stopper

bungalow
5 cabin, lodge **6** chalet **7** cottage

bungle
3 err **4** flub, goof, mess, muff, slip, trip **5** boner, botch, error, fluff, gum up, lapse, misdo, mix up, spoil **6** bollix, bumble, fiasco, foozle, foul up, fumble, goof up, mess up, muck up, muddle **7** blooper, blunder, failure, louse up, misstep, mistake, stumble **9** mishandle, mismanage

bungler
3 oaf **4** clod, dolt, goof **5** klutz **7** screw-up, tomfool **8** bonehead, goofball, shlemiel **9** blunderer, schlemiel **10** stumblebum **11** blunderbuss, incompetent **13** butterfingers

bunglesome
6 clumsy, klutzy **7** awkward **8** bumbling **9** all thumbs **13** uncoordinated

bung up
4 beat, hurt **5** abuse, pound **6** batter, bruise, injure **7** contuse, disable **9** disfigure, manhandle

bunion
4 lump **8** swelling **10** protrusion, tumescence **11** enlargement

bunk
3 bed, cot, kip, rot **4** bosh, bull, guff, jazz **5** bilge, board, crash, hokum, hooey, house, lodge, put up **6** humbug, pallet, piffle **7** eyewash, baloney, hogwash, rubbish, twaddle **8** claptrap, domicile, flimflam, malarkey, nonsense, tommyrot **9** poppycock **10** balderdash

bunker
3 bin **6** dugout **7** bastion, chamber **8** sand trap **10** embankment, stronghold **11** compartment

bunkum
3 rot **4** bosh, bull, guff, jazz **5** bilge, hokum, hooey **6** humbug, piffle **7** baloney, hogwash, rubbish, twaddle **8** claptrap, flimflam, malarkey, nonsense, tommyrot **9** poppycock **10** balderdash

bunting
5 finch, flags **8** songbird **9** streamers

Bunyanesque
4 huge **5** giant, jumbo **7** mammoth, massive, titanic **8** behemoth, colossal, gigantic, towering **9** Herculean **10** gargantuan, prodigious

Bunyan's ox
4 Babe

buoy
4 lift, prop **5** boost, cheer, float, raise **6** assist, beacon, bear up, buck up, signal, solace, uphold, uplift **7** bolster, comfort, gladden, hearten, support, sustain **9** encourage

buoyancy
6 bounce, levity **7** jollity **8** airiness **10** ebullience, exuberance, exuberancy, liveliness, resilience **12** floatability **13** effervescence

buoyant
3 gay **4** airy **5** sunny **6** afloat, bouncy **7** elastic **8** cheerful, floating, volatile **9** expansive, floatable, resilient **10** unsinkable, weightless **12** effervescent, lighthearted

burble
3 gas, yak **4** blab, chat, gush, talk, wash **5** clack, plash, run on, slosh, swash **6** babble, bubble,

gabble, gurgle, murmur, rattle, splash, yammer **7** chatter, prattle, sparkle

burden
3 tax, try **4** care, clog, core, duty, gist, haul, lade, load, onus, pile, pith, task, text **5** brunt, cargo, press, theme, weigh **6** amount, charge, chorus, cumber, hamper, lading, lumber, saddle, strain, stress, thrust, upshot, weight **7** afflict, anxiety, freight, oppress, payload, refrain, purport **8** encumber, handicap, obligate, overload, shiralee **9** millstone, substance, weigh down **10** deadweight **11** encumbrance

burdensome
5 tough **6** taxing, trying **7** arduous, exigent, irksome, onerous, weighty **8** crushing, exacting, grievous **9** demanding, difficult, fatiguing, ponderous **10** exhausting, oppressive **11** troublesome **12** backbreaking, unmanageable

bureau
4 unit **5** chest **6** agency **7** dresser, section **8** ministry **10** department, chiffonier **11** writing desk

bureaucrat
8 mandarin, minister, official **11** functionary **12** civil servant, officeholder

burg
4 city, town **7** borough **8** fortress **10** metropolis, walled town **12** municipality

burgee
4 flag **6** banner, ensign, pennon **7** pendant, pennant **8** standard, streamer

burgeon
4 blow, boom, open **5** bloom, build, mount, run up **6** emerge, expand, flower, sprout, thrive, unfold **7** augment, blossom, develop, enlarge, fill out, prosper, run riot **8** flourish, heighten, increase, multiply, mushroom, snowball **9** germinate **10** burst forth, effloresce

Burgess novel
7 Enderby **13** Earthly Powers **15** Clockwork Orange (A)

burghal
5 civic, urban **8** citified **9** municipal **12** metropolitan

burgher
7 citizen, denizen **8** townsman

burglar
4 yegg **5** thief
loot: **4** swag

burglarize
see **burgle**

burglary
5 heist, theft **7** larceny

burgle
3 rob **4** lift, loot **5** heist, steal, strip **6** rip off, thieve **7** despoil, plunder, ransack **9** break into, knock over **10** housebreak

burgomaster
5 mayor **10** magistrate

Burgundy wine
grape: **5** Gamay **9** Pinot Noir **10** Chardonnay
red: **8** Mercurey **10** Beaujolais
white: **5** Rully **6** Chagny **7** Chablis **10** Montrachet **13** Pouilly-Fuissé

burial
4 tomb **5** grave **7** funeral **9** interment, obsequies, sepulcher, sepulchre, sepulture **10** entombment, inhumation
box: **6** casket, coffin
ceremony: **7** funeral, obsequy **9** obsequies
mound: **6** barrow **7** tumulus
tomb: **9** mausoleum, sepulcher, sepulchre

burial ground
8 boot hill, cemetery **8** boneyard, God's acre **9** graveyard **10** churchyard, necropolis **12** memorial park, potter's field
early Christian: **8** catacomb

Burkina Faso
capital: **11** Ouagadougou
ethnic group: **3** Gur **5** Mossi **7** Voltaic
former name: **10** Upper Volta
language: **4** Moré **5** Dyula **6** French
monetary unit: **5** franc
neighbor: **4** Mali, Togo **5** Benin, Ghana, Niger **10** Ivory Coast
river: **5** Volta (Black, Red) **6** Nazion **7** Mouhoun, Nakanbe **8** Red Volta **10** Black Volta

burlap
5 gunny **6** fabric **7** bagging, sacking
fiber: **4** hemp, jute

burlesque
3 ape **4** mock, sham **5** farce, spoof **6** parody, satire, send-up **7** lampoon, mockery, mocking, takeoff **8** pastiche, skin show, travesty **10** caricature, distortion, girlie show, lampoonery

burly
4 hale **5** beefy, hefty, husky, tough **6** brawny, robust, strong, stocky **8** athletic, heavyset, muscular, powerful, stalwart, thickset, vigorous **9** strapping

Burma
see **Myanmar**

burn
4 bake, char, cook, fire, fume, rage, sear **5** anger, blaze, broil, creek, flame, flare, gleam, roast, scald, singe, smart, smoke, sting, toast **6** ignite, kindle, scorch, seethe **7** bristle, combust, consume, cremate, flare up, inflame, radiate, smolder, swelter **8** smoulder **9** carbonize, cauterize **10** incinerate

burnable
8 volatile **9** flammable, ignitable **10** incendiary **11** combustible, inflammable

burned-out
4 beat, shot **5** spent, weary **6** sapped **7** drained, worn-out **8** consumed, fatigued **9** destroyed, exhausted, played-out **10** broken-down **11** debilitated **12** extinguished

burner
3 hob **4** ring

burning
3 hot **5** afire, aglow, fiery **6** ablaze, aflame, alight, ardent, fervid, heated, hectic, red-hot, torrid, urgent **7** blazing, fervent, fevered, glowing, ignited, kindled, searing **8** broiling, feverish, pressing, sizzling, white-hot **9** scorching **10** imperative, passionate **11** conflagrant, impassioned **12** incandescent
combining form: **4** igni
malicious: **5** arson

burnish
3 rub, wax **4** buff **5** glaze, gloss, scour, sheen, shine **6** luster, patina, polish, smooth **7** furbish, varnish **8** brighten

burnished
5 shiny **6** glossy, satiny, sheeny **7** lambent, radiant, shining **8** gleaming, lustrous, polished **9** brilliant **10** glistening **11** resplendent

burnsides
8 whiskers **9** sideburns **10** sideboards **11** dundrearies, muttonchops **12** side-whiskers

burp
5 belch, eruct, expel

burro
3 ass **6** donkey **7** jackass

Burroughs hero
6 Tarzan

burrow
3 den, dig **4** hole, lair, mine, nook, snug **5** delve, gouge, lodge **6** cavity, cuddle, nestle, nuzzle, tunnel **7** snuggle **10** excavation

burst
3 pop, run **4** bang, boom, clap, gush, gust, rive, rush, slam, wham **5** blast, crack, crash, erupt, flare, go off, lunge, sally, salvo, smash, spasm, split, storm, surge **6** access, blow up, emerge, irrupt, launch, plunge, shiver, spring, shower, volley **7** assault, barrage, dehisce, explode, flare-up, fly open, rupture, shatter, torrent **8** detonate, drumfire, eruption, fragment, outbreak, splinter, splitter **9** broadside, cannonade, explosion, fusillade, onslaught **11** bombardment

Burundi
capital: **9** Bujumbura
ethnic group: **4** Hutu **5** Tutsi
former name: **6** Urundi
lake: **10** Tanganyika
language: **5** Rundi **6** French **7** Kirundi
monetary unit: **5** franc
neighbor: **5** Congo **6** Rwanda **8** Tanzania

bury
4 hide, sink, stow **5** cache, cover, embed, inter, plant, stash **6** absorb, entomb, inhume, mantle, shroud **7** blanket, conceal, cover up, implant, lay away, overlay, put away, secrete **8** ensconce, submerge

bus
5 clear **6** jitney **7** missile, trolley, vehicle **9** hand truck **10** spacecraft

bush
4 rose **5** lilac, shrub, wahoo **6** azalea, cassis, privet **7** currant, thicket, weigela **8** backland, barberry, hazelnut **9** backwater, backwoods, forsythia, manzanita **10** gooseberry, hinterland, wilderness **11** pussy willow **12** rhododendron

bushel
3 ton **4** heap, load, pile **6** basket, hamper **7** pannier

bush-league
5 minor **6** junior, two-bit **8** inferior, mediocre, small-fry **9** small-time **10** inadequate, second-rate **11** lightweight **13** insignificant

bushranger
6 outlaw **8** woodsman **12** frontiersman

bushwhack
4 trap **6** ambush, assail, attack, entrap, waylay **7** assault **8** surprise **9** blindside

bushwhacker
6 bandit, outlaw, raider, sniper **8** guerilla, woodsman **9** guerrilla **10** highwayman

bushy
5 bosky, fuzzy, hairy, leafy **6** fluffy, woolly **7** hirsute, unkempt **9** bristling, luxuriant, overgrown **10** disordered **11** flourishing

business
3 job **4** firm, line, work **5** trade **6** affair, custom, matter, métier, office, outfit, racket **7** calling, company, concern, pursuit, traffic **8** commerce, function, industry **9** patronage **10** employment, enterprise, livelihood, occupation **11** corporation **13** establishment
course: **7** finance **8** modeling **9** marketing **10** accounting
expense: **8** overhead
syndicate: **6** cartel

businesslike
6 formal **7** orderly, serious **8** diligent, thorough **9** competent, efficient, practical, pragmatic **10** impersonal, methodical, no-nonsense, purposeful, systematic **11** disciplined, hardworking **12** professional

businessman
6 broker, dealer, trader, tycoon 7 magnate 8 investor, merchant 9 bourgeois, financier, tradesman, executive 10 capitalist, trafficker 12 entrepreneur, merchandiser 13 industrialist

busker
8 minstrel, musician 11 entertainer

buss
4 kiss, peck 5 smack 6 smooch 8 osculate

bust
3 bag, cop, dud, hit, jag, nab, net 4 bomb, bump, fail, flop, fold, raid, ruin, slug, sock, tear, tour 5 binge, bosom, break, broke, burst, catch, chest, crash, lemon, loser, punch, smash, spell, spree, stint, torso, trash 6 arrest, bender, breast, collar, demote, pick up 7 break up, carouse, degrade, demerit, destroy, exhaust, failure, rupture, wear out 8 bankrupt, demolish, fracture 9 apprehend, break down, destitute, downgrade, penniless 10 impoverish, police raid
opposite: 4 boom

bustle
3 ado, fly, run 4 flit, fuss, rush, stir, tear, teem, to-do 5 hurry, whirl, whisk 6 action, be busy, bestir, clamor, flurry, furore, hassle, hasten, hubbub, hustle, motion, pother, scurry, tumult, uproar 7 ferment, turmoil 8 activity, to-and-fro 9 commotion, whirlpool, whirlwind 10 hurly-burly, excitement, liveliness

bustling
4 busy, rife 5 brisk, fussy, peppy 6 active, hectic, lively 7 dynamic, festive, hopping, humming, jumping 8 animated, swarming, vigorous 9 energetic 10 tumultuous 11 hard-working, industrious

busty
5 ample, buxom, curvy 6 bosomy, chesty, zaftig 7 shapely, stacked 10 curvaceous, voluptuous 11 full-bosomed, well-rounded

busy
5 brisk, fussy, in use 6 active, at work, lively, on duty, tied up 7 crowded, engaged, hopping, humming, swamped, teeming, working 8 bustling, diligent, employed, hustling, meddling, occupied, overdone, sedulous 9 assiduous, congested, elaborate, energetic, intrusive, obtrusive, officious 10 meddlesome 11 distracting, impertinent, industrious, unavailable

busybody
5 prier, pryer, snoop, yenta 6 butt-in, gossip, old hen 7 meddler 8 informer, kibitzer, quidnunc 9 pragmatic 10 chatterbox, newsmonger, pragmatist, talebearer, tattletale 11 nosey parker, rumormonger 12 gossipmonger, rubbernecker, troublemaker

but
3 bar, yet 4 just, only, save 5 alone 6 except, merely, saving, unless 7 barring, besides, however 8 entirely 9 aside from, excepting, excluding, outside of 13 on the contrary

butcher
4 ruin, slay 5 botch, carve, clean, spoil, wreck 6 bollix, killer, mess up, slayer 7 cut meat, destroy, meat man 8 mutilate 9 slaughter 11 slaughterer

butcher-bird
6 shrike

butcherly
5 cruel 6 bloody, clumsy, savage 7 awkward 8 sadistic 9 ferocious, merciless 10 unskillful

butchery
7 carnage 8 abattoir, genocide, massacre 9 bloodbath, bloodshed, holocaust, slaughter 10 mass murder 12 annihilation 13 extermination

buteo
4 hawk 7 buzzard

butler
5 valet 7 steward 10 manservant

Butler, Samuel
novel: 7 Erewhon 13 Way of All Flesh (The)
poem: 8 Hudibras

butt
3 end, keg, tip, ram, tun, vat 4 base, cask, drum, dupe, join, push, rump, stub, tail 5 chump, fanny, patsy, stump, touch, verge 6 adjoin, barrel, border, bottom, firkin, pigeon, sucker, target, thrust, victim 7 collide, fall guy, rear end, run into 8 derriere, hogshead, neighbor 9 cigarette, fundament, lie beside, pilgarlic, posterior, remainder 11 communicate, sitting duck 12 hindquarters 13 laughingstock

butter
artificial: 4 oleo 9 margarine 13 oleomargarine
Indian: 4 ghee
piece: 3 pat
semifluid: 4 ghee
tree: 4 shea

butterball
5 blimp, whale 8 dumpling, elephant 10 bufflehead

butterfish
6 gunnel

butterfly
4 blue 5 diana, satyr, zebra 6 copper, morpho 7 admiral, buckeye, monarch, satyrid, skipper, sulphur, vanessa, viceroy 8 crescent, grayling, milkweed, victoria 9 aphrodite, metalmark,

nymphalid, wood nymph **10** fritillary, hairstreak **11** swallowtail
bush: **8** buddleia
fish: **6** blenny, chiton **7** gurnard
larva: **11** caterpillar
lily: **8** mariposa
order: **11** Lepidoptera
plant: **8** oncidium
pupa: **9** chrysalis
scientist: **13** lepidopterist

butter up
4 coax **5** charm **6** cajole, kowtow, praise, stroke **7** adulate, beguile, blarney, flatter, massage, wheedle **8** blandish, bootlick, soft-soap **9** brownnose, sweet-talk **10** overpraise

butt in
6 kibitz, meddle **7** intrude, obtrude **8** busybody, overstep **9** interfere, interlope, interpose, interrupt

buttinsky
7 meddler **8** busybody, kibitzer, quidnunc **9** loudmouth **10** trespasser **12** troublemaker

buttocks
4 rear, rump, seat, tail **5** fanny, nates **6** behind, bottom, breech, heinie **7** hind end, hunkers, keister, rear end, tail end **8** backside, derriere, haunches **9** fundament, posterior

buttonball
8 sycamore **9** plane tree

button-down
6 square, stuffy **8** decorous, orthodox, straight **10** restrained **11** straitlaced, traditional **12** conservative, conventional

buttonhole
5 lobby **6** accost, chat up, detain, waylay **8** confront

buttonwood
8 sycamore **9** plane tree

buttress
4 pier, prop, stay **5** brace, carry, shore, strut, truss **6** back up, bear up, hold up, column, uphold **7** bolster, bulwark, fortify, shore up, support, sustain **9** reinforce, stanchion **10** strengthen **12** underpinning **13** fortification, reinforcement

buxom
5 ample, busty, curvy **6** bosomy, chesty, zaftig **7** shapely, stacked **10** curvaceous, voluptuous **11** full-bosomed, full-figured, well-rounded

buy
5 bribe **6** obtain, ransom, redeem **7** acquire, bargain, believe **8** purchase

buy back
6 ransom, recoup, redeem, regain **8** retrieve **10** repurchase

buyer
6 client, patron, vendee **7** shopper **8** consumer, customer **9** purchaser

buy off
3 fix, sop **5** bribe **6** settle **7** corrupt, silence **9** influence **10** manipulate, tamper with

buzz
3 fad, hum **4** call, fizz, high, hiss, news, purr, ring, talk, whir, whiz **5** craze, drone, hurry, rumor, strum, thrum, whirr, whish **6** bumble, fizzle, gossip, murmur, natter, report, rumble, sizzle, summon, wheeze, whoosh **7** chatter, scandal, whisper **8** sibilate **9** bombinate **11** reverberate, scuttlebutt

buzzard
5 buteo **7** vulture **13** turkey vulture

by
3 per, via **4** away, near, nigh, past **5** along, aside **6** at hand, beside, next to **7** through **9** alongside **10** incidental **11** according to **12** not later than

by and by
4 anon, soon **5** after, later **7** ere long, shortly **8** directly, latterly **9** afterward, presently **10** before long **12** subsequently

by and large
7 all told, broadly, en masse, overall, usually **8** all in all, normally **9** generally, typically **10** altogether, on the whole, ordinarily **11** principally

by dint of
see **by means of**

bye-bye
4 ciao, ta-ta **5** adieu, adios **6** so long **7** cheerio, toodles **8** au revoir, farewell, sayonara, toodle-oo

bygone
3 old **4** dead, late, lost, once, past **5** dated, of old, olden **6** former, fossil, of yore, remote, whilom **7** antique, archaic, belated, defunct, extinct, old-time, onetime, quondam, vintage **8** departed, sometime, obsolete, outdated, outmoded, vanished **9** erstwhile, out-of-date **10** antiquated, oldfangled **12** antediluvian, old-fashioned

by means of
3 per, via **4** with **5** using **7** through **9** employing, utilizing

byname
6 handle **7** epithet, moniker **8** cognomen **9** sobriquet **10** diminutive, hypocorism **11** appellation

bypass
4 omit, skip **5** avoid, burke, shunt, skirt **6** detour, ignore **7** highway **8** go around, outflank,

ring road, sidestep **10** circumvent, pass around **11** deviate from

by-product
5 yield **6** effect, result **7** outcome, residue, spin-off **8** offshoot **9** outgrowth **10** derivative, descendant **11** aftereffect, consequence **12** repercussion

Byron work
4 Cain, Lara **5** Beppo **6** Giaour (The), Werner **7** Corsair (The), Don Juan, Manfred **12** Childe Harold

bystander
6 gawker, viewer **7** watcher, witness **8** beholder, observer, onlooker, passerby **9** spectator **10** eyewitness **12** rubbernecker

by stealth
5 slyly **7** sub rosa **8** covertly, in secret, secretly **9** furtively, privately **10** under cover **11** insidiously **13** clandestinely

by virtue of
see **by means of**

by way of
see **by means of**

byword
3 saw **5** adage, axiom, maxim, motto, nomen **6** dictum, phrase, saying, slogan, truism **7** epigram, epithet, precept, proverb, refrain **8** aphorism, cognomen, nickname **9** platitude, prescript, sobriquet **10** hypocorism, shibboleth **11** catchphrase, commonplace, rallying cry

Byzantine
6 daedal, knotty **7** complex, devious **8** involved **9** elaborate, intricate **10** convoluted **11** complicated **12** labyrinthine **13** sophisticated, surreptitious
emperor: **3** Leo **4** Zeno **5** Basil **6** Bardas, Justin, Phocas **7** Michael, Romanus **9** Heraclius, Justinian **10** Nicephorus, Theodosius
empress: **3** Zoe **5** Irene **8** Theodora

C

cab
4 hack, taxi **6** jitney **7** hackney **8** carriage

cabal
3 mob **4** clan, club, plot, ring **5** coven, group, junta, mafia **6** cartel, circle, clique **7** coterie, faction, in-group **8** intrigue **9** camarilla **10** conspiracy **11** machination

cabaletta
4 aria, song

cabalistic
6 arcane, mystic, occult **8** esoteric **9** recondite **10** mysterious **11** inscrutable **12** impenetrable

caballero
6 knight **7** paladin **8** cavalier, horseman **9** chevalier

cabana
3 hut **5** shack **7** shelter

cabaret
4 café **6** bistro, nitery **7** hot spot **9** nightclub, nightspot **10** supper club **12** watering hole

cabbage
3 nab, nip **4** cash, hook, lift, palm **5** bread, dough, filch, kraut, money, moola, pinch, steal, swipe **6** dinero, do-re-mi, moolah, pilfer **7** purloin, scratch **10** greenbacks, sauerkraut
disease of: **6** mildew, mosaic **7** root rot, yellows **8** blackleg, club root
family: **4** cole, kale, rape **5** colza, savoy **6** turnip **7** collard, mustard **8** broccoli, colewort, kohlrabi, rutabaga **11** cauliflower
sliced: **4** slaw

cabdriver
4 hack **5** cabby **6** cabbie

cabin
3 hut **4** camp, shed **5** berth, hovel, lodge, shack **6** cabana, chalet, lean-to, shanty **7** bivouac, cottage **9** stateroom

cabin cruiser
5 yacht **9** motorboat, powerboat

cabinet
4 case **6** bureau **7** armoire, chamber, commode, console, council, dresser **8** advisers, advisors, cupboard, ministry **9** presidium **10** chiffonier, collection, counselors

cabinetmaker
American: **5** Eames (Charles, Ray), Phyfe (Duncan) **6** Belter (John Henry) **7** Goddard (John, Stephen, Thomas) **8** McIntire (Samuel), Townsend (Christopher, Edmund, James, Job, John)
English: **4** Adam (James, Robert), Hope (Thomas), Kent (William) **8** Sheraton (Thomas) **11** Chippendale (Thomas), Hepplewhite (George)
French: **6** Boulle (André-Charles) **8** Caffieri (Jacques, Jean-Jacques, Philippe), Cressent (Charles)
German: **10** Weisweiler (Adam)

cable
4 rope, wire **5** braid, chain **6** stitch **8** transmit **9** telegraph

cabriolet
5 coupe **8** carriage

cache
4 bury, hide **5** cover, plant, stash, store, trove **6** memory, wealth **7** arsenal, conceal, lay away, nest egg, put away, reserve, secrete **8** ensconce, treasure **9** stockpile **10** accumulate **11** hiding place

cachet
4 rank, seal **5** motto, state **6** slogan, status **7** dignity, stature **8** approval, position, prestige, standing **11** consequence

cachinnate
4 crow, howl, roar **5** laugh, whoop **6** guffaw, shriek

cackle
3 gab, jaw **4** blab, chat, crow **5** clack, cluck **6** babble, burble, gabble, gaggle, gobble **7** blabber, blatter, chatter, prattle

cacoëthes
4 zeal **5** mania **6** desire **9** obsession

cacomistle
5 civet **7** raccoon **8** civet cat, ringtail

cacophonic
5 harsh **8** tuneless **9** dissonant, unmusical **10** discordant **11** unmelodious **12** unharmonious

cacophony
5 babel, noise **9** confusion, harshness **10** dissonance

cactus
5 nopal **6** cereus, cholla, mescal, peyote **7** opuntia, saguaro **11** prickly pear

cad
3 cur, dog, rat **4** boor, heel, lout, rake **5** creep, knave, louse, rogue **6** rascal, rotter **7** bounder **9** conductor, scoundrel

cadaver
4 body, mort **5** stiff **6** corpse **7** carcass, remains **8** deceased

cadaverous
5 ashen, gaunt, livid **6** pallid, wasted **7** deathly, ghastly, ghostly, shadowy **8** skeletal, spectral **9** deathlike, emaciated, ghostlike **10** corpselike

caddy
3 bin, box **4** aide **5** toter **6** casket **8** canister, tea chest

cadence
4 beat, flow, lilt **5** meter, pulse **6** rhythm **9** pulsation **10** conclusion, inflection, intonation

cadet
4 pimp **5** plebe **7** student, trainee **10** midshipman

cadge
3 beg, bum **5** mooch **6** hustle, sponge **8** freeload, scrounge **9** panhandle

cadmium symbol
2 Cd

Cadmus
daughter: **3** Ino **5** Agave **6** Semele **7** Autonoë
father: **6** Agenor
sister: **6** Europa
victim: **6** dragon
wife: **8** Harmonia

cadre
4 cell, core **5** frame, staff **6** cohort **7** in-group **9** framework

caducity
3 age **6** dotage, old age **8** senility **10** senescence **11** senectitude

Caesar
assassin: **6** Brutus (Marcus Junius) **7** Cassius (Gaius)
battle: **4** Zela **9** Pharsalus
conquest: **4** Gaul **7** Britain
death date: **4** Ides **11** Ides of March
eulogist: **6** Antony (Marc) **7** Anthony (Mark) **8** Antonius (Marcus)
message: **12** Veni vidi vici
river: **7** Rubicon
utterance: **4** Et tu **9** Et tu Brute
wife: **7** Pompeia **8** Cornelia **9** Calpurnia

Caesarism
7 tyranny **9** authority, autocracy, despotism **10** absolutism **12** dictatorship

caesura
5 break, pause **12** interruption

café
5 diner **6** bistro, nitery **7** barroom, beanery, cabaret, hot spot **8** cookshop **9** lunchroom, nightclub, nightspot **10** coffee shop, restaurant, supper club **12** luncheonette, watering hole **13** watering place

café ____
4 noir **5** latte **6** au lait, filtre **7** society

caftan
4 gown, robe **6** muumuu **12** dressing gown

cage
3 hem, pen **4** cell, coop, jail **5** score **6** aviary, corral, immure, lock up, shut in **7** close in, enclose, impound **8** imprison **9** enclosure **11** incarcerate

cagey
3 sly **4** foxy, wary, wily **5** canny, sharp **6** astute, clever, crafty, shrewd

cahier
6 record, report, review **7** journal **8** notebook

cahoots
6 hookup, league **8** alliance **9** collusion **10** complicity **11** partnership

caiman
9 crocodile **11** crocodilian

Cain
brother: **4** Abel, Seth
father: **4** Adam
land: **3** Nod
mother: **3** Eve
nephew: **4** Enos
son: **5** Enoch
victim: **4** Abel

Caine Mutiny
author: **4** Wouk (Herman)
character: **5** Keith (Willie), Maryk (Steve), Queeg (Capt. Francis)

Cain novel
8 Serenade **13** Mildred Pierce **23** Postman Always Rings Twice (The)

cajole
3 con **4** coax, dupe **6** entice, seduce **7** beguile, blarney, deceive, wheedle **8** blandish, inveigle, maneuver, persuade, soft-soap **9** sweet-talk

cake
3 dry, set **4** coat, loaf, rime **5** cover, crust, torte **6** gâteau, harden, pastry **7** congeal, encrust, incrust **8** solidify
almond: **8** macaroon
flat: **5** cooky **6** cookie
oatmeal: **4** farl **5** scone **7** bannock
ring-shaped: **5** donut **6** jumble **8** doughnut
rum-soaked: **4** baba
Scottish: **4** farl **5** scone
shell-shaped: **9** madeleine
topping: **5** icing **8** frosting, streusel
twisted: **7** cruller
without shortening: **6** sponge

Cakes and Ale author
7 Maugham (W. Somerset)

cakewalk
4 romp, rout, snap 5 cinch, dance, strut 6 breeze, prance 8 pushover, walkover

calaboose
3 can 4 brig, coop, jail, tank 5 clink, pokey 6 cooler, lockup, prison 7 slammer 8 hoosegow 9 jailhouse

calamitous
4 dire 5 fatal 6 woeful 7 ruinous 8 grievous 10 disastrous, lamentable 11 cataclysmic, devastating, unfortunate 12 catastrophic 13 heartbreaking

calamity
4 ruin 5 wreck 7 tragedy 8 disaster, downfall 9 cataclysm 11 catastrophe, tribulation

calcium symbol
2 Ce

calculate
4 rely 5 assay, count, gauge, judge, solve, tally, tot up, value 6 assess, cipher, figure, intend, reckon 7 compute, measure, work out 8 appraise, estimate, evaluate, forecast 9 ascertain, determine, figure out

calculated
6 likely 7 planned 8 intended 9 worked out 10 deliberate 12 aforethought, premeditated

calculating
3 sly 4 wary, wily 5 canny, chary, sharp 6 artful, crafty, shrewd 7 careful, cunning, devious, politic 8 cautious, discreet, guileful, scheming 9 designing 11 circumspect

calculating device
6 abacus
Peruvian: 5 quipu

calculation
8 analysis, counting, estimate, figuring, prudence 9 ciphering, reckoning 10 arithmetic, estimation, prediction 11 computation

Caledonia
8 Scotland

calendar
3 log 4 card, sked 6 agenda, docket 7 almanac, program 8 schedule 9 timetable
abbreviation: 3 Apr, Aug, Dec, Feb, Fri, Jan, Mar, Mon, Nov, Oct, Sat, Sep, Sun, Tue, Wed 4 Sept 5 Thurs
ecclesiastical: 4 ordo
unit: 3 day 4 week, year 5 month

calenture
4 fire, zeal 5 ardor, fever 6 fervor 7 passion 10 enthusiasm

calf
hide: 3 kip
leather: 3 elk
meat: 4 veal
stray: 5 dogie
unbranded: 8 maverick

Caliban
5 slave
master: 8 Prospero
witch-mother: 7 Sycorax

caliber
4 bore 5 class, gauge, grade, merit, value, worth 6 virtue 7 ability, quality, stature 8 diameter

calibrate
3 set 6 adjust, polish 7 measure 8 fine-tune, regulate 9 ascertain 11 standardize

California
capital: 10 Sacramento
city: 4 Napa 6 Fresno, Sonoma 7 Anaheim, Oakland, San Jose 8 San Diego, Santa Ana 9 Long Beach, Santa Cruz 10 Los Angeles 12 San Francisco
college, university: 3 USC 4 UCLA 5 Mills 6 Pomona 8 Berkeley, Stanford, Whittier 9 Loma Linda 10 Golden Gate, Occidental, Pepperdine, Santa Clara
desert: 6 Mohave
fault zone: 10 San Andreas
lake: 5 Owens, Tahoe 9 Salton Sea
lowest spot: 11 Death Valley
motto: 6 Eureka
mountain, range: 5 Coast 6 Lassen (Peak), Shasta 7 Whitney 12 Sierra Nevada
nickname: 6 Golden (State)
park: 7 Sequoia 8 Yosemite 11 Kings Canyon 14 Channel Islands
river: 10 Sacramento, San Joaquin
state bird: 5 quail
state flower: 11 golden poppy
state tree: 7 redwood, sequoia
wine region: 4 Napa 6 Sonoma

californium symbol
2 Cf

caliginous
3 dim 4 dark, dusk 5 dusky, foggy, misty, murky 6 gloomy 7 obscure, sunless 8 nebulous 9 lightless, tenebrous

Caligula
mother: 9 Agrippina
predecessor: 8 Tiberius
successor: 8 Claudius

caliph's name
3 Ali 7 Abu Bakr
Calista's seducer
8 Lothario

calisthenics
7 workout 9 exercises

call
3 bid, cry **4** buzz, hail, lure, name, page, ring, yell **5** phone, pop in, shout, visit **6** bellow, come by, drop by, drop in, holler, salute, stop by, stop in, summon **7** convene, convoke, summons **8** estimate **9** designate, telephone

calla
4 lily

call down
5 chide, scold **6** rebuke **7** censure, reprove **8** admonish, reproach **9** reprimand

called
5 named **6** chosen, picked, yclept **7** ycleped **8** selected

caller
5 guest **6** suitor **7** visitor

call for
3 ask, beg **4** page, seek **5** crave, plead **6** demand, entail, pick up **7** beseech, entreat, implore, involve, require **11** necessitate

call forth
5 awake, educe, evoke, rouse **6** arouse, elicit **7** conjure, provoke **9** conjure up

calligrapher
6 penman, scribe **7** copyist **9** engrosser, scrivener

calligraphy
4 hand **6** script **7** writing **8** longhand **10** penmanship **11** handwriting

call in
5 phone **6** summon **7** convene, reclaim **8** retrieve, withdraw **9** repossess, telephone

calling
3 job **4** duty, work **5** craft, trade **6** career, métier **7** mission, pursuit, yelling **8** business, lifework, shouting, vocation **10** employment, obligation, occupation, profession

call in sick
7 book off

Calliope
4 Muse
father: **4** Zeus **7** Jupiter
mother: **9** Mnemosyne
son: **7** Orpheus

Callisto
lover: **4** Zeus **7** Jupiter
son: **5** Arcas

Call It Sleep author
4 Roth (Henry)

call off
4 halt **5** abort, scrub **6** cancel, divert **8** distract

Call of the Wild
author: **6** London (Jack)
dog: **4** Buck

call on
5 visit **6** oblige **7** require

callosity
8 hardness **9** thickness

callous
5 stony **8** hardened, obdurate, uncaring **9** heartless, indurated, unfeeling **10** hard-bitten, hard-boiled **11** coldhearted, hardhearted, insensitive, unemotional **12** case-hardened, stonyhearted **13** unsympathetic

callow
3 raw **5** fresh, green, naive, young **7** puerile **8** immature, juvenile, youthful **9** unfledged **10** unseasoned **13** inexperienced, unexperienced

call up
5 draft, evoke **6** summon **8** mobilize, retrieve **9** conscript

calm
4 cool, ease, hush, lull **5** allay, peace, quiet, relax, salve, still **6** hushed, pacify, placid, poised, repose, sedate, serene, settle, smooth, soothe, stable, steady, stilly **7** appease, assuage, compose, halcyon, mollify, pacific, placate, restful, resting **8** composed, inactive, peaceful, reposing, serenity, tranquil **9** collected, composure, easygoing, impassive, possessed, quiescent, unruffled **10** phlegmatic, untroubled **11** tranquility, tranquilize, unflappable **12** even-tempered, self-composed, tranquillity **13** imperturbable, self-possessed

calmative
8 quietive, relaxing, sedative **9** soporific **12** tranquilizer

calmness
4 lull **5** quiet **6** phlegm **8** coolness, serenity **9** composure, placidity, sangfroid **10** equanimity **11** tranquility **12** tranquillity

calumet
4 pipe **9** peace pipe

calumniate
5 libel, smear **6** defame, malign, vilify **7** asperse, slander, tarnish, traduce **8** besmirch **9** denigrate **10** scandalize

calumnious
8 libelous **9** maligning, traducing, vilifying **10** backbiting, defamatory, detracting, scandalous, slanderous

calumny
7 scandal, slander **9** aspersion **10** backbiting, defamation, detraction **11** denigration **12** backstabbing, belittlement, depreciation **13** disparagement

calvados
6 brandy **9** applejack

calvary
5 agony, cross, trial **6** misery, ordeal **7** anguish **8** distress **9** suffering **10** affliction, visitation **11** tribulation
inscription: **4** INRI

Calvino work
11 Cosmicomics **15** Invisible Cities

Calypso
beloved: **7** Ulysses **8** Odysseus
island: **6** Ogygia

calyx part
3 cup **5** sepal

camaraderie
5 cheer **7** jollity **10** affability, fellowship **12** conviviality

camarilla
3 mob **4** camp, clan, ring **5** cabal, mafia **6** circle, clique **7** coterie, ingroup

Cambodia
9 Kampuchea
capital: **9** Phnom Penh
city: **10** Battambang **11** Kompong Cham
ethnic group: **8** Mon-Khmer
lake: **8** Tonle Sap
language: **5** Khmer
leader: **6** Pol Pot
monetary unit: **4** riel
neighbor: **4** Laos **7** Vietnam **8** Thailand
river: **6** Mekong
ruin: **9** Angkor Wat

camel
one-humped: **9** dromedary
two-humped: **8** Bactrian

camel-hair fabric
3 aba

camelopard
7 giraffe

Camelot
6 palace
lord: **6** Arthur

Camembert
6 cheese

cameo
6 brooch, relief, walk-on **8** portrait

camera type
3 SLR, spy, TLR **5** video **7** digital, folding, pinhole **9** autofocus, single-use **10** viewfinder **11** rangefinder

cameraman
6 photog **7** lensman **12** photographer

Cameroon
capital: **7** Yaoundé
ethnic group: **4** Fang **5** Duala, Pygmy **6** Fulani **8** Bamileke
largest city: **6** Douala
monetary unit: **5** franc
neighbor: **4** Chad **5** Congo, Gabon **7** Nigeria
river: **5** Nyong **6** Sanaga

Camille's creator
5 Dumas (Alexandre)

Camino ___
4 Real

camouflage
4 mask **5** cloak **7** conceal, deceive **8** disguise **9** dissemble **11** dissimulate

camp
3 hut **4** bloc, shed **5** cabin, lodge, shack **6** clique, shanty **7** bivouac, coterie, cottage, faction **10** settlement

campaign
4 push, race **5** blitz, drive, fight, lobby, stump **6** attack **7** agitate, canvass, crusade **8** movement, politick **9** barnstorm, offensive **10** engagement, expedition **11** electioneer, whistle-stop

campaigner
8 activist **9** candidate

campanile
6 belfry **8** carillon **9** bell tower

campesino
6 farmer **7** peasant

campestral
5 rural **6** rustic, sylvan **7** bucolic, country, idyllic **8** agrarian, pastoral **10** provincial **11** countrified

campus
see **college**

Camus work
4 Fall (The) **5** Rebel (The) **6** Plague (The) **8** Caligula, Stranger (The)

can
3 may, tin **4** boot, fire, sack **5** let go, put up **7** dismiss **8** preserve **9** container, discharge **10** receptacle

Canaan
4 Zion **12** Promised Land
father: **3** Ham
grandfather: **4** Noah

Canaanite god
3 Mot **4** Baal **6** Molech, Moloch

Canada
bay: **5** Fundy, James **6** Baffin, Hudson, Ungava **8** Georgian **9** Frobisher
capital: **6** Ottawa
city: **6** London, Oshawa, Quebec, Regina, Surrey **7** Burnaby, Calgary, Halifax, Moncton, Toronto, Windsor **8** Edmonton, Hamilton, Montreal, Moose Jaw, Victoria, Winnipeg **9** Longueuil, North York, Saskatoon, Vancouver **10** Lethbridge, Thunder Bay **11** Fredericton, Scarborough **13** Charlottetown, Mississisauga

district: 6 riding
explorer: 6 Hudson (Henry) 7 Cartier (Jacques) 9 Champlain (Samuel de)
Indian people: 4 Cree, Inuk 5 Blood, Haida, Huron, Inuit, Métis, Niska, Slave 6 Abnaki, Beaver, Eskimo, Micmac, Mohawk, Nootka, Ojibwa, Ojibwe, Ottawa, Piegan, Seneca, Stoney 7 Kutenai, Naskapi, Ojibway, Siksika, Wyandot 8 Algonkin, Chippewa, Iroquois, Kootenai, Kootenay, Kwakiutl, Salishan, Tsattine 9 Algonkian, Algonquin, Blackfeet, Blackfoot, Chipewyan, Tsimshian 10 Algonquian, Athapascan, Gros Ventre, Montagnais 11 Assiniboine
island, island group: 5 Banks, Devon 6 Baffin 7 Belcher 8 Melville, Victoria 9 Anticosti, Ellesmere, Vancouver 10 Cape Breton 11 Southampton 12 Newfoundland, Prince Edward
lake: 6 Louise 7 Nipigon 8 Reindeer, Winnipeg 9 Athabasca, Champlain, Great Bear 10 Great Slave
language: 6 French 7 English
monetary unit: 6 dollar
mountain, range: 5 Coast, Logan, Rocky 10 Laurentian
national park: 5 Banff, Fundy 6 Jasper 7 Glacier, Nahanni 8 Kootenay 9 Gros Morne 10 Grasslands, Point Pelee 11 Georgian Bay, Wood Buffalo
peninsula: 5 Bruce, Gaspé 6 Ungava 8 Labrador
prime minister: 4 King (W. L. Mackenzie) 5 Clark (Joe) 6 Abbott (John), Borden (Robert Laird), Bowell (Mackenzie), Harper (Stephen), Martin (Paul), Tupper (Charles), Turner (John) 7 Bennett (Richard Bedford), Laurier (Wilfrid), Meighen (Arthur), Pearson (Lester), Trudeau (Pierre Elliott) 8 Campbell (Kim), Chrétien (Jean), Mulroney (Brian), Thompson (John) 9 MacDonald (John), Mackenzie (Alexander), St. Laurent (Louis) 11 Diefenbaker (John)
province: 3 Man., NWT, Ont., PEI, Que. 4 Alta, Sask. 6 Quebec 7 Alberta, Nunavut, Ontario 8 Manitoba 10 Nova Scotia 12 New Brunswick, Newfoundland (and Labrador), Saskatchewan 15 British Columbia 18 Prince Edward Island
provincial park: 3 Gas 7 Rondeau 9 Garibaldi
river: 3 Red 5 Liard, Slave, Yukon 6 Albany, Fraser, Nelson, Ottawa, Severn 8 Columbia, Saguenay 9 Athabasca, Churchill, Mackenzie 10 St. Lawrence
sea: 8 Beaufort, Labrador
symbol: 9 maple leaf
territory: 5 Yukon 9 Northwest

Canadian insurgent
4 Riel (Louis)

canaille
3 mob 6 masses, rabble 8 riffraff, unwashed 9 hoi polloi 11 proletarian, proletariat

canal
4 duct 6 course 7 channel, conduit 8 aqueduct 11 watercourse
Africa: 4 Suez 8 Ismailia
Belgium: 6 Albert
Canada: 7 Welland
Central America: 6 Panama
China: 7 Da Yunhe
Florida: 10 Saint Lucie
Germany: 4 Kiel 10 Nord-Ostsee
Greece: 7 Corinth
Michigan: 3 Soo
New York: 4 Erie 6 Oswego 9 Champlain
Ontario: 6 Rideau
Venice: 5 Grand

canapé
6 morsel 9 appetizer 11 hors d'oeuvre
spread: 4 paté
topper: 3 roe 6 caviar

canard
3 fib, lie 4 tale, yarn 5 fraud, rumor, spoof 6 deceit 7 falsity, untruth 8 chestnut 9 falsehood

canary
3 rat 4 fink, wine 5 finch 6 snitch 7 rat fink, stoolie 8 informer, squealer 11 stool pigeon

Canary Islands
5 Ferro, Lobos, Palma 6 Gomera, Hierro 7 Inferno 8 Graciosa, Tenerife 9 Alegranza, Lanzarote

cancel
3 end 4 drop, lift, undo, x out 5 abort, annul, erase, scrub 6 delete, efface, negate, offset, repeal, revoke 7 blot out, call off, destroy, expunge, nullify, rescind, wipe out 8 black out, deletion 9 terminate 10 invalidate, neutralize, obliterate

cancer
5 tumor 9 carcinoma 10 malignancy
treatment: 5 chemo, X rays 9 radiation 12 chemotherapy

cancer-causing
12 carcinogenic
substance: 10 carcinogen

candescent
7 glowing 8 dazzling 9 refulgent

Candia
5 Crete

candid
4 fair, just, open 5 blunt, frank, plain 6 honest 7 sincere 8 unbiased 9 equitable, guileless, impartial, objective 10 aboveboard, forthright, scrupulous, unreserved 11 openhearted, unconcealed, undisguised 12 unprejudiced 13 dispassionate

candidate
6 seeker 7 hopeful, nominee, stumper 8 aspirant

9 applicant, contender 10 campaigner, contestant
unlisted: 7 write-in

Candide
author: 8 Voltaire
lover: 9 Cunegonde
tutor: 8 Pangloss (Dr.)
valet: 7 Cacambo

candle
5 taper 6 bougie
holder: 6 sconce 7 menorah, pricket 9 girandole 10 candelabra 11 candelabrum
material: 3 wax 4 wick 6 tallow 7 beeswax, stearin 8 paraffin
religious: 6 votive 7 paschal

candlefish
8 eulachon
relative: 5 smelt

candlelit service
5 vigil

candlepins
7 bowling

candor
7 honesty 8 fairness, openness 9 frankness, sincerity, whiteness 11 artlessness 13 guilelessness

candy
7 sweeten 9 sugarcoat 10 confection
kind: 4 rock 5 fudge, lolly, sweet, taffy 6 bonbon, comfit, dragée, jujube, nougat, toffee 7 brittle, caramel, fondant, gumdrop, penuche, praline 8 licorice, lollipop, lollypop, marzipan, sourball 9 chocolate, jelly bean, nonpareil, sweetmeat 10 confection 12 butterscotch
medicated: 7 lozenge 9 cough drop

cane
3 rod 4 beat, drub, flog, lash, reed, stem, swat 5 flail, grass, spank, staff, stave, stick, weave, whale 6 batter, buffet, cudgel, larrup, paddle, rattan, thrash, wallop 7 lambast, sorghum 8 lambaste 12 walking stick

Canea's land
5 Crete

canine
3 dog 4 tyke 5 hound, pooch

caning material
5 istle

Canis Major star
6 Sirius

Canis Minor star
7 Procyon

canker
4 rust, sore 5 stain 6 debase, infect 7 corrupt, debauch, deprave, pervert, vitiate 8 necrosis 10 demoralize

cankered
8 infested, infected

canker sore
5 ulcer 6 lesion 10 ulceration

cannabis
3 pot 4 hemp 5 bhang, ganja, grass 7 hashish 9 marijuana

canned
5 drunk, fired 6 potted 11 prerecorded

Cannery Row author
9 Steinbeck (John)

canniness
7 caution, cunning, slyness 8 prudence, wiliness 9 cageyness, foresight 10 artfulness, cleverness, craftiness, discretion, precaution, providence, shrewdness 11 forethought

cannon
6 pom-pom 8 howitzer, ordnance 9 artillery
part: 5 chase 6 breech 8 cascabel, trunnion

cannonade
4 bomb 5 blitz, burst, salvo, shell 6 shower, volley 7 barrage, bombard 8 drumfire, shelling 9 broadside, fusillade 11 bombardment

cannonball
4 dive 5 speed 7 missile

cannoneer
6 gunner

cannon fodder
6 troops 8 infantry, soldiers

canny
3 sly 4 wary, wise 5 acute, cagey, chary, quick, sharp, smart 6 adroit, clever, frugal, saving, shrewd 7 cunning, knowing, prudent, thrifty 9 ingenious, provident 10 economical 11 quick-witted, sharp-witted 12 nimble-witted

canoe
6 dugout 7 pirogue
ancient: 7 coracle
Eskimo: 5 kayak, umiak

canon
3 law 4 list, rule 5 dogma, edict, round, tenet 6 decree 7 precept, statute 8 doctrine, standard 9 clergyman, criterion, ordinance 10 regulation

canonical
5 sound 6 lawful 7 classic 8 accepted, approved, official, orthodox, received 10 authorized, recognized, sanctioned 13 authoritative

canonical hour
4 none, sext 5 lauds, prime, terce 6 matins, tierce 7 vespers 8 compline

canonicals
9 vestments

canoodle
3 hug, pet 5 spoon 6 caress, cuddle, fondle

can opener
9 church key

canopy
5 cover, shade **6** awning, tester **7** marquee, shelter **8** covering, sunshade **9** baldachin **10** baldachino
canvas: **4** tilt

cant
3 tip **4** heel, lean, list, tilt **5** angle, argot, bevel, idiom, lingo, piety, slang, slant, slope **6** humbug, jargon, patois, patter, speech **7** dialect, diction, incline, lexicon, palaver, recline **8** language, singsong **9** hypocrisy **10** dictionary, pharisaism, sanctimony, vernacular **11** inclination, insincerity **12** pecksniffery

cantaloupe
5 melon **9** muskmelon

cantankerous
4 dour, sour **5** cross, huffy, testy, waspy **6** crabby, cranky, crusty, grumpy, morose, ornery **7** bearish, crabbed, grouchy, peevish, prickly, waspish **8** cankered, liverish, petulant, snappish, stubborn, vinegary **9** crotchety, difficult, dyspeptic, irascible, irritable, obstinate **10** ill-natured, irritating, vinegarish **12** cross-grained

canter
3 bum **4** gait, hobo, lope **5** tramp **6** beggar **7** drifter, vagrant **8** derelict, vagabond **11** bindle stiff

Canterbury
Archbishop: **3** Oda **6** Anselm, Becket (Thomas á), Parker (Matthew) **7** Cranmer (Thomas), Dunstan **9** Augustine

Canterbury Tales
author: **7** Chaucer (Geoffrey)
character: **4** host, monk **5** clerk, friar, reeve **6** knight, miller, parson, squire, yeoman **7** plowman, shipman **8** franklin, Griselda, manciple, merchant, pardoner, prioress, summoner **9** physician **10** wife of Bath
inn: **6** Tabard

canticle
3 ode **4** hymn, song **6** Te Deum **10** Benedicite, Benedictus, Magnificat **12** Nunc Dimittis

canticles
11 Song of Songs **13** Song of Solomon

cantilever
4 beam **6** bridge **7** bracket, support

cantillate
4 sing **5** chant **6** intone, recite

cantina
3 bar, pub **6** saloon, tavern **7** barroom

canton
5 state **6** billet **7** quarter, section **8** district, division

cantor
5 hazan **6** singer **9** precentor

canvas
4 duck, sail, tarp, tent **7** tenting **8** painting **9** sailcloth, tarpaulin

canvasback
4 duck

canvass
3 con, vet **5** argue, study **6** debate, survey **7** discuss, dispute, examine, inspect, solicit **8** campaign **9** check over **10** scrutinize **11** electioneer **12** authenticate

canyon
4 Glen, Zion **5** Bryce, chasm, gorge, Grand, gulch, Hells **6** Copper, coulee, ravine, valley

cap
3 tam, top **4** best, coif **5** beret, cover, crest, crown, limit, trump **6** beanie, exceed, top off **7** calotte **9** culminate
clergyman's: **7** biretta **9** zucchetto
hoodlike: **4** coif
hunter's: **7** montero
jester's: **7** coxcomb **9** cockscomb
Jewish: **8** yarmulke
knitted: **5** toque, tuque **9** balaclava
military: **4** kepi
mushroom: **6** pileus
part: **4** bill, brim, flap, peak **5** visor **7** earflap
Roman: **6** pileus
Scottish: **3** tam **8** balmoral **9** glengarry **11** tam-o'-shanter
Turkish: **3** fez **6** calpac **7** calpack

capability
5 craft, means, skill **7** ability, potency **8** adequacy, aptitude, capacity, efficacy, facility **9** potential **10** competence, efficiency **12** potentiality **13** effectiveness, qualification

capable
3 apt **4** able **5** adept **6** adroit, au fait **9** competent, efficient, qualified **10** proficient **11** susceptible

capacious
4 wide **5** ample, roomy **7** sizable **8** abundant, spacious **9** extensive **10** commodious **11** substantial

capacitance
unit of: **5** farad

capacity
4 bent, gift, rank, role, room **5** knack, range, reach, scope, skill, space **6** output, status, talent **7** ability, caliber, faculty **8** adequacy, aptitude, facility, position, standing **10** capability, competence **11** proficiency **13** qualification
unit of: **4** gill, peck, pint **5** liter, litre, minim, quart **6** bushel, gallon **10** fluid ounce, milliliter

Capaneus
slayer: **4** Zeus
wife: **6** Evadne

caparison
5 adorn **6** finery **7** apparel, panoply, raiment **9** adornment, trappings

cape
4 cope, ness **5** cloak, point, talma **6** capote, mantle, tabard, tippet **7** manteau, pelisse **8** foreland, headland, mantelet, mantilla, pelerine **9** peninsula **10** promontory
clergyman's: **8** mozzetta
papal: **5** fanon, orale

Cape
Africa: **4** Juby, Yubi **5** Blanc **6** Blanco **7** Agulhas
Alaska: **3** Icy **4** Nome **11** Krusenstern
Algeria: **3** Fer
Antarctica: **3** Ann **4** Dart **5** Adare
Arctic: **8** Nordkaap
Asia: **5** Aniva
Australia: **5** Byron, Otway, Sandy, Smoky **6** Arnhem **9** Van Diemen
Baffin Island: **4** Dyer
Black Sea: **5** Yasun
Borneo: **4** Datu **6** Datoek
Brazil: **4** Frio, Raso
California: **9** Mendocino
Colombia: **5** Aguja
Costa Rica: **5** Velas
Crete: **5** Plaka
Croatia: **5** Ploca **6** Planka
Cuba: **4** Cruz **5** Maisi
Denmark: **4** Skaw **6** Skagen
Desolación Island: **5** Pilar **6** Pillar
Djibouti: **3** Bir
Egypt: **5** Banas
England: **8** Bolerium, Lands End
Florida: **5** Sable **7** Kennedy **9** Canaveral
Greece: **4** Busa **5** Gallo, Malea, Papas, Vouxa **6** Araxos, Maleas **7** Akritas
Guinea: **5** Verga
Gulf of California: **5** Lobos
Gulf of Guinea: **5** Lopez
Gulf of Mexico: **4** Rojo
Hawaii: **5** Ka Lae **10** South Point **11** Diamond Head
Hispaniola: **5** Beata
Honshu: **3** Iro, Oma **5** Inubo, Kyoga, Nyudo
Indonesia: **4** Vals **5** False
Japan: **4** Esan, Nomo, Sata, Soya **5** Erimo, Kamui
Libya: **3** Tin **4** Milh
Long Island Sound: **10** Throgs Neck
Malay Peninsula: **5** Bulat
Malaysia: **4** Piai **5** Sirik
Massachusetts: **3** Ann, Cod
Mediterranean: **5** Ajdir
Mexico: **4** Buey
Morocco: **3** Sim **4** Guir, Rhir
Namibia: **4** Fria
Newfoundland: **5** Bauld
New Jersey: **3** May
New Zealand: **5** Brett
North Carolina: **4** Fear **7** Lookout **8** Hatteras
Northwest Territories: **8** Bathurst
Nova Scotia: **5** Canso **6** Breton
Oman: **3** Nus **4** Hadd
Ontario: **4** Hurd, Rich
Pakistan: **5** Monze, Muari
Portugal: **4** Roca
Puerto Rico: **4** Rojo
Quebec: **5** Gaspé
Red Sea: **5** Kasar
Sicily: **4** Boeo, Faro **7** Lilibeo, Passero, Pelorus
Solomon Islands: **5** Zelee
Somalia: **4** Asir **5** Assir, Hafun
South Africa: **8** Good Hope
South America: **4** Horn
Spain: **3** Nao **4** Gata **5** Creus, Penas
Syria: **5** Basit
Taiwan: **5** O-luan **7** Garam Bi
Tierra del Fuego: **5** Penas
Tunisia: **5** Blanc
Turkey: **3** Boz **4** Baba, Ince, Kara, Krio **6** Lectum **8** Bozburun **9** Inceburun, Karaburun
Vancouver Island: **5** Scott
Virginia: **5** Henry
Washington: **5** Alava

Căpek, Karel
coinage: **5** robot
play: **3** R.U.R.

caper
4 dido, lark, leap, romp **5** antic, frisk, heist, prank, revel, shine, theft, trick **6** cavort, frolic, gambol, prance **7** roguery, rollick **8** escapade, mischief **10** shenanigan, tomfoolery **11** monkeyshine

Cape Verde
capital: **5** Praia
city: **7** Mindelo
island: **3** Sal **4** Fogo, Maio **5** Brava **8** Boa Vista, São Tiago **10** São Vicente, São Nicolau, Santa Luzia, Santo Antão
language: **7** Crioulo **10** Portuguese
monetary unit: **6** escudo

capillary
4 tube **6** tubule **8** hairlike **11** blood vessel

capital
4 main **5** basic, chief, funds, major, prime **6** assets, lethal, wealth **8** cardinal **9** essential, excellent, financing, first-rate, principal, resources **10** first-class, investment, preeminent, underlying **11** fundamental, outstanding, predominant, wherewithal
Afghanistan: **5** Kabul

Albania: **6** Tirana, Tiranë
Alberta: **8** Edmonton
Algeria: **7** Algiers
Angola: **6** Luanda
Antigua and Barbuda: **7** St. John's **10** Saint John's
Argentina: **11** Buenos Aires
Armenia: **7** Yerevan
Assam: **6** Dispur
Australia: **8** Canberra
Austria: **4** Wien **6** Vienna
Azerbaijan: **4** Baku
Bahamas: **6** Nassau
Bahrain: **6** Manama
Bangladesh: **5** Dacca, Dhaka
Barbados: **10** Bridgetown
Belarus: **5** Minsk
Belgium: **8** Brussels
Belize: **8** Belmopan
Benin: **9** Porto-Novo
Bhutan: **7** Thimphu
Bolivia: **5** La Paz, Sucre
Bosnia and Herzegovina: **8** Sarajevo
Botswana: **8** Gaborone
Brazil: **8** Brasília
Bulgaria: **5** Sofia
Burkina Faso: **11** Ouagadougou
Burma: **6** Yangon **7** Rangoon
Burundi: **9** Bujumbura
Cambodia: **9** Phnom Penh
Cameroon: **7** Yaoundé
Canada: **6** Ottawa
Cape Verde: **5** Praia
Central African Republic: **6** Bangui
Chad: **8** N'Djamena
Chile: **8** Santiago
China: **6** Peking **7** Beijing
Colombia: **6** Bogotá
Comoros: **6** Moroni
Congo (Zaire): **8** Kinshasa
Costa Rica: **7** San José
Côte d'Ivoire: **7** Abidjan **12** Yamoussoukro
Croatia: **6** Zagreb
Cuba: **6** Havana
Cyprus: **7** Nicosia
Czech Republic: **6** Prague
Denmark: **10** Copenhagen
Dominica: **6** Roseau
Dominican Republic: **12** Santo Domingo
East Timor: **4** Dili
Ecuador: **5** Quito
Egypt: **5** Cairo
El Salvador: **11** San Salvador
Equatorial Guinea: **6** Malabo
Eritrea: **6** Asmara
Estonia: **7** Tallinn
Ethiopia: **10** Addis Ababa
Faeroe Islands: **8** Tórshavn
Falkland Islands: **7** Stanley
Fiji: **4** Suva
Finland: **8** Helsinki
France: **5** Paris
French Guiana: **7** Cayenne
Gabon: **10** Libreville
Galápagos Islands: **12** San Cristóbal
Gambia: **6** Banjul
Georgia, Republic of: **6** Tiflis **7** Tbilisi
Germany: **6** Berlin
Ghana: **5** Accra
Greece: **6** Athens
Greenland: **8** Godthaab
Grenada: **9** St. George's **12** Saint George's
Guam: **5** Agana
Guinea: **7** Conakry
Guyana: **10** Georgetown
Haiti: **12** Port-au-Prince
Honduras: **11** Tegucigalpa
Hungary: **8** Budapest
Iceland: **9** Reykjavík
India: **8** New Delhi
Indonesia: **7** Jakarta **8** Djakarta
Iran: **6** Tehran **7** Teheran
Iraq: **7** Baghdad
Ireland: **4** Tara **6** Dublin
Israel: **7** Tel-Aviv **9** Jerusalem
Italy: **4** Rome
Jamaica: **8** Kingston
Japan: **5** Tokyo
Jordan: **5** Amman
Kazakhstan: **6** Astana **7** Alma-Ata
Kenya: **7** Nairobi
Kiribati: **6** Tarawa **11** South Tarawa
Korea, North: **9** Pyongyang
Korea, South: **5** Seoul
Kuwait: **10** Kuwait City
Kyrgyzstan: **7** Bishkek
Laos: **9** Vientiane
Latvia: **4** Riga
Lebanon: **6** Beirut
Lesotho: **6** Maseru
Libya: **7** Tripoli
Liechtenstein: **5** Vaduz
Lithuania: **7** Vilnius
Macedonia: **6** Skopje
Madagascar: **12** Antananarivo
Malawi: **8** Lilongwe
Malaysia: **11** Kuala Lumpur
Maldives: **4** Male
Mali: **6** Bamako
Malta: **8** Valletta
Manitoba: **8** Winnipeg
Marshall Islands: **6** Majuro
Mauritania: **10** Nouakchott
Mauritius: **9** Port Louis
Micronesia: **7** Palikir
Moldova: **8** Chişinău, Kishinev

Mongolia: **9** Ulan Bator **11** Ulaanbaatar
Montenegro: **7** Cetinje **9** Podgorica
Montserrat: **8** Plymouth
Morocco: **5** Rabat
Mozambique: **6** Maputo
Myanmar: **6** Yangon **7** Rangoon
Namibia: **8** Windhoek
Nauru: **5** Yaren
Nepal: **8** Katmandu **9** Kathmandu
Netherlands: **9** Amsterdam
Newfoundland: **10** Saint Johns
New Zealand: **10** Wellington
Nicaragua: **7** Managua
Niger: **6** Niamey
Nigeria: **5** Abuja
Northern Ireland: **7** Belfast
Northern Territory: **6** Darwin
North-West Frontier Province: **8** Peshawar
Northwest Territories: **11** Yellowknife
Norway: **4** Oslo
Nova Scotia: **7** Halifax
Oman: **6** Muscat
Pakistan: **9** Islamabad
Palau: **5** Koror **10** Babelthuap
Papua New Guinea: **11** Port Moresby
Paraguay: **8** Asunción
Peru: **4** Lima
Philippines: **6** Manila
Poland: **6** Warsaw
Portugal: **6** Lisbon
Prince Edward Island: **13** Charlottetown
Puerto Rico: **7** San Juan
Qatar: **4** Doha
Queensland: **8** Brisbane
Réunion: **7** St. Denis **10** Saint Denis
Romania: **9** Bucharest
Russia: **6** Moscow
Rwanda: **6** Kigali
Saint Helena: **9** Jamestown
Saint Kitts and Nevis: **10** Basseterre
Saint Lucia: **8** Castries
Samoa: **4** Apia
Saskatchewan: **6** Regina
Saudi Arabia: **6** Riyadh
Scotland: **9** Edinburgh
Senegal: **5** Dakar
Serbia: **8** Belgrade
Seychelles: **8** Victoria
Shetland: **7** Lerwick
Sicily: **7** Palermo
Sierra Leone: **8** Freetown
Sikkim: **7** Gangtok
Sind: **7** Karachi
Slovakia: **10** Bratislava
Slovenia: **9** Ljubljana
Solomon Islands: **7** Honiara
Somalia: **9** Mogadishu
South Africa: **8** Cape Town, Pretoria **12** Bloemfontein
South Australia: **8** Adelaide
South-West Africa: **8** Windhoek
Spain: **6** Madrid
Sri Lanka: **7** Colombo
Sudan: **8** Khartoum
Suriname: **10** Paramaribo
Swaziland: **7** Mbabane
Sweden: **9** Stockholm
Switzerland: **4** Bern **5** Berne
Syria: **8** Damascus
Tahiti: **7** Papeete
Taiwan: **6** Taipei
Tajikistan: **8** Dushanbe
Tanzania: **6** Dodoma **11** Dar es Salaam
Tasmania: **6** Hobart
Thailand: **7** Bangkok
Tibet: **5** Lhasa
Tirol: **9** Innsbruck
Togo: **4** Lomé
Tonga: **9** Nuku'alofa
Trinidad and Tobago: **11** Port-of-Spain
Tunisia: **5** Tunis
Turkey: **6** Ankara
Turkmenistan: **8** Ashgabat **9** Ashkhabad
Tuvalu: **8** Funafuti
Uganda: **7** Kampala
Ukraine: **4** Kiev
United Arab Emirates: **8** Abu Dhabi
United Kingdom: **6** London
Uruguay: **10** Montevideo
Uttar Pradesh: **7** Lucknow
Uzbekistan: **8** Tashkent
Vanuatu: **4** Vila
Venezuela: **7** Caracas
Victoria: **9** Melbourne
Vietnam: **5** Hanoi
Wales: **7** Cardiff
Western Australia: **5** Perth
Yemen: **4** Sana **5** Sanaa
Yugoslavia: **8** Belgrade
Yukon: **10** Whitehorse
Zambia: **6** Lusaka
Zimbabwe: **6** Harare

capitalist
6 backer, tycoon **7** magnate **8** investor **9** bourgeois, financier, plutocrat **12** entrepreneur

capitalistic
9 bourgeois

capitalize
4 back, fund **5** stake **6** profit **7** convert, finance, promote, sponsor, support **8** bankroll **9** grubstake, subsidize

capital sin
see **deadly sin**

capitation
3 tax **7** payment, poll tax

Capitol Hill sound
3 aye, nay

capitulate
3 bow **4** cave **5** defer, yield **6** cave in, give in, give up, relent, submit **7** concede, succumb **9** acquiesce, surrender **12** knuckle under

capitulation
9 surrender **10** submission

capo
3 bar **4** boss, head **5** chief **9** godfather

capote
4 cope **5** cloak **6** mantle, tabard **7** manteau, pelisse **8** overcoat

Capote work
11 In Cold Blood **19** Breakfast at Tiffany's

capper
4 lure **5** blind, decoy, shill **6** climax, finale **8** clincher

capriccio
4 whim **5** caper, fancy, prank **6** notion, vagary, whimsy **7** impulse

caprice
3 bee **4** mood, vein, whim **5** fancy, freak, humor **6** foible, maggot, megrim, notion, vagary, whimsy **7** conceit **8** crotchet

capricious
4 iffy **5** flaky, moody **6** chancy, fickle **7** erratic, flighty, wayward **8** fanciful, unstable, variable, volatile **9** arbitrary, impulsive, mercurial, uncertain, whimsical **10** changeable, inconstant **12** effervescent, incalculable **13** temperamental, unpredictable

caprid
4 goat

capriole
4 leap **5** caper

capsize
4 keel, roll, sink **5** upset **7** founder, tip over **8** collapse, overturn, turn over

capstone
4 acme, apex, peak **6** apogee, climax, coping, summit, zenith **8** pinnacle **9** high point **11** culmination

capsule
6 canned, pocket, potted **7** compact, outline **9** condensed

capsulize
6 reduce **7** enclose **8** compress, condense **9** summarize, synopsize

captain
6 master **7** skipper
fictional: **4** Ahab, Hook, Kirk, Nemo **5** Queeg **10** Hornblower
historical: **4** Cook (James) **5** Bligh (William)
pirate: **4** Kidd (William) **6** Morgan (Henry)

Captains Courageous author
7 Kipling (Rudyard)

caption
5 title **6** legend, rubric **7** cutline, heading **8** subtitle **9** underline

captious
5 testy **7** carping, peevish **8** caviling, contrary, critical, exacting, petulant, snappish **9** demanding, irritable **10** censorious, nit-picking **12** faultfinding, overcritical **13** hypercritical

captivate
4 draw, grip, hold, take **5** charm **6** allure, dazzle, enamor, please, ravish, seduce **7** attract, beguile, bewitch, delight, enamour, enchant, gratify **8** enthrall **9** enrapture, fascinate, hypnotize, infatuate, magnetize, mesmerize, spellbind

captivating
8 charming, enticing, fetching, magnetic, riveting **9** appealing, glamorous, seductive **10** bewitching, engrossing, intriguing **11** enthralling, fascinating

captive
5 bound, caged, taken **6** jailed **7** hostage **8** confined, detainee, internee, prisoner **10** enthralled, hypnotized, imprisoned

captivity
7 bondage, custody, slavery **9** detention **10** internment **11** confinement **12** imprisonment

capture
3 bag, get, nab, net, win **4** nail, take, trap **5** catch, lasso, prize, seize, snare **6** arrest, collar, entrap, occupy, secure **7** conquer, ensnare **8** preserve

Capuan
4 lush **5** plush **6** deluxe **7** opulent **8** luscious, palatial **9** luxuriant, luxurious, sumptuous **11** upholstered

car
4 auto, heap **5** buggy, coach, crate, sedan, wreck **6** beater, jalopy, junker, wheels **7** clunker, flivver **8** roadster **10** automobile, rattletrap, rust bucket
city: **4** Aygo, Lupo **5** Matiz, Panda, Prime **6** Twingo **7** Picanto
(see also **automobile**)

carafe
4 ewer **5** cruet **6** bottle, flacon, flagon **8** decanter

caravan
6 convoy, safari

caravansary
3 inn **4** khan **5** hotel, lodge, serai **6** hostel, tavern **10** campground

carbohydrate
5 sugar **6** starch **7** amylose, glucose, lactose, maltose, sucrose **8** fructose, glycogen **9** cellulose, galactose

carbolic acid
6 phenol

carbon
4 coal, coke, soot **8** charcoal, graphite, plumbago **9** lampblack

carbonate
6 aerate

carbon copy
4 dupe, twin **5** clone, ditto, mimeo, repro, Xerox **7** replica **8** knockoff **9** duplicate, facsimile **10** dead ringer **11** replication **12** reproduction

carbonize
4 burn, char, sear **5** singe, toast **6** scorch

carbuncle
4 boil, sore **5** ulcer **6** garnet, pimple **7** abscess, pustule **8** cabochon

carcass
4 body, hulk, mort **5** frame, shell, stiff **6** corpse **7** cadaver, remains **8** skeleton

carcinoid
5 tumor **8** neoplasm

carcinoma
5 tumor **6** cancer **8** neoplasm

card
3 wag, wit **4** menu, sked **5** joker **6** agenda, docket **7** program **8** calendar, comedian, humorist, schedule **9** timetable
fortune-telling: **5** tarot
game: **3** gin, loo, Uno, war **4** faro, fish, skat, solo, stud **5** monte, ombre, pitch, poker, rummy, whist **6** Boston, bridge, casino, écarté, euchre, fan-tan, hearts, piquet **7** auction, bezique, canasta, cooncan, old maid, primero **8** baccarat, Canfield, conquian, cribbage, gin rummy, pinochle **9** blackjack, solitaire, twenty-one, vingt-et-un **11** chemin de fer
game authority: **5** Hoyle (Edmond)
high: **3** ace
low: **5** deuce
performer's: **3** cue
spot: **3** pip
wild: **5** deuce, joker

cardboard
5 stiff **6** unreal, wooden **7** bristol, buckram, stilted **8** lifeless **10** unlifelike **11** stereotyped, unrealistic

card-carrying
4 true **7** genuine **8** bona fide **9** authentic, certified **11** full-fledged

cardiac stimulant
7 ouabain **9** digitalis

cardinal
3 key **4** main **5** basic, chief, prime, vital **6** ruling **7** central, leading, pivotal, primary **9** essential, important, principal **10** overriding, overruling **11** fundamental **12** constitutive
point: **4** east, west **5** north, south
suffix: **4** teen
title: **8** Eminence
virtue: **7** justice **8** prudence **9** fortitude **10** temperance

care
4 fear, heed, mind, tend, ward **5** alarm, nurse, serve, trust, worry **6** attend, charge, effort, regard, regret, strain, stress, unease, wait on **7** anguish, anxiety, concern, custody, keeping **8** disquiet, handling **9** attention, curiosity, misgiving, oversight **10** management, solicitude **11** maintenance, safekeeping, supervision **12** guardianship **13** consideration

careen
4 race, sway, tilt **5** lurch, pitch, speed, swing, weave **6** repair, wobble **7** stagger

career
3 job **4** race, rush, tear, work **5** chase, speed **6** charge, course **7** calling, passage **8** lifework, vocation **9** encounter **10** livelihood, profession

care for
4 like, love, mind, tend **5** nurse, treat **6** attend, foster **7** cherish, nurture **8** preserve **9** cultivate, look after

carefree
4 wild **6** blithe, breezy, jaunty **8** reckless **10** insouciant, untroubled **12** happy-go-lucky, lighthearted **13** irresponsible

careful
4 safe, wary **5** chary, exact, fussy **7** dutiful, guarded, precise, prudent, studied **8** accurate, cautious, critical, discreet, gingerly, thorough **9** attentive, provident **10** deliberate, meticulous, particular, scrupulous **11** calculating, circumspect, considerate, foresighted, painstaking, punctilious **13** conscientious

carefully
6 warily **8** gingerly **10** cautiously, discreetly **12** meticulously, scrupulously **13** painstakingly, punctiliously

careless
3 lax **5** hasty, messy, slack **6** casual, remiss, sloppy, untidy **7** cursory, offhand, unkempt **8** feckless, heedless, reckless, slapdash, slipshod, slovenly **9** forgetful, negligent, oblivious, unheeding, unmindful, unstudied **10** disheveled, inaccurate, incautious, neglectful, unthinking, untroubled **11** inadvertent, inattentive, indifferent,

perfunctory, spontaneous, thoughtless, unconcerned **12** uninterested, unreflective **13** irresponsible

caress
3 pat, pet, toy **4** kiss, love **5** dally, touch **6** coddle, cosset, cuddle, dandle, fondle, nuzzle, pamper, stroke **7** cherish, indulge **8** canoodle **10** endearment

caressive
7 calming **8** soothing

caretaker
6 warden **7** curator, janitor **9** custodian

careworn
3 wan **5** drawn, faded, jaded **7** haggard, pinched, wearied **8** fatigued, troubled **9** exhausted **10** distressed

cargo
4 haul, load **6** burden, lading **7** freight, payload **8** shipload, shipment **11** consignment

Caribbean country
4 Cuba **5** Haiti **7** Bahamas, Grenada, Jamaica **8** Dominica **10** Saint Lucia

caribe
7 piranha

caribou
4 deer **8** reindeer
kin: **3** elk **6** wapiti

caricature
4 mock, sham **5** farce, phony **6** parody **7** cartoon, lampoon, mockery, takeoff **8** travesty **9** burlesque **10** distortion, pasquinade **12** exaggeration

Carlsbad feature
4 cave **6** cavern

Carmen
author: **7** Mérimée (Prosper)
composer: **5** Bizet (Georges)
lover: **7** Don José **9** Escamillo

carnage
4 gore **8** butchery, hecatomb, massacre **9** bloodbath, bloodshed, slaughter

carnal
4 lewd **6** animal, bodily, coarse, earthy, sexual, vulgar, wanton **7** earthly, fleshly, lustful, mundane, obscene, sensual, worldly **8** corporal, material, physical, sensuous, temporal **9** corporeal **10** lascivious

carnation
4 pink **5** color **6** flower

carnival
4 fair, fete **6** fiesta
attraction: **4** ride **6** midway **8** sideshow **10** concession
character: **5** shill **6** barker, hawker **7** grifter, spieler
game: **8** Skee-Ball
New Orleans: **9** Mardi Gras
performer: **4** geek

carnivore
9 meat-eater **10** flesh-eater

carol
4 song **6** ballad
Christmas: **4** noel

carom
6 bounce, glance **7** rebound **8** ricochet

Caron role
4 Gigi, Lili **5** Fanny

carotid's relative
5 aorta

carousal
3 bat, jag **4** bash, tear **5** binge, booze, drunk, fling, revel, spree **6** bender, frolic **7** blowout, debauch, shindig **8** wingding **9** brannigan
Scottish: **6** splore

carouse
5 revel **6** cavort, frolic **7** roister
Scottish: **4** birl

carp
3 nag **4** crab, fuss **5** bream, cavil, scold **6** peck at, pester **7** henpeck **8** complain, cyprinid, sea bream **9** complaint, criticize, find fault

carpe ___
4 diem

carpenter
3 ant, bee **6** joiner, wright **7** builder, workman **10** woodworker

carpentry
7 joinery **10** timberwork
tool: **3** saw **5** drill, plane **6** chisel, hammer **11** brace and bit, screwdriver

carper
6 critic, nagger **7** caviler, knocker **9** nitpicker **10** complainer, criticizer **11** faultfinder

carpet
3 mat, rug **4** Agra **5** Herat, Heriz, Koula, Ladik, Sarok, tapis **6** Herati, Kerman, Keshan, Kirman, Sarouk, Tabriz, Wilton **8** moquette **9** Axminster, broadloom

carpet beetle
10 buffalo bug

carping
7 blaming, railing **8** captious, critical **10** censorious **11** reproachful **12** faultfinding, overcritical

carrageen
7 seaweed **9** Irish moss

carrefour
5 plaza **6** square **10** crossroads

carriage
3 gig, rig **4** pose **5** coach **6** stance **7** posture,

transit **8** attitude **9** transport **10** conveyance, deportment
American: **5** buggy **8** rockaway **9** buckboard
attendant: **6** flunky **7** footman
baby: **4** pram **5** buggy **8** stroller **12** perambulator
driver: **4** hack **5** cabby **8** coachman
folding top: **6** calash
four-wheeled: **4** trap **5** buggy, coupe **6** berlin, calash, fiacre, landau, surrey **7** droshky, hackney, phaeton **8** barouche, brougham, carryall, clarence, rockaway, sociable, stanhope, victoria **9** buckboard
Indian: **6** gharry
man-drawn: **8** rickshaw **10** jinricksha, jinrikisha
Russian: **6** troika **7** droshky
stately: **7** caroche
three-horse: **6** troika
two-wheeled: **3** gig **4** shay, trap **5** buggy, sulky, tonga **6** chaise, dennet, hansom **7** calèche, dogcart, tilbury **8** curricle **9** cabriolet
with attendants: **8** equipage

carriage trade
5 elite **6** gentry **7** quality **9** blue blood, gentility **10** upper class, upper crust **11** aristocracy

carrick bend
4 knot

carrier
4 mule **5** envoy **6** bearer, porter, runner, vector **7** airline, courier, shipper, vehicle **8** conveyor, emissary **9** go-between, messenger, stretcher **11** internuncio, transporter

Carroll character
5 Alice, Bruno, snark **6** boojum, Sylvie **8** Dormouse, Red Queen **9** Mad Hatter, March Hare **10** Mock Turtle **11** White Rabbit **12** Humpty Dumpty

carrot
5 prize **6** reward **9** incentive **10** inducement

carry
3 get, lug **4** bear, haul, have, hump, keep, move, pack, send, take, tote, wear **5** bring, ferry, fetch, range, stock **6** affect, bear up, convey, uphold **7** comport, conduct, portage, possess, support, sustain **8** buttress, transfer, transmit **9** influence, transport

carryall
4 tote **7** tote bag

carrying case
7 holdall, satchel

carry off
4 kill **6** abduct, kidnap, remove **7** achieve, destroy, execute, perform, realize **8** complete, conclude, dispatch, shanghai **10** accomplish, spirit away

carry on
3 run **4** go on, keep, rant, rave, wage **6** direct, endure, manage, ordain **7** conduct, operate, persist, prattle, proceed **8** continue, sound off **9** persevere

carry out
6 effect, govern, render **7** achieve, execute, fulfill, oversee, perform, realize **8** bring off, complete, finalize, transact **9** discharge, prosecute **10** accomplish, administer, effectuate **12** administrate

carry over
6 deduct **7** persist **8** postpone, transfer

carry through
4 last **5** abide **6** effect, endure **7** execute, perdure, perform, persist, survive **8** bring off, complete, continue **10** accomplish, effectuate

Carson work
11 Sea Around Us (The) **12** Silent Spring

cart
3 gig **4** dray, haul **5** buggy, carry **6** barrow, convey, schlep **7** schlepp, trundle, tumbrel, tumbril **8** carriage **9** transport **11** wheelbarrow
Indian: **5** tonga
racing: **5** sulky

____ carte
3 à la

____ Carte
5 D'Oyly

carte blanche
3 say **5** power, right, say-so **7** freedom, license **8** free hand, free rein **9** authority **10** blank check **11** prerogative

carte du jour
4 menu

cartel
4 bloc, OPEC, pool **5** trust **7** combine **9** syndicate **10** consortium **12** conglomerate

Carthaginian
goddess of the moon: **5** Tanit **6** Tanith
queen: **4** Dido **6** Elissa

cartilage
7 gristle

cartographer
English: **5** Smith (William)
Flemish: **6** Kremer (Gerhard) **8** Mercator (Gerardus), Ortelius
German: **13** Waldseemüller (Martin)
Greek: **7** Ptolemy
Italian: **8** Vespucci (Amerigo)

cartography
9 mapmaking

carton
3 box **4** pack

cartoon
5 anime, manga **10** comic strip
(see also **comic strip**)

cartoonist
3 Lee (Stan) **4** Arno (Peter), Capp (Al), Kane (Bob), Nast (Thomas), Szep (Paul) **5** Adams (Scott), Booth (George), Chast (Roz), Crumb (R.), Davis (Jim), Gould (Chester), Hanna (Bill), Jones (Chuck), Kelly (Walt), Steig (William), Young (Chic) **6** Addams (Charles), Caniff (Milton), Disney (Walt), Larson (Gary), Martin (Don), Schulz (Charles), Walker (Mort) **7** Barbera (Joe), Feiffer (Jules), Ketcham (Hank), Mauldin (Bill), Thurber (James), Trudeau (Garry) **8** Goldberg (Rube), Groening (Matt), Herblock, Hokinson (Helen), MacNelly (Jeff), Oliphant (Pat) **9** Fleischer (Max) **10** Hirschfeld (Al)

cartouche
5 frame **6** shield **9** cartridge

cartridge
4 case, tube **5** shell **8** cassette, cylinder **9** cartouche, container

cartwheel
4 coin **6** dollar, tumble **10** handspring

carve
3 cut, hew **4** chip, etch, form, hack **5** shape, slice **6** chisel, cleave, incise, sculpt **7** dissect, engrave, whittle **9** sculpture

Casablanca
actor: **5** Lorre (Peter), Rains (Claude) **6** Bogart (Humphrey) **7** Bergman (Ingrid), Henreid (Paul) **11** Greenstreet (Sydney)
character: **4** Ilsa (Lund), Rick (Blaine) **6** Laszlo (Victor)
director: **6** Curtiz (Michael)

Casanova
4 rake, roué, wolf **5** Romeo **6** lecher, masher, tomcat **7** amorist, Don Juan, gallant, playboy, seducer **8** lothario, paramour **9** adulterer, ladies' man, libertine, womanizer **10** lady-killer, voluptuary **11** philanderer

cascade
4 fall, gush, lace, pour, spew **5** chute, falls, flood, spill **6** deluge, plunge, rapids, shower, tumble **7** Niagara, torrent **8** cataract **9** avalanche, waterfall **10** outpouring

Cascade Mountains peak
6 Lassen, Shasta **7** Rainier

case
3 box, con, vet **4** etui, hull, husk, skin, suit **5** cause, event, shell, trunk **6** action, sample, sheath **7** episode, examine, example, inspect, lawsuit **8** argument, covering, incident, instance, sampling, specimen **9** check over, condition, situation **10** occurrence, proceeding, scrutinize **11** eventuality **12** circumstance
grammatical: **6** dative **8** ablative, genitive, vocative **9** objective **10** accusative, nominative, possessive

casebearer
5 larva **11** caterpillar

case-hardened
5 tough **7** callous **8** obdurate **9** indurated, insensate, toughened, unfeeling **11** insensitive **12** thick-skinned

casement
4 sash **6** window

Casey at the Bat poet
6 Thayer (Ernest Lawrence)

cash
4 coin, jack **5** bread, dough, money, scrip **6** dinero, redeem, wampum **7** cabbage, lettuce, scratch **8** currency **10** greenbacks, ready money **11** legal tender
machine: **3** ATM

cashier
2 ax **3** axe, can **4** boot, fire, oust, sack **5** clerk, eject, expel, scrap **6** banker, bounce, bursar, reject, teller **7** boot out, discard, dismiss, kick out **8** jettison, throw out **9** discharge, eliminate, terminate, throw away **10** bookkeeper **11** bean counter, comptroller

cash in
3 die **4** conk, drop **5** croak **6** expire, pop off, redeem, retire **7** kick off, succumb **8** check out, drop dead, pass away, settle up **9** liquidate

casing
4 hull, husk, pipe, rind, skin, tire **5** frame, shell, space **7** wrapper **8** membrane

casino
attendant: **6** dealer **8** croupier
game: **4** faro **5** craps, monte, poker **6** tierce **8** baccarat, roulette **9** blackjack

cask
3 keg, tun **4** butt, drum, pipe **6** barrel, firkin **8** hogshead

casket
3 box **5** chest **6** coffer, coffin **8** jewel box

Caspian Sea
city: **4** Baku
feeder: **4** Kura, Ural **5** Volga

Cassandra
4 seer **7** prophet, seeress **8** doomster **9** doomsayer, pessimist, worrywart **10** prophetess
brother: **7** Helenus
father: **5** Priam
lover: **9** Agamemnon
mother: **6** Hecuba
slayer: **12** Clytemnestra

cassava
4 yuca **5** yucca **6** manioc **7** tapioca

casserole
4 dish **5** crock **6** tureen

Cassiopeia
13 constellation
daughter: **9** Andromeda
husband: **7** Cepheus

Cassio's mistress
6 Bianca

cassock
4 robe **7** soutane **8** vestment

cassowary kin
3 emu, moa

cast
3 add, hue, sum, tot **4** drop, face, fire, form, hurl, kind, look, mold, shed, sort, tint, tone, toss, turn, type **5** color, fling, heave, leave, pitch, range, shade, shape, strew, throw, tinge, total, touch **6** actors, design, devise, direct, figure, nature, reject, slough, troupe, visage **7** arrange, company, quality, replica, scatter **8** abdicate, disperse, jettison, sprinkle **9** character, prognosis, throw away **10** appearance, conjecture, distribute, expression, prediction, strabismus, suggestion **11** countenance
a spell on: **3** hex **5** charm **7** beguile, bewitch **8** enthrall **9** captivate, enrapture, fascinate, hypnotize, infatuate, mesmerize, spellbind
overboard: **7** deep-six **8** jettison

cast about
4 hunt, seek **5** grope **6** search **7** seek out **8** contrive **9** search for, search out

castaway
5 leper, tramp **6** beggar, maroon, pariah **7** Ishmael, outcast, vagrant **8** deadbeat, derelict **10** Ishmaelite

cast down
see **downcast**

caste
5 class **6** degree, estate, status **7** station **8** division, prestige

cast head
4 bust

castigate
4 beat, flay, rail, whip **5** baste, chide, scold, slash **6** berate, pummel, punish, rebuke, scorch, thrash **7** belabor, blister, chasten, chew out, lambast, reprove, scarify, scourge, upbraid **8** chastise, lambaste, penalize **9** criticize, dress down, excoriate, reprimand **10** discipline, tongue-lash

castigation
3 rod **6** rebuke **7** reproof **8** punition, scolding **10** correction, discipline, punishment **12** chastisement

castle
5 manor, villa **7** alcazar, château, citadel, mansion **8** fortress **10** stronghold
adjunct: **4** moat
gate: **10** portcullis
ledge: **7** rampart
structure: **6** turret
tower: **4** keep **6** donjon
wall: **6** bailey **10** battlement

cast off
5 fling, flung, let go, loose, untie **6** jilted, untied **7** unhitch **8** cut loose, forsaken, rejected, unfasten, unmoored **9** discarded, unhitched **10** left behind, unfastened

Castor
brother: **6** Pollux **10** Polydeuces
constellation: **6** Gemini
father: **4** Zeus **9** Tyndareus
mother: **4** Leda
sister: **5** Helen
slayer: **4** Idas

castor oil
8 laxative **9** cathartic, lubricant, purgative

cast out
4 oust **5** egest, eject, evict, exile, expel **6** banish, deport **7** discard **9** eliminate, ostracize

castrate
3 fix **4** geld, spay **5** alter, unman, unsex **6** neuter **7** unnerve **8** enervate, mutilate **9** sterilize **10** emasculate **11** desexualize

castrato singer
9 Farinelli

casual
5 light, minor **6** breezy, chance, random, remote **7** natural, offhand, relaxed, trivial, unfussy **8** detached, informal, laid-back **9** easygoing, impromptu, irregular, uncurious, unplanned, unserious **10** accidental, contingent, fortuitous, improvised, incidental, insouciant, nonchalant, occasional **11** indifferent, low-pressure, spontaneous, unconcerned, unimportant **12** uninterested **13** disinterested, insignificant

casualty
4 prey **5** death **6** mishap, victim **8** accident, calamity, disaster, fatality **9** mischance **10** misfortune **11** catastrophe **12** misadventure

casuistry
7 sophism **9** deception, sophistry **12** equivocation, speciousness **13** deceptiveness

casus ____
5 belli

cat
4 eyra, lion, lynx, pard, puma, puss **5** felid, kitty, liger, moggy, ounce, pussy, tabby, tiger, tigon **6** cougar, feline, jaguar, margay, mouser, ocelot,

serval **7** caracal, cheetah, leopard, panther **10** jaguarundi **12** mountain lion
Alice's: 5 Dinah
Born Free: 4 Elsa
combining form: 5 ailur **6** ailuro
disease: 9 distemper
domestic: 3 Mau, Rex **4** Manx **5** tabby **6** Angora, Birman, calico, exotic, Ocicat, Somali **7** bobtail, Burmese, Persian, Ragdoll, Siamese **8** longhair, Wirehair **9** Himalayan, Maine coon, shorthair, Tonkinese **10** Abyssinian
extinct: 10 saber-tooth
fastest: 7 cheetah
female: 5 queen **7** lioness, tigress **9** grimalkin
genus: 5 Felis
grinning: 8 Cheshire
hybrid: 5 liger, tigon **6** Bengal, Safari **7** Chausie **8** Savannah
lookalike: 5 civet, genet **7** linsang
male: 3 gib, tom
relating to: 6 feline
sound: 3 mew **4** hiss, meow, purr, roar **5** miaou, miaow **9** caterwaul
tailless: 4 Manx
young: 6 kitten

cataclysm
5 flood **6** deluge **7** Niagara, torrent, tragedy **8** calamity, cataract, disaster, flooding **10** inundation **11** catastrophe, devastation

cataclysmic
5 fatal **7** ruinous **10** calamitous, disastrous **11** devastating **12** catastrophic

catacomb
5 crypt, vault **8** cemetery **10** necropolis, undercroft

catafalque
4 bier

catalepsy
6 trance

catalog
4 list, roll **5** enter, index, tally **6** enroll, roster **7** itemize, program **8** classify, inscribe, register, roll call, schedule, syllabus **9** enumerate, inventory **10** prospectus
of books: 11 bibliotheca
of saints: 9 hagiology

catalyst
4 goad, spur **7** impetus, impulse **8** stimulus **9** incentive, stimulant **10** incitation, incitement, motivation

catamaran
4 boat, raft

catamount
4 lynx, puma **6** bobcat, cougar **7** panther, wildcat **12** mountain lion

cataract
5 falls, flood, rapid **6** deluge, rapids **7** cascade, Niagara, torrent **8** downpour **9** waterfall **10** inundation

catastrophe
3 woe **6** deluge, fiasco **7** debacle, tragedy **8** calamity, disaster, meltdown **9** cataclysm, emergency **11** devastation

catastrophic
5 fatal **6** deadly, tragic **7** ruinous **10** calamitous, disastrous **11** cataclysmic

Catawba
4 wine **5** river **6** Indian

catcall
3 boo **4** hiss, hoot, jeer, razz **9** criticism, raspberry **10** Bronx cheer

catch
3 bag, get, nab, net, see, wed **4** dupe, find, fool, grab, grip, gull, haul, hoax, hook, nail, snag, sock, spot, take, trap **5** block, clasp, clout, grasp, hit on, marry, reach, round, seize, smite, snare, stick, stump, trick, watch, whack **6** accept, anchor, arrest, clutch, collar, cut off, descry, detect, engage, entrap, fasten, flurry, follow, put out, rattle, secure, snatch, strike, take in, tangle, turn up **7** capture, confuse, deceive, disturb, ensnare, grapple, hit upon, perplex, receive **8** confound, contract, entangle, flimflam, fragment, hoodwink, kick over, meet with, overhaul, overtake **9** apprehend, bamboozle, embarrass, encounter, intercept **10** comprehend, understand **12** come down with

Catch-22 author
6 Heller (Joseph)

catchall term
3 etc. **4** et al. **5** and/or **7** and so on **10** and so forth

Catcher in the Rye
author: 8 Salinger (J. D.)
character: 9 Caulfield (Holden)

catcher's glove
4 mitt

catching
10 contagious, infectious **12** communicable

catch on
3 see **4** hear **5** learn **7** find out **8** discover **9** ascertain, determine, figure out

catchphrase
see **catchword**

catch up
4 hold **6** gain on **7** close in, ensnare **8** entangle, enthrall **9** fascinate, mesmerize, spellbind

catchword
5 maxim, motto **6** slogan **10** shibboleth

catchy
6 fitful, spotty, tricky **7** erratic **8** sporadic **9** appealing, desultory, irregular, memorable, spasmodic

catechist
7 teacher

catechize
3 ask **4** quiz **5** grill, query, train **7** examine, inquire **8** instruct, question **9** inculcate **11** interrogate

catechumen
6 novice **7** convert, student, trainee **8** initiate, neophyte

categorical
7 certain, decided, express **8** absolute, clear-cut, definite, emphatic, explicit, positive **9** downright **10** definitive, forthright **11** unambiguous, unequivocal, unqualified

categorize
3 peg **4** sort **5** class, group **7** put down **8** classify, identify **10** pigeonhole

category
4 rank, tier **5** class, genre, grade, group, taxon **6** league **7** section **8** division, grouping **10** pigeonhole

catenation
4 link **5** chain **6** series, string **7** linkage **10** connection, succession

catercorner
9 obliquely, slantways, slantwise **10** cornerwise, diagonally

caterpillar
5 larva **7** cutworm, webworm **8** armyworm, silkworm **10** casebearer

cater to
5 humor **6** pamper, supply **7** furnish, gratify, indulge

caterwaul
4 howl, meow, yowl **5** miaow **6** squall

catfish
see **fish**

catharsis
5 purge, tonic **7** purging **8** curative **9** cleansing, purgation, purgative **10** lustration **11** expurgation, restorative **12** purification

cathartic
5 purge, tonic **8** curative **9** castor oil, purgative **11** restorative, therapeutic

Cathay
5 China

cathedral
5 duomo **6** church **8** basilica
feature: 4 apse, nave **5** altar **6** chapel **7** chancel **10** clerestory **8** buttress, transept

cathedral city
3 Ely **4** Bath, York **5** Wells **6** Durham, Exeter, London, Oxford **7** Bristol, Chester, Lincoln, Norwich **8** Carlisle, Coventry, Hereford **9** Lichfield, Liverpool, Salisbury, Worcester **10** Canterbury, Chichester, Gloucester, Winchester **11** Westminster **12** Peterborough

Cather novel
8 Lost Lady (A) **9** My Antonia, One of Ours, O Pioneers **13** Song of the Lark **15** Professor's House (The) **16** Shadows on the Rock

catholic
5 broad **6** global **7** general, liberal **8** eclectic, tolerant **9** expansive, inclusive, undivided, universal, worldwide **10** ecumenical **12** cosmopolitan **13** comprehensive

catholicity
7 breadth **9** tolerance **10** liberality **11** magnanimity **12** universality

catholicon
6 elixir **7** cure-all, nostrum, panacea

catkin
5 ament

catlike
6 feline **7** furtive **8** stealthy

catnap
3 nap **4** doze **6** siesta, snooze **10** forty winks

catnip
3 nep

Cato
title: 6 aedile, censor, consul **7** praetor, tribune **8** quaestor

cat's-paw
4 dupe, knot, pawn, tool **5** patsy **6** puppet, stooge

cattail
4 reed, rush

cattle
4 cows, kine, neat, oxen **7** bovines **9** livestock
breed: 5 Angus, Devon, Kerry **6** Durham, Jersey, Sussex **7** Brahman, Hariana, Red Poll **8** Ayrshire, Galloway, Guernsey, Hereford, Highland, Holstein, Limousin, Longhorn **9** Charolais, Red Polled, Shorthorn, Simmental **10** Brown Swiss **11** Dutch Belted
catching rope: 5 lasso **6** lariat
cry: 3 low, moo
dehorn: 4 poll
disease: 4 loco **5** bloat **6** mad cow, nagana **7** anthrax, locoism, measles, murrain **8** blackleg, lumpy jaw, mastitis, staggers **10** rinderpest, Texas fever **11** brucellosis
dung: 4 tath
extinct breed: 9 Teeswater
family: 7 Bovidae

feed: **6** fodder, silage, stover
genus: **3** Bos
goddess: **6** Bubona
grazing land: **5** range **6** meadow **7** pasture
group: **4** herd **5** drove
herdsman: **6** cowboy, drover, gaucho **7** vaquero **8** neatherd, wrangler **10** cowpuncher
identification: **5** brand
pen: **6** corral
round up: **7** wrangle
stable: **4** barn, byre
steal: **6** rustle
wild flight: **8** stampede

catty
4 mean **5** nasty **6** barbed, bitchy, feline **7** furtive, vicious **8** spiteful, stealthy **9** malicious **10** backbiting, malevolent

Caucasian
capital: **4** Baku **6** Tiflis **7** Tbilisi, Yerevan
republic: **7** Armenia, Georgia **10** Azerbaijan

Caucasus
peak: **6** Elbrus
people: **5** Osset

caucus
4 bloc, sect **5** cabal, lobby **6** parley, powwow **7** faction

caudal appendage
4 tail

caudillo
6 despot, tyrant **8** dictator **9** strongman

cauldron
3 pot **6** boiler, kettle **8** crucible

cause
4 case, make, root **5** evoke, hatch **6** compel, effect, elicit, induce, motive, origin, reason, source, spring **7** produce, provoke **8** engender, generate, movement **9** necessity, principle **10** antecedent, bring about, inducement, originator **11** determinant, precipitate **13** consideration

cause ___
7 célèbre

causerie
4 chat **5** essay **6** column **7** article, feature **8** colloquy, dialogue **12** conversation

caustic
4 acid, keen, tart **5** acerb, acrid, sharp **6** biting, bitter, ironic **7** acerbic, cutting, mordant, pungent **8** scathing, stinging **9** corrosive, sarcastic, trenchant **10** astringent
solution: **3** lye

cauterize
4 burn, numb, sear **6** deaden **11** anesthetize

caution
4 warn **6** caveat **7** warning **8** forewarn, monition, prudence **9** canniness, chariness, foresight, vigilance **10** admonition, discretion, providence **11** carefulness, forethought, forewarning **12** admonishment, discreetness

cautionary
7 warning **8** monitory **10** admonitory

cautious
4 wary **5** alert, cagey, canny, chary, leery **6** shrewd **7** careful, guarded, politic, prudent **8** discreet, gingerly, vigilant, watchful **9** judicious, provident **11** circumspect, considerate, foresighted

cavalcade
6 parade, series **7** cortege **8** sequence **10** procession, succession

cavalier
5 lofty, proud **6** casual, knight, lordly **7** gallant, haughty, offhand **8** arrogant, debonair, horseman, scornful, superior **9** caballero, gentleman **10** disdainful, dismissive, insouciant, nonchalant **12** aristocratic, supercilious

cavalryman
6 lancer **7** dragoon, trooper
Algerian: **5** spahi
horse: **5** waler
Prussian: **5** uhlan
Russian: **7** cossack
Turkish: **5** spahi
weapon: **5** lance, saber **7** carbine

cave
3 bow, den **4** bend, drop, give, grot, lair **5** antre, break, defer, yield **6** fold up, grotto, hollow, submit **7** crumple, knuckle, succumb **8** collapse **9** break down **10** capitulate, subterrane **11** buckle under **12** knuckle under, subterranean
dweller: **3** bat **4** bear, lion **6** hermit **9** Cro-Magnon **10** troglodite **11** Neanderthal
explorer: **9** spelunker
formation: **10** stalactite, stalagmite
France: **7** Lascaux **10** Rouffignac
Iceland: **7** Singing
Indiana: **9** Wyandotte
Iraq: **8** Shanidar
Kentucky: **7** Mammoth
New Zealand: **7** Waitomo
rock: **8** dolomite **9** limestone
Scotland: **7** Fingal's
South Africa: **5** Cango
Spain: **8** Altamira
study of: **10** speleology

caveat
6 notice **7** caution, warning **8** monition **10** admonition **11** explanation, forewarning

caveat ___
6 emptor

caveman
5 brute **6** savage **9** barbarian, Cro-Magnon **10** troglodyte

cavern
6 grotto **12** subterranean
Capri: **10** Blue Grotto
Montana: **13** Lewis and Clark
New Mexico: **8** Carlsbad
Tennessee: **10** Cumberland
Virginia: **5** Luray

cavernous
4 vast **6** gaping, hollow **7** yawning

caviar
3 roe **4** eggs **6** relish
source: **6** beluga **8** sturgeon

cavil
4 carp **7** nitpick, quibble **9** criticize, find fault

caviler
6 carper, critic **7** knocker **8** quibbler **10** criticizer **11** faultfinder

caviling
5 fussy **7** carping, finicky, nagging **8** captious, contrary, critical, exacting, niggling **10** censorious, nitpicking **12** faultfinding **13** hairsplitting

cavity
3 pit **4** bore, hole, void **5** decay, fossa **6** caries, hollow **7** vacuity **10** depression, interstice
body: **5** antra (plural), sinus **6** antrum **8** follicle, hemocoel

cavort
4 leap, romp **5** caper, cut up, frisk, sport **6** frolic, gambol, prance **7** carry on, rollick **10** roughhouse **11** horse around

cavy
4 paca **6** rodent **9** guinea pig

caw
4 crow, yawp **6** squall, squawk

cay
3 key **4** isle, reef **5** islet **6** island

cayenne
6 pepper
genus: **8** Capsicum

cayman
see **caiman**

Cayman Islands
capital: **10** George Town
discoverer: **8** Columbus (Christopher)
territory of: **7** Britain

Cayuga chief
5 Logan (James)

cease
3 die, end **4** halt, quit, stop **5** close **6** desist, ending, finish **8** conclude, give over, knock off, leave off **9** terminate **10** conclusion **11** discontinue, termination

cease-fire
5 truce **9** armistice **10** suspension

ceaseless
7 endless, eternal, nonstop **8** constant, immortal, unending **9** continual, incessant, perennial, perpetual, sustained, unabating **10** continuing, continuous **11** everlasting, never-ending, unremitting **12** interminable **13** uninterrupted

Cecrops' daughter
5 Herse **8** Aglauros, Aglaurus **9** Pandrosos, Pandrosus

cede
4 deed **5** grant, leave, yield **6** assign, convey, give up **7** abandon, concede **8** alienate, hand over, make over, part with, renounce, sign over, transfer **9** surrender, vouchsafe **10** relinquish

ceinture
4 belt, sash **6** girdle **9** waistband

Celaeno
father: **5** Atlas
mother: **7** Pleione
sisters: **8** Pleiades

celebrate
4 fete, hold, hymn, keep, laud **5** bless, cry up, exalt, extol, honor, party, revel **6** praise **7** carouse, glorify, maffick, observe, perform, rejoice **8** eulogize **9** solemnize **11** commemorate

celebrated
5 famed, great, noted **6** famous **7** eminent, notable, partied **8** caroused, rejoiced, renowned **9** prominent, well-known **11** illustrious **13** distinguished

celebration
4 bash, fete, gala **5** beano, party **6** fiesta **7** blowout, jubilee, revelry **8** ceremony, festival, jamboree, wingding **10** observance

celebrity
3 VIP **4** fame, hero, lion, name, star **5** éclat, glory **6** renown, repute **7** notable **8** eminence, luminary, prestige, somebody **9** notoriety, personage, superstar **10** notability, prominence, reputation

celerity
4 pace **5** speed **8** alacrity, dispatch, rapidity, velocity **9** briskness, fleetness, quickness, swiftness **10** speediness

celestial
6 divine **7** blessed, elysian, sublime **8** beatific, empyreal, empyrean, ethereal, heavenly, Olympian, supernal **9** unearthly **12** otherworldly

celestial body
3 sun **4** moon, star **5** comet **6** meteor, nebula, planet **8** asteroid **9** satellite

Celestial Empire
5 China

celibate
5 unwed **6** chaste, single, virgin **8** virginal, virtuous **9** abstinent, continent

cell
4 room **5** cubby, zooid **6** alcove **7** chamber, cubicle **9** corpuscle, cubbyhole **11** compartment
blood: 8 hemocyte
disease: 6 cancer
division: 7 meiosis, mitosis
fertilized egg: 6 zygote
material: 3 DNA, RNA **7** protein **9** chromatin, cytoplasm **10** protoplasm
nerve: 6 neuron
part: 4 gene **7** nucleus, vacuole **8** ribosome **9** centriole **10** chromosome
reproductive: 3 egg **4** germ, ovum **5** sperm **6** gamete **8** gonidium

cellar
5 store **7** shelter **8** basement

cellist
American: 2 Ma (Yo-Yo) **4** Rose (Leonard) **6** Lesser (Laurence), Parnas (Leslie) **7** Nelsova (Zara), Parisot (Aldo), Starker (Janos) **8** Schuster (Joseph) **10** Greenhouse (Bernard)
English: 5 du Pré (Jacqueline)
French: 8 Fournier (Pierre)
Russian: 11 Piatigorsky (Gregor) **12** Rostropovich (Mstislav)
Spanish: 6 Casals (Pablo)

cellophane
4 wrap **7** wrapper **8** wrapping **9** packaging

cell-phone sound
8 ringtone

celluloid
4 film **7** plastic

Celt
4 Gael, Scot **6** Breton **8** Irishman, Welshman **10** Cornishman, Highlander

Celtic
deity: 4 Bran **5** Epona, Lugus, Macha **6** Brigit **8** Rhiannon **9** Cernunnos
festival: 7 Beltane, Samhain
queen: 8 Boadicea, Boudicca

cement
4 bind, glue, join **5** grout, unify, unite **6** mortar, secure **8** concrete
ingredient: 4 lime **6** silica **7** alumina **8** magnesia, pozzolan **9** iron oxide, pozzolana

cemetery
8 boneyard, boot hill **8** God's acre **9** graveyard **10** churchyard, necropolis **12** burial ground, memorial park, potter's field
underground: 8 catacomb

cenacle
7 coterie **9** Upper Room **12** retreat house

cenotaph
4 tomb **6** marker **8** memorial, monument

censer
8 thurible
carrier: 8 thurifer

censor
3 ban, cut **4** blip, edit **5** bleep, purge **6** cut out, delete, excise, purify, screen **7** clean up **8** black out, restrict, suppress, withhold **9** expurgate, red-pencil **10** blue-pencil, bowdlerize

censorious
6 severe **7** carping **8** captious, critical **10** accusatory, condemning **11** reproachful **12** condemnatory, denunciatory, disapproving, faultfinding, overcritical, reprehending **13** hypercritical

censurable
5 wrong **6** guilty, sinful **7** heinous **8** blamable, blameful, culpable, improper, wrongful **9** incorrect **10** deplorable, despicable, detestable **11** blameworthy, disgraceful, impeachable **12** unacceptable **13** discreditable, objectionable, reprehensible

censure
5 blame, chide, scold **6** berate, rebuke, strafe **7** condemn, reprove, upbraid **8** chastise, denounce, disallow, reproach **9** castigate, criticize, reprehend, reprimand, reprobate **10** disapprove

centaur
6 Chiron, Nessus

Centaurus star
4 Beta **5** Alpha

Centennial State
8 Colorado

center
3 hub, mid **4** axis, core, crux, mean, pith, root, seat **5** focus, heart, midst, pivot **6** inside, medial, median, middle, source **7** central, essence **8** interior, midpoint, omphalos **10** focal point **11** equidistant **12** intermediary, intermediate

centerboard
4 keel

centerfold
7 foldout **8** gatefold

centerpiece
7 epergne

central
3 hub, key, mid **4** main, mean **5** basic, chief, focal **6** medial, median, middle **7** leading, pivotal, primary, salient **8** cardinal, dominant, exchange, foremost, moderate **9** essential, paramount, principal **10** overriding **11** fundamental, outstanding, predominant **12** intermediate

Central African Republic
capital: 6 Bangui
former name: 11 Ubangi-Shari
language: 5 Sango, Zande **6** French

monetary unit: **5** franc
neighbor: **4** Chad **5** Congo, Sudan **8** Cameroon

Central America
country: **6** Belize, Panama **8** Honduras **9** Costa Rica, Guatemala, Nicaragua **10** El Salvador
language: **7** Nahuatl, Spanish

centralize
5 focus, unify **11** concentrate, consolidate

centripetal
8 afferent, focusing, unifying **10** converging **11** integrative **12** centralizing **13** concentrating, consolidating

centurion
7 officer **9** commander

century plant
5 agave

cephalopod
5 squid **7** mollusc, mollusk, octopus **10** cuttlefish

Cepheus
daughter: **9** Andromeda
kingdom: **8** Ethiopia
wife: **10** Cassiopeia

cerate
4 balm **5** cream, salve **6** chrism **7** unction, unguent **8** dressing, liniment, ointment **9** demulcent, emollient

Cerberus
5 guard **8** guardian, sentinel, watchdog
father: **6** Typhon
form: **3** dog
mother: **7** Echidna

cereal
4 meal, mush, samp **5** gruel **6** farina **7** oatmeal **8** cornmeal, porridge
disease: **4** bunt, smut **5** ergot
fungus: **5** ergot
grass: **3** rye **4** corn, oats, ragi, rice, teff **5** emmer, maize, spelt, wheat **6** barley, millet **7** sorghum **9** buckwheat
Russian: **5** kasha

cerebral
6 mental **7** bookish **8** highbrow **9** scholarly **10** highbrowed **12** intellectual

cerebrate
5 think **6** reason **7** reflect **8** cogitate **9** speculate **10** deliberate

cerebration
7 thought **9** brainwork **10** cogitation, reflection **11** speculation **12** deliberation

ceremonial
6 august, formal, ritual, solemn **7** courtly, stately, studied **8** mannered, stylized **10** liturgical **11** ritualistic **12** conventional

ceremonious
6 formal, proper, seemly, solemn **7** courtly, stately **8** decorous, imposing, majestic **9** dignified, grandiose **10** impressive **11** punctilious **12** conventional

ceremony
4 form, pomp, rite **6** ritual **7** decorum, liturgy, service **8** protocol **9** formality **10** observance
Jewish: **8** habdalah, havdalah **10** bar mitzvah, bat mitzvah
university: **8** encaenia

Ceres
Greek counterpart: **7** Demeter
daughter: **10** Persephone, Proserpina, Proserpine
father: **6** Cronus, Saturn
mother: **3** Ops **4** Rhea

cerium symbol
2 Ce

certain
3 set **4** firm, sure, true **5** fixed **6** stated **7** assured, settled **8** credible, definite, destined, positive, provable, reliable, specific, surefire **9** authentic, confident, convinced **10** conclusive, dependable, guaranteed, inarguable, inevitable, infallible, stipulated, undeniable, verifiable **11** confirmable, indubitable, unavoidable **12** demonstrable, indisputable, well-grounded **13** incontestable, uncontestable

certainty
5 faith **6** surety **8** sureness **9** assurance, sure thing **10** confidence, conviction **12** definiteness

certificate
7 diploma, license, voucher **8** contract, document **9** affidavit **10** credential

certifier
6 notary **7** auditor **9** registrar

certify
2 OK **4** aver, avow, okay **5** state, swear, vouch **6** assert, assure, attest, verify **7** approve, confirm, endorse, license, testify, warrant, witness **8** accredit, guaranty, notarize **9** authorize, guarantee, recognize **10** commission **12** authenticate

Cervantes character
10 Don Quixote **11** Sancho Panza

cervid
3 elk **4** deer **5** moose **6** wapiti **7** caribou **8** reindeer

cesium symbol
2 Cs

cessation
3 end **4** halt, rest, stop **5** break, cease, close, letup, pause **6** ending, finish, freeze, hiatus, period, recess **7** respite **10** conclusion, suspension **11** termination **12** interruption

cesspool
3 den, pit, sty 4 sink 5 sewer, Sodom 6 cloaca, gutter, pigsty 8 Gomorrah 12 Augean stable

cetacean
5 whale 7 dolphin 8 porpoise

Cetus star
4 Mira

Ceylon
see **Sri Lanka**

cgs unit
3 erg 4 dyne, gram, phot 5 gauss, poise, stilb 6 second, stokes 7 lambert, maxwell, oersted 10 centimeter

Chablis
4 wine 8 Burgundy 9 white wine

Chad
capital: 8 N'Djamena
city: 4 Sarh 6 Abéché 7 Moundou
language: 6 Arabic, French
monetary unit: 5 franc
neighbor: 5 Libya, Niger, Sudan 7 Nigeria 8 Cameroon
river: 5 Chari 6 Logone

chafe
3 irk, rub, vex 4 fret, gall, peel, rage, skin, wear 5 annoy, erode 6 abrade, bother, scrape 7 provoke 8 irritate, vexation

chaff
3 kid, rag, rib 4 jest, joke, josh, razz 5 dregs, husks, tease 6 banter, debris, refuse 7 remains 8 detritus 9 sweepings

chaffer
6 barter, dicker, haggle, higgle, palter 7 bargain, chatter 8 exchange, huckster

chagrin
3 ire, irk, vex 5 abash, annoy, peeve, pique, upset 6 dismay 7 perturb 8 disquiet, distress, unsettle, vexation 9 annoyance, discomfit, displease, embarrass, humiliate, petulance 10 disappoint, discompose, disconcert, irritation 11 frustration, humiliation 12 discomfiture

chagrined
4 hurt 5 upset, vexed 6 shamed 7 ashamed 8 dismayed 9 disturbed, mortified, perturbed, unsettled 10 distressed, humiliated 11 discomposed, embarrassed 12 disappointed, disconcerted

chain
3 row 4 bind, bond, gyve 5 group, train, trust 6 cartel, catena, fetter, hobble, series, string, tether 7 combine, manacle, shackle 8 handcuff, sequence 9 syndicate 10 succession 11 concatenate, progression 12 conglomerate 13 concatenation
adjunct: 8 sprocket
collar: 6 torque
gang: 6 coffle
ornamental: 10 chatelaine
sound: 5 clank

chain ___
3 saw 4 gang, mail 5 store 6 letter 8 reaction

Chained Lady
9 Andromeda

chain store
6 big box

chair
4 seat 5 stool 6 rocker, settee, settle 7 preside
back: 5 splat
bishop's: 8 cathedra
designer: 5 Eames (Charles, Ray) 6 Breuer (Marcel)
maker: 5 caner
portable: 5 sedan
reclining: 6 chaise 12 chaise longue, chaise lounge
royal: 6 throne
type: 4 club, easy 6 morris 7 rocking 8 captain's, electric 9 director's, reclining 10 Adirondack, ladder-back

chaise
4 sofa 5 chair, coach, divan 8 carriage

chalcedony
4 onyx, sard 5 agate, chert 6 jasper, quartz 9 carnelian, cornelian 10 bloodstone 11 chrysoprase

chalet
3 hut 4 camp 5 lodge 7 cottage

chalice
3 cup 5 grail 6 goblet
veil: 3 aer

chalk out
5 draft 6 sketch 7 outline 8 block out, rough out 11 skeletonize 12 characterize

chalk up
3 get, win 4 gain 6 attain, credit, impute, obtain, secure 7 achieve, acquire, ascribe, procure, realize 9 attribute

challenge
3 try 4 dare, defy, face, stir, wake 5 brave, claim, demur, doubt, exact, rouse, waken 6 arouse, awaken, demand, impugn, invite, kindle 7 calling, dispute, protest, require, solicit, venture 8 confront, defiance, demurral, demurrer, question, struggle 9 objection, postulate, stimulate 10 difficulty, insistence 12 remonstrance

challenger
5 rival 8 aspirant, opponent 9 adversary, contender 10 antagonist, competitor, contestant

chamber
4 cell, hall, room 5 haven, house 7 cubicle 9 apartment, enclosure 11 compartment
burial: 4 cist

ceremonial: **4** kiva
underground: **8** hypogeum

chambered seashell
8 nautilus

chamberlain
6 priest **7** officer, servant **9** attendant, treasurer

chameleon
6 lizard

chameleonic
6 fickle **7** protean **9** mercurial **10** changeable, inconstant

chamfer
5 bevel **6** groove

chamois
5 izard **6** shammy **7** leather **8** antelope, ruminant
habitat: **4** Alps
Old Testament: **6** aoudad

chamois-like animal
4 goat, ibex

champ
3 gum **4** bite, chew, mash **5** gnash, munch **7** trample **8** macerate, ruminate **9** masticate

champagne
4 wine **6** bubbly
bucket: **4** icer
center: **5** Reims **6** Rheims
type: **3** sec **4** brut

Champagne capital
6 Troyes

champaign
5 field, plain **7** expanse, terrain **11** battlefield

champignon
6 fungus **8** mushroom

champion
4 back, hero **5** first, prime **6** uphold, victor, winner **7** capital, contend, leading, paladin, premier, support, titlist **8** advocate, defender, exponent, fight for, foremost, medalist, unbeaten **9** excellent, nonpareil, number one, principal, proponent, protector, supporter **11** illustrious, outstanding, titleholder, white knight

championship
5 crown, title **6** laurel, trophy **7** contest, defense, laurels, pennant **8** advocacy **10** blue ribbon

chance
3 hap, hit, lot, odd **4** fate, luck, meet, odds, risk, shot **5** break, fluke, light, wager **6** befall, casual, gamble, happen, hazard **7** fortune, offhand, stumble, venture **8** accident, fortuity, occasion, prospect **9** advantage, transpire **10** accidental, fortuitous, incidental, likelihood **11** contingency, opportunity, possibility, probability
even: **6** toss-up

chancellor
5 judge **8** minister **9** secretary
German: **4** Kohl (Helmut) **6** Brandt (Willy), Erhard (Ludwig), Hitler (Adolf), Merkel (Angela) **7** Schmidt (Helmut) **8** Adenauer (Konrad), Bismarck (Otto von) **9** Schroeder (Gerhard)

chancy
4 iffy **5** dicey, fluky, hairy, risky **6** touchy, tricky **8** perilous, ticklish **9** dangerous, haphazard, hazardous, uncertain **10** capricious, precarious **11** speculative, treacherous **12** incalculable **13** unpredictable

Chandler, Raymond
character: **7** Marlowe (Philip)
novel: **8** Big Sleep (The) **11** Long Good-Bye (The) **13** Murder My Sweet **16** Farewell My Lovely
screenplay: **10** Blue Dahlia (The) **15** Double Indemnity

Chanel, ___
4 Coco

change
3 fix **4** swap, turn, vary **5** add-on, alter, coins, money, morph, shift, trade **6** adjust, evolve, modify, mutate, reform, remake, revamp, revert, revise, switch **7** commute, convert, novelty, replace, reverse **8** exchange, mutation, revision, transfer **9** alternate, deviation, diversify, fluctuate, refashion, transform, transmute, transpose, variation **10** alteration, conversion, divergence, innovation, substitute **11** interchange, permutation, transfigure, vicissitude **12** metamorphose, modification, transmogrify **13** metamorphosis, transmutation
sudden: **8** peripety **10** peripeteia

changeable
5 fluid **6** fickle, labile, pliant, shifty **7** flighty, mutable, plastic, protean, unfixed, varying **8** restless, shifting, slippery, ticklish, unstable, unsteady, variable, volatile **9** adaptable, alterable, impulsive, mercurial, uncertain, unsettled, whimsical **10** capricious, inconstant **11** chameleonic, fluctuating, vacillating **13** kaleidoscopic, temperamental, unpredictable

changeless
5 fixed **6** steady **7** abiding, regular, uniform **8** constant, enduring, resolute **9** immutable, perpetual, steadfast, unvarying **10** invariable

change off
6 rotate **9** alternate

change of heart
8 reversal

change of life
9 menopause **11** climacteric

change of pace
5 pitch, shift **9** slow pitch

changeover
5 shift **10** alteration, conversion, transition

channel
3 way **4** band, duct, kyle, pass, path, pipe **5** agent, canal, carry **6** agency, convey, course, funnel, groove, gutter, medium, siphon, strait, trough, tunnel **7** conduct, conduit, passage, vehicle **8** aqueduct, pipeline, transmit **10** instrument **11** watercourse
Africa-Madagascar: **10** Mozambique
Atlantic-Nantucket Sound: **8** Muskeget
Atlantic-North Sea: **7** English
Ellesmere-Greenland: **7** Robeson
Ganges: **5** Hugli **7** Hooghly
Hawaii: **5** Kaiwi, Kauai
Japan: **5** Bungo
Northwest Territories: **9** M'Clintock
Pakistan: **4** Nara
Scotland: **5** Minch
Tierra del Fuego: **6** Beagle
Tigris-Euphrates: **11** Shatt al Arab
Virginia: **12** Hampton Roads
West Indies: **9** Old Bahama

channel bass
4 drum **7** red drum, redfish

Channel Islands
capital: **8** St. Helier **11** St. Peter Port
dependency of: **7** Britain
island: **4** Herm, Sark **6** Jersey **8** Alderney, Guernsey

chanson
4 song

"Chanson ___"
6 Triste

chanson de ___
5 geste

chant
4 sing, tune **5** drone **6** intone **8** vocalize **10** cantillate
Gregorian: **9** plainsong **12** cantus firmus
Jewish: **6** Hallel

chanteuse
6 singer **7** artiste **10** cantatrice

chanticleer
4 cock **7** rooster

chaos
5 havoc, snafu **6** bedlam, muddle **7** anarchy, clutter, entropy, turmoil **8** disarray, disorder **9** confusion **11** lawlessness, pandemonium

Chaos
daughter: **3** Nox, Nyx **4** Gaea
son: **6** Erebus

chaotic
7 jumbled, lawless **8** anarchic, confused, formless **9** amorphous, haphazard, scrambled **10** disordered, disorderly, topsy-turvy, tumultuous **11** harum-scarum, unorganized **12** disorganized **13** helter-skelter, unpredictable

chap
3 guy **4** gent **5** bloke **6** fellow

chaparral
5 scrub **7** thicket

chaparral cock
10 roadrunner

chapeau
3 hat **6** topper

chapel
6 bethel, church, shrine **7** chantry **9** sanctuary

chaperone
5 guide **6** attend, duenna, escort, matron **7** oversee **9** accompany, companion, supervise **11** superintend

chapfallen
see **crestfallen**

chaplain
5 padre **6** pastor **8** minister, sky pilot

chaplet
5 crown **6** anadem, laurel, rosary, wreath **7** coronal, coronet, garland

chapter
4 unit **5** phase, stage **6** branch, period **7** episode, section **8** division **9** affiliate

char
4 burn, sear **6** scorch **9** carbonize

character
3 ilk **4** bent, case, cast, kind, mark, mind, name, rank, role, rune, sign, sort, type **5** ethos, state, trait **6** cipher, device, letter, makeup, nature, repute, status, symbol, temper, virtue **7** oddball, persona, quality, variety **8** eminence, identity, standing **9** attribute, eccentric, rectitude **10** reputation **11** disposition, personality, temperament
chief: **4** hero **11** protagonist
defect: **8** hamartia

character assassination
5 libel **7** calumny, scandal, slander **10** backbiting, defamation **12** backstabbing

characteristic
4 mark, sign **5** badge, point, token, trait **6** aspect, innate, normal, proper **7** feature, natural, quality, special, typical **8** especial, peculiar, property, specific, tendency **9** attribute, birthmark, component, mannerism, trademark **10** diagnostic, emblematic, individual, particular **11** distinction, distinctive, peculiarity, singularity **12** idiosyncrasy **13** idiosyncratic

characterize
4 mark **5** draft **6** define, sketch, typify **7** outline, portray **8** describe, identify **10** constitute,

pigeonhole **11** distinguish, individuate, personalize **12** discriminate **13** differentiate, individualize

characterless
4 flat **5** mousy **7** humdrum, insipid, vacuous **8** mediocre **9** colorless **10** namby-pamby, wishy-washy **11** nondescript

charade
4 sham **5** farce, put-on **6** parody **8** disguise, pretense, travesty **9** deception **11** make-believe

chare
see **chore**

charge
3 ask, bid, fee, lay, tab, tax **4** bill, care, cost, duty, fill, heap, kick, load, onus, race, rate, rush, task, tell, toll, warn **5** choke, debit, order, place, price, refer, trust **6** accuse, assign, attack, burden, credit, direct, enjoin, exhort, impugn, impute, indict, saddle, thrill **7** arraign, ascribe, bidding, command, conduct, entrust, expense, impeach, mandate, request, solicit **8** accredit, handling, instruct, price tag, reproach, stampede **9** attribute, committal, electrify, inculpate **10** accusation, allegation, commitment, injunction, management, obligation **11** incriminate, instruction, requirement, supervision

chargeable
6 liable **7** subject **11** accountable, responsible

chargeless
4 free **6** gratis **8** costless **10** gratuitous **13** complimentary

charger
5 horse, mount, steed **6** salver **7** courser, platter **8** trencher, warhorse

chariness
7 caution **8** prudence **9** integrity **10** discretion

chariot
8 carriage
four-horse: **8** quadriga

charioteer
6 Auriga, driver

charisma
5 charm **6** allure, appeal, duende **7** glamour **9** magnetism **10** attraction **11** fascination

charitable
6 benign, giving, humane, kindly **7** clement, lenient, liberal **8** generous, merciful, obliging, tolerant **9** forgiving, indulgent **10** altruistic, beneficent, benevolent, forbearing, thoughtful **11** considerate, kindhearted, sympathetic **12** eleemosynary, humanitarian **13** philanthropic

charity
4 alms, love **5** grace, mercy **6** lenity, relief **7** caritas **8** altruism, clemency, donation, goodwill, leniency, offering **10** generosity, humaneness, kindliness **11** benefaction, beneficence, benevolence **12** contribution

charivari
5 babel, melee **6** jangle, jumble, medley, racket, ruckus, uproar **7** farrago **8** serenade, shivaree **9** cacophony, confusion **10** hodgepodge **11** celebration

charlatan
4 sham **5** bluff, faker, fraud, quack **6** con man **8** imposter, impostor, swindler **10** mountebank **11** quacksalver **13** confidence man

Charlemagne
brother: **8** Carloman
capital: **3** Aix **6** Aachen
father: **5** Pepin
knight: **6** Oliver, Roland **7** Olivier, Orlando, paladin **8** douzeper
nephew: **6** Roland **7** Orlando
sword: **7** Joyeuse
traitor: **4** Gano **7** Ganelon

Charles's Wain
9 Big Dipper, Ursa Major

charleston
5 dance

Charlie and the Chocolate Factory author
4 Dahl (Roald)

Charlie Brown
see **Peanuts**

Charlie McCarthy
5 dummy **6** stooge
friend: **5** Snerd (Mortimer)
voice: **6** Bergen (Edgar)

charm
3 hex **4** juju, lure, mojo, rune, take, wile **5** grace, quark, spell **6** allure, amulet, appeal, disarm, enamor, fetish, mascot, seduce, voodoo **7** attract, beguile, bewitch, enchant, glamour **8** enthrall, entrance, talisman, witchery **9** captivate, enrapture, ensorcell, fascinate, hypnotize, magnetism, mesmerize **10** allurement, attraction, phylactery, witchcraft **11** fascination, incantation **13** agreeableness

charmed
5 lucky **7** blessed **8** enamored **9** bewitched, enchanted, entranced, fortunate **10** captivated, fascinated, infatuated

charmer
4 roué **5** magus **6** wizard **7** seducer, warlock **8** conjurer, lothario, magician, sorcerer **9** enchanter **11** spellbinder

charming
7 winsome **8** adorable, alluring, inviting, magnetic **9** appealing, glamorous, seductive **10** attractive, delightful, enchanting, entrancing **11** captivating

Charon
7 boatman **8** ferryman
father: **6** Erebus
mother: **3** Nox
river: **4** Styx

Charpentier opera
5 Médée **6** Louise

charpoy
3 bed, cot

chart
3 map **4** plan, plat, plot **5** graph, table **6** design, lay out, map out, sketch **7** arrange, diagram, outline, project **9** blueprint **10** tabulation

charter
3 let **4** deed, hire, rent **5** grant, lease **10** conveyance **12** constitution

Chartreuse
7 liqueur

chary
4 wary **5** cagey, canny **6** frugal, stingy **7** careful, guarded, miserly, prudent, sparing, thrifty **8** cautious, discreet, gingerly, hesitant **9** provident, reluctant **10** economical, restrained, suspicious, unwasteful **11** calculating, circumspect, constrained, disinclined

Charybdis
9 whirlpool
rock associated with: **6** Scylla

chase
3 run **4** bolt, dash, game, hunt, prey, race, rush, tear **5** chivy, drive, eject, evict, hound, shoot, speed, trail **6** career, charge, course, follow, hasten, pursue, quarry **7** boot out, hunting, kick out, pursuit **8** run after, throw out

chase away
4 rout, shoo

chaser
4 wolf **6** masher **7** Don Juan **8** Casanova **9** ladies' man, womanizer **10** lady-killer **11** philanderer

chasm
3 gap **4** gulf, rift **5** abyss, cleft, clove, flume, gorge, gulch, split **6** ravine **8** crevasse

chasmal
6 gaping **7** echoing, yawning **9** cavernous

chassepot
5 rifle

chaste
4 pure **5** clean, moral **6** decent, modest, proper, seemly, vestal, virgin **7** austere, prudish **8** celibate, decorous, innocent, maidenly, platonic, spotless, virginal, virtuous **9** abstinent, continent, stainless, undefiled, unsullied **10** immaculate **11** unblemished

chasten
5 abase, scold **6** humble, punish, rebuke, refine, subdue **7** correct, upbraid **8** chastise **9** castigate, humiliate, reprimand **10** discipline

chastise
4 beat, flog, whip **5** scold **6** punish, rebuke, thrash **7** belabor, censure, chasten, correct, reprove, scourge, upbraid **9** castigate **10** discipline

chastisement
3 rod **7** reproof **8** punition **10** correction, discipline, punishment **11** castigation

chastity
6 purity, virtue **7** modesty **8** celibacy **9** innocence, integrity, virginity **10** abstention, continence, maidenhood

chasuble
8 vestment

chat
3 gab, jaw, rap, yak, yap **4** blab, gush, talk **5** prate, visit **6** babble, confab, gossip, jabber, natter, parley, patter, yak-yak **7** chatter, palaver, prattle, twaddle **8** causerie, colloquy, converse, dialogue, schmooze **9** tête-à-tête, yakety-yak **11** confabulate **12** conversation, tittle-tattle **13** confabulation

château
5 manor, villa **6** castle, estate **7** mansion **8** fortress **12** country house

chateaubriand
5 steak **10** tenderloin

Chateaubriand novel
4 René **5** Atala

chatelain
6 warden **8** governor **9** castellan

chatelaine
4 hook, wife **5** clasp **8** mistress

chattel
4 serf **5** slave **7** bondman **8** bondsman, property

chatter
3 gab, jaw, yak **4** blab, bull **5** prate **6** babble, gabble, gibber, gossip, jabber, natter, patter, yak-yak, yammer **7** blabber, blather, palaver, prattle, vibrate **9** small talk, yakety-yak **12** tittle-tattle

chatterbox
5 yenta **6** gabber, gossip, magpie, prater **7** blabber **8** jabberer, prattler **12** blabbermouth

chatty
5 gabby **7** voluble **9** garrulous, talkative **10** loquacious

Chaucer pilgrim
4 Cook, Monk **5** Clerk, Friar, Reeve **6** Miller, Parson, Squire **8** Franklin, Manciple, Merchant, Summoner **10** Nun's Priest, Wife of Bath

chauffeur
5 drive **6** driver **9** transport

chauvinism
6 sexism **8** jingoism **10** patriotism **11** nationalism

cheap
4 mean, poor **5** junky, tight **6** cheesy, common, cruddy, flashy, measly, paltry, shabby, shoddy, sleazy, stingy, tawdry, trashy **7** chintzy, cut-rate, low-cost, reduced, thrifty **8** inferior, trifling, uncostly **9** brummagem, low-priced **10** economical **11** inexpensive **12** contemptible, meretricious

cheapen
5 decry, lower **6** debase, reduce **7** devalue **8** mark down **9** devaluate, downgrade **10** depreciate, undervalue

cheapjack
5 junky **6** hawker, cheesy, cruddy, shoddy, sleazy, tawdry, trashy **7** haggler, higgler, packman, peddler **8** huckster, inferior, rubbishy **9** worthless

cheapskate
5 miser **7** niggard, scrooge **8** tightwad **9** skinflint **11** cheeseparer

cheat
3 con, gyp **4** bilk, burn, dupe, fool, gull, hoax, hose, milk, ream, rook, scam **5** bunco, cozen, crook, fraud, fudge, gouge, hocus, put-on, screw, shaft, short, slick **6** chisel, chouse, con man, deceit, delude, diddle, extort, fleece, humbug, rip-off, sucker, take in **7** beguile, chicane, deceive, defraud, diddler, mislead, sharper, shyster, swindle, two-time **8** flimflam, hoodwink, swindler, trickery **9** bamboozle, chicanery, deception, defrauder, imposture, overreach, trickster **11** double-cross **12** double-dealer **13** confidence man
on a check: **4** kite

check
3 tab, try **4** bill, curb, halt, jibe, stay, stop, test, tick **5** block, brake, draft, prove, score, stall **6** accord, arrest, baffle, bridle, damage, desist, hold in, square, thwart, verify **7** compare, conform, control, examine, inhibit, repress, setback **8** dovetail, hold back, hold down, preclude, restrain, reversal, suppress **9** constrain, criterion, interrupt, restraint **10** correspond, inspection **11** examination **13** investigation

checkered
5 plaid **6** motley **7** mutable, spotted **9** patchwork, patterned **10** variegated **11** diversified

checklist
7 catalog **9** catalogue, inventory **11** enumeration

checkmate
4 beat **6** corner, defeat **7** outplay **8** vanquish **9** finish off

check out
3 die, eye **4** case **5** leave **6** assess **7** examine, inspect **8** appraise, evaluate, look over

check over
3 con, vet **4** scan **5** audit, study **6** review, survey **7** analyze, canvass, examine, inspect **10** scrutinize

checkup
4 exam **8** physical **10** inspection **11** examination

cheek
4 gall **5** brass, nerve **8** audacity, chutzpah, temerity **9** brashness, impudence, insolence **10** confidence, effrontery **11** presumption **12** impertinence

cheekbone
5 malar

cheeky
4 bold, flip, pert, wise **5** brash, cocky, fresh, nervy, sassy, saucy, smart **6** brazen **7** forward **8** flippant, impudent, insolent **11** impertinent, smart-alecky **12** presumptuous

cheep
4 peep **5** chirp, tweet **7** chirrup, chitter, twitter

cheer
3 olé, rah, yay **4** buoy, hail, root **5** bravo, huzza, nerve **6** buck up, gaiety, hoorah, hooray, hurrah, hurray, huzzah, rah-rah, solace, spirit **7** animate, applaud, comfort, console, enliven, gladden, hearten **8** embolden, inspirit **9** animation, encourage **10** strengthen

cheerful
3 gay **4** glad, rosy **5** jolly, merry, perky, riant, sunny **6** blithe, bouncy, bright, chirpy, hearty, jaunty, jocund, lively **7** beamish, buoyant, radiant **8** animated, carefree, chirrupy **9** vivacious **12** lighthearted

cheerio
3 bye **4** ciao, ta-ta **5** adieu **6** bye-bye, good-by, so long **7** good-bye, toodles **8** farewell, toodle-oo

cheerless
4 dour, drab, grim **5** bleak **6** dismal, dreary, gloomy, somber, sombre **7** forlorn, joyless **8** desolate, dolorous, funereal, mournful **9** dejecting **10** depressing, melancholy, oppressive, tenebrific **11** dispiriting

cheers
5 salud, skoal **6** cincin, l'chaim, prosit **7** l'chayim, sláinte **8** applause, approval, chinchin **9** bottoms up **10** jubilation **11** acclamation, approbation

Cheers
actor: **4** Long (Shelley) **5** Alley (Kirstie), Wendt (George) **6** Danson (Ted) **7** Grammer (Kelsey), Perlman (Rhea) **8** Neuwirth (Bebe) **9** Harrelson (Woody)

character: 3 Sam 4 Norm 5 Carla, Cliff, Diane, Ernie, Woody 6 Lilith 7 Frasier, Rebecca
creator: 7 Burrows (James), Charles (Glen, Les)

cheery
5 happy, jolly, merry, sunny 6 blithe, bouncy, chirpy, lively, upbeat 7 buoyant, chipper, festive, gleeful 8 animated, carefree, gladsome 9 convivial, sparkling 12 lighthearted

cheese
3 pot 4 bleu, blue, jack 5 brick, cream 6 farmer 7 cottage, process, ricotta 9 smearcase
American: 8 Longhorn 11 Liederkranz 12 Monterey Jack
Belgian: 9 Limburger
curdling agent: 6 rennet, rennin
Danish: 7 Havarti
dish: 6 fondue 7 rarebit, soufflé
Dutch: 4 Edam 5 Gouda 6 Leyden
English: 7 cheddar, Stilton 8 Cheshire 10 Lancashire
French: 4 Brie 7 fromage, Livarot 9 Camembert, Reblochon, Roquefort 10 Neufchâtel 11 Pont l'Évêque, Port du Salut
German: 6 Tilsit 7 Munster 8 Muenster, Tilsiter
Greek: 4 feta
green: 7 sapsago
Italian: 6 Asiago, Romano 7 fontina, ricotta 8 Bel Paese, Parmesan, pecorino 9 provolone 10 Gorgonzola, mozzarella
lover: 9 turophile
main ingredient: 6 casein
Norwegian: 9 Jarlsberg
pickled: 4 feta 5 Ezine 8 Halloumi
protein: 6 casein
Scottish: 6 Dunlop, Orkney 7 kebbock, kebbuck
Swiss: 6 Saanen 7 Gruyère, sapsago 8 Vacherin 10 Emmentaler 11 Emmenthaler
uncured: 7 cottage
Welsh: 10 Caerphilly

cheesecloth
5 gauze

cheeselike
6 caseic 7 caseous

cheeseparer
5 miser 7 niggard, scrooge 8 tightwad 9 skinflint 10 cheapskate, pinchpenny

cheeseparing
4 mean 5 chary, cheap, mingy, tight 6 frugal, shabby, stingy 7 chintzy, miserly, thrifty 8 grudging, skimping 9 niggardly, penurious 11 closefisted, tightfisted 12 parsimonious 13 penny-pinching

cheesy
4 poor 5 cheap 6 common, shabby, shoddy, sleazy, tawdry, trashy 7 caseous 8 rubbishy

Cheever, John
family: 7 Wapshot
novel: 8 Falconer 14 Wapshot Scandal (The) 16 Wapshot Chronicle (The)
story: 7 Swimmer (The)

chef
4 cook

chef d'oeuvre
7 classic 9 showpiece 10 magnum opus, masterwork 11 masterpiece, tour de force

Chekhov, Anton
play: 6 Ivanov 7 Seagull (The) 10 Uncle Vanya 12 Three Sisters 13 Cherry Orchard (The)
story: 9 Black Monk (The)

chelonian
6 turtle 8 tortoise

chemical
agent: 8 catalyst
combining power: 7 valence
compound: 4 acid, base, diol, enol, imid, oxim, salt, tepa, urea 5 amide, amine, diene, ester, imide, imine, indol, orcin, oxime, purin, pyran, salol, tolan, triol 6 alkali, benzin, benzol, diamin, emodin, guanin, halide, hydrid, indole, inulin, ionone, isatin, isolog, isomer, ketone, lactam, maltol, metepa, natron, nitril, pterin, purine, pyrone, pyrrol, quinol, retene, silane, skatol, tannin, tetryl, thiram, thymol, tolane, triene, trimer, uracil, ureide, yttria, zeatin 7 barilla, benzene, benzole, cumarin, diamide, diamine, diazine, diazole, diester, flavone, guanine, heptose, hydride, indamin, indican, indoxyl, isatine, levulin, metamer, monomer, naphtol, nitrile, orcinol, oxazine, phytane, picolin, polyene, polymer, pyrrole, quinoid, quinone, salicin, skatole, steroid, taurine, terpene, thiazin, thiazol, thymine, tolidin, triazin, urethan, uridine, vitamer, xylidin 8 cephalin, cyanamid, disulfid, elaterin, fluorene, furfural, guaiacol, hematein, hexamine, indamine, isologue, kephalin, lichenin, limonene, melamine, naloxone, naphthol, palmitin, phenazin, phosphid, phthalin, picoline, piperine, pristane, quinolin, resorcin, salicine, santonin, siloxane, sodamide, sorbitol, spermine, squalene, stilbene, strontia, tautomer, thiazine, thiazole, thiophen, thiotepa, thiourea, tolidine, triazine, triazole, triptane, tyramine, urethane, vanillin, warfarin, xanthene, xanthine, xanthone, xylidine, ytterbia, zaratite, zirconia
(see also **element**)
quantity: 4 mole
radical: 4 acyl, amyl, aryl, cyan 5 allyl, butyl, ethyl, tolyl 6 acetyl, formyl, methyl, oxalic, phenyl, propyl, toluyl 7 benzoyl
reaction: 5 redox
salt: 5 niter, nitre, urate, ziram 6 haloid, humate, malate, oleate, phytin 7 ferrate, formate, gallate, maleate, pectate, persalt, picrate, tannate, toluate, zincate 8 fumarate, pyruvate,

racemate, selenate, silicate, stearate, tartrate, thionate, titanate, valerate, vanadate, xanthate
suffix: **3** ane, ase, ate, ein, ene, ide, ile, ine, ite, ium, oic, oin, one, ose, ous, yne **4** eine, idin, itol, oate, olic, onic **5** idine, onium, oside, ylene
warfare agent: **7** tear gas **8** vesicant **10** mustard gas

chemin de fer
5 train **7** railway **8** railroad

chemise
4 slip

chemist
7 analyst **8** druggist **10** apothecary, pharmacist
American: **4** Urey (Harold) **6** Remsen (Ira), Sumner (James) **7** Onsager (Lars), Pauling (Linus), Seaborg (Glenn) **8** Hoffmann (Roald), Langmuir (Irving), Mulliken (Robert), Richards (Theodore), Woodward (Robert)
Austrian: **4** Kuhn (Richard) **5** Pregl (Fritz)
British: **4** Abel (Frederick), Davy (Humphry), Todd (Alexander) **5** Boyle (Robert), Soddy (Frederick) **6** Dalton (John), Ramsay (William) **7** Faraday (Michael) **8** Smithson (James) **9** Priestley (Joseph), Wollaston (William) **10** Williamson (Alexander)
Dutch: **8** van't Hoff (Jacobus)
French: **5** Curie (Irene, Marie, Pierre) **7** Moissan (Henri), Pasteur (Louis) **8** Sabatier (Paul) **9** Gay-Lussac (Joseph), Lavoisier (Antoine), Berthelot (Marcellin)
German: **5** Haber (Fritz) **6** Bunsen (Robert), Liebig (Justus von), Nernst (Walther), Wittig (Georg), Wohler (Friedrich) **7** Fischer (Emil, Ernst, Hans), Hofmann (August), Ostwald (Friedrich), Wallach (Otto), Wieland (Heinrich), Windaus (Adolf), Ziegler (Karl) **9** Zsigmondy (Richard) **10** Erlenmeyer (Richard), Staudinger (Hermann) **11** Willstatter (Richard)
Italian: **5** Natta (Giulio) **8** Avogadro (Amedeo)
Russian: **8** Semyonov (Nikolay), Zelinsky (Nikolay) **10** Mendeleyev (Dmitry)
Swedish: **8** Svedberg (The, Theodor) **9** Berzelius (J. J.)
Swiss: **6** Karrer (Paul), Werner (Alfred)
(see also under **Nobel Prize winner**)

chemist's vessel
4 vial **5** flask, phial **6** ampule, beaker, mortar, retort **7** ampoule **8** crucible, test tube

chemoreceptor
8 taste bud

cheongsam
5 dress

Cheops
5 Khufu

cherish
4 keep, save **5** adore, guard, honor, nurse, prize, value **6** admire, cosset, defend, dote on, esteem, foster, harbor, relish, revere, shield **7** apprize, care for, nourish, nurture, shelter, worship **8** conserve, hold dear, preserve, treasure, venerate **9** cultivate, delight in, entertain, reverence, safeguard **10** appreciate

Cherokee
chief: **4** Ross (John)
historian: **7** Sequoia, Sequoya **8** Sequoyah

cherry
dark: **4** bing
family: **4** rose **8** Rosaceae
genus: **6** Prunus
hybrid: **4** Duke
sour: **7** morello
sweet: **4** bing **7** mazzard, oxheart
wild: **7** mazzard **10** maraschino

cherry bomb
11 firecracker

Cherry Orchard author
7 Chekhov (Anton)

cherrystone
4 clam **6** quahog

Chersonese
9 peninsula

cherub
4 babe, baby **5** angel, child, cupid, putto **6** infant **7** bambino **8** amoretto, innocent

cherubic
4 cute, rosy **6** chubby **7** angelic **8** adorable, innocent

chess
champion: **3** Tal (Mikhail) **4** Euwe (Max) **6** Karpov (Anatoly), Lasker (Emanuel) **7** Fischer (Bobby), Kramnik (Vladimir), Smyslov (Vassily), Spassky (Boris) **8** Alekhine (Alexander), Kasparov (Garry), Steinitz (Wilhelm) **9** Botvinnik (Mikhail), Petrosian (Tigran) **10** Capablanca (José)
draw game: **9** stalemate
goal: **4** mate **9** checkmate
move: **6** castle, gambit
opening: **6** gambit
piece: **4** king, pawn, rook **5** queen **6** bishop, knight
risk: **6** gambit
term: **3** pin **4** draw, FIDE, file, fork, luft, rank **5** check **6** skewer **7** battery, capture, endgame **8** blockade, castling, diagonal **9** promotion

chest
3 box **4** arca, cist, kist **5** bosom, torso, trunk **6** breast, bureau, coffer, thorax **7** cabinet **8** cupboard, treasury **9** exchequer
combining form: **5** stern **6** sterno, thorac

chesterfield
4 sofa **5** divan **8** overcoat **9** davenport

chestnut
4 tree **5** color, horse **6** cliché, marron **10** chinquapin
extract: 6 tannin
water: 4 ling

cheval glass
6 mirror

chevalier
5 noble **6** knight **8** horseman **9** caballero, gentleman

chevet
4 apse

chevron
6 stripe

chew
3 eat, gum **4** bite, gnaw **5** champ, chomp, munch **6** crunch, devour, nibble **7** consume **8** ruminate **9** masticate

chewing gum
6 chicle

chew out
3 jaw **5** scold **6** rebuke, revile **7** bawl out, reprove, tell off, upbraid **8** lambaste, reproach **9** castigate, criticize, reprimand **10** tongue-lash, vituperate

Chiang ___
7 Kai-shek

chic
4 mode, rage, tony **5** nobby, smart, style, swank, swish, vogue **6** modish, trendy, with-it **7** dashing, elegant, fashion, stylish **8** elegance **10** dernier cri **11** fashionable

Chicago
7 Chi-Town **9** Windy City **10** Second City
newspaper: 4 Trib **7** Tribune
team: 4 Cubs **5** Bears, Bulls **8** White Sox **10** Black Hawks

chicane
4 dupe, fool, gull, hoax, ploy, ruse, wile **5** cavil, cheat, feint, fraud, trick **6** gambit **8** artifice, flimflam, hoodwink, trickery **9** bamboozle, deception, duplicity, stratagem, victimize **10** dishonesty, hanky-panky **13** double-dealing

chicanery
4 plot, ruse **5** fraud, trick **6** gambit **8** intrigue, trickery **9** deception, duplicity **10** subterfuge **11** machination, skulduggery

chichi
4 arty **5** gaudy, showy, swank **6** dressy, frills, frilly, la-di-da **7** splashy **8** affected, précieux, precious **10** flamboyant, preciosity **11** affectation, fashionable, overrefined, pretentious **12** ostentatious

chick
3 kid, tot **4** girl **5** child **6** moppet, nipper, pullet **7** toddler **8** juvenile **9** youngster

chickadee
8 titmouse
family: 7 Paridae

chicken
4 fowl, funk **5** sissy, timid **6** coward, craven **7** dastard, gutless **8** cowardly, poltroon **11** lily-livered, yellowbelly **13** pusillanimous
breed: 4 Java **6** Cochin **7** Cornish, Leghorn **9** Dominique, Orpington, Wyandotte **11** Jersey Giant, Rock Cornish
castrated: 5 capon
cooking: 5 fryer **7** broiler, roaster
disease: 8 avian flu, pullorum **11** coccidiosis
female: 3 hen **6** pullet
genus: 6 Gallus
male: 4 cock **7** rooster **8** cockerel
pen: 4 coop **7** hennery **10** chick house
small: 6 bantam
sound: 6 cackle

chicken feed
6 bubkes, bupkes, bupkus **7** peanuts **8** pittance **11** chump change

chicken pox
9 varicella

chickpea
4 gram **8** garbanzo

chickweed
4 pink **7** potherb

chicle
3 gum **10** chewing gum

chicory
6 endive **7** witloof **9** radicchio

chide
3 kid **5** scold **6** berate, rebuke **7** chew out, lecture, reprove, upbraid **8** admonish, call down, reproach **9** castigate, reprimand

chiding
6 rebuke **7** reproof **8** reproach **9** reprimand **10** admonition **12** admonishment

chief
3 key **4** arch, boss, duce, emir, head, jefe, lion, main, star **5** first, major, prime **6** führer, honcho, leader, master, primal, ruling, sachem **7** fuehrer, headman, highest, leading, premier, primary **8** cardinal, champion, dictator, dominant, eminence, foremost **9** number-one, principal, prominent **10** preeminent **11** outstanding, predominant
prefix: 4 arch

Chief Justice
3 Jay (John) **4** Taft (William Howard) **5** Chase (Salmon), Stone (Harlan Fiske), Taney (Roger),

Waite (Morrison), White (Edward) **6** Burger (Warren), Fuller (Melville), Hughes (Charles Evans), Vinson (Fred), Warren (Earl) **7** Roberts (John) **8** Marshall (John), Rutledge (John) **9** Ellsworth (Oliver), Rehnquist (William)

chiefly
6 mainly, mostly **7** largely, notably, overall **9** generally, primarily **10** especially **11** principally **12** preeminently **13** predominantly

chief priest
7 primate

chiffchaff
4 bird **7** warbler

chiffonier
5 chest **6** bureau **7** armoire, dresser

chigger
4 mite **6** chigoe, red bug

chignon
3 bun **4** knot

chilblain
4 sore **8** swelling **12** inflammation

child
3 kid **4** brat **5** gamin, minor, youth **6** cherub, infant, moppet, nipper, shaver, urchin **7** bambino, toddler **8** juvenile, small fry **9** youngling, youngster
combining form: **3** ped **4** paed, pedo **5** paedo
gifted: **7** prodigy
homeless: **4** waif
parentless: **6** orphan
Scottish: **5** bairn
spoiled: **4** brat
young: **3** tot **4** baby, tike, tyke **6** infant, kiddie, rug rat **8** bantling, weanling

childish
5 naive **7** puerile **8** arrested, immature, juvenile **9** infantile

childless
6 barren **7** sterile

childlike
5 naive **6** docile, filial **7** natural, puerile **8** innocent, trustful, trusting **9** ingenuous

children
4 kids, seed **5** brood, heirs, issue **6** scions **7** progeny **9** offspring, posterity **11** descendants

child's play
4 snap **5** cinch, setup **6** breeze, picnic **8** cakewalk, duck soup, kid stuff, pushover **11** piece of cake

Chile
capital: **8** Santiago
city: **6** Temuco **10** Concepción, Talcahuano, Valparaíso, Viña del Mar **11** Antofagasta
conqueror: **7** Almagro (Diego de) **8** Valdivia (Pedro de)
desert: **7** Atacama
island: **6** Easter **13** Juan Fernández
lake: **10** Llanquihue
language: **7** Spanish
leader: **7** Allende (Salvador) **8** Pinochet (Augusto)
monetary unit: **4** peso
mountain range: **5** Andes
neighbor: **4** Peru **7** Bolivia **9** Argentina
passage: **5** Drake
poet: **6** Neruda (Pablo) **7** Mistral (Gabriela)
river: **6** Bío-Bío
strait: **8** Magellan

Chileab
father: **5** David
mother: **7** Abigail

chili con ___
5 carne

Chilion
father: **9** Elimelech
mother: **5** Naomi

chill
3 ice, icy, raw **4** ague, cold, cool, hang **5** algid, gelid, nippy **6** arctic, formal, freeze, frigid, frosty, wintry **7** distant, glacial, hostile **8** dispirit, freezing **10** demoralize, discourage, dishearten **11** emotionless, refrigerate

chiller
7 shocker **8** thriller

chilling
5 frore, gelid, scary **6** frigid, frosty **8** alarming **9** unnerving **10** disturbing, terrifying **11** distressing, frightening

chilly
3 raw **4** cold **5** algid, brisk, crisp, nippy **6** frigid **7** bracing, coldish, hostile **10** unfriendly

chilopod
9 centipede

chime
4 bell, bong, dong, peal, ring, toll, tune **5** agree, clang, knell, sound **6** accord, strike **7** concord, harmony **8** carillon **9** agreement, harmonize **10** consonance, correspond

chime in
3 say **4** tell **5** state, utter **6** inject **7** break in, declare **9** interrupt

chimera
5 dream, fancy **7** fantasy, figment, monster, specter, spectre **8** illusion, phantasy **9** nightmare, pipe dream

Chimera
father: **6** Typhon
mother: **7** Echidna
slayer: **11** Bellerophon

chimerical
6 absurd, unreal **7** fictive, utopian **8** delusive, delusory, fabulous, fanciful, illusory, mythical,

spurious **9** ambitious, beguiling, deceptive, fantastic, fictional, imaginary, visionary **10** far-fetched, fictitious, improbable, outlandish **11** extravagant, unrealistic **12** preposterous, suppositious

chiming
8 harmonic **9** consonant **10** harmonious

chimney
3 lum **4** flue, tube, vent **5** stack **10** smokestack
corner: **8** fireside **9** inglenook
output: **4** soot **5** fumes, smoke

chimpanzee
3 ape **7** primate **10** anthropoid
kin: **6** bonobo, gibbon **7** gorilla **9** orangutan

chin
3 gab, jaw, rap, yak **4** blab, chat, talk **8** converse
hair: **5** beard **6** goatee **7** Vandyke **9** soul patch

china
6 dishes **7** ceramic **8** crockery **9** porcelain, tableware **11** earthenware
maker: **3** Bow **5** Hizen, Imari, Spode **6** Doccia, Sèvres **7** Bristol, Chelsea, Dresden, Limoges, Meissen **8** Caughley, Haviland, Wedgwood

China
bay: **8** Hangzhou
capital: **7** Beijing
city: **4** Sian, Xi'an **5** Wuhan **6** Canton, Harbin, Mukden **7** Nanjing, Nanking, Tianjin **8** Shanghai, Shenyang, Tientsin **9** Chongqing, Guangzhou
desert: **4** Gobi **10** Taklimakan
dynasty: **3** Ch'i, Han, Qin, Sui, Wei, Yin **4** Ch'en, Ch'in, Chou, Hsia, Ming, Qing, Song, Sung, T'ang, Tsin, Yüan **5** Ch'ing, Liang, Shang **6** Manchu, Mongol, Shu Han
emperor, legendary: **7** Huangdi, Huang-ti
ethnic group: **3** Han
feudal state: **3** Wei
gulf: **5** Bo Hai
heritage site: **9** Great Wall
island: **6** Hainan **8** Hong Kong
lake: **5** Tai Hu **8** Hongze Hu, Poyang Hu **10** Dongting Hu
language: **3** Han **8** Mandarin
leader: **3** Mao (Tse-tung, Zedong) **9** Kubla Khan, Mao Zedong, Sun Yat-sen **10** Kublai Khan, Mao Tse-tung **12** Deng Xiaoping **13** Chiang Kai-shek, Teng Hsiao-p'ing
monetary unit: **4** jiao, yuan **8** renminbi
monetary unit, former: **4** tael
mountain, range: **6** Kunlun **8** Himalaya **9** Altai Shan, Altay Shan, Himalayan **10** Gongga Shan
old name: **6** Cathay
peninsula: **7** Leizhou **8** Liaodong, Shandong
province: **5** Anhui, Gansu, Hevei, Henan, Hubei, Hunan, Jilin **6** Fujian, Shanxi, Yunnan **7** Guizhou, Jiangsu, Jiangxi, Qinghai, Shaanxi, Sichuan **8** Liaoning, Shandong, Szechuan, Szechwan, Zhejiang **9** Guangdong **12** Heilongjiang
region: **5** Macao, Tibet **6** Xizang **8** Hong Kong **10** Nei Monggol **12** Ningxia Huizu **13** Inner Mongolia, Xinjiang Uygur
river: **4** Amur **5** Chang, Huang, Tarim **6** Mekong, Yellow, Zangbo **7** Salween, Yangtze

china clay
6 kaolin

chinchilla
3 fur **6** rodent

chine
5 crest, ridge, spine **7** hogback **8** backbone

Chinese
aromatic root: **7** ginseng
bamboo: **7** whangee
boat: **4** junk **6** sampan
bow: **6** kowtow
broadsword: **3** dao
cabbage: **7** bok choy, pak choi
calculator: **6** abacus
card game: **6** fan-tan
cauterizing agent: **4** moxa
conveyance: **7** pedicab **8** rickshaw **10** jinricksha, jinrikisha
date: **6** jujube
dialect: **4** Amoy **8** Mandarin **9** Cantonese, Pekingese
distance unit: **2** li
dog: **4** chow, Peke **8** chow chow **9** Pekingese
fabric: **6** pongee, tussah **8** shantung
feminine principle: **3** yin
food: **6** dim sum, lo mein, mantou, subgum, wonton **8** chop suey, chow mein **9** fried rice **10** egg foo yong, egg foo yung, Peking duck **11** egg foo young
fruit: **6** lichee, litchi, lychee, loquat **7** kumquat **8** mandarin
gambling game: **6** fan-tan
gong: **6** tam-tam
gruel: **6** congee
healing art: **6** qigong
herb: **5** ramie **7** ginseng
idol: **4** joss
laborer: **6** coolie
mandarin's residence: **5** yamen
masculine principle: **4** yang
money, silver: **5** sycee
musical instrument: **3** kin **4** pipa
nurse: **4** amah
official: **8** mandarin
official seal: **4** chop
oil: **4** tung
ox: **4** zebu
pagoda: **2** ta
penal system: **6** laogai

porcelain: **4** Ming **7** celadon, Nankeen **8** mandarin **9** cloisonné
pottery: **4** Kuan, Ming **5** Chien
prefix: **4** Sino
puzzle: **7** tangram
race: **9** Mongoloid
religion: **6** Taoism **8** Buddhism **12** Confucianism
sauce: **3** soy
secret society: **4** tong
sheep: **5** urial
silkworm: **6** tussah
tea: **5** bohea, hyson **6** congou, oolong **8** souchong
temple: **2** ta **6** pagoda **9** joss house
tree: **4** tung **6** ginkgo, loquat **7** kumquat
unicorn: **3** lin
vine: **5** kudzu
vital energy: **3** chi

chink
4 rift, slit **5** caulk, cleft, crack, split **6** cranny **7** crevice, fissure, opening **8** aperture

chinquapin
3 nut **8** chestnut

chintzy
5 cheap, gaudy, showy, tacky **6** flashy, garish, stingy, tawdry, vulgar **9** tasteless **12** meretricious

chip
4 flaw, nick **5** flake, notch, shard, slice, split, wafer, wedge **6** chisel, defect, paring, sliver **7** counter

chip in
6 ante up, kick in **7** pitch in **10** contribute **11** come through

chipper
4 spry **5** alert, brisk, perky, zesty **6** bright, lively, nimble **8** animated, spirited **9** sprightly, vivacious

chirk
4 buoy **5** cheer **7** animate, enliven, hearten **8** energize, inspirit **9** encourage **10** strengthen

chirography
6 script **8** longhand **10** penmanship **11** calligraphy, handwriting

chiromancy
9 palmistry

Chiron
7 centaur
father: **6** Cronus
mother: **7** Philyra
pupil: **5** Jason **8** Achilles, Heracles, Hercules **9** Asclepius **11** Aesculapius

chiropody
8 podiatry

chiropractic founder
6 Palmer (Daniel)

chirp
4 chip, peep, sing **5** cheep, trill, tweet **6** warble **7** chirrup, twitter

chirpy
3 gay **5** sunny **6** blithe, cheery, sparky **7** buoyant, sparkly **8** cheerful, sunbeamy **9** lightsome

chirrup
4 chip, peep, sing **5** cheep, tweet **6** warble **7** chipper, twitter

chisel
3 gad, gyp, hew **4** beat, bilk, scam **5** carve, cheat, cozen, cut in, gouge, trick **6** butt in, diddle, fleece, horn in, sculpt **7** defraud, engrave, intrude, swindle

chit
3 IOU, kid **4** memo, note, slip **5** child **6** moppet **7** invoice, voucher **8** notation **9** youngster **10** memorandum

chitchat
3 gab **5** chaff **6** babble, banter, gossip **7** chatter, palaver, prattle **8** badinage **9** small talk **12** tittle-tattle

Chi-Town
7 Chicago

chitter
4 chip, peep, sing **5** cheep, chirp, tweet **6** warble **7** chatter, chirrup, twitter

chivalric
see **chivalrous**

chivalrous
5 lofty, manly, noble **7** courtly, gallant, valiant **8** generous, gracious, knightly **9** honorable **10** benevolent, courageous **11** considerate, gentlemanly, magnanimous

chivy, chivvy
4 bait, ride **5** annoy, tease **6** badger, heckle, hector **7** torment **8** bullyrag

Chloe
11 shepherdess
beloved: **7** Daphnis

chlordane
11 insecticide

chlorine symbol
2 Cl

Chloris
father: **7** Amphion
husband: **6** Neleus **8** Zephyrus
mother: **5** Niobe
son: **6** Nestor

chloroform
7 anodyne, solvent **10** anesthetic **11** anaesthetic

chockablock
4 full **6** jammed, loaded, packed **7** brimful, crammed, crowded, stuffed **9** jam-packed

chocolate
5 brown, cacao, cocoa

Chocolate Soldier composer
6 Straus (Oscar)

chocolate tree
5 cacao

choice
3 top **4** best, pick, rare, vote **5** cream, elite, prime, prize **6** chosen, dainty, option, rating, select **7** elegant, verdict **8** decision, delicate, druthers, election, judgment, selected, superior, volition **9** exquisite, selection **9** selection **10** preference **11** alternative **13** determination
even: **6** toss-up

choir
6 chorus **7** chorale
area: **4** loft **7** chancel, gallery
leader: **6** cantor **8** choragus **9** precentor
member: **9** chorister
section: **4** alto, bass **5** tenor **7** soprano
vestment: **4** gown, robe **5** cotta **8** surplice

choke
3 gag **4** clog, plug, stop **5** block, close **6** stifle **7** congest, occlude, silence, smother **8** obstruct, strangle, throttle **9** constrict, suffocate **10** asphyxiate

choking
8 quashing, stifling **10** repression, smothering, squelching, strangling **11** suppression

choleric
5 angry, fiery, irate **6** fierce, heated **7** enraged **8** incensed, wrathful **9** irascible, splenetic **10** infuriated **11** hot-tempered **13** quick-tempered

cholla
6 cactus **7** opuntia

Chomolungma
7 Everest (Mt.)

chomp
4 bite, chaw, chew **5** munch **6** crunch **9** masticate

choose
3 opt **4** cull, mark, pick, take, want **5** adopt, elect, favor **6** decide, desire, opt for, prefer, select **7** embrace, pick out **8** decide on, handpick **9** single out

choosy
5 fussy, picky **7** finical, finicky **9** finicking, selective **10** fastidious, particular, pernickety **11** persnickety

chop
3 cut, hew **4** dice, fell, hack, hash, seal, veer **5** cut up, grade, mince **7** quality

chop-chop
4 fast **5** quick **6** presto, pronto **7** quickly, rapidly **8** promptly, speedily **9** posthaste **12** lickety-split

chophouse
10 restaurant

Chopin, Frédéric
birthplace: **6** Poland
instrument: **5** piano
lover: **4** Sand (George)
work: **5** étude **7** mazurka, prelude **8** nocturne **9** polonaise **11** Minute Waltz

chopper
10 motorcycle

choppy
4 wavy **5** jerky, rough **6** ripply, stormy, uneven **7** erratic **8** variable **9** turbulent, unsettled

choral section
5 altos **6** basses, tenors **8** sopranos

choral work
5 motet **6** anthem **7** cantata, passion **8** oratorio

chord
5 triad **6** tetrad **7** harmony
sequence: **7** cadence **11** progression

chore
3 job **4** duty, task **5** stint, trial **6** devoir, effort **7** routine **10** assignment, obligation **11** tribulation

choreograph
6 devise, direct, map out **7** arrange, compose **11** orchestrate

choreographer
American: **4** Feld (Elliot), Holm (Hanya), Lang (Pearl) **5** Ailey (Alvin), Fosse (Bob), Limón (José), Shawn (Ted), Tharp (Twyla) **6** Duncan (Isadora), Dunham (Katherine), Fokine (Michel), Graham (Martha), Morris (Mark), Taylor (Paul), Tetley (Glen) **7** de Mille (Agnes), Jamison (Judith), Joffrey (Robert), Martins (Peter), Massine (Leonide), Robbins (Jerome), St. Denis (Ruth), Tamiris (Helen), Weidman (Charles) **8** Champion (Gower, Marge), Humphrey (Doris), Nikolais (Alwin), Villella (Edward) **10** Balanchine (George), Cunningham (Merce)
Australian: **8** Helpmann (Robert)
Cuban: **6** Alonso (Alicia)
Danish: **5** Bruhn (Erik) **7** Martins (Peter) **12** Bournonville (August)
English: **5** Dolin (Anton), Tudor (Antony) **6** Ashton (Frederick), Weaver (John) **7** Markova (Alicia), Rambert (Marie) **8** de Valois (Ninette), Helpmann (Robert) **9** MacMillan (Kenneth)
French: **5** Lifar (Serge) **6** Béjart (Maurice), Perrot (Jules), Petipa (Marius) **7** Camargo (Marie), Massine (Léonide), Noverre (Jean-Georges)
German: **5** Jooss (Kurt)

Hungarian: **5** Laban (Rudolf)
Mexican: **5** Limón (José)
Russian: **5** Lifar (Serge) **6** Fokine (Michel), Petipa (Marius) **8** Nijinska (Bronislava), Nijinsky (Vaslav)

chorography
3 map **7** mapping **8** features **9** mapmaking

chortle
5 laugh **6** giggle, guffaw, hee-haw, titter **7** chuckle, snicker

chorus
5 choir **7** refrain

chorus girl
7 chorine

chosen
4 pick **5** elect, elite, named **6** called, marked, pegged, picked, select **7** blessed **8** selected **9** appointed, delegated, exclusive

Chou ____
5 En-lai

chouse
3 gyp **4** bilk, clip, dupe, herd **5** cheat, cozen, drive, trick **6** diddle, fleece **7** defraud, swindle **8** flimflam

chow
4 eats, feed, food, grub, meal, mess

chowchow
6 medley, relish **7** mélange

chowderhead
4 boob, clod, dodo, dolt, dope, fool **5** chump, dunce, idiot, noddy **6** dimwit, nitwit, noodle **7** halfwit, schnook **8** dumbbell, numskull **9** lamebrain, numbskull

chowhound
7 glutton **8** gourmand

chrism
3 oil **4** balm **5** cream, salve **6** cerate **7** unction, unguent **8** ointment

christen
3 dub **4** call, name, term **5** title **7** asperse, baptize, immerse **8** dedicate, sprinkle **9** designate

christening
7 baptism

Christian
denomination: **6** Mormon, Quaker **7** Baptist, Friends **8** Anglican, Catholic, Lutheran, Moravian, Nazarene, Reformed **9** Calvinist, Episcopal, Mennonite, Methodist, Unitarian **10** Anabaptist **11** Pentecostal **12** Episcopalian, Presbyterian, Universalist
Eastern rite: **5** Uniat **6** Uniate
Egyptian: **4** Copt
love feast: **5** agape
martyr, first: **7** Stephen
symbol: **3** IHS **4** fish, rood **5** cross **6** Chi-Rho **7** ichthus

Christiania
4 Oslo

Christian Science founder
4 Eddy (Mary Baker)

Christie, Agatha
character: **6** Marple (Jane), Poirot (Hercule)
novel: **14** Death on the Nile **16** Ten Little Indians **24** Murder on the Orient Express
play: **9** Mousetrap (The) **24** Witness for the Prosecution

Christina's World painter
5 Wyeth (Andrew)

Christmas
4 Noel, Yule **8** Nativity, yuletide
crumpet: **7** pikelet
song: **4** noel **5** carol
symbol: **7** Yule log

Christmas Carol, A
author: **7** Dickens (Charles)
character: **7** Scrooge (Ebenezer), Tiny Tim **8** Cratchit (Bob)

Christogram
6 Chi-Rho

Christopher Robin creator
5 Milne (A. A.)

chromatic
8 colorful **10** accidental

chromatin thread
7 spireme

chromium symbol
2 Cr

chromosome component
3 DNA **4** gene **8** telomere **10** centromere, chromomere

chronic
5 usual **6** wonted **7** routine **8** constant, enduring, habitual **9** ceaseless, confirmed, continual, customary, incessant, perennial, perpetual, recurrent, recurring **10** accustomed, continuing, habituated, inveterate, persisting **11** unrelenting

chronicle
4 list, tale **6** annals, record, relate, report **7** account, history, narrate, recital, recount **8** describe **9** narration, narrative

chronicler
8 annalist, narrator, recorder, reporter **9** historian

chronograph
5 clock, watch **9** timepiece

chronology
5 annal **6** annals, record **7** history **8** calendar, register, schedule **9** timetable

chronometer
5 clock, watch **9** timepiece

chrysalis
4 pupa **8** covering

Chryseis
captor: **9** Agamemnon
father: **7** Chryses

Chrysippus
father: **6** Pelops
slayer: **6** Atreus **8** Thyestes

chthonic
6 Hadean, nether **7** hellish, satanic **8** accursed, infernal, plutonic **9** plutonian, Tartarean **10** sulphurous

chubby
5 hefty, husky, plump, podgy, pudgy, round, tubby **6** chunky, fleshy, portly, rotund, stocky, zaftig **8** plumpish, roly-poly

chuck
3 pat, tap **4** beef, cast, hurl, junk, oust, shed, toss **5** ditch, fling, heave, nudge, pitch, scrap, throw **6** give up, reject **7** abandon, boot out, discard, dismiss, kick out **8** jettison, throw out **9** throw away

chucker
7 bouncer

chuckle
5 laugh **6** giggle, guffaw, hee-haw, titter **7** chortle, snicker

chucklehead
see **chowderhead**

chuff
3 oaf **4** boor, lout, rube **5** churl, clown, yahoo, yokel **7** bumpkin, hayseed **10** clodhopper

chum
3 pal **4** mate, pard **5** buddy, crony **6** friend, salmon **7** comrade **8** sidekick **9** companion

chummy
4 cozy **5** close, pally, palsy, thick **8** familiar, intimate **10** buddy-buddy, palsy-walsy

chump
3 oaf, sap **4** boob, dolt, dope, dupe, fool, goof, goon, gull, mark **5** booby, dummy, dunce, loser, patsy **6** pigeon, sucker, turkey **7** failure, fall guy, fathead **8** dolthead, lunkhead

chunk
3 sum, wad **4** clod, hunk, lump, slab **5** clump **6** nugget

chunky
5 beefy, dumpy, hefty, husky, plump, pudgy, squat, stout **6** chubby, fleshy, portly, rotund, stocky, stubby, stumpy **8** heavyset, thickset

church
4 cult, fane, kirk, sect **5** creed, faith **6** temple **7** minster **8** basilica, religion **9** cathedral, communion **10** tabernacle **12** denomination
adjunct: **6** belfry **7** steeple **9** bell tower
basin: **4** font **5** stoup
bench: **3** pew
bishop's: **9** cathedral
Buddhist: **2** ta
calendar: **4** ordo
caretaker: **6** sexton
chapel: **7** oratory
code: **8** canon law
council: **5** synod
court: **4** rota **10** consistory
creed: **6** Nicene **8** Apostles'
district: **6** parish **7** diocese
father: **5** Basil **6** Jerome, Justin, Origen **7** Ambrose, Clement **8** Ignatius **9** Augustine **10** Chrysostom, Tertullian, theologian
fund-raiser: **5** bingo **6** bazaar, raffle
governing body: **5** curia **7** classis **10** consistory, presbytery
head: **4** pope **7** pontiff
law: **5** canon
member: **11** communicant
of a monastery: **7** minster
officer: **5** elder, vicar **6** beadle, deacon, sexton, verger, warden **9** presbyter, sacristan
part: **4** apse, bema, loft, nave **5** aisle, altar, choir **6** vestry **7** chancel, gallery, narthex, steeple **8** sacristy, transept **9** baptistry, sanctuary **10** baptistery, clerestory
porch: **6** parvis **7** galilee
reader: **6** lector
recess: **4** apse
response: **4** amen
revenue: **5** tithe
room: **6** vestry **8** sacristy
Scottish: **4** kirk
seats for clergy: **7** sedilia
service: **4** mass **6** matins **7** vespers **8** evensong **9** communion
small: **6** chapel
tribunal: **4** rota
vault: **5** crypt

Churchill, Winston
daughter: **4** Mary **5** Diana, Sarah
estate: **8** Checkers
father: **8** Randolph
gesture: **5** V-sign
mother: **6** Jennie (Jerome)
phrase: **11** Iron Curtain
son: **8** Randolph
trademark: **5** cigar
wife: **10** Clementine

church key
9 can opener

churchman
6 bishop, cleric, divine, parson, pastor, priest **8** minister, preacher, reverend **9** clergyman **12** ecclesiastic

churl
3 oaf **4** boor, clod, lout, rube **5** chuff, clown,

yahoo, yokel **6** mucker **7** bumpkin, hayseed **10** clodhopper

churlish
4 base, curt, dour, rude **5** blunt, crude, gruff, surly **6** coarse, crusty, oafish, vulgar **7** boorish, brusque, loutish, lowbred, uncivil **8** cloddish, clownish **10** unmannerly **11** clodhopping, uncivilized **12** discourteous

churn
4 boil, foam, roil, stir **5** froth, swirl **6** bubble, seethe, simmer, stir up **7** agitate, ferment, smolder

chute
4 fall, ramp **5** falls, rapid, slide, spout **6** rapids **7** cascade, channel, descent **8** cataract **9** spinnaker, waterfall

chutzpah
4 gall **5** brass, cheek, moxie, nerve, spunk **8** audacity, temerity **10** effrontery

CIA predecessor
3 OSS

ciao
4 by-by, ta-ta **5** adieu, adios, aloha, hello, howdy **6** bye-bye, good-by, so long **7** cheerio, goodbye, toodles **8** farewell, toodle-oo **9** greetings

cicatrix
4 scar **13** scarification

Cicero
forte: **7** oratory
speech: **9** philippic
target: **8** Catiline **10** Mark Antony

cicerone
4 guru **5** coach, guide, tutor **6** docent, escort, mentor **7** adviser **9** counselor, tour guide

Cid, El (Le)
4 epic, hero, play, poem **5** opera
composer: **8** Massenet (Jules)
meaning: **4** lord
name: **4** Díaz (Rodrigo, Ruy) **5** Bivar
playwright: **9** Corneille (Pierre)
sword: **6** Colada, Tizona
wife: **6** Jimena, Ximena

cigar
5 claro, stogy **6** corona, Havana, stogie **7** cheroot **8** panatela, perfecto
case: **7** humidor
color: **5** claro **6** maduro **8** colorado

cigarette
3 fag **4** butt **5** smoke **6** gasper **10** coffin nail

cilium
4 hair, lash **7** eyelash

Cimmerian
4 dark **5** dusky, murky **6** gloomy **7** hellish, shadowy, stygian **8** infernal, plutonic **9** plutonian

cinch
4 snap **5** girth, setup **6** assure, breeze, ensure, fasten, insure, picnic, secure, shoo-in **8** duck soup, kid stuff, pushover **9** certainty **10** child's play

cinchona bark extract
7 quinine

cincture
4 band, belt, sash **6** girdle **9** waistband

cinders
3 ash **4** coal, lava, slag **5** ashes, dross **6** embers **8** clinkers

cinema
4 film, nabe, show **5** flick, movie **6** movies **7** picture, theater, theatre **12** silver screen **13** motion picture

cinereous
4 ashy, gray, grey **5** ashen **7** ashlike

cinnabar
3 ore **7** mineral, pigment **9** vermilion
color: **3** red

cinnamon bark
6 cassia

cinnamon stone
6 garnet **8** essonite

cipher
4 code, zero **5** aught, count, digit **6** figure, naught, nobody, number, reckon, symbol **7** compute, integer, numeral **8** estimate, monogram **9** calculate, nonentity **11** whole number

ciphering
8 figuring **9** computing, reckoning **10** arithmetic **11** calculation, computation

circa
4 near, nigh **5** about **6** approx., around **7** roughly **13** approximately

circadian
5 daily **6** cyclic **7** diurnal, regular **9** quotidian

Circe
5 siren, witch **9** sorceress **11** enchantress
brother: **6** Aeëtes
father: **3** Sol **6** Helios
home: **5** Aeaea
lover: **7** Ulysses **8** Odysseus
niece: **5** Medea
son: **5** Comus **9** Telegonus

Circean
6 luring **8** alluring, enticing, fetching, tempting **10** bewitching

circinate
6 coiled **7** rounded

circle
4 belt, gyre, hoop, loop, ring **5** crowd, cycle, group, orbit, wheel, whorl **6** clique, corona,

girdle, gyrate, rotary, rotate **7** compass, coterie, cronies, friends, revolve, rondure **8** surround **9** encompass **10** associates, companions, revolution
bisector: **8** diameter
colored: **6** areola
combining form: **3** gyr **4** cycl, gyro **5** cyclo
graph: **8** pie chart
luminous: **4** aura, halo **6** corona, nimbus **7** aureole
part: **3** arc **6** sector **8** quadrant
small: **4** disk **7** annulet

circlet
4 band, ring **6** bangle, diadem **8** bracelet, headband
for head or helmet: **7** coronal

circuit
3 lap, way **4** loop, tour, trip, turn **5** ambit, cycle, orbit, round, route, track **6** course, hookup, league **7** compass, journey, pathway, travels **8** district, rotation **9** perimeter, periphery, round trip **10** revolution, roundabout **11** association, circulation **13** circumference

circuitous
7 devious, oblique, winding **8** circular, indirect, tortuous **10** collateral, convoluted, meandering, roundabout

circuit rider
5 judge **8** minister, preacher **9** clergyman

circular
4 bill **5** flier, flyer, round **7** annular, cycloid, discoid, handout, leaflet **8** handbill **9** throwaway
file: **11** wastebasket
fort: **8** martello
motion: **4** eddy, gyre, spin **5** whirl **8** gyration, rotation **10** revolution
plate: **4** disc, dish, disk

circularize
4 poll **6** survey **7** canvass **9** advertise, publicize

circulate
4 flow **6** rotate, spread **7** diffuse, radiate, revolve **8** disperse **9** propagate **10** distribute **11** disseminate

circulation
4 flow **6** spread **8** currency **9** diffusion **11** propagation **12** transmission **13** dissemination

circumciser
5 mohel

circumcision, Jewish
4 bris **9** Brit Milah

circumference
3 rim **5** ambit **6** border, bounds, limits, margin **7** circuit, compass **8** boundary, confines **9** perimeter, periphery

circumflex
9 diacritic

circumjacent
11 surrounding

circumlocution
8 pleonasm, verbiage **9** euphemism, loquacity, prolixity, verbosity, wordiness **10** redundancy **11** periphrasis, verboseness

circumnavigate
5 skirt **6** bypass, detour **8** sidestep

circumnavigator
4 Cook (James) **5** Drake (Francis) **8** Magellan (Ferdinand), van Noort (Olivier) **9** Cavendish (Thomas)

circumscribe
5 cramp, limit **6** fetter, hamper **7** confine, delimit, enclose, mark off, outline, trammel **8** restrict, surround **9** constrict

circumscribed
5 bound, fixed **6** finite, narrow, strait **7** bounded, cramped, limited, precise **8** confined, definite, hampered **10** restrained, restricted **11** determinate

circumscription
5 cramp, limit, stint **6** border, margin **8** boundary **9** perimeter, restraint, stricture **10** constraint, definition, limitation **11** confinement, restriction **12** ball and chain, delimitation

circumspect
4 safe, wary **5** chary **7** careful, guarded, prudent **8** cautious, discreet, gingerly **11** calculating

circumstance
4 fact, item **5** event, thing **6** detail, factor **7** adjunct, element, episode, feature **8** accident, incident, occasion **9** component, condition, happening **10** occurrence, particular **11** concomitant, constituent, eventuality
unforeseen: **8** exigency **9** emergency

circumstantial
4 full **5** close, exact **6** strict **7** precise, replete **8** accurate, complete, detailed, thorough **9** elaborate, pertinent **10** blow-by-blow, ceremonial, exhaustive, incidental, particular

circumvent
5 avoid, dodge, elude, evade, hem in, skirt **6** bypass, detour **8** outflank, sidestep

circumvolution
4 gyre, turn **5** wheel, whirl **8** gyration, rotation **10** revolution

circus
4 ring **5** arena **6** big top **9** spectacle **12** amphitheater
animal: **4** bear, flea, lion, seal **5** horse, tiger **8** elephant

attraction: 5 freak 8 sideshow
owner: 6 Bailey (James), Barnum (P. T.) 8 Ringling (Bros.)
performer: 5 clown, tamer 7 acrobat, athlete, juggler, tumbler 9 aerialist, fire eater, strong man
worker: 10 roustabout

Cisco Kid
9 caballero
actor: 4 Beck (Jackson) 6 Baxter (Warner), Roland (Gilbert), Romero (Cesar) 7 Renaldo (Duncan)
horse: 6 Diablo
sidekick: 6 Pancho 7 Gordito

citadel
4 fort 7 redoubt 8 fastness, fortress 10 stronghold
of Carthage: 5 Bursa, Byrsa
Russian: 7 kremlin

citation
5 quote 6 eulogy 7 excerpt, mention, summons, tribute 8 accolade, encomium 9 panegyric, quotation, reference 12 commendation

cite
4 name, tell 5 offer, quote 6 adduce, recall, summon 7 arraign, mention, present, refer to, specify 8 point out, remember 9 recollect

citizen
7 burgess, burgher, subject 8 civilian, national, resident, townsman 10 inhabitant

Citizen Kane director
6 Welles (Orson)

citron
4 tree 5 melon

citrus
family: 3 rue 8 Rutaceae
fruit: 4 lime, ugli 5 lemon 6 citron, orange, pomelo 7 kumquat, tangelo 8 bergamot, mandarin, shaddock 9 tangerine 10 grapefruit

city
4 burg 5 urban 7 burghal 9 municipal 10 metropolis
combining form: 5 polis
Eternal: 4 Rome
fortress: 7 citadel
French: 5 ville
heavenly: 4 Sion, Zion
Latin: 4 urbs
Motor: 7 Detroit
of Bells: 10 Strasbourg
of Bridges: 6 Bruges
of Brotherly Love: 12 Philadelphia
of David: 9 Jerusalem
official: 5 mayor 7 manager 8 alderman 10 councilman
of God: 6 heaven 8 paradise
of Gold: 8 Eldorado
of Kings: 4 Lima
of Lights: 5 Paris
of Lilies: 8 Florence
of Masts: 6 London
of Rams: 6 Canton
of Refuge: 6 Medina
of Saints: 8 Montreal
of Seven Hills: 4 Rome
of the dead: 10 necropolis
of Victory: 5 Cairo
planner: 8 urbanist
section: 4 slum, ward 5 block, plaza 6 barrio, ghetto, square, uptown 8 business, downtown, red-light 11 residential
slicker: 4 dude
windy: 7 Chicago

city-state, Greek
5 Argos, polis 6 Athens, Delphi, poleis (plural), Sparta, Thebes 7 Corinth

city, town, village
(see also **capital**)
Afghanistan: 5 Balkh, Farah, Herat, Kushk 6 Konduz 8 Kandahar, Qandahar 9 Jalalabad
Alabama: 3 Opp 4 Arab, Boaz, Elba 5 Selma 6 Athens, Dothan, Mobile 7 Decatur, Florala 8 Prichard 10 Birmingham, Huntsville, Scottsboro, Tuscaloosa 12 Muscle Shoals
Alaska: 4 Nome 5 Kenai, Sitka 6 Barrow, Bethel, Kodiak, Valdez 9 Anchorage, Fairbanks, Ketchikan 11 Point Barrow
Albania: 4 Fier 5 Berat, Korçë, Kukës, Vlorë
Alberta: 4 Olds 5 Hanna, Leduc, Taber 7 Calgary 10 Lethbridge 11 Medicine Hat
Algeria: 4 Bône, Oran 5 Batna, Blida, Médéa, Saïda, Sétif 6 Annaba, Bechar 11 Constantine
Angola: 6 Huambo 7 Lubango 8 Benguela
Argentina: 4 Azul, Goya 5 Junin, Lanus, Lujan, Merlo, Salta, Tigre 6 Parana 7 Córdoba, La Plata, La Rioja, Mendoza, Rosario, San Juan, Santa Fe 9 Catamarca 11 Bahía Blanca, Mar del Plata
Arizona: 3 Ajo 4 Eloy, Mesa, Yuma 5 Globe, Tempe 6 Tucson 7 Sun City, Winslow 8 Glendale, Prescott 9 Flagstaff, Tombstone 10 Casa Grande, Scottsdale
Arkansas: 4 Mena 5 Beebe, Cabot, Earle, Ozark, Wynne 9 Fort Smith, Pine Bluff, Texarkana 10 Hot Springs
Armenia: 6 Gyumri 8 Vanadzor
Australia: 3 Ayr 5 Dalby, Dubbo, Perth, Unley 6 Darwin, Sydney 8 Adelaide, Brisbane, Randwick 9 Bankstown, Blacktown, Gold Coast, Melbourne, Newcastle 10 Kalgoorlie, Parramatta, Sutherland, Wollongong 12 Alice Springs
Austria: 4 Enns, Graz, Linz, Wels 5 Steyr, Traun 8 Salzburg 9 Innsbruck 10 Klagenfurt
Azerbaijan: 5 Gäncä 8 Sumqayit 9 Kirovabad

Bahamas: **8** Freeport
Bangladesh: **5** Bogra, Pabna **6** Khulna, Sylhet **7** Barisal, Comilla, Jessore, Rangpur, Saidpur **10** Chittagong
Belarus: **5** Brest, Gomel, Mozyr, Pinsk **6** Grodno, Homyel', Hrodna **7** Mogilev, Vitebsk **8** Babruysk, Mahilyow **9** Vitsyebsk
Belgium: **3** Ath, Hal, Huy, Mol **4** Amay, Dour, Geel, Genk, Gent, Hoei, Luik, Mons, Vise **5** Aalst, Arlon, Diest, Evere, Ghent, Halle, Ieper, Jumet, Leuze, Liège, Namur, Ronse, Theux, Wavre, Ypres **6** Bruges, Brugge **7** Antwerp, Hasselt, Louvain **8** Oostende **9** Charleroi
Benin: **5** Kandi **6** Abomey **7** Parakou
Bolivia: **5** Oruro, Uyuni **6** Potosí **9** Santa Cruz **10** Cochabamba
Bosnia and Herzegovina: **5** Bihac, Brcko, Jajce, Tuzla **6** Mostar, Zenica **9** Banja Luka
Botswana: **4** Maun **5** Kanye **11** Francistown
Brazil: **4** Codo, Pará **5** Bahia, Bauru, Belém, Ceara, Natal **6** Campos, Canoas, Caxias, Ilheus, Maceio, Manaus, Olinda, Recife, Santos **7** Aracaju, Caruaru, Goiania, Jundiai, Marilia, Niteroi, Pelotas, São Luis, Uberaba, Vitória **8** Campinas, Colatina, Curitiba, Londrina, Salvador, Santarém, São Paulo, Sorocaba, Teresina **9** Caratinga, Fortaleza, Guarulhos, Rio Grande **10** Guarapuava, Joao Pessoa, Juiz de Fora, Nova Iguaçu, Pernambuco, Petropolis, Piracicaba, Pôrto Velho, Santa Maria, Santo André, São Gonçalo, Uberlândia **11** Campo Grande, Caxias do Sul, Ponta Grossa, Pôrto Alegre **12** Montes Claros, Rio de Janeiro, Teófilo Otoni, Volta Redonda **13** Belo Horizonte
British Columbia: **5** Comox **6** Surrey **7** Burnaby **8** Richmond **9** Vancouver
Bulgaria: **3** Lom **4** Ruse **5** Varna, Vidin **6** Burgas **7** Plovdiv **11** Stara Zagora
Burma: see **Myanmar**
California: **4** Brea, Galt, Lodl, Ojai **5** Arvin, Azusa, Ceres, Chico, Chino, Dixon, Hemet, Indio, Norco, Ripon, Ukiah, Wasco, Yreka **6** Downey, Encino, Fresno, Oxnard, Pomona, Sonoma **7** Anaheim, Burbank, Compton, Fremont, Hayward, Modesto, Oakland, San Jose, Seaside, Soledad, Van Nuys **8** Berkeley, Glendale, Palo Alto, Pasadena, San Diego, Santa Ana, Stockton, Torrance, Yuba City **9** El Segundo, Hollywood, Long Beach, Menlo Park, Riverside, Sausalito **10** Chula Vista, Culver City, Los Angeles, San Leandro, Santa Clara **11** Bakersfield, Laguna Beach, Pebble Beach, Redwood City, San Clemente, Santa Monica **12** Beverly Hills, Mission Viejo, Redondo Beach, San Francisco, Santa Barbara **13** San Bernardino, San Luis Obispo
Cambodia: **8** Siem Reap **10** Battambang **11** Kompong Cham
Cameroon: **4** Buea, Edea **5** Kribi, Lomie **6** Douala **7** Bamenda, Foumban **9** Bafoussam
Canada: **4** York **5** Banff **6** London, Oshawa, Regina, St. John **7** Brandon, Burnaby, Calgary, Halifax, Iqaluit, Red Deer, St. John's, Sudbury, Toronto, Windsor **8** Hamilton, Montreal, Moose Jaw, North Bay, Victoria, Winnipeg **9** Dartmouth, Kitchener, Longueuil, North York, Saint John, Saskatoon, Vancouver **10** Lethbridge, Saint John's, Sherbrooke, Thunder Bay, Whitehorse **11** Fredericton, Medicine Hat, Mississauga, Scarborough, Yellowknife **12** Peterborough, Prince Albert, Prince George **13** Charlottetown, Trois-Rivières
Central African Republic: **5** Bouar **7** Bambari
Chad: **4** Sarh **6** Abéché
Chile: **4** Lebu, Lota, Tomé **5** Ancud, Angol, Arica, Maipu, Penco, Rengo, Talca **6** Temuco **7** Copiapó, Iquique **8** Rancagua **10** Concepción, Talcahuano, Valparaíso **11** Antofagasta
China: **4** Amoy, Jian, Luan, Xi'an, Yaan **5** Hefei, Jilin, Jinan, Lhasa, Qinan, Ssuan, Wuhan, Yibin, Yumen **6** Andong, Anqing, Anshan, Anshun, Anyang, Beihai, Canton, Dalian, Datong, Foshan, Fushun, Fuzhou, Guilin, Haikou, Handan, Harbin, Hohhot, Hoihao, Jilong, Luzhou, Mukden, Ningbo, Pengbu, Suzhou, Ürümqi, Xiamen, Xining, Xuzhou, Yanggu, Yichun, Yining, Zhangi, Zhaoan **7** Baoding, Changan, Chengdu, Dandong, Guiyang, Huainan, Jiamusi, Jiaxing, Kaifeng, Kunming, Lanzhou, Luoshan, Luoyang, Nanking, Nanjing, Nanning, Shantou, Tianjin, Taiyuan **8** Changchi, Changsha, Hangzhou, Hanzhong, Huangshi, Jiangmen, Shanghai, Shaoyang, Shenyang, Shenzhen, Zhenjing **9** Changchun, Chenjiang, Chongqing, Chungking, Guangzhou, Zhengzhou, Zhenjiang
Colombia: **4** Buga, Cali **5** Bello, Mocoa, Neiva, Ocaña, Pasto, Tuluá, Tunja **6** Cúcuta, Ibagué **7** Ciénaga, Palmira, Pereira, Popayán **8** Medellín, Montería **9** Cartagena, Manizales **10** Santa Marta **11** Bucaramanga **12** Barranquilla
Colorado: **6** Arvada, Aurora, Golden, Salida **7** Alamosa, Boulder, Durango, Greeley, La Junta **8** Brighton, Gunnison, Lakewood, Longmont, Loveland, Montrose, Thornton **9** Englewood, Estes Park, Leadville, Littleton, Rocky Ford, Telluride **10** Broomfield, Castle Rock **11** Fort Collins **13** Grand Junction
Congo (Zaire): **4** Boma **6** Bukavu **7** Kolwezi **8** Bandundu **9** Kisangani **10** Lubumbashi **12** Stanleyville
Congo-Brazzaville: **11** Pointe-Noire
Connecticut: **6** Darien, Granby, Groton, Haddam **7** Danbury, Enfield, Meriden, Milford, Newtown, Norwalk, Norwich, Old Lyme, Pomfret, Windham **8** Guilford, New Haven, Simsbury, Stamford, Suffield, Westport **9** Greenwich, New

Canaan, New London, Waterbury, Waterford **10** Bridgeport, Farmington, Kensington, Litchfield, New Britain, Ridgefield, Stonington, Torrington
Costa Rica: 8 Alajuela **10** Puntarenas **11** Puerto Limón
Croatia: 4 Pula **5** Sisak, Split, Zadar **6** Osijek, Rijeka **9** Dubrovnik
Cuba: 5 Banes, Bauta **6** Bayamo **7** Holguín **8** Camagüey, Marianao, Matanzas, Santiago **10** Cienfuegos, Guantánamo **11** Pinar del Río
Cyprus: 7 Kyrenia, Larnaca **8** Limassol **9** Famagusta
Czech Republic: 4 Brno, Zlín **5** Plzen **7** Liberec, Olomouc, Ostrava **10** Bratislava
Delaware: 5 Lewes **7** Seaford **10** Harrington, Wilmington, Winterthur
Denmark: 5 Arhus, Skive, Vejle **6** Alborg, Odense, Viborg **13** Frederiksberg
Dominican Republic: 4 Azua, Bani, Moca **5** Bonao, Nagua **8** Barahona, Santiago
Ecuador: 4 Loja **5** Canar, Daule, Manta, Pinas **7** Machala **8** Riobamba **9** Guayaquil
Egypt: 4 Giza, Idfu, Isna, Qena **5** Aswan, Asyut, Benha, Disuq, Girga, Luxor, Minuf, Tahta, Tanta **6** Helwan **7** El Arish, Zagazig **8** Damanhur, Damietta, El Faiyum, Ismailia, Port Said **10** Alexandria
Eire: see **Ireland, below**
El Salvador: 7 La Unión **8** Santa Ana **9** Sonsonate
England: 4 Bath, Eton, Hove, Ryde, York **5** Brent, Brigg, Colne, Corby, Cowes, Derby, Dover, Egham, Eling, Esher, Eston, Goole, Leeds, Leigh, Lewes, Luton, Poole, Ryton, Wigan **6** Bexley, Bolton, Dudley, Durham, Exeter, Merton, Oldham, Oxford, Torbay, Warley, Welwyn **7** Bristol, Bromley, Croydon, Hackney, Ipswich, Malvern, Norwich, Salford, Seaford, Walsall **8** Abingdon, Basildon, Bradford, Brighton, Coventry, Hastings, Hatfield, Havering, Hertford, Kingston, Lewisham, Plymouth, Wallsend **9** Aylesbury, Blackpool, Cambridge, Islington, Leicester, Liverpool, Newcastle, Sheffield, Stratford **10** Birkenhead, Birmingham, Canterbury, Colchester, Manchester, Nottingham, Portsmouth, Sunderland **11** Bournemouth, Northampton, Southampton **12** Peterborough, Stoke-on-Trent, West Bromwich **13** Southend-on-Sea, Wolverhampton
Estonia: 5 Narva, Pärnu, Tartu
Ethiopia: 5 Aksum, Harer **6** Nazret **8** Dire Dawa
Finland: 4 Kemi, Oulu, Pori **5** Espoo, Hango, Kotka, Lahti, Rauma, Turku, Vaasa **6** Vantaa **7** Tampere
Florida: 5 Largo, Miami, Ocala, Ocoee, Oneco, Tampa **6** DeLand, Naples **7** Hialeah, Key West, Orlando, Sebring **8** Gulfport, Key Largo, Lakeland, Opa-Locka, Sarasota **9** Boca Raton, Bradenton, Fort Myers, Kissimmee, Palm Beach, Pensacola, Vero Beach **10** Clearwater, Cocoa Beach, Miami Beach, Punta Gorda, Titusville **11** Coral Gables, Gainesville, Key Biscayne, St. Augustine, Winter Haven **12** Apalachicola, Daytona Beach, Ft. Lauderdale, Jacksonville, Pompano Beach, St. Petersburg **13** Chattahoochee
France: 3 Dax, Pau **4** Agde, Agen, Albi, Ales, Auch, Caen, Gien, Laon, Lyon, Metz, Nice, Orly, Rezé, Sens, Sète, Vire **5** Arles, Arras, Auray, Auton, Avion, Berck, Blois, Bondy, Brest, Creil, Digne, Dijon, Douai, Dreux, Flers, Gagny, Laval, Le Puy, Lille, Lunel, Lyons, Mâcon, Meaux, Melun, Muret, Nîmes, Niort, Noyon, Reims, Revin, Rodez, Rouen, Royan, Tours, Tulle, Vichy, Vitre **6** Amiens, Angers, Calais, Cannes, Dieppe, Evreux, Le Mans, Nantes, Nevers, Rennes, Rheims, Thiers, Toulon, Troyes **7** Ajaccio, Antibes, Avignon, Béthune, Bourges, Le Havre, Limoges, Lorient, Lourdes, Orléans, Roubaix **8** Beauvais, Besançon, Biarritz, Bordeaux, Chartres, Gentilly, Grenoble, Nanterre, Poitiers, Toulouse **9** Cherbourg, Dunkerque, Marseille, Perpignan **10** Marseilles, Strasbourg, Versailles **11** Carcassonne, Montpellier **13** Aix-en-Provence
Gabon: 4 Oyem **5** Bitam **10** Port-Gentil **11** Franceville
Gambia: 9 Serekunda
Georgia: 4 Adel, Alma, Arco **5** Jesup, Macon, McRae **6** Albany, Athens **7** Augusta, Calhoun **8** Americus, Columbus, Marietta, Savannah, Valdosta **9** Brunswick
Georgia, Republic of: 6 Batumi **7** Kutaisi, Rustavi, Sukhumi
Germany: 3 Aue, Hof, Ulm **4** Bonn, Gera, Goch, Hamm, Jena, Kehl, Kiel, Köln, Marl, Suhl **5** Aalen, Ahlen, Borna, Bruhl, Calbe, Celle, Düren, Emden, Essen, Forst, Fulda, Furth, Gotha, Greiz, Hagen, Halle, Hanau, Herne, Hurth, Kleve, Lemgo, Lobau, Mainz, Trier **6** Aachen, Bremen, Coburg, Dachau, Dessau, Erfurt, Kassel, Lübeck, Munich **7** Cologne, Cottbus, Dresden, Hamburg, Hanover, Koblenz, Krefeld, Leipzig, München, Munster, Potsdam, Rostock, Zwickau **8** Augsburg, Bayreuth, Chemnitz, Cuxhaven, Dortmund, Duisburg, Freiburg, Hannover, Mannheim, Nürnberg, Würzburg
9 Bielefeld, Brunswick, Darmstadt, Frankfurt, Göttingen, Karlsruhe, Magdeburg, Nuremberg, Stuttgart, Wiesbaden, Wuppertal **10** Baden-Baden, Düsseldorf, Heidelberg, Regensburg **11** Brandenburg, Bremerhaven, Saarbrücken **12** Braunschweig **13** Gelsenkirchen
Ghana: 4 Axim, Keta, Tema **5** Lawra, Yendi **6** Kumasi

Greece: **3** Kos **4** Arta **5** Argos, Lamia, Nemea, Volos **6** Sparta, Thebes **7** Corinth, Khalkis, Larissa, Piraeus, Tríkala **8** Salonika **12** Thessaloniki
Guatemala: **5** Cobán **13** Quezaltenango
Guinea: **4** Labé **6** Kankan, Kindia
Haiti: **8** Gonaïves **10** Cap Haitien
Hawaii: **4** Aiea, Hilo, Laie **5** Kapaa, Lihue, Maili **6** Kailua **7** Kaneohe, Waikiki, Wailuku
Honduras: **5** Danlí **7** La Ceiba **12** San Pedro Sula
Hong Kong: **7** Kowloon
Hungary: **3** Ozd **4** Eger, Györ, Pécs **5** Abony, Bekes **6** Szeged **7** Miskolc **8** Debrecen
Idaho: **4** Buhl **5** Nampa **6** Dubois, Moscow **7** Gooding, Payette, Rexburg **8** Caldwell **9** Blackfoot, Pocatello, Sandpoint, Sun Valley, Twin Falls **11** Coeur d' Alene, Grangeville
Illinois: **6** DeKalb, Galena, Hardin, Joliet, Macomb, Moline, Paxton, Peoria, Skokie, Urbana **7** Chicago, Decatur, Glencoe, Oak Lawn, Oak Park, Tuscola, Watseka, Wheaton **8** Carthage, Evanston, Kankakee, La Grange, Monmouth, Rockford, Vandalia, Waukegan **9** Belvidere, Effingham, Galesburg, Park Ridge, Yorkville **10** Belleville, Carbondale, Carrollton, Des Plaines, Northbrook, Rock Island
India: **3** Mau **4** Agra, Ahwa, Bhuj, Durg, Gaya, Kota, Mhow, Pune, Puri, Rewa, Tonk, Ziro **5** Adoni, Aimer, Akola, Alwar, Arcot, Arrah, Banda, Barsi, Bidar, Bihar, Churu, Damoh, Delhi, Dewas, Eluru, Gonda, Jalna, Jammu, Karur, Miraj, Morvi, Nasik, Patan, Patna, Poona, Sagar, Satna, Sikar, Simla, Surat, Thana **6** Baroda, Bhopal, Bombay, Cochin, Guntur, Howrah, Indore, Jaipur, Jhansi, Kanpur, Madras, Meerut, Mysore, Nagpur, Raipur, Rajkot, Ranchi, Ujjain **7** Aligarh, Asansol, Belgaum, Bikaner, Burdwan, Cuttack, Gauhati, Gwalior, Jodhpur, Kurnool, Lucknow, Madurai, Mathura, Nellore, Patiala, Vellore **8** Amritsar, Bhatpara, Calcutta, Dehra Dun, Kolhapur, Ludhiana, Sholapur, Srinagar, Varanasi **9** Ahmadabad, Allahabad, Bangalore, Hyderabad **10** Ahmadnagar, Chandigarh, Trivandrum **11** Pondicherry
Indiana: **4** Gary **5** Berne, Paoli, Vevay **6** Delphi, Kokomo, Marlon, Muncie, Tipton **7** Bedford, Corydon, Elkhart, La Porte, Winamac **8** Bluffton, Kentland **9** Boonville, Fort Wayne, New Albany, Rushville, South Bend, Vincennes **10** Crown Point, Evansville, Logansport, Scottsburg, Terre Haute, Valparaiso **11** Bloomington
Indonesia: **4** Pati **5** Ambon, Bogor, Garut, Kudus, Medan, Tegal, Turen **6** Batang, Kediri, Madiun, Malang, Manado, Padang **7** Bandung, Kendari **8** Semarang, Surabaja, Surabaya, Tjirebon **9** Palembang, Pontianak, Surakarta **10** Pekalongan **11** Tasikmalaja **12** Bandjarmasin
Iowa: **5** Onawa, Pella **6** Eldora, Harlan, Keokuk, Le Mars, Red Oak **7** Allison, Anamosa, Carroll, Clinton, Corydon, Denison, Dubuque, Marengo, Osceola, Waverly **8** Clarinda, Ida Grove, Waterloo **9** Davenport, Fort Dodge, Indianola, Mason City, Muscatine, Oskaloosa, Sioux City, Storm Lake, West Union, Winterset **10** Emmetsburg, Rock Rapids, Spirit Lake **11** Cedar Rapids, Fort Madison **13** Council Bluffs
Iran: **3** Qom, Qum **4** Amul, Arak, Khoi, Sari, Yazd, Yezd **5** Ahvaz, Ahwaz, Babol, Rasht **6** Abadan, Meshed, Shiraz, Tabriz **7** Esfahan, Hamadan, Isfahan, Mashhad **9** Bakhtaran
Iraq: **3** Ana, Kut **4** Kufa **5** Al Kut, Amara, Basra, Erbil, Hilla, Mosul, Najaf, Rutba **6** Amarah, Hillah, Kirkuk, Ramadi, Rutbah **7** Falluja, Samarra **8** Fallujah, Nasiriya **9** Nasiriyah
Ireland: **4** Athy, Birr, Cobh, Cork, Naas, Tuam **5** Ennis, Sligo **6** Carlow, Galway, Tralee **7** Dundalk, Kildare, Wexford, Wicklow **8** Drogheda, Kilkenny, Limerick, Monaghan **9** Castlebar, Killarney, Tipperary, Waterford **10** Balbriggan
Israel: **5** Afula, Haifa, Holon, Jaffa **7** Rehovot **8** Ashqelon, Nazareth, Ramat Gan **9** Beersheba
Italy: **4** Acri, Alba, Asti, Bari, Enna, Este, Fano, Gela, Iesi, Lodi, Lugo, Pisa **5** Adria, Agira, Anzio, Aosta, Arola, Cantù, Capua, Carpi, Crema, Cuneo, Eboli, Fermo, Fondi, Forli, Gaeta, Genoa, Imola, Ivrea, Lecce, Lecco, Lucca, Massa, Melfi, Menfi, Milan, Monza, Padua, Parma, Prato, Siena, Turin **6** Ancona, Assisi, Foggia, Mantua, Milano, Modena, Naples, Napoli, Rimini, Torino, Venice, Verona **7** Bergamo, Bologna, Bolzano, Brescia, Catania, Firenze, Leghorn, Messina, Palermo, Perugia, Pescara, Potenza, Ravenna, Salerno, San Remo, Taranto, Trieste, Venezia **8** Brindisi, Cagliari, Florence, La Spezia, Piacenza, Siracusa, Syracuse
Ivory Coast: **6** Bouaké
Jamaica: **6** May Pen **10** Montego Bay
Japan: **3** Ina, Ise, Ito, Ota, Tsu, Ube, Uji, Yao **4** Ageo, Anan, Gifu, Hagi, Himi, Hofu, Iida, Joyo, Kaga, Kobe, Kofu, Kure, Miki, Mito, Naha, Nara, Noda, Oita, Otsu, Saga, Saku, Soka, Tosu, Ueda, Yono **5** Akita, Atami, Beppu, Chiba, Imari, Itami, Iwaki, Iwata, Izumi, Izumo, Kiryu, Kochi, Kyoto, Minoo, Odate, Ogaki, Okawa, Okaya, Omiya, Omuta, Osaka, Otaru, Oyama, Sabae, Saiki, Sakai, Sanjo, Suita, Tenri, Urawa **6** Akashi, Aomori, Himeji, Kadoma, Kurume, Matsue, Mitaka, Nagano, Nagoya, Numazu, Sasebo, Sendai, Suzuka, Toyama, Yonago **7** Fukuoka, Hitachi, Ibaraki, Imabari, Muroran, Niigata, Niihama, Nobeoka, Obihiro, Odawara, Okayama, Okazaki, Sapporo **8** Ashikaga, Fujisawa, Fukuyama, Hirakata, Hirosaki, Ichihara, Ichikawa,

Kakogawa, Kamakura, Kanazawa, Kawasaki, Miyazaki, Nagasaki, Onomichi, Shizuoka, Takasaki, Toyonaka, Wakayama, Yamagata, Yokohama, Yokosuka **9** Hiroshima
Jordan: 5 Aqaba, Irbid
Kansas: 4 Gove, Iola **5** Colby, Hoxie, Lakin, Leoti, Paola, Pratt **6** Atwood, Beloit, Girard, Holton, Salina **7** Abilene, Emporia, Garnett, Kinsley, Wichita **8** Cimarron, Goodland, La Crosse, Sublette **9** Coldwater, Fort Scott, Great Bend, Oskaloosa **10** Hutchinson **11** Leavenworth **12** Council Grove, Overland Park **13** Medicine Lodge
Kazakhstan: 5 Semey **6** Almaty, Aqtöbe, Guryev, Uralsk **7** Alma-Ata, Zhambyl **8** Balkhash, Chimkent, Dzhambul, Kyzl Orda, Pavlodar, Shymkent **9** Karaganda **10** Aktyubinsk
Kentucky: 4 Inez **5** Cadiz, Hyden, McKee **6** Elkton, Harlan **7** Ashland, Campton, Greenup, Hindman, Paducah, Stanton **8** Fort Knox, Mayfield **9** Bardstown, Covington, Cynthiana, Lexington, Maysville, Owensboro, Pikeville, Pineville, Southgate, Vanceburg **10** Booneville, Hawesville, Louisville, Whitesburg **12** Bowling Green
Kenya: 4 Embu **5** Nyeri **6** Kisumu, Nakuru **7** Mombasa
Kyrgyzstan: 3 Osh **5** Naryn
Laos: 5 Pakse **11** Savannakhet
Latvia: 7 Jelgava, Liepaja **9** Ventspils **10** Daugavpils
Lebanon: 4 Tyre **5** Sidon, Zahlé **7** Juniyah, Tripoli
Libya: 4 Homs **5** Derna, Zawia **6** Tobruk **8** Benghazi, Misratah
Lithuania: 6 Kaunas **8** Klaipeda
Louisiana: 4 Jena **5** Amite, Arabi, Houma, Mamou, Norco, Rayne **6** Colfax, Edgard, Gretna, Minden, Ruston **7** Arcadia, Bastrop, Marrero, Oberlin **8** Bogalusa, De Ridder, Metairie, New Roads, Oak Grove, Westwego **9** Abbeville, Chalmette, Hahnville, Leesville, New Iberia, Opelousas, Port Allen, Thibodaux, Winnfield, Winnsboro **10** New Orleans, Plaquemine, Shreveport **11** Lake Charles **12** Natchitoches
Macedonia: 6 Bitola, Prilep, Tetovo
Maine: 4 Saco **5** Orono **6** Auburn, Bangor, Gorham **7** Berwick, Kittery, Machias, Rumford **8** Lewiston, Portland, Rockland **9** Bar Harbor, Biddeford, Brunswick, Ellsworth, Kennebunk, Skowhegan, Wiscasset **11** Millinocket, Presque Isle **13** Kennebunkport
Malawi: 5 Mzuzu, Zomba **8** Blantyre
Malaysia: 4 Ipoh **5** Gemas, Klang **6** Kelang, Penang, Pinang **11** Johore Bahru
Mali: 5 Kayes, Mopti, Ségou **7** Sikasso
Malta: 10 Birkirkara
Maryland: 5 Bowie **6** Denton, Elkton, Towson **8** Bethesda, Landover, Snow Hill **9** Baltimore, Rockville **10** Beltsville, Hagerstown **11** Chestertown, College Park, Leonardtown **12** Havre de Grace, Silver Spring
Massachusetts: 5 Lenox, Salem **6** Boston, Dedham, Lowell, Malden, Monson, Natick, Saugus, Woburn **7** Amherst, Duxbury, Holyoke, Hyannis, Methuen, Needham, Swansea, Taunton, Walpole, Waltham, Wareham **8** Brockton, Chicopee, Falmouth, Plymouth, Rockport, Yarmouth **9** Brookline, Cambridge, Edgartown, Fall River, Fitchburg, Haverhill, Lexington, Nantucket, Worcester **10** Framingham, Gloucester, Greenfield, Leominster, New Bedford, North Adams, Pittsfield, Somerville **11** Northampton **11** Springfield **12** Provincetown, Williamstown
Mauritania: 4 Atar **5** Kaedi **6** Dakhla
Mexico: 4 León **5** Ameca, Choix, Tepic **6** Cancún, Celaya, Colima, Jalapa, Juárez, Mérida, Oaxaca, Puebla, Toluca, Tuxtla **7** Durango, Guasave, Morelia, Obregón, Reynosa, Tampico, Tijuana, Tlalpán, Torreón, Uruapan, Zapopan **8** Chetumal, Coyoacán, Culiacán, Ensenada, Mazatlan, Mexicali, Saltillo, Tuxtepec **9** Chihuahua, Fresnillo, Ixtacalco, Monterrey, Querétaro, Salamanca, Tapachula, Zacatecas **10** Cuernavaca, Hermosillo, Ixtapalapa, Xochimilco **11** Guadalajara, Nuevo Laredo **13** San Luis Potosí
Michigan: 4 Alma, Holt **5** Flint, Ionia, L'Anse, Niles **6** Otsego, Paw Paw, Warren **7** Allegan, Corunna, Detroit, Gladwin, Livonia, Midland, Saginaw **8** Ann Arbor, Bessemer, Dearborn, Escanaba, Grayling, Hastings, Houghton, Muskegon, Sandusky **9** Cheboygan, Coldwater, Kalamazoo, Menominee, Port Huron, Ypsilanti **10** Charlevoix, Grand Haven **11** Battle Creek, Grand Rapids
Minnesota: 3 Ely **4** Mora **5** Anoka, Edina, Osseo **6** Aitkin, Benson, Duluth, Waseca, Windom, Winona **7** Glencoe, Hibbing, Mankato, Red Wing, St. Cloud, Wabasha **8** Brainerd, Elk River, Moorhead, Shakopee **9** Caledonia, Crookston, Faribault, Pipestone, Rochester, Saint Paul, Silver Bay **10** Park Rapids, Saint Cloud, Saint James, Saint Peter, Stillwater, Two Harbors **11** Bloomington, Fergus Falls, Long Prairie, Minneapolis, Worthington **12** Breckenridge, Granite Falls, Redwood Falls
Mississippi: 4 Iuka **5** Amory **6** Biloxi, Leland, McComb, Purvis, Sardis, Sumner, Tupelo, Winona **7** Belzoni, Brandon, Okolona, Quitman, Wiggins **8** Gulfport, Hernando, Meridian, Paulding, Rosedale, Walthall **9** Greenwood, Indianola, New Albany, Pittsboro, Vicksburg **10** Batesville, Booneville, Brookhaven, Clarksdale, Ellisville, Greenville, Hazlehurst, Pascagoula, Port Gibson, Starkville, Waynesboro **11** Hattiesburg **12** Holly Springs
Missouri: 3 Ava **4** Linn **5** Eldon, Hayti, Ladue,

Rolla **6** Galena, Neosho, Potosi **7** Hermann, Ironton, Kennett, Linneus, Osceola, Palmyra, Sedalia, St. Louis **8** Gallatin, Hannibal **9** Boonville, Hartville, Hillsboro, Maryville, Pineville, Tuscumbia, Warrenton **10** Kansas City, Kirksville, Marble Hill, Marshfield, Perryville, Saint Louis, Springfield **11** Saint Joseph **12** Independence, Saint Charles
Moldova: 5 Balti **7** Tighina **8** Tiraspol
Mongolia: 5 Kobdo **6** Darhan **10** Choybalsan
Montana: 5 Butte, Havre, Libby **6** Hardin, Polson **7** Bozeman **8** Billings, Missoula, Red Lodge **10** Great Falls
Montenegro: 8 Titograd
Morocco: 3 Fès **4** Safi, Salé, Taza **5** Nador, Oujda **6** Agadir, Meknès **7** Kenitra, Tangier **9** Marrakech, Marrakesh **10** Casablanca
Mozambique: 5 Beira **7** Chimoio, Nampula **9** Quelimane, Quilimane
Myanmar: 3 Pyu **4** Paan **5** Akyab, Bhamo, Chauk, Katha, Magwe, Minbu, Mogok, Tavoy **7** Bassein **8** Mandalay, Moulmein
Namibia: 5 Outjo **6** Tsumeb **8** Oshakati **12** Keetmanshoop
Nebraska: 3 Ord **5** Cozad, Omaha, Ponca, Tryon, Wahoo **6** Elwood, Gering, McCook, Minden, Wilber **7** Burwell, Fremont, Kearney, Kimball, Osceola, Tekamah **8** Beatrice, Fairbury, Hastings, Ogallala, Red Cloud, Schuyler, Tecumseh, Thedford **9** Fullerton, Papillion **10** Springview, Stockville **11** Grand Island, Hayes Center, North Platte, Plattsmouth
Netherlands: 3 Ede, Epe, Oss **4** Echt, Tiel, Uden **5** Aalst, Assen, Breda, Delft, Emmen, Hague, Soest, Vaals, Venlo, Vught, Weert, Weesp, Zeist **6** Arnhem **7** Haarlem, Tilburg, Utrecht **8** Enschede, Nijmegen, The Hague **9** Apeldoorn, Eindhoven, Groningen, Rotterdam, Zandvoort **10** Maastricht
Nevada: 3 Ely **4** Elko, Reno **6** Fallon, Minden, Pioche **7** Tonopah **8** Las Vegas, Lovelock **9** Goldfield, Yerington **10** Winnemucca
New Brunswick: 5 Minto **6** St. John **7** Moncton **9** Dalhousie, Saint John **10** Edmundston, Richibucto **12** Hopewell Cape, Perth Andover, Saint Andrews
Newfoundland: 5 Burin **6** Wabana **10** Mount Pearl **11** Corner Brook
New Hampshire: 5 Derry, Dover, Keene **6** Berlin, Exeter, Gorham, Nashua **7** Hanover, Laconia, Lebanon, Ossipee **8** Hinsdale, Seabrook **9** Littleton, Merrimack **10** Manchester, Portsmouth, Woodsville
New Jersey: 4 Atco, Lodi **6** Camden, Newark, Nutley, Rahway, Rumson **7** Bayonne, Cape May, Clifton, Hoboken, Paramus, Passaic, Raritan, Teaneck **8** Freehold, Metuchen, Paterson, Vauxhall, Woodbury **9** Elizabeth, Glassboro, Lakehurst, Menlo Park, Montclair, Princeton, Riverside, Toms River **10** Asbury Park, Bloomfield, Cherry Hill, Hackensack, Jersey City, Morristown, Mount Holly, Perth Amboy, Piscataway, Plainfield, Somerville **11** Mays Landing **12** Atlantic City, New Brunswick **13** Palisades Park
New Mexico: 4 Taos **5** Belen, Hobbs, Raton **6** Clovis, Deming, Grants **7** Roswell, Socorro **8** Estancia, Los Lunas, Portales **9** Carrizozo, Las Cruces, Los Alamos, Lovington, Tucumcari **10** Alamogordo, Bernalillo, Fort Sumner **11** Albuquerque
New York: 4 Elma, Ovid, Troy **5** Depew, Ilion, Islip, Le Roy, Nyack, Olean, Owego, Utica **6** Attica, Cohoes, Delmar, Elmira, Hudson, Ithaca, Oneida **7** Batavia, Buffalo, Corning, Geneseo, Katonah, Mineola, Yonkers **8** Bay Shore, Cortland, Hyde Park, Kingston, Lockport, Ossining, Syracuse, **9** Greenport, Hempstead, Patchogue, Rochester, Scarsdale, Schoharie **10** Binghamton, Glens Falls, Huntington, Lackawanna, Lake George, Lake Placid, Mamaroneck, Massapequa, Mount Kisco, **11** Cooperstown, Plattsburgh, Port Chester, Saint George, Schenectady, Southampton, Watkins Glen, White Plains **12** Poughkeepsie
New Zealand: 4 Hutt, Tawa **5** Levin, Taupo, Waihi **7** Dunedin, Manukau **8** Auckland **12** Christchurch
Nicaragua: 4 León **5** Boaco, Rivas **6** Masaya **7** Granada
Nigeria: 3 Aba, Ado, Ede, Ife, Ila, Iwo, Jos, Owo, Oyo **4** Kano, Ondo **5** Akure, Enugu, Gusau, Lagos, Okene, Zaria **6** Ibadan, Ilesha, Ilorin, Kaduna, Mushin, Sokoto **7** Onitsha, Oshogbo **8** Abeokuta **9** Maiduguri, Ogbomosho **12** Port Harcourt
North Carolina: 4 Dunn **5** Ayden, Elkin, Erwin, Oteen, Sylva **6** Dobson, Durham, Lenoir, Manteo, Marlon, Shelby, Winton **7** Bayboro, Brevard, Edenton, Roxboro, Sanford, Tarboro **8** Asheboro, Beaufort, Gastonia, Hatteras, Snow Hill **9** Albemarle, Asheville, Charlotte, Kitty Hawk, Morganton **10** Chapel Hill, Greensboro, Smithfield, Wilkesboro **12** Murfreesboro, Winston-Salem
North Dakota: 4 Mott **5** Cando, Fargo, Minot, Rolla **6** Amidon, Ashley, Bowman, Formon, Lakota, Linton, Medora, Mohall **8** Wahpeton, Washburn **9** Dickinson, Williston **10** Devils Lake, Grand Forks
Northern Ireland: 5 Derry, Larne, Newry, Omagh **6** Antrim, Armagh **9** Bally-mena, Coleraine, Craigavon, Dungannon **10** Ballymoney **11** Ballycastle, Downpatrick, Enniskillen, Londonderry **13** Carrickfergus
North Korea: 5 Haeju, Nampo **6** Wonsan **7** Hamhung, Kaesong, Sinuiju **8** Ch'ongjin, Kimchaek
Northwest Territories: 6 Dawson **10** Whitehorse

Norway: **4** Bodo **5** Hamar, Skien, Vardo **6** Bergen, Tromso **8** Kirkenes **9** Stavanger, Trondheim **10** Hammerfest **12** Kristiansand
Nova Scotia: **5** Digby **6** Pictou **7** Arichat, Baddeck **8** Port Hood **9** Dartmouth, Kentville, Lunenburg, Shelburne, Westville **10** Antigonish **11** Guysborough
Ohio: **4** Kent **5** Akron, Berea, Bryan, Carey, Eaton, Heath, Logan, Niles, Parma, Piqua, Solon, Xenia **6** Canton, Celina, Dayton, Elyria, Euclid, Kenton, Lorain, Marion, Medina, Sidney, Tiffin, Toledo **7** Ashland, Batavia, Bucyrus, Chardon, Findlay, Ironton, Oakwood, Pomeroy, Ravenna, Wauseon, Wooster **8** Conneaut, Marietta, Sandusky **9** Ashtabula, Cleveland, Coshocton, Mansfield **10** Cincinnati, Gallipolis, Zanesville **11** Chillicothe, Mount Gilead, Port Clinton **12** Steubenville
Oklahoma: **3** Ada **4** Alva, Enid **5** Altus, Atoka, Sayre, Tulsa **6** Durant, El Reno, Guymon, Idabel, Lawton, Okemah, Poteau, Wewoka **7** Antlers, Ardmore, Cordell, Eufaula, Newkirk, Purcell, Sapulpa, Watonga **8** Anadarko, Okmulgee, Pawhuska, Sallisaw, Stilwell **9** Chickasha, Claremore, Frederick, McAlester, Wilburton **10** Stillwater, Tishomingo
Oman: **3** Sur **6** Matrah **7** Salalah
Ontario: **4** Ajax, Wawa, York **6** Barrie, Guelph, Kenora, London, Oshawa, Sarnia, Simcoe **7** Cobourg, Markham, Napanee, Sudbury, Windsor **8** Brampton, Cochrane, Goderich, Hamilton, North Bay, Pembroke, Prescott **9** Brantford, Etobicoke, Kitchener, L'Original, Newmarket, North York, Owen Sound, Walkerton **10** Belleville, Brockville, Burlington, Haileybury, Parry Sound, Thunder Bay **11** Bracebridge, Fort Frances, Mississauga, Scarborough **12** Peterborough, St. Catharines
Oregon: **5** Canby, Nyssa **6** Eugene **8** Coquille, La Grande, Portland, Roseburg **9** Clackamas, Corvallis, Gold Beach, Pendleton, The Dalles, Tillamook **10** Grants Pass **12** Klamath Falls
Pakistan: **5** Bannu, Bhera, Kasur, Kohat **6** Gujrat, Lahore, Mardan, Multan, Quetta, Sukkur **7** Karachi, Sialkot **8** Lyallpur, Peshawar, Sargodha **9** Hyderabad **10** Bahawalpur, Faisalabad, Gujranwala, Rawalpindi
Papua New Guinea: **3** Lae **10** Mount Hagen, Popondetta
Paraguay: **3** Itá **4** Yuty **5** Luque, Pilar **7** Caacupé, Caazapa **9** Paraguarí **10** San Lorenzo
Pennsylvania: **4** Erie, York **5** Avoca, Darby, Muncy, Paoli **6** Easton **7** Altoona, Bedford, Clarion, Hanover, Hershey, Latrobe, Reading, Ridgway, Sunbury **8** Carlisle, Edinboro, Hazleton, Montrose, Scranton, Somerset **9** Allentown, Ebensburg, Honesdale, Jim Thorpe, Lancaster, Lewisburg, Lock Haven, Meadville, New Castle, Wellsboro **10** Bloomsburg, Brookville, Carbondale, Clearfield, Gettysburg, McKeesport, Middleburg, Pittsburgh, Pottsville, Waynesburg **11** Valley Forge, Wilkes-Barre **12** Philadelphia, State College
Peru: **3** Ica, Ilo **5** Ancon, Cuzco, Jauja, Junin, Lamas, Pisco, Piura, Tacna **6** Callao **8** Arequipa, Chiclayo, Chimbote, Trujillo
Philippines: **3** Iba **4** Bago, Bais, Boac, Bogo, Cebu, Daet, Jolo, Lipa, Mati **5** Basco, Bulan, Cadiz, Danao, Davao, Digos, Gapan, Gubat, Iriga, Laoag, Ormoc, Pasay, Silay, Tagum, Vigan **6** Butuan, Iloilo, Quezon **7** Angeles, Bacolod, Basilan **8** Batangas, Calbayog, Caloocan **9** Zamboanga **10** Quezon City
Poland: **4** Lodz, Nysa, Pila, Zary **5** Bytom, Bytow, Chelm, Kutno, Lomza, Luban, Lubin, Plock, Radom, Torun, Tychy **6** Elblag, Gdansk, Gdynia, Kalisz, Kielce, Krakow, Lublin, Poznan, Rybnik, Zabrze **7** Chorzow, Dabrowa, Gliwice, Rzeszow, Wroclaw **8** Gornicza, Katowice, Szczecin **9** Bialystok, Bydgoszcz, Sosnowiec, Walbrzych **11** Czestochowa
Portugal: **4** Faro **5** Braga, Evora, Porto **6** Almada, Oporto, Queluz **7** Amadora **8** Barreiro, Santarém
Prince Edward Island: **10** Summerside
Puerto Rico: **5** Ponce **6** Caguas **7** Arecibo, Bayamón **8** Carolina, Guaynabo, Mayagüez
Quebec: **4** Alma **5** Amqui, Anjou, Gaspé, Laval, Lévis, Magog, Percé, Rouyn **6** Granby, Ham Sud, Matane, Ste.-Foy, Val d'Or **7** Bedford, Lachute **8** Beauport, Cap Santé, Joliette, Lac Brome, Maniwaki, Montreal, Rimouski, Roberval, Sept-Iles, Waterloo **9** Bécancour, Cookshire, Iberville, Inverness, La Malbaie, La Prairie, Longueuil, Montmagny, Sainte-Foy, Saint Jean, Tadoussac, Vaudreuil **10** Baie-Comeau, Chicoutimi **11** Beauharnois, Louiseville, Mont-Laurier **12** Charlesbourg **13** Trois-Rivières
Rhode Island: **7** Newport, Rumford, Warwick **8** Apponaug, Coventry, Cranston, Tiverton, Westerly **9** Hopkinton, Pawtucket **10** Woonsocket **12** Narragansett
Romania: **3** Dej **4** Aiud, Arad, Cluj, Deva, Husi, Iasi **5** Anina, Bacau, Buzau, Carei, Lugoj, Sibiu, Turda **6** Braila, Brasov, Galati, Oradea **7** Craiova **8** Ploiesti **9** Constanta, Timisoara **10** Cluj-Napoca
Russia: **3** Kem, Ufa **4** Inta, Luga, Okha, Omsk, Orel, Orsk, Perm, Tula, Tura, Zima **5** Aldan, Artem, Chita, Ishim, Kansk, Kazan, Lysva, Onega, Penza, Pskov, Rzhev, Salsk, Serov, Sochi, Sokol, Tomsk, Tulun, Volsk, Yurga **6** Bratsk, Grozny, Kaluga, Kovrov, Kurgan, Rostov, Ryazan, Samara, Syzran, Tambov, Tyumen, Vyborg, Yelets **7** Irkutsk, Ivanovo, Izhevsk, Kalinin, Kolomna, Lipetsk, Magadan, Norilsk, Rybinsk, Saransk,

Saratov, Shakhty, Vologda, Yakutsk, Zhdanov **8** Belgorod, Kemerovo, Kostroma, Murmansk, Nakhodka, Novgorod, Orenburg, Smolensk, Taganrog, Vladimir, Volzhski, Voronezh **9** Archangel, Astrakhan, Krasnodar, Stavropol, Ulyanovsk, Volgograd, **10** Dzerzhinsk **11** Arkhangel'sk, Chelyabinsk, Kaliningrad, Krasnoyarsk, Novosibirsk, Vladivostok **12** St. Petersburg **13** Yekaterinburg
Saskatchewan: 8 Moose Jaw **9** Saskatoon **10** Assiniboia **12** Prince Albert
Saudi Arabia: 4 Jauf, Taif **5** Jedda, Jidda, Mecca, Tabuk **6** Jeddah, Jiddah, Medina **8** Buraydah
Scotland: 3 Ayr **4** Alva, Caol, Dyce, Oban **5** Alloa, Annan, Beith, Cowie, Cupar, Dalry, Ellon, Kelso, Kelty, Largs, Leven, Nairn, Patna, Troon **6** Dundee **7** Glasgow, Paisley **8** Aberdeen, Greenock, Hamilton **9** Inverness, Lockerbie **10** Kilmarnock **11** Dunfermline, John o' Groats
Senegal: 5 Thiès **6** Kaolak **7** Kaolack **10** Saint-Louis
Serbia: 3 Bor, Nis, Pec **4** Ruma **5** Becej, Cacak, Pirot, Sabac, Senta, Vrbas, Vrsac **7** Novi Sad **8** Subotica **10** Kragujevac
Slovakia: 5 Nitra **6** Kosice, Presov, Zilina
Slovenia: 4 Bled **5** Celje, Koper, Kranj **7** Maribor
Somalia: 3 Eil **5** Afgoi, Alula, Brava, Burao, Marka, Obbia **7** Berbera, Kismayu **8** Hargeysa, Kismaayo
South Africa: 5 Brits, Ceres, De Aar, Nigel, Paarl **6** Benoni, Durban, Soweto **7** Springs **8** Boksburg, Mafeking **9** Germiston, Kimberley, Ladysmith, Uitenhage **10** East London **11** Krugersdorp, Vereeniging **12** Johannesburg **13** Port Elizabeth
South Carolina: 5 Aiken, Cayce, Saxon **6** Sumter **7** Gaffney, Laurens, Manning, Pickens **8** Beaufort, Newberry, Rock Hill, Walhalla **9** Abbeville, Allendale, Greenwood, Kingstree, McCormick, Winnsboro **10** Charleston, Darlington, Greenville, Hilton Head, Orangeburg, Walterboro **11** Myrtle Beach, Spartanburg
South Dakota: 7 Sturgis, Yankton **8** Deadwood, Elk Point **9** Brookings, Rapid City **10** Sioux Falls
South Korea: 3 Iri **4** Yosu **5** Cheju, Masan, Mokpo, Pusan, Suwon, Taegu, Ulson, Wonju **6** Chinju, Chonju, Inchon, Kunsan, Taejon **7** Kwangju
Spain: 4 Adra, Baza, Elda, Jaca, Jaén, León, Loja, Lugo, Olot, Reus, Vich, Vigo **5** Albox, Alcoy, Alora, Avila, Baena, Cádiz, Ceuta, Cieza, Ecija, Eibar, Elche, Gijón, Ibiza, Jodar, Lorca, Mahon, Oliva, Osuna, Palma, Ronda, Soria, Ubeda **6** Bilbao, Burgos, Cuenca, Huelva, Lérida, Málaga, Mérida, Murcia, Oviedo, Toledo **7** Almadén, Almería, Cáceres, Córdoba, Durango, Granada, Segovia, Sevilla, Seville, Tarrasa, Vitoria **8** Albacete, Alicante, La Coruña, Pamplona, Sabadell, Valencia, Zaragoza **9** Algeciras, Barcelona, Salamanca, Santander, Saragossa, Tarragona **10** Hospitalet, Valladolid **12** San Sebastián
Sri Lanka: 5 Galle, Kandy **6** Jaffna **8** Dehiwala, Moratuwa **10** Batticaloa
Sudan: 4 Juba **5** Kodok, Kosti **7** El Obeid, Kassala **8** Omdurman
Sweden: 4 Lund, Täby, Umea **5** Falun, Gävle, Lulea, Malmö, Växjö, Visby **6** Orebro **7** Uppsala **8** Göteborg, Halmstad **9** Jönköping, Linköping **12** Kristianstad
Switzerland: 3 Zug **4** Biel, Chur, Sion, Thun **5** Aarau, Arbon, Baden, Basel, Koniz **6** Geneva, Lugano, St. Gall, Zürich **7** Lucerne, Zermatt **8** Lausanne, Montreux, St. Moritz **9** Neuchâtel, Saint Gall **11** Saint Moritz
Syria: 4 Hama, Homs **5** Idlib **6** Aleppo, Tartus **7** Latakia
Taiwan: 5 Chia-i **6** T'ai-nan **7** Chi-lung, Hsinchu **8** Feng-shan, Pan-ch'iao, San-ch'ung, T'ai-chung **9** Kao-hsiung
Tanzania: 5 Lindi, Mbeya, Tanga **6** Arusha, Kigoma, Mwanza **8** Morogoro, Zanzibar **11** Dar es Salaam
Tennessee: 5 Alcoa, Erwin, Rives **6** Loudon, Ripley, Selmer **7** Memphis, Waverly **8** Gallatin, Oak Ridge, Rutledge, Tazewell, Wartburg **9** Dandridge, Dyersburg, Jacksboro, Jonesboro, Knoxville, Lewisburg, Maryville **10** Cookeville, Crossville, Somerville, Waynesboro **11** Blountville, Chattanooga, Clarksville, Greeneville, McMinnville, Rogersville, Sevierville, Shelbyville **12** Elizabethton, Lawrenceburg, Madisonville, Murfreesboro
Texas: 4 Azle, Waco **5** Alvin, Anson, Baird, Bowie, Bryan, Clute, Cuero, Emory, Ennis, Freer, Hondo, Marfa, Mexia, Olney, Pampa, Pecos, Pharr, Plano, Sealy, Vidor, Wylie **6** Belton, Boerne, Bonham, Burnet, Dallas, Denton, El Paso, Lamesa, Laredo, Linden, Lufkin, Odessa, Seguin **7** Abilene, Bandera, Denison, Houston, Kaufman, Lubbock, Midland, Wharton **8** Amarillo, Angleton, Beaumont, Eastland, Giddings, Gonzales, Granbury, Groveton, Hemphill, La Grange **9** Fort Worth, Galveston **10** Brownfield, Port Arthur, San Antonio, Sweetwater, Waxahachie **11** Brownsville, Littlefield, Nacogdoches, Weatherford **12** New Braunfels **13** Corpus Christi
Thailand: 3 Nan, Tak **5** Phrae, Roi Et, Surin **8** Songkhla **9** Chiang Mai **10** Nonthaburi
Tunisia: 4 Béja, Sfax **5** Gabès, Gafsa, Susah **6** Ariana **7** Bizerte, Safaqis
Turkey: 5 Adana, Bursa, Izmir, Konya, Sivas

6 Edirne, Erzurm, Samsun 7 Antakya, Antalya, Antioch, Kayseri, Malatya 8 Istanbul 9 Eskisehir, Gallipoli, Gaziantep 10 Diyarbakir
Turkmenistan: 8 Nebit Dag 9 Chardzhou, Dashhowuz
Uganda: 5 Jinja, Mbale 7 Entebbe
Ukraine: 4 Lviv, Lvov, Sumy 5 Lutsk, Rovno, Yalta 6 Odessa 7 Donetsk, Kharkiv, Kharkov, Kherson, Luhansk, Poltava 8 Mariupol, Vinnitsa, Zhitomir 9 Chernigov, Chernobyl, Krivoy Rog, Krivyy Rih, Nikolayev 10 Kirovograd, Sebastopol, Sevastopol, Simferopol, Zaporozhye
United Arab Emirates: 5 Ajman, Dubai 6 Dubayy 8 Fujairah, Fujayrah
Uruguay: 4 Melo 5 Minas, Pando, Rocha, Salto 6 Rivera 8 Paysandú 10 Las Piedras
Utah: 3 Loa 4 Lehi, Orem 5 Manti, Ogden, Provo, Sandy 6 Dugway, Tooele 7 Parowan 8 Duchesne 9 Coalville 11 Saint George
Uzbekistan: 5 Nukus 6 Kokand 7 Bukhara, Fergana 8 Andizhan, Chirchik, Namangan 9 Samarkand, Samarqand
Venezuela: 4 Coro 5 Anaco, Cagua 6 Cumaná, Mérida, Petare 7 Cabimas, Guayana, Maracay 8 Valencia 9 Maracaibo 12 Barquisimeto, San Cristóbal
Vermont: 5 Barre 7 Rutland 8 St. Albans 10 Bennington, Burlington, Middlebury 11 Brattleboro, Saint Albans, St. Johnsbury
Vietnam: 3 Hue 4 Vinh 5 Da Lat, Hoi An, My Tho 6 Can Tho, Da Nang, Saigon 7 Bien Hoa, Nam Dinh, Qui Nhon 8 Haiphong, Nha Trang, Thanh Hoa 9 Long Xuyen
Virginia: 4 Tabb 5 Luray 6 Grundy 7 Accomac, Boydton, Fairfax, Hampton, New Kent, Norfolk 8 Abingdon, Culpeper, Leesburg, Manassas, Montross, Nottoway, Powhatan, Tazewell 9 Arlington, Clintwood, Courtland, Eastville, Farmville, Lunenburg, Lynchburg 10 Alexandria, Appomattox, Front Royal, Hillsville, King George, Portsmouth, Rocky Mount 11 King William, Newport News 12 Prince George, Spotsylvania, Williamsburg
Wales: 4 Rhyl 5 Neath, Risca, Tenby, Tywyn 7 Cwmbran, Denbigh, Harlech, Newport, Swansea 8 Aberdare, Bridgend 10 Caernarfon, Caernarvon, Llangollen 11 Aberystwyth
Washington: 4 Omak 5 Brier, Camas, Kelso, Lacey, Pasco, Selah 6 Asotin, Colfax, Tacoma, Yakima 7 Ephrata, Everett, Prosser, Redmond, Seattle, Spokane 8 Bellevue, Chehalis, Colville, Okanogan 9 Montesano, Ritzville, Snohomish, Wenatchee 10 Bellingham, Coupeville, Ellensburg, Goldendale, Walla Walla, Waterville 11 Port Angeles
West Virginia: 5 Nitro, Welch 6 Elkins, Hamlin, Hinton, Keyser, Ripley 7 Beckley, Weirton 8 Kingwood, Philippi, Wheeling 9 Pineville, Wellsburg 10 Buckhannon, Clarksburg, Huntington, Moorefield, Morgantown, Petersburg, Williamson 11 Harrisville, Martinsburg, Moundsville, Parkersburg 12 Harpers Ferry
Wisconsin: 4 Kiel 5 Ripon, Tomah 6 Antigo, Barron, Oconto, Racine, Wausau 7 Baraboo, Chilton, Elkhorn, Hayward, Kenosha, Mauston, Merrill, Oshkosh, Shawano, Viraqua, Waupaca, Wautoma 8 Appleton, Green Bay, Kewaunee, La Crosse, Washburn, Waukesha, West Bend 9 Eau Claire, Ellsworth, Fond du Lac, Green Lake, Manitowoc, Marinette, Menomonie, Milwaukee, Sheboygan, Whitehall 10 Balsam Lake, Darlington, Dodgeville 12 Stevens Point
Wyoming: 6 Casper, Lander 7 Laramie, Rawlins 8 Gillette, Kemmerer, Sheridan 10 Green River 11 Rock Springs
Yemen: 4 Aden 5 Taizz 7 Hodeida, Mukalla 8 Hudaydah
Zambia: 5 Kabwe, Kitwe, Mansa, Mbala, Mongu, Ndola 6 Kasama 7 Chipata
Zimbabwe: 5 Gweru 6 Hwange, Kadoma, Kwekwe, Mutare, Umtali 7 Mashava 8 Bulawayo, Masvingo

civet
3 cat 5 rasse
Madagascar: 5 fossa
relative: 5 genet

civic
5 urban 6 public, social 8 communal, national, societal 9 municipal

civil
6 polite, public, seemly, urbane 7 affable, cordial, courtly, genteel, refined 8 decorous, gracious, mannerly, national, obliging, well-bred 9 courteous, political 10 diplomatic 12 well-mannered 13 accommodating

civilian clothes
5 mufti

civility
6 comity 7 amenity, decency, decorum, manners 8 courtesy 9 etiquette, gentility, propriety 10 politeness 11 correctness

civilization
7 culture

civilized
6 decent, proper, urbane 7 genteel, refined 8 decorous, mannerly, tasteful 9 courteous 10 cultivated 13 sophisticated

civil rights
organization: 4 CORE, SCLC 5 NAACP
pioneer: 4 King (Martin Luther) 5 Evers (Medgar), Parks (Rosa) 6 Du Bois (W. E. B.), Garvey (Marcus) 7 Jackson (Jesse) 8 Malcolm X, Marshall (Thurgood) 10 Washington (Booker T.)

Civil War
admiral: **8** Buchanan (Franklin), Farragut (David)
battle: **6** Shiloh **7** Bull Run **8** Antietam, Manassas **9** Mobile Bay, Nashville, Vicksburg **10** Cold Harbor, Gettysburg **11** Chattanooga, Chickamauga
general: **3** Lee (Robert E.) **4** Hood (John Bell), Pope (John) **5** Bragg (Braxton), Buell (Don Carlos), Ewell (Richard Stoddart), Grant (Ulysses S.), Meade (George), Sykes (George) **6** Hooker (Joseph) **7** Forrest (Nathan Bedford), Jackson (Thomas "Stonewall"), Sherman (Thomas West, William Tecumseh) **8** Burnside (Ambrose), Johnston (Albert Sidney, Joseph Eggleston), Sheridan (Philip) **9** McClellan (George Brinton), Rosecrans (William), Schofield (John) **10** Beauregard (Pierre)
ship: **7** Monitor **9** Merrimack
soldier: **3** reb **4** yank **9** Billy Yank, Johnny Reb

civil wrong
4 tort

clabber
5 curds

clack
3 gab, jaw, yak **4** blab, chat **5** prate **6** babble, cackle, gabble, gossip, jabber, rattle **7** blabber, chatter, clatter, palaver, prattle **9** yakety-yak

clad
4 face, side, skin **5** dress, faced **6** clothe, decked, garbed, outfit **7** attired, clothed, covered, dressed, overlay, sheathe **8** costumed, overlaid, sheathed **9** outfitted

claim
4 call, dibs, hold, lien, plea, take **5** argue, exact, right, share, stake, title **6** adduce, allege, assert, defend, demand, insist **7** advance, call for, contend, declare, justify, profess, purport, require, solicit, warrant **8** interest, maintain **9** assertion, challenge, postulate, privilege **10** allegation, birthright **11** affirmation, declaration, prerogative, requisition **12** protestation

clairvoyance
3 ESP **7** insight **9** intuition, telepathy **10** sixth sense **11** penetration, second sight **12** precognition

clairvoyant
4 seer **5** sibyl **7** diviner **8** telepath **10** soothsayer

clam
4 buck **5** razor **6** dollar, quahog **7** bivalve, coquina, geoduck, mollusc, mollusk, smacker, steamer **11** cherrystone
genus: **3** Mya

clamant
4 dire **6** crying, urgent **7** blatant, burning, exigent **8** pressing **9** insistent **10** compelling, imperative

clamber
5 climb, crawl, scale, swarm **8** scrabble, scramble, struggle

clammy
4 cool, dank, damp **5** close, moist, slimy **6** sticky

clamor
3 cry, din, row **4** bawl, roar, to-do **5** babel, hoo-ha, noise **6** bellow, demand, hoo-hah, hubbub, jangle, outcry, racket, ruckus, tumult, uproar **7** agitate, dispute, ferment, protest, turmoil **8** brouhaha, foofaraw, shouting **9** agitation, commotion **10** hullabaloo, hurly-burly **11** pandemonium

clamorous
5 noisy, vocal **6** crying, shrill, urgent **7** blatant, exigent, raucous, voluble **8** strident, vehement **9** insistent **10** boisterous, imperative, tumultuous, vociferous **11** importunate **12** obstreperous

clamp
4 grip, hold, vise **5** clasp, grasp **6** clench, clinch, clutch, fasten, secure **7** grapple

clamshell
6 bucket **7** grapple

clan
3 mob **4** camp, folk, ring, sept **5** cabal, house, stock, tribe **6** circle, clique, family **7** coterie, kindred, lineage **9** camarilla
emblem: **5** totem

Clancy novel
12 Patriot Games **13** Sum of All Fears (The) **17** Hunt for Red October (The) **21** Clear and Present Danger

clandestine
6 covert, secret, sneaky **7** furtive, illicit, sub rosa **8** hush-hush, stealthy **10** undercover, under wraps **11** underhanded **12** hugger-mugger, illegitimate **13** surreptitious, under-the-table

clang
3 cry, din **4** ding, peal, slam **6** jangle **8** ding-dong

clangor
3 din **5** noise **6** clamor, jangle, racket, rattle, tumult, uproar **7** clatter, ringing **9** stridency **13** reverberation

clangorous
5 noisy **7** booming, rackety, ringing **8** clattery, sonorous **9** deafening **12** earsplitting

Clan of the Cave Bear author
4 Auel (Jean M.)

clap
3 pat **4** bang, blow, boom, slam, slap **5** blast,

burst, crack, crash, whack **6** strike **7** applaud **8** applause

claptrap
4 bull, bunk **5** cheap, hokum, showy, trash, tripe **6** bunkum, drivel, humbug, vulgar **7** baloney, eyewash, hogwash, twaddle **8** malarkey, nonsense **9** poppycock **10** balderdash, flapdoodle

Clara Bow
6 It girl

claret
3 red **4** wine **8** Bordeaux

clarify
5 clean, clear **6** define, filter, purify **7** analyze, cleanse, clear up, explain, resolve **8** simplify **9** elucidate **10** illuminate **13** straighten out

clarion
5 clear **7** ringing, rousing, trumpet **8** gleaming, stirring **9** brilliant

clarity
6 purity **8** accuracy, lucidity **9** clearness, limpidity, precision **10** exactitude, simplicity **12** transparency

Clarke novel
10 Earthlight **13** Childhood's End **19** Fountains of Paradise (The)

clash
4 bump, jolt **5** brawl, crash, melee, set-to, smash **6** battle, fracas, impact, jangle **7** collide **8** conflict, mismatch, skirmish **9** collision, encounter **10** engagement **11** embroilment

clasp
3 hug, pin **4** clip, grip, hold **5** clamp, grasp, press **6** brooch, buckle, clench, clinch, clutch, enfold **7** embrace, grapple, squeeze **10** chatelaine

class
3 ilk **4** hold, kind, mark, part, rank, rate, sort, tier, type **5** allot, brand, caste, gauge, genre, genus, grade, grain, group, judge, order, score, stamp, style **6** assess, assign, assort, branch, course, league, nature, reckon, regard, stripe **7** bracket, caliber, quality, section, species, variety **8** appraise, category, consider, division, evaluate, grouping, separate **10** categorize, pigeonhole **11** description **12** denomination
middle: 11 bourgeoisie
school: 6 junior, senior **8** freshman **9** sophomore
working: 11 proletariat

classic
5 ideal, model, prime **7** capital, typical, vintage **8** champion, enduring, standard, superior, topnotch **9** authentic, canonical, classical, excellent, exemplary, memorable, tradition **10** magnum opus, masterwork **11** chef d'oeuvre, masterpiece, tour de force, traditional **12** paradigmatic, prototypical **13** authoritative

classical
4 pure **5** Attic, Greek, ideal, Latin, Roman **7** ancient, fitting, Grecian, perfect, typical, vintage **8** Hellenic, standard, sterling **9** canonical, exemplary **10** consummate **11** traditional **13** authoritative

classical musician
4 Böhm (Karl), Hess (Myra), Lind (Jenny), Muti (Riccardo), Pons (Lily), Shaw (Robert) **5** Arrau (Claudio), Biggs (E. Power), Borge (Victor), Boult (Adrian), Davis (Colin), du Pré (Jacqueline), Gould (Glenn), Masur (Kurt), Mehta (Zubin), Melba (Nellie), Ozawa (Seiji), Patti (Adelina), Pinza (Ezio), Price (Leontyne), Ramey (Samuel), Sills (Beverly), Stern (Isaac), Szell (George) **6** Abbado (Claudio), Battle (Kathleen), Boulez (Pierre), Callas (Maria), Caruso (Enrico), Casals (Pablo), Galway (James), Levine (James), Maazel (Lorin), Midori, Norman (Jessye), Peters (Roberta), Previn (André), Rampal (Jean-Pierre), Rattle (Simon), Reiner (Fritz), Serkin (Peter, Rudolf), Terfel (Bryn), Tucker (Richard), Upshaw (Dawn), Walter (Bruno) **7** Bartoli (Cecilia), Beecham (Thomas), Bocelli (Andrea), Brendel (Alfred), Cliburn (Van), Corelli (Franco), Domingo (Plácido), Farrell (Eileen), Fiedler (Arthur), Fleming (Renée), Glennie (Evelyn), Haitink (Bernard), Heifetz (Jascha), Karajan (Herbert von), Menuhin (Yehudi), Nilsson (Birgit), Ormandy (Eugene), Perlman (Itzhak), Pollini (Maurizio), Sargent (Malcolm), Segovia (Andrés), Tebaldi (Renata) **8** Anderson (Marian), Argerich (Martha), Bergonzi (Carlo), Carreras (José), Flagstad (Kirsten), Horowitz (Vladimir), Kreisler (Fritz), Marriner (Neville), Oistrakh (David), Schnabel (Artur), Te Kanawa (Kiri), Zukerman (Pinchas) **9** Barenboim (Daniel), Bernstein (Leonard), Chaliapin (Feodor), Klemperer (Otto), Landowska (Wanda), Pavarotti (Luciano), Stokowski (Leopold), Toscanini (Arturo) **10** Rubinstein (Arthur), Sutherland (Joan), Tetrazzini (Luisa) **11** Furtwängler (Wilhelm), Kostelanetz (André), Schwarzkopf (Elisabeth) **12** Rostropovich (Mstislav)

classification
4 sort, type **5** genre, genus, grade, order **6** family, phylum, rating **7** sorting, species **8** category, division, grouping, ordering, taxonomy, typology **11** arrangement, cataloguing

classified
6 secret, sorted **7** divided, ordered **9** top secret **11** categorized **12** confidential

classified-ad abbreviation
3 ABS, AKC, APR, apt, brm, CDL, CPA, EDP, EOE, est, exc, exp, flr, FSH, FWD, gar, gdn, GWO, ISO, kit, LPN, lux, lwd, max, mgr, min, MLS, neg, OBO, opp, pkg, PWO, rec, ref, rep, sal, sep, sig, spd, TLC, wgn **4** appl, bldg, bdrm,

bsmt, demo, flex, frpl, furn, HVAC, pass, pref, priv, prof, prop, temp, util, vacc, warr **5** specs (see also **real estate term**)

classify
4 rank, rate, sort **5** grade, group **6** assort **7** arrange **9** break down **10** categorize, pigeon-hole

classy
4 chic, tony **5** swank **6** modish **7** dashing, elegant, refined, stylish **8** gracious, tasteful, well-bred **9** courteous **11** fashionable

clatter
4 to-do **6** clamor, hubbub, pother, rattle, tumult, uproar **7** turmoil **9** commotion **10** hurly-burly
Scottish: **7** brattle

clattery
5 noisy **7** rackety **10** clangorous

Claudia's husband
6 Pilate

Claudio's beloved
4 Hero

Claudius
nephew: **6** Hamlet
predecessor: **8** Caligula
slayer: **6** Hamlet **9** Agrippina
successor: **4** Nero
wife: **8** Gertrude **9** Agrippina

Clavell novel
6 Gai-Jin, Shogun, Tai-Pan **7** King Rat

claw
3 dig **4** nail, rake, tear **5** chela, talon, uncus **6** pincer, scrape, ungula **7** scratch

clay
3 cob **4** loam, lute, marl **5** argil, brick, earth, gault, loess, ocher, ochre **6** kaolin **10** terra-cotta
baked: **4** tile **5** adobe, brick
box: **6** saggar, sagger
building: **5** adobe
ceramic: **10** terra-cotta
constituent: **6** silica **8** feldspar, silicate **9** kaolinite
in glass: **4** tear
made of: **7** fictile
porcelain: **6** kaolin
red: **8** laterite
rock: **5** shale
tobacco pipe: **6** dudeen
watery mixture: **4** slip
white: **6** kaolin

clay pigeon
6 target

clean
4 dust, fair, pure, swab, tidy, wash, wipe **5** bathe, fresh, groom, purge, scour, scrub, sweep **6** bright, chaste, decent, neaten, purify, spruce, vacuum, washed **7** clarify, launder, sinless **8** hygienic, innocent, sanitary, sanitize, spotless, unsoiled **9** blameless, faultless, sparkling, stainless, undefiled, unsullied, untainted, wholesome **10** antiseptic, immaculate **11** unblemished **12** spick-and-span

clean-cut
4 trim **7** defined, precise **8** definite, explicit, specific **9** wholesome **10** definitive **11** categorical, unambiguous, well-groomed

cleaner
see **cleanser**

cleanhanded
8 innocent **9** blameless

clean-limbed
4 trim **7** shapely **8** handsome **10** statuesque

cleanse
4 lave, wash **5** purge, rinse **6** purify, refine **7** clarify, deterge, launder **8** lustrate, sanitize **9** disinfect, expurgate, sterilize

cleanser
3 lye **4** soap **9** detergent **10** antiseptic **12** disinfectant

cleansing
7 purging **8** ablution **9** catharsis, purgation **10** lustration **11** expurgation **12** purification

clear
4 earn, fair, fine, pure **5** lucid, overt, plain, repay, solve, stark, sunny **6** acquit, limpid, secure, settle, simple **7** absolve, audible, clarify, clarion, defined, evident, legible, obvious, precise **8** apparent, definite, distinct **9** authorize, cloudless, elucidate, exculpate, exonerate, liquidate, meliorate, unblurred, unclouded, vindicate **10** ameliorate, illuminate, see-through **11** disentangle, open-and-shut, perceptible, transparent, unambiguous, unequivocal **12** unmistakable

clearance
3 gap **4** sale **7** go-ahead, removal **8** approval **10** green light, permission **13** authorization

clear away
6 remove **7** take out

clear-cut
5 crisp, exact, plain **7** decided, precise **8** definite, distinct, explicit, manifest **10** definitive, pronounced, undisputed **11** categorical, indubitable, unambiguous, unequivocal **12** unquestioned

clear-eyed
6 astute **9** judicious, observant **10** discerning, perceptive

clearheaded
4 calm, cool **10** perceptive

clearing
3 gap **5** field, glade **7** opening **10** settlement

clear out
5 scoot, scram, split **6** beat it, begone, bug off,

decamp, depart **7** buzz off, skiddoo, take off, vamoose **8** shove off **9** drive away, skedaddle **10** hightail it

clear-sightedness
6 acuity, acumen **8** keenness, sagacity **10** astuteness, shrewdness **11** discernment, penetration, percipience **12** perspicacity

clear up
5 solve **6** cipher, unfold **7** clarify, dope out, explain, resolve, unravel **8** decipher **9** elucidate, figure out **10** illuminate

clearwing
4 moth

cleat
4 bitt **5** chock **6** batten **7** bollard, dolphin

cleavage
4 rift **5** chasm, cleft, split **6** schism **7** fissure **8** crevasse **9** splitting

cleave
3 cut, hew **4** chop, join, link, rend, rive **5** carve, cling, sever, slice, split, stick, unite **6** adhere, divide, sunder **7** combine **8** dissever, separate

cleft
3 gap **4** rift **5** chasm, chink, clove, crack, gorge, gulch, split **6** clough, ravine, schism **7** crevice, divided, fissure **8** cleavage

clemency
5 grace, mercy **6** lenity **7** caritas, charity **8** kindness, lenience, leniency, mildness **9** tolerance **10** compassion, gentleness, indulgence, sufferance, toleration **11** forbearance

clement
4 fair, kind, mild **5** balmy **6** benign, humane, kindly **7** lenient **8** merciful, tolerant **9** indulgent **10** benevolent, charitable, forbearing **13** compassionate

clench
4 grip, grit, hold **5** clamp, clasp, grasp **6** clutch **7** grapple

Cleopatra
attendant: **4** Iras **8** Charmian
brother: **7** Ptolemy
husband: **7** Ptolemy
killer: **3** asp
lover: **6** Antony (Marc), Caesar (Julius) **7** Anthony (Mark)
river: **4** Nile

Cleopatra's Needle
7 obelisk

clepsydra
9 timepiece **10** water clock

clerestory
7 gallery

clergy
7 canonry **8** ministry **9** churchmen, diaconate, pastorate, rabbinate **10** priesthood **11** cardinalate **13** ecclesiastics

clergyman
5 clerk, padre, vicar **6** bishop, cleric, curate, divine, father, parson, pastor, priest, rector **7** dominie, prelate **8** chaplain, clerical, minister, preacher, reverend, shepherd, sky pilot **9** churchman, pulpiteer **10** evangelist, missionary, sermonizer **12** ecclesiastic
American: **4** Hale (Edward Everett), King (Martin Luther, Thomas Starr) **5** Eliot (John), Moody (Dwight), Stone (Barton Warren), Weems (Parson) **6** Dwight (Timothy), Finney (Charles), Graham (Billy), Holmes (John Haynes), Hooker (Thomas), Mather (Cotton, Increase, Richard), Merton (Thomas), Parker (Samuel, Theodore), Sunday (Billy), Taylor (Edward, Graham, Nathaniel William) **7** Beecher (Henry Ward, Lyman), Edwards (Jonathan), Harvard (John), Russell (Charles Taze) **10** Muhlenberg (Frederick Augustus, Henry Melchior, John Peter Gabriel)
English: **4** Ward (Nathaniel, Seth, William George) **5** Donne (John), Paley (William), Smith (Henry "Silver-Tongued," John "The Se-baptist," Sidney) **6** Cotton (John), Fuller (Andrew, Thomas), Taylor (Jeremy, Rowland), Wesley (Charles, John) **7** Cranmer (Thomas), Parsons (Robert) **8** Kingsley (Charles) **10** Whitefield (George)
home: **5** manse **6** priory **7** rectory **8** vicarage **9** monastery, parsonage
traveling: **12** circuit rider

cleric
see **clergyman**

clerisy
8 literati **10** illuminati **13** intellectuals

clerk
7 cashier **8** salesman **9** secre- tary **10** accountant, bookkeeper **11** salesperson **12** stenographer

clever
3 apt, sly **4** able, deft, good, keen **5** adept, alert, canny, funny, handy, quick, savvy, sharp, smart, witty **6** adroit, astute, brainy, bright, crafty, expert, shrewd, tricky **7** amusing, capable, cunning, knowing, skilled **8** fanciful, humorous, pleasing, skillful, talented **9** competent, dexterous, ingenious **10** proficient **11** intelligent, quick-witted, resourceful **12** entertaining

cliché
3 saw **6** truism **7** bromide **8** banality, buzzword, chestnut **9** platitude **10** shibboleth, stereotype **11** commonplace

clichéd
5 banal, bland, musty, stale, tired, trite, vapid **6** old-hat **7** humdrum, insipid, worn-out

8 bromidic, shopworn, timeworn **9** hackneyed **10** pedestrian, unoriginal **11** stereotyped **13** platitudinous, unimaginative

click
3 fit **4** snap, tick, work **5** agree, match **6** go over, pan out **7** come off, succeed

client
6 patron **7** patient, protégé **8** customer **9** dependent

clientele
4 fans **5** trade, train **6** custom, market, public **7** patrons, traffic **8** audience, patients, regulars, shoppers **9** customers **10** purchasers, supporters **12** constituency

cliff
4 crag **5** bluff, scarp **8** headland, palisade **9** precipice **10** escarpment

climacteric
4 apex, crux, cusp **5** acute **6** crisis **7** crucial **8** critical **9** menopause **11** culmination **12** change of life, turning point

climactic
4 peak **7** crucial, pivotal **8** critical, decisive, dramatic **9** momentous **10** definitive **11** culminating, determining

climate
6 medium, milieu **7** ambient **8** ambience **10** atmosphere **11** environment **12** surroundings

climax
3 cap **4** acme, apex, peak **5** crown **6** apogee, summit, top off **8** capstone, meridian, pinnacle **9** culminate **11** culmination

climb
4 go up, rise, soar **5** mount, scale, slope **6** ascend, ascent **7** clamber **8** escalate, increase

climbing
8 scandent

climbing device
3 cam, nut **5** biner, cinch, piton **7** crampon **9** carabiner

clinch
3 hug, ice **4** grip, hold, seal **5** clamp, clasp, grasp, sew up **6** clutch, decide, ensure, lock up **7** confirm, embrace, grapple, squeeze **8** nail down

clincher
4 tire **5** proof **6** kicker **7** quietus **9** deathblow **10** smoking gun **11** affirmation, attestation, coup de grâce **12** confirmation **13** corroboration

cling
4 bond **5** stick **6** adhere, cleave, clutch, hold on, linger **8** adhesion **9** adherence

clingstone
5 peach

clink
3 can, jug, pen **4** brig, cell, coop, jail, stir **5** pokey, pound **6** cooler, jingle, lockup, prison, tingle, tinkle **7** slammer **8** hoosegow **9** calaboose

clinker
3 dud **4** bomb, bust, flop, goof, slag **5** botch, brick, error, lemon, loser **6** bummer, bungle, fiasco, howler, turkey **7** bloomer, blunder, failure, faux pas, mistake

clinkers
3 ash **4** slag **5** ashes **7** cinders

clinquant
5 gaudy **6** flashy, garish, tawdry, tinsel **8** specious **10** glittering **11** superficial

Clio
see **Muse**

clip
3 bob, cut, mow, pin **4** crop, hasp, pare, snip, sock, trim **5** block, clasp, prune, punch, shave, shear, slash **6** broach, brooch, fleece, reduce **7** curtail, cut back, cut down, shorten **8** magazine, truncate **10** abbreviate, overcharge

clipped
3 cut, hit **4** curt, taut **5** brief, crisp, shorn, short, terse **6** abrupt, cut off, docked, pruned **7** blocked, clasped, cropped, trimmed **8** cut short, fastened **9** curtailed, shortened, truncated

clique
3 set **4** camp, clan, club, gang, ring **5** cabal, crowd, mafia **6** circle **7** coterie, faction, in-group **9** camarilla

cloak
4 cape, mask, robe, veil, wrap **5** cover, guise, talma **6** domino, facade, joseph, mantle, screen, shroud, veneer **7** blanket, conceal, curtain, dress up, manteau, obscure **8** disguise **9** dissemble, semblance **10** camouflage **11** dissimulate
ancient Greek: **7** chlamys
ancient Roman: **7** pallium
Arab: **3** aba
fur: **7** pelisse
hooded: **6** capote **7** burnous **8** burnoose
liturgical: **4** cope
Moroccan: **8** djellaba
over armor: **6** tabard **7** surcoat
Spanish: **5** manta

clobber
4 belt, drub, flay, lick, slam, slug, sock, whip, whup **5** blast, brain, clout, cream, pound, smash **6** hammer, thrash, wallop **7** lambast, shellac, trounce **8** demolish, lambaste

clochard
3 bum, vag **4** hobo **5** tramp **6** beggar, canter **7** drifter, floater, moocher, vagrant **8** deadbeat,

derelict, vagabond **9** transient **10** freeloader, panhandler **11** bindle stiff

cloche
3 hat **5** cover, toque, tuque

clock
4 time **9** timepiece **11** chronometer
water: **9** clepsydra

clocklike
5 exact **6** minute, prompt, strict, timely **7** precise, regular **8** accurate, punctual, reliable, thorough **9** assiduous **10** dependable, meticulous, scrupulous **11** painstaking **13** conscientious

clockmaker
10 horologist

clockwise
6 deasil **7** dextral **11** right-handed

Clockwork Orange author
7 Burgess (Anthony)

clod
3 gob, wad **4** boob, dolt, dope, hunk, lump, soil **5** chump, chunk, clump, dummy, dunce, earth **6** dimwit **8** dumbbell **9** blockhead, lamebrain

cloddish
7 boorish, ill-bred, loutish, uncouth **8** churlish, clownish **9** unrefined **10** uncultured, unpolished **11** uncivilized

clodhopper
4 boor, boot, hick, lout **5** chuff, churl, clown, yokel **6** rustic **7** bumpkin, hayseed, redneck **9** chawbacon

clog
3 gum, jam, tax **4** fill, glut, load, plug, stop **5** block, choke, close, stuff **6** hamper, hinder **7** congest **8** encumber, obstruct, overload **10** impediment **11** encumbrance

cloisonné
6 enamel

cloister
5 abbey, court **6** arcade, garden **7** convent, retreat, seclude, shelter **9** courtyard, monastery, sequester

Cloister and the Hearth author
5 Reade (Charles)

cloistered
7 recluse **8** confined, hermetic, secluded **9** seclusive, withdrawn **11** sequestered

cloistered one
3 nun **4** monk

clone
4 copy **5** ditto **6** double, carbon **7** replica **9** duplicate, facsimile, replicate, reproduce **10** carbon copy, simulacrum **12** reproduction

Clorinda
beloved: **7** Tancred
father: **6** Senapo
guardian: **6** Arsete
slayer: **7** Tancred

close
3 end **4** near, nigh, shut, slam **5** block, cease, choke, humid, muggy, tight **6** ending, finale, finish, narrow, nearby, stuffy, sultry, windup, wrap up **7** airless, compact, crowded, stopper **8** adjacent, complete, conclude, finalize, intimate, obstruct, stifling **9** adjoining, cessation, condensed, terminate **10** conclusion, consummate, convenient, near-at-hand **11** constricted, neighboring, termination **12** confidential

closed-minded
4 deaf **6** narrow **8** obdurate **9** hidebound, obstinate, pigheaded, unbending **10** bullheaded, hardheaded **11** intractable

closefisted
5 cheap, mingy **6** frugal, stingy **7** miserly, thrifty **9** niggardly, penurious **13** penny-pinching

close in
3 hem **4** cage **5** fence, hedge **6** corral, immure **7** advance, confine, enclose, envelop, impound **8** approach, converge, encircle, enshroud, imprison, surround

close-knit
8 intimate

close match
6 toss-up

closemouthed
3 mum **4** mute **6** silent **7** laconic **8** reserved, reticent, taciturn **12** tight-mouthed

closeness
8 intimacy

close off
4 clog, plug **5** block **6** stop up **7** isolate, occlude **8** insulate **9** segregate, sequester

closet
6 covert, inside, office, secret **7** cabinet, chamber, furtive, private **8** wardrobe

closing
3 end **4** last, stop **5** final **6** ending, finish, latest, period, windup, wrap-up **7** curtain **8** eventual, terminal, ultimate **9** cessation **10** concluding **11** termination

closure
3 cap, end, lid **6** ending, finish **8** fastener **9** cessation

clot
3 gel, set **4** curd, glob, jell, lump **5** clump **6** curdle, gelate **7** congeal **8** coagulum, thrombus **9** coagulate **10** gelatinize
combining form: **6** thromb **7** thrombo

cloth
see **fabric**

clothe
3 tog **4** deck, do up, garb, robe **5** array, cloak, couch, drape, dress, endow, endue, equip **6** attire, bedeck, outfit, swathe **7** apparel, costume, dress up **8** accouter

clothes
3 rig **4** duds, garb, rags, togs **5** array, dress, getup, habit **6** attire, outfit, things **7** apparel, costume, raiment, rigging, threads, toggery, vesture **8** garments, glad rags **9** vestments **11** habiliments
basket: 6 hamper
civilian: 5 mufti

clothes-moth genus
5 Tinea

clothespress
7 armoire **8** wardrobe

cloud
3 dim, fog, tar **4** blur, haze, mist, murk **5** addle, befog, brume, gloom, muddy, plume, smear, sully, taint **6** muddle, nebula, puzzle, shadow, smudge **7** besmear, confuse, obscure, perplex, tarnish **8** befuddle, besmirch, discolor, distract, overcast **9** obfuscate
type: 4 nine **6** cirrus, nimbus **7** cumulus, stratus **11** altocumulus, altostratus **12** cirrocumulus, cirrostratus, cumulonimbus, interstellar, nimbostratus **13** stratocumulus

cloudburst
6 deluge, shower **7** monsoon, torrent **8** downpour, drencher, rainfall **10** outpouring

clouded
5 dusky, murky, shady **6** dreary, gloomy, somber, sombre **7** dubious, ominous, sunless, unclear **8** doubtful, overcast **9** ambiguous, equivocal, uncertain, unsettled **11** problematic

cloudless
4 fair, fine **5** clear, sunny **7** clarion **8** pleasant, rainless, sunshiny

cloud-like mass
6 nebula

cloud nine
5 bliss **6** heaven **7** ecstasy, elation, nirvana, rapture **8** euphoria

cloudy
4 dull, hazy **5** dusky, foggy, heavy, misty, murky, vague **6** gloomy, opaque, somber, sombre **7** louring, obscure, tainted, unclear **8** confused, darkened, lowering, nebulous, overcast, vaporous **10** indistinct

clout
3 box, hit, rag **4** blow, cuff, poke, pull, slam, slap, slug, sock, swat, sway **5** paste, power, punch, smack, smite, whack **6** strike **9** influence

clove
4 bulb **5** spice **7** chopped, severed

clove hitch
4 knot

clover
5 lotus **6** alsike, ladino, lucern **7** alfalfa, berseem, lucerne, melilot, trefoil **8** four-leaf, shamrock **9** lespedeza
family: 3 pea
genus: 9 Trifolium

clown
3 wag **4** bozo, mime, zany **5** cutup, joker, Punch **6** jester, mummer **7** buffoon **8** comedian, jokester **9** harlequin, prankster **11** merry-andrew
French: 7 Pierrot
operatic: 5 buffo
Spanish: 8 gracioso

clownish
4 rude **6** clumsy, gauche, oafish **7** awkward, boorish, ill-bred, loutish, lumpish, uncouth **8** churlish, cloddish **9** unrefined

cloy
4 fill, glut, jade, pall, sate **5** gorge **6** sicken **7** satiate, surfeit **8** overfill

cloying
4 icky **5** gushy, mushy, sappy, soppy **6** sticky, sugary **7** fulsome, gushing, maudlin, mawkish **9** excessive, schmaltzy, sickening **10** disgusting, lovey-dovey, nauseating, saccharine **11** distasteful, sentimental

club
3 bat, sap **4** beat, cosh, frat, iron, mace **5** baton, billy, guild, lodge, order, union **6** cudgel, league **7** society **8** bludgeon, sodality, sorority **9** blackjack, truncheon **10** fellowship, fraternity, knobkerrie, nightstick **11** association, brotherhood
Australian: 5 waddy
Irish: 10 shillelagh
Maori: 4 patu

clubfoot
7 talipes

cluck
4 dodo, dolt, dope, fool **5** dunce **6** dimwit, nitwit **7** pinhead

clue
3 cue **4** hint, idea, lead, sign, tell, warn **6** advise, inform, notify, notion, tip-off **7** inkling **8** evidence, telltale **10** indication, intimation, suggestion

Clue character
4 Plum (Prof.) **5** Green (Mr., Rev.) **7** Mustard (Col.), Peacock (Mrs.) **8** Scarlett (Miss)

clueless
4 lost **10** out to lunch

clump
3 gob, wad **4** clod, hunk, lump, mass, mess, plod **5** batch, bunch, chunk, group, stomp, tramp **6** bumble, bundle, lumber, parcel **7** cluster, galumph, stumble
of grass: **4** tuft **6** tuffet **7** tussock

clumsy
5 bulky, gawky, inept, splay **6** clunky, gauche, klutzy, wooden **7** awkward, hulking, lumpish, uncouth, unhandy **8** bumbling, bungling, tactless, ungainly, unsubtle, unwieldy **9** all thumbs, graceless, ham-handed, inelegant, lumbering, maladroit **11** heavy-handed, inefficient
person: **3** oaf **4** clod, goon, lout, slob **5** klutz **6** baboon, galoot, lummox **7** bumpkin, bungler, palooka **13** butterfingers

clunk
4 thud **5** clout, thump, whack **6** thwack, wallop

clunker
3 car **4** bomb, heap **5** crate, lemon, wreck **6** beater, jalopy, junker **7** stinker **10** rattletrap, rust bucket

cluster
3 lot, set **4** band, bevy, crew, knot, pack **5** array, batch, bunch, clump, covey, group **6** bundle, clutch, gather **7** collect, package **8** assemble, assembly **9** aggregate, associate, gathering **10** accumulate

cluster bean
4 guar

clutch
4 grab, grip, hold, keep **5** catch, clamp, clasp, grasp, pinch, seize **6** bundle, clench, clinch, snatch **7** cluster, grapple

clutter
4 hash, mash, mess, muss, ruck **5** chaos, snarl, strew **6** jumble, litter, muddle **7** mélange, rummage **8** disarray, disorder, mishmash, shambles **9** confusion **10** hodgepodge, hotchpotch

Clydesdale
5 horse **10** draft horse

Clymene
father: **7** Oceanus
husband: **7** Iapetus
mother: **6** Tethys
son: **5** Atlas **10** Epimetheus, Prometheus

Clytemnestra
brother: **6** Castor, Pollux **10** Polydeuces
daughter: **7** Electra **9** Iphigenia
father: **9** Tyndareus
husband: **9** Agamemnon
lover: **9** Aegisthus
mother: **4** Leda
slayer: **7** Orestes
son: **7** Orestes
victim: **9** Agamemnon, Cassandra

Clytie
beloved: **6** Apollo
form: **9** sunflower **10** heliotrope

coach
3 bus, car, pro **5** drill, stage, train, tutor **6** chaise, mentor **7** prepare, trainer **8** carriage, instruct **10** instructor

coadjutor
3 aid **4** aide **6** bishop, deputy **9** assistant **10** aide-de-camp, lieutenant

coagulate
3 gel, set **4** clot, jell **6** curdle **7** congeal, jellify, thicken **8** coalesce, condense, solidify **10** gelatinize, inspissate **11** concentrate, consolidate

coal
carrier: **3** hod **7** scuttle
distillate: **3** tar
dust: **4** culm, smut, soot **5** slack
element: **6** carbon
fused leavings: **4** slag **7** clinker
glowing: **5** ember, gleed
hard: **10** anthracite
lump: **3** cob
miner: **7** collier
region: **4** Saar
residue: **4** coke
soft: **6** cannel **10** bituminous

coalesce
3 mix **4** fuse, join, link **5** blend, merge, unite **6** mingle **7** combine, conjoin **10** amalgamate

coalition
4 bloc, ring **5** party, union **6** fusion, league, merger **7** combine, melding, merging **8** alliance **9** anschluss **10** federation **11** affiliation, association, combination, confederacy, integration, unification **13** confederation, consolidation

coarse
3 raw **4** rude **5** bawdy, crass, crude, dirty, gross, harsh, rough, tacky **6** common, filthy, grainy, ribald, smutty, vulgar **7** boorish, obscene, raffish, raunchy, uncouth **8** granular, indecent **9** inelegant, roughneck, unrefined **10** uncultured **11** particulate **12** uncultivated

coast
4 bank **5** beach, drift, shore, slide **6** strand **7** seaside **8** littoral, seashore **9** freewheel
of Antarctica: **4** Knox

coastal
7 seaside **8** littoral, riverine

coaster
4 sled, tray **6** trader

coat
5 crust, glaze, gloss, layer, parka, plate, tunic **6** blazer, duster, finish, jacket, patina, raglan, reefer, ulster, veneer **7** cutaway **8** covering, mackinaw, tegument **9** newmarket, redingote

10 integument, mackintosh 11 windbreaker 12 Prince Albert
animal: 3 fur 4 hide, pelt, wool 6 pelage
fur-lined: 7 pelisse
kind: 3 pea, top 5 frock 6 trench
Levantine: 6 caftan
of arms: 5 crest 6 blazon, emblem, shield, tabard 8 blazonry 10 escutcheon
of egg white: 5 glair 6 glaire
of mail: 7 hauberk
soldier's: 5 frock, tunic 6 capote
waterproof: 7 slicker 10 mackintosh

coating
4 film, leaf, scum, skin 5 glaze, gloss, layer 6 finish, patina, veneer 7 dusting, lacquer, overlay, surface, varnish 8 covering
winter: 3 ice 4 snow 5 sleet

coat rack part
3 leg, peg 4 base, hook 5 stand 6 hanger

coax
4 lure, urge 5 cable, press, tempt 6 cajole, entice, induce 7 blarney, wheedle 8 blandish, butter up, inveigle, persuade, soft-soap 9 importune, sweet-talk

cob
3 ear 4 swan 5 adobe, horse

cobalt symbol
2 Co

cobble
4 make, mend 5 patch, stone 6 repair 11 paving stone

cobbler
3 pie 5 drink 8 cocktail 9 shoemaker
form: 4 last
tool: 3 awl

cobelligerent
4 ally

cobweb
3 net 4 mesh, trap 8 gossamer 9 confusion, spiderweb 12 entanglement

coccyx
8 tailbone

cochineal
3 dye 6 insect

cock
3 tap 4 boss, head, heap, hill, lord, mass, pile, rick, tilt 5 chief, mound, stack, strut, valve 6 faucet, honcho, leader, master, spigot 7 headman, hydrant, rooster, swagger 11 chanticleer

cock-a-hoop
4 awry 5 askew 7 askance, crooked 8 boastful, exultant, exulting, jubilant 9 triumphal 10 triumphant

Cockaigne
6 utopia 7 arcadia 9 Shangri-la 10 wonderland

cockalorum
7 bluster, bombast, bravado 8 blowhard, boasting, braggart, leapfrog 11 braggadocio

cockamamy
5 batty, crazy, daffy, flaky, kooky, loony, nutty, wacky 6 absurd 9 ludicrous 10 incredible, ridiculous 11 harebrained

cock-and-bull story
5 crock 6 canard 7 whopper 9 fairy tale

cockcrow
4 dawn, morn 5 sunup 7 morning, sunrise 8 daybreak, daylight

cocker
4 baby 5 humor, spoil 6 coddle, cosset, pamper 7 indulge, spaniel 11 mollycoddle

cockeyed
4 awry 5 askew 8 lopsided 11 harebrained

cockle
5 shell 6 dimple, furrow, groove, pucker, ripple 7 bivalve, mollusc, mollusk, wrinkle

cockleshell
4 boat

cockscomb
see **coxcomb**

cocksure
5 brash 6 cheeky 9 bumptious 13 overconfident

cocktail
5 Bronx, drink, julep 6 Gibson, gimlet, mai tai, mimosa, mojito, Rob Roy, zombie 7 gin fizz, martini, sidecar, stinger 8 aperitif, daiquiri, pink lady, salty dog, sombrero 9 Cuba libre, manhattan, margarita, mint julep, rusty nail 10 Bloody Mary, Tom Collins, wallbanger 11 grasshopper, screwdriver, whiskey sour 12 black russian, cosmopolitan, old-fashioned
fruit: 9 macedoine
gasoline: 7 Molotov

Cocktail Party author
5 Eliot (T. S.)

cocky
4 bold, sure 5 brash, pushy, sassy, saucy 6 brassy, cheeky, jaunty 8 arrogant, impudent, insolent 9 conceited 10 swaggering 11 self-assured 12 enterprising 13 overconfident, self-confident

coconspirator
7 abettor 9 accessory 10 accomplice 11 confederate

coconut
husk fiber: 4 coir
meat: 5 copra

coda
5 envoi, envoy 6 ending, finale 7 summary 8 epilogue, follow-up 9 afterword 10 conclusion

coddle
4 baby **5** humor, spoil **6** cosset, pamper **7** cater to, indulge

code
6 cipher, symbol **7** encrypt **8** encipher
kind: 3 PIN, zip **4** area **5** Morse, legal, penal
message in: 10 cryptogram **11** cryptograph

code word
see **communications code word**

codger
4 coot, fogy **5** fogey **6** duffer, fellow, fossil, geezer **7** old coot, old fogy **8** old fogey

codicil
5 rider **8** addendum, addition, appendix **10** postscript, supplement

codswallop
see **nonsense**

coefficient
6 factor **7** measure **8** constant

coelenterate
5 coral **7** anemone, hydroid **9** cnidarian, jellyfish **10** sea anemone

coerce
3 cow **5** bully, force, impel, press **6** compel, menace, oblige **8** browbeat, bulldoze, dominate, pressure, threaten **9** blackjack, constrain, strong-arm, terrorize **10** intimidate

coercion
5 force **6** duress, menace, threat **8** pressure **10** compulsion, constraint

Coetzee novel
8 Disgrace

Coeur d'____
5 Alene

coeval
see **contemporary**

coexistent
see **contemporary**

coffee
3 joe, mud **4** java **6** jamoke
alkaloid: 8 caffeine
bean: 3 nib
cake: 6 kuchen
cup: 9 demitasse
French: 4 café
grinder: 4 mill
kind: 4 drip, java **5** decaf, latte, mocha **7** arabica, instant **8** espresso **9** Americano, macchiato **10** café au lait, cappuccino
maker: 10 percolator
pot: 3 urn

coffee shop
4 café **5** diner **8** snack bar **9** cafeteria, hash house, lunchroom **11** greasy spoon **12** luncheonette

coffer
5 chest **6** casket **8** treasury **9** exchequer, strongbox

coffin
3 box **4** kist **6** casket
carrier: 6 hearse **10** pallbearer
nail: 9 cigarette
stand: 4 bier **10** catafalque

cogency
5 force, point, power, punch **7** potency **8** strength, validity **9** relevance **10** conviction, pertinence **13** effectiveness

cogent
5 solid, sound, valid **6** potent **7** telling, weighty **8** forceful, powerful, relevant **9** pertinent **10** compelling, convincing, meaningful, persuasive **11** influential, well-founded **12** well-grounded **13** consequential

cogitate
4 muse **5** think **6** ponder, reason **7** reflect **8** conceive, consider, meditate, mull over, ruminate **9** cerebrate, speculate **10** deliberate

cogitation
7 thought **10** meditation, reflection, rumination **11** cerebration, speculation **12** deliberation **13** consideration

cogitative
7 pensive **10** meditative, reflective, ruminative, thoughtful **11** speculative **13** contemplative

Cogito ____ sum
4 ergo

cognac
6 brandy

cognate
4 akin, like **5** alike **6** allied, common **7** kindred, related, similar **8** parallel **10** affiliated, associated

cognition
9 awareness, knowledge, sentience **10** perception

cognizance
4 heed, note **6** notice **9** attention, awareness, knowledge **12** jurisdiction

cognizant
5 aware **7** knowing, mindful **8** informed, sensible **9** conscious **13** knowledgeable

cognize
4 know **5** grasp **6** fathom **7** realize **8** perceive **9** apprehend **10** appreciate, comprehend, understand

cognomen
4 name **5** alias, title **7** epithet, moniker, surname **8** nickname **11** appellation, appellative, designation **12** denomination

cognoscente
5 judge **6** critic, expert **7** epicure **8** aesthete **9** authority **10** specialist **11** connoisseur

cognoscible
8 knowable **10** fathomable **13** apprehensible

cogwheel
4 gear

cohere
4 fuse, join **5** agree, blend, cling, merge, stick, unite **6** accord **7** combine, comport, conform, connect **8** coalesce, dovetail **10** correspond **11** consolidate

coherence
4 bond **5** union, unity **8** adhesion, cohesion **9** agreement, congruity, integrity **10** conformity, connection, consonance, solidarity **11** consistency, integration

coherent
5 sound **7** logical, ordered, unified **8** rational **10** consistent, integrated, meaningful **11** coordinated

cohesion
see **coherence**

coho
6 salmon **12** silver salmon

cohort
3 pal **4** ally, band, chum, crew, mate **5** buddy, crony, group **6** fellow, friend **7** comrade, partner **8** adherent, confrere, disciple, follower, henchman, sidekick **9** assistant, associate, colleague, companion, supporter **10** accomplice **11** demographic **12** collaborator

coif
3 cap, cut **4** hood, perm **6** hairdo **7** haircut **8** skullcap

coiffeur
6 barber **10** haircutter **11** hairdresser, hairstylist

coiffure
6 hairdo
aid: **3** net, rat **5** snood

coil
4 curl, loop, ring, turn, wind **5** helix, twine, twist **6** rotate, spiral **7** entwine, revolve, wreathe **8** curlicue **9** corkscrew

coiled
6 spiral, volute **7** helical, voluted, whorled **9** circinate

coin
4 mint **6** invent, make up, strike
Afghanistan: **3** pul **7** afghani
Albania: **3** lek **9** quindarka
Algeria: **5** dinar **7** centime
ancient Greek: **4** obol
ancient Muslim: **5** dinar
ancient Roman: **8** denarius
Argentina: **4** peso **7** centavo
Austria: **4** euro **8** groschen **9** schilling
Bahrain: **4** fils **5** dinar
Belgium: **4** euro **5** franc **7** centime
Benin: **5** franc **7** centime
Bhutan: **7** chetrum **8** ngultrum
Bollvla: **7** centavo **9** boliviano
Botswana: **4** pula **5** thebe
Brazil: **4** real **7** centavo **8** cruzeiro
Bulgaria: **3** lev **8** stotinka
Burma: **4** kyat
Burundi: **5** franc **7** centime
Cameroon: **5** franc **7** centime
Canada: **6** loonie, toonie, twonie
Cape Verde Islands: **6** escudo **7** centavo
Chile: **4** peso **7** centavo
China: **3** fen **4** jiao, yuan
Colombia: **4** peso **7** centavo
Costa Rica: **5** colón **7** centimo
Cuba: **4** peso **7** centavo
Czech Republic: **5** haler **6** koruna
defective: **4** fido
Denmark: **3** ore **5** krone
Dominican Republic: **4** peso **7** centavo
Ecuador: **5** sucre **7** centavo
edge: **7** milling
Egypt: **7** piastre
European gold: **5** ducat
Finland: **4** euro **5** penni **6** markka
former: **3** ecu, mil, pie, sol, sou **4** anna, besa, doit, duit, fels, kran, para, pice, reis (plural) **5** fanam, litas, mohur, paisa, rupia, shahi, soldo, taler, toman **6** besant, centas, denier, heller, macuta, pagoda, tangka **7** santims, sapeque **8** maravedi, skilling **9** rigsdaler **10** Indian head, reichsmark **13** reichspfennig
France: **3** ecu, sou **4** euro **5** franc **7** centime
Gambia: **5** butut **6** dalasi
Germany: **4** euro, mark **7** pfennig
Ghana: **4** cedi **6** pesewa
Great Britain: **3** bob **4** quid **5** crown, penny, pound **6** guinea **7** ha'penny **8** farthing, shilling, sixpence **9** halfpenny, sovereign **10** threepence
Greece: **4** euro **6** lepton **7** drachma
Guatemala: **7** centavo, quetzal
Guinea-Bissau: **4** peso
Guyana: **3** bit
Haiti: **6** gourde **7** centime
Honduras: **7** centavo, lempira
Hungary: **5** pengo **6** filler, forint
Iceland: **5** aurar (plural), eyrir, krona
India: **3** pie **4** anna **5** paisa, rupee
Indonesia: **3** sen **6** rupiah
Iran: **4** rial **5** dinar
Iraq: **4** fils **5** dinar
Ireland: **4** euro **5** penny **8** farthing
Israel: **5** agora **6** shekel
Italy: **4** euro, lira **5** scudo

Japan: **3** rin, sen, yen
Jordan: **4** fils **5** dinar
Kenya: **8** shilling
Korea, North and South: **3** won **4** chon
Kuwait: **4** fils **5** dinar
large: **9** cartwheel
Lebanon: **5** livre **7** piastre
Lesotho: **4** loti **7** licente, lisente
Libya: **5** dinar **6** dirham
Luxembourg: **4** euro **5** franc
Macao: **3** avo
Madagascar: **5** franc
Malawi: **6** kwacha **7** tambala
Mauritania: **5** khoum **7** ouguiya
Mauritius: **5** rupee
Mexico: **4** peso **7** centavo
Moldova: **3** leu
Monaco: **4** euro **5** franc
Morocco: **6** dirham
Mozambique: **7** metical
Nepal: **5** paisa, rupee
Netherlands: **4** euro **6** florin, gulden **7** guilder
Nicaragua: **7** centavo, córdoba
Nigeria: **4** kobo **5** naira
Norway: **3** ore **5** krone
Oman: **4** rial **5** baiza
Pakistan: **4** anna **5** paisa, rupee
Palestine: **3** mil
Panama: **6** balboa **9** centesimo
Papua New Guinea: **4** kina, toea
Paraguay: **7** centimo, guarani
Peru: **3** sol **7** centimo
Philippines: **4** peso, piso **7** sentimo
Poland: **5** grosz, zloty
Portugal: **4** euro **6** escudo **7** centavo
Qatar: **5** riyal **6** dirham
Roman: **6** aureus, bezant **7** solidus
Romania: **3** ban, leu
Russia: **5** kopek, ruble **6** kopeck
Samoa: **4** sene, tala
San Marino: **4** lira
Saudi Arabia: **4** rial **6** halala
Scandinavia: **3** ore
Seychelles: **5** rupee
Siam: **3** att
side of a: **7** obverse
Slovakia: **5** haler **6** koruna
South Africa: **4** rand **10** Krugerrand
Spain: **4** euro **6** peseta **7** centimo
Sri Lanka: **5** rupee
stamping metal: **8** planchet
Suriname: **6** florin, gulden **7** guilder
Swaziland: **9** lilangeni
Sweden: **3** ore **5** krona **8** skilling
Switzerland: **5** franc **6** rappen
Syria: **7** piastre
Tanzania: **8** shilling
Thailand: **4** baht **5** tical **6** satang
Timor: **3** avo
Tonga: **6** pa'anga, seniti
Tunisia: **5** dinar
Turkey: **4** lira, para **5** kurus
Uganda: **8** shilling
United Arab Emirates: **6** dirham
United Kingdom: see **Great Britain**
United States: **4** dime **5** penny **6** dollar, nickel **7** quarter **10** half-dollar
Uruguay: **4** peso **9** centesimo
Vatican City: **4** lira
Venezuela: **7** bolivar
Virgin Islands: **3** bit
Zambia: **5** ngwee **6** kwacha

coinage
7 new word **8** creation, currency **9** invention, neologism **10** brainchild **11** contrivance

coincide
4 jibe **5** agree, equal, match, tally **6** accord, concur, square **7** comport, conform **8** dovetail **9** harmonize **10** correspond

coincident
7 similar **9** consonant **10** concurrent **11** concomitant, synchronous **12** accompanying, contemporary, simultaneous

coincidentally
8 by chance, together **12** accidentally, concurrently, fortuitously

coin-shaped
8 nummular

col
4 pass **5** ridge **6** saddle

___ colada
4 piña

colander's cousin
5 sieve **6** sifter **8** strainer

cold ___
3 war **4** call, cash, cuts, feet, fish, sore, wave **5** cream, frame, front, patch, steel, sweat, water **6** turkey **7** comfort, storage **8** shoulder

cold
3 icy, raw **4** cool, dead, iced **5** aloof, chill, crisp, frore, gelid, nippy, polar **6** arctic, biting, chilly, frigid, frosty, frozen, wintry **7** bracing, glacial, shivery **8** chilling, comatose, freezing, lifeless **11** emotionless, passionless, unconscious, unemotional **12** unresponsive
combining form: **4** cryo, kryo
common: **6** coryza
symptom: **5** cough, fever **6** sneeze **7** catarrh

cold-blooded
5 cruel **6** brutal **7** callous **8** hardened, obdurate, pitiless, ruthless **9** heartless, impassive, unfeeling **10** hard-boiled, impersonal **11** ectothermic, emotionless, hard-hearted

12 matter-of-fact, stonyhearted 13 dispassionate, unimpassioned

cold feet
4 fear 5 alarm, doubt, dread, panic, worry 6 dismay, fright, terror 7 anxiety, jitters 8 timidity 9 cowardice 11 trepidation 12 apprehension

coldhearted
see **cold-blooded**

cold-shoulder
3 cut 4 snub 6 ignore, slight 9 ostracize

cold storage
8 abeyance, dormancy 10 quiescence, suspension 12 intermission, interruption

cole
4 kale, rape 7 cabbage 8 brassica, broccoli, kohlrabi 11 cauliflower

Coleridge poem
9 Dejection, Kubla Khan 10 Christabel

Colette character
4 Gigi 5 Chéri 8 Claudine

colewort
4 kale 7 cabbage

colic
5 gripe 9 bellyache 11 stomachache 12 collywobbles

coliseum
4 bowl 5 arena, stade 6 circus 7 stadium

collaborate
6 team up 7 collude 8 conspire 9 cooperate

collaborator
4 ally 6 helper 7 abettor, partner, traitor 8 coworker, henchman, quisling 9 accessory, assistant, associate, auxiliary, colleague 10 accomplice 11 confederate, conspirator

collapse
4 cave, drop, fail, ruin 5 break, crash, plotz, smash, wreck 6 buckle, cave in, fold up 7 breakup, crack-up, crumple, debacle, deflate, failure, founder, give out, give way, pass out, shatter, smashup, succumb 8 condense, downfall 9 breakdown, cataclysm, fall apart, ruination 10 disruption 11 catastrophe, destruction, prostration 12 disintegrate

collar
3 bag, nab 4 grab, hook, nail, take 5 catch, seize 6 arrest, secure 7 capture 9 apprehend
armor: 6 gorget
boy's: 4 Eton
chain: 4 torc 6 torque
jeweled: 8 carcanet
lace-edged: 6 rebato
metal: 4 torc 6 torque
pleated: 4 ruff

collarbone
8 clavicle

collate
5 group, order 7 arrange, collect, compare, compile 8 assemble, contrast, organize 9 integrate

collateral
4 bond 6 allied, lineal, pledge, surety 7 cognate, kindred, oblique, related, subject 8 indirect, parallel, security 9 accessory, ancillary, attendant, auxiliary, dependent, secondary, tributary 10 coincident, coordinate, reciprocal, subsidiary 11 concomitant, subordinate, subservient 12 accompanying, confirmatory, contributory 13 complementary, corresponding, corroborative

colleague
4 aide 6 cohort, fellow, helper 7 partner 8 confrere, coworker, teammate 9 assistant, associate, companion 10 compatriot 11 confederate 12 collaborator

collect
4 draw 5 amass, glean, group, infer, raise 6 deduce, derive, gather, muster, prayer 7 build up, compile, compose, convene, dispose, marshal, round up 8 assemble, conclude, converge 10 accumulate, congregate, rendezvous

collected
4 calm, cool 5 quiet, still 6 poised, serene 7 assured 8 complete, composed, sanguine, tranquil 9 assembled, confident, unruffled 11 unflappable 13 imperturbable, self-possessed

collection
3 ana, kit, lot 4 band, bevy, crew, olio, ruck 5 bunch, crowd, hoard, trove 6 medley, muster 7 cluster, variety 8 assembly, caboodle 9 aggregate, anthology, congeries, gathering, stockpile 10 assemblage, assortment, cumulation, miscellany 11 aggregation 12 accumulation, congregation 13 agglomeration
miscellaneous: 4 hash, olio 6 jumble, medley 7 mélange, mixture 8 mishmash, pastiche 9 potpourri 10 hodgepodge, hotchpotch, salmagundi 11 olla podrida
of anecdotes: 3 ana
of animals: 3 zoo 9 menagerie
of artistic works: 6 museum 7 gallery
of clothes: 8 wardrobe
of dried plants: 9 herbarium
of literary pieces: 8 analects 9 anthology
of reports: 4 file 7 dossier
of trinkets: 10 bijouterie

collective
5 joint 7 commune, kibbutz, kolkhoz 11 cooperative

collector
of bird's eggs: 8 oologist
of books: 11 bibliophile

of coins: **11** numismatist
of fares: **9** conductor
of phonograph records: **10** discophile
of stamps: **11** philatelist

colleen
4 girl, lass **6** maiden
country: **4** Eire, Erin **7** Ireland

college
9 alma mater
building: **3** gym, lab **4** dorm, hall
campus area: **4** quad **10** quadrangle
class meeting: **3** lab **7** lecture, seminar **8** tutorial, workshop
climber: **3** ivy
degree: **2** AA, AB, BA, BD, BS, CE, DD, MA, MM, MS **3** BLS, DST, MBA, MEd, MFA, MLS, PhD **5** LittD
graduate: **6** alumna, alumni (plural) **7** alumnae (plural), alumnus
official: **4** dean **5** prexy **6** bursar, regent **7** proctor, provost **9** registrar
oldest in U.S.: **7** Harvard
oldest women's in U.S.: **12** Mount Holyoke
relating to: **8** academic **10** collegiate
social group: **4** frat **8** sorority **10** fraternity
song: **9** alma mater
student class: **4** soph **5** frosh **6** junior, senior **8** freshman **9** sophomore
teacher: **3** don **4** prof **8** academic **9** professor
term: **7** quarter, session **8** semester **9** trimester
VIP: **4** BMOC
woman: **4** coed

college team
Air Force: **7** Falcons
Alabama: **11** Crimson Tide
Arizona: **8** Wildcats
Arizona State: **9** Sun Devils
Arkansas: **10** Razorbacks
Arkansas State: **7** Indians
Army: **6** Cadets
Auburn: **6** Tigers
Baylor: **5** Bears
Boston College: **6** Eagles
Boston University: **8** Terriers
Brigham Young: **7** Cougars
Brown: **5** Bears
California: **11** Golden Bears
Central Michigan: **9** Chippewas
Cincinnati: **8** Bearcats
Citadel: **8** Bulldogs
Clemson: **6** Tigers
Colgate: **10** Red Raiders
Colorado: **9** Buffaloes
Colorado State: **4** Rams
Columbia: **5** Lions
Connecticut: **7** Huskies
Cornell: **6** Big Red
Dartmouth: **8** Big Green
Davidson: **8** Wildcats
Delaware State: **7** Hornets
Drake: **8** Bulldogs
Duke: **10** Blue Devils
Eastern Kentucky: **8** Colonels
Eastern Michigan: **6** Eagles
Florida: **6** Gators
Florida State: **9** Seminoles
Fresno State: **8** Bulldogs
Furman: **8** Palidans
Georgia: **8** Bulldogs
Georgia Tech: **13** Yellow Jackets
Harvard: **7** Crimson
Hawaii: **15** Rainbow Warriors
Holy Cross: **9** Crusaders
Houston: **7** Cougars
Howard: **6** Bisons
Idaho: **7** Vandals
Idaho State: **7** Bengals
Illinois: **14** Fighting Illini
Illinois State: **8** Redbirds
Indiana: **8** Hoosiers
Indiana State: **9** Sycamores
Iowa: **8** Hawkeyes
Iowa State: **8** Cyclones
Kansas: **8** Jayhawks
Kansas State: **8** Wildcats
Kent State: **13** Golden Flashes
Kentucky: **8** Wildcats
Lehigh: **9** Engineers
Louisiana State: **6** Tigers
Louisiana Tech: **8** Bulldogs
Maine: **10** Black Bears
Maryland: **5** Terps **9** Terrapins
Massachusetts: **9** Minutemen
Miami (Florida): **10** Hurricanes
Miami (Ohio): **8** Redskins
Michigan: **10** Wolverines
Michigan State: **8** Spartans
Minnesota: **7** Gophers
Mississippi: **6** Rebels
Mississippi State: **8** Bulldogs
Missouri: **6** Tigers
Montana: **9** Grizzlies
Montana State: **7** Bobcats
Navy: **10** Midshipmen
Nebraska: **11** Cornhuskers
Nevada: **6** Rebels **8** Wolfpack
New Hampshire: **8** Wildcats
New Mexico: **5** Lobos
New Mexico State: **6** Aggies
North Carolina: **8** Tar Heels
North Carolina State: **8** Wolfpack
Northeastern: **7** Huskies
Northwestern: **8** Wildcats
Notre Dame: **13** Fighting Irish
Ohio State: **8** Buckeyes

Ohio University: 7 Bobcats
Oklahoma: 7 Sooners
Oklahoma State: 7 Cowboys
Oregon: 5 Ducks
Oregon State: 7 Beavers
Pennsylvania: 7 Quakers
Pennsylvania State: 12 Nittany Lions
Pittsburgh: 8 Panthers
Princeton: 6 Tigers
Purdue: 12 Boilermakers
Rhode Island: 4 Rams
Rice: 4 Owls
Rutgers: 14 Scarlet Knights
San Diego State: 6 Aztecs
San Jose State: 8 Spartans
South Carolina: 9 Gamecocks
South Carolina State: 8 Bulldogs
Southern California: 7 Trojans
Southern Illinois: 7 Salukis
Southern Methodist: 8 Mustangs
Stanford: 9 Cardinals
Syracuse: 9 Orangemen
Temple: 4 Owls
Tennessee: 10 Volunteers
Tennessee State: 6 Tigers
Tennessee Tech: 12 Golden Eagles
Texas: 9 Longhorns
Texas A&M: 6 Aggies
Texas Christian: 11 Horned Frogs
Texas Southern: 6 Tigers
Texas Tech: 10 Red Raiders
Toledo: 7 Rockets
Tulane: 9 Green Wave
UCLA: 6 Bruins
UNLV: 12 Runnin' Rebels
Utah: 4 Utes
Utah State: 6 Aggies
Vanderbilt: 10 Commodores
Villanova: 8 Wildcats
Virginia: 9 Cavaliers
VMI: 7 Keydets
VPI: 8 Gobblers
Wake Forest: 12 Demon Deacons
Washington: 7 Huskies
Washington State: 7 Cougars
West Virginia: 12 Mountaineers
William & Mary: 5 Tribe
Wisconsin: 7 Badgers
Wyoming: 7 Cowboys
Yale: 4 Elis 8 Bulldogs

collide
3 hit, ram **4** bump **5** clash, crash, smash **6** impact, strike **7** impinge **8** conflict

collier
4 ship **5** miner **6** choker

Collins novel
9 Moonstone (The) **12** Woman in White (The)

collision
4 bump, jolt **5** clash, crash, shock, smash, wreck **6** impact **7** crack-up, smashup **10** concussion

collocate
7 arrange **8** position **9** juxtapose

collogue
6 confer, huddle, parley, powwow **7** consult

colloid
3 gel, sol **4** agar **7** mixture **8** hydrogel, hydrosol

colloquial
6 casual, vulgar **7** demotic **8** familiar, informal **9** idiomatic **10** vernacular

colloquium
5 forum **7** palaver, seminar **9** symposium **10** conference, roundtable

colloquy
4 chat, talk **5** forum **6** debate, parley **7** palaver, seminar **8** dialogue **9** symposium **10** conference, discussion, roundtable **12** conversation **13** confabulation

collude
4 plot **6** devise, scheme **7** connive **8** conspire, contrive, intrigue **9** machinate

collusion
4 plot **8** intrigue, skin game **10** conspiracy

collywobbles
5 colic, gripe **9** bellyache **11** stomachache

Colombia
capital: 6 Bogotá
city: 4 Cali 6 Ibagué 8 Medellín 9 Cartagena 12 Barranquilla
language: 7 Spanish
liberator: 7 Bolivar (Simón)
monetary unit: 4 peso
mountain, range: 5 Andes, Chita 6 Puracé, Tolima 9 Cristóbal
neighbor: 4 Peru 6 Brazil, Panama 7 Ecuador 9 Venezuela
river: 6 Chauca 7 Orinoco 9 Magdalena
sea: 9 Caribbean

Colonel Blimp
4 fogy, Tory **5** fogey **6** fossil **7** old fogy **8** mossback, old fogey **10** fuddy-duddy **11** reactionary

colonist
6 émigré, nester **7** evacuee, pilgrim, pioneer, settler **8** emigrant, squatter **9** immigrant **10** expatriate **11** homesteader

colonnade
4 stoa **9** peristyle

colony
7 outpost **9** satellite **10** settlement

color
3 dun, dye, hue, red, tan **4** aqua, blue, cast, ecru, glow, gold, gray, grey, jade, lime, navy,

pink, puce, rose, teal, tint, tone **5** amber, azure, beige, belie, black, blush, brown, coral, ebony, flush, green, hazel, henna, ivory, khaki, lilac, mauve, ocher, ochre, olive, paint, peach, rouge, shade, stain, taupe, tinge, umber **6** auburn, bronze, canary, copper, indigo, maroon, orange, purple, redden, salmon, sienna, silver, violet, yellow **7** crimson, emerald, magenta, pigment, saffron, scarlet **8** chestnut, dyestuff, lavender, tincture **9** embellish, embroider, turquoise, vermilion **10** aquamarine, exaggerate, vermillion **12** pigmentation
band: **5** facia, vitta **6** fascia
combining form: **5** chrom **6** chromo **7** chromat **8** chromato
primary: **3** red **4** blue **6** yellow
relating to: **9** chromatic
secondary: **5** green **6** orange, purple
soft: **6** pastel

Colorado
capital: **6** Denver
city: **4** Vail **5** Aspen **6** Aurora, Pueblo **7** Boulder **8** Lakewood **11** Fort Collins
college, university: **5** Regis **9** Fort Lewis
mountain, range: **5** Longs (Peak), Pikes (Peak), Rocky **6** Elbert **7** Rockies
nickname: **10** Centennial (State)
park: **9** Mesa Verde
river: **8** Arkansas **9** Rio Grande
state bird: **11** lark bunting
state flower: **9** columbine
state tree: **10** blue spruce

colorant
3 dye **5** stain **7** pigment **8** dyestuff, tincture

colored
6 biased, warped **8** one-sided, partisan **9** jaundiced **10** prejudiced **11** tendentious

colorful
3 gay **5** gaudy, showy, vivid **6** bright, flashy, florid, garish, motley **7** splashy

coloring
4 cast, tint **5** front, tinge **6** facade, nuance **7** pigment **8** overtone **10** camouflage, complexion **12** embroidering **13** embellishment

colorless
3 wan **4** ashy, drab, dull, flat, pale **5** ashen, pasty, prosy, waxen, white **6** albino, doughy, pallid **7** insipid, neutral, prosaic **8** abstract, blanched, bleached **10** achromatic, lackluster

Color Purple author
6 Walker (Alice)

colossal
4 huge, vast **7** immense, mammoth, massive, titanic **8** enormous, gigantic, towering **9** cyclopean, monstrous **10** gargantuan, stupendous **11** astonishing, elephantine

colossus
5 giant, titan **6** statue **7** goliath, mammoth, monster **8** behemoth **9** leviathan

Colossus of ___
6 Rhodes

colporteur
10 evangelist, missionary **12** propagandist

colt
4 foal, tyro **6** novice, rookie **8** beginner, freshman, neophyte, newcomer **9** fledgling **10** tenderfoot

coltish
6 frisky, impish **7** playful **10** frolicsome

Columbine
beloved: **9** Harlequin
father: **9** Pantaloon

columbium symbol
2 Cb

Columbus, Christopher
birthplace: **5** Genoa
patron: **8** Isabella **9** Ferdinand
ship: **4** Niña **5** Pinta **10** Santa Maria
son: **5** Diego
starting point: **5** Palos

column
3 row **4** pier **5** shaft, stela **6** pillar **7** obelisk **8** pilaster
angle: **5** arris
base: **4** dado, ordo **5** socle **6** plinth **9** stylobate
bulge: **7** entasis
female figure: **8** caryatid
male figure: **5** atlas **7** telamon **8** atlantes (plural)
style: **5** Doric, Ionic **10** Corinthian
top: **7** capital **8** chapiter

coma
6 stupor, torpor **8** blackout, hebetude, lethargy **9** lassitude

comate
3 pal **4** chum **5** buddy, crony **7** comrade, partner **9** associate, colleague, companion

comatose
5 dopey **6** stupid, torpid **7** out cold **8** sluggish **9** lethargic **10** insensible **11** unconscious

comb
4 rake, sift, sort **5** crest, curry, probe, scour, sweep, tease **6** search, winnow **7** ransack **8** untangle **10** straighten **11** investigate

combat
3 war **4** buck, duel, fray **5** fight, repel **6** action, battle, oppose, resist, strife **7** contend, contest, dispute **8** skirmish, struggle **9** withstand **11** controversy

combatant
7 battler, fighter, soldier, warrior **8** militant, opponent **9** adversary, aggressor, assailant, contender, disputant, mercenary **10** antagonist, challenger, competitor, contestant **11** belligerent

combative
6 feisty **7** scrappy, warlike **8** militant **9** agonistic, bellicose, truculent **10** aggressive, pugnacious **11** belligerent, contentious, quarrelsome **12** disputatious, militaristic

combativeness
9 pugnacity **10** aggression, truculence **11** bellicosity **12** belligerence

combe
4 dale, dell, glen, vale **6** dingle, valley

combination
3 mix **4** bloc, pool, ring **5** blend, union **6** fusion, hookup, merger **7** melding, merging **8** alliance **9** aggregate, coalition, composite, synthesis **10** connection **11** affiliation, association, conjunction, partnership, unification **13** consolidation

combine
3 add, mix, wed **4** band, bloc, fuse, join, link, pool, ring **5** blend, chain, group, marry, merge, trust, unify, union, unite **6** cartel, league, mingle **7** bracket, conjoin, connect, faction **8** coadjute, coalesce **9** associate, coalition, commingle, cooperate, integrate, syndicate **10** amalgamate **11** consolidate, incorporate **12** conglomerate
Japanese: **8** keiretsu, zaibatsu
Korean: **7** chaebol, jaebeol

combined action
7 synergy **9** synergism

combo
4 band, trio **5** group, nonet, octet **6** septet, sextet **7** quartet, quintet **8** ensemble

combust
4 burn **6** ignite, kindle **10** incinerate

combustible
4 edgy, fuel **8** burnable, volatile **9** excitable, flammable, ignitable **11** inflammable
material: **3** gas, oil **4** coal, peat, wood **6** tinder

combustion
4 riot **7** burning **8** eruption, ignition, kindling **9** explosion, oxidation **13** thermogenesis

come
4 flow, hail, stem **5** arise, issue, occur **6** arrive, derive, show up, spring, turn up **7** advance, emanate, proceed **8** approach **9** originate
a cropper: **4** fail, fall
across: **4** find, meet **8** discover **9** encounter
apart: **12** disintegrate
at: **6** attack
away: **5** leave **6** depart
before: **7** precede
clean: **7** confess
forth: **5** issue **6** appear, emerge
forward: **7** advance **9** volunteer
into: **5** enter **7** acquire
near: **5** verge **8** approach
round: **5** rally **7** get well, recover
to pass: **5** occur **6** happen
up: **5** arise
upon: **4** find, meet **8** discover **9** encounter

comeback
5 rally **6** answer, retort, return **7** rebound, revival, riposte **8** rebuttal, recovery, repartee, response **11** improvement **12** counterclaim, recuperation

come by
4 call **5** pop in, visit **6** drop in, look in **7** acquire, collect, inherit

comedian
3 wag, wit **4** card **5** clown, comic, droll, joker **6** jester **7** farceur **8** funnyman, humorist, jokester, quipster **11** entertainer
famous: **3** Nye (Louis) **4** Ball (Lucille), Coca (Imogene), Cook (Peter), Dana (Bill), Foxx (Redd), Hope (Bob), Idle (Eric), Leno (Jay), Marx (Chico, Groucho, Gummo, Harpo, Zeppo), Wise (Ernie), Wood (Victoria) **5** Abbot (Bud), Allen (Gracie, Steve, Woody), Berle (Milton), Candy (John), Chase (Chevy), Cosby (Bill), Lewis (Jerry), Lloyd (Harold), Lopez (George), Moore (Dudley), Myers (Mike), Pearl (Minnie) **6** Caesar (Sid), Carrey (Jim), Carson (Johnny), Cleese (John), Diller (Phyllis), Fields (W. C.), Gosden (Freeman), Keaton (Buster), Knotts (Don), Kovacs (Ernie), Lemmon (Jack), Little (Rich), Martin (Steve), Murphy (Eddie), Murray (Bill), O'Brien (Conan), Radner (Gilda), Reiner (Carl), Rivers (Joan), Rogers (Will), Thomas (Danny), Tomlin (Lily), Turpin (Ben) **7** Belushi (John), Buttons (Red), Burnett (Carol), Chaplin (Charlie), Crystal (Billie), Durante (Jimmy), Feldman (Marty), Gleason (Jackie), Grammer (Kelsey), Hackett (Buddy), Matthau (Walter), Moranis (Rick), Newhart (Bob), Nielsen (Leslie), Paulsen (Pat), Rickles (Don), Russell (Mark), Sandler (Adam), Sellers (Peter), Sennett (Mack), Silvers (Phil), Stiller (Ben, Jerry), Winters (Jonathan) **8** Atkinson (Rowan), Costello (Lou), Goldberg (Whoopi), Grenfell (Joyce), Mulligan (Spike), Seinfeld (Jerry), Williams (Robin) **9** Carrot Top, DeGeneres (Ellen), Letterman (David), Morecambe (Eric)

comedo
9 blackhead

comedown
4 dive, fall, ruin **5** crash **7** decline, descent, failure, setback **8** collapse **9** ruination

come down with
3 get **5** catch **7** develop **8** contract

comedy
5 farce, humor **6** levity **8** drollery, hilarity **9** drollness, slapstick, wittiness
show: **3** SNL **6** Hee-Haw **7** Laugh-In **9** Daily Show (The)

come forth
4 grow, rise **5** arise **6** appear **7** emanate

come in
5 enter, reply **6** answer **7** respond

comely
4 fair **5** bonny, sonsy **6** lovely, pretty, proper, sonsie **7** winsome **8** becoming, decorous, handsome, pleasing **9** beauteous, beautiful, befitting **10** attractive **11** good-looking

come off
4 fare, seem **5** click, occur **6** appear, go over, happen, pan out **7** develop, succeed **8** prove out **9** transpire

come-on
4 bait, lure, trap **5** decoy, snare **9** seduction **10** allurement, enticement, inducement, invitation, temptation **12** blandishment, inveiglement, solicitation

come out
4 leak **5** break, debut, end up **6** emerge **9** transpire

come out with
3 say **4** tell **5** state, utter **6** report **7** declare, deliver, publish, release **8** announce, proclaim

comestible
6 edible **7** eatable **8** esculent

comestibles
4 feed, food **6** viands **7** edibles **8** victuals **9** provender **10** provisions

comet
4 West **7** Halley's **8** Hale-Bopp, Kohoutek, McNaught **9** Hyakutake

come through
6 chip in, endure **7** pitch in, prevail, survive **8** transmit **10** contribute

come together
4 mass, meet **5** merge, swarm **6** gather, huddle **7** cluster, collect, combine, convene **8** assemble, converge **10** congregate

come upon
4 find **7** run into, uncover, unearth **8** bump into, discover, trip over **9** encounter, run across

comeuppance
3 due **5** lumps **7** deserts

comfort
3 aid **4** ease, help **5** cheer **6** assist, buck up, luxury, relief, solace, soothe, succor **7** amenity, cheer up, console, relieve, support **8** reassure, sympathy **10** assistance, sympathize **11** commiserate, consolation, contentment

comfortable
4 cozy, easy, homy, snug, soft **5** ample, cushy, homey, roomy **7** content, easeful, restful, well-off **8** adequate, homelike, pleasant, pleasing, spacious, well-to-do **9** agreeable, satisfied, well-fixed **10** commodious, prosperous, sufficient, well-heeled **11** substantial **12** satisfactory

comforter
4 down, pouf, puff **5** duvet, quilt **9** eiderdown

comfy
4 cozy, homy, snug **5** cushy, homey

comic
3 wag, wit **5** antic, droll, funny, joker **6** jester **7** risible **8** comedian, farcical, funnyman, humorist, jokester, quipster **9** laughable, ludicrous **10** ridiculous

comical
4 zany **5** droll, funny, goofy, silly **6** absurd **7** amusing, foolish, risible, waggish **8** farcical **9** laughable, ludicrous **10** ridiculous

comic strip
4 Pogo, Shoe **5** Hazel, Henry, Nancy **6** Archie, Popeye **7** Blondie, Dilbert, Far Side (The), Peanuts **8** Alley Oop, Andy Capp, Garfield, Krazy Kat, Li'l Abner, Superman **9** Betty Boop, Dick Tracy, Marmaduke, Mary Worth, Spider-Man, Yellow Kid (The) **10** Doonesbury, Joe Palooka, Little Nemo **11** Bloom County, Brenda Starr, Flash Gordon, Hogan's Alley, Mutt and Jeff, Rex Morgan M.D., Steve Canyon **12** Beetle Bailey **13** Captain Marvel, Gasoline Alley, Prince Valiant
character: **3** Arn, Jon, Kim, Liz, Owl, Roz **4** Asok, Elmo, Flip, Herb, Irma, Lizz, Loon, Lucy, Odie, Opus, Otto, Phil, Rube, Tess, Thun, Zero **5** Aleta, Alice, Bella, Betty, Carol, Cosmo, Foozy, Honey, Itchy, Lacey, Linus, Mammy, Ooola, Pappy, Patty, Percy, Phred, Plato, Porky, Rerun, Rocky, Rollo, Sally, Shmoo, Spike, Wally **6** Albert, Arlene, Belfry, Cookie, Doc Boy, Dottie, Frieda, Joanie, Junior, Lt. Flap, Lt. Fuzz, Marcie, Nermal, Pig-Pen, Reggie, Skyler, Sluggo, Snoopy, Vultan, Zipper, Zonker **7** Aunt May, Boopsie, Chalkie, Churchy, Dagwood, Dithers, Flattop, Florrie, Jughead, Mr. Butts, Mumbles, Phyllis, Portnoy, Skeezix, Tootsie, Wolf Gal **8** Black Cat, B. O. Plenty, Bull Pupp, Daisy Mae, Dr. Sivana, June Gale, Lana Lang, Lois Lane, Olive Oyl, Pete Ross, Shroeder, Veronica **9** Alexander, Brilliant, Chip Gizmo, Clark Kent, Dale Arden, Diet Smith, Gwen Stacy, Pat Patton, Pruneface, Uncle Duke **10** Aunt Fritzi, Betty Brant, Bill the Cat, Cutter John, Dragon Lady, Hans Zarkov,

Hodge-Podge, Jimmy Olsen, Joe Btfsplk, Louise Lugg, Marryin' Sam, Miss Buxley, Perry White, Sam Catchem, Scott Sloan, Sgt. Snorkel, Walt Wallet **11** Happy Easter, Harry Osborn, Ignatz Mouse, Lola Granola, Mickey Dugan, Peter Parker, Steve Dallas, Summer Olson **12** Charlie Brown, Felicia Hardy, Gen. Halftrack, Gravel Gertie

coming
3 due **4** next **5** fated, onset **6** advent, future **7** arrival, ensuing, nearing **8** approach, expected, foreseen, imminent **9** following, impending **11** approaching
forth: 7 issuant

comity
5 amity **7** concord, harmony **8** goodwill **10** friendship **11** benevolence, camaraderie **12** friendliness

comma
4 lull **5** pause **8** interval

command
3 bid **4** rule, sway **5** order **6** adjure, behest, charge, compel, direct, enjoin **7** bidding, conduct, control, dictate, mandate, mastery, precept **9** authority, direction, directive, expertise, ordinance **10** domination, imperative, injunction **11** instruction **12** jurisdiction
to go: 4 mush **6** avaunt, begone **7** giddyap, giddyup
to stop: 4 whoa **5** avast

commandeer
4 take **5** annex, seize, usurp **6** assume, hijack **7** preempt **8** accroach, arrogate **9** conscript, sequester **10** confiscate **11** appropriate, expropriate, requisition

commander
4 boss, head **6** honcho, leader, master **7** captain, general, headman, officer

commandment
3 law **4** fiat, rule **5** edict, order **6** decree **7** mitzvah, precept, statute

commedia dell' ____
4 arte

comme il faut
6 decent, polite, proper, seemly **7** correct **8** becoming, decorous, suitable

commemorate
4 keep **7** observe **8** eulogize, monument **9** celebrate, solemnize **11** memorialize **13** monumentalize

commemorative
8 memorial **10** dedicatory **11** celebratory

commence
5 begin, start **6** launch, set out **7** kick off **8** embark on, initiate **10** embark upon, inaugurate

commencement
4 dawn **5** birth, onset, start **6** outset **7** dawning, genesis, opening **9** beginning, inception **10** graduation **12** inauguration

commend
4 hail, laud **5** extol **6** commit, kudize, praise, salute, tender **7** acclaim, applaud, approve, consign, entrust **8** hand over, relegate, turn over **10** compliment

commendable
6 worthy **8** laudable **9** admirable, deserving, estimable, meritable, venerable **10** creditable **11** meritorious **12** praiseworthy

commensurable
see **commensurate**

commensurate
4 even **5** equal **10** comparable **11** coextensive **12** proportional **13** corresponding, proportionate

comment
4 note **5** opine **6** remark **7** mention, observe **8** critique, point out **9** criticism, interject **10** animadvert **11** observation **12** obiter dictum

commentary
5 gloss **6** review **8** analysis, critique, exegesis **9** editorial, narration, voice-over **10** annotation, exposition **11** explanation, observation **12** appreciation, obiter dictum

commerce
5 trade **7** contact, traffic **8** business, congress, dealings, exchange, industry **9** communion **11** interchange **13** communication

commercial
2 ad **6** advert **8** economic **10** mercantile **13** advertisement

commie
3 Red **5** pinko **6** bolshy **7** bolshie **9** Bolshevik

commination
5 curse **8** anathema **10** accusation, execration **11** imprecation, malediction **12** denunciation

commingle
3 mix **4** meld **5** blend, merge, unify **8** compound, intermix **9** integrate **10** amalgamate

comminute
4 bray **5** crush, grind **9** granulate, pulverize

commiserate
4 pity **7** condole, feel for **9** empathize **10** sympathize **13** compassionate

commiseration
4 pity, ruth **7** empathy **8** sympathy **10** compassion, condolence

commission
3 bid, fee **4** name **5** board, order, panel **6** agency, assign, charge, enable, engage, enjoin, enlist **7** appoint, command, council, empower, license,

warrant **8** accredit, delegate, deputize **9** authorize, designate **10** delegation, deputation, percentage **11** certificate

commit
4 bind **5** allot, grant, refer **6** assign, convey, invest, ordain, pledge, record, reveal **7** achieve, consign, deposit, entrust, execute, perform, promise, pull off, trustee **8** allocate, carry out, hand over, obligate, relegate, turn over **10** accomplish, perpetrate

commitment
3 vow **4** bond, deal, duty **6** charge, devoir, pledge **7** promise **8** contract **9** agreement, assurance, guarantee **10** obligation **11** undertaking

committal
see **commitment**

commixture
5 blend **6** fusion **7** amalgam, melange **8** compound, mingling **9** composite

commodious
4 wide **5** ample, roomy **8** spacious **9** capacious, expansive, luxurious **11** comfortable

commodities
5 goods, items, wares **8** articles, products **9** vendibles **11** merchandise

common
4 park **5** banal, daily, joint, plaza, trite, usual **6** mutual, normal, shared **7** general, generic, prosaic, regular, routine, typical **8** adequate, communal, conjoint, conjunct, déclassé, everyday, familiar, frequent, habitual, ordinary, standard, workaday **9** customary, prevalent, tolerable, universal **10** collective, pedestrian, prevailing, unexciting, widespread **12** conventional, run-of-the-mill, satisfactory **13** unexceptional, uninteresting

commonalty
3 mob **5** plebs **6** masses, people, plebes, public, rabble **7** commune **8** populace **9** hoi polloi, multitude, plebeians **11** proletariat, rank and file, third estate

commoners
see **commonalty**

commonplace
5 banal, stale, tired, trite, usual **6** cliché, normal, truism **7** bromide, clichéd, humdrum, mundane, obvious, prosaic, regular, routine, typical **8** banality, bromidic, chestnut, everyday, habitual, mediocre, ordinary, well-worn, workaday **9** hackneyed, platitude, prevalent **10** pedestrian, shibboleth, stereotype, uneventful **11** stereotyped **12** conventional, run-of-the-mill, unremarkable **13** stereotypical, unexceptional, uninteresting

common sense
6 wisdom **8** judgment, prudence **10** shrewdness

Common Sense author
5 Paine (Thomas)

commotion
3 ado, din, row **4** flap, fuss, moil, riot, stew, stir, to-do **5** hoo-ha, storm, whirl **6** bustle, clamor, dither, flurry, fracas, furore, hoo-hah, hoopla, hubbub, hurrah, lather, outcry, pother, racket, ruckus, rumpus, shindy, tumult, uproar, upturn **7** ferment, tempest, turmoil **8** brouhaha, foofaraw **9** agitation, confusion **10** convulsion, hullabaloo, hurly-burly, turbulence **11** pandemonium

commove
5 rouse **6** excite **7** agitate, inspire, provoke **9** electrify, galvanize, stimulate

communal
5 civil, joint **6** common, mutual, public, shared **10** collective **11** socialistic

commune
10 collective
Israeli: 7 kibbutz
Russian: 3 mir **7** kolkhoz

communicable
8 catching **10** contagious, infectious **13** transmissible, transmittable

communicate
4 tell **6** convey, impart, inform, pass on, relate, reveal, signal **7** connect, contact, divulge **8** disclose, transmit **9** make known

communication
4 talk **7** contact, message, missive, talking **8** converse, exchange **9** directive **10** discussing, discussion **11** interchange, intercourse **12** conversation
means: 2 IM, TV **3** Web **4** drum, mail, note **5** e-mail, media, phone, radio **6** letter, medium, pigeon, speech **8** Internet **9** telegraph, telephone **10** television

communications code word
4 Alfa, Echo, Golf, Kilo, Lima, Mike, Papa, Xray, Zulu **5** Alpha, Bravo, Delta, Hotel, India, Oscar, Romeo, Tango **6** Quebec, Sierra, Victor, Yankee **7** Charlie, Foxtrot, Juliett, Uniform, Whiskey **8** November

communicative
5 vocal **6** fluent, prolix **7** verbose, voluble **8** eloquent **9** expansive, garrulous, talkative **10** articulate, expressive, loquacious

communion
7 rapport, sharing **9** Eucharist, sacrament **10** connection, fellowship
cloth: 8 corporal
cup: 7 chalice
plate: 5 paten

communism
7 Marxism **8** Leninism **10** bolshevism **12** collectivism

Communist
3 red **5** lefty, pinko **6** bolshy, Maoist **7** bolshie, comrade, Marxist **8** Leninist **9** Bolshevik, Stalinist **10** Bolshevist, Trotskyist

Communist leader
Chinese: 3 Mao **4** Deng **5** Jiang **8** Hu Jintao **9** Mao Zedong **10** Jiang Zemin, Mao Tse-tung **12** Deng Xiaoping **13** Teng Hsiao-p'ing
Cuban: 6 Castro (Fidel)
Russian: 5 Lenin (Vladimir Ilyich) **6** Stalin (Joseph) **7** Kosygin (Aleksey), Trotsky (Leon) **8** Andropov (Yuri), Brezhnev (Leonid) **9** Chernenko (Konstantin), Gorbachev (Mikhail) **10** Khrushchev (Nikita)

community
4 town **7** enclave, society **12** neighborhood
closed: 5 abbey **6** priory **7** convent, nunnery **8** cloister **9** monastery
ecological: 10 biocenosis **11** biocoenosis

commute
5 alter **6** change, make up, modify, soften, travel **7** convert, curtail, shorten, shuttle **8** decrease, exchange, mitigate, transfer **9** transform, translate, transmute, transpose **10** compensate, substitute **11** interchange

Comoros
capital: 6 Moroni
island: 6 Mohéli **7** Anjouan **12** Grande Comore
language: 6 Arabic, French **8** Comorian
monetary unit: 5 franc
volcano: 8 Karthala

compact
4 bond **5** close, dense, unify **7** bargain, bunched, crowded, pressed **8** compress, condense, contract, covenant **9** agreement, concordat **10** convention **11** concentrate, consolidate, transaction

compadre
3 pal **4** chum, mate **5** amigo, buddy, crony **6** cohort, friend **7** comrade, partner **8** confrere, sidekick, intimate **9** associate, colleague, companion

companion
3 pal **4** chum, mate **5** buddy, crony **6** cohort, escort, fellow **7** comrade, consort, partner **8** sidekick **9** associate, attendant, colleague

companionable
6 genial, social **7** affable, amiable **8** outgoing, sociable **9** agreeable, congenial, convivial **10** gregarious **11** good-natured

companionship
7 company, society **8** intimacy **10** fellowship **11** camaraderie

company
4 band, club, crew, firm, gang, team **5** corps, group, party, troop **6** circle, clique, guests, outfit, troupe **7** concern, coterie, retinue, society, visitor **8** assembly, business, ensemble, visitors **9** gathering **10** assemblage, enterprise, fellowship **11** association, camaraderie, corporation **12** congregation **13** companionship, establishment

comparable
4 akin, like **5** alike **6** agnate **7** similar, uniform **8** parallel **9** analogous **10** equivalent, homologous **12** commensurate **13** corresponding

comparative
4 near **8** relative **11** approximate

compare
5 liken, match **6** equate, relate **7** collate **8** contrast, parallel **9** correlate **10** assimilate

comparison
6 simile **7** analogy **8** affinity, contrast, likeness **9** collation, semblance **10** similarity, similitude **11** correlation, resemblance

compartment
3 bay **4** cell, nook, part, slot **5** berth, booth, niche, stall **6** alcove, carrel, locker **7** chamber, cubicle, section **8** division **9** cubbyhole **10** pigeonhole **11** subdivision

compass
3 hem **4** ring **5** ambit, field, grasp, orbit, range, reach, scope, sweep **6** bounds, circle, domain, extent, girdle, limits, radius, sphere **7** circuit, environ, purview **8** boundary, confines, environs **9** enclosure, extension, perimeter, periphery **13** circumference
kind: 4 gyro **5** solar **8** magnetic
stand: 8 binnacle

compassion
4 pity, ruth **5** mercy **7** charity, empathy **8** clemency, humanity, kindness, sympathy **10** condolence, humaneness **11** benevolence **13** commiseration, fellow feeling

compassionate
4 pity, warm **6** humane, tender **7** clement **8** merciful **10** benevolent, charitable, solicitous **11** commiserate, kindhearted, softhearted, sympathetic, warmhearted

compassionless
5 stony **7** callous **8** obdurate **9** heartless, unfeeling **11** coldblooded, hard-hearted, ironhearted **12** stonyhearted

compass point
3 ENE, ESE, NNE, NNW, SSE, SSW, WNW, WSW **4** east, west **5** north, rhumb, south **7** bearing
Scottish: 4 airt

compatible
6 proper **8** suitable **9** agreeable, congenial, congruous, consonant **10** consistent, harmonious, like-minded **11** appropriate, sympathetic

compatriot
7 paesano **8** confrere **9** associate, colleague, companion

compel
4 hale, urge **5** drive, force **6** coerce, impose, oblige **7** enforce **9** constrain

compelling
4 dire **5** acute **6** cogent, crying, urgent **7** clamant, exigent, telling, weighty **8** forceful, pressing **10** convincing, persuasive **11** importunate **12** well-grounded

compendious
5 brief, pithy, short **7** compact, concise, summary **8** succinct **9** condensed **11** abbreviated

compendium
4 list **5** brief, guide **6** aperçu, digest, manual, précis, sketch, survey **7** epitome, summary **8** abstract, Baedeker, handbook, overview, syllabus, synopsis **9** anthology, guidebook, vade mecum **10** abridgment, collection, conspectus **11** abridgement, compilation, enchiridion

compensate
3 pay **5** atone, repay **6** make up, offset, pay off, redeem, set off **7** balance, guerdon, requite, satisfy **8** outweigh **9** indemnify, reimburse **10** counteract, neutralize, recompense, remunerate **11** countervail

compensation
6 amends, reward, salary **7** damages, payment, redress **8** earnings, reprisal, requital, solatium **9** atonement, indemnity, quittance, repayment **10** recompense, reparation **11** restitution **12** remuneration
unexpected: **4** gift **5** bonus **8** windfall

compete
3 vie **4** spar **5** fight **6** battle, strive **7** contend, contest **8** struggle

competence
5 skill **7** ability, know-how **8** adequacy, aptitude, capacity, facility **9** expertise **10** capability **11** proficiency, sufficiency **13** qualification

competent
3 fit **4** able **5** adept **6** au fait, decent, proper **7** capable, skilled **8** adequate **9** efficient, qualified **10** proficient, sufficient **12** satisfactory

competition
4 bout, game, meet, race **5** clash, fight, match, rival **6** strife **7** contest, matchup, rivalry **8** concours, conflict, striving, struggle, tug-of-war **10** antagonism, contention, tournament

competitor
5 enemy, rival **7** entrant **8** opponent **9** adversary **10** antagonist, contestant, opposition

compile
4 edit **5** amass **6** gather, select **7** build up, collate, collect **8** assemble **9** construct **10** accumulate **11** anthologize

complacency
5 pride **7** conceit **8** smugness **10** narcissism

complacent
4 smug **6** serene **7** assured **9** conceited, confident **11** self-assured, unconcerned **13** self-confident, self-contented, self-possessed, self-satisfied

complain
3 nag **4** beef, carp, crab, fret, fuss, moan, wail **5** gripe, grump, whine **6** grouch, grouse, lament, repine, yammer **7** grizzle, grumble, protest **9** bellyache

complainer
4 crab **5** crank **6** griper, grouch **7** grouser **8** grumbler, sourpuss **10** malcontent **11** fault-finder

complaint
4 beef **5** gripe **6** grouse, lament, malady **7** ailment, disease, protest **8** disorder, sickness, syndrome **9** condition, criticism, grievance, infirmity, objection **10** affliction, allegation **12** protestation

complaisant
4 easy, mild **7** amiable, lenient **8** generous, obliging **9** agreeable, compliant, easygoing, indulgent **11** deferential, good-humored, good-natured **12** good-tempered **13** accommodating

complement
4 crew, rest **9** correlate, remainder **10** supplement **11** counterpart

complete
3 end **4** done, full, halt **5** close, ended, total, utter, whole **6** entire, finish, intact, wind up, wrap up **7** achieve, fulfill, perfect, perform, plenary **8** absolute, conclude, finalize, finished, integral, round out, thorough **9** concluded, out-and-out, terminate **10** accomplish, consummate, exhaustive, unabridged **11** categorical, unmitigated **13** thoroughgoing

completed
4 done, over **5** ended **7** through **8** done with, executed, finished **9** concluded, fulfilled **10** terminated **11** consummated **12** accomplished

completely
4 A to Z **5** fully **6** wholly **7** totally, utterly **8** entirely **9** inside out, up and down **10** thoroughly

completion
3 end **6** finish, windup, wrap-up **8** fruition **10** conclusion

complex
6 daedal, knotty, system, varied **7** chelate, gordian, network **8** abstruse, compound, involved, syndrome, tortuous **9** aggregate, Byzantine,

composite, elaborate, intricate **10** convoluted **11** complicated **12** conglomerate, labyrinthine **13** heterogeneous, sophisticated

complexion
3 hue **4** cast, tint, tone **5** color, humor, tinge **6** aspect, makeup, nature, temper **8** tincture **9** character **10** appearance, coloration **11** disposition, temperament **12** pigmentation **13** individuality

compliance
7 consent **8** docility **9** agreement, deference, obedience **10** acceptance, conformity, submission **11** amenability, flexibility, resignation **12** acquiescence, tractability

complicate
5 mix up, ravel, snarl **6** jumble, muddle, tangle **7** confuse, involve **8** confound, disorder, entangle **9** aggravate, convolute **10** disarrange, exacerbate

complicated
6 daedal, knotty **7** complex, gordian, tangled **8** abstruse, involved, tortuous **9** Byzantine, elaborate, intricate, recondite **10** convoluted **12** labyrinthine **13** heterogeneous, sophisticated

complicity
8 abetment **9** collusion **10** connivance **11** involvement

compliment
4 hail, kudo, laud **5** extol, honor, kudos **6** praise, salute **7** acclaim, applaud, bouquet, commend, regards, tribute **8** accolade, encomium **9** laudation, recommend **11** recognition **12** appreciation, commendation, congratulate

complimentary
4 free **6** gratis **8** costless **9** favorable, laudatory **10** chargeless, gratuitous **12** appreciative

comply
4 obey **5** yield **6** accede, submit **7** conform **9** acquiesce

component
4 part **5** piece **6** factor **7** element, segment **10** ingredient **11** constituent

comport
4 bear, jibe **5** agree, carry, fit in, match, tally **6** accord, acquit, behave, demean, square **7** conduct **8** coincide, dovetail **9** harmonize **10** correspond

comportment
3 air **4** mien **7** address, bearing, conduct **8** attitude, behavior, carriage, demeanor, presence

compose
4 calm, cool, form, lull, make **5** forge, quiet, relax, still, write **6** becalm, create, devise, draw up, indite, invent, make up, settle, solace, soothe **7** collect, console, contain, control **8** comprise **9** construct, fabricate, formulate, originate **10** constitute
type: **3** set

composed
4 calm, cool **5** staid **6** poised, sedate, serene **9** collected, unruffled **11** unflappable **13** imperturbable, self-possessed

composer
6 scorer **8** melodist **9** balladist, songsmith, tunesmith **10** songwriter
American: **3** Kay (Hershy, Ulysses) **4** Ager (Milton), Bock (Jerry), Cage (John), Hill (Edward Burlingame), Ives (Charles), Kern (Jerome), King (Carole), Lane (Burton), Monk (Thelonious), Work (Henry Clay) **5** Adams (John), Arlen (Harold), Beach (Amy), Blake (Eubie), Bland (James A.), Bloch (Ernest), Cohan (George M.), Friml (Rudolf), Glass (Philip), Gould (Morton), Grofé (Ferde), Handy (W. C.), Loewe (Frederick), Mason (Daniel Gregory, Lowell), Moore (Douglas), Reich (Steve), Rorem (Ned), Sousa (John Philip), Still (William Grant), Styne (Jule), Zappa (Frank) **6** Barber (Samuel), Berlin (Irving), Carter (Elliott), Cowell (Henry), Emmett (Daniel), Foster (Stephen), Hanson (Howard), Harris (Roy), Herman (Jerry), Joplin (Scott), Kander (John), McHugh (Jimmy), McKuen (Rod), Menken (Alan), Morton ("Jelly Roll"), Oliver ("King"), Parker (Charlie "Bird," Horatio), Piston (Walter), Porter (Cole), Previn (André), Seeger (Pete), Taylor (Deems), Varèse (Edgard), Warren (Harry) **7** Babbitt (Milton), Brubeck (Dave), Copland (Aaron), Gilbert (Henry F.), Gilmore (Patrick), Goldman (Edwin Franko), Herbert (Victor), Loesser (Frank), Mancini (Henry), Menotti (Gian Carlo), Rodgers (Richard), Romberg (Sigmund), Schuman (William), Thomson (Virgil), Tiomkin (Dimitri), Willson (Meredith), Youmans (Vincent) **8** Anderson (Leroy), Billings (William), Burleigh (Henry Thacker), Damrosch (Leopold, Walter), Gershwin (George), Hamlisch (Marvin), Herrmann (Bernard), Korngold (Erich Wolfgang), Kreisler (Fritz), Marsalis (Wynton), Schifrin (Lalo), Schuller (Gunther), Sessions (Roger), Sondheim (Stephen), Williams (John) **9** Bacharach (Burt), Bernstein (Elmer, Leonard), Donaldson (Walter), Ellington (Duke), Hovhaness (Alan), MacDowell (Edward) **10** Blitzstein (Marc), Carmichael (Hoagy), Gottschalk (Louis Moreau)
Argentinian: **9** Ginastera (Alberto)
Australian: **8** Grainger (Percy)
Austrian: **4** Berg (Alban), Wolf (Hugo) **5** Haydn (Franz Joseph) **6** Czerny (Karl), Mahler (Gustav), Mozart (Leopold, Wolfgang Amadeus), Straus (Oscar), Webern (Anton) **7** Strauss (Eduard, Johann, Josef) **8** Bruckner (Anton), Schubert (Franz) **10** Schoenberg (Arnold)

Belgian: **5** Ysaÿe (Eugène) **6** Franck (César)
Brazilian: **5** Jobim (Antonio Carlos) **10** Villa-Lobos (Heitor)
Czech: **3** Suk (Josef) **5** Friml (Rudolf) **6** Dvőrák (Antonín) **7** Janáček (Leoš), Martinu (Bohuslav), Smetana (Bedřich)
Danish: **7** Nielsen (Carl)
Dutch: **9** Sweelinck (Jan Pieterszoon)
English: **4** Arne (Thomas Augustine), Byrd (William) **5** Elgar (Edward), Holst (Gustav) **6** Delius (Frederick), Morley (Thomas), Tallis (Thomas), Walton (William), Wesley (Charles, Samuel) **7** Britten (Benjamin), Dowland (John), Gibbons (Orlando), Purcell (Henry), Tippett (Michael), Weelkes (Thomas) **8** Sullivan (Arthur) **9** Dunstable (John) **11** Lloyd Webber (Andrew)
Finnish: **8** Palmgren (Selim), Sibelius (Jean)
Flemish: **5** Dufay (Guillaume), Lasso (Orlando di) **6** Lassus (Orlande de) **8** Willaert (Adriaan)
French: **4** Indy (Vincent d'), Lalo (Edouard) **5** Auber (Esprit), Bizet (Georges), Dukas (Paul), Fauré (Gabriel), Ibert (Jacques), Jarre (Maurice), Lully (Jean-Baptiste), Ravel (Maurice), Satie (Erik), Widor (Charles-Marie) **6** Boulez (Pierre), Campra (André), Franck (César), Gounod (Charles), Rameau (Jean-Philippe), Thomas (Ambroise) **7** Berlioz (Hector), Debussy (Claude), Delibes (Léo), Machaut (Guillaume de), Milhaud (Darius), Poulenc (Francis) **8** Chabrier (Emmanuel), Couperin (François, Louis), Honegger (Arthur), Massenet (Jules), Messiaen (Olivier) **9** Meyerbeer (Giacomo), Offenbach (Jacques) **10** Saint-Saëns (Camille)
German: **4** Bach (C. P. E., Johann Christian, Johann Sebastian, Wilhelm Friedemann), Orff (Carl) **5** Bruch (Max), Gluck (Christoph Willibald von), Reger (Max), Spohr (Louis, Ludwig), Weber (Carl Maria von), Weill (Kurt) **6** Brahms (Johannes), Handel (George Frideric), Schütz (Heinrich), Vogler (Abt), Wagner (Richard) **7** Hassler (Hans Leo), Strauss (Richard) **8** Korngold (Erich Wolfgang), Schumann (Robert), Telemann (Georg Philipp) **9** Beethoven (Ludwig van), Buxtehude (Dietrich), Hindemith (Paul), Meyerbeer (Giacomo), Pachelbel (Johann) **10** Praetorius (Michael) **11** Humperdinck (Engelbert), Mendelssohn (Felix), Stockhausen (Karlheinz)
Hungarian: **5** Léhar (Franz), Liszt (Franz) **6** Bartók (Béla), Kodály (Zoltán), Ligeti (György) **8** Dohnányi (Erno)
Italian: **4** Peri (Jacopo), Rota (Nino) **5** Berio (Luciano), Boito (Arrigo), Verdi (Giuseppe) **6** Busoni (Ferruccio) **7** Bellini (Vincenzo), Caccini (Giulio), Corelli (Arcangelo), Martini (Padre), Puccini (Giacomo), Rossini (Gioacchino), Salieri (Antonio), Tartini (Giuseppe), Vivaldi (Antonio) **8** Albinoni (Tomaso), Clementi (Muzio), Gabrieli (Andrea, Giovanni), Mascagni (Pietro), Paganini (Niccolò), Respighi (Ottorino) **9** Cherubini (Luigi), Donizetti (Gaetano), Pergolesi (Giovanni Battista), Scarlatti (Alessandro, Domenico), Tommasini (Vincenzo) **10** Boccherini (Luigi), Monteverdi (Claudio), Palestrina (G. P. da), Ponchielli (Amilcare), Zingarelli (Niccolò) **11** Frescobaldi (Girolamo), Leoncavallo (Ruggero) **12** Dallapiccola (Luigi)
Japanese: **4** Taki (Rentaro) **5** Satoh (Somei) **6** Tomita (Isao) **7** Ifukube (Akira) **9** Katsuhisa (Hattori), Takemitsu (Toru)
Mexican: **6** Chávez (Carlos)
Norwegian: **5** Grieg (Edvard)
Polish: **6** Chopin (Frédéric) **7** Gorecki (Henryk) **10** Paderewski (Ignacy Jan), Penderecki (Krzysztof), Wieniawski (Henryk) **11** Lutoslawski (Witold), Szymanowski (Karol)
Romanian: **6** Enescu (Gheorghe, George) **7** Xenakis (Iannis)
Russian: **6** Glinka (Mikhail) **7** Borodin (Aleksandr) **8** Glazunov (Aleksandr), Scriabin (Aleksandr) **9** Balakirev (Mily), Prokofiev (Sergey), Schnittke (Alfred) **10** Kabalevsky (Dmitri), Mussorgsky (Modest), Rubinstein (Anton), Stravinsky (Igor), Tcherepnin (Nikolay) **11** Tchaikovsky (Pyotr Ilich) **12** Khachaturian (Aram), Rachmaninoff (Sergey), Shostakovich (Dmitry)
Spanish: **5** Falla (Manuel de) **7** Albéniz (Isaac), Rodrigo (Joaquin) **8** Granados (Enrique), Victoria (Tomas Luis de)
Swiss: **5** Bloch (Ernest) **6** Martin (Frank) **8** Honegger (Arthur)
(see also **songwriter**)

composite
3 mix **5** blend **6** fusion, hybrid **7** amalgam, complex, mixture **8** compound **11** combination **12** amalgamation

composition
4 opus **5** essay, paper, theme **6** design, layout, makeup **7** article **9** formation **11** arrangement **12** architecture, constitution, construction
choral: **4** mass **5** motet **7** cantata, passion **8** oratorio
for eight: **5** octet
for five: **7** quintet
for four: **7** quartet
for nine: **5** nonet
for one: **4** aria, solo
for seven: **6** septet
for six: **6** sextet
for three: **4** trio
for two: **3** duo **4** duet
instrumental: **3** jig **4** reel **5** étude, fugue, gigue, march, rondo, suite **6** sonata **7** caprice, partita, prelude, scherzo **8** concerto, fantasia, overture, rhapsody, saraband, sinfonia, symphony, tone poem **9** allemande, capriccio, sarabande **10** intermezzo

vocal: 4 aria, lied, mass, song 5 carol, chant, motet, opera, round 6 arioso, ballad, chanty 7 cantata, chanson, chantey, chorale, lullaby, requiem 8 berceuse, madrigal, oratorio 9 plainsong, spiritual 10 plainchant

compos mentis
4 sane 5 lucid, sound 6 normal

composure
4 calm 5 poise 7 balance, dignity 8 calmness, coolness, evenness, serenity, sobriety 9 sangfroid 10 equanimity 11 equilibrium

compound
3 mix 4 join, link 5 admix, alloy, blend, union, unite 6 expand, extend, fusion, make up, mingle 7 amalgam, augment, complex, compost, enlarge, magnify, mixture 8 coalesce, comingle, heighten, increase, intermix, multiply 9 admixture, aggravate, associate, commingle, composite, intensify, synthesis 10 commixture, exacerbate 11 intermingle 12 amalgamation
aroma: 5 neral 6 citral 7 menthol 8 vanillin
chemical:
(see at **chemical**)
protein: 7 peptone

comprehend
4 know 5 catch, grasp 6 absorb, accept, embody, fathom, take in 7 cognize, compass, contain, discern, embrace, include, involve, subsume 8 comprise, perceive 9 encompass 10 appreciate, understand

comprehensible
8 knowable 9 graspable 10 fathomable 12 intelligible

comprehension
3 ken 5 grasp 6 uptake 9 awareness, knowledge 10 cognizance, conception, perception 11 discernment 12 apperception 13 understanding

comprehensive
4 full, wide 5 broad 6 global 7 general, overall 8 catholic, complete, sweeping 9 all-around, extensive, inclusive, universal 10 exhaustive 12 all-inclusive, encyclopedic

comprehensiveness
5 range, reach, scope 7 breadth 8 entirety, fullness, totality 9 amplitude

compress
3 jam 4 cram, push 5 crush, press 6 reduce, shrink, squash, squish, shrink 7 bandage, compact, squeeze 8 condense, contract 11 concentrate

comprise
4 form 6 make up 7 compose, contain, embrace, include, subsume 10 comprehend, constitute

compromise
4 mean, pact, risk 6 settle 7 bargain, compact 8 contract, endanger, trade off 9 agreement, middle way 10 concession, golden mean, jeopardize, settlement 12 middle ground

compulsion
4 itch, need, urge 5 drive, force 6 duress 8 coercion 9 necessity 10 constraint

compulsive
6 driven 7 driving 9 besetting, obsessive 12 irresistible, overwhelming

compulsory
7 binding 8 coercive, enforced, required 9 mandatory, requisite 10 imperative, obligatory

compunction
4 pang 5 demur, qualm 6 regret, unease 7 remorse, scruple 8 distress 9 hesitancy, misgiving 10 conscience, hesitation

compunctious
5 sorry 8 contrite, penitent 9 regretful, repentant 10 apologetic, remorseful 11 penitential

computation
8 figuring 9 ciphering, reckoning 10 arithmetic, estimation 11 calculation

compute
5 tally, total 6 cipher, figure, reckon 8 estimate 9 calculate, determine

computer
6 abacus, laptop 7 desktop 9 mainframe 10 calculator
code: 5 ASCII
component: 3 CPU 4 chip 5 mouse, tower 7 monitor 8 keyboard 9 hard drive
early: 5 Eniac 6 Univac
expert: 4 geek 6 techie
graphics application: 3 CGI, FMV
information: 4 data
instruction: 5 macro
inventor: 7 Babbage (Charles)
key: 3 Alt, Esc, Tab 4 Ctrl 5 Enter, Shift
language: 3 Ada, APL, SQL 4 Java, Lisp, Perl 5 ALGOL, BASIC, COBOL 6 Pascal 7 FORTRAN
see also **programming language**
type: 6 analog 7 digital

computer-game genre
3 FPS, RPG, RTS 6 action, puzzle, racing, sports 8 fighting, platform 9 adventure 10 simulation

comrade
3 pal 4 ally, chum, mate 5 buddy, crony 6 cohort, comate, fellow 7 consort 8 sidekick, tovarich, tovarish 9 associate, colleague, companion

con
3 gyp, vet 4 anti, bilk, coax, dupe, fool, hoax, rook, scam 5 cheat, fraud, learn, study, trick 6 cajole, fleece, gammon, inmate, survey 7 against, blarney, canvass, chicane, convict, deceive, defraud, examine, inspect, swindle,

wheedle **8** blandish, flimflam, hoodwink, inveigle, jailbird, memorize, negative, opponent, persuade, prisoner, soft-soap **9** bamboozle, check over, sweet-talk **10** antithesis, manipulate, scrutinize **11** hornswoggle **12** tuberculosis

concatenate
4 join, link **5** unite **7** connect

concavity
3 dip, sag **4** bowl, dent, sink **5** basin **6** crater, hollow, trough **7** sinkage **8** sinkhole **10** depression

conceal
4 bury, hide, mask, veil **5** cache, cloak, cover, stash **6** screen **7** obscure, secrete **8** ensconce, enshroud, palliate **10** camouflage

concealed
3 hid **5** privy **6** buried, covert, hidden, secret **8** obscured, shrouded, ulterior **11** clandestine

concede
3 own **4** avow, fold **5** admit, allow, award, grant, yield **6** accept, accord **7** confess **9** surrender, vouchsafe **10** capitulate, relinquish **11** acknowledge

conceit
4 idea, whim **5** fancy, pride **6** egoism, megrim, notion, vagary, vanity **7** caprice, egotism, thought **8** crotchet, metaphor, self-love, smugness, snobbery **9** self-pride, vainglory **10** narcissism, self-esteem **11** complacence, complacency, self-opinion, swelled head

conceited
4 vain **6** snobby, snooty, uppish, uppity **7** pompous, stuck-up **8** immodest, puffed up, snobbish **12** narcissistic, vainglorious

conceitedness
6 vanity **8** self-love **9** vainglory **10** narcissism

conceivable
8 possible **9** plausible, thinkable **10** imaginable, supposable

conceive
4 form **5** beget, fancy, grasp, think **6** devise, expect, ideate, ponder **7** dream up, feature, imagine, realize, suppose, suspect, think up **8** envisage, envision **9** formulate, originate, speculate, visualize **10** excogitate, mastermind

concentrate
4 mass **5** focus **6** gather, shrink **7** collect, compact **8** assemble, compress, condense, contract, converge **10** accumulate **11** consolidate

concentrated
5 thick **6** intent, strong **7** focused, intense **8** vehement **9** intensive, undiluted, undivided **12** undistracted

concentration
5 field, major, study **9** attention **10** absorption **11** application

concept
4 idea **5** image **6** notion, theory **7** conceit, thought **10** impression, perception

conception
4 idea **5** birth, image, start **6** notion, origin, outset, theory **7** conceit, genesis, thought **9** beginning **10** impression, perception

conceptual
5 ideal **8** abstract, notional **9** imaginary, visionary **10** ideational **11** theoretical **12** hypothetical, intellectual

concern
4 care, firm, heed **5** doubt, worry **6** affair, bear on, bother, engage, gadget, matter, occupy, outfit, regard, unease **7** anxiety, company, disturb, involve, perturb, trouble **8** business, deal with, disquiet, interest, mistrust **9** attention, curiosity, misgiving, suspicion **10** enterprise, skepticism, solicitude, uneasiness **11** carefulness, contrivance, uncertainty **12** apprehension **13** consciousness, consideration, establishment

concerned
7 anxious, worried **8** affected, involved **10** implicated, interested

concerning
4 as to, in re **5** about, anent, as for **7** apropos **9** as regards, regarding **10** relating to, relative to, respecting

concert
5 agree, union **6** accord, concur, settle, soiree **7** arrange, concord, harmony, recital **8** coincide, musicale **9** agreement, cooperate, harmonize, negotiate **11** performance

concerted
5 joint **6** mutual, united **7** unified **8** combined **11** coordinated **13** collaborative

concert hall
5 arena, odeum **7** theater, theatre **10** auditorium

concession
5 favor, grant **8** giveback **9** admission, allowance, privilege **10** compromise **12** acquiescence

conch
5 shell **7** mollusc, mollusk

concierge
6 porter, warden **7** doorman, janitor **9** custodian **10** doorkeeper

conciliate
4 calm, ease **6** disarm, pacify, soothe **7** appease, assuage, mollify, placate, sweeten, win over **9** reconcile **10** propitiate

concise
5 brief, pithy, short, terse **7** compact, laconic, summary **8** abridged, succinct **9** condensed **10** compressed, contracted **11** compendious **13** short and sweet

conclave
5 synod **6** caucus, powwow **7** meeting, session **8** assembly **9** gathering **10** conference, consistory, convention **11** convocation

conclude
3 end **4** halt, stop **5** close, infer, judge **6** decide, deduce, derive, effect, figure, finish, gather, reason, settle, wind up, wrap up **7** collect, resolve **8** complete **9** determine, terminate

concluding
4 last **5** final **6** latest, latter **7** closing **8** eventual, terminal, ultimate

conclusion
3 end **4** stop **5** cease, close **6** ending, epilog, finale, finish, period, result, windup **7** closing, closure, outcome, verdict **8** decision, epilogue, judgment, sequitur **9** cessation, deduction, inference, summation **10** completion, denouement, resolution, settlement **11** culmination, termination **13** determination
musical: **4** coda
poetic: **5** envoi

conclusive
4 last **5** final **6** cogent **8** deciding, decisive, ultimate **9** clinching **10** compelling, convincing, definitive, undeniable **11** determinant, determinate, irrefutable **12** irrefragable, unanswerable **13** determinative

concoct
3 mix **4** brew, cook **5** frame, hatch **6** cook up, create, devise, invent **7** dream up **8** conceive, contrive **9** fabricate, formulate, originate

concoction
4 brew, plan **5** blend **7** mixture, project **8** compound, creation **9** invention **11** combination, contrivance, fabrication, preparation

concomitant
7 adjunct **8** adjuvant **9** accessory, ancillary, associate, attendant, attending, companion, satellite **10** coincident, collateral **12** accompanying **13** accompaniment, supplementary

concord
4 pact **5** amity, peace, unity **6** accord, comity, treaty, unison **7** concert, entente, harmony, rapport **8** goodwill **9** agreement **10** consonance

concordant
8 agreeing **9** congruous, consonant **10** compatible, consistent, harmonious **11** appropriate

concourse
5 foyer **6** throng **7** joining, meeting **8** junction **9** gathering **10** confluence, crossroads

concrete
5 solid **6** actual **8** specific, tangible **10** particular **11** substantial
component: **4** sand **5** water **6** gravel

concubine
7 hetaera, hetaira **8** mistress **9** courtesan, odalisque

concupiscence
4 lust **5** ardor **6** desire **7** lechery, passion **9** prurience, pruriency **11** lustfulness **13** lickerishness

concupiscent
3 hot **7** aroused, goatish, lustful **8** prurient **9** lecherous, lickerish, salacious **10** lascivious, libidinous, lubricious, passionate

concur
4 jibe **5** agree, unite **6** accord, assent **7** approve, combine, concord, consent, go along **8** coincide **9** cooperate, harmonize

concurrent
6 coeval **8** parallel **10** coexistent, coexisting, convergent, synchronic **11** synchronous **12** contemporary, simultaneous

concurrently
6 at once **8** together **12** coincidently

concuss
3 jar **4** rock, stun **5** shake, shock **7** agitate

concussion
3 jar **4** bump, jolt **5** clout, crash, shock **6** impact **7** jarring, jolting, shaking **8** pounding **9** agitation, collision

condemn
3 rap **4** damn, doom **5** blame, decry, knock, seize **7** censure, convict, deplore **8** denounce, sentence **9** criticize, deprecate, proscribe, reprehend, reprobate **10** denunciate

condensation
3 dew **5** brief **6** digest, précis **7** epitome, outline, summary **8** abstract, synopsis **9** reduction **10** abridgment, conspectus **11** abridgement

condense
5 sum up **6** digest, reduce, shrink **7** abridge, compact, shorten **8** boil down, compress, contract **9** constrict, epitomize, summarize, synopsize **10** abbreviate **11** concentrate, consolidate, precipitate

condensed
7 concise, summary **10** boiled down **11** compendious

condenser
9 capacitor

condescend
5 deign, stoop **6** unbend

condescending
5 lofty **6** lordly, snobby, snooty, uppish, uppity **7** haughty, pompous **8** affected, arrogant, cavalier, snobbish, superior **10** disdainful **11** patronizing, pretentious **12** supercilious

condign
3 apt, due, fit **4** fair, just **5** right **6** proper

7 fitting, merited **8** deserved, rightful, suitable **9** equitable, justified **11** appropriate

condiment
5 curry, sauce, spice **6** catsup, relish, tamari **7** chutney, ketchup, mustard **8** dressing, soy sauce **9** seasoning **10** mayonnaise

____ con Dios!
4 Vaya

condition
5 shape, state, terms **6** fettle, malady, status **7** ailment, disease, fitness, proviso **8** syndrome **9** complaint, essential, exception, necessity, provision, requisite, situation **10** limitation, sine qua non **11** requirement, reservation, stipulation **12** prerequisite **13** qualification

conditional
7 reliant **8** relative **9** dependent, provisory, qualified, tentative, uncertain **10** contingent, restricted **11** provisional

condolence
3 rue **4** pity, ruth **6** solace **7** comfort **8** sympathy **10** compassion **13** commiseration

condonable
7 tenable **9** excusable, tolerable **10** acceptable, defensible, pardonable **11** justifiable

condone
5 remit **6** excuse, pardon **7** forgive **8** overlook

conduce
4 lead, tend **7** redound **10** contribute

conducive
7 helpful, leading, tending **9** favorable **10** beneficial, salubrious **11** efficacious, serviceable, stimulating **12** advantageous, contributory, instrumental **13** accommodating

conduct
3 act, run **4** bear, head, lead, show **5** guide, pilot, steer, usher **6** attend, behave, charge, convey, demean, deport, direct, escort, handle, manage **7** arrange, bearing, comport, control, manners, operate, oversee **8** behavior, demeanor, handling, shepherd, transmit **9** accompany, oversight, supervise **10** administer, deportment, management **11** comportment, supervision

conductor
5 guide **6** escort, leader **7** maestro **8** motorman **10** bandleader
American: **4** Shaw (Robert) **5** Stock (Frederick), Szell (George) **6** Levine (James), Maazel (Lorin), Previn (André), Reiner (Fritz), Thomas (Theodore, Michael Tilson), Walter (Bruno) **7** Fennell (Frederick), Fiedler (Arthur), Monteux (Pierre), Ormandy (Eugene), Schwarz (Gerard), Slatkin (Leonard) **8** Damrosch (Leopold, Walter), Williams (John) **9** Bernstein (Leonard), Leinsdorf (Erich), Rodzinski (Artur), Steinberg (William), Stokowski (Leopold) **11** Kostelanetz (André), Mitropoulos (Dimitri)
Argentinian: **7** Kleiber (Carlos) **9** Barenboim (Daniel)
Australian: **7** Bonynge (Richard)
Austrian: **4** Böhm (Karl) **6** Mahler (Gustav) **7** Karajan (Herbert von) **11** Weingartner (Felix)
Belgian: **5** Ysaÿe (Eugene)
Canadian: **6** Dutoit (Charles) **9** MacMillan (Ernest)
Czech: **7** Kubelik (Jan, Rafael)
Dutch: **7** Haitink (Bernard) **10** Mengelberg (Willem)
English: **4** Wood (Henry) **5** Boult (Adrian), Davis (Colin) **6** Rattle (Simon) **7** Beecham (Thomas), Leppard (Raymond), Malcolm (George), Pinnock (Trevor), Sargent (Malcolm) **8** Goossens (Eugene), Marriner (Neville) **9** Mackerras (Charles) **10** Barbirolli (John)
Finnish: **7** Salonen (Esa-Pekka)
French: **5** Munch (Charles) **6** Boulez (Pierre), Prêtre (Georges) **7** Monteux (Pierre)
German: **4** Muck (Carl, Karl) **5** Masur (Kurt) **6** Jochum (Eugen) **7** Kleiber (Erich) **9** Klemperer (Otto), Scherchen (Hermann) **10** Sawallisch (Wolfgang) **11** Furtwängler (Wilhelm), Mendelssohn (Felix)
Greek: **11** Mitropoulos (Dimitri)
Hungarian: **5** Seidl (Anton), Solti (Georg), Szell (George) **6** Doráti (Antal), Reiner (Fritz) **7** Nikisch (Arthur), Ormandy (Eugene), Richter (Hans)
Indian: **5** Mehta (Zubin)
Italian: **4** Muti (Riccardo) **6** Abbado (Claudio) **7** Chailly (Riccardo), Giulini (Carlo Maria) **8** Cantelli (Guido), Sinopoli (Giuseppe) **9** Toscanini (Arturo)
Japanese: **5** Ozawa (Seiji)
Polish: **9** Rodzinski (Artur)
Russian: **7** Gergiev (Valery) **10** Temirkanov (Yuri) **12** Koussevitzky (Serge)
Spanish: **6** Iturbi (José)
Swiss: **8** Ansermet (Ernest)
stick: **5** baton

conduit
4 duct, main, pipe **5** canal **6** course **7** channel **8** aqueduct, penstock, pipeline **11** watercourse

coney
4 pika **5** hyrax, lapin **6** rabbit **10** butterfish

confab
4 chat, talk **6** confer, huddle, parley, powwow **7** consult **8** collogue, colloquy, dialogue **10** conference, discussion **12** conversation, deliberation

confabulate
see **confab**

confabulation
see **confab**

confection
see **candy**

confederacy
5 cabal, union **6** league **7** compact **8** alliance **9** coalition, syndicate **10** conspiracy, federation

confederate
3 reb **4** ally **5** rebel, unite **6** fellow **7** abettor, partner **9** accessory, associate, colleague, Johnny Reb **10** accomplice **11** conspirator **12** collaborator **13** coconspirator
admiral: 6 Semmes
capital: 8 Richmond
color: 4 gray
general: 3 Lee (Robert E.) **4** Hill (Ambrose), Hood (John Bell) **5** Bragg (Braxton), Ewell (Richard Stoddart), Price (Sterling), Smith (Edmund Kirby) **6** Morgan (John Hunt), Stuart (J. E. B.) **7** Forrest (Nathan Bedford), Hampton (Wade), Jackson (Thomas Jonathan "Stonewall"), Pickett (George) **8** Johnston (Albert Sidney, Joseph Eggleston) **9** Pemberton (John Clifford) **10** Beauregard (Pierre G. T.), Longstreet (James)
president: 5 Davis (Jefferson)
soldier: 9 butternut
spy: 4 Boyd (Belle)
vice-president: 8 Stephens (Alexander)

confederation
see **confederacy**

confer
4 give, meet, talk **5** allot, award, grant, speak **6** accord, advise, bestow, confab, donate, huddle, parley, powwow **7** consult, discuss, present **8** collogue, converse **10** deliberate **11** confabulate

conference
4 talk **5** forum, synod **6** caucus, league, parley, powwow **7** meeting, palaver, seminar **8** assembly, colloquy, congress **9** symposium **10** colloquium, discussion, round-robin, roundtable **11** association, convocation **12** consultation, deliberation **13** confabulation

confess
3 own **4** avow, sing **5** admit, allow, grant, let on, own up **6** reveal **7** concede, divulge, profess **8** disclose **9** come clean **11** acknowledge

confession
5 creed **6** avowal **7** peccavi **9** admission, statement **10** disclosure

confidant
8 familiar, intimate

confide
4 tell **5** trust **6** bestow, commit, reveal **7** commend, consign, entrust, whisper **8** hand over, relegate, turn over

confidence
5 faith, poise, stock, trust **6** aplomb, surety **8** credence, reliance, sureness **9** assurance, certainty, certitude **10** conviction, equanimity
game: 4 scam **5** bunco, bunko, grift, sting **7** swindle **8** flimflam

confidence man
3 gyp **5** shark **7** diddler, grifter, scammer, sharper, sharpie **8** swindler **9** charlatan, defrauder, trickster **11** bunco artist

confident
4 bold, sure **5** brash, brave, cocky **6** secure **7** assured, certain **8** cocksure, fearless, intrepid, positive, sanguine, unafraid **9** dauntless, undaunted **10** courageous, undoubtful **11** self-assured, self-reliant **13** self-assertive, self-possessed

confidential
5 close, privy **6** hushed, inside, secret **7** private **8** familiar, hush-hush, intimate **9** auricular **10** classified

configuration
4 cast, form **5** shape **6** figure, layout, makeup **7** contour, gestalt, outline, pattern **9** structure **12** conformation

confine
3 box, mew, pen **4** cage, coop, crib, jail, term **5** bound, cramp, hem in, limit **6** immure, intern, lock up, shut in, shut up **7** delimit, enclose, impound, put away **8** encircle, imprison, localize, restrict **9** constrain **11** incarcerate **12** circumscribe

confinement
7 custody, lying-in **8** childbed **9** captivity, detention, restraint **10** constraint **12** accouchement, imprisonment **13** incarceration

confines
6 bounds, limits **7** borders, compass **8** boundary, environs, purlieus **9** precincts **10** boundaries

confirm
3 fix, set **5** check, prove, vouch **6** attest, ratify, uphold, verify **7** approve, bear out, certify, concede, endorse, justify, support **8** buttress, check out, validate **9** ascertain, reinforce **10** strengthen **11** corroborate **12** authenticate, substantiate

confirmation
5 proof **7** support, witness **8** approval, evidence **9** testimony **10** validation **11** attestation, endorsement, testimonial **12** ratification, verification **13** certification, corroboration

confirmed
3 set **5** fixed, sworn **6** proven **7** chronic, settled **8** deep-dyed, definite, habitual, hardened,

ratified **10** accustomed, deep-rooted, deep-seated, entrenched, habituated, inveterate, persistent **13** bred-in-the-bone, dyed-in-the-wool

confiscate
4 grab, take **5** annex, seize, usurp **7** escheat, impound, preempt **8** arrogate **9** sequester **10** commandeer **11** appropriate, expropriate

confiture
3 jam **8** conserve, preserve **9** marmalade, preserves

conflagrant
5 afire, fiery **6** ablaze, aflame, alight **7** blazing, burning, flaming

conflagration
3 war **4** fire **5** blaze **7** inferno **8** conflict **9** holocaust

conflate
3 mix **4** fuse, join, meld, weld **5** blend, merge, mix up **6** mingle, muddle **7** combine, confuse, mistake **8** coalesce, confound **9** commingle

conflict
3 row, war **4** bout, duel, rift, vary **5** brawl, clash, fight, melee, set-to **6** battle, combat, differ, fracas, strife **7** contend, contest, discord, dispute, rivalry, warfare **8** argument, disagree, mismatch, struggle, tug-of-war, variance **9** encounter, rencontre **10** contention, engagement **11** competition

conflicting
6 at odds **7** opposed, warring **8** clashing, contrary, opposing **9** dissonant **10** contending, discordant, discrepant **11** incongruent, incongruous, inconsonant **12** antagonistic, antipathetic, incompatible, inconsistent, inharmonious **13** contradictory

confluence
6 merger **7** joining, meeting, merging **8** junction **9** concourse, gathering **11** convergence

conform
3 fit **4** jibe, obey, suit **5** adapt, agree, fit in, match, yield **6** accord, adjust, attune, comply, follow, square, submit, tailor **8** dovetail **9** acquiesce, harmonize, reconcile **10** coordinate, correspond, proportion **11** accommodate

conformable
6 fitted, suited **7** adapted, matched **8** amenable, obedient, suitable **9** agreeable, compliant, congenial, consonant **10** submissive

conformation
4 cast, form **5** shape **6** figure **7** anatomy **9** structure **10** adaptation **11** arrangement **13** configuration

conforming
3 apt **6** decent, proper, seemly **7** correct, uniform **8** becoming, decorous, suitable **9** befitting, civilized **10** compatible, consistent **11** comme il faut

conformity
6 accord **7** decorum, harmony **9** agreement, coherence, congruity, obedience, orthodoxy **10** accordance, allegiance, compliance, consonance, observance, submission **11** consistency **12** acquiescence

confound
4 damn, faze **5** befog, mix up, stump **6** baffle, puzzle, rattle, refute **7** confuse, mistake, mystify, nonplus, perplex, stupefy **8** befuddle, bewilder, disprove **9** discomfit, dumbfound, embarrass, frustrate **10** controvert, disconcert **11** misidentify

confounded
5 utter **6** blamed, cursed, cussed, damned **7** blasted, blessed, doggone, shocked **8** absolute, accursed, dismayed, infernal, outright **9** consarned, dad-blamed, execrable, out-and-out **11** dumbfounded, overwhelmed, unmitigated **13** thunderstruck

confrere
see **colleague**

confront
4 defy, face, meet **5** beard, brave, cross **6** accost, breast, oppose, take on **9** challenge, encounter

confuse
3 fog **4** blur, daze, faze **5** abash, addle, befog, cloud, dizzy, mix up, muddy, stump, upset **6** baffle, ball up, bemuse, flurry, foul up, fuddle, garble, jumble, mess up, muddle, puzzle, rattle **7** agitate, becloud, derange, disrupt, distort, flummox, fluster, mislead, mistake, mystify, nonplus, perplex, perturb, snarl up **8** bedazzle, befuddle, bewilder, confound, disorder, disquiet, distract, throw off, unsettle **9** discomfit, disorient, embarrass **10** complicate, disarrange, discompose, disconcert **11** disorganize, misidentify **12** misrepresent

confused
4 lost **5** dazed, messy, muddy, muzzy, vague **6** addled **7** at a loss, chaotic, mixed up, muddled, puzzled **9** flustered, perplexed, unsettled **10** bewildered, nonplussed, topsy-turvy **11** disoriented **12** disconcerted

confusion
3 ado, din **4** flap, mess, stew **5** babel, chaos, havoc, mix-up, snafu, snarl **6** bedlam, dither, foul-up, hubbub, huddle, jumble, lather, muddle, tumult, unease **7** anarchy, clutter, turmoil **8** disarray, disorder, shambles **9** abashment, agitation, commotion, imbroglio **10** hullabaloo, perplexity,

puzzlement, turbulence, uneasiness **11** derangement, disturbance, pandemonium **12** bewilderment **13** embarrassment

confute
4 deny **5** evert, rebut **6** defeat, negate **8** confound, disprove, puncture **10** controvert, disconfirm

congé
3 bow **5** adieu **6** good-by **7** good-bye, molding, parting, sendoff **8** farewell **9** dismissal **11** leave-taking

congeal
3 dry, gel, set **4** clot, jell **5** jelly **6** curdle, harden **7** stiffen, thicken **8** solidify **9** coagulate **10** gelatinize

congener
6 agnate **7** cognate, sibling **8** relation, relative

congenial
4 nice **6** social **7** affable, amiable, cordial, kindred, welcome **8** amicable, friendly, gracious, pleasant, pleasing, sociable, suitable **9** agreeable, congruous, consonant, favorable **10** compatible, consistent, gratifying, harmonious **11** cooperative, pleasurable, sympathetic **13** companionable

congenital
6 inborn, inbred, innate, native **7** natural **8** inherent **9** essential, ingrained, intrinsic **10** deep-seated, indigenous, indwelling

conger
3 eel

congeries
5 group **7** company **8** assembly **9** gathering **10** assemblage, collection **11** aggregation **12** congregation

congest
3 jam **4** clog, fill, plug, stop **5** block, choke, close, crowd **6** plug up **7** occlude **8** obstruct

conglobate
4 ball **6** sphere **8** ensphere **9** spherical

conglomerate
4 mass, pool **5** chain, group, mixed, trust **6** cartel, motley **7** chaebol, combine **8** keiretsu, zaibatsu **9** aggregate, syndicate **11** aggregation **12** multifarious **13** heterogeneous

conglomeration
5 hoard, trove **8** mishmash **9** aggregate **10** collection, cumulation, hodgepodge, miscellany **11** agglomerate, aggregation **12** accumulation

Congo, Democratic Republic of the
capital: **8** Kinshasa
city: **7** Kolwezi **9** Kisangani, Mbuji-Mayi **10** Lubumbashi
explorer: **7** Stanley (Henry Morton)
former name: **5** Zaire **12** Belgian Congo
lake: **4** Kivu **5** Mweru **6** Albert, Edward **10** Tanganyika
language: **6** French **7** English
monetary unit: **5** franc
neighbor: **5** Sudan **6** Angola, Rwanda, Uganda, Zambia **7** Burundi **8** Tanzania
river: **4** Uele

Congo, Republic of
capital: **11** Brazzaville
city: **11** Pointe-Noire
former name: **11** Middle Congo
language: **6** French
monetary unit: **5** franc
neighbor: **5** Gabon **6** Angola **7** Cabinda **8** Cameroon

congratulate
4 laud **6** salute **10** compliment, felicitate

congregate
4 meet **5** swarm **6** gather, muster **7** collect, convene **8** assemble, converge **9** forgather **10** foregather, rendezvous

congregation
4 mass **5** crowd, flock, group **7** meeting **8** assembly, audience **9** gathering **10** assemblage, collection **11** churchgoers **12** parishioners

congress
4 diet **5** synod **6** league **7** meeting, society **8** assembly, conclave **10** convention, parliament **11** association, Capitol Hill, legislature

congressman
5 solon **7** senator **8** delegate, lawmaker **10** legislator

congruity
9 agreement, coherence **10** conformity **11** consistency

congruous
3 apt, fit **7** fitting **9** agreeable, befitting, congenial, consonant **10** compatible, concordant, consistent, harmonious **11** appropriate, sympathetic

conifer
3 fir, yew **4** pine **5** cedar, larch **6** spruce **7** cypress, hemlock, juniper **8** softwood **9** evergreen **10** arborvitae

conjectural
7 reputed **8** putative, supposed **11** speculative, theoretical **12** hypothetical, suppositious **13** suppositional

conjecture
5 guess, infer **6** assume, theory **7** presume, suppose, surmise, suspect **8** theorize **9** inference, speculate **11** hypothesize, proposition, speculation, supposition

conjoin
3 wed **4** band, link, yoke **5** unite **6** couple **7** combine, connect **8** federate **9** affiliate, associate, cooperate **11** consolidate

conjoint
6 common, mutual, public, shared, united **7** unified **8** combined, communal **9** concerted **10** collective **11** coefficient, cooperative, intermutual

conjointly
8 mutually, together

conjugal
6 wedded **7** marital, married, nuptial, spousal **8** hymeneal **9** connubial **11** matrimonial

conjugality
7 wedlock **8** marriage **9** matrimony

conjugate
4 fuse, join, link, pair, yoke **5** yoked **6** couple, joined, linked **7** bracket, combine, conjoin, connect, coupled **9** associate, connected

conjunct
5 joint **6** common, joined, mutual, shared, united

conjunction
2 as, if, or, so **3** and, but, for, nor, yet **4** lest, once, than, then, when **5** after, since, union, until, where, which, while **6** before, either, though, unless **7** because, however, neither, whereas, whether **8** alliance, although, moreover, whenever **9** therefore **10** connection **11** affiliation, association, combination, concurrence

conjuration
4 oath **5** charm, spell, trick **7** sorcery **10** adjuration, hocus-pocus, invocation **11** abracadabra, incantation

conjure
3 beg **4** urge **6** appeal, invoke, summon **7** beseech, entreat, imagine, implore **8** contrive **9** importune **10** supplicate

conjurer
4 mage, seer **5** magus **6** Magian, wizard **7** warlock **8** magician, sorcerer **9** enchanter, trickster **11** illusionist, necromancer

conjuring
5 magic **7** sorcery **8** wizardry **10** hocus-pocus, necromancy **11** abracadabra, legerdemain, thaumaturgy

conk
3 die, hit, rap **4** belt, swat **5** croak, faint, knock, thump, whack **8** knock out

con man
see **confidence man**

connate
4 akin **6** allied, inborn, native **7** kindred, related **8** inherent **9** congenial, elemental, essential, ingrained, inherited, intrinsic **10** affiliated, congenital, indigenous, indwelling **11** consanguine

connect
3 tie, wed **4** ally, bind, join, link, yoke **5** marry, unite **6** attach, bridge, couple, fasten, relate **7** combine, conjoin **8** transfer **9** affiliate, associate, interlock

Connecticut
capital: **8** Hartford
city: **4** Avon **6** Darien **8** New Haven, Stamford **9** Greenwich, New London, Waterbury **10** Bridgeport
college, university: **4** Yale **7** Trinity **8** Wesleyan **9** Fairfield **10** Quinnipiac
nickname: **6** Nutmeg (State) **12** Constitution (State)
river: **6** Thames **10** Housatonic **11** Connecticut
state bird: **5** robin (American)
state flower: **14** mountain laurel
state tree: **8** white oak

connection
3 tie **4** bond, link **5** joint, nexus, tie-in, union **6** hookup, splice **7** joining, kinship, network **8** affinity, alliance, coupling, junction, juncture **9** coherence, communion, fastening **10** attachment, catenation, continuity **11** affiliation, association, combination, conjunction, partnership **12** relationship

connective
2 or **3** and, nor, not **4** then **6** either **7** neither **8** syndetic **11** conjunction, conjunctive

conniption
3 fit **4** bout, snit **5** furor, spasm, spate, spell, throe **6** attack, frenzy **7** seizure, tantrum **8** outburst, paroxysm **10** convulsion

connivance
8 intrigue **9** collusion **10** complicity, conspiracy

connive
4 plot, wink **5** blink **6** devise, scheme, wink at **7** blink at, collude **8** conspire, contrive, intrigue **9** machinate

connoisseur
4 buff **6** expert **7** epicure, gourmet **8** aesthete, gourmand, highbrow **9** authority, bon vivant **10** dilettante, gastronome **11** cognoscente

connotation
4 hint **7** meaning **8** overtone **9** undertone **10** intimation, suggestion **11** association, implication **13** signification

connote
4 hint, mean **5** imply, spell **6** hint at, intend **7** betoken, express, signify, suggest **8** indicate, intimate **9** insinuate

connubial
6 wedded **7** marital, married, nuptial, spousal **8** conjugal, hymeneal **11** matrimonial

connubiality
7 wedlock **8** marriage **9** matrimony **11** conjugality

conquer
4 beat, best, lick, tame, whip **5** crush **6** defeat, master, subdue **8** overcome, surmount, vanquish **9** checkmate, overpower, overthrow, overwhelm, subjugate

conquest
3 win **4** rout **7** triumph, victory **9** overthrow, seduction **11** subjugation

Conrad, Joseph
character: 3 Jim **4** Axel, Lena **5** Flora, Kurtz **6** Marlow, Verloc **7** Almayer **8** MacWhirr, Nostromo
work: 5 Youth **6** Chance **7** Lord Jim, Typhoon, Victory **8** Nostromo **11** Secret Agent (The) **13** Almayer's Folly **15** Heart of Darkness

Conroy novel
10 Beach Music **11** Water Is Wide (The) **12** Great Santini (The) **13** Prince of Tides (The) **17** Lords of Discipline (The)

consanguineous
4 akin **6** agnate **7** cognate, connate, kindred, related

conscience
5 demur, honor, qualm **6** ethics, virtue **7** decency, remorse, scruple **8** morality, scruples, superego **9** integrity **10** contrition **11** compunction

conscienceless
6 amoral **7** immoral **9** unethical **12** unprincipled, unscrupulous

conscientious
4 fair, just, true **5** exact **6** honest **7** careful, dutiful, upright **8** diligent, reliable, studious **9** honorable **10** high-minded, meticulous, principled, scrupulous **11** hard-working, painstaking, punctilious

conscious
5 alive, awake, aware **7** knowing, mindful, witting **8** sensible, sentient **9** attentive, cognizant **10** deliberate, perceptive

consciousness
4 heed, mind **6** regard **7** concern **9** alertness, awareness, knowledge **10** cognizance, perception **11** realization, recognition

conscribe
5 draft, limit **6** call up, enlist, enroll, muster **7** recruit

conscript
5 draft, elect **6** called, choose, chosen, enlist, enroll, induct, select **7** drafted, dragoon, impress, recruit, soldier **8** selected

consecrate
5 bless **6** anoint, devote, hallow, ordain, pledge **8** dedicate, sanctify

consecrated
4 holy **6** sacred **7** blessed **8** hallowed **10** sanctified
oil: 6 chrism

consecution
see **sequence**

consecutive
4 next **5** later **6** serial **7** ensuing, ordered, sequent **9** following, succedent **10** sequential, subsequent, succeeding, successive **11** progressive **12** successional

consent
3 yes **4** okay **5** agree, allow, leave, yield **6** accede, accord, assent, comply, concur, permit **7** approve, go-ahead **8** approval, sanction **9** acquiesce, agreement, allowance, subscribe **10** compliance, permission **12** acquiescence **13** authorization, understanding

consequence
4 fame, note, rank **5** issue, state **6** cachet, effect, import, moment, renown, repute, result, sequel, status, upshot, weight **7** account, conceit, fallout, outcome, stature **8** eminence, position, prestige, reaction **9** aftermath, magnitude **10** importance, reputation **11** aftereffect, weightiness **12** repercussion, significance

consequent
5 later, sound **7** ensuing, logical **8** rational **9** deduction, following, resulting

consequential
3 big **5** major **7** serious, weighty **8** egoistic, indirect, material **9** conceited, egotistic, important, momentous **10** collateral, incidental, meaningful, subsidiary **11** significant, substantial **12** considerable **13** self-important

consequently
4 ergo, thus **5** hence **9** as a result, therefore, thereupon **10** inevitably **11** accordingly

conservation
4 care **7** control **9** attention, husbandry **10** management, protection **11** safekeeping **12** guardianship, preservation

conservative
4 tory **6** proper **7** diehard, old-line **8** cautious, discreet, old-guard, orthodox, rightist, standpat **9** right-wing, temperate **10** restrained **11** circumspect, reactionary, right-winger, standpatter, traditional

conservatory
6 school **7** academy, nursery **8** hothouse **10** greenhouse **11** music school

conserve
3 can, jam **4** keep, save **5** hoard, lay up, put up, skimp, store **6** keep up **7** husband, protect, support, sustain **8** maintain, set aside, withhold **9** confiture, economize, safeguard, sweetmeat

consider
3 see **4** deem, feel, mind, muse, note, rate, view **5** fancy, judge, sense, study, think, weigh **6** credit, look at, notice, ponder, reason, reckon, regard **7** account, believe, examine, imagine, inspect, reflect, respect, suppose **8** appraise, cogitate, conclude, envisage, meditate, mull over, ruminate **9** speculate, think over **10** deliberate, excogitate, scrutinize, think about **11** contemplate

considerable
3 big **5** ample, hefty, large, major **7** notable, sizable, weighty **8** material, sensible, sizeable **9** extensive, important, momentous, plentiful **10** large-scale, meaningful **11** respectable, significant, substantial **13** consequential

considerably
3 far **4** well **5** quite **6** rather **7** notably **8** somewhat **10** noticeably **11** appreciably **13** significantly, substantially

considerate
4 kind **6** kindly, polite, tender **7** amiable, careful, patient, tactful **8** discreet, generous, obliging **9** attentive **10** chivalrous, forbearing, solicitous, thoughtful **11** circumspect, complaisant, sympathetic, warmhearted **13** compassionate

consideration
3 fee **4** heed, tact **5** cause, favor, issue, study **6** esteem, factor, motive, reason, regard **7** account, concern, payment, respect, thought **8** kindness **9** attention, awareness **10** admiration, cogitation, discussion, reflection, solicitude **11** application, forbearance, mindfulness **12** deliberation

considered
7 advised, studied, weighed **8** studious **10** deliberate, thought-out **11** intentional **12** aforethought, premeditated

consign
4 give, send, ship **5** agree, allot, award, remit, yield **6** commit, convey, devote, submit **7** address, commend, confide, deliver, entrust, forward **8** dispatch, hand over, relegate, transmit, turn over **9** surrender

consist
3 lie **4** rest **5** abide, agree, dwell, exist, fit in **6** accord, inhere, reside **7** comport, conform, consort, subsist **8** dovetail **10** correspond

consistency
7 aptness, concord, density, fitness, harmony, texture **8** evenness, firmness, likeness **9** agreement, coherence, congruity, thickness, viscosity **10** conformity, consonance, similarity **11** suitability

consistent
4 even, true **6** steady **7** regular, uniform **8** constant **9** accordant, agreeable, congenial, congruous, consonant, unfailing, unvarying **10** compatible, conforming, dependable, invariable, unchanging **11** homogeneous, sympathetic, undeviating

consistently
8 wontedly **9** regularly, routinely **10** habitually, invariably **11** customarily

console
4 calm, case **5** cheer **6** buck up, solace **7** cabinet, comfort, hearten **9** sideboard

consolidate
3 mix, set **4** fuse, join, meld, pool **5** blend, merge, unify, unite **6** firm up, secure **7** compact, fortify **8** compress, condense, federate, solidify **9** integrate **10** amalgamate, strengthen **11** concentrate

consolidation
5 union **6** merger **7** melding, merging **9** coalition **11** combination, integration, unification **12** amalgamation

consonance
6 accord **7** concord, harmony **9** agreement, congruity, resonance **10** congruence

consonant
4 akin, like **6** agnate **7** musical, similar **8** blending, harmonic, resonant **9** congruous **10** compatible, harmonious **11** conformable **13** corresponding
kind: 4 stop, surd **5** nasal, velar **6** atonic, voiced **7** lateral, palatal, spirant **8** alveolar, bilabial, unvoiced **9** fricative, voiceless

consort
3 set **4** mate, wife **5** agree, group, tally, unite **6** accord, attend, fellow, spouse, square, troupe **7** company, comport, conform, husband, partner **8** assembly, chaperon, dovetail **9** accompany, associate, companion, harmonize **10** correspond

consortium
4 bloc, club, ring **5** guild, trust, union **6** cartel, league **7** combine, society **8** alliance, congress **9** coalition, syndicate **10** federation **11** association **12** conglomerate

conspectus
5 brief **6** digest, précis, sketch, survey **7** epitome, outline, summary **8** abstract, overview, synopsis

9 reduction **10** abridgment **11** abridgement **12** condensation

conspicuous
5 clear, overt, showy **6** marked, patent, signal **7** blatant, evident, glaring, notable, obvious, pointed, salient **8** apparent, distinct, flagrant, manifest, striking **9** arresting, egregious, notorious, obtrusive, prominent **10** celebrated, noticeable, pronounced, remarkable **11** eye-catching, illustrious, outstanding **12** ostentatious

conspiracy
4 plan, plot **5** cabal **6** scheme **8** intrigue **11** machination

conspirator
7 abettor, plotter, schemer **9** accessory, intriguer **10** accomplice **11** confederate

conspire
4 plot **5** cabal **6** scheme **7** collude, connive **8** intrigue **9** machinate

constable
6 deputy, lawman, warden **7** marshal, sheriff

constancy
5 faith **6** fealty **7** loyalty, resolve **8** adhesion, devotion, fidelity, firmness **9** adherence, diligence, endurance, fortitude **10** allegiance, attachment, dedication, resolution, steadiness **11** staunchness **12** faithfulness, perseverance **13** dependability, steadfastness

constant
4 even, fast, firm, true **5** fixed, loyal **6** dogged, stable, steady, trusty **7** abiding, chronic, endless, equable, lasting, nonstop, staunch, uniform **8** enduring, faithful, habitual, resolute, unending **9** ceaseless, confirmed, continual, immovable, immutable, incessant, obstinate, perpetual, steadfast, sustained, unceasing, unfailing, unmovable, unvarying **10** changeless, consistent, continuous, dependable, inflexible, invariable, inveterate, persistent, persisting, unchanging, unwavering **11** everlasting, inalterable, unalterable, unrelenting, unremitting **12** interminable, unchangeable

Constantine
birthplace: **4** Nish
mother: **6** Helena
son: **7** Crispus
victim: **6** Fausta **7** Crispus
wife: **6** Fausta

constantly
4 ever **5** often **6** always **7** forever **9** eternally **10** frequently, invariably, repeatedly **11** incessantly, perpetually **12** continuously

constellation
5 group **7** pattern **10** assemblage, collection **11** arrangement
Altar: **3** Ara
Archer: **11** Sagittarius
Arrow: **7** Sagitta
Balance: **5** Libra
Bear, Great: **9** Ursa Major
Bear, Little: **9** Ursa Minor
Big Dipper: **9** Ursa Major
Bird of Paradise: **4** Apus
Bull: **6** Taurus
Centaur: **9** Centaurus
Chained Lady: **9** Andromeda
Chameleon: **10** Chamaeleon
Champion: **7** Perseus
Charioteer: **6** Auriga
Clock: **10** Horologium
Colt: **8** Equuleus
Crab: **6** Cancer
Crane: **4** Grus
Cross: **4** Crux
Crow: **6** Corvus
Crown: **6** Corona
Cup: **6** Crater
Dolphin: **9** Delphinus
Dove: **7** Columba
Dragon: **5** Draco
Eagle: **6** Aquila
Fishes: **6** Pisces
Fly: **5** Musca
Flying Fish: **6** Volans
Furnace: **6** Fornax
Graving Tool: **6** Caelum
Great Bear: **9** Ursa Major
Greater Dog: **10** Canis Major
Hare: **5** Lepus
Herdsman: **6** Boötes
Horned Goat: **11** Capricornus
Hunter: **5** Orion
Indian: **5** Indus
Keel: **6** Carina
Lady in the Chair: **10** Cassiopeia
Larger Bear: **9** Ursa Major
Larger Dog: **10** Canis Major
Lesser Dog: **10** Canis Minor
Lion: **3** Leo
Little Bear: **9** Ursa Minor
Little Dipper: **9** Ursa Minor
Little Fox: **9** Vulpecula
Lizard: **7** Lacerta
Lyre: **4** Lyra
Mariner's Compass: **5** Pyxis
Monarch: **7** Cepheus
Net: **9** Reticulum
Painter's Easel: **6** Pictor
Pair of Compasses: **8** Circinus
Peacock: **4** Pavo
Pump: **6** Antlia
Ram: **5** Aries
Rescuer: **7** Perseus
River Po: **8** Eridanus

Sails: 4 Vela
Scorpion: 8 Scorpius
Serpent: 7 Serpens
Serpent Holder: 9 Ophiuchus
Sextant: 7 Sextans
Shield: 6 Scutum
Smaller Bear: 9 Ursa Minor
Square: 5 Norma
Stern: 6 Puppis
Swan: 6 Cygnus
Table: 5 Mensa
Toucan: 6 Tucana
Triangle: 10 Triangulum
Twins: 6 Gemini
Unicorn: 9 Monoceros
Virgin: 5 Virgo
Water Carrier: 8 Aquarius
Water Monster: 5 Hydra
Water Snake: 6 Hydrus
Whale: 5 Cetus
Winged Horse: 7 Pegasus
Wolf: 5 Lupus

consternate
5 alarm, daunt, shake, shock **6** appall, dismay **7** horrify, unnerve **8** distress

consternation
4 fear **5** alarm, dread, panic, shock **6** dismay, fright, horror, terror **11** trepidation **12** bewilderment

constituent
4 part **5** piece, voter **6** factor, member **7** element, portion **8** division, fraction **9** component, elemental, principal **10** ingredient

constitute
4 form, make **5** enact, found, set up, start **6** create, embody, make up **7** appoint, compose **8** complete, comprise, organize **9** establish, institute, represent

constitution
3 law **4** code **5** build, canon **6** design, makeup, nature **7** charter **8** physique **9** formation, structure **11** composition **12** architecture, construction

constitutional
4 walk **6** inborn, inbred, innate, lawful **7** built-in, organic **8** inherent **9** essential, ingrained, intrinsic **10** congenital, deep-seated

Constitution State
11 Connecticut

Constitution, U.S.S.
12 Old Ironsides

constitutive
5 vital **8** cardinal **9** essential **11** fundamental **12** constructive

constrain
3 bar **4** curb, deny, jail **5** chain, check, crush, force, impel, limit, press **6** bridle, coerce, compel, enjoin, oblige, secure, squash, squish **7** confine, deprive, inhibit, refrain, squeeze **8** compress, hold back, hold down, imprison, restrain, restrict **11** incarcerate

constraint
4 bond **5** check, force **6** duress **8** coercion, pressure **9** captivity, detention, restraint **10** compulsion, diffidence, inhibition, limitation, repression **11** confinement, restriction, suppression **13** embarrassment

constrict
4 curb **5** cramp, limit, pinch, strap **6** hamper, narrow, shrink **7** confine, inhibit, squeeze, tighten **8** compress, condense, contract, restrain, strangle, stultify **9** constrain **12** circumscribe

constrictor
3 boa **5** snake **6** muscle **8** anaconda **9** sphincter, strangler

construct
4 form, make **5** build, erect, forge, frame, put up, raise, set up, shape **6** create, devise **7** build up, compile, fashion, produce **8** assemble, engineer **9** establish, fabricate **11** manufacture, put together

construction
6 design, makeup **7** edifice, shaping **8** assembly, building **9** formation **10** fashioning **11** arrangement, engineering, fabrication, manufacture **12** architecture, constitution

constructive
6 useful **7** helpful, implied, virtual **8** implicit, positive, valuable **9** practical **10** beneficial

construe
5 educe, gloss, parse **6** induct **7** analyze, explain, expound **9** explicate, interpret **10** paraphrase, understand

consuetude
5 habit, usage **6** custom, manner **8** practice **10** convention

consult
3 ask **6** advise, confer, huddle, parley **7** examine, refer to **8** collogue, consider **11** confabulate

consume
3 eat, use **4** down, gulp, ruin **5** drain, drink, eat up, gorge, spend, use up, waste **6** absorb, devour, expend, finish, ingest, obsess, take up **7** deplete, destroy, engross, exhaust, put away, put down, swallow **8** squander **9** dissipate, finish off, polish off **10** annihilate, extinguish, monopolize, run through

consumer
4 user **5** buyer **6** client **7** shopper, end user **8** customer **9** purchaser

consumer advocate
5 Nader (Ralph)

consuming
6 ardent **7** fervent, intense **8** gripping, riveting **9** absorbing **10** engrossing **11** enthralling **12** monopolizing

consummate
3 end **4** ripe **5** close, crown, ideal, utter **6** finish, superb, wind up, wrap up **7** achieve, perfect, supreme **8** absolute, complete, conclude, finished, flawless, peerless, ultimate **9** faultless, matchless, perfected, virtuosic **10** accomplish, impeccable, inimitable **11** superlative **12** accomplished **13** thoroughgoing

consumption
2 TB **3** use **5** decay, waste **6** intake **7** wasting **8** phthisis **9** depletion, ingestion **10** absorption **11** dissipation **12** tuberculosis

contact
4 meet **5** reach, touch **8** tangency, touching **9** closeness, communion, proximity **10** connection, contiguity **11** association, contingence **13** communication

contagion
3 pox **4** bane, meme **5** taint, venom, virus **6** miasma, plague, poison **7** disease, scourge **8** epidemic **9** infection, pollution **10** corruption, pestilence **13** contamination

contagious
6 catchy **8** catching, epidemic **9** spreading **10** infectious **12** communicable, pestilential **13** transmissible, transmittable

contain
4 hold, keep **5** check, house **6** embody, take in **7** collect, control, embrace, enclose, include, receive, repress, subsume **8** comprise, restrain **9** encompass **10** comprehend **11** accommodate

container
3 bag, bin, box, can, cup, jar, keg, mug, pod, pot, tin, tub, urn, vat **4** cage, case, cask, drum, etui, ewer, pail, sack, silo, tank, vase, vial, well **5** chest, crate, cruet, flask, glass, gourd, phial, pouch **6** basket, bottle, carafe, carton, casket, coffin, cooler, goblet, hamper, hatbox, holder, inkpot, shaker **7** bandbox, capsule, chalice, inkwell, package, pitcher, thermos **8** canister, catchall, decanter, envelope, hogshead, jerrican, puncheon **10** receptacle
liturgical: **3** pyx **7** chalice **8** ciborium

contaminate
4 foul, soil **5** dirty, spoil, stain, sully, taint **6** befoul, debase, defile, infect, injure, poison **7** corrupt, deprave, pervert, pollute, profane, tarnish, vitiate **9** desecrate **10** adulterate

conte
4 tale **5** story **9** narrative

contemn
4 snub **5** abhor, scorn, spurn **6** deride **7** deplore, despise, disdain **8** ridicule **10** look down on

contemplate
3 eye **4** mull, muse, view **5** study, think, weigh **6** behold, debate, gaze at, intend, look at, ponder, regard **7** examine, inspect, propose, reflect **8** consider, gaze upon, look upon, meditate, mull over, ruminate, think out **9** think over **10** deliberate, excogitate, scrutinize

contemplation
5 study **6** musing **7** thought **8** thinking **9** intention, pondering **10** cogitation, meditation, reflection, rumination **11** cerebration, expectation, speculation **12** deliberation **13** consideration

contemplative
6 musing **7** pensive **10** cogitative, meditative, reflecting, reflective, ruminative, thoughtful **11** speculative **13** introspective

contemporary
3 new **6** coeval, extant, modern, recent **7** current, present, topical **8** existent, existing, up-to-date **9** au courant **10** coexistent, coexisting, coincident, concurrent, present-day, synchronic **11** synchronous **12** simultaneous

contempt
5 scorn, shame **7** despite, disdain, mockery **8** aversion, defiance, disfavor, disgrace, dishonor, distaste, ignominy **9** antipathy, discredit, disesteem, disrepute **10** disrespect, opprobrium, repugnance **12** disobedience, stubbornness

contemptible
3 low **4** base, mean, poor, vile **5** cheap, sorry **6** abject, odious, paltry, scummy, scurvy, shabby, sordid **7** hateful, ignoble, pitiful, squalid **8** inferior, pitiable, shameful, unworthy, wretched **9** abhorrent, loathsome **10** despicable, detestable, disgusting **11** ignominious **12** dishonorable

contemptuous
7 haughty **8** arrogant, derisive, scornful **10** disdainful **12** supercilious **13** condescending, disrespectful

contend
3 vie, war **4** aver, avow, cope, face, urge **5** argue, brawl, claim, fight **6** affirm, allege, assert, battle, charge, combat, debate, defend, insist, oppose, report, strive **7** compete, contest **8** confront, maintain, struggle **9** encounter, withstand

contender
5 match, rival **6** player **8** opponent **9** adversary, candidate, combatant **10** antagonist, challenger, competitor, contestant

___ contendere
4 nolo

content
4 cozy, gist 5 happy 6 at ease, serene 7 appease, gratify, meaning, placate, satisfy 9 gratified, satisfied, substance 11 comfortable 12 significance

contention
3 war 4 beef, feud 6 combat, rumpus, strife, thesis 7 discord, dispute, dissent, quarrel, rivalry, wrangle 8 argument, conflict, disunity, squabble 10 difference, dissension, dissidence 11 altercation, competition, controversy
Scottish: 5 sturt

contentious
5 fiery 7 carping, froward, peppery, scrappy, warlike 8 captious, caviling, contrary, militant, perverse 9 bellicose, combative, hotheaded, litigious, polemical, truculent 10 pugnacious 11 belligerent, quarrelsome 12 disputatious, faultfinding 13 argumentative, controversial

conterminous
10 coincident 11 coextensive

contest
3 vie 4 bout, duel, feud, fray, game, meet, race, tilt 5 clash, fight, match, repel, rival, trial 6 battle, combat, debate, oppose, resist, strife, strive 7 compete, dispute, rivalry, warfare 8 argument, conflict, endeavor, skirmish, struggle, tug-of-war 9 challenge, encounter, rencontre 10 engagement, tournament 11 competition

contestant
5 rival 7 also-ran, entrant, opposer, wannabe 8 opponent 9 adversary, contender 10 challenger, competitor

contiguity
9 adjacency, immediacy, proximity 11 propinquity

contiguous
4 next 8 abutting, adjacent, touching 9 adjoining, bordering 10 juxtaposed

continence
6 purity, virtue 8 chastity, sobriety 9 austerity 10 abnegation, abstinence, asceticism, chasteness, moderation, temperance 11 forbearance 12 renunciation 13 self-restraint

continent
4 Asia, mass 5 sober 6 Africa, chaste, Europe 8 celibate, mainland 9 abstinent, Australia, temperate 10 abstemious, Antarctica, restrained 11 abstentious 12 North America, South America
lost: 8 Atlantis

contingence
5 touch 7 contact 8 tangency, touching

contingency
4 pass 5 event, pinch 6 chance, crisis 8 exigency, juncture, occasion 9 emergency 10 likelihood 11 opportunity, possibility, probability, uncertainty

contingent
3 odd 4 band 5 group, party, troop 6 casual, chance, likely 7 reliant 8 possible, probable, relative 9 dependent, empirical, entourage, uncertain 10 accidental, delegation, deputation, detachment, fortuitous, incidental, unforeseen 11 conditional 13 unanticipated, unforeseeable, unpredictable

continual
6 steady 7 abiding, endless, nonstop, regular, running 8 constant, enduring, timeless, unbroken, unending 9 ceaseless, incessant, perpetual, perennial, recurrent, recurring, unceasing, unfailing, unvarying 10 persistent, persisting, relentless, unchanging, unflagging 11 everlasting, unremitting 12 interminable 13 uninterrupted

continually
4 ever 5 on end 6 always 7 forever 8 steadily, together 9 endlessly 10 constantly 11 incessantly, night and day 12 interminably, persistently, relentlessly, successively 13 consecutively

continuance
3 run 4 stay 5 delay 6 sequel 8 duration, survival 9 longevity 10 permanence 11 adjournment, persistence 12 postponement, prolongation

continuation
3 run 4 coda 6 sequel 8 appendix, duration, epilogue 9 endurance, extension 10 resumption 11 persistence, protraction 12 prolongation

continue
4 go on, last, stay 5 abide, renew, run on, segue 6 endure, hang in, keep at, keep on, keep up, pick up, push on, remain, reopen, resume, retain, take up 7 carry on, persist, press on, proceed, prolong, restart, survive 8 maintain, postpone 9 carry over, persevere 10 recommence

continuing
5 fixed 6 steady 7 abiding, chronic, durable, eternal, lasting, ongoing 8 constant, enduring, lifelong, stubborn 9 long-lived, obstinate, perennial, prolonged, steadfast, tenacious, unabating 10 inveterate, persistent, persisting 11 long-lasting

continuity
4 flow 6 script 8 duration, scenario, sequence 9 endurance 11 persistence, progression

continuous
see **continual**

continuously
see **continually**

contort
4 knot, warp **5** twist, wring **6** deform, wrench, writhe **7** distort, grimace, torture **9** convolute, corkscrew, disfigure

contortionist
7 acrobat

contour
4 form, line **5** curve, lines, shape **6** figure **7** outline, pattern, profile **9** lineament, lineation **10** silhouette **11** delineation

contra
6 facing, toward **7** against, counter, reverse, vis-à-vis **8** converse, fronting, opposite **10** conversely

contraband
3 hot **5** taboo **6** banned **7** bootleg, illegal, illicit, smuggle **8** unlawful **9** forbidden **10** prohibited, proscribed **11** black market, bootlegging, trafficking

contract
4 bond, hire, pact, sink **5** catch, incur, lease **6** engage, induce, lessen, reduce, shrink, treaty, weaken **7** abridge, acquire, afflict, bargain, decline, dwindle, shorten, shrivel **8** compress, condense, covenant, decrease, diminish **9** agreement, constrict, succumb to **11** concentrate, transaction **12** come down with
part: **6** clause **7** article, proviso

contraction
3 he'd, he's, I'll, it's, I've, tic **4** ain't, can't, don't, flex, he'll, isn't, let's, she'd, she's, won't, you'd **5** aren't, cramp, didn't, hadn't, hasn't, she'll, spasm, they'd, wasn't, you'll, you're, you've **6** haven't, mustn't, needn't, they'll, they've, weren't **7** couldn't, elision, mightn't, wouldn't **8** shouldn't **9** reduction, shrinkage **10** abridgment **11** abridgement **12** abbreviation
heart's: **7** systole
poetic: **3** e'en, e'er, o'er, 'tis **4** ne'er, 'twas **5** 'twere, 'twill

contradict
4 deny **5** belie, cross, rebut **6** impugn, negate, refute, take on **7** confute, dispute, gainsay **8** negative, traverse **9** challenge, disaffirm

contradiction
6 denial **7** paradox **8** antinomy, negation, rebuttal, variance **9** disparity **10** gainsaying, opposition, refutation **11** discrepancy, incongruity **12** disagreement, protestation **13** inconsistency

contradictory
7 counter, reverse **8** contrary, converse, negating, opposite **9** antipodal **10** antipodean, antithesis, nullifying **12** antithetical

contraption
3 rig **5** gizmo **6** device, doodad, gadget **7** machine **9** apparatus, doohickey **11** contrivance

contrariety
10 antagonism, antithesis, opposition, perversity, unlikeness

contrariwise
9 vice versa **10** conversely, oppositely

contrary
5 balky **6** averse, ornery, unruly **7** adverse, counter, froward, reverse, wayward **8** converse, opposite, perverse, stubborn **9** antipodal, diametric, dissident, obstinate, vice versa **10** conversely, discordant, headstrong, oppositely, rebellious, refractory **11** conflicting, intractable, wrongheaded **12** antagonistic, antipathetic, antithetical, contumacious, cross-grained, recalcitrant
prefix: **7** counter

contrast
6 differ **7** collate, compare, diverge **8** conflict, disagree **9** disparity **10** comparison, difference, divergence **11** distinction, distinguish

contravene
4 defy, deny **5** break, cross, fight **6** abjure, breach, disown, impugn, negate, offend, oppose, reject **7** disobey, gainsay, violate **8** disclaim, infringe, renege on **9** disaffirm, go against, repudiate **10** contradict, transgress

contravention
6 breach **7** offense **8** trespass **9** violation **10** infraction **12** infringement **13** nonobservance, transgression

contretemps
3 row **4** slip, tiff **5** clash, run-in **6** dustup, mishap, slip-up **7** dispute, quarrel **8** argument **9** mischance **10** falling-out, misfortune

contribute
3 add **4** give, help, tend **5** grant **6** chip in, donate, kick in, submit, supply **7** conduce, pitch in, redound **9** subscribe **11** come through

contribution
4 alms, gift **5** input, share, tithe **7** charity, payment, present **8** donation, offering **11** benefaction, beneficence

contributory
8 adjuvant **9** accessory, ancillary, auxiliary **10** collateral, subsidiary, supporting **11** appurtenant, subservient

contrite
5 sorry **8** penitent **9** regretful, repentant **10** apologetic, remorseful **11** penitential

contrition
3 rue **4** ruth **6** regret **7** penance, remorse **9** penitence **10** repentance **11** compunction **12** self-reproach

contrivance
4 ruse **6** device, gadget **7** gimmick **8** artifice

9 apparatus, expedient, invention, stratagem **10** brainchild **11** contraption

contrive
3 rig **4** fake, make, move, plan, plot **5** frame, hatch **6** cook up, devise, invent, make up, manage, scheme, vamp up, wangle **7** arrange, concoct, connive, develop, dream up, fashion, project, work out **8** cogitate, conspire, engineer, intrigue **9** construct, elaborate, fabricate, formulate, machinate

contrived
5 hokey **6** forced **7** labored **8** strained **9** concocted, insincere **10** artificial, engineered, fabricated, factitious

control
3 run **4** curb, rein, rule, sway **5** guide, power, steer **6** bridle, direct, govern, handle, manage, master, rein in, subdue **7** command, conduct, mastery, oversee, repress, reserve **8** dominate, dominion, regulate, restrain **9** authority, direction, restraint, supervise, supremacy **10** discipline, domination, management **11** supervision **12** jurisdiction

controlled
8 discreet, reserved **9** temperate **10** restrained

controversial
5 risky **6** touchy **7** awkward, charged, eristic **8** delicate, disputed, ticklish **9** explosive, litigious, polemical **11** contentious, problematic **12** disputatious **13** argumentative

controversy
3 row **5** clash **6** debate, rumpus, strife **7** dispute, quarrel, wrangle **8** argument, squabble **10** contention, falling-out **11** altercation, disputation, embroilment

controvert
4 deny **5** rebut **6** debate, oppose, oppugn, refute **7** confute, counter, dispute, gainsay **8** disprove, question **9** challenge, repudiate

contumacious
7 froward **8** contrary, insolent, mutinous, obdurate, perverse **9** obstinate **10** rebellious, refractory **11** disobedient, intractable **12** recalcitrant **13** insubordinate

contumacy
8 contempt, defiance **9** insolence **10** perversity **12** stubbornness **13** recalcitrance

contumelious
7 abusive **8** derisive, insolent, scornful **9** insulting, truculent **10** disdainful, scurrilous **11** opprobrious **12** vituperative

contumely
5 abuse **6** insult **7** affront, mockery, obloquy **8** contempt, ridicule, sneering **9** aspersion, invective **10** scurrility **12** vituperation

contuse
6 batter, bruise, injure **7** blacken

conundrum
5 poser **6** enigma, puzzle, riddle **7** baffler, mystery, problem, puzzler, stumper **10** puzzlement **13** Chinese puzzle

convalesce
4 heal, mend **7** improve, recover **10** recuperate

convene
4 call, meet **6** call in, gather, muster, summon **7** convoke, summons **8** assemble **9** forgather **10** congregate **12** come together

convenience
4 ease **7** amenity, benefit, comfort, leisure **8** facility **9** handiness **10** assistance **13** accessibility

convenient
3 fit **4** near **5** close, handy, ready **6** at hand, nearby, proper, useful **7** close by, helpful **8** suitable **9** available, immediate, opportune **10** accessible **11** appropriate, comfortable **12** advantageous

convent
5 abbey **6** priory **7** nunnery **8** cloister **9** monastery, sanctuary

convention
3 law **4** bond, code, pact, rule **5** canon, usage **6** accord, custom, treaty **7** compact, meeting, precept **8** assembly, congress, contract, covenant, practice, protocol **9** agreement, concordat, formality, gathering, propriety, tradition **11** convocation

conventional
5 trite, usual **6** formal, normal, proper, seemly, solemn, square **7** correct, regular, routine, typical **8** everyday, habitual, moderate, ordinary, orthodox, standard, straight **9** bourgeois, customary **10** button-down, conforming, prevailing, restrained, unoriginal **11** commonplace, traditional **12** conservative

conventionalize
5 adapt **7** conform **9** normalize

converge
4 join, meet **5** focus, merge, unite **11** concentrate **12** come together

conversant
8 familiar **9** au courant **10** acquainted **11** experienced

conversation
4 chat, talk **6** confab, debate, parley **7** palaver, talking **8** causerie, colloquy, dialogue, duologue, exchange, repartee **9** discourse, tête-à-tête **10** discussion **13** confabulation

conversation piece
5 curio **6** oddity **9** curiosity

converse
3 gab **4** chat, chin, talk **5** speak, visit **6** confer, contra, parley **7** chatter, counter, reverse **8** antipode, contrary, opposite **9** antipodal, diametric **10** antithesis **12** antithetical **13** contradictory

conversely
9 vice versa **10** oppositely **12** contrariwise

conversion
5 shift **6** change, switch **7** novelty, rebirth, turning **8** metanoia, mutation, reversal **9** about-face **10** alteration, changeover **11** permutation **12** modification, regeneration **13** metamorphosis, transmutation

convert
4 sway **5** alter **6** change, modify, redeem, reform, switch **7** commute, remodel **8** persuade, renovate **9** proselyte, transform, translate, transmute, transpose **11** transfigure **12** metamorphose, transmogrify
Christian: **10** catechumen

convex
5 bowed, toric **6** arched, curved **7** bulging, curving, gibbous, rounded

convexity
4 arch **6** camber

convey
3 lug **4** bear, cart, cede, deed, pack, send, tell, tote **5** bring, carry, ferry **6** assign, impart, pass on **7** channel, conduct, consign, deliver, express, project **8** make over, sign over, transfer, transmit **9** transport **11** communicate

conveyance
3 car **4** auto, cart, deed, sled **5** coach, sedan, stage, title, wagon **7** charter, trailer, transit, vehicle **8** carriage, carrying **9** transport **10** automobile **12** transporting
public: **3** bus, cab **4** taxi, tram **5** plane, train **6** subway **7** trolley **8** airplane, monorail, railroad, rickshaw **9** streetcar **10** jinricksha, jinrikisha

convict
5 felon, lifer **6** inmate, send up **7** condemn, put away **8** criminal, jailbird, prisoner, sentence, yardbird **10** find guilty

conviction
4 view **5** creed, faith **6** belief, surety **7** opinion **8** doctrine, sentence, sureness **9** assurance, certainty, certitude, sentiment **10** confidence, persuasion **12** condemnation

convince
6 assure, induce, prompt **7** satisfy, win over **8** persuade, talk into **9** influence, prevail on **11** bring around, prevail upon

convincing
5 solid, sound, valid **6** cogent **8** credible, faithful **9** plausible **10** believable, conclusive, persuasive, satisfying **11** trustworthy

convivial
3 gay **5** jolly, merry **6** hearty, jocund, jovial, lively, social **7** festive **8** mirthful, sociable **9** fun-loving, vivacious **10** gregarious **13** companionable

convocation
5 synod **7** council, meeting **8** assembly, conclave **9** gathering **10** assemblage **12** congregation

convoke
4 call **6** gather, invite, muster, summon **7** collect, convene **8** assemble **12** call together

convoluted
6 coiled **7** complex, tangled, winding **8** involved, tortuous **9** intricate **10** circuitous **11** anfractuous, complicated **12** labyrinthine

convoy
6 attend, escort **7** conduct **9** accompany

convulse
4 rock **5** shake **7** agitate, concuss **8** tetanize

convulsion
3 fit **5** spasm **6** attack, tumult, uproar **7** quaking, rocking, seizure, shaking **8** disaster, paroxysm, upheaval **9** commotion, trembling

cook
3 fix, fry **4** bake, boil, chef, heat, melt, stew **5** broil, grill, poach, roast, sauté, steam **6** braise, doctor, simmer **7** falsify, parboil, prepare, swelter

cookbook
abbreviation: **3** tsp **4** tbsp
term: **3** cup, fry, mix **4** bake, beat, boil, chop, pare, peel, roux, sift, stew, stir, toss, whip, zest **5** baste, blend, broil, cream, glaze, grate, grind, knead, mince, pinch, poach, roast, sauté, scald, steam, stock **6** blanch, braise, fillet, season, simmer **7** al dente, deglaze, parboil **8** dissolve, emulsify, julienne, marinate, meringue **10** caramelize

cooked
4 done, sham **5** bogus, faked, phony **6** made-up **7** altered **8** doctored, spurious **10** fictitious

cookery
7 cuisine
expert: **3** Ray (Rachael), Yan (Martin) **4** Chen (Joyce), Kerr (Graham), Puck (Wolfgang), Root (Waverley) **5** Beard (James), Child (Julia), David (Elizabeth), Hines (Duncan), Smith (Jeff) **6** Bocuse (Paul), Carême (Marie-Antoine), Farmer (Fannie), Fisher (M. F. K.), Franey (Pierre), Waters (Alice) **7** Crocker (Betty), Stewart (Martha) **8** Bourdain (Anthony), Rombauer (Irma) **9** Claiborne (Craig), Escoffier (Auguste), Prudhomme (Paul)

cookie
4 Oreo, snap **5** wafer **7** biscuit, brownie **10** gingersnap

cooking
appliance: **4** oven **5** mixer, range, stove **7** blender, toaster **9** microwave **10** rotisserie
implement: **3** cup, pan, pot, wok **4** olla **5** ladle, sieve, spoon, whisk **6** grater, masher, sifter, tureen **7** griddle, skillet, spatula, steamer **8** colander, teaspoon **9** eggbeater, frying pan **10** rolling pin, tablespoon **12** measuring cup
measure: **3** cup, tsp **4** tbsp **8** teaspoon **10** tablespoon
room: **6** galley **7** kitchen

Cook Islands
capital: **6** Avarua
dependency of: **10** New Zealand
island: **9** Rarotonga

cool
3 hep, hip, icy, rad **4** calm, cold, phat **5** abate, aloof, chill, funky, gelid, nippy **6** arctic, chilly, frigid, frosty, with-it **7** assured, compose, control, decline, distant, dwindle, repress, subside **8** composed, decrease, detached, diminish, reserved, suppress **9** collected, confident, impassive, unruffled **10** nonchalant, phlegmatic, unsociable **11** indifferent, standoffish, unflappable **13** dispassionate, imperturbable, self-possessed

cooler
3 fan, jug, pen **4** brig, coop, jail **5** clink, pokey **6** fridge, icebox, lockup, prison **7** freezer, slammer **9** calaboose **11** refrigerant **12** refrigerator

cooling device
3 fan **6** fridge, icebox **7** freezer **12** refrigerator

coolness
5 chill, poise **6** aplomb, phlegm **7** reserve **9** composure, frigidity, sangfroid **10** dispassion, equanimity **11** nonchalance, self-control

coop
3 hem, jug, mew, pen **4** brig, cage, jail **5** cramp, fence, pokey **6** cooler, corral, lockup, prison, shut in **7** close in, confine, enclose, slammer **9** calaboose, enclosure

cooperate
5 agree, unite **6** concur, league **7** combine, conjoin, pitch in **8** coincide, conspire **11** collaborate, participate **12** work together

cooperation
8 alliance, teamwork **13** confederation

cooperative
5 joint **6** common, mutual, shared **8** coactive, conjoint, obliging **9** collegial, concerted **10** collective, synergetic **11** coordinated **13** accommodating, collaborative, uncompetitive
craft society: **5** artel

Cooper hero
7 Hawkeye **10** Deerslayer, Pathfinder **11** Natty Bumppo

coordinate
4 mate, mesh **5** align, equal, match, order **6** adjust, relate **7** coequal, conform **8** organize, parallel **9** companion, correlate, harmonize, integrate, reconcile **10** proportion, reciprocal **11** accommodate, correlative, counterpart
system: **9** Cartesian

coot
4 bird, fogy **5** fogey **6** codger, dotard, duffer, fellow, oddity, scoter, weirdo **7** oddball **9** character, eccentric

cootie
5 louse **9** body louse

cop
3 nab **4** lift, take **5** adopt, catch, filch, pinch, steal, swipe **6** pilfer **7** capture, officer **8** bluecoat **9** patrolman, policeman

copacetic
3 A-OK **4** fine, jake, okay **5** dandy, great, nifty **8** all right **9** excellent **12** satisfactory

cope
4 cape, hack **5** cloak, cover, get by, match, vault **6** canopy, endure, make do, manage, mantle **7** carry on, survive **8** vestment

copestone
5 crown

copious
4 lush, rich **5** ample **6** lavish, plenty **7** liberal, profuse, replete **8** abundant, generous **9** abounding, bounteous, bountiful, exuberant, luxuriant, plenteous, plentiful

Copland work
5 Rodeo **11** Billy the Kid **17** Appalachian Spring

cop-out
5 dodge **6** excuse **7** evasion, pretext, retreat

copper
4 cent, coin **5** metal, penny, token **9** butterfly, policeman
coating: **6** patina
item: **4** cent **5** penny **6** kettle
sulfate: **7** vitriol **9** bluestone **11** blue vitriol
symbol: **2** Cu

copperhead
5 snake, viper **8** pit viper

coppice
4 bosk, wood **5** copse, grove, woods **6** bosque, forest, growth **7** thicket **9** brushwood, underwood

copse
see **coppice**

Copt
8 Egyptian

copula
4 bond, link **5** joint, union **7** coupler

copy
3 ape **4** echo, fake, mock, sham **5** clone, ditto, forge, mimic, model, repro **6** carbon, parrot, repeat **7** emulate, forgery, imitate, replica, takeoff **8** knockoff, likeness, simulate **9** duplicate, facsimile, imitation, replicate, reproduce **10** impression, simulacrum, simulation, transcribe, transcript **11** counterfeit, counterpart, reduplicate, replication **12** reproduction

copycat
3 ape **4** aper **5** mimic **6** parrot **8** imitator

copyist
5 clerk **6** scribe **8** imitator **9** engrosser **10** plagiarist **11** transcriber

copyread
4 edit

coquet
3 toy **4** fool, vamp **5** dally, flirt, tease **6** trifle

coquette
4 vamp **5** flirt, tease

coquettish
3 coy **6** fickle **9** frivolous, kittenish **11** flirtatious

coral
3 red **4** pink, rosy **5** polyp **9** limestone

coral reef
3 cay, key **5** atoll
off Australia: **5** Wreck
world's largest: **12** Great Barrier

cord
3 tie **4** band, lace, pile, rope, whip, yarn **5** cable, nerve, stack **6** strand, string, tendon
twisted: **7** torsade

cordage
4 rope **5** ropes **7** rigging
fiber: **4** bast, hemp, jute, pita **5** sisal

Corday's victim
5 Marat (Jean-Paul)

Cordelia
father: **4** Lear
sister: **5** Regan **7** Goneril

cordial
4 warm **6** genial, hearty, jovial, tender **7** affable, liqueur, sincere **8** cheerful, friendly, gracious, sociable **9** congenial, convivial, heartfelt **10** hospitable **11** sympathetic, warmhearted **12** wholehearted

cordiality
6 warmth **7** amenity **9** geniality **10** amiability **12** agreeability, friendliness

cordon
4 lace, line, ring **5** braid **6** circle, ribbon **7** barrier **8** espalier
bleu: **4** chef, cook **6** ribbon **10** blue ribbon, decoration, master chef

core
3 hub, nub **4** base, crux, gist, meat, pith, root **5** basis, focus, heart, midst **6** center, depths, kernel, middle, upshot **7** essence, nucleus **8** interior, midpoint **9** substance **10** foundation

corium
5 cutis **6** dermis

cork
4 bark, plug, seal, stop **5** float **6** bobber **7** stopper, stopple

corker
4 lulu **5** beaut, dandy, dilly, doozy **6** doozie, killer **8** jim-dandy, knockout **9** humdinger **11** crackerjack **12** lollapalooza

corkscrew
4 coil, wind **5** helix, twist **6** spiral

cormorant
4 bird, shag **7** glutton

corn
5 grain, maize **6** hominy **9** granulate
bread: **4** pone **7** bannock, hoecake
Indian: **5** maize **6** mealie
kind: **3** pop **5** flint, flour, sweet **6** Indian
pest: **5** borer
piece: **3** cob, ear **5** spike **6** kernel, nubbin

Corncracker State
8 Kentucky

corner
3 box, fix, jam, nab **4** hole, nook, trap, tree **5** angle, catch, coign, niche, seize **6** collar, cranny, dogleg, pickle, plight, recess, scrape **7** capture, dilemma, impasse, trouble **8** bottle up, monopoly **10** bring to bay **11** predicament **12** intersection
of eye: **7** canthus

cornerstone
4 base **5** basis **7** support **8** rudiment **10** foundation, groundwork

cornet
4 cone, horn **7** officer, trumpet **10** instrument

Cornhusker State
8 Nebraska

cornice
3 cap **4** band, eave **5** crown **7** molding

cornmeal
4 masa, mush, samp **5** grits **6** hominy **7** hoecake
mush: **7** polenta

cornucopia
4 cone, horn **6** bounty, plenty, wealth **9** abundance, profusion **12** horn of plenty

Cornwallis, Charles
adversary: **6** Greene (Nathanael)
surrender site: **8** Yorktown

corny
5 banal, sappy, stale, trite **6** old hat **7** clichéd, mawkish **8** shopworn **9** hackneyed, schmaltzy **11** sentimental, stereotyped

corollary
6 effect, result, sequel, upshot **8** parallel, sequence **9** resulting **10** associated, end product, equivalent **11** aftereffect, consequence
logical: **9** inference

corona
4 aura, glow, halo **5** cigar, crown, glory **6** circle, nimbus **7** aureola, aureole

coroner
8 examiner

coronet
5 crown, tiara **6** anadem, circle, diadem, wreath **7** chaplet, circlet, garland **8** headband

Coronis
form: **4** crow
son: **9** Asclepius **11** Aesculapius

corporal
3 NCO **6** bodily, carnal **7** fleshly, somatic **8** physical

corporate
7 unified **8** combined **9** aggregate

corporeal
6 bodily, carnal, mortal **7** fleshly, somatic **8** material, physical, tangible **9** objective **10** phenomenal **11** substantial

corposant
11 St. Elmo's fire

corps
4 band, body **5** group, party, troop **6** outfit, troupe **7** company

corpse
4 body **5** bones, stiff **7** cadaver, carcass, carrion, remains
combining form: **4** necr **5** necro

corpselike
4 ashy, dead **5** ashen, gaunt **6** wasted **7** deathly, ghastly, macabre **8** lifeless, skeletal **10** cadaverous

corpulence
7 fatness, obesity **9** adiposity, rotundity **10** fleshiness, overweight, portliness

corpulent
3 fat **5** bulky, gross, heavy, obese, plump, stout **6** fleshy, portly, rotund **7** porcine, weighty **9** overblown **10** overweight

corpus
4 body, bulk, core, mass **6** oeuvre **9** principal, substance **10** collection **11** compilation

corpuscle
4 cell **8** hemocyte, monocyte **9** blood cell, leukocyte **10** lymphocyte **11** erythrocyte, granulocyte

corral
3 mew, pen **5** fence **6** gather, shut in **7** close in, collect, confine, enclose, round up **8** surround **9** enclosure

correct
3 fit, fix **4** edit, just, mend, true **5** amend, emend, exact, right **6** adjust, dead on, decent, proper, punish, reform, remedy, repair, revise, seemly, spot on **7** chasten, fitting, improve, perfect, precise, rectify, redress **8** accurate, becoming, chastise, decorous, flawless, set right **9** castigate, faultless **10** conforming, discipline, impeccable, legitimate, meticulous, scrupulous **11** appropriate, comme il faut, punctilious **12** conventional
combining form: **4** orth **5** ortho

correction
3 rod **6** rebuke **7** reproof **8** revision **9** amendment **10** adjustment, discipline, emendation, punishment **11** castigation

corrective
4 cure **6** remedy **8** antidote, punitive, remedial **10** beneficial **11** counterstep, restorative **12** counteragent **13** counteractive

correctness
7 decorum **8** accuracy, fidelity **9** precision, propriety **10** exactitude

correlate
5 match **6** analog **7** pendant **8** analogue, coincide, dovetail, parallel **9** harmonize **10** complement, correspond **11** counterpart

correlative
2 if, or **3** and, nor **4** both, then **6** either **7** neither, related **10** complement, reciprocal **11** counterpart **13** complementary, corresponding

correspond
4 jibe **5** agree, equal, match, write **6** accord, concur **7** comport, conform **8** dovetail **9** harmonize **11** communicate

correspondence
4 mail **7** analogy, letters **8** symmetry **9** agreement, congruity **10** conformity, similarity **11** consistency, correlation
mathematical: **7** mapping **8** function

correspondent
5 match **6** analog, pen pal, writer **7** fitting **8** analogue, parallel, reporter, suitable **9** correlate **10** conforming, journalist **11** commentator, contributor, counterpart

corresponding
4 akin, like **5** alike **6** agnate **7** related, similar

8 matching, parallel 9 analogous, consonant 10 comparable 11 correlative

correspondingly
4 also 7 equally 8 likewise 9 similarly 11 analogously

corrida
9 bullfight
shout: 3 olé

corridor
4 hall, lane, path 5 aisle, route, strip 6 artery, avenue 7 hallway, passage 10 passageway

corroborate
5 prove 6 uphold, verify 7 approve, bear out, certify, confirm, endorse, justify, support 8 document, validate 9 vindicate 12 authenticate, substantiate

corroborative
9 ancillary, auxiliary 10 collateral, supporting, supportive 12 confirmatory

corrode
4 rust 7 eat away, eat into, oxidize 8 wear away 9 undermine

corrosive
4 acid 5 acerb 6 biting 7 acerbic, caustic, cutting 9 sarcastic

corrosiveness
7 sarcasm 8 acerbity

corrugation
4 fold, ruck 5 plica, ridge 6 crease, furrow, groove 7 crinkle, wrinkle

corrupt
3 rot 5 bribe, decay, spoil, stain, taint, venal 6 befoul, debase, defile, molder, rotten, smirch 7 crooked, debauch, degrade, deprave, pervert, putrefy, tarnish, vitiate 8 bribable, degraded, depraved, infected, perverse 9 decompose, dishonest, miscreant, reprobate, unethical 10 bastardize, degenerate 12 unprincipled, unscrupulous 13 untrustworthy

corruptible
5 venal 7 buyable 8 bribable

corruption
4 vice 5 decay, fraud, graft 7 bribery, jobbery 9 barbarism, depravity, turpitude 10 immorality, wickedness 11 impropriety

corsair
5 rover 6 pirate 8 picaroon, sea rover 9 buccaneer, pickaroon, privateer 10 freebooter

corset
5 stays 6 bodice, girdle 7 support

Corsica
city: 6 Bastia 7 Ajaccio
hero: 8 Napoleon (Bonaparte)
patriot: 5 Paoli (Pasquale)

cortege
5 train 6 parade 7 retinue 9 entourage 10 attendants, procession

cortex
4 bark, husk, peel, rind 6 casing 8 peridium

Cortland
5 apple

corundum
4 ruby 5 emery, topaz 7 emerald 8 abrasive, amethyst, sapphire

coruscate
5 flash, gleam, glint, shine 7 glisten, glitter, sparkle, twinkle 11 scintillate

corvid
3 jay 4 crow 5 raven 6 magpie 9 passerine

Corvino's wife
5 Celia

corybantic
3 mad 4 wild 5 rabid 6 crazed 7 frantic, furious 8 ecstatic, frenetic, frenzied 9 delirious

coryphée
6 dancer 8 danseuse 9 ballerina

Cosí Fan Tutte composer
6 Mozart (Wolfgang Amadeus)

cosine reciprocal
6 secant

cosmetic
4 kohl 5 blush, rouge 6 ceruse, lotion, makeup, powder 7 blusher, bronzer, mascara 8 lip gloss, lipstick 9 eye shadow 10 decorative, nail polish, ornamental 11 beautifying, superficial

cosmetologist
10 beautician

cosmic
4 huge, vast 7 immense 8 infinite 9 planetary, spiritual, unbounded, universal 12 astronomical, metaphysical

cosmopolitan
6 global, urbane 7 worldly 8 catholic, cultured, polished 9 civilized, universal, worldwide 10 cultivated, ecumenical 11 worldly-wise 13 sophisticated

cosmos
6 flower 8 creation, universe

Cossack
army: 3 Don 4 Ural 5 Kuban
land: 7 Ukraine
leader: 5 Razin (Stenka) 6 ataman, hetman, Mazepa (Ivan) 7 Bulavin (Kondraty) 8 Pugachov (Yemelyan)
novel: 10 Taras Bulba

cosset
3 pet 4 baby, lamb, love 5 humor, spoil 6 caress, cocker, coddle, cuddle, dandle, dote on,

fondle, pamper **7** cater to, indulge **11** molly-coddle

cost
3 tab **4** rate, toll **5** price **6** charge, damage, outlay, tariff **7** expense, payment **8** price tag **9** sacrifice **11** expenditure **12** disbursement
business: 8 overhead

Costa Rica
bay: 8 Coronado
capital: 7 San José
city: 8 Alajuela **10** Puntarenas **11** Puerto Limón
discoverer: 8 Columbus (Christopher)
language: 7 Spanish
leader: 5 Arias (Oscar)
monetary unit: 5 colón
neighbor: 6 Panama **9** Nicaragua
peninsula: 3 Osa **6** Nicoya
river: 7 San Juan
volcano: 5 Barba, Irazú **9** Turrialba

costermonger
6 hawker **7** peddler **9** barrow boy

costive
4 mean, slow **5** bound, close, tight **6** frugal, stingy **7** miserly **9** penurious **10** hardfisted, pinchpenny **11** closefisted **12** cheeseparing, parsimonious

costless
4 free **6** gratis **10** gratuitous **13** complimentary

costly
4 dear, rich **5** fancy **6** lavish, pricey **7** opulent, premium **8** precious, splendid, valuable **9** expensive, luxurious, priceless **10** exorbitant, high-priced, invaluable **11** extravagant

costume
3 rig **4** duds, garb, mode **5** dress, getup, guise, habit, style **6** attire, outfit **7** apparel, clothes, fashion, threads, turnout, uniform **8** disguise, ensemble, garments **9** trappings

cot
3 bed, hut **4** camp **5** cabin, lodge, shack **6** shanty
wheeled: 6 gurney

coterie
4 band, camp, clan, club, ring **5** cabal **6** circle, clique **7** in-group **9** camarilla

cotillion
4 ball, prom **5** dance
girl: 3 deb **9** debutante

cottage
3 hut **4** camp **5** cabin, lodge, shack **6** shanty **8** bungalow
Russian: 5 dacha
Swiss: 6 chalet

cotton
cleaner: 3 gin **6** linter
cloth: 4 duck, jean, mull **5** baize, chino, denim, drill, khaki, scrim, terry, wigan **6** calico, canvas, chintz, dimity, muslin, oxford, sateen, velour **7** batiste, etamine, fustian, gingham, jaconet, nankeen, organdy, percale **8** corduroy, dungaree, moleskin, nainsook, tarlatan **9** grenadine, percaline, stockinet, swansdown **10** balbriggan **11** stockinette
cloth, Indian: 5 surah **6** madras **7** dhurrie, khaddar
comb: 4 card
fuzz remover: 6 linter
high-grade: 4 pima
measure: 4 hank, pick, yard **5** count, skein
pad: 7 pledget
pod: 4 boll
refuse: 5 flock
seed separator: 3 gin
sheet: 4 batt
thread: 5 lisle

Cotton State
7 Alabama

cottonwood
5 alamo **6** poplar

cottony
4 soft **6** fluffy

____ Coty
4 René

couch
3 den, put **4** lair, sofa, word **5** divan, lodge **6** burrow, chaise, daybed, lounge, phrase **7** express, lie down, recline **9** davenport, formulate **12** chesterfield

couch potato
7 slacker

cougar
3 cat **4** puma **7** panther **9** catamount **12** mountain lion

cough
4 hack, hawk

cough drop
6 troche **7** lozenge

cough up
3 pay **5** spend **6** lay out, pay out **7** deliver, dole out, fork out **8** fork over, hand over, shell out

couloir
5 chasm, gorge, gulch, gully **6** ravine

council
4 diet **5** board, junta **6** powwow, senate **7** cabinet, meeting **8** assembly, conclave, congress, ministry **10** conference, federation **12** consultation
ancient Greek: 5 boule
church: 5 synod **10** consistory
medieval English: 4 moot **5** gemot **6** gemote **8** hustings

Muslim: **5** divan
Russian: **4** duma **6** soviet
secret: **5** cabal, junto **9** camarilla
Spanish: **7** cabildo

counsel
4 rede, urge, warn **6** advice, advise, charge, direct, enjoin, lawyer **7** consult, suggest **8** advocate, attorney **9** prescribe, recommend **10** advisement **12** deliberation
British: **9** barrister, solicitor

count
3 add, sum, tot **4** bank, earl, mean, rely, tote **5** issue, score, tally, total, tot up, weigh **6** census, charge, depend, expect, figure, matter, number, reckon, result, tote up **7** compute, signify **8** estimate, militate, numerate, quantify **9** calculate, enumerate **10** allegation

countenance
3 mug **4** back, cast, face, look, mien, phiz **5** favor, go for **6** accept, aspect, visage **7** approve, commend, condone, endorse, support **8** advocate, features, hold with, sanction, tolerate **9** approbate, composure, encourage **10** expression **11** physiognomy

counter
3 bar, pit, vie **4** anti, desk **5** asset, check, match, polar, shelf, table **6** contra, offset, oppose **7** adverse, against, hostile, obverse, opposed, reverse **8** antipode, contrary, converse, opposing, opposite **9** antipodal, diametric **10** antipodean, antithesis, contravene **12** antagonistic, antipathetic, antithetical **13** contradictory

counteract
3 fix **4** foil **5** annul **6** cancel, negate, oppose, resist, thwart **7** balance, correct, nullify, prevent, rectify, redress **8** negative **9** cancel out, frustrate **10** balance out, neutralize

counteragent
4 cure **6** remedy **8** antidote **9** antitoxin, antivenin **10** corrective

counterbalance
6 cancel, make up, offset, redeem, set off **7** ballast, correct, even out, rectify, redress **8** equalize, outweigh **10** compensate

counterblow
7 revenge **8** reprisal, requital, revanche **9** vengeance **11** retaliation, retribution

counterclockwise
4 levo **12** levorotatory

counterfeit
4 copy, fake, hoax, sham **5** bluff, bogus, dummy, false, feign, forge, fraud, mimic, phony **6** affect, assume, deceit, ersatz, forged, pseudo **7** feigned, imitate, pretend **8** delusive, delusory, knock off, simulate, spurious **9** brummagem, deception, deceptive, fabricate, imitation, imposture, insincere, pinchbeck, pretended, simulated **10** fraudulent, misleading, simulacrum
prefix: **5** pseud **6** pseudo

counterpane
4 pouf, puff **5** duvet **6** spread **8** bedcover, coverlet **9** bedspread, comforter, eiderdown

counterpart
4 like, twin **5** equal, match **6** analog, double **7** vis-à-vis **8** alter ego, analogue, parallel **9** correlate, duplicate **10** complement, coordinate, equivalent **11** correlative **13** correspondent

counterpoise
6 make up, offset, redeem, set off **7** balance, ballast **8** outweigh **9** stabilize **10** compensate

countersign
8 password **9** watchword

countervail
4 foil **6** cancel, offset, oppose, redeem, set off, thwart **7** balance, correct, nullify, rectify **8** outweigh **9** frustrate **10** compensate, neutralize

countless
6 legion, myriad, untold **7** umpteen **11** innumerable

Count of Monte Cristo
6 Dantès (Edmond)
author: **5** Dumas (Alexandre)

count out
5 expel **6** except **7** exclude **9** disregard, eliminate

countrified
5 rural **6** rustic **7** bucolic **8** homespun, pastoral **10** campestral

country
4 home, land, soil **5** rural **6** nation, region, rustic, sticks **7** boonies, bucolic, outland **8** homeland, pastoral **9** backwoods, boondocks **10** campestral, fatherland, motherland, provincial
dance: **3** jig **4** reel **10** strathspey
home: **5** dacha, manor, ranch, villa **8** hacienda
music: **9** bluegrass
road: **4** lane, path **5** byway
(see also **nation**)

country-music star
4 Cash (Johnny), Ford (Tennessee Ernie), Gill (Vince), Lynn (Loretta), Rich (Charlie), Tubb (Ernest) **5** Acuff (Roy), Autry (Gene), Black (Clint), Cline (Patsy), Davis (Skeeter), Jones (George), Owens (Buck), Pearl (Minnie), Pride (Charley), Twain (Shania), Wells (Kitty), Wills (Bob) **6** Arnold (Eddy), Atkins (Chet), Brooks (Garth), Carter (A. P., June, Maybelle, Sara), Harris (Emmylou), Miller (Roger), Monroe (Bill), Nelson (Willie), Parton (Dolly), Ritter (Tex), Rogers (Kenny, Roy), Skaggs (Ricky), Travis (Randy), Tucker (Tanya), Twitty (Conway) **7** Haggard (Merle), Millsap (Ronnie), Robbins

(Marty), Rodgers (Jimmie), Wynette (Tammy) **8** Jennings (Waylon), McEntire (Reba), Williams (Hank)

coup
4 blow, feat **5** upset **6** putsch, stroke **8** takeover **9** overthrow

coup de ___
5 grâce

couple
3 duo, twa, two **4** bond, dyad, fuse, item, join, link, mate, pair, span, team, yoke **5** brace, hitch, marry, merge, unite **6** hook up, link up **7** bracket, combine, conjoin, connect, doublet, harness, twosome

coupler
4 link, ring **5** hitch, joint **6** hookup **7** shackle **8** ligature
railroad: **7** drawbar

couplet
3 duo **4** dyad, pair **5** twins **7** distich, doublet, twosome

coupling
4 link, seam **5** joint, union **6** yoking **7** joining, pairing **8** junction, juncture **9** connector **10** connection

courage
4 dash, grit, guts **5** heart, moxie, nerve, pluck, spunk, valor **6** daring, mettle, spirit **7** bravery, heroism **8** audacity, backbone, boldness, firmness, temerity, tenacity, valiance, valiancy **9** assurance, fortitude, gallantry **10** resolution **11** doughtiness, intrepidity **12** fearlessness **13** dauntlessness

courageous
4 bold **5** brave, gutsy, nervy, stout **6** daring, heroic, manful, plucky, spunky, strong **7** doughty, gallant, valiant **8** fearless, intrepid, resolute, stalwart, unafraid, valorous **9** audacious, dauntless, tenacious, undaunted **11** venturesome **12** stouthearted

courier
5 envoy, gofer **6** legate, runner **8** emissary **9** go-between, messenger **11** internuncio

course
3 row, run, way **4** dart, dash, duct, flow, line, path, plan, race, road, rush, tack, tear **5** canal, chain, chase, class, hurry, orbit, order, range, route, scoot, scope, speed, surge, track, trend **6** career, design, hasten, hustle, manner, policy, polity, scheme, sequel, series, string, system **7** advance, channel, circuit, conduit, passage, pattern, program, regimen, routine, seminar **8** aqueduct, duration, progress, sequence, syllabus **9** procedure, racetrack **10** curriculum, succession **11** progression
curving: **4** coil, curl, turn, wind **5** swing, twist **6** spiral **9** corkscrew
dinner: **4** soup **5** salad **6** entrée **7** dessert **9** appetizer, blue plate

courser
4 bird **5** horse **7** charger **8** huntsman, warhorse

court
3 bar, woo **4** date, quad, yard **5** atria (plural), charm, motel, spark, suite, tempt **6** allure, atrium, homage, invite, palace, pursue **7** address, flatter, justice, retinue, romance, solicit **8** assembly, cloister, tribunal **9** captivate, curtilage, enclosure, entourage **10** magistrate, parliament, quadrangle **11** legislature
action: **4** suit **5** trial **6** appeal, assize **7** hearing, inquest, lawsuit **10** proceeding
calendar: **6** docket
call to: **7** summons **8** subpoena **11** arraignment
circuit: **4** eyre
crier's call: **4** oyez
decision: **6** assize **7** finding, verdict **8** judgment
ecclesiastical: **4** rota **5** Curia **10** consistory
Indian: **6** durbar
kind: **4** moot **5** civil **6** county, family **7** circuit, customs, federal, supreme **8** chancery, criminal, district, juvenile, kangaroo, superior **9** appellate, municipal **11** territorial
medieval English: **4** eyre, moot **5** geot **6** gemote **8** hustings
of equity: **8** chancery
officer: **2** DA **5** clerk, crier, judge **7** bailiff, justice, marshal, sheriff **10** prosecutor
order: **4** writ **5** edict **6** decree **7** summons **8** mandamus, subpoena
panel: **4** jury
relating to: **8** judicial **9** juridical
session: **6** assize **7** sitting **8** sederunt

courteous
5 civil **6** polite **7** courtly, gallant, genteel **8** mannerly, well-bred **9** attentive **10** chivalrous, thoughtful **11** considerate **12** well-mannered

courtesy
7 amenity, decorum, manners, service **8** chivalry, civility **9** attention, etiquette, gallantry **10** cordiality, indulgence **11** courtliness **12** graciousness **13** attentiveness, consideration

court game
see under **game**

courtly
5 noble **6** august, formal, urbane **7** elegant, gallant, refined, stately **8** gracious **9** dignified **10** chivalrous, flattering **11** ceremonious

courtship
4 suit **6** dating, wooing **7** romance **10** flirtation
former custom of: **8** bundling

courtyard
4 quad **5** atria (plural), garth, patio **6** atrium **9** curtilage **10** quadrangle

cousin
3 kin **7** kinsman **8** relative

Cousteau, Jacques
ship: **7** Calypso
vehicle: **11** bathysphere

couturier
8 clothier, costumer, designer **10** dressmaker

cove
3 arm, bay **4** nook **5** bight, firth, inlet, niche **6** harbor, recess **9** concavity

covenant
3 vow **4** bond, pact **5** agree, swear **6** pledge, treaty **7** compact, promise **8** contract **9** agreement **10** convention

Covent Garden offering
5 opera **6** ballet

cover
3 cap, lid **4** bury, hide, hood, mask, veil, wrap **5** alibi, cloak, front, guise, stash, track **6** clothe, enfold, enwrap, facade, hiding, insure, refuge, screen, secure, shield, shroud, sleeve, travel **7** blanket, conceal, embrace, enclose, envelop, obscure, overlay, protect, secrete, shelter, write up **8** disguise, ensconce, enshroud, traverse **9** encompass, safeguard, sanctuary, superpose **10** overspread **11** concealment, superimpose
rooflike: **6** awning, canopy
the eyes: **4** loup **9** blindfold
the face: **4** mask, veil
the head: **4** hood
the mouth: **6** muzzle
with asphalt: **4** pave
with cloth: **5** drape
with dirt: **7** begrime, blacken **8** besmirch
with straw: **6** thatch

coverall
8 jumpsuit **10** boilersuit

covered wagon
9 Conestoga

covering
anatomical: **5** theca, velum **6** tegmen **7** velamen **8** tegument **10** integument
apex of roof: **3** épi
close-fitting: **6** sheath **9** sheathing
cloth: **5** sheet
flap: **9** operculum
for a book: **4** case **6** jacket
for a cigar: **7** wrapper
for a coffin: **4** pall
for a corpse: **6** shroud **8** cerement
for a package: **7** wrapper
for concealment: **10** camouflage
for food: **4** cosy, cozy
for soil: **5** mulch
metal: **4** mail **5** armor
of a diatom: **6** lorica
of a plant ovary: **8** pericarp
of a seed: **4** aril, case **5** testa
of fruits: **4** peel, rind
of gloom: **4** pall
of grain: **4** hull, husk **5** chaff
shell-like: **7** testudo **8** carapace
thin: **4** film **6** patina, veneer
waterproof: **4** tarp **9** tarpaulin

coverlet
4 pouf, puff **5** duvet **6** spread **8** bedcover **9** bedspread, comforter **11** counterpane

covert
4 lair **5** haven, privy **6** hidden, masked, refuge, secret, veiled **7** feather, furtive, retreat, shelter, sub-rosa, thicket **8** hush-hush, shrouded, stealthy **9** concealed, disguised, sanctuary, sheltered **10** undercover **11** camouflaged, clandestine, hiding place, underhanded **12** hugger-mugger **13** surreptitious, under-the-table

covertly
7 sub-rosa **9** by stealth **12** hugger-mugger

covet
4 want **5** crave **6** desire

covetous
4 avid, keen **5** itchy **6** grabby, greedy **7** envious **8** desirous, esurient, grasping, ravenous **9** rapacious, voracious **10** avaricious, gluttonous **11** acquisitive

covey
4 band, bevy, crew, nest **5** brood, bunch, flock, group, party, troop **6** gaggle, troupe **7** cluster, company

cow
(see also **cattle**)
4 faze, kine (plural), neat **5** abash, bossy, bully, daunt **6** appall, bovine, dismay, hector, rattle **7** bluster, dragoon **8** bludgeon, browbeat, bulldoze, bullyrag **9** discomfit, embarrass, strong-arm **10** disconcert, intimidate
cud: **5** rumen
French: **5** vache
hornless: **5** muley **7** pollard
mammary gland: **5** udder
pen: **6** corral
shed: **4** barn, byre
Spanish: **4** vaca
young: **4** calf **5** stirk **6** heifer

coward
6 craven **7** caitiff, chicken, dastard, milksop, nebbish **8** poltroon, recreant **9** jellyfish **10** scaredy-cat **11** yellowbelly

___ Coward
4 Noël

cowardly
5 timid, wimpy **6** afraid, craven, yellow **7** caitiff, chicken, fearful, gutless **8** poltroon, recreant, timorous **9** dastardly **11** lily-livered, milk-livered, poltroonish **12** apprehensive, fainthearted, poor-spirited, white-livered **13** pusillanimous

cowboy
5 rogue, waddy **6** drover, herder, waddie **7** puncher, rancher **8** buckaroo, herdsman, maverick, wrangler **9** cattleman, ranch hand **10** cowpuncher **12** broncobuster
contest: **5** rodeo
gear: **5** cuffs, quirt, spurs **6** duster **7** bedroll, slicker, Stetson
legendary: **9** Pecos Bill
leggings: **5** chaps
movie: **3** Mix (Tom) **4** Hart (William S.) **5** Autry (Gene), Wayne (John) **6** Gibson (Hoot), McCrea (Joel), Murphy (Audie), Ritter (Tex), Rogers (Roy, Will) **8** Cisco Kid, Eastwood (Clint)
rope: **5** lasso, reata, riata **6** lariat
Spanish-American: **6** charro, gaucho **7** vaquero

cowcatcher
5 pilot

cower
5 quail, wince **6** blench, cringe, flinch, recoil, shrink

cowfish
6 dugong, sea cow **7** grampus, manatee **8** sirenian

cowl
4 cape, hood **5** cloak **6** capote, domino, mantle **7** capuche

cowpox
8 vaccinia

cowpuncher
see **cowboy**

coxcomb
3 fop **4** beau, buck, dude, fool **5** blood, dandy, swell **7** peacock **8** macaroni **9** exquisite **11** Beau Brummel **12** clotheshorse, fashion plate, lounge lizard

coy
3 shy **4** arch, cute, pert **5** saucy, timid **6** demure, modest **7** bashful, evasive, playful **8** blushing, decorous, skittish **9** diffident, kittenish **10** capricious, coquettish **11** flirtatious, mischievous **12** noncommittal

Coyote State
11 South Dakota

coypu
6 rodent
fur: **6** nutria

cozen
3 gyp **4** bilk, scam **5** cheat, trick **6** diddle, fleece, take in **7** beguile, deceive, defraud, swindle, wheedle **8** flimflam **9** bamboozle **11** double-cross

cozy
4 safe, snug, soft **5** comfy, cushy, pally, tight **6** chummy, secure **8** familiar, intimate **11** comfortable

CPR expert
3 EMT

crab
3 nag **4** beef, fuss, yawp **5** gripe, sidle **6** grinch, griper, grouch, kvetch, squawk, yammer **7** decapod, grouser, growler **8** arthopod, complain, grumbler, sourpuss **9** bellyache, shellfish **10** bellyacher, complainer, crosspatch, crustacean, curmudgeon **11** faultfinder
claw: **5** chela **6** nipper
constellation: **6** Cancer
genus: **3** Uca **6** Birgus **7** Limulus, Pagurus
kind: **3** pea **4** blue, king, pine, rock **5** ghost, purse **6** hermit, spider **7** fiddler **9** Dungeness, horseshoe
king, horseshoe: **7** limulus

crabbed
4 dour, glum, grim, sour **5** gruff, surly **6** crusty, gloomy, morose, sullen **9** illegible, irascible, saturnine, splenetic

crablike
8 cancroid

crabwise
8 sidelong, sideward, sideways **9** laterally

crack
3 gag, gap, rap, try **4** bang, barb, bash, belt, blow, boom, clap, flaw, jest, joke, open, peal, quip, rift, roll, shot, slam, slap, snap, stab, wham, whop **5** adept, break, burst, chink, cleft, crash, craze, knock, smack, smash, solve, split, whack, whirl, wreck **6** breach, cranny, decode, expert, master, moment, thwack, zinger **7** break up, crevice, decrypt, destroy, fissure, instant, shatter, skilled **8** crevasse, decipher, disorder, interval, masterly, skillful, superior **9** break into, excellent, interrupt, masterful, witticism **10** percussion, proficient

crackbrain
3 nut **4** kook **5** crank, wacko **6** cuckoo **7** dingbat, lunatic **9** ding-a-ling, fruitcake, screwball

crackdown
5 purge **8** quashing **10** repression **11** suppression

cracked
3 mad **4** daft, nuts **5** balmy, batty, crazy, daffy, loony, nutty **6** broken, crazed, cuckoo, insane,

screwy **7** bonkers, lunatic, smashed **8** demented, deranged

cracker
5 wafer **6** hacker, rustic **7** biscuit, saltine, snapper **8** Georgian **9** Floridian

crackerjack
3 ace **4** lulu **5** dandy, nifty, sharp **6** corker, killer **8** jim-dandy, knockout **9** humdinger **12** lollapalooza

crackle
4 snap **7** glitter, sparkle, twinkle **9** crepitate **10** effervesce **13** effervescence

crackpot
3 nut **4** case, kook, loon **5** crank, loony, wacko **6** cuckoo, madman **7** dingbat, lunatic, oddball **9** ding-a-ling, eccentric, fruitcake, harebrain, screwball

crack-up, crack up
5 crash, smash, wreck **6** fiasco **7** debacle **8** accident, collapse, disaster **9** breakdown **11** catastrophe

cradlesong
7 lullaby **8** berceuse

craft
3 art, job **4** boat **5** guile, knack, skill, trade, wiles **6** career, deceit, métier **7** ability, calling, cunning, know-how, slyness **8** artifice, caginess, foxiness, vocation, wiliness **9** adeptness, canniness, dexterity, duplicity, expertise, ingenuity, technique **10** adroitness, artfulness, competence, occupation, profession, shrewdness **11** proficiency
(see also **boat**)

craftiness
5 guile **7** cunning **8** artifice, subtlety

craftsman
5 smith **6** carter, carver, potter, weaver, wright **7** artisan, builder, cobbler, jeweler **9** carpenter **10** blacksmith

crafty
3 sly **4** foxy, keen, wily **5** acute, cagey, canny, sharp, slick **6** adroit, artful, astute, clever, shrewd, tricky **7** cunning, devious, fawning, vulpine **8** guileful, scheming, skillful, slippery **9** deceitful, designing, ingenious, insidious **11** calculating, duplicitous
Scottish: 7 sleekit

crag
3 tor **4** hill **5** cliff

craggy
5 erose, harsh, rocky, rough **6** jagged, rugged, uneven

cram
3 jam, ram **4** bolt, fill, gulp, heap, load, pack, wolf **5** crowd, crush, drive, force, press, shove, study, stuff, wedge **6** gobble, review, squash, thrust **7** jam-pack, overeat, squeeze

crammed
4 full **5** awash, flush **7** brimful **8** brimming **9** chock-full

cramp
4 kink, pain, pang **5** crick, limit, spasm **6** hamper, stitch **7** confine, inhibit, shackle **8** confined, restrain, restrict **9** restraint, stricture **10** constraint, limitation **11** confinement, restriction

cramped
5 close, tight **6** narrow **9** confining, two-by-four

crane
4 bird, boom, rail **5** heron **7** derrick, stretch
arm: 3 jib
genus: 4 Grus
ship's: 5 davit

Crane hero
12 Henry Fleming

cranium
5 skull **9** braincase

crank
3 nut **4** crab, kook **5** fancy **6** griper, grouch, notion, rotate, turn up, vagary **7** caprice, conceit, fanatic, grouser, oddball **8** crackpot, crotchet, grumbler, sourpuss **9** eccentric, screwball **10** bellyacher, crosspatch

cranky
5 cross, testy **6** crabby, crusty, cussed, grumpy, morose, ornery, tetchy, touchy **7** bearish, crabbed, peevish, prickly **8** contrary, petulant, tortuous, vinegary **9** crotchety, irascible, irritable, obstinate **10** bad-humored, ill-humored **12** cantankerous, disagreeable **13** unpredictable

cranny
3 gap **4** nook, slit **5** chink, crack, niche **6** corner **7** crevice

crash
3 din, jar, ram **4** bang, boom, bump, bust, clap, fail, fold, jolt, peal, slam, wham **5** blast, break, burst, crack, shock, smash, wreck **6** impact, pileup **7** collide, crack-up, debacle, decline, failure, smashup **8** accident, collapse **9** breakdown, collision **10** concussion

crass
4 rude **5** crude, gross **6** coarse, vulgar **7** boorish, loutish, uncouth **8** churlish **9** unrefined **13** materialistic

crate
3 box **4** heap **5** wreck **6** jalopy, junker **7** clunker

crater
3 pit **4** dent, hole, pock **5** crash **6** cavity, dimple, hollow, trough **7** caldera **8** collapse **10** depression
Hawaiian: 7 Kilauea

cravat
3 tie **4** band **5** ascot, scarf **7** necktie

crave
3 ask, beg **4** need, want, wish **5** covet **6** demand, desire **7** call for, entreat, implore, long for, require **8** yearn for

craven
4 funk **6** abject, coward **7** caitiff, chicken, dastard, fearful, gutless, ignoble **8** cowardly, cringing, poltroon, recreant **9** dastardly **11** lily-livered, poltroonish, yellowbelly **13** pusillanimous, yellow-bellied

craving
4 itch, lust, urge **6** desire, hunger, thirst **7** longing, passion **8** appetite, yearning **9** hankering

crawl
4 flow, inch, teem **5** creep, swarm **6** abound, grovel **7** slither, wriggle **9** pullulate

crawling
6 repent

craze
3 fad **4** chic, rage **5** crack, fever, furor, mania, trend, vogue **6** dement, enrage, frenzy, furore, madden **7** derange, fashion, unhinge **9** unbalance **10** dernier cri, enthusiasm

craziness
5 folly, mania **6** lunacy **8** hysteria, insanity **9** absurdity

crazy
3 fey, mad **4** amok, bats, daft, gaga, loco, nuts, wild, zany **5** balmy, barmy, batty, daffy, dotty, goofy, kooky, loony, loopy, nutty, rabid, silly, wacko, wacky **6** absurd, cuckoo, fruity, insane, mental, psycho, screwy, teched, whacky **7** berserk, bonkers, cracked, foolish, frantic, lunatic, meshuga, smitten, tetched, touched, unsound **8** cockeyed, crackpot, demented, deranged, frenetic, frenzied, maniacal, meshugge, unhinged **9** bedlamite, delirious, eccentric, fanatical, foolhardy, ludicrous, possessed, screwball, senseless **10** crackbrain, moonstruck, ridiculous, unbalanced **11** harebrained, nonsensical **12** preposterous
British: **5** potty **6** scatty
Scottish: **3** wud

creak
4 rasp **5** grate, grind **6** scrape, squeak, squeal **7** grating, screech **9** squeaking

creaky
4 aged **5** rusty **7** rickety, run-down, squeaky, unsound, worn-out **8** decrepit **9** tottering **10** broken-down, ramshackle

cream
3 top **4** balm, beat, best, drub, pick, whip, whup **5** blast, elite, prime, salve **6** cerate, choice, defeat, finest, thrash **7** clobber, destroy, trounce, unguent **8** lambaste, liniment, ointment

crease
4 fold, ruck **5** graze, plica, ridge **6** furrow, groove, rumple **7** crinkle, wrinkle

create
3 dub **4** form, make, sire **5** beget, build, cause, forge, found, hatch, set up, spawn, start **6** author, design, devise, father, invent **7** compose, concoct, develop, fashion, produce **8** conceive, engender, generate, occasion **9** construct, establish, fabricate, formulate, institute, originate **10** constitute

creation
5 birth, world **6** cosmos, nature **7** genesis **8** universe **9** inception, macrocosm **10** conception **11** macrocosmos

creative
7 fertile **8** artistic, inspired, original **9** deceptive, demiurgic, ingenious, inventive **10** innovative, innovatory **11** imaginative **12** innovational

creator
3 god **6** author **8** inventor **9** architect, generator, patriarch **10** originator, progenitor

creature
3 man **5** beast, being, brute, human **6** animal, mortal, person **7** critter, varmint
fabled: **3** elf, imp, orc, roc **4** ogre, puck, yeti **5** dwarf, fairy, ghost, giant, gnome, harpy, nymph, pixie, troll **6** dragon, goblin, gorgon, kraken, merman, Nessie, sphinx, sprite, wyvern **7** bigfoot, brownie, bugbear, centaur, chimera, gremlin, griffin, mermaid, monster, unicorn, vampire, wendigo, windigo **8** chimaera, minotaur, werewolf **9** hobgoblin, manticore, sasquatch **10** cockatrice, hippogriff, leprechaun
(see also **monster**)

credence
5 faith, trust **6** belief, credit **8** reliance **9** sideboard **10** acceptance, confidence

credentials
6 papers **9** documents **10** references **12** certificates, testimonials **13** documentation

credenza
6 buffet **7** console **8** bookcase **9** sideboard

credible
5 solid, sound, valid **6** trusty **8** reliable **9** authentic, colorable, plausible **10** believable, convincing, persuasive, reasonable **11** trustworthy **12** satisfactory

credit
4 deem, feel **5** asset, faith, honor, refer, sense, think, trust **6** accept, assign, belief, charge, impute, notice, weight **7** ascribe, believe

8 consider, credence, prestige, reliance **9** attribute, authority, influence **10** confidence, reputation **11** recognition

creditable
6 worthy **8** laudable, reliable **9** colorable, deserving, estimable, plausible, reputable **10** believable **11** commendable, meritorious, respectable **12** praiseworthy

credo
5 canon, creed, dogma, tenet **6** belief, tenets **7** beliefs, precept **8** doctrine, ideology **9** catechism, principle

credulous
5 naive **6** unwary **8** gullible, trustful, trusting **9** believing **12** unsuspecting, unsuspicious **13** unquestioning

creed
4 sect **5** canon, dogma, faith, tenet **6** belief, church, tenets **7** beliefs, precept **8** doctrine, ideology, religion **9** catechism, communion, principle **12** denomination

creek
3 ria **4** burn, rill **5** brook **6** arroyo, rillet, runlet, runnel, stream **7** freshet, rivulet **8** brooklet **9** streamlet

creep
4 drag, edge, inch, jerk, lurk, slip **5** crawl, freak, glide, schmo, shirk, sicko, skulk, slide, slink, snake, sneak, steal **6** shmuck, sickie, spread, tiptoe, weirdo **7** gumshoe, oddball, pervert, schmuck, slither, wriggle **9** pussyfoot

creeping
6 repent **7** gradual **9** prostrate

creepy
5 eerie, weird **6** spooky **7** anxious, macabre, ominous, strange, uncanny **8** ghoulish, menacing, sinister **9** unnerving **10** disturbing, unpleasant, unsettling **11** hair-raising

crème de la crème
4 best **5** elect, elite **6** finest

Cremona family
5 Amati **8** Guarneri **10** Stradivari **12** Stradivarius

Creole
dish: **5** gumbo **9** andouille, dirty rice, jambalaya
music: **6** zydeco

Creon
daughter: **6** Creusa, Glauce, Glauke
sister: **7** Jocasta
son: **6** Haemon
victim: **8** Antigone

crescendo
4 acme, apex, peak, rise **5** crest, surge, swell **6** apogee, climax, growth, height, zenith **8** increase, pinnacle **9** high point **11** culmination

crescent-shaped
5 bowed **6** lunate, sickle **7** falcate
body or surface: **4** lune **8** meniscus

crest
3 cap, top **4** acme, apex, comb, noon, peak, roof, tuft **5** arête, chine, crown, plume, ridge **6** apogee, climax, summit, vertex **7** hogback **8** pinnacle, surmount **9** high point **10** coat of arms, prominence **11** culmination
of a wave: **8** whitecap

crestfallen
3 low **4** blue, down **6** droopy **8** dejected, downcast, drooping **9** depressed **10** dispirited **11** discouraged, downhearted **12** disappointed, disconsolate, disheartened

Crete
ancient city: **7** Cnossus, Knossos **8** Phaistos
ancient name: **6** Candia
capital: **5** Canea
goddess: **8** Dictynna **11** Britomartis
guard: **5** Talos
king: **5** Minos **9** Idomeneus
maze: **9** labyrinth
monster: **8** Minotaur
mountain: **3** Ida
princess: **7** Ariadne

cretin
3 oaf **4** boob, clod, dolt, dope, fool, lout **5** dumbo, dummy, dunce, idiot, moron **6** dimwit, nitwit **7** half-wit **8** imbecile, lunkhead, numskull **9** lamebrain, numbskull, simpleton

Creusa
brother: **6** Haemon
father: **5** Priam
husband: **6** Aeneas
mother: **6** Hecuba
sister: **6** Glauce, Glauke
son: **3** Ion **8** Ascanius

crevice
3 gap **4** seam, slit **5** chink, cleft, crack **6** cranny **7** fissure **8** cleavage **10** interstice

crew
4 band, bevy, gang, team **5** bunch, covey, group, party **6** rowers, rowing **7** company, sailors
leader: **3** cox **8** coxswain

crib
3 bed, bin, box, hut, key **4** pony, trot **5** cheat, crate, hovel, shack, stall, steal, theft **6** cradle, crèche, manger, pilfer **7** barrier, brothel **8** bassinet, bedstead, bordello **9** enclosure **10** plagiarism, plagiarize

Crichton novel
11 Terminal Man (The) **12** Jurassic Park **15** Andromeda Strain (The)

cricket
period of play: **7** innings
team: **6** eleven
term: **3** leg, off, rot **4** bowl **5** pitch **6** bowler, wicket, yorker **7** batsman, striker **9** fieldsman
turn at bat: **4** over

crime
3 sin **4** evil, tort, vice **5** caper **6** breach, delict, felony **7** misdeed, offense **8** atrocity, iniquity **9** diablerie, violation **10** corruption, illegality, infraction, wrongdoing **11** misdemeanor **13** transgression
instructor: **5** Fagin

Crimea
city: **5** Kerch, Yalta **10** Sebastopol, Sevastopol, Simferopol
river: **4** Alma
sea: **4** Azov **5** Black
strait: **5** Kerch

criminal
4 hood, thug **5** crook, felon, shady **6** outlaw **7** convict, corrupt, crooked, hoodlum, illegal, illicit, lawless, mobster **8** culpable, fugitive, gangster, jailbird, offender, scofflaw, unlawful, wrongful **9** desperado, felonious, miscreant, nefarious, racketeer, wrongdoer **10** delinquent, lawbreaker, malefactor, trespasser **12** illegitimate, transgressor
habitual: **8** repeater **10** recidivist
intent: **7** mens rea

criminate
see **incriminate**

crimp
4 bend, curb, wave **5** frizz **6** crease, hamper, hold in **7** crinkle, inhibit, wrinkle **8** hold back, obstacle, restrain **9** constrain, restraint **10** impediment **11** obstruction

crimson
3 red **4** rose **5** blush, color, flush **6** redden

cringe
4 duck **5** cower, hunch, quail, wince **6** blench, flinch, recoil, shrink

crinkle
4 ruck **5** crimp, plica, ridge **6** crease, furrow, pucker, ruck up, rumple, rustle **7** crackle, crumple, scrunch, wrinkle **11** corrugation

crinkly
5 crepy **6** crepey, frizzy **7** frizzed **8** wrinkled

cripple
4 lame, maim **6** mangle **7** disable **8** mutilate, paralyze **9** hamstring, undermine **10** debilitate **12** incapacitate

crippled
4 halt, lame **6** maimed **7** gnarled, mangled **8** battered, deformed, disabled, weakened **9** enfeebled, misshapen, mutilated, paralyzed **11** debilitated, handicapped

crisis
4 crux, pass **5** pinch **6** climax, crunch, height, strait **7** impasse, straits **8** disaster, exigency, juncture, zero hour **9** emergency, extremity **10** crossroads **11** catastrophe, contingency **12** turning point

crisp
4 cold, cool, curl, deft, keen, neat, wavy **5** brisk, clean, crimp, curly, fresh, nippy, pithy, sharp, short **6** biting, chilly, lively, ripple, spruce **7** bracing, brittle, crunchy, cutting, wrinkle **8** clean-cut, clear-cut, incisive **9** trenchant **11** stimulating **12** invigorating

crisscross
3 net **4** grid, mesh **5** weave **7** network, overlap **8** reticule **9** confusion, decussate, intersect, reticular **10** reticulate

criterion
4 norm **5** canon, gauge, ideal, model, tenet **7** measure, precept **8** exemplar, paradigm, standard **9** benchmark, yardstick **10** touchstone

critic
5 judge **6** carper, pundit **7** arbiter, caviler **8** caviller, censurer, quibbler, reviewer **9** belittler, nitpicker **10** disparager, mudslinger **11** commentator, connoisseur, faultfinder

critical
4 dire **5** acute, fussy **7** carping, crucial, finicky, pivotal, weighty **8** captious, caviling, decisive **9** desperate, important, momentous **10** belittling, censorious, conclusive, precarious **11** disparaging, significant **12** faultfinding **13** consequential, determinative, hairsplitting
study: **6** examen **8** exegesis

criticism
4 flak, slap **5** blame, cavil, swipe **6** rebuke, review **7** censure, comment, opinion, reproof **8** analysis, judgment, reproach **9** appraisal, objection **10** assessment, commentary, evaluation, nitpicking **11** examination, observation **12** faultfinding

criticize
3 pan, rap **4** bash, carp, flay **5** blame, blast, cavil, chide, fault, judge, knock, roast, scold **6** assess, rebuke, review, scathe **7** blister, censure, condemn, nitpick, reprove **8** appraise, badmouth, chastise, denounce, evaluate, lambaste **9** castigate, disparage, dress down, excoriate, find fault, reprehend, reprimand, reprobate

critique
see **criticism**

critter
5 beast **6** animal **7** varmint

Crius
father: **6** Uranus
mother: **4** Gaea
son: **8** Astraeus

croak
3 die **6** cackle, cash in, expire, go west, squawk **7** go south, grumble, snuff it **8** check out

croaker
4 drum, fish, frog **6** doctor

croaky
5 gruff, husky, raspy **6** hoarse **8** gravelly

Croatia
capital: **6** Zagreb
city: **5** Split, Zadar **6** Osijek, Rijeka **9** Dubrovnik
monetary unit: **4** kuna
neighbor: **6** Bosnia, Serbia **7** Hungary **8** Slovenia
part of: **7** Balkans
region: **8** Dalmatia, Slavonia

crock
3 jar, lie, pot **4** tale **6** tureen **7** cripple, disable, fiction **9** break down **11** fabrication

crocked
3 lit **4** high **5** drunk, lit up, oiled, tipsy **6** bashed, blotto, bombed, juiced, potted, soaked, soused, stewed, stoned, tanked, wasted, zonked **7** drunken, pickled, pie-eyed, sloshed, smashed **9** plastered **10** inebriated, liquored up **11** intoxicated

crocodile
7 reptile
bird: **6** plover
Indian: **6** gavial **7** gharial
relative: **9** alligator
South American: **6** caiman, cayman
Southeast Asian: **6** mugger

Croesus' kingdom
5 Lydia

croft
4 farm **5** field

crofter
4 hind **6** farmer

Cromwell, Oliver
13 lord protector
battle: **6** Naseby **11** Marston Moor
party: **10** Roundheads
regiment: **9** Ironsides
son: **7** Richard
victim: **7** Charles (I)

crone
3 hag **4** trot **5** biddy, witch **6** beldam **7** beldame

Cronus
5 Titan **6** Saturn
daughter: **4** Hera **6** Hestia **7** Demeter
father: **6** Uranus
mother: **4** Gaea
sister: **4** Rhea **6** Cybele, Tethys
son: **4** Zeus **5** Hades **7** Jupiter, Neptune **8** Poseidon
wife: **4** Rhea **6** Cybele

crony
3 pal **4** chum **5** buddy **6** cohort **7** comrade **8** sidekick **9** associate, companion **10** accomplice **11** confederate

crook
3 bow **4** bend, flex, hook, wind **5** angle, curve, staff, thief **6** bandit, robber **7** burglar, crosier, hoodlum, pothook **8** criminal

crooked
4 awry **5** askew, lying, shady, venal **6** curved, errant, jagged, shifty, skewed, zigzag **7** bending, corrupt, devious, illegal, illicit, slanted **8** cockeyed, criminal, ruthless, tortuous, twisting **9** deceitful, dishonest, nefarious, underhand, unethical **10** fraudulent, mendacious, untruthful **11** duplicitous, underhanded **12** unscrupulous **13** double-dealing

croon
4 sing **6** murmur, warble

crooner
4 Cole (Nat "King"), Como (Perry) **5** Laine (Frankie), Tormé (Mel) **6** Crosby (Bing), Martin (Dean), singer, Vallee (Rudy) **7** Bennett (Tony), Sinatra (Frank) **8** Eckstine (Billy), vocalist, Williams (Andy)

crop
3 bob, cut, hew, lop, mow **4** chop, clip, pare, snip, trim **5** prune, shave, shear, stock, yield **6** gullet, handle, output **7** harvest, produce **8** fruitage, truncate **10** collection

croquet
5 roque

crosier
5 crook, staff

cross
3 mad **4** mule, rood, span **5** angry, surly, testy, trial **6** betray, bridge, crabby, cranky, grumpy, hybrid, negate, oppose, tetchy, touchy **7** athwart, calvary, grouchy, mongrel, peevish **8** captious, choleric, traverse **9** half blood, half-breed, hybridize, intersect, irascible, irritable, querulous, splenetic **10** affliction, contradict, interbreed, transverse **12** cantankerous
a river: **4** ford
bearer: **8** crucifer
decoration: **4** Iron **8** Victoria
kind: **3** tau **4** ankh **5** Greek, Latin, papal **6** Celtic, fleury, formée, moline, pommée, potent **7** avellan, botonée, Calvary, Maltese, saltire

8 crucifix, fourchée, Lorraine, quadrate **11** patriarchal **12** Saint Andrew's **13** Saint Anthony's
section: 5 slice

crossbow
8 arbalest, arbalist

crossbreed
4 mule **6** hybrid **7** bastard, mongrel **9** half blood, hybridize

cross-eye
6 squint **10** strabismus

crossing
8 junction, overpass, traverse **9** traversal, underpass **10** transverse **11** decussation, interchange, transversal **12** intersection

cross out
5 erase **6** cancel, delete, efface, excise **7** expunge

crosspatch
4 crab **5** crank, grump **6** griper, grouch **7** grouser **8** grumbler, sorehead, sourpuss **10** complainer, curmudgeon

crossroads
4 crux, pass **5** pinch **6** crisis, strait **8** exigency, juncture, zero hour **9** carrefour, emergency **11** contingency **12** intersection, turning point
goddess: 6 Hecate, Hekate, Trivia

cross-shaped
8 cruciate **9** cruciform

crossways
6 aslant **7** athwart, oblique **8** diagonal **9** obliquely **10** diagonally, transverse **11** cater-corner, cattycorner, kitty-corner **12** transversely

crotchet
3 bee **4** whim **5** fancy, freak, quirk, trick **6** foible, megrim, notion, vagary **7** caprice, conceit **11** quarter note **12** eccentricity

crotchety
5 testy **6** crabby, cranky, crusty, ornery, tetchy, touchy **7** bearish, peevish, prickly **8** contrary, snappish, vinegary **9** difficult, eccentric, irascible **10** vinegarish **11** ill-tempered **12** cantankerous, cross-grained

crouch
4 bend, duck **5** cower, hunch, squat, stoop **6** cringe, huddle, shrink **10** hunker down

croup
3 bum **4** butt, hack, rear, rump, seat, tail **5** cough, edema, whoop **6** behind **7** keister, rear end, tail end **8** backside, buttocks, derriere, haunches **9** posterior

croupier tool
4 rake

crow
4 blow, brag, puff **5** boast, exult, gloat, prate, vaunt **6** cackle **7** bluster **9** gasconade, humble pie
colony: 7 rookery
cry: 3 caw
family: 6 corvid **8** Corvidae
genus: 6 Corvus
relating to: 7 corvine, corvoid
relative: 3 daw, jay **4** rook **5** raven **6** chough, magpie **7** jackdaw, jaybird

crowbar
3 pry **5** jimmy, lever

crowd
3 jam, mob **4** army, bear, cram, fill, herd, host, mass, pack, pile, push, rout, ruck **5** bunch, crush, drove, flock, flood, group, horde, hurry, press, serry, shove, surge, swarm, troop **6** circle, clique, gaggle, huddle, jostle, legion, rabble, squash, squish, stream, throng **7** cluster, collect, company, coterie, squeeze **8** assembly **9** gathering, multitude **10** assemblage, collection **11** aggregation **12** congregation

crowded
4 full **5** awash, close, dense, thick, tight **6** loaded **7** brimful, compact, teeming **8** brimming, populous, swarming **9** chock-full, congested, jam-packed

crown
3 cap, top **4** acme, apex, peak, roof **5** cover, crest, tiara **6** climax, diadem, laurel, summit, top off, vertex, wreath, zenith **7** chaplet, coronal, coronet, garland, overlay, perfect **8** pinnacle, round off, surmount **9** culminate, finish off **10** consummate **11** culmination

crucial
4 dire **5** acute, vital **6** urgent **7** central, pivotal **8** critical, deciding, decisive **9** desperate, essential, important, momentous, necessary **10** imperative **11** climacteric, significant

crucible
4 test **5** trial **6** ordeal **8** acid test **10** melting pot

crucifix
4 rood **5** cross

crucifixion site
7 Calvary **8** Golgotha

crucify
4 rack **6** impale, martyr **7** mortify, pillory, torment, torture **10** excruciate

crud
3 goo **4** glop, gook, gunk, junk, muck **5** dreck, filth, slime, trash **6** debris, sludge **7** deposit, garbage, rubbish **12** incrustation

crude
3 raw **4** poor **5** crass, dirty, gross, rough **6** coarse, earthy, gauche, impure, ribald, risqué, vulgar **7** boorish, ill-bred, loutish, lowbred, obscene, obvious, raunchy, uncivil, uncouth **8** backward, cloddish, homespun, ignorant, indecent, inferior **9** elemental, graceless, inelegant,

makeshift, primitive, rough-hewn, unrefined **10** amateurish, unfinished, unpolished

cruel
4 fell, grim, mean **5** harsh **6** brutal, fierce, savage **7** bestial, brutish, callous, heinous, vicious **8** inhumane, ruthless, sadistic **9** atrocious, barbarous, ferocious, heartless, merciless, monstrous, truculent **12** bloodthirsty

cruise
4 roam, rove, sail, surf, tour **5** drift, jaunt **6** junket, voyage **9** excursion

cruiser
4 boat **5** yacht **7** warship **8** squad car **9** patrol car, powerboat

crumb
3 bit, ort **4** iota **5** ounce, scrap, shred **6** morsel, sliver **7** smidgen **8** fragment, particle

crumble
5 decay **8** collapse **9** break down, decompose **11** deteriorate **12** disintegrate

crumbly
7 friable

crummy
4 poor **5** dingy, lousy, seedy, tacky **6** cruddy, flimsy, shoddy, sleazy **8** inferior

crumple
3 wad **4** cave **5** crimp **6** buckle, cave in, ruck up **7** crinkle, scrunch, wrinkle **8** collapse

crunch
4 chew **5** champ, chomp, grind, munch, sit-up **6** crisis **7** compute, process, squeeze **8** shortage, showdown

crusade
5 cause, drive **6** appeal **7** holy war **8** campaign, movement **9** offensive **10** expedition **11** undertaking

Crusader
English: **7** Richard (Lionheart)
foe: **7** Saladin, Saracen
French: **5** Louis (IX) **6** Philip, Robert **7** Baldwin, Charles, Godfrey, Raymond, Raymund **8** Boniface, Montfort, Philippe, Theobald
German: **6** Conrad **9** Frederick, Friedrich **10** Barbarossa
Norman: **7** Tancred **8** Bohemund
preacher: **5** Peter (the Hermit), Urban (II) **7** Adhémar, Bernard **8** Innocent (III), Pelagius

crusading
11 evangelical **12** evangelistic

crush
3 jam, mob **4** cram, mash, pulp, push, ruin **5** crowd, drove, grind, horde, pound, press, quash, quell, smash, wreck **6** bruise, burden, defeat, reduce, squash, squish, subdue, throng **7** conquer, destroy, mortify, oppress, passion, put down, repress, scrunch, squeeze, squelch, squoosh, trample **8** bear down, beat down, demolish, overcome, suppress, vanquish **9** humiliate, multitude, overpower, overwhelm, pulverize, puppy love, subjugate **10** annihilate, extinguish, obliterate **11** infatuation

crust
4 cake, coat, rime, scab **7** coating, deposit **8** covering

crustacean
4 crab, flea **5** louse, prawn **6** isopod, shrimp, slater, sow bug **7** copepod, daphnia, decapod, lobster, pill bug **8** amphipod, barnacle, crawfish, crayfish, ostracod, sand flea **9** arthropod, beach flea, shellfish, water flea, wood louse **10** hermit crab, stomatopod, whale louse **11** branchiopod, fiddler crab
aggregate of: **5** krill
appendage: **7** pleopod
body segment: **6** somite, telson **8** metamere
claw: **5** chela **6** pincer
covering substance: **6** chitin
larva: **8** nauplius

crusty
4 curt **5** bluff, blunt, gross, gruff, short, surly **6** cranky **7** brusque, crabbed, prickly **8** choleric **9** irascible, irritable, saturnine, splenetic

crux
3 nub **4** core, gist, meat, pith **5** focus, heart **6** kernel, thrust **7** essence, purport **9** substance

cry
(see also **exclamation**)
3 sob **4** bawl, blub, call, howl, keen, mewl, moan, pule, wail, weep, yawp, yell, yelp, yowl **5** bleat, motto, mourn, shout, whine, whoop **6** boohoo, furore, holler, lament, scream, snivel, squall, squawk, squeak, squeal **7** blubber, screech, ululate, whimper **10** vociferate
bacchanals': **4** evoe
calf: **5** bleat
cat: **3** mew **4** meow **5** miaow
cattle: **3** low, moo
chick: **4** peep **5** cheep
court: **4** oyez
crane: **5** clang
crow: **3** caw
dog: **3** arf **4** bark, woof
donkey: **4** bray **6** hee-haw
duck: **5** quack
frog: **5** croak
goat: **5** bleat
goose: **4** honk **5** clang
hen: **6** cackle
horse: **5** neigh **6** nicker, whinny **7** whicker
lion: **4** roar
owl: **4** hoot
pig: **4** oink **5** grunt
raven: **3** caw **5** croak
rook: **3** caw

sheep: **5** bleat
songbird: **5** chirp, tweet
turkey: **6** gobble

cry down
5 decry **6** defame, deride, malign, revile, vilify **7** condemn **8** belittle, denounce, derogate, diminish **9** denigrate, deprecate, discredit, disparage **10** calumniate, depreciate **11** detract from, opprobriate

crying
4 dire **5** acute, vital **6** urgent **7** blatant, burning, clamant, exigent, heinous **8** flagrant, pressing, shocking **9** atrocious, clamorous, desperate, monstrous, notorious **10** compelling, imperative, outrageous, scandalous **11** importunate

crypt
5 vault **7** chamber **8** catacomb **9** mausoleum **10** undercroft

cryptic
5 vague **6** arcane, occult, opaque, secret **7** Delphic, obscure, unclear **8** abstruse, Delphian, esoteric, puzzling **9** ambiguous, enigmatic, recondite, tenebrous **10** mysterious, mystifying **12** unfathomable

crystal
4 lens **5** clear, lucid **6** limpid, lucent, quartz **8** clear-cut, luminous, pellucid **9** glassware, unblurred **11** translucent, transparent **12** transpicuous
gazer: **4** seer **7** psychic **11** clairvoyant
set: **5** radio

cry up
4 laud, puff **5** boost, extol **6** praise **7** acclaim

cub
3 pup **4** baby, tyro **6** novice, rookie **8** neophyte **9** offspring, youngster **10** apprentice

Cuba
capital: **6** Havana
city: **7** Holguín **8** Camagüey, Santiago **10** Guantánamo, Santa Clara
discoverer: **8** Columbus (Christopher)
language: **7** Spanish
leader: **6** Castro (Fidel) **7** Batista (Fulgencio), Guevara (Che)
monetary unit: **4** peso
sea: **9** Caribbean

cubbyhole
5 niche **6** alcove, recess **7** cubicle

cube
4 dice **5** mince

Cub Scout
rank: **4** Bear, Lion, Wolf **6** Bobcat **7** Webelos
unit: **3** den **4** pack

Cuchulain
father: **3** Lug **4** Lugh **5** Lugus
foe: **4** Medb **5** Maeve
kingdom: **6** Ulster
lord: **9** Conchobar
mother: **8** Dechtire
son: **8** Conlaoch
victim: **8** Conlaoch
wife: **4** Emer

cuckoo
3 mad, nut **4** daft, kook, nuts **5** batty, crank, crazy, daffy, loony, loopy, nutty, potty, silly, wacko, wacky **6** crazed, fruity, insane, screwy, whacky **7** bonkers, cracked, idiotic, lunatic, nutcase **8** crackpot, demented **9** ding-a-ling, harebrain, screwball **12** crackbrained
bird: **3** ani **8** keelbill

cucumber
4 pepo **7** gherkin

cuddle
3 hug, pet **4** neck, snug **5** spoon **6** burrow, caress, clinch, cosset, dandle, fondle, nestle, nuzzle **7** embrace, snuggle, squeeze **8** canoodle

cuddly
7 lovable, snuggly **8** huggable **11** embraceable

cudgel
3 bat, sap **4** club, cosh, mace **5** baton, billy **7** war club **8** bludgeon **9** bastinado, billy club, blackjack, truncheon **10** knobkerrie, nightstick, shillelagh

cue
3 key, nod, rod, tip **4** clue, hint, lead, prod, sign **5** alert **6** insert, notion, prompt, signal, tip-off **7** heads-up, inkling, warning **8** high sign, reminder, telltale **10** indication, intimation, suggestion

cuff
3 box, hit **4** belt, blip, clip, poke, slap, sock **5** clout, fight, punch, smack, whack **6** bangle, buffet, wallop **7** clobber, scuffle **8** bracelet, wristlet

cul-de-sac
5 pouch **6** pocket **7** dead end, impasse **10** blind alley **12** diverticulum

cull
4 pick, sift, thin **5** elect, glean **6** choose, garner, gather, select, winnow **7** extract, thin out

culminate
4 peak **5** crest **6** climax

culmination
3 top **4** acme, apex, peak **6** apogee, capper, climax, height, payoff, summit, zenith **8** capstone, pinnacle **11** ne plus ultra **12** consummation

culpability
4 onus **5** blame, fault, guilt

culpable
6 guilty, liable, sinful 7 at fault 8 blamable, blameful 10 censurable, delinquent 11 blameworthy, impeachable, responsible 13 reprehensible

cult
3 fad 4 sect 5 creed, faith 6 church 8 religion 10 persuasion 12 denomination

cultivable
6 arable 8 tillable

cultivate
4 farm, grow, tend, till 5 breed, nurse, raise 6 enrich, foster, refine 7 cherish, develop, further, improve, nourish, nurture, produce, promote 9 encourage, propagate

cultivated
6 urbane 7 genteel, refined 8 cultured, polished, well-bred

cultivation
6 polish 7 culture, tillage 8 breeding 10 refinement 11 development

culture
4 grow 5 taste 6 foster 7 nurture 9 cultivate, erudition, gentility 10 refinement 11 cultivation 12 civilization 13 enlightenment

cultured
6 urbane 7 erudite, genteel, learned, refined 8 educated, highbrow, literate, polished, well-bred 9 civilized 10 cultivated 11 enlightened

culture medium
4 agar

cum ___ salis
5 grano

cumber
4 clog, lade, load 6 burden, hinder, hobble, impede, saddle 7 clutter 8 handicap 9 hindrance

cumbersome
5 bulky, heavy, hefty 6 clumsy 7 awkward 8 unwieldy 9 lumbering, ponderous 10 slow-moving

cumshaw
3 fee, tip 5 bribe 6 payoff 7 present 8 gratuity, largesse 9 baksheesh, lagniappe, pourboire 10 perquisite

cumulate
4 heap 5 amass, hoard, lay up, store 6 garner, gather, pile up 7 collect, combine, store up 9 stockpile

cumulation
4 heap, mass, pile 5 cache, hoard, trove 9 stockpile 10 collection 11 aggregation 13 agglomeration

cumulative
8 additive, compound 9 summative 10 compounded, increasing

cunning
3 sly 4 cute, foxy, keen, wary, wily 5 acute, cagey, canny, craft, guile, savvy, sharp, skill, slick, smart 6 adroit, artful, astute, clever, crafty, deceit, shifty, tricky 7 finesse, know-how, slyness 8 artifice, caginess, deftness, facility, foxiness, guileful, slippery, subtlety, wiliness 9 adeptness, cageyness, canniness, dexterity, dexterous, duplicity, ingenious, ingenuity, insidious, sharpness, slickness 10 adroitness, artfulness, cleverness, craftiness, shiftiness, shrewdness, trickiness

cup
3 mug 4 toby 5 grail, jorum, stein 6 beaker, goblet, seidel 7 chalice, tankard 8 schooner
handle: 3 ear, lug
holder: 6 saucer
liturgical: 3 ama 5 calix 7 chalice
Scottish: 4 tass
small: 6 noggin 8 cannikin, pannikin 9 demitasse
sports: 5 Davis, Ryder, World 6 Curtis, Nextel 7 Stanley 8 America's, Wightman

cupbearer of the gods
4 Hebe 8 Ganymede

cupboard
5 ambry, cuddy 6 buffet, closet, larder, pantry 7 armoire, cabinet 8 credence, credenza 9 sideboard

Cupid
4 Amor, Eros 5 putto 6 cherub 8 amoretto
beloved: 6 Psyche
brother: 7 Anteros
father: 6 Hermes 7 Mercury
mother: 5 Venus 9 Aphrodite
title: 3 Dan

cupidity
4 lust 5 greed 6 desire 7 avarice, avidity, craving, lechery, passion 8 rapacity, voracity 9 eagerness, esurience 10 greediness 11 infatuation 12 covetousness 13 rapaciousness

cupola
4 dome 5 vault 6 turret 7 furnace, lookout

cur
3 dog 4 mutt 7 mongrel

curate
6 cleric, priest 9 churchman, clergyman

curative
4 pill 5 tonic 6 elixir, relief, remedy 7 healing, nostrum, panacea, therapy 8 antidote, remedial, salutary, sanative, solution 9 healthful, medicinal, remedying, treatment, wholesome 10 beneficial, corrective 11 restorative, therapeutic 12 health-giving

curator
6 keeper, warden **9** caretaker, custodian **11** conservator

curb
3 bit **4** deny, rein **5** check, frame, leash, tie up **6** border, bridle, edging, fetter, hamper, hobble, hold in, rein in, subdue **7** abstain, contain, control, inhibit, refrain, repress **8** hold back, hold down, restrain, suppress, withhold **9** constrain, entrammel, restraint
British: **4** kerb

curdle
4 clot, sour, turn **5** spoil **7** clabber, congeal, thicken **9** coagulate

curdling substance
6 rennet

cure
3 age, spa **4** heal, mend **5** treat **6** elixir, kipper, physic, pickle, relief, remedy **7** rectify, relieve, restore, therapy **8** antidote, medicant, medicine, preserve, recovery, solution **10** ameliorate, corrective **12** counteragent **13** counteractive

cure-all
6 elixir **7** nostrum, panacea **10** catholicon

curio
6 oddity, whimsy **7** novelty, whatsit **9** objet d'art

curiosity
5 freak **6** marvel, oddity, rarity, whimsy, wonder **7** anomaly, concern, novelty **8** interest, nonesuch

curious
3 odd **4** nosy **5** nosey, novel, queer, weird **6** exotic, prying, quaint, snoopy **7** bizarre, oddball, strange, unusual **8** meddling, peculiar, puzzling, singular **9** inquiring, intrusive **11** inquisitive, questioning

curium symbol
2 Cm

curl
4 coil, kink, wind **5** frizz, twine, twist **6** spiral **7** contort, crinkle, entwine, frizzle, ringlet, wreathe **9** corkscrew

curling
match: **8** bonspiel
period of play: **3** end
team: **4** four
term: **3** tee **4** hack, rink **5** house, stone

curly
4 wavy **5** kinky **6** frizzy

currency
4 cash, coin **5** dough, lucre, money, scrip **7** coinage **8** banknote **10** acceptance, prevalence **11** legal tender
unit: see individual country

current
4 eddy, flow, flux, race, rush, tide **5** drift, flood, spate, tenor, trend **6** extant, modern, strain, stream **7** instant, ongoing, popular, present, regnant, topical **8** accepted, existent, existing, tendency, up-to-date **9** prevalent **10** present-day, prevailing, widespread **11** fashionable **12** contemporary
air: **4** gale, gust, wind **5** blast, draft **6** breeze, squall, zephyr **7** cyclone, indraft, updraft **9** downdraft **10** slipstream
ocean: **7** riptide **8** undertow **9** maelstrom, whirlpool
unit: **3** amp **6** ampere

Currier's partner
4 Ives (James)

curry
4 beat, comb, seek, whip **5** groom **6** thrash

curse
3 hex, pox **4** bane, cuss, damn, evil, jinx, oath **5** swear **6** blight, plague, whammy **7** afflict, damning, malison, scourge, torment **8** anathema, cussword, execrate **9** bête noire, blaspheme, blasphemy, expletive, imprecate, profanity, swearword **10** affliction, execration, misfortune, pestilence **11** commination, imprecation, malediction, profanation **12** anathematize, denunciation

cursed
6 damned **7** blasted, dratted **8** damnable, infernal **9** execrable **10** confounded **13** blankety-blank

cursive
6 fluent, smooth **7** flowing, running

cursory
5 hasty, quick, rapid **6** casual **7** hurried, shallow, sketchy **8** careless **10** uncritical **11** perfunctory, superficial

curt
4 rude **5** bluff, blunt, brief, gruff, short, terse **6** abrupt, crusty **7** brusque, concise **8** succinct **10** peremptory

curtail
3 cut **4** clip, dock, trim **5** prune, slash **6** lessen, reduce **7** abridge, cut back, shorten **8** diminish, pare down, retrench, truncate **10** abbreviate

curtain
4 drop, veil **5** drape **6** screen **7** barrier
doorway: **8** portiere
holder: **3** rod
Indian: **6** purdah
material: **4** lace, silk **5** gauze **6** damask, velvet **8** chenille, jacquard
rod concealer: **7** valance
sash: **7** tieback
stage: **4** drop **5** scrim **8** backdrop

curtains
3 end **4** ruin **5** death **6** demise, finish **7** decease **8** disaster

curtilage
4 quad, yard **5** court **8** cloister **9** courtyard, enclosure **10** quadrangle

curvaceous
5 buxom **7** rounded, shapely **9** Junoesque **10** statuesque, voluptuous **13** well-developed

curvature
of the spine: **8** kyphosis, lordosis **9** scoliosis

curve
3 arc, bow **4** arch, bend, coil, curl, turn, veer, wind **5** crook, round, swing, swirl, twist **6** convex, spiral, swerve **7** concave, flexure, rondure **9** corkscrew
of an arch: **8** extrados, intrados
pitcher's: **4** hook
plane: **7** cycloid, limaçon **8** parabola, sinusoid, trochoid **9** hyperbola
S-shaped: **3** ess **4** ogee **7** sigmoid

curved
4 bent **5** arced, bowed, round **6** arched, convex **7** arcuate, bending, embowed, falcate, rounded, sigmoid, sinuous, twisted
implement: **6** sickle
molding: **4** ogee
sword: **5** kukri, saber, sabre **7** cutlass **8** scimitar

curvilinear
see **curved**

curvy
see **curvaceous; curved**

Cush
father: **3** Ham
son: **6** Nimrod

cushion
3 mat, pad **5** squab **6** absorb, buffer, pillow, soften **7** bolster, hassock, pillion **8** palliate, woolsack

cushy
4 cozy, easy, soft **11** comfortable, undemanding

cusp
3 tip **4** apex, edge, peak **5** point, verge **12** turning point

cuspid
6 canine **8** eyetooth

cuspidate
5 sharp **6** peaked, pointy **7** pointed

cuss
3 guy, man **4** chap, damn, dude, oath **5** curse, swear **6** fellow **9** expletive

cussed
4 dour **5** crude, gruff **6** crusty, cursed, grumpy, ornery **7** boorish, brusque, grouchy **8** churlish **9** obstinate **10** unyielding **11** contentious **12** antagonistic, cantankerous

cussword
4 oath **5** curse **9** expletive, swearword

custard
4 flan **7** pudding

custodian
5 super **6** keeper, porter, warden **7** curator, steward **8** guardian, overseer, watchdog, watchman **9** caretaker, concierge, protector **10** supervisor **11** conservator

custody
4 care, ward **5** guard, trust **6** charge **7** keeping **9** captivity, detention **10** caretaking, management, protection **11** confinement, safekeeping, supervision **12** guardianship

custom
3 use **4** norm **5** habit, mores (plural), trade, usage **6** groove, manner, praxis, ritual **7** folkway, precept, routine, traffic **8** business, habitude, practice **9** patronage **10** consuetude, convention

customary
5 usual **6** common, normal, wonted **7** general, regular, routine **8** accepted, everyday, familiar, frequent, habitual, ordinary, orthodox, standard **10** accustomed **11** established, traditional **12** conventional

custom-built
7 bespoke **10** tailor-made **11** made-to-order

customer
5 buyer **6** client, patron **7** shopper **8** consumer **9** purchaser
frequent: **7** habitué

customized
see **custom-built**

custom-made
see **custom-built**

cut
3 bob, hew, lop, mow, saw **4** bite, chop, clip, crop, dice, dock, fell, gash, hack, nick, pare, reap, sawn, skip, slit, snip, snub, trim **5** carve, filet, lathe, lower, mince, notch, piece, prune, quota, sawed, sever, share, shave, shear, slash, slice, split, wound **6** cleave, delete, dilute, divide, excise, fillet, incise, reduce, scythe, sickle, sunder **7** abridge, curtail, dissect, portion, section, segment, shorten **8** division, separate, truncate **9** allotment, allowance, reduction **10** abbreviate
of beef: **3** rib **4** loin, rump **5** chine, chuck, flank, roast, shank, steak, T-bone **6** saddle **7** brisket, sirloin **9** aitchbone **11** porterhouse

cut across
6 bisect **8** transect **9** transcend

cut-and-dried
5 stock **7** routine **9** formulaic **10** unoriginal **11** predictable **13** unimaginative

cutaneous
6 dermal

cutaway
4 coat, dive **5** tails

cut back
3 zag **4** clip, curb, dock, pare, trim **5** lower, prune, shave, slash **6** lessen, reduce **7** abridge, curtail, shorten **8** decrease, retrench, truncate **10** abbreviate

cut down
3 axe **4** chop, clip, fell, pare **5** lower, shave, slash **6** digest, reduce **7** abridge, shorten **10** abbreviate

cute
4 twee **6** dainty, pretty **7** cunning **8** affected **10** attractive **11** impertinent, smart-alecky

cut in
7 include, intrude, obtrude **9** introduce

cutlass
5 saber, sabre, sword **7** machete **8** scimitar

cut off
2 ax **3** axe, bar, end, lop **4** halt, kill, stop **5** abort, block, sever **6** disown **7** curtail, destroy, isolate, suspend **8** amputate, obstruct, renounce, separate, truncate **9** intercept, interrupt, terminate **10** disinherit **11** discontinue

cut out
3 end **4** halt **5** cease, leave, scram, usurp **6** beat it, delete, depart, escape, excise, remove, resect **7** defraud, deprive, take off **8** displace, supplant **9** eliminate, extirpate **10** disconnect

cutpurse
5 thief **10** pickpocket

cut short
3 bob **4** clip, crop, dock, halt, poll **5** abort, check, scrub, shear **7** abridge, curtail **8** break off **9** interrupt, terminate **10** abbreviate

cuttable
7 sectile **8** scissile

cutthroat
5 bravo **6** gunman, hit man, killer **7** torpedo **8** assassin, murderer **10** hatchet man, triggerman

cutting
5 acerb **7** acerbic **8** incisive, piercing **9** sarcastic, trenchant **11** penetrating
edge: **5** blade
remark: **3** dig **4** barb **5** taunt
tool: **2** ax **3** axe, hob, saw **4** adze **5** knife, lathe, mower, plane, razor **6** reaper, scythe, shears, sickle **7** hatchet **8** scissors, tomahawk

cuttlefish
7 mollusc, mollusk **10** cephalopod
ink: **5** sepia
relative: **5** squid **7** octopus

cut up
4 dice, hash, romp **5** caper, clown, mince, slash **6** cavort **7** carry on, show off **9** misbehave **10** roughhouse

cutup
3 wag **4** zany **5** clown, joker **6** madcap **7** buffoon, farceur **8** jokester

cyan
4 blue

Cybele
4 Rhea
beloved: **5** Attis
brother: **6** Cronus
father: **6** Uranus
husband: **6** Cronus
mother: **4** Gaea
son: **4** Zeus **7** Jupiter, Neptune **8** Poseidon

cyber
5 wired **10** electronic

cybernetics founder
6 Wiener (Norbert)

cycle
3 age, lap, set **4** bike, loop, ring **5** chain, orbit, recur, round, wheel **6** course, period, series **7** circuit **8** rotation, sequence **9** vibration **10** revolution, succession, two-wheeler, velocipede **11** oscillation

cycle track
9 velodrome

cyclic
7 regular **8** periodic, repeated, rhythmic **9** iterative, recurring, repeating **10** isochronal **12** intermittent

cyclone
7 tornado, twister

cyclopean
4 huge **7** immense, mammoth, massive, titanic **8** colossal, enormous, gigantic **9** monstrous **10** gargantuan, tremendous **11** elephantine

Cyclops
5 Arges **7** Brontes **8** Steropes **10** Polyphemus

Cycnus
father: **4** Ares, Mars
slayer: **8** Heracles, Hercules

cygnet
4 swan

dam (mother): **3** pen
sire (father): **3** cob

Cygnus
form: **4** swan
friend: **7** Phaeton
star: **5** Deneb

cylinder
4 drum, pipe, tube **5** spool **6** barrel, bobbin, platen, roller

cylindrical
6 terete **7** tubular **8** tubelike

Cymbeline
daughter: **6** Imogen
son: **9** Arviragus, Guiderius
son-in-law: **9** Posthumus

Cymric
5 Welsh **6** Celtic **9** Brythonic
bard: **8** Taliesin
Elysium: **6** Annwfn
god: **5** Lludd
of Elysium: **5** Arawn
of the dead: **5** Pwyll
of the seas: **3** Ler **4** Llyr **5** Dylan
of the sky: **7** Gwydion
of the sun: **4** Lleu, Llew
of the underworld: **4** Gwyn
goddess: **3** Don **9** Arianrhod
magician: **6** Merlin

Cymru
5 Wales

cynical
8 derisive, sardonic, scornful **12** misanthropic

Cynthia
4 Luna, moon **5** Diana **7** Artemis

cyprian
4 bawd, jade, slut, tart **5** hussy, tramp **6** floozy, harlot, hooker, wanton **7** jezebel, trollop **8** slattern, strumpet **10** prostitute

Cyprus
capital: **7** Nicosia **8** Lefkosia
city: **7** Larnaca **8** Limassol
language: **5** Greek **7** Turkish
monetary unit: **4** lira **5** pound
mountain: **7** Olympus
port: **9** Famagusta
sea: **13** Mediterranean

Cyrano de Bergerac
4 poet **7** duelist **8** duellist
author: **7** Rostand (Edmond)
beloved: **6** Roxane **7** Roxanne
feature: **4** nose
rival: **9** Christian

Cyrus
conquest: **5** Lydia, Media **7** Babylon
daughter: **6** Atossa
empire: **7** Persian
father: **8** Cambyses
son: **8** Cambyses

cyst
3 sac, wen **4** sore **5** pouch, spore **6** growth **7** abscess, blister, capsule, vesicle **8** swelling

Cytherea
4 isle **5** Venus **6** island **9** Aphrodite

czar
5 chief, mogul **6** despot, honcho, tycoon, tyrant **7** emperor, kingpin, magnate **8** autocrat
Russian: **4** Ivan **5** Basil, Boris, Peter **6** Alexis, Dmitry, Feodor, Fyodor, Vasily **7** Dimitri, Michael, Romanov **8** Nicholas, Romanoff, Theodore **9** Alexander **12** Boris Godunov
son: **10** czarevitch
wife: **7** czarina

czar's wife
7 czarina

Czech Republic
capital: **6** Prague
city: **4** Brno **7** Ostrava
monetary unit: **6** koruna
neighbor: **6** Poland **7** Austria, Germany **8** Slovakia
region: **7** Bohemia, Moravia
river: **4** Labe, Oder **5** March **6** Morava

D

dab
3 bit, pat **4** blob, blow, daub, peck, poke, spot **5** smear, touch **6** bedaub **7** besmear, plaster, splotch **8** flatfish

dabble
3 dip, dot, toy **4** fool, stud **5** fleck **6** dampen, fiddle, monkey, pepper, putter, splash, tinker **7** freckle, spatter, stipple **8** sprinkle **9** bespeckle, muck about **10** muck around

dabbler
4 duck, tyro **7** amateur **8** putterer, tinkerer **9** smatterer **10** dilettante

dabchick
5 grebe

dacha
5 villa **7** cottage **12** country house

dad
3 pop **4** papa **5** padre, pater **6** father, old man, parent

Dadaist
3 Arp (Jean), Ray (Man) **4** Ball (Hugo) **5** Ernst (Max), Grosz (George), Tzara (Tristan) **7** Duchamp (Marcel), Picabia (Francis) **10** Schwitters (Kurt)

daedal
6 knotty **7** complex **8** artistic, involved, skillful **9** elaborate, intricate **11** complicated **12** labyrinthine **13** sophisticated

Daedalus
7 builder **9** architect, artificer
construction: **9** Labyrinth
father: **6** Metion
son: **6** Icarus
victim: **5** Talos **6** Perdix

daffy
see **daft**

daft
3 mad **4** loco, nuts **5** balmy, crazy, dopey, flaky, loony, nutty, potty, silly, wacko, wacky **6** absurd, crazed, cuckoo, insane, screwy **7** cracked, foolish, idiotic, lunatic, witless **8** demented **10** unbalanced **11** harebrained

Dag
father: **7** Delling
horse: **9** Skinfaksi
mother: **4** Nott

Dagda
chief god of the: **5** Gaels, Irish
daughter: **6** Brigit
instrument: **4** harp
son: **6** Aengus
wife: **5** Boann

dagger
4 dirk, snee **5** skean, skene **6** bodkin, stylet **7** dudgeon, poniard **8** stiletto
handle: **4** hilt
Malay: **4** kris

____ Dahl
5 Roald **6** Arlene

daikon
6 radish

daily
7 diurnal **8** everyday **9** circadian, quotidian
grind: **7** rat race

dainty
5 goody, tasty, treat **6** choice, morsel, select, tidbit **7** elegant, fragile **8** delicacy, delicate, ethereal, graceful, kickshaw **9** exquisite, recherché **10** delightful

dairy
8 creamery

dais
5 stage **6** podium **7** rostrum **8** platform

daisy
5 oxeye **6** Shasta
British: **10** moonflower
Scottish: **5** gowan

Daisy Miller author
5 James (Henry)

Dakota dialect
5 Teton

Daksha's father
6 Brahma

dale
4 dell, glen, vale **6** dingle, valley

Dallas series
character: **3** Liz, Ray **4** Jack, Jock, Lucy **5** April, Bobby, Cally, Cliff, Donna, James, Jenna **6** Carter **7** Clayton, J. R. Ewing, Kristin **8** Michelle, Sue Ellen **9** Miss Ellie
family: **5** Ewing

ranch home: 9 Southfork
star: 4 Gray (Linda), Keel (Howard), Reed (Donna) 5 Davis (Jim), Duffy (Patrick), Rambo (Dack) 6 Crosby (Mary), Hagman (Larry), Howard (Susan), Kanaly (Steve), Tilton (Charlene), Wilson (Sheree) 7 Presley (Priscilla) 9 Bel Geddes (Barbara), Kercheval (Ken), Principal (Victoria)

dally
3 lag, pet, toy 4 drag, idle, play 5 delay, flirt, tarry 6 coquet, dawdle, diddle, linger, loiter, trifle 8 lollygag 9 hang about, waste time 10 fool around

dam
4 weir 5 block, check 7 barrier 8 hold back, restrain
major: 4 Oahe 6 Hoover 7 San Luis 8 Fort Peck, Garrison, Oroville 10 Bonneville, Glen Canyon 11 Grand Coulee

damage
3 mar 4 blot, harm, hurt, loss, maim, ruin 5 abuse, burst, cloud, spoil, stain, wound 6 blight, deface, impair, injure, injury, mangle, ravage, scathe 7 blemish, destroy, marring, tarnish, vitiate 8 maltreat, mischief, mistreat, mutilate, sabotage 9 devastate, vandalism 10 impairment 11 devastation

damaged
4 hurt, rent 6 broken, busted, dinged, flawed, marred 7 injured, spoiled, totaled 8 battered, impaired, ruptured 9 blemished, fractured, imperfect, shattered 10 fragmented

damaging
6 nocent 7 harmful, hurtful, nocuous 9 injurious 11 deleterious, detrimental, prejudicial

dame
4 lady 5 woman 6 gammer, matron 7 dowager 9 matriarch

Damien's island
7 Molokai

Damkina's son
6 Marduk

damn
4 cuss, darn, doom, drat 5 curse, swear 7 condemn, doggone 8 execrate, sentence 9 imprecate 10 vituperate 12 anathematize

damnable
6 blamed, cursed, cussed 7 blasted, dratted 8 accursed, infernal 9 abhorrent, execrable 10 abominable, detestable

damned
5 utter 6 blamed, cursed, cussed, darned, dashed, doomed 7 awfully, blasted, doggone, dratted, goldarn 8 accursed, infernal 9 condemned 10 confounded 13 anathematized

Damocles' ____
5 sword

Damon's friend
7 Pythias

damp
3 wet 4 dank, dewy 5 check, choke, humid, moist, musty 6 clammy 7 bedewed 8 humidify, humidity

dampen
4 cool, curb 5 chill 6 deaden 7 depress, moisten 8 diminish

damsel
3 gal 4 girl, lass, maid, miss 5 filly, wench 6 lassie, maiden

Dan
father: 5 Jacob
mother: 6 Bilhah
son: 6 Hushim

Danaë
father: 8 Acrisius
lover: 4 Zeus
son: 7 Perseus

Danaus
brother: 8 Aegyptus
daughters: 7 Danaïds 8 Danaïdes
father: 5 Belus
founder of: 5 Argos
grandfather: 7 Neptune 8 Poseidon

dance
3 dip, hop, jig, tap 4 ball, flit, foot, heel, hoof, hula, juba, leap, lope, reel, step, trip 5 bamba, brawl, galop, gigue, hover, lindy, mambo, mixer, polka, rumba, stomp, swing, tread 6 ballet, bolero, boogie, Boston, cancan, chassé, foot it, formal, frolic, German, hoof it, rhumba, shimmy 7 beguine, coranto, courant, flicker, flitter, flutter, hoedown, one-step, shuffle 8 cakewalk, flamenco, galliard, glissade, rigadoon, rigaudon 9 allemande, cotillion, jitterbug, pas de deux
Argentinian: 5 tango
art of: 12 choreography
Austrian: 7 ländler
ballroom: 5 rumba, tango 6 cha-cha, rhumba 7 fox-trot, mazurka, two-step 8 merengue 9 cotillion 10 Charleston
Bohemian: 5 polka
Brazilian: 5 samba 6 maxixe 7 carioca, lambada 8 capoeira 9 bossa nova
combining form: 5 chore 6 choreo, chorio
country: 3 hay 4 reel 8 hornpipe
couple: 5 polka 9 cotillion, malaguena 11 square dance
court: 6 canary, pavane 8 saraband 9 allemande, sarabande
Cuban: 5 conga, mambo, rumba 6 rhumba 8 habanera
designer: 13 choreographer
English: 6 morris

formal: 4 ball, prom 9 cotillion
French: 6 cancan 7 bourrée, gavotte 9 allemande 10 carmagnole
garment: 4 tutu 7 leotard
Haitian: 4 juba 8 merengue
Hawaiian: 4 hula
Hungarian: 7 czardas
Indian: 6 nautch 7 bhangra
instrument: 8 castanet
Israeli: 4 hora
Italian: 10 saltarello, tarantella, villanella 11 passacaglia
lively: 3 jig 4 reel, trot 5 galop, gigue, polka, rumba 6 rhumba 7 bourrée 8 fandango, hornpipe, rigadoon, rigaudon 9 farandole, shakedown 10 Charleston, saltarello, tarantella
Maori: 4 haka
movement: 4 plié, step 8 capriole, glissade 9 pirouette
Muse of: 11 Terpsichore
1920's: 10 Charleston
Polish: 5 polka 7 mazurka 9 polonaise
Polynesian: 4 hula
ragtime: 10 turkey trot
Scottish: 3 bob 4 reel 5 fling 10 strathspey 11 schottische 13 Highland fling
shoes: 5 pumps 8 slippers
slipper: 7 toeshoe
slow: 6 adagio, minuet, pavane 8 habanera
Spanish: 4 jota 6 bolero 7 zapateo 8 cachucha, chaconne, fandango, flamenco, saraband 9 malaguena, sarabande 10 seguidilla
spectator: 10 wallflower
springy: 3 jig
square: 7 hoedown, lancers 9 cotillion, quadrille
stately: 5 pavan 6 pavane 8 saraband 9 polonaise, sarabande
step: 3 pas
woman's: 6 cancan

dancer
6 hoofer 7 chorine, clogger, danseur, stepper 8 coryphée, danseuse 9 ballerina, chorus boy 10 cakewalker, chorus girl
American: 4 Feld (Elliot), Holm (Hanya), Lang (Pearl), Tune (Tommy) 5 Ailey (Alvin), Fosse (Bob), Kelly (Gene), Shawn (Ted), Tharp (Twyla) 6 Castle (Irene, Vernon), Duncan (Isadora), Dunham (Katherine), Graham (Martha), Morris (Mark), Taylor (Paul), Verdon (Gwen) 7 Astaire (Adele, Fred), Bujones (Fernando), de Mille (Agnes), Farrell (Suzanne), Gregory (Cynthia), Jamison (Judith), Joffrey (Robert), Martins (Peter), Massine (Leonide), McBride (Patricia), Robbins (Jerome), St. Denis (Ruth), Tamiris (Helen) 8 Champion (Gower, Marge), d'Amboise (Jacques), Humphrey (Doris), Kirkland (Gelsey), Mitchell (Arthur), Nikolais (Alwin), Villella (Edward) 9 Tallchief (Maria) 10 Cunningham (Merce)
Cuban: 6 Alonso (Alicia)
Danish: 5 Bruhn (Erik) 7 Martins (Peter) 8 Tomasson (Helgi)
English: 5 Dolin (Anton), Somes (Michael), Tudor (Antony) 7 Fonteyn (Margot), Markova (Alicia), Rambert (Marie) 8 de Valois (Ninette), Helpmann (Robert)
French: 5 Lifar (Serge) 6 Béjart (Maurice), Perrot (Jules), Petipa (Marius) 7 Camargo (Marie), Massine (Leonide)
German: 5 Jooss (Kurt)
Italian: 5 Grisi (Carlotta)
Mexican: 5 Limón (José)
Russian: 5 Lifar (Serge) 6 Fokine (Michel), Petipa (Marius) 7 Massine (Leonide), Nureyev (Rudolf), Pavlova (Anna), Ulanova (Galina) 8 Danilova (Aleksandra), Makarova (Natalia), Nijinska (Bronislava), Nijinsky (Vaslav), Vaganova (Agrippina) 9 Karsavina (Tamara), Semyonova (Marina) 11 Baryshnikov (Mikhail), Plisetskaya (Maya)
Scottish: 7 Shearer (Moira)

dancing
6 ballet 12 choreography
mania: 9 tarantism

dandle
3 pet 4 play 6 caress, cosset, cradle, cuddle, pamper

dandruff
5 scall, scurf

dandy
3 fop, pip 4 beau, buck, dude, fine, lulu, toff 5 dilly, doozy, nifty, swell 6 doozie, peachy 7 coxcomb, foppish 8 terrific 9 excellent, first-rate, humdinger, hunky-dory 11 Beau Brummel, crackerjack 12 lounge lizard

dang
4 damn, darn 6 cursed, cussed, damned, darned 7 blasted, dratted, goldarn 8 infernal 10 confounded

danger
4 risk 5 peril 6 crisis, hazard, menace, plight, threat 7 pitfall, trouble 8 distress, jeopardy 9 emergency
signal: 4 bell 5 alarm, siren 6 tocsin

dangerous
5 risky 6 unsafe 7 parlous 8 insecure, menacing, perilous, unstable 9 hazardous 10 precarious 11 threatening

dangle
4 hang 5 droop, swing 6 depend 7 suspend

Daniel ____
pioneer: 5 Boone
statesman: 7 Webster

Danish
hero: **5** Ogier
king: **9** Christian, Frederick
queen: **9** Margrethe

dank
3 wet **4** damp **5** humid, moist **6** clammy **8** dripping

Dante
beloved: **8** Beatrice
birthplace: **8** Florence
daughter: **7** Antonia
deathplace: **7** Ravenna
party: **6** Guelph **7** Bianchi
patron: **5** Scala
teacher: **6** Latini
wife: **5** Gemma
work: **5** canto **7** Inferno **8** Commedia, Paradiso **9** Vita Nuova **10** Purgatorio **12** Divine Comedy (The)

Danton's colleague
5 Marat (Jean-Paul) **11** Robespierre (Maximilien)

Danzig
6 Gdańsk

Daphne
father: **5** Ladon **6** Peneus
form: **6** laurel **10** laurel tree
pursuer: **6** Apollo **9** Leucippus

Daphnis' lover
5 Chloe

dapper
4 neat, trim **5** doggy, natty, sassy, smart, swank **6** classy, jaunty, rakish, snazzy, spiffy, spruce, sprucy **7** bandbox, dashing, doggish, foppish, stylish **11** well-groomed

dapple
4 spot **5** fleck, patch **6** mottle **7** speckle, stipple

dappled
4 pied **6** motley **7** flecked, mottled, patched, piebald, spotted **8** brindled **10** variegated **11** varicolored

Dardanelles
10 Hellespont

Dardanus
descendants: **7** Trojans
father: **4** Zeus **7** Jupiter
mother: **7** Electra

dare
3 try **4** defy, risk **5** beard, brave **6** hazard **7** attempt, venture **8** confront, defiance **9** challenge

daredevil
see **daring**

darer
4 hero **6** risker

daring
4 bold, guts, rash **5** brash, brave, gutsy, moxie, nerve, nervy, pluck, valor **6** heroic, plucky **7** bravery, courage, heroism **8** audacity, boldness, fearless, reckless **9** audacious, derring-do, fortitude, venturous **10** courageous **11** adventurous, venturesome **13** adventuresome

Darius
battle: **8** Marathon
father: **9** Hystaspes
country: **6** Persia **7** Parthia
son: **6** Xerxes
wife: **6** Atossa

Darjeeling
3 tea

dark
3 dim **4** dusk, inky, murk **5** black, blind, cloud, dingy, dusky, ebony, murky, night, sable, shady, sooty, swart, umber, unlit, vague **6** brunet, cloudy, dismal, gloomy, opaque, somber, sombre, wicked **7** obscure, ominous, rayless, satanic, shadowy, stygian, subfusc, sunless, swarthy, unclear **8** bistered, brunette, infernal, sinister **9** enigmatic, lightless, secretive, tenebrous, unlighted **10** caliginous, indistinct, mysterious, mystifying, pitch-black **11** crepuscular **13** unilluminated
poetic: **4** ebon

darken
3 dim **5** bedim, cloud, gloom, lower, shade, sully, umber **6** shadow **7** becloud, blacken, eclipse, obscure, tarnish **8** melanize, overcast **9** obfuscate, overcloud **10** overshadow
Scottish: **5** gloam

dark-haired
female: **8** brunette
male: **6** brunet

darkness
4 dusk, evil, murk **5** black, gloom, night, shade **6** shadow **8** blackout **9** nightfall, obscurity

darkroom liquid
3 fix **8** emulsion, hardener

darling
3 gra, hon, pet **4** dear, duck, love **5** angel, deary, ducky, flame, honey, loved, sugar, sweet **7** beloved, dearest, sweetie **8** adorable, charming, favorite, precious **10** sweetheart, sweetie pie

darn
4 drat, knit, mend **5** patch **6** blamed, cursed, cussed, damned, shucks **7** blasted, doggone, dratted **8** infernal **9** embroider **10** confounded
French: **3** zut

Darrow client
4 Debs (Eugene), Loeb (Richard) **6** Scopes (John) **7** Haywood (William), Leopold (Nathan)

dart
3 fly, run, zip **4** barb, bolt, buzz, dash, flit, leap, rush, sail, scud, skim, tear **5** arrow, bound, hurry, lance, pitch, scamp, scoot, shaft, shoot, skirr, spear, speed, spurt **6** glance, hasten, scurry, spring, sprint **7** javelin, missile, scamper
barbed: **10** banderilla

D'Artagnan's friends
5 Athos **6** Aramis **7** Porthos **10** musketeers

Dartmouth location
5 Devon **7** Hanover **12** New Hampshire

darts term
3 leg **4** bust **5** split **6** double, flight, hockey, treble **8** bull's-eye

Darwin, Charles
colleague: **7** Wallace (Alfred Russel)
ship: **6** Beagle
theory: **9** evolution, selection

dash
3 fly, nip, run **4** bolt, brio, cast, damn, dart, élan, foil, hurl, race, ruin, rush, slam, tear, zing **5** break, chase, flair, fling, pinch, smash, style, trace **6** esprit, hyphen, pizazz, scurry, splash, sprint, thrust, thwart **7** bravura, depress, destroy, pizzazz, shatter, smidgen, spatter **8** confound **9** animation, frustrate

dashboard reading
4 fuel **5** speed **7** mileage **8** pressure **11** temperature

dashing
4 bold **5** smart **6** dapper, jaunty, lively, modish **7** gallant, stylish **8** animated, spirited **11** adventurous, fashionable

Das Kapital author
4 Marx (Karl)

dassie
4 pika **5** coney, hyrax

dastard
6 coward, craven **7** chicken, quitter **8** poltroon, recreant **9** scoundrel

dastardly
3 low **4** base, mean **6** craven, yellow **8** cowardly, shameful, skulking **11** treacherous, underhanded **13** pusillanimous

data
4 info **5** facts, input **7** figures **9** documents **11** information
numerical: **5** stats **10** statistics

date
3 age, era, woo **5** court, epoch, tryst **6** cutoff, escort **7** take out **8** deadline **9** accompany **10** engagement, rendezvous **11** anniversary, appointment, assignation

dated
3 old **5** passé **6** démodé, old hat **7** archaic, outworn **8** obsolete, outmoded **10** antiquated **12** old-fashioned **13** unfashionable
fashionably: **5** retro

datum
4 fact

daub
4 blob, blot, spot **5** fleck, paint, smear **6** dapple, smudge, splash **7** besmear, dribble, plaster, speckle, splotch

daughter
Blythe Danner's: **7** Paltrow (Gwyneth)
Bruce Dern's: **5** Laura
Bush's: **5** Jenna **7** Barbara
Carter's: **3** Amy
Cash's: **7** Rosanne
Cher's: **8** Chastity (Bono)
Clinton's: **7** Chelsea
Cole's: **7** Natalie
Coppola's: **5** Sofia
Danny Thomas's: **5** Marlo
Debbie Reynolds's: **6** Carrie (Fisher)
Eddie Fisher's: **6** Carrie
Elizabeth II's: **4** Anne
Elvis's: **9** Lisa Marie
Fonda's: **4** Jane
Ford's (Gerald): **5** Susan
Freud's: **4** Anna
Garland's: **4** Liza (Minnelli)
Goldie Hawn's: **10** Kate Hudson
Ingrid Bergman's: **8** Isabella (Rossellini)
Janet Leigh's: **8** Jamie Lee (Curtis)
Joel Grey's: **8** Jennifer
Johnson's (Lyndon): **4** Lucy **5** Linda
Jon Voight's: **8** Angelina (Jolie)
Kennedy's (John F.): **8** Caroline
Klaus Kinski's: **9** Nastassja
Maureen O'Sullivan's: **3** Mia (Farrow)
Naomi Judd's: **7** Wynonna
Nat King Cole's: **7** Natalie
Nixon's: **5** Julie **6** Tricia
Pat Boone's: **5** Debby
Ravi Shankar's: **10** Norah Jones
Reagan's: **5** Patti **7** Maureen
Richard Burton's: **4** Kate
Ryan O'Neal's: **5** Tatum
Sinatra's: **5** Nancy
Tony Curtis's: **8** Jamie Lee

Daughter of the Moon
7 Nokomis

daunt
3 cow **5** alarm, deter **6** dismay, subdue **7** terrify **8** frighten **10** disconcert, discourage, dishearten, intimidate

daunting
7 awesome 8 imposing 9 dismaying, unnerving 10 forbidding, formidable 11 dispiriting 12 discouraging, intimidating, overwhelming

dauntless
4 bold, game 5 brave 6 daring 7 gallant, valiant 8 fearless, unafraid 9 unfearful, unfearing 10 courageous 11 lionhearted 12 stouthearted

dauntlessness
4 guts 5 heart, nerve, pluck, spunk, valor 6 daring, mettle, spirit 7 bravery, cojones, courage 8 boldness 10 resolution 12 fearlessness

davenport
4 desk, sofa 5 couch, divan 6 daybed 12 chesterfield

David
commander: 4 Joab 5 Amasa
companion: 8 Jonathan
daughter: 5 Tamar
father: 5 Jesse
rebuker: 6 Nathan
son: 5 Amnon 7 Absalom, Solomon 8 Adonijah
song of: 5 psalm
wife: 6 Michal 7 Abigail, Ahinoam 9 Bathsheba

____ David
4 Camp 5 Magen, Mogen 6 Star of

David Copperfield
author: 7 Dickens (Charles)
character: 4 Dora, Heep 5 Uriah 6 Barkis 8 Micawber, Peggotty 9 Murdstone 10 Steerforth

Da Vinci Code author
5 Brown (Dan)

davit
5 crane

dawdle
3 lag 4 idle, laze, loaf, loll 5 dally, delay, tarry 6 diddle, linger, loiter, lounge 8 lollygag 10 dillydally

dawn
4 morn 5 onset, sunup 6 aurora 7 morning, sunrise 8 cockcrow, daybreak, daylight 9 beginning 10 first light
goddess: 3 Eos 6 Aurora
pertaining to: 4 eoan

day
abbreviation: 3 Fri, Mon, Sat, Sun, Thu, Tue, Wed 4 Thur, Tues 5 Thurs
before: 3 eve
church calendar: 5 feria
French: 4 jour
German: 3 Tag
holy: 5 feast
hour: 4 noon
Latin: 4 dies
Spanish: 3 día

daybreak
4 dawn, morn 5 sunup 6 aurora 7 dawning, morning, sunrise 8 cockcrow, daylight

daydream
4 muse 5 fancy 6 vision 7 fantasy, reverie 8 phantasy 9 fantasize 10 woolgather 13 woolgathering

daystar
3 Sol, sun 5 Venus 7 phoebus

daze
3 fog 4 haze, stun 5 amaze, blind 6 dazzle, stupor, trance 7 astound, confuse, stupefy 8 astonish, bedazzle, befuddle, confound 9 dumbfound

dazed
5 woozy 6 groggy, punchy 7 dazzled, stunned 8 confused 9 stupefied 10 punch-drunk

____ d'Azur
4 Côte

dazzle
3 wow 4 stun 5 amaze, blind, éclat, glitz, shine 7 impress 8 astonish, bewilder, confound, outshine 9 overpower

dazzling
6 flashy, garish 7 radiant 8 splendid, stunning 9 brilliant 11 confounding, resplendent 12 overpowering

deacon
6 clergy, cleric, layman 8 reverend 9 churchman

dead
4 cold, gone, late 5 passé, slain, stiff 6 buried, fallen 7 defunct, done for, expired, extinct 8 deceased, departed, lifeless 9 senseless 10 corpselike 11 unconscious 12 extinguished

deadbeat
3 bum 5 idler 6 debtor, loafer, slouch 7 lounger, shirker, slacker 10 delinquent, malingerer

dead duck
5 goner 8 casualty, fatality

deaden
4 dull, kill, mute, numb, stun 5 blunt, quiet 6 benumb, dampen, lessen, muffle, obtund, reduce, stifle 7 smother, stupefy 8 suppress 11 anesthetize, desensitize

dead end
4 halt, stop 6 pocket, unruly 7 impasse 8 cul-de-sac, standoff 9 stalemate, terminate 10 blind alley, bottleneck, standstill

deadened
4 numb **6** asleep, dulled, killed, numbed **7** blunted **8** benumbed, impaired **12** anesthetized

deadeye
5 block **8** marksman **12** sharpshooter

deadfall
4 trap **7** springe **9** booby trap, mousetrap

deadliness
8 fatality **9** lethality, mortality

deadlock
3 tie **4** draw **7** impasse **8** standoff, stoppage **9** checkmate, stalemate **10** standstill

deadly
5 fatal, toxic **6** lethal, mortal **7** capital, killing **8** lethally, unerring **10** implacable **11** destructive, internecine **12** pestilential

deadpan
5 blank, empty **6** vacant **9** impassive **10** poker-faced **11** inscrutable **12** inexpressive, unexpressive

Dead Souls author
5 Gogol (Nikolay)

dead to rights
9 red-handed

deadweight
4 load **6** weight

deal
4 dole, sale, sell **5** allot, serve, shake, share, trade, treat **6** barter, dicker, parcel **7** bargain, deliver, dish out, dole out, mete out, package, portion, traffic, wrestle **8** contract, disburse, dispense, share out **9** agreement, apportion, negotiate **10** administer, compromise, distribute, measure out **11** arrangement, transaction **13** understanding
great: **4** gobs, heap, lots, tons **5** heaps, horde, loads, scads **6** oodles, plenty, stacks
out: **8** disburse, dispense **9** apportion **10** administer, distribute
with: **5** serve, treat **6** handle, regard **7** concern, involve

dealer
5 agent **6** broker, seller, trader, vendor **8** chandler, merchant, operator **9** tradesman **10** negotiator, trafficker **11** businessman, distributer, distributor **12** merchandiser
British: **5** coper **6** draper, jobber, mercer **7** chapman

dealings
5 trade, truck **7** affairs, matters, traffic **8** business, commerce, concerns **11** intercourse **12** interactions, transactions, undertakings

dean
4 head **5** chief, doyen, elder **6** leader

dear
3 gra, pet **4** fond, lamb, love **5** honey, loved, sugar, sweet **6** costly, doting, loving, prized, scarce **7** beloved, darling, devoted, lovable, machree, querida, tootsie **8** favorite, precious, valuable **9** cherished, expensive, heartfelt, treasured **10** fair-haired, honeybunch, sweetheart **12** affectionate
French: **4** cher **5** chère **6** chérie
Scottish: **2** jo

dearth
4 lack, want **6** famine **7** absence, default, paucity **8** scarcity, shortage, sparsity **9** privation, scantness **10** deficiency, meagerness, scantiness

death
3 end **4** exit **6** demise, ending, expiry **7** decease, passing, quietus **8** casualty, curtains, fatality, necrosis, thanatos **9** bloodshed, departure **10** expiration, extinction, grim reaper **11** dissolution, termination **12** annihilation
after: **10** posthumous
combining form: **6** thanat **7** thanato
music: **5** dirge, elegy **8** threnody
notice: **4** obit **8** obituary **9** necrology
of tissue: **8** gangrene
personification: **10** grim reaper
put to: **3** gas, hit, ice, zap **4** do in, hang, kill, slay **5** drown, lynch, snuff, waste **6** murder, poison, rub out **7** bump off, butcher, execute, smother, wipe out **8** blow away, dispatch, immolate, knock off, strangle, throttle **9** slaughter, suffocate **10** asphyxiate **11** assassinate, electrocute
rate: **9** mortality
rites: **7** funeral **8** exequies **9** interment, obsequies

Death in the Family author
4 Agee (James)

deathless
7 abiding, eternal, lasting, undying **8** enduring, immortal **11** everlasting **12** imperishable

deathlike
see **deathly**

deathly
5 fatal **6** lethal, mortal **7** macabre, stygian **12** pestilential

debacle
4 rout **6** defeat, fiasco **7** breakup, failure **8** collapse, disaster **9** breakdown, cataclysm **10** disruption

debar
3 ban **4** stop **6** forbid, outlaw **7** exclude, prevent, rule out **8** preclude, prohibit **9** interdict

debark
4 land **6** alight, get off **11** decorticate

debase
3 mar **4** harm **5** lower, stain **6** damage, defile, demean, dilute, impair, reduce, weaken **7** cheapen, corrupt, degrade, devalue, pervert, pollute, vitiate **8** dishonor **9** undermine **10** adulterate, depreciate **11** contaminate

debatable
4 iffy, moot **7** dubious **8** arguable, doubtful **9** contested, uncertain, undecided **10** disputable, unresolved **11** problematic **12** questionable

debate
4 moot **5** argue, bandy, plead **7** contend, contest, discuss, dispute, quarrel, wrangle **8** argument, consider, forensic, question **9** dialectic, thrash out **10** controvert, toss around **11** application, controversy, disputation **12** deliberation **13** argumentation
again: **6** rehash
art of: **9** forensics
expert: **7** eristic
place for: **5** forum
side: **3** con, pro

debauch
4 orgy, warp **6** seduce **7** corrupt, deprave, pervert, vitiate **9** bacchanal, brutalize **10** lead astray, saturnalia **11** bacchanalia

debauched
6 wanton **8** degraded, depraved, vitiated **9** corrupted, dissolute, libertine, perverted **10** degenerate, licentious

debilitate
3 sap **6** impair, weaken **7** cripple, disable **8** enfeeble **9** attenuate, undermine **10** devitalize

debilitated
4 weak **6** feeble, infirm, sapped **7** run-down, worn-out **8** weakened **9** enfeebled

debility
7 disease, malaise **8** weakness **9** infirmity **10** feebleness, infirmness, sickliness **11** decrepitude

Debir
kingdom: **5** Eglon
slayer: **6** Joshua

debit
4 bill, levy **6** charge **7** deficit **8** drawback **9** liability **11** encumbrance, shortcoming

debonair
5 suave **6** smooth, urbane **7** dashing, elegant **10** nonchalant **12** lighthearted

Deborah's husband
9 Lappidoth

debouch
5 empty, issue **6** emerge

debris
4 junk, slag **5** trash, waste **6** litter, refuse, rubble, spilth **7** garbage, rubbish **8** detritus, riffraff, wreckage
rock: **5** scree, talus **8** colluvia **9** colluvium

debt
3 due, sin **6** arrear, red ink **7** arrears, default, deficit **8** mortgage, trespass **9** arrearage, liability **10** obligation **11** delinquency
acknowledgment: **3** IOU **4** bill **5** check

debtless
7 solvent

debunk
6 expose, reveal, show up, unmask **7** lay bare, lay open, uncloak, uncover, undress **8** unshroud **9** demystify, discredit

Debussy's La ____
3 Mer

debut
3 bow **5** entry **6** entree **7** come out, opening, present **8** entrance, premiere **9** beginning, coming out, introduce **12** introduction, presentation

decadence
5 decay **7** decline **10** degeneracy, regression **11** degradation **12** degeneration **13** deterioration

decadent
6 effete **7** debased **8** decaying, degraded, depraved **9** debauched, declining, dissolute **10** degenerate **13** self-indulgent

Decalogue
12 Commandments
verb: **5** shalt

Decameron, The
author: **9** Boccaccio (Giovanni)
heroine: **8** Griselda

decamp
4 blow, bolt, exit, flee **5** leave, scram, split **6** beat it, begone, cut out, escape, get out, retire **7** abscond, make off, pull out, run away, skiddoo, take off, vamoose **8** clear out, withdraw **9** skedaddle

decant
4 pour **7** draw off, pour out **8** transfer

decanter
5 cruet, flask **6** bottle, carafe, flagon, vessel

decapitate
4 head **6** behead **9** decollate **10** guillotine

decapod
7 mollusc, mollusk **10** crustacean

decathlon champ
6 Jenner (Bruce), Morris (Glenn), O'Brien (Dan), Schenk (Christian), Sebrle (Roman), Toomey (Bill), Zmelik (Robert) **7** Doherty (Ken), Johnson (Rafer), Mathias (Bob) **8** Campbell (Milton), Thompson (Daley)

decay
3 rot **4** ruin, wane **5** spoil, waste **6** molder, wither **7** atrophy, crumble, decline, putrefy, rotting **8** putresce, spoilage **9** decompose **11** deteriorate **12** dilapidation, putrefaction **13** deterioration

decayed
6 putrid, rotted, rotten, ruined **7** carious, spoiled **8** decadent, moldered, overripe **9** putrefied **10** decomposed, degenerate

decease
3 die, end **4** fail, pass **5** death, dying, sleep **6** demise, depart, expire, finish, pass on, perish **7** passing, quietus, release, succumb **8** pass away **9** departure **10** expiration

deceased
4 body, dead, late **6** corpse **7** cadaver, carcass, expired, remains **8** departed, lifeless **9** inanimate

deceit
3 gyp **4** hoax, ruse, sham **5** fraud, guile, trick **6** humbug **7** swindle **8** artifice, flimflam, trickery **9** chicanery, deception, duplicity, imposture **10** dishonesty **13** double-dealing

deceitful
3 sly **4** wily **5** false, lying **6** crafty, sneaky, tricky **7** cunning, knavish, roguish **8** guileful, two-faced **9** deceptive, dishonest, underhand **10** mendacious **11** underhanded **13** double-dealing

deceive
3 con **4** bilk, dupe, fool, gull, hoax **5** bluff, cozen, lie to, trick **6** delude, humbug, palter, take in **7** beguile, mislead, sandbag, two-time **8** flimflam, hoodwink **9** bamboozle, four-flush **11** double-cross

deceiving
5 false **6** tricky **8** deluding, delusive, delusory, guileful, two-faced **9** beguiling, deceptive **10** fallacious, misleading **11** duplicitous, underhanded

decelerate
4 slow **5** delay **6** retard, slow up **7** slacken **8** slow down

decency
7 decorum, dignity, fitness, modesty **8** civility **9** etiquette, propriety **10** conformity, seemliness

decennium
6 decade

decent
4 fair, good **5** right **6** honest, modest, proper, seemly **7** correct, fitting, upright **8** adequate, all right **9** competent, honorable, tolerable **10** acceptable, conforming, sufficient **11** comme il faut, presentable, respectable **12** satisfactory

deception
3 gyp, lie **4** gaff, hoax, hype, ruse, scam, sham, wile **5** cheat, feint, fraud, guile, put-on, trick **6** deceit, dupery, humbug, mirage **7** chicane, cunning, fallacy, fantasm, knavery, sophism **8** flimflam, illusion, intrigue, phantasm, trickery, trumpery, wiliness **9** casuistry, chicanery, duplicity, imposture, sophistry, treachery **10** dishonesty, hanky-panky, subterfuge

deceptive
5 false, phony **6** tricky **8** deluding, delusory, illusory, specious **9** beguiling, deceitful, deceiving **10** fallacious, misleading

decide
3 opt **4** rule, will **5** judge **6** settle **7** adjudge, resolve **8** conclude **9** determine **10** adjudicate

decided
3 set **4** firm **5** fixed **6** intent **7** assured, certain, obvious, settled **8** definite, resolute, resolved **10** determined, pronounced **11** established, unequivocal

decimate
4 raze, ruin **5** wreck **7** abolish, destroy, wipe out **8** demolish, massacre **9** slaughter **10** annihilate, obliterate **11** exterminate

decipher
4 read **5** break, crack, solve **6** decode, reveal **7** decrypt, resolve, unravel **8** unriddle **9** figure out, interpret, puzzle out, translate **12** cryptanalyze

decision
4 fiat **6** choice, ruling **7** finding, resolve, verdict **8** firmness, judgment, sentence **9** selection **10** conclusion, resolution, settlement **13** determination
rabbinical: **9** responsum

decisive
3 set **7** crucial, settled **8** critical, resolute **10** conclusive, convincing, determined, imperative, peremptory **11** determining **12** unmistakable

deck
4 trim **5** adorn, array, dress, equip, floor, level, porch, prank **6** attire, blazon, clothe **7** apparel, appoint, festoon, furnish, garland, garnish, terrace **8** accouter, accoutre, beautify, decorate, emblazon, ornament, platform **9** embellish
chief: **4** bos'n **9** boatswain
high: **4** poop
lowest: **5** orlop
out: **5** array, fix up, slick, spiff, tog up **6** clothe, doll up **7** dress up, gussy up **8** spruce up
part: **7** scupper

deckhand
3 gob **4** jack, swab **6** sailor, seaman **7** jack-tar, rouster, swabbie **10** bluejacket

declaim
4 rant **5** mouth, orate, speak **6** recite **7** deliver, lecture **8** bloviate, harangue, perorate **9** hold forth

declamatory
5 tumid, windy, wordy **6** florid, turgid **7** aureate, flowery, fustian, orotund, pompous, ranting, verbose **8** sonorous **9** bombastic, high-flown, overblown **10** euphuistic, oratorical, rhetorical **12** magniloquent **13** grandiloquent

declaration
5 edict **6** avowal, notice, report **7** promise **8** document, pleading **9** affidavit, manifesto, statement, testimony **10** confession, deposition, disclosure, expression, profession **11** affirmation, attestation **12** announcement, notification, proclamation **13** advertisement, pronouncement

declare
3 say, vow **4** aver, avow, tell, vent **5** claim, sound, state, swear, utter, voice **6** affirm, allege, assert, avouch, blazon, depone, depose, herald, insist, ordain, report, reveal **7** certify, confirm, deliver, divulge, express, profess, signify, testify **8** announce, disclose, indicate, maintain, manifest, proclaim, propound **9** advertise, broadcast, enunciate, predicate, pronounce **10** annunciate, asseverate, promulgate **11** come out with, disseminate
a saint: **8** canonize
in cards: **3** bid **4** meld
invalid: **5** annul

declass
4 bump, bust **5** abase, lower **6** demote, reduce **7** degrade, set back **9** downgrade

déclassé
4 mean, poor **6** common, vulgar **7** ignoble, lowered **8** inferior, lowgrade, mediocre, middling **10** second-rate **11** second-class

declension
5 class, slope **7** decline, descent **8** downfall **9** downgrade **10** inflection **12** dégringolade **13** deterioration

declination
3 ebb **5** slant, slide **6** ebbing **7** refusal, incline **8** downturn **9** downgrade **10** deflection **12** dégringolade, turning aside **13** deterioration

decline
3 dip, ebb, jib, rot, sag, set **4** balk, dive, drop, fade, fail, fall, flag, loss, sink, slip, wane **5** abate, avoid, demur, droop, lapse, lower, say no, slide, slope, slump, spurn **6** ebbing, go down, recede, refuse, reject, renege, waning, weaken, worsen **7** abstain, atrophy, descend, descent, devolve, dismiss, drop-off, dwindle, failure, falloff, forbear, refrain, relapse, sell-off, sinkage, subside **8** comedown, decrease, downfall, downturn, languish, lowering, turn down **9** backslide, decadence, downgrade, downslide, downswing, downtrend, reprobate, repudiate, weakening **10** degeneracy, degenerate, depression, devolution, disapprove, falling off **11** backsliding, deteriorate **12** degeneration, dégringolade **13** deterioration

declivitous
5 steep **6** sloped **7** pitched, sloping **8** inclined **9** inclining **10** descending

declivity
3 dip **4** drop, fall **5** slope **7** de- cline, descent **8** downturn, gradient **9** downgrade **11** inclination

decode
see **decipher**

decollate
4 head, kill **6** behead **10** decapitate, guillotine

decolor
6 blanch, bleach, blench, whiten **7** wash out **11** achromatize

decompose
3 rot **5** decay, spoil, taint **6** fester, molder **7** analyze, break up, crumble, putrefy, resolve **8** dissolve, separate **9** anatomize, break down **12** disintegrate

decor
7 setting **8** backdrop, stage set **11** furnishings **13** ornamentation

decorate
4 do up, pink, trim **5** adorn, dress, frill **6** bedeck **7** bedizen, dress up, enhance, festoon, furnish, garnish **8** appliqué, beautify, emblazon, ornament **9** embellish
a border: **6** purfle

decorated
6 ornate **7** adorned, honored, wrought **9** bemedaled, decked out, garnished **10** beribboned, ornamented **11** embellished

decoration
4 bays **5** award, badge, honor, kudos, medal **6** doodad, plaque **7** garnish, laurels **8** accolade, filigree, fretting, fretwork, frippery, furbelow, ornament, trimming, vignette **11** distinction
cutout: **8** appliqué
furniture: **4** buhl **6** boulle

decorous
3 fit **4** meet, prim **5** right **6** au fait, comely, decent, proper, seemly **7** correct, elegant, fitting **8** becoming, mannerly, suitable, tasteful **9** befitting, civilized, de rigueur, dignified **10** conforming **11** appropriate, respectable, well-behaved

decorously
5 fitly **7** rightly **8** decently, properly, suitably **9** correctly, fittingly **11** befittingly, respectably

decorousness
7 decency **8** civility **9** propriety, rightness **10** seemliness **11** correctness, orderliness **12** correctitude

decorticate
4 bare, bark, flay, hull, husk, pare, peel, skin

5 scale, scalp, shell, shuck, strip **6** denude **7** lay bare, pull off

decorum
5 order **7** decency, dignity, fitness, modesty **8** protocol **9** etiquette, propriety **10** properness, seemliness **11** correctness, orderliness **12** correctitude

decoy
4 bait, fake, lure **5** plant, shill, tempt **6** allure, capper, delude, entice, lead on, pigeon, seduce **7** deceive, mislead **8** inveigle **10** red herring

decrease
3 cut, ebb **4** bate, drop, ease, fall, loss, wane **5** allay, lower **6** lessen, reduce, shrink **7** abridge, curtail, cut back, cutback, cut down, decline, die down, drop off, dwindle, fall off, lighten, shorten, slacken, subside **8** diminish, downturn, moderate, rollback, taper off **9** abatement, alleviate, reduction **10** abbreviate, depreciate, diminution, falling off

decree
4 fiat, rule **5** canon, edict, enact, judge, order, ukase **6** behest, charge, dictum, impose, ordain, ruling **7** adjudge, appoint, bidding, command, declare, dictate, lay down, mandate, precept, statute **8** judgment, proclaim, sentence **9** directive, judgement, ordinance, prescribe, prescript, pronounce **10** adjudicate, injunction, regulation **11** declaration **12** adjudication, announcement, proclamation, promulgation **13** pronouncement
Muslim: 5 fatwa

decrepit
4 aged, weak, worn **5** frail, seedy, tacky **6** creaky, feeble, infirm, senile, shabby, wasted, weakly **7** fragile, run-down, worn-out **8** battered, impaired, weakened **10** bedraggled, broken-down, down-at-heel, ramshackle **11** dilapidated

decrepitude
4 ruin **5** decay **7** frailty, wasting **8** collapse, debility, weakness **9** disrepair, infirmity **10** exhaustion, feebleness, infirmness **12** dilapidation, enfeeblement **13** deterioration

decretal
4 fiat, writ **5** edict, order, ukase **6** assize, dictum, letter, ruling **7** dictate **8** decision, judgment **11** declaration **13** pronouncement

decry
3 boo **4** bash, slam, slur **5** abuse **6** berate, malign, vilify **7** asperse, censure, condemn, degrade, devalue, put down **8** bad-mouth, belittle, denounce, derogate, reproach **9** criticize, deprecate, discredit, disparage, dispraise, reprehend, reprobate **10** depreciate, disapprove **11** rail against

decrypt
see **decipher**

decumbent
4 flat **5** prone **6** supine **9** lying down, prostrate, reclining **10** horizontal

decussate
5 cross **8** crosscut **9** intersect **10** crisscross, intercross

dedicate
3 vow **5** bless **6** commit, devote, hallow, pledge **7** address **8** inscribe, restrict, set apart **10** consecrate

deduce
5 infer, judge, trace **6** derive, evolve, gather, reason, reckon **7** discern, make out, surmise **8** conclude **9** figure out

deduct
4 bate **5** abate, infer, judge **6** gather, remove **7** make out, take off, take out **8** conclude, knock off, perceive, subtract, take away

deduction
3 cut **4** tare **8** discount, illation, judgment, sequitur, write-off **9** abatement, inference, reasoning **10** conclusion **11** subtraction

deductive
7 a priori **8** dogmatic, illative, provable, reasoned **9** derivable, inferable **10** consequent **11** inferential **13** ratiocinative

deed
3 act **4** cede, fact, feat, pact **5** doing, title **6** action, assign, convey, escrow, remise **7** charter, exploit **8** alienate, contract, covenant, make over, sign over, transfer **9** adventure **10** conveyance, enterprise **11** achievement, performance, tour de force
brutal: 8 atrocity
evil: 3 sin **11** malefaction
good: 7 mitzvah

deem
4 feel, hold **5** judge, think **7** account, adjudge, believe **8** consider

de-emphasize
8 downplay, minimize, play down **9** gloss over, soft-pedal, underplay **13** underestimate

deep
3 low **4** bass, rapt, sunk **5** abyss, grave, ocean **6** occult, orphic, secret **7** abyssal, obscure **8** abstruse, esoteric, hermetic, profound **9** engrossed, recondite **10** bottomless, fathomless, mysterious
combining form: 5 bathy

deepen
6 darken, worsen **7** enhance, enlarge, magnify, thicken **8** heighten **9** aggravate, intensify **10** strengthen

deepness
5 abyss **9** intensity **10** profundity

deep-seated
6 inborn, inbred, innate **7** settled **8** inherent, lifelong, profound, stubborn **9** confirmed, ingrained, intrinsic **10** congenital, entrenched, indwelling, inveterate **11** established **12** long-standing **13** bred-in-the-bone, dyed-in-the-wool, thoroughgoing

deep-six
4 dump, toss **5** chuck, scrap **6** unload **7** discard **8** jettison **9** eliminate

deep water
7 trouble **8** distress **10** difficulty

deer
3 elk, roe **4** buck, musk, stag **5** moose **6** wapiti **7** caribou, venison
Asian: 4 axis, maha **6** sambar **7** muntjac
British: 4 hart
female: 3 doe **4** hind
Japanese: 4 sika
male: 4 buck, hart, stag **7** roebuck
meat: 5 jerky **7** venison
path: 3 run **5** trail
red: 7 brocket
relating to: 7 cervine
track: 4 slot **5** spoor
young: 3 kid **4** fawn

Deere rival
4 Case, Ford, Toro **6** Kubota **7** Farmall

Deerslayer, The
author: 6 Cooper (James Fenimore)
character: 5 Harry (Hurry) **6** Hutter (Thomas), Judith (Hutter) **11** Natty Bumppo **12** Chingachgook

deface
3 mar **4** harm, ruin **6** damage, deform, impair, injure **9** disfigure, vandalize

de facto
6 actual, really **8** actually, existing

defalcation
7 default, failing, failure **10** embezzling, inadequacy, negligence **12** embezzlement

defamation
5 libel, smear **7** calumny, obloquy, slander **10** backbiting **11** traducement **12** backstabbing **13** disparagement

defamatory
8 libelous **9** maligning, traducing, vilifying **10** backbiting, calumnious, slanderous **11** denigrating

defame
5 abase, libel, smear **6** malign, vilify **7** asperse, blacken, blemish, slander, traduce **8** dishonor **9** denigrate, discredit **10** calumniate

default
4 fail **5** welsh **7** absence, exclude, failure, forfeit, neglect **9** selection

defeasance
4 deed **6** defeat **9** overthrow **11** termination

defeat
3 tan **4** beat, best, down, drub, edge, foil, lick, loss, rout, sink, undo, whip, whup **5** crush, outdo, skunk, swamp, upset, waste, whomp **6** outgun, reduce, subdue, wallop **7** beating, conquer, destroy, failure, licking, mow down, nose out, nullify, outplay, overrun, setback, shellac, trounce, wipe out **8** confound, knock out, outfight, outflank, overcome, vanquish, waterloo **9** frustrate, overpower, overthrow, overtrump, subjugate, thrashing, trouncing **10** obliterate **11** shellacking

defeatist
8 doomster **9** doomsayer, Gloomy Gus, pessimist, worrywart

defect
3 bug **4** flaw, lack, vice, want **5** botch, error, fault **6** damage, dearth, desert, foible, injury **7** blemish, default, failing **8** drawback, weakness **9** birthmark, deformity **10** apostatize, deficiency **11** shortcoming **12** imperfection, tergiversate
timber: 4 knot
visual: 6 myopia, squint **9** amblyopia, hyperopia **10** presbyopia, strabismus

defection
8 apostasy **9** desertion, forsaking, recreancy **10** disloyalty **11** abandonment

defective
5 amiss **6** broken, faulty, flawed **7** damaged, lacking, unsound, wanting **8** impaired **9** corrupted, deficient, imperfect **10** inaccurate, inadequate, incomplete **12** insufficient

defector
5 Judas **7** traitor **8** apostate, quisling, recreant, renegade, turncoat **9** turnabout **13** double-crosser

defend
4 back, hold, save **5** argue, cover, guard **6** screen, secure, shield, uphold **7** contend, justify, protect, support **8** advocate, champion, maintain, plead for, preserve **9** safeguard

defendable
see **defensible**

defendant
7 accused, libelee **8** libellee

defender
7 paladin, tribune **8** advocate, champion, guardian **9** protector **11** white knight

defense
4 fort, ward **5** aegis, alibi, armor, guard **6** excuse, sconce, shield **7** bulwark, rampart, shelter **8** apologia, armament, fastness, fortress, muniment, security **9** safeguard **10** protection,

stronghold **11** exculpation, explanation **13** justification
organization: **4** NATO **5** ANZUS, NORAD, SEATO **10** Warsaw Pact

defenseless
4 open **7** exposed, unarmed **8** helpless, wide open **9** unguarded **10** vulnerable **11** unprotected

defensible
5 valid **7** tenable **8** passable **9** excusable, plausible **10** condonable, reasonable **11** justifiable

defer
3 bow **4** stay, wait **5** delay, remit, stall, table, yield **6** accede, hold up, put off, shelve, submit **7** hold off, lay over, put over, suspend **8** hold over, postpone, prorogue **9** acquiesce **13** procrastinate

deference
5 honor **6** esteem, homage, regard **7** respect **8** courtesy **9** obeisance **11** recognition

deferential
8 obliging **9** disarming, regardful **10** respectful **11** complaisant

defiance
4 dare **5** moxie **7** bravado **8** audacity, contempt **9** challenge, contumacy, impudence, insolence **10** brazenness, effrontery **12** contrariness, stubbornness

defiant
4 bold **5** brash, gutsy, sassy, saucy **6** brazen, cheeky, daring **8** arrogant, impudent, insolent **9** audacious, obstinate, resistant **10** refractory **12** recalcitrant

deficiency
4 flaw, lack, want **5** fault, minus **6** dearth **7** absence, blemish, demerit, failing, failure, paucity **8** scarcity, shortage, weakness **9** privation **10** inadequacy, scantiness **11** defalcation, shortcoming **12** imperfection
mental: **6** idiocy **7** amentia
pigmentation: **8** albinism

deficient
3 shy **5** minus, scant, short **6** faulty, flawed, meager, meagre, measly, scanty, scarce **7** failing, lacking, unsound, wanting **8** exiguous, impaired **9** defective, imperfect **10** inadequate, incomplete

deficit
4 lack, loss **6** red ink **8** shortage **10** impairment, inadequacy **12** disadvantage **13** insufficiency

defile
3 tar **4** foul, pass, rape, soil **5** dirty, gorge, march, shame, smear, spoil, stain, sully, taint **6** befoul, debase, ravish **7** besmear, corrupt, pollute, profane, tarnish, violate **8** deflower, dishonor **9** desecrate **11** contaminate

defiled
5 raped **6** impure **7** stained, unclean **8** profaned, polluted, ravished, violated **9** corrupted **10** deflowered, desecrated **12** contaminated

define
3 fix, hem, rim, set **4** edge **5** limit **6** assign, border, detail **7** clarify, delimit, lay down, mark off, mark out, outline, specify **9** delineate, demarcate, determine, establish **11** distinguish **12** characterize

definite
3 set **4** sure **5** clear, final, fixed, sharp, solid **7** certain, decided, express, precise, settled **8** clear-cut, distinct, explicit, specific **10** conclusive, pronounced **11** unambiguous, unequivocal **12** unmistakable

definiteness
8 accuracy, sureness **9** certainty, certitude, exactness, precision **10** exactitude

definitive
5 final **7** express **8** clear-cut, complete, explicit, settling, specific, ultimate **10** concluding, conclusive, exhaustive **11** categorical, determining, unambiguous **13** authoritative

deflate
4 dash **6** humble, reduce, shrink **7** devalue, put down **8** contract, ridicule **9** humiliate, shoot down

deflect
5 avert, parry **6** divert **7** deviate, diverge, hold off **9** turn aside

deflection
3 yaw **4** bend, tack, turn, veer **5** carom, curve, shift **6** double, swerve **7** bending, rebound, turning, veering **8** swerving **9** departure, deviation, diversion **10** divergence

deflower
4 rape **5** spoil **6** defile, ravish **7** despoil, violate **9** desecrate

Defoe, Daniel
character: **6** Crusoe (Robinson), Friday, Roxana **12** Moll Flanders

deform
4 warp **5** spoil **6** deface **7** contort, distort **8** misshape **9** disfigure

deformed
4 awry, bent **5** askew, bowed **6** warped **7** buckled, crooked **8** crippled **9** contorted, misshapen, unshapely

deformity
4 flaw **6** defect **7** blemish **11** abnormality **12** imperfection, irregularity, malformation **13** disfigurement

____ de France
3 Île

defraud
3 con, gyp 4 bilk, dupe, rook, scam 5 cheat, cozen, mulct, trick 6 fleece, rip off 7 swindle 8 flimflam 9 bamboozle

deft
3 apt 4 able 5 adept, agile, handy 6 adroit, clever 7 skilled 8 dextrous, skillful 9 dexterous

deftness
5 knack, skill 7 address, prowess 8 facility 9 adeptness, dexterity 10 capability

defunct
4 cold, dead, late 5 kaput 7 extinct 8 deceased, departed, lifeless, vanished

defy
4 dare, face, gibe, jeer, mock 5 beard, brave, flout, stump 6 resist 7 affront, outdare, outface 8 confront 9 challenge, disregard, withstand

dégagé
6 breezy, casual 7 relaxed, unfussy 8 informal 9 easygoing 10 nonchalant, unreserved 13 unconstrained

degeneracy
see **degeneration**

degenerate
4 sink 6 rotten, sunken, worsen 7 corrupt, debased, decayed, decline, descend, immoral, pervert, vicious, vitiate 8 decadent, degraded, depraved 9 backslide, dissolute 11 deteriorate

degeneration
7 atrophy, decline 8 downfall, lowering 9 decadence, depravity, downgrade 10 debasement, perversion, regression 12 dégringolade

degradation
4 fall 7 decline, descent 8 demotion 9 abasement, decadence, depravity, downgrade, reduction 10 corruption, debasement, degeneracy, perversion 11 downgrading 12 degeneration

degrade
4 bump, bust 5 abase, break, decry, lower 6 debase, demean, demote, impair, lessen, reduce 7 corrupt, declass, pervert, put down 8 belittle, cast down, derogate, diminish 9 decompose, discredit, disparage, downgrade, humiliate

degree
3 peg 4 heat, rank, rate, rung, step, term, tier 5 grade, honor, notch, order, pitch, point, ratio, scale, shade, stage, stair 6 amount, extent, status 7 measure, station 8 standing 9 dimension, gradation, intensity, magnitude 10 proportion
academic: 2 BA, BS, MA, MD, MS 3 BFA, BSc, DDS, LLB, LLD, LLM, MBA, MFA, MSc, PhD 5 MPhil 7 master's 9 bachelor's, doctorate
highest: 5 magna, summa 8 cum laude 13 magna cum laude, summa cum laude
seeker: 9 candidate

dégringolade
see **degeneration**

____ de guerre
3 nom

dehydrate
3 dry 4 sear 5 parch 9 desiccate, exsiccate

Deianira
brother: 8 Meleager
father: 6 Oeneus
husband: 8 Heracles, Hercules
mother: 7 Althaea
victim: 8 Heracles, Hercules

deific
5 godly 6 divine 7 godlike

deification
8 idolatry 10 apotheosis, glorifying 13 glorification

deify
5 exalt 7 glorify, idolize, worship 8 sanctify, venerate 11 apotheosize

deign
5 stoop 7 descend 9 vouchsafe 10 condescend

Deiphobus
brother: 5 Paris 6 Hector
father: 5 Priam
mother: 6 Hecuba
wife: 5 Helen

Deirdre
beloved: 5 Noisi
father: 5 Felim

deity
3 god 4 Lord 7 goddess, godhead, godhood 8 Almighty, divinity 12 supreme being
(see also *god* and *goddess* at **Greek; Hindu; Norse; Roman**)

deject
5 chill, cloud, daunt 6 dampen, dismay 7 depress 8 dispirit 9 disparage 10 demoralize, discourage, dishearten

dejected
3 low, sad 4 blue, down, glum, sunk 6 bummed, gloomy, morose, somber, sombre 7 doleful, hangdog, humbled, unhappy 8 downcast, wretched 9 cheerless, depressed, woebegone 10 despondent, spiritless 11 crestfallen, downhearted 12 disconsolate, disheartened

dejection
5 dumps, gloom 7 despair, sadness 10 melancholy 11 despondency, unhappiness 12 mournfulness

Delaware
capital: 5 Dover
city: 10 Wilmington
nickname: 5 First (State) 7 Diamond (State)
state bird: 14 blue hen chicken
state flower: 12 peach blossom
state tree: 13 American holly

delay
3 lag 4 drag, hold, slow, stay, wait 5 dally, defer, stall, tarry, trail 6 dawdle, detain, hang up, hinder, holdup, impede, linger, loiter, put off, retard, slow up 7 bog down, hold off, respite, set back, slacken, suspend 8 hesitate, hold over, postpone, prorogue, reprieve, slow down 10 dilly-dally, moratorium, suspension 13 procrastinate

delaying
8 dawdling, dilatory 10 postponing, putting off

delectable
5 tasty, yummy 6 choice, savory 8 charming, heavenly, luscious, pleasing 9 ambrosial, delicious, enjoyable, exquisite, toothsome 10 delightful, enchanting 11 scrumptious 13 mouth-watering

delectation
3 fun, joy 4 zest 5 gusto 6 relish 7 delight 8 gladness, pleasure 9 enjoyment

delegate
4 name, send 5 agent, envoy, proxy 6 assign, depute, deputy, legate 7 appoint, consign, entrust 8 deputize, emissary, transfer 9 authorize, catchpole, designate, spokesman 10 commission, mouthpiece, procurator

delete
4 drop, omit, x out 5 erase, purge 6 cancel, censor, cut out, efface, excise, remove 7 blot out, destroy, expunge, take out, wipe out 8 black out, cross out 9 eliminate, eradicate, strike out 10 blue-pencil, obliterate

deleterious
3 bad 6 nocent 7 baneful, harmful, hurtful, nocuous, noxious, ruinous 8 damaging 9 injurious 10 pernicious 11 destructive, detrimental, mischievous, prejudicial

deletion
7 erasure, voiding 9 canceling 10 deficiency 11 elimination 12 cancellation

deliberate
4 chaw, cool, muse, pore, slow 5 chary, meant, study, think, weigh 6 chew on, ponder, reason 7 careful, heedful, planned, reflect, studied, willful, willing, witting 8 cautious, cogitate, consider, intended, measured, meditate, mull over, ruminate, talk over 9 cerebrate, conscious, unhurried 10 calculated, considered, purposeful, thought-out 11 circumspect, intentional 12 premeditated

deliberately
9 knowingly, on purpose, purposely, willfully, wittingly 11 consciously 12 purposefully 13 intentionally

deliberation
5 study 6 debate 7 thought 10 conference, discussion, reflection 13 consideration

Delibes, Léo
ballet: 6 Sylvia 8 Coppélia, La Source
opera: 5 Lakmé
waltz: 5 Naila

delicacy
5 goody, treat 6 dainty, luxury, morsel, nicety, tidbit 7 frailty 8 kickshaw, fineness 9 fragility, precision 10 daintiness, difficulty, indulgence, stickiness 11 awkwardness 12 ticklishness

delicate
4 fine, lacy, twee, weak 5 frail 6 choice, dainty, flimsy, petite, queasy, sickly, slight, subtle, tender, touchy, tricky 7 elegant, fragile, refined, tactful, tenuous 8 ethereal, feathery, finespun, gossamer, graceful, pleasing, ticklish 9 exquisite, sensitive, squeamish 10 precarious

delicatessen
11 charcuterie

delicious
5 tasty, yummy 6 choice, divine, savory 8 heavenly, luscious 9 ambrosial, exquisite, toothsome 10 delectable, delightful 11 scrumptious 13 mouthwatering

delight
3 joy 4 glee 5 amuse, bliss, charm, enjoy, exult, glory, mirth, revel 6 divert, please, regale, relish 7 ecstasy, enchant, gladden, gratify, jollity, rapture, rejoice 8 enravish, entrance, fruition, hilarity, pleasure 9 delectate, enjoyment, enrapture, entertain 11 delectation
in: 4 love 5 adore, enjoy, savor 6 admire, relish 7 cherish 10 appreciate

delighted
4 glad 5 happy 6 joyful 8 ecstatic, euphoric

delightful
5 yummy 6 dreamy, lovely 8 charming, heavenly, luscious, pleasant, pleasing 9 congenial, enjoyable 10 delectable, enchanting, satisfying 11 captivating, fascinating, pleasurable, scrumptious 12 entertaining

Delilah's victim
6 Samson

DeLillo novel
5 Libra, Mao II 10 Underworld, White Noise

delimit
3 bar 5 bound, hem in 6 demark, define 7 confine, enclose 8 restrict 9 demarcate, determine 12 circumscribe

delineate
3 map **4** etch, limn **5** chart, image, trace **6** define, depict, detail, render **7** outline, picture, portray **8** describe, spell out **9** elucidate, interpret, represent **10** illustrate

delineation
5 draft, story **6** report **7** account, contour, drawing, outline, picture, profile **9** depiction, rendering **11** presentment

delinquency
4 debt **5** crime, fault, lapse **7** default, failure, misdeed, neglect, offense **8** omission **9** oversight **10** misconduct, nonpayment, wrongdoing **11** dereliction, misbehavior

delinquent
3 lax **5** slack **6** debtor **7** overdue **8** careless, offender **9** defaulter, in arrears, negligent **10** behindhand, neglectful

deliquesce
3 rot, run **4** flux, fuse, melt, thaw **5** decay **6** render, soften **7** liquefy, putrefy **8** dissolve, fluidize **9** decompose, disappear, waste away **12** disintegrate

delirious
3 mad **4** wild **5** crazy **6** crazed, insane, raving **7** frantic, lunatic **8** confused, demented, deranged, ecstatic, frenetic, frenzied, rambling **9** rapturous **10** bewildered, corybantic, distracted, irrational **11** lightheaded, overexcited, overwrought

delirium
5 furor, mania **6** fervor, frenzy **7** ecstasy, jimjams, rapture, seizure **8** dementia, hysteria **13** hallucination

delirium ____
7 tremens

deliver
4 bear, deal, feed, find, give, hand, save, send, ship, sing, take **5** bring, serve, speak, state, throw, utter **6** convey, redeem, rescue, strike, supply **7** consign, present, produce, provide, set free, release **8** hand over, liberate, turn over **9** pronounce, surrender **10** bring forth, emancipate **11** come out with, come through

deliverance
6 rescue **7** freeing, opinion, release, verdict **8** decision **9** acquittal, discharge, salvation **10** absolution, liberation

Deliverance author
6 Dickey (James)

delivery
4 drop **5** birth, labor **6** rescue **7** address, bearing **8** birthing, shipment **9** elocution, rendition, salvation **10** childbirth, conveyance, liberation **11** consignment, parturition, transferral **12** childbearing, transmission

dell
4 dale, glen, vale **6** dingle, hollow, valley

Delphic
4 dark **5** vatic **6** arcane, hidden, mantic, mystic, occult, veiled **7** cryptic, obscure **8** auguring, divining, esoteric, mystical, oracular **9** ambiguous, enigmatic, equivocal, prophetic, recondite, sibylline, vaticinal **10** mystifying, portentous **11** prophesying, prophetical

delta
5 plain **6** letter, symbol **7** deposit **8** triangle **9** increment

delude
3 con **4** dupe, fool, gull, hoax **5** bluff, cozen, trick **6** betray, humbug, juggle, take in **7** beguile, deceive, mislead **8** flimflam, hoodwink **11** double-cross

deluge
5 drown, flood, swamp **6** drench, engulf **7** Niagara, torrent **8** cataract, downpour, drencher, flooding, inundate, overflow **9** cataclysm, overwhelm **10** cloudburst, outpouring, inundation

delusion
4 hoax, sham **5** dream, fancy, snare **6** mirage **7** chimera, fallacy, fantasy, figment, phantom, specter **8** daydream, phantasm **9** deception **10** apparition **11** ignis fatuus **13** hallucination

delusive
5 false **8** fanciful, illusory, specious **9** beguiling, deceiving, deceptive, imaginary **10** chimerical, fallacious, misleading

delusory
see **delusive**

deluxe
4 lush, posh **5** grand, plush, ritzy, swank **6** choice, costly, swanky **7** elegant, opulent **8** luscious, splendid **9** expensive, exquisite, luxuriant, luxurious, sumptuous **10** first class

delve
3 dig, dip **4** mine **5** probe **6** dredge, fathom, hollow, quarry, search, shovel **7** inquire **8** excavate
into: 4 sift **5** probe **7** explore **8** prospect **11** investigate

delving
6 asking **7** inquest, inquiry, probing **8** research **9** inquiring, searching

demagnetize
7 degauss

demagogue
6 leader **7** inciter **8** agitator, fomenter **9** firebrand **10** instigator **11** provocateur **12** rabble-rouser

demand
3 ask, use **4** call, need, urge, want **5** claim,

crave, exact, force, order **6** compel, direct, expect, insist **7** call for, request, require **11** requirement, requisition

demanding
4 hard **5** pushy, tough **6** taxing, trying **7** exigent, onerous, weighty **8** exacting, forceful, rigorous **9** assertive, difficult, insistent, strenuous, stringent **10** aggressive, burdensome, oppressive **11** challenging

demarcate
5 bound, limit **6** define, set off **7** delimit, mark off, outline **8** separate, set apart **9** delineate, determine **11** distinguish **12** circumscribe **13** differentiate

demarcation
9 outlining **10** border line, separation **11** distinction **12** delimitation

démarche
4 plan, ploy, ruse **5** feint **6** action, device, gambit, scheme, tactic **7** protest **8** artifice, maneuver, petition **9** stratagem **10** initiative **11** contrivance, machination

demean
4 bear **5** abase, carry, decry, lower **6** acquit, behave, debase, deport, humble **7** comport, conduct, degrade, detract **8** bad-mouth, belittle **9** disparage, humiliate

demeanor
3 air **4** look, mien **6** aspect, manner **7** address, bearing, conduct **8** behavior, carriage, presence **10** deportment **11** comportment

demented
3 mad **5** crazy, loony, nutty, wacko **6** crazed, insane, psycho **7** lunatic, unsound **8** deranged, frenzied, maniacal **9** delirious **10** hysterical, unbalanced **12** psychopathic

____ de mer
3 mal

demerit
4 mark **5** fault, stain **6** defect **7** blemish, penalty **9** downgrade **10** deficiency, punishment **11** shortcoming **12** imperfection

demesne
5 field, realm **6** domain, estate, region, sphere **7** terrain **8** dominion, province **9** bailiwick, champaign, territory
house: 5 manor

Demeter
see **Ceres**

demigod
4 diva, idol **8** superman **9** superstar

demise
3 die, end **4** drop, pass **5** death, dying, sleep **6** cash in, depart, ending, expire **7** decease, passing, quietus, release, silence, succumb **8** pass away **9** cessation, departure **10** expiration, extinction

demit
4 quit **6** bow out, give up, resign **8** abdicate, renounce, step down, withdraw

demiurgic
8 creative, original **9** formative, inventive **10** innovative **11** originative

demobilize
7 break up, disband, dismiss, scatter **8** disperse, separate **9** discharge, disengage, muster out

democratic
7 popular **8** populist **10** self-ruling **11** egalitarian **13** self-governing

Democrats' symbol
6 donkey

démodé
5 dated, passé **7** antique, archaic **8** old-timey, outdated **9** out-of-date **12** old-fashioned

demoiselle
6 damsel, lassie, maiden **10** damselfish

demolish
4 raze, ruin **5** crush, level, smash, total, wrack, wreck **7** destroy, flatten, wipe out **8** decimate, tear down **9** finish off **10** annihilate, obliterate

demolition
6 razing **8** leveling, wrecking **10** bulldozing **11** destruction **12** annihilation

demolition bomb
11 blockbuster

demon
3 imp **4** jinn **5** devil, fiend, genie, ghoul, jinni, Satan **7** hellion, incubus **9** archfiend
Arabic: 5 afrit **6** afreet
female: 5 lamia **7** succuba, succubi (plural) **8** succubae (plural), succubus

demonic
6 wicked **7** satanic **8** devilish, diabolic, fiendish, infernal **9** possessed **10** diabolical

demonize
6 malign, revile, vilify **7** bedevil, censure, slander **8** denounce **9** diabolize

demonstrate
3 try **4** mark, show, test **5** prove, rally **7** confirm, display, exhibit, explain, make out, protest **8** evidence, manifest, proclaim, validate **9** determine, establish **10** illustrate **12** authenticate

demonstration
4 expo, show, test **5** march, proof, rally, trial **6** picket **7** display, protest **9** spectacle **10** exhibition, exposition, validation **12** presentation **13** corroboration, manifestation

demonstrative
4 open **8** effusive, outgoing, specific

9 emotional, expansive, exuberant, outspoken 10 outpouring, unreserved, validating 12 affectionate, unrestrained 13 unconstrained

demoralize
5 chill, daunt, shake, unman, upset 6 dampen, debase, deject, rattle, weaken 7 corrupt, debauch, deprave, unnerve, vitiate 8 dispirit, psych out 9 undermine 10 discourage, dishearten

Demosthenes
6 orator
oration: 9 Philippic

demote
4 bump, bust 5 lower 6 reduce 7 declass, degrade 9 downgrade

demulcent
4 balm 5 jelly, salve 7 unguent 8 liniment, ointment, soothing 9 softening

demur
5 qualm 6 object, oppose, resist 7 dispute, protest 8 hesitate, question 9 challenge, hesitancy, objection 10 hesitation, indecision, reluctance 11 compunction, remonstrate

demure
3 coy, shy 5 timid 6 modest 7 bashful 8 reserved, reticent, retiring 9 diffident 11 unassertive 12 self-effacing

demurral
7 protest 9 challenge, objection 12 remonstrance 13 remonstration

demurrer
see **demurral**

den
4 base, cave, home, lair, nest, room 5 study 6 burrow, cavern, hollow 7 dayroom, hideout, sanctum 8 hideaway, playroom
rabbit: 6 warren

denial
2 no 3 nay, nix 6 heresy 7 refusal 8 disproof, negation, rebuttal 9 disavowal, rejection 10 abnegation, gainsaying, refutation 11 repudiation 12 renunciation

denigrate
5 decry, libel, smear, stain, sully 6 darken, defame, defile, impugn, malign, vilify 7 asperse, devalue, put down, slander, tarnish, traduce 8 belittle, dishonor, tear down 9 discredit, disparage 10 calumniate, scandalize

denims
5 jeans 8 overalls 9 blue jeans, dungarees

denizen
5 liver 6 native 7 dweller, habitué, haunter, resider 8 habitant, occupant, resident 9 indweller, inhabiter 10 frequenter, inhabitant

Denmark
capital: 10 Copenhagen
city: 5 Århus 6 Ålborg, Odense 11 Helsingborg 13 Frederiksberg
island: 3 Fyn 7 Falster, Zealand 8 Bornholm 9 Sjaelland
monetary unit: 5 krone
neighbor: 6 Sweden 7 Germany
part of: 11 Scandinavia
peninsula: 7 Jutland
possession: 9 Greenland 12 Faroe Islands 13 Faeroe Islands
sea: 5 North 6 Baltic
strait: 5 Lille, Store 9 Langeland

denominate
3 dub 4 call, name, term 5 label, style, title 7 baptize, entitle 8 christen 9 designate

denomination
4 cult, name, sect 5 creed, faith, style, title 6 church 8 category, cognomen, religion 9 communion 10 persuasion
religious: 5 Amish 6 Mormon 7 Baptist 8 Lutheran, Moravian, Reformed 9 Adventist, Episcopal, Mennonite, Methodist, Unitarian 11 Pentecostal 12 Presbyterian, Universalist 13 Roman Catholic

denotation
4 name, sign 5 sense 6 import 7 meaning 10 indication, signifying 11 designation 13 signification, specification

denote
4 mark, mean, name, show 5 spell 6 import 7 add up to, betoken, express 8 announce, indicate 9 designate, represent

denouement
6 effect, result, upshot 7 outcome 10 conclusion 11 consequence, culmination

denounce
3 rap 4 skin 5 blame, blast, decry, knock 6 rebuke, scathe 7 censure, condemn, upbraid 8 derogate, reproach 9 castigate, criticize, dress down, excoriate, reprehend, reprobate 10 denunciate, vituperate 11 incriminate 12 anathematize

de novo
4 anew, over 5 again, newly 6 afresh 8 once more 9 over again 11 from scratch

dense
4 dull, dumb 5 close, heavy, solid, thick, tight 6 obtuse, opaque, stupid 7 compact, crammed, crowded, doltish, serried 9 fatheaded, jampacked 10 numskulled 11 blockheaded, numbskulled, thickheaded 12 impenetrable

dent
4 bash, ding, flaw, nick 5 tooth 6 dimple, hollow 10 depression, impression

dental addition
5 inlay, plate 6 braces, bridge 7 filling

denticulate
6 ridged **7** dentate, notched, serrate, serried, toothed **8** saw-edged, sawtooth, serrated **10** saw-toothed

dentin
6 enamel

dentine
5 ivory

denude
4 bare **5** strip **6** divest **7** disrobe, uncover, undress **8** unclothe

denunciate
see **denounce**

deny
5 cross, rebut **6** disown, forbid, negate, refuse, refute, reject, renege **7** disavow, gainsay **8** abnegate, disallow, disclaim, forswear, renounce, traverse, withhold **9** disaffirm **10** contradict, contravene

depart
2 go **3** die **4** exit, flee, pass, quit **5** leave, scram, split **6** begone, decamp, demise, desert, escape, expire, go away, move on, pass on, perish, skidoo **7** decease, deviate, go forth, move out, pull out, skiddoo, take off, vamoose **8** pass away, shove off, slip away, withdraw **9** skedaddle, take leave

departing
6 egress, exodus **7** good-bye **8** farewell **9** desertion **11** leave-taking, valedictory

department
5 arena **6** branch, domain, sphere **7** section **8** category, division, province **9** bailiwick, territory **11** subdivision

departure
4 exit **5** adieu, break, congé, going **6** egress, exodus, flight **7** leaving **8** farewell **9** deviation, diversion **10** aberration, decampment, deflection, divergence, embarkment, setting-out, withdrawal **11** embarkation, leave-taking
of a ship: **6** sortie
point: **7** outport

dependable
4 sure, true **5** loyal, solid, tried **6** secure, steady, trusty **7** certain, staunch **8** accurate, constant, faithful, reliable, surefire **9** authentic, steadfast, unfailing **11** responsible, trustworthy **12** tried and true **13** authoritative
Scottish: **6** sicker

dependence
4 need **5** faith, habit, stock, trust **8** reliance **9** addiction **11** contingency, habituation

dependent
5 child **6** minion, vassal **7** reliant, relying **9** secondary **10** contingent, equivalent **11** conditional, subordinate

depend on
5 bet on, trust **6** bank on, hang on, look to, rely on, turn on **7** build on, count on, hinge on, stand on, swear by

depict
4 draw, limn, show **5** image, paint **6** relate, render, sketch **7** express, picture, portray **8** describe **9** delineate, represent **10** illustrate

depiction
5 image **6** sketch **7** drawing, picture **9** portrayal, rendering **11** delineation, portraiture, presentment **12** illustration, presentation

deplete
3 sap **4** milk **5** bleed, drain, eat up, empty, leech, use up **6** expend, lessen, reduce **7** consume, draw off, exhaust **8** decrease, diminish, draw down **9** undermine **10** run through

depleted
6 sapped, used up **7** drained, reduced **8** consumed, expended **9** exhausted, washed-out

deplorable
5 awful **6** rotten, woeful **8** dreadful, god-awful, grievous, terrible, wretched **9** execrable, miserable, sickening **10** calamitous, disastrous, lamentable **11** distressing, intolerable **12** contemptible, disreputable, heartrending **13** heartbreaking, reprehensible

deplore
3 rue **5** abhor, mourn **6** bemoan, bewail, grieve, lament, regret **7** condemn **8** denounce, object to **9** deprecate **10** disapprove

deploy
3 use **5** array **6** muster, unfold **7** arrange, display, dispose, marshal, utilize **8** position

___ de plume
3 nom

depone
5 state, swear **6** affirm, assert, attest **7** certify, confirm, declare, testify, warrant **11** corroborate **12** authenticate

deport
3 act **4** bear **5** carry, exile, expel **6** acquit, banish, behave, demean **7** conduct **8** displace, relegate **10** expatriate

deportee
2 DP **5** exile **8** expellee

deportment
3 air, set **4** mien, port **6** aspect, manner **7** address, bearing, conduct, manners **8** behavior, carriage, demeanor, presence

depose
4 aver, avow, oust **5** state, swear **6** affirm, assert, avouch, remove, topple, unmake **7** declare, profess, testify, uncrown **8** dethrone, displace, throw out, unthrone **9** overthrow

deposit
3 lay **4** bank, drop, dump, fund, lees, pawn, save, stow **5** cache, chest, dregs, place, put by, stash, store **6** settle **7** consign, grounds, lay away **8** put aside, security, sediment, sock away **9** settlings **11** precipitate **13** precipitation
alluvial: **5** delta
black: **4** soot
calcium carbonate: **10** stalactite, stalagmite
containing gold: **6** placer
eggs: **5** spawn
geologic: **7** horizon
glacial: **4** till **5** drift, esker **7** moraine
loam: **5** loess
mineral: **4** lode **10** concretion
muddy: **6** sludge
sand: **4** bank **5** beach
sedimentary: **4** silt
skeletal: **5** coral
stream: **8** alluvium, sediment
tooth: **6** tartar

deposition
6 avowal **7** ousting, placing **9** affidavit, dismissal, testimony **10** testifying **11** attestation, declaration

depository
4 bank, dump, safe **5** attic, cache, depot, store, vault **7** archive, arsenal **8** magazine **9** warehouse **10** storehouse
for bones: **7** ossuary

depot
4 dump **5** cache, store **6** armory, garage **7** arsenal, station **8** magazine, terminal, terminus **9** warehouse **10** depository, repository, storehouse **12** station house

deprave
4 warp **6** debase **7** corrupt, debauch, pervert, vitiate **9** brutalize **10** bastardize, bestialize, demoralize

depraved
3 bad, low **4** base, evil, ugly, vile **6** putrid, rotten, wanton, warped, wicked **7** bestial, corrupt, debased, immoral, twisted, vicious **8** degraded, perverse, vitiated **9** corrupted, debauched, miscreant, nefarious, perverted, reprobate **10** degenerate

depravity
4 vice **8** baseness **9** abasement, decadence **10** corruption, debasement, debauchery, degeneracy, immorality, perversion **12** degeneration

deprecate
7 frown on, put down **8** belittle, derogate, disfavor, object to, play down, pooh-pooh **9** disparage **10** disapprove **12** disapprove of

depreciate
4 drop, fall **5** abate, decry, erode, lower **6** lessen, reduce, slight **7** cheapen, devalue, put down **8** belittle, decrease, derogate, diminish, discount, mark down, write off **9** devaluate, disparage, downgrade, underrate **10** devalorize, undervalue **11** detract from

depreciation
8 discount **11** denigration **12** belittlement **13** disparagement

depreciative
9 slighting **10** derogatory, detracting, pejorative **11** disparaging, underrating **12** undervaluing

depredate
4 sack **5** waste **6** ravage **7** despoil, pillage, plunder **8** desolate, lay waste, prey upon, spoliate **9** desecrate, devastate, vandalize

depredation
4 sack **5** havoc **7** pillage, plunder, sacking **8** ravaging **9** marauding, ruination **10** spoliation **11** desecration, destruction, devastation **12** despoliation

depredator
6 looter, raider, vandal **7** forager, spoiler **8** marauder **9** plunderer **10** freebooter

depress
4 damp, dash, dent **5** chill, daunt, lower **6** dampen, deject, dismay, sadden **7** afflict, trouble **8** dispirit, enfeeble **9** disparage, weigh down **10** discourage, dishearten

depressed
3 low, sad **4** blue, down, glum, sunk **6** broody, gloomy, glumpy, lonely, somber **8** cast down, dejected, downcast **9** bummed out, flattened, woebegone **10** dispirited, lugubrious, melancholy, spiritless **11** crestfallen, downhearted, melancholic **12** disconsolate **13** disadvantaged

depressing
3 sad **5** bleak **6** dismal, dreary, gloomy, somber, sombre **7** joyless **8** funereal, mournful **9** saddening **10** melancholy, oppressive **11** melancholic **13** disheartening

depression
3 dip, low, pit, sag **4** bust, drop, funk, glen, hole, sink, vale **5** basin, blues, dolor, dumps, ennui, gloom, scoop, slump **6** cavity, crater, hollow, pocket, valley **7** cyclone, decline, sadness, sinkage **8** downturn, sinkhole **9** concavity, dejection **10** desolation, melancholy **11** melancholia, unhappiness
anatomical: **5** fossa, fovea **6** foveae (plural)
geographic: **7** Qattara
in ridge: **3** col
in snow: **8** sitzmark
small: **4** dent **6** dimple

depressive
4 blue, dour, glum **6** woeful **7** doleful **8** downbeat, downcast, mournful **9** miserable, woebegone **10** despondent, melancholy **11** low-spirited

deprivation
4 lack, loss **6** denial **7** forfeit, removal **10** forfeiture **11** bereavement, divestiture **13** dispossession

deprive
3 rob **5** strip **6** divest **8** disseise, disseize **10** disinherit, dispossess
of brilliancy: **4** dull **6** deaden
of courage: **7** unnerve
of sensation: **6** benumb

depth
4 base, drop, gulf **5** abyss, chasm, gorge **7** lowness **10** profundity
measure: **6** fathom
of water: **5** draft **7** draught

depthless
7 cursory, shallow, sketchy **10** uncritical **11** superficial

Dept. of ___
5 Labor, State **6** Energy **7** Defense, Justice **8** Commerce, Interior, Treasury **9** Education **11** Agriculture

deputize
4 name **6** assign **7** appoint, empower, warrant **8** delegate **9** authorize, designate **10** commission

deputy
4 aide **5** agent, proxy **6** backup, factor **8** delegate **9** assistant, catchpole, surrogate

derange
4 muss **5** craze, upset **6** madden, mess up **7** confuse, perturb, unhinge **8** confound, disarray, disorder, distract, unsettle **9** interrupt, unbalance **10** discompose **11** disorganize

deranged
3 mad **4** loco **5** crazy, wacko **6** crazed, insane, maniac **7** berserk, bonkers, cracked, haywire, lunatic, unsound **8** demented, maniacal, unhinged **9** disturbed **10** disordered, flipped out, unbalanced

derangement
4 mess **5** chaos, mania **6** lunacy, muddle **7** madness **8** dementia, disorder, insanity **9** confusion, unbalance **10** hodgepodge **11** distraction, disturbance, psychopathy

derby
3 hat **4** race **7** contest **9** horse race

derelict
3 bum **4** hobo, lorn **5** tramp **6** remiss, shabby **7** drifter, outcast, run-down, uncouth, vagrant **8** careless, deserted, vagabond **9** abandoned, negligent **10** neglectful **11** dilapidated **12** disregardful, undependable **13** irresponsible

dereliction
5 fault **7** default, failure, neglect **9** deviation, disregard, oversight **11** abandonment, delinquency, shortcoming

deride
3 rag, rap **4** gibe, jeer, jibe, lout, mock, quiz, razz, twit **5** fleer, rally, scoff, scout, sneer, taunt **6** dump on, insult **7** catcall **8** ridicule

de rigueur
5 right **6** au fait, decent, proper **7** correct **8** becoming, decorous, required **9** essential, mandatory, requisite **10** compulsory, obligatory, prescribed **11** comme il faut

derision
5 abuse, scorn **7** disdain, mockery, ribbing **8** contempt, raillery, ridicule, scoffing **9** contumely, invective

derisive
7 abusive, jeering, mocking **8** sardonic, scoffing, scornful, taunting **9** insulting, sarcastic **10** disdainful **12** contemptuous

derivable
7 a priori **9** deducible, deductive, traceable **10** obtainable **11** extractable **12** attributable, determinable

derivation
4 root **6** origin, source **7** descent **8** ancestry **9** etymology **10** provenance, wellspring **11** origination, provenience

derivative
5 banal **7** spin-off **8** acquired, borrowed, offshoot **9** by-product, imitative, outgrowth, secondary **10** descendant, unoriginal

derive
3 get **4** draw, flow, rise, stem, take **5** adapt, arise, educe, infer, issue, trace **6** deduce, deduct, evolve, gather, obtain **7** descend, emanate, extract, proceed, work out **8** arrive at, conclude **9** formulate, originate

dernier cri
3 fad **4** chic, rage **5** craze, vogue **8** last word

derogate
5 decry **6** berate, dump on, insult **7** put down **8** bad-mouth, belittle, diminish, minimize, write off **9** disparage, dispraise **10** depreciate **11** detract from

derogatory
5 snide **8** decrying, scornful, spiteful **9** degrading, demeaning, maligning, slighting **10** belittling, detracting, disdainful, pejorative **11** disparaging **12** contumelious, depreciative

derrick
5 crane, davit, hoist

derriere
3 bum **4** beam, butt, rear, rump, seat, tail **5** fanny **6** behind, bottom **7** rear end **8** backside, buttocks **9** posterior

derring-do
4 guts 5 nerve, pluck, spunk, valor 6 daring, mettle 7 bravado, bravery, bravura, courage 8 boldness 9 gallantry 12 fearlessness 13 dauntlessness

dervish
4 monk, Sufi 9 mendicant
in Arabian Nights: 4 Agib
practice: 7 dancing 8 whirling
wandering: 5 fakir 8 calender

descant
4 sing 6 melody, remark, treble 7 comment, discuss, melisma, melodia, oration, soprano 9 discourse, expatiate 12 counterpoint

Descartes's axiom
13 cogito ergo sum

descend
4 dive, drop, fall, pass, sink 5 slide, stoop, swoop 6 alight, derive, go down, plunge, worsen 7 decline 8 come down, dismount 9 originate 10 degenerate, retrograde
by rope: 6 rappel

descendant
4 heir 5 scion 7 progeny, spin-off 8 offshoot, relative 9 by-product, offspring, outgrowth 10 derivative

descendants
4 seed 5 brood, heirs, issue, spawn 6 litter 7 progeny 8 children 9 offspring, posterity 11 progeniture

descent
3 dip 4 drop, fall 5 birth, blood, slide, slope 6 origin, plunge, tumble 7 decline, drop-off, incline, lineage, sinkage 8 ancestry, comedown, gradient, pedigree 9 declivity, downgrade 10 derivation, devolution, extraction
airplane: 8 approach
parachute: 4 jump 7 bailout

describe
4 limn 6 denote, depict, recite, relate, render, report 7 explain, express, mark out, narrate, outline, picture, portray, recount 9 delineate, represent 10 illustrate 12 characterize

description
3 ilk 4 kind, sort, type 6 nature, report 7 account, picture, species 9 character, depiction, narrative, portrayal 10 recounting

descry
3 see 4 espy, spot 6 behold, detect, spy out, turn up 7 discern, find out, hit upon 8 discover, meet with, perceive 9 encounter, recognize

Desdemona
father: 9 Brabantio
husband: 7 Othello
slanderer: 4 Iago
slayer: 7 Othello

desecrate
4 sack 5 stain, sully, waste 6 befoul, debase, defile, ravage 7 corrupt, degrade, despoil, pillage, pollute, profane, violate 8 spoliate 9 depredate, devastate

desecration
5 abuse 7 impiety 9 blasphemy, sacrilege 10 debasement, defilement, spoliation 11 profanation 12 despoliation

desensitize
4 dull, numb 5 blunt 6 benumb, dampen, deaden, freeze, sedate 11 anesthetize

desert
4 flee, quit 5 leave, waste 6 barren, betray, decamp, defect, escape, go AWOL, maroon, strand 7 abandon, abscond, badland, forsake 8 renounce 9 repudiate, wasteland 10 apostatize, wilderness 12 tergiversate
African: 5 Namib 6 Libyan, Nubian, Sahara 7 Arabian 8 Kalahari
Arizona: 7 Painted
Asian: 4 Gobi, Thar 6 Syrian 7 Kara-Kum 8 Kyzyl Kum, Qizilkum 10 Great Sandy
Australian: 6 Gibson, Tanami 7 Simpson
basin bottom: 5 playa
beast: 5 camel 9 dromedary
California: 6 Mohave, Mojave
Chilean: 7 Atacama
clay: 5 adobe
dweller: 4 bedu 5 nomad 6 Beduin, Berber, Nubian 7 bedouin 8 Maghrebi, Maghribi
Egyptian: 7 Arabian
fertile area: 5 oases (plural), oasis
garb: 3 aba 7 burnous 8 burnoose
hallucination: 6 mirage
Israeli: 5 Negev
region: 3 erg
Saudi Arabia: 7 Al-Nafud, An Nafud 10 Rub Al-Khali
travel group: 7 caravan
wind: 7 sirocco 8 scirocco

deserted
4 bare, lorn 6 barren, vacant 8 derelict, desolate, forsaken, solitary 9 abandoned, neglected 11 uninhabited

deserter
3 rat 4 AWOL 6 bolter 7 runaway 8 apostate, defector, fugitive, renegade, runagate, turncoat

desertion
7 perfidy 8 apostasy 9 defection, forsaking 11 abandonment, dereliction

deserts
3 due 6 reward 8 requital 9 reckoning 10 recompense 11 comeuppance

deserve
3 win **4** earn, gain, rate **5** merit **6** demand **7** justify, warrant

deserved
3 apt, due **4** just **5** right **7** fitting, merited **8** rightful, suitable **9** befitting **11** appropriate **13** rhadamanthine

deserving
3 due **6** worthy **8** laudable **9** admirable, estimable **10** creditable **11** commendable, meritorious, thankworthy **12** praiseworthy

desiccate
3 dry **5** dry up, parch, wizen **6** wither **7** shrivel **9** dehydrate **10** devitalize

desiderate
4 want, wish **5** covet, crave **6** desire **7** long for, wish for **8** yearn for

design
3 aim **4** cast, draw, form, mean, mind, plan, plot, will **5** chart, draft, frame, model, motif **6** create, device, devise, figure, intend, intent, invent, lay out, makeup, map out, motive, scheme, set out, sketch, tailor **7** arrange, diagram, drawing, execute, fashion, meaning, outline, pattern, prepare, project, propose, tracing **8** contrive, creation, game plan, intrigue, strategy, thinking **9** blueprint, construct, delineate, direction, formation, intention, invention **10** decoration, figuration **11** arrangement, composition **12** architecture, construction
book: **8** vignette
carpet: **3** gul **9** medallion
incised: **8** intaglio
Indonesian: **5** batik
inlaid: **6** mosaic
intricate: **9** arabesque
of squares: **5** check
openwork: **8** filigree
perforated: **7** stencil
raised: **8** repoussé
skin: **6** tattoo
textile: **8** polka dot
velvety: **8** flocking

designate
3 dub, tap **4** call, name, pick, term **5** allot, elect, label, style, title **6** assign, choose, denote, depute, select **7** appoint, declare, earmark, reserve, signify, specify **8** allocate, christen, delegate, identify, set aside, stand for **9** apportion, stipulate **10** decide upon **11** appropriate **12** characterize

designation
4 name, sign **5** class, nomen, style, title **6** naming **8** cognomen, monicker **11** appellation

designed
7 devised, planned **8** intended, resolved **9** contrived, patterned **10** considered, deliberate, determined, thought-out **12** premeditated

designedly
9 expressly, knowingly, on purpose, purposely, willfully, wittingly **11** consciously, purposively **12** deliberately **13** intentionally

desirable
8 enviable, fetching **9** advisable, agreeable, preferred **10** attractive, beneficial **12** advantageous

desire
3 aim, yen **4** envy, eros, itch, lust, want, wish **5** covet, crave, fancy, go for, greed **6** pining, thirst **7** avarice, craving, long for, longing, passion **8** appetite, cupidity, petition, yearn for, yearning **9** eroticism, hankering, prurience, pruriency **10** aphrodisia, attraction, preference **11** inclination, lustfulness **13** concupiscence, lickerishness

desired
6 wanted **8** hoped-for **9** preferred, requested

desirous
4 avid **6** greedy **7** athirst, craving, envious, longing, wishful, wishing **8** covetous, grasping **10** solicitous

desist
4 halt, quit, stop **5** cease, yield **7** forbear, hold off, refrain **8** knock off, leave off, surcease **11** discontinue

desistance
3 end **4** halt, stop **5** cease, close **6** ending, finish, period **8** stoppage, stopping **9** cessation **10** conclusion **11** termination

desk
5 booth, stand, table **7** counter, lectern, rolltop **8** lapboard **9** secretary **10** escritoire
adjunct: **8** inkstand, standish
item: **3** pad **7** blotter, inkwell
library: **6** carrel

desolate
4 bare, lorn, sack **5** alone, bleak, drear, stark, waste **6** barren, devoid, dismal, dreary, gloomy, ravage **7** despoil, forlorn, joyless, pillage, plunder **8** dejected, derelict, deserted, desolate, downcast, forsaken, lay waste, lifeless, lonesome, solitary, spoliate **9** abandoned, cheerless, depredate, desecrate, destitute, devastate, sorrowful **10** despondent **11** dilapidated **12** inconsolable **13** disheartening

desolation
3 woe **4** ruin **5** gloom, grief, waste **6** misery, sorrow **7** anguish, despair, sadness **8** bareness **9** bleakness, dejection, wasteland **10** loneliness **11** abandonment, devastation **12** wretchedness

despair
6 give up 8 lose hope

despairing
7 anxious, doleful, forlorn 8 dejected, desolate, hopeless, wretched 9 depressed 10 despondent 11 downhearted 12 disconsolate 13 brokenhearted

desperado
6 bandit, gunman, outlaw 7 bandito, brigand, convict, ruffian 8 criminal 9 cutthroat 10 gunslinger, highwayman, lawbreaker

desperate
4 bold, dire, rash 5 acute, risky 6 daring, futile 7 crucial, forlorn, frantic, useless, violent 8 critical, headlong, hopeless, reckless, shocking 9 foolhardy, impetuous 10 despondent, frustrated, outrageous, scandalous 11 climacteric, precipitate 12 overpowering 13 irretrievable

Desperate Housewives
actress: 5 Cross (Marcia) 7 Hatcher (Teri), Huffman (Felicity) 8 Longoria (Eva), Sheridan (Nicollette)
creator: 6 Cherry (Marc)
character: 4 Bree (Van De Kamp), Edie (Britt), Mike (Delfino) 5 Betty (Applewhite), Orson (Hodge), Susan (Mayer) 7 Lynette (Scavo) 9 Gabrielle (Solis)
narrator: 6 Strong (Brenda)
setting: 8 Fairview 12 Wisteria Lane

desperation
5 agony 7 anguish, despair 8 distress 11 distraction 12 hopelessness, wretchedness

despicable
3 low 4 base, foul, grim, mean, ugly, vile 5 awful, cheap, gross, sorry 6 abject, scurvy, shabby, sordid 7 beastly, hateful, ignoble, pitiful 8 pitiable, shameful, wretched 9 degrading, loathsome 10 deplorable, detestable, disgusting 11 disgraceful, ignominious 12 contemptible, disreputable 13 reprehensible

despise
4 hate, shun, snub 5 abhor, avoid, scorn, spurn 6 detest, loathe, reject 7 contemn 8 execrate 9 abominate

despised one
6 pariah 7 outcast

despisement
4 hate 5 scorn 6 hatred, malice 7 disdain, ill will 8 aversion, contempt, loathing 9 antipathy, contumely 10 abhorrence 11 detestation

despite
8 although 11 in the face of 12 regardless of

despiteful
4 evil, mean 5 catty 6 bitchy, horrid, malign, odious, wicked 7 baleful, baneful, hostile, vicious 8 vengeful 9 malicious, rancorous, repellent 10 despicable, malevolent

despoil
4 sack 5 blast, strip, waste, wreck 6 denude, devour, maraud, ravage 7 pillage, plunder 8 desolate, spoliate 9 depredate, desecrate, devastate, strip away, vandalize 10 wreak havoc

despoiler
6 looter, sacker, vandal 7 ravager, wrecker 8 marauder, pillager 9 plunderer, spoliator 10 depredator, freebooter

despond
4 fret, mope, wilt 5 brood, droop, worry 6 give up, sorrow 8 languish 9 dejection 12 hopelessness

despondency
5 blues, dumps, gloom 6 misery, sorrow 7 anguish, despair, sadness 8 glumness 9 dejection 10 depression, melancholy 11 desperation, unhappiness 12 hopelessness

despondent
3 low, sad 4 blue, down, glum 7 doleful, forlorn 8 cast down, dejected, downcast, grieving, hopeless, mourning 9 depressed, desperate, heartsick, heartsore, sorrowful, woebegone 10 dispairing, dispirited, melancholy 11 discouraged, downhearted 12 disconsolate, disheartened

despot
4 czar, duce, tsar, tzar 5 ruler 6 tyrant 7 autarch, emperor 8 autocrat, dictator 9 oppressor, strong man

despotic
8 absolute 9 arbitrary, autarchic, imperious, tyrannous 10 autocratic, monocratic, tyrannical 11 dictatorial 12 totalitarian

despotism
7 czarism, tsarism, tyranny, tzarism 8 autarchy 9 autocracy 10 absolutism, domination 12 dictatorship

desquamate
4 pare, peel 5 scale 7 peel off 8 flake off, scale off 9 exfoliate

dessert
3 ice, pie 4 cake, flan, fool, tart 5 Betty, bombe, crepe, crisp, fruit, grunt, halva, Jell-O, melba, s'more, sweet, torte 6 afters, blintz, Danish, éclair, fondue, frappe, gâteau, halvah, hermit, junket, kuchen, mousse, pastry, sorbet, sundae, trifle 7 brownie, cobbler, compote, custard, gelatin, parfait, pudding, sabayon, sherbet, soufflé, spumoni, strudel 8 ambrosia, Bismarck, clafouti, crostata, flummery, ice cream, macaroon, meringue, napoleon, pandowdy, streusel, tiramisu, turnover 9 charlotte, cream puff, fruitcake, petit four, shortcake 10 blancmange, brown Betty, cheesecake, frangipane, icebox

cake, peach Melba, zabaglione **11** baked Alaska, banana split, crème brûlée, gingerbread **12** hasty pudding, zuppa inglese
French: **5** bombe **6** éclair, frappe, gâteau, mousse **7** parfait, sabayon **9** petit four **10** blancmange, frangipane
frozen: **5** bombe **7** parfait, sherbet
German: **6** kuchen **7** strudel
Italian: **7** cannoli, spumoni **8** tiramisu **10** zabaglione **12** zuppa inglese
Turkish: **5** halva **6** halvah

destination
3 aim, end, use **6** object, target **7** purpose **8** terminus **9** objective **10** appointing

destine
4 fate **6** assign, direct, intend **8** dedicate, set aside **9** designate, determine, preordain **10** foreordain **12** predetermine

destiny
3 lot **4** doom, fate **5** karma **6** design, future, kismet, Moirai **7** fortune, portion **8** prospect **9** hereafter **12** circumstance

destitute
4 bare, poor, void **5** broke, empty, needy **6** bereft, devoid, ruined **7** drained, lacking **8** bankrupt, depleted, dirt poor, divested, indigent, strapped, stripped **9** deficient, exhausted, penurious **10** bankrupted, stone-broke **11** impecunious **12** impoverished

destitution
6 penury **7** poverty **9** indigence, privation

destroy
3 axe, zap **4** doom, down, kill, nuke, raze, ruin, sack, slay, undo **5** crush, erase, quash, quell, smash, total, trash, waste, wrack, wreck **6** finish, lay low, mangle, ravage, rubble, rub out **7** abolish, atomize, despoil, expunge, nullify, pillage, shatter, wipe out **8** decimate, demolish, dispatch, dynamite, lay waste, pull down, snuff out, stamp out, tear down **9** devastate, dismantle, eradicate, extirpate, liquidate, pulverize **10** annihilate, extinguish, obliterate **11** exterminate

destroyer
4 bane, ruin **6** tin can, vandal **7** undoing, warship **8** downfall

destruction
4 loss, ruin **5** havoc **7** killing, sacking, undoing **8** downfall **9** ruination **10** extinction **11** devastation, liquidation **12** annihilation

destructive
7 baneful, harmful, ruinous **8** damaging **9** corrosive, injurious **10** shattering **11** deleterious, detrimental

desuetude
6 disuse **7** closure, neglect **9** cessation **11** abandonment

desultory
6 casual, chance, fitful, random, spotty **7** aimless, erratic, offhand, vagrant **8** shifting, slipshod, sporadic, wavering **9** haphazard, hit-or-miss, unplanned **10** capricious, digressive, disjointed **11** purposeless **12** unmethodical, unsystematic

detach
4 free, part, undo, wean **5** sever **6** cut off, remove, sunder **7** disjoin, divorce, release **8** separate, uncouple, withdraw **9** disengage **10** disconnect **12** disaffiliate

detached
5 alone, aloof, apart **6** remote **7** distant, neutral, removed, severed **8** abstract, isolated, separate, unbiased **9** incurious, withdrawn **10** impersonal **11** indifferent, unconcerned, unconnected **12** uninterested **13** disinterested, dispassionate, unaccompanied

detachment
5 squad **7** divorce, rupture **8** disunion, division **9** partition **10** neutrality, separation **11** dissolution

detail
4 item, list, part **5** point **6** assign, nicety, relate, report **7** appoint, article, element, itemize, listing, minutia, specify **8** allocate, spell out **9** enumerate, stipulate **10** assignment, particular **12** circumstance **13** particularize

detailed
4 full **6** minute **8** itemized, complete, thorough **10** blow-by-blow, exhaustive, meticulous, particular **13** thoroughgoing

detain
3 nab **4** bust, curb, hold, keep, mire, snag **5** check, delay, run in **6** arrest, collar, hang up, hinder, hold up, impede, pick up, retard, slow up **7** bog down, reserve, set back **8** hold back, keep back, restrain, slow down, withhold **9** apprehend **10** buttonhole
in conversation: **10** buttonhole

detect
4 espy, find, spot **5** catch, dig up, hit on, scent, smell **6** descry, notice, turn up **7** discern, hit upon, uncover, unearth **8** discover, meet with **9** ascertain, encounter, ferret out, track down

detectable
6 patent **7** evident, visible **8** sensible, tangible **10** noticeable, observable **11** discernible, perceptible

detection
9 discovery **10** unearthing
system: **5** radar, sofar

detective
3 tec **4** dick, G-man **6** shamus, sleuth **7** gumshoe **8** hawkshaw, informer, sherlock **9** inspector **10** private eye **12** investigator

fictional: **3** Pym (Lucy) **4** Chan (Charlie), Gray (Cordelia), Moto (Mr.) **5** Banks (Alan), Bosch (Harry), Brown (Father), Dupin (Auguste), Lecoq, Lupin (Arsène), McGee (Travis), Morse (Inspector), Queen (Ellery), Rebus (John), Saint, Spade (Sam), Trent (Philip), Vance (Philo), Wolfe (Nero) **6** Alleyn (Roderick), Archer (Lew), Carter (Nick), Hammer (Mike), Holmes (Sherlock), Marple (Miss Jane), McCone (Sharon), Poirot (Hercule), Wimsey (Peter) **7** Cadfael (Brother), Campion (Albert), Charles (Nick, Nora), Maigret (Jules), Marlowe (Philip) **8** Drummond (Bulldog), Millhone (Kinsey) **9** Dalgliesh (Adam) **10** Robicheaux (Dave), Warshawski (V. I.) **11** Father Brown

detective-story writer
3 Poe (Edgar Allan), Tey (Josephine) **4** Carr (John Dickson), Knox (Ronald) **5** Blake (Nicholas), Block (Lawrence), Cross (Amanda), Doyle (Arthur Conan), Green (Anna Katherine), Innes (Michael), James (P. D.), Marsh (Ngaio), Queen (Ellery), Stout (Rex) **6** Bramah (Ernest), Buchan (John), Dexter (Colin), Hansen (Joseph), McBain (Ed), Mosley (Walter), Parker (Robert), Peters (Ellis), Sayers (Dorothy L.) **7** Bentley (E. C.), Biggers (Earl Derr), Collins (Wilkie), Francis (Dick), Freeman (Austin), Gardner (Erle Stanley), Grafton (Sue), Hammett (Dashiell), Hiaasen (Carl), Hornung (E. W.), Leonard (Elmore), Rendell (Ruth), Simenon (Georges), Van Dine (S. S.), Wallace (Edgar) **8** Chandler (Raymond), Christie (Agatha), Cornwell (Patricia), Gaboriau (Emile), Marquand (John), Mortimer (John), Paretsky (Sara), Rinehart (Mary Roberts), Spillane (Mickey) **9** Allingham (Margery), Highsmith (Patricia), Hillerman (Tony), Lockridge (Frances, Richard), Macdonald (John, Ross) **10** Chesterton (Gilbert Keith)

detent
4 pawl

detention
6 arrest **7** holding **10** internment **11** confinement **12** imprisonment

deter
5 avert, block **6** divert, hamper, hinder, impede, thwart **7** forfend, inhibit, obviate, prevent, rule out, shut out, ward off **8** dissuade, preclude, restrain, stave off **9** forestall, turn aside **10** discourage

deterge
4 wash **7** cleanse, wash off

detergent
4 soap **8** cleanser

deteriorate
3 rot **4** fade, fail, flag, sink, wear **5** decay, lapse, slide, spoil **6** weaken, worsen **7** decline, regress **8** languish **9** decompose, fall apart **10** debilitate, degenerate, depreciate, go downhill, retrograde, retrogress **12** disintegrate

deterioration
4 ruin **5** decay **6** ebbing, waning **7** atrophy, decline, erosion, failing, rotting **8** decaying, spoiling **9** crumbling, decadence, downgrade **10** debasement, degeneracy **12** degeneration, dégringolade

determinant
4 gene **5** agent, basis, cause, trait **6** factor, ground, reason **7** epitope, radical **9** attribute, influence

determinate
5 fixed **6** cymose **7** limited, precise, settled **8** constant, definite **10** definitive, restricted **11** established **13** circumscribed

determination
5 drive, spunk **6** fixing, mettle **7** finding, opinion, purpose, resolve, verdict **8** decision, firmness, judgment, tenacity **9** assurance, hardihood, impulsion, intention, resolving, willpower **10** conclusion, dedication, definition, doggedness, resolution, settlement **11** decidedness, intrepidity **12** perseverance, resoluteness, stubbornness **13** purposiveness

determine
3 fix, set **4** rule **5** bound, limit, prove **6** decide, figure, ordain, settle **7** control, delimit, find out, mark out, measure, preform, unearth **8** conclude, discover, regulate **9** ascertain, demarcate, establish, preordain, resolve on **10** delimitate, foreordain, predestine, predispose

determined
3 set **4** bent **5** fixed **6** driven, intent **7** decided, earnest, serious, settled **8** decisive, hellbent, resolute, resolved, stubborn **9** tenacious **10** persistent, purposeful, unwavering **11** established, persevering, unfaltering **12** foreordained, unhesitating

detest
4 hate **5** abhor, spurn **6** loathe **7** despise, dislike **8** execrate **9** abominate, repudiate

detestable
4 foul, vile **6** damned, horrid, odious **7** hateful, heinous **9** abhorrent, execrable, loathsome **10** abominable, despicable **12** contemptible

detestation
4 hate **6** hatred **8** anathema, aversion, loathing **9** repulsion, revulsion **10** abhorrence, execration, repugnance

dethrone
4 oust **6** depose **7** uncrown **8** displace

detonate
5 blast, burst, go off, spark **6** blow up, set off **7** explode **8** touch off

detonator
3 cap **4** fuse **9** explosive **11** blasting cap
detour
5 avoid, skirt **6** bypass **8** side trip **9** diversion
detract
6 divert, lessen, reduce **8** decrease, diminish, minimize **10** depreciate
detraction
9 aspersion, maligning, traducing **10** backbiting, belittling, derogation, slandering **11** denigration, deprecation, traducement **12** backstabbing, belittlement **13** disparagement
detractive
9 maligning, slighting, traducing, vilifying **10** defamatory, derogatory, pejorative **11** denigrating, disparaging **12** depreciative, depreciatory
detriment
4 harm, loss **6** damage, injury **7** marring **8** drawback **10** impairment **12** disadvantage
detrimental
3 bad, ill **7** adverse, harmful, hurtful, nocuous **8** damaging, negative **9** injurious **11** deleterious, unfavorable
detritus
4 tufa, tuff **5** scree, talus **6** debris, rubble **7** remains **11** odds and ends
Detroit
county: 5 Wayne
founder: 8 Cadillac (Sieur de)
lake: 4 Erie **10** Saint Clair
sobriquet: 6 Motown **9** Motor City
de trop
5 extra, spare **7** too much, surplus **9** excessive, redundant **10** gratuitous **11** superfluous **13** supernumerary
Deucalion
father: 10 Prometheus
kingdom: 6 Phthia
mother: 7 Clymene
son: 6 Hellen
wife: 6 Pyrrha
deuce
3 tie, two **4** card, draw **5** devil **7** dickens **10** even-steven
Deutschland über ____
5 alles
Devaki's son
7 Krishna
____ De Valera
5 Eamon
devaluate
5 abase, decry, lower **6** reduce, weaken **7** cheapen, degrade **8** mark down, write off **9** undermine, underrate, write down **10** depreciate
devaluation
7 decline **10** debasement, declension **11** declination
devalue
see **depreciate**
devastate
4 raze, ruin, sack **5** waste **6** ravage **7** despoil, pillage, plunder **8** demolish, desolate, lay waste, overcome, spoliate **9** depredate, desecrate, overpower, overwhelm
devastation
4 loss, ruin **5** chaos, havoc, waste **6** ravage **7** pillage, plunder **8** disorder **9** confusion, ruination **10** demolition, desolation, spoliation **11** depredation
develop
3 age **4** form, grow **5** occur, reach, ripen **6** attain, dilate, emerge, evolve, expand, grow up, happen, mature, mellow, open up, thrive, unfold, unfurl **7** achieve, acquire, advance, burgeon, enlarge, expound, promote **8** flourish **9** actualize, elaborate, establish, transpire **11** come to light, materialize
development
5 phase **6** growth, result, spread **7** advance, buildup, outcome **8** ontogeny, progress, ripening **9** evolution, expansion, flowering, phylogeny, unfolding **10** maturation **11** elaboration, progression
of life: 10 biogenesis
Devi
7 goddess
consort: 5 Shiva
father: 7 Himavat
name: 3 Uma **4** Kali **5** Durga, Gauri **6** Chandi **7** Parvati
deviant
4 bent **5** kinky, queer **6** off-key **7** twisted, wayward **8** aberrant, abnormal, atypical, perverse **9** anomalous, different, divergent, irregular, unnatural **11** heteroclite
deviate
3 err, yaw **4** turn, vary, veer **5** sheer, stray **6** depart, swerve, wander **7** digress, diverge **8** aberrant **9** eccentric, turn aside
deviation
3 yaw **4** bend, tack, turn **5** error, shift **6** change **7** anomaly, turning, veering **8** variance **9** departure, diversion **10** aberration, alteration, deflection, divergence
device
4 ploy, tool **5** feint, gizmo, means, motif, motto, shift, thing, trick **6** dingus, doodad, emblem, figure, gadget, gambit, hickey, jigger, medium, motive, symbol, widget **7** gimmick, machine, utensil, whatnot, whatsit **8** artifice, creation,

insignia **9** apparatus, appliance, doohickey, expedient, implement, invention, makeshift, mechanism, thingummy **10** instrument **11** contraption, contrivance, inclination, thingamabob, thingamajig, thingumajig
automatic: 5 servo
binding: 5 clamp
fastening: 6 zipper
grasping: 4 tong
heating: 8 radiator
hoisting: 5 crane, lewis **8** windlass
holding: 4 vise **5** clamp
paging: 6 beeper
suction: 4 pump

devil
3 imp **5** beast, cloot, demon, fiend, rogue, Satan, scamp **6** Belial, diablo, dybbuk, rascal, spirit **7** Clootie, dickens, Lucifer, Old Nick, serpent, tempter, villain **8** Apollyon, Mephisto, scalawag, succubus **9** archfiend, Beelzebub, cacodemon, scoundrel, skeezicks **10** blackguard, Old Scratch **11** rapscallion

devilfish
3 ray **5** manta **7** octopus **8** manta ray **10** cephalopod

devilish
3 bad **4** evil **6** cursed, wicked **7** demonic, hellish, roguish, satanic **8** accursed, damnable, diabolic, fiendish, infernal, sinister **9** nefarious **10** diabolical, iniquitous, villainous **11** mischievous

devil-may-care
4 rash, wild **6** rakish, sporty **7** raffish **8** rakehell, reckless **9** easygoing

devilry
7 knavery, roguery, sorcery, waggery **8** mischief **9** diablerie **10** wickedness, witchcraft **11** roguishness, waggishness **12** sportiveness

devious
3 sly **4** foxy, wily **6** artful, crafty, errant, erring, roving, shifty, sneaky, tricky **7** bending, crooked, cunning, curving, erratic, winding **8** aberrant, guileful, indirect, scheming, sneaking, twisting **9** deceptive, underhand, wandering **10** roundabout **11** out-of-the-way, underhanded

devise
4 form, plan, plot, will **5** chart, forge, frame, shape **6** cook up, create, design, invent, legacy, legate, scheme **7** arrange, bequest, concoct, connive, dope out, dream up, hatch up, project **8** bequeath, property **9** determine, formulate **11** inheritance

devitalize
3 sap **5** drain **6** deaden, weaken **7** exhaust **8** enfeeble, etiolate **9** desiccate **10** eviscerate

devoid of
7 lacking, wanting **8** free from

devoir
3 job **4** duty, task, work **5** chore, stint **6** charge **9** committal **10** assignment, commitment, obligation

devolution
5 decay **7** decline, passing **8** receding, transfer **9** conferral, decadence, recession, surrender **10** conveyance, declension, degeneracy, regression, relegation, transferal **11** degradation **12** degeneration, dégringolade, retrograding, transference **13** retrogression

devolve
4 give, pass **6** pass on **8** hand down, hand over, relegate, transfer **10** degenerate

devote
5 apply **6** commit, direct, donate, hallow **7** reserve **8** dedicate, give over, sanctify **9** confirm in, habituate **10** consecrate

devoted
4 dear, fond, true **5** loyal **6** ardent, caring, doting, fervid, loving **7** dutiful, fervent, zealous **8** constant, faithful **9** dedicated **10** thoughtful **12** affectionate
religiously: 6 oblate

devotee
3 fan, nut **4** buff **5** hound, lover **6** addict, votary, zealot **7** admirer, amateur, fanatic, fancier, habitué **8** follower **9** supporter **10** aficionado, enthusiast

devotion
4 love, zeal **5** ardor, piety **6** fealty, fervor, prayer, Rosary **7** loyalty, passion **8** fidelity, fondness **9** adherence, adoration, reverence **10** allegiance, attachment, dedication, enthusiasm **12** faithfulness

devour
3 eat **5** eat up, enjoy **6** absorb, feed on **7** consume, destroy, feast on, pillage **8** prey upon, wolf down **9** delight in, feast upon, polish off, swallow up **10** annihilate

devouring
4 avid **6** greedy **8** esurient, ravenous **9** voracious **10** gluttonous

devout
4 holy **5** godly, loyal, pious **6** ardent **7** earnest, fervent, serious, sincere, zealous **8** faithful, reverent **9** pietistic, prayerful, religious

devoutness
4 zeal **5** ardor, piety **9** reverence **10** commitment

dew
5 sweat, tears **8** moisture **11** precipitate **12** perspiration **13** precipitation

dewy
3 wet **4** damp, pure **5** fresh, moist, naive **7** artless, natural **8** innocent, wide-eyed **9** credulous, guileless, ingenuous, unworldly

dexter
5 right

dexterity
4 ease **5** craft, grace, skill **7** ability, aptness, know-how, prowess, sleight **8** deftness, facility **9** adeptness, expertise, readiness **10** adroitness, nimbleness, smoothness **12** skillfulness

dexterous
3 apt **4** able, deft **5** adept, agile, handy **6** adroit, artful, facile, nimble, smooth **7** skilled **8** masterly, skillful **10** proficient

____ Dhabi
3 Abu

diablerie
7 devilry, roguery, sorcery, waggery **8** deviltry, iniquity, mischief, satanism **9** devilment **10** black magic, wickedness, witchcraft, wrongdoing

diabolical
4 evil **5** awful **6** impish, wicked **7** beastly, demonic, heinous, hellish, puckish, roguish, satanic **8** demoniac, devilish, dreadful, fiendish, godawful, hellborn, infernal, rascally, sinister **9** execrable, malicious, monstrous, nefarious **10** degenerate, demoniacal, horrendous, iniquitous, scandalous, villainous **11** mischievous

diabolism
see **diablerie**

diacritic
5 acute, breve, grave, haček, tilde **6** accent, macron, umlaut **7** cedilla **8** dieresis **9** diaeresis **10** circumflex
Arabic: **5** hamza **6** hamzah

diadem
5 crown, tiara **6** wreath **7** chaplet, coronal, coronet **8** headband

diagnose
4 spot **5** place **8** identify, pinpoint **9** determine, interpret, recognize **11** distinguish

diagnostic
8 analytic **10** analytical, expository, indicating, indicative **11** explanatory, exploratory **12** interpretive

diagonal
4 bias **5** bevel **6** biased **7** beveled, oblique, slanted **8** inclined, slanting **9** inclining, slantways, slantwise

diagonally
7 athwart **9** slantways, slantwise **10** cornerwise **11** catercorner, kitty-corner

diagram
3 map **5** chart, graph **6** design, layout, sketch **7** drawing, isotype **9** represent

dial
4 call, face, knob, tune, turn **5** phone **6** rotate **7** control **10** manipulate

dialect
4 cant, jive **5** argot, idiom, koine, lingo, slang **6** creole, jargon, patois, patter, pidgin, speech, tongue **8** language, localism **10** vernacular **11** regionalism, terminology **13** provincialism
Georgia: **6** Gullah
London: **7** cockney

dialectic
5 logic **6** debate **8** dialogue, forensic **9** reasoning **10** discussion **11** disputation **13** argumentation, investigation

dialogue
4 chat, talk **6** confer, parley, script **8** colloquy, converse **12** conversation **13** confabulation

diameter
4 bore **5** chord, width **7** breadth, caliber **8** bisector, wideness **9** broadness

diametric
7 counter, opposed **8** contrary, converse, opposite **12** antithetical **13** contradictory

diamond
3 gem **5** field, stone **7** rhombus
element: **6** carbon
famous: **4** Hope, Pitt **5** Sancy **6** Orloff, Regent **8** Braganza, Cullinan, Kohinoor **9** Excelsior **10** Great Mogul
holder: **3** dop
inferior: **4** bort
oval: **9** briolette
pattern: **6** argyle
playing card: **7** lozenge
state: **8** Delaware
surface: **5** facet

Diana
see **Artemis**

diapason
4 peal, stop **5** range, scale, scope **7** compass, measure **8** spectrum **10** tuning fork

diaper
5 nappy **7** pattern **8** ornament

diaphanous
5 filmy, gauzy, sheer, vague **6** flimsy **8** ethereal, gossamer **11** transparent **13** insubstantial

diaphragm
4 stop **6** septum **8** membrane **9** partition

diarist
4 Gide (André), Mann (Thomas) **5** Frank (Anne), Inman (Arthur Crew), Kahlo (Frida), Pepys (Samuel), Plath (Sylvia), Rorem (Ned), Scott (Walter), Swift (Jonathan), Woolf (Virginia) **6** Burney (Fanny), Evelyn (John) **7** Boswell (James), Thoreau (Henry David) **8** Robinson

(Henry Crabb) **9** Lindbergh (Anne Morrow) **10** chronicler, journalist

diary
3 log **6** record **7** daybook, diurnal, journal, logbook **8** notebook, register **9** chronicle

diastase
6 enzyme **8** catalyst, reactant

diatribe
4 rant, rave **6** tirade **7** polemic **8** harangue, jeremiad **9** criticism, philippic **11** castigation **12** denunciation

dibs
4 gelt **5** claim, dough, money, title **6** rights **11** reservation

dice
4 cast, cube **5** bones, cubes, ivory, mince **11** devil's-bones
game: **5** craps
losing throw: **7** missout
singular: **3** die
throw: **7** boxcars **9** snake eyes

dicer
5 loser **6** risker **7** gambler

dicey
4 iffy **5** risky **6** chancy, tricky **8** ticklish **9** uncertain, whimsical **10** precarious **11** problematic, speculative **13** unpredictable

dichotomize
5 halve **7** dissect **8** hemisect **9** bifurcate

dichotomous
5 split **6** forked **7** pronged **9** bifurcate **10** bifurcated

dichotomy
7 forking **8** division **9** bisection, branching, splitting **11** bifurcation **13** contradiction

Dickens, Charles
birthplace: **10** Portsmouth
captain: **6** Cuttle
character: **3** Ada (Clare), Pip, Tim **4** Dick (Mr.), Dora, Gamp (Sairey), Heep (Uriah), Nell **5** Drood (Edwin), Emily, Fagin, Lucie (Manette), Sikes (Bill) **6** Barkis, Bumble (Mr.), Carton (Sydney), Cuttle (Capt.), Darnay (Charles), Dombey (Fanny, Florence, Paul), Dorrit (Amy), Oliver (Twist) **7** Barnaby (Rudge), Dedlock (Lady), Defarge, Gargery (Joe), Manette (Dr.), Scrooge (Ebenezer), Tiny Tim **8** Cratchit (Bob), Havisham (Miss), Jarndyce (John), Magwitch (Abel), Micawber (Mr.), Nickleby (Nicholas), Peggotty (Clara, Daniel, Ham), Pickwick (Mr.) **9** Bill Sikes, Gradgrind (Mr.), Murdstone (Mr.), Pecksniff (Mr.), Uriah Heep **10** Chuzzlewit (Anthony, Jonas, Martin), Steerforth **11** Copperfield (David)
hero: **6** Carton (Sydney)
nationality: **7** English
pen name: **3** Boz
villain: **5** Fagin
work: **9** Hard Times **10** Bleak House **11** Oliver Twist **12** Barnaby Rudge, Dombey and Son, Little Dorrit **14** Christmas Carol (A), Pickwick Papers (The) **15** Our Mutual Friend, Tale of Two Cities (A) **16** David Copperfield, Martin Chuzzlewit, Nicholas Nickleby **17** Great Expectations

dicker
4 deal, swap **5** argue, trade **6** barter, haggle, higgle, palter **7** bargain, chaffer **8** contract, huckster **9** negotiate

dickey
10 shirtfront

Dickey novel
11 Deliverance

dictate
3 set **4** lead, rule, word **5** edict, order, tenet **6** behest, decree, direct, enjoin, govern, impose, ordain, recite **7** bidding, command, control, lay down, mandate, read off, summons **9** determine, direction, directive, prescribe, principle, pronounce, verbalize **10** injunction **12** prescription

dictative
5 bossy **8** despotic, dogmatic **9** imperious **10** peremptory **11** doctrinaire, magisterial **13** authoritarian

dictator
4 czar, duce, tsar, tzar **6** caesar, despot, tyrant **8** autocrat, martinet **9** oppressor, strongman
Chinese: **3** Mao **9** Mao Zedong **10** Mao Tsetung
German: **6** Hitler (Adolf)
Italian: **9** Mussolini (Benito)
military: **8** caudillo
Russian: **6** Stalin (Joseph)
Spanish: **6** Franco (Francisco)

dictatorial
5 bossy **8** despotic, dogmatic **9** arbitrary, imperious, masterful **10** autocratic, iron-handed, peremptory, tyrannical **11** doctrinaire, domineering, overbearing **12** totalitarian **13** authoritarian

dictatorship
7 tyranny **9** autocracy, Caesarism, despotism, supremacy **10** absolutism

diction
6 phrase, speech **7** wordage, wording **8** delivery, language, parlance, phrasing, rhetoric, verbiage **9** elocution, verbalism **11** enunciation, phraseology

dictionary
7 lexicon **8** glossary, wordbook **10** repository **13** reference book
compiler: **7** Johnson (Samuel), Webster (Noah) **13** lexicographer
geographical: **9** gazetteer
of synonyms: **8** thesauri (plural) **9** thesaurus

dictum
4 fiat **5** adage, axiom, edict, maxim, moral **6** ruling **7** mandate, opinion, precept, proverb **11** declaration **13** pronouncement

didactic
5 moral **6** teachy **7** donnish, preachy **8** advisory, edifying, pedantic, sermonic, teaching **9** hortative, pedagogic, teacherly **10** moralizing **11** informative, instructive

diddle
3 con, gyp, toy **4** beat, bilk, dupe, hoax, fool, idle, laze, loaf, loll, rook, scam **5** cheat, cozen, delay, drone, trick **6** chisel, chouse, dabble, dawdle, delude, fiddle, fleece, loiter, lounge, rope in, take in **7** deceive, defraud, goof off, mislead, swindle **8** flimflam, fool with, hoodwink, lollygag **9** bamboozle, overreach, victimize, waste time **10** dilly-dally, fool around, hang around

diddler
3 gyp **4** sham **5** cheat, faker, fraud, rogue **6** con man **7** grifter, shammer, sharper **8** swindler **9** con artist, defrauder, trickster **11** flimflammer **12** double-dealer **13** confidence man

dido
4 jest, lark **5** antic, caper, curio, frill, prank **6** bauble, frolic, gewgaw, trifle, whimsy **7** bibelot, novelty, trinket **8** furbelow, gimcrack, kickshaw, mischief **9** bagatelle, plaything **10** knickknack, tomfoolery

Dido
6 Elissa
brother: **9** Pygmalion
city founded by: **8** Carthage
father: **5** Belus **6** Mutton
husband: **7** Acerbas **8** Sichaeus
lover: **6** Aeneas

Dido and Aeneas composer
7 Purcell (Henry)

die
4 drop, fall, mold, pass, stop, wane **5** cease, croak **6** cash in, demise, expire, go west, matrix, pass on, peg out, perish, pop off **7** decease, go south, kick off, snuff it, succumb **8** cash it in, check out, drop dead, pass away **9** disappear **10** buy the farm **12** join the choir **13** kick the bucket
from hunger: **6** starve
loaded: **6** fulham

____ die
4 sine

diehard
7 devoted, fanatic **8** true-blue **9** dogmatist **10** determined **11** bitter-ender, doctrinaire, reactionary, standpatter **12** conservative, intransigent **13** stick-in-the-mud

____ diem
3 per **5** carpe

Dies ____
4 Irae

diet
4 bant, eats, fare, fast, feed, menu **6** ration, reduce, regime **7** regimen **8** assembly, victuals **10** parliament **11** legislature, nourishment

Diet of ____
5 Worms **6** Speyer, Spires **8** Augsburg

Dieu ____ (British motto)
10 et mon droit

____-dieu
4 prie

differ
4 vary **5** demur **7** deviate **8** disagree

difference
3 gap **7** discord, dispute, dissent **8** conflict, contrast, variance **9** departure, deviation, disparity, otherness, variation **10** dissension, divergence, unlikeness **11** controversy, discrepancy, distinction **12** disagreement **13** dissimilarity

different
5 other **6** divers, single, sundry, unlike, varied **7** another, deviant, distant, diverse, several, special, unalike, unequal, unusual, various **8** discrete, distinct, peculiar, separate **9** disparate, divergent **10** dissimilar, individual, particular **11** contrasting, distinctive

differentiate
4 vary **5** adapt **6** change, modify **8** contrast, separate **9** diversify, transform **11** distinguish, individuate **12** characterize, discriminate

difficult
4 hard **5** tight, tough **6** thorny, uphill **7** arduous, awkward, labored, obscure, operose **8** exacting, perverse, puzzling, stubborn **9** demanding, effortful, herculean, laborious, strenuous **10** refractory **11** problematic

difficulty
3 ado, fix, jam **4** beef **4** pass, snag **5** hitch, nodus, pinch, rigor, worry **6** hang-up, hassle, pickle, plight, scrape, strait **7** dilemma, pitfall, problem, trouble **8** distress, hardship, hot water, obstacle, quandary, quagmire, question **9** adversity, challenge **10** impediment **11** aggravation, arduousness, predicament, vicissitude

diffidence
7 modesty, reserve, shyness **8** distrust, meekness, timidity **9** quietness, restraint, timidness **10** hesitation **11** bashfulness

diffident
3 shy **4** meek **5** timid **7** bashful **8** hesitant, reserved, retiring, timorous **9** reluctant, unassured **11** unassertive **12** self-effacing

diffuse
5 strew, vague, wordy **6** prolix, spread **7** scatter, verbose **8** disperse, rambling **9** broadcast, dispersed, propagate, scattered, spreading, spread out **10** distribute, long-winded, widespread **11** disseminate, distributed

diffusion
6 spread **7** osmosis **9** broadcast, dispersal, prolixity, spreading **10** dispersion, scattering **11** circulation, propagation **12** broadcasting, promulgation

dig
3 jab **4** barb, grub, hole, like, mine, poke, prod, root, site, stab **5** delve, ditch, enjoy, gouge, nudge, probe, scoop, spade, taunt **6** burrow, plunge, quarry, relish, rootle, shovel, thrust, trench, tunnel **7** explore, root out, unearth **8** excavate, prospect **10** excavation **11** investigate **up: 6** exhume **7** unearth

digest
5 sum up **6** absorb, codify, précis **7** consume, stomach, summate, swallow **8** abstract, boil down, classify, compress, condense, syllabus, synopsis **9** summarize, summation, synopsize **10** abridgment **12** condensation

digger
4 plow **5** miner **6** shovel **7** soldier

digit
3 toe **5** thumb **6** cipher, figure, finger, number, pinkie **7** integer, numeral **9** character **11** whole number

dignified
4 prim **6** august, formal, proper, seemly **7** courtly, elegant, stately **8** cultured, decorous, ennobled, polished **9** distingué, patrician

dignify
5 adorn, exalt, grace, honor **7** ennoble, elevate, glorify, sublime **11** distinguish

dignitary
3 VIP **4** lion **5** chief, nabob **6** leader, worthy **7** notable **8** eminence, luminary **9** personage **10** notability **11** muckety-muck **13** high-muck-a-muck

dignity
4 rank **5** honor, merit, poise, pride, worth **6** cachet, status, virtue **7** address, decorum, gravity, hauteur, majesty, stature **8** grandeur, nobility, position, prestige, standing **9** propriety **10** augustness, seemliness **11** consequence, self-respect

digress
5 stray **6** depart, ramble, swerve, wander **7** deviate, diverge **8** divagate

digression
5 aside **7** episode, tangent **8** drifting, excursus, rambling, straying **9** deviation, wandering **10** deflection, divagation, divergence **11** parenthesis

dig up
4 find **6** expose, reveal **7** nose out, root out, uncover, unearth **8** discover **9** ferret out, run across, search out, track down

dik-dik
8 antelope

dike
3 dam **4** bank **5** ditch, drain, levee **7** barrier **8** causeway **10** embankment **11** watercourse

dilapidate
4 ruin **5** decay, wreck **7** break up, crumble, decline, neglect **9** break down, decompose, disregard **10** deliquesce **12** disintegrate

dilapidated
5 dingy, seedy **6** beat-up, ragtag, ruined, shabby **7** decayed, run-down **8** battered, crumbled, decrepit **9** crumbling **10** broken-down, down-at-heel, ramshackle **12** deteriorated

dilapidation
4 ruin **5** decay **7** atrophy **8** collapse, decaying **9** crumbling, decadence, disrepair **11** decrepitude **13** decomposition, deterioration

dilate
5 swell, widen **6** expand, extend **7** distend, enlarge, expound **9** discourse, expatiate

dilatory
4 idle, slow **5** slack, tardy **7** laggard **8** dallying, delaying, sluggish **9** leisurely, lingering, unhurried **11** time-wasting

dilemma
3 box, fix, jam **4** bind, hole, spot **6** choice, corner, pickle, plight, scrape **7** catch-22, problem **8** argument, quandary **10** difficulty **11** predicament

dilettante
4 tyro **7** amateur, dabbler **8** aesthete, putterer **9** smatterer

dilettantish
see **amateurish**

diligence
4 zeal **8** industry **9** assiduity **10** commitment **11** application, persistence **12** perseverance, sedulousness **13** assiduousness

diligent
8 sedulous **9** assiduous **10** persistent, persisting, unflagging **11** hardworking, industrious, painstaking, persevering

dilly
3 pip **4** lulu **5** dandy, doozy, peach **6** corker, doozie, pippin, ripper, rouser **8** jim-dandy, knockout **9** humdinger **10** ripsnorter **11** crackerjack

dillydally
see **delay**

dilute
3 cut **4** thin, weak **5** water **6** watery, weaken **8** diminish, weakened **9** attenuate, water down **11** watered-down

dim
4 dull, dumb, hazy, pale, slow **5** befog, blear, blind, cloud, dense, dusky, faint, muddy, murky, muted, thick, vague **6** bleary, gloomy, stupid **7** becloud, low beam, obscure, shadowy, subdued, unclear **9** tenebrous **10** ill-defined, indistinct, lackluster, lusterless **11** unpromising

dime novel
4 pulp **7** chiller, shocker **8** dreadful, thriller **12** bloodcurdler **13** penny dreadful

dimension
4 size **5** reach, scale, scope, width **6** aspect, extent, spread **7** compass, expanse, measure, quality **9** amplitude, magnitude

diminish
3 ebb **4** bate, wane **5** abate, peter, quell, taper **6** lessen, recede, reduce, subdue, temper, weaken **7** curtail, decline, dwindle, subside **8** belittle, decrease, minimize, moderate, restrain, taper off **9** attenuate, disparage, dispraise **10** depreciate **11** detract from

diminutive
3 wee **4** tiny **5** bitsy, dwarf, pygmy, small, teeny, weeny **6** bantam, little, midget, minute, peewee, petite, teensy **9** miniature, pint-sized, undersize **10** teeny-weeny **11** lilliputian **12** teensy-weensy

____ dimittis
4 Nunc

dimple
3 pit **4** dent, dint, fret, nick **5** notch **6** ripple **8** pockmark **10** depression **11** indentation

dimwit
3 oaf **4** clod, dodo, dolt, dope, fool, simp, yo-yo **5** booby, chump, cluck, dummy, dunce, idiot, moron, stupe **6** dum-dum **7** airhead, dullard, fathead, pinhead **8** bonehead, dumbbell, imbecile, lunkhead, meathead, numskull **9** birdbrain, blockhead, dumb bunny, dumb cluck, ignoramus, lamebrain, numbskull, simpleton **10** dunderhead, nincompoop **11** featherhead, knucklehead **12** featherbrain

dim-witted
4 dull, dumb, slow **6** stupid **7** doltish, foolish, idiotic, moronic **8** backward, imbecile, retarded **9** brainless, half-baked, imbecilic **11** birdbrained, lamebrained **12** feebleminded, simpleminded

din
3 row **4** roar **5** babel, clash, noise **6** bedlam, clamor, deafen, hubbub, racket, rattle, tumult, uproar **7** clangor, clatter, resound **8** brouhaha **9** commotion, stridency **10** hullabaloo, hurly-burly **11** pandemonium **13** clamorousness

Dinah
brother: **4** Levi **6** Simeon
father: **5** Jacob
mother: **4** Leah

dine
3 eat, sup **4** feed **5** feast **6** eat out **7** banquet, nourish

diner
4 café **5** eater **6** eatery **7** canteen **8** snack bar **9** hash house **10** coffee shop, restaurant **11** greasy spoon **12** lunch counter, luncheonette, sandwich shop

Dinesen, Isak
6 Blixen (Karen)
work: **11** Out of Africa **12** Winter's Tales **16** Seven Gothic Tales

ding
3 mar **4** dent, nick **5** clang **7** blemish

ding-a-ling
3 nut **4** kook, yo-yo **5** flake, loony, wacko **6** cuckoo, nitwit, weirdo **7** lunatic **8** crackpot **9** fruitcake, harebrain, lamebrain, screwball **10** crackbrain **12** scatterbrain

dinghy
5 skiff **7** rowboat, shallop **8** lifeboat, life raft, sailboat

dingle
4 dale, dell, glen, vale **6** ravine, valley

dingus
5 gizmo **6** doodad, gadget, jigger, widget **7** whatsit **9** doohickey, thingummy **11** thingamabob, thingamajig, thingumajig

dingy
4 foul, mean **5** dirty, seedy, tacky **6** filthy, grubby, grungy, scuzzy, shabby, soiled, sordid **7** rundown, squalid, sullied, unclean **8** begrimed

dinky
3 toy **4** tiny **5** small, teeny **9** undersize **10** locomotive

dinner
4 meal **5** feast **6** regale, repast, spread, supper **7** banquet **8** luncheon **9** collation **10** table d'hôte
course: **4** meat, soup **5** salad **6** entrée **7** dessert **9** appetizer
jacket: **3** tux **6** tuxedo

dinosaur
6 fossil **7** has-been **8** theropod **11** anachronism
fictional: **8** Godzilla

dinosauric
4 huge **5** passé **6** bygone **7** extinct, mammoth **8** colossal, enormous, obsolete, outmoded

9 cyclopean, leviathan, out-of-date 10 antiquated, behemothic, fossilized, gargantuan, mastodonic, oldfangled 11 elephantine 12 antediluvian, old-fashioned, out-of-fashion 13 anachronistic

dint
4 nick 5 force, might, power 6 dimple, virtue 7 drive in, impress 10 impression 11 indentation

diocese
3 see 9 bishopric
Eastern Orthodox: 7 eparchy
subdivision: 6 parish

diode
9 rectifier 10 vacuum tube 12 electron tube
component: 5 anode 7 cathode 9 electrode

Diomedes
city founded by: 4 Arpi
father: 4 Ares, Mars 6 Tydeus
foe: 6 Aeneas, Hector
slayer: 8 Heracles, Hercules
victim: 6 Rhesus

Dione
5 Titan
cult partner: 4 Zeus
daughter: 5 Venus 9 Aphrodite
father: 7 Oceanus
lover: 4 Zeus
mother: 6 Tethys

Dionysus
see **Bacchus**

Dionyza's husband
5 Cleon

Dioscuri
5 twins 6 Castor, Gemini, Pollux
father: 4 Zeus 9 Tyndareus
mother: 4 Leda
sister: 5 Helen

dip
3 sag 4 bail, draw, drop, duck, dunk, fall, lade, sink, skid, slip, slue, swim 5 basin, ladle, lower, pitch, sauce, scoop, slope, slump, spoon, stoop 6 go down, hollow, plunge 7 decline, descend, descent, falloff, immerse, sinkage 8 decrease, downturn, sinkhole, submerge, submerse 9 concavity, declivity, downswing, downtrend, immersion 10 depression

diphthong
7 digraph 8 ligature

diploma
6 degree 7 charter 8 document 9 sheepskin 10 credential

diplomacy
4 tact 7 address, finesse 8 delicacy 10 artfulness, discretion, statecraft 11 negotiation, savoir faire, tactfulness

diplomatic
4 deft 5 bland, suave 6 artful, astute, polite, smooth, urbane 7 courtly, politic, tactful 8 delicate, discreet 9 courteous 12 conciliating, conciliatory, paleographic 13 accommodating

diplomat's office
7 embassy, mission

diplopod
9 millipede

dipper
3 cup 4 bird 5 ladle, ouzel, scoop, stars 6 bucket 10 pickpocket, water ouzel

dippy
4 daft, zany 5 crazy, daffy, flaky, goofy, kooky, loony, nutty, silly, wacky 6 stupid 7 doltish, foolish, witless 9 half-baked 11 harebrained 12 preposterous

dipsomania
10 alcoholism

dire
4 grim 5 acute, awful 6 dismal, horrid, tragic, urgent, woeful 7 baleful, baneful, crucial, extreme, fateful, ominous, ruinous 8 alarming, critical, dreadful, grievous, horrible, horrific, menacing, shocking, sinister, terrible 9 appalling, desperate, frightful, ill-boding 10 calamitous, deplorable, depressing, foreboding, malevolent, oppressing, oppressive, pernicious 11 apocalyptic, distressing, threatening

direct
4 head, lead, show 5 apply, frank, guide, label, level, order, pilot, plain, point, route, steer, train 6 assign, charge, define, devote, divert, enjoin, escort, extend, govern, lineal, linear, manage, ordain, settle 7 address, carry on, command, conduct, control, genuine, nonstop, operate, oversee, preside, project, request 8 dispatch, instruct, regulate, shepherd, straight, unbroken, verbatim 9 determine, firsthand, immediate, prescribe 10 administer, contiguous, continuous, inevitable 11 categorical, undeviating, unequivocal, word for word
a helmsman: 4 conn
proceedings: 7 preside

direction
3 way 4 east, line, path, side, west 5 angle, north, point, south, trend 6 course, design 7 bearing, channel, command, purpose 8 guidance, tendency 9 clockwise, oversight, viewpoint 10 management, standpoint, trajectory 11 instruction, supervision
blowing: 7 leeward 8 windward
horizontal: 7 azimuth
main line of: 4 axis
(see also **compass point**)

directive
4 fiat, memo, word, writ **5** edict, order, ukase **6** charge, decree, dictum, notice, ruling **7** bidding, command, dictate, mandate **8** deciding, managing **9** presiding **10** assignment, injunction, memorandum **11** instruction, supervising, supervisory **12** policy-making **13** communication, pronouncement

directly
3 due **4** anon, soon **5** right, spang **6** at once, pronto **7** bluntly, by and by, shortly **8** first off, in person, promptly, squarely, straight, verbatim **9** forthwith, instanter, instantly, presently, right away **10** face-to-face **11** immediately, straight off, straightway, word for word **12** contiguously, straightaway

director
4 boss, head **5** chief **6** leader, top dog **7** manager **8** overseer **9** conductor, organizer **10** head honcho, supervisor

directory
4 list **5** guide, index **6** folder **7** catalog **8** register **9** catalogue **11** compilation

dirge
6 lament **7** requiem **8** threnody **11** lamentation
Gaelic: **8** coronach

dirigible
5 blimp **7** airship **8** zeppelin **9** steerable

dirk
4 shiv, stab **5** skean, skene, sword **6** bodkin, dagger, stylet **7** poniard

dirt
3 mud **4** clay, dust, land, loam, mire, muck, porn, smut, soil, spot **5** earth, filth, fraud, grime, stain **6** gossip, ground **7** chicane, squalor **9** chicanery, excrement, indecency **10** corruption, hanky-panky **11** pornography

dirt-poor
4 bust **5** broke **8** beggared, indigent **9** destitute, flat broke, penniless, penurious **10** stonebroke **12** impoverished

dirty
3 low, tar **4** base, foul, lewd, racy, smut, soil **5** bawdy, foggy, grimy, messy, mucky, muddy, murky, nasty, smear, sooty, stain, sully, taint **6** basely, befoul, coarse, debase, defile, filthy, grubby, impure, smudge, smutty, soiled, sordid, vulgar **7** begrime, corrupt, defiled, hateful, immoral, naughty, obscene, raunchy, smutchy, spotted, squalid, squally, sullied, tainted, tarnish, unclean, unkempt **8** begrimed, besmirch, indecent, off-color, polluted, unchaste, unwashed **9** ill-gotten, uncleanly **10** abominable, scandalous, scurrilous **11** distasteful, unlaundered **12** contaminated, scatological

Dis
see **Pluto**

disability
7 ailment **8** drawback, handicap **9** detriment, hindrance, infirmity, unfitness **10** affliction, impairment, impediment, incapacity **11** restriction, shortcoming **12** disadvantage

disable
3 sap **4** maim **5** spoil **6** hobble, weaken **7** cripple **8** enfeeble, handicap, paralyze, sabotage **9** hamstring, undermine **10** debilitate, immobilize **12** incapacitate
a racehorse: **6** nobble

disabled
7 hobbled **8** crippled **9** arthritic, paralyzed, rheumatic **11** handicapped **13** incapacitated

disabuse
4 free **5** emend, purge **7** correct, deliver, rectify, redress, release, relieve **8** liberate, unburden **9** enlighten, undeceive **10** illuminate **11** disencumber, disillusion

disaccharide
7 lactose, maltose, sucrose

disaccord
3 jar, war **4** vary **5** brawl, clash **6** combat, debate, differ **7** contest, contend, dispute, dissent, quarrel **8** conflict, disagree **12** disharmonize

disadvantage
3 bar **4** harm, loss **6** burden, damage, hamper **7** barrier, setback **8** drawback, handicap, obstacle **9** detriment, hindrance, liability, prejudice **10** impairment, impediment, imposition, limitation **11** deprivation, obstruction

disadvantaged
7 lacking **8** deprived **11** handicapped

disaffect
4 wean **5** alien, repel **8** alienate, disquiet, disunite, estrange **10** antagonize

disaffirm
4 deny **5** annul, belie, cross **6** abjure, impugn, negate, refute, reject **7** confute, explode, gainsay, reverse **8** disclaim, disprove, negative, traverse **9** repudiate **10** contradict, contravene

disagree
4 vary **5** argue, clash **6** bicker, differ, divide, haggle **7** contend, contest, dispute, dissent **8** conflict

disagreeable
4 ugly **7** peevish **8** annoying, petulant **9** offensive **10** unpleasant **11** disobliging, distressing, ill-tempered

disagreement
5 clash **6** debate **7** discord, dispute, quarrel, wrangle **8** argument, conflict, squabble, variance **9** disparity **10** contention, difference,

dissension, divergence, unlikeness **11** altercation, controversy, discrepancy, incongruity

disallow
4 deny, veto **5** debar **6** enjoin, forbid, refuse, reject **7** disavow, dismiss, exclude, rule out, shut out **8** disclaim, prohibit **9** interdict, proscribe, repudiate

disallowance
4 veto **5** taboo **6** denial **7** refusal **9** disavowal, dismissal, exclusion, rejection **11** prohibition, repudiation **12** interdiction, proscription

____-disant
3 soi

disappear
3 die **5** clear, leave **6** depart, die out, vanish **8** evanesce, fade away, melt away, pass away, slip away **9** evaporate, sneak away, steal away **13** dematerialize

disappoint
4 dash, foil, ruin **6** baffle, defeat, thwart **7** let down **9** frustrate **10** discourage, dishearten

disappointment
4 blow **6** bummer, defeat, downer **7** failure, letdown **8** comedown **9** bringdown **11** frustration

disapproval
4 veto **6** rebuke **7** censure, dislike, obloquy, reproof **8** reproach **9** criticism, objection, rejection
expression of: **3** boo **4** hiss, hoot, jeer **7** catcall **9** raspberry **10** Bronx cheer, thumbs-down

disapprove
4 veto **6** oppose, reject, tut-tut **7** decline, dislike, dismiss, frown on **8** disfavor, turn down **9** dispraise

disarm
5 charm **6** allure **7** win over **8** sideline **9** captivate **10** neutralize

disarming
7 amiable, likable, winning, winsome **8** likeable **9** endearing **10** convincing, persuasive **11** insinuating **12** ingratiating

disarrange
4 mess **5** mix up, upset **6** jumble, mess up, mislay, muddle, muss up **7** confuse, disturb **8** disorder, displace, misplace, unsettle **10** discompose **11** disorganize

disarray
5 chaos **6** bedlam, jumble, mess up, muddle **7** clutter, undress **8** disorder, shambles, unsettle **9** confusion **10** discompose, dishabille

disassemble
6 detach **7** scatter **8** dismount, disperse, separate, take down, tear down **9** break down, come apart, dismantle, dismember, take apart

disassociate
5 sever, unfix **6** detach, sunder **7** back off **8** abstract, alienate, back down, disunite, liberate, separate, uncouple, withdraw **9** disengage **10** disconnect

disaster
3 woe **6** fiasco **7** debacle, failure, tragedy **8** calamity **9** cataclysm, ruination **11** catastrophe, devastation

disastrous
4 dire **5** fatal **6** tragic **7** fateful, ruinous **8** terrible **10** calamitous, horrendous **11** cataclysmic, destructive, devastating **12** catastrophic

disavow
4 deny **6** abjure, disown, impugn, negate, recant, reject **7** forsake, gainsay, retract **8** abnegate, disclaim, forswear, negative, renounce **9** repudiate

disband
3 end **4** part **5** sever **6** divide, sunder **7** break up, dissect, divorce, scatter **8** disperse, dissolve, separate

disbelieve
5 doubt, scorn, scout **6** eschew, reject **7** scoff at, suspect **8** discount, distrust, mistrust, question **9** discredit, repudiate

disbeliever
5 cynic **7** doubter, sceptic, scoffer, skeptic **9** dissenter **10** questioner **11** freethinker

disbelieving
4 wary **5** leery **6** show-me **7** cynical, dubious **8** doubting **9** quizzical, skeptical **11** incredulous, mistrustful, questioning, unconvinced

disburden
4 shed **6** unlade, unload, unship, unstow **7** offload, relieve **8** disgorge **9** discharge

disburse
3 pay **5** allot, issue **6** lay out, pay out, supply **7** deliver, dole out, furnish, mete out, provide **8** dispense, disperse **9** apportion, partition **10** distribute, measure out

disbursement
4 cost **5** funds **6** outlay **7** expense, payment **9** allotment **11** expenditure **12** distribution

discard
4 cast, drop, dump, junk, shed, toss, waif **5** chuck, ditch, eject, let go, scrap **6** reject **7** cast off, castoff, deep-six, wash out **8** get rid of, jettison, shuck off, throw out **9** throw away, toss aside

discarnate
8 bodiless, ethereal, spectral **9** asomatous, unfleshly **10** immaterial, unembodied, unphysical, wraithlike **11** disembodied, incorporeal, nonphysical **12** otherworldly **13** insubstantial

discern
3 see **4** espy, know, note **5** grasp, sense **6** behold, detect, divine, notice **7** glimpse, observe **8** identify, perceive **9** apprehend, ascertain, recognize **10** comprehend **11** distinguish **12** discriminate **13** differentiate

discernible
7 visible **8** apparent, palpable **10** detectable, noticeable, observable **11** appreciable, perceivable **12** recognizable

discerning
4 keen **5** acute, aware **6** astute **7** knowing **9** clear-eyed, insighted, observant, sagacious **10** insightful, perceptive **12** clear-sighted **13** knowledgeable, perspicacious

discernment
6 acuity, acumen **7** insight **8** keenness, sagacity **9** intuition **10** astuteness, perception, shrewdness **11** penetration, percipience **12** perspicacity **13** comprehension, sagaciousness

discharge
2 ax **3** axe, can, pay **4** drop, emit, fire, free, gush, oust, quit, sack, spew, vent, void **5** annul, clear, demob, egest, eject, empty, expel, exude, let go, loose, pay up, quash, salvo, shoot, utter **6** bounce, excuse, exempt, let fly, let off, loosen, outlet, remove, settle, unbind, unload, vacate **7** absolve, boot out, barrage, cashier, deliver, dismiss, exclude, excrete, execute, fulfill, give off, kick out, manumit, off-load, release, relieve, removal, satisfy, unchain **8** abrogate, aquittal, dispense, displace, dissolve, ejection, emission, get rid of, liberate, separate, throw off **9** acquittal, dismissal, eliminate, explosion, expulsion, muster out, pour forth, send forth, terminate, unshackle **10** deactivate, demobilize **11** exoneration, fulfillment
electrical: **5** spark **6** leader **8** streamer **9** lightning

disciple
3 fan **6** minion **7** apostle, devotee, learner **8** adherent, follower, henchman, partisan, retainer **9** supporter **10** enthusiast

disciplinarian
8 enforcer, martinet **10** taskmaster **11** slave driver

disciplinary
8 punitive **9** punishing **10** corrective

discipline
4 curb, rule, will **5** check, drill, field, guide, order, teach, train **6** bridle, direct, ferule, method, punish, school, subdue **7** chasten, conduct, control, correct, educate **8** approach, chastise, instruct, penalize, restrain, training **9** castigate, obedience, subjugate, will-power **10** correction, punishment **11** castigation, self-control, self-mastery **12** chastisement **13** self-restraint

disclaim
4 deny **6** abjure, reject **7** disavow, gainsay, retract **8** disallow, forswear, renounce, traverse **9** repudiate **10** contradict

disclose
3 own **4** avow, tell **5** admit, spill **6** expose, impart, relate, report, reveal, unmask, unveil **7** display, divulge, uncover **8** discover, give away, unclothe **9** make known

disclosure
6 exposé **8** exposure **9** admission **10** revelation **11** declaration

discolor
3 tar **4** blot, dull, fade, smut, soil **5** smear, stain, sully, taint, tinge **6** defile, smudge **7** besmear, bestain, tarnish **8** besmirch

discoloration
4 spot **5** stain, taint **6** blotch, bruise, smudge **7** blemish **9** birthmark

discomfit
3 irk, vex **4** faze **5** abash, annoy, upset **6** baffle, bother, defeat, rattle, thwart **7** fluster, nonplus, perturb, unnerve **8** confound **9** embarrass **10** discompose, disconcert

discomfiture
5 upset **6** unease **8** disquiet **9** abashment, agitation, confusion **10** uneasiness **11** frustration **12** discomposure, perturbation **13** embarrassment, inconvenience

discomfort
3 irk, vex **4** ache, pain **5** annoy **6** bother, unease **7** malaise **8** vexation **9** annoyance **10** uneasiness **13** embarrassment

discommend
5 decry **7** censure, frown on, put down **8** admonish, disfavor, object to **9** criticize, deprecate, disesteem, disparage, reprehend **10** disapprove

discommode
3 irk, vex **5** annoy, upset **6** bother, burden, flurry, put out **7** disturb, fluster, perturb, trouble **8** encumber **9** aggravate, disoblige **13** inconvenience

discompose
3 irk, vex **5** annoy, harry, upset, worry **6** bother, dismay, flurry, harass, pester, plague, ruffle, untune **7** agitate, disturb, fluster, perturb, unhinge **8** disarray, disorder, unsettle **9** embarrass **10** disarrange **11** disorganize

discomposure
5 upset, worry **6** bother, unease **8** vexation **9** abashment, agitation, annoyance, confusion

10 discomfort, irritation, perplexity, uneasiness **11** disquietude **12** discomfiture, perturbation **13** consternation, embarrassment

disconcert
4 faze **5** abash, upset, worry **6** bemuse, bother, puzzle, rattle, ruffle **7** confuse, disturb, nonplus, perplex, perturb, trouble **8** bewilder, confound, disquiet **9** discomfit, embarrass, frustrate

disconfirm
4 deny **5** rebut **6** refute, negate **7** gainsay **8** abnegate, confound, disclaim, disprove **10** contradict, controvert

disconnect
3 cut, gap **5** break, sever, unfix **6** cut off, detach **7** disjoin **8** separate, uncouple **9** disengage **10** dissociate

disconnected
7 muddled **8** detached, separate **10** disjointed, incoherent, unattached **11** fragmentary, unorganized **13** discontinuous

disconsolate
3 low, sad **4** blue, down **5** bleak, drear **6** abject, dreary, gloomy, woeful **7** doleful, forlorn, joyless, unhappy **8** dejected, downcast, wretched **9** cheerless, depressed, miserable, sorrowful, woebegone **10** dispirited, melancholy **11** comfortless, crestfallen, downhearted

discontent
4 envy **7** malaise, unhappy **9** dysphoria **10** depression, inquietude, uneasiness **12** restlessness

discontented
5 upset **6** uneasy **7** annoyed, fretful, unhappy **8** restless **9** disturbed, irritated, perturbed **10** displeased **11** complaining, disgruntled, ungratified, unsatisfied **12** dissatisfied

discontinuation
3 end **4** stop **5** cease, close, pause **6** ending, finish **7** closing **8** abeyance **9** cessation **10** conclusion, desistance, moratorium, suspension **12** postponement

discontinue
3 end **4** halt, quit, stay, stop **5** cease, close, sever **6** desist, give up, wind up, wrap up **8** break off, close out, conclude, knock off, leave off, shut down, surcease **9** terminate

discontinuity
3 gap **4** hole, rent, rift **5** break, cleft, crack, split **6** breach, lacuna **7** fissure, opening, rupture

discontinuous
6 fitful **7** muddled **8** discrete, separate **9** spasmodic **10** incoherent, incohesive **11** unconnected **12** disconnected, intermittent **13** nonsequential

discord
5 clash **6** enmity, rancor, strife **7** rupture **8** conflict, contrast, disunity, division, friction, mismatch, variance **9** animosity, antipathy, hostility **10** antagonism, contention, difference, dissension, dissidence, dissonance, opposition **12** inconsonance, polarization **13** inconsistency
goddess: **3** Ate **4** Eris

discordant
5 harsh **6** at odds **7** grating, jarring **8** clashing, contrary, jangling, strident **9** dissonant, out of tune **10** cacophonic, unpleasant **11** cacophonous, conflicting, disagreeing, inconsonant, quarrelsome, unmelodious **12** unharmonious

discotheque
6 bistro, nitery **7** hot spot **9** dance club, nightclub, night spot

discount
4 agio **5** doubt, lower **6** deduct, ignore, rebate, reduce, slight **7** neglect, take off **8** belittle, derogate, decrease, diminish, knock off, mark down, markdown, minimize, overlook, roll back, rollback, subtract, take away **9** abatement, deduction, disregard, reduction, substract, underrate **13** underestimate

discountenance
4 faze **5** abash **6** rattle **7** frown on **8** confound, disfavor **9** deprecate, discomfit, embarrass **10** disapprove, disconcert, discourage

discourage
4 damp **5** daunt, check, chill, deter **6** dampen, deject, divert, hinder, impede **7** depress, inhibit, trouble **8** disfavor, dissuade, suppress **10** demoralize, dishearten

discouraging
5 bleak **7** unhappy **8** daunting **9** deterring, troubling **10** depressing **11** unfavorable, unpromising **12** unpropitious **13** disappointing, disheartening

discourse
4 talk **5** argue, essay, orate, speak, spiel, voice **6** sermon, speech, thesis **7** amplify, descant, enlarge, explain, expound, lecture **8** converse, harangue, perorate, rhetoric, speaking, treatise **9** expatiate, hold forth, monograph, sermonize, utterance **10** expression **11** interchange **12** conversation **13** verbalization
art of: **8** rhetoric
religious: **6** homily, sermon

discourteous
4 rude **6** unkind **7** boorish, brusque, ill-bred, uncivil, uncouth **8** impolite **10** ungracious, unmannerly **11** ill-mannered, impertinent **13** disrespectful

discover
4 espy, find, spot **5** learn **6** betray, detect, expose, reveal, unmask **7** divulge, find out, observe, unearth **8** come upon, perceive, proclaim, unshroud **9** ascertain, determine, encounter, make known **10** come across

discovery
4 find **5** trove **6** espial, strike **7** finding **8** locating, sighting **9** detection **10** revelation, unearthing

discredit
4 slur, ruin **5** doubt, shame **6** defame, malign, show up **7** asperse, degrade, put down, run down, slander, traduce **8** disgrace, ignominy **9** disparage, disrepute **10** disbelieve, opprobrium

discreditable
5 shady **6** shabby, shoddy **8** shameful, unworthy **9** degrading **10** inglorious **11** blameworthy, disgraceful, ignominious **12** contemptible, dishonorable, disreputable

discreet
4 wary **5** chary, muted, plain **6** modest, simple **7** careful, guarded, prudent, tactful **8** cautious, moderate **9** unadorned **10** controlled, reasonable, restrained **11** circumspect, considerate, unelaborate, unobtrusive **12** unnoticeable **13** unpretentious

discrepancy
3 gap **8** alterity, conflict, variance **9** disparity, otherness, variation **10** difference, divergence, divergency, unlikeness **12** disagreement **13** inconsistency

discrepant
6 unlike **7** diverse, varying **8** contrary **9** different, differing, disparate, divergent **11** conflicting, disagreeing **12** incompatible, inconsistent **13** contradictory

discrete
8 detached, distinct, separate **9** countable, different **10** individual **12** disconnected **13** discontinuous, noncontinuous

discretion
4 care, tact **7** caution, reserve **8** delicacy, judgment, prudence, wariness **9** canniness, chariness, restraint **13** judiciousness

discriminate
5 judge **6** assess **7** compare, discern, make out **8** contrast, disfavor, evaluate, perceive, separate **9** segregate, tell apart **11** distinguish **13** differentiate

discriminating
6 choosy, select **7** finical, finicky **8** eclectic **9** judicious, selective **10** discerning **11** prejudicial

discrimination
5 taste **6** acumen **7** bigotry, insight **8** inequity, judgment **9** prejudice **10** astuteness, favoritism, partiality, perception **11** discernment, intolerance, penetration

discriminatory
6 biased **7** partial, unequal **8** partisan **9** jaundiced **10** prejudiced **11** inequitable, predisposed

discursive
5 windy, wordy **6** chatty, prolix **7** diffuse, logical, verbose **8** rambling, tortuous **9** desultory **10** analytical, circuitous, digressive, long-winded, meandering **11** wide-ranging

discuss
4 moot **5** argue, weigh **6** debate, parley **7** canvass, expound **8** consider, converse, hash over, talk over **9** elucidate, expatiate, interpret, talk about, thrash out, ventilate **10** deliberate, toss around
business: **8** talk shop
lightly: **5** bandy
thoroughly: **7** exhaust

discussion
3 rap **4** chat, talk **6** confab, debate, parley, powwow **7** canvass, palaver **8** argument, colloquy **10** conference, rap session **11** bull session, ventilation **12** conversation, deliberation **13** confabulation

discus thrower
6 Alekna (Virgilijus), Marten (Maritza), Oerter (Al) **10** discobolus **11** Rashchupkin (Viktor)

disdain
5 abhor, scorn, scout, spurn **6** deride, refuse, reject, slight **7** contemn, despise, despite, hauteur, put down **8** aversion, belittle, contempt, disprize, misprize **9** antipathy **10** repugnance, undervalue

disdainful
5 aloof, proud **6** averse, lordly, sniffy, snooty, uppity **7** haughty **8** arrogant, cavalier, derisive, insolent, scorning, snobbish, spurning, superior, toplofty **11** overbearing **12** antipathetic, contemptuous, supercilious **13** high and mighty

disease
3 bug, ill **5** upset, virus **6** blight, malady **7** ailment, anthrax, illness, malaise, mycosis, purpura **8** debility, epidemic, myxedema, pandemic, sickness, syndrome, zoonoses (plural), zoonosis **9** affection, black lung, contagion, ill health, infection, infirmity, sclerosis **10** affliction, blackwater, bronchitis, infirmness, sickliness
animal: **5** mange, surra **6** rabies **7** bighead **8** enzootic, zoonosis **9** distemper, tularemia **10** rinderpest

blood: **8** leukemia, leukoses (plural), leukosis
cabbage: **8** clubroot
cattle: **6** cowpox **7** foot rot, locoism, murrain **8** blackleg, vaccinia **9** vibriosis **10** rinderpest **11** brucellosis
cereal grass: **4** bunt, smut **5** ergot
children's: **5** mumps **7** measles, rubella **10** chicken pox **13** whooping cough
citrus tree: **8** tristeza
classification: **8** nosology
combining form: **4** path **5** patho
communicable: **3** flu **4** mono **5** mumps, polio **6** dengue, herpes, plague, rabies **7** bird flu, cholera, leprosy, malaria, measles, rubella, tetanus, typhoid **8** avian flu, impetigo **9** hepatitis, influenza **10** giardiasis **12** tuberculosis
deficiency: **6** scurvy **7** rickets **8** beriberi, pellagra
disseminator: **6** vector **7** carrier
eye: **6** iritis **8** glaucoma, trachoma **9** retinitis
hair follicle: **7** sycoses (plural), sycosis
heart: **11** cardiopathy
horse: **6** nagana, spavin **7** locosim, sarcoid **8** glanders **9** strangles
identification of: **9** diagnosis
industrial: **10** byssinosis
infectious: **4** mono, yaws **6** dengue, typhus **7** leprosy, malaria, tetanus, typhoid **9** tularemia, vibriosis **10** rinderpest **13** whooping cough
liver: **9** cirrhosis, hepatitis
livestock: **7** locoism **9** vibriosis **10** rinderpest
lung: **8** phthisic, phthisis **9** pneumonia **10** byssinosis **12** tuberculosis
lymph glands: **8** scrofula
metabolic: **4** gout
nervous system: **4** kuru **6** rabies **10** diphtheria
of beets: **8** heartrot
of mammals: **6** rabies **7** malaria **9** distemper **10** babesiosis, rinderpest
parasitic: **3** rot **4** smut **5** mange **7** malaria **8** hookworm, kala-azar **9** heartworm
plant: **4** rust, scab, smut, wilt **5** blast, edema, scald, scurf, stunt **6** blight, blotch, canker, mosaic, streak **7** blister, crinkle, foot rot, frogeye, red leaf, root rot **8** clubroot, curly top, fusarium, gummosis, leaf curl, leaf roll, leaf rust, leaf spot, ring spot, root knot, stem rust **9** chlorosis, crown gall, white rust **10** blackheart, leaf scorch
poultry: **8** leukosis
respiratory: **6** asthma, coryza **10** byssinosis
sheep: **3** gid **7** scrapie **9** vibriosis **10** bluetongue
silkworm: **3** uji
skin: **4** acne, yaws **5** favus, hives, lupus, mange, pinta, tinea **6** eczema, tetter **7** leprosy, prurigo, sarcoid, scabies, serpigo **8** impetigo, miliaria, pyoderma, ringworm, vitiligo **9** pemphigus, psoriasis **10** erysipelas **11** scleroderma
syphilitic: **5** tabes
throat: **5** croup, strep
thyroid: **6** struma
tropical: **4** yaws **5** pinta, sprue, surra **6** dengue **7** malaria **8** kala-azar
venereal: **6** herpes **8** syphilis **9** chancroid, gonorrhea
viral: **3** flu **4** AIDS, noma **5** Ebola, mumps, polio **6** dengue, grippe, herpes, rabies, zoster **7** bird flu, measles, rubella, rubeola, variola **8** avian flu, morbilli, shingles, smallpox **9** hepatitis, influenza, monkey pox, varicella **13** poliomyelitis

diseased
3 ill **6** ailing, infirm, sickly, unwell **7** fevered, unsound **8** feverish, infected

disembark
4 land **6** alight **7** deplane, detrain **8** go ashore

disembarrass
3 rid **4** free **7** release, relieve **8** liberate, unburden, untangle **9** extricate **11** disencumber, disentangle

disembodied
7 ghostly **8** ethereal, spectral **9** asomatous, unfleshly **10** immaterial, unphysical, wraithlike **11** incorporeal, nonmaterial, nonphysical **13** insubstantial

disembogue
4 flow, gush, pour, spew **5** empty **7** pour out **9** discharge

disembowel
3 gut **10** eviscerate, exenterate

disemploy
2 ax **3** axe, can **4** boot, fire, sack **7** cashier **9** discharge, terminate

disenchanted
5 blasé, jaded **6** soured **7** cynical **9** jaundiced **10** undeceived **11** worldly-wise **12** disappointed, dissatisfied **13** disenthralled, disillusioned

disencumber
3 rid **4** free **7** lighten, release, relieve, sort out **8** free from, liberate, unburden **9** alleviate, disburden, extricate

disengage
4 free, part **5** loose, unfix **6** detach, opt out, unbind **7** back out, drop out, release, unloose **8** cut loose, liberate, separate, uncouple, unfasten, unloosen, withdraw **10** disconnect

disentangle
5 untie **6** detach **7** resolve, sort out, unravel, unsnarl, untwine **8** separate **9** extricate **10** unscramble **11** disencumber **13** straighten out

disenthrall
4 free **7** manumit, release **8** liberate **10** emancipate

disfavor
7 dislike **8** aversion, distrust, mistrust **9** deprecate, disesteem, disregard, disrepute **10** disrespect **11** disapproval **12** disadvantage, unpopularity

disfigure
3 mar **4** maim, scar **6** deface, defile, deform, impair, injure, mangle **7** blemish, distort **8** mutilate

disfranchise
3 bar **7** exclude **8** take away **9** deprive of **10** disentitle

disgorge
4 barf, spew **5** belch, eject, eruct, erupt, expel, vomit **6** give up, irrupt, spit up **7** release, throw up, upchuck **9** discharge

disgrace
5 odium, shame **6** stigma **7** attaint, mortify, obloquy **8** black eye, contempt, dishonor, ignominy, reproach **9** discredit, disrepute, humiliate **10** opprobrium, stigmatize **11** degradation, humiliation

disgraceful
7 ignoble **8** shameful **9** degrading **10** deplorable, inglorious, unbecoming **11** humiliating, ignominious, reproachful **12** dishonorable, disreputable

disgruntled
5 vexed **6** cranky, put out **7** annoyed, beefing, griping **8** grousing **9** irritated **10** discontent, displeased, ill-humored, malcontent **11** ungratified **12** discontented, malcontented

disguise
4 hide, mask, sham, veil **5** belie, cloak, feign, put on **6** facade **7** conceal, falsify, obscure **8** artifice, pretense **9** deception **10** camouflage, false front, pretension **12** misrepresent

disguised
6 masked, veiled **7** cloaked, feigned **9** incognito **10** undercover **11** camouflaged

disguisement
4 mask, veil **5** cloak, front **6** facade **8** pretense **9** deception **10** false front, pretention

disgust
6 nausea, offend, revolt, sicken **8** aversion, gross out, loathing, nauseate **9** antipathy, repulsion, revulsion **10** abhorrence, repugnance **11** abomination **13** squeamishness

disgusted
5 fed up **8** offended, repelled, repulsed, revolted, sickened **9** nauseated, squeamish **10** grossed out

disgusting
4 foul, icky, vile **5** gross, nasty, yucky **7** noisome **9** loathsome, offensive, repellent, repugnant, repulsive, revolting, sickening **10** nauseating

dish
4 bowl, buzz, food, talk, tray **5** plate **6** course, gossip, tureen **7** chatter, hearsay, platter, scandal, slander **9** casserole, container **11** scuttlebutt
baked: **7** soufflé
baking: **7** cocotte, scallop **9** casserole **12** scallop shell
cheese: **6** fondue **7** ramekin, rarebit **8** raclette, ramequin
Chinese: **6** dim sum, lo mein, subgum, wonton **8** chop suey, chow mein **10** egg foo yong, egg foo yung **11** egg foo young
deep: **9** casserole
Hungarian: **7** goulash
Italian: **5** pasta, penne, pesto, pizza **6** scampi **7** cannoli, lasagna, polenta, ravioli **8** calamari, linguine, linguini, osso buco, rigatoni **9** foccaccia, manicotti **10** cannelloni, scaloppine, tortellini **11** saltimbocca
Japanese: **5** sushi **7** sashimi, tempura **8** sukiyaki
Mexican: **4** taco **5** chili **6** fajita, flauta, nachos, tamale **7** burrito, chalupa **8** frijoles **9** enchilada, guacamole **10** carne asada **11** chimichanga **12** refried beans **13** chili con carne
Middle Eastern: **5** kebab, kibbe, kibbi **6** hummus, kibbeh **7** falafel **8** couscous, moussaka **10** shish kebab **11** baba ghanouj **12** baba ghanoush
principal: **6** entrée
rice: **5** pilaf **7** risotto
Scottish: **5** brose **6** haggis
shallow: **6** saucer
Thai: **7** pad thai

disharmonize
3 jar, war **5** clash **6** jangle **7** discord **8** conflict, mismatch **9** disaccord

disharmony
6 strife **7** discord **8** conflict, disunion, disunity, friction, variance **9** cacophony **10** contention, difference, dissension, dissonance

dishearten
3 cow **5** chill, crush, daunt, shake **6** dampen, deject, dismay, sadden **7** depress, unnerve **8** dispirit, distress **10** demoralize, discourage, intimidate

dishes
4 ware
clay: **7** pottery
porcelain: **5** china

dishevel
5 touse 6 muss up, rumple, tousle 8 disarray, disorder 10 disarrange, discompose

disheveled
5 messy 6 mussed 7 unkempt 8 ill-kempt, uncombed

dishonest
5 false, lying, rogue, snide 6 tricky, unfair 7 corrupt, crooked, knavish 8 cheating, cozening, two-faced 9 deceitful, deceiving, deceptive, swindling 10 defrauding, fraudulent, mendacious, untruthful 13 double-dealing, untrustworthy

dishonesty
5 fraud, guile 6 deceit 7 falsity, knavery, roguery 8 flimflam, pretense, trickery 9 chicanery, deception, duplicity, falsehood, hypocrisy 10 corruption 11 crookedness 13 double-dealing

dishonor
see **disgrace**

dishonorable
see **disgraceful**

dish out
5 ladle, serve 6 pile on, supply 7 deliver, present, serve up 8 allocate, disburse, dispense 10 distribute

disillusioned
see **disenchanted**

disinclination
7 dislike 8 aversion, distaste 9 antipathy, objection 10 reluctance 13 indisposition, unwillingness

disinclined
5 loath 6 averse 7 opposed 8 hesitant 9 reluctant, resistant, unwilling 10 indisposed

disinfect
6 purify 8 sanitize 9 autoclave, sterilize 13 decontaminate

disingenuous
3 sly 4 foxy, wily 5 false 6 artful, crafty, tricky 7 cunning, devious, feigned 8 delusive, guileful, indirect, specious 9 deceitful, deceiving, deceptive, dishonest, insidious, insincere, sophistic 10 misleading 11 calculating, casuistical, sophistical

disinherit
6 cut off 7 bereave, exclude 9 deprive of, repudiate 10 dispossess

disintegrate
3 rot 4 turn 5 break, burst, decay, spoil, taint 6 molder 7 crumble, scatter, shatter 8 splinter 9 break down, decompose, fall apart 10 deliquesce

disinter
5 dig up 6 exhume, unbury 7 unearth 8 exhumate 9 resurrect

disinterest
6 apathy 7 neglect 8 coolness, lethargy 9 aloofness, disregard, unconcern 10 detachment, dispassion, neutrality 11 impassivity, inattention, insouciance, nonchalance, objectivity 12 indifference

disinterested
4 fair, just 5 aloof 6 candid 7 neutral 8 detached, unbiased 9 impartial, impassive, incurious, objective 10 even-handed, impersonal, neglectful, nonchalant 11 inattentive, indifferent, unconcerned

disjoin
4 part 5 sever, unfix 6 detach, divide, sunder, unlink 7 break up, divorce 8 disunite, separate, uncouple, unfasten 9 disengage, take apart 10 dissociate 12 disaffiliate, disassociate

disjointed
7 jumbled, muddled 8 confused, inchoate, rambling 9 displaced 10 disordered, incoherent, incohesive 11 unconnected, unorganized 13 discontinuous

disk
4 puck 5 wafer 6 record
metal: 4 slug
ornamental: 6 bangle, sequin

dislike
4 shun 5 scorn, spurn 6 animus, oppose, reject, resent 7 deplore, frown on 8 aversion, disfavor, distaste 9 animosity, antipathy 10 alienation, disapprove, repugnance 11 disapproval

dislimn
3 dim 5 bedim 6 darken 7 becloud, obscure 9 obfuscate

dislocate
5 break 7 disrupt, unhinge 9 disengage 10 disconnect 13 disarticulate

dislodge
4 oust 5 eject, evict, expel 6 remove, uproot 8 displace, drive out, force out

disloyal
5 false 6 untrue 8 apostate, recreant 9 alienated, faithless 10 perfidious, traitorous, unfaithful 11 disaffected, treacherous

disloyalty
7 falsity, perfidy, treason 8 apostasy 9 falseness, recreancy, treachery 10 alienation, infidelity 12 disaffection 13 faithlessness

dismal
4 grim 5 bleak, drear 6 dreary, gloomy, horrid, somber, sombre 7 joyless 8 desolate, dreadful, funereal, lowering 9 atrocious, cheerless, depressed, tenebrous 10 depressing, depressive 11 dispiriting 12 discouraging 13 disheartening

dismantle
4 raze, undo **5** strip, unrig, wreck **6** denude, divest **7** break up, destroy **8** demolish, pull down, take down **9** break down, knock down, take apart **11** disassemble

dismay
4 faze, fear **5** abash, alarm, daunt, dread, panic, scare, shake, upset **6** appall, fright, horror, rattle **7** agitate, fluster, horrify, perturb, unnerve **8** affright, bewilder, confound, dispirit, distress, frighten **9** discomfit, dumbfound, embarrass **10** discompose, disconcert, discourage, dishearten **11** trepidation **12** perturbation **13** consternation

dismayed
5 upset **6** afraid, aghast, scared, shaken **7** fearful, shocked **9** disturbed

dismember
4 maim **5** cut up **7** disjoin, dissect **8** mutilate **9** dismantle, take apart

dismiss
2 ax **3** axe, can **4** drop, fire, oust, sack, shed **5** chuck, eject, evict, let go, scorn, spurn **6** bounce, depose, deride, lay off, reject, remove, retire, shelve, unseat **7** boot out, cashier, contemn, decline, disband, kick out, kiss off, turn off **8** displace, furlough, pooh-pooh, ridicule, throw out, turn away, turn down **9** discharge, repudiate, terminate **11** send packing

dismissal
5 congé **6** firing, layoff, ouster **7** removal **8** brush-off, bum's rush **9** discharge, expulsion **10** cashiering

dismount
6 alight, debark, get off **7** deplane, detrain **9** disembark **10** alight from **11** descend from

Disney, Walt
10 cartoonist
character: **4** Gyro, Huey, Lady, Nemo **5** Ariel, Bambi, Daisy, Dewey, Dumbo, Goofy, Louie, Mulan, Pluto, Simba, Tramp **6** Beauty, Donald, Mickey, Minnie, Mowgli **7** Aladdin, Scrooge **9** Gladstone, Pinocchio, Snow White **10** Beagle Boys, Clarabelle, Pocahontas
classic: **5** Bambi, Dumbo **8** Fantasia **9** Pinocchio **10** Jungle Book (The) **15** Lady and the Tramp

disobedient
6 unruly **7** naughty, wayward, willful **8** contrary **10** headstrong, ill-behaved, rebellious, refractory **11** misbehaving, uncompliant **12** contumacious, noncompliant, obstreperous, recalcitrant **13** insubordinate

disoblige
5 annoy **6** bother, offend, put out **7** affront, disturb, trouble **9** displease, incommode **10** discommode **13** inconvenience

disorder
3 ill **4** mess, riot **5** chaos, havoc, mix up, snarl, upset **6** ataxia, hubbub, jumble, malady, mess up, muddle, muss up, ruckus, rumple, tumble, tumult, unrest, uproar **7** ailment, anarchy, clutter, confuse, disease, embroil, illness, misdeed, shuffle, turmoil **8** disarray, sickness, syndrome, unsettle, upheaval **9** affection, agitation, commotion, complaint, confusion, infirmity **10** affliction, turbulence, untidiness
mental: **5** mania **8** delirium, insanity, neurosis, paranoia **9** psychosis **11** psychopathy **13** schizophrenia

disordered
6 roiled **7** chaotic, jumbled, muddled **8** confused, inchoate, shuffled **9** displaced **10** disjointed, dislocated, incoherent, incohesive **11** disarranged, unconnected, unorganized **13** discontinuous

disorderly
5 rowdy **6** unruly, untidy **7** jumbled, raucous, unkempt **8** confused **9** cluttered, offensive, turbulent **10** boisterous, topsy-turvy, tumultuous **12** disorganized, rambunctious, unsystematic

disorganize
5 upset **6** jumble, mess up **7** break up, confuse, derange, disband, disrupt **8** disorder, disperse, unsettle **10** disarrange

disoriented
4 lost **7** mixed up **8** confused **9** displaced, perplexed, unsettled **10** bewildered

disown
4 deny, dump **6** desert, reject **7** cast off, disavow **8** disclaim, renounce **9** repudiate

disparage
5 decry **6** defame, slight **7** condemn, degrade, devalue, dismiss, put down, run down **8** badmouth, belittle, derogate, discount, downplay, minimize, pooh-pooh **9** denigrate, deprecate, discredit, dispraise, downgrade, underrate **10** demoralize, depreciate, undervalue **11** detract from

disparagement
5 scorn **7** calumny, censure, despite, scandal, slander **8** contempt, despisal, reproach **9** aspersion, discredit, stricture **10** backbiting, defamation, derogation, detraction, diminution **11** degradation **12** backstabbing, depreciation **13** animadversion

disparate
6 at odds, divers, unlike, varied **7** diverse, unalike, unequal, various, varying **8** discrete, distinct, separate **9** different, divergent, unsimilar **10** dissimilar **11** distinctive, incongruous, inconsonant **12** incompatible, inconsistent

disparity
3 gap **8** contrast **9** imbalance **10** difference,

divergence, divergency, inequality **11** discrepancy **13** disproportion, dissimilarity

dispassionate
4 calm, fair, just **7** neutral **8** composed, detached, unbiased **9** equitable, impartial, objective, unruffled **10** impersonal **11** unemotional **12** unprejudiced **13** disinterested

dispatch
4 kill, send, ship, slay **5** haste, hurry, scrag, speed **6** defeat, murder **7** bump off, execute, forward, killing, message, put away **8** alacrity, get rid of, shipment, transmit **9** dispose of, eliminate, swiftness **10** expedition, put to death, speediness **11** assassinate, promptitude

dispel
6 banish **7** cast out, scatter **8** disperse **9** clear away, dissipate, drive away

dispensable
5 minor **7** trivial **8** needless, unneeded **10** disposable, expendable, unrequired **11** superfluous, unessential, unimportant, unnecessary **12** nonessential

dispensary
6 clinic

dispensation
4 plan **5** favor, share **7** license, portion, service **8** bestowal, courtesy, kindness, ordering **9** allotment, exception, exemption, privilege, remission **10** indulgence, management **12** disbursement, distribution **13** apportionment, authorization

dispense
5 allot, apply, wield **6** assign, divide, excuse, exempt, ration, supply **7** absolve, deal out, deliver, dish out, dole out, furnish, give out, mete out, portion, provide, release **8** allocate, carry out, disburse, share out, transfer **9** apportion, discharge, partition **10** administer, distribute, measure out, portion out

disperse
3 sow **5** spray, strew **6** dispel, divide, spread, vanish **7** break up, diffuse, disband, radiate, scatter **9** broadcast, dissipate, partition, propagate **10** distribute

dispersion
6 spread **7** breakup, colloid **9** diffusion, spreading **10** scattering **11** dissipation **12** distribution **13** dissemination

dispirit
3 cow **5** chill, daunt **6** deject, dismay, sadden **7** depress, oppress **8** distress **10** demoralize, discourage, dishearten

dispirited
3 low, sad **4** blue, down, glum **5** cowed **6** morose **7** daunted **8** cast down, dejected, dismayed, downcast, saddened **9** bummed out, depressed, oppressed, woebegone **10** distressed, melancholy **11** crestfallen, demoralized, discouraged, downhearted **12** disconsolate, disheartened

dispiriting
4 blue **6** dismal, dreary, gloomy **8** daunting, dolorous, funereal **9** cheerless, dismaying, saddening **10** depressing, oppressive **12** demoralizing, disconsolate, discouraging **13** disheartening

displace
4 oust, sack **5** exile, expel, usurp **6** banish, deport, depose, remove **7** succeed **8** dethrone, supplant **9** supersede, transport **10** expatriate, substitute

display
4 pomp, show **5** array, model **6** evince, expose, flaunt, lay out, parade, reveal, spread, unfold, unfurl, unveil **7** exhibit, panoply, present, showing, show off, trot out, uncover **8** brandish, evidence, manifest, showcase **9** showiness, spectacle **10** exhibiting, exhibition **11** demonstrate, ostentation **13** demonstration, manifestation

displeasing
6 vexing **7** irksome **8** annoying **10** bothersome, unpleasant **12** disagreeable **13** objectionable

displeasure
5 anger **8** aversion, disfavor, vexation **9** annoyance **10** discomfort, discontent, irritation, uneasiness **11** indignation, unhappiness **13** indisposition

disport
4 show **5** amuse **6** acquit, behave, divert, expose, flaunt, frolic, parade **7** conduct, display, exhibit, show off, trot out **9** entertain

disposal
5 order **7** removal **8** bestowal, chucking, jettison, ordering, transfer **9** clearance **10** allocation, assignment, demolition, discarding, regulation, relegation **11** arrangement, consignment, destruction, disposition **12** distribution, transference

dispose
4 bend, bias, rank **5** array, order, range **6** settle **7** arrange, incline, marshal, prepare **8** organize, regulate **9** make ready **11** systematize
of: **4** dump, junk, sell **5** chuck, scrap **6** finish, handle, unload **7** deep-six, destroy, discard **8** deal with, throw out, transfer **9** eighty-six, eliminate **10** distribute

disposed
3 apt **4** fain, game **5** prone, ready **6** biased, minded **7** partial, willing **8** arranged, inclined **9** persuaded

disposition
4 bent, cast, mood, tone, type, vein **5** being, order, stamp **6** makeup, nature, temper **7** control, leaning, mind-set **8** ordering, penchant,

riddance, sequence, tendency, transfer **9** character, direction **10** management, proclivity, propensity, settlement **11** arrangement, inclination, personality, temperament **12** constitution, predilection **13** individuality
favorable: 8 optimism
unfavorable: 9 pessimism

dispossess
3 rob **4** oust **5** eject, evict, strip **6** divest **7** bereave, deprive

dispossession
4 loss **6** ouster **7** seizure **9** privation **10** divestment **11** deprivation, divestiture **13** expropriation

dispraise
3 pan **5** decry **6** censor, deride, dump on **7** put down, run down **8** bad-mouth, belittle, derogate **9** criticize, deprecate, discredit, disparage **10** depreciate, disapprove **11** detract from **12** depreciation

disproportion
8 imparity, mismatch **9** disparity **10** inequality, unevenness **12** lopsidedness

disproportionate
6 uneven **7** unequal **8** lopsided **10** unbalanced

disprove
5 belie, rebut **6** refute, negate **7** confute, explode **8** confound, overturn, puncture, traverse **9** discredit, overthrow **10** invalidate

disputable
4 iffy, moot **7** dubious **8** arguable, doubtful **9** debatable, uncertain, unsettled **10** unresolved **11** problematic **12** questionable **13** controversial

disputation
6 debate **8** argument, forensic, polemics **9** dialectic **11** controversy **13** argumentation

dispute
4 buck, duel, moot, tiff **5** argue, fight, rebut, repel **6** bicker, combat, debate, hassle, impugn, negate, oppose, refute, resist, rumpus, strife **7** confute, contend, contest, discuss, gainsay, quarrel, quibble, wrangle **8** argument, conflict, question, squabble **9** bickering, challenge, thrash out, withstand **10** contention, controvert, falling-out **11** altercation, controversy, embroilment

disputed
7 debated **8** arguable **9** contested, uncertain **12** questionable **13** controversial

disqualified
5 unfit **8** unfitted **10** ineligible, unequipped

disqualify
3 bar **5** debar **6** except **7** exclude, rule out, suspend **9** eliminate
as judge: 6 recuse

disquiet
5 alarm, angst, upset, worry **6** bother, flurry, unease, unrest **7** agitate, anxiety, concern, disturb, ferment, fluster, perturb, trouble, turmoil **10** discompose, uneasiness **11** disturbance, restiveness **12** restlessness **13** Sturm und Drang

disquietude
4 care **5** worry **6** unease, unrest **7** anxiety, concern, ferment, turmoil **9** agitation, misgiving **10** foreboding, uneasiness **11** nervousness, restiveness **12** apprehension, restlessness **13** Sturm und Drang

Disraeli, Benjamin
novel: 5 Sybil **7** Lothair, Tancred **8** Endymion **9** Coningsby
opponent: 4 Peel (Robert) **9** Gladstone (William)
queen: 8 Victoria

disregard
4 skip **6** forget, ignore, slight **7** neglect, tune out **8** overlook **9** unconcern **12** heedlessness, indifference

disregardful
3 lax **5** slack **6** remiss **8** careless, derelict, heedless **9** forgetful, unheeding, negligent, unmindful **10** neglectful, regardless, unthinking **11** indifferent, unconcerned **12** absent-minded

disremember
6 forget

disreputable
4 base **5** dingy, seamy, seedy, shady **6** scurvy, shabby, shoddy, sordid **7** run-down **8** decrepit, infamous, shameful **10** inglorious **11** dilapidated, disgraceful, ignominious **12** contemptible, unprincipled **13** discreditable, unrespectable

disrepute
5 odium, shame **7** obloquy **8** disfavor, disgrace, dishonor, ignominy **9** disesteem **10** opprobrium

disrespect
6 insult **7** disdain **8** boldness, contempt, rudeness **9** disregard, flippancy, impudence, insolence **10** incivility **11** discourtesy, presumption **12** impertinence, impoliteness

disrespectful
4 flip, rude **5** sassy, saucy **7** ill-bred, uncivil **8** flippant, impolite, impudent, insolent **10** ungracious **11** ill-mannered, impertinent **12** contemptuous, discourteous

disrobe
4 bare, peel **5** strip **6** denude, divest **7** undress **8** unclothe

disrupt
5 upset **6** mess up **7** break up, rupture **8** disorder, unsettle

dissatisfaction
6 dismay 9 annoyance, complaint 10 discontent, irritation, uneasiness 11 displeasure, frustration

dissatisfied
5 irked, vexed 7 annoyed, unhappy 8 bothered 10 begrudging, discontent, displeased, malcontent 11 complaining, disaffected, unfulfilled 12 disappointed, discontented, malcontented

dissect
5 probe, study 7 analyze, examine, inspect 9 anatomize, break down, take apart 10 scrutinize

dissection
7 autopsy 8 analysis, necropsy
of animals: 7 zootomy

dissemble
4 hide, mask 5 cloak, feign 7 conceal, cover up, dress up, falsify 8 disguise, simulate 9 whitewash 10 camouflage 11 counterfeit

dissembler
4 fake 5 faker, fraud, phony 8 deceiver, imposter, impostor, pharisee 9 hypocrite, pretender

disseminate
3 sow 5 strew 6 blazon, spread 7 bestrew, diffuse, pass out, publish, scatter, send out 8 announce, disperse, proclaim 9 advertise, broadcast, circulate, propagate, publicize 10 promulgate

dissension
5 fight 6 strife 7 discord, dispute, faction, quarrel, wrangle 8 argument, clashing, conflict, disunity, friction, variance 9 bickering 10 contention, difference, quarreling 11 altercation, controversy 12 disagreement

dissent
5 demur 6 differ, heresy, object 7 protest 8 conflict, variance 9 misbelief 10 contention, difference, heterodoxy, opposition, resistance 11 unorthodoxy 12 nonagreement 13 nonconformism, nonconformity

dissenter
7 heretic 8 apostate, defector, deserter, partisan, recreant 10 schismatic, separatist 11 misbeliever, schismatist 13 nonconformist

dissertation
6 thesis 8 tractate, treatise 9 discourse, monograph 10 commentary, exposition 11 disputation 12 disquisition 13 argumentation

dissever
3 cut, hew 4 hack, part 5 carve, slice, split 6 cleave, detach, divide, sunder 7 disjoin, divorce 8 disjoint, disunite, separate, uncouple 10 disconnect

dissidence
6 heresy, schism, strife 7 discord, dispute, dissent, faction 8 conflict, friction, variance 10 contention, disharmony, dissension, heterodoxy, opposition 11 discordance, unorthodoxy 12 disagreement 13 nonconformism, nonconformity

dissident
7 heretic 8 partisan, recusant 9 differing, dissenter, heretical, heterodox, protestor 10 schismatic, separatist, unorthodox 11 contentious, disagreeing, misbeliever, nonbeliever, quarrelsome, schismatist 12 disputatious, unharmonious 13 nonconformist

dissimilar
6 unlike 7 diverse, unalike, unequal, various 8 distinct 9 different, disparate, divergent 13 heterogeneous

dissimilarity
8 contrast, variance 9 disparity, diversity, variation 10 difference, divergence, divergency, unlikeness 11 incongruity 13 heterogeneity, inconsistency

dissimulate
see **dissemble**

dissimulation
5 fraud, guile, lying 6 deceit 7 cunning 8 artifice, flimflam, pretense 9 deception, duplicity, hypocrisy, mendacity, sophistry 10 craftiness, pharisaism 11 beguilement, smoke screen

dissipate
4 blow 5 use up, waste 6 burn up, spread, vanish 7 break up, scatter 8 disperse, evanesce, melt away, misspend, squander 9 evaporate, throw away 11 fritter away

dissipated
6 rakish, wanton, wasted 8 depraved 9 debauched, reprobate 10 degenerate, licentious, profligate 11 intemperate

dissociate
4 part 5 unfix 6 cut off, detach 7 disband, disjoin 8 alienate, disunite, estrange, separate, uncouple 9 disengage 10 disconnect

dissolute
3 lax 4 fast, wild 5 loose, slack 6 rakish, wanton 7 raffish, wayward 8 decadent, depraved 9 abandoned, debauched, indulgent, reprobate 10 degenerate, dissipated, licentious, profligate 12 unprincipled, unrestrained

dissolution
5 death, decay, split 6 demise 7 breakup, divorce, rupture, split-up 8 division 9 dispersal, partition 10 detachment, disbanding, profligacy 11 evaporation 12 liquefaction

dissolvable
7 soluble 8 meltable

dissolve
3 end **4** flux, melt, thaw, undo, void **5** annul, quash **6** recess, vacate, vanish **7** adjourn, break up, diffuse, liquefy **8** abrogate, disperse, evanesce, fade away, get rid of, melt away, prorogue, separate **9** decompose, dissipate, evaporate, prorogate, terminate, waste away **10** deliquesce, do away with **12** disintegrate

dissonance
6 strife **7** discord **8** clashing, conflict **9** cacophony, harshness **10** contention, difference, disharmony **11** incongruity **12** disagreement **13** inconsistency

dissonant
5 harsh **7** grating, jarring, raucous **8** strident **9** unmusical **10** cacophonic, discordant, inharmonic **11** cacophonous, conflicting, incongruous **12** incompatible, inharmonious

dissuade
5 deter **7** turn off **10** discourage, disincline

distaff
6 female **8** maternal

distance
4 area **5** ambit, lapse, orbit, range, reach, scope, space, sweep **6** course, degree, extent, length, radius, remove, spread **7** breadth, compass, expanse, horizon, mileage, reserve, spacing, stretch **8** interval **9** amplitude, disparity, expansion, extension **10** divergence, divergency, remoteness, separation **11** distinction
between levels: **4** drop
between rails: **4** gage
between supports: **4** span
from bottom to top: **6** height
geometric: **8** altitude
greatest perpendicular: **6** camber
measuring instrument: **8** odometer **9** pedometer, telemeter **11** range finder
perpendicular: **5** depth
shortest: **7** beeline **12** straight line

distant
3 far, shy **4** afar, cold, cool **5** aloof, apart **6** absent, far-off, remote **7** faraway, haughty, obscure, removed, spacial, spatial **8** far-flung, isolated, outlying, reserved, secluded, solitary **9** separated, unsimilar, withdrawn **10** unsociable **11** out-of-the-way, sequestered, standoffish
combining form: **3** tel **4** tele, telo

distaste
7 disgust, dislike **8** aversion, loathing **9** antipathy, hostility, revulsion **10** abhorrence, repugnance **13** indisposition

distasteful
8 unsavory **9** loathsome, obnoxious, offensive, repellent, repugnant, repulsive **10** abominable, unpleasant **11** displeasing, unpalatable **12** disagreeable, unappetizing **13** objectionable

distemper
6 malady **7** ailment, disease **8** disorder **9** contagion, strangles **10** affliction **11** derangement **13** panleucopenia

distend
5 bloat, bulge, swell, widen **6** dilate, expand, extend, puff up **7** amplify, augment, enlarge, inflate, stretch **8** increase, lengthen **10** stretch out

distill
6 refine **7** extract **8** boil down **11** concentrate, precipitate

distinct
4 sole **5** clear, lucid, plain **6** marked, patent, single, unique **7** audible, defined, diverse, evident, express, notable, obvious, special, unusual **8** apparent, clear-cut, definite, discrete, especial, explicit, manifest, palpable, peculiar, separate, specific **9** different, divergent **10** individual, noticeable, particular **11** categorical, unambiguous, unequivocal **12** unmistakable

distinction
4 bays, rank **5** award, badge, grade, honor, kudos **6** nicety, renown **7** laurels **8** accolade, eminence, prestige **10** difference, divergence, divergency, prominence, unlikeness **11** differentia, peculiarity, preeminence, recognition **12** significance **13** dissimilarity

distinctive
6 proper, single, unique **7** special, unusual **8** peculiar, separate, singular **10** individual **13** idiosyncratic

distingué
6 classy, urbane **7** courtly, elegant, eminent, genteel, refined **8** cultured, decorous, highbrow, mannerly, polished, well-bred **9** dignified, high-class **10** cultivated **13** sophisticated

distinguish
4 mark, note, spot, view **5** honor, place **6** descry, notice, set off **7** dignify, make out, mark off, observe, pick out **8** classify, identify, perceive, separate **9** recognize, single out **10** categorize **12** characterize, discriminate **13** differentiate, individualize

distinguished
5 famed, noted **6** famous **7** eminent, notable, stately **8** esteemed, imposing, renowned **9** dignified, prominent **10** celebrated **11** illustrious

distort
4 bend, skew, warp, wind **5** alter, color, twist **6** deform, garble **7** contort, falsify, pervert, torture **8** misstate **11** misconstrue **12** misinterpret, misrepresent

distortion
8 twisting **9** deformity

distract
5 addle, mix up **6** ball up, bemuse, divert, puzzle

7 confuse, fluster, mislead, perplex **8** befuddle, bewilder, confound, throw off **9** sidetrack, unbalance

distracted
8 confused, deranged, maddened, troubled **9** oblivious **10** nonplussed **11** disoriented, inattentive, preoccupied **12** absent-minded

distraction
5 upset **9** agitation, amusement, confusion, diversion **10** perplexity **12** interruption **13** entertainment

distrait
5 upset **7** anxious, bemused, faraway, worried **8** confused, deranged, harassed, maddened, troubled **9** tormented, withdrawn **10** abstracted, distracted, distraught **11** inattentive, preoccupied **12** absentminded, apprehensive

distraught
5 upset **6** addled, crazed **7** anxious, frantic, muddled, rattled, shook up, unglued, worried **8** agitated, confused, demented, deranged, frenzied, harassed, troubled, worked up **9** flustered, perturbed, tormented, wigged-out **10** distressed, bewildered, freaked out, nonplussed **11** overwrought

distress
3 ail, irk, mar, try, vex, woe **4** ache, care, hurt, pain, pang, rack **5** agony, annoy, cross, dolor, grief, rigor, throe, trial, upset, worry **6** bother, grieve, harass, misery, pester, plague, sorrow, strain, strait, twinge **7** afflict, anguish, anxiety, exhaust, torment, torture, trouble **8** aggrieve, calamity, exigency, hardship **9** adversity, constrain, hard times, suffering **10** affliction, difficulty, heartbreak, misfortune, visitation **11** tribulation, vicissitude
call: **6** Mayday
signal: **3** SOS **5** alarm

distressing
4 dire **6** woeful **8** alarming, grievous, shocking **9** offensive **10** deplorable, lamentable **11** dispiriting, regrettable, unfortunate **13** heartbreaking

distribute
4 deal, mete **5** allot, place, strew **6** assign, assort, divide, donate, parcel, ration, spread **7** deal out, deliver, diffuse, dish out, divvy up, dole out, dribble, give out, hand out, mete out, prorate, radiate, scatter, slice up **8** allocate, classify, disburse, dispense, position, separate **9** apportion, circulate, partition, propagate, spread out **10** administer, measure out **11** disseminate

distribution
7 density **8** delivery, dividend, grouping, ordering, sequence **9** allotment, allotting, diffusion, dispersal, marketing, placement, spreading **10** dispersion, scattering **11** arrangement, probability, propagation **12** apportioning, dispensation **13** apportionment, dissemination

distributor
5 agent **6** broker, jobber **7** carrier **9** middleman **10** wholesaler **12** intermediate

district
4 area, ward **5** tract **6** barrio, locale, parcel, region, sector **7** borough, quarter, section **8** division, locality, precinct, vicinage, vicinity **11** subdivision **12** neighborhood
Danish: **3** amt
ecclesiastical: **5** synod **6** parish **7** diocese
Greek: **4** deme
Indian: **6** tahsil
judicial: **7** circuit
London: **4** Soho **7** Chelsea, Mayfair **9** Docklands, Greenwich, Southwark **10** Kensington, Piccadilly **11** Canary Wharf, Notting Hill **13** Knightsbridge
New York: **4** Soho **7** Chelsea, Tribeca
theater: **6** rialto

District of Columbia
college, university: **6** Howard **8** American, Catholic **9** Gallaudet **10** Georgetown
motto: **13** E Pluribus Unum
official bird: **10** wood thrush
official flower: **18** American Beauty rose

distrust
5 doubt **7** suspect **8** question, wariness **9** disbelief, discredit, misgiving, suspicion **10** disbelieve

distrustful
4 wary **5** chary, leery **7** cynical, dubious, jealous **8** doubtful, doubting **10** suspicious **12** questionable

disturb
4 faze **5** alarm, daunt, rouse, upset, worry **6** bother, harass, meddle, mess up, pester, stir up **7** agitate, break up, disrupt, fluster, perplex, trouble, unnerve **8** bewilder, distress, unsettle **9** incommode, interrupt **10** discompose, disconcert, tamper with **13** inconvenience, interfere with

disturbance
4 flap, fuss, stir, to-do **5** stink **6** clamor, hubbub, rumpus, tumult, unrest, uproar **7** bobbery, turmoil **8** disorder **9** agitation, commotion, confusion **10** alteration, disruption, turbulence **11** derangement, distraction **12** interruption
atmospheric: **5** storm **7** cyclone, tornado **9** hurricane
mental: **6** frenzy **8** delirium, neurosis **9** psychosis

disturbed
5 upset **6** insane, shaken **7** anxious, puzzled, rattled, worried **8** bothered, demented, deranged, troubled **9** concerned, psychotic, unsettled **10** distracted, distressed **12** disconcerted

disunion
7 divorce, rupture, split-up **8** division, severing, variance **9** partition **10** detachment, difference, separation **13** disconnection

disunite
4 part **6** divide, sunder **7** break up, disjoin, divorce, split up **8** dissever, separate, uncouple **9** disengage, fall apart **10** disconnect **12** disaffiliate

disunity
6 strife, schism **7** discord **8** conflict, division, variance **10** alienation, contention, disharmony, dissension **12** disaffection, disagreement, estrangement

disused
5 passé **8** obsolete, outdated, outmoded **9** abandoned, discarded **10** antiquated, superseded

ditch
3 dig, pit **4** drop, dump, foss, ha-ha, junk, moat **5** chuck, fosse, leave, scrap, swale **6** reject, trench, trough **7** abandon, cashier, discard, dismiss, forsake, foxhole **8** jettison, throw out **9** crash-land, dispose of, throw away **10** excavation

dither
4 fuss, stew **5** quake, shake, tizzy, waver **6** falter, flurry, quaver, shiver **7** flutter, tremble, twitter, whiffle **8** hesitate **9** agitation, commotion, confusion, vacillate **10** excitement, turbulence **12** shilly-shally

dithyramb
4 hymn, poem **5** chant

dithyrambic
6 ardent, fervid **9** perfervid, rhapsodic **10** boisterous, passionate **11** impassioned

ditto
4 copy, idem, same **5** clone, me too, mimeo, repro, Xerox **6** carbon, repeat **7** replica, reprint, similar **9** duplicate, facsimile, photocopy **10** carbon copy, mimeograph **11** replication **12** reproduction **13** reduplication

ditty
3 air, lay **4** song, tune **5** carol, chant **6** ballad

diurnal
5 daily **7** daytime **8** daylight **9** circadian, ephemeral, quotidian

diva
7 goddess **10** prima donna **11** leading lady

divagate
4 turn, veer **5** drift, stray **6** depart, ramble, wander **7** digress, diverge

divan
4 sofa **5** couch **6** settee **7** chamber, council **9** davenport **12** chesterfield

dive
3 bar, pub **4** dash, dump, hole, jump, leap **5** joint, lunge, pitch, sound, swoop **6** header, lounge, plunge, saloon, tavern **7** barroom, decline, descend, descent, hangout, plummet, taproom **8** submerge **9** honky-tonk, roadhouse **10** cannonball
type: **4** pike, swan, tuck **6** gainer **7** cutaway **9** belly flop, jackknife

diver
4 loon

diverge
4 part, vary **5** stray **6** depart, differ, swerve **7** deflect, deviate, digress **8** disagree, separate **9** bifurcate, branch off, draw apart

divergence
7 parting **9** departure, deviation, differing **10** aberration, deflection, difference, digression, separation **11** disagreeing, discrepancy, distinction **12** disagreement

divergent
6 unlike **8** aberrant, abnormal, atypical **9** anomalous, different, differing, disparate, irregular **10** dissimilar

divers
6 sundry **7** several, various **8** assorted **9** different, disparate **13** miscellaneous

diverse
5 mixed **6** motley, sundry, unlike, varied **7** several, unalike, unequal, various, varying **8** assorted, discrete, distinct, manifold, separate **9** different, differing, disparate, multiform, multiplex, unsimilar **10** contrasted, dissimilar **11** contrasting, contrastive **12** multifarious **13** contradictory, miscellaneous
combining form: **4** vari **5** vario
meanings: **8** polysemy

diversion
5 sport **7** pastime, turning **8** pleasure, sideshow **9** amusement, deviation, enjoyment **10** aberration, deflection, recreation, red herring **11** distraction **13** entertainment

diversity
7 variety **10** assortment, difference, unlikeness **11** variegation **12** multiformity **13** dissimilarity, heterogeneity

divert
4 turn, veer **5** amuse **6** regale, swerve **7** beguile, deflect, delight, deviate, digress **8** distract, redirect **9** entertain, turn aside

divest
3 rid, rob **4** free **5** spoil, strip **6** denude **7** bereave, deprive, despoil, disrobe, undress **8** take away **9** dismantle **10** disinherit, dispossess

divide
3 cut **4** fork, part **5** allot, cut up, sever, share

6 assign, cleave, parcel, ration, schism, sunder **7** break up, dissect, divorce, dole out, isolate, prorate, quarter, share in, split up **8** allocate, classify, dispense, disunite, separate **9** apportion, branch out, partition, watershed **10** distribute, measure out **11** dichotomize, distinguish
into four parts: **7** quarter
into three parts: **7** trisect
into two parts: **5** halve **6** bisect **9** bifurcate

divided
4 rent **5** cleft, riven, split **6** cloven **7** asunder, partite **8** ruptured

dividend
5 bonus, share **6** return, reward **7** benefit, guerdon, portion, premium **9** allotment **12** dispensation

divider
6 border, screen **9** partition

divination
6 augury **7** insight **8** prophecy **11** foretelling, soothsaying
by communication with the dead: **10** necromancy
by figures: **8** geomancy
by lots: **9** sortilege
by numbers: **10** numerology
by rods: **7** dowsing **11** rhabdomancy
by stars: **9** astrology

divine
4 holy **5** clerk, godly, infer **6** cleric, deduce, deific, intuit, parson, priest, sacred, superb **7** foresee, godlike **8** clerical, foreknow, foretell, heavenly, luscious, minister, preacher, prophesy, reverend **9** apprehend, churchman, clergyman, marvelous, religious, visualize **10** anticipate, conjecture, sanctified, superhuman, theologian **11** scrumptious **12** ecclesiastic

Divine Comedy
guide: **6** Vergil, Virgil
poet: **5** Dante (Alighieri)
section: **5** canto **7** Inferno **8** Paradiso **10** Purgatorio

diviner
4 seer **5** augur, sibyl **6** oracle **7** palmist, prophet **8** haruspex **10** forecaster, prophetess, soothsayer

divinity
3 god **5** deity, fudge **7** goddess, godhead, godhood **8** theology

division
3 cut **4** part, unit **5** class, piece, slice, split **6** branch, moiety, parcel, schism, sector **7** breakup, discord, dissent, divorce, parting, portion, rupture, section, segment, split-up **8** category, conflict, district, disunion, disunity, variance **9** partition **10** detachment, difference, disharmony, dissidence, separation **11** dissolution **12** disagreement **13** apportionment
Bible: **5** verse
book: **7** chapter
British territorial: **5** shire
building: **4** wing
cell: **7** meiosis, mitosis
city: **4** ward **7** borough **8** precinct
contest: **4** heat **6** inning, period
corolla: **5** petal
country: **5** state **6** canton **8** province **10** department, prefecture
family: **4** side **6** branch
geologic time: **3** eon, era **5** epoch **6** period
hospital: **4** ward, wing
into two: **9** bisection **11** bifurcation, bipartition
meal: **6** course
music: **3** bar **4** beat **7** measure **8** movement
opera, play: **3** act **5** scena, scene
poem: **5** canto, verse **6** stanza
population: **7** segment, stratum
race: **3** lap **4** heat
social: **5** caste, class, tribe
state: **6** county, parish
term: **8** quotient
time: **3** day, eon **4** week, year **5** month **6** decade, minute, moment, second **7** century, weekend **9** fortnight **10** millennium
tribal: **4** clan
word: **8** syllable
zodiac: **4** sign

divisive
8 factious **11** disunifying

divorce
4 part **5** sever, split **6** divide, sunder **7** break up, breakup, disjoin, rupture **8** disjoint, dissever, disunion, disunite, separate **9** partition, severance **10** detachment, separation **11** dissolution

divot
3 sod **4** turf **5** clump

divulge
4 blab, leak, tell **5** spill **6** betray, expose, gossip, reveal, tattle **7** let slip, uncover **8** disclose, give away

Dixie composer
6 Emmett (Daniel D.)

dizziness
7 vertigo **9** giddiness

dizzy
5 addle, dazed, giddy, mix up, silly, tipsy **6** addled **7** confuse, dazzled, flighty, foolish, fuddled, muddled, puzzled, reeling **8** confused, swimming, whirling **9** befuddled, confusing **10** bewildered, confounded, distracted, exorbitant, immoderate, inordinate **11** extravagant, light-headed, vertiginous

Djibouti
language: **6** Arabic, French
monetary unit: **5** franc
neighbor: **7** Eritrea, Somalia **8** Ethiopia
sea: **3** Red

DNA
component: **7** adenine, guanine, thymine **8** cytosine **10** nucleotide **11** deoxyribose
segment: **4** exon, gene **7** cistron

doable
8 feasible, possible, workable **9** realistic **10** achievable, attainable **11** performable

do away with
3 end, nix, zap **4** kill, slay **5** annul, erase, whack **6** cancel, finish, murder, remove, repeal, revoke, rub out **7** abolish, bump off, deep-six, destroy, discard, expunge, rescind, squelch, wipe out **8** abrogate, blow away, demolish, dispatch, dissolve, massacre, stamp out **9** dispose of, eliminate, eradicate, extirpate, finish off, liquidate, slaughter **10** extinguish, obliterate **11** discontinue, exterminate

docent
5 guide **6** leader **7** teacher **8** lecturer **10** instructor

docile
4 tame **6** pliant **7** ductile, pliable **8** amenable, biddable, obedient, yielding **9** adaptable, compliant, teachable, tractable **10** submissive **11** acquiescent

dock
3 bob, cut **4** crop, fine, pier, quay, rump, slip **5** berth, jetty, levee, tie up, wharf **6** anchor, hangar, lessen, marina, reduce **7** abridge, landing, shorten **8** cut short, platform, truncate
worker: **6** lumper **9** stevedore **12** longshoreman

docket
4 card **6** agenda, lineup, record **7** program **8** abstract, calendar, caseload, register, schedule **9** timetable

doctor
3 fix, vet **4** mend **5** adapt, alter, medic, treat **6** medico, repair **7** croaker, dentist, falsify, scholar, surgeon **8** sawbones **9** clinician, internist, physician **10** adulterate, specialist **11** medicine man, recondition, reconstruct
animal: **3** vet **12** veterinarian
children's: **12** pediatrician
famous: **4** Koop (C. Everett), Weil (Andrew) **5** Galen, Spock (Benjamin) **6** Atkins (Robert), Chopra (Deepak), Ornish (Dean) **9** Kevorkian (Jack) **10** Schweitzer (Albert) **11** Hippocrates, Livingstone (David)
foot: **10** podiatrist **11** chiropodist
heart: **12** cardiologist
organization: **3** AMA
teeth: **7** dentist **10** exodontist
women's: **12** gynecologist

Doctor of the Church
5 Basil **6** Jerome **7** Ambrose, Gregory **9** Augustine **10** Athanasius

Doctorow novel
7 Ragtime **9** City of God (The) **10** Waterworks, World's Fair **12** Book of Daniel (The) **13** Billy Bathgate **18** Welcome to Hard Times

Doctor Zhivago
author: **9** Pasternak (Boris)
character: **4** Lara **7** Larissa
film director: **4** Lean (David)
film star: **6** Sharif (Omar) **8** Christie (Julie)

doctrinaire
5 rigid **8** dogmatic **9** obstinate **10** unyielding **11** domineering, magisterial **13** authoritarian

doctrine
3 ism **5** axiom, basic, canon, credo, creed, dogma, faith, tenet **7** precept **8** teaching **9** principle **11** fundamental

document
4 deed **5** paper **6** record **8** evidence, monument **9** testimony **10** instrument **11** certificate
travel: **8** passport

dodder
4 limp **5** shake **6** falter, hobble, totter **7** shamble, shuffle, stagger, tremble **12** morning glory

doddering
5 shaky **6** doting, feeble, senile **7** fragile **8** unsteady, weakened **9** faltering

dodge
4 duck, jink, ploy, ruse, slip **5** avert, avoid, elude, evade, fence, parry, shirk, skirt, slide, trick **6** escape, scheme, weasel **7** evasion **8** sidestep **9** avoidance, deception, expedient

Dodger
5 Davis (Tommy) **6** Garvey (Steve), Karros (Eric), Koufax (Sandy), Piazza (Michael), Snider (Duke), Sutton (Don) **8** Newcombe (Don), Robinson (Jackie) **9** Hershiser (Orel) **10** Campanella (Roy)
field: **7** Ebbetts
home: **8** Brooklyn **10** Los Angeles
manager: **6** Alston (Walter) **7** Lasorda (Tommy)

dodger
6 outlaw, screen **7** escapee **8** circular, deceiver, deserter, fugitive, handbill, runagate **9** throwaway

dodgy
4 iffy **5** fishy, vague **6** tricky **7** cryptic, obscure **8** doubtful, unproven **9** ambiguous, enigmatic, uncertain **10** indefinite, suspicious, unreliable **11** problematic **12** questionable **13** controversial

dodo
3 oaf **4** bird, boob, clod, dolt, dope, goof, yo-yo **5** chump, dummy, dunce, idiot, moron, ninny, noddy, stupe **6** dimwit, dum-dum, nitwit **7** airhead, dullard, pinhead **8** bonehead, dumbbell, imbecile, lunkhead, meathead, numskull **9** birdbrain, blockhead, ignoramus, lamebrain, numbskull, simpleton **10** dunderhead, nincompoop **11** chowderhead, chucklehead

doe
4 deer **6** female, rabbit **8** kangaroo

doff
4 shed **6** remove **7** take off

dog
3 cur, pom, pug, pup, tag **4** alan, bird, chow, fice, mutt, peke, puli, tail, tyke **5** Akita, boxer, canid, corgi, dhole, dingo, feist, frank, hound, husky, lemon, pooch, puppy, spitz, trail **6** Afghan, beagle, borzoi, bowwow, briard, canine, collie, detent, poodle, pursue, rascal, saluki, setter, shadow, Talbot, vizsla, wiener, wretch **7** andiron, basenji, harrier, Maltese, mastiff, mongrel, pointer, redbone, Samoyed, Scottie, shar-pei, spaniel, terrier, whippet **8** Airedale, Brittany, elkhound, foxhound, inferior, keeshond, komondor, malamute, malemute, papillon, Pekinese, pinscher, sheepdog, Shiba Inu, spurious, wirehair **9** Chihuahua, dachshund, dalmation, deerhound, Great Dane, greyhound, Lhasa apso, Pekingese, retriever, schnauzer, wolfhound **10** bloodhound, Pomeranian, rottweiler, Weimaraner **11** basset hound, bullmastiff, frankfurter, wienerwurst **12** border collie, Newfoundland, Saint Bernard **13** cocker spaniel
Bush's: **6** Millie
Buster Brown's: **4** Tige
Charlie Brown's: **6** Snoopy
command: **3** sit **4** heel, stay
Dagwood's: **5** Daisy
Dorothy's: **4** Toto
family: **7** Canidae
FDR's: **4** Fala
fictional: **3** Max **4** Buck, Lady **5** Astro, Pluto, Scamp, Tramp **6** Big Red **8** McBarker **9** Marmaduke, Old Yeller, Scooby-Doo, White Fang
"Garfield": **4** Odie
genus: **5** Canis
Grinch's: **3** Max
L.B.J.'s: **3** Her
monster: **8** Barghest
movie: **4** Asta, Lady, Toto **5** Benji, Tramp **6** Lassie **9** Beethoven, Old Yeller, Rin Tin Tin
name: **4** Fido, Spot **5** Rover **6** Bowser
Nixon's: **8** Checkers
Odysseus's: **5** Argos
of Hades: **8** Cerberus
Orphan Annie's: **5** Sandy
RCA: **6** Nipper
Roy Rogers's: **6** Bullet
Sgt. Snorkel's: **4** Otto
sled command: **4** mush
space traveler: **5** Laika
Steinbeck's: **7** Charley
television: **4** King **5** Eddie, Tramp **6** Lassie, Murray **8** Wishbone **9** Rin Tin Tin
three-headed: **8** Cerberus
tooth: **4** fang
treat: **4** bone
two-headed: **6** Orthos
Wallace's: **6** Gromit
Welsh: **5** corgi
Wendy's: **4** Nana
wild: **5** dingo
young: **3** pup **5** puppy, whelp

dog days
6 August **9** canicular

dogfight
3 row **4** fray **5** brawl, broil, melee, set-to **6** fracas, ruckus **7** ruction **10** donnybrook, free-for-all

dogfish
6 bowfin, burbot **8** mud puppy

dogged
7 adamant **8** obdurate, resolute, stubborn **9** insistent, steadfast, obstinate, tenacious, unbending **10** bullheaded, determined, hardheaded, persistent, persisting, unshakable, unyielding **11** persevering, unremitting **12** pertinacious

doggone
4 damn, dang, darn, rank **5** utter **6** cursed, damned, darned **7** blasted, blessed, dratted **8** absolute, accursed, infernal, outright **9** out-and-out **10** confounded **11** unmitigated **13** blankety-blank

dogma
4 code, rule **5** canon, credo, creed, tenet **6** belief, gospel **7** precept **8** doctrine, ideology **9** orthodoxy, postulate, teachings **10** conviction, persuasion

dogmatic
8 oracular, orthodox **9** assertive, canonical, doctrinal **11** dictatorial, doctrinaire, magisterial, opinionated

Dog of Flanders author
5 Ouida

dog-paddle
4 swim

dog's age
3 eon **4** aeon **8** blue moon, eternity

Dog Star
6 Sirius

dogwood
6 cornel, Cornus **8** red osier

do in
4 kill, ruin, slay **5** cheat, wreck **6** defeat, finish, murder, rub out **7** blot out, bump off, destroy, execute, exhaust, frazzle, take out, wear out, wipe out **8** dispatch, knock off, knock out **9** eliminate, liquidate, prostrate, run ragged, shipwreck **11** assassinate

doing
3 act **6** action **8** activity
good: **10** beneficent
evil: **10** maleficent

doit
3 bit, jot **4** coin, damn, dram, drop, hoot, iota, mite, whit **6** trifle **8** particle

doldrums
5 blahs, blues, dumps, ennui, gloom, slump **6** apathy, tedium, torpor **7** boredom **9** dejection **10** depression, inactivity, quiescence, stagnation **12** listlessness

doleful
3 sad **4** down **7** forlorn, ruthful **8** cast down, dejected, dolorous, downcast, grieving, mournful, mourning **9** afflicted, cheerless, depressed, miserable, plaintive, sorrowful, sorrowing, woebegone **10** dispirited, lamentable, lugubrious, melancholy **11** crestfallen, downhearted **12** disconsolate

dole out
4 deal **5** allot **6** divide, parcel, ration **7** divvy up **8** disburse, dispense, disperse **9** apportion, partition **10** administer, distribute

doll
3 Ken **6** Barbie, figure, Kewpie, puppet **7** kachina **10** Betsy Wetsy, Raggedy Ann **11** Raggedy Andy
grotesque: **8** golliwog

dollar
3 one **4** bill, buck, clam, oner, peso **5** taler **6** single **7** ringgit, smacker **8** simoleon **9** cartwheel, greenback

dollop
4 blob, glob, lump **7** portion

Doll's House, A
author: **5** Ibsen (Henrik)
heroine: **4** Nora

dolly
4 cart **7** stirrer **8** platform **10** locomotive

dolomite
6 marble **9** limestone

dolor
5 agony, grief **6** misery, sorrow **7** anguish, passion **8** distress **9** suffering **10** affliction

dolorous
6 rueful, woeful **7** ruthful **8** grievous, mournful, wretched **9** afflicted, anguished, miserable, plaintive, sorrowful **10** lamentable, lugubrious, melancholy **13** heartbreaking

dolphin
5 whale **7** bollard **8** porpoise

dolt
3 ass, oaf **4** boob, clod, dodo, dork, fool, goof, goon, lout, yo-yo **5** booby, chump, dunce, idiot **6** nitwit **7** dullard, fathead, halfwit, jughead, saphead, schnook **8** bonehead, dumbbell, dummkopf, imbecile, lunkhead, meathead, numskull **9** blockhead, lamebrain, numbskull, simpleton **11** chowderhead

doltish
4 dull, dumb **5** dense, thick **6** oafish, obtuse, stupid **7** idiotic, moronic **8** ignorant, mindless **9** dim-witted, fatheaded, imbecilic

domain
4 fief, land, rule, turf **5** field, realm **6** estate, sphere **7** fiefdom, kingdom, terrain **8** dominion, province **9** bailiwick, territory

dome
4 head, hill, roof **5** mound **6** cupola **7** ceiling, stadium **8** mountain
shape: **4** cone **5** onion

domestic
4 help, home, maid, tame **6** butler, family, native **7** servant **8** houseboy, internal, national **9** charwoman, household **10** indigenous **11** chambermaid

domesticate
4 tame **5** adapt, adopt, train **10** housebreak

domicile
3 pad **4** home **5** abode, house, lodge, put up **6** bestow, billet, harbor **7** quarter **8** dwelling, quarters **9** residence, residency **10** habitation

domiciliate
4 bunk, tame **5** house, lodge, put up **6** billet, harbor, reside **7** quarter

dominance
4 rule, sway **5** power **7** command, control **7** mastery **9** supremacy **10** ascendancy, prepotency **11** preeminence, sovereignty

dominant
4 main **5** chief, first, major **6** ruling **7** leading, supreme **8** foremost, powerful, reigning **9** ascendant, governing, number-one, paramount, prevalent, principal **10** commanding, preeminent, prevailing, surpassing **11** controlling, overbearing **12** preponderant

dominate
4 rule **5** reign **6** direct, govern, obsess **7** control, prevail, repress **8** bestride, hold sway, look down, loom over, overlook **9** subjugate, tower over, tyrannize **10** tower above

domination
4 rule, sway **5** might, power **7** command, control, mastery **9** authority, supremacy **10** ascendancy, prepotency, suzerainty **11** preeminence, sovereignty **13** preponderancy

dominator
4 boss, head **5** chief, ruler **6** honcho, leader, master, top dog **7** headman **8** director, hierarch, kingfish **9** chieftain, commander

domineer
5 bully **6** hector **7** swagger **8** browbeat, bulldoze **9** tyrannize **10** intimidate

domineering
5 bossy **6** lordly **8** arrogant, despotic **9** imperious, masterful **10** autocratic, high-handed, oppressive, tyrannical **11** dictatorial, magisterial, overbearing

Dominica
capital: **6** Roseau
discoverer: **8** Columbus (Christopher)
location: **10** West Indies
sea: **9** Caribbean

Dominican Republic
capital: **12** Santo Domingo
island: **10** Hispaniola
language: **7** Spanish
location: **10** West Indies
monetary unit: **4** peso
mountain: **6** Duarte
neighbor: **5** Haiti
sea: **9** Caribbean

dominion
3 raj **4** rule, sway, turf **5** realm, power **6** domain, empery, empire, regnum, sphere **7** demesne, kingdom, terrain **8** province **9** ascendant, ownership, supremacy, territory **10** ascendancy, possession **11** preeminence, sovereignty

domino
4 bone, cape, mask **5** amice, cloak, visor **6** vizard **8** disguise
spot: **3** pip

don
3 sir **4** lord **5** get on, put on, tutor **6** assume, fellow, take on **9** professor, undertake

Donalbain
brother: **7** Malcolm
father: **6** Duncan

donate
4 give **5** grant **6** bestow, chip in, supply **7** dish out, hand out, present, provide **8** give away, shell out, transfer **10** contribute

donation
3 aid **4** alms, gift **5** grant **7** bequest, handout **8** offering **9** endowment **11** benefaction, beneficence **12** contribution, philanthropy

Don Carlos
author: **8** Schiller (Friedrich von)
composer: **5** Verdi (Giuseppe)
father: **6** Philip

done
4 over **5** all in, ended, ready, spent **6** bushed, gone by, used up **7** drained, dressed, far-gone, settled, through, worn-out **8** complete, depleted, finished, washed-up **9** completed, concluded, exhausted **10** terminated **12** accomplished
poetic: **3** o'er

donee
7 grantee **8** receiver **9** recipient **11** beneficiary

done for
4 gone, sunk **5** kaput **6** beaten, doomed, ruined **7** wrecked **8** finished, stricken

done in
5 spent **6** bushed, effete, used up **7** drained, far gone, worn-out **8** depleted **9** exhausted, shattered, washed out

Don Giovanni
composer: **6** Mozart (Wolfgang Amadeus)
conquest: **4** Anna (Donna) **6** Elvira (Donna) **7** Zerlina
servant: **9** Leporello

Donizetti, Gaetano
hero: **7** Roberto (Devereux)
opera: **5** Lucia (di Lammermoor) **10** Anna Bolena, La Favorita **11** Don Pasquale **12** Maria Stuarda

Don Juan
4 rake, roué, wolf **5** Romeo **6** chaser, masher **7** amorist, gallant, playboy, seducer **8** Casanova, lothario, paramour **9** ladies' man, libertine, womanizer **10** lady-killer, profligate **11** philanderer
drama: **10** Stone Guest (The)
home: **7** Seville
mother: **4** Inez
poet: **5** Byron (Lord) **7** Pushkin (Alexander)

donkey
3 ass **4** mule **5** burro **7** jackass
female: **5** jenny **6** jennet

donkeywork
4 moil, toil **5** grind, labor **7** travail **8** drudgery

donnybrook
3 row **4** fray, riot **5** brawl, broil, fight, melee, set-to **6** fracas, ruckus, rumpus, tumult, uproar **7** dispute, quarrel, rhubarb, ruction **10** free-for-all **11** altercation

donor
5 giver, Type O **6** patron **7** granter, grantor **8** bestower **9** conferrer, presenter **10** benefactor **11** contributor

do-nothing
3 bum **4** slug **5** idler **6** loafer, slouch **7** goof-off,

slacker **8** deadbeat, fainéant, layabout, slugabed, sluggard **9** lazybones, vegetable **11** couch potato

Don Pasquale composer
9 Donizetti (Gaetano)

Don Quixote
author: **9** Cervantes (Miguel de)
beloved: **8** Dulcinea
companion (squire): **11** Sancho Panza
giant: **8** windmill
home: **8** La Mancha
horse: **9** Rocinante, Rosinante, Rozinante

doodad
5 gizmo, thing **6** bauble, dingus, entity, gadget, gewgaw, jigger, widget **7** trinket, whatsit **8** gimcrack **9** doohickey, thingummy **10** attachment, decoration, knickknack **11** thingamabob, thingamajig, thingumajig

doodle
6 dabble, dawdle, fiddle, potter, putter, sketch, tinker, trifle **7** cartoon, drawing **8** scribble **10** mess around

doodlebug
7 ant lion, missile **8** buzz bomb

doohickey
see **doodad**

doom
4 damn, fate, ruin **5** death **6** decree, demise, kismet **7** condemn, destiny, tragedy **8** calamity, disaster, judgment, sentence **11** catastrophe **12** annihilation, last judgment

doomful
4 dire **7** baleful, baneful, direful, fateful, malefic, ominous, unlucky **8** dreadful, ill-fated, sinister **10** foreboding, portentous **11** apocalyptic

doomsayer
7 killjoy **9** Cassandra, defeatist, Gloomy Gus, pessimist

____ Doone
5 Lorna

door
3 way **4** adit, exit **5** entry **6** access, egress, entrée, portal **7** gateway, ingress, opening **8** entrance, entryway **9** admission **10** admittance **11** entranceway
rear: **7** postern

doorkeeper
5 usher **6** porter **7** ostiary

doorway
5 entry **6** portal **8** entrance, entryway **11** entranceway

doozy
3 ace, pip **4** lulu **5** beaut, dandy, dilly, peach **6** corker **7** paragon **8** standout **9** humdinger **10** ripsnorter **10** phenomenon **11** crackerjack

dope
3 oaf **4** bozo, clod, dodo, dolt, drug, goof, info, news, yo-yo **5** chump, drugs, dummy, dunce, facts, idiot, moron, ninny, noddy, stupe **6** dimwit, doofus, dum-dum, heroin, nitwit, opiate, sedate, skinny **7** airhead, cocaine, details, dullard, lowdown, pinhead **8** bonehead, dumbbell, imbecile, lunkhead, meathead, narcotic, numskull **9** birdbrain, blockhead, ignoramus, lamebrain, marijuana, narcotize, numbskull, simpleton **10** dunderhead, nincompoop **11** anesthetize, chowderhead, chucklehead, information, preparation

doped
4 high **5** dazed **6** stoned, zonked **7** drugged, tuned-in **8** hopped-up, tripping, turned on, wiped out **9** spaced-out, strung out, stupefied **10** narcotized

dopey
4 dumb **5** silly **6** dulled, stupid, torpid **7** fatuous, fuddled, muddled **8** comatose, sluggish **9** lethargic, senseless, stupefied

Doris
brother: **6** Nereus
daughters: **7** Nereids
father: **7** Oceanus
husband: **6** Nereus

dormancy
5 sleep **6** repose **7** latency, slumber **8** abeyance, diapause, doldrums, downtime **9** torpidity **10** inactivity, quiescence, suspension **11** cold storage **12** intermission, interruption

dormant
5 inert **6** asleep, drowsy, fallow, latent, torpid **7** abeyant **8** comatose, inactive, sluggish **9** lethargic, potential, quiescent, suspended **10** slow-moving, slumbering

dormer
3 bay **4** nook **5** niche **6** window

dorsal
6 aboral **7** abaxial

____ d'Orsay
4 Quai

dorsum
4 back

Dorus
brother: **6** Aeolus
father: **6** Hellen

dory
4 bark, boat **5** craft, skiff **6** barque, bateau **7** shallop **8** lifeboat

dose
3 fix, hit **4** dram, shot, slug **7** measure, portion **8** medicate, quantity

Dos Passos trilogy
3 U.S.A.

dossier
4 file **6** folder **9** portfolio

dot
4 mark, mote, stud **5** dower, dowry, point, speck **6** bestud, pepper, period **7** freckle, speckle, stipple **8** flyspeck, sprinkle **9** bespeckle **12** decimal point

dotage
8 senility **11** decrepitude, senectitude

dote on
5 adore, enjoy, fancy, prize **7** cherish, idolize **8** treasure **9** delight in

doting
4 dear, fond, gaga **6** loving **7** adoring, devoted **12** affectionate

dotted
4 semé, sown **6** spotty, strewn **8** punctate, stippled

dotty
4 gaga **5** crazy, loony, wacky **6** absurd, insane **7** foolish, smitten **8** enamored **9** eccentric **10** captivated, enraptured, infatuated **12** preposterous

double
4 copy, dual, fold, mate, tack, twin **5** clone, duple, image, match, twice **6** bifold, binary, duplex, paired, ringer **7** dualize, enlarge, magnify, replica, twofold **8** alter ego, geminate, increase **9** companion, dualistic, duplicate, look-alike, replicate **10** dead ringer, reciprocal, simulacrum, understudy **13** spitting image

double-barreled
4 dual **5** duple **6** bifold, binary, duplex, paired **7** twofold **9** dualistic

double bass
10 bull fiddle

double-cross
3 con **4** dupe **5** cheat, rat on, trick **6** betray, delude, humbug, juggle, take in **7** beguile, deceive, sell out, two-time **8** flimflam, hoodwink **9** four-flush

double dagger
6 diesis

double-dealer
3 gyp **5** cheat, knave **6** con man **7** cozener, diddler, sharper **8** deceiver, swindler **9** defrauder **11** flimflammer **13** confidence man

double-dealing
5 fraud **6** deceit **7** chicane **8** flimflam, trickery **9** chicanery, deceitful, deception, duplicity, two-timing **10** hanky-panky **11** duplicitous

double-dome
7 egghead **8** Einstein, highbrow **10** pointy-head **12** intellectual

double-faced
9 deceitful, deceptive, equivocal, insincere **10** reversible **12** hypocritical **13** untrustworthy

doublet
3 duo **4** dyad, pair, span **5** brace **6** couple, jacket **7** twosome

double-talk
4 bosh, bunk **5** hokum, hooey **6** babble, bunkum, drivel, jabber **7** blather, hogwash, twaddle **8** flimflam, nonsense **9** gibberish, poppycock **10** balderdash **12** gobbledygook

double vision
8 diplopia

doubt
5 qualm **7** concern, dispute, dubiety, suspect **8** distrust, mistrust, question **9** challenge, disbelief, misgiving, suspicion **10** skepticism **11** dubiousness, incertitude, incredulity, uncertainty

doubtable
4 hazy, iffy, moot **7** dubious, suspect **8** arguable **9** ambiguous, debatable, equivocal, uncertain, undecided **10** disputable, borderline, indefinite **11** problematic **12** questionable

doubter
5 cynic **6** Thomas **7** sceptic, skeptic **8** agnostic **10** Pyrrhonist, questioner, unbeliever **11** freethinker

doubtful
4 hazy, iffy, moot **5** fishy, shady, shaky **6** chancy, unsure **7** clouded, dubious, obscure, suspect, unclear **8** arguable, unlikely **9** ambiguous, debatable, dubitable, equivocal, uncertain, undecided, unsettled **10** borderline, disputable, improbable **11** problematic, speculative **12** questionable

doubtfulness
7 concern, dubiety **8** mistrust **9** ambiguity, misgiving, suspicion **10** indecision, skepticism, uneasiness **11** dubiousness, incertitude, uncertainty **13** indeterminacy

doubting Thomas
see **doubter**

doubtless
6 likely, surely **7** certain, clearly **8** of course, probably **10** absolutely, definitely, positively, presumably **11** indubitably **12** indisputably **13** presumptively, unequivocally

douceur
3 tip **4** gift **5** bribe **7** present **8** gratuity **9** bakhsheesh

dough
4 cash **5** bread, money **6** dinero, moolah **7** cabbage, lettuce, scratch **8** currency **11** legal tender
inflator: **5** yeast

doughboy
7 dogface **11** infantryman

doughty
4 bold **5** brave, gutsy, manly, stout **6** daring, heroic, plucky, spunky, strong **7** gallant, valiant **8** fearless, intrepid, resolved, stalwart, unafraid, valorous **9** dauntless, undaunted **10** courageous **12** stouthearted

doughy
3 wan **4** pale **5** pasty, waxen **6** pallid **8** blanched **9** colorless

do up
3 can, fix **4** mend, wash, wrap **5** clean, patch **6** clothe, doctor, fasten, repair, revamp **7** exhaust, festoon, launder, package, prepare, rebuild, wear out **8** decorate, gift wrap, ornament, overhaul **9** embellish **11** recondition, reconstruct

dour
4 glum, grim **5** bleak, harsh, rigid, stern, surly **6** gloomy, morose, severe, strict, sullen **7** austere, crabbed, peevish **9** obstinate, saturnine, stringent **10** forbidding, unyielding

douse
3 sop **4** duck, dunk, soak **5** bathe, drown, plash, slosh, souse **6** drench, put out, quench, splash, strike **7** immerse, slacken **8** inundate, saturate, snuff out, submerge, submerse **10** extinguish

dove
6 culver, pigeon **8** pacifist
call: **3** coo
genus: **7** Columba
pen: **4** cote

dovecote
6 aviary **9** birdhouse

dovetail
3 fit **4** jibe, mesh **5** agree, match, tally **6** accord, splice, square **7** comport, conform **8** check out **9** harmonize, interlock, intermesh **10** correspond

dovish
4 mild **6** gentle **7** antiwar, pacific **8** pacifist **9** peaceable **10** nonviolent, pacifistic **11** peace-loving **12** conciliatory

dowager
4 dame **5** widow **6** matron **9** matriarch **10** grande dame **11** grandmother

dowdy
4 drab **5** dated, frump, passé, seedy, tacky **6** blowsy, bygone, démodé, frowsy, frowzy, frumpy, old hat, shabby **7** rundown, unkempt **8** frumpish, outdated, outmoded, slattern, slovenly **9** out-of-date, unstylish **10** antiquated, bedraggled, slatternly **11** draggle-tail **12** old-fashioned **13** draggletailed

dowel
3 bar, peg, pin, rod **5** stick

dower
4 gift **5** endow, endue **6** legacy, talent **8** bequeath

dowitcher
5 snipe **9** sandpiper

do without
5 forgo, waive **6** abjure, eschew, give up, pass up **8** renounce

down
3 eat, fur, ill, low, off, sad **4** blue, fell, fuzz, lint, pile, sick **5** below, ended, floor, floss, fluff, level, lower, under **6** defeat, fallen, finish, lay low, nether **7** conquer, consume, destroy, flatten, swallow, unhappy **8** bowl over, complete, defeated, dejected, dispatch, feathers, finished, inferior, overcome, sluggish, surmount **9** completed, concluded, depressed, earthward, miserable **10** dispirited, groundward

down-and-out
5 broke, needy **6** hard-up, ruined **8** beggared, derelict, homeless **9** destitute, penniless, penurious **12** impoverished

down-and-outer
3 bum **6** beggar, pauper, wretch **7** have-not **9** mendicant **10** supplicant

down-at-heels
4 mean **5** dingy, ratty, seedy, tacky **6** ragged, ragtag, shabby, shoddy **7** ignoble, run-down, worn-out **8** decrepit, tattered **10** bedraggled, threadbare **11** dilapidated **12** deteriorated, disreputable

downbeat
3 low, sad **4** blue, glum **6** droopy, gloomy, morose **7** decline, doleful **8** dejected **9** depressed **10** dispirited, melancholy **11** discouraged, pessimistic **12** disconsolate, disheartened, heavy-hearted

downcast
3 low, sad **4** blue, glum, sunk **5** moody, mopey **6** droopy, gloomy, morose **7** doleful, forlorn, unhappy **8** dejected, dismayed, listless, soulsick, troubled **9** depressed, heartsick, heartsore, miserable, oppressed, woebegone **10** chapfallen, despondent, dispirited, distressed, melancholy, spiritless **11** crestfallen, discouraged, low-spirited **12** disconsolate, disheartened

downfall
4 bane, ruin **6** demise **7** decline, undoing **8** collapse, Waterloo **9** ruination **10** devolution **11** declination, destruction **12** degeneration, dégringolade **13** deterioration

downgrade
4 bump, bust **5** abase, lower **6** demote **7** decline, demerit, descent, devalue **8** belittle, diminish, discount, minimize, relegate **9** denigrate, deprecate, devaluate, discredit, disparage, humiliate **10** depreciate, undervalue **12** degeneration, dégringolade **13** deterioration

downhearted
see **downcast**

down-in-the-mouth
see **downcast**

down payment
5 token **6** pledge **7** advance, deposit, earnest

downplay
8 belittle, discount, minimize, pooh-pooh **11** deemphasize

downpour
6 deluge **7** monsoon **8** drencher **9** drenching, rainstorm **10** cloudburst, inundation **11** gully washer

downright
5 blunt, gross, total, truly, utter **7** blatant, flat-out **8** absolute, complete, explicit, positive, thorough **9** out-and-out **10** absolutely, sure-enough **11** indubitable, unequivocal, unmitigated, unqualified **13** thoroughgoing

downslide
3 dip, sag **4** drop, slip **5** slump **7** decline, drop-off, falloff **8** decrease **9** declivity, reduction

downstairs
6 cellar **8** basement

down-to-earth
8 rational **9** practical, pragmatic, realistic **10** hard-boiled, hardheaded, no-nonsense, reasonable **11** common-sense, plain-spoken **12** matter-of-fact **13** unpretentious, unsentimental

downtrend
see **downslide**

downtrodden
6 abject, abused **9** oppressed **10** maltreated, mistreated, persecuted, tyrannized

downturn
see **downslide**

downward
8 dropping **9** declining **10** descending

downy
4 soft **5** fuzzy **6** fleecy, fluffy **7** velvety **8** feathery
filler: 5 eider

dowry
4 gift **6** talent
French: 3 dot

doxy
4 bawd, drab, moll, slut, tart **5** wench **6** floozy, harlot **7** trollop **8** mistress, slattern **10** prostitute

doyen
4 dean, head **5** chief, maven **6** expert, leader, master, wizard **7** maestro **8** virtuoso **9** authority, patriarch **10** past master

Doyle's detective
6 Holmes (Sherlock)

D'Oyly Carte offering
8 operetta

doze
3 nap **5** sleep **6** catnap, drowse, nod off, snooze **7** drop off, slumber **8** drift off **10** forty winks

dozy
see **drowsy**

DP
5 exile **6** émigré **7** evacuee, outcast, refugee **8** deportee, emigrant, fugitive **10** expatriate

drab
4 dull, flat **5** bleak, brown, dingy, faded, mousy, muddy, olive, vapid **6** dismal, dreary, mousey **7** subfusc **8** lifeless **9** cheerless, colorless **10** lackluster **11** dispiriting

draconian
5 cruel, harsh, rigid **6** severe, strict **7** callous **8** ironclad, rigorous, ruthless **9** merciless, stringent **10** inflexible, ironfisted, ironhanded

Dracula author
6 Stoker (Bram)

draft
3 tap **4** dose, haul, plan, plot, pull, pump, swig **5** check, claim, drink, frame, press, swill **6** breeze, call up, demand, design, devise, enlist, enroll, induct, potion, scheme, select, siphon, sketch **7** compose, concoct, current, outline, portion, prepare, project, recruit **8** block out, contrive, rough out, skeleton, traction **9** adumbrate, allowance, blueprint, conscribe, conscript, fabricate, formulate, muster out **11** delineation, skeletonize
avoider: 6 dodger
of a law: 4 bill

drag
3 lug, tow, tug **4** bore, haul, puff, pull, swig **5** dally, delay, draft, shlep, tarry, trail **6** burden, dawdle, harrow, loiter, schlep, search, sledge **7** schlepp **8** friction, straggle **9** lag behind **13** procrastinate

dragging
4 beat, long **5** all in, spent, weary **6** pooped **7** drained, lengthy, tedious **8** drawn-out,

extended, fatigued, overlong, sluggish, wiped out **9** exhausted, lethargic, long-drawn, pooped out, prolonged, washed-out, wearisome **10** protracted, slow-moving **12** interminable, long-drawn-out

draggle
3 lag **4** rove **5** stray, trail **8** straggle, trail off **10** fall behind

draggle-tail
4 bawd, drab, slut **5** wench, whore **6** harlot **8** slattern **10** prostitute **11** nightwalker **12** streetwalker

draggletailed
6 blowsy, frowsy, frowzy, sordid, untidy **8** slattern, sluttish **10** slatternly

dragnet
4 trap **5** snare, trawl **7** network

drag off
4 cart, haul

dragon
5 beast **8** basilisk **10** cockatrice
biblical: 5 Rahab
Canaanite: 3 Yam **4** Yamm **5** Lotan
Chinese: 4 lung
French: 8 Tarasque
genus: 5 Draco
Greek: 5 Ladon **9** Eurythion
slayer: 4 Baal, Enki, Zeus **5** Indra **6** Cadmus, George (St.), Marduk, Sigurd **7** Beowulf, Jupiter, Michael (St.), Ninurta, Perseus **8** Margaret (St.)
Sumerian: 3 Kur
Wagnerian: 6 Fafnir

dragoon
3 cow **5** bully **6** badger, coerce, harass, hector **8** bludgeon, browbeat, bulldoze, bullyrag, threaten **9** persecute, strong-arm, terrorize **10** cavalryman, intimidate

drain
3 dry, sap, tap **4** pump, sink, sump, swig, tire, vent, wear **5** bleed, draft, drink, empty, leech, sewer, swill, use up, weary **6** burden, gutter, siphon, trench **7** conduit, culvert, deplete, dwindle, draw off, exhaust, fatigue, outflow **8** bankrupt, draw down, wear down **9** discharge **10** impoverish **11** watercourse

drain away
3 ebb **4** drop, sink, wane **5** abate **6** lessen, reduce, remove **7** draw off, dwindle, retreat, subside **8** decrease, diminish, draw back, taper off, withdraw

drained
4 beat **5** all-in, spent, weary **6** bleary, pooped, used up **7** far-gone, worn-out **8** depleted, dragging, weakened, wiped out **9** exhausted, pooped out, washed-out

drainpipe
4 duct **5** sewer, spout **7** conduit **9** downspout

dram
3 bit, dab, nip, tot **4** atom, dash, drop, iota, jolt, mite, shot, slug, spot, swig, whit **5** crumb, grain, ounce, pinch, scrap, shred, snort, speck **6** morsel, sliver **7** modicum, smidgen, snifter, snippet, soupçon **8** particle

drama
4 play **7** pageant, theater, theatre, tragedy
award: 4 Tony
former English: 6 masque
Japanese: 3 Noh
main part: 8 epitasis
musical: 5 opera **8** operetta, zarzuela
suspenseful: 11 cliff-hanger

dramatic
5 vivid **8** striking, thespian **10** histrionic, theatrical
conflict: 4 agon

dramatis personae
4 cast **5** parts, roles **6** actors, troupe **7** company **10** characters

dramatist
10 playwright
American: 4 Hart (Moss), Inge (William), Rabe (David), Rice (Elmer), Uhry (Alfred) **5** Albee (Edward), Barry (Philip), Foote (Horton), Guare (John), Hecht (Ben), Mamet (David), Odets (Clifford), Parks (Suzan-Lori), Payne (John Howard), Simon (Neil) **6** Ferber (Edna), Gurney (A. R.), Henley (Beth), Miller (Arthur), Norman (Marsha), O'Neill (Eugene), Thomas (Augustus), Wilder (Thornton), Wilson (August, Lanford, Robert) **7** Hellman (Lillian), Kaufman (George S.), Kushner (Tony), Shanley (John Patrick), Shepard (Sam) **8** Anderson (Maxwell, Robert), Caldwell (Erskine), Connolly (Marc), Sherwood (Robert), Williams (Tennessee) **9** Chayefsky (Paddy), Fierstein (Harvey), Hansberry (Lorraine) **11** Hammerstein (Oscar), Wasserstein (Wendy)
Austrian: 10 Schnitzler (Arthur)
Belgian: 11 Maeterlinck (Maurice)
Czech: 5 Havel (Vaclav)
English: 3 Fry (Christopher), Gay (John) **4** Gray (Simon), Hare (David), Rowe (Nicholas), Tate (Nahum) **5** Frayn (Michael), Milne (A. A.), Orton (Joe), Peele (George), Wilde (Oscar) **6** Barrie (James), Coward (Nöel), Dryden (John), Jonson (Ben), Pinero (Arthur Wing), Pinter (Harold), Steele (Richard), Storey (David) **7** Bennett (Alan), Delaney (Shelagh), Marlowe (Christopher), Marston (John), Osborne (John), Shaffer (Anthony, Peter), Webster (John) **8** Congreve (William), Rattigan (Terrence), Shadwell (Thomas), Stoppard (Tom), Tourneur (Cyril), Vanbrugh (John), Zangwill (Israel) **9** Ayckbourn

(Alan), Churchill (Caryl), Goldsmith (Oliver), Middleton (Thomas), Wycherley (William) **11** Shakespeare (William)
French: **5** Camus (Albert), Genet (Jean) **6** Musset (Alfred de), Racine (Jean), Sardou (Victorien), Sartre (Jean-Paul), Scribe (Eugène) **7** Anouilh (Jean), Ionesco (Eugène), Labiche (Eugène), Molière, Rostand (Edmond) **8** Marivaux (Pierre) **9** Corneille (Pierre), Crébillon, Giraudoux (Jean) **12** Beaumarchais (P. A. Caron de)
German: **5** Weiss (Peter) **6** Brecht (Bertolt), Goethe (Johann Wolfgang von), Kleist (Heinrich von) **8** Schiller (Friedrich von) **9** Hauptmann (Gerhart), Zuckmayer (Carl)
Greek: **8** Menander **9** Aeschylus, Euripides, Sophocles **12** Aristophanes
Hindu: **8** Kalidasa
Irish: **4** Shaw (George Bernard) **5** Behan (Brendan), Friel (Brian), Synge (John Millington), Yeats (William Butler) **6** O'Casey (Sean) **7** Beckett (Samuel), Gregory (Lady Augusta) **8** Sheridan (Richard Brinsley)
Italian: **5** Gozzi (Carlo), Verga (Giovanni) **7** Alfieri (Vittorio), Ariosto (Ludovico), Giacosa (Giuseppe), Goldoni (Carlo) **8** Trissino (Gian Giorgio) **9** D'Annunzio (Gabriele) **10** Metastasio (Pietro), Pirandello (Luigi)
Japanese: **5** Zeami
Nigerian: **7** Soyinka (Wole)
Norwegian: **5** Ibsen (Henrik) **8** Bjornson (Bjornstjerne)
Roman: **6** Seneca **7** Plautus, Terence
Romanian: **7** Ionesco (Eugene)
Russian: **7** Chekhov (Anton) **8** Zamyatin (Yevgeny)
South African: **6** Fugard (Athol)
Spanish: **4** Vega (Lope de) **5** Lorca (Federico García) **7** Alberti (Rafael), Arrabal (Fernando) **8** Quintero (Serafín, Joaquín) **9** Benavente (Jacinto) **11** García Lorca (Federico), Valle-Inclán (R. M. del)
Swedish: **5** Sachs (Nelly) **10** Strindberg (August)
Swiss: **6** Frisch (Max)

drape
4 fold, hang, roll **5** adorn, array, cloak, cover **6** clothe, enfold, enwrap, swathe, wrap up **7** curtain, swaddle **8** enswathe, envelope, swathe in

drapery
7 curtain, hanging **8** curtains, hangings

drastic
4 dire **5** harsh **6** severe **7** extreme, radical **9** desperate **10** exorbitant

drat
4 damn, dang, darn **6** phooey, shucks **7** doggone

draw
3 gut, tie, tow, tug **4** etch, haul, limn, lure, puff, pull, pump **5** draft, drain, infer, judge, trace **6** allure, appeal, deduce, depict, derive, elicit, entice, extend, gather, indite, inhale, pencil, siphon, sketch **7** attract, deplete, exhaust, extract, outline, portray, prolong, spin out, win over **8** conclude, contract, convince, dead heat, deadlock, lengthen, protract, standoff **9** delineate, formulate, represent, stalemate **10** allurement, attraction, disembowel, eviscerate, exenterate
forth: **5** educe **6** elicit **7** extract
from: **4** milk, pump **5** bleed
together: **3** tie **4** join, lace

draw back
4 duck **5** cower, quail, wince **6** blench, cringe, flinch, recoil, shrink **7** back off, retreat, take off **9** turn aside

drawback
4 flaw, snag **5** fault, hitch **6** defect, refund **7** failing, trouble **8** weakness **9** detriment, hindrance **10** deficiency, difficulty, impediment **11** shortcoming **12** disadvantage

draw down
4 milk **5** drain, spend, use up **6** expend, reduce **7** deplete, exhaust **8** decrease, diminish **9** reduction, siphon off

drawer
9 draftsman
for money: **4** till

drawers
5 pants **6** undies **8** knickers, trousers **10** underpants

draw in
6 enmesh, entice, induce, prompt **7** involve, retract, win over **8** convince, persuade, pull back **9** prevail on **11** bring around, prevail upon

drawing
6 doodle, sketch **7** cartoon, outline

drawing power
4 lure, pull **6** allure, appeal **9** magnetism **10** attraction

drawn
4 taut, worn **6** peaked **7** fraught, haggard, pinched **8** careworn, fatigued, pictured, strained, stressed **9** attracted **10** delineated

drawn-out
4 long **7** lengthy, tedious **8** extended, overlong **9** prolonged **10** protracted

draw off
3 tap **4** pump **5** bleed, draft, drain **6** siphon

draw out
6 extend **7** prolong, stretch **8** elongate, lengthen, protract

draw up
4 balk, halt, lift, make, stop **5** array, draft, frame, order, raise, write **6** deploy, map out **7** compose, concoct, dispose, marshal, prepare, set down **8** organize, write out **9** formulate

dray
4 cart, drag **5** wagon **6** barrow, sledge **7** travois **9** stoneboat

dread
4 fear **5** alarm, panic **6** dismay, fright, horror, phobia, terror **7** anxiety **10** foreboding **11** trepidation **12** apprehension **13** consternation

dreadful
4 dire **5** awful **6** tragic **7** awesome, extreme, fearful, ghastly, heinous, hideous, ominous **8** alarming, horrible, horrific, shocking, terrible **9** appalling, frightful, revolting **11** distressing, frightening

dreadnought
10 battleship

dream
4 ache, long, wish **5** crave, fancy, ideal **6** aspire, bubble, desire, hanker, vision **7** chimera, fantasy, imagine, rainbow, reverie, specter, spectre **8** ambition, delusion, illusion, phantasm, phantasy **9** fantasize, nightmare **10** aspiration
divination by: **11** oneiromancy
god: **8** Morpheus
sleep: **3** REM

dreamer
7 utopian **8** idealist **9** visionary **10** Don Quixote, lotus-eater **13** castle-builder

dreamlike
5 ideal, vague **6** unreal **7** shadowy, surreal **8** fanciful, illusory, nebulous **9** imaginary, visionary **12** otherworldly

Dream of Gerontius composer
5 Elgar (Edward)

dream up
5 frame, hatch **6** cook up, create, devise, invent **7** concoct, imagine **8** conceive, contrive, envisage, envision **9** formulate, visualize

dreamy
7 pensive **9** unworldly, visionary **10** idealistic **11** impractical **12** otherworldly

dreary
4 blah, drab, dull **5** bleak **6** boring, dismal, gloomy, somber, sombre **7** forlorn, humdrum, joyless, tedious **8** banausic, tiresome, wretched **9** cheerless **10** depressing, depressive, monotonous, oppressive, pedestrian **11** dispiriting

dreck
3 mud **4** junk, muck, slop **5** offal, swill, trash, waste **6** litter, refuse, sewage **7** garbage, rubbish **9** sweepings

dredge
3 dig **5** barge, scoop **6** deepen, dig out, gather **8** excavate, scoop out **9** hollow out, scrape out

dregs
4 lees, scum **5** trash **6** grouts **7** deposit, grounds, remains, residue **8** sediment **9** settlings **11** precipitate

drei
5 three

dreidel
3 top

Dreiser, Theodore
character: **5** Clyde (Griffiths) **6** Carrie (Meeber), Eugene (Witla), Sondra (Finchley) **7** Roberta (Alden) **9** Hurstwood (George) **10** Cowperwood (Frank)
novel: **5** Stoic (The), Titan (The) **6** Genius (The) **9** Financier (The) **12** Sister Carrie **14** Jennie Gerhardt **15** American Tragedy (An)

drench
3 sop **4** dunk, soak **5** douse, souse, steep, swill **6** deluge, seethe **7** immerse **8** inundate, saturate, submerge, waterlog

dress
3 gut **4** bind, clad, deck, doll, duds, garb, gown, sack, togs **5** adorn, align, A-line, array, frock, getup, guise, habit, smock, weeds **6** attire, bedeck, caftan, clothe, dirndl, enrobe, outfit, sacque **7** apparel, bandage, bedizen, chemise, clothes, costume, garment, garnish, raiment, threads, turnout, uniform **8** beautify, clothing, covering, decorate, ensemble, ornament, wardrobe **9** embellish, make ready **11** habiliments
a wound: **7** bandage
designer: **4** Dior (Christian), Erté, Head (Edith) **5** Blass (Bill), Bohan (Marc), Karan (Donna), Klein (Calvin), Prada (Miuccia), Pucci (Emilio), Quant (Mary), Worth (Charles Frederick) **6** Armani (Giorgio), Cardin (Pierre), Jacobs (Marc), Lauren (Ralph), Miyake (Issey), Poiret (Paul) **7** Balmain (Pierre), Cassini (Oleg), Halston, Lacroix (Christian), Mizrahi (Isaac), Versace (Gianni) **8** Galliano (John), Givenchy (Hubert) **9** Courrèges (André), de la Renta (Oscar), Gernreich (Rudi), Lagerfeld (Karl), St.-Laurent (Yves), Valentino **10** Balenciaga (Cristóbal) **12** Saint-Laurent (Yves), Schiaparelli (Elsa)
line: **3** hem
mode of: **5** habit
ordinary: **5** mufti
oriental: **9** cheongsam
part: **5** skirt **6** bodice
South Seas: **6** sarong

dress down
5 chide, scold **6** berate, rail at, rebuke, revile **7** bawl out, reprove, tell off, upbraid **8** admonish,

chastise, reproach **9** castigate, reprimand **10** tongue-lash

dresser
5 chest **6** bureau **7** commode, highboy **10** chiffonier
gaudy: 9 butterfly

dressing
5 sauce **6** catsup **7** bandage, catchup, ketchup **8** stuffing
salad: 5 ranch **6** French **7** Italian, Russian **10** blue cheese **11** vinaigrette **12** green goddess

dressing room
6 vestry **8** vestiary

dressmaker
7 modiste **9** couturier **10** couturiere, seamstress

dress up
6 attire, clothe, rig out, tog out **7** apparel, deck out **8** beautify, disguise, prettify, trick out **9** embellish **10** camouflage

dressy
4 chic **5** showy, smart **6** classy, formal, frilly, ornate **7** duded up, elegant, stylish **9** rigged out

Dreyfus's defender
4 Zola (Emile) **6** Proust (Marcel)

dribble
4 drip, leak, weep **5** drool **6** bounce, drivel, slaver **7** distill, drizzle, slobber, trickle **8** salivate, sprinkle

driblet
4 drop **6** gobbet **7** globule, smidgen **8** particle, pittance

dried grape
6 raisin

dried meat
5 jerky

dried plum
5 prune

drift
3 bat, gad **4** flow, flux, gist, roam, sail, skim, tide, waft, wash **5** amble, coast, creep, float, mosey, range, slide, stray, trend **6** bummel, linger, ramble, stream, stroll, wander **7** current, maunder, meander, meaning, saunter **8** movement, penchant, sideslip, tendency **9** deviation **10** propensity **11** disposition, inclination, progression **12** predilection

drifter
3 bum, vag **4** hobo **5** gypsy, nomad, tramp **7** floater, migrant, vagrant **8** derelict, vagabond **9** transient **11** beachcomber **12** rolling stone

drill
3 bit, dig **4** bore **5** auger, borer, punch, train **6** pierce, trepan, wimble **7** routine, wildcat, workout **8** exercise, practice, practise, rehearse **9** penetrate, rehearsal **10** discipline
command: 6 at ease **8** left face **9** about face, attention, right face

drink
3 ade, lap, nip, sea, sip, tea **4** belt, brew, chug, deep, down, grog, gulp, soak, swig, tope, toss **5** booze, draft, drain, ocean, quaff, slurp, snort, swill, toast **6** absorb, brandy, cassis, cognac, embibe, guzzle, imbibe, jigger, liquid, liquor, pledge, potion, tank up, tipple, tisane **7** consume, potable, schnaps, spirits, swallow, swizzle, toss off **8** aperitif, beverage, libation, liquor up, schnapps **9** aqua vitae
after-dinner: 6 frappé **7** cordial, liqueur
drugged: 6 Mickey **10** Mickey Finn
honey: 4 mead
hot: 5 negus, toddy
liquor: 5 booze, hooch **6** red-eye **9** firewater, moonshine
mixed: 3 kir, nog **5** julep **6** Gibson, gimlet, mai tai, mimosa, mojito, rickey, Rob Roy, zombie **7** gin fizz, martini, sidecar, stinger **8** daiquiri, pink lady **9** alexander, Cuba libre, manhattan, margarita, mint julep, rusty nail **10** Bloody Mary, piña colada, Tom Collins **11** gin and tonic, grasshopper, screwdriver, whiskey sour **12** black Russian, old-fashioned
mixer: 7 swirler
noisily: 5 slurp
of liquor: 4 dram, shot, slug **5** snort **6** bracer **8** highball
of the gods: 6 nectar
soft: 3 pop **4** cola, soda **5** tonic **7** soda pop **8** root beer **9** ginger ale **12** sarsaparilla
stimulating: 6 bracer
Vedic ritual: 4 soma
(see also **beverage**)

drinkable
6 liquor **7** potable **8** beverage, libation, potation

drinking
8 potation
fountain: 7 bubbler
glass: 6 rummer **7** tumbler
horn: 6 rhyton
spree: 3 jag **4** tear, toot **5** binge, spree **6** bender **7** carouse **8** carousal

drip
4 leak, plop, weep **7** dribble, droplet, trickle **8** sprinkle

dripping
3 wet **5** runny, soppy **6** soaked, soused **7** drizzly, soaking, sopping **8** drenched **9** saturated **11** wringing-wet

drippy
5 mushy, rainy, sappy, sobby, soppy, soupy,

teary, weepy **6** slushy, syrupy **7** drizzly, maudlin, mawkish, soaking, sopping, tearful **9** schmaltzy **11** sentimental

drive
3 pep, ram **4** goad, herd, push, spur, taxi, trip, urge **5** chase, force, guide, impel, jaunt, lunge, motor, moxie, oomph, pilot, pound, spunk, steer, surge, vigor **6** compel, convey, exhort, hammer, outing, plunge, propel, strike, thrust **7** actuate, impetus, operate, produce **8** ambition, mobilize, momentum, navigate, shepherd, vitality **9** chauffeur, excursion, urge along **10** enterprise, get-up-and-go, initiative, motivation
away: **4** shoo **5** exile

drive away
see **expel**

drivel
3 rot **4** bosh, bunk **5** drool, hokum, hooey, prate **6** babble, bunkum, gabble, jabber, slaver **7** baloney, blabber, blather, dribble, hogwash, prattle, rubbish, slobber, twaddle **8** claptrap, flimflam, nonsense, salivate **9** gibberish, poppycock **10** balderdash, double-talk, flapdoodle **12** blatherskite, gobbledygook

driver
4 hack, jehu **5** cabby **6** cabbie, cabman, hackie, mallet **7** hackman **8** coachman, motorist, muleteer, operator **9** chauffeur, dowitcher **10** taskmaster **11** tamping iron
of an elephant: **6** mahout
Roman: **10** charioteer
truck: **8** teamster

driving
7 dynamic, powered **8** forceful, vigorous **9** energetic, inspiring **10** compelling

drizzle
4 mist, rain **7** dribble, spatter **8** droplets, sprinkle **10** sprinkling **13** precipitation

Dr. Jekyll and Mr. ____
4 Hyde

droll
3 odd **5** comic, funny, nutty, witty **7** comical, risible **8** farcical, humorous **9** eccentric, laughable, ludicrous, whimsical

drollery
5 humor **6** comedy, joking, whimsy **7** jesting

dromedary
5 camel

drone
3 bee, hum **4** buzz, idle, laze, loaf, loll **5** idler **6** drudge, loiter, lounge, murmur, worker **7** bagpipe **8** aircraft, parasite **9** bombinate **10** pedal point

drool
4 gush, rave **5** froth **6** dote on, drivel, saliva, slaver **7** blather, dribble, enthuse, slobber **8** salivate **10** rhapsodize

droop
3 sag **4** fall, flag, hang, loll, sink, swag, wilt **5** slump **6** dangle, slouch, weaken **7** decline, let down, subside **8** languish

droopy
4 blue, down, limp, weak **5** baggy **6** gloomy **7** doleful, languid, sagging, slouchy, wilting **8** cast down, dejected, downcast **9** depressed **10** dispirited **11** downhearted

drop
3 dip, nip, sag, tot **4** down, drib, dump, fall, fell, jilt, jolt, lose, omit, slip, slug, tear **5** cease, depth, lapse, lower, pitch, plump, scrub, slide, snort, speck, spend **6** cancel, cave in, demise, depart, expire, fumble, give up, go down, ground, plunge, reduce, smitch, topple, unload, vanish **7** abandon, decease, decline, deposit, descend, descent, distill, dribble, driblet, fall off, forfeit, give out, globule, pendant, plummet, trickle **8** bowl over, break off, collapse, comedown, downturn, keel over, nose-dive **9** declivity, discharge, downslide, downswing, downtrend, prostrate, reduction, terminate **10** depository

drop by
4 call **5** pop in, visit **6** stop in **8** come over

droplet
4 bead, drib, tear **7** globule

drop off
3 nap, sag **4** doze, fall, slip **5** slide, slump **6** catnap, drowse, lessen, snooze **7** decline, deliver, deposit, slacken **8** diminish, fall away, hand over **10** fall asleep

dropsical
5 puffy, tumid **6** turgid **7** swollen **8** inflated **9** edematous, tumescent

dropsy
5 edema **8** anasarca

dross
4 junk, scum, slag **5** dregs, offal, waste **6** debris, scoria **7** remains, residue, schlock **8** detritus, impurity, leavings

drossy
4 base **6** impure, scummy **7** trivial **8** inferior, unworthy **9** worthless

drought
4 lack, need, want **6** dearth **7** aridity, dryness **8** scarcity, shortage **10** deficiency

droughty
3 dry **4** arid, sere **7** bone-dry, dried up, parched, thirsty **10** desiccated

drove
3 mob **4** army, herd, host, mass, pack **5** crowd,

flock, horde, troop **6** myriad, pushed, school, throng **7** phalanx **9** multitude

drover
6 cowboy **8** shepherd

drown
4 sink, soak **5** douse, flood, souse, swamp **6** deluge, drench, engulf **7** immerse, repress, smother **8** inundate, submerge **9** overpower, overwhelm, suffocate **10** asphyxiate, extinguish

drowse
3 nod **4** doze **5** sleep **6** catnap, snooze **7** doze off, drop off, shut-eye, slumber **10** forty winks

drowsy
4 dozy **5** dopey **6** droopy, sleepy, torpid **7** languid **8** indolent, sluggish **9** lethargic, somnolent, soporific **10** slumberous **13** lackadaisical

Dr. Seuss
6 Geisel (Theodor Seuss)
book: **11** Cat in the Hat (The) **15** Green Eggs and Ham, Yertle the Turtle **19** Horton Hatches the Egg **26** How the Grinch Stole Christmas

drub
3 tan, wax, zap **4** bash, beat, club, deck, drum, flay, flog, lash, lick, mash, maul, pelt, trim, whip **5** baste, cream, crush, paste, pound, score, slash, smash, smear, spank, stamp, thump, wreck **6** batter, berate, bruise, buffet, deface, hammer, master, pummel, punish, revile, scorch, thrash, thresh, wallop **7** belabor, blister, censure, clobber, cripple, lambast, scourge, shatter, shellac, trounce **8** bulldoze, lambaste, lash into, outclass, outshine **9** castigate, excoriate, overwhelm

drubbing
4 loss, rout **6** defeat **7** setback **10** defeasance **11** shellacking

drudge
4 grub, hack, moil, peon, plod, slog **5** grind, slave **6** menial, slavey **7** grubber, plodder **8** dogsbody

drudgery
4 moil, toil **5** chore, grind **7** travail **9** grunt work **10** donkeywork **11** backbreaker

drudging
6 boring, tiring **7** irksome, tedious **8** dragging, tiresome **9** fatiguing, laborious, wearisome **10** monotonous

drug
4 dope, lull **5** sulfa **6** downer, ipecac, opiate, physic, poison, potion, remedy, statin **7** fen-phen, generic, stupefy **8** biologic, medicine, narcotic, nepenthe, relaxant, sedative **9** ibuprofen, medicinal, methadone **10** antibiotic, medicament, medication **11** thalidomide
addict: **6** junkie
agent: **4** narc
calming: **8** sedative
experience: **4** trip
illicit: **3** ice, kif, LSD, pot **4** acid, coke, dope, hash, meth, scag, snow, weed **5** crack, grass, opium, smack, speed **6** heroin, peyote **7** cocaine, crystal, hashish **8** cannabis, goofball **9** mescaline **10** methadrine, psilocybin
seller: **10** pharmacist
sleep-inducing: **8** hypnotic **9** soporific **11** barbiturate

drugged
4 high **5** dazed, doped, dopey **6** flying, loaded, stoned, zonked **8** benumbed, hopped-up, turned on **9** spaced-out, stupefied **10** narcotized

druggist
7 chemist **10** apothecary, pharmacist

drugstore
8 pharmacy **10** apothecary

druid
4 Celt **6** priest **7** prophet
sacred object: **3** oak **9** mistletoe

drum
3 keg, vat **4** beat, cask **5** conga, naker, tabor, thrum **6** barrel, tom-tom, tympan **7** tambour, timpani (plural), tympani (plural) **8** cylinder, timbales (plural)
Indian: **5** tabla **8** mridanga
Irish: **7** bodhran
large: **4** bass
small: **5** bongo, tabor **7** timbrel
string: **5** snare

drumbeat
4 flam, roll, tuck **6** ruffle, tattoo **7** booming, pit-a-pat, rat-a-tat **8** rataplan

drumfire
5 salvo **6** volley **7** barrage, booming **9** broadside, cannonade, fusillade **11** bombardment

drumhead
4 skin **7** summary

drummer
4 Rich (Buddy) **5** Krupa (Gene), Roach (Max), Starr (Ringo), Watts (Charlie) **6** Blakey (Art), hawker, Puente (Tito), vendor **7** peddler **8** pitchman, salesman

drum up
6 invent **7** canvass, solicit **9** originate
interest: **4** plug, tout **8** ballyhoo

drunk
3 lit, sot **4** lush, soak, wino **5** dipso, lit up, oiled, souse, tight, tipsy **6** blotto, boozer, juiced, soused, stewed, stinko, tiddly, wasted, zonked **7** crocked, guzzler, pie-eyed, sloshed, smashed, squiffy, tippler, tosspot **8** squiffed **9** inebriate, plastered **10** boozehound, inebriated **11** intoxicated

drunkard
3 sot **4** lush, soak, wino **5** dipso, rummy, souse, stiff, toper **6** bibber, boozer, soaker **7** guzzler, swiller, tippler, tosspot **9** alcoholic, inebriate, juicehead **10** boozehound **11** dipsomaniac

Drusilla
brother: **8** Caligula
father: **5** Herod **10** Germanicus
husband: **5** Felix
mother: **9** Agrippina
sister: **8** Berenice **9** Agrippina

dry
3 set **4** arid, brut, dull, sere, sour, tart **5** baked, dusty, parch, stale, wizen **6** barren, desert, harden, stolid, thirst, wither **7** congeal, deadpan, parched, Saharan, shrivel, sterile, thirsty **8** rainless, solidify, tearless, teetotal, withered **9** anhydrous, dehydrate, desiccate, evaporate, unwatered **10** dehydrated, desiccated **11** unemotional **12** matter-of-fact **13** uninteresting
combining form: **3** xer **4** xero
goods: **6** linens, napery **8** clothing, textiles
out: **5** sober **8** soberize
period: **7** drought
wine: **3** sec **4** brut

dryasdust
4 arid, dull **5** banal, inane, vapid **6** boring, stodgy **7** insipid, prosaic, tedious **9** wearisome **10** uninspired **13** uninteresting

dry measure
4 peck, pint **5** quart **6** bushel

Dryope
form: **5** lotus
husband: **9** Andraemon
sister: **4** Iole

dry up
4 wilt **5** wizen **6** wither **7** deplete, exhaust, mummify, shrivel **9** desiccate, disappear, evaporate

dual
3 two **4** twin **5** duple **6** bifold, binary, double, duplex, paired **7** coupled, matched, twofold **8** matching **9** duplicate

dualistic
5 duple **6** bifold, binary, double, duplex, paired **7** twofold **9** Manichean **10** Manichaean

dualize
4 copy, dupe **5** clone **6** double **9** duplicate, replicate, reproduce

dub
4 call, name, term, trim **5** style, title **6** duffer **7** baptize, bungler, entitle, fumbler **8** christen, nickname, rerecord **9** blunderer, designate **10** denominate

dubiety
5 doubt **7** concern **8** mistrust **9** confusion, suspicion **10** skepticism **11** incertitude, incredulity, uncertainty **12** doubtfulness

dubious
4 iffy **5** fishy **6** unsure **7** suspect, unclear **8** doubtful, hesitant, unlikely **9** equivocal, sceptical, skeptical, uncertain, undecided **10** improbable, unreliable **11** mistrustful, problematic, questioning, unconvinced, unpromising **12** questionable, undependable, undetermined

dubitable
5 fishy **7** suspect **8** doubtful, marginal **9** ambiguous, uncertain, unsettled **10** borderline **11** problematic **13** indeterminate

duce
5 ruler **6** despot, leader, tyrant **8** dictator **9** Mussolini (Benito), strongman

duck
3 bob, bow, dip, shy **4** bend, dive, dunk, shun **5** avoid, dodge, douse, elude, evade, fence, parry, shirk, stoop **6** escape, plunge **7** back out, immerse **8** sidestep, submerge, submerse **10** canvasback
Asian: **5** Pekin **8** mandarin
dabbling: **7** gadwall, mallard
diving: **4** smew **7** pochard **9** merganser **10** bufflehead
Eurasian: **4** smew
European: **8** shelduck
genus: **3** Aix **4** Anas
group: **4** team **5** brace, flock, skein **6** flight
hunter's screen: **5** blind
male: **5** drake
red-wattled: **7** Muscovy
river: **4** teal **6** wigeon **7** pintail, widgeon
scaup: **8** bluebill
sea: **5** eider, scaup **6** scoter

duckbill
8 platypus **9** hadrosaur, monotreme

duck soup
4 easy, snap **5** cinch **6** breeze, picnic, simple **8** kid stuff, painless, pushover **10** child's play **11** piece of cake

ducky
4 cute **5** swell **6** lovely, peachy **7** darling **9** hunky-dory **10** peachy-keen

duct
4 flue, pipe, tube **5** canal **6** course, runway **7** channel, conduit **11** watercourse
anatomical: **3** vas **4** vasa (plural)

ductile
6 pliant, supple **7** plastic, pliable **8** flexible, moldable **9** adaptable, compliant, malleable, tractable
metal: **4** wire

ductless gland
see **endocrine gland**

dud
3 dog **4** bomb, bust, flop **5** lemon, loser **6** bummer, misfit, turkey **7** debacle, failure, washout **8** abortion

dude
3 fop, guy **4** beau, buck, rake **5** blood, dandy **6** fellow **7** coxcomb **8** macaroni **9** exquisite **12** Beau Brummell, lounge lizard

dudgeon
3 ire **4** fury, huff, miff, rage **5** anger, pique, wrath **7** chagrin, offense, outrage, umbrage **8** vexation **10** resentment **11** indignation **12** exasperation

duds
3 rig **4** garb, gear, rags, togs **5** dress, getup, weeds **6** attire, things **7** apparel, clothes, raiment, threads, toggery **8** clothing, garments **9** trappings, vestments **11** habiliments

due
4 debt, just, owed **5** lumps, owing **6** direct, earned, lawful, proper, unpaid **7** arrears, condign, deserts, merited, payable, payment, regular **8** adequate, deserved, expected, rightful, suitable **9** deserving, equitable, requisite, scheduled **10** obligatory, receivable, sufficient **11** appropriate, outstanding

duel
4 tilt **5** fight, joust **6** combat **7** contest, dispute **8** conflict **9** smackdown

duenna
8 chaperon **9** chaperone, companion, governess

duet
dancer's: 9 pas de deux

due to
4 over **7** owing to, through **9** because of **11** considering

duff
3 can **4** buns, butt, rear, rump, tail, tush **5** fanny, slack **6** bottom **7** keester, keister, pudding, rear end **8** backside, buttocks, coal dust, derriere **10** leaf litter

duffer
4 boob, clod, dolt, dope, yo-yo **5** chump, dunce, klutz **6** dimwit, dum-dum, lubber, nitwit **7** dullard, fumbler, peddler, pinhead **8** bonehead, dumbbell, lunkhead, numskull **9** blockhead, ignoramus, numbskull, simpleton **10** nincompoop, stumblebum **11** incompetent

dugout
5 canoe **6** trench **7** piragua, pirogue, shelter

duiker
8 antelope

dukedom
5 duchy **6** domain

dulcet
5 sweet **7** melodic, tuneful **8** charming, cheerful, engaging, euphonic, pleasant, pleasing, soothing **9** agreeable, melodious **10** euphonious **11** mellifluous

dulcimer
6 zither **8** psaltery
Hungarian: 8 cimbalom
Persian: 6 santir **7** santour

dull
3 dim, dun, mat **4** arid, blah, blur, drab, flat, numb **5** blunt, dense, dusty, faded, ho-hum, inert, matte, muddy, muted **6** benumb, blurry, boring, deaden, dreary, gloomy, leaden, obtuse, stodgy, stupid **7** blunted, humdrum, insipid, muffled, prosaic, stupefy, subdued, tarnish, tedious **8** banausic, bromidic, deadened, discolor, lifeless, listless, monotone, plodding, sluggish **9** colorless, dim-witted, dryasdust, ponderous, wearisome **10** indistinct, lackluster, lusterless, monotonous, pedestrian **11** commonplace, desensitize, insensitive, thickheaded, thick-witted, unsharpened **12** simpleminded **13** uninteresting

dullard
3 oaf **4** bird, boob, bore, clod, dolt, dope, yo-yo **5** chump, dummy, dunce, idiot, moron, ninny, noddy, stupe **6** dimwit, dum-dum, nitwit **7** airhead, pinhead **8** bonehead, dumbbell, imbecile, lunkhead, meathead, numskull **9** birdbrain, blockhead, ignoramus, lamebrain, numbskull, simpleton **10** dunderhead **11** chowderhead, chucklehead

dullness
5 ennui **6** apathy, stupor, tedium, torpor **7** boredom, languor **8** hebetude, lethargy, monotony **9** bluntness, denseness, lassitude, stupidity, torpidity **12** indifference, listlessness, sluggishness

duly
8 properly, suitably **9** correctly, regularly **12** sufficiently **13** appropriately

duma
7 council **8** assembly, congress **11** legislature

Dumas character
5 Athos **6** Aramis, Dantès (Edmond) **7** Camille, Porthos **9** D'Artagnan

dumb
3 mum **4** dull, mute **5** dense, quiet, thick **6** deaden, obtuse, silent, stupid **7** doltish, foolish, idiotic, moronic **8** ignorant, taciturn, wordless **9** dim-witted, fatheaded, voiceless **10** speechless, tongue-tied **11** blockheaded, thick-witted **12** closemouthed, inarticulate, simple-minded

dumbbell
see **dullard**

dumbfound
5 amaze **6** boggle, puzzle **7** astound, nonplus, perplex, stagger **8** astonish, bewilder, bowl over, confound, distract, surprise **9** take aback **11** flabbergast

dumbfounded
5 agape **6** amazed **7** puzzled, shocked **8** startled **9** astounded, perplexed, staggered, surprised **10** astonished, bewildered, bowled over, confounded, distracted, nonplussed, taken aback **13** thunderstruck

dummkopf
3 oaf **4** boob, clod, dodo, dolt, dope, fool, goof, jerk, mutt, simp, yo-yo **5** chump, dunce, idiot, moron, ninny, noddy, stupe **6** dimwit, donkey, nitwit, noodle **7** airhead, dullard, pinhead, schnook **8** bonehead, clodpoll, dumbbell, dumbhead, imbecile, lunkhead, meathead, numskull **9** birdbrain, blockhead, ignoramus, lamebrain, numbskull, simpleton, thickhead **10** dunderhead, hammerhead, nincompoop **11** chowderhead, chucklehead, knucklehead

dummy
4 boob, clod, dodo, dolt, mock, sham, yo-yo **5** chump, dunce, false, idiot, model, moron, ninny, noddy, stupe **6** dimwit, dum-dum, effigy, ersatz, layout, mock-up, nitwit, puppet, stooge **7** airhead, dullard, manikin, pinhead, stand-in **8** bonehead, dumbbell, imbecile, lunkhead, mannekin, meathead, numskull **9** birdbrain, blockhead, ignoramus, imitation, lamebrain, numbskull, simpleton, simulated **10** artificial, dunderhead, fictitious, nincompoop, substitute **11** chowderhead, chucklehead

dump
4 drop, junk **5** chuck, depot, ditch, scrap **6** armory, midden, pigpen, pigsty, plunge **7** abandon, arsenal, deep-six, discard **8** jettison, landfill, magazine, throw out **9** stockpile, throw away **10** depository

dumpling
5 dough **8** quenelle **10** butterball

dumps
4 funk **5** blues, dolor, gloom, mopes, slump **7** sadness **8** doldrums **9** dejection **10** depression, gloominess, melancholy **11** despondency, unhappiness

dumpy
5 dingy, seedy, squat, stout **6** chubby, chunky, shabby, slummy, stocky, stubby, stumpy **7** rundown **8** heavyset, thickset **9** shapeless

dun
3 dim, fly **4** dull, drab, gray **5** annoy, brown, dusky, horse, murky, press **6** demand, gloomy, mayfly, needle, pester, plague, somber, sombre **9** ephemerid, importune

Duncan's slayer
7 Macbeth

dunce
3 oaf **4** boob, clod, dodo, dolt, dope, goof, mutt, simp, yo-yo **5** booby, chump, dummy, idiot, moron, ninny, noddy, stupe **6** dimwit, donkey, duffer, dum-dum, nitwit, noodle, stupid **7** airhead, dullard, fathead, pinhead **8** bonehead, clodpoll, dumbbell, imbecile, lunkhead, meathead, numskull **9** birdbrain, blockhead, ignoramus, lamebrain, numbskull, simpleton **10** dunderhead, hammerhead, nincompoop **11** chowderhead, chucklehead, knucklehead

Dunciad author
4 Pope (Alexander)

dundrearies
9 burnsides, sideburns **11** muttonchops **12** sidewhiskers

dune
8 sandbank
area: **3** erg **5** beach, shore **6** desert

dung
4 muck **6** manure, ordure **9** excrement
beetle: **6** scarab **9** tumblebug

dungeon
4 jail **5** vault **6** prison **9** black hole, oubliette

dunghill
6 midden

dunk
3 dip, sop **4** soak **5** douse, drown, souse **6** drench **7** immerse **8** saturate, submerge, submerse

dunlin
9 sandpiper

duo
4 dyad, pair **5** brace **6** couple **7** doublet, twosome

dupe
3 con, kid, sap **4** butt, fool, gull, hoax, mark **5** cheat, chump, cozen, patsy, spoof, trick **6** befool, delude, double, outwit, pigeon, sucker **7** chicane, deceive, defraud, mislead **8** flimflam, hoodwink **9** bamboozle, victimize **11** double-cross, hornswoggle

dupery
3 con **4** scam, sham **5** cheat, fraud **6** deceit, humbug, hustle **7** chicane **8** cheating, flimflam, trickery **9** chicanery, deception, duplicity, imposture, swindling **10** dishonesty, hanky-panky **11** hoodwinking **13** double-dealing, sharp practice

duple
4 dual, twin **6** bifold, binary, double, paired **7** coupled, doubled, twofold **9** dualistic

duplex
see **duple**

duplicate
4 copy, fake, mate, redo, same, twin **5** clone, ditto, equal, match, mimeo, repro, Xerox **6** carbon, double **7** dualize, imitate, replica **8** knock-off **9** companion, facsimile, identical, imitation, look-alike, photocopy, replicate, reproduce **10** carbon copy, dead ringer, equivalent, reciprocal **11** counterfeit, counterpart, replication **12** reproduction

duplicitous
5 phony **6** shifty, sneaky **7** devious **8** delusive, guileful, scheming, sneaking, two-faced **9** deceitful, deceiving, deceptive, dishonest, underhand **10** fraudulent **11** underhanded **12** disingenuous **13** double-dealing

duplicity
5 fraud, guile **6** deceit **7** cunning, perfidy **8** scheming, trickery **9** chicanery, deception, treachery **10** dishonesty, doubleness **11** skulduggery **12** dissemblance, skullduggery **13** dissimulation, double-dealing

durability
4 wear **8** firmness **9** endurance, longevity, stability **10** permanence

durable
5 stout **6** stable, strong, sturdy **7** lasting **8** enduring **9** permanent, tenacious **10** dependable **11** long-lasting

durance
7 bondage **9** captivity, detention, restraint **11** confinement **12** enthrallment, imprisonment **13** incarceration

duration
3 run **4** term, time **6** extent, period **7** interim **8** interval **11** persistence

duress
5 force **6** menace, threat **8** bullying, coercion, menacing, pressure **9** restraint **10** compulsion, constraint **11** restriction **12** intimidation

during
4 amid **10** throughout

durra
7 sorghum **12** grain sorghum

Durrell work
4 Cleo **7** Justine **9** Balthazar **10** Mountolive **17** Alexandria Quartet

durum
5 wheat

dusk
4 dark **7** evening **8** darkness, eventide, gloaming, twilight **9** nightfall **12** semidarkness

dusky
3 dim **4** dark **5** murky, swart **6** brunet, gloomy, opaque, twilit **7** obscure, shadowy, swarthy **8** funereal, nubilous, overcast, twilight **9** tenebrous **10** caliginous **11** dark-skinned

dust
4 grit, sand, sift, soot **5** ashes, grime **6** powder **8** sprinkle **10** besprinkle, sprinkling

dust-bowl victim
4 Okie

dustup
3 row **4** spat **5** fight, melee, run-in, set-to **6** battle, fracas, hassle, tussle **7** dispute, quarrel, rhubarb, scuffle **8** argument, skirmish **9** bickering, brannigan **10** falling-out **11** altercation

dusty
3 dry **4** arid, dull **5** stale **7** parched, powdery, tedious, unswept

Dutch
7 trouble **8** hot water
African: **9** Afrikaans
ceramics: **5** delft
cheese: **4** Edam **5** Gouda
dog breed: **7** griffon **8** keeshond
painter: **3** Dou (Gerrit, Gerard) **4** Cuyp (Aelbert Jacobsz), Gogh (Vincent van), Hals (Frans) **5** Bosch (Hieronymus), Hooch (Pieter de), Steen (Jan) **6** Rubens (Peter Paul) **7** de Hooch (Pieter), Hobbema (Meindert), van Gogh (Vincent), Vermeer (Jan) **8** Mondrian (Piet), Ruysdael (Jacob van, Salomon van), Terborch (Gerard) **9** de Kooning (Willem), Honthorst (Gerrit van), Rembrandt (van Rijn)
philosopher: **7** Spinoza (Benedict de)
scholar: **7** Erasmus (Desiderius)

Dutch South African
4 Boer

dutiful
7 devoted **8** faithful **9** compliant **10** respectful **13** conscientious

duty
3 job, tax, use **4** levy, onus, role, task, work **5** chare, chore, stint **6** burden, charge, devoir, impost, office, tariff **7** respect, service **8** function **10** allegiance, assessment, assignment, commitment, dedication, obligation

dwarf
4 runt **5** gnome, pygmy, stunt, troll **6** midget, peewee **7** manikin **8** Tom Thumb **9** miniature **10** diminutive, homunculus
in Snow White: **3** Doc **5** Dopey, Happy **6** Grumpy, Sleepy, Sneezy **7** Bashful
Scottish: **7** blastie

dwarfish
5 pygmy, small **6** midget **7** minikin, stunted **8** inferior, pint-size **9** miniature, pint-sized **10** diminutive, undersized

dweeb
4 dork, drip, geek, nerd, wimp, wuss **5** loser **7** nebbish

dwell
3 lie **4** bide, live, stay **5** abide, exist **6** locate, remain, repose, reside, settle **7** hang out

dweller
7 citizen, denizen, settler **8** habitant, occupant, resident **10** inhabitant

dwelling
3 pad **4** casa, digs, home, nest **5** abode, haunt, house **7** address, habitat, lodging **8** domicile, quarters **9** residence **10** brownstone, habitation
American Indian: **4** tipi **5** hogan, tepee **6** pueblo, teepee, wigwam
clergyman's: **5** manse **7** rectory **8** vicarage **9** parsonage
crude: **3** hut **4** camp **5** cabin, hovel, shack **6** cabana, shanty **7** barrack **8** barracks
Eskimo: **5** igloo
grand: **5** manor, manse, villa **6** palace **7** château, mansion
Hindu: **6** ashram
Navajo: **5** hogan
Russian: **5** dacha
small: **3** cot, hut **5** cabin, hovel, shack **6** shanty **7** cottage **8** bungalow

dwindle
3 ebb **4** fade, fall, wane **5** abate, taper **6** lessen, recede, reduce, shrink, weaken, wither **7** decline, die away, die down, shrivel, slacken, subside **8** decrease, diminish, taper off **9** attenuate, drain away

dyad
3 duo, two **4** pair, yoke **5** brace, twins **6** couple **7** doublet, twosome

dye
4 tint **5** color, stain, tinge **7** pigment **8** colorant, pyronine, tincture
blue: **4** woad **6** indigo **7** cyanine
plant: **4** woad **5** sumac **6** madder
red: **5** eosin, henna **6** kermes, ruddle **7** cudbear, fuchsin, magenta **8** alizarin, fuchsine, amaranth, safranin **9** cochineal, rhodamine, safranine **10** erythrosin
violet: **6** archil
yellow: **7** flavine **8** orpiment
yellowish red: **7** annatto

dyed-in-the-wool
5 loyal, sworn **7** devoted, die-hard, old-line, settled, staunch **8** faithful, hard-core, orthodox, standpat, true-blue **9** confirmed, hard-shell, steadfast **10** deep-rooted, deep-seated, entrenched, inveterate, unwavering **11** established **13** bred-in-the-bone, thoroughgoing

dyewood
6 fustic **10** brazilwood

dying
6 demise **7** done for, quietus **8** moribund **9** departure **10** extinction, in extremis **12** annihilation

dynamic
7 driving, intense **8** forceful, forcible, powerful, vigorous **9** energetic, strenuous **10** compelling, energizing

dynamite
4 raze **5** blast **6** blow up **7** destroy, explode, shatter **8** demolish **9** explosive **10** annihilate
inventor: **5** Nobel (Alfred)

dynamo
8 go-getter, live wire **9** generator **10** ball of fire **11** self-starter

dynasty
Chinese: **3** Han, Qin, Sui **4** Hsia, Ming, Qing, Sung, Tang
Mongol: **4** Yuan

Dynasty series
character: **3** Ben, Dex **4** Adam, Dana **5** Blake, Sable **6** Alexis, Amanda, Fallon, Leslie, Monica, Steven **7** Claudia, Jeffery, Krystie **8** Samantha **9** Dominique
family: **5** Colby **10** Carrington
setting: **6** Denver
spin-off: **6** Colbys (The)
star: **5** Evans (Linda), James (John), Nader (Michael), Samms (Emma) **6** Corley (Al), Garber (Terri), Hunley (Leann), Martin (Pamela Sue) **7** Beacham (Stephanie), Carroll (Diahann), Cellini (Karen), Coleman (Jack), Collins (Joan), Thomson (Gordon) **8** Bellwood (Pamela), Cazenove (Christopher), Forsythe (John), Locklear (Heather), Oxenberg (Catherine), Scoggins (Tracy)

dysentery
4 flux **6** scours **8** diarrhea

dyslogistic
7 adverse **10** derogatory, pejorative **11** deleterious, disparaging, prejudicial, unfavorable

dyspepsia
5 gloom **6** dismay **7** chagrin, pyrosis **8** glumness **9** dejection, heartburn **10** gloominess **11** frustration, indigestion

dyspeptic
5 cross, surly **6** crabby, morose, ornery **9** irritable **10** ill-humored, ill-natured **11** disgruntled, ill-tempered

dysphoria
4 funk **5** blues, dumps, gloom, mopes **6** sorrow **7** sadness **9** dejection **10** depression, gloominess, melancholy **11** unhappiness **12** mournfulness, wretchedness **13** cheerlessness

dysprosium symbol
2 Dy

E

each
3 all, per **4** a pop **5** every **6** apiece **8** everyone **9** per capita, everybody

eager
4 avid, keen **5** antsy, hyper, itchy, ready **6** ardent, fervid, gung ho, intent, raring **7** anxious, athirst, earnest, fervent, restive **8** appetent, aspiring, desirous, restless, yearning **9** ambitious, hankering, impatient **10** breathless **12** enthusiastic

eagerness
4 urge, zeal, zest, zing **5** ardor, gusto **6** desire, fervor, spirit, thirst **7** avidity, craving, itching, longing **8** alacrity, ambition, appetite, fervency **9** intensity **10** enthusiasm, impatience

eagle
4 hawk **9** accipiter
nest: **4** aery **5** aerie, eyrie
North American: **4** bald **6** golden
sea: **3** ern **4** erne **6** osprey

eagle-eyed
8 vigilant, watchful **9** attentive, observant **10** perceptive **12** sharp-sighted

ear
6 notice **7** auricle **9** attention
bone: **5** anvil, incus **6** hammer, stapes **7** malleus, stirrup
canal: **5** scala
combining form: **3** aur, oto **4** auri, otic
doctor: **9** otologist
inner: **9** labyrinth
middle: **8** tympanum
outer: **5** pinna
part: **4** drum, lobe **5** canal **6** tragus **7** cochlea
relating to: **5** aural **9** auricular
science: **7** otology

eardrum
8 tympanum

____ Earhart
6 Amelia

earl
4 lord, peer **5** count, noble **8** nobleman, seigneur **9** patrician **10** aristocrat

earlier
3 ere, yet **4** once **5** as yet, so far **6** before, sooner **7** already, thus far **8** formerly, hitherto, previous **9** erstwhile, preceding **10** beforehand, heretofore, previously

earlier than
3 pre **6** before
Latin: **4** ante

earliest
5 first, prime **6** maiden, primal **7** initial, pioneer, primary **8** original, primeval, pristine **10** aboriginal, primordial

earlike projection
3 lug

early
3 old **5** first, prior **6** primal, timely **7** ancient, betimes **8** original, previous, primeval, pristine, untimely **9** preceding, premature, primitive **10** antecedent, antiquated, precocious, primordial **11** prematurely
prefix: **5** paleo

earn
3 bag, get, net, win **4** gain, make, rate, reap **5** amass, clear, gross, merit, score **6** attain, come by, obtain, pick up, rack up, secure, wangle **7** acquire, bring in, collect, deserve, harvest, procure, produce, realize, receive **8** pull down **9** bring home, knock down

earnest
3 vow **4** bond, busy, firm, keen, pawn, true, warm **5** grave, sober, token **6** active, ardent, intent, pledge, solemn, somber, surety **7** deposit, genuine, intense, serious, sincere, up front, warrant, zealous **8** contract, covenant, diligent, interest, security, sedulous, studious **9** assiduous, heartfelt **10** determined, no-nonsense, passionate, sobersided, thoughtful, unaffected **11** industrious **12** enthusiastic, wholehearted

earnestly
5 madly **7** for real, like mad

earnings
3 net, pay **4** gain **5** lucre, wages **6** EBITDA, income, profit, return, salary **7** profits **8** proceeds, take-home **9** emolument **10** bottom line

earring type
4 cuff, hook, hoop, stud **5** huggy, slave **6** clip-on, dangle **7** barbell, stick-on

ear shell
see **abalone**

earshot
5 range, sound **7** hearing

earsplitting
4 loud **6** shrill **7** blaring, grating, raucous, roaring **8** piercing, strident **9** deafening, dissonant **10** screeching, stentorian **11** fullmouthed

earth
3 orb, sod **4** dirt, land, soil, turf **5** globe, world **6** ground, planet, sphere **7** dry land, terrain **8** creation **10** terra firma
brick: **4** pisé **5** tapia
combining form: **3** geo **4** geog **6** tellur **7** telluro
core: **12** centrosphere
crust: **4** sial, sima **11** lithosphere
god: **3** Geb, Keb, Seb **5** Dagan
goddess: **4** Erda, Gaea **5** Ceres, Nintu **6** Kishar **7** Demeter, Nerthus
pigment: **5** ocher, ochre, umber **6** sienna
relating to: **8** telluric **11** terrestrial
satellite: **4** moon
science: **7** geology **9** geography

earthenware
4 clay **5** china, delft **7** biscuit, faience, pottery **8** clayware, crockery, majolica **9** porcelain, stoneware **10** terra-cotta

earthlike
11 terrestrial

earthling
6 Terran

earthly
6 mortal **7** mundane, worldly **8** material, physical, temporal **9** corporeal **11** terrestrial

earthquake
5 shake, shock **6** tremor **7** temblor
measuring device: **11** seismograph, seismometer
relating to: **7** seismic
science: **10** seismology **11** seismometry

earthwork
4 bank, berm, wall **7** bulwark, rampart **10** embankment **13** fortification

earthworm
7 annelid **12** night crawler

earthy
3 low **4** base, real **5** crude, dirty, dusty, gross, muddy, ocher, ochre, sandy **6** clayey, coarse, common, simple **7** mundane, worldly **8** temporal **9** corporeal, inelegant, practical, pragmatic, realistic, unrefined **10** hard-boiled, hardheaded, indelicate, uncultured, unpolished **11** terrestrial **12** matter-of-fact

earwax
7 cerumen

ease
3 aid **4** bate, calm, dull, free, help, rest **5** allay, loose, peace, poise, relax, slack **6** assist, deaden, loosen, relief, repose, soften **7** assuage, comfort, fluency, improve, leisure, lighten, mollify, relieve, slacken **8** calmness, deftness, diminish, dispatch, facility, idleness, mitigate, moderate, pleasure, serenity **9** abundance, affluence, alleviate, expertise, reduction, untighten, well-being **10** ameliorate, efficiency, facilitate, inactivity, moderation, prosperity, relaxation, smoothness **11** alleviation, contentment, nonchalance, spontaneity
off: **3** ebb **4** bate, fade, fall, flag, wane **5** abate, let up, loose, relax, slack **6** lessen, loosen, relent, unbend, unwind **7** die away, die down, slacken, subside **8** diminish, loosen up, moderate **9** untighten

easel
4 desk **5** frame, stand **7** support **9** workbench, worktable

easement
6 relief **7** comfort **10** mitigation, palliative **11** alleviation, consolation, restorative **13** mollification

easily
6 simply **7** handily, lightly, readily **8** facilely, smoothly **11** dexterously, efficiently **12** effortlessly

East
4 Asia **6** Levant, Orient

Easter
5 Pasch
relating to: **7** paschal
symbol: **3** egg **4** lamb, lily **5** bunny **6** rabbit

Easter Island
7 Rapa Nui

eastern
8 oriental **9** Levantine
countries: **6** Orient
European: **4** Slav

East Indies
country: **8** Malaysia **9** Indonesia, Singapore
plant: **2** da

East Timor
capital: **4** Dili
neighbor: **9** Indonesia

easy
3 lax **4** calm, cozy, mild, soft, snug **5** basic, clear, comfy, cushy, light, loose, naive, plain **6** facile, fluent, placid, polite, secure, serene, simple, smooth **7** amiable, evident, lenient, obvious, patient, relaxed **8** apparent, composed, familiar, graceful, gullible, informal, obliging, peaceful, pleasant, sociable, tolerant, trusting **9** collected, forgiving, indulgent **10** charitable, effortless, elementary **13** uncomplicated

easygoing
3 lax **4** calm, cool, lazy **5** quiet **6** breezy, casual, dégagé, folksy **7** affable, offhand, patient, relaxed, unfussy **8** amenable, carefree, down home, flexible, indolent, informal, laid-back,

together, tranquil **9** apathetic, indulgent, unhurried **10** nonchalant, permissive, unaffected **11** comfortable, complaisant, low-pressure, pococurante, unconcerned, unflappable **12** devil-may-care, even-tempered, happy-go-lucky

easy mark
3 sap **4** butt, dupe, fool, gull **5** chump, patsy, sport **6** pigeon, softie, sucker, turkey, victim **7** fall guy **8** pushover **9** soft touch **11** sitting duck

eat
3 sup, vex **4** bite, chow, dine, gnaw, meal, nosh, pick, take, wolf **5** erode, feast, gorge, graze, lunch, mouth, munch, scarf, scoff, scour, snack, use up **6** devour, feed on, gobble, ingest, inhale, nibble, pester, pick at, pig out, take in **7** banquet, consume, corrode, gorge on, swallow, torment **8** chow down, dissolve, take food, wear away **9** breakfast, decompose, masticate, partake of, polish off **10** break bread, gormandize, nibble away

eatable
6 edible **8** esculent, harmless **9** palatable **10** comestible, digestible

eatery
4 café **5** diner, grill **10** coffee shop, restaurant **11** greasy spoon **12** luncheonette

eating place
3 pub **4** café, mess **5** diner, grill, joint **6** bistro, tavern **7** automat, beanery, canteen, commons, dinette, tearoom **8** cookshop, messroom, pizzeria, snack bar **9** brasserie, cafeteria, chophouse, hash house, lunchroom, trattoria **10** coffee shop, restaurant, steak house **11** greasy spoon **12** luncheonette

eavesdrop
3 bug, tap **4** lurk **5** snoop **7** monitor **8** listen in, overhear

ebb
4 drop, fade, fall, flag, tide, wane **5** abate, droop, let up **6** lessen, recede, reduce, relent, shrink, wither **7** decline, descent, die away, die down, ease off, retreat, slacken, subside **8** decrease, diminish, languish, moderate, withdraw **10** retrograde

Eblis
5 Satan
son: **3** Tir **4** Awar **5** Dasim **8** Zalambur

ebon, ebony
3 jet **4** inky **5** black, jetty, raven, sable **6** brunet **8** brunette, jet-black **9** pitch-dark **10** pitch-black

ebullience
3 vim, zip **4** brio, élan, zing **5** gusto **6** gaiety **7** abandon, elation **8** buoyancy, vitality, vivacity **9** animation **10** enthusiasm, exuberance, liveliness **11** high spirits **13** effervescence

ebullient
5 brash, zingy, zippy **6** bouncy, bubbly, elated, frothy, geeked, pumped, raring **7** boiling, excited, gleeful, gushing, vibrant **8** hopped-up **9** sprightly, vivacious **11** exhilarated **12** enthusiastic, high-spirited **13** irrepressible

eccentric
3 odd, nut **4** coot, kook **5** crank, crazy, droll, flaky, freak, funky, funny, goofy, kooky, nutty, outré, queer, wacky, weird **6** far out, oddity, quaint, quirky, screwy, weirdo, whacko, whacky **7** bizarre, deviant, erratic, heretic, oddball, offbeat, strange, unusual **8** aberrant, abnormal, bohemian, cockeyed, crackpot, goofball, maverick, peculiar, singular, uncommon **9** anomalous, character, deviating, fantastic, fruitcake, grotesque, irregular, off-center, screwball, whimsical **10** elliptical, off-balance, unbalanced, uncentered **11** exceptional **13** idiosyncratic, nonconformist

eccentricity
4 kink **5** quirk, twist **8** crotchet, quiddity **9** deviation, weirdness **10** aberration **11** strangeness **12** idiosyncrasy

ecclesiastic
see **clergyman**

ecclesiastical
4 holy **5** papal **6** church, sacred **8** churchly, clerical, pastoral, priestly **9** apostolic, canonical, episcopal, spiritual, synagogal **10** churchlike, pontifical, rabbinical, sacerdotal **11** ministerial, patriarchal, theological **12** episcopalian, evangelistic, tabernacular

ecdysiast
see **stripteaser**

echelon
3 row **4** file, line, rank, tier **5** grade, group, level, order, queue **6** string **7** chevron **9** formation

echidna
8 anteater **9** monotreme **13** spiny anteater

Echidna
father: **7** Phorcys **8** Chrysaor
mother: **4** Ceto **10** Callirrhoë
offspring: **5** Hydra **6** dragon, Orthus, Sphinx **7** Chimera **8** Cerberus, Chimaera

echinoderm
6 urchin **7** crinoid, sea star **8** starfish **9** coelomate, sea urchin **11** sea cucumber

echo
3 ape **4** mime, ring **5** evoke, mimic, trace **6** mirror, parrot, repeat, result, reverb, second **7** imitate, iterate, reflect, resound, revoice, vestige **8** resonate, response **9** duplicate, imitation, reiterate **10** reflection, repetition **11** reverberate **12** repercussion **13** reverberation

Echo
5 nymph, oread
beloved: **9** Narcissus

echoic
7 mimetic **9** imitative **10** derivative **12** onomatopoeic **13** onomatopoetic

éclat
4 bang, dash, fame, pomp **5** glory, honor, kudos **6** luster, lustre, praise, renown, repute **7** acclaim, display, laurels, stardom, success **8** applause, eminence, prestige, standing **9** celebrity, notoriety, publicity **10** brilliance, brilliancy, exaltation, prominence, reputation **11** distinction, ostentation

eclectic
5 broad, fussy, mixed, picky **6** choosy, select, varied **7** diverse, finicky, mingled **8** assorted, catholic, elective **9** inclusive, selective **10** discerning, fastidious, particular **11** diversified **12** dilettantish, multifarious **13** heterogeneous

eclipse
3 dim **5** bedim, cloud, cover, excel, outdo, shade **6** darken, exceed, shadow **7** becloud, decline, obscure, surpass **8** downfall, outshine **9** adumbrate, obfuscate, overcloud **10** extinguish, overshadow
phenomenon: **5** umbra **6** corona, shadow **7** annulus **8** penumbra **11** Diamond Ring **12** Bailey's Beads

eclogue
3 ode **4** idyl, poem **5** idyll, lyric **8** pastoral

ecological
5 green **8** bionomic
community: **5** biome

ecology
9 bionomics **11** environment

economic
6 fiscal **8** material, monetary **9** budgetary, financial, pecuniary **10** mercantile, profitable
doctrine: **12** laissez-faire
system: **9** communism, socialism **10** capitalism **11** syndicalism **12** mercantilism

economical
4 mean **5** canny, close, spare, tight **6** frugal, saving, stingy **7** careful, miserly, prudent, sparing, thrifty **8** skimping **9** efficient, niggardly, penny-wise, penurious, provident, scrimping **10** unwasteful **12** cheeseparing, parsimonious **13** penny-pinching

economist
American: **5** Arrow (Kenneth), Simon (Herbert, Julian), Solow (Robert), Tobin (James) **6** Becker (Gary), George (Henry), Thurow (Lester), Veblen (Thorstein), Walker (Amasa), Weaver (Robert) **7** Krugman (Paul), Kuznets (Simon), Stigler (George), Volcker (Paul) **8** Friedman (Milton), Stiglitz (Joseph) **9** Galbraith (John Kenneth), Greenspan (Alan), Samuelson (Paul) **10** Schumpeter (Joseph)
Austrian: **5** Hayek (Friedrich von), Mises (Ludwig von)
Canadian: **7** Leacock (Stephen)
Dutch: **9** Tinbergen (Jan)
English: **3** Sen (Amartya) **4** Mill (John Stuart) **5** Coase (Ronald), Hayek (Friedrich von), Pigou (Arthur) **6** Engels (Friedrich), Keynes (John Maynard) **7** Bagehot (Walter), Malthus (Thomas), Ricardo (David)
French: **3** Say (Jean-Baptiste) **6** Monnet (Jean), Turgot (Anne-Robert-Jacques), Walras (Léon) **7** Quesnay (François)
German: **4** Marx (Karl) **5** Weber (Max) **6** Engels (Friedrich) **7** Schacht (Hjalmar)
Indian: **3** Sen (Amartya)
Scottish: **4** Mill (James) **5** Smith (Adam)
Swedish: **6** Myrdal (Gunnar)
Swiss: **8** Sismondi (Simonde de)

economize
4 save **5** skimp, stint **6** manage, scrimp **7** husband **8** conserve **10** cut corners **12** pinch pennies

economy
6 saving, thrift **8** prudence, skimping **9** concision, frugality, husbandry, parsimony, restraint, scrimping **10** discretion, efficiency, providence, stinginess **11** carefulness, conciseness, miserliness, thriftiness **13** niggardliness

Eco novel
9 Baudolino **13** Name of the Rose (The) **17** Foucault's Pendulum

ecru
see **beige**

ecstasy
3 joy **5** bliss **6** frenzy, heaven, trance **7** delight, elation, madness, rapture **8** euphoria, paradise, rhapsody **9** beatitude, transport **10** exaltation, joyfulness **11** blessedness, derangement, enchantment, high spirits, inspiration **12** blissfulness, exhilaration, intoxication **13** seventh heaven

ecstatic
6 elated, joyful **7** gleeful **8** euphoric, exultant, jubilant, thrilled **9** delirious, delighted, entranced, overjoyed, rapturous, rhapsodic **11** exhilarated, transported

ectothermic
11 cold-blooded

Ecuador
capital: **5** Quito
city: **6** Ambato, Cuenca **7** Machala **9** Guayaquil
Indian people: **7** Quechua
island group: **9** Galápagos
language: **7** Spanish
monetary unit: **5** sucre

mountain range: **5** Andes
neighbor: **4** Peru **8** Colombia
volcano: **6** Sangay **7** Cayambe **8** Cotopaxi **10** Chimborazo

ecumenical
6 cosmic, global **7** general, generic **8** catholic **9** inclusive, planetary, universal, worldwide **12** all-inclusive, cosmopolitan **13** comprehensive

ecumenical council
4 Lyon **5** Basel, Lyons, Trent **6** Nicene **7** Ephesus, Ferrara, Lateran, Vatican **8** Florence **9** Chalcedon, Constance

eczema
6 tetter

edacious
see **voracious**

eddy
4 purl **5** swirl, twirl, whirl, whorl **6** vortex **8** backwash **9** backwater, maelstrom, whirlpool **11** counterflow

edema
5 croup, tumor **6** dropsy **8** anasarca, swelling
treatment: **8** diuretic

Eden
6 heaven, utopia **7** arcadia, elysium **8** paradise
river: **5** Gihon **6** Pishon **8** Hiddekel **9** Euphrates

edentate
5 sloth **8** aardvark, anteater, pangolin **9** armadillo, toothless

Edessa's king
5 Abgar

edge
3 cut, end, hem, lip, rim **4** bank, bite, brim, cusp, draw, ease, hone, inch, lead, limb, line, pink, side, whet, worm **5** arris, bound, brink, bulge, force, ledge, picot, point, ridge, sidle, skirt, sting, strop, verge **6** border, fringe, margin, nosing **7** acidity, contour, chamfer, outline, serrate, sharpen, vantage **8** acerbity, acridity, boundary, emborder, handicap, keenness, surround, thinness **9** acuteness, advantage, extremity, harshness, head start, perimeter, periphery, sharpness, threshold, upper hand **10** causticity, shrillness, stringency **11** astringency **12** incisiveness **13** effectiveness

edge city
5 exurb **6** suburb

edged
4 acid, tart **5** acerb, acute, sharp **6** barbed, strong **7** acerbic, cutting **8** incisive, piercing

edge in
6 inject **9** interject, interpose, insinuate **10** infiltrate **11** interpolate

edging
3 hem **4** lace **5** braid, frill, limit **6** border, fringe, lacing, margin, piping **7** flounce, selvage **8** rickrack, selvedge, trimming

edgy
3 hip **5** funky, nervy, sharp, tense, testy, wired **6** daring, touchy, uneasy **7** excited, keyed up, offbeat, restive, uptight **8** Bohemian, out-there, renegade, restless, skittery, skittish, volatile **9** excitable, impatient, irascible, irritable **10** high-strung, outlandish **11** provocative

edible
8 esculent **9** palatable **10** comestible
root: **3** oca, yam **4** beet, taro, yuca **6** carrot, daikon, ginger, jicama, potato, radish, turnip, wasabi **7** burdock, cassava, ginseng, malanga, parsnip, salsify **8** celeriac, galangal, kohlrabi, rutabaga **11** horseradish, sweet potato
seed: **3** nut, pea **4** bean **6** peanut

edibles
4 chow, eats, feed, food, grub **6** viands **7** aliment, goodies, nurture **8** victuals **9** provender **10** provisions, sustenance **11** comestibles

edict
3 law **4** bull, fiat, rule **5** canon, order, ukase **6** decree, dictum, ruling **7** command, dictate, mandate, precept, statute **9** directive, manifesto, ordinance, prescript **10** injunction, regulation **12** proclamation **13** pronouncement
Islamic: **5** fatwa
papal: **4** bull **8** decretal

Edict of ___
5 Milan, Worms **6** Nantes

edifice
4 pile **8** building, erection **9** structure

edify
5 teach **6** better, fill in, illume, inform, update, uplift **7** educate, elevate, enhance, improve **8** illumine, instruct **9** elucidate, enlighten **10** illuminate

edit
3 cut **4** cull, omit **5** adapt, alter, amend, emend, fix up **6** delete, doctor, excise, polish, redact, refine, review, revise, reword, select **7** abridge, compile, correct, rewrite **8** annotate, assemble, condense, copyread, fine-tune **9** proofread, rearrange **10** blue-pencil, bowdlerize

editing term
4 dele, stet **5** caret **7** jump cut

edition
4 copy, form **5** issue, print **7** reissue, reprint, version **8** printing, variorum **10** impression, reprinting **12** reproduction

editor
8 redactor **9** scrivener, wordsmith **10** copyreader **11** proofreader

Edmonton player
5 Oiler

Edomite's ancestor
4 Esau

educate
4 rear 5 brief, coach, drill, edify, nurse, teach, train, tutor 6 inform, school 7 explain, nurture 8 instruct 9 brainwash, enlighten 10 discipline 12 indoctrinate

education
7 culture, tuition 8 breeding, coaching, guidance, learning, literacy, pedagogy, teaching, training, tutelage, tutorage, tutoring 9 erudition, knowledge, schooling, tutorship 11 instruction, learnedness, scholarship 13 enlightenment

educational
11 informative, instructive 13 informational, instructional
institution: 6 school 7 academy, college 10 university 12 conservatory

educator
5 tutor 7 teacher 9 professor 10 instructor
American: 4 Mann (Horace) 5 Dewey (John) 6 Butler (Nicholas Murray), Conant (James Bryant), Harris (William Torrey) 7 Barnard (Henry), Beecher (Catharine), Peabody (Elizabeth) 8 Hutchins (Robert Maynard), McGuffey (William) 10 Washington (Booker T.)
Czech: 8 Comenius (John Amos)
English: 6 Arnold (Thomas) 7 Spencer (Herbert)
German: 7 Froebel (Friedrich), Herbart (Johann)
Italian: 10 Montessori (Maria)
Swiss: 10 Pestalozzi (Johann Heinrich)

educe
4 drag, draw, milk, pull 5 evoke, wrest, wring 6 derive, elicit, evince, evolve, extort, obtain, secure 7 distill, draw out, extract, procure 8 bring out 10 excogitate

eel
5 moray, siren 6 conger 7 hagfish, lamprey, sniggle
young: 5 elver

eelpout
6 blenny, burbot 10 muttonfish

eely
5 slimy 6 slippy, wiggly 7 elusive, wriggly 8 slippery, slithery 9 wriggling

eerie
5 scary, weird 6 creepy, spooky 7 bizarre, strange, uncanny 8 chilling, spectral 9 fantastic, grotesque, unearthly 10 mysterious 11 frightening, hair-raising 12 otherworldly

efface
4 dele, x out 5 annul, erase 6 cancel, delete, rub out 7 blot out, destroy, expunge, scratch, wipe out 8 black out, wear away 9 eliminate, eradicate, extirpate 10 obliterate

effect
3 end 4 make 5 cause, enact, event, fruit 6 create, draw on, induce, intent, invoke, render, result, upshot 7 achieve, execute, fulfill, outcome, perform, produce, realize, turn out 8 bring off, carry out, conceive, generate 9 actualize, aftermath, discharge, implement, outgrowth 10 accomplish, bring about, conclusion, denouement 11 consequence 12 carry through, ramification, repercussion

effective
4 able 5 sound, valid 6 causal, cogent, direct, potent, useful 7 capable, operant 8 adequate 9 competent, operative 10 compelling, convincing, productive

effectiveness
5 clout, force, point, power, vigor 6 weight 7 cogency, potency 8 strength, validity 10 capability

effects
4 gear 5 goods, stuff 6 things 8 chattels, movables, property 9 equipment, moveables, trappings 10 belongings 11 impedimenta, possessions 13 accoutrements

effectual
5 sound, valid 6 potent, strong, useful 7 capable 8 decisive, powerful, workable 10 conclusive, fulfilling, productive 11 influential, practicable 13 authoritative, determinative

effectuate
see **effect**

effeminate
5 sissy 6 swishy 7 epicene 9 sissified 10 old-maidish

effervescence
5 giddy 7 fizzing, foaming, sparkle 8 bubbling, buoyancy, vivacity 9 animation 10 ebullience, ebullition, exuberance, exuberancy, liveliness 12 exhilaration

effervescent
3 gay 4 airy 5 jolly 6 bouncy, bubbly, lively 7 boiling, buoyant, excited 8 animated, mirthful, volatile 9 sparkling, sprightly, vivacious 10 carbonated 12 high-spirited 13 irrepressible

effete
4 soft, weak 5 frail, spent 6 barren 6 sickly 7 decayed, drained, sterile, worn-out 8 decadent, decaying, delicate, depleted, fatigued, pampered 9 declining, dissolute, enfeebled, exhausted, infertile, washed-out 10 degenerate, unfruitful 11 debilitated

efficacious
6 active, potent, strong 8 forceful, powerful, puissant 9 operative 10 productive 11 influential

efficacy
see **effectiveness**

efficiency
see **effectiveness**

efficient
4 able **5** adept **6** expert **7** capable, elegant, skilled **8** economic, masterly, skillful **9** competent **10** economical, productive

effigy
3 guy **4** icon, idol **5** dummy, image **6** figure **7** waxwork **8** likeness

effloresce
4 blow **5** bloom, burst **6** flower, sprout **7** blossom, burgeon **9** bear fruit

effluvium
3 air **4** odor, reek **5** smell, vapor, waste **6** miasma **7** exhaust **8** effusion, emission **9** byproduct, discharge, emanation **10** exhalation

efflux
see **effluvium**

effort
3 job, try **4** feat, push, task, toil, work **5** chore, essay, force, labor, might, nisus, pains, sweat, while **6** energy, strain **7** attempt, travail, trouble, venture **8** endeavor, exertion, industry, struggle **11** application, elbow grease

effortful
4 hard **6** tiring, uphill **7** arduous, labored, operose **8** exacting, toilsome **9** ambitious, difficult, laborious, strenuous **11** challenging

effortless
4 easy **5** adept, light, ready **6** expert, facile, fluent, simple, smooth **8** masterly, skillful **10** proficient **11** undemanding

effrontery
4 face, gall **5** brass, cheek, nerve **8** audacity, boldness, chutzpah, temerity **9** arrogance, assurance, brashness, hardihood, impudence, insolence **10** brazenness **11** presumption **12** impertinence

effulgence
4 glow **5** blaze, glory **6** luster, lustre **8** radiance, splendor **9** splendour **10** brightness, brilliance, brilliancy, luminosity

effulgent
5 vivid **6** bright, lucent **7** beaming, glowing, lambent, radiant, shining **8** dazzling, glorious, luminous, lustrous, splendid **9** brilliant **11** resplendent **12** incandescent

effuse
4 flow, gush, pour, shed **5** exude, issue **6** stream **7** emanate, enthuse, flow out, radiate

effusive
5 gushy **6** lavish, sloppy, smarmy **7** cloying, fulsome, gushing, profuse, verbose **9** expansive, exuberant **10** loquacious, outpouring, unreserved **11** extravagant **12** enthusiastic, unrestrained **13** demonstrative, unconstrained

eft
4 newt **6** triton **10** salamander

e.g.
3 say **10** for example **11** for instance **13** exempli gratia

egad
6 zounds **7** criminy **8** gadzooks **11** odds bodkins

egg
3 ova (plural) **4** ovum, seed **5** ovule
case: **5** shell **7** ootheca
combining form: **3** ovi, ovo
dish: **6** omelet **8** omelette
fertilized: **6** zygote **7** oospore
fish: **3** roe **6** caviar
French: **4** oeuf
immature: **6** oocyte
louse: **3** nit
part: **4** yolk **5** glair, shell, white
shaped: **5** ovate, ovoid
white: **5** glair **7** albumen

egghead
6 pundit **8** highbrow **10** double-dome **12** intellectual

egg on
4 goad, prod, spur, urge **5** prick, rally **6** arouse, exhort, excite, incite, prompt, stir up **7** agitate **9** instigate, stimulate

eggplant
6 purple **9** aubergine **10** nightshade

egg-shaped
4 oval **5** ovate, ovoid **7** oviform

Eglah
husband: **5** David
son: **7** Ithream

eglantine
7 dog rose **10** sweetbriar, sweetbrier

Eglantine
father: **5** Pepin
husband: **9** Valentine

Eglon
king: **5** Debir
slayer: **4** Ehud

ego
4 self **5** pride **6** vanity **7** conceit **10** self-esteem

egocentric
7 selfish **9** conceited **10** self-loving **11** self-seeking **12** narcissistic, self-absorbed, self-affected, self-centered, self-involved, vainglorious **13** individualist, self-conceited, self-concerned, self-indulgent

egoism
5 pride **6** vanity **7** conceit **8** self-love **9** self-glory, self-pride, vainglory **10** narcissism, self-regard **11** selfishness, self-opinion

egoistic
4 smug, vain **7** selfish **9** conceited **12** self-absorbed, self-centered **13** self-concerned, self-contented, self-satisfied

egomaniacal
12 self-exalting, vainglorious

egotism
5 pride **6** vanity **7** conceit **8** boasting, bragging, self-love, vainness, vaunting **9** arrogance, pomposity, self-glory, self-pride, vainglory **10** narcissism, self-esteem **11** megalomania, self-opinion **12** boastfulness **13** conceitedness

egotistic
4 vain **5** cocky, proud **7** selfish, stuck-up **8** arrogant, boastful, inflated, puffed-up **9** conceited **11** pretentious, self-serving **12** self-absorbed, self-centered, self-involved **13** self-concerned, self-satisfied

egregious
4 rank **5** gross, stark **6** arrant, brazen **7** blatant, glaring, heinous **8** flagrant, infamous, outright, shocking **9** atrocious, notorious, shameless **10** deplorable, outrageous **11** conspicuous

egress, egression
4 door, exit **5** issue, leave **6** depart, escape, exodus, outlet **7** doorway, exiting, opening, passage **9** departure, emergence

egret
5 heron, wader

Egypt
ancient city: **6** Thebes **7** Memphis
capital: **5** Cairo
city: **4** Giza **8** Port Said **10** Alexandria
dam: **5** Aswan
desert: **6** Libyan **7** Arabian, Western
gulf: **4** Suez **5** Aqaba
lake: **6** Nasser
language: **6** Arabic
leader: **5** Sadat (Anwar el-) **6** Nasser (Gamal Abdul) **7** Mubarak (Hosni)
monetary unit: **5** pound
neighbor: **5** Libya, Sudan **6** Israel
oasis: **4** Siwa **6** Dakhla, Kharga **7** Farafra
peninsula: **5** Sinai
river: **4** Nile
sea: **3** Red **13** Mediterranean

Egyptian
burial jar: **7** canopic
Christian: **4** Copt
cross: **4** ankh
dynasty: **5** Saite, Xoite **6** Hyksos, Tanite, Theban **7** Persian, Thinite **8** Memphite **9** Bubastite, Ethiopian **10** Diospolite
flower: **5** lotus
god:
chief: **6** Amen-Ra
crocodile-headed: **5** Sebek
falcon-headed: **4** Ment **5** Horus, Mentu **6** Sokari **7** Sokaris
ibis-headed: **5** Thoth **6** Dhouti
jackal-headed: **6** Anubis
of creation: **4** Ptah **5** Phtha
of day: **5** Horus
of death: **6** Anubis
of earth: **3** Geb, Keb, Seb
of evil: **3** Set **4** Seth **5** Sebek
of life: **4** Amen, Amon **5** Ammon
of magic: **5** Thoth **6** Dhouti
of Memphis: **4** Ptah **5** Phtha **6** Sokari **7** Sokaris
of the heavens: **5** Horus
of the morning sun: **5** Horus **7** Khepera
of the sun: **4** Aten, Aton **6** Amen-Ra
of Thebes: **4** Amen **6** Khensu, Khonsu
of the underworld: **6** Osiris
of war: **4** Ment **5** Mentu
of wisdom: **5** Thoth **6** Dhouti
ram-headed: **4** Amen, Amon **5** Ammon, Khnum **6** Khnemu
snake: **4** Apep **5** Apepi
goddess:
cat-headed: **4** Bast **5** Pakht
cow-headed: **5** Athor **6** Hathor
lioness-headed: **4** Bast **5** Pakht **6** Sekhet
of fertility: **4** Isis
of love and mirth: **5** Athor **6** Hathor
of motherhood: **4** Apet, Isis
of Thebes: **3** Mut
of the heavens: **3** Nut
queen of the gods: **4** Sati
vulture-headed: **3** Mut **7** Nekhebt **8** Nekhebet
king:
(see **king** entry)
language: **6** Arabic, Coptic
native: **4** Arab, Copt **5** Nilot
queen: **9** Cleopatra, Nefertiti
sacred bird: **4** ibis **5** bennu
sacred bull: **4** Apis
solar disk: **4** Aten
sultan: **7** Saladin
symbol of life: **4** ankh
talisman: **6** scarab
underworld: **4** Aaru, Duat **6** Amenti
wind: **7** khamsin, sirocco

eider
4 down, duck **7** sea duck

eidetic
5 exact, vivid **7** perfect, precise **8** absolute, lifelike

eidolon
4 icon **5** ghost, ideal, image, model, shade **6** mirage, vision, wraith **7** epitome, fantasm,

figment, paragon, phantom, specter, spectre **8** exemplar, illusion, paradigm, phantasm **9** archetype, prototype **10** apparition

eight
combining form: **4** octa, octo
group of: **5** octad, octet **6** octave

eight bells
4 noon

eighteen-wheeler
3 rig **4** semi **11** semitrailer

eighth note
6 quaver

eighty-six
4 boot, junk, toss **5** chuck, eject, evict, scrap **6** bounce **7** discard, kick out **8** get rid of, jettison, throw out

Einstein, Albert
birthplace: **3** Ulm
theory: **10** relativity

einsteinium symbol
2 Es

Eire
see **Ireland**

Eisenhower, Dwight
3 Ike
home: **7** Abilene
wife: **5** Mamie

eject
4 boot, bump, dump, fire, oust, sack, spew **5** chuck, evict, expel **6** banish, bounce **7** boot out, cast out, dismiss, kick out **8** disgorge, throw out **9** discharge

eke out
6 extend **7** augment, enhance, fill out, squeeze, stretch **8** increase **10** supplement

elaborate
4 busy **5** fancy, showy **6** daedal, dressy, evolve, expand, knotty, minute, ornate, refine, unfold **7** amplify, build up, careful, clarify, comment, complex, develop, discuss, elegant, enlarge, explain, expound, profuse, work out **8** detailed, involved, overdone, thorough **9** Byzantine, decorated, embellish, extensive, interpret, intricate **10** overworked **11** complicated, embellished, extravagant, painstaking **12** labyrinthine

Elaine
father: **6** Pelles
lover: **8** Lancelot **9** Launcelot
son: **7** Galahad

Elam
capital: **4** Susa **7** Shushan
father: **4** Shem
king: **12** Chedorlaomer

élan
3 pep, vim, zip **4** brio, dash, fire, life, zeal, zest, zing **5** ardor, flair, gusto, oomph, verve, vigor **6** energy, esprit, fervor, spirit **7** impetus **8** vivacity **9** animation, eagerness, intensity **10** enthusiasm

élan vital
4 soul **5** anima **6** animus, pneuma, psyche, spirit

elapse
4 go by, pass **6** expire, run out, slip by **8** pass away

elastic
6 bouncy, limber, pliant, rubber, supple **7** ductile, pliable, rubbery, springy **8** animated, flexible, moldable, stretchy, volatile **9** adaptable, expansive, malleable, resilient **10** extendable, extensible, rubber band, rubberlike **11** stretchable

elate
4 buoy **5** cheer, exalt, flush, set up **6** excite, perk up, uplift **7** cheer up, delight, enliven, gladden, gratify, hearten, inspire, overjoy **8** brighten, embolden, inspirit, spirit up **9** encourage **10** exhilarate, invigorate

elated
4 glad, high **5** happy **7** exalted, excited **8** ecstatic, euphoric, exultant, gladsome, jubilant **9** overjoyed **10** enraptured **11** exhilarated, intoxicated, on cloud nine **12** high-spirited

elation
3 joy **4** glee **7** delight, ecstasy, rapture **8** buoyancy, euphoria **9** happiness, transport **10** exaltation, excitement, jubilation **12** exhilaration, intoxication

Elbe tributary
4 Eger, Iser, Ohre **5** Saale **6** Moldau, Vltava

elbow
4 push **5** joint, nudge, shove **6** hustle, jostle

eld
4 yore **6** old age **8** old times

elder
6 senior **8** old-timer **9** patriarch, presbyter **10** golden-ager

elderliness
3 age **6** dotage, old age **8** caducity **10** senescence **11** senectitude

elderly
3 old **4** aged, gray **5** aging, hoary **7** ancient **9** declining, venerable

eldritch
5 eerie, weird **6** creepy, spooky **7** uncanny

Eleanor's husband
7 Henry II **8** Franklin

elect
3 opt, tap **4** name, pick **5** co-opt, saved **6** choice, choose, chosen, decide, opt for, ordain, picked, vote in **7** resolve, vote for **8** destined, nominate,

ordained, redeemed **9** delivered, designate, determine, exclusive, single out **10** designated, singled out

election
6 ballot, choice, voting **7** primary **8** choosing, decision **9** balloting **10** preference, referendum **11** alternative

electioneer
5 stump **7** canvass **8** campaign, politick **9** barnstorm

elective
6 chosen **8** optional **9** voluntary **11** sympathetic **13** discretionary, noncompulsory, nonobligatory

Electra
brother: 7 Orestes
father: 9 Agamemnon
husband: 7 Pylades
mother: 12 Clytemnestra
sister: 9 Iphigenia
victim: 9 Aegisthus **12** Clytemnestra

electric
appliance: 3 fan **4** iron, oven **5** clock, drier, dryer, mixer, range, stove **6** stereo, washer **7** blender, freezer, toaster **10** dishwasher, television **12** refrigerator
coil: 5 tesla **8** solenoid
device: 4 coil, fuse, plug **6** dynamo, magnet, switch **7** battery **8** resistor, rheostat, varistor **9** amplifier, capacitor, condenser, generator **11** transformer
generator: 6 dynamo
particle: 3 ion
unit: 3 amp, ohm **4** volt, watt **5** farad, henry, joule **6** ampere **7** coulomb, faraday **8** kilowatt

electric current
kind: 2 AC, DC **4** AC/DC **6** direct **11** alternating
power: 7 wattage
strength: 8 amperage

electricity
5 juice, spark **7** current **9** galvanism, lightning
kind: 6 static **7** current

electrify
3 jar **4** jolt, stun **5** amaze, power, shock **6** charge, excite, thrill **7** astound, enthuse, inflame, provoke, stagger, startle **8** astonish, energize

electrode
6 dynode
negative: 7 cathode
positive: 5 anode

electron
3 ion **7** polaron
stream: 10 cathode ray
tube: 6 triode **7** tetrode **8** dynatron, klystron

Electryon
brother: 6 Mestor
daughter: 7 Alcmene
father: 7 Perseus
mother: 9 Andromeda
wife: 5 Anaxo

eleemosynary
6 humane **8** generous **10** altruistic, beneficent, benevolent, charitable, munificent, openhanded **12** humanitarian **13** philanthropic

elegance
4 chic, pomp, tone **5** charm, grace, style, taste **6** luxury, polish **7** culture, dignity **8** chicness, poshness, richness, splendor, urbanity **9** gentility, precision **10** ornateness, refinement **11** cultivation **12** tastefulness

elegant
4 chic, fine, posh **5** fancy, grand, noble, swank **6** choice, classy, dainty, lovely, modish, ornate, swanky, urbane **7** courtly, genteel, opulent, refined, stately, stylish **8** cultured, polished, splendid, tasteful **9** exquisite, luxurious, recherché, sumptuous **10** cultivated **11** fashionable

elegiac
7 pensive **8** dactylic **9** lamenting, sorrowful **10** melancholy

elegy
4 poem, song **5** dirge **6** lament, monody **8** threnody

____ eleison
5 Kyrie

Elektra composer
7 Strauss (Richard)

element
4 item, part **5** basic, facet, piece, point **6** aspect, detail, factor, member, sector **7** article, feature, portion, section **8** division, particle, rudiment **9** component, essential, principle **10** ingredient, particular **11** constituent, fundamental
chemical: 3 tin **4** gold, iron, lead, neon, zinc **5** argon, boron, radon, xenon **6** barium, carbon, cerium, cesium, cobalt, copper, curium, erbium, helium, indium, iodine, nickel, osmium, oxygen, radium, silver, sodium **7** arsenic, bismuth, bohrium, bromine, cadmium, calcium, dubnium, fermium, gallium, hafnium, hassium, holmium, iridium, krypton, lithium, mercury, niobium, rhenium, rhodium, silicon, sulphur, terbium, thorium, thulium, uranium, yttrium **8** actinium, aluminum, antimony, astatine, chlorine, chromium, europium, fluorine, hydrogen, illinium, lutecium, masurium, nitrogen, nobelium, platinum, polonium, rubidium, samarium, scandium, selenium, tantalum, thallium, titanium, tungsten, vanadium

9 americium, berkelium, beryllium, columbium, germanium, lanthanum, magnesium, manganese, neodymium, neptunium, palladium, plutonium, potassium, ruthenium, strontium, tellurium, virginium, ytterbium, zirconium **10** dysprosium, gadolinium, lawrencium, meitnerium, molybdenum, seaborgium **11** californium, einsteinium, mendelevium, phosphorous **12** darmstadtium, praseodymium **13** rutherfordium, protoactinium

elemental
3 key **4** pure **5** basal, basic, crude, prime **6** inborn, innate, primal, simple **7** central, connate, primary, radical **8** cardinal, inherent, integral, intimate, simplest **9** beginning, essential, ingrained, intrinsic, primitive **10** deep-seated, primordial, underlying **11** fundamental **13** uncomplicated

elementary
4 easy **5** basal, basic **6** simple **7** initial **9** beginning, essential, primitive **10** rudimental, underlying **11** fundamental, preliminary, rudimentary **12** introductory

elemi
5 resin **9** oleoresin

elephant
5 Babar **6** Horton, tusker **9** pachyderm
boy: 4 Sabu
driver: 6 mahout
enclosure: 5 kraal
extinct: 7 mammoth **8** mastodon
female: 3 cow
group: 4 herd
keeper: 6 mahout
male: 4 bull
maverick: 5 rogue
nose: 5 trunk **9** proboscis
seat: 6 howdah
sound: 6 bellow **7** trumpet
tooth: 4 tusk
tusk: 5 ivory
young: 4 calf

elephant-headed god
6 Ganesa, Ganesh **7** Ganesha

elephantine
4 huge **6** clumsy **7** awkward, hulking, mammoth, massive **8** colossal, enormous, gigantic **9** graceless, humongous, monstrous, ponderous **10** gargantuan, mastodonic, prodigious, ungraceful **11** heavy-footed

Elephant Man
7 Merrick (Joseph)

elevate
4 lift, rear, rise **5** boost, elate, erect, exalt, hoist, raise **6** buoy up, jack up, lift up, pick up, uplift **7** advance, dignify, ennoble, glorify, hearten, improve, inspire, promote, upgrade **8** heighten **10** exhilarate

elevated
4 high **5** grand, lofty, moral, noble **6** aerial, formal, superb **7** ethical, refined, soaring, stately, sublime **8** eloquent, majestic, virtuous **9** dignified, grandiose, high-flown, honorable, righteous

elevation
4 hill, rise **5** boost **6** ascent, height, uplift **7** advance, raising **8** altitude, mountain **9** acclivity, promotion, upgrading **10** apotheosis, preference, preferment **11** advancement, ennoblement
indication: 9 benchmark

elevator
4 cage, lift, silo **5** hoist
maker: 4 Otis

elf
3 fay, imp **4** peri, puck **5** fairy, gnome, pixie, troll **6** goblin, sprite **7** brownie, gremlin **10** leprechaun

elfin
5 antic **6** frisky, impish **7** implike, playful, puckish **8** pixieish **11** mischievous

Elgin ___
7 Marbles

Eli
4 Yale **5** Yalie

Eli ___
4 Yale **5** Lilly **7** Whitney

Elia
4 Lamb (Charles)

Eliab
brother: 5 David
daughter: 7 Abihail
father: 5 Helon, Pallu
son: 6 Abiram, Dathan

Eliada
father: 5 David
son: 5 Rezon

Eliam's daughter
9 Bathsheba

elicit
5 educe, evoke **6** derive, evince, extort **7** extract, provoke **8** bring out **9** call forth, draw forth

elide
4 fail, omit, skip **6** cut off, excise, forget, ignore, remove, slight **7** abridge, curtail, neglect **8** condense, cross out, discount, overlook, pass over, suppress **9** disregard, strike out

eligible
3 fit **6** fitted, likely, nubile, seemly, suited, worthy **7** capable **8** entitled, suitable **9** desirable,

qualified **10** acceptable **11** appropriate **12** marriageable

Elihu ___
4 Root, Yale

Elijah
5 Elias **7** prophet **8** Tishbite
father: 5 Harim **7** Jeroham

Elimelech's wife
5 Naomi

eliminate
3 bar **4** bate, drop, oust, void **5** debar, egest, eject, erase, evict, expel, purge **6** delete, except, remove **7** abolish, discard, dismiss, exclude, expunge, obviate, rule out, take out **8** count out **9** clear away, eradicate, liquidate **11** exterminate

Eliot, George
lover: 5 Lewes (George Henry)
novel: 6 Romola **8** Adam Bede **11** Middlemarch, Silas Marner **13** Daniel Deronda **14** Mill on the Floss (The)
pseudonym of: 5 Evans (Mary Ann)

Eliot, T. S.
character: 8 Prufrock (J. Alfred)
play: 13 Cocktail Party (The) **20** Murder in the Cathedral
poem: 9 Gerontion, Hollow Men (The), Waste Land (The) **12** Ash Wednesday, Four Quartets

Eliphaz
father: 4 Esau
mother: 4 Adah
son: 5 Teman

Elisabeth
husband: 9 Zacharias
son: 4 John (the Baptist)

Elisha
father: 7 Shaphat
servant: 6 Gehazi

Elisheba
brother: 7 Nahshon
father: 9 Amminadab
husband: 5 Aaron
son: 5 Abihu, Nadab **7** Eleazar, Ithamar

elite
3 top **4** best, pick **5** A-list, cream, elect, pride, prime, prize **6** choice, flower, gentry, select **7** quality, society **9** exclusive, gentility, patrician **10** upper class, upper crust **11** aristocracy **12** aristocratic

elixir
4 balm, cure **6** potion **7** arcanum, cure-all, nostrum, panacea, philter, philtre **10** catholicon

Elizabeth I
6 Oriana **8** Gloriana

elk
4 deer **5** moose **6** sambar, wapiti **7** red deer

ell
3 arm **4** wing **5** annex, elbow, joint **8** addition **9** extension

ellipse
4 oval **5** curve, orbit

elliptical
5 brief, ovate, short **6** gnomic **7** concise, cryptic, laconic, obscure, summary **9** condensed, enigmatic **11** abbreviated

Ellison work
10 Juneteenth **12** Invisible Man

elm
5 wahoo

elocution
7 diction, oratory **8** delivery, rhetoric **11** declamation, speechcraft

elongate
4 draw **6** extend **7** draw out, lengthy, spin out, stretch **8** extended, lengthen **10** lengthened

elope
4 flee **6** escape, run off **7** abscond, run away **9** steal away

eloquence
5 force, power **6** fervor, spirit **7** fluency, oratory, passion **8** rhetoric **10** expression **12** expressivity, forcefulness

eloquent
5 lofty **6** ardent, fervid, fluent, moving **7** fervent, voluble **8** elevated, forceful, powerful, stirring **9** affecting **10** articulate, expressive, impressive, meaningful, passionate, persuasive, rhetorical **11** impassioned, sententious **12** smooth-spoken **13** silver-tongued

El Salvador
capital: 11 San Salvador
city: 8 Santa Ana **9** San Miguel
ethnic group: 5 Pipil
lake: 8 Ilopango
language: 7 Spanish
monetary unit: 5 colón **6** dollar
neighbor: 8 Honduras **9** Guatemala
river: 5 Lempa

else
5 if not **7** besides, further **9** otherwise **10** additional **11** differently **12** additionally

elucidate
7 clarify, clear up, explain, expound **8** annotate, spell out **9** exemplify, explicate, interpret **10** illuminate, illustrate

elude
4 defy, duck, flee, foil **5** avert, avoid, dodge, evade **6** baffle, escape, outwit, thwart **8** confound **9** frustrate **10** circumvent

elusive
6 subtle, tricky **7** evasive, phantom **8** baffling, fleeting, fugitive, slippery **10** evanescent, intangible, mysterious **13** insubstantial

elute
7 extract

elver
3 eel

elvish
see **elfin**

Elysium
5 bliss **6** heaven **7** nirvana **8** empyrean, paradise

elytron
4 wing

emaciated
4 bony, lean, thin **5** gaunt **6** skinny, wasted **7** scrawny, starved, wizened **8** skeletal, underfed **10** cadaverous

emaciation
5 tabes **7** atrophy **8** marasmus **10** starvation **11** attenuation

e-mail abbreviation
3 AKA, BAK, BBL, BRB, BTW, FYI, HTH, IMO, IOW, KIT, LOL, NRN, OBO, POV, PDQ, TIA, UKW **4** ASAP, BCNU, BION, FWIW, GMTA, GTGB, IMHO, TTYL, YMMV

emanate
4 emit, flow, rise, stem **5** arise, exude, issue **6** derive, emerge, spring **7** come out, give off, give out, proceed, radiate **9** come forth, originate **10** derive from

emanation
4 aura, flow **6** efflux **8** effusion, emission **9** effluence

emancipate
4 free **5** let go, loose **6** loosen, redeem, unbind **7** manumit, release, set free, unchain **8** liberate, unfetter **9** discharge, unshackle **11** enfranchise

emancipation
7 release **10** liberation **11** deliverance

emancipator
5 Moses **7** Lincoln (Abraham) **9** deliverer, liberator

emasculate
3 fix **4** geld **5** alter, unman **6** neuter, soften, weaken **7** unnerve **8** castrate, enervate, unstring **10** debilitate, devitalize

embalm
7 mummify, perfume **8** preserve

embankment
4 berm, bund, dike, quay **5** levee, mound **6** escarp

embargo
3 ban, bar **5** edict, order **8** blockade, stoppage **10** impediment **11** prohibition

embark
5 board, enter, start **6** set out **7** set sail **8** commence

embarrass
4 faze **5** abash, upset **6** flurry, hamper, hinder, impede, rattle **7** confuse, flummox, fluster, mortify, nonplus, perturb **8** confound, distress **9** discomfit, humiliate **10** complicate, discomfort, discompose, disconcert

embarrassment
5 shame, upset **7** chagrin **8** distress **9** confusion **10** discomfort **11** humiliation **12** discomfiture, perturbation **13** mortification

embassy
5 envoy **7** mission **8** legation **10** ambassador, delegation, deputation

embay
4 trap **5** catch, seize **7** capture **8** encircle, surround

embed
3 fix, set **4** bury, root **5** infix, inlay, lodge **7** implant, ingrain **8** entrench

embellish
3 pad **4** deck, gild, trim **5** adorn, color **6** bedeck, blazon, emboss, enrich **7** amplify, dress up, enhance, festoon, garnish **8** beautify, decorate, ornament **9** elaborate, embroider **10** exaggerate **11** romanticize

embellishment
7 garnish, gilding, melisma, mordent **8** coloring, ornament **9** fioritura, floridity, hyperbole **10** decoration **11** elaboration **12** embroidering, exaggeration **13** ornamentation

ember
3 ash **4** coal **6** cinder

embezzle
4 loot **5** filch, steal **6** pilfer **7** purloin **8** peculate **9** defalcate

embitter
4 sour **6** poison **7** envenom **9** acidulate

emblazon
4 laud **5** extol **7** glorify **8** inscribe **9** celebrate

emblem
4 arms, flag, logo, mace, seal, sign **5** badge, brand, crest, image, token **6** banner, device, symbol **7** pennant **8** colophon, hallmark, insignia, monogram, standard **9** attribute, trademark **10** coat of arms

emblematic
8 symbolic **10** figurative, indicative **11** allegorical **12** illustrative, metaphorical

embodiment
6 avatar **7** epitome **8** exemplar **9** archetype **11** incarnation **13** manifestation

embody
5 reify **6** evince, mirror, typify **7** compose, contain, exhibit, realize, subsume **8** manifest **9** actualize, encompass, epitomize, exemplify, incarnate, integrate, objectify, personify, represent, symbolize **10** constitute, illustrate **11** emblematize, externalize, hypostatize, incorporate, materialize **12** substantiate

embolden
5 steel **7** fortify, hearten, inspire **8** inspirit **9** encourage **10** strengthen

embolus
4 clog, clot

embosom
3 hug **7** embrace, enclose, envelop, shelter

embouchure
10 mouthpiece

embowel
3 gut **4** draw **10** eviscerate, exenterate

embrace
3 hug **4** hold, lock, love, wrap **5** admit, adopt, clasp, cling, press **6** accept, cradle, cuddle, embody, enfold, fondle, nuzzle, take in, take on, take up **7** bear hug, cherish, contain, embosom, enclose, entwine, envelop, espouse, include, receive, snuggle, squeeze, subsume, welcome **8** comprise, encircle **9** encompass **10** comprehend **11** accommodate, incorporate **12** encirclement

embrangle
see **embroil**

embrocation
5 salve **7** unguent **8** liniment

embroider
3 pad, sew, tat **4** gild **5** color **6** expand, overdo, play up, stitch **7** amplify, build up, enhance, garnish, magnify, stretch **8** decorate, ornament **9** dramatize, elaborate, embellish **10** exaggerate **11** hyperbolize, romanticize

embroidery
6 crewel **7** cutwork, orphrey **8** bargello, couching, smocking, tapestry **10** crewelwork, needlework **11** needlepoint

embroil
4 mire **6** tangle **7** confuse, ensnare, involve **8** disorder, entangle **9** implicate

embroilment
4 tiff **6** fracas **7** dispute, quarrel, wrangle **8** squabble **9** bickering **10** falling-out **11** altercation, controversy

embryo
3 bud **4** germ, seed **5** fetus, spark **7** nucleus **8** blastula, gastrula

emend
4 edit **5** alter, right **6** polish, revise **7** correct, improve, rectify, retouch

emerald
3 gem **5** beryl, green, stone **8** gemstone

Emerald Isle
4 Eire, Erin **7** Ireland

emerge
4 flow, loom, rise, stem **5** arise, issue **6** appear, derive, evolve, spring **7** come out, debouch, develop, emanate, proceed, surface **9** originate, transpire **11** come to light, materialize

emergency
3 fix **4** hole, pass **5** pinch **6** climax, clutch, crisis, crunch, strait **7** squeeze **8** accident, exigency

emeritus
7 retired

Emerson, Ralph Waldo
essay: **12** Self-Reliance
forte: **5** essay
friend: **7** Thoreau (Henry David)
home: **7** Concord

emery
6 powder **8** abrasive, corundum

emetic
8 vomitive **9** cathartic, purgative

émeute
4 riot **6** mutiny, revolt, rising, tumult **8** outbreak, upheaval, uprising **9** rebellion **12** insurrection

emigrant
7 pioneer, settler **8** colonist **10** expatriate

émigré
2 DP **5** alien, exile, expat **7** evacuee, migrant, refugee **8** colonist **10** expatriate

Emilia
husband: **4** Iago **7** Palamon
slayer: **4** Iago

eminence
3 VIP **4** fame, peak, rise **5** honor, power **6** bigwig, esteem, height, leader, renown, repute **7** dignity, notable **8** altitude, big-timer, luminary, prestige, standing **9** authority, dignitary, elevation, greatness, loftiness **10** importance, projection, prominence, promontory, reputation **11** distinction, superiority

eminent
4 high **5** famed, grand, great, large, lofty, noble, noted **6** august, famous **7** exalted, notable **8** esteemed, renowned, towering **9** important, well-known **10** celebrated, noteworthy, projecting **11** conspicuous, illustrious, outstanding, prestigious **13** distinguished

eminently
4 very **6** highly **7** notably **9** extremely **10** remarkably, strikingly **11** exceedingly **12** surpassingly **13** exceptionally

emir
5 chief, ruler, sheik, title **6** sheikh **9** chieftain, commander

emissary
see **envoy**

emission
4 flow **7** venting **9** discharge, effluvium, emanation, radiation

emit
4 beam, glow, ooze, pour, shed, spew, vent, void **5** eject, expel, exude, issue, loose, utter **6** exhale, let out **7** emanate, excrete, extrude, give off, give out, radiate, release, secrete, send out **8** evacuate, throw off **9** circulate, discharge

emmer
5 grain, spelt, wheat

emmet
3 ant **7** pismire

emollient
4 aloe, balm **5** salve **7** lenient, unguent **8** aloe vera, lenitive, liniment, ointment, sedative, soothing **9** analgesic, softening **10** mollifying

emolument
3 fee, pay **4** wage **5** wages **6** income, reward, salary **7** guerdon, stipend **8** earnings **10** recompense **11** pay envelope **12** compensation

emotion
3 ire, joy **4** fear, glee, hate, love **5** agony, ardor, grief, shame **6** affect, hatred, relief, sorrow, warmth **7** ardency, despair, disgust, ecstasy, feeling, passion, sadness **8** jealousy, surprise **9** affection, agitation, happiness, sentiment

emotional
4 warm **6** ardent, fervid, heated, moving **7** feeling, fervent, intense, soulful, zealous **8** effusive, stirring, touching, vehement **9** affecting, affective, excitable, heartfelt, impetuous, rhapsodic, sensitive **10** hysterical, passionate **11** impassioned, overwrought, rhapsodical, softhearted, susceptible, sympathetic

emotionless
3 icy **4** cold, cool **5** chill, staid, stoic, stony **6** frigid, remote, torpid **7** callous, deadpan, distant, glacial **8** detached, reserved **9** apathetic, immovable, impassive, unfeeling **10** impersonal **11** cold-blooded, indifferent **12** matter-of-fact **13** dispassionate, unimpassioned

empathy
4 pity **6** lenity, warmth **7** rapport **8** affinity, sympathy **9** communion **10** compassion **12** congeniality **13** compatibility, comprehension, fellow feeling, understanding

emperor
4 czar, shah, tsar, tzar **5** ruler **6** caesar, kaiser **7** monarch **8** autocrat, dictator **9** potentate, sovereign
French: **8** Napoleon (Bonaparte) **9** Bonaparte (Napoleon) **11** Charlemagne
Indian: **5** Babur
Japanese: **6** mikado **7** Akihito **8** Hirohito
Mexican: **8** Iturbide (Agustín de) **10** Maximilian
Roman: **4** Nero, Otho **5** Galba, Nerva, Titus **6** Decius, Julian, Trajan **7** Gratian, Hadrian, Severus **8** Augustus, Aurelian, Caligula, Claudius, Commodus, Domitian, Honorius, Tiberius, Valerian **9** Antoninus, Caracalla, Justinian, Vespasian, Vitellius **10** Diocletian, Elagabalus **11** Constantine

emphasis
5 focus, force **6** accent, stress, weight **9** attention, intensity **10** insistence, prominence **12** accentuation

emphasize
6 accent, play up, stress **7** feature **8** pinpoint **9** highlight, italicize, spotlight, underline **10** accentuate, underscore

emphatic
4 firm **6** marked **7** decided, earnest, pointed **8** accented, decisive, forceful, positive, stressed, vigorous **9** assertive, energetic, insistent **10** resounding, underlined **11** accentuated

empire
5 realm **6** domain **7** demesne, kingdom **8** dominion
ancient:
(see **ancient empire**)

Empire State
7 New York

empirical
7 factual **9** fact-based, pragmatic **12** experiential, experimental **13** observational

emplacement
7 battery **8** position

employ
3 job, use **4** busy, hire, work **5** apply, avail **6** devote, engage, occupy, retain, secure, take on **7** exploit, utilize **8** exercise, practice **9** make use of **10** occupation

employee
4 hand, help **5** agent **6** worker **7** servant **8** factotum **9** underling
bank: **5** clerk, guard **6** teller
hotel: **7** bellboy, bellhop, doorman **9** concierge, desk clerk **11** chambermaid

employer
4 boss **6** master **10** supervisor

employment
3 job, use **4** line, post, task, toil, work **5** trade, usage **6** hiring, métier, office **7** calling, mission, purpose, pursuit **8** business, exercise, function, position, vocation **9** appliance, operation, situation **10** engagement, occupation **11** application, recruitment, utilization **12** exploitation

emporium
4 mall, mart, shop **5** store **6** bazaar, market **8** exchange **11** marketplace

empower
5 endow **6** charge, enable, invest **7** entitle, entrust, license **8** accredit, delegate, deputize, sanction **9** authorize, privilege **10** commission

empress
5 queen
Byzantine: 3 Zoe
French: 7 Eugénie **9** Josephine
Japanese: 5 Suiko
of India: 8 Victoria
Mexican: 7 Carlota
Roman: 6 Fausta
Russian: 4 Anna **7** czarina, tsarina, tzarina **9** Alexandra, Catherine, Elizabeth

empressement
6 fervor, warmth **10** cordiality

emprise
4 feat, gest **5** geste **7** exploit, venture **9** adventure **11** undertaking

emptiness
4 void **5** blank **6** hunger, vacuum **7** inanity, vacancy, vacuity

emptor
5 buyer **6** vendee **8** consumer, customer **9** purchaser

____ emptor
6 caveat

empty
3 rid **4** bare, dump, pour, vain, void **5** blank, clear, drain **6** barren, devoid, hollow, unload, vacant, vacate **7** deplete, drained, exhaust, vacated, vacuous **8** depleted, deserted, evacuate, forsaken **9** abandoned, destitute **10** unoccupied, untenanted
Scottish: 4 toom

empty-headed
6 simple, vacant **7** vacuous, witless **8** ignorant, untaught **9** benighted, brainless, frivolous **10** illiterate, uneducated, unlettered, unschooled **11** know-nothing **12** uninstructed **13** rattlebrained

empyreal
4 airy, holy **6** aerial, divine **7** sublime **8** beatific, ethereal, heavenly **9** celestial, spiritual, unearthly **12** transcendent

empyrean
3 sky **4** Zion **5** bliss, ether **6** heaven, welkin **7** Elysium, heavens, nirvana **8** paradise **9** firmament

EMT's skill
3 CPR

emu
4 bird, rhea **6** ratite **9** cassowary

emulate
3 ape **4** copy **5** equal, mimic, rival **6** follow, mirror **7** compete, imitate **9** challenge

emulation
7 rivalry **8** striving, tug-of-war **9** imitation **10** contention **11** competition

emulous
5 vying **8** aspiring, striving, vaulting **9** ambitious **11** competitive

emulsifier
4 soap **5** algin

enable
3 fit, let **5** allow, ready **6** permit **7** empower, entitle, license, prepare, qualify **8** accredit, sanction **9** authorize, condition **10** commission, facilitate **12** make possible

enact
4 pass, play **6** decree, depict, effect, ordain, ratify **7** execute, perform, portray **8** proclaim **9** authorize, discourse, establish, institute, legislate, represent **10** accomplish, bring about, constitute, effectuate **11** impersonate

enactment
3 law **6** action, decree **7** statute **9** depiction, ordinance, portrayal **11** legislation, performance **12** ratification

enamel
5 glaze, gloss, japan, paint **7** lacquer

enamored
4 fond **6** loving **7** devoted, smitten **8** besotted **9** bewitched, enchanted, entranced, infatuate **10** captivated, infatuated

encamp
4 tent **6** settle **7** bivouac

encampment
6 billet, laager **7** bivouac, hutment

encase
3 box **4** pack **7** confine, enclose, envelop, sheathe

enceinte
6 gravid **8** pregnant **9** expectant, expecting **10** parturient

enchain
4 bind **6** fetter **7** manacle, shackle

enchant
3 hex **4** lure, wile **5** charm, spell, witch **6** allure, enamor, seduce, thrill, voodoo **7** attract, beguile, bewitch, delight **8** ensorcel, enthrall **9** captivate, enrapture, ensorcell, fascinate, hypnotize, magnetize, mesmerize, spellbind

enchanter
4 mage **5** magus **6** wizard **7** charmer, warlock **8** conjurer, conjuror, magician, sorcerer **11** necromancer, spellbinder

enchanting
5 siren 9 glamorous, seductive 10 attractive, delectable, delightful, intriguing

enchantment
3 hex 5 charm, magic, spell 6 allure 7 glamour, sorcery 8 witchery, wizardry 9 conjuring, seduction 10 necromancy, witchcraft 11 incantation

enchantress
3 hex 5 bruja, Circe, lamia, Medea, siren, witch 9 sorceress

enchiridion
4 text 5 guide 6 manual 8 Baedeker, handbook 9 guidebook, vade mecum

encipher
4 code

encircle
3 hem 4 band, gird, halo, hoop, ring 5 girth 6 begird, engird, enlace, girdle 7 compass, embrace, enclose, environ, wreathe 8 surround 9 encompass 12 circumscribe

enclave
6 colony, ghetto, sector 7 quarter 8 district, homeland

enclose
3 box, hem, mew, pen, rim 4 cage, coop, mure, wall, wrap 5 bound, fence, hedge, limit 6 circle, closet, corral, hold in, immure, shroud, shut in, wall in 7 compass, confine, contain, embosom, include 8 fence off, imprison, surround 9 capsulize 12 circumscribe

enclosed
6 obtect

enclosure
3 box, mew, pen, sty 4 boma, cage, camp, cell, coop, cote, fold, jail, pale, quad, SASE, tank, trap, wall, weir, yard 5 court, fence, kraal, pound, stall 6 aviary, corral, cowpen, kennel, paling, prison 7 chamber, enclave, paddock 8 cloister, stockade 9 courtyard 10 quadrangle

encomiast
7 praiser 8 eulogist 10 panegyrist

encomiastic
9 adulatory, laudative, laudatory 10 eulogistic 11 panegyrical

encomium
4 laud 5 kudos, paean 6 eulogy, homage, praise 7 acclaim, plaudit, tribute 8 accolade, citation, plaudits 9 laudation, panegyric 10 compliment, salutation 11 acclamation 12 commendation

encompass
3 hem 4 belt, gird, ring 5 bound 6 begird, circle, girdle, take in 7 contain, embrace, enclose, include, subsume 8 encircle, surround 10 accomplish, bring about, comprehend

encore
6 recall, repeat, return 10 repetition

encounter
4 face, find, fray, meet 5 brush, clash, fight, run-in, scrap, set-to 6 battle, engage, take on 7 collide, contest, meeting, quarrel, run into 8 argument, bump into, come upon, conflict, confront, meet with, skirmish, struggle 10 contention, experience

encourage
3 egg 4 abet, back, buoy, push, spur, stir, urge 5 boost, cheer, egg on, rally, rouse, serve, steel 6 assist, assure, buck up, excite, foster, incite, induce, praise, spur on 7 advance, animate, approve, bolster, cheer up, endorse, fortify, further, hearten, improve, inspire, promote, provoke, quicken, support, sustain 8 advocate, embolden, energize, inspirit, reassure, sanction 9 enhearten, galvanize, instigate, patronize, reinforce, stimulate, subsidize 10 invigorate, strengthen

encouragement
4 lift, push 5 boost 7 backing, support 8 approval 11 inspiration

encouraging
4 rosy 6 bright, likely 7 hopeful 9 favorable, promising 10 auspicious, propitious

encroach
5 poach 6 invade, meddle, trench 7 impinge, intrude 8 entrench, infringe, overstep, trespass

encrypt
4 code 6 cipher, encode 7 convert 8 disguise, encipher

encumber
4 lade, load 6 burden, charge, fetter, hamper, hinder, impede, saddle, weight 7 freight, oppress 8 handicap, obstruct, overload 9 weigh down 10 overburden

encumbrance
4 lien, load, onus 5 claim 6 burden 7 baggage 8 easement, handicap, mortgage 9 albatross, millstone 10 impediment

encyclical
6 letter 7 general 8 circular

encyclopedic
5 broad 7 general 8 complete, thorough 9 extensive, inclusive, universal 11 compendious, wide-ranging 12 all-embracing, all-inclusive 13 comprehensive

encyclopedist
7 Diderot (Denis)

end
3 aim, tip 4 coda, doom, goal, halt, quit, stop, tail, term 5 cease, close, death, finis, lapse, limit 6 demise, expire, finale, finish, object, period, result, scotch, windup, wrap up 7 abolish, closing, closure, extreme, lineman, outcome, purpose 8 complete, conclude, curtains, surcease,

terminal, terminus **9** cessation, extremity, objective, terminate **10** completion, conclusion, denouement, expiration **11** culmination, discontinue, termination **12** consummation

endanger
4 risk **5** peril **6** expose **7** imperil **8** threaten **10** compromise, jeopardize

endearment
term: 3 hon, pet **4** baby, dear, duck, lamb **5** bubby, bunny, honey, romeo, sugar **6** kitten, poopsy, poppet, sparky **7** darling, dearest, gumdrop, ladybug, lambkin, pumpkin, sweetie **8** cutie pie, doll-face, gorgeous, honey-bun, lady-love, lover-boy, precious, princess, pussycat, snookums, snuggles, sunshine, sweet pea, sweetums **9** angel-face, babycakes, buttercup, sugar-lips **10** heartthrob, honey bunch, honeychild, love-muffin, sweetheart, sweetie pie, tootsie pie

endeavor
3 aim, try **4** push, seek, toil, work **5** assay, essay, labor, trial **6** effort, intend, strain, strive **7** attempt, purpose, travail, venture **8** exertion, striving, struggle **9** determine, undertake **10** enterprise **11** undertaking

ended
4 done, over, past **7** through **8** complete

endemic
5 local **6** innate, native **8** homebred, inherent, primeval **9** homegrown, prevalent **10** aboriginal, indigenous, native-born

ending
4 stop **5** close **6** finale, finish, period, windup **7** closing, closure **8** terminus **9** cessation **10** completion, conclusion, denouement **11** termination

endive
7 lettuce, witloof **8** escarole

endless
7 eternal, undying **8** constant, enduring, immortal, infinite, unending **9** ceaseless, continual, incessant, limitless, perpetual, unbounded, unceasing, unlimited **10** continuous, indefinite, unmeasured **11** everlasting, illimitable, measureless **12** immeasurable, interminable

endmost
4 last **5** final **8** farthest, furthest, ultimate **10** concluding

endocrine gland
5 gonad, ovary **6** pineal, testis, thymus **7** adrenal, thyroid **8** pancreas **9** pituitary **11** parathyroid **12** hypothalamus

endomorphic
5 beefy, heavy, husky, plump, pudgy, stout **6** chubby, portly, pyknic, rotund

endorse
2 OK **4** back, okay, sign **5** bless, vouch **6** attest, ratify, second, uphold **7** approve, certify, command, confirm, stand by, support, witness **8** accredit, advocate, champion, inscribe, make over, notarize, sanction **9** autograph, recommend **10** underwrite **12** authenticate

endorsement
2 OK **4** okay **7** backing, support **8** approval, sanction, thumbs-up **9** signature **10** green light **12** confirmation, ratification **13** authorization

endow
4 back, fund **5** found **6** bestow, confer, enrich, supply **7** empower, enhance, finance, furnish, promote, provide, sponsor, support **8** bequeath **9** subsidize

endowment
4 fund, gift **5** award, dower, dowry, grant, power, skill **6** legacy, talent **7** ability, bequest **8** appanage, aptitude, bestowal, capacity, donation **11** benefaction

end product
5 fruit, issue **6** effect, payoff, result, upshot **7** outcome **11** consequence

endue
3 don **4** vest **5** dower, equip, imbue, put on **6** clothe, invest, outfit **7** furnish, provide **8** accouter **9** crown with, transfuse

endurance
4 grit, guts, wind **5** moxie, pluck **6** mettle **7** stamina **8** patience, strength, tenacity **9** fortitude **10** permanence, resolution **11** persistence **12** perseverance

endure
4 bear, bide, go on, last **5** abide, brook, stand **6** accept, hold on, linger, pocket, remain, suffer **7** carry on, persist, ride out, stomach, survive, sustain, swallow, undergo, weather **8** continue, submit to, tolerate, tough out **9** withstand

enduring
3 old **4** fast, firm, sure **6** steady **7** abiding, durable, eternal, lasting, staunch **8** constant, lifelong **9** long-lived, perennial, permanent, steadfast **10** continuing, inveterate, persistent **11** long-lasting, unfaltering **12** never-failing

Endymion
father: 8 Aethlius
lover: 5 Diana **6** Selene
author: 5 Keats (John)

enemy
3 foe **5** rival **8** attacker, opponent **9** adversary, assailant **10** antagonist, competitor

energetic
4 spry **5** brisk, fresh, hardy, lusty, peppy, zippy **6** active, lively **7** driving, dynamic, vibrant

8 spirited, tireless, vigorous 9 sprightly, strenuous, vivacious 13 indefatigable

energize
3 pep 4 fuel, stir 5 liven, pep up, rouse, spark 6 enable, excite, stir up, turn on 7 empower, enliven, fortify, inspire, juice up 8 activate, inspirit, vitalize 9 electrify, galvanize, stimulate 10 invigorate, strengthen

energy
2 qi 3 chi, pep, vim, zip 4 dash, life, tuck 5 drive, force, juice, moxie, pluck, power, steam, verve, vigor 6 effort, muscle, spirit 7 current, potency, stamina, voltage 8 activity, dynamism, exertion, strength, vitality 9 animation, puissance 10 enterprise, get-up-and-go, initiative
unit: 3 erg 4 dyne, volt 5 joule 7 quantum 10 horsepower

enervate
3 sap 4 jade, tire 5 weary 6 soften, weaken 7 disable, exhaust, fatigue, unnerve 8 enfeeble, unstring 10 debilitate, devitalize

enfant terrible
3 imp 5 scamp 6 bad boy, urchin 7 skeezix 9 skeezicks

enfeeble
3 sap 6 soften, weaken 7 deplete, disable, exhaust, fatigue 8 enervate 9 attenuate, undermine 10 debilitate, devitalize

enfold
3 hug 4 wrap 5 clasp, cover, press 6 shroud, swathe 7 contain, embrace, squeeze 8 surround

enforce
5 exact, impel 6 compel, effect, impose, invoke, oblige 7 execute, fulfill 8 carry out 9 constrain, discharge, implement, prosecute 10 accomplish, administer, strengthen

enfranchise
4 free 6 rescue 7 deliver, manumit, release, set free 8 liberate 10 emancipate

engage
4 bind, grip, hire, mesh 5 fight, tie up, troth 6 absorb, attack, battle, commit, employ, enlist, pledge, take on 7 assault, betroth, engross, immerse, involve, promise 8 affiance, interact 9 captivate, encounter, interlace, interlock, intermesh, interplay, preoccupy, undertake

engaged
4 busy, rapt 6 intent 7 working 8 absorbed, employed, immersed, intended, occupied, plighted 9 affianced, betrothed, committed, engrossed, wrapped up 10 contracted 11 preoccupied
person: 6 fiancé 7 fiancée

engage in
4 wage 5 enter 6 pursue, tackle, take up 7 conduct 8 embark on, practice 9 prosecute, undertake

engagement
3 gig 4 date, fray, word 5 fight, troth, tryst 6 action, battle, combat, hiring, pledge, plight 7 booking, meeting, promise 8 espousal, skirmish 9 betrothal, encounter 10 commitment, employment, rendezvous 11 appointment, assignation

engaging
7 likable, winning, winsome 8 charming, pleasant, pleasing 9 appealing 10 attractive 13 prepossessing

engender
4 sire, stir 5 beget, breed, cause, hatch, rouse, spawn 6 arouse, create, excite, father, induce, lead to, work up 7 develop, produce, provoke 8 generate 9 originate, procreate, stimulate

engine
5 motor, turbo 7 turbine 10 locomotive
fluid: 7 coolant 10 antifreeze
kind: 3 gas, jet 5 steam 6 diesel 7 turbine 8 gasoline 9 hydraulic
jet: 8 turbofan, turbojet
part: 3 cam, rod 4 gear, plug, pump 5 choke 6 filter, piston, tappet 8 cylinder, manifold, throttle 9 condenser, crankcase 10 carburetor 12 transmission
siege: 3 ram 6 onager 8 ballista, catapult 9 trebuchet 12 battering ram
sound: 4 chug, roar 6 rattle

engineer
4 plan, plot 5 set up, swing 6 devise, driver, manage, scheme, wangle 7 arrange, finagle 8 contrive, intrigue, maneuver, motorman 9 machinate, negotiate 10 manipulate, mastermind 11 orchestrate
kind: 5 civil 6 mining 8 chemical, sanitary 10 electrical, mechanical 12 aeronautical
military: 6 sapper

engineers' group
4 ASME, IEEE

England
6 Albion 7 Britain 9 Britannia 12 Great Britain
see also **United Kingdom**

English
7 British
cathedral city: 3 Ely 4 York 5 Wells 6 Durham, Exeter 7 Lincoln, Norwich 8 Coventry, Hereford 9 Salisbury, Worcester 10 Canterbury, Winchester
coin: 5 crown, groat, pence 6 florin, guinea 8 farthing, shilling, sixpence, twopence 9 fourpence, half crown, halfpenny, sovereign 10 threepence
combining form: 5 Anglo

farm: **5** croft
forest: **5** Arden **8** Sherwood
letter: **3** zed
measure: **3** rod, tun **4** gill, hand, peck, span **5** chain **6** barrel, bushel, fathom, firkin **7** furlong **8** hogshead **10** barleycorn
military college: **9** Sandhurst
patron saint: **6** George
person: **4** chap, mate **5** bloke **6** Briton
pirate: **4** Kidd (Capt. William) **5** Avery (Henry), Teach (Edward) **6** Morgan (Henry) **7** Dampier (William) **10** Blackbeard
prince: **5** Harry **6** Andrew, Edward, Philip **7** Charles, William
princess: **4** Anne **5** Diana **8** Margaret
professor: **3** don
royal family: **5** Tudor **6** Stuart **7** Hanover, Windsor **11** Plantagenet
saint: **7** Dunstan **8** Cuthbert
school: **4** Eton **6** Harrow
spa: **4** Bath
sport: **5** darts, rugby **7** cricket
tavern: **3** pub
university: **5** Leeds **6** Oxford **9** Cambridge
weight: **5** stone **6** firkin **7** quintal **8** quartern

English Channel
French: **6** Manche (La)
swimmer: **6** Ederle (Gertrude)

engrave
3 cut, fix **4** etch **5** carve, chase **6** incise, scrive **7** instill **8** inscribe

engraver
6 chaser, etcher
German: **5** Dürer (Albrecht) **10** Schongauer (Martin)
Italian: **8** Raimondi (Marcantonio)

engraving
7 etching, linecut, woodcut **8** drypoint, intaglio **9** xylograph

engross
4 bury, busy, copy, grip **5** apply, write **6** absorb, engage, indite, occupy, scribe **7** consume, immerse, involve **8** enthrall, inscribe **9** captivate, preoccupy **10** transcribe

engrossed
4 rapt **6** intent **7** engaged, riveted **8** absorbed, immersed **9** attentive **10** enraptured **11** preoccupied **12** concentrated

engrosser
6 scribe **7** copyist **9** scrivener **12** calligrapher **13** calligraphist

engulf
4 bury **5** drown, flood, swamp, whelm **6** deluge, devour **7** immerse, overrun, swallow **8** flow over, inundate, overflow, submerge **9** overwhelm, swallow up

enhance
4 lift **5** add to, adorn, exalt, raise **6** deepen **7** amplify, augment, build up, elevate, enlarge, flatter, improve, magnify **8** beautify, heighten, increase **9** aggravate, embellish, embroider, intensify, reinforce **10** exaggerate, strengthen

enigma
4 crux, knot **5** poser, rebus **6** puzzle, riddle, sphinx, teaser **7** mystery, problem, puzzler **9** conundrum **10** closed book, perplexity, puzzlement **12** question mark **13** Chinese puzzle, mystification

enigmatic
6 mystic **7** cryptic, Delphic, obscure **8** Delphian, oracular, puzzling **9** ambiguous **10** mysterious, mystifying, perplexing **11** inscrutable

enisle
6 cut off **7** isolate **8** insulate, separate **9** segregate, sequester

enjoin
3 ban, bid **4** deny, rule, tell, urge, warn **5** order, taboo **6** adjure, charge, decree, direct, forbid, impose, outlaw **7** caution, command, counsel, dictate, inhibit **8** admonish, disallow, forewarn, instruct, prohibit **9** interdict, prescribe, proscribe

enjoy
4 like, love **5** eat up, fancy, savor **6** relish **9** delight in **10** appreciate

enjoyable
3 fun **8** pleasant, pleasing **9** agreeable **10** delightful, satisfying **11** pleasurable **12** entertaining

enjoyment
4 zest **5** gusto, savor **6** relish **7** benefit, delight **8** felicity, fruition, pleasure **9** diversion **10** indulgence, recreation, relaxation **11** delectation **12** satisfaction **13** gratification

Enki
consort: **5** Nintu
son: **6** Ninsar

enkindle
4 fire **5** flame, light **6** ignite **7** inflame **8** touch off **9** set fire to

enlarge
3 wax **4** grow, rise **5** add to, boost, build, mount, widen **6** beef up, dilate, expand, extend **7** amplify, augment, broaden, develop, greaten, inflate, magnify, stretch **8** heighten, increase, multiply **9** elaborate, embroider **10** exaggerate

enlargement
4 node **5** tumor **6** blowup, growth, nodule **7** buildup **8** addition, increase, swelling **9** accretion, expansion, extension **12** augmentation **13** amplification

enlighten
5 edify, guide, teach **6** advise, illume, inform, uplift **7** educate, improve **8** illumine, instruct **10** illuminate

enlist
4 join **5** draft, enter **6** employ, enroll, join up, muster, sign on, sign up **7** attract, recruit **8** register **9** volunteer **11** participate

enliven
3 pep **4** buoy, fire, warm **5** amuse, cheer, pep up, renew, rouse **6** excite, jazz up, perk up, vivify, wake up **7** animate, cheer up, inspire, quicken, refresh, restore, spice up **8** energize, recreate **9** entertain, galvanize, stimulate **10** exhilarate, invigorate, rejuvenate

en masse
5 as one **6** bodily **8** together **12** collectively

enmesh
4 hook, mire, trap **5** catch, snare **6** draw in, tangle **7** embroil, ensnarl, involve, trammel **8** drag into, entangle **9** embrangle, implicate

enmity
4 hate **6** animus, hatred, rancor, spleen **7** ill will **8** aversion, bad blood, loathing **9** animosity, antipathy, hostility **10** abhorrence, antagonism **11** detestation

ennoble
5 exalt, honor, raise **6** uplift, uprear **7** dignify, elevate, glorify, magnify, sublime **10** aggrandize **11** distinguish

ennui
6 apathy, tedium **7** boredom, fatigue, languor **8** doldrums, dullness, lethargy **9** jadedness, lassitude, tiredness, weariness **11** languidness **12** listlessness

Enoch
father: **4** Cain
son: **10** Methuselah

Enoch Arden author
8 Tennyson (Alfred)

enormity
6 infamy **7** outrage **8** atrocity, hugeness, rankness, savagery, vastness **9** barbarity, depravity, flagrancy, graveness, greatness, grossness, immensity, magnitude **11** abomination, heinousness, massiveness, monstrosity, seriousness, weightiness

enormous
4 huge, vast **5** great **7** immense, mammoth, massive, titanic **8** colossal, gigantic **9** humongous, monstrous **10** astronomic, gargantuan, prodigious, stupendous, tremendous **12** astronomical

Enos
father: **4** Seth
grandfather: **4** Adam
grandmother: **3** Eve
uncle: **4** Abel, Cain

enough
5 ample **6** fairly, plenty **8** adequate, decently, passably **9** competent, tolerably **10** acceptably, adequately, sufficient **11** comfortable, sufficiency **12** satisfactory, sufficiently
poetic: **4** enow

enounce
3 say **5** state, utter **6** intone **8** proclaim, set forth **10** articulate

enrage
3 ire **4** rile **5** anger **6** madden **7** incense, inflame, steam up **9** infuriate

enrapture
5 charm, elate **6** ravish, trance **7** delight, enchant, rejoice **8** enthrall, entrance **9** captivate, transport

enraptured
6 elated **7** charmed **8** ecstatic, thrilled **9** bewitched, delighted, enchanted, entranced **10** captivated, enthralled, mesmerized, spellbound **11** transported

enrich
5 adorn, endow **6** fatten **7** enhance, improve **8** beautify, ornament **9** embellish, fertilize **10** supplement

enroll
4 book, file, join, list **5** draft, enter **6** enlist, induct, join up, muster, record, sign on, sign up, wrap up **7** catalog, engross, recruit **8** inscribe, register **9** conscript, subscribe **10** transcribe **11** matriculate

ensconce
4 bury, hide **5** cache, cover, place, plant, stash **6** hole up, locate, settle **7** conceal, install, secrete, shelter **9** establish

ensemble
3 duo **4** band, crew, suit, trio **5** choir, combo, decor, group, octet, suite, troop, whole **6** chorus, outfit, septet, sextet, troupe **7** chorale, company, costume, en masse, quartet, quintet **8** together **9** aggregate, orchestra

enshrine
6 hallow, revere **7** cherish **8** dedicate, preserve, sanctify, treasure **10** consecrate **11** memorialize

enshroud
4 hide, veil, wrap **5** cloak **6** clothe, enfold, enwrap, invest **7** blanket, conceal, envelop, obscure

ensign
4 flag, jack, sign **5** badge, crest **6** banner, colors, emblem, pennon **7** officer, pennant **8** gonfalon, insignia, standard, streamer **9** oriflamme

enslave
4 yoke **5** chain **6** fetter, thrall **7** enchain, oppress, shackle, subject **8** dominate, enthrall **9** indenture, subjugate **12** disfranchise

enslavement
4 yoke **6** thrall **7** bondage, helotry, peonage, serfdom, slavery **9** servitude, thralldom

ensnare
3 bag, net **4** hook, lure, mesh, snag, trap **5** benet, catch, decoy **6** enmesh, entrap, tangle **7** capture **8** entangle, inveigle

ensnarl
4 mire **6** enmesh, tangle **7** embroil, perplex, trammel **8** entangle **9** embrangle

ensorcell
3 hex **5** charm, spell, witch **6** allure, voodoo **7** beguile, bewitch, enchant **8** enthrall **9** captivate, enrapture, hypnotize, magnetize, mesmerize, spellbind

ensorcellment
5 magic **7** sorcery **8** witchery, wizardry **9** conjuring **10** necromancy, witchcraft **11** bewitchment, enchantment

ensphere
4 ball **8** conglobe **10** conglobate

ensue
4 stem **5** issue **6** attend, derive, follow, result **7** emanate, proceed, succeed **9** supervene

ensuing
4 next **5** later **9** resultant **10** consequent, subsequent, succeeding

ensure
5 cinch **6** clinch, secure **7** certify, confirm, warrant **9** establish, guarantee

enswathe
4 roll, wrap **5** cloak, drape **6** bundle, enwrap, shroud, wrap up **7** envelop, swaddle

entail
5 imply **6** assign, confer, demand, impose, lead to **7** call for, involve, require **8** occasion, restrict, result in, transmit **11** necessitate

entangle
4 mesh, mire, trap **5** catch, ravel, snare, snarl, tie up, twist **6** enmesh, entrap **7** capture, catch up, embroil, ensnare, ensnarl, involve, perplex, trammel **10** complicate, intertwine, interweave

entanglement
3 web **4** knot, mesh, mess, toil **5** skein, snare **6** affair, cobweb, muddle **8** intrigue **9** confusion, imbroglio **11** embroilment, involvement **12** complication

entente
4 pact **6** league, treaty **7** compact **8** alliance, covenant **9** agreement, coalition, concordat **13** understanding

enter
4 go in, join, list, open **5** admit, begin, key in, start **6** come in, enlist, enroll, go into, insert, join up, muster, record, sign on, sign up **7** intrude **8** come into, embark on, inscribe, register **9** introduce, penetrate **10** embark upon

enterprise
4 deed, feat, firm, push, task **5** cause, drive, pluck, vigor **6** action, daring, effort, energy, hustle, outfit, scheme **7** attempt, company, concern, courage, exploit, project, pursuit, venture **8** activity, ambition, audacity, boldness, business, campaign, endeavor, gumption, industry **9** adventure, eagerness **10** enthusiasm, get-up-and-go, initiative **11** corporation, undertaking **12** organization, self-reliance **13** establishment

enterprising
4 bold **5** eager **6** daring, hungry **7** driving, go-ahead **8** aspiring, hustling **9** ambitious, audacious, energetic **10** aggressive **11** adventurous, hardworking, industrious, up-and-coming, venturesome

entertain
4 host **5** amuse **6** divert, regale **7** delight, receive **8** consider

entertainer
4 mime **5** actor, clown, comic **6** busker, dancer, jester, singer **7** actress, artiste, diseuse, trouper **8** comedian, minstrel **10** comedienne

entertaining
6 lively **7** amusing **8** engaging **9** diverting, enjoyable

entertainment
4 fete, play, show, skit **5** revue, sport **6** circus **7** banquet, concert, pastime, ridotto **8** pleasure **9** amusement, diversion, enjoyment **10** recreation **11** distraction, performance

enthrall
4 grip **5** charm **6** absorb, subdue **7** beguile, bewitch, enchant, engross, enslave **9** fascinate, hypnotize, mesmerize, spellbind, subjugate

enthralling
8 exciting, gripping, riveting **9** absorbing, arresting **10** enchanting, engrossing, entrancing **11** captivating, charismatic, provocative **12** spellbinding

enthuse
4 gush, rave **6** excite, thrill **7** animate, delight, inspire **8** energize **10** rhapsodize

enthusiasm
4 élan, fire, zeal, zest **5** ardor, craze, fever, mania, verve **6** fervor, spirit **7** ardency, passion, rapture **9** eagerness, intensity **10** ebullience, excitement, fanaticism

enthusiast
3 bug, fan, nut **4** buff **5** fiend, freak, lover,

maven **6** addict, junkie, maniac, votary, zealot **7** booster, devotee, fanatic, groupie, habitué **8** believer, partisan **9** extremist **10** aficionado

enthusiastic
4 avid, gaga, keen **5** eager, rabid **6** ardent, fervid, gung ho, hearty, hipped, rah-rah, raring **7** devoted, excited, fervent, intense, zealous **8** hopped-up, obsessed, spirited, vascular **9** fanatical **10** passionate

entice
4 bait, coax, draw, lure, toll, wile **5** charm, decoy, tempt **6** allure, cajole, entrap, invite, lead on, seduce **7** attract, wheedle **8** inveigle, persuade

enticement
4 bait, lure, trap **5** decoy, snare **6** allure, come-on **9** seduction **10** allurement, attraction, seducement, temptation **12** blandishment, inveiglement

enticer
4 bait, vamp **5** Circe, decoy, siren **7** Lorelei **9** attractor, temptress **10** attraction, seductress **11** enchantress, femme fatale

enticing
5 siren **8** fetching, witching **9** seductive **10** attractive, bewitching, intriguing **11** captivating, fascinating

entire
3 all **4** full **5** gross, total, whole **6** intact **7** perfect, plenary, unified **8** complete, integral, outright **10** integrated **12** consolidated
combining form: 3 hol, pan **4** holo

entirely
5 fully, quite **6** wholly **7** utterly **9** perfectly **10** altogether, completely, thoroughly **11** exclusively

entirety
3 sum **5** total, whole **8** sum total, totality **9** aggregate, wholeness **10** everything **12** completeness, universality

entitle
3 dub, let **4** call, name, term **5** allow **6** enable, permit **7** baptize, empower, license, qualify **8** christen **9** authorize, designate **10** denominate

entity
3 sum **4** body, item, unit **5** being, thing, whole **6** object **7** article, integer **8** quiddity, totality **9** existence, something, substance **10** individual

entomb
4 bury **5** inter, inurn **6** immure, inhume, shrine **7** mummify **8** enshrine **9** sepulcher, sepulchre

entombment
6 burial **7** funeral, obsequy **9** obsequies, sepulture **10** inhumation

entourage
5 staff, suite, train **6** escort, milieu **7** cortege, coterie, retinue **8** henchmen **9** courtiers, followers, following, hangers-on, retainers **10** associates, attendants **12** surroundings

entr'acte
8 interval **9** interlude **12** intermission

entrails
4 guts **5** pluck, tripe **6** bowels, tripes, umbles, vitals **7** giblets, innards, insides, viscera **8** stuffing **10** intestines

entrance
4 adit, door, gate, port **5** charm, foyer, inlet, lobby, mouth **6** access, portal, ravish **7** arrival, attract, bewitch, delight, doorway, enchant, gateway, ingress, opening **8** aperture, enthrall, open door **9** admission, captivate, enrapture, fascinate, hypnotize, mesmerize, spellbind, threshold, transport, vestibule **10** admittance, ingression **11** penetration

entrant
7 starter **10** competitor, contestant **11** participant

entrap
3 bag, net **4** bait, lure, toll **5** catch, decoy, snare, tempt **6** allure, ambush, entice, entoil, lead on, seduce, tangle **7** beguile, catch up, ensnare **8** entangle, inveigle

entre ____
4 nous

entreat
3 ask, beg, bid **4** pray, urge **5** crave, plead, press **6** adjure, appeal **7** beseech, implore, wheedle **8** blandish **9** importune **10** supplicate

entreaty
4 plea, suit **6** appeal, orison, prayer **7** request **8** petition **11** application, importunity **12** supplication

entrechat
4 leap

entrée
6 access **7** ingress **8** main dish **9** admission **10** admittance, main course

entrench
3 fix **4** root **5** embed, lodge **6** define, furrow, ground, hole up, invade, settle **7** confirm, impinge, implant, intrude **8** encroach, ensconce, infringe, trespass **9** establish **10** strengthen

entrenched
3 set **4** firm **5** rigid, sworn **8** accepted, deep-dyed **9** hard-shell **10** deep-rooted, deep-seated, inveterate **13** bred-in-the-bone, dyed-in-the-wool

entrepôt
3 hub **4** mart **5** depot **6** bazaar, market **8** emporium, exchange **9** concourse, warehouse **10** depository, storehouse **11** marketplace

entrepreneur
10 capitalist, contractor, impresario
entresol
9 mezzanine
entropy
5 chaos, decay **7** decline **8** disorder **10** randomness **11** degradation
entrust
4 give **5** allot, leave **6** assign, charge, commit, confer, impose **7** commend, confide, consign, deliver, deposit **8** allocate, delegate, hand over, relegate, turn over
entry
3 way **4** adit, door, gate, item, port **5** debit, foyer, inlet, lobby **6** access, credit, portal, record **7** doorway, ingress, opening **8** headword **9** admission, threshold, vestibule **10** admittance, enlistment, enrollment, ingression
entryway
4 door, gate **5** foyer, lobby **6** portal **7** ingress, narthex, portico **9** vestibule
entwine
4 coil, wind **5** braid, plait, twist **6** enmesh **7** wreathe **8** entangle **9** interlace **10** interweave
enumerate
3 sum, tot **4** cite, list, tell, tote **5** add up, count, tally, total, tot up **6** detail, number, recite, reckon, tote up **7** compute, itemize, recount, specify, tick off **8** identify **9** calculate, inventory **13** particularize
enunciate
3 say **5** speak, state, utter, voice **6** affirm, intone **7** declare, express, lay down **8** announce, proclaim, propound, vocalize **9** formulate, postulate, pronounce, verbalize **10** articulate
envelop
3 hem **4** hide, roll, veil, wrap **5** cloak, cover, drape **6** cocoon, enfold, engulf, enwrap, invest, sheath, shield, shroud, swathe, wrap up **7** blanket, embrace, enclose, swaddle **8** encircle, enshroud, enswathe, surround **10** circumfuse
envelope abbreviation
4 ADSR, ATTN
envenom
6 poison **8** embitter **10** exacerbate
envious
7 jealous **8** coveting, covetous, grudging **9** green-eyed, invidious, resentful **10** begrudging
environment
6 medium, milieu **7** ambient, climate, context, habitat, setting, terrain **8** ambiance, ambience, backdrop **9** situation **10** atmosphere, background **11** mise-en-scène **12** surroundings
science: **7** ecology
environmentalist
4 Gore (Al), Muir (John) **6** Brower (David), Carson (Rachel), Nelson (Gaylord), Wilson (Edward O.) **7** Ehrlich (Paul), Thoreau (Henry David) **8** Commoner (Barry), Cousteau (Jacques-Yves) **9** Burroughs (John), ecologist, Roosevelt (Theodore)
environs
4 nabe **6** bounds, limits **7** compass, fringes, suburbs **8** boundary, confines, locality, purlieus, vicinity **9** districts, outskirts, precincts **12** neighborhood, surroundings
envisage
4 view **5** dream, fancy, grasp, image, think **6** ideate, regard, vision **7** dream up, feature, foresee, imagine, picture, realize **8** conceive, look upon, summon up **9** conjure up, objectify, visualize
envoy
5 agent **6** bearer, consul, deputy, legate, nuncio **7** attaché, carrier, courier **8** diplomat, emissary, minister **9** messenger **10** ambassador **11** internuncio **12** intermediary
envy
5 covet **6** grudge **8** begrudge, grudging, jealousy **10** resentment **12** covetousness **13** invidiousness
enwrap
4 roll, veil **5** clasp, drape **6** enfold, invest, shroud, swathe **7** enclose, engross, envelop, sheathe, swaddle **8** enshroud, enswathe
enzyme
3 ase **5** ficin, lyase, renin, urase **6** kinase, ligase, lipase, mutase, papain, pepsin, rennin, urease, zymase **7** amidase, amylase, cyclase, enolase, guanase, hydrase, inulase, isozyme, lactase, maltase, oxidase, pectase, pepsine, plasmin, ptyalin, rennase, sucrase, trypsin, zymogen **8** aldolase, diastase, elastase, esterase, fumarase, lyzozyme, nuclease, protease, steapsin, thrombin, zymogene **9** cellulase, invertase
eon
see **aeon**
Eos
see **Aurora**
épée
5 blade, sword **6** rapier
epergne
5 stand **11** centerpiece
ephemeral
5 brief, short **7** passing **8** episodic, fleeting, fugitive, volatile **9** fugacious, momentary, temporary, transient **10** evanescent, short-lived, transitory **11** impermanent

Ephialtes
5 giant
brother: **4** Otus
father: **6** Aloeus **8** Poseidon
mother: **9** Iphimedia
slayer: **6** Apollo

Ephraim
brother: **8** Manasseh
father: **6** Joseph
grandfather: **5** Jacob
mother: **7** Asenath

epic
4 Edda, poem, saga **5** grand, Iliad **6** Aeneid, heroic **7** Beowulf, Odyssey **8** imposing, sweeping **9** Gilgamesh, narrative **12** Heimskringla

epicene
10 effeminate **11** intersexual **13** hermaphrodite

epicure
7 gourmet **8** aesthete, hedonist, sybarite **9** bon vivant **10** gastronome **11** connoisseur **12** gastronomist

epicurean
7 gourmet, sensual **8** aesthete, hedonist, sensuous, sybarite **9** bon vivant, luxurious **10** gastronome, voluptuous **11** connoisseur **12** gastronomist, sensualistic

epidemic
3 flu **4** rash, wave **6** plague **7** rampant, scourge **8** catching, outbreak **9** contagion, prevalent **10** contagious, pestilence

epidermis
4 skin **7** cuticle **10** integument

epigram
3 saw **4** poem **5** adage, axiom, maxim **6** bon mot, dictum, saying, truism **7** proverb **8** aphorism, apothegm

epigrammatic
5 meaty, pithy, terse, witty **6** cogent **7** compact, concise, marrowy, piquant, pointed

epigraph
5 motto **9** quotation **11** inscription

epilogue
4 coda **5** close **6** ending, finale, windup **7** closing **8** postlude **9** afterword **10** conclusion, postscript

Epimetheus
brother: **10** Prometheus
father: **7** Iapetus
wife: **7** Pandora

epiphany
6 aperçu, vision **7** insight **9** discovery, intuition **10** appearance, disclosure, revelation **11** inspiration, realization **13** manifestation

episode
5 event, phase **7** passage **8** incident, occasion **9** happening, interlude **10** occurrence **12** circumstance

episodic
5 brief **7** passing **8** fleeting, sporadic **9** ephemeral, irregular, temporary, transient **10** evanescent, occasional, short-lived **12** intermittent

epistaxis
9 nosebleed

epistle
4 note **6** letter **7** lection, missive **13** communication

epitaph
3 R.I.P. **5** elegy **6** eulogy **8** hic jacet **11** inscription

epithet
4 name **5** label, title **7** agnomen, moniker **8** cognomen, nickname **9** sobriquet **11** appellation

epitome
3 sum **4** acme, type **5** brief, short **6** digest, précis, résumé **7** essence, example, outline, summary **8** abstract, breviary, exemplar, synopsis, ultimate **9** archetype, summation, summing-up **10** abridgment, apotheosis, conspectus, embodiment **11** abridgement **12** condensation, quintessence

epitomize
5 sum up **6** digest, embody, mirror, typify **7** abridge, outline, summate **8** abstract, boil down, condense, manifest, tabulate **9** capsulize, exemplify, incarnate, inventory, objectify, personify, represent, summarize, symbolize, synopsize **10** abbreviate, illustrate **11** concentrate, emblematize, incorporate, personalize

epoch
3 age, eon, era **4** aeon, term, time **6** period **8** interval, time span

equable
4 calm, even, just **6** serene, stable, steady **7** orderly, regular, stabile, uniform **8** composed, constant **9** immutable, temperate, unvarying **10** consistent, invariable, unchanging **12** unchangeable

equal
3 tie **4** even, fair, like, mate, peer, same, twin **5** agree, alike, match **7** uniform **8** alter ego, amount to, parallel **9** duplicate, identical, impartial, objective **10** fifty-fifty **11** counterpart, symmetrical **12** commensurate, correspond to, proportional **13** commensurable, proportionate
combining form: **3** iso **4** equi, pari
French: **4** égal

equality
3 par **6** equity, parity **7** balance, égalité **8** evenness, fairness, sameness **10** uniformity

Equality State
7 Wyoming

equalize
4 even **5** level **6** square **7** balance **9** harmonize

equalizer
3 gun **6** pistol **8** handicap **10** tying score

equally
10 fifty-fifty **11** impartially

equanimity
4 calm, cool **5** poise **6** aplomb, phlegm **7** balance **8** calmness, coolness, evenness, serenity **9** assurance, composure, equipoise, placidity, sangfroid **10** detachment, steadiness **11** tranquility **12** tranquillity

equate
4 even **5** liken, match, treat **6** adjust, regard, relate, square **7** compare **8** consider, equalize, parallel **10** assimilate

Equatorial Guinea
capital: **6** Malabo
island, island group: **5** Bioko **6** Elobey, Pagulu **7** Corisco
language: **5** Bantu **6** French **7** Spanish
mainland: **5** Mbini **7** Río Muni
monetary unit: **5** franc
neighbor: **5** Gabon **8** Cameroon

equestrian
5 rider **6** horsey **8** horseman, knightly **10** horsewoman

equidistant
3 mid **6** medial, median, middle, midway **7** central, halfway, midmost

equilibrium
5 poise **6** aplomb, stasis **7** balance **8** evenness, symmetry **9** composure, stability **10** steadiness **12** counterpoise **13** stabilization

equine
4 colt, mare **5** filly, horse, steed **6** horsey **8** stallion **9** horselike

equip
3 arm, fit, rig **5** array, dress, endow, rig up **6** attire, fit out, outfit, rig out, supply **7** appoint, furnish, prepare, provide **8** accouter, accoutre **9** provision

equipment
3 rig **4** gear **5** traps **6** attire, outfit, tackle, things **7** baggage, panoply **8** fittings, material, matériel, ordnance, supplies, tackling **9** apparatus, endowment, machinery, trappings **10** provisions **11** accessories, attachments, habiliments, impedimenta **12** accouterment, accoutrement, provisioning **13** accouterments, accoutrements, appurtenances, paraphernalia

equitable
4 even, fair, just **5** level **6** proper, square **7** condign **8** balanced, deserved, unbiased **9** identical, impartial, objective, uncolored **10** evenhanded, impersonal **12** unprejudiced **13** dispassionate

equity
3 law, par **7** justice **8** equality, interest, justness

equivalence
3 par **6** parity, simile **7** analogy **8** equality, identity, likeness, sameness **10** conformity **11** correlation

equivalent
4 akin, copy, like, peer, same, twin **5** alike, match **6** agnate **7** identic, similar **8** parallel **9** analogous, duplicate, identical **10** comparable, homologous, substitute, tantamount **11** convertible, correlative, counterpart **12** commensurate **13** corresponding, proportionate

equivocal
4 hazy **5** fishy, vague **6** unsure **7** clouded, dubious, obscure, suspect, unclear **8** doubtful **9** ambiguous, debatable, enigmatic, uncertain, undecided **10** ambivalent, indecisive, indistinct, irresolute, unresolved **11** problematic **12** disreputable, inconclusive, questionable **13** indeterminate

equivocate
3 fib, lie **5** cavil, dodge, evade, fudge, hedge **6** palter, waffle, weasel **7** shuffle **8** sidestep **9** pussyfoot **11** prevaricate **12** tergiversate

equivocation
3 fib **7** evasion, fibbing, hedging, sophism **8** waffling **9** ambiguity, casuistry, duplicity, sophistry **12** speciousness

equivoque
3 pun **8** wordplay

era
3 age, day, eon **4** aeon, date, term, time **5** epoch, stage **6** period

eradicate
4 dele, raze **5** abate, erase, purge **6** delete, efface, remove, uproot **7** abolish, blot out, destroy, expunge, root out, weed out, wipe out **8** demolish, stamp out **9** eliminate, extirpate, liquidate **10** annihilate, do away with, extinguish, obliterate **11** exterminate

erase
4 dele, void, x out **6** cancel, delete, efface, excise, remove, rub out **7** abolish, blot out, expunge, nullify, scratch, take out, wipe out **8** black out, blank out, cross off, cross out **9** eliminate, extirpate, sponge out, strike out **10** extinguish, obliterate

Erato
see **Muse**

Erbin
father: **9** Custennin
nephew: **6** Arthur
son: **7** Geraint

erbium symbol
2 Er

ere
6 before

Erebus
daughter: **3** Day **6** Hemera
father: **5** Chaos
home: **5** Hades
sister, wife: **3** Nox, Nyx
son: **6** Aether, Charon

Erec et ____
5 Enide

Erechteus
daughter: **8** Chthonia
father: **6** Vulcan **10** Hephaestus
mother: **4** Gaea
slayer: **4** Zeus **7** Jupiter

erect
4 form **5** build, put up, raise, set up **6** create, raised **7** build up, stand-up, upright **8** assemble, elevated, standing, straight, vertical **9** construct, establish **10** upstanding **13** perpendicular

eremite
6 hermit **7** ascetic, recluse, stylite **9** anchoress, anchorite

Erewhon
6 utopia **7** nowhere
author: **6** Butler (Samuel)

ergo
4 then, thus **5** hence **9** therefore **11** accordingly **12** consequently

Erichthonius
father: **8** Dardanus
son: **4** Tros

Eridanus star
8 Achernar

Erin
see **Ireland**

Erinyes
6 Alecto, Furies **7** Megaera **9** Eumenides, Tisiphone

Eris
brother: **4** Ares, Mars
daughter: **3** Ate
fruit: **5** apple
goddess of: **6** strife **7** discord
mother: **3** Nox, Nyx

Eritrea
archipelago: **6** Dahlak
capital: **6** Asmara
island: **5** Zuqar
language: **8** Tigrinya
monetary unit: **5** nakfa
neighbor: **5** Sudan **8** Djibouti, Ethiopia
river: **6** Baraka
sea: **3** Red

ermine
3 fur **5** stoat **6** weasel

erode
3 eat, mar, rot, rub **4** rust, wear **5** decay, scour **6** abrade, rub off **7** consume, corrade, crumble, eat away, oxidize, rub away **8** wear away **9** scrape off **10** scrape away **11** deteriorate **12** disintegrate

Eroica composer
9 Beethoven (Ludwig van)

Eros
see **Cupid**

erose
6 craggy, jagged, uneven **9** irregular

erotic
4 lewd, racy, sexy **5** bawdy, spicy **6** carnal, earthy, ribald, risqué **7** fleshly, obscene, profane, sensual **8** off-color, prurient, sensuous **9** salacious **10** voluptuous **11** aphrodisiac, titillating

err
3 sin **4** goof, slip, trip **5** lapse, stray **6** bollix, bungle, foul up, fumble, mess up, slip up **7** balls-up, blunder, deviate, screw up, stumble **8** trespass **10** transgress

errand
3 job **4** task **5** chore **7** mission **10** assignment

errand boy
4 page **5** gofer **7** bellboy, bellhop, courier **9** go-between

errant
5 stray **6** fickle, roving **7** aimless, deviant, erratic, naughty, ranging, roaming, wayward, willful **8** drifting, fallible, rambling, shifting, straying **9** deviating, itinerant, traveling, wandering **10** meandering, unreliable **11** mischievous

erratic
5 flaky **6** fitful, spotty **7** wayward **8** freakish, shifting, unstable, variable, volatile **9** arbitrary, desultory, eccentric, fluctuant, irregular, mercurial, spasmodic, uncertain, wandering, whimsical **10** capricious, changeable, inconstant, meandering **12** inconsistent **13** idiosyncratic, unpredictable

erring
see **errant**

erroneous
3 off **4** awry **5** amiss, askew, false, wrong **6** untrue **7** unsound **8** mistaken, specious, spurious **9** defective, incorrect, misguided **10** fallacious, inaccurate, misleading

error
4 flub, goof, muff, slip, trip **5** boner, botch, fault, fluff, gaffe, lapse, snafu **6** boo-boo, bungle, fumble, howler, miscue, slipup **7** blooper, blunder, fallacy, falsity, faux pas, misdeed, misstep, mistake, screwup, stumble, untruth **8** delusion, illusion, screamer **9** falsehood, indecorum, oversight **10** inaccuracy, misreading **11** impropriety, misjudgment
printing: **4** typo **6** errata (plural) **7** erratum

ersatz
4 copy, fake, sham **5** bogus, dummy, faked, false, phony, pseud **6** phoney, pseudo **8** spurious **9** imitation, simulated, synthetic **10** artificial, factitious, simulacrum, substitute **11** counterfeit

Erse
5 Irish **6** Celtic, Gaelic

erstwhile
3 old **4** late, once, past **5** prior **6** before, bygone, former, whilom **7** already, earlier, onetime, quondam **8** formerly, previous **10** heretofore, previously

eruct
4 burp, emit, gush, spew **5** belch, eject, expel **7** explode **8** detonate, disgorge

erudite
7 bookish, learned **8** lettered, literate, studious, well-read **9** scholarly **10** scholastic

erudition
7 culture **8** learning, literacy **9** knowledge **11** bookishness, cultivation, learnedness, scholarship **12** studiousness **13** scholarliness

erupt
3 jet **4** spew **5** belch, burst, eject, expel, go off, spout, spurt **7** explode **8** break out, burst out, detonate **9** discharge **10** break forth, burst forth

eruption
4 gust, rush **5** blast, burst, flare, sally **6** access **7** flare-up **8** outbreak, outburst **9** commotion, explosion
skin: **3** zit **4** rash **6** pimple

Esau
brother: **5** Jacob
country: **4** Edom
descendant: **7** Edomite
father: **5** Isaac
father-in-law: **4** Elon
grandson: **6** Amalek
mother: **7** Rebecca, Rebekah
new name: **4** Edom
son: **5** Korha, Reuel **7** Eliphaz
wife: **4** Adah **10** Aholibamah

escalade
5 climb, mount, scale **6** ascend **7** scaling

escalate
4 grow, rise, soar **5** boost, climb, mount, widen **6** expand, extend, spread, step up **7** amplify, augment, broaden, enlarge, inflate **8** heighten, increase, multiply **9** intensify **11** proliferate

escapade
4 lark, romp **5** antic, caper, fling, folly, prank, spree, stunt **6** frolic, vagary **7** roguery, rollick **8** mischief **9** adventure

escape
3 fly, lam **4** bolt, duck, flee, shun, skip, slip **5** avoid, break, dodge, elude, evade, shake **6** bypass, depart, eschew, flight, hegira, outlet **7** abscond, duck out, evasion, get away, make off, release, run away, skip out **8** breakout **9** avoidance, desertion, disappear, steal away **10** circumvent, liberation **11** deliverance, evasiveness
artist: **7** Houdini (Harry)
narrow: **9** close call **10** close shave

escargot
5 snail

escarole
6 endive

escarpment
5 bluff, cliff, slope

eschar
4 scab **5** crust **6** lesion

eschew
4 shun **5** avoid, elude, evade, forgo, spurn **6** abjure, forego, pass up, refuse, reject **7** decline **8** turn down

eschewal
7 elusion, evasion, refusal **8** shunning, spurning **9** avoidance, rejection

escort
4 beau, date, lead, show **5** guard, guide, pilot, steer, usher **6** attend, convoy, direct, gigolo, squire **7** company, conduct, consort, retinue **8** cavalier, chaperon, henchman, shepherd **9** accompany, bodyguard, chaperone, companion, entourage, safeguard **13** accompaniment

escritoire
4 desk **9** secretary **11** writing desk

escrow
4 bond, deed, fund **7** deposit

esculent
6 edible **7** eatable **10** comestible, digestible

escutcheon
6 flange, shield

Eshcol
ally: 7 Abraham
brother: 4 Aner **5** Mamre

esker
2 os **4** kame **5** mound, ridge

Eskimo
4 Inuk **5** Aleut, Inuit
boat: 5 kayak, umiak
boot: 6 mukluk
dog: 5 husky **8** malamute, malemute
dwelling: 5 igloo
outer garment: 5 parka **6** anorak
sledge: 7 komatik

esophagus
6 gullet

esoteric
5 inner **6** arcane, mystic, occult, orphic, secret **7** cryptic, private **8** abstruse, hermetic, profound **9** recondite **10** cabalistic, mysterious **12** confidential

ESP
9 telepathy **10** sixth sense **12** clairvoyance, precognition

espadrille
4 shoe **6** sandal

espalier
7 lattice, railing, trellis

esparto
5 grass

especial
4 main **5** close **7** express, notable, unusual **8** dominant, intimate, peculiar, singular, specific, uncommon **9** paramount **10** individual, particular **11** exceptional

especially
7 notably **8** markedly **9** expressly, primarily, unusually **10** peculiarly, remarkably, singularly **11** principally **12** particularly, specifically **13** distinctively, exceptionally

espial
6 notice **9** detection, discovery **11** observation

espionage
6 spying **9** sleuthing **12** surveillance

espousal
5 troth, union **6** mating **7** embrace, support, wedding **8** adoption, advocacy, approval, ceremony, marriage **9** betrothal, embracing, matrimony, promotion **10** acceptance

espouse
3 wed **4** back **5** adopt, marry **6** accept, take on, take up **7** approve, embrace, support **8** advocate

esprit
3 vim, wit **4** brio, dash, élan, zest, zing **5** oomph, verve, vigor **6** fervor, gaiety, mettle, morale, spirit **7** courage, loyalty, panache, passion, sparkle **8** devotion, vibrancy, vitality **9** animation **10** brightness, enthusiasm, fellowship **11** camaraderie

esprit de corps
see **morale**

espy
3 see **4** mark, spot **5** sight **6** descry, detect, notice **7** discern, make out **9** recognize

____ es Salaam
3 Dar

essay
3 try **4** seek, test **5** labor, paper, piece, study, theme, tract, trial **6** effort, strive, thesis **7** article, attempt, venture **8** endeavor, treatise **9** undertake **10** discussion, exposition **11** composition, undertaking **12** dissertation

essayist
American: 4 Agee (James), Will (George) **5** Baker (Russell), Cooke (Alistair), Gould (Stephen Jay), White (E. B.) **6** Brooks (Cleanth), Fisher (M. F. K.), Holmes (Oliver Wendell), Lowell (James Russell), Sontag (Susan), Thomas (Lewis) **7** Buckley (William F.), Cousins (Norman), Emerson (Ralph Waldo), Mencken (Henry Louis), Thoreau (Henry David) **8** Benchley (Robert), Lippmann (Walter), Repplier (Agnes) **10** Crèvecoeur (Jean de)
English: 4 Elia, Lamb (Charles) **5** Bacon (Francis), Cecil (Lord David), Pater (Walter), Smith (Sydney) **6** Arnold (Matthew), Cowley (Abraham), Morris (Jan), Ruskin (John), Steele (Richard) **7** Addison (Joseph), Hazlitt (William) **8** Beerbohm (Max) **9** De Quincey (Thomas) **12** Chesterfield (Lord)
French: 9 Montaigne (Michel de)
Scottish: 7 Carlyle (Thomas)

essence
3 nub **4** base, core, crux, gist, odor, pith, root, soul **5** attar, basis, being, fiber, fibre, point, stuff **6** center, entity, kernel, marrow, nature, spirit **7** extract, perfume, quality **9** substance **10** distillate **12** distillation, significance

essential
4 main, must, need **5** basal, basic, chief, prime, vital **6** inborn, inbred, innate, primal **7** connate, crucial, element, primary **8** cardinal, foremost, inherent, required, rudiment **9** condition, elemental, intrinsic, necessary, necessity, principal, requisite, substance **10** congenital, deep-seated, elementary, idiopathic, imperative, sine qua non, underlying **11** fundamental, requirement

12 precondition, prerequisite 13 indispensable, part and parcel

essentially
6 almost, au fond, really 7 largely 8 actually, as good as, as much as, well-nigh 9 basically, virtually 11 practically 13 fundamentally, substantially

essonite
6 garnet 13 cinnamon stone

establish
3 fix, lay, put, set 4 base, form, root, show 5 build, enact, endow, erect, found, place, prove, set up, start 6 attest, create, decree, effect, ground, impose, secure, settle, verify 7 build up, certify, clarify, confirm, find out, implant, install, instill, provide, set down 8 document, ensconce, organize 9 authorize, construct, determine, formulate, institute, legislate, originate, prescribe 10 bring about, constitute, inaugurate 11 corroborate, demonstrate 12 authenticate, substantiate

establishment
4 firm 6 outfit 7 company, concern 8 business, old guard 9 institute, workplace 10 enterprise, foundation 11 institution, ruling class

estate
4 farm, land 5 manor, ranch, villa 6 domain, legacy, quinta 7 demesne 8 dominion, hacienda, property 10 plantation
agent: 7 Realtor
feudal: 4 fief 7 fiefdom
first: 6 clergy
fourth: 5 press
manager: 7 steward 8 executor, guardian
second: 6 nobles 8 nobility
third: 7 commons

esteem
4 deem 5 favor, honor, prize, think, value 6 admire, liking, regard, revere 7 account, believe, cherish, idolize, respect, worship 8 approval, consider, treasure, venerate 9 valuation 10 admiration, appreciate 12 appreciation 13 consideration

ester
6 oleate 7 acetate 8 compound 9 phosphate

Esther
cousin: 8 Mordecai
enemy: 5 Haman
father: 7 Abihail
festival: 5 Purim
Hebrew name: 8 Hadassah
husband: 6 Xerxes 9 Ahasuerus

estimable
5 noble 6 august, valued, worthy 7 admired 8 laudable, sterling 9 admirable, deserving, honorable, reputable, respected, venerable 10 creditable 11 commendable, meritorious, respectable 12 praiseworthy

estimate
3 put 4 call, rank, rate 5 assay, gauge, guess, infer, judge, price, set at, value 6 assess, deduce, figure, rating, reckon, survey 7 imagine, opinion, project, suppose, surmise 8 appraise, conclude, discover, evaluate, forecast, judgment, round off 9 appraisal, calculate, determine, reckoning, valuation 10 assessment, conjecture, evaluation, impression, projection 11 approximate, calculation, measurement

estimation
4 fame 5 favor, honor, stock 6 esteem, regard 7 account, opinion, respect 8 figuring, judgment 9 appraisal, reckoning, valuation 10 admiration, assessment, evaluation, impression 11 calculation 13 consideration

Estonia
capital: 7 Tallinn
city: 5 Tartu
gulf: 4 Riga 7 Finland
inhabitant: 4 Balt
island: 4 Muhu 6 Vormsi 7 Hiiumaa 8 Saaremaa
lake: 5 Pskov 6 Peipus 9 Vorts-Jarv
monetary unit: 5 kroon
neighbor: 6 Latvia, Russia
river: 5 Narva, Pärnu 6 Kasari
sea: 6 Baltic

estop
3 bar 6 enjoin, forbid 7 prevent 8 disallow, preclude, prohibit, restrain

estrange
4 part 5 split 7 break up, divorce 8 alienate, disunite, separate 9 disaffect

estrangement
4 rift 5 split 6 breach, schism 7 breakup, cooling, divorce, rupture 8 disunity, division 10 alienation, falling-out, withdrawal 12 disaffection

estuary
5 firth, frith, mouth 10 tidal river

esurient
4 avid 6 greedy, hungry 8 covetous, grasping, ravening, ravenous 9 rapacious, voracious 10 avaricious, gluttonous 11 acquisitive

étagère
7 cabinet, whatnot

Etats-____
4 Unis

etch
3 cut 5 carve, stamp 6 depict, incise 7 engrave, impress, imprint, portray 8 inscribe 9 delineate, represent

etcher
American: 7 Pennell (Joseph) 8 Whistler (James McNeil)

Dutch: **9** Rembrandt (van Rijn)
French: **5** Redon (Odilon) **6** Villon (Jacques)
Italian: **8** Piranesi (Giambattista)
Spanish: **6** Ribera (José)
Swiss: **4** Zorn (Anders)

Eteocles
brother: **9** Polynices **10** Polyneices
father: **7** Oedipus
mother: **7** Jocasta
slayer: **9** Polynices **10** Polyneices

eternal
7 abiding, ageless, endless, lasting, undying **8** constant, enduring, immortal, infinite, timeless, unending **9** ceaseless, continual, deathless, immutable, incessant, permanent, perpetual, unceasing **10** immemorial, unchanging **11** amaranthine, everlasting, illimitable, inalterable, never-ending, unalterable, unremitting **12** imperishable, interminable

Eternal City
4 Rome

eternally
3 e'er **4** ever **6** always **7** forever **8** evermore, for keeps **11** forevermore, in perpetuum **12** in perpetuity

eternity
3 age, eon **4** aeon **7** dog's age **8** blue moon, coon's age, infinity **9** afterlife **10** infinitude, perpetuity **11** endlessness, immortality **12** infiniteness, timelessness

Etesian
4 wind **6** annual

Ethan ___
5 Allen, Brand, Frome

Ethbaal's daughter
7 Jezebel

ether
3 air, gas, sky **6** heaven **7** heavens **8** airwaves, empyrean **10** anesthetic, atmosphere

ethereal
4 aery, airy **5** filmy, light **6** aerial **7** fragile **8** delicate, empyreal, empyrean, gossamer, heavenly, rarefied, vaporous **9** celestial, spiritual, unearthly, unworldly **10** immaterial, intangible **13** unsubstantial

ethical
4 good **5** moral, noble **6** decent **7** upright, virtual **8** elevated, virtuous **9** righteous **10** principled, upstanding **11** right-minded **13** conscientious

ethics
5 mores **6** morals, values **8** morality **9** moral code, standards **10** principles

Ethiopia
battle site: **5** Adowa
biblical name: **4** Cush
capital: **10** Addis Ababa
city: **6** Gonder **8** Dire Dawa
desert: **4** Haud **7** Danakil
emperor: **7** Menelik, Menilek **8** Selassie **9** Ras Tafari **13** Haile Selassie
former name: **9** Abyssinia
language: **5** Oromo **7** Amharic
monetary unit: **4** birr
mountain: **9** Ras Dashen
neighbor: **5** Kenya, Sudan **7** Eritrea, Somalia **8** Djibouti
region: **5** Tigre **6** Ogaden, Tigray **7** Danakil
river: **4** Abay **5** Awash **6** Tekeze **8** Blue Nile

ethnic
6 racial, tribal **8** minority

etiolate
4 fade, pale **6** bleach, weaken **7** lighten, wash out **8** enfeeble

etiquette
4 code, form **5** mores **7** conduct, customs, decency, decorum, manners **8** behavior, protocol **9** amenities, propriety **10** civilities, convention, deportment, seemliness **11** conventions, formalities, proprieties

Etruscan
city, town: **4** Roma, Veii **5** Caere, Vulci **6** Arezzo **7** Clusium, Felsina, Perugia **8** Volsinii **9** Florentia, Tarquinia, Vetulonia
deity: **3** Tin, Tiv, Uni **4** Turm, Usil **5** Tinia, Turan, Turms **6** Menfra, Menrva, Nethun, Trithn **7** Velchan **8** Sethlans, Voltumna
king: **7** Porsena, Tarquin **10** Tarquinius **11** Lars Porsena
kingdom: **7** Etruria

étude
5 study **8** exercise **11** composition

etui
4 case

etymology
11 word history

etymon
4 root **5** radix **6** source **8** morpheme

eucalyptus eater
5 koala

Eucharist
container: **3** pyx
plate: **5** paten
service: **4** Mass **9** Communion
vessel: **8** ciborium
wafer: **4** host **8** viaticum

Euclid
subject: **8** geometry
work: **8** Elements

___ Eulenspiegel
4 Till, Tyll

eulogistic
9 adulatory, laudative, laudatory **11** encomiastic, panegyrical **12** commendatory **13** complimentary

eulogize
4 hymn, laud **5** cry up, exalt, extol **6** praise **7** acclaim, applaud, commend, glorify, magnify **9** celebrate **10** panegyrize

eulogy
5 paean **6** praise **7** oration, tribute **8** accolade, citation, encomium **9** laudation, panegyric **10** salutation **12** commendation **13** glorification

Eumenides
see **Erinyes**

eunuch
7 gelding **8** castrate, castrato

euphony
7 harmony **8** lyricism **9** sweetness **10** consonance

euphoria
3 joy **4** glee **5** bliss **7** ecstasy, elation, rapture **9** transport **10** exaltation, jubilation **11** high spirits **12** exhilaration, intoxication

Euphrosyne
see **Graces**

euphuistic
5 fancy, tumid **6** florid, ornate, prolix, purple, turgid **7** elegant, flowery, fustian, orotund, verbose **8** colorful, elevated, inflated, sonorous **9** bombastic, elaborate, high-flown, overblown **10** figurative, flamboyant, rhetorical **11** highfalutin, overwrought **12** magniloquent **13** grandiloquent

eureka
3 aha

Euridice's husband
7 Orpheus

Euripides play
3 Ion **5** Helen, Medea **6** Hecuba **7** Bacchae (The), Cyclops, Electra, Orestes **8** Alcestis **10** Andromache, Hippolytus, Suppliants (The) **11** Trojan Women (The)

Europa
brother: **6** Cadmus
father: **6** Agenor **7** Phoenix
husband: **8** Asterius
son: **5** Minos **8** Sarpedon

Europe
9 continent
country: **4** Eire **5** Italy, Malta, Spain **6** France, Greece, Latvia, Monaco, Norway, Poland, Russia, Sweden, Turkey **7** Albania, Andorra, Armenia, Austria, Belarus, Belgium, Croatia, Denmark, Estonia, Finland, Georgia, Germany, Hungary, Iceland, Ireland, Moldova, Romania, Rumania, Ukraine **8** Bulgaria, Portugal, Slovakia, Slovenia **9** Lithuania, Macedonia, San Marino **10** Azerbaijan, Luxembourg, Yugoslavia **11** Netherlands, Switzerland, Vatican City **13** Czech Republic, Liechtenstein, United Kingdom
ethnic group: **4** Celt, Finn, Lapp, Lett, Pole, Serb, Sorb, Turk, Wend **5** Croat, Czech, Dutch, Greek, Gypsy, Irish, Latin, Swede, Swiss, Welsh **6** Basque, Celtic, French, German, Magyar, Polish, Scotch, Slovak **7** Bosnian, Catalan, English, Finnish, Fleming, Italian, Lettish, Maltese, Russian, Slovene, Spanish, Swedish, Walloon **8** Albanian, Andorran, Armenian, Croatian, Romanian **9** Belarusan, Bulgarian, Hungarian, Ukrainian **10** Belarusian, Macedonian, Monegasque, Phoenician **11** Belarussian **12** Byelorussian, Scandinavian
language: **4** Lapp **5** Czech, Dutch, Greek, Irish, Latin, Welsh **6** Basque, Breton, Danish, French, Gaelic, German, Magyar, Polish, Slovak **7** Catalan, English, Finnish, Flemish, Italian, Maltese, Romansh, Russian, Serbian, Slovene, Spanish, Swedish, Turkish, Wendish **8** Albanian, Croatian, Lusatian, Romanian, Rumanian **9** Bulgarian, Hungarian, Icelandic, Norwegian **10** Macedonian, Portuguese **13** Serbo-Croatian
mountain range: **4** Alps **8** Pyrenees **11** Carpathians

European Union member
5 Italy, Malta, Spain **6** Cyprus, France, Greece, Latvia, Poland, Sweden **7** Austria, Belgium, Denmark, Estonia, Finland, Germany, Hungary, Ireland, Romania **8** Bulgaria, Portugal, Slovakia, Slovenia **9** Lithuania **10** Luxembourg **11** Netherlands **13** Czech Republic, United Kingdom

europium symbol
2 Eu

Euryale
see **Gorgon**

Eurytus
daughter: **4** Iole
slayer: **8** Hercules

Euterpe
see **Muse**

evacuate
4 exit, void **5** clear, empty, expel, leave **6** decamp, depart, remove, vacate **7** abandon, excrete, exhaust, pull out, retreat **8** clear out, pull back, withdraw **9** eliminate

evacuee
2 DP **6** émigré **7** refugee **8** fugitive

evade
4 duck, flee, foil **5** avoid, dodge, elude, hedge, parry, shirk, skirt **6** baffle, bypass, escape, eschew, outwit, thwart, weasel **7** shuffle **8** sidestep, slip away **9** pussyfoot, turn aside **10** circumvent, equivocate **11** prevaricate **12** tergiversate

evaluate
4 rank, rate **5** assay, class, gauge, grade, set at, weigh **6** assess, figure, reckon, size up, survey **7** eyeball **8** appraise, classify, estimate **9** calculate, criticize

evaluation
6 rating **7** judging, opinion **8** estimate, judgment **9** appraisal **10** assessment **12** appreciation

Evander
father: **6** Hermes **7** Mercury
mother: **8** Carmenta **9** Carmentis
son: **6** Pallas

evanesce
4 fade **5** clear **6** vanish **7** scatter **8** disperse, dissolve, melt away **9** disappear, dissipate, evaporate **13** dematerialize

evanescent
6 fading **7** elusive, melting, passing **8** fleeting, fugitive, volatile **9** ephemeral, fugacious, momentary, transient, vanishing **10** dissolving, short-lived, transitory **12** disappearing

evangelical
6 ardent, fervid **7** fanatic, fervent, zealous **8** militant **9** crusading **10** missionary **13** proselytizing

Evangeline
author: **10** Longfellow (Henry Wadsworth)
beloved: **7** Gabriel
home: **6** Acadia

evangelist
4 John, Luke, Mark **5** Moody (Dwight) **6** Bakker (Jim, Tammy Faye), Dobson (James), Graham (Billy, Franklin), Sunday (Billy), Wesley (John) **7** apostle, Edwards (Jonathan), Falwell (Jerry), Matthew, Roberts (Oral) **8** Schuller (Robert), Swaggart (Jimmy) **9** McPherson (Aimee Semple), missioner, Robertson (Pat) **10** colporteur, missionary, revivalist, Whitefield (George)

evangelistic
9 crusading, reforming **10** missionary, revivalist **13** proselytizing

evangelize
6 preach **7** convert **9** sermonize

evaporate
4 fade, melt **5** clear **6** vanish **8** diminish, disperse, dissolve, evanesce, melt away, vaporize **9** disappear, dissipate

evasion
5 dodge, fudge **6** escape, excuse **7** dodging, elusion, fudging **8** escaping **9** avoidance **13** circumvention

evasive
3 sly **5** cagey, dodgy, vague **6** shifty **7** elusive **8** slippery **9** ambiguous, equivocal

Eve
home: **4** Eden
husband: **4** Adam
son: **4** Abel, Cain, Seth
temptation: **5** apple, fruit

even
3 tie **4** fair, flat, just, same, tied **5** align, equal, exact, flush, grade, level, plane, still, truly **6** as well, equate, smooth, square, stable, steady **7** balance, equable, flatten, uniform **8** balanced, constant, equalize, smoothen, straight **9** equitable, expressly, identical, precisely, unvarying **10** absolutely, comparable, consistent, continuous, fifty-fifty, unchanging **13** fair and square, proportionate

evening
4 dusk **6** soiree, sunset, vesper **7** sundown **8** gloaming, twilight **9** nightfall
French: **4** soir
Italian: **4** sera
service: **7** vespers
star: **5** Venus **6** Vesper **8** Hesperus

evenness
6 equity, parity **7** balance **8** equality **9** stability **10** equanimity, uniformity **11** consistency, equilibrium

event
3 act **4** case, deed, fact, feat, meet **5** issue, match **6** action, affair, chance, effect, result, upshot **7** contest, episode, outcome, product **8** accident, function, incident, occasion **9** aftermath, happening **10** occurrence, phenomenon **11** achievement, competition, consequence, eventuality **12** circumstance, happenstance

eventful
4 busy **6** lively **9** important, momentous

eventual
4 last **5** final **6** ending **7** closing, endmost, ensuing **8** terminal, ultimate **9** resulting **10** concluding, consequent, inevitable, succeeding

eventuality
4 case **6** effect, result **7** outcome **11** consequence, contingency, possibility

eventually
6 at last, in time, one day **7** finally, someday **8** sometime **9** hereafter **10** ultimately **13** sooner or later

eventuate
5 ensue, occur **6** befall, follow, happen, result **9** come about, take place

ever
4 once **5** at all **6** always **7** forever **9** at any time, eternally, regularly **10** constantly, invariably **11** perpetually **12** consistently, continuously
poetic: **3** e'er

evergreen
3 fir, ivy, yew **4** ilex, pine, tree **5** cedar, holly, savin **6** laurel, myrtle, spruce **7** conifer, cypress,

hemlock, juniper, lasting, redwood, sequoia, undying **8** magnolia, mangrove, timeless, unfading **9** mistletoe, perennial **10** arborvitae **12** rhododendron

Evergreen State
10 Washington

everlasting
7 abiding, endless, eternal, forever, lasting, undying **8** constant, immortal, infinite, termless, timeless, unending **9** boundless, ceaseless, continual, deathless, limitless, permanent, perpetual, unceasing **10** continuous, perdurable **11** amaranthine, never-ending, unremitting **12** imperishable

evermore
6 always **7** for good **8** for keeps **9** eternally **12** in perpetuity

every
3 all **4** each
prefix: 3 pan

everybody
3 all **4** each

everyday
5 banal, plain, usual **6** common, normal **7** mundane, prosaic, routine **8** familiar, habitual, ordinary **9** customary, quotidian **11** commonplace **12** conventional, run-of-the-mill, unremarkable

everything
3 all
French: 4 tout
German: 5 alles
Spanish: 4 todo

everywhere
7 all over, overall **8** all round, wherever **9** all around **10** far and near, far and wide, high and low, throughout

evict
3 out **4** boot, oust **5** eject, expel **6** bounce, put out **7** boot out, dismiss, extrude, kick out **8** dislodge, force out, throw out **10** dispossess

evidence
4 clue, mark, show, sign **5** goods, proof, prove **6** attest, evince, expose, reveal **7** confirm, display, exhibit, symptom, testify, witness **8** indicate **9** testament, testimony **10** indication, smoking gun **11** attestation, demonstrate, testimonial **12** confirmation **13** documentation

evident
5 clear, overt, plain **6** marked, patent **7** obvious, visible **8** apparent, distinct, manifest, palpable, tangible **9** prominent **10** noticeable, pronounced **11** conspicuous, perceptible, unambiguous

evidently
9 outwardly, seemingly **10** officially, ostensibly

evil
3 bad, sin **4** foul, vice, vile **5** black **6** infamy, malice, sinful, wicked **7** badness, baleful, baneful, devilry, hateful, heinous, malefic, satanic, vicious **8** damnable, iniquity, satanism, villainy **9** atrocious, diablerie, diabolism, execrable, loathsome, malicious, malignant, nefarious **10** flagitious, iniquitous, maleficent, malevolent, pernicious, sinfulness, wickedness **11** maleficence
combining form: 3 mal

evildoer
6 sinner **7** villain **8** criminal **9** miscreant **10** malefactor

evil spirit
3 imp **5** demon, devil, fiend, Satan **6** daemon

evince
4 mark, show **5** educe, evoke, prove **6** attest, betray, elicit, expose, reveal **7** bespeak, betoken, confirm, display, exhibit, signify **8** evidence, indicate, manifest, proclaim **10** illustrate **11** demonstrate

eviscerate
3 gut **4** draw **5** bowel **7** embowel **8** protrude **10** disembowel, exenterate

evocative
6 moving **8** redolent, stirring **9** affecting, emotional, nostalgic **10** expressive, meaningful, suggestive **11** stimulating

evoke
4 cite, stir **5** educe, raise, waken **6** arouse, awaken, call up, elicit, evince, excite, induce, recall **7** conjure **8** recreate, summon up **9** call forth, conjure up, stimulate **11** summon forth

evolution
6 change, growth **8** progress, upgrowth **9** flowering, phylogeny, unfolding **10** biogenesis, maturation **11** development, progression

evolve
4 grow **5** educe, ripen **6** change, derive, emerge, mature, open up, unfold **7** advance, develop, work out **8** progress **9** elaborate

ewe
5 sheep

ewer
3 jug **4** olpe, vase **7** pitcher

ex
4 from, past **5** out of, prior **6** former **7** earlier, without **9** erstwhile

exacerbate
6 worsen **7** envenom, inflame, provoke **8** embitter, heighten **9** aggravate, intensify

exact
4 levy, true **5** claim, force, gouge, pinch, screw, wrest, wring **6** coerce, compel, dead-on, demand,

extort, spot-on, strict **7** correct, extract, literal, precise, require, solicit, squeeze **8** accurate, rigorous, selfsame **9** identical, postulate, shake down **10** meticulous, scrupulous **11** painstaking, punctilious, requisition

exacting
5 fussy, rigid, stern, tough **6** severe, strict, taxing, trying **7** exigent, finicky, onerous **8** critical, rigorous **9** demanding, stringent **10** fastidious, nitpicking, particular, scrupulous **11** persnickety **13** hypercritical

exactitude
5 rigor **8** accuracy **9** precision **10** definitude **11** correctness, preciseness **12** definiteness

exactly
4 bang, just **5** quite, right, sharp, spang **6** bang on, square, to a tee, wholly **7** totally, utterly **8** entirely, on the dot, smack-dab, squarely **9** on the nose, precisely **10** absolutely, accurately, altogether, completely, positively **12** specifically

exaggerate
6 overdo **7** amplify, enlarge, inflate, magnify, overact, romance **8** overdraw, overrate **9** embellish, embroider, overstate **11** hyperbolize **13** overemphasize

exaggeration
8 travesty **9** hyperbole **10** caricature, stretching **11** enlargement, overdrawing **12** embroidering **13** embellishment, overstatement

exalt
4 fete, laud, lift **5** boost, elate, extol, honor, raise **6** praise, uplift **7** acclaim, adulate, build up, dignify, elevate, enhance, ennoble, glorify, inspire, magnify, promote **8** eulogize, heighten, inspirit **9** intensify **10** aggrandize **11** apotheosize

exaltation
3 joy **5** bliss, glory **6** homage, praise **7** delight, ecstasy, elation, rapture, tribute **8** euphoria, rhapsody **9** panegyric, transport, uplifting **10** apotheosis, jubilation **11** deification **12** exhilaration, intoxication **13** glorification

exalted
4 high **5** grand, lofty, noble **6** august **7** eminent, highest, sublime **9** venerable **11** high-ranking, illustrious, outstanding, prestigious

examination
4 oral, quiz, scan, test **5** assay, final, probe, trial **6** review, survey **7** canvass, checkup, hearing, inquest, inquiry, perusal, sifting, testing **8** analysis, scrutiny **9** breakdown, check-over, diagnosis **10** dissection, inspection **11** inquisition **13** catechization, investigation, perlustration
kind: **3** bar **4** oral **5** final **7** medical, midterm **8** physical
of accounts: **5** audit
of a corpse: **7** autopsy **10** postmortem

examine
3 con, vet **4** pump, quiz, scan, sift, test **5** audit, check, grill, probe, query, study **6** go over, look at, peruse, survey **7** canvass, check up, inquire, inspect, observe **8** check out, look into, look over, question **9** catechize, check over **10** scrutinize **11** interrogate, investigate

examiner
6 censor **7** auditor, coroner **9** inspector **10** inquisitor, prosecutor **12** investigator

example
4 case **5** ideal, model **7** paragon, pattern **8** instance, paradigm, specimen, standard **9** archetype, precedent, prototype **11** case history **12** illustration

exanimate
4 dead **5** inert **8** lifeless, listless, sluggish, stagnant **9** lethargic **10** spiritless

exasperate
3 irk, vex **4** gall, rile, roil **5** anger, annoy, peeve, pique, upset **6** enrage, madden, nettle, rankle **7** agitate, incense, inflame, provoke **8** irritate **9** aggravate, infuriate

exasperation
8 vexation **9** annoyance **10** irritation **11** aggravation

ex cathedra
8 official **9** ex officio **13** authoritative

excavate
3 dig **4** grub **5** scoop, spade **6** dig out, dredge, expose, hollow, quarry, shovel **7** unearth **8** gouge out, scoop out **9** hollow out, scrape out

excavation
3 dig, pit **4** hole, mine **5** ditch, stope **6** dugout, hollow, quarry, trench, trough

exceed
3 cap, top **4** beat, best, pass **5** break, excel, outdo **6** better, outrun, overdo **7** eclipse, outpace, overrun, surpass **8** go beyond, outreach, outshine, outstrip, outweigh, overstep, overtake **9** overreach, transcend

exceedingly
4 very **6** hugely, vastly **7** awfully, notably, vitally **9** extremely **10** remarkably, strikingly **12** surpassingly **13** exceptionally
prefix: **5** ultra

excel
3 cap, top **4** beat, best, pass **5** outdo, shine **6** better, exceed, outrun, overdo **7** eclipse, outpace, overrun, surpass **8** go beyond, outclass, outreach, outshine, outstrip, outweigh, overstep, overtake **9** overreach, transcend

excellence
5 class, merit, value, worth **6** virtue **7** quality

8 fineness 9 greatness 10 perfection 11 distinction, superiority

excellent
3 top 4 A-one, boss, fine 5 bully, model, neato, prime 6 bang-up, banner, famous, Grade A, superb, tip-top, worthy 7 capital, premium, supreme 8 champion, five-star, splendid, stunning, superior, terrific, top-notch 9 classical, exemplary, first-rate, high-class, high-grade, marvelous, number one, top-drawer, wonderful 10 blue-ribbon, first-class 11 exceptional, magnificent, meritorious, sensational, superlative, unsurpassed 12 incomparable

except
3 bar, but, yet 4 omit, only, save 6 beside, exempt, object, reject, unless 7 barring, besides, exclude, however, outside, rule out, suspend 8 pass over 9 apart from, aside from, eliminate, excluding, outside of 11 exclusive of

exception
5 demur 7 anomaly, dissent 8 question 9 allowance, deviation, exclusion, objection 10 aberration

exceptionable
8 unwanted 9 unwelcome 10 unsuitable 11 regrettable, undesirable 12 unacceptable 13 objectionable

exceptional
4 rare 6 scarce, unique 7 notable, special, unusual 8 abnormal, atypical, distinct, singular, superior, uncommon, unwonted 9 anomalous, excellent, marvelous, wonderful 10 infrequent, noteworthy, phenomenal, remarkable 11 outstanding, uncustomary 13 extraordinary

exceptionally
4 very 6 hugely 7 notably 9 extremely 10 especially, remarkably, strikingly 11 exceedingly 12 particularly, stupendously

excerpt
4 cite, clip, cull, pick 5 glean, quote 6 choose, sample, select 7 extract, passage, pick out, portion, snippet 8 fragment 9 quotation

excess
3 fat 4 glut, rest 5 extra, flood, spare, waste 7 nimiety, overage, surfeit, surplus 8 leavings, leftover, overflow, overkill, overmuch 9 indulgent, overstock, redundant, remainder 10 oversupply, surplusage 11 dissipation, prodigality, superfluity, superfluous, unessential 12 extravagance, immoderation, intemperance 13 overabundance, supernumerary

excessive
4 over 5 dizzy, steep, super, undue 6 de trop, too-too 7 extreme, sky-high 8 overmuch, prodigal 10 exorbitant, immoderate, inordinate, profligate 11 extravagant, intemperate, overweening, superfluous 12 supernatural, unrestrained

excessively
3 too 6 overly, unduly 8 overmuch
prefix: 5 hyper

exchange
4 swap, swop 5 bandy, trade, truck 6 barter, market, switch 7 bargain, commute, convert, pay back, replace, traffic 8 displace 9 transpose 10 conversion, substitute 11 reciprocate

exchangerate premium
4 agio

exchequer
5 funds 8 treasury

excise
3 fee, tax 4 toll 5 elide, slash 6 cut out, delete, remove, resect 9 expurgate, extirpate, strike out, surcharge

excision
3 cut 7 removal, surgery 8 deletion 9 resection 11 extirpation

excitable
4 rash 8 volatile 9 impetuous 10 high-strung

excite
4 fire, goad, move, spur, stir 5 elate, evoke, key up, pique, prime, rouse, waken 6 appeal, arouse, elicit, fire up, induce, kindle, stir up, thrill, turn on 7 agitate, animate, commove, inflame, inspire, provoke, quicken 8 activate, charge up, energize, motivate 9 galvanize, impassion, innervate, stimulate 10 exhilarate

excited
3 hot 4 avid 5 eager 6 aflame 7 fevered 8 aflutter, worked up 10 passionate 12 enthusiastic

excitement
3 ado 4 buzz, stir, to-do 5 fever, furor 6 flurry, frenzy, furore, hubbub, thrill 7 turmoil 8 delirium, hysteria 9 agitation, commotion 10 enthusiasm, hullabaloo 11 disturbance, pandemonium 12 exhilaration

exclaim
4 blat, bolt 5 blurt 6 cry out 8 blurt out, burst out 9 ejaculate

exclamation
2 ha, hi, ho, lo 3 aah, aha, bah, boo, cry, eek, feh, fie, gee, hah, hey, huh, oho, ooh, pah, tsk, tut, ugh, wow 4 ahem, alas, amen, damn, dang, darn, drat, egad, gosh, heck, hell, oops, ouch, phew, pish, posh, rats, whew, yell 5 alack, bravo, faugh, golly, humph, pshaw, shout 6 clamor, hurrah, indeed, outcry, phooey, shucks 7 doggone, gee whiz, hosanna, jeepers, whoopee 9 expletive 10 hallelujah 12 interjection
of disappointment: 4 damn, darn, rats
of disapproval: 3 tsk 6 tsk-tsk
of discovery: 3 aha 6 eureka

of disgust: **3** bah, boo, feh, fie, ugh **4** yech, yuck **5** faugh, yecch **6** phooey
of dismay: **4** oh no, uh-oh **5** yikes
of enthusiasm: **4** whee **5** wahoo **7** whoopie
of fear: **3** eek
of pain: **2** ow **4** ouch
of relief: **4** phew
of sorrow: **3** woe **4** alas **5** alack
of surprise: **2** ah, oh **3** wow **4** gosh **5** golly
of triumph: **3** aha, hah **5** yahoo **6** eureka
(see also **interjection**)

exclude
3 ban, bar **4** oust **5** block, debar **6** banish, disbar, reject **7** keep out, lock out, obviate, prevent, rule out, shut out, suspend **8** count out, preclude, prohibit **9** blackball, blacklist, eliminate, ostracize

excluding
3 bar, but **4** less, save **6** except **7** barring, besides **9** apart from, aside from, other than, outside of

exclusion
3 bar **6** ouster **7** barring, lockout, removal **8** ejection, eviction, omission **9** blackball, expulsion, ostracism **10** banishment **12** blackballing, nonadmission

exclusive
4 lone, only, sole **5** elect, elite, prime, scoop, smart, swank, swish **6** choice, chosen, picked, select, single **7** cliquey, high-hat, stylish **8** clannish, cliquish, selected, snobbish **9** preferred, undivided **10** privileged **11** fashionable, prohibitive, restrictive **12** aristocratic, concentrated, preferential

exclusively
4 only **5** alone **6** wholly **8** entirely **10** completely **12** particularly

excogitate
6 derive, devise, invent **7** develop, think up **8** contrive, think out

excommunicate
7 cast out **8** unchurch

excoriate
4 flay, lash, skin **5** roast, slash **6** abrade, scathe, scorch **7** blister, censure, scarify, scourge **8** chastise, lambaste, lash into **9** castigate

excrement
6 ordure
of animals: **4** dung, muck **6** manure
of sea birds: **5** guano

excrescence
4 blot, lump, mole, wart **5** tumor **6** growth, nodule, pimple **7** blemish, process **9** by-product, outgrowth

excrete
4 emit, spew **5** eject, expel, exude **9** discharge

excruciate
4 rack **6** martyr **7** afflict, crucify, torment, torture **9** martyrize

excruciating
5 acute, sharp **6** severe **7** extreme, intense **8** piercing, shooting, stabbing **9** agonizing, harrowing, torturous **10** unbearable **11** unendurable

exculpate
4 free **5** clear, remit **6** acquit, excuse, let off, pardon **7** absolve, amnesty, condone, forgive, justify **9** exonerate, vindicate **11** rationalize

excursion
4 ride, tour, trek, trip, walk **5** aside, drive, jaunt, paseo, sally, tramp **6** cruise, junket, outing, ramble, safari **7** day trip, journey **9** round trip **10** digression, divagation, expedition **11** parenthesis **12** pleasure trip

excusable
6 venial

excuse
3 out **4** plea **5** alibi, clear, remit **6** acquit, cop-out, defend, exempt, let off, pardon, reason, wink at **7** absolve, apology, condone, defense, forgive, justify, pretext, regrets, relieve **8** mitigate, overlook, palliate, pass over, shrug off, tolerate **9** discharge, exculpate, exonerate, extenuate, gloss over, makeshift, vindicate, whitewash **10** substitute **11** explanation, rationalize **13** justification

execrable
4 base, foul, vile **7** heinous **8** accursed, damnable, horrific, infernal, wretched **9** abhorrent, atrocious, loathsome, monstrous, repulsive, revolting **10** abominable, deplorable, despicable, detestable, horrifying

execrate
4 damn, hate **5** abhor, curse **6** detest, loathe, revile, vilify **7** censure, condemn, despise **8** denounce **9** abominate, imprecate **12** anathematize

execute
2 do **3** act **4** do in, kill, play, slay **5** cause, lynch **6** effect, finish, murder, render **7** achieve, bump off, conduct, enforce, fulfill, perform, realize **8** carry out, complete, dispatch, knock off, transact **9** discharge, eliminate, implement, liquidate **10** accomplish, administer, bring about, put through, put to death **11** assassinate **12** administrate

execution
6 murder **7** killing **11** performance

executioner
7 hangman, headman **8** headsman

executive
4 dean, suit **6** leader **7** manager **8** director,

governor **9** president **10** supervisor **13** administrator
ineffective: 9 empty suit

exegesis
5 gloss **8** analysis **9** construal **10** commentary, exposition **11** elucidation, explanation, explication **12** construction

exemplar
4 copy **5** ideal, model **7** epitome, paragon, pattern **8** instance, paradigm, specimen, standard **9** archetype, criterion, prototype **12** illustration

exemplary
4 pure **5** ideal, model **7** classic, typical **8** laudable, monitory, virtuous **9** admirable, blameless, classical, estimable, faultless, honorable, righteous **10** impeccable, inculpable, prototypal **11** commendable, meritorious **12** illustrative, paradigmatic, praiseworthy, prototypical

exemplify
4 copy **6** embody, mirror, typify **7** clarify **9** enlighten, epitomize, personify, represent, symbolize **10** concretize, illuminate, illustrate

exempt
4 free **5** spare **6** except, excuse, let off, spared **7** absolve, excused, relieve **8** dispense **9** discharge

exemption
7 freedom, release **8** immunity, impunity **9** discharge, exception

exenterate
3 gut **4** draw **7** embowel **10** disembowel, eviscerate

exercise
3 use, vex **4** fret, gall, hone **5** alarm, annoy, apply, drill, étude, exert, sit-up, train, upset, wield **6** chin-up, crunch, employ, pull-up, push-up **7** agitate, develop, exploit, improve, prepare, problem, provoke, utilize, work out **8** activity, maneuver, practice, rehearse **9** athletics, condition, cultivate, discharge, operation **10** employment **11** application **12** calisthenics

exert
3 use **5** apply, wield **6** employ, expend, put out, strain **8** exercise, put forth

exertion
4 toil, work **5** labor, pains **6** effort, strain **7** trouble **8** activity, exercise, striving **11** application, elbow grease

exfoliate
4 peel, shed **5** scale **7** cast off, leaf out **8** flake off **10** desquamate

exhalation
6 breath **8** emission **9** breathing, effluvium, emanation

exhale
4 blow, emit **6** expire, let out **7** breathe, respire **10** breathe out
audibly: 4 sigh

exhaust
3 fag, sap **4** do in, tire **5** drain, eat up, empty, spend, use up, waste, weary **6** expend, finish, tucker, wash up, weaken **7** burn out, consume, deplete, fatigue, frazzle, tire out, wear out **8** draw down, enervate, squander, wear down **9** discharge, dissipate, prostrate, tucker out **10** debilitate, overextend, run through

exhausted
4 beat, limp, weak **5** all in, spent, tired **6** bushed **7** run-down, worn out **8** dog-tired

exhaustion
7 burnout, fatigue **8** collapse **9** lassitude, tiredness, weariness **11** prostration

exhaustive
8 complete, sweeping, thorough **9** full-blown, full-scale, intensive **10** scrupulous **11** painstaking **13** comprehensive, thoroughgoing

exhibit
4 fair, show **6** evince, expose, flaunt, parade, reveal **7** display, feature, show off **8** evidence, manifest, proclaim, showcase **10** exposition **11** demonstrate

exhibition
4 expo, fair, show **5** rodeo **7** display, pageant, showing **9** trade show **12** presentation **13** demonstration, manifestation

exhibitionist
3 fop **4** toff **6** hot dog **7** peacock, show-off **8** showboat **12** grandstander

exhilarate
4 buoy, lift **5** boost, cheer, elate, exalt, pep up **6** buck up, excite, thrill, uplift **7** animate, cheer up, commove, delight, enliven, gladden, inspire, refresh **8** inspirit, vitalize **9** stimulate **10** invigorate

exhilaration
3 joy **4** glee **7** ecstasy, elation **8** euphoria, gladness **10** exaltation, excitement **11** inspiration **12** vitalization, vivification **13** galvanization

exhort
4 goad, prod, spur, urge, warn **5** egg on, plead, press, prick **6** adjure, call on, incite, prompt, propel **7** beseech, entreat **8** admonish, call upon **9** stimulate

exhortation
4 plea **6** advice, urging **7** caution, warning **8** entreaty, jeremiad **10** admonition, incitement, injunction **11** inspiration **13** encouragement

exhume
5 dig up **6** redeem **7** reclaim, recover, unearth **8** disinter **9** resurrect

exigency
3 fix, jam **4** need, pass **5** pinch, rigor **6** crisis, demand, pickle, plight, strait **7** urgency **8** juncture, pressure, zero hour **9** extremity, necessity **10** compulsion, constraint, crossroads, difficulty, insistence **11** predicament, requirement

exigent
5 acute, vital **6** crying, taxing **7** burning, clamant, instant, onerous **8** exacting, grievous, pressing **9** clamorous, demanding, insistent, necessary **10** burdensome, imperative **11** importunate

exiguous
4 poor, puny, thin, tiny **5** scant, spare, token **6** meager, meagre, measly, paltry, scanty, shabby, skimpy, slight, sparse **7** minimal, scrimpy **9** miserable **10** inadequate, straitened

exile
4 oust **5** eject, expel **6** banish, deport, emigré **7** cast out, outcast, refugee **8** diaspora, displace, drive out, evacuate, expellee **9** exclusion, expulsion, extradite, migration, ostracism, ostracize **10** banishment, dispossess, expatriate, scattering **11** deportation, extradition **12** displacement, expatriation
place of: **4** Elba **7** Siberia **8** St. Helena

exist
2 am, be, is **3** are, lie **4** live **5** occur

existence
4 esse, life **5** being **7** reality **8** duration **9** actuality

existent
4 live, real **5** being, thing **6** actual, entity, extant, living **7** current, instant, present **10** present-day **12** contemporary

existentialist writer
5 Buber (Martin), Camus (Albert) **6** Marcel (Gabriel), Sartre (Jean-Paul) **7** Jaspers (Karl) **8** Beauvoir (Simone de) **9** Heidegger (Martin), Nietzsche (Friedrich) **11** Kierkegaard (Søren)

existing
5 alive, being, ontic **6** extant, living
from birth: **6** innate **10** congenital
Latin: **6** in esse

exit
2 go **3** die **4** door, gate, quit **5** death, going, leave, scram, split **6** depart, egress, escape, outlet, portal, retire **7** doorway, get away, off-ramp **8** withdraw **9** departure, egression **10** withdrawal

____ ex machina
4 deus

exodus
6 flight **9** migration **10** emigration

Exodus author
4 Uris (Leon)

exonerate
4 free **5** clear, remit **6** acquit, excuse, exempt, let off, pardon **7** absolve **8** reprieve **9** exculpate, vindicate

exorbitant
5 undue **7** extreme **9** excessive **10** immoderate, inordinate, outrageous **11** extravagant, unwarranted **12** preposterous

exordium
5 intro, proem **6** lead-in **7** opening, preface, prelude **8** foreword, overture, preamble, prologue **12** introduction, prolegomenon

exotic
4 rare **5** alien **7** bizarre, foreign, strange, unusual **8** alluring, enticing, imported, romantic **9** different, glamorous, nonnative **10** introduced, mysterious **11** fascinating

expand
3 wax **4** grow, open, rise **5** boost, mount, swell, widen **6** beef up, bulk up, dilate, pad out, spread, unfold **7** amplify, augment, bolster, develop, distend, enlarge, inflate, magnify, prolong, stretch **8** escalate, increase, lengthen, multiply, mushroom, protract **9** discourse, elaborate, expatiate, spread out

expanse
4 area, room **5** field, ocean, range, reach, scope, space, sweep, tract **6** domain, extent, sphere, spread **7** breadth, stretch **8** distance **9** territory

expansion
6 growth, spread **8** increase **9** unfolding **11** enlargement **12** augmentation

expansive
3 big **4** wide **5** ample, broad, large, roomy **6** lavish **7** buoyant, elastic, liberal, sizable **8** effusive, extended, generous, outgoing, spacious **9** capacious, garrulous, talkative **10** gregarious, openhanded, unreserved **11** extroverted **13** demonstrative

expatiate
6 ramble, wander **7** dissert, enlarge **8** dilate on, perorate **9** discourse, elaborate, sermonize **10** dilate upon, dissertate

expatriate
5 exile, expel **6** banish, deport, émigré **8** displace, expellee, relegate

expect
4 feel, hope, take **5** await, sense, think, trust **6** assume, divine, gather, look to **7** believe, count on, foresee, imagine, look for, predict, presume, suppose, surmise **8** forecast, foreknow **9** apprehend, count upon **10** anticipate, presuppose

expectant
5 alert **6** gravid **7** anxious, hopeful **8** enceinte, pregnant, vigilant, watchful **10** breathless, parturient **12** anticipatory, apprehensive

expectation
4 hope **5** hunch **8** prospect **9** assurance, intuition **10** assumption, likelihood **11** presumption, probability **12** anticipation, presentiment

expectorate
4 spit

expediency
5 means **6** resort, tactic **7** aptness, fitness, measure, stopgap **8** meetness, recourse, resource, strategy **9** makeshift, propriety, rightness **11** opportunism, suitability **12** appositeness, practicality, suitableness

expedient
3 fit **5** ad hoc, means, shift **6** resort, timely, useful **7** fitting, politic, prudent, stopgap **8** feasible, recourse, resource, suitable, tactical **9** advisable, judicious, makeshift, opportune, practical, pragmatic, well-timed **10** convenient **11** appropriate, practicable, utilitarian **12** advantageous

expedite
4 send **5** hurry, issue, speed **6** hasten **7** quicken, speed up **8** dispatch **10** accelerate, facilitate

expedition
4 trek, trip **5** hurry, speed **6** voyage **7** journey **8** campaign, dispatch **9** excursion, swiftness **10** efficiency, speediness **11** punctuality

expeditious
4 fast **5** brisk, quick, rapid, swift **6** prompt, speedy **9** efficient **11** efficacious

expeditiousness
5 hurry, speed **6** hustle **8** dispatch

expel
4 boot, oust, spew **5** egest, eject, evict, exile **6** banish, bounce, deport, disbar **7** cast out, dismiss, drum out, kick out, turn out **8** disgorge, displace, throw out **9** discharge, eliminate **10** expatriate

expellee
5 exile **6** émigré **7** outcast **8** deportee, emigrant

expend
3 pay, sap **4** blow **5** drain, spend, use up, waste **6** lay out, outlay, pay out **7** consume, deplete, dig into, dole out, exhaust, fork out, utilize **8** disburse, dispense, shell out, squander **9** dissipate **10** run through

expendable
10 disposable **11** dispensable, inessential, replaceable **12** nonessential

expenditure
4 cost **5** outgo **6** outlay, payoff, payout **12** disbursement

expense
4 cost, loss, toll **5** debit, price **6** burden, charge, outlay **7** forfeit, payment **8** overhead **9** decrement, sacrifice **10** forfeiture **12** disbursement

expensive
4 dear, high, posh **5** fancy, pricy, ritzy, steep, stiff **6** costly, deluxe, lavish, pricey **7** upscale **8** precious, valuable, wasteful **9** big-ticket, luxurious **10** exorbitant, high-priced, overpriced **11** extravagant **12** uneconomical

experience
4 know, live **5** event, savor, skill, trial **6** ordeal, suffer, wisdom **7** episode, know-how, sustain, undergo **8** incident, practice **9** encounter, go through **10** background **11** familiarity, savoir faire
anew: 6 relive

experienced
4 wise **6** mature, versed **7** old-line, veteran, worldly **8** broken in, seasoned **9** practiced, qualified **12** accomplished

experiential
see **empirical**

experiment
3 try **4** test **5** assay, probe, trial **6** try out **7** test out **8** research, trial run **13** trial and error

experimental
9 empirical, tentative **10** innovative **11** exploratory, preliminary, preparatory, provisional **13** developmental, trial-and-error

experimentation
4 test **5** trial **7** testing **8** research, trial run **13** trial and error

expert
3 ace, pro, wiz **4** deft, whiz **5** adept, crack, doyen, maven **6** adroit, master, wizard **7** skilled **8** masterly, skillful, virtuoso **9** authority, dexterous, masterful, virtuosic **10** past master, proficient, specialist **11** crackerjack **12** passed master, professional

expertise
5 craft, skill **7** ability, command, know-how, mastery **8** facility **10** adroitness, competence **11** proficiency **12** skillfulness

expiate
6 offset, pay for, redeem **7** redress **8** atone for

expiation
9 atonement, indemnity **10** recompense, reparation **11** restitution **12** satisfaction

expiatory
7 atoning, lustral **9** purgative **11** penitential, purgatorial **12** propitiatory

expiration
3 end **5** death **10** exhalation **11** termination

expire
3 die, end **4** pass **5** lapse **6** elapse, exhale,

pass on, perish, run out **7** decease **8** pass away **9** terminate **10** breathe out

explain
5 gloss, solve **7** analyze, clarify, clear up, condone, expound, justify, resolve, unravel **8** construe, decipher, spell out, unriddle, untangle **9** break down, elucidate, interpret **10** account for, illuminate, illustrate, unscramble **11** disentangle, rationalize

explain away
6 excuse **7** justify **8** minimize **9** extenuate **10** account for **11** rationalize

explanation
3 key **5** gloss **6** excuse, motive, reason **7** account, example, grounds, meaning **8** exegesis **9** construal, rationale **11** elucidation **12** significance **13** clarification

explanatory
10 discursive, exegetical **12** enlightening, illuminating, illustrative, interpretive

expletive
4 cuss, oath **5** curse, swear **8** cussword **9** swearword **12** interjection (see also **exclamation**)

explicate
7 amplify, develop, explain, expound **8** construe, spell out **9** elucidate, interpret

explication
5 gloss **8** exegesis **9** construal **10** commentary **11** development

explicative
10 discursive, exegetical, scholastic **12** interpretive **13** hermeneutical

explicit
4 open, sure **5** clear, exact, frank, lucid, overt, plain **7** certain, correct, express, obvious, precise **8** clear-cut, definite, distinct, specific **10** definitive **11** categorical, perspicuous, unambiguous, unequivocal

explode
3 pop **4** fire **5** blast, burst, erupt, go off **6** blow up, debunk, negate, refute **7** burgeon, deflate **8** break out, burst out, detonate, disprove, dynamite, mushroom, puncture **9** discharge, discredit **10** burst forth **11** proliferate

exploit
3 act, use **4** coup, deed, feat, gest, play **5** abuse, geste, stunt **6** bestow, effort, employ, parlay, play on **7** emprise, utilize, venture **8** escapade, exercise **9** adventure, cultivate **10** enterprise, manipulate **11** achievement, performance, tour de force

explore
5 probe, scout **6** burrow, go into, search **7** dig into, examine **8** look into, prospect, traverse **9** delve into **11** inquire into, investigate

explorer
African: 3 Cam, Cão (Diogo) **4** Park (Mungo) **5** Grant (James), Laird (Macgregor), Speke (John Hanning) **6** Akeley (Carl, Mary), Burton (Richard), Lander (John, Richard) **7** Covilhâ (Pero da), Stanley (Henry) **8** Covilhâo (Pero da) **10** Clapperton (Hugh) **11** Livingstone (David)
American: 4 Byrd (Richard), Hall (Charles Francis), Kane (Elisha Kent), Pike (Zebulon) **5** Beebe (Charles William), Clark (William), Lewis (Meriwether), Peary (Robert) **6** Henson (Matthew), Powell (John Wesley), Wilkes (Charles) **7** Ballard (Robert), Frémont (John Charles)
Antarctic: 4 Byrd (Richard), Cook (Frederick), Ross (James Clark) **5** Fuchs (Vivian), Ronne (Finn), Scott (Robert Falcon) **6** Palmer (Nathaniel), Rymill (John Riddoch), Wilkes (Charles) **7** Weddell (James), Wilkins (George) **8** Amundsen (Roald), d'Urville (Dumont) **9** Ellsworth (Lincoln) **10** Shackleton (Ernest)
Arctic: 3 Rae (John) **4** Byrd (Richard), Cook (Frederick) **5** Davis (John), Peary (Robert) **6** Baffin (William), Bering (Vitus), Henson (Matthew), Hudson (Henry), Nansen (Fridtjof), Nobile (Umberto) **7** Barents (Willem), Bennett (Floyd), Wilkins (George), Wrangel (Ferdinand von) **8** Amundsen (Roald) **9** Mackenzie (Alexander), MacMillan (Donald) **10** Stefansson (Vilhjalmur)
Australian: 7 Wilkins (George)
Austrian: 9 Weyprecht (Carl)
Canadian: 9 Mackenzie (Alexander) **10** Stefansson (Vilhjalmur)
Danish: 9 Rasmussen (Knud)
Dutch: 6 Tasman (Abel Janszoon)
English: 4 Cook (James) **5** Cabot (John, Sebastian), Drake (Francis), Scott (Robert Falcon), Smith (John) **6** Baffin (William), Burton (Richard), Hudson (Henry) **7** Raleigh (Walter), Stanley (Henry) **9** Vancouver (George) **10** Shackleton (Ernest) **12** Younghusband (Francis)
French: 7 Cartier (Jacques), La Salle (Sleur de), Nicolet (Jean) **8** Cousteau (Jacques-Yves) **9** Champlain (Samuel de), La Perouse (Comte de), Marquette (Jacques)
French Canadian: 6 Joliet (Louis) **7** Jolliet (Louis) **9** Iberville (Sieur d')
German: 6 Peters (Carl) **8** Humboldt (Alexander von)
Italian: 5 Cabot (John) **6** Nobile (Umberto) **8** Vespucci (Amerigo)
New Zealand: 7 Hillary (Edmund)
Norwegian: 6 Nansen (Fridtjof) **8** Amundsen (Roald), Sverdrup (Otto) **9** Heyerdahl (Thor)
Portuguese: 4 Gama (Vasco da) **5** Cunha (Tristão da) **6** Cabral (Pedro) **8** Cabrilho (João Rodrigues), Magellan (Ferdinand)
Scottish: 3 Rae (John) **4** Park (Mungo), Ross (James Clark) **7** Thomson (Joseph) **11** Livingstone (David)

Spanish: **6** Balboa (Vasco Núñez de), Cortés (Hernán, Hernando), de Soto (Hernando), Pinzón (Martín Alonso, Vicente Yáñez) **7** Mendoza (Pedro de), Pizarro (Francisco) **8** Bastidas (Rodrigo de), Coronado (Francisco de) **11** Ponce de León (Juan)

explosion
3 pop, pow **4** bang, boom, clap **5** blast, burst, crack, crash, sally, salvo, storm **6** report, volley **7** barrage, blowout, torrent **8** eruption, outburst, paroxysm **9** discharge **10** detonation
cosmic: **7** big bang

explosive
3 TNT **5** nitro, tense **6** charge, napalm, petard, powder **7** cordite, violent **8** dynamite **9** gunpowder **13** nitroglycerin
device: **3** cap **4** bomb, mine **5** shell **6** petard **7** grenade **8** firework
inventor: **5** Maxim (Hudson), Nobel (Alfred)
sound: **3** pop, pow **4** bang, blam, boom **5** crack

exponent
6 backer **7** booster **8** advocate, champion, defender, partisan, promoter, upholder **9** supporter **12** practitioner

expose
3 air **4** bare, open, show **5** dig up, flash **6** debunk, flaunt, parade, reveal, show up, unmask, unveil **7** abandon, display, exhibit, lay open, publish, show off, subject, uncover, undress **8** brandish, disclose, discover, endanger, unclothe

exposé
10 disclosure, revelation, uncovering

exposed
4 bare, open **5** naked **6** liable **7** evident, subject, visible **8** manifest, stripped, unhidden **9** uncovered **11** susceptible, unconcealed, unprotected

exposition
4 fair, show **6** bazaar **7** display, exhibit **9** trade show

expostulate
5 argue **6** debate, reason **7** discuss, dispute

exposure
4 risk **5** peril **6** airing, baring, danger **8** betrayal, jeopardy, openness **9** liability, publicity **10** revelation **12** helplessness **13** vulnerability

expound
5 state **6** defend **7** clarify, comment, explain, present **8** construe, set forth, spell out **9** discourse, explicate, interpret

expounder
7 teacher **8** advocate, champion, defender, promoter **9** proponent, supporter

express
3 air, say **4** mean, tell, vent **5** couch, crush, frame, state, utter, voice **6** broach, convey, denote, impart, intend, voiced **7** connote, declare, signify, special, uttered **8** announce, clear-cut, definite, disclose, explicit, intended, proclaim, specific **9** enunciate, formulate, high-speed, pronounce, symbolize, ventilate **10** definitive, particular **11** categorical, communicate, intentional, unambiguous
gratitude: **5** thank
regret: **9** apologize

expression
4 cast, face, form, look, mien, sign, vent, word **5** idiom, issue, motto, token, voice **6** symbol, visage **7** diction, gesture **8** locution **9** eloquence, statement, utterance, verbalism, vividness **10** embodiment, indication **11** countenance, enunciation, observation **13** demonstration, manifestation
facial: **4** grin, phiz, pout **5** frown, scowl, smile, smirk, sneer, wince **7** grimace
of assent: **3** aye, nod, yea, yes **4** okay
of sorrow: **4** alas, tear
trite: **6** cliché **7** bromide **8** banality
witty: **4** quip **5** sally **6** bon mot

expressionless
5 blank **6** stolid, vacant, wooden **7** deadpan **9** impassive **10** poker-faced **11** inscrutable

expressive
5 vivid **7** graphic **8** eloquent **9** revealing **10** meaningful, passionate

expressly
9 precisely, purposely **10** explicitly **12** particularly, specifically **13** intentionally

expressway
4 road **7** freeway, highway, parkway **8** turnpike **12** thoroughfare

expropriate
4 take **5** annex, seize **7** impound, preempt **8** arrogate **9** sequester **10** commandeer, confiscate, dispossess

expulsion
5 exile, purge **6** ouster **7** ousting, removal **8** ejection, eviction **9** ostracism **10** banishment, relegation **11** deportation **12** displacement

expunge
4 dele, x out **5** annul, erase **6** cancel, delete, efface **7** blot out, destroy, exclude, wipe out **8** black out **9** eliminate, eradicate, strike out **10** annihilate, obliterate

expurgate
4 blip **5** bleep, purge **6** censor, purify, screen **7** cleanse **8** sanitize **10** bowdlerize

expurgation
8 ablution **9** catharsis, cleansing **10** lustration **12** purification

exquisite
3 fop **4** fine, keen, rare **5** acute, dandy **6** choice, dainty, select, superb **7** coxcomb, elegant, extreme, intense, refined **8** delicate, finished, flawless, macaroni **9** recherché **10** fastidious, immaculate, impeccable

exsiccate
3 dry **4** sear **5** parch **6** wither **7** shrivel **9** dehydrate

extant
4 live **5** alive **6** actual, living **7** current, present **9** surviving **10** present-day **12** contemporary

extemporaneous
5 ad-lib **6** casual **7** offhand **8** ad-libbed, informal **9** impromptu, impulsive, makeshift, unplanned **10** improvised, unprepared, unscripted **11** spontaneous, unrehearsed **12** unthought-out

extempore
see **extemporaneous**

extemporize
5 ad-lib **6** wing it **7** dash off, toss off **8** knock off **9** improvise

extend
4 draw, span, vary **5** award, offer, range, reach **6** bestow, spread, unbend, unfold **7** advance, augment, broaden, drag out, draw out, enlarge, further, hold out, proceed, proffer, project, prolong, spin out, stretch **8** continue, elongate, increase, lengthen, protract **10** outstretch, stretch out

extension
3 arm, ell **4** wing **5** add-on, annex, delay, range, reach, scope, sweep **6** radius, spread **7** adjunct, compass, purview **8** addition, increase **9** appendage, magnitude **10** broadening, elongation **11** enlargement, lengthening, protraction **12** augmentation, continuation, postponement, prolongation

extensity
5 ambit, orbit, range, reach, scope, sweep **6** radius **7** compass, purview

extensive
3 big **4** long, vast, wide **5** broad, large, major **7** general, immense, lengthy, sizable **8** far-flung, sizeable, spacious, sweeping, thorough **9** wholesale **10** large-scale, widespread **11** far-reaching, wide-ranging **12** considerable

extent
4 size **5** ambit, limit, orbit, range, reach, scope, sweep, width **6** amount, degree, domain, radius **7** breadth, compass, measure, purview **8** vicinity **9** magnitude **10** dimensions, proportion

extenuate
6 dilute, excuse, lessen, soften, temper, weaken **7** explain, justify, qualify, varnish **8** diminish, enervate, mitigate, moderate, palliate **9** gloss over **11** rationalize

exterior
4 skin **5** outer, shell **6** facade **7** outmost, outside, outward, surface **8** apparent **9** outermost **11** superficial

exterminate
4 kill **6** rub out **7** destroy, wipe out **8** massacre **9** eliminate, eradicate, finish off, liquidate, slaughter **10** annihilate, extinguish, obliterate

external
3 out **4** over **5** outer **7** foreign, outside, outward, surface **9** outermost **10** peripheral **11** superficial

externalize
4 show **6** embody, evince, excuse, expose, reveal **7** exhibit, justify **8** manifest **9** extenuate, incarnate, objectify, personify **11** rationalize **12** substantiate

extinct
4 cold, dead, gone, late **5** passé **6** bygone **7** archaic, defunct **8** deceased, departed, obsolete, perished, vanished **10** superseded

extinction
3 end **4** doom **5** death **6** demise **11** destruction, eradication, liquidation **12** annihilation, obliteration **13** disappearance, extermination

extinguish
3 end **5** crush, douse, erase, quash, quell, snuff **6** put out, quench, squash, stifle **7** abolish, blot out, blow out, destroy, eclipse, expunge, nullify, put down, wipe out **8** snuff out, stamp out, suppress **9** eliminate, eradicate, extirpate **10** annihilate, obliterate

extirpate
5 erase **6** cut out, efface, excise, resect, uproot **7** abolish, blot out, destroy, expunge, kill off, root out, wipe out **8** demolish **9** eliminate, eradicate **10** annihilate, deracinate, extinguish

extol
4 hymn, laud **5** cry up, exalt **6** praise **7** acclaim, applaud, commend, glorify, magnify **8** eulogize **9** celebrate **10** panegyrize

extort
5 wrest, wring **7** extract

extortion
8 exaction **9** blackmail

extra
3 odd **4** more, over, perk, plus **5** added, add-on, bonus, spare **6** de trop, rarely **7** reserve, surplus **8** leftover **9** lagniappe, redundant, unusually **10** additional, especially, perquisite

11 superfluous 12 particularly, supplemental 13 supernumerary, supplementary

extract
4 pull, yank 5 evoke, glean, quote, wring 6 derive, eke out, elicit, remove 7 abridge, distill, essence, excerpt, passage, pull out, squeeze, take out 8 citation, condense, infusion 9 quotation, selection 11 concentrate

extraction
5 birth, blood, stock 6 origin 7 descent, essence, lineage 8 ancestry, pedigree 9 parentage 10 derivation 12 distillation

extraneous
5 alien, outer 6 exotic 7 foreign, outside 8 external 9 unrelated 10 immaterial, inapposite, incidental, irrelevant, peripheral 11 impertinent, inessential, superfluous, unessential 12 adventitious, inapplicable, nonessential

extraordinary
3 odd 4 rare 6 unique 7 amazing, notable, special, unusual 8 abnormal, atypical, singular, terrific, uncommon, unwonted 9 wonderful 10 noteworthy, phenomenal, remarkable, stupendous, tremendous 11 exceptional, outstanding

extravagance
5 frill, waste 6 excess, luxury 9 hyperbole, profusion 10 indulgence, lavishness 11 ostentation, prodigality, superfluity 12 immoderation, wastefulness

extravagant
4 wild 5 outré, undue 6 lavish 7 bizarre, extreme, profuse 8 overdone, prodigal, reckless, wasteful 9 elaborate, excessive, fantastic, grandiose, overblown 10 exorbitant, hyperbolic, immoderate, inordinate, profligate 11 exaggerated, implausible, intemperate, nonsensical 12 ostentatious, preposterous, unrestrained

extreme
3 max, top 4 apex, dire, last, peak, wild 5 crown, final, limit, ultra, undue 6 climax, excess, height, summit, utmost, zenith 7 drastic, fanatic, intense, maximal, maximum, outmost, radical, violent 8 farthest, furthest, pinnacle, remotest, ultimate 9 desperate, excessive, outermost, uttermost 10 immoderate, inordinate, outlandish, outrageous 11 furthermost, unwarranted 12 unmeasurable, unreasonable 13 revolutionary
degree: 3 nth

extremely
4 mega, most, unco, very 5 ultra 6 highly, hugely, mighty, overly, plenty, wildly 7 acutely, awfully, greatly, utterly 8 severely, terribly 9 immensely, seriously, unusually 10 remarkably, strikingly 11 exceedingly 12 terrifically

extremist
5 rabid, ultra 6 zealot 7 die-hard, fanatic, radical 8 militant, ultraist 9 fanatical 10 monomaniac, ultraistic 11 reactionary 13 revolutionary

extremity
3 arm, end, leg, tip 4 acme, apex, foot, hand, tail 5 limit, verge 6 apogee, vertex, zenith 8 terminal, terminus

extricate
4 free 5 loose 6 detach, redeem, rescue 7 bail out, deliver, resolve, set free, untwine 8 liberate, untangle 9 disengage 11 disencumber, disentangle, distinguish, individuate 12 discriminate, disembarrass 13 differentiate

extrinsic
5 alien, outer 6 exotic 7 foreign, outside, outward 8 exterior, external, imported 10 incidental, extraneous

extrude
4 spew 5 eject 7 push out 8 press out 10 squeeze out

exuberance
4 glee, life, zest 5 ardor 6 gaiety, spirit 7 abandon 8 buoyancy, hilarity, vivacity 9 profusion 10 ebullience, enthusiasm, friskiness, liveliness 11 flamboyance, high spirits, zestfulness 12 exhilaration 13 effervescence, sprightliness

exuberant
3 gay 4 lush, rank 5 happy 6 bouncy, elated, fecund, lavish, lively 7 buoyant, profuse, rampant, riotous, zestful 8 fruitful, prodigal, prolific, spirited 9 ebullient, luxuriant, sprightly, vivacious 10 flamboyant 11 exhilarated 12 effervescent, enthusiastic, high-spirited

exude
4 emit, leak, ooze, seep, shed 5 issue 7 diffuse, display, emanate, excrete, exhibit, give off, ooze out, radiate, secrete 9 discharge

exult
4 crow 5 cheer, gloat, glory, revel 7 delight, rejoice 8 jubilate 9 celebrate

exultant
6 elated, joyful, joyous 7 gleeful 8 ecstatic, euphoric, jubilant 9 cock-a-hoop, overjoyed, rejoicing, triumphal 10 triumphant

exultation
3 joy 4 glee 7 delight, ecstasy, elation, rapture, triumph 8 euphoria, gloating 9 jubilance, rejoicing 10 jubilation

eye
3 orb 4 lamp, ogle, scan, view 5 sight, watch 6 behold, goggle, look at, ocular, oculus, peeper, regard, size up, vision 7 inspect, observe 8 check out, consider, gaze upon, scrutiny 9 headlight 10 scrutinize

combining form: **4** ocul **5** oculo **8** ophthalm **9** ophthalmo
defect: **6** myopia **9** hyperopia **10** emmetropia, presbyopia **11** astigmatism
disease: **8** cataract, glaucoma, trachoma
doctor: **7** oculist **11** optometrist
opening: **5** pupil
part: **4** iris, lens, uvea **5** pupil **6** cornea, retina, sclera
relating to: **5** optic **7** optical
socket: **5** orbit
Spanish: **3** ojo
test: **10** Amsler Grid **12** Snellen Chart

eyeball
4 scan **5** check, study **6** go over, look at, peruse, survey **7** examine, inspect, observe **8** appraise, check out, evaluate, pore over **10** scrutinize

eye-catching
4 bold **5** gaudy, showy **6** flashy **7** salient **8** striking **9** arresting, prominent **10** noticeable, remarkable **11** conspicuous

eyeful
6 looker **7** stunner **8** knockout

eyeglass
7 monocle

eyeglasses
5 specs **6** lenses **7** lorgnon **8** bifocals, pince-nez **9** lorgnette **10** spectacles

eyelash
6 cilium **11** hairbreadth

eyelet
4 hole **7** grommet **8** loophole, peephole

eyelid growth
3 sty **4** cyst, stye **5** nevus **9** chalazion, hordeolum

eyepiece
4 lens **6** ocular

eye-popping
7 amazing **8** exciting, stirring **9** thrilling **10** astounding **11** astonishing, mind-blowing, spectacular **12** breathtaking

eyesore
4 blot, dump, mess **6** blight **7** blemish **8** atrocity **11** monstrosity

eyespot
6 blight, fungus **7** ocellus

eyetooth
6 canine

eyewash
3 rot **4** bunk **5** bilge, hooey, tripe **6** bunkum **7** baloney, garbage, hogwash, rubbish, twaddle **8** malarkey, nonsense **9** poppycock **10** balderdash **13** horsefeathers

eyewitness
8 observer, onlooker **9** bystander, spectator

eyrie
see **aerie**

F

Fabergé product
3 egg 9 Easter egg

Fabian
4 Shaw (George Bernard), Webb (Beatrice, Sidney) 7 politic 8 cautious, dilatory 9 socialist 11 circumspect, calculating

fable
4 myth, tale, yarn 5 story 6 legend 7 fantasy, fiction, figment, parable 8 allegory, tall tale
animal: 8 bestiary

fabled
5 famed 6 famous, unreal 7 storied 8 fanciful, mythical, renowned 9 fictional, imaginary, legendary, pretended 10 fictitious 11 make-believe 12 mythological

fabric
3 aba, rep, web 4 lamé, repp 5 cloth, fiber, grain 7 texture 8 building, material, shirting 9 structure
coarse: 4 tapa 5 crash, gunny 6 burlap, linsey, ratiné 7 cheviot, hopsack 8 homespun
colorer: 4 dyer
corded: 3 rep 4 repp 5 piqué 6 calico, moreen, poplin 7 pinwale 8 corduroy, paduasoy 9 bengaline
cotton: 4 jean, leno 5 baize, chino, denim, domet, drill, lisle, scrim, wigan 6 chintz, dimity, faille, madras, muslin, sateen 7 etamine, gingham, nankeen, percale, ticking 8 chambray, dungaree, nainsook, tarlatan 9 crinoline 10 seersucker
cotton and linen: 4 huck 7 fustian 9 huckaback
crepe: 8 marocain
dealer: 6 draper, mercer
durable: 4 huck, jean 5 chino, denim, drill, scrim 6 frieze, moreen 7 lasting, ticking 8 cretonne, dungaree
embroidered: 9 baldachin 10 baldachino
finishing process: 8 lustring 9 mercerize
flag material: 7 bunting
glazed: 4 ciré 6 chintz 7 cambric, holland
knitted: 6 tricot 10 balbriggan
linen: 7 cambric, lockram
looped: 6 bouclé
lustrous: 4 silk 5 moiré, satin, surah 6 sateen 7 taffeta 12 brilliantine
metallic: 4 lamé
net: 5 tulle 8 bobbinet, illusion
openwork: 4 lace 8 filigree
ornamental: 4 lace 5 braid 6 ribbon 7 bunting
pebbly-surface: 8 barathea
pile-surface: 5 panne, plush, terry 6 velour, velvet 7 duvetyn, velours 8 chenille, moleskin 9 velveteen
plaid: 6 tartan
pleated: 5 ruche
printed: 5 batik, toile 6 calico, chintz, damask 7 allover, challis 8 cretonne, jacquard 11 toile de Jouy
puckered: 6 plissé 10 seersucker
raised pattern: 4 lamé 7 brocade 10 brocatelle
satin weave: 5 panne
sheer: 4 lawn, mull 5 gauze, ninon, voile 6 dimity 7 batiste, chiffon, organdy, organza, tiffany 8 tarlatan
silk: 6 faille, pongee, samite 7 foulard, grogram 8 paduasoy, sarcenet, sarsenet, shantung 9 bombazine
striped: 3 aba 7 ticking 8 bayadere
synthetic: 5 Arnel, ninon, nylon, Orlon, rayon 6 Dacron
trim: 5 ruche
twill: 4 jean 5 chino, drill, serge 7 foulard, nankeen, ticking 8 dungaree, shalloon 9 bombazine 10 broadcloth
unfinished: 6 greige
waterproof: 7 oilskin
wool: 5 baize, loden, tweed 6 alpaca, caddis, camlet, duffel, duffle, melton, merino, wadmal, wadmel, wadmol, woolen 7 woollen 8 mackinaw, prunella 9 cassimere
wool, poor quality: 5 mungo 6 shoddy
wool mixture: 6 saxony 7 drugget, ratteen 8 moquette, shalloon, zibeline 9 zibelline
woven: 4 weft 7 textile

fabricate
4 form, make 5 build, erect, frame, set up, shape 6 cook up, create, devise, invent, make up 7 concoct, dream up, fashion, produce, think up 8 assemble, contrive 9 construct, structure 11 manufacture, put together

fabrication
3 fib, lie 4 bull, jive 6 canard, deceit 7 fiction, figment, hogwash, product, untruth 8 assembly,

building, creation **9** deception, fairy tale, falsehood, invention **10** concoction, production **11** manufacture **12** construction

fabulist
4 liar
French: 10 La Fontaine (Jean de)
Greek: 5 Aesop
Roman: 8 Phaedrus
Russian: 6 Krylov (Ivan)

fabulous
5 super **7** amazing **8** mythical, terrific, wondrous **9** fantastic, legendary, marvelous, wonderful **10** astounding, fictitious, incredible, outrageous, phenomenal, prodigious, remarkable, stupendous **11** astonishing, extravagant, spectacular **12** mythological
animal: 6 dragon **7** centaur, unicorn
bird: 3 roc
serpent: 8 basilisk **10** cockatrice

facade
4 face, mask **5** color, front, guise, put-on **6** veneer **8** disguise, exterior, frontage, pretense **10** appearance, camouflage, false front

face
3 mug, pan **4** dare, defy, dial, meet, phiz, puss, show, side **5** abide, brave, front, guise, honor, image, nerve **6** endure, facade, kisser, makeup, mazard, oppose, resist, suffer, take on, visage **7** compete, contend, dignity, surface **8** confront, cope with, deal with, disguise, features, prestige, war paint **9** assurance, encounter, lineament, semblance, withstand **10** appearance, confidence, experience, expression, maquillage, reputation **11** countenance, self-respect

face-off
5 clash, set-to **13** confrontation

facet
4 edge, item, part, side **5** angle, bezel, front, phase, plane, point, trait **6** aspect, detail **7** element, feature, surface **9** attribute, component **10** appearance, particular

facetious
4 flip **5** comic, droll, jokey, smart, witty **6** blithe, breezy, joking **7** amusing, comical, jesting, jocular, joshing, kidding, risible, waggish **8** flippant, humorous **9** ludicrous, unserious, whimsical **10** irreverent, ridiculous **12** wisecracking **13** tongue-in-cheek

face-to-face
6 direct **7** contact, present, vis-à-vis **8** directly, in person, personal **10** personally

facile
4 deft, easy, glib, snap **5** light, quick, ready **6** adroit, expert, fluent, poised, simple, smooth **7** assured, cursory, offhand, shallow, voluble **8** skillful, untaxing **9** dexterous **10** effortless, simplistic **13** uncomplicated

facilitate
3 aid **4** abet, ease, help **6** assist, enable, smooth **7** advance, forward, further, promote **8** expedite, make easy, simplify

facility
3 aid, wit **4** bent, ease **5** knack, privy, skill **6** talent, toilet **7** ability, amenity, comfort, fluency, leaning **8** aptitude, bathroom, building, capacity, lavatory, washroom **9** advantage, dexterity **10** adroitness, competence, smoothness **11** convenience, institution, proficiency **12** installation **13** accommodation, establishment

facing
5 front, panel **6** contra, lining, toward, veneer **7** surface, vis-à-vis **8** covering, opposite, paneling **11** over against
down: 5 prone
up: 6 supine

facsimile
4 copy, dupe, fake, twin **5** clone, ditto, match, mimeo, repro, Xerox **6** carbon, double **7** replica **8** knockoff, likeness **9** duplicate, imitation, photocopy **10** carbon copy, dead ringer, similitude **11** counterpart, duplication, replication **12** reproduction

fact
4 dope **5** datum, event, truth **6** detail, gospel, truism, verity **7** episode, reality **8** evidence, incident **9** actuality **10** occurrence, particular, phenomenon **11** information **12** circumstance, intelligence

faction
4 band, bloc, camp, part, ring, sect, side, wing **5** cabal, group, party **6** caucus, circle, clique, sector, strife **7** combine, coterie, discord, section **8** alliance, disunity, splinter **10** contingent

factious
7 warring **8** contrary, divisive, partisan **9** dissident, insurgent, sectarian, seditious, turbulent **10** contending, malcontent **11** contentious, disaffected, dissentious, quarrelsome **12** disputatious **13** troublemaking

factitious
4 sham **5** bogus, false, phony **6** ersatz, forced, made-up, unreal **7** assumed, created, feigned, man-made, shammed **8** affected, invented, spurious **9** concocted, contrived, fashioned, pretended, simulated, synthetic, unnatural **10** artificial, fabricated **11** constructed, counterfeit **12** manufactured **13** counterfeited

____ facto
4 ipso **6** ex post

factor
4 gene, item **5** agent, cause, proxy **6** broker, lender, number, symbol **7** divisor, element, exclude, include, resolve **8** attorney, emissary,

quantity **9** component, majordomo, substance **10** antecedent, ingredient, multiplier **11** determinant **12** intermediary

factory
4 mill, shop **5** plant, works **8** workshop **9** sweatshop **11** machine shop

factotum
4 grub **5** gofer **6** drudge **7** servant **9** assistant, gal Friday, man Friday, operative **11** functionary

factual
4 real, true **5** exact, valid **6** actual **7** certain, genuine, literal **8** absolute, positive **9** authentic, undoubted **10** undisputed **12** indisputable

faculty
4 bent, body, gift **5** flair, knack, power **6** talent **7** ability, college **8** aptitude, capacity, facility, function, instinct **9** educators, lecturers **10** department, professors **11** instructors

fad
4 chic, kick, mode, rage, whim **5** craze, furor, mania, style, trend **6** furore, latest, whimsy **7** caprice, fashion **9** bandwagon **10** dernier cri

faddish
3 hot **4** chic **5** today **6** modish, red-hot, trendy, with-it **7** stylish, voguish **8** contempo **9** au courant **11** cutting-edge, fashionable

fade
3 die, dim, ebb **4** fail, pale, wane, wilt **6** lessen, vanish, weaken, wither **7** decline, lighten, wash out **8** decrease, discolor, diminish **9** disappear, evaporate

faded
3 dim, wan **4** drab, dull, pale **6** pallid **8** bleached, vanished, withered **9** etiolated, washed-out

Faerie Queene, The
author: **7** Spenser (Edmund)
character: **3** Ate, Una **4** Alma **5** Guyon, Talus **6** Abessa, Amavia, Amoret, Arthur, Cambel, Duessa, Palmer **7** Artegal, Corceca, Fidessa, Maleger, Sansloy **8** Calidore, Florimel, Fradubio, Gloriana, Lucifera, Orgoglio, Satyrane **9** Archimago, Britomart **11** Britomartis

Faeroes whirlwind
2 oe

Fafnir
6 dragon
brother: **5** Regin **6** Fasolt, Reginn
father: **8** Hreidmar
slayer: **6** Sigurd **9** Siegfried
victim: **6** Fasolt **8** Hreidmar

fag
4 do in, moil, tire, toil **5** serve, smoke, stick, weary **6** drudge, overdo, tucker **7** exhaust, fatigue, servant, wear out **8** drudgery, knock out **9** cigarette

fag end
4 butt, edge, fray **7** remnant

faience
7 pottery **11** earthenware

fail
3 die, end **4** bomb, fade, lack, lose, miss, sink, slip, stop, wane **5** break, flunk **6** fizzle, forget, ignore, lessen, weaken **7** decline, default, founder, give out, go under, neglect **8** fall flat, languish, miscarry **9** break down, fall short **10** disappoint, go bankrupt **11** deteriorate

failing
4 flaw, vice **5** fault **6** defect **8** weakness **9** weak point **10** deficiency **11** shortcoming **12** imperfection

failure
3 bum, dud **4** bomb, bust, flop, miss **5** decay, loser **6** fiasco, fizzle, no-good, outage **7** default, washout **8** collapse, fracture, omission **9** breakdown, cessation, oversight, unconcern **10** bankruptcy, deficiency, insolvency, negligence **11** defalcation, dysfunction, miscarriage **12** interruption **13** deterioration

fain
3 apt **5** eager, prone, ready **6** gladly, minded **7** willing **8** amenable, inclined **9** agreeable

fainéant
3 bum **4** idle, lazy **5** idler, sloth **6** loafer, torpid **7** goof-off, slacker **8** deadbeat, inactive, indolent, layabout, slothful, sluggard, sluggish **9** do-nothing, lazybones, shiftless **11** couch potato, ineffectual **13** lackadaisical

faint
3 dim, low, wan **4** hazy, pale, soft, weak, wilt **5** dizzy, light, plotz, swoon, vague, woozy **6** feeble, subtle **7** conk out, obscure, pass out, shadowy, syncope, unclear **8** black out, collapse, keel over **9** undefined **10** ill-defined, indistinct

fair
2 OK **3** due **4** even, expo, fine, join, just, mild, okay, open, so-so **5** blond, bonny, clear, equal, fresh, light, sunny **6** bazaar, blonde, comely, decent, honest, kermis, lovely, market, pretty, square **7** cricket **8** adequate, all right, balanced, carnival, festival, mediocre, middling, pleasant, pleasing, rational, sunshiny, unbiased **9** beautiful, cloudless, equitable, favorable, fortunate, impartial, objective, tolerable, trade show, unclouded **10** acceptable, attractive, evenhanded, exhibition, exposition, open-minded, reasonable **11** indifferent, nonpartisan, respectable **12** satisfactory, unprejudiced **13** disinterested, dispassionate, sportsmanlike

fair food
10 candy apple, candy floss, fried dough, funnel cake **11** cotton candy, elephant ear

fair-haired
3 pet 5 blond 6 blonde 7 beloved, darling, favored 8 favorite 9 fortunate

fairly
5 quite 6 nearly, rather 7 plainly 8 passably, properly, somewhat 9 tolerably 10 acceptably, deservedly, distinctly, moderately, reasonably 11 practically

fairness
6 candor, equity 7 honesty 8 justness 9 good faith 12 impartiality

fairy
3 elf, imp, nix 4 peri, puck 5 elfin, nixie, nymph, pixie, sylph 6 goblin, kobold, sprite 7 brownie, gremlin 10 leprechaun
king: 6 Oberon
queen: 3 Mab 7 Titania 8 Gloriana
shoemaker: 10 leprechaun

fairy tale
author: 4 Lang (Andrew) 5 Grimm (Jacob, Wilhelm), Wilde (Oscar) 7 Kipling (Rudyard) 8 Andersen (Hans Christian), Perrault (Charles)
character: 4 Jack, Puck 6 Gretel, Hansel 8 Rapunzel, Tom Thumb 9 Snow White 10 Cinderella, Goldilocks, Thumbelina

faith
4 cult, sect 5 credo, creed, stock, troth, trust 6 belief, church, credit 8 credence, reliance, religion 9 certainty, certitude, communion, credulity 10 confidence, persuasion 12 denomination
article of: 5 tenet

faithful
4 fast, just, true 5 liege, loyal, pious, tried 6 steady, trusty 7 devoted, dutiful, staunch 8 constant, follower, reliable, resolute, true-blue 9 religious, steadfast 10 dependable, scrupulous, unwavering 11 truehearted, trustworthy

faithfulness
5 piety, troth 6 fealty 7 loyalty 8 devotion, fidelity 9 adherence, constancy 10 allegiance, attachment

faithless
5 false, Punic 6 fickle, untrue 8 disloyal, recreant 10 perfidious, traitorous 11 treacherous 13 untrustworthy

faithlessness
7 perfidy, treason 8 betrayal 9 falseness, treachery 10 disloyalty, infidelity

fake
3 act, gyp 4 hoax, mock, sham 5 bluff, bogus, false, feign, fraud, phony, pseud, put on, spoof 6 affect, doctor, ersatz, forged, framed, humbug, pseudo 7 falsify, pretend 8 impostor, invented, simulate, spurious 9 brummagem, charlatan, concocted, fabricate, imitation, imposture, pinchbeck, pretended, simulated 10 artificial, fabricated, fictitious, fraudulent, simulation 11 counterfeit
combining form: 5 pseud 6 pseudo

faker
4 sham 5 fraud, phony, quack 6 con man, hoaxer 8 deceiver, impostor 9 charlatan, con artist, pretender 10 mountebank 11 four-flusher 12 double-dealer 13 confidence man

fakir
7 ascetic, dervish 9 mendicant

falafel holder
4 pita, wrap 5 pitta

falcon
4 hawk 5 hobby, saker 6 lanner, merlin 7 kestrel 9 peregrine
eye cover: 4 seel
male: 4 jack 6 tercel 7 tiercel 8 lanneret
mature: 7 haggard
young: 4 eyas

falcon-headed god
see at **Egyptian**

falconry
7 hawking
equipment: 4 bell, hood, jess, lure
procedure: 3 imp 4 cope, seel

Falkland Islands
capital: 7 Stanley
claimant: 9 Argentina
colony of: 7 Britain

fall
3 dip, ebb, sag 4 dive, drip, drop, dump, hang, plop, sink, slip, trip, wane 5 abate, crash, lapse, slide, slump, spill 6 autumn, drowse, give up, go down, header, plunge, sprawl, tumble 7 cascade, decline, descend, descent, devolve, go under, plummet, scatter, stumble, subside 8 collapse, decrease, diminish, keel over, nose-dive 9 hairpiece 10 depreciate 11 precipitate

fallacious
6 untrue 7 invalid 8 delusive, delusory 9 deceitful, deceptive, erroneous, sophistic 10 fraudulent

fallacy
5 error 6 canard 7 falsity, sophism, untruth 8 delusion 9 falsehood 11 non sequitur 13 misconception

fall apart
6 lose it 7 crumble 9 break down, decompose 10 go to pieces 11 come unglued, deteriorate 12 disintegrate

fall back
6 recede, recoil, retire 7 retract, retreat 8 withdraw 9 disengage, retrocede 10 retrograde

fall behind
3 lag 4 drag 5 delay, tarry, trail 6 dawdle, linger, loiter

fall flat
4 bomb, fail, flop, miss **6** fizzle

fall guy
4 dupe, fool, goat, gull **5** chump, front, patsy **6** stooge, sucker **8** front man **9** scapegoat **11** whipping boy

fallible
4 iffy, weak **5** dicey, frail, human **6** errant, erring, faulty **9** imperfect **10** unreliable

falling-out
3 row **4** beef, feud, fuss, spat, tiff **5** break, run-in, words **6** bicker, fracas, hassle **7** dispute, quarrel, rhubarb, wrangle **8** argument, conflict, squabble **9** brannigan **11** altercation, controversy **12** disagreement, estrangement

falloff
3 sag **4** drop, slip **5** slump **7** decline **8** downturn **9** downslide, downswing, downtrend **13** deterioration

fall out
5 argue, break, leave, occur **6** bicker **7** brabble, quarrel, wrangle **8** disagree, squabble

fallow
4 idle **5** inert **6** unsown **7** dormant, resting **8** inactive, unseeded, untilled **9** neglected, quiescent, unplanted **12** uncultivated

false
4 fake, mock, sham **5** bogus, dummy, hokey, lying, phony, wrong **6** ersatz, forged, hollow, pseudo, untrue **7** crooked, devious, feigned, seeming, unloyal **8** apostate, apparent, deluding, delusive, delusory, disloyal, recreant, specious, spurious **9** brummagem, deceitful, deceiving, deceptive, dishonest, distorted, erroneous, faithless, illogical, imitation, incorrect, pinchbeck, simulated **10** artificial, fictitious, fraudulent, inaccurate, misleading, perfidious, traitorous, unfaithful, untruthful **11** counterfeit, treacherous
combining form: **5** pseud **6** pseudo

falsehood
3 fib, lie **5** fable **6** canard **7** fallacy, fiction, untruth, whopper **8** roorback **9** mendacity **11** fabrication **12** misstatement **13** prevarication

falseness
7 fallacy, perfidy **8** apostasy **9** treachery **10** disloyalty, infidelity **11** insincerity

false teeth
8 dentures

falsify
3 fib, lie **4** cook, deny **5** belie, fudge, slant **6** doctor, refute **7** deceive, distort, mislead **8** disprove, misstate **10** contradict **11** prevaricate **12** misrepresent

falsity
3 fib, lie **4** tale, yarn **5** fable **6** canard **7** untruth, whopper **9** falsehood, mendacity **11** fabrication **13** prevarication

Falstaff
companion: **3** Nym **4** Peto **6** Pistol **8** Bardolph
composer: **5** Verdi (Giuseppe)
creator: **11** Shakespeare (William)
drink: **4** sack
play: **7** Henry IV
prince: **3** Hal
tavern: **9** Boar's Head

Falstaffian
3 fat **6** jovial **7** roguish **8** boastful **9** convivial, dissolute

falter
4 halt, limp, reel, sway, trip **5** quail, waver **6** flinch, teeter, totter, wobble **7** give way, stagger, stammer, stumble **8** hesitate **9** vacillate **12** shilly-shally

fame
4 note **5** éclat, glory, honor, kudos **6** esteem, regard, renown, repute **7** acclaim, stardom **8** standing **9** celebrity, notoriety **10** popularity, prominence, reputation **11** acclamation, immortality, recognition

famed
5 noted **6** marked **7** eminent, notable **8** renowned **9** notorious, prominent, well-known **10** celebrated **11** illustrious **13** distinguished

familiar
4 cozy **6** common, folksy **8** domestic, everyday, frequent, informal, intimate, standard **10** accustomed **11** comfortable, commonplace **12** conventional, recognizable **13** garden-variety

familiarity
4 ease **8** intimacy **9** closeness, knowledge **11** informality **12** acquaintance

family
3 kin **4** clan, folk, home, line, race **5** brood, folks, house, issue, stirp, stock, tribe **6** ménage, strain **7** dynasty, kindred, lineage, progeny **8** pedigree **9** bloodline, household, offspring
branch: **5** stirp
lineage: **4** tree **6** stemma **8** pedigree **9** genealogy

famine
4 want **6** dearth, hunger **10** starvation

famished
6 hungry **7** starved **8** ravenous, starving

famous
5 famed, noble, noted **6** fabled **7** eminent, notable, popular **8** historic, renowned **9** legendary, notorious, prominent, well-known **10** celebrated **11** illustrious, prestigious, redoubtable

fan
3 bug, nut **4** blow, buff, open, wind **5** freak, lover, maven, rouse **6** addict, arouse, expand, extend, kindle, rooter, ruffle, spread, stir up, unfold, votary, whip up, winnow **7** admirer, devotee, habitué **8** adherent, enkindle, follower, railbird **9** stimulate **10** aficionado, enthusiast
dance: **11** balletomane
horseracing: **7** turfman
India: **6** punkah
movie: **7** cineast **8** cineaste **9** cinephile

fanatic
3 bug, nut **4** buff **5** fiend, freak, rabid **6** addict, maniac, votary, zealot **7** devotee, die-hard, habitué **10** aficionado, enthusiast

fanatical
5 fiery, rabid **6** ardent, fervid **7** extreme, fervent, zealous **8** frenetic, frenzied, maniacal, obsessed **9** perfervid **10** passionate **11** impassioned

fanaticism
4 zeal **5** mania **6** frenzy **8** zealotry **9** extremism, monomania, obsession

fancier
6 grower **7** amateur, admirer, breeder, devotee

fanciful
6 absurd, unreal **7** bizarre, fictive **8** fabulous, illusory, imagined, mythical, notional, romantic **9** fantastic, fictional, grotesque, imaginary **10** chimerical, fictitious **11** fantastical **12** preposterous

fancy
3 bee, fad **4** idea, like, posh, whim **5** dream, ritzy, shine, smart, taste **6** dressy, liking, megrim, notion, relish, snazzy, swanky, vision, whimsy **7** caprice, chimera, conceit, concept, dream up, elegant, fantasy, feature, imagine, picture **8** conceive, daydream, envision, fondness, judgment, velleity **9** capriccio, elaborate, intricate, inventive, visualize, whimsical **10** decorative, ornamental, partiality, propensity **11** extravagant, highfalutin, imagination, inclination

fandango
5 dance **9** malaguena

fanfare
4 pomp, show, ta-da **5** array, ta-dah **6** hoopla **7** display, hooplah, panoply **8** ballyhoo, flourish
trumpet: **6** tucket **7** tantara

fanlike
7 plicate

fanny
3 bum, can **4** buns, butt, duff, moon, rear, rump, seat, tail, tush **5** booty, nates **6** behind, bottom, breech, heinie **7** caboose, hind end, keister, rear end, tail end **8** backside, buttocks, derriere **9** fundament, posterior

fantasia
6 vision **8** daydream, illusion, rhapsody **9** fairyland **10** apparition

fantasize
4 moon **5** dream, fancy **7** imagine **8** daydream **10** woolgather

fantastic
3 odd **4** wild **6** absurd, unreal **7** bizarre, surreal **8** fanciful, singular **9** eccentric, grotesque, imaginary, marvelous, monstrous, unearthly, whimsical **10** chimerical, far-fetched, improbable, incredible, outlandish, outrageous, prodigious, stupendous, tremendous **11** implausible, nonsensical, sensational, superlative **12** preposterous, unbelievable

fantasy
4 moon, whim **5** dream, fancy, freak **6** vagary, vision, whimsy **7** caprice, chimera, fiction, reverie **8** daydream, delusion, phantasm **9** imagining, invention, pipe dream **10** bizarrerie **11** imagination **12** grotesquerie

far
4 long **6** remote **7** distant **8** outlying
combining form: **3** tel **4** tele, telo

far and wide
7 all over **10** everyplace, everywhere, throughout

faraway
4 lost **5** moony **6** absent, dreamy, remote **7** distant, removed **8** outlying **9** oblivious, unheeding **10** abstracted, distracted **11** preoccupied, inattentive **12** absentminded

farce
5 stuff **6** comedy, satire **7** mockery **8** travesty **9** burlesque, slapstick **10** caricature

farceur
5 clown, cutup, joker **7** buffoon

farcical
5 comic **6** absurd **7** comical, foolish, risible **9** laughable, ludicrous **10** ridiculous **12** preposterous

fare
4 diet, dine, food, pass, rate, toll **5** get on, price, track **6** manage, travel **7** come off, journey, make out, proceed, succeed **8** get along, progress, victuals **9** passenger, surcharge **10** provisions **11** comestibles

farewell
3 ave, bye **4** ciao, ta-ta, vale **5** adieu, adios, aloha, congé **6** bye-bye, pip-pip, shalom, so long **7** aloha oe, cheerio, good-bye, toodles **8** swan song, toodle-oo **9** bon voyage, departure **11** arrivederci, leave-taking, valediction, valedictory

far-fetched
5 fishy **6** absurd **7** dubious **8** doubtful, strained, unlikely **10** improbable, incredible **11** implausible, unrealistic **12** preposterous, unbelievable

far-flung
6 remote **7** distant, removed **8** outlying **10** widespread

farinaceous
5 mealy **6** floury **7** starchy
food: **4** meal **5** flour, grits **6** cereal, hominy **7** polenta, pudding, tapioca

farm
4 till **5** croft, ranch **6** grange, rancho **7** hennery **8** estancia, hacienda, hatchery **9** cultivate, farmstead **10** plantation
building: **4** barn, shed, silo
Dutch: **6** bowery
Israeli collective: **7** kibbutz
Russian: **7** kolkhoz, sovkhoz

farmer
6 grower, tiller, yeoman **7** granger, planter, rancher **8** ranchero, ranchman **13** agriculturist
Russian: **5** kulak
South African: **4** Boer
tenant: **6** cottar, cotter **7** crofter **12** sharecropper

farming
7 tillage **8** agronomy **9** husbandry **11** agriculture, cultivation

faro
5 monte
bet: **7** sleeper
card: **4** case, hock, soda

Faroes whirlwind
2 oe

far-off
6 remote **7** distant, removed **8** outlying

far-out
3 rad **4** cool **5** outré, weird **6** groovy **7** bizarre, offbeat, radical **9** eccentric **10** avant-garde, off-the-wall, outlandish

farrago
4 hash, mess, olio **5** gumbo **6** jumble, medley, muddle **7** goulash, mélange, mixture **8** mishmash, shambles **9** potpourri **10** hodgepodge, miscellany

far-reaching
5 broad **8** sweeping **9** extensive, momentous, pervasive **10** portentous, widespread **11** significant, wide-ranging **13** comprehensive, consequential

farrier
5 smith **10** blacksmith, horseshoer

farsighted
4 sage, wise **9** hyperopic, prescient, sagacious **10** discerning

farthest
6 utmost **7** apogean, extreme, outmost **8** remotest, ultimate **9** outermost, uttermost

Fasching
8 carnival

fascinate
4 draw, wile **5** charm **6** allure, enamor, entice, please **7** attract, beguile, bewitch, enchant **8** enthrall, intrigue, transfix **9** captivate, enrapture, magnetize, mesmerize, spellbind

fascination
5 charm **6** allure, appeal **7** glamour **8** charisma **9** magnetism **10** attraction, witchcraft **11** enchantment **12** enthrallment

Fascist
4 Nazi **6** despot, Hitler (Adolf), tyrant **8** autocrat **9** Falangist, Mussolini (Benito) **10** Blackshirt

fashion
3 fad, fit, ton, way **4** chic, form, mode, mold, suit, tone, vein, wear **5** craze, shape, style, trend, usage, vogue **6** create, custom, design, devise, manner, method, sculpt, tailor **7** compose, costume, pattern **8** contrive **9** bandwagon, construct, fabricate **10** dernier cri **12** haute couture
magazine: **3** WWD **4** Elle **5** Vogue **6** Hilary **7** Glamour, InStyle

fashionable
3 hip **4** chic, cool, posh, tony **5** fresh, ritzy, sharp, smart, swank, swish **6** chichi, du jour, modish, trendy, with-it **7** à la mode, current, dashing, faddish, popular, stylish, voguish **8** up-to-date **9** au courant, exclusive, happening **12** silk-stocking

fashionably nostalgic
5 retro

fashion designer
American: **3** Sui (Anna) **4** Head (Edith) **5** Beene (Geoffrey), Blass (Bill), Dache (Lilly), Ellis (Perry), Karan (Donna), Klein (Anne, Calvin) **6** Jacobs (Marc), Lauren (Ralph), Mackie (Bob) **7** Galanos (James), Halston, Mizrahi (Isaac) **8** Galliano (John), Hilfiger (Tommy) **9** Claiborne (Liz), de la Renta (Oscar), Gernreich (Rudi)
Anglo-French: **5** Worth (Charles Frederick)
Dominican: **9** de la Renta (Oscar)
English: **5** Quant (Mary) **6** Bailey (Christopher) **7** McQueen (Alexander) **8** Westwood (Vivienne)
French: **4** Dior (Christian) **5** Bohan (Marc) **6** Cardin (Pierre), Chanel (Coco), Poiret (Paul) **6** Ungaro (Emanuel) **7** Balmain (Pierre), Lacroix (Christian), Montana (Claude) **8** Gaultier (Jean-Paul), Givenchy (Hubert de) **9** Courrèges (André), Lagerfeld (Karl) **12** Saint-Laurent (Yves), Schiaparelli (Elsa)
German: **9** Lagerfeld (Karl)
Israeli: **7** Mizrahi (Isaac)

Italian: **5** Ferrè (Gianfranco), Prada (Miuccia), Pucci (Emilio), Ricci (Nina) **6** Armani (Giorgio) **7** Cassini (Oleg), Versace (Gianni) **9** Valentino **12** Schiaparelli (Elsa)
Japanese: **6** Miyake (Issey)
Spanish: **10** Balenciaga (Cristóbal)

fast
3 set **4** ASAP, diet, easy, firm, Lent, soon, sure, true, wild **5** apace, fixed, fleet, hasty, hitch, loose, loyal, quick, rapid, swift **6** firmly, presto, prompt, snappy, speedy, stable **7** abstain, hastily, hurried, lasting, quickly, rapidly, staunch, swiftly **8** chop-chop, constant, faithful, full tilt, immobile, promptly, resolute, speedily **9** breakneck, dissolute, immovable, libertine **10** abstinence, profligate, recklessly, stationary **11** expeditious, promiscuous **12** lickety-split **13** expeditiously

fasten
3 fix, peg, pin, set, sew, tie, zip **4** bind, bolt, clip, hook, join, lace, lash, link, lock, moor, nail, seal, shut, weld **5** affix, cable, catch, chain, cinch, clamp, clasp, close, cramp, dowel, girth, hitch, latch, rivet, screw, stake, stick, strap, tie up, truss **6** anchor, attach, batten, buckle, button, couple, secure, skewer, solder, staple, tether **7** connect, mortise **8** buckle up

fastener
3 nut, peg, pin, tie **4** bolt, brad, clip, cord, frog, hasp, link, lock, nail, rope, snap, stud, tack, tape **5** catch, clamp, clasp, dowel, girth, hinge, hitch, latch, rivet, screw, spike, stake, strap **6** buckle, button, cotter, skewer, staple, tether, toggle, Velcro, zipper **7** grommet, padlock, netsuke, shackle **8** coupling, cuff link, handcuff, seat belt, shoelace **9** connector, cotter pin, safety pin, thumbtack **10** clothespin

fastidious
5 fussy, picky **6** choosy, dainty, queasy **7** choosey, finical, finicky, refined **8** exacting **9** demanding, squeamish **10** meticulous, particular, pernickety **11** persnickety

fastness
4 fort, hold, keep **6** bunker, castle, refuge **7** alcazar, bastion, citadel, crannog, redoubt, sanctum **8** casemate, fortress, presidio **10** stronghold, tower house **11** strongpoint

fast-talking
4 glib **5** slick **6** facile **8** slippery **13** silver-tongued

fat
3 big, oil **4** flab, lard, suet, wide **5** beefy, broad, bulky, burly, cream, dumpy, gross, heavy, husky, large, lipid, obese, plump, pudgy, round, stout, thick, tubby **6** chunky, excess, fleshy, grease, portly, rotund, stocky, stubby, tallow **7** adipose, blubber, paunchy, pinguid, porcine, surfeit, surplus, weighty **8** heavyset, oversize, thickset **9** corpulent **10** full-bodied, overweight, potbellied **11** superfluity

fatal
6 deadly, lethal, mortal **7** deathly, ruinous **8** terminal **9** incurable, pestilent **10** pernicious **12** pestilential

fatality
4 doom **5** death **8** casualty **10** deadliness

fata morgana
6 mirage **8** illusion

fat cat
5 mogul, nabob **6** big gun, bigwig, tycoon **7** big shot, magnate, pooh-bah **8** big wheel **9** moneybags, plutocrat **11** muckety-muck **13** high-muck-a-muck

fate
3 end, lot **4** doom, luck, ruin **5** death, karma **6** chance, kismet, upshot **7** destiny, fortune, outcome, portion **13** inevitability

fateful
6 deadly **7** ominous, ruinous **8** decisive **9** momentous, prophetic **10** portentous

Fates
see at **Greek; Norse; Roman**

fathead
3 ass, oaf **4** boob, clod, dodo, dope, dolt, gawk, goof, goon, jerk, lump, mutt, yo-yo **5** cluck, clunk, dummy, dunce, idiot, moron, stock, stupe, yahoo **6** cretin, dimwit, donkey, doofus, dumdum, nitwit, noodle, schlub, turkey **7** buffoon, dullard, jackass, schnook **8** dumbbell, imbecile, numskull **9** birdbrain, ignoramus, lamebrain, numbskull, simpleton

fatheaded
4 dull, dumb **5** dense, dopey, thick **6** obtuse, simple, stupid **7** doltish, idiotic **8** gormless **9** brainless, dim-witted, imbecilic **10** numskulled **11** numbskulled, thick-witted

father
2 pa **3** dad, pop **4** dada, papa, père, sire **5** beget, breed, daddy, hatch, padre, pappy, pater, poppa, spawn **6** author, create, old man, parent, priest **7** builder, creator, founder, produce **8** ancestor, engender, generate, inventor, producer **9** architect, initiator, originate, patriarch, procreate **10** originator, prime mover
combining form: **4** patr **5** patri, patro
French: **4** père
German: **5** Vater
Italian: **5** padre
Portuguese: **3** pai
Spanish: **5** padre

Father Brown creator
10 Chesterton (Gilbert Keith)

fatherland
4 home, soil **7** country

Father Time's implement
6 scythe

fathom
4 know **5** probe, sound **7** discern, explore, measure **9** apprehend, figure out, penetrate **10** comprehend, understand **11** investigate

fathomless
7 abysmal, abyssal **8** profound **12** immeasurable

fatidic
5 vatic **6** mantic **7** Delphic, sibylic **8** Delphian, oracular, sibyllic **9** prophetic, prescient, sibylline, vaticinal **10** divinatory, predictive

fatigue
3 fag **4** poop, tire, wear **5** drain, weary **6** tucker **7** deplete, burn out, exhaust, frazzle, wear out **8** drudgery, wear down **9** tiredness, weariness **10** enervation, exhaustion
combat: **7** frazzle **10** shell shock

Fatima
father: **8** Mohammed, Muhammad
husband: **9** Bluebeard
son: **5** Hasan **6** Husayn
stepbrother: **3** Ali

fatness
7 obesity **9** adiposity **10** corpulence, overweight

fatty
4 oily, rich **6** greasy **7** adipose **8** unctuous **10** oleaginous
combining form: **4** lipo **5** adipo

fatuous
4 dumb, fond **5** inane, sappy, silly **6** jejune, simple **7** asinine, foolish, puerile, witless

faucet
3 tap **4** bung, cock, gate **5** valve **6** spigot **7** hydrant, petcock **8** stopcock

Faulkner, William
character: **3** Ike (Snopes), Joe (Christmas) **4** Eula (Varner Snopes), Flem (Snopes), Mink (Snopes) **5** Benjy (Compson), Caddy (Compson), Gavin (Stevens), Henry (Sutpen), Jason (Compson), Lucas (Beauchamp) **6** Dilsey, Temple (Drake) **7** Candace (Compson), Quentin (Compson) **8** Benjamin (Compson)
county: **13** Yoknapatawpha
family: **6** Benbow, Snopes, Sutpen **7** Compson **8** McCaslin, Sartoris **9** Beauchamp
novel: **4** Town (The) **6** Hamlet (The) **7** Mansion (The), Reivers (The) **8** Sartoris **9** Sanctuary, Wild Palms (The) **11** As I Lay Dying **13** Light in August **14** Absalom Absalom **15** Sound and the Fury (The) **17** Intruder in the Dust

fault
3 err, nag, sin **4** flaw, rift, slip, spot, vice, want **5** blame, break, knock, error, scold **6** accuse, defect, foible, miscue **7** censure, demerit, failing, fissure, frailty, mistake, upbraid **8** fracture, weakness **9** criticize, infirmity **10** San Andreas **11** culpability, dereliction, shortcoming **12** imperfection
line: **4** rift **5** split **6** breach **7** fissure **8** crevasse

faultfinder
4 crab **5** grump **6** critic, griper, grouch, nagger, whiner **7** grouser **8** grumbler **10** bellyacher, complainer, criticizer, crosspatch

faultfinding
7 carping **8** captious, critical, nitpicky **9** criticism **10** censorious, nit-picking, pernickety **11** persnickety **12** overcritical **13** hypercritical

faultless
4 pure **7** perfect **8** innocent, unerring **9** guiltless **10** immaculate, impeccable, inculpable

faulty
4 awry **5** amiss, wrong **6** flawed, marred **7** botched, damaged, defaced, inexact, unsound **8** fallible, specious **9** blemished, defective, deficient, erroneous, imperfect, incorrect **10** fallacious, inaccurate
prefix: **3** dys

faun
5 satyr

fauna
7 animals

Faunus
grandfather: **6** Saturn
son: **4** Acis **7** Latinus

Faust
author: **6** Goethe (Johann Wolfgang von)
beloved: **8** Gretchen
composer: **6** Gounod (Charles)

faux
4 fake, mock, sham **5** bogus, false, phony **6** ersatz **9** imitation, pretended, simulated, synthetic **10** substitute

faux pas
4 flub, goof, slip **5** boner, error, gaffe **6** boo-boo, howler, miscue, slipup **7** blooper, blunder, misstep, mistake, stumble **8** pratfall, solecism **9** gaucherie **11** impropriety

favor
4 baby, back, bias, boon, gift, okay **5** bless, bribe, grace, mercy, token, value **6** accept, behalf, choose, oblige, pamper, prefer, regard **7** indulge, present, support, sustain **8** courtesy, goodwill, interest, keepsake, kindness, resemble, sanction, sympathy **9** attention, patronage, privilege, take after **10** admiration, facilitate, indulgence, partiality **11** approbation, benevolence, countenance

favorable
4 fair **5** lucky **6** benign, biased, golden, timely,

toward, useful **7** helpful, partial **8** pleasant, pleasing, positive **9** agreeable, benignant, fortunate, promising **10** auspicious, benevolent, propitious, prosperous **11** affirmative **12** advantageous **13** complimentary

favoring
4 rosy **6** timely, toward, useful **7** helpful **9** opportune **10** auspicious, beneficial, propitious **12** advantageous
prefix: **3** pro

favorite
3 pet **7** dearest, popular, special **8** precious **9** preferred, well-liked **10** fair-haired, preference **11** front-runner, teacher's pet, white-haired

favoritism
4 bias **8** cronyism, nepotism **10** partiality **12** one-sidedness

fawn
3 kid, tan **4** deer, ecru **5** beige, toady **6** bister, grovel, kowtow **7** flatter, truckle, wheedle **8** blandish, bootlick **9** sweet-talk **11** apple-polish

fawning
6 smarmy **8** unctuous **9** parasitic **10** obsequious **11** sycophantic

fay
3 elf, nix **4** puck **5** elfin, fairy, nixie, pixie **6** elfish, goblin, sprite **7** brownie **10** leprechaun

faze
3 cow **5** abash, daunt, throw **6** dismay, rattle **7** confuse, disturb, nonplus, perturb **8** befuddle, bewilder, confound, unsettle **9** discomfit, dumbfound, embarrass **10** disconcert **11** flabbergast

FBI director
5 Freeh (Louis) **6** Hoover (J. Edgar) **7** Mueller (Robert)

fealty
5 faith, troth **7** loyalty **8** devotion, fidelity **9** adherence, constancy, vassalage **10** allegiance, attachment **11** devotedness **12** faithfulness

fear
3 awe **5** alarm, angst, dread, panic, qualm, scare, worry **6** dismay, fright, horror, phobia, terror **7** anxiety, jitters **8** cold feet, disquiet, timidity **9** agitation, cowardice, misgiving **10** foreboding **11** disquietude, trepidation **12** apprehension, cowardliness, perturbation, presentiment, timorousness
of animals: **9** zoophobia
of being buried alive: **11** taphephobia
of cats: **12** ailurophobia
of crowds: **11** ochlophobia
of darkness: **11** nyctophobia
of dirt: **10** mysophobia
of fire: **10** pyrophobia
of heights: **10** acrophobia
of men: **11** androphobia
of new things: **9** neophobia
of open areas: **11** agoraphobia
of pain: **10** algophobia
of strangers: **10** xenophobia
of thunder: **12** brontophobia
of water: **11** hydrophobia
of women: **10** gynophobia

fearful
5 timid **6** afraid, aghast, scared, trepid **7** alarmed, anxious, jittery, panicky **8** alarmist, paranoid, timorous **9** terrified, tremulous **12** apprehensive

fearless
4 bold **5** brave **6** daring **7** gallant, valiant **8** intrepid, unafraid **9** dauntless **10** courageous **11** lionhearted **12** greathearted, stouthearted

fearmonger
8 alarmist

Fear of Flying author
4 Jong (Erica)

fearsome
3 shy **5** scary, timid **6** afraid **7** extreme, intense **8** daunting, timorous **9** frightful **10** terrifying **11** frightening **12** intimidating

feasible
6 doable, likely, viable **8** possible, suitable, workable **10** reasonable **11** practicable **12** tried-and-true

feast
3 eat **4** dine, meal **5** gorge **6** dinner, regale, repast, spread **7** banquet, indulge **8** potlatch
Hawaiian: **4** luau
Scottish: **3** foy

Feast of Lights
8 Chanukah, Hanukkah

Feast of Lots
5 Purim

Feast of Tabernacles
6 Sukkot **7** Sukkoth

feat
3 act **4** coup, deed, gest **5** stunt, trick **6** action **7** exploit **11** achievement, performance, tour de force

feather
3 ilk **4** down, kind, sort, type **5** breed, order, pinna, plume, quill **6** fledge, fletch, pinion **7** species, variety
kind: **4** down **6** covert **7** contour, plumule, rectrix **8** scapular
part: **3** web **4** barb, vane **5** shaft **7** barbule, calamus **8** barbicel

featherbrained
5 dizzy, giddy, silly **7** flighty, foolish **8** heedless **9** frivolous **11** light-headed, thoughtless

feathered
7 plumose

feathers
4 down **7** plumage

feature
4 item, mark, part **5** add-on, trait **6** aspect, detail, factor **7** article, element, fixture, gimmick, quality **8** hallmark, property **9** attribute, component, lineament **10** attraction, ingredient **11** drawing card, peculiarity

febrile
3 hot **5** fiery **7** fevered, pyretic **8** feverish

feckless
4 weak **7** useless **8** carefree, impotent **11** incompetent, ineffective, ineffectual **12** undependable **13** irresponsible

fecund
4 rich **7** fertile **8** fruitful, prolific **9** inventive **10** productive

fecundity
9 abundance, fertility **11** prodigality **12** fruitfulness, productivity

Federalist writer
3 Jay (John) **7** Madison (James) **8** Hamilton (Alexander)

federation
5 union **6** league, nation **7** council **8** alliance **10** government **11** confederacy

fed up
4 sick **9** disgusted **11** exasperated

fee
3 cut, pay, tax **4** bill, cost, dues, hire, rate, toll, wage **5** price **6** charge **7** expense, payment, rake-off, stipend, tuition **8** retainer **9** emolument **10** commission, recompense
minting: **10** seignorage **11** seigniorage
wharf: **7** quayage

feeble
4 lame, puny, weak **5** anile, frail **6** infirm, senile, sickly, weakly **7** doddery **8** decrepit **9** doddering, unhealthy **10** inadequate

feebleminded
4 daft, dull, slow **5** dense, thick **6** stupid **7** doltish, foolish, idiotic, moronic, witless **8** imbecile, retarded **9** brainless, dim-witted, imbecilic **10** half-witted, slow-witted **11** harebrained, thickheaded

feebleness
7 frailty **8** debility **9** fragility, infirmity **10** enervation, inadequacy **11** decrepitude

feed
3 eat **4** grub, hand, meal **5** feast, gorge, graze, stuff **6** browse, devour, fatten, fodder, ingest, regale, repast, supply, viands **7** banquet, consume, deliver, dish out, edibles, furnish, nourish, nurture, provide, sustain **8** bonemeal, dispense, hand over, victuals **9** partake of, provender, provision, refection **10** provisions

feedback
5 input **8** critique, reaction, response **9** criticism **10** evaluation

feed the kitty
4 ante

feel
5 grope, sense, touch **6** caress, fondle, handle, stroke **7** palpate

feeler
4 palp **5** probe **6** palpus **7** antenna **8** proposal, tentacle **12** trial balloon

feeling
3 air **4** aura, mood, vibe **5** hunch, sense, touch **6** notion, temper **7** emotion, inkling, opinion, outlook, passion, sensate **8** attitude, instinct, sentient **9** affection, emotional, intuition, sensation, sentiment, suspicion **10** atmosphere, impression, persuasion **11** sensibility, sensitivity

feign
3 act **4** fake, play, sham **5** bluff, put on **6** affect, assume **7** pretend **8** simulate **9** dissemble **11** counterfeit, make believe

feigned
4 fake, sham **5** false, phony, put-on **7** assumed **8** imagined **9** imitation, insincere, pretended, simulated **10** fabricated, fictitious **11** counterfeit

feint
4 fake, hoax, play, ploy, ruse, sham, wile **5** trick **6** gambit **8** maneuver **9** stratagem
hockey: **4** deke

feisty
6 frisky, plucky, spunky, touchy **7** bristly, fidgety **8** petulant, snappish, spirited **9** fractious, irascible **10** aggressive **11** quarrelsome

feldspar
6 albite **8** andesine **9** anorthite, moonstone **10** microcline, orthoclase **11** plagioclase
clay: **6** kaolin

felicitate
6 salute **7** commend **10** compliment **12** congratulate

felicitous
3 apt, fit **4** meet **5** happy **6** proper, timely **7** apropos, fitting **8** apposite, pleasant, suitable **9** agreeable **10** delightful **11** appropriate

feline
3 cat, sly, tom **4** lion, lynx, pard, puma, puss **5** catty, felid, pussy, sleek, tiger **6** bobcat, cougar, jaguar, margay, ocelot, serval, slinky, sneaky, tomcat **7** caracal, catlike, cheetah, furtive, leonine, leopard, lioness, panther, tigress, wildcat **8** pussycat, stealthy
hybrid: **5** liger, tigon **6** tiglon

fell
3 cut, hew, mow **4** down, drop, kill, raze **5** floor

6 poleax 7 cut down, flatten 8 knock off 9 bring down, knock down

Fellini film
8 Amarcord, Casanova, La Strada 9 Satyricon 10 I Vitelloni 11 La Dolce Vita 15 Nights of Cabiria 18 Juliet of the Spirits

fellow
3 bub, guy, joe, lad, man 4 buck, chap, dude, gent, mate, peer, twin 5 bloke, match 6 codger, cohort, hombre, person 7 comrade, consort, partner 8 confrere 9 associate, companion, copartner, gentleman 10 coordinate, reciprocal

fellow feeling
5 agape 7 concern, empathy, rapport 8 affinity, kindness, sympathy 9 affection 10 compassion, kindliness 11 consolation 13 understanding

fellowship
4 club 5 guild 6 league 7 coterie, society, stipend 8 sodality 9 communion, community 10 fraternity 11 association, brotherhood

felon
3 con 7 convict, whitlow 8 criminal 10 malefactor

felt
6 groped, sensed

felt hat
3 fez 5 derby, terai 6 fedora, trilby 7 homburg, stetson 8 snap-brim 9 wideawake

female
4 girl 5 woman 7 girlish, womanly 8 feminine
suffix: 3 ess 4 ette, trix

Feminine Mystique author
7 Friedan (Betty)

feminist
10 suffragist 11 suffragette

femme fatale
5 Circe, siren 6 Carmen, Salome 7 Delilah, Lorelei 8 Mata Hari 9 temptress 10 seductress 11 enchantress

femur
9 thighbone

fen
3 bog 4 mire, quag, wash 5 marsh, swale, swamp 6 morass, muskeg, slough 9 marshland

fence
3 bar, pen 4 cage, rail, pale, weir 5 hedge, parry 6 corral, paling, picket 7 barrier, enclose, railing 8 backstop, boundary, hoarding, palisade, receiver, sidestep, stockade 9 barricade, stone wall
sunk: 4 ha-ha

fencer
7 duelist, épéeist 8 foilsman 9 swordsman

fencing
9 swordplay
attack: 5 lunge 6 thrust 7 reprise, riposte
cry: 6 touché 7 en garde
defense: 5 parry
movement: 4 volt
term: 4 jury 5 forte, lunge 6 flèche, foible, touché
touch: 3 cut, hit
weapon: 4 épée, foil 5 blade, guard, saber, sabre 6 pommel

fender
4 skid 5 guard 6 buffer, bumper, shield 7 cushion, railing 8 mudguard

fennec
3 fox

Fenrir
chain: 8 Gleipnir
father: 4 Loki
form: 4 wolf
mother: 9 Angerboda 10 Angerbotha
slayer: 5 Vidar 6 Vithar
victim: 4 Odin 5 Woden

Fenway Park
fence: 12 Green Monster
site: 6 Boston
team: 6 Red Sox

feral
4 wild 5 brute 6 brutal, savage 7 beastly, bestial, brutish, inhuman, untamed

Ferber novel
5 Giant, So Big 8 Cimarron, Show Boat 9 Ice Palace 13 Saratoga Trunk

Ferdinand
beloved: 7 Miranda
father: 6 Alonso

Ferdinand, King
conquest: 7 Granada
daughter: 6 Joanna
wife: 7 Isabela 8 Germaine, Isabella

fermata
4 hold 5 pause

ferment
4 boil, brew, stir 5 rouse, sweat 6 clamor, enzyme, excite, incite, leaven, seethe, simmer, unrest, work up 7 smolder, turmoil 9 agitation, commotion 12 restlessness

fermentation
7 zymosis 13 bioconversion

fern
4 tree 5 brake, holly, royal 6 Boston 7 bracken 8 polypody 10 maidenhair, spleenwort
leaf: 5 frond

ferocious
4 fell, grim, wild 5 brute, cruel 6 brutal, fierce, savage 7 bestial, extreme, inhuman, intense, vicious, violent 8 barbaric, inhumane, ruthless 9 barbarous, rapacious, truculent

ferret out
4 find **5** dig up, flush **6** elicit **7** unearth **8** discover **9** ascertain

ferrule
3 cap, tip **4** band, ring, virl **6** collet

ferry
5 carry **6** convey **7** shuttle **9** transport

ferryman
6 Charon **9** gondolier

fertile
4 lush, rich **6** fecund **8** abundant, creative, fruitful, pregnant, prolific **9** bountiful, ingenious, inventive, luxuriant, plenteous **10** productive **12** reproductive

fertilize
5 beget, breed **6** enrich **8** generate **9** fecundate, pollinate **10** impregnate, inseminate

fertilizer
4 dung **5** guano, mulch **6** manure **7** compost **8** bonemeal **9** plant food

ferule
3 rod **5** stick

fervent
3 hot **4** avid, keen **5** eager, fiery **6** ardent, devout, gung-ho **7** blazing, burning, earnest, glowing, intense, zealous **8** vehement **9** heartfelt **10** hot-blooded, passionate **11** impassioned, warm-blooded **12** enthusiastic, wholehearted

fervor
4 fire, heat, zeal **5** ardor **6** warmth **7** passion **8** devotion, violence **9** vehemence **10** devoutness, enthusiasm

fescennine
7 obscene **10** scurrilous

fess up
3 own **5** admit **9** come clean

fester
3 rot **6** rankle **7** inflame, putrefy **8** ulcerate **9** suppurate

festina ____
5 lente

festival
4 fair, fete, gala **5** feast **6** fiesta **7** jubilee **8** carnival, jamboree **11** celebration, merrymaking

festive
3 gay **4** gala **5** jolly, merry **6** joyful, joyous **7** gleeful **8** mirthful **11** celebratory

festivity
4 bash, fair, fete, gala **5** feast, party, revel **6** affair, frolic, gaiety **7** blowout, revelry, whoopee **8** carnival, jamboree **9** rejoicing, merriment **11** celebration, merrymaking

festoon
4 deck, hang **5** adorn **6** bedeck **7** garland **8** decorate, ornament **9** embellish

fetch
3 get **4** draw, earn **5** bring, yield **6** take in **7** attract, bring in, realize **8** retrieve

fetching
4 fair **6** comely, lovely, pretty **7** winsome **8** alluring, charming, enticing, engaging, handsome, pleasing **9** appealing **10** attractive

fete
4 ball, bash, fair, gala **5** feast, honor, party **6** affair, fiesta, soiree **7** banquet, jubilee, shindig **8** carnival, festival, jamboree, wingding **9** celebrate, entertain **11** celebration, commemorate **13** entertainment

fetid
4 foul, high, rank **5** funky **6** putrid, rancid, smelly, strong **8** mephitic, stinking **10** malodorous

fetish
4 idol, juju, luck **5** charm **6** amulet **7** periapt **8** fixation, gris-gris, talisman **10** phylactery

fetor
4 odor, reek **5** stink **6** stench

fetter
3 tie **4** bind, bond, gyve **5** chain, check, irons **6** hobble, hog-tie, impede **7** enchain, manacle, shackle, trammel **8** handcuff, restrain **9** restraint

fettle
5 shape **6** health **7** fitness **9** condition **12** constitution

feud
6 enmity, strife **7** dispute, quarrel **8** argument, vendetta **9** hostility **11** controversy

feudal
estate: **3** fee **4** feud, fief **6** domain
jurisdiction: **4** soke
laborer: **4** serf
lord: **5** laird, liege, thane **8** suzerain
status: **9** vassalage
tax: **7** tallage
tenant: **6** vassal **7** homager, socager, vavasor **8** vavasour
tenure of land: **6** socage
tribute: **6** heriot
warrior: **5** bushi, ronin **7** samurai

feuilleton
5 essay

fever
4 ague, fire, heat **5** craze, flush, Lassa, mania **6** dengue, frenzy **7** ferment, passion, pyrexia **8** delirium **9** calenture
recurrent: **7** malaria, quartan, tertian
type: **3** hay **6** dengue, hectic **7** scarlet

fevered
6 crazed, heated **7** burning, febrile, flushed **8** agitated, frenetic, restless **9** delirious **10** distracted, overheated **11** overwrought

feverish
3 hot **5** fiery **6** hectic **7** burning, febrile, flushed, pyretic **8** frenetic, frenzied **10** passionate **11** overwrought

fever tree
6 acacia **7** blue gum

few
4 rare **5** scant **6** meager, meagre, scanty, scarce, sparse **7** handful, limited **8** sporadic **9** scattered **10** infrequent, occasional, scattering, smattering, spattering, sprinkling
combining form: **4** olig **5** oligo

fey
4 daft **5** campy, crazy, vatic **7** touched **8** oracular, precious **9** pixilated, prophetic, sibylline, visionary **11** clairvoyant **12** otherworldly

fiasco
3 dud **4** bomb, flop **5** farce, flask **6** bottle, defeat **7** blunder, debacle, failure, washout **8** abortion, disaster **11** miscarriage **13** embarrassment

fiat
5 edict, order **6** decree **7** command, dictate, mandate, warrant **8** sanction **11** endorsement **12** proclamation **13** authorization

fib
3 lie **4** tale **5** story **7** falsify, falsity, untruth **8** white lie **9** falsehood, mendacity **10** taradiddle **11** fabrication, prevaricate

fiber
3 web **4** noil, pita **5** grain, istle **6** fabric, strand, thread **7** texture
basketry: **5** istle
brain: **4** pons
coarse: **4** jute **8** piassava
coconut husk: **4** coir
rope: **4** bast, hemp **5** sisal **8** henequen
silky: **5** kapok
small: **6** fibril
substructure: **7** micelle, spongin
synthetic: **5** nylon, Orlon, rayon, saran, vinal **6** Dacron **7** spandex
woody: **4** bast
woollike: **7** lanital

fibrous
4 ropy, wiry **5** tough, woody **6** sinewy **7** stringy

fibula
4 bone **5** clasp

fichu
5 scarf **8** kerchief

fickle
7 flighty **8** unstable, variable, volatile **9** mercurial **10** capricious, changeable, inconstant, unfaithful, unreliable **12** undependable **13** temperamental, unpredictable

fiction
4 tale, yarn **5** fable, story **7** fantasy, figment **8** pretense **9** falsehood, fish story, invention, narrative **10** concoction **11** fabrication

fictional
6 made-up, unreal **8** notional **9** imaginary **11** make-believe **12** suppositious

fictitious
4 fake, mock, sham **5** bogus, faked, false, phony **6** ersatz, made-up, unreal, untrue **7** assumed, created **8** cooked-up, fanciful, illusory, imagined, invented, mythical, spurious **9** concocted, fantastic, imaginary, simulated, trumped-up **10** apocryphal, artificial, chimerical, fabricated **11** make-believe **12** suppositious

fiddle
3 toy **4** fool, play, rack **5** alter, cheat **6** dawdle, diddle, doodle, finger, meddle, monkey, potter, putter, tamper, tinker, trifle, violin **7** swindle **9** interfere **10** fool around, manipulate, mess around

fiddle-faddle
3 rot **4** bosh, bull, bunk, nuts **5** fudge, drool, hokum, hooey, pshaw **6** bunkum, drivel, hoodoo, humbug, piffle **7** baloney, blarney, hogwash, rubbish, twaddle **8** nonsense, pishposh, tommyrot **9** poppycock **10** applesauce, balderdash, flapdoodle **13** horsefeathers

____ Fideles
6 Adeste

Fidelio
composer: **9** Beethoven (Ludwig van)
hero: **9** Florestan
heroine: **7** Leonora

fidelity
5 ardor, piety, troth **6** fealty **7** loyalty **8** devotion **9** adherence, constancy **10** allegiance, attachment **11** staunchness **12** faithfulness **13** dependability, steadfastness

Fidel's comrade
3 Che

fidget
6 fantod, fiddle, jitter, squirm, twitch **7** wriggle

fidgety
5 antsy, jumpy **6** uneasy **7** jittery, nervous, restive, squirmy, twitchy **8** restless

fiduciary
7 trustee

field
3 lea **4** area, mead, turf **5** green, major, milpa, orbit, range **6** domain, meadow, métier, region, sphere **7** demesne, pasture, purview, terrain **8** dominion, gridiron, precinct, vocation **9** bailiwick, champaign, specialty, territory **10** department, discipline, occupation

field crop
3 hay **4** corn, oats **5** grain, wheat **6** cotton **7** alfalfa **8** soybeans

field deity
3 Pan **4** Faun **5** Fauna **6** Faunus

field glasses
6 binocs **10** binoculars

field hand
4 hoer **5** sower **6** picker **7** laborer, planter

Fielding novel
6 Amelia **8** Tom Jones **13** Joseph Andrews

field marshal
Austrian: **8** Radetzky (Joseph)
British: **6** Napier (Robert), Raglan (Baron), Wavell (Archibald), Wilson (Henry) **7** Roberts (Frederick) **8** Wolseley (Garnet) **9** Kitchener (Horatio) **10** Montgomery (Bernard)
French: **3** Ney (Michel) **4** Foch (Ferdinand) **6** Joffre (Joseph-Jacques-Césaire), Pétain (Philippe)
German: **6** Keitel (Wilhelm), Paulus (Friedrich), Rommel (Erwin), Rupert (Prince) **9** Mackensen (August von), Rundstedt (Karl von), Waldersee (Alfred von) **10** Kesselring (Albert)
Japanese: **8** Sugiyama (Hajime)
Prussian: **6** Moltke (Helmuth von)
Russian: **7** Kutuzov (Mikhail), Suvorov (Aleksandr) **8** Potemkin (Grigory)

field mouse
4 vole

field officer
5 major **7** colonel

fieldwork
5 redan

fiend
3 bug, imp, nut **5** demon, devil, freak, Satan **6** addict, Belial, diablo, maniac, zealot **7** devotee, fanatic, habitué, Lucifer, monster, Old Nick, serpent **8** Apollyon, succubus **9** Beelzebub **10** enthusiast, Old Scratch **13** Old Gooseberry

fiendish
3 bad **4** evil **5** cruel **6** malign, savage, wicked **7** baleful, demonic, hellish, inhuman, malefic, satanic, vicious **8** demoniac, devilish, diabolic, infernal, sinister **9** barbarous, difficult, ferocious, malicious, malignant **10** diabolical

fierce
4 fell, grim, wild **5** cruel **6** brutal, savage, wicked **7** brutish, hostile, inhuman, intense, vicious, violent, wolfish **8** inhumane, pitiless, ruthless, terrible, vehement **9** barbarous, bellicose, ferocious, merciless, truculent **10** aggressive, determined

fiery
3 hot, red **5** afire **6** ablaze, aflame, ardent, fervid, fierce, heated, red-hot, torrid **7** burning, febrile, fervent, flaming, flaring, igneous, intense, peppery **8** broiling, feverish, spirited, vehement, white-hot **9** flammable, hotheaded, irritable, perfervid **10** mettlesome, passionate **11** combustible, inflammable, impassioned

fiesta
4 fete **5** party **6** frolic **8** carnival, festival, jamboree **9** merriment

fife
4 pipe **5** flute

fifth
combining form: **5** quint

fifth columnist
3 spy

fig
genus: **5** Ficus
sacred: **5** pipal
variety: **5** elemi **6** Smyrna

fight
3 row, war **4** bout, buck, duel, feud, fray, spat, tiff **5** brawl, broil, clash, joust, match, melee, repel, scrap, set-to **6** affray, attack, battle, combat, fracas, oppose, oppugn, resist, rumble, scrape, tussle **7** contend, contest, dispute, quarrel, scuffle, wrangle, wrestle **8** conflict, skirmish, slugfest, squabble, struggle, traverse **10** aggression, donnybrook, free-for-all **11** altercation

fighter
2 GI **3** pug **4** swad **5** boxer **7** brawler, soldier, warrior **8** champion, pugilist, scrapper **9** combatant, gladiator, man-at-arms, mercenary **11** interceptor

fighter plane
3 MiG, Roc **4** Zero **5** Sabre **6** bomber, Fokker, Hawker, Mirage, Voodoo **7** Corsair, Harrier **8** Spitfire **11** interceptor

fighting fish
5 betta

figment
5 dream, fable, fancy **7** chimera, fiction **8** daydream, illusion, phantasm **9** invention, unreality **11** contrivance, fabrication

figure
3 add, sum, tot **4** cast, form, mold, rule, tote **5** count, digit, frame, image, model, motif, shape, total **6** cipher, decide, design, device, effigy, motive, number, reckon, settle, symbol **7** compute, integer, numeral, outline, pattern, resolve **8** conclude, estimate, physique **9** calculate, character, determine, enumerate
geometric: **4** cone, cube **5** rhomb **6** circle, isogon, square **7** decagon, ellipse, hexagon,

nonagon, octagon, polygon, rhombus **8** pentacle, pentagon, rhomboid, tetragon, triangle **9** rectangle **10** hexahedron, octahedron **11** icosahedron **12** dodecahedron, rhombohedron
human: **4** nude **5** atlas **7** telamon **8** caryatid
ornamental: **6** statue **8** gargoyle

figurehead
4 pawn, tool **5** front **6** minion, puppet **7** cat's-paw **8** creature **10** instrument, mouthpiece

figure of speech
5 trope **6** aporia, simile **7** litotes **8** metaphor, metonymy **10** synecdoche

figure out
5 crack, learn, solve **6** decide, decode, fathom **7** resolve, unravel **8** decipher, discover, unriddle **9** ascertain, determine

figure skater
see **ice skater**

figure skating
jump: **4** axel, loop, lutz **5** split **6** rocker **7** bracket, counter, salchow **11** spreadeagle
spin: **5** camel

figurine
9 statuette

Fiji
capital: **4** Suva
explorer: **4** Cook (Capt. James) **6** Tasman (Abel)
island: **3** Gau **4** Koro **6** Ovalau **8** Viti Levu **9** Vanua Levu
island group: **3** Lau **6** Yasawa
language: **6** Fijian
neighbor: **5** Samoa **7** Vanuatu

filch
3 cop, nip **4** crib, lift, take **5** boost, pinch, steal, swipe **6** pilfer, snitch **7** purloin

file
3 row, rub **4** line, rank, rasp, tier **5** lodge, march, place, queue **6** smooth **7** archive, arrange, corrupt, dossier **10** emery board

filial
5 sonly **7** duteous, dutiful

filibuster
5 delay, stall **10** adventurer

filigree
4 lace **6** design **7** pattern **8** fretwork, openwork, ornament **10** decoration **13** embellishment, ornamentation

fill
3 jam **4** clog, cloy, cram, glut, heap, lade, load, pack, pile, plug, sate, stop **5** block, choke, close, gorge, stock, stuff **6** charge, stodge **7** congest, engorge, inflate, occlude, pervade, satiate, satisfy, stopper, surfeit **8** permeate
interstices: **4** calk **5** caulk, chink, putty

filled
5 awash, flush, sated **6** packed **7** replete **9** saturated

filler
5 squib **7** packing, padding, tobacco, wadding **8** stuffing

fillet
4 band **5** slice, snood, strip **6** ribbon, stripe **7** bandeau, banding **8** headband
anatomical: **9** lemniscus
architectural: **6** listel, reglet, taenia
meat: **10** tenderloin

fill in
3 sub **4** clew, clue, post **6** advise, detail, insert, notify **7** apprise **8** acquaint, complete **10** substitute

fill-in
3 sub **4** temp **6** backup **7** stopgap **9** alternate, expedient, makeshift, surrogate, temporary **10** substitute **11** locum tenens, pinch hitter, replacement, succedaneum

filling
5 kapok

fillip
3 tap **4** goad, kick, spur **5** boost, tonic **6** buffet, strike **7** impetus, wrinkle **8** catalyst, stimulus **9** incentive, stimulant, stimulate **10** inducement, motivation **13** embellishment

film
4 coat, scum, skim, skin **5** glaze, layer, Mylar **6** lamina, patina **7** tarnish **8** membrane, pellicle
(see also **movie**)

film director
see **movie director**

film producer
see **movie producer**

filmy
4 hazy **5** gauzy, misty, sheer, wispy **6** dainty **8** delicate, gossamer **10** diaphanous **11** transparent

fils
3 son

filter
4 sift **5** clean, leach, sieve **6** purify, refine, screen, strain **7** clarify, cleanse **9** percolate

filth
4 crud, dirt, dung, muck, slop, smut **5** dreck, grime, slime, trash **6** ordure, refuse, sludge **7** squalor **9** obscenity

filthy
4 base, foul, vile **5** black, dirty, grimy, gross, gunky, mucky, muddy, nasty **6** coarse, cruddy, grubby, ribald, scuzzy, skanky, smutty, sordid

7 obscene, raunchy, squalid, unclean **8** indecent **9** loathsome, offensive, repulsive, revolting **12** scatological

filthy lucre
4 cash, loot, pelf **5** bread, bucks, dough, money, moola **6** boodle, riches, moolah, wampum **7** cabbage, scratch **8** currency

fin
3 arm **4** bill **5** fiver, pinna **7** airfoil, flipper
type: **6** caudal, dorsal **7** ventral **8** pectoral

finagle
5 cheat, trick **6** wangle **7** snaffle, swindle, wheedle **8** fast-talk, maneuver, scrounge **9** bamboozle, machinate

final
3 end **4** last **6** ending, latest **7** closing **8** hindmost, terminal, ultimate **10** concluding, conclusive, definitive **11** examination

finale
3 end **4** coda **5** close, finis **6** capper, climax, ending, payoff, windup, wrap-up **7** closing **10** conclusion, denouement **11** culmination, termination

finalize
3 end **5** close, sew up, tie up **6** decide, finish, wind up, wrap up **7** approve **8** complete, conclude, solidify **9** terminate **10** consummate

finally
6 at last, lastly **7** someday **8** at length **9** belatedly **10** at long last, eventually, ultimately **12** subsequently

finance
4 back, bank, fund **5** endow, funds, money, stake **6** credit **7** banking, promote, revenue, sponsor, support **8** bankroll **9** grubstake, patronize, subsidize **10** capitalize, investment, underwrite

financial
6 fiscal, pocket **8** business, economic, monetary **9** pecuniary **10** commercial
plan: **6** budget
statement: **12** balance sheet

financier
American: **4** Hill (James Jerome), Ryan (Thomas Fortune), Sage (Russell) **5** Astor (John Jacob), Baker (George Fisher), Eaton (Cyrus), Field (Cyrus West), Gould (Jay), Grace (William Russell), Green (Hetty), Soros (George) **6** Biddle (Nicholas), Boesky (Ivan), Girard (Stephen), Mellon (Andrew), Morgan (John Pierpont, Junius Spencer), Morris (Robert), Rogers (Henry Huttleston), Yerkes (Charles Tyson) **7** Buffett (Warren), Peabody (George) **10** Vanderbilt (Cornelius, William)
British: **6** Baring (Alexander), Rhodes (Cecil) **7** Gresham (Thomas)
French: **6** Necker (Jacques) **7** Colbert (Jean-Baptiste)
German: **7** Schacht (Hjalmar) **10** Rothschild (Amschel, Jakob, Karl, Mayer, Nathan, Salomon)

finch
4 pape **5** junco, serin, zebra **6** canary, linnet, siskin, towhee **7** bunting, chewink, redpoll, sparrow **8** cardinal, grosbeak, longspur **9** crossbill, seedeater

find
3 gem **4** gain, meet, spot **5** catch, dig up, hit on, reach, sight **6** attain, detect, locate, supply, turn up **7** discern, furnish, scare up, uncover, unearth **8** bump into, come upon, discover, meet with, perceive, treasure **9** determine, discovery, encounter **10** experience **13** treasure trove

find out
4 hear **5** catch, learn **6** detect **7** catch on **8** discover, perceive **9** ascertain, determine

fine
3 A-OK, end, top **4** fair, keen, levy, pure, thin **5** bonny, close, clear, dandy, mulct, sheer **6** amerce, choice, minute, ornate, punish, purify, subtle **7** clarion, damages, elegant, forfeit, penalty **8** all right, delicate, penalize, pleasant, splendid, superior **9** beautiful, enjoyable, excellent, first-rate **10** punishment, reparation

finery
5 array **6** attire **7** apparel, regalia **8** clothing, frippery, glad rags, ornament **9** caparison, full dress, trappings, trimmings **10** decoration, Sunday best

finesse
5 dodge, evade, skill, skirt **6** jockey **7** beguile, cunning, exploit **8** maneuver, subtlety **9** dexterity **10** adroitness, artfulness, manipulate

fine-tune
4 true **5** tweak **6** adjust

Fingal's Cave
composer: **11** Mendelssohn (Felix)
island: **6** Staffa

finger
5 blame, digit, index, pinky, strum, touch **6** accuse, pinkie **7** palpate **8** identify, pinpoint
bone: **7** phalanx
combining form: **6** dactyl

finicky
5 fussy, picky **6** choosy, dainty, prissy **7** choosey **8** exacting **9** squeamish **10** fastidious, meticulous, particular, pernickety **11** persnickety

finis
3 end **5** close **6** finale **10** completion, conclusion

finish
3 end **4** do in, kill, slay, stop **5** cease, close, glaze, use up **6** cut off, ending, finale, murder,

patina, polish, windup, wrap up **7** closing, consume, destroy, execute, exhaust, surface **8** complete, conclude, dispatch, finalize, terminus **9** cessation, liquidate, terminate **10** completion, conclusion, denouement, run through **11** termination
dull: **3** mat **4** matt **5** matte
second: **5** place
third: **4** show

finished
4 done, over, ripe **5** ideal **7** done for, perfect, refined, through **8** achieved, complete, over with, polished, washed-up **9** perfected **10** consummate

finite
5 bound, fixed **7** bounded, limited, precise **9** definable **10** restricted **12** determinable

fink
3 rat **5** Judas **6** betray, snitch, squeal **7** traitor **8** betrayer, informer, quisling, snitcher **11** backstabber, stool pigeon **13** strikebreaker

Finland
5 Suomi
Arctic region: **7** Lapland
capital: **8** Helsinki
city: **5** Espoo, Turku **6** Vantaa **7** Tampere
ethnic group: **4** Lapp, Sami
gulf: **7** Bothnia
invader: **9** Alexander
island: **5** Karlö **6** Kimito **9** Vallgrund
island group: **5** Åland
lake: **5** Inari **6** Saimaa **7** Keitele **8** Pielinen
language: **7** Finnish, Swedish
monetary unit: **4** euro
monetary unit, former: **6** markka
neighbor: **6** Norway, Russia, Sweden

Finlandia composer
8 Sibelius (Jean)

Finnigans Wake
author: **5** Joyce (James)
first word: **8** riverrun
last word: **3** the

Finnish
bath: **5** sauna
epic: **8** Kalevala
god: **6** Jumala

fir
4 pine **6** balsam, Fraser **7** conifer, Douglas **9** evergreen
genus: **5** Abies

fire
2 ax **3** axe, can, pep, vim, zip **4** bake, brio, burn, cast, dash, hurl, sack, stir, toss, zeal, zest, zing **5** ardor, blaze, drive, flame, flare, fling, glare, ingle, light, pitch, rouse, salvo, shoot, spark, throw, torch, verve, vigor **6** arouse, energy, excite, fervor, flames, ignite, kindle, lay off, spirit **7** animate, boot out, dismiss, enthuse, inferno, inflame, inspire, kick out, passion, provoke **8** enkindle **9** calenture, discharge, holocaust, terminate **10** combustion, enthusiasm, liveliness **13** conflagration
combining form: **3** pyr **4** igni, pyro
god: **4** Agni, Loki **6** Vulcan **10** Hephaestus

firearm
see **gun**

firebrand
8 agitator **10** incendiary, instigator

firebug
5 torch **8** arsonist **10** incendiary, pyromaniac

firecracker
5 squib **6** banger **9** explosive **10** cherry bomb, noisemaker

firedog
7 andiron

firedrake
6 dragon

firefly
12 lightning bug

fire opal
7 girasol

fireplace
5 grate, ingle
equipment: **6** fender, screen **7** andiron
part: **3** hob **6** hearth, mantel

fireplug
7 hydrant

fire up
5 anger, annoy, rouse, spark **6** excite, ignite, incite, kindle **7** enliven, inflame, inspire, provoke **8** enkindle, irritate

firework
6 petard, rocket **8** pinwheel, sparkler **11** pyrotechnic, Roman candle
cluster: **9** girandole

firkin
3 keg, tun, vat **4** butt, cask, pipe **6** barrel, vessel **8** hogshead

firm
3 set **4** fast, hard, sure **5** fixed, rigid, solid, sound, stiff, tight, tough **6** harden, outfit, secure, settle, stable, steady, strong, sturdy **7** abiding, adamant, certain, company, concern, improve, settled, staunch, unmoved **8** business, constant, definite, enduring, faithful, resolute, specific, vigorous **9** steadfast, tenacious **10** determined, enterprise, inflexible, stipulated, strengthen, unwavering, unyielding **11** established, partnership, substantial, unfaltering, well-founded **13** establishment

firmament
3 sky **5** vault **6** sphere, welkin **7** expanse, heavens **8** empyrean

firmness
7 resolve **8** decision, security, solidity, strength, tenacity **9** constancy, stability **10** durability, resolution **13** determination

first
4 arch, head **5** alpha, chief, prime **6** maiden, primal **7** highest, initial, leading, lead-off, opening, pioneer, premier, primary, supreme **8** champion, dominant, earliest, foremost, headmost, original **9** inaugural, initially, paramount, principal, sovereign **10** aboriginal, preeminent, primordial
prefix: **4** prot **5** proto

firstborn
4 heir **6** eldest, oldest

first-class
3 top **4** A-one, best, fine **5** prime, primo **6** tiptop **7** capital, supreme **8** five-star, superior, top-notch **9** excellent, top-drawer

firsthand
6 direct **7** primary **9** immediate

first man in space
7 Gagarin (Yury)

first showing
5 debut **7** opening **8** premiere

First State
8 Delaware

firth
3 arm, bay **4** cove, gulf **5** inlet **6** harbor, slough **7** estuary

fiscal
8 monetary **9** budgetary, financial

fish
3 aku, bob, cod, dab, eel, gar, koi, net, ray **4** barb, bass, carp, cast, cero, char, chub, chum, coho, cusk, dace, dory, drum, gata, gill, goby, hake, hint, jack, ling, mero, opah, parr, pike, rudd, scup, shad, sild, sisi, sole, spet, tuna, ulua **5** angle, betta, bream, brill, charr, cisco, cobia, danio, fluke, grunt, guppy, jurel, loach, moray, perch, platy, porgy, roach, scrod, seine, shark, skate, smelt, smolt, snook, sprat, tench, tetra, trawl, troll, trout, tunny, wahoo **6** blenny, bonito, burbot, caribe, conger, dorado, grilse, kipper, marlin, minnow, mullet, permit, plaice, pompon, puffer, remora, salmon, sauger, sebago, shiner, sucker, tarpon, tautog, tomcod, turbot, warsaw, wrasse **7** alewife, anchovy, buffalo, capelin, catfish, cavalla, chimera, chinook, cichlid, corbina, cowfish, crappie, dolphin, escolar, gillnet, gourami, grouper, grunion, haddock, hagfish, halibut, herring, hogfish, jewfish, lamprey, mudfish, oarfish, pigfish, pinfish, piranha, pollack, pollock, pompano, pupfish, rainbow, rasbora, sardine, sawfish, sculpin, sea carp, snapper, sniggle, sockeye, sunfish, tilapia, torpedo, whiting **8** albacore, blowfish, bluefish, bluegill, bocaccio, bonefish, brisling, bullhead, chimaera, crevalle, filefish, flounder, gambusia, goldfish, grayling, halfbeak, hornpout, kingfish, ladyfish, lionfish, lookdown, lumpfish, lungfish, mackerel, menhaden, moonfish, pickerel, pilchard, pipefish, porkfish, rock bass, rockfish, rosefish, sailfish, seahorse, sea trout, skipjack, stingray, sturgeon, tilefish, warmouth, weakfish, wolffish **9** amberjack, angelfish, barracuda, brandling, cutthroat, goosefish, greenling, pilotfish, spadefish, stargazer, swordfish, topminnow, trunkfish, whitebait, whitefish **10** butterfish, flying fish, needlefish, parrotfish, sheepshead, silverside, squeteague, tripletail, victorfish, yellowtail **11** Dolly Varden, hatchetfish, jacksmelt, killifish, lanternfish, mummichog, muskellunge, pumpkinseed, stickleback, triggerfish
basket: **5** creel
character: **4** Nemo **5** Wanda
combining form: **6** ichthy
dish: **7** ceviche, seviche **8** cioppino, matelote **13** bouillabaisse
eggs: **3** roe **5** spawn
genus: **4** Amia, Lota
relating to: **7** piscine
spear: **3** gig **7** harpoon, trident
trap: **4** weir
young: **3** fry **4** parr **5** larva, smolt **6** alevin, grilse

fisherman
6 angler

fish hawk
6 osprey

fishhook
adjunct: **5** snell
part: **4** barb **5** shank

fishing line
4 trot **7** setline **8** longline, trotline
float: **3** bob **5** quill
leader: **5** snell

fishing lure
3 fly **4** bait **5** spoon **7** spinner

fishing net
5 seine, trawl

fishlike mammal
4 orca **5** whale **6** dugong, sea cow **7** dolphin, grampus, manatee, narwhal **8** cetacean, porpoise

fish story
3 fib, lie **4** bunk, yarn **11** fabrication **12** exaggeration **13** overstatement

fishwife
5 harpy, scold, shrew, vixen **6** virago **9** termagant, Xanthippe

fishy
7 dubious, suspect **8** doubtful, unlikely **9** ambiguous, dubitable, equivocal, uncertain **10** suspicious **11** problematic **12** questionable

fission element
7 uranium **9** plutonium

fissure
3 gap **4** gash, hole, part, rent, rift **5** break, chasm, chink, cleft, crack, split **6** breach, cleave, divide, schism **7** crevice, discord, opening, rupture **8** crevasse, fracture **10** disharmony, separation

fist
4 duke, grip, hand **5** clamp, grasp **6** clench, clinch, clutch

fit
3 apt, set **4** able, buff, hale, jibe, just, sane, suit, turn **5** adapt, agree, frame, ready, sound, spasm, spell, tally, throe, toned **6** access, accord, adjust, attack, become, belong, decent, go with, proper, seemly, square, tailor, useful **7** capable, conform, healthy, prepare, qualify, seizure, tantrum **8** assemble, decorous, dovetail, eligible, paroxysm, suitable **9** agree with, congruous, consonant, harmonize, reconcile **10** applicable, convenient, correspond, felicitous, go together **11** accommodate, appropriate

fitful
6 random, spotty **7** erratic **8** periodic, sporadic, variable **9** haphazard, hit-or-miss, irregular, spasmodic, uncertain **10** changeable, convulsive, herky-jerky, inconstant **12** intermittent

fitness
4 trim **5** order, shape **6** fettle, health, kilter, repair **7** account, decorum, service, utility **8** capacity **9** condition, propriety, relevance **11** eligibility, suitability **13** applicability

fit out
3 arm, rig **5** equip **6** outfit **7** appoint, furnish **8** accouter, accoutre

fitting
3 apt, due **4** able, just, meet, part, true **5** happy, right **6** proper, seemly **7** apropos, germane **8** apposite, relevant, suitable **9** accessory, befitting, pertinent, qualified **10** applicable, attachment, felicitous, harmonious **11** appropriate

fit together
4 hook, join, mesh **6** hook up **7** connect **8** dovetail **9** integrate

Fitzgerald novel
10 Last Tycoon (The) **11** Great Gatsby (The) **16** Tender Is the Night **17** Tales of the Jazz Age **18** This Side of Paradise **17** All the Sad Young Men **21** Beautiful and the Damned (The)

five
combining form: **4** pent **5** penta **6** quinqu **7** quinque
group of: **6** pentad **7** quintet

five-dollar bill
3 fin

fivefold
9 quintuple

Five Nations
8 Iroquois
member: **7** Cayugas, Mohawks, Oneidas, Senecas **9** Onondagas

five-sided figure
8 pentagon

five-star
6 deluxe, superb **8** superior, top-notch **9** excellent, first-rate **10** first-class **11** outstanding

five-year period
6 luster, lustre **7** lustrum

fix
3 jam, rig, set **4** cook, cure, geld, mend, mess, moor, root, spay, spot, work **5** affix, alter, catch, patch, ready, renew, rivet, solve, state, stick **6** adjust, anchor, assign, attach, change, decide, doctor, fasten, neuter, pickle, plight, repair, revamp, scrape, secure, settle, square, steady **7** appoint, arrange, correct, dilemma, impress, ingrain, resolve, restore, specify, work out **8** castrate, discover, overhaul, position, renovate, solution **9** condition, establish, stabilize, sterilize **11** predicament

fixation
5 craze, mania **6** fetish **9** obsession **11** fascination, infatuation

____ fixe
4 idée, prix

fixed
3 pat, set **4** fast, firm, sure **6** frozen, secure, stable, stated, steady **7** abiding, certain, limited, precise, settled **8** constant, definite, enduring, immobile, resolute **9** exclusive, immovable, immutable, permanent, steadfast, tenacious **10** inflexible, invariable, restricted, stationary, stipulated, unswerving, unwavering **11** determinate, unalterable **12** concentrated, unchangeable **13** circumscribed

fixture
9 appliance **10** attachment

fizz
4 buzz, foam, hiss **5** froth **6** bubble, spirit **7** bubbles, sparkle, sputter **10** effervesce, liveliness **13** effervescence

fizzle
4 bomb, fail, flop **6** fiasco **7** failure, misfire **8** miscarry, peter out **10** effervesce **11** fall through

fjord
Baffin Island: 9 Admiralty
Denmark: 3 Ise, Lim **5** Lamme
Iceland: 4 Axar, Eyja **5** Horna, Skaga, Vopna
Norway: 3 Tys **4** Bokn, Nord, Salt, Stor, Tana, Vest **5** Lakse, Ranen, Sogne **9** Stavanger, Trondheim
Spitsbergen: 3 Ice
Svalbard: 4 Stor

flab
3 fat **4** bulk, lard **5** flesh **7** blubber, fatness **9** cellulite **10** corpulence **11** love handles

flabbergast
3 awe **4** stun **5** amaze, shock, throw **7** astound, nonplus **8** astonish, bowl over, dumfound, surprise **9** dumbfound, overwhelm

flabby
see **flaccid**

flaccid
4 limp, soft, weak **6** feeble, flabby, floppy **8** flexible

flag
3 ebb, lag, sag, tag **4** fade, fail, hail, iris, jack, sign, swag, tail, tire, waft, wane, wave, wilt **5** abate, color, droop, stone **6** banner, burgee, colors, ensign, falter, guidon, pennon, signal, weaken **7** bunting, decline, pendant, pennant **8** bannerol, gonfalon, languish, Old Glory, penalize, registry, standard, streamer, tricolor, vexillum **9** banderole, blue peter, oriflamme, Union Jack **10** Jolly Roger **11** deteriorate **12** Stars and Bars

flagellate
4 beat, flog, hide, lash, whip **5** whale **6** larrup, lather, stripe, switch, thrash **7** scourge **9** horsewhip

flagitious
4 evil **6** sinful, wicked **7** corrupt, vicious **8** criminal, depraved, infamous, perverse, shameful **9** miscreant, nefarious, perverted **10** degenerate, outrageous, scandalous, villainous **11** disgraceful

flagon
3 jug **4** ewer **5** stein, stoup **6** vessel **7** tankard

flagpole
4 mast **5** staff
rope: 7 halyard

flag-raising site
7 Iwo Jima

flagrant
4 bold, rank **5** gross **6** wanton **7** blatant, glaring, heinous, obvious **8** striking **9** atrocious, egregious, monstrous **10** outrageous **11** conspicuous

flagstone
5 shale, slate

flag-waver
7 patriot **8** jingoist, loyalist **10** chauvinist **11** nationalist **12** superpatriot

flail
4 club, beat, flog, whip **6** strike, thrash, thresh **7** scourge **8** flounder, thresher

flair
4 bent, chic, élan, gift **5** knack, style **6** genius, talent **7** ability, aptness, faculty **8** aptitude, tendency **10** proclivity **11** inclination

flak
4 fire **5** abuse **6** shells **7** censure, vitriol **9** brickbats, criticism, hostility **10** opposition **11** disapproval **12** condemnation, fault-finding

flake
3 bit **4** chip, kook, peel **5** scale **6** lamina **7** oddball **8** crackpot, fragment **9** eccentric

flake off
4 chip, peel **5** scale **9** exfoliate **10** desquamate

flaky
3 odd **5** ditsy, ditzy, goofy, nutty, wacky, weird **6** fickle, screwy **7** bizarre, erratic, offbeat **9** eccentric

flambé
6 ablaze, aflame, alight **7** blazing, flaming

flamboyant
4 loud **5** gaudy, showy **6** flashy, florid, ornate, rococo **7** baroque, splashy **8** colorful, luscious **10** over-the-top **12** ostentatious

flame
4 beau, dear, fire, glow, love **5** ardor, blaze, flare, flash, honey, light, lover **7** beloved, darling, passion, sweetie **8** ladylove, truelove **9** boyfriend, inamorata, inamorato **10** brilliance, brightness, girlfriend, heartthrob, sweetheart

flamen
6 priest

flaming
5 afire, fiery **6** ablaze, alight, ardent, red-hot **7** blazing, burning, fervent, flaring, ignited, intense **10** hot-blooded, passionate **11** conflagrant, impassioned

flammable
8 burnable **9** ignitable **10** incendiary **11** combustible
liquid: 3 gas, oil **7** acetone, alcohol, ethanol **8** gasoline, kerosene **9** petroleum **10** turpentine

Flanders
capital: 5 Lille
language: 7 Flemish

flaneur
5 idler **12** boulevardier, man-about-town

flank
4 abut, side **6** adjoin, border

flap
3 tab, tap **4** beat, flog, fold, slap, stew, wave, wing **5** fling, panel **6** crisis, dither, lather, pother, tumult, uproar **7** aileron, flutter, turmoil **9** agitation, commotion, confusion

flapdoodle
3 rot **4** bosh, bull, nuts **5** drool, fudge, hokum, hooey **6** bunkum, drivel **7** baloney, blarney, hogwash, rubbish **8** malarkey, nonsense, tommyrot **9** poppycock **10** applesauce, balderdash **12** blatherskite, fiddle-faddle, fiddlesticks

flapjack
7 hotcake, pancake **11** griddle cake

flare
4 burn **5** blaze, burst, flame, flash **6** signal **7** flicker **8** outburst
type: **5** Hyder **9** air-assist **11** steam-assist

flare-up
5 blaze, burst, flame, flash, surge **8** eruption, outburst **9** explosion

flaring
5 afire, fiery **6** ablaze, aflame, alight **7** blazing, burning **11** conflagrant

flash
3 ray **4** beam, rush, snap, show **5** blaze, bling, blink, crack, flame, flare, glare, gleam, glint, jiffy, shake, shine, showy, spark, speed **6** dazzle, expose, flaunt, glance, minute, moment, second **7** display, disport, exhibit, flicker, glamour, glimmer, glisten, glitter, instant, pizzazz, shimmer, show off, spangle, sparkle, twinkle **8** brandish **9** coruscate **11** coruscation, scintillate, split second **13** scintillation

flashy
4 loud **5** gaudy, jazzy, showy **6** brazen, florid, garish, glitzy, ornate, snazzy, sporty, tawdry, tinsel **7** blatant, chintzy, glaring, insipid **9** sparkling **10** flamboyant, glittering **12** meretricious, ostentatious

flask
4 olpe, vial **6** bottle, fiasco, flacon **7** ampulla, canteen, costrel, thermos

flat
3 dim, mat **4** dead, drab, dull, even **5** banal, bland, exact, fixed, flush, level, muted, plane, prone, rooms, stale, vapid **7** insipid, prosaic **8** lodgings, tenement, unsavory **9** apartment, colorless, innocuous **10** flavorless, lackluster, monotonous

flatfish
see at **fish**

flatland
4 mesa **5** plain **6** steppe, tundra **7** plateau **9** tableland

flat-out
8 absolute **9** downright **10** absolutely

flatten
4 deck, down, dull, even, fell, raze **5** crush, floor, level **6** smooth, squash **9** knock down, prostrate

flattened at the poles
6 oblate

flatter
4 coax, suit **5** toady **6** become, cajole, praise, stroke **7** adulate, blarney, gratify, wheedle **8** blandish, bootlick, butter up, soft-soap **9** sweet-talk

flattery
5 smarm **6** butter, praise **7** blarney **8** cajolery, soft soap, toadyism **9** adulation, sweet talk **10** sycophancy **11** compliments **12** blandishment, ingratiation, unctuousness

Flaubert, Gustave
birthplace: **5** Rouen
heroine: **4** Emma (Bovary)
novel: **8** Salammbô **12** Madame Bovary

flaunt
4 show, wave **5** flash, flout, vaunt **6** expose, parade **7** display, disport, exhibit, show off **8** brandish, flourish

flavor
4 race, tang, zest, zing **5** sapor, savor, smack, spice, taste, tinge **6** relish, season **7** variety, version

flavorless
4 flat **5** bland, stale **7** insipid **8** unsavory **11** unpalatable

flavorsome
5 sapid, tasty, yummy **6** savory **9** delicious, palatable **10** appetizing, delectable **11** good-tasting

flaw
3 gap, rip, sin **4** blot, chip, tear, vice **5** crack, fault **6** defect **7** blemish **8** weakness **9** deformity **12** imperfection

flawed
5 amiss **6** faulty, marred **7** damaged, spoiled **8** impaired **9** defective, imperfect

flawless
4 pure **5** ideal, model **6** intact **7** perfect **8** seamless, unmarred **9** exquisite **10** immaculate, impeccable **11** unblemished

flax
5 linen
fiber: **3** tow
prepare: **3** ret **4** card **5** dress **6** hackle, scutch

flaxen
4 fair **5** blond, straw **6** blonde, golden, yellow **7** towhead

flay
4 beat, lash, peel, skin **7** blister, censure, lambast, upbraid **8** lambaste **9** castigate, criticize, excoriate

flea
6 chigoe, jigger **7** chigger
water: 7 daphnid

Fleance's father
6 Banquo

flèche
5 spire

fleck
3 dot **4** mark, mote, spot **5** flake, speck **6** dapple, mottle, streak, stripe **7** spatter, speckle, stipple **8** particle **9** bespeckle

Fledermaus, Die
3 bat
character: 5 Adele, Falke, Frank **6** Alfred **9** Rosalinde **10** Eisenstein
composer: 7 Strauss (Johann)

fledge
4 rear **7** feather

fledgling
4 colt, tyro **6** novice, rookie **8** beginner, freshman, neophyte, newcomer **10** apprentice

flee
3 fly, lam, run **4** bolt, scat, skip **5** elude, scoot, scram, skirr, steal **6** decamp, escape **7** abscond, make off, run away, scamper, vamoose **8** stampede, turn tail **9** skedaddle **10** make tracks

fleece
3 rob **4** bilk, clip, gaff, milk, rook, skin, soak, wool **5** bleed, cheat, cozen, mulct, shear, stick, sweat **6** extort, hustle, rip off **7** defraud, swindle **8** flimflam **10** overcharge

fleecy
5 downy **6** fluffy, pilose, woolly **7** hirsute **9** whiskered **10** flocculent

fleer
4 gibe, gird, jeer, jest, mock, quip **5** flout, laugh, scoff, scout, sneer, taunt

fleet
4 fast, navy, spry **5** agile, brisk, group, hasty, quick, rapid, swift **6** argosy, armada, nimble, speedy **8** flotilla **9** breakneck **10** harefooted

fleeting
5 brief **7** passing **8** fugitive, volatile **9** ephemeral, fugacious, momentary, temporary, transient **10** evanescent, short-lived, transitory

Fleming, Ian
see **James Bond**

flesh
4 beef, meat, skin **5** stock **7** kindred **9** offspring, relatives, substance

fleshly
5 obese **6** animal, bodily, carnal **7** lustful, profane, secular, sensual **8** corporal, physical, sensuous, temporal **9** corporeal, epicurean, luxurious, sybaritic **10** voluptuous

fleshy
3 fat **5** ample, beefy, burly, gross, heavy, hefty, husky, meaty, obese, plump, pudgy, stout, tubby **6** chubby, chunky, portly, rotund **7** porcine, weighty **9** corpulent **10** overweight, well-padded
fruit: 4 plum, pome **5** berry, drupe, grape, mango, peach **6** cherry **8** cucumber

Fletcher's partner
8 Beaumont (Francis)

fleur-de-lis
4 iris

flex
4 bend **5** tense

flexible
5 lithe, loose **6** docile, floppy, limber, pliant, supple **7** elastic, pliable, springy, willowy **8** amenable, bendable, stretchy, yielding **9** adaptable, compliant, malleable, tractable

flexion
3 bow **4** bend, fold, turn **5** angle

flexuous
5 fluid, lithe, snaky **7** sinuous, winding **8** tortuous **10** circuitous, convoluted, meandering, serpentine **11** anfractuous

flick
4 film, show **5** movie **13** motion picture, moving picture

flicker
4 bird, film, flit, hint **5** flash, gleam, glint, movie, waver **6** quiver **7** twinkle **10** woodpecker **13** motion picture, moving picture

flickering
7 lambent **8** unsteady

flier
3 ace **5** pilot **6** airman **7** aviator, birdman, handout **8** aviatrix, brochure, circular **9** throwaway

flight
3 hop, lam **4** rout, soar, slip, wing **5** flock, floor, flush, flyby, story **6** escape, flying, series **7** getaway **8** breakout
formation: 7 echelon
overnight: 6 redeye

flighty
5 dizzy, giddy, silly, swift **7** foolish **8** freakish, skittish, unstable, volatile **9** frivolous, mercurial, transient **10** capricious, changeable, inconstant **11** empty-headed, harebrained **13** irresponsible

flimflam
3 con, gyp **4** bilk, dupe, fake, fool, gull, hoax, jazz, sham **5** cheat, cozen, fraud, hokum, trick **6** chouse, deceit, diddle, humbug **7** chicane, deceive, defraud, swindle **8** hoodwink, trickery **9** bamboozle, deception, moonshine **10** balderdash, double-talk **11** hornswoggle

flimflammer
3 gyp **5** cheat **6** con man **7** diddler, sharper **8** swindler **9** defrauder **11** four-flusher **12** double-dealer

flimsy
4 limp, weak **5** cheap, filmy, frail, gauzy, sheer **6** feeble, flabby, sleazy, slight **7** flaccid, fragile, rickety, spindly, tenuous, unsound **8** decrepit, delicate, gossamer **10** diaphanous, improbable **11** implausible, transparent **12** unconvincing **13** insubstantial

flinch
5 quail, start, wince **6** blench, cringe, recoil, shrink

fling
3 peg **4** cast, emit, fire, flap, hurl, plop, rush, shot, slap, stab, tear, toss **5** binge, chuck, heave, pitch, shoot, spree, throw **6** affair, charge, hurtle, launch **7** splurge **8** catapult

Flintstones, The
character: **4** Dino, Fred **5** Betty (Rubble), Wilma **6** Barney (Rubble) **8** Bamm-Bamm
creator: **5** Hanna (Bill) **7** Barbera (Joe)
setting: **7** Bedrock
voice: **5** Blanc (Mel)

flip
4 glib, leaf, pert, riff, toss, wise **6** breezy, invert, riffle, ruffle **8** turn over **10** somersault **11** impertinent, smart-alecky

flip-flop
5 U-turn, waver **6** sandal, switch, waffle **7** reverse **8** reversal **9** about-face, turnabout, vacillate, volte-face **10** turnaround **11** vacillation

flippancy
5 cheek **6** levity **8** archness, pertness **9** cockiness, freshness, frivolity **10** cheekiness, impishness **11** roguishness

flippant
4 glib, pert **5** sassy, saucy **6** breezy, cheeky **11** impertinent, smart-alecky **13** disrespectful

flirt
3 toy **4** flit, fool, minx, ogle, vamp **5** dally, tease **6** coquet, trifle, wanton **8** coquette **10** experiment, mess around

flit
3 fly, zip **4** dart, pass, rush, sail, scud, whiz, wing **5** flash, hurry, scoot, speed **7** flicker, flutter, twinkle

flitter
4 dart, flap, wing **5** hover, waver **6** quiver **7** skitter **9** fluctuate

flivver
6 jalopy **9** tin lizzie

float
3 bob, fly **4** buoy, cork, hang, raft, ride, sail, scud, swim, waft **5** drift, hover **6** wander **7** pontoon, propose **8** levitate **9** negotiate

floater
3 bum, vag **4** hobo, raft **5** tramp **7** drifter, vagrant **8** derelict, vagabond **10** roustabout

floating
5 fluid, loose **6** adrift, natant **7** buoyant, movable **8** moveable, shifting, variable **10** adjustable **11** fluctuating

flocculent
5 flaky **6** fleecy, fluffy, woolly

flock
3 mob **4** army, bevy, herd, host, mass, pack, rout, wisp **5** brood, bunch, cloud, covey, crowd, drove, group **6** flight, gaggle, gather, legion, scores, throng **8** assemble, assembly, converge **9** multitude **11** aggregation **12** congregation

floe
3 ice **4** berg **7** glacier, iceberg **8** ice field

flog
3 tan **4** beat, cane, flap, hide, lash, slog, whip **5** birch, drive, flail, whale **6** larrup, lather, stripe, switch, thrash **7** cowhide, leather, scourge **10** flagellate

flood
4 fill, flow, flux, glut, pour, rush, tide **5** burst, drown, float, spate, swamp **6** deluge, engulf, stream **7** current, freshet, immerse, Niagara, torrent **8** alluvion, cataract, inundate, overflow, submerge **9** avalanche, cataclysm, overwhelm **10** inundation, outpouring

floor
3 awe **4** base, down, drop, fell, stun, tier **5** amaze, level, shock, story **6** ground **7** astound, flatten **8** astonish, audience, bowl down, bowl over, surprise **9** dumbfound, knock down **11** flabbergast

flop
3 dud **4** bomb, bust, fail, fall **5** lemon, loser **6** bummer, fizzle, turkey **7** clinker, failure

floppy
4 disk, limp **6** flimsy **7** flaccid **8** diskette, flexible

flora
6 plants **10** vegetation

flora and fauna
5 biota

Florence
bridge: **12** Ponte Vecchio
cathedral: **5** Duomo
family: **6** Medici
museum: **6** Uffizi **8** Bargello
palace: **5** Pitti
river: **4** Arno

florid
3 red **5** flush, gaudy, ruddy, showy **6** ornate, rococo **7** baroque, flowery, flushed, glowing **8** rubicund, sanguine, sonorous **9** bombastic, elaborate, overblown **10** euphuistic, flamboyant, rhetorical **11** declamatory **12** magniloquent **13** grandiloquent

Florida
capital: **11** Tallahassee
city: **5** Miami, Tampa **6** Naples, Venice **7** Hialeah, Key West, Orlando **8** Sarasota **9** Palm Beach **11** St. Augustine **12** Jacksonville, St. Petersburg
college, university: **7** Rollins, Stetson
county: **3** Lee **4** Dade **6** Orange **7** Broward, Volusia **8** Pinellas, Sarasota
key: **4** Long, Vaca, West **5** Largo **7** Big Pine **9** Matecumbe, Sugarloaf
lake: **9** Kissimmee **10** Okeechobee
nickname: **8** Sunshine (State)
park: **10** Everglades
race site: **7** Daytona
river: **6** Indian **7** St. Johns **8** Suwannee **12** Apalachicola
state bird: **11** mockingbird
state flower: **13** orange blossom
state tree: **9** sabal palm

florilegium
5 album **6** reader **7** garland, omnibus **8** analects **9** anthology **10** collection, miscellany

Florimel's husband
7 Marinel

floss
4 down, fuzz, lint **5** fluff **6** thread

flotilla
5 fleet **6** argosy, armada

Flotow opera
5 Indra **6** L'Ombre, Martha

flotsam
6 debris, jetsam **7** remains **8** wreckage **9** driftwood

flounce
5 frill, mince, strut, waltz **6** bounce, prance, ruffle, sashay

flounder
3 dab **5** slosh **6** fumble, muddle, splash, thrash, wallow **7** blunder, flounce **8** flatfish, struggle

flour
4 meal **6** pinole, powder
beetle: **6** weevil
merchant: **6** miller

flourish
3 wax **4** grow, wave **5** adorn, bloom **6** flower, stroke, thrive **7** blossom, burgeon, develop, fanfare, prosper, succeed **8** brandish, curlicue, ornament **13** embellishment, ornamentation

flout
4 defy, mock **5** scorn, spurn **6** deride, insult **7** scoff at

flow
4 emit, flux, gush, ooze, pour, rill, rise, rush, stem, tide, well **5** arise, drift, flood, issue, spate, spill, surge, swarm **6** course, deluge, onrush, sluice, spring, stream **7** cascade, current, emanate, give off, outflow, proceed **8** inundate, sequence **9** discharge, originate **10** continuity, inundation, succession **11** progression **12** continuation

flower
4 best, blow, pick, posy **5** bloom, cream, elite, pride, prime, prize **6** choice, thrive **7** blossom, burgeon, develop **10** effloresce **13** inflorescence
buttonhole: **11** boutonniere
cluster: **4** cyme **5** spike, umbel **6** corymb, floret, raceme, spadix **7** panicle **8** spikelet **9** capitulum, dichasium, glomerule **11** monochasium **13** inflorescence
cup: **5** calyx
garden: **4** iris, lily, pink, rose **5** aster, canna, daisy, oxlip, pansy, peony, phlox, poppy, tulip **6** azalia, cosmos, crocus, dahlia, orchid, violet **7** jonquil, petunia **8** camellia, daffodil, gardenia, geranium, gloxinia, hyacinth, larkspur, marigold, primrose **9** carnation, gladiolus, narcissus **10** delphinium, heliotrope **13** chrysanthemum
necklace: **3** lei
opening: **8** anthesis
part: **5** bract, calyx, ovary, ovule, petal, sepal, style **6** anther, pistil, spathe, stamen, stigma **7** corolla, nectary, pedicel, petiole **8** calyptra, filament, peduncle, perianth
spike: **5** ament **6** catkin, spadix
stalk: **7** pedicel **8** peduncle
type: **3** ray **4** disk **6** annual, simple **9** composite, perennial
wild: **4** flag **5** bluet, daisy, vetch **6** lupine **7** anemone, arbutus, cowslip, gentian, vervain **8** bluebell, hepatica, trillium **9** buttercup, columbine, dandelion, saxifrage **10** cinquefoil **12** lady's slipper

flower arranging
7 ikebana

flowering
6 growth 8 progress 9 evolution 11 development, florescence, progression

flowerless plant
4 fern, moss 6 lichen 9 liverwort

flowery
5 wordy 6 florid, ornate, prolix 7 aureate, diffuse, verbose 8 sonorous 9 overblown 10 euphuistic, rhetorical 11 declamatory 12 magniloquent 13 grandiloquent

Flowery Kingdom
5 China

flowing
4 easy 5 fluid 6 fluent, liquid, smooth 7 cursive, running 10 effortless
back: 6 reflux 8 refluent
in: 6 influx 8 influent
together: 7 conflux 9 confluent

flow regulator
4 cock, gate 5 valve 8 throttle

flu
6 grippe

flub
4 goof, mess, muff, slip 5 boner, botch, error, fluff, gaffe, lapse, snarl 6 bobble, bollix, bungle, foul up, goof up, mess up 7 blunder, faux pas, louse up

fluctuate
4 sway, yo-yo 5 swing, waver 6 seesaw 8 undulate 9 alternate, oscillate, vacillate

flue
4 duct, pipe, tube, vent 6 funnel, uptake 7 channel, chimney, outtake

fluent
4 easy, glib 5 fluid 6 facile, liquid, smooth, supple 7 cursive, flowing, voluble 8 eloquent, polished 10 articulate, effortless

fluff
4 down, flub, fuzz, goof, lint, mess, muff, slip, trip 5 boner, botch, error, floss, gaffe, lapse, whisk 6 bobble, bollix, bungle, goof up, mess up 7 blooper, blunder, faux pas, louse up, mistake

fluffy
5 downy 6 flossy 7 cursory, shallow 8 puffed up 10 flocculent 11 superficial 13 unsubstantial

fluid
4 free, sera (plural) 5 lymph, serum, water 6 liquid, mobile, molten, serous, watery 7 mutable, protean 8 flexible, shifting, unstable, unsteady, variable 9 adaptable, changeful, unsettled 10 changeable
excessive: 5 edema

fluke
3 hap 4 lobe, worm 5 quirk 6 chance 8 flatfish, fortuity 9 trematode

fluky
3 odd 6 casual, chance, chancy, random 9 arbitrary 10 accidental, fortuitous

flume
5 chute 6 sluice, stream 7 channel 8 aqueduct 11 watercourse

flummox
5 abash, addle 6 baffle, rattle, stymie 7 confuse, fluster, perplex 8 befuddle, bewilder, confound 9 discomfit, embarrass 10 disconcert

flunk
4 fail

flunky
4 peon 5 gofer, toady 6 drudge, lackey, stooge, yes-man 7 footman, servant, steward 8 factotum, follower

flurry
3 ado, fit 4 fuss, gust, spit, stir, to-do 5 haste, whirl 6 bother, bustle, furore, pother, tumult 7 barrage, flutter, turmoil 8 snowfall 9 agitation, commotion, confusion, whirlpool, whirlwind 10 excitement, turbulence

flush
4 even, flat, glow, pink, rich, rose, wash 5 bloom, color, level, plane, raise, rinse, rouge 6 florid, filled, mantle, redden, sluice 7 cleanse, crimson, glowing, inflame, opulent, suffuse, wealthy 8 abundant, abutting, irrigate, rubicund, sanguine, squarely 9 turn color

fluster
5 addle, dizzy, shake, upset 6 ball up, bother, fuddle, muddle, rattle, ruffle 7 agitate, confuse, disturb, nonplus, perturb, unhinge 8 befuddle, bewilder, confound, disquiet, distract 10 discompose

flustered
5 upset 7 abashed, anxious, rattled 8 agitated, confused, troubled 9 chagrined, disturbed, flummoxed, perplexed, perturbed 10 bewildered, disquieted, distracted, distraught, distressed, nonplussed 11 discomposed, embarrassed 12 disconcerted

flute
4 fife, roll 5 pleat 6 goffer, groove 7 chamfer, channel, piccolo 8 recorder 9 wineglass
Japanese: 10 shakuhachi
oval: 7 ocarina
player: 5 piper 7 flutist 8 flautist

flutist
American: 5 Baker (Julius), Baron (Samuel) 7 Robison (Paula) 8 Zukerman (Eugenia)
French: 6 Rampal (Jean-Pierre)
Irish: 6 Galway (James)

flutter
4 beat, flap, flit **5** hover, quake, shake **6** flurry, quaver, quiver, wobble **7** flicker, flitter, pulsate, tremble, vibrate **9** agitation, commotion, confusion, palpitate, vibration **11** fluctuation

flu type
4 bird **5** Asian, avian, swine

flux
3 run **4** flow, fuse, melt, rush, thaw, tide **5** drift, flood, spate **6** change, stream **7** current, flowing, outflow **8** dissolve

fly
3 zip **4** bolt, dart, dash, flee, flit, lure, scud, skip, soar, whiz, wing **5** fleet, float, glide, hover, hurry, pilot, scoot, shoot, skirr, sweep, whish, whisk **6** aviate, escape, hasten, hustle **7** abscond, flutter
insect: **3** ked **4** gnat **5** midge **6** botfly, gadfly, mayfly, tsetse **7** deerfly, sandfly **8** blackfly, dipteron, horsefly, housefly, tachinid **10** bluebottle
larva: **6** maggot

fly-by-night
5 shady **7** passing **9** transient **10** transitory, unreliable **12** disreputable, undependable **13** untrustworthy

flycatcher
5 pewee **6** phoebe, tyrant **8** bellbird, kingbird **9** passerine

flying
5 aloft **6** volant **8** airborne

Flying Dutchman, The
composer: **6** Wagner (Richard)
heroine: **5** Senta

flying fish
7 gurnard

flying fox
3 bat **8** fruit bat

flying horse
7 Pegasus **10** hippogriff

flying island
6 Laputa

flying lemur
6 colugo

flying mammal
3 bat

flying saucer
3 UFO

fly in the ointment
5 catch **8** drawback

foam
4 head, scud, scum, suds, surf **5** churn, froth, spume **6** bubble, lather, seethe **7** bubbles **10** effervesce

fob
4 seal **5** chain **6** pocket, ribbon **8** ornament

fob off
5 foist **6** put off **7** palm off, pass off

focus
3 fix, hub **4** node, zoom **5** heart, rivet **6** adjust, center, fixate, home in **8** converge, emphasis, meditate, polestar **9** concenter, epicenter **10** hypocenter **11** concentrate, nerve center

fodder
4 feed, food **6** forage, silage, stover **9** provender
crop: **3** hay, oat, rye **4** corn **5** maize, vetch, wheat **6** barley, clover, millet **7** alfalfa, sorghum
storage structure: **4** silo
store: **6** ensile

foe
5 enemy, rival **8** opponent **9** adversary **10** antagonist

fog
4 blur, daze, foam, haze, mist, murk, soup **5** brume, cloud, vapor **6** miasma, muddle **7** pea soup, pogonip

foggy
4 hazy **5** dirty, grimy, misty, murky, soupy, vague **7** brumous, muddled, obscure, tenuous **8** confused, pea soupy, vaporous

fogy
6 dotard, fossil, square **7** diehard **8** mossback **10** fuddy-duddy **12** antediluvian, conservative **11** standpatter **13** stick-in-the-mud

fogyish
7 old-line **8** outmoded, standpat **9** hidebound, out-of-date **10** antiquated, fuddy-duddy, mossbacked **11** reactionary **12** conservative, old-fashioned

foible
4 vice **5** fault **6** defect **7** failing, frailty **8** weakness **11** shortcoming **12** imperfection

foil
4 balk, beat, curb, dash, faze **5** check, sword **6** baffle, defeat, rattle, thwart **7** buffalo **8** contrast, restrain **9** discomfit, embarrass, frustrate **10** circumvent, disappoint, disconcert **11** straight man

foist
6 fob off **7** palm off, pass off

fold
3 pen, ply **4** bend, fail, tuck **5** drape, flock, pleat, plica, ridge **6** crease, double, furrow, pucker **7** flexure, plicate **9** plication **11** corrugation
skin: **4** ruga **5** plica, rugae (plural) **6** dewlap, plicae (plural)

folder
4 file **6** binder **9** portfolio

foliage
6 growth, leaves 7 verdure 8 greenery, lushness 10 vegetation

folk
4 race 6 people 9 community

folklore
4 myth, tale 5 fable 6 belief, custom, legend, mythos, wisdom 9 mythology, tradition 12 superstition

folks
6 family 7 parents 9 relatives

folksinger
4 Baez (Joan), Ives (Burl) 5 Dylan (Bob), Niles (John Jacob), White (Josh) 6 Odetta, Seeger (Pete) 7 Collins (Judy), Guthrie (Arlo, Woody), Robeson (Paul) 9 Belafonte (Harry), Ledbetter (Huddie)

folksy
5 homey 6 casual, earthy, mellow, rustic, simple 7 natural 8 down-home, familiar, informal, laid-back, sociable 9 easygoing, ingenuous 10 unaffected, unpolished 13 unpretentious

folktale
4 myth 5 fable 6 legend 7 märchen

follow
3 dog, spy, tag 4 hunt, keep, obey, seek, tail, walk 5 catch, chase, ensue, grasp, hound, trace, track, trail 6 accept, comply, convoy, pursue, search, shadow, travel 7 conform, imitate, proceed, replace, succeed 8 practice, supplant 9 supersede
closely: 5 draft 10 slipstream

follower
3 fan 5 toady 6 addict, cohort, minion, sequel, votary 7 acolyte, apostle, devotee, groupie, habitué, sectary, trailer, wannabe 8 adherent, advocate, disciple, faithful, hanger-on, henchman, myrmidon, parasite, partisan, tagalong 9 dependent, satellite, supporter, sycophant 10 aficionado

following
4 next 5 after, below, later, since 6 behind, public 7 ensuing, retinue 8 audience 9 adherents, afterward, believers, disciples, entourage, partisans 10 afterwards, sequential, supporters, subsequent, succeeding, successive 12 subsequently, subsequent to

follow-up
6 sequel

folly
4 whim 6 lunacy, vanity 7 fatuity, foolery, inanity, madness 8 insanity, nonsense 9 absurdity, craziness, dottiness, silliness, stupidity 10 indulgence 11 foolishness 12 extravagance

foment
3 sow 4 brew, goad, spur 5 rouse, set on 6 arouse, excite, foster, incite, stir up, whip up 7 agitate, nurture, provoke 9 cultivate, encourage, instigate

fond
4 dear, warm 5 silly 6 doting, loving, tender 7 devoted, fatuous, foolish, partial 8 desirous, enamored, romantic 9 indulgent 10 infatuated 11 sentimental 12 affectionate

fondle
3 paw, pet 5 grope, touch 6 caress, cosset, dandle, stroke 7 embrace 8 canoodle

fondness
4 love 5 fancy, taste 6 liking, relish 8 appetite, devotion, penchant, soft spot, weakness 9 affection, tendresse 10 attachment, partiality, preference, propensity 11 inclination 12 predilection

font
4 root, type 6 origin, source 8 fountain 10 receptacle

food
3 pap 4 chow, diet, eats, fare, grub, meal, meat 5 bread, manna 6 fodder, viands 7 aliment, cuisine, edibles, nurture, pabulum, vittles 8 delicacy, victuals 9 nutriment, provender 10 provisions, sustenance 11 comestibles, nourishment
disorder: 7 bulimia 8 anorexia
divine: 8 ambrosia
element: 5 fiber, fibre, sugar 6 starch 7 mineral, protein, vitamin 12 carbohydrate
from heaven: 5 manna
lover: 7 epicure, gourmet 8 gourmand
provision: 4 mess 6 ration 7 serving
scarcity: 6 famine
waste: 7 garbage

foofaraw
3 ado 4 fuss, stir, to-do 5 hoo-ha, stink 6 bother, finery, frills, furore, hoo-hah, hurrah, pother, ruckus, rumpus 8 brouhaha 9 commotion 11 disturbance

fool
3 ass, kid, oaf, rag, rib, sap, toy 4 boob, butt, clod, dolt, dope, dupe, fish, gull, hoax, jerk, jest, joke, josh, mook, zany 5 chump, clown, comic, dally, dummy, dunce, goose, idiot, loser, moron, ninny, patsy, schmo, trick 6 banter, cretin, dawdle, delude, diddle, dimwit, doodle, galoot, gammon, jester, lead on, meddle, monkey, motley, nitwit, pigeon, schmoe, stooge, sucker, tamper, trifle, victim 7 beguile, buffoon, chicane, deceive, fake out, fall guy, fritter, half-wit, jackass, mislead, pinhead, saphead, schmuck 8 bonehead, comedian, dumbbell, flimflam, hoodwink, imbecile, lunkhead, numskull, pushover 9 bamboozle, birdbrain, blockhead, interfere, simpleton

10 nincompoop **11** hornswoggle, merry-andrew, string along **13** laughingstock
around: **4** futz, idle, laze, loaf, loll **5** flirt **6** dawdle, diddle, lounge **8** lollygag, womanize **9** philander

foolhardy
4 bold, rash **6** daring, madcap **8** headlong, reckless **9** audacious, daredevil, impetuous **11** precipitate, temerarious

foolish
3 mad **4** daft, gaga, rash, zany **5** balmy, batty, crazy, dippy, dizzy, dorky, dotty, goofy, inane, inept, kooky, loony, loopy, nutty, sappy, silly, wacky **6** absurd, insane, simple, stupid, unwise **7** asinine, doltish, fatuous, idiotic, lunatic, meshuga, moronic, witless **8** clueless, meshugge, reckless, trifling **9** cockamamy, half-baked, brainless, fantastic, frivolous, half-baked, imbecilic, insensate, laughable, ludicrous, senseless **10** cockamamie, half-cocked, half-witted, irrational, ridiculous **11** harebrained, nonsensical

foolishness
4 bull, bunk **5** folly, fudge **6** bêtise, bunkum, lunacy **7** fatuity, inanity, rubbish **8** claptrap, drollery, insanity, nonsense, tommyrot **9** absurdity, craziness, silliness, stupidity **10** imbecility, imprudence **12** fiddle-faddle **13** horsefeathers

fool's gold
6 pyrite

foot
3 paw, pay **4** hoof
ailment: **4** corn **6** bunion, callus
animal: **3** pad, paw **4** hoof
bones of: **5** talus, tarsi (plural) **6** cuboid, tarsal, tarsus **7** phalanx **9** calcaneus, cuneiform, navicular, phalanges (plural) **10** metatarsal
combining form: **3** ped, pod **4** podo
doctor: **10** podiatrist **11** chiropodist
metric: **4** iamb **5** arsis, paeon **6** dactyl, thesis **7** anapest, pyrrhic, spondee, trochee
part: **3** toe **4** arch, ball, claw, nail **5** ankle, digit, talon **6** hallux, instep

football
4 nerf **5** rugby **6** rugger, soccer **7** pigskin
field: **8** gridiron
foul: **7** holding, offside **8** clipping **12** interference
official: **6** umpire **7** referee **8** linesman **9** back judge, line judge **10** field judge
play: **4** dive, trap **5** sneak, sweep **6** option, screen **7** audible, counter, handoff, rollout, runback **8** dropback **9** crossbuck, off-tackle **10** buttonhook
player position: **3** end **4** back, half, wing **5** guard **6** center, kicker, safety, tackle **7** flanker, lineman, wideout **8** defender, fullback, halfback, linesman, receiver, scatback, slotback, split end, tailback, tight end, wingback **9** noseguard **10** cornerback, linebacker, nose tackle **11** placekicker, quarterback, running back, snapper-back **12** defensive end, strong safety, wide receiver
scoring: **6** safety **9** field goal, touchdown **10** conversion
starting play: **7** kickoff
team: **6** eleven
term: **4** down, kick, pass, punt, rush, snap **5** blitz, block, squad **6** fumble, huddle, kicker, onside, option, player, safety, spiral **7** end zone, handoff, kickoff, offside, pigskin, quarter, spinner, tweener, yardage **8** clipping, crossbar, goal line, goalpost, gridiron, halftime **9** backfield, defensive, field goal, intercept, offensive, placekick, scrimmage, touchback, touchdown **11** ballcarrier, broken field **12** interception, triple threat
(see also **National Football League**)

footballer
4 Kemp (Jack), Long (Howie), Lott (Ronnie), Levy (Marv), Monk (Art), Moon (Warren), Reed (Andre), Rice (Jerry) **5** Allen (Marcus), Baugh (Sammy), Berry (Raymond), Brady (Tom), Brown (Bob, Jim), Clark (Gary), Ditka (Mike), Elway (John), Eller (Carl), Favre (Brett), Gibbs (Joe), Groza (Lou), Jones (Bert, Deacon), Kelly (Jim), Kosar (Bernie), Leahy (Pat), Lomax (Neil), Muñoz (Anthony), Shula (Don), Simms (Phil), Smith (Emmitt), Starr (Bart), Stram (Hank), Swann (Lynn), Young (Steve) **6** Aikman (Troy), Blanda (George), Butkus (Dick), Carter (Chris, Ki-Jana), Csonka (Larry), Dawson (Len), Ellard (Henry), Graham (Otto), Grange (Red), Greene (Joe), Harris (Franco), Jaeger (Jeff), Joiner (Charlie), Lofton (James), Lowery (Nick), Marino (Dan), Murray (Eddie), Namath (Joe), Payton (Walter), Rypien (Mark), Sayers (Gale), Slater (Jackie), Taylor (Lawrence), Thorpe (Jim), Tittle (Y. A.), Turner (Jim), Unitas (Johnny), Walker (Herschel) **7** Bledsoe (Drew), Dorsett (Tony), Esiason (Boomer), Gifford (Frank), Hornung (Paul), Johnson (Norm), Largent (Steve), Luckman (Sid), Manning (Peyton), Montana (Joe), Newsome (Ozzie), Riggins (John), Rozelle (Pete), Sanders (Barry, Deion), Simpson (O. J.), Stabler (Ken), Thurman (Thomas) **8** Andersen (Morten), Anderson (Gary, Ottis), Bradshaw (Terry), Lombardi (Vince), Nagurski (Bronko), Plunkett (Jim), Staubach (Roger) **9** Dickerson (Eric), Jurgensen (Sonny), Hostetler (Jeff), Tarkenton (Fran) **10** Stallworth (John), Singletary (Mike), Stephenson (Dwight), Youngblood (Jack)

Foote play
15 Trip to Bountiful (The) **19** Young Man from Atlanta (The)

footfall
4 step **5** tread

footing
4 base, rank, seat, term 5 basis, place, state 6 bottom, ground, status 7 bedrock, seating, station, warrant 8 basement, capacity, pedestal, position, standing 9 character, situation 10 foundation, groundwork, substratum 12 underpinning

footless
4 dull, dumb 5 crass, dense, inept, unfit 6 apodal, stupid 7 foolish

foot lever
5 pedal 7 treadle

footman
7 servant 10 pedestrian 11 infantryman

footnote abbreviation
4 Ibid., Idem 5 op. cit. 6 loc. cit.

footpad
5 thief 6 mugger, robber 8 criminal 10 highwayman, pickpocket

footprint
3 pug 4 sign, step 5 spoor, trace, track, tract 7 pugmark, vestige

footslog
4 plod, slop, toil 5 tramp, tromp 6 trudge

footstone
6 ledger, marker 8 monument 11 grave marker

footstool
7 cricket, hassock, ottoman

fop
3 jay 4 beau 5 blade, blood, dandy, spark, swell 7 coxcomb, gallant 8 cavalier, macaroni, popinjay 9 exquisite, ladies' man, pretty boy 11 Beau Brummel, petit-maître 12 fashion plate, lounge lizard

foppish
6 chichi 8 dandyish, peacocky 10 peacockish

for
3 pro 7 in favor

forage
4 beat, comb, grub, prog, raid, rake, sack 5 scour 6 browse, fodder, ravage, rustle, search 7 plunder, ransack, rummage 8 finecomb, scrounge 9 pasturage
crop: 5 grass 6 clover, kochia 7 alfalfa, sorghum
(see also **fodder**)

foray
4 raid 6 inroad, sortie 8 invasion 9 incursion, irruption

forbear
4 shun 5 avoid, forgo, spare 6 endure, eschew, resist, suffer 7 abstain, decline, refrain 8 hold back, restrain, tolerate

forbearance
5 grace, mercy 6 lenity 7 charity 8 clemency, lenience, leniency, mildness, patience 9 restraint, tolerance 10 abstinence, toleration 13 consideration

forbearing.
4 easy, kind, mild 6 gentle 7 clement, lenient, patient 8 merciful, tolerant 9 indulgent 10 charitable, thoughtful 11 considerate, magnanimous

Forbes hero
8 Tremaine (Johnny)

forbid
3 ban, bar, nix 4 curb, deny, halt, stop, veto 5 block, check, debar 6 enjoin, hinder, impede, outlaw, refuse 7 inhibit, prevent, rule out, shut out 8 disallow, obstruct, preclude, prohibit, restrain 9 interdict, proscribe

forbidden
5 taboo 6 banned, barred 7 illegal, illicit 8 verboten 10 prohibited

Forbidden City
5 Lhasa 6 Gu Gong 7 Beijing

forbidding
4 grim 5 drear, harsh 6 dreary, severe 8 daunting, menacing, sinister 9 repellent 10 formidable 11 threatening

force
2 od 3 jam 4 cram, dint, push 5 drive, foist, impel, might, power, press, vigor, wreak, wreck, wrest 6 coerce, compel, demand, duress, effort, energy, extort, impose, legion, muscle, oblige 7 command, impetus, inflict, potency, require, sandbag 8 coercion, manpower, momentum, obligate, pressure, shoehorn, strength, violence 9 constrain, intensity, puissance, strong-arm 10 compulsion, constraint
apart: 5 wedge
unit: 4 dyne

forced
8 strained 9 contrived, unnatural 10 artificial, compulsory 11 involuntary

forceful
5 stiff, stout 6 mighty, potent, punchy, strong, virile 7 dynamic 8 emphatic, powerful, puissant, vigorous 9 assertive 10 compelling

forceless
4 lame, weak 5 wimpy 6 feeble 8 impotent, nugatory 9 powerless 10 inadequate 11 ineffective, ineffectual

force out
see **expel**

forcible
8 coercive 9 compelled 10 compulsory, obligatory, peremptory

ford
5 cross

Ford's folly
5 Edsel

for each
3 per 6 apiece

forearm bone
4 ulna 5 radii (plural), ulnae (plural) 6 radius

forebear
8 ancestor 9 precursor 10 antecedent, progenitor 11 predecessor 12 primogenitor

forebode
5 augur 7 betoken, portend, predict, presage 8 foretell, prophesy, soothsay 13 prognosticate

foreboding
4 omen, sign 5 dread 6 augury 7 anxiety, portent, presage, warning 10 prediction, prognostic 11 premonition 12 apprehension, presentiment

forecast
5 augur 6 divine 7 foresee, portend, predict, presage 8 estimate, foretell, indicate, prophecy, prophesy 9 adumbrate, calculate, prevision, prognosis 10 prediction 13 prognosticate

forecaster
4 seer 5 augur 6 oracle 7 diviner, prophet 8 haruspex 9 predictor 10 prophesier, soothsayer, weatherman 11 Nostradamus 13 meteorologist, weatherperson

foreclose
3 bar 5 debar 6 cut off, hinder 7 prevent, shut out 8 preclude

forefather
see **forebear**

forefeel
6 divine 9 apprehend, prevision

forefinger
5 index

forefront
3 van 4 lead 8 vanguard 10 avant-garde, firing line 11 cutting edge

foregoer
6 herald 8 ancestor, forebear 9 harbinger, precursor, prototype 10 antecedent, antecessor, forerunner, progenitor 11 predecessor 12 primogenitor

foregoing
5 prior 6 former 7 earlier 8 anterior, previous 9 precedent, preceding 10 antecedent

forehanded
6 frugal 7 prudent, thrifty 8 sensible, well-to-do 9 provident 10 prosperous

forehead
4 brow 5 frons, front 8 sinciput 9 sincipita (plural)

foreign
5 alien 6 exotic 7 strange 8 external, offshore, overseas 9 extrinsic, nonnative 10 accidental, extraneous, immaterial, irrelevant 11 incongruous 12 adventitious, inapplicable, incompatible, inconsistent 13 inappropriate
prefix: 4 xeno

foreigner
5 alien 8 outsider, stranger 9 outlander 10 tramontane

foreknow
6 divine 9 apprehend, prevision 10 anticipate

foreland
4 beak, cape, head, ness 5 point 10 promontory

forelock
5 bangs, quiff 7 cowlick

foreman
4 bos'n, boss 5 bosun, chief 6 gaffer, ganger, honcho, leader 7 captain, manager, steward 8 overseer 9 boatswain 10 supervisor

foremost
4 arch, head, high, main 5 chief, first, front, grand 7 leading, premier, supreme 9 number one, paramount, principal 10 preeminent 11 cutting-edge, outstanding

forenoon
4 morn 7 morning 12 ante meridiem

forensic
8 judicial 9 debatable 10 rhetorical 13 argumentative

foreordain
4 doom, fate 9 determine 10 predestine 12 predetermine

forerunner
4 omen, sign 5 envoy 6 augury, herald 7 pioneer, portent, presage, symptom, warning 8 ancestor, exemplar, outrider 9 announcer, harbinger, initiator, messenger 10 antecedent, originator, prognostic 11 anticipator, predecessor

foresee
6 divine 7 predict, presage 8 perceive, prophesy 9 apprehend, prefigure, prevision 10 anticipate 13 prognosticate

foreseer
5 augur 6 auspex, oracle 7 diviner, prophet 8 haruspex 9 predictor 10 soothsayer 11 Nostradamus

foreshadow
4 bode, hint 5 augur 6 herald 7 betoken, portend, predict, presage, promise, suggest 8 forecast, intimate 9 adumbrate, prefigure 13 prognosticate

foresight
6 vision 7 caution 8 prudence, sagacity 10 discretion, perception, precaution, prescience, providence

forest
4 bosk, wood **5** copse, grove, weald, woods **6** bosque **7** coppice, thicket, woodlot **8** wildwood, woodland **10** timberland, wilderness
deity: **5** dryad **6** sylvan **8** Sylvanus
English: **4** Dean **5** Arden **8** Sherwood
German: **5** Black **11** Schwarzwald
opening: **5** glade
relating to: **6** sylvan
subarctic: **5** taiga
tropical: **5** selva **6** jungle

forestall
5 avert, block, deter **6** hinder **7** obviate, preempt, prevent, rule out, ward off **8** preclude, stave off **10** anticipate

Forester, C. S.
hero: **10** Hornblower (Horatio)
novel: **12** African Queen (The)

foretell
4 bode, warn **5** augur **6** divine **7** portend, predict, presage, promise **8** proclaim, prophesy, soothsay **9** adumbrate, apprehend, prefigure **10** anticipate, vaticinate **13** prognosticate

forethought
8 judgment, planning, prudence **10** discretion, precaution **12** deliberation **13** premeditation

foretoken
4 bode, hint, omen, sign, warn **5** augur **6** augury, herald **7** portend, portent, presage, promise, symptom, warning **8** forecast **9** harbinger, precursor **10** intimation

forever
3 aye **6** always **7** endless **8** eternity, evermore **9** endlessly, eternally **10** in aeternum **11** ad infinitum, ceaselessly, continually, everlasting, incessantly, permanently, perpetually, unceasingly **12** in perpetuity **13** everlastingly

forewarning
6 caveat, tip-off **7** caution **8** monition **11** premonition

foreword
5 intro, proem **7** preface, prelude **8** exordium, overture, preamble, prologue **12** introduction, prolegomenon

for example
3 say **6** such as

for fear that
4 lest

forfeit
4 fine, lose **5** mulct **6** give up **7** penalty **9** sacrifice **10** amercement

forfend
4 ward **5** avert, deter **6** secure **7** obviate, prevent, protect, rule out, ward off **8** preclude, preserve, stave off

forge
4 copy, fake, form, make **5** pound, shape **6** smithy **7** advance, fashion, imitate, produce, turn out **8** continue **9** construct, fabricate **11** counterfeit, manufacture

forget
4 fail, omit **6** ignore, slight **7** neglect **8** discount, overlook, pass over **9** disregard

forgetful
3 lax **5** slack **6** absent, remiss **7** amnesic **8** amnesiac, careless, heedless **9** negligent, oblivious, unwitting **10** abstracted, neglectful **11** inattentive, thoughtless **12** absentminded

forgetfulness
5 lethe **7** amnesia **8** oblivion **10** negligence **11** inattention

forgivable
6 venial **10** remissible

forgive
5 remit **6** excuse, pardon **7** absolve, condone **8** overlook

forgiveness
6 pardon **7** amnesty **9** remission **10** absolution

forgo
3 bag **5** leave, waive, yield **6** eschew, give up, resign **7** abandon **8** abnegate, jettison, renounce **9** sacrifice, surrender **10** relinquish

fork
6 bisect, branch, crotch **7** diverge, utensil **9** branch off
prong: **4** tine

fork out
3 pay **5** spend **10** contribute

forlorn
5 alone **6** bereft, futile, lonely **8** desolate, forsaken, hopeless, lonesome, solitary, wretched **9** abandoned, depressed, destitute, miserable **10** despairing, despondent **12** disconsolate

form
3 way **4** body, cast, make, mode, mold **5** build, forge, found, frame, image, model, shape, style **6** create, design, devise, figure, make up, manner **7** compose, contour, develop, fashion, outline, process, produce, profile **8** comprise, organize, practice **9** construct, establish, fabricate, framework, procedure, structure, take shape **10** constitute, convention, regulation **11** materialize **13** configuration
combining form: **5** morph
set: **10** stereotype

formal
3 set **4** prim **5** exact, legal, rigid, stiff **6** dressy, lawful, proper, seemly, solemn **7** distant, orderly,

regular, stately, starchy, stilted **8** abstract, black-tie, decorous, elevated, official, reserved **10** ceremonial, methodical, systematic **11** ceremonious, syntactical **12** conventional

formality
4 form, rite **6** ritual **7** liturgy, service **8** ceremony, insignia **10** ceremonial, convention, observance

formalize
6 codify **9** establish, normalize **10** regularize **11** standardize

format
4 plan, size **5** shape, style **6** makeup, method **11** arrangement **12** organization

formation
4 rank **6** design, makeup **9** structure **11** arrangement, composition, development **12** architecture, construction

former
3 old **4** late, once, past **5** prior **6** bygone, whilom **7** earlier, onetime, quondam **8** anterior, previous, sometime **9** erstwhile, precedent, preceding **10** antecedent

formerly
3 née **4** erst, once **6** before, whilom **7** already, earlier **9** erstwhile **10** heretofore, previously

formidable
8 daunting **9** difficult **10** impressive **11** redoubtable

formless
5 vague **7** chaotic, obscure, unclear **8** inchoate, nebulous, unshaped **9** amorphous, undefined, unordered **10** immaterial, indefinite, indistinct **11** unorganized

Formosa
6 Taiwan
capital: 6 Taipei

formula
4 rite, rule **5** canon, maxim, tenet **6** method, recipe, ritual **7** precept, theorem **8** equation **9** algorithm, blueprint, principle, yardstick **10** touchstone **12** prescription

formulate
5 couch, draft, frame, hatch **6** codify, devise, invent, make up, phrase **7** concoct, dream up, express, prepare, work out **8** contrive

forsake
4 quit **5** avoid, leave, spurn **6** defect, depart, desert, give up, reject, resign **7** abandon **8** abdicate, renounce **9** throw over **10** relinquish

forsaken
4 lorn **6** bereft **7** forlorn **8** derelict, deserted, desolate, solitary **9** abandoned

Forseti
father: 6 Balder, Baldur
palace: 7 Glitnir

Forster work
7 Maurice **10** Howards End **13** Room with a View (A) **14** Passage to India (A)

forswear
4 deny **5** unsay **6** abjure, recall, recant, reject **7** perjure, retract **8** renounce, take back, withdraw

fort
4 base **6** castle **7** bastion, bulwark, citadel, redoubt **8** fastness, fortress, garrison, martello, stockade **10** stronghold
Baltimore: 7 McHenry
California: 3 Ord
Kentucky: 4 Knox
New Jersey: 3 Dix
New York: 7 Niagara, Stanwix **8** Schuyler **11** Ticonderoga
Ontario: 9 Frontenac
San Antonio: 5 Alamo
South Carolina: 6 Sumter
Spanish: 7 alcazar **8** presidio

forte
3 bag **4** loud **5** thing **6** métier **8** long suit, strength **9** specialty **10** strong suit **11** strong point

forth
6 onward **7** forward

forthcoming
7 pending **8** imminent **9** impending, proximate **10** responsive **11** approaching

for the most part
9 generally, typically **10** on the whole

for the time being
3 now **6** pro tem **9** at present, currently, presently **10** pro tempore

forthright
4 open **5** blunt, frank, plain **6** candid, direct **7** up-front **8** straight **10** aboveboard, foursquare **11** openhearted, straight-out, undisguised, unvarnished

forthwith
3 now **6** at once **8** directly **9** instantly, right away, thereupon **11** immediately, straightway **12** straightaway

fortification
4 moat, wall **6** abatis, buffer, glacis **7** barrier, bastion, bulwark, citadel, parapet, rampart, redoubt **8** barbican, enceinte, fastness, garrison, palisade, presidio, stockade **9** barricade, earthwork **10** breastwork, stronghold
part: 7 salient

fortify
3 arm **4** gird, stir **5** brace, rally, ready, renew, rouse, steel **6** enrich, secure **7** hearten, prepare, protect, refresh, restore **8** embolden, energize **9** encourage, reinforce **10** invigorate, strengthen

fortitude
4 grit, guts, pith **5** fiber, heart, nerve, pluck, spunk, valor **6** mettle, phlegm, spirit **7** bravery, courage, stamina **8** backbone, boldness, strength, tenacity **9** constancy, endurance, tolerance **10** resolution **11** intrepidity **12** fearlessness, perseverance, resoluteness, staying power **13** dauntlessness, determination

fortress
see **fort**

fortuitous
5 fluky, happy, lucky **6** casual, chance **10** accidental, auspicious **12** providential

fortuity
3 hap **4** luck **5** fluke **6** chance **8** accident **9** happening **10** occurrence

Fortuna
5 Tyche
symbol: 5 wheel **6** rudder

fortunate
5 happy, lucky **9** favorable **10** auspicious, propitious **12** providential

Fortunate Islands
8 Canaries

fortune
3 lot, pot, wad **4** doom, fate, luck, mint, pile, ship **5** worth **6** boodle, bundle, chance, happen, hazard, packet, riches, wealth **7** destiny, success, weather **8** property **9** resources

Fortune founder
4 Luce (Henry)

fortune-teller
4 seer **5** augur, sibyl **7** diviner, palmist **9** wisewoman **10** soothsayer
(see also **foreseer**)

fortune-telling
see **divination**

forty winks
3 nap **6** catnap, siesta, snooze **7** shut-eye

forum
5 court, panel **6** medium **8** congress, tribunal **9** symposium **10** colloquium, conference, roundtable **11** convocation, marketplace

forward
3 aid **4** abet, bold, send, ship **5** ahead, brash, eager, pushy, ready, relay, remit, sassy, saucy **6** cheeky, foster, onward, uphold **7** address, advance, consign, further, promote, support **8** advanced, champion, dispatch, impudent, transmit **9** encourage, in advance **11** smart-alecky **12** presumptuous **13** self-assertive
prefix: 4 ante

For Whom the Bell Tolls
author: 9 Hemingway (Ernest)
character: 5 Maria, Pablo, Pilar **6** Jordan

Forza del Destino composer
5 Verdi (Giuseppe)

fossa
3 pit **5** fovea **6** cavity, groove **10** depression

fosse
4 dike, moat **5** canal, ditch **6** trench **7** acequia, channel

fossil
4 fogy **5** amber, fogey, relic **6** dotard **7** antique **8** calamite, conodont, mossback **10** antiquated, fuddy-duddy **12** antediluvian **13** stick-in-the-mud
fuel: 3 gas, oil **4** coal, peat **9** petroleum **10** natural gas

foster
4 back, help, rear, tend **5** nurse **6** assist, harbor, parent **7** advance, bring up, nourish, nurture, promote, support, sustain **8** champion **9** cultivate, encourage

fou
5 crazy, drunk

foul
4 base, rank, soil, vile **5** botch, dirty, fetid, funky, muddy, nasty, yucky **6** coarse, defile, filthy, grubby, horrid, impure, odious, putrid, rotten, scuzzy, smutty, stormy, turbid, vulgar, wicked **7** abusive, noisome, obscene, pollute, profane, raunchy, squalid, tarnish, unclean **8** indecent, obstruct, polluted, stinking, wretched **9** collision, loathsome, obnoxious, offensive, repellent, repugnant, repulsive, revolting **10** abominable, detestable, disgusting, malodorous **11** contaminate, treacherous **12** dishonorable, scatological

foul play
3 hit **5** blood **6** murder **7** killing, outrage **8** homicide, violence **12** manslaughter

found
4 base, cast, rear **5** begin, erect, raise, set up, start **6** bottom, create, invent **7** fashion, support **8** commence, initiate, organize **9** establish, institute, originate, predicate

foundation
3 bed **4** base, rock **5** basis **6** bottom, corset, makeup **7** bedding, footing, support **8** pedestal **9** endowment **10** groundwork, substratum **11** institution **12** organization, substructure, underpinning

foundational
5 basic **6** bottom **7** primary **10** supportive, underlying **11** fundamental

founder
4 fail, sink **5** wreck **6** author, father, go down **7** creator **8** collapse, inventor, submerge, submerse **9** architect, generator, patriarch, shipwreck **10** originator

foundling
6 infant, orphan
fountain
3 jet **4** head, root **5** spout **6** geyser, origin, source, spring **7** bubbler **8** wellhead **9** inception, reservoir **10** wellspring
nymph: **6** Egeria
four
6 tetrad **7** quartet **10** quaternion
bagger: **5** homer **7** home run
combining form: **4** tetr **5** quadr, tetra **6** quadri, quadru, quater, tessar **7** tessara, tessera
gills: **4** pint
hundred: **5** elite **10** upper crust
inches: **4** hand
pecks: **6** bushel
quarts: **6** gallon
four-flush
4 dupe **5** bluff **6** betray, delude, humbug, take in **7** beguile, deceive **11** doublecross
four-footed animal
8 tetrapod **9** quadruped
Four Horsemen
3 War **5** Death **6** Famine **8** Conquest **10** Pestilence
four-in-hand
3 tie **5** coach **7** necktie
fourpence
5 groat
four-poster
3 bed
fourscore
6 eighty
four-sided figure
5 rhomb **6** square **7** rhombus **9** rectangle **13** quadrilateral, parallelogram
foursquare
8 straight **10** forthright **13** quadrilateral
fourteen pounds
5 stone
fourth
7 quarter **8** quadrant, quartern
combining form: **5** quadr, quart **6** quadri, quadru
fowl
3 hen **4** bird, cock, duck **5** chick, goose, poult **6** bantam, pullet, turkey **7** chicken, rooster (see also **chicken; poultry**)
Fowles novel
5 Magus (The) **9** Collector (The) **22** French Lieutenant's Woman (The)
fox
4 fool **5** trick **6** baffle, outwit **7** confuse, reynard **8** bewilder
African: **4** asse
female: **5** vixen
kind: **3** kit, red **5** swift **6** arctic, fennec, silver **8** bat-eared
Scottish: **3** tod
young: **3** cub
foxglove
9 digitalis
fox grape
9 muscadine **11** scuppernong
foxiness
4 wile **5** craft, guile **7** cunning, slyness **8** wiliness **10** artfulness, craftiness, cleverness
foxlike
7 vulpine
foxy
3 sly **4** wily **5** canny, slick **6** artful, astute, clever, crafty, shrewd, tricky **7** cunning, vulpine **8** guileful **9** insidious
foyer
5 lobby **8** anteroom, entrance **9** vestibule
fracas
3 row **4** feud, fray, spat, to-do **5** brawl, broil, fight, melee, run-in, set-to **6** affray, hassle, shindy, uproar **7** dispute, quarrel, ruction **8** squabble **9** bickering **10** donnybrook, free-for-all **11** altercation
fraction
3 bit, cut **4** part **5** piece, scrap **6** divide, little **7** portion, section **8** fragment
fractious
4 wild **6** unruly **7** peevish, pettish, willful **8** contrary **9** bellicose, irritable **10** headstrong, pugnacious, refractory **11** belligerent, contentious, intractable, quarrelsome **12** recalcitrant, ungovernable, unmanageable
fracture
4 rent, rift, tear **5** break, cleft, crack, split **6** breach, schism **7** rupture
Fra Diavolo composer
5 Auber (Esprit)
fragile
4 weak **5** frail **6** feeble, flimsy, infirm **7** brittle, friable, tenuous, unsound **8** decrepit, delicate **9** breakable, frangible
fragment
3 bit **4** chip, iota, part, rive **5** burst, crumb, flake, grain, piece, scrap, shard, sherd, shred, smash **6** morsel, shiver, sliver **7** break up, flinder, shatter **8** fraction, particle, splinter **9** fall apart **12** disintegrate
fragmentary
6 broken **7** partial **10** fractional, incomplete, unfinished
fragrance
4 musk, nose, odor **5** aroma, attar, scent, smell,

spice **7** bouquet, cologne, incense, perfume **9** redolence **11** eau de parfum, toilet water **13** eau de toilette

fragrant
7 odorous, scented **8** aromatic, perfumed, redolent **11** odoriferous

frail
4 puny, slim, thin, weak **5** petty, reedy, wispy **6** feeble, flimsy, infirm, sickly, slight **7** brittle, fragile, slender, spindly, tenuous, unsound **8** decrepit, delicate **9** breakable, frangible

frailty
4 vice **5** fault **6** foible **7** failing **8** delicacy, weakness **9** infirmity **10** feebleness

frame
4 body, form, mold, plan, sash **5** build, draft, erect, forge, mount, shape, shell **6** border, casing, cook up, devise, draw up, figure, invent, make up, sketch, system **7** arrange, chassis, concoct, fashion, imagine, prepare **8** assemble, casement, conceive, contrive, regulate, skeleton **9** cartouche, construct, fabricate, formulate, structure
part: **4** sill, stud **5** joist, plate

framework
4 rack **5** shell, truss **7** trestle **8** cribbing, cribwork, scaffold, skeleton, studding, studwork, trussing **9** bare bones, structure
of crossed strips: **7** lattice, trellis

France
bay: **6** Biscay
capital: **5** Paris
channel: **6** Manche (La) **7** English
city: **4** Caen, Lyon, Metz, Nice **5** Brest, Lyons **6** Amiens, Calais, Nantes, Rennes **8** Bordeaux, Grenoble, Toulouse **9** Marseille **10** Marseilles, Strasbourg, Versailles **11** Montpellier
conqueror: **6** Caesar (Julius)
department: **3** Var **4** Aude, Gard, Jura, Orne **5** Marne, Rhône, Somme **6** Savoie, Vosges **7** Bas-Rhin **8** Ardennes, Calvados
emperor: **5** Pepin (III, the Short) **8** Napoleon (Bonaparte) **11** Charlemagne
enclave: **6** Monaco
former name: **4** Gaul **6** Gallia
hero: **6** Clovis
heroine: **9** Joan of Arc
historic province: **4** Foix **5** Anjou, Aunis, Bearn, Berry, Maine **6** Alsace, Artois, Marche, Poitou, Vendée **7** Gascony, Guyenne, Picardy **8** Auvergne, Bretagne, Brittany, Burgundy, Dauphine, Flanders, Gascogne, Limousin, Lorraine, Lyonnais, Normandy, Picardie, Provence, Touraine **9** Angoumois, Bourgogne, Champagne, Languedoc, Nivernois, Orléanais, Saintonge, Venaissin **10** Roussillon **11** Bourbonnais, Île-de-France **12** Franche-Comté
island: **3** Yeu **6** Hyères, Oléron, Ushant **7** Corsica **8** Belle-Île **11** Noirmoutier
monarch: **5** Henri, Henry, Louis **6** Philip **7** Charles **8** Philippe
monetary unit: **4** euro
monetary unit, former: **3** sou **5** franc
mountain, range: **4** Alps, Jura **6** Vosges **8** Auvergne, Pyrenees **9** Mont Blanc
neighbor: **5** Italy, Spain **7** Andorra, Belgium, Germany **10** Luxembourg **11** Switzerland
president: **6** Chirac (Jacques) **8** de Gaulle (Charles) **10** Mitterrand (François)
region: **4** Midi **5** Corse **6** Alsace, Centre **7** Corsica, Picardy **8** Auvergne, Bretagne, Brittany, Burgundy, Limousin, Normandy, Picardie **9** Aquitaine, Bourgogne, Champagne, Languedoc, Normandie **10** Rhône-Alpes **11** Île-de-France **12** Franche-Comté, Midi-Pyrénées
river: **4** Aire, Aude, Oise **5** Adour, Isère, Loire, Marne, Rhone, Saône, Seine, Somme, Yonne **7** Garonne
sea: **13** Mediterranean
spa city: **5** Evian
strait: **5** Dover
symbol: **8** Marianne

Francesca's lover
5 Paolo

franchise
4 vote **6** ballot **7** freedom, license **8** suffrage **9** privilege

frangible
7 brittle, fragile, friable **8** delicate **9** breakable

frank
3 dog **4** fair, free, open **5** blunt, plain **6** candid, direct, honest, hot dog, weenie, wiener, wienie **7** upright **8** man-to-man, out-front, straight **9** barefaced, outspoken **10** forthright, scrupulous, unreserved **11** openhearted, plainspoken, transparent, unconcealed, undisguised, uninhibited, unvarnished, wienerwurst **12** heart-to-heart, unmistakable

Frankenstein
author: **7** Shelley (Mary)
helper: **4** Igor

frankfurter
3 dog **6** hot dog, weenie, wiener, wienie **11** wienerwurst

Frankie's lover
6 Johnny

Frankish hero
6 Roland

Franklin, Benjamin
birthplace: **6** Boston
invention: **5** stove **8** bifocals
pen name: **11** Poor Richard

frankness
6 candor **7** honesty

frantic
3 mad **4** wild **5** upset, wired **7** fraught, shook up, unglued **8** feverish, frenetic, frenzied, maniacal, worked up **10** distraught **11** overwrought

Franzen novel
11 Corrections (The)

frappe
7 chilled, liqueur **9** milk shake

fraternal
6 clubby **8** sociable **9** brotherly, comradely, dizygotic **10** like-minded

fraternal society
3 FOE, KOC, SAR **4** BPOE, Elks **5** Lions, Moose **6** Eagles, Masons, Rotary **7** Kiwanis, Woodmen **8** Shriners **10** Freemasons, Hibernians, Odd Fellows

fraternity
4 club **5** guild, order, union **6** league **7** company **8** sodality **10** fellowship **11** association, brotherhood **13** brotherliness

fraud
3 con, gyp **4** fake, gaff, hoax, scam, sham **5** cheat, faker, phony, quack, trick **6** deceit, dupery, humbug, hustle, phoney **7** chicane, con game, swindle **8** cozenage, flimflam, impostor, operator, trickery **9** charlatan, chicanery, deception, imposture, pretender, shell game, trickster **10** dishonesty, mountebank, subterfuge **11** counterfeit **12** double-dealer **13** double-dealing, sharp practice

fraudulence
6 deceit **8** quackery, trickery **9** chicanery, deception, phoniness **10** dishonesty

fraudulent
4 fake **5** false, phony **7** crooked **8** cheating, guileful **9** deceitful, deceptive, dishonest **10** fallacious **11** duplicitous

fraught
4 full **5** laden, tense **6** filled, uneasy **7** charged, replete, stuffed **8** pregnant **9** stressful

fräulein
4 maid, Miss **6** maiden **9** governess **12** mademoiselle

fray
3 row **4** fret **5** brawl, broil, brush, clash, fight, melee, ravel, shred **6** combat, fracas, strain, strife **7** dispute, frazzle, ruction, scuffle **8** irritate, skirmish, struggle **9** commotion, scrimmage **10** donnybrook **11** disturbance

frayed
4 worn **6** tatty **6** ragged, shabby **8** tattered **9** moth-eaten **10** threadbare

frazzle
4 do in, fray, poop, tire, wear **5** upset **6** tucker **7** exhaust, fatigue, wear out

frazzled
4 beat **5** upset **6** bushed, sapped **7** drained, rattled **8** agitated, confused, fatigued, tired out **9** exhausted, fagged out, unsettled **10** distressed **11** overwrought **12** disconcerted

freak
3 bug, nut **4** buff, geek, whim **5** go ape, fancy, fiend, maven **6** addict, hippie, maniac, megrim, oddity, vagary, weirdo, whimsy, zealot **7** anomaly, caprice, chimera, conceit, deviate, fanatic, monster **8** crotchet, flimflam **9** androgyne, curiosity **10** aberration, enthusiast **11** abnormality, monstrosity **12** lusus naturae, malformation

freakish
3 odd **5** kooky, outré, weird **6** far-out, quirky **7** bizarre, erratic, oddball, strange **8** aberrant, abnormal **9** arbitrary, eccentric, grotesque, whimsical **10** capricious, outlandish

freckle
3 dot **4** mole, spot **5** fleck **7** speckle, stipple

free
3 rid **4** comp, open **5** frank, loose, untie **6** acquit, exempt, gratis, loosen, unbind, untied **7** absolve, at large, donated, liberal, manumit, movable, pro bono, release, unbound, unchain, unleash, unloose **8** detached, generous, liberate, separate, unfasten, unloosen **9** at liberty, discharge, exculpate, exonerate, extricate, sovereign, unchained, unchecked, unimpeded, unshackle, unsparing, voluntary **10** autonomous, democratic, emancipate, gratuitous, unconfined, unfettered, unshackled **11** disentangle, emancipated, independent, spontaneous, untrammeled **12** unrestrained, unrestricted **13** complimentary, self-governing, unconstrained

freebie
4 comp, gift, pass **7** present **8** giveaway

freebooter
5 rover **6** bandit, pirate, raider **7** brigand, corsair **8** marauder, picaroon, pillager, rapparee, sea rover **9** buccaneer, pickaroon, plunderer, ransacker

freedom
5 right **7** liberty, license, release **8** autonomy, immunity, latitude **9** exemption, franchise, privilege **11** prerogative **12** emancipation, independence **13** outspokenness
Swahili: 5 uhuru

free-for-all
4 fray **5** brawl, broil, melee **6** affray, fracas, rumble **7** ruction **10** donnybrook

freehanded
7 liberal **8** generous **9** bounteous, bountiful **10** munificent

freeloader
3 bum **5** leech **6** cadger, sponge **7** moocher **8** barnacle, hanger-on, parasite **11** bloodsucker

Free State
8 Maryland

free ticket
4 pass **11** Annie Oakley

freeze
4 halt, stop **5** chill, stall **6** benumb **7** congeal **8** glaciate, solidify, stoppage **10** immobilize

freezing
3 icy **4** cold **5** chill, gelid, nippy, polar **6** arctic, bitter, chilly, frigid, frosty, wintry **7** glacial, shivery
combining form: **4** cryo, kryo

freight
4 haul, lade, load **5** cargo **6** burden, charge, lading **7** payload **9** transport

freighter
4 scow, ship **7** carrier, shipper **9** cargo ship **11** bulk carrier

Freischütz composer
5 Weber (Carl Maria von)

French
article: **2** la, le, un **3** les, une
attendant: **9** concierge
back: **3** dos
bed: **3** lit **6** couche
black: **4** noir
born: **3** née
boy: **6** garçon
brother: **5** frère
cap: **5** beret
cardinal: **7** Mazarin (Jules) **9** Richelieu (Duc de)
castle: **7** château
cathedral city: **4** Albi **5** Paris, Reims, Rouen **6** Amiens, Nantes, Rheims **8** Chartres
clergyman: **4** abbé, curé, père
coin: **3** ecu
cold: **5** froid
combining form: **5** Gallo **6** Franco
conjunction: **2** et, ou **4** mais
daughter: **5** fille
day: **5** jeudi, lundi, mardi **6** samedi **8** dimanche, mercredi, vendredi
dear: **4** cher
department head: **7** prefect
direction: **3** est, sud **4** nord **5** ouest
down with: **4** à bas
dream: **4** rêve
drink: **5** boire
dynasty: **5** Capet **6** Valois **7** Bourbon
egg: **4** oeuf
emblem: **10** fleur-de-lis
empress: **7** Eugénie **9** Joséphine
evening: **4** soir
exclamation: **3** zut **4** eheu, hein **9** sacrebleu
eye: **4** oeil
farewell: **5** adieu **8** au revoir
farmhouse: **5** ferme
father: **4** père
forest: **7** Argonne, Belleau
friend: **3** ami **4** amie
game: **3** jeu **4** jeux (plural)
God: **4** dieu
good: **3** bon **5** bonne
gray: **4** gris
hat: **7** chapeau
head: **4** tête
here: **3** ici
income: **5** rente
island: **3** île
king: **3** roi
language: **9** Provençal
leather: **4** cuir
length: **4** aune
mask: **4** loup
milk: **4** lait
month: **3** mai **4** août, juin, mars, mois **5** avril **7** février, janvier, juillet
mother: **4** mère
nail: **4** clou
national anthem: **12** Marseillaise (La)
nose: **3** nez
nothing: **4** rien
number: **3** dix, six **4** cinq, deux, huit, neuf, onze, sept **5** douze, trois **6** quatre
opera: **5** Faust, Lakmé, Manon, Thaïs **6** Carmen, Mignon **7** Werther
pancake: **5** crêpe
pastry: **6** éclair **8** napoleon
poem: **3** dit
policeman: **4** flic **8** gendarme
porcelain: **6** Sèvres **7** Limoges
preposition: **2** de **3** par, sur **4** avec, dans, pour, sans, sous
pretty: **4** joli **5** jolie
prison: **8** Bastille
pronoun: **2** il, je, te, tu, un **3** eux, ils, mes, moi, toi, une **4** elle, nous, vous
Protestant: **6** Calvin (John) **8** Huguenot
pupil: **5** élève
queen: **5** reine
quick: **4** vite
rabbit: **5** lapin
railroad station: **4** gare
resort: **3** Pau **4** Nice **5** Vichy **6** Cannes, Menton **7** Antibes **8** Biarritz
resort area: **7** Riviera
restaurant: **6** bistro

revolutionist: **5** Marat (Jean-Paul) **6** Danton (Georges) **11** Robespierre (Maximilien)
Revolution party: **7** Gironde, Jacobin **8** Mountain
Revolution song: **5** Ça Ira
roasted: **4** rôti
room: **5** salle
saint: **4** Joan (of Arc) **5** Denis **6** Martin (of Tours) **7** Thérèse (of Lisieux)
school: **5** école, lycée
sea: **3** mer
season: **3** été **5** hiver **7** automne **9** printemps
servant: **5** valet
sherry: **5** xérès
shooting match: **3** tir
shop: **8** boutique
shrine: **7** Lourdes
singer: **4** Piaf (Edith) **8** chanteur **9** chanteuse
sister: **5** soeur
small: **5** petit **6** petite
soldier: **5** poilu **6** soldat, Zouave **8** chasseur
son: **4** fils
song: **3** dit **7** chanson
soup: **6** potage
star: **6** étoile
state: **4** état
stock exchange: **6** bourse
street: **3** rue
subway: **5** metro
summer: **3** été
there!: **5** voilà
too much: **4** trop
very: **4** très
wartime capital: **5** Vichy
water: **3** eau
well: **4** bien
wine: **3** vin
wineshop: **6** bistro
wood: **4** bois
yes: **3** oui
yesterday: **4** hier

French Guiana
capital: **7** Cayenne
ethnic group: **6** Creole
island: **6** Devil's
mountain range: **10** Tumac-Humac
neighbor: **6** Brazil **8** Suriname
river: **4** Mana **6** Maroni **7** Oyapock

French Polynesia
archipelag: **7** Tuamotu
capital: **7** Papeete
island, island group: **6** Tahiti **7** Austral, Gambier, Society **9** Marquesas

frenetic
3 mad **4** loco, wild **5** crazy, wired **6** crazed, hectic **7** berserk, frantic **8** agitated, feverish, frenzied, maniacal **9** delirious, orgiastic **10** corybantic

frenzied
see **frenetic**

frenzy
4 amok, fury, rage **5** amuck, craze, furor, mania **6** madden **7** derange, madness, unhinge **8** delirium, distract, hysteria, insanity, paroxysm **9** unbalance **11** derangement

frequency unit
5 hertz **7** fresnel **9** gigahertz

frequent
5 haunt, often, usual, visit **6** common, hourly **7** regular **8** everyday, familiar, habitual **9** customary

frequenter
7 denizen, habitué, haunter

frequently
4 a lot **5** often **8** commonly **9** routinely **10** oftentimes, repeatedly **11** customarily, recurrently

fresh
3 new, raw **4** rude **5** green, lippy, naive, novel, sassy, saucy, smart **6** callow, cheeky, recent, unused, vernal, virgin **8** brand-new, impudent, insolent, original **9** unspoiled **11** impertinent, smart-alecky **12** invigorating **13** inexperienced

freshet
5 flood, spate **6** influx

freshman
4 pleb, tyro **5** frosh, plebe **6** novice, rookie **8** beginner, neophyte, newcomer **10** apprentice, tenderfoot

fret
4 fume, fuss, stew **5** brood, chafe, worry **6** dither, pother

fretful
5 angry, cross **6** crabby, cranky **7** carping, chafing, peevish, pettish, whining **8** captious, caviling, critical, perverse, petulant, restless, snappish **9** fractious, impatient, irascible, irritable, querulous

Freudian term
2 id **3** ego **5** drive **6** denial, libido **7** complex, Oedipal **8** analysis, cathexis, fixation, neurosis, superego **9** analysand, disavowal, dreamwork, fetishism, psychosis **10** parapraxis, projection, regression, repression **11** association, sublimation, unconscious **12** condensation, displacement, preconscious, transference

Frey
father: **5** Njörd **6** Njörth
god of: **3** sun **4** rain **5** peace **9** fertility
sister: **5** Freya
wife: **4** Gerd **5** Gerda, Gerth

Freya
brother: **4** Frey
domain: **9** Folkvangr
father: **5** Njörd **6** Njörth

friable
5 mealy **7** brittle, crumbly, fragile **9** frangible

friar
7 brother **8** cenobite **9** mendicant

fribble
3 toy **5** dally, flirt **6** coquet, trifle **7** trifler **8** trifling **9** dalliance, frivolity **10** dillydally, fool around

friction
4 drag **7** discord, rubbing **8** abrasion **9** animosity, attrition **10** disharmony, dissension, resistance **12** disagreement

friction match
5 vesta **7** lucifer **8** vesuvian

Friday's rescuer
6 Crusoe (Robinson)

friend
3 pal **4** ally, chum, mate, pard **5** buddy, crony, matey, serve **6** cohort **7** comrade, partner **8** alter ego, compadre, confrere, familiar, intimate, playmate, sidekick **9** colleague, companion, confidant **10** confidante
French: **3** ami **4** amie
Maori: **4** ehoa
Spanish: **5** amiga, amigo

Friend
6 Quaker
founder: **3** Fox (George)

friendly
5 happy **6** amical, chummy, folksy, genial **7** affable, amiable, cordial **8** amicable, cheerful, familiar, sociable **9** congenial, favorable **10** buddy-buddy, compatible, hospitable, neighborly **12** affectionate, well-disposed **13** accommodating

Friendly Islands
5 Tonga

Friends series
character: **4** Joey, Ross **6** Monica, Phoebe, Rachel **8** Chandler
setting: **9** Manhattan
star: **3** Cox (Courteney) **5** Perry (Matthew) **6** Kudrow (Lisa) **7** Aniston (Jennifer), LeBlanc (Matt) **9** Schwimmer (David)

friends and neighbors
4 kith

friendship
5 amity **6** accord, comity **7** concord, empathy, harmony **8** affinity, alliance, goodwill

frigate bird
3 ioa, iwa **8** alcatras **11** man-o'-war bird
genus: **7** Fregata

Frigga, Frigg
husband: **4** Odin **5** Woden
son: **6** Balder, Baldur

fright
4 fear **5** alarm, dread, panic, scare, shock **6** dismay, horror, terror **11** trepidation

frighten
3 cow **5** alarm, bully, daunt, scare, shock, spook **6** appall, dismay **7** horrify, perturb, scarify, startle, terrify, unnerve **9** terrorize **10** intimidate

frightful
4 ugly **5** awful, scary **6** horrid **7** fearful, ghastly, hideous **8** alarming, dreadful, fearsome, horrible, horrific, shocking, terrible, terrific **9** appalling, startling **10** formidable, horrendous, terrifying

frigid
3 icy **4** cold **5** chill **6** arctic, chilly, frosty **7** glacial **8** freezing **11** emotionless, indifferent, passionless, unemotional **12** unresponsive

frijoles
5 beans

frill
4 ruff **5** jabot, ruche **6** doodad, luxury, ruffle **7** flounce, ruching **8** furbelow **11** affectation, superfluity **12** extravagance

fringe
3 hem, rim **4** brim, ruff **5** bound, brink, skirt, thrum, verge **6** border, edging, margin **7** fimbria **8** penumbra, trimming **9** perimeter, periphery **10** borderland

frippery
6 finery, frills, tawdry **7** regalia **8** foofaraw, trumpery **9** trappings **11** ostentation

frisée
6 endive **7** lettuce

frisk
4 leap, play, romp, skip **5** caper, dance **6** cavort, frolic, gambol, search **7** disport, pat down, rollick

frisky
3 gay **5** antic **6** feisty, lively **7** coltish, playful **8** animated, gamesome, sportive **9** sprightly, vivacious **10** frolicsome

fritter away
4 blow **5** spend, waste **7** consume **8** squander **9** dissipate

frivolity
3 fun **4** play **6** gaiety, levity, whimsy **8** nonsense **12** childishness

frivolous
3 gay **4** idle **5** ditsy, ditzy, dizzy, giddy, light, silly **6** breezy, frothy, yeasty **7** flighty, playful, shallow, trivial **8** carefree, careless, heedless, trifling **11** light-headed, superficial

frizzy
5 kinky **6** coiled, curled **7** twisted

frock
4 gown **5** dress, habit **6** jersey, mantle

Frodo's pal
3 Sam

frog
4 toad **5** ranid **6** anuran **7** croaker **9** amphibian **10** batrachian
family: 7 Ranidae
genus: 4 Rana
kind: 4 hyla **5** coqui **6** peeper **7** leopard **8** bullfrog, tree toad
larva: 7 tadpole

frolic
3 fun **4** lark, play, romp **5** antic, caper, dance, frisk, party, prank, revel, sport, spree **6** cavort, didoes, gaiety, gambol, prance **7** disport, skylark **8** escapade, hilarity **9** festivity, merriment **10** shenanigan, tomfoolery

frolicsome
3 gay **5** antic **6** frisky, impish **7** coltish, jocular, playful, roguish **8** sportful, sportive **9** sprightly **10** rollicking **11** mischievous

from
German: 3 von
Scottish: 4 frae

From Here to Eternity author
5 Jones (James)

frondeur
5 rebel **8** mutineer, renegade **9** anarchist, dissident, insurgent **10** malcontent

front
3 bow, van **4** face, fore, lend, look, mask, prow **5** beard **6** facade, facing **7** forward **8** anterior, disguise **9** challenge, encounter **10** appearance, figurehead **11** countenance

frontier
5 bound, field, march **6** border **8** backland, backwash, boundary **9** up-country **10** borderland, hinterland **11** backcountry

frontiersman
5 Boone (Daniel), Clark (George Rogers, William) **6** Carson (Kit) **7** Frémont (J. C.), pioneer, settler **8** Crockett (Davy) **10** bushranger

fronton game
7 jai alai

frontward
8 anterior

frost
4 hoar, rime **6** freeze

frostfish
5 smelt **6** tomcod

frost heave
5 pingo

frosting
5 icing **7** topping **8** trimming

Frost poem
7 Birches **10** Fire and Ice **11** Mending Wall **12** Road Not Taken (The) **18** Death of the Hired Man (The) **30** Stopping By Woods on a Snowy Evening

frosty
3 icy **4** cold, rimy **5** chill, frore, hoary, nippy **6** chilly, frigid **7** glacial **8** freezing **10** unfriendly

Frosty's eyes
4 coal

froth
4 foam, head, suds **5** cream, spume, yeast **6** lather **8** airiness **9** frivolity, lightness

froufrou
6 frills **8** rustling

froward
5 balky **6** mulish, ornery **7** peevish, restive **8** contrary, perverse, petulant, stubborn **9** obstinate **10** headstrong, refractory **11** disobedient

frown
4 pout, sulk **5** glare, lower, scowl **6** glower

frowsy
5 dowdy, funky, fusty, messy, musty, stale **6** shabby, smelly, sordid, untidy **7** squalid, unkempt **8** slattern, slovenly **10** disheveled, disordered, slatternly **13** draggletailed

frozen
4 cold, hard **5** fixed, frore, rigid, stiff **6** frigid, iced up, numbed **7** chilled **8** benumbed, immobile **9** congealed, petrified

frugal
4 mean **5** canny, scant, spare **6** Scotch, stingy **7** careful, prudent, scrimpy, sparing, thrifty **8** discreet, stinting **9** niggardly, penurious, provident **10** economical, unwasteful **12** cheeseparing, parsimonious **13** penny-pinching

frugality
6 thrift **7** economy **8** prudence **9** husbandry **10** providence **11** thriftiness

fruit
3 fig, nut **4** ansu, date, lime, pear, pepo, plum, pome, seed, sloe **5** apple, berry, drupe, gourd, grape, guava, issue, lemon, mango, melon, olive, papaw, peach, prune, young **6** achene, banana, casaba, cherry, citron, durian, legume, loment, loquat, orange, papaya, pawpaw, pomelo, quince, result, samara **7** acerola, apricot,

avocado, capsule, coconut, currant, kumquat, outcome, progeny, silique, syconia (plural), tangelo, utricle **8** bergamot, dewberry, mandarin, rambutan, shaddock, syconium, tamarind **9** blueberry, cherimoya, cranberry, muskmelon, nectarine, offspring, persimmon, pineapple, raspberry, tangerine **10** blackberry, calamondin, gooseberry, grapefruit, loganberry, mangosteen, strawberry **11** boysenberry, hesperidium, huckleberry, pomegranate
dried: **5** prune **6** raisin
drink: **3** ade **5** juice, punch
residue: **4** marc **6** pomace
seed: **3** pip
study of: **8** pomology **9** carpology
sugar: **7** glucose **8** fructose, levulose
undeveloped: **6** nubbin

fruitful
6 fecund **7** copious, fertile **8** abundant, prolific **9** bountiful, fructuous, plenteous, plentiful **10** productive **11** proliferant

fruition
7 delight **8** pleasure **9** enjoyment **10** attainment, conclusion **11** achievement, delectation, fulfillment, realization

fruitless
4 vain **6** barren, futile **7** sterile, useless **8** abortive **10** unavailing **11** ineffective, ineffectual **12** unproductive, unsuccessful

frumpy
4 drab, dull **5** dated, dowdy, tacky **6** stodgy **8** outmoded **9** out-of-date, unstylish **12** old-fashioned

frustrate
4 balk, bilk, dash, foil, halt **5** block, check, stump **6** arrest, baffle, defeat, hinder, impede, stymie, thwart **7** inhibit, prevent **8** confound, obstruct, preclude, prohibit **9** discomfit, forestall, interrupt **10** disappoint

frustration
6 defeat, dismay **7** chagrin, letdown **8** vexation **9** annoyance, hindrance **10** impediment, irritation **11** displeasure, obstruction

fry
4 burn, sear **5** frizz, grill, sauté **6** fishes, picnic **7** frizzle **11** electrocute

frying pan
6 spider **7** griddle, skillet

fuddle
5 befog, booze **6** ball up, jumble, tipple **7** confuse, fluster, stupefy **8** bewilder **10** intoxicate

fuddy-duddy
4 fogy **5** fogey **6** fossil, square, stodgy **8** mossback, outdated, outmoded **12** antediluvian, Colonel Blimp, old-fashioned, stuffed shirt **13** stick-in-the-mud

fudge
3 pad **4** blur, bosh, fake **5** candy, cheat, color, dodge, hedge, hooey, welsh **6** bunkum **7** distort, falsify, hogwash, penuche **8** contrive, divinity, nonsense **9** embellish, embroider, overstate, poppycock **10** equivocate, flapdoodle **11** foolishness

fuel
3 gas, oil **4** coal, coke, fire, peat, wood **5** stoke **6** biogas, diesel, petrol, Sterno **7** ethanol, gasohol, inflame, propane **8** charcoal, gasoline, kerosene **9** biodiesel, petroleum, stimulate **10** natural gas **13** reinforcement
jelled: **6** napalm

Fuentes novel
4 Aura **9** Old Gringo (The)

fugacious
7 brittle, passing **8** fleeting, fugitive, volatile **9** ephemeral, momentary, transient **10** evanescent, short-lived, transitory

fugitive
5 exile **6** outlaw **7** escapee, lamster, nomadic, passing, refugee, runaway **8** deserter, fleeting, runagate, vagabond **9** ephemeral, fugacious, momentary, transient, wandering **10** evanescent, short-lived, transitory

fugue master
4 Bach (Johann Sebastian)

Führer, der
6 Hitler (Adolf)

fulcrum
3 hub **4** axis, prop **5** hinge, nexus, pivot **7** support

fulfill
4 meet **5** honor **6** effect, finish, redeem **7** achieve, execute, perform, satisfy **8** complete **9** discharge, implement **10** accomplish

fulgent
6 bright **7** beaming, glowing, radiant, shining **8** luminous, lustrous **9** brilliant

fuliginous
4 dark **5** dingy, dusky, grimy, murky, sooty **7** obscure

full
5 sated, total, whole **6** entire, gorged, jammed, loaded, packed, utmost **7** crammed, crowded, glutted, maximum, plenary, replete, stuffed **8** brimming, complete, satiated **9** jam-packed, plentiful, surfeited **11** chockablock

full-blooded
4 rich **5** flush, ruddy **6** ardent, florid **7** flushed, genuine, glowing **8** forceful, purebred, rubicund, sanguine **9** pedigreed, pureblood **10** compelling **12** thoroughbred

full-blown
4 lush, ripe **5** adult, total **6** all-out, mature **7** grown-up

full-bodied
4 rich **5** husky, lusty, stout **6** potent, robust, strong **9** corpulent **10** meaningful **11** significant, substantial

full dress
6 finery **7** regalia **8** frippery, glad rags **10** Sunday best

full-figured
5 ample, buxom, plump **6** zaftig **10** curvaceous, Rubenesque, statuesque, voluptuous

full-fledged
4 ripe **5** adult, grown, total **6** mature **7** genuine, grown-up **8** complete **9** full-blown

full-grown
4 ripe **5** adult **6** mature

fullness
6 plenty **7** satiety **9** abundance, amplitude, repletion **10** perfection **12** completeness

full-scale
5 total **6** all-out **8** complete, life-size **9** unlimited

full tilt
7 flat-out, rapidly, swiftly **8** pell-mell, speedily **9** posthaste **12** lickety-split

fulminate
4 boil, burn, foam, fume, rage, rail, rave **5** curse, flare **7** bluster, explode, inveigh

fulsome
4 oily **5** plump, slick, soapy, suave **6** lavish, smarmy, smooth **7** buttery, cloying, copious, profuse **8** abundant, effusive, generous, overdone, unctuous **9** excessive **10** flattering, oleaginous **11** extravagant, pharisaical **12** ingratiating, Pecksniffian

Fulton's steamboat
8 Clermont

fumarole
4 vent

fumble
3 bob, err, paw **4** feel, flub, mess, muff **5** botch, grope **6** bobble, bollix, bungle, muddle **7** blunder, misplay **8** flounder

fume
3 gas **4** boil, burn, odor, rage, rant, rave, reek, snit, stew **5** smoke, vapor **6** seethe, swivet **7** sputter

fun
4 play **5** sport **6** frolic, gaiety **7** amusing, jollity, pastime, whoopee **8** hilarity, pleasant, ridicule **9** amusement, diversion, diverting, enjoyment, frivolity, horseplay, jocundity, joviality, merriment **10** pleasantry **12** entertaining **13** entertainment

function
3 act, job, run, use **4** duty, goal, mark, role, task, work **5** party, power, react, serve **6** affair, behave, object, office, target **7** concern, faculty, operate, perform, purpose, service **8** activity, behavior, business, capacity, ceremony, occasion, province **9** objective, officiate, operation, reception
trigonometric: 4 sine **6** cosine, secant **7** tangent **8** cosecant **9** cotangent

functional
5 handy, utile **6** useful **7** working **9** practical **11** practicable, serviceable, utilitarian **12** occupational

functioning
6 active **7** dynamic **9** operative

fund
4 back, bank, pool **5** endow, stake, stock, store **6** coffer, supply **7** capital, finance, reserve, support **8** bankroll, treasury **9** inventory, subsidize **10** accumulate, capitalize

fundament
3 bum **4** butt, rear, rump, seat **5** basis, fanny **6** behind, bottom **8** backside, buttocks, derriere **9** posterior, principle **10** foundation, groundwork

fundamental
3 key **5** axiom, basal, basic, prime, vital **6** bottom, factor, primal, simple **7** bedrock, organic, primary, radical, theorem **8** absolute, cardinal, dominant, ultimate **9** component, essential, important, necessary, paramount, primitive, principal, principle, requisite **10** deep-rooted, elementary, grassroots, primordial, rock-bottom, underlying **11** constituent, irreducible, nitty-gritty **12** constitutive, foundational

fund-raiser
8 telethon

funeral
6 burial **7** obsequy **9** obsequies
car: 6 hearse
director: 9 mortician **10** undertaker
oration: 6 eulogy **8** encomium **9** panegyric
procession: 7 cortege
service: 7 requiem **9** obsequies
song: 5 dirge, elegy **8** threnody

funereal
3 sad **4** dark **5** black, bleak, grave **6** dismal, dreary, gloomy, solemn, somber, sombre **7** elegiac **8** mournful **9** deathlike, sorrowful **10** depressing, depressive, lugubrious, oppressive, sepulchral

fungus
4 conk, mold, rust, smut **5** ergot, yeast **6** agaric, dry rot, mildew **7** candida, truffle **8** mushroom, puffball **9** earthstar, stinkhorn, toadstool

combining form: **4** myco **5** myces, mycet **6** mycete, myceto
part: **3** cap **4** gill **5** ascus, hypha, stipe, volva **7** annulus **8** basidium, conidium, mycelium
rust: **5** Uredo

fungus disease
3 rot **4** mold, rust, scab, smut **5** ergot, tinea **6** blight, mildew, thrush **7** mycosis **8** lumpy jaw, ringworm **12** athlete's foot

funk
4 odor, reek **5** blues, dolor, dumps, ennui, gloom, smell, stink, slump **6** recoil, stench **7** sadness **9** dejection **10** depression, melancholy

funky
3 hip, odd **4** foul, rank **5** fetid, reeky **6** earthy, frowsy, grungy, quaint, quirky, smelly, stinky **7** natural, noisome, oddball, offbeat **8** down-home **10** malodorous

funnel
4 flue, pipe **5** stack **6** hopper **7** channel, conduct, tornado, tundish, twister **8** transmit **10** smokestack

funny
3 odd **4** joke, zany **5** antic, comic, droll, fishy, queer **7** amusing, bizarre, comical, jocular, risible, strange **8** farcical, humorous, peculiar **9** facetious, fantastic, hilarious, laughable, ludicrous **10** ridiculous

Funny Girl
5 Brice (Fanny)
composer: **5** Styne (Jule)
star: **9** Streisand (Barbra)

funnyman
3 wag, wit **5** clown, comic, cutup, droll, joker **6** gagman, jester **8** comedian, humorist, jokester, quipster **10** comedienne

fur
4 down, hide, pelt, pile **5** floss, fluff, stole **6** pelage, peltry
kind: **3** fox **4** mink, seal **5** coypu, fitch, otter, sable **6** ermine, fisher, marten, nutria, rabbit, tanuki **7** raccoon **10** chinchilla
lamb: **7** caracul, karakul **9** broadtail
medieval: **4** vair **7** miniver

furbelow
5 frill **7** flounce

furbish
4 buff **5** fix up, renew, shine **6** polish, revive **7** burnish, refresh, restore **8** renovate

Furies
6 Alecto **7** Erinyes, Megaera **9** Eumenides, Tisiphone

furious
3 mad **4** wild **5** angry, livid, irate, rabid, upset **6** crazed, fierce, insane, raging, stormy **7** enraged, excited, extreme, frantic, intense, violent **8** feverish, frenetic, frenzied, incensed, maddened, vehement, wrathful **9** impetuous, turbulent **10** boisterous, corybantic

furl
4 curl, fold, roll, wrap **6** take in

furlough
4 pass **5** leave **6** lay off **7** liberty **10** shore leave **13** authorization

furnace
4 kiln, oven **5** forge, stove **6** heater **7** smelter **8** tryworks **11** incinerator
part: **4** port, vent **6** tuyere
tender: **6** stoker

furnish
3 arm, rig **4** give, hand, lend **5** endow, endue, equip **6** fit out, outfit, supply **7** apparel, appoint, deliver, provide, turn out **8** accouter, accoutre, dispense, hand over, transfer **9** provision **10** contribute

furnishings
4 gear **5** decor **9** equipment, trappings **10** housewares **11** appointment **13** accouterments, accoutrements, paraphernalia

furniture designer
American: **5** Eames (Charles, Ray), Phyfe (Duncan) **7** Goddard (John, Stephen, Thomas), Haldane (William) **8** Stickley (Gustav)
British: **6** Morris (William) **7** Gibbons (Grinling), Shearer (Thomas) **8** Sheraton (Thomas) **11** Chippendale (Thomas), Hepplewhite (George)
French: **5** Marot (Daniel) **6** Boulle (André-Charles)
German: **6** Breuer (Marcel)
Scottish: **4** Adam (James, Robert)

furniture style
4 Adam **6** Empire, Shaker **7** Bauhaus, Federal, Mission **8** Colonial, Georgian, Jacobean, Sheraton, Stickley **9** Queen Anne **11** chinoiserie, Chippendale, Duncan Phyfe, Hepplewhite **13** Arts and Crafts

furor
3 ado, cry, fad, wax **4** chic, mode, rage, stir, to-do **5** anger, craze, mania, style, vogue **6** flurry, frenzy, pother, ruckus, rumpus, uproar **7** fashion, madness **8** foofaraw **9** commotion **10** dernier cri, excitement **11** controversy

furrow
3 rut **4** ruck **5** plica, ridge, sulci (plural) **6** course, crease, groove, sulcus, trench **7** channel, crinkle, wrinkle **8** entrench **9** corrugate **11** corrugation

furrowed
5 lined **6** rugose **7** grooved, sulcate **8** wrinkled **10** corrugated

further
4 abet, also, help 5 again, fresh 6 beyond 7 advance, besides, forward, promote 8 engender, moreover 9 encourage, propagate 10 additional, in addition 12 additionally

furthermore
3 and, too 4 also 6 as well, withal 7 besides 8 likewise, moreover 9 what's more 12 additionally

furthermost
4 last 7 extreme 8 farthest, remotest, ultimate

furtive
3 sly 4 foxy, wary, wily 6 artful, covert, crafty, feline, masked, secret, shifty, sneaky, stolen, tricky 7 catlike, cunning, evasive, sub-rosa 8 guileful, hush-hush, scheming, stealthy 9 disguised, insidious 11 circumspect, clandestine 12 hugger-mugger 13 surreptitious, under-the-table
look: 4 peek, peep

fur trader
8 voyageur

furuncle
4 boil 7 abscess

fury
3 ire 4 burn, rage 5 anger, furor, wrath 6 frenzy 7 madness, passion 8 violence 9 vehemence 10 fierceness

furze
4 whin 5 gorse
genus: 4 Ulex 7 Genista

fuse
3 mix 4 flux, meld, melt, weld 5 blend, merge, smelt, unify, unite 6 anneal, solder 7 liquefy 8 coalesce, conflate, dissolve, intermix 9 commingle, integrate 10 amalgamate 11 consolidate, incorporate

fusillade
4 hail 5 burst, salvo 6 shower, volley 7 barrage 8 drumfire, outburst 9 broadside, cannonade 11 bombardment

fusion
5 alloy, blend, union 6 merger 7 amalgam, mixture 8 compound 9 coalition, immixture, synthesis

fuss
3 ado, nag, row 4 beef, crab, flap, fret, miff, stew, stir, to-do 5 gripe, stink, upset, whine, worry 6 bother, bustle, hassle, hurrah, pother, ruckus, rumpus, squawk 7 protest 8 complain, foofaraw, squabble 9 commotion, complaint, kerfuffle, objection 11 controversy

fussbudget
3 hen 6 granny 8 stickler 10 fuddy-duddy 13 perfectionist

fusspot
8 stickler 9 nitpicker, worrywart

fussy
5 picky 6 cranky, dainty, ornate 7 careful, finicky, fretful 9 crotchety, irritable, querulous 10 fastidious, meticulous, particular, pernickety, scrupulous 11 painstaking, persnickety, punctilious 13 conscientious

fustian
4 rant 7 bombast, pompous 8 affected, inflated 9 high-flown 11 exaggerated, highfalutin, pretentious 13 grandiloquent

fusty
4 rank 5 close, dated, fetid, moldy, passé, stale 6 bygone, old-hat, smelly 7 archaic 8 outdated 10 antiquated, malodorous 11 reactionary 12 old-fashioned

futhark letter
4 rune

futile
4 idle, vain 5 empty 6 hollow, otiose 7 useless 8 abortive, bootless, hopeless, nugatory 9 fruitless, worthless 10 unavailing 11 ineffective, ineffectual 12 unproductive, unsuccessful

future
5 later 6 mañana, offing, to come 7 by-and-by 8 oncoming, tomorrow 9 hereafter

Futurism
founder: 9 Marinetti (Filippo Tommaso)
painter: 5 Balla (Giacomo), Carra (Carlo) 7 Russolo (Luigi) 8 Boccioni (Umberto), Severini (Gino)
sculptor: 8 Boccioni (Umberto)

fuzz
3 cop 4 down, lint 6 police

fuzzy
3 dim 5 faint, gauzy, linty, vague, woozy 6 bleary, blurry 7 blurred, muddled, obscure, shadowy, unclear 8 confused 9 distorted, undefined 10 ill-defined, incoherent, indefinite, indistinct

fylfot
8 swastika

G

gab
3 jaw, rap, yak **4** blab, chat, talk **5** clack, drool, prate, speak **6** babble, drivel, gibber, gossip, jabber, natter, yammer **7** blabber, blather, chatter, palaver, prattle, twaddle **8** chitchat, converse, idle talk **9** gibberish, small talk

gabber
5 yenta **6** gossip, magpie **7** blabber **9** chatterer **10** chatterbox **12** blabbermouth, gossipmonger

gabby
4 glib **5** talky, windy **6** chatty **7** voluble **8** effusive **9** garrulous, talkative **10** long-winded, loquacious **11** loose-lipped **12** loose-tongued

gaberdine
4 coat, suit **5** cloak, cloth **6** capote, fabric **7** garment, manteau **8** material

gable
4 wall **8** pediment
ornament: **6** finial

Gabon
capital: **10** Libreville
city: **10** Port-Gentil
ethnic group: **4** Fang **5** Bantu
language: **6** French
monetary unit: **5** franc
neighbor: **5** Congo **8** Cameroon
river: **6** Ogooué

gad
3 bat **4** flit, roam, rove **5** amble, drift, mooch, range, stray, tramp **6** chisel, ramble, wander **7** maunder, meander, traipse **9** gallivant

Gad
brother: **5** Asher
father: **5** Jacob
mother: **6** Zilpah
son: **3** Eri **5** Ezbon, Haggi

Gaddis novel
12 Recognitions (The) **14** Frolic of His Own (A) **16** Carpenter's Gothic

gadfly
3 nag **4** pest, pill **6** bother, critic, insect, nudnik **8** nuisance

gadget
4 tool **5** gizmo, thing **6** device, dingus, doodad, hickey, jigger, widget **7** concern, gimmick, utensil **9** apparatus, appliance, doohickey, implement, mechanism, thingummy **10** instrument **11** contraption, thingamabob, thingamajig, thingumajig

gadwall
4 bird, duck, fowl **9** waterfowl

gadzooks
4 drat, egad **6** crikey, zounds

Gaea
husband: **6** Uranus
offspring: **6** Furies, Giants, Titans, Typhon, Uranus **7** Erinyes **8** Cyclopes **9** Eumenides
parent: **5** Chaos

Gaelic
4 Erse **5** Irish **6** Celtic **8** Scottish
god: **3** Ler **5** Dagda
hero: **5** Oisin **6** Cormac, Ossian **8** Diarmaid **11** Finn MacCool
king: **9** Conchobar, Conchobor
language: **4** Manx
poet: **4** bard **6** Ossian
queen: **4** Medb
soldier: **4** kern **6** Fenian
spirit: **7** banshee

gaff
3 fix, rig **4** hoax, hook, spar, spur **5** abuse, fraud, spear, trick **6** fleece, ordeal **7** deceive, gimmick **8** raillery **12** climbing iron

gaffe
4 flub, goof, muff **5** boner, error, fault, fluff, lapse **6** bollix, boo-boo, bungle, foul-up, howler, slipup **7** blooper, blunder, clinker, faux pas, misstep, mistake **8** solecism **9** gaucherie **11** impropriety, misjudgment **12** indiscretion

gag
4 balk, gasp, hoax, jape, jest, joke, quip **5** choke, crack, heave, prank, retch, trick **6** muffle, muzzle, shtick, stifle, strain **7** repress, silence, squelch **8** throttle **9** restraint, wisecrack, witticism

gaga
4 agog, wild **5** crazy, giddy, nutty, wacky **6** doting, fervid, gung ho **7** foolish, gushing, excited, smitten **8** animated, enamored, obsessed, thrilled **9** ebullient, exuberant **10** captivated, infatuated **12** enthusiastic

gage
3 vow 4 bond 5 token 6 pledge, surety 8 gauntlet, security
(see also **gauge**)

gaggle
4 crew, gang, pack 5 array, bunch, flock, group 6 clutch, number 7 cluster 10 assemblage, collection 11 aggregation

Gaheris
brother: 6 Gareth, Gawain
father: 3 Lot
mother: 8 Margawse, Morgause
uncle: 6 Arthur
victim: 8 Margawse, Morgause

gaiety
3 fun, joy 4 glee 5 mirth, revel 6 finery, frolic, hoopla 7 elation, jollity, revelry, whoopee 8 elegance, hilarity, reveling, vivacity 9 animation, festivity, happiness, joviality, merriment 10 ebullience, exuberance, hullabaloo, joyousness, jubilation, liveliness 11 high spirits, merrymaking 12 conviviality

gain
3 get, net, win 4 earn, land, make, reap 5 clear, cover, reach, score 6 attain, expand, obtain, pick up, profit, rack up, secure 7 achieve, acquire, advance, attract, augment, benefit, bring in, enlarge, procure 8 earnings, increase, persuade, proceeds, windfall 10 accomplish

gainful
6 paying 8 fruitful, generous 9 lucrative, rewarding 10 beneficial, productive, profitable, well-paying, worthwhile 12 advantageous, remunerative

gainsay
4 buck, defy, deny 6 impugn, negate, oppose, refute, resist 7 dispute 8 disclaim, disprove, negative, traverse 9 disaffirm, repudiate, withstand 10 contradict, contravene, controvert

Gainsborough painting
7 Blue Boy

gait
3 air, run 4 clip, dash, lope, pace, rate, step, trot, walk 5 amble, speed, strut, train, tread 6 canter, gallop, stride 7 bearing 8 demeanor

gaiter
4 boot, shoe, spat 7 legging 8 overshoe

gal
4 babe, doll 5 chick

gala
4 ball, bash, fete, prom 5 merry, party 6 lively 7 festive, jubilee, pageant, shindig 8 festival, jamboree, wingding 9 festivity, spectacle 11 celebration 13 entertainment

Galactica commander
5 Adama (Adm. William)

galago
5 lemur 8 bush baby

Galahad
father: 8 Lancelot 9 Launcelot
mother: 6 Elaine
quest: 5 Grail 9 Holy Grail

Galatea
father: 6 Nereus
husband: 9 Pygmalion
lover: 4 Acis
mother: 5 Doris

galaxy
6 nebula 8 Milky Way, universe

Galba
predecessor: 4 Nero
successor: 4 Otho

gale
4 blow, gust, wind 5 blast, storm 6 squall 7 cyclone, tempest, typhoon 8 outburst 9 hurricane

galena
3 ore 4 lead

Galen's forte
7 healing 8 medicine

galilee
5 porch 6 chapel

Galilee town
4 Cana 7 Gergesa 8 Nazareth, Tiberias 9 Bethsaida, Capernaum

Galileo's birthplace
4 Pisa 5 Italy 7 Tuscany

gall
3 irk, nag, rub, vex 4 bile, fray, fret, rile, roil, sore, wear 5 annoy, brass, chafe, cheek, erode, grate, graze, nerve 6 abrade, bother, burn up, harass, pester, plague, rancor, ruffle, scrape 7 conceit, disturb, frazzle, inflame, provoke, scratch, torment 8 audacity, boldness, chutzpah, irritate, temerity 9 aggravate, arrogance, brashness, impudence, insolence 10 bitterness, effrontery
bladder: 9 cholecyst

gallant
3 fop 4 beau, bold, buck, dude, hero 5 blade, blood, brave, civil, dandy, lover, manly, Romeo, showy, suave, swain, wooer 6 daring, heroic, suitor, urbane 7 courtly, coxcomb, dashing, Don Juan, stately, valiant 8 Casanova, gracious, lothario, paramour, spirited, valorous 9 attentive, courteous, dauntless, ladies' man 10 chivalrous, courageous

gallantry
5 honor, poise, valor 6 daring, mettle, spirit 7 amenity, bravery, courage, heroism, prowess,

suavity **8** boldness, chivalry, courtesy, urbanity, valiance, valiancy **9** attention, manliness **10** resolution **11** courtliness **12** fearlessness

galleon
7 warship **12** square-rigger

gallery
5 patio, porch, salon **6** arcade, loggia, museum, piazza **7** balcony, passage, portico, veranda **8** audience, corridor, showroom **9** colonnade, onlookers, promenade
ancient Greek: 4 stoa

galley
3 gig **4** boat, mess, ship, tray **5** cuddy, proof **6** bireme **7** canteen, kitchen, trireme, warship **8** scullery **9** cookhouse

Gallic
6 French

gallimaufry
3 mix **4** hash, mess, olio, stew **5** chaos **6** jumble, medley **7** clutter, goulash, mélange, mixture, variety **8** mishmash, pastiche **9** patchwork, potpourri **10** assortment, hodgepodge, hotchpotch, miscellany, salmagundi

gallinaceous bird
3 hen **5** quail **6** grouse, turkey **7** chicken, hoatzin, peacock **8** curassow, pheasant **9** partridge **10** guinea fowl

galling
6 bitter, vexing **8** rankling **9** upsetting, vexatious **10** afflictive, irritating, nettlesome **11** aggravating, distressing, troublesome **12** exasperating

gallivant
3 bat, bum, gad **4** flit, roam, rove **5** amble, drift, jaunt, mooch, range, stray **6** cruise, ramble, travel, wander **7** meander, traipse **8** vagabond **10** knock about

gallop
4 dash, race **6** sprint

gallows
6 gibbet
bird: 7 villain **8** criminal

galoot
3 ape, guy, oaf **4** dupe, goon, lout, slob **5** chump **6** fellow, lummox **7** palooka

galore
4 full, lush, rich **5** ample, great **6** lavish **7** aplenty, copious, endless, profuse **8** abundant, generous **9** bountiful, expansive, plentiful **11** overflowing

galosh
4 boot, shoe **6** rubber **8** overshoe

Galsworthy work
7 Justice **11** Forsyte Saga (The)

galumph
4 plod **5** barge, clomp, clump, stomp, stump, tramp **6** lumber, trudge

galvanize
3 jar, zap **4** coat, fire, jolt, stir, spur, stun **5** pep up, pique, prime, react, rouse, shock **6** arouse, excite, perk up, thrill **7** animate, enliven, immerse, inspire, provoke, quicken **8** activate, astonish, energize, motivate, vitalize **9** electrify, innervate, magnetize, stimulate **10** invigorate

gam
3 leg, pin, pod, rap **4** chat, flap, limb, talk **5** visit **6** confab **9** drumstick **12** conversation

Gambia
capital: 6 Banjul
city: 9 Serekunda
monetary unit: 6 dalasi
neighbor: 7 Senegal

gambit
3 con, jig **4** move, play, ploy, ruse, wile **5** dodge, topic, trick **6** design, device, remark, tactic **7** gimmick **8** artifice, maneuver, trickery **9** expedient, stratagem **10** subterfuge

gamble
3 bet, lay, set **4** dare, game, play, punt, risk **5** put on, stake, wager **6** chance, hazard, plunge, raffle **7** imperil, lottery, venture **8** cast lots, long shot **9** crapshoot, speculate **10** jeopardize

gambler
5 dicer, shark, sharp **7** sharper **9** cardsharp **10** cardplayer **11** cardsharper

gambling place
3 den **4** club, dive, Reno **5** joint, Vegas **6** casino **8** Las Vegas, pool hall **9** roadhouse **10** Monte Carlo **12** Atlantic City, betting house

gambol
3 hop **4** jump, lark, leap, romp, skip **5** bound, caper, frisk, revel, sport **6** cavort, frolic, prance, spring **7** carry on, roister, rollick

Gambrinus' invention
3 ale **4** beer **5** lager

game
3 bet, fun, lay, RPG **4** bold, jest, joke, lark, play, prey, romp **5** brave, chase, eager, hardy, sport, stake, trick, wager **6** gamble, quarry, spunky **7** contest, pastime, valiant, willing **8** fearless, intrepid, resolute, unafraid, valorous **9** amusement, dauntless, diversion, undaunted **10** courageous, recreation
arcade: 7 Gremlin **8** Carnival, Skee-Ball
ball: 4 golf, polo, pool **5** fives, rogue, rugby **6** hockey, pelota, soccer, squash, tennis **7** cricket, croquet, jai alai **8** baseball, football, handball, hardball, lacrosse, racquets, rounders, softball **9** bagatelle, billiards **10** basketball, volleyball **11** racquetball
Basque: 6 pelota **7** jai alai
bird: 4 duck **5** quail **6** chukar, turkey **7** bustard **8** bobwhite, pheasant **9** partridge

board: **4** Clue, Risk, wari **5** chess, chuba, oware, shogi **7** mancala, pachisi **8** checkers, Monopoly, Scrabble **9** crokinole, Parcheesi **10** backgammon
child's: **3** tag **5** jacks **7** marbles, ringtaw **8** leapfrog, peekaboo **9** hopscotch, tic-tac-toe
confidence: **4** scam **5** bunco, bunko, sting
court: **5** roque **6** pelota, squash, tennis **7** jai alai **8** handball, racquets **9** badminton **10** basketball, volleyball **11** racquetball
electric: **7** pinball
English: **5** rugby **7** cricket **8** draughts
Irish: **7** hurling
of chance: **4** faro, keno **5** beano, bingo, boule, craps, lotto, rondo **6** fan-tan, hazard, policy, raffle **7** lottery, rondeau **8** roulette
parlor: **8** Carnelli, charades
piece: **3** die **4** tile **5** token **6** domino, marble, top hat **7** checker
racket: **6** squash, tennis **8** lacrosse, ping-pong, racquets **9** badminton **11** racquetball, table tennis
roulette-like: **5** boule
rule maker: **5** Hoyle (Edmond)
string: **10** cat's cradle
table: **4** pool **5** craps **7** mah-jong, snooker **8** dominoes, mah-jongg, ping-pong, roulette **9** bagatelle, billiards **11** table tennis
word: **5** rebus **6** crambo **7** anagram, hangman **8** acrostic, charades, Scrabble **9** crossword, logogriph
(see also **card game**)

game plan
6 scheme, tactic **8** scenario, strategy **9** blueprint **10** big picture

gamete
3 egg **4** ovum **5** sperm **8** germ cell

gamin
3 elf, imp, tad **4** brat, tyke, waif **5** scamp **6** monkey, rascal, urchin **11** guttersnipe **12** street urchin

gamine
3 elf, imp **4** brat, waif **5** scamp **6** hoyden, rascal, tomboy, urchin **11** guttersnipe **12** street urchin

gaming cubes
4 dice **5** bones

gammon
3 ham **4** dupe, fool, rook **5** bacon, feign **6** delude, fleece, humbug **7** deceive, pretend, swindle **8** flimflam, hoodwink **9** bamboozle **11** hornswoggle

gamut
4 A to Z **5** range, scale, scope, sweep **6** extent, series, spread **7** compass **8** diapason, spectrum

gamy
3 off **4** foul, racy, rank, vile **5** brave, fetid, funky **6** plucky, putrid, rancid, rotten, smelly, sordid, stinky, strong **7** corrupt, decayed, noisome, noxious, reeking **10** decomposed, malodorous, scandalous **12** disagreeable, disreputable

gander
4 look, peek **5** goose **6** glance **7** glimpse **9** simpleton, waterfowl

____ Gandhi
5 Rajiv **6** Indira **7** Mahatma **8** Mohandas

gandy dancer
10 railroader, tracklayer

ganef
5 thief **6** rascal **9** scoundrel

Ganesa, Ganesh
father: **4** Siva **5** Shiva
head: **8** elephant
mother: **7** Parvati

gang
3 lot, mob, set **4** band, clan, club, crew, pack, ring, team **5** bunch, crowd, group, horde **6** circle, clique, outfit **7** arrange, cluster, collect, combine, company, coterie **8** assemble **10** accumulate, assemblage **11** combination

gangling
4 bony, lean, slim **5** gaunt, lanky, rangy **6** meager, meagre, skinny **7** angular, scrawny, slender, spindly, stringy **8** rawboned **9** spindling

ganglion
5 tumor **7** nucleus

gangrene
3 rot **5** decay **7** mortify, putrefy **8** necrosis **9** decompose

gangster
4 goon, hood, thug **5** cholo, rough, thief, tough **6** bandit, gunman **7** hoodlum, mafioso, mobster, ruffian **8** criminal **9** cutthroat, racketeer
girlfriend: **4** moll

gangway
4 hall, path **5** aisle **7** passage, walkway **8** corridor **10** passageway

ganja
3 kef, kif, pot, tea **4** hemp, herb, weed **5** grass, smoke **7** hashish **8** cannabis, Mary Jane **9** marijuana

gannet
4 bird **5** booby **7** seabird

ganoid fish
3 gar **6** beluga, bowfin **7** dogfish, garfish, teleost **8** billfish, sturgeon **10** paddlefish

Ganymede
abductor: **4** Zeus **7** Jupiter
brother: **4** Ilus
father: **4** Tros
function: **9** cupbearer

gaol
3 jug, pen **4** jail **5** clink, joint, pokey **6** cooler, lockup, prison **7** slammer **8** bastille **9** calaboose, jailhouse **12** penitentiary

gap
3 cut, pit **4** gash, gulf, hole, lull, pass, rent, rift, skip, slit, slot, tear, vent, void, yawn **5** abyss, blank, break, chasm, chink, cleft, clove, crack, gorge, gulch, gully, pause, space, split **6** arroyo, breach, canyon, cavity, cranny, divide, hiatus, hollow, lacuna, ravine, recess, schism, vacuum **7** caesura, crevice, fissure, interim, lacunae (plural), opening, orifice, rupture, vacancy, vacuity **8** aperture, cleavage, division, fracture, interval **9** disparity, interlude **10** deficiency, difference, interstice, separation **12** intermission, interruption **13** discontinuity

gape
3 eye, yaw **4** bore, gawk, gawp, gaze, glom, leer, look, ogle, open, part, peer, yawn **5** crack, glare, gloat, space, split, stare **6** glance, goggle **7** eyeball **10** rubberneck

gaping
4 huge, open, vast, wide **5** broad, great **7** chasmal **9** cavernous

gar
4 fish, pike **8** billfish **10** needlefish

garage
4 shop **7** cabinet, car park, carport, shelter

Garand
5 rifle

garb
4 clad, duds **5** array, cover, dress, getup, style **6** attire, clothe, livery, outfit **7** apparel, clothes, garment, raiment, threads **9** trappings **10** appearance

garbage
4 junk, muck, slop **5** dreck, dregs, filth, offal, trash, waste **6** debris, litter, refuse, sewage **7** rubbish **8** detritus, riffraff
heap: **6** midden

garble
4 sift, warp **5** alter, belie, color, twist **6** jumble, mangle, muddle **7** becloud, confuse, contort, distort, falsify, obscure, pervert **8** miscolor, misstate, mutilate **9** obfuscate **10** impurities **12** misrepresent

garçon
3 boy **6** waiter **7** servant

garden
4 Eden, park **7** nursery
shelter: **5** arbor **6** arbour

gardener
6 grower **7** yardman **9** topiarist

garden house
6 alcove, gazebo **9** belvedere

Garden State
9 New Jersey

garden tool
3 hoe **4** claw, fork, rake **5** edger, mower, spade **6** dibble, pruner, scythe, shears, shovel, sickle, trowel, weeder **8** clippers

Gardner character
10 Perry Mason **11** Della Street

Gareth
brother: **6** Gawain **7** Gaheris
father: **3** Lot
mother: **8** Margawse, Morgause
slayer: **8** Lancelot **9** Launcelot
uncle: **6** Arthur
wife: **6** Liones

Garfield
creator: **5** Davis (Jim)
dog: **4** Odie

Gargamelle's son
9 Gargantua

Gargantua
abbey: **7** Thélème
author: **8** Rabelais (François)
father: **12** Grandgousier
first word: **5** drink
mother: **10** Gargamelle
son: **10** Pantagruel

gargantuan
see **gigantic**

Garibaldi follower
8 redshirt

garish
4 loud **5** gaudy, showy, vivid **6** brassy, brazen, flashy, tawdry, tinsel, vulgar **7** blatant, chintzy, glaring, raffish **12** meretricious

garland
3 ana, lei **5** album, crown **6** anadem, digest, laurel, wreath **7** chaplet, coronal, coronet, laurels, omnibus **8** analects **9** anthology, selection **10** collection, compendium, miscellany **11** florilegium

garlic
4 moly, ramp **5** aglio, clove **6** allium
mayonnaise: **5** aioli

garment
4 garb, gear **5** array, habit **6** attire **7** apparel, raiment **8** clothing, vestment **10** habiliment
African: **6** kaross **7** dashiki
Arab: **3** aba **4** haik
British: **10** mackintosh
clergy's: **3** alb **4** cope **7** cassock, soutane **8** vestment
close-fitting: **6** girdle, tights **7** leotard
for sleeping: **6** pajama **7** nightie **9** nightgown
Greek: **5** tunic **6** chiton, peplos **7** chlamys **8** himation

Hindu: **4** sari **6** patola
hooded: **8** djellaba
Japanese: **6** kimono
lace: **10** chemisette
Malay: **6** sarong
Mexican: **6** sarape, serape
outer: **4** cape, coat, robe, wrap **5** apron, cloak, parka, shawl, smock, stole **6** capote, jacket, kimono, poncho, sarong, ulster, wammus **7** overall, pelisse, surtout, sweater, topcoat **8** overcoat, pinafore, pullover, scapular **9** coveralls, gaberdine, polonaise
Polynesian: **5** pareo, pareu
rain: **6** poncho **7** oilskin, slicker
Roman: **4** toga **5** tunic
Scottish: **4** jupe, kilt **7** sporran
sleeveless: **3** aba **4** cape **6** mantle, tabard
Turkish: **6** dolman
women's: **4** gown **5** dress, skirt, teddy **6** blouse, vestee **7** blouson, chemise, nightie, partlet **8** camisole, negligee, peignoir, pelerine

garner
4 cull, earn, hive, reap **5** amass, glean, hoard, lay up, store **6** gather, pick up, roll up **7** collect, extract, harvest, store up **8** cumulate, ingather **9** stockpile **10** accumulate

garnet
5 jewel, stone **6** pyrope **8** essonite **9** hessonite
black: **8** melanite
red: **9** almandine, almandite

garnish
4 deck, trim **5** adorn **6** bedeck **7** dress up, enhance **8** beautify, decorate, ornament **9** embellish

garret
4 loft, room **5** attic **8** cockloft

garrison
4 camp, fort, post **6** assign, billet, occupy, troops **7** station **8** fortress **10** stronghold

garrote
5 choke **8** strangle, throttle **11** strangulate

garrulous
see **gabby**

garter
4 band, belt **5** strap **7** support **9** supporter

garth
4 yard **5** close **9** enclosure

gas
4 fuel, fume **5** fumes, steam, vapor **6** petrol **8** gasoline **9** petroleum
atmospheric: **4** neon **5** argon, oxide, ozone, xenon **6** helium, oxygen **7** krypton, methane **8** hydrogen, nitrogen
flammable: **6** butane, ethane, ethyne **7** methane, propane, propene **8** ethylene
inert: **4** neon **5** argon, radon, xenon **6** helium **7** krypton
mine: **8** firedamp **9** black damp
oxygen: **5** ozone
toxic: **5** sarin, soman, tabun **6** arsine, ketene **7** mustard **8** phosgene **9** phosphine

gasconade
4 brag **7** bravado **8** boasting, bragging **11** braggadocio

gash
3 cut, rip **4** rend, slit, tear **5** carve, cleft, gouge, slash, slice, split **6** incise **8** lacerate **10** depression, laceration

gasket
4 ring, seal **5** O-ring **6** sealer

gasoline
4 fuel **6** petrol
rating: **6** octane

gasp
4 blow, huff, pant, puff **5** heave **6** wheeze **11** exclamation

Gaspar
companion: **8** Melchior **9** Balthazar
gift: **12** frankincense

gassy
5 windy **7** verbose **8** inflated, vaporous **9** flatulent

gastronome
7 epicure, gourmet **8** gourmand **9** bon vivant **11** connoisseur

gastropod
4 slug **5** conch, murex, snail, whelk **6** cowrie, limpet, volute **7** abalone, mollusc, mollusk, sea slug **8** pteropod, univalve **10** periwinkle

gat
3 gun, rod **6** pistol, roscoe **7** channel, firearm, handgun, passage **8** revolver

gate
3 tap **4** cock, door, exit, port **5** entry, hatch, toril, valve **6** faucet, portal, spigot, switch, wicket **7** hydrant, opening, petcock **8** entrance, entryway, stopcock **9** turnstile **10** attendance

gâteau
4 cake

gatefold
6 insert **7** foldout

Gates of Hercules
9 Gibraltar **12** promontories

gateway
4 arch, door, exit **5** pylon, toril **6** portal **7** archway, doorway, opening **8** entrance

gather
4 brew, cull, gain, grow, heap, herd, loom, mass, meet, pick, pile, pool, reap **5** amass, bunch, flock, glean, group, horde, infer, judge, pluck, shirr, swarm **6** assume, deduce, derive, expect, garner, muster, pick up, pucker, summon, take in

7 cluster, collect, convene, extract, harvest, marshal, round up, suppose, surmise, suspect **8** assemble, conclude, converge, increase **9** aggregate, intensify **10** accumulate, congregate, understand **11** concentrate

gathering
4 bevy, crew, gang, herd, mass, ruck **5** bunch, crowd, crush, drove, flock, group, horde, party, press, rally, swarm **6** caucus, klatch, muster, throng **7** company, harvest, klatsch, meeting, reunion, turnout **8** assembly, congress, junction **9** concourse, congeries **10** assemblage, collection, conference, confluence **11** aggregation, get-together **12** congregation

Gath's giant
7 Goliath **10** Philistine

gauche
5 crude, gawky, inept **6** clumsy **7** awkward, halting, loutish, uncouth **8** bumbling, tactless **9** graceless, ham-handed, inelegant, maladroit **10** blundering

gaucho
6 cowboy **8** herdsman
weapon: **4** bola **5** bolas **7** machete

gaudeamus ___
6 igitur

gaudy
4 loud **5** showy **6** brassy, brazen, coarse, flashy, garish, tawdry, tinsel, vulgar **7** blatant, chintzy, glaring **9** brummagem, tasteless **10** outlandish **12** meretricious, ostentatious

Gaugamela
loser: **6** Darius, Persia
victor: **9** Alexander (the Great)

gauge
4 bore, rule, size **5** check, judge, meter, scale, weigh, width **6** assess, degree **7** compute, measure **8** diameter, estimate, evaluate, quantify, standard **9** benchmark, criterion, dimension, thickness, yardstick **10** instrument, touchstone **11** measurement

Gauguin's island
6 Tahiti

Gaul
4 Celt **6** France **9** Frenchman
ancient inhabitants: **4** Remi **6** Belgae

Gaulish
6 French
god: **4** Esus **7** Taranis
goddess: **8** Belisama
priest: **5** druid

gaunt
4 bare, bony, grim, lank, lean, thin **5** harsh, lanky, spare **6** barren, gangly, skinny, wasted **7** angular, scraggy, scrawny **8** gangling, rawboned, skeletal **9** emaciated **10** cadaverous

gauntlet
4 dare, test **5** glove, trial **6** attack, ordeal **9** challenge, onslaught

Gautama
6 Buddha **10** Siddhartha
mother: **4** Maya **8** Mahamaya
son: **6** Rahula
wife: **9** Yasodhara

gauze
4 film, haze, leno, mesh, mist **5** cloth, crepe, tulle **6** fabric, tissue **7** bandage, chiffon, tiffany **8** compress, dressing **11** cheesecloth

gauzy
4 thin **5** filmy, fuzzy, sheer, vague **6** flimsy **8** delicate, pellucid **9** gossamery **10** diaphanous **11** transparent

gavel
6 hammer, mallet

gavial
7 gharial, reptile **9** crocodile

gavotte
4 tune **5** dance

Gawain
brother: **6** Gareth **7** Gaheris
father: **3** Lot
mother: **8** Margawse, Morgause
slayer: **8** Lancelot **9** Launcelot
uncle: **6** Arthur
victim: **6** Uwayne **7** Lamerok **9** Pellinore

gawk
3 oaf **4** bore, gape, gaze, hick, look, lout, lump, peer, rube **5** churl, glare, gloat, klutz, looby, stare, yokel **6** goggle, lubber

gawky
5 inept, splay **6** clumsy, coarse, gauche, oafish **7** awkward, loutish, lumpish, uncouth **8** bumbling, bungling, lubberly, ungainly **9** graceless, ham-handed, lumbering, maladroit

gay
4 glad **5** happy, jolly, merry, queer, showy, sunny, vivid **6** blithe, bouncy, bright, cheery, festal, frisky, jocund, jovial, joyful, lively **7** excited, festive, gleeful, lesbian, playful, raffish **8** animated, cheerful, colorful, mirthful, spirited, sportive **9** exuberant, sparkling, vivacious **10** frolicsome, homosexual, insouciant, nonchalant **12** lighthearted

___ Gay
4 John **5** Enola

Gaza victor
7 Allenby (Edmund)

gaze
3 eye **4** bore, gape, gawk, leer, look, ogle, peer, pore, scan, view **5** glare, gloat, stare, watch **6** goggle **7** eyeball, observe **8** consider **10** rubberneck **11** contemplate

gazebo
6 alcove **8** pavilion **9** belvedere **11** garden house, summerhouse

gazelle
3 goa **4** cora, kudu, mohr, oryx **5** eland, nyala **6** koodoo **7** gemsbok **8** antelope

gazette
5 paper **6** record **7** journal, publish **9** newspaper **10** periodical **11** publication **12** announcement

gazetteer
5 atlas, guide, index

Ge
see **Gaea**

gear
3 cam, cog, rig **5** dress, goods, shift, stuff, wheel **6** adjust, tackle, things **7** apparel, harness, rigging **8** clothing, cogwheel, garments, materiel, property, sprocket, tackling, trapping **9** apparatus, equipment, machinery **10** belongings **11** accessories, habiliments, possessions **13** accouterments, accoutrements, paraphernalia

Geats
king: **7** Hygelac
prince: **7** Beowulf

Geb
daughter: **4** Isis **8** Nephthys
father: **3** Shu
mother: **6** Tefnut
sister: **3** Nut
son: **3** Set **6** Osiris
wife: **3** Nut

gecko
6 lizard **7** reptile

Gedaliah
father: **6** Ahikam **7** Pashhur **8** Jeduthun
slayer: **7** Ishmael

gee
3 wow **4** gosh, turn **5** golly, right **8** goodness, gracious **9** turn right

geek
4 buff, guru, nerd, whiz **5** carny, fiend, freak **6** carney, carnie, expert, pundit, weirdo **7** devotee, egghead, fanatic, oddball **9** authority, eccentric **10** enthusiast **12** intellectual

geezer
4 coot, fogy **5** bloke, crank, fogey **6** codger, dotard, fossil

Gehenna
3 pit **4** hell **5** abyss, hades, Sheol **6** Tophet **7** inferno **8** Tartarus **9** perdition **10** underworld **11** netherworld

Geisel pseudonym
7 Dr. Seuss

geisha wear
3 obi **6** kimono

gel
3 dry, set **4** agar, clot **6** harden, mousse **7** colloid, congeal, thicken **8** solidify **9** coagulate

gelatin
3 jam **4** agar **5** jelly **7** sericin

geld
3 cut, fix, tax **5** alter, desex, unsex **6** change, neuter **7** deprive **8** castrate, mutilate **9** sterilize **10** emasculate **11** desexualize

gelid
3 icy **4** cold **5** chill, nippy, polar **6** arctic, chilly, frigid, frosty, frozen, steely **7** glacial **8** freezing

gelt
5 money

gem
3 jet **4** jade, onyx, opal, rock, ruby, sard **5** agate, amber, beryl, bijou, coral, jewel, lapis, pearl, stone, topaz **6** amulet, garnet, jasper, scarab, sphene, spinel, zircon **7** bejewel, cat's-eye, citrine, diamond, emerald, enjewel, olivine, peridot **8** amethyst, corundum, diopside, fluorite, intaglio, lazurite, obsidian, sapphire, sardonyx, sparkler, tigereye **9** brilliant, carnelian, jadestone, moonstone, phenakite, scapolite, spodumene, tiger's-eye, turquoise **10** aquamarine, cordierite, tourmaline **11** alexandrite, chrysoberyl, chrysoprase, lapis lazuli, masterpiece
blue: **6** zircon **8** sapphire **9** turquoise **10** aquamarine **11** lapis lazuli
carved: **5** cameo **8** intaglio
changeable: **9** chatoyant
cut: **7** marquis **8** baguette, cabochon, marquise **9** brilliant
face: **5** culet, facet
green: **4** jade **7** emerald, peridot, smaragd **10** chrysolite **11** chrysoprase
red: **4** ruby, sard **6** garnet, pyrope, spinel **9** carnelian
support: **7** setting
weight: **5** carat
yellow: **5** amber, topaz **6** sphene **7** citrine

Gemini star
6 Castor, Pollux

gemmule
3 bud

gemsbok
4 oryx **8** antelope

Gem State
5 Idaho

gemütlich
see **genial**

gendarme
3 cop **5** bobby **7** officer, soldier **8** flatfoot **9** constable, patrolman, policeman

gender
3 sex **4** kind, male, sort, type **5** class **6** female, neuter **8** feminine **9** masculine

genealogy
5 roots, stirp, stock **6** origin, stemma **7** descent, history, lineage **8** ancestry, heredity, pedigree **9** bloodline **10** family tree

general
4 wide **5** broad, usual, vague **6** common, global, normal, public **7** blanket, generic, overall, regular, routine, typical **8** catholic, everyday, sweeping **9** all-around, prevalent, universal **10** collective, prevailing, unspecific, widespread **11** commonplace **13** comprehensive
American: **3** Lee (Robert E.) **4** Haig (Alexander), Pike (Zebulon), Wood (Leonard) **5** Clark (Mark, Wesley, William), Grant (Ulysses S.), Meade (George), Scott (Charles, Hugh, Winfield), Smith (Andrew Jackson, Giles, Holland, Morgan, Samuel, Walter, Bedell), Stark (John), Worth (William) **6** Abrams (Creighton), Custer (George Armstrong), Franks (Tommy), Hooker (Joseph), Kearny (Philip, Stephen), Patton (George S.), Porter (Fitz-John), Powell (Colin), Slocum (Henry), Spaatz (Carl), Taylor (Maxwell, Richard, Zachary) **7** Bradley (Omar), Frémont (John Charles), Houston (Samuel), Jackson (Andrew, Thomas "Stonewall"), Lejeune (John), Ridgway (Matthew B.), Sherman (William Tecumseh), Twining (Nathaniel), Wallace (Lewis), Wheeler (Joseph) **8** Burnside (Ambrose), Goethals (George Washington), Marshall (George), Mitchell (Billy), Pershing (John J.), Sheridan (Philip), Stilwell (Joseph) **9** MacArthur (Arthur, Douglas), McClellan (George), Rosecrans (William), Schofield (John), Wilkinson (James) **10** Beauregard (P. G. T.), Eisenhower (Dwight D.), Vandegrift (Alexander), Wainwright (Jonathan) **11** Schwarzkopf (Norman) **12** Westmoreland (William)
American Revolutionary: **4** Knox (Henry), Ward (Artemas) **5** Gates (Horatio), Wayne ("Mad Anthony") **6** de Kalb (Baron), Greene (Nathanael), Morgan (Daniel), Putnam (Israel, Rufus) **8** Moultrie (William), Sullivan (John) **10** Washington (George)
Austrian: **11** Wallenstein (Albrecht von)
British: **4** Gage (Thomas), Howe (William) **5** Clive (Robert), Monck (George), Wolfe (James) **6** Rupert (Prince) **7** Amherst (Jeffery), Wingate (Orde Charles, Reginald) **8** Burgoyne (John), Cromwell (Oliver) **10** Abercromby (Ralph, Robert), Cornwallis (Charles), Wellington (Duke of)
Carthaginian: **8** Hamilcar, Hannibal **9** Hasdrubal
Chinese: **3** Yan (Xishan), Yen (Hsi-shan) **4** Feng (Guozhang, Kuo-chang, Yü-hsiang, Yuxiang) **5** Chang (Tso-lin), Zhang (Zuolin)
Confederate: **3** Lee (Robert E.) **4** Hill (Ambrose), Hood (John Bell) **5** Bragg (Braxton), Ewell (Richard Stoddart), Price (Sterling), Smith (Edmund Kirby) **6** Morgan (John Hunt), Stuart (Jeb) **7** Forrest (Nathan Bedford), Hampton (Wade), Jackson (Thomas "Stonewall"), Pickett (George) **8** Johnston (Albert Sidney, Joseph Eggleston) **9** Pemberton (John) **10** Beauregard (Pierre G. T.), Longstreet (James)
French: **3** Ney (Michel) **4** Foch (Ferdinand) **6** Moreau (Victor), Pétain (Philippe) **7** Weygand (Maxime) **8** de Gaulle (Charles), Lefebvre (Pierre), Montcalm (Marquis de), Saint-Cyr (Laurent de Gouvion-) **9** Frontenac (Comte de) **10** Rochambeau (Comte de)
German: **4** Jodl (Alfred) **6** Kleist (Paul Ludwig von), Rommel (Erwin) **9** Rundstedt (Gerd von) **10** Kesselring (Albert), Ludendorff (Erich)
Greek: **6** Nicias **9** Miltiades **10** Alcibiades **12** Themistocles
Japanese: **4** Tojo (Hideki) **5** Koiso (Kuniaki) **6** Yasuda (Yoshisada) **8** Yamagata (Aritomo) **9** Yamashita (Tomoyuki)
Mexican: **9** Santa Anna (Antonio López de)
Prussian: **11** Scharnhorst (Gerhard von)
Roman: **5** Sulla (Lucius Cornelius) **6** Caesar (Julius), Fabius (Quintus), Marius (Gaius), Pompey (the Great), Scipio (Gnaeus Cornelius, Publius Cornelius) **7** Regulus (Marcus Atilius), Ricimer (Flavius) **8** Agricola (Gnaeus Julius), Lucullus (Lucius Licinius), Stilicho (Flavius) **9** Marcellus (Marcus Claudius), Sertorius (Quintus) **10** Theodosius (the Great) **11** Cincinnatus (Lucius Quinctius)
Russian: **6** Zhukov (Georgy) **7** Kutuzov (Mikhail), Trotsky (Leon), Wrangel (Pyotr), Zhdanov (Andrey) **9** Yeremenko (Andrey)
Spanish: **4** Alba (Duke of), Alva (Duke of) **6** Franco (Francisco)
Swedish: **7** Wrangel (Karl Gustav)

general assembly
4 diet **6** plenum **8** congress **10** parliament **11** legislature

generalize
5 infer, widen **6** derive, extend, induce, spread **7** broaden **8** conclude **12** universalize

generally
6 mainly, mostly, widely **7** all told, as a rule, broadly, chiefly, en masse, largely, overall, usually **8** all in all, commonly, normally **9** on average, primarily, typically **10** altogether, by and large, frequently, on the whole, ordinarily **11** customarily, principally

generate
4 bear, make, sire **5** beget, breed, cause, hatch,

spawn, yield **6** create, effect, father, induce, work up **7** achieve, develop, produce, provoke **8** engender, initiate, multiply **9** originate, procreate, propagate, reproduce **10** bring about, bring forth

generic
5 broad **6** common, global **7** blanket **9** inclusive, unbranded, universal **10** indistinct **12** nonexclusive

____ generis
3 sui

generosity
7 charity **8** altruism, kindness, largesse **9** abundance **10** liberality **11** beneficence, benevolence, magnanimity, munificence **12** philanthropy **13** unselfishness

generous
4 free, kind **5** ample **6** lavish **7** copious, helpful, liberal, profuse, willing **8** abundant **9** bounteous, bountiful, plenteous, plentiful, unselfish, unsparing **10** altruistic, benevolent, bighearted, charitable, munificent, openhanded, ungrudging, unstinting **11** considerate, kindhearted, magnanimous, overflowing **12** greathearted

genesis
4 dawn, root **5** alpha, birth, start **6** origin, outset, source **7** dawning, opening **8** creation **9** beginning, formation, inception **10** provenance **12** commencement

Genet play
5 Maids (The) **6** Blacks (The) **7** Balcony (The)

genetic
10 congenital, hereditary
material: **3** DNA, RNA **7** cistron **9** chromatid **10** chromosome
term: **8** synapsis **9** backcross

genial
4 kind, warm **5** jolly, merry **6** benign, blithe, hearty, jocund, jovial, kindly, mellow, social **7** affable, amiable, cordial **8** amicable, friendly, gracious, pleasant, sociable **9** agreeable, congenial, convivial, easygoing **10** neighborly **11** good-humored, good-natured, warmhearted

genie
3 imp **4** jann, jinn, puck **5** afrit **6** afreet, spirit, sprite

geniture
4 dawn **5** birth, start **6** origin **8** nativity **9** beginning, inception

genius
3 wiz **4** bent, gift, head, turn, whiz **5** flair, jinni, knack **6** acumen, brains, master, spirit, talent, wizard **7** aptness, faculty, prodigy **8** aptitude, brainiac, capacity, penchant **9** ingenuity, intellect **10** brilliance, creativity, mastermind, propensity **12** intelligence **13** inventiveness

Genoa's liberator
5 Doria (Andrea)

genre
3 ilk **4** kind, sort, type **5** class, style **6** family, stripe **7** species, variety **8** category, division

gens
3 kin **4** clan **5** group **6** family, people **7** kinfolk **9** relations, relatives

Genseric's subjects
7 Vandals

genteel
4 nice, prim **5** civil **6** formal, polite, prissy, strict, stuffy, urbane **7** courtly, elegant, prudish, refined, stilted, stylish **8** affected, cultured, graceful, gracious, ladylike, mannerly, polished, priggish, well-bred **9** courteous **10** cultivated **11** gentlemanly, pretentious, straitlaced, well-behaved

gentile
3 goy **5** pagan **7** heathen **9** Christian, non-Jewish

gentility
5 elite **6** gentry **7** decorum, manners, quality, society **8** breeding, courtesy, nobility **9** blue blood **10** aristocrat, refinement, upper class, upper crust **11** aristocracy

gentle
4 calm, easy, kind, meek, mild, soft, tame **5** balmy, quiet, tamed **6** benign, docile, genial, kindly, mellow, placid, serene, smooth, tender **7** amiable, lenient **8** delicate, peaceful, pleasant, soothing, tranquil **9** agreeable **11** softhearted, sympathetic, warmhearted **13** compassionate
creature: **4** lamb

gentleman
3 sir **6** aristo, fellow, mister **8** cavalier **9** blue blood, chevalier, patrician **10** aristocrat
English: **6** milord
French: **8** monsieur
Hindu: **4** babu
Spanish: **3** don **5** señor

gentleman friend
4 beau **5** lover, swain **6** fiancé, squire, suitor **7** gallant

gentlemanly
5 civil, noble, suave **6** polite, urbane **7** elegant, gallant, genteel, refined **8** mannerly, well-bred **9** courteous, honorable **10** chivalrous, cultivated **11** considerate

Gentlemen Prefer Blondes author
4 Loos (Anita)

gentry
5 elite, folks **7** quality, society **8** nobility **9** gentility, patrician **10** gentlefolk, patriciate, upper class, upper crust **11** aristocracy, high society, ruling class

genuflect
3 bow **4** fawn **5** kneel **6** kowtow

genuine
4 echt, pure, real, true **5** plain, pucka, pukka, valid **6** actual, dinkum, honest, tested **7** factual, natural, sincere **8** absolute, bona fide, positive, trueborn **9** authentic, certified, unalloyed, undoubted, unfeigned, veritable **10** sure-enough, unaffected

genus
3 ilk **4** kind, mode, sort, type **5** class, group, order **6** family **7** species, variety **8** category
amphibian: **4** Hyla, Rana
antelope: **4** Oryx
bee: **4** Apis
bird: **4** Alca, Anas, Chen, Olor, Pavo, Pica, Rhea, Sula, Uria, Xema **5** Sitta
fish: **4** Amia, Lota
herb: **4** Arum, Geum
insect: **4** Nepa
lily: **4** Aloe
orchid: **4** Disa
owl: **4** Bubo, Otus
palm: **4** Nipa
sheep: **4** Ovis
shrub: **4** Ilex, Itea, Ulex
snake: **4** Eryx
tree: **4** Acer, Cola, Maba, Olea
turtle: **4** Emys

geode
4 rock **5** stone **6** cavity, nodule

geoduck
4 clam

geographer
American: **10** Huntington (Ellsworth)
Flemish: **8** Mercator (Gerardus)
German: **6** Ratzel (Friedrich)
Greek: **6** Strabo **7** Ptolemy
Itallan: **8** Vespucci (Amerigo)

geologic period
5 azoic **6** Eocene, Hadean **7** Archean, Miocene, Permian **8** Cambrian, Cenozoic, Devonian, Holocene, Jurassic, Mesozoic, Pliocene, Silurian, Triassic **9** Oligocene, Paleocene, Paleozoic **10** Cretaceous, Ordovician **11** Phanerozoic, Pleistocene, Precambrian, Proterozoic **13** Mississippian, Pennsylvanian

geometer
6 Euclid **13** mathematician

geometric
coordinate: **8** abscissa, ordinate
curve: **3** arc **6** spiral **7** ellipse, evolute **8** parabola
figure: **5** rhomb **6** circle, oblong, square **7** ellipse, hexagon, octagon, polygon, rhombus **8** heptagon, pentagon, rhomboid, triangle **9** rectangle
solid: **4** cone, cube **5** prism **6** sphere **7** pyramid **8** cylinder, spheroid, spherule
surface: **5** nappe, torus **6** toroid

geometry letters
3 QED

geophagy
4 pica

Georgia
capital: **7** Atlanta
city: **5** Macon **6** Albany, Athens **7** Augusta **8** Columbus, Marietta, Savannah
college, university: **5** Clark, Emory **6** Mercer **7** Spelman **8** Valdosta **9** Morehouse
founder: **10** Oglethorpe (James)
nickname: **5** Peach (State)
river: **8** Ocmulgee **13** Chattahoochee
state bird: **13** brown thrasher
state flower: **12** Cherokee rose
state tree: **7** live oak
swamp: **10** Okefenokee

Georgia, Republic of
ancient kingdom: **6** Iberia **7** Colchis
capital: **6** Tiflis **7** Tbilisi
city: **7** Kutaisi, Rustavi
includes: **6** Ajaria **8** Abkhazia, Adzharia **12** South Ossetia
monarch: **6** Tamara (Queen)
monetary unit: **4** lari
mountain range: **8** Caucasus
neighbor: **6** Russia, Turkey **7** Armenia **10** Azerbaijan
river: **4** Kura **5** Rioni
sea: **5** Black

Georgics author
6 Vergil, Virgil

Geraint's wife
4 Enid

Gerda's husband
4 Frey

geriatric
3 old **4** aged **5** aging **6** senior **7** elderly **8** outmoded **12** old-fashioned **13** superannuated

germ
3 bud, bug **4** seed **5** spark, spore, virus **6** embryo, origin, source **7** microbe, nucleus **8** pathogen **9** bacterium
cell: **3** egg **4** ovum **5** sperm

German
3 Hun **4** Goth **6** Teuton
after: **4** nach
airport: **9** Flughafen
always: **5** immer
article: **3** das, der, des, die, ein **4** eine
attention: **7** Achtung
bad: **8** schlecht
battle: **4** Kampf **8** Schlacht
bomber: **5** Gotha, Stuka

beneath: **5** unter
border: **6** Grenze
breakfast: **9** Frühstück
cabbage: **5** Kraut
child: **4** Kind
city: **5** Stadt
coin: **4** Mark **5** Taler **6** Thaler **7** Pfennig
count: **4** Graf
day: **3** Tag
doctor: **4** Arzt
dog: **4** Hund
empire: **5** Reich
entire, whole: **4** ganz
fairy tale: **7** Märchen
fast: **7** schnell
forbidden: **8** verboten
fruit: **4** Obst
good: **3** gut **4** gute
hardly, scarcely: **4** kaum
head: **4** Kopf
hero: **4** Held
highway: **8** Autobahn
history, story: **10** Geschichte
honor: **4** Ehre
hope: **8** Hoffnung
horse: **5** Pferd
I: **3** ich
labor: **6** Arbeit
leader: **6** Führer, Kaiser
lightning: **5** Blitz
liquor: **8** Schnapps
little: **5** klein **6** kleine
love: **5** Liebe
measles: **7** rubella
Miss: **8** Fräulein
money: **4** Geld
moon: **4** Mond
mountain: **4** Berg
musical: **9** Singspiel
no: **4** nein
Mr.: **4** Herr
Mrs.: **4** Frau **4** nein
nobleman: **6** Junker
nothing: **6** nichts
numbers: **3** elf **4** acht, drei, eins, fünf, neun, vier, zehn, zwei **5** sechs, zwölf **6** sieben
over: **4** über
picture: **4** Bild
please: **5** bitte
portion: **4** Teil
prince: **5** Fürst
pronoun: **2** du, er, es **3** ich, sie, wir **4** dich, mich, sich
proud: **5** stolz
railroad: **9** Eisenbahn
rifle: **6** Gewehr, Mauser
rule: **5** Regel
silence: **4** Ruhe **6** Stille
song: **4** Lied **6** Lieder (plural)
space: **4** Raum
spirit: **5** Geist
strength, power **5** Kraft, Macht
submarine: **5** U-boat, U-boot
success: **6** Erfolg
tank: **6** Panzer
television: **9** Fernseher
thank you: **5** danke
today: **5** heute
tomorrow: **6** morgen
train: **3** Zug
train station: **7** Bahnhof
tree: **4** Baum
truth: **8** Wahrheit
valley: **3** Tal
value: **4** Wert
victory: **4** Sieg
war: **5** Krieg
weight: **3** Lot **5** Pfund, Stein **8** Vierling
with: **3** mit
work: **6** Arbeit
world: **4** Welt
woman: **4** Frau **8** Fräulein
youth: **6** Jugend

germane
3 apt **5** ad rem **7** apropos, fitting, related **8** material, relevant **9** pertinent **10** applicable **11** appropriate

Germany
11 Deutschland
capital: **6** Berlin
city: **3** Ulm **4** Bonn, Jena, Kiel **5** Essen, Mainz **6** Bremen, Erfurt, Lübeck, Munich **7** Cologne, Dresden, Hamburg, Hanover, Leipzig, München, Potsdam **8** Augsburg, Dortmund, Duisburg, Freiburg, Hannover, Schwerin **9** Frankfurt, Nuremberg, Stuttgart, Wiesbaden **10** Baden Baden, Düsseldorf
leader: **4** Kohl (Helmut) **6** Brandt (Willy), Hitler (Adolf), Merkel (Angela) **7** Schmidt (Helmut), Wilhelm (Kaiser) **8** Bismarck (Otto)
monetary unit: **4** euro
monetary unit, former: **4** mark **5** taler **6** thaler **12** deutsche mark
mountain, range: **4** Harz **7** Brocken
neighbor: **6** France, Poland **7** Austria, Belgium, Denmark **10** Luxembourg **11** Netherlands, Switzerland **13** Czech Republic
region: **4** Ruhr **6** Saxony **7** Bavaria **11** Black Forest
river: **4** Eder, Elbe, Isar, Main, Oder, Ruhr, Saar **5** Fulda, Mosel, Rhein, Rhine, Weser **6** Danube **7** Moselle
sea: **5** North **6** Baltic
state: **5** Hesse **6** Saxony **7** Bavaria **8** Saarland **9** Thuringia **11** Brandenburg

germinate
3 bud **6** evolve, spring, sprout **7** blossom, develop **9** originate, pullulate

Gershom, Gershon
father: **4** Levi
son: **5** Libni **6** Shimei

Gershwin
3 Ira **6** George
opera: **12** Porgy and Bess
piece: **14** Rhapsody in Blue **15** American in Paris (An)
show: **5** Oh Kay **9** Funny Face, Girl Crazy **10** Lady Be Good **11** Of Thee I Sing **15** Strike Up the Band
song: **10** I Got Rhythm, Summertime

Gertrude
husband: **8** Claudius
son: **6** Hamlet

Gervaise's daughter
4 Nana

Geryon
dog: **6** Orthus
father: **8** Chrysaor
mother: **10** Callirrhoë
slayer: **8** Hercules

gestalt
4 form **5** shape **6** figure **7** pattern **9** structure **13** configuration

Gestapo chief
7 Himmler (Heinrich)

geste
4 deed, feat **7** emprise, exploit, romance, venture **9** adventure **10** enterprise **11** undertaking

gesticulate
3 nod **4** move, wave **6** beckon, motion, signal

gesticulation
4 wave **6** motion **7** gesture **8** high sign **9** pantomime **12** body language, sign language

gesture
3 nod **4** sign, wave **5** shrug, token **6** motion, salute, signal **8** reminder **9** signalize **10** expression, indication
graceful: **9** beau geste

get
3 bag **4** draw, earn, gain, land **5** catch, cause, seize **6** access, attain, become, elicit, extort, obtain, pick up, secure **7** achieve, acquire, bring in, capture, chalk up, deliver, extract, procure, receive **8** contract **10** understand **12** come down with

get around
4 roam, rove, tour, trek, walk **5** avoid, dodge, elude, evade, skirt **6** cruise, detour, escape, ramble, travel, wander **8** ambulate, outflank, sidestep **10** circumvent

get away
see **get out**

getaway
3 lam **4** exit, slip **6** escape, flight **7** retreat **8** breakout, vacation

get back
6 go home, recoup, regain, return, revert **7** recover, reclaim, revenge, revisit **8** retrieve **9** repossess, retaliate

get by
4 cope, fare, pass **5** slide **6** eke out, endure, manage **7** carry on, survive **8** maintain

get off
4 walk **5** leave **6** alight, depart, go free, launch **7** pull out **8** dismount **9** disembark **10** beat the rap

get out
2 go **4** exit, kite, leak **5** break, issue, leave, scram, split **6** alight, beat it, begone, decamp, depart, egress, escape **7** buzz off, publish, skiddoo, take off, vamoose **8** dispatch, hightail **9** circulate, skedaddle **10** make tracks

Gettysburg general
3 Lee (Robert E.) **5** Meade (George)

get up
4 gain **5** arise, breed, cause, dress, hatch, mount, raise, stand **6** create, induce, summon **7** acquire, prepare, produce **8** engender, generate **12** rise and shine

getup
3 rig **4** duds, garb, togs **5** array, dress, guise **6** outfit **7** costume, threads

get-up-and-go
3 pep, vim, zip **4** bang, push, snap, zeal, zest **5** drive, moxie, oomph, punch, spunk, steam, verve, vigor **6** energy, spirit, starch **8** ambition **10** enterprise, initiative

gewgaw
3 toy **4** dido **5** bijou, curio **6** bangle, bauble, doodad, trifle **7** bibelot, novelty, trinket, whatnot **8** gimcrack, kickshaw **9** bagatelle, objet d'art **10** knickknack

geyser
3 jet **5** fount, spout, spurt **6** gusher, spring **8** fountain **10** wellspring **11** Old Faithful

Ghana
capital: **5** Accra
city: **4** Tema **6** Kumasi, Tamale
ethnic group: **4** Akan **5** Mossi
former name: **9** Gold Coast
gulf: **6** Guinea
lake: **5** Volta
monetary unit: **4** cedi
neighbor: **4** Togo **10** Ivory Coast **11** Burkina Faso
river: **5** Volta

ghastly
4 grim, pale **5** awful, lurid **6** grisly, horrid, pallid **7** ghostly, hideous, macabre **8** dreadful, ghoulish, gruesome, horrible, shocking, spectral, terrible **9** appalling, deathlike, frightful, ghostlike, repulsive, sickening **10** cadaverous, corpselike, disgustful, disgusting, horrifying, nauseating, terrifying **11** frightening

ghee
3 fat **6** butter

gherkin
4 vine **6** pickle **8** cucumber

ghetto
4 slum

ghost
4 soul **5** demon, haunt, shade, spook, trace **6** kelpie, shadow, spirit, wraith, zombie **7** eidolon, phantom, specter **8** phantasm **10** apparition **11** poltergeist
cartoon: 6 Casper

ghostly
5 eerie, scary **6** spooky **7** shadowy **8** ethereal, spectral **9** deathlike, spiritual, unearthly, unworldly **10** cadaverous, corpselike, phantasmal **12** supernatural

Ghosts author
5 Ibsen (Henrik)

ghoul
4 ogre **5** fiend **7** monster **11** grave robber

GI
5 grunt **7** dogface, fighter, soldier, warrior **8** doughboy **9** man-at-arms **10** serviceman

Gianni Schicchi composer
7 Puccini (Giacomo)

giant
4 huge, hulk, ogre, Otus, vast **5** gross, Gyges, Hymir, jumbo, titan, whale **6** Cottus, Typhon **7** Aloadae (plural), Antaeus, Cyclops, Goliath, immense, mammoth, monster, titanic, whopper **8** behemoth, Briareus, colossal, colossus, enormous, gigantic, Orgoglio **9** cyclopean, Enceladus, Ephialtes, Gargantua, humongous, leviathan, monstrous **10** gargantuan, prodigious **11** elephantine
biblical: 4 Anak **7** Goliath
cactus: 7 saguaro
hundred-armed: 9 Enceladus
hundred-eyed: 5 Argus
killer: 4 Jack **5** David
movie monster: 6 Mothra **8** Godzilla, King Kong
one-eyed: 5 Arges **7** Cyclops **10** Polyphemus
rime-cold: 4 Ymer, Ymir
sea god: 5 Aegir

Giant author
6 Ferber (Edna)

giaour
7 infidel **10** unbeliever **11** nonbeliever

gib
3 tom **6** tomcat

gibber
3 gab, yak **4** blab **5** prate **6** babble, drivel, gabble, jabber, yammer **7** blabber, blather, chatter, palaver, prattle, twaddle

gibberish
3 gab **5** Greek, hokum **6** babble, bunkum, burble, drivel, gabble, jabber, yammer **7** blabber, blather, chatter, palaver, prattle, twaddle **8** claptrap, flimflam, nonsense **10** balderdash, doubletalk, hocus-pocus, mumbo jumbo **11** abracadabra, jabberwocky **12** gobbledygook

gibbet
4 hang **5** lynch, noose, scrag **7** execute, gallows **8** string up

gibbon
3 ape, lar **7** primate, siamang **10** anthropoid

gibbous
6 arched, convex, humped **7** bulging, rounded, swollen **10** humpbacked **11** protuberant

gibe
4 gird, jape, jeer, jest, mock, quip, rail **5** fleer, flout, scoff, scorn, scout, sneer, taunt, tease **6** deride, insult **8** ridicule

Gibraltar
colony of: 7 Britain, England
conqueror: 5 Tarik, Tariq
neighbor: 5 Spain
opposite: 5 Ceuta

Gibran work
7 Prophet (The)

giddy
4 gaga **5** dizzy, inane, light, silly, woozy **6** elated, yeasty **7** flighty, foolish, vacuous **8** euphoric **9** frivolous, slaphappy **10** hoity-toity **11** empty-headed, harebrained, light-headed, vertiginous

___ Gide
5 André

Gideon
father: 5 Joash
servant: 5 Purah
son: 9 Abimelech

gift
3 set, tip **4** alms, bent, boon, head, turn **5** award, bonus, endow, favor, flair, forte, grant, knack **6** genius, legacy, reward, talent **7** ability, aptness, cumshaw, faculty, freebie, handout, present, subsidy **8** aptitude, bestowal, capacity, donation, gratuity, largesse, oblation, offering

9 endowment, lagniappe **11** benefaction, benevolence **12** contribution, presentation

gifted
4 able **5** smart **6** expert **7** hotshot, skilled **8** masterly, skillful, talented **9** ingenious, masterful

gig
3 jab, job, top **4** boat, fool, goad, prod, spur **5** annoy, freak, rotor, spear **6** chaise, harass **7** booking, demerit, provoke, rowboat **8** carriage **10** engagement

gigantic
4 huge, vast **5** giant, jumbo **7** hulking, immense, mammoth, massive, titanic **8** behemoth, colossal, enormous, king-size, whopping **9** cyclopean, humongous, king-sized, monstrous, walloping **10** gargantuan, prodigious, stupendous **11** elephantine

giggle
5 laugh **6** guffaw, hee-haw, titter **7** chortle, chuckle, snicker, snigger, twitter

Gigi author
7 Colette

Gilbert and Sullivan opera
6 Mikado (The) **8** Iolanthe, Patience, Sorcerer (The) **9** Grand Duke (The), Ruddigore **10** Gondoliers (The) **11** H.M.S. Pinafore, Princess Ida, Trial by Jury

Gil Blas author
6 Lesage (Alain-René)

gild
4 coat, deck **5** adorn, cover, tinge **6** bedeck, tinsel **7** enhance, overlay **8** brighten, ornament **9** embellish, embroider

Gilda's father
9 Rigoletto

Gilead
father: **6** Machir
grandfather: **8** Manasseh
son: **7** Jephtha **8** Jephthah

Gilgamesh
4 epic
companion: **6** Eabani, Enkidu
goddess: **5** Aruru **6** Ishtar, Siduri
home: **4** Uruk **5** Erech
mother: **6** Ninsun
victim: **6** Huwawa **7** Humbaba

gill
4 race **5** brook, creek **6** runnel, stream, wattle **7** rivulet
relating to: **9** branchial

gillyflower
4 pink **9** carnation, clove pink

Gilroy play
15 Subject Was Roses (The)

gilt
3 hog, pig, sow **4** bond, gold **5** swine **6** gilded, golden **10** brilliance

gimcrack
5 cheap **6** bauble, gewgaw, shoddy, trifle **7** bibelot, chintzy, trinket **8** kickshaw **10** knickknack

gimlet
4 tool **5** drill, drink **8** cocktail
ingredient: **3** gin **5** vodka **9** lime juice

gimmick
3 con **4** ploy, ruse, wile **5** angle, catch, dodge, feint, gizmo, trick **6** device, gadget, gambit, jigger, scheme, widget **8** artifice, maneuver **9** stratagem **10** subterfuge

gimp
3 vim **4** cord, halt **5** braid, hitch **6** dodder, falter, hobble, spirit **7** cripple **8** lameness

gimpy
4 game, halt, lame **7** hobbled, limping **8** crippled

gin
3 net **4** sloe, trap **5** catch, rummy, snare **6** device, liquor **7** springe **8** beverage, generate, separate

ginger
3 fig, pep, vim, zip **4** herb, stir, zing **5** liven, spice, verve, vigor **6** energy, mettle, revive, spirit **7** sparkle
cookie: **4** snap

gingerly
4 safe, wary **5** canny, chary **7** careful, guarded **8** cautious, delicate, discreet

gingery
4 tart **5** fiery, peppy, sharp, spicy, tangy, zesty **6** snappy, spunky **7** peppery, piquant, pungent **8** spirited **10** mettlesome **12** high-spirited

gingham
5 cloth **6** fabric **7** textile **8** material

gingiva
3 gum

gin mill
3 bar, pub **4** dive **5** joint **6** saloon, tavern **7** barroom, taproom **8** alehouse **9** roadhouse **11** public house **12** watering hole

Ginsberg poem
4 Howl **7** Kaddish

ginseng
4 herb, root

Gioconda, La
8 Mona Lisa
composer: **10** Ponchielli (Amilcare)
painter: **7** da Vinci (Leonardo) **8** Leonardo (da Vinci)

giraffe
8 ruminant **9** quadruped **10** camelopard

girandole
7 earring **10** candelabra **11** candelabrum, candlestick, composition

girasol
3 gem **4** opal **5** jewel, stone **7** mineral **8** fire opal **9** artichoke

gird
3 hem **4** band, belt, bind, ring, wrap **5** brace, equip, hem in, ready, round, steel **6** circle **7** bolster, enclose, fortify, prepare, provide, shore up, wreathe **8** buttress, cincture, encircle, surround **9** encompass, reinforce **10** strengthen

girder
4 beam **5** brace, I-beam **7** support **8** crossbar **9** crossbeam **10** crosspiece, transverse

girdle
4 band, belt, ring, sash **6** cestus, circle **8** ceinture, cincture, encircle, surround **9** encompass, waistband
of Aphrodite: 6 cestus

girl
4 babe, bird, coed, doll, lass, maid, miss **5** chick, filly, missy, wench **6** damsel, lassie, maiden **8** daughter **10** sweetheart

girth
4 band, belt, bind, size **5** brace, cinch, strap **6** circle, fasten, girdle **7** measure **8** cincture, encircle, surround **9** thickness **10** dimensions **13** circumference

Giselle composer
4 Adam (Adolphe)

gist
3 nub, sum **4** core, meat, pith **5** sense **6** burden, ground, kernel, marrow, matter, thrust, upshot **7** essence **9** main point, substance

give
3 pay **4** deal, hand **5** allot, allow, award, grant, issue, offer, remit **6** accord, afford, assign, bestow, commit, confer, convey, devote, direct, donate, extend, market, pony up, render, supply, tender **7** deliver, dish out, display, dole out, fall out, fork out, furnish, hand out, mete out, present, produce, proffer, provide **8** allocate, bequeath, disburse, dispense, give away, hand over, shell out, turn over **9** apportion, sacrifice **10** administer, contribute, distribute

give-and-take
6 banter **8** exchange, repartee, trade-off **10** compromise **11** cooperation, reciprocity

give away
4 blab, leak **5** award, grant, spill **6** bestow, betray, confer, devote, donate, expose, reveal, tattle **7** deliver, divulge, hand out, let slip, present **8** bequeath, disclose

giveaway
4 deal, gift, leak **5** steal, value **6** tip-off **7** bargain, freebee, freebie, premium, present, sellout **8** betrayal, exposure **10** disclosure, revelation

give back
6 refund, retire, return **7** replace, restore, retreat **8** withdraw **9** reinstate

give in
4 cave, fold, quit, stop **5** yield **6** assent, comply, desist, relent, submit **7** concede, deliver, indulge, succumb **8** back down, cry uncle **9** surrender **10** relinquish

given
5 prone **6** donnée **7** assumed, granted **8** inclined **9** presented, specified **10** particular **11** considering, susceptible

give off
4 beam, emit, flow, vent **5** exude, issue **6** effuse **7** emanate, radiate, release **9** discharge

give out
4 deal, dole, emit, fail, mete, vent **5** issue **6** cave in **7** declare, release, succumb **8** collapse, throw off **9** break down **10** distribute

giver
5 donor **7** donator, grantor

give up
4 cede, quit **5** allow, cease, forgo, waive, yield **6** abjure, devote, resign, vacate **7** abandon, despair **8** abdicate, hand over, renounce, withdraw **9** sacrifice, surrender **10** relinquish

give way
5 yield **6** buckle, cave in **7** retreat, succumb **8** collapse **9** surrender

gizmo
see **gadget**

glabrous
4 bald, bare **6** shaven, smooth **8** hairless **9** beardless **10** bald-headed **12** smooth-shaven

glacial
3 icy, raw **5** chill, gelid, nippy, polar **6** arctic, biting, chilly, frigid, frosty, frozen, wintry **8** freezing **11** Pleistocene

glacier
3 ice **6** ice cap **8** ice field, ice sheet
Alaska: 4 Muir, Taku **6** Bering **10** Mendenhall
Antarctica: 9 Beardmore
deposit: 4 kame **5** esker **6** placer **7** moraine
fissure: 8 crevasse
fragment: 4 berg **7** iceberg
Greenland: 8 Humboldt
hill: 7 drumlin
Karakoram: 5 Biafo **7** Baltoro
New Zealand: 6 Tasman
pinnacle: 5 serac
surface: 4 névé

glacis
5 grade, slope **7** incline **10** buffer zone **11** buffer state

glad
3 gay **4** fain **5** happy, jolly, merry **6** blithe, bright, cheery, genial, jocund, jovial, joyful, joyous **7** beaming, gleeful, pleased, radiant, tickled, willing **8** cheerful, mirthful, pleasant, rejoiced **9** delighted, gratified

gladden
4 buoy **5** cheer, elate **6** buck up, perk up, please, uplift **7** cheer up, delight, gratify, hearten

glade
6 meadow **8** clearing **9** open space

gladiator
7 fighter **9** combatant, Spartacus

gladly
4 fain, lief **6** freely **7** happily, readily **8** heartily **9** willingly **10** cheerfully, with relish **12** with pleasure

gladness
3 joy **4** glee **5** bliss, cheer, mirth **6** gaiety **7** delight, jollity **9** happiness, merriment

gladstone
3 bag **8** suitcase

glamorous
7 elegant **8** alluring, charming, dazzling, enticing, magnetic **9** seductive **10** attractive, bewitching, enchanting **11** captivating, fascinating **13** sophisticated

glamour
5 charm, magic, spell **6** allure, appeal **7** romance **8** charisma, witchery **9** magnetism, sex appeal **10** attraction, witchcraft **11** fascination **12** razzle-dazzle

glance
4 peek, peep, skim, skip **5** brush, carom, flash, glaze, graze, shine **6** bounce, careen **7** glimpse **8** ricochet
lascivious: **4** leer

gland
5 gonad, liver, organ **6** pineal, thymus **7** adrenal, mammary, parotid, thyroid **8** exocrine, pancreas, prostate, salivary **9** endocrine, pituitary **11** parathyroid
secretion: **7** hormone
swelling: **4** bubo

glare
4 gaze, glow, peer **5** blaze, flame, flash, frown, gleam, light, lower, scowl, shine, stare **6** dazzle, glower **7** obtrude **8** stand out **10** garishness

glaring
4 loud, rank **5** gaudy, plain, vivid **6** brazen, flashy, garish, tawdry, tinsel **7** blatant, obvious **8** blinding, flagrant **9** audacious, egregious, obtrusive **10** noticeable **11** conspicuous, outstanding **12** ostentatious

glass
4 lens, pane **5** image, lense, prism **6** mirror **7** reflect **9** barometer, telescope
combining form: **5** vitro
container: **3** jar **6** beaker, bottle
decorative: **7** schmelz **8** schmelze
drinking: **4** pony **5** flute **6** goblet, jigger, rummer, seidel **7** snifter, tumbler **8** schooner, stemware
gem: **5** paste **6** strass
magnifying: **5** loupe
milky: **7** opaline
volcanic: **7** perlite **8** obsidian

glasses
5 specs **6** shades **7** goggles **8** bifocals, pince-nez, tumblers **9** lorgnette, trifocals **10** spectacles

glass-like
5 clear **6** glazed, limpid, smooth **8** pellucid, vitreous **9** vitrified **11** translucent, transparent

glassmaker
6 Blenko (William) **7** Lalique (René), Tiffany (Louis Comfort) **9** Waterford

glassmaking tool
5 punty **6** pontil **8** blowpipe

Glass Menagerie author
8 Williams (Tennessee)

glassy
5 blank, dazed, shiny **6** glazed, smooth, vacant **7** hyaloid **8** polished, vitreous **9** burnished

glaucous
4 waxy **7** frosted, powdery

Glaucus
beloved: **6** Scylla
father: **5** Minos **8** Sisyphus
mother: **6** Merope **8** Pasiphaë
son: **11** Bellerophon

glaze
3 rub **4** buff, coat, film **5** cover, glint, gloss, sheen, shine **6** enamel, finish, luster, patina, polish **7** burnish, coating, furbish, lacquer, overlay, varnish

glazed
5 blank **6** glassy

gleam
3 ray **4** beam, burn, glow **5** flare, flash, glint, sheen, shine **6** glance **7** glimmer, glisten, glitter, radiate, shimmer, sparkle, twinkle **8** radiance **11** coruscation, scintillate **13** scintillation

gleaming
5 aglow, shiny **6** glossy, sheeny **7** beaming, burning, glowing, lambent, radiant, shining **8** flashing, luminous, lustrous, polished **9** brilliant, burnished, refulgent, sparkling, twinkling **10** glimmering, glistening, glittering, shimmering **13** scintillating

glean
4 cull, reap, sift **5** amass, learn **6** garner, gather, pick up **7** extract, find out, harvest

glebe
4 land **5** field, tract **7** acreage **8** cropland, farmland

glee
3 joy **5** mirth **6** gaiety, levity **7** delight, elation, jollity **8** gladness, hilarity, part-song **9** enjoyment, festivity, good cheer, happiness, jocundity, joviality, merriment **10** exuberance, joyfulness, jubilation **12** exhilaration

gleeful
3 gay **5** jolly, merry **6** blithe, elated, jocund, jovial, joyous **8** cheerful, exultant, jubilant, mirthful **9** exuberant **12** lighthearted

glen
4 dale, vale **5** swale **6** dingle, valley
deep: 5 gorge **6** ravine

glengarry
3 cap **6** bonnet

glib
4 easy **5** slick **6** facile, fluent, smooth **7** offhand, shallow, voluble **8** eloquent, flippant **10** articulate, nonchalant **11** superficial

glide
3 fly **4** flow, sail, skim, slip, soar, waft **5** coast, creep, drift, float, skate, skirr, skulk, slide, slink, sneak, steal **7** descend, slither **8** glissade, volplane **10** portamento

glimmer
4 glow, hint **5** blink, flash, gleam, glint, shine, spark, trace **6** glance **7** flicker, glisten, glitter, inkling, shimmer, sparkle, twinkle **9** coruscate **10** suggestion **11** coruscation, scintillate **13** scintillation

glimpse
4 espy, peek, peep **5** flash, glint, stime **6** glance

glint
3 ray **5** flash, glaze, gleam, sheen, shine, trace **6** glance, luster **7** glimmer, glisten, glitter, shimmer, sparkle, twinkle **9** coruscate **11** coruscation, scintillate **13** scintillation

glissade
4 skim, slip **5** glide, slide

glissando
3 run **5** slide **7** gliding, sliding

glisten
4 glow **5** flash, gleam, glint, shine **6** glance **7** flicker, glimmer, glitter, shimmer, spangle, sparkle, twinkle **9** coruscate **11** coruscation, scintillate **13** scintillation

glitch
3 bug **4** flaw, snag **5** fault, snafu **6** defect **7** failing, failure, gremlin, problem **8** obstacle **10** difficulty **11** malfunction

glitter
5 flash, gleam, glint, shine **7** glimmer, glisten, shimmer, spangle, sparkle, twinkle **9** coruscate **11** coruscation, scintillate **13** scintillation

glittering
5 gaudy, shiny, showy **6** flashy **7** fulgent **9** brilliant, clinquant, coruscant, effulgent **11** spectacular

gloaming
3 eve **4** dusk **5** gloom **7** evening **8** eventide, twilight **9** nightfall

gloat
4 crow **5** exult, revel, vaunt **6** relish **7** triumph **9** celebrate

glob
4 clot, lump **6** dollop

global
5 grand **6** cosmic **7** blanket, general, overall **8** all-round, catholic **9** inclusive, planetary, spherical, universal, worldwide **12** encyclopedic **13** comprehensive

globe
3 orb **4** ball **5** earth, round, world **6** planet, sphere **7** rondure
half: 10 hemisphere

globule
4 ball, bead, drip, drop **6** gobbet, pellet **7** driblet, droplet **8** spherule

glom
4 grab, take **5** catch, latch, seize, steal

gloom
3 dim **4** dusk, funk, loom, murk **5** bedim, blues, cloud, dumps, frown, lower, mopes, scowl **6** darken, glower, shadow **7** becloud, despair, dimness, obscure, sadness **8** darkness, overcast, twilight **9** adumbrate, bleakness, dejection **10** blue devils, depression, melancholy, overshadow **11** despondency, unhappiness **12** mournfulness

gloomy
3 dim, dun, sad **4** cold, dark, dour, down, drab, dull, glum **5** black, bleak, drear, dusky, mopey, murky, muzzy, sulky, surly **6** dismal, dreary, morose, solemn, somber, sullen **7** forlorn, joyless, obscure, stygian, unhappy **8** dejected, desolate, downcast, funereal, mournful **9** cheerless, depressed, mirthless, oppressed, saturnine, tenebrous, woebegone **10** caliginous, chapfallen, depressing, depressive, dispirited, despondent, forbidding, lugubrious, melancholy, oppressive, tenebrific **11** dispiriting, pessimistic **12** disconsolate, discouraging

glorify
4 hymn, laud **5** bless, cry up, erect, exalt, extol, honor **6** admire, praise, revere **7** acclaim, dignify, elevate, ennoble, light up, lionize, magnify, sublime, worship **8** eulogize, venerate **9** celebrate **10** aggrandize

glorious
5 grand, great, noble, proud **6** august, divine, superb **7** eminent, exalted, radiant, sublime **8** esteemed, gorgeous, lustrous, majestic, renowned, splendid, stunning **9** beautiful, brilliant, effulgent, excellent, marvelous, ravishing, wonderful **11** illustrious, magnificent, resplendent, splendorous

glory
4 crow, fame, halo, pomp **5** exalt, exult, gloat, honor, revel **6** heaven, praise, relish, renown **7** acclaim, aureole, delight, majesty, rejoice, triumph **8** eminence, eternity, grandeur, jubilate, radiance, splendor **9** greatness, hereafter **10** effulgence, exaltation, exultation **11** distinction **12** magnificence, resplendence

gloss
4 buff **5** glaze, glint, sheen, shine **6** define, enamel, facade, finish, luster, patina, polish, veneer **7** burnish, comment, explain, furbish, varnish **8** annotate **9** interpret, sleekness, slickness, translate **10** annotation, appearance, brilliance, commentary, definition **11** elucidation, explanation, translation

glossary
7 lexicon **8** wordbook **9** word-hoard **10** dictionary, vocabulary

gloss over
4 mask **5** slant **6** veneer **7** conceal, cover up, distort, falsify, varnish **8** disguise, palliate **9** dissemble, extenuate, sugarcoat, whitewash **10** camouflage

glossy
5 glacé, shiny, sleek, slick **7** shining **8** gleaming, lustrous, polished **9** burnished **10** glistening
fabric: **4** silk **5** satin
paint: **6** enamel

glove
4 gage, mitt **5** catch, cover **6** mitten, sheath **8** covering, gauntlet

glow
4 burn, pink, rose **5** bloom, blush, flush, gleam, rouge, shine **6** mantle, redden **7** blossom, crimson, fox fire, glisten, glitter, radiate **8** brighten, radiance **10** brilliance, luminosity **13** incandescence

glower
5 frown, scowl, stare **11** look daggers

glowing
3 hot, red **4** avid **5** flush, ruddy, shiny **6** ardent, fervid, florid, heated, red-hot **7** beaming, burning, fervent, flushed, lambent, radiant, vibrant **8** blushing, dazzling, gleaming, luminous, lustrous, rubicund, sanguine, suffused **9** brilliant **10** candescent, hot-blooded, passionate **11** impassioned **12** enthusiastic, incandescent

Gluck opera
5 Orfeo **6** Armide **7** Alceste

glucose
5 sugar, syrup

glue
3 fix, gum **4** bind, join **5** epoxy, paste, stick **6** adhere, attach, cement, fasten **7** plaster, stickum **8** adhesive, mucilage

gluey
5 gummy, tacky **6** sticky, viscid **7** viscous **8** adhesive **12** mucilaginous

glum
3 sad **4** blue, dour, down **5** moody, sulky, surly **6** dismal, dreary, gloomy, morose, sullen, woeful **7** crabbed **8** brooding, dejected, downcast, taciturn **9** depressed, oppressed, saturnine, sorrowful, woebegone **10** despondent, dispirited, melancholy **11** downhearted, melancholic

glut
4 clog, cloy, cram, fill, pack, pall, sate **5** feast, flood, gorge, stuff **6** deluge, excess, stodge **7** satiate, surfeit, surplus, swallow **8** saturate **10** oversupply **13** overabundance

glutinous
4 ropy **5** gluey, gooey, gummy, pasty, tacky, thick **6** sticky, viscid **7** viscous **10** gelatinous **12** mucilaginous

glutton
3 hog, pig **8** gourmand **9** chowhound, wolverine **11** gormandizer

gluttonous
7 hoggish, piggish **8** edacious, ravening, ravenous **9** dissolute, indulgent, rapacious, voracious **10** insatiable **11** intemperate

gluttony
6 excess **7** edacity **8** gulosity, rapacity, voracity **11** piggishness

glyph
6 figure, groove, symbol **7** graphic **9** character

G-man
3 fed **4** narc, Ness (Eliot) **5** agent **6** Hoover (J. Edgar) **10** gangbuster

gnarl
4 bend, knot, warp **5** growl, snarl, twist **6** deform **7** contort, distort

gnash
4 bite **5** grind

gnat
3 bug, fly **4** pest **5** midge **6** insect, punkie **7** no-see-um

gnaw
3 eat, nag, vex **4** bite, chaw, chew **5** annoy, chomp, erode, munch, scour, tease, worry **6** bother, crunch, nibble, pester, plague, rankle **7** bedevil, corrode, eat away **8** irritate, wear away **9** masticate

gnome
3 elf, saw **4** rule **5** adage, axiom, dwarf, maxim, moral, troll, truth **6** dictum, goblin, saying, truism **7** proverb **8** aphorism, apothegm **10** shibboleth

gnostic
6 occult, secret **8** abstruse **10** mysterious

gnu
10 wildebeest

go
against: **4** defy **5** fight **6** oppose, resist **7** counter, protest **10** contradict
ahead: **4** lead **7** precede, proceed **8** continue, progress
along: **5** agree, yield **6** accede, comply, concur **7** consent **9** acquiesce
around: **5** avoid, skirt **6** bypass, detour **7** compass **8** outflank, sidestep **10** circumvent
ashore: **6** debark **9** disembark
at: **6** assail, attack, tackle **7** assault
away: **3** git **4** exit, scat, shoo **5** leave, scram, split **6** beat it, begone, cut out, depart, move on, retire **7** buzz off, get lost, pull out, take off **8** clear out, run along, shove off, withdraw **9** skedaddle
back: **6** recede, return, revert **7** regress, retreat
back on: **6** betray, renege **7** abandon **8** abrogate
back over: **6** rehash, review, rework **7** recheck, retrace
before: **4** lead **7** precede, predate **8** antedate
beyond: **4** pass **5** excel, outdo **6** exceed, outrun **7** eclipse, surpass **8** outshine, outstrip, overtake **9** transcend
forward: **6** move on, push on **7** advance, press on, proceed **8** continue, progress
in: **5** enter **9** penetrate
out: **4** exit **5** leave **6** expire
Scottish: **3** gae
through: **4** bear **5** audit, brave, check, spend **6** endure, suffer **7** consume, deplete, examine, exhaust, ride out, survive, sustain, undergo **8** squander **9** penetrate, withstand **10** experience
together: **3** fit **4** date, jibe, suit **5** agree, match, tally **6** accord, square **7** conform **8** dovetail **9** accompany, harmonize **10** correspond
with: **4** suit **5** befit, match **9** accompany

goad
3 egg, rod, sic **4** prod, push, spur, urge **5** drive, egg on, impel, prick, thorn **6** coerce, exhort, incite, motive, needle, prompt, propel **7** impetus, impulse **8** catalyst, motivate, stimulus **9** encourage, impulsion, incentive, stimulant, stimulate **10** inducement

go-ahead
4 okay **7** consent **8** spirited **9** ambitious, authority, clearance, energetic **10** green light, permission **11** progressive, up-and-coming **12** enterprising **13** authorization

goal
3 aim, end, use **4** duty, hope, mark **5** score **6** design, intent, object, target **7** mission, purpose **8** ambition, function **9** intention, objective

goat
3 kid, ram **4** lech **5** billy, letch, nanny **6** alpaca, angora, lecher, Saanen **8** cashmere **10** Toggenburg
female: **3** doe **5** nanny
genus: **5** Capra
Himalayan: **4** tahr, thar
male: **4** buck **5** billy
neutered: **6** wether
relating to: **7** caprine
wild: **4** ibex
wool: **6** mohair **8** cashmere, pashmina

goat antelope
5 serow **7** chamois

goatee
5 beard **7** Vandyke **8** imperial, whiskers

goatfish
6 mullet

goatish
3 hot **4** lewd **6** carnal **7** caprine, lustful, satyric **8** prurient **9** indulgent, lecherous, lickerish **10** lascivious, libidinous, passionate **12** concupiscent

goat-man deity
3 Pan **5** satyr **7** silenus

goat nut
6 jojoba, pignut

gob
3 wad **4** blob, clod, glob, hunk, lump, mass **5** chunk, mouth **6** nugget, sailor **7** extract

gobbet
4 drib, drip, drop, hunk, lump, mass **5** chunk, piece **7** driblet, droplet, globule, portion **8** fragment

gobble
3 eat **4** bolt, cram, grab, glut, gulp, slop, wolf **5** gorge **6** devour, guzzle **7** swallow **11** ingurgitate

gobbledygook
see **gibberish**

go-between
5 agent, envoy, proxy **6** broker, deputy, factor **7** courier, liaison **8** emissary, mediator, procurer **9** middleman **10** arbitrator, interagent, interceder, matchmaker, negotiator, procurator **11** intercessor **12** intermediary, intermediate

goblet
3 cup **5** glass, grail **6** vessel **7** chalice

goblin
3 elf, fay, hob, imp **4** puck **5** bogey, bogle, fairy, ghost, gnome **6** sprite **7** brownie, bugbear **8** bogeyman

___ go bragh
4 Erin

gobs
4 lots, tons, wads **5** heaps, loads, lumps, piles, rafts, reams, scads **6** oodles **8** slathers **10** quantities

god
4 idol **5** deity **7** creator **8** Almighty, divinity, immortal
combining form: 4 theo
false: 4 baal
French: 4 dieu
Hebrew: 6 Elohim, Yahweh
Latin: 4 deus
Spanish: 4 dios
see specific entries— **Greek, Roman,** etc.—for names of specific gods and goddesses

god-awful
4 foul **6** horrid, rotten **7** beastly **8** dreadful, horrible, shameful, shocking, terrible, wretched **9** appalling, atrocious, miserable **10** abominable, deplorable, despicable, detestable, disgusting, outrageous

God Bless America composer
6 Berlin (Irving)

goddess
4 idol **5** deity **8** divinity, immortal
Italian: 4 diva
Latin: 3 dea
(see note at **god**)

godfather
3 don **4** boss, capo **6** leader **7** sponsor

Godfather, The
8 Corleone (Don)
actor: 6 Brando (Marlon), De Niro (Robert), Pacino (Al)
author: 4 Puzo (Mario)
director: 7 Coppola (Francis Ford)

God-fearing
5 pious **6** devout **8** faithful, reverent **9** pietistic, religious, righteous

godforsaken
4 bare **5** bleak **6** barren, dismal, gloomy, remote **7** pitiful **8** deserted, desolate, pitiable, wretched **9** miserable, neglected **11** unfortunate

Godiva's husband
7 Leofric

godless
5 pagan **6** unholy, wicked **7** atheist, heathen, impious, infidel, profane **8** agnostic **9** atheistic **11** irreligious, unreligious

godlike
4 holy **6** divine **7** blessed, supreme **8** almighty, immortal **10** omniscient **11** all-powerful

godliness
5 piety **6** purity **8** devotion, divinity, holiness, sanctity **9** beatitude, reverence **10** devoutness, sacredness **11** religiosity, saintliness **12** spirituality, virtuousness

godly
4 holy **5** pious **6** devout, divine **7** angelic, blessed, saintly, supreme **8** almighty, hallowed, immortal, virtuous **9** pietistic, prayerful, religious **10** omniscient **11** all-powerful

go down
3 dip, set **4** drop, fall, fold, lose, sink **5** ensue, lower, occur, pitch, slide, slump **6** cave in, happen, plunge, settle, topple, tumble **7** crumple, decline, descend, founder, succumb **8** collapse, keel over, submerge, submerse **9** surrender, take place

God's acre
8 boneyard, catacomb, cemetery **9** graveyard **10** churchyard, necropolis **12** burial ground, memorial park, potter's field

godsend
4 boon, gift, good **5** manna **7** benefit **8** blessing, windfall **9** advantage **11** benevolence, serendipity

Goethe work
5 Faust **6** Egmont, Stella **7** Clavigo **10** Prometheus

gofer
4 aide, peon **5** toady **6** drudge, flunky, helper, lackey, menial **7** courier, servant **8** factotum **9** assistant, attendant

goffer
5 crimp, flute, pinch, plait, pleat

go-getter
6 dynamo **7** hustler, rustler **8** live wire **10** ball of fire, powerhouse **11** self-starter

goggle
3 eye **4** bore, gape, gawk, gaze, look, ogle, peer **5** glare, gloat, stare **10** rubberneck

goggles
5 specs **7** glasses **10** eyeglasses, spectacles

go-go
5 hyper **6** hectic **7** frantic **8** frenetic, frenzied

Gogol novel
novel: 9 Dead Souls
story: 8 Overcoat (The) **10** Taras Bulba
14 Diary of a Madman

goiter
6 struma **8** swelling

Golconda
see **gold mine**

gold
4 gilt **5** money **6** riches, wealth, yellow **7** bullion **8** treasure
bar: 5 ingot
combining form: 4 auri, auro **5** chrys **6** chryso
fool's: 6 pyrite
heraldic: 2 or
imitation: 6 ormolu
measure: 5 carat, karat
Spanish: 3 oro
symbol: 2 Au

goldbrick
3 bum **4** idle, laze, lazy, loaf, loll **5** cheat, dally, dog it, idler, shirk, slack **6** dawdle, loafer, loiter, lounge **7** lounger, shirker, slacker, swindle **8** lollygag, malinger, sluggard **9** lazybones **10** dillydally, malingerer

Gold Bug author
3 Poe (Edgar Allan)

gold cloth
4 lamé

gold-covered
4 gilt **6** gilded

golden
4 gilt, rich **5** auric, blond, shiny, straw **6** blonde, flaxen, gilded, mellow, superb, yellow **7** aureate, honeyed, shining **8** glorious, lustrous, resonant **9** favorable **10** auspicious, prosperous **11** flourishing

golden-ager
5 elder **6** senior **7** ancient, oldster, retiree **8** old-timer **13** senior citizen

golden-apples guardian
5 Ithun **6** Ithunn

golden bough
9 mistletoe

Golden Bough author
6 Frazer (James George)

Golden Boy playwright
5 Odets (Clifford)

golden-crowned accentor
7 warbler **8** ovenbird

goldeneye
3 bug **4** duck, fowl **6** insect **8** lacewing

Golden Fleece seeker
5 Jason **8** Argonaut

Golden Hind captain
5 Drake (Francis)

Golden Horde
6 Tatars **7** Mongols
leader: 4 Batu

golden horse
7 Trigger **8** palomino

golden shiner
4 dace, fish

Golden State
10 California

goldfinch
4 bird **8** songbird **12** yellowhammer

Golding novel
14 Lord of the Flies

gold mine
7 bonanza, pay dirt **8** El Dorado, Golconda, treasure, treasury **13** treasure trove

golem
3 oaf **4** clod, dolt, dope **5** dunce, idiot, robot **6** nitwit **7** halfwit, machine **8** imbecile **9** automaton, blockhead **10** nincompoop **11** blunderhead

golf
assistant: 5 caddy **6** caddie
ball material: 6 balata **11** gutta-percha
club: 4 iron, wood **5** billy, spoon, wedge **6** driver, mashie, putter **7** niblick, pitcher **9** metal wood, sand wedge
club part: 3 toe **4** face, grip, head, heel, neck, sole **5** hosel, shaft
course: 5 links
cup: 5 Ryder **6** Curtis, Walker
hazard: 4 trap **6** bunker **8** sand trap
score: 3 ace, par **5** bogey, eagle **6** birdie
stroke: 4 baff, chip, draw, fade, hook, putt **5** drive, pitch, shank, slice **6** sclaff
target: 3 cup, par, pin **4** flag **5** green **7** fairway
term: 3 lie, tee **4** club, fore, hole, loft **5** divot, rough, swing **6** dormie, hazard, marker, stance, stroke **8** foursome, handicap **9** backswing, downswing, flagstick

golfer
8 linksman
man: 3 Els (Ernie) **4** Aoki (Isao), Daly (John), Ford (Doug), Haas (Jay), Kite (Tom), Lyle (Sandy), Mize (Larry), Tway (Bob) **5** Boros (Julius), Faldo (Nick), Floyd (Ray), Grady (Wayne), Green (Hubert), Hagen (Walter), Hogan (Ben), Jones (Bobby), Irwin (Hale), North (Andy), Pavin (Corey), Peete (Calvin), Price (Nick), Shute

(Denny), Singh (Vijay), Snead (Sam), Woods (Tiger) **6** Casper (Billy), Graham (David), Janzen (Lee), Langer (Bernhard), Miller (Johnny), Nelson (Byron, Larry), Norman (Greg), Ouimet (Francis), Palmer (Arnold), Player (Gary), Sluman (Jeff), Sutton (Hal), Vardon (Harry), Watson (Tom) **7** Azinger (Paul), Couples (Fred), Guldahl (Ralph), Mayfair (Billy), Sarazen (Gene), Simpson (Scott), Stewart (Payne), Strange (Curtis), Trevino (Lee), Woosnam (Ian), Zoeller (Fuzzy) **8** Crenshaw (Ben), Nicklaus (Jack), Olazabal (José), Weiskopf (Tom) **9** Rodriguez (Chi Chi), Elkington (Steve) **10** Middlecoff (Cary) **11** Ballesteros (Seve)
woman: **3** Pak (Se Ri) **4** Berg (Patty), King (Betsy) **5** Baker (Kathy), Lopez (Nancy), Rawls (Betsy), Stacy (Hollis), Suggs (Louise) **6** Alcott (Amy), Carner (Joanne), Daniel (Beth), Davies (Laura), Geddes (Jane), Mallon (Meg), Merten (Lauri), Wright (Mickey) **7** Bradley (Pat), Inkster (Juli), Mochrie (Dottie), Sheehan (Patty) **8** Zaharias (Babe) **9** Didrikson (Babe), Sorenstam (Annika), Whitworth (Kathy) **10** Stephenson (Jan)

Golgotha
7 Calvary

Goliath
5 giant **10** Philistine
deathplace: **4** Elah
home: **4** Gath
slayer: **5** David

Gollum creator
7 Tolkien (J. R. R.)

gonad
5 gland, ovary **6** testis **8** testicle

gondola
3 car **4** boat **7** ski lift **11** railroad car

gone
4 away, dead, left, lost, past **5** flown **6** absent **7** defunct, extinct, lacking, missing **8** departed, vanished

gonef
see **ganef**

goner
8 dead duck **9** lost cause

Goneril
father: **4** Lear (King)
husband: **6** Albany
sister: **5** Regan **8** Cordelia
victim: **5** Regan

Gone with the Wind
author: **8** Mitchell (Margaret)
character: **5** Rhett (Butler) **6** Ashley (Wilkes) **7** Melanie (Wilkes) **8** Scarlett (O'Hara)
plantation: **4** Tara

gonfalon
4 flag, jack **6** banner, ensign **7** pendant, pennant **8** banderol, standard **9** banderole

gong
6 cymbal, tam-tam

gonzo
6 far-out **7** bizarre, offbeat **9** wigged-out **10** outrageous

goo
4 crud, glop, guck, gunk, muck **5** slime

goober
6 peanut

good
4 pure **5** right, sound, whole **6** decent, humane, kindly, worthy **7** benefit, upright, welfare **8** innocent, virtuous **9** admirable, blameless, exemplary, favorable, honorable, righteous, well-being, wholesome **10** altruistic, beneficent, beneficial, benevolent, charitable, worthwhile **11** respectable, well-behaved
French: **3** bon **5** bonne
German: **3** gut **4** gute
Spanish: **5** buena, bueno

good-bye
4 ciao, ta-ta **5** adieu, congé, later **6** so long **7** cheerio, parting, send-off, toodles **8** farewell, toodle-oo **9** departing, departure **11** leave-taking, valediction, valedictory
French: **5** adieu **8** au revoir **9** bon voyage
German: **8** lebe wohl
Italian: **11** arrivederci
Japanese: **8** sayonara
Spanish: **5** adios **10** hasta luego **12** hasta la vista

Good Earth
author: **4** Buck (Pearl S.)
heroine: **4** O-lan

good-for-nothing
3 bum **6** rascal, waster **7** inutile, rounder, useless, wastrel **8** fainéant, feckless, rascally, unworthy **9** dissolute, scoundrel, valueless, worthless **10** ne'er-do-well, profligate, scapegrace **11** purposeless

good-looking
4 cute, fair, foxy **5** bonny, dishy, hunky **6** comely, lovely, pretty **8** alluring, drop-dead, fetching, handsome, stunning **9** beauteous, beautiful, bodacious, ravishing **10** attractive

goodly
4 fair, tidy **5** ample, hefty, large **7** sizable **8** generous **9** bountiful, plentiful **11** significant, substantial **12** considerable

good-natured
4 easy, kind, mild, warm **6** genial, jovial, mellow **7** affable, amiable, cordial, lenient **8** cheerful,

friendly, laid-back, obliging, pleasant, pleasing, sanguine **9** agreeable, congenial, easygoing, gemütlich **10** altruistic, benevolent, charitable **11** complaisant

goodness
5 honor, merit, worth **6** purity, virtue **7** decency, honesty, probity, quality **8** morality **9** integrity, rectitude **11** benevolence

goods
4 gear **5** cargo, stock, stuff, wares **7** effects **8** chattels, movables, property **9** vendibles **10** belongings **11** commodities, merchandise, possessions **13** paraphernalia
smuggled: **10** contraband
stolen: **4** loot, swag **5** booty **6** boodle, spoils **7** plunder
thrown overboard: **5** lagan **6** jetsam

good-tasting
5 sapid, yummy **6** delish, savory, toothy **8** luscious **9** delicious, palatable, relishing, toothsome **10** appetizing, delectable, flavorsome **11** scrumptious **13** mouthwatering

goodwill
5 amity, favor **6** comity **7** charity, rapport **8** altruism, kindness, sympathy **9** tolerance **10** compassion, friendship, generosity, kindliness **11** benevolence, helpfulness **12** friendliness

goody
5 candy, treat **6** bonbon, dainty, morsel, tidbit **8** delicacy, kickshaw

goody-goody
4 prig **5** prude **6** Grundy **7** prudish, puritan, uptight **8** bluenose, Comstock, priggish **9** Mrs. Grundy, nice-nelly **11** puritanical

gooey
5 gluey, gummy, mushy, sappy, soupy **6** cloggy, drippy, slushy, sticky, viscid **7** maudlin, viscous **8** adhesive **9** glutinous **11** sentimental **12** mucilaginous

goof
3 err, kid **4** boob, dolt, flub, fool, mess, muff, slip **5** boner, booby, botch, chump, dunce, error, fluff, gaffe, gum up, idiot, put on **6** bobble, boggle, bollix, boo-boo, bumble, bungle, fumble, mess up, slip-up **7** blooper, blunder, fathead, louse up, mistake **8** dolthead, lunkhead **9** blockhead

go off
4 blow **5** blast, burst, erupt, leave, sound **6** blow up, depart **7** explode **8** detonate

goofy
5 balmy, batty, crazy, daffy, dippy, loony, nutty, potty, silly **6** simple, stupid **7** foolish, idiotic **9** ludicrous **10** ridiculous **11** harebrained

gook
4 crud, glop, gunk, muck **5** gumbo, slime **6** debris, sludge

go on
4 last, stay **5** occur **6** endure, happen, keep up **7** persist, proceed **8** continue **9** persevere

goon
3 oaf, sap **4** boob, dodo, dolt, dope, fool, hood, thug **5** dummy, idiot **6** dimwit, hit man, nitwit **7** hoodlum **8** dumbbell, enforcer **10** triggerman

gooney
7 seabird **9** albatross

goop
4 crud, gunk, muck **5** gumbo, tripe

Goops author
7 Burgess (Gelett)

goose
4 poke, spur **9** stimulate
cry: **4** honk **5** clang
formation: **3** vee **5** skein, wedge **6** gaggle
genus: **5** Anser
Hawaiian: **4** nene
male: **6** gander
wild: **5** brant **7** greylag **8** barnacle
young: **7** gosling

gooseberry
7 currant

Goosebumps author
5 Stine (R. L.)

goose egg
3 nil, nix, zip **4** nada, zero **5** aught, zilch **6** bubkes, bupkes, bupkus, cipher, naught, nought **7** no score, nothing

gooseflesh
5 bumps **7** pimples

go over
4 scan, skim **5** study **6** peruse, review **7** examine, inspect

gopher
6 rodent **8** tortoise

Gopher State
9 Minnesota

Gordian knot cutter
9 Alexander

Gordius' son
5 Midas

gore
3 jab **4** stab **5** blood, slime, wound **6** gusset, pierce **7** carnage **12** gruesomeness

gorge
3 gap **4** cloy, fill, glut, jade, pall, sate **5** abyss, chasm, cleft, clove, flume, gulch, stuff **6** arroyo, canyon, clough, defile, pig out, ravine **7** couloir, overeat, satiate, surfeit **11** overindulge
Arizona: **11** Grand Canyon
Colorado: **5** Royal

gorgeous
5 grand, plush **6** comely, lavish, lovely, pretty, superb **7** opulent, sublime **8** alluring, dazzling, glorious, splendid **9** beautiful, brilliant, exquisite, luxurious, sumptuous **10** attractive, glittering **11** magnificent, resplendent, splendorous

gorgon
3 hag **5** crone, harpy, witch **6** Medusa, ogress, virago **8** battle-ax, fishwife, harridan, slattern **9** battle-axe, termagant
father: 7 Phorcus, Phorcys
mother: 4 Ceto

gorilla
3 ape **4** goon, hood, thug **5** tough **6** simian **7** primate **8** gangster **10** anthropoid

Gorky drama
11 Lower Depths (The)

gormless
4 dumb, slow **6** stupid

gorse
4 whin **5** furze, shrub **6** legume

gory
5 lurid **6** bloody, grisly **8** gruesome, sanguine **10** sanguinary **11** ensanguined, sanguineous, sensational **12** bloodstained **13** bloodcurdling

gosh
3 gee, wow **4** dang, darn, drat, egad, geez, heck **5** golly **6** crikey, cripes, shucks **7** doggone **8** goodness, gracious

gospel
5 truth **6** truism **7** message **8** doctrine **9** scripture **11** evangelical

gossamer
4 airy, film, fine, webs **5** filmy, gauzy, sheer **6** flimsy **7** cobwebs, tenuous **8** delicate **10** diaphanous **11** transparent

gossip
4 blab, buzz, chat, dirt, dish, talk **5** clack, prate, rumor, yenta **6** babble, rumble, tattle **7** babbler, chatter, hearsay, prattle, tattler **8** bigmouth, busybody, informer, prattler, quidnunc, telltale **10** talebearer **11** rumormonger, scandalizer, scuttlebutt **12** blatherskite

gossipy
5 gabby, talky **6** chatty **8** babbling, blabbing **9** garrulous, talkative

Gotham
7 New York (City)

Gothic
4 dark, wild **5** crude **6** brutal, coarse, savage **7** uncouth **8** barbaric, Germanic, medieval, Teutonic **9** barbarian, barbarous, sans serif **11** black letter, uncivilized

Götterdämmerung composer
6 Wagner (Richard)

Gouda
6 cheese

gouge
3 dig **4** milk, ream, tool **5** cheat, exact, pinch, screw, wrest, wring **6** chisel, coerce, extort, groove, wrench **7** squeeze **8** scoop out **9** blackmail, extortion, shake down **10** overcharge

goulash
4 olio, stew **6** jumble, medley **7** mélange **8** mishmash **9** potpourri **10** bridge hand, hodgepodge, hotchpotch, salmagundi **11** gallimaufry

go under
4 fall, flop, fold, lose, sink **5** drown **6** plunge, submit **7** founder, immerse, succumb **8** collapse, submerge, submerse **9** surrender **10** capitulate

Gounod work
5 Faust **8** Ave Maria

gourd
4 pepo **5** fruit, melon **6** bottle, squash, vessel **7** chayote, gherkin, pumpkin **8** calabash, cucumber, cucurbit
instrument: 6 maraca

gourmand
see **glutton; gourmet**

gourmet
7 epicure **9** bon vivant, epicurean **10** gastronome **11** connoisseur **12** gastronomist

gout
4 blob, clot, gush **5** spurt **6** splash **7** disease, podagra **8** eruption, swelling

govern
4 head, lead, rule **5** guide, order, reign, steer **6** direct, manage, master **7** command, conduct, control, execute, oversee **8** dominate, hold sway, regulate **9** supervise **10** administer **11** superintend

governess
5 nanny, nurse **6** duenna **8** mistress **9** nursemaid **10** babysitter **11** Mary Poppins

government
4 rule **5** power **6** polity, regime **7** regency, regimen **8** monarchy, republic, Uncle Sam **9** authority, autocracy, democracy, hierarchy, oligarchy **10** Big Brother **11** aristocracy, sovereignty
autocratic: 7 czarism, fascism, tyranny **9** despotism **10** absolutism **12** dictatorship
by a few: 9 oligarchy
by one: 8 monarchy
by three: 8 triarchy **11** triumvirate
by women: 8 gynarchy
official: 10 bureaucrat **11** functionary
without: 7 anarchy

government agency
3 ATF, BIA, BLM, CDC, CIA, DEA, EPA, FAA, FBI, FCC, FDA, FEC, FHA, GAO, GPO, HUD, ICC, INS, IRS, NBS, NEA, NIH, NRC, TVA **4** FDIC, FEMA, FEPC, NASA, NOAA, NTSB, OSHA

governor
3 bey, dey **4** head **5** chief, nabob, ruler **6** leader, regent **7** manager, viceroy **8** director **9** executive, regulator **10** commandant, magistrate
Chinese: **6** tuchun
of a fort: **7** alcaide, alcayde **9** castellan, chatelain
Persian: **6** satrap

gown
4 robe, toga **5** dress, frock, habit, tunic **6** camise, kimono, kirtle, mantua **7** cassock, chemise **8** peignoir
dressing: **8** bathrobe
hospital: **6** johnny

goy
6 non-Jew **7** gentile

grab
3 nab **4** glom, grip, snag, take **5** catch, clasp, grasp, pluck, seize **6** clutch, collar, snatch, tackle **7** capture, grapple, seizure

grabby
6 greedy **8** covetous, desirous, grasping **9** rapacious **10** avaricious, prehensile **11** acquisitive

grace
4 ease **5** adorn, charm, favor, mercy, poise **6** allure, lenity, pardon, polish, prayer, thanks, virtue **7** charity, dignify, dignity, enhance **8** approval, blessing, clemency, easiness, elegance, goodness, kindness, leniency, petition, reprieve **9** embellish, privilege **10** indulgence, invocation, refinement **11** benediction, forbearance **12** thanksgiving

graceful
4 airy, deft, easy **5** lithe **6** nimble, poised, smooth **7** elegant, flowing **8** debonair, polished

graceless
4 rude **5** crude, gawky, inept **6** clumsy, coarse, gauche, klutzy, vulgar **7** awkward, boorish, uncouth **8** barbaric, ungainly **9** barbarian, barbarous **10** outlandish, unmannered **12** infelicitous

Graces
6 Charis **8** Charites (plural)
brilliance: **6** Aglaia
bloom: **6** Thalia
joy: **10** Euphrosyne
mother: **5** Aegle

gracious
4 kind **5** suave **6** benign, genial, kindly, urbane **7** affable, amiable, cordial, courtly, gallant, stately, tactful **8** charming, generous, mannered, merciful, obliging, sociable **9** congenial, courteous **11** complaisant, good-natured **13** compassionate

grackle
4 myna **5** mynah **7** jackdaw **8** starling **9** blackbird

gradation
4 rank, step **5** order, range, scale, shade, stage **6** ablaut, change, degree, nuance, series **8** ordering, position, spectrum **9** continuum, variation **10** difference, succession

grade
3 peg **4** cant, form, kind, lean, mark, rank, rate, rung, sort, step, tier, tilt **5** blend, class, group, level, notch, order, pitch, place, slant, slope, stage **6** assess, assort, degree, league, rating **7** arrange, caliber, echelon, incline, leaning, quality **8** appraise, category, classify, division, evaluate, grouping, position, standard **10** categorize **11** inclination

Grade A
3 ace, top **4** best, boss, fine, tops **5** grand, great, prime, primo, super **6** choice, tip-top **7** capital, supreme **8** five-star, superior, top-notch **9** excellent, first-rate, nonpareil, number one, top-drawer **10** first-class **11** outstanding **13** par excellence

gradient
4 lean, ramp, rise, tilt **5** angle, pitch, slant, slope **7** incline, leaning **9** acclivity, declivity **11** inclination

gradual
4 even, slow **6** Psalms, steady **7** ongoing **8** bit-by-bit, creeping **9** piecemeal, prolonged **10** continuous, developing, protracted, step-by-step **11** progressive

gradually
6 slowly **7** by steps **8** bit by bit **9** by degrees, piecemeal **10** step by step **12** deliberately **13** imperceptibly, incrementally

graduate
4 alum
acquisition: **6** degree **7** diploma
female: **6** alumna **7** alumnae (plural)
male: **6** alumni (plural) **7** alumnus

Graeae, Graiae
4 Enyo **5** Deino **8** Pephredo
father: **7** Phorcus, Phorcys
mother: **4** Ceto
sisters: **7** Gorgons

graffiti artist
6 tagger
signature: **3** tag

graft
3 imp **4** join, mend, scam, skim **5** affix, crime, fraud, scion, unite **6** attach, boodle, fasten, payola, splice **7** implant, swindle, topwork **8** kickback **10** corruption

Grafton character
8 Millhone (Kinsey)

Grahame, Kenneth
character: **3** Rat **4** Toad, Mole **6** Badger
novel: **16** Wind in the Willows (The)

grail
3 cup, end **4** goal **6** goblet, object, target **7** chalice **9** objective
seeker: **7** Galahad

grain
3 bit, jot, rye **4** corn, flax, iota, meal, mite, oats, rice **5** crumb, fiber, kamut, maize, speck, spelt, trace, wheat **6** barley, cereal, millet, quinoa, tittle **7** granule, smidgen, sorghum, texture **8** amaranth, molecule, particle **9** buckwheat, triticale
beard: **3** awn
bundle: **4** bale **5** sheaf
chute: **6** hopper
ear: **5** spike
elevator: **4** silo
mixture: **6** fodder
row: **5** swath **7** windrow

grainy
5 rough **6** coarse **8** granular **10** unfinished, unpolished

grammarian
7 Donatus (Aelius)

grammatical case
6 dative **7** oblique **8** ablative, genitive, locative, vocative **9** objective **10** accusative, nominative, possessive, subjective

grampus
3 orc **5** whale **7** dolphin **8** cetacean, porpoise, scorpion **9** blackfish **12** whip scorpion

Granada
building: **8** Alhambra
citadel: **8** Alcazaba
last Moorish king: **7** Boabdil

granary
3 bin **4** silo **10** repository, storehouse

grand
3 fab **4** epic, fine, huge, vast **5** gaudy, lofty, noble, regal, royal, showy, super **6** august, garish, lavish, lordly, mighty, ornate, superb **7** exalted, opulent, pompous, stately, sublime **8** baronial, elevated, gorgeous, imposing, majestic, princely, splendid **9** first-rate, inclusive, luxurious, sumptuous, wonderful **10** first-class, impressive, monumental, prodigious, stupendous, tremendous **11** magnificent **12** ostentatious

Grand Canyon
explorer: **6** Powell (John Wesley)
state: **7** Arizona

grande dame
5 queen **6** matron **7** dowager, doyenne **9** matriarch

grandee
4 duke, earl, king, lord, peer **5** baron, noble, pasha **6** bashaw, prince **8** mandarin, marquess, nobleman, viscount **10** panjandrum **11** muckety-muck

grandeur
4 pomp **5** glory **7** dignity, majesty **8** nobility, opulence, splendor, vastness **9** greatness, immensity, largeness, loftiness, nobleness, sublimity **10** augustness **11** stateliness **12** magnificence

grandiloquent
5 lofty **7** aureate, bloated, fustian, orotund, pompous **8** inflated **9** bombastic, flatulent, high-flown, overblown **10** histrionic, portentous **11** declamatory, highfalutin, pretentious **12** magniloquent

grand inquisitor
10 Torquemada (Tomás de)

grandiose
4 epic, vast **5** lofty, noble, regal, royal, showy **6** august, cosmic, lavish, lordly **7** pompous, stately, sublime, utopian **8** affected, imposing, majestic, princely, splendid **9** ambitious, high-flown **11** extravagant, highfalutin, magnificent, pretentious **12** ostentatious

grand mal
7 seizure **8** epilepsy

grandmother
4 nana
Russian: **8** babushka

grange
4 farm **9** farmhouse, farmstead

granite
3 ore **4** rock **5** stone **6** aplite **7** mineral **11** igneous rock

Granite State
12 New Hampshire

grant
3 aid **4** alms, avow, cede, dole, gift, give **5** admit, allow, award, endow, yield **6** accord, assert, assign, assume, bestow, confer, convey, donate, permit **7** charity, concede, consent, entitle, handout, present, subsidy, suppose **8** bequeath, donation, property, transfer **9** endowment, vouchsafe **10** assistance, concession, relinquish, subvention **11** acknowledge, benefaction **12** contribution **13** appropriation

granular
5 rough, sandy **6** coarse, grainy **7** powdery **8** powdered **10** unfinished, unpolished

granule
3 bit, jot **4** iota, pill, spot **5** grain **6** pellet **8** fragment, particle

grape
3 fox, uva **4** Bual **5** Gamay, Pinot, Syrah **6** Arinto, Burger, Gentil, merlot, muscat, Shiraz **7** Albillo, Aligote, Barbera, Catawba, Concord, Furmint, Niagara, sultana **8** Aleatico, Cabernet, Charbono, Delaware, Friularo, Grenache, Isabella, malvasia, muscadel, Muscadet, Nebbiolo, Riesling, Semillon, Sylvaner, Thompson, Traminer, vinifera, Viognier **9** Carmenère, Chasselas, Lambrusco, Malvoisie, muscadine, Pinot Gris, pinot noir, Sauvignon, Trebbiano, zinfandel **10** chardonnay, Grignolino, muscadelle, pinot blanc, Sangiovese, Verdicchio **11** Chenin Blanc, Petite Sirah, pinot grigio, scuppernong
disease: **4** esca
dried: **6** raisin
drink: **4** wine
pulp: **4** rape **6** pomace
residue: **4** marc

grapefruit
6 pomelo

Grapes of Wrath, The
author: **9** Steinbeck (John)
family: **4** Joad
people: **5** Okies

grapevine
4 buzz **5** rumor **6** gossip **7** hearsay **9** rumor mill **11** scuttlebutt

graph
3 map **4** plot **5** chart **6** sketch **7** diagram, outline **8** nomogram, pie chart

graphic
3 map **5** clear, lucid, photo, vivid **6** cogent, visual **7** picture, precise, telling, written **8** clear-cut, definite, detailed, explicit, incisive, striking **9** pictorial, realistic **10** compelling, photograph **11** descriptive, picturesque

graphite
4 lead **6** carbon **8** plumbago

grapnel
4 hook **6** anchor

grappa
6 brandy

grapple
3 nab **4** bind, cope, grab, grip, hold **5** catch, clamp, clasp, fight, grasp, seize **6** battle, bucket, clench, clinch, clutch, fasten, tackle, tussle **7** contest, scuffle, wrestle **8** struggle

grasp
3 dig, ken, see **4** glom, grip, hold, know, take **5** catch, clamp, clasp, cling, seize **6** accept, clench, clinch, clutch, fathom, follow, handle, take in, tenure **7** cognize, compass, control, embrace, grapple, realize **8** envisage, perceive **9** apprehend, awareness **10** appreciate, comprehend, take hold of, understand **12** apprehension **13** comprehension, understanding

graspable
5 clear, lucid **6** lucent **8** coherent, knowable, palpable **10** fathomable **11** perspicuous **12** intelligible **13** apprehensible

grasping
4 avid **6** grabby, greedy **8** covetous, desirous **9** rapacious **10** avaricious, prehensile **11** acquisitive

grass
3 Poa, pot, sod, tea, Zea **4** lawn, reed, turf, weed **6** redtop **7** herbage, panicum, pasture **8** cannabis, Mary Jane **9** cocksfoot, marijuana
African: **6** imphee
annual: **6** darnel **8** teosinte
Asian: **7** vetiver, whangee
Australian: **8** spinifex
beach: **6** marram
cereal: **3** oat, rye, Zea **4** milo, teff **5** kafir, maize, proso, sorgo, wheat **6** millet **7** sorghum **8** triticum
clump: **4** tuft **7** tussock
cover: **3** dew
dried: **3** hay **5** straw
European: **7** Bermuda, timothy
fiber: **4** flax
fragrant: **10** citronella
meadow: **3** Poa
pasture: **5** Bahia, grama
perennial: **6** fescue, quitch, zoysia **7** esparto, galleta
prairie: **8** bluestem
second growth: **5** rowen
tropical: **5** cogon **6** bamboo

grasshopper
6 locust **7** katydid **8** cocktail

grassland
3 lea **5** field **6** meadow **7** pasture, prairie
African: **4** veld **5** veldt
flat: **7** savanna **8** savannah
South American: **5** pampa **6** pampas

Grass novel
7 Tin Drum (The) **8** Dog Years, Flounder (The) **11** Cat and Mouse

grate
3 irk, jar, rub, vex **4** file, fray, fret, gall, rasp, rile **5** annoy, chafe, gnash, grill, grind, peeve, pique **6** abrade, grille, nettle, rankle, scrape **7** provoke, scratch **8** irritate **9** aggravate, fireplace

grateful
7 obliged, pleased, restful, welcome **8** beholden, indebted, pleasant, pleasing, thankful **9** agreeable, congenial, favorable **10** refreshing **11** restorative **12** appreciative

Gratiano
brother: **9** Brabantio
friend: **7** Antonio **8** Bassanio
niece: **9** Desdemona
wife: **7** Nerissa

gratify
4 baby, sate **5** favor, humor, spoil **6** coddle, oblige, pamper, pander, please **7** appease, cater to, content, delight, gladden, indulge, satisfy

gratin
5 crust

grating
3 dry **4** grid, rasp **5** grill, harsh, rough **6** grille, hoarse **7** irksome, jarring, lattice, rasping, raucous **8** gridiron, strident **9** vexatious **10** stridulous

gratis
4 comp, free **6** comped **8** costless **10** chargeless **13** complimentary

gratitude
6 thanks **12** appreciation, gratefulness, thankfulness

gratuitous
6 wanton **8** baseless **9** unfounded, voluntary **10** groundless, reasonless, ungrounded **11** uncalled-for, unnecessary, unwarranted **12** indefensible

gratuity
3 tip **4** gift, perk **5** bonus **6** reward **7** cumshaw, douceur **8** donation, largesse, offering **9** baksheesh, lagniappe, pourboire **10** perquisite **11** benefaction **12** contribution

grave
3 pit, sad **4** dire, dour, fell, grim, tomb **5** acute, awful, crypt, fatal, heavy, major, sober, staid, vault **6** burial, deadly, gloomy, sedate, severe, solemn, somber, sombre, urgent **7** austere, ghastly, ominous, ossuary, serious, subdued, weighty **8** catacomb, critical, dreadful, perilous, pressing, terrible **9** dangerous, mausoleum, momentous, ponderous, saturnine, sepulcher, sepulchre, sepulture, unsmiling
marker: **5** stela, stele **8** memorial, monument **9** footstone, headstone, tombstone **11** sarcophagus
mound: **6** barrow **7** tumulus
robber: **5** ghoul

gravel
4 dirt, grit, sand
ridge: **5** esker

gravelly
5 raspy, rough **6** gritty, hoarse **7** rasping, grating **8** abrasive, granular, guttural, scratchy

graven image
4 icon, idol

graver
4 tool **5** burin **8** sculptor

graveyard
8 boot hill, catacomb, cemetery, God's acre **10** necropolis **12** burial ground, memorial park, potter's field

gravid
5 heavy **8** enceinte, pregnant **9** expectant, expecting, with child **10** parturient **12** childbearing

gravity
5 force **6** weight **7** dignity, urgency **8** sobriety **9** heaviness, solemnity **10** importance, somberness **11** consequence, seriousness **12** significance

gravlax
3 lox **6** salmon

gravy
4 perk **5** bonus, bribe, graft, juice, sauce **6** payola **8** dressing, windfall
French: **3** jus

gray
3 ash, old **4** aged, ashy, blah, drab, dull **5** ashen, bleak, color, hoary, slate, slaty **6** dismal, gloomy, leaden **7** elderly, grizzly, neutral **8** grizzled, gunmetal, overcast **9** cinereous, colorless
brownish: **3** dun **5** taupe **7** fuscous

gray duck
7 gadwall, pintail

grayfish
5 shark **7** dogfish

gray matter
3 wit **4** head, mind **5** brain **6** brains, noddle, noggin, noodle **8** cerebrum **9** intellect **10** encephalon **12** intelligence, neural tissue

graze
3 eat, rub **4** feed, gall, kiss, skim, skip, wear **5** brush, chafe, erode, shave, touch **6** abrade, browse, bruise, forage, glance, scrape **7** contuse, corrade, pasture **8** abrasion, ricochet

grazier
7 rancher

grease
3 fat, oil **4** lard **5** smear **6** smooth **7** lanolin **9** lubricant, lubricate
combining form: **4** sebi, sebo

greasy
4 oily **5** fatty, slick **8** slippery, unctuous **10** lubricious, oleaginous

greasy spoon
4 café **5** diner, grill **6** eatery **7** beanery, hashery **9** chophouse, hash house, lunchroom **10** coffee shop **12** luncheonette

great
3 big, fat **4** huge, vast **5** boffo, grand, jumbo, large, noble, socko **6** famous, heroic **7** awe-

some, eminent, exalted, immense, mammoth, notable, sublime, supreme, titanic **8** colossal, enormous, gigantic, glorious, renowned, terrific, towering **9** excellent, fantastic, humongous, paramount, prominent, wonderful **10** celebrated, impressive, noteworthy, prodigious, remarkable, stupendous, tremendous **11** illustrious, magnificent, outstanding, superlative **13** distinguished
combining form: **4** mega **6** megalo

Great Bear
9 Big Dipper, Ursa Major **13** constellation

Great Britain
see **England, United Kingdom**

Great Commoner, the
4 Pitt (William) **5** Bryan (William Jennings) **7** Lincoln (Abraham)

Great Emancipator, the
7 Lincoln (Abraham)

greater
4 more **5** metro **6** better, bigger, higher, larger **8** superior **9** exceeding **10** surpassing **12** metropolitan

greatest
4 best, most **6** utmost **7** maximum, supreme **8** foremost

Great Expectations
author: **7** Dickens (Charles)
character: **3** Joe (Gargery), Pip **5** Biddy **7** Estella, Jaggers **8** Havisham (Miss), Magwitch (Abel)

greathearted
4 bold, kind **5** brave, lofty, noble **6** heroic **7** gallant **8** fearless, generous, princely **10** benevolent, chivalrous, courageous, high-minded **11** considerate, magnanimous

Great Lake
4 Erie **5** Huron **7** Ontario **8** Michigan, Superior
acronym: **5** HOMES

Great Lake State
8 Michigan

greave
7 legging

grebe
4 bird, fowl **8** dabchick **10** diving bird

Greece **6 Hellas**
ancient city-state: **5** Argos **6** Athens, Sparta, Thebes **7** Corinth
ancient town: **6** Delphi
capital: **6** Athens
city: **6** Patras **7** Larissa, Piraeus **8** Salonika **12** Thessaloníki
conqueror: **6** Philip (of Macedonia) **9** Alexander (the Great)
island, island group: **5** Crete **6** Aegean, Euboea, Ionian **8** Cyclades, Sporades
monetary unit: **4** euro
monetary unit, former: **6** lepton **7** drachma
mountain, range: **3** Ida **4** Ossa **5** Athos **6** Pelion, Pindus **7** Olympus **9** Parnassus
neighbor: **6** Turkey **7** Albania **8** Bulgaria **9** Macedonia
part of: **7** Balkans
peninsula: **6** Balkan **10** Chalcidice **11** Peloponnese
region: **6** Attica, Epirus, Thrace **8** Thessaly
sea: **6** Aegean, Ionian **13** Mediterranean
vale: **5** Tempe

greed
4 lust **6** excess, hunger **7** avarice, avidity, craving **7** edacity, longing **8** cupidity, gluttony, rapacity, voracity **12** covetousness, ravenousness

greedy
4 avid **5** itchy **6** grabby **7** hoggish, miserly, selfish **8** covetous, desirous, edacious, esurient, grasping **10** avaricious, gluttonous **11** acquisitive

Greek
6 Argive, babble, drivel, jabber **7** Achaean, Hellene **8** Hellenic, nonsense **9** gibberish
assembly: **5** agora, boule
cheese: **4** feta
coin: **4** obol **6** lepton, stater
column: **5** Doric, Ionic **10** Corinthian
contest: **4** agon
counselor: **6** Nestor
dictator: **7** Metaxas (Ioannis)
dragon: **9** Eurythion
drink: **4** ouzo
epic: **5** Iliad **7** Odyssey
Fates: **6** Clotho, Moirae **7** Atropos **8** Lachesis
gift: **11** Trojan Horse
god:
chief: **4** Zeus
messenger: **6** Hermes
of agriculture: **6** Cronus
of death: **8** Thanatos
of dreams: **8** Morpheus
of fire: **10** Hephaestus
of healing: **9** Asclepius **11** Aesculapius
of love: **4** Eros
of marriage: **5** Hymen
of the sun: **6** Apollo
of physicians: **6** Hermes
of sleep: **6** Hypnos
of the sea: **6** Nereus, Triton **7** Oceanus **8** Poseidon
of the sun: **6** Helios
of the underworld: **5** Pluto
of the winds: **5** Eurus, Notus **6** Aeolus, Boreas **8** Zephyrus
of war: **4** Ares
of wine: **8** Dionysus
of woods: **3** Pan

goddess:
of agriculture: **7** Demeter
of beauty: **9** Aphrodite
of dawn: **3** Eos
of discord: **4** Eris
of fertility: **6** Cybele
of flowers: **7** Chloris
of fortune: **5** Tyche
of harvests: **4** Rhea
of hunting: **7** Artemis
of justice: **7** Astraea
of love: **9** Aphrodite
of marriage: **4** Hera
of night: **3** Nyx
of peace: **5** Irene
of retribution: **7** Nemesis
of ruin: **3** Ate
of the earth: **4** Gaea, Gaia
of the hearth: **6** Hestia
of magic: **6** Hecate, Hekate
of the moon: **6** Hecate, Hekate, Selena, Selene **7** Artemis, Astarte
of the rainbow: **4** Iris
of the seasons: **5** Horae
of the underworld: **6** Hecate, Hekate **10** Persephone
of vengeance: **7** Nemesis
of victory: **4** Nike
of wisdom: **6** Athena
of witchcraft: **6** Hecate, Hekate
of womanhood: **4** Hera
of youth: **4** Hebe
hero: **4** Aias, Ajax **5** Jason **7** Theseus **8** Achilles, Argonaut, Heracles, Hercules, Odysseus **9** Achilleus
historian: **8** Xenophon **9** Herodotus **10** Thucydides
lawgiver: **5** Draco, Solon
leader: **9** Agamemnon
letter: **2** mu, nu, pi, xi **3** chi, eta, phi, psi, rho, tau **4** beta, iota, zeta **5** alpha, delta, gamma, kappa, omega, sigma, theta **6** lambda **7** epsilon, omicron, upsilon
magistrate: **6** archon
marketplace: **5** agora
physician: **5** Galen
porch: **4** stoa
sandwich: **4** gyro
soldier: **7** hoplite
theater: **5** odeon, odeum
underworld: **5** Hades
war cry: **5** alala
warrior: **4** Ajax **7** Ulysses **8** Achilles, Diomedes, Odysseus **9** Agamemnon, Palamedes
weeper: **5** Niobe
wine: **7** retsina

green
3 raw **4** jade, lime, moss **5** alive, fresh, kelly, leafy, naive, virid, young **6** callow, forest, unripe **7** avocado, celadon, emerald, envious, untried, verdant **8** immature, juvenile, unversed, youthful **9** unfledged **10** unseasoned **11** unpracticed **13** inexperienced
bluish: **8** glaucous
combining form: **4** verd **6** chloro
grayish: **5** olive
heraldry: **4** vert
yellowish: **7** luteous **10** chartreuse

greenbacks
4 cash, jack, loot **5** bread, bucks, dough, lucre, money, moola **6** moolah, wampum **7** dollars, scratch **8** currency, smackers **11** legal tender

green beryl
7 emerald

greenery
7 foliage, leafage **8** verdancy

green-eyed
7 envious, jealous **9** invidious
monster: **8** jealousy

greenfly
5 aphid

greengage
4 plum

greenhead
3 fly **8** horsefly

greenheart
6 laurel **9** evergreen

greenhorn
4 babe, hick, jake, naïf, rube, tiro, tyro **6** newbie, novice, rookie **7** ingenue **8** beginner, neophyte, newcomer **10** provincial

greenhouse
7 nursery **12** conservatory

Greenland
capital: **4** Nuuk **7** Godthåb
city: **5** Thule
ethnic group: **5** Inuit **6** Eskimo
explorer: **4** Eric (the Red), Erik (the Red), Leif (Eriksson) **9** Rasmussen (Knud)
language: **6** Danish
monetary unit: **5** krone
possession of: **7** Denmark

green light
2 OK **3** nod **4** okay **5** leave **6** assent **7** consent, go-ahead, mandate **8** approval, blessing, sanction, thumbs-up **9** authority, clearance **10** permission **11** endorsement **13** authorization

Green Mansions
author: **6** Hudson (W. H.)
character: **4** Rima

green monkey
6 guenon, simian, vervet

Green Mountain State
7 Vermont
greenness
5 youth **6** spring **7** puberty **8** verdancy, viridity **9** youthhood **10** immaturity, juvenility, pubescence, springtide, springtime **11** adolescence **12** inexperience
green osier
6 willow **7** dogwood
green plover
7 lapwing **9** shorebird
greenroom
6 lounge
greenstone
4 jade **7** diabase **8** nephrite **9** tremolite **10** actinolite
greet
3 bow **4** hail, meet **6** accost, call to, salaam, salute **7** address, react to, receive, welcome
greeting
3 ave, bow, nod **4** ahoy, ciao, g'day, hail **5** aloha, hello, howdy **6** salaam, salute **7** address, welcome **9** handshake, reception **10** salutation
gregarious
6 clubby, genial, social **7** affable **8** outgoing, sociable **9** clubbable, congenial, convivial **11** extroverted **13** companionable
gremlin
3 bug, elf, imp **5** dwarf, gnome **6** defect, glitch **7** brownie
Grenada
capital: 9 St. George's
discoverer: 8 Columbus (Christopher)
former name: 10 Concepción
location: 10 West Indies
nickname: 11 Isle of Spice
grenade
4 bomb **5** shell **7** missile **9** explosive, pineapple
grenadier
7 rattail, soldier
grenadine
4 pink, yarn **5** syrup **6** fabric **9** carnation
Grendel's slayer
7 Beowulf
Gretchen's lover
5 Faust
greylag
5 goose
grid
3 net **5** grate, grill **6** grille **7** grating, lattice, network, trellis
griddle
3 pan **5** grill
griddle cake
7 hotcake, pancake **8** flapjack
gridiron
3 net **5** field, grate, grill **7** grating, network
grief
3 rue, woe **4** care **5** agony, dolor, gloom, tears **6** mishap, regret, sorrow **7** anguish, chagrin, sadness, trouble **8** disaster, distress, hardship **9** adversity, heartache, suffering **10** affliction, heartbreak, misfortune **11** despondency
Grieg work
8 Peer Gynt
grievance
4 beef **5** cross, gripe, trial, wrong **6** burden, grouse, injury, squawk **8** hardship, jeremiad **9** complaint, injustice **10** affliction, allegation, unfairness **11** tribulation
grieve
3 cry **4** ache, keen, moan, wail, weep **5** mourn **6** burden, lament, sadden, sorrow, suffer **7** afflict, agonize **8** distress
grievous
3 sad **4** dire, fell, sore **5** cruel, grave, great, major **6** bitter, severe, taxing, tragic, woeful **7** galling, heinous, onerous, painful, serious, weighty **9** egregious **10** abominable, burdensome, calamitous, deplorable, lamentable, oppressive **11** distressing, regrettable, troublesome, unfortunate **12** heartrending
grift
3 con, gyp **4** bilk, rook **7** defraud, swindle **8** flimflam
grifter
3 gyp **5** cheat, crook, thief **6** con man, gouger **7** cheater, scammer, sharper, slicker **8** swindler **9** defrauder, trickster **13** confidence man
grill
3 fry, vex **4** cook, grid, pump, quiz **5** broil, grate, sauté, toast **6** eatery **7** afflict, debrief, grating, griddle, torment **8** gridiron, question **10** restaurant **11** interrogate **12** cross-examine
grilse
6 salmon
grim
3 set **4** cold, dour, fell, firm, hard **5** bleak, cruel, fixed, grave, harsh, rigid, stern **6** dismal, dogged, dreary, fierce, grisly, intent, savage, severe, somber **7** adamant, austere, inhuman, joyless, ominous **8** gruesome, inhumane, obdurate, resolute, ruthless, stubborn **9** merciless, offensive, truculent **10** determined, forbidding, implacable, inevitable, inexorable, inflexible, melancholy, relentless, unyielding, vindictive **11** unforgiving, unrelenting

grimace
3 mow, mug **4** face, moue, pout **5** frown, lower, mouth, scowl, sneer

grimalkin
3 cat **5** tabby **6** feline **9** female cat

grime
4 crud, dirt, gunk, muck, smut, soot **5** filth

grim reaper
5 death

grimy
5 dingy, dirty **6** filthy, grubby, grungy, soiled, scuzzy, smutty **10** besmirched

grin
4 beam **5** smile, smirk

grind
3 rut, vex **4** chew, grub, mill, moil, pace, plod, plug, rote, slog, toil, whet **5** crank, crush, gnash, grate, labor, slave, sweat **6** abrade, crunch, drudge, groove, harass, kibble, powder, rotate **7** oppress, routine, travail **8** drudgery, monotony, wear down **9** pulverize, treadmill **10** donkey-work

grinder
3 sub **4** gyro, hero **5** molar, tooth **6** hoagie **8** sandwich **9** submarine

grinding
5 harsh **6** severe **7** arduous, grating, wearing **9** fatiguing, strenuous
stone: **4** mano **6** mortar, muller, pestle

griot
11 storyteller

grip
4 glom, hold, take **5** clamp, clasp, grasp, seize **6** clench, clinch, clutch, handle, tenure, valise **7** grapple **8** enthrall, suitcase **9** fascinate, mesmerize, restraint, spellbind, stagehand **10** constraint

gripe
3 bug, vex **4** beef, carp, crab, fuss, yawp **5** annoy, bitch, bleat, cavil, croak, groan, whine **6** bother, grouch, grouse, kvetch, murmur, mutter, object, squawk, yammer **7** afflict, grumble **8** complain, distress, irritate **9** bellyache, complaint, grievance, objection

griper
see **grumbler**

grippe
3 flu **9** influenza

gripper
4 clip, hand, vise **5** clamp, clasp, tongs **6** pliers

gris-gris
4 juju **5** charm, spell **6** amulet, fetish **8** talisman **11** incantation

Grisham novel
4 Firm (The) **6** Broker (The), Client (The) **7** Chamber (The), Partner (The) **8** Brethren (The) **12** Pelican Brief (The)

grisly
4 gory, grim **5** awful, lurid **6** horrid **7** ghastly, hideous, macabre **8** fearsome, god-awful, gruesome, horrible, terrible **9** frightful, repellent, repulsive, sickening **10** disgusting, horrifying, terrifying

grist
3 lot **5** grain, input, stint **6** amount, output **7** product **8** quantity

gristle
9 cartilage

grit
4 guts, sand **5** grate, grind, heart, moxie, nerve, pluck, spunk **6** gravel, mettle, powder, smooth, spirit **7** bravery, courage, granule **8** backbone, tenacity **9** fortitude **10** doggedness **13** determination

gritty
4 game **5** dirty, gutsy, rough, sandy **6** dogged, plucky, spunky **8** abrasive, gravelly, resolute, spirited **9** steadfast, tenacious **10** courageous, determined

groan
4 beef, carp, moan **5** cavil, creak, gripe **6** bemoan, grouse, lament, object, repine **7** grumble **8** complain **9** bellyache

grocery
5 store **11** supermarket
Spanish: **6** bodega

grog
3 rum **5** booze, drink, hooch, juice, sauce **6** liquor, tipple **7** alcohol, spirits **9** firewater

groggy
4 dull, hazy, logy, weak **5** dazed, dopey, foggy, muzzy, tired, woozy **6** dulled, sleepy **7** muddled **8** befogged, confused, sluggish **9** befuddled, slaphappy, stupefied **10** punch-drunk

groin
4 fold **6** crotch

grok
6 intuit

grommet
6 eyelet **7** cringle

groom
4 comb, tend, tidy **5** brush, clean, curry, primp, ready, shave **6** neaten, ostler, polish **7** hostler, prepare, servant **8** benedict **9** attendant
Indian: **4** syce

groove
3 rut **4** dado, pace, rote, slot **5** canal, flute, glyph, gouge, grind, niche, score, stria **6** furrow, gutter,

hollow, rabbet, rhythm **7** chamfer, channel, routine, top form **8** monotony **10** depression

groovy
3 hip **4** cool, neat **5** ducky, great, nifty, sharp, slick, super, swell **6** choice, gnarly, peachy **7** right-on **8** smashing **9** copacetic, excellent, hunky-dory, marvelous, wonderful **10** delightful, marvellous, peachy keen

grope
4 feel, grub, poke, root **6** fondle, fumble, search **7** grabble **8** scrabble

grosbeak
5 finch **8** hawfinch, songbird

gross
3 fat, raw, sum **4** earn, foul, mass, rude **5** brute, bulky, crude, obese, rough, utter, whole **6** carnal, coarse, entire, vulgar **7** blatant, boorish, capital, extreme, glaring, hulking, obscene, overall, porcine, uncouth **8** absolute, complete, flagrant, ignorant, improper, indecent, outright, sum total, tangible, totality **9** aggregate, before tax, corporeal, corpulent, downright, egregious, excessive, loathsome, offensive, out-and-out, repulsive, revolting, unrefined **10** disgusting, exorbitant, immoderate **11** twelve dozen

grotesque
6 absurd, rococo, unreal **7** baroque, bizarre, extreme **8** aberrant, abnormal, deformed, fanciful, freakish **9** distorted, fantastic, ludicrous, misshapen, monstrous **11** incongruous

grotto
4 cave, hole **5** crypt, vault **6** cavern
Capri: **4** Blue

grouch
4 beef, carp, crab, kick, sulk, yawp **5** crank, croak, growl, grump, pique **6** carper, griper, grouse, grudge, kicker, kvetch, murmur, mutter, repine, squawk, whiner, yawper **7** crabber, grouser, growler, grumble **8** complain, grumbler, kvetcher, sorehead, sourpuss, squawker **9** bellyache, complaint **10** bellyacher, complainer, crosspatch, malcontent

ground
3 bed, sod **4** base, dirt, land, root, seat, soil, turf **5** basis, cause, earth, floor, proof **6** bottom, reason **7** bedrock, dry land, footing, support, sustain, terrain **8** argument, buttress, evidence **9** establish, testimony **10** foundation, terra firma

groundbreaking
10 innovative, innovatory, pioneering **11** cutting-edge, leading-edge

grounded
6 stable **7** beached **8** marooned, sensible, stranded **9** realistic **13** unpretentious

groundhog
6 marmot **9** woodchuck

grounding
8 practice, training, tutelage **11** instruction, preparation

groundless
4 idle **5** empty, false **6** hollow **8** baseless **9** causeless, unfounded **10** gratuitous **11** uncalled-for, unjustified, unwarranted

groundwork
3 bed **4** base, foot, root **5** basis **6** bottom **7** bedrock, footing, support **8** basement **10** foundation, substratum **11** cornerstone, preparation **12** substruction, substructure, underpinning

ground zero
5 focus, get-go **6** center, outset, target **8** bull's-eye **9** epicenter, square one

group
3 lot, set **4** band, bevy, body, club, crew, gang, pack, ruck, sect, team, tier **5** array, batch, bunch, class, clump, combo, covey, crowd, horde, panel, squad, taxon, troop **6** assort, bundle, cartel, circle, clique, clutch, huddle, klatch, league, passel **7** battery, brigade, cluster, combine, company, coterie, council, echelon, klatsch, platoon **8** assemble, assembly, category, classify, ensemble, organize **9** congeries, gathering, syndicate **10** assemblage, categorize, collection
of angels: **4** host
of ants: **6** colony
of bees: **4** hive **5** swarm
of birds: **6** flight
of cats: **7** clowder, clutter
of cattle: **5** drove
of chicks: **5** brood **6** clutch
of clams: **3** bed
of crows: **6** murder
of ducks: **5** brace
of eight: **5** octad, octet
of elephants: **4** herd
of elks: **4** gang
of fish: **5** shoal **6** school
of five: **5** quint **6** pentad **7** quintet
of four: **6** tetrad **7** quartet
of foxes: **5** leash, skulk
of geese: **5** flock, skein **6** gaggle
of gnats: **5** cloud, horde
of goats: **5** tribe
of gorillas: **4** band
of greyhounds: **5** leash
of grouse: **5** covey
of hares: **4** down, husk
of hawks: **4** cast
of hounds: **3** cry **4** mute, pack
of kangaroos: **3** mob **5** troop
of kittens: **6** litter
of larks: **10** exaltation

of lions: **5** pride
of locusts: **6** plague
of monkeys: **5** troop
of mules: **4** span
of nine: **5** nonet **6** ennead
of oysters: **3** bed
of partridges: **5** covey
of peacocks: **6** muster
of pheasants: **4** nest
of plovers: **4** wing **12** congregation
of quail: **4** bevy **5** covey
of seals: **3** pod **5** patch
of seven: **6** pleiad, septet
of sheep: **5** drove, flock
of six: **6** sextet
of swans: **4** bevy
of teals: **6** spring
of ten: **6** decade
of three: **4** trio **5** triad **7** ternary, trinity, triplet
of vipers: **4** nest
of whales: **3** gam, pod
of wolves: **4** pack

grouper
8 rockfish

grouse
4 beef, carp, crab **5** croak, gripe, quail, scold **6** mutter, yammer **7** grumble **8** complain, pheasant **9** bellyache, blackcock, ptarmigan **12** capercaillie
extinct: **8** heath hen
red: **8** moorfowl
strut: **3** lek

grout
4 lees, lute **5** dregs **6** cement, filler, mortar **7** grounds, plaster **8** concrete

grove
4 holt, wood **5** copse **7** boscage, coppice, orchard, thicket

grovel
4 fawn **5** abase, cower, crawl, creep, toady **6** cajole, cringe, kowtow, snivel, wallow **7** eat dirt, truckle **8** blandish, bootlick **9** brownnose **10** curry favor, ingratiate **11** apple-polish

grow
3 age, wax **4** flow, gain, rise, tend **5** amass, breed, nurse, raise, ripen, swell **6** abound, become, expand, foster, mature, sprout, thrive **7** burgeon, care for, develop, enlarge, gestate, nurture, produce **8** escalate, flourish, increase, multiply, mushroom, spring up **9** cultivate, propagate

growl
4 beef, carp, crab, fuss, gnar, roar **5** bitch, gripe, gnarr, groan, snarl **6** grouse, kvetch, mutter, repine, rumble, yammer **7** grumble **8** complain **9** bellyache

growler
3 can **4** crab, floe **5** crank, grump **6** grouch, vessel **7** ice floe, iceberg, pitcher **8** sorehead, sourpuss **9** container **10** crosspatch, malcontent **11** faultfinder

grown-up
5 adult **6** mature **8** seasoned **9** developed **11** full-fledged

grow old
3 age **4** wane **5** ripen, wizen **6** mature, mellow

growth
4 gain, rise **5** surge, swell, tumor **7** buildup **8** increase, progress, swelling **9** accretion, evolution, expansion, flowering, unfolding **11** development, enlargement, progression
malignant: **6** cancer
skin: **3** tag, wen **4** corn, cyst, mole, wart **5** nevus **6** bunion, callus, keloid **7** verruca

grow up
3 age **5** ripen **6** evolve, mature, mellow **7** advance, develop **8** maturate **9** come of age

grub
3 dig **4** chow, comb, eats, feed, food, hack, moil, plod, poke, rake, root, slog, toil **5** grind, larva, scour, slave, spade, stump **6** burrow, drudge, forage, menial, shovel, slavey, uproot, viands **7** edibles, ransack, rummage, unearth, vittles **8** excavate, hireling, victuals **9** provender **11** comestibles

grubby
4 foul **5** dirty, grimy, messy, seedy **6** filthy, frowsy, frowzy, grungy, scuzzy, shabby, sloppy, soiled **7** scruffy, squalid, unclean, unkempt **8** slovenly, unwashed

grubstake
3 aid **4** back, fund, help, loan **5** funds **6** assist **7** backing, capital, finance, support **8** bankroll **9** financing **10** assistance, capitalize, underwrite

grudge
4 deny, envy **5** spite **6** refuse, spleen **7** ill will **9** grievance **10** resentment **12** hard feelings, spitefulness

gruel
4 mush **5** atole, kasha **6** burgoo, congee, sowens **8** flummery, loblolly, porridge **9** stirabout

gruesome
see **grisly**

gruff
4 curt, dour **5** bluff, blunt, cross, harsh, husky, stern, surly **6** abrupt, crabby, crusty, hoarse, morose, sullen **7** bearish, brusque, crabbed, grating, grouchy **8** churlish, croaking, snappish, snippety **9** saturnine **10** ill-natured **11** bad-tempered

grumble
4 beef, carp, crab, fuss, moan, yawp **5** bitch, croak, gripe, groan, growl, snarl, whine **6** bemoan, grouch, grouse, murmur, mutter, repine, squawk **8** complain **9** bellyache

grumbler
4 crab **5** crank, grump **6** grouch **8** sorehead **10** crosspatch, malcontent

grump
3 pet **4** beef, carp, crab, pout, sulk **5** crank, gripe, growl **6** griper, grouch **7** growler, grumble **8** complain, sorehead, sourpuss **9** bellyache **10** bellyacher, malcontent

grumpy
4 dour, sour **5** cross, moody, sulky, surly, testy **6** crabby, cranky, sullen **7** crabbed, peevish **8** petulant, vinegary **9** crotchety, irascible **11** bad-tempered, ill-tempered **12** cantankerous

grunion
10 silverside

grunt
5 groan, growl, snort **7** dogface, draftee, soldier

G sharp
5 A flat

guacharo
7 oilbird

Guadeloupe
capital: 10 Basse-Terre
department of: 6 France
dependency: 8 Désirade, St. Martin **12** Marie-Galante, St. Barthélemy
discoverer: 8 Columbus (Christopher)
island: 10 Basse-Terre **11** Grande-Terre
location: 10 West Indies
volcano: 9 Soufrière

Guam
capital: 5 Agana
ethnic group: 8 Chamorro
island group: 7 Mariana

guanaco
5 llama **6** alpaca
kin: 5 camel

guano
6 manure **9** excrement

guarantee
3 vow **4** bail, bond, oath, seal, word **5** token, vouch **6** assert, assure, ensure, insure, pledge, surety **7** certify, earnest, promise, warrant **8** security, warranty **9** agreement, assurance, insurance, undertake **11** stand behind, undertaking

guarantor
5 angel **6** backer, patron, surety **7** ensurer, insurer, sponsor **8** bondsman **11** underwriter

guard
4 fend, mind, tend, ward **5** aegis, alert, armor, cover, watch **6** convoy, defend, escort, jailer, keeper, minder, patrol, picket, police, screen, secure, sentry, shield, warden, warder **7** bulwark, defense, lookout, oversee, protect, turnkey **8** chaperon, overseer, preserve, security, sentinel, shepherd, watchdog, watchman **9** chaperone, custodian, look after, patrolman, protector, watch over **10** protection

guarded
4 safe, wary **5** cagey, chary, leery **7** careful, politic, prudent **8** cautious, discreet, gingerly, reserved **11** circumspect, considerate

guardhouse
4 brig, jail, keep **5** clink **6** lockup, prison **8** stockade

guardian
6 escort, keeper, patron, warden, warder **7** curator, trustee **8** Cerberus, defender, overseer, watchdog **9** custodian, protector **10** genius loci **11** conservator

guardianship
4 care, keep, ward **5** aegis, trust **6** charge **7** custody, keeping **8** auspices **10** protection **11** safekeeping

Guare play
17 House of Blue Leaves (The) **22** Six Degrees of Separation

Guatemala
capital: 9 Guatemala (City)
ethnic group: 4 Maya **5** Mayan
lake: 6 Izabal **7** Atitlán **9** Petén Itzá
language: 7 Spanish
monetary unit: 7 quetzal
mountain, range: 6 Tacaná **9** Tajumulco **10** Acatenango, Santa María **11** Sierra Madre
neighbor: 6 Belize, Mexico **8** Honduras **10** El Salvador
peninsula: 7 Yucatán
river: 7 Motagua **8** Polochic, Sarstoon **10** Usumacinta

guck
3 bog, goo, mud **4** clay, crud, dirt, glop, goop, mire, ooze, smut **5** filth, slime **7** stickum

gudgeon
3 pin **4** fish **5** pivot **6** socket **7** journal

Gudrun
brother: 6 Gunnar **7** Gunther
father: 5 Hetel
husband: 4 Atli **5** Etzel **6** Sigurd **9** Siegfried

guerrilla
8 partisan **9** irregular
Greek: 6 klepht

guess
4 call, shot, stab **5** fancy, hunch, infer **7** believe, predict, presume, suppose, surmise **8** estimate **9** speculate **10** conjecture, prediction **11** presumption, supposition, speculation

guest
6 caller, lodger, roomer **7** boarder, company, visitor **9** sojourner

guff
3 jaw, lip **4** bosh, sass **5** bilge, cheek, hokum, hooey, mouth, sauce, trash **6** bunkum, drivel, hot air, humbug **7** baloney, hogwash, palaver, twaddle **8** back talk, claptrap, malarkey, nonsense, tommyrot **9** poppycock **10** balderdash **13** horsefeathers

guffaw
6 cackle, hee-haw **7** chortle

guidance
6 advice **7** control, counsel **8** handling **9** direction, oversight **10** leadership, management **11** instruction, supervision

guide
4 dean, guru, help, lead, show **5** doyen, pilot, route, steer, usher **6** beacon, convoy, direct, docent, escort, handle, leader, manage, manual, mentor **7** adviser, conduct, control, marshal, oversee **8** Baedeker, chaperon, director, handbook, instruct, maneuver, navigate, shepherd, signpost **9** accompany, chaperone, conductor, vade mecum, Sacagawea **10** bellwether, compendium, instructor, pathfinder **11** enchiridion

guidebook
6 Fodor's, manual **8** Baedeker, Frommer's, handbook, Michelin **9** itinerary, vade mecum **10** compendium **11** enchiridion

guided missile
3 ABM **4** Hawk, ICBM, IRBM, Nike, Scud, Thor, Zuni **5** Atlas, drone, Snark, Titan **6** Bomarc, cruise, Exocet, Falcon, Navaho, rocket **7** Bullpup, Matador, Polaris, Regulus, Terrier **8** Redstone, Tomahawk **9** Minuteman **10** projectile, Sidewinder

Guiderius
brother: **9** Arviragus
father: **9** Cymbeline

guidon
4 flag **6** banner, burgee, ensign, pennon

guild
4 club **5** lodge, order, union **6** cartel, league **7** society **8** sodality **10** fellowship, fraternity **11** association, brotherhood
medieval: **5** Hansa, Hanse

guile
4 wile **5** craft, fraud **6** deceit **7** cunning **8** artifice, trickery, wiliness **9** deception, duplicity, stratagem **10** cleverness **13** dissimulation

guileful
3 sly **4** foxy, wily **5** cagey, canny, slick **6** artful, astute, crafty, shifty, shrewd, sneaky, tricky **7** cunning, devious **8** indirect, slippery, sneaking **9** designing, insidious, underhand **11** calculating, duplicitous, underhanded

guileless
4 open **5** frank, naive **6** candid, direct, honest **7** genuine, natural, sincere, up-front **8** innocent, truthful **9** ingenuous **10** aboveboard, forthright

guillemot
3 auk **5** murre **7** seabird

guillotine
6 behead **9** decollate **10** decapitate

guilt
4 onus **5** blame, fault, shame **6** regret, stigma **7** offense, remorse **10** contrition **11** culpability **12** self-reproach

guiltless
4 pure **5** clean **6** chaste **8** innocent, virtuous **9** blameless, exemplary, faultless, righteous, stainless **10** immaculate, inculpable

guilty
6 liable, rueful, sinful **7** ashamed, at fault **8** blamable, contrite, culpable, indicted, penitent **9** impeached, regretful **10** answerable, remorseful **11** accountable, blameworthy, responsible

guimpe
6 blouse

Guinea
capital: **7** Conakry
city: **4** Labé **6** Kankan, Kindia
ethnic group: **6** Fulani **7** Malinke
island, island group: **3** Los **5** Tombo
language: **6** French
monetary unit: **5** franc
mountain: **5** Nimba
neighbor: **4** Mali **7** Liberia, Senegal **10** Ivory Coast **11** Sierra Leone **12** Guinea-Bissau
river: **5** Niger **6** Gambia **7** Senegal

Guinea-Bissau
archipelago: **7** Bijagós
capital: **6** Bissau
ethnic group: **6** Fulani **7** Malinke **8** Mandyako
language: **10** Portuguese
monetary unit: **5** franc
neighbor: **6** Guinea **7** Senegal
river: **4** Gêba

guinea fowl
genus: **6** Numida
young: **4** keet

guinea pig
4 cavy **6** rodent
genus: **5** Cavia

Guinevere
court: **7** Camelot
husband: **6** Arthur
lover: **8** Lancelot **9** Launcelot

guise
4 mask **5** cloak, cover, dress, getup **6** aspect,

facade, outfit, veneer **7** costume, pretext **8** coloring, pretense **9** posturing, semblance **10** appearance, false front

guitar
accessory: **4** capo
Mexican: **5** tiple **6** cuatro **8** charango
part: **3** nut, peg **4** fret, neck **5** brace **6** bridge, string **7** peghead
small: **3** uke **7** ukulele
tool: **4** pick **8** plectrum

guitarist
American: **4** Byrd (Charlie), King (B. B., Freddie), Page (Jimmy), Pass (Joe), Paul (Les) **5** Berry (Chuck), Ellis (Herb), Isbin (Sharon) **6** Allman (Duane), Kessel (Barney), Kottke (Leo), Watson (Doc) **7** Burrell (Kenny), Hendrix (Jimi), Johnson (Robert), Metheny (Pat), Vaughan (Stevie Ray) **9** Christian (Charlie), Parkening (Christopher) **10** Montgomery (Wes), Pizzarelli (Bucky, John)
Australian: **8** Williams (John)
British: **4** Beck (Jeff) **5** Bream (Julian) **7** Clapton (Eric) **8** Richards (Keith)
French: **9** Reinhardt (Django)
Italian: **7** Ghiglia (Oscar)
Spanish: **5** Yepes (Narciso) **6** Romero (Celedonio) **7** Segovia (Andrés)

guitarlike instrument
3 uke **4** lute, vina **5** banjo, sitar **7** bandore, pandora, samisen, ukulele **8** mandolin, shamisen

gulch
3 gap **4** glen **5** gorge, gully **6** arroyo, canyon, coulee, hollow, ravine, valley **7** couloir

gules
3 red

gulf
3 bay, pit **4** cove **5** abysm, abyss, bayou, bight, chasm, firth, gorge, gulch, inlet **6** cavity, harbor, hollow, ravine, slough **8** crevasse
Adriatic Sea: **6** Venice
Aegean Sea: **7** Saronic **8** Salonika
Africa: **6** Guinea
Arabian Sea: **4** Oman **7** Persian
Australia: **9** Van Diemen **11** Carpentaria
Baltic Sea: **4** Riga **6** Danzig, Gdansk **7** Bothnia, Finland
Bering Sea: **6** Anadyr
Canada: **13** Saint Lawrence
Central America: **7** Fonseca
Djibouti: **6** Tajura **8** Tadjoura
Europe: **7** Bothnia, Gascony **8** Gascogne
Greece: **7** Corinth, Lepanto
Indian Ocean: **4** Aden
Ionian Sea: **4** Arta **7** Taranto
Iran: **7** Arabian
Italy: **5** Genoa
Mediterranean Sea: **5** Sidra, Tunis **8** Valencia **10** Khalij Surt **11** Syrtis Major
Middle East: **7** Persian
New Guinea: **5** Papua **7** McCluer
New Zealand: **7** Hauraki
North America: **6** Mexico
Northwest Territories: **7** Boothia **8** Amundsen **9** Queen Maud
Philippines: **4** Asid **5** Davao, Leyte, Panay, Ragay
Red Sea: **4** Suez **5** Aqaba **11** Aelaniticus
Russia: **8** Sakhalin
Solomon Sea: **4** Huon, Kula **5** Vella
South China Sea: **4** Siam **6** Tonkin **8** Lingayen
Tyrrhenian Sea: **7** Paestum
Yellow Sea: **6** Chihli

Gulf State
5 Texas **7** Alabama, Florida **9** Louisiana **11** Mississippi

gull
3 con, mew, sap **4** bird, dupe, fool, hoax, scam, Xema **5** chump, cozen **6** fleece, pigeon, stooge, sucker, take in **7** chicane, fall guy **8** flimflam, hoodwink **9** bamboozle **11** hornswoggle

gullet
3 maw **4** crop, tube **6** dewlap, throat **7** channel **9** esophagus

gullible
4 easy **5** green, naive **8** innocent, trusting **9** believing, credulous **11** susceptible **12** unsuspecting

Gulliver's Travels
author: **5** Swift (Jonathan)
horses: **10** Houyhnhnms
land: **6** Laputa **8** Lilliput **11** Brobdingnag
people: **6** Yahoos

gully
3 gap **4** glen, wadi, wash **5** gorge, gulch **6** arroyo, coulee, hollow, nullah, ravine, valley **7** couloir

gulp
4 bolt, chug, cram, glut, slop, swig, wolf **5** gorge, quaff, scarf, scoff, stuff, swill **6** devour, gobble, guzzle **7** swallow **8** mouthful **11** ingurgitate

gum
4 chew **5** botch **6** bobble, bollix, bungle, chicle, gluten, goof up, tupelo **7** exudate, gingiva, louse up **8** adhesive, mucilage **9** sapodilla **10** eucalyptus
kind: **6** acacia, Arabic, balata, bubble **7** chewing, dextrin
resin: **5** myrrh **7** gamboge **8** ammoniac, galbanum, scammony **9** asafetida **10** asafoetida **12** frankincense

gumbo
3 mud **4** okra, olio, soil, soup, stew **6** creole **7** mélange, mixture
ingredient: **4** crab, duck, filé, okra **5** quail, tasso **6** shrimp **8** crawfish

gummy
5 gooey, pasty **6** cloggy, sticky, viscid **7** viscous **8** adhesive **9** glutinous **10** gelatinous **12** mucilaginous

gumption
5 drive, moxie, nerve, savvy **6** energy **8** industry **10** enterprise, get-up-and-go, initiative

gumshoe
3 cop, tec **4** bull, dick, fuzz, G-man, heat, narc **6** copper, peeler, shamus, sleuth **7** officer **8** flatfoot, hawkshaw, Sherlock **9** detective, policeman **10** bloodhound, private eye **12** investigator

gun
3 gat, rev, rod **4** Colt **5** rev up, rifle **6** cannon, Garand, heater, mortar, musket, pistol, weapon **7** bazooka, carbine, firearm **8** Browning, howitzer, revolver **9** derringer, Remington **10** Winchester **11** Springfield
antiaircraft: **6** ack-ack, Bofors
Austrian: **5** Glock
British: **4** Sten
French: **8** arquebus **9** harquebus
German: **5** Luger
Israeli: **3** Uzi
Italian: **7** Beretta
mount: **6** turret
part: **3** pin **4** bolt, bore, butt, lock **5** sight, stock **6** barrel, breech, hammer, muzzle, safety **7** chamber, trigger **8** cylinder, magazine **9** buttstock
stun: **5** Taser

gunfire
4 shot **5** blast, salvo **6** volley **7** barrage **9** broadside, discharge, fusillade

gung ho
4 avid, keen **6** ardent, fervid, raring **7** fervent, zealous **9** exuberant **11** impassioned **12** enthusiastic

Guni's father
8 Naphtali

gunk
3 goo **4** crud, glop, gook, goop, muck **5** slime

gunman
5 bravo **6** hit man, killer **7** shooter, torpedo **8** assassin, enforcer

Gunnar
brother-in-law: **6** Sigurd
father: **5** Hetel
sister: **6** Gudrun
wife: **8** Brunhild, Brynhild

gunner
6 sniper **7** shooter **8** marksman, rifleman **9** musketeer **11** infantryman **12** artilleryman

Gunther
sister: **7** Gutrune **9** Kriemhild
slayer: **5** Hagen
uncle: **5** Hagen
wife: **8** Brunhild **9** Brynhilde

gurgle
3 lap **4** flow, purl, wash **5** plash, slosh, swash **6** babble, bubble, burble, ripple

Gurkha knife
5 kukri

gurney
3 cot **9** stretcher

guru
4 sage **5** guide, swami, tutor **6** expert, leader, master, mentor **7** teacher **9** maharishi

gush
3 jet **4** emit, flow, pour, rave, roll, rush, spew, teem, well **5** burst, flood, flush, issue, spout, spurt, surge **6** babble, effuse, sluice, spring, stream **7** cascade, emanate **10** effervesce, outpouring

gushy
5 gooey, mushy, sappy, soppy **6** sloppy, slushy, sticky **7** cloying, maudlin, mawkish, tearful **8** bathetic, effusive **9** schmaltzy, sickening **10** nauseating, saccharine **11** sentimental

gusset
4 fold, gore, tuck **5** armor, plate, pleat **6** insert **7** bracket

gussy up
5 adorn **6** bedeck **7** furbish **8** decorate, renovate

gust
3 fit **4** blow, gale, rush, wind **5** blast, burst, draft, sally, surge, whiff **6** breeze, flurry, squall **7** bluster, delight, flare-up **8** eruption, outburst, paroxysm

gusto
3 vim **4** brio, élan, zeal, zest **5** ardor, heart, oomph, taste, verve **6** fervor, palate, relish, spirit **7** delight, passion **9** enjoyment **10** enthusiasm

gusty
5 blowy, windy **6** breezy **8** blustery

gut
4 draw, loot, silk **5** belly, bowel, dress, empty, tummy **6** bowels, paunch **7** abdomen, ransack, stomach **8** clean out, entrails, visceral **9** intestine **10** disembowel, eviscerate, exenterate, intestines **11** instinctive

Gutenberg, Johannes
city: **5** Mainz
invention: **11** movable type
partner: **4** Fust (Johann)

gutless
5 sissy, wimpy, wussy **6** coward, craven, yellow **7** chicken, unmanly **8** cowardly, timorous **9** spineless, spunkless, weak-kneed **11** lily-livered, poltroonish **12** fainthearted **13** pusillanimous

guts
4 grit, sand **5** bowel, heart, moxie, nerve, pluck, spunk, tripe **6** bowels, mettle, spirit **7** bravery, courage, innards, insides, stamina, viscera **8** backbone, entrails, stuffing **9** fortitude, intestine **10** intestines, resolution

gutsy
4 bold **5** brave **6** plucky, spunky **7** valiant **8** intrepid, resolute **10** courageous, determined, mettlesome

gutter
5 chase, ditch, flume, gully **6** furrow, groove, trench, trough **7** channel, conduit

guttersnipe
3 bum **4** hobo, scum, waif **5** gamin **6** beggar, gamine, urchin **7** outcast, vagrant, wastrel **8** derelict, riffraff, vagabond **10** ragamuffin

guttural
4 deep **5** gruff, harsh, husky, rough, velar **6** croaky, hoarse **7** grating, palatal, rasping, throaty **8** gravelly
warning: **5** growl

guy
3 cat, joe, lad, man **4** buck, chap, dude, male, rope, stud, wire **5** bloke, brace, chain, guide **6** effigy, fellow, steady **7** support

Guyana
capital: **10** Georgetown
mountain range: **9** Pacaraima
neighbor: **6** Brazil **8** Suriname **9** Venezuela
river: **9** Essequibo

Guys and Dolls
author: **6** Runyon (Damon)
character: **3** Sky (Masterson) **6** Nathan (Detroit) **8** Adelaide (Miss)
composer: **7** Loesser (Frank)

guzzle
4 belt, chug, gulp, slop, soak, swig, toss, tope **5** booze, drink, quaff, slosh, swill **6** imbibe, tank up, tipple **7** consume, swizzle

Gwendolen's husband
7 Locrine

gymnast
7 acrobat, athlete, tumbler
American: **4** Hamm (Paul) **5** Rigby (Cathy) **6** Conner (Bart), Miller (Shannon), Retton (Mary Lou), Thomas (Kurt)
Romanian: **8** Comaneci (Nadia)
Russian: **3** Kim (Nelly) **6** Korbut (Olga)
Ukrainian: **5** Baiul (Oksana)

gymnastics
5 sport **8** exercise, tumbling **9** athletics **10** acrobatics **12** calisthenics
apparatus: **3** bar **4** bars, beam, buck, ring, rope **5** horse **11** balance beam
feat: **3** kip **4** flip **5** vault **6** tumble **9** handstand, headstand **10** handspring, headspring, somersault

gyp
3 con **4** bilk, dupe, fake, hoax, rook, scam, sham **5** bunco, cheat, cozen, cross, fraud, spoof, trick **6** chisel, chouse, con man, diddle, fleece, humbug, rip-off, rip off **7** cheater, deceive, defraud, diddler, finagle, sharper, swindle **8** chiseler, hoodwink, swindler **9** bamboozle, defrauder, imposture, trickster **10** mountebank **11** double-cross, flimflammer **12** double-dealer

gypsum
7 drywall, mineral **8** selenite **9** alabaster, wallboard

gypsy
3 Rom **5** caird, nomad, rover **6** roamer, Romany, tinker **7** drifter, tzigane **8** Bohemian, vagabond, wanderer
Spanish: **6** gitano

gyrate
4 coil, purl, roll, spin, turn, wind **5** orbit, twirl, whirl **6** circle, rotate **7** revolve **9** oscillate, pirouette

gyration
4 coil, turn **5** cycle, orbit, twirl, wheel, whirl **6** circle **7** circuit, turning **8** rotation **10** revolution

gyre
4 coil, gird, ring, spin, wind **5** cycle, orbit, twirl, whirl **6** circle, girdle, rotate, spiral, vortex **7** circuit, revolve **8** rotation **10** revolution

gyro
8 sandwich

gyve
4 bond, iron **5** chain **6** fetter **7** shackle **8** restrain **9** restraint

H

Habakkuk
7 prophet

habeas corpus
4 writ **5** right **7** mandate

habiliments
4 gear **5** dress **6** attire, outfit **7** apparel, clothes **8** clothing **9** apparatus, equipment, trappings

habilitate
5 dress **6** clothe **7** qualify

habit
3 rut **4** bent, form, garb, mode, rote, wont **5** dress, quirk, style, usage **6** attire, clothe, custom, groove, manner, outfit **7** costume, fashion, pattern, routine **8** behavior, clothing, practice, tendency **9** addiction, mannerism **10** consuetude, convention, proclivity **11** disposition, inclination
riding: **8** jodhpurs
wearer: **3** nun **5** rider

habitable
7 livable

habitant
5 liver **7** denizen, dweller, resider **8** occupant, resident

habitat
4 home, site, turf **5** abode, haunt, range **6** locale, milieu **7** terrain **8** domicile **9** territory **11** environment **12** surroundings

habitation
3 pad **4** digs, flat, home, nest, seat **5** abode, haunt, haven, house, place, roost **7** housing, lodging, tenancy **8** domicile, dwelling, lodgment, quarters **9** homestead, residence, residency **10** settlement

habitual
3 set **5** fixed, usual **6** addict, inborn, native, normal, steady, wonted **7** chronic, regular, routine, settled **8** accepted, addicted, constant, familiar, frequent, inherent **9** automatic, confirmed, continual, customary, ingrained **10** accustomed, inveterate, persistent **11** established, instinctive, involuntary

habitually
8 commonly, normally, wontedly **9** generally, regularly, routinely **10** ordinarily **11** customarily **12** consistently

habituate
4 bear **5** inure, train **6** addict, adjust, endure, harden, school, season, take to **7** break in, prepare, support **8** accustom, tolerate **9** acclimate, condition **11** familiarize

habitué
3 fan **4** buff, user **5** hound, lover **6** addict, patron **7** denizen, devotee, haunter **8** adherent, customer **10** enthusiast, frequenter

hacienda
4 farm **5** ranch, villa **6** estate, quinta **8** estancia **10** plantation

hack
3 cab, cut, hew, try, vex **4** blow, chip, chop, dull, gash, grub, jade, loaf, mean, ride, taxi **5** annoy, cabby, cough, grind, horse, petty, sever, usual **6** cabbie, cliché, drudge, lackey, mangle, stroke, writer **7** clichéd, machine, plodder, taxicab, trivial **8** inferior, low-grade, mediocre, tolerate **9** cabdriver, mercenary, potboiler **10** second-rate, uninspired

hacker
4 geek, nerd **6** duffer

hackney
3 cab **4** taxi **5** horse **6** jitney **7** taxicab **8** carriage

hackneyed
4 dull, worn **5** banal, corny, stale, stock, tired, trite **6** cliché, common, old hat, old saw **7** archaic, clichéd, worn-out **8** everyday, obsolete, outdated, overused, outmoded, timeworn **9** out-of-date **10** antiquated, overworked, pedestrian

Hadad
father: **5** Bedad **7** Ishmael
victim: **6** Midian

Hades
4 Hell **5** Pluto, Sheol **6** blazes, Tophet **7** Gehenna, inferno **8** Tartarus **9** perdition **10** underworld **11** netherworld
Babylonian: **5** Aralu
god: **3** Dis **5** Orcus, Pluto
goddess: **10** Persephone
guard: **8** Cerberus
lake: **7** Avernus
river: **4** Styx **5** Lethe **7** Acheron, Cocytus **10** Phlegethon

haft
4 grip, hilt, knob **5** helve **6** handle

hag
3 hex **5** biddy, crone, harpy, shrew, vixen, witch **6** beldam, gorgon, virago **8** battle-ax, fishwife, harridan, slattern **9** hobgoblin

Hagar
9 concubine
lover: **7** Abraham
rival: **5** Sarah, Sarai
son: **7** Ishmael

Hagen
father: **8** Alberich
nephew: **7** Gunther
slayer: **9** Kriemhild
victim: **9** Siegfried

haggard
3 wan **4** hawk, lank, pale, thin, weak, wild, worn **5** ashen, drawn, faded, gaunt, tired **6** fagged, pallid, skinny, wasted **7** angular, pinched, scraggy, scrawny, starved, wearied **8** careworn, fatigued, shrunken, worn-down **9** emaciated, exhausted

Haggard, H. Rider
novel: **3** She **17** King Solomon's Mines

Haggith
husband: **5** David
son: **8** Adonijah

haggle
4 deal **5** argue, cavil, trade **6** barter, bicker, dicker **7** bargain, chaffer, dispute, quibble, stickle, wrangle **8** squabble **10** horse-trade

hagiography subject
5 saint

hail
3 ave **4** ahoy, call **5** greet, salvo, shout, storm **6** accost, call to, holler, praise, salute, shower, volley **7** acclaim, address, applaud, barrage, call out, commend **8** greeting **9** broadside, cannonade, fusillade, originate, recommend **10** salutation **11** acclamation, bombardment

Haile Selassie
9 Ras Tafari
follower: **11** Rastafarian
nation: **8** Ethiopia

hair
3 bit, jot **4** hint, mite, wool **5** cilia (plural), pilus, trace **6** cilium, trifle **7** eyelash, whisker **8** fraction, particle
animal: **3** fur **4** mane, pelt, wool **8** vibrissa **9** vibrissae (plural)
braid: **5** plait, queue **7** pigtail
clip: **8** barrette
coarse: **7** bristle
combining form: **3** pil **4** pili, pilo **5** trich **6** tricho
covering of: **3** wig
dressing: **3** gel **6** mousse **6** pomade **7** pomatum **8** macassar **12** brilliantine
facial: **5** beard, patch **6** goatee **7** Vandyke **8** mustache, whiskers **9** burnsides, handlebar, moustache, sideburns, soul patch **11** muttonchops
fine: **6** lanugo
fringe: **5** bangs
head of: **9** chevelure
knot: **3** bun
lock of: **4** curl **5** tress **7** cowlick
loose roll: **4** pouf
matted: **6** dreads **10** dreadlocks
net: **5** snood
ornament: **7** topknot
preparation: **3** gel **6** mousse, pomade **12** brilliantine
root: **6** fibril
set: **4** perm
stiff: **4** seta **5** setae (plural)
tangled: **7** elflock
tuft of: **5** quiff **7** cowlick, fetlock
unruly: **3** mop
without: **4** bald

haircutter
6 barber **7** stylist **8** coiffeur **9** coiffeuse

hairdo
2 DA **3** bob, bun **4** afro, flip, perm, pomp, shag, trim, updo **5** bangs, braid, butch, taper, wedge **6** Caesar, Mohawk, mullet **7** beehive, bowl cut, buzz cut, chignon, crew cut, flattop, pageboy, tonsure **8** brush cut, coiffure, cornrows, ducktail, pigtails, ponytail, razor cut **9** permanent, pompadour **10** dreadlocks

hairdresser
see **haircutter**

hair-raising
5 eerie, scary **6** spooky **7** amazing, awesome **8** exciting **9** thrilling **10** terrifying **11** astonishing, fright ening

hairsplitting
7 finicky **8** exacting **9** quibbling **10** nit-picking **12** overcritical **13** hypercritical

hairstyle
see **hairdo**

hairy
5 bushy, downy, furry, fuzzy, nappy, risky, rough **6** chancy, fleecy, fluffy, shaggy, tufted, woolly **7** bristly, hirsute, scraggy, unshorn, villous **8** perilous, strigose **9** dangerous, difficult, hazardous, tomentose, whiskered **11** treacherous

Haiti
capital: **12** Port-au-Prince
island: **7** Tortuga **10** Hispaniola
language: **6** Creole, French
leader: **8** Aristide (Jean-Bertrand), Duvalier (François, Jean-Claude)

location: **10** West Indies
monetary unit: **6** gourde
passage: **8** Windward
peninsula: **7** Tiburon
river: **10** Artibonite

hajj
5 Umrah **10** pilgrimage
site: **4** Mina **5** Mecca **6** Arafat **10** Muzdalifah

hake
4 fish, ling **7** codling, whiting
relative: **3** cod

halcyon
4 calm **5** happy, lucky, quiet, still **6** golden, hushed, placid, serene **8** affluent, peaceful, tranquil **9** favorable **10** auspicious, felicitous, kingfisher, prosperous, untroubled

Halcyone
father: **6** Aeolus
husband: **4** Ceyx

hale
3 fit **4** sane, well **5** sound, stout **6** hearty, robust **7** healthy **8** vigorous **9** strapping, wholesome

Hale character
5 Nolan (Philip)

Haley epic
5 Roots

half
6 moiety
prefix: **4** demi, hemi, semi

half-baked
8 slapdash, slipshod **9** imbecilic, senseless, underdone **11** harebrained, impractical, nonsensical, unrealistic **12** ill-conceived, shortsighted **13** irresponsible

half-cocked
4 rash **5** brash **8** reckless **9** foolhardy, imprudent, impulsive, misguided, premature **10** incautious, unprepared **11** precipitate

halfhearted
4 weak **5** tepid **6** feeble **8** lukewarm **12** uninterested

half-moon
4 arch **5** curve **6** lunule **8** crescent

halfway
3 mid **6** center, medial, median, middle **7** midmost **10** centermost **11** equidistant **12** intermediate

half-wit
4 dolt, dope, fool **5** dunce, idiot, moron **6** cretin **8** imbecile **9** blockhead, simpleton

half-witted
4 dull, slow **7** moronic **8** backward, imbecile **9** imbecilic **12** feebleminded, simpleminded

hall
4 dorm **5** foyer, lobby **6** lyceum **7** passage **8** corridor **9** dormitory **10** auditorium, passageway
exhibition: **5** salon
Salvation Army: **7** citadel

Halley's ____
5 comet

hallmark
4 logo, seal, sign **5** badge, stamp, trait **6** device, emblem, symbol, virtue **7** feature, imprint, quality **8** logotype **9** attribute **11** distinction

hallow
5 bless, honor **6** anoint, devote, revere **8** dedicate, make holy, sanctify, venerate **10** consecrate

hallowed
4 holy **6** sacred

hallucination
4 trip **5** ghost **6** mirage, vision, wraith **7** fantasy, phantom, specter, spectre **8** delusion, illusion, phantasm **10** apparition **11** fata morgana, ignis fatuus

hallucinogen
3 LSD **9** mescaline **10** psilocybin **11** scopolamine

halo
4 aura, nimb **5** nimbi (plural) **6** corona, nimbus **7** aureole

halogen
6 iodine **7** bromine, element **8** astatine, chlorine, fluorine

halt
3 bar, end **4** lame, limp, quit, stay, stop **5** avast, cease, check, close, hitch, lapse, stall, waver **6** arrest, desist, dither, falter, finish, pull up **7** adjourn, bring up, stagger, suspend **8** conclude, cut short, hesitate, knock off, leave off **9** determine, interrupt, terminate, vacillate **10** standstill **11** discontinue

halter
3 bit **4** hang, rope **5** noose **6** blouse, bridle, hamper **8** restrain, trammels **9** hackamore, headstall, restraint

halvah base
6 sesame

ham
4 hock **5** bacon, emote, thigh **7** buttock, overact **8** overplay, strutter **10** scene-eater **13** exhibitionist

Ham
brother: **4** Shem **7** Japheth
father: **4** Noah
son: **4** Cush, Phut **6** Canaan **7** Mizraim

Haman's adversary
6 Esther

ham-handed
5 inept **6** clumsy, gauche **8** bumbling **9** all thumbs, graceless, inelegant, maladroit **10** blundering, unskillful

Hamilcar
conquest: **5** Spain
home: **8** Carthage
son: **8** Hannibal
surname: **5** Barca

hamlet
4 dorp **7** village
Irish, Scottish: **7** clachan

Hamlet
author: **11** Shakespeare (William)
beloved: **7** Ophelia
castle: **8** Elsinore
country: **7** Denmark
friend: **7** Horatio
mother: **8** Gertrude
slayer: **7** Laertes
uncle: **8** Claudius
victim: **7** Laertes **8** Claudius, Polonius

Hamlet, The
author: **8** Faulkner (William)
family: **6** Snopes

hammer
4 drub, maul, peen **5** forge, gavel, pound **6** batter, mallet, pummel, sledge **7** malleus **8** lambaste
end: **4** peen
type: **3** air **4** claw, maul **6** sledge **8** ball-peen **9** pneumatic

hammerhead
4 dolt, dope, fool **5** dunce, idiot, shark **8** clodpoll, numskull **9** numbskull **10** thickskull

hamper
3 bin, tie **4** balk, curb, snag **5** block, check, cramp, crimp, leash, limit **6** baffle, basket, fetter, hinder, hobble, hold up, impede, retard, stymie, thwart **7** inhibit, manacle, pannier, prevent, trammel **8** encumber, handicap, obstacle, obstruct, restrain, restrict, slow down **9** frustrate

hamstring
4 lame **6** muscle, tendon **7** cripple, disable **10** immobilize **12** incapacitate

Hamutal
father: **8** Jeremiah
husband: **6** Josiah
son: **8** Jehoahaz, Zedekiah

hand
3 aid, paw **4** fist, mitt, pass **5** manus **6** script, worker **7** deliver, dish out, laborer, workman **8** employee, transfer **10** assistance, penmanship **11** calligraphy, chirography
clenched: **4** fist
combining form: **4** chir **5** chiro
counting zero: **8** baccarat
covering: **5** glove **6** mitten
down: **8** bequeath
gesture: **5** mudra
on hip: **6** akimbo
part: **4** palm **5** thumb **6** finger
poker: **5** flush **8** straight **9** full house
protector: **5** glove **7** gantlet **8** gauntlet

handbag
4 grip **5** purse **6** clutch **8** reticule, suitcase **10** pocketbook

handbill
5 flier, flyer **6** poster **7** affiche, leaflet, placard **8** circular

handbook
5 guide **6** manual **8** Baedeker **9** vade mecum **10** compendium **11** enchiridion
religious: **9** catechism

handcuff
6 fetter **7** manacle, shackle
British: **7** darbies (plural)

hand down
4 will **6** bestow, pass on **7** deliver **8** bequeath, transmit

Handel, George Frideric
aria: **5** Largo
birthplace: **5** Halle **7** Germany
opera: **4** Nero **5** Serse **6** Admeto, Alcina, Almira, Ottone, Xerxes **7** Arminio, Orlando, Rinaldo, Rodrigo **8** Berenice **9** Agrippina, Ariodante **12** Giulio Cesare, Julius Caesar
oratorio: **4** Saul **6** Esther, Joshua, Samson, Semele **7** Athalia, Deborah, Jephtha, Messiah, Solomon **8** Theodora

handicap
4 edge, load, odds **6** burden, hamper, hinder, impede **8** drawback, encumber, restrict **9** advantage, allowance, detriment, head start, hindrance **10** disability, limitation **11** encumbrance **12** disadvantage

handicraft
5 skill **8** artefact, artifact

hand in
6 submit, tender **7** deliver, present

handkerchief
5 hanky **6** hankie **7** bandana **8** bandanna, mouchoir **9** accessory

handle
3 paw, use **4** ansa, feel, grip, haft, hilt, knob, name, test **5** crank, see to, touch, trade, treat, wield **6** manage **7** control, moniker, operate **8** deal with, doorknob, exercise, maneuver, nickname **10** manipulate
scythe: **5** snath **6** snathe

handling
4 care 6 charge 9 packaging, treatment
partner: 8 shipping

hand out
4 give, mete 6 bestow, donate 7 deliver, present, provide 8 disburse, dispense, give away 10 administer, distribute

hand over
4 cede, feed, give 5 leave, yield 6 commit, donate, fork up, give up, supply 7 commend, confide, consign, deliver, entrust, present 8 dispense, give back, relegate, transfer 9 deliver up, surrender 10 relinquish

handrail
8 banister

handsome
4 buff, cute, fair 5 hunky, noble 6 comely 7 dashing 10 attractive 11 good-looking

handspring
6 tumble
lateral: 9 cartwheel

handwriting
6 script 8 longhand 10 autography, manuscript, penmanship 11 calligraphy, chirography, copperplate
bad: 10 cacography
study of: 10 graphology

handy
4 able, deft, near, yare 5 adept, close, utile 6 adroit, clever, nearby, nimble, useful 7 close-by, skilled 8 adjacent, skillful 9 adaptable, available, dexterous 10 accessible, convenient, proficient 11 practicable, within reach

handyman
6 helper 7 go-to guy 8 factotum

hang
3 jut, sag 4 hook, idle, loll 5 cling, drape, droop, float, hoist, knack, lynch, sling, swing 6 dangle, depend 7 suspend
back: 3 lag 4 drag, poke 5 trail 6 dawdle, schlep 7 schlepp 8 straggle
loosely: 3 sag 6 dangle

hang around
4 stay, wait 5 abide, dally, tarry 6 dawdle, linger, loiter 7 goof off 8 frequent

hangdog
3 sad 4 blue, glum 5 cowed 6 guilty 7 abashed, ashamed, pitiful, unhappy 8 dejected, sheepish 9 chagrined, depressed 11 embarrassed

hanger-on
5 leech 6 sponge, sucker 7 sponger 8 barnacle, follower, parasite 9 sycophant 10 freeloader 11 bloodsucker

hanging
5 arras, slope 7 curtain, drapery, pendant, pendent 8 covering, tapestry 9 declivity, execution, pendulous, suspended

Hanging Gardens site
7 Babylon

hang on
4 grip 5 grasp 6 clutch, endure, remain 7 persist, survive 8 continue, hold fast 9 persevere

hang out
4 idle, loaf 5 chill, dally, relax 6 loiter, lounge 7 goof off

hangout
5 haunt, joint 6 resort 7 purlieu, retreat 10 rendezvous 12 watering hole

hang up
4 mire, snag 5 delay 6 detain, impede, retard 7 bog down, set back, suspend 8 slow down

hang-up
5 block 7 dilemma, problem 9 obsession 10 difficulty, inhibition

hank
4 clip, coil, loop, ring 6 bundle

hanker
3 yen 4 ache, itch, long, lust, want, wish 5 covet, crave, yearn 6 desire, hunger, thirst

hankering
3 yen 4 ache, itch, lust, urge 5 ardor 6 desire, hunger, pining, thirst 7 craving, longing, passion 8 appetite, yearning

hanky-panky
5 fraud, trick 7 chicane 8 mischief, trickery 9 chicanery, dalliance, deception 13 double-dealing, sharp practice

Hannibal
defeat: 4 Zama
father: 8 Hamilcar
home: 8 Carthage
surname: 5 Barca
vanquisher: 6 Scipio
victory: 6 Cannae

Hansa
5 guild 6 league

Hans Brinker author
5 Dodge (Mary Mapes)

Hanseatic League city
6 Bremen, Lübeck, Wismar 7 Cologne, Hamburg, Rostock

Hänsel und Gretel composer
11 Humperdinck (Engelbert)

Hansen's disease
7 leprosy

hansom
3 cab 5 coach 8 carriage

haole
5 white 9 Caucasian

haphazard
6 casual, chance, random **7** aimless **8** at random, careless, slipshod **9** desultory, hit-or-miss, irregular, unplanned **10** accidental, willy-nilly **11** unorganized **12** unsystematic **13** helter-skelter

hapless
4 poor **6** woeful **7** unhappy, unlucky **8** ill-fated, wretched **9** miserable **10** ill-starred **11** star-crossed, unfortunate

happen
4 pass **5** occur **6** befall, betide **7** develop, fall out, turn out **8** bechance **9** transpire
again: **5** recur
together: **6** concur **8** coincide

happening
3 new **5** event, scene, thing **7** episode **8** incident, occasion **9** adventure **10** experience, occurrence, phenomenon **11** fashionable **12** circumstance

happen on
4 find **8** bump into, discover

happenstance
5 event **6** chance **8** incident, occasion **9** condition, situation **11** coincidence

happiness
3 joy **4** glee **5** bliss, cheer, mirth **6** gaiety **7** aptness, content, delight, elation, jollity **8** felicity, gladness, pleasure **9** enjoyment, well-being **11** contentment **12** satisfaction

happy
4 glad **5** jolly, lucky, merry **6** joyful, joyous, upbeat **7** blessed, content, pleased **8** friendly, jubilant **9** contented, favorable, satisfied **12** enthusiastic, lighthearted

Happy Days
character: **5** Chuck **6** Chachi, Fonzie, Howard, Joanie, Marion, Potsie, Richie
family: **10** Cunningham
site: **9** Milwaukee
star: **4** Baio (Scott), Ross (Marion) **5** Moran (Erin) **6** Bosley (Tom), Howard (Ron) **7** Winkler (Henry) **8** O'Herlihy (Gavan), Williams (Anson)

happy-go-lucky
4 easy **6** blithe, breezy, casual **8** carefree, careless, cheerful, heedless, laid-back, reckless **9** easygoing, unworried **10** insouciant, nonchalant **11** unconcerned **12** devil-may-care, lighthearted

hara-kiri
7 seppuku, suicide **8** felo-de-se

Haran
brother: **7** Abraham
daughter: **5** Iscah **6** Milcah
father: **5** Terah **6** Shimei
son: **3** Lot

harangue
4 rant, rave **5** orate, spiel **6** exhort, hassle, tirade **7** declaim, lecture, oration **8** bloviate, diatribe, jeremiad **9** discourse, philippic **11** declamation, exhortation

harass
3 irk, vex **4** bait, raid, ride **5** annoy, beset, bully, chivy, harry, hound, tease, worry **6** badger, chivvy, hassle, heckle, hector, pester, plague, stress **7** bedevil, exhaust, fatigue, torment, trouble **8** bullyrag, distress **9** beleaguer, persecute

harbinger
4 omen, sign **5** augur **6** augury, herald **7** apostle, portent **9** messenger, precursor **10** forerunner, indication

harbor
3 bay **4** cove, port **5** haven, inlet, lodge, put up **6** billet, refuge, shield, take in **7** nurture, protect, seaport, shelter **9** anchorage, safeguard, sanctuary
Hawaii: **5** Pearl

hard
4 firm, iron **5** cruel, harsh, solid, tough **6** brutal, knotty, packed, rugged, tiring, trying **7** arduous, callous, onerous **8** absolute, concrete, exacting, granitic, grinding, indurate, pitiless, rigorous **9** demanding, difficult, fatiguing, intensely, intensive, laborious, unfeeling **10** adamantine, exhausting, spirituous, thoroughly, vigorously **11** complicated, intensively, intractable, troublesome, unrelenting, unremitting **12** backbreaking
cover: **5** crust
to please: **7** finicky

hard-boiled
4 grim **5** rough, stoic, tough **6** coarse **7** callous **8** seasoned **9** impassive, pragmatic, unfeeling **11** insensitive, unemotional **12** stonyhearted, thick-skinned **13** unsympathetic

harden
3 dry, set **5** enure, inure, steel **6** anneal, freeze, ossify, season, temper **7** calcify, compact, congeal, densify, lithify, petrify, stiffen, toughen **8** solidify **9** acclimate, fossilize, habituate **10** strengthen

hardfisted
4 mean **5** close, tight **6** stingy, strict **13** penny-pinching

hardheaded
5 sober, tough **6** mulish, shrewd **7** willful **8** obdurate, perverse, stubborn **9** obstinate, practical, pragmatic, realistic **10** determined **11** down-to-earth, intractable

hardhearted
4 cold **5** stony **8** pitiless, uncaring **9** merciless, unfeeling

hard-hitting
6 strong 8 emphatic, forceful, powerful 9 effective

hardihood
3 pep 4 gall, grit, guts 5 cheek, moxie, nerve, pluck, vigor 6 daring 7 courage 8 audacity, boldness, temerity 9 assurance, brashness, cockiness, fortitude, impudence, insolence 10 brazenness, robustness

hard-line
4 firm 5 fixed, rigid, tough 8 obdurate 9 obstinate, unbending 10 inflexible, unyielding 11 stiff-necked 12 intransigent

hardness
5 rigor 7 density 8 rigidity, severity 10 difficulty, resistance

hardscrabble
6 barren 8 marginal 9 infertile, unbearing, unfertile 12 impoverished, unproductive

hardship
4 need, toil 5 rigor, trial 6 burden 7 travail 8 asperity, distress, drudgery 9 adversity, privation, suffering 10 affliction, difficulty, discomfort, misfortune 11 tribulation

Hard Times author
7 Dickens (Charles)

hard up
4 poor 5 broke, needy 6 bad off 8 beggared, bankrupt, deprived, indigent, strapped 9 desperate, destitute, penniless 10 down-and-out 11 necessitous 12 impoverished

hardy
4 bold, hale 5 brave, tough 6 daring, robust, rugged, strong 7 healthy 8 intrepid, resolute 9 audacious

Hardy, Thomas
character: 3 Sue (Bridehead) 4 Alec (D'Urberville), Clym (Yeobright), Jude (Fawley), Tess (Durbeyfield) 5 Angel (Clare) 7 Gabriel (Oak) 8 Arabella (Donn), Eustacia (Vye), Henchard (Michael) 9 Bathsheba (Everdene)
novel: 11 Woodlanders (The) 14 Jude the Obscure 17 Return of the Native (The) 19 Mayor of Casterbridge (The) 21 Tess of the D'Urbervilles 22 Far from the Madding Crowd
setting: 6 Wessex

Hardy Boys
author: 5 Dixon (Franklin W.) 9 McFarlane (Leslie)
character: 3 Joe 4 Biff (Hooper), Chet (Morton), Iole 5 Frank, Laura 6 Callie, Fenton 12 Aunt Gertrude
city: 7 Bayport
jalopy: 5 Queen
motorboat: 6 Napoli, Sleuth

hare
5 lapin 6 rabbit
female: 3 doe
genus: 5 Lepus
male: 4 buck
tail: 4 scut
young: 7 leveret

harebrained
5 crazy, loony, silly, wacky 6 absurd, insane, stupid 7 asinine, foolish 9 frivolous 10 ridiculous 12 preposterous

harem
5 serai 6 zenana 8 seraglio
attendant: 6 eunuch
concubine: 9 odalisque

haricot
3 pod 4 bean 10 kidney bean

hark
4 hear, heed, mind, note 6 attend, listen, notice

harlequin
5 clown, joker 6 jester, mottle 7 buffoon 9 prankster

Harlequin
beloved: 9 Columbine
rival: 7 Pierrot

harm
3 mar 4 hurt, maim, ruin 5 abuse, spoil, wound, wrong 6 damage, ill-use, impair, injure, injury, misuse, molest 7 tarnish 8 ill-treat, maltreat, mischief, mistreat 9 undermine 10 disservice, misfortune

harmful
3 bad 4 evil 5 risky, toxic 6 malign, unsafe 7 noisome, noxious 8 damaging 9 dangerous, hazardous, injurious, malignant, unhealthy 10 pernicious 11 deleterious, detrimental, unhealthful

harmless
4 safe 6 benign 8 innocent, nontoxic 9 innocuous 11 inoffensive

Harmonia
daughter: 3 Ino 5 Agave 6 Semele 7 Autonoë
father: 4 Ares, Mars
husband: 6 Cadmus
mother: 5 Venus 9 Aphrodite
son: 9 Polydorus

harmonious
5 sweet 7 chiming, chordal, musical, pacific 8 blending, friendly, in accord, peaceful, pleasing 9 agreeable, congenial, congruous, consonant, symphonic 10 compatible, concordant 11 cooperative, symmetrical, sympathetic

harmonize
3 fit 4 jibe, sing 5 agree, blend, match 6 accord, attune 7 arrange, concert, conform

8 coincide, dovetail 9 integrate 10 coordinate, correspond, synthesize 11 orchestrate

harmony
4 sync 5 grace, peace, unity 6 accord 7 balance, concert, concord, oneness, rapport 8 affinity, sonority, symmetry 9 agreement, congruity, polyphony 10 accordance, concinnity, conformity, consonance, proportion 11 concordance, consistency, cooperation
lack of: 7 discord 10 dissonance
of movement: 8 eurythmy

harness
4 curb, gear, yoke 5 hitch, leash 6 bridle, tackle 7 utilize 11 domesticate
part: 3 bit 4 rein 5 girth, trace 6 collar 7 blinder, crupper 9 bellyband, breeching, checkrein 12 breast collar
ring: 6 terret

harp
4 lyre 9 harmonica
Greek: 7 cithara, kithara
Japanese: 4 koto

harpsichord
7 cembalo 8 clavecin

harpsichordist
American: 6 Fuller (Albert, David), Kipnis (Igor), Newman (Anthony) 7 Marlowe (Sylvia), Pinkham (Daniel), Valenti (Fernando) 11 Kirkpatrick (Ralph)
Dutch: 9 Leonhardt (Gustav)
English: 7 Malcolm (George), Pinnock (Trevor)
German: 7 Richter (Karl)
Italian: 7 Sgrizzi (Luciano)
Polish: 9 Landowska (Wanda)

harpy
3 nag 5 leech, scold, shrew, vixen 6 virago 8 fishwife, harridan 9 termagant

Harpy
5 Aello 7 Celaeno, Ocypete
father: 7 Thaumas
mother: 7 Electra
sister: 4 Iris

harridan
3 hag 4 fury 5 biddy, harpy, shrew, vixen, witch 6 dragon, gorgon, ogress, virago 7 hellcat 8 battle-ax, fishwife 9 battle-axe, termagant

harrier
3 dog 4 hawk 6 hector, runner 10 persecutor

Harris, Joel Chandler
character: 7 Brer Fox 8 Brer Bear 10 Brer Rabbit
narrator: 10 Uncle Remus

harrow
3 try, vex 4 bait, rack 5 devil, tease 6 badger, heckle, hector, needle, pester, suffer 7 afflict, bedevil, torment, torture, trouble 8 distress, irritate 9 cultivate 10 excruciate

harry
3 dog, irk, vex 4 gnaw, raid, ride, sack 5 annoy, tease, upset, worry 6 attack, badger, harass, hassle, maraud, pester, plague, ravage 7 assault, bedevil, despoil, perturb, pillage, plunder, torment 8 desolate, maltreat 9 beleaguer, depredate

harsh
5 cruel, gruff, rough, stern 6 biting, brutal, coarse, severe, uneven, unkind 7 austere, caustic, grating, jarring, painful, pungent, raucous, stubbly 8 exacting, grinding, jangling, scraping, scratchy, strident, unsmooth 9 dissonant, inclement 10 discordant, irritating, unpleasant

harshness
8 asperity 9 roughness

hart
4 deer, stag 7 red deer
mate: 4 hind

hartebeest
4 tora 8 antelope
family: 7 Bovidae

Harte story
17 Luck of Roaring Camp (The) 19 Outcasts of Poker Flat (The)

Hartford
college: 7 Trinity
specialty: 9 insurance

Hart, Moss
autobiography: 6 Act One
collaborator: 7 Kaufman (George S.)
musical: 13 Lady in the Dark
play: 15 Once in a Lifetime 18 Man Who Came to Dinner (The) 20 You Can't Take It with You

haruspex
4 seer 5 augur 7 diviner, prophet 8 foreseer 9 predictor 10 forecaster, foreteller, soothsayer

harvest
4 crop, pick, reap 5 amass, cache, glean, hoard, stash, yield 6 garner, gather 7 collect, reaping, store up, vintage 8 ingather, squirrel, stow away 9 garnering, gathering
bug: 4 mite 7 chigger
fly: 6 cicada
festival: 6 Lammas 7 Cerelia 10 Michaelmas 12 Thanksgiving
god, goddess: 3 Ops 5 Ceres 6 Consus 7 Demeter

harvester
7 gleaner
grain: 6 binder, header
of grapes: 8 vintager

Harvey
5 pooka 6 rabbit
author: 5 Chase (Mary)
character: 6 Elwood (P. Dowd)

hash
4 chop, mess, stew **5** botch, mince, mix-up **6** jumble, medley, muddle, review **7** clutter, confuse, mélange, mixture **8** consider, shambles **9** patchwork **10** assortment, hodgepodge, miscellany

hash house
4 café **5** diner **6** bistro, eatery **7** beanery, pit stop **10** coffee shop **11** greasy spoon **12** luncheonette

hashish
5 bhang, ganja **6** charas **8** cannabis, narcotic
plant: **4** hemp

hash out
6 review **7** discuss **8** talk over **9** talk about

hasp
5 catch **6** fasten **8** fastener **9** fastening

hassle
3 row **4** beef, to-do **5** annoy, argue, brawl, fight, run-in **6** bicker, clamor, harass, hubbub, tumult, uproar **7** dispute, problem, quarrel, rhubarb, turmoil, wrangle **8** argument, squabble, struggle **9** commotion **11** altercation, controversy

hassock
4 pouf **7** cushion, kneeler, ottoman **9** footstool

haste
3 hie, run **4** dash, rush **5** hurry, speed **6** barrel, bustle, flurry, hustle **7** beeline, hotfoot **8** celerity, dispatch, rapidity, velocity **9** fleetness, quickness, swiftness **10** speediness **11** hurriedness, impetuosity

hasten
3 fly, hie, run **4** rush, urge **5** hurry, press, speed **6** barrel, hustle, step up, urge on **7** hurry up, quicken, speed up **8** expedite **10** accelerate

hasty
4 fast, rash **5** brisk, eager, fleet, quick, rapid, swift **6** abrupt, rushed, speedy, sudden **7** cursory, hurried, rushing **8** careless, fleeting, headlong, heedless, reckless, slapdash **9** hotheaded, impatient, impetuous, irritable, quickened **10** ill-advised, incautious **11** expeditious, perfunctory, precipitate, precipitous, superficial, thoughtless

hat
5 derby, toque, tuque **6** boater, cloche, fedora, panama, topper **7** bicorne, chapeau, homburg, porkpie, Stetson, tricorn **8** sombrero, tricorne **9** headpiece **11** deerstalker
ancient Greek: **7** petasos, petasus
brimless: **7** pillbox
close-fitting: **4** kufi **5** toque, tuque **6** cloche, turban
felt: **5** busby, derby **6** bowler, trilby
fur: **5** busby **6** castor
helmetlike: **4** topi **5** topee
maker: **7** modiste **8** milliner
Middle Eastern: **3** fez
military: **4** kepi **5** busby, shako **8** bearskin
Muslim: **3** fez **6** turban **8** tarboosh
Scottish: **3** tam **9** glengarry **11** tam-o'-shanter
sheepskin: **6** calpac **7** calpack
soft: **5** toque, tuque
straw: **6** boater, panama, sailor **7** bangkok, leghorn, skimmer **8** sombrero
sun: **5** terai
tall: **9** stovepipe
waterproof: **9** sou'wester
woman's: **4** coif **5** toque, tuque **6** bonnet **7** pillbox

hatch
4 door, plan, plot **5** breed, brood, cover, inlay, spawn **6** cook up, create, design, devise, emerge, invent, make up, work up **7** concoct, dream up, opening, produce, think up **8** contrive, engender, generate, incubate, occasion **9** floodgate, formulate, give birth, give forth, originate, procreate **11** compartment

hatchet
3 axe **8** tomahawk

hatchet man
5 bravo **6** killer **7** torpedo **8** assassin, enforcer, murderer **9** attack dog, cutthroat **10** eliminator

hate
5 abhor, scorn **6** animus, detest, enmity, loathe, malice, rancor **7** despise **8** aversion, execrate, loathing **9** abominate, animosity, antipathy **10** abhorrence, repugnance

hateful
4 evil, foul, mean, vile **5** nasty **6** horrid, malign, odious, scurvy **7** vicious **8** accursed, damnable, infamous **9** abhorrent, execrable, malicious, obnoxious, repellent, repulsive **10** abominable, despicable, detestable, malevolent **11** blasphemous, opprobrious, unspeakable **13** reprehensible

Hatfields vs. ___
6 McCoys

hatred
5 odium, spite **6** animus, enmity, rancor **7** dislike **8** aversion, loathing **9** animosity, antipathy, hostility, repulsion, revulsion **10** abhorrence, repugnance **11** abomination, detestation, malevolence
of change: **9** misoneism
of humankind: **11** misanthropy
of marriage: **8** misogamy
of men: **8** misandry
of women: **8** misogyny

hats
9 millinery

hauberk
5 armor **9** chain mail, habergeon

haughtiness
4 airs **5** pride, scorn **7** conceit, disdain, hauteur **9** arrogance, insolence, pomposity **12** snobbishness

haughty
5 aloof, proud **6** lordly, sniffy **7** distant **8** arrogant, cavalier, scornful, snobbish, superior **9** egotistic **10** disdainful **11** overbearing **12** contemptuous, supercilious

haul
3 lug, tow, tug **4** cart, drag, draw, hump, lift, load, loot, pull, swag, take, tote **5** boost, booty, cargo, hoist, raise, truck **6** burden, lading, schlep, spoils **7** freight, payload, schlepp
with a tackle: **5** bowse

haul up
5 hoise, hoist
with a rope: **5** trice

haunch
3 hip **11** hindquarter

haunches
4 butt, rump **7** hind end, rear end **8** backside, buttocks **9** posterior **12** hindquarters

haunt
4 site **5** spook **6** obsess, prey on **7** habitat, hang out, inhabit, torment, trouble **8** frequent **9** preoccupy **10** hang around, rendezvous, stay around, visit often

haunter
5 ghost **7** denizen, habitué

hautbois
4 oboe

hauteur
see **haughtiness**

haut monde
5 elite **6** jet set **7** society, who's who **10** glitterati, upper crust **11** aristocracy, high society **13** carriage trade

have
3 own **4** hold **7** contain, include, possess

haven
4 port, roof **5** house, oases (plural), oasis **6** asylum, harbor, refuge **7** retreat, shelter **9** anchorage, sanctuary

haversack
3 bag **4** pack **8** backpack

havoc
4 loss, ruin, sack **5** chaos, waste **6** mayhem **8** calamity, disorder, ravaging **9** confusion, ruination **11** catastrophe, destruction, devastation, pandemonium

haw
4 left, tree **5** berry, fruit, shrub **8** turn left **10** equivocate

Hawaii
author: **8** Michener (James A.)
beach: **7** Waikiki
capital: **8** Honolulu
city: **4** Hilo
coast: **4** Kona
discoverer: **4** Cook (Capt. James)
island: **4** Maui, Oahu **5** Kauai, Lanai **6** Niihau **7** Molokai
mountain: **7** Kilauea **8** Mauna Kea, Mauna Loa
nickname: **5** Aloha (State)
park: **9** Haleakala
state bird: **4** nene
state flower: **8** hibiscus
state tree: **5** kukui **9** candlenut

Hawaiian
dance: **4** hula
feast: **4** luau
food: **3** poi
god: **4** Kane, Lono **5** Wakea **7** Kanaloa
goddess: **4** Pele
goose: **4** nene
gooseberry: **4** poha
grass: **4** hilo
instrument: **3** uke **7** ukulele
lava: **2** aa
neckwear: **3** lei
nonnative: **5** haole **8** malihini
resident: **8** kamaaina
shaman: **6** kahuna
soup: **6** saimin
thrush: **4** omao
tree: **3** koa

hawk
4 kite, sell, vend **5** buteo **6** falcon, monger, osprey, peddle **7** Cooper's, goshawk, haggard, harrier **8** caracara, huckster, roughleg **9** accipiter, red-tailed, warmonger **10** militarist **11** ferruginous, rough-legged
Hawaiian: **2** io
male: **6** tercel **7** tiercel
young: **4** eyas

hawker
6 coster, monger, seller, vendor **7** packman, peddler **8** pitchman **12** costermonger

hawkeyed
11 keen-sighted **12** sharp-sighted

Hawkeye State
4 Iowa

hawkish
7 martial, warlike **9** combative **10** aggressive **11** belligerent **12** militaristic

____ Hawley Tariff
5 Smoot

Hawthorne, Nathaniel
birthplace: **5** Salem

character: **6** Hester (Prynne) **8** Clifford (Pyncheon), Hepzibah (Pyncheon), Pyncheon (Judge) **10** Dimmesdale (Rev. Arthur) **13** Chillingworth (Roger)
novel: **10** Marble Faun (The) **13** Scarlet Letter (The) **21** House of the Seven Gables (The)

hay
3 bed **4** feed **5** grass **6** fodder, reward **7** herbage
crops: **6** clover **7** alfalfa, timothy

Haydn oratorio
7 Seasons (The) **8** Creation (The)

hay fever
7 allergy **10** pollenosis, pollinosis
cause: **6** pollen **7** ragweed

haying machine
5 baler

haymaker
3 box **4** blow, sock **5** clout, punch **6** wallop

hayseed
see **hick**

haywire
4 amok, awry **5** amuck, crazy, upset **6** faulty **8** confused **10** out of order **12** out of control

hazard
3 bet, try **4** dare, game, luck, risk **5** peril, shoal, wager **6** chance, danger, gamble, menace **7** fortune, imperil, venture **8** accident, endanger, jeopardy, obstacle

hazardous
5 hairy, risky **6** chancy, unsafe **7** unsound **8** perilous **9** dangerous, unhealthy **10** precarious

haze
3 fog **4** film, mist, murk, smog **5** brume, cloud, drive, smoke, vapor **6** harass **7** dimness, obscure **8** dullness, initiate, overcast **9** mistiness, murkiness, vagueness **10** cloudiness

hazel
4 wood **5** birch, shrub **7** filbert

hazy
3 dim **5** faint, filmy, foggy, fuzzy, misty, murky, smoky, vague **6** cloudy, unsure **7** blurred, clouded, obscure, unclear **8** nebulous, vaporous **9** uncertain **10** indefinite, indistinct

head
3 nob, nut, top **4** bean, boss, capo, foam, john, main, mind, pate, poll **5** brain, caput, chief, first, gourd, poise, prime, privy, scalp, skull **6** honcho, leader, master, noggin, noodle, talent, toilet **7** cranium, faculty, latrine, premier, supreme **8** director, foremost, lavatory **9** chieftain, principal **10** promontory
area: **5** crown **6** temple
back part: **7** occiput
bone: **5** skull **7** cranium **8** parietal
combining form: **6** cranio **7** cephalo
covering: **3** cap, hat **6** bonnet **8** kerchief
monastery: **4** dean **5** abbot **8** superior
nunnery: **6** abbess **8** superior
of hair: **4** mane **6** fleece **9** chevelure
relating to: **8** cephalic
shaving of: **7** tonsure
skin: **5** scalp
top: **4** pate **5** crown

headache
4 pain **5** worry **6** bother, megrim **7** problem **8** migraine, nuisance, vexation **9** annoyance **10** irritation

headband
7 bandeau, circlet, coronal
ancient Greek: **6** taenia **7** taeniae (plural)

headdress
7 topknot
American Indian: **9** warbonnet
Arab: **8** kaffiyeh, keffiyeh
bishop's: **5** miter, mitre
medieval: **4** barb
Eastern: **6** turban
nobleman's: **7** coronet
royal: **5** crown, tiara **6** diadem
Spanish women's: **8** mantilla
women's: **6** bonnet
(see also **hat**)

headland
4 cape **5** point **10** promontory

headline
6 banner **7** feature, promote **8** screamer **9** emphasize, publicize, spotlight **10** noteworthy

headlong
4 rash **5** brash, hasty **6** abrupt, daring, rashly, sudden **7** hurried, rushing **8** heedless, reckless **9** foolhardy, impetuous, impulsive **10** heedlessly, recklessly **11** precipitate, precipitous

headmaster
6 leader **9** principal

head off
4 stop **5** avert, block **6** thwart **7** deflect, obviate, prevent, ward off **8** stave off, turn back **9** forestall, intercept

headquarters
3 hub **4** base, seat **6** center

head start
4 edge, jump, lead, odds **5** boost **7** advance, vantage **8** handicap **9** advantage, allowance

headstone
6 marker **8** memorial, monument **11** grave marker

headstrong
6 dogged, mulish, unruly **7** willful **8** contrary,

perverse, stubborn **9** obstinate **10** bullheaded, refractory, self-willed **11** intractable, stiff-necked

heads-up
5 alarm, alert **6** signal, tip-off **7** warning **8** high sign **11** resourceful

headway
4 gain **6** growth **7** advance **8** anabasis, progress **11** advancement, improvement

heady
4 rash, rich **5** giddy **6** elated, potent **7** willful **8** exciting **9** impetuous **11** exhilarated, intoxicated **12** intoxicating

heal
3 fix **4** cure, mend **5** sew up, treat **6** cement, remedy, repair **7** patch up, restore **8** make well

healer
6 doctor, shaman

healing
8 curative, remedial, salutary, sanative **9** vulnerary, wholesome **10** salubrious **11** restorative, therapeutic **12** convalescent
goddess of: 3 Eir

health
7 fitness, welfare **8** haleness, vitality, wellness **9** soundness, well-being, wholeness
club: 3 gym, spa

healthful
8 curative, hygienic, remedial, salutary **9** favorable, wholesome **10** beneficial, corrective, profitable, salubrious **11** restorative

healthy
3 fit **4** hale, spry, well **5** sound, tonic **6** benign, robust, strong, sturdy **7** chipper **8** blooming, hygienic, positive, salutary, thriving, vigorous **9** wholesome **10** able-bodied, beneficial, prosperous, salubrious **11** flourishing

Heaney work
5 North **9** Field Work **12** Wintering Out
translation: 7 Beowulf

heap
3 lot **4** cock, fill, gobs, hill, load, lump, mass, much, pack, pile, rick, scad **5** amass, bunch, clump, crate, loads, mound, shock, stack, wreck **6** barrel, charge, gather, jalopy, junker, lumber, oodles **7** clunker, collect, deposit, jillion **8** assemble, mountain, slathers **9** abundance, profusion, stockpile

hear
4 heed, oyez **5** catch, learn **8** listen to, perceive **9** apprehend

hearing
4 oyer, test **5** trial **6** tryout **7** earshot, inquiry **8** audience, audition **9** interview **10** conference, discussion
distance: 7 earshot

hearken
4 heed, mind, note **6** attend, listen, notice **7** observe

hearsay
4 buzz, news, talk **5** rumor **6** gossip, report **7** account, chatter **9** grapevine **11** scuttlebutt

heart
3 cor, hub **4** core, crux, gist, guts, love, pith, root, seat, soul, zest **5** ardor, bosom, focus, gusto, moxie, pluck, spunk **6** breast, center, kernel, mettle, relish, spirit, ticker **7** courage, resolve **8** feelings, sympathy **9** character, fortitude **10** compassion
chart: 3 ECG, EKG
combining form: 6 cardio
contraction: 7 systole
dilation: 8 diastole
part: 5 valve **6** atrium, septum **9** ventricle

heartache
3 rue, woe **4** care, pain, pang **5** grief **6** regret, sorrow **7** anguish, sadness **8** distress **10** affliction

heartbeat
5 flash, jiffy, pulse, throb, trice **6** moment, second **9** pulsation
irregular: 10 arrhythmia

heartbreak
3 rue, woe **5** agony, grief **6** misery, regret, sorrow **7** anguish, despair, torment, torture **9** suffering **10** desolation **12** wretchedness

heartbreaking
6 bitter, tragic **8** grievous **9** agonizing **10** calamitous, deplorable, lamentable **11** devastating, distressing

heartbroken
7 crushed, grieved **8** mournful, overcome, wretched **9** sorrowful **10** despairing, despondent **12** disconsolate

heartburn
7 pyrosis

hearten
4 buoy, stir **5** cheer, rally, rouse **6** arouse, buck up, buoy up, perk up **7** animate, cheer up, enliven, inspire **8** embolden, energize, inspirit **9** encourage

heartfelt
4 deep, true **6** honest **7** earnest, fervent, genuine, sincere **8** profound **9** unfeigned

hearth
4 home **5** abode **8** domicile, dwelling, fireside **9** fireplace, residence

heartily
6 wholly **9** sincerely, with gusto, zestfully **10** completely, thoroughly

heartless
4 cold, hard 5 cruel 6 unkind 7 callous 8 uncaring 9 unfeeling 10 hard-boiled 11 insensitive, unemotional 13 unsympathetic

Heart of Dixie
7 Alabama

heartsease
5 pansy, viola 6 violet 11 peace of mind, tranquility 12 johnny-jump-up, tranquillity

heart-shaped
7 cordate

heartsick
4 blue, down 8 dejected, desolate, dismayed, downcast 9 depressed 10 despondent, dispirited 11 demoralized 12 disconsolate

heartthrob
4 idol, love 5 flame, honey, sweet 7 beloved, darling, passion 9 dreamboat 10 sweetheart

heart-to-heart
4 open, talk 5 frank 6 candid, honest 7 sincere 8 truthful 12 conversation

hearty
4 hale, warm 5 ample 6 jovial, robust, sailor, strong 7 cordial, healthy, profuse, sincere 8 abundant, vehement, vigorous 9 approving, energetic, exuberant, flavorful, unfeigned 12 enthusiastic, unrestrained

heat
4 cook, rage, warm, zeal 5 ardor, fever 6 fervor, simmer, warmth 7 caloric, inflame, passion, swelter 8 pyrolyze
combining form: 4 pyro 6 calori, thermo 7 thermia
measuring device: 11 calorimeter, thermometer
quantity: 3 BTU

heated
3 hot, mad 5 angry, fiery, irate 6 ardent, fervid, fierce, ireful, raging, steamy 7 boiling, burning, fevered, furious 8 broiling, feverish, scalding, sizzling, vehement, wrathful 9 indignant, scorching 10 passionate 11 acrimonious

heater
3 gun, rod 4 etna 5 stove 6 boiler, pistol 7 furnace, handgun 8 fastball, radiator

heath
4 ling, moor 5 broom, Erica, shrub 7 Calluna 9 crowberry, wasteland

heathen
5 pagan 7 infidel 8 barbaric 11 irreligious, uncivilized

heat-producing
9 calorific

heave
3 lob 4 cast, draw, fire, gasp, haul, heft, huff, hurl, lift, pant, puff, pull, push, toss 5 fling, hoist, labor, pitch, raise, retch, sling, surge, throw, vomit 6 launch

heave-ho
4 boot 6 ouster 8 bum's rush 9 dismissal

heaven
4 Eden, Zion 5 bliss, glory 6 utopia 7 arcadia, ecstasy, elysium, nirvana, rapture 8 empyrean, eternity, paradise 9 firmament, Shangri-la 10 wonderland 11 immortality, kingdom come 12 promised land

heavenly
4 lush 6 divine, sacred 7 blessed 8 beatific, empyreal, empyrean, ethereal 9 ambrosial, celestial, delicious 10 delectable, delightful, enchanting

heavy
3 big, fat 5 beefy, bulky, gross, hefty, obese, stout, thick 6 bad guy, chunky, fleshy, leaden, portly 7 labored, porcine, villain, weighty 8 cumbrous, sluggish, unwieldy 9 corpulent, laborious, lumbering, ponderous, strenuous 10 burdensome, cumbersome, oppressive, overweight

heavy-handed
5 crude, harsh, inept 6 clumsy, gauche, klutzy 7 awkward 8 bumbling, despotic 9 maladroit 10 oppressive 11 domineering, overbearing

heavyhearted
3 sad 4 glum 5 sorry 7 unhappy 8 dejected, downcast, mournful, saddened 9 depressed, miserable, sorrowful 10 despondent, dispirited, melancholy

heavyset
5 beefy, husky, stout, thick 6 chunky, portly, stocky 11 thick-bodied

heavyweight
3 VIP 4 lion 5 boxer, chief 6 big gun, bigwig, honcho, leader 7 big shot, notable 8 big-timer

Hebe
father: 4 Zeus 7 Jupiter
husband: 8 Hercules
mother: 4 Hera, Juno
successor: 8 Ganymede

hebetude
6 stupor, torpor 7 languor 8 dullness, lethargy 9 lassitude, torpidity 10 drowsiness

hebetudinous
4 dull, logy 5 dopey 6 drowsy, stupid, torpid 8 listless, sluggish 9 lethargic

Hebrew
3 Jew 6 Jewish
coin: 6 lepton, shekel
festival: 5 Purim 6 Pesach, Sukkot 7 Hanukah, Sukkoth 8 Chanukah, Lag b'Omer, Passover,

Shabuoth **9** Tishah-b'Ab, Yom Kippur **12** Rosh Hashanah, Simchas Torah
God: **6** Adonai, Elohim, Yahweh **7** Jehovah
judge: **6** Gideon
lawgiver: **5** Moses
leader: **4** Saul **5** Moses **6** Joshua **7** Solomon
letter:
(see at **alphabet**)
lyre: **6** kinnor
measure: **4** beka, omer **5** bekah, cubit, ephah
month: **2** Ab **4** Abib, Adar, Elul, Iyar **5** Nisan, Sivan, Tebet **6** Kislev, Shebat, Tammuz, Tishri **6** Veadar (in leap year) **7** Heshvan
patriarch: **3** Dan, Gad **4** Cain, Levi, Seth **5** Asher, David, Isaac, Jacob, Judah **6** Joseph, Lamech, Reuben, Simeon **7** Abraham, Zebulun **8** Benjamin, Issachar, Naphtali
sacred city: **5** Safad, Safed **6** Hebron **8** Tiberias **9** Jerusalem
tribe: **3** Dan, Gad **4** Levi **5** Asher, Judah **6** Reuben, Simeon **7** Ephraim, Zebulon **8** Benjamin, Issachar, Manasseh, Naphtali
(see also **Jewish**)

Hebrides island
4 Eigg, Rhum, Skye, Uist **5** Lewis **6** Harris

Hecate
father: **6** Perses
goddess of: **5** night **10** underworld, witchcraft
mother: **7** Asteria

hecatomb
7 killing, slaying **8** butchery **9** bloodbath, sacrifice, slaughter

heck
4 darn, drat, geez, gosh, hell, jeez **5** golly **6** shucks

heckle
3 nag **4** bait, faze, gibe, ride **5** annoy, chivy, hound, tease, worry **6** badger, bother, harass, hassle, hector, molest, needle, pester, plague, rattle **7** disrupt, disturb, torment **9** interrupt **10** disconcert

hectic
3 red **6** fervid **7** burning, excited, fevered, flushed **8** confused, exciting, feverish, frenetic, restless **9** turbulent **10** persistent

hector
3 cow, nag **4** bait, ride **5** bully, chivy, hound **6** badger, harass, lean on **7** bedevil, swagger **8** browbeat, bullyrag, domineer **10** intimidate

Hector
brother: **5** Paris **7** Helenus, Troilus **9** Deiphobus, Polydorus
father: **5** Priam
mother: **6** Hecuba
sister: **6** Creusa **8** Polyxena **9** Cassandra
slayer: **8** Achilles
victim: **9** Patroclus
wife: **10** Andromache

Hecuba
daughter: **6** Creusa **8** Polyxena **9** Cassandra
father: **5** Dymas
husband: **5** Priam
son: **5** Paris **6** Hector **7** Helenus, Troilus **9** Deiphobus, Polydorus
victim: **11** Polymnestor

hedge
4 trim **5** avoid, evade, fence, guard, hem in, limit **6** hinder **7** barrier, defense, enclose, evasion, protect **8** boundary, encircle, restrict **9** shrubbery **10** protection

hedgehog
9 porcupine **10** stronghold

hedonist
4 rake **7** epicure, gourmet **8** gourmand, sybarite **9** bon vivant, epicurean, libertine **10** sensualist, voluptuary

heebie-jeebies
5 jumps **6** creeps, nerves, shakes **7** jitters, shivers, willies **11** nervousness

heed
4 care, hark, mark, mind, note, obey **5** watch **6** attend, harken, listen, notice, regard, remark **7** be aware, concern, hearing, hearken, observe, respect **8** consider, interest, listen to **9** attention **10** observance

heedful
5 alert, aware **7** on guard **8** vigilant **9** attentive, observant, observing **10** interested, meticulous, scrupulous **13** conscientious

heedless
9 negligent, oblivious, unmindful **10** unthinking **11** inadvertent, inattentive, unobservant **12** unreflective **13** inconsiderate

heedlessness
7 neglect **9** disregard, unconcern **11** disinterest, inattention, insouciance **12** indifference

hee-haw
4 bray **5** laugh **6** guffaw **10** horse laugh

heel
3 bum, cad, tip **4** cant, hock, lean, list, tilt **5** creep, knave, louse, rogue, skunk, slope **6** rascal, rotter **7** bounder, incline, lowlife, villain **9** scoundrel
bone: **8** calcanea (plural), calcanei (plural) **9** calcaneum, calcaneus

heft
4 bulk, lift, load **5** hoist, raise, weigh **6** weight **7** heave up **9** heaviness, influence **10** importance

hefty
3 big **5** beefy, burly, bulky, heavy, husky, large, major **6** brawny, mighty, rugged, strong **7** massive, sizable **8** imposing, powerful **9** extensive, good-sized, plentiful, ponderous, strapping **11** substantial

hegira
6 escape, exodus, flight **7** journey **10** emigration, evacuation **11** deliverance

Heidi
author: **5** Spyri (Johanna)
goatherd: **5** Peter
setting: **4** Alps

heifer
4 calf

____ Heifetz
6 Jascha

height
3 top **4** acme, apex, cusp, peak, rise **6** apogee, climax, heyday, summit, vertex, zenith **7** stature **8** altitude, pinnacle **9** elevation, loftiness **10** prominence
combining form: **4** acro

heighten
3 wax **5** boost, mount, raise **6** beef up, expand, extend **7** amplify, augment, build up, elevate, enhance, enlarge, improve, magnify **8** increase **9** highlight, intensify **10** aggrandize

heinie
3 bum **4** butt, rear, rump, tush **5** fanny **6** bottom **7** hind end, rear end **8** backside

heinous
4 evil **6** odious **7** hateful **8** infamous, shocking **9** abhorrent, atrocious, execrable, monstrous **10** abominable, detestable, outrageous

heinousness
4 evil **6** horror, infamy **8** atrocity, enormity **13** monstrousness

heir
5 scion **7** grantee, heritor, legatee **9** inheritor, successor **11** beneficiary
joint: **8** parcener **10** coparcener

heist
3 cop, rob **4** lift, loot **5** boost, caper, filch, pinch, steal, swipe, theft **6** holdup, rip off **7** larceny, purloin, robbery **8** burglary **9** strong-arm

Helen of Troy
abductor: **5** Paris
husband: **8** Menelaus

Helenus
brother: **5** Paris **6** Hector **7** Troilus **9** Deiphobus, Polydorus
father: **5** Priam
mother: **6** Hecuba
sister: **6** Creusa **8** Polyxena **9** Cassandra
wife: **10** Andromache

Hel, Hela
father: **4** Loki
hall: **7** Niflhel **8** Niflheim
mother: **9** Angerboda

helical
6 spiral

helicopter
7 chopper **9** eggbeater **10** whirlybird
armed: **7** gunship **9** Black Hawk
blade: **5** rotor
manufacturer: **8** Sikorsky (Igor)

Helios
6 Apollo
daughter: **5** Circe **8** Pasiphaë
father: **8** Hyperion
mother: **5** Theia
sister: **3** Eos **6** Aurora, Selene
son: **8** Phaethon

heliotrope
4 herb **5** shrub **6** borage **10** bloodstone

helium symbol
2 He

hell
5 hades, Sheol **6** blazes, Tophet **7** Gehenna, inferno **9** perdition, tarnation **10** blue blazes

hell-bent
6 driven, intent **8** obsessed, resolved **10** determined

Hellen
father: **9** Deucalion
mother: **6** Pyrrha
son: **5** Dorus **6** Aeolus, Xuthus

hellhole
3 pit **8** dystopia, snake pit **9** mare's nest

hellion
3 elf, imp **4** puck, punk **5** demon, rogue, scamp **6** rascal **7** gremlin

hellish
6 horrid **7** ghastly, hideous, satanic, stygian **8** damnable, diabolic, dreadful, gruesome, horrible, infernal, terrible **9** appalling, frightful, monstrous, plutonian **10** diabolical

Hellman play
11 Little Foxes (The) **13** Children's Hour (The) **15** Watch on the Rhine

hello
3 hey **4** ciao, hail **5** aloha, howdy **7** hi there, welcome **8** greeting **9** greetings

helm
4 head **5** wheel **7** cockpit **8** controls

helmet
6 casque, sallet, tin hat **7** morrion **8** burgonet, headgear
medieval: **6** sallet **7** basinet
part: **5** nasal **7** ventail **8** aventail
sun: **4** topi **5** topee

helmsman
5 pilot

Heloïse
husband: **7** Abelard (Peter)
son: **9** Astrolabe

helot
4 peon, serf **5** slave **6** vassal **7** laborer, peasant, servant

helotry
4 yoke **6** thrall **7** bondage, peonage, serfdom, slavery **9** servitude, thralldom **11** enslavement

help
3 aid **4** abet, back, mend **5** avail, boost, guide, serve **6** assist, relief, remedy, succor **7** advance, benefit, bolster, further, promote, relieve, secours, service, support **8** mitigate, palliate **9** alleviate, meliorate **10** ameliorate, assistance, facilitate **11** cooperation
forward: **7** further
hired: **5** labor

helper
4 aide, ass't **6** deputy, server **7** ancilla, servant **8** employee **9** assistant, associate, attendant, auxiliary **10** apprentice **11** subordinate

helpful
5 of use **6** usable, useful **8** salutary, valuable **9** effective, favorable, practical **10** beneficial, profitable, propitious **11** encouraging **12** advantageous, constructive

helping
4 dose **5** share **7** portion, serving **9** auxiliary

helpless
4 weak **6** feeble, futile, unable **7** forlorn **8** desolate **9** abandoned, dependent **11** unprotected

helter-skelter
6 anyhow **7** anywise, flighty, hastily, turmoil **8** at random, disorder, pell-mell, randomly **9** confusion, haphazard, hit-or-miss **11** any which way, haphazardly, in confusion, precipitate

helve
4 haft **6** handle

Helvetian
5 Swiss

hem
3 pen, rim **4** brim, edge, gird, ring, seam, shut **5** bound, brink, fence, hedge, skirt, verge **6** border, circle, corral, edging, fringe, immure, margin, stitch **7** close in, enclose, selvage, shorten **8** encircle, surround **9** encompass, perimeter, periphery
turned-back: **4** cuff

he-man
4 hunk, stud **5** macho

Heman
father: **4** Joel
grandfather: **6** Samuel

hematite
3 ore **7** mineral **12** black diamond

Hemingway, Ernest
work: **9** In Our Time **12** Sun Also Rises (The) **13** Moveable Feast (A) **14** Farewell to Arms (A) **15** Old Man and the Sea (The) **16** To Have and Have Not **18** Islands in the Stream, Snows of Kilimanjaro (The) **19** For Whom the Bell Tolls
sobriquet: **4** Papa

hemipterous insect
3 bug

hemlock
4 drug, herb, tree, wood **6** poison

hemophiliac
7 bleeder

hemp
3 kef, kif **7** hashish **8** cannabis **9** marijuana
fiber: **5** oakum
kind: **4** aloe

hen
5 biddy, layer
broody: **6** sitter
spayed: **8** poularde
young: **6** pullet

hence
4 away, ergo, thus **5** since **6** hereat **9** as a result, from now on, therefore, thereupon **11** accordingly **12** consequently

henceforth
9 from now on, hereafter

henchman
6 cohort, lackey, minion, stooge **7** abettor **8** adherent, disciple, follower, partisan, retainer **9** attendant, supporter **10** accomplice

Henley poem
8 Invictus

henpeck
3 nag **4** carp, fuss **5** annoy **6** badger, carp at, harass, hector **8** domineer **9** find fault

Henry II
adversary: **6** Becket (Thomas à)
son: **4** John (Lackland) **7** Richard (Lionheart)
surname: **5** Anjou **11** Plantagenet
wife: **7** Eleanor

Henry IV **11** **Bolingbroke**
surname: **9** Lancaster
victim: **10** Richard III

Henry VIII
archbishop: **7** Cranmer (Thomas) **10** Thomas More
daughter: **9** Elizabeth
son: **6** Edward
surname: **5** Tudor
victim: **4** Anne (Boleyn) **9** Catherine (Howard) **10** Thomas More
wife: **4** Anne (Boleyn, of Cleves), Jane (Seymour) **9** Catherine (Howard, of Aragon, Parr)

hepatic
9 liverwort

Hephaestus
6 Vulcan
father: **4** Zeus **7** Jupiter
mother: **4** Hera, Juno
wife: **5** Venus **6** Charis **9** Aphrodite

Hephzibah
husband: **8** Hezekiah
son: **8** Manasseh

hepped up
5 eager **7** charged, excited, fervent **8** enthused **12** enthusiastic

Hera
4 Juno
father: **6** Cronus, Saturn
husband: **4** Zeus **7** Jupiter
messenger: **4** Iris
mother: **4** Rhea

Heracles
beloved: **4** Iole
brother: **8** Iphicles
charioteer: **6** Iolaus
father: **4** Zeus **7** Jupiter
mother: **7** Alcmene
son: **6** Hyllus
victim: **5** Hydra, Ladon **6** Geryon, Megara, Orthus **10** Nemean lion
wife: **4** Hebe **6** Megara **8** Deianira

herald
4 hail, tout **5** crier, greet **6** signal **7** courier, declare, portend, precede, presage, trumpet **8** announce, ballyhoo, exponent, outrider, proclaim **9** advertise, harbinger, messenger, precursor, publicize, spokesman **10** forerunner, foreshadow

heraldic
border: **7** bordure
cross: **6** fleury, formée, moline, pommée **8** fourchée
term: **4** aile, bend, fess, orle, pale, semé, vair, vert **5** crest, flank, gules **6** argent, blazon, canton, charge, device, dexter, emblem, impale, manche, sejant, voided, volant **7** chevron, nombril, passant, purpure, rampant, saltire, statant, urinant **8** guardant, sinister, tincture **9** regardant **10** escutcheon

heraldry
6 armory **9** pageantry

herb
3 Iva, oca, pia, udo **4** arum, dill, flax, forb, geum, hemp, leek, mint, nard, sage, wort **5** basil, canna, chive, cumin, tansy, thyme **6** allium, arnica, borage, catnip, endive, eryngo, fat hen, fennel, garlic, hyssop, lovage, orpine, squill, yarrow **7** boneset, caraway, catmint, chervil, chicory, comfrey, episcia, ginseng, milfoil, mullein, oregano, parsley, pinesap, pussley, salsify, sanicle **8** angelica, camomile, capsicum, cardamom, centaury, cilantro, costmary, feverfew, freewort, hepatica, lungwort, mandrake, marjoram, origanum, pokeweed, purslane, rapeseed, selfheal, tarragon, turmeric, euphrasy, valerian, woodruff, wormwood **9** birthwort, bush basil, chamomile, goosefoot, patchouli, spikenard **10** basil thyme, cuckoo pint **12** balm of Gilead
beverage: **6** tisane
genus: **4** Arum, Geum
mythical: **4** moly
poisonous: **4** atis **7** aconite, dogbane, hemlock, henbane **8** veratrum **9** hellebore, monkshood

herbicide
6 dioxin, diquat, diuron **7** monuron **8** picloram, simazine **11** Agent Orange

Herculean
4 huge, vast **5** giant **7** arduous, immense, mammoth, titanic **8** colossal, enormous, gigantic, powerful **10** formidable, superhuman

Hercules
see **Heracles**

herd
3 mob **4** bevy, lead **5** covey, crowd, drive, drove, flock, swarm **6** gather, throng **9** associate, multitude

herdsman
6 Boötes, cowboy **7** breeder **8** shepherd

here and there
6 passim **7** at times **9** sometimes **11** irregularly

hereditary
6 inborn, inbred, innate, lineal **7** genetic **9** ancestral, inherited **10** congenital **11** traditional, transmitted

heredity
7 lineage **8** ancestry **9** tradition **11** inheritance
unit: 4 gene

heresy
6 schism **7** dissent, fallacy, impiety **9** defection, deviation, misbelief **10** dissidence, heterodoxy, infidelity, radicalism **11** revisionism, unorthodoxy **13** nonconformism, nonconformity

heretic
7 infidel **8** apostate, defector, recusant, renegade **9** dissenter, dissident **10** iconoclast, schismatic, separatist, unbeliever **11** misbeliever, nonbeliever, revisionist **13** nonconformist

heretical
7 infidel **8** apostate **9** dissident, heterodox, miscreant, sectarian **10** dissenting, schismatic, unorthodox **11** revisionist **12** misbelieving **13** nonconformist

heretofore
6 ere now **7** up to now

heritage
6 legacy **7** bequest **9** patrimony, tradition **10** birthright

Hermes
7 Mercury
attribute: 7 petasos, petasus **8** caduceus
father: 4 Zeus **7** Jupiter
mother: 4 Maia

hermetic
6 arcane, closed, occult, sealed, secret **7** recluse **8** abstruse, airtight, profound, secluded, solitary **9** recondite **10** cloistered, impervious **11** sequestered

Hermia
beloved: 8 Lysander
father: 5 Egeus

Hermione
father: 8 Menelaus
husband: 7 Orestes, Pyrrhus **11** Neoptolemus
mother: 5 Helen

hermit
5 loner **6** cookie **7** eremite, recluse **8** solitary **9** anchorite

hermitage
7 retreat **8** cloister, hideaway **9** monastery

hernia
6 breach **7** rupture **10** protrusion
support: 5 truss
type: 6 cystic, hiatal **7** femoral **9** umbilical **10** incisional

hero
4 idol, lion **6** knight **7** demigod, paladin **8** champion **11** protagonist
American: 6 Bunyan (Paul) **8** Superman
Armenian: 10 Skanderbeg
Babylonian: 9 Gilgamesh
Celtic-French: 7 Tristan **8** Tristram
Crusades: 7 Tancred **8** Tancredi
English: 6 Arthur **7** Beowulf **9** Robin Hood
French: 6 Roland **11** Charlemagne
German: 5 Etzel **8** Arminius **9** Siegfried
Greek: 4 Ajax **5** Jason **7** Perseus, Ulysses **8** Achilles, Heracles, Hercules, Leonidas, Odysseus **11** Bellerophon
Hebrew: 5 David **6** Daniel, Samson
Hungarian: 5 Arpad **7** Hunyadi (János)
Irish: 9 Cuchulain, Cuchulinn, Cuchullin
Italian: 7 Orlando
Roman: 7 Romulus **8** Horatius
Scandinavian: 6 Sigurd **9** Siegfried
Scottish: 5 Bruce (Robert) **6** Rob Roy
Spanish: 3 Cid **5** El Cid
Spartan: 8 Leonidas
Trojan: 6 Aeneas, Hector

Herod
daughter: 6 Salome
father: 7 Antipas **9** Antipater
kingdom: 5 Judea **6** Judaea
mother: 6 Cyprus
son: 5 Herod (Antipas) **6** Joseph **7** Pheroas **9** Phasaelus

Herodias
daughter: 6 Salome
father: 11 Aristobulus
husband: 5 Herod (Antipas)

heroic
4 bold, epic **5** brave, noble **6** daring **7** drastic, extreme, radical, valiant **8** fearless, intrepid, unafraid, valorous **9** dauntless, Herculean, undaunted **10** courageous

heroin
4 gear, skag, snow **5** horse, smack **8** narcotic **11** diamorphine

heroism
5 valor **6** daring, spirit **7** bravery, courage, prowess **8** boldness, chivalry, nobility, valiance **9** gallantry **11** intrepidity

heron relative
5 egret **7** bittern

Hero's lover
7 Leander

herring
7 sardine **8** brisling, pilchard
measure: 4 cran
smoked: 7 bloater

Herse
father: 7 Cecrops
sister: 8 Aglauros
son: 8 Cephalus

Hersey
novel: **4** Wall (The) **12** Bell for Adano (A)
town: **5** Adano

Hesione
brother: **5** Priam
father: **8** Laomedon
husband: **7** Telamon
rescuer: **8** Heracles, Hercules
son: **6** Teucer

hesitant
4 slow **5** chary, loath, timid **6** afraid, averse, unsure **7** halting, uneager **9** faltering, reluctant, tentative, uncertain, unwilling **10** irresolute **11** disinclined, vacillating

hesitate
4 balk **5** delay, demur, hedge, pause, stall, stick, waver **6** dawdle, dither, falter, waffle **7** stammer, stutter **8** hang back, hold back **9** temporize, vacillate **12** shilly-shally

Hesperides
6 nymphs

Hesperus
5 Venus **11** evening star
father: **8** Astraeus
mother: **3** Eos

Hesse novel
6 Demian **10** Siddhartha **11** Steppenwolf **12** Magister Ludi

Hestia
5 Vesta
father: **6** Cronus, Saturn
mother: **4** Rhea

heterodox
9 dissident, heretical, sectarian **10** schismatic, unorthodox **13** nonconformist

heterodoxy
6 heresy, schism **7** dissent **9** misbelief **10** dissidence **13** nonconformism, nonconformity

heterogeneous
5 mixed **6** motley, sundry, varied **7** diverse, various **8** assorted **9** disparate **12** conglomerate

het up
5 irate, upset **7** excited **8** agitated

hew
3 axe, cut **4** chop, fell, form **5** shape, stick **6** adhere **7** conform, cut down

hex
4 jinx **5** charm, curse, spell, witch **6** voodoo, whammy **7** bad luck, bewitch, enchant **9** sorceress **11** enchantment, enchantress

hey
4 psst

heyday
4 acme, peak **5** prime **6** height, zenith **9** high point

Hezekiah
father: **4** Ahaz **7** Neariah
mother: **3** Abi
son: **8** Manasseh
wife: **9** Hephzibah

hiatus
3 gap **5** break, space **6** breach, lacuna **7** interim **8** aperture, downtime, interval **10** suspension **12** interruption **13** discontinuity

Hiawatha
author: **10** Longfellow (Henry Wadsworth)
craft: **5** canoe
grandmother: **7** Nokomis
mother: **7** Wenonah
tribe: **6** Ojibwa, Ojibwe **8** Onondaga **7** Ojibway
wife: **9** Minnehaha

hibernal
6 wintry **8** winterly

Hibernia
4 Eire, Erin **7** Ireland

hick
4 rube **5** yokel **6** rustic **7** bumpkin, hayseed **8** cornball **10** clodhopper, provincial

hidden
5 privy **6** buried, covert, occult, secret, veiled **7** obscure **8** obscured, shrouded, ulterior **9** concealed **11** undisclosed
combining form: **6** crypto, krypto

hide
3 fur **4** bury, lurk, mask, pelt, skin, veil **5** cache, cloak, cover, inter, shade, stash **6** harbor, lie low, screen, shroud **7** conceal, cover up, leather, obscure, seclude, secrete, shelter **8** ensconce

hideaway
see **hideout**

hidebound
8 obdurate **9** parochial **10** inflexible, provincial **11** reactionary, straitlaced **12** conservative, narrow-minded **13** straightlaced

hideous
4 ugly **5** awful, gross, lurid, nasty **6** grisly, horrid **7** ghastly, hateful **8** gruesome, horrible, shocking, terrible **9** appalling, dismaying, frightful, loathsome, monstrous, offensive, repellent, repugnant, repulsive, revolting, sickening **10** disgusting, horrifying

hideout
3 den **4** lair **5** cache, haven **6** covert, refuge **7** retreat, shelter **9** hermitage, safe house, sanctuary

hie
3 run **4** dash, push, trot **5** hurry, scoot **6** hasten, hustle

hierarch
4 boss, head **5** chief **6** honcho, leader, master **7** headman **9** chieftain **10** high priest

hierarchy
5 group, order, ranks **6** ladder, system **7** pyramid **9** food chain, structure **11** bureaucracy **12** pecking order

hieratic
6 formal **8** priestly, stylized **10** priestlike, sacerdotal

high
4 tall **5** drunk, giddy, grand, lofty, noble, tipsy **6** elated, raised, stoned, treble, zonked **7** drugged, keyed up, soaring, supreme **8** abstruse, elevated, eloquent, euphoric, hopped-up, piercing, towering **9** climactic, delirious, prominent, spaced-out **11** extravagant, intoxicated
combining form: 4 alti

high ___
3 hat, tea **4** card, five, noon, road, sign, tech, tide, time **5** chair, heels, hopes, jinks **6** priest, roller, school

high-and-mighty
5 bossy, proud **6** lordly **7** haughty **8** arrogant, cavalier, insolent, superior **9** imperious **10** disdainful **11** domineering, overbearing **12** supercilious

highball
3 fly, run **4** dash, rush, whiz **5** hurry, speed **6** barrel, hustle, signal **7** hotfoot **8** cocktail

highboy
5 chest **6** bureau **7** dresser **9** furniture

highbrow
4 snob **7** egghead **8** cerebral, cultured, educated **9** intellect **12** intellectual

high-class
7 elegant **8** five-star, superior **9** exclusive, exquisite, first-rate, patrician **11** fashionable **12** aristocratic **13** sophisticated

highest
3 top **5** chief **6** apical, upmost **7** exalted, supreme, topmost **9** top-drawer, uppermost **10** top-ranking
point: 4 acme, apex **5** crest **6** summit, zenith **8** pinnacle

highfalutin
5 fancy, windy **6** florid **7** aureate, flowery, fustian, orotund, pompous **8** affected **9** bombastic, grandiose, overblown, rhapsodic **10** oratorical, rhetorical **11** declamatory, pretentious

high-flown
5 showy, tumid, windy **6** turgid **7** aureate, flowery, fustian, orotund, pompous, swollen **8** elevated, inflated, sonorous **9** bombastic, grandiose, overblown **10** flamboyant **11** declamatory, pretentious **12** magniloquent, ostentatious **13** grandiloquent

high-handed
5 bossy **8** arrogant, dogmatic, imperial **9** arbitrary, imperious **10** autocratic, disdainful, imperative, peremptory **11** dictatorial, domineering, magisterial, overbearing

high-hat
4 snub **6** slight, snobby, snooty **7** disdain, haughty **8** arrogant, snobbish **9** conceited, disregard **11** pretentious **12** supercilious

high jinks
3 fun **6** antics **7** fooling, revelry **9** horseplay, rowdiness, whoop-de-do

Highlander
4 Gael, Scot

highlight
4 mark **5** focus **6** accent, stress **7** feature **8** point out **9** emphasize, underline **10** accentuate, focal point

high-minded
5 lofty, moral, noble **7** ethical, upright **8** elevated **10** principled

high-muck-a-muck
3 VIP **5** nabob **6** bigwig **7** big shot, notable

high-pitched
6 shrill **7** excited **8** agitated, feverish, frenetic, piercing

high point
3 top **4** acme, peak **6** apogee, summit, zenith **8** best part, pinnacle

high-powered
6 driven, strong **7** dynamic **8** animated, forceful, vigorous **9** energetic, strenuous **10** aggressive, compelling **12** enterprising

high-pressure
7 intense **8** forceful **9** insistent, stressful **10** aggressive

high roller
7 gambler, spender, wastrel **8** prodigal **10** big spender, profligate, squanderer **11** spendthrift

high sign
3 nod, tip **4** wink **5** alarm **6** signal, tipoff **7** gesture, warning **8** thumbs-up

Highsmith novel
11 Ripley's Game **16** Talented Mr. Ripley (The)

high-sounding
7 fustian, pompous **8** affected, imposing, inflated, puffed-up **9** grandiose, overblown **11** pretentious

high-spirited
4 bold **5** brash, fiery, jolly, merry **6** bubbly, daring, joyful, lively, plucky, spunky **7** excited, gleeful **9** ebullient, energetic, exuberant, vivacious **12** effervescent, lighthearted

high-strung
4 edgy, taut **5** hyper, jumpy, nervy, tense, tight, wired **6** touchy **7** fidgety, jittery, keyed up, nervous, uptight **8** restless **9** excitable, sensitive

hightail it
3 run **4** bolt, dash, flee **5** scoot, scram **6** get out, run off **7** take off **8** clear out **9** skedaddle

highway
4 pike, road **5** track **6** artery **8** corridor, turnpike **10** interstate **12** thoroughfare
German: **8** autobahn
Italian: **10** autostrada

highwayman
5 thief **6** bandit, robber **7** brigand

hijack
5 seize, steal **6** abduct, kidnap **8** take over **10** commandeer **11** appropriate

hike
2 up **4** jump, rove, snap, trek, walk **5** boost, raise, tramp, tromp **6** jack up, rise up, travel **7** journey, traipse, upgrade **8** backpack, increase

hilarious
5 funny, merry **7** comical **8** humorous, mirthful **9** laughable, priceless **10** rollicking

hilarity
4 glee **5** cheer, mirth **6** gaiety **7** delight **8** jocosity, laughter **9** merriment **12** cheerfulness

hill
4 bank, brae, bump, cock, dune, heap, knob, pile, rick, rise **5** bluff, butte, knoll, mound, ridge, shock, slope, stack **6** cuesta, height **7** hummock, incline **8** mountain **9** elevation, monadnock
African veld: **5** kopje **6** koppie
Boston: **6** Bunker
craggy: **3** tor
Cuba: **7** San Juan
D.C.: **7** Capitol
elongate: **7** drumlin
level-topped: **4** mesa **5** butte
of stratified drift: **4** kame
rounded: **5** swell
sand: **4** dune
small: **5** knoll, kopje, mound **6** koppie
surrounded by ice: **7** nunatak

hillbilly
4 rube **5** yokel **6** rustic **7** bumpkin, hayseed **10** clodhopper **12** backwoodsman

hillock
4 rise **5** knoll, mound

hillside
5 slope
Scottish: **4** brae

hilt
4 grip, haft **6** handle **8** handgrip

Himalayan
country: **5** Nepal **6** Bhutan
creature: **4** yeti
peak: **6** Makalu **7** Everest **9** Annapurna **10** Dhaulagiri **11** Nanga Parbat **13** Kangchenjunga

hind
3 doe **4** back, deer, rear **5** after **7** grouper **9** posterior
mate: **4** hart

hinder
4 balk, curb, mire **5** block, check, delay, deter **6** baffle, burden, fetter, hamper, hold up, impede, retard, thwart **7** inhibit, prevent, shackle, trammel **8** handicap, hold back, obstruct, restrain **9** frustrate, hamstring, interfere, interrupt

hindmost
3 end **4** back, last, rear **5** after, final **6** latter **7** closing **8** farthest, terminal, ultimate **9** posterior **10** concluding

hindquarters
8 haunches

hindrance
3 bar **4** snag **6** hurdle **7** barrier **8** obstacle **9** impedance **10** impediment **11** obstruction

Hindu
age: **4** yuga
ascetic: **4** yogi **5** fakir, swami
camel: **4** oont
caste (varna): **5** Sudra **6** Vaisya **7** Brahman **9** Kshatriya
class: **5** caste, varna
community: **6** ashram
demon: **4** Rahu **6** Ravana
essence: **5** atman
force: **5** karma
garment: **4** sari
gentleman: **4** babu
god: **4** deva, Rama, Siva **5** Shiva **6** Brahma, Vishnu
goddess: **4** devi
goddess of beauty: **7** Lakshmi
goddess of destruction: **4** Kali
goddess of speech: **4** Vach
god of destruction: **4** Siva **5** Shiva
god of fire: **4** Agni
god of love: **4** Kama
god of the heavens: **7** Krishna
god of the wind: **4** Vayu

god of war: 6 Skanda 10 Karttikeya
god of wisdom: 6 Ganesa, Ganesh
hell: 6 Naraka
holy man: 5 sadhu
honorific: 3 Sri 5 Swami 6 Pandit
hundred thousand: 4 lakh
instrument: 5 sitar, tabla
leader: 6 Gandhi (Mahatma)
lowest caste: 5 Sudra
nobleman: 4 raja 5 rajah
philosophy: 7 Vedanta
precept: 5 sutra
prince: 4 raja 5 rajah 8 maharaja 9 maharajah
queen: 4 rani 5 ranee 8 maharani 9 maharanee
salvation: 7 nirvana
scripture: 4 Veda 6 Purana 12 Bhagavad Gita
social group: 5 caste, varna
teacher: 4 guru 5 swami 9 maharishi
term of respect: 5 sahib
treatise: 9 Upanishad
twice-born: 6 Vaisya 7 Brahman 9 Kshatriya
weaver: 5 tanti

hinge
4 pawl 5 joint, mount 12 turning point
kind: 4 butt 5 piano 10 hook-and-eye

hint
3 cue, tip 4 clue, dash, sign, wisp 5 imply, taste, tinge, touch, trace 6 allude, notion, shadow, tipoff 7 inkling, soupçon, suggest 8 allusion, indicate, innuendo, intimate 9 insinuate, scintilla, suspicion 10 indication, intimation, suggestion 11 implication, insinuation

hinterland
4 bush 6 sticks 8 frontier, interior 9 backwater, backwoods, boondocks, up-country 10 wilderness 11 backcountry

hip
3 hot 4 chic, coxa 5 aware, savvy 6 haunch, trendy, with-it 7 tuned in 11 fashionable
bone: 5 ilium, pubis 6 pelvis 7 ischium
cattle: 5 thurl
disorder: 8 sciatica

hip-hop
star: 3 DMC, DMX, Nas 4 Dash (Damon), Jay-Z, West (Kanye), Zola 5 Combs (Sean "Diddy"), Dr. Dre, Kelis 6 Eminem, Franti (Michael), Ja Rule, Lil' Kim 7 Ice Cube, LL Cool J, OutKast, Simmons (Russell) 8 Jadakiss, Ludacris 9 Biz Markie, Fifty Cent, Foxy Brown, Snoop Dogg 11 Busta Rhymes, Tupac Shakur
term: 3 dap, def, dip, dis 4 bima, simp, wack 5 busta, chill, crunk, floss, freak, homey, peeps, props, sherm, stilo, whodi 6 gaffle, hottie, nucker, step to 7 all that, be geese, down low, homeboy, hooptie, puff lye, shizzle, wangsta 9 dukey rope, freestyle, throw bows 10 bling bling, ghetto bird, scrap a lick 12 South Central

hippie
8 bohemian, longhair 11 flower child 13 nonconformist

Hippocratic ____
4 oath

Hippodamia
father: 8 Oenomaus
husband: 6 Pelops 9 Pirithous 10 Peirithous
son: 6 Atreus 8 Thyestes

Hippolytus
father: 7 Theseus
mother: 7 Antiope 9 Hippolyte
stepmother: 7 Phaedra

hire
3 fee, let, pay 4 rent, wage 5 lease, wages 6 employ, engage, retain, sign on, take on 7 charter, payment, recruit 8 contract 10 employment 11 contract for

hireling
4 hack 6 worker 7 servant 8 employee 9 mercenary

Hirschfeld's daughter
4 Nina

hirsute
5 hairy 6 shaggy, woolly 9 whiskered

Hispania
6 Iberia 9 peninsula
part: 5 Spain 8 Portugal

Hispaniola country
5 Haiti

hiss
3 boo 4 hoot, jeer 5 decry 6 deride, revile, sizzle, wheeze 7 catcall, whisper, whistle 8 sibilate

historian
8 annalist 10 chronicler
American: 4 Webb (Charles Richard) 5 Adams (Brooks, Charles Kendall, Hannah, Henry, Herbert Baxter), Beard (Charles, Mary), Foote (Shelby) 6 Brooks (Van Wyck), Catton (Bruce), DeVoto (Bernard), Durant (Ariel, Will), Malone (Dumas), Miller (Perry), Muzzey (David), Nevins (Allen), Sarton (George Alfred), Shirer (William), Sparks (Jared), Turner (Frederick Jackson) 7 Ambrose (Stephen), Morison (Samuel Eliot), Parkman (Francis), Ridpath (John Clark), Tuchman (Barbara), Woodson (Carter G.) 8 Bancroft (George), Boorstin (Daniel), Channing (Edward), Commager (Henry Steele), Prescott (William H.), Robinson (James Harvey), Woodward (C. Vann) 10 McCullough (David) 11 Schlesinger (Arthur)
Arab: 10 Ibn Khaldun
Danish: 4 Saxo (Grammaticus)
Dutch: 8 Huizinga (Johan)

English: 4 Bede (Venerable), Stow (John), Ward (Adolphus) 5 Acton (Lord), Grote (George), Wells (Herbert George) 6 Camden (William), Gibbon (Edward), Keegan (John), Namier (Lewis Bernstein), Stubbs (William), Taylor (A. J. P.) 7 Hakluyt (Richard), Raleigh (Walter), Toynbee (Arnold), Whewell (William) 8 Geoffrey (of Monmouth), Macaulay (Thomas Babington) 9 Holinshed (Raphael), Trevelyan (George)
French: 5 Bloch (Marc), Renan (Ernest), Taine (Hippolyte) 6 Guizot (François), Thiers (Louis-Adolphe), Volney (Comte de) 7 Braudel (Ferdinand) 8 Hanotaux (Gabriel), Michelet (Jules)
German: 5 Ranke (Leopold von) 7 Mommsen (Theodor), Niebuhr (Barthold Georg) 8 Spengler (Oswald)
Greek: 8 Plutarch, Polybius, Xenophon 9 Dionysius, Herodotus 10 Thucydides
Italian: 4 Vico (Giovanni) 5 Croce (Benedetto) 9 Salvemini (Gaetano)
Jewish: 8 Josephus (Flavius)
Roman: 4 Livy 7 Sallust, Tacitus (Cornelius) 9 Suetonius
Scottish: 7 Carlyle (Thomas) 9 Robertson (William)
Swiss: 6 Müller (Johannes von)
Welsh: 7 Nennius

historical period
3 age, era 5 epoch

history
4 past, saga 5 diary 6 annals, memoir, record 7 account, done for, journal 9 chronicle, narrative, treatment 10 chronology

histrionic
5 showy, stagy 6 staged 8 affected, dramatic 10 artificial, theatrical

hit
3 bop, jab, rap 4 bang, bash, bean, biff, blow, bump, bunt, butt, conk, cuff, ding, lick, slap, slug, sock, swat 5 clout, knock, paste, pound, punch, smack, smash, smite, swipe, whack 6 batter, buffet, chance, larrup, strike, stroke, thwack, wallop 7 clobber, sellout, success 8 bludgeon, lambaste 9 collision, sensation
baseball: 5 homer, liner 6 double, single, triple 7 home run 9 line drive
topposite: 4 bomb, flop, miss
golf ball: 5 shank

hitch
4 jerk, join, halt, hook, knot, lift, limp, snag, yoke 5 delay, thumb, unite 6 attach, couple, fasten, hobble, tether 7 connect, harness 8 make fast, stoppage 10 connection, difficulty, impediment 11 obstruction 12 entanglement

Hitchcock, Alfred
film: 4 Rope 5 Birds (The), Topaz 6 Frenzy, Marnie, Psycho 7 Rebecca, Vertigo 8 Lifeboat, Sabotage 9 Notorious, Suspicion 10 Rear Window, Spellbound 12 Lady Vanishes (The) 13 To Catch a Thief 14 Shadow of a Doubt 16 North by Northwest
forte: 8 suspense

hitchhike
5 thumb

hither
4 here 6 nearer 11 to this place

hitherto
5 as yet, so far 7 earlier, thus far, till now 8 formerly, until now 10 previously

Hitler, Adolf
follower: 4 Nazi
title: 6 Führer 7 Fuehrer
wife: 5 Braun (Eva)

hit man
5 bravo 6 killer 7 torpedo 8 assassin, enforcer, hired gun, murderer 9 cutthroat

hit-or-miss
6 casual, chance, random 7 aimless, erratic 8 careless 9 desultory, haphazard, irregular, unplanned

hive
6 apiary, colony 7 cluster 9 stockpile

HMS Pinafore
composer: 8 Sullivan (Arthur)
librettist: 7 Gilbert (W. S.)

hoagie
3 sub 4 hero 5 po'boy 7 grinder, torpedo 8 sandwich 9 submarine

hoar
4 rime 5 frost

hoard
4 save 5 amass, cache, lay by, lay up, stash, stock, store, trove 6 supply 7 collect, lay away, nest egg, reserve 8 squirrel, treasure 9 stockpile 10 accumulate, collection, cumulation 11 aggregation 12 accumulation

hoarder
5 miser 7 scrooge

hoarse
5 gruff, husky, raspy, rough, thick 6 croaky 7 grating, rasping, raucous, throaty 8 croaking, gravelly, guttural

hoary
3 old 4 aged 5 stale 6 age-old 7 ancient, antique, graying 8 grizzled, timeworn 9 venerable

hoax
3 con 4 dupe, fake, fool, gull, sham 5 fraud, phony, trick 6 befool, delude, humbug, take in 7 deceive, mislead 8 flimflam, hoodwink, trickery 9 bamboozle, deception, imposture

Hobbit creator
7 Tolkien (J. R. R.)

hobble
4 lame, limp **6** fetter, hamper, hinder, hog-tie, impede **7** cripple, trammel **8** handicap

hobby
6 falcon **7** pastime, pursuit **8** activity, sideline **9** avocation, diversion

hobgoblin
4 Puck **5** bogey
6 sprite **7** bugaboo

hobnob
3 mix **6** mingle **7** consort **9** associate, rub elbows, socialize **10** fraternize **11** get together

hobo
3 bum **5** gypsy, tramp **7** drifter, floater, swagman, vagrant **8** derelict, vagabond

hock
4 debt, pawn **5** ankle **6** prison

hockey
6 shinny
arena: 4 rink
cup: 7 Stanley
implement: 4 puck **5** stick
official: 7 referee **8** linesman
player: 3 Orr (Bobby), Roy (Patrick) **4** Bure (Pavel), Fuhr (Grant), Howe (Gordie), Hull (Bobby, Brett), Jagr (Jaromir), wing **5** Bossy (Mike), Bucyk (John), Hasek (Dominik), Kurri (Jari), Maruk (Dennis), Sakic (Joe), Shore (Eddie), Shutt (Steve) **6** center, Clarke (Bobby), Coffey (Paul), Dionne (Marcel), Dryden (Ken), goalie, Harvey (Doug), Juneau (Joe), Kariya (Paul), Leetch (Brian), Mikita (Stan), Morenz (Howie), Parent (Bernie), Potvin (Denis), Recchi (Mark), Savard (Denis), Sundin (Mats) **7** Belfour (Ed), Bourque (Ray), Brodeur (Martin), Chelios (Chris), Fedorov (Sergei), forward, Francis (Ron), Gretzky (Wayne), Lafleur (Guy), Lemieux (Claude, Mario), Lindros (Eric), Messier (Mark), Mogilny (Alexander), Richard (Maurice), Richter (Mike), Selanne (Teemu), Stastny (Peter), Yzerman (Steve) **8** Beliveau (Jean), Esposito (Phil, Tony), Forsberg (Peter), Nicholls (Bernie), pointman, Shanahan (Brendan), Trottier (Bryan), Ysebaert (Paul) **9** Hawerchuk (Dale) **10** Carbonneau (Guy), defenseman, goalkeeper
term: 3 box **4** cage, deke, goal, puck, rink **5** bandy, bench, check, icing, stick **6** charge, crease, shinny **7** face-off, offside **8** blue line **9** back-check, body-check **10** center line, penalty box
variation of: 9 broomball
(see also **National Hockey League**)

hocus-pocus
4 sham **8** artifice, nonsense, trickery **9** conjuring, deception, imposture **10** mumbo jumbo **11** abracadabra, incantation, legerdemain **13** sleight of hand

hod
4 tray **6** trough **7** scuttle **11** coal scuttle

Hoder, Hoth
brother: 6 Balder, Baldur
slayer: 4 Vali
victim: 6 Balder, Baldur

hodgepodge
4 hash, olio **6** jumble, medley **7** mélange, mixture **8** mishmash, mixed bag **9** patchwork, potpourri **10** assortment, miscellany, salmagundi **11** gallimaufry

hoe
4 till, weed **6** tiller, weeder **9** cultivate

hoedown
9 barn dance **11** contra dance, square dance

hog
3 pig, sow **4** boar, suid **5** swine
family: 6 Suidae
female: 3 sow **4** gilt
genus: 3 Sus
red: 5 duroc
young: 5 shoat

hogback
5 crest, ridge

hogshead
3 keg, tun **4** butt, cask **6** barrel **9** container

hog-tie
4 bind **6** fetter **7** shackle, trammel

Hogwarts lesson
6 charms, spells **7** Muggles, potions

hogwash
3 rot **4** bosh, bunk, slop **5** bilge, hokum, hooey, swill **6** piffle **7** baloney, garbage, rubbish **8** nonsense, tommyrot **9** moonshine, poppycock **10** applesauce, balderdash, flapdoodle, taradiddle **12** gobbledygook

hog wild
5 crazy **6** crazed, madcap **7** berserk

ho-hum
4 dull **5** bored **6** boring **7** tedious **8** tiresome **10** unexciting **11** indifferent

hoi polloi
3 mob **5** horde **6** masses **8** populace **9** multitude **10** lower class **11** proletariat

hoist
4 lift **5** drink, raise, winch **6** lift up, pick up, take up **7** derrick, elevate **8** windlass

hoity-toity
4 smug **5** dizzy, giddy, silly **7** flighty, pompous **9** conceited, frivolous **11** highfalutin

hokey
4 fake, mock, sham **5** banal, bogus, corny, hammy, phony, stale, stagy, trite **6** ersatz,

pseudo **7** clichéd **8** cornball, outdated **9** contrived, hackneyed **12** melodramatic

hokum
4 bosh **5** hooey **7** baloney, hogwash **8** malarkey, nonsense **9** moonshine, poppycock **10** applesauce, balderdash, flapdoodle, taradiddle **11** foolishness **12** gobbledygook

hold
3 own **4** bear, deem, grab, grip, keep **5** carry, clamp, clasp, cling, grasp, gripe, judge, sense, think, value **6** arrest, clench, clinch, clutch, detain, harbor, regard, retain **7** contain, convene, convoke, fermata, grapple, keep out, possess, reserve, support, sustain **8** keep back, maintain, preserve, restrict
close: 6 cuddle
dear: 7 cherish
in check: 7 repress
in common: 5 share
out: 4 last **6** endure
together: 4 bond **5** clamp **6** fasten
wrestling: 6 nelson **8** headlock, scissors **10** full nelson, half nelson

hold back
4 curb, keep, stop **5** check, delay **6** bridle, detain, impede, retain **7** inhibit, keep out, prevent, refrain, reserve **8** restrain, suppress, withhold **9** constrain

holder
3 cup, pot **4** bowl, cone, vase **5** owner **6** tenant **7** pitcher

hold forth
4 rant **5** orate, speak, spout **7** declaim, expound, lecture **8** harangue, proclaim **9** expatiate **10** dilate upon

hold off
4 stay, wait **5** defer, delay, pause, repel **6** rebuff, resist **7** abstain, adjourn, repulse, suspend **8** hesitate, postpone, prorogue **9** withstand **11** discontinue

holdup
5 heist, theft **7** mugging, robbery

hold up
3 rob **4** halt, lift, stay **5** check, defer, delay, raise **6** hinder, impede, put off, retard **7** support, suspend **8** postpone, prorogue, slow down

hole
3 den, gap, jam, pit **4** cave, flaw, lair, rent, spot, void **5** fault, niche **6** breach, burrow, cavity, cranny, defect, eyelet, lacuna, outlet **7** dilemma, opening, orifice **8** aperture, weakness **9** perforate **10** excavation, interstice **11** perforation, predicament

hole in one
3 ace

holiday
4 Xmas **5** leave **6** May Day **7** Flag Day **8** Labor Day, New Year's, vacation **9** Christmas, Hallowmas, Halloween **10** Father's Day, Mother's Day **11** Memorial Day, Veterans Day **12** All Saints' Day, Groundhog Day, Thanksgiving **13** Presidents' Day, St. Patrick's Day, Valentine's Day
British: 9 Boxing Day
Canadian: 11 Dominion Day, Victoria Day
Jewish: 8 Passover
Vietnamese: 3 Tet

holiness
5 piety **6** purity **8** devotion, divinity, sanctity **9** beatitude **11** religiosity **12** consecration, spirituality

Holland
see **Netherlands**

holler
3 cry **4** call, yell **5** shout **6** bellow, clamor, cry out, outcry **7** call out **8** complain **9** complaint

hollow
3 dip, sag **4** void **5** basin, empty, false **6** cavity, ravine, sunken, vacant **7** concave, echoing, sinkage **8** sinkhole, thorough **9** cavernous, concavity **10** depression, sepulchral
out: 3 dig, gut **4** mine **5** gouge **8** excavate

holly
4 tree **5** shrub
genus: 4 Ilex

Hollywood
10 Tinseltown
street: 4 Vine

holocaust
4 fire **7** inferno **8** genocide **9** sacrifice **10** mass murder **11** destruction **13** conflagration

Holofernes' slayer
6 Judith

holy
6 adored, divine, sacred **7** angelic, blessed, revered, sainted, saintly, sublime **8** hallowed **9** glorified, religious, spiritual, venerated, worshiped **10** reverenced, sacrosanct, sanctified **11** consecrated
combining form: 5 hagio, hiero
communion: 9 Eucharist
oil: 6 chrism
person: 5 saint **6** zaddik **7** tzaddik
Spirit: 9 Paraclete
vessel: 5 grail **7** chalice **8** ciborium

holy place
6 church, shrine, temple **7** sanctum **9** sanctuary

Holy Roman Emperor
4 Karl, Otto **5** Adolf, Franz, Henry, Louis **6** Albert, Arnulf, Conrad, Joseph, Lothar, Ludwig, Philip, Rudolf, Rupert, Wenzel **7** Charles, Francis, Leopold, Lothair **8** Heinrich **9** Ferdinand, Frederick, Friedrich, Sigismund **10** Maximilian **11** Charlemagne

Holy Thursday
6 Maundy (Thursday) **9** Ascension (Day)

holy war
5 jihad **7** crusade

holy writ
5 Bible **9** Scripture

homage
5 honor **6** praise **7** respect, tribute **9** deference, obeisance, reverence

hombre
3 cat, guy, lad, man **4** buck, chap, dude, gent, stud **6** fellow, honcho **7** comrade

home
3 den **4** digs, lair, land, site **5** abode, haunt, house, range **6** family, hearth **7** country, habitat, housing **8** domicile, dwelling, locality **9** household, residence **10** fatherland, habitation, motherland **12** headquarters
country: **5** cabin **7** cottage **8** bungalow

homeless
5 stray **6** exiled **7** outcast, vagrant **8** derelict **9** abandoned, displaced, wandering **12** dispossessed

homely
4 cozy **5** plain **6** direct, modest, simple **7** natural **8** familiar, ordinary **11** comfortable, commonplace **12** unattractive **13** unpretentious

Homer epic
5 Iliad **7** Odyssey

homesickness
7 longing **9** nostalgia

homespun
5 plain **6** fabric, folksy, russet, simple **8** ordinary **9** practical **13** unpretentious

Home, Sweet Home
music: **6** Bishop (Henry)
words: **5** Payne (John Howard)

homicidal
6 bloody **8** sanguine **9** murdering, murderous **10** sanguinary **11** sanguineous **12** bloodthirsty

homicide
5 blood **6** killer, murder, slayer **7** killing **8** foul play, murderer **9** manslayer **12** manslaughter

homily
6 sermon **7** lecture **9** discourse

homogeneous
7 uniform **10** consistent

Homo sapiens
3 man **7** mankind **8** humanity **9** humankind, human race

homunculus
5 dwarf, pygmy **6** midget, peewee **7** manikin **8** Tom Thumb

honcho
4 boss, head **5** chief, Mr. Big **6** bigwig, leader, master, top gun **7** big shot, foreman, headman **8** hierarch, overseer **9** chieftain, Mister Big

Honduras
capital: **11** Tegucigalpa
city: **7** La Ceiba **9** Choluteca **10** El Progreso **12** San Pedro Sula
coast: **8** Mosquito
discoverer: **8** Columbus (Christopher)
Indian people: **4** Maya **5** Mayan
language: **7** Spanish
monetary unit: **7** lempira
neighbor: **9** Guatemala, Nicaragua **10** El Salvador
river: **4** Coco, Ulúa **5** Aguán **6** Patuca
sea: **9** Caribbean

hone
4 edge, whet **6** finish, polish, refine, smooth **7** perfect, sharpen **9** whetstone

honest
4 fair, just, open, real, true **5** frank, plain **6** candid **7** genuine, sincere, upright **8** innocent, reliable, truthful **9** objective, reputable, unfeigned, veracious **10** creditable, forthright, legitimate, scrupulous **13** conscientious, unimpeachable

honesty
4 herb **5** honor **6** candor, virtue **7** probity **8** fairness, goodness, justness, veracity **9** integrity, rectitude, sincerity **11** uprightness **12** truthfulness

honey
combining form: **3** mel **4** meli, mell **5** melli
drink: **4** mead

honeybee genus
4 Apis

honeycomb
3 pit **4** fill, fret **5** cells **6** impair, infest, riddle, weaken **7** subvert **9** perforate

honeydew
5 melon

honeyed
5 sweet **6** golden, liquid, mellow **9** sweetened **10** flattering **11** mellifluous

Honeymooners, The
bus company: **6** Gotham
character: **5** Alice (Kramden) **6** Trixie (Norton) **8** Ed Norton **12** Ralph Kramden
lodge: **7** Raccoon
setting: **8** Brooklyn **11** Bensonhurst
star: **6** Carney (Art) **7** Gleason (Jackie), Meadows (Audrey) **8** Randolph (Joyce)

honeysuckle
6 azalea **9** columbine **13** pinxter flower

honk
4 blow, toot **5** blare, blast **7** trumpet

honky-tonk
4 dive **5** joint **7** hangout **9** juke joint, roadhouse **11** barrelhouse

honor
4 fete, laud **5** adorn, asset, award, badge, exalt, glory, kudos, medal **6** credit, esteem, homage, praise, purity, regard, trophy **7** commend, dignify, ennoble, fulfill, glorify, laurels, respect **8** accolade, approval, carry out, chastity, decorate, devotion, good name **9** adulation, deference, integrity, privilege, recognize, reverence **10** admiration, decoration, reputation, veneration **11** distinction, distinguish, recognition **12** commendation

honorable
4 just, true **5** moral, right **6** honest, worthy **7** ethical, upright **8** laudable **9** dignified **10** creditable, scrupulous **11** illustrious **13** conscientious

honorarium
7 payment **8** gratuity **10** recompense **12** compensation **13** consideration

hooch
6 liquor, rotgut **7** bootleg **8** dwelling, home brew **9** firewater, moonshine **10** bathtub gin

hood
4 cowl, thug **5** tough **6** bonnet, helmet **7** capuche **8** covering, gangster, hooligan **10** delinquent

hoodlum
4 punk, thug **5** bully **7** mobster, ruffian **8** criminal, gangster, hooligan **10** delinquent

hoodoo
3 hex **4** jinx, juju, rock **5** curse, haunt, hokum, magic, spell, spook **6** harass, whammy **7** bewitch, evil eye, sorcery, terrify, torment **8** nonsense **9** conjuring **10** black magic, hocus-pocus, mumbo jumbo, witchcraft

hoodwink
3 con **4** bilk, dupe, fool, gull, hoax, rook **5** trick **6** befool **7** deceive, mislead **8** flimflam **9** bamboozle

hooey
3 rot **4** bunk **5** bilge **6** bunkum **7** baloney, eyewash, hogwash **8** claptrap, malarkey, nonsense, tommyrot **10** balderdash

hoof
4 foot, walk **5** troop **6** ungula **7** traipse **8** ambulate
cloven: **5** cloot
sound: **4** clop **8** clip-clop

hoofer
6 dancer **7** danseur **8** coryphée, danseuse, showgirl **9** ballerina, tap dancer

hooflike
6 ungual

hook
3 nab, nip **4** gore, hasp **5** catch, curve, hitch, pinch, steal **6** anchor, fasten, pilfer **7** hamulus **8** crotchet
a fish: **4** gaff, snag
for keys: **10** chatelaine

hooklike
7 falcate **8** unciform, uncinate
part: **5** uncus **7** hamulus

hookup
7 circuit, linkage **8** alliance **10** assemblage, connection **11** affiliation, association, combination, conjunction, partnership

hooky
6 truant **7** truancy **8** truantry

hooligan
see **hoodlum**

hoop
4 band, ring **6** circle **7** circlet

hoopla
4 bash, fuss, stir, to-do **6** bustle, frolic **7** revelry, shindig, whoopee **8** ballyhoo, wingding **9** commotion, festivity, merriment, promotion

hoops
5 b-ball **10** basketball

hooray
3 rah, yay **5** cheer, huzza **6** huzzah, yippee **7** acclaim, whoopee **10** hallelujah

hoosegow
3 jug, pen **4** brig, cage, coop, jail, keep, stir **5** clink, pokey **6** cooler, lockup, prison **7** slammer **8** bastille, big house **9** calaboose, jailhouse **12** penitentiary

Hoosier State
7 Indiana

hoot
3 bit, boo, jot **4** hiss, iota, jeer, whit **5** laugh, scrap, shout, whoop **6** assail, deride, heckle **7** catcall, modicum **8** particle

hooter
3 owl **5** owlet

Hoover Dam lake
4 Mead

hop
4 jump, leap, trip, vine **5** bound, dance **6** bounce, spring, wait on **7** rebound **8** jump over

hope
4 goal, wish **5** await, dream, faith, trust **6** aspire, desire, expect **7** count on, longing, promise **8** ambition, optimism, prospect **9** count upon **10** anticipate, aspiration, confidence
loss of: **7** despair

hopeful
4 rosy **5** eager, sunny **6** bright, cheery, golden, seeker, upbeat **7** assured **8** aspirant, aspiring **9** candidate, confident, expectant, promising **10** auspicious, contestant, optimistic, propitious **11** encouraging **12** advantageous

hopeless
4 glum, lost, vain **6** futile, gloomy, morose **7** forlorn **8** downcast **9** desperate, incurable, insoluble **10** despairing, despondent, impossible **11** ineffectual, irreparable, pessimistic **12** incorrigible, irredeemable, irremediable

hoper
7 truster **8** optimist **9** expectant, Pollyanna

hopped-up
4 high **5** giddy **6** stoned, zonked **7** drugged, excited **9** delirious **12** enthusiastic

hopper
3 box, mix **4** frog, hare, tank, toad **5** bunny, chute **6** rabbit **7** cricket **10** freight car, receptacle

____ Hopper
5 Grace (Murray), Hedda **6** Edward

hopping
4 busy **5** irate, livid **6** lively **7** furious **9** extremely, violently **10** infuriated

Horae
4 Dike **6** Eirene **7** Eunomia, seasons

Horam
kingdom: **5** Gezer
slayer: **6** Joshua

horde
3 mob **4** army **5** crowd, crush, drove, press, swarm **6** throng **9** multitude

horizon
4 goal **5** limit, range, reach, scope, vista **6** extent **7** purview, skyline **8** prospect **11** perspective

horizontal
4 flat **5** level **8** parallel

hormone
4 ACTH **5** kinin **6** estrin **7** estriol, estrone, gastrin, insulin, relaxin **8** autacoid, estrogen, glucagon, kallidin, secretin
female: **8** estrogen
insect: **8** ecdysone
pituitary: **8** oxytocin

horn
4 toot **5** cornu **6** antler, klaxon, shofar **7** trumpet **10** cornucopia, projection
ancient Greek: **5** rhyta (plural) **6** rhyton
animal: **6** antler

Hornblower, Horatio
creator: **8** Forester (C. S.)
ship: **6** Le Reve **7** Atropos, Hotspur **10** Sutherland

horn in
6 meddle **7** intrude, obtrude **9** insinuate, interfere, interlope, interrupt

hornlike
8 corneous **10** keratinous

hornswoggle
3 con **4** dupe, fool, gull, hoax, hose **5** trick **7** deceive **8** flimflam, hoodwink **9** bamboozle

horrendous
5 awful **7** fearful, ghastly, heinous, hideous **8** alarming, dreadful, gruesome, horrible, horrific, shocking, terrible **9** abhorrent, appalling, execrable, frightful, repugnant, revolting **11** distressing, unspeakable

horrible
4 grim **5** awful, lurid **6** grisly **7** fearful, ghastly, hateful, hellish, hideous **8** dreadful, gruesome, shocking **9** abhorrent, appalling, frightful, loathsome, repellent, repugnant, repulsive, revolting **10** abominable, disgusting, terrifying

horrid
5 nasty **7** noisome **8** shocking **9** loathsome, offensive, repulsive, sickening **10** detestable, disgusting

horrific
5 awful **7** fearful **8** dreadful, shocking, terrible **9** appalling, dismaying, frightful, harrowing

horrified
6 aghast **8** appalled

horrify
5 daunt, shock **6** appall, dismay

horrifying
4 grim **5** awful, lurid **6** grisly **7** ghastly, hideous **8** gruesome, terrible **9** appalling, atrocious

horror
4 fear, hate, pain **5** alarm, dread, panic, shock **6** dismay, fright, hatred, terror **7** disgust **8** aversion, loathing **9** repulsion, revulsion **10** abhorrence, repugnance **11** abomination, detestation, trepidation

hors d'oeuvre
4 whet **5** snack **6** canape, tidbit **7** crudité **9** antipasto, appetizer

horse
3 nag **4** buck **5** bronc, mount, pacer, steed **6** bronco, brumby, equine **7** cavalry, palfrey, sawbuck, trestle, trotter **8** footrope, jackstay, stallion, traveler
Australian-bred: **5** waler
battle: **7** charger
breed: **4** Arab **5** pinto **6** Morgan **7** Arabian, Belgian, Iceland **8** Palomino, Shetland **9** Appaloosa, Percheron **10** Lippizaner **12** standardbred, Thoroughbred
champion: **7** Barbaro, Man o' War **8** Affirmed,

Citation **10** Seabiscuit **11** Seattle Slew, Secretariat, Smarty Jones
collar part: 4 hame
color: 3 bay, dun **4** roan **6** grullo, sorrel **8** buckskin, chestnut, palomino
combining form: 4 hipp **5** hippo
covering: 8 trapping
draft: 5 shire **10** Clydesdale
extinct: 8 eohippus
farm: 6 dobbin
female: 4 mare **5** filly
foot part: 7 pastern
gait: 4 trot **6** canter, gallop
gear: 3 bit **4** rein **6** saddle **7** harness **9** checkrein
leg joint: 7 fetlock
leg part: 6 gaskin **7** gambrel
male: 4 colt **8** stallion
mark: 5 blaze
of the movies: 4 Fury **6** Flicka, Silver **7** Trigger **8** Champion **11** Black Beauty
race: 5 Ascot, derby **7** Belmont **9** Preakness
rump: 7 crupper
small: 4 pony **6** garron, jennet
spotted: 5 pinto **7** piebald
talking: 4 Mr. Ed
tan: 8 palomino
thoroughbred: 8 hotblood
tooth: 4 tush
war: 8 destrier
wild: 7 mustang

horsefeathers
3 rot **4** bull, bunk **5** bilge, hokum, hooey, trash **6** bunkum, drivel, piffle **7** baloney, garbage, hogwash, rubbish, twaddle **8** claptrap, flimflam, nonsense, tommyrot **9** poppycock **10** applesauce, balderdash

horseman
5 rider **6** cowboy **7** vaquero **8** cavalier **9** caballero, chevalier **10** equestrian

horsemanship
6 manège **10** equitation

horse opera
5 oater **7** western

horseplay
7 fooling **8** clowning, rowdyism **9** high jinks, rowdiness **10** buffoonery, roughhouse **11** shenanigans **12** roughhousing

horse-racing term
3 bug, cup **4** bolt, calk, gait, oaks, pill, prop, show, tack **5** float, place, purse, silks, washy **6** bobble, closer, exacta, impost, mudder, router, stayer **7** also-ran, blowout, clocker, paddock, spit box **8** breakage, claiming, climbing, dead heat, handicap, hand ride, off track, perfecta, post time, quiniela **9** hot walker **10** allowances, in the money, parimutuel, shadow roll **11** backstretch, daily double, morning line, triple crown **12** morning glory

horseshoer
6 smithy **10** blacksmith

hortative
8 advisory **9** exhorting, homiletic

horticulturist
6 Carver (George Washington) **7** Burbank (Luther)

Horus
brother: 6 Anubis
father: 6 Osiris
mother: 4 Isis
victim: 3 Set **4** Seth

hose
4 sock, tube, wash **5** cheat, spray, trick, water **6** tights **8** stocking

hoser
6 barfly, boozer **7** redneck

hospice
see **hostel**

hospitable
4 kind, open **6** social **7** cordial **8** friendly, generous, gracious **9** convivial, receptive, welcoming **10** gregarious

hospital
6 clinic **7** lazaret **9** infirmary, lazaretto
attendant: 7 orderly
ship's: 7 sickbay

Hospitallers' island
5 Malta **6** Rhodes

host
2 MC **4** army **5** array, cloud, crowd, emcee, flock, horde **6** angels, legion, myriad, scores, server **7** compere, present, receive **8** assemble **9** innkeeper, introduce, moderator, multitude, presenter

hostage
4 pawn **5** token **6** pledge, surety **7** captive, earnest **8** guaranty, prisoner, security **9** guarantee

hostel
3 inn **4** stay **5** lodge **6** tavern, travel **7** auberge, lodging **11** caravansary, public house

hostile
4 anti, mean **5** enemy **6** bitter, fierce **7** adverse, opposed, warlike **8** contrary, inimical, opposite **9** bellicose, combative, resistant, resisting **10** malevolent, pugnacious, unfriendly **11** belligerent, contentious **12** antagonistic **13** argumentative

hostility
3 war **6** animus, enmity, hatred, rancor **7** ill will **8** conflict **9** antipathy **10** aggression, antagonism, opposition, resistance **12** belligerence

hot
3 new **4** fast, heat, sexy **5** angry, close, eager, fiery, lucky, spicy **6** ardent, baking, banned, heated, hectic, on fire, raging, stolen, sultry, torrid, urgent **7** boiling, burning, excited, fevered, illicit, lustful, peppery, popular, pungent, zealous **8** broiling, feverish, in demand, scalding, sizzling, tropical, vehement **9** energized, lecherous, scorching **10** blistering, contraband, passionate, sweltering **11** radioactive

hot air
4 bosh **6** bunkum **7** blather, prattle, twaddle **8** malarkey, nonsense **9** empty talk, poppycock **10** double-talk

hotbed
3 hub **4** core, seat **5** heart **6** center **7** nucleus **10** focal point **11** nerve center

hot-blooded
5 fiery **6** ardent **7** burning, fervent, flaming **9** excitable, impetuous, impulsive **10** passionate **11** impassioned **12** high-spirited

hotchpotch
see **hodgepodge**

hot dog
5 frank **6** weenie, wiener, wienie **7** sausage, show-off **11** frankfurter, wienerwurst

hotel
3 inn **5** lodge **6** tavern **7** auberge, hospice, pension **8** motor inn **11** public house **12** lodging house, rooming house **13** boardinghouse
chain: **5** Hyatt **6** Hilton, Ramada, Westin **7** Days Inn **8** Marriott, Radisson, Sheraton, Stouffer **10** Holiday Inn **11** Best Western, Four Seasons
inferior: **7** fleabag **9** flophouse

hothead
5 rebel **7** fanatic, inciter, radical **8** agitator **9** demagogue, firebrand **10** incendiary **12** rabble-rouser, troublemaker **13** revolutionary

hotheaded
4 rash **5** brash, fiery, hasty **6** madcap **8** reckless **9** excitable, impetuous, imprudent, impulsive, irritable

hotshot
3 ace **4** star, whiz **5** comer **6** expert, master, wizard **8** virtuoso **10** powerhouse **11** heavyweight

hot-tempered
see **quick-tempered**

hot water
3 box, fix, jam **4** bind, hole **6** corner, pickle **7** dilemma, trouble **9** tight spot **11** predicament
in: **10** up the creek

____ Houdini
5 Harry

hound
3 dog, fan **4** bait, buff, ride **5** chivy **6** badger, basset, beagle, bowwow, canine, harass, hassle, heckle, hector, pester, pursue, Talbot **7** devotee **8** bullyrag **9** dachshund, persecute **10** aficionado
Russian: **6** borzoi

hourglass
5 timer

house
3 cot, hut, ken **4** home, shed **5** abode, board, cabin, dwell, hovel, lodge, put up, shack **6** billet, chalet, harbor, shanty **7** contain, cottage, enclose, mansion, quarter, saltbox, shelter, theater **8** audience, bungalow, domicile, dwelling, quarters **9** residence
clergyman's: **5** manse **7** rectory **9** parsonage
country: **5** manor **7** cottage **8** bungalow
dog: **6** kennel
earth: **5** adobe
Eskimo: **5** igloo
mean: **5** hovel, shack
of prostitution: **4** crib **6** bagnio **7** brothel **8** bordello
religious: **5** abbey **6** priory **7** convent, nunnery **9** monastery
rooming: **5** lodge
Russian: **5** dacha
small: **4** camp **5** cabin, shack **6** shanty **7** cottage **8** bungalow
Spanish: **4** casa

housebreaker
4 yegg **5** thief **7** burglar, prowler **8** picklock

household
4 home **5** folks **6** family, ménage **8** domestic, familiar
gods (Roman): **5** lares **7** penates

house of worship
6 bethel, chapel, church, mosque, pagoda, shrine, temple **7** chantry, minster, oratory **8** basilica **9** cathedral, sanctuary, synagogue **10** tabernacle **11** conventicle

housing
4 case, room **7** shelter **8** barracks, quarters **9** enclosure

hovel
3 hut, sty **4** dump, shed **5** hutch, shack **6** burrow, pigpen, pigsty, shanty **7** shelter

hover
4 flit, hang, loom **5** dance, drift, float, poise, waver **7** flitter, flutter, suspend **9** fluctuate, hang about

howbeit
3 yet **4** when **5** still, while **6** even if, much as, though **7** whereas **8** after all, although **11** nonetheless **12** nevertheless

however
3 but, yet **4** only **5** still **6** except, though **8** after all **11** nonetheless

howl
3 bay, cry **4** bark, keen, wail, yell, yelp **6** cry out **9** caterwaul

howler
4 flub, gaff, goof **5** boner, fluff, gaffe **6** boo-boo **7** blooper, blunder

huarache
6 sandal

hub
4 axis, core **5** focus, heart, pivot **6** center **8** polestar **10** focal point **11** nerve center
opposite: 3 rim

hubbub
3 din **4** fuss, stir, to-do **5** babel, furor, hoo-ha, noise **6** clamor, furore, hassle, jangle, pother, racket, rumpus, tumult, uproar **7** turmoil **8** brouhaha, foofaraw **9** commotion, confusion **10** hullabaloo, hurly-burly **11** disturbance, pandemonium

hubris
3 ego **4** gall **5** brass, cheek, nerve, pride **7** conceit, hauteur, swagger **8** audacity, chutzpah **9** arrogance, cockiness, vainglory **11** braggadocio

hubristic
4 vain **5** cocky, proud **7** haughty **8** arrogant, insolent, superior **11** overbearing, overweening **13** overconfident

Huckleberry Finn
author: 5 Twain (Mark) **7** Clemens (Samuel)
character: 3 Jim, Tom (Sawyer) **4** Duke, King
river: 11 Mississippi

huckster
4 hawk, plug, tout, vend **5** pitch **6** dicker, haggle, hawker, peddle, vendor **7** bargain, chaffer, haggler, packman, peddler, promote **8** pitchman

huddle
4 lump, mass **5** bunch, crowd, group, hunch **6** confab, confer, crouch, curl up, gather, parley, powwow **7** cluster, consult, meeting **8** assemble **10** conference, discussion

Hudson's ship
8 Half Moon

hue
4 cast, tint, tone **5** color, shade, shape, tinge, value **6** aspect, manner **8** coloring, tincture **10** coloration, complexion

huff
3 pet **4** blow, gasp, pant, rile, roil, snap, snit, tiff **5** annoy, grate, heave, peeve, pique, storm **6** nettle, put out **7** bluster, inflate **8** irritate

huffy
5 angry, proud, testy **6** piqued, touchy **7** annoyed, fretful, haughty, peevish, prickly, waspish **8** arrogant, petulant, snappish **9** irritable, irritated, querulous

hug
4 hold **5** clasp, press, prize, value **6** clinch, clutch, cuddle, enfold **7** cherish, embrace, envelop, squeeze **8** hold fast, hold onto **12** congratulate

huge
4 epic, vast, wide **5** bulky, giant, grand, great, jumbo, mondo **6** heroic, mighty, untold **7** immense, mammoth, massive, titanic **8** colossal, enormous, gigantic, whopping **9** extensive, monstrous **10** monumental, prodigious, stupendous, tremendous **11** magnificent, mountainous

hugeness
8 enormity **9** immensity, magnitude

hugger-mugger
4 hash **6** jumble, muddle, secret, tangle **7** clutter, furtive, jumbled, secrecy **8** confused, covertly, disorder, secretly **9** by stealth, confusion, furtively **10** disordered, disorderly, stealthily, undercover **11** clandestine **13** clandestinely

Hugo, Victor
character: 6 Javert (Inspector) **7** Cosette, Fantine, Valjean (Jean) **9** Esmeralda, Quasimodo
novel: 13 Les Misérables **20** Hunchback of Notre Dame (The)

Huguenot
10 Protestant
leader: 5 Condé (Prince de), Rohan (Henri) **6** Mornay (Philippe) **7** Coligny (Gaspard II de)

Huguenots composer
9 Meyerbeer (Giacomo)

hulk
4 body, loom, ship **5** shell, wreck **8** skeleton **9** shipwreck

hulking
4 huge **5** beefy, bulky, burly, husky **7** immense, mammoth, massive **8** colossal, enormous, gigantic, oversize **9** humongous, lumbering, monstrous, ponderous, strapping **11** heavyweight

hull
3 pod **4** bark, body, case, husk, peel, rind, skin **5** chaff, frame, shell, shuck **6** casing **8** covering **11** decorticate

hullabaloo
3 ado, din **4** roar, to-do **5** hoo-ha, noise **6** clamor, hoo-hah, hubbub, jangle, pother, racket, tumult, uproar **8** ballyhoo, foofaraw **9** commotion, hue and cry **11** pandemonium

hum
4 buzz, purr, sing, zing **5** drone **6** murmur **7** vibrate

human
5 being, party **6** mortal, person **7** hominid **8** hominoid **10** individual
race: **7** mankind

Human Comedy author
6 Balzac (Honoré de) **7** Saroyan (William)

humane
4 kind **6** gentle, kindly, tender **8** merciful **10** altruistic, benevolent, charitable **11** considerate, kindhearted, soft-hearted, sympathetic, warmhearted **13** compassionate, philanthropic

humanitarian
5 giver **8** generous **10** altruistic, benefactor, beneficent, benevolent, charitable **13** compassionate, philanthropic

humanity
6 people **7** mankind **8** kindness, sympathy **10** compassion, generosity **11** benevolence, Homo sapiens

humble
3 low **4** meek **5** abase, abash, crush, lowly, quiet **6** demean, modest, simple **7** chagrin, deflate, degrade, subdued **8** cast down, disgrace, ordinary **9** compliant, diffident, discomfit, embarrass, humiliate **10** submissive, unassuming **11** acquiescent, deferential **13** insignificant, unpretentious

humbug
3 con, rot **4** fake, fool, hoax, sham **5** faker, fraud, hokum, phony, spoof, trick **6** bunkum, delude, drivel, take in **7** beguile, deceive, mislead **8** flimflam, impostor, malarkey, nonsense, pretense, quackery **9** deception, hypocrite, imposture, pretender, trickster **10** balderdash

humdinger
3 ace, gem, pip **4** lulu **5** beaut, dandy, dilly, doozy, jewel, peach, prize **6** doozie **8** jim-dandy, knockout **11** crackerjack

humdrum
4 blah, dull, flat **6** boring, dreary, stodgy **7** prosaic, tedious **8** monotone, monotony, plodding, unvaried, workaday **10** monotonous, uneventful **13** uninteresting

humid
3 wet **4** damp, dank **5** close, moist, muggy, soggy **6** clammy, sodden, steamy, sticky, stuffy **10** oppressive

humidify
6 dampen **7** moisten

humiliate
5 abase, crush, lower, shame **6** bemean, debase, demean, humble **7** chagrin, degrade, mortify **8** belittle, cast down, disgrace **9** embarrass

humiliation
5 shame **7** chagrin, put-down **8** disgrace, ignominy, reproach **9** abasement, disrepute, indignity **11** degradation **13** embarrassment, mortification

humility
7 modesty, shyness **8** meekness **9** abasement, lowliness **10** diffidence, submission **12** subservience **13** self-abasement

humming
4 busy **5** brisk **6** active, lively **8** bustling, hustling **9** energetic

hummock
4 hump **5** couch, knoll, mound **7** hillock

humongous
4 huge, vast **5** giant, jumbo **7** immense, mammoth, massive, titanic **8** colossal, enormous, gigantic **9** monstrous **10** gargantuan, prodigious, tremendous

humor
3 wit **4** baby, bent, mind, mood, tone, vein, whim **5** fancy, fluid, spoil, yield **6** banter, coddle, comedy, cosset, esprit, joking, levity, nature, pamper, temper **7** caprice, cater to, conceit, gratify, indulge, jesting, kidding **8** crotchet, drollery, jocosity, repartee **9** character, drollness, flippancy, funniness, witticism, wittiness **10** complexion, jocularity, pleasantry **11** disposition, temperament

humorist
3 Ade (George), wag, wit **4** card, Nash (Ogden), Shaw (Henry Wheeler), Ward (Artemus, Edward) **5** Adams (Franklin Pierce), Allen (Fred), Barry (Dave), clown, comic, cutup, droll, Dunne (Finley Peter), joker, Twain (Mark), White (E. B.) **6** Blount (Roy), Browne (Charles Farrar), Diller (Phyllis), gagman, jester, kidder, Martin (Steve), Parker (Dorothy), Rogers (Will), Rourke (P. J.), Runyon (Damon), Thorpe (Thomas Bangs) **7** buffoon, Bombeck (Erma), Burgess (Gelett), Clemens (Samuel Langhorne), gagster, Hubbard (Kin), Keillor (Garrison), Marquis (Don), punster, Sedaris (David), Thurber (James), Trillin (Calvin) **8** Aleichem (Shalom), Benchley (Robert), comedian, funnyman, jokester, Perelman (S. J.), quipster **9** jokesmith, prankster, Wodehouse (P. G.)
Canadian: **7** Leacock (Stephen)

humorous
5 comic, droll, funny, jokey, merry, witty **6** jocose **7** amusing, comical, jocular, risible, waggish **8** mirthful **9** facetious, laughable, whimsical

hump
3 lug **4** bump, race, tote **5** bulge, carry, hunch, mound, range **6** hustle, schlep **7** hummock, schlepp **8** mountain, obstacle, swelling **9** transport **10** protrusion

humpback
5 whale **8** kyphosis **10** pink salmon

humpbacked
6 convex, curved **7** gibbous

Humperdinck opera
15 Hansel and Gretel

humus
3 mor **4** mull, soil **7** compost **8** material

hunch
4 arch, clod, idea, lump, hump, push **5** chunk, clump, crook, squat, stoop **6** crouch, curl up, huddle, jostle, notion, nugget **7** feeling, inkling **9** intuition

Hunchback of Notre Dame
author: **4** Hugo (Victor)
character: **9** Esmeralda, Quasimodo

hundred
combining form: **5** centi, hecto
dollar bill **5** C-note

Hungary
capital: **8** Budapest
city: **4** Pécs **6** Szeged **7** Miskolc **8** Debrecen
ethnic group: **6** Magyar
lake: **7** Balaton
monetary unit: **6** forint
mountain range: **10** Carpathian
national hero: **5** Árpád
neighbor: **6** Serbia **7** Austria, Croatia, Romania, Ukraine **8** Slovakia, Slovenia
plain: **11** Great Alföld
river: **4** Eger **5** Tisza **6** Danube

hunger
3 yen **4** ache, itch, long, lust, need, pine, want **5** crave, greed, yearn **6** desire, hanker, thirst **7** craving, longing

hungry
4 avid, keen, poor **5** eager **6** barren **7** craving, starved, thirsty **8** desirous, famished, ravenous, starving, underfed, yearning **9** hankering, motivated

hunk
3 gob, wad **4** clod, lump, stud **5** chunk, clump, himbo, piece, wedge **6** nugget **7** portion

hunker down
5 dig in, squat **6** crouch **8** settle in

hunky
4 buff **5** burly **6** buffed **8** athletic, muscular **9** strapping, well-built

hunky-dory
4 fine, okay **5** dandy, ducky, nifty, swell **6** peachy **10** peachy keen **12** satisfactory

Hunnish
4 rude, wild **6** savage **7** fearful, uncivil **9** barbarian, barbarous, ferocious **11** uncivilized

hunt
3 dog, run **4** hawk, seek **5** chase, hound, prowl, quest, shoot, snare, stalk, track, trail **6** battue, course, dig out, prey on, pursue, safari, search **7** explore, pursuit, rummage **9** ferret out, search for, search out
birds: **4** fowl
illegally: **5** poach

hunter
6 jaeger, nimrod **8** predator
biblical: **6** Nimrod
cap: **7** montero
constellation: **5** Orion
mythological: **5** Orion **7** Actaeon

hunting
5 chase **6** venery **7** gunning, hawking **8** coursing, falconry **9** predatory **10** predacious
bird: **6** falcon
call: **7** recheat
cry: **6** yoicks **7** tallyho **10** view halloo
dog: **5** hound **6** basset, beagle, borzoi, saluki, setter, vizsla **7** harrier, pointer, spaniel **9** ridgeback, wolfhound **10** bloodhound
expedition: **6** safari
garb: **4** camo **10** camouflage
horn: **5** bugle

huntress
5 Diana **7** Artemis **8** Atalanta

hurdle
3 bar **4** leap, snag **5** bound, clear, vault **6** hamper, spring **7** barrier **8** leap over, obstacle, overcome, overleap, surmount, traverse **9** negotiate **10** difficulty, impediment **11** obstruction

hurl
4 cast, fire **5** chuck, fling, heave, pitch, sling, throw, vomit **6** launch, thrust **8** catapult

hurly-burly
3 din **4** riot, to-do **5** melee **6** clamor, furore, hassle, hubbub, racket, rumpus, tumult, uproar **7** turmoil **8** confused **9** commotion, confusion

hurrah
3 olé, yay **4** fuss, to-do, zeal **5** cheer **6** fervor, rumpus **7** fanfare, ovation **8** approval **9** commotion **10** enthusiasm **11** acclamation

hurricane
7 typhoon

hurried
4 fast, sped **5** hasty, quick, swift **6** abrupt, rushed, sudden **7** cursory, rushing **8** headlong **9** impetuous **11** precipitant, precipitate

hurry
3 fly, hie, jog, run, zip **4** post, prod, push, rush **5** fleet, haste, scoot, speed, whirl, whish, whisk **6** barrel, breeze, bullet, bustle, hasten, hustle, rocket, rustle, step up, tumult **7** beeline, hotfoot, quicken, shake up, skelter, speed up, swiften **8** celerity, dispatch, expedite, highball, make time **9** commotion, make haste, swiftness **10** accelerate, speediness

hurt
3 mar **4** ache, blow, harm, pain **5** smart, wound, wrong **6** damage, grieve, hamper, harmed, impair, injure, injury, in pain, misuse, offend, pained, suffer **7** afflict, anguish, blemish, damaged, wounded **8** aggrieve, distress, mischief, mistreat **9** constrain, detriment, prejudice, resentful, suffering **10** resentment

hurtful
4 mean, sore **6** aching, unkind **7** harmful, painful **8** damaging, wounding **9** injurious **11** deleterious, destructive, detrimental, distressing, prejudicial

hurtle
3 fly **4** race, rush, tear **5** fling, shoot, speed, throw **6** charge, plunge, rocket

husband
3 man **4** mate, save **6** manage, mister, spouse **7** consort, partner **8** conserve, helpmate, helpmeet **9** economize, other half **10** bridegroom

husbandry
6 thrift **7** control, economy, farming **8** prudence **9** frugality **10** management **11** agriculture, thriftiness **12** conservation, preservation

hush
4 calm **5** quell, quiet **6** shut up, stifle **7** cover up, mollify, secrecy, silence **8** choke off, suppress **9** cessation, quietness, stillness

hush-hush
6 covert, secret **7** private, sub-rosa **9** top secret **11** clandestine **12** confidential **13** surreptitious, under-the-table

husk
3 pod **4** case, hull, peel, rind, skin **5** shell, shuck, strip **6** casing

husky
3 big, dog **5** beefy, burly, great, hefty, large, rough, stout **6** brawny, croaky, hoarse, mighty, robust, strong, sturdy **7** throaty **8** muscular, oversize, stalwart, thickset **9** strapping

hustings
5 stump

hustle
3 fly, rob, run **4** earn, move, push, rush, sell, urge, work **5** cheat, elbow, fraud, haste, hurry, press, shove, speed **6** hasten **7** hotfoot, promote, solicit, swindle **8** bulldoze, dispatch **9** deception, swiftness

hustler
4 doer **6** dynamo, vendor **8** go-getter, live wire **10** powerhouse

hustling
4 busy **5** eager **6** active, lively, speedy **7** hopping, humming **9** energetic **10** aggressive

hut
3 cot **4** camp, crib, shed **5** cabin, dacha, hooch, hovel, hutch, jacal, lodge, roost, shack **6** cabana, chalet, lean-to, shanty **7** cottage **8** bungalow
American Indian: **6** wigwam **7** wickiup
Scottish: **5** bothy, shiel **8** shieling

hutch
3 bin, pen **4** cage, coop **5** chest, shack **6** locker, shanty **8** cupboard **9** enclosure

Huxley novel
8 Antic Hay **11** Crome Yellow **13** Brave New World, Eyeless in Gaza

Hyacinthus
father: **7** Amyclas
slayer: **6** Apollo

hybrid
5 blend, cross, mixed, Prius, spork **7** amalgam, mixture **8** combined, compound **9** composite, crossbred **10** crossbreed **11** combination
animal: **4** mule **5** hinny, liger, tigon
fruit: **4** Ugli **7** tangelo

hybridize
4 join **5** blend, cross **7** combine **10** crossbreed, interbreed, intercross

Hydra
5 polyp **6** plague **7** monster, serpent **13** constellation
father: **6** Typhon
mother: **7** Echidna
slayer: **8** Heracles, Hercules

hydrant
3 tap **4** pipe **5** valve **6** faucet, spigot **7** petcock **8** fireplug

hydraulic device
3 ram **4** jack, lift, pump **5** brake, press **8** elevator

hydrocarbon
5 xylol **6** dioxin, ethane, xylene **7** benzene, methane, styrene, toluene **8** biphenyl, butylene, ethylene, paraffin
liquid: **6** octane **7** retinol, styrene **8** menthene

hydroid
5 polyp **6** medusa, obelia **9** jellyfish

hydrometer scale
4 Brix **5** Baumé

hydrophobia
5 lyssa **6** rabies

hyena
5 dingo **6** jackal **9** scavenger

Hygeia
5 Salus
father: **9** Asclepius **11** Aesculapius
goddess of: **6** health

hygiene
6 health **10** sanitation **11** cleanliness

hygienic
5 clean **7** aseptic, healthy, sterile **8** sanitary **9** healthful **10** antiseptic, unpolluted

Hyllus' father
8 Heracles, Hercules

hymeneal
6 bridal, wedded **7** marital, married, nuptial, spousal **8** conjugal **9** connubial **11** matrimonial

hymn
4 laud, song **5** bless, carol, chant, extol, paean, psalm **6** anthem, choral, praise, Te Deum **7** chorale, glorify **8** canticle, doxology, eulogize

hype
4 plug, tout **5** boost, thump **7** acclaim, enliven, glorify, promote, puffery, trumpet **8** ballyhoo, increase **9** advertise, excellent, publicity, publicize, stimulate **11** advertising

hyper
4 edgy **5** antsy, jumpy, wired **6** on edge **7** anxious, frantic **8** agitated, frenetic, hopped-up **9** excitable **10** high-strung, overactive **11** overwrought

hyperbole
6 excess **12** embroidering, exaggeration **13** embellishment, overstatement

hypercritical
6 severe **7** carping **8** captious, exacting **10** censorious, nit-picking **12** faultfinding

Hyperion
daughter: **3** Eos **6** Aurora, Selene
father: **6** Uranus
mother: **4** Gaea
son: **6** Helios
wife: **5** Theia

hypnotic
6 opiate, sleepy **8** mesmeric, narcotic, sedative **9** somnolent, soporific **11** mesmerizing, somniferous **12** somnifacient, spellbinding

hypnotize
4 drug **5** charm **6** dazzle, trance **8** enthrall, entrance, overcome **9** captivate, fascinate, mesmerize, overpower, spellbind

hypocorism
7 pet name **8** nickname **9** sobriquet

hypocrisy
4 cant, sham **6** deceit, humbug **7** falsity, pietism **8** quackery **9** deception, duplicity, phoniness **10** sanctimony **11** insincerity, religiosity

hypocrite
4 fake, sham **5** actor, faker, fraud, phony, poser **6** humbug, poseur **7** bluffer, pietist **8** deceiver, impostor, pharisee **9** charlatan, pretender **10** dissembler **11** masquerader **12** dissimulator

hypocritical
5 false **7** canting **8** affected, specious, two-faced **9** deceitful, insincere, pietistic **10** Janus-faced **11** dissembling, double-faced, duplicitous **12** mealymouthed, pecksniffian **13** sanctimonious

hypothesis
6 belief, theory **7** premise **8** position, supposal **9** condition, inference **10** antecedent, assumption, conjecture **11** explanation, speculation, supposition

hypothetical
7 assumed **8** abstract, academic, supposed **10** assumptive **11** conditional, conjectural, suppositous, theoretical **12** suppositious **13** suppositional

hyrax
4 cony **5** coney **6** dassie, mammal **8** ungulate

hysteria
4 fear **5** craze, furor, mania, panic **6** excess, frenzy **7** madness **8** delirium

hysterical
5 rabid **6** crazed, raving **7** berserk, frantic **8** agitated, frenzied, neurotic **9** delirious, hilarious **10** convulsive, distraught, uproarious **11** overexcited, overwrought **13** side-splitting

I

Iago
general: **7** Othello
victim: **6** Cassio, Emilia **7** Othello **9** Desdemona
wife: **6** Emilia

Iapetus
father: **6** Uranus
mother: **4** Gaea
son: **5** Atlas **9** Menoetius **10** Epimetheus, Prometheus
wife: **7** Clymene

Iasion
brother: **8** Dardanus
father: **4** Zeus **7** Jupiter
lover: **5** Ceres **7** Demeter
mother: **7** Electra
son: **6** Plutus

ibex
4 tahr **8** wild goat
family: **7** Bovidae
genus: **5** Capra

Ibhar's father
5 David

ibis-headed god
5 Thoth

ibis relative
5 heron, stork

Ibsen, Henrik
character: **3** Ase **4** Nora (Helmer) **5** Brack (Judge), Brand, Hedda (Gabler), Helen (Alving), Werle (Gergers) **6** Ejlert (Lovberg), Hedvig (Ekdal), Jorgen (Tesman), Oswald (Alving) **7** Solness (Halvard), Solveig, Torvald (Helmer) **8** Peer Gynt **9** Stockmann (Thomas)
country: **6** Norway
play: **6** Ghosts **8** Peer Gynt, Wild Duck (The) **10** Doll's House (A) **11** Hedda Gabler, Little Eyolf, Rosmersholm **13** Master Builder (The) **16** Enemy of the People (An)

Icarus' father
8 Daedalus

ICBM part
4 MIRV **7** booster, warhead

ice
area: **4** rink
dessert: **6** sorbet **7** sherbet
floating: **4** berg, floe
hanging: **6** icicle
pinnacle: **5** serac
sheet: **7** glacier

icebox
6 cooler, fridge **12** refrigerator

ice cream
6 gelato **7** spumoni, tortoni
brand: **4** Edy's **7** Breyers **8** Klondike **9** Good Humor
dish: **6** sundae **11** baked Alaska
drink: **4** soda **6** frappe
headache: **11** brain freeze
holder: **4** cone

iced
5 glacé **6** glazed **7** chilled

ice field
4 floe **7** glacier

ice game
6 hockey **7** curling

ice house
5 igloo

Iceland
capital: **9** Reykjavik
monetary unit: **5** krona
possession: **9** Greenalnd
sea: **9** Norwegian
snowfield: **11** Vatnajökull
strait: **7** Denmark
volcano: **5** Hekla

Icelandic
epic: **4** Edda, saga
hero: **5** Njáll **6** Gunnar **7** Grettir

ice skater
figure skater: **4** Witt (Katarina) **5** Baiul (Oksana), Henie (Sonja), Kulik (Ilia) **6** Hughes (Sarah), Umanov (Alexei) **7** Arakawa (Shizuka), Cousins (Robin), Fleming (Peggy), Yagudin (Alexei) **8** Hamilton (Scott), Lipinski (Tara) **9** Plushenko (Evgeny)
speed skater: **4** Koss (Johann Olav), Ohno (Apolo Anton), Yang (Yang) **5** Blair (Bonnie), Davis (Shani) **6** Heiden (Eric), Timmer (Marianne) **7** Hedrick (Chad), Klassen (Cindy), Zhurova (Svetlana) **9** Pechstein (Claudia)

ice smoother
7 Zamboni

Ichabod Crane's beloved
7 Katrina

icing
7 topping 8 frosting

icky
4 vile 5 awful, gross, nasty 9 loathsome, offensive, repellent, repulsive, revolting, sickening 10 disgusting 11 distasteful

icon
4 idol, sign 5 image 6 emblem, symbol

iconoclastic
9 dissident, heretical 10 rebellious, unorthodox 13 nonconformist

icy
4 cold 5 gelid, polar 6 arctic, chilly, frigid, frosty, frozen, steely 7 glacial 8 freezing 11 emotionless, unemotional

Idaho
capital: 5 Boise
city: 6 Moscow 9 Pocatello, Twin Falls 10 Idaho Falls 11 Coeur d'Alene
mountain: 5 Borah (Peak)
nickname: 3 Gem (State)
river: 5 Snake 6 Salmon
state bird: 8 bluebird
state flower: 7 syringa
state tree: 9 white pine

Idas
brother: 7 Lynceus
father: 8 Aphareus
slayer: 4 Zeus
victim: 6 Castor
wife: 8 Marpessa

idea
4 whim 5 fancy, guess, motif 6 belief, notion, theory, thesis, vagary 7 caprice, conceit, concept, inkling, meaning, opinion, subject, surmise, thought 8 estimate 9 sentiment, suspicion 10 assumption, brainchild, brainstorm, conception, conclusion, conjecture, conviction, estimation, hypothesis, impression, perception, reflection 11 abstraction, formulation, supposition

ideal
4 best, goal 5 model 7 chimera, classic, epitome, paragon, perfect, utopian 8 absolute, ensample, exemplar, flawless, nonesuch, paradigm, standard, ultimate 9 archetype, classical, exemplary, nonpareil 10 archetypal, conceptual, consummate 11 theoretical

idealist
7 dreamer, quixote, utopian 9 ideologue, visionary

idealistic
6 dreamy 7 utopian 8 poetical, quixotic, romantic 9 visionary 10 starry-eyed 11 impractical, unrealistic

idealize
5 deify, exalt, extol 7 elevate, ennoble, glorify, worship 8 venerate

ideate
5 think 7 imagine 8 conceive, envisage, envision

idée fixe
5 mania 6 fetish, phobia 7 complex 8 fixation 9 obsession 13 preoccupation

identical
3 one 4 like, same, very 5 alike, equal, exact 8 selfsame 9 duplicate 10 equivalent, synonymous

identification mark
4 logo 5 badge, brand, label 6 emblem

identify
3 peg, tag 4 mark, name, spot 5 brand, place 6 finger, select 7 make out, pick out 8 pinpoint 9 determine, recognize 11 distinguish

identity
4 name, self 7 oneness 8 sameness, selfhood 9 character 10 congruence, uniformity, uniqueness 11 personality, singularity 13 individuality, particularity

ideological
8 notional 10 conceptual, ideational 11 speculative 13 philosophical

ideologue
8 believer, idealist, partisan, theorist

ideology
3 ism 5 credo, creed 7 beliefs 8 doctrine 10 philosophy, principles

idiocy
7 fatuity 9 cretinism, stupidity 10 imbecility 11 foolishness

idiomatic
7 demotic 8 peculiar 9 dialectal 10 colloquial, vernacular

idiosyncrasy
3 tic 5 quirk 6 oddity 7 anomaly 11 peculiarity, singularity 12 eccentricity

idiosyncratic
3 odd 5 kooky, queer, weird 6 quirky 7 erratic, oddball, offbeat, unusual 8 peculiar, singular 9 eccentric 11 distinctive

idiot
3 ass 4 dolt, fool, jerk, simp 5 dummy, dunce, moron, ninny 6 cretin, doofus, nitwit, stupid 7 airhead, dullard, half-wit, jackass, natural, tomfool 8 dumbbell, imbecile, numskull 9 ignoramus, numbskull, simpleton 10 nincompoop

idiotic
5 dopey 6 stupid 7 foolish, moronic 8 ignorant 9 brainless, imbecilic, senseless

idle
3 bum **4** laze, lazy, loaf, loll, rest, vain **5** dally, drone, empty, inert, slack, tarry **6** asleep, dawdle, diddle, fallow, futile, linger, loiter, lounge, otiose, unused, vacant **7** aimless, dormant, passive **8** inactive, indolent, slothful **9** shiftless **10** unoccupied

idleness
4 ease **5** sloth **6** vanity **7** leisure, loafing **8** lethargy **9** indolence **10** inactivity

idler
3 bum **4** slug **5** drone **6** loafer, slouch **7** dawdler **8** deadbeat, fainéant, loiterer, slugabed, sluggard **9** do-nothing, lazybones **11** couch potato

Idmon
daughter: 7 Arachne
father: 6 Apollo
mother: 6 Cyrene

idol
3 god **4** hero, icon, star **5** deity, image, totem **6** fetish, minion, symbol **8** likeness
Chinese: 4 joss

idolatry
7 worship **8** devotion **9** adoration **10** exaltation, veneration **11** deification **13** glorification

idolize
5 adore, deify, exalt **6** revere **7** glorify, worship **8** venerate

Idomeneo composer
6 Mozart (Wolfgang Amadeus)

idyllic
5 ideal **6** rustic **7** bucolic, halcyon, perfect, utopian **8** arcadian, heavenly, pastoral, peaceful, romantic **9** idealized, unspoiled **11** picturesque, sentimental

Idylls of the King
author: 8 Tennyson (Alfred)
character: 4 Enid **6** Arthur, Elaine, Gareth, Merlin, Vivien **7** Geraint, Lynette **8** Lancelot

iffy
5 dicey, risky **6** chancy, unsure **7** dubious, erratic **8** doubtful **9** uncertain **10** unreliable **12** inconsistent **13** unpredictable

igneous rock
4 lava **5** magma **6** basalt, gabbro **7** diabase, granite **8** porphyry

ignis fatuus
6 mirage **7** chimera **8** delusion, illusion, phantasm **9** pipe dream **12** will-o'-the-wisp **13** hallucination

ignitable
8 burnable **9** excitable, flammable **10** incendiary **11** combustible, inflammable

ignite
4 fire **5** light, spark **6** excite, kindle **7** inflame **8** enkindle, touch off

ignited
3 lit **5** afire, fiery **6** ablaze, aflame, alight **7** blazing, burning, flaming, flaring **11** conflagrant

ignoble
3 low **4** base, mean, poor, vile **5** lowly **6** abject, coarse, common, scurvy, sordid, vulgar **7** lowborn, servile **8** baseborn, indecent, inferior, plebeian, shameful, unwashed, wretched **10** despicable, inglorious **11** disgraceful **12** contemptible, dishonorable

ignominious
6 odious **8** infamous, shameful **9** degrading **10** despicable, inglorious **11** disgraceful, humiliating, opprobrious **12** contemptible, dishonorable, disreputable **13** discreditable, unrespectable

ignominy
5 odium, shame **6** infamy **7** obloquy, scandal **8** disgrace, dishonor **9** discredit, disesteem, disrepute **10** opprobrium **11** humiliation **13** mortification

ignoramus
4 dolt **5** dummy, dunce, idiot, moron **6** dimwit, nitwit, stupid **7** airhead, dullard, half-wit **8** dumbbell, imbecile, numskull **9** numbskull, simpleton

ignorance
7 naiveté **9** innocence, nescience, stupidity **10** illiteracy, simpleness, simplicity **11** unawareness **12** incognizance

ignorant
5 naive **6** simple **7** unaware **8** clueless, nescient, untaught **9** benighted, ingenuous, oblivious, unknowing, unlearned, untutored, unwitting **10** illiterate, uncultured, uneducated, uninformed, unlettered, unschooled **11** incognizant, know-nothing **12** uninstructed **13** unenlightened

ignore
4 omit, snub **5** avoid **6** forget, reject, slight **7** neglect **8** overlook **9** disregard

Igraine
husband: 5 Uther **7** Gorlois
son: 6 Arthur

iguana
5 anole **6** lizard **8** basilisk **10** chuckwalla

ilex
4 maté **5** holly **6** yaupon **7** holm oak **8** inkberry

Iliad
4 epic
author: 5 Homer
character: 4 Ajax **5** Helen, Paris, Priam **6** Aeneas, Hector **8** Achilles, Diomedes, Odysseus **9** Agamemnon, Patroclus
city: 4 Troy

Ilium
4 Troy

ilk
4 kind, sort, type 5 breed, class, genre 6 family, kidney, nature, stripe 7 variety

ill
4 sick 6 ailing, infirm, laid up, malady, peaked, queasy, unwell 7 ailment, disease, trouble, unlucky 8 diseased, disorder, distress, feverish, nauseous, scarcely, sickness, syndrome 9 afflicted, infirmity, nauseated, unhealthy 10 misfortune

ill-adapted
8 unfitted, unsuited 10 unsuitable

ill-advised
4 rash 5 brash, hasty 6 madcap, unwise 7 foolish 8 careless, heedless, reckless 9 foolhardy, impolitic, imprudent 10 incautious, indiscreet, unthinking 11 inexpedient, injudicious, thoughtless

ill at ease
3 shy 4 edgy 6 on edge 7 anxious, awkward, fidgety, nervous 8 insecure, restless 9 unsettled 11 discomfited 12 apprehensive 13 self-conscious, uncomfortable

ill-boding
4 dire 7 baleful, doomful, fateful, ominous, unlucky 8 sinister 10 portentous 11 apocalyptic 12 inauspicious, unpropitious

ill-bred
4 rude 5 crude 7 boorish, loutish, uncivil, uncouth 8 impolite 9 unrefined 10 uncultured, ungracious, unmannered, unmannerly, unpolished 11 uncivilized 12 discourteous

ill-defined
5 faint, fuzzy, vague 7 shadowy 10 indistinct

illegal
3 hot 6 banned 7 bootleg, lllIclt, lawless 8 criminal, outlawed, unlawful, wrongful 9 felonious, forbidden 10 actionable, prohibited, proscribed, unlicensed 12 illegitimate
act: 5 crime 6 felony
payment: 5 bribe 6 payola
scheme: 4 scam

illegible
8 scrawled 10 unreadable 11 inscrutable

illegitimacy
8 bastardy 11 bar sinister 12 unlawfulness

illegitimate
7 bastard, bootleg, erratic, invalid, lawless, natural 8 criminal, improper, spurious, unlawful 11 misbegotten 12 unauthorized

ill-fated
6 cursed, doomed 7 unhappy, unlucky 8 accursed, luckless, untoward 10 disastrous 11 star-crossed, unfortunate

ill-favored
4 ugly 5 plain 6 homely 12 unattractive

ill-humored
4 dour, sour 5 cross, surly, testy 6 crabby, cranky, crusty, grumpy, morose, ornery, sullen, tetchy, touchy 7 crabbed, grouchy, peevish, prickly 8 choleric, churlish, snappish 9 dyspeptic, irascible, irritable, saturnine, splenetic 12 cantankerous, disagreeable, misanthropic

illiberal
6 biased, narrow 7 bigoted, insular 9 hidebound, parochial, penurious 10 intolerant, prejudiced, provincial 11 reactionary, small-minded 12 conservative, narrow-minded, uncharitable

illicit
7 bootleg, crooked, lawless 8 criminal, unlawful 9 forbidden 10 contraband, prohibited 11 black-market, clandestine 12 unauthorized

illimitable
7 endless 8 infinite, unending 9 boundless 11 measureless

Illinois
capital: 11 Springfield
city: 6 Aurora, Cicero, Joliet, Peoria 7 Chicago 8 Rockford
college, university: 4 Knox 6 DePaul 7 Wheaton 12 Northwestern
nickname: 7 Prairie (State)
river: 6 Wabash
state bird: 8 cardinal
state flower: 6 violet
state tree: 8 white oak

illiterate
6 unread 8 untaught 9 untutored 10 uneducated, unlettered, unschooled

ill-mannered
4 rude 6 coarse 7 boorish, loutish, uncivil, uncouth 8 churlish, impolite 10 ungracious 12 discourteous

ill-natured
4 sour 5 cross, huffy, surly, testy 6 bitchy, crabby, grumpy, ornery, tetchy 7 grouchy, peevish, waspish 8 choleric, churlish, snappish, spiteful 9 dyspeptic, fractious, irascible, irritable 10 malevolent 11 belligerent, contentious, quarrelsome 12 cantankerous, disagreeable

illness
6 malady 7 ailment, disease, malaise 8 cachexia, disorder, sickness 9 infirmity 10 affliction 13 indisposition

illogical
6 absurd 7 invalid, unsound 8 specious 9 plausible, senseless, sophistic 10 fallacious, irrational, unreasoned 11 nonrational 12 preposterous, unreasonable

ill-starred
6 cursed, doomed, malign 7 fateful, ominous,

unhappy, unlucky **8** luckless, untoward **10** disastrous, foreboding, portentous **11** unfavorable, unfortunate, unpromising **12** inauspicious, unpropitious

ill-tempered
4 sour **5** cross, huffy, surly **6** crabby, bitchy, grumpy, ornery, snippy **7** grouchy, peevish, waspish **8** choleric, churlish, petulant, shrewish, snappish, spiteful **9** dyspeptic, fractious, irascible, irritable **11** belligerent, contentious, quarrelsome **12** cantankerous, disagreeable

ill-timed
11 inopportune **12** unseasonable

ill-treat
4 harm, hurt **5** abuse **6** injure, misuse, molest **7** torment **8** aggrieve **10** traumatize

illuminate
5 clear, edify, exalt, gloss, light **6** uplift **7** clarify, clear up, explain, lighten **8** brighten, decorate **9** elucidate, embellish, enlighten, highlight, irradiate, spotlight

illuminati
5 elite **7** clerisy, scholar **8** academic **11** academician **13** intellectuals

illumination
5 light **8** lighting
unit of: **3** lux **4** phot **5** lumen **6** candle **7** candela **10** footcandle

illusion
4 myth **5** dream, fancy, ghost **6** facade, mirage **7** chimera, fantasy **8** phantasm, phantasy **9** invention, pipe dream, semblance **11** ignis fatuus **12** will-o'-the-wisp **13** hallucination

illusionist
8 conjurer, magician **9** trickster

illusive
see **illusory**

illusory
4 sham **6** unreal **7** seeming **8** apparent, fanciful **9** deceptive, fictional, imaginary, visionary **10** chimerical, fallacious, fictitious, misleading, ostensible

illustrate
4 mark, show **6** depict, evince, expose, reveal **7** clarify, display, exhibit, explain, picture, portray **8** decorate, describe, evidence, instance, manifest **9** elucidate, epitomize, exemplify **11** demonstrate

illustration
4 case **6** sample **7** diagram, drawing, example, picture, problem **8** instance

illustrative
7 graphic **9** pictorial **10** clarifying **11** descriptive **12** iconographic

illustrator
American: **4** Kent (Rockwell), Pyle (Howard) **5** Abbey (Edwin Austin), Flagg (James Montgomery), Smith (Jessie Willcox), Wyeth (Newell Convers) **6** Gibson (Charles Dana) **7** Burgess (Gelett), Parrish (Maxwell) **8** Rockwell (Norman) **9** Remington (Frederic)
English: **5** Crane (Walter) **6** Morris (William), Potter (Beatrix) **7** Nielsen (Kay), Rackham (Arthur), Tenniel (John) **9** Beardsley (Aubrey), Caldecott (Randolph), du Maurier (George), Greenaway (Kate)
French: **4** Doré (Gustave) **5** Dulac (Edmund)
German: **5** Dürer (Albrecht)

illustrious
5 famed, great, lofty, noted **6** famous **7** eminent, exalted, notable, sublime **8** glorious, renowned, splendid **9** acclaimed, prominent **10** celebrated, preeminent **11** outstanding, prestigious **13** distinguished

illustriousness
4 fame **5** glory **6** renown **8** eminence, prestige **9** celebrity **10** prominence **11** distinction, preeminence

ill will
5 spite, venom **6** animus, enmity, malice, rancor, spleen **7** despite, dislike **8** acrimony, aversion, bad blood **9** animosity, antipathy, hostility, malignity **10** resentment **11** malevolence **12** spitefulness **13** maliciousness

Ilus
father: **4** Tros
grandson: **5** Priam
mother: **10** Callirrhoë
son: **8** Laomedon

image
4 copy, form, icon, idea, idol, ikon **5** equal, match **6** double, effigy, figure, mirror, notion, ringer, vision **7** concept, fantasm, feature, picture **8** likeness, phantasm, portrait **9** facsimile, semblance **10** conception, equivalent, impression, reflection, simulacrum **12** illustration
Polynesian: **4** tiki
Semitic: **6** teraph **8** teraphim (plural)

imaginary
5 ideal **6** made-up, unreal **7** fancied, fictive **8** abstract, fabulous, fanciful, illusive, illusory, notional, quixotic **9** dreamlike, fantastic, fictional, legendary, visionary **10** apocryphal, chimerical, fictitious, phantasmal **11** make-believe **12** hypothetical, suppositious

imagination
5 fancy **7** fantasy **8** phantasy **9** invention **10** creativity **11** inspiration **13** inventiveness

imaginative
5 false **7** blue-sky, fictive **8** artistic, creative,

fanciful, original, poetical **9** ingenious, inventive, visionary, whimsical **11** resourceful **12** enterprising

imagine
5 dream, fancy **6** assume, invent, make up **7** dream up, feature, picture, suspect **8** conceive, envisage, envision **9** fabricate, visualize **10** conjecture

imbecile
4 dodo, dolt, dull, fool, jerk **5** dunce, idiot, moron, ninny **6** cretin, dimwit, nitwit **7** half-wit, jackass, moronic, pinhead, tomfool **8** numskull **9** birdbrain, blockhead, numbskull **10** dunderhead, nincompoop

imbibe
3 sip, sup **4** chug, soak, swig, tope, toss **5** booze, drink, quaff, swill **6** absorb, guzzle, tipple **7** consume, swallow, swizzle **10** assimilate

imbricate
3 lap **7** overlap, shingle **11** overlapping

imbroglio
3 row **4** maze, mess, spat, to-do **5** brawl, broil, mix-up **6** fracas, muddle, tangle **7** dispute, quarrel, rhubarb, scandal, wrangle **8** argument, disorder, squabble **9** confusion, intricacy **10** falling-out **11** altercation, predicament **12** complication, entanglement

imbrue
4 soil **5** stain **8** discolor

imbue
3 dye **4** soak **5** bathe, endow, steep, tinge **6** infuse, invest, leaven **7** ingrain, instill, pervade, suffuse **8** permeate, saturate **9** influence, inoculate

imitate
3 ape **4** copy, echo, mime, mock **5** forge, mimic, spoof **6** parody **7** emulate, take off **8** resemble, simulate, travesty **9** burlesque, duplicate, replicate, reproduce **11** counterfeit, impersonate

imitation
4 copy, fake, mock, sham **5** clone, ditto, dummy, false, match, phony **6** ersatz, parody, ringer **7** forgery, replica **8** likeness, parallel, spurious, travesty **9** duplicate, semblance, simulated **10** artificial, simulacrum, simulation, substitute **11** counterfeit, counterpart **12** reproduction, substitution

imitative
4 mock **5** apish **6** echoic **7** copycat, mimetic, parodic, slavish **11** counterfeit **12** onomatopoeic **13** onomatopoetic

imitator
4 aper, mime **5** mimic **6** parrot **7** copycat

immaculate
4 pure **5** clean **6** chaste, virgin **7** cleanly, perfect, sinless **8** flawless, spotless, unsoiled, virtuous **9** stainless, undefiled, unsullied **11** spic-and-span, unblemished **12** spick-and-span

immaterial
7 trivial **8** bodiless, ethereal **10** extraneous, inapposite, intangible, irrelevant **11** disembodied, incorporeal, nonphysical, unimportant **12** inapplicable **13** insignificant, insubstantial, unsubstantial

immature
3 raw **5** crude, green, young **6** callow, infant, unripe **7** puerile **8** childish, juvenile, youthful **9** infantile, primitive, unfledged **10** unfinished **11** undeveloped

immaturity
6 nonage **7** infancy **8** minority **9** childhood, salad days **11** adolescence **12** juvenescence

immeasurable
4 vast **6** untold **7** endless **8** infinite **9** boundless, extensive, limitless, unbounded, unlimited **11** illimitable, inestimable, uncountable **12** incalculable, unfathomable

immediate
4 next, nigh **5** close **6** at hand, direct, nearby, urgent **7** current, instant, ongoing, primary **9** firsthand, proximate **10** unmediated **12** straightaway **13** instantaneous

immediately
3 now, PDQ **4** anon, ASAP, stat **6** at once, presto, pronto **8** directly, promptly **9** forthwith, instanter, instantly, right away **11** straightway **12** straightaway

immense
4 huge, mega, vast **5** great, large, mondo **6** mighty **7** mammoth, massive, titanic **8** colossal, enormous, gigantic **9** humongous, monstrous **10** gargantuan, monumental, prodigious, tremendous **11** elephantine

immensely
4 a lot **8** terribly **9** extremely **11** exceedingly **12** inordinately

immensity
8 enormity, hugeness, vastness **9** greatness **12** enormousness

immerse
3 dip **4** duck, dunk, sink, soak **5** bathe, douse **6** drench, engage, plunge **7** baptize, engross, involve **8** saturate, submerge

immigrant
5 alien **7** settler **8** newcomer **10** transplant
Japanese: 5 issei

imminent
4 near **6** at hand **6** coming **7** brewing, nearing, ominous, pending **8** upcoming **9** gathering, proximate **11** approaching, overhanging

immobile
3 set **5** fixed, inert, still **6** frozen, stable, static **9** unmovable **10** motionless, stationary

immobilize
5 still **7** cripple, disable **8** paralyze **9** hamstring **12** incapacitate

immoderate
5 undue **7** extreme **9** excessive **10** exorbitant, inordinate, untempered **11** extravagant, intemperate **12** unreasonable, unrestrained **13** extraordinary, overindulgent

immoderation
6 excess **11** exorbitance, prodigality **12** extravagance, intemperance

immodest
4 lewd, vain **7** stuck-up **8** arrogant, boastful, indecent, puffed-up, unchaste **9** conceited, egotistic **11** pretentious

immolate
4 burn, kill **7** destroy **9** sacrifice

immoral
4 evil, vile **5** dirty, wrong **6** sinful, wanton, wicked **7** corrupt, unclean, vicious **8** depraved, indecent, unchaste **9** dissolute, reprobate, uncleanly **10** degenerate, iniquitous, licentious

immorality
3 sin **4** vice **8** iniquity **9** depravity **10** corruption, unchastity, wickedness

immortal
7 endless, eternal, godlike, undying **8** timeless, unending **9** ceaseless, deathless, perpetual **11** amaranthine, everlasting, sempiternal

immotile
5 fixed, inert **6** rooted, static **9** paralyzed **10** stationary

immovable
3 pat, set **4** fast, firm **5** fixed, rigid **6** rooted, stable **7** adamant **8** constant, obdurate, stubborn **9** steadfast **10** inflexible, invariable, stationary, unyielding

immune
4 free, safe **6** exempt, secure **9** protected **10** impervious **12** invulnerable, unassailable

immunity
7 defense, freedom **9** exemption, privilege **10** protection

immure
3 pen **4** cage, coop, jail, wall **6** entomb, intern, shut in **7** confine, enclose **8** imprison **11** incarcerate

immutable
4 firm **5** fixed **8** constant **9** permanent, steadfast **10** changeless, inflexible, invariable, unchanging **11** inalterable, unalterable **12** unchangeable

Imogen
father: **9** Cymbeline
husband: **9** Posthumus

imp
3 elf **4** brat, puck **5** demon, devil, fiend, gamin, gnome, pixie, scamp **6** goblin, kobold, rascal, sprite, urchin **7** gremlin **9** hobgoblin

impact
3 hit, jar, rap **4** blow, bump, jolt, rock, slam, slap **5** brunt, embed, pound, punch, shock, smash, smite **6** affect, buffet, effect, strike, wallop **9** collision, influence **10** concussion, percussion

impair
3 mar, sap **4** harm, hurt **5** spoil **6** damage, injure, lessen, weaken, worsen **7** cripple, tarnish, vitiate **8** enfeeble **9** prejudice, undermine **10** debilitate

impala
8 antelope

impale
4 gore, spit, stab **5** lance, prick, spear, spike, stick **6** pierce, skewer **8** puncture, transfix **11** transpierce

impalpable
4 fine **7** powdery **8** ethereal **10** intangible **11** disembodied, incorporeal **12** imponderable **13** imperceptible, indiscernible

impart
4 cede, give, lend, tell **5** grant, share, yield **6** afford, bestow, confer, convey, pass on, relate, render **8** disclose, transmit **11** communicate
knowledge: **5** teach **6** inform **7** educate **8** instruct

impartial
4 even, fair, just **5** equal **7** neutral **8** detached, unbiased **9** equitable, objective, uncolored **10** evenhanded **12** unprejudiced **13** disinterested, dispassionate

impassable
6 closed **7** blocked **10** obstructed **12** impenetrable

impasse
3 box, fix, jam **6** aporia, corner, logjam, pickle, pocket **7** dead end, dilemma **8** cul-de-sac, deadlock, standoff **9** stalemate **10** blind alley, bottleneck

impassioned
3 hot **5** fiery **6** ardent, fervid, fierce, heated, red-hot, torrid **7** burning, fervent, intense, zealous **8** feverish, romantic, vehement, white-hot **9** emotional, perfervid **10** hot-blooded, overheated **11** dithyrambic **12** melodramatic

impassive
4 calm, cold, cool **5** stoic **6** serene, stolid, vacant **7** deadpan **8** composed, hardened,

reserved, reticent, taciturn **9** heartless **10** insensible, insentient, phlegmatic, poker-faced **11** cold-blooded, emotionless, insensitive, unconcerned, unemotional, unexcitable, unflappable **12** inexpressive, unexpressive, unresponsive **13** dispassionate, self-possessed

impassivity
6 apathy, phlegm **8** stoicism **9** sangfroid, stolidity **12** indifference **13** insensibility

impatient
4 edgy **5** antsy, eager, hasty **7** anxious, fretful, restive **8** restless

impeach
5 blame, doubt **6** accuse, charge, indict **7** censure **9** inculpate, reprehend **11** incriminate

impeccable
4 pure **5** exact **7** perfect, precise **8** absolute, accurate, flawless, unerring **9** blameless, errorless, faultless, guiltless **10** infallible **11** unblemished

impecunious
4 poor **5** broke, needy **7** pinched **8** bankrupt, beggarly, indigent **9** destitute, insolvent, penniless, penurious **10** down-and-out **11** necessitous

impecuniousness
4 need, want **6** penury **7** poverty **9** indigence, neediness, pauperism, privation **11** destitution

impedance
3 bar **4** clog **5** block **8** blockage, obstacle **9** hindrance **10** opposition **11** obstruction

impede
3 bar, dam **4** clog, slow **5** block, check, debar, delay, deter, stall **6** hinder, hang up, hold up, stymie, thwart **7** bog down **8** encumber, obstruct **9** embarrass, interfere, stonewall

impediment
3 bar **4** clog, snag **5** block, hitch **6** hurdle **7** barrier **8** obstacle **9** barricade, hindrance, roadblock **10** difficulty **11** encumbrance, obstruction

impel
4 goad, prod, push, spur, urge **5** drive, force, rouse **6** excite, incite, prompt **7** actuate, inspire **8** mobilize, motivate **9** instigate, stimulate

impend
4 loom, near **6** menace **8** approach, overhang, threaten

impenetrable
5 dense **6** arcane **7** obscure **9** enigmatic, recondite **10** impervious, invincible, mysterious, unknowable **11** impermeable, bulletproof, inscrutable, ungraspable **12** unfathomable

imperative
4 duty, need, rule, writ **5** acute, vital **6** crying, urgent **7** burning, clamant, command, crucial, exigent **8** critical, pressing, required **9** clamorous, essential, insistent, mandatory, necessary, necessity, requisite **10** compulsory, obligation, obligatory **11** fundamental, necessitous **12** prerequisite

imperceptible
3 dim **5** faint, vague **6** slight, subtle **7** gradual **9** invisible **10** impalpable, indistinct, insensible, intangible, unapparent **12** undetectable, unnoticeable, unobservable **13** inappreciable, inconspicuous, indiscernible

imperceptive
4 dull **7** shallow, unaware **11** inattentive, insensitive

imperfect
6 faulty, flawed **9** defective, deficient, irregular **10** defeasible, inadequate

imperfection
3 sin **4** flaw, wart **5** fault **6** defect, foible **7** blemish, demerit, failing, frailty **8** weakness **10** deficiency **11** shortcoming

imperial
5 regal, royal **6** kingly, lordly **7** haughty **8** absolute, majestic **9** masterful, sovereign **10** high-handed, peremptory **11** domineering, magisterial, monarchical

imperil
4 risk **6** hazard, menace **7** venture **8** endanger, threaten **10** jeopardize

imperious
5 bossy **6** urgent **7** haughty **8** absolute, arrogant, despotic, dominant **9** arbitrary, masterful **10** autocratic, commanding, high-handed, oppressive, peremptory, tyrannical **11** dictatorial, domineering, heavy-handed, magisterial, overbearing

impermanent
7 passing **8** fleeting, fugitive **9** ephemeral, fugacious, momentary, temporary, transient **10** evanescent, short-lived, transitory

impersonal
4 cold **5** aloof **8** abstract, detached **11** cold-blooded, emotionless **13** dispassionate, unimpassioned

impersonate
3 ape **4** play **5** mimic **6** act out **7** imitate, play-act, portray **9** represent **11** counterfeit

impersonator
3 ape **4** aper, mime **5** actor, mimic **6** mummer, player, ringer **7** actress, copycat **8** thespian
female: **9** drag queen

impertinence
3 lip **4** gall, guff, sass **5** brass, cheek **8** audacity, boldness, chutzpah, rudeness, temerity

9 brashness, impudence, insolence **10** brazenness, effrontery, incivility **11** discourtesy, irrelevance

impertinent
4 bold, busy, rude **5** brash, fresh, sassy, saucy **6** brazen, cheeky **7** uncivil **8** insolent, meddling **9** audacious, intrusive, obtrusive, officious **10** inapposite, irrelative, irrelevant, meddlesome **11** ill-mannered **12** discourteous, inapplicable, presumptuous

imperturbability
5 poise **6** aplomb, phlegm **8** calmness, coolness, serenity, stoicism **9** composure, placidity, sangfroid **10** dispassion, equanimity **11** equilibrium, nonchalance, tranquility **12** tranquillity

imperturbable
4 calm, cool **5** stoic **6** placid, poised, serene, smooth, steady, stolid **7** unmoved **8** composed, tranquil **9** collected, unruffled **10** nonchalant, phlegmatic, unaffected **11** unflappable

impervious
4 safe **6** immune **8** hardened **10** inviolable **12** inaccessible, invulnerable

impetuous
3 hot **4** rash, wild **5** fiery, hasty **6** ardent, fervid, madcap, sudden **8** headlong, vehement, volatile **9** hotheaded, mercurial **10** irrational, passionate **11** precipitant, precipitate, precipitous, spontaneous **13** temperamental

impetus
4 goad, push, spur **5** force **6** motive **8** catalyst, momentum, stimulus **9** incentive, stimulant **10** incitement, motivation **13** encouragement

impinge
5 press **6** border **7** intrude, obtrude **8** encroach

impious
6 sinful, unholy, wicked **7** godless, infidel, profane, secular, ungodly **8** agnostic, apostate **9** atheistic **10** irreverent, unfaithful, unhallowed **11** blasphemous, irreligious, unrighteous **12** iconoclastic, sacrilegious **13** unconsecrated

impish
4 arch **5** elfin **6** elvish **7** playful, puckish, roguish, waggish **11** mischievous

impishness
7 devilry, roguery, waggery **8** deviltry, mischief **9** devilment **11** roguishness, waggishness

implacable
4 grim **8** ruthless **9** merciless **10** inexorable, unyielding **11** intractable **12** unappeasable

implant
3 fix **4** root **5** embed, graft, infix **6** enroot, infuse, insert **7** ingrain, inspire, instill **9** establish, inculcate, inoculate, introduce **10** inseminate **12** augmentation

implausible
5 fishy **6** flimsy **7** dubious, suspect **8** doubtful, fanciful, unlikely **10** far-fetched, incredible **12** questionable, unbelievable, unconvincing

implement
4 tool **6** device, effect, enable, gadget **7** enforce, execute, fulfill, perform, realize, utensil **8** carry out, complete, make good **9** actualize, apparatus, appliance **10** accomplish, instrument, supplement **11** contraption, contrivance
carpentry: **3** adz, die, saw **4** adze, file **5** brace, clamp, drill, punch, tongs **6** chisel, hammer, pliers, reamer, sander, wrench **7** hacksaw, scraper **9** blowtorch **11** screwdriver
cleaning: **3** mop **5** broom, brush, whisk **6** duster, vacuum **7** sweeper **10** whiskbroom
cutting: **5** knife, mower, razor **6** scythe, shears, sickle **8** scissors
digging: **5** spade **6** dibber, dibble, shovel
drawing: **3** pen **6** eraser, pencil **7** compass **8** template
eating: **4** fork **5** knife, spoon **9** chopstick
engraving: **5** burin **6** graver
farm: **4** plow **6** binder, harrow, plough, scythe, seeder, sickle **8** gangplow, reaphook, spreader, thresher **9** pitchfork **10** cultivator
fireplace: **5** poker, tongs **7** andiron
fishing: **3** rod **4** hook, lure, reel **6** sinker **7** harpoon, trident
garden: **3** hoe **4** rake **5** edger, spade **6** dibber, dibble, digger, tiller, trowel **7** mattock
grooming: **4** comb, file **5** brush, razor **7** clipper **8** clippers, nail file, tweezers **10** toothbrush
kitchen: **3** pan, pot **4** mold **5** mixer, whisk **6** grater, kettle, mortar, pestle **7** blender, skillet, spatula **8** colander, saucepan, stockpot
logging: **5** peavy **6** peavey **8** cant hook
measuring: **3** cup **4** gage, rule **5** gauge, ruler, scale **7** caliper, divider, trammel, T-square **10** micrometer, protractor
stone: **5** burin **7** neolith **9** paleolith

implicate
4 link, mire **5** blame **6** tangle **7** concern, embroil, entwine, include, involve **8** entangle, intimate **11** incriminate

implication
4 hint **8** allusion, overtone **9** inference, undertone **10** connection, intimation, suggestion **11** association, connotation **12** significance

implicit
5 tacit **6** unsaid **8** inherent, unspoken **9** doubtless, potential, unuttered **10** undeclared, understood **11** unexpressed

implied
5 tacit **6** unsaid **8** inherent, unspoken **9** suggested **10** undeclared, understood **11** unexpressed

implore
3 ask, beg **4** coax, pray **5** crave, plead **6** adjure, appeal **7** beseech, entreat, solicit **10** supplicate

imply
4 hint, mean **5** get at **7** connote, include, involve, signify, suggest **8** indicate, intimate **9** insinuate

impolite
4 rude **5** crude **7** ill-bred, uncivil, uncouth **10** ungracious, unladylike, unmannered, unmannerly **11** ill-mannered **12** discourteous **13** ungentlemanly

impolitic
5 brash **6** unwise **8** tactless **9** imprudent, maladroit, untactful **10** ill-advised, indiscreet **11** inadvisable, inexpedient, injudicious **12** shortsighted, undiplomatic

import
4 bear, gist, mean, pith **5** sense, value, worth **6** convey, denote, intend, intent, matter, moment, stress, thrust, weight **7** concern, connote, express, meaning, message, purpose, signify **8** emphasis, indicate, transfer **9** magnitude, substance **10** intendment **11** acceptation, consequence **12** significance **13** signification

importance
4 mark, note, pith **5** value, worth **6** moment, weight **7** account, gravity **8** eminence, priority, salience, standing **9** greatness, magnitude, substance **10** prominence, worthiness **11** consequence, distinction, seriousness, weightiness **12** significance

important
3 big **5** chief, grave, great, heavy, major, noted, vital **6** famous, marked, potent, urgent, worthy **7** big-time, capital, crucial, eminent, fateful, notable, salient, serious, telling, weighty **8** critical, eventful, foremost, material, powerful, pressing, valuable **9** essential, estimable, imperious, memorable, momentous, prominent **10** meaningful, noteworthy, preeminent, worthwhile **11** outstanding, significant, substantial **12** considerable **13** consequential, distinguished, indispensable

importune
3 beg **4** pray, urge **5** annoy, plead, worry **6** appeal, invoke, plague **7** beseech, besiege, entreat, solicit, trouble **8** petition

impose
3 fob **4** lade, levy **5** abuse, enact, exact, foist, force, order, place, put on, visit, wreak **6** assess, burden, charge, compel, decree, demand, enjoin, fob off, ordain, saddle **7** command, dictate, exploit, inflict, intrude, lay down, obtrude, palm off, pass off, require **8** encroach, encumber, infringe, trespass **9** authorize, constrain, establish

imposing
4 huge **5** grand, noble, regal, royal **6** august **7** awesome, massive, pompous, stately **8** baronial, majestic, towering **9** dignified **10** commanding, monumental **11** magnificent, outstanding **12** high-sounding **13** distinguished

imposition
3 tax **4** duty, fine, levy **6** burden, demand **7** penalty **9** deception **13** inconvenience

impossible
6 absurd **8** hopeless **10** infeasible, unfeasible, unworkable **11** unthinkable **12** preposterous, unacceptable, unattainable, unbelievable, unimaginable, unrealizable, unreasonable **13** inconceivable

impost
3 fee, tax **4** duty, levy, toll **6** charge, tariff **7** tribute **9** surcharge **10** assessment

impostor
4 fake, sham **5** actor, cheat, faker, fraud, mimic, phony, poser, quack **6** humbug, poseur **8** deceiver **9** charlatan, con artist, hypocrite, pretender **10** dissembler, mountebank **11** masquerader **12** impersonator

imposture
4 fake, hoax, sell, sham, wile **5** cheat, fraud **6** deceit, humbug **8** flimflam **9** deception, mare's nest, stratagem **11** counterfeit

impotence
8 weakness **9** sterility **10** inadequacy **12** helplessness **13** powerlessness

impotent
4 lame, weak **6** effete, feeble **7** sterile **8** helpless **9** forceless, incapable, powerless **11** ineffective, ineffectual **12** invertebrate

impound
5 seize **6** immure, lock up **7** confine, enclose, put away **8** imprison **10** confiscate

impoverish
4 bust, ruin **5** break **6** beggar **8** bankrupt **9** pauperize

impoverished
4 poor **5** broke, needy **8** bankrupt, indigent **9** destitute, penniless, penurious

impoverishment
4 need, want **6** penury **9** indigence, neediness, privation **11** destitution

impracticable
8 unusable **10** infeasible, unfeasible, unworkable **11** insuperable, unrealistic **12** inaccessible, unattainable

impractical
7 utopian **8** quixotic, romantic, unusable **9** visionary **10** idealistic, infeasible, ivory-tower, starry-eyed, unfeasible, unworkable **11** theoretical, unrealistic

imprecation
3 hex **4** cuss **5** curse **7** malison **8** anathema **11** malediction

imprecise
5 rough, vague **7** inexact **9** estimated **10** indefinite **11** approximate, unspecified

impregnable
4 safe **6** immune, secure **9** protected **10** invincible, inviolable, unbeatable **11** indomitable, insuperable **12** unassailable **13** unconquerable

impregnate
3 sop **4** fill, soak **5** imbue, souse, steep **6** drench, infuse **7** pervade **8** conceive, permeate, saturate **9** fecundate, fertilize, penetrate, transfuse **10** inseminate

impresario
4 Bing (Rudolf) **5** Carte (Richard D'Oyly), Hurok (Sol) **6** Pastor (Tony) **7** manager **8** director, Kirstein (Lincoln), producer, promoter **9** Diaghilev (Sergei) **10** D'Oyly Carte (Richard)

impress
3 fix, set **4** dent, etch, mark, move, seal, sway **5** brand, carry, drive, exert, force, grave, infix, print, stamp, touch **6** affect, effect, excite, strike **7** engrave, ingrain, inspire **8** inscribe, transfer, transmit **9** establish, influence, stimulate

impressible
8 gullible, immature, moldable **9** malleable, receptive, sensitive **10** affectable, susceptive, vulnerable **11** persuadable, suggestible, susceptible

impression
4 dent, idea, mark, sign **5** image, print, stamp, trace, track **6** effect, hollow, notion **7** concept, edition, feeling, reissue, thought, vestige **8** printing, reaction **9** influence

impressionable
8 sensible, sentient **9** malleable, receptive, sensitive **10** responsive **11** suggestible, susceptible

impressionist
composer: **5** Ravel (Maurice) **7** Debussy (Claude)
mimic: **6** Carvey (Dana), Little (Rich)
painter: **5** Degas (Edgar), Manet (Edouard), Monet (Claude) **6** Renoir (Auguste), Sisley (Alfred) **7** Cassatt (Mary), Morisot (Berthe) **8** Pissarro (Camille)
(see also **postimpressionist**)

impressive
5 grand, noble **6** moving, superb **7** amazing, awesome, notable, stately, sublime **8** dazzling, dramatic, gorgeous, majestic, powerful, splendid, stirring, striking, touching **9** admirable, affecting, arresting, inspiring **11** magnificent

imprimatur
6 permit **7** license **8** approval, sanction **10** permission **13** authorization

imprint
3 fix **4** dent, etch, mark **5** grave, press, stamp **6** dimple, effect **7** engrave **8** inscribe **9** engraving, influence **10** depression **11** indentation, inscription

imprison
3 jug **4** cage, jail **6** coop up, detain, immure, intern, send up **7** confine, enclose **8** restrain, restrict, stockade **9** constrain **11** incarcerate

improbable
5 fishy **7** dubious **8** doubtful, fanciful, unlikely **10** far-fetched **11** implausible

impromptu
5 ad-lib **7** offhand **9** extempore, makeshift, unplanned, unstudied **10** off-the-cuff, unprepared, unscripted **11** extemporary, spontaneous, unrehearsed

improper
5 inapt, inept, outré, undue, wrong **6** gauche, risqué **7** illicit, naughty **8** ill-timed, indecent, tactless, unseemly, untimely, untoward **9** incorrect, unethical, unfitting **10** inaccurate, inapposite, indecorous, indelicate, malapropos, unbecoming, undecorous, unsuitable **11** impertinent, unbefitting **12** illegitimate, inadmissible, inapplicable, infelicitous, unseasonable **13** inappropriate

impropriety
5 gaffe **7** blooper, blunder, faux pas **8** solecism **9** barbarism, gaucherie, indecorum, vulgarism **12** unseemliness **13** incorrectness

improve
4 edit, help, mend **5** amend, boost, edify, emend, raise **6** better, enrich, look up, perk up, refine, reform, remedy, revise, revive, update, uplift **7** advance, amplify, augment, build up, correct, develop, enhance, enlarge, further, perfect, recover, rectify, upgrade **8** increase, progress **9** cultivate, intensify, meliorate **10** ameliorate, recuperate, strengthen

improvident
4 rash **6** lavish **8** careless, feckless, heedless, prodigal, reckless, wasteful **9** impetuous, negligent, unthrifty **10** profligate **11** extravagant, spendthrift **12** shortsighted

improvise
4 scat **5** ad-lib **6** cook up, invent, make up, wing it **7** concoct **8** contrive **9** fabricate **11** extemporize

improvised
7 offhand **9** extempore, unstudied **10** off-the-cuff, unprepared, unscripted **11** extemporary, unrehearsed

imprudent
4 rash **6** unwise **7** foolish **8** reckless **9** foolhardy **10** ill-advised, incautious, indiscreet **11** inadvisable, inexpedient, injudicious **12** shortsighted

impudence
4 gall **5** brass, cheek, nerve **8** audacity, boldness, chutzpah, temerity **9** brashness, cockiness, hardihood, insolence, nerviness **10** disrespect, effrontery **11** presumption

impudent
4 bold, flip, pert, rude, wise **5** brash, cocky, fresh, lippy, nervy, sassy, saucy, smart **6** brassy, brazen, cheeky **7** blatant, forward **8** flippant, insolent, overbold **9** audacious, barefaced, boldfaced **11** brazen-faced, smart-alecky **12** contumelious **13** disrespectful

impugn
5 cross **6** assail, attack, defame, malign, oppose, vilify **7** asperse, gainsay, impeach **8** chastise, reproach, traverse **9** castigate, denigrate, deprecate, disparage, reprehend **9** criticize, denigrate

impugnable
5 fishy, shady **6** guilty **7** suspect **8** doubtful **9** equivocal, uncertain **10** assailable, suspicious **11** problematic **12** disreputable

impulse
4 goad, push, spur, urge, whim **5** drive, force **6** motive, thrust, whimsy **7** caprice, passion **8** catalyst, excitant, stimulus **9** actuation, incentive, stimulant **10** incitation, incitement, motivation **11** inspiration, instigation
conductor: 4 axon

impulsive
4 rash **5** brash, hasty **6** abrupt, fickle, sudden **7** erratic, flighty, offhand **8** headlong, volatile **9** extempore, mercurial, unplanned, whimsical **10** capricious **11** instinctive, precipitate, spontaneous

impunity
7 freedom, liberty, license **8** immunity **9** exception, exemption, indemnity, privilege **10** absolution, protection

impure
3 raw **5** mixed **6** soiled, sordid, unholy **7** alloyed, defiled, profane, sullied, unclean **8** indecent, polluted, unchaste **9** uncleanly, unrefined **10** desecrated, unhallowed **11** adulterated

impute
3 lay **4** cite **5** blame, refer **6** accuse, adduce, assign, charge, credit, indict **7** ascribe **8** accredit **9** attribute, implicate

inaccessible
5 aloof **6** arcane, closed, far-off, remote **7** cryptic, distant, faraway, obscure **8** abstruse, esoteric, hermetic **9** recondite **11** unavailable, unreachable **12** unattainable, unobtainable

inaccurate
5 false, wrong **6** all wet, faulty, untrue **7** unsound **8** specious **9** distorted, erroneous **10** fictitious

inaction
6 repose **7** latency **8** dormancy, idleness, lethargy **9** indolence, passivity, slackness, torpidity **10** quiescence

inactive
4 idle, lazy **5** inert, quiet, slack, still **6** asleep, latent, sleepy, static, torpid **7** abeyant, dormant, passive, resting **8** slothful, sluggish **9** do-nothing, lethargic, quiescent, sedentary

in addition
4 also **6** as well, to boot, withal **7** besides, further **8** moreover **11** furthermore

inadequacy
4 lack, want **6** dearth **7** deficit, failure, paucity **8** shortage, weakness **9** impotence **10** deficiency, scantiness **11** shortcoming

inadequate
3 shy **5** scant, short **6** meager, scanty, scarce, skimpy **7** lacking, scrimpy, wanting **8** impotent **9** defective, deficient

inadmissible
5 unapt, unfit **8** unusable, unworthy **9** unwelcome **10** unsuitable **11** unqualified **12** unacceptable

inadvertent
8 careless, heedless **9** negligent, unmindful, unplanned, unwitting **10** accidental, unintended, unthinking **13** unintentional

inadvisable
4 rash **6** unwise **7** foolish **8** careless, reckless **9** foolhardy, impolitic, imprudent, pointless **10** ill-advised **11** harebrained

inalterable
5 fixed **6** stable **8** constant **9** immovable, immutable, steadfast, unmovable, unvarying **12** unchangeable

inamorata, inamorato
4 beau, dear **5** flame, honey, lover **6** steady **7** beloved, darling, squeeze, sweetie **8** ladylove, mistress, paramour, truelove **9** boyfriend **10** girlfriend, heartthrob, sweetheart

inane
4 idle, vain **5** blank, dotty, empty, silly, vapid **6** absurd, jejune, vacant **7** asinine, fatuous, foolish, idiotic, insipid, trivial, vacuous, witless **8** mindless **9** frivolous, laughable, pointless, senseless

inanimate
4 dead, dull **5** inert **5** still **6** asleep, torpid

7 dormant **8** immotile, lifeless **9** quiescent **10** motionless **11** unconscious

inanity
5 folly **6** idiocy, lunacy **7** fatuity, vacuity **8** vapidity **9** absurdity, dottiness, emptiness, silliness **10** hollowness **11** foolishness, vacuousness, witlessness **13** senselessness

inappreciable
6 meager, scanty, skimpy, slight **10** impalpable, unapparent **13** imperceptible

inappropriate
5 amiss, undue, unfit **6** unmeet **8** improper, unseemly, untimely, untoward **9** ill-suited **10** malapropos, unsuitable **11** impertinent

inapt
5 unfit **6** clumsy, gauche, jejune, unmeet **7** awkward, unhandy **8** improper, unfitted, unsuited, untimely **9** maladroit, unfitting, unskilled **10** amateurish, irrelevant, malapropos, unskillful, unsuitable

inarticulate
4 dumb, mute **5** tacit **6** silent **7** halting, unvocal **8** mumbling, unspoken, wordless **9** voiceless **10** maundering, speechless, tongue-tied, undeclared **11** unexpressed

inasmuch as
5 since **7** because, whereas **11** considering

inattentive
6 absent, remiss **8** distrait, heedless **9** forgetful, negligent, unheeding, unmindful **10** abstracted, distracted, unthinking **12** absentminded

inaugural
5 first **6** maiden, speech **7** address, initial, leading, opening, premier **8** foremost **9** beginning

inaugurate
5 begin, set up, start **6** launch **7** kick off **8** commence, dedicate, initiate **9** establish, institute, originate **10** consecrate

inauspicious
4 dire **7** adverse, baleful, direful, fateful, ominous, unlucky **8** sinister **9** ill-boding **11** threatening, unfavorable, unpromising **12** unpropitious

inborn
6 innate, native **7** connate, natural **8** inherent **9** intrinsic **10** congenital, connatural, hereditary, unacquired

inbred
7 connate, genetic, natural **8** inherent **9** intrinsic **10** congenital, connatural, deep-seated, hereditary

Inca
capital: **5** Cuzco
conqueror: **7** Pizarro (Francisco)
god: **4** Inti **9** Viracocha **10** Pachacamac
language: **7** Quechua
record: **5** quipu
ruin: **11** Machu Picchu
ruler: **9** Atahualpa, Pachacuti **10** Atahuallpa

incalculable
4 huge, iffy, vast **6** untold **8** enormous **9** boundless, countless, limitless, uncertain **10** tremendous, unnumbered **11** illimitable, measureless, uncountable **12** immeasurable, unmeasurable **13** unpredictable

in camera
7 privily, sub rosa **8** covertly, secretly **9** furtively, privately **10** stealthily **13** clandestinely

incandescent
3 hot **5** lucid **6** ardent, bright, lucent **7** beaming, fulgent, glowing, intense, lambent, radiant **8** dazzling, luminous **9** brilliant, effulgent, refulgent **11** resplendent

incantation
3 hex **4** rune **5** chant, charm, magic, spell **10** hocus-pocus, mumbo-jumbo, necromancy **11** abracadabra, conjuration, enchantment
Buddhist, Hindu: **6** mantra

incapable
5 unfit **6** unable **8** impotent, unexpert, unfitted **9** powerless, unskilled **10** unequipped, unskillful **11** unqualified **12** disqualified

incapacitate
6 disarm **7** cripple, disable **8** paralyze **10** debilitate, devitalize, disqualify, immobilize

incapacity
9 impotence, unfitness **10** impairment **11** disablement **12** fecklessness

incarcerate
3 jug **4** jail **6** coop up, immure, intern, send up **7** confine, enclose, impound **8** imprison

incarnadine
3 red **4** rosy **5** ruddy **6** redden **7** pinkish **8** bloodred

incarnate
5 human, reify **6** embody **7** realize **8** embodied, manifest **9** actualize, corporeal, personify **11** materialize, personalize **12** substantiate

incarnation
6 avatar **10** embodiment **11** reification
of Christ: **7** kenosis
of Vishnu: **4** Rama

incautious
4 rash **5** brash, hasty **6** daring, madcap, unwary **8** careless, heedless, reckless **9** daredevil, foolhardy, impetuous, imprudent, negligent, unmindful **10** ill-advised, neglectful, regardless **11** precipitate, thoughtless

incendiary
5 fiery, torch **7** firebug **8** agitator, arsonist, arsonous **9** explosive, firebrand, ignitable **10** pyromaniac **12** pyromaniacal

incense
3 ire, mad, oil **4** balm, burn, rile **5** anger, aroma, scent, spice **6** arouse, enrage, homage, incite, madden **7** inflame, provoke **8** irritate **9** infuriate
vessel: **6** censer **8** thurible

incentive
4 goad, spur **5** spark **6** motive **7** impetus, impulse **8** catalyst, stimulus **9** stimulant **10** inducement, motivation **11** provocation **13** encouragement

inception
4 root **5** birth, start **6** origin, outset, source **7** genesis, kickoff, opening **9** beginning **10** derivation, provenance **11** provenience **12** commencement

inceptive
7 initial, leadoff, nascent **9** beginning **10** initiatory

incertitude
5 doubt **7** dubiety **8** mistrust **9** suspicion **10** skepticism **11** dubiousness, uncertainty, vacillation **12** irresolution

incessant
6 steady **7** endless, eternal, nonstop **8** constant **9** ceaseless, continual, perpetual, unceasing **10** continuous **11** everlasting, unremitting **12** interminable **13** uninterrupted

inch
3 bit **5** crawl, creep **7** modicum

inchoate
8 formless, immature, unformed, unshaped **9** amorphous, embryonic, incipient, potential, shapeless **10** disjointed, incoherent **11** rudimentary, unorganized **12** disconnected

incident
5 event **7** episode **8** occasion **9** happening **10** affiliated, collateral, occurrence **11** concomitant

incidental
5 fluky, minor **6** casual, chance **9** accessory **10** contingent, fortuitous **11** subordinate **12** nonessential

incidentally
7 by the by **8** by the bye, by the way, casually **12** fortuitously

incinerate
4 burn **7** cremate

incipient
7 nascent **9** beginning, embryonic **10** commencing

incipit
5 start **7** opening **9** beginning

incise
3 cut **4** etch, gash, kerf, slit **5** carve **6** chisel **7** engrave

incision
3 cut **4** gash, slit **5** blaze, notch **10** laceration

incisive
4 keen **5** acute, crisp, sharp, terse **6** direct **7** cutting, mordant **8** clear-cut, piercing, slashing, succinct **9** trenchant **11** penetrating **13** perspicacious

incite
3 egg **4** abet, goad, prod, spur, urge **5** egg on, raise, rouse, set on **6** arouse, exhort, foment, kindle, set off, spur on, stir up, whip up **7** actuate, agitate, provoke, trigger **8** motivate **9** instigate, stimulate

incitement
see **incentive**

inclement
3 raw **5** harsh, rough **6** bitter, brutal, severe, stormy **8** rigorous

inclination
3 bow, nod **4** bent, bias, lean, tilt, will **5** fancy, grade, pitch, slant, slope, taste, trend **6** ascent, liking **7** descent, incline, leaning **8** affinity, appetite, fondness, gradient, penchant, soft spot, tendency, velleity, weakness **9** affection **10** attachment, partiality, proclivity, propensity **11** disposition **12** predilection

incline
3 tip **4** bend, bias, cant, cast, heel, lean, list, sway, tend, tilt, turn **5** grade, impel, slant, slide, slope **6** affect, induce **7** dispose, leaning **8** gradient, persuade **9** influence, prejudice

inclined
3 apt **5** atilt, given, leant, prone, raked, ready **6** liable, likely, minded **7** dipping, leaning, oblique, sloping, tilting, willing **8** diagonal, pitching **11** predisposed
way: **4** ramp

include
5 admit, bound, cover **6** enfold, number, take in **7** confine, contain, embrace, enclose, receive, subsume **8** comprise, encircle **9** encompass **10** comprehend **11** accommodate

inclusive
5 all up, broad **6** global **7** general, overall **8** complete, sweeping **9** all-around, embracive **11** compendious **12** encompassing, encyclopedic **13** comprehensive

incognito
6 veiled **7** cloaked **9** anonymous, disguised **11** camouflaged

incognizant
7 unaware **8** ignorant **9** oblivious, unknowing, unmindful, unwitting **10** unfamiliar, uninformed **11** unconscious **12** unacquainted

incoherent
5 loose **6** broken, raving **7** muddled, unclear **8** confused **9** illogical **10** disjointed, disordered, irrational, maundering, tongue-tied **11** unconnected, unorganized **12** disconnected, disorganized **13** discontinuous

incombustible
9 fireproof **10** unburnable **12** nonflammable

income
4 gain, take **5** wages **6** profit **7** revenue **8** entrance, proceeds, receipts **9** emolument

incommode
3 irk, vex **5** annoy, upset **6** bother, burden, hinder, plague, put out **7** disturb, perturb, trouble **8** disquiet, distress, irritate **9** disoblige **10** disconcert

incommodious
7 awkward, cramped, crowded **8** confined **9** congested

incommunicable
8 reserved, taciturn **9** ineffable, withdrawn **11** unspeakable, unutterable **13** undescribable, unexpressible

incomparable
6 unique **7** supreme **8** peerless, singular, ultimate **9** matchless, nonpareil, paramount, unequaled, unmatched, unrivaled **10** preeminent, surpassing, unequalled, unrivalled **11** outstanding, superlative, unequalable, unmatchable **12** transcendent, unparalleled **13** unsurpassable

incompatible
7 adverse, counter **8** contrary, opposite **9** dissonant, unmixable **10** discordant, discrepant **11** conflicting, disagreeing, uncongenial, unfavorable **12** antagonistic, antithetical **13** contradictory, unsympathetic

incompetence
9 unfitness **10** disability, ineptitude **12** fecklessness

incompetent
5 inept, unfit **6** clumsy **8** helpless, inexpert, unfitted **9** incapable, maladroit, unskilled **10** unequipped **11** inefficient, unqualified

incomplete
4 part **5** short **6** broken, undone **7** partial, sketchy **8** abridged, immature **9** truncated **10** unfinished **11** fragmentary

incompliant
5 rigid, stiff **6** mulish **7** defiant **8** perverse, stubborn **9** obstinate, pigheaded, resistant, unbending **10** bullheaded, headstrong, inflexible, self-willed, unyielding **11** intractable **12** pertinacious, recalcitrant

incomprehensible
7 cryptic, obscure, unclear **8** abstruse, baffling, esoteric **9** fantastic **10** fathomless, mysterious, mystifying, unknowable **11** ungraspable **12** impenetrable, unfathomable, unimaginable

inconceivable
10 improbable, unknowable **11** implausible, unthinkable **12** unbelievable, unconvincing, unimaginable

in conclusion
6 lastly **7** finally

inconclusive
4 open **9** equivocal, uncertain, undecided, unsettled **10** unfinished

incongruous
5 alien **6** absurd **7** foreign, variant **9** anomalous, dissonant **10** discordant, discrepant, unsuitable **11** conflicting, disagreeing **12** disconsonant

inconsequential
5 petty, small **6** measly, paltry **7** trivial **8** picayune, trifling **9** illogical, small-time **10** immaterial, irrelevant, negligible **11** impertinent, superficial, unimportant

inconsiderable
4 puny **5** minor, petty **6** meager, meagre, paltry, scanty, skimpy, slight **7** scrimpy, trivial **8** picayune, trifling **9** frivolous, small-beer **10** negligible **11** unimportant

inconsiderate
4 rash **5** brash, hasty **6** unkind **8** careless, heedless, impolite, reckless **9** hotheaded, impulsive **10** ill-advised, ungracious **11** precipitate, thoughtless **12** discourteous, uncharitable

inconsistent
6 fickle **8** contrary **9** dissonant, illogical, mercurial **10** capricious, changeable, discordant, discrepant **11** conflicting **13** contradictory

inconsolable
7 forlorn **8** desolate **9** heartsick **11** comfortless, heartbroken

inconspicuous
6 hidden, subtle **7** obscure **9** concealed **11** unobtrusive **12** unnoticeable

inconstant
6 fickle, untrue **7** erratic, mutable, protean, vagrant **8** unstable, unsteady, variable, volatile, wavering **9** changeful, faithless, fluctuant, irregular, mercurial, uncertain, unsettled

10 capricious, changeable, irresolute, perfidious, unfaithful **11** chameleonic, vacillating **13** temperamental

incontestable
4 sure **7** certain **8** absolute, clear-cut, ironclad, positive **9** apodictic, undoubted **10** conclusive, inarguable, undeniable **11** irrefutable, unequivocal **12** unassailable, undisputable **13** unimpeachable

incontinent
5 loose **6** wanton **9** dissolute **10** licentious, profligate **12** unrestrained

incontrovertible
4 sure **7** certain **8** absolute, clear-cut, definite, positive **10** conclusive, undeniable **11** irrefutable, unequivocal **12** undisputable

inconvenience
3 irk, vex **5** annoy **6** bother, meddle, put out **7** disrupt, disturb, trouble **8** handicap, vexation **9** annoyance **10** discomfort, discommode, disruption, exasperate **11** aggravation

inconvenient
7 awkward, unhandy **8** annoying **10** bothersome, unsuitable **11** pestiferous, troublesome

incorporate
3 mix **4** form, fuse, join **5** blend, merge, unite **6** absorb, embody, imbibe, mingle **7** combine **8** organize **9** establish **10** amalgamate, assimilate

incorporeal
8 bodiless, formless **9** spiritual **10** discarnate, immaterial, unphysical **11** disembodied, nonmaterial, nonphysical **12** metaphysical **13** unsubstantial

incorrect
5 false, wrong **6** faulty, untrue **7** unsound **8** improper, specious **9** erroneous, imprecise **10** fallacious, inaccurate, unbecoming

incorrigible
6 unruly **8** depraved **9** incurable **10** delinquent, inveterate **11** unalterable **12** irredeemable

increase
2 up **3** add, wax **4** gain, grow, hike, jump, plus, rise, soar, teem **5** add to, boost, build, mount, raise, run up, surge, swarm, swell **6** accrue, amount, beef up, dilate, expand, extend, growth, jack up, markup, step up **7** accrual, advance, amplify, augment, burgeon, enhance, enlarge, inflate, magnify, prolong, upsurge **8** addition, compound, escalate, flourish, heighten, lengthen, manifold, multiply, protract, snowball **9** accession, accretion, expansion, extension, increment, inflation, intensify, reinforce **10** accelerate, accumulate, aggrandize, appreciate **11** enlargement **12** augmentation **13** amplification

incredible
7 amazing, awesome **8** unlikely **9** cockamamy, fantastic **10** astounding, cockamamie, far-fetched, impossible, improbable, outlandish, phenomenal, remarkable **11** astonishing, implausible **12** preposterous, unbelievable, unconvincing, unimaginable **13** extraordinary

incredulity
7 unfaith **8** distrust, mistrust, unbelief **9** disbelief, nonbelief, suspicion **10** skepticism

incredulous
6 show-me **7** dubious **8** doubting **9** quizzical, sceptical, skeptical **10** suspicious **11** distrustful, mistrustful, questioning, unbelieving, unconvinced **12** disbelieving

increment
4 gain, hike, rise, step **5** raise **6** degree, growth **7** quantum **8** addition **9** accession, accretion **11** enlargement **12** augmentation

incriminate
6 accuse, charge **7** arraign, impeach **9** implicate

incrustation
4 film, rime, scab **5** scale **6** tartar **7** coating

incubate
5 hatch

incubus
5 demon, fiend **9** nightmare

inculcate
5 teach, train **6** impart **7** educate, implant, impress, instill

inculpable
4 pure **5** clean **8** innocent, spotless, virtuous **9** blameless, guiltless, righteous **10** impeccable

incumbent
7 leaning, resting **8** occupant, required **9** overlying **10** obligatory **12** officeholder

incur
7 acquire, bring on **8** contract

incurable
5 fatal **6** deadly, lethal **8** hopeless, terminal **9** immutable **11** immedicable, irreparable **12** irremediable, unchangeable **13** uncorrectable

incursion
4 raid **5** blitz, foray, sally **6** attack, sortie **7** assault **9** irruption

incus
4 bone **5** anvil

indebted
5 bound **7** obliged **8** beholden **9** obligated

indebtedness
3 due, IOU **7** arrears **9** arrearage, gratitude, liability **10** obligation **11** delinquency **12** thankfulness

indecent
4 blue, lewd, racy **5** bawdy, dirty, gross **6** coarse, filthy, impure, risqué, smutty, vulgar **7** obscene, profane, raunchy **8** immodest, improper, off-color, unseemly, untoward **9** offensive **10** scurrilous **13** objectionable

indecision
5 doubt **8** wavering **9** hesitancy **11** ambivalence, uncertainty, vacillation **12** equivocation, irresolution, shilly-shally

indecisive
5 vague **6** unsure **7** dubious, unclear **8** wavering **9** equivocal, tentative, uncertain, undecided, unsettled **10** irresolute **11** problematic, vacillating

indecorous
4 rude **5** gross, rough **6** coarse, vulgar **7** uncivil **8** impolite, improper, unseemly, untoward **9** graceless, irregular, offensive, tasteless, unrefined **10** unbecoming **11** ill-mannered, undignified **12** discourteous

indecorum
5 gaffe **6** breach **7** blooper, blunder, faux pas, offense **8** solecism **11** impropriety

indeed
4 amen **5** truly **6** really, surely, verily **8** forsooth, honestly **9** assuredly, certainly **10** positively, undeniably **11** doubtlessly, undoubtedly **13** unequivocally

indefatigable
6 dogged **8** tireless, untiring, vigorous **9** energetic, tenacious **10** persistent, relentless, unflagging, unwearying **11** unrelenting

indefensible
9 unguarded, untenable **10** assailable, vulnerable **11** unprotected **12** unforgivable, unpardonable **13** unjustifiable

indefinable
5 vague **7** elusive **9** uncertain **11** unspeakable, unutterable **13** undescribable

indefinite
4 wide **5** broad, loose, vague **7** endless, general, inexact, obscure, unclear, unfixed **8** infinite **9** ambiguous, boundless, imprecise, limitless, unbounded, uncertain, undefined, unlimited **10** indistinct, inexplicit, unmeasured, unspecific **12** inconclusive **13** indeterminate
article: **2** an
pronoun: **3** all, any, few **4** each, many, most, none, some **6** anyone, nobody **7** anybody, several, someone **8** everyone, somebody **9** everybody

indehiscent fruit
3 key, nut **4** pepo **5** berry, grain, grape, melon **6** achene, loment, samara, squash **7** pumpkin **8** cucumber **9** caryopsis **10** schizocarp

indelible
4 fast **5** fixed **7** lasting **8** enduring **9** memorable, permanent **13** unforgettable

indelicate
3 raw **4** lewd, rude **5** crude, gross, rough **6** coarse, vulgar **7** uncouth **8** impolite, immodest, improper, tactless, unseemly, untoward **9** unrefined **10** unbecoming

indemnify
5 repay **6** secure **7** redress, requite **9** reimburse **10** compensate, recompense, remunerate

indemnity
6 amends **7** redress **8** requital, security **9** exemption, quittance, reprisals **10** protection, recompense, reparation **11** restitution **12** compensation, remuneration **13** fee-for-service

indentation
4 dent, nick, pock **5** notch **6** dimple, recess **10** depression

indenture
4 nick **5** notch **8** contract **9** agreement **11** certificate

indentured
5 bound **10** controlled **11** apprenticed

independent
4 free **8** absolute, autarkic, separate **9** autarchic, sovereign **10** autonomous **11** self-reliant **13** self-contained

indescribable
11 unspeakable, unutterable **13** unexplainable

indestructible
7 lasting **8** enduring, immortal **9** permanent **12** imperishable, irrefragable, unperishable

indeterminate
5 vague **9** imprecise, uncertain, unlimited

index
4 list, mark, sign **5** ratio, table **7** catalog, symptom **8** classify, evidence, regulate **9** catalogue **11** systematize

India
bay: **6** Bengal
capital: **8** New Delhi
city: **5** Delhi **6** Bombay, Kanpur, Madras, Mumbai, Nagpur **7** Benares, Chennai, Kolkata, Lucknow **8** Calcutta **9** Ahmadabad, Bangalore, Hyderabad
coast: **7** Malabar **10** Coromandel
European discoverer: **4** Gama (Vasco da)
language: **5** Hindi
leader: **3** Rao (P. V. N.) **5** Nehru (Jawaharlal) **6** Gandhi (Indira, Mohandas, Rajiv)
monetary unit: **5** rupee
mountain range: **7** Vindhya **9** Himalayas
neighbor: **5** Burma, China, Nepal **6** Bhutan **7** Myanmar **8** Pakistan **10** Bangladesh

pass: **5** Bolan, Gumal **6** Khyber
plateau: **6** Deccan
river: **5** Indus **6** Ganges, Yamuna **7** Krishna **11** Brahmaputra
sea: **7** Arabian

Indian
bread: **3** nan **4** naan **7** chapati
butter: **3** ghi **4** ghee
caste: **4** Bahr **5** Sudra **6** Vaisya **7** Brahman **9** Kshatriya
cattle: **4** dhan
cavalry commander: **8** risaldar
crop-related: **4** rabi **6** kharif
female dancer: **8** bayadere
groom: **4** syce
harem: **6** zenana
instrument: **4** vina **5** sarod, sitar, tabla **7** tambura
lady: **4** bibi **5** begum **8** memsahib
musical term: **4** raga, tala
musician: **7** Shankar (Ravi)
nurse: **4** amah, ayah
outcast: **6** pariah
peasant: **4** ryot
prince: **4** raja, rana **5** rajah **8** maharaja **9** maharajah
princess: **5** begum
queen: **4** rani **5** ranee
scholar: **6** pandit, pundit
screen: **6** purdah
seal, stamp: **4** chop
soldier: **4** peon **5** sepoy
steps: **4** ghat
teacher: **4** guru
title: **5** sahib
viceroy: **5** nabob, nawab
weight unit: **3** ser **4** cash, dhan, pank, pice, powe, rati, tank, tola **5** adpao, fanam, hubba, masha, maund, pally, pouah, ratti **6** dhurra, pagoda, pollam **7** chinnam, chittak

Indian, American
baby: **7** papoose
ball game: **8** lacrosse
carrier: **7** travois
Central and South American: **3** Mam, Ona **4** Cuna, Inca, Maya **5** Arara, Aztec, Carib, Huave, Olmec, Taino, Yagua **6** Arawak, Aymara, Jivaro, Omagua, Toltec, Yahgan **7** Chibcha, Quechua, Zapotec **8** Tarascan, Yanomamo **10** Araucanian **11** Tupi-Guaraní
food: **4** samp **5** maize **8** pemmican
home: **5** hogan, lodge, tepee **6** pueblo, teepee, wigwam **7** wickiup
leader: **4** Popé **6** Wovoka **7** Cochise, Osceola, Pontiac, Sequoia, Sequoya **8** Geronimo, Hiawatha, Powhatan, Sequoyah, Tecumseh **9** Black Hawk, Massasoit **10** Crazy Horse **11** Cornplanter, Sitting Bull
money: **6** wampum
North American: **3** Aht, Fox, Hoh, Kaw, Oto, Sac, Sia, Ute, Wea **4** Coos, Cora, Cree, Crow, Erie, Hopi, Hupa, Iowa, Otoe, Pima, Pomo, Sauk, Taos, Yuma, Zuni **5** Aleut, Caddo, Creek, Haida, Huron, Kansa, Kiowa, Maidu, Miami, Modoc, Omaha, Osage, Sioux, Uinta **6** Apache, Cayuga, Dakota, Lenape, Mandan, Micmac, Mohawk, Munsee, Navaho, Navajo, Nootka, Oglala, Ojibwa, Oneida, Paiute, Pawnee, Pueblo, Quapaw, Salish, Santee, Seneca, Siwash **7** Anasazi, Arapaho, Arikara, Bannock, Chilkat, Chinook, Choctaw, Dakotah, Esselen, Klamath, Kutenai, Mohican, Naskapi, Natchez, Ojibway, Pontiac, Shawnee, Tlingit **8** Cherokee, Cheyenne, Chippewa, Comanche, Delaware, Illinois, Iroquois, Kickapoo, Kwakiutl, Nez Percé, Onondaga, Powhatan, Seminole, Shoshoni **9** Blackfoot, Chickasaw, Menominee, Tsimshian, Tuscarora, Wampanoag, Winnebago **10** Assiniboin, Chiricahua, Gros Ventre, Potawatomi **11** Massachuset, Narraganset
pipe: **7** calumet
spirit: **5** totem **6** manitu **7** kachina, manitou

Indiana
capital: **12** Indianapolis
city: **4** Gary **6** Muncie **9** Fort Wayne, South Bend **10** Evansville, Terre Haute **11** Bloomington
college, university: **6** DePauw, Purdue **9** Ball State, Notre Dame
nickname: **7** Hoosier (State)
river: **5** White **6** Wabash
state bird: **8** cardinal
state flower: **5** peony
state tree: **5** tulip

Indian paintbrush
8 hawkweed **10** painted cup

indicate
4 bode, hint, mark, mean, show **5** augur, imply, point, prove **6** attest, convey, denote, evince, import, reveal **7** bespeak, betoken, connote, display, exhibit, express, presage, signify, suggest **8** disclose, evidence, foretell, manifest, register **9** designate **10** foreshadow, illustrate **11** demonstrate

indication
3 cue **4** clue, hint, mark, sign **5** proof, token, trace **6** augury, signal **7** gesture, inkling, portent, symptom **8** evidence, reminder, telltale **9** testimony **10** expression, suggestion **13** foreshadowing, manifestation

indicative
10 expressive, suggestive **11** evidentiary, symptomatic **12** illustrative **13** demonstrative

indicia
5 marks, signs **8** imprints, markings

indict
5 blame **6** accuse, charge **7** arraign, censure, impeach **9** criticize
indifference
6 apathy **9** aloofness, unconcern **10** detachment, dispassion **11** disinterest **12** carelessness, impartiality
indifferent
4 cold, cool, numb, so-so **5** aloof, blasé, stoic **6** casual, remote **7** average, neutral **8** careless, detached, mediocre, middling, moderate, ordinary, passable, unbiased, uncaring **9** apathetic, impartial, impassive, objective **10** nonchalant, unaffected **11** unconcerned, unemotional **12** uninterested, unprejudiced **13** disinterested, dispassionate
indigence
4 need, want **6** penury **7** poverty **9** neediness, pauperism, privation **11** deprivation, destitution
indigene
6 native **9** aborigine **10** aboriginal
indigenous
6 native **7** endemic, natural **10** aboriginal, congenital, connatural, unacquired **13** autochthonous
indigent
4 poor **5** broke, needy **9** destitute, penniless **11** impecunious, necessitous **12** impoverished
indigestion
9 dyspepsia, heartburn
indignant
3 mad **5** irate, riled, upset, vexed **6** galled, heated **7** annoyed **8** offended, outraged, provoked **9** affronted, irritated, resentful
indignation
5 pique **7** dudgeon **10** irritation, resentment
indignity
3 cut **4** slap **6** injury, insult, slight **7** affront, outrage **9** contumely, grievance **10** disrespect **11** humiliation **13** disparagement, embarrassment
indigo
4 anil, blue **8** deep blue
indigo bird
5 finch **7** bunting
Indira's father
5 Nehru (Jawaharlal)
indirect
7 devious, oblique, vagrant, winding **8** circular, sidelong, tortuous **9** deceitful, underhand, wandering **10** backhanded, circuitous, collateral, meandering, roundabout **11** duplicitous, underhanded
indiscreet
5 gabby **6** unwise **7** foolish, gossipy **8** tactless **9** impolitic, imprudent, untactful **10** ill-advised **11** loose-lipped
indiscretion
4 slip **5** folly, gaffe, lapse **7** blunder, faux pas, mistake, misstep **8** solecism **10** imprudence **11** impropriety
indiscriminate
5 mixed **6** hybrid, motley, random, varied **7** aimless, jumbled, vagrant **8** assorted, careless **9** arbitrary, desultory, haphazard, hit-or-miss, unplanned, wholesale **10** uncritical **11** promiscuous **12** conglomerate, multifarious, unrestrained **13** heterogeneous, miscellaneous
indispensable
5 basic, vital **6** needed **7** crucial, needful, pivotal **8** cardinal, critical **9** essential, necessary, requisite **10** imperative, obligatory **11** fundamental
indisposed
3 ill **4** down, sick **5** loath **6** ailing, averse, poorly, sickly, unwell **7** uneager **8** hesitant **9** reluctant, resistant, unwilling **11** disinclined
indisposition
6 malady **7** ailment, dislike, illness, malaise **8** aversion, disfavor, distaste, sickness, unhealth **10** affliction, reluctance
indisputable
4 sure, true **7** certain, evident, obvious **8** absolute, ironclad, positive **9** apodictic **10** undeniable **11** irrefutable, unequivocal **12** irrefragable, unassailable
indistinct
3 dim **4** hazy **5** faint, foggy, misty, murky, vague **6** bleary, blurry, cloudy **7** blurred, obscure, shadowy, unclear **8** confused **9** uncertain, undefined **12** undetermined
indistinguishable
4 same **5** alike, equal, vague **7** unclear **9** duplicate, identical **10** equivalent
indite
3 pen **5** write **6** record, scribe **7** compose, engross **10** transcribe
individual
3 one **4** body, lone, self, sole, soul, unit **5** being, human, party, thing **6** entity, mortal, person, proper, single **7** special **8** creature, discrete, distinct, peculiar, personal, separate, singular, solitary, specific **10** particular, respective **11** distinctive **13** idiosyncratic
combining form: 4 idio
individualist
5 loner **6** hermit **8** lone wolf, maverick **13** nonconformist
individuality
4 self **7** essence, oneness **8** identity, selfhood

9 character 10 uniqueness 11 personality, singularity 12 idiosyncrasy, separateness

individualize
4 mark 7 specify 9 customize 10 specialize 11 distinguish, personalize, singularize 12 characterize 13 differentiate, particularize

Indochinese country
4 Laos 5 Burma 7 Myanmar, Vietnam 8 Cambodia, Thailand 9 Kampuchea

indoctrinate
5 teach, tutor 7 educate, program 8 convince, persuade 9 brainwash, inculcate

indolence
4 laze 5 sloth 7 inertia, languor 8 idleness, laziness, lethargy 9 torpidity 12 slothfulness, sluggishness 13 shiftlessness
fruit of: 5 lotus

indolent
4 idle, lazy 6 torpid 8 fainéant, slothful, sluggish 9 lethargic, shiftless

indomitable
7 staunch 9 steadfast 10 invincible, unbeatable 11 impregnable 13 unconquerable

Indonesia
archipelago: 5 Malay
capital: 7 Jakarta 8 Djakarta
city: 5 Medan 7 Bandung, Cilacap 8 Semarang, Surabaja, Surabaya 9 Palembang
island group: 5 Sunda 8 Moluccas
language: 6 Bahasa
leader: 7 Suharto, Sukarno
monetary unit: 6 rupiah
regions: 4 Bali, Java 5 Ceram, Timor 6 Bangka, Borneo, Flores, Lombok, Madura 7 Celebes, Sumatra 8 Sulawesi 9 Irian Jaya
volcano: 8 Krakatau, Krakatoa

indubitable
4 sure 6 patent 7 certain, evident, obvious 8 definite, ironclad, positive 9 apodictic, veritable 10 undeniable 11 irrefutable, self-evident, unequivocal 12 irrefragable

induce
5 cause 6 effect, elicit, prompt 7 actuate, procure 8 convince, engender, generate, motivate, occasion, persuade 9 encourage

inducement
4 bait, lure 6 come-on, motive 10 attraction, motivation 13 consideration

induct
4 lead 5 admit 6 enlist, enroll 7 appoint, install

inductance unit
5 henry

induction
8 entrance 9 accession, reasoning 10 enlistment 11 appointment 13 ratiocination

inductive
7 logical 9 prefatory, prelusive 11 a posteriori

indulge
3 pet 4 baby, bask 5 allow, favor, humor, spoil 6 cocker, coddle, cosset, oblige, pamper, permit, please, wallow 7 cater to, delight, gratify, satisfy 9 luxuriate 11 mollycoddle

indulgence
5 favor, mercy, treat 6 luxury 7 charity 8 clemency, courtesy, kindness, lenience, leniency 9 allowance, remission, tolerance 10 compassion, kindliness, permission, toleration 11 forbearance, forgiveness 12 dispensation, mercifulness 13 gratification

indulgence seller
5 Tezel (Johann) 6 Tetzel (Johann)

indulgent
4 easy, kind 7 clement, lenient 8 generous, merciful, tolerant 9 forgiving 10 charitable, permissive

indurate
6 harden 7 callous, confirm, congeal 8 hardened, solidify, stubborn 9 unfeeling 11 hardhearted

industrialist
6 tycoon 7 magnate 12 manufacturer

industrious
4 busy 8 diligent, sedulous 9 assiduous, laborious

industry
4 work 5 labor 8 business, commerce 9 assiduity, diligence 10 enterprise

Indy 500 winner
4 Foyt (A. J.) 5 Mears (Rick), Unser (Al, Bobby) 8 Andretti (Mario)

inebriant
see **intoxicant**

inebriate
3 sot 4 lush, soak 5 drunk, souse, tight, tipsy, toper 6 bibber, boozer 7 stupefy, tippler, tosspot 8 drunkard 10 intoxicate

inebriated
3 lit 5 drunk, lit up, oiled, stiff, tight, tipsy 6 blotto, juiced, loaded, plowed, potted, soused, stewed, tanked, wasted 7 crocked, pickled, pie-eyed, sloshed, smashed 8 polluted 9 plastered

inedible
9 poisonous 12 unappetizing

ineffable
5 taboo 9 forbidden 11 unspeakable, unutterable 13 undescribable

ineffaceable
7 lasting 8 enduring 9 indelible, permanent

ineffective
4 vain, weak **6** futile **7** useless **8** abortive, bootless, feckless, impotent **9** fruitless, powerless **10** emasculate, unavailing **12** unproductive, unsuccessful

ineffectiveness
8 futility **9** impotence

ineffectual
see **ineffective**

inefficient
5 slack **6** clumsy **8** careless, slipshod, wasteful **9** negligent

inelastic
5 rigid, stiff **7** brittle **9** unbending **10** unyielding

inelegant
5 crass, crude, gross, rough **6** coarse, gauche, vulgar **7** awkward, uncouth **9** graceless, unrefined **10** uncultured, ungraceful **12** uncultivated

ineligible
5 unfit **8** unfitted, unworthy **10** unequipped, unsuitable **11** unqualified **12** disqualified

ineluctable
4 sure **5** bound, fated **6** doomed **7** certain **8** destined **9** necessary **10** inevitable, unevadable **11** unavoidable, unescapable **13** unpreventable

inept
5 unfit **6** clumsy, gauche, klutzy **7** artless, awkward, foolish, halting, unhandy **8** bumbling, bungling **9** all thumbs, ham-handed, maladroit, unskilled **10** malapropos, unskillful, unsuitable **11** heavy-handed, undexterous, unfortunate

inequality
8 imparity **9** disparity **10** unevenness **12** irregularity, variableness **13** disproportion, heterogeneity

inequitable
6 biased, unfair, unjust **7** partial **10** prejudiced **11** unjustified, unrighteous

inequity
4 bias **5** wrong **9** prejudice **10** unfairness, unjustness

ineradicable
6 innate **7** chronic **8** constant, inherent, stubborn **9** ingrained **10** deep-rooted, deep-seated, entrenched, inveterate **11** established, ever-present, never-ending

inert
4 calm, dead, idle **5** quiet, still **6** asleep, sleepy **7** dormant, passive **8** immobile, lifeless, sluggish **9** apathetic, lethargic **10** motionless

inert gas
4 neon **5** argon, radon, xenon **6** helium **7** krypton

inertia
5 sloth **6** apathy, stupor, torpor **7** languor **8** idleness, laziness, lethargy **9** indolence, inertness, lassitude, passivity, torpidity **10** immobility, inactivity **11** disinterest **12** listlessness, sluggishness

inescapable
see **inevitable**

inessential
see **unessential**

inestimable
9 priceless **11** measureless **12** immeasurable, unmeasurable, unfathomable

inevitable
4 sure **5** bound, fated **6** doomed **7** certain **8** destined **9** necessary **11** unavoidable, unescapable **12** foreordained **13** unpreventable

inevitably
8 perforce **10** willy-nilly **11** like it or not, unavoidably

inexcusable
6 guilty **8** blamable, culpable **9** untenable **10** censurable **11** blameworthy, condemnable **12** criticizable, unforgivable, unpardonable **13** reprehensible, unjustifiable

inexhaustible
8 tireless, untiring **9** unfailing, weariless **10** bottomless, unflagging **13** indefatigable

inexorable
5 rigid **6** strict **7** adamant **8** immobile, obdurate, stubborn **9** immovable, unbending **10** relentless, unyielding **11** unrelenting

inexpensive
3 low **5** cheap **7** cut-rate **8** moderate **10** reasonable

inexperience
7 naïveté, rawness **8** verdancy **9** freshness, greenness **10** callowness

inexperienced
3 raw **5** fresh, green, naive, young **6** callow **7** untried **8** unversed **9** unskilled, untrained, unworldly **10** amateurish, unseasoned

inexpert
9 maladroit, unskilled, untrained **10** amateurish

inexplicable
6 arcane, obtuse, opaque **7** cryptic **9** enigmatic **10** mysterious, mystifying, unsolvable **12** impenetrable, unfathomable **13** unaccountable, unexplainable

inexpressible
8 nameless **11** unspeakable, unutterable **13** undescribable, unexplainable

inexpressive
5 blank, stoic **6** stolid, vacant, wooden **7** deadpan **9** impassive **10** poker-faced **13** straight-faced

inextricable
9 insoluble **10** unsolvable

infallible
4 sure **5** exact **6** trusty **7** certain, correct, perfect **8** absolute, accurate, flawless, surefire, unerring **9** errorless, unfailing **10** dependable, impeccable **11** trustworthy **12** tried-and-true **13** unimpeachable

infamous
4 evil, vile **6** odious **7** hateful, heinous **8** flagrant, shameful **9** abhorrent, miscreant, nefarious, notorious **10** abominable, despicable, detestable, flagitious, scandalous, villainous **11** disgraceful, ignominious, opprobrious **12** contemptible, disreputable

infamy
5 odium, shame **7** obloquy **8** disgrace, dishonor, ignominy **9** disrepute, notoriety **10** opprobrium

infancy
6 nonage **8** babyhood **9** childhood

infant
4 babe, baby **5** bairn, child, green **7** bambino, neonate, newborn, papoose, toddler **8** bantling, immature, nursling **9** unfledged
bed: 4 crib **6** cradle **8** bassinet
condition: 5 colic
food: 3 pap **4** milk **7** pabulum
room: 7 nursery

infanta
8 princess

infantile
7 babyish, puerile **8** childish, immature

infantryman
7 dogface **8** doughboy **11** foot soldier
Algerian: 6 Zouave

infatuated
4 gaga **5** dotty, silly **7** foolish **8** besotted, enamored, obsessed **9** bewitched, rapturous **10** captivated, passionate

infatuation
4 rage **5** ardor, craze, crush, folly **7** passion, rapture **8** devotion **9** obsession, puppy love **11** fascination

infect
5 taint **6** defile, poison **7** corrupt, pollute **11** contaminate

infection
3 bug **6** sepses (plural), sepsis
carrier: 6 vector
fungous: 8 mycetoma

infectious
8 catching, epidemic, virulent **9** pestilent **10** contagious, corrupting **12** communicable **13** contaminating, transmittable

infelicitous
5 unapt, unfit **6** unmeet **7** awkward, unhappy **8** improper **9** imperfect **10** malapropos, unsuitable **11** regrettable, unfortunate

infer
5 judge **6** deduce, deduct, derive, gather, reason **7** collect, make out, suppose, surmise **8** conclude, construe **10** conjecture **11** extrapolate, hypothesize

inference
7 surmise **8** illation, sequitur **9** deduction **10** assumption, conclusion, conjecture, derivation **11** presumption, supposition

inferior
3 low **4** base, fair, hack, mean, poor, puny **5** cheap, lousy, lower, minor, petty, scrub, sorry, under, worse **6** common, deputy, feeble, impure, junior, lesser, nether, no-good, paltry, satrap, shoddy, sleazy, tawdry, tinpot, vassal **7** average, subject, unequal **8** declassé, low-grade, mediocre, middling, ordinary, unworthy, wretched **9** attendant, auxiliary, no-account, satellite, secondary, subaltern, subjacent, underling, worthless **10** inadequate, second-rate **11** substandard
prefix: 3 sub **4** demi **5** infra

infernal
6 Hadean **7** demonic, hellish, satanic **8** chthonic, damnable, demoniac, devilish, diabolic, plutonic **9** chthonian, plutonian, Tartarean **10** diabolical, sulphurous

inferno
3 pit **4** fire, hell **5** Hades, Sheol **6** blazes, Tophet **7** Gehenna **9** holocaust, perdition **10** underworld **11** netherworld **13** conflagration

Inferno
division: 5 canto
poet: 5 Dante (Alighieri)
verse form: 9 terza rima

infertile
6 barren, effete **7** sterile **8** impotent **10** unfruitful **12** hardscrabble, unproductive

infest
4 teem **5** beset, swarm **6** plague **7** overrun **10** parasitize

infidel
5 pagan **7** atheist, heathen, heretic, skeptic **8** agnostic **10** unbeliever

infidelity
7 perfidy, treason **8** adultery, betrayal, cheating **9** disbelief, treachery **10** disloyalty **13** faithlessness

infinite
4 vast **7** endless, eternal, immense **8** unending **9** boundless, countless, limitless, perpetual, unlimited **11** everlasting, illimitable, measureless, sempiternal **12** immeasurable

infinity
8 eternity **10** perpetuity **11** endlessness **12** sempiternity **13** boundlessness, limitlessness

infirm
4 lame, sick, weak **5** frail **6** ailing, feeble, sickly **7** failing, fragile, unsound **8** decrepit, unstable **9** doddering **11** debilitated

infirmity
3 ill **4** flaw **5** decay **6** malady **7** ailment, disease, frailty, illness, malaise **8** debility, disorder, sickness, syndrome, weakness **9** complaint, condition **10** affliction, feebleness, sickliness **11** decrepitude **12** debilitation, enfeeblement

infix
4 root **5** embed, lodge **6** fasten, pierce **7** engrave, implant, impress

inflame
4 fire, gall, goad, rile, roil **5** anger, light, rouse **6** arouse, enrage, excite, foment, ignite, kindle, madden, redden, stir up **7** provoke **8** enkindle, irritate **9** aggravate **10** exacerbate, exasperate

inflammable
5 fiery **6** ardent **8** burnable, volatile **9** excitable, ignitable, irascible **11** combustible

inflammation
4 gout, sore **6** otitis, quinsy **7** catarrh, colitis **8** adenitis, bursitis, cystitis, neuritis, pleurisy, rachitis, swelling **9** arthritis, chilblain, gastritis, nephritis, phlebitis **10** bronchitis, cellulitis, combustion, dermatitis, gingivitis, laryngitis, tendinitis **12** encephalitis **13** poliomyelitis
eye: **6** iritis **7** pinkeye **9** keratitis
horse: **7** fistula, quittor
intestines: **7** ileitis **9** enteritis
suffix: **4** itis

inflammatory
8 exciting **9** explosive, seditious **11** provocative **13** rabble-rousing, revolutionary

inflate
4 fill **5** bloat, elate, swell **6** expand **7** amplify, distend **9** supersize **10** aggrandize

inflated
5 tumid, windy **6** turgid **7** bloated, swollen, verbose **9** bombastic, distended, dropsical, flatulent, overblown **10** heightened **11** exaggerated, pretentious

inflection
4 bend, tone **5** curve, pitch **6** accent, change, stress, timbre **8** emphasis, tonality **9** accidence **10** modulation

inflexible
3 set **4** grim, hard, iron **5** fixed, rigid, stiff **6** strict **7** adamant, die-hard **8** granitic, hard-line, ironclad, obdurate, stubborn **9** immovable, immutable, obstinate, steadfast, unbending **10** adamantine, brassbound, implacable, rock-ribbed, unbendable, unyielding **11** unalterable, unrelenting **12** unchangeable

inflict
5 visit, wreak **7** mete out, subject **8** dispense **10** administer

inflow
4 rush **7** arrival

influence
4 move, pull, sway **5** alter, bribe, clout, force, impel, lobby, touch **6** affect, compel, impact, modify, moment, strike, weight **7** command, control, impress, mastery **8** dominate, militate, persuade, prestige **9** authority, dominance

influenceable
8 gullible **9** malleable, receptive, tractable **11** persuadable, persuasible, suggestible

influential
6 potent **8** forceful, powerful **9** effective **10** persuasive **13** authoritative

influx
7 arrival **8** entrance, invasion **9** accession

inform
3 rat, tip **4** blab, clue, leak, post, tell, warn **5** brief, edify, endow, endue, imbue, teach **6** advise, betray, fill in, impart, leaven, notify, reveal, snitch, squeal, tattle, turn in, update **7** animate, apprise, caution, educate **8** acquaint, disclose, forewarn **9** advertise, enlighten **11** familiarize

informal
6 casual, dégagé, folksy **7** natural, offhand, relaxed **8** down-home, familiar, laid-back **9** easygoing **10** colloquial, unofficial **13** unceremonious

information
3 tip **4** data, fact, lore, news, poop, word **5** scoop **6** advice, notice, skinny, wisdom **7** lowdown, tidings **9** knowledge **12** intelligence
manager: **9** cybrarian
secondhand: **7** hearsay

information bureau
abbreviation: **4** USIA, USIS

informative
8 edifying, exegetic **10** exegetical **11** educational, elucidative, explanatory **12** enlightening, illuminating

informed
4 wise **5** aware **6** au fait, versed **7** abreast, knowing **8** apprised, educated **9** au courant, cognizant **10** acquainted, conversant **11** enlightened **13** knowledgeable

informer
3 rat, spy **4** fink, mole, narc **5** stool **6** canary, gossip, snitch **7** rat fink, stoolie, tattler, tipster **8** squealer, telltale **10** deep throat, talebearer, tattletale **11** stool pigeon **13** whistle-blower

infra
5 after, below, later, under **7** beneath

infract
3 sin **6** breach, offend **7** violate **8** trespass **10** contravene, transgress

infraction
3 sin **4** foul **5** crime, error **6** breach **7** faux pas, misdeed, offense **8** trespass **9** violation **12** encroachment **13** contravention, transgression

infrastructure
4 base **5** basis **9** framework **10** foundation, groundwork, substratum **12** underpinning

infrequent
3 odd **4** rare **6** scarce, seldom **7** unusual **8** isolated, sporadic, uncommon, unwonted **10** occasional **11** exceptional

infringe
6 breach, impose, meddle, offend **7** disturb, obtrude, violate **8** encroach, entrench, trespass **10** transgress

infuriate
3 ire, mad **4** rile **5** anger, pique **6** enrage, madden, rankle **7** incense, inflame, outrage, provoke, steam up

infuse
4 fill, soak **5** imbue, steep **6** leaven **7** animate, implant, pervade, suffuse **8** permeate, saturate **10** impregnate

ingenious
5 acute, canny, sharp, smart, witty **6** adroit, clever, crafty **7** cunning, fertile **8** creative, original **11** imaginative, resourceful

ingenuity
5 knack, savvy, skill **6** acumen, smarts, talent **7** know-how, mastery **8** deftness, keenness **9** adeptness, handiness **10** adroitness, capability, cleverness, perception, shrewdness **11** proficiency **12** intelligence, skillfulness **13** inventiveness

ingenuous
4 open **5** naive **6** simple **7** artless, natural **8** innocent **9** childlike, guileless, unstudied **10** unaffected

ingest
3 eat **4** feed **6** devour **7** consume, partake, swallow

Inge work
6 Picnic **7** Bus Stop **18** Splendor in the Grass **19** Come Back Little Sheba

inglorious
8 shameful **11** disgraceful, ignominious, opprobrious **12** dishonorable, disreputable **13** discreditable, unrespectable

ingot
3 bar, pig, rod **4** mold **6** billet

ingrain
4 etch **5** imbue

ingrained
6 innate **8** inherent **9** essential **10** congenital, deep-rooted, deep-seated

ingratiating
5 silky **6** silken, smarmy **7** fawning **8** pleasing, unctuous **9** adulatory **10** flattering **11** sycophantic

ingredient
4 part **5** piece **6** factor **7** element **9** component **11** constituent

ingress
4 door **5** entry **6** access, entrée, portal **7** doorway, passage **8** entrance, entryway **9** admission, vestibule **10** admittance **11** entranceway

ingurgitate
4 bolt, cram, gulp, slop, wolf **5** gorge, scarf, stuff, swill **6** devour, gobble, guzzle **7** swallow

inhabit
4 live **5** dwell, haunt **6** occupy, people, settle, tenant **8** populate

inhabitant
5 liver **6** inmate, native **7** citizen, denizen, dweller, resider **8** indigene, resident **9** aborigine **10** autochthon
foreign: **5** alien
indigenous: **6** native **9** aborigine

inhale
7 breathe, consume, respire, swallow

inharmonious
6 atonal **7** jarring **9** dissonant, unmusical **10** discordant **11** cacophonous, conflicting, conflictive, disagreeing, quarrelsome, uncongenial **12** antagonistic

inhere
3 lie **5** dwell **6** belong, reside

inherent
4 born **5** basic, per se **6** inborn, native **7** built-in, connate, natural **8** immanent **9** elemental, essential, intrinsic **10** congenital, deep-seated **11** fundamental

inherit
7 acquire, receive, succeed

inheritance
3 DNA **4** gene, gift **6** devise, estate, legacy **7** bequest **8** heirloom, heritage **9** patrimony, tradition **10** birthright **13** primogeniture

inherited
6 native **7** connate, genetic, natural **10** bequeathed, congenital, connatural, handed-down, hand-me-down

inheritor
4 heir **7** heiress, legatee **11** beneficiary

inhibit
4 curb, slow **5** check **6** arrest, bridle, enjoin,

fetter, hamper, hinder, hobble, impede **7** prevent, repress, trammel **8** hold back, obstruct, restrain, suppress, withhold **9** constrain **10** discourage

inhibition
4 curb **5** taboo **6** hang-up **7** barrier **9** hindrance, restraint, stricture **10** impediment, repression **11** suppression

inhuman
5 cruel, feral **6** brutal, savage **7** beastly, bestial, brutish **8** fiendish **9** barbarous, monstrous **10** diabolical

inhumane
4 fell, grim **5** cruel **6** brutal, fierce, malign, savage **8** ruthless, sadistic **9** barbarous, ferocious, heartless, merciless, truculent

inhumation
6 burial **9** interment, sepulture **10** entombment

inhume
4 bury **5** plant **6** entomb **7** put away **9** lay to rest

inimical
7 adverse, harmful, hostile **10** malevolent, unfriendly **11** belligerent, contentious **12** antagonistic, antipathetic

iniquitous
3 bad **4** base, evil, vile **5** wrong **6** sinful, unjust, wicked **7** immoral, vicious **9** nefarious

iniquity
3 sin **4** evil **5** crime, wrong **7** offense **9** turpitude **8** trespass **10** immorality, wickedness, wrongdoing **13** transgression

initial
5 first, prime **6** anlage, letter, maiden **7** approve, engrave, leading, opening, primary **8** earliest, foremost, monogram, original **9** beginning

initiate
4 open **5** begin, enter, set up, start **6** enroll, get off, induct, invest, launch, take up **7** install, kick off, usher in **8** commence **9** originate **10** inaugurate

initiation
5 debut **7** baptism **9** admission, beginning, induction **10** admittance **11** investiture, origination **12** commencement, introduction

initiative
4 push **5** drive, spunk **6** energy **8** ambition, aptitude, gumption **9** beginning **10** enterprise, get-up-and-go

inject
3 add **6** insert **7** implant, instill **9** inoculate, introduce, vaccinate

injection
3 fix **4** hypo, shot **5** serum **7** booster, vaccine **10** hypodermic **11** inoculation, vaccination

injudicious
4 rash **5** hasty **6** unwise **8** heedless, reckless **9** ill-judged, impolitic, imprudent **10** ill-advised, indiscreet **11** inexpedient **12** shortsighted

injunction
3 ban, bar **4** writ **5** order **6** behest, charge **7** bidding, command, dictate, mandate **9** direction **11** prohibition

injure
3 mar **4** foul, harm, hurt, maim **5** spoil, wound, wrong **6** blight, bruise, damage, deface, deform, impair, mangle **7** contort, cripple, disable, torture **8** maltreat, mutilate **9** disfigure **12** incapacitate

injurious
6 nocent **7** abusive, adverse, harmful, hurtful **8** damaging **9** offensive **10** defamatory **11** detrimental

injury
3 ill **4** harm, hurt **5** wound, wrong **6** bruise, damage, trauma **8** distress **9** detriment

injustice
4 tort **5** crime, wrong **6** breach, damage **7** outrage **8** inequity, trespass **9** grievance, violation **10** favoritism, wrongdoing

ink
3 dye, pen **4** sign **8** inscribe **9** autograph, signature, subscribe
roller: **6** brayer

inkling
3 cue, tip **4** clue, hint, idea, lead, wind **5** hunch **6** notion, tip-off **8** telltale **9** suspicion **10** indication, intimation, suggestion

inky
3 jet **4** ebon **5** black, ebony, jetty, raven, sable **9** Cimmerian, pitch-dark **10** pitch-black

inlaid
5 piqué **6** boolle **7** hatched **8** enchased, nielloed **9** damascene, incrusted

Inland Empire
8 Illinois

inlet
3 arm, bay, ria **4** cove, gulf, loch **5** bayou, bight, creek, fiord, firth, fjord, sound **6** harbor, slough, strait **7** estuary
Admiralties: **4** Kali
Adriatic Sea: **5** Vlorë
Aegean Sea: **7** Saronic
Alaska: **4** Cook **5** Cross, Taiya **8** Chilkoot
Aleutians: **5** Holtz, Nazan
Angola: **5** Bengo, Tiger **6** Tigres
Antarctica: **7** McMurdo **8** Amundsen **10** Shackleton
Arabian Sea: **4** Qamr **5** Kamar
Australia: **4** King **7** Repulse **10** Broad Sound
Baffin Island: **9** Admiralty
Baltic Sea: **6** Gdansk

Barents Sea: **4** Kola **7** Pechora
Bismarck Sea: **5** Kimbe
Canada: **9** Howe Sound
Cape Breton Island: **4** Mira
Chile: **5** Otway
Crete: **4** Suda **5** Canea
Denmark: **3** Ise
Djibouti: **6** Tajura **8** Tadjoura
Ecuador: **5** Manta
Florida: **10** Saint Lucie
Georgia: **8** Altamaha
Gulf of Alaska: **3** Icy **5** Woman
Gulf of Mexico: **8** Suwannee **9** Matagorda **10** Terrebonne
Hawaii: **11** Pearl Harbor
Honshu: **3** Ise **5** Owari **6** Atsuta
Iceland: **4** Axar, Eyja, Huna **5** Horna, Skaga, Vopna **8** Hunafloi
Indonesia: **4** Bima **5** Saleh
Ionian Sea: **7** Taranto
Java: **4** Lada **5** Peper
Kara Sea: **6** Enisei **7** Yenisei
Labrador: **8** Hamilton
Lake Erie: **8** Put-in-Bay, Sandusky
Long Island: **8** Rockaway
Madagascar: **8** Antongil
Massachusetts: **9** Annisquam
Massachusetts Bay: **10** Lynn Harbor
Mediterranean Sea: **8** Valencia **9** Famagusta **10** Khalij Surt **11** Syrtis Major
Mozambique: **5** Memba, Pemba
Nantucket Sound: **5** Lewis
New Guinea: **3** Oro **5** Berau, Hansa **11** McCluer Gulf
New Jersey: **9** Little Egg
New Zealand: **5** Hawke **6** Tasman
North Carolina: **9** Albemarle
Northern Ireland: **12** Belfast Lough
North Sea: **4** Lyse **9** Hardanger
Northwest Territories: **5** Wager **8** Bathurst, Franklin **9** Frobisher **12** Prince Albert
Norway: **3** Tys **4** Bokn, Tana **5** Lakse, Sogne
Norwegian Sea: **4** Nord, Salt, Stor, Vest **5** Ranen **8** Scoresby **9** Trondheim
Ontario: **4** Owen
Potomac: **10** Tidal Basin
Philippines: **5** Baler, Pilar, Sogod **6** Butuan **9** Davao Gulf, Leyte Gulf, Panay Gulf
Puget Sound: **4** Carr, Case
Quebec: **6** Ungava
Red Sea: **4** Foul
Russia: **5** Chaun **8** Sakhalin
Santa Cruz Islands: **8** Basilisk
Solomon Islands: **4** Deep **8** Huon Gulf
South Africa: **5** Table
South Carolina: **4** Bull
South China Sea: **4** Bias, Datu, Siam, Taya **5** Dasol **6** Brunei, Paluan **8** Lingayen
Spitsbergen: **3** Ice **4** Bell **5** Kings
Sumatra: **5** Bajur **10** Koninginne
Wales: **5** Burry
Washington: **11** Grays Harbor
(see also **bay**)

inmate
7 convict **8** occupant, prisoner, resident **10** inhabitant

inmost part
4 core, pith **5** heart **6** center, depths, kernel, marrow **7** nucleus

inn
5 hotel, lodge, motel, serai **6** hostel, tavern **7** auberge, hospice, pension **8** hostelry **9** roadhouse **11** caravansary, public house **12** caravansarai **13** boardinghouse
French: **7** auberge
German: **7** Gasthof **8** Gasthaus
Spanish: **5** fonda **6** posada **7** parador
Turkish: **6** imaret

innards
4 guts **5** belly **6** bowels, tripes **7** viscera **8** entrails, stuffing **10** intestines

innate
see **inherent**

inner
3 gut **5** focal **6** hidden, middle, secret **7** central, nuclear, private **8** familiar, interior, internal, personal, visceral **9** concealed, essential
prefix: **3** ent **4** ento

innervate
4 jolt, move **5** pique, rouse **6** excite **7** animate, provoke, quicken **8** motivate, vitalize **9** electrify, galvanize, stimulate

Innisfail
4 Eire, Erin **7** Ireland

innkeeper
4 host **8** boniface, hosteler, hotelier, landlord, publican

innocence
6 purity **7** naiveté **8** chastity **10** simplicity **11** artlessness, sinlessness

innocent
4 good, lamb, naïf, pure, void **5** clean, legal, licit, naive **6** chaste, devoid, lawful **7** artless, natural, unaware **8** harmless, ignorant, virtuous **9** blameless, childlike, exemplary, faultless, guileless, guiltless, ingenuous, innocuous, righteous, stainless, unstained, unsullied, untainted **10** inculpable, legitimate **12** unsuspecting

innocuous
5 banal, bland **6** pallid **7** insipid **8** harmless **11** inoffensive, unoffending **13** insignificant

innovation
6 change **7** novelty

innovative
3 new **5** novel **8** creative, original **9** inventive **10** newfangled **11** cutting-edge, leading-edge **12** trailblazing

innovator
9 architect, developer **10** originator **11** trailblazer **13** revolutionary

innuendo
4 clue, hint, slur **7** calumny **8** allusion **9** aspersion **10** backbiting, intimation **11** implication, insinuation

innumerable
4 many **6** legion, myriad, untold **7** umpteen **9** countless, uncounted **10** numberless **13** multitudinous

Ino
brother: **9** Polydorus
father: **6** Cadmus
grandfather: **6** Agenor
husband: **7** Athamas
mother: **8** Harmonia
sister: **5** Agave **6** Semele **7** Autonoë
son: **8** Learchus, Palaemon **10** Melicertes

inobtrusive
4 meek **5** muted, quiet **6** modest **7** subdued **8** discreet, tasteful **10** restrained

inoculate
5 imbue, shoot, steep **6** infuse **7** implant, suffuse **9** vaccinate

inoffensive
5 bland **7** neutral **8** harmless **9** innocuous, peaceable

inopportune
8 ill-timed, mistimed, untimely **12** unseasonable

inordinate
5 undue **6** wanton **7** extreme **8** overmuch **9** excessive **10** exorbitant, gratuitous, immoderate, irrational **11** extravagant, intemperate, superfluous, uncalled-for **12** unreasonable **13** extraordinary

inorganic
7 mineral **10** artificial

in passing
5 aside **6** obiter **7** by the by **8** by the bye, by the way **12** incidentally

in perpetuum
4 ever **6** always **7** forever, for good **8** evermore, for keeps **9** eternally **10** enduringly **11** forevermore

input
4 data **6** advice, energy **7** comment, counsel, opinion **8** feedback, guidance, material, stimulus **11** information

inquest
5 probe **7** hearing, inquiry **11** examination **13** investigation

inquietude
5 angst **6** unease, unrest **7** anxiety, ferment, turmoil **8** distress **10** uneasiness **11** restiveness **12** restlessness **13** Sturm und Drang

inquire
3 ask, pry **4** seek **5** probe, query **7** examine **8** question **9** catechize **11** interrogate, investigate

inquiry
5 audit, probe, query **7** hearing **8** grilling, question, research, scrutiny **11** examination, questioning **13** investigation

inquisition
4 hunt **5** probe, quest, trial **6** search **7** inquiry **8** grilling, research **11** examination **13** interrogation, investigation

inquisitive
4 nosy **5** nosey **6** prying, snoopy **7** curious **8** meddling, snooping **9** intrusive **10** meddlesome **11** questioning

inquisitor
10 Torquemada (Tomás de)

in re
4 as to **5** about, as for **7** apropos **9** as regards, regarding **10** as respects, concerning, respecting **12** with regard to **13** with respect to

in respect to
see **in re**

inroad
4 raid **5** foray **7** advance **8** invasion **9** incursion **12** encroachment

ins and outs
5 ropes **6** quirks **7** details **8** minutiae, oddities **11** incidentals, particulars **12** lay of the land

insane
3 mad, off **4** daft, nuts **5** batty, crazy, daffy, dotty, loony, manic, nutsy, nutty, rabid, silly, wacky **6** absurd, crazed, cuckoo, maniac, raving, schizo, screwy, teched **7** berserk, bonkers, cracked, haywire, lunatic, tetched, touched, unsound **8** demented, deranged, unhinged **9** eccentric, psychotic **10** disordered, irrational, moonstruck, unbalanced **11** harebrained **12** crackbrained, preposterous, unreasonable

insane asylum
6 bedlam **8** loony bin, madhouse, nuthouse, snake pit **10** sanatorium, sanitarium

insanity
5 folly, mania **6** frenzy, lunacy **7** madness **8** delirium, delusion, dementia, hysteria, illusion **9** craziness, dottiness, psychosis **11** derangement, psychopathy

insatiable
6 crying, greedy, urgent **7** exigent **8** pressing, ravenous **9** clamorous, demanding, voracious **10** quenchless **11** importunate **12** unappeasable, unquenchable

inscribe
4 etch, list **5** carve, enter, print, write **6** enroll, record **7** engrave, engross, impress, imprint **8** dedicate, enscroll, register

inscription
5 title **6** legend **7** epigram, epitaph, heading **8** epigraph **10** dedication
Calvary: 4 INRI

inscrutable
6 arcane **7** deadpan **10** mysterious, poker-faced, sphinxlike, unknowable, unreadable **12** impenetrable, unfathomable

insect
3 bee, bug, fly **6** beetle
adult: 5 imago
antenna: 4 palp **6** feeler, palpus
combining form: 5 entom **6** entomo
covering: 6 chitin
genus: 4 Nepa
immature: 4 grub, pupa **5** larva, nymph **6** larvae (plural), maggot **8** wriggler **9** chrysalis **11** caterpillar
kind: 3 ant, bee **4** flea, moth, wasp **5** aphid, scale **6** bedbug, beefly, beetle, cicada, earwig, hornet, mantid, mantis, mayfly **7** ant lion, cricket, firefly, June bug, katydid, ladybug, termite **8** honeybee, horsefly, housefly, lacewing, mosquito, stinkbug **9** bumblebee, butterfly, damselfly, dragonfly **10** silverfish, springtail **11** grasshopper **12** walkingstick
luminous: 7 firefly **8** glowworm
molt: 7 ecdysis
moth: 4 luna **5** gypsy **6** miller, sphinx **7** noctuid, pyralid, tortrix, tussock **8** cecropia, cinnabar, forester, sphingid **9** clearwing, geometrid, saturniid, tortricid **10** Polyphemus
multi-legged: 8 diplopod **9** centipede, millipede
noisy: 6 cicada
part: 4 palp **5** cerci (plural) **6** arista, cercus, labium, labrum, ocelli (plural), palpus, thorax **7** antenna, maxilla, ocellus **8** antennae (plural), mandible, maxillae (plural) **9** proboscis, spiracles **10** ovipositor **11** exoskeleton
pest: 4 flea, lice (plural), mite **5** louse, midge, scale **7** blowfly, termite **8** horsefly, housefly, mealybug **9** cockroach, gypsy moth **10** boll weevil, Hessian fly, silverfish
science: 10 entomology
stage: 6 instar
sucking: 5 aphid
winged: 5 alate
wingless: 4 flea, lice (plural) **5** louse **8** firebrat **10** silverfish, springtail **11** bristletail

insecticide
3 DDT **5** mirex, naled **6** aldrin, endrin **7** lindane, phorate **8** carbaryl, dieldrin, rotenone **9** chlordane, malathion, parathion **10** permethrin

insecure
5 shaky **6** unsafe, unsure, wobbly **7** anxious **8** unstable **9** uncertain **10** precarious **11** unconfident **12** apprehensive

inseminate
7 implant, instill **9** fertilize, pollinate **10** impregnate

insensate
4 dull, hard, numb **5** stony **6** brutal, numbed **7** callous **8** comatose **9** bloodless, heartless, impassive, unfeeling

insensibility
4 coma **6** apathy, torpor **8** lethargy, stoicism **12** indifference

insensible
4 cold, dead, dull, hard, numb, rapt **5** stoic **6** asleep, intent, numbed, obtuse, stolid **7** callous **8** absorbed, comatose, deadened, hardened, obdurate **9** apathetic, bloodless, engrossed, impassive, unfeeling **11** unconscious **12** anesthetized

insensitive
4 dull, hard, numb, rude **5** crass **6** numbed, obtuse, unkind **7** callous **8** benumbed, deadened, hardened, tactless, uncaring **9** bloodless, heartless, unfeeling **10** anesthetic, impossible **11** indifferent, unconcerned **12** anesthetized, unresponsive

insert
5 enter **7** implant, obtrude **9** interpose **10** interleave **11** intercalate, interpolate

insertion
8 addendum, addition **13** interpolation
symbol: 5 caret

in short
7 briefly, tersely **9** concisely **10** succinctly

inside
6 closet, secret, within **7** private **8** hush-hush, interior **12** confidential
combining form: 4 endo

insidious
3 sly **4** foxy, wily **6** artful, crafty, subtle, tricky **7** cunning, gradual **8** creeping, guileful **9** deceitful **13** surreptitious

insight
6 acumen, aperçu, wisdom **8** sagacity, sapience **9** intuition **11** discernment, penetration **13** understanding

insightful
4 keen, sage, wise **7** gnostic, knowing **9** intuitive, sagacious **10** discerning, perceptive **11** penetrating

insignia
4 mark, sign **5** badge **6** emblem **8** brassard **10** decoration

insignificant
4 mere, puny **5** dinky, minor, petty, small **6** casual, little, minute, paltry **7** minimal, trivial **8** nugatory, trifling **9** secondary, small-time **10** negligible **11** Mickey Mouse, minor-league, unimportant

insincere
5 false, lying, phony **6** double, forced, hollow, phoney, shifty, tricky **7** feigned **8** mala fide, slippery, spurious **9** deceitful, deceptive, dishonest, pretended, simulated **10** left-handed, mendacious, untruthful **11** dissembling, double-faced **12** hypocritical

insinuate
4 hint **5** imply **6** inject, insert, work in, worm in **7** implant, instill, suggest **9** introduce

insipid
4 drab, dull, mild, pale, thin, weak **5** banal, bland, vapid **6** jejune, watery **7** mundane, prosaic, tedious **8** bromidic, lifeless, ordinary **9** innocuous, tasteless **10** flavorless, monotonous, namby-pamby, wishy-washy **11** commonplace

insist
4 hold **5** argue, claim, swear **6** affirm, assert, demand, stress **7** certify, contend, declare, require, testify **8** maintain

insistent
6 crying, dogged, urgent **7** adamant, burning, clamant, exigent **8** emphatic, forceful, pressing, resolute **9** assertive, clamorous, obtrusive **10** determined, imperative, relentless **11** persevering

insolence
4 gall, guff, sass **5** brass, cheek, nerve **8** audacity, boldness, chutzpah, contempt, rudeness **9** arrogance, impudence **10** brazenness, disrespect, effrontery **11** haughtiness, presumption **12** impertinence

insolent
4 bold, flip, pert, rude **5** cocky, lofty, sassy, saucy **6** brazen, cheeky **7** haughty, uncivil **8** arrogant, cavalier, flippant, impolite, impudent, superior **9** audacious, barefaced, bold-faced **10** disdainful, peremptory **11** impertinent **12** contumelious, discourteous

insouciance
6 aplomb **9** disregard, unconcern **10** breeziness **11** disinterest, nonchalance **12** carelessness, heedlessness, indifference

insouciant
4 airy, flip **6** blithe, breezy, casual, jaunty **8** carefree, flippant, heedless **9** easygoing **10** nonchalant, untroubled **11** indifferent, thoughtless, unconcerned **12** devil-may-care, happy-go-lucky, lighthearted

inspect
3 con, vet **4** scan, view **5** audit, check, probe, study **6** review, size up, survey **7** canvass, examine, observe **8** appraise, check out, look over, question **9** check over **10** scrutinize **11** investigate

inspiration
4 idea, muse **6** animus, genius, vision **7** insight **8** afflatus **9** brainwave, influence **10** brainchild, brainstorm, creativity **13** enlightenment

inspire
4 fire, stir **5** elate, exalt, imbue, rouse **6** arouse, excite, foment, incite, prompt, strike **7** animate, enliven, impress, instill, quicken **8** motivate **9** encourage, galvanize, influence, stimulate **10** exhilarate

inspiring
6 moving **7** awesome, rousing **8** exalting, stirring **9** animating, uplifting **10** vitalizing

inspirit
4 fire, lift, spur, stir **5** cheer, elate, exalt, liven, rally, rouse, spark, steel **6** arouse, excite, incite, kindle, revive, uplift, vivify **7** animate, comfort, console, delight, enliven, gladden, hearten, nourish, quicken, refresh, restore **8** activate, embolden, energize, revivify, vitalize **9** encourage, stimulate **10** invigorate, strengthen

instability
8 fluidity **9** shakiness **10** insecurity, volatility **11** inconstancy **12** unsteadiness

install
4 seat, vest **5** put in, set up **6** induct, invest **8** ensconce, enthrone, entrench **9** establish

instance
4 case, cite, item **6** detail, ground, reason, sample **7** example **8** specimen **10** particular **12** illustration

instant
3 sec **4** wink **5** flash, jiffy, point, shake, trice **6** moment, second, urgent **7** current, exigent, present **8** existent, occasion, pressing **9** heartbeat, immediate, insistent, twinkling **10** imperative, present-day

instantaneous
4 fast **5** quick, rapid **9** immediate, ligntning, momentary **11** hair-trigger, split-second

instantly
3 now, PDQ **4** ASAP, stat **6** at once, pronto **8** directly **9** forthwith, right away **11** immediately

instead
4 else 6 in lieu, rather 11 alternately 13 alternatively

instigate
4 abet, fire, goad, plan, plot, prod, spur, urge 5 egg on, impel, raise 6 excite, foment, incite, stir up, whip up 7 provoke, suggest 8 motivate 9 stimulate 10 bring about

instill
5 imbue 6 impart, infuse, inject 7 implant, suffuse 8 engender 9 inculcate, introduce

instinct
4 nose 5 hunch, sense 7 feeling, impulse 8 aptitude, behavior 9 intuition 10 proclivity, sixth sense 11 gut reaction

instinctive
3 gut 6 inborn, innate, normal 7 natural 8 habitual, inherent, visceral 9 automatic, ingrained, intrinsic, intuitive, reflexive, unlearned 10 congenital, unprompted 11 involuntary, spontaneous, unmeditated

instinctual
6 reflex 7 natural, routine 8 habitual, knee-jerk, untaught 9 automatic, impulsive, intuitive, reflexive 10 mechanical, unthinking 11 involuntary, spontaneous, unconscious

institute
5 begin, found, set up, start 6 decree, launch, ordain 7 academy, pioneer, usher in 8 initiate, organize 9 establish, introduce, originate 10 inaugurate 12 organization

institution
4 firm, rite 5 habit 6 custom 9 enactment 10 foundation 13 establishment
kind: 6 asylum, school 7 academy, college 8 hospital 10 sanatorium, sanitarium, sanitorium, university

instruct
4 show 5 coach, drill, guide, order, steer, teach, train, tutor 6 direct, enjoin, inform, school 7 apprise, command, counsel, educate, lecture 9 enlighten, prescribe

instruction
5 drill 6 advice, lesson 7 precept 8 coaching, guidance, teaching, training, tutelage 9 catechism, education, schooling 10 directions
place of: 6 school 7 academe, academy, college 10 university

instructive
8 didactic, edifying, pedantic 9 pedagogic 11 educational, explanatory, explicative, informative 12 enlightening

instructor
3 don 4 guru 5 coach, guide, swami, tutor 6 mentor 7 teacher, trainer 8 educator, lecturer 9 pedagogue, preceptor

instrument
4 deed, gear, mean, tool 5 agent, means, organ 6 agency, device, gadget, medium 7 utensil, vehicle 9 apparatus, appliance, machinery, mechanism 11 contraption, contrivance 13 paraphernalia
aircraft: 5 radar, radio 7 compass 9 altimeter, gyroscope 10 altazimuth, tachometer 11 transponder
calculating: 6 abacus 8 computer 9 slide rule
graphic: 6 camera 8 otoscope 9 telescope 10 binoculars, microscope 11 fluoroscope, stethoscope, stroboscope 12 bronchoscope, oscilloscope, spectrograph, spectroscope
measuring: 4 gage 5 clock, gauge, radar, scale, sonar 7 alidade, ammeter, balance, caliper, sextant, transit 8 quadrant 9 altimeter, astrolabe, barometer, bolometer, manometer, pedometer, sonometer, voltmeter 10 anemometer, Fathometer, hydrometer, hygrometer, micrometer, radiometer, radiosonde, spirometer, tachometer, theodolite 11 chronometer, lie detector, range finder, seismograph, speedometer, thermometer 12 electroscope, galvanometer, oscillograph, oscilloscope 13 Geiger counter, potentiometer
medical: 6 lancet, trocar 7 curette, forceps, specula (plural) 8 tenacula (plural) 9 tenaculum
radiation-producing: 5 laser, maser
(see also **implement; musical instrument; tool**)

instrumental
5 vital 6 useful 7 crucial, helpful 9 conducive, essential, necessary, requisite 10 imperative 13 indispensable

instrumentality
5 agent, force, means, organ 6 agency, energy, medium 7 channel, vehicle 8 ministry 9 mechanism

insubordinate
6 unruly 8 factious, mutinous 9 fractious, seditious 10 headstrong, rebellious, refractory 11 disobedient, intractable, uncompliant 12 contumacious, recalcitrant, ungovernable

insubstantial
4 airy, weak 5 frail 6 feeble, flimsy, jejune 7 fragile, tenuous 8 bodiless, ethereal 9 unfleshly 10 intangible 11 disembodied 12 aparitional

insufferable
10 unbearable 11 intolerable, unendurable 13 insupportable

insufficiency
4 lack 6 dearth 7 paucity, poverty 8 scarcity, shortage 10 deficiency, inadequacy, scantiness, scarceness 11 defalcation

insufficient
5 scant **6** scanty, scarce, skimpy **7** lacking, wanting **10** inadequate, incomplete

insular
5 local **6** narrow **7** bigoted, limited **8** confined, isolated, secluded **9** illiberal, parochial, sectarian, small-town **10** prejudiced, provincial, restricted

insulate
6 cut off, enisle **7** isolate **8** close off **9** segregate, sequester

insult
4 gibe, jeer, mock, slap, slur **5** abuse, fleer, scoff, scorn, shame, sneer, taunt **6** debase, deride, offend, revile **7** affront, disdain, obloquy, offense, outrage **8** derision, disgrace, ignominy, ridicule **9** contumely, humiliate **10** opprobrium **12** vituperation

insurance
8 guaranty, warranty **10** protection
agency: 7 actuary **8** adjuster **11** underwriter
term: 6 policy **7** annuity **8** coverage **9** bordereau **11** beneficiary
type: 4 crop, fire **5** crime, flood, title **6** dental **7** no-fault **8** accident, casualty **9** liability **10** disability, homeowner's **11** workers' comp

insure
5 cinch, guard **6** shield **7** confirm, protect **9** guarantee, safeguard **10** underwrite

insurgent
5 rebel **6** anarch **8** factious, frondeur, mutineer, mutinous, revolter **9** anarchist, seditious **10** incendiary, rebellious **12** contumacious **13** insubordinate, revolutionary

insurrection
4 coup **6** mutiny, putsch, revolt, rising **8** uprising **9** rebellion

insurrectionist
5 rebel **6** anarch **8** frondeur, mutineer, revolter **10** malcontent

insusceptible
6 exempt, immune **9** resistant **10** impervious **11** unreceptive

intact
5 sound, whole **6** entire, unhurt, virgin **7** perfect **8** complete, unbroken, unmarred, virginal **9** undamaged, uninjured, untouched **10** unimpaired

intangible
4 airy **5** vague **7** elusive, ghostly **8** ethereal **10** evanescent, immaterial, impalpable **11** incorporeal

integer
4 unit **5** digit **6** entity, figure, number **7** numeral **11** whole number

integral
4 full **5** whole **6** entire **7** perfect **8** complete, inherent **9** composite, elemental, essential, necessary, requisite **11** constituent **13** indispensable

integrate
3 mix **4** fuse, join, link **5** blend, merge, unify, unite **6** embody, mingle **7** combine, conjoin **8** coalesce **9** harmonize, reconcile **10** amalgamate, assimilate, coordinate, synthesize **11** consolidate, desegregate

integrity
5 honor **6** virtue **7** honesty, probity **8** cohesion **9** coherence, constancy, rectitude, soundness, wholeness **12** completeness

integument
4 coat **5** testa **7** coating, cuticle **8** covering, envelope

intellect
3 wit **4** mind **5** brain **6** acumen, brains, genius, reason, smarts **9** intuition, mentality **12** intelligence **13** comprehension, understanding

intellectual
5 brain **6** brainy, mental, pundit **7** bookish, egghead, erudite, psychic, thinker **8** academic, cerebral, highbrow, longhair **9** scholarly

intelligence
3 wit **4** dope, info, mind, news, word **5** brain, savvy, sense **6** acuity, acumen, brains, notice, reason, smarts, wisdom **7** hearsay, tidings **8** aptitude, judgment, learning, sagacity **9** knowledge, mentality, mother wit **10** brainpower, shrewdness

intelligent
4 keen, wise **5** acute, alert, aware, quick, sharp, smart, sound **6** adroit, astute, brainy, bright, clever, shrewd **7** cunning, knowing, logical **8** rational, sensible **9** brilliant, ingenious, sagacious **10** reasonable **11** quick-witted, ready-witted **13** perspicacious

intelligentsia
7 clerisy **8** literati, vanguard **10** avant-garde, illuminati

intelligible
5 clear, lucid, plain

intemperance
6 excess **7** license **9** depravity **10** debauchery, profligacy **11** dissipation, drunkenness **12** immoderation, incontinence

intemperate
5 harsh **6** bitter, brutal, severe **7** drunken, extreme, violent **8** bibulous **9** crapulous, dissolute, excessive **10** dissipated, exorbitant, gluttonous, immoderate, inordinate, profligate **12** unrestrained **13** overindulgent

intend
3 aim, try **4** mean, plan **5** essay, spell **6** assign, denote, design, scheme, strive **7** attempt, connote, propose, purpose, signify **8** endeavor **9** designate

intended
6 fiancé **7** engaged, fiancée **8** destined, plighted, promised, proposed **9** affianced, betrothed **10** calculated, deliberate

intense
4 keen **5** acute, vivid **6** ardent, fervid, fierce, severe, strong **7** extreme, fervent, furious, violent, zealous **8** powerful, vehement **9** assiduous, excessive, exquisite **10** heightened **12** concentrated

intensify
4 rise **5** mount, rouse **6** accent, heat up, stress **7** enhance, sharpen **8** escalate, heighten, increase, redouble **9** aggravate, emphasize **10** accentuate, aggrandize, exacerbate **11** concentrate

intensity
6 energy, fervor **7** passion **8** emphasis, ferocity, fervency, loudness **9** vehemence

intensive
6 all-out **7** zealous **8** sweeping, thorough **10** exhaustive **12** concentrated
pronoun: **6** itself, myself **7** herself, himself **8** yourself **9** ourselves **10** themselves, yourselves

intent
3 aim, set **4** bent, goal, plan, rapt, will **5** eager, fixed **6** design, import, object **7** decided, earnest, engaged, meaning, purport, purpose, riveted, wrapped **8** absorbed, conation, decisive, diligent, immersed, resolute, resolved, sedulous, volition **9** engrossed, objective, wrapped up **10** determined

intention
3 aim, end **4** goal, hope, plan, wish **6** design, desire, object **7** meaning, purpose **8** ambition **9** objective **10** aspiration

intentional
5 meant **7** advised, studied, willful, willing, witting **8** designed, proposed **9** voluntary **10** considered, deliberate **12** premeditated

intentionally
9 on purpose, purposely

inter
4 bury **5** plant **6** entomb, inhume **9** lay to rest

interact
9 cooperate **11** collaborate

interbreed
5 cross **9** hybridize **10** mongrelize

intercede
6 step in **7** mediate **9** arbitrate

intercept
4 grab **5** catch, seize, steal **6** cut off, hijack

intercessor
5 agent **6** broker **8** advocate, mediator **9** go-between, middleman

interconnect
4 join, link, mesh **5** unite **6** couple, hook up, link up

intercourse
3 sex **5** trade, truck **7** contact, dealing, traffic **8** business, commerce, dealings **9** communion **10** connection, networking **11** give-and-take **12** conversation **13** communication

intercross
9 hybridize **10** mongrelize

interdict
3 ban, bar **4** veto **5** block, taboo **6** cut off, enjoin, forbid, outlaw **7** censure, condemn, embargo **8** disallow, prohibit, sanction **9** proscribe **11** prohibition

interest
4 gain, grab, hook, lure, pull **5** pique, stake, tempt **6** appeal, arouse, behalf, engage, profit, regard **7** attract, concern, engross, involve, welfare **8** appeal to, intrigue **9** attention, curiosity, fascinate, tantalize, well-being **10** prosperity

interested
4 rapt **5** drawn **7** curious, partial **8** invested, partisan **9** attentive

interface
3 GUI **6** border **8** boundary **9** cooperate **11** communicate

interfere
6 butt in, horn in, meddle, step in **7** barge in, intrude

interim
3 gap **5** break, pause **6** acting, breach, hiatus, lacuna, pro tem **7** stopgap, time-out **8** downtime, meantime **9** makeshift, temporary **10** pro tempore **11** provisional

interior
3 gut **4** pith **5** belly, bosom, heart, inner **6** center, inland, inside, inward, marrow **8** visceral **9** heartland **10** hinterland

interject
3 add **6** fill in, insert **7** throw in

interjection
agreement: **4** amen **5** roger **6** righto **7** right on
attention-getter: **3** hey **4** ahem, ahoy, psst **6** yoo-hoo
cheer: **3** rah, yay **5** wahoo **6** hooray, hurrah, hurray

contempt: **4** pooh **5** pshaw
disappointment: **4** rats **5** shoot **6** shucks
disapproval: **3** boo, fie
disbelief: **2** aw **3** huh
disgust: **3** bah, boo, pah, ugh **4** rats, yuck **5** faugh, yecch **6** phooey
dismay: **2** oy **4** oh no, uh-oh
dismissal: **3** git **4** shoo
in golf: **4** fore
in hunting: **6** yoicks
in marching: **3** hup, hut
joy: **4** whee **6** hooray, hurrah, hurray, yippee **7** hosanna, whoopee **8** alleluia **10** hallelujah
mild apology: **4** oops **6** whoops
mild oath: **3** gad **4** darn, drat, egad, geez, gosh, heck, jeez **5** egads, golly, zooks **6** jiminy, zounds **7** begorra, gee whiz, jeepers **8** gadzooks **13** gee whillikers
O.K.: **5** roger, wilco
pain: **2** ow **4** ouch
regret: **3** woe **4** alas **5** alack **8** lackaday
relief: **4** phew
silence: **2** sh **3** shh
sneeze: **5** achoo **6** atchoo **7** kerchoo
sorrow: **4** alas **5** alack **8** lackaday
stop: **4** whoa **5** avast
surprise: **2** ah, ho, lo, oh **3** aha, huh, oho, wow **4** gosh, oops **5** blimy, yikes, yipes, zowie **6** blimey
triumph: **3** aha, hah **6** eureka
(see also **exclamation**)

interlace
3 mix **5** braid, plait, twine, weave **7** entwine **9** alternate

interlard
3 mix **6** mingle

interlock
4 mesh **5** unite **6** enmesh

interlocuter
4 host **5** emcee

interlope
6 butt in, horn in, meddle **7** intrude **8** encroach, infringe **9** interfere

interlude
4 halt, lull, rest **5** break, idyll, letup, pause, spell **6** hiatus, recess **7** episode, respite **8** breather, entr'acte, meantime, stoppage **9** meanwhile **10** suspension

intermediary
3 mid **4** mean **5** agent, envoy, organ **6** agency, broker, center, medium, middle, midway **7** central, channel, vehicle **8** delegate, emissary, mediator, ministry **9** go-between, middleman

intermediate
3 mid **4** fair, mean, so-so **5** mesne **6** broker, center, middle, midway, step in **7** arbiter, average, between, central, halfway **8** middling **9** arbitrate, go-between, middleman

intermediator
6 broker **7** arbiter, liaison, referee **9** go-between, middleman

interment
6 burial **9** sepulture **10** inhumation

intermesh
4 lock **6** engage **8** dovetail

interminable
7 endless, eternal, lasting **8** constant, infinite, unending **9** boundless, ceaseless, continual, limitless, permanent, perpetual, unceasing **10** protracted **11** everlasting, never-ending

intermission
4 lull, rest, stop **5** break, pause, spell **6** hiatus, recess **7** latency, respite, time-out **8** abeyance, dormancy, interval **10** quiescence, suspension **11** parenthesis

intermit
4 halt, stay **5** break, defer, delay **6** arrest, hold up, put off **7** suspend **8** postpone, prorogue **9** interrupt **11** discontinue

intermittent
6 broken, cyclic, fitful, serial **8** cyclical, metrical, periodic, seasonal, sporadic **9** irregular, recurrent, recurring, spasmodic, stop-and-go **10** occasional

intermix
4 meld **5** blend **6** mingle **8** comingle, compound **9** commingle, integrate **10** amalgamate

intermixture
4 brew **5** blend **7** amalgam **8** compound **9** composite, synthesis **12** amalgamation **13** miscegenation

intern
4 jail **6** immure **7** confine, impound, put away, trainee **8** imprison **11** incarcerate

internal
6 native **7** private **8** visceral **10** subjective
concretion: **9** gallstone
prefix: **5** intra

internal organs
4 guts **6** bowels, vitals **7** innards, viscera **8** entrails **10** intestines, penetralia

international organization
2 UN **3** FAO, IAM, ICJ, IFC, ILO, ITO, ITU, OAS, WHO, WMO, WTO **4** IAAF, IABA, IAEA, IARU, IATA, ICAO, IFIP, IMCO, NATO **5** ICFTU, SEATO **6** UNESCO, UNICEF

Internet forum
9 newsgroup

internuncio
5 envoy **6** bearer, legate **7** carrier, courier **8** delegate, emissary **9** go-between, messenger, middleman

interpolate
3 add **5** admit, annex, enter **6** append, fill in, inject, insert **7** throw in **9** introduce

interpose
6 butt in, fill in, insert, meddle, step in **7** intrude, mediate, obtrude, throw in **8** moderate **9** arbitrate, insinuate, introduce, negotiate **11** come between

interpret
5 gloss **6** decode **7** explain, expound **8** annotate, construe **9** elucidate, explicate **10** paraphrase

interpretation
5 gloss **7** meaning, reading, version **8** exegesis **9** construal, rendering **11** explanation, translation

interpretive
8 exegetic **10** diagnostic, exegetical, expository **11** explanatory, explicatory

interregnum
5 break, lapse, pause **6** hiatus **7** time-out

interrogate
3 ask **4** pump, quiz **5** grill, query **7** examine **8** question **9** catechize **12** cross-examine

interrupt
4 halt, stay, stop **5** abort, break, cut in **7** break in, chime in, suspend **8** cut short

interruption
3 gap **4** halt **5** break, pause, split **6** breach, cutoff, hiatus, lacuna, recess **7** caesura **8** stoppage

intersect
4 meet **5** cross **9** decussate **10** crisscross

intersection
3 hub **4** node **8** crossing, junction, juncture **10** crossroads

intersperse
7 diffuse, scatter **8** sprinkle

interstice
3 gap **4** slit, slot, vent **5** chink, cleft, crack, space **6** breach, cavity, cranny **7** crevice, fissure, opening, orifice **8** aperture

intertwine
4 mesh **5** braid, plait, twist, weave **6** enlace **7** network **9** convolute **10** crisscross

interval
3 gap **4** lull, wait **5** break, comma, delay, letup, pause, space **6** breach, hiatus, lacuna **7** caesura, interim, respite, time-out **8** downtime **9** pausation **11** parenthesis
music: **4** rest

intervene
6 butt in, meddle, step in **7** intrude, mediate, obtrude

interweave
3 mix **4** fuse, join, knit, link, mesh **5** blend, plait, twine **6** enmesh **7** entwine, wreathe

intestinal
5 ileal **7** colonic, jejunal **8** duodenal

intestinal fortitude
4 grit, guts **5** nerve, pluck, spunk **6** mettle, spirit **7** courage **8** backbone **10** resolution

intestine
3 gut **4** tube **5** bowel, canal **7** viscera (plural)
combining form: **4** coli, colo **6** entero
part: **5** cecum, colon, ileum **7** jejunum **8** duodenum

in the same place
6 ibidem

intimacy
9 closeness **11** familiarity **12** acquaintance

intimate
3 gut **4** cozy, dear, fond, hint **5** amigo, close, crony, imply, inner, privy **6** attest, friend, impart, loving, secret **7** comrade, connote, devoted, nearest, suggest **8** familiar, inherent **9** close-knit, companion, confidant, ingrained, insinuate, intrinsic **12** confidential

intimation
3 cue **4** clue, hint **5** shade, tinge, trace **6** breath **7** inkling **8** telltale **10** suggestion

intimidate
3 awe, cow **4** bait **5** bully, chivy, daunt, scare **6** badger, coerce, hector **7** buffalo, overawe **8** browbeat, bulldoze, bullyrag **9** strong-arm, terrorize

intolerable
10 unbearable **11** unendurable **12** insufferable **13** insupportable

intolerant
6 biased, narrow **7** bigoted **8** dogmatic **9** hidebound, illiberal **10** inflexible, prejudiced **11** small-minded **12** narrow-minded

intonation
5 chant, pitch **6** accent, timbre **7** cadence **8** chanting **10** inflection, modulation, recitation

intone
5 chant, croon, drone **10** cantillate

in toto
3 all **6** wholly **7** all told, en masse **10** altogether

intoxicant
5 booze, drink, hooch, sauce **6** hootch, liquor, rotgut **7** alcohol, spirits **9** aqua vitae, firewater, moonshine

intoxicated
3 lit, wet **4** high **5** blind, drunk, fried, giddy, lit up, oiled, stiff, tight, tipsy **6** blotto, bombed, canned, elated, juiced, loaded, looped, potted, sodden, soused, stewed, stoned, tanked, tiddly, zonked **7** blitzed, crocked, drunken, excited, maudlin, muddled, pickled, pie-eyed, sloshed, smashed, sozzled **8** cockeyed, polluted, squiffed **9** crapulous, plastered **11** exhilarated

intoxication
3 joy **5** bliss **6** frenzy **7** ecstasy, elation, rapture **8** delirium, euphoria **9** transport **10** exaltation **11** drunkenness, inebriation

intractable
4 wild **5** balky **6** mulish, ornery, unruly **7** froward, willful **8** mutinous, obdurate, perverse, stubborn **9** fractious, obstinate, pigheaded, unbending **10** bullheaded, headstrong, inflexible, rebellious, refractory, unyielding **12** pertinacious, recalcitrant, ungovernable **13** undisciplined

intransigent
5 rigid, tough **7** willful **8** obdurate, perverse, resolute, stubborn **9** obstinate, unbending, unpliable **10** refractory, self-willed, unyielding **12** contumacious, pertinacious

intrepid
4 bold, game **5** brave, gutsy, hardy **6** daring, heroic **7** doughty, gallant, valiant **8** fearless, resolute, stalwart, unafraid, valorous **9** audacious, dauntless, undaunted **10** courageous **11** adventurous, temerarious

intricate
4 mazy **6** daedal, knotty **7** complex, gordian, tangled **8** abstruse, involved, tortuous **9** Byzantine, elaborate **10** circuitous, convoluted **11** complicated **12** labyrinthine **13** sophisticated

intrigue
4 plot, wile **5** amour, cabal, cheat, pique, trick **6** affair, appeal, excite, scheme **7** attract, beguile, collude, connive, liaison, romance **8** cogitate, conspire, contrive, interest **9** machinate **10** conspiracy **11** machination

intriguing
8 enticing **9** absorbing, beguiling **10** engrossing, entrancing **11** captivating, fascinating, stimulating

intrinsic
see **inherent**

intrinsically
5 per se **6** as such **7** at heart **10** inherently

introduce
5 begin, enter, found, set up **6** broach, fill in, insert, launch, unveil, work in **7** bring up, implant, install, instill, precede, preface, present, propose, throw in, usher in **8** initiate, innovate **9** insinuate, institute, interject, interpose, originate **10** inseminate

introduction
5 debut, proem **6** lead-in **7** introit, opening, preface, prelude **8** entrance, exordium, foreword, overture, preamble, prologue, protases (plural), protasis **12** prolegomenon

introductory
5 basic **7** initial, nascent, opening **8** proemial **9** beginning, prefatory **10** elementary **11** preliminary, preparatory

intrude
5 cut in **6** butt in, horn in, impose, invade, meddle **7** barge in, burst in, presume **8** encroach, infringe, trespass **9** interfere, interlope, interrupt

intrusive
4 busy, nosy **5** nosey **6** prying, snoopy **7** curious **8** meddling, snooping **9** officious **10** meddlesome **11** impertinent

in truth
6 indeed, really, verily **8** actually, candidly **9** veritably

intuit
5 infer, sense **6** deduce, divine **7** surmise

intuition
5 hunch **7** feeling, inkling, insight **8** instinct **10** sixth sense **11** second sight **12** presentiment

intuitive
6 innate **7** natural **8** unwilled, visceral **10** unthinking **11** instinctive, instinctual, involuntary, spontaneous, unconscious

Inuit
6 Eskimo

inundate
4 glut **5** drown, flood, swamp, whelm **6** deluge, engulf **7** overrun **8** overflow, submerge **9** overwhelm

inundation
5 flood, spate **6** deluge **7** Niagara, torrent **8** cataract, flooding, overflow **9** avalanche, cataclysm, landslide **10** cloudburst

inure
5 steel, train **6** harden, season **7** prepare, toughen **8** accustom **9** acclimate, habituate **10** discipline **11** familiarize

inutile
6 no-good **7** useless **8** unusable **9** valueless, worthless

invade
4 loot, raid **6** breach, occupy, ravage **7** overrun, pillage, plunder **8** encroach, infringe, trespass **9** penetrate

invader
8 intruder **10** encroacher, interloper, trespasser **11** infiltrator

invalid
3 bad **4** null, sick, void **5** false **6** ailing, infirm, shut-in, sickly **7** expired, unsound **8** baseless, disabled **9** bedridden, illogical, sophistic **10** fallacious, irrational **11** null and void **12** convalescent

invalidate
4 undo, void **5** annul, quash **6** cancel, offset,

vacate **7** abolish, nullify **9** discredit, repudiate **10** counteract, disqualify, neutralize

invaluable
7 crucial **8** precious **9** essential, priceless **11** beyond price, inestimable **13** irreplaceable

invariable
4 same **5** fixed **6** static, steady **7** uniform **8** constant **9** continual, immovable, immutable, unfailing, unvarying **10** changeless, consistent, unchanging **11** inalterable, unalterable **12** unchangeable

invariably
4 ever **6** always **7** forever

invasion
4 raid **5** foray **6** attack, inroad **7** assault, offense **8** trespass **9** incursion, intrusion, offensive, onslaught **12** encroachment

invective
5 abuse **6** tirade **7** abusive, obloquy **8** diatribe, jeremiad **9** contumely, philippic, truculent **10** opprobrium, scurrility, scurrilous **11** opprobrious **12** billingsgate, contumelious, vituperation, vituperative

inveigh
4 kick, rail, rant **6** object **7** protest **8** complain **9** fulminate **11** expostulate, remonstrate

inveigle
4 coax, lure **5** decoy, snare, tempt **6** allure, cajole, entice, entrap, lead on, rope in, seduce, wangle **7** blarney, win over **8** blandish, butter up, maneuver, persuade

invent
4 coin, mint **6** cook up, create, design, devise, make up, patent, vamp up **7** concoct, dream up, fashion, hatch up, pioneer, think up **8** conceive, contrive, discover, engineer, envision **9** fabricate, formulate, originate

invention
7 coinage, fiction **8** creation **10** brainchild, innovation **11** contrivance

inventive
7 fertile, teeming **8** creative, fruitful, original **9** demiurgic, ingenious **10** innovative, innovatory **11** imaginative

inventor
5 maker **6** author, father, mother **7** creator, founder **8** engineer **9** architect, generator, innovator **10** discoverer, introducer, originator
air brake: **12** Westinghouse (George)
air conditioning: **7** Carrier (Willis)
automobile: **7** Daimler (Gottlieb)
ballpoint pen: **4** Loud (John)
barbed wire: **7** Glidden (Joseph Farwell)
barometer: **10** Torricelli (Evangelista)
bifocal lens: **8** Franklin (Benjamin)
camera: **7** Eastman (George)
cash register: **5** Ritty (James)
cotton gin: **7** Whitney (Eli)
cylinder lock: **4** Yale (Linus)
dirigible: **8** Zeppelin (Ferdinand von)
dynamite: **5** Nobel (Alfred)
electric battery: **5** Volta (Alessandro)
electric fan: **7** Wheeler (George)
electric organ: **7** Hammond (Laurens)
electric razor: **6** Schick (Jacob)
electric stove: **7** Hadaway (W. S.)
elevator: **4** Otis (Elisha)
fountain pen: **8** Waterman (Lewis)
friction match: **6** Walker (John)
gyrocompass: **6** Sperry (Elmer)
helicopter: **8** Sikorsky (Igor)
hot-air balloon: **11** Montgolfier (Jacques, Joseph)
incandescent lamp: **6** Edison (Thomas Alva)
induction motor: **5** Tesla (Nikola)
lawn mower: **5** Hills (Amariah)
Linotype: **12** Mergenthaler (Ottmar)
logarithm: **6** Napier (John)
machine gun: **7** Gatling (Richard)
microphone: **8** Berliner (Emile)
microwave oven: **7** Spencer (Percy)
movable type: **9** Gutenberg (Johannes)
parachute: **9** Blanchard (Jean-Pierre)
pendulum clock: **7** Huygens (Christiaan)
phonograph: **6** Edison (Thomas Alva)
photography: **6** Niepce (Nicéphore), Talbot (W. H. Fox) **8** Daguerre (Louis)
piano: **10** Cristofori (Bartolomeo)
radio: **7** Marconi (Guglielmo)
reaper: **9** McCormick (Cyrus)
revolver: **4** Colt (Samuel)
rocket engine: **7** Goddard (Robert)
safety pin: **4** Hunt (Walter)
safety razor: **8** Gillette (King)
sewing machine: **4** Howe (Elias)
sleeping car: **7** Pullman (George)
spinning jenny: **10** Hargreaves (James)
steamboat: **5** Fitch (John) **6** Fulton (Robert), Miller (Patrick), Rumsey (James) **8** Jouffroy (Claude de)
steam engine: **4** Watt (James)
steam locomotive: **10** Stephenson (George)
stethoscope: **7** Laënnec (René)
submarine: **7** Holland (John Philip)
synthesizer: **4** Moog (Robert)
tank: **7** Swinton (Ernest)
telegraph: **5** Morse (Samuel F. B.)
telephone: **4** Bell (Alexander Graham)
telescope: **10** Lippershey (Hans)
television: **5** Baird (John) **6** Nipkow (Paul) **8** Zworykin (Vladimir) **10** Farnsworth (Philo)
thermometer: **7** Galileo (Galilei)
torpedo: **9** Whitehead (Robert)

tractor: **5** Deere (John)
transistor: **7** Bardeen (John) **8** Brattain (Walter), Shockley (William)
vulcanized rubber: **8** Goodyear (Charles)
writing for the blind: **7** Braille (Louis)
zipper: **6** Judson (Whitcomb)

inventory
3 sum **4** fund, list **5** hoard, stock, store, tally **6** assets, digest, record, supply, survey **7** account, backlog, catalog, itemize, reserve, specify, summary **8** register, tabulate **9** catalogue, checklist, enumerate, reservoir, stockpile, summarize, synopsize

inverse
8 contrary, opposite

inversion
7 reverse **8** flipping, reversal, upending **9** about-face, turnabout, volte-face

invert
4 flip **5** upend **7** reverse **8** overturn, turn over **9** transpose

invertebrate
4 weak **5** timid **7** chicken, doormat, milksop **8** boneless, impotent, weakling **9** jellyfish, spineless **10** namby-pamby **11** ineffectual, milquetoast
kind: **4** worm **6** insect, sponge **7** mollusc, mollusk **8** arachnid **9** arthropod **12** coelenterate

invest
4 gird, veil, wrap **5** adorn, array, dress, endow, imbue **6** clothe, confer, enfold, induct, infuse, ordain **7** empower, enclose, envelop, ingrain, install, suffuse

investigate
3 pry **4** sift **5** audit, probe, study **6** go into, search **7** dig into, examine, explore, inquire, inspect **8** check out, look into, muckrake, prospect, research **9** delve into **10** scrutinize **11** inquire into

investigation
5 audit, probe **6** survey **7** inquest, inquiry **8** research, scrutiny **11** fact-finding, inquisition

investigator
3 spy, tec **4** dick **5** hound **6** shamus, sleuth **7** gumshoe **8** hawkshaw, sherlock **9** detective **10** private eye

investiture
9 inaugural, induction **10** initiation, ordination **12** inauguration, installation, ratification

inveterate
3 old, set **5** fixed, sworn **6** rooted **7** abiding, chronic, settled **8** deep-dyed, enduring, habitual, hard-core, hardened, lifelong **9** confirmed, ingrained, perennial **10** continuing, deep-rooted, deep-seated, entrenched, habituated, persistent, persisting **11** established **12** incorrigible **13** dyed-in-the-wool

Invictus author
6 Henley (William Ernest)

invidious
7 envious, envying, jealous **9** green-eyed, obnoxious, resentful

invigorate
4 stir **5** brace, liven, pep up, rally, renew, rouse **6** perk up, vivify **7** animate, brace up, enliven, fortify, juice up, refresh, restore **8** energize, vitalize **9** reinforce, stimulate **10** rejuvenate, revitalize, strengthen

invincible
10 inviolable, unbeatable **11** impregnable, indomitable, insuperable **12** invulnerable, unassailable, undefeatable **13** unconquerable

in vino ____
7 veritas

inviolable
4 safe **6** secure **10** impervious, sacrosanct **11** consecrated, impregnable **12** unassailable **13** incorruptible

invisible
6 hidden **9** concealed **10** intangible **12** unnoticeable **13** imperceptible

Invisible Man
author: **5** Wells (H. G.) **7** Ellison (Ralph)
character: **7** Griffin (Herbert)

invitation
4 call, lure **6** come-on **7** bidding, proffer **8** entreaty, proposal **10** enticement **11** proposition **12** solicitation

invite
3 ask, bid **4** call, lure **5** tempt **6** allure, call in, entice, summon **7** propose, request, solicit

inviting
8 engaging, enticing, tempting **9** appealing, beguiling, seductive **10** attractive, intriguing

invocation
6 appeal, prayer **8** entreaty, petition **11** conjuration, incantation **12** supplication

invoice
3 tab **4** bill, list **5** score **7** account **8** manifest **9** reckoning, statement **11** consignment

invoke
3 beg **4** pray **5** crave, plead **6** appeal, call on, effect **7** beseech, conjure, enforce, entreat, implore, solicit **8** call upon, petition **9** call forth, conjure up, implement, importune **10** supplicate

involuntary
6 forced, reflex **8** knee-jerk **9** automatic, impulsive, reflexive, unwitting **10** compulsory, unintended, unprompted **11** instinctive, spontaneous, unconscious, unmeditated **13** unintentional

involve
4 mire 6 affect, embody, engage, entail, take in 7 call for, concern, contain, embrace, embroil, include, require, subsume 8 comprise, entangle 9 encompass, implicate 10 complicate, comprehend 11 necessitate

involved
6 daedal, knotty 7 complex, gordian 8 confused 9 Byzantine, elaborate, intricate 10 convoluted 11 complicated 12 labyrinthine

invulnerable
6 immune, secure 10 impervious, invincible, unbeatable 11 impregnable, indomitable 12 unassailable

Io
father: 7 Inachus
guard: 5 Argus
son: 7 Epaphus

iodine source
4 kelp

Iolanthe
composer: 8 Sullivan (Arthur)
librettist: 7 Gilbert (W. S.)

Iolcus king
5 Aeson 6 Pelias

Iole
captor: 8 Heracles, Hercules
father: 7 Eurytus
husband: 6 Hyllus

ion
6 ligand
kind: 5 anion 6 cation 8 thermion

Ion
father: 6 Apollo
mother: 6 Creusa
stepfather: 6 Xuthus

Ionesco, Eugène
play: 6 Chairs (The), Lesson (The) 10 Rhinoceros 11 Bald Soprano (The)

iota
3 bit, jot, ray 4 atom, hint, mite, whit 5 crumb, grain, ounce, scrap, shred, speck, trace 6 smidge, tittle 7 smidgen, smidgin 8 molecule, particle, smidgeon 9 scintilla

IOU
4 chit, debt
part: 3 owe, you

Iowa
capital: 9 Des Moines
city: 4 Ames 7 Dubuque 8 Waterloo 9 Davenport, Sioux City 11 Cedar Rapids 13 Council Bluffs
college, university: 5 Drake 8 Grinnell
nickname: 7 Hawkeye (State)
river: 9 Des Moines
state bird: 9 goldfinch
state flower: 15 wild prairie rose
state tree: 3 oak

Iphicles
brother: 8 Heracles, Hercules
mother: 7 Alcmene
son: 6 Iolaus

Iphigenia
avenger: 12 Clytemnestra
brother: 7 Orestes
father: 9 Agamemnon
mother: 12 Clytemnestra
sister: 7 Electra

Iran
ancient civilization: 4 Elam 5 Medes, Media 6 Persia
capital: 6 Tehran 7 Teheran
city: 3 Qom, Qum 6 Shiraz, Tabriz 7 Esfahan, Isfahan, Mashhad
conqueror: 9 Alexander (the Great)
gulf: 4 Oman 7 Persian
island: 5 Qeshm
language: 3 Tat 5 Farsi 7 Persian
leader: 7 Pahlavi (Mohammad Reza, Reza Shah) 8 Khomeini (Ayatollah Ruholla)
monetary unit: 4 rial
mountain, range: 6 Elburz, Zagros 8 Damavand 9 Hindu Kush
neighbor: 4 Iraq 6 Turkey 7 Armenia 8 Pakistan 10 Azerbaijan 11 Afghanistan 12 Turkmenistan
river: 5 Atrek, Karun, Safīd 7 Karkheh
sea: 7 Caspian
strait: 6 Hormuz

Iranian
7 Persian
parliament: 6 Majlis
religious movement: 5 Baha'i
sect: 4 Shia
sect member: 6 Shiite

Iraq
ancient civilization: 5 Akkad, Sumer 8 Akkadian, Sumerian 9 Babylonia 10 Babylonian
ancient name: 11 Mesopotamia
capital: 7 Baghdad
city: 5 Basra, Mosul, Najaf 6 Kirkuk 7 Falluja, Karbala 8 Fallujah
conqueror: 9 Alexander (the Great)
desert: 6 Syrian
gulf: 7 Persian
leader: 6 Faisal 7 Hussein (Saddam)
monetary unit: 5 dinar
neighbor: 4 Iran 5 Syria 6 Jordan, Kuwait, Turkey 11 Saudi Arabia
port: 5 Basra 7 Umm Qasr
river: 6 Tigris 9 Euphrates

irascible
4 tart **5** huffy, surly, testy **6** crabby, cranky, feisty, tetchy, touchy **7** bristly, grouchy, peevish, peppery, prickly **8** choleric, petulant, snappish **9** crotchety, fractious, irritable, querulous, splenetic **11** hot-tempered **12** cantankerous **13** quick-tempered

irate
3 mad **5** angry, livid, riled, vexed, wroth **6** fuming **7** enraged, furious, steamed **8** choleric, incensed, provoked, wrathful **9** indignant **10** infuriated

ire
4 fury, rage, rile **5** anger, wrath **6** choler, enrage, madden, temper **7** incense, steam up, umbrage **9** infuriate **10** exasperate **11** indignation **12** exasperation

Ireland
4 Eire, Erin **8** Hibernia
capital: 6 Dublin
city: 4 Cork **5** Kerry, Louth, Meath, Sligo **6** Galway **7** Donegal, Kildare, Wexford, Wicklow **8** Kilkenny, Limerick **9** Waterford **12** Dun Laoghaire
county: 4 Cork, Mayo **5** Clare, Kerry, Louth, Meath, Sligo **6** Galway **7** Donegal, Kildare, Wexford **8** Limerick
flag color: 5 green, white **6** orange
flower: 8 shamrock
island group: 4 Aran **8** Hibernia
lake: 3 Ree (Lough) **4** Derg (Lough) **5** Neagh (Lough) **6** Corrib (Lough)
language: 4 Erse **5** Irish **6** Gaelic **7** English
legislature: 4 Dail
monetary unit: 4 euro
nickname: 11 Emerald Isle
province: 7 Munster **8** Connacht, Leinster
river: 4 Erne, Nore **5** Boyne **6** Barrow, Liffey **7** Shannon
symbol: 4 harp

Irene
3 Pax
father: 4 Zeus **7** Jupiter
mother: 6 Themis

irenic
4 calm **7** pacific **8** pacifist **9** peaceable, placative, placatory **10** nonviolent **12** conciliatory, propitiatory

iridescent
8 gleaming, lustrous **10** opalescent
gem: 4 opal **5** pearl **7** apatite **8** ammolite **9** fire agate, moonstone
shell: 7 abalone

iridium symbol
2 Ir

Iris
father: 7 Thaumas
mother: 7 Electra

Irish
4 Erse **6** Celtic, Gaelic
accent: 6 brogue
airline: 9 Aer Lingus
cattle: 5 Kerry
chief heir-elect: 6 tanist
clan: 4 sept
combining form: 7 Hiberno
coronation stone: 7 Lia Fail
cudgel: 9 shillalah **10** shillelagh
death spirit: 7 banshee
design: 8 claddagh
dog: 6 setter **7** terrier
elf: 10 leprechaun
fortification: 4 liss
girl: 4 lass **6** lassie **7** colleen
god: 3 Ler **5** Dagda **6** Aengus
goddess: 4 Badb, Bodb **6** Brigit **8** Morrigan
hero: 9 Cuchulain **10** Cú Chulainn
heroine: 7 Deirdre
king: 9 Brian Boru
lake: 5 lough
language: 4 Erse
militant force: 3 IRA
nationalist: 4 Tone (Wolfe) **6** Pearse (Padraig) **7** Collins (Michael), Parnell (Charles) **8** De Valera (Eamon), O'Connell (Daniel) **9** Sarsfield (Patrick)
nationalist society: 8 Sinn Fein
patron saint: 7 Patrick
police officer: 5 garda
singer: 4 Enya **5** Makem (Tommy), Margo **6** Clancy (Bobby, Liam, Paddy, Patrick, Tom) **8** O'Donnell (Daniel)
symbol: 4 harp
theater: 5 Abbey
writing system: 4 ogam **5** ogham
(see also **Gaelic; Celtic**)

Irish moss
7 seaweed **9** carrageen

irk
3 try, vex **4** fret, gall, miff, pain, rile **5** annoy, peeve, pique, upset **6** abrade, bother, harass, nettle, ruffle, strain, stress **7** provoke, trouble **8** exercise, irritate **10** exasperate

irksome
6 vexing **7** tedious **8** annoying, rankling **9** provoking, upsetting, vexatious **10** bothersome, irritating, nettlesome, unpleasant **11** aggravating, troublesome, unpalatable

iron
4 firm, gyve, hard **5** press, rigid **6** fetter, strong **7** adamant, manacle, shackle **8** handcuff, obdurate **9** unbending **10** inexorable, inflexible
combining form: 5 ferro **6** sidero

German: 5 Eisen
relating to: 6 ferric 7 ferrous 11 ferruginous
symbol: 2 Fe

ironbound
5 harsh, rocky, rough, stern 6 craggy, jagged, rugged, severe, strict, uneven 7 scraggy 8 asperous, exacting, rigorous, scabrous 9 stringent 10 inflexible

Iron City
10 Pittsburgh

ironclad
5 fixed 7 binding 8 constant 9 immovable, immutable 10 inflexible, invariable 11 inalterable, irrefutable, unalterable 12 indisputable, irrefragable, unchangeable 13 unimpeachable

ironfisted
4 grim, hard, mean 5 harsh 6 brutal, severe, stingy 7 callous, miserly 8 pitiless, ruthless 9 penurious 10 implacable, unmerciful 11 hardhearted, intractable, remorseless 12 unappeasable

ironhanded
5 harsh, rigid 6 severe, strict 8 despotic, rigorous 9 draconian, stringent 10 tyrannical 12 unpermissive

ironhearted
5 stony 7 callous 8 hardened, obdurate, ruthless 9 merciless, unfeeling 10 hard-boiled 11 cold-blooded 13 unsympathetic

iron horse
10 locomotive

ironic
3 wry 6 biting 7 caustic, cutting, cynical, mordant, satiric 8 sardonic 9 sarcastic, trenchant

iron ore
8 goethite, hematite, limonite, siderite, taconite 9 magnetite

Iron Pants
6 Patton (George)

irons
5 bonds, gyves 6 chains 7 bilboes, darbies, fetters 8 manacles, shackles

Iroquois tribe
6 Cayuga, Mohawk, Oneida, Seneca 8 Onondaga 9 Tuscarora

irradiate
4 beam, glow 5 edify, light, shine 6 uplift 7 light up 8 illumine 9 enlighten 10 illuminate

irrational
3 mad 5 crazy 6 absurd, insane 7 invalid 8 demented 9 cockamamy, illogical, senseless, sophistic 10 cockamamie, fallacious, ridiculous 12 preposterous, unreasonable
number: 4 surd

irrefutable
4 sure 6 proven 7 certain 8 airtight, ironclad, positive 9 apodictic, veracious 10 conclusive, inarguable 11 indubitable 12 indisputable 13 incontestable

irregular
3 odd 5 erose, queer 6 fitful, patchy, random, spotty, uneven 7 aimless, erratic, unequal 8 aberrant, abnormal, atypical, informal, lopsided, peculiar, singular, sporadic, unstable, unsteady, variable 9 anomalous, desultory, divergent, eccentric, guerrilla, haphazard, hit-or-miss, spasmodic, unregular, unsettled 10 asymmetric, capricious, changeable, inconstant, off-balance, unbalanced, unofficial 11 exceptional, fluctuating 12 intermittent, unsystematic

irregularity
5 freak, quirk 6 oddity, vagary 7 anomaly 8 deviance 9 deviation, roughness 10 aberration, inequality, unevenness 11 abnormality

irrelevant
5 inapt 9 unrelated 10 extraneous, immaterial, inapposite, peripheral 11 inessential, unessential, unimportant 12 inapplicable 13 insignificant

irreligious
6 unholy 7 godless, impious, profane, ungodly 11 blasphemous

irreparable
8 cureless, hopeless 9 incurable 11 immedicable 12 irredeemable, irremediable 13 irretrievable, unrecoverable

irreproachable
4 pure 8 flawless, innocent, spotless, virtuous 9 blameless, errorless, exemplary, faultless, guiltless, righteous 10 immaculate, impeccable, inculpable, unblamable

irresolute
5 shaky 6 fickle, unsure, wobbly 7 halting 8 doubtful, hesitant, unstable, waffling, wavering 9 equivocal, faltering, tentative, uncertain, undecided 10 ambivalent, changeable, inconstant, wishy-washy 11 fluctuating, half-hearted, vacillating

irresponsible
4 rash, wild 8 carefree, careless, feckless, reckless 10 incautious, unreliable 12 undependable 13 unaccountable, untrustworthy

irreverent
4 flip 7 impious, profane, ungodly 8 flippant 9 satirical 11 blasphemous 12 sacrilegious

irrevocable
4 firm 5 final 9 immutable 11 unalterable 12 irreversible, unchangeable 13 nonreversible

irrigate
3 wet 4 soak 5 flush, water

irrigation ditch
5 flume 6 sluice 7 acequia

irritability
5 pique 6 choler 8 edginess 9 petulance 10 crabbiness, impatience 11 fretfulness, peevishness
abnormal: 8 erethism

irritable
4 edgy, sour 5 cross, huffy, ratty, testy, waspy, whiny 6 crabby, cranky, crusty, grumpy, ornery, snappy, tetchy, touchy 7 fretful, grouchy, peevish, pettish, prickly, waspish 8 captious, choleric, petulant, snappish 9 crotchety, fractious, impatient, irascible, querulous, splenetic 12 cantankerous, disagreeable

irritant
4 itch, pest 5 nudge, peeve 6 bother, gadfly, noodge, nudnik, pester, plague 7 nudnick 8 headache, nuisance, vexation 9 annoyance 11 botheration

irritate
3 bug, irk, rub, vex 4 fret, gall, goad, rile, roil 5 anger, annoy, chafe, grate, peeve, pique, spite 6 abrade, badger, bother, burn up, harass, hector, madden, needle, nettle, offend, ruffle 7 inflame, provoke 9 aggravate, stimulate 10 exacerbate, exasperate

irritated
5 irate, testy 7 fretful, peevish 8 choleric 9 impatient, irascible

irritation
4 itch, pest, rash, sore 6 bother, plague 7 chagrin 8 nuisance, vexation 9 annoyance

irrupt
5 belch, eruct, surge 6 invade 7 intrude

irruption
4 raid 5 foray 6 inroad 7 upsurge 8 invasion 9 incursion, intrusion

I.R.S. employee
7 auditor 10 accountant

Irving novel
15 Cider House Rules (The) 17 Hotel New Hampshire (The) 20 World According to Garp (The)

Isaac
father: 7 Abraham
mother: 5 Sarah
son: 4 Esau 5 Jacob
wife: 7 Rebekah

Isabella I
country: 5 Spain
home: 7 Castile
husband: 9 Ferdinand

Isaiah
7 prophet
father: 4 Amoz

Iscah
brother: 3 Lot
father: 5 Haran
sister: 6 Milcah

Iseult, Isolde
beloved: 7 Tristan 8 Tristram
husband: 4 Mark

Ishbak
father: 7 Abraham
mother: 7 Keturah

Ishbosheth's father
4 Saul

Ishmael
6 pariah 7 outcast 8 castaway, outsider 11 untouchable
captain: 4 Ahab
father: 7 Abraham
mother: 5 Hagar
ship: 6 Pequod

Ishtar
brother: 7 Shamash
father: 3 Anu, Sin
lover: 6 Tammuz

Ishui's father
4 Saul 5 Asher

Isis
brother: 6 Osiris
father: 3 Geb
husband: 6 Osiris
mother: 3 Nut
son: 4 Sept 5 Horus

Islam
adherent: 6 Moslem, Muslim
founder: 8 Mohammed, Muhammad
god: 5 Allah
holy city: 5 Mecca
holy month: 7 Ramadan
law: 6 Sharia
place of worship: 6 mosque
priest: 4 imam
scriptures: 5 Koran, Quran
sect: 4 Shia, Sufi 5 Sunni 6 Salafi, Shiite, Sufism 7 Ismaili, Wahhabi 8 Salafism
(see also **Muslim**)

island
3 ait, cay, key 4 holm 5 atoll, oasis 6 skerry 7 crannog
Adriatic Sea: 3 Vis 4 Brac, Cres, Hvar 5 Brach, Ciovo, Mljet, Solta 6 Lesina, Pharus
Aegean Sea: 4 Scio 5 Chios, Khios, Samos, Thira 6 Ikaria, Lemnos, Lesbos, Limnos 7 Nikaria 8 Mitilini, Mytilene, Santorin 10 Sakis-Adasi, Susam-Adasi
Alaska: 4 Adak, Atka, Attu, Kuiu 8 Wrangell
American Samoa: 3 Ofu, Tau 4 Rose 6 Swains
Andaman Sea: 4 Mali 5 Tavoy
Antarctica: 5 Scott, Young

Arafura Sea: **5** Dolak
Arctic Archipelago: **6** Baffin **8** Victoria
Arctic Ocean: **5** Senja
Australian: **5** Cocos **8** Tasmania
Azores: **4** Pico **5** Corvo, Faial
Bahamas: **3** Cat, Rum **4** Long **5** Abaco, Exuma **6** Andros, Inagua **7** Acklins, Crooked **8** Watlings **9** Eleuthera, Mayaguana **11** San Salvador
Bahrain: **5** Sitra **8** Muharraq
Baltic Sea: **4** Moon, Muhu **5** Faron, Mukhu, Rugen, Worms **6** Vormsi **7** Gotland **8** Bornholm, Gothland, Gottland
Barents Sea: **4** Bear
Bay of Naples: **5** Capri
Bay of Panama: **4** Naos
Bering Sea: **5** Medny **7** Nunivak **10** Big Diomede **13** Little Diomede
Bismarck Archipelago: **5** Lihir **10** New Britain
Bristol Channel: **5** Lundy
Buzzards Bay: **9** Cuttyhunk
Canadian: **5** Banks, Devon **6** Baffin **8** Bathurst, Melville, Somerset, Victoria **9** Anticosti, Ellesmere **10** Cape Breton **11** Axel Heiberg, Southampton **12** Newfoundland, Prince Edward
Canaries: **6** Gomera **7** La Palma **8** Tenerife **9** Lanzarote
Cape Verde: **4** Fogo, Maio, Mayo **5** Brava, Rombo
Caribbean Sea: **4** Cuba **5** Aruba, Utila, Vache **6** Tobago **7** Antigua, Curaçao, Jamaica **8** Barbados, Dominica, Trinidad **10** Guadeloupe, Martinique, Puerto Rico (see also **Virgin group**)
Carolines: **3** Uap, Yap **4** Truk **5** Chuuk, Nomoi, Sorol **6** Ponape **7** Hogoleu, Pohnpei **9** Ascension
Chagos Archipelago: **11** Diego Garcia
Chesapeake Bay: **4** Deal, Kent **5** Smith, Watts
Chukchl Sea: **6** Herald
Comoro group: **7** Mayotte
Congo River: **4** Bamu
Croatia: **3** Krk, Pag, Rab **5** Susak, Unije
Cyclades: **3** Ios, Kea, Nio **4** Ceos, Keos, Milo **5** Delos, Melos, Milos, Naxos, Paros, Siros, Syros **6** Andros, Dhilos **7** Amorgos, Cythnos, Kithnos, Kythnos, Mykonos
Denmark: **3** Als, Fyn, Mon **4** Aero, Fano, Moen, Mors **5** Alsen, Funen, Moers, Samso **8** Bornholm **9** Greenland **13** Fanum Fortunae
East River: **5** Ward's **7** Welfare **9** Roosevelt
England's: **7** Britain **9** Britannia **12** Great Britain
English Channel: **5** Wight
Fiji: **4** Koro **5** Mango, Vatoa
French: **7** Corsica **12** New Caledonia
French Polynesia: **4** Rapa, Reao, Ua Pu **5** Ua Pau
Futunas: **5** Alofi
Galápagos: **5** Pinta **7** Chatham, Isabela **8** Abingdon **10** Albermarle
Georgia: **5** Tybee
Germany: **4** Fohr **7** Fehmarn **9** Helgoland **10** Heligoland
Greater Antilles: **4** Cuba **7** Jamaica **10** Hispaniola, Puerto Rico
Greece: **4** Milo, Rodi **5** Creta, Crete, Hydra, Idhra, Kriti, Rodos, Tenos, Tinos **6** Euboea, Evvoia, Hydrea, Lesbos, Rhodes, Rhodus **9** Negropont **10** Negroponte
Grenadines: **5** Union
Gulf of Alaska: **6** Kodiak
Gulf of Bothnia: **5** Karlö
Gulf of Carpentaria: **5** Maria **6** Groote **7** Eylandt
Gulf of Guinea: **7** Sao Tomé **8** Príncipe, Sao Thomé **11** Saint Thomas
Gulf of Mexico: **3** Cat **5** Lobos
Gulf of Panama: **3** Rey
Gulf of St. Lawrence: **5** Brion
Gulf of Thailand: **3** Kut **5** Samui
Haiti: **6** Gonâve
Hawaii: **4** Maui, Oahu **5** Kauai, Lanai **6** Niihau **7** Molokai **9** Kahoolawe
Hudson Bay: **5** Coats
Indian Ocean: **4** Mahé, Nias **5** Heard, Pemba **7** La Dique, Praslin, Réunion **8** Sri Lanka, Zanzibar **9** Mauritius **10** Madagascar
Indonesia: **4** Bali, Biak, Java, Maja, Muna, Nias, Rhio, Riau, Roma, Roti, Savu, Sawu **5** Batam, Boano, Buton, Djawa, Japen, Lakor, Moena, Riouw, Rotti, Rupat, Sawoe, Solor, Sumba, Wetar, Wokam **6** Butung, Flores, Jappen, Lombok, Madura, Padang, Roepat, Romang, Soemba **7** Celebes, Madoera, Sumatra, Sumbawa **8** Boetoeng, Soembawa, Sulawesi **10** Bandanaira, Banda Neira, Sandalwood
Iran: **5** Shahi
Ireland: **4** Aran
Irish Sea: **3** Man
Italy: **4** Elba **6** Sicily **8** Sardinia
Japan: **3** Iki, Uku **4** Naru, Yezo **5** Awaji, Fukae, Fukue, Hondo, Shodo **6** Honshu, Kyushu **7** Shikoku **8** Hokkaido **10** Shodoshima
Java Sea: **4** Laut
Kiribati: **6** Tarawa
Lake Champlain: **5** Grand
Lake Erie: **9** North Bass, South Bass **10** Middle Bass
Lake Huron: **8** Drummond **10** Manitoulin
Lake Michigan: **3** Hog **4** High **6** Beaver
Lake Ontario: **5** Wolfe
Lake Superior: **4** Sand **6** Royale **7** Manitou
Lake Winnipeg: **5** Hecla
largest: **9** Greenland
Leeward group: **5** Nevis **7** Antigua, Barbuda, Redonda **8** Anguilla, Sombrero **10** Montserrat, Saint Kitts **13** St. Christopher

legendary: **7** Cipango
Lesser Sundas: **4** Alor **5** Ombai
Long Island Sound: **4** City, Hart **5** Goose, Harts
Malay Archipelago: **5** Kisar, Larat, Timor **6** Borneo **9** New Guinea
Malaysia: **6** Penang, Pinang **13** Prince of Wales
Malta: **4** Gozo
Massachusetts: **9** Nantucket
Mediterranean Sea: **4** Elba **5** Corfu, Crete, Malta **6** Cyprus, Euboea, Rhodes, Sicily **7** Corsica **8** Sardinia
Moluccas: **4** Buru **5** Ambon, Ceram, Seram **6** Boeroe
Mozambique channel: **10** Juan de Nova
Myanmar: **5** Daung, Kadan, Lanbi
Narragansett Bay: **5** Rhode **8** Prudence **9** Aquidneck, Conanicut
Netherlands: **5** Texel **7** Ameland **8** Vlieland
Netherlands Antilles: **7** Curaçao
New York: **4** Fire, Long **5** Ellis **6** Staten **7** Liberty **9** Gardiners, Governors, Manhattan, Roosevelt
New York Bay: **5** Ellis **6** Staten **7** Liberty **9** Governors, Manhattan
New Zealand: **5** South, White **7** Chatham, Stewart **8** D'Urville
Niagara River: **4** Goat
Nile River: **4** Argo, Roda, Ruda **5** Rhoda **6** Rawdah **11** Elephantine
North Channel: **3** Mew **8** Manihiki **9** Tongareva
North Pacific: **4** Wake
Northwest Territories: **5** Banks, Bylot, Devon **8** Bathurst, Melville **9** Ellesmere **10** Cornwallis, Resolution **13** Prince of Wales
Norwegian: **8** Jan Mayen
Norwegian Sea: **5** Donna, Smola, Vikna
Nova Scotia: **5** Sable **10** Cape Breton
off Alaska: **4** Dall **5** Kayak
off Albania: **5** Sazan **6** Saseno
off Australia: **4** Dunk
off Belize: **9** Ambergris
off Brazil: **4** Apeu **5** Rocas
off British Columbia: **4** King, Pitt **9** Vancouver
off Cape Cod: **8** Muskeget **9** Nantucket
off Chile: **5** Guafo, Mocha
off China: **4** Amoy **5** Ma-tsu **6** Hainan, Quemoy, Taiwan
off Crete: **3** Dia
off Ecuador: **4** Puna
off England: **3** Man **4** Sark **5** Wight **6** Jersey, Walney **8** Alderney, Guernsey
off Florida: **3** Dog **4** Pine **6** Amelia **7** Pelican, Sanibel **9** Anastasia
off French Guiana: **6** Devil's
off Georgia: **10** Cumberland **11** Saint Simons
off Germany: **4** Sylt
off Greenland: **5** Disko
off Guinea: **5** Tombo
off Hispaniola: **5** Beata
off Honduras: **5** Tigre
off Iceland: **7** Surtsey
off India: **5** Sagar
off Ireland: **4** Tory **5** Clare, Clear
off Kenya: **4** Lamu
off Long Island: **7** Fishers
off Louisiana: **5** Marsh
off Maine: **4** Deer, Orrs **5** Swans **8** Monhegan **11** Mount Desert
off Malay Peninsula: **6** Phuket **9** Singapore
off Maryland: **10** Assateague
off Massachusetts: **4** Plum **7** Naushon
off Mexico: **7** Cozumel
off Mississippi: **4** Horn, Ship
off Mozambique: **3** Ibo
off New Brunswick: **10** Campobello
off Newfoundland: **4** Bell
off Nigeria: **5** Lagos
off North Carolina: **5** Bodie
off Norway: **5** Bomlo, Froya, Hitra, Sotra, Stord, Vardo **8** Hitteren
off Panama: **4** Naos **5** Coiba **6** Parida
off Poland: **5** Wolin **6** Wollin
off Puerto Rico: **4** Crab **7** Culebra, Vieques
off Rhode Island: **5** Block
off Scotland: **4** Bute, Iona, Jura **5** Arran, Islay
off South Carolina: **5** North **6** Parris **10** Hilton Head
off Sri Lanka: **5** Delft
off Staten Island: **7** Hoffman
off Sumatra: **3** Weh
off Sweden: **5** Graso, Oland, Vaddo
off Syria: **5** Arvad, Arwad, Rouad **6** Aradus
off Tanzania: **5** Mafia, Pemba
off Tasmania: **5** Bruni, Bruny
off Tunisia: **5** Jerba **6** Djerba, Meninx
off Venezuela: **5** Aruba **7** Bonaire **8** Buen Aire
off Virginia: **5** Wreck
off Wales: **5** Caldy **6** Caldey
Orkneys: **3** Hoy
Outer Hebrides: **5** Barra, Scarp
Palmer Archipelago: **6** Anvers **7** Antwerp, Brabant
Pearl Harbor: **4** Ford
Persian Gulf: **4** Qeys **5** Kharg, Khark
Philippines: **4** Buad, Cebu, Fuga, Ilin, Poro, Sulu **5** Balut, Batan, Bohol, Coron, Daram, Leyte, Luzon, Panay, Samal, Samar, Sugbu, Talim, Ticao, Verde **6** Negros **7** Masbate, Mindoro, Palawan, Paragua **8** Limasawa, Mindanao **10** Corregidor
Puerto Rico: **4** Mona
Quebec: **4** Alma
Red Sea: **5** Tiran, Zugur, Zuqar
Russia: **7** Wrangel
St. Lawrence River: **4** Hare **5** Jesus **8** Montreal

San Francisco Bay: **5** Angel
Santa Cruz: **5** Anuda, Ndeni **6** Cherry
Sea of Japan: **4** Sado **5** Rebun
Sea of Marmara: **4** Avsa
second largest: **9** New Guinea
Senegal: **5** Gorée
Seychelles: **4** Mahé **7** La Digue, Praslin
Shetland archipelago: **4** Unst, Yell **5** Foula
Sierra Leone: **5** Tasso
South Atlantic: **5** Gough **6** Gough's **11** Saint Helena
South Korea: **5** Cheju
South of Tokyo: **3** Iwo **7** Iwo Jima, Naka Iwo
South Orkneys: **10** Coronation
South Pacific: **3** Hiu **4** Niue **5** Raoul **6** Savage, Sunday **7** Norfolk **8** Pitcairn
Spitsbergen archipelago: **4** Edge
Strait of Hormuz: **5** Qeshm, Qishm
Sulu Archipelago: **4** Jolo **5** Lapac
Svalbard: **4** Hope
Sverdrup: **11** Axel Heiberg **12** Amund Ringnes
Swedish: **3** Ven **4** Hven **5** Hveen, Orust
Tanzania: **8** Zanzibar
Texas: **5** Padre
Thames River: **7** Sheppey
third largest: **6** Borneo
Tierra del Fuego: **5** Hoste
Tonga: **3** Eua, Foa **4** Uiha **5** Haano
Tuamotu Archipelago: **4** Anaa **5** Chain
Turkish: **5** Imroz **6** Imbros
Tuvalu: **7** Nanumea **9** Nukufetau
Tyrrhenian Sea: **6** Ischia **11** Montecristo
Vanuatu: **3** Api, Epi, Oba **4** Aoba, Gaua, Tana, Vate **5** Efate, Maewo, Tanna
Venezuelan: **5** Patos **9** La Tortuga
volcanic: **5** Tofua **7** Iwo Jima
Wales: **8** Anglesea, Anglesey, Holyhead
Weddell Sea: **4** Ross **6** Hearst
Western Samoa: **5** Upolu **6** Savaii
West Indies: **4** Mona, Saba, Salt **5** Nevis, Peter, Saona **6** Tobago, Tortue **7** Grenada, Tortuga **8** Trinidad **9** Santa Cruz **10** Concepción, Hispaniola, Montserrat, Saint Croix (see also **Bahamas; Greater Antilles; Leeward group; Virgin group; Windward group**)
West of England: **7** Ireland
West Pacific: **5** Dyaul, Fauro, Ocean **6** Banaba, Marcus **7** Iwo Jima, Kita Iwo **9** Minami Iwo
with former penitentiary: **8** Alcatraz

island group
Admiralty: **5** Manus
Alaska: **3** Rat **8** Aleutian, Pribilof **9** Andreanof, Catherine
Aleutians: **4** Near
Aleutian: **3** Rat **4** Adak, Akun, Attu **5** Amlia, Kiska, Umnak **6** Kanaga, Tanaga, Unimak **8** Amchitka, Unalaska
American Samoa: **5** Manua
Apostle: **3** Oak **4** Long, Sand **5** Outer **8** Madeline, Michigan, Stockton
Arabian Sea: **9** Laccadive
Arctic Archipelago: **8** Sverdrup
Arctic Ocean: **8** Svalbard **12** Novaya Zemlya
Bahamas: **5** Berry, Exuma **6** Bimini
Balearic: **5** Ibiza **7** Majorca, Menorca, Minorca **8** Mallorca
Banda Sea: **5** Damar
Bangladesh: **5** Hatia, Hatya
Bay of Bengal: **7** Andaman, Nicobar
between England and France: **7** Channel
Bismarck Archipelago: **4** Feni **5** Tabar, Tanga
Bismarck Sea: **4** Vitu
British: **7** Bermuda
Caribbean Sea: **4** Swan **5** Pearl **6** Cayman, Perlas, Pigeon **8** Pichones **10** Grenadines, West Indies
Central Pacific Ocean: **4** Line **5** Samoa, Union **6** Danger, Midway **7** Phoenix, Tokelau **8** Manihiki **9** Polynesia **12** Northern Cook
Channel: **4** Herm, Sark **5** Lihou, Sercq **6** Jersey **8** Guernsey
Cook: **4** Atiu **5** Mauke
Coral Sea: **4** Huon
Cuba: **8** Camagüey
Denmark: **6** Faroes **7** Faeroes
D'Entrecasteaux: **8** Kaluwawa **9** Fergusson
Dodecanese: **3** Coo, Cos, Kos **4** Caso, Lero, Simi, Syme **5** Kasos, Leros, Lipso, Lisso, Patmo, Telos **6** Calino, Lipsos, Nisiro, Patmos **7** Calimno, Nisiros, Nisyros **8** Kalymnos
east of Philippines: **10** Micronesia
East Siberian Sea: **4** Bear **8** Medvezhi
Ecuador: **5** Colón **9** Galápagos
England: **5** Farne
Faeroes, Faroes: **4** Vago **5** Bordo, Sando
Fiji: **3** Lau **7** Eastern
Florida Keys: **4** Long, Vaca, West **5** Largo **7** Big Pine **9** Matecumbe, Sugarloaf
Formosa Strait: **4** Hoko **6** Peng hu **10** Pescadores
Fox: **5** Umnak **6** Akutan, Unimak **8** Unalaska
France: **5** Salut **6** Safety **9** Kerguelen
French Polynesia: **3** Low **6** Tubuai **7** Austral, Paumotu, Société, Society, Tuamotu **9** Marquesas, Touamotou
Frisian: **3** Rom **4** Föhr, Sylt **5** Amrum, Juist, Mando, Texel **6** Borkum **7** Ameland **8** Langeoog, Pellworm, Vlieland **9** Helgoland, Norderney
Germany: **8** Halligen
Greece: **6** Aegean, Ionian **8** Cyclades **10** Dodecanese **11** Dodecanesus
Hudson Bay: **7** Belcher
Indian Ocean: **7** Aldabra
Indonesia: **4** Asia, Batu, Pagi, Sula **5** Babar, Batoe, Pagai, Pageh, Penju, Spice, Wakde **6** Maluku

Inner Hebrides: **4** Coll, Eigg, Iona, Jura, Muck, Mull, Skye **5** Canna, Gigha, Islay, Tiree, Tyree
Ionian: **5** Corfu, Paxos, Zante **6** Cerigo, Ithaca, Leukas, Levkas **10** Santa Maura
Ireland: **4** Aran
Italy: **6** Lipari
Japan: **5** Osumi
Kuril: **4** Urup **5** Ketoi, Matua **6** Iturup **7** Etorofu, Matsuwa **8** Kunashir **9** Kunashiri
largest: **5** Malay **8** Malaysia
Lesser Antilles: **8** Windward
Leti: **3** Moa **5** Lakor
Line: **5** Flint **6** Malden, Vostok **7** Fanning, Palmyra **8** Starbuck **9** Christmas
Loyalty: **3** Uea **4** Lifu, Maré, Uvea **5** Lifou
Malay Archipelago: **5** Sunda **6** Soenda
Marianas: **4** Maug, Rota **5** Pagan **6** Saipan
Marquesas: **4** Eiào, Ua Pu **6** Hatutu, Hiva Oa, Ua Huka **7** Tahuata **8** Fatu Hiva, Nuku Hiva
Marshall: **5** Wotho, Wotje **8** Eniwetok **9** Kwajalein
Mediterranean Sea: **8** Baleares, Balearic
Midway: **4** Sand **7** Eastern
Moluccas: **3** Kai, Kei, Obi **4** Buru, Leti **5** Ambon, Banda, Letti, Seram **6** Boeroe **8** Tanimbar **9** Timorlaut
New Caledonia: **7** Loyalty **9** Loyalties
Northern Cook: **7** Penrhyn
north of Australia: **9** Melanesia
north of British Isles: **5** Faroe **7** Faeroes
north off Fiji: **5** Hoorn **6** Futuna
north of Madagascar: **7** Aldabra **8** Farquhar
north of New Caledonia: **5** Belep
north of New Guinea: **8** Bismarck **9** Admiralty **11** Admiralties
Northwest Territories: **5** Parry
off Alaska: **3** Fox
off Alaska Peninsula: **8** Shumagin
off Cape Cod: **9** Elizabeth
off eastern Asia: **5** Kuril **6** Kurile
off England: **6** Scilly
off Florida: **11** Dry Tortugas
off Guinea: **3** Los **4** Loos
off Honduras: **5** Bahia
off Morocco: **7** Madeira
off New Guinea: **3** Aru **4** Aroe
off Nicaragua: **4** Corn
off northern Africa: **6** Canary **8** Canaries
off northern Australia: **6** Wessel **7** Dampier
off Sicily: **5** Egadi **8** Aegadian
Okinawa: **4** Kume
Outer Hebrides: **4** Uist
Papua New Guinea: **5** Green
Persian Gulf: **4** Tunb
Philippines: **4** Cuyo **5** Tapul **6** Lubang **7** Basilan, Bisayas, Visayan
Phoenix: **4** Hull, Mary **6** Birnie, Canton **9** Enderbury
Portuguese: **6** Azores
Quebec: **8** Magdalen **9** Madeleine
Queen Charlotte: **7** Moresby
Ryukyus: **5** Amami **7** Okinawa
St. Lawrence River: **8** Thousand
Sea of Japan: **3** Oki
Sea of Marmara: **5** Kizil **7** Princes **11** Kizil Adalar
Shumagin: **4** Unga
Society: **5** Eimeo, Tahaa, Tahao, Taiti **6** Moorea, Tahiti **8** Otaheite
Solomon: **4** Buka, Gizo, Savo **7** Malaita **11** Guadalcanal **12** Bougainville
South Atlantic Ocean: **8** Falkland, Malvinas
South China Sea: **6** Hirata **7** Paracel, Spratly
south of New Zealand: **8** Auckland
South Pacific: **11** Austronesia
Sulu Sea: **7** Cagayan **9** Cagayanes
Tonga: **5** Vavau
Treasury: **4** Mono
Truk: **3** Tol **4** Haru, Moen, Udot, Uman **5** Fefan
Tyrrhenian Sea: **5** Ponza
Venezuelan: **4** Aves, Bird **9** Los Roques
Virgin, American: **9** Saint John **10** Saint Croix **11** Saint Thomas
Virgin, British: **5** Peter **6** Norman **7** Anegada, Tortola **11** Jost Van Dyke
West Europe: **12** British Isles
West Indies: **6** Virgin **10** Guadeloupe
west of French Polynesia: **4** Cook
west of Scotland: **7** Western **8** Hebrides
west Pacific Ocean: **4** Duff **5** Belau, Bonin, Mapia, Palau, Pelew **7** Ladrone, Mariana, Solomon, Vanuatu **8** Marshall, Treasury **9** Ogasawara **10** Saint David
Windward: **10** Martinique

island nation
Atlantic Ocean: **9** Cape Verde
Indian Ocean: **8** Malagasy, Malgache, Sri Lanka **9** Mauritius **10** Madagascar, Seychelles
Mediterranean Sea: **6** Cyprus
Mozambique Channel: **6** Comoro **7** Comores
off southern China: **6** Taiwan
south of Greenland: **7** Iceland
West Indies: **4** Cuba **7** Jamaica **8** Barbados **10** Saint Lucia
West Pacific Ocean: **4** Fiji **5** Belau, Nauru, Palau, Samoa **6** Tuvalu **7** Vanuatu
Windward group: **8** Dominica

island province
12 Prince Edward

island state
6 Hawaii

isle
see **island**

Ismene
brother: **9** Polynices **10** Polyneices

father: 7 Oedipus
mother: 7 Jocasta
sister: 8 Antigone
uncle: 5 Creon

isochronous
7 regular 8 cyclical, periodic, rhythmic 9 recurrent, recurring 10 periodical 12 intermittent

isolate
6 cut off, detach, enisle 7 seclude 8 close off, insulate, pinpoint, separate, set apart 9 segregate, sequester 10 quarantine

isolated
5 alone 6 random, remote, unique 7 unusual 8 solitary, sporadic 9 separated, withdrawn 11 exceptional, quarantined

Isolde
see **Iseult**

Israel
airline: 4 El Al
ancient name: 4 Zion 5 Judea 6 Canaan, Judaea 9 Palestine
capital: 9 Jerusalem
city: 4 Acre 5 Haifa, Jaffa 7 Tel Aviv 9 Beersheba
desert: 5 Negeb, Negev
gulf: 5 Aqaba
lake: 8 Tiberias 12 Sea of Galilee
language: 6 Arabic, Hebrew
monetary unit: 6 shekel
neighbor: 5 Egypt, Syria 6 Jordan 7 Lebanon
plain: 9 Esdraelon
river: 6 Jordan
sea: 4 Dead 13 Mediterranean

Israeli
5 sabra
dance: 4 hora 5 horah
gun: 3 Uzi

Israelite
see **Hebrew; Jewish**

Issachar
father: 5 Jacob
mother: 4 Leah

issue
4 emit, flow, gush, pour, rise, seed, stem, vent 5 arise, birth, brood, child, empty, fruit, scion, topic 6 affair, appear, effect, emerge, get out, matter, put out, result, scions, sequel, source, spring, upshot 7 concern, debouch, descent, edition, emanate, give off, give out, outcome, problem, proceed, progeny, publish, release, subject 8 bulletin, children, question, throw off 9 come forth, offspring, originate, posterity 10 derive from, distribute, end product, promulgate 11 consequence, descendants, progeniture, publication

Istanbul
ancient name: 9 Byzantium
business section: 6 Galata
country: 6 Turkey
foreign quarter: 4 Pera 7 Beyoglu
park: 8 Seraglio
residential section: 7 Uskudar

isthmus
Africa-Asia: 4 Suez
America: 6 Panama
Greece: 7 Corinth
Malay Peninsula: 3 Kra

Italian
after: 4 dopo
against: 6 contro
ahead: 6 avanti
apple: 4 mela
article: 2 il, la
aunt: 3 zia
automobile: 4 Fiat 6 Lancia 7 Ferrari 8 Maserati 9 Alfa Romeo 11 Lamborghini
be: 6 essere
book: 5 libro
brandy: 6 grappa
brother: 8 fratello
cake: 5 torta
cat: 5 gatto
cathedral: 5 duomo
cheers: 6 cin cin
chicken: 5 pollo
child: 7 bambino
coffee: 5 caffè
come: 6 venire
day: 6 giorno
deer: 5 cervo
dialect: 6 Tuscan 8 Sicilian
dictator: 9 Mussolini (Benito)
die: 6 morire
dinner: 6 pranzo
do, make: 4 fare
dog: 4 cane
enough: 5 basta
evening: 4 sera
everyone: 5 tutti
family: 4 Este 5 Cenci, Savoy 6 Borgia, Medici, Orsini, Pepoli, Savoia, Sforza 7 Colonna, Gonzaga, Spinola 8 Visconti
fascist: 10 Blackshirt
game: 5 bocce, bocci 6 boccie
gentleman: 6 signor 7 signore
give: 4 dare
go: 6 andare
goat: 5 capra
good-bye: 4 ciao
grape: 3 uva
hear: 7 sentire
hello: 4 ciao

highway: **10** autostrada
honey: **5** miele
how much: **6** quanto
ice cream: **6** gelato
lady: **5** donna **7** signora **9** signorina
leave: **7** partire
magistrate: **7** podestà
maybe: **5** forse
meat: **5** carne **6** salami **8** pancetta **9** pepperoni, salsiccia **10** mortadella, prosciutto
man: **4** uomo
milk: **5** latte
mountain soldier: **6** Alpino
much: **5** molto
mushroom: **5** fungo
night: **5** notte
nothing: **6** niente
numbers: **3** due, sei, tre, uno **4** nove, otto **5** dieci, sette **6** cinque **7** quattro
often: **6** spesso
oil: **4** olio
open: **6** aprire
opera house: **7** La Scala
over: **5** sopra
patriot: **6** Cavour (Conte di), Rienzo (Cola di) **7** Mazzini (Giuseppe) **9** Garibaldi (Giuseppe)
peach: **5** pesca
pencil: **6** matita
please: **9** per favore
red: **5** rosso
religious reformer: **10** Savonarola (Girolamo)
resort: **4** Lido **5** Abano, Capri **8** Sorrento, Taormina
road: **6** strada
sandwich: **6** panino
sell: **7** vendere
shrimp: **6** scampi
sing: **7** cantare
sister: **7** sorella
soldier: **7** soldato
soup: **5** zuppa **10** minestrone
speak: **7** parlare
square: **6** piazza
squid: **8** calamari
star: **6** stella
street: **3** via **5** corso
summer: **6** estate
sun: **4** sole
tell, say: **4** dire
thanks: **6** grazie
think: **7** pensare
toward: **5** verso
uncle: **3** zio
under: **5** sotto
voice: **4** voce
weight: **5** libra, oncia
white: **6** bianco
wine: **4** vino
with: **3** con
without: **5** senza
write: **8** scrivere

Italy
bay: **6** Naples
capital: **4** Roma, Rome
city: **4** Asti, Bari, Pisa **5** Aosta, Genoa, Milan, Padua, Parma, Siena, Turin **6** Genova, Mantua, Milano, Modena, Naples, Napoli, Padova, Torino, Venice, Verona **7** Bergamo, Bologna, Bolzano, Catania, Cremona, Firenze, Leghorn, Livorno, Mantova, Palermo, Perugia, Ravenna, Salerno, Taranto, Trieste, Venezia **8** Florence, Siracusa, Syracuse
enclave: **9** San Marino **11** Vatican City
gulf: **5** Gaeta **7** Salerno, Taranto **11** Sant' Eufemia
island, island group: **4** Elba, Lido **5** Capri **6** Ischia, Lipari, Sicily **7** Aeolian, Capraia **8** Sardinia
lake: **4** Como **5** Garda **7** Bolsena **8** Maggiore **9** Bracciano
leader: **9** Mussolini (Benito)
monetary unit: **4** euro
monetary unit, former: **4** lira **5** scudi (plural), scudo, soldi (plural), soldo
mountain, range: **4** Alps, Etna **9** Apennines, Mont Blanc, Monte Rosa **10** Monte Corno
neighbor: **6** France **7** Austria **8** Slovenia **11** Switzerland
peninsula: **9** Salentina
river: **4** Arno, Liri **5** Adige, Piave, Tiber **6** Isonzo, Tevere **8** Volturno
sea: **6** Ionian **8** Adriatic, Ligurian **10** Tyrrhenian **13** Mediterranean
strait: **7** Messina, Otranto
volcano: **4** Etna **8** Vesuvius
wine region: **4** Asti

itch
3 yen **4** ache, long, lust, pine, urge **5** crave, yearn **6** desire, hanker, hunger, thirst **7** craving, longing **8** appetite, pruritus, yearning **9** hankering

itchy
4 avid, edgy, keen **5** antsy, eager, jumpy **7** fidgety, restive **8** prurient, pruritic, restless **9** impatient

item
3 bit **5** entry, point, scrap, story, thing, topic **6** detail, matter **7** account, article, element, feature, product **8** clipping **9** commodity **10** particular

itemize
4 list **5** count, tally **6** number **7** catalog, run down, specify, tick off **8** document, spell out **9** catalogue, enumerate, inventory

iterate
5 drill, recap, renew **6** rehash, repeat, replay, retell **7** reprise, restate **12** recapitulate

Ithaca king
8 Odysseus

Ithamar's father
5 Aaron

itinerant
5 gypsy, nomad **6** roving **7** migrant, nomadic, roaming, vagrant **8** drifting, rambling, traveler, vagabond, wanderer **9** migratory, transient, unsettled, wandering, wayfaring **11** peripatetic

itty-bitty
3 wee **4** tiny **5** teeny, weeny **6** teensy **10** teeny-weeny **12** teensy-weensy

Ivanhoe
author: **5** Scott (Walter)
character: **5** Isaac **6** Cedric, Rowena, Ulrica **7** Rebecca, Wilfred **9** Robin Hood

Ivory Coast
11 Côte d'Ivoire
capital: **7** Abidjan **12** Yamoussoukro
city: **6** Bouaké
language: **6** French
monetary unit: **5** franc
mountain: **5** Nimba
neighbor: **4** Mali **5** Ghana **6** Guinea **7** Liberia **11** Burkina Faso
river: **7** Bandama **9** Sassandra

ivory-tower
8 academic **11** conjectural, impractical, theoretical, unrealistic

Ivy League
4 Penn, Yale **5** Brown **7** Cornell, Harvard **8** Columbia **9** Dartmouth, Princeton **12** Pennsylvania

J

jab
3 hit **4** barb, blow, poke, prod, sock, stab **5** nudge, prick, punch **6** pierce, strike, thrust **8** puncture

jabber
3 gab, jaw, yak **6** babble, drivel, gabble **7** blather, chatter, prattle **8** nonsense **9** gibberish

jabberer
6 gabber, magpie **7** babbler, blabber, gabbler **8** prattler **9** chatterer **10** chatterbox

Jabberwocky author
7 Carroll (Lewis), Dodgson (Charles)

jabot
4 fall **5** frill **6** ruffle

___ jacet
3 hic

jack
3 tar **4** bird, card, fish, flag, hike, lift, move, salt **5** boost, brace, bread, dough, knave, knife, money, put up, raise **6** brandy, cheese, device, donkey, rabbit, sailor, seaman **7** laborer, mariner, servant **8** increase, standard **9** criticize, mechanism **10** take to task

jackal
4 dupe, pawn **5** agent, canid, patsy **6** canine, flunky, lackey, minion, stooge **7** cat's-paw **9** accessory, auxiliary **10** accomplice **11** stool pigeon
god: **4** Anpu **6** Anubis

jackanapes
3 ape, imp **4** brat, fool **6** monkey

jackass
4 dolt, dope, fool, jerk **5** burro, dunce, idiot, schmo **6** donkey, nitwit **7** nebbish **8** bonehead, imbecile, numskull **9** blockhead, numbskull **10** nincompoop
deer: **3** kob **8** antelope

jackdaw
7 grackle **9** blackbird

jacket
3 tux **4** Eton **5** parka, tunic **6** anorak, blazer, bolero, jerkin, reefer, sacque, tuxedo **7** doublet, Norfolk, peacoat, spencer **8** camisole **10** roundabout
armored: **7** hauberk **9** habergeon
sleeveless: **4** vest **6** bolero, jerkin **9** waistcoat

jackhammer
5 drill **9** rock drill

jack-in-the-pulpit
4 arum

jackknife
4 dive **6** barlow
game: **11** mumblety-peg

jackleg
6 make-do, novice **7** amateur, shyster, stopgap **9** dishonest, greenhorn, makeshift, temporary, unskilled **10** substitute **11** pettifogger **12** unscrupulous

jack-of-all-trades
6 tinker **7** go-to guy **8** factotum, handyman

jack-o'-lantern
6 fungus **7** pumpkin

jackpot
3 sum **4** pool **5** award, kitty, prize **6** reward, stakes **7** bonanza, success **8** windfall

jackrabbit
4 hare

jackstay
3 bar, rod **4** rope **7** rigging, support

Jacob
brother: **4** Esau
daughter: **5** Dinah
father: **5** Isaac
father-in-law: **5** Laban
mother: **7** Rebekah
new name: **6** Israel
son: **3** Dan, Gad **4** Levi **5** Asher, Judah **6** Joseph, Reuben, Simeon **7** Zebulun **8** Benjamin, Issachar, Naphtali
variant: **5** James
wife: **4** Leah **6** Rachel

Jacobin
7 radical **9** Dominican, extremist

Jacob's ladder
4 herb **5** phlox **9** perennial

jade
3 gem, nag **4** bore, cloy, dull, minx, pall, tire, wear **5** color, drain, flirt, green, hussy, jewel, stone, tramp, weary, wench **6** wanton **7** fatigue, jezebel, mineral, trollop, wear out **8** gemstone, nephrite, strumpet, wear down

jaded
4 worn **5** blasé, bored, sated, tired, weary **6** dulled **7** cynical, wearied, worn-out **8** fatigued, satiated, worn down **9** apathetic, exhausted, surfeited **10** overworked

jaeger
4 skua **6** hunter **8** huntsman

Jael
husband: **5** Heber
victim: **6** Sisera

jag
3 cut **4** barb, jerk, load, pink, tear **5** binge, notch, prick, spell, spree **6** bender, indent, thrill, thrust **7** serrate

jagged
5 erose, harsh, rough, sharp **6** broken, craggy, rugged, spiked, uneven **7** scraggy **8** serrated, unsmooth **9** irregular

Jaguar model
3 XKE

jai alai
6 pelota
basket: **5** cesta
court: **6** cancha **7** fronton

jail
3 can, jug, pen **4** coop, gaol, poky **5** clink, pokey **6** cooler, lockup, prison **7** confine, freezer, slammer **8** hoosegow, imprison, stockade **9** constrain **11** confinement, incarcerate

jailbird
3 con **5** felon, loser **7** convict **8** criminal, prisoner, repeater **10** recidivist

jailer
5 guard, screw **6** keeper, warden **7** turnkey **8** overseer

jakes
3 loo **5** privy **7** latrine **8** outhouse **9** backhouse

jalopy
3 car **4** auto, heap **5** crate, wreck **6** beater, junker **7** clunker, vehicle **10** automobile, rattletrap

jalousie
5 blind **6** window **7** shutter

jam
3 box, fix **4** bind, clog, cram, dunk, pack, push **5** block, crowd, crush, force, jelly, press, stuff, wedge **6** bruise, impede, plight, scrape, squash, squish **7** dilemma, squeeze **8** compress, conserve, obstacle, preserve **9** confiture, preserves **10** difficulty **11** predicament

Jamaica
capital: **8** Kingston
cay: **5** Pedro **6** Morant
city: **10** Montego Bay **11** Spanish Town
discoverer: **8** Columbus (Christopher)
location: **10** West Indies
mountain range: **4** Blue **10** Dry Harbour
sea: **9** Caribbean

Jamaican
export: **3** rum **5** sugar
hair style: **6** dreads **10** dreadlocks
music: **3** dub, ska **6** reggae
musician: **5** Cliff (Jimmy) **6** Marley (Bob, Ziggy) **7** Wailers
nationalist: **6** Garvey (Marcus)

jambalaya
4 olio **5** gumbo **6** medley **7** mélange, mixture **8** mishmash **10** hodgepodge, hotchpotch, salmagundi

jamboree
4 gala **5** revel **6** fiesta, frolic **7** carouse, shindig **8** carnival, festival, wingding **9** merriment **11** celebration **13** entertainment

James
brother: **4** John **5** Jesus, Joses
cousin: **5** Jesus
father: **7** Zebedee **8** Alphaeus
mother: **4** Mary **6** Salome

James novel
8 American (The) **9** Europeans (The) **10** Bostonians (The), Confidence, Golden Bowl (The), Tragic Muse (The) **11** Ambassadors (The), Daisy Miller **14** Turn of the Screw (The), Wings of the Dove (The) **15** Portrait of a Lady (The) **16** Washington Square

James, P. D.
detective: **9** Dalgliesh (Adam)
novel: **11** Original Sin **12** Mind to Murder (A)

James Bond
actor: **5** Craig (Daniel), Moore (Roger) **6** Dalton (Timothy) **7** Brosnan (Pierce), Connery (Sean), Lazenby (George)
author: **7** Fleming (Ian)
cocktail: **12** vodka martini
film: **4** Dr. No **9** GoldenEye, Moonraker, Octopussy **10** Goldfinger **11** Thunderball, View to a Kill (A) **12** Casino Royale **13** Die Another Day, License to Kill, Live and Let Die, Spy Who Loved Me (The) **15** For Your Eyes Only, Living Daylights (The) **16** World Is Not Enough (The), You Only Live Twice **17** Tomorrow Never Dies **18** Diamonds Are Forever, From Russia with Love **19** Man with the Golden Gun (The) **26** On Her Majesty's Secret Service
gun: **7** Beretta, Walther **8** Lilliput
novel: **4** Dr. No **9** Moonraker **10** Goldfinger **11** Thunderball **12** Casino Royale **13** Live and Let Die, Spy Who Loved Me (The) **15** For Your Eyes Only **16** You Only Live Twice **18** Diamonds Are Forever, From Russia with Love **19** Man with the Golden Gun (The) **26** On Her Majesty's Secret Service

secretary: **10** Moneypenny (Miss)
villain: **4** Drax (Sir Hugo), Dr. No, Khan (Kamal), King (Elektra) **5** Klebb (Rosa), Largo (Emilio), Mr. Big, Zorin **6** Carver (Elliot), Graves (Gustav), Renard **7** Blofeld (Ernst Stavro), Mr. White, Sanchez (Franz) **8** Gen. Orlov, Whitaker (Brad) **9** Dr. Kananga, Gen. Koskov, Kristados (Aristotle), Le Chiffre, Stromberg (Karl), Trevelyan (Alec) **10** Goldfinger (Auric), Scaramanga (Francisco)

Jammu and ___
7 Kashmir

Jane Eyre
author: **6** Brontë (Charlotte)
lover: **9** Rochester

jangle
3 jar **4** ring **5** babel, clash **6** clamor, excite, hubbub **7** discord, quarrel **8** conflict **11** discordance, discordancy **12** disharmonize

jangling
5 harsh, noisy, tense **7** grating **9** dissonant **10** discordant, quarreling

janitor
5 super **6** porter **7** cleaner **9** caretaker, concierge, custodian **10** doorkeeper

japan
4 coat **7** coating, varnish **11** lacquerware

Japan
5 Nihon **6** Nippon
capital: **3** Edo **5** Tokyo
city: **4** Kobe **5** Kyoto, Osaka, Otaru **6** Nagoya **7** Fukuoka, Okinawa, Sapporo **8** Kawasaki, Nagasaki, Yokohama **9** Hiroshima
island: **6** Honshu, Kyushu **7** Shikoku **8** Hokkaido
lake: **4** Biwa **8** Chuzenji
monetary unit: **3** yen
mountain: **4** Fuji **8** Fujiyama

Japanese
aborigine: **4** Ainu
art: **6** bonsai, ukiyo-e **7** origami
baron: **6** daimyo
battle cry: **6** banzai
Buddha: **5** Amida, Amita
business alliance: **8** keiretsu
cartoons: **5** anime
coin: **2** bu
comics: **5** manga
dancing girl: **6** geisha
dish: **4** miso, soba **5** gyoza, katsu, kombu, sushi **7** sashimi, tempura **8** sukiyaki, teriyaki
drama: **3** Noh **6** Bugaku, Kabuki **7** Bunraku
drink: **4** sake, saki
emperor: **6** Mikado **7** Akihito **8** Hirohito
fencing: **5** kendo
festival: **3** Bon
fish: **4** fugu
flower arrangement: **7** ikebana
garment: **6** kimono
gateway: **5** torii
god: **5** Ebisu, Hotei **7** Daikoku, Jurojin **8** Bishamon
goddess: **6** Benten **9** Amaterasu
governor: **6** shogun
grill: **7** hibachi
honorific: **3** san
immigrant: **5** issei
instrument: **4** biwa, koto **7** samisen **8** shamisen **10** shakuhachi
language: **4** Ainu
martial art: **4** judo **5** kendo **6** aikido, karate **7** jujitsu
martial artist: **5** ninja
mat: **6** tatami
measure: **2** bu, ri
money: **3** sen, yen
plum: **6** loquat
poem: **5** haiku, tanka
porcelain: **5** imari
pottery: **4** raku **7** satsuma
race: **4** Ainu
radish: **6** daikon
religion: **6** Shinto **8** Buddhism **9** Shintoism
rice wine: **4** sake, saki
robe: **6** kimono
samurai clan: **5** Taira **8** Minamoto
sash: **3** obi
song: **3** uta
suicide: **7** seppuku **8** hara-kiri, hari-kari, kamikaze
theater: **2** No **3** Noh **6** Bugaku, Kabuki **7** Bunraku
tidal wave: **7** tsunami
vehicle: **8** rickshaw
warrior: **7** samurai
warrior code: **7** bushido
weight: **2** mo
wrestling: **4** sumo
writing: **4** kana **5** kanji **8** hiragana, katakana
zither: **4** koto

Japanese-American
5 Issei, Nisei
second-generation: **6** Sansei

jape
3 gag, kid, rib **4** gibe, jest, jibe, joke, mock, quip **5** crack, laugh, prank, tease **7** waggery **8** drollery **9** wisecrack, witticism

Japheth
brother: **3** Ham **4** Shem
father: **4** Noah
son: **5** Gomer, Javan, Madai, Magog, Tiras, Tubal **7** Meshech

jar
4 bump, jolt, olla 5 cruse, quake, shake, shock, upset 6 jangle, jounce 7 tremble, vibrate 8 mismatch 9 container
ancient: 6 krater 7 amphora, canopic

jardiniere
5 stand 6 holder 7 garnish

jargon
4 cant 5 argot, idiom, lingo, slang 6 patois, pidgin 7 dialect, lexicon, palaver 8 language 9 gibberish 10 mumbo-jumbo, vernacular, vocabulary 11 terminology
lawyer's: 8 legalese
tinkers': 6 shelta

jarl
4 earl 5 noble 8 nobleman 12 Scandinavian

jarring
5 harsh, rough 6 hoarse, jangly 7 grating, rasping, raucous 8 strident 9 dissonant 10 discordant, unsettling

jasmine
3 tea 4 vine 5 shrub 6 flower, yellow 7 perfume

Jason
father: 5 Aeson
helper: 5 Medea
lover: 6 Creusa, Glauce, Glauke
quest: 6 Fleece 12 Golden Fleece
ship: 4 Argo
shipmate: 8 Argonaut
teacher: 6 Chiron 7 Cheiron
uncle: 6 Pelias
wife: 5 Medea

jasper
6 morlop, quartz 9 stoneware 10 chalcedony

jaundice
4 bias 7 disease, icterus 9 prejudice

jaundiced
6 biased, warped, yellow 7 colored, cynical, envious, hostile, jealous 9 distorted 10 suspicious

jaunt
4 ride, trip 5 drive, sally 6 junket, outing, ramble 7 journey 9 excursion

jaunty
4 airy, pert 5 fresh, light, peppy, perky 6 breezy, lively 7 buoyant 8 debonair 9 sprightly 10 nonchalant

java
6 coffee

Java
almond: 7 talisay
cotton: 5 kapok
jute: 5 kenaf
lake: 4 Ijen 5 Dieng, Kelut
plum: 5 jaman 6 jambul 7 jambool
strait: 4 Bali 5 Sunda
volcano: 4 Gede, Kawi, Lawu 5 Bromo, Kelut, Raung 7 Ciremai

Javanese
civet: 5 rasse
orchestra: 7 gamelan
tree: 4 upas

Javan squirrel
8 jelerang

javelin
5 lance, shaft, spear 7 assagai, assegai, harpoon

Javert's prey
7 Valjean (Jean)

jaw
3 gab, yak 4 chat, rail, talk 5 chops, clack, prate 6 babble, gabble 7 chatter, prattle 9 yakety-yak

jawbone
7 maxilla 8 arm-twist, mandible, persuade, talk into

jawbreaker
9 hard candy

jay
4 bird, blue, hick, rube 5 dandy 6 rustic 7 bumpkin, hayseed 9 chatterer, greenhorn

Jayhawker
9 guerrilla
State: 6 Kansas 8 Missouri

jazz
3 bop 4 guff, jive 5 bebop, swing 6 boogie 7 ragtime 8 malarkey, nonsense
group: 5 combo
term: 3 axe 4 blow, riff, scat, tune, vamp 5 bebop, chart, chops 6 bridge, groove, improv 7 changes 8 stop time 9 front line 10 broken time
up: 5 rouse 6 vivify 7 animate, enliven 9 stimulate

jazz musician
3 Ory (Kid) 4 Cole (Nat "King"), Getz (Stan), Hirt (Al), Monk (Thelonious), O'Day (Anita), Rich (Buddy), Shaw (Artie) 5 Baker (Chet), Basie (Count), Brown (Clifford), Corea (Chick), Davis (Miles), Evans (Bill, Gil), Hines (Earl "Fatha"), Jones (Hank), Krall (Diana), Krupa (Gene), McRae (Carmen), Roach (Max), Smith (Jimmy), Sun Ra, Tatum (Art), Tormé (Mel), Young (Lester) 6 Bechet (Sidney), Blakey (Art), Burton (Gary), Carter (Benny), Dorsey (Jimmy, Tommy), Farmer (Art), Garner (Erroll), Gordon (Dexter), Herman (Woody), Hodges (Johnny), Jordan (Louis), Kenton (Stan), Miller (Glenn), Mingus (Charles), Morton (Jelly Roll), Oliver (King), Parker (Charlie "Bird"), Pepper (Art), Powell (Bud), Puente (Tito), Silver (Horace), Waller (Fats) 7 Brubeck (Dave), Coleman (Ornette), Connick (Harry), Goodman (Benny), Hampton (Lionel), Hancock (Herbie),

Hawkins (Coleman), Holiday (Billie), Jarrett (Keith), Metheny (Pat), Rollins (Sonny), Rushing (Jimmy), Shorter (Wayne), Vaughan (Sarah), Webster (Ben) **8** Adderley (Cannonball), Calloway (Cab), Coltrane (John), Eldridge (Roy), Marsalis (Wynton), Mulligan (Gerry), Peterson (Oscar), Williams (Mary Lou) **9** Armstrong (Louis), Blanchard (Terence), Christian (Charlie), Ellington (Duke), Gillespie (Dizzy), Lunceford (Jimmie), Reinhardt (Django) **10** Fitzgerald (Ella), Montgomery (Wes), Washington (Dinah) **11** Beiderbecke (Bix)

jazzy
5 gaudy **6** brassy, flashy, glitzy, lively, rakish, sporty **7** raffish, splashy **8** animated, colorful, exciting, spirited **9** vivacious **10** flamboyant

jealous
5 green **7** envious **9** green-eyed, invidious, resentful **10** possessive

jeans brand
3 Lee **5** Levi's **8** Wrangler

jeer
4 gibe, jibe, mock **5** fleer, flout, scoff, scorn, sneer, taunt **6** deride, heckle, hector, insult **7** contemn, laugh at, mockery **8** derision, ridicule

Jeeves
creator: **9** Wodehouse (P. G.)
employer: **7** Wooster (Bertie)
position: **5** valet **6** butler

jeez
4 gosh, heck **5** golly, shoot **6** shucks **7** jeepers

jefe
4 boss, head, lord **5** chief, ruler **6** honcho, leader **9** chieftain, commander

Jefferson, Thomas
home: **10** Monticello
lover: **5** Sally (Hemings)
state: **8** Virginia

Jehoram
brother: **7** Ahaziah
father: **4** Ahab **11** Jehoshaphat
kingdom: **5** Judah
slayer: **4** Jehu
wife: **8** Athaliah

Jehoshaphat
father: **3** Asa **6** Ahilud, Nimshi, Paruah
father-in-law: **4** Ahab
son: **4** Jehu **7** Jehoram
wife: **8** Athaliah

Jehovah
3 God **6** Adonai, Elohim, Yahweh

Jehu
6 driver
father: **6** Hanani **11** Jehoshaphat
grandfather: **6** Nimshi
son: **8** Jehoahaz
victim: **5** Joram **7** Jehoram

jejune
4 dull, flat **5** banal, bland, empty, inane, silly, trite, vapid **7** insipid, puerile **8** lifeless **9** colorless **13** uninteresting

Jekyll's alter ego
4 Hyde (Mr.)

jell
3 set **4** form **6** cohere, gelate **7** congeal, thicken **8** coalesce **9** coagulate, take shape

jelly
3 set **4** mass **5** aspic **6** spread **7** congeal, thicken **9** coagulate

jellyfish
6 coward, medusa **7** doormat, medusan **8** medusoid, pushover, weakling **10** ctenophore **12** coelenterate, invertebrate, siphonophore

jennet
3 ass **5** hinny, horse **6** donkey

jenny
4 bird **6** donkey, female

jeopardize
4 risk **5** peril **6** chance, expose, hazard **7** imperil **8** endanger

jeopardy
4 risk **5** peril **6** danger, hazard, menace **8** exposure **9** liability **12** endangerment

jeremiad
6 lament, screed, tirade **7** lecture **8** diatribe, harangue **9** complaint, philippic **11** declamation, lamentation

Jeremiah's scribe
6 Baruch

Jericho's conqueror
6 Joshua

jerk
3 ass, lug, tic, tug **4** dolt, dope, fool, jolt, pull, push, snap, twit, yank **5** brute, creep, idiot, lurch, ninny, spasm, twist, wrest **6** bounce, nitwit, thrust, twitch, wrench **7** jackass **8** preserve **10** nincompoop

jerkin
6 jacket

jerky
4 meat **5** inane **6** abrupt, stupid, sudden **7** foolish, idiotic, jolting **8** saccadic **9** senseless

Jerome's Bible
7 Vulgate

jersey
3 cow **6** fabric **7** sweater **8** pullover

Jerusalem
4 Sion, Zion **5** Salem **8** Holy City

hill: **4** Sion, Zion **6** Moriah
mosque: **4** Omar **6** Al-Aqsa **13** Dome of the Rock
pool: **6** Siloam **8** Bethesda

Jerusalem artichoke
5 tuber **8** girasole **9** sunflower

Jerusalem thorn
9 horsebean

jess
5 strap

Jesse
daughter: **7** Abigail, Zeruiah
father: **4** Obed
grandfather: **4** Boaz
son: **4** Ozem **5** David, Eliab, Elihu **6** Raddai **7** Shammah **8** Abinadab, Nethanel
youngest son: **5** David

Jessica
father: **7** Shylock
husband: **7** Lorenzo

jest
3 fun, gag, kid, rag, rib **4** butt, game, gibe, jape, jeer, joke, josh, mock, quip, razz **5** crack, fleer, flout, humor, prank, scoff, sneer, spoof, sport, tease **6** banter, gaiety **7** mockery, waggery **8** derision, drollery, ridicule **9** merriment, wisecrack, witticism

jester
3 wag, wit **4** fool **5** actor, clown, comic, joker **7** buffoon **8** comedian, funnyman, humorist, jokester, quipster **9** prankster **11** entertainer

Jesuit
founder: **6** Loyola (Ignatius)
leader: **6** Xavier (St. Francis)

jet
4 coal, ebon, emit, gush, inky, Lear, rush, spew **5** black, ebony, plane, spout, spurt **6** engine, nozzle, squirt, stream, travel **7** current, jewelry **8** airplane **9** pitch-dark **10** pitch-black

Jethro
daughter: **8** Zipporah
son-in-law: **5** Moses

jetsam
7 flotsam **8** wreckage **9** driftwood

jet set
5 A-list, elite **9** beau monde, haut monde **10** glitterati

jettison
4 drop, dump, junk, omit **5** eject, forgo, scrap **6** reject, remove **7** deep-six, discard **8** disposal, get rid of, throw out **9** sacrifice, throw away

jetty
4 dock, ebon, inky, pier, quay **5** black, ebony, groin, wharf **7** project, seawall **9** pitch-dark **10** breakwater, pitch-black

Jew
6 Essene, Hebrew, Semite **7** Israeli, Judaist **9** Israelite

jewel
3 gem **4** rock **5** adorn, bijou, ideal, prize, stone **7** bearing **8** gemstone, ornament, treasure **9** embellish

jeweler
8 lapidary
famous: **7** Cartier (Jacques, Louis, Pierre), Fabergé (Carl), Lalique (René), Tiffany (Charles Lewis)

jewelry
5 bling **10** bijouterie, bling-bling
artificial: **5** glass, paste **6** strass **7** costume
piece: **3** pin **4** ring **6** brooch **7** earring **8** bracelet, cufflink, necklace, tieclasp **9** lavaliere
set: **6** parure

Jewish
bread: **5** matzo **6** matzoh
ceremony: **4** bris **8** havdalah **10** bar mitzvah, bas mitzvah, bat mitzvah
combining form: **5** Judeo **6** Judaeo
credo: **5** shema
doctrine: **6** Mishna **7** Mishnah
New Year: **12** Rosh Hashanah
organization: **8** Hadassah **9** B'nai B'rith
prayer: **7** kaddish, kiddush
prayer book: **6** siddur
sabbath: **8** Saturday
scripture: **5** Torah **6** Talmud
synagogue: **4** shul
teacher: **5** rabbi, rebbe **6** Hillel
village: **6** shtetl
(see also **Hebrew**)

Jezebel
4 slut **5** hussy, tramp, trull, wench **6** wanton **7** trollop **8** slattern, strumpet
father: **7** Ethbaal
home: **5** Sidon
husband: **4** Ahab
slayer: **4** Jehu
victim: **6** Naboth

jib
3 arm, shy **4** balk, boom, sail, stop **5** demur **6** refuse **9** stop short

jibe
5 agree, fit in, match, shift, tally **6** accord, concur, square **7** conform **8** dovetail **9** harmonize **10** correspond, go together **12** change course

jiffy
3 sec **4** snap, tick, wink **5** flash, hurry, shake, trice **6** minute, moment, second **7** instant **11** split second

jig
4 fish, game, hoax, hook, jerk, play, ploy, ruse,

sham, wile **5** catch, dance, feint, trick **6** device, gambit **7** gimmick **9** deception

jigger
4 jerk, mold, sail **5** alter, gismo, gizmo **6** device, dingus, doodad, gadget, widget **7** gimmick, machine, measure **9** doohickey, rearrange, shot glass, thingummy **10** manipulate

jiggle
4 jerk **5** shake **7** agitate **9** oscillate

jigsaw
3 cut **4** tool **6** puzzle **7** arrange, machine

jihad
3 war **6** strife **7** crusade, holy war **8** campaign, struggle

jilt
4 drop **5** ditch, leave **6** desert, reject **7** abandon, cast off, discard

jim-dandy
3 ace, gem, pip **4** A-one, lulu **5** doozy, great, ideal, nifty, peach, super, swell **6** doozie **7** perfect **8** knockout **9** excellent, first-rate, humdinger **11** outstanding

jimmy
3 bar, pry **4** open **5** crack, force, lever **7** crowbar **9** break open, force open

jimsonweed
6 datura **10** thorn apple

jingle
4 call, ring, song **5** clink, rhyme, sound, verse **6** tinkle

jingoistic
7 hawkish **11** belligerent **12** chauvinistic, militaristic **13** nationalistic

jinn
5 afrit, genie **6** afreet, spirit

jinx
3 hex **5** charm, curse, spell **6** plague, whammy **7** bad luck, evil eye **8** foredoom **10** affliction, misfortune

jitters
5 jumps, panic **6** nerves, shakes **7** anxiety, shivers, willies **9** whim-whams **11** nervousness, stage fright **13** heebie-jeebies

jittery
4 edgy **5** jumpy, nervy **6** goosey, spooky **7** anxious, fearful, fidgety, nervous, panicky **10** high-strung

jive
3 kid **4** fool, jazz, talk **5** dance, music, swing, tease **6** cajole, hot air, jargon

Joab
brother: **6** Asahel **7** Abishai
father: **7** Seraiah, Zeruiah
slayer: **7** Benaiah
uncle: **5** David
victim: **5** Abner, Amasa

Joan of Arc
birthplace: **7** Domremy
epithet: **7** Pucelle (La) **13** Maid of Orléans
king: **7** Charles (VII)
victory: **7** Orléans

Joan's husband
5 Darby

Joash
father: **4** Ahab **7** Ahaziah **8** Jehoahaz
son: **6** Gideon **7** Amaziah **8** Jeroboam
victim: **9** Zechariah

job
3 gig **4** duty, hire, item, post, role, spot, task, work **5** chore, stint, trade **6** effort, office **7** calling, posting, pursuit, robbery **8** business, function, position, vocation **9** situation **10** assignment, employment, engagement, livelihood, occupation, profession **11** undertaking

Job
daughter: **6** Keziah **7** Jemimah
father: **8** Issachar
friend: **6** Bildad, Zophar **7** Eliphaz

jobber
6 broker, dealer, seller, trader **8** merchant **10** contractor, wholesaler

job-safety agency
4 OSHA

job-training program
4 JTPA

Jocasta
daughter: **6** Ismene **8** Antigone
husband: **5** Laius **7** Oedipus
son: **7** Oedipus **8** Eteocles **9** Polynices **10** Polyneices

jock
5 pilot **7** athlete

jockey
4 play **5** rider, trick **7** beguile, exploit, finesse **8** maneuver **10** manipulate
famous: **5** Baeza (Braulio), Krone (Julie) **6** Arcaro (Eddie), Bailey (Jerry), Murphy (Isaac), Pincay (Laffit) **7** Cauthen (Steve), Cordero (Angel), Hartack (Bill), Longden (Johnny), Stevens (Gary) **8** McCarron (Chris), McHargue (Darrel), Turcotte (Ron) **9** Shoemaker (Willie)

jocular
5 comic, funny, jolly, merry, witty **6** jocose, jocund, jovial, lively **7** amusing, comical, jesting, playful **8** cheerful, humorous **9** facetious

jocularity
3 fun, wit **4** glee **5** humor, mirth **6** gaiety **7** jollity **8** hilarity **9** joviality, merriment **11** high spirits, playfulness

jocund
3 gay 5 happy, jolly, merry 6 elated, jovial, lively 7 festive, gleeful, playful 8 mirthful 12 lighthearted

joe
3 guy 4 dude, java 6 coffee, fellow

jog
3 dig, jab, run 4 lope, move, pace, poke, prod, push, ride, stir, trot 5 nudge, punch, rouse, shake 6 bounce, change, jounce, prompt, remind

joggle
4 join, trot 5 dowel, joint, notch, shake, tooth 6 jostle

john
2 WC 3 lav, loo 4 head 5 jacks, privy 6 toilet 7 latrine 8 bathroom, lavatory 11 water closet

John Hancock
9 autograph, signature

Johnson, Samuel
biographer: 7 Boswell (James)
work: 8 Rasselas 10 dictionary

John the Baptist
father: 9 Zacharias
mother: 9 Elisabeth

John the Evangelist
brother: 5 James
father: 7 Zebedee
mother: 6 Salome

joie de vivre
4 elan, zest 5 gusto 6 esprit 10 love of life

join
3 tie, wed 4 abut, ally, bind, bond, fuse, line, link, mate, yoke 5 affix, align, blend, marry, merge, piece, touch, unify, union, unite 6 attach, border, couple, engage, enlist, enroll, sign on, sign up, splice 7 combine, connect 8 compound, federate, side with 9 affiliate, associate, integrate 12 come together

joint
3 bar, ell, hip, tie 4 butt, crux, dive, knee, link, node, seam 5 ankle, elbow, hinge, nexus, union, wrist 6 common, mutual, public, shared, suture, united 7 hangout, knuckle, shiplap 8 abutment, combined, communal, conjunct, coupling, junction, juncture, shoulder 9 concerted, honky-tonk 10 collective, connection 11 cooperative 12 articulation
combining form: 5 arthr 6 arthro, condyl 7 condylo
disease: 9 arthritis 10 rheumatism

joist
4 beam 6 rafter, timber 7 support

joke
3 gag, kid, pun, rag, rib, yak 4 fool, jape, jest, josh, quip, razz 5 crack, humor, prank, sally 6 banter, corker, parody 7 mockery, sarcasm, waggery 8 drollery, one-liner 9 burlesque, wisecrack, witticism 11 monkeyshine
hilarious: 12 sidesplitter
stale: 8 chestnut

joker
3 guy, wag, wit 4 card, fool 5 catch, clown, comic, cutup 6 fellow, jester, kicker 7 proviso 8 comedian, humorist 9 condition 10 limitation 11 stipulation

jollity
3 fun 4 glee 5 cheer, mirth 6 gaiety, revels 7 revelry, whoopee 8 hilarity 9 festivity, jocundity, joviality, merriment 10 ebullience, jocularity 11 high spirits, merrymaking 12 cheerfulness, conviviality

jolly
3 fun, gay, kid 4 glad, jest, josh, very 5 humor, merry 6 banter, jocund, jovial, joyful, joyous 7 festive, gleeful, jocular, playful, roguish, waggish 8 cheerful, mirthful 9 convivial 10 frolicsome 12 lighthearted

Jolly Roger
4 flag 6 ensign
user: 6 pirate

jolt
3 hit, jar 4 blow, bump, jerk, shot, slug, stun 5 check, clash, crash, knock, lurch, shake, shock, upset 6 impact, jounce, rattle 7 disturb, shake up, startle 8 astonish, surprise 9 collision

Jonah
7 prophet
swallower: 4 fish 5 whale

Jonathan
brother: 7 Johanan
father: 4 Saul
friend: 5 David

Jones, John Paul
ship: 15 Bonhomme Richard
victim: 7 Serapis

Jones novel
11 Thin Red Line (The) 15 Some Came Running 18 From Here to Eternity

jongleur
4 bard 6 singer 7 juggler 8 minstrel 10 troubadour 11 entertainer

jonquil
8 daffodil 9 narcissus, perennial

Jonson play
7 Volpone 9 Alchemist (The) 15 Bartholomew Fair

Joplin creation
3 rag 7 ragtime 11 Entertainer (The) 12 Maple Leaf Rag

Joram
brother: 7 Ahaziah
father: 3 Toi 4 Ahab 11 Jehoshaphat
slayer: 4 Jehu
son: 7 Ahaziah

Jordan
capital: 5 Amman
city: 5 Irbid, Zarqa
gulf: 5 Aqaba
language: 6 Arabic
monarch: 7 Hussein 8 Abdullah
monetary unit: 5 dinar
mountain: 4 Ramm
neighbor: 4 Iraq 5 Syria 6 Israel 11 Saudi Arabia
sea: 4 Dead

jorum
3 cup, jug 6 vessel

Joseph
brother:
(see **Jacob** son)
buyer: 8 Potiphar
father: 5 Asaph, Jacob 9 Zacharias 10 Mattathias
mother: 6 Rachel
son: 5 Jesus 7 Ephraim 8 Manasseh
wife: 4 Mary 7 Asenath

josh
3 kid, rag, rib 4 jest, joke, razz 5 chaff, jolly, tease 6 banter

Joshua's victory
7 Jericho

Joshua tree
5 yucca

joss
4 idol 5 image

Jo's sister
3 Amy, Meg 4 Beth

jostle
3 jar, jog 4 bump, push 5 crowd, elbow, nudge, press, shove 7 agitate, collide, compete, contend, vie with 8 shoulder

jot
3 bit 4 atom, iota, note, whit 5 grain, minim, speck, write 6 tittle 7 smidgen 8 particle

joule component
3 erg

jounce
3 bob, jar, jog 4 bump, jolt 5 shake, shock, thump 6 impact

journal
3 log 4 blog 5 diary, organ 6 ledger, record 7 account, gazette, minutes 8 magazine, register 9 chronicle, newspaper 10 periodical

journalist
3 Bly (Nellie) 4 Dowd (Maureen), Drew (Elizabeth), King (Larry), Pyle (Ernie), Reed (John), Rose (Charlie), Will (George F.), Zahn (Paula) 5 Baker (Russell), Brown (George), Cooke (Alistair), Dunne (Finley Peter), Evans (Rowland), Hersh (Seymour), Novak (Robert), Rowan (Carl), Royko (Mike), Safer (Morley), Smith (Hedrick), Stahl (Lesley), Stone (I. F.), Szulc (Tad), White (William Allen), Wolfe (Tom) 6 Arnett (Peter), Bierce (Ambrose), Broder (David), Brokaw (Tom), Couric (Katie), Ephron (Nora), Koppel (Ted), Gibson (Charles), Kuralt (Charles), Lehrer (Jim), Moyers (Bill), Murrow (Edward R.), Osgood (Charles), Rather (Dan), Reston (James), Reuter (Paul Julius), Rivera (Geraldo), Runyon (Damon), Safire (William), Shirer (William L.), Thomas (Helen, Lowell), Zenger (John Peter) 7 Blitzer (Wolf), Bradlee (Benjamin), Breslin (Jimmy), Cousins (Norman), Greeley (Horace), Gunther (John), Huntley (Chet), Kempton (Murray), McGrory (Mary), Mencken (H. L.), Pearson (Drew), Royster (Vermont), Russert (Tim), Tarbell (Ida), Trillin (Calvin), Wallace (Chris, Mike), Walters (Barbara) 8 Amanpour (Christiane), Anderson (Jack, Terry), Atkinson (Brooks), Brinkley (David), Cronkite (Walter), Garrison (William Lloyd), Jennings (Peter), Lippmann (Walter), Pulitzer (Joseph), Salinger (Pierre), Sevareid (Eric), Steffens (Lincoln), Thompson (Dorothy, Hunter), Williams (Brian), Winchell (Walter), Woodward (Bob) 9 Bernstein (Carl), Donaldson (Sam), Frederick (Pauline), Salisbury (Harrison), Schieffer (Bob)

journey
3 hie 4 hike, roam, tour, trek, trip 5 jaunt, quest 6 cruise, junket, safari, travel, voyage 7 caravan, odyssey, proceed, travels 8 progress 9 excursion 10 expedition, pilgrimage
route: 9 itinerary
stage: 3 leg

joust
4 duel, feud, spar, tilt 5 clash, fight 6 combat 7 contest 8 conflict 10 tournament
arena: 5 lists 8 tiltyard

Jove
see **Jupiter**

jovial
5 happy, jolly, merry 6 cheery 7 amiable 8 cheerful 9 convivial 11 good-humored, good-natured

jowl
3 jaw 5 cheek 6 dewlap, wattle 8 mandible

joy
4 glee 5 bliss, mirth 6 gaiety 7 delight, elation 8 felicity, fruition, gladness, pleasure 9 enjoyment, happiness, merriment 11 delectation

Joyce, James
birthplace: 6 Dublin

character: 5 Bloom (Leopold), Bloom (Molly) 7 Dedalus (Stephen)
work: 6 Exiles 7 Ulysses 9 Dubliners 13 Finnegans Wake

joyful
3 gay 4 glad 5 happy, jolly, merry 6 elated, jocund 7 buoyant, gleeful, pleased 8 ecstatic, jubilant, mirthful 9 delighted, rapturous 12 lighthearted

jubilant
5 happy 6 elated, joyful, joyous 8 euphoric, exultant, exulting 9 cock-a-hoop, delighted, overjoyed, triumphal 10 triumphant

jubilate
5 exult, glory 7 delight, rejoice 9 celebrate

jubilation
3 joy 4 glee 7 ecstasy, rapture 8 euphoria, rhapsody 9 rejoicing, transport 10 exaltation, exultation, joyfulness, joyousness 11 celebration 12 exhilaration

jubilee
6 flambé 8 festival 9 festivity 10 indulgence 11 anniversary, celebration 13 commemoration

Judah
brother:
(see **Jacob** son)
father: 5 Jacob
king: 3 Asa 4 Ahaz, Amon 5 Joash 6 Abijam, Josiah, Jotham, Uzziah 7 Ahaziah, Amaziah, Jehoram 8 Hezekiah, Jehoahaz, Manasseh, Rehoboam, Zedekiah 9 Jehoiakim 10 Jehoiachin 11 Jehoshaphat
mother: 4 Leah
son: 4 Onan 6 Shelah

Judas
7 traitor 8 informer, turncoat
father: 5 Simon 7 Chalphi 10 Mattathias
replacement: 8 Matthias
suicide place: 8 Aceldama, Akeldama

judge
3 ref, try, ump 4 call, deem, rate, rule, test 5 infer 6 critic, decide, deduce, jurist, reckon, settle, umpire 7 arbiter, justice, mediate, referee 8 assessor, critique, estimate, mediator 9 arbitrate, criticize, determine, moderator 10 adjudicate, arbitrator, chancellor, magistrate, negotiator 11 conciliator 12 intermediary
bench: 4 banc
chamber: 6 camera
in Hades: 5 Minos 6 Aeacus 12 Rhadamanthus
mallet: 5 gavel
Muslim: 4 cadi, qadi 5 mufti

judgment
5 award, dicta (plural), sense 6 acumen, decree, dictum, ruling, result, wisdom 7 finding, insight, opinion, verdict 8 decision, sagacity, sentence 9 appraisal, deduction, good sense, inference 10 assessment, conclusion, discretion, estimation, evaluation, horse sense, punishment 11 common sense, discernment 13 determination

judgmental
7 carping 8 captious, critical 10 belittling, censorious, derogatory 11 disparaging, reproachful 12 disapproving, faultfinding 13 hypercritical

Judgment Day
8 doomsday

____ judicata
3 res

judicial
assembly: 5 court
document: 4 writ
order: 10 injunction

judicious
3 apt 4 fair, just, sage, sane, wise 5 right, sound 6 astute 7 careful, prudent, sapient 8 accurate, discreet, rational, sensible 9 equitable, objective, sagacious 10 discerning, reasonable

Judith
father: 5 Beeri
home: 8 Bethulia
husband: 4 Esau
victim: 10 Holofernes

judo
10 martial art
school: 4 dojo
teacher: 6 sensei

Judy's husband
5 Punch

jug
3 jar, pen 4 coop, ewer, gaol, jail, olla, olpe, stew, stir, toby 5 clink, pokey 6 cooler, flagon, immure, intern, lockup, prison, vessel 7 confine, pitcher, slammer 8 demijohn, imprison 9 constrain, container 11 incarcerate

jug-band instrument
5 kazoo 6 bottle 7 washtub 9 stovepipe, washboard

juggernaut
11 steamroller

juggle
3 fix 4 fool, toss 5 bluff, trick 6 change, delude, doctor, handle, humbug, take in 7 balance, beguile, deceive, mislead, shuffle 9 rearrange 10 manipulate

juice
3 sap 4 fuel, must 5 fluid 7 current, essence 8 vitality 10 succulence 11 electricity
fermented: 4 wine 5 cider, perry

juicy
4 racy 5 lusty 7 piquant 8 dripping 9 succulent 10 profitable 11 sensational

juju
4 luck **5** charm, magic **6** amulet, fetish, grigri, mascot **8** gris-gris, talisman **10** lucky charm

jujube
4 tree **5** fruit **7** gumdrop, lozenge

julep
5 drink

Juliet
betrothed: 5 Paris
father: 7 Capulet
lover: 5 Romeo

July 14
11 Bastille Day

jumble
3 mix **4** cake, hash, mess, olio **5** chaos, mix up, shake **6** cookie, medley, mess up, muddle, muss up **7** clutter, confuse, disturb, mélange, rummage, shuffle **8** disarray, disorder, mish-mash, pastiche, scramble **9** confusion, patch-work, potpourri **10** assortment, hodgepodge, hotchpotch, miscellany

jumbo
4 huge, vast **5** giant **6** mighty **7** immense, mammoth, massive **8** colossal, enormous, gigantic, oversize **9** humongous, oversized **10** prodigious **11** elephantine

jump
3 hop **4** bolt, hike, leap, move, trip **5** avoid, begin, boost, bound, clear, flush, hurry, leave, put up, raise, shift, start, vault **6** attack, bounce, bustle, change, hurdle, hustle, jack up, pounce, spring **7** bail out, elevate, startle **8** increase, leap over

jumper
4 sled **5** dress, horse, smock **6** blouse, jacket

jumping-frog county
9 Calaveras

jumpy
4 edgy **6** on edge **7** anxious, jittery, nervous **9** excitable **10** high-strung

junction
4 seam **5** joint, union **7** joining, meeting **8** coupling **9** interface **10** confluence, connection, crossroads **12** intersection

juncture
4 seam **5** joint, point, union **6** crisis, moment **7** instant, joining **8** coupling **10** connection, crossroads **11** concurrence, convergence **12** turning point

jungle
3 web, zoo **4** hash, mash, maze **5** selva, snarl **6** jumble, morass, muddle, tangle **7** clutter, thicket **8** mishmash **9** labyrinth

Jungle Books, The
author: 7 Kipling (Rudyard)
bear: 5 Baloo
boy: 6 Mowgli
panther: 8 Bagheera
python: 3 Kaa
tiger: 9 Shere Khan
wolf: 5 Akela

Jungle, The
author: 8 Sinclair (Upton)
locale: 7 Chicago **10** stockyards

junior
3 son **5** lower, minor, sonny, youth **6** lesser **7** student, younger **8** inferior, young man, youthful **9** secondary, youngster **11** subordinate

juniper
4 cade, cone **5** cedar, fruit, savin, shrub **7** conifer **9** evergreen

junk
4 boat, dope, drug, ship **5** scrap, trash, waste **6** debris, heroin, litter, refuse, reject **7** cashier, clutter, discard, rubbish, rummage **8** get rid of, jettison, throw out **9** narcotics, throw away
e-mail: 4 spam

junker
4 heap **5** crate, wreck **6** beater, jalopy **10** rattletrap, rust bucket

junket
4 trip **5** feast, jaunt, spree **6** outing, picnic **7** banquet, dessert, journey **9** excursion

junk mail
4 spam

Juno
bird: 7 peacock
epithet: 6 Moneta
Greek equivalent: 4 Hera
husband: 7 Jupiter
(see also **Hera**)

Junoesque
7 stately **10** curvaceous, statuesque

junta
5 cabal, group **7** council, faction **9** committee

Jupiter
4 Jove, Zeus
angel: 7 Zadkiel
cupbearer: 8 Ganymede
daughter: 5 Venus **7** Minerva
epithet: 6 Fidius, Fulgur, Stator, Tonans **7** Pluvius
father: 6 Saturn
lover: 6 Europa **8** Callisto
mother: 3 Ops
satellite: 6 Europa **8** Callisto, Ganymede
son: 5 Arcas **6** Castor, Pollux
temple: 7 Capitol
wife: 4 Juno

juridical
5 legal **6** lawful **8** juristic **10** legalistic

jurisdiction
3 law, see **4** sway, zone **5** might, orbit, power, range, reach, scope, venue **6** county, domain, parish, sphere **7** circuit, command, compass, control, diocese, mastery, purview **8** dominion, hegemony, province **9** authority, bailiwick, territory **10** domination **11** supervision

jurisprudence
3 law

jurist
5 judge

jury
5 panel
decision: **7** verdict

jury-rigged
6 make-do **7** stopgap **9** makeshift, temporary **10** improvised

just
3 apt, due, fit **4** even, fair, good, meet, only, true **5** equal, legal, right **6** barely, hardly, honest, lawful, proper, simply, square **7** correct, ethical, exactly, fitting, merited, precise, upright **8** accurate, deserved, rightful, suitable, unbiased **9** equitable, honorable, impartial, objective, requisite, righteous **10** legitimate, reasonable, scrupulous **11** appropriate, well-founded **12** unprejudiced

justice
3 law **5** court, judge, right **6** equity **7** honesty **8** evenness, fairness, fair play **10** lawfulness, magistrate **11** correctness **12** impartiality

justification
6 excuse, reason **7** account, apology, defense, grounds **8** apologia **9** rationale **10** validation **11** explanation, vindication

justify
5 argue, claim, prove **6** assert, defend, uphold, verify **7** account, bear out, confirm, contend, explain, support, warrant **8** maintain, make even, validate **9** vindicate **10** legitimate, legitimize **11** corroborate, rationalize **12** authenticate, legitimatize, substantiate

jut
4 hang, poke **5** bulge, pouch **6** beetle, thrust **7** project **8** extend up, overhang, protrude, stand out, stick out **9** extend out, extension **10** projection, protrusion **12** protuberance

jute
5 gunny **6** burlap **7** hessian, sacking

Juvenal
4 poet **5** Roman
forte: **6** satire

juvenile
3 kid **5** actor, child, green, young, youth **6** callow, jejune, junior, moppet **7** preteen, puerile **8** childish, immature, youthful **9** childlike, fledgling, unfledged, youngling, youngster **11** undeveloped

juvenility
5 youth **9** childhood, greenness **10** immaturity, springtide, springtime **12** youthfulness

juxtaposed
4 next **8** abutting, adjacent, neighbor, proximal, touching **9** adjoining, bordering **10** appositive, contiguous, side-by-side **11** coterminous, neighboring **12** conterminous

K

kabob
see **kebab**
kachina
4 doll **6** spirit **12** impersonator
kaddish
6 prayer
Kafka, Franz
character: **4** Olga **6** Gregor (Samsa), Joseph (K.)
novel: **5** Trial (The) **6** Castle (The) **7** Amerika
story: **8** Judgment (The) **12** Hunger Artist (A) **13** Metamorphosis (The)
kaiser
5 ruler **7** emperor, monarch **8** autocrat **9** sovereign
kaka
6 parrot
kale
4 cash, cole **5** bucks, lucre, money, moola **6** moolah **7** cabbage **8** Brassica, colewort
kaleidoscopic
8 changing, colorful **10** variegated
Kali
aspect: **5** Durga **7** Parvati
husband: **4** Siva **5** Shiva
Kama
god of: **4** love
mount: **6** parrot **7** sparrow
wife: **4** Rati
Kama ___
5 Sutra
kamikaze
7 suicide **8** suicidal
kampong
6 hamlet **7** village
Kampuchea
see **Cambodia**
kangaroo
6 hopper, leaper **7** wallaby **8** wallaroo **9** marsupial
herd: **3** mob
young: **4** joey
Kansas
capital: **6** Topeka
city: **4** Iola **6** Olathe, Salina **7** Abilene, Emporia, Shawnee, Wichita **8** Lawrence
nickname: **9** Jayhawker (State), Sunflower (State)
prison: **11** Leavenworth
river: **8** Arkansas
state bird: **10** meadowlark
state flower: **9** sunflower
state tree: **10** cottonwood
kaolin
4 clay
kaput
5 spent **6** ruined **7** done for, useless **8** defeated, finished, outmoded **9** destroyed
karakul
5 sheep **9** broadtail
karate
level: **4** belt
school: **4** dojo
teacher: **6** sensei
karma
4 fate **7** destiny **9** emanation
kaross
3 rug **7** garment
kasha
5 grain **8** porridge **9** buckwheat
Katharina
father: **8** Baptista
suitor: **9** Petruchio
Katrina's suitor
9 Brom Bones **12** Ichabod Crane
katydid
3 bug **6** insect **11** grasshopper
katzenjammer
3 din **5** hoo-ha, noise **6** clamor, hoo-hah, hubbub, racket, rumpus **8** brouhaha, distress, foofaraw, hangover, headache **9** commotion
kava
5 shrub **6** pepper **8** beverage
kayo
6 defeat, finish **8** knockout **9** finish off **11** coup de grace
Kazakhstan
capital: **6** Akmola, Astana
city: **5** Semey **8** Pavlodar, Shymkent
lake: **6** Tengiz **8** Balkhash
language: **6** Kazakh **7** Russian
monetary unit: **5** tenge

mountain: **10** Khan-Tengri
neighbor: **5** China **6** Russia **10** Kyrgyzstan, Uzbekistan **12** Turkmenistan
river: **4** Ural **6** Irtysh **8** Syr Dar'ya
sea: **4** Aral **7** Caspian

Kazantzakis hero
5 Zorba (Alexis)

kea
6 parrot

Keats poem
5 Lamia **8** Endymion, Hyperion, Isabella, To Autumn **11** Ode to Psyche **12** Eve of St. Agnes (The) **16** Ode on a Grecian Urn **17** Ode to a Nightingale

kebab
8 shashlik

kedge
6 anchor

keel
4 boat, lean, ship **5** barge, pitch, ridge, slump **6** carina **7** capsize **8** overturn **11** centerboard

keen
4 avid, fine, wail, yowl **5** acute, alert, eager, honed, mourn, neato, nifty, sharp, smart, super **6** ardent, astute, bewail, bright, clever, gung ho, intent, lament, peachy, shrewd **7** anxious, fervent, intense, whetted, zealous **8** animated, spirited **9** fine-edged, impatient, sensitive, wonderful **10** perceptive, razor-sharp **11** lamentation, penetrating, quick-witted, sharp-witted **12** enthusiastic, sharp-sighted

keenness
3 wit **4** edge, zeal **6** acuity, acumen **10** enthusiasm **11** discernment, penetration **12** incisiveness, perspicacity

keep
3 own **4** hold, jail, mind, obey, save, stay, stet, tend **5** lodge, stock **6** castle, comply, detain, living, lockup, manage, prison, retain **7** abstain, conduct, confine, forbear, fulfill, possess, refrain, reserve **8** conserve, fortress, maintain, preserve, withhold **9** constrain **10** livelihood, sustenance **11** maintenance, subsistence

keep back
3 bar, dam **4** curb, hold, save, stay **6** detain, retain, retard, stifle **7** contain, inhibit, repress, reserve **8** restrain, restrict, suppress, withhold

keeper
5 guard **6** warden **7** big fish, curator **8** Cerberus, guardian, watchdog **9** custodian, protector

keeping
4 care, ward **5** aegis, trust **6** charge **7** custody, support **8** wardship **9** provision **10** caretaking, conformity, observance **11** maintenance **12** conservation, guardianship

keep on
4 last **5** abide **6** endure **7** persist **8** continue **9** hang tough, persevere

keep out
3 ban, bar **4** hold, stop **5** block, check, debar **6** forbid **7** embargo, exclude **8** prohibit, turn back **9** blackball

keepsake
5 token **6** trophy **7** memento **8** memorial, reminder, souvenir **11** remembrance

keep up
7 persist, prolong, sustain **8** continue, maintain, preserve **9** persevere

kef
3 pot **4** hash, hemp **5** grass **7** hashish **9** marijuana **10** dreaminess **12** tranquillity

keg
3 tun **4** butt, cask, pipe **6** barrel, firkin, vessel **8** hogshead **9** container

kegler
6 bowler

keister
3 bum, end **4** buns, butt, duff, rear, rump, seat, tail, tush **5** fanny **6** behind, bottom, heinie **8** backside, buttocks, derriere **9** posterior

keloid
4 scar

kelp
4 alga **7** seaweed

kelpie
3 dog **5** naiad, nixie **6** sprite

Kemo Sabe
10 Lone Ranger

ken
4 view **5** grasp, range, reach, scope, sight **7** horizon, purview **9** knowledge **10** perception **13** comprehension, understanding

kenaf
5 fiber **8** hibiscus

Kenilworth author
5 Scott (Walter)

Kennedy novel
8 Ironweed

kennel
4 pack **5** board **6** gutter **7** shelter **9** enclosure

keno
4 game
similar to: **5** beano, bingo, lotto

Kentucky
capital: **9** Frankfort
city: **9** Lexington **10** Louisville **12** Bowling Green
nickname: **9** Bluegrass (State)
park: **11** Mammoth Cave
racecourse: **14** Churchill Downs

river: **4** Ohio
state bird: **8** cardinal
state flower: **9** goldenrod
state tree: **11** tulip poplar

Kentucky bluegrass
3 Poa

Kenya
capital: **7** Nairobi
city: **6** Kisumu, Nakuru **7** Mombasa
lake: **7** Turkana **8** Victoria
monetary unit: **8** shilling
mountain: **5** Elgon, Kenya
neighbor: **5** Sudan **6** Uganda **7** Somalia **8** Ethiopia, Tanzania
river: **4** Tana

kepi
3 cap

kerchief
6 hankie **7** bandana **8** babushka, bandanna, kaffiyeh
Scottish: **5** curch

kerf
3 cut **4** nick, slit **5** cleft, notch **6** groove

kerfuffle
3 ado, row **4** flap, fuss, stir, to-do **5** hoo-ha **6** dust-up, hoo-hah, ruckus, rumpus **7** turmoil **8** foofaraw **9** commotion **11** disturbance

kermis
4 fair **8** carnival, festival

kernel
3 nub, nut **4** core, crux, gist, meat, pith, seed **5** grain **6** nubbin, upshot **7** essence, nucleus **9** substance

Kerouac novel
6 Big Sur **9** On the Road **10** Dharma Bums (The) **13** Subterraneans (The)

Kesey novel
21 Sometimes a Great Notion **25** One Flew over the Cuckoo's Nest

kestrel
4 bird, hawk **6** falcon **9** windhover

ketch
4 boat **6** vessel **8** sailboat **10** watercraft

ketone
7 acetone, camphor

kettle
3 pot **6** hollow, vessel **7** caldron, marmite, pothole **8** cauldron
handle: **4** bail

kettledrum
5 naker **7** timpani (plural), timpano
Moorish: **6** atabal

key
4 clue, isle, reef **5** basic, islet, vital **6** cotter, island, legend, master, opener, samara, spline, ticket, tip-off **7** central, crucial, digital, pivotal **8** critical, password, solution, tonality **9** essential, important **10** open sesame **11** fundamental
combining form: **5** clavi, clavo
notch: **4** ward
type: **8** skeleton

keyboard
6 manual **7** clavier

key fruit
6 samara

Key Largo
director: **6** Huston (John)
star: **6** Bacall (Lauren), Bogart (Humphrey)

key man
5 chief **7** kingpin **9** locksmith

keynote
4 core, crux, gist, pith, tone **5** theme, tonic

keynoter
6 orator **7** speaker

Keystone Kops director
7 Sennett (Max)

Keystone State
12 Pennsylvania

khaki
3 tan **5** brown, cloth, color **7** garment, uniform

khamsin
4 wind

khan
5 chief, ruler **9** chieftain, sovereign **11** caravansary

khedive
5 ruler **7** viceroy

Khomeini
4 imam **9** ayatollah

Ki
mother: **5** Nammu
son: **5** Enlil

kiang
3 ass

kibble
4 meal **5** grain, grind **9** pulverize

kibbutz
4 co-op, farm **7** commune **10** collective, settlement **11** cooperative

kibe
4 heel, sore **8** swelling **9** chilblain

kibitz
4 chat **6** banter, butt in, meddle **7** comment, intrude, obtrude **9** interfere

kibitzer
7 meddler **8** busybody, observer **9** buttinsky, spectator **10** rubberneck

kibosh
3 hex **4** jinx, stop **5** check, curse

kick
4 bang, boot, punt 6 recoil, thrill, wallop
kicker
5 catch 6 clause, punter 9 condition, fine print
kick in
3 die, pay 4 give 5 begin, put up, start 6 donate, pony up 7 cough up, fork out 8 fork over, hand over 10 contribute
kick off
3 die 4 open 5 begin, croak, start 6 launch 8 commence, drop dead, embark on, initiate 10 inaugurate
kick out
2 ax 3 axe, can 4 fire, oust, sack 5 eject, evict, expel 6 bounce 7 cashier, dismiss 9 discharge
kickshaw
5 curio, goody, treat 6 bauble, dainty, gewgaw, morsel, tidbit, trifle 7 bibelot, trinket 8 delicacy 9 bagatelle
kid
3 guy, rag, rib 4 dupe, fool, gull, hoax, jest, joke, josh, razz 5 bairn, child, jolly, trick, youth 6 banter, befool, moppet, nipper 7 deceive, younger 8 flimflam, hoodwink, juvenile 9 bamboozle, youngling, youngster
kidnap
6 abduct, snatch 8 shanghai
kidney
3 ilk 4 kind, sort, type 5 gland, organ
combining form: 4 reni, reno 5 nephr 6 nephro
kidney-shaped
8 reniform
delicacy: 6 cashew
kielbasa
7 sausage
kilderkin
3 keg 4 cask 6 barrel
kilim
3 mat, rug 6 carpet
kill
2 ax 3 axe, end, ice, nix, off, zap 4 do in, prey, slay, stop, veto 5 creek, croak, erase, quash, scrag, snuff, waste 6 defeat, delete, finish, murder, quarry, stifle 7 bump off, butcher, channel, destroy, execute 8 blow away, carry off, dispatch, knock off, massacre 9 sacrifice, slaughter 10 annihilate 11 assassinate, exterminate
killer
5 bravo 6 gunman, hit man 7 butcher, torpedo 8 assassin, homicide
combining form: 4 cide
Killer Angels author
6 Shaara (Michael)
killer whale
4 orca 8 cetacean
killing
5 blood, fatal 6 deadly, lethal, mortal, murder 7 carnage 8 butchery, foul play, homicide 9 bloodbath, bloodshed, slaughter 12 manslaughter
of a race: 8 genocide
of bacteria: 11 bactericide
of a brother: 10 fratricide
of a father: 9 patricide
of a king: 8 regicide
of a mother: 9 matricide
of a relative: 9 parricide
of a sister: 10 sororicide
of oneself: 7 suicide
of plants: 9 herbicide
killjoy
6 downer, grinch, grouch 7 spoiler 8 doomster, sourpuss 9 Cassandra, defeatist, doomsayer, gloomy Gus, pessimist, worrywart 10 spoilsport, wet blanket
Kilmer poem
5 Trees
kiln
4 oast, oven 7 furnace
kilt
5 skirt
accessory: 7 sporran
fabric: 5 plaid 6 tartan
kilter
4 trim 5 order, shape 6 fettle, repair 7 fitness 9 condition
kimono
4 gown, robe
sash: 3 obi
kin
3 sib 4 clan, folk, sept 5 blood, flesh, house, stock, tribe 6 family 7 lineage, related 8 relation, relative
kind
3 ilk 4 good, like, sort, type, warm 5 breed, class, genre 6 benign, gentle, humane, loving, nature, stripe, tender 7 affable, amiable, clement, essence, feather, lenient, quality, species, variety 8 category, merciful, tolerant 9 character 10 altruistic, benevolent, charitable, forbearing, responsive 11 considerate, good-hearted, good-humored, good-natured, openhearted, softhearted, sympathetic, warmhearted
kindle
4 bear, fire, stir, wake, whet 5 light, rally, rouse, spark, start, waken 6 arouse, awaken, bestir, excite, foment, ignite, incite 7 inflame, provoke 8 activate 9 galvanize, instigate, stimulate 10 illuminate
kindliness
8 goodwill, sympathy 9 affection 10 solicitude 11 benevolence

kindly
6 benign, gentle **7** benefic **8** friendly, generous, gracious, pleasant **9** agreeable, benignant **10** beneficent, beneficial **11** considerate, goodhearted, sympathetic

kindness
5 favor, mercy **7** service **8** clemency, courtesy, goodwill, sympathy **10** compassion, generosity, indulgence **11** benevolence **13** consideration

kind of
5 quite **6** fairly, pretty, rather **8** passably, somewhat **9** tolerably **10** more or less, reasonably, relatively

kindred
3 sib **4** clan, folk, like, sept **5** alike, blood, flesh, house, stock, tribe **6** agnate, allied, family **7** cognate, connate, lineage, related, similar **9** relatives **10** affiliated, connatural **11** consanguine

king
3 rex **4** czar, tsar, tzar **5** mogul, ruler **6** tycoon **7** magnate, monarch **9** sovereign
Albanian: **3** Zog **7** William
Assyrian: **6** Sargon **11** Sennacherib, Shalmaneser
Babylonian: **6** Sargon **9** Hammurabi **10** Belshazzar
Belgian: **6** Albert **7** Leopold **8** Baudouin
Bohemian: **9** Wenceslas **10** Wenceslaus
Bulgarian: **5** Boris **6** Simeon
Damascus: **8** Benhadad
Danish: **4** Abel, Eric, Gorm, Hans, John, Olaf **5** Sweyn **6** Canute, Harold, Magnus **8** Nicholas, Waldemar **9** Christian, Frederick **11** Christopher
Dutch: **7** William
Egyptian: **3** Tut **4** Pepi, Seti **5** Khufu, Menes, Necho **6** Cheops, Ramses **7** Harmhab, Osorkon, Psamtik, Ptolemy **8** Ikhnaton, Thothmes, Thutmose **9** Amenhotep, Sesostris **11** Tutankhamen
English: **4** John **5** Henry, James **6** Alfred, Canute, Edmund, Edward, Egbert, George, Harold **7** Charles, Richard, Stephen, William **8** Ethelred **9** Athelstan, Ethelbald, Ethelbert
French: **3** Odo, roi **4** Jean, John **5** Henri, Henry, Louis, Pepin, Raoul **6** Philip, Robert, Rudolf **7** Charles, Francis, Lothair **8** François **9** Hugh Capet **11** Charlemagne
German: **4** Carl, Karl **5** König, Louis **6** Lothar, Ludwig **7** Charles, Lothair
Greek (modern): **4** Paul **6** George **9** Alexander **11** Constantine
Hawaiian: **10** Kamehameha
Hungarian: **6** Attila
Indian: **4** raja **5** rajah
Irish: **9** Brian Boru
Italian: **7** Humbert, Umberto
Jordanian: **5** Talal **7** Hussein **8** Abdullah
Judah:
(see at **Judah**)
Judean: **5** Herod
legendary: **3** Lud **4** Atli, Cole
Lydian: **5** Gyges **7** Croesus **8** Alyattes
Norwegian: **4** Eric, Erik, Inge, Olaf **5** Sweyn **6** Haakon, Harald, Harold, Magnus, Sigurd, Sverre
Ostrogothic: **9** Theodoric
Persian: **5** Cyrus **6** Darius, Xerxes
Portuguese: **4** John **5** Henry, Louis, Peter **6** Carlos, Edward, Manuel, Sancho **7** Alfonso **9** Ferdinand, Sebastian
Prussian: **7** Wilhelm, William **9** Frederick, Friedrich
relating to: **5** regal, royal
Saudi Arabian: **4** Saud **6** Faisal **9** Abdul-Aziz
Scottish: **4** John **5** David, Edgar, James **6** Duncan **7** Macbeth, Malcolm, William **9** Alexander, Donalbane **10** David Bruce **11** Robert Bruce
Spanish: **3** rey **5** Louis **6** Philip **7** Alfonso, Amadeus, Charles **9** Ferdinand **10** Juan Carlos
Spartan: **8** Leonidas
Swedish: **4** Eric, John **5** Oscar **6** Birger, Gustav, Haakon, Magnus **7** Charles **8** Gustavus, Waldemar **9** Frederick, Sigismund, Sten Sture
Visigothic: **6** Alaric

King Arthur
birthplace: **8** Tintagel
chronicler: **8** Geoffrey (of Monmouth)
court site: **7** Camelot **8** Caerleon
deathplace: **6** Camlan
father: **5** Uther
father-in-law: **9** Laodogant, Leodegran **11** Leodegrance
foster father: **5** Ector
jester: **7** Dagonet
knight: **3** Kay **4** Bors **5** Balan, Balin **6** Gareth, Gawain, Modred **7** Galahad, Geraint, Lamerok, Mordred, Tristan **8** Bedivere, Lancelot, Parsifal, Percival, Tristram **9** Launcelot
lance: **3** Ron
last abode: **6** Avalon
last name: **9** Pendragon
magician: **6** Merlin
mother: **6** Ygerne **7** Igraine
nephew: **6** Gareth, Modred **7** Mordred
queen: **9** Guinevere
shield: **7** Pridwin
sister: **7** Morgain **11** Morgan le Fay
slayer: **6** Modred **7** Mordred
son: **6** Modred **7** Mordred
steward: **3** Kay
sword: **9** Excalibur
victim: **6** Modred **7** Mordred
wife: **9** Guinevere

king crab
7 limulus

kingdom
5 realm **6** domain, empire **7** demesne **8** monarchy

kingdom come
4 Zion **6** heaven **8** paradise **9** hereafter **10** afterworld

kingfish
4 boss **6** bigwig, honcho, master **7** big shot, croaker **8** mackerel

kingfisher
7 halcyon **10** kookaburra

King Kong
character: **4** Dwan **6** Darrow (Ann), Denham (Carl), Wilson (Fred) **8** Driscoll (Jack), Prescott (Jack)
director: **6** Cooper (Merian C.) **7** Jackson (Peter) **10** Guillermin (John)
home: **11** Skull Island
star: **4** Wray (Fay) **5** Black (Jack), Brody (Adrien), Cabot (Bruce), Lange (Jessica), Watts (Naomi) **6** Grodin (Charles) **7** Bridges (Jeff) **9** Armstrong (Robert)

King Lear
actor: **3** Cox (Brian) **4** Holm (Ian) **5** Booth (Edwin), Jones (James Earl), Magee (Patrick) **7** Burbage (Richard), Garrick (David), Gielgud (John), Olivier (Laurence) **8** Scofield (Paul)
author: **11** Shakespeare (William)
daughter: **5** Regan **7** Goneril **8** Cordelia
servant: **6** Oswald
son: **5** Edgar **6** Edmund

kingly
5 regal, royal **6** august, lordly, regnal **7** exalted **8** imperial, majestic **9** imperious, masterful, monarchal, sovereign **10** monarchial **11** monarchical

King novel
6 Carrie **7** Shining (The) **8** Dead Zone (The) **9** Dark Tower (The), Green Mile (The), Salem's Lot **11** Firestarter, Pet Sematary

King Philip
9 Metacomet

kingpin
4 boss, guru, head **5** chief, mogul **6** bigwig, top dog **7** magnate **9** top banana **10** mastermind

Kings Peak range
5 Uinta

Kingu
consort: **6** Tiamat
slayer: **6** Marduk

kink
4 bend, curl, knot, whim **5** cramp, crick, quirk, snarl, spasm, twist **6** tangle **11** peculiarity **12** eccentricity, imperfection

kinky
3 odd **4** bent **5** curly, outré, ultra, weird **6** curled, far-out, frizzy, quirky **7** bizarre, deviant, knotted, strange, twisted **9** eccentric **10** outlandish

kiosk
5 booth, stand **8** pavilion **9** newsstand **11** summerhouse

kip
3 bed, nap **4** hide, pelt, skin **5** sleep

Kipling work
3 Kim **6** L'Envoi **8** Gunga Din, Mandalay **10** Fuzzy Wuzzy **11** Jungle Books (The), Recessional **13** Just So Stories, Soldiers Three **15** Light That Failed (The), Puck of Pook's Hill **18** Captains Courageous

Kiribati
capital: **6** Tarawa
island, island group: **4** Line **6** Banaba **7** Gilbert, Phoenix
location: **7** Oceania

kirk
6 church

kirsch
6 brandy, liquor

kirtle
4 coat, gown **5** dress, tunic **7** garment

Kish
father: **3** Ner **4** Abdi **5** Abiel, Jeiel **6** Jehiel
son: **4** Saul

kismet
3 lot **4** doom, fate, luck **5** weird **6** Moirai **7** destiny, fortune

kiss
4 buss, neck, peck **5** graze, smack, spoon **6** cookie, glance, smooch **7** lip-lock **8** osculate, pucker up **10** osculation

kisser
3 mug **4** face, lips **5** mouth

Kiss sculptor
5 Rodin (Auguste)

kit
3 set **4** gear, pelt **5** group **6** outfit, tackle, violin **7** package **8** caboodle **9** container **10** collection

kitchen
4 mess **6** galley **7** cuisine **8** scullery
appliance:
(see at **appliance**)
boss: **4** chef
(see also **cooking**)

kite
4 hawk, sail, soar **5** check, glede, hurry, mosey **7** saunter, take off **8** clear out, hightail, predator **9** spinnaker

kith
3 kin, sib **4** clan, folk **6** family **7** friends, kindred, kinfolk **9** neighbors, relatives

kitsch
4 camp, junk **9** vulgarity

kittenish
3 coy **6** elvish, frisky, impish **7** coltish, playful **10** frolicsome **11** mischievous

kitty
3 cat, pot **4** ante, fund, pool, puss **5** pussy **6** feline, stakes **7** jackpot

kiwi
4 bird **5** fruit **7** Apteryx **12** New Zealander

klatch
5 bunch, group **7** meeting **9** gathering **11** get-together

kleptomaniac
5 thief **7** booster **10** shoplifter

klutz
3 oaf **4** boob, clod, gawk, lout, lump **5** looby **6** lubber, lummox **7** bungler, palooka **8** shlemiel **9** schlemiel **10** stumblebum

klutzy
5 inept **6** clumsy **7** awkward **9** all thumbs, maladroit **10** blundering

knack
4 bent, gift, head **5** flair, forte, skill, trick **6** genius, talent **7** ability, aptness, command, faculty, know-how, mastery **8** aptitude, capacity, facility **9** dexterity, expertise, stratagem

knapsack
4 pack **8** backpack

knave
3 cad **4** heel, jack **5** fraud, rogue, scamp **6** rascal, varlet **7** bounder, lowlife, villain **8** scalawag, swindler **9** scoundrel **10** blackguard **11** rapscallion

knavery
5 fraud **6** deceit **8** mischief, trickery, villainy **9** chicanery, deception, rascality **10** dishonesty

knavish
5 lying **6** shifty, tricky **7** devious, roguish **8** rascally **9** deceitful, deceptive, dishonest **10** mendacious **12** unscrupulous

knead
4 form, mold, work **5** press, shape **7** massage **10** manipulate

knee
5 joint
bend: **9** genuflect **12** genuflection
bone: **7** patella

kneeler
5 stool **7** cushion **8** prie-dieu **9** footstool

knell
4 bong, peal, ring, toll **5** chime **6** summon **7** warning **8** announce, proclaim

knickknack
3 toy **4** dido **5** curio **6** bauble, gadget, gewgaw, trifle **7** bibelot, novelty, trinket, whatnot, whatsit **8** gimcrack, ornament, souvenir **9** bagatelle, bric-a-brac, objet d'art

knife
3 ulu **4** bolo, kris, shiv, snee **5** blade, bowie, panga, shank, sword **6** barong, cutter, dagger, lancet, parang, sickle **7** cleaver, machete, scalpel **8** stiletto, yataghan **11** switchblade
case: **6** sheath
handle: **4** haft, hilt
maker: **6** cutler **7** grinder

knifelike
4 keen **5** acute, sharp **7** cutting **8** piercing, stabbing **11** penetrating

knight
3 dub, sir **5** eques **8** cavalier, chessman, horseman **9** caballero, chevalier
code: **8** chivalry
competition: **7** listing, tilting **8** jousting **10** tournament
German: **6** Ritter
servant: **4** page **5** valet **6** squire
title: **3** sir
wife: **4** lady

knighthood
8 chivalry

knightly
4 bold **5** brave, noble **6** heroic **7** gallant, valiant **10** chivalrous

Knight of the Round Table
see **King Arthur**

Knight of the Rueful Countenance
10 Don Quixote

knit
4 bind, heal, join, link, mend, purl **5** plait, unite, weave **6** fabric, stitch **7** conjoin, crochet **8** contract **9** interlace **10** intertwine

knitting
material: **4** yarn
stitch: **3** rib **4** purl **6** garter
tool: **6** needle

knob
3 bun, bur, nub **4** bump, burl, burr, dial, hill, hump, lump, node, umbo **5** bulge, gnarl, knoll, mound **6** button, finial, handle, nubble, pommel **7** hillock **12** protuberance

knobkerrie
3 bat **4** club, mace **5** billy **6** cudgel, weapon **7** war club **8** bludgeon **9** billy club, shillalah, truncheon **10** shillelagh

knock
3 bob, hit, rap, tap **4** bash, blow, bump, cuff, lick, swat **5** blame, clout, fault, pound, swipe, thump **6** strike **7** censure, condemn, setback **8** denounce, reversal **9** criticize **10** denunciate

knockabout
5 rough, rowdy, sloop, tough **7** roaming, vagrant **10** boisterous

knock down
4 drop, earn, fell, gain, raze **5** floor, level, lower **6** lay low, reduce **7** acquire, bring in, flatten **9** dismantle **11** disassemble

knocker
6 carper, critic **7** caviler **8** quibbler **10** complainer, criticizer **11** fault-finder

knock off
3 rob **4** copy, do in, halt, kill, quit, slay, stop **5** cease **6** deduct, defeat, desist, finish, murder **7** execute, imitate, take out, take ten **8** discount, overcome, subtract, take five **9** liquidate **11** assassinate, call it quits, counterfeit

knockout
2 KO **4** kayo, lulu **5** dandy, doozy, final **6** beauty, doozie, eyeful, looker, lovely **7** stunner **8** decisive, jim-dandy, striking, stunning **9** deathblow, finishing, humdinger **10** attractive **11** coup de grace, crackerjack

knock over
3 rob **4** down, drop, fell **5** amaze, floor, steal, upset **6** boggle, hijack, hold up, lay low, topple **7** flatten, stick up **9** bring down, eliminate, overpower, overthrow, overwhelm, prostrate

knoll
4 hill, knob, rise **5** mound **7** hillock

knot
3 bow, tie **4** bond, burr, link, loop, lump, node **5** bunch, gnarl, hitch, nexus **6** jungle, tangle **8** ligament, ligature, vinculum
hair: **7** chignon
in fiber: **3** nep
kind: **4** bend, loop, slip **5** hitch **6** granny, splice, square **7** bowline **9** sheet bend **10** clove hitch, sheepshank

knotty
4 hard **6** sticky **7** complex, gnarled, Gordian **8** involved **9** byzantine, difficult, elaborate, intricate **10** formidable **11** complicated, problematic

knout
4 flog, lash, whip **7** scourge

know
3 wot **5** grasp **6** fathom, intuit **7** discern, realize **9** apprehend, recognize **10** comprehend, understand
Scottish: **3** ken

knowable
9 graspable **10** cognizable, fathomable **12** intelligible **13** apprehensible

know-how
5 craft, knack, skill **6** talent **7** ability, cunning, faculty, mastery **8** aptitude **9** dexterity, expertise **10** adroitness, expertness **11** proficiency

knowing
3 hep, hip **4** sage, wise **5** aware, blasé, canny, savvy, smart **6** bright, clever **7** witting, worldly **8** sentient **9** cognizant, conscious, sagacious **10** conversant, discerning, insightful, perceptive **11** worldly-wise **13** sophisticated

know-it-all
6 smarty **7** wise guy **8** wiseacre **10** smart aleck **11** smarty-pants, wisenheimer

knowledge
3 ken **4** data, info, lore, news **5** facts **6** wisdom **7** science **8** learning **9** cognition, education, erudition **10** cognizance **11** information, scholarship **12** intelligence
lack of: **9** ignorance
mystical: **6** gnosis

knowledgeable
5 savvy **8** educated, informed

know-nothing
4 dolt, dope, fool **5** dummy, dunce, idiot, yahoo **6** dimwit **7** pinhead **8** agnostic, ignorant, numskull **9** benighted, blockhead, brainless, ignoramus, lamebrain, numbskull **10** illiterate, uneducated **11** empty-headed

knuckle
5 joint
combining form: **6** condyl **7** condylo

knucklehead
4 dolt, dope, fool **5** dummy, dunce, idiot, yahoo **6** dimwit **8** clodpole, numskull **9** ignoramus, lamebrain, numbskull

knuckle under
3 bow **4** cave **5** yield **6** cave in, give in, submit **7** succumb **8** say uncle **9** surrender **10** capitulate

knurl
3 nub **4** bead, knob **5** ridge **12** protuberance

KO
8 knockout

koan
7 paradox

kobold
3 nis **5** dwarf, gnome **6** goblin, spirit, sprite
Kohinoor
3 gem **7** diamond
kohlrabi
7 cabbage **8** Brassica
kola
3 nut **4** tree
komatik
4 sled **6** sledge
kook
3 nut **5** crank, loony, wacko **6** cuckoo, weirdo **7** dingbat, lunatic, oddball **8** crackpot **9** ding-a-ling, fruitcake, screwball **10** crackbrain
kooky
4 bats, daft, nuts **5** batty, crazy, daffy, ditsy, ditzy, dotty, flaky, loony, nutty, silly, wacky, weird **6** freaky, fruity, insane, screwy **7** bizarre, idiotic, lunatic, offbeat, touched **8** demented **9** eccentric, fantastic **10** flipped out, freaked-out, off-the-wall, outlandish
kopeck
4 coin
one hundred: **5** ruble
Koran
chapter: **4** sura
revealer of: **7** Gabriel
scholar: **5** ulama, ulema
Korea, North
capital: **9** P'yongyang
city: **7** Hamhung **8** Ch'ongjin
leader: **9** Kim Il-sung, Kim Jong Il **10** Kim Chong-Il
monetary unit: **3** won
mountain: **6** Paektu
neighbor: **5** China **6** Russia **10** South Korea
sea: **6** Yellow
Korea, South
captial: **5** Seoul
city: **5** Pusan, Taegu **6** Inch'on, Taejon **7** Kwangju
island: **5** Cheju
monetary unit: **3** won
neighbor: **10** North Korea
river: **3** Han **7** Naktong
sea: **5** Japan **6** Yellow
Korean
dynasty: **5** Silla **7** Koguryo
national dish: **6** kimchi
kosher
3 fit **4** pure **5** clean **6** proper **10** acceptable, legitimate, sanctioned **12** satisfactory
not: **4** tref **7** terefah
Kosinski novel
5 Steps **10** Being There **11** Painted Bird (The)
Kosovo
capital: **8** Priština
city: **7** Prizren
lake: **6** Badovc **8** Gazivoda
monetary unit: **4** euro **5** dinar
neighbor: **6** Serbia **7** Albania **9** Macedonia **10** Montenegro
river: **3** Lab **4** Ibar **6** Erenik **7** Sitnica **9** White Drin
kowtow
3 bow **4** fawn **5** cower, defer, kneel, toady **6** cringe, grovel **7** honey up, truckle **8** bootlick **11** apple-polish
kraal
3 pen **6** corral **7** village **9** enclosure
kraken
5 squid **9** leviathan **10** giant squid, sea monster
krater
3 jar **4** vase **6** vessel
Kriemhild
brother: **7** Gunther
husband: **5** Etzel **6** Attila **9** Siegfried
slayer: **10** Hildebrand
victim: **5** Hagen
kris
6 dagger
Krishna
avatar of: **6** Vishnu
brother: **8** Balarama
father: **8** Vasudeva
mother: **6** Devaki
uncle: **5** Kansa
victim: **5** Kansa
Krupp works site
5 Essen
krypton symbol
2 Kr
Kubla Khan
author: **9** Coleridge (Samuel Taylor)
intruder's home: **7** Porlock
palace: **6** Xanadu
river: **4** Alph
kudos
4 bays, fame **5** award, glory, honor **6** honors, praise, renown **7** acclaim, bouquet, laurels **8** accolade, bouquets **10** compliment **11** distinction, recognition
kudu
8 antelope
kukri
5 sword

Kumin work
9 Up Country **12** Long Marriage (The)

kumquat
5 fruit
kin: 6 orange

Kushner play
15 Angels in America

Kuwait
gulf: 7 Persian
island: 7 Bubiyan **8** Faylakah
language: 6 Arabic **7** Persian
monetary unit: 5 dinar
neighbor: 4 Iraq **11** Saudi Arabia
oasis: 8 Al-Jahrah

kvass
4 beer

kvetch
4 beef, crab, fret, fuss **5** gripe, whine **6** grouch, grouse **7** grumble **8** complain **9** bellyache

kyphosis
8 humpback **9** curvature, hunchback

Kyrgyzstan
capital: 7 Bishkek
city: 3 Osh
conqueror: 9 Jöchi Khan
lake: 8 Issyk-Kul
language: 6 Kyrgyz **7** Russian
monetary unit: 3 som
mountain, range: 4 Alai **6** Pobedy **7** Victory **8** Tian Shan **10** Khan-Tengri **11** Kok Shaal-Tau
neighbor: 5 China **10** Kazakhstan, Tajikistan, Uzbekistan
river: 5 Naryn

L

Laadah
father: **6** Shelah
grandfather: **5** Judah

laager
4 camp **6** encamp **7** bivouac

lab
see **laboratory**

Laban
daughter: **4** Leah **6** Rachel
father: **7** Bethuel
grandfather: **5** Nahor
sister: **7** Rebekah

label
3 tag **4** band, mark **6** marker, ticket **7** epithet, sticker **8** classify, hallmark, identify, insignia

labium
3 lip

La Bohème
composer: **7** Puccini (Giacomo)
librettist: **6** Illica (Luigi) **7** Giacosa (Giuseppe)
role: **4** Mimi **6** Benoit **7** Colline, Musetta, Rodolfo **8** Marcello **9** Alcindoro, Schaunard
setting: **5** Paris
source author: **6** Murger (Henri)

labor
4 moil, task, toil, work **5** chore, grind, sweat **6** drudge, effort, strain, strive **7** slavery, travail **8** drudgery, endeavor, exertion, struggle **10** birth pangs, childbirth, donkeywork **12** childbearing
camp: **5** gulag
group: **3** AFL, CIO **5** ILGWU, union **6** AFL-CIO
leader: **5** Hoffa (James, Jimmy), Lewis (John L.), Meany (George) **6** Chavez (Cesar) **7** Gompers (Samuel), Reuther (Walter), Sweeney (John J.) **8** Kirkland (Lane), Randolph (A. Philip)

laboratory
device: **5** flask **6** beaker, mortar, pestle, retort **7** burette, pipette **8** crucible, test tube **9** petri dish **12** Bunsen burner **13** proving ground

labored
4 hard **6** forced, taxing, tiring **7** arduous **8** strained **9** difficult, effortful, fatiguing, strenuous

laborer
4 esne, hack, hand, peon **5** grind, navvy, prole **6** coolie, menial **7** workman **10** roustabout, workingman
Mexican: **7** bracero

laborious
4 hard **6** tiring, uphill **7** arduous, onerous, operose **8** diligent, grueling, sedulous, toilsome **9** assiduous, difficult, effortful, strenuous **10** burdensome, unflagging **11** hardworking, industrious, persevering **12** backbreaking

La Brea
4 pits **7** tar pits
fossil: **7** mammoth **8** mastodon **10** saber-tooth

labyrinth
3 web **4** coil, knot, maze, mesh **5** skein, snarl **6** jungle, morass, tangle
builder: **8** Daedalus
hero: **7** Theseus
monster: **8** Minotaur

labyrinthine
4 mazy **6** daedal, knotty **7** complex, gordian **8** involved, mazelike, tortuous **9** Byzantine, elaborate, intricate **10** convoluted, perplexing **11** bewildering, complicated

lace
3 net, tat, tie **4** cord, trim **5** adorn, braid, frill, plait, twine **6** fasten, string **7** entwine, netting, tatting **8** filigree, openwork **9** embroider **10** embroidery, intertwine **11** needlepoint
edge: **5** picot
fall: **5** jabot
ground: **6** reseau
into: **5** abuse **6** attack **7** condemn
kind: **6** bobbin **7** Alençon, guipure, macramé, Maltese, Mechlin, torchon **8** Brussels, Venetian **9** Chantilly **11** needlepoint **12** Valenciennes
make: **3** tat
pattern: **5** toilé

Lacedaemon
6 Sparta

lacerate
3 cut, rip **4** gash, rend, tear **5** slash, wound **6** mangle, pierce **7** afflict, mangled, torment **8** distress

lacework
7 tatting

lachrymose
3 sad **5** teary, weepy **7** doleful, tearful, weeping **8** dolorous, mournful **11** tear-jerking

lack
4 need, want **6** dearth, defect **7** absence,

default, deficit, failure, paucity, poverty, require **8** scarcity, shortage **9** privation **10** deficiency, inadequacy, scantiness **13** insufficiency

lackadaisical
4 idle, lazy, limp, slow **5** moony **6** dreamy **7** languid, passive **8** fainéant, indolent, listless, slothful **9** apathetic, enervated **10** languorous, spiritless **11** halfhearted

lackey
5 toady **6** fawner, flunky, minion, vassal **7** footman, servant **8** truckler **9** attendant, sycophant

lacking
3 shy **4** sans **5** minus, short **6** absent, flawed, needed **7** missing, needing, omitted, wanting, without **8** devoid of, impaired **9** defective, deficient **10** deprived of, inadequate, incomplete **11** halfhearted **12** insufficient

lackluster
3 dim **4** arid, blah, drab, dull, flat **5** blind, ho-hum, matte, muted, prosy, rusty, vapid **6** boring, leaden **7** prosaic **8** lifeless, mediocre **9** colorless, tarnished **10** uninspired **13** unimaginative

Laconian
7 Spartan
king: 5 Lelex, Myles **8** Menelaus

laconic
4 curt **5** bluff, blunt, brief, pithy, short, terse **7** brusque, concise **8** succinct

lacquer
5 glaze, gloss **6** enamel, finish **7** shellac, varnish

lacrosse
related game: 7 jai alai
term: 5 clamp **6** crease, crosse, pocket **7** face-off
team: 3 ten

lactate
4 salt **5** ester, nurse **6** suckle **7** secrete **8** wet-nurse **10** breast-feed

lacteal
5 milky **6** cloudy, pearly

lacuna
3 gap, pit **4** void **5** blank, break, space **6** breach, cavity, hiatus **7** caesura **10** deficiency **12** interruption

lacy
4 fine **5** meshy **6** dainty **7** netlike **8** delicate, gossamer **9** filigreed

lad
3 boy, son, tad **4** tike, tyke **5** youth **6** shaver **9** shaveling, stripling
Irish: 4 boyo **5** bucko
Scottish: 5 chiel **7** callant

ladder
3 run **5** ranks, scale **6** series **7** ranking **9** hierarchy
piece: 4 rung **6** rundle

ladderlike
6 scalar, scaled **7** stepped **11** scalariform

lade
3 dip, tax **4** bail, load, pack, ship, stow **5** ladle, scoop **6** burden, saddle, weight **8** encumber

la-di-dah
6 chichi, too-too **7** elegant, genteel, stuck-up **8** affected, snobbish **9** conceited, grandiose, high-flown **10** hoity-toity **11** pretentious

ladies' man
4 stud, wolf **5** Romeo **7** amorist, Don Juan, gallant **8** lothario **9** womanizer

lading
4 haul, load **5** cargo, goods **6** burden **7** bailing, dipping, freight, loading, payload **8** shipment **11** consignment

ladle
3 dip **4** bail **5** scoop, spoon **6** dipper

Ladon
6 dragon
father: 7 Phorcus, Phorcys
mother: 4 Ceto
slayer: 8 Heracles, Hercules

lady
4 dame **5** madam, woman **6** female, matron
French: 4 dame
German: 4 Frau
Italian: 5 donna **7** signora
Muslim: 5 begum
Spanish: 4 doña **6** señora

lady ___
4 luck **5** apple **6** beetle, chapel

ladybug
6 beetle
Australian: 7 vedalia

Lady Chatterley's Lover
author: 8 Lawrence (David Herbert)
character: 6 Connie **7** Mellors (Oliver) **9** Constance

lady-killer
4 dude, hunk, roué, stud **7** playboy, seducer **8** Casanova, lothario **12** heartbreaker

Lady of the Lake, The
5 Ellen (Douglas), Nimue **6** Vivien
author: 5 Scott (Walter)

Lady Windermere's Fan author
5 Wilde (Oscar)

Laertes
father: 8 Acrisius, Polonius
sister: 7 Ophelia
son: 7 Ulysses **8** Odysseus
victim: 6 Hamlet
wife: 8 Anticlea

La Fontaine's forte
5 fable

lag
4 drag, flag, last, poke, slow, tire **5** dally, delay, tarry, trail **6** dawdle, linger, loiter **7** slacken **8** hang back, hindmost, interval **10** dillydally **13** procrastinate

lager
4 beer, brew, malt, suds **7** brewski

laggard
3 lax **4** slow **5** tardy **6** loafer **7** dawdler **8** dallying, dawdling, delaying, dilatory, flagging, lingerer, loiterer, slowpoke, sluggish, tarrying **9** apathetic, lazybones, lethargic, loitering, straggler **10** behindhand

La Gioconda
8 Mona Lisa
composer: **10** Ponchielli (Amilcare)
painter: **7** da Vinci (Leonardo) **8** Leonardo (da Vinci)

lagniappe
3 tip **4** gift, perk **5** bonus, extra **7** cumshaw, largess **8** dividend, gratuity **9** baksheesh, pourboire **10** perquisite

lagomorph
4 hare, pika **6** rabbit

lagoon
4 pond, pool **5** bayou, sound **6** strait **7** channel, narrows
rim: **5** atoll

____ La Guardia
8 Fiorello

Lahmi
brother: **7** Goliath
slayer: **7** Elhanan

laid-back
4 cool **6** breezy, casual **7** relaxed **8** carefree, informal **9** easygoing, hang-loose **10** nonchalant

lair
3 den **4** cave **5** haunt, lodge **6** burrow, refuge **7** hideout, retreat **8** hideaway **9** sanctuary

Laius
father: **8** Labdacus
slayer, son: **7** Oedipus
wife: **7** Jocasta

lake
4 loch, mere, pond, pool, tarn **5** lough **6** lagoon
Adriatic: **6** Varano
Alberta: **6** Louise
Algeria: **5** Hodna
Alps: **6** Annecy
Arizona-Nevada: **4** Mead
Armenia: **5** Sevan **6** Gokcha, Sevang **9** Lychnitis
Aswan's: **6** Nasser
Australia: **4** Eyre **5** Carey, Cowan, Frome, Wells **6** Barlee **7** Amadeus, Everard, Torrens **8** Gairdner
Austria: **5** Atter, Traun **6** Kammer **8** Attersee **9** Kammersee
Bolivia: **5** Poopó
Botswana: **5** Ngami
British Columbia: **4** Pitt **5** Atlin
California: **4** Mono, Tule **5** Clear, Eagle, Honey
Cambodia: **8** Tonle Sap
Canada: **4** Dyke **8** Manitoba
central Africa: **4** Kivu **5** Mweru **6** Albert
Central America: **5** Guija
central Europe: **5** Leman **6** Geneva, Lugano **7** Ceresio **8** Bodensee **9** Constance
central North America: **5** Rainy
Chile: **4** Laja **5** Ranco
China: **6** Poyang **8** Dongting
Colorado: **5** Grand
Denmark: **5** Esrum
east Africa: **6** Rudolf **7** Turkana
east Asia: **6** Khanka **7** Xingkai **8** Hsingkai
east central Africa: **8** Victoria **10** Tanganyika
east China: **3** Tai **5** Dalai, Hulun
Ethiopia: **4** Tana, Zwai **5** Abaya, Shala, Shamo, Tsana **8** Stefanie **9** Chew Bahir
Finland: **5** Inari
Florida: **5** Worth **10** Okeechobee
Germany: **5** Ammer, Chiem **8** Ammersee, Chiemsee
Ghana: **5** Volta
Great: **4** Erie **5** Huron **7** Ontario **8** Michigan, Superior
Greece: **5** Bolbe, Volvi
Guatemala: **7** Atitlán
Honduras: **5** Yojoa
Honshu: **3** Omi **4** Biwa, Suwa, Yodo
Hungary: **7** Balaton **10** Plattensee
Idaho: **4** Waha **5** Grays **6** Priest **11** Coeur d'Alene, Pend Oreille
India: **3** Dal **5** Wular **6** Chilka
Indonesia: **4** Poso, Toba **5** Ranau
Iowa: **5** Storm
Iran: **5** Niriz, Shahi, Urmia **8** Matianus, Urumiyeh **9** Bakhtigan
Ireland: **3** Gur, Ree **4** Conn, Derg, Mask **5** Allen, Arrow, Leane
Israel: **12** Bahr Tabariya, Sea of Galilee
Israel-Jordan: **7** Dead Sea
Italy: **4** Como, Iseo, Nemi **5** Garda **6** Albano **7** Bolsena, Perugia **8** Maggiore **9** Trasimene
Japan: **4** Imba **8** Imbanuma
Kazakhstan: **7** Balqash **8** Balkhash
Louisiana: **4** Soda **9** Catahoula **13** Pontchartrain
Maine: **6** Sebago **9** Moosehead
Mali: **4** Debo
Manitoba: **4** Gods **5** Cedar, Moose **8** Winnipeg

Mexico: **7** Chapala
Michigan: **4** Burt
Minnesota: **3** Red **4** Cass, Gull, Swan **5** Leech **6** Itasca **9** Mille Lacs **10** Minnetonka, of the Woods **11** Lac qui Parle
Minnesota-Wisconsin: **5** Pepin
Mongolian: **3** Har **5** Har Us, Khara **8** Khara Usu
Montana: **8** Medicine
mountain: **4** tarn
Myanmar: **4** Inle
Nevada: **4** Ruby **7** Pyramid
New Hampshire: **5** Squam **13** Winnipesaukee
New Jersey: **5** Union
New York: **4** Long **5** Chazy, Keuka **6** Cayuga, George, Oneida, Otsego, Owasco, Placid, Seneca **7** Crooked, Saranac **8** Onondaga, Saratoga **9** Champlain **10** Chautauqua **11** Canandaigua, Skaneateles
New Zealand: **4** Ohau **5** Hawea, Taupo **6** Pukaki, Wanaka **8** Wakatipu
Nicaragua: **7** Managua
North Africa: **4** Chad
Northern Ireland: **5** Neagh
Northwest Territories: **4** Gras **5** Baker, Garry, Pelly **9** Great Bear **10** Great Slave
Norway: **5** Mjosa
Nova Scotia: **7** Bras d'Or
Ontario: **4** Rice, Seul **5** Trout
Oregon: **5** Abert **6** Crater **7** Malheur, Wallowa
Paraguay: **4** Ypoá
Peru: **5** Junín **13** Chinchaycocha
Philippines: **4** Bato, Taal **5** Lanao **6** Bombon
Poland: **5** Mamry, Mauer
Quebec: **5** Minto, Payne
Russia: **3** Seg **5** Chany, Ilmen, Lacha, Onega **6** Baikal, Ladoga **7** Rybinsk **10** Eltonskoye **11** Ladozhskoye
Saskatchewan: **4** Cree **5** Ronge
Scotland: **3** Ard, Awe **4** Doon, Earn, Ness, Oich, Shin, Sloy **5** Leven, Lochy, Maree, Morar, Shiel **6** Lomond
Siberia: **6** Baikal, Baykal
South Africa: **4** Kosi
South America: **5** Merin, Mirim **8** Titicaca
South Carolina: **7** Wateree
South Dakota: **5** Andes
southeast Africa: **5** Nyasa **6** Nyassa
southwest Europe: **5** Ohrid **7** Okhrida
Sweden: **5** Asnen, Roxen **6** Siljan, Vänern, Vetter **7** Malaren, Vattern
Switzerland: **3** Zug **4** Biel, Joux **5** Zuger **6** Bieler, Bienne, Brienz, Sarnen, Sarner, Zurich **7** Lucerne, Lungern **8** Brienzer, Züricher **9** Neuchâtel, Zürichsee
Tajikistan: **7** Karakul
Tanzania: **5** Rukwa
Texas-Louisiana: **5** Caddo
Tibet: **4** Na-mu **6** Nam Tso, Tengri
Turkey: **3** Tuz, Van **4** Bafa, Nice **5** Iznik, Sugla **6** Nicaea
Uganda: **5** Kyoga
Utah: **6** Powell, Sevier **9** Great Salt
Vermont: **9** Champlain
Wales: **4** Bala
Washington: **4** Omak **5** Moses **6** Chelan **9** Wenatchee
western China: **4** Ai-pi **6** Ebinur
western United States: **4** Bear **5** Tahoe
Wisconsin: **5** Green **9** Winnebago
Yellowstone National Park: **5** Heart, Lewis **8** Shoshone
Zaire: **5** Tumba
Zambia: **9** Bangweolo, Bangweulu

lake group
central North America: **5** Great
Egypt: **5** Balah
Maine: **8** Rangeley
New York: **6** Finger
Saskatchewan: **5** Quill
Twin: **8** Washinee **9** Washining

lake herring
5 cisco

Lake poet
7 Southey (Robert) **9** Coleridge (Samuel Taylor) **10** Wordsworth (William)

Lake Wobegon Days author
7 Keillor (Garrison)

Lakmé
aria: **8** Bell Song
composer: **7** Delibes (Léo)

Lakshmi
husband: **6** Vishnu
son: **4** Kama

L. A. Law
actor: **3** Dey (Susan) **5** Drake (Larry), Smits (Jimmy) **6** Dysart (Richard), Greene (Michele), Hamlin (Harry), Ruttan (Susan), Tucker (Michael) **7** Bernsen (Corbin), Rachins (Alan) **10** Eikenberry (Jill)
character: **5** Kuzak (Michael) **6** Becker (Arnie), Kelsey (Ann), Melman (Roxanne) **7** Van Owen (Grace), Perkins (Abby) **8** Brackman (Douglas), McKenzie (Leland) **9** Markowitz (Stuart), Sifuentes (Victor)
creator: **6** Bochco (Steven)

lam
3 hit **4** beat, blow, bolt, drub, flay, flee, flog, pelt, skip, whip **5** baste, paste, pound, scram, smack, split, whale **6** batter, beat it, buffet, cut out, decamp, escape, flight, hammer, pummel, strike, thrash, wallop **7** getaway, take off, vamoose **8** breakout, escaping **9** skedaddle

La Mancha's knight
10 Don Quixote

lamb
4 cade **5** sheep **6** cosset **8** yeanling
leg of: 5 gigot
parent: 3 ewe, ram

lambaste
3 pan **4** beat, drub, flay, flog, lash, lick, pelt, slam, slap, trim, whip **5** paste, pound, roast, scold, score, slash, smear **6** assail, attack, berate, cudgel, hammer, pummel, scathe, scorch, thrash, wallop **7** assault, blister, censure, clobber, reprove, scourge, shellac, upbraid **8** bludgeon, denounce, harangue, lash into **9** castigate, excoriate **10** tongue-lash

lambent
5 aglow **6** ardent, bright, lucent **7** beaming, glowing, radiant, shining **8** gleaming, luminous, lustrous **9** brilliant, effulgent, refulgent, twinkling **10** flickering, glittering, shimmering **12** incandescent

lamblike
4 meek **6** docile

lamb of God
5 Jesus **6** Christ **8** Agnus Dei

Lamb's pseudonym
4 Elia

lame
4 gimp, halt, limp **5** gimpy, stiff **6** feeble, flimsy **7** cripple, disable, halting, limping **8** crippled, disabled, hobbling, inferior **10** inadequate **11** ineffectual **12** contemptible, unconvincing

lamebrain
3 oaf **4** dolt, dope, goof, mutt, simp, yo-yo **5** chump, dummy, dunce, idiot, moron, ninny, noddy, stupe **6** dimwit, donkey, dum-dum, nitwit, noodle **7** airhead, dullard, pinhead, schnook **8** bonehead, clodpoll, dumbbell, dumbhead, imbecile, lunkhead, meathead, numskull **9** blockhead, ignoramus, numbskull, simpleton, thickhead **10** dunderhead, hammerhead, nincompoop **11** chowderhead, chucklehead, knucklehead

Lamech
daughter: 6 Naamah
father: 10 Methuselah
son: 4 Noah **5** Jabal, Jubal **9** Tubalcain
wife: 4 Adah **6** Zillah

lament
3 cry, rue **4** keen, moan, pine, wail, weep **5** dirge, elegy, mourn **6** bemoan, bewail, grieve, plaint, regret, repent, sorrow **7** deplore, elegize, wailing **8** jeremiad, threnody **9** complaint, ululation

lamentable
6 rueful, woeful **7** doleful, pitiful **8** dolorous, grievous, mournful **9** plaintive, sorrowful **10** afflictive, deplorable, lugubrious, melancholy **11** distressing, regrettable, unfortunate **13** heartbreaking

lamentation
5 elegy, grief **7** anguish, remorse, wailing **8** grieving, mourning, threnody **9** sorrowing, ululation

Lamerok
father: 9 Pellinore
lover: 8 Margawse
slayer: 6 Gawain

lamia
3 hex **5** witch **7** hellcat, vampire **8** succubus **9** sorceress **11** enchantress

Lamia
country: 5 Libya
form: 7 serpent
lover: 4 Zeus

lamina
5 blade, flake, layer, plate, scale

lamp
3 arc **4** bulb, davy **5** klieg, light, torch **7** lantern **10** candelabra **11** candelabrum
floor: 8 torchère **9** torchiere
hanging: 10 chandelier

lampblack
4 soot **6** carbon

Lampetia
father: 6 Apollo, Helios
husband: 9 Asclepius
mother: 6 Neaera
sister: 9 Phaethusa

lampoon
4 mock **5** roast, spoof, squib **6** parody, satire, send-up **7** take off **8** ridicule, satirize **9** burlesque **10** caricature, pasquinade

lamprey
3 eel **8** nine-eyes

lanai
5 patio, porch **6** piazza **7** terrace, veranda

lance
4 gash, hurl, open **5** slash, spear **6** impale, pierce, skewer **7** javelin **8** transfix

Lancelot, Launcelot
father: 3 Ban
lover: 6 Elaine **9** Guinevere
son: 7 Galahad
victim: 6 Gawain

lancer
10 cavalryman
Prussian: 5 uhlan

lancet
4 arch **5** blade, knife **6** cutter, window **7** scalpel

land
4 dirt, dock, gain, soil **5** acres, berth, earth, light, manor, shore, terra, tract **6** alight, estate, ground, obtain, pick up, secure **7** acquire, acreage, country, expanse, grounds, procure, set down, terrain, terrene **9** touch down **10** terra firma
alluvial: **5** delta
barren: **5** waste **6** desert
cultivated: **4** farm **5** glebe, tilth **7** tillage
for grazing: **3** lea, ley **5** range **6** meadow **7** pasture
high: **4** hill, mesa **7** plateau **8** mountain
level: **4** mesa **5** plain **7** plateau
low: **4** vale **6** valley **9** intervale
measure: **3** rod **4** acre
open: **3** lea **5** field, green, plain **6** meadow **7** pasture
piece: **3** lot **4** plot **5** tract **6** estate, parcel
reclaimed: **6** polder
sloping: **6** cuesta
strip: **7** isthmus
wet: **3** bog, fen **5** marsh, swamp **6** marish

land east of Eden
3 Nod

landed
4 alit

landlord
6 lessor, squire **9** innkeeper **10** freeholder

landmark
5 cairn, guide **9** benchmark, milestone, watershed **11** achievement **12** breakthrough, turning point

Land of Enchantment
9 New Mexico

Land of Lakes
8 Michigan

Land of Opportunity
3 USA **8** Arkansas **12** United States

Land of the Midnight Sun
6 Norway

landowner
6 squire, yeoman
Anglo-Saxon: **5** thane, thegn
Dutch: **7** patroon
Scottish: **5** laird

landscape
5 scene, vista **7** scenery, setting, terrain **8** backdrop, prospect

lane
3 way **4** path, road **5** aisle, alley, byway, track **6** street **7** pathway, roadway **8** footpath **10** passageway

Langland work
12 Piers Plowman

lang syne
4 past, yore **10** yesteryear

language
4 cant **5** argot, idiom, lingo, prose, slang **6** jargon, patois, speech, tongue **7** dialect, lexicon, palaver **10** vernacular, vocabulary **11** terminology
ambiguous: **8** newspeak **10** double-talk
ancient: **5** Greek, Latin **6** Hebrew **8** Etruscan, Sanskrit
artificial: **3** Ido **7** Volapük **9** Esperanto
Bantu: **3** Ila
classical: **5** Greek, Latin
combining form: **5** gloss, glott **6** glosso, glotto
expert: **8** linguist, polyglot
informal: **4** jive **5** lingo, slang
meaningless: **6** babble, jabber **7** blather **9** gibberish **10** mumbo-jumbo
mixed: **6** creole, pidgin
pretentious: **7** bombast, fustian **8** claptrap
regional: **7** dialect
relating to: **10** linguistic
Romance: **6** French **7** Catalan, Italian, Spanish **8** Romanian, Rumanian **10** Portuguese
Scotch-Irish: **4** Erse **6** Gaelic
secret: **4** cant, code **5** argot
Siamese: **3** Lao, Tai
structure: **6** syntax **7** grammar
suffix: **3** ese
written: **5** prose

languid
4 lazy, limp **5** inert **6** draggy, supine, torpid **8** drooping, flagging, inactive, listless, slothful, sluggish **9** apathetic, enervated, impassive, lethargic **10** languorous, phlegmatic, spiritless **13** lackadaisical

languish
4 fade, fail, pine, tire, wilt **5** brood, droop **6** weaken **7** decline **9** waste away

languishing
4 limp, weak **6** feeble, pining **7** languid **8** fainéant, indolent, listless, weakened **9** depressed, enervated, enfeebled **10** dispirited, spiritless **11** debilitated, devitalized **13** lackadaisical

languor
3 kef, kif **5** ennui **6** stupor, tedium, torpor **7** fatigue **8** doldrums, dullness, hebetude, lethargy **9** heaviness, inertness, lassitude, torpidity, weariness **10** exhaustion

languorous
4 lazy, limp **5** inert **6** draggy, supine, torpid **7** laggard, languid, passive, relaxed **8** dilatory, drooping, fainéant, flagging, inactive, indolent, indulged, listless, pampered, slothful, sluggard **9** apathetic, enervated, impassive, lethargic **10** phlegmatic, spiritless **13** lackadaisical

lank
4 bony, lean, thin **5** rangy, spare **6** gangly **7** angular, scraggy, slender **8** gangling
lanky
4 bony, lean, thin **5** gaunt, spare **6** gangly **7** scraggy, scrawny **8** gangling, rawboned
lanyard
4 cord, line, rope **7** cordage
Laocoön
city: 4 Troy
killer: 8 serpents
Laodamia
father: 7 Acastus
husband: 11 Protesilaus
Laomedon
daughter: 7 Hesione
father: 4 Ilus
kingdom: 4 Troy
mother: 8 Eurydice
slayer: 8 Heracles, Hercules
son: 5 Priam **8** Tithonus
Laos
capital: 9 Vientiane
city: 11 Savannakhet
ethnic group: 5 Hmong
monetary unit: 3 kip
neighbor: 5 Burma, China **7** Myanmar, Vietnam **8** Cambodia, Thailand **9** Kampuchea
river: 6 Mekong
lap
3 sip **4** fold, join, wind **5** drink **6** cuddle, splash, swathe **7** circuit, control, custody, shingle **9** imbricate
lapidary
6 cutter **7** elegant, jeweler **8** engraver, polisher
lapillus
4 lava **6** cinder
lapin
6 rabbit
Lapiths
foes: 8 centaurs
king: 5 Ixion
lappet
4 flap, fold **5** lapel
lapse
3 err, gap, sin **4** fall, flub, goof, sink, slip, vice **5** boner, cease, error, fluff, gaffe, slide **6** breach, bungle, expire, foible, miscue **7** blooper, blunder, decline, failing, failure, faux pas, forfeit, frailty, mistake, screwup, subside **8** abeyance, apostasy, interval, trespass **9** backslide, deviation, oversight, violation **10** apostatize **11** backsliding, impropriety **12** indiscretion, interruption
lapsed
4 sunk **5** ended **6** ceased **7** expired **8** obsolete **9** forfeited
Laputan
6 absurd **9** visionary
Lar
3 god **6** spirit **12** household god
larboard
4 left, port **8** leftward
larcenist
5 thief **6** bandit, robber **7** burglar, filcher, stealer **8** pilferer **9** embezzler, plunderer, purloiner **10** pickpocket, shoplifter
larcenous
7 robbing **8** thieving **9** pilfering **10** plunderous **13** light-fingered
larceny
5 theft **7** looting, robbery **8** burglary, stealing, thievery, thieving
kind: 5 grand, petty
lard
3 fat **6** fatten, grease **10** shortening
larder
6 pantry
large
3 big, fat **4** bull, huge, vast **5** ample, bulky, giant, grand, great, gross, hefty, jumbo, major **6** goodly **7** copious, immense, mammoth, massive, outsize, sizable **8** colossal, enormous, gigantic, king-size, oversize, spacious, whopping **9** capacious, excessive, extensive, humongous, monstrous **10** exorbitant, large-scale, monumental, prodigious, stupendous, tremendous, voluminous **11** extravagant, substantial
combining form: 4 macr, mega **5** macro **6** megalo
largesse
4 alms, gift **6** bounty **7** bequest, charity, cumshaw, gifting, present **8** donation, gratuity **9** endowment, pourboire **10** almsgiving, generosity, liberality **11** benefaction, beneficence, benevolence, magnanimity, munificence **12** philanthropy
largo
4 slow **5** broad, tempo
lariat
4 bola, bolo, rope **5** lasso, noose, reata, riata
user: 6 cowboy, drover **10** cowpuncher
lark
4 bird, dido, romp **5** antic, caper, prank, shine, stunt, trick **6** frolic **7** rollick **8** escapade, songbird **9** diversion **10** tomfoolery **11** distraction, shenanigans **12** monkeyshines
larrup
3 tan **4** beat, cane, drub, dust, flay, flog, hide, lash, lick, whip, whup **5** pound, spank, whale **6** cudgel, lather, paddle, thrash, wallop **7** clobber, scourge, shellac, trounce **8** lambaste **10** flagellate

larva
3 bot **4** grub, worm **6** dobson, maggot **8** cercaria, hornworm, mealworm **10** casebearer **11** caterpillar **12** hellgrammite
amphibian: 7 tadpole
crustacean: 4 zoea
flatworm: 5 redia
free-swimming: 7 planula
mollusk: 7 veliger
moth: 8 leafworm
tapeworm: 6 measle

larynx
7 trachea **8** voice box

lasagna
5 pasta **7** noodles

lascivious
4 lewd **5** bawdy, loose, randy **6** carnal, coarse, rakish, wanton **7** fleshly, goatish, immoral, lustful, satyric **8** depraved, prurient **9** lecherous, libertine, lickerish, salacious **10** libidinous, licentious, lubricious, profligate **12** concupiscent

lash
4 beat, bind, dash, flay, flog, hide, whip **5** baste, birch, fling, pound, scold, slash, whale **6** assail, berate, buffet, pummel, scathe, strike, stripe, switch, thrash **7** blister, scarify, scourge, upbraid **8** lambaste **9** castigate, excoriate, horsewhip **10** flagellate

lass
3 gal **4** girl, maid **5** wench **6** damsel, maiden **7** colleen

lassitude
5 ennui, sloth **6** apathy, stupor, tedium, torpor **7** fatigue, languor **8** debility, doldrums, dullness, hebetude, laziness, lethargy **9** indolence, tiredness, torpidity, weariness **10** exhaustion **11** insouciance **12** heedlessness, indifference, listlessness, sluggishness

lasso
see **lariat**

last
3 end, lag, nth **5** abide, final **6** endure, latest, latter, utmost **7** closing, extreme, perdure, persist **8** continue, crowning, eventual, farthest, furthest, hindmost, rearmost, remotest, terminal, ultimate **9** umpteenth, uttermost **10** concluding, conclusive **11** terminating
French: 7 dernier
next to: 6 penult **11** penultimate

last-ditch
5 final **7** defiant **8** ultimate **9** desperate **10** concluding

lasting
6 stable **7** abiding, durable, undying **8** enduring, lifelong, long-term, longtime **9** continual, indelible, perennial, permanent, unceasing **10** continuing, continuous, perdurable, persisting **12** indissoluble, long-standing

Last of the Mohicans, The
5 Uncas
author: 6 Cooper (James Fenimore)
character: 4 Cora **5** Alice, Magua, Uncas **11** Natty Bumppo **12** Chingachgook

Last Supper, The
painter: 7 da Vinci (Leonardo) **8** Leonardo (da Vinci)
location: 5 Milan

latch
4 bolt, glom, hasp, hook **5** catch **6** fasten, secure **8** fastener
British: 5 sneck

latchet
4 band, cord, lace **5** strap, thong **8** shoelace

late
4 dead, past, slow **5** tardy **6** former, recent, whilom **7** defunct, delayed, onetime, overdue, quondam **8** deceased, departed, sometime **9** preceding

latent
4 idle **5** inert **6** covert, fallow, hidden, innate, unripe **7** abeyant, dormant, lurking **8** immature, inactive, inherent **9** concealed, intrinsic, potential, quiescent

later
4 anon, soon **5** after, infra **6** behind **7** by and by, ensuing **9** afterward, following, posterior **10** subsequent, succeeding **12** subsequently

lateral
4 pass, side **6** branch **8** crabwise, flanking, sidelong, sideward, sideways, sidewise

laterally
8 crabwise, sideward, sideways, sidewise

latest
6 newest, red-hot **7** current **8** contempo **9** au courant **10** dernier cri **13** up-to-the-minute

latex
6 balata **8** emulsion
product: 5 paint **6** chicle, rubber **11** gutta-percha

lath
4 slat **5** board, frame, stave, stick, strip

lather
4 flap, flog, foam, hide, lash, soap, stew, suds, whip **5** froth, spume, tizzy, yeast **6** dither, hoopla, pother, thrash, welter **7** scourge, turmoil **8** soapsuds

Latin
5 Roman **7** Italian **8** Hispanic
after: 4 post
always: 6 semper

and: **2** et
as directed: **6** ut dict
be, being: **4** esse
before: **4** ante, prae
behold: **4** ecce
believe: **5** credo
book: **5** liber
boy: **4** puer
brother: **6** frater
but: **3** sed
day: **4** dies
dog: **5** canis
earth: **5** terra
egg: **3** ova
father: **5** pater
foot: **3** pes
friend: **6** amicus
girl: **6** puella
god: **4** deus
goddess: **3** dea
good-bye: **4** vale **5** salve
grammarian: **7** Donatus (Aelius)
greeting: **3** ave
hail and farewell: **12** ave atque vale
hand: **5** manus
hello: **3** ave
horse: **5** equus
house: **5** domus
is: **3** est
law: **3** ius, jus, lex
let it stand: **4** stet
life: **4** vita
light: **3** lux
love: **3** amo **4** amas, amat, amor
man: **4** homo
mother: **5** mater
moon: **4** luna
night: **3** nox
nothing: **5** nihil
now: **4** nunc
peace: **3** pax
pronoun: **2** tu **3** ego, nos, vos
road: **3** via
same: **4** idem
sea: **4** mare
see: **4** vide
sister: **5** soror
step: **6** gradus
sun: **3** sol
that is: **5** id est
thing: **3** res
this: **3** hic, hoc **4** haec
thus: **3** sic
truth: **7** veritas
war: **6** bellum
welcome: **5** salve
wife: **4** uxor
woman: **6** femina
year: **4** anno **5** annus

Latin American
country: **4** Cuba, Peru **5** Chile **6** Belize, Brazil, Guyana, Mexico, Panama **7** Bolivia, Ecuador, Uruguay **8** Colombia, Honduras, Paraguay, Suriname **9** Argentina, Costa Rica, Guatemala, Nicaragua, Venezuela **10** El Salvador
dance: **4** juba **5** conga, mambo, rumba, samba **6** maxixe, rhumba **7** carioca, lambada **8** capoeira, habanera, merengue **9** bossa nova
revolutionary: **6** Castro (Fidel) **7** Bolívar (Simón), Guevara (Ché), Hidalgo (Father Miguel) **8** O'Higgins (Bernardo) **9** San Martín (José de)

Latinus
daughter: **7** Lavinia
father: **6** Faunus **8** Odysseus
son-in-law: **6** Aeneas
wife: **5** Amata

latitude
4 play, room **5** range, scope, space, width **6** leeway, margin **7** breadth, compass, freedom, liberty, license **9** elbowroom **10** discretion **12** independence

latke
7 pancake **13** potato pancake

Latona
4 Leto
daughter: **5** Diana **7** Artemis
father: **5** Coeus
mother: **6** Phoebe
son: **6** Apollo

Latter-day Saint
6 Mormon

lattice
4 grid, mesh **5** grate, grill **7** grating, network, trellis **12** reticulation

Latvia
capital: **4** Riga
city: **7** Liepaja **10** Daugavpils
gulf: **4** Riga
language: **7** Lettish
monetary unit: **3** lat
native: **4** Lett
neighbor: **6** Russia **7** Belarus, Estonia **9** Lithuania
river: **7** Daugava **12** Western Dvina
sea: **6** Baltic

Latvian
4 Balt, Lett **7** Lettish

laud
5 adore, bless, cry up, extol, glory, honor **6** admire, praise, revere **7** acclaim, flatter, glorify, magnify, worship **8** eulogize, venerate **9** celebrate, reverence

laudable
6 worthy **9** admirable, deserving, estimable **11** commendable, meritorious, thankworthy **12** praiseworthy

laudatory
7 glowing 9 adulatory, approving 10 eulogistic, flattering 11 approbative, encomiastic, panegyrical 12 commendatory 13 complimentary

laugh
3 yuk 4 ha-ha, roar, yuck 5 tehee, whoop 6 cackle, giggle, guffaw, hee-haw, titter 7 chortle, chuckle, snicker 10 cachinnate

laughable
4 rich 5 comic, droll, funny, goofy, witty 6 absurd, jocose 7 amusing, comical, jocular, mocking, risible 8 derisive, derisory, farcical, humorous 9 ludicrous 10 ridiculous

Laugh-In
cast: 4 Sues (Alan), Hawn (Goldie) 5 Buzzi (Ruth), Carne (Judy), Owens (Gary) 6 Dawson (Richard), Gibson (Henry), Tomlin (Lily) 7 Johnson (Arte)
catch phrase: 10 sock it to me 12 go to your room
guest: 6 Wilson (Flip) 7 Tiny Tim 8 Youngman (Henny)
host: 5 Rowan (Dan) 6 Martin (Dick)

laughing
5 merry, riant 6 blithe 8 mirthful 9 sparkling

laughingstock
4 butt, dupe, fool, jest, joke, mark, mock 5 sport 6 target 7 mockery 8 derision

launch
4 boat, cast, fire, hurl 5 begin, debut, fling, heave, pitch, sling, start, throw 6 get off 7 jump off, kick off, lift off, release, take off, usher in 8 blast off, catapult, commence, embark on, initiate 9 inception, institute, introduce, motorboat, set afloat 10 inaugurate, initiation 12 inauguration

launder
4 wash 5 clean 6 trough 7 cleanse 8 sanitize, transfer

Laura's lover
8 Petrarch

laurels
4 bays, fame 5 award, honor, kudos, prize 6 awards, badges, honors, prizes, renown 7 acclaim 8 accolade, citation 9 accolades, citations 10 decoration, reputation 11 decorations, distinction 12 achievements, distinctions

laurel-tree nymph
6 Daphne

lava
2 aa 4 slag 5 magma 6 scoria 8 andesite, trachyte
fragment: 8 lapillus
stream: 4 flow 6 coulee

lavalava
5 cloth, skirt 6 sarong

lavaliere
7 pendant 8 necklace

lavatory
2 WC 3 loo 4 head, john 5 basin, jakes, potty, privy 6 johnny, toilet 7 latrine 8 bathroom, restroom, washroom 11 water closet

lave
4 pour, wash 5 bathe

Lavinia
father: 7 Latinus
husband: 6 Aeneas
mother: 5 Amata

Lavinium's founder
6 Aeneas

lavish
4 lush, posh, pour 5 plush, spend, waste 6 swanky 7 liberal, opulent, profuse 8 effusive, prodigal, splendid, squander 9 bountiful, excessive, exuberant, luxuriant, luxurious, sumptuous 10 immoderate, inordinate, munificent 11 extravagant

law
3 act, lex 4 bill, code, rule 5 axiom, canon, edict, Torah 6 assize, decree, equity 7 dictate, justice, mandate, precept, statute, theorem 8 exigency 9 enactment, ordinance, principle 10 principium, regulation 11 commandment, fundamental 12 prescription
body of: 4 code 7 pandect 12 constitution
degree: 2 JD 3 LLB, LLD
expert: 5 judge 6 jurist 7 justice
practitioner: 6 lawyer 7 counsel 8 attorney 9 barrister, solicitor
relating to: 5 jural, legal 7 canonic 8 forensic, juristic 9 judiciary
violation of: 4 tort 5 crime 6 felony 11 misdemeanor

law-abiding
6 decent 7 duteous, dutiful, orderly, upright 8 obedient, obliging, straight 9 compliant, peaceable 10 forthright, respectful 11 respectable, well-behaved

Law & Order
actor: 4 Röhm (Elisabeth) 6 Govich (Milena), Martin (Jesse), Orbach (Jerry) 7 Hendrix (Leslie) 8 Thompson (Fred) 9 Merkerson (S. Epatha), Waterston (Sam)
character: 5 Green (Ed), McCoy (Jack) 6 Branch (Arthur) 7 Briscoe (Lennie), Cassady (Nina), Rodgers (Elizabeth) 8 Van Buren (Anita) 10 Southerlyn (Serena)
creator: 4 Wolf (Dick)

lawbreaker
3 con 4 hood, thug 5 crook, felon 6 outlaw, sinner 7 convict, hoodlum, mobster 8 criminal, gangster, hooligan, jailbird, offender, scofflaw,

violator **9** desperado, wrongdoer **10** malefactor, trespasser **12** transgressor

lawful
3 due **4** just **5** legal, legit, licit, valid **6** kosher **7** condign **8** bona fide, innocent, mandated, ordained **9** allowable, canonical, juridical, legalized **10** authorized, legitimate **11** permissible

lawgiver
5 Draco, Moses, solon **7** senator **8** alderman **10** councilman, legislator **11** congressman, thesmothete

lawlessness
5 chaos **6** strife **7** anarchy, discord, misrule, turmoil **8** conflict, disorder **9** mobocracy **10** illegality, misconduct, ochlocracy, unruliness, wrongdoing **11** criminality, pandemonium

lawman
7 marshal, officer, sheriff **9** policeman

Lawrence novel
7 Rainbow (The) **8** Kangaroo, Lost Girl (The) **9** Aaron's Rod **11** Women in Love **13** Plumed Serpent (The), Sons and Lovers

lawrencium symbol
2 Lr

lawsuit
4 case **5** cause, claim **6** action **8** replevin **9** assumpsit **10** litigation, proceeding **11** presentment, prosecution

lawyer
6 jurist, legist **7** counsel, pleader **8** advocate, attorney **9** barrister, counselor, solicitor
dishonest: **7** shyster **11** pettifogger
fictional: **5** Finch (Atticus) **7** Matlock (Ben), Rumpole (Horace) **10** Perry Mason
French: **6** avocat
title: **3** Esq. **7** Esquire

lax
5 loose, slack **6** casual, remiss, sloppy **7** lenient **8** careless, derelict, lacrosse **9** deficient, forgetful, negligent **10** neglectful, permissive **11** inattentive

lay
3 bet, put, set **5** apply, hatch, place, wager **6** assert, assign, ballad, charge, credit, devise, impute, settle, spread **7** amateur, arrange, ascribe, concoct, deposit, prepare, present **11** nonclerical

lay by
4 keep, save **5** amass, hoard, store **7** deposit, discard, store up **8** preserve, salt away, set aside **10** accumulate

lay down
3 set **4** rule **5** order, store, yield **6** assert, decree, define, give up, impose, ordain, record, resign **7** abandon, command, dictate, specify **8** hand over, preserve, proclaim **9** establish, prescribe, surrender **10** relinquish

layer
3 hen, ply **4** coat, film, seam, tier **5** paver, sheet **6** folium, lamina, strata (plural), veneer **7** coating, stratum **8** covering, laminate, membrane, sandwich, stratify
inner: **6** lining
of skin: **6** dermis **9** epidermis
outer: **4** skin **6** veneer

lay for
6 ambush **8** surprise

lay in
see **lay by**

layman
6 novice, oblate **7** amateur, secular **11** parishioner

lay off
4 fire, halt, quit, stop **5** avoid, cease, let go, lie by **6** desist **7** abstain, dismiss, measure, release **9** discharge, terminate **10** inactivity **11** discontinue

lay out
3 pay **4** give, plan **5** chart, dummy, place, spend **6** design, expend **7** arrange, display, exhibit, prepare **8** disburse

lay waste
4 ruin **5** wreck **6** ravage **7** destroy **8** desolate **9** devastate

lazar
5 leper

Lazarus' sister
4 Mary **6** Martha

laze
3 bum, lag **4** bask, hang, idle, loaf, loll **5** chill **6** dawdle, loiter, lounge, slouch **7** goof off, hang out **8** chill out **9** goldbrick **10** hang around

laziness
5 sloth **6** torpor **7** inertia, languor, laxness, loafing **8** idleness, lethargy, otiosity **9** indolence, lassitude, loitering, slackness **10** inactivity **11** languidness **12** listlessness

lazy
3 lax **4** idle **5** inert, slack **6** droopy, remiss, supine, torpid **7** languid, loafing, passive **8** fainéant, inactive, indolent, listless, slothful, sluggish **9** lethargic, negligent, shiftless, slowgoing **10** languorous

lazy Susan
4 tray **9** turntable

leach
4 drip, leak, ooze, perk, seep, suck, weep **5** bleed, drain, exude, issue **7** draw out, dribble, trickle **8** filtrate, perspire **9** discharge, lixiviate, percolate

lead
3 tip **4** head, hint, show, star **5** guide, metal, plumb, route, steer, trace, usher **6** bullet, ceruse, direct, escort, leader **7** captain, conduct, precede, preface **8** graphite, persuade, shepherd **9** spearhead **10** bellwether
combining form: **5** plumb **6** plumbo
ore: **6** galena **9** anglesite
oxide: **6** sinter
sounding: **5** plumb **7** plummet
symbol: **2** Pb

lead astray
6 seduce **7** corrupt

leaden
4 drab, dull, flat, gray **5** heavy, inert **6** gloomy, somber **7** languid, weighty **8** dragging, lifeless, sluggish **9** ponderous

leader
4 boss, dean, duce, guru, head, jefe, lord **5** chief, guide, pilot **6** despot, honcho, rector **7** captain, foreman, general, headman, manager, warlord **8** chairman, director, hierarch, superior **9** chieftain, commander, conductor, demagogue, harbinger, precursor, president, principal, straw boss **10** bellwether, forerunner, pacesetter
authoritarian: **10** Big Brother
Cossack: **6** ataman, hetman
German: **6** führer **7** fuehrer
Japanese: **6** shogun
military: **7** admiral, general, warlord **9** commander **12** field marshal
Muslim: **3** aga **4** agha, amir, emir, imam **5** ameer **6** caliph, mullah
national: **7** premier **9** president **12** chief of state

leading
4 arch, head, main **5** ahead, chief, first, major **6** famous, master **7** premier, primary **8** champion, foremost, headmost, peerless **9** paramount, principal, prominent, well-known **10** preeminent

lead on
3 con **4** bait, dupe, fool, gull, hoax, lure, scam, tole, toll, wile **5** cozen, flirt, tempt **6** allure, betray, cajole, coquet, delude, entice, entrap, humbug, seduce, suck in, take in, trifle **7** beguile, deceive, toy with **8** coquette, hoodwink, inveigle **9** bamboozle **11** string along

leaf
4 flip, foil, page, riff, scan, skim **5** blade, bract, folio, frond, petal, scale, sepal, thumb **6** browse, glance, riffle, spathe
angle: **4** axil
aperture: **5** stoma
axis: **6** rachis
combining form: **5** phyll **6** phyllo **7** phyllum
edge: **9** crenation
lily: **3** pad
part: **4** lobe, vein **5** blade, costa, stoma **7** petiole, stipule, tendril
pine: **6** needle
vein: **5** costa

leafage
7 foliage, umbrage, verdure

leaflet
5 flier, flyer, pinna, sheet, tract **6** folder **7** handout **8** brochure, circular, handbill, pamphlet

leafy
4 lush **5** green, shady **6** shaded, wooded **7** foliate, verdant **8** foliated, laminate **9** verdurous

league
4 band, bond, club, crew **5** class, grade, group, guild, order, union, unite **6** circle **7** circuit, combine, society **8** alliance, category, division, grouping, sodality **9** coalition **10** conference, consortium, federation, fellowship, fraternity **11** association, brotherhood, confederacy **13** confederation

Leah
daughter: **5** Dinah
father: **5** Laban
husband: **5** Jacob
sister: **6** Rachel
son: **4** Levi **5** Judah **6** Reuben, Simeon **7** Zebulun **8** Issachar

leak
4 drip, ooze, seep **5** break, crack, spill **6** escape, get out, reveal, source **7** come out, divulge, seepage **8** disclose **9** discharge **10** make public

leaky
6 broken, faulty, porous **7** cracked, damaged

lea, ley
4 veld **5** field, veldt **6** fallow, meadow **7** pasture **9** grassland, pasturage

lean
3 sag, tip **4** bend, bony, cant, heel, lank, list, slim, thin, tilt **5** gaunt, lanky, shift, slant, slope, spare **6** meager, meagre, skinny, slight, wasted **7** angular, deviate, haggard, incline, pinched, scraggy, scrawny, slender, stringy, wizened **8** gradient, rawboned **9** deficient **11** inclination

Leander's beloved
4 Hero

Leaning Tower site
4 Pisa

lean-to
3 hut **4** shed **5** shack **6** shanty **7** bivouac, shelter

leap
3 hop **4** buck, jump, loup, lutz, rise, soar **5** bound,

caper, clear, mount, vault **6** ascend, gambol, hurdle, spring **7** saltate **8** capriole, surmount
ballet: **4** jeté **9** entrechat
by a horse: **7** gambado

Lear, King
daughter: **5** Regan **7** Goneril **8** Cordelia
son: **5** Edgar **6** Edmund

learn
3 con **4** hear **5** grasp, study **6** attain, detect, master, pick up **7** acquire, catch on, discern, find out, realize, uncover, unearth **8** discover, memorize **9** apprehend, ascertain, determine **10** comprehend, understand **11** stumble onto

learned
4 sage, wise **6** expert, versed **7** bookish, erudite, sapient, studied **8** abstruse, academic, cultured, educated, esoteric, highbrow, lettered, pedantic, well-read **9** recondite, scholarly **10** cultivated, scholastic **12** intellectual

learner
4 tiro, tyro **5** pupil **6** novice, rookie **7** student, trainee **8** beginner, disciple, initiate, neophyte **9** greenhorn, postulant **10** apprentice, catechumen **11** abecedarian

learning
4 lore **6** wisdom **7** science, tuition **8** booklore, pedantry **9** education, erudition, knowledge **11** scholarship
person of: **7** egghead, scholar **9** professor **12** intellectual

lease
3 let **4** hire, rent **6** sublet **7** charter, compact **8** contract, covenant, document **11** continuance

leash
3 tie **4** bind, cord, curb, rein, rope **5** strap **6** bridle, fetter, hamper, tether **7** shackle, trammel **8** restrain **9** entrammel

least
6 fewest **7** minimal, minimum **8** smallest

leather
3 tan **4** hide, skin, whip **6** thrash
kind: **3** kid, kip, oak **4** bock, buff, calf, roan **5** crown, grain, mocha, strap, suede, whang **6** castor, latigo, oxhide, patent, roller, saddle, skiver **7** buffalo, chamois, morocco, ostrich, peccary **8** capeskin, cordovan, cordwain, shagreen
maker: **5** tawer **6** tanner **7** tannery
piece: **4** welt **5** strap, thong
prepare: **3** tan, taw **5** curry
soft: **5** mocha, suede **8** cabretta

leatherneck
6 marine

Leatherstocking Tales, The
author: **6** Cooper (James Fenimore)
hero: **5** Natty (Bumppo)
title: **7** Prairie (The) **8** Pioneers (The) **10** Deerslayer (The), Pathfinder (The) **17** Last of the Mohicans (The)

leave
2 go **3** fly, let **4** blow, cede, exit, flee, move, part, quit, will **5** allow, scram, split **6** assent, assign, beat it, begone, commit, cut out, decamp, depart, desert, devise, escape, get off, legate, permit, resign, retire, set out, vacate **7** abandon, abscond, absence, consent, consign, entrust, forsake, get away, liberty, pull out, take off, vamoose **8** bequeath, clear out, farewell, furlough, hand down, transmit, vacation, withdraw **9** departure, disappear, surrender, terminate **10** permission, relinquish, sabbatical **13** authorization

leaved
5 green **7** foliate, verdant **8** foliated

leaven
5 imbue, steep, yeast **6** infuse, invest, modify, temper, vivify **7** enliven, ingrain, lighten, suffuse **8** moderate **9** alleviate, inoculate, sourdough **12** baking powder

leavening
5 yeast **9** sourdough **10** baking soda **12** baking powder

leave of absence
8 furlough

leave off
3 end **4** halt, quit, stop **5** cease **6** desist, give up **7** abstain **8** give over, surcease **9** terminate **11** discontinue

leave out
4 omit, skip **5** elide **7** exclude

Leaves of Grass author
7 Whitman (Walt)

leavings
4 lees, orts, rest **5** dregs, scrap **6** debris, grouts **7** balance, remains, remnant, residue, rubbish **8** discards, oddments, remnants, residual, residuum **9** fragments, leftovers, remainder

Lebanon
capital: **6** Beirut
city: **4** Tyre **5** Sidon **6** Zahlah **7** Tripoli
language: **6** Arabic, French
monetary unit: **5** pound
mountain: **6** Hermon
neighbor: **5** Syria **6** Israel
river: **6** Litani **7** Orontes
sea: **13** Mediterranean
valley: **5** Bekaa

Le Carré, John
character: **6** Smiley (George)
novel: **11** Russia House (The) **17** Little Drummer Girl (The) **22** Tinker Tailor Soldier Spy **23** Spy Who Came in from the Cold (The)

lecher
4 rake, roué, wolf 7 Don Juan, seducer 8 Casanova, lothario 9 debauchee, reprobate, libertine, womanizer 10 degenerate, profligate, voluptuary 11 philanderer

lecherous
4 lewd 5 bawdy, loose, randy 6 carnal, coarse, rakish, wanton 7 fleshly, goatish, immoral, lustful, satyric 8 depraved, prurient, scabrous 9 debauched, libertine, lickerish, salacious 10 lascivious, libidinous, licentious, lubricious, profligate 11 promiscuous 12 concupiscent

lectern
4 desk 5 podia (plural), stand 6 podium

lecture
4 talk 5 chide, scold, speak 6 berate, preach, rebuke, sermon, speech 7 address, declaim, expound, oration, reproof, reprove, upbraid 8 admonish, briefing, harangue, scolding 9 chalk talk, criticism, criticize, discourse, hold forth, reprimand, talking-to 10 allocution 12 disquisition, dressing-down

lecturer
3 don 6 docent, fellow, master, orator, reader 7 scholar, speaker, teacher, trainer 9 pedagogue, preceptor, professor 10 instructor 11 academician

Leda
daughter: 5 Helen 12 Clytemnestra
father: 8 Thestius
husband: 9 Tyndareus
lover: 4 swan, Zeus
son: 6 Castor, Pollux

ledge
3 bar, rim 4 berm, lode, reef, sill, vein 5 bench, ridge, shelf 6 mantle 7 bedrock, molding 10 projection

ledger
4 book 5 tally 6 record 7 account, balance 8 notebook, register 9 reckoning

lee
5 haven 7 shelter 9 protected, sheltered

leech
4 milk, worm 5 bleed, drain 6 sponge, sucker 7 exhaust, sponger 8 barnacle, hanger-on, parasite 10 freeloader 11 bloodsucker 12 lounge lizard

leer
3 eye 4 ogle 5 fleer, gloat, smirk, sneer, stare 6 glance, goggle, squint 7 grimace

leery
4 wary 5 chary 6 unsure 7 dubious, guarded 8 cautious, doubtful, doubting 10 suspicious 11 circumspect, distrustful, mistrustful

lees
5 dregs 6 grouts, refuse 7 deposit, grounds, residue 8 leavings, residual, residuum, sediment 9 settlings 11 precipitate

leeward
8 downwind
opposite: 8 windward

leeway
4 play, room 5 scope, space 6 margin 7 breadth, compass, freedom, liberty 8 latitude 9 elbowroom, tolerance

left
4 port 7 liberal, radical 8 departed, deserted, larboard, residual, sinister 9 abandoned, discarded, remaining, sinistral

left-handed
5 inept 6 clumsy, gauche 7 awkward, dubious 8 fumbling, southpaw 9 ambiguous, equivocal, insincere, maladroit 10 morganatic

left-hand page
5 verso

leftover
5 extra, spare 6 excess, unused 7 remnant, reserve, residue, surplus, uneaten, vestige 8 residual, unneeded 9 redundant, remainder, remaining 10 unconsumed 11 superfluous

leftovers
see **leavings**

leftward
4 levo 5 aport
go: 3 haw

leg
3 bow, gam 4 limb 5 shank, stage 6 branch 7 support, upright 8 cabriole 9 appendage, drumstick
bone: 4 shin 5 femur, tibia 6 fibula 7 patella
part: 4 calf, crus, foot, knee, shin 5 ankle, thigh

legacy
4 gift 5 trust 6 devise, estate 7 bequest 8 heirloom, heritage 9 endowment, patrimony, tradition 10 birthright 11 benefaction, inheritance

legal
5 legit, licit 6 lawful 7 allowed 8 innocent 9 juridical, statutory 10 legitimate, sanctioned
matter: 3 res 4 case, suit
order: 4 writ 7 summons 8 subpoena
organization: 3 ABA
party: 6 suitor 8 litigant 9 defendant, plaintiff
restraint: 8 estoppel

legal tender
3 wad 4 cash 5 bread, dough, money, moola, notes 6 moolah, specie 7 coinage 8 banknote, currency 9 long green

legate
4 will 5 endow, envoy, grant, leave 6 bestow, commit, devise, deputy, devise, pass on 7 entrust, leave to 8 bequeath, delegate, emissary, hand down, transmit 10 ambassador

legatee
4 heir **7** devisee **9** inheritor

legato
5 fluid **6** smooth **7** flowing

legend
3 key **4** lore, myth, saga, tale, yarn **5** fable, motto, story **6** mythos **7** caption, fiction **8** epigraph, folklore, folktale, tall tale **9** mythology, tradition **11** inscription

legendary
5 famed **6** fabled, famous, mythic **7** fabular, fancied, fictive, storied **8** fabulous, mythical, renowned, supposed **9** well-known **10** apocryphal, celebrated **11** illustrious, traditional **12** mythological

legerdemain
5 magic **8** prestige, trickery **9** chicanery, conjuring, deception **13** sleight of hand

leggings
5 chaps **7** puttees **9** gambadoes

leghorn
3 hat **4** fowl **5** straw **7** chicken

legible
5 clear **8** distinct, readable **12** decipherable, intelligible

legion
4 army, host, many, mass, rout **5** cloud, crowd, drove, flock, horde **6** myriad, scores, sundry, throng **7** phalanx, various **8** numerous, populous **9** countless, multitude **10** numberless

legislate
5 enact, order **6** codify, decree, ordain, permit, ratify **7** empower, mandate **8** legalize, regulate, sanction **9** establish

legislation
3 act, law **4** acts, bill, code, laws **5** bills, codes, rules **6** edicts **7** statute **8** charters, dictates, statutes **9** enactment, lawmaking **10** enactments, ordinances, regulation **11** regulations **12** codification

legislator
5 solon **7** senator **8** alderman, lawgiver, lawmaker **10** councilman **11** assemblyman, congressman, thesmothete

legislature
4 diet **5** house, junta **6** senate **7** council **8** assembly, congress **10** parliament
Communist: **6** soviet **9** politburo, presidium
Danish: **9** Folketing
Finnish: **9** Eduskunta
German: **9** Bundesrat, Bundestag
Iceland: **7** Althing
Ireland: **4** Dáil
Israel: **7** Knesset
Norway: **8** Storting
one-house: **10** unicameral
Poland: **4** Sejm
Russian: **4** duma
Spain: **6** Cortes
Sweden: **7** Riksdag
two-house: **9** bicameral
Ukraine: **4** Rada

legitimate
4 fair, just, true **5** legal, licit, sound, usual, valid **6** kosher, lawful, normal, proper **7** genuine, regular, typical **8** accepted, innocent, orthodox, rightful **9** allowable, authentic, canonical, customary **10** admissable, authorized, reasonable, recognized **11** justifiable, well-founded

Le Guin, Ursula K.
novel: **7** Telling (The) **8** Solitude (The) **12** Dispossessed (The) **18** Left Hand of Darkness (The)
series: **8** Earthsea

legume
3 dal, pea, pod **4** bean, dhal, guar, seed **5** pulse **6** clover, lentil **7** soybean

leg up
3 aid **4** edge, lift **5** boost **6** assist **9** advantage, head start

lei
6 wreath **7** garland **8** necklace

Leibniz's invention
8 calculus

Leif Eriksson
discovery: **7** Vinland
father: **4** Eric, Erik (the Red)

leisure
4 ease, rest, time **6** casual, chance, repose **7** freedom, liberty **8** downtime **10** relaxation **11** opportunity

leisurely
4 easy, slow **6** lazily, slowly **7** relaxed, restful **8** laid-back **9** unhurried

leitmotiv
4 idea **5** theme, topic **6** burden, motive, thesis **7** subject **8** idée fixe

lemma
5 bract, theme **7** heading, premise, theorem **8** argument **11** proposition

lemon
3 dud **4** bomb, bust, flop **5** fruit, loser, scent **6** flavor, yellow **7** failure

lemur
4 lori **5** indri, loris, potto **6** aye-aye, colugo, galago **7** tarsier **8** bush baby

lend
4 give, loan **5** allow, grant **6** afford, oblige, supply **7** advance, furnish, provide **11** accommodate

L'Engle novel
10 Many Waters **13** Wind in the Door (A), Wrinkle in Time (A)

length
4 span **5** ambit, range, reach, realm, scope **6** extent, radius **7** compass, expanse, measure, purview, section, stretch, yardage **8** distance, duration

lengthen
6 expand, extend, let out **7** draw out, prolong, spin out, stretch **8** elongate, increase, protract **9** string out
Scottish: **3** eke

lengthy
4 long **8** dragging, drawn-out, extended, overlong **9** elongated, prolonged **10** long-winded, protracted, voluminous **12** interminable

leniency
5 mercy **7** quarter **8** clemency **9** tolerance **10** indulgence, toleration **11** forbearance

lenient
4 easy, kind, mild, soft **6** benign, gentle, kindly **7** amiable, clement **8** merciful, obliging, tolerant **9** benignant, forgiving, indulgent **10** forbearing, permissive

lenity
5 mercy **7** quarter **8** clemency **9** tolerance **10** humaneness, indulgence **11** forbearance

lens
5 glass **6** lentil **8** meniscus
kind: **5** toric **6** convex **7** bifocal, concave **8** trifocal

lento
4 slow **5** tempo

Leofric's wife
6 Godiva

Leoncavallo opera
9 Pagliacci (I) **10** Chatterton

leonine
8 lionlike

Leonora
7 heroine
alias: **7** Fidelio
husband: **9** Florestan

leopard
3 cat **4** pard **5** ounce **7** panther

leper
6 pariah **7** Ishmael, outcast **8** castaway, derelict **9** incurable **10** Ishmaelite **11** untouchable
hospital: **9** lazaretto
island: **7** Molokai
priest: **6** Damien (Father)

Leper Priest
6 Damien (Father)

lepers' hospital
9 lazaretto

lepers' island
7 Molokai

lepidoptera
5 moths **8** skippers **11** butterflies **12** caterpillars

Leporello's master
11 Don Giovanni

leprechaun
3 elf **5** dwarf, fairy **6** sprite **7** brownie
trade: **8** cobbling

lepton
4 coin, muon **8** electron, neutrino

Lesage hero
7 Gil Blas

Lesbos poet
6 Sappho **7** Alcaeus

____ LeShan
3 Eda

lesion
3 cut **4** boil, flaw, harm, sore **5** ulcer, wound **6** injury **7** blister

Lesotho
capital: **6** Maseru
ethnic group: **5** Sotho
former name: **10** Basutoland
language: **5** Sotho
monetary unit: **4** loti
mountain: **9** Ntlenyana
neighbor: **11** South Africa
river: **6** Orange **7** Caledon

less
5 lower, minus **7** reduced, without

lessen
3 cut **4** clip, crop, ease, thin, wane **5** abate, erode, lower, taper **6** dilute, impair, minify, recede, reduce, shrink, weaken **7** abridge, assuage, curtail, degrade, dwindle, lighten, relieve, subside **8** decrease, diminish, minimize, mitigate, taper off **9** attenuate

lessening
4 drop, fall **5** letup **8** decrease, slowdown **9** abatement, reduction **10** curtailing, diminution **11** degradation

lesser
5 lower, minor **7** smaller **8** inferior **9** secondary, small-time, subjacent **11** minor-league, subordinate **13** insignificant

lesson
4 text **5** chide, moral, study **6** rebuke **7** example, lecture, reading, reprove, warning **8** admonish, exercise, homework, reproach **9** reprimand **10** admonition, assignment **11** instruction

lessor
8 landlady, landlord 9 landowner 10 freeholder
let
4 make, rent 5 allow, grant, lease, leave 6 assign, permit, suffer 9 authorize 11 obstruction
letdown
5 slump 6 defeat 7 decline, descent, failure, reverse, setback 10 anticlimax, depression, misfortune 11 frustration
let go
3 can 4 boot, fire, free, sack 5 remit 6 unhand 7 dismiss, neglect, release, set free 8 liberate 9 discharge, terminate
lethal
4 fell 5 fatal 6 deadly, mortal, poison 7 baleful, deathly 8 poisoned, virulent 9 murderous, poisonous 11 destructive, devastating
lethargic
4 dull, idle, slow 5 dopey, heavy, inert 6 draggy, supine, torpid 7 dormant, laggard, languid, passive 8 comatose, dilatory, inactive, listless, slothful, sluggish 9 apathetic, impassive 10 languorous, phlegmatic, spiritless 11 indifferent 12 hebetudinous 13 lackadaisical
lethargy
5 sloth 6 apathy, phlegm, stupor, torpor 7 inertia, languor, slumber 8 dullness, hebetude, idleness, laziness 9 disregard, inanition, indolence, inertness, lassitude, torpidity 10 inactivity, supineness 11 impassivity, passiveness 12 listlessness
lethe
7 amnesia 8 oblivion 13 forgetfulness
Leto
see **Latona**
let off
5 spare 6 excuse, exempt 7 absolve, relieve 8 dispense 9 discharge
let on
3 own 5 admit, allow, grant, own up, spill 6 betray, fess up, reveal 7 concede, confess, confirm, divulge, pretend 8 disclose, give away
let out
5 blurt, loose 6 exhale 7 release, set free, unloose 8 lengthen, liberate, set loose 9 discharge, turn loose
letter
2 ar, ef, el, em, en, ex 3 bee, cee, cue, dee, eff, ell, ess, gee, jay, kay, pee, tee, vee, wye, zed, zee 4 line, mail, memo, note, rune 5 aitch, print, vowel 6 report, screed, symbol 7 epistle, message, missive 8 dispatch, inscribe 9 consonant
airmail: 8 aerogram
Anglo-Saxon:
(see **Anglo-Saxon**)
Arabic:
(see **alphabet**)
Greek:
(see **alphabet**)
Hebrew:
(see **alphabet**)
kind: 4 open 5 chain, roman 6 italic, uncial 8 Dear John
large: 7 capital 9 majuscule, uppercase
papal: 4 bull 10 encyclical
small: 9 lowercase, minuscule
start: 4 Dear
lettuce
3 cos 4 Bibb, head 6 Boston 7 iceberg, romaine, Simpson 10 butterweed
let up
3 ebb 4 fall, stop, wane 5 abate, cease 6 lessen, relent 7 die away, die down, ease off, slacken, subside 8 decrease, diminish, moderate, taper off
letup
4 lull 5 break, pause 7 respite 9 abatement, cessation, lessening, reduction 10 slackening
levee
4 dike, dock, pier, quay 5 jetty, ridge, wharf 7 seawall 8 assembly, function 9 reception 10 breakwater, embankment, riverfront
level
3 aim, lay, par 4 calm, even, flat, raze, same, tier, true 5 equal, floor, flush, grade, plane 6 direct, ground, smooth, status, steady 7 aligned, flatten, mow down 8 balanced, bulldoze, demolish, equalize, parallel, smoothen, standing 9 bring down, intensity, knock down, magnitude 10 equivalent, horizontal, reasonable 11 equilibrium
lever
3 bar, pry 4 jack, tool 5 jimmy, peavy, prize 6 peavey, tappet 7 crowbar
leverage
5 clout, power 7 exploit 9 advantage, dominance, influence 11 superiority 13 effectiveness
leveret
4 hare
Levi
father: 5 Jacob
mother: 4 Leah
son: 6 Kohath, Merari 7 Gershon
leviathan
4 huge 5 giant, jumbo, large, titan, whale 7 Goliath, immense, mammoth, massive, monster, titanic 8 behemoth, colossal, colossus, enormous, gigantic 9 cyclopean, monstrous 10 formidable, gargantuan 11 elephantine, monstrosity
Leviathan author
6 Hobbes (Thomas)

levitate
4 lift, rise **5** float, raise **7** elevate, suspend

levity
5 folly, humor **8** buoyancy **9** absurdity, flippancy, frivolity, giddiness, lightness, silliness **10** jocularity, volatility

levy
3 tax **4** duty, toll, wage **5** exact, lay on **6** assess, charge, custom, enlist, impose, impost, tariff **7** carry on, collect **9** conscript **10** assessment, enlistment **12** conscription

lewd
5 bawdy, gross **6** coarse, ribald, smutty, vulgar **7** fleshly, goatish, lustful, obscene, satyric **8** depraved, improper, indecent, prurient, unchaste **9** debauched, lecherous, libertine, lickerish, salacious **10** indelicate, lascivious, libidinous, licentious, lubricious

Lewis and Clark interpreter
9 Sacagawea, Sacajawea

Lewis work
7 Babbitt **9** Dodsworth **10** Arrowsmith, Main Street **11** Elmer Gantry **16** Screwtape Letters (The) **18** Chronicles of Narnia (The)

lexicographer
8 compiler
American: 6 Porter (Noah) **7** Webster (Noah) **9** Worcester (Joseph)
English: 4 Wyld (Henry) **6** Fowler (Francis, Henry), Murray (James), Onions (Charles) **7** Craigie (William), Johnson (Samuel) **9** Partridge (Eric)
French: 6 Littré (Paul-Emile) **8** Larousse (Pierre)
German: 5 Grimm (Jakob, Wilhelm)

lexicon
4 cant **6** jargon **8** glossary, language, wordbook **9** inventory, word-hoard **10** dictionary, repertoire, vocabulary **11** terminology

liable
3 apt **4** open **5** given, prone **6** likely **7** exposed, subject **8** inclined **9** sensitive **10** answerable, assailable, vulnerable **11** accountable, responsible, susceptible

liaison
4 bond, link **5** amour, fixer **6** affair, broker, hookup **7** contact, romance **8** intrigue **9** go-between **10** connection **12** entanglement, intermediary, relationship **13** communication

liana
4 vine

liar
6 fibber **7** Ananias **8** fabulist, perjurer **9** falsifier **12** prevaricator
female: 8 Sapphira

libation
5 drink **6** liquid, liquor **7** potable **8** beverage, oblation, offering, potation

libel
4 slur **5** smear **6** defame, malign, vilify **7** asperse, calumny, obloquy, slander, traduce **8** bad-mouth, tear down **9** aspersion, denigrate **10** calumniate, defamation, scandalize **11** denigration

libelous
6 untrue **9** injurious, invidious, maligning, traducing, vilifying **10** backbiting, calumnious, defamatory, derogative, derogatory, detracting, detractive, malevolent, pejorative, scandalous, slanderous

liberal
4 full, open **5** ample, broad, loose **6** lavish **7** copious, profuse, radical **8** abundant, generous, prodigal, tolerant **9** bounteous, bountiful, indulgent, plentiful, unsparing **10** benevolent, bighearted, charitable, freehanded, munificent, openhanded, permissive, unorthodox **11** broad-minded

liberal arts
quadrivium: 5 music **8** geometry **9** astronomy **10** arithmetic
trivium: 5 logic **7** grammar **8** rhetoric

liberate
4 free **5** loose **7** manumit, release, unchain **9** discharge, unshackle **10** commandeer, emancipate **11** appropriate, expropriate

liberator
6 savior **7** messiah **9** deliverer
of Argentina: 9 San Martín (José de)
of Chile: 8 O'Higgins (Bernardo)
of Ecuador: 5 Sucre (Antonio José de)
of Scotland: 5 Bruce (Robert the)
of South America: 7 Bolívar (Simón)

Liberia
capital: 8 Monrovia
coast: 3 Kru **5** Grain
neighbor: 6 Guinea **10** Ivory Coast **11** Côte d'Ivoire, Sierra Leone

Liberian
language: 3 Kwa
native: 3 Kru, Vai **4** Gola, Toma **5** Bassa, Grebo **6** Kruman

libertine
4 lewd, rake, roué **5** bawdy, loose, randy **6** carnal, rakish, wanton **7** Don Juan, lustful, raffish, satyric **8** Casanova **9** debauched, debauchee, dissolute, lecherous, salacious **10** degenerate, dissipated, lascivious, libidinous, licentious, profligate **11** promiscuous

liberty
4 risk **5** leave **6** chance **7** freedom, license

8 autonomy 9 franchise, privilege 10 permission 11 familiarity 12 emancipation, independence

libidinous
4 lewd 5 bawdy, loose, randy 6 carnal, rakish, wanton 7 fleshly, goatish, lustful, satyric 8 depraved, prurient 9 debauched, lecherous, libertine, lickerish, salacious 10 lascivious, licentious, lubricious, profligate 11 promiscuous 12 concupiscent

librarian
5 Dewey (Melvil)

library
7 archive 8 atheneum 9 athenaeum 11 bibliotheca
desk: 6 carrel

Libya
capital: 7 Tripoli
city: 8 Benghazi
desert: 6 Sahara
gulf: 5 Sidra
language: 6 Arabic 7 Hamitic
leader: 7 Gadhafi, Qaddafi (Mu'ammar)
monetary unit: 5 dinar
neighbor: 4 Chad 5 Egypt, Niger, Sudan 7 Algeria, Tunisia
sea: 13 Mediterranean

lice
7 cooties

license
3 let, tag 5 allow, grant, leave 6 enable, laxity, permit, suffer, ticket 7 certify, empower, freedom, go-ahead, liberty 8 accredit, document, sanction, variance 9 authority, authorize, slackness 10 permission, profligacy 11 certificate, impropriety 12 carte blanche 13 authorization

licentious
4 lewd 5 bawdy, loose, randy 6 amoral, carnal, rakish, wanton 7 fleshly, goatish, immoral, lustful, satyric 8 depraved, prurient, scabrous 9 abandoned, debauched, dissolute, lecherous, libertine, salacious 10 lascivious, libidinous, lubricious, profligate 11 promiscuous 12 concupiscent

lichen
4 moss 6 archil, litmus 7 oakmoss
genus: 5 Usnea

licit
4 okay 5 legal 6 lawful 7 allowed 8 approved, innocent, licensed 9 allowable, permitted 10 admissible, authorized, legitimate, sanctioned 11 permissible

lick
3 bit, dab, dig, hit, lap, rap, tan 4 beat, dash, deck, down, drub, hint, swat, whip, wipe 5 cream, pinch, pound, smack, smear, spank, taste, touch, trace, whiff 6 defeat, master, punish, thrash, tongue, wallop 7 clobber, conquer, shellac, trounce 8 lambaste, outstrip, overcome, surmount 9 overwhelm

lickerish
see **libidinous**

lickety-split
4 fast 5 apace 6 presto, pronto 7 flat out, hastily, quickly, rapidly, swiftly 8 chop-chop, full tilt, headlong, pell-mell, speedily 9 posthaste 13 expeditiously, precipitately

licorice
4 root 5 candy
pill: 6 cachou

lid
3 cap, top 5 cover 8 covering
moss: 9 operculum

lie
3 fib 4 rest, tale 5 exist, fable, libel 6 belong, canard, covert, delude, extend, inhere, remain, repose, reside 7 consist, falsify, falsity, perjure, recline, untruth, whopper 8 misspeak, misstate, tall tale 9 dissemble, falsehood, fish story, mendacity 10 inaccuracy, taradiddle 11 prevaricate 12 misstatement

Liechtenstein
capital: 5 Vaduz
language: 6 German
monetary unit: 4 euro
mountain range: 4 Alps
neighbor: 7 Austria 11 Switzerland
river: 5 Rhein, Rhine

lied
4 song 7 art song

lief
4 fain, soon 6 freely, gladly 7 happily, readily 9 willingly 11 contentedly

liege
4 lord, true 5 loyal 6 ardent, master, vassal 7 abiding, staunch 8 constant, enduring, faithful, reliable, resolute, stalwart 9 dedicated, steadfast 10 dependable

lien
5 claim 6 charge, demand 8 interest, mortgage 10 imposition

lieu
5 place, stead

lieutenant
4 aide 5 looey, looie 6 backup, deputy 7 officer 9 assistant, coadjutor 10 aide-de-camp, coadjutant 11 subordinate

life
3 vim 4 brio, dash, élan, soul 5 verve 6 energy, esprit, spirit 8 vitality 9 animation, existence
animal: 5 fauna
animal and plant: 5 biota

combining form: 3 bio
plant: 5 flora
relating to: 5 vital 8 biologic 10 biological
science: 7 biology

life jacket
7 Mae West

lifeless
4 dead, drab, dull 5 inert 6 asleep, barren, torpid, wasted 7 defunct, extinct 8 comatose, deceased, departed 9 inanimate, inorganic, insensate 10 lackluster

lifelike
5 exact 7 natural, precise 8 accurate, faithful, veristic 9 realistic

life of ___
5 Riley 8 the party

lift
4 heft, hike, jack, load, rear, rise 5 boost, exalt, filch, heave, hoist, pinch, raise, steal, swipe, theft 6 assist, pick up, pilfer, repeal, revoke, snitch, take up 7 elevate, purloin, rescind, reverse, support 8 levitate, stealing, thievery 10 plagiarize

lift-off
6 ascent, launch 7 takeoff 9 launching

ligament
3 tie 4 band, bond, link, yoke 5 nexus 8 ligature, vinculum 10 connection

ligature
see **ligament**

Ligeia author
3 Poe (Edgar Allan)

light
4 airy, dawn, deft, easy, fair, fire, lamp, land, luck, neon 5 blond, flash, minor, perch, roost, sunny, torch 6 beacon, blithe, bright, candle, casual, facile, flimsy, fluffy, ignite, kindle, settle, simple, slight, strobe 7 lantern, sunrise, trivial 8 cheerful, daybreak, enkindle, illumine, luminous, trifling 9 frivolous, touch down 10 chandelier, effortless, illuminate
and shade interplay: 11 chiaroscuro
combining form: 4 luci, phot 5 lumin, photo 6 lumini, lumino
indicator: 3 LED
measure: 3 lux 4 phot 5 lumen 6 candle 7 candela
refractor: 5 prism
relating to: 6 photic
ring: 4 halo 6 corona 7 aureola, aureole
science: 6 optics
source: 3 sun 4 lamp

light-emitting
6 lasing, lucent 7 beaming, fulgent, glowing, lambent, shining 8 luminous 9 effulgent, refulgent

lighten
4 dawn, ease, fade 5 allay, cheer 6 bleach, lessen, reduce 7 assuage, gladden, hearten, mollify, relieve 8 decrease, mitigate, unburden 9 alleviate, attenuate, extenuate 11 disencumber

light-headed
5 dizzy, faint, giddy, silly 6 swimmy 7 flighty 9 frivolous, slaphappy 10 unbalanced 11 disoriented, vertiginous

lighthearted
3 gay 4 glad 5 happy, jolly, merry, sunny 6 blithe, jocund, jovial, joyful, joyous, lively, upbeat 7 buoyant, festive, gleeful, playful 8 carefree, cheerful, mirthful, volatile 9 easygoing, expansive, sprightly, vivacious 10 blithesome, insouciant 12 effervescent, happy-go-lucky, high-spirited

lighthouse
6 beacon 7 warning

lighting crew member
6 gaffer

lightless
4 dark 5 unlit 7 aphotic, stygian 9 tenebrous, pitch-dark 10 caliginous, pitch-black 11 unillumined

lightness
6 bounce, gaiety, levity 8 buoyancy, vivacity 9 animation, frivolity 10 cheeriness, liveliness, resiliency, volatility 12 cheerfulness 13 effervescence

lightning bug
7 firefly

lignite
4 coal 9 brown coal

likable
4 nice 6 genial 7 affable, amiable, popular, winning, winsome 8 charming, engaging, friendly, pleasant, pleasing 9 agreeable, appealing, congenial 10 attractive, personable 11 good-natured

like
3 à la, dig 4 akin, same, such 5 close, enjoy, equal, match 6 admire, agnate, akin to, allied, prefer, relish 7 approve, cognate, kindred, related, similar, uniform 8 parallel, selfsame 9 analogous, consonant, identical 10 appreciate, comparable, comprehend, equivalent, resembling

likelihood
6 chance 8 prospect 11 eventuality, possibility, presumption, probability

likely
3 apt 5 given, prone 6 liable, odds-on 7 assumed 8 credible, inclined, possible, presumed, probable, probably, reliable, suitable 9 doubtless, plausible, promising 10 achievable, attractive, believable, presumably

liken
5 match **6** equate **7** compare **8** parallel **10** assimilate

likeness
4 copy, twin **5** clone, image **6** double, effigy **7** analogy, picture, replica **8** affinity, portrait, sameness **9** depiction, facsimile, look-alike, semblance **10** appearance, photograph, similarity, similitude, uniformity **11** resemblance

likewise
3 and, too **4** also **5** ditto **6** as well, withal **7** besides **8** moreover **9** similarly **10** in addition **11** furthermore

liking
4 bent **5** fancy, taste **6** desire **8** affinity, appetite, fondness, penchant, pleasure, soft spot, weakness **9** affection **10** attraction, partiality **11** inclination **12** appreciation, predilection

Lilith
husband: 4 Adam
successor: 3 Eve

lilliputian
3 wee **4** runt, tiny **5** dwarf, petty, pygmy, small **6** bantam, little, midget, peanut, peewee, shrimp **7** manikin **8** mannikin, pint-size, Tom Thumb **9** miniature, pint-sized, undersize **10** diminutive, homunculus

lilt
3 air **4** flow, purl, sing, song, tune **5** carol, pulse, swing, tempo **6** melody, rhythm **7** cadence **8** buoyancy

lily
3 pad **4** aloe, sego **5** calla, tiger, yucca **6** flower **7** leopard **8** mariposa
genus: 4 Aloe

lily-livered
5 sissy, wimpy **6** craven, yellow **7** caitiff, chicken, fearful, gutless **8** cowardly, cowering, poltroon, recreant, timorous **9** spineless, spunkless, weak-kneed **12** fainthearted, poor-spirited **13** pusillanimous

lily-white
4 pure **6** chaste **7** upright **8** innocent, virtuous **9** blameless, estimable, exclusive, exemplary, guiltless, righteous, untainted **10** inculpable **11** uncorrupted

limb
3 arm, fin, gam, leg **4** lobe, twig, wing **5** bough, shoot, spray, sprig **6** branch, member, pinion **7** flipper **8** offshoot **9** appendage, dismember, extremity

limber
4 spry **5** agile, lithe, loose **6** nimble, pliant, supple **7** elastic, lissome, pliable, springy **8** flexible **9** lithesome, resilient

limbo
5 dance **7** neglect **8** oblivion **9** detention, purgatory **11** confinement, uncertainty

lime
4 tree **5** color, fruit, green **6** citrus, linden **7** calcium

limen
8 doorsill, doorstep **9** threshold

limerick
4 poem **5** verse
writer: 4 Lear (Edward)

limestone
4 tufa, tuff **5** chalk **6** marble, oolite **7** coquina **10** travertine

lime tree
6 linden

limit
3 bar, cap, end, fix, max, set **4** curb **5** check, quota **6** border, bounds, curfew, define, extent, hinder, lessen **7** confine, curtail, enclose, extreme, mark out, measure **8** boundary, deadline, restrain, restrict **9** constrict, demarcate, determine, extremity, prescribe **12** circumscribe

limitless
4 vast **7** endless **8** infinite, wide-open **9** boundless, unbounded **10** indefinite **11** illimitable, innumerable, measureless **12** immeasurable, incalculable **13** inexhaustible

limn
4 draw **5** image, paint **6** depict, render, sketch **7** outline, picture, portray **8** describe **9** delineate, interpret, represent

Limoges product
5 china **9** porcelain

limp
3 lax **4** bent, halt, lame, wilt **5** hitch, loose, slack, spent, weary **6** dodder, droopy, falter, hobble **7** flaccid, languid, shamble, shuffle, slumped **8** drooping **9** enervated, exhausted **10** spiritless

limpid
4 pure **5** clear, lucid **6** glassy, serene **8** pellucid **10** see-through, untroubled **11** crystalline, translucent, transparent **12** crystal clear

limping
4 halt, lame **5** gimpy **7** halting **8** hobbling, lameness **9** faltering **12** claudication

linchpin
8 backbone, mainstay

Lincoln
assassin: 5 Booth (John Wilkes)
biographer: 8 Sandburg (Carl)
debater: 7 Douglas (Stephen)
law partner: 7 Herndon (William)
mother: 5 Nancy (Hanks)

nickname: **9** Honest Abe **12** Railsplitter
photographer: **5** Brady (Mathew)
secretary of state: **6** Seward (William)
secretary of war: **7** Stanton (Edwin)
wife: **8** Mary Todd

Lindsay poem
5 Congo (The)

line
3 row **4** file, rank, rope **5** array, goods, queue, route **6** border, column, cordon, series, strain, string **7** contour, descent **8** business, pedigree, sequence **10** employment, occupation, succession
curved: **3** arc
mathematical: **6** vector
metrical: **5** verse **6** verset **8** versicle
of rulers: **7** dynasty
weather map: **6** isobar

lineage
3 kin **4** clan, folk, race **5** birth, blood, breed, house, stirp, stock, tribe **6** family, origin, strain **7** descent, kindred **8** ancestry, breeding, pedigree **9** forebears, genealogy **10** derivation, extraction, succession **11** forefathers, progenitors

lineal
6 direct **8** familial **9** ancestral, inherited **10** bequeathed, hereditary

lineament
4 form **6** figure, relief **7** contour, feature, outline, profile **10** figuration, silhouette

lined
5 drawn, ruled **7** aligned, striate, striped **8** streaked, wrinkled

linen
4 lawn **5** cloth, toile **6** byssus, damask, fabric, napery, sheets **7** batiste, bedding, cambric, taffeta **8** cretonne, lingerie
fiber: **3** tow
source: **4** flax

lineup
6 roster

linger
3 lag **4** bide, drag, loll, mope, poke, stay, wait **5** abide, dally, delay, mosey, tarry **6** dawdle, loiter, put off, remain **7** saunter **10** dillydally **11** stick around **13** procrastinate

lingerie
8 negligee

lingo
4 cant **5** argot, idiom, slang **6** jargon, patois, patter, speech, tongue **7** dialect **10** vernacular, vocabulary

linguist
8 polyglot **11** philologist

linguistics
9 philology

liniment
3 oil **4** aloe, balm **5** salve **6** lotion **7** anodyne, unction, unguent **8** aloe vera, lenitive, ointment **9** demulcent **11** embrocation

lining
6 facing, insert **8** wainscot

link
3 tie **4** bind, bond, join, knot, ring, yoke **5** hitch, nexus, unite **6** attach, copula, couple, hookup, relate, splice **7** bracket, combine, conjoin, connect, contact, joining **8** catenate, division, vinculum **9** associate, conjugate **10** attachment, connection **11** association **12** relationship

linksman
6 golfer

linnet
5 finch

lint
3 fur, nap **4** down, fuzz, pile **5** floss, fluff **9** ravelings

lion
3 cat **4** puma **6** cougar **7** notable **8** eminence, luminary **9** carnivore, personage
group: **5** pride
young: **3** cub

lionhearted
4 bold **5** brave **6** heroic **7** valiant **8** fearless, intrepid, stalwart, unafraid, valorous **9** dauntless **10** courageous

lionize
4 fete **5** exalt, extol, honor **7** glorify **8** venerate **9** celebrate

Lion King, The
character: **4** Nala, Scar, Zazu **5** Simba, Timon **6** Banzai, Mufasa, Pumbaa, Rafiki, Sarabi, Shenzi **8** Sarafina
composer: **4** John (Elton)
film score: **6** Zimmer (Hans)
lyricist: **4** Rice (Tim)
setting: **10** Pride Lands
voice: **5** Irons (Jeremy), Jones (James Earl), Marin (Cheech) **8** Atkinson (Rowan), Goldberg (Whoopi) **9** Broderick (Matthew)

lion monkey
7 tamarin **8** marmoset

Lion of Judah
8 Selassie (Haile)

lip
3 rim **4** brim, edge, guff, kiss, sass **6** labium, labrum, margin **8** back talk
relating to: **6** labial

lipid
3 fat, wax

lipped
7 labiate **9** bilabiate

liquefy
3 run **4** flux, melt, thaw **5** smelt **6** render **8** dissolve **10** deliquesce

liqueur
4 arak, ouzo, raki **5** crème **6** arrack, brandy, Kahlua, kirsch, kummel, pastis, Pernod **7** Campari, Cinzano, cordial, curaçao, ratafia, sambuca, sloe gin **8** absinthe, amaretto, anisette, Drambuie, Galliano, Tía Maria **10** Chartreuse, pousse-café

liquid
5 drink, fluid, sauce, water **6** watery **7** flowing **8** beverage, emulsion **11** mellifluous
container: **3** cup, jug, keg, mug **4** vial **5** glass **6** bottle, goblet **7** pitcher, tumbler
flammable: **3** gas, oil **5** ether, furan **6** butane, toluol **7** alcohol, toluene **8** gasoline, pyridine
measure: **2** cc, ml, oz, pt, qt **3** cup, gal **4** pint **5** liter, litre, ounce, quart **6** gallon
thick: **5** syrup **8** molasses

liquidate
3 pay **4** do in, kill **5** pay up, purge **6** murder, remove, rub out, settle, square **7** bump off, convert, satisfy **8** amortize, dispatch, dissolve, knock off **9** eliminate, terminate **10** annihilate **11** assassinate

liquor
5 booze, drink, hooch **7** alcohol, potable, spirits **8** potation **9** firewater, inebriant **10** intoxicant
add: **4** lace **5** spike
Asian: **4** arak **6** arrack
homemade: **5** hooch **9** moonshine **10** bathtub gin
inferior: **5** hooch **6** red-eye, rotgut
Japanese: **4** sake, saki
kind: **3** gin, rum, rye **5** vodka **6** brandy, geneva, scotch, whisky **7** aquavit, bourbon, schnaps, whiskey **8** schnapps, vermouth **9** aqua vitae **10** barley-bree
malt: **3** ale **4** beer **5** nappy, stout **6** porter
measure: **4** dram, shot **6** jigger **7** shooter
Mexican: **5** sotol **6** mescal **7** tequila

lissome
5 agile, lithe **6** limber, nimble, supple, svelte **7** slender **8** flexible, graceful

list
3 tip **4** book, cant, file, heel, lean, menu, note, post, roll, tilt **5** arena, count, index, slant, slate, slope, tally **6** agenda, census, docket, lineup, record, roster **7** catalog, incline, itemize, specify **8** calendar, glossary, manifest, register, roll call, schedule, tabulate **9** chronicle, enumerate, inventory **13** particularize
type: **3** hit **4** life, to-do, wish **5** punch, short **6** linked **7** laundry, mailing, waiting **8** shopping **10** best-seller

listen
4 hark, hear, heed, hist, note **5** audit **6** attend, harken **7** hearken, monitor **8** overhear **9** eavesdrop

listeners
8 audience

listless
4 dull, limp, weak **5** inert, slack **6** torpid, vacant **7** languid **8** indolent, sluggish **9** apathetic, enervated, lethargic, lymphatic **10** languorous, phlegmatic, spiritless **11** indifferent, languishing **13** lackadaisical

listlessness
6 apathy, stupor, torpor **7** fatigue, inertia, languor **8** doldrums, lethargy **9** indolence, lassitude, torpidity **10** enervation

litany
4 list **5** chant **6** prayer **7** account, listing, recital, refrain **8** petition, rogation **9** catalogue **10** invocation, recitation **11** enumeration **12** supplication

literal
4 bald, bare **5** blunt, exact, stark **6** actual, simple, strict **7** precise **8** accurate, bona fide, faithful, verbatim **9** authentic **11** unvarnished, word-for-word **13** unembellished

literally
5 truly **6** direct, indeed, openly, simply **7** plainly, totally, utterly **8** candidly, directly, verbatim **9** genuinely, virtually **11** word for word

literary
7 bookish, erudite, learned **8** lettered, well-read **9** authorial, scholarly **12** belletristic

literary work
4 book, opus, play, poem **5** drama, essay, novel **10** short story

literature
5 prose **6** poetry **7** fiction **13** belles-lettres

lithe
4 lean, slim **5** agile, spare **6** limber, supple, svelte **7** lissome, pliable, slender **8** flexible, graceful

lithium symbol
2 Li

lithographer
4 Ives (James Merritt) **7** Currier (Nathaniel)

Lithuania
capital: **7** Vilnius
city: **6** Kaunas **8** Klaipeda
monetary unit: **5** litas
neighbor: **6** Latvia, Poland, Russia **7** Belarus
river: **5** Neman, Venta **7** Lielupe
sea: **6** Baltic

litigant
4 suer **6** suitor **9** defendant, disputant, plaintiff

litigate
3 sue **6** indict **7** arraign, contest, dispute **9** prosecute

litigation
4 case, suit **7** lawsuit **11** prosecution, proceedings

litter
3 bed **4** cubs, junk **5** brood, couch, issue, strew, trash, waste, young **6** clutch, debris, refuse **7** bedding, clutter, garbage, kittens, piglets, progeny, puppies, rubbish, scatter **8** detritus **9** offspring, stretcher **10** scattering

little
3 bit, dab, toy, wee **4** dash, hint, mean, puny, tiny **5** brief, dinky, minor, petty, pinch, runty, short, small, taste, trace, young **6** bantam, meager, meagre, minute, narrow, paltry, petite, skimpy **7** limited, trivial **8** dwarfish, slightly, smallish, trifling **9** miniature, small-beer **10** diminutive, short-lived, undersized **11** microscopic, unimportant

Little Bighorn
state: 7 Montana
victim: 6 Custer (George Armstrong)
victor: 11 Sitting Bull

little by little
6 slowly **8** inchmeal, steadily **9** gradually, piecemeal

Little Dipper
constellation: 9 Ursa Minor
star: 5 North **7** Polaris

Little Women
author: 6 Alcott (Louisa May)
character: 3 Amy, Meg **4** Beth **6** Laurie, Marmee
surname: 5 March

littoral
5 beach, coast, shore **6** strand **7** coastal, seaside **8** seaboard, sea front, seashore **9** shoreline **10** oceanfront

liturgy
4 rite **6** ritual **7** service **8** ceremony **9** sacrament **10** ceremonial, observance, repertoire

livable
6 viable **8** adequate, bearable, passable **9** endurable, habitable, tolerable **11** inhabitable, supportable

live
4 fare, stay **5** abide, dwell, exist, on air, vital, vivid **6** actual, reside, thrive **7** breathe, current, subsist, survive

livelihood
3 job **4** game, keep, work **5** craft, trade **7** support **8** business, vocation **10** employment, handicraft, occupation, profession, sustenance **11** subsistence

liveliness
3 pep, zip **4** brio, élan, zing **5** verve, vigor **6** energy, hustle, spirit **8** dispatch, vibrance, vibrancy, vitality, vivacity **9** animation

lively
3 gay **4** busy, keen, pert, spry, yare **5** agile, alert, brisk, fresh, jazzy, jolly, merry, peppy, zippy **6** active, bouncy, bright, chirpy, frisky, jocund, nimble **7** animate, buoyant, chipper, intense, rousing **8** animated, bustling, hustling, spirited, vigorous, volatile **9** energetic, resilient, sparkling, sprightly, vivacious **11** stimulating

liven
5 pep up **6** jazz up, vivify **7** animate, freshen, quicken **8** energize, inspirit, vitalize **10** invigorate

liver
7 denizen **8** habitant, occupant, resident **10** inhabitant
combining form: 5 hepat **6** hepato
disease: 9 cirrhosis, hepatitis
French: 4 foie
lobster's: 8 tomalley

liverwort
8 hepatica **9** bryophyte

livestock
4 cows, hogs, pigs **5** bulls, goats, sheep **6** beasts, calves, cattle **7** animals
feed: 6 silage **8** ensilage

live wire
6 dynamo **7** hustler, rustler **8** go-getter, promoter **9** energizer, generator **11** self-starter

livid
3 hot, mad, wan **4** ashy, pale **5** ashen, lurid, waxen **6** fuming, leaden, pallid, sultry **7** boiling, bruised, enraged, furious, reddish **8** blanched, contused, incensed **9** colorless **10** discolored, infuriated **12** black-and-blue **13** beside oneself

living
5 means, vital **6** extant, income **8** animated, existent **10** livelihood, sustenance
combining form: 3 bio

living room
6 parlor **10** lebensraum

lizard
3 eft, Uta **4** gila, newt, uran **5** agama, anole, gecko, skink, teiid **6** dragon, goanna, iguana **7** monitor, reptile, saurian **8** basilisk, mosasaur, slowworm, squamate, whiptail **9** alligator, blindworm, chameleon, crocodile **10** chuckwalla, salamander
combining form: 4 saur **5** saura, sauro

llama
7 camelid
country: 4 Peru 7 Bolivia, Ecuador
habitat: 5 Andes
relative: 6 alpaca, vicuña 7 guanaco

Lloyd's business
9 insurance

lo
4 ecce, hark, heed, look, mark, mind 6 attend, behold 7 observe

load
3 tax 4 bias, copy, fill, haul, heap, lade, onus, pack, pile, stow, task 5 cargo, laden, swamp, weigh 6 burden, debase, doctor, dope up, eyeful, lading, saddle, weight 7 freight 8 encumber, shipment, transfer 9 liability, millstone, transport 11 consignment, encumbrance

loaded
4 full, high, rich 5 awash, doped 6 aboard, biased, filled, packed, stoned 7 boarded, brimful, crowded, wealthy 8 affluent, brimming, chockful, tripping, turned on 9 chock-full

loaf
3 bum, bun 4 idle, laze, lazy, loll 5 bread, dough 6 dawdle, lounge 7 goof off 8 lollygag 9 bum around, goldbrick 10 fool around

loafer
3 bum 4 shoe, slug 5 idler 6 slouch 7 goof-off, lounger 8 deadbeat, dolittle, fainéant, slugabed, sluggard 9 do-nothing, goldbrick, lazybones 11 beachcomber, lollygagger

loam
4 clay, dirt, sand, silt, soil 7 topsoil
deposit: 5 loess

loan
3 pay 4 lend 6 credit 7 advance, imprest 9 grubstake
figure: 3 APR

loan shark
6 lender, usurer 7 Shylock 10 pawnbroker 11 moneylender

loath
6 afraid, averse 8 hesitant 9 reluctant, unwilling 10 indisposed 11 disinclined 12 antipathetic

loathe
4 hate 5 abhor, scorn, spurn 6 detest, refuse, reject 7 despise 8 execrate 9 abominate

loathsome
4 foul, ugly, vile 5 gross, nasty 6 odious 7 beastly, hateful, hideous 8 horrible 9 abhorrent, execrable, obnoxious, offensive, repellent, repugnant, repulsive, revolting 10 abominable, deplorable, detestable, disgusting, nauseating

lob
4 loft, toss 5 chuck, fling, heave, pitch, sling, throw 6 propel

lobby
4 hall 5 foyer 7 promote 8 anteroom, corridor 9 influence, vestibule 10 passageway 11 waiting room

lobe
4 flap 7 pendant

lobo
4 wolf 8 gray wolf 10 timber wolf

lobster
8 crawfish 10 crustacean
claw: 5 chela 6 pincer
female: 3 hen
male: 4 cock
trap: 3 pot 5 creel

local
6 native 7 endemic, insular, topical 9 parochial 10 provincial

locale
4 area, belt, site, turf, ward 5 place, scene, venue 6 milieu, parish, region, sector 7 commune, quarter, setting 8 district, precinct, vicinage, vicinity 9 community, territory 11 mise-en-scène 12 neighborhood

locality
4 area, belt, city, site, turf, zone 5 block, field, haunt, place, tract 6 county, domain, hamlet, region, sector, sphere, square 7 habitat, section 8 district, environs, precinct, province, purlieus, township, vicinage, vicinity 9 bailiwick, situation, territory 12 neighborhood

localize
4 mass 5 amass, focus 7 cluster, collect 8 coalesce, pinpoint 10 accumulate 11 concentrate, consolidate 12 conglomerate

locate
3 fix, spy 4 espy, find, site, spot 5 dwell, place, trace 6 detect, reside, settle 7 nose out, situate, station, uncover 8 come upon, discover, pinpoint, position 9 establish, ferret out, search out 10 come across

location
4 area, site, post, spot 5 locus, place, point, scene, venue, where 7 bearing, habitat, setting 8 position 9 situation 11 mise-en-scène, whereabouts

loch
3 bay 4 lake

lock
4 bolt, curl, hank, hold, tuft 5 latch, tress 6 fasten, secure 7 ringlet 8 fastener 9 enclosure, fastening

lockjaw
7 tetanus, trismus

lock up
3 ice 4 seal 5 sew up 6 assure, clinch, ensure,

ratify, secure, settle **7** confirm **8** complete, conclude, finalize, validate **9** guarantee

lockup
3 jug, pen **4** brig, cell, coop, gaol, jail, stir, tank **5** clink, pokey, pound **6** cooler, prison **7** slammer **8** bastille, hoosegow

loco
3 ape, mad **4** bats, nuts **5** balmy, batty, crazy, kooky, loony, nutty **6** crazed, insane, screwy **7** bananas, berserk, bonkers, cracked, flipped, lunatic **8** demented, deranged, frenzied, unhinged **10** flipped out

locomotive
5 cheer, dolly, train **6** engine
small: 5 dinky **6** dinkey
type: 5 steam **6** diesel **8** electric

locum tenens
3 sub **5** proxy **6** backup, fill-in, supply **7** stand-in **9** alternate, auxiliary, surrogate **10** substitute **11** pinch hitter, replacement, succedaneum

locus
3 hub **4** seat, site **5** focus, heart, stage **6** center **7** setting **8** cynosure, location, polestar **10** focal point **11** nerve center **12** headquarters

locust
4 tree, wood **5** carob **6** cicada, insect **11** grasshopper

locution
4 word **5** argot, idiom, lingo **6** jargon, patois, phrase **7** dialect **8** parlance, phrasing **9** utterance **10** expression **11** phraseology

lode
4 seam, vein **5** store **6** source, supply **7** deposit
mother: 7 bonanza

lodestar
4 guru **5** gauge, guide, ideal, model **6** beacon, leader, mentor **7** epitome **8** exemplar, paradigm **9** archetype, guidepost **11** inspiration

lodestone
6 magnet **9** magnetite

lodge
3 den, fix, inn **4** bunk, camp, club, file, lair, nest, root, stay **5** abide, abode, board, cabin, couch, dwell, embed, guild, hotel, house, motel, order, put up **6** billet, burrow, hostel, league, remain, shanty, tavern, wigwam **7** auberge, contain, cottage, deposit, hospice, quarter, receive, shelter **8** domicile, hostelry, sodality **9** gatehouse **10** fellowship **11** accommodate, brotherhood, caravansary, public house

lodger
5 guest **6** renter, roomer, tenant **7** boarder, resider

lodging
3 inn, pad **4** dorm, room **5** abode, hotel, motel, place **7** shelter **8** chambers, diggings, domicile, dwelling, quarters **9** apartment, residence **10** pied-à-terre **13** accommodation

loess
4 clay, loam, marl **7** deposit

loft
4 rise **5** attic, raise **6** dormer, garret, propel **7** gallery

loftiness
5 pride **6** height **7** disdain, hauteur, stature **8** altitude, eminence **9** aloofness, arrogance, elevation, pomposity, sublimity **11** haughtiness, superiority **13** condescension

lofty
4 airy, epic, high, tall **5** grand, noble, proud **6** aerial, august, raised, remote, superb **7** exalted, haughty, soaring, stately, sublime, utopian **8** arrogant, cavalier, elevated, eloquent, imposing, insolent, majestic, superior, towering **9** ambitious, grandiose, visionary **10** disdainful **11** overbearing, pretentious, skyscraping **12** supercilious

log
5 diary, tally **6** record, timber **7** journal **8** register
cutter: 8 chain saw
mover: 5 peavy **6** peavey **7** cant dog

loge
3 box **5** booth, stall **7** balcony **9** mezzanine

logger
9 lumberman **10** lumberjack, woodcutter
legendary: 10 Paul Bunyan

loggerhead
6 shrike, turtle

loggia
6 arcade **7** balcony, gallery, veranda

logic
6 reason **9** reasoning **10** syntactics
specious: 7 sophism **9** sophistry

logical
5 sound, valid **6** cogent **8** analytic, sensible **9** deducible, deductive, plausible **10** analytical, compelling, convincing, diagnostic, reasonable, scientific, systematic

logjam
5 crowd **7** impasse **8** blockage, deadlock, stoppage **11** obstruction

logo
5 badge, brand, motto **6** cipher, device, emblem, symbol **8** colophon, hallmark, monogram **9** trademark

logogriph
6 puzzle **7** anagram

logroll
4 birl

logy
4 dull, slow **5** dopey, heavy **6** drowsy, groggy, torpid **8** listless, sluggish

Lohengrin
composer: **6** Wagner (Richard)
father: **8** Parsifal, Parzival
wife: **4** Elsa

loincloth
5 dhoti **11** breechcloth, breechclout

Loire city
5 Blois, Tours **6** Nantes **7** Orléans

loiter
3 bum, lag **4** drag, idle, laze, lazy, loaf, loll, poke **5** dally, delay, tarry, trail **6** dawdle, diddle, linger, lounge, put off, putter **8** lollygag **10** dillydally, fool around, hang around **11** screw around **13** procrastinate

Loki
father: **8** Farbauti
mother: **3** Nal **6** Laufey
offspring: **3** Hel **4** Hela **6** Fenris **7** Midgard
slayer: **8** Heimdall
victim: **6** Balder, Baldur
wife: **5** Sigyn **9** Angurboda

Lolita
author: **7** Nabokov (Vladimir)
suitor: **7** Humbert (Humbert)

loll
3 bum, lag **4** drag, idle, laze, lazy, loaf, poke **5** chill, dally, delay, droop, slump, tarry, trail **6** dawdle, diddle, linger, lounge, putter, slouch **8** chill out **10** dillydally, fool around, hang around **13** procrastinate

lollapalooza
4 lulu **5** beaut, doozy **6** doozie **8** knockout **9** humdinger

Lollards' leader
8 Wycliffe (John)

lollygag
4 idle, loaf, loll, poke, drag **5** chill **6** dawdle, diddle, loiter, piddle, putter **10** dilly-dally, fool around

Lombard
6 banker **11** moneylender
king: **5** Cleph **6** Alboin, Audoin **7** Aistulf, Aripert, Authari **9** Liudprand

London
attraction: **3** Eye **5** Tower
borough: **5** Brent **6** Barnet, Bexley, Ealing, Harrow, Sutton **7** Barking, Bromley, Chelsea, Croydon, Enfield, Hackney, Lambeth **8** Haringey, Havering, Hounslow, Lewisham **9** Greenwich, Islington, Redbridge **10** Kensington **11** Westminster
cathedral: **7** St. Paul's
clock: **6** Big Ben
district: **4** Soho **5** Acton **7** Chelsea, Mayfair **9** Belgravia, Southwark
gallery: **4** Tate
gardens: **3** Kew
policeman: **5** bobby
prison: **7** Newgate
river: **6** Thames
square: **9** Leicester, Trafalgar
street: **4** Bond **5** Fleet **6** Strand **7** Downing **9** Whitehall **10** Piccadilly
subway: **4** tube

London novel
7 Sea Wolf (The) **8** Iron Heel (The) **9** White Fang **10** Martin Eden **13** Call of the Wild (The)

lone
4 only, sole, solo **5** alone **6** single, unique **8** deserted, forsaken, isolated, secluded, separate, singular, solitary **13** unaccompanied

lonely
4 left, lorn **5** alone **7** forlorn **8** deserted, forsaken, homesick, lonesome, rejected, solitary **9** abandoned

loneness
8 solitude **9** isolation **10** detachment **12** separateness, solitariness

loner
6 hermit **7** isolate, outcast, recluse **8** outsider, solitary **13** individualist

Lone Ranger, The
creator: **7** Striker (Fran)
companion: **5** Tonto
epithet: **8** Kemo Sabe
horse: **6** Silver
trademark: **4** mask **12** silver bullet

Lone Star State
5 Texas

long
3 far, yen **4** ache, itch, pine, tall **5** wordy, yearn **6** hanker, hunger, prolix, thirst **7** endless, lengthy **8** dragging, drawn-out, extended, unending **9** extensive **10** full-length, protracted

long ago
4 yore

long-drawn-out
7 endless, lengthy **8** dragging, unending **10** protracted **12** interminable

Longfellow poem
8 Christus, Hiawatha, Hyperion, Kavanagh **10** Evangeline **11** My Lost Youth, Psalm of Life (A)

long for
4 want **5** covet, crave, mourn **6** desire, repine **8** aspire to

longing
3 yen **4** itch, lust, urge, wish **5** greed **6** desire, hunger, thirst **7** avidity, craving, passion **8** appetite

longshoreman
9 stevedore **10** roustabout

long-suffering
7 patient, stoical **8** enduring, resigned **9** compliant **10** forbearing, submissive **13** accommodating, uncomplaining

long suit
3 bag **4** gift **5** forte **6** métier, talent **8** strength **9** specialty

long-winded
5 wordy **6** prolix **7** diffuse, lengthy, verbose **8** rambling **9** garrulous, redundant **10** loquacious

loo
2 WC **3** lav **4** head, john **5** jakes, privy **6** toilet **7** latrine **8** bathroom, outhouse

look
3 air, eye **4** gape, gawk, gaze, leer, mien, ogle, peek, peep, peer, seem, view **5** glare, stare, watch **6** admire, appear, aspect, behold, expect, eyeful, glance, glower, goggle, regard, squint, survey, visage **7** bearing, examine, eyeball, glimpse, observe **8** demeanor, once-over **10** appearance, rubberneck

look after
4 mind, tend **5** nurse, serve, watch **6** attend, wait on **7** care for, husband **8** wait upon **9** watch over **10** provide for

look-alike
4 twin **5** clone **6** double **7** similar **8** matching **9** duplicate

look at
3 eye, see **4** face, ogle, scan, view **5** check **6** behold, ponder, regard **7** examine, inspect **8** confront, consider **11** investigate

look back
6 recall, review **7** reflect **8** remember **9** reminisce

look down on
5 abhor, scorn, scout, spurn **7** contemn, despise, disdain **8** dominate **9** tower over **10** tower above

looker
6 beauty, eyeful, lovely, vision **7** stunner, witness **8** knockout, ornament **9** bystander, sightseer, spectator **10** eyewitness

looker-on
5 gaper **6** viewer **7** watcher, witness **8** beholder, observer **9** bystander, spectator **10** eyewitness **12** rubbernecker

look for
4 seek **5** await **6** expect, plan on **9** search out **10** anticipate

looking glass
6 mirror **9** reflector

look into
5 check, probe, study **6** pursue, survey **7** examine, explore, inspect **8** check out, question, research **10** scrutinize **11** investigate

look out
4 mind **6** beware

lookout
4 aery, view **5** aerie, guard, scout, tower, vista, watch **6** cupola, picket, sentry **7** spotter **8** panorama, prospect, sentinel, watchman **9** belvedere, crow's nest, firetower **10** watchtower, widow's walk **11** observatory, perspective

look over
3 vet **4** read **5** check **6** review, size up **7** examine, inspect **8** appraise, evaluate

loom
4 brew, bulk, near, rear **5** hover, mount, tower **6** appear, come on, emerge, gather, impend **7** portend **8** approach, overhang, stand out, threaten **9** take shape
part: 6 heddle **7** harness, shuttle, treadle, trundle

loon
3 nut, oaf **4** bird, clod, dodo, dolt, goof, lout, yo-yo **5** chump, dummy, dunce, ninny, noddy, stupe, yokel **6** dimwit, dum-dum, nitwit **7** airhead, buffoon, dullard, pinhead **8** bonehead, dumbbell, crackpot, imbecile, lunkhead, meathead, numskull **9** birdbrain, blockhead, ignoramus, lamebrain, numbskull, simpleton **10** dunderhead, nincompoop **11** chowderhead, chucklehead

loony
3 nut **4** bats, loco **5** balmy, batty, crazy, daffy, dippy, goofy, nutty, silly, wacky **6** absurd, insane, madman, screwy **7** fatuous, foolish, idiotic **8** demented **9** bedlamite, half-baked, ludicrous, senseless **10** ridiculous **11** harebrained **12** preposterous

loony bin
6 asylum, bedlam **8** bughouse, madhouse, nuthouse **9** funny farm **10** booby hatch, crazy house

loop
3 arc, eye **4** ansa, ring **5** curve, noose, picot **6** circle, eyelet, league, staple **7** circlet, circuit **8** doubling

looped
4 high **5** bowed, drunk, stiff **6** blotto, bombed, curved, juiced, loaded, potted, stewed, tanked,

zonked **7** crocked, pickled, pie-eyed, sloshed, smashed **9** plastered **10** inebriated **11** curvilinear, intoxicated

loophole
3 out **6** escape, outlet **7** opening

loopy
4 bats, daft, nuts, wavy **5** arced, batty, bowed, crazy, daffy, dotty, flaky, nutty, silly, snaky, wacky **6** arched, curved, freaky, fruity, screwy, swirly **7** bizarre, idiotic, lunatic, offbeat, sinuous, touched **8** demented **9** eccentric **10** flipped out, off-the-wall, outlandish

loose
3 lax **4** easy, fast, free, lewd, limp **5** baggy, slack, untie, vague **6** flabby, wanton **7** flaccid, relaxed **8** flexible **9** debauched, desultory, dissolute, imprecise **10** disjointed, dissipated, ill-defined, licentious, unattached, unconfined **12** disconnected, unrestrained

loose end
6 detail **8** fragment

loose-lipped
see **loquacious**

loosen
4 ease, free, undo **5** relax, slack, untie **6** unbind **7** ease off, manumit, release, slacken, unchain **8** liberate, unbuckle, unfasten **10** emancipate

loosen up
5 relax **6** unbend, unwind **7** ease off, stretch

loot
3 rob **4** haul, lift, pelf, raid, sack, swag **5** boost, booty, dough, lucre, money, moola, reave, rifle, spoil **6** boodle, moolah, ravish, spoils **7** despoil, pillage, plunder, ransack, stick up **9** knock over

looter
5 thief **7** brigand **8** marauder

lop
3 cut **4** chop, clip, crop, snip, trim **5** prune, sever **6** excise **8** amputate, truncate **9** dismember **10** guillotine

lope
3 jog, run **4** gait, romp, trot **5** amble **6** canter

lopsided
4 awry **5** askew **6** aslant, uneven **7** crooked, leaning, tilting **8** top-heavy **10** asymmetric, off-balance, unbalanced **12** asymmetrical **13** unsymmetrical

loquacious
5 gabby, talky, wordy **6** chatty, mouthy, prolix **7** verbose, voluble, yakking **8** babbling **9** garrulous, jabbering, talkative **10** blathering, chattering, long-winded **11** loose-lipped **12** motor-mouthed

Lorca play
5 Yerma **12** Blood Wedding

lord
3 sir **4** boss, duke, earl, peer **5** noble, ruler **6** master **7** marquis **8** governor, marquess, nobleman, viscount **9** sovereign, tyrannize
feudal: **5** liege **8** seigneur, suzerain
Muslim: **6** sayyid

Lord High Executioner
4 Koko

Lord Jim author
6 Conrad (Joseph)

lordly
5 grand, lofty, noble, proud **6** august, uppity **7** exalted, haughty, pompous, stately, swollen **8** affected, arrogant, cavalier, gracious, imposing, insolent, majestic, princely, snobbish, superior **9** dignified, egotistic, grandiose **10** disdainful, high-handed **11** dictatorial, magisterial, magnificent, overbearing, patronizing **12** aristocratic, supercilious **13** authoritarian, high-and-mighty

Lord of the Flies
author: **7** Golding (William)
character: **4** Jack **5** Piggy, Ralph

Lord of the Rings
author: **7** Tolkien (J. R. R.)
book: **9** Two Towers (The) **15** Return of the King (The) **19** Fellowship of the Ring (The)
character: **3** Sam **5** Arwen, Frodo, Gimli **6** Elrond, Gollum, Sauron **7** Aragorn, Baggins (Bilbo, Frodo), Boromir, Gandalf, Legolas, Saruman, Théoden **9** Galadriel, Treebeard
film director: **7** Jackson (Peter)
illustrator: **3** Lee (Alan) **4** Howe (John)
race: **4** ents, orcs **5** wargs **6** huorns **7** hobbits **11** ringwraiths
realm: **5** Arnor, Moria, Rohan **6** Gondor, Mordor **10** Lothlórien **11** Middle-earth **12** Undying Lands
site: **5** Shire (The) **8** Isengard **9** Mount Doom, Rivendell
star: **3** Lee (Christopher) **4** Hill (Bernard), Holm (Ian), Wood (Elijah) **5** Astin (Sean), Baker (Sala), Bloom (Orlando), Tyler (Liv) **6** Serkis (Andy) **7** Weaving (Hugo) **8** McKellen (Ian), Monaghan (Dominic) **9** Blanchett (Cate), Mortensen (Viggo)
sword: **5** Sting **6** Narsil **7** Andúril **9** Glamdring

Lord's Prayer
9 Our Father **11** Paternoster

lore
6 mythos, wisdom **7** history **8** folkways, learning **9** knowledge, mythology, tradition **11** information **12** superstition

Lorelei
5 siren **9** temptress **10** seductress **11** femme fatale

poet: 5 Heine (Heinrich)
river: 5 Rhein, Rhine
victim: 6 sailor **7** mariner

lorgnette
10 eyeglasses, spectacles **12** opera glasses

Lorna Doone
author: 9 Blackmore (Richard)
hero: 4 Ridd (John)

____ Lorraine
6 Alsace

lorry
3 rig, van **4** semi **5** truck

lose
4 miss, shed **5** evade, shake, waste, yield **6** escape, give up, mislay **7** destroy, forfeit, succumb **8** misplace, shake off, throw off **9** sacrifice, surrender

lose it
5 go ape **7** crack up, flip out, go crazy, run amok **8** freak out, run amuck

loser
3 dud **4** bomb, bust, flop **5** lemon **6** bummer, fiasco, misfit, turkey **7** also-ran, debacle, failure, washout **8** deadbeat **11** incompetent

loss
4 bath, harm, ruin **5** waste **6** damage, defeat, injury **7** deficit, failure, forfeit **8** casualty, decrease, fatality **9** depletion, privation, sacrifice, shrinkage **10** divestment, forfeiture, misfortune, misplacing **11** bereavement, deprivation, destruction

lost
4 asea, dead, gone, rapt **6** absent, astray, bygone, damned, doomed, futile, hidden, wasted **7** defunct, faraway, lacking, mislaid, missing **8** absorbed, departed, distrait, helpless, hopeless, vanished **9** condemned, desperate, destroyed **10** abstracted, insensible, overlooked **11** irrevocable, preoccupied **12** irredeemable, unregenerate

Lost Horizon
author: 6 Hilton (James)
character: 6 Conway (Hugh)
land: 9 Shangri-La

lot
3 cut, ilk **4** doom, fate, heap, kind, mass, plat, yard **5** batch, block, bunch, field, moira, patch, quota, share, slice, tract, weird **6** assign, barrel, bundle, parcel, stripe **7** acreage, cluster, destiny, fortune, mete out, portion, species **8** allocate, clearing, frontage **9** aggregate, allowance, apportion

Lot
father: 5 Haran
sister: 5 Iscah **6** Milcah
son: 4 Moab **5** Ammon
uncle: 7 Abraham

lothario
4 lech, stud, wolf **5** letch, Romeo **6** lecher, tomcat **7** amorist, Don Juan, gallant, seducer **8** Casanova, paramour **9** debaucher, ladies' man, womanizer **10** lady-killer **11** philanderer

lotion
3 oil **4** balm **5** cream, salve **6** cerate **7** unguent **8** ablution, cosmetic, lenitive, liniment, ointment **9** demulcent **11** embrocation

lottery
6 raffle **7** drawing **11** sweepstakes

lotus-eater
7 dreamer **8** escapist, romantic **10** daydreamer **13** castle-builder

loud
5 forte, gaudy, noisy, showy **6** brassy, brazen, flashy, garish, glitzy, tawdry, vulgar **7** blaring, blatant, booming, chintzy, glaring, pealing, raucous, roaring **8** piercing, resonant, sonorous, strident **9** clamorous, deafening, obnoxious, obtrusive, offensive, tasteless **10** bigmouthed, boisterous, flamboyant, fortissimo, resounding, stentorian, thunderous, vociferous **12** earsplitting

loudmouth
6 ranter **7** stentor **8** blowhard, braggart **9** blusterer

loudspeaker
3 amp **6** Tannoy, woofer **7** tweeter **9** amplifier

Louisiana
capital: 10 Baton Rouge
city: 10 New Orleans, Shreveport
college, university: 6 Tulane
county: 6 parish
lake: 13 Pontchartrain
nickname: 7 Pelican (State)
river: 11 Mississippi
state bird: 12 brown pelican
state flower: 8 magnolia
state tree: 11 bald cypress

lounge
3 bar, bum, lie, pub, tap **4** idle, laze, loaf, loll, sofa **5** couch, dally, drift, lobby, relax **6** dawdle, loiter, parlor, repose, saloon **7** barroom, goof off, lie down, recline, taproom **8** restroom, kill time **10** living room

lounge lizard
3 fop **4** rake, toff **5** blade, dandy, leech **6** gigolo, sponge **9** ladies' man

Lourdes saint
10 Bernadette

louse
3 cad, cur, dog, rat **4** toad **5** aphid, creep, skunk,

snake **6** cootie, psylla, rotter, slater, wretch **7** bounder, stinker
egg: **3** nit

louse up
4 blow, flub, muff, ruin **5** botch, spoil, wreck **6** bobble, bollix, bumble, bungle, fumble

lousy
3 ill **4** poor, rife **5** awful **6** crummy, shoddy, rotten **7** replete, teeming **8** crawling, horrible, inferior, infested, terrible **9** miserable, repulsive **10** despicable **12** contemptible

lout
3 oaf **4** boob, boor, dolt, gawk, hick, rube **5** brute, chuff, churl, klutz, looby, scorn, yahoo, yokel **6** galoot, lubber, lummox, rustic **7** bumpkin, hayseed, palooka **9** simpleton **10** clodhopper

Louvre masterpiece
8 Mona Lisa **11** Venus de Milo

lovable
4 dear **5** sweet **6** cuddly **7** winning, winsome **8** adorable **9** appealing, endearing **11** embraceable

love
4 zeal **5** adore, ardor, crush, Cupid, prize, value **6** desire, dote on, fervor, revere **7** adulate, cherish, idolize, passion, romance, worship **8** devotion, fondness, idolatry, treasure, venerate, yearning **9** adoration, adulation, delight in **10** attachment **11** amorousness, infatuation
combining form: **4** phil **5** philo, phily **6** philia
French: **5** amour
Italian: **5** amore
tennis: **3** nil **4** zero **7** nothing

love apple
6 tomato

lovebird
6 budgie, parrot **10** budgerigar

love-bite
3 nip **6** hickey

love feast
5 agape

love god
4 Amor, Eros, Kama **5** Bhaga, Cupid

love goddess
5 Athor, Freya, Venus **6** Hathor, Inanna, Ishtar **7** Astarte **9** Aphrodite, Ashtoreth

love letter
8 mash note **9** valentine **10** billet-doux

lovely
4 fair **5** sweet, swell **6** comely, dainty, pretty **7** elegant **8** adorable, alluring, charming, delicate, engaging, graceful, knockout **9** beauteous, beautiful, exquisite **10** attractive, delightful, enchanting, entrancing **11** captivating, good-looking

love potion
7 philter, philtre **11** aphrodisiac

lover
3 fan **4** beau, buff **5** flame, leman, Romeo, swain **6** addict, steady, suitor, votary **7** amorist, darling, devotee, Don Juan, gallant, habitué, squeeze **8** fancy man, lothario, mistress, paramour **9** boyfriend, inamorata, inamorato **10** aficionado, girlfriend, sweetheart

lovey-dovey
5 mushy **6** doting **7** amorous **12** affectionate

loving
4 dear, fond **6** ardent, erotic, tender **7** amatory, amorous, cordial, devoted, fervent **8** attached, enamored, faithful **10** benevolent, infatuated, passionate, solicitous **11** impassioned **12** affectionate

low
3 moo **4** base, blue, dead, deep, flat, mean, neap **5** cheap **6** abject, ailing, humble, hushed, lesser, nether, poorly, sickly, sordid, unwell **7** cut-rate, reduced, scrubby **8** cast down, dejected, depleted, downcast, inferior, mediocre, wretched **9** declining, depressed, miserable, subnormal, woebegone **10** inadequate, indisposed **11** crestfallen, downhearted, unfavorable

lowbred
4 base, rude **6** coarse, oafish, vulgar **7** boorish, brutish, loutish, uncouth **8** churlish, cloddish, lubberly **11** uncivilized

low-cost
5 cheap **6** budget, cheapo **7** bargain, cut-rate **10** affordable, reasonable **11** inexpensive

low-down
4 base, mean, ugly, vile **6** grubby, odious, scurvy, sleazy, sordid **7** ignoble, squalid **8** shameful, wretched **9** abhorrent, worthless **10** despicable, disgusting **11** ignominious **12** contemptible

lowdown
4 dope, info **5** facts, goods, scoop, specs **6** skinny **8** briefing **11** information

lower
3 cut **4** clip, drop, fall, sink **5** frown, gloom, scowl, shave, slash, under **6** debase, demean, demote, humble, lesser, menace, nether, reduce **7** cut down, deflate, degrade, demerit, depress, descend, devalue, let down **8** inferior, mark down, overcast, submerge, threaten **9** devaluate, downgrade
prefix: **5** infra

Lower Depths author
5 Gorki, Gorky (Maksim, Maxim)

lowest point
5 nadir
in the U.S.: **11** Death Valley
on earth's crust: **13** Mariana Trench
on earth's surface: **7** Dead Sea

low-grade
4 hack **5** junky, lousy **6** cheesy, cruddy, shabby, shoddy, sleazy, tawdry **8** below par, déclassé, inferior, mediocre **9** deficient **10** second-rate **11** second-class, substandard **12** second-drawer

low-key
4 soft **5** muted, quiet **7** relaxed, subdued **8** laid-back, softened, tasteful **9** easygoing, minimized, temperate, toned down **10** played down, restrained **11** understated

lowland
4 flat, sump, vale **5** basin **6** bottom, slough, valley **7** bottoms
Scottish: **6** lallan **7** lalland

lowlife
4 fink, heel **5** knave, rogue **6** no-good, outlaw, rascal, wretch **7** hoodlum, ruffian, villain **9** miscreant, reprobate, scoundrel **10** blackguard, black sheep, sleazeball **11** rapscallion, slimebucket **12** bottom-feeder

lowly
4 base, mean, meek **6** abject, humble, menial, modest **7** ignoble, mundane, obscure, prosaic, servile **8** baseborn, plebeian, unwashed

low-pressure
4 calm **6** casual, dégagé, folksy, mellow **7** relaxed **8** flexible, informal, laid-back **9** easygoing **10** nonchalant

low-spirited
3 sad **4** blue, down, glum **6** abject, droopy, gloomy, morose **7** doleful **8** cast down, dejected, downcast, saddened **9** bummed out, cheerless, depressed, woebegone **10** dispirited, melancholy **11** discouraged, downhearted **12** disheartened, heavyhearted

low tide
3 ebb **4** neap

loyal
4 firm, true **5** liege **6** ardent, trusty **7** devoted, dutiful, staunch **8** constant, faithful, resolute, true-blue **9** allegiant, steadfast, unfailing **10** dependable **11** trustworthy

loyalist
4 Tory **7** patriot **8** partisan **10** countryman **11** nationalist

loyalty
6 fealty **8** adhesion, devotion, fidelity **9** adherence, constancy **10** allegiance, attachment, dedication **11** staunchness **12** faithfulness **13** dependability, steadfastness

lozenge
4 pill **6** troche **7** diamond, rhombus **8** pastille

LSD
4 acid
user: **8** acidhead

lubricate
3 oil **6** grease, smooth **7** moisten

lubricious
4 lewd, oily **5** slick **6** carnal, greasy, slippy, wanton **8** prurient, slippery, slithery, ticklish **9** lecherous, salacious **10** lascivious, libidinous **12** concupiscent

lucent
5 clear **6** bright, limpid **7** beaming, crystal, glowing, lambent, radiant, shining **8** clear-cut, luminous, pellucid **9** brilliant, effulgent, refulgent **11** unambiguous

Lucia di Lammermoor
character: **7** Edgardo
composer: **9** Donizetti (Gaetano)
novelist: **5** Scott (Walter)

lucid
4 sane **5** clear **6** bright, limpid **7** crystal, lambent, radiant **8** clear-cut, knowable, luminous **9** brilliant, effulgent, graspable, refulgent, unblurred **10** articulate, fathomable **11** translucent, transparent, unambiguous **12** compos mentis, incandescent, intelligible, transpicuous

lucidity
6 acumen, sanity **7** clarity **8** sagacity, saneness **9** clearness, plainness, soundness **10** cognizance, perception **12** clairvoyance

Lucifer
5 devil, fiend, Satan, Venus **7** Old Nick **8** Apollyon **9** archfiend, Beelzebub **10** Old Scratch **13** Old Gooseberry

Lucinde
beloved: **7** Leandre **9** Clitandre
father: **7** Geronte **10** Sganarelle

luck
3 hap, hit **4** juju, meet **5** fluke, light **6** chance, happen, hazard, kismet **7** fortune, godsend, stumble **8** fortuity, occasion, windfall **9** advantage **11** opportunity
token: **5** charm **6** amulet, clover, fetish, mascot **8** talisman **9** horseshoe **11** rabbit's foot

luckless
7 adverse, hapless, unhappy **8** ill-fated, untoward, wretched **9** miserable **10** ill-starred **11** star-crossed, unfavorable, unfortunate **12** misfortunate, unpropitious

lucky
6 golden, timely **7** favored **9** favorable, fortunate **10** auspicious, beneficial, felicitous, fortuitous, propitious **12** advantageous, providential **13** serendipitous
Scottish: **5** canny

Lucky Jim author
4 Amis (Kingsley)

lucrative
6 paying **7** gainful **8** fruitful **10** high-income,

productive, profitable, well-paying, worthwhile **11** moneymaking **12** advantageous, remunerative

lucre
3 pay **4** cash, gain, jack, loot, pelf, swag **5** booty, dough, green, money, moola **6** boodle, dinero, do-re-mi, moolah, profit, wampum **7** cabbage, revenue **9** long green **10** greenbacks

Lucrezia ___
6 Borgia

Lucy's husband
4 Desi **5** Arnaz (Desi)

ludicrous
4 zany **5** antic, comic, droll, funny, goofy, nutty, silly **6** absurd **7** amusing, bizarre, comical, foolish, risible **8** farcical **9** fantastic, grotesque, laughable **10** off-the-wall, outlandish, ridiculous **11** incongruous **12** preposterous

Ludlum novel
14 Bourne Identity (The) **15** Bourne Supremacy (The) **16** Holcroft Covenant (The)

lug
3 nut, oaf, tow, tug **4** bear, buck, drag, draw, haul, hump, jerk, pull, tote **5** carry, ferry, shlep **6** convey, schlep **7** bruiser, schlepp **9** transport

luggage
4 bags, gear **7** baggage

lugubrious
3 sad **4** blue, dour, down, glum **5** bleak **6** dismal, dreary, gloomy, morose, rueful, somber, sullen, woeful **7** doleful, joyless **8** cast down, dejected, dolesome, downcast, mournful **9** cheerless, depressed, plaintive, saturnine, sorrowful, woebegone **10** depressing, despondent, lamentable, melancholy, oppressive **11** discouraged, dispiriting, downhearted **12** disconsolate

lukewarm
5 blasé, tepid **7** dubious, offhand **8** hesitant **9** uncertain, undecided **10** wishy-washy **11** halfhearted, indifferent

lull
3 ebb **4** balm, calm, hush, wane **5** letup, pause, quiet, still **6** becalm, pacify, soothe, temper **7** compose, decline, ease off, slacken **8** abeyance, interval **9** stillness **10** quiescence **11** tranquilize

lullaby
8 berceuse **10** cradlesong

lulu
3 ace, gem, pip **5** beaut, dandy, dilly, doozy, dream, honey **6** doozie, wonder **7** delight **8** jimdandy, knockout **9** humdinger, sensation

lumber
3 tax **4** clog, lade, load, logs, plod, slog, wood **5** barge, clump, stump, weigh **6** burden, charge, rumble, saddle, timber, trudge **8** encumber

lumberjack
see **logger**

luminance
10 brightness

luminary
3 sun, VIP **4** lion, name, star **5** celeb, light, nabob **6** leader, worthy **7** big name, notable **8** big-timer, eminence, somebody **9** celebrity, dignitary, superstar **10** notability **12** leading light

luminous
5 clear, lucid **6** bright, lucent **7** beaming, crystal, fulgent, lambent, radiant, shining **8** clear-cut, lustrous, pellucid **9** brilliant, effulgent, refulgent **11** illustrious, translucent, transparent **12** enlightening, incandescent

lummox
3 oaf **4** boor, clod, gawk, goon, hulk, lout **5** klutz, looby **6** lubber **7** palooka

lump
3 gob, lot, oaf, wad **4** blob, bulk, chip, clod, gawk, glob, heap, hunk, lout, mass, pile, welt **5** abide, batch, block, brook, bulge, bunch, chunk, hunch, klutz, knurl, looby, piece, scrap, stand, tumor **6** digest, endure, entire, lubber, morsel, nugget **7** handful, palooka, portion, stomach, swallow **8** swelling, totality **9** aggregate **10** protrusion, tumescence **12** protuberance

lumpy
5 crude, gawky, rough **6** choppy, clumsy, coarse, oafish **8** clumpish, unformed **9** roughhewn

lunacy
5 folly, mania **6** idiocy **7** fatuity, foolery, inanity, madness **8** delirium, dementia, insanity **9** absurdity, craziness, silliness, stupidity **10** imbecility **11** derangement, foolishness **13** senselessness

lunar
dark area: **4** mare **5** maria (plural)
valley: **4** rill **5** rille

lunatic
3 mad, nut **4** bats, daft, kook, loco, yo-yo, zany **5** balmy, batty, crank, crazy, nutty, raver, wacko, wacky **6** absurd, crazed, cuckoo, insane, madman, maniac, nitwit, psycho, screwy **7** bonkers, cracked, foolish **8** crackpot, demented, demoniac, deranged, frenzied, maniacal, paranoid, schizoid, unhinged **9** bedlamite, ding-a-ling, fruitcake, harebrain, screwball **10** crackbrain **11** nonsensical

lunch
3 eat **4** meal, nosh **5** snack

luncheonette
4 café **5** diner **6** bistro, eatery **7** beanery, canteen, tearoom **8** snack bar **9** cafeteria **10** coffee shop, restaurant **11** greasy spoon

lune
3 bow 5 curve 6 sickle 8 crescent, meniscus

lung
combining form: 5 pneum, pulmo 6 pneumo, pulmon
disease: 9 emphysema, pneumonia 10 byssinosis 12 tuberculosis

lunge
3 jab 4 dash, dive, stab 5 bound, drive, pitch, surge 6 charge, plunge, pounce, thrust

lunkhead
3 oaf 4 boob, clod, dodo, dolt, goof, yo-yo 5 booby, chump, dummy, dunce, idiot, moron, ninny, noddy, stupe 6 dimwit, dum-dum, nitwit 7 dullard 8 dumbbell, imbecile, numskull 9 birdbrain, ignoramus, lamebrain, numbskull, simpleton 10 nincompoop

lupine
5 feral 6 brutal, fierce 7 wolfish 8 ravening 9 predatory, rapacious 10 bluebonnet, sanguinary

lurch
3 bob, yaw 4 jerk, lean, list, reel, rock, roll, sway, tilt, toss 5 heave, pitch, slide, swing 6 bumble, careen, falter, plunge, seesaw, swerve, teeter, totter 7 blunder, stagger, stumble 8 flounder

lure
3 bag 4 bait, call, draw, fake, hook, pull, rope, toll, trap, wile 5 blind, catch, charm, decoy, snare, tempt, trick 6 appeal, cajole, come-on, draw in, draw on, entice, entrap, invite, lead on, seduce 7 attract, beguile, bewitch, capture, con game, enchant, ensnare, gimmick, wheedle 8 blandish, delusion, illusion, inveigle 9 captivate, fascinate, incentive, seduction, siren song 10 attraction, camouflage, enticement, inducement, seducement, temptation
fishing: 3 fly 4 worm 5 spoon 6 minnow 8 bucktail

lurid
4 ashy, gory, gray, grim, pale 5 ashen, fiery, gross, livid, waxen 6 grisly, malign, sultry 7 baleful, ghastly, graphic, hideous, macabre, malefic, tabloid 8 blanched, gruesome, horrible, shocking, sinister, terrible 9 colorless 10 horrifying, maleficent, terrifying 11 sensational 12 melodramatic

Lurie novel
14 Foreign Affairs 18 War Between the Tates (The)

lurk
4 hide, slip 5 creep, prowl, skulk, slide, slink, sneak, snoop, steal 9 pussyfoot

luscious
4 rich, sexy 5 sapid, sweet, tasty, yummy 6 delish, divine, ornate, savory 7 opulent, piquant, sensual 8 sensuous 9 ambrosial, epicurean, exquisite, flavorful, luxurious, seductive, sumptuous, toothsome 10 delectable, delightful, flamboyant, flavorsome, voluptuous 11 scrumptious 13 mouth-watering

lush
3 sot 4 rank, rich, wino 5 dense, drink, drunk, yummy 6 bibber, boozer, deluxe, lavish, savory 7 fertile, opulent, profuse, sensual, teeming, tippler 8 abundant, drunkard, palatial, prodigal, sensuous, thriving 9 ambrosial, epicurean, exuberant, inebriate, luxuriant, luxurious, plentiful, sumptuous, toothsome 10 boozehound, delectable, delightful, profitable, prosperous, voluptuous 11 extravagant, flourishing

Lusitania
8 Portugal

lust
3 rut, yen 4 ache, itch, pine, urge, wish, zeal, zest 5 ardor, crave, drive, greed, letch, yearn 6 desire, fervor, hanker, hunger, libido 7 avidity, craving, lechery, longing, passion 8 appetite, coveting, cupidity, lewdness, priapism, salacity, satyrism, yearning 9 carnality, eagerness, eroticism, lubricity, prurience, pruriency 10 enthusiasm, excitement, satyriasis, wantonness 11 nymphomania 13 concupiscence, lecherousness, salaciousness

luster
4 glow 5 glaze, gleam, glint, gloss, sheen, shine 6 polish 7 burnish, shimmer 8 lambency, radiance 9 afterglow 10 brightness, brilliance, brilliancy, effulgence, luminosity, refulgence 11 candescence, iridescence

lusterless
3 dim, wan 4 blah, drab, dull, flat, gray, matt 5 brown, dingy, dusky, faded, matte, muddy, muted, vapid 6 boring 10 uninspired

lustful
3 hot 4 lewd 5 bawdy, horny 6 carnal, erotic, wanton 7 burning, goatish, itching, ruttish, satyric 8 prurient 9 debauched, lecherous, libertine, lickerish, salacious 10 hot-blooded, lascivious, libidinous, licentious, lubricious, passionate 12 concupiscent

lustrate
5 purge 6 purify 7 cleanse

lustration
6 ritual 8 ablution 9 catharsis, cleansing, purgation 10 sprinkling 12 purification

lustrous
4 naïf 5 nitid, shiny 6 bright, gleamy, glossy, pearly, sheeny 7 fulgent, glowing, lambent, radiant, shining 8 gleaming, luminous, polished, splendid 9 brilliant, burnished, effulgent, refulgent 10 glimmering, glistening 11 resplendent 12 incandescent

lusty
4 hale **5** hardy, vital **6** brawny, hearty, mighty, potent, robust, strong, virile **7** dynamic, healthy, rousing **8** vigorous **9** energetic, strapping, strenuous **10** prodigious, red-blooded **12** enthusiastic

lute
4 clay, seal **5** grout **6** cement **7** bandora **8** mandolin **10** chitarrone, instrument
Arabic: **3** oud
Indian: **5** sitar
Japanese: **4** biwa **7** samisen **8** shamisen
Oriental: **3** tar
two-necked: **7** theorbo

lutenist
5 Bream (Julian) **7** Dowland (John) **8** Gaultier (Denis)

Lutetia
5 Paris

Luxembourg
capital: **10** Luxembourg
monetary unit: **4** euro
monetary unit, former: **5** franc
mountain range: **8** Ardennes
neighbor: **6** France **7** Belgium, Germany
river: **4** Sûre **7** Alzette

luxuriant
4 lush, rank, rich **5** dense **6** fecund, lavish **7** copious, fertile, opulent, profuse, rampant, riotous, teeming **8** abundant, fruitful, luscious, prodigal, prolific **9** excessive, exuberant, sumptuous

luxuriate
4 bask **5** bloom, enjoy, feast, revel **6** abound, relish, thrive, wallow **7** delight, indulge **8** flourish

luxurious
4 lush, posh, rich **5** fancy, grand, plush, ritzy, showy **6** costly, deluxe, lavish, plushy **7** opulent, sensual, stately **8** imposing, majestic, palatial, splendid **9** elaborate, epicurean, expensive, grandiose, sumptuous **10** impressive **11** extravagant, magnificent
situation: **7** fat city **10** bed of roses, easy street

luxury
5 frill, treat **6** dainty **7** amenity, comfort **8** delicacy, opulence **9** abundance, affluence **10** indulgence **11** superfluity **12** extravagance

lycée
6 school **10** high school

lyceum
4 hall **6** school **7** academy, chamber **9** institute

Lycidas author
6 Milton (John)

Lycomedes
daughter: **8** Deidamia
victim: **7** Theseus

Lycus
brother: **7** Nycteus
father: **7** Pandion
slayer: **6** Zethus **7** Amphion
wife: **5** Dirce

Lydian
king: **5** Gyges **7** Croesus **8** Alyattes
queen: **7** Omphale

lye
7 caustic **9** hydroxide

lynch
4 hang **5** scrag **6** gibbet, murder **7** execute **8** string up

Lynette
see **Line**

lynx
4 puma **6** bobcat, cougar **7** caracal, wildcat **9** catamount

Lyra star
4 Vega

lyre
4 harp

lyric
3 ode **4** odic, poem **5** melic, verse **6** poetic **7** melodic, musical **8** operatic **9** exuberant, rhapsodic

lyrical
7 lilting, melodic, musical, songful, tuneful **8** operatic **9** melodious

lyricist
4 poet **10** librettist
see **songwriter**

Lysander's beloved
6 Hermia

M

Maacah
father: **5** Nahor **6** Talmai **7** Absalom
husband: **5** David **6** Jehiel, Machir **8** Rehoboam
son: **5** Hanan **6** Abijam, Achish **7** Absalom **10** Shephatiah

macabre
4 grim **5** lurid **6** grisly, horrid, morbid **7** deathly, ghastly, hideous **8** ghoulish, gruesome, horrible **9** deathlike **10** horrifying

macadam
3 tar **7** asphalt, roadway **8** pavement

macaque
6 monkey, rhesus

macaroni
3 fop **4** beau, buck, dude, toff **5** dandy, pasta, swell **7** coxcomb, gallant

macaw
3 Ara **6** parrot

Macbeth
character: **4** Ross **5** Angus **6** Hecate, Lennox **7** Fleance
slayer: **7** Macduff
successor: **7** Malcolm
title: **5** thane
victim: **6** Banquo, Duncan

mace
4 club **5** baton, staff **6** cudgel, nutmeg **8** bludgeon

Macedonia
capital: **6** Skopje
city: **6** Tetovo
monetary unit: **5** denar
neighbor: **6** Greece, Serbia **7** Albania **8** Bulgaria
part of: **7** Balkans
peninsula: **6** Balkan

macerate
3 ret **4** soak **5** steep **6** drench, soften **7** immerse, suffuse **8** saturate

machete
4 bolo **5** knife **6** scythe

Machiavellian
4 wily **6** shrewd **7** cunning, devious **8** guileful, scheming **9** conniving, deceitful, insidious **10** conspiring **11** duplicitous, treacherous **12** unscrupulous

Machiavelli work
6 Prince (The) **8** Mandrake (The) **10** Mandragola (La)

machinate
4 plot **6** scheme **7** connive, finagle **8** conspire, intrigue, maneuver

machination
4 plot, ploy, ruse **5** cabal, dodge **6** gambit, scheme **8** artifice, intrigue, maneuver, scheming, trickery **9** chicanery, collusion, deception, dirty work, expedient, stratagem **10** hanky-panky, subterfuge **11** contrivance, skulduggery **12** gamesmanship, skullduggery

machine
6 device, engine, gadget **9** apparatus, appliance, automaton **11** contraption
part: **3** cam **4** gear **5** lever, shaft, valve **6** caster, flange, router, switch **7** bearing

machine-gun
4 rake **6** strafe **8** enfilade **9** rapid-fire

machine-gun inventor
7 Gatling (Richard)

machinery
5 works **9** apparatus, equipment, mechanism

machismo
7 swagger **8** virility **9** manliness **11** masculinity

macho
4 stud **5** he-man, manly **6** virile **9** masculine

Machu Picchu resident
4 Inca

mackinaw
4 coat **5** cover, trout **7** blanket

mackintosh
7 slicker **8** raincoat

macrocosm
5 world **6** cosmos **8** creation, universe

mad
4 daft, nuts, rash, sore, wild **5** angry, crazy, irate, irked, kooky, livid, loony, loopy, nutty, rabid, upset, wacky **6** absurd, crazed, cuckoo, heated, insane, ireful, screwy **7** berserk, bonkers, cracked, enraged, foolish, frantic, furious, lunatic **8** choleric, demented, deranged, frenetic,

frenzied, incensed, offended, outraged, seething, unhinged, worked up, wrathful **9** delirious, fanatical, fantastic, hilarious, illogical, senseless **10** distracted, infuriated, irrational, unbalanced

Madagascar
capital: **10** Tananarive **12** Antananarivo
channel: **10** Mozambique
city: **9** Mahajanga, Toamasina
language: **6** French **8** Malagasy
monetary unit: **6** ariary
mountain range: **9** Ankaratra

madame
3 Mrs. **4** wife **6** milady, missus
German: **4** Frau
Spanish: **3** Sra. **6** Señora

Madame Bovary
author: **8** Flaubert (Gustave)
character: **4** Emma (Bovary) **7** Charles (Bovary) **8** Rodolphe

Madame Butterfly
character: **9** Cho-Cho-San, Cio-Cio-San, Pinkerton, Sharpless
composer: **7** Puccini (Giacomo)

madcap
4 rash, wild, zany **5** antic **7** foolish **8** reckless **9** frivolous, hotheaded **10** capricious, incautious

Mad Cavalier
6 Rupert (Prince)

madden
3 ire, vex **4** goad **5** anger, craze **6** enrage **7** derange, incense, inflame, outrage, possess, steam up, unhinge **9** infuriate, unbalance

Madeira Islands
capital: **7** Funchal
export: **4** wine
part of: **8** Portugal

mademoiselle
4 girl, Miss **6** maiden **9** governess **10** yellowtail **11** silver perch

made-to-order
6 custom **7** bespoke **10** customized **11** custom-built

made-up
5 bogus, faked, false, phony **6** phoney **7** painted **8** invented, mythical, specious **9** fictional, imaginary, pretended, trumped-up **10** apocryphal, fabricated, fictitious **11** make-believe **12** cosmeticized

madhouse
6 asylum, bedlam **8** loony bin **9** funny farm **10** booby hatch

madman
3 nut **4** kook, loon **5** loony, raver **6** cuckoo, maniac, psycho **7** lunatic, nutcase **9** bedlamite, psychotic, fruitcake

madness
4 rage **5** folly **6** lunacy **8** insanity **9** psychosis **11** derangement

Madonna initials
3 BVM

Madras
9 Tamil Nadu
founder: **3** Day (Francis)

Madrid museum
5 Prado

madrigal
4 glee, poem, song **8** part-song

madrigalist
English: **4** Byrd (William) **6** Morley (Thomas), Wilbye (John) **7** Tomkins (Thomas), Weelkes (Thomas)
Flemish: **8** Willaert (Adriaan)
Italian: **5** Lasso (Orlando di) **6** Lassus (Orlandus) **8** Marenzio (Luca) **10** Monteverdi (Claudio)

maelstrom
4 eddy **5** whirl, whorl **6** vortex **7** turmoil **9** whirlpool

maenad
9 bacchante, priestess
cry: **4** evoe

maestro
see **conductor**

Mafia
3 mob **4** ring **6** clique **7** rackets **8** gangland **9** Black Hand, syndicate **10** Cosa Nostra, underworld
code: **6** omertà

mafioso
4 capo, goon **6** hit man **7** goombah, made man, mobster **8** gangster **9** racketeer

magazine
4 dump **5** cache, depot, organ, store **6** armory, digest, review, weekly **7** arsenal, gazette, journal, monthly **8** biweekly **9** bimonthly, quarterly, warehouse **10** depository, periodical, repository, storehouse **11** publication
type: **3** box, pan **4** drum, news, tube **5** humor, trade **6** glossy, little, rotary **7** popular **8** literary

mage
6 priest **8** magician, sorcerer

maggot
3 bee **4** grub, whim **5** fancy, larva **6** megrim, vagary **7** caprice, conceit

Magi
6 Caspar, Gaspar **8** Melchior **9** Balthasar, Balthazar
gift: **4** gold **5** myrrh **7** incense **12** frankincense

magic
4 juju **5** obeah, wicca **6** hoodoo, voodoo **7** alchemy, devilry, sorcery **8** satanism, witchery,

witching, wizardry **9** conjuring, diablerie, diabolism, occultism, sortilege **10** hocus-pocus, mumbo jumbo, necromancy, witchcraft **11** abracadabra, bewitchment, enchantment, legerdemain, thaumaturgy

magical
5 runic **6** occult **8** wizardly **10** bewitching, entrancing **11** necromantic **12** thaumaturgic
expression: **6** presto, shazam **8** alakazam **11** abracadabra

Magic Flute composer
6 Mozart (Wolfgang Amadeus)

magician
5 brujo, witch **6** shaman, wizard **7** Houdini, warlock **8** conjurer, satanist, sorcerer **9** diabolist, enchanter, trickster, voodooist **11** medicine man, necromancer, thaumaturge
Arthurian: **6** Merlin
Shakespearean: **8** Prospero
stage: **5** Randi (James) **11** Copperfield (David), illusionist
Tolkien's: **7** Gandalf

Magic Mountain, The
author: **4** Mann (Thomas)
character: **7** Castorp (Hans)

magisterial
6 lordly **7** pompous **8** dogmatic **9** imperious, masterful **10** high-handed **11** doctrinaire, domineering, overbearing **13** authoritative, self-important

Magister Ludi author
5 Hesse (Hermann)

magistrate
5 court, judge **7** bencher, justice **8** official
ancient Greek: **5** ephor **6** archon
ancient Roman: **6** aedile **7** duumvir, praetor, questor **8** quaestor
Italian: **4** doge **7** podesta
Scottish: **6** bailie

Magna Carta
king: **4** John
place signed: **9** Runnymede

magnanimous
5 noble **7** liberal **8** generous, princely **9** forgiving, unselfish **10** benevolent, bighearted, charitable, chivalrous, high-minded, munificent

magnate
5 baron, mogul, nabob **6** fat cat, prince, tycoon **9** personage, plutocrat

magnesium symbol
2 Mg

magnet
9 lodestone **10** attraction

magnetic
8 alluring **9** appealing, seductive **10** attractive **11** captivating, charismatic, fascinating **12** irresistible
substance: **4** iron **7** ferrite

magnetism
4 draw, lure, pull **5** charm **6** allure, appeal **7** glamour **8** charisma **10** attraction **11** fascination

magnetize
4 draw, lure, wile **5** charm **6** seduce **7** attract, bewitch, enchant **9** captivate, fascinate

magnification unit
8 diameter

magnificence
4 pomp **7** majesty **8** grandeur, splendor **9** pageantry **13** sumptuousness

magnificent
5 grand, noble, regal, royal **6** august, lavish, lordly, superb **7** exalted, opulent, stately, sublime **8** glorious, imposing, majestic, palatial, princely, splendid **9** brilliant, grandiose, luxurious, sumptuous **11** extravagant, resplendent, splendorous **13** splendiferous

magnifier
4 lens **9** telescope
jeweler's: **5** loupe

magnify
4 hymn, laud **5** add to, boost, cry up, exalt, extol, swell **6** expand, extend, praise **7** amplify, augment, enhance, enlarge, ennoble, glorify, inflate **8** heighten, increase, maximize, multiply, overplay **9** aggravate, celebrate, embellish, embroider, intensify, overstate **10** aggrandize, exaggerate **13** overemphasize

magniloquent
5 tumid, windy **6** florid, turgid **7** aureate, flowery, fustian, orotund, pompous, swollen **8** sonorous **9** bombastic, high-flown, overblown, rhapsodic **10** euphuistic, rhetorical **11** declamatory

magnitude
4 size **5** order, range **6** extent, import, number, volume **7** bigness, caliber, measure, quality **8** enormity, hugeness, quantity, vastness **9** greatness, immensity, largeness **10** dimensions, importance, proportion **11** consequence

Magnolia State
11 Mississippi

magnum opus
7 classic **10** masterwork **11** chef d'oeuvre, masterpiece, tour de force

Magog's king
3 Gog

magpie
3 jay **4** bird **6** gabber, prater **7** blabber, hoarder **8** jabberer, prattler **9** chatterer, collector **10** chatterbox **12** blabbermouth

maguey
5 agave, fiber **7** cantala
relative: **4** aloe

magus
6 wizard **7** diviner, warlock **8** conjurer, magician, sorcerer **9** enchanter **10** astrologer **11** necromancer

Magyar
9 Hungarian
leader: **6** Attila

Mahalath
father: **7** Ishmael **8** Jerimoth
husband: **4** Esau **8** Rehoboam

Mahfouz work
12 Cairo Trilogy

mah-jongg piece
4 tile

Mahlon
father: **9** Elimelech
mother: **5** Naomi
wife: **4** Ruth

Maia
father: **5** Atlas
mother: **7** Pleione
sisters: **8** Pleiades
son: **6** Hermes **7** Mercury

maid
4 girl, lass, miss **5** biddy, bonne, wench **6** au pair, damsel, lassie, live-in, virgin **7** servant **8** domestic **9** charwoman, hired girl **10** au pair girl
Indian: **4** ayah
lady's: **7** abigail
stage: **9** soubrette

maiden
3 gal **4** girl, lass, miss **5** first, fresh, missy, prime, wench **6** damsel, lassie, unused, virgin **7** initial, pioneer, primary **8** earliest, original, spinster, virginal **10** spinsterly
Norse mythological: **8** valkyrie

maidenhair tree
6 ginkgo

maidenhead
5 hymen **6** purity **9** virginity

maidenhood
9 virginity

Maid of Astolat
6 Elaine

Maid of Orleans, The
7 Pucelle (La) **9** Joan of Arc
author: **8** Schiller (Friedrich von)

mail
4 post **5** armor **7** hauberk, letters **8** messages

____ mail
3 air **5** chain, snail

maim
4 maul **6** mangle **7** cripple, disable **8** mutilate, paralyze **9** disfigure

main
3 sea **5** chief, great, major, ocean, prime, trunk **7** central, high sea, leading, premier, primary **8** cardinal, foremost, high seas **9** paramount, principal **10** preeminent, prevailing **11** fundamental, outstanding, predominant

Maine
capital: **7** Augusta
city: **6** Bangor **8** Lewiston, Portland
college, university: **5** Bates, Colby **7** Bowdoin
lake: **6** Sebago
motto: **6** Dirigo
mountain: **8** Cadillac, Katahdin
nickname: **8** Pine Tree (State)
park: **6** Acadia
river: **8** Kennebec **9** Penobscot
state bird: **9** chickadee
state flower: **22** white pine cone and tassel
state tree: **9** white pine

mainly
6 mostly **7** chiefly, largely **8** above all **9** primarily **10** especially **11** principally **13** predominantly

mainstay
4 prop **5** brace **6** pillar **7** bulwark, standby, support **8** backbone, buttress **9** supporter, sustainer

Main Street author
5 Lewis (Sinclair)

maintain
4 aver, avow **5** argue, claim **6** affirm, allege, assert, back up, defend, insist, keep up, manage, stress, uphold **7** care for, carry on, contend, declare, justify, persist, profess, support, sustain, warrant **8** continue, preserve **9** cultivate, emphasize, look after **10** provide for

maintenance
4 care, keep **6** living, upkeep **7** alimony, support **10** livelihood **11** subsistence **12** alimentation
worker: **7** janitor **9** custodian

maize
4 corn, milo **10** Indian corn

majestic
5 grand, noble, regal, royal **6** august, kingly, lordly, superb **7** exalted, stately **8** elevated, imperial, imposing, princely, splendid **9** dignified, grandiose **11** ceremonious, magnificent

majesty
4 pomp **5** glory **8** eminence, grandeur, splendor **9** greatness, loftiness **11** stateliness **12** magnificence

major
3 big **4** main, star **5** chief, grave, large **6** higher, larger **7** capital, greater, notable, primary, serious, sizable **8** sizeable, superior **9** principal, prominent **10** large-scale, preeminent **11** outstanding, predominant, significant **12** considerable

Major Barbara author
4 Shaw (George Bernard)

majority
4 bulk, edge **6** margin **13** preponderance

make
3 net **4** earn, form, mold **5** build, cause, erect, forge, frame, hatch, shape, spawn **6** create, effect, output **7** achieve, bring in, compose, fashion, prepare, produce **8** comprise, conclude, generate **9** construct, establish, fabricate, originate **10** constitute **11** manufacture, put together
amends: **5** atone
believe: **7** pretend
certain: **6** assure **8** convince
fast: **3** fix **4** gird **6** secure
good: **7** succeed **9** indemnify
known: **3** air **6** expose, reveal, spread **7** declare, divulge, uncover **8** announce, disclose, proclaim
use of: **6** employ

make-believe
4 mock, sham **7** charade, fantasy, feigned, fiction **8** disguise, pretense **9** fictional, imaginary, insincere, pretended, simulated **10** fictitious

make do
4 cope **5** get by, get on, shift **6** endure, fake it, manage, wing it **7** survive **8** get along **9** improvise **11** extemporize **13** muddle through

make off
3 fly, run **4** flee, skip **5** leave, scoot, scram **6** decamp, depart, escape **7** abscond, run away **9** skedaddle

make out
3 pet, see **4** fare, neck **5** grasp, infer, spoon **6** accept, cuddle, deduce, derive, follow, gather, manage, take in, thrive **7** discern, prosper, succeed **8** conclude, flourish, get along, perceive **9** apprehend, determine, establish, interpret **10** comprehend, understand

make over
4 cede, deed **6** assign, convey, reform **7** remodel, reshape **8** renovate, transfer

maker
7 builder, creator **8** borrower, designer, inventor, producer **10** originator **11** constructor **12** manufacturer

makeshift
6 resort **7** stopgap **8** recourse, resource **9** expedient, temporary **10** expediency, jerry-built, jury-rigged, substitute **11** provisional **13** quick-and-dirty, rough-and-ready

make up
4 form **5** atone **6** devise, invent **7** arrange, compile, compose, concoct, fashion, prepare **8** comprise, contrive **9** apologize, construct, fabricate, formulate, improvise, reconcile **10** compensate

makeup
4 cast, form, kohl, mold **5** blush, fiber, gloss, grain, paint, rouge, shape, stamp, style **6** design, nature, powder, stripe, temper **7** blusher, mascara **8** eyeliner, lip gloss, war paint **9** character, eye shadow, formation **10** complexion, maquillage **11** arrangement, composition, disposition, greasepaint, personality, temperament **12** architecture, constitution, construction, organization

maladroit
5 inept **6** clumsy, gauche, klutzy **7** awkward, unhandy **8** bumbling, bungling, tactless **9** ham-handed, impolitic **10** blundering, ungraceful **11** heavy-handed **12** undiplomatic

malady
3 ill **7** ailment, disease, illness **8** disorder, sickness, syndrome **9** complaint, condition, infirmity **10** affliction

malaise
4 funk **5** dumps, ennui **8** debility, doldrums **10** enervation

Malamud, Bernard
novel: **5** Fixer (The) **7** Natural (The) **9** Assistant (The)
story: **11** Magic Barrel (The)

malapert
4 rude **5** brash, fresh, nervy, sassy, saucy, smart **6** brassy, brazen, cheeky **7** forward **8** impudent, insolent **12** presumptuous

Malaprop creator
8 Sheridan (Richard Brinsley)

malapropos
5 inapt, undue **8** improper, unseemly, untimely **10** unsuitable **11** inopportune **13** inappropriate, inopportunely

malaria
4 ague **6** miasma
medicine: **7** quinine **8** Atabrine, cinchona **10** quinacrine
mosquito: **9** anopheles

malarkey
4 bosh, bunk, guff **5** bilge, hokum, hooey, tripe **6** bunkum, drivel **7** baloney, eyewash, hogwash, rubbish, twaddle **8** nonsense, tommyrot **9** poppycock **10** balderdash **12** blatherskite

Malawi
capital: **8** Lilongwe
city: **8** Blantyre
explorer: **11** Livingstone (David)
former name: **9** Nyasaland
lake: **5** Nyasa **6** Malawi
language: **8** Chichewa
monetary unit: **6** kwacha
neighbor: **6** Zambia **8** Tanzania **10** Mozambique
river: **5** Shire

Malaysia
capital: **11** Kuala Lumpur
city: **4** Ipoh **6** Penang **11** Johor Baharu
island: **6** Borneo
monetary unit: **7** ringgit
neighbor: **8** Thailand **9** Indonesia
peninsula: **5** Malay
sea: **10** South China
strait: **7** Malacca

malcontent
5 rebel **6** griper, grouch, unruly **8** agitator, factious, frondeur, grumbler, mutinous, restless **9** alienated **10** bellyacher, complainer, rebellious **11** disaffected, disgruntled **12** contumacious, dissatisfied

mal de mer
6 nausea **8** vomiting **10** queasiness **11** seasickness

Maldives
capital: **4** Male
language: **6** Divehi
monetary unit: **7** rufiyaa

male
3 guy, tom **4** gent **5** macho, manly **6** manful, virile **7** manlike **9** masculine, staminate

malediction
4 jinx, oath **5** curse **7** malison **8** anathema **10** execration **11** imprecation

malefactor
5 felon, knave, rogue **6** sinner **8** criminal, evildoer, offender **9** miscreant, reprobate, scoundrel, wrongdoer **10** blackguard, lawbreaker

maleficent
4 evil, vile **5** toxic **6** malign, sinful, wicked **7** baleful, baneful, beastly, harmful, noxious, vicious **8** damnable, sinister, virulent **9** execrable, injurious, nefarious, repugnant **10** pernicious, villainous **11** destructive

malevolence
4 evil **5** spite **6** grudge, malice, spleen **7** ill will **9** hostility, malignity **12** spitefulness **13** maliciousness

malevolent
4 evil **6** malign, wicked **7** baleful, hateful, hurtful, vicious **8** sinister, spiteful, venomous **9** injurious, malicious, malignant, poisonous

malfunction
6 glitch **7** misfire

Mali
capital: **6** Bamako
city: **5** Mopti, Ségou **7** Sikasso **8** Timbuktu **10** Tombouctou
desert: **6** Sahara
former name: **11** French Sudan
language: **6** French
monetary unit: **5** franc
neighbor: **5** Niger **6** Guinea **7** Algeria, Senegal **10** Ivory Coast, Mauritania **11** Burkina Faso, Côte d'Ivoire
river: **5** Niger

malice
4 bile, hate **5** spite, venom **6** animus, enmity, grudge, hatred, poison, spleen **7** ill will **8** meanness **9** animosity, antipathy **10** bitterness, resentment **11** hatefulness, malevolence **12** spitefulness **13** invidiousness

malicious
4 evil, mean **5** nasty, petty **6** wicked **7** baneful, hateful, heinous, jealous **8** spiteful, vengeful, venomous, virulent **9** poisonous, poison-pen, rancorous **10** malevolent

maliciousness
see **malevolence**

malign
4 evil, soil **5** abuse, decry, libel, smear, stain, sully, taint **6** befoul, defame, defile, revile, smirch, vilify, wicked **7** asperse, baleful, baneful, blacken, detract, hateful, hostile, noxious, slander, tarnish, traduce, vicious **8** besmirch, derogate, inimical, sinister, spiteful, tear down, virulent **9** denigrate, disparage, injurious, rancorous **10** calumniate, depreciate, maleficent, malevolent, pernicious, scandalize, vituperate **11** deleterious, opprobriate **12** antagonistic, antipathetic

malignant
4 evil **5** fatal **6** deadly, lethal, wicked **7** baleful, hateful, vicious **8** devilish, fiendish, spiteful **9** injurious, rancorous **10** diabolical, malevolent

malison
5 curse **8** anathema **11** commination, imprecation, malediction

mall
4 lane **5** alley, plaza, strip **7** passage **9** concourse, esplanade, promenade **10** passageway **11** median strip

malleable
6 pliant, supple **7** ductile, plastic, pliable **8** flexible **9** adaptable

mallet
6 hammer

malodorous
4 foul, gamy, rank **5** fetid, fuggy, funky, fusty, musty, stale **6** frowsy, putrid, rancid, rotten,

smelly, stinky **7** noisome, noxious, reeking, spoiled **8** mephitic, stinking **9** offensive **10** nauseating **11** ill-smelling **12** pestilential

Malraux novel
8 Man's Fate

Malta
capital: **8** Valletta
city: **5** Qormi **10** Birkirkara
island: **4** Gozo **6** Comino
language: **6** French **7** Maltese
monetary unit: **4** lira
sea: **13** Mediterranean

Maltese Falcon, The
actor: **5** Astor (Mary), Lorre (Peter) **6** Bogart (Humphrey) **11** Greenstreet (Sydney)
author: **7** Hammett (Dashiell)
detective: **5** Spade (Sam)
director: **6** Huston (John)

maltreat
5 abuse **6** ill-use, misuse, molest

Mamet, David
film: **5** Heist **7** Verdict (The) **9** Wag the Dog **12** House of Games, Untouchables (The)
play: **7** Oleanna, Romance **14** Boston Marriage **15** American Buffalo **17** Glengarry Glen Ross

mammal
2 ox **3** ass, bat, cat, cow, dog, elk, fox, pig, rat **4** bear, deer, goat, Homo, lion, mink, mole, oxen (plural), pika, seal, tahr, unau, urva, wolf **5** camel, civet, coati, fossa, genet, hippo, hyena, hyrax, koala, lemur, llama, moose, okapi, otter, panda, ratel, sable, sheep, shrew, sloth, takin, tapir, tiger, tigon, zebra **6** alpaca, badger, beaver, colugo, dassie, grison, jackal, marten, ocelot, rabbit, racoon, rodent, sifaka, tenrec, tiglon, vicuña, wombat **7** caracal, giraffe, guanaco, hyraces (plural), leopard, lioness, opossum, linsang, peccary, polecat, primate, raccoon, tigress **8** aardvark, aardwolf, edentate, elephant, hedgehog, kangaroo, kinkajou, mongoose, pangolin, pinniped, ruminant, squirrel, starnose, ungulate **9** armadillo, bandicoot **10** cacomistle **12** hippopotamus
aquatic: **4** orca, seal **6** dugong, sea cow, walrus **7** cowfish, dolphin, grampus, manatee, narwhal, platypi (plural) **8** cetacean, platypus, porpoise, sirenian
extinct: **6** quagga **8** mastodon, stegodon

mammon
4 pelf **5** lucre **6** riches, wealth **8** treasure **9** abundance, affluence **10** prosperity **11** possessions

mammoth
4 huge, vast **5** giant, jumbo **6** mighty **7** immense, massive, monster, titanic **8** colossal, enormous, gigantic **9** leviathan, monstrous **10** gargantuan, mastodonic, monumental **9** humongous **11** elephantine

man
2 Mr. **3** guy **4** buck, chap, cuss, dude, gent, male **5** being, bloke **6** fellow, mister, mortal, person **7** husband **8** creature, paramour **9** boyfriend, mortality, personage **10** individual **11** Homo sapiens
castrated: **6** eunuch
combining form: **4** andr **5** andro, homin **6** homini
common: **7** Joe Blow, John Doe **11** John Q. Public
French: **5** homme
Italian: **4** uomo
Latin: **3** vir **4** homo
old: **6** codger, geezer
Spanish: **6** hombre
Yiddish: **6** mensch

manage
3 run **4** cope, fare, head, keep, mind, tend **5** get by, get on, shift **6** afford, direct, effect, govern, handle **7** achieve, carry on, conduct, control, execute, finagle, operate, oversee, succeed **8** carry out, contrive, cope with, deal with, dominate, engineer, get along, maintain **9** cultivate, supervise **10** accomplish, administer, bring about **11** orchestrate, superintend

manageable
6 docile, pliant **8** amenable, bearable, biddable, passable **9** agreeable, compliant, endurable, tractable **10** responsive **11** cooperative, supportable, sustainable **13** accommodating

management
4 care **5** brass **6** charge **7** conduct, control, running **8** guidance, handling **9** direction, oversight **10** conducting **11** front office, supervising, supervision

manager
4 boss, exec **6** gerent **7** handler, officer **8** director, official, overseer, producer **9** conductor, executive **10** impresario, supervisor **13** administrator
museum: **7** curator

mañana
7 someday **8** sometime, tomorrow

Man and Superman author
4 Shaw (George Bernard)

Manassas battle
7 Bull Run

Manasseh, Manasses
brother: **7** Ephraim
father: **6** Hashum, Joseph **8** Hezekiah **10** Pahathmoab
grandfather: **5** Jacob
grandson: **6** Gilead
mother: **7** Asenath
son: **6** Machir

man-at-arms
2 GI **7** fighter, soldier, warrior **10** serviceman
Mandalay author
7 Kipling (Rudyard)
mandarin
5 elder **6** orange **8** official **9** tangerine **10** bureaucrat, panjandrum
mandate
4 fiat, word **5** edict, order, ukase **6** behest, charge, decree **7** bidding, command, dictate **9** authority, directive **10** imperative, injunction **13** authorization
mandatory
6 forced **7** binding **8** required **9** de rigueur, necessary, requisite **10** compulsory, imperative, obligatory **11** involuntary
mandible
3 jaw **8** lower jaw
man-eater
4 lion, ogre **5** shark, tiger **8** cannibal **13** mackerel shark
Manette's daughter
5 Lucie
maneuver
3 ply **4** move, plan, plot, ploy, step **5** feint, trick, wield **6** design, device, gambit, handle, jockey, scheme, tactic, wangle **7** exploit, finagle, finesse **8** artifice, démarche, engineer, exercise, intrigue, movement, navigate **9** machinate, procedure, stratagem **10** manipulate, proceeding, subterfuge **11** contrivance, machination **12** manipulation
maneuvering room
8 latitude
Man for All Seasons, A
author: **4** Bolt (Robert)
subject: **4** More (Thomas)
manganese
ore: **10** pyrolusite
symbol: **2** Mn
manger
4 rack **6** cratch, feeder, trough
mangle
3 mar **4** iron, maim, maul **5** press **6** damage, deface, deform, impair, injure **7** butcher, contort, distort **8** lacerate, mutilate **9** disfigure
mangy
5 seedy **6** ragtag, shabby **7** scruffy, squalid **8** decrepit, tattered **9** moth-eaten **10** down-at-heel, threadbare
manhandle
5 abuse **6** batter **7** rough up **8** maltreat, mistreat **10** push around, slap around
Manhattan
building: **8** Chrysler **11** Empire State
district: **4** Soho **6** Harlem **7** Chelsea, Tribeca
entertainment district: **11** Times Square
financial district: **10** Wall Street
museum: **3** Met **4** MOMA **7** Whitney **10** Guggenheim **12** Metropolitan
opera house: **3** Met **12** Metropolitan
purchaser: **6** Minuit (Peter)
river: **4** East **6** Hudson
school: **3** NYU **6** Hunter **8** Columbia **9** Juilliard
mania
4 rage, zeal **5** craze, fancy **6** frenzy, lunacy **7** madness, passion **8** fixation, idée fixe, insanity **9** cacoëthes, obsession **10** compulsion, enthusiasm **11** infatuation
maniac
3 bug, nut **4** loon **5** fiend, freak **6** madman, psycho, zealot **7** fanatic, lunatic, nutcase **8** crackpot **9** bedlamite **10** enthusiast
manifest
4 show **5** clear, overt, plain, shown, utter, voice **6** appear, embody, evince, expose, patent, reveal **7** display, evident, evinced, exhibit, express, invoice, obvious, visible **8** apparent, distinct, evidence, palpable, proclaim, revealed **9** evidenced, incarnate, objectify, prominent **10** illustrate, noticeable, observable **11** demonstrate, exteriorize, externalize, perceptible, unambiguous
manifestation
4 show, sign **5** proof **7** display, symptom **8** epiphany **10** appearance, revelation
manifesto
4 fiat, rule, writ **5** credo, creed, edict, ukase **6** decree, dictum, gospel, notice, policy, ruling **7** mandate **8** doctrine, document, platform **9** directive, statement, testament, testimony, ultimatum **10** deposition, injunction, resolution **11** declaration **12** announcement, notification, proclamation **13** pronouncement
manifold
7 diverse, various **8** compound, multiple, multiply, numerous **9** multiform, multiplex **10** multiphase **12** multifarious
manikin
4 runt **5** dummy, dwarf, gnome, model, pygmy **6** midget, peewee **8** Tom Thumb **10** homunculus
Manila
founder: **7** Legazpi (Miguel López de)
site: **5** Luzon **11** Philippines
victor: **5** Dewey (George)
manioc
4 yuca **5** yucca **6** casava **7** cassava, tapioca
manipulate
3 ply, rig **4** play **5** steer, swing, tweak, wield **6** adjust, direct, doctor, handle, jockey, juggle, manage **7** beguile, conduct, control, exploit,

finagle, finesse, massage **8** engineer, maneuver **9** machinate **10** tamper with

Man, Isle of
capital: 7 Douglas
cat: 4 Manx
possession of: 7 Britain
sea: 5 Irish

Manitoba
capital: 8 Winnipeg
lake: 8 Winnipeg **12** Winnipegosis
mountain: 5 Baldy
provincial flower: 13 prairie crocus
river: 6 Nelson **9** Churchill

mankind
6 humans, people **8** humanity **11** Homo sapiens

manlike
4 male **6** virile **8** hominoid, humanoid **9** masculine **10** anthropoid

manly
4 male **5** macho **6** virile **9** masculine

man-made
9 synthetic **10** artificial, factitious
object: 8 artefact, artifact

Mann character
6 Joseph **9** Leverkühn (Adrian) **10** Aschenbach (Gustav von), Felix Krull **11** Hans Castorp, Tonio Kröger

manner
3 air, way **4** form, kind, mien, mode, sort, vein, wont **5** habit, modus, style, usage **6** aspect, custom, method **7** bearing, conduct, fashion **8** behavior, demeanor, habitude, practice, presence **9** demeanour, etiquette, technique **10** consuetude, deportment **11** affectation, comportment **12** idiosyncrasy

mannered
7 stilted **8** affected, precious **10** artificial **13** self-conscious

mannerism
3 tic **4** pose **5** quirk **10** preciosity **11** affectation, peculiarity, singularity **12** eccentricity, idiosyncrasy **13** artificiality

mannerless
4 rude **6** coarse **7** boorish, ill-bred, uncivil, uncouth **8** impolite **12** discourteous

mannerly
5 civil **6** polite **7** genteel, refined **8** decorous, gracious, well-bred **9** civilized, courteous **10** respectful

Manon composer
8 Massenet (Jules)

Manon Lescaut
author: 7 Prévost (Abbé)
composer: 7 Puccini (Giacomo) **8** Massenet (Jules)
lover: 9 des Grieux

manor
5 villa **6** estate, quinta **7** château, demesne **12** landed estate

manservant
5 valet **6** butler

mansion
4 hall **5** villa **6** palace **7** château

manslayer
6 killer **8** homicide, murderer

manta
3 ray **5** cloak, cloth, shawl **7** blanket

manteau
4 coat, robe, wrap **5** cloak **6** capote, domino, mantle, tabard

mantic
5 vatic **6** orphic **7** Delphic, fatidic **8** Delphian, oracular **9** prophetic, sibylline, vaticinal **10** divinatory

mantilla
4 cape, wrap **5** cloak, fichu, scarf, shawl **8** kerchief

mantle
4 cope, glow, pink, robe, rose **5** blush, cloak, color, cover, flush, rouge **6** capote, casing, pinken, redden **7** crimson

man-to-man
4 open **5** frank, plain **6** candid, direct, honest **10** forthright, unreserved **11** openhearted

mantra
2 om **5** chant, motto **6** prayer, slogan **9** watchword **10** invocation **11** incantation

manual
4 text **5** guide **6** primer **8** Baedeker, handbook, hornbook, textbook **9** guidebook, vade mecum **10** compendium **11** abecedarium, enchiridion
religious: 9 catechism
worker: 6 menial **7** laborer

manufacture
4 form, make **6** create **7** fashion, produce **8** assemble **9** construct, fabricate **11** put together

manumit
4 free **6** unbind **7** release, set free, unchain **8** liberate **9** unshackle **10** emancipate

manure
4 dung **6** ordure **7** excreta **9** excrement **10** fertilizer

manuscript
4 hand **6** scrawl **8** longhand **9** autograph **10** penmanship **11** calligraphy, handwriting
ancient: 5 codex **6** scroll **7** codices (plural)
red part: 6 rubric
style: 6 uncial
symbol: 6 obelus

many
5 scads **6** divers, legion, myriad, sundry **7** copious, diverse, umpteen, various **8** abundant,

manifold, multiple, numerous **9** abounding, bounteous, bountiful, countless, multitude, plentiful **12** multifarious **13** multitudinous
combining form: 4 poly **5** multi, pluri

many-sided
7 diverse **8** all-round, talented **9** all-around, versatile **10** variegated **11** diversified **12** multifaceted, multifarious **13** comprehensive

Mao's successor
3 Hua (Guofeng, Kuo-feng) **4** Deng (Xiaoping), Teng (Hsiao-p'ing)

map
4 plan, plat **5** chart, draft, globe, graph **6** design, lay out, set out, sketch, survey **7** arrange, diagram, drawing, outline, tracing **9** delineate
collection: 5 atlas
line: 6 isobar **7** contour, isogram, isohyet **8** isogloss, isogonic, isopleth, isotherm
maker: 12 cartographer
making: 11 cartography

maple
genus: 4 Acer
product: 5 syrup
type: 3 red **5** sugar **8** box elder

map projection
5 conic **8** Mercator **9** polyconic **10** sinusoidal **12** orthographic **13** stereographic

maquillage
6 makeup

mar
4 ding, harm, hurt, scar, warp **5** spoil, stain **6** bruise, damage, deface, deform, impair, injure **7** blemish, scratch, tarnish, vitiate **9** disfigure

marabou
5 stork

Marat/Sade author
5 Weiss (Peter)

Marat, Jean-Paul
colleague: 6 Danton (Georges) **11** Robespierre (Maximilien)
slayer: 6 Corday (Charlotte)

maraud
4 loot, raid, sack **5** foray, harry **6** harass, ravage, ravish **7** despoil, pillage, plunder, ransack

marauder
6 bandit, pirate **7** brigand, spoiler, wrecker **9** buccaneer, desperado **10** freebooter

marble
3 mib, mig, taw **4** immy, migg **5** agate, aggie, alley, rance **6** blotch, miggle, mottle, streak **7** cipolin, glassie, steelie **9** limestone

marbled
6 veined **7** dappled, flecked, mottled **8** speckled, streaked

Marble Faun, The
author: 9 Hawthorne (Nathaniel)
character: 5 Hilda **6** Kenyon, Miriam **9** Donatello
setting: 4 Rome

marcel
4 wave

march
3 hem, rim **4** abut, file, line **5** skirt **6** adjoin, border, parade **7** advance, headway, proceed **8** anabasis, boundary, frontier, outlands, progress, traverse **9** periphery **10** borderland

March
date: 4 ides
mother: 6 Marmee
sisters: 3 Amy, Meg **4** Beth

March King
5 Sousa (John Philip)

Mardi Gras
8 carnival **10** Fat Tuesday
city: 10 New Orleans

Marduk
city: 7 Babylon
consort: 8 Zarbanit, Zarpanit
victim: 5 Kingu **6** Tiamat

mare
3 sea **5** horse **6** equine

mare's nest
3 con, din **4** hoax, scam **5** babel, cheat, fraud, put-on, spoof **6** bedlam, clamor, hubbub, humbug, racket, ruckus, tumult, uproar **7** swindle, turmoil **8** brouhaha, flimflam, illusion **9** confusion, imposture **10** hullabaloo **11** pandemonium

margarine
4 oleo

margin
3 hem, rim **4** brim, edge, join, line, play, room, side **5** bound, brink, frame, scope, shore, skirt, verge **6** border, fringe, leeway **7** minimum, outline, selvage **8** boundary, latitude, selvedge, surround, trimming **9** elbowroom, perimeter, periphery **13** circumference
tiny: 4 hair

marginal
5 minor **7** limited, minimal **9** bordering **10** borderline, negligible, peripheral, subsidiary **13** insignificant

Marguerite's lover
5 Faust

Maria ____
5 Elena **7** Stuarda

Marianas
discoverer: 8 Magellan (Ferdinand)
island: 4 Guam, Rota **5** Pagan **6** Guguan, Saipan, Tinian **7** Agrihan, Aguijan

marijuana
3 kef, kif, pot **4** hash, hemp, weed **5** bhang, grass **6** reefer **7** hashish **8** cannabis

marina
4 dock, pier, quay **5** basin, berth, wharf **8** boatyard

marinate
4 soak **5** steep **6** drench, pickle **7** immerse **8** macerate

marine
5 naval **7** abyssal, aquatic, deep-sea, oceanic, pelagic **8** nautical, seagoing, seascape **9** seafaring, thalassic **10** oceangoing **12** hydrographic **13** oceanographic
crustacean: 6 shrimp **7** lobster **8** barnacle
deposit: 5 coral
plant: 4 kelp, nori **5** dulse **6** wakame **7** seaweed

mariner
3 gob, tar **4** jack, salt, swab **5** limey **6** hearty, rating, sailor, sea dog, seaman **7** jack-tar, old salt, swabbie **8** seafarer **9** sailorman, shellback, tarpaulin **10** bluejacket

marital
6 wedded **7** married, nuptial, spousal **8** conjugal, hymeneal **9** connubial

maritime
7 oceanic, pelagic **8** nautical **9** thalassic **12** navigational

mark
3 aim, jot, sap, tee **4** butt, dupe, fool, goal, gull, heed, look, nick, note, pick, show, sign, view **5** blaze, bound, brand, chart, chump, elect, grade, label, notch, stamp, token, trait **6** behold, choose, denote, evince, lay off, notice, object, opt for, rating, record, select, sucker, target, victim, virtue **7** betoken, delimit, discern, exhibit, fall guy, feature, gudgeon, indicia, initial, measure, observe, qualify, scratch, signify, symptom **8** function, indicate, perceive, register **9** attribute, character, designate, objective, single out **10** indication **11** differentia, distinction, distinguish **12** characterize
distinctive: 7 indicia **8** indicium
identifying: 4 logo, seal **6** emblem, signet, symbol **8** colophon, logotype
of insertion: 5 caret
of omission: 4 dele **8** ellipsis **10** apostrophe
of retention: 4 stet
over a vowel: 5 breve, haček **6** accent, macron, umlaut **8** dieresis **9** diaeresis **10** circumflex
over n: 5 tilde
punctuation: 4 dash **5** brace, colon, comma, slant, slash **6** hyphen, period **7** bracket, solidus **9** backslash, guillemet, semicolon **10** apostrophe
under a letter: 7 cedilla

Mark
6 Gospel
cousin: 8 Barnabas
mother: 4 Mary

mark down
3 cut **4** pare **5** shave, slash **6** reduce **7** devalue **8** discount **9** devaluate **10** depreciate, undervalue

marked
5 noted **6** patent, signal **7** evident, notable, obvious, pointed, salient **8** distinct, manifest, striking **9** arresting, prominent **10** noticeable, remarkable **11** conspicuous, outstanding **12** considerable **13** distinguished
man: 4 Cain

marker
3 IOU, run **5** score **7** felt-tip

market
3 suq **4** fair, mall, sell, shop, souk, vend **5** store **6** bazaar, outlet, retail, rialto **8** emporium, exchange, showroom **9** advertise, traffic in, wholesale **11** merchandise
kind: 4 flea **5** money, stock

marketable
5 sound **7** salable **8** vendible **10** commercial

marketplace
3 suq **4** mall, souk **5** agora **6** bazaar, rialto **8** emporium

marksman
4 shot **6** sniper **7** deadeye, shooter **12** sharpshooter

marl
4 clay, silt

marlin
8 billfish **9** spearfish

Marlowe play
8 Edward II **9** Dr. Faustus **10** Jew of Malta (The) **11** Tamburlaine **13** Doctor Faustus

marmot
6 rodent **9** woodchuck **10** prairie dog

maroon
3 red **6** claret, desert, strand **7** abandon, crimson, forsake, isolate, outcast **8** burgundy, castaway

Marquand character
4 Gray (Charles), Moto (Mr.) **5** Apley (George), Wayde (Willis) **6** Pulham (H.M.) **7** Goodwin (Melville)

Marquis, Don
cat: 9 Mehitabel
cockroach: 5 Archy

marriage
5 match, union **6** bridal **7** nuptial, spousal, wedding, wedlock **8** coupling, espousal, monogamy,

nuptials, polygamy **9** matrimony **11** conjugality **12** connubiality
combining form: **4** gamy **6** gamous
notice: **5** banns
outside a group: **7** exogamy
within a group: **8** endogamy

marriageable
6 nubile **8** eligible

marriage broker
5 yenta **9** go-between **10** matchmaker

Marriage of Figaro composer
6 Mozart (Wolfgang Amadeus)

marrow
4 core, meat, pith, soul **5** heart, stuff **6** kernel **7** essence **12** quintessence

marry
3 tie, wed **4** join, link, mate, wive, yoke **5** hitch, merge, unite **6** couple, splice, spouse **7** combine, conjoin, espouse **9** conjugate

Mars
4 Ares **6** planet
combining term: **4** areo
feature: **4** face **5** basin **6** canyon, crater **7** volcano **8** polar cap
lover: **5** Venus
mission: **6** Viking **7** Mariner **10** Pathfinder
moon: **6** Deimos, Phobos
relating to: **7** martian
(see also **Ares**)

Marseillaise composer
13 Rouget de Lisle (Claude-Joseph)

marsh
3 bog, fen **4** mire, ooze, quag **5** bayou, glade, swale, swamp **6** morass, muskeg, slough **7** wetland **8** quagmire **9** swampland

marshal
5 align, array, guide, order, rally, usher **6** deploy, direct, escort, muster **7** arrange, officer, round up **8** assemble, mobilize, organize, shepherd **9** methodize, systemize
(see also **field marshal**)

Marshall Islands
atoll: **6** Bikini **8** Enewetak **9** Kwajalein
capital: **6** Majuro
ethnic group: **11** Micronesian
island chain: **5** Ralik, Ratak **6** Sunset **7** Sunrise **11** Marshallese

marshy
4 miry **5** boggy, mucky **6** quaggy, swampy **7** sloughy

marsupial
3 roo **4** euro **5** koala **6** possum, wombat **7** opossum, wallaby **8** kangaroo, wallaroo **9** bandicoot

marten
6 fisher, weasel

Martha
brother: **7** Lazarus
sister: **4** Mary

martial
7 warlike **8** militant, military, spirited **9** bellicose, combative, soldierly **11** belligerent **12** militaristic

martial art
4 judo **5** kendo **6** aikido, karate, kung fu, neijia, tai chi **7** shaolin **8** capoeira, jiujitsu **9** tae kwon do **11** tai chi chuan
expert: **5** ninja
school: **4** dojo
teacher: **6** sensei

Martial's forte
7 epigram

Martin Chuzzlewit author
7 Dickens (Charles)

Martinique
capital: **12** Fort-de-France
department of: **6** France
discoverer: **8** Columbus (Christopher)
island group: **8** Windward
location: **10** West Indies
neighbor: **8** Dominica **10** Saint Lucia
volcano: **5** Pelée

martyr
4 Paul, rack **5** Agnes, Alban, James, Peter, saint, wring **6** George, harrow, Justin **7** afflict, agonize, Clement, crucify, Cyprian, Stephen, torment, torture **8** Ignatius, Lawrence, Polycarp, sufferer **9** Joan of Arc, Sebastian **10** excruciate, Thomas More
Protestant: **6** Ridley (Nicholas) **7** Cranmer (Thomas), Latimer (Hugh)

marvel
4 gape **6** wonder **7** miracle, portent, prodigy, stunner **9** curiosity, sensation **10** phenomenon **12** astonishment

marvelous
5 super, swell **6** divine **7** amazing, awesome, ripping **8** glorious, striking, stunning, superior, terrific, wondrous **9** excellent, wonderful **10** astounding, incredible, miraculous, phenomenal, prodigious, remarkable, staggering, stupendous, surprising **11** astonishing, exceptional, sensational, spectacular **12** awe-inspiring, supernatural **13** extraordinary

Marx brother
5 Chico, Gummo, Harpo, Zeppo **7** Groucho

Marxist
9 socialist **9** communist

Marx, Karl
book: **7** Kapital (Das)
collaborator: **6** Engels (Friedrich)

Mary
husband: **6** Clopas, Joseph **8** Alphaeus
kinswoman: **9** Elisabeth
son: **4** Mark **5** James, Jesus

Maryland
bay: **10** Chesapeake
capital: **9** Annapolis
city: **9** Baltimore, Frederick
college, university: **6** Towson **7** Goucher **9** Annapolis **12** Johns Hopkins **12** Naval Academy (U.S.)
fort: **7** McHenry
nickname: **7** Old Line (State)
river: **7** Potomac **8** Patuxent
state bird: **15** Baltimore oriole
state flower: **14** black-eyed Susan
state tree: **8** white oak

mascot
4 juju **5** charm **6** amulet, fetish, symbol **8** gris-gris, talisman

masculine
4 male **5** macho, manly **6** manful, virile **7** manlike

masculinity
8 machismo, virility **9** manliness

Masefield work
7 Cargoes **8** Sea Fever

mash
4 pulp **5** crush, smash **6** squash, squish **7** squoosh **8** macerate **9** pulverize

masher
4 wolf **5** flirt **6** chaser **7** Don Juan, seducer **8** Casanova, lothario **9** ladies' man, womanizer **10** lady-killer **11** philanderer, skirt chaser

mash note
10 billet-doux, love letter

mask
4 hide, pose, sham, veil **5** cover, front, guard, guise, visor **6** facade, screen, vizard **7** dress up, frisket, pretext **8** coloring, disguise, pretense **9** dissemble, semblance **10** appearance, camouflage, false front, simulation **11** dissimulate

masonry
9 brickwork, stonework
in a frame: **7** nogging

masquerade
4 pose **6** facade **7** costume, posture **8** carnival, disguise **10** camouflage, masked ball **11** costume ball

mass
3 lot, sum, wad **4** bank, body, bulk, clot, core, glob, heap, hill, lump, pack, peck, pile **5** clump, mound **6** corpus, volume **7** expanse, globule, wadding **8** assemble, quantity **9** aggregate, stockpile, substance **11** aggregation **12** conglomerate
compacted: **4** cake
for the dead: **7** requiem
of individuals: **3** mob **4** host **5** crowd, crush, flock, horde, swarm **6** throng **12** congregation **13** agglomeration
part: **5** Kyrie **6** proper **8** Agnus Dei, ordinary

Massachusetts
cape: **3** Ann, Cod
capital: **6** Boston
city: **6** Lowell, Quincy **9** Cambridge, Worcester **10** New Bedford **11** Springfield
college, university: **3** MIT **5** Clark, Smith, Tufts **7** Amherst, Berklee, Harvard, Wheaton **8** Brandeis, Williams **9** Hampshire, Holy Cross, Radcliffe, Wellesley **12** Mount Holyoke, Northeastern
island: **9** Nantucket **15** Martha's Vineyard
mountain, range: **8** Greylock **9** Berkshire
nickname: **3** Bay (State) **9** Old Colony (State)
river: **11** Connecticut
state bird: **9** chickadee
state flower: **9** mayflower
state tree: **3** elm (American)
symbol: **3** cod

massacre
4 kill **6** mangle, murder, pogrom **7** butcher, carnage **8** butchery, decimate, genocide, mangling, mutilate **9** bloodbath, bloodshed, slaughter **10** annihilate, blood purge, decimation, mutilation **11** exterminate **12** annihilation

massage
3 rub **5** knead **7** flatter, rubdown, shiatsu **8** blandish **10** manipulate

Massenet opera
5 Le Cid, Manon, Sapho, Thaïs **7** Werther

massive
4 huge, mega, vast **5** bulky, giant, jumbo, mondo, solid **6** mighty **7** hulking, immense, mammoth, weighty **8** colossal, cumbrous, enormous, gigantic, towering **9** humongous, monstrous **10** gargantuan, monumental, prodigious, stupendous, tremendous **11** elephantine, mountainous

master
4 best, boss, guru, head, lick, rule, tame **5** adept, bwana, chief, crack, learn, ruler, sahib, tutor **6** artist, expert, genius, honcho, leader, subdue, victor **7** captain, conquer, headman, maestro, padrone, prevail, skilled, triumph **8** dominant, dominate, employer, governor, overcome, overlord, overseer, regulate, skeleton, skillful, superior, surmount, virtuoso **9** authority, chieftain, conqueror, dominator, paramount, principal, sovereign **10** proficient **11** predominant
of ceremonies: **4** host **5** emcee **7** compere

masterful
4 deft **5** adept **6** adroit, expert **7** skilled **8** skillful **10** high-handed, proficient **11** magisterial **13** authoritative

masterly
5 adept, crack **6** adroit, expert **7** skilled **8** skillful **9** dexterous **10** proficient **11** crackerjack **12** accomplished

Master of Ballantrae, The
6 Durrie
author: 9 Stevenson (Robert Louis)

masterpiece
7 classic **10** magnum opus **11** chef d'oeuvre, tour de force

mastery
5 knack, skill **7** ability, command, control, know-how, prowess **8** dominion **9** authority, expertise **10** ascendancy, domination, expertness, virtuosity **11** proficiency, superiority

masticate
4 chaw, chew, pulp **5** champ, chomp, crush, munch **6** crunch **7** scrunch **8** macerate, ruminate **9** break down

mat
3 rug **4** felt **6** border, carpet, tatami

matador
6 torero **8** toreador **11** bullfighter
adjunct: 6 muleta
move: 4 pase **5** faena **8** veronica

Mata Hari
3 spy **10** seductress **11** femme fatale

match
3 pit **4** bout, game, meet, peer, suit, twin **5** array, equal, rival, touch, union **6** double, equate, oppose **7** compare, contest, counter, paragon, play off **8** alliance, analogue, marriage, opponent, parallel **9** adversary, correlate, duplicate, encounter, measure up, smackdown **10** antagonist, complement, coordinate, engagement, equivalent, reciprocal, supplement, tournament **11** counterpart **12** correspond to
a bet: 3 see
friction: 7 lucifer

matchless
6 unique **7** supreme **8** peerless, singular **9** nonpareil, unequaled, unrivaled **10** inimitable **12** incomparable, unparalleled

matchmaker
see **marriage broker**

mate
3 bud, pal, tie, wed **4** chum, pair, twin **5** amigo, breed, buddy, crony, equal, hitch, marry **6** cohort, couple, double, fellow, friend, helper, splice, spouse **7** compeer, comrade, consort, partner **8** confrere, sidekick **9** associate, companion, copartner, duplicate, procreate **10** complement, equivalent, reciprocal **11** concomitant

maté
3 tea **5** holly **8** beverage

mater
3 mom, mum **6** mother **9** matriarch

____ mater
4 alma

material
4 real, true **5** cloth, stuff **6** actual, fabric, matter, object **7** element, germane, worldly **8** palpable, physical, relevant, sensible, tangible **9** component, corporeal, essential, important, objective, pertinent, substance **10** applicable, ingredient, meaningful, phenomenal **11** appreciable, constituent, fundamental, perceptible, significant, substantial
building: 5 adobe, brick **6** stucco **7** lagging, plaster, plywood, shingle **8** concrete

materialistic
7 secular, worldly **11** acquisitive

materialize
4 loom, rise **5** arise, issue **6** appear, embody, emerge, evolve, show up **7** develop, surface **8** manifest **9** come about, incarnate, take shape **12** substantiate

matériel
4 gear **5** stock **8** supplies **9** apparatus, equipment, machinery **10** provisions **13** accouterments, accoutrements, paraphernalia

maternal
8 motherly

matey
5 pally, tight **6** clubby **7** affable **8** amicable, familiar, friendly, intimate, sociable **9** congenial

mathematician
American: 5 Wiles (Andrew) **6** Peirce (Charles S.), Veblen (Oswald), Wiener (Norbert)
Austrian: 5 Gödel (Kurt)
British: 6 Stokes (George)
Dutch: 7 Huygens (Christiaan)
English: 6 Newton (Isaac), Taylor (Brook), Turing (Alan), Wallis (John) **7** Pearson (Karl), Russell (Bertrand) **8** Hamilton (James Rowan) **9** Sylvester (James Joseph), Whitehead (Alfred North, Henry)
French: 4 Weil (André) **5** Borel (Emile), Comte (Auguste), Viète (François) **6** Galois (Evariste), Pascal (Blaise), Picard (Charles-Emile) **7** Fourier (Jean-Baptiste), Laplace (Marquis de), Vernier (Pierre) **8** Painlevé (Paul), Poincaré (Jules-Henri) **9** Descartes (René)
German: 5 Gauss (Carl Friedrich), Wolff (Freiherr von) **6** Staudt (Karl von) **7** Leibniz (Gottfried Wilhelm), Riemann (Georg) **11** Weierstrass (Karl)

Greek: 6 Euclid 10 Archimedes, Pythagoras
Hungarian: 5 Erdos (Paul)
Italian: 8 Volterra (Vito) 10 Torricelli (Evangelista)
Norwegian: 7 Stormer (Fredrik)
Russian: 11 Lobachevsky (Nikolay)
Scottish: 4 Tait (Peter) 6 Napier (John) 8 Stirling (James)
Swiss: 5 Euler (Leonhard), Sturm (Jacques) 7 Steiner (Jakob)

mathematics
branch: 4 trig 7 algebra 8 calculus, geometry, topology 10 arithmetic, statistics 12 trigonometry
proven statement in: 7 theorem

___ Mather
6 Cotton 7 Richard 8 Increase

mating arena
3 lek

matriarch
4 dame 6 mother 7 dowager 10 grande dame

matriculate
4 join 5 enter 6 enroll, sign on 8 register

matrimonial
6 bridal, wedded 7 marital, married, nuptial, spousal 8 conjugal, hymeneal 9 connubial 11 epithalamic

matrimony
7 wedlock 8 marriage 11 conjugality 12 connubiality

matrix
3 die, net, web 4 grid, mesh 5 array 6 cradle, gangue 7 complex, network 10 groundmass, truth table

matron
4 dame 7 dowager 8 chaperon 9 chaperone 10 grande dame

Mattathias
father: 5 Simon 6 Ananos 7 Absalom, Boethus 10 Theophilus
son: 8 Josephus

matter
4 body, core, gist, meat, pith, text 5 being, cause, order, point, sense, stuff, theme, thing, topic, value, weigh 6 affair, amount, burden, entity, import, object 7 concern, signify, subject 8 argument, material 9 grievance, magnitude, substance 11 constituent 12 circumstance

matter-of-fact
3 dry 5 plain, prose, sober, stoic 6 stolid 7 prosaic 9 impassive, objective, practical, pragmatic, realistic 10 hard-boiled, hardheaded, impersonal, phlegmatic 11 down-to-earth 13 unimpassioned, unsentimental

mattress
3 pad 4 sack
case: 4 tick
fabric: 7 ticking
straw: 6 pallet

mature
3 age, due 4 grow, ripe 5 adult, grown, owing, ready, ripen 6 flower, grow up, mellow, season, unpaid 7 advance, blossom, decline, develop, grown-up, overdue, payable, ripened 8 progress 9 developed, full-blown, full-grown 11 full-fledged

maudlin
5 gushy, mushy, silly, sappy, soppy 6 slushy, sticky 7 cloying, gushing, mawkish 8 bathetic 11 sentimental, tear-jerking

Maugham character
4 Kear, Liza 5 Carey, Rosie, Sadie 7 Mildred 8 Ashenden, Craddock 10 Strickland

maul
4 bang, bash, beat, club, drub, flog, whip 5 abuse, flail, pound 6 batter, bruise, buffet, cudgel, hammer, injure, mangle, molest, pummel, sledge, thrash 7 clobber, rough up 8 bludgeon, lambaste 9 manhandle

Mauna ___
3 Kea, Loa

maunder
3 bat, gad 4 rove 5 drift, mooch, range 6 mumble, mutter, ramble, wander 7 blather, digress, traipse 8 divagate

Mauritania
capital: 10 Nouakchott
desert: 6 Sahara
language: 5 Wolof 6 Arabic, Fulani 7 Soninke
monetary unit: 7 ouguiya
neighbor: 4 Mali 6 Guinea 7 Senegal 7 Algeria 13 Western Sahara
river: 7 Senegal

Mauritius
capital: 9 Port Louis
island group: 9 Mascarene
language: 6 Creole
monetary unit: 5 rupee

mauve
5 lilac 6 purple, violet

maven
3 ace 4 buff, whiz 5 adept, freak, shark 6 addict, expert, master, savant 7 devotee, fanatic, hotshot 8 virtuoso 9 authority 10 enthusiast 11 connoisseur

maverick
5 rogue, stray 7 heretic 8 unmarked 9 dissident, unbranded 10 iconoclast 11 independent, loose cannon 13 nonconformist

maw
4 crop **5** chasm, mouth **6** cavity, gullet **7** stomach

mawkish
5 gushy, mushy, sappy, soppy **6** sloppy, slushy, sticky, syrupy **7** cloying, gushing, insipid, maudlin **8** bathetic, romantic **9** schmaltzy, sickening **10** lovey-dovey, nauseating **11** sentimental, tear-jerking

maxilla
3 jaw **4** bone

maxim
3 law, saw **4** rule **5** adage, axiom, gnome, moral, motto, tenet, truth **6** byword, dictum, saying, truism **7** precept, proverb, theorem **8** aphorism, apothegm **9** platitude, prescript, principle **11** commonplace

maximal
3 nth, top **6** utmost **7** highest, largest, supreme, topmost **8** complete, greatest, ultimate **9** paramount

maximum
3 nth, top **6** utmost **7** highest, largest, supreme, topmost **8** extremum, greatest, ultimate **9** paramount

may
5 might, shrub **6** spirea **8** hawthorn

maybe
7 perhaps **8** possibly **9** perchance **11** conceivably, uncertainty

Mayberry resident
4 Andy (Taylor), Opie (Taylor) **5** Gomer (Pyle) **6** Barney (Fife) **7** Aunt Bee

Mayflower
document: **7** Compact
passengers: **8** Pilgrims

mayhem
4 maim, riot **5** chaos, havoc **7** cripple, dislimb **8** mutilate **9** dismember **10** mutilation

mayor
11 burgomaster
Boston: **6** Curley (James Michael)
Chicago: **5** Daley (Richard)
New York: **4** Koch (Edward) **6** Walker (Jimmy) **7** Lindsay (John) **8** Giuliani (Rudolph) **9** Bloomberg (Michael), La Guardia (Fiorello)
Spanish: **7** alcalde

Mayor of Casterbridge, The
author: **5** Hardy (Thomas)
character: **8** Henchard (Michael)

maze
3 web **4** knot, mesh **5** skein, snarl **6** jungle, morass, tangle **7** confuse, network, perplex **8** bewilder, mishmash **9** labyrinth

Mazel ___!
3 tov

McCarthy novel
8 Crossing (The) **16** Cities of the Plain **18** All the Pretty Horses

McCourt memoir
3 'Tis **10** Teacher Man **12** Angela's Ashes

McCullers, Carson
novel: **18** Ballad of the Sad Cafe (The) **18** Member of the Wedding (The) **20** Heart Is a Lonely Hunter (The) **23** Reflections in a Golden Eye

McCullough novel
10 Thorn Birds (The)

McEwan novel
8 Saturday **9** Amsterdam, Atonement, Black Dogs **12** Enduring Love

McMurtry novel
12 Buffalo Girls, Lonesome Dove **14** Horseman Pass By **15** Last Picture Show (The) **17** Terms of Endearment

McTeague author
6 Norris (Frank)

MD
3 doc **6** doctor, medico **8** sawbones **9** physician

mea culpa
5 error, fault **7** apology **9** admission **10** concession, confession

meadow
3 lea, ley **4** vega **5** field, green **7** pasture **9** grassland
historic: **9** Runnymede
low-lying: **5** haugh

meadow mushroom
6 agaric

meager
4 bare, bony, lean, mere, thin **5** gaunt, lanky, scant, short, spare **6** paltry, scanty, shabby, skimpy, skinny, slight, sparse **7** angular, minimum, scraggy, scrawny, scrimpy **8** exiguous, rawboned **9** deficient, miserable **10** inadequate **12** insufficient

meal
4 chow, fare, feed, grub **5** board, feast, lunch, snack **6** brunch, dinner, farina, picnic, repast, spread, supper **7** high tea, nooning **8** luncheon, victuals **9** breakfast, collation, elevenses, refection
army: **3** MRE **4** mess

mealy
6 spotty, uneven **11** farinaceous

mean
3 low, mid, par **4** base, fair, hint, norm, poor, want, wish **5** cheap, cruel, imply, lousy, lowly, mingy, petty, rough, small, snide, spell, tight, weigh **6** attest, center, common, denote, design, humble, intend, matter, medial, medium, middle, paltry, scummy, scurvy, shabby, shoddy, sleazy,

stingy, unwell **7** average, betoken, connote, express, lowborn, miserly, pitiful, portend, propose, purport, signify, suggest, vicious **8** déclassé, indicate, inferior, mediocre, middling, midpoint, moderate, ordinary, pitiable, plebeian, stand for **9** designate, penurious, represent, symbolize **10** despicable, second-rate **11** closefisted, tightfisted **12** contemptible, intermediary, intermediate

meander
4 roam, rove, turn, wind **5** amble, drift, range, snake, stray, twist **6** ramble, wander **7** traipse, winding **8** vagabond **9** gallivant, labyrinth

meandering
5 snaky **7** sinuous **8** flexuous, tortuous **10** convoluted, serpentine **11** anfractuous

meaning
3 aim **4** gist, pith **5** drift, force, point, sense **6** effect, import, intent **7** essence, message, purport **9** intention, substance **10** definition, denotation, intimation **11** connotation, implication **12** significance **13** signification

meaningful
5 valid **7** pointed, serious, weighty **8** eloquent, material **9** important, momentous **10** expressive **11** sententious, significant, substantial **13** consequential

meaningless
5 empty, inane **6** absurd, futile, hollow, jejune **7** trivial **8** nugatory **11** nonsensical **13** insignificant

meanings
diverse: **8** polysemy
study of: **9** semantics

means
5 funds, money **6** assets, avenue, income **7** backing, capital **8** finances, holdings, property, reserves **9** equipment, resources, substance **11** wherewithal

meantime
7 interim **8** interval

measly
4 poor, puny **5** petty, scant **6** meager, meagre, paltry, scanty, skimpy **7** pitiful, trivial **8** niggling, pathetic, picayune, piddling, trifling **9** miserable **10** picayunish **13** insignificant

measure
3 bar, ken **4** bill, size, step, test **5** bound, gauge, index, quota, scale, share, weigh **6** amount, bounds, effort, extent, figure, ration, reckon, resort, size up, survey **7** caliper, compute, delimit, mark out, portion **8** calliper, estimate, regulate, resource, standard **9** allotment, benchmark, calculate, calibrate, criterion, demarcate, determine, expedient, magnitude, yardstick **10** dimensions, indication, proportion, touchstone
area: **3** are, cho, mou, tan **4** acre **7** hectare
capacity: **3** cab, cor, pin, zak **4** fass, gill, peck, pint **5** liter, minim, quart, stere **6** bushel, gallon **8** fluidram **9** fluid dram **10** fluid ounce, milliliter
cloth: **3** ell
combining form: **6** metric **8** metrical
depth: **5** plumb, sound
dry: **4** peck **6** bushel
electrical: **3** amp, mho, ohm **4** volt, watt **6** ampere **7** coulomb
energy: **3** erg
force: **4** dyne
horse height: **4** hand
interstellar space: **6** parsec
length: **3** mil, pik, rod **4** alen, aune, foot, hiro, inch, link, mile, tsun, vara, yard **5** chain, cubit, meter **6** league **7** braccio, furlong **9** kilometer **10** centimeter, hectometer
liquid: **3** hin, tun **4** gill, pint **5** minim, quart **6** gallon
mixed drinks: **6** jigger
of comparison: **8** standard
paper: **4** ream
printer's: **2** em, en **4** pica **5** point
radioactive decay: **8** halflife
rotation: **5** angle
strength of solution: **7** titrate
surface: **3** are
thermodynamic: **7** entropy **8** enthalpy
yarn: **3** lea
(see also **weight**)

measured
7 regular, stately **8** metrical **9** regulated, temperate, unhurried **10** calculated, controlled, deliberate, restrained **13** proportionate

Measure for Measure
character: **6** Angelo, Juliet **7** Claudio, Mariana **8** Isabella **9** Vincentio
setting: **6** Vienna

measurement
4 area **6** degree **8** capacity, quantity **9** dimension, magnitude **11** calibration, mensuration

measure up to
3 tie **4** meet **5** equal, match, rival, touch **7** emulate **10** qualify for

measuring device
4 gage, tape **5** buret, gauge, ruler, scale, timer **7** burette, caliper, sextant, venturi **8** calipers **8** dipstick **9** altimeter, barometer, dosimeter, pedometer, yardstick **11** tensiometer, velocimeter

meat
4 core, food, gist, pith, pork, veal **5** flesh, jerky, steak **6** thrust, upshot **7** edibles **8** victuals **9** foodstuff, provender, substance **10** provisions **11** comestibles
broth: **8** bouillon

cake: **6** burger **9** hamburger
cured: **7** biltong
cut: **3** rib **4** loin, rump **5** chuck, flank, plate, round, shank **7** brisket, sirloin **8** rib roast **9** club steak, rump roast, short loin, short ribs **10** blade roast, flank steak, round steak, T-bone steak **12** sirloin steak
dealer: **7** butcher
deer: **7** venison
dried: **5** jerky
fastening pin: **6** skewer
holding rod: **4** spit **10** rotisserie
juices: **5** gravy
packer: **5** Swift **6** Armour
raw: **6** gobbet
roasted: **8** barbecue
roasting shop: **10** rotisserie
seasoned: **7** sausage **8** pastrami, scrapple
sheep: **6** mutton
side: **8** sowbelly
skewered: **5** kebab, kebob
slice: **6** cutlet, rasher
small portion: **6** collop
tough part: **7** gristle

meat-eating
11 carnivorous

meathead
3 lug, oaf **4** clod, dodo, dolt, gawk, goon, lout **5** chump, klutz, looby **6** dimwit, lubber **7** bungler, palooka **8** dumbbell, numskull **9** birdbrain, ignoramus, lamebrain, numbskull **10** nincompoop

Mebd
husband: **6** Ailill
victim: **10** Cuchulainn

Mecca
4 goal
country: **11** Saudi Arabia
pilgrim: **5** hadji, hajji
pilgrimage: **4** hadj, hajj
port: **5** Jedda, Jidda **6** Jeddah, Jiddah
shrine: **5** Kaaba

mechanic
7 artisan **9** machinist

mechanical
4 cold **7** cursory, pasteup, robotic **8** lifeless **9** automated, automatic, unfeeling **10** impersonal **11** emotionless, instinctive, involuntary, perfunctory, unemotional

mechanism
4 gear **5** gizmo, means, works **6** agency, doodad, jigger, medium, widget **7** whatsit **8** dohickey **9** apparatus, appliance, procedure, technique, thingummy **10** instrument **11** contraption, contrivance, thingamabob, thingamajig, thingumajig

medal
5 badge, honor, prize **6** reward **7** laurels **8** accolade **10** decoration **13** commemoration

meddle
3 pry **4** fool, nose **5** snoop **6** butt in, dabble, horn in, kibitz, monkey, putter, tamper, tinker **7** intrude, obtrude **8** trespass **9** interfere, interlope, intervene **10** mess around

meddler
5 snoop, yenta **7** snooper **8** busybody, intruder, kibitzer **9** buttinsky **12** troublemaker

meddlesome
4 busy, nosy **5** nosey **6** prying **9** intrusive, obtrusive, officious **11** impertinent, interfering

Medea
5 witch **9** sorceress **11** enchantress
aunt: **5** Circe
brother: **8** Absyrtus
father: **6** Aeëtes
husband: **5** Jason **6** Aegeus
sister: **5** Circe
son: **6** Medeus
victim: **6** Creusa, Glauce, Glauke

medial
3 mid **4** mean **6** center, middle **7** average, central, halfway, midmost **8** middling, moderate **10** centermost, middlemost **11** equidistant **12** intermediary, intermediate

median
see **medial**

mediate
5 judge **6** broker, convey, liaise, settle, step in, umpire **7** adjudge, referee, resolve **8** moderate, transmit **9** arbitrate, intercede, interfere, interpose, intervene, negotiate **10** conciliate

mediator
3 ref, ump **5** judge **6** broker, umpire **7** arbiter, liaison, referee **9** go-between, middleman **10** interceder, negotiator, peacemaker **11** intercessor

medical instrument
6 needle **7** forceps, scalpel, scanner, syringe **8** otoscope, speculum **9** endoscope **11** cardiograph, stethoscope

medical practitioner
2 PA, RN **3** doc, LPN **5** nurse **6** doctor, intern **7** interne, surgeon **9** physician

medicament
4 cure, pill **6** elixir, physic, remedy **7** nostrum **8** antidote, curative **10** palliative
inert: **7** placebo

medicate
4 cure, dose, drug, heal **5** treat

medicinal
8 curative, remedial, salutary, sanative **9** healthful **12** health-giving, pharmaceutic

medicine
4 cure, pill **5** bromo **6** physic, remedy **7** anodyne, nostrum **8** busulfan, poultice **11** antipyretic
African: **4** muti
bottle: **4** vial
branch: **7** surgery **8** oncology **9** neurology, pathology **10** bariatrics, cardiology, geriatrics, gynecology, nephrology, obstetrics, pediatrics, psychiatry
cathartic: **8** evacuant **9** purgative
combining form: **5** iatro **8** pharmaco
quantity of: **4** dose **6** dosage
shell: **7** capsule
soothing: **7** anodyne **8** lenitive, narcotic, sedative **9** calmative, soporific

medicine man
6 doctor, kahuna, shaman **9** curandero

medieval study
5 logic **7** grammar, trivium **8** rhetoric **10** quadrivium

mediocre
4 dull, fair, hack, so-so **6** common **7** average, fairish **8** inferior, middling, moderate, ordinary, passable **9** tolerable **10** pedestrian, uninspired **11** commonplace, indifferent **12** run-of-the-mill **13** unexceptional

meditate
4 mull, muse **5** weigh **6** intend, ponder **7** purpose, reflect, revolve **8** cogitate, consider, mull over, ruminate, turn over **9** reflect on **10** deliberate **11** contemplate

meditative
6 broody **7** pensive **8** brooding **10** reflective, ruminative, thoughtful

meditator
4 yogi

Mediterranean
11 Mare Nostrum **12** Mare Internum
coastal region: **7** Riviera
eastern shores: **6** Levant
island:
(see at **island**)
wind: **7** mistral, sirocco **8** scirocco

medium
3 par **4** fair, mean, so-so **5** agent, organ **6** agency, métier, milieu, normal **7** ambient, average, channel, climate, culture, neutral, vehicle **8** ambience, middling, moderate, passable, standard **9** tolerable **10** atmosphere **11** clairvoyant, environment **12** run-of-the-mill
of exchange: **5** money **8** currency **11** legal tender

medley
4 brew, olio, stew **5** combo, gumbo **6** jumble, ragout **7** farrago, mélange, mixture **8** mishmash, pastiche **9** pasticcio, patchwork, potpourri **10** assortment, hodgepodge, hotchpotch, miscellany, salmagundi **11** gallimaufry

Medusa
6 Gorgon
father: **7** Phorcus, Phorcys
hair: **6** snakes
mother: **4** Ceto
offspring: **7** Pegasus **8** Chrysaor
sister: **6** Stheno **7** Euryale
slayer: **7** Perseus

medusa
9 jellyfish

meed
3 due **4** part **5** quota, share **6** amount, desert, ration, return, reward **7** guerdon, measure, portion **8** dividend **9** allotment, allowance **10** recompense

meek
3 shy **4** mild, tame **5** lowly, timid **6** docile, gentle, humble, modest **7** patient **8** tolerant **10** submissive, unassuming **11** deferential **13** long-suffering

meerschaum
4 pipe **9** sepiolite

meet
3 apt, fit **4** face, fair, fill, find, join, just, open, spot **5** cross, event, hit on, match, right, touch, unite **6** answer, chance, engage, oppose, proper, settle, take on **7** contest, convene, fitting, fulfill, hit upon, satisfy, stumble **8** approach, assemble, come upon, concours, conflict, confront, converge, suitable **9** encounter, measure up **10** congregate **11** competition
a bet: **3** see
a need: **7** suffice
athletic: **8** gymkhana **10** tournament
by appointment: **10** rendezvous

meeting
4 moot, talk **5** tryst **6** huddle, parley, powwow **7** session **8** assembly, conclave, concours, congress, junction **9** concourse, encounter, gathering, rencontre **10** conference, confluence, convention, rendezvous **11** competition, convocation, get-together **12** intersection
Anglo-Saxon: **5** gemot **6** gemote
place: **5** forum
spiritual: **6** séance

Mefistofele composer
5 Boito (Arrigo)

Megaera
see **Erinyes**

megaphone
8 bullhorn **10** mouthpiece

Megara
father: **5** Creon
husband: **8** Heracles, Hercules
king: **5** Nisus

megillah
5 story **7** account

megrim
3 bee **4** urge, whim **5** fancy, freak, humor **6** notion, vagary, whimsy **7** caprice, conceit, impulse, vertigo **8** crotchet, migraine **9** dizziness

Mehitabel
3 cat
creator: **7** Marquis (Don)
friend: **5** Archy

Mein Kampf author
6 Hitler (Adolf)

meiosis
7 litotes **12** cell division

Meissen
5 china **8** ceramics **9** porcelain

Meistersinger
5 Sachs (Hans) **9** Frauenlob

Meistersinger, Die
beloved: **3** Eva
composer: **6** Wagner (Richard)
hero: **6** Walter
mentor: **5** Sachs (Hans)

melancholia
5 gloom **6** sorrow **7** despair, sadness **9** dejection, morbidity **10** depression, desolation, gloominess **11** despondency, dolefulness

melancholic
3 low, sad **4** blue, glum **6** gloomy, morose, triste **7** joyless **8** dejected, downcast, mournful **9** depressed, saddening **10** depressing, despondent, dispirited

melancholy
3 low, sad **4** blue, funk, glum **5** blues, dumps, ennui, gloom **6** dismal, dreary, gloomy, misery, morose, rueful, somber, tedium, triste, woeful **7** boredom, despair, doleful, joyless, sadness, unhappy **8** dejected, dolorous, downcast, funereal, mournful, saddened **9** black bile, dejection, depressed, plaintive, saddening, sorrowful **10** depressing, depression, despondent, dispirited, lachrymose, lugubrious **11** despondency, unhappiness **12** heavyhearted, wretchedness

mélange
see **medley**

Melanippus
father: **7** Theseus
slayer: **10** Amphiaraus
victim: **6** Tydeus

Melchior
companion: **6** Caspar, Gaspar **9** Balthasar, Balthazar
gift: **4** gold

Melchizedek's kingdom
5 Salem

meld
3 mix **4** fuse **5** blend, merge **6** mingle **7** combine, mixture **8** compound **9** commingle, interfuse **10** amalgamate **11** intermingle

Meleager
beloved: **8** Atalanta
father: **6** Oeneus
mother: **7** Althaea
victim: **4** boar

melee
3 row **4** fray, riot **5** brawl, broil, clash, fight, set-to **6** affray, fracas, ruckus, rumpus **7** scuffle **8** skirmish **9** scrimmage **10** donnybrook, free-for-all

meliorate
4 help **5** amend **6** better, soften **7** improve **8** mitigate, palliate

Mélisande's lover
7 Pelléas

melisma
7 cadenza, descant

mellifluous
5 sweet **6** dulcet, fluent, golden, liquid, smooth **7** flowing, honeyed, silvery **8** euphonic, soothing **10** euphonious **13** silver-tongued

mellow
3 age **4** aged, ripe **5** ripen **6** genial, golden, grow up, mature, season, smooth **7** honeyed, matured, ripened **8** laid-back, pleasant, seasoned **9** agreeable

melodic
5 sweet **6** dulcet **7** musical, songful, tuneful **8** canorous, euphonic **10** euphonious

melodious
5 lyric, sweet **6** dulcet **7** musical, songful, tuneful **8** euphonic **9** cantabile **10** euphonious

melody
3 air, lay **4** aria, lilt, song, tune **5** canto, music, theme **6** chorus, strain, warble **7** descant, refrain **11** tunefulness

melon
4 pepo **5** gourd **6** casaba, profit **8** crenshaw, honeydew, windfall **10** cantaloupe

Melpomene
see **Muse**

melt
3 run **4** flux, fuse, thaw **6** relent, soften **7** liquefy **8** dissolve, liquesce, unfreeze **9** disappear **10** deliquesce
down: **6** render
together: **4** fuse

Melville, Herman
character: **3** Pip **4** Ahab, Toby **5** Bembo, Chase **6** Cereno (Benito), Jermin, Pierre **7** Fayaway, Ishmael **8** Bartleby, Queequeg, Starbuck

work: **4** Omoo **5** Mardi, Typee **6** Pierre **7** Redburn **8** Moby Dick **11** White-Jacket **12** Benito Cereno **13** Confidence-Man (The)

member
3 cut **4** part **5** piece **6** clause, parcel **7** portion, section, segment **8** division **9** appendage, component **10** ingredient
Parliament: **2** MP
political party: **4** Tory, Whig **7** Liberal **8** Democrat, Laborite **9** Labourite **10** Republican **12** Conservative
service club: **3** Elk **4** Lion **8** Kiwanian, Rotarian

membrane
4 film, tela **5** velum **6** pleura **7** pleurae (plural)
bodily: **6** serosa
brain: **3** pia
diffusion through: **7** osmosis
dividing: **5** septa (plural) **6** septum
ear: **8** tympanum
enclosing: **5** tunic **8** indusium
thin: **6** lamina **7** lamella, laminae (plural) **8** lamellae (plural)
wing: **8** patagium

memento
5 relic, token, trace **6** trophy **7** vestige **8** keepsake, reminder, souvenir **11** remembrance

Memnon
father: **8** Tithonus
mother: **3** Eos **6** Aurora
slayer: **8** Achilles

memoir
3 bio **4** life **5** diary **6** record, report, thesis **7** account, journal **8** anecdote **9** biography **11** confessions **12** recollection, reminiscence **13** autobiography

memoirist
7 Boswell, diarist **10** biographer

memorable
7 lasting, notable **8** historic **9** deathless, indelible, momentous, red-letter **10** noteworthy **11** significant **13** distinguished

memorandum
4 chit, note **6** minute, notice, record **7** tickler **8** notation, reminder **12** announcement

memorial
4 note **5** relic, token, trace **6** record, trophy **7** relique **8** keepsake, monument, reminder, souvenir **10** dedicatory **11** celebrative, remembrance **12** consecrative, remembrancer **13** commemoration, commemorative
mound: **5** cairn

memorial park
see **cemetery**

memorize
3 con, get **6** retain **8** remember

memory
6 recall **8** mind's eye, souvenir **9** anamnesis, awareness, flashback, retention **10** reflection **11** remembrance **12** recollection, reminiscence **13** retentiveness, retrospection
assisting: **8** mnemonic
loss: **7** amnesia
trace: **6** engram
unit: **3** meg

menace
4 risk **5** alarm, peril, scare **6** danger, hazard, threat **7** imperil, jeopard, torment **8** endanger, frighten, jeopardy, threaten **9** terrorize **10** intimidate, jeopardize

ménage
4 clan **5** house **6** family **8** quarters **9** household **12** housekeeping

menagerie
3 zoo **7** mixture

mend
3 fix, sew **4** cure, darn, heal, knit **5** patch, renew **6** cobble, doctor, look up, perk up, reform, remedy, repair, revamp **7** correct, improve, patch up, rebuild, rectify, redress, restore **8** overhaul, renovate **9** condition, refurbish **10** ameliorate, convalesce, recuperate **11** recondition, reconstruct

mendacious
5 false, lying **6** shifty **7** fibbing **9** deceitful, deceptive, dishonest, paltering **10** untruthful **11** dissembling **13** prevaricating

mendacity
3 lie **6** deceit **9** deception, duplicity, falsehood **10** dishonesty **12** equivocation **13** truthlessness

mendelevium symbol
2 Md

mendicancy
7 beggary, begging, bumming, cadging **8** mooching, sponging **11** panhandling

mendicant
5 friar **6** beggar **7** begging

Mending Wall author
5 Frost (Robert)

Menelaus
brother: **9** Agamemnon
father: **6** Atreus
kingdom: **6** Sparta
mother: **6** Aerope
wife: **5** Helen

menial
4 dull **5** lowly **6** humble **7** servant, servile, slavish **8** obeisant, retainer **9** unskilled **10** obsequious **11** subservient, undignified

meniscus
4 lens **9** cartilage

Menlo Park inventor
6 Edison (Thomas Alva)

menopause
11 climacteric **12** change of life

menorah
10 candelabra

Menotti, Gian Carlo
character: 5 Amahl
opera: 6 Consul (The), Medium (The) **9** Telephone (The)

men's store
12 haberdashery

mental
5 inner **7** psychic **8** cerebral, rational, thinking **9** reasoning, spiritual **10** immaterial, telepathic **11** intelligent **12** intellective, intellectual **13** psychological
faculty: 6 memory

mentalist
6 Geller (Uri) **7** Kreskin **8** Banachek

mentality
3 wit **5** sense **6** brains **7** mindset, outlook **9** intellect, mother wit **10** brainpower **12** intelligence

mention
4 cite, name, note **7** refer to, specify **8** advert to, allude to, citation, instance **9** reference

mentor
4 guru **5** coach, guide, tutor **7** teacher **9** counselor **10** counsellor

Mentor's pupil
10 Telemachus

menu
4 card, diet **5** carte **10** bill of fare **11** carte du jour
item: 4 soup **5** salad **6** entrée **7** dessert **9** appetizer

Mephibosheth
father: 4 Saul **8** Jonathan
mother: 6 Rizpah

Mephistophelian
7 satanic **8** devilish, diabolic **10** diabolical

mephitic
4 rank **5** fetid, funky, musty **6** putrid, smelly **7** noisome, noxious, reeking **8** stinking **9** poisonous **10** malodorous

Merab
father: 4 Saul
husband: 6 Adriel

mercenary
4 hack **5** ninja, ronin, venal **6** greedy **7** corrupt, soldier **8** hireling **10** gun for hire

merchandise
4 line, sell **5** cargo, goods, stock, trade, wares **6** deal in, job lot, market, retail **7** effects, promote, staples, traffic **8** products **9** publicize, vendibles **11** commodities

merchandiser
6 dealer, trader, vendor **8** retailer **9** tradesman **10** wholesaler **11** businessman **13** businesswoman

merchant
5 buyer **6** dealer, jobber, seller, trader, vendor **7** peddler **8** purveyor, retailer **9** tradesman **10** trafficker, wholesaler **11** businessman, storekeeper
guild: 5 Hansa, Hanse
League: 9 Hanseatic
ship: 5 oiler **6** argosy, coaler, galiot, packet, tanker, trader **7** collier, galliot, steamer **8** Indiaman **9** freighter
wine: 7 vintner

Merchant of Venice, The
7 Antonio
character: 6 Portia **7** Jessica, Lorenzo, Nerissa, Shylock **8** Bassanio

merciful
4 kind **6** benign, humane, kindly **7** clement, lenient **8** tolerant **9** forgiving, indulgent **10** charitable, forbearing **11** softhearted **13** compassionate

merciless
4 grim **5** cruel, harsh **6** brutal, savage, wanton **9** cutthroat, ferocious, unfeeling **10** gratuitous, implacable, ironfisted, unyielding **11** hardhearted, unrelenting **12** unappeasable

mercurial
5 flaky **6** fickle, mobile **7** erratic **8** unstable, variable, volatile **9** impulsive **10** capricious, changeable, inconstant **13** temperamental, unpredictable

mercury
5 azoth **11** quicksilver
ore: 8 cinnabar
symbol: 2 Hg

Mercury
6 planet
(see also **Hermes**)

Mercutio
friend: 5 Romeo
slayer: 6 Tybalt

mercy
4 pity, ruth **5** grace **6** lenity **7** caritas, charity **8** clemency, goodwill, kindness, leniency **9** benignity, tolerance **10** compassion, generosity, kindliness **11** benevolence, forbearance **13** commiseration
petition for: 5 kyrie **8** miserere

mere
4 bare, lake, pool, pure **6** meager, meagre,

paltry **7** trivial **8** boundary, landmark, piddling **9** undiluted

merely
4 just, only **6** simply, solely, wholly

meretricious
4 loud, sham **5** gaudy, phony, showy **6** flashy, garish, glitzy, sleazy, tawdry, tinsel, trashy **7** chintzy **8** delusive, delusory, illusory **9** contrived, deceptive **10** misleading **11** counterfeit, pretentious

merganser
4 duck, smew

merge
3 mix **4** fuse, join **5** blend, unify, unite **6** mingle **7** combine **8** coalesce, compound **9** commingle, interfuse **10** amalgamate, assimilate **11** consolidate, intermingle

merger
5 union **6** fusion **7** melding **8** alliance, takeover **9** coalition **10** absorption **11** combination, unification **12** amalgamation **13** consolidation

meridian
4 acme, apex, peak **6** apogee, climax, summit, zenith **8** pinnacle

merit
3 due **4** earn, rate **5** arete, value, worth **6** virtue **7** caliber, deserts, deserve, entitle, justify, quality, stature, warrant **10** excellence, perfection, recompense **11** achievement

merited
3 due **4** fair, just **5** right **7** condign, fitting **8** deserved, rightful, suitable **9** justified, requisite **11** appropriate

meritorious
6 worthy **8** laudable **9** admirable, deserving, estimable, honorable **10** creditable **11** commendable, thankworthy **12** praiseworthy

Merlin
4 seer **5** augur, magus **6** shaman, wizard **7** prophet **8** magician **10** soothsayer **11** necromancer, thaumaturge

merlin
6 falcon **10** pigeon hawk

mermaid
3 nix **5** Ariel, nixie **7** manatee **8** sirenian **10** water nymph **11** water sprite

Merope
father: **5** Atlas **8** Oenopion
husband: **7** Polybus **8** Sisyphus **11** Cresphontes
lover: **5** Orion
mother: **7** Pleione
sisters: **8** Pleiades
son: **7** Aepytus, Glaucus

merriment
4 glee **5** mirth, revel **6** gaiety **7** jollity, revelry, whoopee **8** hilarity, reveling **9** festivity, jocundity, joviality **10** jocularity, jubilation **13** entertainment

merry
3 gay **4** glad **5** happy, jolly **6** blithe, jocund, jovial, joyful, joyous, lively **7** festive, gleeful **8** animated, cheerful, mirthful **9** hilarious, sprightly, vivacious **12** high-spirited, lighthearted

merry-andrew
4 fool, zany **5** clown, joker **6** jester, madcap **7** buffoon **9** harlequin **10** mountebank

merrymaker
7 partyer, reveler **8** carouser

merrymaking
5 party, revel **6** frolic, gaiety **7** jollity, revelry, whoopee **8** hilarity **9** festivity **12** conviviality

Merry Widow composer
5 Lehár (Franz)

Merry Wives of Windsor character
3 Nym **4** Ford, Page **5** Caius **6** Fenton, Pistol **7** Slender **8** Falstaff

mesa
5 bench, butte **7** plateau **9** tableland

mescal
5 agave **6** cactus, liquor, maguey, peyote

mesh
3 net, web **4** jibe, maze **5** skein, snare, snarl **6** engage, morass, tangle **7** entwine, netting, network **8** dovetail, entangle **9** harmonize, interlock, labyrinth **10** coordinate **12** reticulation

meshuga
3 mad **4** nuts **5** crazy, goofy, kooky, loony, nutty, wacky **6** insane, screwy **7** foolish

mesmeric
8 alluring, hypnotic **9** glamorous, seductive **10** bewitching, enchanting **11** captivating, fascinating

mesmerize
4 vamp **6** dazzle, seduce **7** bewitch **8** ensorcel, enthrall, entrance **9** captivate, ensorcell, fascinate, hypnotize, spellbind

Mesopotamia
4 Iraq
civilization: **4** Elam **5** Akkad, Sumer **7** Assyria, Elamite **8** Akkadian, Assyrian, Sumerian **9** Babylonia **10** Babylonian
river: **6** Tigris **9** Euphrates

mess
4 hash **5** botch, snafu **6** fright, jumble, muddle **7** eyesore **8** botchery, disarray, disorder, shambles, wreckage **9** confusion **10** hodgepodge, hotchpotch, miscellany
around: **4** hang, idle **5** chill, dally **6** dawdle,

doodle, fiddle, potter, putter **7** goof off, hang out **8** chill out, lollygag **10** dilly-dally
up: **3** err **4** blow, flub, muff, ruin **5** botch, fluff, fudge, spoil, touse **6** bungle, fumble, tousle **7** butcher

message
4 note, post **5** sense, theme **6** letter, report **7** epistle, meaning, mission, missive, purport **8** bulletin, dispatch, telegram **9** directive, telegraph **10** communiqué **12** significance **13** communication, signification

Messalina's husband
8 Claudius

mess around
4 fool, idle **5** flirt **6** dabble, dawdle, fiddle, meddle, monkey, potter, putter, tamper, tinker **8** womanize **9** associate, interfere, interlope, philander

messenger
4 post **5** envoy **6** herald, runner **7** apostle, courier **8** emissary **9** go-between, harbinger **10** ambassador **11** internuncio **12** intermediary
God's: **5** angel
of the gods: **4** Iris **6** Hermes **7** Mercury
Turkish: **6** chiaus

messiah
6 savior **7** saviour **8** defender **9** deliverer, liberator

Messiah composer
6 Handel (George Frideric)

messy
6 frowsy, frowzy, sloppy, unneat, untidy **7** chaotic, rumpled, unkempt **8** careless, confused, ill-kempt, slapdash, slipshod, slovenly **10** disheveled, disorderly **11** dishevelled
abode: **3** sty **6** pigpen, pigsty

mestizo
5 métis **6** ladino **10** mixed-blood

Mestor
father: **7** Perseus
mother: **9** Andromeda

metal
4 gold, iron **5** steel **6** bronze
alloy:
(see **alloy**)
casting mold: **5** ingot
corrosion: **4** rust
fuse: **6** solder
in mass: **7** bullion
layer: **7** plating
lump: **6** nugget
magnetic: **4** iron
refuse: **4** slag **5** dross **6** scoria
sheath: **5** armor
source: **3** ore
thin: **4** foil, leaf **5** plate
worker: **5** smith **10** blacksmith

metallic element
3 tin **4** gold, iron, lead, zinc **6** barium, cobalt, copper, nickel, radium, silver, sodium **7** arsenic, bismuth, cadmium, calcium, lithium, mercury, uranium **8** aluminum, chromium, platinum, titanium, tungsten, vanadium **9** magnesium, manganese, potassium, strontium **10** molybdenum

metamere
6 somite **7** segment

metamorphic rock
5 slate **6** gneiss, marble, schist **9** quartzite, soapstone

metamorphose
6 change, mutate **7** convert, develop **9** transform, translate, transmute **11** transfigure **12** transmogrify

metamorphosis
6 change **8** changing, mutation **9** evolution, sea change **10** changeover **13** transmutation

Metamorphosis author
5 Kafka (Franz)

___ me tangere
4 noli

metaphor
5 trope **6** simile, symbol **7** analogy **8** allegory **10** comparison, similitude

metaphorical compound
7 kenning

metaphysical
8 bodiless, numinous **9** unearthly, unfleshly **10** immaterial, suprahuman **12** supermundane, supramundane, supranatural, transcendent **13** preternatural
poet: **5** Donne (John) **6** Cowley (Abraham) **7** Crashaw (Richard), Herbert (George), Marvell (Andrew), Vaughan (Henry) **9** Cleveland (John)

mete
4 deal, dole, give **5** allot, bound **6** border, parcel, ration **7** portion **8** allocate, boundary, disburse, dispense **9** apportion **10** distribute

meteor
8 fireball **12** shooting star
exploding: **6** bolide
shower: **5** Lyrid **6** Leonid, Taurid **7** Aquarid, Geminid, Orionid, Perseid **10** Quadrantid

meteorite
8 aerolite **10** siderolite

meter
4 beat, scan **6** rhythm **7** cadence, measure, pattern

meter maid
4 Rita

metheglin
4 mead **8** beverage
ingredient: **5** honey

method
3 way **4** mode, modi (plural), plan **5** means, modus, order, style **6** course, design, manner, schema, scheme, system **7** fashion, formula, pattern, process, routine, wrinkle **8** practice **9** procedure, technique **11** orderliness **13** modus operandi
careful: 8 strategy
of employing troops: 6 tactic **7** tactics
of procedure: 4 game

methodical
5 exact **7** careful, logical, orderly, precise, regular **9** efficient, organized **10** deliberate, scrupulous, systematic, systemized **12** systematized

Methuselah
father: 5 Enoch
grandson: 4 Noah
son: 6 Lamech

meticulous
5 exact, fussy, picky **6** strict **7** careful, finicky, precise **8** detailed, thorough **10** fastidious, nitpicking, pernickety, scrupulous **11** microscopic, painstaking, persnickety, punctilious **13** conscientious

métier
4 work **5** craft, field, forte, trade **7** calling, pursuit **8** business, strength, vocation **9** specialty **10** employment, occupation, profession

metrical foot
4 iamb **5** ionic, paeon **6** cretic, dactyl, iambic, iambus **7** anapest, pyrrhic, pyrrhus, spondee, triseme, trochee **8** bacchius, choriamb, dactylic, spondaic, tribrach, trochaic **9** anapestic **10** tribrachic

metric unit
area: 3 are **7** hectare
capacity: 5 liter, litre **9** decaliter, deciliter, kiloliter **10** centiliter, hectoliter, milliliter
length: 5 meter **9** decameter, decimeter, dekameter, kilometer **10** centimeter, hectometer, millimeter
mass and weight: 4 gram **7** quintal **8** decagram, decigram, dekagram, kilogram **9** centigram, hectogram, metric ton, milligram
volume: 5 liter, litre

metro
4 tube **6** subway **11** underground

metropolis
4 city **7** capital

metropolitan
5 urban **6** urbane **7** primate **9** municipal **10** archbishop

mettle
4 fire, grit, guts **5** heart, moxie, nerve, pluck, spunk, steel, valor, vigor **6** daring, spirit, starch, temper **7** cojones, courage, resolve, stamina **8** backbone, boldness, tenacity, vitality **9** fortitude **10** resolution

mettlesome
4 bold, game **5** brave, fiery, gutsy **6** plucky, spunky **7** staunch, valiant **8** intrepid, resolute, spirited, vigorous **9** tenacious **10** courageous, determined

mew
3 hem, pen **4** cage, coop, gull **5** alley, fence **6** corral, immure, shut in, stable **7** enclose **8** hideaway

mewl
4 moan, pule **5** whine **6** snivel **7** whimper

Mexican
crop: 5 sisal **8** henequen
estate: 8 hacienda
food: 4 masa, taco **5** chili, salsa **6** fajita, tamale **7** burrito, panocha, penuche, tostada **8** frijoles, tortilla **9** enchilada, guacamole **10** quesadilla **11** chimichanga
hut: 5 jacal
liquor: 6 mescal, mezcal **7** tequila

Mexico
ancient city: 12 Tenochtitlán
ancient culture: 4 Maya **5** Aztec, Mayan, Olmec **6** Toltec
bay: 8 Campeche
capital: 10 Mexico City
city: 4 León **6** Juárez, Mérida, Oaxaca, Puebla **7** Nogales, Tijuana **8** Acapulco, Mexicali, Saltillo **9** Chihuahua, Matamoros, Monterrey **10** Cuernavaca **11** Guadalajara **12** Ciudad Juárez
conqueror: 6 Cortés (Hernán, Hernando)
discoverer: 7 Córdoba (Fernández de)
emperor: 10 Maximilian
gulf: 10 California
island: 7 Cozumel
island group: 13 Revillagigedo
lake: 7 Chapala, Cuitzeo, Texcoco **9** Pátzcuaro
language: 7 Spanish
leader: 4 Díaz (Porfirio) **6** Juárez (Benito) **8** Carranza (Venustiano)
monetary unit: 4 peso
mountain, range: 8 Malinche **11** Sierra Madre
neighbor: 6 Belize **9** Guatemala
peninsula: 4 Baja **7** Yucatán
port: 7 Tampico **8** Ensenada, Mazatlán, Veracruz
resort: 6 Cancún **8** Acapulco
revolutionist: 5 Villa (Pancho) **6** Zapata (Emiliano) **7** Hidalgo (Padre Miguel)
river: 4 Mayo **5** Bravo, Yaquí **6** Balsas, Grande, Pánuco **7** Conchos **8** Grijalva, Río Bravo, Santiago **9** Rio Grande **10** Usumacinta
ruined city: 5 Tulum, Uxmal **7** Mayapán **8** Palenque **11** Chichén Itzá
state: 6 Oaxaca, Puebla, Sonora **7** Chiapas, Durango, Hidalgo, Tabasco, Yucatán **8** Veracruz

sea: **9** Caribbean
volcano: **6** Colima **9** Paricutín **11** Ixtacihuatl **12** Citlaltépetl, Ixtaccihuatl, Popocatépetl

mezzanine
4 loge **5** story **7** balcony **8** entresol

mezzo
4 half **6** singer **7** soprano

mezzo-soprano
American: **5** Elias (Rosalind), Horne (Marilyn), Jones (Sissieretta) **6** Bumbry (Grace), Graves (Denyce) **7** Stevens (Risë), Verrett (Shirley) **8** Troyanos (Tatiana), von Stade (Frederica)
Austrian: **6** Ludwig (Christa)
English: **5** Baker (Janet)
Italian: **7** Bartoli (Cecilia) **8** Cossotto (Fiorenza)

Miami
bowl: **6** Orange
chief: **12** Little Turtle
county: **4** Dade
stadium: **9** Joe Robbie
team: **4** Heat **7** Marlins **8** Dolphins, Panthers

miasma
3 fog **4** haze, mist, murk, smog **5** brume, vapor **9** effluvium

mica
7 biotite **8** silicate **9** isinglass, muscovite

Michelangelo Buonarotti
painting: **10** Holy Family (The) **12** Last Judgment (The)
statue: **5** David, Moses, Pietà **7** Bacchus

Michener novel
5 Space, Texas **6** Hawaii, Poland, Source (The) **8** Caravans, Covenant (The), Drifters (The), Sayonara **10** Centennial, Chesapeake **13** Fires of Spring (The) **15** Bridges at Toko-Ri (The)

Michigan
capital: **7** Lansing
city: **5** Flint **7** Detroit, Pontiac **8** Ann Arbor, Dearborn **9** Kalamazoo **11** Grand Rapids **13** Sault Ste. Marie
college, university: **6** Calvin **9** Kalamazoo **10** Wayne State
lake: **4** Erie **5** Huron **8** Michigan, Superior
nickname: **9** Wolverine (State) **10** Great Lakes (State)
state bird: **5** robin
state flower: **12** apple blossom
state tree: **9** white pine

mickey
5 flask, split

Mickey Mouse
5 dinky, petty **7** trivial **8** trifling **9** pointless, small-time, worthless **10** irrelevant

microbe
3 bug **4** germ **5** virus **8** bacillus, pathogen **9** bacterium **13** microorganism
see **microorganism**

microfilm sheet
5 fiche

Micronesia
capital: **7** Palikir
island, island group: **3** Yap **5** Chuuk **6** Kosrae **7** Pohnpei **8** Caroline

microorganism
3 bug **4** germ **5** ameba, virus **6** aerobe, amoeba **7** bacilli (plural), microbe, protist **8** bacillus, bacteria (plural), pathogen, protozoa (plural) **9** bacterium, protozoan, protozoon

microphone
3 bug **4** mike
shield: **4** gobo

microscope
9 magnifier
inventor: **11** Leeuwenhoek (Antoni van)
part: **5** stage **6** mirror **8** eyepiece **9** objective

microscopic
4 tiny **5** small **6** minute **13** infinitesimal

Microsoft founder
5 Gates (Bill)

microwave
3 zap **4** nuke

Mid-Atlantic state
7 New York **8** Delaware, Maryland, Virginia **9** New Jersey **12** Pennsylvania, West Virginia

midday
4 noon, sext **8** high noon, noontide, noontime

middle
4 core, mean **5** mesne, waist **6** center, medial, median **7** average, central, halfway **8** interior **10** centermost **11** equidistant, intervening **12** intermediary, intermediate
combining form: **3** mes **4** meso

Middle American country
4 Cuba **5** Haiti **6** Belize, Mexico, Panama **7** Bahamas, Grenada, Jamaica **8** Barbados, Dominica, Honduras **9** Costa Rica, Guatemala, Nicaragua **10** El Salvador

middlebrow
7 Babbitt

middle class
11 bourgeoisie

middle-class
9 bourgeois

middle ear
bone: **5** incus **6** stapes **7** malleus
membrane: **7** eardrum **8** tympanum

Middle Eastern country
4 Iran, Iraq, Oman **5** Egypt, Qatar, Sudan, Syria, Yemen **6** Cyprus, Israel, Jordan, Kuwait, Turkey **7** Bahrain, Lebanon **11** Saudi Arabia

Middle Kingdom
5 China

middleman
5 agent **6** broker **8** mediator **9** go-between **11** distributor, intercessor **12** intermediary, intermediate

Middlemarch author
5 Eliot (George), Evans (Mary Ann)

middle-of-the-road
7 neutral **8** moderate **9** impartial **11** nonpartisan

middling
4 fair, okay, so-so **6** decent, fairly, medium, rather **7** average, fairish, typical **8** adequate, mediocre, moderate, ordinary, passable **9** tolerable **10** moderately, second-rate **11** indifferent **12** intermediate, run-of-the-mill

midge
3 fly **4** gnat **6** punkie **7** no-see-um **8** dipteran **10** chironomid
larva: **9** bloodworm

midget
4 runt **5** dwarf, pygmy **6** bantam, peewee **7** manikin **8** Tom Thumb **10** homunculus **11** hop-o'-my-thumb, Lilliputian

Midian
father: **7** Abraham
mother: **7** Keturah
son: **5** Abida, Ephah, Epher **6** Eldaah, Hanoch

midpoint
3 par **4** mean, norm **6** center, median, middle **7** average, centrum, halfway **8** bull's-eye, standard

midwife
4 dhai **5** doula **6** granny, Lucina **10** accoucheur

mien
3 air, set **4** look **6** aspect, manner **7** address, bearing **8** carriage, demeanor, presence **9** mannerism **10** appearance, deportment, expression **11** comportment

miff
3 fit, irk, vex **4** beef, flap, spat **5** annoy, pique, run-in, upset **6** bother, fracas, nettle, offend, put out **7** dispute, provoke, quarrel, rhubarb **8** irritate, squabble **10** conniption, falling-out **11** altercation

might
3 may **4** sway **5** brawn, clout, force, means, power **6** energy, muscle **7** ability, command, control, mastery, potency **8** capacity, strength **9** authority, resources **12** forcefulness

mighty
4 huge, very **5** grand, great **6** heroic, potent, strong **7** eminent, immense, massive, titanic **8** enormous, forceful, gigantic, imposing, powerful, puissant **10** impressive, monumental, prodigious, stupendous, tremendous

Mignon composer
6 Thomas (Ambroise)

mignonette
4 herb **5** sauce **6** annual **6** reseda

migrant
5 exile, mover, nomad **7** drifter, nomadic, refugee **8** traveler, wanderer **9** itinerant, transient **10** expatriate

migrate
4 move, trek **5** drift, range, shift **6** wander **8** transfer

migration
6 exodus **8** diaspora
of professionals: **10** brain drain

migratory
5 nomad **6** errant, mobile, moving, roving **7** nomadic, ranging **9** wandering

Mikado, The
character: **4** Ko-Ko **6** Yum-Yum **7** Pooh-Bah **8** Nanki-Poo **9** Pitti-Sing
composer: **8** Sullivan (Arthur)
librettist: **7** Gilbert (W. S.)

milady
6 madame **10** noblewoman **11** gentlewoman

Milan
family: **6** Sforza **8** Visconti
opera house: **7** La Scala

Milcah
brother: **3** Lot
father: **5** Haran **10** Zelophehad
husband: **5** Nahor
son: **7** Bethuel

mild
4 calm, easy, meek, soft, tame **5** balmy, bland, faint, tepid **6** benign, docile, gentle, placid, serene, smooth, tender **7** amiable, clement, equable, insipid, lenient, patient, subdued **8** moderate, obliging **9** benignant, temperate **10** forbearing, submissive

mildew
4 mold, rust **6** fungus, growth

___ mile
7 country, statute **8** nautical

mileage recorder
8 odometer

milestone
5 event **6** marker **8** landmark, occasion

milieu
5 scene 6 medium, sphere 7 ambient, climate, setting 8 ambiance, ambience 10 atmosphere, background 11 environment, mise-en-scène 12 surroundings

militant
7 fighter, martial, warlike, warrior 8 activist, fighting 9 assertive, bellicose, combatant, combative, truculent 10 aggressive, pugnacious 11 belligerent, contentious, quarrelsome 12 gladiatorial

military
5 troop 6 forces, troops 7 martial, warlike 8 soldiery 9 soldierly 10 servicemen 11 armed forces, soldierlike
alert protocol: 6 DEFCON
alliance: 4 NATO
base: 4 camp, fort, post 5 depot, field 6 billet 8 barracks, garrison, quarters 10 encampment
officer: 5 major 7 captain, colonel, general 9 brigadier 10 lieutenant
prisoner: 3 POW
school: 3 OCS, OTS 4 ROTC, USMA 9 Annapolis, West Point
sector: 10 combat zone, front lines 11 battlefront
store: 2 BX, PX 10 commissary
storehouse: 5 depot 6 armory 7 arsenal
supplies: 8 matériel, ordnance
unit: 5 corps, squad, troop 7 company, platoon 8 division, regiment 9 battalion 11 battle group
vehicle: 4 jeep, tank 6 Abrams, Humvee 7 Bradley 9 Black Hawk, half-track

militate
4 tell 5 count, weigh 6 matter 11 carry weight

militia
7 reserve

milk
4 pump, rook, suck 5 drain, educe, empty, evoke, exact, mulct, nurse, wring 6 elicit, extort, fleece 7 exhaust, exploit, extract
coagulated: 4 curd
combining form: 4 lact 5 lacti, lacto
curdled: 7 clabber
fermented: 5 kefir 6 kumiss, yogurt 7 koumiss, yoghurt
liquid part: 4 whey
store: 5 dairy
sugar: 7 lactose

milkfish
3 awa

milk shake
6 frappe 7 frosted

milky
4 fair, meek, mild, pale, tame 5 white 6 chalky, cloudy, gentle 7 lacteal, whitish 8 timorous
lymph: 5 chyle

mill
5 grind, plant, shape, works 7 factory, machine 9 circulate, pulverize 11 manufactory

millenary
8 thousand

Miller, Arthur
film: 7 Misfits (The)
play: 5 Price (The) 9 All My Sons 8 Crucible (The) 12 After the Fall 16 Death of a Salesman 17 View from the Bridge (A)
salesman: 5 Loman (Willy)

milliner
6 hatter

million
combining form: 3 meg 4 mega

millionth
combining form: 4 micr 5 micro

Mill on the Floss author
5 Eliot (George), Evans (Mary Ann)

millstone
4 duty, load, onus 6 burden, charge, weight 9 albatross 10 affliction, deadweight

Milne character
3 Roo 4 Pooh (Winnie the) 5 Kanga 6 Eeyore, Piglet, Tigger

milord
8 nobleman 9 gentleman, patrician 10 aristocrat 12 silk stocking

milquetoast
see **milksop**

Miltiades' victory
8 Marathon

Milton work
5 Comus 7 Lycidas 8 L'Allegro 12 Areopagitica, Paradise Lost

mime
3 act 5 actor 6 act out 7 Marceau (Marcel) 9 performer, represent 11 impersonate 12 impersonator

mimic
3 act, ape, tui 4 aper, copy, mock, play 5 actor, enact 6 mummer, parody, parrot, player 7 copycat, imitate 8 resemble, simulate, travesty 9 burlesque, pantomime 11 impersonate 12 impersonator

mimicry
4 echo 6 parody 8 travesty 9 imitation, parroting 10 caricature 13 impersonation

minatory
4 dire, grim 7 baleful, baneful, direful, hostile, malefic, ominous 8 menacing, sinister 9 ill-boding 10 forbidding, foreboding, maleficent 11 frightening, threatening 12 intimidating

mince
4 chop, dice, hash **5** cut up, strut **6** prance, sashay, soften **8** moderate, restrain, tone down **9** euphemize

mincing
5 fussy **6** dainty, la-di-da, too-too **7** finical, finicky, stilted **8** affected, delicate **10** fastidious, pernickety **11** persnickety

mind
3 wit **4** mood, obey, soul, tend, will, wits **5** brain, fancy, watch, weigh **6** attend, belief, beware, brains, follow, memory, notice, psyche, reason, senses, spirit **7** care for, discern, dislike, feeling, observe, oversee, purpose **8** consider **9** intellect, intention, mentality, supervise **10** brainpower, gray matter **11** disposition, temperament **12** intelligence **13** consciousness
combining form: **5** psych **6** psycho

mindful
5 alert, awake, aware **7** knowing **8** sensible, vigilant **9** attentive, cognizant, conscious, observant **10** conversant **13** conscientious

mindless
4 rash **5** ditsy, ditzy, inane, silly **6** jejune, simple, stupid **7** asinine, foolish, unaware, vacuous **9** nitwitted, oblivious **10** irrational, unthinking **13** unintelligent

mine
3 dig, pit, sap **4** fund, lode, vein, well **5** delve, drill, hoard, stock, store, trove **6** burrow, quarry, spring **7** bonanza, deposit, extract **8** eldorado, excavate, Golconda **10** excavation, wellspring **13** treasure trove
coal: **8** colliery
entrance: **4** adit

miner
6 pitman **7** collier

mineral
5 beryl, topaz, trona **6** augite, barite, garnet, iolite, pinite, rutile, sphene, spinel, sulfur, zircon **7** apatite, axinite, azurite, bornite, calcite, citrine, coesite, cyanite, jadeite, kernite, kunzite, olivine, zeolite **8** boracite, cinnabar, dolomite, epsomite, fayalite, feldspar, fluorite, hematite, lazulite, lazurite, siderite, sodalite, stibnite, triplite, wellsite **9** aragonite, celestite, cerussite, danburite, fosterite, kaolinite, lawsonite, magnetite, malachite, muscovite, phenakite, scapolite, tridymite, turquoise, wulfenite **10** chalcedony, orthoclase, pyrrhotite, tourmaline **11** alexandrite, chrysoberyl, melanterite **12** brazilianite, chalcopyrite, tincalconite **13** rhodochrosite
flaky: **4** mica
greasy: **4** talc **10** serpentine
hard: **6** spinel **7** diamond **8** corundum
iridescent: **4** opal
nonmetallic: **5** boron **6** gypsum, halite **8** asbestos, graphite
shiny: **4** gold **6** galena, pyrite, silver
soft: **4** talc **6** gypsum **8** graphite
transparent: **6** quartz

mineral water
7 seltzer **8** club soda

Minerva
see **Athena**

mingle
3 mix **4** meld **5** blend, merge **6** commix **7** combine **8** intermix **9** associate, socialize

mingy
4 mean **5** cheap, tight **7** chintzy, miserly, scrimpy **8** grudging, ungiving **9** niggardly, penurious **10** pinchpenny **11** closefisted, tightfisted

miniature
3 wee **4** tiny **5** small, teeny, weeny **6** little, minute, petite, teensy **9** itsy-bitsy, itty-bitty **10** diminutive, small-scale, teeny-weeny **11** Lilliputian **12** illumination

minify
4 trim **6** lessen, shrink **7** abridge, curtail **8** decrease, diminish **10** abbreviate

minim
3 bit, jot **4** atom, iota **5** grain, speck **7** modicum, smidgen **8** particle
music: **8** half note

minimal
5 basic, least, token **6** lowest **7** nominal **8** littlest, smallest **9** slightest

minimize
5 decry **6** reduce **7** run down **8** belittle, derogate, discount, downplay, play down **9** disparage, soft-pedal, underrate **10** depreciate **13** underestimate

minimum
3 dab, jot **4** iota, whit **5** least, speck **6** lowest, margin **7** smidgen **8** particle, pittance, smallest

minion
4 idol **5** toady **6** flunky, lackey, vassal, yes-man **7** devotee, flunkey, flunkie, spaniel **8** favorite, follower, parasite, truckler **9** sycophant, toadeater, underling **10** bootlicker **11** lickspittle, subordinate

minister
4 tend **5** agent, clerk, serve **6** cleric, curate, divine, parson **8** clerical, preacher, reverend **9** churchman, clergyman **10** ambassador **12** ecclesiastic
of state: **10** chancellor
plenipotentiary: **5** envoy **6** consul **8** diplomat, emissary

ministry
5 agent, organ **6** agency, clergy, medium **7** cabinet **10** department, instrument **11** bureaucracy

mink kin
5 otter, skunk, stoat **6** ermine, ferret, fisher, weasel

Minnehaha's husband
8 Hiawatha

Minnesota
capital: **6** St. Paul
city: **5** Edina **6** Duluth **9** Rochester **11** Minneapolis
college, university: **8** Carleton **9** Saint Olaf **10** Macalester
nickname: **6** Gopher (State) **9** North Star (State)
park: **9** Voyageurs
river: **7** St. Croix **9** Minnesota **11** Mississippi
state bird: **4** loon (common)
state flower: **12** lady's slipper
state tree: **7** red pine

minor
5 lower, petty, small, youth **6** casual, lesser, little, paltry, slight **7** trivial **8** inferior, mediocre, piddling, small-fry, trifling, underage **9** dependent, secondary, small-beer, small-time **10** bush-league, second-rate, shoestring **11** indifferent, unimportant **13** insignificant

minority
5 youth **6** nonage **7** infancy **9** childhood **10** immaturity

minor-league
5 small **6** lesser **9** secondary, small-time **11** unimportant

Minos
daughter: **7** Ariadne, Phaedra
father: **4** Zeus **7** Jupiter
kingdom: **5** Crete
monster: **8** Minotaur
mother: **6** Europa
son: **9** Androgeos
wife: **8** Pasiphaë

Minotaur
father: **4** bull
home: **9** labyrinth
mother: **8** Pasiphaë
slayer: **7** Theseus

minstrel
4 bard, wait **6** harper, singer **7** gleeman **8** jongleur **9** balladist **10** troubadour
end man: **5** Bones (Mr.), Tambo (Mr.)
instrument: **4** lute, lyre **5** naker, rebec, shawm, tabor **8** crumhorn, psaltery **9** krummhorn **10** tambourine

mint
3 pot **4** cast, coin, heap, pile, sage **5** basil, bugle, forge, issue, stamp, trove **6** boodle, bundle, create, intact, packet, savory, strike, unused **7** fortune, like-new, menthol, perfect, produce **8** brand-new, lavender, marjoram, original **9** blue curls, bugleweed, undamaged **10** pennyroyal

Minuit's purchase
9 Manhattan

minus
4 flaw, lack, less, sans **6** absent, defect **7** lacking, missing, wanting, without **8** drawback, negative, subtract **10** deficiency

minuscule
4 tiny **5** small **6** letter, little, minute **7** trivial **9** lowercase, miniature **10** negligible, small-scale **11** meaningless, microscopic **13** imperceptible, inappreciable, insignificant

minute
3 wee **4** jiff, memo, note, tiny **5** draft, flash, jiffy, small, teeny, weeny **6** little, moment, record, teensy **7** careful, instant, precise, trivial **8** detailed, itemized, thorough, trifling **9** itsy-bitsy, itty-bitty, miniature, minuscule **10** diminutive, memorandum, meticulous, scrupulous, teeny-weeny **11** Lilliputian, punctilious **13** infinitesimal

minutes
3 log **6** annals, record **7** summary **10** transcript **11** proceedings

minutiae
6 trivia **7** details **10** fine points, triviality **11** particulars

minx
4 bawd, moll, slut, tart **5** bimbo, tramp, wench, whore **6** floozy, harlot, hooker **7** hustler, trollop **8** strumpet **10** prostitute

miracle
4 boon, feat **6** marvel, wonder **7** godsend, portent, prodigy, stunner **8** windfall **9** sensation **10** phenomenon

miraculous
7 amazing **8** wondrous **9** marvelous, unearthly, wonderful **10** astounding, prodigious, superhuman **11** astonishing, spectacular **12** inexplicable, supernatural **13** preternatural

mirage
6 vision, wraith **8** delusion, illusion, phantasm **11** fata morgana, ignis fatuus **13** hallucination

Miranda
father: **8** Prospero
lover: **9** Ferdinand

mire
3 bog, fen, mud **4** muck, ooze, sink, trap **5** delay, marsh, slush, swamp **6** detain, enmesh, entrap, hang up, morass, slough, tangle **7** bog down, embroil, ensnare, involve, set back **8** entangle **9** imbroglio, implicate, quicksand

Miriam's brother
5 Aaron, Moses
mirror
5 glass **6** embody, typify **7** reflect **8** speculum **9** exemplify, personify, reflector **10** illustrate **11** cheval glass **12** looking glass
signaling: 10 heliograph
mirth
3 fun, joy **4** glee **5** cheer **6** gaiety, levity **7** jollity, revelry **8** gladness, hilarity **9** festivity, frivolity, happiness, jocundity, joviality, merriment **10** jocularity **11** merrymaking **12** cheerfulness
mirthful
3 gay **5** jolly, merry, riant **6** jocund, jovial **7** festive **9** exuberant, hilarious **12** lighthearted
miry
4 oozy **5** boggy, mucky, muddy **6** marshy, slushy, swampy
misadventure
4 slip **5** boner, error, lapse **6** howler, mishap **7** blunder, faux pas **8** accident, calamity, casualty, disaster **9** cataclysm **10** misfortune **11** catastrophe
misanthrope
5 cynic, grump, loner **6** grinch **7** killjoy, recluse, scoffer **10** curmudgeon
misanthropic
7 cynical **10** antisocial
misappropriate
5 filch, steal **6** pilfer **7** purloin **8** embezzle, peculate **9** defalcate
misbegotten
7 bastard, illicit, natural **8** baseborn, deformed, spurious **10** fatherless, unfathered **12** contemptible, disreputable, ill-conceived, illegitimate
misbehave
5 act up, cut up, lapse, rebel, stray **6** act out, offend **7** carry on, disobey **8** trespass **10** roughhouse, transgress
misbehavior
7 misdeed **8** rudeness **9** high jinks **10** misconduct, wrongdoing **11** delinquency, dereliction, naughtiness **13** transgression
miscalculate
3 err **8** miscount, misgauge
miscarry
4 fail, flop **5** abort **6** fizzle **7** go wrong
miscellaneous
3 odd **5** mixed **6** motley, sundry, varied **7** diverse **8** assorted **9** different, disparate, scrambled **13** heterogeneous
miscellany
3 ana **4** hash, olio, stew **5** salad **6** jumble, medley, motley, muddle **7** farrago, mélange, mixture, omnibus **8** mixed bag, pastiche **9** anthology, congeries, pasticcio, patchwork, potpourri **10** assortment, hodgepodge, hotchpotch, salmagundi **11** aggregation, gallimaufry, odds and ends, olla podrida, smorgasbord
mischance
6 mishap **7** bad luck, tragedy **8** accident, casualty **9** adversity **10** misfortune **11** contretemps
mischief
3 ill **4** evil, harm **5** prank **6** damage, strife **7** devilry, roguery, trouble, waggery **8** deviltry, sabotage **9** devilment, diablerie, vandalism **10** wrongdoing **11** naughtiness, shenanigans **12** monkeyshines
mischief-maker
3 imp **4** puck **5** devil, knave, rogue, scamp **6** rascal **7** villain **8** agitator, scalawag **9** prankster, trickster **11** rapscallion **12** rabble-rouser
mischievous
3 sly **4** arch, foxy **5** antic, saucy **6** artful, bratty, impish, tricky, vexing **7** harmful, irksome, larkish, naughty, playful, puckish, roguish, tricksy, waggish **8** annoying, damaging, perverse, prankish, rascally, sportive **9** injurious, malicious **10** bothersome, frolicsome, ill-behaved
misconception
5 error **7** fallacy, mistake **8** delusion, illusion
misconduct
8 adultery **10** wrongdoing **11** dereliction, impropriety, malfeasance, malpractice, misbehavior **12** malversation **13** transgression
miscreant
4 heel **5** felon, knave, rogue **6** outlaw, rascal, sinner, wretch **7** corrupt, culprit, heretic, hoodlum, infidel, lowlife, vicious, villain **8** apostate, criminal, depraved, infamous, perverse **9** heretical, nefarious, scoundrel, unhealthy, wrongdoer **10** blackguard, degenerate, delinquent, unbeliever, villainous
miscue
4 goof, miss, slip, trip **5** error, fluff, lapse **6** slip-up **7** blooper, blunder, mistake
misdeed
3 sin **5** crime, wrong **6** breach **7** offense **9** violation **10** infraction **13** transgression
misdoubt
4 fear **5** dread **7** suspect
mise-en-scène
3 set **4** site **6** locale, medium, milieu **7** ambient, climate, context, scenery, setting **8** ambiance, ambience, stage set **10** atmosphere, background **11** environment **12** stage setting, surroundings
miser
5 piker **7** hoarder, niggard, scrooge **8** tightwad **9** skinflint **10** cheapskate, pinchpenny

miserable
6 gloomy, meager, meagre, paltry, rueful, sordid, woeful **7** doleful, forlorn, piteous, pitiful, squalid **8** desolate, dolorous, downcast, hopeless, shameful, tortured, wretched **9** afflicted, destitute, sorrowful, worthless **10** despairing, despondent, melancholy

Miserables, Les
author: **4** Hugo (Victor)
character: **6** Javert (Inspector) **7** Cosette, Fantine, Valjean (Jean)

miserly
4 mean **5** close, tight **6** greedy, stingy **7** scrimpy **8** covetous, grasping **9** niggardly, penurious, scrimping **10** avaricious **11** closefisted, tightfisted **12** cheeseparing, parsimonious **13** penny-pinching

misery
3 woe **5** agony, dolor, grief **6** sorrow **7** anguish, squalor **8** calamity, distress **9** adversity, dejection, suffering **10** affliction, depression, desolation **11** despondency **12** wretchedness

misfit
6 oddity, weirdo **7** oddball **8** maverick **9** eccentric, screwball

misfortune
3 ill, woe **4** blow, harm, loss **5** cross, trial **7** reverse, setback, tragedy, trouble **8** accident, calamity, casualty, disaster, hardship **9** adversity, cataclysm **10** affliction, visitation **11** catastrophe, contretemps, tribulation

misgiving
4 fear **5** doubt, dread, qualm **6** unease **7** anxiety, scruple **8** distrust **9** suspicion **10** foreboding **11** premonition, trepidation **12** apprehension, presentiment

misguided
5 wrong **9** erroneous **10** ill-advised **11** injudicious **12** short-sighted

mishandle
4 flub **5** abuse, botch **6** bungle, fumble, mess up **7** rough up **8** maltreat **10** knock about, slap around

mishap
7 bad luck, tragedy **8** accident, casualty **9** adversity **11** contretemps

mishmash
4 olio, stew **6** jumble, litter, medley, motley, muddle **7** clutter, farrago, mélange, mixture, rummage **8** pastiche, scramble **9** pasticcio, patchwork, potpourri **10** hodgepodge, hotchpotch, salmagundi **11** gallimaufry

misidentify
5 mix up **7** confuse **8** confound

misinterpret
7 confuse, misread

mislay
4 lose

mislead
4 dupe, fool, gull, lure **5** bluff, cheat **6** betray, delude, entice, seduce, take in **7** beguile, deceive **8** hoodwink, inveigle **11** double-cross

misleading
5 false, wrong **8** delusive, delusory, specious **9** deceitful, deceptive **10** fallacious, inaccurate **11** casuistical, sophistical

mismatch
3 jar **5** clash **6** jangle **7** discord **8** conflict

misplace
4 lose

misprint
4 typo

misprision
5 scorn **7** despite, disdain, neglect **8** contempt, sedition **9** contumely, disregard **10** misconduct, negligence **11** concealment, dereliction, impropriety, malpractice

misrepresent
4 warp **5** twist **6** garble **7** distort, falsify, varnish **8** disguise **9** embellish, embroider **10** camouflage **11** counterfeit

misrepresentation
3 fib, lie **4** tale **5** story **6** canard **7** falsity, untruth **9** falsehood **10** distortion

miss
3 err, gal **4** fail, girl, lass, maid, omit, skip **5** avoid **6** damsel, escape, forget, ignore, lassie, maiden **7** failure, misfire, neglect **8** discount, leave out, overlook **9** disregard
French: **4** Mlle. **12** Mademoiselle
German: **8** Fräulein
Spanish: **4** Srta. **8** Señorita

Missa Solemnis composer
9 Beethoven (Ludwig van)

misshape
4 warp **6** deform **7** contort, distort, torture **9** disfigure

missile
4 bolt, dart **5** arrow, shell, spear **6** bullet, rocket **10** cannonball, projectile
shelter: **4** silo
underwater: **7** torpedo
(see also **guided missile**)

missing
4 AWOL, lost **6** absent

mission
3 aim, job **4** duty, goal, task **5** quest, recon **6** charge, errand, object, sortie **7** calling, embassy, purpose **8** legation, lifework, ministry, vocation **9** objective **10** assignment

missionary
7 apostle **8** emissary **10** evangelist, revivalist **12** propagandist, proselytizer

Mississippi
capital: **7** Jackson
city: **6** Biloxi **8** Gulfport **10** Greenville
college, university: **12** Jackson State **8** Millsaps
nickname: **8** Magnolia (State)
river: **5** Pearl **11** Mississippi
state bird: **11** mockingbird
state flower: **8** magnolia
state tree: **8** magnolia

missive
4 memo, note **6** letter, report **7** epistle, message **8** dispatch

Miss Julie author
10 Strindberg (August)

Miss Lonelyhearts author
4 West (Nathanael)

Missouri
capital: **13** Jefferson City
city: **7** St. Louis **10** Kansas City **11** Springfield **12** Independence
college, university: **10** Washington
lake: **15** Lake of the Ozarks
nickname: **6** Show Me (State)
river: **8** Missouri **11** Mississippi
state bird: **8** bluebird
state flower: **8** hawthorn
state tree: **7** dogwood

misstate
4 warp **5** color, twist **6** garble **7** distort, falsify

misstatement
3 fib, lie **4** tale **7** falsity, untruth **9** falsehood **13** prevarication

misstep
4 flub, goof, slip **5** boner, error, fluff, gaffe, lapse **6** slipup **7** blooper, blunder, faux pas

mist
3 dim, fog **4** blur, film, haze, murk **5** befog, brume, cloud **7** becloud, obscure

mistake
4 flub, slip **5** boner, error, fluff, folly, gaffe, lapse, snafu **6** boo-boo, bungle, howler, slipup **7** blooper, blunder, confuse, faux pas, take for **8** confound **10** inaccuracy

mistaken
5 false, wrong **6** all wet, faulty, flawed, untrue **7** invalid **8** specious **9** defective, erroneous, incorrect, misguided, unfounded **10** fallacious, fraudulent, inaccurate **11** misinformed

mister
3 sir **7** husband
French: **8** Monsieur
German: **4** Herr
Italian: **6** Signor
Spanish: **5** Señor

mistreat
5 abuse **6** ill-use, molest **7** rough up **9** brutalize, manhandle

mistress
4 doxy, moll **5** lover, woman **7** hetaira **8** dulcinea, ladylove, paramour **9** concubine, courtesan, inamorata, kept woman **10** chatelaine, girlfriend
of Charles II: **4** Gwyn (Nell) **8** Villiers (Barbara)
of Edward III: **7** Perrers (Alice)
of Henry II (England): **8** Clifford (Rosamund)
of Henry II (France): **10** de Poitiers (Diane)
of Louis XV: **9** Pompadour (Madame de)
of Ludwig I: **6** Montez (Lola)

mistrust
5 doubt **7** concern, dispute, dubiety, surmise, suspect **8** wariness **9** apprehend, misgiving, suspicion **10** foreboding, skepticism **11** incertitude, uncertainty **12** apprehension

mistrustful
4 wary **5** leery **6** uneasy **7** dubious, jealous **8** doubting **9** skeptical **10** suspicious

misty
3 dim **4** hazy **5** foggy, vague **6** cloudy, vapory **7** blurred, obscure, tearful, unclear **8** confused, nebulous, vaporous **10** indistinct

misunderstanding
4 rift, spat, tiff **5** mix-up **6** breach **7** dispute, quarrel, rupture **8** squabble **10** falling-out **12** disagreement

misuse
5 waste
of a word: **8** malaprop **11** malapropism

Mitchell novel
15 Gone with the Wind

mite
3 bit, jot **4** atom, iota **5** grain, minim, ounce, speck **6** acarid, tittle **7** chigger, modicum, smidgen **8** molecule, particle
family: **8** oribatid

miter
5 crown, joint **9** headdress

mitigate
4 ease **5** abate, allay, relax, slake **6** lessen, soften, subdue, temper **7** assuage, lighten, mollify, relieve **8** palliate, moderate, tone down **9** alleviate, extenuate, meliorate

mitigation
4 ease **6** relief **8** easement

mitosis
12 cell division, karyokinesis
stage: **8** anaphase, prophase **9** metaphase, telophase

mix
4 fuse, link, lump, meld, stir **5** blend, merge, unite **6** fusion, jumble, mingle, tangle, work in **7** amalgam, combine, concoct, confuse, conjoin **8** coalesce, compound, confound **9** associate, commingle, interfuse **10** amalgamate, crossbreed **11** intermingle **12** amalgamation

mixed
6 hybrid, impure, motley, sundry, varied **7** diluted, diverse, mongrel **8** assorted, compound **9** composite, crossbred, interbred, irregular **12** multifarious **13** heterogeneous, miscellaneous

mixed bag
4 hash, olio **5** gumbo, salad **6** jumble, medley **7** mélange **8** mishmash, pastiche **9** potpourri **10** assortment, hodgepodge, hotchpotch, miscellany, salmagundi **11** gallimaufry

mixed-up
5 fazed **6** addled **7** jumbled **8** confused **9** flustered, nonplused, perplexed **10** bewildered, disjointed, distracted, incoherent, nonplussed **12** disconcerted

mixologist
6 barman **7** tapster **9** barkeeper, bartender

mixture
4 brew, hash, olio, stew **5** alloy, blend, gumbo **6** fusion, hybrid, jumble, medley **7** amalgam, farrago, mélange **8** compound, mishmash, solution **9** composite, potpourri **10** concoction, confection, miscellany, salmagundi **11** combination **12** amalgamation

mix up
5 addle **6** fuddle, jumble, muddle **7** confuse, fluster, mistake **8** befuddle, bewilder, confound **10** disarrange, discompose **11** disorganize, misidentify

mix-up
4 hash, mess, muss **5** botch, chaos, error, melee **6** muddle, tangle **7** mistake **8** shambles **9** commotion, confusion

MKS unit
3 lux, ohm **4** mole, volt, watt **5** farad, henry, hertz, joule, lumen, meter, metre, tesla, weber **6** ampere, kelvin, newton, pascal, second **7** candela, coulomb, siemens **8** kilogram

Mnemosyne
6 Memory
daughters: **5** Muses
father: **6** Uranus
lover: **4** Zeus
mother: **4** Gaea

Moabite
city: **3** Kir
god: **7** Chemosh
king: **5** Eglon, Mesha

Moab's father
3 Lot

moan
4 wail, weep **5** gripe, groan, whine **6** bewail, grieve, grouse, lament **7** deplore **8** complain

mob
3 jam **4** clan, gang, herd, pack, push, ring, riot **5** crowd, crush, horde, mafia, press, swarm **6** jostle, masses, rabble, throng **8** canaille, riffraff **9** hoi polloi, multitude **11** proletariat

mobile
5 fluid **6** moving **7** migrant, movable **8** cellular, moveable, variable **9** itinerant, migratory, unsettled, versatile **10** ambulatory **11** peripatetic

mobile home
4 tent **6** camper **7** trailer **9** Airstream

mobile-phone area
4 cell

mobilize
5 drive, impel, rally, ready, rouse **6** arouse, call up, muster, prompt, propel **7** actuate, animate, marshal **8** activate, assemble, organize **9** circulate

mobster
4 capo, goon, thug **6** hit man **7** goombah, made man, mafioso **8** criminal, gangster **9** godfather, racketeer

Moby Dick
5 whale **10** white whale
author: **8** Melville (Herman)
character: **3** Pip **6** Daggoo, Parsee **7** Ishmael **8** Queequeg, Starbuck, Tashtego
pursuer: **4** Ahab
ship: **6** Pequod

moccasin
6 loafer **7** slipper **8** larrigan

mock
3 ape **4** defy, fake, gibe, jape, jeer, razz, twit **5** bogus, chaff, dummy, false, feign, mimic, phony, quasi, sneer, taunt, tease **6** deride, ersatz, parody, pseudo, send up **7** deceive, feigned, imitate, lampoon, mislead **8** ridicule, satirize, so-called, spurious **9** imitation, simulated **10** artificial **11** counterfeit

mockery
4 sham **5** farce, scorn, sport **6** japery, parody, satire **7** take-off **8** contempt, derision, raillery, ridicule, travesty **9** burlesque, imitation **10** caricature **13** laughingstock

mocking
8 derisive, sardonic, scornful **9** sarcastic

mode
3 fad, way **4** chic, rage **5** state, style, vogue **6** custom, manner, method, status, system

7 fashion 9 condition, procedure, situation, technique 10 convention, dernier cri

model
4 copy, type 5 dummy, ideal, shape 6 design, effigy, mirror, mockup, symbol 7 classic, epitome, example, imitate, manikin, paragon, pattern, perfect, replica, typical 8 ensample, exemplar, flawless, mannikin, maquette, nonesuch, paradigm, standard 9 archetype, beau ideal, blueprint, classical, criterion, exemplary, miniature, nonpareil 10 apotheosis, embodiment, prototypal, touchstone 12 paradigmatic, prototypical, reproduction
famous: 4 Moss (Kate) 5 Banks (Tyra) 6 Hutton (Lauren), Parker (Suzy), Twiggy 8 Campbell (Naomi), Crawford (Cindy), Schiffer (Claudia) 9 Shrimpton (Jean) 10 MacPherson (Elle), Turlington (Christy)

moderate
3 ebb 4 bate, curb, even, fair, mild, so-so, wane 5 abate, sober 6 lessen, medium, reduce, relent, soften, steady, subdue, temper 7 average, control, ease off, equable, lighten, limited, neutral, relieve, subside, trivial 8 centrist, constant, discreet, middling, mitigate, restrain 9 alleviate, constrain, temperate 10 abstemious, controlled, reasonable, restrained 11 indifferent 12 conservative

moderation
7 control, measure 9 restraint 10 abstinence, constraint, limitation, temperance 13 temperateness

moderator
5 judge 7 arbiter 8 chairman, examiner, governor, mediator 10 peacemaker 11 chairperson

modern
3 new 5 fresh, novel 6 recent 7 current 8 neoteric, up-to-date 10 newfangled, present-day 12 contemporary

modernize
4 redo 5 renew 6 update 7 remodel 8 renovate 9 refurbish 10 rejuvenate

modest
3 coy, shy 4 meek, prim 5 plain, timid 6 decent, demure, humble, proper, seemly, simple 7 bashful, prudish 8 decorous, discreet, moderate, reserved, reticent, retiring 9 diffident 10 unassuming 11 straitlaced, unassertive 12 self-effacing 13 unpretentious

Modest Proposal author
5 Swift (Jonathan)

modesty
7 decency, reserve 8 chastity, humility, timidity 9 propriety, reticence 10 diffidence

modicum
3 bit, jot, tad 4 atom, iota, mite, whit 5 grain, minim, ounce, pinch, scrap, speck, trace 7 smidgen, soupçon 8 particle

modify
4 vary 5 adapt, alter, amend, limit, tweak 6 adjust, change, mutate, revise, rework, temper 7 qualify 8 mitigate, moderate, restrain 9 refashion

modish
4 chic 5 smart, swank 6 chichi, trendy, with-it 7 dashing, stylish 11 fashionable

Modred
father: 6 Arthur
mother: 8 Margawse
slayer, victim: 6 Arthur

module
4 item, unit 7 element 9 component 11 constituent

modulate
4 vary 5 tweak 6 adjust, attune, temper 8 fine-tune, regulate, restrain

modus operandi
5 style 6 custom, manner, method, system 7 process, program, routine 8 approach, practice, strategy 9 procedure, technique

modus vivendi
9 way of life

mogul
4 czar, king, lord 5 baron, nabob, ruler 6 bigwig, honcho, prince, sachem, top gun, tycoon 7 kingpin, magnate 9 plutocrat, potentate

Mohammed
see **Muhammad**

Mohawk chief
5 Brant (Joseph) 8 Hiawatha

Mohican chief
5 Uncas

moiety
3 cut 4 half, part 5 piece 7 element, portion, section, segment 8 division 9 component

moil
3 tug, wet 4 grub, to-do, work 5 churn, dirty, drive, grind, labor, swirl 6 bustle, clamor, drudge, hubbub, lather, seethe, strain, strive, uproar 7 ferment, travail, trouble, wrangle 8 drudgery 9 agitation, commotion, confusion 10 hurly-burly, turbulence

moist
3 wet 4 damp, dank, dewy 5 humid 6 clammy, steamy, sticky 7 dampish, maudlin, tearful, wettish

moisten
3 wet 6 dampen 8 humidify, saturate

moisture
4 damp **5** vapor **7** wetness **8** humidity **13** precipitation

mojo
3 hex **4** jinx **5** charm, magic, power, spell **6** hoodoo, whammy

molar
5 tooth **7** grinder
neighbor: **6** canine

molasses
7 treacle **10** blackstrap

mold
3 die **4** cast, form, sort, type **5** forge, ingot, knead, shape, stamp **6** design, fungus **7** fashion, pattern **8** template **9** construct

moldable
6 pliant, supple **7** ductile, plastic, pliable **9** adaptable, malleable

molder
3 rot **5** decay, waste **7** crumble **9** break down, decompose **11** deteriorate **12** disintegrate

molding
4 bead, gula, ogee **5** congé, ogive, talon, torus **6** reglet **7** annulet, beading, cavetto, cornice, reeding **8** cincture **9** baseboard
compound: **4** beak, cyma, ogie **10** serpentine
edge: **5** arris
flat: **5** splay **6** fascia, fillet, listel, regula **7** chamfer
simple curve: **4** roll **5** flute, ovolo, torus **6** scotia **8** astragal

Moldova
capital: **8** Chisinau, Kishinev
former name: **8** Moldavia
language: **8** Romanian
monetary unit: **3** leu
neighbor: **7** Romania, Ukraine
river: **8** Dniester

moldy
5 dated, fusty, musty, passé **6** bygone, old hat **7** ancient, antique, archaic, outworn **8** mildewed, outdated **9** crumbling, moth-eaten **10** antiquated **12** old-fashioned

mole
3 spy **4** pier, quay **5** jetty, nevus **6** burrow, tunnel **9** birthmark **10** breakwater

molecule
3 bit, jot **4** iota **5** minim, speck **7** modicum **8** particle

molest
3 vex **4** bait **5** abuse, annoy, harry, tease **6** badger, bother, harass, heckle, hector, pester, plague **7** disturb, torment, trouble **9** persecute

Moll Flanders author
5 Defoe (Daniel)

mollify
4 calm, ease **5** allay **6** pacify, soften, soothe, temper **7** appease, assuage, lighten, placate, relieve, sweeten **8** mitigate **9** alleviate **10** ameliorate, conciliate, propitiate

mollusk
6 chiton
bivalve: **4** clam **6** cockle, mussel, oyster, teredo **7** geoduck, scallop **8** shipworm
cephalopod: **5** squid **7** octopus **8** argonaut, nautilus **10** cuttlefish
part: **6** mantle, radula, siphon
tooth shell: **9** dentalium
univalve: **4** slug **5** conch, cowry, murex, snail, whelk **6** cowrie, limpet, triton **7** abalone **10** nudibranch, periwinkle

Molly ___
7 Maguire, Pitcher

mollycoddle
3 pet **4** baby **5** humor, spoil **6** cocker, cosset, dandle, pamper **7** cater to, indulge, milksop **8** mama's boy **11** milquetoast

Moloch's pit
6 Tophet

molt
4 cast, shed, slip **6** change, slough **7** cast off, discard, ecdysis **9** slough off

molted skins
7 exuviae

molten
6 melted **7** glowing **9** liquefied

molten rock
4 lava **5** magma

molybdenum symbol
2 Mo

moment
3 sec **4** jiff **5** flash, jiffy, point, shake, trice **6** import, minute, second **7** instant **8** juncture, occasion **9** magnitude **10** importance **11** consequence, split second **12** significance

momentary
5 brief, quick **8** fleeting, fugitive **9** ephemeral, fugacious, transient **10** evanescent, short-lived, transitory

momentous
5 grave **7** epochal, fateful, serious, weighty **9** important **10** meaningful **11** significant, substantial **12** considerable **13** consequential

momentousness
6 import, weight **9** magnitude **10** importance **11** consequence, weightiness **12** significance

momentum
5 drive **6** energy, thrust **7** impetus, impulse **10** propulsion

Momo author
4 Ende (Michael)

momus
6 carper, critic, mocker **7** caviler **8** caviller **9** detractor **11** faultfinder

Monaco
commune:
language:
monetary u
monetary u
neighbor: 6
prince: 6 A
princess: 5

monad
3 one **4** ato

Mona Lisa
10 La Gioco
painter: 7 d
(da Vinci)

monarch
4 czar, king,
6 kaiser, prin
9 butterfly, p
daughter: 7
heir: 7 daug
son: 6 princ

monarchical
5 regal, roya
jestic **9** sove

monarchy
4 rule **5** real
9 autocracy,

monastery
5 abbey **6** fri
8 cloister
Buddhist: 8
Eastern Orth
head: 5 abb

monastic
4 abbé, monk
secluded **9** r
tered

____ Mondrian
4 Piet

monetary
6 fiscal **9** fina

monetary rate
7 millage

monetary uni
see at individ

money
4 cash, coin,
5 bread, chips, dough, funds, lolly, lucre, moola, rhino, scrip **6** boodle, change, dinero, do-re-mi, mammon, moolah, riches, specie, wampum, wealth **7** cabbage, capital, coinage, lettuce, needful, scratch, stipend **8** bankroll, currency, finances, treasure **9** resources **10** greenbacks **11** filthy lucre, legal tender

moneyed
4 rich **5** flush **6** loaded **7** opulent, wealthy, well-off **8** affluent, well-to-do **10** prosperous, well-heeled

money-gr...**ber**
5 miser **7** hoarder, niggard, scrooge **8** tightwad **9** skinflint **10** cheapskate **12** penny-pincher

...**g**
...ainful **9** lucrative **10** profitable, ...worthwhile **12** advantageous, re-

...vend **6** broker, dealer, hawker, ...r, vendor **7** higgler, packman, ...ckster

...**9** Tamerlane **10** Kublai Khan ...han, Tamburlaine

...Daur, Olöt, Urat **5** Ordos **6** Bargut, ...wa, Chahar, Dorbet, Torgut **7** Kar- ..., Monguor

...an Bator **11** Ulaanbaatar
...**6** Ögödei **11** Genghis Khan
...bi
...l
...**it: 6** tugrik
...**nge: 5** Altai, Altay **6** Kentai **7** Hen- ...han, Altay Shan
...China **6** Russia
...**5** Orhun **7** Selenga

...mutt **5** cross **6** hybrid **7** bastard, ...f-bred **9** crossbred, half blood, ...crossbreed

...**6** handle **8** cognomen, nickname ...**1** appellation, designation

...ution, portent, warning **11** fore-

..., watch **6** screen **7** adviser, ob- ...e **8** watchdog **11** keep track of

Monitor
designer: 8 Ericsson (John)
opponent: 8 Virginia **9** Merrimack

BORDERS®

BORDERS
BOOKS AND MUSIC
2173 ZEIER RD
MADISON, WI 53704
608-240-0080

STORE: 0210 REG: 02/37 TRAN#: 1144
SALE 07/29/2009 EMP: 00615

MERRIAM WEBSTER CROSSWORD PUZZ
9034495 QP T 19.95

Subtotal 19.95
BR: 8260636041

Subtotal 19.95
WISCONSIN 5.5% 1.10
1 Item Total 21.05
CASH 22.00
Cash Change Due .95

07/29/2009 01:00PM

Shop online
24 hours a day
at Borders.com

monitory
7 warning **8** advisory **10** cautionary

monk
4 abbé **5** friar **7** brother **8** cenobite, monastic **9** anchorite
Buddhist: **4** lama **5** bonze
Hindu: **8** sannyasi
Roman Catholic: **8** Capuchin, Salesian, Trappist **9** Carmelite, Dominican **10** Carthusian, Cistercian, Franciscan **11** Augustinian
room: **4** cell
shaven crown: **7** tonsure
title: **3** Dom, Fra **5** Padre

monkey
3 imp **4** mess **5** gamin **6** meddle, simian, tamper, urchin **8** busybody **9** interfere, interlope
Ceylon: **4** maha
Cochin China: **4** douc
New World: **4** mico, saki, titi **6** howler, spider, uakari, woolly **7** sapajou, tamarin **8** capuchin, marmoset, squirrel **11** douroucouli
Old World: **4** mona **5** Diana, drill **6** guenon, langur, rhesus, vervet **7** colobus, hanuman, macaque **8** mandrill, mangabey **9** proboscis **10** Barbary ape

monkeyshine
3 gag **4** dido, jape, lark **5** antic, caper, prank, stunt, trick **6** frolic **10** shenanigan, tomfoolery

monocratic
8 absolute, despotic **9** arbitrary, autarchic, tyrannous **10** autocratic, tyrannical

monogram
8 initials

monograph
5 study **6** thesis **8** tractate, treatise **9** discourse **12** disquisition, dissertation

monopolize
3 hog **5** sew up **6** absorb, corner **7** control, engross **8** dominate, take over

monopoly
5 trust **6** cartel, corner **7** control **9** ownership, syndicate **10** consortium, domination **11** exclusivity

monotone
5 drone, thrum **8** sameness

monotonous
4 blah, dull **6** boring, dreary **7** droning, humdrum, one-note, uniform **8** singsong, unvaried **9** unvarying **10** pedestrian, repetitive **11** repetitious

monotony
6 tedium **7** humdrum **8** flatness, sameness **10** uniformity

monsoon
6 deluge **8** downpour **9** rainstorm **10** cloudburst

monster
3 orc **4** ogre **5** beast, freak, giant, whale **6** mutant, ogress **8** behemoth, bogeyman, colossus, giantess **9** hellhound, leviathan, manticore
biblical: **5** Rehab **8** Behemoth **9** Leviathan
female: **6** Gorgon, Medusa, Scylla
fire-breathing: **6** dragon, Typhon **7** Chimera **8** Chimaera
fowl-dragon: **10** cockatrice
French: **8** Tarasque
Hebrew: **5** golem
horse-fish: **11** hippocampus
hundred-armed: **9** Enceladus
hundred-eyed: **5** Argus
hundred-handed: **8** Briareus
lion-eagle: **7** griffin
nine-headed: **5** Hydra
serpent-headed: **6** gorgon
study of: **10** teratology
three-bodied: **6** Geryon
three-headed dog: **8** Cerberus
two-headed dog: **6** Orthos
water: **6** kraken
woman-bird: **5** Harpy
woman-lion: **6** Sphinx
woman-serpent: **7** Echidna
(see also **dragon, giant**)

monstrosity
5 freak **6** horror **7** eyesore, outrage, prodigy **8** atrocity, enormity **11** abomination **12** malformation

monstrous
4 huge, vast **5** awful, giant, large **7** glaring, heinous, hellish, hideous, immense, inhuman, mammoth, massive, titanic **8** aberrant, abnormal, colossal, deformed, dreadful, enormous, fiendish, freakish, gigantic, god-awful, gruesome, horrible, infamous, shocking, towering **9** atrocious, egregious, fantastic, frightful, grotesque, humongous, loathsome, malformed, unnatural **10** diabolical, flagitious, gargantuan, horrendous, impressive, monumental, outrageous, prodigious, scandalous, stupendous, tremendous

montage
4 olio **6** jumble, medley **7** mélange, mixture **9** composite, patchwork, potpourri **10** assortment, miscellany **12** conglomerate

Montagues' enemies
8 Capulets

Montaigne's forte
5 essay

Montana
capital: **6** Helena
city: **5** Butte **7** Bozeman **8** Billings, Missoula **10** Great Falls
lake: **8** Flathead
motto: **9** Oro y plata

mountain: **7** Granite (Peak)
nickname: **8** Treasure (State)
park: **7** Glacier
river: **8** Missouri **11** Yellowstone
state bird: **10** meadowlark
state flower: **10** bitterroot
state tree: **13** ponderosa pine

Montenegro
capital: **7** Cetinje **9** Podgorica
language: **7** Serbian
monetary unit: **4** euro
park: **8** Durmitor
river: **3** Lim **4** Piva, Tara, Zita **6** Morača
sea: **8** Adriatic

Monteverdi opera
5 Orfeo **7** Arianna

Montezuma
capital: **12** Tenochtitlán
conqueror: **6** Cortés, Cortéz (Hernán, Hernando)
people: **6** Aztecs
revenge: **8** diarrhea

month
Hindu: **3** Pus **4** Asin, Jeth, Magh **5** Aghan, Chait, Sawan **6** Asargh, Bhadon, Kartik, Phagun **7** Baisakh
Jewish: **2** Ab **4** Adar, Elul, Iyar **5** Nisan, Sivan, Tebet **6** Kislev, Shebat, Tammuz, Tishri **7** Heshvan
Muslim: **4** Rabi **5** Rajab, Safar **6** Jumada, Sha'ban **7** Ramadan, Shawwal **8** Muharram **9** Dhu'l-Hijja, Dhu'l-Qa'dah

Montmartre church
10 Sacré Coeur

Montserrat
capital: **8** Plymouth
discoverer: **8** Columbus (Christopher)
location: **10** West Indies
territory of: **7** Britain
volcano: **9** Soufrière

monument
5 cairn, stela, stupa **7** memento, tribute **8** archives, cenotaph, document, memorial **9** footstone, headstone, tombstone **10** gravestone **11** grave marker, testimonial
prehistoric: **6** dolmen, menhir **8** cromlech, megalith

monumental
4 epic, huge, vast **6** mighty, mortal **7** awesome, immense, mammoth, massive **8** enormous, gigantic, historic, majestic, towering **9** monstrous **10** prodigious, stupendous, tremendous **11** mountainous, outstanding **12** overwhelming

mooch
3 bat, beg, bum **4** grub, roam, rove **5** amble, cadge, drift, range, slink, sneak, steal, stray **6** ramble, sponge, wander **7** maunder, meander, saunter **8** freeload, scrounge **9** panhandle

mooching
7 beggary **9** mendicity **10** mendicancy

mood
3 air **4** aura, feel, tone, whim **5** fancy, humor **6** spirit, temper, vagary **7** caprice, emotion, feeling, mind-set **8** ambiance, ambience **9** character, semblance **10** atmosphere **11** disposition, personality, temperament

moody
4 glum **5** mopey **6** fickle, gloomy **7** pensive **8** unstable **9** mercurial, whimsical **10** capricious, changeable, depressive, inconstant, melancholy **13** temperamental

moola
4 cash, coin, pelf, swag **5** bread, dough, money **6** dinero, specie, wampum **7** cabbage, scratch **9** long green

moon
4 gape, mope **5** dream **6** dawdle **8** languish **9** satellite
dark area: **4** mare **5** maria (plural) **7** farside
god: **3** Sin **5** Nanna **6** Meztli
goddess: **4** Luna **5** Diana, Tanit **6** Hecate, Hekate, Selena, Selene, Tanith **7** Artemis, Astarte
period: **5** phase
valley: **4** rill
vehicle: **3** LEM
(see also **satellite**)

Moon and Sixpence author
7 Maugham (W. Somerset)

mooncalf
4 dolt, fool **5** dunce, ninny **7** jackass, tomfool **9** simpleton

moonfish
4 opah **5** platy

Moon River composer
7 Mancini (Henry)

moonshine
4 bosh, jake **5** hokum **6** bunkum, humbug **7** bootleg, eyewash, hogwash **8** homebrew, malarkey, nonsense, tommyrot **9** poppycock **10** balderdash, bathtub gin, contraband, flapdoodle **11** mountain dew **12** blatherskite

Moonstone, The
author: **7** Collins (Wilkie)
detective: **4** Cuff

moonstruck
4 daft, nuts **5** batty, corny, flaky, kooky, mushy, nutty, sappy, wacko, wacky **6** crazed, cuckoo, fruity, insane, screwy **7** berserk, bonkers, lunatic, maudlin, touched **8** romantic **9** nostalgic, schmaltzy **10** lovey-dovey, saccharine, unbalanced **11** sentimental

moor
3 bog, fen **4** dock, fell **5** berth, catch, tie up **6** anchor, Berber, fasten, Muslim, secure, tether **7** peat bog **8** make fast, Moroccan
fictional: **7** Othello

moose
6 cervid
female: **3** cow
male: **4** bull
relative: **3** elk **4** deer **6** wapiti **7** caribou **8** reindeer

moot
5 argue, plead **6** broach, debate **7** agitate, bring up, canvass, discuss, dispute, dubious, suggest, suspect **8** abstract, academic, arguable, disputed, doubtful **9** debatable, introduce, thrash out, uncertain, unsettled, ventilate **10** disputable, unresolved **11** problematic **12** questionable **13** controversial

mop
4 swab, wipe

mope
4 fret, idle, moon, pine, pout, sigh, stew, sulk **5** brood, drift, mosey **6** dawdle, linger **7** maunder, meander, saunter **8** languish

mopes
4 funk **5** blues, dumps, ennui, slump **7** dismals, malaise, sadness **8** dolefuls **10** depression, melancholy **11** unhappiness

mopey
3 low **4** blue, down, glum **6** broody, droopy, morose **7** doleful **8** cast down, dejected, downcast **9** depressed **10** dispirited, melancholy, spiritless

moppet
3 kid, tot **4** tike, tyke **5** chick, child **7** toddler **8** juvenile **9** youngster

mop up
4 beat, drub, dust, lick, whip **6** absorb, garner, gather **7** shellac, trounce **8** complete, lambaste **9** overwhelm

moral
3 saw **4** good, just, pure, rule **5** adage, axiom, gnome, maxim, noble, right **6** chaste, decent, dictum, honest, lesson, proper, saying, truism **7** epigram, ethical, preachy, precept, proverb, upright, virtual **8** aphorism, apothegm, didactic, elevated, sermonic, virtuous **9** honorable, righteous **10** high-minded, principled, scrupulous, upstanding **11** right-minded **13** conscientious

morale
4 mood **5** heart **6** esprit, mettle, spirit, temper **7** resolve **10** confidence **13** esprit de corps

moralistic
5 noble, pious **7** canting, ethical **8** didactic, virtuous **9** righteous **10** principled **11** pharisaical, right-minded **13** sanctimonious

morality
5 ethic, honor, mores **6** purity, virtue **7** decency, probity **8** goodness **9** integrity, rectitude, rightness **11** saintliness, uprightness **13** righteousness

moralize
6 preach **7** lecture **9** preachify, sermonize **11** pontificate

morals
5 mores **6** ethics, ideals **8** scruples **9** integrity, standards **10** principles

morass
3 bog, fen, web **4** knot, maze, mesh, mire, quag, trap **5** marsh, skein, snarl, swamp **6** jungle, muddle, tangle **8** quagmire **9** imbroglio

moratorium
3 ban **5** delay **8** interval **10** suspension

moray
3 eel

morbid
4 dark, sick **5** moody **6** gloomy, grisly, morose, sickly, sullen **7** unsound **8** diseased, gruesome **9** saturnine, unhealthy **11** melancholic, unwholesome **12** pathological

mordancy
7 acidity **8** acerbity, acridity, acrimony, asperity, pungency **9** harshness, sharpness **10** causticity, trenchancy **11** astringency

mordant
4 acid, keen **5** acerb, acrid, salty, sharp **6** biting **7** acerbic, burning, caustic, cutting, pungent **8** incisive, sardonic, scathing **9** sarcastic, trenchant

Mordecai
cousin: **6** Esther
father: **4** Jair
mother: **6** Esther

more
3 new, too **4** also, else, plus **5** added, again, along, extra, fresh, older, other, spare **6** as well, better, nearer, withal **7** another, besides, farther, further, greater **8** likewise, moreover **9** increased **10** additional

More book
6 Utopia

more or less
5 about, circa **7** roughly **13** approximately

moreover
3 and, too **4** also **6** as well, withal **7** besides, further **8** likewise **10** in addition **11** furthermore **12** additionally

mores
6 ethics, habits, values **7** beliefs, customs, manners **8** folkways **9** amenities, etiquette **10** civilities **11** proprieties

Morgan le Fay
9 sorceress
brother: 6 Arthur (King)

moribund
5 dying **6** ebbing, fading **7** dormant, outworn **8** decaying, expiring, inactive **9** declining **11** obsolescent **13** deteriorating

Mormon Church
administrative unit: 4 ward **5** stake
founder: 5 Smith (Joseph)
leader: 5 Young (Brigham)
priest: 5 elder

Mormon State
4 Utah

morning
4 dawn **5** sunup **6** aurora **7** dawning, sunrise **8** cockcrow, daybreak, daylight, forenoon
moisture: 3 dew **8** dewdrops
song: 6 aubade

Morocco
capital: 5 Rabat
city: 3 Fès **6** Agadir, Meknès **7** Tangier **9** Marrakech, Marrakesh **10** Casablanca
coast: 7 Barbary
language: 6 Arabic, Berber
monetary unit: 6 dirham
mountain, range: 3 Rif **5** Atlas **7** Toubkal
neighbor: 5 Spain **7** Algeria **13** Western Sahara
sea: 13 Mediterranean

moron
4 dodo, dolt, dope, fool **5** dummy, dunce, idiot **6** cretin, dimwit, stupid **7** dullard, half-wit **8** dumbbell, imbecile, numskull **9** ignoramus, lamebrain, numbskull, simpleton

moronic
4 dull, dumb **6** simple, stupid **8** backward, retarded **9** brainless, dim-witted, imbecilic **10** half-witted, slow-witted **12** feebleminded, simpleminded

morose
4 dour, glum, sour **5** moody, sulky **6** cranky, crusty, gloomy, morbid, sullen **7** crabbed, unhappy **9** depressed, saturnine **10** depressive, ill-humored, melancholy

morph
6 change, mutate **7** convert **9** transform, transmute **12** metamorphose, transmogrify

Morpheus
father: 6 Hypnos
god of: 5 sleep

Morrison novel
4 Jazz, Love, Sula **7** Beloved **9** Bluest Eye (The) **13** Song of Solomon

Morse code
dash: 3 dah
dot: 3 dit

morsel
3 bit, ort **4** bite **5** crumb, goody, piece, scrap, snack, taste, treat **6** dainty, nibble, tidbit **7** soupçon **8** delicacy, fragment, kickshaw, mouthful

mortal
3 man **5** awful, being, fatal, frail, human, party **6** deadly, lethal, person **7** deathly, earthly, extreme, fleshly, tedious, worldly **8** creature, ruthless, temporal **9** merciless, personage **10** implacable, individual, perishable **11** conceivable

mortality
5 flesh **7** mankind **8** fatality, humanity **9** death rate, humankind, lethality **10** deadliness

mortar
5 grout **6** binder, cannon, cement, vessel **7** plaster, sealant **8** howitzer, ordnance

Morte d'Arthur author
6 Malory (Thomas)

mortgage
4 hock, lien, pawn **6** pledge **10** obligation

mortician
8 embalmer **10** undertaker

mortified
6 shamed **7** ascetic, ashamed, austere **8** redfaced **9** chagrined **10** humiliated, shamefaced **11** embarrassed

mortify
5 abash, shame **6** deaden, dismay **7** chagrin, perturb **8** disgrace **9** discomfit, embarrass, humiliate

mortuary
8 funereal **10** sepulchral **11** funeral home

mosaic
5 inlay **7** chimera **8** terrazzo **9** composite, patchwork **12** tessellation
piece: 6 smalto **7** tessera **8** tesserae (plural)

Moscow
cathedral: 8 St. Basil's **11** Saint Basil's
citadel: 7 Kremlin
resident: 9 Muscovite

Moses
brother: 5 Aaron
brother-in-law: 5 Hobab
deathplace: 4 Nebo
father-in-law: 6 Jethro
sister: 6 Miriam
son: 7 Eliezer, Gershom
spy: 5 Caleb
successor: 6 Joshua
wife: 8 Zipporah

mosey
4 mope **5** amble, drift **6** dawdle, linger, ramble, stroll, wander **7** maunder, meander, saunter

mosh
4 slam **9** slam-dance

Moslem
see **Muslim**

mosque
6 masjid
niche: 6 mihrab
prayer caller: 7 muezzin
turret: 7 minaret

mosquito
5 culex **7** skeeter
eater: 3 bat **4** bird, frog **9** dragonfly
genus: 5 Aëdes, Culex **9** Anopheles

moss
9 bryophyte
kind: 4 peat **8** sphagnum
part: 4 seta **7** capsule, rhizoid
study of: 8 bryology

mossback
4 fogy **6** fossil **10** fuddy-duddy **11** reactionary **12** antediluvian, conservative **13** stick-in-the-mud

mostly
6 mainly **7** chiefly, largely, overall, usually **9** generally, primarily **11** principally **13** predominantly

mote
3 bit, dot, jot **4** iota, whit **5** grain, point, speck, trace **8** flyspeck, particle

moth
immature: 5 larva **6** larvae (plural) **11** caterpillar
kind: 4 luna **7** codling, tussock **8** Cecropia, silkworm **9** browntail
order: 11 Lepidoptera

moth-eaten
4 worn **5** dated, dingy, faded, mangy, moldy, musty, passé, ratty, seedy **6** bygone, old hat, patchy, shabby **7** antique, archaic, raggedy, run-down, unkempt **8** decrepit, outdated, outmoded, tattered, timeworn **10** antiquated, down-at-heel, threadbare **11** dilapidated

mother
2 ma **3** dam, mom **4** mama, root **5** fount, mammy, mater, momma, mommy, mummy, nurse **6** matrix, origin, source **7** care for, nurture **9** prototype, rootstock **10** provenance, wellspring
combining form: 4 matr **5** matri, matro
French: 4 mère
German: 6 Mutter
Italian: 5 madre
Portuguese: 3 mãe
Spanish: 5 madre

mother country
8 homeland **10** fatherland

Mother Courage author
6 Brecht (Bertolt)

motherly
8 maternal **9** nurturing **10** protective

mother-of-pearl
5 nacre

Mother of Presidents
8 Virginia

Mother of the Gods
3 Ops **4** Rhea **6** Cybele

motif
4 idea, text **5** point, theme, topic **6** design, device, figure, matter **7** pattern, subject **8** idée fixe **13** subject matter

motion
4 stir, sway **6** signal **7** gesture **8** movement, proposal, stirring **9** agitation

motionless
5 fixed, inert, still **6** frozen, static **7** stalled **8** becalmed, immobile, stagnant, unmoving **9** immovable, steadfast **10** stationary, stock-still

motion picture
see **movie**

motivate
4 fire, goad, move, spur **5** impel, pique, rouse **6** arouse, excite, incite, induce, prompt **7** actuate, inspire, provoke, quicken, trigger **8** inspirit, persuade **9** galvanize, influence, stimulate

motivation
4 spur **5** drive **7** impetus, impulse **8** ambition, catalyst, stimulus **9** impulsion, incentive, stimulant **10** incitation, incitement **11** inspiration, instigation, provocation

motive
3 aim, end **4** spur **5** cause, point, theme, topic **6** design, device, figure, intent, matter, object, reason, spring **7** impulse, pattern, purpose, subject **8** stimulus **9** incentive, intention, rationale **10** incitement, inducement **11** inspiration

motley
4 olio, stew **5** mixed, salad **6** jumble, medley, varied **7** dappled, diverse, piebald **8** assorted, pastiche **9** disparate, multihued **10** assortment, hodgepodge, hotchpotch, miscellany, multicolor, salmagundi, variegated **11** gallimaufry, varicolored **12** conglomerate, multicolored, multifarious, parti-colored **13** heterogeneous, miscellaneous, polychromatic

motor
3 car **4** auto, ride **5** buggy, drive **6** cruise, engine **7** machine **10** automobile

motorboat
6 launch **7** cruiser, inboard **8** outboard, runabout **12** cabin cruiser

motorcycle
7 chopper 8 minibike 9 trail bike
adjunct: 7 sidecar

Motown
7 Detroit
founder: 5 Gordy (Berry)
group: 8 Four Tops, Miracles, Supremes 9 Vandellas 11 Temptations

mottle
4 spot 5 fleck 6 blotch, dapple, marble 7 spatter, speckle, stipple, splotch

mottled
5 tabby 7 blotchy, dappled, flecked, spotted 8 blotched, brindled, speckled 9 checkered 10 variegated

motto
3 cry 5 adage, axiom, maxim 6 byword, saying, slogan, war cry 7 precept, proverb 8 aphorism 9 battle cry, catchword, watchword 10 shibboleth 11 catchphrase

moue
3 mow, mug 4 face, pout 7 grimace

mound
4 bank, berm, cock, heap, hill, hump, mass, pile 5 cairn, drift, knoll, shock, stack 6 barrow, tumuli (plural) 7 bulwark, hillock, rampart, tumulus 9 elevation 10 embankment
Buddhist: 5 stupa
burial, Eastern Europe: 6 kurgan
of detritus: 4 kame
of sand: 4 dune
of stones: 5 cairn

mount
3 alp, wax 4 lift, peak, rise, show, soar 5 arise, build, climb, frame, horse, put on, raise, rouse, scale, set up, stage, steed, swell 6 ascend, aspire, deepen, expand, launch, uprear 7 advance, augment, display, enhance, enlarge, install, magnify, produce, support, upsurge 8 bestride, escalade, escalate, heighten, increase, multiply, redouble 9 aggravate, intensify 10 promontory

mountain
3 alp, lot 4 bank, crag, dome, heap, hill, hulk, lump, mass, mesa, much, peak, pile, slew 5 bluff, butte, drift, mound, shock, stack 6 height, massif
Adirondack: 9 Whiteface
Africa's highest: 4 Kibo
Alaska: 4 Bona 6 Denali 7 Foraker, Sanford 8 McKinley, Wrangell
Alaska-Canada: 10 Saint Elias
Alberta: 6 Castle 10 Eisenhower
Alps: 4 Rosa (Monte) 5 Blanc, Eiger 8 Jungfrau 10 Matterhorn
Andes: 4 Ruiz 5 Torrá
Angola: 4 Moco
Antarctica: 4 Mohl 6 Vinson (Massif) 7 Gardner 9 Elizabeth
Apennines: 5 Amaro
Appalachians: 8 Mitchell 10 Kittatinny 10 Washington 13 Clingmans Dome
Argentina: 4 Azul 5 Negra, Payún 9 Aconcagua
Asia Minor: 3 Ida
Australia: 4 Ziel 5 Bruce 6 Cradle 9 Kosciusko
Bavaria: 5 Arber
Berkshires: 8 Greylock
biblical: 5 Horeb, Sinai, Tabor 6 Ararat, Carmel, Gilboa, Gilead, Hermon, Moriah, Olivet, Pisgah 7 Lebanon 8 Har Tavor
Black Hills: 6 Harney (Peak) 8 Rushmore
Bolivia: 5 Cuzco, Tahua, Ubina 6 Sajama, Sorata 8 Illimani
Borneo: 4 Raja 8 Kinabalu, Kinabulu
California: 5 Guyot 6 Shasta, Sonora 7 Palomar, Whitney 8 Half Dome, Tuolumne 9 Excelsior 10 Buena Vista, Stanislaus
Canada: 5 Keele, Logan
Canaries: 5 Telde 8 Tenerife
Carpathian: 4 Rysy
Cascades: 7 Rainier
Catskill: 6 Pisgah
Caucasus: 5 Ushba 6 Elbrus
Chile: 4 Mayo, Pili 5 Paine, Pular
China: 4 Emei, Song
Colombia: 4 Tama 5 Neiva
Colorado: 3 Ute 5 Eolus, Pikes (Peak) 9 Purgatory (Peak)
Costa Rica: 6 Blanco 14 Chirripó Grande
Cuba: 8 Turquino
Cyprus: 7 Olympus, Troodos
depression: 3 col
Dominican Republic: 6 Duarte 8 Trujillo
Ecuador: 10 Chimborazo
Egypt: 4 Musa 5 Sinai
England: 11 Scafell Pike
Ethiopia: 4 Guna 5 Holla
Fiji: 8 Victoria 9 Tomaniivi
foot: 8 piedmont
France: 5 Blanc (Mont), Pilat
French Guiana: 5 Amana
Gabon: 8 Iboundji
Georgia: 8 Springer 10 Oglethorpe
Germany: 7 Zollern 9 Zugspitze 11 Fichtelberg
Glacier National Park: 8 Kootenal
Greece: 3 Ida 4 Ossa 5 Athos, Levka 6 Pelion 7 Helicon, Olympus 9 Parnassus, Psiloriti 10 Pendelikon, Pentelicus
Greenland: 9 Gunnbjorn
Himalayas: 3 Api 6 Khamet, Lhotse 7 Everest 9 Annapurna 10 Gasherbrum
Honshū: 4 Yari 10 Yarigatake

Idaho: **11** Pend Oreille
India: **5** Japvo
Indonesia: **4** Lawu **5** Kwoka, Lawoe, Raung **6** Raoeng, Semeru **7** Kerinci
Iran: **8** Damavand
Israel: **5** Meron **6** Carmel
Italy: **4** Etna **8** Vesuvius
Ivory Coast: **5** Nimba
Japan: **4** Fuji, Sobo **5** Iwate, Oyama **7** Fujisan, Sobozan **8** Fujiyama
Java: **5** Liman **6** Slamet
Jordan: **3** Hor **5** Hārūn **6** Gilead
Karakoram Range: **7** Dapsang **10** Masherbrum **12** Godwin Austen
Maine: **8** Katahdin **10** Saddleback
Malaysia: **5** Ophir, Tahan **6** Ledang
Mediterranean entrance: **5** Calpe **9** Gibraltar
Mexico: **7** Orizaba (Pico de)
Montana: **8** Gallatin
Nevada: **3** Ely
Newfoundland: **9** Gros Morne
New Hampshire: **9** Monadnock
New York: **4** Bear **5** Marcy
New Zealand: **3** Una **4** Cook **7** Aorangi **8** Aspiring
North America's highest: **6** Denali **8** McKinley
North Carolina: **8** Mitchell
Oahu: **5** Kaala
Oman: **4** Sham
Oregon: **4** Hood
Pakistan: **9** Tirich Mir
Papua New Guinea: **7** Wilhelm **8** Victoria
peak: **3** top **4** acme, apex, roof **5** crest, crown **6** summit, vertex, zenith **8** pinnacle
Pennine Alps: **4** Rosa (Monte) **10** Matterhorn, Mont Cervin
Philippines: **3** Apo, Iba **4** High, Labo **5** Silay
Pyrenees: **11** de Vignemale
ridge: **4** spur **5** arête, crest **7** sawbuck
Romania: **11** Moldoveanul
Russia's highest: **6** Elbrus
Scotland: **8** Ben Nevis
Sicily: **4** Etna
South America: **7** Roraima **9** Aconcagua
South Dakota: **6** Custer (Peak)
Spain: **5** Yelmo **8** Mulhacén **11** Pico de Aneto
Switzerland: **3** Dom **4** Dôle, Rosa (Monte), Tödi **5** Eiger, Mönch **6** La Dôle, Rusein **7** Pilatus **8** Jungfrau **10** Matterhorn
Syria: **4** Druz **5** Duruz
Tanzania: **11** Kilimanjaro
Tasmania: **4** Ossa
Tennessee: **13** Clingmans Dome
Togo: **4** Agou
Turkey: **3** Ida
Utah: **5** Kings
Vermont: **8** Ascutney, Haystack, Stratton **9** Mansfield
Vietnam: **8** Ngoo Linh
Virginia: **6** Rogers
Washington: **7** Olympus, Rainier **11** Saint Helens
Western Hemisphere's highest: **9** Aconcagua
White Mts.: **10** Washington
world's highest: **7** Everest
Wyoming: **3** Elk **5** Cloud **7** Gannett (Peak) **10** Grand Teton
Yukon: **4** King **5** Logan

mountain climbing
equipment: **2** ax **3** axe, nut **5** piton **7** crampon **9** carabiner
maneuver: **6** rappel **10** rappelling

mountain dew
see **moonshine**

mountain formation
7 orogeny **10** orogenesis

mountainous
4 huge, vast **6** alpine, mighty **7** immense, mammoth, massive **8** enormous, gigantic, towering **10** monumental, prodigious

mountain pass
3 col, gap
Afghanistan-Pakistan: **6** Khyber
Alps: **5** Gries
California: **4** Muir **6** Sonora
China-Myanmar: **5** Namni
Colorado: **3** Ute **5** Mosca, Muddy, Music, Raton
Europe: **8** Moravian
Greece: **5** Rupel
Hindu Kush Mts.: **5** Dorah, Durah
Pakistan: **5** Bolan, Gomal, Gumal
Sierra Nevada: **4** Mono
Switzerland: **5** Furka, Gemmi **7** Grimsel **8** Lötschen
Tunisia: **4** Faïd
Ukrainian: **5** Uzhok
Wyoming: **5** Union

mountain range
Asia: **5** Altai, Altay **8** Himalaya, Tien Shan **9** Altai Shan, Altay Shan, Himalayan, Himalayas, Hindu Kush
Australia: **8** Flinders
Europe: **4** Alps **10** Carpathian
Germany: **4** Harz **5** Hartz
Greece: **4** Oeta
India: **5** Ghats
Iran: **6** Zagros
Italy: **9** Apennines, Dolomites
Mexico: **11** Sierra Madre
North Africa: **5** Atlas
North America: **5** Rocky **7** Rockies **11** Appalachian
Russia: **4** Ural

Scotland: **9** Grampians
Sinai: **9** Gebel Musa
Slovakia: **5** Tatra, Tatry **9** High Tatra
South America: **5** Andes
Spain: **8** Pyrenees
Turkey: **3** Ida **6** Taurus **7** Kazdagi
United States: **5** Rocky, White **6** Brooks **7** Cascade, Olympic, Rockies, Sawatch, Wasatch **8** Absaroka, Aleutian, Catskill, Wrangell **9** Blue Ridge, Wind River **10** Adirondack, Bitterroot, Black Hills, Clearwater, Grand Teton
Zimbabwe: **6** Matopo (Hills) **7** Matoppo (Hills)

Mountain State
7 Montana **12** West Virginia

mountebank
5 quack **6** con man **8** swindler **9** charlatan **11** flimflammer, quacksalver **13** confidence man

Mount St. Helens
7 volcano

mourn
3 rue **6** bemoan, bewail, grieve, lament, sorrow **7** deplore, protest

mournful
3 sad **6** dismal, gloomy, rueful, triste, woeful **7** doleful, forlorn, unhappy **8** dejected, desolate, dolorous, funereal, grievous, wretched **9** dirgelike, plaintive **10** depressing, despondent, dispirited, lugubrious, melancholy **11** melancholic **12** heavyhearted

mournfulness
5 blues, dumps, gloom **7** dismals, sadness **9** dejection **10** blue devils, depression, melancholy

mourning
5 grief **7** keening, remorse, wailing, weeping **8** grieving **9** lamenting, morbidity, sorrowing, ululation **10** heartbreak **11** bereavement, lamentation

Mourning Becomes Electra author
6 O'Neill (Eugene)

mourning period, Jewish
5 shiva **6** shivah

mourning symbol
7 armband

mouse
6 rodent, shiner **8** black eye
meadow: **4** vole

mousy
3 shy **4** drab, dull **5** plain, quiet, timid **7** bashful **8** retiring, timorous **9** colorless, diffident, shrinking **11** unassertive **12** self-effacing

mouth
3 gob, maw **4** trap **5** chops **6** kisser **8** entrance **10** embouchure

mouthlike opening
5 stoma **7** stomata (plural)

mouthpiece
5 organ **6** puppet **7** speaker **8** front man **9** spokesman **10** figurehead **11** spokeswoman **12** spokesperson

mouthwatering
5 sapid, tasty, yummy **6** savory, toothy **9** delicious, palatable, succulent, toothsome **10** appetizing, delectable **11** good-tasting

mouthy
4 glib **5** gabby, talky, windy **7** verbose, voluble **8** effusive **9** bombastic, garrulous, talkative

movable
5 loose **6** mobile, motile, roving **8** portable **10** changeable

movables
5 goods **7** effects **8** chattels **10** belongings **11** furnishings

move
4 relo **5** budge, leave, march, shift, start, touch **6** affect, depart, incite, induce **7** advance, conduct, inspire, migrate, proceed, propose, request **8** dislodge, displace, motivate, persuade, progress, relocate, resettle, transfer, withdraw **9** influence, instigate, stimulate, transport **10** relocation

movement
4 flow, stir **5** tempo, trend **6** action, motion **7** crusade **8** activity, campaign, dynamism, maneuver, progress, stirring, tendency, velocity **9** migration
music: **4** moto
reflex: **5** taxis
stimulated: **7** kinesis

movie
4 cine, film, show **5** flick **6** cinema, talkie **7** picture **9** photoplay **11** picture show **13** motion picture **7** western
genre: **3** war **4** cult, epic **5** adult, anime, crime, oater **6** action, comedy, cowboy, family, horror, silent **7** cartoon, fantasy, Western **9** adventure, animation **11** documentary, martial arts **12** mockumentary
short: **4** clip **8** newsreel

movie director
American: **3** Lee (Spike), Ray (Nicholas) **4** Coen (Joel), Ford (John), Hill (George Roy), Mann (Anthony), Penn (Arthur), Ritt (Martin), Ross (Herbert), Sirk (Douglas), Wise (Robert) **5** Allen (Woody), Ashby (Hal), Brown (Clarence), Capra (Frank), Cukor (George), Demme (Jonathan), Donen (Stanley), Fosse (Bob), Hawks (Howard), Ivory (James), Jonze (Spike), Kazan (Elia), LeRoy (Mervyn), Logan (Joshua), Lucas (George), Lumet (Sidney), Lynch (David), Moore (Michael),

Roach (Hal), Stone (Oliver), Vidor (King), Walsh (Raoul), Whale (James), Wyler (William), Zwick (Ed) **6** Altman (Robert), Beatty (Warren), Benton (Robert), Brooks (Richard), Burton (Tim), Cimino (Michael), Corman (Roger), Curtiz (Michael), Fuller (Samuel), Gibson (Mel), Hanson (Curtis), Howard (Ron), Huston (John), Kramer (Stanley), Malick (Terrence), Pakula (Alan), Parker (Alan), Seaton (George), Waters (John), Welles (Orson), Wilder (Billy) **7** Borzage (Frank), Cameron (James), Chaplin (Charlie), Coppola (Francis Ford, Sofia), Costner (Kevin), De Mille (Cecil B.), De Palma (Brian), Fleming (Victor), Gilliam (Terry), Jewison (Norman), Kubrick (Stanley), McCarey (Leo), Nichols (Mike), Pollack (Sydney), Redford (Robert), Siodmak (Robert), Stevens (George), Sturges (Preston), Van Sant (Gus), Wellman (William) **8** Avildsen (John), Eastwood (Clint), Flaherty (Robert), Friedkin (William), Griffith (David Wark), Grosbard (Ulu), Jarmusch (Jim), Levinson (Barry), Lubitsch (Ernst), Marshall (Penny), Minnelli (Vincente), Mulligan (Robert), Scorsese (Martin), Zemeckis (Robert) **9** Carpenter (John), Hitchcock (Alfred), Milestone (Lewis), Peckinpah (Sam), Preminger (Otto), Spielberg (Steven), Sternberg (Josef von), Streisand (Barbra), Tarantino (Quentin), Zinnemann (Fred) **10** Cassavetes (John), Heckerling (Amy), Mankiewicz (Joseph), Soderbergh (Steven) **11** Bogdanovich (Peter) **13** Frankenheimer (John)
Australian: **4** Weir (Peter) **6** Noonan (Chris) **9** Armstrong (Gillian), Beresford (Bruce)
Austrian: **4** Lang (Fritz) **8** Stroheim (Erich von) **9** Sternberg (Josef von)
British: **4** Lean (David), Reed (Carol) **5** Leigh (Mike), Loach (Ken), Losey (Joseph), Reisz (Karel), Scott (Ridley) **6** Figgis (Mike), Frears (Stephen), Jordan (Neil), Newell (Mike), Parker (Alan), Powell (Michael) **7** Boorman (John), Branagh (Kenneth), Forsyth (Bill) **8** Anderson (Lindsay) **9** Hitchcock (Alfred) **10** Richardson (Tony) **11** Schlesinger (John)
Chinese: **3** Lee (Ang) **4** Chen (Kaige) **5** Zhang (Yimou)
French: **4** Demy (Jacques), Tati (Jacques), Vigo (Jean) **5** Malle (Louis) **6** Godard (Jean-Luc), Ophüls (Marcel), Renoir (Jean), Rohmer (Eric) **7** Bresson (Robert), Chabrol (Claude), Cocteau (Jean), Resnais (Alain), Rivette (Jacques) **8** Truffaut (François)
German: **6** Herzog (Werner), Ophüls (Max) **7** Wenders (Wim) **8** Petersen (Wolfgang) **10** Fassbinder (Rainer Werner) **11** Riefenstahl (Leni), Schlöndorff (Volker)
Italian: **5** Leone (Sergio) **6** De Sica (Vittorio) **7** Fellini (Federico) **8** Pasolini (Pier Paolo), Visconti (Luchino) **9** Antonioni (Michelangelo) **10** Bertolucci (Bernardo), Rossellini (Roberto), Wertmüller (Lina), Zeffirelli (Franco)
Japanese: **3** Ozu (Yasujiru) **5** Itami (Juzo) **8** Kurosawa (Akira), Miyazaki (Hayao) **9** Mizoguchi (Kenji)
Mexican: **6** Cuarón (Alfonso)
New Zealand: **7** Campion (Jane)
Polish **5** Wajda (Ardrzej) **7** Holland (Agnieszka) **8** Polanski (Roman)
Russian: **9** Tarkovsky (Andrei) **10** Eisenstein (Sergei)
Spanish: **6** Buñuel (Luis) **9** Almodóvar (Pedro)
Swedish: **7** Bergman (Ingmar) **10** Zetterling (Mai)

movie producer
American: **3** Fox (William) **4** Cohn (Jack) **5** Lasky (Jesse), Mayer (Louis B.), Zukor (Adolph) **6** Warner (Jack L.), Zanuck (Darryl, Richard) **7** Goldwyn (Samuel), Laemmle (Carl) **8** Selznick (David O.) **9** Weinstein (Bob, Harvey)
Austrian: **9** Reinhardt (Max)

moving
5 astir **6** mobile **7** emotive, rousing **8** arousing, exciting, gripping, pathetic, poignant, stirring, touching **9** affecting, emotional, inspiring, transient **11** stimulating

moving stairs
9 escalator

mow
3 cut **4** clip, crop, fell, heap, moue, pile, raze, rick **5** level, shave, shear, stack **7** grimace **9** knock down

moxie
3 pep, vim, zip **4** grit, guts **5** brass, heart, nerve, oomph, pluck, savvy, spunk, vigor **6** energy, mettle, spirit, starch **7** cojones, courage, know-how **8** backbone **9** fortitude **10** get-up-and-go, resolution **13** determination

Mozambique
capital: **6** Maputo
language: **5** Bantu **7** Swahili **10** Portuguese
monetary unit: **7** metical
neighbor: **6** Malawi, Zambia **8** Tanzania, Zimbabwe **9** Swaziland **11** South Africa
river: **6** Ruvuma **7** Limpopo, Zambezi

Mozart, Wolfgang Amadeus
birthplace: **8** Salzburg
cataloger: **6** Köchel (Ludwig)
deathplace: **6** Vienna
opera: **8** Idomeneo **10** Magic Flute (The) **11** Don Giovanni, Il Rè Pastore **12** Così Fan Tutte **16** Marriage of Figaro (The)

MP's prey
4 AWOL **8** deserter

Mr.
French: **8** Monsieur

German: **4** Herr
Italian: **6** Signor
Spanish:
5 Señor

Mr. Moto star
5 Lorre (Peter)

Mrs.
French: **3** Mme. **6** Madame
German: **4** Frau
Italian: **3** Sra. **7** Signora
Spanish: **3** Sra. **6** Señora

Mrs. Grundy
4 prig **5** prude **7** puritan **8** bluenose

much
3 oft **4** long, many, most **5** often **6** highly, hugely, plenty **7** greatly, notably **8** abundant **9** eminently, extremely
combining form: **4** poly **5** multi

Much Ado About Nothing character
4 Hero **7** Claudio, Don John **8** Beatrice, Benedick, Dogberry

muck
3 goo, mud **4** crap, crud, dirt, dung, glop, gook, goop, grub, gunk, junk, mess, mire, murk, plod, slog, slop, soil, toil **5** dirty, dreck, filth, grime, gumbo, slave, slime, swill, trash, waste **6** drudge, litter, manure, meddle, putter, sleaze, sludge, smirch, tinker **7** garbage, rubbish **8** nonsense **9** interfere

muckety-muck
3 VIP **5** nabob **6** bigwig, fat cat, honcho **7** big shot, kingpin, notable **8** kingfish, somebody **9** dignitary

mucky
4 foul **5** dirty, grimy, muddy, muggy, murky, nasty, soggy **6** cruddy, filthy, grubby, grungy **7** squalid, unclean

mucous
5 slimy **6** viscid

mud
4 dirt, mire, muck, ooze **5** dregs, slime **6** depths, sludge

muddle
3 mix **4** hash, mess, muck, rile, roil **5** addle, botch, mix up, snarl **6** ataxia, bungle, drivel, foul up, fumble, jumble, jungle, litter, mess up, tangle, tumble **7** clutter, confuse, fluster, perplex, rummage, shuffle, snarl up, stumble, stupefy **8** befuddle, bewilder, confound, disarray, disorder, distract, entangle, mishmash, scramble, shambles, throw off, unsettle **9** confusion, throw away **10** complicate, disarrange, discompose **11** disorganize

muddled
5 drunk, tight, tipsy, vague **7** mixed-up **8** inchoate **10** disjointed, disordered, incoherent, inebriated **11** intoxicated, unorganized

muddle through
4 cope, fare **5** get by, get on **6** manage **7** carry on, make out **8** get along

muddy
3 dim, fog **4** base, blur, drab, dull, fade, foul, hazy, oozy, roil, soil **5** befog, cloud, dingy, dirty, grime, grimy, murky **6** cloudy, gloomy, grubby, sordid, turbid **7** becloud, begrime, confuse, obscure, squalid, tarnish, unclean, unclear **8** confused

muff
4 blow, flub **5** botch, fluff **6** bobble, bollix, bungle, fumble, goof up, mess up **7** louse up, misplay, screw up **9** mishandle

muffle
3 gag **4** dull, mute, veil **5** shush **6** dampen, deaden, lessen, shroud, soften, stifle, subdue, wrap up **7** envelop, repress, silence, smother, squelch **8** bundle up, suppress, tone down

muffled
5 muted **6** dulled **7** stifled, subdued **8** deadened, obscured, silenced **9** distorted, enveloped **10** indistinct, suppressed

muffler
4 mask, veil **5** cloak, scarf

mug
3 cup, ham, mop, mow, rob **4** boob, dolt, dope, face, fool, moue, phiz, punk, puss, thug **5** dunce, idiot, mouth, rowdy, stein, tough **6** ambush, dimwit, kisser **7** assault, grimace, tankard **8** bullyboy, dumbbell, features, numskull **9** blockhead, bushwhack, ignoramus, roughneck

mugger
4 thug **6** robber **9** assailant, crocodile

muggy
4 damp **5** humid, moist **6** sticky, sultry **7** dampish

Muhammad
adopted son: **3** Ali
birthplace: **5** Mecca
camel: **5** Kaswa
daughter: **6** Fatima
deathplace: **6** Medina
deity: **5** Allah
father: **8** Abdallah, Abdullah
father-in-law: **7** Abu Bakr
flight: **6** hegira, hejira
follower: **6** Moslem, Muslim
horse: **5** Buraq **7** Alborak
religion: **5** Islam
scripture: **5** Koran
son: **7** Ibrahim
son-in-law: **3** Ali
successor: **6** caliph **7** Abu Bakr

tribe: **7** Koreish, Quraysh
uncle: **8** Abu Talib
wife: **5** Aisha **6** Ayesha **7** Khadija

mulatto
5 métis, mixed **7** mestizo **9** half-breed, half-caste **10** crossbreed

mulberry
3 fig **10** breadfruit
type: **6** banyan **11** India rubber, osage orange

mulct
4 fine, milk, rook **5** bleed, cheat, gouge **6** extort, fleece **7** deceive, defraud, forfeit, penalty, swindle **8** penalize **9** blackmail

mule
5 cross, scuff **6** bagman, hybrid **7** bastard, courier, mongrel **8** smuggler **9** crossbred, half blood, half-breed **10** crossbreed

mulish
8 contrary, perverse, stubborn **9** obstinate, pigheaded **10** bullheaded, headstrong, inflexible, refractory, unyielding **11** stiff-necked

mull
4 hash, muse **5** brood, think, weigh **6** ponder **7** reflect **8** cogitate, consider, meditate, ruminate, turn over **9** pulverize **10** deliberate **11** contemplate

multicolored
4 pied **6** motley **7** dappled **9** prismatic **10** variegated **13** polychromatic

multifarious
5 mixed **6** motley, sundry, varied **7** diverse, various **8** assorted, manifold **13** heterogeneous, miscellaneous

multiform
6 sundry, varied **7** diverse, various **8** assorted, manifold **9** disparate **12** multifarious

multilateral
9 many-sided

multiple
4 many **6** shared, sundry **7** diverse, several, various **8** assorted, manifold, numerous **9** composite

multiplicity
3 lot **4** heap, load, mass, peck **5** flood, hoard, horde **6** barrel **7** variety **8** mountain, plethora **9** diversity, great deal, profusion

multiply
3 wax **4** rise **5** boost, breed, build, mount **6** expand, extend, spread **7** amplify, augment, enlarge, magnify **8** generate, heighten, increase **9** procreate, propagate, reproduce **10** aggrandize **11** proliferate

multitude
3 mob **4** army, herd, host, mass, slew **5** crowd, crush, drove, flock, horde, swarm **6** legion, myriad, public, throng **8** populace

multitudinous
4 many **6** legion, myriad, sundry **7** copious, various **8** abundant, manifold, numerous, populous **9** countless **10** numberless, voluminous **11** innumerable

mum
4 dumb, mute **5** quiet **6** silent **8** wordless **10** speechless, tongue-tied

mumble
6 murmur, mutter **7** maunder

mumbo jumbo
4 juju **6** fetish **9** gibberish **10** hocus-pocus **11** abracadabra **12** gobbledygook, superstition

mummer
4 mime **5** actor, mimic **12** impersonator

mummify
5 dry up, wizen **6** embalm, wither **7** shrivel **9** desiccate

munch
3 eat **4** chaw, chew **5** champ, chomp, snack **6** crunch **9** masticate

mundane
5 lowly **6** earthy, normal **7** earthly, humdrum, prosaic, routine, terrene, worldly **8** banausic, day-to-day, everyday, familiar, ordinary, telluric, workaday **9** practical, sublunary, tellurian **11** commonplace, terrestrial, uncelestial **13** materialistic

municipal
5 civic, local, urban **12** metropolitan

munificent
6 lavish **7** liberal **8** generous, handsome **9** bounteous, bountiful **10** benevolent, freehanded, openhanded **11** magnanimous **13** philanthropic

munitions maker
5 Krupp

muralist
4 Sert (José María) **6** Benton (Thomas Hart), Giotto, Orozco (José Clemente), Rivera (Diego) **7** La Farge (John) **9** Siqueiros (David Alfaro) **12** Michelangelo (Buonarotti)

murder
3 hit, off **4** do in, kill, slay **5** blood, lynch, scrag, snuff, waste **6** rub out **7** bump off, execute, garrote, killing, smother, take out **8** foul play, homicide, knock off, strangle **9** eradicate, liquidate, slaughter **10** annihilate, asphyxiate, decapitate, extinguish **11** assassinate, electrocute, exterminate **12** manslaughter
brother: **10** fratricide
father: **9** patricide
king: **8** regicide
mother: **9** matricide
parent: **9** parricide
sister: **10** sororicide

murderer
6 hit man, killer, slayer **7** butcher **8** assassin, homicide **9** cutthroat, manslayer **11** slaughterer

Murder in the Cathedral
author: **5** Eliot (Thomas Stearns)
character: **5** Henry (II) **6** Becket (Thomas à)

murderous
6 deadly, lethal **10** sanguinary **12** bloodthirsty

murk
3 fog **4** haze, mist **5** brume, gloom **6** miasma **8** darkness **9** obscurity

murky
3 dim **4** dark, dull, foul, gray **5** dirty, dusky, foggy, misty, muddy, roily, vague **6** cloudy, gloomy, opaque, somber, turbid **7** obscure **8** nebulous **9** ambiguous, equivocal, tenebrous **10** caliginous

murmur
3 hum **4** buzz, purr **5** drone, rumor **6** grouch, grouse, mumble, mutter, rumble **7** grumble, whisper **8** complain **9** grumbling, undertone **11** scuttlebutt, susurration

Muscat sultanate
4 Oman

muscle
4 beef, thew **5** brawn, force, might, power, sinew **6** energy **7** potency **8** strength **9** strong arm
abdomen: **3** abs **7** abdomen
arm: **3** bis **4** tris **6** biceps **7** triceps
back: **4** lats **5** traps **9** trapezius
buttock: **6** glutes
calf: **6** soleus
chest: **4** pecs **10** pectoralis
jaw: **8** masseter
kind: **6** flexor, tensor **7** dilator, evertor, levator, rotator **8** abductor, adductor, extensor
leg: **4** hams
loin: **5** psoas
neck: **5** traps **8** platysma **9** trapezius
shoulder: **5** delts **7** deltoid **10** deltoideus
side: **4** lats
stomach: **3** abs
straight: **6** rectus
study of: **7** myology
thigh: **5** quads **8** gracilis **9** sartorius

muscle-bound
5 rigid, stiff **6** wooden

muscular
4 ropy **5** beefy, burly, husky **6** brawny, mighty, robust, sinewy, strong, sturdy **8** athletic, forceful, powerful, resolute, stalwart, vigorous **9** Herculean, strapping, well-built

muse
5 angel, brood, guide, think **6** genius, ponder, trance **7** reflect, reverie **8** cogitate, meditate, mull over, ruminate, turn over **10** deliberate **11** contemplate

Muse
father: **4** Zeus **7** Jupiter
home: **7** Helicon
leader: **6** Apollo
mother: **9** Mnemosyne
of astronomy: **6** Urania
of choral song: **11** Terpsichore
of comedy: **6** Thalia
of dancing: **11** Terpsichore
of epic poetry: **8** Calliope
of history: **4** Clio
of love poetry: **5** Erato
of lyric poetry: **5** Erato
of music: **7** Euterpe
of pastoral poetry: **6** Thalia
of sacred poetry: **8** Polymnia **10** Polyhymnia
of tragedy: **9** Melpomene

museum
5 salon **7** archive, exhibit, gallery **8** atheneum **10** collection, repository
famous: **3** Met **4** Fogg, MoMA, Tate **5** Field, Frick, Getty, Orsay, Prado **6** Louvre **7** Peabody, Walters, Whitney **9** Henry Ford, Hermitage, Hirshhorn **10** Guggenheim **11** Norton Simon, Smithsonian

mush
4 slop **5** grits, gruel, hokum **6** bathos, drivel, hominy **8** porridge, schmaltz

mushroom
4 grow **6** expand, spread **7** burgeon, explode, inflate **8** snowball **11** proliferate
combining form: **3** myc **4** myco **5** mycet **6** myceto
edible: **5** enoki, morel **6** bolete **7** cremini, crimini, porcini **8** shiitake **9** mousseron **10** champignon, portabella, portabello, portobello **11** chanterelle
kind: **6** agaric, bolete **7** inky cap, russula
part: **3** cap **4** gill, ring **5** stipe, volva **6** pileus **7** annulus **8** mycelium
poisonous: **7** amanita **8** death cap **9** fly agaric, toadstool

mushy
4 soft **5** pulpy, soppy, vague **6** quaggy, spongy **7** amorous, maudlin, mawkish, squashy, squishy **8** bathetic, effusive, romantic, squooshy **9** schmaltzy **10** lovey-dovey, saccharine **11** sentimental

music
abbreviation: **3** fff, ppp, sfz **5** cresc
bass staff lines: **5** GBDFA
bass staff spaces: **4** ACEG
characteristic phrase: **9** leitmotif, leitmotiv
chord: **5** major, minor, tonic **7** harmony **8** dominant **9** augmented **10** diminished
closing: **4** coda
embellishment: **3** run **4** turn **5** trill **7** cadenza,

mordent, roulade **8** arpeggio, flourish **9** grace note
for eight: 5 octet
for five: 7 quintet
for four: 7 quartet
for nine: 5 nonet
for one: 4 solo
for seven: 6 septet
for six: 6 sextet
for three: 4 trio
for two: 3 duo **4** a due, duet
god: 6 Apollo
hall: 5 odeum **7** cabaret, theater
instrumental form: 3 jig, rag **4** jazz, reel **5** étude, fugue, gigue, march, polka, rondo, suite, waltz **6** minuet, pavane, sonata **7** bourrée, gavotte, mazurka, prelude, toccata **8** chaconne, concerto, courante, fantasia, galliard, nocturne, overture, rhapsody, ricercar, saraband, serenade, symphony, tone poem **9** allemande, polonaise
morning: 6 aubade
Muse: 7 Euterpe
night: 8 nocturne, serenade
note: 4 half **5** breve, minim, neume, whole **6** eighth, quaver **7** quarter **8** crotchet **9** sixteenth **10** semiquaver
patron saint: 7 Cecilia
period: 6 Modern, Rococo **7** Baroque **8** Medieval, Romantic **9** Classical
symbol: 3 bar, key **4** clef, flat, note, rest, slur, turn **5** G clef, neume, sharp, staff **7** fermata, mordent **8** bass clef **9** alla breve **10** accidental, treble clef
treble staff lines: 5 EGBDF
treble staff spaces: 4 FACE
vocal form: 3 air **4** aria, hymn, lied, mass, song **5** chant, motet, opera, round **6** anthem, ballad **7** cantata, chanson, chorale **8** cavatina, madrigal, operetta, oratorio, serenade **9** cabaletta

musical
4 show **5** revue **6** choral **7** lyrical, melodic, songful, tuneful **8** harmonic, operetta, zarzuela **9** melodious, symphonic **10** euphonious, harmonious
famous: 4 Cats, Hair, Mame, Rent **5** Annie, Evita, Gypsy **6** Grease, Kismet, Oliver **7** Cabaret, Camelot, Chicago, Company, Follies **8** Carousel, Fiorello, Godspell, King and I (The), Lion King (The), Music Man (The), Oklahoma, Show Boat **9** Brigadoon, Funny Girl, Girl Crazy, On the Town, Over There, State Fair **10** Chorus Line (A), Dreamgirls, Hello Dolly, Kiss Me Kate, Miss Saigon, My Fair Lady, Pajama Game (The) **11** Damn Yankees, Of Thee I Sing, Sweeney Todd **12** Anything Goes, Bye Bye Birdie, Guys and Dolls, Sound of Music (The), South Pacific, Sweet Charity **13** Les Misérables, Man of La Mancha, Silk Stockings, West Side Story, Wonderful Town **14** Finian's Rainbow, Flower Drum Song, Paint Your Wagon **15** Annie Get Your Gun **16** Fiddler on the Roof **17** Phantom of the Opera (The) **20** Jesus Christ Superstar

musical composition
4 aria, coda, hymn, lied, opus, song, trio **5** chant, canon, carol, dirge, étude, fugue, march, motet, opera, rondo, suite **6** anthem, ballad, sextet, sonata **7** cantata, chanson, chorale, prelude, quartet, quintet, requiem, scherzo, toccata **8** concerto, fantasia, madrigal, nocturne, operetta, oratorio, overture, postlude, serenade, sonatina, symphony **9** bagatelle, barcarole, cabaletta, interlude **10** intermezzo, recitative

musical direction
accented: 7 marcato **8** sforzato **9** sforzando
all: 5 tutti
bowed: 4 arco
brisk: 4 brio, vivo **6** vivace **7** allegro, animato
connected: 6 legato
detached: 8 spiccato, staccato
dignified: 8 maestoso
disconnected: 8 staccato
emotional: 12 appassionato
emphatic: 7 marcato
excited: 7 agitato
fast: 4 vite, vivo **6** presto, veloce, vivace **7** allegro
faster: 7 stretto **11** accelerando
fluctuating tempo: 6 rubato
forcefully: 7 furioso
freely: 9 ad libitum
from the beginning: 6 da capo
gay: 7 giocoso
gentle: 5 dolce **7** amabile, amoroso **10** affettuoso
graceful: 8 grazioso
half: 5 mezzo
heavy: 7 pesante
held firmly: 6 tenuto
less: 4 meno
little: 4 poco
little by little: 9 poco a poco
lively: 4 vite, vivo **6** vivace **7** allegro, animato, giocoso
loud: 5 forte
louder: 9 crescendo
majestic: 8 maestoso
moderate: 7 andante **8** moderato
moderately loud: 10 mezzo forte
moderately soft: 10 mezzo piano
playful: 10 scherzando

plucked: 9 pizzicato
quick: 4 vite, vivo 6 presto, veloce, vivace 7 allegro
quickening: 11 affrettando
repeat: 3 bis 6 da capo
run: 8 arpeggio 9 glissando
sad: 7 dolente 8 doloroso
separate: 6 divisi
silent: 5 tacet
singing: 9 cantabile
sliding: 9 glissando
slow: 5 grave, largo, lento 6 adagio 7 andante 9 larghetto
slowing: 3 rit 6 ritard 10 ritardando 11 rallentando
smooth: 6 legato
soft: 5 dolce, piano
softening: 10 diminuendo 11 decrescendo
solemn: 5 grave
spirited: 4 vivo 6 vivace 7 animato 9 spiritoso
stately: 7 pomposo 8 maestoso
sustained: 6 tenuto 9 sostenuto
sweet: 5 dolce
tender: 7 amabile, amoroso 10 affettuoso
together: 4 a due 5 tutti
very: 5 assai
very fast: 11 prestissimo
very loud: 10 fortissimo
very soft: 10 pianissimo

musical drama
5 opera 8 operetta, zarzuela 9 singspiel

musical group
4 band, trio 5 choir, combo 6 chorus, sextet 7 quartet, quintet 8 ensemble, glee club 9 orchestra

musical instrument
African: 5 mbira, rebab 7 kalimba
ancient: 4 lyre, rote 5 crwth 6 syrinx 7 cithara, kithara, sistrum, timbrel 8 psaltery
Arabic: 3 oud
bagpipe: 7 musette, pibroch 8 psaltery
brass: 4 horn, tuba 5 bugle 6 cornet 7 althorn, clarion, helicon, saxhorn, trumpet 8 trombone 10 flugelhorn, French horn, sousaphone
Indian: 4 vina 5 sarod, sitar, tabla
Japanese: 4 biwa, koto 7 samisen 8 shamisen 10 shakuhachi
keyboard: 5 organ, piano 6 spinet 7 celesta, cembalo, clavier 8 calliope, melodeon, virginal 9 accordion 10 clavichord, concertina, pianoforte 11 harpsichord
medieval: 4 lute 5 naker, rebab, rebec, shawm, tabor 7 gittern, mandola 8 cornetto, gemshorn, hornpipe, oliphant 9 monochord 10 hurdy-gurdy
percussion: 4 bell, drum 5 anvil, güiro, piano 6 cymbal, maraca 7 maracas, marimba, timpani, tympani 8 bass drum, castanet, triangle 9 castanets, snare drum, xylophone 10 kettledrum, tambourine, vibraphone
Persian: 6 santir
reed: 4 oboe 7 bassoon 8 clarinet 9 harmonica, saxophone 11 English horn
Renaissance: 4 viol 5 regal, shawm 6 curtal, spinet 7 bagpipe, bandora, cittern, rackett, sackbut, serpent, theorbo, vihuela, violone 8 crumhorn, recorder, virginal 9 krummhorn 10 chitarrone, colascione 11 harpsichord
Russian: 9 balalaika
stringed: 3 uke 4 harp, lute, lyre, viol 5 banjo, cello, piano, rebab, viola 6 fiddle, guitar, violin, zither 7 bandora, cittern, gittern, kantele, pandura, ukulele 8 autoharp, dulcimer, mandolin 10 contrabass, double bass 11 harpsichord, violoncello
toy: 5 kazoo 7 ocarina
woodwind: 4 oboe 5 flute 7 bassoon, piccolo 8 clarinet 9 saxophone 11 English horn

musical interval
5 fifth, major, minor, sixth, third 6 fourth, octave, second 7 perfect, seventh, tritone

musical syllable
2 do, fa, la, mi, re, si, ti, ut 3 sol

musician
4 bard 5 piper 6 player 7 jazzman, maestro 8 minstrel, virtuoso 9 performer 10 troubadour

muskeg
3 bog, fen 4 mire, quag 5 marsh, swamp 6 morass, slough 8 quagmire

musket
5 fusil 9 flintlock, matchlock 12 muzzleloader

Musketeer
5 Athos 6 Aramis 7 Porthos
author: 5 Dumas (Alexandre)
friend: 9 d'Artagnan

muskmelon
10 cantaloupe

Muslim
ascetic: 4 Sufi 5 fakir 7 dervish 8 marabout
body of scholars: 5 ulama, ulema
branch: 4 Shia 5 Sunni 6 Shiite
caller to prayer: 7 muezzin
decree: 5 fatwa, irade
devil: 5 Iblis
garment: 5 burka, burqa 6 chador
god: 5 Allah
heavenly virgin: 5 houri
holy city: 5 Mecca 6 Medina
holy war: 5 jihad
judge: 4 qadi 5 mufti
lady: 5 begum
law: 6 Sharia

leader: 3 aga 4 agha, amir, emir, imam 5 ameer 6 caliph, sayyid, sultan 9 ayatollah
lord: 5 omrah
mendicant: 5 fakir
messiah: 5 Mahdi
month:
(see at **month**)
month of fasting: 7 Ramadan
mosque: 6 masjid
mystic: 4 Sufi
official: 3 dey 6 mullah, vizier
pilgrim: 5 hajji
pilgrimage: 4 hadj, hajj 5 omrah
prayer: 5 salat
priest: 4 imam
prophet: 8 Mohammed, Muhammad
religion: 5 Islam
scripture: 5 Koran, Quran
school: 7 madrasa 8 madrasah, madrassa 9 madrassah
shrine: 5 Kaaba
spirit: 4 jinn 5 djinn, jinni 6 djinni
temple: 6 masjid, mosque
theological student: 5 softa
title: 3 aga 4 emir 6 caliph
tradition: 5 sunna
veil: 7 yashmak
(see also **mosque; Muhammad**)

muss
3 row 4 mess 5 botch, chaos, mix-up, upset 6 jumble, mess-up, muddle, rumple, tousle 7 disrupt, rummage 8 disarray, dishevel, disorder, shambles 9 confusion 10 disarrange 11 disorganize

mussel
5 naiad
genus: 4 Unio 7 Mytilus 8 Anodonta
larva: 9 blackhead

Mussolini, Benito
4 Duce (Il)
son-in-law: 5 Ciano (Galeazzo)

mussy
6 sloppy, untidy 7 tousled, unkempt 8 slovenly 9 cluttered 10 disheveled

must
4 duty, mold, need, want 5 gotta, juice, ought 6 devoir, should 9 condition, essential, necessity, requisite 10 obligation, sine qua non 11 requirement 12 precondition, prerequisite

muster
4 call, roll 5 crowd, group, raise, rally, rouse 6 enlist, enroll, gather, induce, invoke, join up, roster, sample, sign on, sign up, summon, work up 7 collect, convene, develop, include, marshal, produce 8 assemble, assembly, comprise, congress, generate, mobilize, organize, roll call, specimen 9 gathering, inventory, nose count 10 accumulate, assemblage, collection, congregate, rendezvous 12 accumulation, congregation

muster out
5 demob, let go 9 discharge 10 demobilize

musty
4 dank 5 funky, moldy, stale, tired, trite 6 frowsy, frowzy, old hat, smelly 7 airless, antique, mildewy, squalid 8 shopworn, timeworn 10 antiquated, malodorous, threadbare

Mut
husband: 4 Amen, Amon
son: 5 Chons 6 Chonsu, Khonsu

mutable
5 fluid 6 fickle, mobile, shifty 7 erratic, protean 8 slippery, unstable, unsteady, variable, volatile, wavering 9 changeful, mercurial, unsettled 10 capricious, changeable, inconstant 11 fluctuating, vacillating 12 inconsistent

mutate
4 vary 5 alter, morph 6 change, modify 9 refashion, transform, transmute 11 transfigure 12 metamorphose, transmogrify

mutation
5 sport 6 change 7 novelty 9 deviation, variation 10 alteration 11 vicissitude 12 modification 13 metamorphosis

mute
3 mum 4 dumb 5 quiet 6 dampen, deaden, muffle, muzzle, reduce, silent, soften, stifle, subdue 7 silence 8 silencer, wordless 9 voiceless 10 speechless, tongue-tied

muted
3 dim, mat 4 dull 6 low-key, silent 10 speechless

mutilate
3 mar 4 maim 6 damage, deface, injure, mangle 7 cripple 9 disfigure, dismember

mutineer
5 rebel

mutinous
6 unruly 8 factious 9 insurgent, seditious, turbulent 10 rebellious 12 contumacious 13 insubordinate

mutiny
5 rebel 6 revolt, rise up 8 uprising 9 rebellion 12 insurrection

mutt
3 cur, dog 4 mule 5 cross 6 hybrid 7 mixture, mongrel 9 half blood, half-breed 10 crossbreed

Mutt and ___
4 Jeff

mutter
5 growl **6** grouch, grouse, mumble, murmur **7** grumble **9** undertone

muttonchops
9 burnsides, sideburns **10** sideboards **11** dundrearies **12** side-whiskers

mutual
5 joint **6** common, public, shared, united **7** related **8** communal, conjoint, conjunct **9** bilateral, connected **10** associated, reciprocal, respective
prefix: 5 inter

muumuu
6 caftan

muzzle
3 gag **4** hush, mute, nose, phiz **5** snout **7** silence, squelch

muzzy
3 dim **4** dull, hazy **5** faint, vague **6** blurry, gloomy **7** blurred, muddled, unclear **8** confused, nebulous **9** imprecise

myalgia
4 ache, pain **5** cramp **6** strain **8** soreness

Myanmar
5 Burma
bay: 6 Bengal
capital: 6 Yangon **7** Rangoon
monetary unit: 4 kyat
neighbor: 4 Laos **5** China, India **8** Thailand **10** Bangladesh
peninsula: 9 Indochina
river: 7 Salween **9** Irrawaddy
sea: 7 Andaman

My Antonia author
6 Cather (Willa)

My Last Duchess author
8 Browning (Robert)

My Lost Youth author
10 Longfellow (Henry Wadsworth)

Myra Breckenridge author
5 Vidal (Gore)

myriad
3 lot **4** heap, host, raft, slew **5** flood, horde, swarm **6** throng **9** countless, multitude **10** infinitude, numberless **11** innumerable **12** incalculable **13** multitudinous

myrmecology subject
3 ant **4** ants

myrmidon
6 minion **8** follower, retainer **9** attendant, underling **11** subordinate

Myron's statue
10 Discobolos, Discobolus **13** Discus Thrower (The)

Myrrha's son
6 Adonis

mysterious
6 arcane, mystic, occult, secret **7** cryptic, obscure, strange **8** abstruse, esoteric, numinous **9** ambiguous, enigmatic, equivocal, recondite **10** cabalistic, unknowable **11** inscrutable **12** impenetrable, inexplicable, unfathomable **13** unaccountable

mystery
5 poser **6** enigma, puzzle, riddle, secret **7** arcanum, problem, stumper **8** whodunit **9** conundrum **10** closed book, perplexity, puzzlement **13** Chinese puzzle
writer: 3 Poe (Edgar Allan), Tey (Josephine) **5** Blake (Nicholas), Cross (Amanda), Doyle (Arthur Conan), Innes (Michael), James (P. D.), Lynds (Dennis), Marsh (Ngaio), Oates (Joyce Carol), Queen (Ellery), Stout (Rex), Waugh (Hillary) **6** Dexter (Colin), Parker (Robert B.), Peters (Ellis), Sayers (Dorothy) **7** Barnard (Robert), Collins (Michael, Wilkie), Gardner (Erle Stanley), Grafton (Sue), Hammett (Dashiell), MacLeod (Charlotte), Rendell (Ruth), Upfield (Arthur) **8** Chandler (Raymond), Christie (Agatha), Paretsky (Sara), Spillane (Mickey) **9** MacDonald (John D.), Macdonald (Ross) **10** Chesterton (G. K.)

mystic
4 seer **6** arcane, medium, occult, oracle, secret **7** obscure **8** anagogic, esoteric, hermetic, numinous **9** enigmatic, visionary **10** cabalistic, unknowable **11** inscrutable, necromantic **12** impenetrable, thaumaturgic **13** unaccountable

mystical
4 holy **6** arcane, covert, divine, occult, orphic, sacred, secret **7** cryptic, sub-rosa **8** anagogic, esoteric, hermetic, oracular, profound **9** recondite, spiritual **10** miraculous, symbolical **11** clandestine **12** supernatural, supranatural

mysticism
7 Orphism **8** cabalism, quietism **11** hermeticism

mystify
6 baffle, puzzle **7** confuse, obscure, perplex **8** befuddle, bewilder, confound **9** obfuscate

mystifying
7 cryptic, delphic **8** Delphian **9** enigmatic

mystique
4 aura **5** charm, magic **6** glamor **7** glamour **8** charisma **9** magnetism

myth
4 lore, saga, tale **5** fable, story **6** legend **7** fiction, figment, parable **8** allegory, folklore **9** tradition **11** fabrication

mythical
6 fabled, made-up, unreal **7** created, fictive **8** fabulous, fanciful, invented **9** fantastic, fictional, imaginary, legendary **10** apocryphal, fictitious

mythologist
4 Jung (Carl Gustav), Ovid **5** Tylor (Edward Burnett) **6** Eliade (Mircea), Frazer (James George), Müller (Friedrich Max) **8** Campbell (Joseph) **9** Euhemerus **10** Malinowski (Bronislaw)

mythology
see **myth**

N

Naamah
brother: **9** Tubalcain
father: **6** Lamech
husband: **7** Solomon
mother: **6** Zillah
son: **8** Rehoboam

nab
4 grab **5** catch, pinch, run in, seize **6** arrest, clutch, collar, pick up, pull in, snatch **7** capture **9** apprehend

nabob
3 VIP **5** mogul, noble **6** bigwig, fat cat, tycoon **7** big shot, magnate, notable **8** big chief, eminence, governor **9** big cheese, dignitary, personage **10** notability

Nabokov novel
3 Ada **4** Gift (The), Pnin **6** Lolita **7** Defense (The), Despair **8** Pale Fire **14** King Queen Knave

nacre
13 mother-of-pearl

nada
3 nil, nix, zip **4** zero **5** zilch **6** naught **7** nothing, nullity **11** nothingness

nadir
4 base, foot **5** depth **6** bottom **8** low point
opposite: **6** zenith

nag
3 irk, vex **4** bait, carp, goad, ride **5** annoy, chivy, harry, horse, hound, shrew, worry **6** badger, bother, carp at, harass, heckle, hector, needle, peck at, pester, plague **7** henpeck, torment **8** complain, harangue, irritate

naiad
5 nymph

naïf
7 ingenue

nail
3 bag, get, nab **4** brad, grab, spad, stud, tack, trap **5** catch, clone, spike, sprig **6** arrest, collar, secure **7** capture **9** apprehend

naive
6 simple **7** artless, natural **8** gullible, innocent, wide-eyed **9** childlike, credulous, guileless, ingenuous, unstudied **10** self-taught, unaffected, unschooled **11** susceptible

naked
3 raw **4** bald, bare, mere, nude, pure **5** clear, sheer **6** peeled, scanty, simple, unclad **7** denuded, evident, exposed, obvious **8** revealed, starkers, stripped **9** au naturel, disclosed, unclothed, uncovered, undressed
combining form: **4** gymn **5** gymno

Naked and the Dead author
6 Mailer (Norman)

namby-pamby
4 weak **5** banal, bland, inane, sissy, vapid **6** effete, jejune **7** insipid, milksop, nebbish **8** nebbishy, weakling **9** spineless **10** effeminate, indecisive, pantywaist, wishy-washy **11** milquetoast **12** milk-and-water **13** characterless

name
3 dub, nom, tab, tag, tap **4** cite, term **5** alias, label, nomen, title **6** finger, repute, rubric **7** appoint, baptize, epithet, moniker, specify **8** christen, identify, nominate **9** designate, incognito, sobriquet **10** denominate, reputation **11** appellation, appellative, designation
ancient Rome: **7** agnomen **8** prenomen
assumed: **5** alias **9** sobriquet
family: **8** cognomen
fictitious: **9** pseudonym
giver: **6** eponym

nameless
6 unsung **7** obscure, unknown **9** anonymous **11** indefinable, unutterable **12** uncelebrated, unidentified

namely
3 viz. **5** id est, to wit **6** that is **8** scilicet **9** expressly, specially, videlicet **10** especially **12** particularly, specifically

Name of the Rose author
3 Eco (Umberto)

Namibia
capital: **8** Windhoek
city: **8** Oshakati, Rehoboth
desert: **5** Namib **8** Kalahari
language: **5** Bantu **6** German **9** Afrikaans
neighbor: **6** Angola **8** Botswana **11** South Africa
river: **6** Cunene, Orange **8** Okavango

nana
7 grandma 11 grandmother

Nana
author: 4 Zola (Emile)
mother: 8 Gervaise

Nancy Drew
aunt: 6 Eloise
author: 5 Keene (Carolyn)
boyfriend: 3 Ned
creator: 11 Stratemeyer (Edward)
dog: 4 Togo
father: 6 Carson
friend: 4 Bess 5 Helen 6 George
housekeeper: 6 Hannah

Nanna
brother: 6 Nergal, Ninazu
father: 5 Enlil
husband: 6 Balder, Baldur
mother: 6 Ninlil
son: 3 Utu
wife: 6 Ningal

nanny
5 nurse 9 caregiver, governess, nursemaid

Naomi
4 Mara
daughter-in-law: 4 Ruth 5 Orpah
husband: 9 Elimelech
son: 6 Mahlon 7 Chilion

nap
4 doze, pile, rest, shag, wale, warp, weft, woof 5 sleep, weave 6 drowse, nod off, siesta, snooze 7 drop off, surface 10 forty winks

nape
6 scruff

Naphtali
brother: 3 Dan
father: 5 Jacob
mother: 6 Bilhah
son: 4 Guni 5 Jezer 7 Jahzeel, Jahziel, Shallum

naphtha
7 solvent 9 petroleum

napkin
5 cloth, doily, towel 9 serviette

napoleon
4 boot 6 pastry 8 card game 9 solitaire
bid: 7 blucher 10 wellington

Napoleon
adversary: 6 Nelson (Horatio) 7 Kutuzov (Mikhail) 10 Wellington (Duke of)
birthplace: 7 Ajaccio, Corsica
brother: 5 Louis 6 Jérome, Joseph, Lucien
brother-in-law: 5 Murat (Joachim)
deathplace: 8 St. Helena
defeat: 7 Leipzig 8 Waterloo 9 Trafalgar
doctor: 11 Antommarchi (Francesco)
father: 5 Carlo
island of exile: 4 Elba 8 St. Helena
marshal: 3 Ney (Michel) 5 Murat (Joachim), Soult (Nicolas-Jean) 6 Suchet (Louis-Gabriel)
sister: 5 Maria 8 Carlotta, Carolina
victory: 3 Ulm 4 Jena, Lodi 5 Ligny 6 Abukir, Abu Qir, Arcole, Wagram 7 Bautzen, Dresden, Marengo 8 Borodino 10 Austerlitz
wife: 9 Josephine 11 Marie Louise

narcissism
6 egoism, vanity 7 conceit, egotism 8 self-love, vainness 9 vainglory 11 egocentrism, self-conceit 13 conceitedness

narcissistic
4 vain 7 stuck-up 9 conceited, egotistic 10 self-loving 11 egotistical 12 self-absorbed, self-admiring, self-centered, vainglorious

Narcissus
admirer: 4 Echo
father: 9 Cephissus
mother: 7 Liriope

narcotic
3 hop 4 dope, drug, junk 5 opium 6 heroin, opiate 7 anodyne, cocaine, hashish 8 hypnotic, morphine, nepenthe 9 somnolent, soporific 10 somnorific 11 somniferous
peddler: 6 dealer, pusher

narrate
4 tell 5 state 6 detail, recite, relate, report 7 express, outline, recount 8 describe 9 chronicle

narrative
4 epic, myth, saga, tale, yarn 5 fable, story 6 legend, report 7 account, history, recital, version 8 anecdote 9 chronicle
medieval French: 5 roman 7 romance
prose: 5 novel 7 novella

narrator
6 teller 7 reciter 8 reporter 9 describer, performer 10 chronicler

narrow
5 close, small, taper 6 lessen, strait 7 bigoted, limited, precise, slender 8 contract, decrease, straiten 9 confining, constrict, hidebound, illiberal 10 brassbound, inflexible, intolerant, prejudiced, restricted

narrowly
6 barely 7 closely 8 scarcely, strictly

narrow-minded
5 petty 7 bigoted, insular 9 hidebound, illiberal 10 brassbound, intolerant, prejudiced, provincial

nasal
6 rhinal, twangy 9 nosepiece
combining form: 4 rhin 5 rhino
sprayer: 9 nebulizer

NASCAR champion
5 Busch (Kurt) **6** Gordon (Jeff), Martin (Mark), Newman (Ryan) **7** Jarrett (Dale), Johnson (Jimmie), Kenseth (Matt), Labonte (Bobby, Terry), Stewart (Tony) **9** Earnhardt (Dale)

nascency
5 birth **6** origin **7** genesis **8** birthing, creation, nativity **9** inception **11** parturition

nascent
7 budding, growing, newborn **8** emergent **9** beginning, embryonic, fledgling, incipient, sprouting **10** blossoming, burgeoning, initiative, initiatory

Naseby victor
7 Fairfax (Thomas) **8** Cromwell (Oliver)

___ Nastase
4 Ilie

nasty
4 evil, foul, icky, mean, vile **5** awful, dirty, gross, snide **6** filthy, grubby, horrid, malign, odious, wicked **7** beastly, harmful, hateful, ill-bred, painful, raunchy, squalid, vicious **8** god-awful, indecent, spiteful **9** loathsome, malicious, malignant, obnoxious, offensive, repugnant, repulsive **10** disgusting, malevolent **11** distasteful **12** disagreeable

natant
8 floating, swimming

Nathan
father: 4 Bani **5** Attai, David
son: 5 Zabad

nation
4 race **5** realm, state, tribe **6** domain, people, polity **7** country, kingdom, society **8** dominion, populace, republic **11** sovereignty **12** commonwealth, principality
Africa: 4 Chad, Mali, Togo **5** Benin, Congo, Egypt, Gabon, Ghana, Kenya, Libya, Niger, Sudan **6** Angola, Gambia, Guinea, Malawi, Rwanda, Uganda, Zambia **7** Algeria, Burundi, Comoros, Eritrea, Lesotho, Liberia, Morocco, Namibia, Nigeria, Senegal, Somalia, Tunisia **8** Botswana, Cameroon, Djibouti, Ethiopia, Tanzania, Zimbabwe **9** Cape Verde, Mauritius, Swaziland **10** Ivory Coast, Madagascar, Mauritania, Mozambique, Seychelles **11** Burkina Faso, Côte d'Ivoire, Sierra Leone, South Africa **12** Guinea-Bissau **16** Equatorial Guinea **18** São Tomé and Principe **22** Central African Republic
Americas: 4 Peru **5** Chile **6** Belize, Brazil, Canada, Guyana, Mexico, Panama **7** Bolivia, Ecuador, Uruguay **8** Colombia, Honduras, Paraguay, Suriname **9** Argentina, Costa Rica, Guatemala, Nicaragua, Venezuela **10** El Salvador **12** United States
Asia: 4 Laos **5** Burma, China, India, Japan, Korea, Nepal **6** Bhutan, Brunei, Ceylon, Taiwan **7** Armenia, Georgia, Myanmar, Vietnam **8** Cambodia, Malaysia, Maldives, Mongolia, Pakistan, Sri Lanka, Thailand **9** East Timor, Indonesia, Singapore **10** Azerbaijan, Bangladesh, Kazakhstan, Kyrgyzstan, North Korea, South Korea, Tajikistan, Timor-Leste **11** Afghanistan, Philippines **12** Turkmenistan
Caribbean: 4 Cuba **5** Haiti **7** Bahamas, Grenada, Jamaica **8** Barbados, Dominica **10** Saint Lucia **15** St. Kitts and Nevis **17** Antigua and Barbuda, Dominican Republic, Trinidad and Tobago **18** Saint Kitts and Nevis **25** St. Vincent and the Grenadines **28** Saint Vincent and the Grenadines
Europe: 5 Italy, Malta, Spain **6** Bosnia, Cyprus, France, Greece, Latvia, Monaco, Norway, Poland, Russia, Serbia, Sweden, Turkey **7** Albania, Andorra, Austria, Belarus, Belgium, Croatia, Denmark, Estonia, Finland, Germany, Hungary, Iceland, Ireland, Moldova, Romania, Ukraine **8** Bulgaria, Portugal, Slovakia, Slovenia **9** Lithuania, Macedonia, San Marino **10** Luxembourg, Montenegro, Yugoslavia **11** Netherlands, Switzerland **13** Czech Republic, Liechtenstein, United Kingdom
Middle East: 3 UAE **4** Iraq, Iran, Oman **5** Qatar, Syria, Yemen **6** Israel, Jordan, Kuwait **7** Bahrain, Lebanon **11** Saudi Arabia **18** United Arab Emirates
Oceania: 4 Fiji **5** Samoa, Tonga **7** Vanuatu **8** Kiribati **9** Australia **10** Micronesia, New Zealand **14** Papua New Guinea, Solomon Islands **15** Marshall Islands

national
6 native **7** citizen, federal, subject **8** resident **10** countryman **11** countrywide

National Basketball Association
Atlanta: 5 Hawks
Boston: 7 Celtics
Charlotte: 7 Bobcats
Chicago: 5 Bulls
Cleveland: 9 Cavaliers
Dallas: 9 Mavericks
Denver: 7 Nuggets
Detroit: 7 Pistons
Golden State: 8 Warriors
Houston: 7 Rockets
Indiana: 6 Pacers
Los Angeles: 6 Lakers **8** Clippers
Memphis: 9 Grizzlies
Miami: 4 Heat
Milwaukee: 5 Bucks
Minnesota: 12 Timberwolves
New Jersey: 4 Nets
New Orleans: 7 Hornets
New York: 6 Knicks
Orlando: 5 Magic

Philadelphia: 13 Seventy-sixers
Phoenix: 4 Suns
Portland: 12 Trail Blazers
Sacramento: 5 Kings
San Antonio: 5 Spurs
Seattle: 11 SuperSonics
Toronto: 7 Raptors
Utah: 4 Jazz
Washington: 7 Wizards

National Football League
Arizona: 9 Cardinals
Atlanta: 7 Falcons
Baltimore: 6 Ravens
Buffalo: 5 Bills
Carolina: 8 Panthers
Chicago: 5 Bears
Cincinnati: 7 Bengals
Cleveland: 6 Browns
Dallas: 7 Cowboys
Denver: 7 Broncos
Detroit: 5 Lions
Green Bay: 7 Packers
Houston: 6 Texans
Indianapolis: 5 Colts
Jacksonville: 7 Jaguars
Kansas City: 6 Chiefs
Miami: 8 Dolphins
Minnesota: 7 Vikings
New England: 8 Patriots
New Orleans: 6 Saints
New York: 4 Jets **6** Giants
Oakland: 7 Raiders
Philadelphia: 6 Eagles
Pittsburgh: 8 Steelers
St. Louis: 4 Rams
San Diego: 8 Chargers
San Francisco: 11 Forty-niners
Seattle: 8 Seahawks
Tampa Bay: 4 Bucs **10** Buccaneers
Tennessee: 6 Titans
Washington: 8 Redskins

National Hockey League
Anaheim: 5 Ducks
Atlanta: 9 Thrashers
Boston: 6 Bruins
Buffalo: 6 Sabres
Calgary: 6 Flames
Carolina: 10 Hurricanes
Chicago: 10 Blackhawks
Colorado: 9 Avalanche
Columbus: 11 Blue Jackets
Dallas: 5 Stars
Detroit: 8 Red Wings
Edmonton: 6 Oilers
Florida: 8 Panthers
Los Angeles: 5 Kings
Minnesota: 4 Wild
Montreal: 9 Canadiens
Nashville: 9 Predators
New Jersey: 6 Devils
New York: 7 Rangers **9** Islanders
Ottawa: 8 Senators
Philadelphia: 6 Flyers
Phoenix: 7 Coyotes
Pittsburgh: 8 Penguins
St. Louis: 5 Blues
San Jose: 6 Sharks
Tampa Bay: 9 Lightning
Toronto: 10 Maple Leafs
Vancouver: 7 Canucks
Washington: 8 Capitals

nationalism
8 jingoism **10** chauvinism, patriotism

National League
Arizona: 12 Diamondbacks
Atlanta: 6 Braves
Chicago: 4 Cubs
Cincinnati: 4 Reds
Colorado: 7 Rockies
Florida: 7 Marlins
Houston: 6 Astros
Los Angeles: 7 Dodgers
Milwaukee: 7 Brewers
New York: 4 Mets
Philadelphia: 8 Phillies
Pittsburgh: 7 Pirates
St. Louis: 9 Cardinals
San Diego: 6 Padres
San Francisco: 6 Giants
Washington: 9 Nationals

national military park
Alabama: 13 Horseshoe Bend
Arkansas: 8 Pea Ridge
Mississippi: 9 Vicksburg
Pennsylvania: 10 Gettysburg
South Carolina: 13 Kings Mountain
Tennessee: 6 Shiloh

national monument
Alabama: 11 Russell Cave
Alaska: 9 Aniakchak
Arizona: 5 Tonto **6** Navajo **7** Saguaro, Wupatki **8** Tuzigoot **10** Chiricahua, Pipe Spring, Tumacacori **11** Hohokam Pima **12** Sunset Crater, Walnut Canyon
California: 8 Cabrillo, Lava Beds **9** Muir Woods, Pinnacles **10** Joshua Tree **11** Death Valley
Colorado: 10 Yucca House
Colorado-Utah: 8 Dinosaur **9** Hovenweep
Florida: 12 Fort Matanzas **13** Fort Jefferson
Georgia: 8 Ocmulgee **11** Fort Pulaski **13** Fort Frederica
Iowa: 12 Effigy Mounds
Louisiana: 12 Poverty Point
Maryland: 11 Fort McHenry
Minnesota: 9 Pipestone **12** Grand Portage
Nebraska: 9 Homestead **11** Scotts Bluff

New Mexico: **5** Pecos **7** El Morro **9** Bandelier, El Malpais, Fort Union **10** Aztec Ruins, White Sands
New York: **11** Fort Stanwix **13** Castle Clinton
South Carolina: **10** Fort Sumter **13** Congaree Swamp
South Dakota: **9** Jewel Cave
Utah: **11** Cedar Breaks **13** Rainbow Bridge
Wyoming: **11** Devils Tower, Fossil Butte

national park
Alaska: **6** Denali, Katmai **9** Lake Clark **10** Glacier Bay **11** Kenai Fjords, Kobuk Valley
Angola: **4** Iona, Mupa
Arizona: **11** Grand Canyon
Arkansas: **10** Hot Springs
Botswana: **5** Chobe
California: **7** Redwood, Sequoia **8** Yosemite **11** King's Canyon
Chad: **5** Manda
Colombia: **5** Uraba
Colorado: **9** Mesa Verde **13** Rocky Mountain
eastern Africa: **10** Mount Kenya
Florida: **8** Biscayne **10** Everglades
Hawaii: **9** Haleakala
India: **5** Kanha
Japan: **5** Nikko
Kentucky: **11** Mammoth Cave
Kenya: **4** Meru **5** Tsavo **10** Royal Tsavo
Lake Superior: **10** Isle Royale
Maine: **6** Acadia
Malaysia: **8** Kinabalu
Minnesota: **9** Voyageurs
Montana: **7** Glacier
Nevada: **10** Great Basin
Oregon: **10** Crater Lake
Poland: **5** Ojcow, Tatra
South Africa: **6** Kruger
South Dakota: **8** Badlands, Wind Cave
Sri Lanka: **4** Yala
Sweden: **5** Sarek
Tanzania: **5** Ruaha **9** Serengeti
Texas: **7** Big Bend
Utah: **4** Zion **6** Arches **11** Bryce Canyon, Canyonlands, Capitol Reef
Virginia: **10** Shenandoah
Washington: **7** Olympic **12** Mount Rainier **13** North Cascades
Wyoming: **10** Grand Teton
Wyoming-Idaho-Montana: **11** Yellowstone
Zambia: **5** Kafue
Zimbabwe: **13** Rhodes Inyanga, Victoria Falls

native
3 raw **4** wild **5** local **6** inborn, innate **7** connate, endemic, natural **8** domestic, indigene, inherent, internal, national **9** inherited **10** aboriginal, congenital, connatural, indigenous, unacquired
Acadian Louisiana: **5** Cajun
China: **3** Han **9** Celestial
India: **5** sepoy
Japan: **9** Nipponese
London: **7** Cockney
Mindanao: **3** Ata
New England: **4** Yank **6** Yankee
New York: **13** Knickerbocker

Native American
see **Indian, American**

Native Son author
6 Wright (Richard)

Nativity
4 Noel, Xmas, yule **8** yuletide **9** Christmas
scene: **6** crèche

nativity
5 birth, start **6** origin, outset **7** genesis **8** delivery **9** beginning, horoscope, inception **11** parturition

natter
3 gab, jaw, yak, yap **4** blab, buzz, chat, go on **5** prate, run on **6** babble, gabble, gossip, tattle **7** chatter, prattle, twaddle **8** chitchat, converse

natty
4 neat, tidy, trim **5** doggy, nobby, sassy, smart, swank **6** classy, dapper, jaunty, snazzy, spiffy, spruce, sprucy, swanky **7** bandbox, doggish, stylish **9** turned out **11** well-groomed

natural
4 pure, wild **5** naive, usual **6** candid, inborn, innate, native, normal, simple **7** artless, connate, organic **8** homespun, inherent, innocent **9** childlike, ingenuous, ingrained, primitive **10** congenital, indigenous, legitimate, unaffected **11** commonplace, instinctive, spontaneous

naturalist
American: **4** Muir (John) **5** Gould (Stephen Jay), Hyatt (Alpheus) **6** Carson (Rachel) **7** Agassiz (Louis), Audubon (John James), Thoreau (H. D.), Verrill (Addison, Alpheus) **9** Burroughs (John)
English: **3** Ray (John) **5** White (Gilbert) **6** Darwin (Charles) **7** Wallace (Alfred Russel) **10** Williamson (William)
French: **5** Fabre (Jean-Henri) **7** Lamarck (Chevalier de), Réaumur (René-Antoine)
German: **8** Humboldt (Alexander von)
Scottish: **6** Wilson (Alexander) **10** Richardson (John)

nature
3 ilk, way **4** kind, sort, type **6** makeup, manner, stripe, temper **7** essence, scenery **8** creation, tendency, universe **9** character, landscape **10** complexion **11** description, disposition, personality, temperament **12** constitution

naught
3 nil, nix, zip **4** love, nada, zero **5** zilch **6** cipher **7** nothing, nullity **8** goose egg **11** nothingness

naughty
3 bad **4** lewd **5** bawdy **6** unruly, ribald, risqué, smutty, vulgar **7** froward, obscene, raunchy, wayward, willful **8** contrary, improper, perverse, rascally **10** ill-behaved **11** disobedient, mischievous **12** obstreperous, recalcitrant

Nauru
capital: **5** Yaren
former name: **8** Pleasant (Island)

nauseate
5 repel **6** offend, sicken **7** disgust, repulse

nauseated
6 queasy **7** carsick **8** qualmish **9** disgusted, squeamish **10** grossed out

nauseating
6 putrid **7** noisome **9** loathsome, offensive, repellant, repugnant, repulsive, revolting, sickening **10** disgusting

Nausicaa
father: **8** Alcinous
mother: **5** Arete

nautical
5 naval **6** marine **7** oceanic **8** maritime **12** navigational
instrument: **3** aba **7** compass, pelorus, sextant

Navajo dwelling
5 hogan

naval hero
5 Drake (Francis), Jones (John Paul), Perry (Matthew, Oliver Hazard) **6** Nelson (Horatio) **8** Farragut (David, George), Lawrence (James)

navel
6 middle **7** nombril **9** umbilicus **11** belly button
combining form: **6** omphal **7** omphalo
type: **5** innie, outie

navigate
4 helm, plot, sail **5** guide, pilot, steer **6** cruise **8** maneuver, traverse

navigation
8 piloting **10** seamanship **12** helmsmanship

navigational system
5 loran

navigator
5 flyer, pilot **6** airman **7** copilot
Danish: **6** Bering (Vitus)
Dutch: **6** Tasman (Abel) **7** Barents (Willem)
English: **4** Cook (Captain James) **5** Cabot (John, Sebastian), Drake (Francis) **6** Hudson (Henry) **7** Gilbert (Humphrey), Raleigh (Walter) **9** Vancouver (George)
French: **7** Cartier (Jacques) **9** La Perouse (Comte de)
Italian: **6** Caboto (Giovanni) **8** Columbus (Christopher), Vespucci (Amerigo) **9** Verrazano (Giovanni) **10** Verrazzano (Giovanni)
Norwegian: **4** Eric (the Red), Erik (the Red) **8** Ericsson (Leif), Eriksson (Leif) **12** Leif Ericsson, Leif Eriksson
Portuguese: **4** Dias (Bartolomeu, Dinis) **6** Cabral (Pedro Alvares), da Gama (Vasco) **8** Magellan (Ferdinand)
Spanish: **9** Fernández (Juan)

navy
4 blue **5** fleet **6** argosy, armada **8** flotilla
officer: **3** ADM, CWO, ENS **4** CAPT, LCDR, LTJG, RADM, VADM **6** ensign **7** admiral, captain **9** commander **10** lieutenant

Nazi
9 Hitlerite **10** brownshirt
admiral: **6** Dönitz (Karl), Raeder (Erich) **7** Doenitz (Karl)
air force: **9** Luftwaffe
armed forces: **9** Wehrmacht
cheer: **8** Siegheil
collaborator: **5** Laval (Pierre) **8** Quisling (Vidkun)
concentration camp: **6** Belsen, Dachau **9** Auschwitz, Treblinka **10** Buchenwald, Nordhausen
field marshal: **5** Model (Walter) **6** Keitel (Wilhelm), Paulus (Friedrich), Rommel (Erwin) **9** Rundstedt (Karl von) **10** Kesselring (Albert)
greeting: **4** heil **10** heil Hitler
leader: **3** Ley (Robert) **4** Hess (Rudolf), Röhm (Ernst) **5** Roehm (Ernst) **6** Führer, Göring (Hermann), Hitler (Adolf) **7** Fuehrer, Goering (Hermann), Himmler (Heinrich) **8** Goebbels (Joseph), Heydrich (Reinhard) **9** Rosenberg (Alfred)
police: **7** Gestapo
propagandist: **8** Goebbels (Joseph)
submarine: **5** U-boat
surrender signer: **4** Jodl (Alfred) **6** Keitel (Wilhelm)
symbol: **6** fylfot **8** swastika
tactic: **10** blitzkrieg
tank: **6** Panzer

NCO
3 cpl, sgt **8** corporal, sergeant

neap
3 low **4** tide

near
4 nigh **5** about, circa, close, round **6** almost, around **7** close by, close on **8** adjacent, approach **9** immediate, proximate **11** approximate

nearby
4 nigh **5** about, aside, close, handy **6** around, beside **8** adjacent **9** adjoining, proximate **10** contiguous, convenient **11** neighboring

nearest
4 next **7** closest **8** adjacent, proximal **9** proximate **10** contiguous

nearsighted
6 myopic

neat
4 deft, nice, prim, snug, tidy, trig, trim **5** clean, clear, kempt **6** bovine, cattle, clever, smooth, spruce **7** orderly, precise, unmixed **8** straight, well-kept **9** shipshape, undiluted **10** methodical, systematic **11** spic-and-span, uncluttered, well-groomed **12** spick-and-span **13** unadulterated

neb
3 tip **4** beak, bill, nose, prow **5** snoot, snout **9** proboscis

Nebraska
capital: 7 Lincoln
city: 5 Omaha
college, university: 9 Creighton
nickname: 10 Cornhusker (State)
river: 6 Platte **8** Missouri
state bird: 10 meadowlark
state flower: 9 goldenrod
state tree: 10 cottonwood

nebula
6 galaxy

nebulous
4 hazy **5** vague **6** cloudy, turbid **7** clouded, obscure, unclear **9** ambiguous, amorphous, uncertain **10** indefinite, indistinct **13** indeterminate

necessary
5 basic, vital **6** needed **7** crucial, needful **8** cardinal, integral, required **9** de rigueur, essential, mandatory, requisite **10** compulsory, imperative, inevitable, obligatory, undeniable **11** fundamental, ineluctable, inescapable, unavoidable **12** all-important, prerequisite **13** indispensable

necessitate
5 cause, exact, force **6** compel, demand, entail **7** call for, involve, require **8** occasion

necessity
4 must, need **6** crisis, duress **7** poverty **8** exigency **9** essential, privation, requisite **10** compulsion, imperative, obligation, sine qua non **11** dire straits, needfulness, requirement **12** precondition, prerequisite

neck
3 pet **4** kiss **5** spoon **6** fondle, smooch
back of: 4 nape **5** nucha, nuque **6** scruff
ornament: 6 gorget, torque

necklace
5 chain **6** choker **7** rivière **8** carcanet
floral: 3 lei

necktie
4 bolo **5** ascot **6** cravat **10** four-in-hand

necrology
4 obit **8** obituary

necromancy
4 juju, mojo **5** magic, vodun **6** hoodoo, voodoo **7** devilry, sorcery **8** witchery, wizardry **9** conjuring, diabolism, magicking **10** black magic, witchcraft **11** bewitchment, conjuration, enchantment, incantation, thaumaturgy

necropolis
8 boneyard, boot hill, cemetery, God's acre **9** graveyard **10** churchyard **12** memorial park, potter's field

necropsy
7 anatomy, autopsy **10** dissection, postmortem

née
4 born **10** originally

need
3 use **4** call, duty, lack, must, want **5** crave **6** demand, devoir, hunger, penury, thirst **7** poverty, require **8** distress, exigency, occasion, shortage **9** indigence, necessity, privation, requisite **10** compulsion, deficiency, obligation **11** deprivation, destitution, requirement

neediness
4 want **6** penury **7** poverty **9** essential, indigence, privation **11** deprivation, destitution **13** insufficiency

needle
3 rib **5** annoy, tease **6** harass, pester, plague **7** bedevil, hagride, obelisk, pricker, syringe **10** hypodermic
case: 4 etui
hole: 3 eye

needlefish
3 gar **8** pipefish

needlelike
7 styloid **8** belonoid
part: 7 acicula

needlepoint
4 lace **7** alençon, crochet, tatting **8** bargello **10** embroidery **11** cross-stitch

needlework
4 lace **6** sewing **7** alençon, crochet, sampler, tatting **8** bargello, knitting **9** stitching **10** crocheting, embroidery **11** cross-stitch

needy
4 poor **5** broke **6** hard up **8** beggared, dirt-poor, indigent, strapped **9** destitute, penniless, penurious **10** down-and-out **11** impecunious, necessitous **12** impoverished

ne'er-do-well
3 bum, dud **5** loser **6** loafer, no-good **7** failure, wastrel **8** derelict, fainéant **9** shiftless **10** profligate, scapegrace

nefarious
4 evil, vile **6** savage, wicked **7** heinous, impious, noxious **8** depraved, dreadful, flagrant,

infamous, perverse **9** execrable, miscreant, monstrous, offensive **10** abominable, degenerate, detestable, iniquitous, outrageous, villainous **11** opprobrious **13** reprehensible

negate
4 deny, undo, void **5** annul, belie, quash, rebut **6** cancel, impugn, refute, vacate **7** abolish, gainsay, nullify, redress, vitiate **8** abrogate, disallow, disprove, overturn, traverse **9** cancel out, disaffirm, repudiate **10** contradict, contravene, counteract, invalidate, neutralize

negative
2 no **3** nay, nix **4** deny, kill, veto **5** annul, cross, minus **6** impugn **7** adverse, gainsay, nullify, redress, refusal **8** abrogate, disprove, traverse **9** cancel out, frustrate **10** contradict, contravene, counteract, invalidate, neutralize **11** detrimental, unfavorable
battery terminal: **5** anode
ion: **5** anion
Scottish: **3** nae
sign: **5** minus

neglect
4 fail, omit **5** let go, shirk **6** forget, ignore, laxity, slight **7** failure, laxness **8** omission, overlook, overpass, pass over **9** avoidance, disregard, oversight, pretermit **10** negligence **11** dereliction, inattention **12** carelessness

neglectful
see **negligent**

negligee
4 gown **5** teddy **7** chemise, nightie **8** camisole, peignoir **9** nightgown

negligent
3 lax **5** slack **6** remiss **8** careless, derelict, heedless **9** forgetful, imprudent **10** delinquent, neglectful, nonchalant, regardless, unthinking **11** inattentive, pococurante, unconcerned **13** irresponsible, lackadaisical

negligible
4 puny, slim **5** minor, petty, small **6** meager, meagre, minute, remote, paltry, skimpy, slight **7** minimal, slender, trivial **8** nugatory, picayune, trifling **9** minuscule **11** meaningless, unimportant **13** imperceptible, insignificant

negotiable
8 passable **11** convertible **12** transferable

negotiate
4 cash **6** confer, dicker, hurdle, manage, parley, settle **7** arrange, bargain, develop, mediate, work out, wrangle **8** contract, covenant, moderate, surmount, transact, transfer **9** arbitrate **10** horse-trade

neigh
6 nicker, whinny

neighbor
4 abut **5** flank, frame, skirt, touch **6** adjoin, border **7** abutter **8** border on

neighborhood
4 area, nabe, turf, ward **5** block, range **6** parish **8** district, environs, locality, precinct, purlieus, vicinage, vicinity **9** community, proximity

neighborly
6 genial **7** amiable, cordial, helpful **8** amicable, friendly, obliging, sociable **9** congenial **10** gregarious, hospitable **11** considerate, cooperative, good-natured **13** accommodating

nematode
4 worm **7** eelworm **9** roundworm

Nemean predator
4 lion

nemesis
4 bane, doom **5** curse, enemy, rival **8** opponent **9** bête noire **11** retribution

neologism
7 coinage, new word

neon symbol
2 Ne

neophyte
see **newcomer**

Neoptolemus
7 Pyrrhus
father: **8** Achilles
slayer: **7** Orestes
victim: **5** Priam
wife: **8** Hermione

neoteric
6 modern, recent

Nepal
capital: **8** Katmandu **9** Kathmandu
city: **7** Pokhara **8** Lalitpur
monetary unit: **5** rupee
mountain, range: **7** Everest **8** Himalaya **9** Himalayan, Himalayas **10** Dhaulagiri **11** Gauri Sankar **12** Kanchenjunga
neighbor: **5** China, India
river: **6** Ganges

nepenthe
6 opiate, potion **7** anodyne **8** lenitive, narcotic **9** analgesic **10** anesthetic, painkiller **11** anaesthetic

Nephthys
brother, husband: **3** Set **4** Seth

nepotism
10 favoritism, partiality

Neptune
6 planet
satellite: **6** Nereid, Triton
(see also **Poseidon**)

nerd
4 drip, geek **5** dweeb **6** misfit, weenie **7** egghead, nebbish, oddball **10** pointy-head

Nereid
6 Thetis **7** Galatea **10** Amphitrite
father: 6 Nereus
mother: 5 Doris

Nereus
daughters: 8 Nereides
emblem: 7 trident
father: 6 Pontus
mother: 4 Gaea
wife: 5 Doris

Nergal
brother: 5 Nanna **6** Ninazu
father: 5 Enlil
mother: 6 Ninlil

Nero
birthplace: 4 Rome
mother: 9 Agrippina
successor: 5 Galba
tutor: 6 Seneca
victim: 5 Lucan **6** Seneca **7** Octavia, Poppaea **9** Agrippina
wife: 7 Octavia, Poppaea

Nero Wolfe creator
5 Stout (Rex)

nerve
4 face, gall, grit, guts **5** brass, cheek, crust, heart, moxie, spunk **6** daring **7** sciatic **8** audacity, backbone, boldness, chutzpah, temerity **9** assurance, brashness, fortitude, hardihood, hardiness **10** confidence, effrontery **11** presumption
cell: 6 neuron
cell group: 7 ganglia (plural) **8** ganglion
cell part: 4 axon **8** dendrite, receptor
combining form: 4 neur **5** neura, neuro
cranial: 4 vagi (plural) **5** optic, vagus **8** abducens
lesion: 8 neuritis

nerve center
3 hub **4** core, seat **5** focus, heart, locus **7** capital **8** cynosure, polestar **10** crossroads, focal point **12** headquarters

nerve gas
5 sarin, soman, tabun

nervous
4 edgy **5** antsy, jerky, jumpy, tense, timid **6** fitful, goosey, on edge, spooky, uneasy **7** erratic, fidgety, fretful, jittery, restive, twitchy, uptight **8** aflutter, agitated, skittery, skittish, spirited, twittery, unsteady, vigorous, volatile **9** excitable, irritable **10** high-strung **12** apprehensive

nervy
4 bold, edgy, flip, pert **5** brash, cocky, fresh, jerky, jumpy, sassy, tense **6** brassy, cheeky, goosey, plucky, uneasy **7** fidgety, forward, jittery, restive, twitchy, uptight **8** flippant, impudent, intrepid, twittery **9** excitable **10** high-strung **11** smart-alecky

ness
4 cape **8** foreland, headland **9** peninsula **10** promontory

Nessus' victim
8 Heracles, Hercules

nest
3 den **4** aery, home, lair, nidi (plural) **5** aerie, eyrie, nidus **7** hangout, shelter **11** aggregation
eagle's: 4 aery **5** aerie, eyrie
pheasant's: 4 nide
wasp's: 8 vespiary

nest egg
5 cache, funds, hoard, kitty, stash **6** assets **7** reserve

nestle
4 snug **6** bundle, burrow, cuddle, huddle, nuzzle **7** snuggle

Nestor
father: 6 Neleus
kingdom: 5 Pylos

net
4 gain, gist, mesh **5** basic, catch, clear, seine, tulle, yield **6** maline **7** clean up, essence, malines
conical: 5 trawl
fishing: 5 seine
hair: 5 snood

Nethanel
brother: 5 David
father: 5 Jesse **7** Pashhur **8** Obededom
son: 8 Shemaiah

nether
3 low **4** down **5** below, lower, under **6** lesser **8** chthonic, inferior **9** subjacent **10** underworld **11** underground **12** subterranean

Netherlands
7 Holland
capital: 9 Amsterdam
city: 5 Hague (The) **7** Utrecht **8** The Hague **9** Rotterdam
former inlet: 9 Zuider Zee
island group: 11 West Frisian
lake: 10 IJsselmeer
language: 5 Dutch
monetary unit: 4 euro
monetary unit, former: 6 gulden, stiver **7** guilder
neighbor: 7 Belgium, Germany
river: 4 Maas **5** Meuse, Rhein, Rhine **7** Scheldt
sea: 5 North

Netherlands Antilles
capital: **10** Willemstad
discoverer: **8** Columbus (Christopher)
former name: **7** Curaçao
island: **4** Saba **7** Bonaire **7** Curaçao
location: **10** West Indies

netherworld
3 pit **4** hell **5** abyss, hades, Sheol **6** blazes, Tophet **7** Gehenna, inferno **8** hellfire **9** perdition **10** no-man's-land, underworld **11** underground

netlike
9 reticular **10** reticulate

nettle
3 irk, nag, vex **4** gall, huff, rile, roil **5** annoy, chafe, peeve, pique, upset **6** abrade, badger, harass, incite, put out, pester, ruffle, stir up **7** agitate, disturb, perturb, provoke **8** irritate **10** exasperate

nettle rash
5 hives **9** urticaria

nettlesome
5 pesky **6** vexing **7** galling, irksome, prickly **8** annoying, rankling **9** irritable, upsetting, vexatious **10** irritating

network
3 ABC, CBS, CNN, CTV, Fox, HBO, NBC, PBS, QVC, TBS, TNT, web **4** ESPN, grid, INHD, mesh, NESN, rete **8** gridiron, Internet **9** reticulum
anatomical: **4** rete **5** retia (plural)

neurotic
6 phobic, touchy **7** anxious **8** abnormal, unstable **9** disturbed, obsessive **10** compulsive, disordered

neuter
3 fix **4** geld, spay **5** alter, unsex **7** sexless **8** castrate, mutilate **9** sterilize **11** desexualize **12** intransitive

neutral
7 hueless **8** detached, middling, unbiased **9** colorless, impartial, unaligned **10** achromatic, disengaged, even-handed, impersonal, nonaligned, pokerfaced **11** indifferent, nonpartisan **13** disinterested, dispassionate

neutralize
4 undo **5** annul **6** negate, offset **7** balance, nullify, redress, reverse **9** cancel out **10** counteract, invalidate **11** countervail **12** countercheck, counterpoise

Nevada
capital: **10** Carson City
city: **4** Elko, Reno **8** Las Vegas
dam: **6** Hoover **7** Boulder
lake: **4** Mead **5** Tahoe
mountain: **8** Boundary (Peak)
nickname: **6** Silver (State)
river: **8** Humboldt
state bird: **8** bluebird (mountain)
state flower: **9** sagebrush
state tree: **5** piñon **6** pinyon **15** bristlecone pine

névé
4 firn, snow

never-ending
7 eternal **8** immortal **9** ceaseless **11** everlasting

Never-Ending Story author
4 Ende (Michael)

nevertheless
3 but, yet **5** still **6** anyhow, anyway, though, withal **7** howbeit, however **8** after all **10** regardless **11** nonetheless, still and all

nevus
4 mole **9** birthmark

new
5 fresh, novel **6** modern, recent **7** another, revived **8** neoteric, pristine **9** fledgling **10** additional, unfamiliar **11** modernistic **12** contemporary
combining form: **3** neo, nov **4** novo
word: **7** coinage **9** neologism

New Age
belief: **5** karma **6** cabala, holism, kabala **7** kabbala **8** kabbalah **9** occultism, pantheism, shamanism, theosophy, wholeness **10** numerology, soul travel **12** spiritualism **13** reincarnation, synchronicity
community: **6** Esalen, Sedona, Totnes **7** Dornach **8** Byron Bay, Damanhur, Findhorn **9** Arcosanti, Auroville
healing technique: **5** auras **8** Ayurveda, crystals **9** iridology **10** homeopathy **11** acupressure, acupuncture, biofeedback **12** aromatherapy
practice: **4** yoga **5** reiki **7** fasting **10** channeling, meditation, syncretism
teacher: **3** Orr (Leonard) **4** Dass (Ram), Long (Barry), Myss (Caroline) **5** Cohen (Andrew) **6** Chopra (Deepak), Walsch (Neale Donald), Wilber (Ken) **7** Kabbani (Hisham), Quanjer (Johan) **8** Cottrell (Douglas James), Rajneesh (Bhagwan Shree), Spangler (David) **9** Castaneda (Carlos), Helminski (Kabir) **10** Williamson (Marianne)

New Brunswick
capital: **11** Fredericton
city: **6** St. John **7** Moncton
mountain: **8** Carleton

provincial flower: **12** purple violet
river: **9** Miramichi, Saint John **10** Nepisiguit **11** Restigouche

New Caledonia
capital: **6** Nouméa
department of: **6** France
discoverer: **4** Cook (Capt. James)
island: **7** Loyalty, Walpole **11** Isle of Pines

newcomer
4 colt, tiro, tyro **6** novice, rookie **7** trainee **8** beginner, freshman, initiate, neophyte **9** greenhorn, immigrant, novitiate **10** apprentice, tenderfoot

New Deal agency
3 CCC, NRA, REA, RFC, SEC, TVA, WPA **4** FDIC, NLRB

Newfoundland and Labrador
capital: **7** St. John's
mountain: **8** Caubvick
provincial flower: **12** pitcher plant
river: **6** Gander **8** Exploits **9** Churchill

New Hampshire
capital: **7** Concord
city: **6** Nashua **10** Manchester, Portsmouth
college, university: **9** Dartmouth
motto: **13** Live Free or Die
mountain, range: **5** White **10** Washington
nickname: **7** Granite (State)
river: **9** Merrimack **11** Connecticut
state bird: **11** purple finch
state flower: **11** purple lilac
state tree: **10** white birch

New Jersey
capital: **7** Trenton
city: **6** Camden, Newark **7** Cape May **8** Paterson **9** Elizabeth **10** Jersey City
college, university: **4** Drew **7** Rutgers **9** Princeton, Seton Hall
nickname: **6** Garden (State)
river: **6** Hudson **7** Raritan **8** Delaware
state bird: **9** goldfinch
state flower: **6** violet
state tree: **6** red oak

New Mexico
capital: **7** Santa Fe
caverns: **8** Carlsbad
city: **4** Taos **7** Roswell **9** Las Cruces, Los Alamos **10** Farmington **11** Albuquerque
mountain, range: **7** Wheeler (Peak) **14** Sangre de Cristo
nickname: **17** Land of Enchantment
river: **5** Pecos **9** Rio Grande
state bird: **10** roadrunner
state flower: **5** yucca
state tree: **5** piñon **6** pinyon

news
4 dope, poop, word **5** rumor **6** advice, gossip, report, tattle **7** lowdown, tidings **9** knowledge, speerings **11** information, scuttlebutt **12** announcement, intelligence
agency: **2** AP **3** AFP, UPI **4** TASS **7** Reuters **8** ITAR-TASS

newspaper
3 rag **5** daily, organ **6** review **7** gazette, journal, tabloid **8** magazine **10** periodical
goof: **4** typo
publisher: **6** Hearst (William Randolph) **7** Murdoch (Rupert) **11** Beaverbrook (Lord)
section: **4** arts, op-ed **6** comics, sports **8** business **10** classified

newt
3 eft **6** triton
green: **5** ebbet

New Testament
see at **Bible**

New York
capital: **6** Albany
city: **4** Rome, Troy **5** Utica **6** Elmira, Ithaca **7** Buffalo, Yonkers **8** Saratoga, Syracuse **9** Rochester
college, university: **3** RPI **4** Pace, CUNY, SUNY **5** Pratt, Siena **6** CW Post, Hunter, Vassar **7** Adelphi, Barnard, Colgate, Cornell, Fordham, Hofstra, St. Johns, Yeshiva **8** Columbia, Skidmore, Syracuse **9** Juilliard, West Point **13** Sarah Lawrence
county: **5** Tioga **6** Albany, Oneida, Queens **7** Clinton, Niagara **8** Dutchess, Onandaga
island: **4** Long, Fire
lake, lake group: **4** Erie **6** Cayuga, Finger, Oneida **7** Saranac **9** Champlain
motto: **9** Excelsior
mountain, range: **5** Marcy **8** Catskill **10** Adirondack
nickname: **6** Empire (State)
prison: **6** Attica
river: **6** Hudson **7** Niagara **10** St. Lawrence
state bird: **8** bluebird
state flower: **4** rose
state tree: **10** sugar maple

New York City
6 Gotham **8** Big Apple
borough: **5** Bronx **6** Queens **8** Brooklyn, Richmond **9** Manhattan **12** Staten Island
neighborhood: **4** Soho **6** Harlem **7** Tribeca

New Zealand
capital: **10** Wellington
city: **8** Auckland **12** Christchurch
ethnic group: **5** Maori
evergreen: **4** tawa

explorer: **4** Cook (Capt. James) **6** Tasman (Abel)
island: **7** Chatham, Stewart
island group: **4** Cook **8** Manihiki **12** Northern Cook
lake: **5** Taupo
language: **5** Maori
mountain, range: **4** Cook **6** Egmont **12** Southern Alps
native: **4** Kiwi
parrot: **4** kaka
shrub: **4** tutu
strait: **4** Cook
volcano: **7** Ruapehu **9** Ngauruhoe

next
4 then **5** after, later **6** behind, beside, second **7** closest, ensuing, nearest **8** abutting, adjacent, touching **9** adjoining, afterward, alongside, following, proximate **10** contiguous, subsequent, succeeding **11** neighboring

next to
4 near **6** almost, beside **7** abreast, close by **8** abutting, adjacent, opposite, touching **9** adjoining, alongside, bordering **11** neighboring

nexus
3 tie **4** bond, knot, link, yoke **5** focus **6** center **8** ligament, ligature, vinculum **10** connection

Nez Percé chief
6 Joseph

Niagara
5 flood, spate **6** deluge **7** torrent **8** alluvion, cataract, flooding, overflow **9** cataclysm, waterfall **10** inundation

nib
3 tip **4** beak, bill, nose, prow **5** prong, snoot, snout, tooth **8** pen point **9** proboscis

nibble
3 eat, nip **4** bite, chew, crop, gnaw, nosh, peck, pick **5** graze, munch, snack, taste **6** morsel, tidbit

Nicaragua
capital: **7** Managua
city: **4** León **6** Masaya **7** Grenada
coast: **8** Mosquito
ethnic group: **4** Maya **5** Mayan
discoverer: **8** Columbus (Christopher)
language: **7** Spanish
monetary unit: **7** córdoba
neighbor: **8** Honduras **9** Costa Rica
sea: **9** Caribbean

nice
4 fine, good, kind, mild, neat **5** right **6** benign, decent, polite, proper, seemly **7** affable, cordial, correct, fitting, refined **8** becoming, charming, decorous, obliging, pleasant, pleasing, suitable, virtuous, well-bred **9** admirable, agreeable, courteous, congenial, enjoyable, favorable **10** attractive, personable **11** appropriate, respectable

niche
4 nook **6** alcove, corner, cranny, recess **7** calling **8** vocation **9** cubbyhole **11** compartment

Nicholas Nickleby author
7 Dickens (Charles)

nick
3 cut **4** chip, gash **5** cheat, notch, score **6** groove, record **10** overcharge **11** indentation

nickel symbol
2 Ni

nickname
3 tag **5** label **6** byword, handle **7** agnomen, epithet, moniker **8** cognomen **9** sobriquet **10** diminutive, hypocorism

Nicomede
conquest: **10** Cappodocia
dramatist: **9** Corneille (Pierre)
half-brother: **6** Attale
stepmother: **7** Arsinoë

nictitate
3 bat **4** wink **5** blink **7** flutter, twinkle

nifty
4 cool, keen, neat **5** dandy, ducky, super, swell **6** clever, groovy, peachy **7** stylish **8** jim-dandy, splendid, terrific **9** ingenious

Niger
capital: **6** Niamey
city: **6** Maradi, Zinder
desert: **5** Sahel **6** Sahara
ethnic group: **5** Hausa
language: **5** Hausa **6** Arabic, French
monetary unit: **5** franc
neighbor: **4** Chad, Mali **5** Benin, Libya **7** Algeria, Nigeria **11** Burkina Faso
river: **5** Niger

Nigeria
capital: **5** Abuja, Lagos
city: **4** Kano **6** Ibadan, Ilorin **7** Oshogbo **9** Ogbomosho
ethnic group: **4** Igbo **5** Hausa **6** Fulani, Yoruba
gulf: **6** Guinea
lake: **4** Chad
language: **5** Hausa
monetary unit: **5** naira
neighbor: **4** Chad **5** Benin, Niger **8** Cameroon
river: **5** Benue, Niger **6** Kaduna

niggard
5 churl, miser, piker, screw **7** hoarder, scrooge **8** tightwad **9** skinflint **10** cheapskate, curmudgeon **12** money-grubber, penny-pincher

niggardly
5 tight **6** scanty, stingy **7** chintzy, miserly **9** penurious **10** begrudging **11** closefisted, tightfisted **12** cheeseparing, parsimonious **13** penny-pinching

niggling
5 minor, petty **6** measly, paltry, two-bit **7** trivial **8** picayune, piddling, tiresome, trifling **9** small-time **10** bothersome, picayunish **11** Mickey Mouse, small-minded

nigh
4 near **5** about, close, round **6** all but, almost, around, beside, nearby, nearly **7** close to **8** approach **9** immediate, just about, proximate, virtually **10** near at hand **11** practically

night blindness
10 nyctalopia

nightclub
5 disco **6** bistro, casino **7** cabaret **9** honky-tonk, speakeasy **11** discotheque

nightfall
3 eve **4** dusk, even **6** sunset **7** evening, sundown **8** eventide, gloaming, twilight

nighthawk
6 petrel **7** bullbat **10** goatsucker

nightjar
9 nighthawk **10** goatsucker **12** whip-poor-will

nightly
9 nocturnal

nightmare
5 dream, fancy, worry **6** fright, horror, ordeal, vision **7** bugbear, fantasy, incubus, torment **8** phantasm, phantasy, succubus **12** apprehension **13** hallucination

nightshade
6 tomato **7** henbane **8** eggplant **10** belladonna **11** bittersweet

nightstick
3 bat **4** club, mace **5** baton, billy, staff **6** cudgel **8** bludgeon **9** billy club, blackjack, shillalah, truncheon **10** shillelagh

Nike
father: **6** Pallas
goddess of: **7** victory
mother: **4** Styx

nil
3 nix, zip **4** love, nada, wind, zero **5** zilch **6** naught **7** nothing

Nile
6 Al-Bahr
dam: **5** Aswan **6** Makwar **10** Gebel Aulia
enclave: **4** Lado
explorer: **5** Baker (Sir Samuel), Bruce (James), Grant (James Augustus), Speke (John Hanning)
queen: **4** Cleo **9** Cleopatra
section: **4** Abay **5** Abbai
source lake: **4** Tana

nilgai
8 antelope

nimble
4 deft, spry, yare **5** agile, alert, fleet, handy, light, quick, zippy **6** adroit, limber, lively **7** lissome **9** dexterous, sprightly **10** responsive **11** quick-witted

nimbus
4 aura, halo **5** glory **6** corona **7** aureole

Nimrod
6 hunter
father: **4** Cush

Nin, Anaïs
father: **7** Joaquin
friend: **6** Miller (Henry)

Ninazu
brother: **5** Nanna **6** Nergal
father: **5** Enlil
mother: **6** Ninlil

nincompoop
3 oaf **4** boob, clod, dodo, fool, goof, mutt, simp, yo-yo **5** chump, dummy, dunce, idiot, moron, ninny, noddy, stupe **6** dimwit, donkey, dum-dum, nitwit **7** airhead, dullard, pinhead, schnook, tomfool **8** bonehead, clodpoll, dumbbell, dumbhead, imbecile, lunkhead, meathead, numskull **9** bird-brain, blockhead, ignoramus, lamebrain, numbskull, simpleton, thickhead **10** dunderhead, hammerhead **11** chowderhead, chucklehead, knucklehead, ninnyhammer

nine
12 baseball team
combining form: **3** non **4** nona **5** ennea
goddesses: **5** Muses
group: **6** ennead
inches: **4** span
instruments: **5** nonet

nine-eyes
7 lamprey

Nine Worlds
3 Hel **6** Asgard **7** Alfheim, Midgard **8** Niflheim, Vanaheim **10** Jotunnheim **12** Muspellsheim **13** Svartalfaheim

ninny
see **nincompoop**

Ninsum's son
9 Gilgamesh

Nintu
consort: **4** Enki
son: **6** Ninsar

Ninurta
father: **5** Enlil
victim: **3** Kur

Ninus
father: **5** Belus
wife: **9** Semiramis

Niobe
brother: **6** Pelops
father: **8** Tantalus
husband: **7** Amphion
sister-in-law: **5** Aedon

nip
3 bit, nab, sip **4** bite, dart, dash, dram, drop, jolt, peck, shot, slug, swig **5** chill, clamp, hurry, pinch, sever, snort, steal **6** imbibe, snatch, thwart, tipple **7** cabbage, snifter, swallow **9** frustrate

nipper
3 kid **4** tike, tyke **5** child **6** moppet, shaver **7** pincers **9** youngling, youngster

nipple
3 pap **4** teat **7** mammila

Nippon
5 Japan

nippy
3 icy, raw **4** cold, cool **5** algid, chill, crisp, sharp **6** arctic, biting, bitter, chilly, frosty, wintry **7** caustic, glacial, numbing, shivery **8** chilling, freezing

nirvana
5 bliss, dream **6** heaven **7** Elysium, rapture **8** empyrean, euphoria, oblivion, paradise **9** Shangri-la

Nisus
betrayer, daughter: **6** Scylla
father: **7** Pandion

nitid
6 bright, glossy, lucent **7** fulgent, glowing, shining **8** gleaming, glinting, luminous, lustrous, polished **9** burnished

nitpick
4 carp **5** cavil **7** quibble **10** split hairs

nitrogen
5 azote
combining form: **3** azo

nitty-gritty
4 core, gist, meat, pith **5** heart, stuff **6** burden, kernel **7** essence **9** substance **10** bottom line, brass tacks

nitwit
3 oaf **4** boob, clod, dodo, dolt, dope, goof, mutt, simp **5** chump, cluck, dummy, dunce, idiot, moron, ninny, noddy, stupe **6** donkey, dum-dum **7** airhead, dullard, pinhead, schnook **8** bonehead, clodpoll, dumbbell, imbecile, lunkhead, meathead, numskull **9** birdbrain, blockhead, ignoramus, lamebrain, numbskull, simpleton, thickhead **10** dunderhead, hammerhead, nincompoop **11** chowderhead, chucklehead, knucklehead

nix
2 no **3** nay, nil, zap **4** kill, nada, nope, veto, zero **5** quash **6** cancel, naught, reject, scotch, sprite **7** call off, nothing, nullify

Njord, Njorth
daughter: **5** Freya
son: **4** Frey
wife: **6** Skadhi, Skathi

no
3 nay, nix **4** uh-uh **6** denial **7** refusal **8** negative **10** thumbs-down
German: **4** nein
Scottish: **3** nae

no-account
see **no-good**

Noachian
3 old **4** aged **5** fusty, hoary **6** age-old **7** ancient, antique, archaic **8** timeworn **9** venerable **10** antiquated, oldfangled **12** antediluvian, old-fashioned **13** superannuated

Noah
father: **6** Lamech **10** Zelophehad
grandson: **4** Aram **6** Canaan
great-grandson: **3** Hul
landing place: **6** Ararat
son: **3** Ham **4** Shem **6** Canaan **7** Japheth

Nobel Prize winner
chemistry:
1901: **8** van't Hoff (Jacobus)
1902: **7** Fischer (Emil)
1903: **9** Arrhenius (Svante)
1904: **6** Ramsay (William)
1905: **9** von Baeyer (Adolf)
1906: **7** Moissan (Henri)
1907: **7** Buchner (Eduard)
1908: **10** Rutherford (Ernest)
1909: **7** Ostwald (Wilhelm)
1910: **7** Wallach (Otto)
1911: **5** Curie (Marie)
1912: **8** Grignard (François), Sabatier (Paul)
1913: **6** Werner (Alfred)
1914: **8** Richards (Theodore)
1915: **11** Willstatter (Richard)
1918: **5** Haber (Fritz)
1920: **6** Nernst (Walther)
1921: **5** Soddy (Frederick)
1922: **5** Aston (Francis)
1923: **5** Pregl (Fritz)
1925: **9** Zsigmondy (Richard)
1926: **8** Svedberg (Theodor)
1927: **7** Wieland (Heinrich)
1928: **7** Windaus (Adolf)
1929: **6** Harden (Athur) **12** Euler-Chelpin (Hans von)
1930: **7** Fischer (Hans)

1931: **5** Bosch (Karl) **7** Bergius (Friedrich)
1932: **8** Langmuir (Irving)
1934: **4** Urey (Harold)
1935: **11** Joliot-Curie (Frédéric, Irene)
1936: **5** Debye (Peter)
1937: **6** Karrer (Paul) **7** Haworth (Walter)
1938: **4** Kuhn (Richard)
1939: **7** Ruzicka (Leopold) **9** Butenandt (Adolf)
1943: **6** Hevesy (Georg de)
1944: **4** Hahn (Otto)
1945: **8** Virtanen (Artturi)
1946: **6** Sumner (James) **7** Stanley (Wendell) **8** Northrop (John Howard)
1947: **8** Robinson (Robert)
1948: **8** Tiselius (Arne)
1949: **7** Giauque (William)
1950: **5** Alder (Kurt), Diels (Otto)
1951: **7** Seaborg (Glenn) **8** McMillan (Edwin)
1952: **5** Synge (Richard) **6** Martin (Archer)
1953: **10** Staudinger (Hermann)
1954: **7** Pauling (Linus)
1955: **10** du Vigneaud (Vincent)
1956: **7** Semenov (Nikolay) **11** Hinshelwood (Cyril)
1957: **4** Todd (Alexander)
1958: **6** Sanger (Frederick)
1959: **9** Heyrovsky (Jaroslav)
1960: **5** Libby (Willard)
1961: **6** Calvin (Melvin)
1962: **6** Perutz (Max) **7** Kendrew (John)
1963: **5** Natta (Giulio) **7** Ziegler (Karl)
1964: **7** Hodgkin (Dorothy) **8** Woodward (Robert)
1966: **8** Mulliken (Robert)
1967: **5** Eigen (Manfred) **6** Porter (George) **7** Norrish (Ronald)
1968: **7** Onsager (Lars)
1969: **6** Barton (Derek), Hassel (Odd)
1970: **6** Leloir (Luis)
1971: **8** Herzberg (Gerhard)
1972: **5** Moore (Stanford), Stein (William) **8** Anfinsen (Christian)
1973: **7** Fischer (Ernst) **9** Wilkinson (Geoffrey)
1974: **5** Flory (Paul)
1975: **6** Prelog (Vladimir) **9** Cornforth (John)
1976: **8** Lipscomb (William)
1977: **9** Prigogine (Ilya)
1978: **8** Mitchell (Peter)
1979: **5** Brown (Herbert) **6** Wittig (Georg)
1980: **4** Berg (Paul) **6** Sanger (Frederick) **7** Gilbert (Walter)
1981: **5** Fukui (Kenichi) **8** Hoffmann (Roald)
1982: **4** Klug (Aaron)
1983: **5** Taube (Henry)
1984: **10** Merrifield (R. Bruce)
1985: **5** Karle (Jerome) **8** Hauptman (Herbert)
1986: **3** Lee (Yuan) **7** Polanyi (John) **10** Herschbach (Dudley)
1987: **4** Cram (Donald), Lehn (Jean-Marie) **8** Pedersen (Charles)
1988: **5** Huber (Robert) **6** Michel (Hartmut) **11** Deisenhofer (Johann)
1989: **4** Cech (Thomas) **6** Altman (Sidney)
1990: **5** Corey (Elias)
1991: **5** Ernst (Richard)
1992: **6** Marcus (Rudolph)
1993: **5** Smith (Michael) **6** Mullis (Kary)
1994: **4** Olah (George)
1995: **6** Molina (Mario) **7** Crutzen (Paul), Rowland (F. Sherwood)
1996: **4** Curl (Robert) **5** Kroto (Harold) **7** Smalley (Richard)
1997 **4** Skou (Jens) **5** Boyer (Paul) **6** Walker (John)
1998: **4** Kohn (Walter) **5** Pople (John)
1999: **6** Zewail (Ahmed)
2000: **6** Heeger (Alan) **9** Shirakawa (Hideki) **10** MacDiarmid (Alan)
2001: **6** Noyori (Ryoji) **7** Knowles (William) **9** Sharpless (K. Barry)
2002: **4** Fenn (John) **6** Tanaka (Koichi) **8** Wüthrich (Kurt)
2003: **4** Agre (Peter) **9** MacKinnon (Roderick)
2004: **4** Rose (Irwin) **7** Hershko (Avram) **11** Ciechanover (Aaron)
2005: **6** Grubbs (Robert) **7** Chauvin (Yves), Schrock (Richard)
2006: **8** Kornberg (Roger)

economics:
1969: **6** Frisch (Ragnar) **9** Tinbergen (Jan)
1970: **9** Samuelson (Paul)
1971: **7** Kuznets (Simon)
1972: **5** Arrow (Kenneth), Hicks (John)
1973: **8** Leontief (Wassily)
1974: **5** Hayek (Friedrich von) **6** Myrdal (Gunnar)
1975: **8** Koopmans (Tjalling) **11** Kantorovich (Leonid)
1976: **8** Friedman (Milton)
1977: **5** Meade (James), Ohlin (Bertil)
1978: **5** Simon (Herbert)
1979: **5** Lewis (Arthur) **7** Schultz (Theodore)
1980: **5** Klein (Lawrence)
1981: **5** Tobin (James)
1982: **7** Stigler (George)
1983: **6** Debreu (Gerard)
1984: **5** Stone (Richard)
1985: **10** Modigliani (Franco)
1986: **8** Buchanan (James)
1987: **5** Solow (Robert)
1988: **6** Allais (Maurice)
1989: **8** Haavelmo (Trygve)
1990: **6** Miller (Merton), Sharpe (William) **9** Markowitz (Harry)
1991: **5** Coase (Ronald)
1992: **6** Becker (Gary)

1993: **5** Fogel (Robert), North (Douglass)
1994: **4** Nash (John) **6** Selten (Reinhard) **8** Harsanyi (John)
1995: **5** Lucas (Robert)
1996: **7** Vickrey (William) **8** Mirrlees (James)
1998: **3** Sen (Amartya)
1999: **7** Mundell (Robert)
2000: **7** Heckman (James) **8** McFadden (Daniel)
2001: **6** Spence (Michael) **7** Akerlof (George) **8** Stiglitz (Joseph)
2002: **5** Smith (Vernon) **8** Kahneman (Daniel)
2003: **5** Engle (Robert) **7** Granger (Clive)
2004: **7** Kydland (Finn) **8** Prescott (Edward)
2005: **6** Aumann (Robert) **9** Schelling (Thomas)
2006: **6** Phelps (Edmund)

literature:
1901: **9** Prudhomme (Sully)
1902: **7** Mommsen (Theodor)
1903: **8** Bjornson (Bjornstjerne)
1904: **7** Mistral (Frédéric) **9** Echegaray (José)
1905: **11** Sienkiewicz (Henryk)
1906: **8** Carducci (Giosue)
1907: **7** Kipling (Rudyard)
1908: **6** Eucken (Rudolf)
1909: **8** Lagerlof (Selma)
1910: **5** Heyse (Paul)
1911: **11** Maeterlinck (Maurice)
1912: **9** Hauptmann (Gerhart)
1913: **6** Tagore (Rabindranath)
1915: **7** Rolland (Romain)
1916: **10** Heidenstam (Verner von)
1917: **9** Gjellerup (Karl) **11** Pontoppidan (Henrik)
1919: **9** Spitteler (Carl)
1920: **6** Hamsun (Knut)
1921: **6** France (Anatole)
1922: **9** Benavente (Jacinto)
1923: **5** Yeats (William Butler)
1924: **7** Reymont (Wladyslaw)
1925: **4** Shaw (George Bernard)
1926: **7** Deledda (Grazia)
1927: **7** Bergson (Henri)
1928: **6** Undset (Sigrid)
1929: **4** Mann (Thomas)
1930: **5** Lewis (Sinclair)
1931: **9** Karlfeldt (Erik Axel)
1932: **10** Galsworthy (John)
1933: **5** Bunin (Ivan)
1934: **10** Pirandello (Luigi)
1936: **6** O'Neill (Eugene)
1937: **12** Martin du Gard (Roger)
1938: **4** Buck (Pearl)
1939: **9** Sillanpää (Frans Eemil)
1944: **6** Jensen (Johannes)
1945: **7** Mistral (Gabriela)
1946: **5** Hesse (Hermann)
1947: **4** Gide (André)
1948: **5** Eliot (Thomas Stearns)
1949: **8** Faulkner (William)
1950: **7** Russell (Bertrand)
1951: **10** Lagerkvist (Pär)
1952: **7** Mauriac (François)
1953: **9** Churchill (Winston)
1954: **9** Hemingway (Ernest)
1955: **7** Laxness (Halldór)
1956: **7** Jiménez (Juan Ramón)
1957: **5** Camus (Albert)
1958: **9** Pasternak (Boris)
1959: **9** Quasimodo (Salvatore)
1960: **5** Perse (Saint-John)
1961: **6** Andric (Ivo)
1962: **9** Steinbeck (John)
1963: **7** Seferis (George)
1964: **6** Sartre (Jean-Paul)
1965: **9** Sholokhov (Mikhail)
1966: **5** Agnon (Shmuel Yosef), Sachs (Nelly)
1967: **8** Asturias (Miguel Angel)
1968: **8** Kawabata (Yasunari)
1969: **7** Beckett (Samuel)
1970: **12** Solzhenitsyn (Alexander)
1971: **6** Neruda (Pablo)
1972: **4** Böll (Heinrich)
1973: **5** White (Patrick)
1974: **7** Johnson (Eyvind) **9** Martinson (Edmund)
1975: **7** Montale (Eugenio)
1976: **6** Bellow (Saul)
1977: **10** Aleixandre (Vicente)
1978: **6** Singer (Isaac Bashevis)
1979: **6** Elytis (Odysseus)
1980: **6** Milosz (Czeslaw)
1981: **7** Canetti (Elias)
1982: **13** García Márquez (Gabriel)
1983: **7** Golding (William)
1984: **7** Seifert (Jaroslav)
1985: **5** Simon (Claude)
1986: **7** Soyinka (Wole)
1987: **7** Brodsky (Joseph)
1988: **7** Mahfouz (Naguib)
1989: **4** Cela (Camilo José)
1990: **3** Paz (Octavio)
1991: **8** Gordimer (Nadine)
1992: **7** Walcott (Derek)
1993: **8** Morrison (Toni)
1994: **2** Oe (Kenzaburo)
1995: **6** Heaney (Seamus)
1996: **10** Szymborska (Wislawa)
1997: **2** Fo (Dario)
1998: **8** Saramago (José)
1999: **5** Grass (Günter)
2000: **3** Gao (Xingjian)
2001: **7** Naipaul (V. S.)
2002: **7** Kertész (Imre)
2003: **7** Coetzee (J. M.)
2004: **7** Jelinek (Elfriede)

2005: **6** Pinter (Harold)
2006: **5** Pamuk (Orhan)
peace:
1901: **5** Passy (Frédéric) **6** Dunant (Jean-Henri)
1902: **5** Gobat (Charles Albert) **8** Ducommun (Elie)
1903: **6** Cremer (William)
1905: **7** Suttner (Bertha von)
1906: **9** Roosevelt (Theodore)
1907: **6** Moneta (Ernesto) **7** Renault (Louis)
1908: **5** Bajer (Fredrik) **9** Arnoldson (Klas Pontus)
1909: **9** Beernaert (Auguste) **13** d'Estournelles (Paul)
1911: **5** Asser (Tobias), Fried (Alfred)
1912: **4** Root (Elihu)
1913: **10** La Fontaine (Henri)
1919: **6** Wilson (Woodrow)
1920: **9** Bourgeois (Léon)
1921: **5** Lange (Christian Louis) **8** Branting (Karl Hjalmar)
1922: **6** Nansen (Fridtjof)
1925: **5** Dawes (Charles) **11** Chamberlain (Austen)
1926: **6** Briand (Aristide) **10** Stresemann (Gustav)
1927: **6** Quidde (Ludwig) **7** Buisson (Ferdinand)
1929: **7** Kellogg (Frank)
1930: **9** Soderblom (Nathan)
1931: **6** Addams (Jane), Butler (Nicholas Murray)
1933: **6** Angell (Norman)
1934: **9** Henderson (Arthur)
1935: **9** Ossietzky (Carl von)
1936: **13** Saavedra Lamas (Carlos de)
1937: **5** Cecil (Robert)
1945: **4** Hull (Cordell)
1946: **4** Mott (John) **5** Balch (Emily Greene)
1949: **3** Orr (John Boyd)
1950: **6** Bunche (Ralph)
1951: **7** Jouhaux (Léon)
1952: **10** Schweitzer (Albert)
1953: **8** Marshall (George)
1957: **7** Pearson (Lester)
1958: **4** Pire (Dominique Georges)
1959: **9** Noel-Baker (Philip)
1960: **7** Luthuli (Albert John)
1961: **12** Hammarskjöld (Dag)
1962: **7** Pauling (Linus)
1964: **4** King (Martin Luther)
1968: **6** Cassin (René)
1970: **7** Borlaug (Norman)
1971: **6** Brandt (Willy)
1973: **8** Le Duc Tho **9** Kissinger (Henry)
1974: **4** Sato (Eisaku) **8** MacBride (Sean)
1975: **8** Sakharov (Andrey)
1976: **8** Corrigan (Mairead), Williams (Betty)
1978: **5** Begin (Menachem), Sadat (Anwar el-)
1979: **12** Mother Teresa
1980: **8** Esquivel (Adolfo Pérez)
1982: **6** Myrdal (Alva) **12** García Robles (Alfonso)
1983: **6** Walesa (Lech)
1984: **4** Tutu (Desmond)
1986: **6** Wiesel (Elie)
1987: **12** Arias Sánchez (Oscar)
1989: **9** Dalai Lama
1990: **9** Gorbachev (Mikhail)
1991: **13** Aung San Suu Kyi
1992: **6** Menchú (Rigoberta)
1993: **7** de Klerk (F. W.), Mandela (Nelson)
1994: **5** Peres (Shimon), Rabin (Yitzhak) **6** Arafat (Yasir)
1995: **7** Rotblat (Joseph)
1996: **10** Ramos-Horta (José) **11** Ximenes Belo (Carlos Felipe)
1997: **8** Williams (Jody)
1998: **4** Hume (John) **7** Trimble (David)
2000: **3** Kim (Dae-jung)
2001: **5** Annan (Kofi)
2002: **6** Carter (Jimmy)
2003: **5** Ebadi (Shirin)
2004: **7** Maathai (Wangari)
2005: **9** ElBaradei (Mohamed)
2006: **5** Yunus (Muhammad)
physics:
1901: **8** Roentgen (Wilhelm)
1902: **6** Zeeman (Pieter) **7** Lorentz (Hendrik Antoon)
1903: **5** Curie (Marie, Pierre) **9** Becquerel (Antoine-Henri)
1904: **6** Strutt (John) **8** Rayleigh (Lord)
1905: **6** Lenard (Philipp von)
1906: **7** Thomson (Joseph)
1907: **9** Michelson (Albert)
1908: **8** Lippmann (Gabriel)
1909: **5** Braun (Karl) **7** Marconi (Guglielmo)
1910: **11** van der Waals (Johannes)
1911: **4** Wien (Wilhelm)
1912: **5** Dalen (Nils)
1914: **4** Laue (Max von)
1915: **5** Bragg (William)
1917: **6** Barkla (Charles)
1918: **6** Planck (Max)
1919: **5** Stark (Johannes)
1920: **9** Guillaume (Charles)
1921: **8** Einstein (Albert)
1922: **4** Bohr (Niels)
1923: **8** Millikan (Robert)
1924: **8** Siegbahn (Karl)
1925: **5** Hertz (Gustav) **6** Franck (James)
1926: **6** Perrin (Jean-Baptiste)
1927: **6** Wilson (Charles) **7** Compton (Arthur)
1928: **10** Richardson (Owen)

1929: **7** Broglie (Louis-Victor de)
1930: **5** Raman (Chandrasekhara)
1932: **10** Heisenberg (Werner)
1933: **5** Dirac (Paul) **11** Schrödinger (Erwin)
1935: **8** Chadwick (James)
1936: **4** Hess (Victor) **8** Anderson (Carl)
1937: **7** Thomson (George) **8** Davisson (Clinton)
1938: **5** Fermi (Enrico)
1939: **8** Lawrence (Ernest)
1943: **5** Stern (Otto)
1944: **4** Rabi (Isidor Isaac)
1945: **5** Pauli (Wolfgang)
1946: **8** Bridgman (Percy)
1947: **8** Appleton (Edward)
1948: **8** Blackett (Patrick)
1949: **6** Yukawa (Hideki)
1950: **6** Powell (Cecil)
1951: **6** Walton (Ernest) **9** Cockcroft (John)
1952: **5** Bloch (Felix) **7** Purcell (Edward)
1953: **7** Zernike (Frits)
1954: **4** Born (Max) **5** Bothe (Walther)
1955: **4** Lamb (Willis) **5** Kusch (Polykarp)
1956: **7** Bardeen (John) **8** Brattain (Walter), Shockley (William)
1957: **3** Lee (Tsung Dao) **4** Yang (Chen Ning)
1958: **4** Tamm (Igor) **5** Frank (Ilya) **9** Cherenkov (Pavel)
1959: **5** Segrè (Emilio) **11** Chamberlain (Owen)
1960: **6** Glaser (Donald)
1961: **9** Mossbauer (Rudolf) **10** Hofstadter (Robert)
1962: **6** Landau (Lev)
1963: **5** Mayer (Maria) **6** Jensen (J. Hans), Wigner (Eugene)
1964: **5** Basov (Nikolay) **6** Townes (Charles) **9** Prochorov (Alexander)
1965: **7** Feynman (Richard) **8** Tomonaga (Shinichiro) **9** Schwinger (Julian)
1966: **7** Kastler (Alfred)
1967: **5** Bethe (Hans)
1968: **7** Alvarez (Luis)
1969: **8** Gell-Mann (Murray)
1970: **4** Néel (Louis) **6** Alfven (Hannes)
1971: **5** Gabor (Dennis)
1972: **6** Cooper (Leon) **7** Bardeen (John) **10** Schrieffer (John)
1973: **5** Esaki (Leo) **7** Giaever (Ivar) **9** Josephson (Brian)
1974: **4** Ryle (Martin) **6** Hewish (Antony)
1975: **4** Bohr (Aage) **9** Mottelson (Ben), Rainwater (L. James)
1976: **4** Ting (Samuel) **7** Richter (Burton)
1977: **4** Mott (Nevill) **8** Anderson (Philip), Van Vleck (John)
1978: **6** Wilson (Robert) **7** Kapitsa (Pyotr), Penzias (Arno)
1979: **5** Salam (Abdus) **7** Glashow (Sheldon) **8** Weinberg (Steven)
1980: **5** Fitch (Val) **6** Cronin (James)
1981: **8** Schawlow (Arthur), Siegbahn (Kai) **11** Bloembergen (Nicholaas)
1982: **6** Wilson (Kenneth)
1983: **6** Fowler (William) **13** Chandrasekhar (Subrahmanyan)
1984: **6** Rubbia (Carlo) **11** van der Meere (Simon)
1985: **8** Klitzing (Klaus von)
1986: **5** Ruska (Ernst) **6** Binnig (Gerd), Rohrer (Heinrich)
1987: **6** Müller (K. Alex) **7** Bednorz (J. Georg)
1988: **8** Lederman (Leon), Schwartz (Melvin) **11** Steinberger (Jack)
1989: **4** Paul (Wolfgang) **6** Ramsey (Norman) **7** Dehmelt (Hans)
1990: **6** Taylor (Richard) **7** Kendall (Henry) **8** Friedman (Jerome)
1991: **8** De Gennes (Pierre-Gilles)
1992: **7** Charpak (Georges)
1993: **5** Hulse (Russell) **6** Taylor (Joseph)
1994: **5** Shull (Clifford) **10** Brockhouse (Bertram)
1995: **4** Perl (Martin) **6** Reines (Frederick)
1996: **3** Lee (David) **8** Osheroff (Douglas) **10** Richardson (Robert) **3** Chu (Steven) **8** Phillips (William) **14** Cohen-Tannoudji (Claude)
1998: **4** Tsui (Daniel) **7** Störmer (Horst) **8** Laughlin (Robert)
1999: **6** 't Hooft (Gerardus) **7** Veltman (Martinus)
2000: **5** Kilby (Jack) **7** Alferev (Zhores), Kroemer (Herbert)
2001: **6** Wieman (Carl) **7** Cornell (Eric) **8** Ketterle (Wolfgang)
2002: **5** Davis (Raymond) **7** Koshiba (Masatoshi) **8** Giacconi (Riccardo)
2003: **7** Leggett (Anthony) **8** Ginzburg (Vitaly) **9** Abrikosov (Alexei)
2004: **5** Gross (David) **7** Wilczek (Frank) **8** Politzer (David)
2005: **4** Hall (John) **6** Hänsch (Theodor) **7** Glauber (Roy)
2006: **5** Smoot (George) **6** Mather (John)
physiology or medicine:
1901: **7** Behring (Emil von)
1902: **4** Ross (Ronald)
1903: **6** Finsen (Niels Ryberg)
1904: **6** Pavlov (Ivan)
1905: **4** Koch (Robert)
1906: **5** Golgi (Camillo) **11** Ramón y Cajal (Santiago)
1907: **7** Laveran (Alphonse)
1908: **7** Ehrlich (Paul) **11** Metchnikoff (Elie)
1909: **6** Kocher (Emil)

1910: **6** Kossel (Albrecht)
1911: **10** Gullstrand (Allvar)
1912: **6** Carrel (Alexis)
1913: **6** Richet (Charles)
1914: **6** Barany (Robert)
1919: **6** Bordet (Jules)
1920: **5** Krogh (August)
1922: **4** Hill (Archibald) **8** Meyerhof (Otto)
1923: **7** Banting (Frederick), Macleod (John)
1924: **9** Einthoven (Willem)
1926: **7** Fibiger (Johannes)
1927: **13** Wagner-Jauregg (Julius)
1928: **7** Nicolle (Charles)
1929: **7** Eijkman (Christiaan), Hopkins (Frederick)
1930: **11** Landsteiner (Karl)
1931: **7** Warburg (Otto)
1932: **6** Adrian (Edgar) **11** Sherrington (Charles)
1933: **6** Morgan (Thomas)
1934: **5** Minot (George) **6** Murphy (William) **7** Whipple (George)
1935: **7** Spemann (Hans)
1936: **4** Dale (Henry) **5** Loewi (Otto)
1937: **12** Szent-Györgyi (Albert)
1938: **7** Heymans (Corneille)
1939: **6** Domagk (Gerhard)
1943: **3** Dam (Henrik) **5** Doisy (Edward)
1944: **6** Gasser (Herbert) **8** Erlanger (Joseph)
1945: **5** Chain (Ernst) **6** Florey (Howard) **7** Fleming (Alexander)
1946: **6** Muller (Hermann)
1947: **4** Cori (Carl, Gerty) **7** Houssay (Bernardo)
1948: **7** Mueller (Paul)
1949: **4** Hess (Walter) **5** Moniz (Antonio)
1950: **5** Hench (Philip) **7** Kendall (Edward) **10** Reichstein (Tadeus)
1951: **7** Theiler (Max)
1952: **7** Waksman (Selman)
1953: **5** Krebs (Hans) **7** Lipmann (Fritz)
1954: **6** Enders (John), Weller (Thomas) **7** Robbins (Frederick)
1955: **8** Theorell (Hugo)
1956: **8** Cournand (André), Richards (Dickinson) **9** Forssmann (Werner)
1957: **5** Bovet (Daniel)
1958: **5** Tatum (Edward) **6** Beadle (George) **9** Lederberg (Joshua)
1959: **5** Ochoa (Severo) **8** Kornberg (Arthur)
1960: **6** Burnet (Macfarlane) **7** Medawar (Peter)
1961: **6** Bekesy (Georg von)
1962: **5** Crick (Francis) **6** Watson (James) **7** Wilkins (Maurice)
1963: **6** Eccles (John), Huxley (Andrew) **7** Hodgkin (Alan)
1964: **5** Bloch (Konrad), Lynen (Feodor)
1965: **5** Jacob (Francois), Monod (Jacques) **5** Lwoff (André)
1966: **4** Rous (Francis) **7** Huggins (Charles)
1967: **4** Wald (George) **6** Granit (Ragnar) **8** Hartline (H. Keffer)
1968: **6** Holley (Robert) **7** Khorana (H. Gobind) **9** Nirenberg (Marshall)
1969: **5** Luria (Salvador) **7** Hershey (Alfred) **8** Delbruck (Max)
1970: **4** Katz (Bernard) **5** Euler (Ulf von) **7** Axelrod (Julius)
1971: **10** Sutherland (Earl)
1972: **6** Porter (Rodney) **7** Edelman (Gerald)
1973: **6** Frisch (Karl von), Lorenz (Konrad) **9** Tinbergen (Nikolaas)
1974: **4** Duve (Christian) **6** Claude (Albert), Palade (George)
1975: **5** Temin (Howard) **8** Dulbecco (Renato) **9** Baltimore (David)
1976: **8** Blumberg (Baruch), Gajdusek (D. Carleton)
1977: **5** Yalow (Rosalyn) **7** Schally (Andrew) **9** Guillemin (Roger)
1978: **5** Arber (Werner), Smith (Hamilton) **7** Nathans (Daniel)
1979: **7** Cormack (Allan) **10** Hounsfield (Godfrey)
1980: **5** Snell (George) **7** Dausset (Jean) **10** Benacerraf (Baruj)
1981: **5** Hubel (David) **6** Sperry (Roger), Wiesel (Torsten)
1982: **4** Vane (John) **9** Bergstrom (Sune) **10** Samuelsson (Bengt)
1983: **10** McClintock (Barbara)
1984: **5** Jerne (Niels) **7** Koehler (Georges) **8** Milstein (Cesar)
1985: **5** Brown (Michael) **9** Goldstein (Joseph)
1986: **5** Cohen (Stanley) **14** Levi-Montalcini (Rita)
1987: **8** Tonegawa (Susumu)
1988: **5** Black (James), Elion (Gertrude) **9** Hitchings (George)
1989: **6** Bishop (J. Michael), Varmus (Harold)
1990: **6** Murray (Joseph), Thomas (E. Donnall)
1991: **5** Neher (Erwin) **7** Sakmann (Bert)
1992: **5** Krebs (Edwin) **7** Fischer (Edmond)
1993: **5** Sharp (Phillip) **7** Roberts (Richard)
1994: **6** Gilman (Alfred) **7** Rodbell (Martin)
1995: **5** Lewis (Edward) **9** Wieschaus (Eric) **15** Nüsslein-Volhard (Christiane)
1996: **7** Doherty (Peter) **11** Zinkernagel (Rolf)
1997: **8** Prusiner (Stanley)
1998: **5** Murad (Ferid) **7** Ignarro (Louis) **9** Furchgott (Robert)
1999: **6** Blobel (Günter)
2000: **6** Kandel (Eric) **8** Carlsson (Arvid) **9** Greengard (Paul)

2001: **4** Hunt (Tim) **5** Nurse (Paul) **8** Hartwell (Leland)
2002: **7** Brenner (Sydney), Horvitz (Robert), Sulston (John)
2003: **9** Lauterbur (Paul), Mansfield (Peter)
2004: **4** Axel (Richard), Buck (Linda)
2005: **6** Warren (J. Robin) **8** Marshall (Barry)
2006: **4** Fire (Andrew) **5** Mello (Craig)

Nobel's invention
8 dynamite

nobility
6 virtue **7** dignity, peerage, royalty **8** eminence, noblesse **9** loftiness **10** exaltation, excellence, worthiness **11** aristocracy, superiority, uprightness

noble
4 lord, peer **5** grand, lofty, moral **6** august, lordly, titled, worthy **7** courtly, eminent, exalted, notable, stately, sublime, upright **8** baronial, elevated, generous, gracious, highborn, highbred, imposing, magnific, majestic, princely, sterling, virtuous, wellborn **9** dignified, estimable, excellent, grandiose, honorable, righteous **10** high-minded, impressive, principled **11** illustrious, magnanimous, magnificent, outstanding, right-minded **12** aristocratic

nobleman
4 duke, earl, lord, peer **5** baron, count **6** aristo, prince **7** baronet, marquis **8** marquess, viscount **10** aristocrat
French: **5** comte **7** vicomte
German: **4** Graf **8** margrave **9** landgrave
Indian: **6** sardar, sirdar **8** maharaja **9** maharajah
Islamic: **4** amir, emir **5** ameer
Italian: **8** marchese
Japanese (former): **6** daimyo
Scandinavian: **4** jarl
Spanish: **7** hidalgo

noblewoman
4 lady **7** duchess, peeress **8** baroness, countess, princess **11** marchioness, viscountess
French: **7** baronne **8** marquise
Italian: **8** marchesa

nobody
4 zero **6** cipher **7** nothing, nullity, upstart **9** nonentity **11** lightweight, small potato

nocturnal
7 nightly **9** nighttime

nocuous
3 bad **6** nocent **7** harmful, hurtful **8** damaging **9** injurious **11** deleterious, destructive, detrimental, mischievous

nod
3 bob, err **4** doze, okay **5** agree, droop, slump **6** assent, invite, signal **7** approve **8** approval **10** acceptance

nodding
6 casual, slight **7** passing **8** drooping **9** pendulous **11** superficial

noddle
3 nob, nut **4** bean, head, pate, poll **6** noggin

noddy
3 oaf **4** boob, clod, dodo, dolt, dope, fool, goof, mutt, simp, yo-yo **5** chump, dummy, dunce, moron, ninny, stupe **6** dimwit, donkey, dum-dum **7** airhead, dullard, pinhead, schnook **8** bonehead, clodpoll, dumbbell, dumbhead, imbecile, lunkhead, meathead, numskull **9** birdbrain, blockhead, ignoramus, lamebrain, numbskull, simpleton, thickhead **10** dunderhead, hammerhead, nincompoop **11** chowderhead, chucklehead, knucklehead

node
4 bump, burl, knob, knot, lump, mass **5** bulge, point **6** growth, vertex **8** swelling **11** enlargement, predicament **12** entanglement, protuberance

Noel
4 Xmas **5** carol **9** Christmas

nog
3 ale **4** beer, brew, malt, suds **5** lager, stout

noggin
3 cup, mug, nip, nob, nut **4** bean, gill, head, pate, poll **6** noddle, noodle

no-good
3 bum, dud **4** base, vile, worm **5** loser **6** scurvy, wretch **7** dirtbag, inutile, lowlife, rounder, wastrel **8** deadbeat, fainéant, shameful, unworthy, wretched **9** no-account, valueless, worthless **10** ne'er-do-well, profligate, scapegrace **11** ignominious **12** contemptible, disreputable **13** reprehensible

noise
3 din **4** blab, talk **5** babel, rumor, sound **6** clamor, gossip, hubbub, racket, ruckus, rumpus, tattle, uproar **7** ruction, sonance, stridor **8** resonant **11** pandemonium

noiseless
4 hush, mute **5** muted, quiet, still, whist **6** hushed, silent, stilly

noisemaker
4 horn **6** rattle **7** clapper, whistle

noisome
4 foul, rank, vile **5** fetid, funky, fusty, musty, nasty **6** filthy, horrid, putrid, rancid, smelly **7** harmful, noxious, squalid **8** stinking **9** obnoxious, offensive, repulsive, revolting, sickening **10** disgusting, malodorous, nauseating

noisy
4 loud **5** rowdy **7** blatant, booming, clamant, rackety, raucous, squeaky **8** clattery, strident

9 clamorous, deafening, turbulent 10 boisterous, chattering, clangorous, tumultuous, uproarious, vociferous 11 conspicuous 12 earsplitting, obstreperous

nomad
4 bedu, hobo 5 gipsy, gypsy, rover 6 beduin, Tuareg 7 bedouin, migrant, rambler, Touareg 8 vagabond, wanderer, wayfarer

nomadic
5 gipsy, gypsy 6 roving 7 roaming, vagrant 8 drifting, vagabond 9 itinerant, migratory, wandering, wayfaring 11 peripatetic 13 perambulatory

nom de plume
see **pen name**

nomen
4 name 7 moniker 11 appellation, designation

nomenclature
4 list, name 7 catalog 8 glossary, taxonomy 11 appellation, designation, phraseology, terminology 12 codification

nominal
3 low 5 given, named, rated, small 6 formal, puppet 7 alleged, minimal, seeming, titular 8 apparent, so-called, trifling 9 pretended, professed 10 ostensible 11 approximate, inexpensive 12 satisfactory 13 insignificant

nominate
3 tap 4 call, name 5 offer, put up 7 appoint, propose, suggest 9 designate, recommend

nominee
6 choice 8 aspirant 9 candidate, contender 10 contestant

nonage
5 youth 7 infancy 8 minority 9 childhood 10 immaturity, juvenility

nonchalant
4 cool, easy 5 blasé 6 casual, mellow, serene 7 offhand 8 carefree, careless, cheerful, laidback 9 easygoing 10 effortless, insouciant, untroubled 11 unconcerned, unflappable, unperturbed 12 lighthearted 13 lackadaisical

noncommittal
7 neutral 8 reserved 9 impassive 10 disengaged

nonconformist
5 loner, rebel 7 beatnik, heretic, oddball, offbeat, radical 8 bohemian, maverick 9 dissenter, dissident, eccentric, heretical, heterodox, protester, sectarian 10 schismatic, separatist, unorthodox 11 misbeliever, schismatist

nonconformity
6 heresy, schism 7 dissent 9 misbelief, recusancy 10 dissidence, heterodoxy, opposition 11 unorthodoxy 13 individualism

nonentity
4 zero 5 aught, zilch 6 cipher, nobody 7 nothing, nullity, whiffet 8 unperson 10 figurehead, mouthpiece

nonesuch
5 ideal 7 epitome, paragon, pattern 8 exemplar, paradigm, standard 9 archetype, beau ideal, matchless, nonpareil, unequaled, unrivaled 10 apotheosis

nonetheless
3 yet 5 still 6 anyway, though, withal 7 howbeit, however 8 although, after all 10 regardless 11 still and all

nonexistence
4 nada, void 7 nullity, vacuity 11 nothingness

nonflammable
9 fireproof 10 unburnable 13 incombustible

non-Hawaiian
5 haole

non-Jewish
3 goy 6 goyish 7 gentile

non-Muslim
6 giaour

no-nonsense
5 grave, sober 6 solemn 7 earnest, serious 8 resolute 9 pragmatic, realistic 10 hardheaded, sobersided 11 plainspoken 12 businesslike 13 unsentimental

nonpareil
see **nonesuch**

nonpartisan
7 neutral 8 unbiased 9 equitable, impartial, objective, uncolored 10 nonaligned 11 independent 12 unprejudiced

nonplus
4 faze 5 stump 6 baffle, boggle, muddle, puzzle, rattle, stymie 7 buffalo, confuse, dilemma, flummox, fluster, mystify, perplex, stagger 8 bewilder, confound, distract, overcome, paralyze, quandary 9 discomfit, dumbfound, frustrate 10 disconcert

nonresistant
6 docile, pliant 7 passive, pliable 8 resigned, yielding 9 complying, malleable, tractable 10 conforming, submissive 11 acquiescent, conformable 13 accommodating

nonsense
3 rot 4 blah, bosh, bull, bunk, crap, gook, guff, jazz, punk, tosh 5 bilge, crock, drool, folly, fudge, Greek, hokum, hooey, trash, tripe 6 babble, blague, bunkum, drivel, hot air, humbug, jabber, piffle 7 baloney, blather, eyewash, flubdub, foolery, fooling, hogwash, inanity, rubbish, trifles, twaddle 8 buncombe, claptrap, falderal, folderol, flimflam, malarkey, pishposh, slipslop, tommyrot, trumpery 9 gibberish, moonshine,

poppycock **10** applesauce, balderdash, double-talk, flapdoodle, tomfoolery **11** jabberwocky **12** blatherskite, fiddle-faddle, fiddlesticks **13** horsefeathers
British: **10** codswallop

nonsensical
5 crazy, daffy, flaky, goofy, inane, kooky, loony, nutty, silly, wacky **6** absurd, screwy **7** foolish, idiotic, risible **9** illogical, laughable, ludicrous, senseless **10** irrational **12** preposterous, unreasonable

nonviolent
6 irenic **7** pacific **8** pacifist **9** peaceable **10** pacifistic

noodle
3 oaf **4** bean, boob, clod, dodo, dope, goof, head, mutt, poll, simp, yo-yo **5** chump, dummy, dunce, idiot, moron, ninny, noddy, stupe **6** dimwit, donkey, dum-dum, nitwit, noggin **7** airhead, dullard, pinhead, schnook **8** bonehead, clodpoll, dumbbell, dumbhead, imbecile, lunkhead, meathead, numskull **9** birdbrain, blockhead, ignoramus, lamebrain, numbskull, simpleton **10** dunderhead, hammerhead, nincompoop **11** chowderhead, chucklehead, knucklehead
dish: **5** pasta **7** lasagna, lasagne **8** linguine, linguini **10** fettuccine, fettuccini **11** pappardelle

nook
3 bay **4** cove **5** hutch, niche **6** alcove, cavity, corner, cranny, recess **9** cubbyhole **11** compartment

noose
3 tie **4** bait, bind, hang, loop, lure, trap **5** lasso, snare **6** entrap, secure

norm
3 par **4** mean, rule, type **5** gauge, maxim, model **6** median **7** average, measure, pattern **8** paradigm, standard **9** benchmark, criterion **10** touchstone

Norma
composer: **7** Bellini (Vincenzo)
librettist: **6** Romani (Felice)

normal
4 sane **5** usual **6** common **7** average, general, natural, regular, typical **8** ordinary, standard **9** customary, prevalent **11** commonplace, traditional **12** conventional **13** perpendicular

Normandy's capital
5 Rouen

Norns
5 fates, Skuld, Urdur **9** Verthandi

Norris novel
3 Pit (The) **4** Blix **7** Octopus (The) **8** McTeague

Norse
abode of the dead: **8** Niflheim
alphabet: **5** Runic
archer: **4** Egil
bard: **5** scald, skald
chieftain: **4** jarl, Rolf **5** Rollo
demon: **4** Mara, Surt **5** Surtr
dragon: **6** Fafnir **8** Nithhogg
epic: **4** Edda
explorer: **4** Eric, Erik, Leif **8** Ericsson (Leif), Eriksson (Leif)
first man: **3** Ask **4** Askr
first woman: **5** Embla
giant: **4** Egil, Wade, Wate, Ymer, Ymir **5** Aegir, Egill, Hymir, Jotun, Mimir **6** Fafnir, Jotunn
giantess: **4** Egia, Norn, Nott
god: **3** Asa, Ass **4** Surt, Vali, Vili **5** Aesir (plural), Surtr, Vanir (plural) **6** Hoenir, Vithar **7** Vitharr
blind: **4** Hoth **5** Hoder, Hodur, Hothr
chief: **4** Oden, Odin **5** Othin, Wodan, Woden, Wotan
guardian: **7** Heimdal **8** Heimdall **9** Heimdallr
messenger: **6** Hermod **7** Hermodr
of beauty: **5** Baldr **6** Balder, Baldur
of evil: **4** Loke, Loki
of fertility: **4** Frey **5** Freyr
of fire: **4** Loke, Loki
of justice: **7** Forsete, Forseti
of light: **3** Dag
of peace: **5** Baldr **6** Balder, Baldur
of poetry: **5** Brage, Bragi
of the hunt: **3** Ull **4** Ullr
of the seas: **5** Njord **6** Njoerd, Njorth **4** Hler **5** Aegir, Gymir
of the sky: **4** Odin **5** Othin, Wodan, Woden, Wotan
of thunder: **4** Thor **5** Donar
of war: **3** Tiu, Tiw, Tyr, Zio, Ziu
wolf: **6** Fenrir
goddess: **3** dis **4** Saga **5** disir (plural) **7** Asynjur
of fate: **3** Urd **4** Norn, Urth, Wyrd **5** Skuld **9** Verthandi
of healing: **3** Eir
of love: **5** Freya
of marriage: **5** Frigg **6** Frigga
of night: **4** Natt, Nott
of storms: **3** Ran
of the earth: **4** Erda **5** Joerd, Jorth
of the moon: **5** Nanna
of the sea: **3** Ran
of the sky: **5** Frigg **6** Frigga
of the underworld: **3** Hel **4** Hela
of youth: **4** Idun **5** Ithun **6** Ithunn
gods' abode: **6** Asgard
hall of heroes: **8** Valhalla
king: **4** Atli, Olaf
nobleman: **4** jarl
patron saint: **4** Olaf
poem: **4** rune

poet: **5** scald, skald
rainbow bridge: **7** Bifrost
sea serpent: **4** Wade, Wate **6** kraken **7** Midgard
smith: **6** Völund
tale: **4** saga
toast: **5** skoal
watchdog: **4** Garm **5** Garmr
world's destruction: **8** Ragnarok
world tree: **8** Ygdrasil **10** Yggdrasill

north
combining form: **4** arct **5** arcto

North African
country: **5** Egypt, Libya **7** Algeria, Morocco, Tunisia
fruit: **3** fig **4** date
garment: **4** haik **7** burnous **8** burnoose
grass: **4** alfa **7** esparto
jackal: **4** dieb
language: **6** Arabic, Berber
Muslim sect: **6** Sanusi **7** Senussi
people: **4** bedu **6** beduin, Berber, Hamite **7** bedouin
seaport: **4** Oran, Sfax **6** Annaba **7** Tangier **10** Casablanca

North America
country: **6** Belize, Canada, Mexico, Panama **8** Honduras **9** Costa Rica, Guatemala, Nicaragua **10** El Salvador **12** United States

North Carolina
capital: **7** Raleigh
city: **6** Durham **9** Asheville, Charlotte **10** Greensboro **12** Winston-Salem
college, university: **4** Duke, Elon **10** Chapel Hill, Wake Forest
mountain, range: **8** Mitchell **9** Blue Ridge **10** Great Smoky
nickname: **7** Tar Heel (State)
state bird: **8** cardinal
state flower: **7** dogwood
state tree: **4** pine

North Dakota
capital: **8** Bismarck
city: **5** Fargo, Minot **10** Grand Forks
nickname: **5** Sioux (State) **11** Flickertail (State)
river: **3** Red **8** Missouri
state bird: **10** meadowlark
state flower: **11** prairie rose
state tree: **3** elm (American)

North Korea
see **Korea, North**

northern
4 pike **6** boreal **11** hyperborean

Northern Ireland
capital: **7** Belfast
city: **5** Derry, Newry **6** Armagh **7** Lisburn
conflict: **8** Troubles (The)
county: **4** Down **6** Antrim, Armagh, Tyrone **9** Fermanagh **11** Londonderry
lake: **10** Lough Neagh
language: **3** BSL, ISL **5** Irish **11** Ulster Scots
monetary unit: **5** pound
mountains: **6** Mourne **7** Sperrin
prison, former: **4** Maze
province: **6** Ulster
university: **6** Queens

Northern Mariana Islands
commonwealth of: **12** United States
discoverer: **8** Magellan (Ferdinand)
island: **4** Rota **6** Saipan, Tinian

North Star State
9 Minnesota

Northwest Territories
capital: **11** Yellowknife
gulf: **8** Amundsen
island: **5** Banks **8** Victoria
lake: **9** Great Bear **10** Great Slave
river: **9** Mackenzie
sea: **8** Beaufort

north wind
see at **wind**

Norway
Arctic region: **7** Lapland
cape: **7** Nordkyn
capital: **4** Oslo
city: **5** Hamar **6** Bergen **9** Stavanger, Trondheim
inlet: **9** Skagerrak
island: **5** Senja **6** Sørøya **8** Magerøya, Steinsøy **10** Nord-Kvaløy, Ringvassøy
island group: **7** Lofoten **10** Vesterålen
king: **4** Eric, Olaf, Olav **5** Oscar **6** Haakon, Harald, Magnus **7** Charles **9** Christian, Frederick **11** Christopher
lake: **5** Mjøsa
monetary unit: **5** krone
mountain range: **6** Kjølen **11** Jotunheimen
neighbor: **6** Russia, Sweden **7** Finland
part of: **11** Scandinavia
patron saint: **4** Olaf, Olav
port: **5** Vardø **6** Tromsø **8** Kirkenes **10** Hammerfest
river: **4** Tana **5** Glåma, Lågen **9** Dramselva
sea: **5** North

Norwegian
goblin: **5** nisse
language: **5** Norse **6** Bokmal **7** Bokmaal, Nynorsk, Riksmal **8** Landsmal, Riksmaal **9** Landsmaal

nose
3 pry **4** beak, bent, bump, head, poke **5** aroma, flair, knack, scent, smell, sniff, snift, snoop, snoot,

snout, snuff **6** muzzle, nuzzle, schnoz, talent **7** aptness, faculty, schnozz, smeller, sneezer **8** smell out **9** olfaction, proboscis, schnozzle
combining form: **4** naso, rhin **5** rhino
French: **3** nez
kind: **3** pug **5** Roman **8** aquiline
lengthener: **3** lie
opening: **5** nares (plural) **7** nostril

nosebleed
9 epistaxis

nosedive
4 drop, fall **6** header, plunge **7** plummet

nosegay
4 posy **6** flower **7** bouquet, corsage **11** boutonniere

nosh
4 bite **5** graze, munch, snack **6** nibble

Nostradamus
4 seer **7** prophet
birthplace: **6** St. Remy

Nostromo author
6 Conrad (Joseph)

nostrum
4 cure **6** elixir, remedy **7** cure-all, panacea **8** antidote, medicine **10** catholicon, corrective **11** restorative

nosy
6 prying, snoopy **7** curious, peeping **8** snooping **9** intrusive **11** inquisitive, inquisitory

not
4 nary

notable
3 VIP **4** lion, star **5** celeb, chief, famed, mogul, nabob, power **6** big boy, biggie, big gun, bigwig, famous, fat cat, honcho, leader, prince, worthy **7** big name, big shot, eminent, magnate, poohbah **8** big chief, big-timer, big wheel, eminence, luminary, renowned, somebody, striking **9** big cheese, celebrity, character, chieftain, dignitary, distingué, personage, prominent, superstar **10** celebrated, celebrious, noteworthy, remarkable **11** conspicuous, heavyweight, illustrious, muckety-muck, personality **13** distinguished, high-muck-a-muck

notarize
7 certify, endorse **8** validate **12** authenticate

not at all
5 nohow, noway **6** noways, nowise

notch
3 cut, gap, jag **4** gash, kerf, mark, nick, nock, rung, slit, step **5** cleft, grade, score, stage **6** degree, groove, indent, rabbet, record **7** achieve, scratch **8** incision, undercut **11** indentation

notched
5 erose

note
3 jot **4** bond, chit, heed, mark, memo, show, sign, tone **5** catch, sound, token **6** letter, notice, record, regard **7** comment, discern, jotting, missive, observe, promise, set down **8** eminence, indicate, perceive, reminder **9** attention, knowledge **10** cognizance, memorandum, reputation **11** distinction, distinguish, observation

notebook
3 log **5** diary **7** journal

noted
5 famed **6** famous **7** eminent, leading, popular **8** esteemed, renowned, striking **9** acclaimed, prominent, well-known **10** celebrated, recognized, remarkable **11** illustrious **13** distinguished

noteworthy
7 salient **8** singular, striking **9** arresting, bodacious, memorable, prominent, red-letter **10** impressive, meaningful, remarkable **11** conspicuous, exceptional, high-profile, major-league, outstanding, significant **12** considerable **13** extraordinary

nothing
3 nil, nix, zip **4** nada, zero **5** aught, nihil, zilch **6** cipher, naught, nobody, nought, trifle **7** nullity, whiffet **8** goose egg, whipster **9** no-account, nonentity
French: **4** rien
German: **6** nichts
Latin: **5** nihil
Spanish: **4** nada

nothingness
4 nada, void **5** death **6** vacuum **7** nullity, vacuity **9** emptiness **12** nonexistence

notice
2 ad **3** eye, see **4** espy, heed, mark, memo **5** catch, sight **6** descry, regard, review **7** discern, observe, respect **8** handbill, perceive **9** attention, directive, recognize **10** cognizance, evaluation **11** declaration, information, observation **12** announcement, proclamation

noticeable
6 marked, patent, signal **7** evident, obvious, pointed, salient **8** apparent, manifest, striking **9** arresting, prominent **10** noteworthy, observable, remarkable **11** appreciable, conspicuous, eye-catching, outstanding, perceptible, significant **12** unmistakable

notify
3 cue **4** tell, warn **5** alert, brief **6** advise, clue in, fill in, inform **7** apprise **8** acquaint **9** enlighten

notion
4 clue, hint, idea, whim **5** fancy **6** belief, maggot, theory, vagary **7** caprice, conceit, concept,

inkling, thought **8** crotchet **10** conception, impression, intimation, perception **11** inclination

notional
5 ideal **6** unreal **7** fancied, fictive **8** fanciful, illusory, imagined **9** imaginary, visionary, whimsical **10** capricious, conceptual **11** speculative, theoretical **12** hypothetical

notoriety
4 fame **6** infamy, renown **7** obloquy **9** disrepute **10** opprobrium, prominence **11** recognition

notorious
5 noted **6** famous **8** ill-famed, infamous **9** prominent, well-known **10** outrageous, scandalous **12** disreputable

Notus
6 Auster
brother: **5** Eurus **6** Boreas **8** Zephyrus
father: **6** Aeolus **8** Astraeus
mother: **3** Eos

noun
4 name **7** nominal **11** substantive
inflectional form: **4** case
verbal: **6** gerund

nourish
4 feed, rear **5** nurse, raise **6** foster **7** bring up, build up, nurture, promote, support **8** maintain **9** cultivate, encourage **10** provide for, strengthen

nourishment
3 pap **4** diet, eats, feed, food, grub **6** viands **7** aliment, pabulum, vittles **8** victuals **9** nutriment, provender **10** sustenance

____ nous
5 entre

nouveau riche
7 climber, parvenu, upstart **9** arriviste

Nova Scotia
capital: **7** Halifax
city: **9** Dartmouth
island: **10** Cape Breton
lake: **7** Bras D'Or
provincial flower: **9** mayflower

novel
3 new, odd **4** book **5** fresh **6** unique **7** fiction, offbeat, unusual **8** atypical, original, peculiar, singular, uncommon **9** different, narrative **10** avant-garde, innovative, newfangled

novelist
see **author**

Novello, ____
4 Ivor

novelty
5 curio **6** bauble, gewgaw, oddity, trifle **7** bibelot, gimmick, newness, trinket, whatnot **8** gimcrack, souvenir **9** bagatelle, curiosity, objet d'art **10** innovation, knickknack

novice
3 cub **4** colt, punk, tyro **5** plebe **6** newbie, rookie **7** amateur, learner, recruit, student, trainee **8** aspirant, beginner, freshman, neophyte, newcomer, prentice **9** fledgling, greenhorn, novitiate, postulant **10** apprentice, tenderfoot **11** probationer

Novum Organum author
5 Bacon (Francis)

now
3 PDQ **4** ASAP, soon, stat **5** today **6** at once, pronto **7** anymore, present **8** directly, first off, promptly **9** forthwith, instanter, instantly, presently, right away, sometimes **11** immediately, straightway **12** straightaway

now and then
7 at times, betimes **9** sometimes **12** infrequently, occasionally, periodically, sporadically

Nox
brother: **6** Erebus
daughter: **3** Day **4** Eris **5** Light
father: **5** Chaos
husband: **6** Erebus
son: **6** Charon, Hypnos **8** Thanatos

noxious
4 foul **5** fetid, toxic **6** deadly, putrid **7** baneful, harmful, noisome **8** stinking **9** dangerous, pestilent, poisonous, unhealthy **10** corrupting, pernicious **11** deleterious, destructive, detrimental, pestiferous **12** disagreeable, pestilential

nozzle
4 nose, vent **5** spout **7** channel

nth
4 last **6** utmost **7** extreme, highest, maximal, maximum, supreme **8** greatest, ultimate

nuance
4 hint **5** shade, tinge, touch, trace **6** nicety **7** shading, soupçon **8** overtone, subtlety **9** gradation, suspicion **10** refinement, suggestion **11** distinction

nub
4 bump, core, crux, gist, knob, knot, lump, meat, node, pith **5** bulge, point, short **6** kernel, upshot **8** swelling **9** substance **10** projection **12** protuberance

Nubian
5 Mahas **6** Birked, Kenuzi, Midobi **7** Dongola **8** Cushitic **9** Chari-Nile

nubile
4 ripe **10** attractive **12** marriageable

nuchal
4 nape

nuclear agency
3 AEC, NRC

nuclear particle
5 meson **6** proton **7** neutron

nucleus
3 bud **4** core, germ, head, kern, ring, seed **5** focus, spark **6** embryo
material: **8** karyotin

nude
3 raw **4** bald, bare **5** naked, stark **6** barren, peeled, unclad **8** disrobed, starkers, stripped **9** au naturel, buck naked, unattired, unclothed, uncovered, undressed **10** stark naked

nudge
3 dig, jab, jog **4** near, poke, prod, push **5** elbow, shove **8** approach

nudnik
4 bore, drip, pest, pill, twit **8** nuisance

nugatory
4 idle, vain **5** empty, inane, vapid **6** futile, hollow, otiose **7** invalid, vacuous **8** trifling **9** fruitless, worthless **11** inoperative, meaningless

nugget
4 hunk, lump, plum **5** chunk **6** tidbit

nuisance
4 pain, pest, pill **6** bother, nudnik **7** nudnick **8** headache, irritant, pesterer, vexation **11** botheration

nuke
3 zap **4** bomb **5** crush, smash **6** attack **7** destroy **8** demolish **9** eradicate, microwave **10** annihilate **11** exterminate

null
4 void, zero **5** annul, empty **6** futile **7** invalid, useless **8** nugatory **9** worthless **10** invalidate, obliterate, unavailing **11** ineffective, ineffectual, inoperative

nullify
3 zap **4** undo, veto, void **5** abate, annul, limit, quash, scrub, trash **6** cancel, efface, negate, offset, repeal, revoke, squash **7** abolish, rescind, scratch, take out, wipe out **8** abrogate **10** annihilate, compensate, counteract, invalidate, neutralize **11** countervail

nullity
4 nada, zero **5** zilch **6** cipher, nobody **7** nothing, vacuity, whiffet **9** annulment, nonentity **11** nothingness **12** nonexistence

numb
5 chill, dazed **6** deaden, freeze **7** callous **8** deadened **9** insensate, paralyzed, stupefied, unfeeling **10** insensible, insentient **11** desensitize **12** anesthetized, desensitized

number
5 add up, count, digit, run to, sum to, tally, total **6** amount, cipher, figure **7** chiffer, include, integer, numeral, ordinal, several **8** cardinal, paginate **9** aggregate, enumerate
added to another: **6** augend
great: **4** army, host **5** horde **6** googol, legion **9** multitude **10** googolplex
irrational: **4** surd
resulting from division: **8** quotient
resulting from multiplication: **7** product
resulting from subtraction: **10** difference
science: **11** mathematics

number one
3 top **4** best, main **5** chief, first, major **6** finest, Grade A, tip-top, top dog **7** capital, highest, leading, primary, stellar **8** dominant, five-star, foremost, superior **9** excellent, first-rate, front-rank, numero uno, principal, top-drawer **10** blue-ribbon, first-class, preeminent **11** first-string, outstanding, predominant

numbness
5 shock **6** stupor **10** anesthesia **11** anaesthesia **12** stupefaction
combining form: **4** narc **5** narco

numeral
5 digit **6** cipher, figure, number **7** integer **11** whole number

numerate
4 list **5** count, tally **6** number **7** compute, itemize, tick off **8** tabulate **9** calculate

numerous
4 many **6** legion **7** profuse, umpteen **8** abundant, populous **9** plentiful **10** voluminous **13** multitudinous

Numitor
brother: **7** Amulius
daughter: **9** Rea Silvia **10** Rhea Silvia
grandson: **5** Remus **7** Romulus

numskull
3 oaf **4** boob, clod, dodo, dolt, dope, goof, mutt, simp **5** chump, dummy, dunce, idiot, moron, ninny, noddy, stupe **6** dimwit, donkey, dum-dum, nitwit **7** airhead, dullard, pinhead, schnook **8** bonehead, clodpate, clodpoll, dumbbell, dumbhead, imbecile, lunkhead, meathead **9** birdbrain, blockhead, ignoramus, lamebrain, simpleton, thickhead **10** dunderhead, hammerhead, nincompoop **11** chowderhead, chucklehead, knucklehead

nun
4 buoy **6** sister
headcloth: **6** wimple

Nunavut
capital: **7** Iqaluit
island: **5** Devon **6** Baffin **9** Ellesmere **11** Southampton
mountain: **7** Barbeau (Peak)

peninsula: 7 Boothia 8 Melville
provincial flower: 11 Arctic poppy

nunnery
7 convent 8 cloister 10 sisterhood
head: 8 superior

nuptial
6 bridal, wedded 7 marital, married, spousal, wedding 8 conjugal, espousal, hymeneal, marriage 9 connubial 11 matrimonial

nurse
3 LPN, LVN 4 feed, nana, rear, suck 5 nanny, serve 6 attend, foster, pamper, suckle 7 care for, cherish, nourish, nurture 9 cultivate 10 minister to
children's: 5 nanny
English: 11 Nightingale (Florence)
Indian: 4 ayah
Chinese: 4 amah

nursemaid
4 nana 5 nanny 6 minder, sitter 9 governess 10 babysitter
Indian: 4 ayah
Chinese: 4 amah

nursery
6 crèche 7 brooder 8 hothouse 9 fosterage 10 greenhouse 12 conservatory

nurture
4 care, feed, rear, tend 5 nurse, raise, train 6 cradle, foster, parent, suckle 7 bring up, care for, develop, educate, nourish, rearing 8 breeding, instruct, training, tutelage 9 cultivate 10 upbringing

nut
3 bug 4 cola, kola, kook, loon, pili 5 acorn, betel, crank, fiend, freak, hazel, loony, pecan, piñon 6 almond, cashew, cuckoo, madman, maniac, walnut, zealot 7 buckeye, fanatic, filbert, hickory, lunatic 8 crackpot 9 bedlamite, ding-a-ling, macadamia, pistachio, screwball 10 enthusiast, Tom o' Bedlam
of a violin bow: 4 frog, heel

Nut
consort: 3 Geb, Keb
daughter: 4 Isis 8 Nephthys
son: 6 Osiris

nuthouse
6 asylum, bedlam 8 loony bin 9 funny farm 10 booby hatch 11 institution 12 insane asylum

Nutmeg State
11 Connecticut

nutria
5 coypu

nutriment
4 diet, fare, food, grub, keep 6 viands 7 aliment, pabulum 8 victuals 9 provender 10 provisions, sustenance 11 comestibles, nourishment, subsistence

nutrition
4 diet 7 vittles 8 victuals 10 sustenance 11 nourishment

nutritious
9 healthful, wholesome 10 alimentary, nourishing

nuts
3 mad 4 daft, keen, wild, zany 5 batty, crazy, dotty, kooky, loony, rabid, wacky 6 absurd, cuckoo, insane, screwy 7 bonkers, cracked, excited, foolish, idiotic 8 animated, demented, deranged 9 exuberant, fanatical, screwball 10 passionate, unbalanced 12 enthusiastic
on forest floor: 4 mast

nutty
see **nuts**

nuzzle
3 rub 4 root, snug 5 nudge 6 burrow, cuddle, nestle 7 snuggle

Nycteus
brother: 5 Lycus
daughter: 7 Antiope

nymph
3 nix 5 dryad, larva, naiad, nixie, oread, sylph 6 kelpie, maiden, sprite 7 mermaid
changed into a bear: 8 Callisto
changed into a laurel: 6 Daphne
changed into a rock: 4 Echo
mountain: 5 oread
sea: 6 Nereid 7 Calypso
water: 5 naiad 6 undine
wood: 5 dryad

Nyx
see **Nox**

O

oaf
3 ape, dub, lug **4** boob, boor, bull, clod, dodo, dolt, goof, goon, hulk, lout, lump, slob **5** booby, chump, clown, dummy, dunce, klutz **6** dum-dum, galoot, lubber, lummox **7** fathead, palooka **8** bonehead, lunkhead, meathead **9** blockhead, blunderer, lamebrain, simpleton

oafish
5 dense **6** clumsy, klutzy, rustic **7** boorish, doltish, loutish **8** bungling, churlish, clownish, lubberly

oak
African: 7 turtosa
fruit: 5 acorn
genus: 7 Quercus
kind: 3 bur, pin, red **4** bear, cork, holm, ilex, live **5** black, holly, roble, white **6** barren, cerris, encina **7** durmast, English, moss-cup, valonia **9** blackjack
Mexican: 8 chaparro
young: 8 flittern

oar
3 row **4** pole, pull **5** rower, scull **6** paddle **7** paddler
part: 4 loom, palm **5** blade, shaft **6** button, collar
pin: 5 thole

oarsman
3 bow **5** rower **6** stroke **7** sculler
captain: 3 cox **8** coxswain

oasis
3 spa **4** wadi **6** refuge, relief
ancient: 4 Merv
Egypt: 4 Siwa **5** Gafsa **6** Dakhla **7** Farafra **8** Ammonium
Libya: 5 Mizda, Sebha **6** Sabhah **7** Gadames **8** Ghudamis
Niger: 5 Bilma
Saudi Arabia: 5 Hofuf, Taima **7** Al-Hufuf

oast
4 kiln, oven

oat
5 grain, grass **6** cereal
genus: 5 Avena
Scottish: 3 ait

oater
7 western **10** horse opera

oath
3 vow **4** cuss **5** curse, swear **6** pledge **7** promise **8** cussword **9** expletive, profanity, swearword
mild: 4 darn, drat, egad **6** jiminy, zounds

oatmeal
5 gruel **6** burgoo **8** porridge
Scottish: 8 drammock

obdurate
3 set **4** firm, hard **5** harsh, rigid, stony **6** dogged, mulish **7** adamant, callous **8** stubborn **9** heartless, immovable, unbending, unfeeling **10** hard-boiled, inflexible, unshakable, unyielding **11** coldhearted, hardhearted, insensitive **12** intransigent, stonyhearted **13** unsympathetic

obeah
5 charm, magic
relative: 5 vodun **6** vodoun, voodoo **8** Santeria **9** Candomblé

Obed
father: 4 Boaz **6** Ephlal **8** Shemaiah
mother: 4 Ruth
son: 5 Jesse **7** Azariah

obedient
5 loyal **6** docile **7** devoted, duteous, dutiful, willing **8** amenable, biddable, obliging, yielding **9** compliant, tractable **10** law-abiding, manageable, respectful, submissive **11** acquiescent, cooperative, deferential, subservient

obeisance
3 bow **5** honor **6** curtsy, esteem, fealty, homage, kowtow, salaam **7** gesture, loyalty, respect **9** deference, reverence **10** allegiance, submission

obelisk
6 dagger, pillar, symbol

Oberon
9 fairy king
messenger: 4 Puck
wife: 7 Titania

obese
3 fat **5** bulky, gross, heavy, tubby **6** fleshy, portly **7** adipose, outsize, porcine **9** corpulent **10** overweight

obey
3 bow **4** heed, keep, mind **5** agree, defer, serve, yield **6** accede, accept, assent, comply,

follow, regard, submit **7** abide by, conform, execute, fulfill, observe, satisfy **9** acquiesce

obfuscate
4 blur **5** cloud, muddy **6** darken **7** becloud, conceal, confuse, cover up, obscure **9** adumbrate

obi
4 sash

obiter dictum
4 note **6** remark **7** comment, opinion **10** commentary, incidental **11** observation

obituary
9 necrology **11** death notice

object
3 aim, end, use **4** goal, item, kick, view, wish **5** demur, focus, frown, point, thing **6** design, entity, except, intent, matter, motive, oppose, target **7** article, dissent, protest, purpose **8** complain, disagree, material **9** criticize, intention, something **10** disapprove

objection
5 demur **7** protest **8** argument, demurral, demurrer, question **9** challenge, complaint, exception **10** difficulty, opposition **11** disapproval **12** disagreement, remonstrance **13** remonstration

objectionable
5 unfit **8** unwanted **9** invidious, obnoxious, offensive, unwelcome **10** unpleasant **11** displeasing, distasteful, undesirable **12** disagreeable

objective
3 aim, end **4** fair, goal, just, lens, mark **6** actual, design, intent, target **7** mission, purpose **8** ambition, function, material, physical, sensible, unbiased **9** corporeal, equitable, impartial, intention **10** impersonal **11** independent, substantial **12** unprejudiced **13** dispassionate

objet d'art
5 curio, virtu (plural) **7** bibelot, novelty **8** kickshaw **10** knickknack

objurgate
5 chide, decry, scold **6** rebuke **7** censure, reprove, upbraid **8** admonish, reproach **9** castigate, reprimand

oblate
7 lay monk **9** flattened, religious

oblation
4 gift **6** corban **8** holy gift, offering **9** sacrifice **12** presentation

obligate
4 bind **7** require **8** encumber, restrict **9** constrain

obligated
5 bound, owing **6** liable **8** beholden, indebted **11** accountable, responsible

obligation
3 IOU, vow **4** bond, call, debt, dues, duty, need, oath **5** cause **6** burden, charge, pledge **7** promise **8** business, contract **9** committal, liability, necessity, restraint **10** commitment, compulsion, constraint **11** requirement **12** indebtedness

obligatory
7 binding **8** required **9** essential, mandatory, necessary, requisite **10** compulsory, imperative **11** unavoidable

oblige
3 aid **4** bind, help, make **5** avail, favor, force **6** assist, coerce, compel, please, profit **7** benefit, command, gratify, require **9** constrain **10** contribute **11** accommodate, necessitate

obliged
4 made **5** bound **6** forced **8** beholden, grateful, indebted, thankful **11** constrained **12** appreciative

obliging
4 kind **5** civil **7** amiable, helpful, willing **8** friendly, pleasant **11** complaisant, considerate, cooperative, good-humored, good-natured **12** good-tempered

oblique
6 sloped, tilted **7** devious, leaning, obscure, slanted, sloping, tilting **8** diagonal, inclined, indirect **9** inclining **10** roundabout

obliterate
4 raze, x out **5** erase **6** cancel, delete, efface, remove, rub out **7** blot out, destroy, expunge, wipe out **8** black out, cross out **9** extirpate, liquidate **10** annihilate

oblivion
5 lethe, limbo **7** amnesia, nirvana, nowhere **9** emptiness **11** nothingness **13** forgetfulness

oblivious
4 lost **5** blind **7** unaware **8** absorbed, heedless, ignorant **9** unknowing, unmindful, unwitting **10** unfamiliar, uninformed **11** incognizant, unconscious

oblong
4 oval **5** ovate **7** ellipse **8** elongate **9** elongated, rectangle **11** rectangular

obloquy
4 slam, slur **5** abuse, odium, shame **6** infamy, rebuke **7** calumny, censure **8** disgrace, dishonor, ignominy **9** aspersion, contumely, discredit, disrepute, invective, stricture **10** defamation, opprobrium, scurrility **11** disapproval **12** billingsgate, condemnation, vituperation

obnoxious
4 vile **5** awful **6** odious, rotten **7** hateful **9** abhorrent, invidious, loathsome, offensive, repellant, repellent, repugnant, revulsive, sickening **10** abominable, detestable, disgusting

oboe
4 reed **7** hautboy **8** hautbois, woodwind **10** double reed
early: 5 shawm
relative: 7 bassoon **10** cor anglais **11** English horn

O'Brian character
6 Aubrey (Jack) **7** Maturin (Stephen)

obscene
4 foul, lewd, rank, vile **5** bawdy, crude, dirty, gross, lurid, taboo **6** coarse, filthy, ribald, risqué, smutty, vulgar **7** immoral, noisome, profane, raunchy **8** indecent, scabrous **9** abhorrent, appalling, offensive, repellent, repugnant, repulsive, salacious **10** disgusting, lascivious, scurrilous **11** foulmouthed, unprintable **12** pornographic, scatological

obscure
3 dim **4** blur, hide, mask, veil **5** blind, cloak, cloud, cover, dusky, faint, minor, murky, shade, shady, vague **6** cloudy, darken, hidden, opaque, remote, screen, secret, shadow, shroud, veiled **7** clouded, conceal, cryptic, eclipse, removed, shadowy, unclear, unknown, unnoted **8** disguise, nameless, overcast, puzzling, secluded, shrouded **9** ambiguous, enigmatic, tenebrous, uncertain, undefined **10** camouflage, ill-defined, indefinite, indistinct, mysterious, overshadow **11** out-of-the-way, unimportant **12** inaccessible **13** inconspicuous

obscurity
3 fog **4** haze, mist, murk **5** gloom **6** enigma, miasma, puzzle **7** dimness, mystery, shadows **8** darkness **9** ambiguity

obsequies
4 rite **5** rites **6** burial **7** funeral **10** burial rite

obsequious
4 oily **6** abject, smarmy **7** fawning, fulsome, servile, slavish **8** obedient, obeisant, toadying, unctuous **9** parasitic **10** flattering, submissive **11** deferential, subservient, sycophantic

observance
4 rite, rule **6** custom, notice, regard, ritual **7** liturgy, service **8** ceremony, practice **9** adherence, attention, formality **10** ceremonial

observant
4 keen **5** alert, awake, aware, sharp **7** heedful, mindful **8** watchful **9** advertent, attentive **10** perceptive

observation
4 note **6** notice, record, remark **7** comment, finding, opinion **8** judgment, notation **9** attention, inference **10** commentary **12** obiter dictum

observatory
5 tower **7** lookout, outlook **8** overlook
famous: 4 Lick **6** Wilson, Yerkes **7** Palomar
instrument: 9 telescope

observe
3 eye, see **4** espy, keep, look, mark, mind, note, obey, twig, view **5** honor, opine, sight, state, study, watch **6** behold, comply, follow, look at, notice, remark **7** abide by, comment, conform, discern, respect **8** perceive **9** celebrate, solemnize **10** comply with **11** commemorate

obsess
5 beset, haunt, hound, rivet **6** absorb, plague **7** consume, possess **9** captivate, preoccupy

obsessed
6 dogged, driven, hipped, hooked **7** gripped, haunted, plagued **8** overcome, troubled **9** dominated, possessed **11** preoccupied **12** prepossessed

obsession
5 craze, mania **6** fetish, hang-up **8** fixation, idée fixe **11** infatuation **13** preoccupation

obsessive
5 rabid **8** frenetic, maniacal, neurotic **9** fanatical, possessed **10** passionate **11** preoccupied

obsolete
3 old **5** dated, passé, stale **6** old hat **7** disused, worn-out **8** outmoded, time-worn **9** out-of-date **10** antiquated, superseded **12** antediluvian, old-fashioned

obstacle
3 bar **4** bump, clog, snag **5** block, catch, check, crimp, hitch **6** hurdle **7** barrier **8** handicap, hardship **9** hindrance, impedance, roadblock **10** difficulty, impediment **11** encumbrance, vicissitude **12** interference

obstinate
4 deaf, firm **5** balky, fixed **6** dogged, mulish, ornery **7** staunch, willful **8** obdurate, perverse, resolute, stubborn **9** pigheaded, resistant, unbudging, immovable **10** hardheaded, headstrong, inflexible, persistent, refractory, unyielding **11** intractable, stiff-necked, wrongheaded **12** intransigent, pertinacious, recalcitrant

obstreperous
4 loud **5** noisy, rowdy **6** unruly **7** blatant, raucous **8** strident **9** clamorous, insistent **10** boisterous, disorderly, vociferant, vociferous **11** disobedient, loudmouthed **12** rambunctious

obstruct
3 bar, dam **4** clog, hide, plug, stop **5** block, check, choke, close **6** cut off, hamper, hinder, impede, stymie, thwart **7** congest, occlude, prevent, shut off, shut out, trammel **9** interfere

obstruction
3 bar **4** snag **5** hitch **6** hamper, hurdle **7** barrier **8** blockage, obstacle, stoppage **9** hindrance, impedance **10** impediment

obtain
3 buy, get, win **4** earn, gain, have, reap **5** annex,

reach **6** pick up, secure **7** achieve, acquire, chalk up, procure **8** purchase

obtrude
5 cut in **6** butt in, horn in, impose, meddle **7** presume, push out **8** chisel in, infringe **9** interfere, thrust out

obtrusive
4 nosy **5** pushy **6** prying **7** forward **8** meddling **9** bumptious, officious **10** meddlesome, protruding **11** impertinent, interfering

obtuse
4 dull, dumb, slow **5** blunt, dense, thick **6** stupid **7** rounded, unclear **11** insensitive

obverse
4 face, side **5** front **8** opposite **9** other side **10** complement **11** counterpart

obviate
4 ward **5** avert, deter, block **7** forfend, prevent, rule out **8** preclude, stave off **9** forestall, interfere, interpose, intervene **10** anticipate

obvious
5 clear, overt, plain **6** patent, simple **7** blatant, evident, glaring **8** apparent, clear-cut, distinct, manifest, palpable **10** undeniable **11** conspicuous, self-evident, transparent, unambiguous, unequivocal

oca
5 tuber **6** sorrel

O'Casey, Sean
9 dramatist **10** playwright
plays: **17** Juno and the Paycock, Plough and the Stars (The)

occasion
4 call, need, shot, show, time **5** basis, break, cause, event **6** chance, demand, effect, excuse, ground, lead to, moment, reason **7** episode, instant, opening, produce **8** ceremony, incident, instance **9** condition, happening, necessity **10** bring about, foundation, occurrence **11** celebration, opportunity **12** circumstance **13** justification

occasional
3 few, odd **4** rare **6** casual, fitful, random, scarce, seldom **7** special, unusual **8** specific, sporadic, uncommon **9** irregular **10** incidental, infrequent

occasionally
7 at times

Occidental
7 Western **8** European **9** Westerner

occlude
4 clog, fill, hide, plug, stop **5** block, choke, close, cover **6** screen, stop up **7** close up, conceal, congest **8** block off, obstruct

occult
5 eerie, magic **6** arcane, orphic, secret **8** abstruse, esoteric, hermetic, mystical **9** recondite, unearthly **10** cabalistic, mysterious **12** supernatural

occupant
5 liver **6** inmate, tenant **7** denizen, dweller, resider **8** habitant, resident **10** inhabitant

occupation
3 job, use **4** line, work **5** trade **6** career, métier, office **7** calling, control, pursuit, seizure **8** activity, business, position, vocation **9** occupancy, residence **10** employment, habitation, possession, settlement

occupy
3 use **4** busy, fill, hold, take **5** seize, tie up **6** absorb, employ, engage, live in, people, take up, tenant **7** control, engross, immerse, inhabit, involve, possess **8** populate, reside in, take over

occur
3 hap **4** pass **5** arise, ensue, pop up **6** appear, befall, betide, chance, dawn on, happen, result, strike **7** come off, develop **9** take place, transpire

occurrence
3 hap **4** pass **5** event, state **7** episode **8** exigency, incident, juncture, occasion **9** adventure, condition, emergency, happening, situation

ocean
3 sea **4** blue, deep, main **5** brine, drink **6** Arctic, Indian **7** Pacific **8** Atlantic **9** Antarctic
movement: **4** tide, wave

Oceania
country: **4** Fiji **5** Belau, Nauru, Palau, Samoa, Tonga **6** Tuvalu **7** Vanuatu **8** Kiribati **9** Australia **10** New Zealand
territory: **7** Tokelau **12** New Caledonia **13** American Samoa
ethnic group: **6** Fijian, Papuan, Samoan **10** Melanesian, Polynesian **11** Micronesian
language: **5** Maori **6** Fijian, Papuan, Pidgin, Samoan **10** Melanesian

oceanic
4 huge, vast **5** great **6** marine **7** immense, pelagic **8** enormous, maritime **9** saltwater, thalassic

Ocean State
11 Rhode Island

Oceanus
daughter: **5** Doris **7** Oceanid **8** Eurynome
father: **6** Uranus
mother: **4** Gaea
sister: **6** Tethys
son: **6** Peneus **7** Alpheus
wife: **6** Tethys

ocellus
3 eye **7** eyespot

ocelot
3 cat **7** wildcat

O'Connor novel
9 Wise Blood

octave
5 eight, scale 6 eighth, stanza 8 interval

Octavia
brother: 8 Augustus
grandson: 8 Caligula
husband: 4 Nero 6 Antony

octopus
7 mollusc, mollusk 9 devilfish 10 cephalopod
arm: 8 tentacle
genus: 7 Polypus
kin: 5 squid 10 cuttlefish

ocular
4 seen 5 optic 6 visual 7 eyelike, optical, visible 8 eyepiece, viewable 9 perceived

Odalisque painter
6 Ingres (Jean-Auguste-Dominique) 7 Matisse (Henri)

odd
4 lone, rare 5 extra, fluky, queer, rummy, weird 6 casual, chance, single, uneven 7 curious, erratic, strange, unusual 8 peculiar, singular 9 eccentric, unmatched 13 idiosyncratic

oddball
4 kook 5 kooky, weird 6 weirdo 7 bizarre, curious, offbeat, strange, unusual 8 original, peculiar 9 character, eccentric 10 outlandish 13 idiosyncratic

Odd Couple, The
author: 5 Simon (Neil)
character: 5 Felix, Oscar
director: 4 Saks (Gene) 7 Nichols (Mike)
star: 6 Carney (Art), Lemmon (Jack) 7 Klugman (Jack), Matthau (Walter), Randall (Tony)

oddity
5 freak, quirk 6 weirdo 7 anomaly 9 character, curiosity, departure, deviation, eccentric, weirdness 10 aberration, difference 11 abnormality, peculiarity, strangeness 12 eccentricity, idiosyncrasy, irregularity

odds
4 edge 5 favor, ratio 7 benefit, chances 8 handicap, variance 9 advantage, allowance, disparity 10 difference, likelihood, partiality 11 probability 12 disagreement

odds and ends
4 bits, olio 6 jumble, medley, motley, scraps 7 mélange, mixture 8 remnants, sundries 9 etceteras, leftovers, potpourri 10 assortment, hodgepodge, hotchpotch, miscellany 13 paraphernalia

ode
4 hymn, poem 5 lyric, psalm, verse
part: 5 epode 7 strophe 11 antistrophe

Odets play
9 Golden Boy 11 Country Girl (The) 12 Awake and Sing 15 Waiting for Lefty

odeum
4 hall 7 theater 11 concert hall

Odin
brother: 4 Vili
daughter-in-law: 5 Nanna
father: 3 Bor
hall: 8 Valhalla
horse: 8 Sleipnir
maiden: 8 Valkyrie
mansion: 9 Gladsheim
mother: 6 Bestla
raven: 5 Hugin, Munin
ring: 8 Draupnir
son: 3 Tyr 4 Thor, Vali 6 Balder, Baldur
spear: 7 Gungnir
sword: 4 Gram
wife: 4 Fria, Rind 5 Frigg 6 Frigga
wolf: 4 Geri 5 Freki

odious
4 foul, vile 6 horrid 7 hateful, heinous, noxious 8 horrible 9 abhorrent, execrable, invidious, loathsome, malicious, repellent, repugnant 10 abominable, despicable, detestable, disgusting

odium
4 hate, onus 5 shame 6 hatred, infamy, stigma 7 censure, obloquy 8 contempt, disgrace, dishonor, ignominy, loathing 9 disrepute 10 abhorrence, opprobrium 11 detestation 12 condemnation

odor
4 funk 5 aroma, scent, smell, stink, whiff 6 stench 7 bouquet, perfume 9 fragrance, redolence

odorous
5 heady, sweet 6 smelly, strong 7 pungent, scented 8 aromatic, fragrant, perfumed, redolent, unsavory 9 offensive

Odysseus
7 Ulysses
dog: 5 Argos
enchantress: 5 Circe
father: 7 Laertes
friend: 6 Mentor
harasser: 8 Poseidon
herb: 4 moly
kingdom: 6 Ithaca
mother: 8 Anticlea
rescuer: 3 Ino 8 Nausicaa
son: 9 Telegonus 10 Telemachus
swineherd: 7 Eumaeus
voyage: 7 odyssey
wife: 8 Penelope

odyssey
4 trek **5** quest **6** voyage **7** journey **9** wandering **13** peregrination

Odyssey author
5 Homer

Oedipus
brother-in-law: 5 Creon
daughter: 6 Ismene **8** Antigone
father: 5 Laius
foster father: 7 Polybus
foster mother: 8 Periboea
kingdom: 6 Thebes
mother: 7 Jocasta
son: 8 Eteocles **9** Polynices **10** Polyneices
victim: 5 Laius
wife: 7 Jocasta

Oeneus
kingdom: 7 Calydon
son: 8 Meleager
wife: 7 Althaea

Oenomaus
charioteer: 8 Myrtilus
daughter: 10 Hippodamia
kingdom: 4 Pisa
slayer: 6 Pelops

Oenone
husband: 5 Paris
rival: 5 Helen

oeuvre
4 work **6** corpus, output **8** lifework **10** collection **11** compilation

of
German: 3 aus, von
Italian: 5 degli, della, delle

off
4 away, kill, slay **5** aside **6** depart, murder, remote, slight **7** seaward, spoiled **8** dispatch **9** eccentric, incorrect

offal
4 guts **4** junk **5** gurry, trash, waste **6** debris, litter, refuse, spilth **7** carrion, garbage, innards, rubbish, viscera **8** entrails **9** sweepings **10** intestines

offbeat
3 odd **5** fresh, outré, weird **6** way out **7** bizarre, oddball, strange, unusual **8** bohemian, peculiar, singular, uncommon **9** different, eccentric, whimsical **10** outlandish, unorthodox **11** distinctive **13** idiosyncratic

off-color
3 ill, low **4** blue, racy **5** bawdy, broad, salty, shady **6** ailing, peaked, poorly, risqué, sickly, unwell **7** dubious, naughty **8** improper, indecent **10** indisposed, suggestive

offend
3 sin, vex **4** gall, hurt, miff, pain **5** anger, annoy, pique, repel, shock, upset **6** appall, breach, insult, nettle **7** affront, disturb, provoke, violate **8** aggrieve, distress, irritate **9** displease **10** antagonize, transgress

offender
5 felon **6** sinner **7** culprit **8** criminal, violator **9** wrongdoer **10** lawbreaker, malefactor **12** transgressor

offense
3 sin **4** huff, hurt, miff, tort, vice **5** crime, fault, pique, wrong **6** attack, breach, felony, injury, insult **7** affront, assault, dudgeon, misdeed, mistake, outrage, umbrage **9** indignity, onslaught, violation **10** aggression, infraction, resentment **11** misdemeanor

offensive
3 bad **4** foul, rank, vile **5** drive, onset **6** attack, odious **7** assault, fulsome, noisome, obscene, painful **8** nauseous, unsavory **9** loathsome, obnoxious, onslaught, repellent, repugnant, repulsive, sickening **10** aggression, aggressive, disgusting, nauseating, unpleasant **12** disagreeable, unappetizing **13** objectionable

offer
3 bid, try **4** seek, show **5** assay, essay, pitch, put up **6** afford, extend, submit, tender **7** advance, attempt, display, exhibit, hold out, present, propose, provide, suggest **8** endeavor, proposal, threaten **9** sacrifice **10** submission **11** proposition

offering
3 IPO **4** alms, gift **5** grant **6** course, corban **7** charity, present **8** donation, oblation **9** sacrifice **11** benefaction, beneficence **12** contribution

offhand
5 ad-lib **6** blithe, breezy, casual **8** informal **9** extempore, impromptu, unstudied **10** improvised, nonchalant, unprepared **11** extemporary, spontaneous, unrehearsed

office
3 job **4** duty **5** berth, suite **6** agency, billet, bureau **7** station **8** business, cube farm, function, province **9** situation, workplace **10** department
head: 4 boss **7** manager
holder: 9 incumbent **11** functionary
machine: 3 fax **6** copier **7** printer **8** computer **10** calculator, fax machine **11** photocopier
seeker: 9 candidate **10** politician
without work: 8 sinecure
worker: 5 clerk **6** typist **9** file clerk, secretary **10** bookkeeper

officer
3 cop **4** exec **6** noncom, police **7** John Law, manager **8** official **9** executive
abbreviation: **2** Lt. **3** Adm., Col., Ens., Gen., Maj. **4** Capt., Cmdr. **5** Comdr., Lieut.
army: **5** looey, looie, major **7** captain, colonel, general **10** lieutenant
British: **9** brigadier
court: **7** bailiff
king's: **11** chamberlain
law-enforcement: **3** cop **6** deputy, police **7** marshal, sheriff **9** constable, patrolman, policeman
naval: **4** mate **6** ensign **7** admiral, captain **9** commander, commodore **10** lieutenant
noncommissioned: **5** sarge **8** corporal, sergeant
petty: **4** bos'n **5** bosun **6** yeoman **9** boatswain
prison: **5** guard **6** warden

official
4 exec **7** cleared, manager **8** approved, bona fide, endorsed **9** authentic, canonical, cathedral, certified, executive **10** accredited, authorized, ex cathedra, magistrate, sanctioned **13** administrator, authoritative
city or town: **5** mayor **8** alderman **9** councilor, selectman **10** councillor
diplomatic: **5** envoy **6** consul **7** attaché **10** ambassador
governmental: **6** syndic
parish: **6** beadle
sports: **3** ref, ump **6** umpire **7** referee **8** linesman
university: **4** dean **6** bursar **7** provost **9** registrar **10** chancellor

officiate
5 chair, serve **6** direct, umpire **7** conduct, oversee, preside, referee **9** supervise **11** superintend

officious
4 busy, nosy **5** nosey, pushy **7** forward **8** meddling **9** assertive, intrusive, obtrusive **10** meddlesome **11** impertinent **13** self-important

offing
6 future **7** by-and-by **9** aftertime, hereafter **10** near future

off-key
3 odd **4** sour **7** jarring **9** anomalous, dissonant, unnatural **10** discordant **12** inharmonious

off-putting
8 daunting **9** dismaying, offensive, repellent **10** forbidding **11** distasteful **12** disagreeable, discouraging **13** disconcerting, disheartening, objectionable

offscouring
5 leper, trash **6** pariah, refuse, reject **7** outcast **8** castaway, derelict **11** untouchable

offset
6 square **7** balance **8** equalize **10** balance out, compensate, neutralize **11** counterpose, countervail **12** counterpoise, displacement

offshoot
4 twig **5** scion **6** branch **7** product, spin-off **9** affiliate, by-product, outgrowth **10** derivative, descendant

offspring
3 cub, kid **4** kids, seed **5** brood, child, hatch, issue, scion, spawn, swarm, young **7** produce, product, progeny **8** children **9** posterity **10** descendant **11** progeniture

off-the-wall
3 odd **5** kooky, weird **6** far-out, way-out **7** bizarre, oddball, unusual **8** freakish **9** eccentric, fantastic, grotesque **10** outlandish

off-white
4 bone **5** cream, ivory **6** oyster, vellum **9** parchment

Of Human Bondage author
7 Maugham (W. Somerset)

Of Mice and Men
author: **9** Steinbeck (John)
character: **6** George (Milton), Lennie (Small)

often
9 generally **10** frequently, habitually, repeatedly **11** recurrently

ogee
3 ess **4** arch **5** curve **7** molding

Ogier the ___
4 Dane

ogive
3 rib **4** arch **5** graph

ogle
3 eye **4** gape, gaze, leer, look **5** stare **6** goggle **7** stare at **10** rubberneck

ogre
3 orc **5** bogey, giant, Shrek **6** Grinch **7** bugbear, monster **8** bogeyman **9** boogeyman
Algonquian: **7** wendigo, windigo

ogress
5 harpy, scold, shrew, vixen **6** amazon, virago **8** fishwife **9** termagant, Xanthippe

O'Hara novel
7 Pal Joey **16** Butterfield Eight **17** Ten North Frederick

Ohio
capital: **8** Columbus
city: **5** Akron, Xenia **6** Canton, Dayton, Toledo **9** Cleveland **10** Cincinnati
college, university: **5** Miami **6** Kenyon **7** Antioch, Denison, Oberlin **9** Kent State **12** Bowling Green
nickname: **7** Buckeye (State)
river: **4** Ohio **6** Maumee **8** Sandusky

state bird: **8** cardinal
state flower: **16** scarlet carnation
state tree: **7** buckeye

Oholibamah
father: **4** Anah
husband: **4** Esau

oil
3 fat, gas **4** balm, fuel, lube, oleo **5** oleum, slick **6** anoint, grease, pomade **7** blarney, incense, lanolin **8** flattery, soft soap **9** adulation, lubricant, lubricate, petroleum
combining form: **3** ole **4** olei, oleo
company: **3** Sun **4** Arco, Esso, Gulf, Hess, Hunt, Pure **5** ADNOC, Amoco, Citgo, Exxon, Getty, Mobil, Pemex, Shell, Sohio, Union, YUKOS **6** Aramco, Conoco, Lukoil, Sunoco, Texaco, Valero **7** Ashland, Chevron **8** Marathon, Pennzoil, Phillips, Sinclair, Standard **9** Petrobras **10** ExxonMobil, Occidental, PetroChina
consecrated: **6** chrism
fragrant: **5** attar **6** neroli
fuel: **3** gas **6** butane, petrol **7** benzene, propane **8** gasoline, kerosene
relating to: **5** oleic
ship: **6** tanker
source: **4** rape **5** olive, shale **6** canola **7** linseed **8** flaxseed, rapeseed **9** sunflower
well: **6** gusher

oilbird
8 guacharo

oily
5 fatty, slick, soapy, suave **6** greasy, smarmy, smooth **7** fulsome **8** slippery, unctuous **10** lubricious, obsequious, oleaginous

ointment
4 balm, nard **5** cream, salve **6** lotion **7** unction, unguent **8** calamine, liniment **9** emollient, spikenard **11** embrocation

OK, okay
3 aye, yea, yes **4** fine, good, safe, well, yeah **5** agree, allow, favor, licit **6** agreed, assent, decent, permit **7** approve, certify, endorse, support **8** accredit, adequate, all right, approval, blessing, high sign, passable, sanction, thumbs-up **9** authorize, hunky-dory **10** acceptable, permission **11** endorsement, permissible **12** satisfactory

Okinawa capital
4 Naha

Oklahoma
capital: **12** Oklahoma City
city: **3** Ada **4** Enid **5** Tulsa **6** Norman
college, university: **11** Oral Roberts
mountain: **9** Black Mesa
nickname: **6** Sooner (State)
river: **3** Red **8** Arkansas, Canadian
state bird: **10** flycatcher
state flower: **9** mistletoe
state tree: **6** redbud

okra
4 soup **5** gumbo **6** mallow

old
4 aged, gray, late, past **5** dated, hoary, passé, stale **6** bygone, démodé, former, mature, senior, whilom **7** ancient, antique, archaic, elderly, lasting, onetime, overage, quondam, veteran **8** enduring, lifelong, Noachian, outmoded, timeworn **9** erstwhile, geriatric, long-lived, perennial, perpetual, primitive, venerable **10** antiquated, inveterate **13** superannuated
Scottish: **4** auld

old age
3 eld **6** dotage **8** caducity **10** senescence **11** decrepitude, elderliness, senectitude

Old Bailey
5 court

Old Colony State
13 Massachusetts

Old Curiosity Shop
author: **7** Dickens (Charles)
character: **4** Nell **10** Little Nell

Old Dominion State
8 Virginia

Old Faithful
6 geyser

old-fashioned
4 aged **5** dated, dowdy, fusty, moldy, passé, stale, tired **6** bygone, démodé, quaint, stodgy **7** ancient, antique, archaic, outworn, vintage **8** obsolete, outdated, outmoded **9** out-of-date, unstylish **10** antiquated

old hand
3 pro, vet **6** expert, master **7** veteran **9** authority **10** past master, specialist

old hat
5 dated, passé, stale, tired, trite **6** démodé **7** antique, clichéd, vintage **8** outmoded, timeworn, well-worn **9** hackneyed, out-of-date **10** antiquated

Old Ironsides
12 Constitution (U.S.S.)
poet: **6** Holmes (Oliver Wendell)

Old Line State
8 Maryland

old maid
6 fusser **7** fusspot **8** spinster **10** fussbudget

Old North State
13 North Carolina

Old Rough and Ready
6 Taylor (Zachary)

Olds' car
3 Reo

old-time
5 dated **6** bygone **7** antique, vintage **10** antiquated **12** long-standing

old-timer
3 vet **5** elder **6** senior **7** ancient, antique, veteran

Old World
6 Europe

oleaginous
see **oily**

oleaster
5 shrub **12** Russian olive

olecranon
9 funny bone

oleo
9 margarine

oleoresin
10 turpentine

oleum
3 oil

olfaction
5 sense, smell **8** smelling

olid
4 rank **5** fetid **6** putrid, rancid, rotten **7** stenchy **8** stinking **9** offensive **10** malodorous

olio
3 mix **4** hash, stew **5** gumbo, umble **6** medley **7** grab bag, mélange, mixture **8** mishmash, mixed bag **9** potpourri **10** assortment, collection, hodgepodge, hotchpotch, miscellany, salmagundi **11** gallimaufry

Oliver Twist
author: **7** Dickens (Charles)
character: **5** Fagin, Nancy, Sikes (Bill) **6** Bumble (Mr.) **12** Artful Dodger

Ollie's partner
4 Stan

Olympian
3 god **5** lofty, noble **6** lordly **7** athlete, exalted, godlike **8** majestic, superior **10** competitor

Olympics site
1972: **6** Munich **7** Sapporo
1976: **8** Montreal **9** Innsbruck
1980: **6** Moscow **10** Lake Placid
1984: **10** Los Angeles **8** Sarajevo
1988: **5** Seoul **7** Calgary
1992: **9** Barcelona **11** Albertville
1994: **11** Lillehammer
1996: **7** Atlanta
1998: **6** Nagano
2000: **6** Sydney
2002: **12** Salt Lake City
2004: **6** Athens
2006: **5** Turin **6** Torino
2008: **7** Beijing
2010: **9** Vancouver
2012: **6** London

Oman
capital: **6** Masqat, Muscat
language: **6** Arabic **7** Baluchi
monetary unit: **4** rial
mountain range: **7** Al-Hajar
neighbor: **5** Yemen **11** Saudi Arabia
peninsula: **7** Arabian
sea: **7** Arabian

Omar
4 poet **7** Khayyám
country: **6** Persia
father: **7** Eliphaz
poem: **8** Rubaiyat

omega
3 end **6** ending, finale, letter
kin: **3** zed, zee

omen
4 sign **5** augur, token **6** augury, boding **7** auspice, portent, presage, warning **8** bodement, prophecy **9** foretoken **10** foreboding, prediction, prognostic

ominous
4 dark, dire, grim **6** dismal **7** baleful, direful, doomful, fateful **8** alarming, lowering, menacing, sinister **9** ill-boding, prophetic **10** forbidding, foreboding, portentous **11** frightening, threatening **12** inauspicious, unpropitious

omission
3 cut, gap **4** lack, skip, slip **5** blank, break, chasm, error, lapse **6** hiatus, lacuna **7** elision, failure **8** eclipsis, ellipsis, overlook **9** exclusion
mark: **5** caret **8** ellipsis **10** apostrophe

omit
4 drop, fail, skip **5** elide **6** except, forget, ignore, slight **7** exclude, neglect **8** leave out, overlook, pass over

omnibus
3 ana **4** posy **5** album **7** garland **8** analects, treasury **9** anthology **10** miscellany **11** florilegium

omnipotent
6 divine **7** godlike, supreme **8** almighty **9** unlimited **11** all-powerful

omnipresent
7 allover, endless **8** infinite, unending **9** boundless, limitless, universal **10** ubiquitous

omniscient
4 wise **7** learned **9** know-it-all **10** all-knowing

omnium-gatherum
see **olio**

Omphale
domain: **5** Lydia
slave: **8** Heracles, Hercules

omphalos
3 hub 5 focus, navel 9 umbilicus 10 focal point 11 belly button

on
4 atop, over 5 above, along, going 7 working 9 operating 11 functioning

onager
3 ass 5 kiang 8 catapult

Onan's father
5 Judah

once
4 ever, late, past 5 at all 6 before, bygone, former, whilom 7 already, earlier, long ago, onetime, quondam 8 formerly, sometime

once-over
4 look 5 check 6 gander, glance, survey 10 inspection 11 examination

one
4 lone, only, sole, unit 5 monad 6 single, unique 7 numeral 8 separate, singular, solitary 9 undivided 10 individual, particular
combining form: 4 mono
French: 2 un 3 une
German: 3 ein 4 eine
prefix: 3 uni
Scottish: 2 ae 3 ane, yin
Spanish: 2 un 3 una, uno

one and a half
combining form: 6 sesqui

one-eyed giant
7 Cyclops 10 Polyphemus

one-handed god
3 Tiu, Tyr

one-horse town
4 burg 5 thorp 6 hamlet, Podunk 7 village 11 whistle-stop

one hundred
6 centum
years: 7 century

O'Neill, Eugene
daughter: 4 Oona
heroine: 4 Anna, Nina
play: 3 Ile 4 Gold 8 Hairy Ape (The) 12 Ah Wilderness, Anna Christie, Emperor Jones, Iceman Cometh (The) 13 Great God Brown (The), Marco Millions 16 Strange Interlude 18 Desire Under the Elms 22 Mourning Becomes Electra 24 Long Day's Journey into Night

oneiric
6 dreamy 8 anagogic 9 dreamlike

oneness
3 all 5 union, unity, whole 7 harmony 8 entirety, identity, sameness, totality 9 integrity, unanimity 10 singleness, uniformity 11 singularity, unification 13 individuality

onerous
4 hard 5 heavy, tough 6 taxing, trying 7 arduous, exigent, wearing, weighty 8 exacting, grievous, imposing, pressing, toilsome 9 demanding, difficult, laborious 10 burdensome, cumbersome, oppressive 11 troublesome

one-sided
6 biased, uneven 7 colored, partial, unequal 8 inclined, partisan, weighted 10 prejudiced, unbalanced, unilateral

onetime
3 old 4 once, past 6 bygone, former, whilom 7 quondam 8 previous 9 erstwhile

ongoing
7 current, growing 8 evolving 9 advancing, in process 10 continuing, continuous, developing, in progress, unfinished 11 progressing

on hand
4 here 5 ready 6 nearby 7 pending, present 9 available

onion
4 bulb 7 shallot
bulb: 3 set
genus: 6 Allium
kin: 4 leek 6 garlic
kind: 7 Bermuda, Danvers, Spanish
roll: 5 bialy
young: 8 scallion

online
5 wired 9 connected
business: 5 e-tail
guffaw: 3 LOL
pages: 7 Web site
system: 3 Web 8 Internet

onlooker
6 viewer 7 watcher, witness 8 beholder, kibitzer, observer 9 bystander, kibbitzer, spectator 10 eyewitness 12 rubbernecker

only
3 but, few, one, yet 4 just, lone, mere, save, sole, solo 5 alone 6 and yet, at most, except, merely, simply, single, solely, unique 7 however, utterly 8 entirely, singular, solitary 11 exclusively

onomasticon
7 lexicon 8 wordbook

onomatopoeic
5 mimic 6 echoic 7 mimetic 9 emulative, imitative 10 simulative

onset
4 dawn, rush 5 birth, get-go, start 6 attack, coming, origin 7 arrival, assault, dawning, offense, opening 8 invasion 9 beginning, inception, offensive 10 aggression 12 commencement

onslaught
5 blitz **6** attack, charge, deluge **7** assault, barrage, offense, torrent **8** invasion **9** offensive **10** aggression

on-target
3 apt, fit **5** exact, right **7** correct, perfect, precise **8** accurate **11** appropriate

Ontario
bay: **8** Georgian
capital: **7** Toronto
city: **4** York **6** London, Ottawa **7** Markham, Windsor **8** Hamilton **9** Etobicoke, Kitchener, North York **10** Thunder Bay **11** Mississauga, Scarborough **13** Sault Ste. Marie
lake: **4** Erie **5** Huron **7** Nipigon, Ontario **8** Superior
provincial flower: **13** white trillium
river: **5** Moose **6** Albany, Severn, Winisk

on the go
4 busy **6** active

on the house
4 free **6** comped, gratis **13** complimentary

on the nose
5 bingo **6** dead-on, spot-on **7** exactly **8** accurate **9** precisely **10** accurately

on the other hand
3 but **7** however **11** nonetheless **12** nevertheless

on the rocks
4 iced **7** with ice, wrecked

on the whole
6 mainly, mostly **7** usually **8** all in all **9** generally, in general, typically **10** altogether, by and large

onus
3 tax **4** duty, load, task **5** blame, brand, fault, guilt, odium, stain **6** burden, charge, stigma, weight **8** black eye **9** liability **10** obligation, oppression

onward
5 ahead, along, forth **7** forward **9** advancing

onyx
5 agate **10** chalcedony

oodles
4 gobs, lots, tons, wads **5** heaps, loads, piles, rafts, reams, scads **6** plenty

oolong
3 tea

oomph
3 pep, vim, zip **4** brio, dash, élan, push, zest, zing **5** drive, punch, verve, vigor **6** esprit, pizazz, spirit **7** pizzazz **8** strength, vitality **9** sex appeal

ooze
3 goo, mud **4** emit, goop, leak, seep, weep **5** bleed, exude, issue, marsh, slime, sweat **7** secrete, seepage **8** transude

opacity
9 murkiness, obscurity **10** obtuseness

opal
3 gem **5** jewel, stone **6** silica **7** girasol, hyalite **8** gemstone

opaque
3 dim **4** dull, hazy **5** dense, filmy, murky, vague **6** cloudy **7** clouded, obscure, unclear **8** abstruse

OPEC nation
3 UAE **4** Iran, Iraq **5** Libya, Qatar **6** Kuwait **7** Algeria, Nigeria **9** Indonesia, Venezuela **11** Saudi Arabia

open
4 ajar, bare, free, wide **5** frank, lance, overt, unzip **6** broach, candid, expand, expose, public, reveal, spread, unfold, unlock, unseal, unveil **7** convene, outdoor, uncover, unlatch **8** disclose, outdoors, unlocked, unsealed **9** available, uncovered, undecided **10** unfastened **11** susceptible, unconcealed, undisguised **12** unrestricted

open-air
7 outdoor, outside **8** alfresco, outdoors **9** out-of-door **10** out-of-doors

open-and-shut
4 easy **5** clear, plain **6** patent, simple **7** evident, obvious

openhanded
6 giving, lavish **7** liberal **8** generous **9** bounteous, bountiful, unselfish, unsparing **10** beneficent, bighearted, charitable, munificent **11** magnanimous

openhearted
4 kind, warm **5** frank, plain **6** candid, honest **8** generous **10** responsive **11** sympathetic

opening
2 os **3** gap **4** dawn, door, gate, hole, pass, pore, slit, slot, vent **5** break, chasm, chink, cleft, crack, debut, intro, mouth, onset, start, stoma **6** breach, chance, lacuna, outlet, outset **7** crevice, dawning, fissure, orifice, pinhole **8** aperture, overture **9** beginning **11** opportunity
ship's: **5** hatch **8** hatchway, porthole

open-minded
7 liberal **8** tolerant, unbiased **9** receptive **12** freethinking, unprejudiced

openmouthed
4 agog, awed, rapt **5** agape **6** amazed, gaping **7** stunned **9** astounded, surprised **10** astonished, speechless

open sesame
3 key **5** charm **6** ticket **8** passport, password

open up
4 fire, talk **5** shoot **6** reveal **7** cut into, divulge **8** disclose **9** make plain, spread out **11** communicate

opera
comic: 5 buffa 6 bouffe
glasses: 9 lorgnette
house: 3 Met 7 La Scala 12 Covent Garden, Metropolitan
kind: 4 soap 5 comic, grand, horse, space
part: 3 act 4 aria 5 scena
solo: 4 aria
star: 4 diva 10 prima donna
text: 8 libretto
(see also individual titles and composers)

opera (famous)
4 Aida 5 Faust, Manon, Norma, Tosca 6 Carmen, Otello, Salome 7 Elektra, Fidelio, Macbeth, Nabucco, Walküre (Die), Wozzeck 8 Don Carlo, Falstaff, Idomeneo, La Bohème, Turandot 9 Don Carlos, Lohengrin, Rheingold (Das), Rigoletto, Siegfried 10 I Pagliacci, La Gioconda, La Traviata, Magic Flute (The), Prince Igor, Tannhäuser 11 Don Giovanni, William Tell 12 Così Fan Tutte, Manon Lescaut, Pearl Fishers (The) 14 Flying Dutchman (The) 15 Barber of Seville (The), Götterdämmerung, Madama Butterfly 16 Marriage of Figaro (The), Tristan und Isolde

operant
8 behavior 9 effective 10 measurable, observable, productive 12 conditioning

operate
3 act, run, use 4 work 5 drive, exert, steer 6 behave, direct, effect, handle, manage 7 carry on, conduct, control, perform, produce 8 function, maneuver 9 influence 10 manipulate

operation
3 use 4 step 6 action 7 concern, mission, process, surgery 8 activity, business, exercise, exertion, function, maneuver 9 procedure 10 employment, engagement, enterprise 11 performance, transaction

operative
3 key 5 agent, alive 6 active, moving, usable 7 dynamic, in force, running, working 8 relevant 9 effective 10 functional 11 efficacious, secret agent

operator
4 user 5 agent, fixer, pilot 6 doctor, driver 7 schemer, surgeon 9 conductor

operculum
3 lid 4 flap 8 covering

operetta composer
5 Friml (Rudolf), Lehár (Franz), Suppé (Franz von) 6 Straus (Oscar) 7 Herbert (Victor), Romberg (Sigmund), Strauss (Johann) 8 Sullivan (Arthur) 9 Offenbach (Jacques)

operose
4 dull 6 boring, tiring 7 tedious 8 tiresome, toilsome, weariful 9 difficult, laborious, wearisome

Ophelia
beloved: 6 Hamlet
brother: 7 Laertes
father: 8 Polonius

ophidian
5 snake 9 snakelike

opiate
4 dope, drug 7 anodyne 8 hypnotic, narcotic, nepenthe, sedative 9 analgesic, soporific 10 anesthetic, painkiller 11 somniferous 12 somnifacient, tranquilizer
type: 7 codeine 8 morphine

opine
4 aver, deem, hold, view 5 claim, judge, state, think 6 advise, assert 7 believe, express, suppose 8 point out 9 recommend

opinion
4 idea, view 5 tenet 6 belief, notion, theory 7 feeling, thought 8 attitude, estimate, judgment, reaction 9 sentiment 10 assumption, conclusion, conjecture, conviction, estimation, hypothesis, persuasion 11 speculation, supposition
express an: 4 vote 5 judge 9 criticize

opium
4 dope, drug 8 narcotic
derivative: 6 heroin 7 codeine 8 laudanum, morphine 9 paregoric
source: 5 poppy

opossum
9 marsupial
kin: 8 kangaroo

opponent
3 con, foe 4 anti 5 enemy, rival 6 muscle 7 nemesis 9 adversary, assailant, combatant 10 antagonist, challenger, competitor 12 counteragent

opportune
3 apt, fit 6 timely 8 suitable 9 favorable, well-timed 10 auspicious, convenient, felicitous, propitious 11 appropriate

opportunity
4 turn 5 break, space, spell 6 chance 7 opening 8 juncture, occasion, prospect 12 circumstance

oppose
4 buck, defy, deny, duel 5 cross, fight, repel 6 attack, combat, debate, differ, object, refute, resist 7 assault, contest, counter, dispute, prevent, protest 8 confront, contrast, disagree, obstruct 9 withstand 10 contradict, contravene, controvert, disapprove

opposed
3 con 4 agin, anti 6 contra 7 adverse, against 11 adversarial 12 antagonistic, antipathetic

opposite
4 foil 5 polar 6 contra, facing 7 antonym, counter,

inverse, obverse, opposed, reverse **8** antipode, antipole, contrary, contrast, converse **9** antipodal, diametric **10** antipodean, antithesis **11** contrasting, counterpole **12** antithetical, counterpoint **13** contradictory
prefix: **3** dis **5** retro **6** contra **7** counter

opposition
3 con, foe **5** enemy **7** rivalry **8** conflict, defiance **9** adversary, animosity, hostility **10** antagonism, antithesis, resistance **11** contrariety, disapproval

oppress
5 abuse, crush, wrong **6** burden, injure, sadden, subdue **7** afflict, torment, torture, trouble **8** aggrieve, distress, overload **9** persecute, subjugate, weigh down

oppressive
5 harsh, heavy **6** brutal, dismal, gloomy, severe, somber, sombre, taxing **7** exigent, onerous, weighty **8** crushing, exacting, grievous, stifling **9** demanding **10** burdensome, depressing, tyrannical **11** dispiriting, overbearing, suffocating **12** discouraging, overwhelming
force: **4** onus, yoke **6** burden, weight

oppressor
5 bully **6** despot, tyrant **8** autocrat, dictator **9** strongman

opprobrious
4 evil, vile **6** odious, vulgar **7** abusive, hateful **8** infamous **9** notorious, truculent **10** despicable, scurrilous **11** disgraceful, ignominious **12** contemptible, contumelious, vituperative

opprobrium
5 abuse, blame, odium, scorn, shame **6** infamy **7** obloquy **8** contempt, disgrace, dishonor, ignominy, reproach **9** contumely, discredit, disesteem, disrepute **10** scurrility **12** vituperation

oppugn
5 argue, fight **6** battle, combat **7** contend, contest, dispute **8** question

Ops
4 Rhea
consort: **6** Cronus, Saturn
daughter: **5** Ceres **7** Demeter

opt
3 tap **4** pick **5** elect, favor **6** choose, decide, prefer, select

optical
6 ocular, visual **8** visional
debris: **7** floater
instrument: **4** lens **5** scope **7** transit **9** magnifier, periscope, telescope **10** microscope

optimal
4 best **5** ideal **6** choice, finest **7** perfect, supreme **8** choicest

optimist
4 bull **5** hoper **7** dreamer **8** idealist, Micawber **9** Pollyanna **10** positivist

optimistic
4 rosy **5** happy, merry, sunny **6** bright, hoping, upbeat **7** assured, buoyant, hopeful, roseate **8** cheerful, positive, sanguine, trusting **9** confident, promising **11** rose-colored **12** Pollyannaish

option
4 pick **5** claim, extra, grant, right **6** choice **7** license **8** contract, election **9** accessory, privilege, selection **10** preference **11** alternative, prerogative

optional
4 free **5** extra **8** elective **9** voluntary **11** alternative **13** discretionary
item: **5** add-on, extra

opulence
4 luxe **6** bounty, luxury, plenty, riches, wealth **7** fortune **9** abundance, affluence, plenitude, profusion **10** luxuriance **12** extravagance

opulent
4 lush, rich **5** plush, showy, swank **6** deluxe, lavish **7** moneyed, profuse, wealthy **8** affluent, palatial **9** luxuriant, luxurious, plentiful, sumptuous **11** extravagant **12** ostentatious

opuntia
6 cactus

opus
4 work **5** piece **6** oeuvre **7** product **8** creation **11** composition

or
4 else, gold **6** golden, yellow **9** otherwise

oracle
4 sage, seer **5** augur, sibyl **6** augury, medium, Pythia, vision **7** prophet **8** haruspex, prophecy **10** apocalypse, revelation, soothsayer
site: **6** Claros, Delphi, Didyma, Dodona **7** Olympia **9** Epidaurus

oracular
5 vatic **6** mantic, orphic **7** cryptic, Delphic, fatidic, obscure **8** Delphian, dogmatic **9** ambiguous, arbitrary, prophetic, sibylline, vaticinal

oral
4 exam **5** vocal **6** spoken, verbal, voiced **8** narrated, viva voce **9** unwritten **11** examination

orange
6 citrus
brownish: **6** Titian
deep: **11** bittersweet
gem: **7** jacinth
genus: **6** Citrus
kin: **4** lime **5** lemon **7** kumquat, satsuma **8** mandarin **9** tangerine **10** grapefruit

kind: **4** sour **5** blood, chino, navel, Osage, sweet **7** Seville **8** bergamot, mandarin, Valencia
oil: **6** neroli
seed: **3** pip
skin: **4** rind

orangutan
3 ape **6** pongid **7** primate **10** anthropoid

Oranjestad island
5 Aruba

orate
4 rant **5** mouth, speak, spiel **6** preach **7** address, declaim, lecture **8** bloviate, harangue, perorate **9** discourse, sermonize, speechify **11** pontificate

oration
6 homily, sermon, speech **7** address, lecture **9** discourse
funeral: **6** eulogy

orator
7 speaker
American: **4** Clay (Henry) **5** Bryan (William Jennings), Henry (Patrick) **7** Calhoun (John C.), Douglas (Stephen), Webster (Daniel)
British: **5** Burke (Edmund) **8** Disraeli (Benjamin) **9** Churchill (Winston), Gladstone (William)
French: **8** Mirabeau (Comte de)
Greek: **5** Corax **8** Pericles **11** Demosthenes
Roman: **6** Cicero

oratory
6 chapel, speech **7** bombast **8** rhetoric **9** discourse, elocution, eloquence **10** expression **11** exhortation, speechcraft

orb
3 eye **4** ball **5** globe, round **6** circle, sphere

orbit
4 path **5** ambit, range, reach, scope, sweep, track **6** extent, radius **7** ellipse
farthest point: **4** apse **5** apsis **6** apogee **8** aphelion
nearest point: **4** apse **5** apsis **7** perigee **10** perihelion

orchard
5 trees **10** plantation

orchestra
4 band **7** gamelan **8** ensemble, symphony **12** philharmonic
instrument: **4** harp, oboe, tuba **5** cello, flute, viola **6** chimes, violin **7** bassoon, cymbals, piccolo, timpani, trumpet **8** bass drum, clarinet, triangle, trombone **9** castanets, snare drum, xylophone **10** double bass, French horn, tambourine **11** English horn, violoncello **12** glockenspiel
leader: **9** conductor
section: **5** brass **6** string **7** brasses, strings **8** woodwind **9** woodwinds **10** percussion

orchestrate
5 blend, score, unify **6** manage **7** arrange, compose **8** organize **9** harmonize, integrate **10** coordinate

orchid
genus: **4** Disa
kind: **7** calypso, pogonia **8** cattleya, oncidium **9** cymbidium **11** cypripedium
petal: **3** lip **8** labellum
product: **5** salep
tuber: **5** salep

ordain
4 will **5** enact, order **6** decree, direct, impose, invest **7** appoint, command, conduct, destine, dictate, install, lay down **9** establish, prescribe, pronounce **10** predestine

ordeal
4 test **5** agony, cross, trial **7** calvary, torment, trouble **8** crucible **9** suffering **10** affliction, difficulty, visitation **11** tribulation

order
4 book, fiat, rank **5** array, caste, class, genre, range **6** decree, lineup, method, scheme, series, system **7** command, harmony, mandate, marshal, pattern, reserve **8** classify, neatness, position, shipment, tidiness **9** directive, hierarchy, procedure, structure **10** injunction, regularity **11** progression
lack of: **5** chaos **6** ataxia **7** anarchy, clutter **9** confusion **11** pandemonium
of business: **6** agenda, docket
of preference: **8** priority

orderly
4 aide, calm, neat, tidy, trim **6** batman **7** correct, precise, regular, soldier, uniform **8** methodic, peaceful **9** attendant, organized, peaceable, regulated, shipshape **10** methodical, systematic **11** uncluttered, well-behaved **12** businesslike

ordinance
3 law **4** code, rule **5** edict **6** decree **7** precept, statute **9** direction, prescript **10** regulation

ordinary
4 so-so **5** banal, cheap, judge, plain, trite, usual **6** common, normal **7** average, humdrum, mundane, natural, popular, prelate, prosaic, regular, routine, typical **8** everyday, familiar, inferior, mediocre, workaday **9** clergyman, customary, quotidian **10** uneventful, unoriginal **11** commonplace

ordnance
4 arms, guns **6** cannon **7** weapons **8** armament, supplies, weaponry **9** artillery, munitions **10** ammunition

ore
4 gold, rock 5 metal 6 copper, silver 7 mineral 8 platinum
analysis: 5 assay
deposit: 4 lode, vein
excavation: 5 stope
iron: 5 ocher, ochre 8 goethite, hematite, limonite
lead: 6 galena
process: 8 leaching, smelting
refuse: 4 slag 5 dross, matte 6 scoria
smelted: 7 regulus

oread
5 nymph

Oregon
capital: 5 Salem
city: 4 Bend 6 Eugene 7 Coos Bay, Medford 8 Portland
college, university: 4 Reed
lake: 6 Crater
mountain, range: 4 Hood 7 Cascade
nickname: 6 Beaver (State)
river: 5 Snake 8 Columbia
state bird: 10 meadowlark
state flower: 11 Oregon grape
state tree: 10 Douglas fir

Orestes
father: 9 Agamemnon
friend: 7 Pylades
mother: 12 Clytemnestra
sister: 7 Electra 9 Iphigenia
victim: 9 Aegisthus 12 Clytemnestra
wife: 8 Hermione

organ
5 agent, means 6 agency, medium, review 7 channel, journal, vehicle 8 magazine, ministry 9 newspaper 10 instrument, periodical
ancient: 9 hydraulus
barrel: 10 hurdy-gurdy
bodily: 3 ear, eye 4 lung, nose, skin 5 gland, heart, liver 6 kidney, larynx, spleen, tongue, tonsil, viscus 9 intestine
displacement: 8 prolapse
mouth: 9 harmonica
part: 4 pipe, reed, stop 5 pedal, valve 6 blower 7 console, tremolo 8 keyboard 9 wind chest
reed: 8 melodeon 9 harmonium
stop: 4 oboe, sext 5 gamba, quint, viola 6 dulcet 7 bassoon, celesta, melodia, subbass, tertian 8 carillon, diapason, dulciana, gemshorn
tactile: 6 feeler 8 tentacle

organ cactus
7 saguaro

organic
5 basic 6 innate 7 natural, primary 8 inherent, integral 9 essential 10 structural 11 fundamental

organism
5 being, plant 6 animal
disease-producing: 4 germ 5 virus 8 pathogen 9 bacterium
single-celled: 5 monad 6 amoeba 9 protozoan

organist
American: 3 Fox (Virgil) 5 Biggs (E. Power) 6 Newman (Anthony)
Dutch: 9 Sweelinck (Jan)
English: 6 Wesley (Samuel) 7 Gibbons (Christopher, Edward, Ellis, Orlando)
French: 5 Alain (Marie-Claire), Widor (Charles) 6 Franck (César) 8 Messiaen (Olivier) 10 Schweitzer (Albert)
German: 4 Bach (Johann Sebastian) 6 Handel (George Frideric), Walcha (Helmut) 7 Richter (Anton, Ernst, Ferdinand, Johann, Karl)
Swiss: 4 Rogg (Lionel)

organization
4 body, club, unit 5 group, guild, setup 6 agency, system 7 pattern 9 framework, structure 11 arrangement, association, corporation, institution 13 establishment
college: 4 frat 8 sorority 10 fraternity
criminal: 3 Mob 4 gang 5 Mafia
fraternal:
(see **fraternal society**)
government:
(see **government agency**)
lack of: 5 chaos
political: 4 bloc 5 party 7 apparat, machine
service: 3 USO, VFW

organize
4 form 5 array, group, order, rally, set up, start 6 create, line up 7 arrange 8 classify, unionize 9 construct, establish, institute, integrate 10 constitute, coordinate 11 put together

orgulous
5 proud

orgy
4 rite 5 binge, revel, spree 7 blowout, carouse, debauch, rampage, revelry, splurge 8 carousal 9 bacchanal 10 indulgence, saturnalia 11 bacchanalia

oriel
3 bay 6 window

orient
3 set 4 face 5 adapt, align, pearl, sheen 6 adjust, direct, inform, locate, luster 7 arrange 8 acquaint, lustrous 9 sparkling 11 accommodate, familiarize

Orient
4 Asia, East **7** Far East

Oriental
3 rug **5** Asian **6** carpet **7** Eastern **10** Far Eastern

orientation
7 bearing **8** location, position **9** alignment, direction **10** adjustment **11** arrangement

orifice
see **opening**

oriflamme
4 flag **5** ideal **6** banner, pennon, symbol **7** pendant, pennant **8** standard, streamer

origami
12 paper folding
bird: **5** crane

origin
4 root, seed, well **5** birth, blood, start **6** source **7** descent, genesis, lineage **8** ancestry, fountain, pedigree **9** beginning, inception, maternity, parentage, paternity **10** derivation, extraction, provenance, wellspring

original
3 new **5** first, model, novel, prime **6** native, unique **7** initial, pattern, pioneer, primary **8** creative, earliest **9** archetype, ingenious, innovator, inventive, precursor, primitive, prototype **10** archetypal, forerunner, innovative, primordial

originally
5 first **7** at first **8** formerly **9** initially, primarily

originate
4 coin, flow, hail, make, rise, stem **5** arise, begin, found, hatch, issue, set up, start **6** create, derive, invent, launch, spring **7** emanate, proceed, produce, think up **8** commence, generate, initiate, innovate **9** institute, introduce

originator
5 maker **6** author **7** creator, founder, planner **8** inventor, producer **9** initiator, innovator **10** institutor, introducer

oriole
4 bird **8** troupial
European: **6** loriot
genus: **7** Icterus
golden: **6** loriot
kind: **6** golden **7** orchard **8** Bullock's **9** Baltimore

Orion
6 hunter **13** constellation
beloved: **3** Eos
belt: **7** Ellwand
father: **7** Hyrieus **8** Poseidon
slayer: **5** Diana **7** Artemis
star: **5** Rigel **9** Bellatrix **10** Betelgeuse

orison
6 prayer **8** entreaty, petition **12** supplication

Orithyia
lover: **6** Boreas
son: **5** Zetes **6** Calais

Orlando author
5 Woolf (Virginia)

Orlando Furioso author
7 Ariosto (Ludovico)

Orléans heroine
9 Joan of Arc

orlop
4 deck

ormolu
5 brass **6** bronze

ornament
3 gem **4** bead, deck, trim **5** adorn, jewel **6** bedeck, finial, tassel **7** dress up, garnish, jewelry, pendant, whatnot **8** beautify, decorate, filigree **9** embellish, embroider, lavaliere
Christmas tree: **4** bulb **5** angel **6** tinsel
lip: **6** labret
shoulder: **7** epaulet

ornamental case
4 etui

ornate
4 lush, rich **5** fancy, gaudy, showy **6** florid, frilly, gilded, glitzy, rococo **7** baroque, flowery, opulent **8** overdone **9** elaborate, luxuriant, sumptuous **10** flamboyant

ornery
5 balky, cross, testy **6** crabby, cranky, crusty, grumpy **7** bearish, froward, grouchy **8** contrary, perverse, stubborn, vinegary **9** crotchety, difficult, irascible, irritable **10** inflexible, vinegarish **12** cantankerous

ornithic
5 avian **8** birdlike

ornithologist
American: **4** Bond (James) **7** Audubon (John James), Bartram (William) **8** Peterson (Roger Tory)
English: **5** Gould (John)
Scottish: **6** Wilson (Alexander)

orotund
4 full, loud **5** round **7** flowery, fustian, pompous, ringing **8** resonant, sonorous **9** bombastic, high-flown, overblown **10** euphuistic, oratorical, resounding, rhetorical, stentorian **11** declamatory **12** magniloquent **13** grandiloquent

Orpah
husband: **7** Chilion
sister-in-law: **4** Ruth

orphan
4 waif **5** Annie, gamin, stray **6** bereft, gamine, urchin **7** cast-off, ignored **8** forsaken, homeless **9** abandoned, foundling, neglected **10** motherless, parentless

Orpheus
father: **6** Apollo **7** Oeagrus
home: **6** Thrace
instrument: **4** lyre
mother: **8** Calliope
wife: **8** Euridice

orphic
6 arcane, mystic, occult **7** cryptic, Delphic, obscure **8** abstruse, Delphian, esoteric, hermetic, mystical, oracular, profound **9** enigmatic, recondite

ort
3 bit **4** bite **5** crumb, piece, scrap **6** morsel **7** remnant **8** leftover

orthodox
6 proper **8** accepted, approved, official, received, standard **9** canonical, customary **10** conformist, recognized, sanctioned **11** established, traditional **12** acknowledged, conservative, conventional **13** authoritative

orthography
7 writing **8** spelling

ortolan
7 bunting

Orwell novel
10 Animal Farm **18** Nineteen Eighty-four

oryx
7 gemsbok **8** antelope

os
3 ora (plural) **4** bone, ossa (plural) **5** mouth **7** orifice

Osborne play
6 Luther **11** Entertainer (The) **15** Look Back in Anger

oscillate
3 wag **4** sway, vary **5** swing, waver **6** change, seesaw **7** vibrate **9** alternate, fluctuate

oscillation
4 sway **5** swing **9** variation, vibration **10** undulation **11** fluctuation, periodicity

osculate
3 lip **4** buss, kiss, peck **5** smack **6** smooch

osculation
4 buss, kiss, peck **6** smooch **7** lip-lock

osier
3 rod **6** willow **7** dogwood

Osiris
brother: **3** Set **4** Seth
father: **3** Geb, Keb, Seb
mother: **3** Nut
scribe: **5** Thoth
sister: **4** Isis
slayer: **3** Set **4** Seth
son: **5** Horus **6** Anubis
wife: **4** Isis

osmium symbol
2 Os

osmosis
4 flow **8** transfer **9** diffusion **10** absorption **12** assimilation **13** incorporation

osprey
4 hawk **8** fish hawk

osseous
4 bony **8** bonelike

ossicle
4 bone **5** incus **6** stapes **7** malleus

ossify
3 set **6** harden **7** stiffen **8** solidify **9** fossilize

osso ____
4 buco

ossuary
4 tomb **5** vault **8** boneyard, cemetery **9** sepulcher, sepulchre

ostensible
6 stated **7** alleged, seeming **8** apparent, asserted, illusive, illusory, so-called, supposed **9** pretended, professed, purported, semblable **11** superficial

ostentation
4 pomp, show **5** flash, swank **7** display **9** pomposity, showiness, vainglory **10** flashiness, pretension **11** flamboyance

ostentatious
4 loud **5** gaudy, showy, swank **6** flashy, garish, swanky **7** pompous, splashy **8** overdone, peacocky **10** flamboyant, peacockish **11** pretentious **12** vainglorious

ostiole
4 pore **7** orifice **8** aperture

ostracism
5 exile **7** removal **9** exclusion **10** banishment, relegation **11** deportation

ostracize
3 bar, cut **4** shun, snub **5** exile **6** banish, deport **7** exclude, keep out, shut out **8** throw out **9** blackball **10** expatriate **12** cold-shoulder

ostrich
4 rhea **6** ratite

Ostrogoth king
9 Theodoric

Oswego tea
7 bee balm

otalgia
7 earache

Otello composer
5 Verdi (Giuseppe) **7** Rossini (Gioacchino)

O tempora! O ____!
5 mores

Othello
ancient / ensign: 4 Iago
author: 11 Shakespeare (William)
lieutenant: 6 Cassio
maid: 6 Emilia
victim, wife: 9 Desdemona

others
4 rest **9** remainder
and: 4 et al **6** et alia, et alii **7** et aliae

other than
3 but **4** save **6** except **7** besides **9** apart from, aside from, except for, excepting, excluding

otherwise
3 not **4** else **5** if not **6** or else **7** changed **9** different **11** differently **12** anything else **13** alternatively

otic
5 aural **8** auditory **9** auricular

otiose
4 idle, vain **5** empty **6** futile, hollow **7** surplus, useless **8** nugatory **9** fruitless, pointless, worthless **11** ineffective, purposeless, superfluous **12** functionless **13** supernumerary

Ottawa chief
7 Pontiac

ottoman
4 seat **5** couch **6** fabric **9** footstool

Ottoman
4 Turk **7** Turkish
council: 5 divan
governor: 3 bey
official: 3 aga, dey **6** vizier
ruler: 3 bey **5** Osman, Selim **8** Suleiman, Süleyman

Otus
5 giant
brother: 9 Ephialtes
father: 6 Aloeus **8** Poseidon
mother: 9 Iphimedia
slayer: 6 Apollo

ouch
5 bezel, jewel **6** brooch, buckle **7** setting **8** ornament **11** exclamation

ounce
3 bit, cat **4** dram **5** pinch, scrap, shred **6** amount, splash, weight **7** measure, modicum, smidgen **8** fraction, particle **11** snow leopard

our
French: 5 notre
Italian: 6 nostra
Spanish: 7 nuestro

Our Town author
6 Wilder (Thornton)

oust
4 fire, sack **5** eject, evict, expel **6** banish, deport, remove, topple, unseat **7** boot out, cast out, deprive, dismiss, kick out **8** displace, drive out, force out, relegate, supplant, take away, throw out **10** dispossess

ouster
7 removal **8** ejection, eviction **9** discharge, dismissal, expulsion **10** banishment

out
4 away, exit **5** forth, loose **6** absent, excuse
of control: 4 amok, wild **5** amuck **7** chaotic
of gas: 5 tired **7** drained **9** exhausted
of line: 4 awry, rude **5** askew, fresh
of place: 13 inappropriate
of sorts: 5 cross **7** grouchy, peevish **9** irritable
of the ordinary: 3 odd **7** bizarre, strange, unusual

outage
4 loss **5** break **7** failure **8** blackout **12** interruption

out-and-out
5 gross, sheer, total, utter **7** perfect **8** absolute, complete, positive **9** downright **10** consummate **11** unmitigated, unqualified **13** thoroughgoing

outback
4 bush **6** sticks **7** boonies **9** boondocks **10** hinterland, wilderness

Outback call
5 cooee

outboard
4 boat **5** motor **6** engine

outbreak
4 rash, rise, rush **5** burst, flare, spike, surge **6** attack, blowup, plague, revolt **7** flare-up **8** epidemic, eruption, increase, uprising **9** rebellion **12** insurrection

outbuilding
4 barn, shed

outburst
3 fit **4** gush, gust **5** flare, sally, scene, spasm, storm, surge **6** frenzy, tirade **7** flare-up, tantrum, torrent **8** eruption, paroxysm, upheaval **9** explosion

outcast
4 hobo **5** exile, leper, tramp **6** pariah **7** Ishmael, vagrant **8** castaway, derelict, vagabond **9** reprobate **10** expatriate, Ishmaelite **11** offscouring, untouchable

outclass
3 top **4** best **5** excel **6** exceed **7** surpass

outcome
3 end **5** event, fruit, issue **6** effect, result,

sequel, upshot **9** aftermath **10** conclusion **11** aftereffect, consequence, development

outcrop
4 rock **5** ledge **6** appear **7** project **8** protrude **10** projection, protrusion **12** protuberance

outcry
3 hue **4** yell **5** noise, shout **6** clamor, tumult, uproar **7** auction, ferment, protest **8** upheaval **9** commotion, objection **11** exclamation

outdated
3 old **5** passé **6** bygone, démodé, old hat **7** antique, archaic, vintage **10** antiquated, old-fangled **12** old-fashioned

outdistance
3 top **4** beat, best, pass **5** excel, trump **6** better, exceed **7** eclipse, surpass

outdo
3 top **4** beat, best, pass **5** excel, trump **6** better, defeat, exceed **7** eclipse, surpass, triumph **8** overcome **9** transcend

outdoor
7 open-air **8** alfresco

outer
6 remote **7** surface **8** exoteric, exterior, external **9** extrinsic **10** extraneous **11** superficial

outermost
4 last **5** final **6** far-off **7** distant, extreme **8** farthest, furthest, remotest

outfit
3 kit, rig, set **4** band, firm, gear, suit, team, togs, unit **5** corps, dress, equip, getup, group, squad, troop **6** clothe, supply, tackle, troupe **7** appoint, company, concern, costume, furnish **8** accouter, accoutre, business, clothing, ensemble, matériel, tackling **9** equipment, provision **10** enterprise **12** organization **13** accouterments, accoutrements, establishment

outflank
5 evade **6** bypass **9** get around **10** circumvent

outflow
6 efflux **8** drainage, effluent **9** effluence

out-front
4 open **5** frank **6** candid, honest **10** forthright

outgoing
4 open **7** affable **8** friendly, sociable **9** departing, expansive **10** gregarious, responsive **11** extroverted

outgrowth
6 effect, result **7** product, spin-off **8** offshoot **9** by-product, offspring **10** derivative **11** aftereffect, consequence

outhouse
5 jakes, privy **7** latrine

outing
4 spin, trip **5** drive, jaunt, sally **6** junket, picnic **9** excursion **10** appearance, disclosure

outlandish
3 odd **4** wild **5** alien, outré, ultra, weird **6** exotic **7** bizarre, curious, extreme, foreign, offbeat, strange, uncouth, unusual **8** peculiar, singular **9** eccentric, fantastic, tasteless **10** ridiculous, unorthodox **11** extravagant

outlast
6 endure **7** survive, weather **9** withstand

outlaw
3 ban, con **4** wild **5** crook **6** bandit, banned, enjoin, forbid **7** exclude, illegal **8** criminal, disallow, fugitive, prohibit, renegade, restrict **9** desperado, interdict, proscribe **10** illegalize, rebellious

outlay
3 pay, tab **4** cost, give **5** spend **6** amount, expend **7** expense, payment **8** disburse **11** expenditure **12** disbursement

outlet
4 exit, hole, mart, shop, vent **5** issue, store **6** avenue, egress, escape, market **7** channel, opening, passage, release **8** aperture **10** discounter, receptacle

outline
4 edge, form, limn, plan **5** brief, draft, shape, trace **6** bounds, border, précis, schema, sketch **7** contour, profile, summary **8** abstract, boundary, skeleton, syllabus, synopsis **9** delineate, summarize **10** figuration, silhouette **11** skeletonize

outlive
7 survive, weather

outlook
4 side, view **5** angle, scope, sight, slant, vista **6** aspect, future **7** promise **8** attitude, forecast, position, prospect **9** direction, viewpoint **10** standpoint **11** expectation, observatory, perspective, point of view

outlying
3 far **6** far-off, remote **7** distant, faraway, removed **8** far-flung

outmoded
4 dead **5** dated, passé, tired **6** old hat **7** antique, archaic **8** obsolete **9** moth-eaten, unstylish **10** oldfangled **11** obsolescent **12** old-fashioned

Out of Africa author
7 Dinesen (Isak)

out-of-date
3 old **4** past **5** passé, stale **6** démodé, old hat, square **7** antique, archaic, old-time, vintage

8 obsolete **9** unstylish **10** antiquated, oldfangled **12** old-fashioned

out of it
4 lost **5** dazed, spacy **6** addled, spacey **7** muddled **8** confused, demented **10** bewildered

out-of-the-way
4 rare **6** remote **7** distant, obscure, removed, unusual **8** secluded, uncommon

outpost
4 base **6** branch, colony **7** station **8** foothold **10** detachment, settlement

outpouring
4 flow, gush, rush **5** burst, flood, spate, spurt **6** deluge, stream **7** torrent **8** effusion

output
4 crop, gain, take **5** power, yield **6** amount, profit **7** harvest, produce, product **10** production **11** achievement, information

outrage
4 fury, rape **5** abuse, shock, wrong **6** injury, insult, offend **7** affront, incense, violate **8** aggrieve, atrocity, ill-treat, mischief, violence **9** brutality, infuriate **10** resentment, scandalize

outrageous
5 awful, gross **6** horrid, insane, odious, unholy, wicked **7** beastly, ghastly, heinous, ignoble, obscene **8** dreadful, flagrant, horrible, indecent, shocking, terrible **9** atrocious, egregious, excessive, fantastic **10** abominable, inordinate, scandalous **11** intolerable

outré
3 odd **5** ultra **6** far-out **7** bizarre, extreme, offbeat, strange **8** peculiar **9** eccentric **10** off-the-wall

outrigger
4 boat, beam, prau, proa, spar

outright
4 pure **5** total, utter, whole **6** entire **7** perfect **8** absolute, complete, entirely, positive **9** on the spot **10** completely, consummate **11** unequivocal, unmitigated, unqualified **13** thoroughgoing

outrun
3 top **4** beat, pass **6** exceed **7** surpass

outset
4 dawn **5** birth, get-go, start **7** opening **9** beginning, inception **12** commencement

outshine
3 top **4** beat, best **5** excel **6** better, exceed **7** eclipse, surpass

outside
5 alien **7** foreign, open-air **8** alfresco, exterior, external
combining form: **3** ect, exo **5** extra

outsider
5 alien **7** inconnu **8** newcomer, stranger **9** foreigner

outsmart
see **outwit**

outspoken
4 free, open **5** blunt, frank, plain, vocal **6** candid, direct, honest **7** up front **8** explicit **10** forthright, point-blank, unreserved **11** unequivocal

outstanding
3 due **4** A-one, star **5** boffo, noted, owing, socko **6** signal, superb, tip-top, unpaid **7** capital, eminent, notable, salient, stellar **8** dominant, striking, superior, top-notch **9** arresting, excellent, first-rate, prominent, unsettled **10** noticeable, preeminent, remarkable, unresolved **11** conspicuous, distinctive, exceptional, magnificent, superlative, uncollected **13** extraordinary

outstrip
3 top **4** beat, best, pass **5** excel **6** better, exceed **7** surpass **8** distance, go beyond, overtake **9** transcend **11** leave behind

outward
5 overt **7** evident, visible **8** apparent, exterior, external **10** noticeable, ostensible **11** superficial

outweigh
6 exceed **8** overbear **10** overshadow **11** overbalance **12** preponderate

outworn
see **outmoded**

ouzel
6 dipper, thrush **9** blackbird

oval
5 track **6** oblong **7** ellipse **8** elliptic **9** egg-shaped, racetrack **10** elliptical **11** ellipsoidal

ovation
5 kudos **6** homage, praise **7** acclaim, tribute **8** applause, approval, cheering, clapping, plaudits **11** acclamation

oven
4 kiln, oast **5** range, stove

over
4 anew, atop, done, past, upon **5** above, again, aloft, ended **6** across, beyond **8** done with, finished, once more
French: **3** sur
German: **4** über
prefix: **3** epi, sur **5** extra, hyper, super, supra
Spanish: **5** sobre

overabundance
4 glut **6** excess **7** surfeit, surplus **8** plethora **10** surplusage **11** superfluity

overact
3 ham, mug **4** rant **5** emote **10** exaggerate

overage
6 excess **7** surplus

overall
5 smock, total **6** global, mainly, mostly **7** chiefly, general, largely **8** as a whole, sweeping **9** generally, inclusive, in general, primarily **10** far and wide **11** principally **13** comprehensive, predominantly

overalls
5 pants **8** trousers

over and above
4 also **6** as well, beyond **7** besides **8** as well as **10** in addition

over and over
3 oft **5** often **8** ofttimes **10** frequently, oftentimes, repeatedly **11** continually, recurrently

overbearing
5 bossy **6** lordly **7** haughty, pompous **8** absolute, arrogant, despotic, dominant, imperial, insolent, scornful, superior **9** imperious, tyrannous **10** autocratic, disdainful, dominating, high-handed, oppressive, peremptory, tyrannical **11** dictatorial, domineering, magisterial **12** supercilious **13** high-and-mighty

overblown
6 turgid **7** flowery, hyped up, orotund, pompous **8** inflated **9** bombastic, excessive, high-flown **10** euphuistic, oratorical, rhetorical **11** declamatory, exaggerated, pretentious **12** magniloquent **13** grandiloquent

overcast
3 sew **4** dull, gray, hazy **5** cloud, cover **6** cloudy, darken, shadow **7** becloud, blanket, clouded, obscure **8** covering, lowering **9** adumbrate

overcharge
3 pad **4** bilk, clip, rook, skin, soak **5** cheat, stick **6** fleece **7** inflate

overcoat
5 paint **6** capote, raglan, ulster **7** surtout **9** balmacaan, outerwear **12** chesterfield

overcome
4 beat, best, lick **5** drown, throw **6** defeat, hurdle, master **7** conquer, prevail, triumph **8** surmount **9** prostrate

overconfident
4 rash **5** brash, cocky, pushy **8** arrogant, cocksure, reckless **9** hubristic, presuming **12** presumptuous

overdo
7 exhaust, fatigue, wear out **9** embellish **10** exaggerate

overdue
4 late **5** owing, tardy **6** behind, unpaid **7** belated, delayed, payable **8** dilatory **9** unsettled **10** behindhand, delinquent, unpunctual **11** outstanding

overemphasize
7 magnify **8** heighten **9** dramatize, embellish **10** exaggerate

overflow
4 pour **5** cover, drown, flood, slosh, spate, spill, swamp **6** deluge, engulf, excess, outlet **7** surfeit, surplus, torrent **8** flooding, inundate, spillage, submerge **10** inundation, surplusage **11** superfluity

overgrown
4 lush **5** dense, thick **6** brushy **7** hulking **8** ungainly **9** excessive, ponderous **10** junglelike

overhang
3 jut **4** loom **5** bulge **6** beetle, extend, impend **7** project **8** protrude, stick out, threaten **10** projection

overhaul
3 fix **4** mend, redo **5** patch, renew **6** doctor, remake, repair, revamp, revise **7** rebuild, restore **8** renovate **11** recondition, reconstruct

overhead
4 atop **5** above, aloft, smash **7** ceiling, expense **8** expenses

overheated
5 fiery **7** fervent **8** inflated **9** perfervid **11** impassioned

overindulgence
6 excess **7** surfeit **8** gluttony **11** dissipation **12** immoderation, intemperance

overjoyed
6 elated **7** gleeful **8** blissful, ecstatic, euphoric, exultant, jubilant, thrilled **9** rapturous **11** transported

overkill
4 glut **6** excess **7** surfeit, surplus, too much **8** plethora **10** obliterate, redundancy, surplusage **11** superfluity

overlap
7 shingle **9** imbricate

overlay
3 cap **4** coat **5** cover, glaze **6** finish, veneer **7** blanket, coating, lacquer, varnish **8** covering **11** superimpose **12** transparency

overload
4 glut **5** stuff **6** burden, excess, pile on, strain **7** surfeit

overlook
4 fail, miss, omit, skip **5** check, let go **6** excuse, forget, ignore, pass by, slight, slip up, survey, wink at **7** blink at, condone, forgive, inspect, let pass, neglect **8** discount, dominate, surmount **9** disregard, supervise **11** superintend

overlord
4 czar, tsar, tzar **5** chief, mogul, ruler **6** tycoon **7** magnate **8** suzerain **9** potentate, sovereign

overly
3 too **6** too-too, unduly **11** exceedingly, excessively **12** immoderately, inordinately

overpass
5 cross **6** bridge **8** crossing, traverse **9** traversal **11** interchange

overplay
4 hype **6** expand **7** enlarge, inflate, magnify, point up, stretch **8** maximize **9** dramatize **10** exaggerate **11** hyperbolize

overpower
4 rout **5** crush, swamp, whelm **6** defeat, master, subdue **7** conquer **8** vanquish **9** prostrate, subjugate **11** steamroller

overreach
3 con **4** beat, bilk **5** cheat, outdo **6** defeat, outfox, outwit **7** defraud **8** flimflam, outsmart **10** exaggerate **11** outmaneuver

override
4 veto **5** annul **6** cancel **7** nullify **10** counteract, neutralize

overriding
3 key **4** main **5** chief, major, prime, vital **7** central, crucial, pivotal, primary, supreme **8** cardinal, dominant, foremost **9** paramount, principal

overrule
4 undo, veto **5** upset **6** negate, revoke **7** reverse **8** set aside **11** countermand

overrun
4 beat, raid, teem, whip **5** swamp, swarm **6** defeat, excess, infest, invade, occupy, ravage, spread, thrash **7** clobber, conquer

overseas
6 abroad **11** transmarine, ultramarine **12** transoceanic, transpacific **13** transatlantic

oversee
3 run **4** boss, tend **5** watch **6** direct, manage, survey **7** command, examine, inspect **9** supervise **11** superintend

overseer
4 boss, exec, head **5** chief **7** foreman, manager **8** director **9** executive **10** supervisor **13** administrator

overshadow
4 veil **5** cloud, dwarf, shade **6** darken, exceed **7** becloud, eclipse, obscure, surpass **8** dominate, outshine, outweigh **9** adumbrate

overshoe
4 boot **6** arctic, galosh, patten, rubber

oversight
4 care, slip **5** aegis, check, error, lapse **6** charge, slip-up **7** control, failure, mistake, neglect **8** omission **10** intendance, management **11** supervision

overspread
3 cap **5** beset, cover, flood, swarm **6** infest, invade **7** blanket, obscure, pervade **8** permeate

overstate
3 pad **7** amplify, enlarge, magnify **9** embellish, embroider **10** exaggerate

overstep
6 exceed, offend **7** surpass, violate **8** infringe, trespass **10** transgress

overstock
4 glut **5** extra **6** excess **7** surplus **9** remainder **10** surplusage

overstress
7 magnify **8** maximize **10** exaggerate

overt
4 open **5** clear **6** patent **7** evident, obvious, outward, visible **8** apparent, manifest **10** observable

overtake
4 pass **5** catch **6** pass by **7** outpace, surpass **8** come upon, outstrip **11** outdistance

Over the Rainbow
composer: **5** Arlen (Harold)
lyricist: **7** Harburg (E. Y.)
movie: **10** Wizard of Oz (The)
singer: **7** Garland (Judy)

over there
3 yon **6** yonder

over-the-top
5 outré **7** extreme **8** reckless **9** egregious, excessive **10** exorbitant, flamboyant, outrageous **11** extravagant

overthrow
4 fell, oust, rout **5** evert, purge, upset **6** defeat, depose, remove, topple, unseat **7** conquer **8** dethrone, downfall **9** bring down

overtone
4 hint **5** sense **8** coloring, harmonic **9** inference **10** suggestion **11** association, connotation, implication **12** undercurrent

overture
3 bid **5** proem **7** advance, preface, prelude, present **8** approach, foreword, preamble, prologue, proposal **9** prelusion **10** initiative **11** proposition **12** introduction, presentation

overturn
3 tip **4** flip, void **5** upend, upset **6** topple, tumble **7** capsize, nullify, reverse **8** set aside **10** invalidate

overused
5 banal, musty, stale, tired, trite **7** clichéd, worn-out **9** hackneyed **10** threadbare

overview
6 aperçu, précis, survey **7** epitome, summary **10** conspectus

overweening
5 brash, pushy **6** lordly, uppish, uppity **7** forward **8** arrogant **9** conceited, presuming **10** immoderate **11** exaggerated **12** presumptuous

overweight
3 fat **5** beefy, burly, dumpy, gross, heavy, husky, obese, plump, pudgy, stout **6** chubby, chunky, flabby, fleshy, portly, rotund **7** outsize **8** heavyset, thickset **9** corpulent

overwhelm
4 beat, bury, rout, ruin, sink, whip **5** crush, drown, flood, swamp, upset, wreck **6** boggle, defeat, deluge, engulf, thrash **7** conquer, destroy, oppress, shatter, shellac, smother **8** inundate, submerge **9** devastate, prostrate **10** demoralize **11** steamroller, subordinate

overwhelmed
6 aghast **7** shocked, stunned, touched **8** defeated, helpless **10** distressed **13** thunderstruck

overwhelming
4 huge **5** great **7** extreme **8** numerous

overwrought
5 hyper, upset **7** anxious, frantic, wound up **8** agitated, frenetic, stressed, troubled **9** disturbed, emotional **10** distracted, freaked out, high-strung, hysterical **11** discomposed

Ovid work
5 Fasti **6** Amores **7** Tristia **8** Heroides **13** Metamorphoses

ovine
5 sheep **9** sheeplike

ovoid
9 egg-shaped

ovule
3 egg
fertilized: 4 seed

ovum
3 egg **6** gamete **7** egg cell **11** macrogamete

owing
3 due **6** in debt, mature, unpaid **7** overdue, payable **9** unsettled **11** outstanding

owing to
4 over **7** through **9** because of **10** by reason of **11** on account of

owl
cry: 4 hoot
genus: 4 Bubo, Otus
kind: 3 elf **4** barn, gray, lulu **5** eagle, gnome, madge, pygmy, snowy **6** barred, horned **7** saw-whet, screech **9** long-eared **10** short-eared **11** great horned

Owl and the Pussycat author
4 Lear (Edward)

own
4 avow, have, hold **5** admit, allow, enjoy, grant, let on **6** accept, fess up, retain **7** concede, confess, possess **8** disclose **9** recognize **11** acknowledge

owner
6 holder **8** landlady, landlord **9** possessor, purchaser **10** proprietor

ownership
4 hand **5** title **8** dominion, property **10** possession **11** proprietary
perpetual: 8 mortmain

ox
3 yak **4** anoa, gaur, musk, zebu **5** bison, steer **6** bovine **7** banteng, buffalo
Asian: 4 zebu
attachment: 4 yoke
extinct: 4 urus **7** aurochs
family: 7 Bovidae
relating to: 6 bovine
wild: 4 anoa, gaur **7** banteng

oxeye
5 daisy **6** flower

oxford
4 shoe **5** cloth, sheep **6** cotton, fabric

oxide
calcium: 4 lime **9** quicklime
ferric: 4 rust
sodium: 4 soda

oxidize
4 rust

oxygen
3 air, gas **5** ozone **7** element
discoverer: 9 Lavoisier (Antoine)
form: 5 ozone
liquid: 3 lox

oyster
7 bivalve, mollusc, mollusk
bed: 4 park **6** claire, cultch
eggs: 5 spawn
genus: 6 Ostrea
lining: 5 nacre
Long Island: 9 bluepoint
product: 5 pearl
shell: 4 test **5** shuck
young: 4 spat

oyster plant
7 salsify

Oz
9 Australia, Down Under
creator: **4** Baum (L. Frank)
inhabitant: **8** Munchkin
princess: **4** Ozma

Ozark State
8 Missouri

Ozem
brother: **5** David
father: **5** Jesse **9** Jerahmeel

Ozymandias author
7 Shelley (Percy Bysshe)

P

pabulum
3 pap **4** food **7** aliment **8** nutrient **9** blandness, nutriment **10** insipidity, sustenance **11** nourishment

paca
4 cavy

pace
3 set **4** beat, clip, gait, lead, rate, step, time, walk **5** speed, tempo, tread, troop **6** motion, stride, timing **7** example, fluency, measure, precede, proceed, routine, step off **8** ambulate, antecede, movement, progress, regulate

pachyderm
8 elephant

pacific
4 calm, mild **6** gentle, irenic, placid, serene **8** dovelike, peaceful, soothing, tranquil **9** peaceable, temperate **12** conciliatory

Pacific
island: **3** Yap **4** Wake **6** Easter, Jarvis, Saipan, Tahiti, Tarawa **7** Iwo Jima, Tokelau **8** Pitcairn, St. Helena **11** Guadalcanal
nation: **4** Fiji **5** Belau, Japan, Nauru, Palau, Tonga **6** Tuvalu **7** Vanuatu **8** Kiribati

Pacificator, Great
4 Clay (Henry)

Pacific Ocean discoverer
6 Balboa (Vasco Núñez de)

pacifist
4 dove **6** irenic **8** appeaser, peaceful, peacenik **9** peaceable **10** nonviolent **11** peacemonger

pacify
4 calm, cool, ease, lull **5** allay, quell, quiet, still **6** disarm, settle, soften, soothe, subdue, temper **7** appease, assuage, mollify, placate **9** subjugate **10** conciliate, propitiate

pack
3 jam, kit, lot, lug, ram, set, wad **4** band, bear, cram, deck, fill, gang, heap, load, lump, mass, pile, stow, tamp, tote, unit **5** bunch, carry, cover, crowd, ferry, group, store, stuff, troop **6** bundle, charge, clique, convey, depart, gather **7** possess **8** assemble, compress, knapsack **9** container, equipment, influence, transport **10** collection, congregate

package
3 box **4** bale, deal, unit, wrap **5** array, combo, whole **6** bundle, parcel **7** enclose, present, wrapper **8** shipment **9** container **10** collection **11** combination

pack animal
3 ass **4** mule **5** burro, camel, horse, llama **6** donkey **7** jackass **13** beast of burden

packed
4 full **5** awash, dense, flush **6** filled, jammed **7** brimful, crowded, stuffed **8** brimming **9** chockfull **10** compressed

packet
3 wad **4** boat, mass, pile **5** group **6** bundle, parcel **7** cluster

pact
4 bond, deal **6** accord, treaty **7** bargain, concord **8** alliance, contract, covenant **9** agreement

pad
3 bed, mat, wad **4** foot, mute **5** fudge, guard, paper, stuff **6** buffer, expand, muffle, shield, tablet **7** augment, bolster, cushion, stretch **8** dressing, increase **9** embellish, embroider, overstate **10** exaggerate, overcharge

paddle
3 oar, row **4** beat, stir **5** spank **6** propel, thrash

paddock
5 field **7** pasture **9** enclosure

paddy wagon
10 Black Maria

padre
3 Fra **6** father, priest **8** chaplain, minister **9** clergyman, confessor

paean
4 hymn, song **6** anthem, eulogy, praise **7** tribute **8** accolade, encomium **9** panegyric

page
4 book, call, leaf **5** folio, sheet **6** locate, summon **7** bellhop, equerry
left-hand: **5** verso
right-hand: **5** recto

pageant
4 sham, show **7** charade, display, tableau **8** pretense **9** spectacle **10** exhibition

pageantry
4 pomp, show **7** display, panoply **8** flourish, splendor **9** spectacle **10** exhibition **11** flamboyance, ostentation **12** magnificence

Pagliacci, I
character: **5** Canio, Nedda, Tonio **6** Silvio
composer: **11** Leoncavallo (Ruggero)

pagoda
2 ta **6** temple

pail
3 hod **6** bucket, piggin, vessel **7** scuttle

pain
3 irk **4** ache, care, hurt, pang **5** agony, cramp, grief, throe, upset **6** grieve, harass, stitch, twinge **7** afflict, anguish, torture, travail, trouble **8** aggrieve, distress **9** suffering **10** affliction, discomfort
back: **7** lumbago
muscular: **7** myalgia

painful
3 raw **4** hard, sore **5** acute, sharp **6** aching, trying **7** arduous, irksome **8** annoying, piercing, stinging **9** agonizing, difficult, laborious, torturous, upsetting, vexatious **10** afflictive, tormenting

painkiller
4 drug **6** opiate **7** anodyne, codeine **8** morphine, narcotic **9** analgesic **10** anesthetic

painstaking
5 exact **7** careful, heedful **8** diligent, exacting, thorough **9** assiduous, diligence, laborious **10** meticulous, scrupulous **11** punctilious

paint
4 coat, daub, limn, swab, tint **5** adorn, brush, color, cover, horse, pinto, rouge, stain **6** depict, makeup **7** coating, pigment, portray, produce, touch up **8** cosmetic, decorate **9** delineate, represent **10** maquillage

painter
6 artist
American: **4** Cole (Thomas), Haas (Richard), West (Benjamin), Wood (Grant) **5** Abbey (Edwin Austin), Davis (Stuart), Gorky (Arshile), Grosz (George), Henri (Robert), Hicks (Edward), Homer (Winslow), Johns (Jasper), Kline (Franz), Kroll (Leon), Marin (John), Marsh (Reginald), Moses (Grandma), Peale (Anna, Charles Willson, James, Raphaelle, Rembrandt, Sarah, Titian), Ryder (Albert Pinkham), Shahn (Ben), Sloan (Eric, John), Weber (Max), Wyeth (Andrew, Jamie, Newell Convers) **6** Albers (Josef), Benton (Thomas Hart), Catlin (George), Church (Frederick Edwin), Coburn (Alvin Langdon), Copley (John Singleton), Durand (Asher), Eakins (Thomas), Hassam (Childe), Hopper (Edward), Inness (George), Leutze (Emanuel), Martin (Agnes, Homer), Newman (Barnett), Rivers (Larry), Rothko (Mark), Stella (Frank), Stuart (Gilbert), Tanguy (Yves), Thorpe (Thomas), Warhol (Andy) **7** Allston (Washington), Bearden (Romare), Bellows (George), Bingham (George Caleb), Cassatt (Mary), Duchamp (Marcel), Harnett (William), Hartley (Marsden), Kinkade (Thomas), La Farge (John), O'Keeffe (Georgia), Parrish (Maxfield), Pollock (Jackson), Sargent (John Singer), Sheeler (Charles), Tiffany (Louis Comfort), Tworkov (Jack), Wiggins (Carleton) **8** Melchers (Gari), Rockwell (Norman), Sullivan (Patrick), Trumbull (John), Whistler (James McNeill) **9** Bierstadt (Albert), de Kooning (Willem), Feininger (Lyonel), Reinhardt (Ad), Remington (Frederic), Twachtman (John Henry), Vanderlyn (John), Walkowitz (Abraham) **10** Motherwell (Robert), Whittredge (Thomas) **12** Lichtenstein (Roy), Rauschenberg (Robert)
Austrian: **5** Klimt (Gustav) **9** Kokoschka (Oskar)
Belgian: **5** Ensor (James) **6** Campin (Robert) **8** Magritte (René)
Canadian: **4** Kane (Paul) **6** Harris (Lawren), Watson (Homer) **7** Jackson (Alexander Young), Thomson (Tom) **9** MacDonald (James Edward Hervey)
Chinese: **4** Wu Li **6** Ma Yüan **7** Wang Wei **8** Yen Li-pen
Dutch: **3** Dou (Gerrit) **4** Hals (Frans), Lely (Peter), Maas (Nicolas) **5** Bosch (Hieronymus), Hooch (Pieter de), Steen (Jan) **6** Potter (Paul) **7** de Hooch (Pieter), de Witte (Emanuel), Hobbema (Meindert), van Gogh (Vincent), Vermeer (Jan) **8** Mondrian (Piet), Ruisdael (Jacob van, Salomon), Ruysdael (Salomon), Terborch (Gerard) **9** de Kooning (Willem), Rembrandt (van Rijn), Wouwerman (Philips) **11** Terbrugghen (Hendrik)
English: **4** Hunt (William Holman), John (Augustus), Lear (Edward) **5** Bacon (Francis), Blake (William), Brown (Ford Madox), Lewis (Wyndham), Watts (George Frederick) **6** Fuseli (Henry), Romney (George), Stubbs (George), Turner (Joseph Mallord William), Wilson (Richard), Wright (Joseph) **7** Hockney (David), Hogarth (William), Kneller (Godfrey), Millais (John), van Dyke (Anthony) **8** Landseer (Edwin), Lawrence (Thomas), Reynolds (Joshua), Rossetti (Dante Gabriel) **9** Constable (John), Nicholson (Ben, William) **10** Alma-Tadema (Lawrence), Burne-Jones (Edward) **12** Gainsborough (Thomas)
Finnish: **9** Järnefelt (Edvard)
Flemish: **4** Eyck (Hubert van, Jan van), Goes (Hugo van der) **6** Rubens (Peter Paul), Weyden (Rogier van der) **7** Memling (Hams), Teniers

(David), Van Dyck (Anthony), van Eyck (Hubert, Jan) **8** Breughel, Brueghel (Abraham, Ambrose, Jan, Pieter)
French: **3** Arp (Hans) **4** Doré (Gustave), Dufy (Raoul), Erté, Gros (Antoine-Jean) **5** Corot (Camille), David (Jacques-Louis), Degas (Edgar), Léger (Fernand), Manet (Edouard), Monet (Claude), Redon (Odilon), Vouet (Simon) **6** Braque (Georges), Breton (André), Claude (of Lorrain), Clouet (François, Jean), Gérôme (Jean-Léon), Greuze (Jean-Baptiste), Ingres (Jean-Auguste-Dominique), Le Brun (Charles), Le Nain (Antoine, Louis, Mathieu), Millet (Jean-François), Renoir (Pierre-Auguste), Seurat (Georges), Sisley (Alfred), Tanguy (Yves), Vernet (Carle, Horace, Joseph) **7** Balthus, Bonheur (Rosa), Bonnard (Pierre), Boucher (François), Cézanne (Paul), Chagall (Marc), Chardin (Jean-Baptiste), Courbet (Gustave), Daumier (Honoré), Duchamp (Gaston, Marcel), Gauguin (Paul), Matisse (Henri), Morisot (Berthe), Poussin (Nicolas), Rouault (Georges), Utrillo (Maurice), Watteau (Antoine) **8** Dubuffet (Jean), Magritte (René), Pissarro (Camille), Rousseau (Henri, Théodore), Vlaminck (Maurice de), Vuillard (Edouard) **9** Delacroix (Eugène), Fragonard (Jean-Honoré), Géricault (Théodore), Laurencin (Marie) **10** Bouguereau (William), Meissonier (Jean-Louis) **11** Caillebotte (Gustave) **13** Claude Lorrain
German: **5** Dürer (Albrecht), Ernst (Max), Grosz (George), Nolde (Emil) **6** Albers (Josef), Müller (Friedrich "Maler") **7** Cranach (Lucas), Holbein (Hans), Lochner (Stefan), Schwind (Moritz von), Zoffany (Johann) **8** Kirchner (Ernst), Kollwitz (Käthe) **9** Grünewald (Matthias), Kandinsky (Wassily) **10** Schongauer (Martin), Wohlgemuth (Michael)
Greek: **6** Zeuxis **7** Apelles **10** Polygnotus
Irish: **5** Yeats (Jack, John Butler)
Italian: **4** Reni (Guido), Rosa (Salvator), Tura (Cosme) **5** Campi (Antonio, Bernardino, Giulio, Vincenzo), Lippi (Fra Filippo, Filippino, Lorenzo), Piero (della Francesca, di Cosimo), Sarto (Andrea del) **6** Andrea (del Sarto), Cosimo (Agnolo di, Piero di), Giotto, Romano (Giulio), Sodoma (Il), Titian, Vasari (Giorgio) **7** Bellini (Gentile, Giovanni, Jacopo), Chirico (Giorgio De), Cimabue, da Vinci (Leonardo), Fiesole (Giovanni da), Martini (Simone), Orcagna, Peruzzi (Baldassare), Raphael, Tiepolo (Giovanni), Uccello (Paolo), Zuccari (Taddeo) **8** del Sarto (Andrea), Fabriano (Gentile da), Giordano (Luca), Leonardo (da Vinci), Mantegna (Andrea), Masaccio, Montagna (Bartolommeo), Perugino, Pontorno (Jacopo da), Severini (Gino), Veronese (Paolo), Vivarini (Alvise, Antonio, Bartolomeo) **9** Carpaccio (Vittore), Correggio, Francesca (Piero della) **10** Caravaggio, Modigliani (Amedeo), Signorelli (Luca), Tintoretto, Verrocchio (Andrea del), Zuccarelli (Francesco) **11** Ghirlandaio (Domenico), Ghirlandajo (Domenico) **12** Michelangelo (Buonarotti), Parmigianino
Japanese: **5** Korin **6** Sesshu
Lithuanian: **7** Soutine (Chaim)
Mexican: **6** Orozco (José Clemente), Rivera (Diego), Tamayo (Rufino) **9** Siqueiros (David Alfaro)
Norwegian: **5** Munch (Edvard)
Russian: **7** Chagall (Marc), Roerich (Nikolay) **9** Kandinsky (Wassily)
Scottish: **6** Ramsay (Allan) **7** Nasmyth (Alexander), Raeburn (Henry)
Spanish: **4** Dalí (Salvador), Goya (Francisco), Gris (Juan), Miró (Joan), Sert (José Maria) **6** Ribera (José), Rincón (Antonio del), Tapiés (Antonio) **7** El Greco, Herrera (Francisco de), Murillo (Bartolomé Esteban), Picasso (Pablo), Zuloaga (Ignacio) **8** Zurbarán (Francisco de) **9** Velázquez (Diego)
Swedish: **4** Zorn (Anders) **6** Roslin (Alexander)
Swiss: **4** Klee (Paul), Witz (Konrad) **6** Fuseli (Henry)

painting
3 oil **7** acrylic, picture **10** watercolor
circular: **5** tondo
one-color: **8** monotint **10** monochrome
plaster: **5** secco **6** fresco
style: **4** Dada **5** fauve **6** cubism, cubist, Gothic, pop art, rococo **7** baroque, Bauhaus, dadaism, fauvism, fauvist, realism, realist **8** Barbizon, futurism, futurist, romantic **9** Byzantine, geometric, mannerism, mannerist **10** classicism, classicist, surrealism, surrealist **11** romanticism **13** expressionism, expressionist, impressionism, impressionist
technique: **3** oil **6** fresco, pastel **7** gouache, polymer, tempera **9** encaustic **10** watercolor
tool: **5** brush, easel, knife, paint **6** canvas **7** palette
wall: **5** mural

pair
3 duo, two **4** dyad, item, join, mate, span, team, twin, yoke **5** brace, match, twins, unite **6** couple **7** doublet, twosome **8** geminate

Pakistan
capital: **9** Islamabad
city: **6** Lahore, Multan **7** Karachi **9** Hyderabad **10** Faisalabad, Rawalpindi
language: **4** Urdu
leader: **6** Bhutto (Benazir) **9** Musharraf (Pervez)
monetary unit: **5** rupee
mountain, range: **8** Himalaya **9** Himalayan, Himalayas **11** Nanga Parbat
neighbor: **4** Iran **5** China, India **11** Afghanistan
sea: **7** Arabian

pal
3 bud **4** chum, mate, pard **5** amigo, buddy, crony **6** comate, friend **7** comrade, partner **9** companion

palace
5 court, manor, manse **6** castle **7** alcazar, château, mansion **8** seraglio

paladin
6 leader **8** advocate, champion, defender, official

Palamedes
brother: **6** Sforza **8** Achilles
father: **8** Nauplius
slayer: **7** Corinda, Ulysses **8** Odysseus

palatable
5 sapid, tasty **6** savory **8** pleasing, savorous, tasteful **9** agreeable, appealing, delicious, toothsome **10** acceptable, appetizing **12** satisfactory

palate
5 taste **6** liking **6** relish

palatial
4 rich **5** grand, large, noble, plush, regal **6** deluxe, ornate **7** opulent, stately **8** imposing, majestic, splendid **9** grandiose, luxuriant, luxurious, sumptuous **10** impressive **11** magnificent

Palau
capital: **5** Koror
former name: **5** Pelew
island: **5** Koror **6** Angaur **7** Eli Malk **10** Babelthuap, Urukthapel
language: **7** Palauan

palaver
3 gas, yak **4** blab, cant, chat, guff, talk **6** babble, cajole, hot air, jargon, parley, powwow, speech **7** chatter, prattle **8** colloquy, converse, dialogue **10** conference, discussion, rap session **12** conversation

pale
3 dim, wan **4** area, ashy, dull, fade, sick, weak **5** ashen, faded, faint, fence, field, light, livid, pasty, stake, waxen **6** anemic, blanch, chalky, doughy, feeble, pallid, picket, sallow, sickly, weaken, whiten **7** enclose, ghastly, insipid **8** blanched, district, encircle **9** bloodless, colorless, enclosure

palindrome
3 aha, bib, dad, dud, DVD, eke, ere, eve, ewe, eye, gag, gig, huh, mem, mom, mum, nun, pap, PCP, pep, pip, pop, pup, sis, SOS, tat, TNT, tot, tut, wow **4** deed, kook, ma'am, noon, peep, poop, toot **5** alula, civic, imami, kayak, Kazak, level, madam, minim, put-up, radar, refer, rotor, stats, Tebet, tenet, we few **6** pull-up, terret **7** deified, race car, reviver, top spot **9** Malayalam, never even **11** borrow or rob, drawn inward, Kinnikinnik, Madam I'm Adam

palinode
10 retraction **11** recantation

pall
4 bore, cloy, damp, jade, sate, tire **5** cloak, cloth, cloud, drape, ennui, gloom, weary **6** coffin, damper, mantle, shadow **7** dwindle, satiate, surfeit **8** covering

palladium
9 safeguard
symbol: **2** Pd

Pallas
6 Athena
brother: **6** Aegeus
father: **7** Pandion
slayer: **7** Theseus
wife: **4** Styx
(see also **Athena**)

palliate
4 ease, help **5** cover, salve **6** excuse, lessen, reduce, soften, soothe, temper **7** assuage, cover up, lighten **8** mitigate, moderate **9** alleviate, sugarcoat, whitewash **10** ameliorate

pallid
3 wan **4** ashy, dull, pale, weak **5** ashen, pasty, waxen **6** anemic, doughy, sickly **8** blanched, lifeless **9** bloodless, colorless

pallor
8 lividity, paleness **9** pastiness, whiteness **10** etiolation **12** glaucousness

pally
4 cozy **5** close, matey **6** chummy **7** devoted **8** familiar, friendly, intimate

palm
5 prize, steal, swipe **6** trophy **7** conceal, triumph, victory
beverage: **4** nipa
fiber: **4** bass, bast, coir **8** piassava
fruit: **4** date **7** coconut **11** coquilla nut
kind: **3** fan, wax **4** atap, coco, date, doom, hemp, nipa, sago **5** areca, betel, ivory, royal, sabal **6** miriti, raffia, rattan **7** cabbage, feather, palmyra **8** carnauba, palmetto, piassava **12** Washingtonia
leaf: **4** olla **5** frond
lily: **2** ti
starch: **4** sago
vine: **6** rattan

palmer
7 pilgrim

Palmetto State
13 South Carolina

palmistry
6 augury **8** prophecy **10** divination **11** soothsaying

palm off
5 foist **7** deceive, pretend **8** disguise

palmy
6 golden 7 booming, halcyon, opulent 8 affluent, thriving 10 prospering, prosperous 11 flourishing

Palmyra's queen
7 Zenobia

palooka
3 oaf 4 boob, dolt, goon, lout, lump 5 boxer, klutz 6 baboon, galoot, lummox 7 bruiser

palpable
4 real, sure 5 clear, plain 6 patent 7 certain, evident, obvious, tactile 8 apparent, concrete, definite, distinct, manifest, material, positive, tangible 10 noticeable 11 discernible, perceptible, unequivocal

palpate
4 feel 5 touch 6 finger 7 examine

palpitate
4 beat 5 pulse, throb 6 quiver 7 flutter, pulsate 12 pitter-patter

palsy-walsy
4 cozy 5 close, thick, tight 6 chummy 8 intimate 10 buddy-buddy

palter
3 fib, lie 5 evade 6 dicker, haggle 7 bargain, chaffer, deceive, falsify, wrangle 10 equivocate 11 prevaricate 12 misrepresent

paltry
3 low 4 base, mean, poor, puny, vile 5 cheap, petty, tatty 6 meager, measly, narrow, shabby, shoddy, sleazy, trashy 7 low-down, pitiful, trivial 8 beggarly, inferior, picayune, piddling, rubbishy, trifling 9 worthless 10 despicable, picayunish 11 unimportant 12 contemptible 13 insignificant

paludal place
3 fen 5 marsh

Pamela author
10 Richardson (Samuel)

pampa
5 plain 7 prairie 9 grassland

pamper
3 pet 4 baby 5 humor, spoil 6 caress, cocker, coddle, cosset, cuddle, dandle, fondle 7 cater to, cherish, gratify, indulge 9 spoon-feed 11 mollycoddle

pamphlet
5 flier, flyer, tract 6 folder 7 leaflet 8 brochure, circular 9 throwaway 10 broadsheet

pan
3 pot, rap 4 slam, wash 5 basin, knock, roast, trash 6 attack, vessel 7 censure, condemn, skillet 8 denounce, ridicule 9 betel leaf, container, criticism, criticize 10 receptacle

Pan
5 Inuus 6 Faunus
father: 6 Hermes
invention: 6 syrinx
lower part: 4 goat
mother: 8 Penelope
pipe: 6 syrinx
seat of worship: 7 Arcadia
son: 7 Silenus

panacea
4 cure 6 elixir, remedy 7 cure-all, nostrum 10 catholicon

Panacea's father
9 Asclepius 11 Aesculapius

panache
4 brio, dash, élan, tuft, zest 5 ardor, crest, flair, style, verve, vigor 6 esprit, polish, spirit 8 aigrette, flourish, vivacity 11 flamboyance

panama
3 hat

Panama
discoverer: 6 Balboa (Vasco Núñez de) 8 Columbus (Christopher)
gulf: 7 San Blas 8 Mosquito
language: 7 Spanish
leader: 7 Noriega (Manuel)
monetary unit: 6 balboa
neighbor: 8 Colombia 9 Costa Rica
peninsula: 6 Azuero
sea: 9 Caribbean
volcano: 8 Chiriquí

pancake
8 flapjack, slapjack
chain: 4 IHOP
French: 5 crepe
Jewish: 5 latke 6 blintz 7 blintze
Russian: 4 blin 5 blini

Pandarus
6 archer 8 procuror
father: 6 Lycaon
slayer: 8 Diomedes

pandect
4 code, laws 8 treatise 10 compendium 11 compilation

pandemic
4 rife 7 general, rampant 9 contagion, extensive, prevalent 10 contagious, widespread 11 wide-ranging

pandemonium
3 din 5 babel, chaos, furor 6 bedlam, clamor, hubbub, tumult, uproar 7 anarchy, discord, inferno, misrule, turmoil 8 disorder 9 confusion 10 hullabaloo

pander
4 pimp 5 cater 9 exploiter, go-between

Pandion
daughter: 6 Procne 9 Philomela
son: 6 Pallas

Pandora
creator: **10** Hephaestus
husband: **10** Epimetheus

pane
4 side **5** sheet **7** section

panegyric
6 eulogy, praise **7** tribute **8** citation, encomium **9** laudation **10** compliment **12** commendation

panegyrical
8 praising **9** laudative, laudatory **10** eulogistic **11** encomiastic **12** commendatory **13** complimentary

panel
4 jury **5** board, frame **6** hurdle **7** console, section **9** dashboard

panfry
5 sauté

pang
4 ache, pain, stab **5** agony, prick, spasm, throe **6** stitch, twinge **7** anguish, torment **8** distress

Pangloss's pupil
7 Candide

panhandle
3 beg, bum, tap **5** cadge, hit up, touch **6** hustle **7** solicit

panhandler
6 beggar

panic
4 fear, riot, rush **5** alarm, scare **6** dismay, frenzy, fright, horror, terror **7** anxiety, terrify **8** frighten, hysteria, stampede

pannier
4 hoop, pack **6** basket, hamper **9** overskirt

panoply
4 pomp, show **5** armor, array **6** attire **7** display, fanfare **9** trappings

panorama
4 view **5** range, reach, scene, scope, sweep, vista **7** display, expanse, picture, purview **12** presentation

panoramic
8 sweeping, synoptic **12** all-inclusive, unobstructed **13** comprehensive

pan out
4 work **5** click, prove, score **7** come off, succeed

pant
4 blow, gasp, gulp, huff, puff **5** chuff, heave **6** wheeze

Pantagruel
5 giant
companion: **7** Panurge
father: **9** Gargantua
mother: **7** Badebec

pantaloon
7 buffoon, trouser

Pantaloon's daughter
9 Columbine

pantheon
4 gods **5** Aesir **6** temple **9** hierarchy **10** hall of fame

panther
4 pard, puma **6** cougar, jaguar **7** leopard **12** mountain lion

pantomime
5 drama, mimic **6** act out, ballet, dancer **7** charade **12** harlequinade
clown: **7** Pierrot

pantry
6 closet, larder **7** buttery **9** storeroom

pants
5 jeans **6** slacks **7** drawers, garment **8** breeches, britches, knickers, trousers

Panurge's companion
10 Pantagruel

Paolo's lover
9 Francesca

pap
4 food, mash, mush **7** aliment, pabulum **8** soft food **9** blandness, nutriment **10** sustenance **11** nourishment

papal
8 pontific **9** apostolic **10** pontifical
court: **5** Curia
decree: **8** decretal
envoy: **6** nuncio
letter: **4** bull **10** encyclical

paper
5 essay, sheet, theme **6** letter, report **7** article **8** document **9** monograph, newsprint **10** memorandum **11** composition, publication **12** dissertation
measure: **4** ream **5** quire
roll: **6** scroll
scrap: **4** chad
size: **3** cap **5** atlas, crown, folio, legal, royal, sexto, sixmo **6** octavo, quarto **7** emperor **8** elephant, foolscap, imperial
stiff: **7** bristol **9** cardboard **12** bristol board
strong: **5** kraft **6** manila
thin: **6** tissue **9** onionskin
transparent: **8** glassine
writing: **3** rag **6** vellum **9** parchment

paper folding
7 origami

paperwork
7 red tape

papillon
7 spaniel **9** butterfly

Papua New Guinea
archipelago: **8** Bismarck
capital: **11** Port Moresby
city: **3** Lae
island: **12** Bougainville
language: **4** Motu **8** Tok Pisin
monetary unit: **4** kina
neighbor: **9** Indonesia, Irian Jaya

par
4 mean, norm **5** equal, score, usual **6** median, normal **7** average, typical **8** equality, standard

parable
4 myth, tale **5** fable, moral, story **7** example **8** allegory

parachute
7 bailout, skydive
part: **5** riser **6** canopy **7** harness, ripcord

Paraclete
9 Holy Ghost **10** Holy Spirit

parade
4 brag, pomp **5** array, boast, flash, march, shine, strut **6** expose, flaunt, review **7** display, exhibit, fanfare, marshal, panoply, show off **8** brandish, ceremony, proclaim **9** advertise, cavalcade, pageantry, promenade **10** masquerade, procession

paradigm
5 ideal, model **6** mirror **7** example, pattern **8** exemplar, standard **9** archetype, beau ideal, framework, prototype

paradise
4 Eden, Zion **5** bliss **6** heaven, utopia **7** arcadia, elysium, nirvana **8** empyrean **9** Shangri-la **10** wonderland **12** New Jerusalem, promised land

Paradise Lost author
6 Milton (John)

paragon
3 gem **4** tops **5** champ, cream, ideal, jewel, match, model, peach, saint **6** beauty **7** compare, epitome **8** champion, exemplar, last word, nonesuch, parallel, ultimate **9** archetype, beau ideal, nonpareil **10** apotheosis

Paraguay
capital: **8** Asunción
lake: **4** Ypoá
language: **7** Guarani, Spanish
monetary unit: **7** guarani
neighbor: **6** Brazil **7** Bolivia **9** Argentina
river: **9** Pilcomayo

parallel
4 akin, copy, even, like **5** agree, align, alike, along, equal, liken, match **6** double, equate, line up **7** aligned, compare, similar **8** analogue **9** alongside, analogous, companion, consonant, corollary, correlate, duplicate **10** comparable, comparison, correspond, equivalent, similarity **11** coextensive, counterpart, duplication, resemblance **13** correspondent, corresponding

parallelogram
5 rhomb **6** oblong, square **7** rhombus **8** rhomboid **9** rectangle **13** quadrilateral

paralysis
5 palsy **7** inertia **9** impotence

paralyze
3 awe **4** daze, numb, stun **6** benumb, deaden, dismay **7** cripple, disable, nonplus, petrify, stupefy **8** shut down **10** immobilize **12** incapacitate

paramount
5 chief, ruler **6** master **7** capital, leading, primary, regnant, supreme **8** cardinal, crowning, dominant, foremost, headmost, superior **9** principal, sovereign, uppermost **10** commanding, preeminent **11** predominant

paramour
5 lover, Romeo **7** Don Juan, gallant **8** Casanova, lothario, mistress **9** courtesan, inamorata, inamorato

parapet
4 wall **7** bastion, bulwark, rampart **10** battlement, breastwork
part: **6** merlon **12** crenellation

paraphernalia
4 gear **5** items **6** outfit, tackle **7** effects **8** property **9** equipment, trappings **10** belongings **11** accessories, furnishings **13** accouterments, accoutrements, appurtenances

paraphrase
6 reword **7** restate, version **9** interpret, rendering, translate **11** restatement, translation

parasite
5 leech, toady **6** sponge, sucker **7** sponger **8** barnacle, deadbeat, hanger-on **9** dependent, exploiter, sycophant **10** freeloader, self-seeker **11** bloodsucker

parasitic
8 sponging, toadying **9** leechlike **11** freeloading, sycophantic **12** bloodsucking
flatworm: **5** fluke **9** trematode

parasol
8 umbrella

____ paratus
6 semper

Parcae
5 Fates, Norns **6** Moirai
name: **4** Nona **5** Morta **6** Decuma

parcel
3 box, cut, lot **4** deal, dole, land, mete, pack, part, plot, wrap **5** allot, array, batch, bunch,

group, share, tract **6** assign, bundle, divide, packet, ration **7** package, partial, portion, prorate, section, segment **8** allocate, disburse, disperse, division **9** apportion, partition **10** distribute

parch
3 dry **4** burn, sear **5** dry up, roast, toast **6** dry out, scorch **7** shrivel **9** dehydrate, desiccate

parched
3 dry **4** arid, sere **5** dusty **7** bone-dry, thirsty **8** scorched, withered **9** shriveled, waterless **10** dehydrated

parchment
4 skin **5** paper **6** vellum **7** diploma **8** document

pardon
4 free **5** remit, spare **6** excuse, let off **7** absolve, amnesty, condone, forgive, release **8** liberate, reprieve, tolerate **9** acquittal, exculpate, indemnity, remission **10** absolution, indulgence **11** exculpation, exoneration, forgiveness

pardonable
6 venial **9** allowable, excusable **11** permissible

pare
3 cut **4** clip, crop, peel, trim **5** lower, prune, shave **6** reduce, remove **7** curtail, cut back, cut down, trim off, whittle **8** diminish

parent
4 make, rear **5** beget, cause, hatch, raise, spawn **6** author, create, father, mother, origin **7** bring up, care for, produce **8** begetter, generate **9** originate, procreate **10** progenitor

parenthetically
7 by the by **8** by the bye, by the way **9** in passing **12** incidentally

parentless
6 orphan **8** orphaned

par excellence
3 top **5** prime **6** superb **7** premier, supreme **8** foremost, peerless, superior **9** matchless, number one, unmatched **10** first-class, preeminent **11** outstanding

pariah
5 leper **7** Ishmael, outcast **8** castaway **10** Ishmaelite **11** offscouring, untouchable
Japanese: **3** eta

Paris
airport: **4** Orly
ancient name: **7** Lutetia
avenue: **13** Champs-Elysées
basilica: **10** Sacré Coeur
cathedral: **9** Notre Dame
city hall: **12** Hôtel de Ville
college: **8** Sorbonne
garden: **9** Tuileries **10** Luxembourg
island: **11** Île de la Cité
museum: **5** Cluny **6** Louvre
palace: **6** Louvre **7** Bourbon
patron saint: **9** Geneviève
racecourse: **7** Auteuil
river: **5** Seine
section: **8** Left Bank **9** Right Bank **10** Montmartre, Rive Gauche **12** Latin Quarter
stock exchange: **6** Bourse
subway: **5** Métro
tower: **6** Eiffel

Paris
beloved: **5** Helen
betrothed: **6** Juliet
father: **5** Priam
mother: **6** Hecuba
slayer: **11** Philoctetes
wife: **6** Oenone

parish
6 county **8** district **9** community **12** congregation, neighborhood

Parisina
author: **5** Byron (Lord)
husband: **3** Azo
lover: **4** Hugo
slayer: **3** Azo

parity
8 equality, sameness, symmetry **10** similarity, similitude **11** equivalence, equivalency, parallelism

park
4 stop **5** green, plaza **7** deposit, funfair, reserve **8** carnival, preserve **9** esplanade **11** reservation

parka
6 anorak, jacket **7** garment **8** pullover **9** outerwear

park designer
4 Vaux (Calvert) **6** Paxton (Joseph) **7** Alphand (Jean), Le Nôtre (André), Olmsted (Frederick Law)

parlance
4 cant, talk **5** argot, idiom, lingo, style, usage **6** jargon, patois, phrase, speech **7** wording **8** language, locution, phrasing **9** verbalism **11** phraseology

parlay
3 bet **4** risk **5** bid up, boost, stake, wager **6** expand, extend, hazard **7** build up, enhance, enlarge, exploit, venture **8** increase, leverage **9** transform

parley
4 talk **5** speak **6** confab, confer, huddle, powwow **7** discuss, meeting **8** colloquy, converse, dialogue **9** discourse, negotiate **10** conference, discussion **11** confabulate **12** conversation **13** confabulation

parliament
see **legislature**

parlor
4 room **5** salon **11** drawing room **13** reception room

parlous
5 dicey, hairy, risky **6** chancy, touchy, tricky, unsafe **8** critical, ticklish **9** dangerous, hazardous **10** precarious

Parnassian
4 poet **6** poetic

parochial
5 local **6** narrow **7** insular, limited **9** sectarian, small-town **10** provincial, restricted

parody
3 rib **4** mock **5** mimic, spoof **6** satire **7** imitate, lampoon, mockery, takeoff **8** ridicule, travesty **9** burlesque, imitation **10** caricature

parole
4 free, word **6** let out, pledge **7** promise, release **9** discharge, probation, watchword **11** performance

paronomasia
3 pun **11** play on words

paroxysm
3 fit **4** bout **5** spasm, throe **6** attack, frenzy **7** flare-up, seizure **8** eruption, outbreak, outburst **9** explosion **10** conniption, convulsion

parrot
3 ape **4** aper, copy, echo **5** mimic **6** repeat **7** chatter, copycat, imitate
kind: 3 ara, kea **4** jako, kaka, lory **5** macaw **6** Amazon, budgie, kakapo **8** cockatoo, lorikeet, lovebird, parakeet **9** cockatiel **10** budgerigar **11** African gray

parrot fever
11 psittacosis

parry
4 duck, fend **5** avert, avoid, block, dodge, elude, evade **7** counter, deflect, evasion, fend off, prevent, respond, ward off **8** sidestep, stave off **9** turn aside **10** circumvent

parse
4 scan **7** analyze, dissect, examine, resolve **8** construe **9** anatomize, explicate, interpret

Parsi
11 Zoroastrian

Parsifal
composer: 6 Wagner (Richard)
magician: 8 Klingsor
quest: 5 Grail
son: 9 Lohengrin
temptress: 6 Kundry

parsimonious
4 mean **5** cheap, close, tight **6** frugal, stingy **7** chintzy, miserly, sparing, thrifty **9** penurious **10** restrained **11** closefisted, tightfisted **12** cheese-paring **13** penny-pinching

parsley
4 herb **7** garnish
family: 6 carrot
piece: 5 sprig

parson
6 cleric, pastor, rector **8** clerical, minister, preacher, reverend **9** clergyman **12** ecclesiastic

parsonage
5 manse **7** rectory

part
3 bit, cut **4** chip, role, unit **5** chunk, piece, quota, scrap, sever, share, slice **6** detail, divide, member, moiety, ration, sector **7** element, measure, portion, quantum, quarter, section, segment **8** division, fraction, fragment, function, separate **9** component

partake of
3 eat **5** savor, share **6** accept, sample **7** acquire, consume, receive **9** enter into **11** participate

Parthenon
sculptor: 7 Phidias **8** Pheidias
sculpture: 6 frieze
site: 9 Acropolis

partial
6 biased, unfair, warped **7** colored, half-way **8** inclined, one-sided **9** jaundiced **10** fractional, incomplete, prejudiced **11** fragmentary, predisposed

partiality
4 bent, bias **5** favor, taste **6** liking **7** leaning **8** affinity, fondness, tendency **10** favoritism, preference **11** inclination **12** one-sidedness, predilection

participant
5 party **6** fellow, member, player, sharer **7** partner, sharing **11** contributor, shareholder

participate
4 join, play **5** share **6** engage, join in **7** partake **8** take part

particle
3 ace, bit, dab, dot, jot, ort, tad **4** atom, doit, dram, drop, hint, hoot, iota, mite, mote, spot, whit **5** atomy, crumb, fleck, grain, minim, ounce, scrap, shred, speck **6** morsel, tittle **7** granule, modicum, smidgen, smidgin, soupçon **8** fragment, smidgeon **9** scintilla
atomic: 3 ion **5** anion **6** baryon, cation
elementary: 3 psi, tau **4** kaon, muon, pion **5** boson, meson **6** baryon, hadron, lambda, lepton, photon, proton **7** fermion, hyperon, neutron, nucleon, upsilon **8** electron, mesotron, neutrino, positron

hypothetical: **5** gluon, quark **6** parton **8** graviton
virus: **6** virion
with negative charge: **8** electron
with positive charge: **6** proton **8** positron

particular
4 fact, full, item **5** exact, fussy, picky, point **6** detail, minute, single, unique **7** careful, correct, element, feature, finicky, precise, special, unusual **8** accurate, detailed, distinct, especial, exacting, itemized, separate, solitary, specific **10** fastidious, individual, meticulous, pernickety, scrupulous **11** distinctive, exceptional, persnickety, punctilious **12** circumstance

particularize
4 list **6** detail **7** catalog, itemize, specify **8** spell out **9** enumerate, inventory **13** individualize

parting
4 last **5** adieu, break, congé, final **6** good-by **7** good-bye **8** division, farewell **10** divergence, separation **11** leave-taking, valedictory

partisan
6 backer, biased, warped **7** devotee, die-hard, fanatic, patriot, sectary **8** adherent, advocate, disciple, follower, guerilla, one-sided, stalwart, upholder **9** factional, guerrilla, irregular, satellite, sectarian, supporter

partition
4 wall **6** divide, screen **7** divider, section, wall off **8** disunion, division, fence off, separate **10** separation

partner
4 ally, chum, mate **5** buddy, crony **6** cohort, fellow **7** comrade **8** confrere, sidekick **9** assistant, associate, colleague, companion **10** accomplice **11** confederate

partnership
4 axis, firm **5** union **7** cahoots, company, sharing **8** alliance, business, marriage, relation **11** affiliation, association, combination **12** consociation, togetherness **13** participation

parturient
6 gravid, parous **8** enceinte, pregnant **9** expecting

parturition
5 birth **8** delivery **10** childbirth **12** childbearing

party
4 ball, band, bash, bevy, bloc, crew, fete, gala, luau, orgy, rave, side **5** actor, corps, covey, feast, group, revel, troop **6** fiesta, frolic, kegger, mortal, person, social, soiree, troupe **7** blowout, carouse, faction, roister, shindig **8** carousal, litigant, wingding **9** bacchanal, gathering, make merry, raise hell **10** detachment, individual, saturnalia **11** bacchanalia, celebration, participant

parvenu
7 upstart **9** arriviste **12** nouveau riche

Pascal essay
6 Pensée

pasha
3 dey

Pasiphaë
daughter: **7** Ariadne, Phaedra
husband: **5** Minos
son: **8** Minotaur

pass
3 bye, die, end **4** fare, hand **5** cease, enact, get by, lapse, occur, relay, spend, while **6** crisis, depart, elapse, exceed, expire, hand on, happen, permit, push on, slight, slip by, strait **7** come off, develop, journey, proceed, succumb **8** bequeath, fork over, hand down, juncture, outshine, outstrip, transmit **9** while away
Afghanistan: **5** Murgh
Afghanistan-Pakistan: **6** Khyber
Alaska: **5** White
Alps: **5** Cenis, Loibl **7** Brenner, Ljubelj, Simplon **9** St. Bernard
California: **5** Cajon
China-India: **9** Karakoram
Colorado: **3** Ute
mountain: **3** col, gap **4** ghat **5** notch
Pakistan: **5** Kilik
Russian: **12** Caspian Gates
Tennessee: **10** Cumberland
Turkey: **13** Cilician Gates

passable
4 okay, open, so-so **6** decent **8** adequate, all right **9** tolerable, unblocked **10** accessible, good enough **12** satisfactory

passably
6 enough **8** all right, somewhat **10** moderately

passage
3 way **4** exit, fare, hall, iter, path, text **5** route, shift **6** access, arcade, avenue, course, egress, strait, travel, tunnel, voyage **7** channel, excerpt, hallway, journey, transit **8** corridor, transfer, traverse **9** enactment, quotation **10** transition **11** transmittal **12** transference, transmission
air: **7** windway
arched: **6** arcade
Atlantic-Pacific: **9** Northwest
narrow: **3** gut
roofed: **6** arcade **9** breezeway

Passage to India author
7 Forster (E. M.)

pass away
3 die, end **6** demise, depart, elapse, expire, perish **7** decease, succumb **9** disappear

pass by
4 miss, omit **6** forget, ignore **7** neglect **8** overlook **9** disregard

passé
4 dead **5** dated, stale **6** démodé, old hat **7** demoded, disused, extinct, outworn **8** obsolete, outdated, outmoded **9** out-of-date **10** antiquated, oldfangled, superseded **12** old-fashioned

passel
3 lot **4** heap, pack **5** bunch **6** bundle **9** multitude

passenger
4 fare

passing
5 brief, death, quick **6** demise, highly **7** cursory, decease **8** fleeting **9** ephemeral, fugacious, extremely, momentary, transient **10** evanescent, short-lived, transitory **11** exceedingly, superficial

passion
4 fire, heat, itch, love, lust, zeal **5** agony, amour, ardor, craze, crush, drive **6** desire, fervor, hunger **7** avidity, craving, ecstasy, emotion, rapture **8** appetite, devotion, yearning **9** eagerness, suffering, transport **10** enthusiasm, excitement **11** amorousness, infatuation

passionate
3 hot **5** angry, fiery **6** ardent, fervid, heated **7** amorous, aroused, blazing, burning, excited, fervent, furious, intense **8** incensed, vehement **9** impetuous, steamed up **10** hot-blooded, stimulated **11** hot-tempered **12** enthusiastic **13** quick-tempered

passive
4 idle **5** inert **6** docile, latent **8** enduring, immobile, inactive, listless, resigned, yielding **9** apathetic, compliant, lethargic, quiescent **10** motionless, nonviolent, phlegmatic, submissive **11** acquiescent, complaisant, indifferent, unresistant

pass out
3 die **5** faint, swoon **7** divvy up **8** disburse, keel over **10** distribute

pass over
4 miss, omit, skip **6** forget, ignore **7** dismiss, neglect **8** discount, leave out **9** disregard

Passover
5 Pasch **6** Pesach
bread: **5** matzo **6** matzoh
meal: **5** seder

pass up
5 forgo **6** refuse, reject **7** decline

past
3 ago, old **4** gone, late, once, yore **5** above, after, prior **6** beyond, bygone, former, whilom **7** onetime, quondam **8** anterior, foretime, lang syne, previous, sometime **9** antiquity, erstwhile, foregoing, precedent, preceding, yesterday **10** antecedent, yesteryear

pasta
5 dough
kind: **4** orzo, ziti **5** penne, ruote **6** rotini **7** fusilli, gemelli, gnocchi, lasagna, lasagne, mafalda, noodles, ravioli **8** farfalle, linguine, linguini, macaroni, rigatoni **9** canneloni, capellini, cavatappi, fettucine, fettucini, manicotti, radiatore, spaghetti, tubettini **10** cannelloni, conchiglie, fettuccine, fettuccini, tortellini, vermicelli **11** cappelletti, orecchiette, pappardelle

paste
3 fix, hit **4** beat, clay, drub, food, glue, sock **5** affix, dough, pound, stick, stuff **6** adhere, attach, cement, defeat, fasten, thrash, wallop **7** trounce **8** adhesive, material

Pasternak character
4 Lara **7** Zhivago (Dr.)

pastiche
4 olio **6** jumble, medley **7** farrago, mélange, mixture **8** mishmash **9** potpourri **10** assortment, hodgepodge, hotchpotch, miscellany, salmagundi **11** gallimaufry

pastime
4 game **5** hobby, sport **9** amusement, diversion **10** recreation **13** entertainment

past master
3 ace, pro, wiz **4** whiz **5** adept, maven **6** expert, wizard **8** virtuoso **9** authority

pastor
5 padre **6** cleric, parson **8** minister, preacher, reverend, sky pilot **9** clergyman

pastoral
4 idyl **5** idyll, rural **6** rustic **7** bucolic, country, crosier, idyllic **8** agrarian, clerical, innocent, peaceful **10** campestral

pastor's assistant
6 curate

pastry
3 bun, pie **4** baba, cake, flan, tart **5** torte **6** cornet, Danish, éclair, gâteau **7** baklava, beignet, bouchée, dariole, gâteaux (plural), palmier, savarin, strudel, tartlet **8** napoleon, papillon, piroshki, pirozhki, turnover **9** barquette, cream puff, madeleine, petit four, vol-au-vent **10** cheesecake **11** profiterole **12** millefeuille
kind: **4** filo, puff **5** flaky **6** phyllo
shell: **7** timbale **8** meringue

pasture
3 lea, ley **4** feed, land **5** field, grass, graze **6** browse, meadow **9** grassland

pasty
3 wan **4** pale **6** doughy, pallid, sickly **7** meat pie **8** turnover **9** unhealthy

pat
3 apt, dab, set **4** firm **5** fixed, slice, stiff, trite

6 dead-on 7 apropos, fitting 8 apposite, standard, suitable 9 contrived, pertinent, rehearsed

patch
3 bit, fix 4 area, fill, mend, plot 5 cover, piece, scrap, spell 6 doctor, emblem, fill up, repair, shield 7 connect, plaster 8 material 10 connection

patchwork
4 olio 5 quilt 6 jumble 7 mixture 8 covering, mishmash, mixed bag 10 assortment, hodgepodge, hotchpotch, miscellany, salmagundi

patchy
6 fitful, random, spotty, uneven 7 erratic 8 sporadic 9 haphazard, hit-or-miss, irregular 12 intermittent

pate
4 bean, dome, head, poll 5 brain, crown 6 noddle, noggin, noodle

patella
7 kneecap, kneepan

patent
4 open 5 clear, plain, right 6 secure 7 evident, license, obvious, visible 8 apparent, distinct, manifest 9 exclusive, privilege, prominent, protected 11 proprietary

paternal
8 fatherly
relative: 6 agnate

paternity
7 lineage 8 ancestry 10 fatherhood, provenance 11 progenitors

Pater Noster
9 Our Father 11 Lord's Prayer

path
3 way 4 lane, line, road, tack, walk 5 byway, orbit, route, track, trail 6 avenue, bridle, course 7 passage, walkway 9 direction 10 trajectory

pathetic
3 sad 4 poor 5 sorry 6 absurd, moving, paltry 7 piteous, pitiful, risible, useless 8 inferior, pitiable, poignant, touching 9 affecting, laughable, miserable 10 lamentable, ridiculous

Pathfinder, The
author: 6 Cooper (James Fenimore)
hero: 6 Bumppo (Natty)

pathogen
4 germ 5 E. coli, virus 9 bacterium

pathological
7 deviant 8 aberrant, abnormal, diseased, maniacal, schizoid 9 psychotic

pathos
4 pity 7 emotion 8 sympathy 9 poignance, poignancy

pathway
4 line, walk 5 route, track, trail 6 course 7 channel, conduit, network, passage

patience
4 cool 8 calmness, stoicism 9 composure, endurance 10 equanimity, sufferance 11 forbearance, resignation, self-control

Patience
composer: 8 Sullivan (Arthur)
librettist: 7 Gilbert (W. S.)

patient
4 case, meek 8 enduring 9 easygoing 10 persistent 11 susceptible 13 long-suffering
man: 3 Job

patina
4 aura, coat, film 6 finish, polish 7 coating 8 covering 10 appearance, coloration

patio
5 atria (plural), court 6 atrium 7 terrace 9 courtyard

patois
4 cant 5 argot, lingo, slang 6 jargon 7 dialect 10 colloquial, vernacular

patriarch
4 sire 6 father, nestor 7 creator, founder 9 architect, graybeard
biblical: 5 David, Isaac, Jacob 7 Abraham

patrician
5 noble 6 aristo 9 blue blood, gentleman 10 aristocrat, upper-class

patriciate
5 elite 6 gentry 9 blue blood, gentility 10 upper crust 11 aristocracy

patrimony
6 estate, legacy 8 heritage 9 endowment 10 birthright 11 inheritance

patriot
5 jingo 8 jingoist, loyalist 9 flag-waver 10 chauvinist 11 nationalist

patriotism
8 jingoism 10 chauvinism 11 nationalism

Patroclus
friend: 8 Achilles
slayer: 6 Hector

patrol
5 guard, round, scout, troop, watch 7 protect 8 sentinel 9 keep watch

patrolman
3 cop 5 guard 6 police 7 officer

patrol wagon
see **paddy wagon**

patron
5 angel 6 backer, client 7 sponsor 8 customer, guardian 9 protector, supporter 10 benefactor

patronage
4 help **5** aegis, trade **6** custom **7** backing, subsidy, support, traffic **8** activity, advocacy, auspices, business, cronyism **9** clientage, clientele, influence **10** pork barrel, protection **11** benefaction, sponsorship **12** guardianship

patronize
3 aid, use **4** back **5** deign, favor **6** assist, shop at **7** protect, support **8** frequent **10** condescend

patron saint
of beggars, cripples: **5** Giles
of children: **8** Nicholas
of England: **6** George
of fishermen: **5** Peter
of France: **5** Denis
of Ireland: **7** Patrick
of lawyers: **4** Ives
of musicians: **7** Cecilia
of Norway: **4** Olaf
of physicians: **4** Luke
of sailors: **4** Elmo **8** Nicholas
of Scotland: **6** Andrew
of shoemakers: **7** Crispin
of Spain: **5** James **8** Santiago
of travelers: **11** Christopher
of Wales: **5** David
of winegrowers: **7** Vincent
of workers: **6** Joseph

patsy
3 sap **4** dupe, fool, mark **5** chump **6** pigeon, sucker, victim **8** easy mark, pushover

patter
4 cant **5** argot, lingo, slang, spiel **6** babble, jargon, patois **7** chatter, prattle

pattern
4 copy, form, plan **5** guide, ideal, model, motif, order, plaid, shape **6** argyle, design, figure, floral, follow, method, mirror, system **7** diagram, emulate, example, imitate, paisley **8** exemplar, grouping, paradigm, standard, template **9** archetype, incidence, prototype **10** flight path, stereotype **11** arrangement, orderliness **12** distribution **13** configuration

paucity
4 lack, want **6** dearth **7** poverty **8** scarcity, shortage **9** scantness, smallness **10** deficiency, meagerness, meagreness **13** insufficiency

Paul the Apostle
birthplace: **6** Tarsus
companion: **5** Silas, Titus **7** Artemas, Timothy **8** Barnabas
original name: **4** Saul
place of conversion: **8** Damascus
prosecutor: **9** Tertullus
teacher: **8** Gamaliel
tribe: **8** Benjamin

paunch
3 gut, pot **5** belly, tummy **7** abdomen, stomach **8** potbelly **9** bay window, beer belly **11** breadbasket, corporation

paunchy
3 fat **5** beefy, plump, tubby **6** chunky, portly, rotund **8** thickset **10** overweight, potbellied

pauper
6 beggar **7** have-not **8** bankrupt, indigent **9** mendicant

pauperism
4 need, ruin, want **6** penury **7** beggary, poverty **9** indigence, neediness, privation **11** destitution

pause
3 gap **4** halt, hush, lull, rest, stop, wait **5** break, comma, delay, lapse, letup **6** hiatus, linger, recess **7** caesura, respite, take ten, time out **8** breather, hesitate, inaction, interval, take five **9** cessation, interlude **10** hesitation, suspension **12** intermission, interruption

pave
3 lay, tar **5** cover **7** asphalt, surface **8** blacktop, concrete

pavement
6 tarmac **7** asphalt, macadam, surface **8** concrete, sidewalk

pavilion
4 tent **5** kiosk **6** canopy, gazebo **9** belvedere **11** summerhouse

paw
4 feel, foot, grab, hand, mitt **5** grope, touch **6** fondle, handle, molest, scrape

pawn
4 hock, tool **6** pledge, puppet, stooge, victim **7** deposit, hostage, warrant **8** guaranty, security **9** guarantee **10** chess piece, instrument

pax
5 peace **6** tablet

Pax ___
3 Dei **6** Romana **10** Britannica

pay
3 fee **4** ante, wage **5** remit, serve, spend **6** answer, ante up, defray, expend, kick in, lay out, pony up, profit, render, salary, settle, tender, reward **7** benefit, bring in, cough up, forfeit, fork out, satisfy, stipend **8** disburse, earnings, shell out **9** discharge, emolument, indemnify, reimburse **10** compensate, recompense, remunerate **12** compensation, remuneration

payable
3 due **4** owed **5** owing **6** mature, unpaid **7** overdue **9** unsettled **10** obligatory **11** outstanding, uncollected

paycheck
5 wages **6** salary

payload
4 haul **5** cargo, goods **6** burden, lading, weight **7** freight, tonnage **8** shipment

payment
3 fee **4** dues **5** award, money **6** amends, outlay, return, reward **7** penance **8** defrayal, requital **11** restitution **12** compensation, remuneration, satisfaction

payoff
3 fix **5** bribe **6** climax, profit, result, reward, upshot **7** outcome **8** clincher, decisive **10** conclusion, conclusive, denouement **11** retribution

payola
5 bribe

PDQ
4 ASAP, stat **6** at once, pronto **8** directly, right now, right off **9** forthwith, instanter, instantly, right away **11** immediately, straightway **12** straightaway

peace
3 pax **4** calm, ease, pact **5** amity, order, quiet **6** accord, repose **7** concord, harmony, silence **8** serenity **11** tranquility **12** tranquillity

peaceable
6 dovish, irenic **7** amiable, pacific **8** amicable, friendly, pacifist, tranquil **10** nonviolent **11** complaisant **12** conciliatory

peaceful
4 calm **5** still, quiet **6** irenic, placid, serene **7** equable, halcyon, pacific **8** composed, tranquil **9** unruffled **10** harmonious, nonviolent, untroubled

peacemaker
7 arbiter **8** mediator, pacifier, placater **10** arbitrator, negotiator **11** conciliator, pacificator

peace officer
3 cop **6** police **9** policeman **11** policewoman

peach
3 ace, pip, rat **4** blab, lulu, tree **5** fruit, honey **6** betray, inform, reveal, snitch, squeal **7** Elberta **8** knockout **9** freestone, humdinger, nectarine **10** clingstone **11** crackerjack
family: **4** rose

Peach State
7 Georgia

peachy
4 fine, good, neat, nice **5** dandy, neato, nifty, super, swell **8** pleasant, pleasing **9** excellent, hunky-dory, marvelous, wonderful

peacockish
5 showy, swank **6** chichi, flashy, swanky **7** splashy **8** show-offy **10** flamboyant **11** pretentious **12** ostentatious

peak
3 top **4** acme, apex, roof **5** crest, crown **6** summit, vertex, zenith **8** pinnacle
Arizona: **9** Humphreys
Bighorn Mtns.: **5** Cloud
Black Hills: **6** Harney
California: **6** Lassen **9** Telescope
Cascade Range: **6** Lassen
Colorado: **5** Grays, Longs, Pikes **6** Blanca **7** La Plata **11** Uncompahgre
Idaho: **5** Borah
Kyrgyzstan: **5** Lenin **6** Pobeda
Montana: **7** Granite **8** Electric
Nevada: **7** Wheeler **8** Boundary **10** Charleston
New Mexico: **7** Truchas, Wheeler **12** Sierra Blanca
South Dakota: **6** Harney
Sri Lanka: **5** Adam's **8** Samanala
Tajikistan: **5** Lenin **9** Communism
Utah: **5** Kings
White Mtns.: **8** Boundary
Wyoming: **5** Cloud **6** Franks **7** Gannett
(see also **mountain**)

peaked
3 ill, wan **4** ashy, pale, sick **5** acute, ashen, drawn, sharp **6** ailing, pallid, sickly **7** pointed **9** emaciated

peal
4 bell, bong, ring, toll **5** chime, knell, sound **7** ring out, ringing **8** ding-dong

peanut
4 mani **6** goober, legume, peewee, shrimp **9** pipsqueak

Peanuts
character: **4** Lucy (van Pelt) **5** Linus, Patty (Peppermint), Rerun, Sally (Brown), Spike **6** Frieda, Marcie, Pig-Pen, Snoopy **8** Franklin **9** Schroeder, Woodstock **12** Charlie Brown
creator: **6** Schulz (Charles M.)
expression: **4** rats
forerunner: **8** Li'l Folks

pear
4 Bosc, pome **5** Anjou, Hardy **6** Comice, Garber, Seckel **7** Kieffer, LeConte **8** Bartlett
cider: **5** perry

pearl
3 gem **4** dear **5** jewel **7** paragon **8** treasure

Pearl Mosque site
4 Agra

pearly
8 lustrous, nacreous, precious **10** iridescent, opalescent

pear-shaped
8 pyriform

peasant
4 carl, kern, peon, serf **5** churl **6** rustic **7** bumpkin, hayseed, villein
Arab: **6** fellah
Indian: **4** ryot
Latin-American: **9** campesino
Philippine: **3** tao
Russian: **5** mujik **6** moujik, muzhik

peccary
8 javelina
genus: **7** Tayassu

peck
3 lot, nag **4** buss, carp, fuss, heap, kiss, load, mess, pile, poke **6** carp at, nibble, pick at, pick up, pierce, strike **8** quantity

pecking order
6 ladder **7** pyramid **9** food chain, hierarchy

peculate
5 steal **8** embezzle **9** defalcate **11** appropriate

peculiar
3 odd **4** rare **5** queer, weird **6** unique **7** bizarre, curious, oddball, offbeat, special, strange, unusual **8** abnormal, singular, specific, uncommon **9** eccentric **10** individual, particular **11** distinctive

peculiarity
3 tic **4** mark **5** quirk, trait **6** oddity **7** feature, quality **8** property **9** attribute, character, mannerism **12** eccentricity, idiosyncrasy

pecuniary
6 fiscal **8** economic, monetary **9** financial

pedagogue
5 tutor **6** pedant **7** teacher **8** educator **12** schoolmaster

pedagogy
8 teaching **9** education

pedal
5 lever **7** bicycle, treadle
digit: **3** toe

pedant
7 teacher **9** formalist **10** schoolmarm **12** precisionist

pedantic
3 dry **4** arid, dull **6** stodgy **7** bookish, donnish, erudite, learned, tedious **8** academic, didactic, priggish **9** ponderous **10** pedestrian, scholastic **11** pedagogical **13** unimaginative

peddle
4 hawk, push, sell, vend **5** pitch **6** monger **8** huckster

peddler
6 coster, dealer, hawker, monger, vendor **8** huckster, merchant, promoter **9** tradesman **12** costermonger

pedestal
4 base, foot **5** stand **7** footing, support **10** foundation **12** underpinning
part: **4** dado **6** plinth **7** subbase

pedestrian
4 blah, dull **5** banal **6** dreary, stodgy, walker **7** humdrum, mundane, prosaic **8** everyday, ordinary **11** commonplace **13** unimaginative
crossing: **5** zebra **10** footbridge

pedigree
6 origin, purity **7** descent, history, lineage **8** ancestry, purebred **9** bloodline, genealogy **10** background, extraction, family tree

peduncle
4 stem **5** stalk **7** pedicel

peek
3 spy **4** look **6** glance **7** glimpse

peel
4 bark, pare, rind, skin **5** flake, scale, strip **7** take off **8** flake off **9** break away, exfoliate

peeled
4 bare, open **5** naked **7** denuded, exposed **8** stripped **9** uncovered

peep
3 see, spy **4** look **5** chirp, tweet, watch **6** glance, squeak **7** glimpse, twitter **9** sandpiper

Peeping Tom
5 snoop **6** voyeur **7** prowler, snooper

peer
3 pry **4** gaze, lord **5** equal, glare, noble, stare **6** goggle, squint **9** associate
British: **4** duke, earl **5** baron **7** marquis **8** marquess, viscount

Peer Gynt
author: **5** Ibsen (Henrik)
beloved: **7** Solveig
character: **6** Anitra
composer: **5** Grieg (Edvard)
mother: **3** Ase **4** Aase

peerless
4 best **6** unique **7** perfect, supreme **8** superior **9** matchless, nonpareil, paramount, unequaled, unmatched, unrivaled **12** incomparable, unparalleled

peeve
3 bug, irk, vex **4** miff, rile **5** anger, annoy, pique **6** bother, nettle, put out **7** disturb, provoke **8** irritate, nuisance, vexation **9** aggravate, annoyance, grievance **10** exasperate **11** aggravation

peevish
4 sour **5** cross, testy **6** cranky, grumpy, ornery **7** fretful, whining **8** petulant **9** fractious, irritable, obstinate, querulous **11** ill-tempered

peewee
4 runt, tike, tyke **5** dwarf, pigmy, pygmy, small

6 midget, shaver, shrimp, squirt 9 miniature 10 diminutive, flycatcher 11 lilliputian

peg
3 fix, pin, tee 4 mark, plug, step 5 dowel, prong, stake, throw 6 attach, fasten, marker 7 pin down, pretext, support 8 identify

Pegasus
5 horse, steed
rider: 11 Bellerophon

pejorative
7 adverse 8 critical, debasing 9 slighting 10 belittling, derogatory, detractive 11 denigrating, deprecatory, disparaging, opprobrious, unfavorable 12 depreciatory

pelagic
6 marine 7 oceanic 8 maritime

Peleus
brother: 7 Telamon
father: 6 Aeacus
half brother: 6 Phocus
son: 8 Achilles
victim: 8 Eurytion
wife: 6 Thetis

pelf
4 loot, swag 5 booty, lucre, money, moola 6 boodle, moolah, riches, spoils 7 plunder

Pelias
country: 6 Iolcus
father: 8 Poseidon
half brother: 5 Aeson
son: 7 Acastus

Pelican State
9 Louisiana

Pelléas
beloved: 9 Mélisande
brother, slayer: 6 Golaud

Pelles
daughter: 6 Elaine
grandson: 7 Galahad

pellet
3 wad 4 ball, shot 6 sphere 10 projectile

Pellinore
slayer: 6 Gawain
son: 5 Torre 6 Dornar 7 Lamerok 8 Percival 9 Agglovale

pell-mell
5 chaos, snarl 6 muddle, rashly 7 chaotic, clutter, hastily 8 confused, disarray, disorder, headlong, reckless 9 confusion, haphazard, hurriedly 10 carelessly, heedlessly 11 hurry-scurry 13 helter-skelter

pellucid
5 clear, plain, sheer 6 limpid 7 crystal, evident, obvious 8 clear-cut, luminous 9 unblurred 10 see-through 11 crystalline, transparent

Pelops
father: 8 Tantalus
son: 6 Atreus 8 Pittheus, Thyestes
wife: 10 Hippodamia

pelota
4 ball 7 jai alai

pelt
3 fur, run 4 beat, blow, dash, drub, hide, hurl, rush, skin, whop 5 hurry, pound, scoot, speed, strip, throw, whack 6 assail, batter, pepper, pummel, strike, wallop 7 bombard, hotfoot

pen
3 sty 4 cage, coop, jail, swan 5 pound, quill, write 6 cooler, corral, indite, prison, shut in, stylus, writer 7 close in, confine, enclose, fence in 9 ballpoint, enclosure

penal
8 punitive 12 correctional, disciplinary

penalize
4 dock, fine 5 mulct 6 punish 7 deprive 8 handicap 10 discipline 12 disadvantage

penalty
4 fine, loss 5 mulct 7 damages, forfeit 8 hardship 10 amercement, forfeiture, punishment 12 disadvantage

penance
4 rite 7 penalty 8 hardship 9 atonement 10 punishment

penchant
4 bent 5 taste 6 liking 7 leaning 8 affinity, fondness, tendency 9 inclining 10 partiality, proclivity, propensity 11 inclination 12 predilection

pendant
4 flag, jack, rope 7 fixture 8 lavalier, ornament 10 supplement

pendent
7 hanging 9 suspended, undecided, unsettled 11 overhanging 12 undetermined

pending
6 during 8 awaiting, imminent 9 undecided, unsettled 12 undetermined

___ Pendragon
5 Uther

pendulous
7 hanging 8 dangling, drooping, wavering 9 faltering, suspended, tentative, uncertain 10 hesitating, indecisive 11 vacillating

Penelope
father: 7 Icarius
father-in-law: 7 Laertes
husband: 7 Ulysses 8 Odysseus
mother: 8 Periboea
son: 10 Telemachus
suitor: 7 Agelaus

penetrable
6 porous **8** pervious **9** permeable

penetrate
3 jab **4** bore, go in, stab **5** break, drive, enter, probe, touch **6** affect, charge, invade, pierce **7** pervade **8** discover, encroach, perceive, permeate, puncture, saturate **9** percolate, perforate **10** understand

penetrating
4 keen **5** acute, sharp **6** astute, shrewd **8** incisive, piercing **9** trenchant **10** discerning, insightful, perceptive **11** quick-witted, sharp-witted **12** sharp-sighted

Peneus
daughter: **6** Daphne
father: **7** Oceanus
mother: **6** Tethys

penguin type
6 Adélie

____ Penh
5 Phnom

peninsula
4 neck **10** chersonese
Alaska: **5** Kenai **6** Seward
Australia: **6** Tasman
Barents Sea: **5** Kanin
British colony: **9** Gibraltar
Canada: **5** Bruce, Gaspé **6** Ungava **8** Labrador
Chile: **5** Swett
China: **8** Shandong
Costa Rica: **3** Osa
Croatia: **6** Istria
Denmark: **7** Jutland
eastern United States: **8** Delmarva
Estonia: **5** Sorve
Florida: **8** Pinellas **9** Canaveral
France: **5** Giens
Greece: **4** Acte **10** Chalcidice **11** Peloponnese **12** Peloponnesus
Guam: **5** Orote
Hong Kong: **7** Kowloon
Honshu: **3** Izu **5** Miura
Massachusetts: **7** Cape Ann, Cape Cod
Mexico: **4** Baja **7** Yucatan **14** Baja California
Michigan: **8** Keweenaw
Middle East: **5** Sinai
New Guinea: **4** Huon
New Jersey: **9** Sandy Hook
New Zealand: **5** Banks, Mahia
Nunavut: **7** Boothia **8** Melville
Ontario: **5** Bruce
Persian Gulf: **9** Ras Tanura
Quebec: **5** Gaspé
Russia: **4** Kola **5** Taman, Yamal **6** Kolski, Taimyr **9** Kamchatka
Scotland: **7** Kintyre
South Australia: **4** Eyre **5** Yorke
Southeast Asia: **5** Malay **9** Indochina
southeastern Europe: **6** Balkan
southwestern Asia: **6** Arabia **7** Arabian
southwestern Europe: **7** Iberian
Texas: **9** Matagorda
Tierra del Fuego: **5** Mitre
Turkey: **8** Anatolia **9** Asia Minor
Ukraine: **5** Kerch **6** Crimea **7** Crimean
Wales: **5** Gower, Lleyn
Washington: **7** Olympic
Wisconsin: **4** Door

Peninsular State
7 Florida

penitence
3 rue **4** ruth **6** regret, sorrow **7** anguish, remorse **8** distress, humbling **10** contrition, repentance **11** compunction, self-reproof **12** self-reproach

penitent
5 sorry **6** rueful **8** contrite **9** regretful, repentant **10** apologetic, remorseful

penitentiary
see **prison**

penman
5 clerk **6** author, scribe, writer **7** copyist **9** scrivener **12** calligrapher

penmanship
4 hand **5** style **6** script **7** writing **11** calligraphy, chirography, handwriting

pen name
6 anonym **9** pseudonym **10** nom de plume
Addison, Joseph: **4** Clio
Arouet, François-Marie: **8** Voltaire
Beyle, Marie-Henri: **8** Stendhal
Blair, Eric: **12** George Orwell
Blixen, Karen: **11** Isak Dinesen
Brontë, Anne: **9** Acton Bell
Brontë, Charlotte: **10** Currer Bell
Brontë, Emily: **9** Ellis Bell
Clemens, Samuel: **9** Mark Twain
Dickens, Charles: **3** Boz
Dodgson, Charles Lutwidge: **12** Lewis Carroll
Dupin, Amandine-Aurore: **10** George Sand
Evans, Mary Ann: **11** George Eliot
Faust, Frederick: **8** Max Brand
Franklin, Benjamin: **11** Poor Richard
Geisel, Theodore: **7** Dr. Seuss
Glidden, Frederick: **9** Luke Short
Lamb, Charles: **4** Elia
Lederer, Esther: **10** Ann Landers
Munro, Hector Hugh: **4** Saki
Poquelin, Jean-Baptiste: **7** Molière
Porter, William Sidney: **6** O. Henry
Ramé, Maria Louise: **5** Ouida
Thibault, J.-A.-F.: **13** Anatole France
Viaud, L.-M.-J.: **10** Pierre Loti
Wofford, Chloe Anthony: **12** Toni Morrison

pennant
4 flag, jack **5** color **6** banner, ensign **8** standard, streamer **9** banderole **12** championship

penniless
4 poor **5** broke, needy **8** bankrupt, indigent **9** destitute, insolvent **11** impecunious

pennon
4 flag, jack, wing **5** color **6** banner, ensign **8** bannerol, gonfalon, streamer **9** banderole, oriflamme

Pennsylvania
capital: 10 Harrisburg
city: 4 Erie **7** Reading **8** Scranton **9** Allentown **10** Pittsburgh **12** Philadelphia
college, university: 6 Drexel, Lehigh, Temple **7** LaSalle **8** Bryn Mawr, Bucknell **9** Dickinson, Haverford, Lafayette, Penn State, Villanova **10** Swarthmore **14** Carnegie Mellon
mountain range: 6 Pocono
nickname: 8 Keystone (State)
river: 9 Allegheny **10** Schuylkill **11** Monongahela, Susquehanna
state bird: 12 ruffed grouse
state flower: 14 mountain laurel
state tree: 7 hemlock

penny-pincher
5 miser **7** niggard, scrooge **8** tightwad **9** skinflint **10** cheapskate

penny-pinching
4 mean **6** frugal, stingy, thrift **7** miserly, thrifty **9** frugality, niggardly, parsimony, penurious **11** tightfisted **12** cheeseparing, parsimonious

penny-wise
5 canny, tight **6** frugal, stingy **7** prudent, sparing, thrifty **9** provident **10** economical **12** parsimonious

pen point
3 neb, nib

pension
3 inn **5** hotel, lodge **6** hostel, reward **7** annuity, auberge, payment, stipend **8** gratuity **9** allowance **12** room and board, roominghouse **13** boardinghouse

pensioner
7 retiree

pensive
3 sad **6** dreamy, musing **7** wistful **10** meditative, melancholy, reflective, ruminative, thoughtful **11** preoccupied **13** contemplative

Pentateuch
5 Torah
books: 6 Exodus **7** Genesis, Numbers **9** Leviticus **11** Deuteronomy

Penthesilea
queen of: 7 Amazons
slayer: 8 Achilles

Pentheus
grandfather: 6 Cadmus
king of: 6 Thebes
mother: 5 Agave

penumbra
4 veil **5** cover, shade **6** fringe, screen, shadow, shroud **7** curtain

penurious
4 mean, poor **5** needy, tight **6** frugal, stingy **7** miserly **8** indigent, stinting **9** destitute, niggardly **11** impecunious, tightfisted **12** impoverished, parsimonious **13** penny-pinching

penury
4 need, want **7** beggary, poverty **8** distress **9** indigence, privation, pauperism **11** destitution, needfulness

peon
4 serf **5** prole, slave **6** drudge, toiler, worker **7** laborer, peasant **11** galley slave
Anglo-Saxon: 4 esne

peonage
4 yoke **6** thrall **7** bondage, helotry, serfdom, slavery **9** servitude, thralldom, villenage **11** enslavement

people
3 kin **4** folk **5** folks, peeps, plebs **6** public **7** society **8** populace **9** commoners, community, plebeians **10** commonalty **11** inhabitants, rank and file, third estate
combining form: 5 ethno

pep
3 vim, zip **4** brio, dash **5** gusto, moxie, punch, verve, vigor **6** energy, spirit **7** sparkle **8** vitality, vivacity **10** get-up-and-go, liveliness **11** high spirits

pepo
5 gourd, melon **6** squash **7** pumpkin **8** cucumber

pepper
4 kava, pelt **5** chili **6** season, shower **7** cayenne, paprika, pimento, tabasco **8** capsicum, cascabel, chipotle, habanero, jalapeño, pimiento, sprinkle **9** condiment, seasoning **12** Scotch bonnet

peppery
3 hot **5** cross, fiery, sharp, spicy, testy, zesty **6** biting, lively, snappy, touchy **7** piquant, pungent **8** choleric, poignant, seasoned, stinging **9** irascible, irritable **11** hot-tempered **13** quick-tempered

peppy
4 spry **5** alert, perky **6** active, bright, lively **7** vibrant **8** animated, spirited, vigorous **9** energetic, sprightly, vivacious

Pequod
cabin boy: 3 Pip

captain: 4 Ahab
harpooner: 6 Daggoo 8 Queequeg, Tashtego
mate: 8 Starbuck
seaman: 7 Ishmael

per
3 via 4 a pop, each, with 6 apiece 7 by way of, for each, through 9 by means of 12 individually

perambulate
4 walk 6 ramble, stroll 8 traverse 9 promenade

per capita
4 each 6 apiece, by each 7 equally, for each

perceive
3 see 4 espy, feel, know, mark, note 5 grasp, seize, sense 6 detect, notice, remark 7 discern, observe, realize 8 identify 9 apprehend, recognize 10 comprehend, understand

percentage
3 cut 4 part 5 piece, share, slice 6 profit 7 portion 9 advantage 10 commission, proportion 11 probability

perceptible
5 clear 6 marked 7 visible 8 apparent, definite, distinct, palpable, sensible, tangible 10 detectable, noticeable, observable 11 appreciable, discernible 12 recognizable

perception
3 ken 4 idea 5 grasp, image 6 acumen, notion 7 concept, feeling, insight, thought 9 awareness, cognition 10 impression 11 discernment, observation

perceptive
4 keen, sage, wise 5 acute, alert, aware, sharp 7 knowing 9 intuitive, observant, sagacious, sensitive 10 discerning, insightful, responsive 13 understanding

perch
3 bar, peg, set 4 fish, land, rest, seat 5 light, roost, sit on 6 alight, settle 7 set down, sit atop, sit down

perchance
5 maybe 6 mayhap 7 perhaps 8 possibly 11 conceivably

percipience
6 acumen 8 keenness 9 cognition, intuition 10 astuteness 11 discernment 12 appreciation, perspicacity 13 comprehension

percolate
4 drip, ooze, seep 5 exude, leach 6 charge, filter, simmer, spread 7 pervade, trickle 9 penetrate

percussion
3 jar 4 bump, jolt 5 clash, crash, shock 6 impact 9 collision 10 concussion
instrument:
(see at **musical instrument**)

Perdita
father: 7 Leontes
mother: 8 Hermione

perdition
4 hell 5 hades 7 inferno 9 damnation 10 underworld 11 netherworld

Père Goriot author
6 Balzac (Honoré de)

peregrination
4 trek, trip, walk 7 journey, travels 9 traversal 10 expedition

peremptory
5 bossy, final 7 haughty 8 absolute, arrogant, decisive, dogmatic, imperial 9 imperious, masterful 10 autocratic, commanding, disdainful, high-handed, imperative 11 dictatorial, domineering, magisterial, overbearing

perennial
7 durable 8 constant, enduring, lifelong 9 continual, long-lived, permanent, perpetual, recurrent, unceasing 10 continuing, persistent, persisting, unchanging 11 long-lasting

Perez
brother: 5 Zerah
father: 5 Judah
mother: 5 Tamar

perfect
4 full, pure 5 exact, ideal, model, right, sound, total, utter, whole 6 entire, expert, intact, polish, proper, refine 7 correct, improve, precise 8 absolute, accurate, complete, finished, flawless, peerless, spotless, unbroken, unflawed 9 downright, excellent, faultless, matchless, stainless, unalloyed, undiluted 10 consummate, impeccable, proficient 11 unequivocal, unmitigated, unqualified

perfection
4 acme 5 ideal 6 purity, virtue 7 paragon 9 integrity, wholeness 10 excellence, excellency 12 flawlessness

perfectly
5 fully, quite 6 wholly 7 to a turn, utterly 8 entirely 10 altogether, completely, thoroughly

perfidious
5 false 6 untrue 8 disloyal 9 deceitful, dishonest, faithless 10 treasonous, traitorous, unfaithful, unreliable 11 treacherous

perfidy
6 deceit 7 falsity, sellout, treason 8 betrayal 9 falseness, treachery 10 disloyalty, infidelity 13 faithlessness

perforate
3 pit 4 bore 5 drill, prick, punch 6 pierce 8 puncture 9 penetrate

perform
2 do **3** act **4** play, work **5** enact **6** behave, comply, effect **7** achieve, execute, fulfill, operate, playact, present, satisfy **8** bring off, carry out, complete, function **9** discharge, entertain, implement **10** accomplish

performance
3 act **4** deed, feat, show, work **6** acting, action **7** conduct, display **8** behavior, efficacy, exercise **9** discharge, execution, operation **10** efficiency, exhibition **11** achievement, fulfillment **12** presentation

performer
4 doer, mime **5** actor, mimic **6** mummer, player **7** actress, artiste, trouper **8** thespian **9** play-actor **12** impersonator

perfume
4 balm **5** aroma, cense, scent, smell, spice **6** sachet **7** bouquet, incense, odorize **9** aromatize, fragrance, redolence
source: **4** musk **5** attar, myrrh, orris **8** bergamot

perfumer
4 Dior (Christian), Nose (The) **5** Estée **6** Chanel (Coco), Lanvin, Lauder **8** Guerlain (Aimé, Jacques), Guichard (Aurelien, Jean)

perfunctory
7 cursory, routine **8** careless **9** automatic **10** impersonal, mechanical **11** superficial

pergola
5 arbor, bower **7** trellis

perhaps
5 maybe **8** feasibly, possibly **9** perchance **11** conceivably

periapt
see **amulet**

Pericles
father: **10** Xanthippus
mistress: **7** Aspasia
mother: **8** Agariste

peril
4 risk **6** danger, hazard, menace **8** exposure, jeopardy **9** liability **12** endangerment

perilous
5 hairy, risky **6** chancy, unsafe **7** unsound **9** dangerous, desperate, hazardous, uncertain **11** treacherous

____ Perilous
5 Siege

perimeter
4 edge **5** limit, verge **6** border, bounds, margin **8** boundary

period
3 age, end, era **4** span, stop, term, time **5** cycle, phase, point, spell, stage **6** extent **8** division, duration, interval, sentence

periodic
6 cyclic, fitful **7** regular **8** cyclical, repeated, sporadic **9** recurrent, recurring **10** occasional **11** fluctuating **12** intermittent

periodical
3 mag **5** organ **6** cyclic, review **7** journal **8** cyclical, magazine **9** alternate, newspaper, recurrent, recurring **10** isochronal **11** isochronous, publication **12** intermittent

peripatetic
6 moving, roving **7** nomadic, walking **8** ambulant, vagabond **9** itinerant, traveling, wayfaring **10** ambulatory, pedestrian, travelling **13** perambulatory

peripheral
6 remote **7** lateral, surface **8** far-flung, marginal, outlying **9** auxiliary, secondary **10** borderline, tangential **11** out-of-the-way **13** supplementary

perish
3 die, end **4** pass **5** cease **6** be lost, demise, depart, expire, vanish **7** decease, decline, go under, succumb **8** collapse, pass away **9** disappear

perjure
3 lie **6** delude **7** deceive, distort, falsify, mislead **8** forswear **9** misinform **10** equivocate **11** prevaricate

perk
4 gain, mend, plus **5** bonus, cheer, extra **7** benefit, freshen, improve, refresh, smarten **8** brighten

perky
5 alert, cocky, happy **6** bouncy, bubbly, cheery, chirpy, frisky, jaunty, lively, upbeat **7** buoyant, chipper **8** animated, cheerful, spirited, sportive **9** energetic, sparkling, sprightly, vivacious **12** effervescent, high-spirited

permanent
5 fixed **6** stable **7** abiding, durable, lasting **8** constant, enduring, hair wave **9** continual, perennial **10** changeless, invariable, unchanging **11** established, everlasting **12** imperishable

permeable
6 porous, spongy **8** pervious **9** absorbent, diffusive **10** penetrable

permeate
5 imbue **6** drench, infuse, spread **7** diffuse, pervade, suffuse **8** saturate **9** penetrate, percolate **10** impregnate, infiltrate **11** pass through

permissible
4 okay **5** legal **7** allowed **8** approved **9** allowable, tolerable, tolerated **10** acceptable, authorized, sanctioned

permission
5 leave **6** assent, permit **7** consent, license **8** approval, sanction **9** agreement, allowance **11** approbation, endorsement **12** acquiescence **13** authorization

permissive
3 lax **4** open **7** lenient, liberal **8** tolerant **9** easygoing, forgiving, indulgent **10** forbearing **11** acquiescent, complaisant

permit
3 let **4** okay, pass **5** agree, allow, grant, leave **6** accede, enable, say yes, suffer **7** consent, license, warrant **8** sanction, tolerate **9** allowance, authorize, give leave **10** permission **13** authorization

permutation
6 change **7** variety, version **9** variation **10** alteration, innovation **11** arrangement, vicissitude **12** modification

pernicious
4 evil **5** fatal, toxic **6** deadly, lethal, malign, wicked **7** baleful, baneful, harmful, hurtful, killing, malefic, noxious, ruinous **8** damaging, sinister, virulent **9** injurious, malignant, offensive, poisonous **10** maleficent **11** deleterious, destructive, detrimental, devastating

Pernod flavor
5 anise **8** licorice

perorate
5 speak **7** declaim, lecture **8** bloviate, harangue, proclaim **9** hold forth, speechify

perpend
5 study, weigh **6** ponder **7** examine, reflect **8** consider, think out **9** reflect on, think over **10** excogitate, think about **11** contemplate

perpendicular
5 plumb, sheer, steep **7** upright **8** straight, vertical **11** precipitate, precipitous

perpetrate
6 commit, effect **7** inflict, execute, perform **8** carry out **10** bring about

perpetual
7 endless, eternal, undying **8** constant, unending **9** ceaseless, continual, incessant, perennial, recurrent, unceasing **10** continuous **11** everlasting, unremitting

perpetuate
7 sustain **8** conserve, continue, eternize, maintain, preserve **9** keep alive **10** eternalize **11** immortalize

perplex
5 befog, mix up, stump **6** baffle, bemuse, muddle, puzzle **7** buffalo, confuse, mystify, nonplus, perturb **8** befuddle, bewilder, confound, distract, entangle **9** dumbfound **10** discompose

perplexed
7 at a loss, mixed up, puzzled **8** confused

Perry Mason
author: 7 Gardner (Erle Stanley)
character: 5 Drake (Paul), Drumm (Lt. Steve), Mason (Perry), Tragg (Lt. Arthur) **6** Burger (Hamilton), Street (Della) **8** Anderson (Lt. Andy)
TV star: 4 Burr (Raymond), Hale (Barbara)

perquisite
3 tip **4** gain **5** right **6** profit **7** benefit, payment **8** gratuity **9** privilege

per se
6 as such, solely **8** in itself **11** essentially **13** intrinsically

persecute
4 bait, ride **5** annoy, harry, hound, worry, wrong **6** badger, harass, hector, injure, molest, pester, pick on, plague, punish, pursue **7** afflict, oppress, torment, torture **8** aggrieve

Persephone
4 Kore **10** Proserpina
father: 4 Zeus **7** Jupiter
husband: 5 Hades, Pluto
mother: 5 Ceres **7** Demeter

Perseus
father: 4 Zeus **7** Jupiter
grandfather: 8 Acrisius
mother: 5 Danaë
victim: 6 Medusa **8** Acrisius
wife: 9 Andromeda

perseverance
8 tenacity **9** diligence, endurance **10** dedication **11** persistence **13** steadfastness

persevere
see **persist**

Persia
4 Iran

Persian
ancient: 4 Mede
fairy: 4 peri
governor: 6 satrap
language: 5 Farsi, Parsi
mystic: 4 sufi
New Year's: 6 Nowruz
poet: 4 Omar **5** Hafez, Hafiz **7** Firdusi **8** Ferdowsi, Firdausi, Firdawsi, Firdousi **11** Omar Khayyám
prophet: 9 Zoroaster
robe: 6 caftan
sacred books: 6 Avesta
sun-god: 7 Mithras
title: 4 shah
writing: 9 cuneiform

persiflage
6 banter, joking **7** jesting, kidding, ribbing **8** badinage, raillery, repartee

persist
4 go on, last **5** abide **6** endure, hang on, keep on, linger **7** carry on, prevail **8** continue **9** persevere

persistence
8 duration **9** endurance **10** continuity **11** continuance **12** continuation

persistent
6 dogged **7** lasting **8** enduring, obdurate, stubborn **9** continual, steadfast, tenacious **10** continuing, determined, relentless, unshakable **11** persevering, unremitting

persnickety
5 fussy, picky **6** choosy **7** finicky **8** exacting **10** fastidious, particular

person
3 guy **4** self, soul **5** being, human **6** entity, mensch, mortal **8** creature, specimen **10** individual

personable
4 nice **6** genial **7** affable, amiable **8** charming, friendly, pleasant, pleasing **9** appealing, congenial **10** attractive

personage
3 VIP **5** human, mogul **6** bigwig, figure, honcho **7** big shot, magnate, notable **8** creature, luminary, somebody **9** celebrity, character, dignitary **10** individual

personal
3 own **5** privy **7** private, special **8** peculiar **10** individual, particular

personal effects
5 stuff **10** belongings **11** possessions

personality
3 ego, VIP **4** self **6** makeup, nature, temper **7** notable **8** identity, selfhood **9** celebrity, character **10** complexion **11** disposition, singularity, temperament **13** individuality

personate
3 act **4** play **5** enact **6** embody, typify **7** perform **9** epitomize, exemplify, represent **10** illustrate

personify
6 embody, typify **8** stand for **9** actualize, epitomize, exemplify, incarnate, represent, symbolize **11** emblematize

perspective
4 view **5** angle, scene, slant, vista **7** outlook **8** position, prospect **9** viewpoint **10** standpoint **11** point of view

perspicacious
4 keen **5** acute, quick, savvy, sharp **6** astute, clever, shrewd **9** observant, sagacious **10** discerning, insightful, perceptive **11** penetrating

perspicacity
6 acumen **7** insight **8** keenness **10** astuteness, shrewdness **11** discernment, penetration, percipience

perspicuous
5 clear, lucid, plain **6** lucent, simple **7** crystal, precise **8** clear-cut, pellucid **11** unambiguous

perspiration
5 sweat

perspire
see **sweat**

persuadable
4 open **7** willing **9** receptive **11** suggestible, susceptible

persuade
3 win **4** coax, lead, sell, sway, urge **5** argue **6** entice, induce, prompt **7** convert, impress, win over **8** convince **9** influence, prevail on **11** bring around

persuasion
4 kind, mind, sort, type, view **5** group **6** belief, school **7** faction, opinion **8** argument **9** character, prejudice, sentiment **10** connection, conviction **11** affiliation, description

Persuasion author
6 Austen (Jane)

persuasive
6 cogent **7** telling, winning **8** credible **10** compelling, convincing **11** influential

pert
4 bold, chic, flip, trim **5** alert, cocky, fresh, lippy, sassy, saucy, smart **6** brazen, bright, cheeky, jaunty, lively **7** forward **8** animated, flippant, spirited **9** audacious, sprightly, vivacious

pertain
5 apply, refer **6** affect, bear on, belong, regard, relate **7** concern **8** bear upon **9** touch upon

pertinacious
4 firm **5** fixed **6** dogged, mulish **7** willful **8** resolute, stubborn **9** obstinate, tenacious **10** inflexible, persistent, unshakable, unyielding

pertinent
3 apt, fit **5** ad rem **7** apropos, fitting, germane **8** apposite, material, relevant **10** applicable **11** appropriate

perturb
5 upset, worry **6** bother **7** agitate, disturb, fluster, trouble **8** disorder, disquiet, unsettle **10** discompose, disconcert

Peru
ancient civilization: **4** Inca
capital: **4** Lima
city: **5** Cusco, Cuzco **6** Callao **8** Arequipa, Trujillo
conqueror: **7** Pizarro (Francisco)

ethnic group: **7** Quechua
lake: **8** Titicaca
language: **6** Aymara **7** Quechua, Spanish
leader: **8** Fujimori (Alberto)
monetary unit: **3** sol
mountain, range: **5** Andes **9** Huascarán
neighbor: **5** Chile **6** Brazil **7** Bolivia, Ecuador **8** Colombia
river: **6** Amazon **7** Marañón
volcano: **5** Misti **7** El Misti **8** Yucamani

peruse
4 read, scan **5** study **6** survey **7** examine **8** consider, look over, pore over

Peruvian singer
5 Sumac (Yma)

pervade
5 imbue **6** spread **7** diffuse **8** permeate, saturate **9** penetrate, percolate, transfuse **10** impregnate

perverse
5 balky **6** cranky, mulish, ornery **7** corrupt, deviant, froward, peevish, wayward, willful **8** contrary, depraved, improper, stubborn **9** incorrect, irritable, obstinate **10** degenerate, headstrong, refractory **11** stiff-necked, wrong-headed **12** cross-grained, unreasonable

pervert
4 ruin, skew, warp **5** abuse, twist **6** debase, divert, garble, misuse **7** corrupt, debauch, deprave, distort, deviant, falsify, vitiate **8** misstate, mistreat **9** misdirect

pervious
4 open **6** porous **9** permeable **10** accessible, penetrable

pesky
6 vexing **7** irksome **8** annoying **9** vexatious **10** bothersome **11** troublesome

pessimist
5 cynic **9** Cassandra, defeatist, doomsayer, worrywart **11** misanthrope

pessimistic
6 gloomy, morose **7** cynical **10** despairing **11** distrustful **12** misanthropic

pest
4 bane **5** trial, worry **6** bother, nudnik, plague, vermin **7** nudnick, trouble **8** irritant, nuisance, vexation **9** annoyance, tormentor

pester
3 bug, irk, nag **4** ride **5** annoy, harry, tease, worry **6** badger, bother, harass, hassle, plague **7** bedevil, disturb, torment **8** irritate

pestiferous
7 baneful, noxious **8** annoying, infected **9** infective, pestilent **10** pernicious **11** troublesome

pestilence
5 curse **6** plague **7** scourge

pestilential
5 fatal **6** deadly, lethal, vexing **7** baneful, deathly, noxious, ruinous **8** annoying **10** pernicious

pestle
4 mano **6** muller
vessel: **6** mortar

pet
3 cat, dog, hug **4** dear, kiss, love, neck, pout, sulk **5** loved, spoon **6** caress, cosset, dandle, fondle, pamper, stroke **7** beloved, cherish, darling, indulge **8** favorite, treasure **9** cherished

petcock
3 tap **5** valve **6** faucet, spigot

Peter Grimes composer
7 Britten (Benjamin)

peter out
4 fade, wane **5** abate, cease **6** lessen, recede, run dry **7** dwindle **8** decrease, diminish, taper off **9** drain away

Peter Pan
author: **6** Barrie (James)
character: **5** Wendy **7** Michael **9** Tiger Lily **10** Tinker Bell
dog: **4** Nana
family: **7** Darling
pirate: **4** Hook, Smee

Peter the Apostle
brother: **6** Andrew
father: **5** Jonah
original name: **5** Simon

Peter the Great
father: **6** Alexis
mother: **8** Nataliya
wife: **7** Eudoxia **9** Catherine

petite
5 small **6** little **8** smallish **10** diminutive

petition
3 ask **4** plea **5** plead **6** appeal **7** beseech, entreat, implore, request, solicit **8** entreaty **10** supplicate **11** application **12** supplication

Petrarch's beloved
5 Laura

Petrified Forest author
8 Sherwood (Robert)

petrify
4 daze, numb, stun **5** chill, scare **6** benumb, deaden, harden **7** startle **8** confound, frighten, paralyze

Petruchio's wife
9 Katharina, Katharine

pettifogger
7 shyster **8** quibbler **9** nitpicker

petty
4 mean **5** minor, small **6** measly, narrow, paltry

7 trivial **8** niggling, picayune, piddling, trifling **9** frivolous, secondary **10** irrelevant, negligible **11** small-minded, subordinate, unimportant **13** insignificant

petty officer
6 noncom

petulant
5 huffy, moody, sulky, testy, whiny **6** touchy **7** grouchy, peevish **8** snappish **9** irascible, irritable, querulous **10** ill-humored

pew
3 row **4** seat **5** bench

peyote
6 cactus, mescal
drug: 9 mescaline

Phaedra
father: 5 Minos
husband: 7 Theseus
mother: 8 Pasiphaë
sister: 7 Ariadne
stepson: 10 Hippolytus

Phaëthon's father
6 Helios **7** Phoebus

phalanx
4 army, host, mass **5** horde **6** myriad, throng **6** troops

phantasm
5 dream, fancy, ghost **6** spirit, vision **7** fantasy, fiction, figment, specter, spectre **8** daydream, delusion, illusion **9** invention **10** apparition **11** fabrication **13** hallucination

phantom
5 dummy, ghost, shade, spook **6** goblin, shadow, spirit, vision **7** bugbear, chimera, eidolon, specter, spectre **8** illusory, spectral **9** imaginary **10** apparition, fictitious **12** will-o'-the-wisp

pharaoh
3 Tut **4** Seti **5** Menes, ruler **6** Ahmose, Ramses, tyrant **7** Harmhab **8** Ikhnaton, Thutmose **9** Amenhotep, Merneptah **11** Tutankhamen, Tutankhaten

pharisee
9 hypocrite

pharmacist
8 druggist **10** apothecary
British: 7 chemist

pharos
6 beacon **10** lighthouse

Pharsalus, battle of
vanquished: 6 Pompey
victor: 6 Caesar (Julius)

phase
4 part, side, view **5** point, stage, state **6** adjust, aspect **7** conduct **8** carry out, position **9** condition, situation, viewpoint **10** appearance

PhD exam
5 orals

Phèdre author
6 Racine (Jean)

phenomenal
6 actual **7** unusual **8** material, physical, sensible, singular, tangible, uncommon **9** corporeal, fantastic, objective **10** astounding, remarkable **11** astonishing, exceptional, outstanding, perceivable, perceptible, substantial **13** extraordinary

phenomenon
4 fact **5** event **6** marvel, object, rarity, wonder **7** miracle, reality **9** actuality, sensation **10** experience, uniqueness **11** peculiarity, singularity

philander
8 womanize

philanthropic
6 giving, humane **8** generous **10** altruistic, benevolent, bighearted, charitable **11** magnanimous **12** eleemosynary, humanitarian

philanthropist
American: 5 Gates (Bill) **6** Cooper (Peter), Girard (Stephen), Mellon (Andrew) **7** Buffett (Warren), Cornell (Ezra), Eastman (George), Packard (David), Whitney (Gertrude Vanderbilt) **8** Carnegie (Andrew), Stanford (Leland) **9** Rosenwald (Julius) **10** Vanderbilt (Cornelius) **11** Rockefeller (J. D.)
English: 11 Wilberforce (William)
Swedish: 5 Nobel (Alfred)

Philemon's wife
6 Baucis

philharmonic
8 symphony **9** orchestra, symphonic

Philip of Macedonia
father: 7 Amyntas
son: 9 Alexander

philippic
4 rant **6** tirade **8** diatribe, harangue, jeremiad **12** condemnation

Philippics author
6 Cicero

Philippines
capital: 6 Manila
city: 4 Cebu **5** Davao **10** Quezon City
discoverer: 8 Magellan (Ferdinand)
guerrilla: 3 Huk **10** Hukbalahap
island: 4 Cebu **5** Leyte, Luzon, Panay, Samar **6** Negros **7** Masbate, Mindoro, Palawan **8** Mindanao
language: 7 Ilocano, Tagalog **8** Filipino, Pilipino
leader: 6 Aquino (Corazon), Marcos (Ferdinand)
liberator: 9 MacArthur (Douglas)
patriot: 5 Rizal (José)

monetary unit: **4** peso
people: **3** Ati **4** Moro
sea: **4** Sulu **5** Samar **7** Celebes, Sibuyan, Visayan **8** Mindanao **10** Philippine, South China
volcano: **4** Taal **5** Mayon

Philippi victor
6 Antony (Marc, Mark) **8** Octavian

Philip the Tetrarch
father: **5** Herod
mother: **9** Cleopatra

philistine
4 boob **7** Babbitt **9** bourgeois, vulgarian **10** capitalist **11** materialist

Philistine
champion: **7** Goliath
city: **4** Gath, Gaza **5** Ekron **6** Ashdod **8** Ashkelon
foe: **5** David **6** Samson
god: **5** Dagon

Philoctetes
father: **5** Poeas
victim: **5** Paris

Philomela
11 nightingale
father: **7** Pandion
ravisher: **6** Tereus
sister: **6** Procne

philosopher
American: **5** Adler (Mortimer), Dewey (John), James (William), Quine (Willard), Rorty (Richard), Royce (Josiah) **6** Langer (Susanne), Peirce (C. S.) **7** Marcuse (Herbert), Mumford (Lewis), Strauss (Leo) **9** Santayana (George)
Arab: **8** Averroës, Avicenna
Austrian: **6** Popper (Karl) **12** Wittgenstein (Ludwig)
Chinese: **5** Laoxi **6** Lao-tsu **7** Dai Zhen, Mencius, Tai Chen **9** Confucius
Danish: **11** Kierkegaard (Soren)
Dutch: **7** Erasmus (Desiderius), Spinoza (Baruch de)
English: **4** Ayer (A. J.), Joad (C. E. M.), Mill (John Stuart), More (Henry, Thomas), Watt (James) **5** Bacon (Francis), Burke (Edmund), Locke (John), Moore (G. E.), Occam (William of), Paine (Thomas) **6** Berlin (Isaiah), Hobbes (Thomas), Huxley (Thomas), Ockham (William), Popper (Karl) **7** Bentham (Jeremy), Russell (Bertrand), Spencer (Herbert), Whewell (William) **9** Whitehead (Alfred North) **12** Wittgenstein (Ludwig)
Finnish: **11** Westermarck (Edward)
French: **4** Weil (Simone) **5** Comte (Auguste), Taine (Hippolyte) **6** Pascal (Blaise), Sartre (Jean-Paul), Valéry (Paul) **7** Abelard (Peter), Bergson (Henri), Derrida (Jacques), Diderot (Denis), Fourier (Charles) **8** Foucault (Michel), Maritain (Jacques), Rousseau (Jean-Jacques), Voltaire **9** Descartes (René), Montaigne (Michel de) **10** Saint-Simon (Comte de) **11** Montesquieu (Baron de) **12** Merleau-Ponty (Maurice)
German: **4** Kant (Immanuel), Marx (Karl) **5** Frege (Gottlob), Hegel (Georg Wilhelm Friedrich), Wolff (Christian von) **6** Carnap (Rudolf), Fichte (Immanuel, Johann), Herder (Johann von) **7** Husserl (Edmund), Jaspers (Karl), Leibniz (Gottfried) **8** Spengler (Oswald) **9** Heidegger (Martin), Nietzsche (Friedrich), Schelling (Friedrich von) **12** Schopenhauer (Arthur) **14** Albertus Magnus
Greek: **4** Zeno **5** Plato, Timon **6** Thales **7** Gorgias, Proclus **8** Diogenes, Epicurus, Longinus, Socrates **9** Aristotle, Epictetus **10** Anaxagoras, Democritus, Empedocles, Heraclitus, Parmenides, Protagoras, Pythagoras, Xenocrates, Xenophanes **11** Anaximander **12** Theophrastus
Irish: **8** Berkeley (George)
Italian: **5** Croce (Benedetto) **6** Ficino (Marsilio) **11** Machiavelli (Niccolo)
Jewish: **5** Buber (Martin), Philo **10** Maimonides (Moses) **12** Philo Judaeus
Roman: **6** Seneca (Lucias Annaeus) **8** Boethius (Anicius), Plotinus **9** Lucretius
Scottish: **4** Hume (David), Mill (James), Reid (Thomas) **7** Stewart (Dugald)
Spanish: **6** Suárez (Francisco) **7** Unamuno (Miguel de) **13** Ortega y Gasset (José)
Swedish: **10** Swedenborg (Emanuel)

philosopher's stone
3 key **6** elixir

philosophical
4 calm **7** stoical **8** composed, rational, resigned **9** unruffled **10** thoughtful

philosophy
6 system, theory, values **7** beliefs, inquiry **8** attitude, calmness **10** discipline
component: **5** logic **6** ethics **10** aesthetics **11** metaphysics **12** epistemology

philter
4 drug **5** charm, tonic **6** potion **9** stimulant **10** love potion **11** aphrodisiac, restorative

Phineas
beloved: **9** Andromeda
tormentors: **7** Harpies
wife: **9** Cleopatra

phlegm
5 humor, mucus **6** apathy **8** calmness, coolness, dullness **9** composure, sangfroid **10** equanimity **11** impassivity, nonchalance **12** indifference

phlegmatic
4 calm, cool, dull **5** aloof, stoic **6** stolid **8** detached **9** apathetic, impassive, lethargic **11** indifferent, unconcerned

Phlegyas
daughter: **7** Coronis
father: **4** Ares, Mars
son: **5** Ixion

phobia
see **fear**

Phobos
4 moon **9** satellite
brother: **6** Deimos
father: **4** Ares, Mars

Phocus
father: **6** Aeacus **8** Ornytion
half brother: **6** Peleus **7** Telamon
mother: **8** Psamathe
slayer: **6** Peleus **7** Telamon
wife: **7** Antiope

Phoebe
5 Diana **7** Artemis
daughter: **4** Leto
father: **9** Leucippus
mother: **4** Gaea

Phoebus
see **Apollo**

Phoenician
city: **4** Acre, Tyre **5** Sidon
colony: **8** Carthage
god: **4** Baal **6** Eshmun
goddess: **6** Baltis **7** Astarte

Phoenix
pupil: **8** Achilles
sister: **6** Europa
team: **4** Suns **7** Coyotes **9** Cardinals **12** Diamondbacks

phony
4 fake, sham **5** bogus, cheat, faker, false, fraud **6** ersatz, humbug, pseudo **8** impostor, specious, spurious **9** charlatan, dishonest, pretender **10** ficticious, suspicious **11** counterfeit **12** hypocritical

photograph
3 pic **4** film, snap **5** shoot **6** glossy **7** picture, tintype **8** snapshot
color: **5** sepia
three-dimensional: **8** hologram

photographer
8 photoist **9** cameraman **10** shutterbug
famous: **3** Ray (Man) **4** Capa (Cornell, Robert), Haas (Ernst), Hine (Lewis), Penn (Irving), Riis (Jacob) **5** Adams (Ansel), Arbus (Diane), Atget (Eugène), Brady (Mathew), Evans (Frederick, Walker), Frank (Robert), Horst (Horst Peter), Karsh (Yousuf), Lange (Dorothea), Model (Lisette), Nadar, Parks (Gordon), Ritts (Herb), Smith (W. Eugene), Weber (Bruce), White (Clarence, Minor) **6** Abbott (Berenice), Avedon (Richard), Beaton (Cecil), Brandt (Bill), Coburn (Alvin), Curtis (Edward S.), Newton (Helmut), Porter (Eliot), Rowell (Galen), Siegel (Eliot), Strand (Paul), Talbot (William Henry Fox), Weegee, Wegman (William), Weston (Brett, Edward) **7** Brassaï, Cameron (Julia Margaret), Emerson (Peter), Halsman (Philippe), Jackson (William Henry), Kertész (André), Salomon (Erich), Siskind (Aaron), Snowdon (Earl of), Thomson (John), Watkins (Carleton) **8** Callahan (Harry), Cosindas (Marie), Daguerre (Louis-Jacques-Mandé), Kasebier (Gertrude), Scavullo (Francesco), Steichen (Edward), Steinert (Otto) **9** Caponigro (Paul), Feininger (Andreas), Leibovitz (Annie), Meyrowitz (Joel), Muybridge (Eadweard), O'Sullivan (Timothy), Rejlander (Oscar), Rothstein (Arthur), Stieglitz (Alfred), Winogrand (Garry) **10** Cunningham (Imogen), Heartfield (John), Moholy-Nagy (Laszlo) **11** Bourke-White (Margaret), Eisenstaedt (Alfred) **12** Mapplethorpe (Robert)

photographic
5 exact, vivid **7** graphic **8** accurate, detailed **9** pictorial **11** picturesque
solution: **4** hypo **5** fixer, toner **7** reducer **9** developer

phrase
5 couch, frame, idiom **6** slogan **7** diction, express, styling, wording **8** locution, verbiage **9** catchword, formulate, verbalism, watchword **10** expression

Phrygian
god: **4** Atys **5** Attis
goddess: **6** Cybele
king: **5** Midas **7** Gordius

phthisis
2 TB **11** consumption **12** tuberculosis

phylactery
5 charm **6** amulet **7** periapt **8** talisman

physic
4 cure, heal **5** purge **6** remedy **8** medicine **9** cathartic, purgative **10** medication

physical
4 real **5** lusty, rough **6** actual, bodily, carnal, sexual **7** fleshly, natural, somatic **8** concrete, corporal, material, sensible, tangible **9** corporeal, objective **10** phenomenal **11** perceivable, perceptible, substantial

physician
2 MD **3** doc **5** medic **6** doctor, medico **7** surgeon **8** sawbones
American: **4** Koop (C. Everett), Rush (Benjamin), Salk (Jonas) **5** Minot (George), Spock

(Benjamin), Still (Andrew) **6** Jarvik (Robert), Murphy (John), Weller (Thomas) **7** Huggins (Charles), Robbins (Frederick), Theiler (Max) **8** Richards (Dickinson) **9** Sternberg (George Miller)
Arab: 8 Avicenna
Canadian: 5 Osler (William)
English: 4 Ross (Ronald) **6** Harvey (William), Jenner (Edward, William), Willis (Thomas) **8** Sydenham (Thomas)
French: 5 Widal (Fernand) **7** Laveran (Charles) **10** Schweitzer (Albert)
German: 7 Sylvius (Franciscus)
Greek: 5 Galen **11** Hippocrates
Italian: 7 Galvani (Luigi)
organization: 3 AMA
South African: 7 Barnard (Christiaan)
Swiss: 10 Paracelsus
(see also **Nobel Prize winner** *physiology or medicine;* **surgeon**)

physicist
American: 4 Rabi (I. I.), Ting (Samuel) **5** Fermi (Enrico), Gibbs (J. Willard), Kusch (Polykarp), Mayer (Maria-Goeppert), Pauli (Wolfgang), Pupin (Michael), Segré (Emilio), Smyth (Henry DeWolf), Stern (Otto) **6** Teller (Edward), Townes (Charles), Wigner (Eugene) **7** Alvarez (Luis), Feynman (Richard), Goddard (Robert), Purcell (Edward) **8** Einstein (Albert), Gell-Mann (Murray), McMillan (Edwin), Millikan (Clark, Robert), Mulliken (Robert), Shockley (William), Van Allen (James) **9** Michelson (Albert), Schwinger (Julian) **11** Oppenheimer (J. Robert)
Austrian: 4 Mach (Ernst) **7** Doppler (Christian) **11** Schrödinger (Erwin)
British: 4 Snow (C. P.) **5** Dirac (B. A. M.), Jeans (James), Joule (James) **6** Dalton (John), Kelvin (Baron), Newton (Isaac), Powell (Cecil), Stokes (George) **7** Faraday (Michael), Hodgkin (Dorothy), Thomson (George, Joseph, William) **7** Tyndall (John) **8** Rayleigh (Lord), Robinson (Robert), Thompson (Benjamin, Silvanus) **9** Wollaston (William) **10** Richardson (Owen), Rutherford (Ernest), Wheatstone (Charles)
Chinese: 4 Yang (Chen-Ning)
Danish: 4 Bohr (Aage, Niels)
Dutch: 6 Zeeman (Pieter) **7** Huygens (Christian), Lorentz (Hendrik), Zernike (Frits) **11** Van der Waals (Johannes)
French: 4 Néel (Louis) **5** Arago (François) **6** Ampère (André-Marie), Perrin (Jean-Baptiste) **7** Coulomb (Charles-Augustin de), Kastler (Alfred), Réaumur (René-Antoine de) **8** Lippmann (Gabriel)
German: 3 Ohm (Georg) **4** Laue (Max von), Wien (Wilhelm) **5** Hertz (Gustav, Heinrich), Stark (Johannes), Weber (Wilhelm) **6** Jensen (Hans), Lenard (Philipp), Nernst (Walther), Planck (Max) **7** Meitner (Lise) **8** Roentgen (Wilhelm) **9** Helmholtz (Hermann von), Kirchhoff (Gustav), Mossbauer (Rudolf) **10** Fahrenheit (Daniel), Hofstadter (Robert)
Indian: 5 Raman (Chandrasekhara)
Irish: 6 Walton (Ernest)
Italian: 5 Rossi (Bruno), Volta (Alessandro) **7** Galileo (Galilei), Galvani (Luigi) **10** Torricelli (Evangelista)
Japanese: 6 Yukawa (Hideki) **8** Tomonaga (Shinichiro)
Mexican: 8 Vallarta (Manuel)
Russian: 4 Tamm (Igor) **6** Landau (Lev) **9** Prokhorov (Aleksandr)
Scottish: 4 Tait (Peter) **6** Wilson (Charles) **7** Maxwell (James Clerk)
Swedish: 7 Rydberg (Johannes) **8** Angstrom (Anders), Siegbahn (Kai, Karl)
Swiss: 6 Zwicky (Fritz) **7** Piccard (Auguste)
(see also **Nobel Prize winner** *physics*)

physiognomy
3 mug **4** face **5** front **6** aspect, visage **7** profile **8** features **9** character **10** lineaments **11** countenance, temperament

physiologist
English: 8 Starling (Ernest)
German: 5 Weber (Ernst), Wundt (Wilhelm) **7** Schwann (Theodor) **9** Helmholtz (Hermann von)
Italian: 11 Spallanzani (Lazzaro)
(see also **Nobel Prize winner** *physiology or medicine*)

physique
3 bod **4** body, form **5** build, shape **6** figure, makeup **7** anatomy **9** structure **12** constitution

pianist
American: 4 Nero (Peter), Tesh (John), Wild (Earl) **5** Janis (Byron), Watts (André) **6** Duchin (Peter), Joplin (Scott), Serkin (Peter, Rudolf) **7** Cliburn (Van), Istomin (Eugene), Ohlsson (Garrick), Perahia (Murray), Winston (George) **8** Graffman (Gary), Horowitz (Vladimir), Pennario (Leonard) **9** Fleischer (Leon) **10** Johannesen (Grant), Rubinstein (Arthur)
Argentinian: 8 Argerich (Martha) **9** Barenboim (Daniel)
Austrian: 6 Czerny (Karl) **7** Brendel (Alfred) **8** Schnabel (Artur)
Bulgarian: 11 Weissenberg (Alexis)
Canadian: 5 Gould (Glenn)
Chilean: 5 Arrau (Claudio)
Cuban: 5 Bolet (Jorge)
English: 4 Hess (Myra) **5** Ogdon (John) **6** Curzon (Clifford)
French: 6 Cortot (Alfred) **7** Cziffra (Gyorgy) **9** Casadesus (Robert), Entremont (Philippe) **10** Saint-Saëns (Camille)

German: **6** Kempff (Wilhelm) **8** Schumann (Clara) **9** Gieseking (Walter)
Hungarian: **5** Liszt (Franz) **7** Cziffra (Gyorgy)
Italian: **6** Busoni (Ferruccio) **7** Pollini (Maurizio) **8** Clementi (Muzio)
Japanese: **6** Uchida (Mitsuko)
Polish: **6** Chopin (Frédéric) **7** Hofmann (Josef) **10** Paderewski (Ignacy), Rubinstein (Arthur)
Romanian: **4** Lupu (Radu) **7** Lipatti (Dinu)
Russian: **6** Berman (Lazar), Gilels (Emil), Kissin (Evgeny) **7** Richter (Sviatoslav) **8** Horowitz (Vladimir), Pachmann (Vladimir von) **9** Ashkenazy (Vladimir) **10** Rubinstein (Anton) **12** Rachmaninoff (Sergey)
Spanish: **6** Iturbi (José) **8** Granados (Enrique) **10** de Larrocha (Alicia)
Swiss: **4** Anda (Geza)
(see also **jazz musician**)

piano
5 grand **6** softly, spinet **7** quietly, upright **9** baby grand
builder: **5** Knabe (William), Stein (Johann), Zumpe (Johann) **7** Baldwin (Dwight) **8** Steinway (Henry) **9** Bechstein (Friedrich) **10** Chickering (Jonas), Silbermann (Johann)
inventor: **10** Cristofori (Bartolomeo)
keys: **7** ivories
pedal: **6** damper **9** sostenuto

piazza
5 patio, plaza, porch **6** square **7** balcony, gallery, portico, terrace, veranda **9** courtyard

picaro
5 rogue, rover, thief **6** pirate **7** brigand, corsair **8** bohemian, sea rover **9** buccaneer **10** freebooter

picayune
5 petty **6** measly, paltry, trifle **7** trivial **8** piddling **11** small-minded **13** insignificant

pick
3 rob, tap **4** best, carp, cull, open, pull, take, tool **5** elect, pluck, probe, prize **6** choice, choose, chosen, option, pierce, pilfer, remove, select, unlock **7** harvest, provoke **8** selected **9** exclusive, single out

picket
4 pale, post **5** fence, guard, stake, watch **6** sentry, tether **7** enclose, lookout, protest **8** palisade, sentinel, watchman **11** demonstrate

pickle
3 fix, jam **4** dill, spot **5** brine, treat **6** plight, scrape **7** dilemma, gherkin, trouble **8** marinate, preserve **10** difficulty **11** predicament

pick on
5 bully, harry, taunt, tease **6** hector, pester **9** criticize, single out

pick out
4 espy, name, spot **6** choose, descry, detect, select, take in **7** discern **8** identify, perceive **9** apprehend, ascertain, recognize **11** distinguish

pickpocket
3 dip **5** thief **6** dipper **8** cutpurse

pick up
3 buy, get **4** cull, gain, earn, land, lift, tidy **5** catch, glean, hoist, learn, raise, run in **6** arrest, detain, gather, notice, obtain, pull in, resume, revive **7** acquire, clean up, collect, restart **8** perceive **9** apprehend **10** appreciate, understand

pickup
3 ute **5** truck **9** detention **10** hitchhiker **11** improvement **12** acceleration

picky
5 fussy **6** choosy **7** finicky **10** fastidious, particular, pernickety **11** persnickety

picnic
4 snap **5** cinch **6** breeze, outing **7** cookout **8** cakewalk **11** piece of cake

picture
4 limn, show **5** image, photo, pinup **7** drawing, tableau **8** describe, painting, portrait **9** depiction, portrayal **10** simulacrum **11** delineation, description **13** spitting image
stand: **5** easel

picturesque
5 vivid **6** quaint, scenic **8** artistic, charming

piddling
4 puny **5** petty **6** meager, meagre, measly, paltry **7** trivial **8** picayune, trifling **11** Mickey Mouse, unimportant **13** insignificant

pie
4 flan, tart **5** pasty **6** pastry **7** cobbler, dessert **8** turnover

piebald
5 mixed **6** motley **7** mottled **10** multicolor, variegated

piece
4 part **5** patch, slice **6** member, parcel **7** firearm, portion, section, segment **8** division, fraction, fragment **9** allotment **10** allocation

pièce de résistance
8 main dish **9** showpiece **11** centerpiece, chef d'oeuvre, masterpiece

piecemeal
5 apart **6** slowly **7** gradual **8** bit by bit **9** by degrees, gradually **11** fragmentary

piece of cake
4 snap **5** cinch **6** breeze, picnic, shoo-in **8** duck soup, kid stuff, pushover

pied
6 motley **7** blotchy, brindle, dappled, mottled **8** brindled, speckled **9** multihued **10** variegated **11** varicolored **12** parti-colored

pier
4 anta, dock, quay, slip **5** berth, jetty, levee, wharf **6** column, pillar **8** pilaster
architectural: **4** anta

pierce
3 cut **4** stab **5** probe, spear **6** impale, incise, skewer **8** puncture **9** penetrate, perforate **10** run through

piercing
4 high, keen **5** acute, sharp **6** piping, shrill **8** shooting, stabbing, strident **9** knifelike **12** earsplitting
tool: **3** awl

piety
6 fealty **7** loyalty **8** devotion, fidelity, sanctity **9** reverence **10** allegiance, dedication, devoutness **12** faithfulness

piffle
4 bosh, bunk **5** bilge, hokum, hooey **6** bunkum, drivel **7** baloney, eyewash, hogwash, rubbish, twaddle **8** malarkey, nonsense, tommyrot **9** poppycock **10** balderdash, codswallop

pig
3 hog **4** Babe, slob **5** Porky, shoat, swine **6** farrow, piglet, porker **7** casting, glutton
breed: **5** Duroc **8** Tamworth **9** Berkshire, Hampshire, Yorkshire
female: **3** sow **4** gilt
feral: **9** razorback
litter: **6** farrow
male: **4** boar **6** barrow
meat: **3** ham **4** pork **5** bacon **7** sausage **8** chitlins **12** chitterlings
sound: **3** wee
wild: **4** boar **7** peccary, warthog **8** babirusa

pigeon
3 Nun, sap **4** dupe, fool, gull, mark **5** chump, decoy, patsy **6** culver, stooge, sucker **7** fall guy, stoolie **8** rock dove
genus: **7** Columba
house: **4** cote, loft
kind: **4** barb, rock **5** homer **6** homing, pouter, roller **7** carrier, crowned, fantail, tumbler
relative: **4** dove
young: **5** squab

pigeon hawk
6 merlin

pigeonhole
4 slot, sort **5** class, cubby, grade, group, niche **6** recess, shelve **7** catalog **8** category, classify, grouping **10** categorize **11** compartment

piggish
6 greedy **7** selfish, swinish **10** gluttonous

pigheaded
5 rigid **6** dogged, mulish **7** willful **8** contrary, perverse, stubborn **9** obstinate **10** inflexible, unyielding

piglet
5 shoat

pigment
3 dye **4** tint **5** color, paint, stain **8** colorant, dyestuff, tincture
black: **9** lampblack
blue: **4** cyan **5** azure, smalt **6** indigo **7** cyanine **8** cerulean **9** verdigris **11** ultramarine
brown: **5** sepia
umber: **6** bister, sienna
combining form: **5** chrom **6** chromo
dark: **7** melanin
green: **7** celadon **8** viridian **10** biliverdin
orange: **7** realgar **8** carotene
red: **4** lake **5** eosin
toxic: **8** gossypol
yellow: **5** ocher, ochre **6** flavin, lutein **7** flavine, xanthin

pigpen
3 sty **4** dump, mess **5** hovel

pigskin
6 saddle **8** football

pike
4 dive, Esox, fish **5** spear **7** highway **8** pickerel

piker
5 miser **7** scrooge **8** tightwad **9** skinflint **10** cheapskate **12** penny-pincher

pilaster
4 pier **6** column, pillar

pilchard
7 herring, sardine

pile
3 fur, lot, nap **4** coat, fill, heap, hill, load, mass, much, pack, peck, pyre, rick **5** amass, crowd, drive, mound, stack **6** bundle, column, jumble **7** collect, fortune, reactor **8** quantity **9** great deal **10** assemblage, collection **11** aggregation **12** accumulation

pileup
4 mass **5** crash, smash **8** accident **9** collision **12** accumulation

pilfer
3 rob **4** lift, take **5** filch, pinch, steal, swipe **6** finger, snitch, thieve **7** purloin **11** appropriate

pilgarlic
4 butt **8** baldhead **13** laughingstock

Pilgrim
5 Alden (John) **6** Carver (John) **7** Puritan,

Winslow (Edward) **8** Bradford (William), Brewster (William), Standish (Myles)
interpreter: **7** Squanto
ship: **9** Mayflower

pilgrim
5 hadji, hajji **6** palmer **8** traveler, wanderer, wayfarer

pilgrimage
4 hadj, hajj, trip **7** journey
destination: **5** Mecca **6** Assisi, Delphi, Dodona, Fátima, Medina **7** Lourdes **8** Bodh Gaya **10** Canterbury, Kusinagara

Pilgrim's Progress
8 allegory
author: **6** Bunyan (John)
hero: **9** Christian

pill
4 ball, bore, pain, pest **5** bolus **6** pellet **7** capsule, lozenge **8** medicine, nuisance **9** annoyance

pillage
4 lift, loot, sack **5** booty, prize, reave, reive, spoil, steal **6** maraud, ravage, thieve **7** despoil, plunder, purloin **8** spoliate **9** depredate, desecrate

pillar
4 pier, post, prop **5** pylon, shaft, stela, stele **6** column, stelae (plural) **7** obelisk, support, upright **8** backbone, mainstay, pedestal, pilaster

pillory
6 stocks

pillow
3 pad **4** rest **7** bolster, cushion, support

pillowcase
4 sham

pilot
3 ace **4** lead, show, tool **5** drive, flier, guide, steer **6** airman, direct, leader **7** aviator, conduct, guiding, tracing **8** aviatrix, helmsman, shepherd
seat: **7** cockpit

pimple
3 dot, zit **4** acne, boil, spot, stud **6** papule **7** blemish, blister, pustule, speckle **8** sprinkle, swelling

pin
3 leg, peg **4** clip, hold, join **5** affix, blame, rivet, stake **6** attach, broach, brooch, cotter, emblem, fasten, secure, trifle **8** fastener, hold down, ornament, restrain

pinafore
5 apron, dress, frock

pinch
3 bit, nab, nip **4** dash, lift, pain, take **5** filch, press, prune, run in, skimp, steal, swipe, taper, theft, tweak **6** arrest, crisis, narrow, pilfer, snatch, stress **7** confine, deficit, larceny, squeeze, straits **8** compress, exigency, hardship, juncture, pressure, stealing, straiten **9** apprehend, constrict, emergency, privation, tight spot **10** substitute

pinchbeck
4 fake, sham **5** alloy, bogus, false, phony **6** pseudo **8** spurious **9** brummagem **11** counterfeit

pinch hitter
3 sub **6** backup, fill-in, relief **7** stand-in **9** alternate, surrogate **10** substitute **11** alternative, replacement

pinchpenny
4 mean **5** cheap, close, mingy, tight **6** stingy **7** chintzy, costive, miserly, scrimpy **9** niggardly, penurious **11** closefisted, tightfisted **12** parsimonious

Pindar
home: **6** Thebes
poem: **3** ode

pine
4 ache, long, mope, sigh, tree, wish, wood **5** brood, crave, dream, yearn **6** desire, grieve, hanker, hunger, lament, thirst **7** conifer **8** languish **9** evergreen
textile screw: **3** ara **4** hala **7** lauhala

Pine Tree State
5 Maine

pinhead
4 dolt, dope, fool **5** dunce **6** dimwit, doofus, nitwit **7** dullard **8** dumbbell **9** birdbrain

pinion
3 cog **4** bind, gear, wing **5** quill, tie up, truss **6** fetter, tether **7** disable, feather, shackle **8** cogwheel, restrain **9** hamstring

pink
3 cut **4** best, peak, stab **5** blush **6** flower, height, pierce **7** excited, paragon **9** perforate

pinna
3 ear, fin **4** wing **7** feather, leaflet

pinnacle
3 top, tor **4** acme, apex, peak **5** crest, crown, serac, spire **6** apogee, climax, height, summit, zenith **7** steeple **8** capsheaf, meridian **11** culmination

pinniped
4 seal **6** walrus

Pinocchio author
7 Collodi (Carlo) **9** Lorenzini (Carlo)

pinochle
card: **3** ace, ten **4** jack, king, nine **5** queen
term: **4** meld **5** widow **7** auction
two-handed: **7** goulash

pinpoint
3 aim, fix **4** spot, tiny **5** exact, place **6** locate **7** precise **8** identify, stand out **9** determine, highlight, recognize **11** distinguish

Pinter play
8 Betrayal **9** Caretaker (The) **10** Homecoming (The)

pinto
4 pied, pony **5** horse, paint **7** mottled, piebald **8** skewbald

pint-size
3 wee **5** dwarf, small **6** midget, pocket **9** miniature **10** diminutive

pioneer
5 first, prime **6** maiden **7** explore, founder, initial, primary, settler **8** colonist, earliest, explorer, original **9** innovator **10** avant-garde, pathfinder **11** trailblazer **12** frontiersman
famous: **5** Boone (Daniel), Bowie (Jim), Clark (William), Lewis (Meriwether) **6** Carson (Kit), Colter (John) **7** Bridger (Jim), Chapman (John), Frémont (John C.), Whitman (Marcus) **8** Crockett (Davy)

pious
4 holy **5** godly **6** devout, worthy **7** devoted, dutiful **8** reverent, virtuous **9** hypocrite, pietistic, prayerful, religious **10** devotional **12** hypocritical

pip
3 dot **4** blip, peep, seed, spot **5** speck **9** break open

pipe
3 keg, tun **4** butt, cask, duct, flue, hose, tube **5** briar **6** barrel, convey, funnel, siphon **7** channel, conduct, conduit **8** aqueduct, hogshead **10** meerschaum
ceremonial: **7** calumet
part: **4** bowl, stem

pipe down
4 hush **5** dry up, quiet **6** shut up **7** be quiet

pipe dream
4 wish **7** chimera, fantasy **8** illusion

pipeline
5 works **6** system **7** channel, conduit, process **8** activity, supplier **10** connection

pipsqueak
6 shaver, squirt **7** tadpole **8** half-pint, small fry

piquancy
4 zest **5** gusto **6** relish

piquant
4 racy, tart **5** sharp, spicy, tangy, zesty **6** biting, lively, savory, snappy **7** peppery, pungent **8** poignant, spirited **9** flavorful, sparkling **10** appetizing **11** provocative, stimulating

pique
3 irk, vex **4** huff, miff, move **5** anger, annoy, peeve, pride, rouse **6** arouse, excite, nettle, offend, put out **7** dudgeon, offense, provoke, quicken **8** irritate, motivate, vexation **9** aggravate, annoyance, challenge, stimulate **10** exasperate, irritation, resentment

piracy
5 theft **7** lifting, looting, pillage, plunder, robbery **8** stealing, thievery **10** plagiarism

piranha
6 caribe

pirate
5 rover **6** looter, picaro, raider, robber, sea dog **7** brigand, corsair, sea wolf **8** marauder, picaroon, pillager, sea rover **9** buccaneer, plunderer, privateer, sea robber **10** freebooter
address: **5** matey
English: **4** Read (Mary) **5** Bonny (Anne), Teach (Edward) **6** Morgan (Henry) **7** Dampier (William) **10** Blackbeard
flag: **10** Jolly Roger
French: **7** Laffite (Jean), Lafitte (Jean)
Scottish: **4** Kidd (William)

Pirates of Penzance, The
composer: **8** Sullivan (Arthur)
librettist: **7** Gilbert (W. S.)

pirogue
5 canoe **6** dugout

pirouette
4 spin, turn **5** twirl, wheel, whirl

piscator
6 angler **9** fisherman

pismire
3 ant

pistol
3 gat, rod **4** Colt **5** Glock, Luger **6** Magnum, Mauser, roscoe **7** bulldog, handgun **8** revolver, small arm **9** derringer, pepperbox
case: **7** holster

pit
3 vie **4** dent, hell, hole, scar **5** arena, hades, match, shaft, stone **6** cavity, hollow, oppose **7** counter, play off **8** pockmark **11** indentation

Pit and the Pendulum author
3 Poe (Edgar Allan)

pitch
3 dip, set **4** buck, dive, drop, fall, hurl, line, play, plug, tilt, tone, toss **5** erect, fling, heave, lurch, put up, resin, slant, sling, slope, spiel, throw **6** encamp, go down, plunge **7** discard, incline, present, promote, sidearm **8** distance **9** advertise, declivity **13** advertisement
uneven: **3** rub

pitch-dark
3 jet **4** ebon, inky **5** black, ebony, jetty

pitcher
4 ewer, olla, olpe, toby **5** cruse **6** beaker, flagon **7** creamer
area: **5** mound
handle: **3** ear **4** ansa
see also **baseballer**

pitch in
3 aid **4** help **5** begin, set to, start **6** fall to **8** commence, get going, start off **9** subscribe, volunteer **10** contribute

piteous
3 sad **4** poor **8** pathetic **9** affecting **10** lamentable **11** distressing

pitfall
4 risk, snag, trap **5** catch, peril, snare **6** danger, hazard **9** booby trap **10** difficulty **12** entanglement

pith
3 nub **4** core, kill, meat, pulp **5** focus, heart **6** center, import, kernel **7** essence, nucleus **9** substance **10** importance **12** significance

pith helmet
4 topi **5** topee

pithy
5 brief, crisp, meaty, short, terse **6** cogent **7** compact, concise, pointed **8** succinct **12** epigrammatic **13** short and sweet

pitiable
4 poor **5** cheap, sorry **8** shameful **10** deplorable, lamentable **12** contemptible

pitiful
3 sad **4** mean, poor **5** cheap, sorry **6** meager, meagre, paltry, shabby **7** forlorn **8** beggarly, pathetic, wretched **9** miserable **10** despicable, inadequate **12** contemptible **13** heartbreaking

pitiless
4 cold, hard **5** cruel, harsh, stony **6** brutal **8** inhumane, uncaring **9** barbarous, unfeeling **10** unmerciful **11** coldhearted, hardhearted

pittance
4 wage **5** scrap, trace **6** trifle **7** modicum, peanuts **9** allowance

pity
3 rue **4** ache, ruth **5** mercy **6** regret, sorrow **7** empathy, feel for, sadness **8** distress, sympathy **10** compassion, condolence, sympathize **11** commiserate **13** commiseration

pivot
3 pin **4** slew, slue, turn **5** hinge, shaft, swing, wheel **6** center, swivel

pivotal
3 key **5** chief, vital **7** central, crucial **8** critical, decisive **9** essential, important

pixie
3 elf, fay, imp **5** antic, fairy, scamp **6** elvish, impish, rascal, sprite **7** brownie, coltish, playful, puckish **8** prankish **11** mischievous

pixilated
3 fey **7** bemused, erratic, flighty, muddled, touched **9** eccentric, whimsical **10** capricious

Pizarro, Francisco
brother: **7** Gonzalo
city founded: **4** Lima
conquest: **4** Peru
victims: **5** Incas **9** Atahualpa **10** Atahuallpa

pizzazz
3 pep, vim, zip **4** bang, brio, dash, élan, snap, zest, zing **5** éclat, flair, flash, gusto, moxie, oomph, punch, verve **6** dazzle, energy, hoopla, sizzle, spirit **7** glamour, panache **8** vitality **10** excitement

placard
4 bill, post **6** notice, plaque, poster **7** affiche **8** handbill

placate
4 calm, ease **6** pacify, soothe **7** appease, assuage, comfort, mollify, satisfy, sweeten, win over **10** conciliate, propitiate

place
3 lay, put, set **4** area, lieu, loci (plural), post, rank, site, spot, zone **5** locus, point, stead, tract **6** region, status **7** situate, station **8** district, identify, locality, location, pinpoint, position, standing **9** establish, recognize
combining form: **3** top **4** loco, topo, topy

placid
4 calm, easy, mild **5** quiet, still **6** gentle, serene **7** halcyon **8** composed, peaceful, tranquil, waveless, windless **9** unruffled **10** complacent, unagitated, untroubled **11** undisturbed **13** imperturbable

plagiarize
4 copy, crib **5** steal **6** pirate **11** appropriate

plague
3 vex **4** bane, evil, pest **5** annoy, beset, curse, harry, hound, smite, trial, worry **6** blight, bother, infest, harass, hassle, hector, pester **7** afflict, bedevil, disease, disturb, scourge, torment, trouble **8** calamity, distress, epidemic, invasion, irritant, irritate, nuisance, outbreak, pandemic **9** annoyance, beleaguer **10** affliction, black death, pestilence **11** infestation

plaid
6 tartan

plain
3 lea **4** bald, bare, open, pure, veld **5** blunt, clear, field, frank, llano, pampa, usual, veldt **6** candid, common, homely, modest, pampas, patent, severe, simple, steppe, tundra **7** expanse, evident, obvious, prairie, savanna **8** apparent,

distinct, everyday, homespun, manifest, ordinary, savannah, straight **9** outspoken, unadorned **10** absolutely, forthright, unaffected **11** undecorated, unvarnished **13** uncomplicated

plainclothesman
3 tec **4** dick **6** shamus, sleuth **7** gumshoe **8** hawkshaw **9** detective **12** investigator

plainness
6 candor, purity **7** clarity, honesty **8** lucidity **10** simplicity

plainsong
5 chant **12** cantus firmus

plainspoken
4 open **5** frank **6** candid, direct, honest **8** straight, truthful **10** forthright **11** undisguised, unvarnished

plaintive
3 sad **4** glum **6** woeful **7** doleful, piteous, pitiful **8** dolorous, downcast, mournful **9** sorrowful **10** dispirited, lamentable, lugubrious, melancholy

plait
4 fold **5** braid, pleat, weave **7** pigtail **10** intertwine, interweave

plan
3 aim, map, way **4** cast, goal, idea, mean, plot **5** chart, frame **6** design, devise, intend, intent, lay out, map out, method, scheme, set out **7** arrange, diagram, drawing, outline, pattern, program, project, propose, purpose, work out **8** contrive, engineer, organize, strategy, think out **9** blueprint, formulate, intention, procedure **11** arrangement, formulation

plane
3 fly **4** even, flat, tool, tree **5** flush, level **6** smooth
(see also **airplane**)

planet
4 Mars **5** Earth, Venus **6** Saturn, Uranus **7** Jupiter, Mercury, Neptune
dwarf: **4** Eris **5** Ceres, Pluto
path: **5** orbit
satellite: **4** moon
shadow: **5** umbra
small: **8** asteroid

planetary
4 vast **6** global **7** erratic, immense **8** colossal, enormous **9** universal, wandering, worldwide **11** terrestrial

plangent
7 orotund, ringing, vibrant **8** resonant, sonorous **9** consonant, plaintive **10** expressive, resounding **11** reverberant

plank
4 item, wood **5** board, floor **6** lumber, timber **7** article, support

plant
3 fix, pot, set, sow **4** bury, grow, hide, mill, park, root, seed, tomb **5** cache, cover, imbed, inter, place, plunk, put in, stash, works **6** entomb, inhume, occult, screen **7** conceal, factory, install, lay away, put away, secrete **8** colonize, populate **9** cultivate
angiosperm: **5** dicot **7** monocot
aquatic: **4** reed **5** lotus, sedge **7** awlwort, cattail, fanwort, papyrus **8** duckweed, eelgrass, hornwort, pondweed **9** water lily **10** watercress **11** bladderwort **12** pickerelweed
aromatic: **4** nard **6** lovage **9** spikenard
Australian: **6** mallee **7** banksia **8** blackboy **10** eucalyptus
body: **4** stem **7** thallus
bulbous: **4** Ixia, lily **5** camas, onion, tulip **7** jonquil **8** hyacinth **9** narcissus
carnivorous: **6** sundew **10** butterwort **12** pitcher plant, Venus flytrap
cell layer: **7** phellem
climbing: **3** ivy **4** vine **5** betel, liana, vetch **6** bryony, derris, smilax **7** creeper, jasmine **8** bignonia, fumitory, moonseed, scammony, wisteria **12** morning glory
coloring agent: **8** carotene **11** chlorophyll, xanthophyll
combining form: **4** phyt **5** phyto
cone-bearing: **3** fir, yew **4** pine **5** cedar, cycad **6** ginkgo, spruce **7** conifer, cypress, redwood **10** arborvitae, gymnosperm
desert: **4** aloe **5** agave **6** cactus, cholla **8** mesquite, ocotillo **9** paloverde **11** brittlebush
disease: **3** rot **4** gall, mold, rust, scab, smut, wilt **5** ergot **6** blight, mildew, mosaic **7** blister **8** clubroot **9** black spot **10** black heart
extinct: **8** calamite
flowerless: **4** alga, fern, kelp, moss **5** algae (plural), fungi (plural) **6** fungus, lichen **7** seaweed **8** clubmoss **9** bryophyte, equisetum, horsetail, liverwort
fluid: **3** gum, sap **4** milk **5** latex, resin
gland: **7** nectary
hallucinogenic: **4** hemp **5** poppy **6** mescal **8** cannabis **9** marijuana
hard-to-grow: **5** miffy
largest: **7** sequoia
life: **5** flora
marine: **4** kelp, nori **5** dulse, fucus **6** wakame **7** seaweed **8** gulfweed **10** sea lettuce
marsh: **4** reed **5** carex, sedge **7** bogbean, bulrush, calamus, cattail **8** red maple, sphagnum **10** rose mallow **11** loosestrife
medicinal: **4** aloe, sage **5** poppy, senna, tansy **6** catnip, fennel, garlic, hyssop, ipecac, nettle **7** aconite, boneset, burdock, camphor, comfrey, ginseng, hemlock, henbane, juniper, lobelia, mullein, mustard, parsley **8** camomile, capsicum,

cinchona, feverfew, licorice, pilewort, plantain, wormwood **9** asafetida, chamomile, dandelion, echinacea, fenugreek, monkshood **10** asafoetida, goldenseal, peppermint
microscopic: **4** mold **6** diatom **7** euglena **8** bacteria (plural) **9** bacterium
oldest: **11** bristlecone
onion-like: **4** leek **5** chive **7** shallot **8** scallion
opening: **5** stoma **7** stomata (plural)
parasitic: **6** dodder, fungus **7** pinesap **8** gerardia **9** broomrape, mistletoe, rafflesia, witchweed **10** beechdrops
part: **3** bud, nut, sap **4** bark, bulb, cell, cone, corm, leaf, pome, root, seed, stem, wood **5** bract, drupe, fruit, grain, spore, stool, thorn, tuber, xylem **6** catkin, flower, nectar, phloem, raceme, spadix **7** rhizome **8** lenticel **9** cellulose, cotyledon **11** chlorophyll, chloroplast **13** inflorescence
pepper: **3** ava **4** kava
pest: **5** aphid, scale **6** chafer, thrips, weevil **7** cutworm **8** fruit fly, wireworm **9** gypsy moth **10** cankerworm, leafhopper, phylloxera **11** codling moth
poisonous: **4** poke, upas **5** sumac **6** castor, croton, datura **7** amanita, cassava, cowbane, henbane, lobelia, tobacco **8** foxglove, larkspur, locoweed, mayapple, oleander, pokeweed **9** baneberry, monkshood **10** belladonna, jimsonweed, manchineel, nightshade
saprophytic: **5** fungi (plural) **6** fungus **7** pinesap **9** pinedrops, snow plant **10** beechdrops, Indian pipe
succulent: **4** aloe **5** agave **6** cactus **10** bitterroot
thorny: **4** rose **5** briar **6** cactus, nettle, teasel **7** caltrop, thistle **9** cocklebur
tissue: **5** xylem **6** phloem **7** cambium, medulla **8** meristem
young: **5** scion, shoot **6** sprout **7** cutting **8** seedling

plantain
5 fruit **6** banana

plantation
5 manor **6** colony, estate, quinta **7** acreage, demesne **8** hacienda **10** encampment, habitation, settlement

plant louse
5 aphid

plaque
4 film **5** badge, patch **6** brooch, lesion, tablet **7** tribute **8** bacteria, memorial **13** commemoration

plaster
3 dab **4** coat **5** affix, cover, gesso **6** stucco **7** coating, conceal, overlay **8** dressing
of paris: **5** gesso **6** gypsum

plastered
3 lit **4** high **5** drunk, lit up, oiled **6** bashed, blotto, bombed, juiced, potted, soaked, soused, stewed, stoned, tanked, wasted, zonked **7** crocked, drunken, pickled, pie-eyed, sloshed, smashed, sottish **10** inebriated, liquored up **11** intoxicated

plastic
4 soft **5** vinyl **6** pliant, supple **7** ductile, pliable **8** creative, flexible, moldable, workable **9** adaptable, formative, malleable, synthetic **10** artificial, credit card, sculptural

plat
3 lot, map **4** plan **5** chart, tract **6** parcel **7** quadrat

plate
4 base, coat, disc, dish, disk, gild, tile **5** layer, paten, scute, slice **6** enamel, fascia, lamina, plaque **7** anodize, lamella, overlay

plateau
4 mesa **5** table **6** upland **9** altiplano, tableland
arid: **4** puna
barren: **5** field **6** paramo
dry: **5** karoo **6** karroo

platform
3 map **4** bank, base, dais, deck, plan **5** bimah, forum, ledge, riser, shelf, stage, stump **6** design, pallet, perron, podium, pulpit, scheme **7** balcony, pattern, rostrum **8** hustings, scaffold **9** banquette, manifesto **11** declaration
temporary: **7** staging **8** scaffold
wooden: **9** boardwalk

Plath, Sylvia
novel: **7** Bell Jar (The)
poem: **5** Ariel, Daddy

platinum symbol
2 Pt

platitude
6 cliché, truism **7** bromide **8** banality, prosaism **10** shibboleth

Plato
father: **7** Ariston
literary form: **6** dialog **8** dialogue
original name: **10** Aristocles
school: **7** Academy
work: **3** Ion **4** Meno **5** Crito, Lysis **6** Laches, Phaedo **7** Apology, Gorgias **8** Phaedrus, Republic (The) **9** Charmides, Symposium

platter
5 plate **6** record **8** trencher

platypus
8 duckbill

plaudits
5 kudos **6** cheers, praise **7** acclaim, ovation **8** applause, approval, encomium **9** accolades **11** acclamation

plausible
8 credible, specious **10** believable, convincing, creditable, persuasive, reasonable

play
3 act, fun **4** game, jest, joke, romp **5** drama, feint, serve, sport, treat, trick, wager **6** cavort, comedy, fiddle, frolic, gambit, gambol, leeway, margin **7** delight, disport, perform **8** latitude, pleasure **9** amusement, diversion, enjoyment, stratagem **10** manipulate, recreation
an instrument: **3** bow **4** beat, blow, pick **5** pluck, sound, strum **6** strike **7** squeeze
kind: **5** farce **6** comedy **7** musical, tragedy **8** one-acter **9** melodrama, pantomime
part: **3** act **5** scene **8** epilogue, prologue
passionate: **9** melodrama
site: **8** stage set

playact
5 put on **7** perform, posture, pretend **9** personate **11** impersonate, make believe

playboy
4 rake, roué **7** swinger **8** hedonist, lothario **9** bon vivant, libertine

play down
8 minimize **9** deprecate, soft-pedal, underrate **11** de-emphasize

player
5 actor **6** mummer **7** actress, athlete, trouper **8** musician, thespian **9** contender, performer **10** competitor, contestant **11** participant
reserve: **11** benchwarmer

player piano
7 Pianola **10** Disklavier

play for time
5 stall

playful
5 antic, jolly, ludic, merry, pixie **6** elvish, frisky, impish, jocund, joking, jovial, lively **7** coltish, jocular, puckish, waggish **8** humorous, sportive **9** kittenish, sprightly **10** frolicsome

play off
3 pit, vie **5** match **6** oppose **7** counter **8** contrast

plaything
3 toy

play up
6 stress **7** feature **9** dramatize, emphasize, highlight, overstate, underline **10** accentuate, exaggerate, underscore

playwright
9 dramatist **10** dramaturge
(see also **dramatist**)

plaza
6 circus, common, square, zocalo **9** carrefour **11** marketplace

plea
4 suit **5** alibi **6** appeal, excuse, orison, prayer **7** apology, defense, pretext, request **8** entreaty, overture, petition **11** application, imploration **12** supplication
defendant's: **4** nolo **6** guilty **8** innocent **9** not guilty

plead
3 beg **4** pray **5** argue **6** allege, answer, appeal **7** beseech, entreat, implore **8** advocate, maintain **9** importune **10** supplicate

pleasant
4 fair, fine, good, nice **5** clear, sunny, sweet **6** cheery, genial, pretty **7** amiable, clarion, likable, welcome **8** amicable, charming, cheerful, engaging, gracious, grateful, likeable, pleasing, sunshine, sunshiny **9** agreeable, appealing, cloudless, congenial, convivial, enjoyable, favorable, unclouded **10** delightful, gratifying

pleasantry
3 fun **4** jest, joke **6** banter, levity **8** badinage, repartee **9** wittiness **10** jocularity

please
4 like, suit, wish **5** agree, amuse, enjoy, serve **6** choose **7** content, delight, gladden, gratify, indulge, satisfy
French: **12** s'il vous plait
German: **5** bitte
Spanish: **8** por favor

pleasing
4 good, nice **6** pretty **7** welcome **8** suitable **9** agreeable, congenial, favorable, palatable **10** attractive, delightful, gratifying **12** satisfactory

pleasure
3 fun, joy **4** will **5** bliss, fancy **6** desire, liking, relish **7** delight, gladden, gratify **8** felicity, gladness, hedonism **9** amusement, diversion, enjoyment, happiness, merriment **11** inclination

pleat
4 fold **5** crimp **6** crease

plebe
5 frosh **8** freshman

plebeian
3 low **4** base **5** crude, lowly **6** coarse, common, humble, menial **8** commoner, everyday, ordinary **10** lower-class

plebiscite
4 vote

plectrum
4 pick

pledge
3 vow **4** bail, bind, bond, gage, hock, oath, pawn, seal, sign, word **5** drink, swear, toast, token **6** parole, plight, surety **7** chattel, earnest,

promise, warrant **8** bailment, contract, covenant, guaranty, security, warranty **9** agreement, assurance, certainty, guarantee, undertake **11** hypothecate

pledget
3 pad **8** compress

Pleiades
4 Maia **6** Merope **7** Alcyone, Celaeno, Electra, Sterope, Taygeta **8** Asterope
brightest star: **7** Alcyone

plenary
4 full **5** whole **6** entire **7** general **8** absolute, complete **9** inclusive **11** unqualified **12** unrestricted

plenitude
4 glut **6** excess **7** satiety, surfeit **8** fullness **9** abundance, profusion, repletion **11** copiousness, sufficiency, superfluity **12** completeness

plenteous
7 fertile **8** abundant, fruitful, prolific **9** abounding **10** productive

plentiful
4 full, rich, rife **5** ample, flush **7** copious, profuse **8** abundant, affluent, generous **9** abounding, bounteous, unstinted **10** sufficient

plenty
3 lot **4** heap, lots, pack, peck, pile **6** stacks, wealth **8** adequacy, fullness, mountain **9** abundance, affluence, great deal **10** cornucopia

pleonasm
8 verbiage **9** prolixity, tautology, verbosity, wordiness **10** redundancy **11** periphrasis, superfluity

plethora
4 glut **5** flood **6** excess **7** overrun, surfeit, surplus **8** fullness, overflow **9** abundance, profusion, repletion **11** superfluity **13** overabundance

plexus
4 rete **7** network

pliable
6 supple **7** plastic **9** adaptable **10** adjustable **11** complaisant, manipulable

pliant
5 lithe **6** limber, supple **7** ductile, plastic, springy **8** flexible, moldable, workable, yielding **9** adaptable, malleable, tractable **10** manageable

plica
4 fold **6** crease, groove

plight
3 fix, jam, vow **4** hole, spot, word **5** swear **6** engage, pickle, pledge, scrape **7** betroth, dilemma, promise **8** quandary **9** betrothal **10** difficulty, engagement **11** predicament

plod
4 slog, toil **5** grind, slave, tramp, tread, tromp **6** drudge, lumber, trudge **8** plug away

plot
3 map **4** area, land, mark, note, plan, ruse **5** cabal, chart, story, tract **6** design, devise, invent, lay out, locate, parcel, scheme **7** collude, compact, connive, diagram, outline **8** conspire, contrive, intrigue, scenario **9** collusion, conniving, machinate **10** complicity, connivance, conspiracy **11** machination

plover
5 pewit, stilt **6** peewit **7** lapwing **8** dotterel, killdeer
relative: **9** sandpiper, turnstone

plow
3 dig **4** till, turn **5** break **6** furrow, harrow, trench **8** turn over **9** cultivate
part: **4** beam, frog **5** share **7** coulter **8** landside **9** moldboard

ploy
4 ruse, scam, wile **5** feint, trick **6** device, frolic, gambit, tactic **7** gimmick **8** artifice, escapade, maneuver **9** stratagem **11** contrivance

pluck
3 rob, tug **4** grit, guts, pick, pull, yank **5** cheek, grasp, heart, moxie, nerve, spunk **6** daring, fleece, mettle, remove, snatch, spirit, tweeze **7** bravery, courage, pull out

plucky
4 bold, game **5** brave **6** feisty, spunky **7** doughty **8** fearless, spirited, unafraid **9** dauntless **10** courageous

plug
3 tap **4** bung, clog, core, cork, fill, hype, pack, push, stop, tout **5** block, blurb, boost, choke, close, cry up, shoot, spile **6** device, remedy **7** congest, fitting, hydrant, promote, stopper **8** obstruct **9** advertise, publicity, publicize **10** connection

plug-ugly
4 goon, thug **5** bully, rowdy, tough **7** goombah, hoodlum, ruffian **8** enforcer **9** roughneck

plum
5 prize **6** purple, reward **7** guerdon, premium **8** dividend
dried: **5** prune
kind: **6** damson **7** bullace **9** greengage
spiny: **4** sloe **10** blackthorn

plumage
8 feathers
early: **4** down

plumb
5 delve, probe, sound **6** fathom, weight **7** examine, explore, install, measure **8** vertical **10** vertically **13** perpendicular

plume
4 tail **5** array, preen, pride, prize **6** column **7** feather **8** aigrette

plummet
4 dive, drop, fall **5** crash **6** plunge, tumble **8** collapse, nose-dive **11** precipitate

plump
3 fat **4** drop, fall, full **5** ample, buxom, favor, pudgy, round, stout, tubby **6** chubby, portly, rotund, zaftig **7** rounded, support **8** roly-poly **9** pneumatic **10** Rubenesque

plumply
7 frankly, plainly **8** candidly **12** forthrightly

plunder
3 rob **4** loot, sack, swag, take **5** booty, prize, seize, spoil, steal, strip **6** boodle, rapine, spoils **7** despoil, pillage, ransack, relieve, stick up **9** pillaging

plunge
3 bet, ram, run **4** dive, drop, fall, jump, rush, sink, stab, swim **5** drive, lunge, pitch, stick **6** charge, gamble, hasten, hurtle, thrust, topple, tumble **7** descend, immerse, plummet **8** nose-dive, submerge **9** penetrate

plus
3 and **4** also, more, perk **5** added, asset, bonus, boost, extra **6** excess **7** benefit **8** addition, increase, positive

plush
4 full, rich **6** deluxe, fabric, lavish, velvet **7** opulent **8** luscious, palatial **9** expensive, luxuriant, luxurious, sumptuous

Pluto
3 Dis **5** Hades
brother: 4 Zeus **7** Jupiter, Neptune **8** Poseidon
father: 6 Cronus, Saturn
mother: 3 Ops **4** Rhea
wife: 10 Persephone, Proserpina

plutocrat
5 mogul **6** fat cat, tycoon **7** magnate **9** financier, moneybags **10** capitalist

plutonian
8 infernal **10** underworld

plutonium symbol
2 Pu

Plutus
father: 6 Iasion
god of: 6 riches, wealth
mother: 5 Ceres **7** Demeter

ply
3 use **4** bias, sail **5** apply, exert, layer, wield **6** employ, handle, strand, supply, travel, voyage **7** furnish, perform **8** maneuver, practice **11** inclination

pneuma
4 soul **5** anima **6** psyche, spirit

pneumatic
4 airy **5** ample, buxom, plump **6** aerial, zaftig **9** spiritual **10** curvaceous **11** atmospheric

poach
4 cook **5** steal **6** coddle, simmer **7** intrude **8** encroach, trespass **9** interlope **11** appropriate

Pocahontas
father: 8 Powhatan
husband: 5 Rolfe (John)

pock
3 pit **4** hole, spot **7** pustule

pocket
3 bag **4** lift, sack **5** filch, pinch, pouch, purse, steal, swipe **6** cavity **7** capsule, dead end, impasse **8** cul-de-sac **9** condensed **10** blind alley
billiards: 4 pool

pocketbook
3 bag **4** poke **5** purse **6** clutch, income, wallet **7** handbag **8** billfold **9** clutch bag

pocket bread
4 pita **5** pitta

pocket money
6 change **9** petty cash **11** small change

pocket-size
4 tiny **5** small **9** miniature **10** diminutive

pod
3 bag, gam, sac **4** boll, case, hull, husk, skin **5** shell, shuck **6** cocoon **7** capsule, silique **8** seedcase
plant: 3 pea **4** bean, okra **5** chili, gumbo **6** cassia, cowpea, legume, lentil, peanut, pepper **8** capsicum, mesquite, milkweed **9** lespedeza

pod-bearing tree
5 carob **6** locust **7** catalpa

podiatry
9 chiropody

podium
4 dais **6** pulpit **7** lectern, rostrum **8** platform

___ podrida
4 olla

Poe, Edgar Allan
detective: 5 Dupin (C. Auguste)
poem: 5 Bells (The), Raven (The) **6** Lenore **7** Israfel, To Helen, Ulalume **8** Eldorado, For Annie **10** Annabel Lee
tale: 6 Ligeia, Shadow **7** Gold-Bug (The), Morella, Silence **8** Black Cat (The) **13** Tell-tale Heart (The) **15** Purloined Letter (The) **17** Cask of Amontillado (The), Pit and the Pendulum (The) **19** Masque of the Red Death (The) **21** Fall of the House of Usher (The)

poem
3 ode **4** epic, epos, idyl, rime, rune, song **5** ditty, elegy, epode, idyll, lyric, rhyme, verse **6** ballad, epopee, jingle, rondel, sonnet **7** eclogue, rondeau **8** limerick, madrigal
closing: **5** envoi, envoy
division: **4** foot, line **5** canto, epode, stich, verse **6** stanza **7** refrain **8** epilogue, prologue
Japanese: **5** haiku, tanka
of eight lines: **6** octave **7** triolet
of four lines: **8** quatrain
of fourteen lines: **6** sonnet
of three lines: **7** triplet
pastoral: **7** eclogue, georgic
short: **5** ditty **7** epigram

poet
4 bard, muse, scop **5** skald **6** lyrist **7** elegist **8** idyllist, lyricist **9** balladist, sonneteer **10** Parnassian
American: **3** Poe (Edgar Allan) **4** Dove (Rita), Hass (Robert), Nash (Ogden), Read (Thomas), Rich (Adrienne), Tabb (John Banister), Tate (Allen) **5** Auden (Wystan Hugh), Benét (Stephen Vincent), Crane (Hart), Field (Eugene), Frost (Robert), Guest (Edgar), Moore (Marianne), Plath (Sylvia), Pound (Ezra), Riley (James Whitcomb), Wylie (Elinor) **6** Barlow (Joel), Bishop (Elizabeth), Brooks (Gwendolyn), Bryant (William Cullen), Ciardi (John), Dickey (James), Dunbar (Paul Laurence), Hughes (Langston), Kilmer (Joyce), Lanier (Sidney), Lowell (Amy, James Russell, Robert), McKuen (Rod), Millay (Edna St. Vincent), Pinsky (Robert), Ransom (John Crowe), Seeger (Alan), Strand (Mark), Taylor (Edward), Warren (Robert Penn), Wilbur (Richard) **7** Angelou (Maya), Ashbery (John), Emerson (Ralph Waldo), Freneau (Philip), Halleck (Fitz-Greene), Jeffers (Robinson), Lindsay (Vachel), Markham (Edwin), Merrill (James), Nemerov (Howard), Roethke (Theodore), Shapiro (Karl), Stevens (Wallace), Whitman (Walt) **8** Berryman (John), Cummings (E. E.), Ginsberg (Allen), MacLeish (Archibald), Robinson (Edwin Arlington), Sandburg (Carl), Teasdale (Sara), Wheatley (Phillis), Whittier (John Greenleaf), Williams (C. K., William Carlos) **9** Dickinson (Emily), Santayana (George) **10** Bradstreet (Anne), Longfellow (Henry Wadsworth) **12** Wigglesworth (Michael)
Anglo-Saxon: **7** Caedmon, Cynwulf **8** Cynewulf, Kynewulf
Arab: **5** Jarir **6** Hariri **8** al-Hariri
Australian: **8** Paterson (Andrew Barton)
Belgian: **11** Maeterlinck (Maurice)
Canadian: **5** Pratt (Edwin John) **6** Hébert (Anne) **7** Roberts (Charles G. D.), Service (Robert) **8** Drummond (William Henry) **9** Fréchette (Louis-Honoré)
Chilean: **6** Neruda (Pablo) **7** Mistral (Gabriela)
Chinese: **4** Li Po, Tu Fu **7** Wang Wei
Danish: **4** Rode (Helge) **5** Ewald (Johannes)
English: **3** Gay (John) **4** Gray (Thomas), Owen (Wilfred), Pope (Alexander), Rowe (Nicholas), Tate (Nahum), Wyat (Thomas) **5** Blake (William), Byron (Lord), Carew (Thomas), Clare (John), Donne (John), Eliot (Thomas Stearns), Gower (John), Hardy (Thomas), Keats (John), Noyes (Alfred), Wilde (Oscar), Wyatt (Thomas), Young (Edward) **6** Arnold (Matthew), Austin (Alfred), Belloc (Hilaire), Brooke (Rupert), Butler (Samuel), Clough (Arthur Hugh), Cowper (William), Dryden (John), Graves (Robert), Larkin (Philip), Milton (John), Savage (Richard), Sidney (Philip), Surrey (Earl of), Symons (Arthur), Waller (Edmund), Warton (Thomas), Watson (William), Wotton (Henry) **7** Bridges (Robert), Campion (Thomas), Chaucer (Geoffrey), Gilbert (W. S.), Herbert (George), Herrick (Robert), Hopkins (Gerard Manley), Housman (A. E.), Kipling (Rudyard), Layamon, Marvell (Andrew), Patmore (Coventry), Quarles (Francis), Shelley (Percy Bysshe), Skelton (John), Southey (Robert), Spender (Stephen), Spenser (Edmund) **8** Betjeman (John), Browning (Elizabeth Barrett, Robert), de la Mare (Walter), Langland (William), Lovelace (Richard), Meredith (George), Rossetti (Christina, Dante Gabriel), Suckling (John), Tennyson (Alfred Lord), Thompson (Francis) **9** Coleridge (Samuel Taylor), Masefield (John), Swinburne (Algernon Charles) **10** Chatterton (Thomas), FitzGerald (Edward), Wordsworth (William) **11** Shakespeare (William)
Finnish: **8** Runeberg (Johan Ludvig)
French: **5** Marot (Clément) **6** Musset (Alfred de), Valéry (Paul), Villon (François) **7** Bourget (Paul), Chénier (André de, Marie-Joseph), Gautier (Théophile), Rimbaud (Arthur), Ronsard (Pierre de) **8** Malherbe (François de), Mallarmé (Stéphane), Verlaine (Paul) **9** Lamartine (Alphonse de) **10** Baudelaire (Charles) **11** Apollinaire (Guillaume)
German: **5** Heine (Heinrich), Rilke (Rainer Maria), Sachs (Hans), Storm (Theodor) **6** Brecht (Bertolt), Goethe (Johann Wolfgang von), Uhland (Ludwig) **7** Walther (von der Vogelweide), Wolfram (von Eschenbach) **8** Schiller (Friedrich von) **9** Klopstock (Friedrich Gottlieb) **10** Tannhäuser
Greek: **5** Arion, Homer **6** Elytis (Odysseus), Erinna, Hesiod, Pindar, Ritsos (Yannis), Sappho **7** Agathon, Alcaeus, Orpheus, Seferis (George), Thespis **8** Anacreon **9** Simonides **10** Apollonius, Theocritus

Hindu: **5** Naidu (Sarojini) **6** Tagore (Rabindranath) **8** Kalidasa, Tulsidas
Hungarian: **6** Petofi (Sandor), Zrinyi (Miklos)
Irish: **5** Moore (Thomas), Wolfe (Charles), Yeats (William Butler) **6** Heaney (Seamus) **7** Dunsany (Lord) **8** Drummond (William Henry), MacNeice (Louis)
Italian: **4** Rosa (Salvator), Vida (Marco) **5** Dante (Alighieri), Tasso (Torquato) **7** Ariosto (Ludovico), Manzoni (Alessandro), Montale (Eugenio) **8** Carducci (Giosuè), Leopardi (Giacomo), Petrarch **9** Boccaccio (Giovanni), D'Annunzio (Gabriele), Marinetti (Filippo Tommaso), Quasimodo (Salvatore), Ungaretti (Giuseppe)
Japanese: **5** Basho **6** Matsuo
medieval: **8** minstrel, trouvère **10** troubadour
Mexican: **3** Paz (Octavio)
nonsense: **4** Lear (Edward) **7** Dr. Seuss
Norwegian: **8** Bjornson (Bjornstjerne), Welhaven (Johan) **9** Wergeland (Henrik)
Persian: **4** Sadi **5** Attar, Hafez, Hafiz **11** Omar Khayyám
Roman: **4** Ovid **6** Horace, Vergil, Virgil **7** Juvenal, Martial, Statius **8** Catullus, Tibullus **9** Lucretius
Russian: **4** Blok (Aleksandr) **7** Brodsky (Joseph), Pushkin (Aleksandr), Yesenin (Sergey) **9** Akhmatova (Anna), Kheraskov (Mikhail), Pasternak (Boris), Tsvetaeva (Marina) **10** Mandelstam (Osip), Mayakovsky (Vladimir) **11** Yevtushenko (Yevgeny)
Saint Lucian: **7** Walcott (Derek)
Scottish: **4** Hogg (James), Muir (Edwin) **5** Burns (Robert), Scott (Alexander, Walter) **6** Dunbar (William), Ramsay (Allan) **7** Thomson (James) **10** MacDiarmid (Hugh)
Spanish: **5** Lorca (Federico García) **7** Jiménez (Juan Ramón) **8** Figueroa (Francisco) **10** Aleixandre (Vicente) **11** García Lorca (Federico)
Swedish: **5** Sachs (Nelly) **6** Tegner (Esaias) **8** Snoilsky (Carl Johan) **9** Karlfeldt (Erik Axel)
Swiss: **5** Amiel (Henri Frédéric) **9** Spitteler (Carl)
Welsh: **6** Thomas (Dylan) **7** Aneurin, Watkins (Vernon)

poetic
5 lyric **6** dreamy **8** romantic **9** aesthetic, beautiful
word: **3** ere, e'er, thy **4** dost, doth, hast, hath, kine, ne'er, thee, thou, wert, wilt **5** thine **8** forsooth **9** beauteous

poet laureate
British: **3** Pye (Henry) **4** Rowe (Nicholas), Tate (Nahum) **6** Austin (Alfred), Cibber (Colley), Dryden (John), Hughes (Ted), Jonson (Ben), Motion (Andrew) **7** Bridges (Robert), Southey (Robert) **8** Betjeman (John), Davenant (William), Day-Lewis (Cecil), Shadwell (Thomas), Tennyson (Alfred) **9** Masefield (John), Whitehead (William) **10** Wordsworth (William)
American: **4** Dove (Rita), Hall (Donald), Hass (Robert) **5** Glück (Louise) **6** Kooser (Ted), Kunitz (Stanley), Merwin (W. S.), Pinsky (Robert), Strand (Mark), Warren (Robert Penn), Wilbur (Richard) **7** Brodsky (Joseph), Collins (Billy), Nemerov (Howard), Van Duyn (Mona)

poetry
5 verse

poetry term
4 iamb, mora, scan **5** arsis, canto, envoi, ictus, ionic, paeon, rhyme, stave, stich **6** dactyl, septet, sestet, stanza, thesis **7** anapest, cadence, elision, euphony, quintet, refrain, spondee, strophe, trochee **8** chiasmus, choriamb, cinquain, end rhyme, eye rhyme, quatrain, rhopalic **9** decameter, dithyramb, hexameter, near rhyme, octameter, terza rima **10** enjambment, fourteener, heptameter, ottava rima, rhyme royal **11** Alexandrine, antistrophe, heroic verse, rhyme scheme, shaped verse **12** sprung rhythm

Pogo creator
5 Kelly (Walt)

poi
4 taro

poignancy
6 pathos **7** emotion, sadness **9** sentiment

poignant
3 sad **4** keen **5** acute, sharp **6** biting, moving **7** painful, piquant, pointed, pungent **8** incisive, piercing, stirring, touching **9** affecting

point
3 aim, dot, end, jag, nib, tip **4** apex, crux, item, mark, show, site, spot, step, tine, turn, unit **5** motif, place, stage, theme, topic, trace, verge **6** detail, direct, intent, moment, motive, object, period, reason **7** decimal, essence, instant, meaning, purpose, subject **8** headland, juncture, locality, location, particle, position **9** direction **10** promontory **12** significance

pointed
5 acute, sharp **6** barbed, marked, signal **7** salient **8** incisive, striking **9** arresting, pertinent, prominent **11** conspicuous, penetrating

pointer
3 dog, tip **4** clue, hint **5** arrow, guide **6** gundog **9** indicator **10** suggestion

pointillist
6 Seurat (Georges), Signac (Paul) **8** Pissarro (Camille)

pointless
4 idle, vain **5** inane, silly **6** futile **7** useless **8** bootless **9** fruitless, senseless, worthless **10** immaterial, irrelevant, unavailing, unfruitful **11** meaningless **12** unprofitable

point of view
5 angle, slant **7** outlook **8** position, prospect **11** perspective

poise
4 ease, hang, tact **5** brace, grace, hover, skill **6** aplomb, steady **7** address, balance, bearing, dignity, support, suspend **8** carriage, elegance, serenity **9** assurance, composure, diplomacy, sangfroid **10** confidence, equanimity **11** delicatesse, equilibrium, savoir faire, tactfulness

poised
4 calm **6** at ease, serene, steady **7** assured, equable **8** composed, tranquil **9** collected, confident **13** self-possessed

poison
4 bane, upas **5** toxin, venom **6** toxoid **7** arsenic, botulin, cyanide, envenom **8** toxicant **9** botulinum, contagion **10** strychnine **13** contamination
arrow: **4** inée, upas **6** curare **7** ouabain
combining form: **3** tox **4** toxi, toxo **6** toxico

poisoning
food: **8** botulism
lead: **8** plumbism

poisonous
5 toxic **7** baneful, miasmal, nocuous, noxious **8** mephitic, venomous, virulent **9** pestilent **10** pernicious

poke
3 dig, hit, jab, jut, lag, pry **4** cuff, nose, prod, push, sock, stab, stir, urge **5** bulge, dally, delay, elbow, nudge, punch, snoop, tarry **6** dawdle, meddle, pierce, putter, thrust **7** intrude, project, rummage **8** stick out **9** interfere, interject, interpose

poker
bet total: **3** pot
bullet: **3** ace
form: **4** stud
hand: **4** pair **5** flush **8** straight **9** full house **10** royal flush **13** straight flush
ploy: **5** bluff
stake: **4** ante
term: **3** see **4** call, draw, open **5** raise
token: **4** chip

poker-faced
5 blank, staid **7** deadpan, neutral **9** impassive **11** inscrutable, noncommital **12** inexpressive

pokey
3 can, jug, pen **4** brig, coop, jail, stir **5** clink **6** cooler, prison **7** slammer **9** calaboose

poky
4 slow **5** dingy, seedy **6** dreary, shabby **7** cramped, laggard, run-down **8** dilatory, plodding, sluggish

Poland
capital: **6** Warsaw
city: **4** Lódz **6** Gdansk, Kraków, Poznan **7** Wroclaw **8** Katowice, Szczecin
leader: **6** Walesa (Lech)
monetary unit: **5** zloty
mountain range: **10** Carpathian
national hero: **10** Kosciuszko (Thaddeus)
neighbor: **6** Russia **7** Belarus, Germany, Ukraine **8** Slovakia **9** Lithuania **13** Czech Republic
river: **4** Oder **7** Vistula
sea: **6** Baltic

polar
6 arctic **7** pivotal **8** opposite **9** diametric

pole
3 rod **4** punt, spar **5** anode, shaft, staff, stick, stilt **7** cathode
Indian: **5** totem
Scottish: **5** caber

polecat
5 fitch, skunk **6** ferret **7** fitchet

polemic
6 attack, debate, screed, tirade **7** defense, dispute **8** argument, diatribe, harangue, jeremiad **9** assertion, philippic **10** contention, refutation **11** controversy, disputation **12** denunciation, remonstrance

polemical
11 contentious, opinionated **12** disputatious **13** argumentative, controversial

polestar
3 hub **5** focus, guide **10** focal point

police
3 law, man **4** fuzz, heat **6** govern, patrol **7** control, monitor **8** regulate
officer: **3** cop **4** flic, fuzz, heat **5** bobby **6** copper, lawman, peeler **7** John Law, sheriff, trooper **8** bluecoat, Dogberry, flatfoot, gendarme **9** constable, patrolman **11** carabiniere

policy
4 plan **6** course, method, number **7** lottery, program **8** contract, practice **9** procedure **10** management

polio vaccine developer
4 Salk (Jonas) **5** Sabin (Albert)

polish
3 rub, wax **4** buff **5** glaze, glint, gloss, sheen, shine **6** luster, refine, smooth, soften **7** burnish, culture, enhance, improve, perfect, touch up **8** brighten **10** refinement

Polish
dumpling: **6** pirogi **7** pierogi
leader: **6** Walesa (Lech)
patriot: **9** Kosciusko (Thaddeus)
pope: **8** John Paul
sausage: **8** kielbasa, kielbasy
soldier: **7** Pulaski (Casimir)

polish off
5 eat up **6** devour **7** consume, put away **8** dispatch **9** dispose of

polite
5 civil **7** courtly, genteel, refined **8** cultured, mannerly, polished, well-bred **9** attentive, courteous **10** thoughtful **11** considerate **12** well-mannered

politeness
7 manners **8** civility, courtesy **10** refinement

politic
4 wise **5** suave **6** adroit, shrewd, smooth **7** prudent, tactful **8** tactical **9** advisable, expedient, judicious, sagacious **10** diplomatic

political
meeting: **6** caucus
party: **3** GOP **10** Democratic, Republican
system: **7** fascism **9** communism, democracy, socialism

poll
4 cast, clip, crop, head, nape, pate **5** count, shear, tally, votes **6** noggin, record, sample, survey **7** canvass, pollard **8** question **9** interview **10** canvassing
type: **4** exit **5** straw

pollack
4 fish **6** saithe **8** bluefish
family: **3** cod

pollard
3 top **4** crop, tree **7** cut back

pollen-producing organ
6 stamen

pollex
5 thumb

____ polloi
3 hoi

pollster
5 Zogby (John) **6** Gallup (George), Harris (Lou)

pollute
4 foul, soil **5** dirty, spoil, stain, sully, taint **6** befoul, damage, debase, defile **7** corrupt, profane **10** adulterate **11** contaminate

pollution
4 smog **5** abuse **8** impurity **10** defilement

Pollux
10 Polydeuces
brother: **6** Castor
father: **4** Zeus
mother: **4** Leda
sister: **5** Helen **12** Clytemnestra

Pollyanna
8 optimist
author: **6** Porter (Eleanor)

Pollyannaish
6 blithe, cheery, upbeat **8** cheerful, positive **10** optimistic **11** rose-colored

pollywog
7 tadpole

Polonius
daughter: **7** Ophelia
hiding place: **5** arras
slayer: **6** Hamlet
son: **7** Laertes

poltergeist
5 ghost **6** spirit

poltroon
6 coward, craven, yellow **7** chicken, dastard, gutless **8** cowardly **9** dastardly **11** lily-livered

Polydorus
father: **5** Priam **6** Cadmus
mother: **6** Hecuba **8** Harmonia
slayer: **8** Achilles **10** Polymestor **11** Polymnestor

polygon
eight-sided: **7** octagon
five-sided: **8** pentagon
four-sided: **8** tetragon
nine-sided: **7** nonagon
seven-sided: **8** heptagon
six-sided: **7** hexagon
ten-sided: **7** decagon
three-sided: **8** triangle
twelve-sided: **9** dodecagon

Polyhymnia
4 Muse
invention: **4** lyre

polymer
5 amber, nylon **6** rubber, Teflon **7** shellac **8** Bakelite, silicone

Polynesian
5 Maori **6** Samoan, Tongan **8** Hawaiian, Tahitian **9** Marquesan

Polynices
brother: **8** Eteocles
father: **7** Oedipus
mother: **7** Jocasta
wife: **5** Argia **6** Argeia

polyp
5 tumor, zooid **6** growth **7** hydroid
freshwater: **5** hydra

Polyphemus
7 Cyclops
beloved: 7 Galatea
father: 8 Poseidon
victim: 4 Acis

pome
4 pear 5 apple, fruit

pommel
4 knob 6 handle

pomp
4 show 5 array 6 parade, ritual 7 display, fanfare, panoply 8 ceremony, grandeur, splendor 9 pageantry, vainglory 11 ostentation

pompano
4 fish 8 carangid 10 butterfish

Pompeii's volcano
8 Vesuvius

pompous
4 vain 5 proud, showy 6 lordly, ornate, stuffy 7 stuck-up 8 arrogant, boastful, inflated 9 bombastic, conceited, important, overblown 10 egocentric, flamboyant, pontifical 11 magisterial, pretentious 12 ostentatious, vainglorious

pond
4 mere, pool, tarn 5 stank 6 lagoon
growth: 4 scum 5 algae

ponder
4 mull, muse 5 study, think, weigh 6 reason 7 examine, perpend, reflect 8 appraise, cogitate, consider, evaluate, meditate, mull over, ruminate 9 reflect on, speculate 10 deliberate, think about 11 contemplate

ponderous
4 dull 5 heavy 6 clumsy, dreary, stodgy, wooden 7 labored, massive, weighty 8 cumbrous, lifeless, plodding, unwieldy 9 lumbering 10 burdensome, cumbersome, oppressive

poniard
6 dagger

Ponte Vecchio
city: 8 Florence
river: 4 Arno

Pontiac
5 chief
tribe: 6 Ottawa

pontiff
4 pope

pontifical
7 pompous 8 dogmatic 9 episcopal 11 magisterial

pony
4 crib, trot 5 horse 6 bronco, cayuse 7 mustang
breed: 6 Exmoor 8 Shetland

pony up
3 pay 6 lay out, pay out 7 dish out, dole out, fork out 8 hand over, shell out, turn over 10 compensate, remunerate

pooch
3 dog, pup 4 tyke 5 hound, puppy 6 bowwow, canine

Pooh
creator: 5 Milne (A. A.)
friend: 5 Kanga 6 Eeyore, Piglet, Tigger
illustrator: 7 Shepard (Ernest)

pooh-bah
3 VIP 4 czar, king, star, tsar, tzar 5 baron, heavy, mogul 6 big gun, bigwig, honcho, kahuna, prince, worthy 7 big name, big shot, kingpin, magnate, notable 8 big wheel, eminence, luminary 9 big cheese, personage, superstar 11 heavyweight

pooh-pooh
5 scorn 6 deride 7 disdain, dismiss, sneer at 8 minimize, play down

pool
3 pot 4 mere, pond, tarn 5 chain, group, kitty, merge, trust 6 cartel, lagoon, laguna, puddle 7 combine, jackpot 9 syndicate
player: 7 Mosconi (Willie) 13 Minnesota Fats
(see also **billiards**)

poop
4 dirt, info, tire 7 fatigue

poor
4 base, mean 5 broke, needy, scant, skimp, spare 6 humble, meager, meagre, paltry, scanty, skimpy, sparse 8 bankrupt, beggarly, indigent, strapped 9 destitute, insolvent, penniless, penurious 10 down-and-out, pauperized, stone-broke 11 impecunious, necessitous

poorly
3 ill, low 4 sick 5 badly 6 ailing, sickly, unwell 10 indisposed 11 imperfectly

pop
3 dad, dot, gun, hit, try 4 dada, dart, ding, shot, slap, slog, sock, soda 5 catch, crack, daddy, drink, fling, shoot, whack, whirl 6 attack, bug out, effort, father, strike 7 assault, attempt, explode 8 backfire

pop artist
5 Blake (Peter), Johns (Jasper) 6 Warhol (Andy) 7 Hockney (David), Indiana (Robert) 9 Oldenburg (Claes), Wesselman (Tom) 10 Rosenquist (James) 12 Lichtenstein (Roy)
(see also **pop singer**)

pope
3 Leo 4 John, Mark, Paul, Pius 5 Caius, Conon, Donus, Felix, Gaius, Lando, Linus, Peter, Soter, Urban 6 Adrian, Agatho, Fabian, Julius, Lucius,

Martin, Sixtus, Victor **7** Anterus, Clement, Damasus, Gregory, Hadrian, Hyginus, Marinus, Paschal, Pontian, Romanus, Sergius, Stephen, Zosimus **8** Agapetus, Anicetus, Benedict, Boniface, Calixtus, Eugenius, Eusebius, Formosis, Gelasius, Hilarius, Honorius, Innocent, John Paul, Liberius, Nicholas, Pelagius, Siricius, Theodore, Vigilius, Vitalian **9** Adeodatus, Alexander, Anacletus, Callistus, Celestine, Cornelius, Densdedit, Dionysius, Eutychian, Evaristus, Hormisdas, Marcellus, Miltiades, Severinus, Silverius, Silvester, Sisinnius, Sylvester, Symmachus, Valentine, Zacharias **10** Anastasius, Melchiades, Sabinianus, Simplicius, Zephyrinus **11** Christopher, Constantine, Eleutherius, Eutychianus, Marcellinus, Telesphorus

Pope poem
7 Dunciad (The) **10** Essay on Man (An) **13** Rape of the Lock (The)

Popeye
accessory: **4** pipe
baby: **7** Swee'Pea **8** Sweet Pea
creator: **5** Segar (E. C.)
energizer: **7** spinach
friend: **5** Wimpy **8** Olive Oyl
occupation: **6** sailor
rival: **5** Bluto

pop in
4 call **5** visit **6** drop by, look up, stop by **8** come over

popinjay
3 fop **4** toff **5** dandy, swell **7** peacock **8** macaroni

poplar
5 abele, alamo, aspen **6** balsam **9** tulip tree **10** cottonwood **12** balm of Gilead

Poppaea's husband
4 Nero

poppycock
3 rot **4** bosh, bunk, guff **5** bilge, hokum, hooey **6** bunkum **7** baloney **8** malarkey, nonsense, tommyrot **10** balderdash

pop singer
3 Lee (Brenda), Ray (Johnnie), Vee (Bobby) **4** Cher, Como (Perry), Enya, Gore (Lesley), Joel (Billy), Page (Patti), Ross (Diana) **5** Abdul (Paula), Aiken (Clay), Arden (Toni), Cline (Patsy), Lopez (Trini), Simon (Carly, Paul), Valli (Frankie) **6** Avalon (Frankie), Brewer (Teresa), Crosby (Bing), Fisher (Eddie), Martin (Dean, Tony), Mathis (Johnny), Midler (Bette), Murray (Billy), Pitney (Gene), Spears (Britney), Summer (Donna), Vallee (Rudy), Vinton (Bobby) **7** Bennett (Tony), Buffett (Jimmy), Diamond (Neil), Estefan (Gloria), Francis (Connie), Houston (Whitney), Jackson (Michael), Loggins (Kenny), Madonna, Rodgers (Jimmie), Simpson (Jessica), Sinatra (Frank), Warwick (Dionne) **8** Aguilera (Christina), Williams (Andy) **9** Streisand (Barbra)

populace
5 plebs **6** masses, people, public **9** citizenry, commonage, commoners, plebeians **10** commonalty **11** commonality, rank and file, third estate

popular
5 cheap, noted **6** common, famous **7** admired, current, favored, general, leading **8** accepted, approved, favorite, ordinary **9** preferred, prevalent, prominent, well-known, well-liked **10** democratic, prevailing, widespread **11** inexpensive

populate
6 occupy, people, settle **7** inhabit

populous
6 packed **7** crowded, teeming **8** numerous **9** congested **13** multitudinous

porcelain
Chinese: **9** Lowestoft
English: **3** Bow **5** Derby, Spode **6** Minton **7** Aynsley, Belleek, Bristol, Chelsea **8** Caughley, Wedgwood
French: **6** Sèvres **7** Limoges
German: **7** Dresden, Meissen
ingredient: **6** kaolin
Italian: **6** Doccia
Japanese: **5** Imari

porch
4 deck **5** lanai **6** piazza **7** gallery, veranda **8** verandah

porcupine
8 hedgehog

pore
6 outlet **7** opening, orifice, reflect **8** meditate **10** interstice

pore over
4 read, scan **5** study **6** peruse **10** scrutinize

porgy
3 tai **4** fish, scup **6** sparid **8** menhaden

Porgy and Bess
composer: **8** Gershwin (George)
librettist: **7** Heyward (DuBose) **8** Gershwin (Ira)

Po River city
5 Milan, Padua, Turin **6** Milano, Padova, Torino, Verona **7** Brescia

pork
3 ham, pig **5** bacon, swine **8** sowbelly
cut: **3** ham **4** jowl, loin, side **7** fatback **8** forefoot, hind foot, spare rib **9** picnic ham **10** Boston butt

pork-barreling
9 patronage

pornographic
7 obscene

porous
5 leaky **6** spongy **8** pervious **9** permeable **10** penetrable

porpoise
5 whale **7** dolphin

porridge
4 mush **5** gruel, kasha **6** burgoo, cereal, congee, pablum, sowens **7** oatmeal, pabulum **8** flummery, loblolly **9** stirabout

port
4 hole, jack, left, wine **5** cover, haven **6** harbor, refuge **7** bearing, opening, retreat, shelter **8** larboard, left side **9** anchorage, harborage, roadstead, sanctuary **11** comportment
opposite: **9** starboard

portable
5 handy **6** mobile, wieldy

portal
4 door, gate **5** entry **7** doorway, gateway **8** approach, entrance, entryway

portcullis
4 gate **5** orgue **7** grating, lattice

portend
4 bode **5** augur **6** signal **7** betoken, predict, presage, promise, signify **8** forebode, forecast, foretell, indicate, prophesy **9** adumbrate, foretoken **10** foreshadow, vaticinate

portent
4 omen, sign **6** augury, boding **7** presage, prodigy **9** foretoken, sensation **10** foreboding, indication **11** premonition

portentous
5 grave **6** solemn **7** ominous, pompous, serious, weighty **8** inflated **9** marvelous, momentous, ponderous **10** prodigious

porter
5 hamal, stout **6** bearer, redcap, skycap **7** bellboy, bellhop, carrier **9** transport **10** doorkeeper

Porter novel
11 Ship of Fools

Portia
6 lawyer
husband: **6** Brutus **8** Bassanio
maid: **7** Nerissa

portico
4 stoa **9** colonnade

portion
3 cut, lot **4** bite, part **5** dower, moira, piece, quota, share, slice **6** moiety, parcel **7** measure, quantum, segment **8** division
largest: **10** lion's share
unused: **8** leftover

portly
3 fat **5** bulky, heavy, large, stout **6** fleshy **7** rotound, stately, weighty **8** imposing **9** corpulent **10** overweight

portmanteau
7 holdall **8** carryall, suitcase

portrait
4 bust **5** image **6** figure, statue **7** picture **8** painting **9** depiction

portray
4 draw, limn, play **5** enact, paint **6** depict, render **7** picture **8** describe **9** delineate, interpret, represent

portrayal
5 image **7** account, picture **8** likeness, painting **9** depiction **11** delineation, description, performance **12** illustration

Portugal
capital: **6** Lisbon
city: **5** Porto **6** Oporto **7** Amadora
former colony: **3** Goa **5** Macao **6** Angola, Brazil
former name: **9** Lusitania
island group: **6** Azores **7** Madeira
leader: **4** Luís **7** Salazar (Antonio de)
monetary unit: **4** euro
monetary unit, former: **6** escudo
neighbor: **5** Spain
peninsula: **6** Iberia **7** Iberian
river: **5** Tagus

pose
3 act, air, ask, set, sit **4** airs, fake, role, sham **5** feign, front, offer, place, stand, state, strut **6** affect, assume, pass as, stance **7** pass for, pass off, present, pretend, show off, suggest **8** attitude, pretense, set forth **9** mannerism **10** pretension **11** affectation

Poseidon
7 Neptune
brother: **4** Zeus **5** Hades, Pluto **7** Jupiter
consort: **4** Tyro **6** Medusa **7** Demeter
father: **6** Cronus
mother: **4** Rhea
offspring: **7** Pegasus
son: **5** Orion **6** Neleus, Pelias, Triton **7** Antaeus **10** Polyphemus
weapon: **7** trident
wife: **10** Amphitrite

poser
6 puzzle, riddle **7** problem **9** conundrum **11** brainteaser

poseur
4 fake **5** bluff, decoy, fraud, phony, pseud, quack **6** phoney **7** bluffer **8** deceiver, imposter **9** charlatan, hypocrite, pretender **10** mountebank **11** masquerader **12** impersonator

posh
4 chic, rich, tony **5** fancy, grand, smart, swank **7** elegant, stylish **9** exclusive, expensive, luxurious **11** fashionable, highfalutin, pretentious

posit
3 fix **5** offer **6** affirm, assert, assume **7** premise, present, presume, propose, suggest **9** postulate

position
3 job **4** rank, site, spot **5** locus, place, point, situs, stand, state **6** belief, locate, stance **7** emplace, footing, stature **8** attitude, capacity, location, prestige, standing **10** standpoint
without work: **8** sinecure

positive
4 firm, real, sure **6** actual, useful **7** assured, certain, decided, factual, genuine, reality **8** absolute, complete, definite, forceful, outright **9** confident, doubtless, effective, favorable **10** beneficial, inarguable, optimistic, undeniable **11** categorical, irrefutable, unequivocal, unqualified **12** indisputable, unmistakable **13** incontestable

possess
3 own **4** have, hold, keep **5** carry **6** retain **7** acquire, control

possessed
3 mad **6** crazed, hooked **8** frenzied **9** bewitched

possession
7 control **8** property **9** occupancy, ownership **10** occupation

possessive
7 jealous **8** watchful **10** protective **11** proprietary

possibility
2 if **4** odds **6** chance **8** instance **9** potential **10** likelihood **11** contingency, feasibility

possible
6 doable, likely, viable **7** earthly **8** feasible **9** expedient, potential **10** imaginable, realizable **11** practicable

possibly
5 maybe **7** perhaps **8** by chance **9** perchance **11** conceivably

post
3 set **4** camp, mail, pole, ride, send, spot, stem, task **5** affix, after, hurry, newel, place, put up, score, stage, stake **6** advise, column, fill in, inform, notify, office, pillar **7** apprise, express, placard, publish, station **8** announce, denounce, position **9** advertise **10** assignment

poster
4 bill, sign **6** notice **7** affiche, placard **9** broadside, signboard **12** announcement **13** advertisement

posterior
4 back, butt, hind, rear, rump, seat, tail **5** after, fanny, later **6** behind, caudal, dorsal, heinie, hinder **7** ensuing, rear end, tail end **8** backside, buttocks, derriere, hindmost, rearward **9** following **10** subsequent

posterity
6 future **7** progeny **8** children **9** offspring **11** descendants

posthaste
4 fast **6** at once, pronto **7** fleetly, quickly, rapidly, swiftly **8** promptly, speedily **11** immediately

Postimpressionist painter
6 Seurat (Georges) **7** Cezanne (Paul), Gauguin (Paul), Van Gogh (Vincent) **8** Pissarro (Camille), Rousseau (Henri)

postmortem
7 autopsy **8** necropsy

postpone
5 defer, delay, table **6** hold up, put off, shelve **7** hold off, lay over, suspend **8** hold over, prorogue

postulate
5 axiom, claim **6** assert, assume, demand, thesis **7** premise, suppose **10** assumption, hypothesis, presuppose **11** hypothesize, presumption, supposition

posture
4 mode, pose **5** state **6** affect, assume, manner, stance, status **7** bearing, outlook **8** attitude, carriage, position **9** condition, situation **12** attitudinize

posy
5 bloom **6** flower **7** blossom, bouquet, corsage, nosegay **9** sentiment

pot
3 bet, pan, wad **4** ante, hemp, olla, weed **5** grass, kitty, stake, wager **6** boodle, bundle, pipkin **7** marmite **8** cannabis **9** marijuana

potable
5 clean, drink, fresh **6** liquid, liquor **8** beverage **9** drinkable

potassium ore
7 sylvite

potato
3 yam **4** spud **5** tater
bud: **3** eye

pot-au-____
3 feu **5** creme

potbelly
3 gut **5** stove **6** paunch **9** bay window, spare tire **11** corporation

Potemkin mutiny site
6 Odessa

potency
3 pep **5** force, might, power, vigor **6** energy, muscle **8** strength **9** influence, puissance **10** capability **13** effectiveness

potent
4 rich **6** mighty, robust, strong, virile **7** dynamic **8** forceful, forcible, powerful **9** effective **10** persuasive **11** influential

potential
6 latent, likely **7** ability, promise **8** capacity, possible **9** plausible, promising **10** imaginable **11** conceivable, possibility

pother
3 ado **4** flap, fret, fuss, stir, to-do **5** furor, whirl, worry **6** bustle, flurry, furore, hassle, hubbub, tumult, uproar **7** fluster, turmoil **9** agitation, annoyance, commotion, confusion

potion
6 liquid **7** mixture, philter, philtre **8** medicine **10** concoction

Potiphar's slave
6 Joseph

Potiphera
daughter: **7** Asenath
son-in-law: **6** Joseph

Potok novel
6 Chosen (The) **16** My Name Is Asher Lev

potpourri
4 olio **5** blend **6** medley, sachet **7** grab bag, mélange, variety **8** mishmash, pastiche **10** assortment, collection, hodgepodge, hotchpotch, miscellany, salmagundi **11** gallimaufry

potshot
3 cut, dig **4** barb, gibe, jibe **5** crack, shoot, swipe **6** attack, insult **9** criticism

potter
see **putter**

Potter character
5 Mopsy, Mr. Tod **6** Flopsy, Jemima (Puddle-duck) **10** Cotton-tail, Hunca Munca **11** Peter Rabbit **12** Jeremy Fisher

potter's field
8 cemetery, God's acre **9** graveyard

pottery
4 raku **5** delft, Imari **7** redware **8** ceramics, clayware, slipware **10** lusterware, terra-cotta, yellowware **11** earthenware

pouch
3 bag, sac **4** sack **5** bulge, bursa, burse **6** pocket **7** saccule **8** sacculus

pouf
5 quilt **7** ottoman **9** comforter

poultry
4 fowl
type: **4** duck, swan **5** goose, quail **6** grouse, pigeon, turkey **7** chicken, ostrich, peacock **8** pheasant **9** partridge

pounce
5 seize, swoop, talon **6** attack, powder **7** assault, stencil

pound
4 bang, bash, beat, slam, slug, sock **5** drive, money, smite, stamp, throb, thump, tramp **6** batter, buffet, hammer, pummel, strike, thrash, wallop **7** belabor, impress, pulsate **9** enclosure

Pound work
6 Cantos (The)

poupée
4 doll

pour
4 flow, gush, rain, rill, rush, teem **5** flood, issue, skink, spate, surge, swarm **6** decant, deluge, drench, sluice, spring, stream **7** cascade, torrent **8** inundate, overflow

pourboire
3 tip **7** cumshaw **8** gratuity **9** baksheesh

pout
3 pet **4** fish, moue, sulk **5** grump **8** protrude **10** expression, protrusion

poverty
4 need, want **6** dearth, penury **7** beggary, paucity **8** hardship, poorness, scarcity, shortage **9** indigence, neediness, pauperism, privation **10** mendicancy, scarceness **11** destitution **13** pennilessness

POW camp
6 stalag

powder
4 bray, dust, talc **5** crush **6** talcum **8** sprinkle **9** comminute, pulverize, triturate **10** besprinkle

power
3 vis **4** sway **5** force, might, sinew, steam, vigor, vires (plural) **6** energy, muscle **7** command, ability, control, potency, voltage **8** dominion, dynamism, imperium, strength **9** authority, influence, privilege, puissance, strong arm **10** ascendancy, domination **11** prerogative, sovereignty, superiority **12** jurisdiction, potentiality
combining form: **5** dynam **6** dynamo
unit: **4** watt

powerful
5 great **6** mighty, potent, strong **7** dynamic **8** dominant, puissant, vigorous **9** energetic, strenuous **10** convincing, impressive, invincible, persuasive

powerless
4 weak **5** inert **6** feeble, unable **7** passive

8 impotent **9** incapable **11** incompetent, ineffective

powwow
4 chat, talk **6** confab, confer, huddle, parley **7** discuss, meeting **8** ceremony **9** gathering **10** discussion **11** confabulate, get-together

practicable
5 utile **6** doable, likely, usable, useful **8** feasible, possible **9** operative **10** functional

practical
5 handy, utile **6** active, useful, versed **7** applied, skilled, trained, virtual **8** sensible **9** pragmatic, realistic **10** functional **11** down-to-earth, experienced **12** businesslike

practically
5 about **6** all but, almost, near to, nearly **7** close to **8** in effect **9** in essence, just about

practice
3 ply, use, way **4** form, mode, wont **5** drill, habit, usage **6** custom, manner, method, repeat, system, tryout, warm up **7** perform, process, workout **8** drilling, engage in, exercise, habitude, rehearse **9** procedure, rehearsal **10** convention

pragmatic
7 factual, logical **8** rational **9** practical, realistic **11** down-to-earth

prairie
4 veld **5** pampa, plain, veldt **6** pampas **7** plateau **9** grassland

prairie chicken
6 grouse

prairie wolf
6 coyote

praise
4 hail, hymn, laud, puff **5** bravo, cry up, exalt, extol, honor, kudos **6** belaud, kudize **7** acclaim, adulate, applaud, commend, flatter, glorify, hosanna, magnify, ovation, plaudit, puffery **8** accolade, applause, approval, citation, encomium, eulogize, flattery **9** celebrate, laudation, panegyric, recommend **10** aggrandize, compliment, panegyrize **11** acclamation **12** commendation

praiseworthy
8 laudable **9** admirable, deserving, estimable **11** commendable, meritorious

prance
4 step **5** mince, strut **6** sashay, spring **8** cakewalk

prank
3 gag **4** deck, dido, lark, whim **5** adorn, antic, caper, fancy, spiff, sport, trick **6** doll up, frolic, gambol, levity, shavie, vagary, whimsy **7** caprice, deck out, doll out, dress up, garnish, rollick, spiff up **8** beautify, decorate, escapade, ornament, spruce up **9** embellish, frivolity, horseplay, smarten up **10** shenanigan, tomfoolery **11** monkeyshine

prankster
3 wag **5** cutup, joker

prate
3 gab, jaw, yak **4** blab, chat, go on **5** run on **6** babble, gabble, jabber **7** blabber, blather, chatter **9** yakety-yak

prater
5 yenta **6** gossip, magpie **10** chatterbox **12** blabbermouth

pratfall
6 mishap, tumble **7** blunder, stumble **11** humiliation

prattle
3 gab **4** blab **5** prate **6** babble, gabble, jabber, natter **7** blabber, chatter

prawn
6 shrimp **11** langoustine
French: **8** crevette

praxis
5 habit **6** action, custom, manner **7** conduct **8** exercise, habitude, practice

Praxiteles statue
5 Satyr **6** Hermes **9** Aphrodite

pray
3 ask, beg **5** plead **6** appeal **7** beseech, entreat, implore, request **8** petition **10** supplicate

prayer
4 plea, suit **6** appeal, litany, orison **7** angelus, begging, worship **8** blessing, devotion, entreaty, petition, pleading, rogation **9** adoration **11** application, imploration, imprecation **12** supplication
beads: **6** rosary
ending: **4** amen
for the dead: **7** requiem
Jewish: **7** kaddish, kiddush
period: **6** novena **7** triduum
shawl: **7** tallith

prayer book
6 missal, siddur **8** breviary

prayerful
4 holy **5** godly, pious **6** devout **7** earnest, sincere

preach
4 urge **6** exhort **7** address, deliver, lecture **8** admonish, advocate, moralize **9** sermonize **10** evangelize

preacher
5 padre **6** cleric, divine, parson, pastor

8 chaplain, clerical, minister, reverend **9** churchman, clergyman **10** evangelist, sermonizer **12** ecclesiastic

preaching friar
9 Dominican

preachy
4 smug **7** donnish **8** didactic, pedantic, sermonic, unctuous **9** homiletic, hortative, pedagogic, pietistic **10** moralizing **11** exhortative, sermonizing **13** sanctimonious, self-righteous

preamble
5 intro, proem **8** exordium, foreword, overture, prologue **12** introduction

precarious
4 iffy **5** dicey, risky, shaky **6** chancy, touchy, tricky, unsafe **7** dubious **8** delicate, doubtful, insecure, ticklish, unstable **9** dangerous, hazardous, sensitive, uncertain **10** unreliable

precaution
4 care **8** prudence **9** foresight, insurance, provision, safeguard **11** forethought

precede
4 lead, rank **5** usher **6** herald **7** forerun, outrank, surpass **8** announce, antedate, go before **9** introduce

precedence
5 order **8** priority **9** seniority

precedent
4 past, rule **5** model, prior **6** former **7** earlier, example **8** anterior **9** foregoing **10** convention

preceding
4 past **5** prior **6** before, former **7** ahead of, prior to **8** anterior, hitherto **9** erstwhile **10** heretofore **11** in advance of
prefix: **4** ante

precept
3 law **4** rule **5** axiom, edict, order, tenet **6** behest, decree **7** bidding, command **8** doctrine **9** principle **10** injunction, regulation **11** fundamental

preceptive
8 didactic

preceptor
4 head **5** tutor **7** teacher **9** principal **10** headmaster

precinct
4 area **6** domain, region, sector, sphere **7** quarter, section **8** district, division, township **9** bailiwick, enclosure

precious
3 pet **4** dear, nice, rare, rich, very **5** fussy, great, loved, showy **6** adored, choice, costly, la-di-da, prized **7** beloved, darling **8** affected, esteemed, favorite, valuable **9** cherished, exquisite, extremely, priceless **10** invaluable

precipice
5 brink, cliff **8** overhang

precipitancy
4 rush **5** haste, hurry **9** hastiness **10** abruptness, suddenness **11** hurriedness

precipitate
4 fall, hurl **5** hasty, sheer, steep, throw **6** abrupt, madcap, sudden, upshot **7** bring on, deposit, grounds, hurried, outcome, product **8** condense, headlong, sediment, separate **9** breakneck, impatient **10** unexpected, unforeseen **11** consequence

precipitation
4 hail, mist, rain, snow **5** sleet **7** deposit **8** sediment

precipitous
4 rash **5** hasty, sheer, steep **6** abrupt, sudden **7** hurried, rushing **8** headlong, heedless, plunging **9** breakneck **13** perpendicular

précis
6 digest, survey **7** summary **8** abstract, overview, syllabus **10** abridgment, compendium **11** abridgement **12** condensation

precise
4 nice **5** exact, fixed, right **6** narrow, strict **7** correct, limited **8** accurate, clear-cut, definite, rigorous, specific **9** clocklike, stringent **10** particular

precisely
4 just **5** right **7** exactly **8** strictly

precision
4 care **5** rigor **6** nicety **8** accuracy **9** exactness **10** exactitude, refinement **11** correctness

preclude
5 avert, deter **7** forfend, obviate, prevent, rule out **8** prohibit, stave off **9** forestall

precocious
5 smart **6** brainy, bright, mature **7** forward **8** advanced

precondition
4 must, need **7** proviso **9** essential, necessity, provision, requisite **10** sine qua non **11** requirement, stipulation

precursor
6 herald **8** ancestor, forebear **9** harbinger, indicator, prototype **10** antecedent, forerunner

predator
6 hunter, preyer, raptor **7** stalker **8** devourer **9** destroyer **10** bird of prey

predatory
6 greedy **8** ravening, ravenous **9** pillaging, rapacious **10** plundering **12** exploitative

predecessor
8 ancestor, forebear **9** precursor, prototype **10** antecedent, forerunner

predicament
3 fix, jam **4** bind, hole, spot **5** pinch, state **6** corner, muddle, pickle, plight, puzzle, scrape, strait **7** dilemma, impasse, trouble **8** hardship, nuisance, quagmire **9** condition, situation **10** difficulty

predicate
4 aver, avow, base, rest **5** found, imply **6** affirm, assert, avouch **7** declare, profess **9** establish

predict
5 augur, guess, infer **6** expect **7** forbode, foresee, portend, surmise **8** announce, conclude, forebode, forecast, foretell, indicate, prophesy, soothsay **10** conjecture, vaticinate **13** prognosticate

prediction
6 augury **8** forecast, prophecy **9** prognosis **10** expectancy **11** expectation

predilection
4 bent, bias **5** fancy, taste **6** liking **7** leaning **8** fondness, penchant, tendency **9** inclining **10** partiality, proclivity, propensity **11** inclination

predispose
4 bend, bias, tend, sway **5** prime **6** affect **7** incline **9** influence

predisposed
5 prone, ready **6** biased **7** partial, willing **8** inclined **11** susceptible

predisposition
4 bent, bias **7** leaning **8** penchant, tendency **9** inclining **10** partiality, proclivity, propensity **11** inclination

predominant
3 top **4** main **5** chief, major **6** master, ruling **7** capital, general, leading, primary, supreme **8** reigning, superior **9** number one, paramount, principal, sovereign **10** prevailing **11** outstanding

predominate
4 rule **5** reign **6** govern, master **7** command, control, prevail **8** outweigh

preeminence
6 renown **7** primacy **8** dominion, prestige **9** supremacy **10** ascendancy, domination, excellence, importance **11** distinction, superiority

preeminent
3 top **4** main **5** chief, first **7** capital, stellar, supreme **8** dominant, foremost, peerless, towering, ultimate **9** matchless, number-one, paramount, principal, unrivaled **10** surpassing, unrivalled **11** outstanding, unmatchable **12** incomparable, transcendent
prefix: **4** arch

preempt
4 bump, take **5** annex, seize, usurp **6** assume **7** acquire, replace **8** arrogate **9** forestall **10** confiscate, substitute **11** appropriate, expropriate

preen
5 gloat, groom, pride, primp, swell **6** smooth

preface
4 lead, open **5** begin, intro, proem, usher **6** herald **8** exordium, foreword, overture, preamble, prologue **9** introduce **11** preliminary **12** introduction

prefatory
7 opening **8** proemial **12** introductory

prefect
7 head boy, monitor **8** head girl **10** magistrate

prefer
5 elect, favor **6** choose, opt for, select **7** advance, elevate, promote, upgrade

preferable
5 finer **6** better **8** superior, worthier

preference
4 pick **6** choice, option **8** election, priority **9** advantage, elevation, promotion, selection, upgrading **10** favoritism, partiality

prefigure
4 hint **7** foresee **8** indicate **9** adumbrate **10** foreshadow

pregnancy
9 gestation, gravidity

pregnant
4 full, rich **5** heavy **6** gravid, parous **7** teeming, weighty **8** eloquent, enceinte, profound **9** expectant, expecting, gestating, inventive, momentous, with child **10** expressive, meaningful, parturient **11** significant

prehensile
8 grasping

prejudice
3 mar **4** bias, harm, hurt, sway **5** color, favor **6** damage, injure, injury, racism, sexism **7** bigotry, leaning **8** aversion **9** antipathy, hostility, influence **10** partiality **11** intolerance **12** one-sidedness

prejudicial
6 biased **7** bigoted **8** damaging **9** injurious **11** deleterious, detrimental

prelate
5 abbot **6** bishop **7** primate **8** cardinal, diocesan **9** patriarch **10** archbishop **12** ecclesiastic

preliminary
4 heat **5** basic, match, trial **7** initial, opening **8** proemial **9** beginning **10** qualifying **11** fundamental **12** introductory

prelude
5 intro, proem **7** opening **8** exordium, foreword, overture, prologue **12** introduction, prolegomenon

premature
5 early **8** untimely **10** beforehand

premeditated
5 set up **7** planned, studied, willful **8** designed, intended **9** conscious **10** calculated, considered, deliberate, thought-out **11** intentional

premier
4 head, main **5** chief, first **7** leading, primary **8** earliest, foremost, original **9** principal **13** prime minister

premiere
5 debut **7** opening **8** earliest, original **9** beginning **10** first night

premise
4 base **5** posit **6** assume, thesis **8** building, property, set forth **9** postulate **10** assumption **11** postulation, proposition, supposition

premium
4 agio **5** bonus, extra, prize **6** reward **8** dividend, superior **9** excellent **10** recompense **11** exceptional

premonition
4 omen **9** misgiving, suspicion **10** foreboding **11** forewarning **12** apprehension, presentiment

preoccupied
4 deep, lost, rapt **6** absent, intent **7** engaged, faraway, worried **8** absorbed, immersed **9** concerned, engrossed, wrapped up **10** abstracted, distracted **11** inattentive **12** absentminded

prep
5 basic, coach, drill, equip, groom, prime, ready, train, trial **8** get ready **11** preliminary **12** introductory

preparation
4 base, plan **5** study **7** fitness, measure **8** compound, medicine, training **9** alertness, foresight, readiness **10** background, concoction

preparatory
5 basic **11** preliminary, rudimentary **12** introductory

prepare
3 fit, fix, set **4** gird **5** draft, groom, prime, ready, train **6** draw up, make up, outfit **7** fortify, furnish **9** formulate

prepared
3 set **4** up on **5** fixed, ready **6** primed **7** treated **9** processed

preponderance
4 bulk **8** dominion, majority, main part **9** ascendant, dominance, supremacy **10** ascendancy, domination **11** superiority

preponderant
7 supreme **8** dominant, superior **9** paramount **10** prevailing

preponderate
4 rule **5** reign **6** exceed **7** command, dictate, outrank, prevail **8** dominate, outweigh

preposition
2 at, by, in, of, on, to, up **3** for, off **4** down, from, into, like, near, onto, over, past, upon, with **5** about, above, after, along, among, below, since, under, until **6** across, around, before, behind, beside, during, except, inside, toward, within **7** against, beneath, between, outside, through, without

prepossess
4 bias, sway **5** favor **6** absorb, engage, occupy **7** engross, immerse, involve **9** influence

prepossessing
7 likable **9** appealing **10** attractive

preposterous
4 wild **5** crazy, wacky **6** absurd, insane **7** asinine, foolish, idiotic **9** fantastic, laughable, senseless **10** irrational, ridiculous **11** harebrained **12** unreasonable

prerequisite
4 must, need **5** vital **8** required **9** condition, essential, mandatory, necessary, necessity **10** imperative, sine qua non **11** requirement **13** indispensable

prerogative
5 power, right **8** appanage, immunity **9** authority, exemption, privilege **10** birthright, perquisite

presage
4 bode, omen, warn **5** augur, sense **6** augury, boding, herald, intuit **7** portend, portent, predict, promise, warning **8** announce, forebode, forecast, foretell, forewarn, indicate, prophesy, soothsay **9** foretoken, harbinger, intuition, misgiving **10** foreboding, foreshadow, prediction, prognostic, vaticinate

presbyter
5 elder **6** priest

prescience
9 foresight **12** anticipation, clairvoyance **13** foreknowledge

prescribe
3 fix, set **4** rule **5** guide, order **6** assign, choose, decide, decree, define, direct, impose, ordain, select **7** dictate, lay down, pick out, require, specify **9** designate, determine, stipulate

prescript
3 law **4** rule **5** edict, order **6** decree **10** regulation

prescription
3 med **4** drug, rule **5** claim, right, title **6** custom, remedy **8** medicine **9** direction **10** medication

presence
3 air **4** look, mien **5** poise **6** aspect, spirit **7** address, bearing **8** carriage, demeanor **9** composure

present
3 act, aim, now **4** boon, gift, give, here, pose, show **5** award, bring, favor, offer, point, stage, tense, today **6** at hand, bestow, confer, convey, direct, donate, extend, in view, modern, render, submit, tender **7** hand out, largess, perform, proffer **8** existing, nominate **9** introduce **12** contemporary

presentable
3 fit **6** decent, proper **8** becoming **9** befitting **10** acceptable **11** appropriate **12** satisfactory

present-day
6 living, recent **7** current, ongoing, popular, topical **8** contempo, existent, existing, pressing, up-to-date **9** prevalent, surviving **10** prevailing **12** contemporary

presently
3 now **4** anon, soon **5** today **6** in time, one day **7** by and by **9** forthwith, these days **10** before long

preservation
4 care **6** saving, shield **7** defense, keeping **8** pickling **10** husbanding, protection **11** conservancy, maintenance, safekeeping

preserve
3 can, jam **4** save **5** jelly, put up **6** embalm, ensile, keep up, pickle **7** protect, shelter, sustain **8** keep safe, maintain **9** confiture

preside
3 run **4** head, lead **5** chair **6** direct, handle, manage **7** conduct, control, operate, oversee **8** moderate **9** officiate

president, U. S.
3 Abe, DDE, FDR, HST, Ike, JFK, LBJ, RMN **4** Bush (George, George W.), Ford (Gerald R.), Polk (James K.), Taft (William H.) **5** Adams (John, John Quincy), Grant (Ulysses S.), Hayes (Rutherford B.), Nixon (Richard M.), Tyler (John) **6** Arthur (Chester A.), Carter (Jimmy), Hoover (Herbert), Monroe (James), Pierce (Franklin), Reagan (Ronald), Taylor (Zachary), Truman (Harry S.), Wilson (Woodrow) **7** Clinton (Bill), Harding (Warren), Jackson (Andrew), Johnson (Andrew, Lyndon), Kennedy (John F.), Lincoln (Abraham), Madison (James) **8** Buchanan (James), Coolidge (Calvin), Fillmore (Millard), Garfield (James), Harrison (Benjamin, William Henry), McKinley (William), Van Buren (Martin) **9** Cleveland (Grover), Jefferson (Thomas), Roosevelt (Franklin D., Theodore) **10** Eisenhower (Dwight D.), Washington (George)

presidential nominee
4 Dole (Robert J.), Gore (Albert) **5** Dewey (Thomas), Kerry (John) **7** Dukakis (Michael), Mondale (Walter) **8** Humphrey (Hubert), McGovern (George) **9** Goldwater (Barry), Stevenson (Adlai)

presidio
4 fort **7** bastion, citadel **8** fastness, fortress, garrison **10** stronghold **13** fortification

Presley, Elvis
4 King (The) **6** Pelvis (The)
daughter: 9 Lisa Marie
manager: 6 Parker (Col. Tom)
middle name: 4 Aron **5** Aaron
property: 9 Graceland
wife: 9 Priscilla

press
3 hug, jam, ram **4** cram, iron, mass, pack, pile, push, rush, urge **5** clasp, crowd, crush, drive, force, horde, hurry, media, shove **6** demand, hustle, insist, jostle, propel, squash, stress, throng, thrust **7** beseech, entreat, imprint, printer, squeeze **9** constrain, influence, multitude

pressing
5 acute, vital **6** urgent **7** crucial, earnest, exigent, serious **8** critical **9** immediate, important, insistent **10** compelling, imperative

pressure
4 push, rush **5** drive, impel **6** burden, coerce, strain, stress **7** tension **10** constraint
combining form: 5 piezo
instrument: 9 barometer
unit: 3 bar **6** pascal

prestige
4 fame, rank, sway **5** power **6** cachet, credit, esteem, regard, renown, repute, status, weight **7** dignity, stature **8** eminence, position, standing **9** authority, influence **10** importance, prominence **11** consequence, distinction

prestigious
5 famed, great **6** famous **7** eminent, honored, notable **8** esteemed, renowned **9** prominent, respected **10** celebrated **11** influential **13** distinguished

presto
4 fast **7** hastily, quickly, rapidly **8** suddenly **9** posthaste **11** immediately

presumably
6 likely, surely **8** probably **9** doubtless

presume
4 dare **5** guess, imply, infer, think, trust **6** expect,

gather, impose, reason **7** believe, intrude, suppose, surmise, venture **8** infringe **9** postulate **10** conjecture

presumption
4 gall **5** brass, cheek, nerve **6** belief, daring, ground, reason, thesis **7** conceit **8** audacity, chutzpah, evidence **9** brashness, inference, postulate **10** confidence, effrontery

presumptuous
4 bold, smug **5** brash, fresh, pushy **6** cheeky, uppity **7** forward **8** arrogant **9** audacious, confident **11** overweening, self-assured

presuppose
5 posit **6** assume, expect **7** imagine, require, surmise **9** postulate

pretend
3 act **4** fake, pose, sham **5** bluff, claim, false, feign, guess, put on **6** affect, assume, delude, invent **7** deceive, imitate, mislead, playact, profess, purport, suppose, surmise **8** simulate **9** imaginary **11** counterfeit, make-believe

pretender
4 fake, sham **5** actor, faker, fraud, phony **6** humbug **8** claimant, impostor **9** hypocrite

pretense
3 act, air **4** face, fake, mask, pose, sham **5** claim, cloak, cover, front, guise **6** deceit, facade, humbug **7** charade, fiction **8** disguise **9** deception, false show, imposture **10** masquerade, simulation **11** affectation, make-believe, ostentation

pretension
5 claim, right **6** vanity **8** ambition **10** allegation, aspiration **11** affectation

pretentious
4 arty **5** lofty, put-on, showy **6** chichi, la-de-da, la-di-da, too-too **7** pompous, stilted **8** affected, inflated, lah-de-dah, lah-di-dah, puffed up, snobbish, specious **9** bombastic, conceited, grandiose, lah-dee-dah, overblown **10** euphuistic, rhetorical **11** highfalutin **12** high-sounding, magniloquent, vainglorious

preternatural
7 psychic, unusual **8** abnormal, atypical **9** anomalous, unearthly, untypical **10** mysterious **12** inexplicable, supernatural **13** extraordinary

pretext
4 mask, ploy **5** alibi, cloak, cover, front, guise **6** device, excuse **7** apology **10** subterfuge

pretty
4 cute, fair **5** bonny, quite **6** comely, fairly, lovely, rather, sort of **7** cunning **8** graceful, pleasant, pleasing, somewhat **9** appealing, beautiful **10** attractive, more or less **11** good-looking **12** considerable

prevail
4 beat, rule **5** reign **6** master **7** conquer, impress, persist, triumph **8** convince, dominate, domineer, overcome, override, persuade **9** influence

prevalent
4 rife **6** ruling **7** favored, popular, regnant **8** accepted, dominant, superior **9** ascendant, customary, paramount, sovereign **10** accustomed, widespread

prevaricate
3 fib, lie **5** avoid, evade **6** palter **7** confuse, deceive, distort, falsify, quibble **12** misrepresent

prevarication
3 fib, lie **4** tale **5** lying, story **6** canard, deceit **7** falsity **9** deception, falsehood

prevent
3 bar, dam **4** balk, foil, ward **5** avert, avoid, block, check, debar, deter, estop **6** arrest, baffle, forbid, hinder, impede, thwart **7** forfend, head off, inhibit, obviate **8** obstruct, preclude, prohibit, stave off **9** forestall, frustrate, interdict **10** anticipate

previous
4 fore, past **5** early, prior **6** before, former **7** earlier, onetime **8** anterior **9** erstwhile, foregoing, in advance **10** antecedent, beforehand

previously
4 once **5** afore, ahead **6** before **7** already, earlier **8** formerly **9** erstwhile **10** heretofore

prewar
10 antebellum

prey
4 feed, game, mark **5** chase **6** quarry, target, victim **8** casualty, distress

Priam
daughter: **6** Creusa **8** Polyxena **9** Cassandra
father: **8** Laomedon
grandfather: **4** Ilus
kingdom: **4** Troy **5** Ilium
slayer: **7** Pyrrhus **11** Neoptolemus
son: **5** Paris **6** Hector, Lycaon **7** Helenus, Troilus **9** Deiphobus, Polydorus
wife: **6** Arisbe, Hecuba

Priapus
father: **7** Bacchus **8** Dionysus
mother: **5** Venus **9** Aphrodite

price
3 fee, fix, tab **4** cost, fare, rate, toll **6** amount, assess, charge, figure, outlay, reward, tariff **7** expense, payment **8** appraise

priceless
4 rare, rich **5** droll, funny, witty **6** absurd, costly, prized, valued **7** amusing **8** precious, valuable **9** cherished, treasured **10** invaluable

pricey
4 dear **5** steep **6** costly **9** expensive

prick
3 jab **4** goad, mark, prod, spur, urge **5** egg on, point, sting, thorn **6** affect, excite, exhort, pierce, prompt **7** pinhole **8** puncture **9** perforate

prickly
5 burry, sharp, spiny **6** briary, thorny, tetchy, tingly, touchy, trying **7** brambly, waspish **8** annoying, nettling, snappish, stinging **9** difficult, fractious, irritable, vexatious **10** bothersome, irritating, nettlesome **11** troublesome

pride
3 ego, top **4** best, brag, pack, pick **5** boast, cream, elite, exult, group, preen, prime, prize, vaunt **6** choice, egoism, hubris, vanity **7** conceit, delight, elation, dignity, disdain, egotism **8** smugness, treasure **9** arrogance, cockiness, vainglory **10** self-esteem, self-regard **11** self-respect **12** congratulate

Pride and Prejudice author
6 Austen (Jane)

prideful
6 elated **7** haughty **8** exultant **10** disdainful

prier
5 snoop **7** meddler **8** busybody, quidnunc **9** buttinsky

priest
5 padre **6** cleric, divine, father, rector **8** chaplain **9** clergyman, presbyter
ancient Roman: **6** flamen **8** pontifex
Biblical: **3** Eli
Buddhist: **4** lama
Celtic: **5** druid
French: **4** abbé, curé
Muslim: **4** imam
prop: **4** bell, book **6** candle
tribal: **6** shaman

priestly
8 clerical, hieratic **10** sacerdotal

prig
5 prude, thief **6** pedant **8** bluenose **9** Mrs. Grundy **10** goody-goody

priggish
5 fussy **6** stuffy **7** genteel, pompous, prudish **8** affected, pedantic **11** puritanical, straitlaced

prim
4 neat, nice, snug, tidy, trig **5** stiff **6** formal, proper, strict, stuffy, wooden **7** correct, genteel, orderly, precise, prudish **8** decorous, priggish **11** straitlaced

prima donna
4 diva, snob, star **7** artiste **9** chanteuse **10** narcissist **11** leading lady

prima facie
4 true **5** valid **8** apparent **11** self-evident

primal
5 basic **6** age-old **7** ancient, premier **8** cardinal, original **9** atavistic, paramount, primitive **10** preeminent **11** prehistoric

primary
4 main **5** basal, basic, chief, first **6** direct **7** initial, pioneer, radical **8** cardinal, earliest, original **9** elemental, essential, firsthand, immediate, number-one, paramount, principal **10** aboriginal, underlying **11** fundamental, rudimentary **12** foundational, introductory
combining form: **4** prot **5** proto
prefix: **4** arch **5** archi

primate
3 ape, man **5** human, lemur, loris **6** aye-aye, bishop, bonobo, monkey **7** gorilla **10** anthropoid, archbishop, chimpanzee, human being **11** Homo sapiens
nocturnal: **5** loris **7** tarsier
small: **6** galago

prime
3 top **4** best, dawn, fill, load, morn, peak, pick, rate **5** coach, cream, elite, first, paint, sunup, tonic, youth **6** choice, excite, height, spring, symbol **7** capital, highest, initial, morning, prepare, provoke, quicken **8** earliest, motivate, original, superior **9** excellent, first-rate, principal, stimulate **10** first-class

primer
4 book **5** guide **6** manual, reader **8** hornbook

primeval
7 ancient **8** earliest, original **10** aboriginal

primitive
3 raw **4** rude **5** basic, crude, early **6** savage **7** archaic, Spartan **8** barbaric, original, primeval **9** atavistic, barbarian, barbarous, elemental, essential, unevolved **10** elementary, primordial, underlying **11** fundamental, preliterate, uncivilized, undeveloped **12** uncultivated
combining form: **5** palae, paleo **6** archae, archeo, palaeo **7** archaeo
prefix: **4** arch **5** arche, archi

primogenitor
4 sire **8** ancestor, forebear **9** precursor **10** forefather

primordial
5 basic, early, first **7** ancient **8** earliest, original

primp
4 fuss **5** adorn, dress, fix up, preen **7** dress up

prince
Anglo-Saxon: **8** atheling
Arab: **4** amir, emir **5** ameer
Austrian: **8** archduke
Ethiopian: **3** ras
Indian: **4** raja, rana **5** rajah
of demons: **9** Beelzebub

of Monaco: 6 Albert 7 Rainier
of the church: 8 cardinal
of Wales: 7 Charles

Prince and the Pauper author
5 Twain (Mark) 7 Clemens (Samuel)

Prince Edward Island
capital: 13 Charlottetown
provincial flower: 12 lady's slipper

Prince Igor composer
7 Borodin (Aleksandr)

princely
5 grand, noble, royal 8 generous, imposing, majestic 9 dignified 11 magnificent

princess
7 infanta
fictional: 3 Ida, Mia 4 Aura, Leia, Miyu, Ozma, Xena 5 Ariel, Belle, Fiona, She-Ra, Storm, Vespa, Zelda 6 Anelle, Aurora, Kadiya 7 Camilla, Jasmine 8 Angelica, Starfire 9 Belphoebe, Blackfire, Britomart, Buttercup, Gwenevere, Snow White 10 Bradamante, Cinderella, Pocahontas 11 Casamassima
mythical: 3 Ino 5 Medea
of Monaco: 5 Grace

Prince Valiant
artist: 6 Foster (Hal)
son: 3 Arn
wife: 5 Aleta

principal
4 arch, dean, head, main, star 5 chief, first, major, prime 6 assets 7 capital, leading, premier, primary, stellar 8 cardinal, champion, dominant, foremost 9 paramount 10 headmaster, preeminent 11 outstanding, predominant
combining form: 4 prot 5 proto
prefix: 4 arch 5 archi

principium
3 law 5 axiom, basis 7 element, theorem 10 foundation 11 fundamental

principle
3 law 4 code, form, rule 5 axiom, basis, canon, ethic, tenet 6 ground, origin, source 7 conduct, faculty, precept 8 doctrine, polestar, rudiment 10 assumption, convention, foundation 11 fundamental

principled
5 moral, noble 6 honest 7 ethical, upright 8 virtuous 9 righteous 10 moralistic

print
4 type 5 issue, litho, stamp, write 7 engrave, impress, publish, typeset 10 impression
style: 4 bold 5 roman 6 italic 7 cursive 8 boldface

printer
English: 6 Caxton (William)
German: 9 Gutenberg (Johann, Johannes)
Italian: 6 Bodoni (Giambattista) 8 Manutius (Aldus)

printing
7 edition, reissue 10 impression
measure: 4 pica 5 agate
plate: 10 stereotype
process: 4 roto 7 gravure 11 lithography
tool: 6 brayer

priority
4 lead 5 order 8 ordering 9 supremacy 10 importance, precedence, preference

prison
3 can, pen 4 brig, coop, jail, keep 5 clink 6 cooler, lockup 7 dungeon, slammer 8 bastille, big house, stockade 9 calaboose 11 reformatory 12 penitentiary
British: 4 gaol
California: 8 Alcatraz 10 San Quentin
New York: 6 Attica 8 Sing Sing 12 Rikers Island
Northern Ireland: 4 Maze
resident: 6 inmate 7 convict 8 jailbird
Russian: 5 gulag

prisoner
7 captive, convict, hostage 8 criminal, detainee, jailbird

prissy
5 picky 7 finicky, precise, prudish 8 exacting 10 fastidious, particular 11 straitlaced

pristine
4 pure 5 clean, fresh 8 earliest, original 9 unspoiled

privacy
6 secret 7 retreat, secrecy 9 seclusion 11 concealment

private
5 inner 6 secret 7 soldier 8 eyes-only, hush-hush, intimate, personal 9 concealed 10 closed-door, restricted, unofficial 11 independent, sequestered 12 confidential

privateer
4 ship 6 pirate 7 gunship 9 mercenary

private eye
3 spy, tec 4 tail 6 sleuth, shamus 7 gumshoe 8 sherlock 9 detective 12 investigator

privately
7 sub rosa 8 covertly, in camera, in secret, secretly

privation
4 lack, loss, need, want 6 dearth, penury 7 absence, poverty 8 distress 9 indigence, neediness, suffering

privilege
4 boon 5 favor, grant, right 7 license 8 appanage 9 allowance, exemption 10 birthright,

concession, perquisite **11** entitlement, opportunity, prerogative
pope-granted: **6** indult

privy
2 WC **3** can, loo **4** head, john **5** jakes **6** secret, toilet **7** latrine **8** bathroom, informed, lavatory, outhouse, personal **9** concealed, withdrawn **11** water closet

prize
3 pry, top **4** best, loot, pick, plum, rate, swag **5** award, booty, cream, elite, force, lever, purse, spoil, value **6** choice, esteem, reward, spoils, trophy **7** capture, cherish, jackpot, plunder, premium **8** treasure **10** appreciate **11** outstanding

prizefighting
6 boxing **8** pugilism

pro
3 for **6** expert, master **8** skillful **9** authority, in favor of **11** affirmative
opposite: **3** con **4** anti

probable
6 likely **7** seeming **8** apparent, credible, expected, feasible, rational, reliable **10** reasonable

probe
4 poke, quiz, test **5** query, sonde, study **6** search **7** dig into, examine, explore, feel out, inquest, inquire, inquiry **8** check out, look into, research, sound out **9** delve into, penetrate **11** exploration, investigate, reconnoiter **13** investigation

probity
5 honor **6** virtue **7** honesty **8** fairness, goodness **9** integrity, rectitude **11** uprightness

problem
4 mess, snag **5** hitch, issue, poser **6** enigma, hassle, puzzle, riddle **7** dilemma, example, mystery, puzzler, trouble **8** hardship, headache, question **10** difficulty

problematic
4 iffy, moot, open **7** dubious **8** arguable, doubtful **9** debatable, uncertain, unsettled **10** precarious **12** questionable

proboscis
4 beak, nose **5** snoot, snout, trunk

procedure
4 plan, step **6** course, custom, method, policy, system **7** formula, measure, routine **8** protocol **9** operation **11** instruction

proceed
2 go **4** flow, move, rise, stem, wend **5** arise, get on, issue, segue **6** emerge, push on, spring, travel **7** advance, carry on, emanate, journey **8** continue **9** originate

proceedings
8 goings-on
recorded: **4** acta **6** annals **7** minutes

proceeds
4 gain, take **5** yield **6** profit, result, return **8** earnings

process
3 way **4** mode, wise **5** modus, treat **6** handle, manner, method, refine, system **7** fashion, prepare, recycle, routine **8** workings **9** evolution, operation, outgrowth, procedure, technique **11** development
nerve cell: **4** axon

procession
5 march, order, train **6** parade, series, string **7** caravan, cortege **8** sequence **9** cavalcade, march-past, motorcade **11** consecution

proclaim
5 extol **6** assert, insist **7** declare, exhibit, glorify, publish **8** announce, evidence, manifest **9** advertise, broadcast, make known **10** annunciate, bruit about

proclivity
4 bent **5** taste **6** liking **7** leaning **8** affinity, fondness, penchant, tendency **9** proneness **11** inclination **12** predilection

Procne
father: **7** Pandion
husband: **6** Tereus
sister: **9** Philomela
son: **4** Itys

procrastinate
5 dally, delay **6** dawdle

procreate
5 beget, breed **7** produce **8** conceive, generate, multiply **9** reproduce

Procris' husband
8 Cephalus

Procrustean ___
3 bed

proctor
7 monitor, oversee **9** supervise **10** supervisor

procure
3 buy, get **4** gain **6** obtain, pick up **7** achieve, acquire **8** purchase **10** bring about

prod
3 dig, jab, jog **4** goad, poke, push, spur, stir, urge **5** egg on, elbow, nudge, point, prick, rouse **6** excite, exhort, incite, thrust **8** motivate **9** stimulate **10** incitement

prodigal
4 lush **6** lavish **7** opulent, profuse, riotous, spender, wastrel **8** reckless, wasteful **9** exuberant, luxuriant **10** profligate, squanderer **11** extravagant, spendthrift

prodigious
4 huge, vast **6** mighty, unreal **7** amazing, immense, mammoth, massive, strange, unusual **8** colossal, enormous, gigantic **9** fantastic, marvelous, wonderful **10** astounding, impressive, monumental, phenomenal, remarkable, staggering, stupendous, surprising **11** astonishing **13** extraordinary

produce
4 bear, form, grow, make, show, sire **5** beget, breed, build, cause, erect, frame, hatch, mount, put on, raise, spawn, stage, yield **6** create, effect, father, output, parent, secure, work up **7** deliver, fashion, turn out **8** engender, generate, multiply **9** construct, fabricate, originate, procreate, propagate **10** bring about **11** manufacture, put together

product
5 fruit, issue, yield **6** effect, legacy, output, result, upshot **7** harvest, outcome, turnout **8** artifact, creation, multiple, offshoot **9** handiwork, outgrowth **11** consequence, manufacture **combining form: 3** gen

production
5 fruit, yield **6** output **7** staging, turnout **8** artifact, assembly, creation **9** execution, handiwork, rendering **11** achievement, manufacture, realization

productive
4 rich **6** fecund, useful **7** fertile **8** abundant, fruitful, prolific **9** rewarding **10** beneficial

proem
5 intro **7** preface, prelude **8** exordium, foreword, overture, prologue **11** preliminary **12** introduction

profane
3 lay **4** damn, foul **5** abuse, dirty, pagan **6** coarse, debase, defile, filthy, impure, unholy, vulgar **7** impious, obscene, secular **8** indecent, temporal, unsacred **9** desecrate **10** irreverent, unhallowed **11** blasphemous, irreligious **12** sacrilegious, unsanctified

profanity
4 oath **5** abuse, curse **7** cursing, cussing **8** swearing **9** blasphemy, sacrilege **10** execration **11** imprecation, irreverence

profess
4 aver, avow **5** claim, teach **6** affirm, allege, assert, avouch **7** declare, pretend, protest, purport **8** maintain, practice

profession
3 art, job, vow **5** craft, trade **6** avowal, career, métier **7** calling **8** business, vocation **9** assertion, specialty, statement, testimony **10** handicraft, occupation, walk of life **11** affirmation

professional
4 paid **6** expert, master **7** learned, skilled **9** authority **10** proficient, specialist **11** experienced **12** businesslike

professor
3 don **6** expert **7** teacher **8** academic, educator

proffer
4 give, pose **6** extend, submit, tender **7** hold out, present, suggest **10** invitation, suggestion

proficiency
5 savvy, skill **7** ability, advance, mastery, prowess **8** facility, progress **9** adeptness, dexterity, expertise, knowledge **10** competence

proficient
4 able **5** adept **6** expert **7** capable, skilled **8** advanced, masterly, skillful **9** authority, competent, effective, masterful, qualified **11** crackerjack, experienced **12** accomplished

profile
3 bio **5** chart **6** sketch, survey **7** contour, diagram, outline **8** exposure, portrait, side view **9** biography **10** silhouette **11** description

profit
3 net **4** gain, take **5** serve, yield **6** excess, income, payoff, return **7** benefit, receipt **8** earnings, proceeds **10** percentage **12** compensation **sudden: 7** killing

profitable
6 paying, useful **7** gainful **8** fruitful **9** lucrative, rewarding **10** beneficial, well-paying, worthwhile **11** moneymaking **12** advantageous, remunerative

profligate
4 wild **6** waster **7** immoral, spender, wastrel **8** prodigal, reckless, wasteful **9** abandoned, dissolute, indulgent, reprobate **10** dissipated, immoderate, licentious, squanderer **11** extravagant, promiscuous, spendthrift **13** self-indulgent

profound
4 deep, wise **5** heavy, total, utter **7** abysmal, intense **8** absolute, abstruse, complete, esoteric, thorough **9** intensive **10** deep-seated, insightful

profundity
5 depth **6** wisdom **7** insight **8** deepness **12** abstruseness

profuse
4 lush **6** lavish **7** copious, fulsome, liberal, opulent **8** abundant, generous, prodigal **9** abounding, bounteous, bountiful, excessive, exuberant, luxuriant, plentiful **10** munificent **11** extravagant

profusion
4 glut, riot **5** flood, spate, surge **6** bounty, deluge, excess, wealth **7** nimiety, satiety, surfeit,

surplus, torrent **8** overflow, overload, plethora **9** abundance, plenitude **10** lavishness, luxuriance, oversupply, plentitude, redundancy **11** copiousness, prodigality, sufficiency, superfluity **12** extravagance **13** overabundance

progenitor
4 sire **6** author, father, mother **8** ancestor, forebear **9** initiator, precursor **10** antecessor, forefather, forerunner, originator **11** predecessor

progeny
4 line **5** issue **6** litter, result, scions **7** outcome, product **8** children **9** offspring, posterity **11** descendants

prognosis
8 estimate, forecast, prophecy **9** prevision **10** estimation, prediction **11** expectation **12** anticipation

prognostic
4 omen, sign **6** augury **7** portent, presage **10** foreboding, indication

prognosticate
6 divine **7** foresee, predict, presage **8** forecast, foretell, prophesy

program
4 bill, book, plan, show **5** plans, slate **6** agenda, course, docket, lineup, policy **7** listing **8** calendar, playbill, schedule, syllabus **9** broadcast, procedure, timetable **10** bill of fare, curriculum

programming language
3 SQL **4** DASL, JADE, Java, LISP, Perl, Thue **5** Algol, BASIC, COBOL, CORAL **6** Euclid, Groovy, Inform, Pascal, Prolog, Python, Scheme, Simula **7** FORTRAN, Haskell, Miranda **10** JavaScript, PostScript **11** Visual Basic

progress
4 fare, gain, grow **5** get on, march **6** course, growth **7** advance, headway, passage, proceed **8** anabasis, get along, momentum **9** evolution, flowering, unfolding **11** advancement, development, improvement
planned: 7 telesis

progressing
5 afoot **7** en route **8** under way

progression
4 path **5** chain **6** course, growth, series **7** advance **8** sequence **9** evolution, unfolding **10** trajectory **11** development

progressive
6 modern **7** growing, liberal, radical **8** advanced, tolerant **9** advancing **10** developing, increasing

prohibit
3 ban, bar **4** stop **5** block, debar **6** enjoin, forbid, outlaw **7** prevent **8** preclude **9** interdict

prohibited
4 tabu **5** taboo **6** banned, barred **7** illegal, illicit **8** verboten **9** forbidden

prohibition
3 ban, bar **5** taboo **7** embargo **8** sanction **9** interdict **10** constraint, forbidding, injunction **12** disallowance, interdiction, proscription

prohibitive
5 steep **6** costly **7** sky-high **9** excessive **10** exorbitant, forbidding **11** restrictive

project
3 jut **4** cast, feat, plan **5** bulge **6** affair, design, devise, extend, intend, scheme, vision **7** arrange, concern, emprise, exploit, feature, imagine, propose, purpose, venture **8** business, conceive, envisage, envision, game plan, overhang, protrude, stand out, stick out, strategy **9** blueprint, visualize **10** enterprise **11** proposition, undertaking

projection
3 jut **4** bump, knob, view **5** bulge **7** display **8** estimate, forecast, overhang, scheming, swelling **9** extension **10** jutting out, perception **11** expectation
vaulted: 4 apse

prolapse
3 sag

proletariat
6 masses **7** workers **8** laborers **9** commoners, hoi polloi **12** working class

prolific
4 rich **6** fecund, gifted, lavish **7** fertile **8** abundant, creative, fruitful **9** abounding, bountiful, inventive **10** generating, generative **11** reproducing **12** reproductive

prolix
4 long **5** windy, wordy **7** diffuse, lengthy, tedious, verbose **8** drawn out, rambling, tiresome **9** redundant, wearisome **10** long-winded

prologue
7 opening, preface, prelude **8** exordium, foreword, overture, preamble **9** beginning **12** introduction

prolong
6 extend **7** drag out, draw out, spin out, stretch **8** continue, elongate, lengthen

prolonged
7 lasting, lengthy **8** drawn-out **9** lingering **10** continuing, persistent, persisting

prom
4 ball, fete, gala **5** dance **6** formal

promenade
4 deck, walk **6** parade, stroll **9** boardwalk

Prometheus
brother: 5 Atlas **9** Menoetius **10** Epimetheus
creation: 3 man **7** mankind
father: 7 Iapetus
gift: 4 fire

mother: **7** Clymene
muralist: **6** Orozco
rescuer: **8** Heracles, Hercules
tormentor: **5** eagle

prominence
4 crag, fame, rise, spur **5** bulge **6** height, renown, status **8** eminence, headland, prestige, salience, standing **9** celebrity, elevation **10** importance, projection **11** distinction

prominent
5 famed, great, noted **6** famous, marked, signal **7** eminent, jutting, leading, notable, popular, salient **8** renowned, striking **9** arresting, notorious, well-known **10** celebrated, noticeable, pronounced, remarkable **11** conspicuous, eye-catching, illustrious, outstanding **13** distinguished
person: **3** VIP **4** BMOC, lion **5** mogul, nabob **6** bigwig, honcho **7** big shot, grandee **8** luminary, mandarin, somebody **9** dignitary **13** high-muck-a-muck

promiscuous
5 mixed **6** casual, random, varied **7** immoral **8** careless **9** haphazard, hit-or-miss, irregular **10** licentious **11** unselective **12** unrestrained

promise
3 vow **4** bode, bond, oath, word **5** agree, augur, swear, vouch **6** assure, engage, ensure, expect, insure, parole, pledge, plight **7** betroth, compact, consent, declare, outlook, portend, presage, suggest **8** contract, covenant, indicate **9** assurance, betrothal, potential, undertake **11** declaration, expectation

promised land
4 Zion **6** Canaan, heaven **8** paradise **11** kingdom come

promising
6 likely **7** hopeful **9** favorable **10** auspicious **11** encouraging

promissory note
3 IOU

promontory
4 beak, bill, cape, head, ness **5** bulge, point **8** foreland, headland

promote
3 aid **4** help, hype, plug, puff, push, sell, tout **5** boost, favor, raise **6** foster, launch, prefer **7** advance, build up, elevate, endorse, forward, further, nurture, present, support **8** advocate, champion **9** advertise, encourage, publicize, recommend

promotion
6 step up **7** advance, buildup, puffery **9** elevation, publicity, upgrading **10** preference, preferment **11** advancement, advertising, improvement **13** advertisement

prompt
3 apt, cue, jog **4** fast, goad, help, hint, move, spur, urge **5** alert, quick, rapid, ready **6** assist, incite, induce, on time, remind, speedy, stir up, timely **7** suggest **8** convince, persuade, punctual, reminder **10** responsive

promulgate
5 issue **6** decree **7** declare, publish **8** announce, proclaim **9** advertise, broadcast **10** annunciate **11** disseminate

prone
3 apt **4** flat, open **5** given, level **6** liable, likely, supine **7** subject, tending, willing **8** disposed, facedown, inclined **9** lying down, reclining, prostrate, recumbent **10** horizontal **11** predisposed, susceptible

prong
4 barb, fang, fork, spur, stab, tine **5** point, thorn **6** pierce

pronghorn
8 antelope

____ pro nobis
3 ora

pronoun
archaic: **2** ye **3** thy **4** thou **5** thine
demonstrative: **4** that, this **5** these, those
indefinite: **3** all, any, few, one **4** both, each, none, some **5** no one, other **6** anyone, either, nobody **7** another, anybody, neither, nothing, someone **8** anything, somebody **9** everybody, something **10** everything
personal: **2** he, it, my, we **3** her, him, she, you **4** them, they
possessive: **2** my **3** her, his, its, our **4** hers, mine, ours, your **5** their, yours **6** theirs
reflexive: **6** itself, myself **7** herself, himself, oneself, ourself **8** yourself **9** ourselves **10** themselves, yourselves
relative: **3** who **4** that, what, whom **5** which, whose, whoso **6** whomso **7** whoever **8** whatever, whomever **9** whichever, whosoever **10** whatsoever, whomsoever **11** whichsoever

pronounce
3 say **5** judge, sound, speak, state, utter **6** affirm, assert, decree, recite **7** declare **9** enunciate **10** articulate

pronounced
5 clear **6** marked, strong **7** assured, decided, evident, obvious **8** clear-cut, definite, distinct **12** unmistakable

pronouncement
5 edict **6** decree **9** manifesto, statement **11** declaration, publication **12** notification

pronto
3 now, PDQ **4** ASAP, fast, stat **6** at once **7** quickly **8** directly **9** forthwith, instanter, instantly, posthaste, right away **11** immediately

pronunciation
distinctive: **4** burr, lilt **5** drawl, twang **6** accent, brogue
study: **8** orthoepy **9** phonetics

proof
4 test **5** facts, goods, repro **6** galley **8** argument, evidence **9** testament, testimony **10** impression **11** attestation **12** confirmation

proofreaders' mark
4 dele, stet **5** caret

prop
4 stay **5** brace, shore **6** buoy up, hold up **7** bolster, shore up, support, sustain **8** buttress **10** strengthen **12** underpinning

propaganda
4 hype **8** agitprop, lobbying

propagandize
4 tout **5** boost, extol **7** advance, promote, trumpet **9** brainwash, catechize, inculcate **10** promulgate **11** proselytize **12** indoctrinate

propagate
5 beget, breed, raise, strew **6** extend, spread **7** diffuse, publish, radiate **8** disperse, generate, increase, multiply, transmit **9** circulate, cultivate, publicize, reproduce **10** distribute **11** disseminate

propel
4 goad, move, push, spur, urge **5** drive, egg on, power, shoot, shove **6** exhort, launch, thrust **7** actuate **8** activate

propellant
3 gas **4** fuel, spur **7** impetus, impulse **8** catalyst, stimulus **9** explosive, incentive, stimulant **10** motivation

propensity
7 leaning **8** penchant **10** preference **11** inclination

proper
3 apt, due, fit **4** good, just, meet, nice, prim, true **5** exact, right **6** au fait, decent, prissy, seemly, useful **7** correct, desired, fitting, genteel **8** becoming, decorous, priggish, rightful, rigorous, suitable **9** befitting **10** felicitous **11** appropriate, comme il faut, distinctive
combining form: **4** orth **5** ortho

property
4 land, mark **5** acres, trait, worth **6** assets, estate, realty, riches, virtue, wealth **7** acreage, chattel, effects, feature, fortune, quality **8** chattels, dominion, hallmark, holdings, premises **9** attribute, ownership, resources, substance **10** belongings, possession, real estate
conveyor: **7** alienor
recipient: **7** alienee
seller: **7** Realtor
transfer: **8** alienate

prophecy
6 vision **8** forecast **10** divination, prediction **11** foretelling

prophesy
5 augur **6** divine, preach **7** foresee, portend, predict, presage **8** forecast, foretell, instruct, soothsay **9** adumbrate, prefigure **10** vaticinate **13** prognosticate

prophet
4 seer **5** augur, sibyl **6** auspex, oracle **7** diviner, seeress **8** foreseer, haruspex **9** predictor **10** forecaster, foreteller, prophesier, soothsayer **11** Nostradamus **13** fortune-teller
Arthurian: **6** Merlin
Major: **6** Daniel, Isaiah **7** Ezekiel **8** Jeremiah
Minor: **4** Amos, Joel, Osee **5** Hosea, Jonah, Micah, Nahum **6** Haggai **7** Malachi, Obadiah **8** Habakkuk **9** Zechariah, Zephaniah

Prophet author
6 Gibran (Khalil)

prophetess
5 sibyl **6** Pythia **7** Deborah **9** Cassandra

prophetic
5 vatic **6** orphic **7** Delphic **8** Delphian, oracular **9** presaging, prescient, sibylline, vaticinal **10** predictive, revelatory **11** apocalyptic, foretelling

propinquity
7 kinship **8** nearness **9** closeness, proximity **10** contiguity

propitiate
5 adapt, atone **6** adjust, pacify, soothe **7** appease, assuage, gratify, mollify, placate, satisfy **9** intercede, reconcile **10** conciliate

propitious
4 good, rosy **5** lucky **6** benign, bright **7** benefic, helpful **8** favoring **9** favorable, fortunate, opportune, promising **10** auspicious, beneficent, beneficial, benevolent **12** advantageous

proponent
6 backer **8** advocate, champion, defender **9** expounder, supporter **10** enthusiast

proportion
4 rate, size **5** allot, ratio, quota, share **6** adjust, divide **7** balance, conform, harmony **8** symmetry **9** dimension **10** percentage **12** relationship

proportional
5 scale **7** in scale, pro rata **8** relative **9** equalized **10** contingent, equivalent, reciprocal **11** correlative, symmetrical **12** commensurate **13** commensurable, corresponding

proposal
3 bid **4** idea, plan **6** motion, scheme **7** outline, proffer, project **8** scenario **10** invitation, suggestion **11** proposition
final: **9** ultimatum

propose
3 aim, ask, put **4** name, plan, pose **5** offer **6** design, intend, submit, tender **7** advance, move for, present, request, solicit, suggest **8** nominate, put forth, set forth, theorize **9** recommend **10** put forward

proposition
4 plan **5** offer **6** scheme, thesis **7** premise, suggest, theorem **8** proposal **10** invitation, suggestion

propound
3 put **4** pose **5** offer **7** present, suggest **8** put forth

proprietor
5 owner **8** landlord **9** possessor

propriety
7 aptness, decency, decorum, manners **8** behavior, civility, good form **9** etiquette, rightness **10** seemliness **11** correctness, fittingness, suitability **12** decorousness

propulsion
4 fuel, push **5** drive, force, power **6** energy, thrust

prorate
5 allot, divvy, quota, share, split **6** assess, divide, parcel, ration **7** divvy up, portion **9** apportion, partition **10** distribute

prorogue
3 end **4** rise, stay **5** defer, delay **6** hold up, put off, recess, shelve **7** adjourn, hold off, suspend **8** dissolve, hold over, postpone **9** terminate

prosaic
4 dull, flat **5** banal, prose, prosy, trite, vapid **6** boring, common **7** factual, literal, mundane, tedious **8** everyday, lifeless, ordinary, workaday **9** colorless **10** lackluster, uneventful **11** commonplace **13** unimaginative

proscenium
5 frame, stage **9** forestage **10** foreground

proscribe
3 ban **4** damn **6** enjoin, forbid, outlaw **7** condemn **8** prohibit, sentence **9** interdict

proscription
3 ban **4** tabu **5** taboo **8** sanction **11** prohibition **12** condemnation, interdiction

prosecute
3 sue **4** wage **5** press **6** charge, indict, pursue **7** carry on, perform **8** continue **9** bring suit, persevere

prosecutor
2 DA

proselyte
7 convert, recruit **8** neophyte

proselytize
5 draft **6** enlist, enroll, sign up **7** convert, recruit, win over **8** convince **9** brainwash, catechize **11** prevail upon **12** indoctrinate

____ prosequi
5 nolle

prospect
4 mine, view **5** scene, vista **6** chance, survey, vision **7** dig into, explore, lookout, outlook **8** customer, exposure **9** candidate **10** expectancy **11** expectation, possibility **12** anticipation

prospective
6 coming, future, likely **7** awaited, ensuing, nearing, pending, planned, would-be **8** destined, eventual, expected, hoped-for, intended, proposed, soon-to-be **9** impending, looked-for, potential, scheduled **10** consequent, succeeding **11** anticipated, approaching, predestined, forthcoming

prospectus
4 list, plan **6** design, layout, précis **7** epitome, outline, program, summary **8** bulletin, synopsis **9** catalogue, timetable **10** projection **11** description **12** announcement

prosper
5 score, yield **6** arrive, do well, thrive **7** make out, produce, succeed, turn out **8** flourish, grow rich

prosperity
4 ease **6** riches, wealth **7** success **8** thriving **9** abundance, advantage, affluence, well-being

Prospero
daughter: **7** Miranda
servant: **5** Ariel
slave: **7** Caliban

prosperous
4 rich, well **5** happy, lucky **6** robust, strong **7** booming, halcyon, opulent, wealthy, well-off **8** affluent, thriving, well-to-do **9** desirable, favorable, fortunate, promising, well-fixed **10** auspicious, successful, well-heeled **11** comfortable, flourishing

prostitute
4 bawd, doxy, drab, moll **5** abuse, B-glrl, madam, quean, whore **6** callet, debase, floozy, harlot, hooker, misuse, wanton **7** chippie, cocotte, corrupt, cyprian, floozie, hustler, Paphian **8** call girl, meretrix, strumpet **9** courtesan, party girl **11** fille de joie, nightwalker **12** camp follower, streetwalker
reformed: **8** magdalen **9** magdalene

prostitution
8 harlotry, whoredom **13** streetwalking
house of: **4** crib, stew **6** bagnio **7** brothel, lupanar **8** bordello, cathouse **10** bawdy house **13** sporting house

prostrate
4 fell, flat **5** abase, level, prone **6** humble, lay low, submit, supine **7** exhaust, wear out **8** helpless, overcome **9** decumbent, exhausted, overpower, overwhelm, powerless, recumbent **10** procumbent, submissive

protagonist
4 hero, lead, star **5** actor **6** leader **7** heroine, sponsor **8** advocate, champion **9** principal

protean
6 mobile, varied **7** diverse, mutable **8** variable **9** adaptable, versatile **10** changeable

protect
4 save **5** cover, guard **6** defend, screen, secure, shield **7** shelter **8** preserve, restrict **9** safeguard

protection
4 care **5** aegis, armor, bribe, graft, guard **6** safety, shield **7** bulwark, defense, shelter, support **8** armament, coverage, immunity, security **9** extortion, insurance, safeguard **11** supervision

protector
5 armor, guard **6** patron, regent, shield **8** guardian **9** caretaker

protégé
4 ward **5** pupil **7** student, trainee **8** disciple

protein
4 zein **5** actin, opsin **6** avidin, enzyme, fibrin, globin **7** albumin, elastin, fibroin, histone, keratin, legumin, sericin **8** creatine, globulin, glutelin, prolamin, protamin, proteose, vitellin
complex: 6 mucoid
derivative: 7 peptide, peptone
poisonous: 5 abrin, ricin

pro tem
6 acting **7** interim **9** ad interim, temporary

protest
4 aver, avow, beef **5** sit-in **6** affirm, assert, avouch, except, object, oppose, picket, resist **7** declare, dissent, profess **8** maintain **9** challenge, complaint, objection **10** disapprove **11** demonstrate, disapproval **13** demonstration

Protestant
5 Amish **6** Mormon, Quaker, Shaker **7** Baptist, Lollard, Pilgrim, Puritan **8** Anglican, Lutheran, Moravian **9** Adventist, Mennonite, Methodist, Unitarian **11** Pentecostal **12** Episcopalian, Presbyterian
Bohemian: 7 Hussite
French: 8 Huguenot

protocol
4 code, form, rule **6** custom, ritual **7** compact, conduct, decorum, manners **8** courtesy **9** concordat, etiquette, politesse, propriety **11** conventions, formalities

prototype
4 norm **5** model, pilot **6** design **7** example, pattern **8** original, paradigm, standard

prototypical
5 ideal, model **7** classic **9** classical, exemplary **10** archetypal

protozoan
4 cell **5** ameba **6** amoeba **7** ciliate, stentor **10** flagellate, paramecium

protract
6 drag on, extend **7** drag out, draw out, prolong, stretch **8** continue

protrude
3 jut **4** poke, pout **5** bulge **6** jut out **7** project **8** overhang, stand out, stick out

protrusion
3 jut, nub **4** bump **5** bulge **8** swelling **10** projection

protuberant
5 bulgy **7** bulging **9** prominent **11** conspicuous

proud
4 vain **5** huffy, lofty, noble **6** lordly, stuffy, superb **7** haughty, pleased, pompous, stuck-up, stately **8** arrogant, exultant, glorious, scornful, snobbish, spirited, splendid, superior, vigorous **9** conceited, delighted, imperious **10** disdainful, high-handed **11** magnificent, pretentious, resplendent **12** ostentatious, supercilious

Proulx novel
9 Postcards **12** Shipping News (The)

Proust character
5 Swann (Charles) **6** Marcel, Odette (Swann) **7** Charlus (Baron de) **8** Gilberte (Swann) **9** Albertine

prove
3 try **4** show, test **5** argue, check **6** attest, pan out, verify **7** bear out, certify, confirm, examine, explain, turn out **8** document, indicate, validate **9** determine, establish **11** corroborate, demonstrate **12** substantiate

provenance
4 root, well **6** origin, source **7** history **9** inception **10** derivation

provender
4 feed, food **8** victuals **10** provisions

proverb
3 saw **5** adage, axiom, maxim **6** byword, saying **7** epigram **8** aphorism

provide
4 give, hand **5** endow, endue, equip, serve, state **6** afford, outfit, render, supply **7** deliver, furnish, prepare, specify, support **8** dispense, hand over, maintain **9** stipulate

provided
5 given **6** if only **8** equipped, supplied

providence
4 care **6** thrift **7** caution, economy **8** prudence **9** foresight, frugality **11** forethought, thriftiness

provident
5 canny, chary **6** frugal, saving **7** careful, prudent, sparing, thrifty **8** prepared **10** economical, unwasteful **11** foresighted

providential
5 happy, lucky **9** benignant, fortunate **10** auspicious, fortuitous

province
4 area, duty, role, work **5** field, shire **6** canton, county, domain, office, region, sphere **7** demesne, pursuit, terrain **8** district, dominion, function **9** bailiwick, champaign, territory **10** department **12** jurisdiction

provincial
5 local, rural **6** narrow, rustic, simple **7** country, insular, limited **8** pastoral **9** parochial, sectarian, small-town **11** countrified

proving ground
10 laboratory, White Sands

provision
5 stock, store **6** supply **9** condition **11** preparation, requirement, reservation, stipulation

provisional
5 stamp **6** acting, pro tem **9** temporary **10** contingent **11** conditional

provisions
4 feed, food, grub **5** stock **6** viands **7** aliment, edibles, nurture, vittles **8** supplies, victuals **9** provender **10** sustenance **11** comestibles
dealer: **8** chandler

proviso
6 clause **7** article **9** condition **11** stipulation

provocation
5 cause, wrong **7** offense **8** stimulus, vexation **9** annoyance, incentive **10** incitement **11** instigation

provocative
4 edgy **5** heady **8** alluring, annoying, arousing, exciting **9** offensive **10** intriguing **11** challenging, stimulating

provoke
3 bug, irk, vex **4** abet, rile, stir, wake **5** anger, annoy, cause, evoke, pique, rouse, upset, waken **6** arouse, awaken, bother, excite, foment, harass, incite, induce, kindle, nettle, stir up, whip up **7** incense, inflame, inspire, outrage, quicken **8** generate, irritate, motivate, occasion **9** challenge, galvanize, instigate, stimulate

provost
4 head **6** keeper **7** marshal **8** director **10** magistrate **13** administrator

prow
3 bow **4** stem **5** front **10** projection

prowess
5 skill, valor **7** bravery, command, courage, heroism, mastery **9** expertise, gallantry **10** excellence

prowl
4 hunt, roam **5** skulk, slink, sneak, steal **6** search, wander

proximate
4 near, next **5** close **6** nearby **8** adjacent, imminent **9** following, immediate, preceding **10** near-at-hand **11** forthcoming

proximity
8 nearness, vicinity **9** adjacency, closeness, immediacy **10** contiguity **11** propinquity

proxy
5 agent **6** deputy **7** stand-in **8** attorney **9** surrogate **10** substitute

pro ___
3 tem **4** bono, rata **5** forma, tanto **7** tempore

prude
4 prig **7** old maid, Puritan **8** bluenose **9** Mrs. Grundy

prudence
4 care **5** skill **6** acumen, reason, thrift, wisdom **7** caution, economy **8** sagacity **9** foresight, frugality **10** astuteness, discretion, expediency, precaution, providence, shrewdness **11** calculation, forethought, thriftiness

prudent
4 sage, sane, wary, wise **5** canny, chary **6** frugal **7** careful, politic **8** cautious, discreet, sensible **9** expedient, judicious **11** circumspect

prudish
4 prim **5** stern **6** narrow, prissy, proper, severe, strict, stuffy **7** austere, genteel **8** affected, decorous, priggish **11** puritanical, straitlaced

prune
3 cut, lop **4** clip, crop, pare, plum, thin, trim **5** shear **6** cut off, reduce, remove **7** cut away, cut back, shorten **8** pare down, truncate

prurience
4 lust **6** desire, libido **7** lechery, passion **8** cupidity **9** carnality, eroticism **11** lustfulness **13** concupiscence

prurient
4 lewd **5** bawdy **6** erotic **7** goatish, lustful, satyric, sensual **9** lickerish **10** lascivious, libidinous, passionate **12** concupiscent

pruritic
5 itchy

Prussian
aristocrat: **6** Junker **12** Hohenzollern
prime minister: **8** Bismarck (Otto von)
ruler: **7** Wilhelm **9** Frederick (the Great)

pry
4 nose, open, poke **5** jimmy, lever, snoop **6** meddle **7** inquire **9** interfere

prying
4 nosy **6** snoopy **7** curious **8** meddling, snooping **9** intrusive, obtrusive, officious **10** meddlesome **11** impertinent, inquisitive

psalm
3 ode **4** hymn, poem, song **5** paean
book: 7 psalter
selection: 6 Hallel
word: 5 selah

psalmist
4 poet **5** Asaph, David **6** cantor

pseudo
4 fake, mock, sham **5** bogus, false, phony **7** pretend **8** spurious **9** imitation **10** artificial **11** counterfeit

pseudonym
5 alias **7** pen name **9** false name, stage name **10** nom de plume **11** nom de guerre

psyche
4 mind, soul **5** anima **6** animus, pneuma, spirit
part: 2 id **3** ego **8** superego

Psyche's beloved
4 Eros **5** Cupid

psychiatrist
6 shrink **8** alienist **11** neurologist
American: 3 May (Rollo) **5** Reich (Wilhelm) **6** Kramer (Peter), Rogers (Carl) **7** Erikson (Erik) **8** Sullivan (Harry Stack) **9** Menninger (Karl)
Austrian: 5 Adler (Alfred), Freud (Anna, Sigmund), Reich (Wilhelm)
British: 5 Laing (R. D.)
French: 5 Lacan (Jacques)
German: 5 Fromm (Erich) **6** Horney (Karen)
Swiss: 4 Jung (Carl) **9** Rorschach (Hermann)

psychic
4 seer **6** medium, mental, occult **8** cerebral **9** mentalist, prophetic, spiritual **10** mind reader, telepathic **11** clairvoyant, telekinetic **12** intellectual, supersensory
American: 5 Cayce (Edgar), Dixon (Jeane) **10** Montgomery (Ruth)
power: 3 ESP

psycho
3 nut **5** crazy, sicko, wacko **6** madman, maniac, mental, schizo, weirdo **7** berserk, haywire, lunatic, nutcase **8** crackpot, demented, deranged, head case **9** fruitcake, screwball, sociopath

psychoanalyst
4 Jung (Carl Gustav), Rank (Otto) **5** Adler (Alfred), Freud (Sigmund), Fromm (Erich), Klein (Melanie), Kohut (Heinz), Lacan (Jacques) **6** Horney (Karen) **7** Erikson (Erik) **8** Ferenczi (Sandor)

psychologist
6 shrink **9** therapist
American: 5 James (William) **6** Terman (Lewis), Watson (John), Yerkes (Robert) **7** Skinner (B. F.) **9** Thorndike (Edward L.)
English: 4 Ward (James) **8** Spearman (Charles), Tichener (Edward)
German: 5 Wundt (Wilhelm) **6** Müller (Georg), Stumpf (Carl) **10** Wertheimer (Max)

psychotic
3 mad **5** crazy **6** insane **8** demented, deranged, schizoid **13** schizophrenic

ptarmigan
6 grouse

ptomaine
6 poison

pub
3 bar, inn **4** dive **5** joint **6** tavern **7** barroom, gin mill, taproom **8** grogshop **9** roadhouse **11** rathskeller

puberty
11 adolescence

public
4 open **5** civic, civil, state **6** common, mutual, people, shared, social **7** general, popular, society **8** communal, national, populace **9** community, municipal, universal **10** accessible, government

publican
7 barkeep **8** landlord, licensee, taverner **9** bartender, collector, innkeeper **12** tax collector

publication
4 book **7** article, journal **8** magazine, pamphlet **9** broadside, newspaper **10** periodical
list: 12 bibliography

public house
3 bar, inn **6** hostel, saloon, tavern **7** auberge, hospice **8** hostelry

publicity
3 ink **4** hype, plug **5** blurb, press, promo **6** hoopla, notice **7** billing, fanfare, write-up **8** ballyhoo **9** attention, promotion **11** advertising **12** announcement **13** advertisement

publicize
3 air **4** bill, hype, plug, puff, push, tout **5** boost **7** promote, trumpet **8** announce **9** advertise, broadcast **10** press-agent, promulgate

publish
3 air **5** issue, print **6** get out, inform, put out, report **7** release **8** announce, bring out, proclaim **9** advertise, broadcast, make known **10** distribute, promulgate **11** disseminate

Puccini opera
5 Tosca **7** Le Villi **8** La Bohème, Turandot **12** Manon Lescaut **15** Madame Butterfly

puck
3 elf, imp **4** disk **5** fairy **6** spirit, sprite **9** hobgoblin, prankster

pucker
4 fold **5** purse **6** cockle, crease **7** wrinkle **8** compress, contract **9** constrict

puckish
5 antic, elfin, larky, pixie **6** elvish, impish **7** playful **8** prankish **9** whimsical **11** mischievous

Puck's master
6 Oberon

pudding
4 duff **6** burgoo **7** custard, tapioca
baked: **5** kugel **10** brown Betty

pudgy
3 fat **5** plump, round, stout, tubby **6** chubby, chunky, flabby, rotund **8** plumpish, roly-poly

pueblo
4 town **7** village **8** dwelling
ceremonial room: **4** kiva

Pueblo tribe
3 Zia **4** Hopi, Taos, Zuñi **5** Acoma, Jemez, Keres, Tigua **6** Laguna **7** Cochiti

puerile
5 inane, silly **6** jejune **7** foolish **8** childish, immature, juvenile

Puerto Rico
capital: **7** San Juan
city: **5** Ponce **7** Bayamon **8** Mayagüez
discoverer: **8** Columbus (Christopher)
language: **7** Spanish
location: **10** West Indies

puff
3 pad **4** blow, brag, crow, drag, emit, huff, pant, plug, pouf, push, tout, waft **5** blurb, boast, boost, elate, expel, quilt, swell, vaunt, whiff **6** exhale, pastry, praise **7** flatter, inflate **8** swelling **9** advertise, comforter, publicize **10** exaggerate

puffer
8 blowfish **9** globefish, swellfish

puffery
4 buzz, hype, plug **7** fanfare **8** ballyhoo **9** promotion, publicity **11** advertising **12** exaggeration, press-agentry

puffin
4 bird **7** seabird **9** sea parrot **10** shearwater
cousin: **3** auk

puffy
7 swollen **8** inflated

pug
3 bun, dog **4** nose **5** boxer, track **9** footprint

Puget Sound port
6 Tacoma **7** Seattle

pugilism
6 boxing **13** prizefighting

pugilist
5 boxer **7** fighter **12** prizefighter

pugnacious
7 defiant, scrappy **8** brawling, fighting, militant **9** bellicose, combative, truculent **10** aggressive, rebellious **11** belligerent, contentious, quarrelsome **13** argumentative

pugnacity
9 hostility **10** aggression, truculence, truculency **12** belligerence **13** combativeness

puisne
6 junior **8** inferior

puissance
5 force, might, power **6** energy **7** potency **8** strength

puissant
6 mighty, potent, strong **8** forceful, powerful

pukka
4 real, tops **7** genuine **8** bona fide **9** authentic **10** first-class

pule
3 cry **4** mewl **5** whine **7** whimper

Pulitzer Prize fiction winner
1918: **5** Poole (Ernest)
1919: **10** Tarkington (Booth)
1921: **7** Wharton (Edith)
1922: **10** Tarkington (Booth)
1923: **6** Cather (Willa)
1924: **6** Wilson (Margaret)
1925: **6** Ferber (Edna)
1926: **5** Lewis (Sinclair)
1927: **9** Bromfield (Louis)
1928: **6** Wilder (Thornton)
1929: **8** Peterkin (Julia)
1930: **7** La Farge (Oliver)
1931: **6** Barnes (Margaret)
1932: **4** Buck (Pearl)
1933: **9** Stribling (T. S.)
1934: **6** Miller (Caroline)
1935: **7** Johnson (Josephine)
1936: **5** Davis (Harold)
1937: **8** Mitchell (Margaret)
1938: **8** Marquand (John)
1939: **8** Rawlings (Marjorie Kinnan)
1940: **9** Steinbeck (John)
1942: **7** Glasgow (Ellen)
1943: **8** Sinclair (Upton)
1944: **6** Flavin (Martin)
1945: **6** Hersey (John)
1947: **6** Warren (Robert Penn)
1948: **8** Michener (James)
1949: **7** Cozzens (James Gould)
1950: **7** Guthrie (A. B.)
1951: **7** Richter (Conrad)

1952: **4** Wouk (Herman)
1953: **9** Hemingway (Ernest)
1955: **8** Faulkner (William)
1956: **6** Kantor (MacKinlay)
1958: **4** Agee (James)
1959: **6** Taylor (Robert Lewis)
1960: **5** Drury (Allen)
1961: **3** Lee (Harper)
1962: **7** O'Connor (Edwin)
1963: **8** Faulkner (William)
1965: **4** Grau (Shirley Ann)
1966: **6** Porter (Katherine Anne)
1967: **7** Malamud (Bernard)
1968: **6** Styron (William)
1969: **7** Momaday (N. Scott)
1970: **8** Stafford (Jean)
1972: **7** Stegner (Wallace)
1973: **5** Welty (Eudora)
1975: **6** Shaara (Michael)
1976: **6** Bellow (Saul)
1978: **9** McPherson (James Alan)
1979: **7** Cheever (John)
1980: **6** Mailer (Norman)
1981: **5** Toole (John Kennedy)
1982: **6** Updike (John)
1983: **6** Walker (Alice)
1984: **7** Kennedy (William)
1985: **5** Lurie (Alison)
1986: **8** McMurtry (Larry)
1987: **6** Taylor (Peter)
1988: **8** Morrison (Toni)
1989: **5** Tyler (Anne)
1990: **8** Hijuelos (Oscar)
1991: **6** Updike (John)
1992: **6** Smiley (Jane)
1993: **6** Butler (Robert Olen)
1994: **6** Proulx (E. Annie)
1995: **7** Shields (Carol)
1996: **4** Ford (Richard)
1997: **10** Millhauser (Steven)
1998: **4** Roth (Philip)
1999: **10** Cunningham (Michael)
2000: **6** Lahiri (Jhumpa)
2001: **6** Chabon (Michael)
2002: **5** Russo (Richard)
2003: **9** Eugenides (Jeffrey)
2004: **5** Jones (Edward P.)
2005: **8** Robinson (Marilynne)
2006: **6** Brooks (Geraldine)

pull
3 oar, row, tow, tug **4** drag, draw, haul, lure, root, yank **5** clout, draft, drive, force, pluck, put on, wrest **6** appeal, assume, entice **7** attract, draw out, extract, stretch **9** advantage, influence **10** attraction

pull back
6 rein in **7** retreat **8** withdraw

pull down
4 draw, earn, raze, ruin **5** lower, wreck **6** reduce **7** depress, destroy **8** demolish, overcome **9** dismantle

pullet
3 hen **5** chick **7** chicken

pulley
5 wheel **6** sheave
watch's: **5** fusee

pull in
3 nab **4** stop **5** check, pinch **6** arrest, arrive, collar, detain, pick up **7** inhibit **8** hold back, restrain **9** apprehend

pulling
6 towage **7** draught, haulage **8** traction
cable: **7** towline

Pullman
3 car **7** sleeper **8** suitcase **11** railroad car

pull off
6 attain, manage **7** achieve, succeed **8** carry out **10** accomplish

pull out
4 exit, quit **5** leave **6** depart **7** abandon, retreat, take off **8** shove off, withdraw

pull through
5 rally **7** get over, recover, ride out, survive, weather **9** get better

pullulate
4 teem **5** breed, crawl, swarm **6** abound, sprout **7** produce **9** germinate

pull up
4 halt, stop **5** check **6** rebuke **8** draw even **9** reprimand

pulp
4 mash, pith **5** crush **6** bruise, squash **7** tabloid **8** soft part

pulpit
4 ambo, dais **6** podium **7** lectern, rostrum **8** ministry, platform

pulpy
4 soft **5** cheap, juicy, lurid, mushy **6** spongy **11** sensational

pulsate
4 beat, pump **5** pound, throb **7** vibrate **9** oscillate, palpitate

pulse
4 beat **5** throb **6** rhythm

pulverize
4 beat, ruin **5** crush, grind, smash, wreck **6** crunch, powder **7** atomize, destroy **8** demolish **9** micronize **10** annihilate

puma
3 cat **6** cougar **7** panther **12** mountain lion

pummel
3 hit **4** beat, drub **5** pound, punch **6** batter, buffet, hammer, thrash, wallop **7** belabor

pump
4 draw, shoe, quiz **5** exert, grill, heart, raise **6** device, elicit **7** operate **8** energize, question

pumpernickel
3 rye **5** bread

pumpkin
4 pepo **6** orange, squash **12** jack-o'-lantern
family: **5** gourd

pump up
4 fill **6** excite, expand **7** enthuse, inflate **8** energize, increase, motivate **9** stimulate

pun
4 joke **11** paronomasia, play on words **13** double meaning

punch
3 box, cut, die, dig, hit, jab, jog, pep **4** bang, blow, cuff, poke, prod, push, snap, sock **5** clout, drive, notch, smack, vigor **6** buffet, emboss, energy, impact, pummel, strike, thrust **8** uppercut, vitality **9** emphasize, perforate

punch bowl
8 monteith

punch-drunk
5 dazed, dizzy, woozy **6** addled, groggy **8** unsteady **9** befuddled, slaphappy **10** staggering **11** disoriented

puncheon
3 log **4** cask, slab, tool **6** timber

puncher
5 boxer **6** cowboy

Punch's wife
4 Judy

punchy
5 dazed, dizzy, vivid **6** addled, lively **7** dynamic, vibrant **8** forceful, spirited, vigorous **9** befuddled, energetic, slaphappy **11** light-headed

punctilious
5 exact, fussy **7** careful, precise **9** attentive, observant **10** meticulous, particular, scrupulous **11** painstaking

punctual
5 ready **6** on time, prompt, timely

punctuate
4 mark **5** point **6** accent, divide, stress **8** separate **9** emphasize, interrupt **10** accentuate

punctuation mark
4 dash **5** brace, colon, comma, slant, slash **6** hyphen, parens, period **7** bracket, solidus, virgule **8** diagonal, ellipsis **9** backslash, guillemet, semicolon **10** apostrophe **11** parenthesis

puncture
3 jab **4** bore, flat, hole, stab **5** burst, drill, prick, punch **6** blow up, debunk, pierce, riddle **7** deflate, explode **8** disprove **9** discredit, perforate **11** perforation

pundit
4 guru, sage **5** maven, swami **6** critic, expert **7** teacher, wise man **9** authority, columnist **11** talking head

pungency
4 bite **5** sting **8** piquancy **9** intensity, sharpness

pungent
5 acrid, acute, harsh, sharp, spicy, tangy, zesty **6** barbed, biting **7** caustic, cutting, intense, mordant, painful, peppery, piquant, pointed **8** exciting, incisive, poignant, stinging **9** trenchant **10** irritating **11** provocative, stimulating

punish
4 fine, hurt **5** mulct, spank **6** amerce, avenge **7** chasten, correct, put down, reprove, revenge, scourge, torture **8** chastise, penalize **9** castigate, criticize **10** discipline

punishment
3 rod **4** fine **5** lumps, mulct **7** penalty, reproof **10** amercement, chastening, correction, discipline **11** castigation, comeuppance, just deserts **12** chastisement
instrument: **7** scourge

punitive
5 penal **11** castigating, vindicative **12** correctional, disciplinary

punk
4 hood, thug **5** cholo, rowdy, tough **6** novice, rookie, tinder **7** hoodlum, ruffian, toughie **8** beginner, gangster, inferior **9** roughneck **10** delinquent
rock group: **7** Ramones **10** Sex Pistols

punkah
3 fan

punt
4 boat, boot, kick, play **6** gamble, propel

Punta del ____
4 Este

puny
4 weak **5** dinky, petty, small **6** feeble, little, measly, paltry, slight **7** trivial **8** inferior, niggling, picayune, piddling, trifling

pupa
9 chrysalid, chrysalis

pupil
5 cadet, tutee **7** learner, scholar, student **8** disciple **9** schoolboy **10** apprentice, schoolgirl
French: **5** élève

puppet
4 doll, dupe, pawn, tool **6** figure, stooge **10** figurehead, marionette

puppy
3 dog **5** whelp

Purcell opera
13 Dido and Aeneas

purchase
3 buy **4** hold **6** obtain, pay for **7** acquire, procure **9** advantage **11** acquisition

pure
5 clean, fresh, plain, sheer, total, utter **6** chaste, decent **7** a priori, genuine, perfect, unmixed **8** absolute, abstract, innocent, spotless, virtuous **9** authentic, continent, exemplary, inviolate, stainless, unalloyed, undiluted, untainted **10** immaculate **11** theoretical, unblemished, unmitigated, unqualified **13** unadulterated

purebred
8 pedigree **9** full-blood, pedigreed **10** registered **11** full-blooded

puree
4 soup **5** paste

purely
4 just **5** quite **6** merely, simply, wholly **7** exactly, totally, utterly **8** entirely **10** altogether, completely **11** exclusively

purfle
4 trim **6** border **8** decorate, ornament

purgation
9 catharsis, cleansing **10** lustration

purgative
5 jalap **7** lustral **9** cathartic

purge
3 rid **4** oust **5** clear, expel **6** purify, remove **7** cleanse, wipe out **8** get rid of, lustrate **9** eliminate, liquidate

purification
8 ablution **9** catharsis, cleansing, expiation, purgation **10** absolution, lustration **11** expurgation **12** regeneration
sacrament: **7** baptism

purify
5 clean, purge **6** filter, refine **7** clarify, cleanse

Purim
11 Feast of Lots
queen: **6** Esther

puritan
4 prig **5** prude **8** bluenose **9** Mrs. Grundy

puritanical
4 prim **5** rigid **6** severe, strict **7** ascetic, austere, prudish **8** priggish **9** bluenosed **11** straitlaced

purity
8 chastity **9** innocence

purl
4 eddy, edge, knit **5** swirl, whirl **6** border, murmur, stitch **9** embroider

purlieu
5 haunt **7** hangout

purlieus
6 bounds, limits **7** suburbs **8** boundary, confines, environs **9** outskirts, precincts **12** neighborhood

purloin
3 nip **4** lift, take **5** filch, pinch, steal, swipe **6** pilfer, remove, rip off, snitch **11** appropriate

purloiner
5 crook, thief **8** larcener **9** larcenist

purple
4 plum, robe **5** cloth, grape, lilac, mauve, regal **6** florid, maroon, orchid, ornate, turgid, violet **7** flowery, pigment, pompous **8** imperial, lavender **9** bombastic, high-flown, overblown **10** rhetorical

Purple Heart
5 award, medal **10** decoration

purport
4 gist, mean **5** claim, drift, sense, tenor **6** allege, intend, thrust **7** meaning, message, profess, purpose **8** maintain **9** substance **11** connotation, implication **12** significance, significancy

purported
7 alleged, reputed, seeming **8** apparent, so-called, supposed **9** professed **10** ostensible

purpose
3 aim, end, use **4** goal, plan **5** point **6** action, design, intent, object **7** meaning, mission, resolve, subject **8** ambition, function, proposal **9** direction, intention, objective **10** aspiration, resolution **13** determination

purposeful
5 telic **6** driven, intent **7** earnest, planned, studied, willful **8** resolute **9** conscious, dedicated **10** calculated, considered, deliberate, determined **11** intentional **12** premeditated

purposeless
6 random **9** desultory, haphazard, hit-or-miss, irregular, unplanned

purposely
9 expressly **10** explicitly **12** deliberately **13** intentionally

purr
3 hum **6** murmur

purse
3 bag, sum **4** knit **5** money, pouch, prize **6** pucker, wallet **7** handbag **8** reticule **9** clutch bag **10** pocketbook, prize money
Scottish: **7** sporran

pursue
3 woo **4** hunt, seek **5** chase, haunt, hound, stalk, track, trail **6** badger, follow **7** afflict, go after, proceed **8** continue, engage in **9** persecute, persevere

pursuit
3 job **4** hunt, work **5** chase, quest, trade **6** search **8** activity, business, vocation **9** avocation, following **10** employment, occupation, profession

purvey
6 obtain, peddle, supply **7** furnish, provide **9** provision

purview
3 ken **5** ambit, limit, orbit, range, reach, scope, sweep **6** extent **8** boundary

push
3 pep **4** goad, plug, prod, sell, spur, urge **5** boost, drive, elbow, exert, force, impel, press, punch, shove, vigor **6** attack, effort, energy, expand, peddle, propel, throng, thrust **7** advance, assault, impetus, promote **8** ambition, pressure, vitality **9** incentive, influence, offensive **10** enterprise, get-up-and-go, initiative

Pushkin, Alexander
novel: **12** Eugene Onegin
play: **10** Stone Guest (The) **12** Boris Godunov
story: **13** Queen of Spades (The)

push off
4 exit **5** leave, start **6** depart, set out

push on
6 travel **7** advance, journey, proceed **8** continue, progress

pushover
4 snap **5** chump, cinch, softy **6** breeze, picnic, stooge, sucker **9** soft touch

pushy
4 bold **5** brash, nervy **7** forward **8** forceful **9** assertive, obnoxious **10** aggressive **12** presumptuous

pusillanimous
5 timid **6** coward, craven **7** chicken, gutless **8** cowardly, poltroon, timorous **9** spineless **11** lily-livered

puss
3 cat, mug **4** face **6** kisser, kitten

pussycat
5 sissy, softy **6** softie **8** pushover, weakling **9** soft touch **10** namby-pamby **13** bleeding heart

pussyfoot
5 creep, dodge, evade, glide, skulk, slink, sneak, steal **6** tiptoe **10** equivocate

pustule
4 boil **6** pimple **7** abscess, blister **8** furuncle **9** carbuncle

put
3 lay, set **4** park **5** place **8** position

putative
7 assumed, reputed **8** accepted, believed, presumed, supposed **11** conjectural **12** hypothetical

put away
3 eat **4** stow **5** eat up, swill **6** commit, devour, lock up **7** confine, consume **9** polish off **11** incarcerate

put by
4 save **5** lay in, store **7** lay away **8** lay aside, salt away

put down
5 crush, quash, quell **6** demean, demote, depose, squash, subdue **7** squelch **8** belittle, suppress **9** criticize, disparage, downgrade, humiliate

put forth
5 issue **6** assert **7** present, propose

put off
5 defer, delay **7** suspend **8** hold over, postpone

put on
3 act, don, kid **4** fake **5** apply, bluff, feign, mount, stage **6** affect, assume **7** mislead, perform, pretend, produce

put-on
3 act **4** fake, sham, show **5** faked, phony, spoof **6** parody **7** assumed, feigned **8** affected, disguise **9** pretended **10** artificial, false front

put out
3 vex **4** gall **5** annoy, douse, evict, issue, upset **6** bother, quench **7** disturb, produce, publish, trouble **8** irritate **9** aggravate, displease, embarrass **10** disconcert, exasperate, extinguish **13** inconvenience

putrefy
3 rot **5** decay, spoil, taint **6** molder **7** corrupt **9** break down, decompose

putrid
4 foul **5** fetid **6** rancid, rotten **7** corrupt, decayed, noisome, spoiled

putsch
4 coup **6** revolt **8** takeover, uprising **9** coup d'état, overthrow, rebellion **10** usurpation

putter
4 club, idle **6** fiddle, golfer, tinker **8** golf club

putting area
5 green

putto
5 cupid **6** cherub **8** amoretto

put together
4 form, join, make **5** build, unite **7** combine, connect, fashion, produce **8** assemble **9** construct, fabricate

putty
3 mud **4** clay **6** cement

put up
4 bunk **5** board, build, erect, house, lodge, raise **6** billet, harbor **7** quarter **8** domicile **9** construct

put up with
4 bear **5** stand **6** endure **8** tolerate

Puzo novel
6 Omerta **7** Last Don (The) **8** Fools Die, Sicilian (The) **9** Godfather (The)

puzzle
3 why **4** foil, koan **5** poser, rebus **6** baffle, enigma, fuddle, muddle, riddle **7** anagram, confuse, mystery, mystify, nonplus, paradox, perplex, problem, tangram **8** acrostic, befuddle, bewilder, confound **9** conundrum, crossword, dumbfound, frustrate **10** disconcert **11** brain-teaser
number: **6** Sudoku

puzzle out
5 solve **6** answer, decode **7** clarify, clear up, explain, unravel **8** decipher, unriddle

puzzling
6 knotty **7** cryptic **8** baffling **9** confusing, difficult, enigmatic **10** mystifying, perplexing **11** bewildering, paradoxical **12** inexplicable

Pygmalion
beloved: **7** Galatea
character: **5** Eliza (Doolittle) **7** Higgins (Henry)
father: **5** Belus
musical: **10** My Fair Lady
playwright: **4** Shaw (George Bernard)
sister: **4** Dido
victim: **8** Sichaeus

pygmy
4 tiny **5** dwarf **6** bantam, little, midget **8** dwarfish **10** diminutive, homunculus **11** lilliputian

Pylades
companion: **7** Orestes
father: **9** Strophius
wife: **7** Electra

pylon
4 post **5** tower **6** marker **7** gateway

Pym's creator
3 Poe (Edgar Allan)

Pynchon novel
13 Mason and Dixon **15** Gravity's Rainbow

pyramid builder
5 Khufu **6** Cheops

Pyramus' beloved
6 Thisbe

pyre
4 heap, pile

pyretic
3 hot **7** burning, febrile, fevered **8** feverish

pyromaniac
5 torch **8** arsonist **10** incendiary

pyrosis
9 heartburn

pyrotechnics
7 display **9** fireworks, spectacle

Pyrrha's husband
9 Deucalion

Pyrrhonist
7 doubter, skeptic **10** unbeliever

Pyrrhus
kingdom: **6** Epirus
victory: **7** Asculum

Pythias' friend
5 Damon

python
3 boa **5** snake
slayer: **6** Apollo

pyx
3 box **4** case **6** vessel **9** container **10** receptacle

Q

Qatar
capital: **4** Bida, Doha
gulf: **7** Persian
language: **6** Arabic
monetary unit: **4** rial **5** riyal
neighbor: **11** Saudi Arabia
peninsula: **7** Arabian

QED word
4 erat, quod **13** demonstrandum

q.t., on the
7 sub rosa **8** covertly, secretly **13** under the table

quack
3 cry **4** honk, sham **6** con man, humbug **7** shammer **9** charlatan **10** mountebank **12** saltimbanque

quackery
4 hoax, scam **5** fraud, hokum **6** deceit **8** flim-flam, pretense **9** deception, duplicity, imposture **11** dissembling

quad
see **quadrangle**

quadrangle
4 yard **5** close, court, patio **6** square **7** polygon **9** courtyard, curtilage, enclosure

quadrant
3 arc **6** fourth **9** one-fourth **10** instrument

quadratic
4 boxy **6** square **7** boxlike **10** foursquare

quadriga
7 chariot

quadrille
5 dance, ombre **8** card game **11** square dance

quadrivium subject
5 music **8** geometry **9** astronomy **10** arithmetic

quaestor
6 bursar **8** official **9** paymaster, treasurer

quaff
3 sip **4** swig, toss **5** drink, sup up **6** guzzle, imbibe, sup off **7** carouse, swallow

quagga
3 ass

quaggy
4 soft **5** boggy, mushy, pulpy **6** flabby, marshy, spongy **7** flaccid, squashy, squishy **8** squooshy, yielding

quagmire
3 bog, fen, fix, jam **4** mire **5** marsh, pinch, swamp **6** morass, pickle, plight, scrape, slough **7** dilemma **8** quandary **9** imbroglio, marshland, swampland **11** predicament

quahog
4 clam **7** mollusc, mollusk **9** shellfish **11** cherrystone

quail
5 cower, wince **6** blanch, blench, cringe, flinch, recoil, shrink **7** shudder, squinch, tremble **8** bobwhite
flock of: **4** bevy

quaint
3 odd **5** funny, queer **7** antique, archaic, curious, oddball, strange, unusual **8** peculiar, singular **9** different, eccentric, whimsical **10** antiquated, unfamiliar **12** old-fashioned

quake
5 shake, waver **6** dither, quaver, quiver, shiver, tremor **7** shudder, temblor, tremble, twitter, vibrate **8** trembler

Quaker
6 Friend
city: **12** Philadelphia
colonizer: **4** Penn (William)
color: **4** gray
founder: **3** Fox (George)
poet: **6** Barton (Bernard) **8** Whittier (John Greenleaf)
pronoun: **3** thy **4** thee, thou **5** thine
State: **12** Pennsylvania

qualification
6 caveat **7** ability, fitness **8** adequacy, aptitude, capacity, standard **9** condition, criterion **10** capability, competence **11** requirement, restriction, stipulation

qualified
3 fit **4** able **6** au fait, proper, proved, proven, tested **7** capable, limited, partial, skilled, trained **8** eligible, modified, reserved **9** competent **10** restricted **11** conditional **12** accomplished

qualify
3 fit **5** limit **6** lessen, modify, reduce, soften,

temper **7** certify, entitle, license, mollify, prepare **8** describe, mitigate, moderate **9** authorize **12** characterize

quality
4 rank **5** class, elite, grade, merit, prime, savor, state, trait, value, worth **6** factor, flower, gentry, status, virtue **7** caliber, element, feature, stature **8** position, property, standing **9** attribute, blue blood, character, gentility, parameter **10** excellence, patriciate, perfection

qualm
4 fear **5** demur, doubt **6** nausea, unease **7** illness, scruple **8** mistrust **9** faintness, misgiving, objection **10** conscience, foreboding, reluctance, uneasiness **11** compunction, nervousness, uncertainty **12** apprehension, remonstrance **13** unwillingness

qualmish
3 ill **4** sick **6** queasy, uneasy, unwell **8** hesitant, nauseous **9** nauseated, reluctant, squeamish, uncertain **10** scrupulous **12** apprehensive

quandary
3 fix, jam **4** bind, hole, spot **5** pinch **6** pickle, plight, scrape **7** dilemma **8** quagmire **10** difficulty **11** predicament

quantity
4 body, bulk, dose **5** total **6** amount, degree, volume **9** abundance, aggregate, magnitude
fixed: **8** constant
small: **3** bit **7** modicum, smidgen

quantum
5 quota, share, total **6** amount, budget, ration **7** measure, portion **9** aggregate, allotment, allowance, increment **13** apportionment
of gravity: **8** graviton
of radiant energy: **6** photon
of vibrational energy: **6** phonon
theory originator: **6** Planck (Max)

quarantine
6 detain **7** confine, isolate **8** restrain **9** isolation, restraint **10** detainment **11** confinement

quarrel
3 row **4** beef, bolt, dust, fray, fuss, miff, spar, spat, tiff **5** argue, arrow, brawl, broil, clash, fight, melee, run-in, scrap, set-to **6** affray, battle, bicker, differ, dustup, fracas, ruckus, squall, strife **7** brabble, discord, dispute, dissent, fall out, rhubarb, ruction, scuffle, wrangle **8** argument, catfight, conflict, disagree, skirmish, squabble **9** altercate, bickering, brannigan, lock horns, imbroglio, scrimmage **10** contention, difference, dissension, falling-out **11** altercation, embroilment **12** disagreement

quarrelsome
6 brawly **7** adverse, counter, hostile, scrappy, warlike **8** brawling, choleric, inimical, militant **9** bellicose, combative, irascible, irritable, rancorous, truculent **10** pugnacious **11** bad-tempered, belligerent, contentious **12** cantankerous, disputatious **13** argumentative

quarry
3 dig, pit **4** game, mine, pane, prey **5** chase, delve **6** source, victim **8** excavate **10** excavation

quarter
4 area, bunk, part **5** board, house, lodge, mercy, put up **6** barrio, billet, canton, fourth, ghetto, harbor, sector **7** barrack, section, shelter **8** clemency, district, division, locality, precinct, quadrant
circle: **8** quadrant
note: **8** crotchet
pint: **4** gill
ship's: **6** fo'c'sle **10** forecastle

quarterback
4 boss, head, lead **6** direct, leader, player **7** athlete, oversee **8** director, overseer **9** supervise **10** footballer, supervisor

quartet
4 four **5** group **6** tetrad **8** ensemble, foursome **10** quadruplet, quaternion **11** composition

quart, metric
5 liter, litre

quartz
4 onyx, sard **5** agate **6** jasper **7** citrine, mineral **8** amethyst, sardonyx **9** cairngorm, carnelian **10** chalcedony

quash
2 ax **3** axe, nix **4** undo, veto, void **5** annul, crush, quell **6** defeat, negate, quench, stifle, subdue **7** abolish, nullify, put down, repress, smother, squelch **8** abrogate, dissolve, suppress **10** extinguish, invalidate

quasi
6 almost **7** nominal, seeming, virtual **8** apparent

Quasimodo
9 hunchback
creator: **4** Hugo (Victor)
occupation: **10** bell ringer
residence: **5** Paris **9** Notre Dame

quaver
4 note **5** quake, shake, trill, waver **6** dither, shiver, tremor **7** shudder, tremble, twitter **10** eighth note

quay
4 dock, pier, slip **5** berth, jetty, levee, wharf **6** marina **7** moorage

quean
4 bawd, slut, tart **5** tramp, wench, whore **6** harlot, hooker **7** chippie, hustler **8** strumpet **9** courtesan **10** prostitute **12** streetwalker

queasy
3 ill **4** sick **6** qualmy, uneasy, unwell **7** dubious **8** delicate, doubtful, hesitant, nauseous, qualmish, troubled **9** hazardous, nauseated, reluctant, squeamish

Quebec province
capital: **6** Quebec
city: **5** Laval **8** Montreal **9** Longueuil
island: **9** Anticosti
mountain: **9** Tremblant **10** D'Iberville
peninsula: **5** Gaspé
provincial flower: **10** fleur-de-lys **11** madonna lily
river: **10** St. Lawrence

Queeg's ship
5 Caine

queen
Austria-Hungary: **12** Maria Theresa
Belgian: **6** Astrid
Danish: **8** Margaret, Margrete
Egyptian: **9** Cleopatra **10** Hatshepsut
English: **4** Anne, Mary **8** Victoria **9** Elizabeth
French and English: **7** Eleanor
Netherlands: **7** Beatrix, Juliana **10** Wilhelmina
of Carthage: **4** Dido
of heaven: **4** Mary, moon **7** Astarte
of Isles: **6** Albion
of Ithaca: **8** Penelope
of Navarre: **8** Margaret
of Scots: **4** Mary
of Sheba: **6** Balkis
of the Adriatic: **6** Venice
of the Antilles: **4** Cuba
of the East: **7** Zenobia
of the fairies: **3** Mab **7** Titania
of the gods: **4** Hera, Juno, Sati
of the Nile: **9** Cleopatra
of the North: **9** Edinburgh
of the underworld: **3** Hel **4** Hela **10** Persephone, Proserpina
Spanish: **7** Isabela **8** Isabella
Spartan: **4** Leda
Swedish: **9** Christina

Queen Anne's lace
6 carrot **10** wild carrot

Queen of Spades
author: **7** Pushkin (Alexander)
composer: **11** Tchaikovsky (Peter Ilyich)

Queensland
capital: **8** Brisbane
explorer: **4** Cook (Captain James)

queer
3 odd **5** bogus, weird **7** bizarre, curious, deviant, dubious, oddball, strange, touched, unusual **8** doubtful, peculiar, singular **9** eccentric, worthless **10** homosexual, outlandish, suspicious **11** counterfeit

quell
4 calm, stop **5** allay, check, crush, quash, quiet **6** pacify, quench, squash, subdue **7** conquer, put down, squelch **8** overcome, suppress, vanquish **9** overwhelm, subjugate **10** extinguish

Quemoy's neighbor
4 Amoy **5** Matsu

quench
4 sate **5** allay, douse, quash, quell, slake **6** lessen, put out, reduce **7** appease, assuage, gratify, lighten, put down, relieve, satiate, satisfy **8** mitigate, suppress **9** alleviate, eliminate **10** extinguish

quenelle
8 dumpling, meatball **9** forcemeat

quern
4 mill

querulous
5 whiny **7** fretful, peevish, pettish, whining **8** petulant **9** lamenting **10** whimpering **11** complaining

query
3 ask **4** quiz **5** doubt, grill **7** dubiety, inquire, inquiry **8** question **9** catechize **11** interrogate **13** interrogation

quest
4 hunt **5** probe **6** pursue, search **7** delving, inquire, inquiry, probing, pursuit, seeking **8** research **9** pursuance **11** inquisition **13** investigation
object: **5** grail

question
3 ask, pry **4** poll, pump, quiz **5** doubt, grill, issue, probe, query **6** chance, matter **7** debrief, dispute, examine, inquire, inquiry, problem, suspect **8** distrust, mistrust **9** catechize, challenge, objection **10** difficulty, puzzle over **11** interrogate, possibility **13** interrogation, interrogatory

questionable
4 iffy, moot **5** shady, vague **6** unsure **7** dubious, obscure, suspect **8** arguable, doubtful, unproven **9** debatable, equivocal, refutable, uncertain **10** disputable, fly-by-night, improbable, unreliable **11** problematic **12** undependable

questioning
5 probe, query **6** show-me **7** delving, dubious, inquiry, probing **8** doubtful, grilling **9** inquiring, quizzical, skeptical, uncertain **11** incredulous, inquisitive, unbelieving **12** disbelieving **13** interrogation, interrogatory, investigative

quetzal
4 bird, coin **6** trogon

queue
3 row **4** file, line, rank, wait **5** braid **6** column **8** sequence

quibble
4 carp **5** argue, cavil **6** argufy, bicker, niggle, object **7** dispute, evasion, nitpick, wrangle **8** squabble **9** criticism, criticize, objection **10** split hairs

quick
4 core, deft, fast, keen, pith, root **5** acute, adept, agile, brisk, fleet, hasty, rapid, sharp, smart, swift **6** abrupt, bright, clever, nimble, prompt, speedy, sudden **7** hurried **9** breakneck, impetuous **10** harefooted **11** expeditious **12** lickety-split
combining form: **5** tachy

quick bread
6 muffin **7** biscuit

quicken
4 goad, grow, move, spur, stir, wake **5** hurry, liven, pique, rouse, speed **6** arouse, awaken, excite, hasten, incite, induce, kindle, revive, step up, vivify **7** actuate, animate, enliven, provoke, shake up, sharpen, speed up **8** activate, energize, motivate, vitalize **9** galvanize, stimulate **10** accelerate, exhilarate, invigorate

quickly
5 apace **6** at once, pronto **9** forthwith, posthaste **12** straightaway

quickness
5 haste, speed **8** alacrity, celerity, dispatch, legerity, rapidity, velocity **9** fleetness, rapidness, swiftness **10** promptness

quicksand
3 bog **4** mire **6** morass

quicksilver
7 mercury **9** mercurial **10** inconstant

quick-tempered
5 cross, fiery, ratty, testy **6** cranky, touchy **7** peppery **8** choleric, petulant **9** irascible, irritable, splenetic **10** passionate

quick-witted
3 apt **4** keen **5** acute, agile, alert, canny, ready, sharp, smart **6** astute, brainy, bright, clever, prompt **9** brilliant **10** perceptive **11** intelligent, penetrating

quid
3 cut, wad **4** chew, coin **5** money, pound **9** sovereign

quiddity
3 nub **4** gist, meat, pith **6** trifle **7** essence, quibble **8** crotchet **12** eccentricity, quintessence

quidnunc
see **rumormonger**

quiescent
4 calm **5** quiet, still **6** benign, hushed, latent, placid, serene, stilly **7** abeyant, dormant, halcyon, lurking **8** inactive, tranquil **10** untroubled

quiet
4 calm, hush, idle, lull, mute, stop **5** abate, allay, inert, muted, shush, still, whist **6** asleep, becalm, gentle, hushed, lessen, placid, serene, settle, silent, soothe, subdue **7** compose, halcyon, pacific, passive, restful, silence, subdued **8** decrease, inactive, peaceful, reserved, secluded, taciturn, tranquil **9** noiseless, soundless, stillness, unruffled **11** tranquility, tranquilize, unobtrusive **12** tranquillity

quietus
3 end **5** death, sleep **6** damper, demise, finish **7** decease, passing, silence **8** curtains **10** inactivity, settlement **11** termination

quill
3 pen **5** float, shaft, spine, spool **6** bobbin **7** feather, spindle

quilt
4 pouf, puff **5** duvet **8** coverlet **9** comforter, eiderdown **11** counterpane
design: **8** trapunto

quince
3 bel

quintessence
4 gist, meat, pith, soul **5** ideal, model, stuff **6** marrow **7** epitome **8** exemplar, last word, quiddity, ultimate **9** substance **10** apotheosis **12** essentiality

quintessential
5 ideal, model **7** classic, typical **8** ultimate **9** classical, exemplary **10** archetypal, consummate, prototypal **12** prototypical

quintillionth combining form
4 atto

quintuple
8 fivefold

quip
3 dig, gag, kid **4** gibe, gird, jape, jeer, jest, jibe, joke **5** crack, fleer, sally, scoff, sneer, tease **6** banter, oddity, retort, zinger **7** quibble **8** drollery, repartee **9** wisecrack, witticism **12** equivocation

quipster
3 wag, wit **4** card **5** clown, comic, droll, joker **6** jester **8** comedian, funnyman, humorist, jokester **11** wisecracker

quirk
3 tic **4** bend, kink, quip, whim **5** crook, curve, twist **6** groove, oddity, vagary **7** caprice

8 accident, crotchet **9** mannerism **11** peculiarity **12** idiosyncrasy

quirky
3 odd **7** erratic, offbeat **8** peculiar **9** eccentric, irregular, whimsical **10** capricious **13** idiosyncratic

quirt
4 lash, whip

quisling
5 Judas, rebel **7** traitor **8** apostate, betrayer, defector, turncoat **10** copperhead **11** backstabber **12** collaborator

quit
3 end, pay **4** drop, free, halt, stop **5** cease, chuck, leave **6** depart, desert, desist, give up, resign, retire, settle **7** abandon, drop out, forsake, release, relieve, satisfy **8** knock off, leave off, released, renounce, withdraw **9** discharge, liquidate, surrender, terminate **10** relinquish **11** discontinue

quite
3 all **4** just, very, well **5** fully, in all **6** in toto, purely, rather, wholly **7** exactly, totally, utterly **8** entirely **9** perfectly **10** absolutely, altogether, completely, positively, thoroughly **12** considerably

quittance
6 amends **7** redress **8** reprisal, requital **9** atonement, discharge, expiation, repayment **10** recompense, reparation **11** restitution **12** compensation

quitter
4 funk **6** coward, craven **7** chicken, dastard **8** poltroon, recreant **9** defeatist **11** yellowbelly

quiver
4 beat, case **5** pulse, quake, shake, throb, waver **6** arrows, dither, jitter, quaver, shiver, tremor **7** pulsate, shudder, tremble, twitter, vibrate **9** palpitate, vibration

qui vive
5 alert **7** lookout

Quixote
see **Don Quixote**

quixotic
7 foolish **8** fanciful, illusory, romantic **9** fantastic, imaginary, visionary **10** capricious, chimerical, idealistic **11** impractical

quiz
3 ask **4** exam, test **5** grill, query **7** examine, inquire **8** question **9** catechize **11** interrogate **12** cross-examine

quizzical
3 odd **5** queer **6** quaint, show-me **7** curious, dubious, mocking, probing, puzzled, teasing **8** doubtful, doubting, sardonic **9** inquiring, skeptical **11** incredulous, inquisitive, questioning, unbelieving **12** disbelieving

quodlibet
5 issue, point **6** debate, medley **7** mélange **8** fantasia, question **11** disputation

quoin
5 angle, block, wedge **6** corner **8** keystone, voussoir

quoit
4 hoop, ring **6** circle

quoits peg
3 hob

quondam
4 late, once, past **6** bygone, former, whilom **7** defunct, onetime **8** sometime **9** erstwhile **10** occasional

quorum
4 body **5** group **7** council **8** majority

quota
3 cut, lot **4** bite, meed, part **5** share, slice, whack **6** amount, parcel, ration **7** measure, portion, quantum **9** allotment, allowance **10** allocation, percentage, proportion

quotation
3 bid **5** offer, price **7** excerpt, extract, passage **8** citation

quotation mark, French
9 guillemet

quote
3 bid **4** cite, list **5** blurb, offer, price, refer **6** adduce, borrow, repeat **7** excerpt, extract, passage **8** citation

quotidian
5 daily, plain, usual **6** common **7** average, diurnal, prosaic, regular, routine, vanilla **8** day-to-day, everyday, ordinary, workaday **9** circadian **11** commonplace **12** unremarkable

quotient
5 ratio, share **7** caliber, portion **9** allotment, magnitude **10** percentage, proportion

Quo Vadis
author: **11** Sienkiewicz (Henryk)
character: **4** Nero **5** Lygia, Peter **8** Vinicius **9** Petronius

R

Ra
son: **6** Khonsu
wife: **3** Mut

Raamah
father: **4** Cush
son: **5** Dedan, Sheba

Rabbi Ben Ezra author
8 Browning (Robert)

rabbit
4 cony, hare **5** bunny, coney
female: **3** doe
fictional: **5** Fiver, Hazel, Mopsy, Peter **6** Flopsy, Harvey **7** Thumper **8** Crusader, Ricochet **9** Bugs Bunny **10** Cotton-tail **11** Easter Bunny
food: **5** salad **6** carrot **7** lettuce
neutered: **5** lapin
tail: **4** scut

rabble
3 mob **4** mass, rout **5** crush, horde **6** masses **8** canaille, populace, riffraff, unwashed **9** hoi polloi **10** lower class **11** proletariat, rank and file

rabble-rouser
7 inciter **8** agitator, fomenter **9** demagogue **10** incendiary **12** troublemaker

Rabelais character
7 Panurge **9** Gargantua **10** Pantagruel

rabid
3 mad **4** wild **5** crazy, ultra **6** crazed, insane **7** extreme, fanatic, frantic, furious, radical, zealous **8** demented, deranged, frenetic, frenzied, obsessed, ultraist **9** delirious, extremist **10** corybantic **11** hydrophobic

rabies
11 hydrophobia

raccoon
8 ringtail
dog: **6** tanuki
relative: **5** civet, coati, panda **8** civet cat, kinkajou **10** cacomistle, coatimundi

race
3 rev **4** bolt, dart, dash, gill, lash, meet, rush, tear, type **5** brook, chase, creek, fling, hurry, match, rally, relay, shoot, speed, spurt **6** charge, course, gallop, runnel, scurry, sprint, stream **7** channel, contest, rivalry, rivulet, scamper **8** marathon **9** grand prix **11** competition, watercourse
zigzag: **6** slalom

race car
4 Elva, Lola, Ralt **5** Lotus, March, Swift **6** Abarth, Cooper, Merlyn, Royale, Turner **7** Avenger, Brabham, Chevron, Crosslé, Ferrari, Mallock, McLaren, Reynard, TransAm, Triumph **8** Corvette **9** Van Diemen **12** Austin Healey

racecourse
4 oval, turf **5** track **8** speedway

racehorse
5 Alsab, Kelso **6** Forego **7** Assault, Barbaro, Man O' War **8** Affirmed, Citation **9** Riva Ridge, War Emblem **10** War Admiral **11** Forward Pass, Seattle Slew, Secretariat, Smarty Jones **12** Native Dancer

Rachel
father: **5** Laban
husband: **5** Jacob
servant: **6** Bilhah
sister: **4** Leah
son: **6** Joseph **8** Benjamin

rachis
4 back **5** chine, spine **8** backbone **12** spinal column

rachitic
5 shaky **6** wobbly **7** rackety, rickety, tenuous **9** tremulous **10** ramshackle, rattletrap

___ Rachmaninoff
6 Sergei, Sergey

racing enthusiast
8 railbird

racism
7 bigotry, jim crow **9** apartheid, prejudice **11** segregation

racist
4 nazi **5** bigot **7** bigoted **10** intolerant, prejudiced **11** supremacist

rack
3 bed **4** buck, bunk, pace, pain, sack, scud **5** frame, wring **6** harass, harrow, martyr, strain, wrench **7** afflict, agonize, antlers, crucify, ratchet, sawbuck, stretch, torment, torture **8** distress, sawhorse **9** framework, persecute **10** excruciate

racket
3 con, din **4** game **5** babel, fraud, hoo-ha, noise **6** clamor, hubbub, rattle, scheme, tumult, uproar **7** pursuit, swindle **8** ballyhoo, brouhaha, foofaraw **10** hullabaloo **11** pandemonium

racketeer
7 goombah, mafioso, mobster **8** extorter, gangster **9** godfather
law: **4** RICO (Act)

rack up
3 win **4** gain **5** reach, score **6** attain **7** achieve, realize **10** accomplish

raconteur
11 storyteller

racy
4 blue, gamy **5** bawdy, broad, juicy, salty, spicy, vampy, zesty **6** purple, risqué, smutty, snappy, vulgar, wicked **7** piquant, pungent **8** indecent, off-color, vigorous **10** suggestive

Radames' beloved
4 Aïda

radar image
3 pip **4** blip, spot **5** trace

Raddai
brother: **5** David
father: **5** Jesse

radiance
3 ray **4** glow **5** glory, shine **6** luster **7** aureola, aureole **8** splendor **10** brightness, brilliance

radiant
4 glad **5** aglow, beamy, shiny **6** bright, cheery, lucent **7** beaming, fulgent, glowing, lambent **8** cheerful, luminous, lustrous **9** brilliant, effulgent **10** effulgence **12** incandescent

radiate
4 beam, glow **5** gleam, shine, strew **6** spread **7** diverge **8** illumine **10** illuminate

radiation unit
3 rad, rem, rep **7** langley, sievert **8** roentgen

radiator
6 cooler, heater **9** convector **11** transmitter **13** heat exchanger

radical
4 acyl, root **5** basal, basic, rebel, ultra **7** extreme, fanatic, primary **8** agitator, cardinal, inherent, militant, ultraist **9** anarchist, essential, extremist, intrinsic **10** subversive, underlying **11** fundamental **12** foundational, iconoclastic **13** revolutionary
mathematical: **4** surd

radicle
4 root **5** radix **9** hypocotyl

radio
4 AM-FM **8** wireless
frequency range: **8** waveband
shortwave: **3** ham **7** amateur

radioactive
3 hot **7** nuclear

radium
discoverer: **5** Curie (Marie, Pierre)
symbol: **2** Ra

radius
5 ambit, orbit, range, reach, sweep **6** extent **7** compass, purview **9** extension

radix
4 base, root **6** source

radon symbol
2 Rn

raffish
6 coarse, jaunty, rakish, sporty, vulgar **9** dissolute **12** devil-may-care

raffle
7 drawing, lottery

raft
3 lot, ton **4** heap, mess, pile, scad, slew **5** balsa, float **6** bundle
Maori: **4** moki

rafter
4 balk, beam, viga

rag
3 jaw, kid, rib **4** bait, jive, josh, rail, razz, rock **5** baste, cloth, scold, tease **6** berate, harass, hector, needle, pester **7** tabloid, torment **9** newspaper

ragamuffin
3 bum **4** hobo, waif **5** gamin, tramp **6** beggar, gamine, orphan, urchin **7** wastrel **8** vagabond **9** scarecrow **11** guttersnipe

rage
3 cry, fad, ire, mad, wax **4** chic, fume, fury, mode, rant **5** anger, craze, fancy, furor, go ape, mania, storm, style, vogue, wrath **6** blow up, frenzy, furore, lose it, seethe **7** fashion, madness, passion **8** boil over, hysteria, violence **10** dernier cri **11** indignation

ragged
4 rent, torn **5** seedy **6** frayed, jagged, shabby, uneven **7** unkempt, worn-out **8** frazzled, straggly, tattered **10** threadbare

raging
4 wild **6** stormy **7** furious, extreme, intense, violent **8** blustery **9** ferocious, turbulent **10** blustering **11** tempestuous

ragout
4 stew **5** salmi **6** burgoo, jumble, medley **7** farrago, goulash, mélange, mixture **8** mishmash **9** potpourri **10** hodgepodge, salmagundi **11** gallimaufry

rags
4 duds, garb **5** dress **6** attire, shreds **7** apparel, clothes, raiment, threads **8** clothing **10** attirement **11** habiliments

ragtag
see **rabble**

ragwort
7 senecio **9** cineraria, groundsel **10** butterweed

raid
4 bust, loot, sack **5** foray, harry **6** attack, forage, harass, inroad, invade, maraud, ravage, sortie **7** assault, despoil, overrun, plunder **8** invasion, spoliate **9** incursion, onslaught

raider
6 pirate **10** freebooter

rail
3 bar, jaw **5** fence, scold, track **6** berate, revile **7** barrier, inveigh, upbraid **8** banister **10** tongue-lash, vituperate

rail bird
4 coot, sora **5** crake **7** clapper **8** marsh hen, water hen
extinct: **4** moho

railing
8 banister **10** balustrade
part: **8** baluster

raillery
5 scorn **6** banter **7** mockery, teasing **8** badinage, derision, ridicule, taunting **10** lampoonery, persiflage

railroad
branch: **6** siding
car: **5** coach, diner, stock **6** hopper **7** caboose, gondola, Pullman
engine: **10** locomotive
locomotive: **9** iron horse
station: **5** depot
underground: **4** tube **5** metro **6** subway
worker: **6** porter **7** fireman **8** brakeman, engineer **9** conductor **11** gandy dancer

raiment
4 duds, garb, gear, togs **5** array, dress **6** attire **7** apparel, clothes, threads, vesture **8** clothing, garments, glad rags, vestiary **9** caparison, vestments **10** attirement **11** habiliments

rain
4 spit **6** deluge, mizzle, shower **7** drizzle **8** downpour, sprinkle **10** cloudburst **13** precipitation

rainbow
3 arc **4** irid, iris **5** array, gamut **7** fantasy **8** illusion, spectrum **9** pipe dream
bridge: **7** Bifrost
chaser: **9** visionary
goddess: **4** Iris

rainbow fish
5 guppy, trout **6** wrasse

raincoat
3 mac **4** mack **6** poncho, trench **7** oilskin, slicker **10** mackintosh

rain leader
9 downspout

rain tree
9 monkeypod

raise
2 up **4** ante, grow, hike, jack, jump, lift, pump, rear **5** boost, breed, erect, exalt, hoist, put up **6** foment, incite, jack up, leaven, muster, uplift **7** augment, bring up, collect, elevate, enhance, inflate, produce **8** heighten, increase **9** construct, cultivate, increment, propagate

raisin
5 grape **7** currant, sultana **10** dried grape

Raisin in the Sun author
9 Hansberry (Lorraine)

raison d' ____
4 état, être

raja
4 king **5** chief, ruler **6** prince **9** dignitary

rake
3 rip **4** comb, roué, scan **5** angle, blood, pitch, rifle, scamp, scour, slope **6** forage, glance, lecher, rascal, scrape, search, strafe **7** incline, playboy, ransack, rummage, scratch **8** enfilade, lothario **9** debauchee, libertine **10** profligate

rakehell
4 fast, wild **5** blood, rogue, scamp **6** rascal, sporty **7** playboy, raffish **8** lothario, rascally **9** debauchee, dissolute, lecherous, libertine **10** licentious, profligate

rake-off
3 cut **4** bite, take **5** chunk, share **7** portion **9** baksheesh, lagniappe **10** commission, percentage

rake's look
4 leer, ogle

Rake's Progress artist
7 Hogarth (William)

rakish
see **rakehell**

rally
4 race, stir, wake **5** harry, renew, rouse, waken **6** arouse, awaken, bestir, kindle, muster, perk up, pick up, repair, volley **7** convene, enliven, marshal, rebound, recover **8** assemble, clambake, comeback, mobilize, recovery **9** challenge, re-collect **10** invigorate, reorganize

rallying cry
5 motto **6** byword, slogan **9** watchword **10** shibboleth **11** catchphrase

ram
5 Aries, crash, crowd, drive, pound, sheep, stuff **6** batter, plunge, strike, thrust **7** warship

Rama's wife
4 Sita

ramble
3 gad **4** roam, rove **5** drift, range, run on, stray, troll **6** stroll, wander **7** blather, digress, diverge, maunder, meander, saunter, traipse **8** divagate, straggle **9** gallivant

rambler
4 rose **5** gypsy, hiker, nomad, rover **6** roamer, walker **7** drifter, vagrant **8** stroller, vagabond, wanderer **9** itinerant **10** ranch house

rambunctious
5 rowdy **6** unruly **7** raucous, willful **10** boisterous, headstrong **11** intractable **12** recalcitrant, ungovernable

ramification
5 shoot **6** branch, offset **8** offshoot **9** outgrowth, offspring **11** consequence

ramify
6 branch, divide, extend **7** develop, radiate **9** branch out, propagate **11** proliferate

Ramona author
7 Jackson (Helen Hunt)

ramose
8 branched

ramp
5 apron **7** incline

rampage
4 rage, riot, tear **5** binge, fling, spree, storm

rampageous
4 wild **6** unruly **7** riotous

rampant
4 rank, rife, wild **7** rearing, regnant **9** prevalent, unbridled **10** widespread **12** uncontrolled, unrestrained

rampart
4 wall **5** ridge **7** bulwark, parapet **9** barricade **10** breastwork

ramshackle
6 flimsy **7** rickety, run-down **8** decrepit **10** tumbledown **11** dilapidated

ram's mate
3 ewe

ranch
5 finca **6** quinta, spread **8** estancia, hacienda
worker: **6** cowboy, gaucho **7** cowgirl, cowhand, cowpoke **10** cowpuncher

rancher
6 cowboy **7** breeder **9** cattleman

rancid
4 high, rank, sour **5** fetid **6** putrid, skunky, smelly **7** noisome, spoiled **8** stinking **9** offensive **10** malodorous

rancor
4 gall **6** animus, enmity, hatred **7** ill will **9** animosity, antipathy, hostility **10** antagonism, bitterness

rancorous
6 bitter **7** hateful, hostile **8** spiteful, venomous **9** malicious, malignant, vitriolic **10** malevolent **11** acrimonious **12** antagonistic

Rand, Ayn
novel: **6** Anthem **12** Fountainhead (The) **13** Atlas Shrugged

random
6 casual **7** aimless **8** slapdash **9** arbitrary, desultory, haphazard, hit-or-miss, unplanned **10** accidental, contingent, hit-and-miss, incidental **11** purposeless

randy
4 lewd **5** bawdy, lusty **7** lustful, satyric **9** lecherous, libertine, lickerish, salacious **10** lascivious, libidinous, licentious

range
3 row, run **4** area, band, roam, rove, shot, site, sort, span, vary **5** align, ambit, carry, drift, field, gamut, orbit, order, reach, realm, ridge, scale, scope, space, stove, stray, sweep, width **6** assort, domain, extent, length, limits, ramble, sierra, sphere, spread, wander **7** compass, earshot, expanse, eyeshot, habitat, meander, purview, stretch **8** confines, distance, latitude, locality, panorama, province, stovetop, traverse, vicinity **9** amplitude, extension, gallivant, magnitude, territory **12** distribution

range finder
9 telemeter

ranger
3 spy **5** scout **6** lawman, patrol, warden **8** overseer **9** caretaker, protector

rangy
4 lean **5** lanky **6** gangly **7** spindly **8** gangling

rani's mate
4 raja **5** rajah

rank
3 row **4** file, foul, lush, rate, seed, sort, tier **5** class, fetid, funky, grade, gross, humid, order, place, queue **6** assort, cachet, coarse, filthy, lavish, putrid, rancid, rating, smelly, status **7** arrange, dignity, echelon, footing, noisome, profuse, rampant, reeking, station, stature **8** classify, evaluate, flagrant, outright, position, standing, stinking **9** downright, egregious, loathsome, luxuriant, overgrown, repulsive **10** consummate, malodorous **11** conspicuous, unmitigated

rank and file
5 plebs **6** people, plebes **8** populace **9** commonage, commoners, plebeians **10** commonalty **11** enlisted men

rankle
3 irk, vex **4** rile **5** annoy **6** bother, fester, nettle, seethe **8** embitter, irritate **9** aggravate **10** exasperate

ransack
3 rob **4** comb, grub, loot, rake **5** rifle, scour **6** forage, ravage **7** plunder, rummage

Ran's husband
5 Aegir

ransom
3 buy **4** free **6** redeem, regain, rescue **7** deliver, recover **8** liberate **13** consideration

rant
3 jaw, rag **4** huff, rage, rail, rate, rave **5** mouth, scold **6** screed, tirade **7** bluster, bombast, declaim, fustian **8** bloviate, harangue, perorate **10** vituperate **11** rodomontade

ranula
4 cyst

rap
3 hit, tap **4** blow, chat, swat, talk, wipe **5** blame, chide, knock, swipe **6** charge, patter, rebuke **7** censure, condemn, reproof **8** causerie, denounce, reproach, sentence **9** criticize, criticism, reprehend, reprimand, reprobate **10** discussion **12** conversation

rapacious
6 greedy **8** covetous, grasping, ravening, ravenous **9** predatory, raptorial, voracious **10** gluttonous, predaceous

rapacity
5 greed **7** avarice, avidity **8** cupidity, voracity **10** greediness **12** covetousness, ravenousness

rape
4 ruin **5** colza, force, spoil **6** canola, defile, ravage, ravish **7** assault, debauch, despoil, outrage, plunder, violate **9** violation **10** ravishment, spoliation

Rape of the Lock, The
author: 4 Pope (Alexander)
heroine: 7 Belinda

Raphael
birthplace: 6 Urbino
subject: 7 Madonna
teacher: 8 Perugino

rapid
4 fast **5** brisk, chute, fleet, hasty, quick, swift **6** speedy **7** hurried **9** breakneck **11** expeditious

rapidity
5 haste, hurry, speed **8** celerity, velocity

rapids
5 chute **8** cataract **10** white water

rapier
4 épée **5** blade, sword

rapine
4 loot, pelf, swag **5** booty, prize, spoil **6** boodle, spoils **7** pillage, plunder **10** spoliation

Rappaccini's Daughter
8 Beatrice
author: 9 Hawthorne (Nathaniel)

rapper
3 DMX, Eve, GZA, Jin **4** Ice T, Jay-Z **5** Cee-Lo, Rakim **6** Eminem, Heavy D, KRS-ONE, Mac Dre, Mos Def, Run DMC, Twista **7** Caushun, LL Cool J, OutKast **8** Ludacris, Snoop Dog, Melle Mel, Paul Wall **9** Kanye West, Method Man **10** Kool Moe Dee, Lupe Fiasco, Spoonie Gee, Vanilla Ice **11** Busta Rhymes, Public Enemy

rapport
5 unity **6** accord **7** concord, harmony **8** affinity **9** communion **13** communication

rapscallion
see **rascal**

rap session
6 confab, parley **7** palaver **8** colloquy **10** discussion

rapt
6 intent **7** engaged **8** absorbed, immersed **9** engrossed **10** enthralled **11** carried away, preoccupied, transported

raptor
3 owl **4** hawk **5** eagle **6** condor, falcon, merlin, osprey **7** kestrel, vulture **9** gyrfalcon **10** bird of prey **11** deinonychus

rapture
5 swoon **6** heaven **7** delight, ecstasy, nirvana **9** transport **10** exaltation **13** seventh heaven

rara ____
4 avis

rare
3 few, red **4** pink, thin **6** choice, dainty, exotic, scarce, seldom, select **7** elegant, unusual **8** delicate, singular, sporadic, superior, uncommon, unwonted **9** exquisite, recherché, underdone **10** infrequent, occasional **11** distinctive, exceptional **13** extraordinary

rarefied
4 fine, thin **7** tenuous **8** esoteric **10** attenuated

rarefy
4 thin **6** refine **9** attenuate

rarely
6 little, seldom **9** extremely, unusually **12** infrequently

raring
4 avid, keen **5** eager **6** gung-ho **12** enthusiastic

rarity
5 curio **6** oddity **7** curiosa **8** scarcity **9** curiosity **10** aberration **11** collectible

rascal
3 imp **4** rake **5** devil, knave, rogue, scamp

7 lowlife, villain, wastrel 8 scalawag 9 miscreant, reprobate, scoundrel, skeezicks 10 blackguard 11 rapscallion
Irish: 8 spalpeen

rash
5 hasty, heady 6 abrupt, brazen, daring, madcap, plague, sudden, unwary, unwise 7 foolish 8 careless, epidemic, eruption, headlong, heedless, outbreak, reckless 9 audacious, daredevil, foolhardy, hotheaded, impetuous, imprudent, impulsive 10 ill-advised, incautious, indiscreet, unthinking 11 injudicious, precipitate, temerarious, thoughtless

rasp
4 file, fret 5 annoy, chafe, grate 6 abrade, scrape 7 scratch 8 irritate

raspberry
7 catcall 8 blackcap 10 Bronx cheer

raspy
3 dry 5 harsh, rough 6 hoarse 7 grating, jarring, raucous 8 scrabbly, scratchy

rat
4 blab, fink, heel, scab, sing 5 louse 6 defect, desert, inform, rodent, snitch, squeak, squeal, tattle 7 stoolie 8 apostate, defector, informer, recreant, renegade, squealer, turncoat 9 bandicoot, repudiate, turnabout 11 stool pigeon 12 tergiversate
female: 3 doe

ratchet
4 pawl 6 detent

rate
3 fee, set, tab 4 cost, earn, rank 5 assay, class, grade, merit, price, scale, set at, value 6 amount, assess, charge, degree, esteem, regard, survey, tariff 7 apprize, deserve, valuate 8 appraise, classify, consider, estimate, evaluate, price tag 9 valuation 10 proportion

rather
4 a bit 5 quite 6 fairly, in lieu, kind of, pretty, sort of 7 instead 8 somewhat 10 more or less, preferably 11 alternately 13 alternatively

rathskeller
3 bar, inn, pub 4 dive 6 saloon, tavern 7 barroom, taproom 8 alehouse, basement

ratify
4 seal 5 enact 7 approve, certify, confirm, endorse, license 8 accredit, sanction, validate

rating
4 mark, rank 5 class, grade 6 number 8 estimate, standing

ratio
5 scale 7 percent 8 fraction, quotient 10 percentage, proportion

ratiocination
8 judgment, sequitur 9 inference, reasoning 10 conclusion

ration
4 dole, food, meal, mete 5 allot, divvy, quota, share 6 divide, parcel 7 measure, mete out, prorate 8 allocate 9 allotment, allowance 10 provisions 13 apportionment

rational
4 calm, cool, sane 5 lucid, sober, sound 6 stable 7 logical, prudent 8 sensible, thinking 9 judicious 10 consequent, reasonable 11 circumspect, intelligent, level-headed 12 intellectual

rationale
5 basis, logic 6 reason 7 grounds 9 reasoning 11 explanation 13 justification

rationalize
7 explain, justify 10 account for 11 externalize

ratite
3 emu, moa 4 kiwi, rhea 7 ostrich

rattail
3 cod 9 grenadier

rattan
4 cane, palm 6 switch 7 malacca

Rattigan play
10 Winslow Boy (The) 14 Separate Tables

rattle
3 gab, jaw, yak 4 chat, faze, rale 5 abash, addle, clack, noise, rouse, run on, upset 6 babble, gabble, jangle, racket 7 chatter, clatter, confuse, disturb, flummox, perplex, unnerve 8 bewilder, confound, distract 9 discomfit, embarrass 10 disconcert, noisemaker

rattlebrained
5 dizzy, giddy, silly 7 flighty 8 skittish 9 frivolous

rattling
4 very 5 brisk, quick 6 damned, lively, mighty 8 whacking, whopping 9 energetic, extremely 11 exceedingly

ratty
4 mean 5 dowdy, dumpy, seedy, tacky 6 cheesy, scurvy, shabby 7 unkempt 8 slovenly 9 irritable 10 despicable 11 treacherous 12 contemptible

raucous
4 loud 5 harsh, noisy, rough, rowdy 6 hoarse, unruly 7 grating, jarring, squawky 8 rowdyish, strident 9 termagant, turbulent 10 boisterous, disorderly, stridulent, stridulous, tumultuous 11 cacophonous 12 rambunctious

raunchy
4 foul 5 dirty, nasty 6 coarse, filthy, sloppy, smutty, vulgar 7 obscene 8 indecent 9 salacious

ravage
4 loot, raze, ruin, sack 5 foray, harry, spoil, strip, waste, wreck 6 forage, invade, ravish 7 despoil, overrun, pillage, plunder, ransack, scourge 8 desolate, spoliate 9 depredate, desecrate, devastate

rave
4 gush, rant 5 storm 6 babble, jabber 7 enthuse 10 rhapsodize

ravel
3 run 4 fray 5 snarl 6 muddle, tangle 7 perplex, untwine 8 entangle 9 extricate 10 complicate 11 disentangle

ravelings
4 lint 7 threads

Ravel work
6 Boléro 7 La Valse 14 Daphnis et Chloé 17 Rapsodie espagnole

raven
3 jet 4 ebon, inky, prey 5 black, ebony, jetty, sable 7 despoil, plunder 9 pitch-dark 10 pitch-black
relative: 3 jay 4 crow 6 magpie 7 blue jay

Raven, The
author: 3 Poe (Edgar Allan)
lost love: 6 Lenore
refrain: 9 Nevermore

ravenous
6 greedy, hungry 7 starved 8 edacious, famished, starving 9 rapacious, voracious 10 gluttonous

ravine
3 cut, gap 4 gulf, pass, wadi 5 abyss, chasm, cleft, clove, flume, gorge, gulch, gully, notch 6 arroyo, canyon, clough, coulee, defile, gutter, nullah 7 crevice, fissure 8 barranca, crevasse
Mt. Washington's: 9 Tuckerman

raving
3 mad 5 manic, rabid, upset 6 crazed 7 frantic, lunatic, unglued 8 demented, deranged, frenetic, frenzied, maniacal, obsessed, unhinged, worked up 9 ravishing 10 distraught, flipped out, hysterical, irrational 11 overwrought

ravish
4 rape 5 force, spoil 6 defile 7 assault, despoil, outrage, pillage, plunder, violate 8 deflower, entrance, overcome 9 enrapture, transport

raw
4 cold, nude, rude 5 bleak, chill, crass, crude, fresh, green, naked, rough, young 6 callow, coarse, impure, native, unclad, unripe, vulgar 7 uncouth 8 immature, uncooked, unformed 9 au naturel, inelegant, irritated, run-of-mine, unbridled, unclothed, undressed, unrefined 10 unfinished, unpolished 13 inexperienced

rawboned
4 bony, lank, lean 5 gaunt, gawky, lanky, spare 6 skinny 7 angular, scraggy, scrawny

ray
4 beam 5 gleam, manta, shaft, skate, trace 6 radius, streak, stream 7 radiate, sawfish, sunbeam, torpedo 8 moonbeam 9 devilfish, thornback 10 guitarfish

raze
4 ruin 5 level 7 destroy 8 demolish, pull down, tear down

razor
4 Atra 6 shaver

razz
3 rag, rib 4 bait, josh, mock, twit 5 scout, taunt 6 badger, banter, deride, heckle, hector 8 ridicule
(see also **raspberry**)

RBI
11 run batted in 12 runs batted in

re
4 as to 5 about, as for 7 apropos 9 apropos of, as regards, regarding 10 as respects, concerning, relating to, respecting 12 with regard to 13 with respect to

reach
4 beat, gain, pass, span, tack 5 carry, get at, get to, grasp, level, range, scope, sweep, touch 6 arrive, attain, extend, extent, rack up, thrust 7 achieve, contact, horizon, project, stretch 9 encompass, influence 10 accomplish, get through

____ reaction
4 dark 5 alarm, chain, light 7 nuclear 8 chemical

reactivate
5 renew 6 revive 8 rekindle, revivify 9 resurrect 10 revitalize 11 resuscitate

read
4 scan, skim 6 peruse 8 pore over
inability to: 8 dyslexia

readable
7 legible

reader
6 lector, primer 7 proofer, scanner 8 bookworm 9 anthology

readily
4 well 6 easily, freely 7 lightly 9 willingly 12 effortlessly

readiness
4 ease 5 skill 6 DEFCON 7 aptness 8 alacrity, dispatch, facility 9 dexterity, quickness 10 promptness 11 inclination, promptitude 12 preparedness

reading
6 lesson **7** lection, version, vulgate **9** rendition **10** recitation

ready
3 set **4** prep, ripe, yare **5** equip **6** active, gear up, make up, primed, prompt **7** prepare **8** inclined, prepared **9** available

real
4 true, very **5** pukka, sound, valid **6** actual, honest **7** certain, genuine, sincere **8** bona fide, concrete, existent, tangible **9** authentic, undoubted, veridical **10** sure-enough, undeniable **11** substantive **12** indisputable

real-estate abbreviation
3 ARM, apt, flr, gar, gdn, kit, lux, mbr, MLS, TLC, vic **4** bsmt, bdrm, frpl, FSBO, furn, HVAC, PITI, util, wbfp **5** RESPA

realism
6 verism **7** verismo **10** naturalism, pragmatism **11** objectivism, objectivity

realistic
4 sane **5** sober, sound **7** genuine, natural **8** lifelike, rational, sensible, veristic **9** practical, pragmatic **10** bottom-line, hard-boiled, hard-headed, reasonable, unromantic **11** down-to-earth **12** matter-of-fact **13** unsentimental

reality
4 fact, true **5** being, sooth, truth **9** actuality, existence, substance **13** flesh and blood

realize
4 gain, reap **5** grasp, reach, score **6** attain, rack up **7** achieve, feature, imagine, reflect **8** conceive, envisage, envision **9** actualize, recognize **10** accomplish, comprehend

really
4 very **5** truly **6** indeed, verily **7** awfully, clearly **8** actually, honestly **9** assuredly, certainly, decidedly, genuinely **10** definitely, positively **11** exceedingly, indubitably, undoubtedly **12** unmistakably

realm
5 orbit, range, scope, sweep **6** domain, empire, estate, extent, radius, sphere **7** compass, demesne, kingdom, purview **8** dominion

ream
4 load, scad **5** widen **7** enlarge **11** countersink

reanimation
7 rebirth, revival **10** renascence, resurgence **11** reawakening, renaissance **12** risorgimento

reap
3 cut **4** earn, gain **5** glean, shear **6** garner, gather, obtain, sickle, thresh **7** harvest

rear
3 aft **4** back, butt, hind, lift, ramp, rump, seat, tail **5** after, breed, build, erect, fanny, hoist, nurse, put up, raise, set up, stern **6** behind, bottom, fledge, foster, heinie, uphold **7** bring up, caboose, elevate, nurture **8** backside, buttocks, hindmost **9** construct, posterior

rear end
3 bum, bun, can **4** butt, duff, moon, rump, seat, tail, tush **5** booty, fanny, stern **6** behind, bottom, heinie **7** caboose, keister **8** backside, buttocks, derriere **9** posterior

rearmost
3 end **4** last **5** final **8** terminal, ultimate

rearrange
see **readjust**

rearward
3 aft **4** back **6** behind **8** backward **9** posterior **10** retrograde

Rea Silvia
father: **7** Numitor
son: **5** Remus **7** Romulus

reason
3 why, wit **4** mind, nous **5** basis, cause, infer, proof, think **6** excuse, ground, motive, sanity, senses **7** account, reflect **8** argument, cogitate, conceive, persuade **9** inference, intellect, rationale, soundness, speculate, wherefore **10** deliberate **11** explanation **12** intelligence **13** consideration, justification, ratiocination, understanding

reasonable
4 fair, just **5** cheap, level, sound **6** modest **7** logical, low-cost, tenable **8** credible, feasible, moderate, rational, sensible **9** equitable, plausible **10** acceptable, affordable, restrained **11** inexpensive, intelligent

reasoning
4 case **5** logic **8** argument **9** deduction

reasonless
7 invalid **8** baseless **9** illogical, senseless, unfounded **10** fallacious, groundless, irrational **11** meaningless, purposeless

reawaken
5 renew **6** revive **7** refresh **8** revivify **9** reanimate **10** regenerate **12** reinvigorate

rebate
6 lessen, refund, return **8** decrease, diminish, give back **9** deduction, reduction

Rebecca
beloved: **7** Ivanhoe
father: **5** Isaac

Rebekah
brother: **5** Laban
father: **7** Bethuel
husband: **5** Isaac
nurse: **7** Deborah
son: **4** Esau **5** Jacob

rebel
6 anarch, mutiny, resist, revolt **7** disobey **8** frondeur, mutineer **9** insurgent **10** malcontent **13** revolutionary, revolutionist

rebellion
6 émeute, mutiny, revolt, rising **8** defiance, intifada, sedition, uprising **10** insurgence, insurgency, resistance, revolution **12** insurrection

rebellious
6 unruly **8** mutinous, stubborn **9** insurgent **10** refractory **11** disaffected, disobedient **12** contumacious, unmanageable **13** insubordinate

rebirth
7 revival **9** awakening **10** conversion, renascence, resurgence **11** reanimation, reawakening, renaissance **12** resurrection, risorgimento

rebound
5 rally **6** bounce, reecho, recoil, repeat **7** recover **8** comeback, recovery, ricochet, snap back **10** convalesce

rebozo
5 scarf, shawl

rebuff
4 slap, snub **5** repel **6** reject **7** fend off, repulse, ward off **8** turn away

rebuild
6 repair, revamp **7** remodel, restore **8** overhaul, renovate, retrofit **9** modernize, refurbish **11** recondition, reconstruct **12** rehabilitate

rebuke
3 rap **4** snub **5** chide, scold, scorn **6** berate, earful, lesson, rebuff **7** bawl out, lecture, reproof, reprove **8** admonish, call down, reproach, scolding **9** reprimand, talking-to **10** tongue-lash **11** comeuppance, objurgation **12** admonishment, dressing-down **13** tongue-lashing

rebut
5 repel **6** refute, reject **7** confute, fend off, repulse, ward off **8** confound, disprove, stave off **10** controvert, disconfirm

rebuttal
5 reply **6** answer, retort **7** defense, riposte **8** argument, comeback, response **9** rejoinder **10** refutation **11** repudiation

recalcitrant
6 unruly **7** froward, willful **8** contrary, perverse, stubborn, untoward **9** fractious, obstinate, resistant **10** headstrong **11** intractable **12** ungovernable, unmanageable

recall
4 stir **5** evoke, renew, rouse, waken **6** arouse, awaken, cancel, memory, remind, repeal, revive, revoke **7** bethink, rescind, restore, retract, reverse **8** callback, remember, resemble, take back, withdraw **9** anamnesis, recollect, reinstate, reminisce, represent, reproduce **10** revocation **11** bring to mind, countermand, remembrance **12** recollection, reminiscence

recant
5 unsay **6** abjure, revoke **7** retract **8** forswear, renounce, take back, withdraw **9** backtrack, repudiate

recap
5 sum up **6** précis, résumé, review **7** reprise, retread, summary **8** overview **9** summarize **10** retrograde

recapitulate
5 sum up **6** resume, review **9** summarize **10** retrograde

recapitulation
5 sum-up **6** précis, résumé, review **7** epitome, reprise, summary **9** summing-up

recede
3 ebb **4** back **5** abate, taper **6** lessen, reduce, retire **7** dwindle, regress, retract, retreat **8** decrease, diminish, fall back, withdraw **10** retrograde, retrogress

receipts
4 gate, take **5** sales **6** income **7** revenue, takings **8** earnings, proceeds

receive
4 host **5** admit, catch, greet **6** accept, endure, suffer, take in **7** acquire, sustain, welcome **10** experience

received
5 plain, sound **6** common **7** popular **8** accepted, familiar, ordinary, orthodox **12** acknowledged, conventional

receiver
4 dish **5** donee, fence, pager **6** aerial **7** antenna, catcher, scanner **9** recipient, treasurer

recent
3 new **4** late **5** fresh, novel **6** latest, modern **8** neoteric

receptacle
6 hamper, holder, hopper, trough, vessel **9** container **10** repository

receptive
4 open **7** passive **8** amenable **9** sensitive **10** accessible, hospitable, open-minded, responsive **11** persuadable, persuasible, suggestible, susceptible

recess
4 cove, nook **5** break, cleft, niche **6** alcove, grotto, hiatus **7** adjourn **8** prorogue **9** prorogate, terminate **11** indentation

Recessional author
7 Kipling (Rudyard)

recessive
3 shy 8 retiring 9 reclusive, withdrawn 10 unsociable

recherché
4 rare 5 novel 6 choice, dainty, exotic, select 7 elegant, unusual 8 affected, delicate, original, superior, uncommon 9 exquisite 11 pretentious

recipe
7 formula 9 procedure 12 prescription

recipient
5 donee 7 grantee 8 receiver 11 beneficiary

reciprocal
4 mate, twin 5 match 6 double, fellow, mutual 8 requited 9 bilateral, companion, duplicate 10 coordinate 11 interactive
prefix: 5 inter

reciprocate
5 repay 6 retort, return 7 requite 8 exchange 9 retaliate 10 compensate, recompense 11 interchange

recital
5 story 6 soiree 7 concert, reading 9 discourse, narration 10 recounting 11 enumeration, performance

recite
4 tell 5 chant, count, state 6 detail, number, relate, repeat, report, set out 7 declaim, narrate, recount, reel off 8 describe, rehearse 9 pronounce

reckless
4 rash, wild 5 brash, hasty 6 daring, madcap 8 carefree, heedless 9 audacious, daredevil, foolhardy, hotheaded 10 ill-advised, incautious 11 harebrained, temerarious, thoughtless 12 devil-may-care 13 irresponsible

reckon
3 sum 5 count, gauge, guess, judge, opine, tally, total 6 cipher, figure, number, regard 7 account, compute, suppose, surmise 8 consider, estimate 9 calculate, enumerate 10 conjecture 11 approximate

reckoning
3 tab 4 bill 5 tally, score 7 account, invoice 9 statement 10 arithmetic, estimation 11 calculation, computation

reclaim
4 save, tame 6 redeem, reform, rescue 7 deliver, recover, restore 9 restitute 11 recondition, reconstruct 12 rehabilitate

recline
3 lie 4 rest, tilt 5 couch, slant, slope 6 lounge, repose 7 lie down 10 stretch out

reclining
4 flat 5 prone 6 supine 9 decumbent, prostrate, recumbent

recluse
5 loner 6 hermit, shut-in 7 eremite 8 cenobite, solitary 9 anchorite
female: 7 ancress 9 anchoress

reclusive
8 eremitic, hermetic, reserved, solitary 9 withdrawn 10 antisocial, eremitical, unsociable 12 misanthropic

recognition
6 credit, esteem, notice 9 attention, awareness, gratitude 10 cognizance, perception 11 realization 12 appreciation

recognize
4 note, spot 5 admit 6 notice 7 observe, realize 8 accredit, diagnose, identify 9 apprehend 10 appreciate 11 acknowledge, determinate, distinguish

recoil
4 balk, kick 5 cower, dodge, quail, start, wince 6 blench, cringe, flinch, shrink 7 rebound, retract, squinch 8 reaction

recollect
5 evoke 6 recall, remind, revive 7 bethink 8 remember 9 reminisce

recollection
6 memory, recall 9 anamnesis, flashback 11 remembrance 12 reminiscence

recommence
5 renew 6 pick up, reopen, resume, take up 7 restart 8 continue

recommend
4 tout 6 advise, praise, prefer 7 acclaim, commend, counsel, endorse, entrust, propose, suggest 8 advocate

recommendation
4 plug 5 pitch 6 advice 7 counsel 11 endorsement, testimonial

recompense
3 pay 4 wage 5 repay 6 amends, reward 7 guerdon, premium, redress, requite 8 gratuity, requital 9 indemnify, indemnity, quittance, reimburse, repayment 10 compensate, remunerate, reparation 11 reciprocate, restitution, retribution 12 compensation, remuneration 13 consideration, gratification

reconcile
4 suit, tune 5 adapt 6 accept, accord, adjust, attune, make up, resign, settle, square, submit, tailor 7 conform, get over, resolve 9 harmonize, integrate 10 conciliate, coordinate 11 accommodate

recondite
4 deep **6** arcane, hidden, mystic, occult, orphic, secret **7** cryptic, erudite, learned, obscure **8** abstruse, academic, esoteric, hermetic, profound **9** concealed, difficult, enigmatic, scholarly

recondition
3 fix **4** mend **6** doctor, repair, revamp **7** rebuild, restore **8** make over, overhaul, retrofit **9** restitute **10** rejuvenate **12** rehabilitate

reconnoiter
5 scout **6** survey

reconsider
6 review, revise **7** rethink, reweigh **8** reassess **9** reexamine **10** reevaluate **13** think better of

reconstruct
6 recast, re-form, remake, revamp **7** rebuild, reclaim, remodel, restore **8** make over, overhaul, readjust, renovate **9** refashion, restitute **10** reassemble, reorganize

record
4 disc, disk, tape **5** album **6** annals, enroll **7** archive, journal, platter **8** archives, document, register **9** chronicle **10** transcript
of a meeting: **7** minutes
of proceedings: **4** acta
ship's: **3** log **7** logbook

recorder
4 TiVo **5** flute **9** registrar
flight: **8** black box

record player
4 hi-fi **5** phono **8** Victrola **9** turntable **10** gramophone, phonograph

recount
4 tell **5** state **6** recite, relate, report, retail **7** narrate **8** describe, rehearse **9** enumerate

recoup
6 regain **7** get back, reclaim, recover **8** retrieve **9** repossess

recourse
6 backup, refuge, resort **7** standby, stopgap, support **8** resource **9** expedient, makeshift

recover
4 heal, mend **5** evict, rally, renew **6** recoup, redeem, regain, revive **7** get back, get over, improve, rebound, reclaim, recycle, restore **8** retrieve, snap back **9** come round, reacquire, recapture, re-collect, repossess, restitute **10** bounce back, convalesce, recuperate

recreant
3 rat **5** false **6** coward, craven, untrue **7** chicken, dastard, unloyal **8** apostate, cowardly, defector, deserter, disloyal, poltroon, renegade, turncoat **9** dastardly, faithless, turnabout **10** perfidious, traitorous, unfaithful **13** pusillanimous

recreate
4 play **5** evoke, renew **7** freshen, refresh, restore **11** reconstruct

recreation
4 play **5** hobby, sport **7** leisure, pastime **8** activity **9** avocation, diversion **10** relaxation **13** entertainment

recrudesce
5 recur **6** return, revert, revive **7** reoccur **8** break out

recruit
4 boot, hire **5** raise **6** engage, enlist, enroll, muster, novice, rookie **7** draftee **8** beginner, enlistee, freshman, headhunt, neophyte, newcomer **9** conscript, fledgling, reinforce, replenish **10** apprentice, tenderfoot

rectifier
4 tube **5** diode **8** detector, ignitron

rectify
3 fix **4** mend **5** amend, emend **6** adjust, remedy, repair **7** correct

rectitude
6 virtue **7** honesty, probity **8** morality **9** rightness **11** uprightness **13** righteousness

rector
6 parson, pastor, priest **9** clergyman **10** headmaster

rectory
5 manse **8** benefice **9** parsonage

recumbent
4 flat **5** prone **6** supine **7** leaning, resting **8** reposing **9** lying down, prostrate, reclining

recuperate
4 heal, mend **5** rally **6** regain, revive **7** rebound, recover **8** snap back **10** convalesce

recur
5 cycle, haunt **6** repeat, resort, return **7** iterate, revolve **8** turn back

recurring
7 chronic **8** periodic **10** continuous, isochronal, periodical, persistent **11** isochronous **12** intermittent

red
4 puce, ruby **5** coral, gules, rouge, ruddy **6** cerise, claret, florid, maroon **7** carmine, crimson, flushed, glowing, magenta, oxblood, scarlet, vermeil **8** burgundy, sanguine **9** vermilion
combining form: **4** rhod **5** rhodo

Red
6 Bolshy, commie **7** Bolshie, comrade **9** Bolshevik, Communist

redact
4 edit **6** censor, revise

Red and the Black author
8 Stendhal

red ape
9 orangutan

red arsenic
7 realgar

red-backed sandpiper
6 dunlin

Red Badge of Courage, The
author: 5 Crane (Stephen)
hero: 7 Fleming (Henry)

red-bellied snipe
9 dowitcher

redbird
7 tanager **8** cardinal **13** summer tanager

red blood cell
11 erythrocyte

red-blooded
5 juicy, lusty, manly **6** hearty, robust, virile **8** vigorous **9** energetic

redbreast
4 knot **5** robin **7** sunfish

red-breasted snipe
9 dowitcher

Redburn author
8 Melville (Herman)

red carp
8 goldfish

red cobalt
9 erythrite

red copper ore
7 cuprite

Red Cross
founder: 6 Barton (Clara), Dunant (Henri)
Knight: 6 George

redden
5 blush, color, flush, rouge **6** mantle, ruddle **11** incarnadine

red dog
5 blitz

redecorate
4 redo **5** fix up **9** refurbish

redeem
4 free, save **5** atone, loose, renew **6** offset, pay off, ransom, reform, rescue **7** expiate, reclaim, recover, restore **9** exonerate

redeemer
5 Jesus **6** Christ, savior **7** messiah, saviour

redemption
6 ransom **7** release **9** atonement, expiation, salvation **11** deliverance

red-eye
5 hooch **6** flight, rotgut **7** whiskey **8** home brew, rock bass **9** moonshine

red-faced
5 ruddy **6** florid, shamed **7** abashed, flushed, glowing **8** blushing, rubicund, sanguine, sheepish **9** mortified **11** embarrassed

red felt hat
3 fez

redfish
4 bass, drum **5** perch **6** salmon **10** ocean perch **11** channel bass

red hickory
6 pignut

red-hot
5 fiery **6** ardent, fervid **7** blazing, boiling, burning, fervent, flaming, glowing **8** brand-new, scalding, sizzling **9** scorching **10** blistering, passionate, sweltering **11** impassioned

red Indian paint
9 bloodroot **11** sanguinaria

red ink
7 arrears, deficit **8** shortage

red inkberry
8 pokeweed

red ironbark
8 eucalypt **10** eucalyptus

red iron ore
5 ocher, ochre **8** hematite

red lauan
8 mahogany

red-legged crow
6 chough

red-legged sandpiper
9 turnstone

red-letter
7 notable **8** historic **9** important, memorable **10** noteworthy, observable, remarkable **11** significant

red-light district
5 stews **10** tenderloin

red mite
7 chigger

redneck
4 clod, hick, rube **5** Bubba, yahoo, yokel **6** rustic **7** bumpkin, hayseed **9** hillbilly **10** clodhopper, good old boy, good ole boy

redo
5 renew **6** repeat, revamp **7** remodel, restyle **8** make over, overhaul, refinish, renovate **9** refurbish **10** redecorate

red ocher
8 hematite

redolence
4 balm, odor **5** aroma, attar, scent, spice **7** bouquet, incense, perfume **9** fragrance

redolent
5 balmy, spicy, sweet **7** odorous, scented **8** aromatic, fragrant, perfumed **9** ambrosial, evocative **10** suggestive **11** reminiscent

redouble
4 dupe **7** dualize, enhance, magnify **8** heighten **9** duplicate, intensify, reinforce **10** strengthen

redoubt
4 fort **7** bastion, citadel **8** fastness, fortress **10** stronghold

redoubtable
5 famed, great **6** famous, mighty **7** awesome, eminent **8** imposing, puissant, renowned **9** prominent **10** celebrated, formidable, impressive **11** illustrious **12** intimidating, overwhelming **13** distinguished

redound
6 accrue, recoil **7** conduce, reflect **10** contribute

red pigment
4 lake **5** eosin, ocher, ochre **6** ruddle

Red Planet
4 Mars

redpoll
5 finch **6** linnet

redraft
6 revamp, revise, rework **7** restyle, rewrite **8** make over, overhaul, rescript, revision, work over **9** recension

redress
4 heal **6** amends, avenge, negate, offset, relief, remedy **7** correct **8** reprisal, requital **9** cancel out, indemnity, quittance, vindicate **10** compensate, counteract, correction, neutralize, recompense, reparation **11** restitution, retribution **12** compensation

red roe
5 coral **6** caviar

redroot
7 alkanet, pigweed **9** bloodroot **12** New Jersey tea

red sable
8 kolinsky

red silver ore
9 proustite

red squirrel
9 chickaree

reduce
2 ax **3** axe, cut **4** cull, diet, melt, pare **5** abate, force, lower, shade, shave, slash, smelt **6** humble, lessen, recede, weaken **7** abridge, curtail, cut back, cut down, dwindle, liquefy, squeeze **8** boil down, compress, contract, decrease, diminish, discount, mark down, minimize, simplify, taper off **10** depreciate, slenderize **11** consolidate

reductio ad ___
8 absurdum

reduction
6 digest, précis, rebate **7** cutback, cutdown, epitome, summary **8** abstract, discount, markdown, synopsis **9** abatement **10** shortening **11** curtailment **12** condensation

redundancy
6 excess **7** nimiety, surfeit **8** pleonasm **9** abundance, profusion, prolixity, tautology **10** repetition **11** periphrasis, reiteration, superfluity **13** supernumerary

redundant
5 extra, spare, windy, wordy **6** de trop, prolix **7** surplus, verbose **9** duplicate, excessive, iterative **11** duplicative, reiterative, repetitious, superfluous, tautologous **13** supernumerary

redux
7 revived **8** restored

redwing
6 thrush **9** blackbird

redwood
7 amboyna, sequoia **8** mahogany

reed
4 di mo, pipe **5** arrow, grass

reed instrument
3 sax **4** dizi, oboe **5** shawm **6** curtal **7** bagpipe, bassoon, dulcian **8** bagpipes, clarinet, crumhorn, melodeon **9** accordion, harmonica, krummhorn, saxophone **10** concertina **11** English horn

reedy
4 thin **6** skinny, stalky, twiggy **7** spindly

reef
3 bar, cay, key **4** lode, vein **5** atoll, ledge **6** reduce, skerry **7** sandbar

reek
4 funk **5** fetor, smell, stink **6** stench **9** effluvium

reeking
4 rank **5** fetid, funky, fusty **6** putrid, rancid, smelly, stinky **7** noisome, stenchy **10** malodorous

reel
4 spin, sway, turn **5** lurch, spool, weave, whirl **6** bobbin, careen, teeter, totter, waggle, wobble **7** stagger, stumble **8** fall back

reestablish
5 renew **6** revive **7** restore **9** reinstate **10** reinscribe **11** reintroduce

reevaluate
6 review **7** rethink, reweigh **8** reassess **9** reexamine **10** reconsider

reeve
4 ruff **6** thread **9** sandpiper **10** magistrate

reexamine
see **reevaluate**

refashion
5 alter **6** change, modify, recast, remake, revamp **7** remodel **8** make over, overhaul **9** transmute

refection
4 feed, meal **6** repast **11** nourishment, refreshment

refectory
7 commons **10** dining hall

refer
6 advert, allude, assign, relate, submit **7** ascribe **9** attribute

referee
3 ump **5** judge **6** umpire **7** adjudge, arbiter, mediate **8** mediator **9** arbitrate, officiate **10** adjudicate, arbitrator

reference
6 credit, source **7** meaning, mention **8** allusion, citation, innuendo, relation, resource **11** testimonial
guide: 5 index **12** bibliography
work: 5 atlas, bible, guide **6** manual **7** almanac **8** handbook **9** directory, guidebook, thesaurus **10** dictionary **11** enchiridion **12** encyclopedia

referendum
4 poll, vote **10** plebiscite

refine
5 prune, smelt **6** polish, purify, smooth **7** elevate, improve, perfect, process **8** civilize **9** cultivate

refined
4 pure **6** subtle, urbane **7** elegant, genteel, raffiné **8** cultured, elevated, ladylike, raffinée, well-bred **9** civilized **10** cultivated, fastidious **13** sophisticated

refinement
5 couth, grace, taste **6** finish, polish **7** culture, finesse, suavity **8** breeding, civility, courtesy, elegance, subtlety, urbanity **9** politesse **10** politeness **11** cultivation **12** civilization, distillation, purification **13** clarification

reflect
4 echo, pore, show **5** weigh **6** bounce, mirror, ponder, reason, return **7** redound **8** chew over, cogitate, consider, ruminate **9** cerebrate **10** deliberate, retrospect **11** contemplate, demonstrate

reflection
4 slur **5** image **6** musing **7** replica, thought **8** reproach **9** aspersion **10** cogitation, meditation, rumination, simulacrum **11** cerebration **12** deliberation, reproduction **13** animadversion, consideration, contemplation

reflective
7 pensive **9** reflexive **10** cogitative, indicative, meditative, ruminative, thoughtful **12** deliberative **13** contemplative

reflux
3 ebb **4** GERD **8** backflow

reform
5 amend, emend **6** redeem, revise **7** correct, improve, reclaim, shape up **8** make over **10** correction, houseclean, regenerate

Reformation leader
4 Knox (John) **6** Calvin (John), Luther (Martin) **7** Zwingli (Huldrych)

reformatory
3 pen **6** prison **7** borstal **8** big house, remedial **10** corrective **12** penitentiary

refractory
6 mulish, unruly **7** froward, restive **8** contrary, perverse, stubborn **9** obstinate **10** bullheaded, headstrong, rebellious, unyielding **11** intractable, stiff-necked **12** unmanageable

refrain
4 fa-la, keep, la-la, stop **5** eieio, tra-la **6** burden, chorus, fa-la-la, shrink **7** abstain, forbear, tra-la-la **8** hold back

refresh
5 renew **6** revive **7** animate, enliven, quicken, restore **8** irrigate, recreate, renovate **9** replenish, stimulate **10** rejuvenate

refresher
5 drink, tonic **6** bracer **8** reminder **9** stimulant **11** restorative

refreshing
5 brisk, tonic **7** bracing **8** reviving **9** analeptic, animating **10** delightful, energizing **11** restorative, stimulating **12** invigorating, rejuvenating

refrigerant
3 ice **5** freon **7** coolant, cryogen **12** fluorocarbon **13** sulfur dioxide

refrigerator
6 cooler, fridge, icebox, walk-in **9** condenser **10** Frigidaire

refuge
3 den **4** lair, port **5** cover, haven **6** asylum, covert, harbor, resort **7** hideout, protect, retreat, shelter **8** hideaway, recourse, resource **9** expedient, harborage, sanctuary, safe house

refugee
2 DP **5** exile **6** émigré **7** evacuee **8** emigrant, fugitive **10** boat person, expatriate
refulgent
6 bright **7** glowing, radiant **8** luminous **9** brilliant
refund
5 repay **6** rebate **8** give back **9** reimburse, repayment, restitute **11** restitution
refurbish
4 redo **5** fix up, renew **6** revamp **7** restore **8** make over, overhaul, renovate, retrofit **10** redecorate, rejuvenate **11** recondition
refusal
4 veto **6** denial **7** regrets **8** negative, negation **9** disavowal **10** abnegation, thumbs-down **11** declination, repudiation
refuse
3 jib, nix **4** chum, deny, junk, scum **5** dreck, dross, offal, spurn, swill, trash, waste **6** debris, litter, reject, scraps, spilth **7** decline, garbage, residue, rubbish **8** disallow, leavings, remnants, turn down, withhold **9** reprobate, repudiate, sweepings **10** disapprove
refutation
8 disproof, elenchus, rebuttal
refute
4 deny **5** rebut **7** confute **8** confound, disprove **10** controvert, disconfirm
regain
6 recoup **7** get back, recover **8** reoccupy, retrieve **9** recapture, repossess
possession: **7** replevy **8** replevin
regal
5 grand **6** august, kingly, purple **7** queenly, stately, sublime **8** glorious, imperial, imposing, kinglike, majestic, princely, splendid **9** monarchal, sovereign **10** monarchial **11** magnificent, monarchical, resplendent
regale
4 feed **5** amuse, feast **6** dinner, divert, spread **7** banquet **9** entertain
regalia
5 array **6** finery **8** frippery, insignia **9** caparison, full dress, trappings **10** decoration **11** habiliments
Regan
father: **4** Lear
husband: **8** Cornwall
sister: **7** Goneril **8** Cordelia
regard
4 deem, heed, mark, note, rate, view **5** assay, favor, honor, judge, value **6** admire, assess, esteem, homage, liking, look at, notice, reckon, repute **7** account, concern, respect **8** approval, consider, devotion, estimate, fondness **9** attention **10** admiration, cognizance, estimation, observance, solicitude **11** approbation, contemplate, observation **12** appreciation, satisfaction **13** consideration
regardful
7 heedful **8** watchful **9** advertent, attentive, observant **10** perceptive, respectful
regarding
4 as to, in re **5** about, anent, as for **7** apropos **8** touching **9** apropos of **10** as respects, concerning, relative to, respecting **11** in respect to **13** with respect to
regatta
4 race
site: **6** Henley **10** Argenteuil
regenerate
5 renew **6** reform, revive **7** rebirth, restore **8** recreate **9** reproduce
regent
5 ruler **6** warden **8** governor **9** protector
regicide's victim
4 king **7** monarch
regime
4 rule, term **5** reign **6** empire, tenure **7** dynasty **10** government, leadership
regimen
4 diet, plan, rule **6** course **10** government
region
4 area, belt, part, zone **5** field, tract **6** domain, locale, sector, sphere **7** demesne, terrain **8** locality, province, vicinity **9** bailiwick, territory **12** neighborhood
regional
5 local **9** localized, sectional **10** provincial **11** territorial
register
4 file, list, note, roll, till **5** enter, range, tally **6** annals, docket, enroll, ledger, record, roster **7** catalog, check in, express **8** indicate **9** catalogue
regnant
4 rife **6** ruling **7** current, popular **8** dominant, reigning **9** paramount, prevalent, sovereign **10** prevailing, widespread
regress
6 revert **9** backslide **10** retrograde
regret
3 rue, woe **4** care **5** grief, mourn **6** bemoan, bewail, excuse, grieve, lament, repent, sorrow **7** anguish, apology, deplore, remorse **9** heartache, penitence **10** contrition, heartbreak **11** compunction
regretful
5 sorry **6** rueful **8** contrite, mournful, penitent

9 repentant, sorrowful 10 apologetic, remorseful 11 penitential

regrettable
3 sad 6 too bad, woeful 8 grievous 10 lamentable 11 distressing, unfortunate 13 heartbreaking

regular
3 due, set 4 even 5 fixed, usual 6 common, normal, steady 7 average, equable, general, natural, orderly, typical, uniform 8 complete, constant, everyday, methodic, ordinary, standard 9 clocklike, customary, prevalent 10 methodical, systematic 11 commonplace 12 run-of-the-mill

regulate
5 order, scale 6 adjust, direct, govern, police, square, temper 7 arrange, control 8 organize 9 methodize, systemize 11 systematize

regulation
3 law 4 rule 5 canon, edict, order 6 decree 7 precept, statute 9 ordinance, prescript 11 restriction 12 codification

regulator
8 governor

rehabilitate
4 cure, heal 7 reclaim, recover, restore 8 renovate 9 reeducate, restitute 11 recondition

rehash
5 reuse 6 repeat, review, rework 7 restate, version 8 chew over, rehearse, talk over 9 rendering, rendition, rewording 11 restatement 12 recapitulate

rehearsal
5 trial 6 dry run, tryout 7 recital 8 dummy run, practice 10 run-through, simulation 11 reiteration 12 woodshedding

rehearse
5 drill, train 6 repeat 7 run over 8 exercise, practice 10 run through

Rehoboam
father: 7 Solomon
kingdom: 5 Judah 6 Israel
mother: 6 Naamah

reign
4 rule, sway 6 govern 7 prevail 8 dominate, dominion 11 predominate, sovereignty

reimburse
3 pay 5 repay 6 recoup, refund 7 pay back, requite 9 indemnify 10 compensate, remunerate

rein
4 curb, stem 5 check 6 bridle 7 compose, control, repress 8 hold back, restrain, suppress

reinforce
4 prop 5 brace 7 augment, bolster, enlarge, fortify, recruit, sustain 8 buttress, increase, redouble 10 invigorate, strengthen

reinstate
6 recall 7 restore 11 reestablish, reintroduce 12 rehabilitate

reintroduce
6 recall, revive 7 restore 9 reinstate 11 reestablish

reinvestment
4 DRIP 8 plowback

reiterate
5 renew, resay 6 repeat, resume, retell 7 reprise

reject
3 nix 4 jilt, junk, shed 5 debar, scorn, scrap, spurn 6 abjure, pariah, pass up, rebuff, refuse 7 cashier, castoff, decline, discard, dismiss, exclude, outcast, repulse, shut out 8 castaway, jettison, throw out, turn away, turn down 9 eliminate, repudiate, shoot down, throw away 10 disapprove

rejoice
5 cheer, exult, glory 7 delight, gladden 8 jubilate

rejoinder
5 reply 6 answer, retort 8 comeback, rebuttal, repartee, response

rejuvenate
5 green, renew 7 refresh 8 renovate 9 modernize 10 revitalize

rekindle
5 renew 6 revive 7 restart 8 reawaken, reignite, revivify 10 reactivate, revitalize

relate
4 link, tell 5 apply, refer 6 assign, detail, recite, report 7 connect, express, narrate, pertain, recount 8 describe, disclose, interact, rehearse 9 appertain, chronicle

related
4 akin 5 alike, enate 6 agnate, allied 7 cognate, connate, germane, kindred 8 incident 9 analogous, connected, identical, pertinent 10 associated, connatural, homologous 11 consanguine

relation
3 kin 6 agnate 7 hinship, kinsman 8 affinity 9 kinswoman, reference 11 propinquity

relationship
3 tie 4 bond, link 5 ratio, tie-in, union 6 affair 7 analogy, contact, liaison 8 affinity, alliance 10 connection 11 affiliation, association 13 confederation, consanguinity

relative
2 ma, pa 3 mom, pop, sib, sis, son 4 aunt, mama, papa 5 blood, madre, mamma, momma, niece, pappy, pater, poppa, uncle 6 agnate, cousin, father, mother, nephew, parent, sister 7 apropos, brother, cognate, germane, kinsman, sibling 8 ancestor, daughter, grandson, relation,

relevant **9** ascendant, dependent, kinswoman, pertinent **10** applicable, collateral, descendant, grandchild **11** comparative, conditional, grandfather, grandmother, grandparent **13** granddaughter

relatives
3 kin **4** kith **5** folks **7** kindred, kinfolk **8** kinfolks **9** relations

relax
4 bask, ease, laze, loaf, loll, rest **5** chill, let go, loose, remit **6** loosen, lounge, modify, unbend, unkink, unwind **7** slacken **8** chill out, kick back, loosen up, unbuckle, wind down **9** untighten **10** decompress

relaxation
3 fun **4** ease, rest **5** hobby **6** repose **7** leisure, pastime **9** amusement, diversion, enjoyment **10** recreation

relaxed
5 loose, slack **6** casual, dégagé, mellow **8** informal **9** easygoing **11** low-pressure

release
4 emit, free, vent **5** issue, let go, loose, untie, yield **6** acquit, let out, loosen, pardon, ransom, unbind, uncage **7** give off, give out, manumit, set free, unchain, unleash **8** liberate, unfetter **9** acquittal, discharge, exculpate, exonerate, surrender **10** emancipate **11** manumission **12** emancipation
conditional: **6** parole

relegate
5 exile, expel **6** assign, banish, charge, commit, demote, resign **7** commend, confide, consign, entrust **8** delegate, hand over, transfer, turn over

relent
3 ebb **4** cave, ease, wane **5** abate, let up, yield **6** give in, submit **7** die away, die down, ease off, slacken, subside **8** moderate **9** acquiesce **10** capitulate

relentless
5 cruel, rigid, stern **6** dogged **7** adamant, nonstop **8** constant, obdurate, rigorous, unabated **9** ferocious, incessant, stringent **10** implacable, inexorable, inflexible, unyielding **11** remorseless, unfaltering

relevant
3 apt, fit **5** ad rem **6** cogent **7** apropos, germane **8** apposite, material, relative **9** pertinent **10** admissible, applicable **11** applicative, appropriate **12** proportional

reliable
4 safe, sure **5** solid, sound, tried, valid **6** proven, secure, trusty **7** bedrock, certain **8** constant, verified **9** foolproof, validated **10** dependable **11** trustworthy **12** tried-and-true

reliance
4 hope **5** faith, stock, trust **10** dependence

relic
5 token **6** corpse **7** antique, memento, remains, remnant, vestige **8** artifact, fragment, keepsake, memorial, reminder, souvenir **11** remembrance

relict
5 widow **8** survivor

relief
3 aid **4** ease, fret, hand, help, lift **5** break, cameo **6** assist, raised, remedy, succor **7** comfort, redress, respite, support, welfare **8** breather, fretwork, repoussé **9** abatement, diversion **10** assistance, mitigation **11** alleviation, deliverance
pitcher: **6** closer **7** fireman, stopper

relieve
3 rid **4** calm, ease, free, help, quit, vent **5** allay, relax, spell **6** assist, exempt, lessen, loosen, reduce, remedy, soften, solace, soothe, succor, supply **7** absolve, assuage, comfort, deprive, lighten, mollify, release **8** diminish, dispense, mitigate, moderate, palliate, unburden **9** alleviate

religion
4 cult, Jain, sect, Sikh **5** Baha'i, cause, creed, dogma, faith, Hindu, Islam **6** belief, church, Jewish, Mormon, Muslim, Shinto **7** Friends, Jainism, Judaism, Quakers, Sikhism **8** Buddhism, Buddhist, devotion, doctrine, Hinduism **9** Christian, Mormonism, Shintoism **11** Zoroastrian **12** Christianity

religious
3 nun **4** holy, monk **5** friar, godly, pious **6** devout, priest, sacred, votary **7** staunch, upright **8** cenobite, faithful, monastic, priestly, reverent **9** pietistic, prayerful, spiritual, steadfast **10** scriptural, scrupulous, worshipful

relinquish
4 cede, quit, shed **5** forgo, leave, waive, yield **6** desert, give up, resign **7** abandon, discard, lay down, release **8** abdicate, hand over, renounce **9** quitclaim, sacrifice, surrender

relish
4 like, tang, zest **5** enjoy, fancy, flair, gusto, savor, taste **6** flavor, liking, palate **7** chutney, delight **8** chowchow, fondness, penchant, pleasure, sapidity **9** appetizer, condiment, enjoyment **10** appreciate, piccalilli **11** delectation, hors d'oeuvre

relucent
6 bright **7** glaring, radiant, shining **10** reflecting

reluctant
3 shy **4** wary **5** chary, loath **6** afraid, averse **8** cautious, grudging, hesitant **9** unwilling **10** indisposed **11** disinclined
prophet: **5** Jonah

rely
3 bet **4** bank, plan **5** count **6** depend, gamble, reckon

rely on
5 trust **6** expect **10** anticipate

remain
4 bide, last, live, stay, wait **5** abide, stand, tarry **6** endure, linger, loiter **7** persist, survive **8** continue **10** hang around **11** stick around

remainder
4 rest **5** dregs, trace **6** excess **7** balance, residue, remnant, surplus, vestige **8** leavings, leftover, residual, residuum

remains
4 body **5** ashes, bones, ruins **6** corpse, debris, relics **7** balance, cadaver, carcass, flotsam **8** leavings, remnants **9** reliquiae

remand
8 send back

remark
4 gibe, note **5** aside, crack **7** comment, mention **9** utterance, wisecrack, witticism **10** annotation **11** observation **12** obiter dictum

remarkable
4 rare **5** great **6** signal, unique **7** salient, strange, unusual **8** singular, striking, uncommon **9** arresting, bodacious, momentous, prominent **10** impressive, noteworthy, noticeable **11** conspicuous, exceptional, outstanding, significant **13** extraordinary

remarkably
4 unco

remedial
8 curative, salutary, sanative **9** medicinal **10** corrective **11** restorative, therapeutic **12** recuperative

remedy
3 fix **4** cure, drug, heal **5** salve, solve **6** elixir, relief, repair **7** correct, cure-all, nostrum, panacea, rectify, redress, relieve **8** antidote, medicine, specific **9** alleviate, treatment **10** corrective, medicament, medication

remember
5 educe, evoke **6** recall, record, relive, retain, reward **7** bethink **9** flash back, recollect, reminisce **10** bear in mind **11** commemorate, memorialize

remembrance
4 gift **5** favor, relic, token **6** déjà vu, memory, recall, trophy **7** memento, present, thought **8** keepsake, memorial, reminder, souvenir **9** anamnesis, flashback **12** recollection, reminiscence

remind
6 advise, prompt **7** bethink **8** admonish

reminder
4 hint, memo **5** relic, token **6** prompt, trophy **7** memento **8** keepsake, memorial, monument, souvenir **9** refresher **10** admonition, memorandum **11** remembrance

reminisce
see **remember**

reminiscence
6 memory, recall **8** anecdote **9** anamnesis, flashback **11** remembrance **12** recollection

remise
4 cede, deed **5** alien, grant **6** assign, convey **8** make over, transfer **9** quitclaim

remiss
3 lax **4** lazy **5** slack **8** careless, derelict, heedless, indolent, slothful **9** negligent **10** delinquent, neglectful, slatternly **11** inattentive

remit
4 send, ship, stay, stop **5** abate, defer, delay, relax **6** desist, hold up, pardon, put off, remand, shelve **7** condone, consign, forgive, forward, hold off **8** dispatch, moderate, postpone

remnant
3 end **4** heel, husk, part, rest, rump **5** relic, trace, wrack **6** fag end, relict **7** balance, oddment, residue **8** leavings, leftover, residuum **9** remainder

remodel
4 redo **6** recast, revamp **8** make over, overhaul, redesign **9** refashion **11** reconstruct

remonstrance
5 demur **7** protest **8** demurral, demurrer, scolding **9** challenge, objection

remonstrate
5 argue, demur, plead, scold **6** combat, object, oppose, reason **7** protest **9** challenge

remora
4 clog, drag **6** sucker **9** hindrance **10** impediment **11** encumbrance, shark sucker

remorse
3 rue **4** ruth **5** guilt, smart **6** regret, sorrow **9** penitence **10** contrition, repentance **11** compunction **12** self-reproach

remorseful
see **regretful**

remote
3 far, off **4** slim **5** aloof **6** far-off, slight **7** distant, faraway, obscure, outside, slender **8** detached, far-flung, frontier, isolated, lonesome, off-lying, outlying, secluded **9** backwoods, withdrawn **10** negligible **11** godforsaken, out-of-the-way
combining form: **3** tel **4** tele

remotest
6 utmost **7** extreme, outmost **8** farthest **9** outermost, uttermost **11** furthermost

remove
4 doff, skim **5** purge **6** delete, unseat **7** extract, take off, take out **8** dislodge, evacuate, take away, withdraw **9** clear away, eliminate
from office: **6** depose
hair: **8** depilate
surgically: **6** resect

removed
5 aloof, apart **6** far-off, remote **7** devious, distant, faraway, obscure **8** detached, far-flung, isolated, outlying, separate **10** distracted **11** unconnected

remunerate
3 pay **5** repay **7** requite **9** indemnify, reimburse **10** compensate, recompense

remunerative
6 paying **7** gainful, payable **9** lucrative **10** productive, profitable **11** moneymaking

Remus
brother: **7** Romulus
father: **4** Mars
mother: **9** Rea Silvia **10** Rhea Silvia
slayer: **7** Romulus

renaissance
see **rebirth**

renal
7 nephric **9** nephritic

rend
3 rip **4** rive, tear **5** split **6** cleave, divide

render
3 pay **4** cede, limn **5** yield **6** depict, give up, impart, return, submit **7** deliver, execute, pay back, picture, portray, present, proffer, provide, restore **8** carry out, describe, hand over, turn over **9** delineate, interpret, represent, translate, transpose **10** administer, relinquish **12** administrate

rendering
4 copy **7** version **9** depiction **10** paraphrase **11** description, performance, restatement, translation **12** reproduction

rendezvous
4 date **5** haunt, tryst **6** gather, muster **7** collect, hangout, meeting **8** assemble **10** congregate, engagement **11** appointment, assignation, get-together

rendition
7 reading, version **10** adaptation **11** performance, translation

renegade
3 rat **5** rebel **6** outlaw **7** heretic **8** apostate, defector, deserter, maverick, recreant, turncoat **9** turnabout **10** schismatic

renege
4 deny **5** welch, welsh **6** cry off, recall, recant, revoke **7** back off, back out, retract **8** renounce, withdraw **9** backpedal

renew
6 redeem, reform, revamp, revive **7** freshen, refresh, remodel **8** make over, overhaul, recharge, recreate, rekindle, renovate, revivify **9** refurbish, resurrect **10** reactivate, recommence, regenerate, rejuvenate, revitalize

rennet
8 abomasum

renounce
4 deny, quit **5** demit **6** abjure, defect, desert, give up, recant, renege, resign **7** abandon, decline, forsake, put away, retract **8** abdicate, abnegate, disclaim, forswear, swear off **9** repudiate, sacrifice **10** apostatize

renovate
4 redo **5** renew **6** remake, repair, revamp, revive **7** furbish, refresh, restore **8** overhaul, revivify **9** modernize, refurbish, resurrect **10** rejuvenate, revitalize **12** rehabilitate

renown
4 fame **5** éclat, glory, kudos **6** repute **7** acclaim **8** eminence, prestige **9** celebrity, notoriety **10** prominence, reputation **11** distinction

renowned
5 famed, great, noted **6** fabled, famous **7** eminent, notable **8** extolled **9** acclaimed, legendary, notorious, prominent, well-known **10** celebrated **11** illustrious, outstanding **13** distinguished

rent
3 let, rip **4** hire, rift, tear, torn **5** lease, split **6** breach, sublet **7** charter, fissure, rupture **8** fracture

rental
4 hire **7** tenancy

renter
6 lessee, tenant **11** leaseholder

renunciation
6 denial **7** refusal **8** apostasy, eschewal, forgoing **9** disavowal, sacrifice, surrender **10** abdication, abnegation, disclaimer, self-denial **11** abandonment, forswearing, repudiation, resignation

reorder
5 shift **7** permute **9** rearrange, reshuffle

reorganization
7 shake-up **8** turnover

repair
3 fix **4** mend **5** patch **6** cobble, doctor **7** fitness, service **8** overhaul **9** condition **11** recondition

reparations
6 amends **7** redress **9** indemnity, quittance

10 recompense, settlement **11** restitution **12** satisfaction

repartee
4 quip **6** banter, retort **7** riposte **8** backchat, badinage, comeback **9** cross talk, rejoinder **10** persiflage

repast
3 eat **4** feed, meal **5** feast **9** refection

repay
6 offset, return, reward **7** requite **9** indemnify, reimburse **10** compensate, recompense, remunerate **11** get even with

repeal
4 lift, null, void **5** annul **6** recall, revoke **7** abandon, abolish, nullify, rescind, reverse **8** abrogate, renounce

repeat
4 copy, echo **5** recap, recur, rerun, resay **6** go over, parrot, reecho, recite, rehash, relate, retell **7** imitate, iterate, reprise, restate **9** duplicate, reiterate, replicate **11** reduplicate **12** recapitulate

repeater
7 firearm **10** recidivist

repeating
7 iterant **9** perennial, recurrent **11** reiterative, repetitious

repel
5 rebut **6** rebuff, reject, revolt, sicken **7** disgust, fend off, hold off, repulse, ward off **8** nauseate, stave off

repellent
4 foul, vile **5** nasty **7** noisome **8** aversive **9** abhorrent, loathsome, obnoxious, offensive, repulsive, revolting **10** forbidding, disgusting, off-putting **11** rebarbative

repent
3 rue **6** regret

repentance
3 rue **4** ruth **6** sorrow **7** remorse **10** contrition **11** compunction

repentant
see **regretful**

repetition
4 copy, echo **5** rerun **7** recital, reprise **11** duplication

rephrase
6 recast, reword **7** restate

repine
4 beef, fuss, kick, long, moan, wail **5** gripe, yearn **6** grouse, hanker, murmur **7** grumble **8** complain

replace
7 put back, restore **8** exchange, supplant **9** supersede **10** substitute

replacement
3 sub **6** fill-in, loaner, makeup **7** stand-in **9** alternate, surrogate, temporary **10** substitute **11** locum tenens, pinch hitter, succedaneum

replenish
4 fill **5** renew, stock **6** refill **7** refresh, restock, restore

replete
4 full, rife **5** awash, lousy **6** packed **7** brimful, crammed, stuffed **8** brimming **9** chock-full **11** overflowing

replica
4 copy, dupe, fake **5** clone, ditto **6** carbon **9** duplicate, facsimile, imitation **10** carbon copy, simulacrum **12** reproduction

replicate
4 copy **5** clone **6** repeat **9** reproduce

reply
4 echo, RSVP **6** answer, rejoin, retort **7** respond **8** comeback, repartee, response **9** rejoinder

report
4 bang, boom, news, tell **5** crack, relay, rumor, study **6** record, relate, return, review, show up **7** account, article, check in, hearsay, narrate, recount, rundown **8** advisory, bulletin, describe, dispatch **9** broadcast, chronicle, narrative, statement **11** compte rendu

reporter
7 newsman **8** pressman **9** newshound, newswoman **10** journalist
inexperienced: 3 cub

repose
3 lie **4** calm, rest **5** peace, poise, quiet, sleep **7** lie down, recline **8** quietude **9** composure, stillness **10** inactivity, quiescence, relaxation **11** restfulness, tranquility **12** tranquillity

repository
3 ark **5** depot, store **7** archive, arsenal **8** magazine, treasury **10** storehouse

repossess
see **regain**

reprehend
3 rap **4** rate, skin **5** blame, chide, fault, knock, scold **6** berate, rebuke **7** censure, condemn, upbraid **8** admonish, denounce **9** criticize **10** denunciate

reprehensible
4 base, evil **6** guilty, sinful, unholy, wicked **8** blamable, criminal, culpable **10** censurable **11** blameworthy, disgraceful

represent
3 act **6** denote, depict, embody, mirror, recall, relate, render, sketch, typify **7** display, exhibit, express, hold out, imitate, make out, narrate, outline, picture, portray, present, protest, realize,

signify, suggest **8** describe, stand for **9** delineate, epitomize, exemplify, interpret, personify, symbolize **10** constitute, illustrate, substitute **11** emblematize, impersonate

representation
5 draft, image **6** effigy, symbol **7** picture **8** likeness **9** portrayal, statement **10** caricature, delegation

representative
5 agent, envoy, model, proxy **6** deputy, sample **7** burgess, example, typical **8** delegate, emissary, sampling, specimen **9** exemplary, spokesman **10** ambassador, legislator, prototypal, substitute **11** congressman **12** illustrative, prototypical **13** congresswoman

repress
4 curb **5** check, sit on **6** bridle, muffle, stifle, subdue **7** smother, squelch, swallow **8** keep down, restrain, suppress

repression
4 curb **7** amnesia, control **8** stifling **9** clampdown, crackdown, restraint **10** constraint

reprieve
4 stay **5** grace **7** respite, suspend

reprimand
3 rap **4** rate, ream, task **5** chide, scold **6** rebuke **7** bawl out, censure, chew out, reproof, reprove **8** admonish, call down, reproach, scolding **9** reprimand, talking-to **10** admonition **12** admonishment, dressing-down **13** tongue-lashing

reprisal
7 redress, revenge **8** revanche **9** vengeance **11** counterblow, retaliation, retribution

reprise
5 recap **6** repeat **9** reiterate **10** recurrence, repetition

reproach
3 rap **4** rail **5** blame, chide, scold **6** berate, rebuke **7** bawl out, censure, chew out, remorse, reprove, upbraid **8** admonish, call down **9** reprimand **10** admonition, opprobrium **12** admonishment

reprobate
3 rap **4** skin **5** blame, scamp, spurn **6** refuse, reject, sinner **7** censure, condemn, lowlife, villain **8** denounce, scalawag **9** miscreant, scoundrel **10** blackguard, degenerate

reproduce
4 bear, copy, sire **5** beget, breed, spore **7** imitate **8** multiply **9** duplicate, procreate, propagate, replicate **10** regenerate **11** reduplicate

reproduction
see **replica**

reproductive cell
3 egg **4** ovum **5** sperm, spore **6** gamete **12** spermatozoid, spermatozoon

reproof
3 rap **6** rebuke **7** censure, lecture **8** scolding **9** criticism, reprimand **10** admonition **11** castigation **12** admonishment, reprehension **13** remonstration

reprove
5 chide, scold **6** rebuke **7** censure, chasten **8** admonish, call down, lambaste, reproach **9** criticize, dress down, reprimand

reptile
4 croc **5** gator, skink, snake **6** caiman, cayman, gavial, iguana, lizard, turtle **7** tuatara **8** tortoise **9** alligator, crocodile, sphenodon
combining form: **6** herpet **7** herpeto
extinct: **8** dinosaur

republic
5 state **6** nation **9** democracy

Republican Party
3 GOP
symbol: **8** elephant

Republic author
5 Plato

repudiate
4 deny **5** spurn **6** abjure, disown, recant, refuse, reject **7** decline, disavow, dismiss **8** disclaim, renounce **9** disaffirm **10** apostatize, disapprove

repugnance
6 horror **7** disgust **8** aversion, loathing **9** repulsion, revulsion **10** abhorrence, antagonism, odiousness **11** abomination, detestation

repugnant
4 foul, vile **5** nasty, yucky **6** creepy, horrid, skanky **7** noisome **8** aversive, gruesome **9** abhorrent, loathsome, obnoxious, offensive, repulsive, revolting **10** disgusting

repulse
5 rebut, repel, spurn **6** rebuff, reject, revolt, sicken **7** disgust, fend off, hold off, ward off **8** nauseate, stave off

repulsion
see **repugnance**

repulsive
see **repugnant**

reputable
7 eminent, upright **8** esteemed **9** estimable, honorable **10** creditable, legitimate, recognized, sanctioned **11** respectable, trustworthy **13** well-thought-of

reputation
4 fame, name, note **5** éclat, honor **6** esteem, renown, report **8** position, prestige, standing **9** celebrity, character, notoriety

reputed
6 honest 7 alleged 8 putative, supposed 9 estimable, purported 10 creditable, ostensible 11 respectable 12 hypothetical

request
3 ask, dun, sue 4 pray, seek, wish 5 plead, press 6 appeal, ask for, demand, invite 7 entreat, solicit 8 entreaty, petition 10 invitation

Requiem for a Nun author
8 Faulkner (William)

require
3 ask, beg 4 lack, need, want 5 claim, crave 6 demand, desire 7 call for, dictate, mandate, solicit 8 insist on 11 necessitate

required
3 due 5 vital 7 crucial 9 essential, mandatory, necessary, requisite 10 compulsory, obligatory 11 fundamental

requirement
4 must, need, want 5 claim 6 charge, demand 9 condition, essential, necessity, requisite 10 imperative, sine qua non 11 stipulation

requisite
3 due 4 must 5 vital 7 crucial, needful 8 cardinal 9 condition, essential, necessity 10 imperative, sine qua non 11 fundamental 12 precondition 13 indispensable

requisition
4 call 5 claim, exact 6 demand 7 solicit 11 application

requite
3 pay 5 repay 6 return 7 revenge, satisfy 9 indemnify, reimburse 10 compensate, recompense, remunerate 11 reciprocate

reredos
6 screen 9 partition

rescind
4 lift 5 annul 6 cancel, recall, repeal, revoke 7 retract, reverse 8 roll back, take back

rescue
4 free, save 6 ransom, redeem 7 bailout, deliver, reclaim, recover, release, salvage 8 liberate, preserve 9 extricate 11 deliverance

rescuer
6 savior 7 saviour

research
5 probe, study 7 inquest, inquiry 8 look into 9 delve into 10 experiment 11 examination, inquisition, investigate 13 investigation

resect
6 cut out, excise 8 amputate 9 extirpate

resemblance
7 analogy 8 likeness 9 alikeness 10 comparison, similarity, similitude 11 parallelism

resemble
5 favor 6 recall 8 look like, simulate 9 take after 11 approximate

resembling
3 à la 4 like 6 akin to

resentful
4 sore 6 bitter, piqued, sullen 7 envious

resentment
5 pique 6 animus, grudge, malice, rancor 7 dudgeon, offense, umbrage 9 animosity 11 indignation

reservation
5 doubt 7 booking, enclave, proviso 8 homeland, preserve 9 condition, misgiving, sanctuary 10 limitation

reserve
4 book, fund, hold, keep 5 hoard, put by, stash, stock, store, tract 6 retain, supply 7 nest egg, savings, standby 8 contract, distance, fallback, hold back, postpone, set aside, squirrel, withhold 9 inventory, restraint, reticence, stockpile 10 constraint, discretion, diffidence 13 qualification

reserved
4 cool 5 aloof, stiff 6 demure, formal, remote 7 distant 8 reticent, retiring, taciturn 9 diffident, reclusive, secretive, withdrawn 10 unsociable 11 tight-lipped 12 closemouthed 13 self-contained

reservoir
5 hoard, stock, store 6 supply 7 nest egg 9 inventory, stockpile

reside
3 lie 4 hive, live, stay 5 dwell, exist 6 inhere 7 consist

residence
4 home, stay 5 abode, house 7 address 8 domicile, dwelling 9 occupancy 10 habitation

resident
5 liver 6 inmate, lodger, native, tenant 7 citizen, denizen, dweller, present 8 inherent, occupant 10 inhabitant 11 householder

residential area
9 community 12 neighborhood

residual
7 balance, payment, remnant 8 leavings, leftover 9 remainder

residue
3 ash 4 heel, lees, marc, rest, silt, slag 5 ashes, dregs, grout 6 debris, excess, scraps 7 balance, grounds, remains, remnant, surplus 8 leavings, remnants, residuum 9 leftovers, remainder, scourings

resign
4 cede, quit 5 demit, leave, yield 6 give up, retire, submit 7 abandon, consign 8 abdicate,

hand over, relegate, renounce, step down **9** reconcile, surrender **10** relinquish

resignation
8 meekness **9** demission, surrender **10** abdication, compliance, submission **12** acquiescence, renunciation

resigned
9 compliant **10** submissive **11** acquiescent, complaisant

resile
6 recede, recoil, spring **7** rebound, retract, retreat **8** draw back, snap back

resilient
6 bouncy, supple, whippy **7** buoyant, elastic, springy **8** flexible, stretchy **9** adaptable

resin
4 balm **5** copal, damar, roset **6** dammar **7** acrylic, copaiba
aromatic: 6 balsam, mastic **8** sandarac
fragrant: 5 elemi **6** storax, styrax **7** ladanum **8** labdanum
gum: 5 myrrh **7** benzoin
medicinal: 6 guaiac **8** guaiacum
of an insect: 3 lac
synthetic: 8 phenolic
used by bees: 8 propolis

resist
4 buck, defy, kick **5** rebel **6** baffle, combat, oppose, revolt **7** contest, counter, gainsay **8** traverse **10** contradict, contravene

resistance
7 dissent **8** defiance, variance **10** dissension, dissidence, opposition **11** contrariety, obstruction

resistance unit
3 ohm

resistor
8 rheostat, varistor **10** thermistor

resolute
3 set **4** bent, bold, fast, firm, true **6** intent, steady, sturdy **7** decided, staunch **8** constant, decisive, faithful, intrepid, stubborn **9** obstinate, steadfast, tenacious, undaunted **10** determined, persistent **12** pertinacious, single-minded

resolution
4 guts **5** heart, nerve, pluck, spunk **6** mettle, spirit **7** courage, outcome **8** decision, firmness, tenacity **10** conclusion **12** perseverance **13** determination, steadfastness

resolve
5 clear, crack **6** decide, settle **7** clear up, iron out, unravel, work out **8** boldness, conclude, decipher, firmness **9** breakdown, determine, intention, reconcile **10** unscramble **13** determination, steadfastness

resonant
4 deep, full, rich **6** silver **7** booming, echoing, orotund, vibrant **8** powerful, sonorous **11** reverberant

resonate
4 echo, peal, ring **7** resound, vibrate **11** reverberate

resort
3 spa **4** lido **5** haven, hotel, lodge, shift **6** harbor, refuge **7** retreat, riviera, stopgap **8** recourse **9** expedient, makeshift **10** substitute
last: 8 pis aller

resound
4 boom, echo, peal, ring **11** reverberate

resounding
7 booming, echoing, orotund, vibrant **8** emphatic, sonorous **10** clangorous, resonating, thunderous **11** unequivocal

resource
3 aid **5** asset, means, shift **6** supply **7** standby

resourceful
5 adept **6** adroit, artful, clever, shrewd **7** capable, cunning **8** creative, skillful **9** ingenious, inventive **10** innovative **11** imaginative **12** enterprising

resources
5 funds, means, money, purse **6** assets, riches, wealth **7** capital, fortune, reserve **8** bankroll, finances, property, reserves **9** substance **11** wherewithal

respect
3 awe **5** favor, honor, props **6** admire, detail, devoir, esteem, homage, regard, revere **7** account, concern **8** venerate **9** deference **10** admiration, estimation, particular, veneration

respectable
4 fair **5** ample **6** decent, proper, worthy **8** adequate **9** admirable, estimable, honorable **10** sufficient **11** appropriate, presentable **12** satisfactory **13** well-thought-of

respectful
5 civil **6** polite **8** obeisant, reverent **9** courteous **11** deferential, reverential

respecting
3 per **4** as to, in re **5** about **7** apropos **9** as regards, regarding **10** as concerns, concerning, relating to **11** considering

respire
7 breathe

respite
4 lull, rest **5** break, delay, pause, spell, truce **6** hiatus, recess, relief **8** breather, reprieve, surcease **12** intermission

resplendent
5 regal **7** glowing, shining **8** glorious, gorgeous **9** brilliant, refulgent **11** magnificent

respond
5 react, reply 6 answer, rejoin, retort 8 come back

response
5 reply 6 answer, retort, return 7 riposte 8 antiphon, comeback, reaction 9 rejoinder
involuntary: 6 reflex 7 tropism

responsibility
4 buck, duty, onus 5 blame, brief, fault 6 burden, charge, devoir 10 obligation 11 reliability

responsible
6 liable 8 amenable, reliable 10 answerable, chargeable, dependable 11 accountable, trustworthy

responsive
4 open 8 sentient 9 sensitive 11 susceptible, sympathetic

rest
3 nap, sit 4 calm, ease, laze, loaf, loll, lull, stay 5 let up, pause, peace, quiet, relax, spell 6 catnap, depend, excess, lounge, repose 7 balance, leisure, lie down, recline, remains, remnant, surplus 8 breather, leavings, vacation 9 interlude, predicate, remainder

restate
4 echo 6 reword 8 rephrase 9 translate 10 paraphrase 12 recapitulate

restatement
10 paraphrase 11 translation

restaurant
4 café 5 diner 6 eatery 7 beanery 9 brasserie, cafeteria 10 coffee shop 11 coffeehouse, greasy spoon
price: 8 à la carte, prix fixe 10 table d'hôte
worker: 4 chef, cook 6 busboy, server, waiter 7 maître d', waitron 8 waitress 10 dishwasher, headwaiter, waitperson 12 maître d'hôtel

restful
4 calm 5 quiet 6 placid 8 peaceful, tranquil

restitute
6 refund, return 7 reclaim, recover, restore 8 give back 11 recondition, reconstruct 12 rehabilitate

restitution
6 amends, refund, return 7 redress 8 reprisal 9 indemnity, quittance 10 recompense, reparation 11 restoration 12 remuneration, satisfaction

restive
4 edgy 5 balky, nervy, tense 6 ornery, uneasy 7 fidgety, froward, uptight, wayward 8 contrary, perverse, skittish

restiveness
7 anxiety, ferment, turmoil 8 disquiet 9 balkiness 10 inquietude, perversity 11 contrariety, disquietude, waywardness 12 contrariness

restless
5 antsy, itchy, jumpy 6 fitful, uneasy 7 anxious, fidgety, fretful, jittery, nervous, unquiet 8 agitated, troubled 9 disturbed, perturbed, unsettled 12 discontented, dissatisfied

restorative
4 balm 5 tonic 7 healing 8 curative, remedial, sanative 12 recuperative

restore
4 cure, heal, mend, stet 5 amend, remit, renew, right 6 recall, recoup, reform, remedy, render, repair, return, revive 7 get back, improve, reclaim, recover, rectify, refresh, replace 8 give back, recreate, renovate, revivify 9 refurbish, reinstate, replenish, restitute 10 regenerate, rejuvenate 11 recondition, reestablish 12 rehabilitate

restrain
3 bit, gag 4 bate, curb, rein 5 check, leash 6 arrest, bridle, halter, hamper, hinder, hold in, impede, muzzle, temper 7 collect, control, harness, inhibit, repress 8 hold back, hold down, moderate, suppress

restrained
4 cool 6 low-key 5 canny, quiet 6 modest 7 subdued 8 discreet, reserved, reticent, retiring, tasteful 9 contained, inhibited, temperate 10 controlled, reasonable

restraint
5 stint 6 bridle 7 durance, embargo, reserve 8 estoppel, pullback 9 hindrance 10 deterrence, inhibition, limitation, moderation 11 confinement, forbearance 12 straitjacket

restrict
3 bar, tie 4 bind, curb 5 hem in, limit 6 hamper, hobble, impede, narrow, shrink 7 confine, curtail, delimit, inhibit, trammel 8 hold back, prelimit 10 delimitate 12 circumscribe
a will: 6 entail

restriction
4 curb 5 check, limit, stint 7 control 9 restraint 10 constraint, limitation, regulation 11 confinement, prohibition 12 proscription 13 qualification

restyle
4 redo 6 revamp, revise, rework 8 make over

result
3 end 4 flow, stem 5 close, ensue, fruit, issue 6 effect, emerge, finish, follow, payoff, sequel, upshot 7 outcome, product 8 sequence, solution 9 aftermath, come about, eventuate 10 conclusion, denouement, production 11 aftereffect, consequence, eventuality
incidental: 7 spinoff

resume
4 go on 5 renew 6 pick up, reopen 7 carry on, proceed, restart 8 continue 10 recommence

résumé
2 CV **4** vita **5** sum-up **6** précis **7** summary **9** summation, summing-up

resurgence
5 rally **7** rebirth, revival **8** comeback, recovery **10** renascence **11** renaissance **12** risorgimento

resurrect
5 raise, renew **6** come to, revive **8** retrieve, revivify **10** reactivate

resurrection
7 rebirth, revival **10** renascence **11** renaissance **12** risorgimento

resuscitate
see **resurrect**

retail
4 sell, tell, vend **6** market **7** narrate **11** merchandise

retailer
6 dealer, seller, trader, vendor **8** merchant **9** tradesman **10** shopkeeper **11** storekeeper **12** merchandiser

retain
3 own **4** hire, hold, keep **6** detain **7** reserve **8** hold over, preserve, remember, withhold

retainer
3 fee **6** lackey, menial, minion, yeoman **7** deposit, servant **8** employee, follower **9** bite plate, dependent, pensioner

retaliate
7 get back, get even **10** strike back

retaliation
see **reprisal**

retaliatory
8 punitive, vengeful **10** vindictive

retard
4 clog, mire, slow **5** delay, stunt **6** detain, fetter, hamper, hang up, hinder, impede, slow up **7** set back, slacken **8** decrease, hold back, restrain **10** decelerate

retarded
3 dim **4** dull, dumb, slow **6** opaque, simple, stupid **8** backward **9** dim-witted **10** half-witted, slow-witted **11** exceptional

retch
3 gag **4** barf, hurl, puke, spew **5** heave, vomit **6** spit up **7** bring up, throw up, upchuck **8** disgorge

retention
6 memory **7** storage

reticent
see **reserved**

reticulate
4 vein **5** veiny **6** meshed, netted **7** netlike **10** crisscross

retinue
4 band, tail **5** suite, train **6** livery **7** company, cortege **9** entourage, following

retire
4 exit, quit **5** leave, yield **6** bow out, depart, recede, resign, turn in **7** dismiss, pension **8** step down, withdraw **9** discharge, strike out, terminate **10** relinquish

retired person
7 emerita **8** emeritus **9** pensioner

retiree
6 senior **9** pensioner **10** golden-ager **13** senior citizen

retirement allowance
3 SEP **7** pension

retiring
3 shy **5** mousy, timid **6** demure, modest **7** bashful **8** reserved **9** diffident, withdrawn **11** unassertive

retool
7 reequip **10** reengineer

retort
5 reply, sally **6** answer, rejoin **7** counter, respond, riposte **8** comeback, repartee, response **9** rejoinder, retaliate, wisecrack

retouch
5 alter, emend, renew **6** repair **7** correct, enhance, improve, restore

retract
4 deny **5** unsay **6** abjure, recall, recant, recede, renege, resile, revoke **7** disavow, rescind, retreat, swallow **8** forswear, renounce, take back, withdraw

retreat
3 den, ebb **4** flee, quit **5** cover, haven, leave **6** ashram, asylum, bow out, covert, decamp, depart, escape, recede, recoil, refuge, shrink, vacate **7** abandon, back off, back out, pull out, shelter **8** back down, draw back, evacuate, fall back, hideaway, withdraw **9** backtrack, climb down, sanctuary **10** give ground, withdrawal

retrench
3 cut **4** pare **5** slash **6** excise, lessen, reduce **7** abridge, curtail **9** economize

retribution
6 return, reward **7** deserts, revenge **8** avenging, reprisal, requital, revanche **9** vengeance **10** punishment, recompense **11** counterblow, retaliation
goddess of: 3 Ate **4** Fury **7** Nemesis

retrieve
5 fetch **6** recall, recoup, redeem, rescue **7** get back, recover, restore, salvage **9** resurrect

retro
5 campy **7** antique, revival, vintage **9** nostalgic **12** old-fashioned

retrograde
4 back **7** inverse, reverse **8** backward, inverted, rearward

retrogress
see **revert**

retrospect
9 hindsight **12** recollection **13** reexamination

retrospective
6 review **8** backward **10** exhibition, reflective, ruminative

return
5 recur, repay, reply, yield **6** answer, rebate, regain, rejoin, render, repeat, retort, revert **7** bring in, get back, rebound, recover, reprise, requite, respond, reverse, riposte **8** comeback, dividend, earnings, give back, proceeds, reappear, response **9** rejoinder, repayment, reversion **10** recompense, recurrence **11** reciprocate, restitution

Return of the Native
author: **5** Hardy (Thomas)
character: **4** Clym (Yeobright) **8** Eustacia (Vye)

Reuben
brother: **6** Joseph
father: **5** Jacob
mother: **4** Leah
son: **5** Carmi **6** Hanoch, Hezron, Phallu

Réunion
capital: **7** St.-Denis
city: **6** St.-Paul **7** St.-Louis **8** St.-Pierre
department of: **6** France
ethnic group: **6** Creole
former name: **7** Bourbon **9** Bonaparte
island group: **9** Mascarene

revamp
4 redo **5** renew **6** remake, repair, revise, rework **7** remodel, restyle, rewrite **8** make over, overhaul, redesign, renovate **9** refurbish **11** recondition

reveal
4 bare, blab, jamb, leak, open, show, tell **5** admit, let on, peach, spill **6** betray, evince, expose, impart, unmask, unveil **7** confess, declare, display, divulge, exhibit, publish, uncover, undress **8** announce, decipher, disclose, discover, give away, unclothe **9** broadcast, made known **11** acknowledge, communicate **12** bring to light

revel
4 bask, orgy, riot **5** binge, feast, party, spree **6** boogie, frolic, gaiety, hoopla, wallow **7** carouse, delight, indulge, jollity, roister, rollick, wassail, whoopla **8** carnival, carousal, festival **9** bacchanal, celebrate, festivity, luxuriate, merriment, whoop-de-do **11** bacchanalia, celebration, merrymaking

revelation
6 kicker **8** epiphany, giveaway, prophecy, surprise **9** discovery **10** apocalypse, disclosure **13** manifestation

reveler
7 orgiast **8** bacchant, carouser **9** bacchante, wassailer **10** merrymaker

revelry
4 orgy, riot **6** gaiety **7** carouse, jollity, wassail, whoopee, whoopla **8** carousal, partying **9** festivity, high jinks, merriment, whoop-de-do **10** whoop-de-doo **11** merrymaking

revenant
5 ghost, haunt, shade, spook **6** shadow, spirit, undead, wraith, zombie **7** phantom, specter, spectre **8** phantasm, prodigal, visitant **10** apparition

revenge
5 right **6** defend **7** get back, get even, redress, requite **8** reprisal, requital, revanche **9** retaliate, vindicate **11** retaliation, retribution

revenue
4 rent **5** gains, issue, yield **6** income, profit, return **7** comings **8** earnings, interest, proceeds, receipts, taxation

reverberant
6 hollow **7** booming, echoing **8** resonant **10** resounding

reverberate
4 echo, gong, ring **6** reecho **7** resound

revere
4 laud **5** adore, exalt, extol, honor, prize, value **6** admire, esteem, regard **7** cherish, magnify, respect, worship **8** treasure, venerate **10** appreciate

revered
6 sacred **9** estimable, venerable

reverence
3 awe **5** adore, dread, honor, piety **6** esteem, fealty, homage **7** loyalty, respect, worship **8** devotion, venerate **9** deference, obeisance, solemnity **10** veneration
gesture of: **3** bow **6** kowtow **8** kneeling **12** genuflection

reverend
4 abbé, holy **5** clerk, vicar **6** clergy, cleric, deacon, divine, parson, rector **8** chaplain, clerical, minister, preacher **9** churchman, clergyman **11** clergywoman **12** ecclesiastic

reverent
5 godly, pious **6** devout **7** dutiful **9** prayerful **10** God-fearing, respectful, worshipful

reverie
4 muse **5** dream **6** trance, vision **7** fantasy **8** daydream **10** absorption, brown study, meditation **11** abstraction **13** woolgathering

reversal
4 turn **5** U-turn **6** double, switch **7** setback, undoing **8** backfire, flip-flop **9** about-face, inversion, turnabout, volte-face **10** switcheroo **12** solarization **13** change of heart

reverse
4 lift, undo **6** change, contra, defeat, invert, recall, repeal, revoke **7** capsize, counter, rescind, setback **8** antipode, backward, contrary, disaster, exchange, opposite, overrule, overturn **9** about-face, backwards, diametric, overthrow, transpose, turnabout, volte-face **10** antithesis, misfortune

reversion
4 turn **5** lapse **6** return **7** atavism, escheat **9** about-face, throwback, turnabout, volte-face **10** regression, succession

revert
4 turn **6** return **7** decline, devolve, escheat, inverse, regress **8** turn back **9** backslide **10** degenerate, retrograde, retrogress

revetment
4 berm **6** bunker, riprap **9** barricade, earthwork **10** embankment

review
4 scan **5** audit, recap, study **6** assess, go over, parade, report, revise, survey **7** analyze, journal, rethink **8** analysis, critique, magazine, revision, scrutiny, talk over **9** criticism, reexamine, refresher **10** evaluation, inspection, periodical, reconsider, reevaluate **11** examination **13** reexamination, retrospective

revile
4 rail, rate **5** abuse, scold **6** attack, berate, defame, malign, vilify **7** asperse, bawl out, chew out, upbraid **8** belittle, disgrace, execrate **9** blaspheme **10** tongue-lash, vituperate

revise
4 edit **5** alter, amend, emend, proof, renew **6** change, polish, redraw, reform, retool, revamp, rework **7** correct, improve, redraft, restore, restyle, rewrite **8** overhaul, redesign, work over **9** red-pencil **10** blue-pencil

revision
6 change, revamp, update **7** redraft **8** facelift, overhaul, updating **10** alteration, correction, emendation **11** overhauling **12** modification

revitalize
see **revive**

revival
7 rebirth, renewal **8** comeback **10** renascence, resurgence **11** reanimation, renaissance, restoration **12** regeneration, rejuvenation, resurrection, risorgimento **13** recrudescence, resuscitation

revive
4 wake **5** rally, renew, rouse **6** arouse, awaken, come to, recall **7** bring to, enliven, freshen, quicken, refresh, restore **8** reawaken, rekindle, renovate, retrieve **9** reanimate, resurrect **10** reactivate, recuperate, regenerate, rejuvenate **11** bring around, reintroduce, resuscitate **12** reinvigorate

revoke
4 lift, void **5** annul, erase **6** abjure, cancel, recall, recant, renege, repeal **7** abolish, nullify, rescind, retract, reverse **8** abrogate, call back **10** invalidate **11** countermand

revolt
4 riot **5** rebel, repel, shock **6** mutiny, resist, sicken **7** disgust, repulse **8** nauseate, outbreak, uprising **9** jacquerie, rebellion **10** insurgence, insurgency **12** insurrection

revolter
5 rebel **6** anarch **8** frondeur, mutineer **9** anarchist, insurgent **10** malcontent

revolting
4 foul, ugly, vile **5** nasty **6** horrid **7** hideous, noisome, obscene **8** shocking **9** atrocious, loathsome, repellent, repugnant, repulsive **10** disgusting, nauseating

revolution
4 gyre, reel, riot, roll, spin, turn **5** cycle, orbit, twirl, wheel, whirl **6** mutiny **7** circuit **8** gyration, rotation, uprising **9** pirouette, rebellion **10** barrel roll, changeover, somersault **12** insurrection

revolutionary
5 rebel, ultra **7** extreme, radical **8** mutineer, rotating, ultraist **9** extremist, insurgent
American: **4** Hale (Nathan), Reed (John) **5** Adams (Samuel), Allen (Ethan), Henry (Patrick), Shays (Daniel) **6** Revere (Paul)
English: **5** Paine (Thomas)
French: **5** Marat (Jean-Paul) **6** Danton (Georges) **8** Mirabeau (Comte de) **9** Saint-Just (Louis) **11** Robespierre (Maximilien)
Irish: **4** Tone (Wolfe) **6** Pearse (Padraig, Patrick) **7** Collins (Michael), Parnell (Charles Stewart) **8** Casement (Roger), de Valera (Eamon), Griffith (Arthur), O'Connell (Daniel)
Mexican: **5** Villa (Pancho) **6** Zapata (Emiliano) **7** Hidalgo (Padre Miguel)
Russian: **5** Kirov (Sergey), Lenin (Vladimir Ilyich) **7** Trotsky (Leon) **8** Kerensky (Aleksandr) **9** Kropotkin (Pyotr)

revolutionize
9 transform **11** transfigure

revolve
4 spin, turn **5** twirl, wheel, whirl **6** circle, gyrate, rotate

revolver
3 gat, gun, rod **4** Colt **5** Glock, Luger, Ruger **6** Magnum, pistol, six-gun **7** firearm, handgun, shooter, sidearm **10** six-shooter

revue
4 show **9** burlesque **10** production, vaudeville **13** entertainment

revulsion
4 hate **6** hatred, horror **7** disgust **8** aversion, loathing **10** abhorrence, repugnance **11** abomination, detestation

reward
5 bonus, booty, crown, medal, price, prize **6** bounty, carrot, payoff, trophy **7** guerdon, jackpot, premium **8** dividend **10** compensate, honorarium, recompense, remunerate **12** compensation, remuneration

rewarding
7 gainful **8** edifying, fruitful, valuable **9** lucrative **10** beneficial, fulfilling, gratifying, productive, profitable, satisfying, worthwhile **12** advantageous, remunerative

reword
see **restate**

rework
6 revamp, revise **7** restyle, rewrite

Reynard
3 fox

rhadamanthine
3 due **4** just **5** right **6** strict **7** condign, fitting, merited **8** deserved, rigorous, rightful, suitable **9** requisite, stringent **11** appropriate

Rhadamanthus
5 judge
brother: 5 Minos
father: 4 Zeus **7** Jupiter
mother: 6 Europa

rhapsodic
5 lyric **8** ecstatic, effusive **9** emotional, exuberant

rhapsodize
4 gush, rave **5** drool **6** effuse **7** enthuse

Rhea
3 Ops
daughter: 4 Hera, Juno **5** Ceres, Vesta **6** Hestia **7** Demeter
father: 6 Uranus
husband: 6 Cronus, Saturn
mother: 4 Gaea
son: 4 Zeus **5** Hades, Pluto **7** Jupiter, Neptune **8** Poseidon

Rheingold, Das
character: 4 Loge, Loki **5** Freya, Wotan **6** Fafner, Fafnir, Fasolt **8** Alberich
composer: 6 Wagner (Richard)

rheostat
8 resistor

rhesus
6 monkey **7** macaque

rhetoric
4 rant **6** speech **7** bombast, fustian, oratory **8** rhapsody **9** elocution, eloquence, verbosity **11** rodomontade, speechcraft
term: 6 aporia, simile **7** litotes **8** metaphor **10** apostrophe, digression **12** alliteration, onomatopoeia

rhetorical
4 glib **5** gassy, grand, tumid, windy **6** florid, fluent, ornate, purple, turgid **7** aureate, flowery, orotund, pompous, stilted **8** eloquent, forensic, inflated, overdone, sonorous **9** bombastic, grandiose, high-flown, overblown, tumescent **10** euphuistic, flamboyant, oratorical **11** declamatory, highfalutin, overwrought, pretentious **12** high-sounding, magniloquent **13** grandiloquent

rhetorician
6 orator, writer **7** speaker
Roman: 10 Quintilian

Rhine River
city: 4 Bonn, Köln **5** Basel, Mainz **7** Coblenz, Cologne, Koblenz **8** Duisburg, Mannheim **9** Rotterdam, Wiesbaden **10** Düsseldorf
nymph: 7 Lorelei
tributary: 3 Aar, Ill, Lek **4** Aare, Lahn, Main, Ruhr, Waal

rhizome
4 root **5** tuber

Rhode Island
bay: 12 Narragansett
capital: 10 Providence
city: 7 Newport, Warwick **9** Pawtucket
college, university: 4 RISD **5** Brown
island: 5 Block
nickname: 5 Ocean (State) **11** Little Rhody
river: 8 Pawtuxet
state bird: 14 Rhode Island red
state flower: 6 violet
state tree: 8 red maple

Rhodesia
8 Zimbabwe

rhombus
7 diamond, lozenge **13** parallelogram

rhonchus
5 snore

Rhône River
city: 4 Lyon **5** Arles, Lyons **6** Geneva **7** Avignon
lake: 6 Geneva
mountain range: 4 Jura
tributary: 5 Isère, Saône

rhubarb
3 row **4** flap **5** run-in **6** ruckus, tangle **7** dispute, quarrel, wrangle **8** argument, pieplant **11** altercation, controversy

rhyme
4 poem, song **5** agree, ditty, verse **6** accord, jingle, poetry **7** conform **8** dovetail **9** harmonize **10** coordinate, correspond
scheme: **4** ABAB

rhymer
4 bard, poet **5** odist **7** metrist **8** lyricist **9** poetaster, rhymester, sonneteer, versifier

rhythm
4 beat, flow, lilt, time **5** meter, pulse, swing **6** accent, groove **7** cadence, measure, pattern **8** sequence

rhythmic
7 pulsing, regular **8** measured, metrical

rialto
6 market **8** district, exchange **11** marketplace

riant
3 gay **5** jolly, merry **6** blithe, bright, jocund, jovial **7** buoyant, gleeful **8** cheerful, mirthful **10** blithesome

riata
4 rope **5** lasso **6** lariat

rib
3 fun, kid, rag **4** band, bone, dike, fool, jape, jest, joke, josh, purl, razz, stay, wale **5** chaff, costa, ridge, tease **6** banter, costae (plural), lierne, needle

ribald
3 raw **4** blue, racy, rude, sexy **5** bawdy, crude, dirty, salty, spicy **6** coarse, earthy, filthy, purple, risqué, smutty, vulgar **7** naughty, obscene, profane, raunchy **8** indecent, off-color **9** offensive, reprobate, salacious **10** suggestive

ribbon
3 bow **4** band, tape **5** braid, shred, strip **6** cordon, fillet, stripe, tatter **7** bandeau

rice
7 arborio, basmati, risotto
dish: **5** pilaf **6** congee **7** risotto **9** jambalaya
drink: **4** sake, saki **5** mirin **6** arrack
field: **5** paddy
husk: **5** lemma

rich
4 dear, lush, oily, posh **5** ample, fatty, flush, grand, heavy, plush, swank, vivid **6** costly, creamy, deluxe, fecund, gilded, lavish, loaded, monied, ornate, potent, rococo **7** baroque, copious, elegant, fertile, filling, moneyed, opulent, orotund, profuse, wealthy, well-off **8** abundant, affluent, eloquent, fruitful, palatial, well-to-do **9** abounding, bountiful, elaborate, luxuriant, luxurious, plentiful, sumptuous, well-fixed **10** productive, prosperous, well-heeled **11** extravagant
person: **4** have **5** Midas, mogul, nabob **6** fat cat **7** Croesus, magnate **9** moneybags, plutocrat

Richardson work
6 Pamela **8** Clarissa

Richelieu's successor
7 Mazarin

riches
4 gold, pelf **5** booty, lucre, worth **6** mammon, wealth **7** fortune **8** opulence, property, treasure **9** resources
demon of: **6** Mammon

rick
4 cock, heap, pile **5** shock, stack

rickety
4 weak **5** shaky **6** flimsy, wobbly **7** unsound **8** decrepit, insecure, rachitic, unstable, unsteady **10** ramshackle, rattletrap

ricochet
4 ping, skim, skip **5** carom **6** bounce, glance **7** rebound **9** boomerang

rid
6 divest **7** relieve **8** unburden **11** disencumber

riddle
5 rebus **6** enigma, puzzle **7** mystery, perplex, problem **9** conundrum, perforate **10** closed book, puzzlement **11** brainteaser

ride
4 spin, tour, trip **5** drive, jaunt, mount **6** travel **7** journey **8** carousel **9** excursion

ride out
6 endure **7** outlast, survive, weather **9** withstand

rider
6 clause, cowboy, jockey **7** codicil **8** addendum, addition, appendix, horseman, reinsman **9** amendment **10** equestrian, horsewoman, supplement

ridge
3 rib, top **4** bank, berm, brow, fold, keel, reef, roll, ruck, seam, wave **5** arête, arris, chine, crest, esker, knurl, plica, spine **6** crease, divide, furrow, rimple, saddle, summit **7** annulet, breaker, crinkle, hogback, wrinkle **8** shoulder **9** razorback **11** corrugation
gravelly: **5** esker
on the skin: **4** wale, weal, welt
sharp: **7** hogback

ridicule
3 pan, rib **4** gibe, haze, jape, jeer, mock, razz, ride, twit **5** chaff, flout, mimic, roast, scoff, scout, sneer, squib, taunt **6** deride, satire **7** lampoon,

mockery, pillory, sarcasm **8** derision, raillery, satirize, travesty **9** burlesque **10** caricature
god of: **5** Momus
object of: **4** butt **13** laughingstock

ridiculous
5 comic, daffy, dotty, goofy, silly, wacky **6** absurd, insane **7** bizarre, comical, foolish, risible **8** derisory, farcical **9** cockamamy, fantastic, grotesque, laughable, ludicrous, monstrous, senseless **10** cockamamie, outrageous **11** for the birds, harebrained **12** preposterous, unbelievable

riding
academy: **6** manège
costume: **5** habit
pants: **8** jodhpurs
whip: **3** bat **4** crop **5** quirt

Rienzi composer
6 Wagner (Richard)

rife
4 full **5** flush **6** common **7** replete, teeming **8** abundant, swarming **9** abounding, plentiful, prevalent **10** widespread **11** overflowing

riff
4 flip, leaf, scan, skim **5** theme, thumb **6** browse **8** ostinato

riffle
4 flip, leaf, fret, scan, skim, wave **5** shoal, thumb **6** browse, sluice **7** shallow, shuffle **10** interstice

riffraff
3 mob **5** trash, waste **6** debris, kelter, litter, masses, rabble, refuse **7** garbage, rubbish **8** canaille, unwashed **9** hoi polloi, multitude **11** proletariat

rifle
3 arm, gun, rob **4** loot, sack **5** steal **6** burgle, groove, weapon **7** carbine, despoil, firearm, pillage, plunder, ransack, rummage **9** chassepot
accessory: **6** ramrod
attachment: **5** scope **8** silencer
kind: **6** Garand, Mauser **7** Enfield **8** Browning **9** Remington **10** Winchester **11** Springfield

rift
3 gap **4** rent **5** break, chasm, chink, cleft, crack, fault, space, split **6** breach, cleave, divide, hiatus, schism **7** fissure, opening, rupture **8** crevasse, division, fracture, interval **9** fault line **10** separation **12** estrangement

rig
3 arm, fit, fix **4** fake, gear, semi **5** dress, equip, getup, trick **6** adjust, clothe, doctor, outfit, tackle **7** apparel, arrange, costume, derrick, furnish, turn out **8** accouter, accoutre, clothing, equipage **9** apparatus, construct, equipment **10** manipulate

rigging
3 net **4** duds, gear, togs **5** dress, lines, ropes **6** attire, chains, tackle, things **7** apparel, clothes, raiment **8** clothing **9** apparatus, equipment

right
3 apt, due, fit **4** fair, just, sane, true, well **5** amend, amply, claim, droit, emend, exact, sound, title **6** at once, common, decent, dexter, direct, equity, honest, lawful, proper, square, strict **7** condign, correct, exactly, fitting, freedom, genuine, healthy, liberty, license, merited, old-line, rectify, redress **8** accurate, bona fide, orthodox, smack-dab, suitable **9** authentic, befitting, equitable, privilege, veracious, veritable **10** perquisite **11** appropriate, correctness, prerogative
combining form: **4** orth, rect **5** dextr, ortho, recti **6** dextro
feudal: **4** soke
legal: **5** droit **8** usufruct
royal: **7** regalia (plural)

right away
3 now **6** at once, pronto **8** directly, promptly **9** forthwith, instanter, instantly **11** immediately, straight off, straightway **12** then and there

righteous
4 good, holy, just, pure **5** godly, moral, noble, pious **6** devout, worthy **7** ethical, genuine, sinless, upright **8** innocent, virtuous **9** blameless, guiltless **10** inculpable, principled

righteousness
5 honor **6** equity, virtue **7** honesty, justice, probity **8** holiness, morality **9** integrity, rectitude

rightful
3 apt, due, fit **4** fair, just, true **5** legal **6** honest, lawful, proper **7** condign, fitting **8** deserved, suitable **9** befitting, equitable, impartial **10** applicable, legitimate **11** appropriate

right-handed
6 dexter **7** dextral **9** clockwise

right-hand page
5 recto

rightist
4 tory **11** reactionary **12** conservative

right-minded
5 moral, noble **6** decent, honest **7** ethical **8** virtuous **10** upstanding

Rights of Man author
5 Paine (Thomas)

rigid
3 set **4** firm, hard, taut **5** fixed, stiff, tense **6** severe, strict **7** austere, precise, hard-set **8** cast-iron, ironclad, obdurate, rigorous **9** draconian, immovable, inelastic, rockbound,

stringent, unbending **10** adamantine, brass-bound, inflexible, relentless, unyielding **11** unbudgeable **13** rhadamanthine

rigidity
6 turgor **7** buckram **8** hardness **9** stiffness
muscular: **8** myotonia

rigmarole
6 bunkum, drivel, ramble **7** blather **8** nonsense **9** gibberish, procedure **10** balderdash, mumbo jumbo **12** gobbledygook

Rigoletto
composer: **5** Verdi (Giuseppe)
daughter: **5** Gilda
setting: **6** Mantua

rigor
7 cruelty **8** asperity, hardness, hardship, severity **9** austerity, exactness, harshness, roughness, sharpness, sternness **10** affliction, difficulty, exactitude, strictness **11** tribulation **13** inflexibility

rigorous
5 exact, harsh, rigid, rough, stern, stiff **6** bitter, brutal, proper, rugged, severe, strict **7** ascetic, drastic, onerous, precise **8** accurate, exacting **9** draconian, ironbound, stringent **10** burdensome, inflexible, ironhanded, oppressive **11** punctilious **13** rhadamanthine

rile
3 bug, rub, vex **4** roil **5** anger, annoy, grate, muddy, peeve, pique, upset **6** muddle, nettle, put out, rankle **7** agitate, disturb, fluster, inflame, perturb, provoke **8** disorder, disquiet, irritate **9** aggravate **10** discompose, exasperate

rill
3 run **4** burn, purl **5** bourn, brook, creek **6** runnel, stream, valley **7** freshet, rivulet **8** brooklet **9** streamlet **11** watercourse

rim
3 hem, lip **4** bank, boss, brim, edge, ring **5** bezel, bezil, bound, brink, skirt, verge **6** border, flange, fringe, margin, shield **7** annulus, horizon, outline **8** boundary, surround **9** perimeter, periphery
of a basket: **4** hoop
of a cask: **5** chime
of an insect's wing: **6** termen
of a spoked wheel: **5** felly **6** felloe

Rimbaud work
12 Season in Hell (A) **13** Illuminations (Les)

rime
3 ice **4** hoar **5** crust, frost **7** coating, encrust **9** hoarfrost, Jack Frost **12** incrustation

Rinaldo
beloved: **8** Angelica
cousin: **7** Orlando
father: **5** Aymon
horse: **6** Bayard
mother: **3** Aya
sister: **10** Bradamante
uncle: **11** Charlemagne

rind
4 bark, husk, peel, skin **5** crust **9** crackling

ring
3 eye, hem, rim **4** band, bloc, bong, echo, gird, gyre, hoop, loop, peal, toll **5** arena, bezel, cabal, chime, clang, cycle, group, knell, knoll, round, sound **6** circle, clique, collar, girdle, staple **7** annulus, clangor, combine, compass, resound, vibrate **8** bracelet, cincture, encircle, surround **9** coalition, encompass **11** combination, reverberate
around sun or moon: **6** corona
curtain: **3** eye
for a compass: **6** gimbal
harness: **3** dee **6** button, terret
heraldic: **7** annulet
in a hinge: **7** gudgeon
of chain: **4** link
of color: **8** stocking
of leaves or flowers: **6** wreath **7** garland
of light: **4** halo **5** glory **6** corona, nimbus **7** aureole **8** halation
of rope or metal: **4** hank **6** becket **7** garland, grommet, thimble
of two hoops: **6** gimmal
relating to: **7** annular
used as a valve or diaphragm: **5** wafer
wedding: **4** band

Ring and the Book author
8 Browning (Robert)

ringed
8 annulate, bordered **9** encircled **10** surrounded

ringer
4 fake, spit **5** clone, image **6** double **7** clapper, picture **8** impostor, portrait **10** simulacrum **13** spitting image

ringing
7 orotund, vibrant **8** decisive, emphatic, plangent, resonant, sonorous **10** clangorous, resounding **11** reverberant, unequivocal

ringleader
4 boss **5** chief **6** honcho, top dog **7** kingpin **9** godfather, top banana **10** head honcho, instigator, mastermind

ringlet
4 curl, lock **5** crimp, tress **7** circlet, earlock, tendril

Ring of the Nibelung composer
6 Wagner (Richard)

ringworm
5 tinea

rinse
4 dunk, lave, wash **5** bathe, douse, swill **6** shower, sluice **7** cleanse
the mouth: **6** gargle

riot
5 brawl, broil, melee, revel, spree **6** bedlam, émeute, jumble, revolt, tumult, uproar **7** carouse, debauch, rampage, revelry, roister, wassail **8** carousal, disorder, uprising **9** commotion **10** debauchery, donnybrook, revolution **11** disturbance

riotous
4 lush, wild **6** stormy, unruly, wanton **7** bacchic, profuse, untamed **8** abundant **9** abounding, clamorous, exuberant, luxuriant, plentiful, turbulent, unchecked **10** boisterous **11** saturnalian, tempestuous **12** unrestrained

rip
4 gash, hole, rend, rent, rive, spit, tear **5** shred, slash, split **6** attack, cleave **7** current, sputter **8** lacerate, undertow **9** criticize, disparage **12** undercurrent
into: **5** go for **6** assail, attack **8** lambaste
off: **3** con, rob **4** copy **5** cheat, steal, theft **7** defraud, imitate, swindle **9** imitation

ripe
4 aged, full, late **5** adult, grown, ready, ruddy, plump **6** mature, mellow, smelly, timely **7** grown-up **8** prepared, suitable **9** developed, full-blown, full-grown, offensive, opportune **10** seasonable **11** appropriate, full-fledged

ripen
3 age **4** cure, grow **6** better, grow up, mature, mellow, season **7** develop, enhance, improve, perfect **8** heighten, maturate

rip off
3 con, rob **4** copy **5** cheat, steal **7** defraud, imitate, swindle

rip-off
4 copy, scam **5** fraud, theft **7** swindle **8** stealing **9** deception, imitation **12** exploitation

riposte
5 parry, reply **6** retort, return, thrust **8** back talk, comeback, repartee **13** counterattack

ripping
4 fine **5** grand, nifty, super, swell **6** divine, peachy **7** capital **8** glorious, splendid, terrific **9** admirable, delicious, excellent, fantastic, marvelous, wonderful **10** delightful, delectable, remarkable **11** scrumptious, sensational

ripple
3 lap **4** curl, fret, riff, wave **6** cockle, dimple, lipper, popple, ruffle, spread, wimple **7** crinkle, wavelet, wrinkle **8** undulate

rip-roaring
5 noisy **6** lively **8** exciting **9** hilarious **10** boisterous, rollicking, uproarious

ripsnorter
3 ace, pip **4** lulu **5** dandy, doozy **6** doozie, hummer **8** jim-dandy, knockout **9** humdinger **11** crackerjack

riptide
7 current **8** undertow **12** undercurrent

Rip Van Winkle
author: **6** Irving (Washington)
dog: **4** Wolf

rise
3 wax **4** grow, hill, lift, rear, soar **5** awake, get up, issue, mount, stand, surge, swell **6** ascend, ascent, awaken, emerge, expand, growth, origin, spring, uprear **7** advance, augment, develop, emanate, enhance, enlarge, hilltop, stand up, succeed, surface, upsurge **8** eminence, heighten, increase **9** ascension, beginning, increment, intensify, originate, terminate
above: **8** surmount
again: **7** resurge **9** resurrect
against: **5** rebel **6** mutiny, revolt
and fall: **4** tide **5** heave **6** welter
and shine: **5** get up
gradually: **4** loom

Rise of Silas Lapham author
7 Howells (William Dean)

riser
4 dais, step **8** platform

risible
4 rich **5** comic, droll, funny, jokey **6** absurd **7** comical **8** farcical **9** laughable, ludicrous **10** ridiculous

risk
4 ante, dare, defy **5** peril, stake, throw, wager **6** chance, danger, gamble, hazard, menace, stakes **7** imperil, jeopard, venture **8** endanger, exposure, jeopardy **9** adventure, encounter, liability **10** jeopardize

risky
4 bold **5** dicey, hairy **6** chancy, daring, touchy, tricky **7** parlous, unsound **8** delicate, perilous, ticklish **9** dangerous, hazardous, unhealthy **10** jeopardous, precarious **11** adventurous, speculative, treacherous

risqué
4 blue, lewd, racy, sexy **5** broad, crude, dirty, salty, spicy, vampy **6** coarse, daring, earthy, purple, ribald, vulgar **7** naughty, obscene, raunchy **8** indecent, off-color, scabrous **9** salacious **10** indecorous, indelicate, suggestive

rite
6 office **7** liturgy, mystery, service **8** ceremony

9 **formality**, ordinance, sacrament, solemnity 10 ceremonial, initiation, observance 11 celebration, sacramental
funeral: 6 exequy 7 obsequy 8 exequies 9 obsequies
Jewish: 4 bris
of initiation or purification: 7 baptism
of knighthood: 8 accolade
(see also **sacrament**)

ritual
see **rite**

ritzy
4 posh 5 fancy, swank 6 chichi, classy, modish, snazzy, swanky 7 elegant, high-hat, stylish 9 au courant, exclusive, expensive, luxurious 11 fashionable 12 ostentatious

rival
3 tie, try, vie 4 even, peer, side 5 equal, match 6 strive 7 attempt, compete, contend, contest, emulate 8 approach, opponent 9 adversary, competing, contender, measure up 10 antagonist, competitor, contending, contestant 11 comparative, competition

rivalry
6 strife 7 contest, warfare 8 conflict, jealousy, tug-of-war 9 emulation 10 contention, opposition 11 competition

rive
3 rip 4 rend, tear 5 break, burst, crack, sever, smash, split 6 cleave, divide, shiver, sunder 7 fissure, shatter 8 fracture, fragment, lacerate, separate, splinter

river
Afghanistan: 5 Kabul
Africa: 4 Bomu, Juba, Nile, Uele 5 Chari, Congo, Shari, Tsavo, Zaire 6 Atbara, Mbomou, Songwe, Ubangi 7 Aruwimi, Limpopo, Zambesi, Zambezi 9 Astaboras, Crocodile
Alabama: 5 Coosa 6 Mobile 7 Conecuh, Perdido 9 Tombigbee 10 Tallapoosa
Alaska: 5 Kobuk 6 Copper, Noatak, Tanana 7 Koyukuk, Susitna 9 Kuskokwim
Albania: 4 Drin 5 Drini
Argentina: 5 Negro 6 Paraná 7 Matanza
arm: 6 branch 9 tributary
Asia: 3 Ili 4 Amur, Lena, Oxus 5 Indus 6 Jayhun, Sutlej 7 Oedanes 8 Amu Darya 9 Dyardanes 11 Brahmaputra
Australia: 4 Daly 5 Roper, Yarra 6 Barwon, Culgoa, Dawson, DeGrey, Murray 7 Darling, Fitzroy, Lachlan 8 Victoria 10 Yarra Yarra
Austria: 4 Enns
bank: 5 levee
Belgium: 4 Leie, Yser 5 Rupel, Senne, Weser 6 Dender, Dindar, Ourthe 8 Visurgis
Bolivia: 4 Beni 5 Abuná 6 Mamoré
Borneo: 5 Kajan
bottom: 3 bed
Brazil: 3 Ica 4 Pará, Paru 5 Negro, Xingu 6 Paraná 7 Madeira, Tapajos, Tapajoz
British Columbia: 6 Skeena 10 Bella Coola
Burma: 4 Pegu 7 Irawadi 8 Chindwin 9 Irrawaddy
California: 3 Eel, Pit 4 Kern, Yuba 6 Merced 7 Feather, Salinas, Trinity 8 Tuolumne
Cambodia: 8 Tonle Sap
Canada: 3 Bow 4 Back 5 Moose, Peace, Slave 6 Beaver, Fraser, Nelson 8 Gatineau, Saguenay 9 Athabasca, Great Fish, Mackenzie, Richelieu 11 Assiniboine
Carolinas: 7 Catawba
central United States: 3 Fox 5 Grand 6 Neosho, Platte, Wabash 8 Keya Paha, Missouri, Niobrara 9 Tennessee, Verdigris 10 Republican, Saint Croix 11 Mississippi
channel: 6 alveus
Chile: 3 Loa 5 Itata, Maule 6 Bío-Bío 8 Valdivia
China: 3 Bei, Han, Hun, Nen, Wei 4 Amur, Dong 5 Baihe, Chang, Huang, Tarim 6 Yellow 7 Kashgar, Yangtze
China-North Korea: 4 Yalu
Colombia: 4 Meta, Tomo 6 Atrato 9 Magdalena
Colorado: 5 Yampa 8 Gunnison
Connecticut: 6 Thames 7 Niantic, Shepaug 9 Naugatuck 10 Farmington, Housatonic, Quinnipiac 11 Willimantic
Crimea: 4 Alma
crossing: 4 ford
current: 4 eddy 6 rapids
Czech Republic: 4 Iser 6 Jizera, Moldau, Vltava
dam: 4 weir
Denmark: 4 Stor
dried bed: 4 wadi
East Asia: 4 Yalu 5 Amnok 7 Oryokko
Ecuador: 4 Napo 10 Esmeraldas
England: 3 Esk, Exe, Nen, Ure 4 Aire, Avon, Eden, Nene, Ouse, Tees, Tyne, Wear, Yare 5 Swale, Trent 6 Mersey, Ribble, Thames
Ethiopia: 3 Omo 4 Baro, Dawa
Europe: 4 Eger, Elbe, Labe, Oder, Ohre, Saar 5 Albis, Meuse, Saale 6 Danube, Ticino
Florida: 6 Indian 9 Kissimmee 10 Saint Johns 12 Apalachicola
Foster's: 6 Swanee
France: 3 Ain, Lot, Lys, Var 4 Aire, Aude, Cher, Eure, Gers, Loir, Oise, Orne, Saar, Tarn, Yser 5 Adour, Aisne, Drôme, Indre, Isère, Loire, Marne, Rhône, Saare, Sâone, Seine, Somme, Yonne 6 Allier, Ariège, Scarpe, Vienne 7 Durance, Garonne, La Riège, Moselle 8 Charente, Dordogne
Georgia: 6 Etowah, Oconee 8 Altamaha, Ocmulgee 13 Chattahoochee

Germany: 3 Ems, Rur 4 Eder, Eger, Elbe, Isar, Main, Rems, Ruhr, Saar 5 Hunte, Lippe, Mosel, Rhine, Spree, Werra, Weser 6 Neckar
Germany-Poland: 4 Oder
Ghana: 5 Volta
god: 7 Alpheus, Inachus 8 Achelous
Greece: 3 Iri 4 Arta 5 Lerna, Lerne 7 Alpheus, Eurotas 8 Achelous 9 Arakhthos
Honduras: 4 Ulúa 5 Aguán 6 Patuca
Iberian: 5 Douro, Duero
Idaho: 5 Lemhi
Illinois: 8 Mackinaw
India: 4 Sind 5 Sindh, Tapti 6 Chenab, Ganges, Jhelum, Kaveri, Kistna 7 Cauvery, Krishna 8 Acesines, Godavari
inlet: 5 bayou 6 slough
Iran: 3 Kor 4 Mand, Mund 5 Karun 8 Safid Rud, Sefid Rud
Ireland: 3 Lee 4 Deel, Erne, Suir 5 Boyne, Clare, Foyle 6 Barrow, Liffey 7 Shannon
Italy: 4 Adda, Arno, Liri, Nera 5 Adige, Arnus, Etsch, Liris, Oglio, Padus, Piave, Tiber 6 Ollius, Rapido, Tevere, Trebia 7 Athesis, Rubicon, Secchia, Tiberis, Trebbia 8 Rubicone, Volturno
Kansas: 6 Pawnee
Kazakhstan-Russia: 4 Emba, Ural 5 Tobol 6 Irtysh
Kenya: 4 Athi, Tana
Kubla Khan's: 4 Alph
land: 4 holm 5 flats 7 bottoms
Latvia: 5 Gauja
Latvia-Lithuania: 7 Lielupe
Lebanon: 6 Litani
Little Rock's: 8 Arkansas
living on the bank of: 8 riparian
longest: 4 Nile
Louisiana: 11 Atchafalaya
Maine: 8 Kennebec 9 Aroostook, Penobscot
Malaysia: 9 Trengganu
Maryland: 8 Monocacy, Patapsco, Patuxent 9 Nanticoke
Massachusetts: 7 Charles, Taunton 9 Merrimack, Westfield 10 Housatonic
Mexico: 6 Pánuco, Sonora 7 Tabasco 8 Grijalva
Michigan: 4 Cass 5 Huron 7 Saginaw 8 Manistee, Muskegon 9 Cheboygan, Kalamazoo 10 Michigamme, Shiawassee
Mississippi: 5 Pearl, Yazoo 10 Pascagoula
Moldova-Ukraine: 8 Dneister
Missouri: 5 Osage
mouth: 5 delta
Myanmar: 4 Pegu 7 Irawadi 8 Chindwin 9 Irrawaddy
Nebraska: 4 Loup 6 Nemaha, Platte 7 Elkhorn
Netherlands: 4 Maas, Waal 5 Issel, Yssel 6 Amstel, IJssel 7 Vahalis
New England: 4 Saco 6 Nashua 9 Merrimack 10 Blackstone 11 Connecticut 12 Androscoggin
New Jersey: 6 Rahway 7 Passaic, Raritan 8 Tuckahoe
New York: 5 Tioga 6 Hudson, Mohawk, Oneida, Oswego, Seneca 7 Chemung, Niagara 8 Chenango
New Zealand: 7 Waikato
Nicaragua: 4 Coco 7 Segovia
Nigeria: 5 Benin
North Carolina: 3 Haw, Tar 5 Neuse 6 Chowan 8 Alamance
northeast United States: 4 Ohio 6 Hoosic 7 Genesee, Hocking 8 Delaware, Mahoning 9 Allegheny 11 Monongahela, Susquehanna
Northern Ireland: 4 Bann 6 Mourne
North Korea: 4 Yalu 5 Daido 7 Taedong
northwest United States: 5 Snake 7 Klamath 8 Columbia 11 Pend Oreille
Norway: 4 Otra, Tana, Teno
nymph: 5 naiad
of fire: 10 Phlegethon
of forgetfulness: 5 Lethe
of ice: 7 glacier
of woe: 7 Acheron
Ohio: 5 Miami 8 Cuyahoga, Sandusky 9 Muskingum 10 Tuscarawas
Oklahoma: 8 Cimarron
Oregon: 5 Rogue 6 Owyhee 7 Malheur 8 McKenzie 9 Clackamas, Deschutes 10 Willamette
Nevada: 7 Truckee
Pakistan: 4 Ravi
Panama: 5 Tuira 7 Chagres
Papua New Guinea: 3 Fly 5 Sepik
Paraguay: 3 Apa 9 Pilcomayo
Pennsylvania: 6 Lehigh 10 Schuylkill
Peru: 5 Rímac, Santa 7 Marañón 8 Apurímac, Huallaga, Urubamba
Philippines: 4 Abra, Agno 5 Pasig 7 Cagayan 8 Cotabato, Mindanao, Pampanga
Poland: 3 San 7 Vistula
Portugal: 4 Sado 7 Mondego
relating to: 7 fluvial
Rhode Island: 7 Seekonk 8 Sakonnet 10 Providence
Romania: 5 Arges
Russia: 3 Don, Oka, Ufa, Usa 4 Kama, Kara, Lena, Msta, Neva, Sura, Svir 5 Onega, Terek, Volga 6 Anadyr, Angara, Belaya, Kolima, Kolyma, Ussuri, Vyatka 7 Dnieper, Pechora, Yenisey 8 Barguzin, Kostroma, Voronezh, Vychegda
Russia-Ukraine: 6 Donets
sacred: 6 Ganges
Scotland: 3 Dee, Don, Esk, Tay 4 Doon, Nith, Spey, Tyne 5 Afton, Annan, Clyde, Forth, Tweed 6 Teviot 7 Deveron 8 Findhorn
Shanghai's: 7 Huangpu, Hwang Pu
Sicily: 5 Salso 6 Simeto
siren: 7 Lorelei

Slovakia: 3 Vag, Vah 4 Gran, Hron, Waag 5 Garam, Nitra 6 Neutra, Nyitra
South Africa: 4 Vaal 6 Orange
South America: 3 Apa 6 Amazon 8 Amazonas, Orellana 9 Pilcomayo
South Carolina: 6 Saluda, Santee 7 Wateree 8 Congaree
South Dakota: 3 Bad
Southeast Asia: 6 Dza-chu, Mekong 7 Salween 8 Lan-ts'ang
southeast United States: 6 Pee Dee 7 Noxubee, Washita 8 Escambia, Ouachita, Suwannee 10 Okanoxubee
southern United States: 6 Sabine
South Korea: 3 Kum
southwest United States: 3 Red 4 Gila, Zuni 5 Pecos 8 Canadian, Colorado
Spain: 4 Ebro 5 Tagus 6 Aragon 12 Guadalquivir
Sweden: 4 Göta 5 Kalix
Switzerland: 3 Aar 4 Aare 5 Reuss 7 Obringa
Syria: 6 Khabur 7 Orontes
Tasmania: 4 Huon
Tbilisi's: 4 Kura
Texas: 5 Llano 6 Brazos, Nueces 7 San Saba, Trinity 9 Guadalupe
Texas-Mexico: 8 Rio Bravo 9 Rio Grande
tidal: 7 estuary
Tokyo's: 6 Sumida
Turkey: 4 Aras 5 Araks 6 Seihun, Seyhan
Ukrainian: 3 Bug 4 Alma, Styr
underworld: 4 Styx 5 Lethe 7 Acheron, Cocytus 10 Phlegethon
Uruguay: 5 Negro
Utah: 5 Provo, Uinta, Weber 6 Jordan, Sevier
valley: 6 strath
Venezuela: 5 Apure, Caura 6 Caroní 7 Orinoco
Vermont: 3 Mad 5 Onion, White 8 Winooski
Virginia: 3 Dan 5 James 7 Rapidan 9 Nansemond 10 Appomattox, Shenandoah 12 Chickahominy, Rappahannock
wailing: 7 Cocytus
Wales: 4 Dyfi 5 Clwyd, Dovey, Teifi
Washington: 6 Skagit, Yakima 9 Klickitat, Snohomish, Wenatchee
West Africa: 5 Niger 6 Gambia 7 Senegal
western United States: 7 Laramie 8 Columbia, Flathead 11 Yellowstone
West Virginia: 7 Kanawha
Wisconsin: 8 Kickapoo 9 Menominee
Wyoming: 8 Shoshone 10 Gros Ventre 11 Medicine Bow

Rivera's wife
5 Kahlo (Frida)

river duck
4 teal 6 wigeon 7 dabbler, mallard, widgeon 8 shoveler 9 greenwing

river horse
5 hippo 12 hippopotamus

riverine
8 riparian

river island
3 ait 4 eyot

rivet
3 fix, pin 4 bolt, brad, stud 5 affix 6 absorb, attach, clinch, fasten 7 engross 8 fastener

Riviera city
4 Nice 6 Cannes, Monaco 7 Antibes, San Remo 8 St. Tropez 10 Monte Carlo

rivulet
3 run 4 beck, burn, gill, race, rill 5 bourn, brook, creek 6 runlet, runnel, stream 9 streamlet

Rizpah
father: 4 Aiah
lover: 4 Saul
son: 6 Armoni 12 Mephibosheth

roach
3 hog 6 shiner 7 sunfish

road
3 way 4 fare, lane, line, path 5 drive, going, route, track 6 artery, avenue, career, causey, course, street 7 highway, journey, passage 8 causeway, chaussée, crossway, highroad, pavement, speedway, turnpike 9 boulevard 12 thoroughfare
along a cliff: 8 corniche
around a city: 6 bypass 7 beltway
bend: 7 hairpin
edge: 4 berm 8 shoulder
French: 6 chemin
Irish: 6 boreen
machine: 5 paver 6 grader 9 bulldozer
Roman: 3 via 4 iter
shoulder: 4 berm
side: 6 branch 8 shunpike
Spanish: 6 camino
surface: 3 tar 6 gravel 7 asphalt, macadam 8 pavement

roadblock
7 barrier 8 blockade 9 barricade 11 obstruction

road book
3 map 5 atlas 9 gazetteer, itinerary

roadhouse
3 bar, inn 4 dive 5 hotel, lodge 6 tavern 9 nightclub

roadrunner
6 cuckoo 13 chaparral cock

road rut
6 kettle 7 pothole 9 chuckhole

roam
3 bat, bum, gad, run 4 rove, walk 5 drift, prowl, range, stray 6 ramble, stroll, travel, wander

7 meander, traipse 8 straggle, vagabond 9 gallivant

roamer
3 bum 5 gipsy, gypsy, nomad, rover 6 ranger, walker 7 drifter, prowler, rambler, vagrant 8 marauder, stroller, traveler, vagabond, wanderer 11 nightwalker

roar
3 din 4 bawl, bell, boom, bray, howl, yell 5 shout 6 bellow, clamor, outcry 7 bluster 10 vociferate
bullring: 3 olé

roast
4 bake, mock, rack, sear 5 broil, grill, joint, parch 6 scathe, scorch 7 banquet, blister, mockery, swelter 8 barbecue, ridicule 9 criticize

rob
3 cop, mug 4 lift, loot, nick, raid, roll, sack 5 boost, filch, heist, pinch, pluck, reave, steal 6 burgle, fleece, hijack, hold up, pilfer, rip off, snitch, thieve 7 defraud, deprive, despoil, pillage, plunder, purloin, ransack, stick up, swindle 8 knock off 9 knock over 10 burglarize

robber
4 yegg 5 crook, thief 6 bandit, looter, mugger, pirate, reiver 7 brigand, burglar, footpad, rustler 8 hijacker, swindler 9 holdup man 10 cat burglar, highwayman, sandbagger, stickup man 12 housebreaker
grave: 5 ghoul

robbery
5 heist, theft 6 holdup, piracy 7 larceny, mugging, stickup 8 banditry

robe
3 aba 4 cape, gown, wrap 5 cloak, habit 6 caftan, mantle 7 garment, manteau 8 covering, dalmatic, vestment
baptismal: 7 chrisom
bishop's: 7 chimere
of Roman emperors: 6 purple
Turkish: 6 dolman

Robin Goodfellow
4 Puck 6 sprite

Robinson Crusoe
author: 5 Defoe (Daniel)
character: 6 Friday

robot
5 droid, golem 7 android 8 automata (plural) 9 automaton

Rob Roy author
5 Scott (Walter)

robust
4 hale, rude 5 hardy, husky, lusty, rough, sound, stout 6 hearty, potent, rugged, sinewy, strong, sturdy 7 healthy 8 athletic, muscular, vigorous 9 energetic, strapping 10 boisterous, red-blooded, full-bodied, prosperous

robustious
4 rude 5 lusty, rough, rowdy, wooly 6 rugged 7 boorish, ill-bred, loutish 8 churlish, clownish 9 unrefined 10 boisterous, unpolished

rock
4 crag, reel, roll, sway, toss 5 geode, pitch, quake, shake, swing 6 totter 7 boulder, breccia 8 astonish, convulse, undulate 9 oscillate
basaltic: 5 wacke
cavity: 3 vug
combining form: 4 lite, lith, lyte, petr 5 clast, petri, petro
decomposed: 6 gossan
fissile: 5 shale
formation: 4 sill 5 butte, nappe 6 pluton 7 rimrock, terrane 8 isocline, syncline
fragment: 8 xenolith
igneous: 4 lava, sial, sima 5 magma 6 basalt, gabbro, pumice 7 diabase, diorite, granite 8 eruptive, felstone, obsidian, porphyry, traprock 10 travertine
layer: 10 mantlerock
mass: 5 scree 9 batholith
metamorphic: 5 slate 6 gneiss, marble, schist 9 quartzite, soapstone
molten: 4 lava
sedimentary: 4 clay, coal 5 chalk, chert, coral, flint, shale 8 mudstone 9 limestone, sandstone, siltstone
volcanic: 4 tuff 6 basalt

rock band
3 Who (The) 5 Byrds (The), Cream, Doors (The), Kinks (The), Queen 6 Eagles (The), Police (The) 7 Animals (The), Beatles (The), Bee Gees (The), Blondie, Bon Jovi, Nirvana, Ramones (The), Rascals (The), Santana 8 Drifters (The), Pearl Jam, Platters (The), Supremes (The), Van Halen 9 Aerosmith, Beach Boys (The), Metallica, Pink Floyd, Steely Dan, Yardbirds (The) 10 Duran Duran, Sex Pistols (The), Spice Girls 11 Four Seasons (The), Led Zeppelin 12 Black Sabbath, Fleetwood Mac, Grateful Dead (The), Talking Heads (The) 13 Nine Inch Nails, Rolling Stones (The)

rock bass
7 sunfish

rock-bottom
4 root 6 lowest 8 cheapest 9 lowermost 11 fundamental

rocket
3 fly, zip 4 soar, whiz, zoom 5 mount 6 ascend, bullet 7 missile, shoot up 8 firework, starship 10 projectile
European: 6 Ariane

landing: **7** reentry **10** splashdown
launcher: **7** bazooka
launching: **7** liftoff **8** blastoff
scientist: **5** Braun (Wernher von) **7** Goddard (Robert)
section: **5** stage

rockfish
4 cony, hind **5** coney **7** grouper, jewfish, sea bass **8** bocaccio **10** scorpaenid **11** striped bass

Rockies resort
4 Vail **5** Aspen **8** Snowmass **9** Telluride

___ Rockne
5 Knute

rock rabbit
4 cony, pika **5** coney, hyrax **6** dassie

rock-ribbed
5 rigid **8** dogmatic, obdurate **9** unbending **10** inflexible, unyielding

rock star
3 J. Lo, Pop (Iggy) **4** Bono, Cher, Crow (Sheryl), Dion (Celine), Joel (Billy), John (Elton), King (Carole), Love (Courtney), Roth (David Lee) **5** Abdul (Paula), Berry (Chuck), Bowie (David), Haley (Bill), Holly (Buddy), Lewis (Jerry Lee), Lopez (Jennifer), Smith (Patti), Starr (Ringo), Wyman (Bill), Young (Neil) **6** Cobain (Kurt), Domino (Fats), Eminem, Garcia (Jerry), Jagger (Mick), Joplin (Janis), Lennon (John), Manson (Marilyn), Prince, Spears (Britney), Vedder (Eddie) **7** Bon Jovi (Jon), Clapton (Eric), Cochran (Eddie), Diddley (Bo), Lavigne (Avril), Madonna, Mercury (Freddie), Michael (George), Perkins (Carl), Presley (Elvis), Shannon (Del), Stefani (Gwen), Stewart (Rod), Vincent (Gene) **8** Costello (Elvis), Harrison (George), Morrison (Jim, Van), Richards (Keith), Van Halen (Eddie) **9** Boy George, McCartney (Paul), Townshend (Pete) **10** Mellencamp (John) **11** Springsteen (Bruce) **13** Little Richard

rockweed
5 algae, fucus **7** seaweed **12** bladder wrack

rocky hill
3 tor **5** kopje

rococo
4 busy **5** showy **6** florid, frilly, ornate **7** baroque, elegant, opulent **9** elaborate, intricate **10** decorative, flamboyant **11** overwrought

rod
3 bar, gat **4** cane, pole, wand **5** baton, dowel, spoke, staff, stave, stick **6** pistol **7** scepter **8** revolver **10** correction, discipline, punishment **11** castigation **12** chastisement
bundle of: **6** fasces

rodent
3 rat **4** cavy, cony, mole, paca, pika, vole **5** cavie, coney, coypu, mouse, shrew **6** agouti, beaver, gerbil, gopher, jerboa, marmot, murine, nutria, rabbit **7** hamster, lemming, leveret, muskrat **8** capybara, chipmunk, dormouse, squirrel, tuco tuco, viscacha, vizcacha, water rat **9** guinea pig, porcupine **10** chinchilla, field mouse, prairie dog **11** kangaroo rat, meadow mouse, pocket mouse **12** pocket gopher
aquatic: **5** coypu **6** beaver, nutria **7** muskrat **8** musquash
burrowing: **4** mole, paca **6** gerbil, gopher **7** hamster **8** viscacha, vizcacha
family: **5** murid **6** murine **7** sciurid
genus: **3** Mus **5** Lepus
tropical: **6** agouti

rodeo
7 contest, roundup **9** enclosure **10** exhibition **11** competition
animal: **5** horse, steer **10** Brahma bull
event: **10** calf roping **11** bulldogging **12** bronco riding
performer: **5** clown **6** cowboy

___ Rodin
7 Auguste

rodomontade
4 blow, brag, rant **5** boast, swash, vaunt **7** bluster, swagger **9** gasconade **11** braggadocio

Rodomonte
beloved: **8** Doralice
slayer: **8** Ruggiero

Rodrigo Díaz de Bivar
5 El Cid

rod-shaped
7 virgate **8** bacillar **9** bacillary

roe
4 deer, eggs **6** beluga, caviar, osetra **7** sevruga

Roentgen's discovery
4 X-ray

Roethke work
6 Waking (The) **8** Far Field (The)

rogation
6 litany, prayer **8** entreaty, petition **10** beseeching **12** supplication

___ Rogers
3 Roy **4** Carl, Fred, Will **6** Ginger, Robert

rogue
5 cheat, gypsy, knave, scamp **6** rascal **7** lowlife, sharper, villain **8** picaroon, scalawag, swindler **9** defrauder, miscreant, reprobate, scoundrel, skeezicks, trickster **10** blackguard, mountebank **11** rapscallion
relating to: **10** picaresque

roguery
5 fraud **7** devilry, knavery, waggery **8** deviltry, mischief, trickery **9** devilment, diablerie **11** waggishness **12** sportiveness

roguish
3 sly **4** arch **6** impish, wicked **7** knavish **8** devilish, espiègle, scampish **10** picaresque **11** mischievous

roil
3 mud, vex **4** foul, rile, romp **5** annoy, dirty, grate, muddy, peeve, upset **6** befoul, muddle, nettle, stir up **7** agitate, disturb **8** disorder, irritate **9** aggravate **10** exasperate

roily
5 muddy, riley **6** turbid **9** turbulent

roister
4 riot **5** revel **6** frolic **7** carouse, reveler, wassail **9** wassailer

Roland
7 Orlando
battle site: **9** Roncevaux **12** Roncesvalles
beloved: **4** Aude
betrayer: **4** Gano **7** Ganelon
friend: **6** Oliver **7** Olivier
horn: **7** Olivant
sword: **8** Durandal, Durendal
uncle: **11** Charlemagne

role
3 bit **4** duty, lead, part, pose **5** cameo, cloak, guise, niche **6** aspect, office **7** quality **8** capacity, function, position **9** character **13** impersonation

roll
3 bun, rob **4** bolt, coil, flow, furl, gyre, list, pour, rock, toss, turn, wind, wrap **5** heave, pitch, surge **6** bundle, roster, rotate, stream, swathe, wallow, wrap up **7** biscuit, brioche, envelop, revolve, swaddle, trundle **8** involute, register, schedule, turn over
ring-shaped: **5** bagel

roll about
6 wallow, welter

roll back
5 lower **6** reduce, repeal **7** curtail, rescind

roller
3 rod **4** bowl, drum, wave **6** canary, caster, platen **7** breaker, carrier, tumbler **8** cylinder

Roller Derby round
3 jam

rollick
4 lark, play, romp **5** caper, frisk, party, revel, sport **6** cavort, frolic, gambol **7** disport, skylark **8** escapade **9** merriment

rollicking
4 wild **5** antic, merry **6** frisky, lively **8** sportive **10** boisterous, frolicsome **12** high-spirited

rolling stock
4 cars **7** coaches, engines **8** cabooses, Pullmans, sleepers, trailers **11** locomotives

rolling stone
4 hobo **5** gipsy, gypsy, nomad, rover, tramp **6** roamer **7** drifter, rambler, vagrant **8** vagabond, wanderer

Rolling Stones
4 Wood (Ron) **5** Jones (Brian), Watts (Charlie), Wyman (Bill) **6** Jagger (Mick), Taylor (Dick, Mick) **7** Stewart (Ian) **8** Richards (Keith)

roly-poly
see **rotund**

Roman
5 Latin **7** Italian
amphitheater: **9** Colosseum
assembly: **5** forum **6** senate **7** comitia
building: **5** Forum **6** Circus **8** basilica, Pantheon
clan: **4** gens
comedy writer: **7** Plautus (Titus), Terence
conspirator: **6** Brutus (Marcus Junius) **7** Cassius (Gaius) **8** Catiline
date: **4** Ides **7** calends, kalends
Doric: **6** Tuscan
emperor: **4** Nero, Otho **5** Galba (Servius Sulpicius), Nerva (Marcus Cocceius), Titus, Verus (Lucius Aurelius) **6** Julian, Trajan **7** Hadrian, Maximus (Magnus Clemens, Marcus Clodius, Petronius), Severus (Lucius Septimius) **8** Augustus, Caligula, Claudius, Commodus (Lucius Aelius), Domitian, Tiberius, Valerian **9** Caracalla, Vespasian **10** Diocletian, Theodosius **11** Constantine, Valentinian
entrance hall: **5** atria (plural) **6** atrium
epic: **6** Aeneid
epigrammatist: **7** Martial
family: **7** Gracchi
Fates: **4** Nona **5** Morta **6** Decuma, Parcae
festival: **10** Saturnalia
founder: **5** Remus **7** Romulus
fountain: **5** Trevi **6** Triton
garment: **4** toga **5** tunic
general: **5** Sulla (Lucius Cornelius), Titus **6** Antony (Marc), Marius (Gaius), Scipio (Publius Cornelius) **8** Agricola (Gnaeus Julius)
god: **3** Lar **4** deus
blind: **6** Plutus
chief: **4** Jove **7** Jupiter
messenger: **7** Mercury
of agriculture: **6** Saturn
of animals: **6** Faunus
of death: **4** Mors
of dreams: **8** Morpheus
of fire: **6** Vulcan
of gates and doors: **5** Janus
of healing: **9** Asclepius **11** Aesculapius
of heaven: **6** Uranus
of households: **3** Lar **5** Lares **7** Penates
of love: **4** Amor **5** Cupid
of medicine: **9** Asclepius **11** Aesculapius

of mirth: **5** Comus
of regeneration: **7** Priapus
of sleep: **6** Somnus
of the sea: **6** Pontus **7** Neptune, Proteus
of the sun: **3** Sol **6** Apollo
of the underworld: **3** Dis **5** Orcus, Pluto **8** Dispater
of the wind: **5** Eurus, Notus **6** Aeolus, Aquilo, Auster, Boreas **8** Favonius, Zephyrus
of war: **4** Mars **8** Quirinus
of wealth: **6** Plutus
of wine: **7** Bacchus
of woods: **6** Faunus
two-faced: **5** Janus
goddess: **3** dea
of agriculture: **5** Ceres
of beauty: **5** Venus
of dawn: **6** Aurora
of death: **5** Morta
of flowers: **5** Flora
of handicrafts: **7** Minerva
of harvests: **3** Ops
of health: **7** Minerva
of hope: **4** Spes
of hunting: **5** Diana
of justice: **7** Astraea
of love: **5** Venus
of marriage: **4** Juno
of night: **3** Nox
of peace: **3** Pax
of springs: **7** Juturna
of strife: **9** Discordia
of the earth: **5** Terra **6** Tellus
of the hearth: **5** Vesta
of the moon: **4** Luna
of the sea: **10** Amphitrite
of the underworld: **10** Proserpina
of victory: **6** Vacuna
of war: **7** Bellona
of wisdom: **7** Minerva
of womanhood: **4** Juno
greeting: **3** ave
hero: **6** Caesar (Julius) **11** Cincinnatus (Lucius Quinctius)
hill: **7** Caelian, Viminal **8** Aventine, Palatine, Quirinal **9** Esquiline **10** Capitoline
historian: **4** Livy **5** Nepos **7** Sallust, Tacitus **9** Suetonius
king: **7** Romulus, Servius, Tullius **12** Ancus Martius **13** Numa Pompilius
marketplace: **5** agora
military formation: **3** ala **6** alares (plural) **7** phalanx
miltary unit: **6** cohort, legion **7** maniple
officer: **9** centurion
official: **5** augur, edile **6** aedile, censor, consul, lictor **7** praetor, prefect, tribune **8** quaestor **9** proconsul
people: **5** Laeti, plebs **6** populi (plural) **7** populus, Sabines **9** plebeians
philosopher: **4** Cato **6** Seneca **8** Apuleius **9** Epictetus, Lucretius
physician: **9** Asclepius **11** Aesculapius
port: **5** Ostia
procurator: **6** Pilate (Pontius)
province: **4** Asia **5** Lycia, Syria **6** Achaea, Africa, Arabia, Cyprus, Raetia **7** Baetica, Belgica, Galatia, Numidia, Sicilia, Thracia **8** Aegyptus, Dalmatia **9** Aquitania, Britannia, Lusitania **10** Cappadocia, Mauretania
racecourse: **6** circus
road: **4** iter
slave: **9** Spartacus
statesman: **4** Cato **5** Pliny **6** Caesar, Cicero, Pompey, Seneca **7** Agrippa **8** Augustus, Gracchus, Maecenas **9** Flaminius
symbol of authority: **6** fasces

roman à ___
4 clef

romance
3 woo **4** gest, love **5** amour, court, fling, geste, novel **6** affair **7** fantasy, fiction **8** stardust **10** love affair **12** bodice ripper

Romance language
6 French **7** Catalan, Italian, Spanish **8** Romanian, Rumanian **9** Sardinian **10** Portuguese

romance writer
4 Holt (Victoria) **5** Brown (Sandra), Clark (Mary Higgins), Heyer (Georgette), Steel (Danielle) **6** Dailey (Janet), Graham (Heather), Howard (Linda), Krantz (Judith), Krentz (Jayne Ann), Stuart (Anne) **7** Baldwin (Faith), Collins (Jackie), Cookson (Catherine), Coulter (Catherine), Estrada (Rita Clay), Hatcher (Robin Lee), Maxwell (Anne), Osborne (Maggie), Roberts (Nora), Stewart (Mary), Whitney (Phyllis) **8** Bradford (Barbara Taylor), Cartland (Barbara), Deveraux (Jude), Phillips (Susan Elizabeth) **9** Alsobrook (Rosalyn), Evanovich (Janet), Woodiwiss (Kathleen)

Romania
capital: **9** Bucharest
city: **4** Iasi **6** Brasov, Galati **7** Craiova **9** Constanta, Timisoara
monetary unit: **3** leu **4** bani
mountain range: **10** Carpathian
neighbor: **6** Serbia **7** Hungary, Moldova, Ukraine **8** Bulgaria
part of: **7** Balkans
peninsula: **6** Balkan
river: **5** Siret, Tisza **6** Danube
sea: **5** Black

romantic
5 gauzy, ideal, idyll, mushy **6** ardent, dreamy,

exotic, gothic, poetic, unreal **7** amorous, maudlin, mawkish **8** fanciful, quixotic **9** fantastic, imaginary, visionary **10** idealistic, lovey-dovey **11** sentimental

Romany
5 Gipsy, Gypsy

Romeo
5 lover, swain **7** amorist, Don Juan, gallant **8** Casanova, lothario, paramour
beloved: **6** Juliet
enemy: **6** Tybalt
father: **8** Montague
friend: **8** Mercutio

Rommel, Erwin
9 Desert Fox

romp
4 lark, play **5** caper, frisk, sport **6** cavort, frolic, gambol, hoyden **7** rollick, runaway, skylark **8** escapade

Romulus
brother: **5** Remus
father: **4** Mars
mother: **9** Rea Silvia **10** Rhea Silvia
victim: **5** Remus

rondure
3 arc, orb **4** arch, ball, ring **5** curve, globe, round **6** circle, sphere **9** curvature

rood
5 cross **8** crucifix

roof
3 hip, top **4** apex, peak **5** cover, crest, crown **6** summit **7** ceiling **8** covering, housetop
material: **3** tar, tin **4** tile **5** slate, straw, terne **6** copper, thatch **7** shingle
of a cavern: **4** dome
of the mouth: **6** palate
part: **3** hip **4** eave **5** eaves **6** soffit **8** overhang **9** ridgepole
structure: **9** penthouse
type: **5** gable **6** hipped **7** gambrel, lamella, mansard **9** butterfly
vaulted: **4** dome

roofer
5 tiler

rook
4 bilk, colt, crow, scam, tyro **5** cheat, mulct, raven, stick **6** castle, fleece, novice **7** amateur, defraud, recruit, swindle, trainee **8** beginner, flimflam, freshman, neophyte, newcomer **10** apprentice, tenderfoot

rookery
5 roost **6** colony

rookie
4 colt, tyro **5** plebe **6** novice **7** amateur, recruit, trainee **8** beginner, freshman, neophyte, newcomer **10** apprentice, tenderfoot

room
3 den **4** cell, hall, play, rein **5** divan, house, lodge, put up, salon, scope, space **6** alcove, billet, leeway, margin, reside, studio **7** chamber, cubicle, expanse, gallery, lodging **9** clearance
ancient Roman: **5** atria (plural) **6** atrium
eating: **4** nook **6** alcove **7** commons, kitchen **8** mess hall **9** refectory
food storage: **6** larder, pantry
for paintings: **7** gallery
in a harem: **3** oda
in a monastery: **4** cell **9** refectory **11** calefactory
in a prison: **4** cell
on a ship: **5** cabin **6** galley
round: **7** rotunda

roomer
5 guest **6** lodger, renter, tenant **7** boarder

roomy
4 wide **5** ample, broad, large **8** spacious **9** capacious **10** commodious

Roosevelt, Franklin D.
birthplace: **8** Hyde Park
dog: **4** Fala
message: **12** fireside chat
mother: **4** Sara
predecessor: **6** Hoover (Herbert)
program: **7** New Deal
successor: **6** Truman (Harry)
vacation home: **10** Campobello
wife: **7** Eleanor

roost
3 sit **4** land, nest, rest **5** perch **6** alight, settle **7** rookery **8** dovecote

rooster
4 cock **5** capon **8** cockerel, gamecock **10** cockalorum **11** chanticleer

root
3 dig, fix **4** base, bulb, core, grub, pith, stem, well **5** basis, cheer, embed, grout, lodge, plant, radix, tuber **6** bottom, etymon, ground, marrow, origin, settle, source **7** applaud, bedrock, essence, footing, radical **8** radicate **9** beginning, establish, inception **10** foundation
aromatic: **7** ginseng
edible: **3** oca, yam **4** beet, taro, yuca **5** yucca **6** carrot, daikon, ginger, jicama, manioc, potato, radish, turnip **7** burdock, cassava, parsnip, salsify **8** celeriac, kohlrabi, rutabaga, tuckahoe **11** horseradish
fragrant: **5** orris **7** vetiver
main: **7** taproot
medicinal: **5** jalap **7** ginseng

relating to: **7** radical
starch: **4** arum **7** tapioca
word: **6** etymon

rootlet
7 radicle, rhizoid

root out
4 grub **9** eradicate, extirpate **10** deracinate

Roots
author: **5** Haley (Alex)
character: **3** Lea (George, Tom) **4** Toby **5** Haley (Alex, Simon Alexander) **6** Bertha, Waller (Bell, John, Kizzy, Dr. William) **7** Cynthia, Matilda **8** Kintango **9** Missy Anne **10** Kunta Kinte

rope
3 guy, tie **4** bind, cord, line, stay **5** belay, bight, brace, cable, chord, lasso, riata, sheet **6** binder, fasten, halter, hawser, lariat, marlin, shroud, strand, string, tether **7** halyard, lashing, marline, painter, towline **8** buntline, lifeline
fiber: **4** coir, hemp, jute **5** abaca, sisal **6** Manila **8** henequen
loop: **7** cringle
mooring: **6** hawser
ship's: **4** vang **5** sheet **6** marlin, parral, parrel, shroud **7** lanyard, marline, ratline **9** mainsheet

ropedancer
11 funambulist

rope off
6 cordon

ropes
10 ins and outs, procedures, techniques

ropy
4 wiry **6** sinewy **7** stringy, viscous **8** muscular

roque
7 croquet

rorqual
5 whale **7** finback **8** fin whale **11** baleen whale

Rosalind's beloved
7 Orlando

rosary
5 beads **7** chaplet **8** beadroll, devotion **11** prayer beads

rose
4 glow, pink **5** blush, color, flush, rouge **6** mantle, pinken, redden **7** crimson **10** erysipelas
Chinese: **8** Cherokee
cotton: **7** cudweed
feature: **5** thorn
kind: **4** moss **5** Peace, Vogue **6** Circus, damask **7** Fashion, Granada, Iceberg, New Dawn, Pascali, Tiffany **8** Rubaiyat **9** Floradora, Montezuma, polyantha, Tropicana **10** Floribunda **11** grandiflora, Mount Shasta **12** Crimson Glory

roseate
see **rosy**

rose-colored
see **rosy**

Rosenkavalier composer
7 Strauss (Richard)

rose of ____
6 Sharon

rose oil
5 attar

Rose Tattoo author
8 Williams (Tennessee)

rosette
7 cockade **8** ornament

Rosinante's master
7 Quixote (Don)

Rosmersholm author
5 Ibsen (Henrik)

____ Rossetti
5 Dante (Gabriel) **9** Christina
work: **8** Sing-Song **11** Annus Domini, House of Life (The), Seek and Find, Sister Helen **12** Beata Beatrix, Goblin Market

Rossini opera
6 Otello **8** Tancredi **11** Cenerentola (La), William Tell **14** Siege of Corinth (The) **15** Barber of Seville (The)

Rostand hero
6 Cyrano (de Bergerac)

roster
4 list, roll, rota **5** slate **6** muster, scroll **8** register, roll call, schedule **9** honor roll **10** muster roll **11** waiting list

rostrum
4 dais **5** bimah **6** pulpit **7** lectern, tribune **8** platform

rosy
3 red **4** pink **5** sunny **6** bright, upbeat **7** beamish **8** cheerful, sanguine **10** optimistic

rot
4 bosh, bull, mold **5** decay, hooey, spoil, taint, trash **6** fester, molder **7** corrupt, crapola, crumble, eyewash, garbage, hogwash, putrefy, rubbish **8** gangrene, nonsense **9** break down, decompose, poppycock **10** balderdash, degenerate **11** deteriorate, putrescence **12** disintegrate, putrefaction **13** decomposition

rotary
6 circle **8** gyratory, spinning, whirling **10** roundabout **11** vertiginous **13** traffic circle

rotate
4 gyre, roll, spin, turn **5** pivot, twirl, wheel, whirl **6** gyrate, swivel **7** revolve, trundle **9** alternate, pirouette
a log: **4** birl

rotation
4 gyre, loop, turn **5** cycle, orbit, pivot, round, wheel, whirl **7** circuit, turning **8** gyration **10** revolution, succession

rote
5 crowd, grind **6** custom, groove, memory **7** routine **8** practice **9** automatic, treadmill **10** mechanical, repetition **12** memorization

Roth novel
11 Call It Sleep **15** Goodbye Columbus **16** American Pastoral **17** Portnoy's Complaint

rotten
4 foul **5** fetid, lousy **6** crummy, putrid **7** corrupt, decayed, spoiled, tainted **9** nefarious, offensive, putrified **10** decomposed, degenerate, putrescent

rotter
3 cad, cur **4** heel, lout **5** creep, louse **7** bounder **9** scoundrel **10** blackguard

rotund
3 fat **5** obese, plump, podgy, pudgy, round, stout, thick, tubby **6** chubby, chunky, portly, stocky **7** rounded **8** heavyset, roly-poly, thickset **9** corpulent **10** potbellied

roué
4 lech, rake, wolf **6** lecher **7** amorist, Don Juan, gallant, seducer, swinger **8** Casanova, lothario, sybarite **9** bon vivant, debauchee, libertine, womanizer **10** sensualist, voluptuary **11** philanderer

rouge
3 red **4** glow, pink, rose **5** blush, color, flush **6** mantle, pinken, redden **7** crimson

rough
3 raw **4** rude, wild **5** brute, bumpy, crass, crude, hairy, harsh, raspy, rowdy, yahoo **6** choppy, coarse, craggy, crusty, hoarse, jagged, rugged, stormy, uneven **7** cragged, grating, jarring, rasping, raucous, ruffian, scraggy, uncivil, uncouth **8** bullyboy, churlish, impolite, scabrous, unformed **9** difficult, imperfect, strenuous, turbulent, unrefined **10** boisterous, tumultuous, unfinished, unpolished **11** approximate, tempestuous

rough-and-ready
5 crude **6** make-do **7** stopgap **8** slapdash **9** expedient, impromptu, makeshift **10** improvised **11** provisional **13** quick-and-dirty

rough-hewn
4 rude **5** crude, plain **10** unfinished, unpolished **12** uncultivated

roughly
5 about, circa **9** virtually **10** more or less **13** approximately

roughneck
see **ruffian**

rough out
5 block, chalk, draft **6** sketch **7** outline **9** adumbrate **11** skeletonize

rough up
4 beat, maul **6** batter, pummel **8** maltreat **9** brutalize, manhandle **10** slap around

roulette
bet: 4 noir, trio **5** rouge, split **7** sixline **10** straight up
term: 5 passe, tiers **6** impair, manque, mucker **7** orphans **8** croupier **9** house edge

round
4 gyre, tour, turn **5** bowed, cycle, globe, wheel **6** circle, curved, rotund **7** annular, circuit **8** circular, globular, roly-poly, rotation, sequence **9** orbicular, spherical **10** conglobate

roundabout
6 circle, detour, rotary **7** circuit, compass, curving, devious, oblique, winding **8** circular, indirect **10** circuitous, meandering **13** traffic circle

rounded
5 bowed, plump **6** arched, convex, curved, rotund, zaftig **7** concave **9** developed **10** curvaceous, Rubenesque **13** well-developed

rounder
4 rake, roué, waif **6** no-good, waster **7** wastrel **8** prodigal, vagabond **9** libertine **10** ne'er-do-well, profligate

roundly
4 well **5** fully, quite **6** widely, wholly **7** bluntly, sharply, smartly, utterly **8** candidly, entirely **9** brusquely **10** altogether, completely, rigorously, scathingly, thoroughly, vigorously

round off
3 cap, top **5** crown **6** climax, finish **8** conclude **9** culminate

round-robin
6 appeal, letter, series **7** protest **8** petition, sequence **9** statement **10** tournament

round trip
4 tour **7** circuit **9** excursion

round up
4 herd **5** drive, group **6** gather **7** cluster, collect **8** assemble

rouse
3 jog **4** call, goad, rock, stir, wake, whet **5** alarm, awake, pique, rally, roust, waken **6** awaken, bestir, excite, foment, incite, kindle, muster, rattle, recall, revive, vivify, work up **7** agitate, animate, commove, disturb, enliven, provoke, quicken **8** motivate **9** aggravate, challenge, galvanize, instigate, stimulate

rousing
5 brisk, peppy **6** lively **8** animated, exciting,

spirited, stirring **9** inspiring **11** stimulating **12** exhilarating, intoxicating

Rousseau work
5 Émile

roustabout
4 hand **6** worker **7** laborer, workman **8** deckhand **10** workingman **12** longshoreman, troublemaker

route
3 way **4** path, road, send, ship **5** guide, pilot, steer, track, trail **6** avenue, bypass, course, detour, direct, divert, escort, flyway, seaway, skyway **7** channel, circuit, conduct, consign, forward, highway, journey, passage, portage, sea-lane **8** corridor, dispatch, transmit, traverse **9** direction, itinerary

routine
3 act, bit, rut **4** dull, pace, rote **5** chore, drill, grind, habit, ho-hum, plain, round, trial, usual **6** course, groove, improv, shtick, wonted **7** chronic, formula, program, regimen, regular, utility **8** accepted, everyday, habitual, ordinary, standard, workaday **9** customary, monologue, procedure, quotidian, treadmill **10** accustomed, donkeywork, mechanical **11** commonplace, cut-and-dried, perfunctory **12** housekeeping, unremarkable

rove
3 gad **4** roam **5** drift, range, stray **6** ramble, wander **7** meander, traipse **8** straggle, vagabond **9** gallivant

rover
5 gipsy, gypsy, nomad, stray **6** picaro, pirate, roamer, viking **7** corsair, drifter, floater, rambler, vagrant **8** picaroon, runabout, traveler, vagabond, wanderer **9** buccaneer, meanderer **10** freebooter **12** rolling stone

roving
6 errant, mobile **7** movable, nomadic, vagrant **8** straying, vagabond **9** itinerant, migratory, wayfaring **11** peripatetic

row
3 oar, way **4** bank, crew, file, fray, fuss, line, muss, rank, spat, tier, tiff **5** align, brawl, broil, chain, fight, melee, order, queue, range, run-in, scrap, scull, strip, swath **6** bicker, clamor, column, dustup, fracas, kickup, paddle, propel, ruckus, series, string, stroke **7** brabble, dispute, quarrel, rhubarb, wrangle **8** argument, diagonal, sequence, squabble **9** commotion **10** falling-out, single file, succession **11** altercation, disturbance, progression

rowdy
4 punk, rude **5** bully, crude, rough, yahoo **6** unruly **7** hoodlum, rackety, raffish, raucous, ruffian **8** bullyboy, hooligan **9** roughneck **10** boisterous, disorderly, robustious **11** rumbustious **12** rambunctious

Rowena
father: **7** Hengist
guardian: **6** Cedric
husband: **7** Ivanhoe **9** Vortigern

Rowling character
3 Ron (Weasley) **5** Harry (Potter), Snape (Severus) **6** Malfoy (Draco), Sirius (Black) **8** Hermione (Granger) **9** Voldemort (Lord) **10** Dumbledore (Albus)

Roxana
husband: **9** Alexander
rival: **7** Statira

royal
5 grand, noble, regal **6** kingly, lordly **7** stately **8** glorious, imperial, imposing, majestic, princely, splendid **9** grandiose, monarchal, sovereign **10** monarchial **11** magnificent, monarchical

rub
4 buff **5** chafe, grate, shine **6** abrade, polish, smooth, stroke **7** burnish, massage

Rubaiyat author
4 Omar (Khayyám)

rubber
4 buna **5** crepe **6** caucho, eraser **10** caoutchouc
basis: **5** latex
hard: **7** ebonite
synthetic: **8** neoprene
tree: **3** Ule **4** Para

Rubber City
5 Akron

rubberneck
3 eye **4** gape, gawk, gaze **5** snoop, stare **6** goggle **8** sightsee

rubber-stamp
2 OK **4** okay **7** approve, certify, endorse **9** authorize

rubbish
3 rot **4** bosh, crap, crud, junk, muck, slop, tosh **5** bilge, dreck, hooey, offal, trash, truck, waste **6** debris, litter, refuse, raffle, rubble, spilth **7** crapola, garbage, hogwash **8** nonsense, riffraff, tommyrot **9** poppycock, sweepings **11** foolishness

rubbishy
5 cheap, tatty **6** paltry, shoddy, sleazy, trashy **9** worthless

rubble
5 ruins, scree **6** debris, litter **8** detritus, wreckage

rube
4 boor, hick, naïf **5** churl, cluck, swain, yahoo, yokel **6** rustic **7** bumpkin, hayseed, redneck

9 greenhorn, hillbilly **10** clodhopper **12** apple-knocker, backwoodsman

rubicund
3 red **5** flush, ruddy **6** florid **7** glowing, reddish **8** sanguine **11** full-blooded, incarnadine

rubidium symbol
2 Rb

____ Rubik
4 Erno

rub out
3 ice, off, zap **4** do in, kill, slay **5** erase, smoke, waste, whack **6** finish, murder **7** bump off, destroy, put away **8** dispatch, knock off **9** liquidate, terminate **10** extinguish, obliterate **11** assassinate

rubric
4 name, rule **5** canon, class, gloss, style, title **6** custom **7** concept, heading **8** category, headline **9** tradition **11** appellation, designation **13** interpolation

ruck
3 mob **4** fold, heap, mass, pile **5** crimp, crowd, group, purse, ridge **6** cockle, crease, furrow, gather, jumble, pucker, rumple **7** crinkle, crumple, scrunch, wrinkle **10** generality **11** corrugation

rucksack
4 pack **6** kit bag **7** musette **8** backpack

ruckus
3 ado, row **4** fuss, to-do **5** brawl, melee, scrap **6** fracas, furore, hassle, pother, rumpus, shindy, uproar **7** dispute, quarrel, rhubarb, shindig, wrangle **8** squabble **9** commotion **10** falling-out **11** altercation, controversy, disturbance

ruddle
see **redden**

ruddy
3 red **4** ripe, rosy **5** flush **6** blowsy, florid **7** flushed, glowing **8** rubicund, sanguine **11** full-blooded, incarnadine

rude
3 raw **4** curt **5** crass, gross, gruff, harsh, rough, rowdy, surly **6** abrupt, callow, clumsy, coarse, crusty, robust, rugged, rustic, sturdy, unhewn, vulgar **7** boorish, brusque, ill-bred, loutish, lowbred, uncivil, uncouth **8** arrogant, churlish, clownish, impolite, tactless **9** barbarian, barbarous, elemental, inelegant, primitive, rough-hewn, unrefined **10** ungracious, unmannered, unmannerly, unpolished **11** ill-mannered, impertinent, uncivilized **12** discourteous, uncultivated **13** disrespectful

rudimentary
5 basal, basic **6** simple **7** initial, primary **8** simplest **9** beginning, elemental, vestigial **10** elementary **11** fundamental, undeveloped **12** introductory

rudiments
4 ABCs **6** basics **10** essentials **12** fundamentals

rue
3 woe **4** pity, ruth **5** dolor, grief, mourn, prick **6** grieve, lament, regret, repent, sorrow **7** anguish, deplore, remorse **8** sympathy **9** heartache, penitence **10** affliction, compassion, contrition, heartbreak, repentance **11** compunction

rueful
5 sorry **6** woeful **8** contrite, penitent **9** regretful, sorrowful **10** remorseful

ruff
5 frill, perch, trump **6** collar, fringe **9** sandpiper **11** pumpkinseed
female: 5 reeve

ruffian
4 goon, hood, punk, thug **5** beast, brute, bully, rowdy, tough, yahoo **6** Apache, hector **7** gorilla, hoodlum **8** bullyboy, hooligan **9** muscleman, roughneck, swaggerer

ruffle
3 bug, irk, rub, vex **4** fret, gall, wear **5** annoy, brawl, chafe, frill, graze, jabot, pleat, ruche **6** abrade, bother, nettle, ripple **7** agitate, bristle, disturb, flounce, provoke, trouble, wrinkle **8** drumbeat, furbelow, irritate, skirmish **9** commotion

rug
3 mat **6** carpet, runner, toupee **7** laprobe
kind: 3 rag, rya **6** hooked **7** braided, dhurrie, drugget, flokati, Persian **8** Aubusson, bearskin, Oriental **10** Savonnerie

rugby
formation: 5 scrum **9** scrummage
goal: 7 dropped, penalty
period: 4 half
player: 6 center, hooker, winger **8** standoff **9** scrum half
scoring: 3 try **4** goal **10** conversion
team: 7 fifteen
term: 4 heel **5** match **7** convert, dribble, hand off, knock on **9** fair catch
time-out: 8 stoppage
version: 5 union **6** league

rugged
5 burly, hardy, harsh, heavy, husky, rough, tough **6** brawny, coarse, craggy, jagged, robust, severe, stable, stormy, strong, sturdy, uneven **7** arduous, austere, scraggy **8** leathery, muscular, rigorous, scabrous, stalwart, vigorous **9** difficult, inclement, strenuous, unrefined, weathered **10** formidable, unpolished **11** tempestuous

Ruggiero
guardian: 7 Atlante
sister: 7 Marfisa
slayer: 11 Tisaphernes
wife: 10 Bradamante

rug rat
3 tot 4 tyke 6 moppet 7 toddler

Ruhr city
5 Essen 8 Dortmund

ruin
4 bane, bust, dash, do in, doom, fall, loss, rape, raze, sack, undo 5 decay, havoc, smash, spoil, trash, use up, waste, wrack, wreck 6 beggar, finish, pauper, perish, ravage 7 corrupt, deplete, despoil, destroy, exhaust, failure, nemesis, pillage, shatter, undoing, wipe out 8 bankrupt, collapse, decimate, demolish, downfall, spoliate 9 depredate, devastate, disrepair, overthrow, pauperize, shipwreck 10 desolation, impoverish 11 destruction, devastation, dissolution 12 degeneration 13 deterioration

ruination
4 bane, loss, rack 5 havoc 7 undoing 8 calamity, disaster, downfall 10 decimation 11 destruction, devastation

ruinous
5 fatal 7 baneful 10 calamitous, disastrous, pernicious 11 cataclysmic, destructive 12 catastrophic

rule
3 law, Raj 4 lead, sway 5 axiom, bylaw, canon, edict, habit, judge, maxim, moral, order, reign 6 assize, custom, decree, deduce, dictum, direct, govern, regime, truism 7 brocard, command, control, precept, prevail, regency, regimen, resolve, statute 8 decretum, doctrine, dominate, domineer, dominion 9 authority, determine, etiquette, ordinance, principle, procedure 10 regulation
absolute: 7 autarky 8 autarchy
by a god: 8 theonomy

Rule Britannia composer
4 Arne (Thomas)

rule out
3 bar 5 block, debar 6 forbid, refuse, reject 7 dismiss, exclude, forfend, head off, obviate, prevent 8 preclude, prohibit, stave off 9 eliminate

ruler
4 king, lord 5 queen 6 archon, dynast, ferule, gerent, prince, regent, satrap, sultan 7 emperor, monarch, viceroy 8 governor, hierarch, oligarch, pentarch, princess, theocrat 9 dominator, imperator, matriarch, patriarch, potentate, sovereign 12 straightedge
absolute: 6 despot, tyrant 8 autocrat, dictator, overlord
Arab: 4 amir, emir 5 ameer, sheik 6 sharif, sheikh, sultan
Asian: 4 khan
Byzantine Empire: 6 exarch
Egyptian: 7 pharaoh
family: 7 dynasty
Iranian: 4 shah
one of four: 8 tetrarch
one of seven: 8 heptarch
one of three: 7 triarch 8 triumvir
Persian: 6 satrap
Russian: 4 czar, tsar, tzar
Turkish: 3 bey, dey 6 sultan

ruling
3 law 4 call 5 chief, edict, order, ukase 6 decree 7 current, finding, popular, regnant, verdict 8 decision, judgment 9 directive, judgement, prevalent, statement 10 prevailing, widespread 11 predominant 12 adjudication

Rumania
see **Romania**

rumble
4 buzz, roar, roll 5 brawl, drone, fight, growl, rumor 6 murmur, report 7 hearsay, quarrel, resound, thunder 8 feedback 9 complaint 11 altercation, disturbance, reverberate, scuttlebutt

ruminant
3 Bos, cow, yak 4 deer, goat, tahr 5 bison, camel, llama, okapi, serow, sheep, takin 6 alpaca, cattle, musk ox, vicuña 7 buffalo, chamois, chewing, giraffe, guanaco 8 antelope 9 pronghorn
stomach: 5 rumen 6 omasum 8 abomasum 9 reticulum

ruminate
4 chew, mull, muse 5 champ, chomp, weigh 6 ponder 7 reflect 8 cogitate, consider, meditate 9 masticate 10 deliberate 11 contemplate

ruminative
7 pensive 8 thinking 9 pondering 10 cogitative, meditative, reflective, thoughtful 11 speculative 13 contemplative, introspective

rummage
4 comb, fish, grub, hash, hunt, poke, rake, rout, seek 5 delve, scour 6 ferret, forage, jumble, litter, search 7 clutter, ransack 8 mishmash 9 potpourri 10 hodgepodge, hotchpotch, miscellany

rummy
3 gin, odd, sot 4 lush, soak, wino 5 drunk, souse, toper 6 boozer 7 bizarre, canasta, curious, guzzler, strange, swiller, tippler, tosspot 8 drunkard, peculiar 9 eccentric, inebriate 10 boozehound

rumor
4 blab, buzz, talk **5** bruit, noise, story **6** canard, gossip, murmur, mutter, report, rumble, tattle **7** hearsay, tidings, whisper **9** grapevine **11** scuttlebutt, susurration
personified: 4 Fama

rumormonger
5 yenta **6** gossip **8** gossiper, informer, quidnunc, telltale **9** whisperer **10** talebearer, tattletale

rump
3 can **4** beam, butt, duff, hind, rear, tush **5** fanny **6** behind, bottom, breech, heinie **7** keester, keister, rear end **8** backside, buttocks, derriere, haunches **9** posterior

rumple
4 fold, muss, ruck **5** crimp, screw, touse **6** pucker, tousle **7** crimple, crinkle, scrunch, wrinkle **8** dishevel, disorder

rumpus
see **ruckus**

run
3 fly, hie, jog **4** bolt, dart, dash, flee, flow, race, rush, scud, tear **5** chase, haste, hurry, scoot, skirr, speed **6** career, gallop, hasten, scurry, sprint, streak, stream **7** scamper, scuttle, smuggle **9** skedaddle

run across
4 meet **8** bump into, discover **9** encounter, stumble on

runagate
4 hobo **5** gipsy, gypsy, nomad, tramp **6** outlaw **7** drifter, floater, lamster, vagrant, wastrel **8** bohemian, fugitive, rapparee, vagabond, wanderer **11** guttersnipe

run along
2 go **5** leave, scram **6** beat it, begone, cut out, depart **7** buzz off, get lost, skiddoo, take off, vamoose **8** shove off **9** skedaddle **10** make tracks

runaround
4 duck, slip **5** dodge **7** elusion, evasion

run away
4 bolt, flee, skip **5** elope, leave, scram, skirr, split, steal **6** depart, desert, escape **7** abscond, make off **8** clear out, light out, stampede **9** skedaddle **10** make tracks

runaway
4 romp, wild **5** loose **6** outlaw **7** escapee, lamster **8** deserter, fugitive **10** delinquent **12** uncontrolled

run down
3 hit, ram, tag **5** catch, knock, trace **6** pursue **7** decline **8** belittle, derogate, diminish **9** apprehend, disparage **10** depreciate **11** catch up with

run-down
5 dingy, seedy, tacky, tired **6** beat-up, bushed, shabby **7** rickety, ruinous, worn-out **8** decrepit, tattered, untended **9** burned-out, exhausted, neglected **10** bedraggled, down-at-heel, ramshackle, uncared-for **11** dilapidated

rundown
4 dope, poop **5** recap, scoop **6** report, review, skinny, update **7** outline, summary **8** briefing, synopsis

runes
4 ogam **5** ogham **7** futhark

rung
3 bar **4** step **5** grade, notch, round, spoke, staff, stage, stair, tread **6** degree, rundle **10** crosspiece

run-in
3 row **4** tiff **5** brush, fight, set-to **6** hassle, scrape, tangle **7** dispute, quarrel, rhubarb, wrangle **8** skirmish, squabble **9** encounter **10** falling-out **11** altercation

run into
3 hit, ram **4** meet **9** encounter, stumble on **11** collide with

runner
3 rug **5** gofer, miler, racer **6** carpet, stolon **7** carrier, courier, tendril **8** smuggler, sprinter **9** go-between, messenger **10** marathoner **11** ballcarrier
see **track star**

running
6 active, fluent **7** cursive, dynamic, flowing, working **9** operative **10** continuous **11** functioning

run-of-the-mill
4 dull, so-so **5** usual **6** common, normal **7** average, humdrum, regular, typical **8** everyday, familiar, mediocre, middling, moderate, ordinary **9** prevalent **10** monotonous **11** commonplace, indifferent **12** intermediate **13** unexceptional

run on
3 gab, yak **4** blab **5** clack **6** babble, cackle, gabble, jabber, ramble, rattle **7** chatter, prattle **8** continue

run out of
5 use up **6** finish **7** exhaust

run over
5 spill **6** exceed, repeat **7** examine **8** overfill, overflow, rehearse

runt
5 dwarf, pygmy **6** midget, peanut, peewee, shrimp, squirt **7** manikin **8** mannikin, Tom Thumb **10** homunculus **11** hop-o'-my-thumb, lilliputian

run through
3 jab 4 blow, gore, read, scan, stab 5 spend, use up, waste 6 expend, finish, impale, pierce 7 consume, examine, exhaust 8 rehearse, squander, transfix

runty
3 wee 4 puny 6 peewee 7 stunted 8 dwarfish 10 diminutive, undersized

run up
5 build, erect, mount 6 expand 7 augment, enlarge 8 increase, multiply 9 construct 10 accumulate

runway
4 duct, path 5 strip, track, trail 6 sluice, tarmac 7 channel, conduit 8 airstrip, platform

rupture
4 rend, rent, rift, rive 5 break, burst, cleft, sever, split 6 breach, cleave, hernia, schism, sunder 7 blowout, break up, disrupt, divorce, fissure, parting, split-up 8 division, fracture, separate 9 partition 10 separation 11 dissolution 12 estrangement

R.U.R.
author: 5 Capek (Karel)
character: 5 robot

rural
6 rustic 7 bucolic, country, idyllic 8 agrarian, arcadian, down-home, pastoral 10 campestral 11 countrified

ruse
3 con, jig 4 hoax, ploy, wile 5 dodge, feint, fraud, stall, trick 6 deceit, gambit 7 gimmick, swindle 8 artifice, maneuver, trickery 9 deception, stratagem 10 subterfuge 13 double-dealing

rush
3 fly, rip, run 4 boil, bolt, dart, dash, flit, flow, hurl, lash, race, roar, scud, tear, tide, whiz 5 blitz, break, carry, chase, court, daily, flash, haste, hurry, lunge, onset, sally, scoot, sedge, shoot, spate, speed, storm, surge 6 attack, barrel, beat it, bustle, career, charge, course, hasten, hurtle, hustle, irrupt, plunge, streak, stream, thrill, whoosh 7 assault, cattail, current, rampage, torrent 8 stampede 9 whirlwind, wire grass 13 precipitation

Rushdie novel
5 Shame 13 Satanic Verses (The) 17 Midnight's Children

rushing
5 hasty 6 abrupt, sudden 7 hurried 8 headlong 9 impetuous 11 precipitate, precipitous

rusk
7 biscuit 8 biscotto

Russia
capital: 6 Moscow
city: 3 Ufa 4 Omsk, Orel, Perm' 5 Kazan', Kursk 6 Grozny, Samara 7 Groznyy, Izhevsk, Ivanovo 8 Murmansk 9 Leningrad, Volgograd 10 Stalingrad 11 Chelyabinsk, Novosibirsk, Vladivostok 12 St. Petersburg 13 Yekaterinburg
czar: 4 Ivan 5 Basil, Boris (Godunov), Peter (the Great) 6 Alexis, Dmitry, Feodor, Vasily 7 Dimitri, Godunov (Boris), Michael (Romanov), Romanov (Michael) 8 Nicholas, Romanoff, Theodore 9 Alexander
empress: 4 Anna (Ivanovna) 9 Catherine (the Great), Elizabeth (Petrovna)
ethnic group: 7 Cossack
island: 8 Sakhalin
island group: 5 Kuril 6 Kurile
lake: 5 Il'men', Onega 6 Baikal, Ladoga
leader: 5 Lenin (Vladimir), Putin (Vladimir) 6 Stalin (Joseph) 7 Trotsky (Leon) 8 Brezhnev (Leonid) 10 Khrushchev (Nikita)
legislature: 4 Duma
monetary unit: 5 kopek, ruble 6 kopeck
mountain, range: 4 Ural 5 Altai, Altay, Sayan 6 Elbrus, Kolyma, Koryak 8 Caucasus, Stanovoy
neighbor: 5 China 6 Latvia, Norway 7 Belarus, Estonia, Finland, Georgia, Ukraine 8 Mongolia 9 Kazakstan 10 Azerbaijan, Kazakhstan, North Korea
peninsula: 4 Kola 5 Gydan, Kanin, Yamal 6 Taymyr 7 Chukchi 9 Kamchatka
region: 7 Siberia 9 Circassia 11 Golden Horde
revolution: 9 Bolshevik
river: 3 Don 4 Amur, Lena, Neva, Ural 5 Desna, Dvina, Vitim, Volga 6 Belaya, Kolyma, Vilyui, Vilyuy 7 Pechora, Yenisey 9 Indigirka
sea: 4 Azov, Kara 5 Black, White 6 Laptev 7 Barents, Caspian, Chukchi, Okhotsk
secret police: 3 KGB, MVD 4 NKVD
strait: 6 Bering

Russian
aristocrat: 5 boyar
caviar: 6 beluga
comrade: 8 tovarich, tovarish
country house: 5 dacha
dog: 6 borzoi 7 Samoyed
drink: 5 kvass, vodka
family: 7 Romanov 9 Stroganov
farmer: 5 kulak
forest: 5 taiga
grandmother: 8 babushka
instrument: 9 balalaika
monk: 8 Rasputin
no: 4 nyet
pancakes: 5 blini
peasant: 5 kulak, mujik 6 moujik, muzhik

republic: **6** oblast
saint: **15** Alexander Nevsky
urn: **7** samovar
vehicle: **6** troika
villa: **5** dacha

rustic
4 hick, rube, rude **5** churl, clown, plain, rough, rural, swain, yokel **6** farmer **7** bucolic, bumpkin, country, granger, hayseed, peasant, plowboy, plowman, redneck, uncouth **8** agrarian, pastoral **9** chawbacon, hillbilly **10** campestral, clodhopper, countryman, husbandman **11** countrified **12** apple-knocker, backwoodsman

rustle
5 haste, hurry, speed, steal, swish **6** forage, swoosh **7** crackle, crinkle **8** susurrus

rustler
5 thief **6** duffer, robber **7** forager **8** marauder

Rustum's son
6 Sohrab

rusty
4 slow **6** bygone, creaky **7** outworn **8** outdated, outmoded **10** antiquated, discolored **12** old-fashioned

rut
5 gouge, grind, track **6** furrow, groove **7** channel, routine **9** treadmill

rutabaga
5 swede **6** turnip

ruth
3 rue, woe **4** pity **5** grief, mercy **6** regret, sorrow **7** anguish, remorse, sadness **8** distress, sympathy **9** attrition, penitence **10** compassion, contrition, repentance **11** compunction **13** commiseration

Ruth
husband: **4** Boaz **6** Mahlon
mother-in-law: **5** Naomi
son: **4** Obed

ruthful
6 woeful **7** doleful **8** dolorous, wretched **9** miserable, sorrowful

ruthless
4 hard **5** cruel, harsh **6** brutal, savage **7** inhuman **8** pitiless **9** barbarous, cutthroat, dog-eat-dog, ferocious, heartless, merciless, unsparing **10** implacable, ironfisted **11** cold-blooded

ruttish
4 lewd **5** lusty, randy **6** wanton **7** goatish, lustful, satyric **9** lecherous, lickerish, salacious **10** lascivious, libidinous **12** concupiscent

Rwanda
capital: **6** Kigali
ethnic group: **4** Hutu **5** Tutsi
language: **6** French, Rwanda
monetary unit: **5** franc
neighbor: **5** Congo **6** Uganda **7** Burundi **8** Tanzania

S

____ Saarinen
4 Eero 5 Eliel

Sabatini novel
11 Scaramouche 12 Captain Blood

sabbatical
4 rest 5 leave 7 time off 8 vacation

saber
5 sword 7 cutlass 8 scimitar

sabertooth
3 cat 5 tiger

sable
3 fur 4 dark, inky 5 black, ebony, raven 6 gloomy, somber, sombre, weasel 8 mourning

sabot
4 clog, shoe 10 wooden shoe

sabotage
5 wreck 6 damage, hamper, hinder 7 cripple, disable, subvert, torpedo 8 obstruct, wreckage, wrecking 9 frustrate, undermine, vandalize 10 subversion 11 undermining

Sabra
father: 7 Ptolemy
rescuer: 8 St. George
son: 3 Guy 5 David 9 Alexander

sac
4 caul, cyst 5 pouch 7 vesicle

saccharine
5 mushy, sweet 6 sugary, syrupy 7 candied, cloying, honeyed, maudlin, mawkish, sugared 9 oversweet, schmaltzy 11 sentimental, sugar-coated 12 ingratiating

sacerdotal
8 hieratic, pastoral, priestly 10 priestlike 11 ministerial

sachem
4 boss 5 chief 6 leader

sachet
3 bag 6 powder 7 perfume 9 potpourri

sack
2 ax 3 axe, bag, bed, can 4 bunk, drop, fire, loot, raid, wine 5 expel, pouch, strip, waste 6 pocket, ravage, tackle 7 boot out, cashier, despoil, dismiss, hammock, kick out, pillage, plunder 8 desolate, spoliate 9 container, depredate, desecrate, devastate, white wine

sackbut
8 trombone

sacque
6 jacket

sacrament
4 rite 6 ritual 7 baptism, penance 8 ceremony, marriage 9 Communion, Eucharist, matrimony 10 holy orders 12 confirmation

sacrarium
6 chapel, shrine 7 oratory, piscina 8 sacristy 9 sanctuary

sacred
4 holy 5 godly 6 divine, immune 7 angelic, blessed, saintly 8 hallowed, numinous 9 inviolate, spiritual 10 inviolable, sacrosanct, sanctified 11 consecrated, sacramental
combining form: 4 hagi, hier, sacr 5 hagio, hiero, sacro
monkey: 6 baboon, rhesus 7 hanuman
place: 7 sanctum
song: 4 hymn
weed: 7 vervain

sacrifice
4 bunt, cede, lamb, lose, loss 5 forgo, yield 6 devote, donate, eschew, give up, martyr, victim 7 forfeit, offer up 8 dedicate, hecatomb, immolate, oblation, offering 12 renunciation

sacrilege
6 heresy 7 impiety, offense 9 blasphemy, violation 11 desecration, irreverence, profanation

sacrilegious
7 impious, profane, ungodly 10 irreverent 11 blasphemous

sacristan
6 sexton

sacristy
6 vestry

sacrosanct
9 inviolate 10 inviolable

sad
4 blue, down, glum 5 sorry 6 dismal, dreary, gloomy, morose, triste, woeful 7 doleful, joyless, piteous, pitiful, unhappy 8 dejected, desolate, dolorous, downbeat, downcast, grieving, mournful, pathetic, pitiable 9 depressed,

sorrowful, woebegone **10** depressing, dispirited, lamentable, melancholy **11** melancholic **12** heavyhearted

sadden
7 depress, oppress, trouble **8** aggrieve, dispirit **9** weigh down **10** discourage

saddle
3 tax **4** lade, load, task **5** weigh **6** burden, charge, hamper, impede, impose, weight **7** aparejo, inflict **8** encumber, restrict
adjunct: **7** stirrup
part: **6** cantle, pommel
strap: **5** cinch, girth **6** latigo **7** harness

sadness
3 woe **4** funk **5** blues, dolor, dumps, gloom, grief, mopes **6** misery, sorrow **7** dismals, megrims **8** doldrums, glumness, mourning **9** dejection, dysphoria, heartache **10** blue devils, depression, desolation, melancholy **11** despondency, melancholia, unhappiness

safari
4 hunt, trek, trip **7** caravan, journey **10** expedition

safe
4 snug, wary **5** chary **6** secure, unhurt **7** careful, guarded **8** cautious, defended, shielded, unharmed **9** innocuous, protected, sheltered, strongbox, uninjured, unscathed **10** inviolable, sheltering **11** impregnable **12** invulnerable, unassailable

safecracker
4 yegg **8** picklock **9** cracksman

safeguard
4 ward **6** convoy, defend, escort, shield, surety **7** bulwark, defense, protect **8** armament, preserve **10** precaution, protection

safety
6 asylum, refuge **7** defense, shelter **8** immunity, security **9** assurance, sanctuary **10** protection **13** inviolability

sag
3 dip **4** bend, drop, flag, flap, flop, hang, sink, slip, wilt **5** droop, slide, slump **6** dangle, hollow, slouch **7** decline, drop off, falloff, sinkage, sinking **8** downturn, prolapse, settling, sinkhole **9** concavity, downswing **10** depression

saga
4 Edda, epic, myth, tale **5** story **6** legend **9** chronicle, narrative **12** Heimskringla

sagacious
4 keen, wise **5** acute, smart **6** astute, clever, shrewd **7** knowing, prudent, sapient **8** critical **9** far-seeing, judicious **10** discerning, insightful, perceptive **11** intelligent **13** perspicacious

sagacity
5 grasp **6** acuity, acumen, wisdom **7** insight **8** judgment, keenness, prudence, sapience **10** perception, shrewdness **11** discernment, penetration, percipience, perspicuity **12** perspicacity **13** comprehension, judiciousness, understanding

sagamore
5 chief **6** sachem

Sagan work
6 Cosmos **16** Bonjour tristesse

sage
4 Bias, guru, mint, wise **5** Solon, Vyasa **6** Buddha (Gautama), Chilon, expert, Gandhi (Mohandas), Lao Tzu, master, Narada, Nestor, nestor, pundit, savant, shrewd, Thales **7** gnostic, knowing, learned, prudent, sapient, scholar, Solomon, Valmiki, wise man **8** polymath, profound, sensible **9** Confucius, judicious **10** discerning, insightful, perceptive **11** penetrating, philosophic
Hindu: **6** pandit, pundit **7** mahatma

Sage
of Chelsea: **7** Carlyle (Thomas)
of Concord: **7** Emerson (Ralph Waldo)
of Emporia: **5** White (William Allen)
of Ferney: **8** Voltaire
of Monticello: **9** Jefferson (Thomas)
of Pylos: **6** Nestor

Sagebrush State
6 Nevada

Sagittarius
6 archer **7** centaur **13** constellation

sago
4 palm **6** starch

saguaro
6 cactus

sahib
3 sir **6** master **9** gentleman

sail
3 fly **4** dart, flit, scud, skim, wing **5** fleet, float, shoot, skirr, sweep **6** cruise, mizzen **7** spencer **9** spinnaker
into wind: **4** luff
support: **4** mast
triangular: **3** jib **5** genoa

sailing term
3 aft, bow, lee, yaw **4** alee, beam, boom, port, tack, trim **5** abaft, abeam, aloft, belay, brale, stern **6** astern, adrift, fouled, pay out **7** cast off, heading, rigging, sea room **8** downhaul, overhaul, sounding, underway **9** starboard **10** batten down, Cunningham, lubber line, scandalize **11** self-tacking

sailing vessel
4 bark, brig, moth, yawl **5** xebec, yacht **6** barque, cutter **7** clipper, frigate, galleon **8** schooner, skipjack **10** barkentine, brigantine **11** barquentine

sailor
3 gob, tar **4** jack, mate, salt, swab **6** hearty, sea dog, seaman **7** jack-tar, mariner, matelot, old salt, swabbie **8** flatfoot, seafarer, shipmate, water dog **9** shellback, tarpaulin, yachtsman **10** bluejacket
British: **5** limey
East Indian: **6** lascar
fictional: **6** Sinbad
patron saint: **4** Elmo
song: **6** chanty **7** chantey **9** barcarole

saint
7 paragon
biography: **11** hagiography
list: **9** hagiology
Muslim: **3** pir
(see also **patron saint**)

Saint, The
12 Simon Templar
creator: **9** Charteris (Leslie)

Saint Anthony's cross
3 tau

Saint Elmo's Fire
9 corposant

Saint Helena
capital: **9** Jamestown
colony of: **7** Britain
island: **9** Ascension

Saint Joan author
4 Shaw (George Bernard)

Saint John's bread
5 carob

Saint Kitts and Nevis
capital: **10** Basseterre
island group: **7** Leeward
location: **10** West Indies

Saint Louis attraction
11 Gateway Arch

Saint Lucia
capital: **8** Castries
island group: **8** Windward
location: **10** West Indies
volcano: **8** Quilabou

saintly
4 holy, pure **5** godly, pious **6** devout, worthy **7** angelic, blessed, upright **8** beatific, seraphic, virtuous **9** righteous

Saint Paul's architect
4 Wren (Christopher)

Saint Peter's Basilica
architect: **7** Bernini (Gian Lorenzo) **12** Michelangelo (Buonarotti)
sculpture: **5** Pietà

Saint-Pierre and Miquelon
capital: **8** St.-Pierre
department of: **6** France

Saint Teresa birthplace
5 Avila

Saint Vincent and the Grenadines
capital: **9** Kingstown
island group: **8** Windward
location: **10** West Indies
volcano: **9** Soufrière

Saint Vitus' dance
6 chorea

sake
3 end **4** good **5** drink **7** benefit, purpose, welfare

Saki
5 Munro (H. H.)

salaam
3 bow **6** kowtow **8** greeting **9** obeisance

salacious
4 blue, fast, lewd, racy **5** bawdy **6** erotic, ribald, risqué, smutty **7** lustful, obscene, satyric **8** indecent, off-color, prurient **9** lecherous, libertine **10** lascivious, libidinous, licentious

salad
item: **3** egg, udo **4** bean, cuke, herb **5** cress, olive, onion, pasta **6** carrot, celery, cheese, endive, pepper, potato, radish, tomato **7** anchovy, arugula, cabbage, crouton, lettuce, mesclun, niçoise, parsley, spinach **8** chickpea, cucumber, garbanzo, mushroom, scallion **9** radicchio **10** watercress
dressing: **5** ranch **6** French **7** Italian, Russian **10** blue cheese, buttermilk, gorgonzola **11** vinaigrette
type: **4** Cobb **5** chef's **6** Caesar **7** Waldorf **8** coleslaw

salamander
3 eft, olm **4** newt **7** urodele **8** mud puppy, water dog **10** hellbender
Mexican: **7** axolotl

salary
3 pay **4** take, wage **6** income **7** stipend **8** earnings **9** emolument **10** recompense **12** compensation, remuneration

sale
6 bazaar, demand **7** auction **8** closeout, disposal, transfer **9** clearance **11** transaction

salesperson
3 rep

salient
6 marked, signal **7** obvious, weighty **8** striking **9** arresting, important, obtrusive, pertinent, prominent **10** impressive, noticeable, projecting, pronounced, remarkable **11** conspicuous, outstanding, significant

saline
5 briny, salty **8** brackish

Salinger, J. D.
character: 4 Esmé 6 Holden (Caulfield)
novel: 14 Franny and Zooey 15 Catcher in the Rye

saliva
4 spit 6 slaver, sputum 7 spittle

salivate
5 drool 6 drivel, slaver 7 slobber

____ Salk
5 Jonas

sallow
3 wan 4 pale, waxy 5 pasty 6 pallid, sickly, willow, yellow 7 bilious 9 jaundiced

sally
3 gag 4 gust, jape, jest, joke, quip 5 blast, burst, crack, jaunt 6 depart, junket, outing, set out, sortie, volley, zinger 7 barrage, flare-up 8 drollery, eruption, outbreak, outburst, paroxysm 9 discharge, excursion, explosion, wisecrack, witticism

salmagundi
see **hodgepodge**

salmon
3 dog 4 chum, coho, kelt, parr, pink 5 smolt 6 grilse, Sebago 7 chinook, sockeye 9 brandling
cured: 4 nova 7 gravlax 8 gravlaks
male: 6 kipper
smoked: 3 lox

Salome
composer: 7 Strauss (Richard)
father: 5 Herod
husband: 6 Philip 7 Zebedee 11 Aristobulus
mother: 8 Herodias
son: 4 John 5 James
victim: 4 John (the Baptist)

salon
4 hall, shop 5 suite 6 parlor 7 gallery 9 apartment, reception 10 exhibition

saloon
3 bar, pub 6 tavern 7 barroom, cantina, gin mill, taproom 9 beer joint 12 watering hole

salt
3 gob, tar 4 jack, keep, NaCl, swab 5 brine, limey 6 sailor, saline, sea dog, seaman 7 jack-tar, mariner 8 salinize, seafarer 9 sailorman

salt away
4 bank, save 5 hoard, lay by, lay up, put by, stash, store 7 deposit 8 lay aside, squirrel

saltpeter
5 niter, nitre

salty
4 blue, racy 5 briny, crude, spicy, tangy 6 earthy, purple, risqué, saline 7 caustic, mordant, pungent 8 brackish, off-color, scathing 9 trenchant

salubrious
5 tonic 7 bracing, healthy 8 hygienic, salutary 9 healthful, wholesome 10 beneficial 11 restorative 12 invigorating

Salus
see **Hygeia**

salutary
5 tonic 6 benign 7 bracing, healing 8 curative, remedial, sanative 9 analeptic, healthful, vulnerary, wholesome 10 beneficial, salubrious 11 restorative, therapeutic 12 advantageous, health-giving

salutation
2 hi 4 hail 5 hello, howdy 7 welcome 8 greeting
Arab: 6 salaam
French: 5 salut
Hawaiian: 5 aloha
Italian: 4 ciao
Latin: 3 ave
Spanish: 4 hola

salute
4 hail 5 greet, honor 6 praise 7 address, commend 8 greeting 12 congratulate

salvage
4 save 6 ransom, recoup, redeem, regain, rescue 7 deliver, reclaim, recover 8 retrieve

salvation
6 saving 7 keeping 10 redemption 11 deliverance 12 conservation, preservation

Salvation Army founder
5 Booth (General William)

salve
4 balm 5 cream, quiet 6 cerate, chrism, lotion, remedy 7 assuage, unction, unguent 8 ointment 9 emollient

salver
4 tray

salvo
4 hail 5 burst, spray, storm 6 attack, shower, volley 7 barrage, proviso 9 broadside, cannonade, discharge, fusillade 11 bombardment

Samaritan
6 helper 10 benefactor

same
4 idem, like, very 5 equal, exact 7 coequal, similar 8 constant 9 duplicate, identical, unvarying 10 consistent, equivalent, invariable, unchanging
combining form: 3 hom 4 homo

Samoa
capital: 4 Apia
island: 5 Upolu 6 Savai'i
monetary unit: 4 tala

samovar
3 urn

samp
6 cereal, hominy

sampan
4 boat **5** skiff

sample
3 try **4** case, part, test, unit **5** piece, taste **7** dip into, element, example, excerpt, portion, segment **8** fragment, instance, specimen **10** indication **11** case history, constituent **12** illustration

Samson
betrayer: 7 Delilah
birthplace: 5 Zorah
deathplace: 4 Gaza
father: 6 Manoah
tribe: 3 Dan

Samson Agonistes author
6 Milton (John)

Samuel
father: 7 Elkanah
grandson: 5 Heman
mentor: 3 Eli
mother: 6 Hannah

samurai code
7 Bushido

San Antonio
team: 5 Spurs
landmark: 5 Alamo

sanatorium
3 spa **8** hospital, rest home

sanctify
5 bless **6** hallow, ordain, purify **8** dedicate **10** consecrate

sanctimonious
5 pious **7** canting, preachy **8** unctuous **9** pharisaic **11** pharisaical **12** hypocritical, Pecksniffian **13** self-righteous

sanction
2 OK **4** fiat, okay **5** bless, leave **6** assent, decree, permit, ratify **7** approve, backing, boycott, certify, consent, embargo, endorse, license, penalty, support **8** accredit, approval **9** allowance, authorize **10** commission, permission, sufferance **11** approbation, endorsement **12** confirmation, ratification **13** authorization, encouragement

sanctity
8 holiness **9** godliness **11** saintliness, uprightness **13** inviolability, righteousness

sanctuary
5 haven, oasis **6** asylum, covert, harbor, refuge, shrine, temple **7** reserve, retreat, shelter **8** preserve **9** holy place

sanctum
4 lair **6** shrine **7** retreat, shelter **9** holy place, sanctuary

sand
3 tan **4** buff, ecru, fawn, grit **5** beach, beige, camel, grind, khaki, scour, shore **6** gravel, polish, smooth **7** burnish **8** granules

sandal
4 clog, zori **5** sabot, thong **6** patten **8** flip-flop, huarache **10** espadrille

sandbag
3 hit **4** stun **6** ambush, waylay **7** deceive

sandbar
4 reef, spit **7** tombolo

Sandburg, Carl
biographical subject: 7 Lincoln (Abraham)
work: 9 People Yes (The) **12** Chicago Poems, Harvest Poems **13** Smoke and Steel **16** Rootabaga Stories

Sand County Almanac author
7 Leopold (Aldo)

sandpiper
4 knot, ruff **5** reeve **6** dunlin **9** shorebird

sandstone deposit
6 flysch

sandwich
3 BLT, sub **4** club, gyro, hero, roti **5** butty, Cuban, po'boy **6** Denver, hoagie, Reuben **7** grinder, Western **9** submarine **10** muffuletta
shop: 4 deli

sandy
4 fair **5** blond **6** blonde, grainy, gritty

sane
3 fit **4** good, hale, sage, well, wise **5** lucid, right, sober, sound **6** cogent, normal **7** healthy, logical, prudent, sapient **8** all there, balanced, oriented, rational, sensible **9** judicious, wholesome **10** reasonable **11** levelheaded **12** compos mentis

San Francisco
hill: 3 Nob **7** Russian
tower: 4 Coit

sangfroid
4 calm **5** poise **6** aplomb, phlegm **8** serenity **9** composure **10** equanimity **11** self-control

sanguinary
4 gory **6** bloody **9** homicidal, murdering, murderous **12** bloodstained, bloodthirsty

sanguine
4 gory **5** flush, ruddy **6** bloody, florid, secure, upbeat **7** assured, buoyant, flushed, glowing, hopeful **8** bloodred, cheerful, rubicund **9** confident, homicidal, murdering, murderous **10** optimistic **11** self-assured **12** blood-stained, bloodthirsty, Pollyannaish **13** self-confident

sanitary
5 clean **7** sterile **8** hygienic **9** healthful **10** antiseptic, salubrious

sanitize
5 clean, purge **6** bleach, censor, purify **7** cleanse, launder **8** black out **9** disinfect, expurgate, sterilize **10** bowdlerize

sanity
6 health, reason **7** balance **8** lucidity, prudence **9** normality, soundness, stability

San Marino
capital: **9** San Marino
monetary unit: **4** euro
monetary unit, former: **4** lira
neighbor: **5** Italy

sans
7 lacking, missing, wanting, without

Sanskrit
dialect: **4** Pali
epic: **8** Ramayana
Scripture: **4** Veda **6** Purana

Santa Lucia composer
5 Denza (Luigi)

São Tomé and Príncipe
capital: **7** São Tomé
language: **10** Portuguese
location: **12** Gulf of Guinea
monetary unit: **5** dobra

sap
4 dupe, fool, gull, mark **5** chump, drain, ninny **6** pigeon, sucker, weaken **7** cripple, deplete, disable, exhaust, fall guy **8** enervate, enfeeble **9** attenuate, schlemiel, undermine **10** debilitate
pine: **5** resin, rosin

sapid
5 tasty **6** savory **9** delicious, flavorful, palatable, toothsome **10** appetizing **11** scrumptious

sapience
see **sagacity**

sapient
see **sagacious**

sapling
4 tree **5** child, youth **9** youngster

Sapphira's husband
7 Ananias

Sappho
forte: **6** poetry
island: **6** Lesbos
student: **6** Erinna

sappy
5 ditzy, flaky, mushy, silly, soupy **6** drippy, slushy, sticky, syrupy **7** cloying, foolish, maudlin, mawkish **8** bathetic **11** sentimental

Saracen hero
9 Rodomonte

Sarah
husband: **7** Abraham
maid: **5** Hagar
son: **5** Isaac

sarcasm
3 wit **4** gibe **5** irony, scorn **6** satire **7** mockery **8** acerbity, mordancy, ridicule, sneering **10** causticity

sarcastic
4 acid, tart **5** acerb, sharp **6** biting, ironic **7** acerbic, caustic, cutting, cynical, jeering, mocking, mordant, satiric **8** sardonic, scathing, scornful, stinging **9** corrosive

sarcophagus
4 tomb **6** coffin

sardine
4 sild **7** anchovy, herring **8** pilchard

Sardinia
capital: **8** Cagliari
neighbor: **7** Corsica

sardonic
3 wry **6** ironic **7** caustic, cynical, jeering, mocking, satiric **8** derisive, scornful, sneering **9** corrosive, sarcastic **10** disdainful **12** contemptuous

sarong
5 skirt **7** garment

Sarpedon
brother: **5** Minos **12** Rhadamanthus
father: **4** Zeus **7** Jupiter
mother: **6** Europa **8** Laodamia

Sartor ___
8 Resartus

Sartre work
4 Wall (The) **5** Flies (The) **6** Nausea, No Exit **8** Huis Clos **10** Saint Genet

sash
3 obi **4** belt **6** girdle **8** ceinture, cincture **9** waistband **10** cummerbund

sashay
5 mince, strut **6** prance **7** flounce, saunter, swagger

Saskatchewan
capital: **6** Regina
city: **8** Moose Jaw **9** Saskatoon **12** Prince Albert
mountain range: **12** Cypress Hills
provincial flower: **7** red lily **11** prairie lily
river: **9** Churchill **11** Assiniboine

sass
3 lip **4** guff **5** brass, cheek, mouth, sauce **8** back talk **9** impudence, insolence **12** impertinence

sassy
4 bold, flip, pert, wise **5** fresh, lippy, nervy,

smart **6** brazen, cheeky **7** forward **8** flippant, impudent, insolent, malapert **9** audacious, unabashed **11** smart-alecky

Satan
5 demon, devil, fiend **6** diablo **7** Lucifer, Old Nick, serpent, villain **9** archfiend, Beelzebub **10** Old Scratch

satanic
4 evil **6** wicked **7** demonic, hellish **8** demoniac, devilish, diabolic, fiendish, infernal

satanism
9 diabolism

satchel
3 bag **4** case, tote **5** pouch **6** valise **7** handbag **9** briefcase

sate
4 cloy, fill, glut, jade, pall **5** gorge, stuff **6** stodge **7** appease, overeat, placate, surfeit **8** overfill **9** overstuff **10** conciliate

sated
4 full **6** filled, gorged **7** glutted, overfed, replete, stuffed **8** appeased, chockful **9** chock-full, surfeited

satellite
4 moon **5** toady **6** cohort, minion **7** Sputnik **8** adherent, disciple, follower, henchman, partisan **9** attendant, supporter, sycophant, tributary
of Jupiter: **6** Europa **8** Callisto, Ganymede
of Mars: **6** Deimos, Phobos
of Neptune: **6** Nereid, Triton
of Saturn: **4** Rhea **5** Dione, Janus, Mimas, Titan **6** Phoebe, Tethys **7** Iapetus **8** Hyperion **9** Enceladus
of Uranus: **5** Ariel **6** Oberon **7** Miranda, Titania, Umbriel

satiate
see **sate**

satire
3 wit **5** irony, spoof, squib **6** parody **7** lampoon, mockery, takeoff **8** raillery, ridicule, spoofery, travesty **9** burlesque **10** caricature, lampoonery, pasquinade, persiflage

satiric
6 ironic **7** mocking **8** farcical, ironical

satirist
American: **5** Twain (Mark) **6** Bierce (Ambrose)
English: **4** Pope (Alexander) **5** Swift (Jonathan), Waugh (Evelyn) **7** Marston (John)
French: **7** Molière **8** Rabelais (François), Voltaire
Greek: **8** Menippus **12** Aristophanes
Italian: **7** Aretino (Pietro)
Roman: **6** Horace **7** Juvenal, Martial, Persius **8** Apuleius **9** Petronius

satirize
4 mock **5** spoof **6** parody, send up **7** lampoon **8** ridicule **10** caricature

satisfaction
6 amends **7** redress **8** pleasure, serenity **9** atonement **10** reparation **11** contentment, fulfillment, restitution, vindication **12** propitiation **13** gratification

satisfactory
4 fair, good, okay **5** sound **6** decent **7** alright **8** adequate, all right, passable **9** agreeable, competent, tolerable **10** acceptable, sufficient **13** unexceptional

satisfy
3 pay **4** fill, meet, sate, suit **5** clear, humor, pay up, serve **6** answer, assure, dispel, pacify, please, settle, square **7** appease, content, fulfill, gladden, gratify, indulge, placate, satiate, suffice, win over **8** convince, persuade **9** conform to, discharge, indemnify **10** comply with

satori
12 illumination **13** enlightenment

satrap
5 ruler **6** cohort **7** viceroy **8** governor, henchman, sidekick **11** subordinate

saturate
3 sop, wet **4** fill, soak **5** bathe, douse, imbue, souse, steep **6** charge, drench, infuse **7** pervade, suffuse **8** permeate, waterlog **9** transfuse

Saturday Night Live
cast member: **4** Sanz (Horatio) **5** Chase (Chevy), Myers (Mike), Vance (Danitra) **6** Carvey (Dana), Dratch (Rachel), Farley (Chris), Kattan (Chris), Morgan (Tracy), Murphy (Eddie), Murray (Bill), Nealon (Kevin), Radner (Gilda), Rocket (Charles) **7** Aykroyd (Dan), Belushi (John), Ferrell (Will), Franken (Al), Hammond (Darrell), Hartman (Phil), Meadows (Tim), Parnell (Chris), Rudolph (Maya), Sandler (Adam) **9** MacDonald (Norm), O'Donoghue (Michael)
creator: **8** Michaels (Lorne)

Saturn
moon: **4** Rhea **5** Dione, Janus, Mimas, Titan **6** Phoebe, Tethys **7** Iapetus **8** Hyperion **9** Enceladus
see also **Cronus**

saturnalia
4 orgy **5** party, revel **6** excess **7** debauch **9** bacchanal **11** bacchanalia, dissipation

saturnine
4 dour, glum, grim **5** sulky, surly **6** gloomy, moping, morose, somber, sombre, sullen **7** crabbed **8** funereal, sardonic

satyr
4 faun, goat, lech, rake, wolf **5** letch **6** lecher **8** Casanova, lothario **9** butterfly

satyric
4 lewd **5** randy **6** wanton **7** goatish, lustful **8** prurient **9** lecherous, libertine, lickerish, salacious **10** lascivious, libidinous, licentious, lubricious **11** promiscuous **12** concupiscent

sauce
3 lip **4** guff, sass **5** mouth **6** relish **7** topping **8** back talk **9** condiment, impudence
kind: **3** soy **4** hard, mole, roux **5** aioli, chili, curry, gravy, melba, pesto, ponzu, salsa **6** Mornay, panada, tamari, tartar **7** chutney, marengo, Newburg, piquant, soubise, tartare, velouté **8** béchamel, duxelles, marinara, matelote, noisette, normande **9** béarnaise, lyonnaise, rémoulade **10** bordelaise, Provençale **11** hollandaise, vinaigrette

saucy
see **sassy**

Saudi Arabia
capital: **6** Riyadh
city: **5** Jedda, Jidda, Mecca **6** Jeddah, Jiddah, Medina
desert: **7** Arabian **10** Rub Al-Khali **12** Empty Quarter
gulf: **7** Persian
monetary unit: **4** rial **5** riyal
neighbor: **3** UAE **4** Iraq, Oman **5** Qatar, Yemen **6** Jordan
peninsula: **7** Arabian
sea: **3** Red

Saul
concubine: **6** Rizpah
cousin: **5** Abner
daughter: **5** Merab **6** Michal
father: **4** Kish
general: **5** Abner
son: **8** Jonathan
successor: **5** David
uncle: **3** Ner
wife: **7** Ahinoam

saunter
4 mope, roam, rove **5** amble, drift, mosey **6** loiter, ramble, sashay, stroll, wander **7** meander, traipse

sausage
5 wurst **6** banger, kishke, salami, Vienna, wiener **7** baloney, bologna, boloney, chorizo, saveloy **8** cervelat, kielbasa, kielbasy **9** andouille, bratwurst, frankfurt, pepperoni, Thuringer **10** knackwurst, knockwurst, liverwurst, mortadella **11** frankfurter

sauté
3 fry **4** sear **5** brown, grill **6** sizzle **7** frizzle

savage
4 grim, wild **5** brute, cruel, feral **6** bloody, brutal, fierce, Gothic, rugged **7** bestial, brutish, inhuman, untamed, vicious, wolfish **8** barbaric, inhumane, primeval, ravenous, unbroken **9** barbarian, barbarous, ferocious, heartless, murderous, primitive, rapacious, truculent, voracious **10** implacable, relentless **11** uncivilized **12** bloodthirsty, uncontrolled, uncultivated, unsocialized

savagery
7 cruelty **8** atrocity **9** barbarity, brutality, depravity **10** bestiality, inhumanity **11** abomination, monstrosity, viciousness **12** ruthlessness

savanna
4 veld **5** plain, veldt **9** grassland

savant
4 sage **7** scholar, thinker, wise man

save
3 bar, but, yet **4** bank, keep, only, stow **5** amass, avoid, cache, guard, hoard, lay by, lay in, lay up, put by, set by, skimp, spare, store **6** defend, except, gather, keep up, manage, ransom, redeem, rescue, scrimp, shield, unless **7** barring, besides, collect, deliver, deposit, however, husband, lay away, protect, reclaim, reserve, salvage, set free, store up **8** conserve, lay aside, liberate, maintain, preserve, salt away, set aside, squirrel **9** aside from, economize, excluding, safeguard, stash away, stockpile **10** accumulate

savior
7 messiah, paladin, rescuer **8** defender **9** deliverer, liberator, preserver, protector, salvation **11** white knight

savoir faire
4 tact **5** grace, poise **6** aplomb **7** address, dignity, finesse, manners **8** urbanity **10** confidence, refinement **13** self-assurance

savor
4 odor, tang **5** enjoy, scent, smack, smell, spice, taste, tinge **6** flavor, relish, season **8** sapidity

savory
5 sapid, spicy, tangy, tasty **7** piquant **9** flavorful, palatable, toothsome **10** appetizing

savvy
4 deft **5** adept, craft, handy, knack, skill **6** clever, talent **7** ability, know-how, skilled **8** deftness **9** adeptness, expertise, handiness, ingenuity **10** capability, cleverness, competence

saw
3 cut, hew **5** adage, axiom, maxim **6** byword, cliché, cutter, saying **7** precept, proverb **8** aphorism, apothegm

___ saw
3 bow, jig, pit, rip **4** band, buck, buzz, fret, hack, whip **5** chain, crown, saber **6** coping, scroll **7** compass, keyhole **8** circular, crosscut

sawbones
3 doc **6** doctor **7** surgeon **9** physician

sawbuck
6 tenner **7** trestle

sawhorse
see **sawbuck**

saw-toothed
7 serrate, serried **8** serrated **11** denticulate

Saxon
assembly: 4 moot **5** gemot **6** gemote
nobleman: 8 atheling
serf: 4 esne **6** thrall
warrior: 5 thane

say
4 talk, tell **5** mouth, speak, state, utter, voice **6** affirm, assert, assume, recite, remark **7** comment, declare, express **8** announce, proclaim **9** enunciate, pronounce **10** articulate

Sayers character
6 Wimsey (Lord Peter)

saying
3 mot, saw **5** adage, axiom, maxim, motto **6** byword, dictum, truism **7** precept, proverb **8** aphorism, apothegm

scab
5 crust **6** eschar **8** blackleg **13** strikebreaker

scabbard
6 sheath

scabrous
4 lewd **5** bawdy, harsh, rough, salty, scaly **6** craggy, crusty, grubby, jagged, knobby, knotty, ribald, rugged, scurfy, sordid, uneven **7** bristly, prickly, scraggy, squalid **8** indecent, prurient **9** salacious **10** scandalous

scads
4 gobs, lots, tons, wads **5** heaps, loads, piles, rafts, reams **6** oodles, plenty **8** slathers **10** quantities

scaffold
5 stage, truss **7** staging **8** platform **9** framework

Scala, La
city: 5 Milan **6** Milano
production: 5 opera

scalawag
see **scamp**

scald
4 boil, burn **6** scorch

scale
4 peel, rate, skin **5** climb, flake, gamut, gauge, mount, ratio, scute, strip **6** ascend, degree, extent, ladder, lamina, scutum, squama **7** measure, ranking **8** escalade, flake off, spall off **9** exfoliate, hierarchy **10** desquamate, proportion **11** decorticate
auxiliary: 7 vernier
earthquake: 7 Richter
musical: 2 do, fa, la, mi, re, ti, ut **3** sol
temperature: 6 Kelvin **7** Celsius, Réaumur **10** centigrade, Fahrenheit
wind: 8 Beaufort

scallion
4 leek **5** onion **7** shallot **10** green onion

scalp
4 flay, skin **5** cheat **6** resell, trophy

scam
3 con, gyp **4** bilk, dupe, fool, hoax **5** cheat, fraud, stick, trick **6** delude, diddle, take in **7** beguile, deceive, defraud, swindle **8** flimflam, hoodwink, phishing **11** double-cross

scamp
3 imp **4** brat, rake, tyke **5** devil, joker, knave, rogue **6** rascal, urchin **7** hellion **8** scalawag, slyboots **9** prankster, scoundrel, skeezicks **11** rapscallion

scamper
3 run **4** dash, skip **5** scoot **6** scurry **7** scuttle

scan
3 eye, MRI **4** skim, view **5** audit, check **6** browse, review, survey **7** examine, eyeball, inspect **8** glance at **10** run through, scrutinize

scandal
5 rumor **6** gossip, infamy **7** calumny, obloquy, offense, slander **8** disgrace, dishonor, reproach **9** aspersion, discredit, disrepute **10** backbiting, defamation, detraction, opprobrium

scandalize
5 libel, shock, smear **6** defame, malign **7** asperse, slander **9** denigrate **10** calumniate

scandalmonger
6 gossip **8** busybody, gossiper, quidnunc, telltale **9** backbiter, muckraker **10** talebearer

scandalous
7 heinous **8** infamous, libelous, shameful, shocking **9** notorious, offensive **10** defamatory, outrageous, scurrilous **11** disgraceful

Scandinavian
see **Norse**

Scandinavian country
6 Norway, Sweden **7** Denmark, Finland, Iceland

scant
5 short, skimp, spare, stint, tight **6** meager, meagre, paltry, scarce, scrimp, skimpy, slight, sparse **7** scrimpy, wanting **8** exiguous **10** inadequate **12** insufficient

scantiness
4 lack **6** dearth **7** deficit, paucity **8** scarcity, shortage, sparsity **10** deficiency, inadequacy, scarceness, sparseness **13** insufficiency

scanty
see **scant**

scapegoat
6 target, victim **7** fall guy **9** sacrifice **11** whipping boy

scapegrace
5 knave, rogue, scamp **6** bad egg, rascal, sinner **7** ruffian, varmint, villain **8** hooligan, recreant, scalawag **9** miscreant, reprobate, scoundrel **10** blackguard, black sheep, delinquent **11** rapscallion

Scapin
5 rogue, valet **6** rascal
author: **7** Molière
employer: **7** Léandre

scar
3 mar **4** flaw **5** score **6** deface, defect, keloid **7** blemish, scratch **8** cicatrix, pockmark **9** cicatrize, disfigure
on a seed: **5** hilum

scarab
6 beetle

scaramouch
see **scamp**

scarce
3 few **4** rare **5** scant **6** barely, hardly, scanty, sparse **7** limited, wanting **8** sporadic, uncommon **9** deficient **10** inadequate, infrequent, occasional **12** insufficient

scarcity
see **scantiness**

scare
5 alarm, panic, spook **6** fright **7** horrify, petrify, shake up, startle, terrify **8** frighten, paralyze **9** terrorize

scaredy-cat
4 wimp, wuss **5** mouse, sissy **6** coward **7** chicken, dastard **8** alarmist, poltroon **11** milquetoast, yellowbelly

scare up
4 find, snag **5** rally **6** corral, gather, locate, obtain, secure **7** acquire, collect, procure, unearth **8** smoke out **9** ferret out, track down

scarf
3 boa **4** gulp, wolf **5** ascot, fichu, plaid, shawl, stole **6** cravat, devour, gobble, inhale **8** babushka, liripipe, mantilla, puggaree **10** lambrequin
Mexican: **6** rebozo

Scarlet Letter, The
author: **9** Hawthorne (Nathaniel)
character: **5** Pearl **6** Hester (Prynne) **10** Dimmesdale (Arthur) **13** Chillingworth (Roger)

Scarlet Pimpernel author
5 Orczy (Baroness Emmuska)

Scarlett's home
4 Tara

scary
6 creepy, spooky **8** chilling **9** frightful
cry: **3** boo

scathe
4 burn, flay, flog, harm, lash, sear **5** roast, slash **6** assail, berate, scorch, thrash **7** blister, scarify, scourge, upbraid **8** lambaste **9** castigate, excoriate

scathing
6 biting, brutal **7** caustic, mordant **8** stinging **9** trenchant

scatter
3 sow, ted **4** cast, part, shed **5** strew **6** divide, spread **7** bestrew, break up, diffuse, disband, diverge **8** disperse, sprinkle **9** broadcast, dissipate **10** besprinkle, distribute **11** disseminate

scatterbrained
5 dizzy, giddy, silly **7** flighty, foolish **8** heedless **9** frivolous

scattering
8 diaspora **10** dispersion

scavenger
5 hyena **6** jackal **7** vulture

scenario
4 plot **6** script **7** outline **8** libretto, synopsis **10** screenplay

scene
3 row, set **4** fuss, site, spot, view **5** arena, field, place, sight, vista **6** locale, milieu, sphere **7** episode, outlook, setting, tableau, tantrum **8** backdrop, locality, location, stage set **9** commotion, landscape, situation **10** background **11** environment **12** stage setting

scenery
3 set **5** decor, props **7** setting **8** stage set **10** properties **11** furnishings **12** stage setting

scent
4 nose, odor **5** aroma, smell, sniff, snuff, whiff **7** bouquet, essence, incense, odorize, perfume **9** aromatize, fragrance, redolence

scepter
4 mace **5** baton, staff **11** sovereignty

schedule
4 list, roll **5** chart, slate, table **6** agenda, docket, record, roster **7** catalog, program, reserve **8** calendar, register, roll call **9** catalogue, timetable

scheme
4 plan, plot, ploy, ruse **5** bunco, bunko, cabal, order **6** design, device, devise **7** collude, connive, diagram, program, project **8** cogitate, conspire, contrive, game plan, intrigue, proposal, strategy **9** blueprint, expedient, machinate **10** conspiracy, strategize **11** arrangement, contrivance, machination
type: 5 Ponzi **7** pyramid

schism
4 rent, rift **5** break, chasm, cleft, split **6** breach, divide, heresy **7** discord, dissent, fissure, rupture **8** cleavage, division, fracture **10** disharmony, dissidence, divergence, falling-out, heterodoxy, separation **11** unorthodoxy **12** estrangement

schlemiel
4 fool **5** chump, klutz **7** bungler

schlep
3 lug, tow **4** drag, haul, hump, plod, pull, slog, tote **5** carry, truck **6** trudge **7** shamble, shuffle **8** straggle

schlock
4 junk, mean **5** cheap, dreck, gaudy, junky, tacky, tatty **6** cheesy, common, kitsch, shoddy, sleazy, tawdry, trashy **8** inferior, low-grade **11** second-class, substandard

schmaltzy
5 mushy, soppy **6** drippy **7** maudlin, mawkish **11** sentimental, tear-jerking

schmo
4 dolt, dope, dork, fool, goof, jerk, mutt, simp, twit, yo-yo **5** brute, chump, idiot, moron, ninny, noddy, scamp **6** dimwit, donkey, dumdum, nitwit, noodle, nudnik, rascal **7** dullard, halfwit, jackass, schmuck, schnook **8** bonehead, clodpoll, imbecile, lunkhead, meathead, numskull **9** birdbrain, blockhead, ignoramus, lamebrain, numbskull, thickhead **10** dunderhead, hammerhead, nincompoop **11** chowderhead, chucklehead, knucklehead

schmooze
3 gab, yak **4** chat **6** chat up **8** converse

schnoz
4 beak, nose **5** snout **6** honker

scholar
4 sage, wonk **5** pupil **6** savant **7** bookman, egghead, student, wise man **8** bookworm, polymath **12** intellectual
Hindu: 6 pandit, pundit
Muslim: 5 ulama, ulema

scholarly
7 bookish, erudite, learned **8** academic, educated, studious **10** scholastic **12** intellectual

scholarship
5 award, grant **7** stipend **8** learning **9** education, erudition, knowledge **11** learnedness

scholastic
7 bookish, erudite, learned **8** academic, lettered, literary, pedantic **9** scholarly
life: 8 academia

school
3 gam, pod **5** shoal, teach, train, tutor **7** academy, college, educate **8** instruct **9** alma mater, institute **10** discipline, university
English: 4 Eton **6** Harrow
French: 5 école, lycée
grounds: 6 campus
Jewish: 5 heder **7** yeshiva
judo: 4 dojo
organization: 3 PTA, PTO
religious: 8 seminary
term: 7 quarter **8** semester **9** trimester
type: 4 coed

schoolbook
4 text **6** primer, reader **7** speller

School for Scandal author
8 Sheridan (Richard Brinsley)

schooner
4 ship **5** stoup **6** goblet, seidel **7** tumbler **8** sailboat

Schubert forte
4 lied, song

science
of agriculture: 8 agronomy
of animals: 7 zoology
of criminal punishment: 8 penology
of environment: 7 ecology
of fermentation: 8 zymology
of health: 7 hygiene **9** hygienics
of heredity: 8 genetics
of human behavior: 10 psychology
of measuring time: 8 horology **11** chronometry
of motion: 8 kinetics
of mountains: 7 orology
of plants: 6 botany
of projectiles: 10 ballistics
of the earth: 7 geology

scientific classification
8 taxonomy

sci-fi writer
3 Lem (Stanislaw) **4** Card (Orson Scott), Dick (Philip K.), Pohl (Frederik) **5** Disch (Thomas M.), Lewis (C. S.), Niven (Larry), Verne (Jules), Wells (H. G.) **6** Aldiss (Brian), Asimov (Isaac), Bester (Alfred), Bishop (Michael), Butler (Octavia), Clarke (Arthur C.), Delany (Samuel), Farmer (Philip José), Gibson (William), Le Guin (Ursula), Leiber (Fritz), Miller (Walter), Norton (Andre) **7** Ballard (J. G.), Clement (Hal), Ellison (Harlan), Herbert (Frank), Hubbard (L. Ron), Van Vogt (A. E.), Zelazny (Roger) **8** Anderson (Poul), Bradbury (Ray), Heinlein (Robert A.), Sterling (Bruce), Sturgeon (Theodore), Vonnegut

(Kurt) **9** Gernsback (Hugo), Kornbluth (C. M.) **10** Silverberg (Robert)

scimitar
5 saber, sabre, sword **7** cutlass

scintilla
3 bit, jot **4** atom, iota, whit **5** grain, spark, speck, trace **7** smidgen **8** particle

scintillate
5 flash, gleam, glint, spark **6** glance **7** glimmer, glisten, glitter, shimmer, sparkle, twinkle **9** coruscate

scion
4 heir **5** child, graft, issue **7** progeny **8** offshoot **9** inheritor, offspring, successor **10** descendant

scoff at
4 mock, twit **5** fleer, scorn **6** deride **7** contemn, disdain **8** belittle, pooh-pooh, ridicule

scold
3 rag **4** chew, lash, rail, rant **5** baste, blame, chide, grill, harpy, hound, shrew, vixen **6** berate, grouch, grouse, harass, murmur, mutter, rebuke, revile, virago **7** bawl out, blister, censure, chasten, chew out, grumble, lecture, reprove, tell off, upbraid **8** admonish, execrate, fishwife, lambaste, reproach, Xantippe **9** criticize, dress down, excoriate, objurgate, reprehend, reprimand, termagant, Xanthippe **10** tongue-lash, vituperate

scoop
3 dig, dip **4** bail, beat, lift **5** gouge, ladle, spade **6** dig out, pick up, shovel **8** excavate **9** exclusive

scoot
3 fly, run, zip **4** dash, flee, race, rush, skip **5** hurry, scram, skirr, slide **6** hustle, scurry, sprint **7** scamper **9** skedaddle

scope
3 ken **4** area, room **5** ambit, gamut, orbit, range, reach, sweep **6** extent, leeway, margin, radius **7** breadth, compass, purview **8** capacity, fullness, latitude **9** amplitude, extension

Scopes trial lawyer
5 Bryan (William Jennings) **6** Darrow (Clarence)

scorch
4 bake, burn, char, flay, sear **5** broil, roast, singe **6** scathe **7** blacken, blister, scarify, scourge, swelter **8** lambaste **9** castigate, excoriate

score
3 cut, tab, win **4** bill, gain, goal, line, mark, nick, slit **5** cleft, count, notch, reach, tally, total **6** attain, furrow, groove, grudge, rack up, record, thrive, twenty **7** account, achieve, invoice, prosper, scratch, succeed **8** flourish **9** reckoning **10** accomplish

scorn
4 gibe, jeer, mock **5** abhor, flout, scoff, spurn, taunt **6** deride **7** contemn, despise, despite, disdain, jeering, mockery **8** contempt, derision, ridicule, scoffing, taunting **9** contumely

Scorpius star
7 Antares

Scot
4 Celt, Gael

Scotch cocktail
6 Rob Roy **9** Rusty Nail

scoter
7 sea coot, sea duck

Scotland
capital: 9 Edinburgh
church: 11 the Auld Kirk
city: 6 Dundee **7** Glasgow **8** Aberdeen **9** Inverness **11** Dunfermline
emblem: 7 thistle
firth: 5 Clyde, Forth, Moray **6** Solway
former capital: 5 Perth
island, island group: 4 Iona, Jura, Mull, Skye, Uist **5** Arran, Islay **7** Orkneys **9** Shetlands **8** Hebrides
lake: 8 Loch Ness **10** Loch Lomond
mountain, range: 8 Ben Nevis **9** Grampians
patron saint: 6 Andrew
river: 3 Dee, Esk **5** Clyde

Scott, Sir Walter
novel: 5 Abbot (The) **6** Rob Roy **7** Ivanhoe **8** Talisman (The), Waverley **9** Woodstock **10** Kenilworth **11** Redgauntlet **12** Old Mortality **14** Quentin Durward
poem: 7 Marmion **13** Lady of the Lake (The)

____ Scott case
4 Dred

Scottish
4 Erse **6** Gaelic
cap: 3 tam **9** glengarry **11** tam-o'-shanter
child: 5 bairn
coin: 6 bawbee
dance: 4 reel **5** fling **10** strathspey
Gaelic: 4 Erse
guide: 6 gillie
hero: 5 Bruce (Robert) **7** Wallace (William)
hill: 4 brae
lake: 4 loch
landowner: 5 laird
language: 4 Erse **6** Gaelic
no: 3 nae
outlaw: 6 Rob Roy
plaid: 6 tartan
pudding: 6 haggis
skirt: 4 kilt
spirit: 6 kelpie **7** banshee
sword: 8 claymore
trousers: 5 trews

scoundrel
3 cad **4** heel **5** knave, rogue, scamp **6** bad guy, rascal **7** lowlife, villain **9** miscreant, reprobate **10** blackguard

scour
4 comb, rake **5** erode, purge, range, scrub **6** forage, search **7** corrode, eat away, ransack, rummage **8** wear away **9** ferret out

scourge
4 bane, flay, flog, hide, lash, whip, whop **5** curse, flail, slash, whale **6** plague, ravage, scathe, stripe, thrash **7** afflict, blister, despoil, pillage, scarify **8** chastise, lambaste **9** castigate, depredate, desecrate, devastate, excoriate **10** affliction, flagellate, pestilence

Scourge of God
6 Attila

scout
3 spy **6** ranger, survey **7** explore, lookout **8** searcher, watchman **11** investigate, reconnoiter

scouting group
3 BSA, GSA

scow
3 hoy **5** barge **6** garvey **7** lighter

scowl
5 frown, glare, lower **6** glower

scrabble
5 grope **6** scrawl **7** clamber **8** flounder

scraggly
6 ragged, shaggy, uneven **7** unkempt **9** irregular

scraggy
4 bony, lank, lean **5** gaunt, harsh, lanky, rocky, rough **6** jagged, rugged, skinny, uneven **7** angular, scrawny, spindly, unlevel **8** gangling, rawboned, scabrous

scram
3 git **4** scat, shoo **5** scoot, split **6** beat it, begone, get out **7** buzz off, get lost, skiddoo, take off, vamoose **8** clear out **9** skedaddle

scramble
4 hash **6** jumble, jungle, muddle, scurry, tumble **7** clamber, clutter, rummage, scuttle, shuffle **8** mishmash, scrabble, straggle **9** confusion

scrambled
7 chaotic, jumbled, mixed-up **8** confused **9** corrupted **10** disordered, disorderly

scrap
3 bit, jot, ort, row **4** chip, dump, fray, iota, junk, spat, tiff, whit **5** abort, brawl, chuck, crumb, fight, melee, piece, set-to, shred, speck **6** bicker, fracas, reject, sliver, tittle **7** brabble, cutting, discard, fall out, quarrel, scuffle, smidgen, wrangle **8** fragment, jettison, leftover, particle, squabble, throw out **9** throw away

scrape
3 fix, jam, rub **4** mess, rasp, spot **5** chafe, fight, grate, graze, pinch, scour, scuff, shave, skimp, spare, stint **6** abrade, pickle, plight, scrimp **7** dilemma, scratch, trouble **8** abrasion, struggle **11** predicament

scrappy
6 feisty **8** brawling **9** combative, truculent **10** pugnacious **11** belligerent, contentious, quarrelsome

scratch
4 claw, rake, rasp **5** grate, money, score, scrup **6** scotch, scrape, scrawl **7** call off **8** scrabble, scribble

scratchy
5 rough **6** gritty **7** itching, prickly, rasping **8** abrasive, granular, tingling **10** irritating

scrawl
6 doodle **7** scratch **8** scrabble, scribble

scrawny
4 bony, lank, lean **5** gaunt, lanky **6** skinny **7** scraggy **8** rawboned

scream
3 cry **4** riot, yell, yowl **5** shout **6** screak, shriek, shrill, squeal **7** screech

screech
6 screak, scream, shriek, shrill, squeal

screed
4 rant **5** level, spiel **6** letter, tirade **8** diatribe, harangue, jeremiad **9** discourse, philippic **11** disputation **12** disquisition

screen
4 cull, hide, sift, veil **5** blind, sieve **6** facade, filter, movies, shroud, winnow **7** conceal, obscure, pick out **9** partition **10** camouflage
Japanese: 5 shoji

screw
9 propeller

screwball
3 nut, wag **4** kook, zany **5** clown, crazy, cutup, flake, flaky, freak, gonzo, joker, kooky, loony, loopy, nutty, silly, wacko, wacky **6** madcap, weirdo **7** buffoon, dingbat, farceur **8** crackpot, jokester **9** ding-a-ling, eccentric, fruitcake, whimsical

Screwtape Letters author
5 Lewis (C. S.)

screwy
3 mad **4** daft, nuts **5** batty, crazy, goofy, loony, nutty, wacky **6** absurd, insane **7** bizarre, cracked, lunatic **9** eccentric **10** unbalanced

scribble
5 write **6** scrawl **7** scratch **8** squiggle

scribe
5 clerk, write **6** author, penman, writer **7** copyist **9** scrivener, secretary **10** amanuensis

scrimmage
4 fray **5** brawl, broil, clash, fight, melee, scrap, scrum, set-to **6** battle, fracas, ruckus, rumpus **7** scuffle **8** skirmish **10** donnybrook, free-for-all

scrimp
4 save **5** stint **6** save up, scrape **8** conserve **9** economize

script
4 hand, text **5** write **8** longhand, scenario **10** penmanship, screenplay **11** calligraphy, chirography, handwriting, orchestrate

scrivener
5 clerk **6** notary, scribe, writer **7** copyist **10** amanuensis

scrooge
5 miser **7** niggard **8** tightwad **9** skinflint **10** cheapskate **12** moneygrubber

scrounge
3 beg, bum, tap **4** grub, hunt, loot **5** cadge, filch, mooch, pinch, steal, swipe, touch **6** forage, hustle, pilfer, snitch, sponge, thieve **7** finagle, solicit, wheedle **8** freeload **9** panhandle

scroungy
5 dirty, seedy **6** grubby, grungy, scurvy, scuzzy, shabby, sleazy, sordid **7** scruffy, squalid, unkempt **8** slovenly **10** slatternly

scrub
3 rub **4** buff, drop, wash **5** abort, brush, scour **6** cancel, mallee, maquis, polish **7** abandon, call off, cleanse, scratch **9** chaparral, eliminate

scrubby
4 drab, mean **5** dingy, dowdy, runty **6** paltry, ragged, shabby, shoddy **7** rundown, runtish, stunted **8** inferior **9** neglected **10** bedraggled, broken-down

scruff
4 nape, neck

scruffy
5 mangy, seedy, tacky **6** frowsy, frowzy, shabby, shaggy **7** run-down, scrubby, unkempt **8** slovenly, tattered **10** down-at-heel, threadbare

scrumptious
5 tasty, yummy **8** heavenly, luscious **9** ambrosial, delicious, succulent, toothsome **10** delectable, delightful **13** mouthwatering

scruple
3 bit, jot **4** balk, iota **5** demur, doubt, grain, qualm, scrap, shred, worry **7** concern, modicum **8** particle, question **9** hesitancy **11** compunction

scrupulous
5 exact, fussy **6** honest, minute, strict **7** careful, heedful, upright **8** critical, punctual, rigorous **9** honorable **10** fair-minded, fastidious, meticulous, principled, upstanding **11** painstaking, punctilious **12** conscionable **13** conscientious

scrutinize
4 comb, scan **5** audit, probe, study **6** peruse **7** analyze, canvass, dig into, dissect, examine, eyeball, inspect **8** look over, pore over **9** check over **11** contemplate, investigate

scrutiny
4 scan **5** audit **6** review, survey **7** perusal **8** analysis **10** inspection **11** examination **12** surveillance

scuba diver
7 frogman **8** aquanaut

scud
3 fly **4** race, rain, rush, sail, skim **5** brume, froth, scoot, speed, spray, spume **6** clouds, scurry, shower

scuff
6 scrape **7** scratch, shamble, shuffle

scuffle
3 row **4** fray **5** brawl, broil, fight, scrap, set-to **6** affray, fracas, hubbub, tussle **7** bobbery, grapple, shamble, shuffle, wrestle **10** rough-house

scull
3 oar, row **4** boat **5** shell **6** propel

sculpt
3 hew **5** carve, shape **6** chisel

sculptor
American: **3** Lin (Maya) **4** Gabo (Naum), Judd (Donald), Taft (Lorado) **5** Andre (Carl), Koons (Jeff), Pratt (Bela), Segal (George), Serra (Richard), Smith (David), Story (William) **6** Aitkin (Robert), Calder (Alexander), Fraser (James Earle), French (Daniel Chester), Powers (Hiram), Zorach (William) **7** Borglum (Gutzon), Cornell (Joseph), Noguchi (Isamu) **8** Lachaise (Gaston), Lipchitz (Jacques), Nadelman (Elie), Nevelson (Louise) **9** Bourgeois (Louise), Mestrovic (Ivan), Oldenburg (Claes), Remington (Frederic) **12** Saint-Gaudens (Augustus)
Czech: **6** Stursa (Jan)
Danish: **11** Thorvaldsen (Bertel), Thorwaldsen (Bertel)
Dutch: **6** Sluter (Claus)
English: **5** Moore (Henry), Watts (George) **7** Epstein (Jacob), Flaxman (John) **8** Hepworth (Barbara)
French: **3** Arp (Hans, Jean) **4** Bloc (André) **5** Rodin (Auguste) **6** Dubois (Paul), Houdon (Jean-Antoine) **7** Maillol (Aristide), Pevsner (Antoine) **9** Bartholdi (Frédéric-Auguste), Roubillac (Louis-François)
German: **5** Hesse (Eva)
Greek: **5** Myron **7** Phidias **8** Pheidias **10** Polyclitus, Praxiteles **11** Polycleitus
Italian: **5** Leoni (Leone), Salvi (Niccolò, Nicola) **6** Canova (Antonio), Pisano (Andrea, Nino), Robbia (Andrea, Giovanni, Girolamo, Luca della)

7 Bernini (Gian Lorenzo), Cellini (Benvenuto), da Vinci (Leonardo), Orcagna, Quercia (Jacopo della) **8** Ghiberti (Lorenzo), Leonardo (da Vinci), Vittoria (Alessandro) **9** Donatello, Sansovino (Jacopo) **10** Giocometti (Alberto), Verrocchio (Andrea del) **12** Michelangelo (Buonarroti)
Rhodian: **9** Polydorus
Romanian: **8** Brancusi (Constantin)
Russian: **7** Zadkine (Ossip)
Swedish: **6** Milles (Carl) **9** Oldenburg (Claes)
Swiss: **10** Giacometti (Alberto)

scum
5 algae, dregs, dross **6** refuse, vermin **8** riffraff

scummy
3 low **4** base, mean, vile **5** dirty, mucky, slimy **6** grubby, odious, sleazy, sordid **7** squalid **10** despicable **12** contemptible

scurrilous
4 foul **5** dirty, gross, nasty **6** coarse, filthy, vulgar **7** abusive, obscene, profane **8** indecent **9** insulting, offensive **10** outrageous **11** opprobrious **12** contumelious, vituperative

scurry
3 run **4** dart, dash **5** scoot, shoot **6** bustle **7** scamper, scuffle, scuttle

scurvy
see **scummy**

scut
4 tail

scuttle
3 run **4** hole, pail, sink **5** abort, scrap, wreck **6** basket, scurry **7** destroy, opening

scuttlebutt
4 buzz, talk **5** rumor **6** gossip, report **7** chatter, hearsay **9** grapevine

Scylla
4 rock
counterpart: **9** Charybdis
father: **5** Nisus
lover: **5** Minos

scythe handle
5 snath **6** snathe

sea
4 blue, deep, main **5** brine, drink, ocean
Antarctica: **4** Ross **5** Davis **7** Weddell **8** Amundsen
Arctic: **4** Kara **7** Chukchi **8** Beaufort, Karskoye **9** Chuckchee, Norwegian **11** Chukotskoye **12** East Siberian
Asia-Europe: **5** Black
Asia Minor: **7** Icarian
Atlantic: **5** North **7** Weddell **9** Caribbean
Australia-Indonesia: **7** Arafura
Balkan Peninsula-Italy: **8** Adriatic
Bay of Bengal: **7** Andaman
China-Korea: **5** Huang, Hwang **6** Yellow
combining form: **3** mer **4** mari **5** pelag **6** pelago **7** thalass **8** thalasso
Corsica-Italy: **10** Tyrrhenian
Denmark-Norway: **9** Skagerrak
Denmark-Sweden: **8** Kattegat
England-Ireland: **5** Irish
Fiji: **4** Koro
France-Italy: **8** Ligurian
Greece: **5** Crete
Greece-Italy: **6** Ionian
Greece-Turkey: **6** Aegean **8** Thracian
Honshu: **6** Sagami
Indian Ocean: **5** Timor **7** Arabian
Indonesia: **4** Bali **6** Flores
inland: **3** Red **4** Aral **7** Caspian
Japan: **3** Suo **6** Inland
Kazakhstan: **4** Aral
Malay Archipelago: **5** Banda
Mexico: **6** Cortés
Netherlands: **6** Wadden
North Atlantic: **8** Sargasso
Northern Europe: **6** Baltic, Ostsee **8** Suevicum
North Pacific: **6** Bering
off Scotland: **8** Hebrides
off Sweden: **5** Aland
Pacific: **4** Java **5** China, Coral **6** Maluku **7** Celebes, Eastern, Molucca, Solomon **9** East China **10** South China
Philippine: **4** Sulu
Russia: **5** White **7** Okhotsk
Russia-Ukraine: **4** Azov
South Pacific: **4** Ross **6** Tasman **8** Amundsen
Turkey: **7** Marmara **9** Propontis
Uzbekistan: **4** Aral
West Pacific: **5** Ceram, Japan **8** Bismarck **10** Philippine

sea anemone
5 polyp

seabird
see **bird** *aquatic*

seacoast
5 beach, coast, shore **6** strand **8** littoral **9** shoreline

sea cucumber
7 trepang **11** holothurian

sea dog
see **sailor**

sea duck
5 eider, scaup **6** scoter **9** merganser

sea eagle
4 erne **6** osprey **8** fish hawk

seafarer
3 tar **4** salt **6** sailor **7** jack-tar, mariner

seafood dish
4 clam, crab **5** clams, squid **6** cockle, mussel,

oyster, scampi, shrimp **7** ceviche, lobster, mussels, oysters, scallop, seviche **8** calamari, scallops

seagoing
8 maritime, nautical

seal
5 sigil, stamp **6** cachet, signet **7** sticker
female: **3** cow
herd: **3** pod **5** patch
joint: **6** gasket
young: **3** pup

sealant
4 lute **5** caulk, grout **6** luting, mastic **8** caulking

sea lily
7 crinoid

seam
4 bond **5** joint, union **8** coupling, juncture **10** connection

seaman
see **sailor**

sea monster
3 Orc **6** kraken **9** leviathan

seamount
5 guyot

seamy
5 dirty, rough, seedy **6** sordid **7** squalid **12** disreputable

séance
7 meeting, session, sitting
holder: **6** medium

seaport
Alaska: **6** Juneau **9** Anchorage
Albania: **5** Vlorë **6** Durres, Valona
Algeria: **4** Bône, Oran **6** Annaba
Angola: **6** Lobito, Luanda **7** Cabinda **8** Benguela
Argentina: **11** Buenos Aires, Mar del Plata
Australia: **4** Eden **5** Bowen, Perth **6** Darwin, Hobart, Sydney **8** Brisbane **9** Melbourne **10** Wollongong
Azores: **5** Horta
Balearic: **5** Ibiza
Belgium: **6** Ostend **7** Antwerp
Benin: **7** Cotonou **9** Porto-Novo
Black Sea: **5** Varna **6** Burgas, Odessa **9** Constanta
Brazil: **3** Rio **4** Pará **5** Bahia, Belém, Natal **6** Recife, Santos **7** Vitoria **8** Salvador **9** Fortaleza **10** Pernambuco **11** Pôrto Alegre, São Salvador **12** Rio de Janeiro
Bulgaria: **5** Varna **6** Burgas
Cameroon: **6** Douala
Canaries: **8** Arrecife **9** Las Palmas
Chile: **5** Arica **8** Coquimbo **10** Valparaíso
China: **4** Amoy **6** Dalian, Fuzhou, Lüshun, Xiamen **7** Foochow, Hsia-men, Qingdao, Tianjin **8** Shanghai, Shenzhen, Tientsin, Tsingtao **9** Guangzhou, Zhenjiang **10** Chen-chiang, Port Arthur
Colombia: **6** Lorica **9** Cartagena **12** Barranquilla
Corsica: **5** Calvi **7** Ajaccio
Costa Rica: **5** Limón **10** Puntarenas
Crimean: **5** Kerch, Yalta **10** Sebastopol, Sevastopol
Croatia: **5** Rieka, Split **6** Rijeka **9** Dubrovnik
Cuba: **6** Havana **8** La Habana, Matanzas, Santiago
Cyprus: **9** Famagusta
Denmark: **5** Arhus **6** Aarhus, Alborg **7** Aalborg **8** Elsinore **10** Copenhagen
Ecuador: **9** Guayaquil
Egypt: **4** Said **10** Alexandria
England: **4** Hull **5** Dover **9** Liverpool **10** Portsmouth **11** Southampton
Equatorial Guinea: **4** Bata
Eritrea: **4** Aseb
Estonia: **5** Pärnu **7** Tallinn
Finland: **3** Abo **4** Kemi, Oulu, Pori, Vasa **5** Hango, Kotka, Rauma, Turku, Vaasa **6** Vyborg
Florida: **5** Miami, Tampa **9** Pensacola **12** Apalachicola, Jacksonville
France: **4** Nice **5** Brest, Havre **6** Calais, Cannes, Toulon **7** Dunkirk, Le Havre **8** Bordeaux, Boulogne **9** Cherbourg, Dunkerque, Marseille **10** Marseilles
French Polynesia: **7** Papeete
Georgia: **8** Savannah **9** Brunswick
Georgia, Republic of: **4** Pot'i
Germany: **4** Kiel **5** Emden **6** Bremen, Lübeck, Wismar **7** Hamburg, Rostock **8** Cuxhaven **11** Bremerhaven
Ghana: **4** Tema **5** Accra
Greece: **5** Pylos, Syros, Volos **7** Piraeus
Guatemala: **7** San José **10** Livingston
Haiti: **5** Cayes **10** Cap Haitien
Honduras: **7** La Ceiba **8** Trujillo
India: **3** Goa **4** Puri **5** Marud **6** Bombay, Madras, Mumbai, Old Goa **7** Calicut, Chennai **8** Calcutta **9** Jagannath **10** Trivandrum
Iran: **4** Jask **7** Bushehr
Iraq: **5** Basra
Ireland: **4** Cork **5** Sligo **6** Dingle, Dublin, Galway, Tralee **8** Drogheda, Limerick **9** Waterford **10** Balbriggan
Israel: **4** Acre, Akko, Elat, Yafo **5** Accho, Eilat, Haifa, Jaffa, Joppa **6** Ashdod **8** Ashqelon
Italy: **4** Bari **5** Anzio, Gaeta, Genoa **6** Genova, Naples, Napoli, Pesaro, Rimini, Venice **7** Leghorn, Livorno, Marsala, Messina, Rapallo, Salerno, Taranto, Trieste, Venezia **8** Brindisi, Siracusa, Sorrento, Syracuse

Ivory Coast: **5** Tabou **7** Abidjan
Jamaica: **8** Kingston **10** Montego Bay
Japan: **4** Kobe, Oita **5** Kochi, Osaka, Rumoi, Ujina, Uraga **6** Sasebo **7** Fukuoka **8** Nagasaki, Yokohama **9** Hiroshima
Java: **5** Tegal, Tuban **7** Cilacap, Jakarta **8** Semarang, Surabaya
Jordan: **5** Aqaba, Elath **6** Aelana
Latvia: **4** Riga
Lebanon: **4** Tyre **5** Saida, Sidon **6** Beirut **7** Tripoli
Libya: **6** Tobruk **7** Tripoli **8** Benghazi
Lithuania: **5** Memel **8** Klaipeda
Madagascar: **8** Tamatave
Maine: **7** Belfast **8** Portland
Malaysia: **4** Miri, Weld **5** Pekan **6** Melaka, Pinang **7** Malacca **10** George Town
Massachusetts: **6** Boston **9** Fall River **10** New Bedford
Mauritius: **9** Port Louis
Mediterranean: **4** Gaza, Oran **5** Genoa, Haifa, Jaffa **6** Beirut, Naples, Venice **7** Algiers, Bizerte, Catania, Palermo, Piraeus, Tripoli **8** Benghazi, Port Said **9** Barcelona, Marseille **10** Alexandria, Marseilles
Mexico: **7** Tampico **8** Acapulco, Mazatlán, Veracruz
Minorca: **5** Mahón
Moluccas: **5** Ambon
Montenegro: **5** Kotor
Morocco: **4** Safi, Salé **5** Ceuta **6** Agadir **7** Tangier, Tétouan **10** Casablanca
Mozambique: **5** Beira, Pemba **6** Amelia, Maputo, Xai Xai **11** Porto Amelia
New Hampshire: **10** Portsmouth
New Zealand: **8** Auckland **10** Wellington
Nicaragua: **5** Brito
Nigeria: **5** Lagos **8** Harcourt
Niger mouth: **5** Bonny
North Korea: **4** Yuki **5** Nampo, Unggi **6** Wonsan
Norway: **4** Bodo, Moss **5** Vadso **6** Bergen, Tromso **9** Stavanger, Trondheim **11** Fredrikstad
Oman: **6** Masqat, Muscat **7** Salalah
Pakistan: **5** Pasni **6** Gwadar **7** Karachi
Papua New Guinea: **3** Lea
Peru: **3** Ilo **4** Eten **5** Paita, Pisco **6** Callao
Philippines: **4** Cebu **5** Davao, Laoag **6** Aparri, Cavite, Iloilo, Manila **7** Legaspi **8** Tacloban **9** Zamboanga
Poland: **6** Danzig, Gdansk, Gdynia **7** Stettin **8** Szczecin
Portugal: **4** Faro **5** Porto **6** Oporto **7** Funchal, Setúbal
Puerto Rico: **5** Ponce **7** Arecibo, San Juan **8** Mayagüez
Russia: **6** Vyborg **8** Murmansk **11** Kaliningrad, Vladivostok
Ryukyu: **4** Naha, Nawa
Sakhalin Island: **8** Korsakov
Saudi Arabia: **5** Jedda, Jidda, Yanbu, Yenbo **6** Jeddah, Jiddah, Jubail
Scotland: **3** Ayr **5** Leith, Leven **6** Dundee **7** Glasgow **8** Aberdeen
Sicily: **7** Catania, Marsala, Messina, Palermo **8** Syracuse
Slovenia: **5** Kopar, Koper, Piran
Somalia: **7** Berbera **9** Mogadishu
South Africa: **5** Natal **6** Durban **8** Cape Town
South Carolina: **8** Savannah **10** Charleston
South Korea: **5** Masan, Mokpo, Pusan **6** Inchon **7** Incheon, Masampo
Spain: **4** Vigo **5** Cádiz, Gijón **6** Abdera, Málaga **8** Alicante **9** Algeciras, Barcelona, Cartagena, Las Palmas
Sri Lanka: **7** Colombo **10** Batticaloa
Sumatra: **5** Medan **6** Padang **9** Banda Aceh
Sweden: **4** Umea **5** Gavle, Lulea, Malmö, Pitea, Ystad **8** Göteborg **9** Stockholm **10** Gothenburg **11** Helsingborg
Tanzania: **5** Lindi, Tanga **8** Zanzibar **11** Dar es Salaam
Thailand: **4** Trat **8** Bang Phra
Tunisia: **4** Sfax **5** Gabès **6** Sousse **7** Bizerta, Bizerte
Turkey: **4** Rize **5** Izmir, Sinop **6** Samsun, Smyrna **7** Antalya **8** Istanbul
Ukraine: **5** Kerch, Yalta **6** Odessa **7** Kherson
Vanuatu: **4** Vila **8** Port-Vila
Vietnam: **3** Hue **6** Da Nang **7** Tourane **8** Haiphong, Nha Trang
Virginia: **7** Norfolk **10** Portsmouth
Yemen: **4** Aden **5** Mocha

seaport capital
4 Aden, Apia, Dili, Lomé, Suva **5** Accra, Adana, Dakar, Lagos **6** Banjul, Belize, Bissau, Dublin, Havana, Kuwait, Lisbon, Maputo, Masqat, Muscat, Roseau **7** Algiers, Batavia, Colombo, Jakarta, Moresby, San Juan **8** Castries, Djakarta, Freetown, Hamilton, Helsinki, Honolulu, Kingston, Monrovia, Valletta **9** Mogadishu, Nuku'alofa, Porto-Novo, Reykjavík, Singapore **10** Bridgetown, Daressalem, Libreville, Mogadiscio, Paramaribo **11** Dar es Salaam, Port of Spain **12** Port-au-Prince

sear
3 dry **5** brand, parch, singe **6** burn up, scorch, sizzle **7** shrivel **9** cauterize, dehydrate, desiccate

search
4 beat, comb, grub, hunt, scan, seek **5** chase, check, delve, frisk, grope, quest, rifle, scour **6** ferret, forage, google **7** fossick, hunting, manhunt, pursuit, ransack, rummage, run down **8** finecomb, scavenge, scout out **9** cast about, ferret out **10** scrutinize

searing
3 hot 5 harsh 6 severe 7 blazing, burning, intense 8 scathing 9 agonizing, scorching 10 blistering 12 excruciating

sea robber
5 rover 6 pirate 7 corsair 8 picaroon 9 buccaneer 10 freebooter

seasickness
6 nausea 8 mal de mer

season
3 fit 4 fall, term, time, Yule 5 spice, train, treat 6 autumn, flavor, harden, pepper, period, school, spring, summer, winter 7 prepare, toughen 8 marinade, marinate 9 acclimate, Christmas 10 case-harden, discipline 11 acclimatize

seasonable
3 apt 6 timely 7 welcome 9 favorable, opportune, pertinent, well-timed 10 auspicious, convenient, propitious 11 appropriate

seasoned
6 inured, mature, tested, versed 7 adapted, matured, veteran 8 flavored, hardened 9 flavorful, practiced 10 acclimated, habituated 11 experienced 12 acclimatized, accomplished

seasoning
3 bay 4 dill, herb, mace, sage, salt 5 anise, basil, chili, clove, cumin, spice, thyme 6 cloves, fennel, garlic, ginger, nutmeg, pepper, savory 7 cayenne, chervil, mustard, oregano, paprika, parsley, saffron 8 allspice, cardamom, cinnamon, rosemary, tarragon, turmeric 9 condiment, coriander

seat
3 hub 4 base, beam, duff, rear, rest, rump 5 basis, chair, place, usher 6 behind, bottom, center, settee 7 fulcrum 8 backside, buttocks, derriere 9 fundament, posterior 10 foundation
church: 3 pew
on a camel or elephant: 6 howdah
upholstered: 9 banquette

sea urchin
7 echinus 8 echinoid

seaweed
4 agar, alga, kelp, limu, nori, tang, ulva 5 dulse, fucus, kombu 6 fucoid, wakame 8 sargasso 9 carrageen, Irish moss 12 bladder wrack

Sea Wolf, The
author: 6 London (Jack)
captain: 10 Wolf Larsen
ship: 5 Ghost

Sebastian
brother: 6 Alonso
sister: 5 Viola

secco
3 dry 8 painting, staccato

secede
4 quit 5 leave 8 separate, withdraw

seclude
4 hide 6 closet, immure, retire, screen 7 confine, enclose, isolate, shut off 8 cloister, separate, withdraw 9 sequester

secluded
6 hidden, remote 7 private, recluse, shut off 8 hermetic, isolated, screened, solitary 9 concealed, reclusive, withdrawn 10 cloistered, tucked away 11 out-of-the-way, quarantined, sequestered

seclusion
7 privacy 8 solitude 9 isolation 10 separation, withdrawal

second
4 wink 5 flash, jiffy, place, trice 6 moment 7 endorse, instant, support 9 twinkling

secondary
3 sub 6 lesser 7 derived 8 borrowed, inferior 9 resultant, tributary 10 collateral, derivative, subsequent 11 subordinate, subservient

second-class
6 common 8 déclassé, inferior, low-grade, mediocre

secondhand
4 used, worn 7 derived 8 borrowed 10 derivative

second-string
3 sub 6 backup 9 alternate 10 substitute

secrecy
7 silence, stealth 10 covertness, subterfuge 11 concealment, furtiveness

secret
5 sneak 6 arcane, closet, covert, hidden, occult 7 cryptic, furtive, obscure, sub-rosa 8 abstruse, backdoor, discreet, hermetic, hush-hush, stealthy 9 concealed, recondite 10 classified, restricted, undercover 11 clandestine, out-of-the-way, underhanded 12 confidential, hugger-mugger 13 surreptitious, under-the-table
combining form: 5 crypt, krypt 6 crypto, krypto

secret agent
3 spy 8 emissary

secretary
4 aide, desk 5 clerk 6 scribe 9 assistant 10 amanuensis, escritoire
king's: 10 chancellor

Secretary-General
3 Ban (Ki-moon), Lie (Trygve) 4 Jebb (Gladwyn) 5 Annan (Kofi), Thant (U) 8 Waldheim (Kurt) 12 Boutros-Ghali (Boutros), Hammarskjöld (Dag)

secrete
4 bury, emit, hide 5 cache, exude, plant, stash 6 screen 7 conceal, deposit, emanate

secretion
3 pus **5** mucus

secretive
7 furtive **8** reticent, taciturn **10** backstairs, buttoned-up **11** tight-lipped **12** close-mouthed **13** unforthcoming

secretly
7 sub rosa **9** furtively **10** stealthily

secret police
East Germany: 5 Stasi
Soviet Union: 3 KGB, MGB, MVD **4** NKVD, OGPU **5** Cheka

secret society
3 KKK **4** tong **5** cabal, Mafia, Triad **6** Mau Mau, Yakuza **7** camorra **9** camarilla, Carbonari **10** Cosa Nostra, Freemasons, Ku Klux Klan

sect
4 cult **5** creed, party **7** faction **8** division, religion **12** denomination

sectarian
5 local **8** splinter **9** dissident, heretical, heterodox, parochial **10** provincial, schismatic, unorthodox **13** nonconformist

sectary
5 rebel **7** heretic **8** adherent, disciple, follower, partisan **9** dissenter, dissident **10** schismatic, separatist **13** nonconformist, revolutionary

section
3 cut **4** area, belt, part, unit, zone **5** chunk, piece, slice, tract **6** member, moiety, parcel, region, sector, sphere **7** portion, quarter, segment **8** district, division, locality, precinct **11** subdivision

sector
4 area, zone **7** quarter, section **8** district, precinct **11** subdivision

secular
3 lay **4** laic **7** earthly, profane, worldly **8** temporal, unsacred **11** nonclerical, terrestrial **12** nonreligious

secure
3 fix, ice, tie **4** bind, fast, firm, gain, land, lock, moor, nail, safe, seal **5** catch, cinch, clamp, cover, fixed, guard, solid, sound, tried **6** anchor, assure, cement, clinch, defend, effect, ensure, fasten, insure, obtain, shield, stable **7** acquire, assured, capture, procure, protect, tie down **8** reliable, sanguine **9** confident, safeguard **10** batten down, bring about **11** established, impregnable

security
4 bail, bond, pawn **5** guard, T-note, token **6** pledge, safety, shield, surety **7** defense, earnest, warrant **8** guaranty, immunity, warranty **9** assurance, guarantee, safeguard, soundness, stability **10** collateral, protection, steadiness **13** certification

sedate
4 calm **5** grave, sober, staid **6** placid, proper, seemly, serene, steady **7** earnest, serious **8** composed, decorous, tranquil **9** collected, dignified, unruffled **10** sobersided **13** dispassionate, imperturbable

sedative
4 balm **6** downer, Valium **7** calmant, Librium, Miltown, Seconal **8** barbital, hyoscine, Nembutal **9** calmative, soporific **10** depressant **11** barbiturate **12** sleeping pill, tranquilizer **13** tranquillizer

sedentary
4 lazy **6** seated **7** alluvia, settled, sitting **8** inactive **10** stationary

sediment
4 lees, silt **5** dregs, dross **7** bottoms, deposit, grounds, heeltap, residue **8** residuum **9** settlings **11** precipitate
layer: 5 varve

sedition
4 coup **6** mutiny, putsch, revolt, strike **7** protest, treason **8** intrigue, uprising **9** coup d'état, rebellion **10** revolution **12** insurrection

seditious
8 disloyal, factious, mutinous **9** dissident, insurgent **10** rebellious, traitorous **11** treacherous

seduce
4 bait, coax, lure **5** decoy, tempt **6** allure, betray, delude, entice, entrap, lead on, ravish **7** corrupt, debauch, deceive **8** entrance, inveigle

seducer
4 rake, roué, vamp **7** Don Juan, playboy **8** Casanova, lothario **9** libertine, womanizer **11** philanderer

seduction
4 lure **8** conquest **9** siren song **10** allurement, attraction, ravishment, temptation

seductive
5 siren **8** alluring, magnetic, tempting **9** beguiling **10** attractive, bewitching, enchanting **11** captivating

seductress
5 siren **7** Lorelei **9** temptress **11** femme fatale

sedulous
8 diligent, tireless **9** assiduous, laborious **10** persistent **11** industrious, persevering, unremitting

see
4 call, espy, gaze, look, mark, peer, scan, view **5** sight, watch **6** behold, descry, divine, notice,

take in **7** discern, find out, glimpse, make out, observe, realize **8** consider, envisage, envision, perceive **9** apprehend, ascertain, recognize, visualize

seed
3 pip, sow **4** core, germ **5** brood, grain, issue, ovule, plant, spark, spawn, spore **6** embryo, kernel, notion **7** concept, nucleus, progeny **8** children **9** offspring **11** descendants
aromatic: 5 anise **6** fennel
coating: 5 testa **6** testae (plural)
covering: 4 aril
of a bean: 7 haricot
of a vine: 6 peanut
poisonous: 10 castor bean
poppy: 3 maw
scar: 5 hilum
small: 3 pip
vessel: 3 pod **5** fruit, pyxis **7** silicle, silique

seedcase
3 pod **4** aril

seedy
5 dingy, faded, mangy, ratty, tired **6** droopy, frowsy, frowzy, shabby, used up, wilted **7** run-down, scruffy, squalid, unkempt, wilting **8** decaying, decrepit, drooping, flagging, inferior, slovenly, tattered **9** neglected, overgrown **10** bedraggled, down-at-heel, threadbare **12** disreputable

seek
3 try **4** fish, hunt, root **5** assay, delve, essay, offer, quest, sniff **6** pursue, strive **7** attempt, inquire, look for, request **8** endeavor, smell out **9** search for, search out, undertake

seem
3 act **4** look **5** imply **6** appear, behave **7** suggest **8** resemble

seemly
3 fit **6** decent, proper, suited **7** apropos, correct, fitting **8** becoming, decorous, suitable **9** befitting, congenial, congruous **10** compatible, conforming **11** appropriate, comme il faut

seep
4 drip, leak, ooze, weep **5** bleed, exude, leech, sweat **6** filter, strain **7** diffuse, dribble, trickle **8** transude **9** percolate

seer
5 augur, sibyl **6** oracle **7** diviner, prophet **8** foreseer, haruspex **9** predictor **10** forecaster, foreteller, soothsayer **11** clairvoyant, Nostradamus, vaticinator **13** fortune-teller

seesaw
3 yaw **4** rock, veer **5** lurch, pitch, swing **6** teeter **7** bascule **8** flip-flop **9** alternate, fluctuate, oscillate **11** teeterboard **12** teeter-totter

seethe
3 sop **4** boil, burn, foam, fret, fume, rage, soak, stew **5** churn, erupt, froth, souse, steam, steep **6** bubble, drench, simmer, sizzle **7** bristle, ferment, parboil, smolder **8** saturate, smoulder, waterlog

see-through
5 clear **6** limpid **8** pellucid **11** translucent, transparent

segment
3 bit, cut, lap, leg **4** clip, part **5** phase, piece **6** divide, member, moiety **7** portion, section **8** division, fragment, separate **10** categorize

sego
4 lily

segregate
6 enisle, select **7** isolate **8** separate **9** sequester **10** disconnect

segregation
9 apartheid, isolation **10** jim crowism, separatism **13** ghettoization

segue
7 proceed **8** continue **10** transition **11** progression

seidel
5 stoup **8** schooner

seine
3 net **5** trawl

Seine tributary
4 Oise **5** Marne, Yonne

seismologist
7 Richter (Charles)

seize
3 bag, nab **4** glom, grab, take **5** annex, catch, clasp, grasp, usurp **6** abduct, arrest, clinch, clutch, kidnap, occupy, secure, snatch **7** capture, grapple, impound **8** arrogate, carry off **9** apprehend, sequester **10** commandeer, confiscate **11** appropriate, expropriate

seizure
3 fit **4** turn **5** spasm, spell, throe **6** access, attack, taking **7** capture **8** paroxysm, takeover **9** breakdown **10** annexation, convulsion, usurpation **12** confiscation

seldom
6 hardly, rarely **8** scarcely **10** hardly ever **12** infrequently, occasionally, sporadically

select
4 best, cull, fine, pick, rare **5** A-list, cream, elite, prime **6** choice, choose, chosen, culled, opt for, picked **7** favored, pick out **8** screened, superior **9** exclusive, exquisite, preferred, recherché, single out

selection
6 choice 7 culling, excerpt, picking 8 choosing 10 assortment, preference

selective
5 fussy, picky 6 choosy 7 choosey, finicky 8 specific 10 discerning, particular, scrupulous 11 persnickety

Selene
4 Luna 6 Hecate 7 Artemis
beloved: 8 Endymion
brother: 6 Helios
father: 8 Hyperion
mother: 4 Thea
sister: 3 Eos

selenium symbol
2 Se

self
3 ego
combining form: 3 aut 4 auto

self-absorbed
4 smug 8 egoistic 9 conceited, egotistic 10 complacent, egocentric 11 egotistical, introverted 12 narcissistic 13 inner-directed

self-acting
9 automatic

self-assertive
4 bold 5 brash, pushy 6 cheeky 7 forward 8 cocksure, militant 9 audacious, obtrusive, officious 10 aggressive 11 impertinent, overweening 12 presumptuous

self-assurance
5 poise 6 aplomb 8 coolness 9 composure, sangfroid 10 confidence, equanimity 13 collectedness

self-assured
4 smug 6 poised 8 sanguine 9 confident

self-centered
9 conceited, egotistic 10 egocentric 11 egotistical 12 narcissistic

self-composed
4 calm 6 poised, serene 7 assured 9 collected, confident, possessed 10 controlled

self-confidence
5 poise 6 aplomb 9 assurance

self-confident
5 cocky 6 jaunty, poised 7 assured 8 sanguine

self-conscious
4 prim 5 stiff 6 formal, uneasy 7 awkward, stilted, studied 8 affected, mannered 9 contrived, ill at ease 10 artificial

self-contained
6 closed, formal 7 built-in 8 composed, enclosed, reserved, reticent 9 exclusive 10 restrained 11 independent

self-control
7 balance, dignity, reserve 9 restraint, stability, willpower 10 abstinence, constraint, discipline, temperance 11 forbearance

self-defense art
4 judo 6 aikido, karate, kung fu 7 jujitsu 9 tai kwan do

self-destruction
7 seppuku, suicide 8 felo-de-se, hara-kiri, hari-kari

self-discipline
4 will 8 stoicism 9 willpower 10 abstinence

self-educated
12 autodidactic

self-effacing
3 shy 5 timid 6 modest 7 bashful 8 retiring, sheepish 9 diffident, unassured 11 unassertive

self-esteem
5 pride 6 vanity 7 conceit, dignity, egotism 10 narcissism 11 amour propre

self-evident
5 clear, plain 6 patent 7 obvious 8 manifest, palpable 10 prima facie, undeniable 12 demonstrable, unmistakable
truth: 5 axiom

self-explanatory
5 clear, plain 7 evident, obvious 8 manifest 11 perspicuous, transparent

self-governing
7 popular 9 sovereign 10 autonomous, democratic

self-importance
3 ego 5 pride 6 egoism, hubris 7 conceit, egotism 9 arrogance, pomposity, vainglory

self-important
4 smug, vain 6 lordly 7 bloated, haughty, pompous 8 arrogant 9 conceited, egotistic 10 pontifical 11 magisterial, pretentious

self-indulgent
9 libertine, sybaritic 10 hedonistic

self-interest
6 egoism

selfish
6 stingy 8 egoistic 9 egotistic 10 egocentric, ungenerous 11 egomaniacal 12 self-centered 13 self-indulgent

selfless
8 generous 10 altruistic, benevolent, charitable

self-love
6 egoism, vanity 7 conceit, egotism 8 vainness 9 vainglory 10 narcissism 11 amour propre 13 conceitedness

self-possessed
4 calm **6** poised, serene **7** equable **8** composed, sanguine **9** collected, unruffled **11** unflappable **13** imperturbable

self-proclaimed
8 so-called **9** soi-disant **10** self-styled

Self-Reliance author
7 Emerson (Ralph Waldo)

self-respect
5 pride **7** dignity **11** amour propre

self-restraint
8 chastity, sobriety **9** willpower **10** abnegation, abstention, abstinence, continence, discipline **11** forbearance

self-righteous
5 pious **7** canting, preachy **8** unctuous **9** pharisaic **10** complacent, goody-goody **11** pharisaical **12** hypocritical, pecksniffian **13** sanctimonious

self-sacrificing
8 generous, selfless **9** unselfish

self-satisfied
4 smug **8** priggish **10** complacent

self-seeking
6 greedy **7** selfish **8** egoistic **9** egotistic **10** egocentric **11** egotistical

self-serving
see **self-seeking**

self-starter
7 hustler **8** go-getter

self-styled
7 nominal, would-be **8** so-called **9** soi-disant

self-taught
12 autodidactic

sell
4 hawk, vend **5** trade **6** barter, deal in, hustle, market, peddle, retail, unload **7** auction **8** exchange

sell out
4 dump, move **6** betray, turn in, unload **7** deceive **8** inform on **11** double-cross

selvage, selvedge
3 hem **4** edge **6** border

semblance
3 air **4** face, look, mask, pose, show, veil **5** front, guise, image **6** aspect, facade, simile, veneer **7** analogy, feeling, modicum **8** affinity, disguise, likeness, pretense **10** apparition, appearance, comparison, false front, masquerade, similarity, similitude, simulacrum **11** countenance

Semele
father: **6** Cadmus
mother: **8** Harmonia
sister: **3** Ino **5** Agave **7** Autonoë
son: **7** Bacchus **8** Dionysus

semi
3 rig **4** demi, half, hemi **5** truck **6** partly

seminar
5 forum **8** colloquy **10** colloquium, conference, roundtable

Seminole chief
7 Osceola

Semiramis
husband: **5** Ninus
kingdom: **7** Babylon

Semite
3 Jew **4** Arab **6** Hebrew **7** Moabite **8** Akkadian, Assyrian **9** Canaanite **10** Babylonian, Phoenician

Senapo
daughter: **8** Clorinda
kingdom: **8** Ethiopia

senate
7 chamber, council **8** assembly **11** legislature

senator
5 solon **8** lawmaker **10** legislator

send
4 mail, post, ship **5** relay, remit, route **6** commit, export, launch **7** address, advance, airmail, consign, forward, traject **8** dispatch, transmit
back: **6** remand

Sendak book
17 In the Night Kitchen **21** Where the Wild Things Are

send in
6 submit

send-up
5 roast, spoof **6** parody, satire **7** lampoon, takeoff **9** burlesque **10** caricature, pasquinade

Senegal
capital: **5** Dakar
enclave: **6** Gambia
ethnic group: **5** Wolof **6** Fulani **7** Malinke
language: **6** French
monetary unit: **5** franc
neighbor: **4** Mali **6** Guinea **10** Mauritania **12** Guinea-Bissau
river: **6** Gambia

senescence
6 old age **8** caducity **11** elderliness, senectitude

senility
6 dotage

senior
5 doyen, elder, older, prior **7** ancient, doyenne, oldster **8** higher-up, old-timer, superior **10** golden-ager
Sennacherib
domain: 7 Assyria
father: 6 Sargon
kingdom: 7 Assyria
slayer, son: 8 Sharezer **11** Adrammelech
sensation
4 bomb **5** éclat **6** marvel, tingle, wonder **7** feeling, miracle, prodigy, stunner **8** response **9** bombshell **10** impression, perception, phenomenon **13** consciousness
sensational
3 hot **5** boffo, juicy, lurid **6** purple, vulgar **7** tabloid **8** dramatic, exciting, fabulous, glorious, slambang, smashing, stunning **9** hunky-dory, marvelous, thrilling **10** astounding, impressive, incredible, remarkable, scandalous **11** astonishing, extravagant, outstanding, spectacular **12** electrifying
sense
3 wit **4** feel **5** sight, smell, taste, touch **6** divine, intuit, pick up **7** believe, discern, feeling, hearing, meaning, message, realize **8** consider, judgment, perceive, prudence **9** awareness, foresight, intuition **10** anticipate, cognizance, discretion, perception **12** intelligence, significance **13** comprehension, consciousness, understanding
sixth: 3 ESP
Sense and Sensibility author
6 Austen (Jane)
senseless
4 cold, numb **5** silly **6** absurd, numbed, simple, stupid **7** fatuous, foolish, idiotic, moronic, trivial, witless **8** benumbed, comatose, deadened, mindless **9** brainless, pointless **10** irrational **11** meaningless, purposeless, unconscious
senselessness
5 folly **7** inanity **8** insanity **9** absurdity, stupidity **12** illogicality
sense organ
3 ear, eye **4** nose, skin **6** tongue **8** receptor
sensibility
5 taste **7** emotion, feeling, insight **8** judgment, keenness **9** affection, awareness, sensation **11** discernment, penetration **12** appreciation
sensible
4 sage, sane, wise **5** solid, sound **6** astute, shrewd **7** logical, prudent, sapient **8** rational **9** judicious, objective, sagacious **10** reasonable
sensitive
4 keen, sore **5** aware, prone **6** liable, tender, touchy, tricky **7** feeling, nervous **8** delicate, sensible, sentient, ticklish **9** emotional **10** high-strung, perceptive, precarious, responsive **11** susceptible **13** understanding
sensitive plant
6 mimosa
family: 3 pea
sensual
4 lush **6** animal, carnal, earthy **7** fleshly, mundane, worldly **8** temporal **9** epicurean, luxurious, sybaritic **10** hedonistic, voluptuous **11** irreligious, unspiritual
sensuality
4 lust **6** desire, luxury **7** lechery, license **8** hedonism, lewdness, pleasure **9** carnality, depravity, eroticism, prurience **10** debauchery, degeneracy, immorality, indulgence, perversion, profligacy, sybaritism **11** dissipation **13** dissoluteness, gratification, salaciousness
sensuous
4 lush **6** carnal **7** fleshly **8** luscious **9** epicurean, luxurious, sybaritic **10** hedonistic, voluptuous **13** self-indulgent
sentence
3 rap **4** damn, doom **5** blame, judge **6** dictum, ordain, punish **7** adjudge, condemn, convict, verdict **8** decision, denounce, judgment, penalize **10** adjudicate, punishment
sententious
5 crisp, pithy, terse **7** concise, piquant, pointed **8** eloquent, pregnant, succinct **10** aphoristic, expressive, meaningful, moralistic, moralizing
sentient
5 alert, aware, savvy **7** knowing **8** sensible **9** attentive, cognizant, conscious, receptive, sensitive **10** conversant, discerning, perceptive, percipient, responsive **12** appreciative
sentiment
4 view **5** ethos **6** belief **7** emotion, feeling, leaning, opinion, passion, posture **8** penchant, position, tendency **9** affection, inclining, sensation **10** conception, conviction, partiality, persuasion, propensity **11** disposition, inclination, sensibility
sentimental
4 soft **5** corny, gooey, gushy, mushy, sappy, soupy, sweet **6** dreamy, drippy, slushy, sticky, sugary, syrupy, tender **7** cloying, gushing, insipid, maudlin, mawkish **8** bathetic, effusive, romantic **9** misty-eyed, nostalgic, schmaltzy **10** idealistic, lovey-dovey, moonstruck, namby-pamby, saccharine, soft-boiled **11** tear-jerking **12** affectionate
sentimentality
4 mush **8** schmaltz
sentinel
see **sentry**

sentry
5 guard, watch **6** picket **7** lookout **8** sentinel, watchman

separate
4 comb, only, part, sift, sole, sort **5** apart, sever, split **6** cut off, detach, divide, single, unique **7** asunder, diverse, divided, divorce, isolate, several, split up, unravel, various **8** alienate, detached, discrete, disjoint, distinct, insulate, isolated, solitary, splinter, uncouple **9** different, divergent, extricate, segregate **11** compartment, distinctive, distinguish, independent, unconnected **12** disconnected, discriminate **13** differentiate

separation
3 gap **4** rift **5** break, split **6** schism **7** breakup, divorce, parting, rupture, split-up **8** disunion, disunity, division **9** apartheid, dichotomy, partition **11** disjunction, dissolution, segregation **12** dissociation, estrangement **13** disconnection, sequestration

separatism
9 apartheid **11** segregation

separatist
10 schismatic **12** secessionist

sepia
3 ink **5** brown, umber **6** sienna

sepulchral
4 grim **5** bleak, grave **6** dismal, gloomy, solemn, somber **7** doleful, macabre **8** funereal, ghoulish, mortuary **9** tenebrous

sepulchre
4 tomb **5** grave, vault **9** mausoleum

sequel
3 end **5** close **6** effect, ending, finish, result, upshot **7** closing, outcome **8** epilogue **9** aftermath **10** succession **11** aftereffect, consequence, development, eventuality, progression, termination **12** continuation

sequence
3 row, run, set **4** flow **5** chain, order, train **6** course, series, string **8** disposal, ordering **9** placement **10** procession, succession **11** arrangement, disposition, progression **12** distribution

sequential
6 serial **9** succedent **10** continuous, succeeding, successive **11** consecutive **12** successional **13** chronological

sequester
4 hide, take **5** annex, seize **6** attach, cut off, enisle **7** impound, isolate, preempt, seclude, secrete **8** accroach, arrogate, cloister, close off, insulate, separate, set apart, withdraw **9** segregate **10** commandeer, confiscate, dispossess **11** appropriate, expropriate

sequoia
7 big tree, redwood **12** coast redwood

seraglio
5 harem

serape
5 shawl

seraph
5 angel **8** guardian **9** messenger

seraphic
4 pure **7** angelic, sublime **8** beatific, cherubic, ethereal

Serbia
capital: **8** Belgrade
city: **3** Bar, Niš **7** Novi Sad, Pancevo **10** Kragujevac
former leader: **9** Milošević (Slobodan)
monetary unit: **4** euro **5** dinar
neighbor: **6** Bosnia, Kosovo **7** Albania, Croatia, Hungary, Romania **8** Bulgaria **9** Macedonia **10** Montenegro
part of: **7** Balkans
peninsula: **6** Balkan
province: **9** Vojvodina
province, former: **6** Kosovo
river: **4** Sava **6** Danube
sea: **8** Adriatic

sere
3 dry **4** arid **5** dried **7** parched, thirsty **8** withered **9** shriveled, unwatered

serenade
7 lullaby **8** shivaree **9** charivari

serene
4 calm **5** quiet, still **6** limpid, placid, poised, sedate **7** halcyon **8** composed, tranquil **9** unruffled **10** untroubled

serenity
4 calm **5** peace **8** calmness, quietude **9** composure, placidity, stillness **10** equanimity **11** contentment, tranquility **12** peacefulness, tranquillity

serf
4 esne, peon **5** churl, helot, slave **6** thrall **7** bondman, villein
freeborn: **7** colonus

sergeant
3 NCO **6** noncom

serial
4 soap **10** sequential, successive **11** consecutive, installment

series
3 row, run, set **4** list, tier **5** chain, range, scale, train **6** catena, column, parade, sequel, string **8** sequence **9** cavalcade, gradation **10** procession, succession **11** progression **12** continuation

serious
4 grim, hard **5** grave, heavy, major, sober, staid, stern, tough **6** intent, sedate, severe, solemn, somber, sombre, steady **7** austere, earnest, intense, pensive, sincere, unfunny, weighty **8** funereal, menacing, resolute, sobering **9** difficult, humorless, important, laborious, strenuous, unamusing **10** determined, formidable, meditative, no-nonsense, poker-faced, purposeful, reflective, sobersided, thoughtful, unhumorous **11** significant, threatening **12** businesslike **13** contemplative

sermon
6 homily, speech, tirade **7** address, lecture, oration **8** harangue **9** preaching **10** preachment **11** exhortation

sermonize
5 orate **6** dilate, exhort, preach **7** dissert, lecture **8** moralize **9** discourse, expatiate, preachify **10** dissertate, evangelize **11** pontificate

serpent
5 fiend, Satan, snake
fabled: 8 basilisk
mythical: 10 cockatrice
sound: 4 hiss

serpentine
4 rock, wily **5** snaky **6** snakey **7** cunning, devious, mineral, sinuous, winding **8** flexuous, tempting, tortuous **9** snakelike **10** circuitous, convoluted, meandering

serrated
7 notched, toothed **8** saw-edged, sawtooth **10** saw-toothed **11** denticulate

servant
4 maid, peon **5** slave, valet **6** butler, flunky, helper, lackey, menial **7** famulus, footman **8** domestic, handmaid, hireling, houseboy **9** attendant **11** chamberlain, chambermaid
India: 4 syce
kitchen: 8 scullion
Wodehouse: 6 Jeeves

serve
3 act, fit, use **4** help, make, play, suit, work **5** avail, nurse, spend, treat **6** foster, handle, wait on **7** advance, benefit, care for, present, promote, provide, satisfy, suffice, work for **8** deal with, function **9** encourage, officiate **10** minister to

service
3 use **4** duty, help, rite **5** favor **6** employ, repair, ritual **7** account, benefit, fitness, liturgy **8** ceremony, courtesy, disposal, maintain **10** active duty, assistance, ceremonial, observance, usefulness **11** maintenance **12** dispensation

serviceable
5 handy, utile **6** decent, usable, useful **7** durable, helpful **8** adequate, suitable **9** efficient, practical **10** acceptable, beneficial, convenient, dependable, functional **11** utilitarian **12** satisfactory

servile
6 abject, craven, humble, menial **7** fawning, slavish **8** obedient, obeisant **9** groveling **10** obsequious, submissive **11** subservient

servility
7 bondage, helotry, peonage, serfdom, slavery **9** thralldom **11** enslavement

serving
6 dollop **7** helping, portion

servitude
5 labor **6** corvée, thrall **7** bondage, helotry, peonage, serfdom, slavery **9** captivity, indenture, thralldom, villenage **10** subjection **11** enslavement **12** enthrallment

sesame
3 til **4** teel
grass: 4 gama
seed paste: 6 tahini

Sesame Street
human character: 3 Bob, Tom **4** Alan, Gabi, Luis **5** David, Linda, Maria, Miles, Susan **6** Gordon, Savion **8** Mr. Hooper (Harold)
Muppet: 3 Zoe **4** Abby, Bert, Biff, Elmo **5** Count (The), Ernie, Oscar, Sully, Telly **6** Fluffy, Grover, Kermit, Rosita, Slimey, Snuffy **7** Barkley, Big Bird **9** Guy Smiley, Miss Piggy **13** Cookie Monster, Count von Count
puppeteer: 6 Henson (Jim)

sessile
5 fixed **6** rooted **7** settled **8** attached **11** established

session
6 assize, séance **7** meeting, sitting

set
3 aim, dry, fix, gel, lay, lot, put **4** firm, jell **5** array, batch, bunch, fixed, group, place, put on, ready, rigid, scene **6** belong, harden, impose, placed, rooted, secure, stated **7** arrange, certain, cluster, congeal, decided, deposit, dictate, jellify, lay down, located, prepare, scenery, situate, specify, station **8** prepared, resolute, resolved, situated, solidify, specific **9** confirmed, designate, establish, prescribe, specified, stipulate, tenacious **10** assortment, determined, gelatinize, inflexible, positioned, prescribed, stipulated **11** established, mise-en-scène
a gem: 6 collet
right: 7 redress

set aside
4 void **5** annul **7** discard, dismiss, reserve **8** overrule

set back
4 mire **5** delay **6** detain, hang up, hinder, retard, slow up

setback
4 snag **5** check, hitch **6** defeat, glitch, holdup, rebuff **7** reverse **8** obstacle, reversal **9** hindrance **10** impediment, regression

set down
4 land **5** light, perch, roost **6** alight, record **9** establish, touch down

set fire to
4 burn **5** light, spark **6** ignite, kindle **7** emblaze, inflame **8** enkindle, touch off

set forth
4 cite **5** state **6** adduce, affirm, allege, avouch, depart, embark, launch, submit **7** advance, declare, express, present, proffer, propose, take off **8** proclaim, spell out **9** introduce **10** account for

set free
5 loose **6** redeem, rescue, unbind **7** deliver, manumit, unchain, unloose **8** liberate, unloosen **9** unshackle **10** emancipate

Seth
brother: **4** Abel, Cain
father: **4** Adam
mother: **3** Eve
son: **4** Enos

set out
5 start **6** embark, intend **7** take off **9** undertake

Set
brother: **6** Osiris
mother: **3** Nut
opponent: **5** Horus
victim: **6** Osiris

settee
4 seat, sofa **5** bench, divan **6** lounge

setting
5 scene **7** context, scenery **8** ambience **10** background **11** mise-en-scène
for a stone: **4** ouch

settle
3 fix, lay, pay, put **4** calm, sink **5** allay, judge, light, pay up, perch, place, quiet, roost, still **6** alight, clinch, decide, soothe, square, verify, wind up **7** arrange, clarify, compose, confirm, dispose, install, mediate, resolve, satisfy, work out **8** colonize, conclude, ensconce, nail down **9** determine, discharge, establish, negotiate, reconcile, touch down

settlement
4 deal, mise **6** colony, hamlet **7** outpost, quietus, village **8** decision **9** agreement **10** conclusion, encampment, habitation, resolution **11** arrangement **13** determination
Israeli: **6** moshav

settler
7 pioneer **8** colonist, squatter **9** colonizer

set-to
3 row **4** fray, spat **5** brawl, broil, brush, fight, run-in, scrap **6** affray, blowup, fracas, tussle **7** dispute, quarrel, rhubarb, scuffle **8** argument, skirmish **9** encounter **10** falling-out **11** altercation

set up
4 open **5** erect, found, raise, start **6** create, launch **7** arrange, install **8** assemble, generate, initiate, organize **9** construct, establish, institute, originate

setup
4 plan, trap **5** array, trick **6** layout, scheme, shoo-in **7** pattern, project, setting **8** assembly, carriage, position, slam dunk **9** alignment, apparatus, structure, sure thing **11** arrangement, preparation **12** constitution

Seuss, Dr.
6 Geisel (Theodore)
character: **6** Grinch, Horton, Sam-I-Am, Yertle
work: **11** Cat in the Hat (The) **15** Green Eggs and Ham, Horton Hears a Who, Yertle the Turtle

seven
combining form: **4** hept, sept **5** hepta, septi
group of: **6** heptad **8** hebdomad

seventeenth century
8 seicento

sever
3 cut, lop **4** part, rend **5** slice, split **6** cleave, cut off, detach, divide, lop off, sunder **7** break up, divorce **8** amputate, disjoint, separate

several
4 a few, many, some **6** divers, plural, sundry, varied **7** certain, diverse, various **8** assorted, discrete, distinct, manifold, numerous, separate, specific **9** different **10** respective

severe
4 dour, grim, hard **5** acute, grave, harsh, heavy, rigid, sober, stern, tough **6** bitter, brutal, rugged, strict **7** arduous, ascetic, austere, extreme, intense, onerous, serious, weighty **8** exacting, pitiless, rigorous **9** demanding, difficult, laborious, strenuous, stringent, unbending **10** forbidding, implacable, inflexible, iron-willed, oppressive, unyielding **11** disciplined, heavy-handed

severity
5 rigor **7** gravity, urgency **8** exigency, grimness, obduracy, rigidity **9** austerity, harshness, intensity, plainness, privation, restraint, spareness, starkness, sternness **10** strictness, stringency **11** seriousness

sew
4 darn, mend, seam **5** baste **6** needle, stitch, suture

Seward's Folly
6 Alaska

sewer
4 duct **5** ditch, drain **6** tailor **7** cesspit, conduit **8** cesspool, stitcher

sewing
aid: **7** thimble
case: **4** etui
kit: **9** housewife

sewing-machine inventor
4 Howe (Elias)

sew up
3 ice **4** darn, mend, seal **5** patch **6** clinch, decide, ensure, secure, settle, stitch, tailor **7** confirm **8** complete, conclude, finalize, nail down **9** determine

sexless
6 neuter **7** epicene **8** neutered

sex manual
9 Kama-sutra

sexton
6 deacon **9** custodian, sacristan

sexual
4 blue, lewd, racy **6** carnal, erotic, ribald, risqué, smutty **7** obscene **8** venereal **9** salacious **12** pornographic

sexual desire
4 eros, lust **6** libido

sexy
4 blue, racy **5** bawdy, spicy **6** erotic, purple, ribald, risqué, steamy, sultry **7** naughty **8** alluring, off-color, sensuous **9** appealing, salacious, seductive **10** attractive, suggestive

Seychelles
capital: **8** Victoria
island: **4** Mahé **7** La Digue, Praslin
language: **6** Creole, French
monetary unit: **5** rupee

Sganarelle
brother: **6** Ariste
daughter: **7** Lucinde
ward: **7** Leonore **8** Isabelle
wife: **7** Martine

shabby
5 dingy, dowdy, faded, mangy, ratty, seedy, sorry, tacky, tatty, tired **6** frayed, scurvy, shoddy, sleazy, sordid **7** outworn, rickety, run-down, scrubby, scruffy, squalid, worn-out **8** beggarly, decaying, decrepit, dog-eared, tattered **9** miserable, moth-eaten, neglected, worm-eaten **10** bedraggled, down-at-heel, ramshackle, threadbare **11** dilapidated **12** deteriorated, disreputable **13** deteriorating, unrespectable

shack
3 cot, hut **4** camp, shed **5** cabin, hovel, lodge **6** shanty **7** cottage

shackle
4 gyve **5** bilbo, chain, leash, strap **6** fetter, hobble, hog-tie, impede, pinion, secure **7** enchain, leg-iron, manacle, trammel **8** handcuff **9** entrammel

shad
7 clupeid, herring

shade
3 bit, hue, tad **4** cast, tint, tone, veil **5** ghost, tinge, trace, umbra **6** awning, darken, nuance, screen **7** dimness, eclipse, phantom, shelter, specter, spectre, umbrage **8** darkness, penumbra, phantasm, tincture **9** gradation, intensity, obscurity **10** apparition **11** distinction

shadow
3 dim, dog, tag **4** haze, hint, tail **5** cloud, shade, tinge, touch, trace, trail, umbra **6** screen, spirit, wraith **7** eidolon, obscure, phantom, specter, umbrage, vestige **8** overcast, penumbra, phantasm, revenant, tincture **9** inumbrate, overcloud, suspicion **10** apparition, intimation, suggestion **11** adumbration

shadowy
3 dim **4** dark **5** dusky, faint, murky, vague **6** gloomy, shaded **7** ghostly, obscure **9** tenebrous **10** indistinct

shady
4 dark **5** bosky, dusky, fishy **6** purple, shabby, shoddy **7** clouded, dubious, suspect **8** doubtful, screened **9** equivocal, sheltered, uncertain **10** suggestive, suspicious, umbrageous, unreliable **12** disreputable

Shaffer play
5 Equus **7** Amadeus

shaft
3 jab, ray, rod **4** axle, barb, beam, dart, pole, stem **5** arrow, lance, shoot, spear, stalk, thill **6** thrust **7** chimney, spindle **8** short end

shag
3 nap, rug **4** pile **5** chase, fetch **7** thicket, tobacco **9** cormorant

shaggy
5 bushy **7** unkempt **8** uncombed

shake
3 jar, jog, rid **4** deal, jerk, jolt, lose, rock, roil, sway **5** avoid, churn, daunt, elude, jiffy, quake, shock, waver, worry **6** escape, frappe, jiggle, joggle, quaver, quiver, shimmy, shiver, tremor **7** agitate, shingle, shudder, temblor, tremble, unnerve, vibrate **8** brandish, convulse, unsettle **9** palpitate **10** earthquake

shake down
5 frisk, gouge, screw, wrest, wring **6** coerce, extort, fleece, search **7** squeeze **9** blackmail

shakedown
3 bed **4** test **5** dance, trial **6** pallet, search,

tryout **7** pursuit, testing **8** exaction **9** blackmail, extortion **10** inspection

Shaker leader
3 Lee (Ann) **9** Mother Ann

Shakespearean actor
4 Kean (Edmund) **5** Booth (Edwin), Dench (Judi), Evans (Maurice), Terry (Ellen) **6** Irving (Henry), Jacobi (Derek) **7** Branagh (Kenneth), Burbage (Richard), Garrick (David), Gielgud (John), Olivier (Laurence), Siddons (Sarah) **8** Ashcroft (Peggy), Macready (William), McKellen (Ian), Redgrave (Michael), Scofield (Paul) **9** Barrymore (Ethel, John, Lionel, Maurice) **10** Richardson (Ralph)

Shakespeare, William
4 bard
character: **3** Hal **4** Doll (Tearsheet), Hero, Iago, Kent, Lear, Puck **5** Ariel, Edgar, Feste, Harry, Percy (Henry), Poins (Ned), Regan, Romeo, Timon, Titus (Andronicus), Viola **6** Antony, Banquo, Bottom, Brutus, Caesar, Cassio, Duncan, Edmund, Emilia, Fabian, Hamlet, Hecate, Hermia, Jaques, Juliet, Oberon, Olivia, Orsino, Pistol, Portia **7** Antonio, Caliban, Cassius, Claudio, Fleance, Goneril, Horatio, Hotspur, Jessica, Laertes, Lavinia, Macbeth, Macduff, Malcolm, Miranda, Ophelia, Orlando, Othello, Perdita, Shylock, Sir Toby (Belch), Theseus, Titania, Troilus **8** Bassanio, Beatrice, Benedick, Claudius, Cordelia, Cressida, Dogberry, Falstaff (Sir John), Gertrude, Hermione, Lysander, Malvolio, Mercutio, Mortimer, Pericles, Polonius, Prospero, Rosalind **9** Cleopatra, Cymbeline, Demetrius, Desdemona, Hippolyta, Katherine, Petruchio, Sir Andrew (Aguecheek), Vincentio **10** Fortinbras, Holofernes **11** Bolingbroke, John of Gaunt, Lady Macbeth, Lady Macduff, Peter Quince **13** Queen Gertrude, Queen Margaret
contemporary: **6** Jonson (Ben) **7** Marlowe (Christopher)
forest: **5** Arden
mother: **9** Mary Arden
play: **6** Hamlet, Henry V **7** Henry IV, Henry VI, Macbeth, Othello, Tempest (The) **8** King John, King Lear, Pericles **9** Cymbeline, Henry VIII, Richard II **10** Coriolanus, Richard III **11** As You Like It, Winter's Tale (The) **12** Julius Caesar, Twelfth Night **13** Timon of Athens **14** Comedy of Errors (The), Romeo and Juliet **16** Love's Labour's Lost, Merchant of Venice (The), Taming of the Shrew (The) **17** Measure for Measure **18** Antony and Cleopatra **19** Much Ado About Nothing **20** All's Well That Ends Well, Midsummer Night's Dream (A)
theater: **5** Globe
wife: **12** Anne Hathaway

shaky
4 weak **6** infirm, unsure, wobbly **7** aquiver, dubious, jittery, quaking, rackety, rickety, suspect, trembly, unsound **8** doubtful, insecure, rachitic, unstable, unsteady, wavering **9** quivering, tottering, trembling, tremulous, uncertain, unsettled **10** indecisive, precarious, rattletrap, unreliable **11** problematic, vacillating

shale
4 rock **5** slate

shallot
4 herb **5** onion **10** green onion

shallow
4 idle, vain **5** petty, shoal **7** cursory, sketchy, trivial **8** trifling **9** depthless, frivolous **11** perfunctory, superficial

shallows
6 lagoon, shoals

Shallum
father: **5** Shaul, Zadok **6** Jabesh, Josiah, Sismai, Tikvah **8** Colhozeh, Naphtali **9** Hallohesh
mother: **6** Bilhah
nephew: **8** Jeremiah
slayer: **7** Menahem
son: **6** Mibsam **7** Hilkiah **8** Maaseiah
victim: **9** Zechariah

shalom
5 peace

sham
3 act, ape **4** fake, hoax, mock **5** bluff, bogus, bunco, cheat, dummy, false, farce, feign, fraud, phony, pseud, put on, spoof **6** deceit, ersatz, facade, fakery, forged, invent, pseudo **7** assumed, feigned, forgery, imitate, mislead, mockery, pretend **8** affected, flimflam, simulate, spurious, travesty **9** brummagem, burlesque, deception, hypocrisy, imitation, imposture, pinchbeck, simulated **10** artificial, caricature, false front, fictitious, fraudulent, sanctimony, substitute **11** counterfeit, make-believe **12** pecksniffery
combining form: **5** pseud **6** pseudo

shaman
6 healer, priest, wizard **7** diviner **8** conjurer, conjuror, magician, sorcerer **9** enchanter, priestess **10** high priest, soothsayer **11** faith healer, necromancer, thaumaturge, witch doctor

Shamash
6 sun-god
father: **3** Sin
sister: **6** Ishtar
wife: **3** Aya

shamble
see **shuffle**

shambles
4 mess 5 chaos 6 jumble, muddle 8 disarray, disorder, wreckage 9 confusion

shame
4 pity 5 abash, guilt, odium 6 infamy, stigma 7 chagrin, mortify, obloquy, remorse, scandal 8 disgrace, dishonor, ignominy 9 disrepute, embarrass, humiliate, ill repute 10 opprobrium 11 humiliation 12 self-reproach 13 embarrassment, mortification

shamefaced
7 abashed 8 blushing, sheepish 9 mortified 10 humiliated 11 crestfallen, embarrassed

shameless
6 arrant, brazen, wanton 7 blatant, immoral 8 depraved, flagrant, immodest, impudent 9 abandoned, bald-faced, barefaced, dissolute, unabashed 10 outrageous, profligate, unblushing 11 brazen-faced, disgraceful 12 presumptuous

Shammah
brother: 5 David
father: 4 Agee 5 Jesse, Reuel
grandfather: 4 Esau 7 Ishmael
son: 7 Jonadab 8 Jonathan

Shammua
father: 5 David, Galal 6 Bilgah, Zaccur
mother: 9 Bathsheba
son: 4 Abda

shamus
3 cop 4 dick, tail 6 copper, shadow, sleuth 7 gumshoe 8 flatfoot, sherlock 9 constable, detective, operative, policeman 10 private eye 12 investigator 13 police officer

shanghai
6 abduct, hijack, kidnap

Shangri-la
5 Tibet 6 utopia 7 arcadia 8 paradise 9 Cockaigne, fairyland 10 wonderland

shank
3 leg 4 shin, stem 5 stalk, tibia

shanty
3 cot, hut 4 camp, shed 5 cabin, hovel, lodge, shack 7 cottage

shape
3 fit 4 case, cast, form, mold, plan, trim 5 forge, frame, state, whack 6 aspect, devise, fettle, figure, kilter, repair, sculpt, tailor, work up 7 contour, fitness, outline, pattern, profile 8 assemble 9 condition, construct, fabricate, semblance 10 appearance, silhouette 12 conformation 13 configuration
combining form: 5 morph 6 morpho
dark: 6 shadow 10 silhouette

shapeable
6 pliant, supple 7 ductile, plastic, pliable 8 flexible 9 tractable

shapeless
8 inchoate, unformed 9 amorphous

shapely
4 trim 5 buxom 9 Junoesque 10 curvaceous, statuesque, well-turned 11 clean-limbed

shard
4 chip 5 chunk, scale, scrap, shell 6 sliver 7 elytron 8 carapace, fragment

share
3 cut, lot 4 part 5 chunk, claim, quota, slice, stake 6 divide, parcel, ration 7 dole out, give out, helping, partake, portion, prorate, quantum 8 dispense, fraction, interest, quotient 9 allotment, allowance, apportion 10 experience, percentage, proportion 11 participate

shared
5 joint 6 common, mutual, public 8 communal, conjoint, conjunct 9 concerted 10 collective 11 cooperative

Sharezer
father, victim: 11 Sennacherib

shark
5 cheat 8 swindler
kind: 4 gata, mako, sand, tope 5 nurse, tiger 7 basking, dogfish, leopard 8 mackerel, maneater, thresher 9 porbeagle 10 great white, hammerhead
skin: 8 shagreen

sharp
3 sly 4 acid, keen, tony, trig 5 acerb, acrid, acute, alert, canny, crisp, honed, quick, slick, smart, swank 6 astute, biting, brainy, bright, clever, jagged, nimble, peaked, shrewd, shrill, snappy, snazzy 7 caustic, dashing, intense, pointed, prickly, stylish, whetted 8 clean-cut, clear-cut, incisive 9 brilliant, ingenious, knifelike, vitriolic 10 astringent, perceptive 11 intelligent, penetrating, quick-witted, resourceful

sharpen
4 edge, file, hone, whet 5 grind, strop

sharper
6 con man 7 diddler 8 chiseler, swindler 9 defrauder, trickster 10 mountebank 12 double-dealer

sharp-eyed
4 keen 5 alert 8 vigilant, watchful 9 attentive, observant 10 discerning, perceptive

sharpie
see **sharper**

sharpness
4 edge 6 acuity, acumen 9 precision

sharpshooter
6 sniper **7** deadeye **8** marksman

sharp-sighted
8 hawk-eyed, lynx-eyed **9** eagle-eyed

sharp-witted
4 keen **5** acute, canny, quick, smart **6** astute, clever, shrewd **11** intelligent

shatter
4 dash **5** break, burst, crush, smash **6** shiver **8** demolish, fragment, splinter **9** pulverize **10** annihilate **11** fragmentize **12** disintegrate

shatterable
7 brittle, fragile **9** breakable, frangible

shave
3 cut **4** clip, crop, pare, peel, skim, trim **5** lower, plane, prune, shear, skive **6** barber, cut off, deduct, reduce, scrape, sliver **7** cut back, whittle **8** mark down

shaver
3 boy, kid, lad, tad **4** tike, tyke **5** child, razor **6** barber, laddie, squirt **9** stripling, youngster

shawl
4 wrap **5** fichu, manta **6** afghan, chador, serape **7** tallith **8** mantilla

shawm's descendant
4 oboe

Shawnee chief
8 Tecumseh, Tecumtha **9** Cornstalk

Shaw play
6 Geneva **7** Candida **9** Pygmalion, Saint Joan **11** Misalliance **12** Major Barbara **13** Arms and the Man

shay
6 chaise **8** carriage

shear
3 cut, mow **4** clip, crop, pare, snip, trim **5** prune, shave, skive **6** barber

shears
8 scissors

shearwater
4 bird **6** petrel **7** skimmer

sheath
4 case, skin **5** cover **7** holster **8** scabbard

sheathe
4 case, clad, face, side, skin, wrap **5** cover, panel **6** encase, jacket

Sheba
father: 6 Bichri
queen: 6 Balkis

shebang
4 mess **6** affair **7** schmear **8** business, caboodle **9** ball of wax, enchilada

shed
3 hut **4** cast, doff, drop, emit, molt **5** exude, hovel, hutch, scrap, shack, stall **6** divest, lean-to, reject, slough **7** cast off, diffuse, discard, radiate, take off **8** jettison, throw out **9** throw away

sheen
5 glaze, gleam, glint, gloss, shine **6** finish, luster, lustre, polish **7** burnish, glitter, shimmer **8** radiance **9** shininess **10** brightness

sheeny
see **shiny**

sheep
5 ovine
breed: 5 Tunis **6** Dorper, Dorset, Exmoor, Merino, Navajo, No-Tail, Oxford, Panama, Romney **7** Cheviot, Colbred, Karakul, Lincoln, Ryeland, Suffolk **8** Columbia, Cotswold, Polwarth **9** Hampshire, Leicester, Montadale, Southdown **10** Corriedale, Debouillet **11** Rambouillet
coat: 4 wool **6** fleece
disease: 3 gid, orf
female: 3 ewe
genus: 4 Ovis
male: 3 ram **6** wether
meat: 6 mutton
relating to: 5 ovine
Scottish: 9 blackface
sound: 5 bleat
tender: 8 shepherd
wild: 3 sha **5** urial **6** aoudad, argali, bharal **7** bighorn, mouflon
young: 4 lamb

sheepish
4 meek **5** timid **7** abashed, ashamed, bashful **8** timorous **9** diffident **10** shamefaced **11** embarrassed

sheepskin
4 roan **6** mouton **7** diploma **9** parchment
prepare: 3 taw

sheer
4 pure, skew, thin, turn, veer **5** filmy, gauzy, steep, utter **6** abrupt, arrant, flimsy, simple, swerve **7** chiffon, deflect, deviate, perfect, unmixed **8** absolute, complete, gossamer, outright **9** out-and-out, unalloyed, undiluted **10** diaphanous, see-through **11** precipitate, precipitous, transparent, unmitigated

sheet
3 ply **4** film, leaf, page, sail, slab **5** cover, linen, paper **6** lamina, veneer **8** membrane **9** newspaper

sheet ___
3 ice **4** film **5** glass, metal, music **6** anchor

shelf
3 hob **4** bank, edge, reef, sill **5** ledge, shoal **6** mantel **7** counter **8** sandbank

shell
3 pod **4** boat, bomb, case, hull, husk, rake, skin **5** blitz, conch, shuck **6** pepper **7** bombard, capsule, grenade, mollusc, mollusk **8** carapace **9** cannonade, cartridge
defective: **3** dud
explosive: **4** bomb
layer: **5** nacre
ornamental: **6** cowrie
study: **10** conchology

shellac
4 beat, drub, flay, lick, rout, trim, whap, whip, whop, whup **5** resin, smear, whomp **6** defeat, thrash **7** clobber, smother, trounce **8** lambaste, vanquish

Shelley, Percy Bysshe
friend: **5** Byron (Lord), Keats (John)
poem: **5** Cloud (The) **7** Adonais, Alastor **8** Queen Mab **10** Ozymandias, To a Skylark **16** Ode to the West Wind
wife: **4** Mary

shellfish
4 clam, crab **5** conch, cowry, prawn, snail, whelk **6** cockle, limpet, mussel, oyster, quahog, triton **7** abalone, crawdad, geoduck, lobster, mollusc, mollusk, scallop **8** barnacle, crayfish, escargot **10** crustacean, periwinkle

shell out
3 pay **4** give **5** spend **8** fork over, hand over

shell-shaped
6 spiral **9** cochleate

shelter
3 den, hut, lee **4** cote, fold, hide, port, roof, shed, tent **5** bower, cloak, cover, haven, house, shack **6** asylum, burrow, covert, defend, harbor, refuge, shield **7** defense, foxhole, hideout, hospice, housing, lodging, pillbox, protect, retreat **8** hideaway, hidy-hole, security **9** dwellings, hermitage, hidey-hole, sanctuary
for aircraft: **6** hangar
for cows: **4** barn, byre
toward: **4** alee

shelve
4 dish, drop, stay, tilt **5** defer, delay, slope, stock, waive **6** freeze, give up, hold up, put off **7** hold off, suspend **8** hold over, mothball, postpone, prorogue, set aside

Shem
brother: **3** Ham **7** Japheth
father: **4** Noah

Shema's father
4 Joel **6** Hebron

Shemida's father
6 Gilead

shenanigan
4 dido, lark **5** antic, caper, prank, stunt, trick **6** frolic **8** escapade, mischief **10** tomfoolery **11** monkeyshine

Sheol
see **hades**

shepherd
4 lead, show, tend **5** guide, pilot, route, steer, watch **6** direct, escort, leader **7** conduct **8** guardian
dog: **6** collie **12** border collie
stick: **5** crook, staff

Sheridan, Richard Brinsley
character: **8** Bob Acres, Malaprop (Mrs.) **10** Lady Teazle **13** Lady Sneerwell, Lydia Languish
play: **6** Critic (The), Rivals (The) **7** Pizarro **16** School for Scandal (The)

sheriff
5 reeve **6** lawman **7** marshal, officer
aide: **6** deputy

sherlock
4 dick, tail **5** snoop **6** shadow, shamus, sleuth **7** gumshoe **8** hawkshaw **9** detective **10** private eye **12** investigator

Sherlock Holmes
address: **11** Baker Street
creator: **5** Doyle (Arthur Conan)
sidekick: **6** Watson (Dr.)

sherry
4 fino, wine **7** oloroso **10** manzanilla **11** amontillado

shibboleth
3 saw, tag **5** axiom, maxim **6** byword, cliché, phrase, saying, slogan, truism **7** bromide **8** banality, chestnut, password, prosaism **9** catchword, platitude, watchword **11** catchphrase, commonplace

shield
4 fend, roof, ward **5** aegis, armor, cover, guard, haven, house, pavis **6** buffer, defend, harbor, screen, secure **7** buckler, bulwark, defense, protect, shelter **8** defilade **9** safeguard **10** escutcheon
band: **4** fess
bullfighter's: **9** burladero
light: **5** targe
part: **4** boss, umbo **7** bordure
Roman: **7** testudo

shield-like
7 peltate

shift
3 yaw **4** bend, bout, move, stir, tack, time, tour, turn, vary, veer **5** alter, budge, get by, spell, stint, trick **6** change, make do, manage, remove,

resort, swerve **7** deviate, replace, shuffle, stopgap **8** get along, relocate, resource, transfer **9** deviation, expedient, fluctuate **10** alteration, changeover, conversion, transition **11** fluctuation

shiftless
4 idle, lazy **5** inept **8** feckless, indolent, slothful **11** inefficient

shifty
3 sly **4** foxy, wily **5** cagey, lying, shady, slick **6** crafty, sneaky, tricky **7** cunning, devious, elusive, evasive, furtive **8** guileful, slippery, sneaking **9** conniving, deceitful, deceptive, dishonest, insidious, underhand **10** inconstant, untruthful **11** duplicitous, underhanded **12** equivocating

shill
5 blind, decoy, pitch **6** capper **8** promoter **10** accomplice, sales pitch

shillelagh
3 bat **4** club, cosh, mace **5** baton, billy, stick **6** cudgel **8** bludgeon **9** bastinado, billy club, blackjack, truncheon **10** nightstick

shilling
3 bob

shilly-shally
5 fudge, hedge, stall, waver **6** dawdle, dither, waffle **7** whiffle **8** hesitate **9** temporize, vacillate **11** prevaricate **12** tergiversate

Shimea
brother: **5** David
father: **5** David, Jesse
son: **7** Jonadab **8** Jonathan

shimmer
5 flash, gleam, glint, sheen **6** luster, lustre **7** glimmer, glisten, glitter, spangle, sparkle, twinkle **9** coruscate **11** coruscation, scintillate **13** scintillation

shimmy
5 dance, shake **6** quiver, shiver, tremor **7** chemise, shudder, tremble, vibrate **9** vibration

shin
3 run **4** dash **5** scoot, tibia **6** scurry, sprint **7** scamper

shindig
4 ball, bash, fête, gala **5** binge, dance, party, revel **6** affair, frolic **7** blowout **8** wingding

shine
3 ray, rub **4** beam, buff, burn, glow **5** blaze, flare, flash, glare, glaze, gleam, glint, gloss, sheen **6** luster, lustre, polish **7** burnish, glimmer, glisten, glitter, radiate, shimmer, sparkle, twinkle **9** luminesce **10** incandesce

shiner
4 fish **8** black eye, cyprinid

shingle
5 beach, coast, shore **7** haircut, overlap, overlay **8** detritus **9** signboard

shiny
6 agleam, bright, glossy **7** fulgent, radiant **8** dazzling, gleaming, lustrous, polished **9** burnished, effulgent **10** glistening

ship
4 boat, send **5** remit, route **6** export **7** consign, forward, freight **8** dispatch, transfer, transmit
ancient: **6** bireme, galley **7** galleon, trireme
attendant: **7** steward
beam: **7** keelson
berth: **4** dock, slip
boat: **6** dinghy **7** lighter
body: **4** hull
cabin: **9** stateroom
commercial: **5** liner, oiler **6** argosy, tanker, trader **9** freighter
crew member: **4** hand, mate **6** sailor
deck: **4** boat, main, poop **5** orlop **6** bridge **10** forecastle
fishing: **6** lugger **7** trawler
fleet: **6** armada
floor: **4** deck
front: **3** bow **4** prow, stem **8** cutwater
hoister: **4** boom **5** davit **7** capstan
kitchen: **6** galley
left side: **4** port **8** larboard
military: **6** cutter, PT boat **7** carrier, cruiser **9** destroyer, submarine
officer: **4** mate **5** bosun **6** purser **7** captain, steward **9** boatswain
part: **3** bow **4** beam, deck, helm, hold, hull, keel, mast, skeg, stem **5** bilge, hatch, stern **6** bridge, rudder **7** scupper
partition: **7** bulwark **8** bulkhead
personnel: **4** crew
platform: **9** crow's nest, gangboard, gangplank
poetic: **4** bark
post: **4** bitt, mast **7** bollard
prison: **4** brig
projection: **7** sponson
rear: **5** stern
record: **3** log
right side: **9** starboard
room: **4** brig **5** cabin **6** galley
rope: **4** line **5** sheet **7** halyard
sailing: **3** hoy **4** brig, dhow, prau, proa, yawl **5** ketch, sloop, xebec, yacht **6** lugger **7** caravel, galleon **8** schooner
steerer: **4** helm **6** tiller
storage area: **4** hold
to the rear of: **3** aft **5** abaft **6** astern
valve: **7** seacock
window: **4** port **8** porthole

shipment
5 cargo **6** lading **7** freight, payload **8** delivery **11** consignment

Ship of Fools author
6 Porter (Katherine Anne)

Shipping News author
6 Proulx (Annie)

ships, group of
4 navy **5** fleet, flota **6** armada **8** flotilla

shipshape
4 neat, snug, tidy, trig, trim **7** orderly **11** spic-and-span, uncluttered **12** spick-and-span

shipworm
6 teredo

shire
5 horse **6** county **8** district **10** draft horse

shirk
4 duck, lurk, shun **5** avoid, creep, dodge, elude, evade, skulk, slink, sneak, steal **8** sidestep

shirker
see **slacker**

shirt
3 tee **4** polo, sark **5** dress, kurta, sport **6** blouse, jersey **9** guayabera

shirty
3 mad **5** angry, cross, irate **6** heated, ireful **7** annoyed **8** choleric, incensed, offended **9** indignant, irritated

shiv
5 blade, knife, shank **6** dagger **8** stiletto

Shiva
consort: **3** Uma **4** Devi, Kali **5** Durga, Gauri **6** Ambika, Chandi **7** Parvati **9** Haimavati
son: **6** Ganesa, Ganesh, Skanda **7** Ganesha **10** Karttikeya

shiver
5 burst, quake, shake, smash **6** quaver, quiver, tremor **7** shatter, shudder, tremble, twitter **8** fragment, splinter, splitter

shlep
see **schlep**

shoal
3 bar **4** bank, hook, reef, spit **6** school **7** barrier, sandbar, shallow, tombolo **8** sandbank, sand reef

shoat
3 hog, pig **4** gilt **5** swine **6** piglet, porker

Shobab
father: **5** Caleb, David
mother: **6** Azubah **9** Bathsheba

shock
3 jar **4** blow, bump, daze, jolt, pile, rick, stun **5** amaze, clash, crash, mound, quake, shake, sheaf **6** appall, dismay, impact, insult, offend, trauma, tremor **7** astound, disgust, horrify, outrage, stagger, startle, stupefy, temblor **8** astonish, surprise **9** collision, electrify **10** concussion, earthquake, percussion, scandalize, traumatize **11** flabbergast **12** stupefaction

shock absorber
6 spring **7** dashpot, snubber

shocker
4 blow **7** stunner **8** surprise, thriller **9** bombshell, eye-opener, sensation **11** showstopper

shocking
5 awful, lurid **6** horrid **7** glaring, heinous **8** dreadful, horrible, horrific, shameful, terrible **9** appalling, atrocious, frightful, monstrous, revolting, traumatic **10** outrageous, scandalous **11** disgraceful, distressing, unspeakable

shoddy
4 base, mean, poor **5** cheap, dingy, gaudy, junky, seedy, tacky, tatty **6** cheesy, common, flimsy, paltry, shabby, sleazy, tawdry, trashy **7** run-down, scruffy **8** inferior, rubbishy, shameful **9** makeshift **10** broken-down, down-at-heel, jerry-built, jury-rigged **11** dilapidated, disgraceful, ignominious, pretentious **12** dishonorable, disreputable **13** discreditable

shoe
3 pac **4** boot, clog, geta, mule, pump **5** sabot, wedge **6** brogan, brogue, buskin, gaiter, galosh, gillie, loafer, oxford, patten, sandal, slip-on **7** chopine, ghillie, slipper, sneaker **8** balmoral, moccasin, platform, plimsoll **10** clodhopper, espadrille
armored: **8** solleret
athlete's: **7** sneaker
form: **4** last, tree
kind: **8** elevator, open-toed **10** high-heeled
part: **3** tip, toe **4** arch, heel, lace, lift, sole, vamp **5** cleat, shank, upper **6** box toe, collar, foxing, insole, lining, throat, tongue **7** counter, outsole **8** backstay
protective: **6** galosh, rubber
shiner: **6** polish **9** bootblack
wooden: **5** sabot **7** chopine

shoelace tip
5 aglet

shoeless
6 unshod **8** barefoot **9** discalced

shoemaker
7 cobbler
patron saint: **7** Crispin
Scottish: **6** souter

Shogun author
7 Clavell (James)

Sholem Aleichem character
5 Golde, Tevye, Yente

shoo
4 scat **5** drive, leave, scare, scram, split **6** beat it, begone, bug off, skidoo **7** buzz off, get lost, skiddoo, vamoose **8** clear out **9** skedaddle, take a hike **10** hit the road

shoo-in
6 winner **7** sure bet **8** slam dunk **9** sure thing

shoot
3 bud, fly, gun, ray **4** beam, bolt, dart, dash, fire, lash, race, rush, sail, scud, skim, spew, tear **5** blast, chase, fling, photo, plink, shaft, skirr, snipe, spurt **6** branch **7** project **9** discharge **10** photograph

shoot down
3 pan, rap **4** bash, kill, slam **5** blast, decry, knock, scorn, trash **6** assail, deride, dump on, reject, squash **7** deflate, squelch, torpedo **8** bad-mouth, belittle, derogate, discount, disprove, puncture, ridicule **9** discredit

shooting
4 keen **5** acute, sharp **7** gunplay **8** piercing, stabbing

shooting star
6 meteor **8** fireball

shoot up
4 soar **6** inject, rocket **7** burgeon **8** mushroom **9** skyrocket

shop
4 hunt **5** store **6** browse, market, outlet, search **8** boutique, emporium, showroom

shoplift
3 bag, cop **4** lift, palm **5** boost, filch, pinch, steal, swipe **6** pilfer, rip off, snitch

shop owner
8 merchant, retailer **9** tradesman **10** proprietor

shopworn
5 banal, faded, stale, tired, trite **6** cliché, soiled **7** clichéd **8** overused **9** hackneyed **10** threadbare

shore
4 bank, prop, stay **5** beach, brace, brink, coast **6** bear up, strand, uphold **7** bolster, shingle, support, sustain **8** buttress, littoral, seacoast **9** coastland, coastline, riverbank, riverside, waterside **10** embankment, waterfront

shorebird
see at **bird**

short
3 shy **4** curt **5** blunt, brief, crisp, scant, skimp, spare, squat, stint, terse **6** abrupt, meager, meagre, scanty, scarce, skimpy, stubby **7** brusque, compact, concise, lacking, laconic, stunted, wanting **8** abridged, succinct **9** deficient **10** inadequate **11** abbreviated **12** insufficient

shortage
4 lack **5** pinch **6** dearth, ullage **7** deficit, paucity **8** scarcity **10** deficiency, inadequacy, scantiness

shortcoming
3 bug, sin **4** flaw, lack **5** fault, lapse **6** defect **7** demerit, failing **8** weakness **9** weak point **10** deficiency **12** imperfection

shortcut
5 macro **6** bypass, cutoff

shorten
3 bob, cut **4** clip, dock **5** elide, slash **6** lessen, reduce, shrink **7** abridge, curtail, cut back, cut down, excerpt **8** boil down, compress, condense, contract, decrease, diminish, minimize, truncate **10** abbreviate

shorthand
11 stenography
method: **5** Gregg **6** Pitman

shorthanded
7 wanting **11** undermanned **12** understaffed

short-lived
5 brief **7** passing **8** fleeting **9** ephemeral, fugacious, momentary, temporary **10** evanescent, transitory

shortly
4 anon, soon **6** pronto **7** briefly, by and by, in brief, quickly, tersely **8** directly **9** concisely, presently **10** succinctly **11** laconically

shortness
7 brevity **9** concision

shortsighted
6 myopic **8** heedless, reckless **10** astigmatic

short-spoken
4 curt **5** bluff, blunt, brief, gruff, terse **6** abrupt, crusty, snippy **7** brusque **8** snippety

short-tempered
5 testy **6** touchy **7** prickly **8** snappish **9** irascible, irritable

Shoshone chief
8 Washakie **9** Pocatello

shot
3 nip, pop, try **4** dose, dram, drop, jolt, stab **5** blast, break, carom, crack, fling, guess, ounce, photo, range, reach, snort, swipe, whack, whirl **6** chance, effort, stroke **7** attempt, snifter **8** marksman, occasion **9** discharge **11** opportunity

shoulder
4 bear, edge, push, side **5** elbow, press, shove **6** assume, hustle, jostle, take on **8** bulldoze
bone: **7** scapula **8** clavicle
covering: **6** tippet **8** scapular
muscle: **7** deltoid
relating to: **7** humeral **8** scapular

shoulder blade
7 scapula

shout
3 cry **4** bark, bawl, bray, call, roar, yell **5** blare, whoop **6** bellow, clamor, holler, scream **7** exclaim **10** vociferate

shove
3 dig, jab, jam **4** cram, prod, push **5** crowd, drive, elbow, press **6** jostle, propel, thrust **8** bulldoze, shoulder

shovel
3 dig **4** grub **5** delve, scoop, spade **6** dig out, dredge, trowel **8** excavate

shoveler
4 duck **9** broadbill

shove off
2 go **3** git **4** blow, exit **5** leave, scoot, scram, split **6** beat it, cut out, decamp, depart, move on **7** move out, pull out, vamoose **8** clear out, run along

show
4 fair, film, lead, pomp, sham **5** array, flick, front, guide, mount, movie, offer, prove, revue, sport, stage **6** appear, arrive, direct, effect, evince, expose, flaunt, lay out, parade, reveal, set out, submit, unveil **7** conduct, display, divulge, exhibit, explain, fanfare, panoply, picture, present, produce, project, trot out **8** brandish, disclose, evidence, illusion, indicate, instruct, manifest, proclaim **9** determine, establish, pageantry, represent, semblance, spectacle **10** appearance, exhibition, exposition, illustrate, production **11** demonstrate, materialize, performance **13** demonstration, manifestation

Show Boat
author: **6** Ferber (Edna)
composer: **4** Kern (Jerome)
lyricist: **11** Hammerstein (Oscar)

showcase
6 flaunt, parade **7** cabinet, exhibit, feature, vitrine

shower
4 hail, rain, wash **5** bathe, burst, party, salvo, spray, storm **6** deluge, lavish, volley **7** barrage, cascade, shatter, spatter **8** cataract, downpour, fountain, rainfall **9** broadside, cannonade, fusillade **10** cloudburst **11** bombardment

showman
8 producer, promoter **10** impresario
famous: **4** Cody (William F.) **6** Barnum (Phineas T.)

Show Me State
8 Missouri

show off
4 brag **5** boast, flash, model, strut, vaunt **6** expose, flaunt, hotdog, parade **7** display, exhibit, swagger, trot out **8** brandish **10** grandstand

show-off
3 ham **6** hotdog **7** boaster, hotshot, peacock **8** blowhard, braggart **9** swaggerer **13** exhibitionist

showpiece
3 gem **5** jewel, prize **10** magnum opus, masterwork **11** chef d'oeuvre, masterpiece

show up
4 come **6** appear, arrive, debunk, expose, reveal, unmask **8** discover **9** discredit, embarrass **10** invalidate **11** materialize

showy
4 loud **5** gaudy, jazzy **6** flashy, garish, ornate, sporty, tawdry **7** opulent, splashy **8** gorgeous, overdone, striking **9** luxurious, sumptuous **10** flamboyant **11** overwrought, pretentious, resplendent, sensational **12** meretricious, orchidaceous, ostentatious

shred
3 bit, dag, jot, rag **4** chip, iota, whit **5** crumb, grain, grate, ounce, scrap, shave, speck, trace **6** sliver, tatter **7** modicum, smidgen, snippet **8** demolish, fragment, particle **9** scintilla

shrew
3 erd, nag **4** mole **5** harpy, scold, vixen, witch **6** dragon, gorgon, ogress, rodent, virago **7** hellcat **8** battle-ax, fishwife, harridan, she-devil, spitfire, Xantippe **9** battle-axe, termagant, Xanthippe

shrewd
3 sly **4** cagy, foxy, keen, wily, wise **5** acute, cagey, canny, savvy, sharp, slick, smart **6** artful, astute, clever, crafty, smooth **7** knowing, prudent **8** sensible **9** ingenious, judicious, sagacious **10** discerning **11** intelligent, penetrating, quick-witted **13** perspicacious

shrewish
5 cross, testy **6** cranky, snappy **7** nagging, peevish, peppery **8** choleric, petulant **9** crotchety, fractious, irascible, splenetic **10** ill-natured **11** contentious, intractable, quarrelsome **12** disputatious **13** quick-tempered, short-tempered

shriek
3 cry **4** yell **6** screak, scream, shrill, squawk, squeal **7** screech

shrill
4 keen **5** acute, sharp **6** piping **8** piercing, strident **9** deafening **12** earsplitting

shrimp
4 runt **5** prawn **6** peanut, peewee, scampi, shorty **9** pipsqueak **10** crustacean

shrine
5 altar **6** temple **7** sanctum **9** reliquary, sacrarium, sanctuary
Buddhist: **4** tope **5** stupa **7** chorten

shrink
3 shy **4** wane **5** cower, quail, slink, start, wince **6** blench, boggle, cringe, flinch, huddle, recede, recoil, wither **7** analyst, dwindle, refrain **8** compress, condense, contract, draw back, withdraw **9** constrict, shrivel up, therapist, waste away **12** psychiatrist, psychologist

shrinking
3 shy **5** mousy, timid **7** bashful **8** retiring, skittish **9** withdrawn

shrive
5 purge **6** pardon, purify **7** absolve, confess, expiate **8** lustrate

shrivel
4 wilt **5** dry up, parch, wizen **6** shrink, wither **7** dwindle, wrinkle **9** dehydrate, desiccate

Shropshire Lad author
7 Housman (A. E.)

shroud
4 hide, rope, veil, wrap **5** cloak, cover, shade **6** enfold, enwrap, screen **7** conceal, enclose, envelop, obscure **8** cerement, obstruct **9** cere-cloth **12** winding-sheet

shrouded
5 privy **6** covert, hidden, secret **7** obscure **10** mysterious

shrub
4 bush **5** elder, erica, hazel **6** muskit, privet **7** arboret, dyeweed, guayule **8** barberry, blue-wood, boxthorn, inkberry, ironweed, rosebush **9** bearberry **10** bladdernut
Asian: **4** bago **6** kerria **8** caragana, japonica
desert: **4** jhow **7** ephedra **8** tamarisk
dwarf: **6** bonsai
East Indian: **3** aal **4** sunn
European: **4** cade **8** woodbine
evergreen: **3** box, kat, yew **4** ilex, khat, titi **5** furze, heath, holly, pyxie, savin, taxus **6** kalmia, laurel, myrtle, nandin, protea, sabine, savine **7** boxwood, heather, jasmine, juniper, rosebay **8** lambkill, oleander, rosemary, tamarisk
flowering: **5** ribes, tiara, wahoo **6** daphne, laurel, myrtle, spirea **7** chamise, chamiso, mahonia, maybush, rhodora, spiraea, weigela **8** magnolia, mezereon, nineback, oleander, oleaster, shadblow, shadbush, snowball, snowbush, tornillo, viburnum, wisteria
genus: **3** Iva **4** Ilex, Inga, Itea, Rhus, Rosa, Ulex **7** Solanum **8** Euonymus
hardwood: **4** pelu **6** cornel, kowhai
Mexican: **8** ocotillo
New Zealand: **4** tutu
ornamental: **6** privet **7** syringa **9** bluebeard
pasture: **8** cowberry
prickly: **4** Ulex **5** briar, chico, furze, gorse **7** bramble **8** hawthorn, mesquite **9** buckthorn
thicket: **6** maquis **7** macchia **9** chaparral
tropical: **4** kava, Sida **5** henna **7** lantana **8** buddleia **10** frangipani
West Indian: **4** anil **7** acerola

shrug off
8 belittle, downplay, minimize

shtick
3 act, bag, bit **5** spiel **6** number **7** routine **9** specialty **11** performance

Shuah
father: **7** Abraham
mother: **7** Keturah

shuck
3 pod **4** case, cast, hull, husk, junk, peel, shed, skin **5** ditch, scrap, shell, strip **6** reject, remove, slough **7** discard, peel off, take off **8** jettison **11** decorticate

shudder
5 quake, shake **6** quaver, quiver, shimmy, shiver, tremor **7** frisson, tremble, twitter, vibrate

shuffle
3 mix **4** hash **5** dodge, evade, hedge, scuff, shift **6** jumble, mess up, muddle, weasel **7** clutter, reorder, rummage, shamble **8** disarray, disorder, intermix, mishmash **9** rearrange **10** disarrange, equivocate **11** disorganize

shun
3 cut **4** duck, snub **5** avoid, dodge, elude, evade, scorn **6** escape, eschew, refuse, reject **7** decline, disdain

shunt
4 turn **5** avert, shift **6** change, divert, switch **7** deflect, shuttle **8** transfer **9** sidetrack

shush
4 hush **5** quiet, still **6** muffle, muzzle, shut up, stifle **7** repress, silence, squelch **8** suppress

shut
3 bar **4** lock, seal, slam **5** close **6** fasten **9** close down **10** batten down

Shute novel
10 On the Beach

shut in
3 hem, mew, pen **4** cage, coop, wall **5** fence **6** coop up, immure **7** confine, enclose **8** imprison

shut-in
7 invalid **8** confined **9** withdrawn **12** convales-cent

shut out
3 bar **6** screen **7** exclude **9** ostracize

shutter
5 blind **6** screen

shuttle
5 ferry, shunt **6** bobbin **7** commute, spindle **9** alternate

shuttlecock
4 bird **5** bandy

shut up
3 gag, mew, pen **4** cage, hush, jail, mute **5** burke, choke, quiet, shush, still **6** muzzle, stifle **7** confine, enclose, impound, silence, squelch **8** choke off, imprison, pipe down, suppress **9** quiet down **11** incarcerate

shy
3 coy **4** balk, duck, meek, shun, wary **5** avoid, chary, elude, evade, mousy, quail, scant, short, timid **6** averse, blench, demure, modest, recoil, scanty, scarce, shrink **7** bashful, fearful, lacking, wanting **8** hesitant, reserved, reticent, retiring, sheepish, timorous **9** diffident, withdrawn **11** introverted, unassertive **12** apprehensive, insufficient, self-effacing **13** self-conscious

Shylock
6 usurer **9** loan shark
daughter: **7** Jessica

shyster
11 pettifogger

Siam
see **Thailand**

sib
3 bro, kin, sis **4** akin **6** sister **7** brother, kindred, kinsman, related **8** relation, relative **9** relatives

Sibelius composition
9 Finlandia **11** Valse Triste

Siberian
dog: **5** husky **7** Samoyed
native: **5** Tatar, Yakut **6** Tartar, Tungus **7** Chukchi **9** Mongolian
plain: **6** steppe
tent: **4** yurt

sibilate
4 buzz, fizz, hiss, whiz **6** fizzle, sizzle **7** whisper

sibling
3 bro, sis **6** sister **7** brother

sibyl
4 seer **6** oracle **7** prophet **10** prophetess, soothsayer **13** fortune-teller

sic
3 set **4** thus **5** chase **6** attack

Sicilian secret organization
5 Mafia **10** Cosa Nostra

Sicily
capital: **7** Palermo
city: **4** Enna **7** Catania, Messina **8** Siracusa, Syracuse, Taormina
volcano: **4** Etna

sick
3 ill **5** fed up, tired, weary **6** ailing, laid up, morbid, peaked, rotten, unwell, wobbly **7** fevered, invalid **8** confined, diseased **9** bedridden, defective, disgusted, unhealthy **10** indisposed **11** debilitated

sicken
5 upset **7** afflict, disgust, fall ill **8** nauseate

sickle
5 blade, mower **6** scythe **8** crescent

sickle-shaped
7 falcate

sickly
3 ill, low, wan **4** puny, weak **5** frail **6** ailing, anemic, feeble, infirm, morbid, peaked, poorly, unwell **8** delicate, diseased **9** unhealthy **10** indisposed **11** unhealthful, unwholesome **12** insalubrious

sickness
3 bug **6** malady **7** ailment, disease, illness **8** disorder, syndrome **9** complaint, condition, infirmity **10** affliction **13** indisposition

sick-out
7 blue flu

sic transit gloria ____
5 mundi

side
4 clad, team **5** angle, facet, flank **6** aspect **9** direction **10** standpoint
combining form: **5** later **6** lateri, latero
exposed: **8** windward
of a coin: **7** obverse, reverse
sheltered: **3** lee

sideboard
5 table **6** buffet **8** credence, credenza
for wine: **8** cellaret **10** cellarette

sideburns
9 burnsides **10** sideboards **11** dundrearies, muttonchops

sidekick
3 pal **4** chun **5** buddy, crony **7** partner **9** assistant, companion **10** accomplice

sideline
5 eject, hobby **6** injure **7** disable, pastime, take out **9** avocation, diversion **10** recreation **11** distraction **12** incapacitate

sidereal
6 astral, starry **7** stellar

side road
5 byway **8** bystreet, shunpike

sideshow
9 diversion **11** distraction

sidestep
4 duck **5** avoid, burke, dodge, evade, hedge,

skirt **6** bypass, swerve, weasel **10** circumvent, equivocate **12** tergiversate

sideswipe
5 brush, carom, graze, shave **6** glance, scrape

sidetrack
5 shunt **6** divert, switch **7** deflect

sidewhiskers
see **sideburns**

side with
4 back **5** favor **6** second, uphold **7** endorse, support **8** backstop, champion

sidle
4 edge, inch, slip

siege
4 bout **5** spell **6** attack **7** assault, seizure **8** blockade **9** onslaught

Siegfried
composer: **6** Wagner (Richard)
lover: **8** Brunhild
mother: **9** Sieglinde
slayer: **5** Hagen
sword: **7** Balmung
vulnerable spot: **4** back **8** shoulder
wife: **9** Kriemhild

Sienkiewicz novel
8 Quo Vadis

sierra
3 saw **4** fish **5** range **8** mackerel **13** mountain range

Sierra ___
4 Club **5** Ancha, Leone, Madre **6** Blanca, Nevada

Sierra Leone
capital: **8** Freetown
ethnic group: **5** Mende, Temne
language: **4** Krio **7** English
monetary unit: **5** leone
neighbor: **6** Guinea **7** Liberia

Sierra Nevada lake
5 Tahoe

siesta
3 nap **4** doze **5** sleep **6** catnap, snooze **10** forty winks

sieve
4 sift **6** filter, screen, winnow **8** colander, filtrate, strainer

Sif's husband
4 Thor

sift
3 pan **4** comb, cull, sort **5** glean, sieve **6** filter, screen, strain, winnow **8** filtrate, separate

sigh
3 sob **4** gasp, long, moan, pine **5** groan, sough, whine, yearn **6** exhale, grieve, hanker, murmur **7** breathe, respire, suspire

sight
3 aim, eye, spy **4** espy, view **5** scene, vista **6** notice, vision **7** make out, outlook
relating to: **5** optic **6** ocular, visual **7** optical

sightseer
7 tourist **10** rubberneck **12** rubbernecker

sign
3 cue, ink **4** flag, hint, mark, omen **5** index, proof, token, trace **6** motion, signal, symbol **7** endorse, gesture, indicia, initial, symptom, vestige, warning **8** evidence, exponent, reminder **9** autograph, indicator **10** expression, indication, suggestion
box office: **3** SRO
magic: **4** rune
directional: **5** arrow
of the zodiac:
(see **zodiac sign**)

signal
3 cue, nod **4** flag **5** alarm, alert **6** beckon, wigwag **7** gesture **8** high sign **9** indicator, semaphore
distress: **3** SOS **6** Mayday

signature
4 name **9** autograph **11** John Hancock
flourish: **6** paraph

signet
4 ring, seal **5** stamp **6** device **8** hallmark, intaglio

significance
4 pith **5** merit, point, sense **6** credit, import, moment, weight **7** gravity, meaning **9** authority, magnitude **10** importance **11** consequence, weightiness

significant
5 major, sound, valid **7** notable, telling, weighty **8** material, powerful **9** important, momentous **10** compelling, convincing, meaningful, note-worthy **11** substantial **12** considerable **13** consequential

signification
4 gist **5** point, sense **6** import **7** essence, meaning, message, purport **9** substance **10** intendment **11** implication **12** notification **13** understanding

signify
4 mean, show **5** count, imply, spell, weigh **6** convey, denote, intend, matter **7** add up to, bespeak, connote, express, purport, suggest **8** indicate

sign on
4 book, hire, join **5** draft **6** engage, enlist, enroll, induct, join up, retain, secure **7** recruit **9** conscript

sign over
4 cede, deed 5 alien, grant 6 assign, convey, remise 7 consign 8 alienate, transfer

sign up
4 join 5 enrol, enter 6 enlist, enroll, muster

Sigurd
horse: 5 Grani
slayer: 5 Hogni
victim: 6 Fafner, Fafnir
wife: 6 Gudrun

Sigyn's husband
4 Loki

Sikhism
deity: 4 Akal
founder: 5 Nanak 9 Guru Nanak
leader: 5 Arjan 9 Guru Arjan 11 Gobind Singh
scripture: 9 Adi Granth
shrine: 12 Golden Temple

silage
6 fodder

silence
3 gag 4 calm, hush, lull, mute 5 quash, quell, quiet, shush, still 6 dampen, deaden, muffle, muzzle, shut up, squash, stifle 7 secrecy, squelch 8 choke off, muteness, quietude, suppress 9 quietness, reticence, stillness

silent
3 mum 4 dumb, mute 5 muted, quiet, still, tacit, whist 6 hushed, stilly 8 reticent, taciturn, unspoken, wordless 9 noiseless, soundless, voiceless 10 speechless 11 close-lipped, tight-lipped 12 closemouthed, tight-mouthed

Silent Night writer
4 Mohr (Joseph) 6 Gruber (Franz)

silhouette
6 shadow 7 contour, outline, profile 9 lineament, lineation 10 figuration 11 delineation

silicon symbol
2 Si

Silicon Valley city
7 San Jose 8 Palo Alto

silk
5 fiber 7 foulard 8 sarcenet, sarsenet
fabric: 4 gros 5 caffa, ninon, Pekin, satin, surah, tulle 6 mantua, pongee, samite, sendal, tussah 7 taffeta
factory: 8 filature
hat: 6 topper
maker: 4 worm
raw: 6 greige
source: 6 cocoon
waste: 4 noil 5 floss
wild: 6 tussah

sill
5 bench, ledge, shelf 9 threshold

silliness
5 folly 6 idiocy 7 inanity 9 absurdity, stupidity

silly
4 daft 5 balmy, crazy, daffy, dippy, dizzy, funny, giddy, inane, loony, sappy, wacky 6 absurd, simple 7 asinine, fatuous, flighty, foolish, idiotic, vacuous, witless 9 brainless, frivolous, ludicrous, nitwitted, senseless 10 irrational, ridiculous, weak-minded 11 empty-headed, harebrained, light-headed 12 preposterous, simpleminded 13 rattlebrained

silt
4 marl 5 dregs 7 deposit, residue 8 alluvium, sediment

silver
4 coin 5 money, shiny 6 argent, dulcet 7 bullion, element 8 flatware, lustrous, sterling 9 argentine, tableware
relating to: 9 argentine
symbol: 2 Ag

silverfish
6 insect, tarpon

silversmith
6 Revere (Paul) 11 metalworker

silver-tongued
4 glib 6 fluent 7 voluble 8 eloquent

silvery
6 argent 7 shining 9 argentine, brilliant 10 glittering, shimmering

Silvia's beloved
9 Valentine

____ Simbel
3 Abu

Simenon character
7 Maigret (Inspector)

Simeon
father: 5 Jacob
mother: 4 Leah
son: 4 Ohad 6 Nemuel

simian
3 ape 5 chimp, lemur, loris 6 baboon, bonobo, galago, monkey 7 apelike, gorilla, primate, tarsier 9 orangutan 10 anthropoid, chimpanzee, monkeylike

similar
4 akin, like 5 alike 6 agnate 7 uniform 8 parallel, suchlike 9 analogous, consonant 10 comparable, reciprocal 11 correlative 13 complementary, corresponding

similarity
6 parity 7 analogy, harmony, kinship 8 affinity, likeness, parallel, sameness 9 alikeness, closeness, congruity, semblance 10 conformity, congruence 11 coincidence, correlation, homogeneity, parallelism, resemblance

similarly
8 likewise

simile
7 analogy 8 affinity, likeness, metaphor 9 alikeness, semblance 10 comparison 11 correlation, resemblance
word: 2 as 4 like

similitude
4 copy 5 image 6 double 7 analogy, kinship, replica 8 affinity, likeness, metaphor, relation, sameness 9 alikeness, congruity, semblance 10 comparison, similarity 11 correlation, counterpart, equivalence, resemblance

simmer
4 boil, fret, fume, stew, stir 5 churn 6 bubble, seethe 7 ferment, smolder

simmer down
5 relax

Simon
brother: 5 Jesus 6 Andrew
father: 5 Jonah
new name: 5 Peter
son: 5 Judas, Rufus 9 Alexander

Simon ___
5 Magus 6 Legree 8 of Cyrene 9 the Zealot

Simon Maccabaeus
father: 10 Mattathias
nickname: 6 Thassi
slayer: 7 Ptolemy

Simon play
9 Odd Couple (The) 10 Chapter Two, Plaza Suite 11 Biloxi Blues 12 Sunshine Boys (The) 13 Lost in Yonkers 16 Come Blow Your Horn 17 Barefoot in the Park 20 Brighton Beach Memoirs 21 Last of the Red Hot Lovers 22 Prisoner of Second Avenue (The)

simp
4 dope 5 dunce, idiot, moron 6 dimwit, nitwit 7 pinhead 8 bonehead, imbecile, lunkhead, numskull 9 blockhead, lamebrain, numbskull 10 nincompoop

simple
4 easy, mere, pure 5 basic, lucid, naive, plain, sheer 6 modest 7 artless, natural, unmixed 8 absolute, trusting 9 childlike, credulous, ingenuous, unadorned 10 effortless, elementary, unaffected 11 fundamental, undecorated, unelaborate 13 unpretentious
combining form: 4 hapl 5 haplo

simpleminded
4 dull, slow 5 naive 6 stupid 7 foolish, idiotic, moronic 8 gullible, retarded 9 dim-witted, imbecilic 10 half-witted, slow-witted

simpleton
4 dolt, dope, fool 5 dummy, dunce, idiot, moron 6 cretin, dimwit, nitwit 7 dullard, half-wit, pinhead 8 bonehead, dumbbell, imbecile, lunkhead 9 blockhead, ignoramus, lamebrain 10 nincompoop

simplify
4 ease 7 clarify, clear up 8 boil down 10 facilitate, streamline, unscramble 11 disentangle 13 straighten out

simply
4 just, only 6 merely

Simpsons, The
catchphrase: 3 d'oh 12 don't have a cow
character: 3 Abe, Apu, Moe 4 Bart, Lisa 5 Homer, Marge, Patty, Selma, Snake 6 Barney, Krusty, Maggie, Martin, Willie 7 Bouvier, Mr. Burns, Skinner (Principal Seymour) 8 Chalmers (Supt.), Milhouse, Smithers 9 Dr. Hibbert, Joe Quimby (Mayor) 11 Chief Wiggum (Clancy), Ned Flanders, Nelson Muntz, Sideshow Bob, Sideshow Mel, Troy McClure 12 Kent Brockman, Mrs. Krabappel
creator: 8 Groening (Matt)
Lisa's instrument: 3 sax 9 saxophone
setting: 11 Springfield
voice: 5 Smith (Yeardley) 6 Azaria (Hank), Kavner (Julie) 10 Cartwright (Nancy) 12 Castellaneta (Dan)

simulacrum
4 copy 5 clone, ditto, guise, image, trace 6 double, ersatz, mirror, ringer 7 picture, replica 8 likeness, portrait 9 facsimile, imitation, semblance 10 appearance 12 reproduction 13 impersonation, spitting image

simulate
3 ape 4 fake, sham 5 feign, mimic 6 embody, mirror, parody, parrot 7 imitate 8 resemble 9 incarnate 11 counterfeit

simulated
4 fake, mock, sham 5 bogus, dummy, false, phony 6 ersatz 8 spurious 9 imitation, insincere, pretended 10 artificial, fictitious, substitute 11 counterfeit

simultaneous
6 coeval 10 coexistent, coexisting, coincident, coinciding, concurrent, synchronic 11 synchronous 12 contemporary

simultaneously
6 at once 7 jointly 8 together 9 meanwhile

sin
3 err 4 debt, evil, no-no, tort, vice 5 crime, fault, guilt, lapse, misdo, stray, wrong 6 offend 7 demerit, misdeed, offense 8 hamartia, iniquity, trespass 10 deficiency, peccadillo, transgress, wickedness, wrongdoing 11 shortcoming 12 imperfection
deadly: 4 envy, lust 5 anger, greed, pride, sloth 8 gluttony 12 covetousness

Sin
7 moon-god
daughter: 6 Ishtar
son: 7 Shamash
wife: 6 Ningal

since
3 ago **5** after **6** behind **7** because, whereas **8** as long as **9** following **10** inasmuch as **11** considering
Scottish: 4 syne

sincere
4 real, true **5** frank, plain **6** actual, candid, devout, honest **7** artless, earnest, genuine, serious **8** bona fide, truthful **9** authentic, heartfelt, ingenuous, unfeigned **10** aboveboard, forthright **12** wholehearted **13** unpretentious

sincerity
6 candor **7** honesty **8** goodwill, openness **9** frankness, good faith **11** artlessness, earnestness

Sinclair novel
6 Jungle (The)

sine qua non
4 must **9** condition, essential, necessity, requisite **11** requirement **12** precondition, prerequisite

sinew
6 tendon

sinewy
4 ropy, wiry **5** tough **6** brawny **7** fibrous, stringy **8** muscular

sinful
3 bad **4** base, evil, vile **5** wrong **6** guilty, unholy, wicked **7** immoral, peccant, vicious **8** blamable, culpable, damnable, depraved, shameful **9** reprobate **10** iniquitous **11** blameworthy, disgraceful **13** reprehensible

sing
3 rat **4** fink, hymn **5** carol, chant, chirp, croon, troll, yodel **6** inform, intone, snitch, squeal, warble **7** confess, descant, lullaby **8** serenade, vocalize **10** cantillate

singe
4 burn, char, sear **6** scorch

singer
4 alto, bass **5** mezzo, tenor **6** canary **7** crooner, soloist, soprano **8** baritone, choirboy, songbird, songster, vocalist **9** balladeer, chorister, contralto **10** troubadour **12** mezzo-soprano
cabaret: 11 chansonnier
female: 9 chanteuse
opera: 4 diva **10** cantatrice, prima donna
religious: 6 cantor
(see also **alto, baritone, bass, folksinger, mezzo-soprano, pop singer, rock star, soprano**)

singing
exercise: 7 solfège
group: 5 choir **6** chorus **7** chorale **8** glee club

single
3 hit, odd, one **4** free, lone, only, sole **5** unwed **6** maiden, unique **7** base hit, unitary **8** distinct, isolated, separate, solitary, specific **9** exclusive, unmarried **10** individual, particular, unattached
combining form: 3 mon **4** hapl, mono **5** haplo
prefix: 3 uni

single-minded
5 rigid **6** dogged, driven, intent **7** adamant, devoted, diehard **8** hell-bent, obdurate, resolute, resolved, stubborn **9** dedicated, steadfast, unbending **10** brassbound, determined, inexorable, inflexible, purposeful, relentless, unyielding

single out
4 cull, mark, pick **5** elect, favor **6** choose, opt for, select **9** designate **11** distinguish

singsong
4 cant

singular
3 odd **4** lone, only, rare, sole, solo **5** weird **6** unique **7** bizarre, oddball, strange, unusual **8** peculiar, solitary, uncommon **9** exclusive **10** individual, outlandish, particular, unexampled **11** exceptional **13** extraordinary

singularity
5 quirk, unity **6** oddity **7** anomaly, oneness **8** identity **9** exception **11** peculiarity, personality **12** idiosyncrasy **13** individuality, particularity

singularize
4 mark **11** distinguish, individuate **12** characterize **13** differentiate, individualize

sinister
4 dark, dire, evil, left **6** creepy, malign **7** baleful, fateful, malefic, ominous **8** lowering, menacing **9** ill-omened, malicious **10** foreboding, maleficent, portentous **11** apocalyptic, threatening **12** inauspicious, unpropitious

sink
3 dip, pit, sag **4** bore, bury, dive, drop, fall, sump, wane **5** basin, drill, droop, lower, sewer, slope, slump, stoop, swamp **6** hollow, invest, plunge, settle, thrust, worsen **7** capsize, cesspit, decline, depress, descend, founder, go under, immerse, let down, scuttle, subside, torpedo **8** cesspool, hellhole, submerge, submerse **9** concavity, disappear **10** depression

sinker
3 bob **5** plumb **6** weight **8** doughnut, fastball, plumb bob

sinkhole
3 dip, sag **4** bowl **5** basin **6** hollow **8** cesspool **9** concavity **10** depression

sinless
4 pure **6** chaste **8** innocent **9** righteous **10** impeccable

sinner
5 rogue, scamp **6** bad egg, outlaw, rascal, wretch **7** lowlife, villain **8** criminal, evildoer, offender **9** libertine, miscreant, reprobate, scoundrel, wrongdoer **10** black sheep, delinquent, profligate, malefactor **11** rapscallion

Sinn ___
4 Fein

sinuous
4 wavy **5** lithe, snaky **7** winding **8** flexuous, tortuous **10** convoluted, meandering, serpentine **11** anfractuous, snake-shaped

sinus
6 cavity, hollow, recess

Sioux
6 Dakota
chief: **8** Red Cloud **10** Crazy Horse **11** Sitting Bull
language: **6** Dakota, Lakota
people: **3** Ofo **4** Crow **6** Biloxi, Tutelo **7** Catawba, Hidatsa **9** Winnebago

sip
5 drink, savor, taste **6** imbibe

siphon
3 tap **4** draw, pipe, pump **5** draft, drain **6** convoy, divert, funnel **7** channel, conduct, draw off **8** transmit

sir
4 lord **5** title **6** knight, mister **9** gentleman

sire
4 lord **5** beget, breed, hatch, spawn **6** father, parent **7** founder **8** engender **9** patriarch, procreate, propagate, reproduce **10** forefather

siren
4 vamp **5** alarm **7** Lorelei **9** temptress **10** seductress **11** femme fatale
film: **4** Bara (Theda)

Siren
5 Ligea **8** Leucosia **10** Parthenope
German: **7** Lorelei

sirenian
6 dugong, sea cow **7** manatee

siren song
4 lure **5** decoy, snare **6** come-on **10** allurement, enticement, temptation

Sirius
7 Dog Star

sister
3 nun **7** sibling
French: **5** soeur
Latin: **5** soror
Spanish: **7** hermana

Sister Carrie author
7 Dreiser (Theodore)

sisterly
7 sororal

Sisyphus
brother: **7** Athamas **9** Salmoneus
father: **6** Aeolus
mother: **7** Enarete
son: **7** Glaucus

sit
4 pose **5** perch, roost

Sita
abductor: **6** Ravana
husband, rescuer: **4** Rama

sitarist
7 Shankar (Ravi)

sitcom
3 ALF **4** MASH, Mr. Ed, Soap **5** Maude **6** Batman, Cheers **7** Frasier, Friends, Jetsons (The), Newhart **8** Get Smart, Love Boat (The), Mister Ed, Munsters (The), Simpsons (The), Roseanne, Seinfeld **9** Bewitched, Cosby Show (The), Full House, Happy Days, I Love Lucy, Odd Couple (The) **10** Brady Bunch (The), Green Acres, Jeffersons (The), Night Court **11** Flintstones (The), Golden Girls (The), Murphy Brown, My Three Sons, Wonder Years (The) **12** Addams Family (The), Barney Miller, Fawlty Towers, Hogan's Heroes, Honeymooners (The), King of Queens (The), Mork and Mindy, Will and Grace **13** One Day at a Time, Our Miss Brooks, Sanford and Son, Three's Company **14** All in the Family **15** Diff'rent Strokes, Father Knows Best, Gilligan's Island, Home Improvement, Leave It to Beaver, Ozzie and Harriet **17** Are You Being Served, Laverne and Shirley, My Favorite Martian, Petticoat Junction **18** Beverly Hillbillies (The) **19** Married with Children **20** Keeping Up Appearances **21** Everybody Loves Raymond

site
3 dig **4** home, spot **5** haunt, locus, place, point, scene, venue **6** locale **7** station **8** locality, location, position

sit-in
7 protest

sitting
6 séance **7** session
prolonged: **8** sederunt

Sitting Bull's tribe
5 Sioux **6** Dakota

sitting duck
4 butt, mark **6** target

situate
3 put, set **5** place **6** locate **7** install **8** position

situation
3 job **4** post, rank **5** point, state **6** plight, status **7** footing, setting, station **8** location, position, standing **9** condition **13** circumstances

situs
5 place, venue **6** locale

Siva
see **Shiva**

six
combining form: 3 hex, sex **4** hexa, sexi **5** sexti
group of: 6 sestet, sextet **9** sextuplet
relating to: 6 senary

sixfold
8 sextuple

six-pack
3 abs

six-shooter
3 gun **6** pistol **8** revolver

sixth sense
3 ESP **5** hunch **7** insight **9** intuition, telepathy **12** clairvoyance

sizable
3 big **5** ample, hefty, large, major, roomy **8** spacious **9** capacious, extensive **10** commodious, large-scale **11** substantial **12** considerable

size
2 sm, xl **3** lge, med **4** area, bulk, mass **5** range, scope, width **6** extent, height, length, spread, volume **7** bigness, breadth, caliber, expanse, measure, stature **9** amplitude, dimension, extension, greatness, largeness, magnitude **10** dimensions, proportion **11** measurement, proportions

size up
3 peg **4** rate, read **5** assay, gauge, judge, value **6** assess, review, survey **7** adjudge, dope out **8** appraise, estimate, evaluate **9** figure out

sizzle
3 fry **4** buzz, fizz, hiss, whiz **5** grill **6** hoopla, seethe **7** pizzazz **8** sibilate **10** excitement

sizzling
3 hot **6** red-hot, torrid **7** burning **8** scalding, white-hot **9** scorching

skald
4 bard, poet

Skanda
6 war-god
brother: 6 Ganesa, Ganesh **7** Ganesha
father: 4 Siva **5** Shiva

skate
3 nag, ray **4** skid, skim **5** glide, skirr, slide **8** glissade
blade: 6 runner
kind: 6 figure, hockey, in-line **11** Rollerblade

skateboard maneuver
3 air **4** bail, hang **5** carve, grind, ollie, pivot **8** kickflip

skater
see **ice skater**

skating
area: 10 kiss and cry
game: 8 ringette **9** broomball, ice hockey **12** in-line hockey, roller hockey
site: 3 ice **4** rink
term: 3 COP **4** axel, lobe, lutz, quad **5** T-stop **6** Mohawk, rocker, spiral **7** bracket, choctaw, gliding, salchow, sit spin, swizzle, toe loop, twizzle **8** heel stop, star lift, striding, stroking, toe picks **9** camel spin, crossover, free dance, free skate, waltz jump, Zayak Rule **11** death spiral, falling leaf, hydrant lift
type: 3 ice **5** trail **6** in-line, roller

skedaddle
3 run **4** bolt, flee, skip **5** scoot, scram, split **6** beat it, begone, bug off, cut out, decamp, get out **7** make off, run away, scamper, skiddoo, take off, vamoose **8** clear out **10** make tracks

skein
4 coil, hank **5** flock, snarl, twist **6** tangle **12** entanglement

skeletal
4 bony **5** gaunt **6** wasted **7** angular, scraggy, starved **8** rawboned **9** emaciated **10** cadaverous

skeleton
5 bones, draft, frame **6** sketch **7** diagram, outline **9** bare bones, framework
marine: 5 coral, shell

skeptic
5 cynic **7** doubter, scoffer **8** agnostic **10** Pyrrhonist, questioner, unbeliever **11** disbeliever

skeptical
4 wary **5** leery **6** show-me **7** cynical, dubious **8** doubtful, doubting **9** quizzical **10** dissenting, suspicious **11** mistrustful, questioning, unbelieving **12** disbelieving, freethinking

skepticism
5 doubt **7** dubiety **8** distrust, mistrust, wariness **9** dubiosity, misgiving, suspicion **11** incertitude, uncertainty

skerry
4 isle, reef **6** island

sketch
4 draw, plot **5** draft, rough, trace **6** depict, design, doodle, lay out, map out, précis **7** develop, diagram, outline, portray **8** block out, chalk out, rough out **9** blueprint, delineate **12** characterize

sketchy
4 iffy **5** crude, rough, vague **6** skimpy, slight **7** cursory, shallow **8** skeletal **10** incomplete **11** preliminary, superficial **12** questionable

skew
4 bias, veer **5** angle, fudge, slant, slide **6** swerve **7** distort

skewer
3 rod **4** spit **5** lance, spear, spike **6** impale, pierce **8** puncture, ridicule, transfix **9** brochette, criticize

ski
5 glide, slide
lift: **4** J-bar, T-bar **5** chair **7** gondola

skid
5 glide, skate, slide **6** pallet, runner **7** spinout **8** sideslip

skiddoo
4 scat **5** leave, scram, split **6** beat it, begone, bug off, decamp, depart, vacate **7** buzz off, take off, vamoose **8** clear out, shove off **9** skedaddle, take a hike **10** hit the road, make tracks

skid row
6 bowery

skier
American: **3** Moe (Tommy) **4** Kidd (Billy) **5** Mahre (Phil, Steve) **6** Miller (Bode) **7** Johnson (Bill)
Austrian: **5** Maier (Hermann) **6** Proell (Annemarie), Sailer (Toni) **7** Klammer (Franz), Schranz (Karl) **10** Girardelli (Marc) **11** Moser-Proell (Annemarie)
French: **5** Killy (Jean-Claude)
Italian: **5** Tomba (Alberto) **6** Thoeni (Gustavo)
Luxembourg: **10** Girardelli (Marc)
Swedish: **8** Stenmark (Ingemar)
Swiss: **10** Zurbriggen (Pirmin)

skiff
4 boat **7** rowboat

skiing
area: **3** run **5** slope
cross-country: **7** touring
event: **6** schuss, slalom **8** downhill **11** giant slalom
horse-drawn: **9** skijoring
kind: **6** Alpine, Nordic
position: **7** vorlage
technique: **6** wedeln **8** snowplow, traverse
turn: **7** christy **8** christie

skill
3 art **5** craft, knack **7** ability, address, command, cunning, finesse, know-how, mastery, prowess, sleight **8** deftness, facility **9** dexterity, expertise, ingenuity, readiness, technique **10** adroitness, competence **11** proficiency

skilled
3 apt **4** able **5** adept **6** expert **7** capable, trained **8** masterly, talented **9** competent, masterful, practiced **10** proficient **12** accomplished

skillet
3 pan **6** spider **9** frying pan

skillful
4 able, deft **5** adept, crack, handy **6** adroit, clever, daedal, expert **7** skilled **8** masterly **9** competent, dexterous, masterful, practiced, workmanly **10** proficient **11** crackerjack, workmanlike **12** accomplished

skim
4 sail, scan, scud, skip **5** brush, carom, glide, graze, skirr **6** browse **8** embezzle, ricochet

skimp
4 save **5** pinch, scant, spare, stint **6** meager, scanty, scrape, sparse **7** slender **8** begrudge, conserve, retrench, withhold **9** economize

skimpy
5 scant, spare **6** meager, meagre, paltry, scanty, scarce, sparse **7** limited, wanting **8** exiguous **9** deficient **10** inadequate **12** insufficient

skim through
4 scan **6** browse

skin
3 fur, gyp, pod, rap **4** clad, clip, flay, husk, hide, pare, peel, pelt, rind, soak **5** blame, cheat, cover, scale, shell, stiff, strip **6** fleece, sheath, slough **7** censure, condemn, sheathe **8** denounce **9** epidermis, sheathing **10** integument, overcharge **11** decorticate
animal: **4** coat, hide, pelt **6** hackle, peltry
beaver: **4** plew
combining form: **3** cut **4** cuti, derm **5** derma, dermo, dermy **6** dermat, dermia, dermis **7** cutaneo, dermata (plural), dermato, epiderm **8** epidermo
depression: **6** dimple
disease: **4** acne **5** hives, mange **6** eczema, herpes, tetter **8** ringworm **10** dermatitis
dry: **5** scurf
fold: **5** plica
layer: **5** derma **6** corium, dermis **7** cuticle **9** epidermis
opening: **4** pore
protuberance: **3** tag, wen **4** mole, wart **6** pimple
rabbit: **5** coney
relating to: **6** dermal **9** cuticular, epidermal
spot: **7** freckle

skin-deep
7 shallow, trivial **11** superficial

skinflint
5 miser **7** niggard, scrooge **8** tightwad **10** cheapskate, pinchpenny

skin game
3 con **4** scam **5** bunco, bunko, cheat, fraud, sting, trick **6** hustle, racket **7** swindle **8** flimflam

skink
4 adda **6** lizard

skinny
4 bony, dope, info, lank, lean, thin **5** gaunt, lanky, scoop, spare, weedy **6** twiggy **7** angular, lowdown, scraggy, scrawny **8** rawboned, skeletal **9** emaciated

Skin of Our Teeth author
6 Wilder (Thornton)

skip
3 hop, run **4** flee, jump, leap, omit, trip **5** bound, caper, carom, frisk, leave, scoot, skirr **6** cavort, gambol, ignore, pass up, spring **7** abscond, misfire, scamper, skitter **8** leave out, overlook, pass over, ricochet **9** skedaddle

skipjack
4 boat, fish, tuna **8** bluefish, ladyfish, sailboat

skipper
5 pilot **6** leader **7** captain **9** butterfly, commander

ski resort
Austrian: **9** Kitzbühel
Canadian: **5** Banff **8** Big White, Sun Peaks, Whistler **9** Tremblant (Mont) **10** Lake Louise
French: **8** Chamonix
Italian: **7** Cortina
Swiss: **5** Davos **6** Gstaad **7** Verbier, Zermatt **8** St. Moritz **9** Engelberg, Sugarloaf
U. S.: **4** Alta, Taos, Vail **5** Aspen, Stowe **6** Big Sky **8** Snowbird, Snowmass **9** Camelback, Lake Tahoe, Snowbasin, Sun Valley, Telluride **10** Killington **11** Jackson Hole, Squaw Valley **12** Breckenridge

skirmish
3 row **4** fray **5** broil, brush, clash, melee, run-in, scrap, set-to **6** affray, battle, fracas **7** assault, dispute **8** conflict, struggle **9** encounter, scrimmage

skirr
3 run **4** bolt, flee, sail, scud, skim, skip **5** float, scoot, shoot **7** make off, scamper **9** skedaddle

skirt
3 hem, rim **4** brim, duck, edge **5** avoid, bound, brink, burke, dodge, elude, evade, hedge, verge **6** border, bypass, define, detour, escape, fringe, ignore, margin **8** sidestep, surround **9** perimeter, periphery **10** circumvent
ballet: **4** tutu
feature: **3** hem **4** slit
long: **4** maxi
Polynesian: **5** pareo, pareu
Scottish: **4** kilt
short: **4** mini
style: **5** A-line **6** sheath **9** crinoline
support: **11** farthingale

skit
6 shtick, sketch **9** burlesque
show: **5** revue

skitter
3 hop **4** flit, skip, trip **6** scurry, spring **7** scamper

skittery
see **skittish**

skittish
3 coy, shy **4** edgy, wary **5** chary, dizzy, jumpy, leery **6** fickle **7** bashful, fidgety, flighty, nervous, rabbity, restive **8** unstable, volatile **9** excitable, frivolous, impulsive, mercurial, whimsical **10** capricious, unreliable

skive
4 pare **5** carve, shave, slice

skivvies
9 underwear

skoal
5 toast **6** health

skua
4 bird **6** jaeger **7** seabird

skulduggery
5 fraud **8** foul play, trickery **9** chicanery, duplicity **10** hanky-panky

skulk
4 lurk, slip **5** creep, prowl, shirk, slink, sneak, steal

skull
4 head, mind **5** brain **7** cranium **8** brainpan **9** braincase
back of: **7** occiput
bone: **5** vomer **6** zygoma **7** ethmoid, frontal **8** parietal, sphenoid, temporal
jawless: **9** calvarium
joint: **6** suture
part: **3** jaw **5** inion

skullcap
6 beanie, pileus **7** calotte **8** yarmulke **9** calvarium, zucchetto

skunk
4 beat, drub, lick, scum, whip, whup **6** thrash, wallop **7** clobber, polecat, shellac, stinker, trounce **8** civet cat, lambaste **9** overwhelm, slaughter
genus: **8** Mephitis

sky
5 azure **6** heaven, welkin **7** heavens **8** empyrean **9** firmament

sky-blue
5 azure **8** cerulean

skylarking
5 revel **7** revelry, whoopee **9** high jinks, horseplay, rowdiness, whoop-de-do **10** roughhouse **12** roughhousing

skylight
6 window

skyline
7 horizon, outline

sky pilot
5 padre **6** cleric, parson, pastor **8** chaplain, minister, preacher **9** churchman, clergyman

skyrocket
4 rise, soar **7** shoot up **8** catapult

sky sighting
3 UFO

slab
5 block, chunk, slice, strip **8** pavement

slack
3 lax **4** lazy, slow, soft **5** inert, loose, relax **6** remiss **7** ease off, laggard, passive, relaxed **8** careless, derelict, dilatory, inactive, indolent, slothful, sluggish, stagnant **9** leisurely, lethargic, negligent **10** neglectful

slacken
3 ebb, lax **4** ease, slow, wane **5** abate, let up, loose, relax **6** detain, ease up, lessen, loosen, relent, retard, slow up **7** die down, dwindle, ease off, subside **8** diminish, moderate, slow down **9** untighten **10** decelerate

slacker
3 bum **4** slug **5** idler, sloth **6** loafer **7** goof-off, shirker, wastrel **8** deadbeat, layabout, slugabed, sluggard **9** goldbrick, lazybones **10** delinquent **11** couch potato

slag
4 lava **5** dross **6** cinder, debris, scoria

slake
5 allay **6** deaden, quench **7** crumble, hydrate, relieve, satisfy **9** alleviate

slam
3 bat, hit, jab, pan, rap **4** bang, bash, beat, belt, blow, boom, dash, drub, flay, slug, slur, swat, wham **5** blast, crack, crash, fling, knock, pound, slash, smack, smash, swipe, whack **6** batter, cudgel, hammer, scathe, strike, thwack, wallop **7** clobber, potshot **8** lambaste **9** castigate

slam-dance
4 mosh

slam dunk
5 cinch, setup **6** shoo-in **7** safe bet **9** certainty, sure thing

slammer
3 can, jug, pen **4** brig, coop, jail, stir **5** clink, pokey **6** cooler, lockup, prison **9** calaboose **12** penitentiary

slander
4 slur, tale **5** libel, slime, smear, sully **6** defame, malign, smirch, vilify **7** asperse, calumny, scandal, tarnish, traduce **8** besmirch **9** denigrate **10** backbiting, calumniate, defamation, detraction, scandalize **11** mud-slinging **12** back-stabbing

slang
4 cant, jive **5** argot, lingo **6** jargon, patois, patter **7** dialect **10** vernacular

slant
3 tip **4** bank, bias, cant, heel, lean, list, skew, tilt, veer, warp **5** angle, aside, bevel, grade, slope, splay **7** distort, incline, leaning, outlook **8** gradient **9** prejudice, viewpoint **10** standpoint **11** inclination **12** predilection
combining form: **4** clin **5** clino

slap
3 hit, pop **4** bash, blow, cuff, shot, slam, swat **5** clout, smack, spank, whack **6** buffet, insult, rebuff, strike **7** affront, putdown **8** brickbat, lambaste, penalize **9** castigate

slapdash
5 hasty, messy **6** random, sloppy **7** cursory **8** careless, slipshod **9** half-baked, haphazard, hit-or-miss, makeshift

slap down
5 quell **6** kibosh **7** squelch **8** prohibit, suppress

slaphappy
5 dazed, dizzy, woozy **6** punchy **10** punch-drunk

slash
3 cut **4** clip, gash, hack, pare, slit **5** lower, shave, slice **6** reduce, scathe, scorch **7** abridge, blister, curtail, cut back, cut down, scarify, scourge, shorten **8** lacerate, lambaste, mark down **9** castigate, excoriate **10** abbreviate

slat
4 lath **5** board, stave, strip **6** louver, louvre **7** airfoil

slate
4 gray, list, rock, tile **6** lineup, record, tablet, ticket **7** shingle **8** schedule **9** designate

slather
5 smear **6** spread **8** squander

slattern
4 bawd, moll, slut, tart **5** hussy, tramp, wench **6** floozy, harlot **7** chippie, jezebel, trollop **8** strumpet **10** prostitute **11** painted lady **12** scarlet woman, streetwalker

slaughter
4 kill, slay **6** murder **7** butcher, carnage, killing, wipe out **8** butchery, decimate, demolish, hecatomb, massacre **9** bloodbath, bloodshed, liquidate **10** annihilate, butchering **11** destruction, exterminate, liquidation **12** annihilation

slaughterhouse
8 abattoir, shambles

Slav
4 Pole, Serb, Sorb, Wend **5** Croat, Czech **6** Bulgar, Slovak **7** Russian, Serbian, Slovene

8 Bohemian, Croatian, Moravian 9 Bulgarian, Ruthenian, Ukrainian

slave
4 grub, help, peon, plod, serf, slog, toil 5 grind, helot, swink 6 drudge, menial, thrall, toiler, vassal 7 bondman, chattel, servant
feudal: 4 serf
harem: 9 odalisque
liberated: 8 freedman
Muslim: 6 Mamluk 8 Mameluke
Spartan: 5 helot

slave driver
6 tyrant 7 foreman 8 martinet, overseer 10 taskmaster 11 Simon Legree

slaver
4 spit 5 drool, froth 6 drivel, saliva 7 dribble, slobber, spittle 8 salivate

slavery
6 thrall 7 bondage, helotry, peonage, serfdom 9 indenture, servitude, thralldom 11 subjugation

Slavic apostle
5 Cyril 9 Methodius

slavish
6 abject, menial 7 servile 8 obeisant, wretched 9 groveling, imitative, laborious 10 obsequious, unoriginal 11 subservient

slay
4 do in, kill 6 murder 7 bump off, butcher, execute, put away 8 dispatch, knock off 9 liquidate, slaughter 11 assassinate

slayer
7 butcher 11 executioner

sleazy
3 low 5 cheap, dingy, seedy, tacky, tatty 6 cheesy, flimsy, shabby, shoddy, trashy 7 run-down, squalid 8 gimcrack 10 down-at-heel 11 dilapidated 12 disreputable

sled
4 luge, pung 6 sleigh 7 coaster, travois 8 toboggan
Russian: 6 troika

sled dog
5 husky 8 malamute

sledge
4 maul 6 hammer, sleigh
Eskimo: 7 komatik
Lapp: 5 pulka

sleek
4 oily 6 glassy, glossy, smooth 7 elegant, stylish 8 lustrous, polished 10 glistening

sleep
3 nap 4 doss, doze, rest 6 catnap, repose, siesta, snooze 7 shut-eye, slumber 11 slumberland
bringer: 7 sandman
combining form: 4 hypn, narc 5 hypno, narco, somni
god: 6 Hypnos, Somnus
noise: 5 snore

sleeper
3 tie 4 beam, mole 7 Pullman 8 long shot 11 double agent, stringpiece

sleeping
7 dormant 8 comatose
disease: 10 narcolepsy

sleepless
7 wakeful 8 vigilant 9 insomniac

sleeplessness
8 insomnia

sleepwalker
12 somnambulist

sleepy
4 dozy 6 drowsy 7 nodding 9 somnolent 10 slumberous

sleigh
4 pung 6 sledge

sleight
4 ploy, ruse, wile 5 skill, trick 7 gimmick, prowess 8 artifice, deftness, maneuver 9 dexterity, stratagem 10 adroitness

sleight of hand
11 legerdemain

slender
4 lean, slim, thin, trim 5 lithe, reedy, spare 6 skinny, slight, svelte, twiggy 7 spindly, willowy

sleuth
4 dick, Drew (Nancy) 5 Brown (Encyclopedia, Father), Hardy (Frank, Joe), Kojak, Morse, Queen (Ellery), Saint (The), snoop, Spade (Sam), Tracy (Dick), Wolfe (Nero) 6 Hammer (Mike), Holmes (Sherlock), Marple (Miss), Poirot (Hercule), shamus, Wimsey (Peter) 7 Cadfael (Brother), Columbo, Fansler (Kate), gumshoe, Maigret, Marlowe (Philip) 8 hawkshaw, Millhone (Kinsey), Rockford (Jim), sherlock 9 Dalgliesh (Adam), detective, Scarpetta (Kay) 10 private eye, Warshawski (V. I.) 12 investigator

slew
3 lot, mob, ton 4 army, heap, host, load, mess, pile, raft, skid, turn, veer 5 batch, bunch, crowd, flock, pivot, twist 6 myriad, passel, swerve, throng 9 abundance, multitude

slice
3 cut 4 gash, slit 5 allot, carve, divvy, quota, sever, share, slash, split, wedge 6 cleave, divide, incise, sample 7 dissect, portion, segment 8 allocate 9 allotment, allowance

slick
4 film, glib, oily, slip, wily 5 sharp, sleek, soapy 6 crafty, glossy, greasy, shrewd, smarmy,

smooth, tricky **7** cunning **8** slippery, slithery, unctuous **10** lubricious, oleaginous

slicker
4 dude **5** dandy, shark **6** con man **7** cheater, diddler, grifter, oilskin, sharper **8** raincoat, swindler **9** trickster **11** flimflammer

slide
3 dip, sag **4** flow, ramp, skid, slip **5** chute, coast, chute, drift, glide, skate, slump, spill **6** scooch, stream **7** decline, slither **8** downturn **9** downswing, downtrend **12** transparency

slight
4 omit, skip, slim, snub, thin **5** frail, reedy, scorn, small **6** flimsy, ignore, meager, meagre, modest, offend, paltry, remote, skinny **7** contemn, neglect, outside, put-down, slender, tenuous, trivial **8** brush-off, delicate, discount, overlook, smallish, trifling **9** disregard, pint-sized **10** disrespect, negligible

slightly
4 a bit, a tad **6** a touch **7** a little

slim
4 thin **5** lithe, reedy, small, spare **6** meager, meagre, minute, narrow, paltry, remote, skinny, slight, svelte, twiggy **7** lissome, outside, slender, tenuous **9** lithesome **10** negligible

slim down
4 diet, fast **6** reduce **10** slenderize

slime
3 goo, mud **4** glop, gook, guck, gunk, muck, ooze, scum **5** filth **6** sleaze, sludge **7** slander

slimy
4 oozy **6** mucous **7** viscous

sling
3 lob **4** cast, fire, hang, hurl, sock, toss **5** chuck, heave, march, pitch, throw **6** dangle, launch **7** suspend **8** catapult

slink
4 lurk **5** creep, prowl, skulk, slide, sneak, steal **7** gumshoe

slinky
4 sexy **5** lithe, sleek **6** svelte **7** furtive, lissome, sinuous, slender, willowy **8** graceful, sensuous, stealthy

slip
3 sag **4** dock, drop, fall, flow, flub, goof, lurk, shed, sink, skid **5** berth, boner, creep, error, fluff, gaffe, glide, lapse, slide, slink, slump, sneak, steal **6** escape **7** blooper, blunder, decline, drop off, fall off, faux pas, mistake, slither **8** downturn, throw off **9** downswing, downtrend

slipper
4 mule, shoe **5** scuff **6** bootee, bootie, sandal **8** flip-flop, pantofle

slippery
3 icy **4** eely, oily **5** slick **6** greasy, shifty, smooth **7** devious, evasive **8** illusive, slithery **10** lubricious

slipshod
6 blowsy, blowzy, flimsy, frowsy, frowzy, shabby, shoddy, sloppy, untidy **7** rumpled, scrubby, scruffy, unkempt **8** careless, ill-kempt, slapdash, slovenly, tattered **9** haphazard, makeshift, negligent **10** bedraggled, disheveled, down-at-heel

slipup
4 goof **5** boner, error, fluff, lapse **6** bungle, glitch, miscue, mishap **7** blooper, blunder, faux pas, misstep, mistake, setback, stumble **8** accident **9** mischance, oversight **10** misfortune **11** misjudgment

slit
3 cut, gap **4** gash, rent **5** chink, crack, slash, slice **6** cranny, incise **7** crevice, fissure, opening

slither
4 slip **5** creep, glide, sidle, slide, slink, snake, sneak, steal **7** wriggle **8** undulate

slithery
see **slippery**

sliver
5 scrap, shard, shave, shred, slice **6** paring **7** shaving, snippet **8** splinter

slob
3 oaf **4** boor, clod, goon, lout **6** galoot, sloven

slobber
4 gush **5** drool, froth **6** drivel, effuse, slaver **7** dribble, enthuse **8** salivate

sloe
4 plum **10** blackthorn

slog
4 grub, moil, plod, plug, toil **5** chore, grind, labor, shlep, slave, sweat **6** drudge, schlep, trudge **7** schlepp

slogan
5 maxim, motto **6** byword **9** battle cry, catchword, watchword **10** shibboleth **11** catchphrase

sloop
4 boat **5** yacht **8** sailboat

slop
3 mud, pap **4** gush, muck **5** douse, dreck, dregs, offal, slosh, slush, spill, swill **6** guzzle, pablum, refuse, splash, sludge **7** garbage, pabulum, rubbish **8** splatter

slope
3 tip **4** bend, brae, cant, heel, lean, list, rise, skew, swag, sway, tilt **5** grade, pitch, scarp, slant **6** ascent, glacis **7** descent, incline, leaning, recline **8** gradient **9** acclivity, declivity, obliquity **11** inclination
combining form: **5** cline **6** clinal

sloppy
5 dowdy, gushy, messy **6** slushy, untidy **7** gushing, unkempt **8** careless, effusive, ill-kempt, slapdash, slipshod, slovenly **10** bedraggled, disheveled **11** dishevelled

slosh
4 gush, slop, wash **5** churn, swash **6** gurgle, splash **8** flounder, splatter

slot
4 vent **5** niche, notch **6** groove, keyway **7** keyhole, opening, passage **8** aperture **10** pigeonhole

sloth
4 laze, unau **5** idler **6** acedia, apathy, idling, lazing, loafer, slouch, torpor **7** goof-off, languor, loafing, slacker **8** idleness, laziness, lethargy **9** heaviness, indolence, lassitude, lazybones, torpidity **11** couch potato **12** listlessness, sluggishness **13** shiftlessness
three-toed: **2** ai

slothful
4 idle, lazy **8** fainéant, indolent **9** shiftless

slouch
3 bum, oaf, sag **4** laze, loaf, loll, lout, mope, slug **5** droop, idler, sloth, slump, stoop **6** loafer, loiter, lounge **7** saunter, shamble, shuffle **8** fainéant, slugabed, sluggard **9** do-nothing, lazybones

slough
3 bog, fen **4** cast, mire, molt, quag, shed, sump **5** inlet, marsh, scrap, swamp **6** morass, reject **7** discard **8** jettison, quagmire, throw out **9** backwater, marshland, swampland, throw away

Slovakia
capital: **10** Bratislava
city: **6** Kosice
monetary unit: **6** koruna
mountain range: **10** Carpathian
neighbor: **6** Poland **7** Austria, Hungary, Ukraine **13** Czech Republic
river: **3** Váh **4** Hron **6** Danube, Morava

Slovenia
capital: **9** Ljubljana
city: **7** Maribor
monetary unit: **4** euro
monetary unit, former: **5** tolar
neighbor: **5** Italy **7** Austria, Croatia, Hungary
part of: **7** Balkans
peninsula: **6** Balkan

slovenly
5 dingy, messy, mussy, seedy, slack **6** frowsy, frowzy, grubby, grungy, scuzzy, shabby, skanky, sleazy, sloppy, untidy **7** squalid, unkempt **8** careless, slapdash, slipshod **10** bedraggled, slatternly

slow
4 late, poky **5** brake, check, lento, pokey, tardy **6** adagio, hinder, impede, leaden, retard, torpid **7** halting, lagging, slacken **8** dilatory, dragging, plodding, sluggish, stagnant **9** leisurely, snail-like, unhurried **10** decelerate, snail-paced, straggling

slowpoke
5 snail **6** lagger **7** dawdler, laggard **8** lingerer, loiterer **9** straggler

sludge
3 mud **4** crud, gook, guck, gunk, mire, muck, ooze, slop **5** slime **6** sewage **8** sediment

slug
3 bum, hit, nip, tot **4** bash, belt, dram, drop, jolt, shot, slam, swat **5** blast, clout, idler, larva, pound, punch, smack, smash, snail, snort, thump **6** buffet, bullet, loafer, slouch, thwack, wallop **7** clobber, goof-off, slacker **8** fainéant, toothful **9** do-nothing, lazybones **11** couch potato
genus: **5** Limax

slugfest
4 bout **5** brawl, set-to **6** rumble **8** dogfight **10** donnybrook, prizefight

sluggard
3 bum **5** idler **6** loafer, slouch **7** dawdler, goof-off, laggard, shirker, slacker **8** deadbeat, fainéant, slowpoke **9** do-nothing, goldbrick, lazybones

slugger
5 boxer **6** batter, hitter **7** palooka

sluggish
4 lazy, logy, slow **5** inert, slack **6** draggy, leaden, stupid, torpid **7** lumpish **8** dragging, indolent, listless, slothful **9** apathetic, lethargic

sluice
4 duct, flow, gush, pour, race, wash **5** flush, surge **6** trough **7** channel **8** spillway **9** floodgate

slum
6 ghetto **7** skid row

slumber
3 nap **4** doze **5** sleep **6** catnap, drowse, snooze, stupor, torpor **8** dormancy, hebetude, lethargy **9** lassitude, torpidity

slumberous
see **sleepy**

slumgullion
4 stew **6** burgoo, ragout **7** goulash

slump
3 dip, sag **4** drop, fall, flag, funk, loll, sink, slip **5** droop, hunch, slide **6** slouch, trough **7** decline, drop off, falloff **8** collapse, downturn **9** downslide, downswing, downtrend, recession **10** depression, stagnation

slur
4 blot, blur, lisp, onus, slam, spot **5** brand, knock, libel, odium, smear, stain **6** befoul, defame, insult, malign, stigma, vilify **7** blacken, calumny, obloquy, obscure, slander, spatter, traduce **8** black eye, brickbat, innuendo, tear down **9** aspersion, bespatter, denigrate, discredit, disparage **10** accusation, calumniate

slurp
3 lap **4** gulp, suck **5** lap up, swill **6** guzzle

slush
3 mud **4** mire, muck, slop **6** drivel **8** schmaltz

sly
4 arch, foxy, wily **5** cagey, saucy, shady, slick **6** artful, clever, crafty, shifty, shrewd, smooth, sneaky, subtle, tricky **7** cunning, devious, furtive, roguish, vulpine **8** guileful, scheming, slippery, stealthy **9** designing, insidious, underhand **11** mischievous, underhanded

slyboots
see **scamp**

slyness
4 wile **5** guile **7** cunning **8** caginess, foxiness, wiliness **9** canniness **10** craftiness

smack
3 bat, bop, box **4** bang, bash, belt, biff, blow, buss, chop, clip, cuff, dash, hint, kiss, peck, reek, slam, slap, sock, tang, whop **5** clout, crack, plumb, punch, right, savor, smell, spang, spank, stink, taste, tinge, trace, whack **6** buffet, heroin, relish, smooch, square, strike, thwack **7** clobber, soupçon

smack-dab
4 bang, just **5** plumb, right, spang **6** square **7** exactly **8** squarely **9** perfectly, precisely

small
3 wee **4** mean, mini, puny, tiny **5** bitty, dinky, dwarf, micro, minor, petty, runty, short, teeny **6** bantam, little, meager, meagre, minute, monkey, narrow, paltry, petite, slight, teensy **7** cramped, stunted, trivial **8** picayune, piddling, pint-size, trifling **9** miniature, minuscule, pint-sized **10** diminutive, negligible, undersized **11** ineffectual, unimportant
combining form: **4** micr, mini **5** micro

small fry
4 kids, tots **8** children **10** youngsters

small-minded
4 mean **5** petty **6** narrow **7** bigoted **9** hidebound, illiberal, parochial **10** brassbound, intolerant, provincial

smallpox
7 variola

small talk
4 chat **6** banter **7** chatter, palaver, prattle **8** badinage, chitchat, raillery, repartee **10** persiflage

small-time
5 minor, petty **6** paltry, two-bit **7** trivial **8** picayune, piddling, trifling **10** bush-league, negligible, shoestring **11** minor-league, unimportant **13** insignificant

smalt
4 blue

smarmy
4 glib, oily **5** slick **6** sleazy **7** buttery, fawning, fulsome **8** unctuous **10** obsequious, oleaginous **12** ingratiating

smart
3 apt **4** ache, chic, keen **5** acute, alert, canny, fresh, natty, nobby, quick, sassy, saucy, savvy, sharp, slick, sting, swank, throb **6** brainy, bright, cheeky, clever, dapper, shrewd, spiffy, spruce, suffer **7** dashing, stylish **8** impudent **11** fashionable, intelligent, quick-witted, ready-witted, sharp-witted

smart aleck
7 show-off, wise guy **8** wiseacre **9** know-it-all **11** wisecracker, wisenheimer

smart-alecky
4 wise **5** fresh, sassy, saucy **6** cheeky **8** impudent, insolent **9** bold-faced **11** impertinent

smart set
5 elect, elite **6** bon ton, gentry **7** in crowd, quality, society, who's who **9** beau monde, haut monde **10** blue bloods, upper crust **11** aristocracy, Four Hundred, high society

smarty-pants
7 wise guy **9** know-it-all, swellhead **11** wisenheimer

smash
3 hit, jar **4** bang, bash, belt, blow, boom, clap, jolt, raze, ruin, slam, slug, sock, wham, whop **5** blast, boffo, burst, clash, crack, crash, crush, shock, whack, wreck **6** batter, impact, pileup, shiver, wallop **7** clobber, crack-up, debacle, destroy, shatter, success **8** collapse, decimate, demolish, knockout, overhand, splinter **9** breakdown, collision, pulverize, sensation, succès fou **10** annihilate **12** disintegrate

smashup
5 crash, wreck **6** fiasco, pileup **7** crack-up, debacle **8** accident, collapse, disaster **9** breakdown, collision

smattering
3 few **7** handful **10** sprinkling

smear
3 dab, tar **4** beat, coat, daub, drub, lick, slur, soil, whip **5** cover, libel, stain, sully, taint **6** befoul, defame, defile, malign, smirch, smudge, spread,

thrash, vilify **7** asperse, blacken, calumny, plaster, shellac, slander, tarnish, traduce **8** besmirch **9** bespatter, denigrate **10** calumniate

smell
4 funk, nose, odor, reek **5** aroma, scent, sense, smack, sniff, snuff, stink, trace, whiff **6** detect, stench **7** bouquet, perfume **9** fragrance, redolence
rotten egg: **6** sulfur

smell, sense of
9 olfaction

smelly
4 rank **5** fetid, funky, reeky **6** foetid, putrid, rancid, stinky **7** noisome, reeking, stenchy **8** mephitic, stinking **10** malodorous

smelt
4 flux, fuse, slag **6** reduce, refine, tomcod **8** sparling **9** sand lance, whitebait

smidgen
3 bit, dab, jot **4** atom, iota, mite **5** crumb, speck, touch **6** morsel

smile
4 beam, grin **5** smirk **6** simper

smirch
see **smudge**

smirk
4 grin, leer **5** fleer, sneer **6** simper **7** grimace

smite
3 hit **4** belt, kill, sock **5** clout, whack **6** assail, attack, strike **7** afflict, assault, clobber, torment

smithereens
4 bits **6** pieces **9** fragments, particles

smitten
4 gaga **5** taken **6** hooked **8** besotted, enamored **9** enamoured, enchanted, entranced **10** captivated, enraptured, infatuated **11** intoxicated

smock
5 apron, dress, frock **8** pinafore

smoke
4 cure, fume **5** fumes, vapor **8** fastball, fumigate **9** cigarette

smoky
4 fumy, gray, hazy **5** murky, sooty **6** turbid **7** reeking **10** caliginous, smoldering

smolder
4 fume, glow, stew **5** churn **6** bubble, seethe, simmer **7** ferment **9** fulminate

smooch
4 buss, kiss, neck, peck **5** smack **8** osculate

smooth
4 easy, even, flat, oily **5** fluid, flush, level, plane, sleek, slick, suave **6** facile, fluent, glassy, glossy, polish, urbane **7** cursive, flatten, flowing, running **8** glabrous, hairless, soothing, unbroken **10** effortless, unwrinkled

smooth-spoken
4 glib **6** fluent **8** eloquent **10** articulate **13** silver-tongued

smorgasbord
4 hash, olio **6** buffet, jumble, medley **7** farrago, grab bag, mélange **8** mishmash, mixed bag, pastiche **9** potpourri **10** hodgepodge, hotchpotch, miscellany, salmagundi **11** gallimaufry

smother
5 choke, douse, quell **6** hush up, muffle, quench, stifle **7** blanket, repress, squelch **8** inundate, restrain, suppress **9** overwhelm, suffocate **10** asphyxiate

smudge
3 dab **4** blot, blur, daub, foul, soil **5** dirty, smear, stain, sully, taint **6** bedaub, blotch, defile, smirch **7** begrime, besmear, blacken, blemish, splotch, tarnish **8** besmirch

smug
8 priggish **9** conceited **10** complacent **13** self-satisfied

smuggle
3 run **7** bootleg

smut
4 porn **5** filth **9** obscenity **11** pornography

smutty
4 blue, foul, lewd, racy **5** bawdy, dirty, nasty, sooty **6** coarse, filthy, risqué, vulgar **7** obscene, raunchy **8** indecent, off-color, prurient **9** salacious **12** pornographic, scatological

Smyrna
5 Izmir

snack
3 tea **4** bite, nosh, tapa **6** morsel, nibble **11** refreshment

snaffle
3 bit, cop **4** lift **5** filch, pinch, swipe **6** pilfer, pocket **7** purloin

snafu
5 botch, error, mix-up, snarl **6** bungle, foul up, mess up, muddle **7** chaotic, screwup **9** confusion

snag
3 nab **4** curb, grab, hook, nail, tear **5** catch, hitch **6** glitch, holdup, hurdle, obtain, secure **7** capture **8** drawback, obstacle **9** apprehend **10** impediment **11** obstruction

snail
5 whelk **6** limpet **7** mollusc, mollusk **8** escargot, ramshorn, slowpoke **9** gastropod **10** periwinkle

snake
3 boa **4** fink **5** crawl, creep, racer, slide **6** python, writhe **7** hognose, serpent, slither **8** anaconda, ophidian, undulate
genus: 4 Eryx
poisonous: 3 asp **5** adder, cobra, coral, krait, mamba, viper **6** elapid, taipan **7** rattler **8** pit viper **10** bushmaster, copperhead, fer-de-lance **11** cottonmouth **13** water moccasin

snakebird
6 darter **7** anhinga

snake-eater
8 mongoose **13** secretary bird

snakelike
7 sinuous **8** ophidian **10** serpentine

snakeroot
7 bugbane **10** wild ginger **11** blazing star

snakeweed
7 bistort **13** poison hemlock

snaky
7 sinuous, winding **8** flexuous, tortuous **10** convoluted, meandering, serpentine **11** anfractuous

snap
4 bang, bark **5** break, cinch, crack **6** breeze, lose it, picnic **7** crackle **8** duck soup, kid stuff, pushover **10** child's play

snap back
6 revive **7** rebound, recover **10** convalesce, recuperate

snappy
4 edgy, fast, tart **5** brisk, hasty, huffy, natty, quick, rapid, sharp, smart, swank, swift, testy **6** lively, prompt, speedy, touchy **7** dashing, stylish, waspish **8** animated, petulant, vigorous **9** breakneck, fractious, irritable, vivacious

snapshot
4 view **5** image, photo **6** précis, sketch, visual **7** picture **8** overview, synopsis **10** shadow copy

snare
3 bag, get, net **4** bait, hook, lure, trap **5** catch, decoy, noose, tempt **6** come-on, enmesh, entice, entrap, seduce, tangle **7** capture, catch up, chicane, embroil, ensnare, ensnarl, involve, mantrap, pitfall, trammel **8** entangle, inveigle **9** chicanery, deception **10** enticement, temptation

snarl
3 jam, web **4** bark, gnar, knot, maze, mesh **5** chaos, growl, ravel, skein **6** jungle, morass, muddle, tangle **7** perplex **8** disarray, disorder, entangle, gridlock, mishmash **9** confusion, labyrinth **10** complexity, complicate **12** complication, entanglement

snatch
3 bit, nab **4** grab, jerk, take, yank **5** catch, pluck, seize, swipe **6** abduct, clutch, kidnap, wrench **8** fragment

snazzy
4 chic **5** fancy, gaudy, jazzy, nobby, ritzy, sassy, sharp, smart, showy, swank **6** chichi, classy, flashy, garish, glitzy, jaunty, spiffy, swanky **7** elegant

sneak
3 cur, pad **4** lurk, slip, worm **5** crawl, creep, glide, mooch, prowl, shirk, skulk, skunk, slide, slink, steal **6** covert, secret, tiptoe, weasel **7** furtive, gumshoe, slither, smuggle **8** hush-hush, slyboots, stealthy **9** pussyfoot, scoundrel **10** undercover **11** clandestine

sneaky
4 foxy **6** shifty, tricky **7** devious, furtive **8** guileful, indirect, slippery, stealthy **9** underhand **11** duplicitous, underhanded

sneer
4 gibe, jeer **5** fleer, scoff, smirk **7** grimace, snigger

sneeze
5 achew, achoo **6** ahchoo
cause: 5 snuff **6** dander, pollen **7** allergy **8** dust mite
French: 7 atchoum
German: 7 hatschi
Spanish: 6 atchís

snicker
5 laugh **6** giggle, titter **7** chortle, chuckle

snide
4 mean **5** nasty **8** spiteful **9** malicious **11** insinuating

sniff
4 jeer, nose **5** scent, scoff, smell, snoop **6** inhale

sniffy
4 smug **5** aloof, lofty **6** lordly, snooty, uppity **7** haughty, pompous, stuck-up **8** scornful, superior **10** disdainful, hoity-toity **12** contemptuous, supercilious

snifter
3 nip, sip, tot **4** dram, drop, jolt, shot, slug **5** glass, snort **6** finger, goblet

snip
3 bit, cut **4** clip, crop, trim **5** notch, scrap **8** fragment

snipe
4 carp **9** sandpiper

sniper
6 gunman, killer **7** shooter **8** marksman, rifleman **12** sharpshooter

snippety
see **snippy**

snippy
4 curt, tart **5** bluff, blunt, brief, gruff, short, terse **6** abrupt, crusty **7** brusque **8** snappish

snit
3 fit **4** flap, fume, huff, stew **5** panic, pique, sweat, tizzy **6** dither, frenzy, lather, pother, swivet **10** conniption

snitch
3 cop, nip, rat **4** beak, blab, fink, hook, lift, palm, sing, tell **5** filch, peach, pinch, spill, steal, swipe **6** inform, pilfer, pocket, squeal, tattle **7** purloin, rat fink, stoolie, tattler, tipster **8** betrayer, informer, squealer **11** stool pigeon

snivel
3 sob **4** weep **5** cower, whine **6** cringe, whinge **7** blubber, snuffle, whimper

snob
5 snoot **6** poseur **7** parvenu

snobbish
6 la-de-da, la-di-da, snooty, uppity **7** elitist, haughty, high-hat, stuck-up **8** lah-de-dah, lah-di-dah **9** lah-dee-dah **10** hoity-toity **11** patronizing, pretentious **12** supercilious **13** condescending

snook
5 cobia **6** robalo **12** sergeant fish

snooker
3 con **4** dupe, fool, hoax, pool **5** trick **6** delude **7** beguile, deceive, defraud **8** flimflam, hoodwink **9** bamboozle **11** hornswoggle

snoop
3 pry, spy **4** nose, peek, peep, peer, poke **5** prier, pryer **6** ferret, meddle, sleuth **7** gumshoe, intrude, meddler **8** busybody, quidnunc **9** detective, inspector, interfere **10** rubberneck

snooper
3 spy **9** detective, inspector **12** investigator

snoopy
4 nosy **6** prying **7** curious **8** meddling **9** intrusive **10** meddlesome **11** inquisitive

snoot
see **snout**

snooty
see **snobbish**

snooze
3 kip, nap **4** doze **5** sleep **6** catnap, drowse, nod off, siesta **7** drop off, slumber **10** forty winks

snore
8 rhonchus

snort
3 nip, tot **4** dram, drop, jolt, shot, slug **5** scoff, snarl **6** exhale, inhale **7** snifter

snout
3 neb **4** beak, nose **6** muzzle, schnoz **7** schnozz **9** proboscis

snow
glacial: 4 firn, névé
melted: 5 slush
pellet: 7 graupel
ridge: 8 sastruga

snow apple
8 mushroom

snowball
5 mount, run up **6** expand **7** augment, burgeon, explode, inflate **8** increase, multiply, mushroom, viburnum **10** accumulate **11** proliferate

snowbird
5 finch, junco **6** thrush **7** bunting **9** fieldfare, ivory gull

Snow-Bound author
8 Whittier (John Greenleaf)

snow finch
9 brambling

snow grouse
9 ptarmigan

snow leopard
5 ounce

Snow Leopard author
11 Matthiessen (Peter)

snowstorm
8 blizzard

snub
3 cut **4** shun **5** blunt, scorn, spite, spurn **6** rebuff, rebuke, slight, stubby **7** put down **9** ostracize, repudiate **12** cold-shoulder

snuff
3 ice, off **4** kill, nose **5** pinch, scent, smell **6** murder, rappee **7** execute **10** extinguish **11** exterminate

snug
4 cozy, neat, taut, tidy, trim **5** comfy, cushy, tight **6** burrow, cuddle, nestle, nuzzle, secure **7** orderly **9** sheltered, shipshape **11** comfortable

snuggle
5 spoon **6** burrow, cuddle, curl up, huddle, nestle, nuzzle

so
3 sae **4** ergo, then, thus, true **5** hence **6** indeed **9** similarly, therefore **11** accordingly **12** consequently

soak
3 ret, sop, sot, wet **4** bilk, clip, lush, skin, swig, wino **5** douse, drink, gouge, imbue, souse, steep **6** boozer, drench, fleece, infuse, rip off,

seethe **7** drinker, guzzler, immerse **8** drunkard, permeate, saturate, submerge **9** alcoholic, penetrate **10** boozehound, impregnate, overcharge
flax: **3** ret

soap
4 suds **6** stroke **7** flatter, wheedle **8** blandish, butter up, inveigle **9** sweet-talk
hard: **7** castile
ingredient: **3** lye, oil **5** scent **9** fragrance

soapbox
4 dais **6** podium **7** rostrum **8** hustings, platform, scaffold

soap plant
5 amole

soapstone
4 talc **8** steatite

soapwort
7 cowherd **11** bouncing bet

soar
3 fly **4** lift, rise **5** arise, climb, glide, hover, mount, shoot **6** ascend, rocket **7** shoot up **8** increase **9** skyrocket

sob
3 cry **4** bawl, blub, wail, weep **7** blubber, whimper

sober
4 calm, cool **5** grave, staid **6** low-key, proper, sedate, solemn **7** austere, earnest, serious, subdued **8** composed, low-keyed, moderate, rational, reserved **9** abstinent, collected, practical, pragmatic, realistic, temperate **10** abstaining, abstemious, controlled, hardheaded, no-nonsense, reasonable, restrained **11** disciplined, down-to-earth **12** matter-of-fact **13** imperturbable, self-possessed

sobriety
7 gravity **10** abstinence, continence, sedateness, temperance **11** seriousness

sobriquet
3 tag **5** alias **6** byname **7** epithet, moniker **8** cognomen, nickname **10** hypocorism

so-called
6 formal **7** alleged, nominal, titular **8** supposed **9** pretended, professed, purported **10** ostensible, self-styled

soccer
cup: **5** World
official: **7** referee **8** linesman
player: **6** booter, goalie, kicker, winger **7** forward, link man, striker, sweeper **8** defender, fullback, halfback **10** goalkeeper
star: **4** Hamm (Mia), Pelé **5** Akers (Michelle), Henry (Thierry), Klose (Miroslav) **6** Zidane (Zinedine) **7** Beckham (David), Ronaldo **8** Chastain (Brandi), Maradona (Diego) **10** Ronaldinho **11** Beckenbauer (Franz)
term: **3** net **4** boot, chip, kick, trap **6** corner, header, tackle, volley **7** dribble, kickoff, throw-in **8** back-heel, free kick, goal kick, goal line **9** touchline **10** center spot, corner flag, corner kick **11** dropped ball, halfway line, penalty kick, penalty spot

sociable
5 close **6** genial **7** affable, amiable, cordial **8** familiar, gracious **9** clubbable, congenial, convivial **10** gregarious, hospitable **11** good-natured

social
5 civic, civil **8** communal **9** clubbable, convivial **10** collective, gregarious, hospitable **11** extroverted **13** companionable
class: **5** caste

Social Contract author
8 Rousseau (Jean-Jacques)

socialist
American: **4** Debs (Eugene) **6** Ripley (George), Thomas (Norman)
British: **4** Owen (Robert, Robert Dale), Webb (Beatrice, Sidney) **6** Morris (William)
French: **7** Fourier (Charles), Viviani (René) **10** Saint-Simon (Henri de)
German: **4** Marx (Karl) **6** Engels (Friedrich) **9** Luxemburg (Rosa) **10** Liebknecht (Wilhelm)

socialize
3 mix **5** party, visit **6** hobnob, mingle **7** consort **9** associate **10** fraternize

social worker
4 Riis (Jacob), Wald (Lillian D.) **6** Addams (Jane) **7** Alinsky (Saul), Lathrop (Julia C.)

society
4 club **5** elite, guild **6** gentry, league, people, public **7** company, quality, who's who **8** populace, sodality **9** beau monde, community, haut monde **10** fellowship, fraternity, upper class, upper crust **11** aristocracy, association, brotherhood **13** companionship
branch: **7** chapter

sociologist
American: **4** Bell (Daniel), Ward (Lester Frank) **5** Balch (Emily Green), Whyte (William H.) **6** Du Bois (W. E. B.), Glazer (Nathan), Sumner (William Graham) **7** Johnson (Charles Spurgeon), Riesman (David)
English: **7** Spencer (Herbert)
French: **8** Durkheim (Emile)
German: **5** Weber (Max)
Italian: **6** Pareto (Vilfredo)
Swedish: **6** Myrdal (Alva, Gunnar)

sock
3 bop, box, hit **4** bash, belt, blow, chop, cuff, ding, slap, slog **5** clout, punch, smack, smash, whack **6** argyle, buffet, strike, thwack, wallop **7** clobber **8** stocking

sock away
4 bank, save, stow **5** cache, hoard, lay by, put by, stash **8** lay aside

socks
4 hose **7** hosiery

Socrates
birthplace: 6 Athens
poison: 7 hemlock
pupil: 5 Plato
wife: 8 Xantippe **9** Xanthippe

Socratic
8 maieutic

sod
4 land, peat, turf **5** earth, grass **6** ground

soda
3 pop **4** cola **5** tonic **7** seltzer

sodality
4 club **5** guild, lodge, order, union **6** league **7** society **9** community **10** fellowship, fraternity **11** association, brotherhood

sodden
3 wet **5** soggy, soppy **6** soaked, soused **7** soaking, sopping **8** drenched, dripping **9** saturated **11** waterlogged, wringing-wet

sodium symbol
2 Na

Sodom and ___
8 Gomorrah
visitor: 3 Lot

sofa
5 couch, divan **7** ottoman **9** banquette, davenport

so far
3 yet **5** as yet, still **6** to date **7** till now **8** hitherto, until now **10** heretofore

Sofia native
6 Bulgar **9** Bulgarian

soft
4 cozy, easy, mild, snug **5** balmy, comfy, cushy, downy, faint, mushy, silky **6** doughy, flabby, gentle, low-key, pliant, satiny, silken, simple, smooth, spongy, tender **7** cottony, lenient, pillowy, pliable, squashy, squishy, subdued, velvety **8** cushiony, workable, yielding **9** malleable **11** comfortable

softcover
9 paperback

soften
4 ease, tame **5** abate, allay, relax **6** dampen, lessen, mellow, soothe, subdue, temper, weaken **7** assuage, lighten, mollify **8** diminish, mitigate, moderate, palliate, tone down **9** alleviate

soft hail
7 graupel

softhearted
4 kind, warm **6** humane, kindly, tender **7** lenient **10** responsive **11** sympathetic **13** compassionate

soft palate
5 velum

soft-pedal
4 mute **6** dampen, hush up, muffle, subdue **8** minimize, play down, suppress, tone down **9** underplay **11** de-emphasize

soft-soap
3 con **4** coax **6** cajole, soothe, wangle **7** blarney, flatter, wheedle **8** blandish, butter up, inveigle **9** sweet-talk

soggy
3 wet **6** doughy, soaked, sodden **7** soaking, sopping **8** drenched, dripping **9** saturated **10** bedraggled **11** waterlogged

Sohrab and Rustum author
6 Arnold (Matthew)

soi-disant
7 alleged **8** putative, so-called, supposed **9** pretended, professed, purported **10** ostensible, self-styled

soil
3 mud, tar **4** daub, dirt, foul, land, loam, mess, muck, murk **5** dirty, earth, grime, muddy, smear, stain, sully, taint **6** defile, ground, smirch, smudge **7** begrime, blacken, country, pollute, tarnish **8** besmirch, discolor, homeland **10** fatherland, motherland, terra firma **11** contaminate
aggregate: 3 ped
clay: 5 gault
combining form: 3 geo **4** agro
dark: 9 chernozem
deposit: 5 loess **7** eluvium
infertile: 6 podzol
layer: 4 gley, sola (plural) **5** solum
rich: 6 hotbed
tropical: 7 latosol

soiree
4 fete, gala **5** party **6** affair, social **7** evening, shindig **8** function **9** festivity, reception **11** celebration **13** entertainment

sojourn
4 bide, stay, stop **5** abide, lodge, tarry, visit **6** linger **7** layover **8** stopover

Sol
3 sun **7** daystar, phoebus
horse: 4 Eous **5** Ethon **9** Erythreos
(see also **Helios**)

solace
5 allay, amuse, cheer **6** buck up **7** comfort, console, hearten **8** inspirit **10** condolence
solar disk
4 Aten, Aton
solarium
7 sunroom
solar-system model
6 orrery
solder
4 fuse, weld **5** braze
soldier
2 GI **5** grunt, sepoy **7** dogface, draftee, fighter, private, recruit, trooper, veteran, warrior **8** bluecoat, doughboy, fusilier, rifleman **9** free lance, guerrilla, man-at-arms, mercenary **10** carabineer, carabinier, serviceman **11** condottiere, infantryman
ancient Greece: **7** hoplite
British: **5** Tommy **7** redcoat
cavalry: **6** hussar **8** chasseur
Confederate: **3** reb
French: **5** poilu **6** Zouave
German: **5** jerry
irregular: **8** guerilla **9** guerrilla
Prussian: **5** uhlan
Turkish: **9** janissary
sole
3 one **4** lone, only **5** alone **6** bottom, single, unique **8** flatfish, singular **9** exclusive
solecism
4 goof, slip **5** boner, error, gaffe, lapse **6** misuse **7** blooper, blunder, faux pas, mistake **9** barbarism, indecorum, vulgarism **11** impropriety
solemn
5 grand, grave, sober, staid, stern **6** august, formal, ritual, sedate, somber, sombre **7** earnest, plenary, serious, stately, weighty **8** funereal, imposing, majestic **9** dignified **10** ceremonial, impressive, no-nonsense, sobersided **11** ceremonious, magnificent
solemnize
4 keep **5** bless, honor **6** hallow **7** dignify, observe **8** venerate **9** celebrate, ritualize **10** consecrate **11** commemorate
solicit
3 ask, beg **4** lure, tout, urge **5** apply **6** demand, drum up, entice **7** beseech, bespeak, canvass, entreat, implore, request **8** petition **9** importune **11** proposition, requisition
solicitor
6 jurist, lawyer, suitor **7** pleader **8** advocate, attorney **9** counselor
solicitous
4 avid, keen **5** eager, fussy **6** ardent, tender **7** anxious, careful, devoted, fearful, finicky, worried **8** rigorous **9** assiduous, attentive, concerned, impatient **10** fastidious, meticulous, scrupulous **11** considerate, punctilious, sympathetic **12** apprehensive **13** conscientious
solicitude
4 care, heed **5** qualm, worry **6** unease **7** anxiety, concern, scruple **9** attention, vigilance **10** uneasiness **11** compunction **12** watchfulness **13** consideration
solid
4 firm, hard **5** dense, sound, valid **6** cogent, secure, stable, sturdy, united **7** compact **8** reliable, unbroken **9** steadfast, unanimous, undivided **10** convincing **11** substantial
solidarity
5 union, unity **6** cement, esprit **7** concord, oneness **8** cohesion **9** integrity **10** singleness **12** cohesiveness, togetherness **13** esprit de corps
solidify
3 dry, fix, gel, set **4** cake, jell **6** freeze, harden, secure **7** compact, congeal **8** compress, contract, indurate **11** consolidate
solitary
4 lone, lorn, only, solo **5** alone **6** hermit, lonely, single, unique **7** recluse **8** derelict, deserted, desolate, eremitic, forsaken, isolated, lonesome, separate, singular **9** abandoned, reclusive, withdrawn **10** antisocial, particular, unsociable **11** standoffish **12** misanthropic **13** unaccompanied
solitude
7 privacy **8** loneness **9** aloneness, isolation, seclusion **10** detachment, loneliness, quarantine, retirement, withdrawal **11** confinement **12** separateness
solo
4 aria, lone **5** alone **6** single **7** unaided **8** solitary **13** independently, unaccompanied
Solomon
brother: **8** Adonijah
daughter: **7** Taphath **8** Basemath
father: **5** David
kingdom: **6** Israel
mother: **9** Bathsheba
son, successor: **8** Rehoboam
victim: **4** Joab **8** Adonijah
Solomon Islands
capital: **7** Honiara
ethnic group: **10** Melanesian
island: **7** Florida, Malaita, Rennell **8** Choiseul **11** Guadalcanal, Santa Isabel **12** San Cristóbal
solon
8 lawgiver **10** legislator

so long
4 by-by, ciao, ta-ta 5 adieu, adios 6 bye-bye, good-by 7 cheerio, good-bye, toodles 8 farewell, Godspeed, toodle-oo

solution
6 answer, result
salt: 6 saline

solve
3 fix 5 break, crack 6 decode, reveal, settle 7 clarify, clear up, dope out, explain, unravel, work out 8 construe, decipher, unriddle, untangle 9 elucidate, figure out, interpret, puzzle out 11 disentangle

Somalia
capital: 9 Mogadishu
gulf: 4 Aden
language: 6 Arabic, Somali
location: 12 Horn of Africa
monetary unit: 8 shilling
neighbor: 5 Kenya 8 Djibouti, Ethiopia

somatic
6 bodily, carnal 7 fleshly 8 corporal, parietal, physical 9 corporeal

somber
3 dim 4 dark, drab, dull, grim 5 bleak, dusky, grave, heavy, murky, staid 6 dismal, dreary, gloomy, sedate, solemn 7 doleful, joyless, obscure, serious, weighty 8 funereal, mournful 9 tenebrous 10 caliginous, depressing, depressive, lugubrious, melancholy, sepulchral, sobersided, tenebrific 11 dispiriting

somersault
4 flip

somewhat
4 a bit, a tad 5 quite 6 fairly, kind of, rather, sort of 7 a little 8 slightly 9 partially, tolerably 10 moderately

sommelier's offering
4 wine

____ Sommer
4 Elke

somniferous
see **sleepy**

somnolent
see **sleepy**

Somnus
brother: 4 Mors
god of: 5 sleep
mother: 3 Nox

son
French: 4 fils
Italian: 6 figlio
Spanish: 4 hijo

song
3 air, lay 4 aria, glee, hymn, lied, tune 5 carol, chant, ditty, lyric, paean 6 ballad, melody, number 7 chanson 8 madrigal
biblical: 8 canticle
boat: 9 barcarole 10 barcarolle
French: 7 chanson
German: 4 lied 6 lieder (plural)
lamentation: 5 dirge 8 threnode, threnody
medieval: 8 sirvente 9 sirventes
morning: 6 aubade
of joy: 5 paean
operatic: 4 aria 7 arietta 8 cavatina 9 cabaletta
Portuguese: 4 fado
sacred: 5 psalm
sailor's: 6 chanty, shanty 7 chantey
short: 8 canzonet
wedding: 8 hymeneal

song and dance
5 pitch, spiel

songbird
see at **bird**

Song of Myself author
7 Whitman (Walt)

Song of Solomon
9 Canticles

songwriter
8 composer, lyricist
famous: 3 Ebb (Fred) 4 Anka (Paul), Bock (Jerry), Cahn (Sammy), Duke (Vernon), Hart (Lorenz), Kern (Jerome), King (Carole), Nyro (Laura), Webb (Jimmy), Wolf (Hugo) 5 Arlen (Harold), Berry (Chuck), Byrne (David), Cohan (George M.), Cohen (Leonard), Cooke (Sam), David (Hal), Dietz (Howard), Dylan (Bob), Evans (Ray), Green (Adolph), Holly (Buddy), Loewe (Frederick), Simon (Carly, Paul), Styne (Jule), Waits (Tom), Weill (Kurt) 6 Berlin (Irving), Comden (Betty), Denver (John), Dozier (Lamont), Fields (Dorothy), Foster (Stephen), Goffin (Gerry), Herman (Jerry), Kander (John), Leiber (Jerry), Lennon (John), Lerner (Alan Jay), Lovett (Lyle), McHugh (Jimmy), Mercer (Johnny), Newman (Randy), Parton (Dolly), Porter (Cole), Sedaka (Neil), Seeger (Pete), Taupin (Bernie), Taylor (James), Travis (Merle), Warren (Harry), Wonder (Stevie) 7 Diamond (Neil), Guthrie (Woody), Harburg (E. Y.), Harnick (Sheldon), Holland (Brian, Eddie), Loesser (Frank), Mancini (Henry), Manilow (Barry), Novello (Ivor), Orbison (Roy), Rodgers (Richard), Romberg (Sigmund), Spector (Phil), Stoller (Mike), Youmans (Vincent) 8 Costello (Elvis), Gershwin (George, Ira), Hamlisch (Marvin), Mayfield (Curtis), Mitchell

(Joni), Morrison (Van), Robinson (Smokey), Schubert (Franz), Schwartz (Arthur), Sondheim (Stephen) **9** Bacharach (Burt), Donaldson (Walter), McCartney (Paul), Strayhorn (Billy), Von Tilzer (Albert, Harry), Van Heusen (Jimmy) **10** Carmichael (Hoagy) **11** Hammerstein (Oscar), Springsteen (Bruce)

Sonja ___
5 Henie

Sonnambula composer
7 Bellini (Vincenzo)

sonnet
developer: 8 Petrarch
part: 5 octet **6** octave, sestet

sonorous
7 ringing, vibrant **8** resonant **10** oratorical, resounding, rhetorical **11** declamatory **12** magniloquent **13** grandiloquent

Sons and Lovers hero
5 Morel (Paul)

Sontag novel
9 In America **12** Volcano Lover (The)

soon
4 anon **6** any day, pronto **7** betimes, by and by, quickly, rapidly, shortly **8** directly, promptly, speedily **9** forthwith, presently, right away **10** before long

Sooner State
8 Oklahoma

soothe
4 balm, calm, ease, hush, lull **5** allay, quiet, salve, still **6** becalm, pacify, settle, solace, subdue **7** appease, assuage, comfort, compose, console, massage, mollify, placate, relieve **8** calm down, reassure **9** alleviate **10** conciliate, propitiate **11** tranquilize

soothsay
5 augur **8** prophesy **9** adumbrate **10** vaticinate **13** prognosticate

soothsayer
4 seer **5** sibyl **6** oracle **7** diviner, prophet **8** foreseer **9** predictor **10** forecaster, foreteller
ancient Roman: 5 augur **6** auspex **8** haruspex
blind: 8 Tiresias
(see also **prophet**)

sop
3 wet **4** gift, soak **5** bribe, douse, goody, souse, steep **6** deluge, drench, reward, seethe **7** douceur **8** gratuity, saturate, waterlog **9** incentive, lagniappe, sweetener **10** enticement

sophism
see **sophistry**

sophistic
5 false, phony **7** invalid, seeming, unsound **8** delusive, illusory, spurious **9** beguiling, casuistic, deceptive, plausible **10** fallacious, fraudulent, misleading, ostensible

sophisticated
5 blasé, jaded, suave **6** smooth, svelte, urbane **7** complex, knowing, refined, worldly **8** cultured, involved, schooled, seasoned **9** Byzantine, elaborate, intricate, practiced **10** world-weary **11** complicated, experienced, worldly-wise **12** cosmopolitan

sophistry
9 casuistry **12** equivocation **13** dissimulation, prevarication

Sophocles play
4 Ajax **7** Electra **8** Antigone **10** Oedipus Rex

Sophonisba
brother: 8 Hannibal
father: 9 Hasdrubal
husband: 6 Syphax

soporific
4 dozy **6** drowsy, opiate, sleepy **7** anodyne, calming, numbing **8** hypnotic, narcotic, sedative **9** calmative, deadening, somnolent **10** anesthetic, slumberous **11** somniferous **12** somnifacient **13** tranquilizing

soprano
American: 4 Pons (Lily) **5** Costa (Mary), Gluck (Alma), Moffo (Anna), Moore (Grace), Price (Leontyne), Sills (Beverly) **6** Arroyo (Martina), Battle (Kathleen), Callas (Maria), Curtin (Phyllis), Donath (Helen), Farrar (Geraldine), Garden (Mary), Munsel (Patrice), Norman (Jessye), Peters (Roberta), Piazza (Marguerite), Resnik (Regina), Upshaw (Dawn) **7** Farrell (Eileen), Fleming (Renée), Kirsten (Dorothy), Stevens (Risë), Traubel (Helen) **8** Ponselle (Rosa)
Australian: 5 Melba (Nellie) **10** Sutherland (Joan)
Austrian: 4 Popp (Lucia) **7** Rysanek (Leonie) **8** Sembrich (Marcella)
Canadian: 7 Stratas (Teresa)
French: 7 Crespin (Régine)
German: 6 Leider (Frida) **7** Lehmann (Lilli, Lotte) **11** Schwarzkopf (Elisabeth)
Italian: 5 Freni (Mirella), Grisi (Giuditta, Giulia), Patti (Adelina) **6** Scotto (Renata) **7** Bartoli (Cecilia), Tebaldi (Renata) **10** Tetrazzini (Luisa) **11** Ricciarelli (Katia)
Korean: 6 Sumi Jo
Mexican: 8 Cruz-Romo (Gilda)
New Zealand: 8 Te Kanawa (Kiri)
Norwegian: 8 Flagstad (Kirsten)

Romanian: **8** Cotrubas (Ileana)
Russian: **8** Netrebko (Anna)
Spanish: **7** Caballé (Montserrat) **8** Berganza (Teresa) **12** de los Angeles (Victoria)
Swedish: **4** Lind (Jenny) **7** Nilsson (Birgit)
(see also **mezzo-soprano**)

sorcerer
4 mage **5** magus **6** wizard **7** warlock **8** conjurer, conjuror, magician **9** enchanter **11** necromancer, thaumaturge **13** thaumaturgist

sorceress
3 hag, hex **5** Circe, witch

sorcery
5 magic **8** diablery, wizardry **9** conjuring **10** necromancy, witchcraft **11** bewitchment, enchantment, thaumaturgy
West Indian: **5** obeah

sordid
3 low **4** base, foul, mean, vile **5** dirty, nasty, seamy, shady, venal **6** blowsy, blowzy, filthy, frowsy, frowzy, grubby, scurvy, shabby, sleazy **7** ignoble, low-down, squalid, unclean **8** degraded, shameful, wretched **9** loathsome, mercenary **10** despicable, scandalous, slatternly **11** disgraceful **12** contemptible, disreputable **13** reprehensible

sore
3 raw **4** achy, boil **5** angry, irked, ulcer, upset, vexed **6** aching, bitter, canker, peeved, tender **7** abscess, chancre, hurting, painful **8** inflamed, smarting **9** chilblain, irritated, rancorous, resentful, sensitive **10** affliction

sorehead
4 crab **5** grump **6** griper, grouch **7** grouser **8** grumbler, sourpuss **10** bellyacher, complainer, crosspatch, malcontent

sorrel
3 oca **4** dock **8** chestnut, sourwood

sorrow
3 rue, sob, woe **4** moan, ruth **5** dolor, grief, mourn **6** grieve, lament, misery, regret **7** anguish, remorse, sadness **8** distress, grieving, mourning **9** dejection, heartache, suffering **10** affliction, heartbreak, melancholy **11** lamentation, unhappiness **12** mournfulness

sorrowful
3 sad **6** rueful, triste, woeful **7** doleful, forlorn, piteous, ruthful, unhappy **8** dolorous, downcast, grieving, mournful, tristful, wretched **9** afflicted, miserable, plaintive, woebegone **10** lamentable, lugubrious, melancholy **11** heartbroken **12** disconsolate

sorry
3 bad, sad **4** mean, poor **5** cheap **6** cheesy, paltry, scummy, scurvy, shabby, shoddy **7** scruffy, unhappy **8** beggarly, contrite, mournful, penitent, pitiable, saddened, trifling, wretched **9** miserable, regretful, repentant **10** apologetic, despicable, inadequate, melancholy, remorseful **11** disgraceful, penitential **12** contemptible, heavyhearted

sort
3 ilk, lot, set **4** comb, cull, kind, pick, sift, type **5** class, order **6** choose, screen, select, stripe, winnow **7** arrange, catalog, species, variety **8** classify, separate **9** catalogue, character **10** categorize, pigeonhole

sortie
4 dash, raid **5** foray, sally **7** assault, mission **9** excursion **10** expedition

sortilege
6 augury **7** sorcery **8** divining, witchery **10** divination, necromancy, witchcraft **11** thaumaturgy

so-so
4 fair, okay **6** decent, enough, fairly, medium, rather **7** average, fairish **8** adequate, mediocre, middling, moderate, passable, passably **9** tolerably **10** moderately **11** indifferent **12** run-of-the-mill

sot
4 lush, wino **5** drunk, souse **6** bibber, boozer **7** guzzler, tippler, tosspot **8** drunkard **9** alcoholic, inebriate **10** boozehound

sotto voce
3 low **5** aside **6** softly **7** faintly, mutedly, quietly **9** privately

souchong
3 tea

sough
4 sigh **7** suspire, whisper

soul
4 pith **5** anima, being, heart, stuff **6** animus, breast, marrow, pneuma, psyche, spirit **7** essence **9** élan vital, substance **10** conscience, vital force **12** quintessence
combining form: **5** psych **6** psycho

soulful
6 moving, tender **7** emotive, fervent **8** poignant, stirring, touching **9** affecting, emotional **11** impassioned, sentimental

soul singer
4 Gaye (Marvin) **5** Bland (Bobby), Brown (James), Cooke (Sam), Flack (Roberta), Green (Al), Hayes (Isaac) **6** Butler (Jerry), Knight (Gladys), Sledge (Percy) **7** Charles (Ray), Pickett (Wilson), Redding (Otis) **8** Franklin (Aretha), Mayfield (Curtis)

sound
3 fit **4** firm, hale, kyle, safe, sane **5** audio, legit, noise, plumb, probe, right, sober, solid, valid,

whole **6** cogent, fathom, intact, secure, stable, sturdy, unhurt **7** correct, earshot, healthy, logical, prudent **8** rational, reliable, sensible, unharmed **9** judicious, resonance, undamaged, vibration, wholesome **10** convincing, reasonable **11** well-founded **12** satisfactory, well-grounded **13** reverberation
combining form: 3 son **4** phon, soni, sono **5** audio, audit, phone, phono, phony **6** audito, phonia
gentle: 6 rustle
high-pitched: 4 ping, ting
pleasant: 7 euphony
quality: 6 timbre
repeating: 7 rat-a-tat **8** rataplan **10** rat-a-tat-tat
science: 6 sonics **7** phonics **9** acoustics

Sound
Alaska: 5 Cross
Antarctica: 7 McMurdo
Australia: 4 King **5** Broad
Bahamas: 5 Exuma
Canada: 4 Howe **6** Nansen
Connecticut-New York: 10 Long Island
English Channel: 8 Plymouth
Georgia: 8 Altamaha
Greenland: 5 Smith
Gulf of Mexico: 8 Suwannee **11** Mississippi
Massachusetts: 8 Vineyard **9** Nantucket
New England: 11 Block Island
North Carolina: 4 Core **5** Bogue **7** Pamlico, Roanoke **9** Albemarle, Currituck
Northwest Territories: 4 Peel **8** Melville **9** Lancaster **12** Prince Albert
Norwegian Sea: 8 Scoresby
Ontario: 4 Owen
Scotland: 3 Hoy **4** Jura, Mull **5** Inner
Spitsbergen: 4 Bell
Washington: 5 Puget

Sound and the Fury, The
author: 8 Faulkner (William)
character: 5 Benjy (Compson), Caddy (Compson), Jason (Compson) **6** Dilsey **7** Quentin (Compson)

soundness
6 health, sanity **7** balance **8** lucidity, prudence, security, solidity, strength **9** integrity, stability **11** reliability **12** practicality

sound off
7 speak up **8** speak out

soup
beet: 6 borsch **7** borscht
bowl: 6 tureen
clear: 5 broth **8** bouillon, consommé, julienne
cold: 8 gazpacho **11** vichyssoise
curry: 12 mulligatawny
okra: 5 gumbo
seafood: 7 chowder
soy: 4 miso
thick: 5 gumbo, puree **6** bisque, burgoo, potage
vegetable: 10 minestrone

soupçon
see **particle**

soupy
5 foggy, gooey, gushy, murky, mushy **6** drippy, slushy, smoggy **7** cloying, maudlin, mawkish **8** cornball **9** schmaltzy **10** saccharine **11** sentimental, tear-jerking

sour
4 acid, dour, tart **5** acerb, acrid, tangy, testy **6** acidic, bitter, crabby, cranky, curdle, grumpy, morose, rancid, rotten, sullen, turned **7** acerbic, grouchy, peevish, prickly, spoiled, unhappy **8** embitter, vinegary **9** acidulous, fermented **12** disagreeable

source
4 font, root, well **5** basis, cause, fount, model, onset, start **6** mother, origin, spring **7** dawning, genesis **8** begetter, fountain, wellhead **9** beginning, inception, informant, precursor, prototype, reference, rootstock **10** antecedent, authorship, birthplace, derivation, originator, progenitor, provenance, wellspring **11** origination, provenience **12** fountainhead

sourness
7 acidity **8** acerbity, asperity

sourpuss
4 crab **5** crank, grump **6** griper, grouch **7** grouser, killjoy **8** grumbler, sorehead **10** bellyacher, complainer, crosspatch, curmudgeon **11** misanthrope

souse
3 dip, sop, sot **4** lush, soak, wino **5** binge, drown, steep **6** boozer, drench, pickle, plunge, seethe **7** immerse **8** drunkard, inundate, marinate, preserve, saturate, submerge, submerse **9** alcoholic, immersion, inebriate **10** boozehound, intoxicate **11** dipsomaniac

soused
3 lit **4** high **5** drunk, lit up, oiled **6** bashed, blotto, bombed, juiced, potted, soaked, soused, stewed, stoned, tanked, wasted, zonked **7** crocked, drunken, pickled, pie-eyed, sloshed, smashed, sottish **8** polluted **9** plastered **10** inebriated, liquored up **11** intoxicated

south
combining form: 5 austr **6** austro
French: 3 sud
Spanish: 3 sur

South Africa
capital: 8 Cape Town, Pretoria **12** Bloemfontein
city: 6 Durban **12** Johannesburg
desert: 8 Kalahari

enclave: **7** Lesotho
grassland: **4** veld **5** veldt
language: **5** Bantu **7** English **9** Afrikaans
monetary unit: **4** rand
mountain range: **11** Drakensberg
native: **3** San **4** Khoi, Zulu **5** Pondo, Sotho, Swazi, Venda, Xhosa **6** Tswana **7** Bushmen, Khoisan **9** Hottentot
neighbor: **7** Namibia **8** Botswana **9** Swaziland **10** Mozambique, Zimbabwe
plateau: **5** Karoo **6** Karroo
province: **7** Gauteng **8** Northern **9** Free State **10** Mpumalanga
river: **6** Molopo, Orange
settlers: **5** Boers

South America
country: **4** Peru **5** Chile **6** Brazil, Guyana **7** Bolivia, Ecuador, Uruguay **8** Colombia, Paraguay, Suriname **9** Argentina, Venezuela
ethnic group: **6** Aymara, Creole, Indian **7** mestizo, mulatto, Quechua, Spanish **10** Amerindian, Portuguese
language: **6** Aymara **7** Guaraní, Quechua, Spanish **10** Portuguese

South Carolina
capital: **8** Columbia
city: **10** Charleston, Greenville
college, university: **7** Citadel, Clemson
fort: **6** Sumter
island, island group: **3** Sea **6** Edisto, Parris **10** Hilton Head
nickname: **8** Palmetto (State)
river: **6** Edisto, Pee Dee, Santee **7** Tugaloo **8** Savannah
state bird: **12** Carolina wren
state flower: **13** yellow jasmine
state tree: **8** palmetto

South Dakota
capital: **6** Pierre
city: **9** Rapid City **10** Sioux Falls
mountain: **6** Harney (Peak) **8** Rushmore **10** Black Hills
nickname: **6** Coyote (State) **10** Mt. Rushmore (State)
park: **8** Badlands, Wind Cave
river: **8** Missouri **11** Belle Forche
state bird: **18** ring-necked pheasant
state flower: **12** pasqueflower
state tree: **6** spruce

southerly
7 austral

South Korea
see **Korea, South**

southpaw
5 lefty

South-West Africa
7 Namibia

south wind
see at **wind**

souvenir
5 relic, token **6** trophy **7** memento **8** keepsake, memorial, reminder **11** remembrance

sovereign
4 coin, czar, free, king, tsar **5** queen, regal, royal, ruler **6** kingly, ruling **7** emperor, empress, highest, monarch, regnant, supreme **8** absolute, autarkic, autocrat, dominant, imperial, kinglike, majestic **9** ascendant, autarchic, monarchal, number one, paramount, potentate **10** autonomous, monarchial **11** independent, monarchical, predominant **12** self-governed

soviet
7 council **9** committee

Soviet Union
4 CCCP, USSR

sow
4 seed, toss **5** drill, fling, plant, strew **7** bestrew, scatter **9** broadcast **11** disseminate

soybean paste
4 miso

spa
5 baths, hydro, wells **6** hot tub, resort, spring, waters **7** springs **13** watering place
Czech: **6** Bilina **8** Karlsbad
English: **4** Bath **6** Buxton **9** Harrogate
French: **3** Dax **5** Evian
German: **3** Ems **5** Baden **6** Bad Ems **9** Kissingen

space
3 gap **4** area, room **5** blank, ether, plena (plural), scope **6** cavity, extent, plenum, spread, volume **7** breadth, expanse, stretch **8** capacity, distance, interval, universe **9** amplitude, expansion

spaced-out
4 high **5** doped **6** stoned, zonked **7** drugged **8** hopped-up, turned on

space station
3 Mir **6** Salyut, Skylab

spacious
3 big **4** vast, wide **5** ample, large, roomy **7** immense **8** enormous, extended **9** boundless, capacious, cavernous, expansive, extensive **10** commodious, voluminous

spade
3 dig, loy **4** grub **5** dig up, scoop **6** dig out, shovel **8** excavate

Spade, Sam
4 dick **6** shamus, sleuth **7** gumshoe **9** detective **10** private eye
creator: **7** Hammett (Dashiell)
novel: **13** Maltese Falcon (The)

Spain
ancient name: **8** Hispania
capital: **6** Madrid
city: **6** Málaga **7** Seville **8** Pamplona, Valencia, Zaragoza **9** Barcelona, Saragossa
island group: **6** Canary **8** Balearic
king: **10** Juan Carlos
leader: **6** Franco (Francisco)
monetary unit: **4** euro
monetary unit, former: **4** real **6** peseta
mountain: **8** Mulhacén **11** Pico de Aneto
mountain range: **8** Pyrenees
neighbor: **6** France **8** Portugal
peninsula: **7** Iberian
region: **6** Aragon, Murcia **7** Galicia **8** Valencia **9** Andalusia, Catalonia
river: **4** Ebro **12** Guadalquivir
sea: **13** Mediterranean
strait: **9** Gibraltar

spall
4 chip **5** flake **7** shaving **8** fragment **9** exfoliate

span
4 arch, term, time **5** cross, reach **6** extent, length, period, spread **7** compass, measure, stretch **8** duration, interval, lifetime, straddle, traverse

spangle
4 trim **5** flash, gleam **6** sequin **7** glitter, shimmer, sparkle, twinkle **9** coruscate **11** scintillate

Spaniard
9 Castilian

Spanish
aunt: **3** tia
bay: **5** bahia
bed: **4** cama **5** lecho
bird: **6** pájaro
boss: **7** cacique
bread: **3** pan
bridge: **6** puente
bull: **4** toro **6** el toro
chaperone: **6** duenna
church: **7** iglesia
combining form: **7** hispano
crossword puzzle: **10** crucigrama
dance: **4** jota **5** baile, salsa **6** bailar **8** fandango, flamenco **9** zapateado
devil: **6** diablo
dictator: **8** caudillo
door: **6** puerta
dress: **7** vestido
folksong: **6** tonada
fortress: **7** alcazar
game: **5** juego
garrison: **8** presidio
gift: **6** regalo
gold: **3** oro
good-bye: **5** adiós
hello: **4** hola
hors d'oeuvre: **4** tapa
house: **4** casa
husband: **6** esposo, marido
ice cream: **6** helado
inn: **6** posada
journey: **5** viaje
library: **10** biblioteca
light: **3** luz
mayor: **7** alcalde
milk: **5** leche
money: **5** plata **6** dinero
movie: **8** pelicula
movies: **4** cine
number: **3** dos, uno **4** diez, doce, ocho, once, seis, tres **5** cinco, nueve, siete **6** cuatro
national hero: **3** Cid (El) **5** El Cid
nobleman: **7** grandee
operetta: **8** zarzuela
penal settlement: **8** presidio
plain: **4** vega **5** llano, pampa
plantation: **8** hacienda
please: **8** por favor
princess: **7** infanta
ranch: **5** finca **8** estancia
river: **3** rio
room: **4** sala **6** cuarto
saint: **7** Dominic **8** Ignatius
sale: **5** venta
scarf: **7** pañuelo **8** mantilla
school: **7** colegio, escuela
shawl: **6** rebozo, serape
shirt: **6** camisa
shoe: **6** zapato **7** calzado
singer: **8** cantante
skirt: **5** falda
soccer: **6** fútbol
street: **5** calle
thank you: **7** gracias
title: **3** don, Sra. **4** doña, Srta. **5** señor **6** señora **8** señorita
tree: **5** árbol
trousers: **10** pantalones
uncle: **3** tío
wife: **6** esposa
wine: **4** sack **6** sherry

Spanish fly
9 cantharis

spank
4 cane, flog, lash, slap **5** smack **6** larrup, paddle, punish, thrash **7** scourge **8** chastise

spar
3 box, vie **4** pole **5** joust, sprit, stall **7** dispute, wrangle **8** longeron
ship's: **4** boom, gaff, mast, yard **7** yardarm **8** bowsprit

spare
4 lank, lean, pity, save, slim **5** avoid, extra, gaunt, lanky **6** backup, excess, excuse, exempt,

let off, meager, meagre, pardon, scanty, scrape, scrimp, skimpy, skinny, slight, unused **7** absolve, relieve, reserve, scrawny, scrimpy, surplus **8** leftover **10** additional **11** superfluous

sparing
4 bare, wary **5** canny, chary, tight **6** frugal, meager, meagre, saving, stingy **7** prudent, thrifty **9** provident **10** economical, restrained, unwasteful **11** tightfisted **12** parsimonious

spark
3 woo **5** court, ember, glint **6** foment, incite, kindle, set off **7** provoke, trigger **8** activate, touch off **9** instigate, scintilla

sparkle
4 zing **5** flash, gleam, glint, verve **7** glimmer, glisten, glitter, shimmer, twinkle **8** vivacity **9** animation, coruscate **10** effervesce, liveliness **11** coruscation, scintillate **13** scintillation

sparkling
6 bubbly, lively **8** animated, bubbling **9** brilliant **12** effervescent

Spark novel
11 Memento Mori **21** Prime of Miss Jean Brodie (The)

sparse
4 rare, thin **5** scant **6** meager, meagre, scanty, scarce, skimpy **7** limited, scrimpy **8** exiguous, sporadic, uncommon **9** dispersed, scattered **10** inadequate, infrequent, occasional **12** insufficient

Sparta
10 Lacedaemon
country: **7** Laconia
king: **8** Leonidas, Menelaos
opponent: **6** Athens
queen: **4** Leda

Spartacus
author: **4** Fast (Howard)
slayer: **7** Crassus

spasm
3 fit, tic **4** pang **5** burst, crick, throe **6** twitch **8** paroxysm **10** convulsion
muscular: **6** clonus

spasmodic
5 jerky **6** fitful, spotty **7** erratic **8** sporadic **9** desultory, excitable **10** convulsive **12** intermittent

spat
3 row **4** flap, miff, tiff **5** fight, scene, scrap **6** bicker, gaiter, hassle, oyster **7** brabble, dispute, fall out, quarrel, rhubarb, wrangle **8** argument, outburst, squabble **10** falling-out **11** altercation

spate
4 flow, flux, gush, pour, rain, rush, tide **5** flood, river, spurt, surge **6** deluge, series, shower, stream **7** current, freshet, torrent **8** cataract, outburst, overflow **10** inundation, outpouring

spatter
4 slop, slur, spit **5** douse, fleck, plash, slosh, smear, spray, spurt, swash **6** befoul, defame, malign, splash, splosh, vilify **7** asperse, blacken, handful, slander, speckle, splurge, stipple, traduce **8** besmirch, sprinkle **9** denigrate, disparage

spawn
4 eggs, sire **5** beget, breed, brood, hatch, issue **6** create, father, parent **7** produce, product, progeny, provoke **8** engender, generate **9** offspring, originate, procreate, propagate, reproduce, stimulate

speak
3 gab, jaw, say, yak **4** blab, chat, chin, talk **5** blurt, drawl, mouth, orate, spiel, spout, utter, voice **6** assert, convey, intone, mumble, murmur, mutter, parley **7** address, declaim, declare, lecture, phonate, whisper **8** converse, dilate on, perorate, vocalize **9** discourse, enunciate, expatiate, hold forth, verbalize
combining form: **4** phon
confusedly: **7** stammer, stutter **8** splutter
for: **7** testify

speaker
5 voice **6** orator **9** spokesman **10** mouthpiece **12** spokesperson

spear
3 gig **4** pike, spit **5** gouge, lance, spike **6** impale, pierce, skewer **7** assagai, assegai, harpoon, leister, trident **8** puncture, transfix **9** penetrate

spearhead
4 lead **5** front **6** direct

spear-thrower
6 atlatl **7** woomera

special
4 rare **6** unique **7** express, notable, unusual **8** peculiar, uncommon **10** designated, individual, noteworthy, particular **11** distinctive, exceptional, outstanding

species
4 kind, sort, type **5** breed, class, order

specific
3 set **5** exact **6** strict, unique **7** express, limited, precise, special **8** clean-cut, clear-cut, definite, distinct, especial, explicit **10** individual, particular **11** categorical, unambiguous

specify
3 fix, set **4** cite, list, name **6** detail **7** itemize, mention, pin down, tick off **8** instance, spell out **9** determine, enumerate, establish, inventory, stipulate **13** particularize

specimen
4 case, sort, type **6** sample **7** example, neotype, variety **8** exemplar, holotype, instance, sampling **12** illustration

specious
5 empty, false **6** hollow **8** spurious **9** casuistic, plausible, sophistic **10** misleading, ostensible **11** sophistical

speciousness
7 sophism **9** casuistry, sophistry

speck
3 bit, dot, jot **4** atom, iota, mite, mote, spot, tick, whit **5** crumb, fleck, grain, point, shred, trace **7** freckle, smidgen **8** molecule, particle, pinpoint

speckle
3 dot **4** spot **5** flake, fleck **6** dapple, pepper **7** stipple **8** sprinkle

spectacle
4 pomp, show **5** drama, sight **6** parade **7** display, pageant, panoply, tableau **10** exhibition, exposition **12** extravaganza

spectacular
5 stagy **7** amazing, pageant **8** dazzling, dramatic, striking, wondrous **9** marvelous, thrilling, wonderful **10** astounding, eye-popping, histrionic, miraculous, phenomenal, prodigious, staggering, stupefying, stupendous, theatrical **11** astonishing, sensational **12** extravaganza

spectator
5 gazer **6** viewer **7** watcher, witness **8** beholder, observer, onlooker **9** bystander **10** eyewitness

Spectator author
6 Steele (Richard) **7** Addison (Joseph)

specter
5 ghost, shade **6** shadow, spirit, wraith **7** eidolon, phantom **8** phantasm, revenant, visitant **10** apparition

spectral
6 spooky **7** ghastly, ghostly, phantom **9** ghostlike, unearthly **10** shadowlike **11** disembodied, phantomlike

spectrum
5 ambit, gamut, range, scale, sweep **7** compass **8** diapason **9** continuum
producer: **5** prism

speculate
4 muse **5** study, think, weigh **6** ponder, reason, review, wonder **7** reflect **8** cogitate, consider, meditate, ruminate, theorize **9** cerebrate **10** conjecture, deliberate **11** contemplate

speculation
5 guess, hunch **6** gamble, review, theory **7** surmise **9** brainwork **10** conjecture

speculative
5 risky **7** curious, pensive **8** academic **10** thoughtful **11** conjectural, theoretical **12** hypothetical

speech
4 talk **5** idiom, spiel, voice **6** debate, homily, parley, sermon, tirade, tongue **7** address, dialect, diction, lecture, monolog, oration, palaver **8** dialogue, diatribe, harangue, language, parlance, rhetoric **9** discourse, monologue, utterance **10** allocution, expression, vernacular **11** declamation **12** articulation, disquisition, vocalization **13** verbalization
defect: **4** lisp **7** stutter

speechcraft
7 oratory **8** rhetoric **9** elocution

speechless
3 mum **4** dumb, mute **6** silent **7** aphonic **10** dumbstruck, tongue-tied

speed
3 fly, hie, run, zip **4** clip, gait, pace, race, rush, tear, whiz **5** chase, haste, hurry, tempo **6** barrel, burn up, career, hasten, hustle, whoosh **7** quicken **8** alacrity, celerity, dispatch, expedite, highball, legerity, momentum, rapidity, velocity **9** fleetness, quickness, swiftness **10** accelerate, cannonball, facilitate, promptness

speed skater
see **ice skater**

speedway
5 track **8** turnpike **9** racetrack **10** racecourse

speedy
4 fast **5** brisk, fleet, hasty, quick, rapid, swift **6** nimble, prompt **8** headlong **9** breakneck **11** expeditious

spell
3 hex **4** bout, jinx, mojo, rune, time, tour, turn **5** charm, hitch, shift, stint, throe, while **6** attack, period, streak, voodoo **7** relieve, stretch **11** conjuration, incantation

spellbind
3 hex **4** grip, vamp **5** charm **7** bewitch, catch up, enchant **8** enthrall, entrance **9** enrapture, fascinate, hypnotize, mesmerize

spelling
11 orthography
bad: **10** cacography

spell out
7 clarify, explain, expound **8** construe, set forth **9** elucidate, explicate, interpret

spelunker
5 caver

spend
3 pay **4** blow, drop, pass **5** use up, waste **6** lavish, lay out, outlay **7** consume, exhaust,

fork out, hand out, splurge **8** disburse, shell out, squander **9** dissipate, go through, throw away, while away **10** contribute, run through

spender
7 wastrel **8** prodigal **10** high roller, profligate, squanderer **11** scattergood

spendthrift
see **spender**

Spenser poem
11 Faerie Queen (The)

spent
4 shot **5** all in **6** effete, pooped, used-up, wasted **7** drained, worn-out **8** burnt out, consumed, depleted, washed-up **9** exhausted, washed-out

spew
4 gush, ooze **5** belch, eject, eruct, erupt, expel, exude, flood, heave, shoot, spray, vomit **6** irrupt, spit up, squirt **7** throw up, upchuck **8** disgorge

sphagnum
4 moss

sphere
3 orb **4** area, ball, star, turf, zone **5** arena, field, globe, range, realm, round, scope **6** circle, domain, planet **7** demesne, rondure, terrain **8** dominion, province **9** bailiwick, territory **12** jurisdiction

spherical
5 round **6** global **7** globose **8** globular **9** orbicular

Sphinx
builder: **6** Khafre
father: **6** Typhon
mother: **7** Echidna
query: **6** riddle
site: **4** Giza **6** Thebes

spice
3 pep, zip **4** kick, mace, tang, zest **5** anise, aroma, clove, cumin, poppy, savor, scent, smack, smell, taste **6** cloves, fennel, ginger, nutmeg, pepper, relish, sesame **7** bouquet, caraway, perfume **8** cardamom, cinnamon, piquancy **9** fragrance, redolence, seasoning

Spice Islands
8 Moluccas

spick-and-span
3 new **4** mint, neat, snug, tidy, trig, trim **5** clean, fresh **6** spruce **7** orderly **8** brand-new, spotless **9** shipshape **10** immaculate **11** well-groomed

spicy
3 hot **4** racy **5** bawdy, fiery, salty, tangy, zesty **6** lively, purple, ribald, risqué, savory, snappy, wicked **7** gingery, peppery, piquant, pungent, scented, zestful **8** aromatic, fragrant, off-color, perfumed, redolent, seasoned, spirited **9** flavorful, salacious **10** scandalous, suggestive **11** titillating

spider
6 Aranea, frypan **7** skillet **8** arachnid **9** frying pan **10** black widow

spiel
4 jive, line **5** pitch **6** patter **12** song and dance

Spielberg film
4 Hook, Jaws **6** Always, Munich **7** Amistad **8** Terminal (The) **9** Lost World (The) **11** Color Purple (The) **12** Jurassic Park, Twilight Zone (The) **14** Empire of the Sun, Minority Report, Schindler's List, War of the Worlds **15** Catch Me if You Can **16** Sugarland Express (The) **17** Saving Private Ryan **19** Raiders of the Lost Ark

spieler
4 tout **6** barker, hawker, talker **8** huckster

spigot
3 tap **4** cock, gate **5** valve **6** faucet **7** hydrant, petcock, shutoff **8** stopcock

spike
3 pin **4** brob, heel, lace, nail **5** lance, piton, spear **6** antler, impale, needle, skewer **7** spindle **8** increase, mackerel, puncture, transfix

spile
4 bung **5** spout

spill
4 blab, drip, drop, fall, flow, slop, tell **5** spray **6** betray, inform, reveal, splash, squeal, tattle **7** divulge, dribble, run over, spatter **8** disclose, overflow

Spillane detective
10 Mike Hammer

spilth
5 dregs, dross, swill, trash, waste **6** debris, refuse, scraps **7** garbage, rubbish **8** leavings

spin
4 gyre, reel, ride, swim, turn **5** dizzy, swirl, twirl, wheel, whirl **6** gyrate, rotate **7** revolve **8** rotation **9** pirouette, whirligig **10** revolution
a log: **4** birl
out: **4** draw **6** extend **7** prolong, stretch **8** elongate, lengthen, protract **10** prolongate

spinal column
5 chine **6** rachis
curvature: **8** lordosis
part: **8** vertebra
(see also **spine**)

spindle
3 pin, rod **5** newel, shaft, spike **6** impale, rachis

spindly
5 frail, lanky, rangy, shaky, weedy **6** flimsy, gangly, skinny, twiggy, wobbly **7** fragile, rickety, tottery **8** gangling, skeletal, unsteady **9** emaciated **10** jerry-built

spine
4 back **6** rachis **7** spicule **8** backbone **9** vertebrae

spineless
5 timid **8** cowardly, timorous **9** weak-kneed **10** weak-willed **12** invertebrate

spin-off
8 offshoot **9** by-product, outgrowth **10** derivative, descendant

____ Spinoza
6 Baruch

spinster
7 old maid **10** maiden lady

spiny
6 barbed, thorny **7** prickly **8** echinate **10** nettlesome

spiral
4 coil, curl, wind **5** helix, twine, twist **6** volute **7** helical, helices (plural) **8** gyroidal, volution **9** cochleate, corkscrew
combining form: **3** gyr **4** gyro **5** helic **6** helico

spire
4 coil **5** twist, whorl **7** steeple **8** pinnacle

spirit
3 pep, vim, zip **4** brio, dash, élan, gimp, grit, guts, life, mood, snap, soul, zeal, zest, zing **5** anima, ardor, drive, force, heart, moxie, oomph, pluck, shade, spunk, tenor, verve, vigor **6** animus, daimon, energy, esprit, fervor, ginger, mettle, morale, pneuma, psyche, starch, temper, wraith **7** courage, passion, phantom, specter, spectre **8** phantasm, revenant, vitality **9** animation, élan vital, substance **10** apparition, enthusiasm, get-up-and-go, liveliness
away: **6** abduct, kidnap, snatch
bottled: **5** genie
evil: **3** ker **4** aitu **5** afrit, demon **6** afreet **7** erlking, shaitan
female: **5** nymph **7** banshee
Hopi: **7** kachina
of a place: **10** genius loci
Persian: **4** peri

spirited
4 bold, game, keen **5** eager, fiery, peppy **6** ardent, gritty, lively, plucky, spunky **7** chipper, fervent, gingery, peppery, valiant, zealous **8** animated, cheerful, intrepid, resolute **9** audacious, dauntless, energetic, sprightly, vivacious **10** courageous, mettlesome, passionate **12** enthusiastic

spirits
5 booze, drink **6** liquor, tipple **9** aqua vitae, firewater
low: **5** blues, dumps, ennui **8** doldrums **10** blue devils, depression, melancholy

spiritual
6 sacred **7** saintly **8** churchly, mystical, numinous, platonic **9** religious **10** high-minded, immaterial, unphysical **11** disembodied, incorporeal, nonmaterial, nonphysical **12** metaphysical, supernatural, transcendent

spiritualist
6 medium, mystic **7** psychic

spit
5 spear **6** impale, saliva, skewer, slaver, sputum **7** spatter, sputter **8** splutter **9** brochette **11** expectorate

spite
5 venom **6** grudge, malice, rancor, spleen **7** ill will, revenge **9** pettiness, vengeance **11** malevolence **13** maliciousness

spiteful
4 mean **5** catty, nasty, snide **6** malign, wicked **7** vicious, waspish **8** venomous **9** malicious, malignant, rancorous **10** malevolent, vindictive

spitfire
4 fury **5** harpy, shrew, vixen **6** dragon, virago **7** hellcat, tigress **8** fishwife, harridan **9** termagant

spitting image
4 twin **5** clone **6** double, ringer **9** duplicate **10** carbon copy, dead ringer, simulacrum

spittoon
8 cuspidor

splash
3 sop, wet **4** slop, soak **5** douse, slosh, spray, swash **6** drench **7** spatter **8** sprinkle

splashy
5 gaudy, jazzy, showy **6** flashy, garish, glitzy, tawdry **7** blatant, dashing **8** colorful, dazzling, striking **10** flamboyant, theatrical **11** sensational **12** meretricious, ostentatious

splatter
4 slop **5** douse, plash, slosh, spray, swash **6** splash **8** sprinkle

splay
4 cant, tilt **5** angle, bevel, gawky, slant, slope **6** clumsy, extend, spread **7** awkward, incline **8** ungainly **9** expansion **11** inclination

spleen
see **spite**

splendid
4 fine **5** grand, showy **6** superb **7** elegant, shining **8** glorious, gorgeous **9** brilliant,

excellent, marvelous, wonderful **10** first-class, impressive **11** illustrious, magnificent, outstanding **12** transcendent

splendor
4 pomp **5** glory **6** dazzle **7** panoply **8** grandeur, richness **9** pageantry, spectacle **10** brilliance, brilliancy **12** magnificence

splenetic
5 cross, surly **6** fuming **8** incensed, spiteful **9** malicious **10** ill-natured, malevolent **11** ill-tempered

splice
3 tie **4** join, mate, mesh **5** braid, graft, plait, unite

splint
5 brace, strip **7** support **10** immobilize

splinter
4 rive **5** burst, smash **6** shiver, sliver **7** faction, shatter **8** fragment **12** disintegrate

split
3 rip **4** part, rend, rent, rift, rima, rime, rive, tear **5** break, carve, chasm, chink, cleft, crack, sever, slice **6** breach, cleave, cloven, divide, schism, sunder **7** break up, disjoin, dissect, diverge, divorce, divvy up, fission, fissure, rupture **8** cleavage, dissever, fracture, separate **11** dichotomize
combining form: **5** schiz **6** schizo **7** schisto

splotch
4 blob, blot, spot **5** fleck, stain **6** smudge

splurge
4 orgy **5** binge, fling, spree **7** blowout, rampage **10** indulgence **12** extravagance

splutter
4 spit **6** babble, jabber **7** stammer

spoil
3 mar, rob, rot **4** baby, harm, prey, ruin, sack **5** decay, humor, taint, waste, wreck **6** coddle, cosset, curdle, damage, defile, impair, molder, pamper, ravish **7** blemish, cater to, destroy, indulge, pillage, putrefy, tarnish, vitiate **8** demolish **9** break down, decompose **11** mollycoddle

spoiled
4 rank, sour **6** putrid, rancid, rotten, ruined **7** coddled, decayed, gone bad **8** impaired, indulged, pampered **9** indulgent

spoils
4 haul, loot, swag **5** booty **7** pillage, plunder

spoilsport
7 killjoy

spoken
4 oral, said, told **6** verbal, voiced **7** uttered **8** phonetic, viva voce **9** delivered, unwritten **11** articulated

sponge
4 grub **5** cadge, leech, mooch **6** absorb, loofah **7** moocher **8** freeload, parasite, scrounge **10** freeloader
material: **8** mesoglea
opening: **6** oscula (plural) **7** osculum, ostiole

sponger
5 leech **7** moocher **8** parasite **10** freeloader

spongy
4 soft **5** mushy, pulpy **6** porous, quaggy **7** squashy, squishy **9** absorbent

sponsor
4 back, fund **5** angel, stake **6** backer, patron, surety **7** endorse, finance **8** advocate, bankroll, champion, Maecenas, mainstay, promoter, vouch for **9** grubstake, guarantee, guarantor, patronize, subsidize, supporter **10** benefactor, underwrite **11** underwriter

sponsorship
5 aegis **7** backing, support **8** advocacy, auspices **9** patronage

spontaneous
5 ad-lib **7** natural, offhand **8** ad-libbed, unforced **9** automatic, extempore, impromptu, impulsive, unstudied **10** improvised, off-the-cuff, unprompted **11** instinctive, unmeditated **13** unconstrained

spontoon
4 pike **5** lance, spear

spoof
4 sham **5** farce, put-on **6** parody, satire, send-up **7** lampoon, takeoff **8** travesty

spook
3 spy **5** agent, alarm, ghost, haunt, scare **7** specter, spectre, startle, terrify **8** frighten

spooky
5 eerie, weird **6** creepy **7** ghostly, ominous, uncanny **8** eldritch **9** unearthly

spool
4 reel, wind **6** bobbin

spoon
3 pet, woo **4** neck **5** court, ladle, scoop **6** cuddle

spoonbill
4 ibis **8** shoveler **9** ruddy duck **10** paddlefish

Spoon River poet
7 Masters (Edgar Lee)

spoony
5 mushy, silly **6** simple, slushy, syrupy **7** fatuous, foolish, mawkish, smitten, witless **9** schmaltzy **10** saccharine **11** sentimental

spoor
5 scent, trace, track, tract, trail **7** vestige **8** footstep **9** droppings, footprint

sporadic
4 rare **6** catchy, fitful, random, scarce, sparse, spotty **7** erratic **8** episodic, isolated, uncommon

9 desultory, irregular, scattered, spasmodic **10** infrequent, occasional

sport
3 fun **4** game, jest, joke, mock, play **6** frolic, racing, trifle **7** mockery, show off **9** diversion, high jinks, horseplay **10** recreation
indoor: 6 boxing, hockey, squash **7** bowling **8** handball **9** wrestling **10** acrobatics, basketball, gymnastics **11** racquetball, table tennis
Olympic: 4 judo **6** boxing, diving, hockey, rowing **7** archery, cycling, fencing, shot put **8** canoeing, football, high jump, long jump, marathon, shooting, swimming, yachting **9** decathlon, pole vault, water polo, wrestling **10** basketball, gymnastics, pentathlon, triple jump, volleyball **11** discus throw, hammer throw **12** javelin throw, steeplechase **13** weightlifting
water: 6 diving, rowing **7** sailing, surfing **8** canoeing, swimming, yachting
winter: 4 luge **6** hockey, skiing **7** curling, lugeing, skating **8** biathlon, sledding **10** ski jumping **11** bobsledding, tobogganing

sporting house
6 bagnio **7** brothel **8** bordello

sportive
5 antic **6** frisky, impish **7** playful, roguish, waggish **10** frolicsome **11** mischievous

sportiveness
7 devilry, roguery, waggery **8** deviltry, mischief **9** devilment, rascality

sporty
4 fast **5** peppy **6** breezy, casual, jaunty, lively **7** dashing, relaxed **8** debonair, informal **10** insouciant **11** streamlined

spot
3 fix, jam, nip, pip, see **4** espy, post, site **5** fleck, hit on, locus, place, point, speck **6** blotch, detect, pickle, plight, scrape **7** dilemma, smidgen, spatter, speckle **8** diagnose, flyspeck, identify, location, pinpoint, position **9** recognize, situation **11** predicament

spotless
4 pure **5** clean **6** chaste **8** hygienic, sanitary, unsoiled **9** undefiled, unstained, unsullied **10** immaculate **11** unblemished

spotlight
5 focus **6** notice **7** feature, point up **8** interest, point out **9** attention, emphasize, public eye, publicity **10** illuminate **12** illumination

spotted
4 seen **6** calico, motley **7** brindle, dappled, flecked, piebald **8** brindled, speckled, stippled

spouse
4 mate, wife **5** bride, groom, hubby **7** consort, husband

spout
3 jet **4** gush **5** chute, eject, spray, spurt **6** nozzle, squirt

sprain
4 pull, tear, turn **5** twist **6** wrench **7** stretch

sprawl
4 flop, loll **5** drape, slump **6** extend, lounge, slouch, spread **7** stretch **11** spread-eagle

spray
3 fog **4** hose, mist **6** shower, spritz **7** aerosol, atomize, diffuse, spatter **8** atomizer, droplets, fumigate, nebulize **9** spindrift

spread
3 jam, lay, set, sow, ted **4** deal, oleo, open, pâté, push **5** apply, feast, jelly, space, splay, strew, sweep **6** butter, expand, extend, fan out, pass on, retail **7** banquet, breadth, diffuse, expanse, overrun, pervade, radiate, scatter, slather, stretch, suffuse **8** bedcover, coverlet, dispense, disperse, mushroom, permeate **9** amplitude, broadcast, circulate, diffusion, dissipate, expansion, extension, profusion, propagate, radiation **10** dispersion, distribute, outstretch **11** counterpane, disseminate **12** transmission **13** proliferation

spree
3 jag **4** bash, bust, lark, orgy, riot, tear **5** binge, drunk, fling, revel **6** bender, frolic **7** blowout, carouse, rampage, splurge **8** carousal, wingding **10** indulgence **11** bacchanalia

sprig
4 brad, heir, twig **5** scion, shoot **7** pintail **9** ruddy duck

sprightly
3 gay **4** keen, spry, yare **5** agile, alert, antic, brisk, peppy, perky, zesty, zingy, zippy **6** active, breezy, chirpy, frisky, jaunty, lively, nimble **7** animate, chipper, coltish, piquant, playful, pungent **8** animated, cheerful, spirited, sportive **9** energetic, vivacious **10** frolicsome, rollicking

spring
3 hop **4** flow, free, jump, leap, lope, rise, root, skip, stem, trip, well **5** arise, begin, bound, cause, fount, issue, start **6** appear, bounce, emerge, hurdle, pounce, reason, source, uncoil, vernal **7** come out, emanate, proceed, rebound, startle **8** commence, fountain, stimulus, wellhead **9** originate **10** incitement, resilience **12** fountainhead
back: 6 resile
mineral: 3 spa

springe
4 trap **5** noose, snare **7** pitfall **9** booby trap

springlike
6 vernal

springy
6 supple **7** elastic **8** flexible, stretchy **9** recoiling, resilient

sprinkle
3 dot **4** rain, spot **5** shake, speck, spray, strew **6** pepper, powder, spritz **7** asperse, drizzle, freckle, scatter, speckle, stipple **9** bespeckle

sprint
3 run **4** dart, dash, race, shin, tear **5** scoot **6** gallop, hurtle, scurry **7** scamper

sprite
3 elf, fay, nix **4** puck **5** dryad, fairy, naiad, nixie, nymph, oread, pixie, sylph **6** kelpie **7** brownie **9** hamadryad, hobgoblin

spritz
3 jet **5** spray, spurt **6** shower, squirt

sprout
3 bud **4** grow **5** scion, shoot **6** ratoon, sucker **7** burgeon **8** offshoot **9** germinate

spruce
4 trim **5** natty, sassy, spiff **6** dapper, spiffy **11** well-groomed

spry
4 yare **5** agile, brisk, sound, zesty, zippy **6** active, lively, nimble, robust **7** healthy **8** animated, spirited, vigorous **9** energetic, vivacious

spud
5 tater **6** potato

___ Spumante
4 Asti

spume
4 fizz, foam, head, scum, suds **5** froth, spray, yeast **6** lather

spunk
4 grit, guts **5** heart, moxie, nerve, pluck **6** mettle, spirit, tinder **7** cojones, courage **8** backbone, gumption **9** fortitude, toughness **10** liveliness, resolution

spunky
4 bold **5** brave, fiery **6** daring **7** doughty, gingery, peppery **8** fearless, spirited **9** dauntless **10** courageous, mettlesome **12** high-spirited

spur
4 goad, prod, stir, urge **5** egg on, impel, prick, rally, rouse, spine **6** arouse, branch, exhort, motive, prompt, propel **7** impetus, impulse **8** buttress, catalyst, excitant, stimulus **9** actuation, incentive, instigate, stimulant, stimulate **10** incitement, inducement, motivation, projection
part: **5** rowel

spurious
4 fake, mock, sham **5** bogus, dummy, false, phony, put-on **6** ersatz, pseudo **7** assumed, feigned, pretend **8** affected **9** brummagem, imitation, pinchbeck, pretended, simulated **10** apocryphal, artificial, substitute **11** counterfeit, make-believe **12** illegitimate
combining form: **5** pseud **6** pseudo

spurn
4 snub **5** flout, scoff, scorn, scout, sneer **6** rebuff, refuse, reject **7** contemn, decline, despise, disdain, dismiss, repulse **8** turn down **9** disregard, reprobate, repudiate **10** disapprove **12** cold-shoulder

spurt
3 jet **4** gush, jump **5** burst, expel, spout, surge **6** shower, spritz, squirt **7** upsurge **8** eruption, increase **9** discharge

sputter
4 fizz, fume, rage, rant, rave, spew, spit **6** gibber, jabber **7** bluster, stammer

spy
5 agent, scout, snoop, spook **6** beagle, sleuth **7** gumshoe **8** informer, saboteur **9** detective **12** investigator **13** undercover man
name: **4** Ames (Aldrich), Boyd (Belle) **5** André (John), Blunt (Anthony), Fuchs (Klaus) **6** Philby (Kim), Smiley (George) **7** Burgess (Guy), Hanssen (Robert), Maclean (Donald), Pollard (Jonathan) **8** Mata Hari

spyglass
9 telescope

spying
9 espionage

Spyri's heroine
5 Heidi

squab
5 couch **6** pigeon **7** cushion

squabble
3 row **4** miff, spat, tiff **5** argue **6** bicker, dustup **7** brabble, dispute, quarrel, wrangle

squad
4 crew, side, team, unit **5** cadre **6** detail, lineup, patrol

squalid
3 low **4** base, foul, mean, vile **5** dingy, dirty, nasty, seedy **6** filthy, frowsy, frowzy, grubby, scurvy, shabby, shoddy, sleazy, slummy, sordid **7** ignoble, low-down, run-down, scrubby, unclean, unkempt **8** slovenly, wretched **10** despicable, disheveled **11** dilapidated **12** disreputable

squall
3 caw, row, yap, yip **4** bark, bawl, beef, feud, fuss, gust, howl, roar, tiff, wail, yawp, yell, yelp, yowl **5** brawl, fight, hoo-ha, shout **6** bellow, clamor, flurry, fracas, hubbub, ruckus, rumpus, scream, shriek, squeal, yammer **7** dispute, flare-up, quarrel, rhubarb, screech **8** brouhaha, squabble **9** bickering, caterwaul, commotion **10** falling-out, hullabaloo **11** altercation

squalor
5 filth **6** misery **7** neglect, poverty **8** baseness, iniquity **9** depravity, dirtiness **10** sordidness **11** degradation **12** wretchedness

squander
4 blow **5** spend, waste **7** consume, exhaust, fritter, scatter **9** dissipate, throw away **10** trifle away **11** fritter away

squanderer
see **spender**

square
3 fit, fix **4** bang, boxy, even, fair, jibe, just, tied **5** adapt, agree, align, clear, equal, exact, match, pay up, plaza, sharp, spang, tally **6** accord, adjust, settle **7** balance, conform, satisfy, settled **8** check out, dovetail, orthodox, quadrate, smack-dab, straight, unbiased **9** equitable, liquidate, objective, quadratic, reconcile, rectangle

squash
3 jam **4** cram, mash, pepo, pulp **5** crush, gourd, press, quell **7** flatten, put down, squeeze, squelch **8** suppress
variety: 5 acorn **6** cushaw, Sibley, turban **7** Hubbard, scallop **8** pattypan, zucchini **9** butternut, crookneck **10** Marblehead

squat
3 low **5** dumpy, hunch, stoop, stout, thick **6** chunky, crouch, hunker, stocky, stubby **8** heavyset, thickset **10** hunker down **11** thick-bodied

squawfish
4 chub **8** cyprinid **10** pikeminnow

squawk
3 caw, yap, yip **4** beef, crab, fuss, yawp **5** bleat, gripe **6** yammer **7** protest, screech **8** complain **9** bellyache, complaint

squeak
3 rat **4** blab, fink, peep, pipe, sing **5** cheep, creak **6** escape, inform, snitch, tattle **10** tattletale

squeal
3 rat, yip **4** blab, howl, sing, yell, yelp, yowl **5** bleat, creak, grate, gripe, peach **6** inform, screak, scream, shriek, shrill, snitch, squawk, tattle **7** protest, screech **8** complain **10** tattletale

squealer
3 rat **4** fink **6** canary, snitch, weasel **7** ratfink, stoolie, tattler, tipster **8** betrayer, informer **10** talebearer, tattletale **11** stool pigeon

squeamish
5 fussy, upset **6** queasy **7** finical, finicky **8** nauseous **9** nauseated **10** fastidious, particular, pernickety **11** persnickety

squeeze
3 hug, jam **4** bind, cram, grip, milk, pack, push **5** clasp, crowd, crush, exact, gouge, juice, pinch, press, screw, wring **6** clutch, coerce, compel, crunch, eke out, enfold, extort, jostle, squash, squish **7** dilemma, embrace, extract **8** compress, contract, pressure, quandary **9** shake down **11** compression, predicament

squelch
5 quell, shush, sit on **6** muffle, muzzle, squash, squish, stifle, subdue **7** repress, silence, smother **8** strangle, suppress **10** extinguish

squib
4 fire **6** filler **7** lampoon **8** shoot off **9** detonator **11** firecracker

squid
7 mollusc, mollusk **8** calamari, calamary **10** cephalopod
kin: 7 octopus **10** cuttlefish

squiggle
4 worm **6** doodle, scrawl, squirm, writhe **7** scratch **8** curlicue, scrabble, scribble

squinch
5 quail, start, wince **6** blench, crouch, recoil, shrink

squint
4 peek, peep, peer **10** hagioscope, strabismus

squire
6 attend, escort, lawyer **7** consort, gallant **8** cavalier, chaperon **9** accompany, landowner

squirm
4 worm **6** fidget, wiggle, writhe **7** wriggle

squirrel
4 stow **5** cache, hoard, stash **7** secrete
red: 9 chickaree

squirt
3 jet, kid, pup, tot **4** brat, tyke **5** sprat, spray, spurt, twerp **6** shaver, shrimp, splurt, spritz **7** spatter

squish
3 jam **4** cram, mash, mush, pack, push **5** crush, press, quash, smash **7** flatten, scrunch, squeeze, squelch, trample

squishy
4 soft **6** flabby, quaggy, slushy, spongy

Sri Lanka
aborigine: 5 Vedda
bay: 6 Bengal
capital: 7 Colombo
city: 5 Kandy **8** Moratuwa
ethnic group: 9 Sinhalese
former name: 6 Ceylon
language: 5 Tamil **9** Sinhalese
monetary unit: 5 rupee
shoals: 11 Adam's Bridge
strait: 4 Palk

SRO
7 sellout

SS chief
7 Himmler (Heinrich)

S-shaped
7 sigmoid
arch, molding: 4 ogee

stab
3 dig, pop, try 4 pang, poke, shot 5 crack, drive, fling, guess, prick, spear, stick, whack, whirl 6 effort, pierce, thrust, twinge 7 attempt 8 puncture 9 penetrate

Stabat ____
5 Mater

stabile
6 steady 9 sculpture 10 stationary

stabilize
3 fix, set 4 prop 5 brace, poise 6 cement, firm up, fixate, prop up, secure, settle, steady 7 balance, ballast, support, sustain 8 solidify 9 reinforce

stable
3 set 4 barn, fast, firm, mews, safe, sure 5 fixed, solid, sound 6 secure, steady, sturdy 7 abiding, durable, lasting, staunch 8 balanced, constant, enduring, resolute 9 immutable, permanent, steadfast, unvarying 10 perdurable, stationary, unchanging, unshakable

stack
4 cock, heap, hill, load, mass, pile, pipe, rick 5 mound, sheaf 7 chimney, pyramid

stack up
3 add 5 equal, total 6 equate, gather 7 compare, measure

stadium
4 bowl, dome, rink, ring 5 arena 6 garden 8 coliseum 10 hippodrome 12 amphitheater
level: 4 tier

staff
3 rod 4 cane, club, prop, rung, team, wand 5 baton, billy 6 cudgel 7 faculty, support 9 personnel
bishop's: 7 crosier, crozier
medical: 8 caduceus
of office: 4 mace

stag
4 male, solo 5 alone

stage
3 lot 4 dais, play, rung, show, step 5 grade, level, mount, notch, phase, put on 6 degree, period, status 7 execute, perform, present, produce 8 platform
direction: 4 exit 5 enter 6 exeunt
scenery: 3 set 8 backdrop
show: 4 play 5 drama, revue 7 musical 9 burlesque 10 vaudeville
signal: 3 cue
whisper: 5 aside

stage set
5 decor, scene 7 scenery 8 backdrop 11 mise-en-scène

stagger
4 daze, reel, stun, sway 5 amaze, floor, lurch, pitch, stump, waver, weave 6 boggle, careen, dither, falter, teeter, topple, totter, wobble, zigzag 7 astound, nonplus, perplex, shatter, stumble, stupefy 8 astonish, bowl over 9 dumbfound, overwhelm, vacillate 11 flabbergast

stagnant
5 musty, stale 6 static 8 immobile, unmoving 10 motionless, stationary

stagnate
4 idle 5 stall 6 fester 8 languish, stultify, vegetate

stagy
10 artificial, histrionic, theatrical 11 pretentious 12 melodramatic

staid
5 grave, sober 6 formal, sedate, solemn, somber, sombre, stuffy 7 earnest, serious, starchy 8 composed, decorous, priggish 9 dignified

stain
3 dye, tar 4 blot, daub, onus, slur, soil, spot 5 brand, color, odium, shame, smear, sully, taint, tinge 6 blotch, defile, embrue, imbrue, smirch, smudge, stigma 7 blemish, pigment, tarnish 8 besmirch, colorant, discolor, dishonor, dyestuff, tincture

staircase
handrail: 8 banister 9 bannister
outdoor: 6 perron
post: 5 newel 8 baluster

stake
3 bet, lay, pot, set 4 ante, back, game, pale, play, post, risk 5 claim, put on, share, wager 6 gamble, paling, picket, pledge, tether 7 finance 8 bankroll, interest 10 capitalize, investment

stalag
7 POW camp 10 prison camp

stale
5 banal, dusty, faded, fusty, moldy, musty, passé, tired, trite 7 clichéd, tedious, worn-out 8 over-used, shopworn, stagnant, timeworn 9 hack-neyed, tasteless 11 commonplace, stereotyped

stalemate
3 tie 4 draw 7 impasse 8 deadlock, gridlock, standoff

stalk
4 hunt, prey 5 chase, track 6 ambush, follow, pursue, stride 8 flush out
flower: 8 peduncle
leaf: 7 petiole
short: 5 stipe

stall
3 bay, pew **4** halt **5** booth, brake, check, delay, hedge, kiosk, stand **6** arrest, put off **7** conk out, counter, hold off **8** obstruct **9** stonewall **10** filibuster **11** compartment, prevaricate

stalwart
4 bold **5** brave, gutsy, hardy, husky, stout, tough **6** brawny, robust, sinewy, strong, sturdy **7** valiant **8** fearless, intrepid, unafraid, valorous, vigorous **9** dauntless, tenacious, undaunted **10** courageous

stamen part
6 anther **8** filament

stamina
8 tenacity **9** endurance, fortitude, tolerance **11** persistence **12** staying power

stammer
6 gibber, jabber **7** sputter, stutter **8** hesitate, splutter

stamp
3 ilk, lot **4** etch, kind, mark, mint, mold, seal, sort, type **5** clomp, clump, pound, print, tromp **6** hammer, stripe **7** impress, imprint, trample **8** hallmark, inscribe **9** character **10** impression **12** characterize

stampede
4 bolt, dash, rout, rush, tear **5** crush, panic, rodeo **6** charge

stamps
7 postage

stance
4 pose **7** bearing, posture **8** attitude, carriage, position **10** deportment

stanch
4 stem, stop **5** check **6** stop up **8** hold back

stanchion
4 post, prop **5** brace **7** support

stand
4 bear **5** abide, booth, brook, kiosk, stall, treat **6** endure, handle, suffer **7** counter, stomach, swallow, weather **8** attitude, platform, position, tolerate
artist's: **5** easel
three-legged: **6** tripod, trivet
ornamental: **7** étagère

standard
3 law, par **4** flag, jack, mean, norm, rule **5** color, gauge, ideal, model, stock, usual **6** banner, common, ensign, median, normal, pennon **7** average, classic, example, general, labarum, measure, pattern, pennant, regular, typical, uniform **8** accepted, everyday, exemplar, familiar, ordinary, orthodox, paradigm **9** archetype, benchmark, criterion, customary, principle, yardstick **10** recognized, regulation, touchstone **11** established, fundamental

standardize
6 adjust **7** conform **8** regulate **9** reconcile

stand for
4 bear, mean **5** allow **6** denote, permit **7** signify **8** indicate, tolerate **9** put up with, represent, symbolize

stand-in
3 sub **5** proxy **6** backup, second **9** alternate, surrogate **10** substitute, understudy **11** pinch hitter, replacement **12** impersonator

standing
4 rank, term **5** erect, fixed, place **6** cachet, credit, repute, status **7** dignity, footing, station, stature, upright **8** capacity, duration, eminence, position, prestige, stagnant **9** character, permanent, situation **10** estimation, reputation **11** consequence, established

standoff
see **stalemate**

standoffish
5 aloof **6** chilly **7** distant, haughty **8** detached, reserved **9** reclusive, withdrawn **10** unfriendly, unsociable **12** misanthropic

stand out
3 jut **4** bulk, loom **5** bulge **7** project **8** protrude

standpatter
4 fogy, tory **5** fogey **7** diehard **8** mossback **11** bitter-ender **12** conservative

standpoint
4 side **5** angle, slant **7** outlook **9** direction **11** perspective

standstill
4 halt, stop **5** check, pause **7** impasse **8** deadlock, dead stop **9** cessation, stalemate

Stanford site
8 Palo Alto

Stanley Kowalski's wife
6 Stella

Stanleys' car
7 steamer

Stan's partner
5 Ollie

stanza
7 strophe
combining form: **5** stich
final: **5** envoi
of eight lines: **6** octave
of four lines: **6** ballad **8** quatrain
of six lines: **6** sestet
of three lines: **6** tercet **7** triplet
Persian: **8** rubaiyat

star
4 icon, idol, lead, main, nova **5** actor, chief, major **6** étoile **7** actress, capital **8** asterisk, dominant, luminary **9** celebrity, headliner, principal **10** preeminent **11** outstanding

bright: **4** Vega **5** Algol, Deneb, Rigel, Spica **6** Altair, Castor, Pollux, Sirius **7** Antares, Canopus, Capella, Polaris, Procyon, Regulus **8** Arcturus **9** Aldebaran, Archernar, Fomalhaut **10** Beta Crucis, Betelgeuse **11** Alpha Crucis **12** Beta Centauri **13** Alpha Centauri
combining form: **4** astr **5** aster, astro **6** astero, sidero
envelope: **6** corona
exploding: **4** nova
five-pointed: **8** pentacle, stellate **9** pentagram
giant: **10** Betelgeuse
North: **7** Polaris
six-pointed: **8** hexagram

starch
3 pep **4** push, snap **5** drive, moxie, punch, spunk, vigor **7** stiffen **8** gumption, vitality **9** formality
combining form: **4** amyl **5** amylo

starchy
4 prim **5** aloof, stiff **6** doughy, formal, wooden **7** stilted

star-crossed
6 doomed **7** hapless, unlucky **8** ill-fated, luckless **10** ill-starred **11** unfortunate **12** misfortunate

Stardust composer
10 Carmichael (Hoagy)

stare
3 eye **4** gape, gawk, gaze, ogle, peer **6** goggle **10** rubberneck

stark
3 raw **4** bare, nude, pure **5** bleak, blunt, clear, harsh, naked, quite, rigid, sheer, utter **6** barren, strict, unclad, vacant, wholly **8** absolute, complete, desolate, stripped **9** au naturel, out-and-out **10** absolutely

starry
6 astral **7** stellar **8** sidereal

starry-eyed
6 dreamy, unreal **7** utopian **8** ecstatic **9** rapturous, visionary **11** impractical, unrealistic **13** impracticable

Star-Spangled Banner writer
3 Key (Francis Scott)

start
4 bolt, dawn, draw **5** arise, begin, crank, found, get-go, issue, onset, quail, react, set up, wince **6** blench, create, embark, flinch, launch, outset, recoil, shrink, spring, take up **7** actuate, genesis, infancy, kickoff, opening, trigger **8** activate, commence, embark on, initiate, organize, reaction **9** beginning, establish, institute, originate **10** inaugurate **12** commencement

startle
4 jolt, jump **5** alarm, scare, shock, spook **8** astonish, frighten, surprise

Star Trek
captain: **4** Kirk (James T.) **5** Sisko (Benjamin) **6** Archer (Jonathan), Picard (Jean-Luc) **7** Janeway (Kathryn)
character: **3** Dax (Jadzia), Kim (Harry), Nog, Odo, Rom, Yar (Natasha) **4** Data, Kurn, Lore, Sulu, Troi (Deanna, Lwaxana), Worf **5** Adami (Kai Winn), Dukat, Duras (Lursa, B'Etor), McCoy ("Bones"), Nerys (Kira), Paris (Tom), Quark, Riker (Will), Sarek, Scott, Spock, Tuvok, Uhura **6** Bashir (Julian), Chekov, Doctor (The), Guinan, Gowron, O'Brien (Keiko, Miles), Torres (B'Elanna), Weyoun **7** Crusher (Dr. Beverly, Wesley), La Forge (Geordi) **8** Chakotay **9** Borg Queen **11** Seven of Nine
creator: **11** Roddenberry (Gene)
fan: **7** Trekker, Trekkie
race: **4** Borg, Gorn, Voth **5** Breen, Human, Trill, Vorta **6** Lurian, Pakled, Terran, Vulcan **7** Bajoran, Ferengi, Iconian, Klingon, Romulan, Tribble **8** Andorian, Betazoid, El-Aurian, Jem'Hadar **9** Nausicaan, Tellarite **10** Cardassian, Changeling
actor: **5** Nimoy (Leonard), Takei (George) **6** Kelley (DeForest) **7** Mulgrew (Kate), Shatner (William), Stewart (Patrick) **8** Fletcher (Louise), Goldberg (Whoopi) **11** Auberjonois (René)
starship: **10** Enterprise

starved
6 hungry **8** famished, ravenous, underfed

Star Wars
3 SDI
actor: **3** Lee (Christopher) **4** Ford (Harrison) **5** Jones (James Earl) **6** Fisher (Carrie), Hamill (Mark), Neeson (Liam) **7** Jackson (Samuel L.), Portman (Natalie) **8** Guinness (Alec), McGregor (Ewan), Williams (Billy Dee) **9** McDiarmid (Ian)
character: **4** Fett (Boba, Jango), Jinn (Qui-Gon), Leia (Princess), Maul (Darth), Solo (Han), Yoda (Master) **5** Binks (Jar Jar), Dooku (Count), Vader (Darth) **8** Grievous (General) **9** Chewbacca, Palpatine (Senator, Chancellor, Emperor), Skywalker (Anakin, Luke) **10** Calrissian (Lando) **12** Jabba the Hutt
composer: **8** Williams (John)
creator: **5** Lucas (George)
film: **7** New Hope (A) **13** Phantom Menace (The) **15** Return of the Jedi **16** Revenge of the Sith **17** Attack of the Clones, Empire Strikes Back (The)
group: **4** Jedi, Sith **5** Ewoks **6** Clones, Droids **8** Wookiees **13** Rebel Alliance
parody: **6** Troops **10** Spaceballs **12** Hardware Wars
planet: **4** Hoth **5** Naboo **7** Dagobah **8** Alderaan, Tatooine **9** Coruscant
threat: **9** Death Star

stash
4 bury, hide, pile **5** cache, hoard, plant, store **7** conceal, lay away, nest egg, secrete **8** lay aside, sock away, squirrel **9** stockpile

stasis
7 balance, inertia **9** equipoise **10** immobility, stagnation **11** equilibrium

stat
3 now, PDQ **4** ASAP **6** at once, pronto

state
3 air, put, say **4** aver, mode, rank, tell, vent **5** utter **6** affirm, assert, recite, relate, report **7** declare, dignity, explain, expound, express, posture, recount **8** attitude, capacity, describe, position, set forth, standing **9** condition, enunciate, situation, ventilate
subdivison: **6** county

state
easternmost: **5** Maine
largest: **6** Alaska
smallest: **11** Rhode Island
southernmost: **6** Hawaii

state abbreviation
Alabama: **3** Ala.
Alaska: **4** Alas.
Arizona: **4** Ariz.
Arkansas: **3** Ark.
California: **3** Cal. **5** Calif.
Colorado: **3** Col. **4** Colo.
Connecticut: **4** Conn.
Delaware: **3** Del.
Florida: **3** Fla.
Idaho: **3** Ida.
Illinois: **3** Ill.
Indiana: **3** Ind.
Kansas: **3** Kan. **4** Kans.
Kentucky: **3** Ken.
Massachusetts: **4** Mass.
Michigan: **4** Mich.
Minnesota: **4** Minn.
Mississippi: **4** Miss.
Montana: **4** Mont.
Nebraska: **3** Neb. **4** Nebr.
Nevada: **3** Nev.
New Mexico: **4** N. Mex.
North Carolina: **4** N. Car.
North Dakota: **4** N. Dak.
Oklahoma: **4** Okla.
Oregon: **3** Ore. **4** Oreg.
Pennsylvania: **4** Penn. **5** Penna.
South Carolina: **4** S. Car.
South Dakota: **4** S. Dak.
Tennessee: **4** Tenn.
Texas: **3** Tex.
Vermont: **4** Verm.
Virginia: **4** Virg.
Washington: **4** Wash.
West Virginia: **3** W. Va.
Wisconsin: **3** Wis. **4** Wisc.
Wyoming: **3** Wyo.

stately
5 grand, lofty, noble, regal, royal **6** august, formal, kingly, lordly, solemn **7** courtly, elegant, gallant, haughty **8** gracious, imperial, imposing, majestic, palatial, princely **9** dignified **10** ceremonial, impressive, monumental **11** ceremonious, magnificent

statement
3 tab **4** bill **5** score **6** avowal, charge, dictum, remark, report **7** account, comment, invoice, recital **8** averment **9** affidavit, assertion, manifesto, narrative, reckoning, testimony, utterance **10** deposition, expression **11** description
introductory: **7** preface **8** foreword, prologue

stateroom
5 cabin

statesman
10 politician
American: **3** Hay (John Milton) **4** Clay (Henry), Hull (Cordell), Otis (James), Root (Elihu) **5** Adams (Samuel), Henry (Patrick), Lodge (Henry Cabot), Vance (Cyrus) **6** Bunche (Ralph), Bunker (Ellsworth), Dulles (John Foster), Kennan (George F.), Morris (Gouverneur), Powell (Colin), Sumner (Charles) **7** Acheson (Dean), Hancock (John), Kellogg (Frank B.), Lansing (Robert), Sherman (John, Roger), Stimson (Henry L.), Webster (Daniel) **8** Franklin (Benjamin), Hamilton (Alexander), Harriman (Averell), Pinckney (Charles, Thomas), Randolph (Edmund Jennings, John, Payton), Rutledge (John), Trumbull (Jonathan, Joseph) **9** Kissinger (Henry), Stevenson (Adlai) **10** Stettinius (Edward Reilly)
Australian: **9** Wentworth (William Charles)
Austrian: **6** Renner (Karl) **7** Kaunitz (Wenzel von) **8** Dollfuss (Engelbert) **10** Metternich (Klemens von) **13** Schwarzenberg (Felix zu)
Canadian: **4** King (W. L. Mackenzie) **7** Laurier (Wilfrid) **8** Thompson (John Sparrow) **9** Macdonald (John Alexander, John Sandfield), Mackenzie (Alexander, William Lyon)
Chinese: **3** Yen (Hsishan) **4** Deng (Xiaoping), Kung (Hsiang-hsi), Teng (Hsiao-p'ing), Wang (Anshih, Chingwei), Yuan (Shih-kai) **9** Sun Yat-Sen
Dutch: **6** de Witt (Johan de) **7** Grotius (Hugo), Stikker (Dirk)
East German: **8** Ulbricht (Walter)
English: **3** Fox (Charles, Henry) **4** Eden (Anthony, George, William), More (Thomas), Peel (Arthur, Robert, William), Pitt (William),

Vane (Henry) **5** Cecil (Robert, William), North (Francis, Frederick, Roger) **6** Morley (John), Sidney (Algernon, Henry, Philip, Robert), Temple (Henry, William), Wolsey (Thomas) **7** Halifax (Earl of), Reading (Marquis of), Russell (John, William), Stanley (Edward George, Edward Henry), Stewart (Robert), Warwick (Earl of) **8** Cromwell (Oliver, Thomas), Disraeli (Benjamin), Robinson (George Frederick Samuel), Villiers (George) **9** Cavendish (Spencer, William), Churchill (Randolph, Winston), Gladstone (William), Salisbury (Earl, Marquis of), Strafford (Earl of), Wellesley (Arthur, Richard Colley) **10** Palmerston (Lord), Rockingham (Marquis of), Sunderland (Earl of), Walsingham (Francis), Wellington (Duke of) **11** Chamberlain (Austen, Joseph, Neville), Shaftesbury (Earl of) **12** Chesterfield (Earl of)
Finnish: **9** Stahlberg (Kaarlo Juho)
French: **5** Sully (Duc de) **6** Guizot (François-Pierre-Guillaume), Thiers (Louis-Adolphe), Turgot (Anne-Robert-Jacques) **7** Herriot (Edouard), Mazarin (Jules), Schuman (Robert), Viviani (René) **8** Hanotaux (Gabriel) **9** Lafayette (Marquis de), Millerand (Alexandre), Richelieu (Duc de) **10** Clemenceau (Georges) **11** Tocqueville (Alexis de)
German: **5** Wirth (Joseph) **10** Stresemann (Gustav)
German-Danish: **9** Struensee (Johann Friedrich)
Greek: **6** Zaimis (Alexandros) **8** Pericles **9** Aristides **11** Cleisthenes, Demosthenes **12** Themistocles
Israeli: **4** Eban (Abba) **5** Begin (Menachem), Dayan (Moshe), Peres (Shimon), Rabin (Yitzhak) **7** Sharett (Moshe) **9** Ben-Gurion (David)
Italian: **6** Cavour (Conte di), Crispi (Francesco) **7** Orlando (Vittorio Emanuele) **11** Machiavelli (Niccolo)
Japanese: **3** Ito (Hirobumi) **5** genro, Kanoe **6** Kanoye
Norwegian: **6** Nansen (Fridtjof)
Polish: **7** Zaleski (August) **9** Pilsudski (Jozef) **10** Paderewski (Ignacy)
Prussian: **5** Stein (Karl)
Roman: **4** Cato (Marcus Porcius) **6** Cicero (Marcus Tullius), Pompey, Seneca (Lucius Annaeus) **7** Agrippa (Marcus Vipsanius) **8** Gracchus (Gaius, Tiberius), Maecenas (Gaius) **9** Symmachus (Quintus Aurelius)
Russian: **5** Witte (Sergey) **7** Molotov (Vyacheslav) **8** Potemkin (Grigory) **9** Vyshinsky (Andrey)
Scottish: **4** Knox (John)
South American: **7** Bolívar (Simón) **9** San Martín (José de)
Swiss: **4** Ador (Gustave) **5** Welti (Emil)

static
5 fixed, inert **6** stable, steady **7** stabile, stalled, stopped **8** constant, immobile, inactive, stagnant, unmoving **9** immovable, unvarying **10** changeless, unchanging

station
4 post, rank, site, spot **5** depot, locus, place, point **6** assign **7** footing **8** capacity, standing **9** character **10** white noise

stationary
5 fixed **6** static **8** immobile, stagnant, unmoving **9** immovable **10** motionless, stock-still

statue
base: **6** plinth **8** pedestal
gigantic: **8** Colossus
Greek: **5** atlas **7** telamon **8** caryatid
religious: **5** Pietà
small: **8** figurine

stature
see **status**

status
4 rank **5** merit, place, worth **6** cachet, rating, renown **7** caliber, dignity, footing, posture, quality **8** capacity, eminence, position, prestige, standing **9** character, condition, situation **10** prominence **11** consequence, distinction

statute
3 act, law **4** bill **5** canon, edict **9** enactment, ordinance

staunch
4 fast, firm, sure, true **5** liege, loyal, solid, sound **6** secure, stable, strong, trusty **8** constant, faithful, reliable, resolute, stalwart **9** steadfast **10** dependable **11** substantial, trustworthy

stave off
4 foil **5** avert, block, deter, dodge, elude, parry, rebut, repel **6** rebuff, thwart **7** forfend, obviate, prevent, repulse **8** preclude **9** forestall **10** circumvent

stay
3 guy, lag **4** bide, halt, prop, rest, stop, wait **5** abide, brace, check, defer, delay, dwell, lodge, tarry, visit **6** linger, put off, remain **7** sojourn, support, suspend **8** hold over, postpone, stop over **9** interrupt **10** suspension **11** stick around

stead
4 lieu **5** place **9** advantage

steadfast
4 firm, sure, true **5** fixed, liege, loyal **7** abiding, adamant, patient, staunch **8** constant, enduring, faithful, immobile, reliable, resolute, stubborn **9** immovable, unbending, unmovable **10** dependable, unwavering, unyielding **11** unfaltering, unflinching **12** never-failing, single-minded, wholehearted **13** unquestioning

steady
3 set **4** beau, even, fast, firm, sure **5** fixed, liege, loyal, sober **6** stable, static **7** abiding, ballast, certain, durable, equable, nonstop, regular, stabile, staunch, uniform **8** constant, enduring, faithful, habitual, reliable, resolute, unbroken, unshaken **9** ceaseless, incessant, stabilize, unvarying **10** changeless, consistent, continuous, dependable, persistent, sweetheart, unchanging, unswerving, unwavering **11** unfaltering **12** unchangeable, wholehearted

steak
4 club, cube, loin **5** chuck, flank, round, T-bone **6** rib eye **7** brisket, sirloin **9** Delmonico, hamburger, Salisbury **10** tenderloin **11** filet mignon, London broil, porterhouse **13** chateaubriand

steal
3 bag, cop, nab, nip, rob **4** glom, grab, hook, kite, lift, loot, lurk, slip, take **5** boost, creep, filch, glide, heist, pinch, poach, prowl, seize, shirk, sidle, skulk, slide, slink, sneak, swipe **6** burgle, fleece, hijack, pilfer, pocket, snatch, snitch, thieve, tiptoe **7** bargain, pillage, plunder, purloin **8** embezzle, shanghai, shoplift **9** pussyfoot **10** burglarize, plagiarize **11** appropriate
a vehicle: **6** hijack **8** highjack

stealing
5 theft **6** piracy **7** larceny, robbery **8** burglary

stealthy
3 sly **4** wily **6** covert, crafty, feline, secret, shifty, silent, slinky, sneaky **7** catlike, cunning, furtive, sub-rosa **8** hush-hush, skulking, slinking, sneaking **9** noiseless **10** undercover **11** clandestine **13** surreptitious

steam
3 gas, pep, zip **4** foam, fume, mist, rage **5** anger, force, might, power, vapor **6** energy, seethe **8** momentum

steam bath
5 sauna

steamboat structure
5 texas

steamer
4 boat, clam, ship

steam organ
8 calliope

steamy
3 hot **5** humid, muggy **6** erotic, sticky, sultry, torrid **8** stifling

steed
5 horse, mount **7** charger

steel
4 gird **5** brace, nerve, rally **6** buck up, harden **7** fortify, hearten, stiffen **8** embolden, inspirit **9** reinforce **10** strengthen

steep
3 sop **4** high, soak **5** bathe, dizzy, imbue, sheer **6** abrupt, drench, infuse **7** arduous, extreme, immerse, suffuse **8** elevated, marinate, saturate **9** excessive **10** exorbitant, immoderate, impregnate, inordinate **11** precipitate, precipitous

steeple
5 spire, tower **6** flèche

steer
4 helm, lead **5** guide, pilot, point, route **6** direct, escort, tip-off **7** channel, conduct, skipper **8** shepherd
a ship: **4** conn, helm, luff

steersman
3 cox **7** captain **8** coxswain

Stegner novel
13 Angle of Repose, Spectator Bird (The)
20 Big Rock Candy Mountain (The)

stein
3 mug **5** stoup **6** goblet **7** tankard

Steinbeck novel
5 Pearl (The) **10** Cannery Row, East of Eden **12** Of Mice and Men, Tortilla Flat **13** Grapes of Wrath (The)

Stein's companion
6 Toklas (Alice B.)

Steinway product
5 piano

stellar
6 astral, starry **7** leading, shining **8** sidereal, standout, starlike **10** preeminent **11** outstanding, predominant, superlative

stem
4 flow, head, rise, stop **5** abate, arise, check, issue **6** arrest, derive, spring, stanch **7** control, develop, emanate, proceed **8** peduncle **9** originate
plant: **4** axis **5** haulm
underground: **5** tuber **7** rhizome

stench
4 funk, reek **5** smell, stink

stentorian
4 loud **7** blaring, booming, orotund, raucous, roaring **8** sonorous, strident **9** clamorous, deafening **10** thundering **12** earsplitting

step
4 hoof, pace, rung, walk **5** grade, level, notch, stage, stair, stile, track, tread **6** degree **7** measure, traipse **8** footfall **9** gradation
dance: **3** pas

step-by-step
7 gradual **9** piecemeal

steppe
5 plain **6** tundra

Steppenwolf author
5 Hesse (Hermann)

stereotype
4 mold **5** plate **7** pattern **10** categorize, pigeonhole **11** standardize

stereotypical
4 hack **5** banal, stale, trite **7** clichéd **8** shop-worn, timeworn **9** hackneyed **11** commonplace

sterile
4 arid, bare, vain **6** barren, fallow **7** aseptic, worn-out **8** desolate, hygienic, impotent, lifeless, sanitary **9** fruitless, infertile **10** antiseptic, unfruitful, uninspired **11** disinfected **12** unproductive

sterilize
3 fix **4** geld, spay **5** alter **6** neuter, purify **7** cleanse **8** sanitize **9** disinfect **10** emasculate

sterilized
7 aseptic

sterling
4 pure, true **5** noble **6** worthy **8** virtuous **9** estimable, exemplary, honorable

stern
4 grim **5** harsh, rigid, sober, stony **6** gloomy, severe, strict **7** ascetic, austere **8** obdurate **10** forbidding, implacable, inexorable, inflexible **11** unrelenting

Sterne novel
14 Tristram Shandy

sternutation
8 sneezing

sternward
3 aft **5** abaft

Sterope
father: **5** Atlas
mother: **7** Pleione
sisters: **8** Pleiades

Stevenson, Robert Louis
character: **3** Jim (Hawkins) **4** Hyde (Mr.) **5** David (Balfour) **6** Jekyll (Dr.), Silver (Long John)
novel: **9** Kidnapped **14** Treasure Island

stew
4 boil, brew, flap, fret, fume, fuss, hash, olio, olla, snit **5** daube, gumbo, salmi, sweat, tizzy, worry **6** burgoo, dither, jumble, lather, medley, menudo, pother, ragout, seethe, simmer, swivet, tumult **7** brothel, goulash, mélange, mixture, parboil, swelter, turmoil **8** bordello, mishmash, mulligan, pot-au-feu **9** Brunswick, cassoulet, commotion, confusion, pasticcio, potpourri **10** hodgepodge, hotchpotch, miscellany, turbulence **11** gallimaufry, olla podrida, ratatouille, slumgullion **13** bouillabaisse

steward
6 manage **7** manager **8** overseer **10** supervisor

stewed
3 lit **4** high **5** drunk, lit up, oiled **6** bashed, blotto, bombed, cooked, juiced, potted, soaked, soused, stewed, stoned, tanked, wasted, zonked **7** crocked, drunken, pickled, pie-eyed, sloshed, smashed, sottish **8** simmered **9** plastered **10** inebriated, liquored up **11** intoxicated

Stheno
see **Gorgon**

stick
3 put, rod **4** glue, pole, stab **5** affix, baton, cling **6** adhere, attach, cleave, cohere, fasten **7** scruple **10** overcharge

stick around
4 bide, stay, wait **5** abide, dally, tarry **6** linger, remain

sticker
3 pin **4** barb, seal, shiv, spur **5** decal, point, prong, shank, spike, spine, stamp **6** dagger **8** stiletto

stick-in-the-mud
4 fogy **5** fogey **6** fossil **8** mossback **10** fuddy-duddy

stick out
3 jut **5** bulge **6** beetle **7** project **8** overhang, protrude

stick up
3 mug, rob **6** waylay **7** project **8** protrude

sticky
5 gluey, gooey, gummy, humid, muggy, mushy, soggy, tacky **6** clammy, knotty, slushy, sultry, thorny, viscid **7** awkward, cloying, maudlin, mawkish, viscous **8** adhesive, bathetic, clinging, romantic **9** difficult **11** problematic, sentimental, tear-jerking

stiff
3 lit, set **4** body, firm, hard, lush **5** cheat, drunk, harsh, oiled, rigid, stark, steep, stick, tense, tight, tipsy **6** buzzed, corpse, frozen, jelled, juiced, person, plowed, potent, potted, severe, soused, stewed, wooden **7** cadaver, carcass, sloshed, starchy, stilted **8** hardened, reserved, stubborn **9** cardboard, inelastic, petrified, plastered, unbending **10** inflexible, mechanical, unyielding **11** intoxicated, intractable

stiffen
5 tense **6** harden **7** thicken **8** rigidify, solidify **9** stabilize **10** immobilize

stifle
3 gag **4** hush, mute **5** burke, choke, deter **6** dampen, deaden, hush up, muffle, muzzle **7** repress, silence, smother, squelch **8** stultify, suppress **9** suffocate **10** asphyxiate, discourage

stigma
4 blot, onus, spot **5** brand, odium, shame, stain,

taint **6** smudge, smutch **8** black eye, disgrace, dishonor, petechia, tainting

stigmatize
5 brand, label, stamp

still
3 but, yet **4** calm, even, hush, lull **5** allay, inert, quiet, shush, whist **6** even so, hushed, placid, serene, settle, silent, though, withal **7** alembic, halcyon, silence **8** peaceful, stagnant, tranquil **9** noiseless, quietness, soundless **10** motionless, stationary **11** furthermore, nonetheless, tranquility **12** nevertheless

stilt
4 bird, pile, pole **8** longlegs **9** shorebird

stilted
4 prim **5** stiff **6** formal, wooden **7** pompous, starchy **8** affected **9** cardboard

stilt-like bird
6 avocet

Stimpy's pal
3 Ren

stimulant
4 goad, spur **5** tonic **7** impetus, impulse **8** caffeine, catalyst, excitant **9** analeptic, energizer, incentive **10** incitement, motivation

stimulate
4 fire, goad, move, prod, spur, urge, whet **5** impel, pique, rouse, set up, spark **6** arouse, excite, fire up, foment, incite, prompt, vivify, work up **7** agitate, enliven, inspire, provoke, quicken, trigger **8** activate, energize, motivate, vitalize **9** galvanize **10** exhilarate

stimulus
4 goad, kick, push, spur **5** boost, cause **6** charge, motive **7** impetus, impulse **8** catalyst **9** incentive **10** incitement, inducement, motivation **11** instigation, provocation **13** encouragement

sting
3 con **4** scam, trap **5** cheat, prick, smart, snare **6** hustle, tingle **7** con game **8** skin game

stinging
8 aculeate

stingy
4 mean **5** close, tight **6** frugal, narrow, paltry, skimpy **7** chintzy, costive, miserly, niggard, scrimpy, sparing, thrifty **8** grudging **9** niggardly, penny-wise, penurious **10** economical, iron-fisted, pinchpenny, ungenerous **11** tightfisted **12** cheeseparing, parsimonious **13** penny-pinching

stink
4 flap, funk, fuss, reek **5** smell **6** stench **7** malodor

stinker
3 dog, dud **4** bomb, bust, flop **5** lemon, loser, skunk **6** petrel, turkey **7** washout

stinking
see **smelly**

stinky
see **smelly**

stint
3 job **4** bout, task, time, tour, turn **5** chore, cramp, pinch, scant, share, shift, skimp, spare, spell **6** amount, scrape, scrimp **8** quantity, restrict **9** allotment, stricture **10** assignment, limitation **11** restriction

stipend
3 fee, pay **4** hire, wage **5** award **6** salary **7** payment **9** allowance, emolument **13** consideration

stipple
3 dot **5** fleck, speck **6** pepper **7** freckle, speckle **8** sprinkle

stipulate
5 state **6** detail **7** specify **8** contract, spell out **13** particularize

stipulation
5 limit, terms **7** proviso, strings **9** condition, provision **11** requirement

stir
3 ado, din, mix **4** fuss, rout, to-do, wake, whet **5** blend, budge, churn, impel, rally, rouse, roust, spark, waken **6** arouse, bustle, excite, flurry, foment, hubbub, incite, kindle, pother, seethe, simmer, tumult, whip up **7** agitate, disturb, ferment, inspire, provoke, quicken **8** activity **9** agitation, commotion, galvanize, stimulate **11** disturbance

stirrup
6 stapes **8** footrest

stithy
5 anvil

stoat
6 ermine, weasel

stock
4 butt, fund, hope, race **5** brace, carry, faith, goods, hoard, store, talon, trunk, trust **6** family, supply **7** furnish, lineage **8** pedigree, reliance **9** inventory, selection **10** confidence, dependence **11** merchandise

stockade
4 jail **5** fence **6** paling, prison **8** palisade **9** enclosure, guardroom

stock exchange
4 AMEX, FTSE, NYSE **6** bourse, NASDAQ

stockings
4 hose **5** socks **7** hosiery

stockpile
4 bank, heap, mass **5** amass, cache, hoard, lay up, store **6** garner, supply **7** backlog, collect, nest egg, reserve, store up **9** inventory, reservoir **10** accumulate, repository

stocky
3 fat **5** beefy, burly, dumpy, husky, plump, pudgy, squat, stout, thick **6** chunky, stubby, stumpy **8** heavyset, thickset **9** corpulent

stodge
4 fill, sate **5** gorge, stuff **7** overeat, surfeit

stodgy
5 fusty **6** stuffy **9** hidebound, out-of-date **12** old-fashioned

stogie
4 shoe **5** cigar **6** brogan

stoic
4 Zeno **6** stolid **7** Spartan **9** apathetic, impassive **10** phlegmatic **11** indifferent, unconcerned

stoicism
9 stolidity **11** impassivity
founder: **4** Zeno

stoke
3 fan **4** feed, fuel, poke, stir, tend **6** supply

Stoker novel
7 Dracula

stolid
3 dry **4** dull, flat **5** stoic **6** wooden **8** rocklike **9** apathetic, impassive, unruffled **10** phlegmatic **11** unemotional

stomach
3 gut, maw **4** bear, craw **5** abide, belly, brook, stand, taste, tummy **6** digest, endure, paunch, venter **7** abdomen, swallow **8** appetite, tolerate
combining form: **5** gastr **6** gastro, ventri, ventro
enzyme: **6** pepsin, rennin
muscle: **7** pylorus
ruminant: **6** omasum **8** abomasum **9** reticulum
Scottish: **4** kyte

stomachache
5 colic, gripe **12** collywobbles

stomp
5 clomp, clump, pound, tramp, tromp **7** trample

stone
3 gem **4** rock **5** lapis **6** pebble **7** boulder
base: **6** plinth
block of: **8** monolith
carving: **7** epitaph
chip: **5** spall
combining form: **4** lite, lith, lyte
cosmic: **6** meteor **9** chondrite, meteorite
facing: **6** ashlar
for grinding grains: **6** metate
fruit: **5** drupe
memorial: **5** cairn, stela **7** obelisk
monument: **6** dolmen **8** megalith
of a fruit: **3** pit
paving: **3** set **4** sett

____ Stone
7 Blarney, Rosetta

Stone novel
11 Lust for Life **18** Agony and the Ecstasy (The)

stonecrop
5 sedum

stoned
3 lit **4** high **5** boozy, doped, drunk, fried, oiled, tight, tipsy **6** buzzed, canned, juiced, loaded, plowed, potted, soused, stewed, tanked, wasted, zonked **7** crocked, drugged, muddled, pickled, pie-eyed, sloshed, smashed **8** hopped-up, turned on, wiped out **9** pixilated, plastered, spaced-out, strung out **10** inebriated, tripped out **11** intoxicated

stonewall
5 delay, stall **6** hamper, hinder, impede, stymie **8** obstruct

stooge
3 act, sap **4** dupe, foil, gull, mark, pawn, tool **5** chump, dummy, patsy, proxy **6** puppet, sucker, victim **7** fall guy **8** sidekick **9** represent **11** stool pigeon, straight man **12** second banana

Stooge
3 Moe (Howard) **5** Curly (Howard), Larry (Fine)

stool pigeon
3 rat **4** fink, nark **5** decoy **6** canary, snitch **7** ratfink, tipster **8** informer

stoop
3 dip **4** bend, duck, sink **5** deign, hunch, porch, slump **6** resort, slouch **7** descend, portico, veranda **8** stairway **10** condescend

stop
3 bar, can, dam, end **4** clog, fill, halt, plug, quit, stay, stem **5** block, brake, cease, check, close, stall, tarry **6** arrest, desist, ending, kibosh, stanch **7** disrupt, occlude, prevent, sojourn, suspend **8** knock off, obstruct **9** cessation, interrupt, terminate **10** conclusion, standstill **11** discontinue, termination
up: **4** cork, plug **7** occlude

stopgap
5 shift **6** resort **8** recourse, resource **9** expedient, makeshift **10** expediency, substitute

stopover
4 stay **5** visit **7** sojourn

stoppage
4 halt **6** cutoff, strike **7** walkout **8** shutdown **10** standstill **11** obstruction

Stoppard play
7 Jumpers **9** Real Thing (The) **10** Travesties **13** Coast of Utopia (The)

stopper
4 bung, cork, fill, plug **5** close

store
3 bin **4** fund, mart, pack, shop, stow, tank **5** amass, cache, depot, hoard, lay up, stash **6** ensile, garner, market, outlet, shoppe, supply **7** arsenal, backlog, bootery, deposit, reserve **8** boutique, cumulate, emporium, mothball, showroom, squirrel **9** abundance, chandlery, inventory, reservoir, stockpile, warehouse **10** accumulate, depository, five-and-ten, repository **11** five-and-dime **12** accumulation
display: **6** endcap **8** showcase

storehouse
5 depot **7** arsenal, granary **8** magazine **9** stockpile **10** depository, repository

storekeeper
8 merchant, retailer **9** tradesman

storeroom
6 larder, pantry **7** buttery

storm
3 row **4** fury, gale, hail, rage, rant, rave, roar, rush, to-do **5** beset, blast, blitz, burst, furor, onset, salvo **6** assail, attack, charge, clamor, fall on, flurry, furore, hubbub, outcry, pother, racket, shower, squall, tumult **7** assault, bluster, cyclone, monsoon, ruction, tempest, thunder, tornado, turmoil, twister, typhoon **8** blizzard, downpour, fall upon, outbreak, outburst, paroxysm, upheaval **9** broadside, commotion, discharge, hurricane, nor'easter, onslaught **10** cloudburst, hurly-burly **11** northeaster, northwester

storm trooper
10 brownshirt

stormy
4 foul **5** rainy, rough **6** raging **7** furious **8** blustery **9** turbulent **10** tumultuous **11** tempestuous, threatening

story
3 fib, lie **4** epic, saga, tale, yarn **5** conte, fable **6** canard, legend, report **7** account, fiction, märchen, parable, version **8** allegory, anecdote, folktale, megillah, tall tale **9** chronicle, fairy tale, narration, narrative **11** description, fabrication

storyteller
4 liar **6** fibber **8** fabulist **9** raconteur

stoup
4 font **5** basin **6** flagon, goblet **7** chalice, tankard

stout
3 ale, fat **4** brew **5** beefy, bulky, burly, heavy, husky, obese, plump, thick **6** fleshy, porter, portly, strong, sturdy **9** corpulent **10** overweight

Stout detective
5 Wolfe (Nero)

stouthearted
4 bold, game **5** brave, gutsy **7** doughty, gallant, valiant **8** fearless, intrepid, resolute, stalwart, stubborn, unafraid **9** audacious, dauntless, undaunted **10** courageous

stove
4 kiln, oven **5** range **8** Franklin, potbelly

stow
3 bin **4** lade, load, pack **5** stash, store **7** arrange, deposit

stower
9 stevedore

Stowe work
4 Dred

strabismus
6 squint

straddle
4 span **6** sprawl **8** bestride **11** spread-eagle

strafe
4 rake **6** attack **8** enfilade **10** machine-gun

straggle
3 lag **4** poke, roam, rove **5** drift, range, stray **6** dawdle, loiter, ramble, wander **7** maunder, meander **8** trail off **9** string out

straight
4 even, fair, neat, pure, true **5** erect, plain, plumb, right **6** at once, candid, direct, honest, linear, square **7** unmixed, upright **8** orthodox **9** bourgeois, forthwith, undiluted **10** aboveboard, button-down, forthright **12** conventional **13** unadulterated
combining form: **4** orth, rect **5** ortho, recti

straightaway
3 now **6** at once **7** stretch **8** directly, first off, promptly **9** forthwith, instanter **11** immediately

straighten
4 even, tidy **5** align **6** neaten, unbend, uncurl **7** rectify

straightforward
5 frank, lucid **6** candid, direct, honest **7** genuine, precise, sincere **8** clear-cut **9** outspoken **10** forthright **11** undeviating

strain
3 air, tax, try **4** hint, kind, pull, sort, toil, tune, vein **5** exert, stock, sweat, tinge, touch, trace, twist **6** filter, melody, screen, streak, stress, strive, wrench **7** lineage, overtax, tension, trouble **8** ancestry, exertion, overwork, pedigree, pressure, struggle **9** overexert

strait
4 bind, kyle, pass **5** pinch **6** crisis, plight **7** channel, dilemma, narrows, squeeze **8** exigency, hardship, juncture **9** crossroad, emergency **10** difficulty **11** contingency

Adriatic Sea-Ionian Sea: 7 Otranto
Alaska: 3 Icy
Alaska-Russia: 6 Bering
Albania-Greece: 5 Corfu
Asia-Europe: 11 Dardanelles
Atlantic-Baffin Island: 5 Davis
Atlantic-Mediterranean: 9 Gibraltar
Atlantic-Nantucket Sound: 8 Muskeget
Atlantic-North Sea: 7 English
Atlantic-Pacific: 5 Drake 8 Magellan
Atlantic-Saint Lawrence: 5 Cabot
Baffin Island-Quebec: 6 Hudson
Bering Sea-Sea of Okhotsk: 5 Kuril 6 Kurile
Bismarck Sea-Solomon Sea: 6 Vitiaz
Canada: 3 Rae 5 Dease
East China Sea: 5 Korea 8 Tsushima
East China-South China: 6 Taiwan 7 Formosa
England-France: 5 Dover
Flores Sea-Indian Ocean: 4 Sape
Flores Sea-Savu Sea: 4 Alor
Indian Ocean-Java Sea: 5 Sunda
India-Sri Lanka: 4 Palk
Indonesia: 4 Alas, Alor, Bali 5 Tioro 6 Lombok 7 Dampier 8 Macassar, Makassar, Surabaya
Inner Hebrides: 5 Tiree
Iran-Oman: 6 Hormuz
Italy: 7 Messina
Japan: 4 Yura 5 Bungo, Kitan 7 Hayasui
Japan-Sakhalin Island: 4 Soya
Lake Huron: 10 Mississagi
Lake Huron-Lake Michigan: 8 Mackinac
Malay Archipelago: 5 Wetar
Malaysia-Singapore: 6 Johore
Malay-Sumatra: 7 Malacca
New Jersey-Staten Island: 7 van Kull
New South Wales-Tasmania: 4 Bass
New Zealand: 4 Cook
Northwest Territories: 6 Barrow 8 Franklin, Victoria 13 Prince of Wales
Nova Scotia: 5 Canso
Pacific-San Francisco Bay: 10 Golden Gate
Pacific-South China Sea: 5 Luzon
Philippines: 5 Bohol, Tanon 6 Iloilo 7 Basilan
Russia: 4 Kara
Suvu Sea-Timor Sea: 4 Roti
Sea of Azov-Black Sea: 5 Kerch 7 Enikale
Sea of Japan: 5 Tatar
Solomon Islands: 12 Bougainville
South China Sea: 7 Mindoro 9 Singapore
Turkey: 8 Bosporus 9 Bosphorus, Karadeniz
Vancouver-Washington: 10 Juan de Fuca
Wales: 5 Menai
Washington Sound: 4 Haro

straitened
7 lacking, pinched, wanting **8** deprived, strapped **9** deficient, destitute **10** distressed, inadequate **12** impoverished

straitlaced
4 prim **5** staid, stiff **6** formal, narrow, prissy, strict, stuffy **7** genteel, prudish, starchy, stilted **8** priggish **9** hidebound, Victorian **11** puritanical

strand
4 bank **5** beach, coast, fiber, leave, shore, wreck **6** desert, maroon, thread **7** abandon, shingle **8** cast away, filament, littoral, seacoast, seashore **9** shipwreck **10** run aground, waterfront

strange
3 odd **5** alien, crazy, eerie, fishy, funny, kinky, kooky, nutty, outré, queer, weird **6** exotic, far-out, freaky **7** bizarre, curious, oddball, offbeat, uncanny, unknown, unusual **8** aberrant, abnormal, atypical, peculiar, singular **9** eccentric, fantastic, grotesque **10** mysterious, off-the-wall, outlandish, unfamiliar **11** exceptional **12** unaccustomed

Strange Interlude author
6 O'Neill (Eugene)

stranger
5 alien, guest **7** visitor **8** newcomer, outsider, wanderer **9** auslander, foreigner, immigrant, transient

strangle
5 burke, choke, shush **6** muffle, quelch, stifle **7** garotte, garrote **8** suppress, throttle **10** asphyxiate

strap
4 band, beat, belt, bind, rein **5** leash **6** attach, punish, secure, suffer **7** binding, leather **8** distress **9** constrict

strapping
5 beefy, burly, hardy, husky **6** brawny, robust, rugged, sturdy **8** muscular, vigorous **10** able-bodied

stratagem
4 play, plot, ploy, ruse, wile **5** feint, trick **6** device, gambit, scheme, tactic **8** artifice, intrigue, maneuver **10** conspiracy, subterfuge **11** machination

strategy
4 plan **6** design, method, scheme **7** project, tactics **8** game plan **9** blueprint

stratum
3 bed **4** rank **5** class, grade, layer, level

Strauss, Richard
opera: **6** Salome **7** Elektra **13** Rosenkavalier (Der) **15** Ariadne auf Naxos **16** Frau ohne Schatten (Die)
tone poem: **7** Don Juan **10** Don Quixote **11** Heldenleben (Ein) **20** Thus Spake Zarathustra **23** Death and Transfiguration

straw
3 hay 5 blond 6 flaxen, golden, thatch
braided: 6 sennit
mat: 6 tatami
plaited: 7 leghorn

straw man
4 dupe, foil, sham

stray
3 err, gad 4 lost, roam, rove, waif 5 drift, range 6 depart, errant, ramble, random, wander 7 deviate, digress, diverge, erratic, meander, runaway, traipse, vagrant 8 divagate, homeless, sporadic 9 gallivant

streak
4 hint, vein 5 fleck, tinge, trace 6 dapple, marble, mottle, strain, stripe 7 striate 8 tincture 9 suspicion, variegate 10 intimation, suggestion

streaked
5 upset 7 brindle, marbled, striped 8 brindled, grizzled 9 disturbed

stream
3 run 4 beck, burn, flow, flux, gill, gush, pour, race, rill, rush, sike, tide 5 bourn, brook, creek, spate, surge 6 bourne, branch, rindle, runnel, sluice 7 current, freshet, rivulet, torrent 8 affluent

streambed
4 wadi, wash 5 gully

streamer
4 flag, jack 6 banner, burgee, ensign, pennon 7 pennant 8 banderol, bannerol, standard 9 banderole

streamline
7 contour 8 organize, simplify 9 modernize

street
3 way 4 drag, road, wynd 5 alley, drive 6 artery, avenue 7 roadway 9 boulevard 12 thoroughfare
border: 4 curb 7 curbing
material: 6 cobble 7 asphalt, macadam 11 cobblestone
name: 3 Elm 4 Main, Park 5 Maple, State

streetcar
4 tram 7 trolley

Streetcar Named Desire, A
author: 8 Williams (Tennessee)
character: 6 Stella (Kowalski) 7 Blanche (DuBois), Stanley (Kowalski)

Street Scene author
4 Rice (Elmer)

strength
5 brawn, force, forte, might, power, sinew, vigor 6 energy, muscle 7 potency 8 firmness, security 9 fortitude, intensity, soundness, stability, toughness 10 steadiness, sturdiness

strengthen
4 gird 5 brace, steel 6 anneal, beef up, harden, prop up 7 bolster, enhance, fortify, support, toughen 8 buttress, embolden, energize 9 intensify, reinforce, undergird 10 invigorate, rejuvenate

strenuous
4 hard 5 tough 6 taxing, uphill 7 arduous, operose 9 demanding, difficult, effortful, Herculean, laborious 12 backbreaking

Strephon
8 shepherd
beloved: 5 Chloe 6 Urania

stress
6 accent, burden, import, play up, strain, weight 7 anxiety, feature, tension, trouble, urgency 8 emphasis, pressure 9 emphasize, italicize, underline 10 accentuate, underscore 12 accentuation
in poetry: 5 ictus

stretch
4 area, draw, time 5 crane, range, reach, scope, space, spell, sweep, tract, while 6 extend, extent, length, limber, region, spread 7 breadth, compass, draw out, expanse, magnify, prolong, purview, spin out, tighten 8 distance, elongate, lengthen, protract 9 embellish, embroider, expansion, overstate 10 exaggerate
on a frame: 6 tenter
out: 6 sprawl 7 lie down, recline

stretchable
7 ductile, elastic, tensile

stretched
4 taut

stretcher
4 yarn 6 gurney, litter 8 tall tale

strew
3 sow 4 dust 5 cover 6 pepper, spread 7 scatter 8 disperse, sprinkle 9 broadcast, circulate, propagate 10 distribute 11 disseminate

stricken
3 hit, ill 4 hurt, sick 6 bereft 7 injured, wounded 9 afflicted 11 overwhelmed

strict
4 firm 5 exact, harsh, rigid, stern, tough 6 narrow, severe 7 precise 8 exacting, faithful, rigorous 9 draconian, stringent, unsparing 10 inflexible, ironhanded, meticulous, scrupulous 11 punctilious

stricture
5 cramp, stint 7 censure, reproof 8 reproach 9 aspersion, criticism, reprimand 10 constraint, limitation 11 restriction 13 animadversion

stride
4 gait, pace, step **5** march, stalk **7** advance **8** straddle

strident
4 loud **5** harsh **6** shrill **7** grating, jarring, rasping, raucous, squawky **8** piercing **9** clamorous, insistent, obtrusive **10** boisterous, discordant, stentorian, vociferous **11** loud-mouthed **12** earsplitting, obstreperous

strife
4 fray **5** broil, fight **6** battle, combat **7** discord, dispute, dissent, quarrel, rivalry, warfare, wrangle **8** argument, conflict, disunity, friction, struggle, tug-of-war **10** contention, difference, dissension, dissidence **11** altercation, competition, controversy

strike
3 hit, pop, rap **4** bash, beat, find, poke, slam, slap, slug, sock, swat, whap, whop **5** clout, knock, punch, smack, smite, swipe, thump, whack **6** affect, assail, attack, cudgel, delete, hammer, pummel, thrash **7** assault, impress, inflict, inspire, wildcat **8** discover, stoppage

strike out
4 dele **5** elide **6** delete, efface **7** expunge

striking
5 showy, vivid **6** cogent, marked, signal **7** salient, telling **8** forceful **9** arresting, prominent **10** compelling, noticeable, remarkable **11** conspicuous, outstanding

Strindberg play
6 Easter, Father (The) **8** Comrades **9** Creditors (The), Dream Play (A), Miss Julie **10** Master Olaf **11** Ghost Sonata (The) **12** Dance of Death (The), Gustavus Vasa

string
3 row **4** file, line, rank, tier **5** chain, order, queue, train, twine **6** sequel, series **7** echelon **8** recourse, resource, sequence **10** succession
together: **4** bead
up: **4** hang **5** noose, scrag **6** gibbet

stringent
see **strict**

stringy
4 lean, ropy, wiry **6** sinewy **7** fibrous **8** muscular

strip
4 band, bare, doff, flay, husk, peel, sack, skin **5** scale **6** billet, denude, divest, expose, fillet, ravage, ribbon **7** bandeau, deprive, disrobe, pillage, uncover, undress **8** unclothe
leather: **5** thong
of wood: **4** lath, slat
skin, blubber: **5** scarf **6** flense

stripe
3 ilk **4** band, kind, lash, sort, type **5** order **6** strake, streak **7** banding, chevron, lineate, striate, variety

stripling
3 boy, lad **5** youth **9** youngster **10** adolescent

stripper
6 peeler, teaser **9** ecdysiast

stripteaser
see **stripper**

strive
3 try, vie **4** seek **5** labor **6** strain **7** attempt, contend **8** endeavor, struggle **9** undertake

stroke
3 fit, hit, pet, rub **4** blow, hone, whet **5** swing **6** attack, caress, fondle, soothe **7** flatter **8** apoplexy, ischemia **9** heartbeat

stroll
4 rove, turn, walk **5** amble, drift, mosey, paseo **6** cruise, linger, ramble, wander **7** saunter, traipse **9** promenade

stroller
4 pram **6** go-cart **8** carriage **12** baby carriage, perambulator

strong
4 fast, firm, hard **5** burly, hardy, lusty, solid, sound, stout, tough **6** brawny, hearty, heroic, mighty, potent, robust, rugged, secure, sinewy, stable, sturdy **7** durable, intense, staunch **8** forceful, muscular, powerful, stalwart, vigorous **9** resilient, strapping, tenacious **10** able-bodied, full-bodied, spirituous **12** concentrated

strong-arm
5 bully **6** bounce, coerce, hector, lean on **7** assault, dragoon **8** browbeat, bulldoze, bullyrag **9** terrorize **10** intimidate

strongbox
4 arca, safe **5** chest **6** coffer **9** reliquary **13** treasure chest

stronghold
4 fort **7** bastion, bulwark, citadel, redoubt **8** fastness, fortress

strongman
4 Amin (Idi), Tito **5** Assad (Hafez), Perón (Juan) **6** Castro (Fidel), Chávez (Hugo), despot, Marcos (Ferdinand), Mobutu (Sese Seko), Samson, Taylor (Charles), tyrant **7** Batista (Fulgencio), Hussein (Saddam), Noriega (Manuel), Suharto **8** caudillo, Pinochet (Augusto) **9** Milošević (Slobodan), Mussolini (Benito)

strong point
5 forte **6** métier

strong suit
see **strong point**

strontium symbol
2 Sr

strophe
5 verse 6 stanza

struck
3 hit 5 smote

structure
4 form 5 frame 6 format, makeup, system 7 anatomy, complex, edifice, network 8 building, erection, skeleton 9 framework 10 morphology 11 arrangement, composition

struggle
3 try, vie 4 agon 5 trial 6 battle, effort, hassle, strain, strife, strive, tussle 7 attempt, compete, contend, contest, grapple, scuffle 8 endeavor, exertion, flounder, skirmish, striving 9 undertake 11 undertaking

strumpet
4 bawd, jade, slut, tart 5 hussy, tramp, trull, wench 6 floozy, harlot, hooker, wanton 7 jezebel, trollop 8 slattern

strut
6 flaunt, parade, prance, sashay 7 flounce, peacock, show off, swagger

stub
3 end 4 butt, tail 5 stump 6 put out, strike 7 remnant 10 extinguish

stubborn
5 balky, rigid 6 cussed, dogged, mulish, ornery 7 adamant, lasting, willful 8 obdurate, perverse 9 obstinate, pigheaded, steadfast, unbending 10 bullheaded, determined, headstrong, inexorable, inflexible, persistent, rebellious, refractory, relentless, unyielding 11 intractable 12 contumacious, pertinacious, single-minded

stubby
5 dumpy, short, squat, stout 6 stocky, stumpy 8 heavyset, thickset

stuck
5 clung, glued 6 jammed, wedged 7 adhered, baffled, blocked, saddled, stabbed, stopped, stumped 8 attached, held fast 11 overcharged

stuck-up
4 vain 6 sniffy, snippy, snooty 7 haughty 8 snobbish 9 conceited 12 narcissistic, supercilious

stud
3 guy 4 dude, hunk, male, nail, post 5 cleat, he-man, himbo, macho 6 button, pillar 7 earring, speckle, upright 8 sprinkle, stallion

student
4 tiro, tyro 5 pupil, tutee 6 novice 7 protégé, scholar 8 disciple, neophyte 10 apprentice
college: 9 undergrad 13 undergraduate
female: 4 coed
first-year: 5 frosh 8 freshman
fourth-year: 6 senior
French: 5 élève 8 étudiant
military: 5 cadet, middy 10 midshipman
second-year: 4 soph 9 sophomore
third-year: 6 junior
wandering: 7 goliard

studio
4 shop 7 atelier 8 workroom, workshop

studious
7 bookish, learned 9 scholarly

Studs Lonigan creator
7 Farrell (James T.)

study
3 con, den, vet 4 case, cram, muse 5 étude 6 ponder, survey 7 analyze, examine, inspect, reverie 8 consider 9 attention, think over 10 excogitate, scrutinize

stuff
3 jam, ram 4 cram, fill, glut, junk, pack, sate, tamp 5 crowd, gorge, shove 6 matter, things 7 essence, jam-pack, squeeze, surfeit 8 material, overfill 9 substance 11 possessions

stuffy
4 dull, prim 5 close, fuggy, heavy, humid, stale, thick 6 narrow, stodgy 7 airless, bloated, genteel, humdrum, pompous, prudish, stilted 8 priggish, stagnant, stifling 9 hidebound, Victorian 10 oppressive, pontifical 11 puritanical, suffocating 12 narrow-minded 13 self-important, self-righteous

stultify
4 dull 6 deaden, impair, stifle, weaken 7 inhibit, nullify, repress, smother, trammel 8 restrain, stagnate, suppress 9 suffocate 10 discourage, invalidate

stumble
3 err 4 reel, slip, trip 5 error, fluff, gaffe, lapse, lurch 6 falter, muddle, slipup, totter 7 blunder, faux pas, mistake, stagger, stammer 8 flounder

stump
3 end 4 beat, butt, dare, defy, plod, stub 5 barge, clomp, clump, stick 6 baffle, outwit, puzzle, stymie, trudge 7 buffalo, flummox, galumph, mystify, nonplus, perplex 8 bewilder, campaign, confound, hustings, politick 9 barnstorm, challenge 11 electioneer

stun
4 daze 5 amaze, floor, shock 6 dazzle 7 astound,

nonplus, stagger, stupefy **8** astonish, bewilder, bowl over, knock out, paralyze **9** dumbfound **11** flabbergast

stunning
6 superb **7** amazing, awesome **8** gorgeous, striking **9** excellent, wonderful **10** astounding, impressive, remarkable, staggering, surprising **11** astonishing

stunt
4 curb, feat **5** antic, caper, check, dwarf, prank, trick **6** hinder, impair, retard **8** escapade, hold back, suppress

stupefy
4 daze, dull, faze, stun **5** addle, amaze **6** muddle, rattle **7** astound, nonplus, petrify, stagger **8** astonish, bewilder, paralyze **9** disorient, dumbfound **11** flabbergast

stupendous
4 huge **7** amazing, awesome, massive, titanic **8** colossal, enormous, gigantic, stunning, towering, wondrous **9** fantastic, humongous, marvelous, monstrous, wonderful **10** astounding, miraculous, monumental, phenomenal, prodigious, staggering, tremendous **11** astonishing, spectacular **12** breathtaking, mind-boggling, overwhelming

stupid
3 dim **4** dull, dumb, slow **5** dense, dopey, inane, silly, thick **6** oafish, obtuse, simple, torpid **7** asinine, brutish, doltish, fatuous, foolish, idiotic, moronic, witless **8** backward, ignorant, mindless, retarded **9** brainless, fatheaded, imbecilic, laughable, ludicrous, pinheaded, senseless, vexatious **10** half-witted, slow-witted **11** blockheaded, thickheaded, thick-witted **12** exasperating **13** chuckleheaded

stupor
6 torpor, trance **7** languor **8** dullness, hebetude, lethargy, narcosis **9** lassitude, torpidity **10** anesthesia, somnolence **13** insensibility
combining form: **4** narc **5** narco

sturdy
5 hardy, solid, sound, stout, tough **6** robust, rugged, secure, strong **7** durable, healthy, staunch **8** stalwart, vigorous **9** strapping

sturgeon
6 beluga
roe: **6** caviar

Sturm und Drang
5 angst **6** unease, unrest **7** anxiety, ferment, turmoil **8** disquiet **9** agitation **10** inquietude, turbulence **11** disquietude, restiveness **12** restlessness

St. Vitus' ____
5 dance

sty
3 pen **4** coop, cyst **6** pigpen **7** piggery

stygian
4 dark **6** gloomy **7** hellish, sunless **8** infernal, plutonic **9** Cimmerian, plutonian

style
3 fad, way **4** chic, élan, mode, rage, vein **5** craze, decor, flair, trend, vogue **6** manner **7** fashion, panache **10** dernier cri **11** savoir-faire
hair: **4** coif **8** coiffure

stylish
3 mod **4** chic, posh, tony, trig **5** doggy, natty, ritzy, sassy, sharp, showy, sleek, slick, smart, swank, swell **6** chichi, dapper, dressy, modern, modish, snappy, snazzy, spiffy, trendy, with-it **7** à la mode, dashing, doggish **8** spiffing, up-to-date **10** newfangled **11** fashionable

stymie
4 stop **5** block **6** hamper, hinder, impede, thwart **7** flummox, prevent **8** confound, obstruct **9** frustrate, hamstring

Stymphalides' slayer
8 Heracles, Hercules

Styron novel
13 Sophie's Choice **22** Confessions of Nat Turner (The)

Styx
father: **7** Oceanus
ferryman: **6** Charon
location: **5** Hades
mother: **6** Tethys

Styx's counterpart
5 Lethe **7** Acheron, Cocytus **10** Phlegethon

suave
4 oily **5** slick **6** smarmy, smooth, urbane **7** cordial, courtly, gallant, politic, refined, tactful, worldly **8** debonair, gracious, polished, unctuous, well-bred **9** courteous **10** cultivated, diplomatic **12** ingratiating **13** sophisticated

sub
5 below, proxy, under **6** backup, fill-in **7** standby, stand-in **8** pinch-hit **9** alternate, secondary, surrogate **10** understudy **11** locum tenens, pinch hitter, replacement

subaltern
8 inferior **9** secondary, underling

subdue
4 curb, tame **5** crush, quash, quell **6** defeat, master, quench **7** conquer, control, put down, repress, squelch **8** beat down, overcome, suppress, tone down, vanquish **9** overpower, overthrow, subjugate

subdued
4 soft, tame 5 muted, quiet, sober 6 low-key, mellow, subtle 7 neutral, serious 8 low-keyed, softened, tasteful, tempered 9 moderated, toned down 10 controlled, restrained, submissive 11 unobtrusive

subjacent
3 low 5 lower, under 6 lesser, nether 8 inferior

subject
3 apt 4 core, open 5 liege, motif, point, prone, theme, topic 6 expose, liable, likely, matter, motive, vassal 7 citizen, exposed, lay open, problem 8 argument, inferior, material, question 9 dependent, leitmotif, secondary, sensitive, subjugate, substance, tributary 11 subordinate, subservient, susceptible

subjective
6 biased 10 prejudiced

subjugate
see **subdue**

sublime
4 holy 5 ideal, lofty, noble, proud 6 august, divine, sacred, superb 7 blessed, exalted 8 elevated, glorious, heavenly, majestic, splendid 9 celestial, spiritual 11 magnificent, resplendent 12 transcendent

submarine
4 hero 5 po'boy, U-boat 6 hoagie 7 grinder
detector: 5 sonar

submerge
3 dip 4 duck, dunk, sink 5 drown, flood, swamp 6 deluge, engulf, plunge 7 founder, go under, immerse 8 inundate, overflow

submerse
see **submerge**

submissive
4 meek, tame 6 abject, docile, pliant 7 servile, slavish, subdued 8 amenable, obedient, obeisant, yielding 9 compliant, tractable 10 obsequious 11 acquiescent, deferential, subservient, unresisting 12 nonresisting

submit
3 bow 4 cave, fold, obey 5 defer, offer, yield 6 accede, comply, give in, hand in, relent, send in, tender 7 concede, deliver, go under, present, proffer, provide, subject, succumb, suggest 9 acquiesce, surrender 10 capitulate 11 buckle under 12 knuckle under

subordinate
5 minor, scrub, under 6 junior 7 adjunct, subject 8 inferior 9 accessory, ancillary, auxiliary, dependent, secondary, subaltern, tributary, underling 10 collateral, submissive, subsidiary 11 subservient

sub rosa
6 covert, secret 7 furtive, private 8 covertly, in camera, secretly, stealthy 9 by stealth, furtively, privately, secretive, underhand 10 stealthily 11 clandestine, underhanded 13 clandestinely, surreptitious

subscribe
3 ink 4 sign 5 agree 6 accede, adhere, assent, attest, pledge 7 approve, consent, endorse, support 8 sanction 9 acquiesce

subsequent
4 next 5 after, later 6 serial 7 ensuing 9 following, resultant, resulting 10 sequential, succeeding, successive 11 consecutive
prefix: 4 post

subsequently
4 next, then 5 after, later, since 9 afterward 10 afterwards, thereafter

subservient
6 abject, docile 7 fawning, ignoble, servile, slavish 8 adjuvant, obeisant 9 accessory, ancillary, auxiliary, compliant, truckling 10 collateral, obsequious, submissive 11 acquiescent, deferential, subordinate, sycophantic

subside
3 die, ebb 4 ease, fall, lull, sink, wane 5 abate, let up, taper 6 ease up, recede, settle 7 decline, descend, die away, die down, dwindle, ease off, slacken 8 decrease, diminish, moderate

subsidiary
5 minor 6 backup, branch 7 subject 8 adjuvant 9 accessory, ancillary, auxiliary, secondary, tributary 10 collateral 11 subordinate 12 supplemental 13 supplementary

subsidize
4 back, fund 5 endow, stake 7 finance, promote, sponsor, support 8 bankroll 9 grubstake 10 underwrite

subsidy
4 gift 5 grant 6 reward 10 subvention 13 appropriation

subsistence
4 keep, salt 5 bread, means 6 income, living 7 support 9 resources 10 livelihood, sustenance 11 maintenance, wherewithal 12 alimentation

substance
3 nub 4 bulk, core, crux, gist, mass, meat, pith, soul 5 being, drift, focus, heart, point, sense, stuff, tenor 6 amount, burden, entity, import, kernel, marrow, matter, nubbin, object, thrust, upshot, wealth 7 essence, meaning, nucleus, purport 8 material, property, sum total 9 resources 12 essentiality, quintessence

substantial
3 big **4** full **5** ample, hefty, large, meaty, solid **6** strong, sturdy **7** massive, sizable, weighty **8** abundant, concrete, material, physical, sensible, tangible **9** corporeal, important, objective **10** meaningful, phenomenal **11** significant **12** considerable

substantiate
5 prove **6** embody, evince, verify **7** bear out, confirm, justify **8** evidence, manifest, validate **9** establish, incarnate, objectify, vindicate **11** corroborate, demonstrate **12** authenticate

substantive
4 firm, noun, real **5** solid **8** definite **9** essential

substitute
4 mock, sham, swap **5** dummy, locum, proxy, trade **6** acting, backup, deputy, double, ersatz, fill-in, refuge, resort, second, switch **7** replace, reserve, standby, stand-in, stopgap **8** exchange, recourse, resource, spurious **9** alternate, expedient, imitation, makeshift, simulated, surrogate, temporary **10** artificial, expediency, understudy **11** alternative, locum tenens, pinch hitter, replacement, succedaneum

substratum
4 base **5** basis **6** bottom, ground **7** bedrock, footing **10** foundation, groundwork **12** underpinning

substructure
4 base, seat **5** basis **6** bottom **7** footing **10** foundation, groundwork **12** underpinning

subsume
6 embody, take in **7** contain, embrace, include, involve **8** comprise **9** encompass **10** comprehend

subterfuge
4 ploy, ruse, scam, sham **5** cheat, feint, fraud **6** deceit, dupery **7** chicane **8** trickery **9** chicanery, deception **10** dishonesty

subterranean
11 underground

subtle
4 fine **5** faint **6** artful, astute **7** cunning, refined **8** delicate, finespun, guileful, skillful **9** insidious **10** indistinct **13** inconspicuous

subtract
6 deduct, remove **7** take off **8** discount, knock off, take away, withdraw, withhold

subtraction
6 rebate **8** discount **9** abatement, deduction **10** diminution, withdrawal
term: **7** minuend **9** remainder **10** subtrahend

suburb
5 slurb **8** edge city

suburbs
7 fringes **8** environs, purlieus **9** outskirts

subversion
8 sabotage **11** undermining **12** undercutting

subvert
5 upset **6** debase **7** corrupt, deprave, vitiate **8** overturn, sabotage **9** overthrow, undermine

subway
British: **4** tube **11** underground
French: **5** métro

succeed
3 win **4** boom **5** click, ensue, go far, score **6** arrive, follow, go over, make it, pan out, thrive, win out **7** catch on, come off, make out, prevail, prosper, replace, triumph **8** displace, flourish, get ahead, make good, supplant **9** supervene

succes ___
3 fou **7** d'estime

success
3 hit **4** fame **5** smash, éclat **6** wealth **7** arrival, fortune, killing, triumph, victory **8** fruition **10** attainment, prosperity **11** achievement, fulfillment

successful
5 boffo, smash, socko **7** booming **8** fruitful, thriving **9** effective, lucrative **10** prosperous, triumphant, victorious **11** flourishing

succession
3 row **5** chain, cycle, march, order, round, suite, train **6** course, sequel, series, string **8** sequence **11** progression

successive
4 next **7** ensuing **9** following **10** subsequent

successor
4 heir **8** claimant, follower **9** inheritor **11** beneficiary

succinct
4 curt **5** blunt, brief, pithy, short, terse **7** brusque, compact, concise, laconic, summary **11** compendious

succor
3 aid **4** help, lift **6** assist, relief **7** comfort, relieve, support **10** assistance, sustenance

succulent
5 juicy **8** luscious
plant: **4** aloe, hoya **5** agave, ficus, yucca **6** cactus, cereus, hoodia, viscum **7** begonia

succumb
3 bow, die **4** cave, fold, wilt **5** defer, yield **6** accede, buckle, cave in, expire, give in, perish, relent, resign, submit **7** give out, go under, knuckle **8** collapse **9** break down, surrender **10** capitulate **11** buckle under **12** knuckle under

sucker
3 con, gyp, sap **4** bilk, dupe, fool, gull, mark, rook **5** cheat, chump, patsy, shoot **6** diddle, pigeon **7** defraud, fall guy, swindle **8** hoodwink, pushover **9** bamboozle

suckle
5 nurse **7** nourish, nurture **10** breast-feed

Sudan
capital: **8** Khartoum
desert: **6** Libyan
language: **6** Arabic
monetary unit: **5** dinar
neighbor: **4** Chad **5** Congo, Egypt, Kenya, Libya **6** Uganda **7** Eritrea **8** Ethiopia
river: **4** Nile
sea: **3** Red

sudden
4 rash **5** hasty, swift **6** abrupt, prompt **7** hurried **8** headlong **9** impetuous, impromptu, impulsive **10** unexpected, unforeseen **11** precipitant, precipitate, precipitous

suddenly
5 aback **7** hastily, shortly, unaware **8** abruptly, promptly, unawares **9** all at once **10** by surprise **12** unexpectedly

suds
4 beer, fizz, foam, head, soap **5** froth, spume **6** lather

sue
8 litigate

suer
8 litigant

suet
3 fat **4** lard **6** tallow

Suez Canal
builder: **7** Lesseps (Ferdinand de)
city: **8** Ismailia, Port Said

suffer
4 ache, bear, lump **5** abide, admit, allow, brook, leave, stand, yield **6** accept, endure, permit, submit **7** agonize, anguish, stomach, sustain, swallow, undergo **8** tolerate **10** experience **11** countenance

sufferer
6 victim

suffering
4 ache **5** agony, dolor **6** misery, ordeal **7** anguish, passion, torment, torture **8** distress **10** affliction, misfortune

suffice
5 avail, serve

sufficient
3 due **5** ample **6** common, decent, enough, plenty **8** adequate, all right **9** competent, tolerable **10** acceptable **11** comfortable **12** commensurate, satisfactory **13** commensurable, proportionate
poetic: **4** enow

suffocate
5 burke, choke **6** stifle **7** smother **8** snuff out, strangle **10** asphyxiate

suffrage
4 vote **5** voice **6** ballot **9** franchise

suffragist
4 Catt (Carrie Chapman), Howe (Julia Ward), Mott (Lucretia), Paul (Alice) **5** Stone (Lucy) **7** Anthony (Susan B.), Bloomer (Amelia), Stanton (Elizabeth Cady) **8** Woodhull (Victoria Claflin) **9** Pankhurst (Emmeline)

suffuse
4 fill **5** bathe, flush, imbue, steep **7** pervade **8** permeate, saturate **10** impregnate

sugar
6 aldose, fucose, ribose, xylose **7** glucose, lactose, maltose, mannose, pentose, sorbose, sucrose, sweeten **8** fructose, furanose, levulose **10** saccharose
burnt: **7** caramel
combining form: **4** gluc, glyc, sucr **5** gluco, glyco, sucro **7** sacchar **8** sacchari, saccharo
from palm sap: **7** jaggery
Mexican: **7** panocha, penuche
source: **4** beet, cane, corn **5** maple

sugarcane refuse
7 bagasse

sugarcoat
5 candy **6** veneer **7** sweeten, varnish **8** palliate **9** extenuate, gloss over, gloze over, whitewash

sugary
6 syrupy **7** cloying, honeyed, mawkish **10** saccharine **11** sentimental

suggest
4 hint **5** evoke, imply **6** submit **7** connote, propose, signify **8** indicate, intimate **9** adumbrate, insinuate

suggestion
3 cue **4** clue, hint **5** shade, smack, tinge, trace **6** advice **7** inkling **8** allusion, innuendo, overtone, proposal, reminder **9** suspicion, undertone **10** indication, intimation **11** implication, insinuation

suggestive
4 racy **5** salty, spicy **6** ribald, risqué **8** off-color **9** evocative **10** indicative **11** reminiscent

suicidal pilot
8 kamikaze

suicide
8 felo-de-se **10** self-murder **13** self-slaughter
Japanese: **7** seppuku **8** hara-kiri, hari-kari

suit
3 fit **4** case, jibe, plea **5** adapt, agree, befit, cause, check, serve, tally **6** accord, action, adjust, appeal, become, go with, please, prayer, square, tailor **7** conform, enhance, flatter, lawsuit, request, satisfy **8** entreaty, petition **9** agree with, reconcile **10** go together **11** accommodate,

application, imploration, imprecation **12** solicitation, supplication
card: **5** clubs **6** hearts, spades **8** diamonds
type: **4** zoot **6** monkey, vested **9** paternity **10** pin-striped **11** class-action

suitable
3 apt, due, fit **4** just, meet **5** right **6** proper, seemly, useful **7** condign, fitting **8** apposite, becoming, deserved, eligible **9** pertinent, qualified, requisite **10** acceptable, felicitous **11** appropriate

suitcase
3 bag **4** grip **6** valise **7** carry-on, holdall **8** carryall

suite
3 lot, row, set **4** flat **5** array, group, rooms, staff, train **6** sequel, series, string **7** lodging, retinue **8** chambers, sequence **9** apartment, entourage, following

suitor
4 beau **5** lover, spark, swain, wooer **7** admirer, gallant, sparker **8** cavalier, paramour **9** boyfriend **10** petitioner

sulfur
9 brimstone

sulk
4 mope, pout **5** brood, gloom

sulky
4 cart, dour, glum **5** moody **6** gloomy, morose, sullen **7** crabbed **9** saturnine

sullen
4 dour, glum, mean, sour **5** moody, pouty, surly **6** crabby, dismal, gloomy, grumpy, morose, somber, sombre **7** crabbed, pouting **8** lowering, scowling **9** glowering, saturnine **10** ill-humored **11** pessimistic

Sullivan's partner
7 Gilbert (William Schwenk)

sully
3 tar **4** soil **5** dirty, shame, smear, stain, taint **6** defame, defile, malign, vilify **7** asperse, blacken, pollute, slander, tarnish, traduce **8** besmirch, disgrace, dishonor **9** denigrate

Sultan of Swat
8 Babe Ruth

sultry
3 hot **4** sexy **5** close, humid, muggy **6** steamy, sticky, stuffy, torrid **7** airless **8** stifling **9** seductive **10** passionate, sweltering, voluptuous

sum
3 add, all, tot **4** mass, tote **5** gross, total, whole **6** amount, digest, entity, figure, resumé **7** epitome **8** entirety, integral, nutshell, totality **9** aggregate, epitomize

Sumatra
country: **9** Indonesia
highest peak: **7** Kerinci **8** Kerintji
largest city: **5** Medan
shrew: **4** tana

Sumerian
city: **4** Kish, Umma **5** Erech **6** Lagash, Nippur
dragon: **3** Kur
god: **3** Abu, Kur, Utu **4** Enki **5** Enlil, Lahar, Nanna, Nintu **6** Dumuzi, Nergal, Ninazu **7** Enkimdu
goddess: **6** Ningal, Ninlil

summarize
5 recap **6** digest **7** abridge, outline **8** boil down, condense **9** epitomize, synopsize **11** encapsulate **12** recapitulate

summary
5 recap **6** aperçu, digest, précis, résumé, review, wrap-up **7** compend, epitome, outline, roundup, rundown **8** abstract, overview, scenario, synopsis **9** inventory **10** abridgment, compendium, conspectus **11** abridgement **12** condensation

summer
French: **3** été
Spanish: **6** verano

summerhouse
6 alcove, gazebo, pagoda **9** belvedere

summery
7 estival

summit
3 top **4** acme, apex, peak, roof **5** crest, crown **6** apogee, climax, height, vertex, zenith **8** capstone, meridian, pinnacle **11** culmination

summon
3 bid **4** call, cite **5** evoke, order **6** beckon, call in, invite, muster **7** arraign, command, conjure, convene, convoke, send for **8** assemble, subpoena

sump
4 sink **8** cesspool

sumptuous
4 lush, rich **5** grand **6** costly, deluxe, lavish, superb **7** opulent **8** gorgeous, luscious, palatial, splendid **9** grandiose, luxurious **11** extravagant, resplendent **12** awe-inspiring

sun
3 orb, Sol **4** bask, star **7** daystar, phoebus **8** daylight, luminary, radiance **9** radiation
combining form: **4** heli **5** helio
disk: **4** Aten
god: **3** Lug, Sol, Tem, Utu **4** Amen, Atmu, Atum, Inti, Lleu, Llew, Lugh, Utug **5** Horus, Sunna, Surya **6** Apollo, Babbar, Helios, Marduk **7** Khepera, Ninurta, Phoebus, Shamash **8** Hyperion, Merodach

Sun Also Rises, The
author: **9** Hemingway (Ernest)
character: **6** Ashley (Brett), Barnes (Jake)

sunder
3 cut **4** rend, rive **5** break, sever, slice, split **6** cleave, divide **8** dissever, disunite, separate

sundial part
6 gnomon

sundown
4 dusk **7** evening **8** eventide, gloaming, twilight

sundries
7 notions **8** oddments **9** etceteras **11** odds and ends

sundry
4 many, some **6** varied **7** diverse, several, various **8** assorted, manifold, numerous **9** different, disparate **12** multifarious **13** miscellaneous, multitudinous

sunfish
4 opah **7** pompano **8** bluegill **11** pumpkinseed

Sunflower State
6 Kansas

sun-god
see at **sun**

Sun King
8 Louis XIV

sunny
4 fair, fine, warm **5** clear, happy **6** blithe, bright, cheery, chirpy, golden **7** beaming, clarion, radiant **8** cheerful, pleasant, rainless **9** brilliant, cloudless, unclouded **10** optimistic

sunrise
4 dawn, morn **6** aurora **7** dawning, morning **8** cockcrow, daybreak, daylight
goddess: **3** Eos **6** Aurora

sunroom
8 solarium

sunset
3 eve **4** dusk **7** evening **8** gloaming, twilight

Sunset State
6 Oregon

Sunshine State
7 Florida

sunup
see **sunrise**

sup
3 eat **4** dine **5** feast

super
4 very **5** great **8** powerful, splendid, terrific **9** excellent, extremely, fantastic, first-rate, wonderful **11** outstanding

superannuated
4 aged **5** hoary, passé **6** bygone **7** ancient, archaic, elderly, outworn **8** obsolete, outdated, outmoded **9** out-of-date **10** antiquated **11** obsolescent **12** old-fashioned

superb
4 A-one, rich **5** grand, lofty, noble, prime, primo, super **7** elegant, exalted, optimal, optimum, opulent, stately, sublime, supreme **8** glorious, gorgeous, imposing, majestic, peerless, splendid, standout **9** excellent, marvelous, matchless, wonderful **11** magnificent, outstanding, resplendent, sensational, splendorous **13** splendiferous

supercilious
5 lofty **6** lordly, sniffy, snippy **7** haughty, stuck-up **8** cavalier, snobbish, superior **10** disdainful **11** patronizing **13** condescending, high-and-mighty

superficial
5 hasty **6** breezy, casual, slight **7** cursory, shallow, sketchy, surface, trivial **8** external, skin-deep **9** depthless, frivolous **11** perfunctory

superfluity
4 glut **5** frill **6** excess **7** nimiety, overrun, surfeit, surplus **8** overflow, overkill, overload, overmuch, overplus, plethora **10** oversupply, redundancy, surplusage **11** prodigality **12** extravagance **13** overabundance

superfluous
5 extra, spare **6** de trop, excess, otiose **7** surplus **8** needless **9** excessive, redundant **10** gratuitous **11** uncalled-for, unnecessary

superintend
4 boss **6** direct, manage **7** control, oversee **10** administer

superintendence
4 care **6** charge **7** conduct, running **8** handling **9** authority, direction, oversight **10** management

superior
4 rare **5** above, lofty, major, prime, proud, upper **6** better, choice, higher, lordly, select, sniffy, snippy, snooty **7** capital, greater, haughty, premium, stuck-up **8** arrogant, brass hat, cavalier, dominant, higher-up, insolent **9** excellent, first-rate, marvelous **10** disdainful, first-class, preeminent, preferable, remarkable **11** exceptional, overbearing, patronizing, predominant **13** condescending, high-and-mighty

superiority
9 advantage, dominance, seniority, supremacy, upper hand **10** ascendancy

superjacent
4 over **6** higher **7** greater **9** overlying

superlative
3 ace **4** A-one, best **8** peerless, standout **9** matchless **10** consummate **11** magnificent, outstanding

Superman
9 Clark Kent
actor: 4 Alyn (Kirk), Cain (Dean) 5 Reeve (Christopher), Routh (Brandon) 6 Reeves (George) 7 Collyer (Bud)
bane: 10 kryptonite
birthplace: 7 Krypton
creator: 7 Shuster (Joe)
employer: 11 Daily Planet (The)
father: 5 Jor-El
foe: 3 Zod (General) 6 Luthor (Lex) 7 Bizarro 8 Brainiac, Darkseid, Doomsday, Mxyzptlk (Mr.)
friend: 5 Olsen (Jimmy)
girlfriend: 8 Lois Lane
mother: 4 Lara
original name: 5 Kal-El

supernatural
5 magic 6 divine, mystic 7 magical, psychic, uncanny 8 heavenly 9 celestial, unearthly 10 miraculous, paranormal, phenomenal 12 metaphysical, transcendent 13 extraordinary

supernatural being
3 elf, fay, god, hob, imp, nix 4 jinn, ogre, peri, puck 5 afrit, angel, bogle, deity, demon, fairy, gnome, jinni, lamia, naiad, nixie, nymph, pixie, satyr, sylph, Titan, troll 6 afreet, goblin, kelpie, seraph, spirit, sprite 7 banshee, brownie, bugbear, goddess, incubus, silenus, vampire, wendigo, windigo 8 bogeyman, demiurge, succubus 9 boogeyman, hobgoblin 10 leprechaun

supernumerary
5 extra, spare 6 de trop, excess, walk-on 7 reserve, surplus 8 leftover 9 redundant

supersede
5 usurp 7 replace, succeed 8 displace, supplant

supervene
5 ensue, occur 6 befall, follow, result 7 succeed 9 eventuate, transpire

supervise
3 run 4 boss 5 steer 6 direct, govern, manage 7 conduct, control, monitor, oversee, proctor, referee 8 chaperon, overlook 10 administer

supervision
4 care 6 charge 7 control, running 8 auspices, handling 9 direction, oversight 10 intendance, management 11 stewardship

supervisor
7 foreman, manager 8 director, overseer 13 administrator

supine
5 inert, prone, slack 7 passive 8 inactive, indolent 9 prostrate, recumbent 10 horizontal 12 outstretched

supper club
6 nitery 7 cabaret 9 night spot

supplant
4 oust 5 usurp 6 cut out, unseat 7 replace, succeed 8 crowd out, displace, force out 9 overthrow, supersede

supple
5 agile, lithe, withy 6 limber, nimble, pliant, whippy 7 ductile, elastic, lissome, plastic, pliable, springy, willowy 8 flexible, graceful, moldable 9 adaptable, malleable, resilient

supplement
3 add, pad 4 coda 5 rider 6 append, beef up, enrich, extend, sequel 7 adjunct, augment, codicil, enhance, fill out, fortify 8 addendum, addition, appendix, buttress, increase 9 accessory, reinforce 10 postscript, strengthen

suppliant
5 asker 6 beggar, suitor 9 solicitor 10 petitioner

supplicant
see **suppliant**

supplicate
3 ask, beg, sue 4 pray 5 crave, plead 6 appeal, invoke 7 beseech, entreat, implore, solicit 8 petition 9 importune

supplication
4 plea, suit 6 appeal, orison, prayer 8 entreaty, petition 11 application

supplies
6 stores 8 matériel 9 equipment, materials 10 provisions

supply
3 man 4 feed, fund, hand, help 5 cache, equip, hoard, stock, store 6 afford, outfit, purvey 7 deliver, fulfill, furnish, provide, reserve, satisfy, surplus 8 dispense, hand over, transfer, turn over 9 inventory, provision, reservoir, stockpile 10 contribute 12 accumulation

support
3 aid 4 back, base, bear, hand, help, lift, prop, root, side, stay 5 abide, adopt, boost, brace, bread, brook, carry, favor, shore, strut, truss 6 anchor, assist, bear up, buoy up, column, crutch, defend, endure, girder, pillar, prop up, second, suffer, uphold, verify 7 alimony, applaud, approve, backing, bolster, comfort, confirm, embrace, endorse, espouse, fortify, fulcrum, nourish, nurture, pull for, shore up, stiffen, sustain, trestle 8 abutment, advocate, backstop, buttress, champion, mainstay, maintain, sanction, side with, tide over, underpin 9 encourage, reinforce, underprop 10 assistance, foundation, livelihood, provide for, strengthen, sustenance 11 corroborate, handholding, maintenance, subsistence 12 underpinning

supporter
3 fan 4 ally 6 patron 7 booster, sectary

8 adherent, advocate, champion, disciple, exponent, follower, henchman, partisan **9** proponent

suppose
4 deem **5** allow, guess, infer, opine, posit, think **6** assume, expect, gather, reckon **7** believe, imagine, presume, pretend, surmise, suspect **8** consider **9** postulate, speculate **10** conjecture **11** hypothesize

supposed
7 alleged, seeming **8** apparent, putative **10** ostensible

supposition
2 if **5** guess, hunch, posit **6** notion, theory, thesis **7** premise, surmise **9** postulate **10** assumption, conjecture, hypothesis **11** postulation, presumption, speculation

supposititious
6 unreal **7** dubious, fictive, reputed **8** doubtful, fanciful, illusory, putative, spurious **9** fantastic, fictional, imaginary, pretended, simulated **10** chimerical, fictitious, fraudulent **11** conjectural **12** hypothetical, illegitimate, questionable

suppress
4 curb, stop **5** burke, check, choke, crush, drown, quash, quell, shush, spike, stunt **6** arrest, censor, cut off, hush up, muffle, muzzle, quench, retard, squash, stifle, subdue **7** abolish, collect, conceal, control, prevent, put down, silence, smother, squelch, swallow **8** prohibit, restrain, snuff out, withhold **9** overthrow **10** extinguish

suppurate
6 fester

supra
5 above

supremacy
7 control, mastery **8** dominion **9** authority, dominance **10** ascendancy, domination, mastership, prepotency **11** preeminence, sovereignty **12** predominance **13** preponderance

supreme
4 best **5** chief, final, prime **6** superb, utmost **7** highest, leading, maximum, perfect **8** absolute, cardinal, crowning, foremost, greatest, peerless, towering, ultimate **9** matchless, paramount, principal, sovereign, unequaled, unmatched, unrivaled **10** preeminent, surpassing **11** culminating, predominant, superlative, unmatchable, unsurpassed **12** incomparable, transcendent, unparalleled **13** unsurpassable

Supreme Being
3 God **5** Allah **7** creator, Jehovah **8** Almighty
belief in: 5 deism

Supreme Court justice
3 Jay (John) **4** Taft (William Howard) **5** Alito (Samuel), Black (Hugo), Chase (Salmon P.), Stone (Harlan Fiske), Story (Joseph), Taney (Roger B.) **6** Breyer (Stephen G.), Burger (Warren), Holmes (Oliver Wendell), Hughes (Charles Evans), Scalia (Antonin), Souter (David), Thomas (Clarence), Vinson (Fred), Warren (Earl) **7** Brennan (William), Cardozo (Benjamin), Douglas (William O.), O'Connor (Sandra Day), Roberts (John G.), Stevens (John Paul), Kennedy (Anthony M.) **8** Blackmun (Harry), Brandeis (Louis), Ginsburg (Ruth Bader), Marshall (John, Thurgood) **9** Rehnquist (William) **11** Frankfurter (Felix)

surcease
3 end **4** halt, quit, rest, stay, stop **6** desist **7** refrain, respite, suspend **8** knock off, leave off, postpone, stoppage **9** cessation, remission **10** suspension **11** discontinue **12** postponement

sure
3 set **4** fast, firm, safe **5** fixed **6** indeed, secure, stable, steady, strong **7** certain, staunch **8** absolute, definite, enduring, positive, reliable, unerring **9** confident, convinced, steadfast **10** convincing, dependable, inevitable, infallible, undeniable, unshakable, unwavering **11** indubitable, trustworthy, unequivocal, unfaltering **12** indisputable **13** incontestable, unquestioning

surefire
7 assured, certain **8** reliable **10** dependable, guaranteed

sure thing
6 shoo-in, winner **9** certainty

surety
4 bail, bond **5** angel **6** backer, patron, pledge **7** sponsor **8** guaranty, security, warranty **9** certainty, certitude, guarantee, guarantor **10** confidence, conviction

surf
4 scan, skim **6** browse **9** bodyboard, kneeboard

surfing term
4 deck, tube **5** leash **6** A-frame, barrel, drop in, hollow, turtle **7** bail out, carving, cutback, grommet, hang ten, snaking, wipeout **8** backdoor, blown out **9** goofy foot **10** impact zone **12** kneeboarding

surface
3 top **4** face, pave, rise, skin **5** cover **6** appear, come up, emerge, facade, facing, finish, patina, show up, veneer **7** outside **8** covering, exterior **11** superficial

surfeit
4 cloy, fill, glut, jade, pall, sate **5** gorge, stuff **6** excess **7** replete, satiate, surplus **8** overfill, overflow, overkill, overmuch, overplus, plethora **10** surplusage **11** overindulge, superfluity **13** overabundance

surge
4 flow, gush, pour, rise, roll, rush, soar, tide, wave **5** flood, swell **6** billow, deluge, sluice, stream **7** torrent

surgeon
8 sawbones
American: **4** Mayo (Charles, William), Reed (Walter) **6** Thorek (Max) **7** Cushing (Harvey), DeBakey (Michael) **8** McDowell (Ephraim)
English: **5** Paget (James) **6** Lister (Joseph)
French: **4** Paré (Ambroise) **5** Broca (Paul)
South African: **7** Barnard (Christiaan)

surgery
9 operation
instrument: **5** clamp, curet, laser **6** gorget, lancet, splint, stylet, trocar **7** forceps, scalpel

surgical removal
8 ablation
combining form: **6** ectomy

Suriname
capital: **10** Paramaribo
former name: **11** Dutch Guiana
monetary unit: **7** guilder
mountain range: **10** Tumac-Humac
neighbor: **6** Brazil, Guyana **12** French Guiana
river: **6** Maroni **8** Suriname **10** Courantyne

surly
4 dour, glum **5** cross, gruff, sulky **6** crusty, grumpy, morose, sullen **7** bearish, crabbed, grouchy **8** churlish, menacing, snappish **9** irritable, saturnine **10** ungracious **11** ill-mannered, threatening **12** discourteous

surmise
see **suppose**

surmount
3 cap, top **4** best, down, leap, lick **5** clear, climb, crest, crown, excel, outdo, vault **6** better, hurdle, master **7** conquer, surpass **8** outstrip, overcome, vanquish **9** negotiate, transcend

surpass
3 cap, top **4** beat, best **5** excel, outdo, trump **6** better, exceed, outrun **7** eclipse, outpace **8** go beyond, outclass, outshine, outstrip, outweigh, overstep **9** transcend **10** overshadow

surplice
5 cotta, ephod **8** vestment

surplus
5 extra, spare **6** excess **7** overage, overrun, reserve, surfeit **8** leftover, overflow, overkill, overmuch, plethora **9** overstock, remainder **10** oversupply **11** superfluity, superfluous

surprise
4 faze, stun **5** amaze, floor **6** ambush, dismay, rattle, waylay, wonder **7** astound, capture, nonplus, stagger, startle, stupefy **8** astonish, bewilder, bowl over **9** amazement, dumbfound, overpower, take aback **11** flabbergast **12** astonishment, stupefaction

surreal
5 weird **7** bizarre **9** dreamlike, fantastic **10** outlandish **12** unbelievable

surrealist
3 Arp (Jean), Ray (Man) **4** Dalí (Salvador), Népo **5** Ernst (Max) **6** Breton (André), Tanguy (Yves) **8** Magritte (René) **9** de Chirico (Giorgio)

surrender
4 cave, cede, fold **5** waive, yield **6** cave in, give in, give up, resign, submit **7** abandon, concede, succumb **8** cry uncle, hand over **10** abdication, capitulate, relinquish, submission **12** capitulation
sign: **7** hands up **9** white flag

surreptitious
see **stealthy**

surrogate
3 sub **5** proxy **6** acting, deputy, fill-in **7** stand-in, stopgap **9** makeshift **10** substitute **11** locum tenens, pinch hitter, replacement

surround
3 hem, rim **4** edge, gird, loop, ring **5** beset, bound, hem in, limit, round, skirt, verge **6** border, circle, fringe, girdle, margin **7** besiege, compass, confine, enclose, envelop, outline **8** encircle **9** encompass **12** circumscribe

surrounding
5 about **7** ambient **12** circumjacent
prefix: **4** peri **6** circum

surroundings
6 milieu **7** ambient **8** ambience **11** environment

surveillance
3 eye, tab **4** tail **5** vigil, watch **7** lookout **8** scrutiny, stakeout **9** vigilance **11** supervision

survey
3 con, vet **4** case, poll, scan, view **5** assay, audit **6** assess, précis, review, size up **7** canvass, examine, inspect, pandect, perusal, preview **8** analysis, appraise, estimate, evaluate, look over, overlook, overview, scrutiny, syllabus **9** check over **10** scrutinize **11** reconnoiter

survive
4 keep, last **6** endure **7** carry on, hold out, outlast, outlive, outwear, persist, recover, ride out, weather **8** continue, live down **9** withstand **11** come through, live through, pull through

Surya
6 sun-god
son: **4** Manu, Yama **5** Karna **6** Asvins
temple site: **7** Konarak

susceptible
4 open **5** naive, prone **6** liable **7** exposed, pliable, subject **8** disposed, inclined, sensible **9** malleable, receptive, sensitive **10** responsive, vulnerable **11** impressible, persuadable

suspect
5 doubt, fishy, guess 6 assume, unsure 7 believe, dubious, imagine, suppose, surmise 8 distrust, doubtful, mistrust 9 doubtable, uncertain 10 disbelieve 11 problematic

suspend
3 bar 4 bate, halt, hang, stay, stop 5 debar, defer, delay, hover, sling 6 dangle, depend, hold up, put off, shelve 7 adjourn, hold off 8 intermit, postpone, prorogue 9 eliminate 11 discontinue

suspended
6 frozen 7 hanging, pendant, pendent, stopped 8 dangling, swinging 9 pendulous

suspenders
6 braces 8 galluses

suspense
7 anxiety, mystery, tension 10 expectancy 11 expectation, uncertainty 12 apprehension

suspension
4 halt, stay, stop 5 delay, letup, pause 6 cutoff, freeze 7 latency, respite, time-out 8 abeyance, dormancy, stoppage 9 remission 10 moratorium, quiescence 11 cold storage, withholding 12 intermission, interruption, postponement

suspicion
4 hint 5 doubt, dread, guess, hunch, qualm, shade, smell, tinge, touch, trace, whiff 7 concern, dubiety, surmise 8 distrust, mistrust, wariness 9 chariness, misgiving 10 foreboding, intimation, skepticism, suggestion 11 incertitude, premonition, supposition, uncertainty

suspicious
4 wary 5 chary, fishy, leery 7 dubious, jealous, suspect 8 doubtful, watchful 9 doubtable, skeptical 11 distrustful, mistrustful, problematic 12 apprehensive, questionable

suspire
4 sigh 5 sough

sustain
4 bear, feed, prop, save 5 brace, carry, stand 6 bear up, buoy up, endure, foster, hold up, keep up, succor, suffer, uphold 7 bolster, confirm, nourish, nurture, prolong, relieve, shore up, support, undergo 8 buttress, preserve

sustenance
3 pap 4 food, keep, meat 5 bread, means 6 living, viands 7 aliment, alimony, pabulum, support 8 victuals 9 nutriment, provender 10 livelihood, provisions 11 maintenance, nourishment, subsistence, wherewithal

susurration
4 purr 6 mumble, murmur, mutter, rustle 7 whisper 9 undertone

suture
3 sew 4 seam 6 stitch

suzerain
5 ruler 8 overlord 9 sovereign

svelte
4 slim 5 lithe, sleek, suave 6 smooth, urbane 7 elegant, slender 8 graceful

swab
3 mop 4 Q-Tip 5 clean 6 sponge

swaddle
4 roll, wrap 5 drape 6 enfold, swathe, wrap up 7 blanket 8 enshroud, enswathe

swag
3 sag, yaw 4 loot, sway, tilt 5 booty, droop, lurch, money, prize 6 boodle, spoils 7 festoon, garland, pillage, plunder 10 contraband

swagger
4 brag 5 boast, bully, strut, swank, swash, swell 6 sashay 7 bluster, bravado, peacock, saunter 9 arrogance, cockiness, gasconade 11 braggadocio, swashbuckle

swagman
4 hobo 5 rover, tramp 7 drifter, vagrant 8 vagabond, wanderer

swain
4 beau 5 lover, spark, wooer 6 rustic, suitor 7 admirer 8 shepherd 9 boyfriend

swallow
3 buy, sip 4 bear, belt, bolt, down, gulp, swig, take, toss, wolf 5 abide, brook, drink, quaff, slurp, stand, swill 6 absorb, accept, digest, endure, guzzle, imbibe, ingest, inhale 7 believe, consume, fall for, repress, retract, stomach 8 chugalug, take back, tolerate 11 ingurgitate

swamp
3 bog, fen 4 holm, mire, moss, muck, quag 5 drown, flood, glade, marsh, whelm 6 deluge, engulf, morass, muskeg, slough 7 bottoms 8 inundate, overcome, overflow, quagmire, submerge 9 everglade, marshland, overwhelm
Everglades: 10 Big Cypress
Georgia: 10 Okefenokee
North Carolina-Virginia: 6 Dismal

swamped
5 awash 7 brimful, flooded, overrun 8 engulfed 9 inundated, submerged 11 overflowing, overwhelmed

Swamp Fox
6 Marion (Francis)

swan
female: 3 pen
genus: 4 Olor 6 Cygnus
male: 3 cob 4 cobb
young: 6 cygnet

swank
4 posh, tony, trig 5 boast, fancy, ritzy, sharp, showy, smart, swell, swish 6 chichi, classy, dapper, deluxe, lavish, plushy, snappy, trendy

7 elegant, peacock, show off, splashy, stylish, swagger 8 peacocky 9 glamorous, luxurious 10 flamboyant, peacockish

Swan Lake
character: 5 Odile 6 Odette 9 Siegfried (Prince) 11 Von Rothbart
composer: 11 Tchaikovsky (Pyotr Ilyich)

swap
5 trade, truck 6 barter, change, switch 7 bargain, traffic 8 exchange 10 substitute

swarm
3 jam, mob 4 army, bevy, herd, host, mass, pack, push, shin, teem 5 crawl, crowd, crush, drove, flock, group, horde, mount, press 6 abound, gather, myriad, throng 7 climb up, cluster, overrun 9 multitude, pullulate 10 congregate

swarthy
4 dark 5 dusky, sooty 6 brunet 8 bistered

swash
3 lap 4 brag, dash, gush, rush, slop 5 boast, churn, douse, froth, plash, slosh 6 bubble, burble, gurgle, seethe, splash 7 bluster, channel, saunter, spatter, splurge, swagger

swat
3 bat, box, hit, rap 4 bash, belt, blow, cuff, lick, slap, slog, slug, sock 5 blast, clout, homer, knock, smack, smash, smite, swipe, whack 6 buffet, larrup, strike, wallop 7 clobber

swath
4 belt, path 5 strip, sweep 6 stroke

swathe
see **swaddle**

sway
4 bend, bias, rock, rule 5 lurch, range, reach, scope, sweep, swing, waver, weave 6 affect, careen, direct, govern, totter, wobble 7 command, control, dispose, impress, incline, mastery, stagger, win over 8 dominate, dominion, overrule, persuade, undulate 9 authority, dominance, fluctuate, influence, oscillate, vacillate 10 domination, predispose

Swaziland
capital: 7 Lobamba, Mbabane
language: 5 Swazi
monetary unit: 9 lilangeni
neighbor: 10 Mozambique 11 South Africa
river: 5 Usutu 6 Komati 8 Umbeluzi

swear
3 vow 4 avow, bind, cuss, damn, oath, rail, rant 5 abuse, curse, vouch 6 adjure, affirm, assert, attest, depone, depose, pledge, plight 7 declare, promise, testify, warrant 8 covenant, maintain 9 blaspheme, imprecate 10 asseverate

swearword
4 cuss, oath 5 curse 9 expletive, obscenity

sweat
4 emit, glow, moil, ooze, seep, toil, weep 5 exude, grind, labor 6 strain, swivet 7 excrete 8 perspire, transude 12 perspiration

sweater
8 cardigan, pullover, slipover 10 turtleneck

sweaty
6 clammy, sticky 7 glowing 10 perspiring

Sweden
Arctic region: 7 Lapland
capital: 9 Stockholm
city: 5 Malmö 8 Göteborg
gulf: 7 Bothnia 8 Kattegat
island: 5 Öland 7 Gotland
lake: 6 Vänern 7 Mälaren, Vättern 9 Hjälmaren
monetary unit: 5 krona
mountain range: 5 Kölen
neighbor: 6 Norway 7 Finland
part of: 11 Scandinavia
river: 3 Dal
sea: 6 Baltic

Swedish Nightingale
4 Lind (Jenny)

Swedish pop group
4 ABBA

sweep
3 arc, fly, mop, win 4 flit, sail, scud, skim, wing 5 ambit, broom, brush, clean, clear, curve, drive, orbit, range, reach, scope, surge, whisk 6 extent, radius, search 7 compass, purview, victory 9 extension

sweeping
5 broad 6 all-out 7 blanket, general, overall, radical 8 thorough, whole-hog 9 extensive, inclusive, out-and-out, universal, wholesale 11 far-reaching 12 all-embracing

sweepings
4 dust 5 trash, waste 6 debris, litter, refuse 7 garbage, residue, rubbish 8 detritus

sweet
5 candy, honey 6 bonbon, dulcet, lovely, sugary, syrupy 7 angelic, cloying, dessert, melodic, scented, sugared, winning, winsome 8 aromatic, fragrant, heavenly, luscious, perfumed 9 ambrosial, delicious 10 delectable, saccharine
combining form: 4 glyc 5 glyco

Sweet ___
7 Adeline, Charity 8 Caroline 12 Georgia Brown

sweeten
5 candy, honey, sugar 6 soften 7 appease, assuage, enhance, mollify, placate 9 sugarcoat, sugar over 10 conciliate, propitiate

sweetheart
3 gra 4 dear, love 5 flame, honey 7 beloved, darling, tootsie 10 heartthrob, honeybunch

sweetmeat
5 candy **6** comfit **8** delicacy, preserve **10** confection

sweet potato
3 yam **7** boniato

sweet-talk
4 coax **5** charm **6** banter, cajole, wangle **7** blarney, flatter, wheedle **8** blandish, butter up, inveigle, soft-soap

swell
4 fine, grow, keen, neat, pout, puff **5** bloat, bulge, dandy, neato, nifty, pouch, super, surge, swank **6** abound, billow, blow up, dilate, expand, groovy, peachy **7** amplify, augment, balloon, distend, enlarge, inflate, peacock, swagger, upsurge **8** increase, jim-dandy, terrific **9** crescendo, marvelous, wonderful
British: 3 nob **4** toff

swelled head
5 pride **6** egoism, vanity **7** conceit, egotism **8** smugness **9** arrogance, vainglory **10** narcissism **11** amour propre, self-conceit

swelling
3 sty **4** boil, bubo, bump, corn, gall, node **5** bulge, edema, tumid, tumor **6** bunion, growth, nodule **7** gibbous **8** tubercle **9** carbuncle, chilblain, expansion, tumescent **10** tumescence **11** excrescence **12** inflammation, protuberance

sweltering
3 hot **5** fiery **6** baking, sultry, torrid **7** burning **8** broiling, roasting, sizzling **9** scorching

swerve
3 yaw **4** skew, turn, veer **5** sheer, shift, stray, waver **6** depart, wander **7** deflect, deviate

swift
4 fast **5** fleet, hasty, quick, rapid, ready **6** prompt, snappy, speedy, sudden **8** full-tilt, headlong **9** breakneck

____ Swift
3 Tom **8** Jonathan
character: 8 Gulliver

swiftness
4 gait, pace **5** haste, hurry, speed **8** celerity, dispatch, legerity, rapidity, velocity

swig
4 belt, down, drag, gulp, pull, slug **5** booze, draft, drain, drink, quaff, swill **6** guzzle, imbibe, tipple **7** swallow, swizzle

swill
4 bolt, gulp, slop, swig, tope, wolf **5** booze, draft, drink, gorge, scarf, scoff, slops **6** debris, gobble, guzzle, inhale, spilth, tank up, tipple **7** consume, garbage, hogwash, rubbish, swizzle

swim
3 dip **4** reel, spin, turn **5** bathe, crawl, float, swoon, whirl **9** dizziness, dog-paddle

swimmingly
6 easily **8** smoothly **10** splendidly

swimming stroke
5 crawl **7** dolphin, trudgen **9** butterfly, dog paddle

swindle
3 con, gyp **4** bilk, clip, dupe, fake, hoax, rook, scam, sell, sham, skin, soak **5** bunco, bunko, cheat, cozen, fraud, gouge, phony, rogue, shaft, skunk, sting **6** chouse, diddle, fleece, humbug, hustle, take in **7** con game, defraud **8** flimflam, hoodwink **9** bamboozle, imposture, victimize **11** hornswoggle

swindler
5 cheat, crook, ganef, gonif, shark **6** con man, goniff **7** sharper, shyster **8** deceiver **9** charlatan, defrauder **10** mountebank

swine
see **hog**

swing
4 jive, slew, slue, sway, veer **5** flail, lurch, pivot, twirl, waver, weave, whirl, wield **6** dangle, divert, rhythm, rotate, seesaw, stroke, swerve, switch **7** revolve, suspend **8** brandish **9** alternate, fluctuate, oscillate, vacillate

swinish
5 feral **6** coarse **7** beastly, bestial, porcine

swipe
3 cop, hit, nab, rap **4** blow, clip, conk, grab, hook, lick, lift, nick, sock, swat, wipe **5** clout, filch, heist, knock, pinch, smack, steal **6** pilfer, snatch, snitch, strike, wallop

swirl
4 eddy, purl, roil **5** curve, twist, whirl, whorl **6** swoosh, vortex **9** whirlpool **11** convolution

swish
4 buzz, chic, fizz, hiss, posh, tony, whiz **5** ritzy, smart, swank, whisk **6** classy, dressy, sizzle, trendy, whoosh **7** elegant, stylish **8** sibilate

Swiss Family Robinson author
4 Wyss (Johann David)

switch
3 rod, wag **4** beat, flay, flog, lash, swap, veer, wand, whip **5** shift, shunt, trade, whisk **6** change, strike, waggle **7** scourge **8** exchange, flip-flop, reversal **9** about-face, sidetrack **10** substitute **12** substitution

Switzerland
canton: 3 Uri, Zug **4** Jura, Vaud **5** Berne **6** Geneva, Ticino, Valais
capital: 4 Bern **5** Berne
city: 5 Basel **6** Geneva, Zürich **8** Lausanne
lake: 6 Geneva, Wallen **7** Lucerne **9** Constance, Neuchâtel, Thunersee, Zürichsee
language: 6 French, German **7** Italian

monetary unit: **5** franc
mountain, range: **4** Alps, Jura **9** Monte Rosa
neighbor: **5** Italy **6** France **7** Austria, Germany **13** Liechtenstein
resort: **5** Davos, Vevey **7** Zermatt **8** Montreux, St. Moritz **10** Interlaken
river: **3** Aar **4** Aare **5** Rhine, Rhône
state: **6** canton

swivel
4 spin, turn **5** pivot, swing, twirl, whirl **6** rotate **7** revolve **9** pirouette

swivet
see **snit**

swizzle
3 mix **4** stir **5** swill **6** guzzle, tipple

swollen
5 puffy, tumid **6** turgid **7** bloated, bulbous, bulging, pompous **8** enlarged, inflated, varicose **9** bombastic, distended, tumescent **10** rhetorical

swoon
4 coma, daze, fade **5** droop, faint **6** torpor **7** pass out, rapture, syncope **8** black out

swoosh
4 eddy, gush, purl, rush **5** swirl, whirl, whorl

sword
4 épée, foil **5** saber, sabre **6** barong, bilboa, rapier, Toledo **7** cutlass **8** claymore, falchion, scimitar, yataghan

sword-shaped
6 ensate **8** ensiform

sworn
6 avowed **7** devoted **8** affirmed **9** committed, confirmed **10** deep-rooted, deep-seated, entrenched, inveterate

sybarite
7 epicure **8** hedonist **9** libertine **10** sensualist, voluptuary

sybaritic
6 carnal **7** sensual **8** sensuous **9** epicurean, libertine, luxurious **10** hedonistic, voluptuous

sycophancy
7 fawning **8** flattery, toadying **9** truckling **11** bootlicking

sycophant
5 leech, toady **6** flunky, lackey, minion, yes-man **8** groveler, hanger-on, parasite, truckler **9** easy rider, flatterer, toadeater **10** bootlicker, self-seeker **11** lickspittle **13** apple-polisher

sycophantic
7 fawning, servile, slavish **8** toadying, unctuous **9** groveling, kowtowing, parasitic, truckling **10** obsequious **11** bootlicking

Sycorax's son
7 Caliban

syllable
deletion: **7** apocope
last: **6** ultima
lengthening of: **7** ectasis
musical: **2** do, fa, la, mi, re, si, ti, ut **3** sol
next to last: **6** penult
shortening: **7** elision, systole
stressed: **5** arsis

syllabus
6 aperçu, digest, précis, sketch, survey **7** epitome, outline, pandect, summary **8** abstract, headnote, synopsis **10** compendium

sylph
5 fairy, nymph **6** sprite

sylvan
5 bosky, woody **6** rustic, wooded
deity: **3** Pan **4** Faun **5** dryad, satyr **6** Faunus **7** Silenus **8** Arethusa, Silvanus, Sylvanus

symbol
4 icon, logo, mark, sign **5** badge, glyph, motif, stamp, token **6** design, device, emblem, mascot
chemical:
see individual element
musical: **4** clef, flat, hold, note, rest, turn **5** shake, sharp **7** fermata, mordent, natural

symbolic
5 token **10** emblematic **11** allegorical

symbolist poet
7 Rimbaud (Arthur) **8** Mallarmé (Stéphane), Verlaine (Paul)

symbolize
4 mean **6** embody, mirror, typify **7** signify **8** stand for **9** epitomize, exemplify, personify, represent **10** illustrate **11** emblematize

symmetrical
5 equal **7** regular **8** balanced

symmetry
5 order **6** parity **7** balance, harmony **8** equality, evenness **9** agreement, congruity **10** conformity, proportion, regularity **11** arrangement

sympathetic
4 kind, warm **6** benign, caring, humane, kindly, tender **8** amenable, friendly **9** agreeable, approving, benignant, congenial, congruous, consonant, favorable, receptive **10** compatible, consistent, responsive **11** considerate, kind-hearted, softhearted, warmhearted

sympathize
4 pity **7** condole **11** commiserate

sympathy
4 pity, ruth **5** heart **6** accord, solace, warmth **7** comfort, harmony, rapport **8** affinity, kindness **9** agreement **10** benignancy, compassion, condolence, kindliness, tenderness **11** consolation, sensitivity **13** commiseration

symphonic
10 orchestral

symphony
9 orchestra **12** philharmonic
movement: 5 rondo **6** minuet

symposium
5 forum **7** meeting, seminar **9** gathering **10** conference, discussion

symptom
4 mark, sign **5** index, token **8** evidence **10** indication

symptoms
7 indicia **8** syndrome

synagogue
4 shul **6** temple
platform: 5 bimah

sync
4 jibe **5** agree, match **7** harmony **8** coincide **9** harmonize **10** concurrent **12** simultaneous

synchronize
5 agree **6** concur **8** coincide

synchronous
6 coeval **10** coetaneous, coexistent, coexisting, coincident, concurrent **11** concomitant **12** contemporary, simultaneous **13** geostationary

syncope
4 coma **5** faint, swoon **8** blackout

syndicate
3 mob **4** pool **5** chain, group, mafia, trust, union **6** cartel, league **7** combine **11** association, partnership **12** conglomerate, organization

syndrome
3 ill **6** malady **7** ailment, disease **8** disorder, sickness **9** complaint, condition, infirmity

synergic
5 joint **6** shared **8** coacting, coactive, conjoint **9** collusive, concerted **11** cooperating, cooperative, coordinated

synod
4 body, diet **7** council, meeting **8** assembly, conclave, congress **10** conference, convention **11** convocation

synopsis
5 brief, recap **6** aperçu, digest, précis, review **7** capsule, epitome, outline, rundown, summary **8** abstract, breviary, syllabus **10** abridgment, compendium, conspectus **12** condensation

synopsize
5 recap, sum up **6** digest **7** outline, summate **8** abstract, boil down, compress, condense **9** epitomize, inventory, summarize

synthesis
5 blend, union **6** fusion, merger **7** amalgam **8** blending, compound **9** composite **11** combination **12** amalgamation **13** incorporation

synthesize
4 fuse, meld **5** blend, merge, unify **7** combine **8** compound **9** harmonize, integrate **10** amalgamate **11** incorporate

synthetic
6 ersatz **7** man-made, plastic **9** imitation, unnatural **10** artificial, fabricated **11** counterfeit
fiber: 3 PBI, PLA **5** Modal, Mylar, Nomex, nylon, Orlon, saran, Zylon **6** Kevlar, olefin, sulfar, Twaron, vinyon **7** acetate, acrylic, lyocell, spandex, vectran, vinalon **9** polyester **10** modacrylic

Syria
capital: 8 Damascus
city: 4 Homs **6** Aleppo
language: 6 Arabic, French
monetary unit: 5 pound
neighbor: 4 Iraq **6** Israel, Jordan, Turkey **7** Lebanon

syringe
4 hypo **6** needle **10** hypodermic

Syrinx
5 nymph
pursuer: 3 Pan

syrinx
7 panpipe **8** panpipes

syrup
6 orgeat **9** grenadine

syrupy
5 gooey, mushy, sappy, sweet **6** drippy, dulcet, slushy, sticky, sugary **7** cloying, maudlin, mawkish **9** schmaltzy **10** saccharine **11** sentimental

system
3 way **4** mode, plan **5** modus, order, setup **6** entity, manner, method, scheme **7** complex, network, pattern, process, regimen, routine **8** strategy **9** procedure, structure, technique

systematic
7 logical, ordered, orderly, regular **8** arranged **9** organized **10** analytical, methodical

systematize
5 array, order **6** codify **7** arrange, catalog, dispose, marshal **8** classify, organize, regiment **9** catalogue, methodize

system of weights
4 troy **11** avoirdupois **12** apothecaries

T

tab
4 bill, cost, flap, list, loop, rate **5** check, count, price, score **6** charge, record **7** account, invoice **8** eagle eye, price tag, scrutiny **9** appendage, designate, extension, reckoning, statement **12** surveillance

tabard
4 cape, coat **5** tunic **10** coat of arms

tabby
3 cat **6** feline, cement **8** brindled

tabernacle
4 tent **5** hovel **6** church, temple

tabes
7 atrophy, wasting **12** degeneration

Tabitha's Greek name
6 Dorcas

table
4 fare, list **5** bench, board, chart, defer, stand **6** buffet, put off, record, shelve, teapoy **7** counter **8** mahogany, postpone **9** sideboard
ornament: 7 epergne **11** centerpiece
writing: 4 desk **9** secretary **10** escritoire

table d' ___
4 hôte

tableland
4 mesa **5** butte **6** upland **7** plateau
Alabama-West Virginia: 10 Cumberland
Arizona: 5 Kanab **6** Kaibob
England: 8 Dartmoor
India: 5 Malwa
(see also **plateau**)

tablet
3 bar, pad **4** cake, disk, pill, slab **5** panel, slate **6** pellet, plaque, troche **7** lozenge, notepad **8** steno pad

tableware
4 cups **5** bowls, china, forks **6** dishes, knives, plates, silver, spoons **7** glasses, saucers **8** settings, utensils **9** stainless

tabloid
3 rag **5** lurid, pulpy **6** digest **7** summary **9** condensed, newspaper **11** sensational **12** scandal sheet

taboo
3 ban **4** no-no **6** banned, enjoin, forbid, outlaw **7** inhibit, obscene **9** forbidden, ineffable, interdict, off-limits, restraint **10** inhibition **11** restriction, unspeakable **12** interdiction

tabor
4 drum

tabulate
4 list **5** count, order **6** codify, figure, record **7** arrange **9** enumerate **11** systematize

tabulation
4 list **5** chart, tally **6** record **7** account

tabula ___
4 rasa

tacit
6 silent, unsaid **7** assumed, implied **8** implicit, inferred, unspoken **9** intimated, suggested **10** subtextual, undeclared, underlying, understood **11** acquiescent, unexpressed **12** inarticulate

taciturn
4 dumb **6** silent **7** laconic **8** reserved, reticent, wordless **9** secretive **11** tight-lipped **12** close-mouthed

Tacitus work
7 Annales **8** Dialogus, Germania **9** Historiae

tack
3 pin, yaw **4** beat, brad, gear, join, nail, stay, turn **5** baste, reach, shift **6** attach, course, double, stitch, swerve, turn up, zigzag **7** tangent **8** put about **9** come about, deviation **10** alteration, deflection, digression, sea biscuit **11** ship biscuit **12** pilot biscuit

tackle
3 cat, rig **4** gear, sack **6** outfit, take on, take up **7** halyard, lineman, rigging **8** set about **9** apparatus, equipment, machinery, undertake **10** footballer, linebacker, plunge into **13** paraphernalia

tacky
5 cheap, crude, dingy, dowdy, gaudy, messy, seedy, ratty, tatty **6** blowsy, frowsy, frumpy, kitsch, shabby, sleazy, sloppy, sticky, frumpy, tawdry, untidy, vulgar **7** run-down, unkempt **8** adhesive, frumpish, slovenly **9** inelegant, tasteless, unstylish **10** down-at-heel, threadbare

tact
5 poise, touch **6** acumen **7** address, finesse, suavity **8** civility, courtesy, delicacy, urbanity **9** diplomacy, politesse **10** adroitness, politeness, smoothness **11** savoir faire, sensitivity

tactful
5 civil, suave **6** adroit, urbane **7** politic **8** delicate, discreet, polished **9** courteous, sensitive **10** diplomatic, perceptive, thoughtful **11** considerate

tactic
4 hoax, plan, play, ploy, ruse, scam **5** dodge, feint, means, stunt, trick **6** device, gambit, method **7** sleight **8** approach, artifice, maneuver, strategy **9** procedure, stratagem

tactical
7 politic, prudent **9** advisable, expedient, strategic

tactics
4 plan **6** method, scheme **8** maneuver, playbook, strategy **9** stratagem

tactile
8 palpable, tangible **9** touchable

taction
4 feel **5** touch **7** contact **9** palpation

tactless
4 rude **5** blunt, crude, inept **6** candid, clumsy, gauche **7** awkward **8** impolite **9** impolitic, maladroit **10** indiscreet **11** insensitive

tad
3 bit, boy, lad, son **4** lick, mite, snap, spot, whit **5** child, crumb, shade, sonny, speck **6** laddie, nipper, shaver **7** smidgen **8** fraction

tadpole
8 polliwog, pollywog

taffy
5 candy **8** flattery

tag
3 bit, dog, end **4** cost, flag, game, logo, mark, name, tail **5** aglet, brand, label, price, trail **6** append, charge, follow, select, shadow, slogan, tassel, tatter, ticket **7** license, run down **8** graffito, identify, insignia

tagline
5 motto **6** byword, slogan

Tahiti
city: **7** Papeete
painter: **7** Gauguin (Paul)
war god: **3** Oro

tail
3 dog, end, tag **4** butt, rear **5** hound, stalk **6** follow, pursue, shadow **7** hind end, rear end **8** backside, buttocks **9** posterior
bone: **6** coccyx
relating to: **6** caudal
short: **4** scut

tailed
7 caudate

tailor
3 fit, hem, sew **4** suit **5** adapt, alter, style **7** fashion **8** clothier, seamster **11** haberdasher

tailor-made
6 fitted, suited **7** bespoke, fitting **8** suitable **10** well-suited **11** appropriate

taint
3 rot **4** blot, blur, foul, harm, hurt, smut, soil, spot, turn, vice **5** brand, cloud, color, decay, dirty, fault, smear, spoil, stain, sully, touch **6** befoul, darken, defile, poison, smudge, smutch **7** blacken, blemish, corrupt, pollute, putrefy, tarnish **8** besmirch, discolor **9** discredit **10** adulterate, stigmatize **11** contaminate

taipan
5 snake **8** merchant **11** businessman

Taiwan
7 Formosa
capital: **6** Taipei
channel: **5** Bashi
city: **6** T'ai-nan **8** Pan-ch'iao, T'ai-chung **9** Kao-hsiung
language: **8** Mandarin
leader: **13** Chiang Kai-shek
mountain: **6** Yü Shan

Tajikistan
capital: **8** Dushanbe
monetary unit: **5** diram **6** somoni
monetary unit, former: **5** ruble, tanga
mountain, range: **6** Pamirs **9** Communism (Peak), Trans Alai **10** Revolution (Peak)
neighbor: **5** China **10** Kyrgyzstan, Uzbekistan **11** Afghanistan
river: **8** Amu Dar'ya, Syr Dar'ya

Taj Mahal
9 mausoleum
builder: **9** Shah Jahan
site: **4** Agra

take
3 cop, get, nab **4** glom, grab **5** annex, catch, seize, steal, swipe **6** endure, gather, obtain, secure **7** capture, receive **8** proceeds, receipts
account of: **6** notice
advantage of: **5** abuse **7** exploit
after: **6** follow **8** resemble
apart: **7** analyze, dissect **9** dismantle
care: **6** beware
care of: **3** fix **4** tend **5** nurse **6** attend
exception: **6** object
five: **4** rest **5** break, relax
from: **7** deprive, detract **8** subtract
it easy: **5** relax
on the: **7** corrupt, crooked
part: **4** join **5** share **11** participate
place: **5** occur **6** happen

to task: 5 scold 7 reprove
turns: 9 alternate
unawares: 8 surprise

take away
4 grab 5 wrest 6 arrest, commit, deduct, detach, detain, remove, revoke 7 deprive, detract 8 diminish, discount, minimize, subtract, withdraw

take back
5 unsay 6 abjure, recall, recant, return, revoke 7 replace, restore, retract, swallow 8 forswear, withdraw 9 repossess

take down
4 note 5 lower, write 6 humble, record, reduce 7 deflate 8 dismount 9 dismantle 11 disassemble

take in
3 con 4 dupe, fool, furl, jail 5 admit, bluff, board, house, trick 6 absorb, accept, arrest, attend, betray, delude, embody 7 beguile, compass, contain, deceive, embrace, include, involve, mislead, observe, receive, shelter, snooker, subsume 8 flimflam, hoodwink, perceive 9 apprehend, bamboozle, encompass, four-flush 10 assimilate, comprehend, understand 11 double-cross

take off
2 go 4 doff, exit, quit, soar 5 leave, scram 6 begone, deduct, depart, remove, set out 7 pull out, skiddoo, vamoose 8 clear out, discount, hightail, light out, subtract, withdraw 9 skedaddle

takeoff
5 spoof 6 launch, parody, satire, send-up 7 lampoon 8 travesty 9 burlesque 10 caricature
area: 3 pad 6 runway

take on
3 don 4 face, hire, meet 5 adopt, annex, fight 6 accept, append, assume, attack, battle, employ, engage, strike, tackle 7 contest, embrace, espouse, venture 8 endeavor, set about 9 encounter, undertake

take out
4 date, dele, kill, omit 5 loose, whack 6 deduct, excise, remove 7 destroy, release, unleash 8 discount, knock off, separate, subtract, withdraw, withhold 9 eliminate 10 annihilate

take over
5 seize, spell, usurp 6 assume 7 capture, relieve

take up
3 use 4 fill, open 5 adopt, begin, enter, raise, renew, set to, start 6 absorb, accept, assume, gather, occupy, resume, shrink, tackle 7 embrace, espouse, kick off, restart, shorten, tighten 8 commence, continue, initiate 10 recommence

talc
6 powder 8 steatite 9 soapstone

tale
3 fib, lie 4 myth, saga, yarn 5 fable, rumor, story 6 canard, legend 7 fiction 8 anecdote 9 narration, narrative

talebearer
3 rat 4 fink 5 yenta 6 canary, gossip, snitch 7 rat fink, tattler 8 busybody, gossiper, informer, quidnunc, squealer, telltale 9 informant 10 newsmonger, tattletale 11 rumormonger, stool pigeon 12 blabbermouth 13 scandalmonger

talent
4 bent, gift, head, nose 5 craft, dowry, flair, forte, knack, skill 6 genius 7 ability, aptness, faculty 8 aptitude 9 endowment, expertise

talented
4 able 6 clever, expert, gifted 8 skillful

Tale of Two Cities, A
author: 7 Dickens (Charles)
character: 5 Lucie (Manette) 6 Carton (Sidney), Darnay (Charles) 7 Defarge (Madame), Manette (Alexander)

Tales of a Traveller author
6 Irving (Washington)

Tales of a Wayside Inn author
10 Longfellow (Henry Wadsworth)

Tales of Hoffman composer
9 Offenbach (Jacques)

talisman
4 juju, luck 5 charm 6 amulet, fetish, grigri, mascot, scarab 7 periapt 8 gris-gris 10 phylactery

Talisman author
5 Scott (Walter)

talk
3 gab, rap, yak 4 blab, buzz, chat, chin, yarn 5 prate, rumor, run on, speak, utter, voice 6 babble, gabble, gossip, parley, patter, report, speech 7 address, chatter, declaim, hearsay, lecture, prattle 8 colloquy, converse, dialogue, harangue 9 discourse, utterance 10 discussion 12 conversation
about: 7 discuss
back: 4 sass
empty: 3 gas 6 hot air 7 bombast
foolish: 4 bunk 6 babble 7 chatter, palaver
indistinctly: 6 mumble, mutter
over: 7 discuss
shop: 5 argot
slowly: 5 drawl
small: 6 banter 8 chitchat 10 persiflage
wildly: 4 rant, rave

talkative
4 glib **5** gabby, vocal **6** chatty, fluent **7** gossipy, voluble **9** garrulous **10** loquacious **13** communicative

talk over
6 debate **7** discuss, hash out **8** consider **9** thrash out **10** deliberate

talky
5 gabby, windy, wordy **6** chatty, prolix **7** verbose, voluble

tall
4 high, long **5** lanky, large, lofty, rangy **6** absurd **7** pompous **8** towering **9** high-flown **10** far-fetched **11** skyscraping **12** altitudinous

tallow
3 fat **4** lard, suet **6** grease

tally
3 tab **4** jibe, list, tale **5** agree, count, match, score, total **6** accord, census, number, reckon, square **7** account, balance, catalog, compute, conform, itemize **8** check off, register, tabulate **9** agreement, catalogue, enumerate, harmonize, inventory, reckoning **10** complement, correspond

talon
4 claw, hand **5** stock **6** finger

talus
5 ankle, scree, slope **9** anklebone **10** astragalus

tam
3 cap

Tamar
brother: **7** Absalom
father: **5** David **7** Absalom
father-in-law: **5** Judah
half brother: **5** Amnon
seducer: **5** Amnon
son: **5** Perez, Zerah

tamarisk
9 salt cedar

tambour
3 cup **4** drum **9** embroider **10** embroidery

Tamburlaine the Great author
7 Marlowe (Christopher)

tame
4 bust, dull, meek, mild **5** break, train, vapid **6** bridle, docile, gentle, humble, soften, subdue **7** harness, insipid, reclaim, subdued **8** domestic, familiar, obedient **9** tractable **10** housebreak, submissive **11** domesticate, housebroken **12** domesticated

Taming of the Shrew, The
character: **6** Bianca **8** Baptista **9** Katharina, Petruchio
locale: **5** Padua

Tammany boss
5 Tweed (William)

Tammuz's lover
6 Ishtar

tam-o'-shanter
3 cap

tamp
3 ram **4** pack **5** pound, press, stuff

tampion
4 plug **5** cover

tan
3 sun, taw **4** beat, ecru, flog, whip **5** beige, brown, taupe, tawny, toast **6** bronze, darken, thrash **7** biscuit

Tan novel
11 Joy Luck Club (The) **15** Kitchen God's Wife (The) **19** Bonesetter's Daughter (The)

tanager
7 redbird

Tancred, Tancredi
beloved: **8** Clorinda
composer: **7** Rossini (Gioacchino)
father: **3** Odo
mother: **4** Emma
victim: **8** Clorinda

tandem
4 pair **7** bicycle, concert **8** carriage

tang
3 nip **4** bite, fang, odor, ring, zest **5** aroma, clang, prong, sapor, savor, shank, smack, taste, trace **6** flavor, relish **8** piquancy, pungency, sapidity **9** spiciness

tangible
4 real **7** tactile **8** concrete, material, palpable, physical, sensible **9** corporeal, touchable **10** detectable, observable, phenomenal **11** appreciable, discernible, perceptible, substantial

tangle
3 mat, web **4** foul, knot, maze, mesh, shag **5** ravel, skein, snare, snarl **6** entrap, hamper, jumble, jungle, morass, muddle, pileup, raffle **7** dispute, embroil, ensnare, ensnarl, involve, thicket **8** obstruct **9** implicate **10** complicate **11** altercation, predicament **12** complication

Tanglewood Tales author
9 Hawthorne (Nathaniel)

tango
5 dance **8** circuity **11** indirection **13** deceitfulness

tangy
5 sharp **6** lively **7** piquant, pungent, zestful **9** flavorful

tank
3 vat **5** basin **7** cistern **8** aquarium **9** reservoir
American: **6** Abrams **7** Bradley, Sherman
German: **6** panzer
part: **6** turret

tankard
3 mug **5** stein, stoup **6** flagon **9** blackjack

tanked
3 lit **4** high, lost **5** drunk, lit up, oiled **6** bashed, blotto, bombed, failed, gave up, juiced, potted, soaked, soused, stewed, stoned, tanked, wasted, zonked **7** crocked, drunken, pickled, pie-eyed, sloshed, smashed, sottish **9** collapsed, plastered **10** inebriated, liquored up **11** intoxicated

tanker
4 ship **5** oiler

Tannhäuser
character: **5** Venus **9** Elisabeth
composer: **6** Wagner (Richard)
locale: **8** Wartburg **9** Venusberg

tantalize
3 rag **4** bait, lure **5** tease, tempt **6** entice, needle **7** torment **9** frustrate

Tantalus
daughter: **5** Niobe
father: **4** Zeus
son: **6** Pelops

tantamount
4 same **5** alike, equal **8** parallel, selfsame **9** duplicate, identical **10** equivalent **12** commensurate

tantara
5 blare **7** fanfare

tantivy
3 run **6** gallop

tantrum
3 fit **6** blowup **8** outburst, paroxysm **9** hysterics **10** conniption

Tanzania
capital: **6** Dodoma **11** Dar es Salaam
city: **6** Arusha
former name: **10** Tanganyika
island: **5** Mafia, Pemba **8** Zanzibar
lake: **5** Rukwa **6** Malawi **8** Victoria **10** Tanganyika
language: **7** Swahili
monetary unit: **8** shilling
mountain: **11** Kilimanjaro
neighbor: **5** Congo, Kenya **6** Malawi, Rwanda, Uganda, Zambia **7** Burundi **10** Mozambique
plain: **9** Serengeti
river: **6** Kagera, Rufiji, Ruvuma **7** Pangani
volcano: **6** Lengai

Taoism founder
5 Laozi **6** Lao-tzu

tap
3 hit, pat **4** cock, draw, flap, name, plug, tick **5** chuck, draft, drain, nudge, touch, valve **6** faucet, select, siphon, spigot, strike **7** appoint, draw off, hydrant, percuss, petcock **8** drumbeat, half sole, nominate, stopcock **9** designate

tape
4 band, belt, bind **5** strip **6** fillet, ribbon **7** bandage
kind: **5** inkle **6** ferret **7** masking **8** adhesive
machine: **4** deck **8** recorder

taper
4 wane, wick **5** abate, close, draft, pinch, spire **6** candle, lessen, narrow, reduce **7** dwindle, glimmer **8** decrease, diminish

tapering
5 conic, spiry **6** spired, terete **7** conical **8** ensiform, fusiform, napiform, subulate **9** acuminate, attenuate **10** lanceolate

tapestry
5 arras, kilim **6** dossal **7** curtain, Gobelin, hanging
pattern: **7** cartoon
subject: **4** hunt **7** unicorn

Taphath's father
7 Solomon

tapioca
4 yuca **5** yucca **6** manioc **7** cassava, farinha, pudding

tapir
4 anta

taproom
3 bar, pub **4** café **6** bodega, saloon, tavern **7** cantina **8** dramshop **9** roadhouse

tapster
6 barman **7** barkeep, barmaid, skinker **9** barkeeper, bartender **10** mixologist

tar
3 gob **4** jack, salt, soil, swab **5** pitch, smear, stain, sully, taint **6** defile, hearty, sailor, seaman **7** asphalt, besmear, mariner, shipman **8** besmirch, creosote, deckhand, flatfoot **9** shellback

taradiddle
3 fib, lie **5** hooey, story, trash **6** bunkum, canard **7** baloney, falsity **8** claptrap, nonsense **9** falsehood **10** balderdash **13** prevarication

tarantella
5 dance

tarantula
6 spider **10** wolf spider

Taras Bulba author
5 Gogol (Nikolai)

tarboosh
3 fez, hat

tardy
4 dull, late, lazy, slow **7** belated, delayed, laggard, overdue **8** dilatory, sluggish **10** behindhand, delinquent, unpunctual

tare
4 seed, weed **5** vetch, weigh **6** darnel, weight **11** undesirable **13** counterweight

target
3 aim **4** butt, goal, mark, prey **5** aim at **6** object, quarry, victim **9** objective **11** sitting duck
center: **8** bull's-eye
shooter's: **10** clay pigeon

Tar Heel State
13 North Carolina

tariff
3 tax **4** cost, duty, levy, rate **5** price **6** charge, impost **7** tribute **10** assessment

Tarkington character
6 Penrod **10** Alice Adams

tarn
4 lake, pool

tarnish
3 dim, mar **4** dull, foul, harm, hurt, soil **5** dirty, muddy, smear, spoil, stain, sully, taint **6** damage, darken, defile, injure, smirch, smudge, smutch **7** begrime, besmear, blemish, vitiate **8** besmirch, discolor

taro
3 yam **4** eddo **5** aroid **6** yautia **7** dasheen, malanga
product: **3** poi
root: **4** eddo

tarpaulin
3 gob **4** jack, salt, swab **5** cover, sheet **6** hearty, sailor, seaman **7** mariner, shipman **9** shellback

tarpon
8 ladyfish **10** silverfish

tarry
3 lag **4** bide, drag, stay, wait **5** abide, dally, delay, visit **6** dawdle, linger, loiter, pitchy, remain **7** sojourn

tarsus
5 ankle

tart
3 pie **4** acid, bawd, moll, slut, sour **5** acerb, quean, sharp, tramp, trull, whore **6** biting, harlot, pastry **7** acerbic, cutting, piquant, pungent, tootsie **8** chess pie, strumpet **10** prostitute

tartar
5 argol **6** plaque **8** calculus

Tartar
see **Tatar**

Tartuffe author
7 Molière

Tarzan
chimpanzee: **7** Cheetah
creator: **9** Burroughs (Edgar Rice)
mate: **4** Jane
son: **3** Boy **4** Jack **5** Korak

task
3 job **4** duty, lade, load, post, slog, toil, work **5** chare, chore, labor, stint **6** assign, burden, charge, detail, devoir **7** mission, project **8** business, encumber, function **9** challenge, dress down, reprimand **10** assignment, commission **11** undertaking **12** dressing-down

Tasmanian
4 wolf **5** devil
capital: **6** Hobart
pine: **4** Huon

tassel
3 tag **4** tuft **5** adorn **6** fringe **7** pendant, tzitzit **8** ornament **13** inflorescence

Tasso, Torquato
patron: **4** Este (Alfonso II d')
work: **6** Aminta **7** Rinaldo **18** Jerusalem Delivered

taste
3 eat, sip, try **4** tang, zest **5** savor, smack **6** flavor, liking, palate, relish **7** stomach **8** appetite, elegance, fondness, sapidity, soft spot, weakness **10** experience, partiality, preference, refinement **11** inclination
kind: **4** salt, sour **5** sweet **6** bitter
organ: **3** bud

tasteful
4 fine **7** elegant, genteel, refined, stylish **8** artistic, becoming **9** aesthetic

tasteless
4 dull, flat **5** bland, crass, gaudy, showy, stale, tacky, vapid **6** vulgar **7** insipid **8** off-color, unsavory **9** inelegant, savorless, unrefined **10** flavorless

tasty
5 sapid, yummy **6** dainty, delish, savory **8** luscious **9** delicious, flavorful, palatable, succulent, toothsome **10** appetizing, delectable, flavorsome **11** scrumptious

Tatar
6 Mongol, Turkic **7** Turkish **9** Mongolian
leader: **4** Vatu

tattered
4 torn **5** dingy, seedy **6** frayed, ragged, ripped, shabby **7** raggedy, run-down, worn-out **10** bedraggled, threadbare **11** dilapidated

tattle
3 rat, wag, yak **4** blab, buzz, dish, talk, tell **5** clack, prate, rumor **6** gossip, inform, report, snitch, squeal **7** chatter, hearsay, prattle **8** chitchat **9** grapevine **11** scuttlebutt

tattletale
see **talebearer**
tatty
5 cheap, dingy, dowdy, dumpy, seedy, tacky **6** beat-up, cheesy, paltry, scuzzy, shabby, shoddy, sleazy, trashy **7** run-down, scrubby **8** rubbishy **10** threadbare **11** dilapidated
taunt
3 jab **4** gibe, jeer, mock, quip, razz, skit, twit **5** scout, tease **6** deride, insult **7** affront, provoke **8** reproach, ridicule **9** challenge
taurine
6 bovine **8** bull-like
Taurus
4 bull
star: **9** Aldebaran
taut
4 firm, snug, trim **5** rigid, tense, tight **6** corded **10** high-strung
tautology
8 iterance, pleonasm **9** iteration **10** redundancy, repetition
tavern
3 bar, inn, pub **4** café, dive **6** bistro, bodega, saloon **7** barroom, cantina, gin mill, taproom **8** alehouse, pothouse, wineshop **9** roadhouse **11** public house, rathskeller **12** watering hole **13** watering place
taverner
7 barkeep **8** boniface, publican **9** barkeeper, bartender, innkeeper **12** saloonkeeper
taw
3 tan **6** marble **7** partner
tawdry
4 loud **5** cheap, gaudy, tacky **6** brazen, flashy, garish, tinsel **7** chintzy, glaring, ignoble **9** brummagem, dime-store **12** meretricious
tawny
3 tan **4** buff **5** beige, brown, sandy **6** copper, tanned
tax
4 cess, duty, lade, levy, load, onus, scot, toll **5** drain, tithe **6** assess, burden, cumber, impost, saddle, strain, tariff, weight **7** tribute **8** encumber **10** imposition
agency: **3** IRS
feudal: **7** scutage, tallage
kind: **4** geld **5** sales, tithe **6** excise, income **8** property **9** ad valorem, surcharge
on salt: **7** gabelle
rate: **10** assessment
taxi
3 cab, car **4** hack **5** cyclo
taxi driver
5 cabby **6** cabbie, hackie **7** hackman
taxing
5 tough **6** trying **7** exigent, onerous, wearing **8** exacting, grievous, grueling **9** demanding, difficult **10** burdensome, oppressive
Taygeta
father: **5** Atlas
mother: **7** Pleione
sisters: **8** Pleiades
tazza
3 cup **4** vase
Tchaikovsky, Pyotr Ilyich
ballet: **8** Swan Lake **10** Nutcracker (The) **14** Sleeping Beauty
opera: **12** Eugene Onegin **13** Queen of Spades (The)
tea
5 party **6** repast **8** beverage **9** reception
black: **5** bohea, pekoe **8** souchong
box: **5** caddy
cake: **6** cookie
genus: **4** Thea
herbal: **6** ptisan, tisane
kind: **4** herb, Java **5** Assam, black, bohea, green, hyson, pekoe **6** Ceylon, congou, oolong **7** cambric, rooibos **8** Earl Grey, souchong **9** chamomile, sassafras **10** Darjeeling
teach
5 coach, edify, guide, train, tutor **6** impart, school **7** educate, instill, profess **8** instruct **9** enlighten, inculcate **12** indoctrinate
teacher
4 guru, prof **5** coach, guide, tutor **6** docent, master, mentor, pedant **7** maestro, trainer **8** educator **9** pedagogue, preceptor, professor **10** instructor **12** schoolmaster
Hindu: **5** swami
Jewish: **5** rabbi, rebbe
Muslim: **6** mullah
organization: **3** NEA
religious: **9** catechist **10** mystagogue
Tea for Two composer
7 Youmans (Vincent)
team
4 band, club, crew, gang, join, pair, side, yoke **5** group, squad, troop, wagon **6** stable, troupe **8** carriage
baseball: **4** nine
basketball: **4** five **7** quintet
football: **6** eleven
kind: **2** JV **6** jayvee **7** varsity
teamster
6 driver **7** trucker
tear
3 cry, cut, fly, rip, run **4** bolt, claw, dash, drop, flaw, gash, hole, lash, pull, race, rend, rift, rive, rush, slit, snag, weep **5** chase, hurry, shoot,

shred, slash, speed, split, spree **6** career, charge, course, sunder, tatter, wrench **7** droplet, fissure, rupture **8** lacerate **10** laceration

tear down
4 raze, ruin, slur **5** knock, smash, smear, wreck **6** defame, malign, vilify **7** asperse, traduce, destroy, shatter, slander **8** demolish **9** denigrate, disparage, take apart **10** annihilate, calumniate **11** disassemble

tearful
3 sad **5** misty, moist, weepy **6** crying, watery, woeful **7** bawling, sobbing, weeping **8** mournful, pathetic **9** lamenting, sniveling, sorrowful **10** blubbering, lachrymose

tear-jerking
5 mushy **6** drippy, sticky **7** maudlin, mawkish **8** touching **9** schmaltzy **11** sentimental

teary-eyed
5 blear, moist

tease
3 bug, kid, rag, rib, rip **4** bait, coax, comb, gibe, jive, josh, ride, tear, twit **5** annoy, chaff, chivy, harry, shred, taunt, worry **6** cajole, harass, needle, pester, pick on, plague **7** bedevil, torment **8** ridicule **9** tantalize

teaser
4 lure **5** promo **7** preview

teched
3 mad **4** daft **5** batty, crazy **6** insane **7** cracked, lunatic **8** demented

technicality
6 detail **8** loophole

technique
4 mode **5** modus **6** method, system **8** approach **9** procedure **13** modus operandi

ted
5 strew **6** spread **7** scatter

tedious
3 dry **4** dull **5** ho-hum, stale **6** boring, dreary, trying **7** irksome, operose **8** drudging, tiresome **9** dryasdust, wearisome **10** monotonous **11** mind-numbing **13** uninteresting

tedium
4 yawn **5** ennui **7** boredom **8** doldrums, dullness, monotony, sameness

teem
4 flow, pour **5** crawl, empty, swarm **6** abound, bustle **7** produce **9** pullulate

teeming
4 lush, rife **5** alive **6** aswarm **7** replete **8** abundant, swarming, thronged **9** abounding **11** overflowing

teen
5 youth **10** adolescent

tee off
4 open **5** begin, drive, enter, start **8** commence, initiate

teeter
4 rock, sway **5** waver **6** falter, seesaw, wobble **9** vacillate

telamon
5 atlas
counterpart: **8** caryatid

Telamon
brother: **6** Peleus
father: **6** Aeacus
half-brother: **6** Phocus
son: **4** Ajax **6** Teucer

Telegonus
father: **7** Ulysses **8** Odysseus
mother: **5** Circe

telegraph
4 wire **5** cable **6** signal
code: **5** Morse
inventor: **5** Morse (Samuel F. B.)

Telemachus
father: **7** Ulysses **8** Odysseus
mother: **8** Penelope

telephone
4 buzz, call, cell, dial, ring **6** mobile, ring up **8** cordless, landline
inventor: **4** Bell (Alexander Graham)

Telephus
father: **8** Heracles, Hercules
mother: **4** Auge

telescope
5 glass **6** finder **7** compact **8** compress, condense, contract, spyglass **9** reflector, refractor

television
2 TV **4** tube **5** video **8** boob tube, idiot box
antenna: **10** rabbit ears
award: **4** Emmy
British: **5** telly
children's: **6** kidvid
frequency: **3** UHF, VHF
interference: **4** snow
network: **3** ABC, BBC, CBS, Fox, HBO, NBC, NET, PBS, QVC, TNT **4** ESPN, INHD
pioneer: **5** Baird (John Logie) **8** De Forest (Lee), Goldmark (Peter Carl), Zworykin (Vladimir) **10** Farnsworth (Philo T.)
program: **4** news **5** pilot, rerun **6** series, sitcom **7** western **8** game show, talk show **9** broadcast, docudrama, soap opera **11** infomercial
tube: **9** kinescope

tell
3 rat, say **4** blab, clue **5** count, mound, order, spill, state, utter **6** advise, betray, fill in, inform, notify, relate, report, retail, reveal, tattle **7** confess, declare, divulge, narrate, recount **8** disclose, give away **9** come clean

teller
5 clerk **6** banker **7** cashier, counter **8** informer, narrator **12** communicator

telling
5 solid, sound, valid **6** cogent **7** weighty **8** powerful **9** effective **10** convincing, expressive

tell off
4 flay, rate, ream **5** chide, scold **6** berate, rebuke **7** bawl out, chew out, reprove, upbraid **8** admonish, call down **9** dress down, excoriate, reprimand **10** take to task, tongue-lash, vituperate

tell on
6 inform, snitch, tattle

telltale
3 cue **4** clue, fink, lead, sign **5** proof **6** canary, gossip, signal, snitch, tip-off **7** rat fink, tattler **8** evidence, gossiper, informer, quidnunc, signpost, squealer **9** indicator **10** indication, newsmonger **12** blabbermouth, gossipmonger **13** scandalmonger

telluric
6 earthy **7** earthly, mundane, terrene, worldly **9** sublunary **11** terrestrial

tellurium symbol
2 Te

temblor
5 quake, shake, shock **6** tremor **8** upheaval **10** aftershock, earthquake

temerarious
4 rash **6** daring **8** heedless, reckless **9** audacious, daredevil, foolhardy, venturous **11** adventurous, venturesome **13** adventuresome

temerity
4 gall **5** cheek, nerve **6** daring **8** audacity, chutzpah, rashness **9** assurance, brashness, hardihood, hardiness **10** effrontery **12** recklessness **13** foolhardiness

temper
4 heat, mean, mind, mood, tone, vein **5** admix, alloy, anger, blood, grain, humor, trend **6** anneal, attune, dander, dilute, govern, hackle, makeup, medium, season, soften, spirit, strain **7** courage, mollify, passion, quality, toughen **8** hardness, moderate, modulate, restrain **9** character, composure, condition **10** resilience, resiliency **11** disposition, personality

temperament
4 mood **5** humor **6** manner, makeup, mettle, nature **9** character **10** complexion **11** disposition, personality

temperamental
5 moody **6** ornery, touchy **7** erratic **8** contrary, ticklish, unstable, variable, volatile **9** mercurial **10** capricious, changeable, high-strung, inconstant **13** unpredictable

temperance
8 sobriety **9** austerity, restraint **10** abstinence, continence, moderation, self-denial **11** self-control
advocate of: **6** Nation (Carry) **7** Willard (Frances)

temperate
4 calm, even, mild, soft **5** balmy, sober **6** modest, steady **7** clement **8** discreet, moderate **9** abstinent, continent **10** abstemious, controlled, reasonable, restrained **11** abstentious

temperature
4 heat, mood **5** fever **6** degree, warmth **7** hotness **8** coldness **9** intensity

tempered
7 diluted, treated **8** adjusted, hardened, softened **9** mitigated, moderated, qualified **12** strengthened

tempest
3 din **4** blow, gale, rage, wind **5** furor, hurly, storm **6** hubbub, squall, tumult, uproar **8** brouhaha, foofaraw **9** commotion, hurricane **10** hullabaloo, hurly-burly

Tempest character
5 Ariel **6** Alonso **7** Caliban, Miranda **8** Prospero **9** Ferdinand

tempestuous
4 wild **5** roily, rough **6** raging, stormy **7** furious, moiling, violent **8** blustery **9** turbulent **10** tumultuous

temple
4 fane **6** church **9** synagogue **10** tabernacle
ancient: **8** pantheon
Aztec: **8** teocalli
Buddhist: **2** ta **3** wat
Eastern: **6** pagoda
Greek: **9** Parthenon
sanctuary: **4** naos **5** cella, Nemea **6** adytum **10** penetralia

tempo
4 pace, rate, time **5** speed **6** rhythm
fast: **6** presto, vivace **7** allegro
moderate: **7** andante
slow: **5** grave, lento **6** adagio

temporal
3 lay 5 civil 6 carnal 7 earthly, mundane, profane, secular, worldly 13 chronological, synchronistic

temporary
6 acting 7 Band-Aid, interim 8 fleeting 9 ad interim, makeshift, transient 10 short-lived, substitute, transitory 11 provisional

temporize
5 delay, stall, yield 6 palter 7 draw out 8 gain time 10 equivocate 11 prevaricate

tempt
3 woo 4 bait, lure, risk, sway 5 court, decoy 6 allure, entice, entrap, invite, lead on, seduce 7 provoke 8 inveigle 9 tantalize

temptation
4 bait, lure, trap 5 decoy, siren, snare 6 allure, come-on 9 seduction 10 attraction, enticement

tempting
8 alluring 9 appealing, delicious, seductive 10 attractive, come-hither

temptress
4 vamp 5 siren 7 Lorelei 10 seductress 11 femme fatale

ten
cents: 4 dime
combining form: 3 dec, dek 4 deca, deka 5 decem
dollars: 7 sawbuck
mills: 4 cent
thousand: 6 myriad
years: 6 decade

tenable
5 sound 8 rational 10 defendable, defensible, reasonable 12 maintainable

tenacious
3 set 4 fast, firm, true 5 fixed, stout 6 dogged, secure, sturdy 8 adhesive, clinging, resolute, stalwart, stubborn 9 obstinate, steadfast 10 persistent 11 persevering

tenacity
4 grit, guts 5 moxie, pluck, spunk 6 mettle, spirit 7 courage 8 firmness 10 resolution 11 persistence 13 determination

tenant
6 holder, lessee, lodger, renter 7 boarder, dweller 8 occupant
feudal: 6 vassal

tenantable
7 livable 9 habitable 11 inhabitable

Ten Commandments
9 Decalogue
director: 7 DeMille (Cecil B.)

tend
4 lean, mind, till, work 5 guard, labor, nurse, serve, watch 6 foster 7 babysit, care for, conduce, incline, nurture, oversee 8 minister 9 cultivate, look after, watch over

tendency
4 bent, bias 5 drift, tenor, trend 7 current, leaning 8 penchant 10 partiality, proclivity, propensity 11 disposition, inclination 12 predilection

tendentious
6 biased 7 colored, partial 8 one-sided, partisan 10 prejudiced

tender
3 bid 4 fond, mild, soft, sore, warm 5 green, money, mushy, offer 6 extend, gentle, humane, loving, submit, touchy 7 fragile, lenient, painful, present, proffer, propose 8 delicate, proposal 9 sensitive, succulent 11 considerate, warm-hearted 12 affectionate 13 compassionate

tenderfoot
4 colt, punk, tiro, tyro 6 novice, rookie 7 amateur 8 beginner, freshman, neophyte, newcomer 9 cheechako, fledgling, greenhorn, novitiate 10 apprentice

tenderhearted
6 kindly 11 sympathetic 13 compassionate

Tender Is the Night author
10 Fitzgerald (F. Scott)

tendon
4 band, cord 5 nerve, sinew 6 leader 9 hamstring

tendril
4 curl, vine 6 cirrus, spiral 7 ringlet

tenebrific
4 dark, glum, gray, grim 5 black, bleak, sable 6 dismal, dreary, gloomy, somber, sombre 8 desolate, funereal 10 depressing, oppressive 11 dispiriting

tenebrous
3 dim 4 dark, deep, dusk, hazy 5 dusky, foggy, muddy, murky, vague 6 cloudy, gloomy 7 cryptic, obscure, shadowy, unclear 9 ambiguous, lightless 10 caliginous

tenement
4 flat 6 rental, walk-up, warren 7 lodging, rookery 8 building 9 apartment, residence

tenet
3 ism 5 canon, creed, dogma 6 belief 7 paradox 8 doctrine 9 principle 10 empiricism

tenfold
7 decuple

Tennessee
capital: 9 Nashville
city: 7 Memphis 9 Knoxville 11 Chattanooga
college, university: 10 Vanderbilt

mountain, range: **7** Lookout **10** Great Smoky **13** Clingmans Dome
nickname: **9** Volunteer (State)
public works: **3** TVA **9** Norris Dam
river: **9** Tennessee **11** Mississippi
state bird: **11** mockingbird
state flower: **4** iris
state tree: **11** tulip poplar

tennis
award: **8** Davis Cup
item: **3** net **4** ball **6** racket **7** racquet
kind: **5** table **7** doubles, singles **8** platform
score: **4** ad-in, love **5** add-in, ad-out, deuce **6** add-out
serve: **3** ace
shoe: **7** sneaker
stroke: **3** cut, lob **4** chop, drop **5** serve, slice **6** volley **8** backhand, forehand
term: **3** let, set **5** court, fault **7** service **9** advantage, backcourt

tennis champ
4 Ashe (Arthur), Borg (Bjorn), Cash (Pat), Graf (Steffi), King (Billie Jean), Noah (Yannick), Wade (Virginia) **5** Budge (Don), Chang (Michael), Court (Margaret Smith), Evert (Chris), Gómez (Andres), Laver (Rod), Lendl (Ivan), Nadal (Rafael), Perry (Fred), Safin (Marat), Seles (Monica), Stich (Michael), Vilas (Guillermo), Wills (Helen) **6** Agassi (André), Austin (Tracy), Becker (Boris), Casals (Rosie), Edberg (Stefan), Fraser (Neale), Gibson (Althea), Hewitt (Lleyton), Hingis (Martina), Kramer (Jack), Muster (Thomas), Pierce (Mary), Stolle (Fred), Tilden (Bill) **7** Connors (Jimmy), Courier (Jim), Emerson (Roy), Federer (Roger), Lacoste (René), McEnroe (John), Nastase (Ilie), Novótna (Jana), Sampras (Pete) **8** Connolly (Maureen), González (Pancho), Martínez (Conchita), Newcombe (John), Rosewall (Ken), Sabatini (Gabriela), Wilander (Mats), Williams (Serena, Venus) **9** Davenport (Lindsay) **10** Mandlikova (Hana) **11** Navratilova (Martina)

Tennyson poem
4 Maud **7** Ulysses **8** Princess (The), Tiresias **10** Enoch Arden, In Memoriam **12** Locksley Hall **23** Charge of the Light Brigade (The)

tenor
4 mood, tone **5** drift, voice **6** singer **7** meaning, purport **8** tendency **9** substance
American: **5** Lanza (Mario) **6** Hadley (Jerry), Peerce (Jan), Tucker (Richard) **9** McCracken (James)
Belgian: **6** Maison (René)
Canadian: **7** Vickers (Jon)
Czech: **6** Slezak (Leo)
Danish: **8** Melchior (Lauritz)
English: **5** Pears (Peter)
German: **10** Wunderlich (Fritz)
Irish **9** McCormack (John)
Italian: **5** Gigli (Beniamino) **6** Alagna (Roberto), Caruso (Enrico) **7** Bocelli (Andrea), Corelli (Franco) **8** Bergonzi (Carlo) **9** del Monaco (Mario), di Stefano (Giuseppe), Pavarotti (Luciano)
Spanish: **5** Kraus (Alfredo) **7** Domingo (Plácido) **8** Carreras (José)
Swedish: **5** Gedda (Nicolai) **8** Björling (Jussi) **9** Bjoerling (Jussi)

tenpins
7 bowling

tense
4 edgy, taut **5** nervy, rigid, tight, wired **6** uneasy **7** anxious, jittery, nervous, restive, uptight **8** strained, stressed **10** high-strung
grammatical: **4** past **6** future **7** perfect, present **8** preterit **9** preterite **10** pluperfect **11** progressive

tension
5 state, steam **6** nerves, strain, stress, unease **7** anxiety, balance **8** edginess, pressure, tautness **9** agitation, hostility, stiffness **10** discomfort, opposition, uneasiness **11** nervousness, uptightness

tent
4 camp **6** canopy, encamp, laager **7** bivouac, shelter
kind: **3** ger, pup **4** yurt **5** Baker, tepee **6** teepee **7** marquee **8** pavilion, umbrella
maker: **4** Omar
material: **6** canvas
part: **3** fly, guy, peg **4** pole **5** stake

tentacle
3 arm **6** barbel, feeler

tentative
4 test **5** chary, loath, probe, trial **6** averse **7** halting **8** hesitant, insecure **9** diffident, makeshift, reluctant, uncertain, undecided, unsettled **10** irresolute **11** conditional, disinclined, problematic, provisional

tenth
5 tithe
combining form: **4** deci

tenuous
4 slim, thin, weak **5** reedy, shaky **6** feeble, flimsy, slight, stalky **7** fragile, sketchy, slender **8** gossamer **10** precarious **11** implausible **13** insubstantial, unsubstantial

tenure
4 term **6** estate **10** incumbency
feudal: **7** burgage

tepid
4 mild, warm **7** warmish **8** lukewarm **9** apathetic **11** halfhearted, indifferent

tequila source
5 agave

terbium symbol
2 Tb

Terentia's husband
6 Cicero

Tereus
son: **4** Itys
wife: **6** Procne

tergiversate
3 haw, hem, rat **5** dodge, evade, hedge **6** defect, desert, waffle, weasel **7** abandon, shuffle **8** renounce, sidestep **9** pussyfoot, repudiate **10** apostatize, equivocate

term
3 dub, end **4** call, name, span, tour, word **5** label, spell, stint, title **6** detail, period, tenure **7** quarter, session **8** duration, semester **9** designate **10** conclusion, denominate, expression, limitation, particular **11** appellation, designation

termagant
5 harpy, scold, shrew, vixen **6** ogress, virago **8** fishwife, harridan **9** Xanthippe

terminable
6 finite

terminal
3 end, lag **4** last **5** anode, depot, fatal, final **6** finial, latest, latter, lethal **7** cathode, closing, extreme, station **8** eventual, hindmost, junction, ultimate **9** extremity **10** concluding
negative: **7** cathode
positive: **5** anode

terminate
2 ax **3** end **4** boot, drop, fire, halt, kill, quit, sack, stop **5** abort, cease, close, issue, leave **6** cut off, finish, wind up **7** abolish, dead-end, dismiss **8** complete, conclude, dissolve **9** determine, discharge **10** extinguish **11** assassinate, discontinue

terminology
4 cant **5** argot, idiom, lingo **6** jargon, patois **7** lexicon **8** language, shoptalk **10** vernacular, vocabulary **12** nomenclature

termite
5 alate **8** white ant

ternary
5 third **6** triple **9** threefold

Terpsichore
see **Muse**

terrace
4 bank, deck, mesa, park, roof, step **5** bench, porch, shelf **6** street **7** balcony, sundeck **8** platform **9** promenade

terra-cotta
4 clay **7** pottery

terra firma
4 dirt, land, soil **5** earth **6** ground

terrain
4 area, land, turf **5** field **6** domain, ground, milieu, sphere **8** province **9** bailiwick, territory **10** topography **11** environment

terrapin
6 turtle

terrestrial
4 land **6** earthy, ground **7** earthly, mundane, worldly **8** everyday, ordinary, telluric, workaday **9** earthlike, planetary, sublunary **10** earthbound

terrible
4 dire **5** awful, dread **6** grisly, horrid **7** dreaded, fearful, ghastly, heinous, hideous, intense, macabre, vicious, violent **8** dreadful, gruesome, horrible, horrific, shocking, vehement **9** abhorrent, appalling, atrocious, frightful, harrowing, loathsome, monstrous **10** disastrous, formidable, horrendous, horrifying

terrier
3 dog
kind: **3** fox **4** blue, bull, Skye **5** cairn, Irish, Welsh **6** Boston **8** Airedale, Lakeland **9** Yorkshire

terrific
5 boffo, socko, super, swell **6** superb **7** amazing, awesome **8** dreadful, dynamite, glorious **9** appalling, fantastic, frightful, marvelous, upsetting, wonderful **10** formidable, incredible **11** magnificent, sensational **13** extraordinary

terrify
5 alarm, scare **7** scarify, startle **8** affright, frighten **10** intimidate

terrifying
4 grim **5** scary **6** grisly, horrid **7** ghastly, hideous, macabre **8** alarming, dreadful, fearsome, gruesome, horrible, horrific, terrible **9** frightful **10** formidable, horrifying

territory
4 area, belt, land, turf, zone **5** field, route, state, tract **6** domain, region, sphere **7** country, demesne, terrain **8** conquest, district, dominion, province **9** bailiwick **10** borderland **12** jurisdiction

terror
4 fear **5** alarm, dread, panic, worry **6** dismay, fright, horror **7** scourge **9** nightmare **11** fearfulness, trepidation

terrorize
3 cow **5** alarm, bully, scare **6** coerce, fright, menace **7** scarify **8** browbeat, bulldoze, frighten, threaten **9** strong-arm **10** intimidate

terry
4 loop **5** cloth **6** fabric **12** Turkish towel

terse
4 curt **5** brief, crisp, pithy, short **6** abrupt **7** brusque, compact, concise, elegant, laconic, summary **8** polished, succinct **11** compendious, sententious, telegraphic **12** monosyllabic

tertiary
5 third

terza ___
4 rima

tessera
3 die **4** tile **6** tablet, ticket

test
3 try **4** exam, quiz **5** assay, check, essay, final, proof, prove, taste, touch, trial, try on **6** sample, tryout, verify **7** confirm, examine, midterm **8** evaluate, gut check, sounding, trial run **9** benchmark, criterion **10** evaluation, experiment, touchstone **11** examination

testa
6 cupule **7** coating **8** envelope, seed coat, tegument **10** integument

testament
4 will **5** credo, creed, proof **7** tribute, witness **8** evidence **9** scripture **11** attestation **12** confirmation

tester
4 coin **6** canopy, prover **7** analyst, assayer **8** examiner **12** investigator

testifier
7 witness **8** deponent

testify
5 prove, swear **6** affirm, attest, depone, depose, evince **7** certify, witness **11** certificate

testimonial
5 proof **6** salute **7** tribute, witness **8** evidence, memorial, monument **9** affidavit, character, reference **11** attestation **12** appreciation, commendation, confirmation **13** commemoration

testimony
5 proof **6** avowal **7** witness **8** evidence **9** affidavit, authority **10** deposition, profession **11** affirmation, attestation, declaration **12** confirmation **13** corroboration, documentation

testy
4 edgy **5** cross, fussy, hasty **6** cranky, ornery, tetchy, touchy **7** fretful, grouchy, peevish **8** choleric **9** crotchety, irascible, irritable **10** ill-humored, out of sorts **12** cantankerous **13** quick-tempered

tetanus
7 lockjaw, trismus

tetchy
see **testy**

tête-à-tête
4 chat, talk **5** à deux **7** private, vis-à-vis **8** causerie **10** face-to-face **12** conversation

tether
3 tie **4** bind, rope **5** cable, chain, stake **6** fasten, fetter, lariat, picket **8** restrain **9** restraint

Tethys
daughters: **9** Oceanides
father: **6** Uranus
husband: **7** Oceanus
mother: **4** Gaea **5** Terra

tetrad
4 four **7** quartet **8** foursome **10** quaternion

Teutonic
6 German **8** Germanic
language: **5** Dutch **6** Danish, German, Gothic **7** English, Flemish, Frisian, Swedish **9** Afrikaans, Norwegian

Texas
capital: **6** Austin
city: **4** Waco **6** Dallas, El Paso **7** Houston **8** Amarillo **9** Arlington, Fort Worth **10** San Antonio
college, university: **3** SMU **4** Rice **5** Lamar **6** Baylor **9** Texas Tech
island: **5** Padre
mountain: **9** Guadalupe (Peak)
nickname: **8** Lone Star (State)
park: **7** Big Bend
river: **3** Red **5** Pecos **6** Brazos **8** Colorado **9** Rio Grande
state bird: **11** mockingbird
state flower: **10** bluebonnet
state tree: **5** pecan

text
6 script

textbook
6 primer

textile
5 cloth **6** fabric
dealer: **6** mercer
machine: **8** calender
pattern: **7** paisley **11** houndstooth
shop: **7** mercery
starch: **4** sago
treat: **9** mercerize

texture
3 web **4** feel, hand, wale, woof **5** weave **6** fabric

Thackeray novel
9 Pendennis **10** Vanity Fair **11** Barry Lyndon, Henry Esmond

Thailand
capital: **7** Bangkok
city: **9** Chiang Mai

former name: 4 Siam
island: 6 Phuket
monetary unit: 4 baht
neighbor: 4 Laos 5 Burma 7 Myanmar 8 Cambodia, Malaysia
river: 10 Chao Phraya
sea: 7 Andaman

Thaïs
7 hetaera, hetaira 9 courtesan
author: 6 France (Anatole)
composer: 8 Massenet (Jules)
husband: 7 Ptolemy
lover: 9 Alexander (the Great)

thalassic
6 marine 7 oceanic 8 maritime

Thalia
see **Graces; Muse**

thallium symbol
2 Tl

Thanatopsis author
6 Bryant (William Cullen)

Thanatos
5 death
brother: 6 Hypnos
mother: 3 Nyx

thankful
4 glad 8 grateful 12 appreciative

thanks
5 grace 8 blessing 9 gratitude 11 benediction 12 appreciation, gratefulness

Thanksgiving
5 feast 7 holiday
first celebrant: 6 Indian 7 Pilgrim
food: 6 turkey

thatch
3 mop 4 hair, roof 5 cover

that is
Latin: 5 id est

Thaumas
daughter: 4 Iris 5 Aello, Harpy 7 Celaeno, Ocypete
daughters: 7 Harpies
father: 6 Pontus
mother: 4 Gaea
wife: 7 Electra

thaumaturgic
5 magic 6 Magian, mystic, witchy 7 magical 8 wizardly 9 marvelous 10 miraculous 11 necromantic 12 supernatural

thaumaturgy
5 magic 7 sorcery 8 cabbalah, kabbalah, witchery, wizardry 10 necromancy

thaw
4 melt 5 deice, relax 6 unbend 7 defrost, liquefy 8 dissolve, unfreeze 10 condescend, deliquesce

the
7 article
French: 2 la, le, un 3 les, une
German: 3 das, der, die, ein 4 eine
Italian: 2 il, la 3 una, uno
Spanish: 2 el, la, un 3 las, los, una, uno

Thea
daughter: 6 Selene
father: 6 Uranus
husband: 8 Hyperion
mother: 4 Gaea

theater
4 nabe 5 drama, stage 6 boards 9 playhouse 10 footlights
award: 4 Obie, Tony
district: 6 rialto
drop: 5 scrim
entrance: 5 foyer, lobby
Greek: 5 odeum
movie: 6 cinema 8 cineplex, megaplex 9 multiplex
outdoor: 7 drive-in
part: 3 box, pit 4 loge 5 apron, stage, wings 6 stalls 7 balcony, parquet 8 parterre 9 greenroom, mezzanine, orchestra 10 proscenium 11 dress circle, grand circle, royal circle, upper circle

theatrical
5 stagy 6 staged 8 dramatic, thespian 10 artificial, flamboyant, histrionic 11 dramaturgic 12 melodramatic
agent: 6 Morris (William)
device: 4 prop
group: 6 troupe

Theban Eagle
6 Pindar

Thebes
founder: 6 Cadmus
king: 5 Laius 7 Oedipus
queen: 5 Niobe 7 Jocasta

Theda ____
4 Bara

theft
5 heist, pinch 6 holdup, piracy 7 break-in, larceny, robbery 8 burglary, stealing, thievery 9 pilferage
combining form: 5 klept 6 klepto

theme
4 stem, text, tune 5 essay, lemma, motif, paper, point, topic, topos 6 burden, matter, melody, mythos, thesis 7 article, conceit, message, subject 8 argument 11 composition 12 dissertation

Themis
father: **6** Uranus
goddess of: **3** law **7** justice
husband: **4** Zeus **7** Jupiter
mother: **4** Gaea

then
4 also, anon, ergo, next, thus, when **5** again, hence, later **7** besides, further **8** moreover **9** therefore, thereupon **10** in addition **11** accordingly, furthermore **12** additionally, consequently

thence
4 away **7** thereof **9** from there, therefrom

Theogony poet
6 Hesiod

theologian
American: **6** Merton (Thomas) **7** Edwards (Jonathan), Niebuhr (Reinhold), Tillich (Paul), Walther (Carl)
Dutch: **6** Jansen (Cornelis)
English: **4** Bede (Venerable) **5** Pusey (Edward), Watts (Isaac) **6** Alcuin, Wesley (John) **7** Langton (Stephen) **8** Pelagius, Wycliffe (John)
French: **6** Calvin (John) **7** Abelard (Peter), William (of Auvergne, of Auxerre) **8** Maritain (Jacques), Sabatier (Auguste), Teilhard (de Chardin, Pierre)
German: **6** Rahner (Karl) **7** Eckhart (Meister) **8** Albertus (Magnus) **9** Niemöller (Martin) **10** Bonhoeffer (Dietrich)
Greek: **9** Zygomalas (Theodore)
Italian: **6** Thomas (Aquinas) **7** Aquinas (Thomas), Socinus (Fausto, Laelius)
Scottish: **10** Duns Scotus (John)
Spanish: **6** Suárez (Francisco) **7** Vitoria (Francisco de) **8** Servetus (Michael)
Swedish: **9** Soderblom (Nathan)
Swiss: **4** Küng (Hans) **5** Barth (Karl), Vinet (Alexandre-Rodolphe) **6** Calvin (John), Cauvin (Jean)

theological
school: **8** seminary
virtue: **4** hope **5** faith **7** charity

___ Theologica
5 Summa

theorbo
4 lute

theorem
3 law **4** rule **5** axiom **7** formula, inverse, stencil **8** converse **9** principle **10** principium **11** fundamental, proposition

theoretical
4 pure **5** ideal **8** abstract, academic, notional, unproved **11** conjectural, speculative **12** hypothetical **13** problematical, suppositional

theorize
5 guess **6** submit **7** suggest **9** formulate, postulate, speculate **10** conjecture **11** hypothesize

theory
7 perhaps, premise, surmise **8** supposal **10** conjecture, hypothesis **11** speculation, supposition
astronomical: **7** big bang
suffix: **3** ism

therapeutic
5 tonic **7** healing, helpful **8** curative, remedial, salutary, sanative **9** healthful, medicinal, vulnerary, wholesome **10** beneficial, corrective **11** restorative **12** health-giving

therapy
9 treatment

therefore
4 ergo, then, thus **5** hence **6** hereat, thence **11** accordingly **12** consequently

therefrom
4 away **6** thence

thereupon
4 ergo, then, thus **6** at once, at that, thence **8** directly **9** right away, therefore, wherefore **11** accordingly, straightway **12** consequently

thermal unit
3 Btu **6** degree **7** calorie

thermometer
5 gauge **9** indicator
kind: **7** Celsius, Réaumur **10** centigrade, Fahrenheit

thermos
5 dewar **10** Dewar flask

Theroux work
9 Saint Jack **13** Mosquito Coast (The) **14** Half Moon Street **18** Great Railway Bazaar (The)

Thersites' slayer
8 Achilles

thesaurus editor
5 Roget (Peter Mark)

Theseus
beloved: **7** Ariadne
father: **6** Aegeus
mother: **6** Aethra
slayer: **9** Lycomedes
son: **10** Hippolytus
victim: **6** Sciron **8** Minotaur **10** Procrustes
wife: **7** Phaedra

thesis
5 essay, point, theme **6** belief **7** premise **8** downbeat, position, tractate, treatise **9** discourse, monograph, postulate, synthesis **10** contention, exposition **11** postulation, proposition, supposition **12** disquisition, dissertation

thespian
5 actor **6** mummer, player **7** actress, trouper **8** dramatic **9** performer **10** histrionic, theatrical **11** dramaturgic **12** impersonator, melodramatic

Thespis' forte
5 drama **7** tragedy

Thessalian hero
5 Jason **8** Achilles

Thetis
6 Nereid
father: 6 Nereus
husband: 6 Peleus
mother: 5 Doris
son: 8 Achilles

theurgist
5 witch **7** warlock **8** magician, sorcerer **12** wonder-worker

thew
4 beef **5** brawn, might, power, sinew, vigor **6** muscle **8** strength, vitality

thick
3 fat **4** wide **5** broad, bulky, burly, close, dense, dumpy, husky, squat, stout **6** chummy, chunky, packed, stocky **7** compact, crammed, crowded, viscous **8** familiar, heavyset, intimate **11** inspissated

thicken
3 set **4** blur, clot, jell **6** curdle **7** broaden, compact, congeal **8** condense **9** coagulate **10** inspissate **11** concentrate

thicket
4 bosk, bush, shaw, wood **5** clump, copse, grove, hedge **6** bosket, covert, mallee, tangle **7** boscage, bosquet, coppice, spinney **8** hedgerow, quickset **9** brushwood, canebrake, chaparral

thickness
3 ply **4** bulk, loft **5** depth, gauge, layer, sheet **7** density **9** viscosity

thickset
5 bulky, burly, heavy, husky, plump, pudgy, stout, tubby **6** chubby, chunky, portly, stocky, sturdy **7** compact **9** corpulent

thief
3 dip **4** prig, yegg **5** ganef, gonif **6** bandit, goniff, lifter, looter, pirate, rascal, robber **7** booster, burglar, filcher, stealer **8** hijacker, larcener, pilferer, water rat **9** larcenist, purloiner **10** cat burglar, highwayman, pickpocket, shoplifter **12** housebreaker

thieve
3 rob **4** hook, lift, pick, roll **5** boost, filch, pinch, pluck, steal, swipe **6** hijack, hold up, pilfer, rip off, snitch **7** purloin **8** knock off **9** knock over

thievery
see **theft**

thievish
7 corrupt, crooked **9** larcenous **13** light-fingered

thigh
3 ham **5** flank **6** gammon
bone: 5 femur
relating to: 6 crural **7** femoral

thimble
3 cup **5** cover

thin
4 fine, lank, lean, slim **5** gaunt, lanky, reedy, scant, sharp, sheer, spare **6** dilute, flimsy, meager, meagre, rarefy, scanty, skimpy, skinny, slight, sparse, stalky, treble, twiggy, watery **7** diluted, scraggy, scrawny, slender, spindly, squinny, subtile, tenuous **8** rarefied, skeletal **9** attenuate, extenuate **10** attenuated **11** watered-down **13** unsubstantial

thing
4 item, unit **5** being, event **6** entity, matter, object **7** article, concern, element **10** occurrence, phenomenon
in law: 3 res

thingamajig
5 gismo, gizmo **6** dingus, doodad, gadget, hickey, jigger, widget **7** whatsit **9** doohickey

things
4 gear **5** goods, stock, stuff **7** baggage, clothes, effects, luggage **8** chattels, clothing, matériel, movables, property, supplies **10** belongings, provisions **11** impedimenta, merchandise **13** accoutrements, paraphernalia

think
4 mull, muse **5** brood, study, weigh **6** ideate, ponder, reason **7** believe, imagine, reflect, suppose, surmise **8** cogitate, consider, meditate, ruminate **9** cerebrate, speculate **10** conjecture, deliberate, excogitate **11** contemplate

Thinker sculptor
5 Rodin (Auguste)

Thin Man, The
actor: 3 Loy (Myrna) **6** Powell (William), Skippy **9** O'Sullivan (Maureen)
author: 7 Hammett (Dashiell)
character: 4 Nick (Charles), Nora (Charles) **6** Wynant (Clyde, Dorothy)
dog: 4 Asta

third
4 show **8** tertiary
combining form: 3 tri
power: 4 cube

third degree
7 torture **8** grilling **11** inquisition, questioning **13** interrogation

third estate
5 plebs **6** people, plebes **8** populace **9** commonage, commoners, plebeians **10** commonalty **11** rank and file

Third Man author
6 Greene (Graham)

Third of May painter
4 Goya (Francisco)

thirst
3 yen **4** itch, long, lust, pine **5** crave, yearn **6** desire, hanker, hunger **7** craving, dryness, longing **8** appetite

thirsty
3 dry **4** arid, avid **5** eager **6** ardent **7** anxious, bone-dry, parched **8** droughty **9** absorbent, waterless

this and that
8 oddments, sundries **9** etceteras **11** miscellanea, odds and ends

Thisbe's lover
7 Pyramus

This Side of Paradise author
10 Fitzgerald (F. Scott)

thistle
4 weed **7** caltrop
Russian: **10** tumbleweed

thistlebird
9 goldfinch

thither
3 yon **5** there **6** yonder

thole
3 peg, pin **6** endure

Thomas à ____
6 Becket, Kempis

Thomas's Greek name
7 Didymus

Thomas opera
6 Mignon

____ Thompson
4 Emma **5** Sadie **6** Hunter **7** Dorothy, Francis, J. Walter **8** Benjamin

thong
4 band, lace, lash, rein, zori **5** lasso, strap, strip, whang **6** sandal **7** latchet **8** flip-flop

Thor
5 Donar
father: **4** Odin **5** Wotan
god of: **7** thunder
hammer: **8** Mjollnir
mother: **5** Jordh, Jorth

thorax
5 chest, trunk **6** pereon

Thoreau, Henry David
friend: **7** Emerson (Ralph Waldo)
pond: **6** Walden
town: **7** Concord
work: **6** Walden

thorium symbol
2 Th

thorn
4 barb **5** briar, spike, spine **7** prickle, spinule **9** annoyance **10** irritation

thorny
5 sharp, spiny **6** briary, touchy, tricky **7** awkward, prickly, spinous **8** ticklish **9** difficult, vexatious **10** nettlesome **11** troublesome

thorough
4 full **6** minute **7** careful, in-depth **8** complete, detailed, diligent, whole-hog **9** downright **10** blow-by-blow, exhaustive, meticulous **11** painstaking **13** conscientious

thoroughbred
5 racer **8** pedigree, purebred **9** pedigreed, pureblood **10** bloodstock **11** full-blooded

thoroughfare
3 way **4** road **5** track **6** artery, avenue, street **7** highway, parkway **8** corridor **9** boulevard

thoroughgoing
5 utter **6** all-out **7** extreme **8** absolute, complete, outright, whole-hog **9** out-and-out **10** consummate, exhaustive **11** straight-out, unmitigated **13** dyed-in-the-wool

thou
3 you **5** grand
French: **5** mille

though
3 yet **5** still, while **6** albeit **7** however, whereas **8** after all **11** nonetheless **12** nevertheless

thought
4 idea **6** notion, reason **7** concept, opinion **8** ideation **9** brainwork **10** cogitation, conception, meditation, reflection, rumination **11** cerebration, speculation **12** deliberation, intellection **13** contemplation

thoughtful
6 polite **7** gallant, heedful, mindful, pensive, serious **8** gracious, studious, thinking **9** attentive, courteous **10** cogitative, meditative, reflective, ruminative, solicitous **11** considerate **12** deliberative, intellectual **13** contemplative

thoughtless
4 rash, rude **5** brash, hasty **6** madcap **7** selfish **8** careless, feckless, heedless, impolite, reckless,

uncaring **9** insensate **10** incautious, ungracious **12** discourteous **13** inconsiderate

thousand
combining form: **4** kilo
cubed: **7** billion
dollars: **5** grand
squared: **7** million
years: **10** millennium

thousandth
10 millesimal
combining form: **5** milli

thrall
4 peon, serf, yoke **5** helot, slave **7** bondage, bondman, helotry, peonage, serfdom, slavery, villein **9** servitude, villenage **10** absorption **11** enslavement

thrash
3 tan **4** beat, belt, drub, flog, hide, lash, lick, maul, pelt, trim, whip **5** baste, flail, pound, smear, swing, thump, whale, whang **6** batter, buffet, larrup, pummel, stripe, wallop **7** scourge, shellac, trounce **8** flounder, lambaste, work over **10** flagellate

thrash out
4 moot **5** argue **6** debate **7** discuss, dispute **10** deliberate, kick around

thread
4 line, vein, yard **5** fiber, trail, weave **6** strand, stream, string **8** filament
ball of: **4** clew
dental: **5** floss
holder: **6** bobbin
kind: **4** silk, yarn **5** floss, lisle **6** cotton **8** surgical
loose: **8** raveling **9** ravelling
surgical: **6** catgut, suture

threadbare
4 hack, worn **5** dingy, faded, seedy, stale, tacky, tatty, tired, trite **6** beat-up, cheesy, cliché, frayed, ragged, shabby, shoddy **7** clichéd, run-down, tedious, worn-out **8** shopworn, slipshod, tattered, timeworn, well-worn **9** destitute, hackneyed **10** down-at-heel **11** commonplace, dilapidated, down-at-heels, stereotyped **13** down-at-the-heel

threadlike
6 filate **11** filamentous

threads
4 duds **7** clothes **8** clothing, garments

threat
6 danger, duress, menace **7** assault, warning **8** big stick, coercion **11** thunderbolt

threaten
3 cow **4** warn **5** augur, lower **6** coerce, menace **7** caution, portend, presage **8** endanger, forebode, forewarn, overhang **10** intimidate

three
4 trey **5** crowd
combining form: **3** ter, tri

threefold
5 trine **6** thrice, treble, trinal, triple **7** triplex

Three Musicians artist
7 Picasso (Pablo)

Three Musketeers
5 Athos **6** Aramis **7** Porthos
author: **5** Dumas (Alexandre)
friend: **9** D'Artagnan

Threepenny Opera, The
author: **6** Brecht (Bertolt)
composer: **5** Weill (Kurt)

threescore
5 sixty

Three Sisters, The
4 Olga **5** Irina, Masha
author: **7** Chekhov (Anton)

threesome
4 trio **5** triad, trine **6** triple, triune, troika **7** trinity **8** triangle **11** triumvirate

three-wheeler
5 cycle, trike **7** pedicab **8** tricycle **10** velocipede

threnody
5 dirge, elegy **6** lament

thresh
3 lam, tan **4** beat, belt, drub, flog, hide, lash, lick, pelt, trim, wave, whip **5** baste, forge, flail, pound, slate, smear, swing, thump, whale, whang **6** batter, buffet, larrup, pummel, strike, stripe, wallop, winnow **7** scourge, shellac, trounce **8** lambaste, work over **10** flagellate

threshold
3 eve **4** door, edge, gate, sill **5** brink, limen, verge **6** outset **8** boundary

thrift
6 saving **7** economy, sea pink **8** prudence **9** frugality, parsimony

thrifty
5 canny **6** frugal, saving **7** sparing **9** provident **10** economical **12** cheeseparing, parsimonious **13** penny-pinching

thrill
3 wow **4** bang, boot, kick, rush, send **5** blast, throb **6** charge, excite, shiver, tingle, wallop **7** frisson, tremble, vibrate **9** electrify **10** excitement **11** titillation

thriller
6 gothic **7** chiller, mystery, shocker **8** whodunit **9** dime novel **10** hair-raiser **13** penny dreadful

thrive
4 boom, grow **7** advance, burgeon, develop, prosper, succeed **8** flourish, get ahead

throat
3 maw **4** tube **5** gorge **6** groove, gullet **7** channel, weasand
infection: 5 strep **12** epiglottitis
inflammation: 5 croup **6** angina, quinsy **10** laryngitis **11** pharyngitis
relating to: 8 guttural
warmer: 5 scarf

throaty
5 gruff, husky, thick **6** hoarse **8** gravelly, guttural

throb
4 ache, beat, drum **5** pound, pulse **6** thrill **7** pulsate, vibrate **9** palpitate

throe
3 fit **4** pain, pang **5** agony, spasm **6** attack **7** seizure **9** suffering **10** convulsion **11** contraction

thrombus
4 clot **8** blockage, coagulum

throne
4 seat **5** chair, crown, power, reign **8** cathedra, dominion **11** sovereignty

throng
3 jam, mob **4** host, pack, push, rout **5** bunch, crowd, crush, drove, flock, group, horde, press, scrum, shoal, swarm **6** resort **9** multitude **10** assemblage

throttle
3 gun **5** choke **6** throat **7** garrote, trachea **8** strangle, suppress **11** accelerator, strangulate

through
3 per, via **4** done, past **5** due to, ended **6** direct **7** by way of, done for, nonstop, owing to **8** by dint of, complete, finished, washed-up **9** because of, by means of, completed, concluded **10** by virtue of, terminated, throughout
prefix: 3 dia, per

throughout
3 mid **4** amid **5** midst **6** during **7** all over, overall **10** everywhere, far and near, far and wide, high and low

Through the Looking Glass
author: 7 Carroll (Lewis)
character: 5 Alice

throve
9 burgeoned, prospered **10** flourished

throw
3 lob, peg, put **4** cast, fire, hurl, toss **5** chuck, fling, heave, pitch, sling **6** afghan, launch, propel **7** buck off, project
in the towel: 4 quit **6** give up

throw away
4 blow, cast, junk, shed **5** scrap, waste **7** discard, fritter **8** jettison, squander

throwback
7 atavism **9** reversion **11** anachronism

throw off
4 lose, shed **5** addle, shake **7** confuse, fluster **8** befuddle, bewilder, distract
the track: 6 derail **7** confuse, mislead

throw out
4 emit, junk, shed **5** chuck, eject, evict, scrap **6** reject **7** discard **8** jettison

throw up
4 barf, cast, hurl, lose, puke, quit, spew, toss **5** heave, retch, vomit **7** upchuck **8** disgorge **11** regurgitate

thrush
4 omao **5** mavis, ouzel, robin, veery **6** mistle **8** bluebird **9** blackbird, fieldfare, mistletoe **11** nightingale

thrust
3 dig, jab, ram **4** barb, butt, core, cram, dash, dive, duck, gist, hurl, kick, pith, poke, prod, push, stab, tilt **5** barge, crowd, cut in, drive, force, lunge, press, punch, sense, shoot, shove, spear, stick, stuff **6** burden, extend, insert, pierce, plunge, propel, upshot **7** assault, obtrude, project, purport, riposte **8** pressure **9** substance

thud
3 jar **4** bump, jolt, plop **5** clunk, throb, thump **6** impact **10** concussion

thug
3 mug **4** goon, hood, punk **5** bully, rough, rowdy, tough **6** Apache, Capone, gunman, hit man **7** hoodlum, mobster, ruffian **8** enforcer, gangster, hooligan, plug-ugly **9** cutthroat, roughneck

thulium symbol
2 Tm

thumb
4 leaf, turn **5** digit, hitch, ovolo **6** pollex, riffle **8** pollices (plural) **9** hitchhike

thumbs-up
3 AOK, nod **4** okay **7** go-ahead **10** green light

thumb through
4 scan **6** browse, riffle **7** dip into

thump
3 bop, hit **4** bash, beat, belt, blow, drub, jolt, pelt, whip, whup **5** knock, paste, pound, punch, shock, smack, sound, whack **6** batter, buffet, defeat, impact, pummel, strike, thrash, thwack, wallop **7** clobber, endorse, promote, shellac, trounce **8** advocate

thunder
4 bang, boom, clap, peal, roar **6** rumble **7** resound **8** rumbling **9** fulminate

thunderbolt
9 lightning

thunder lizard
11 apatosaurus **12** brontosaurus

thunderstruck
5 agape **6** amazed **7** shocked, stunned **8** dismayed **9** astounded, staggered **10** astonished, bewildered, confounded **11** dumbfounded **13** flabbergasted

Thurber character
5 Mitty (Walter)

thurible
6 censer

thus
3 sic **4** ergo, then **5** hence **9** therefore **11** accordingly **12** consequently
French: **5** ainsi

Thus Spake Zarathustra author
9 Nietzsche (Friedrich)

thwack
3 bop **4** belt, biff, blow, pelt, sock, whop **5** crack, pound, smack, thump, whack **6** wallop **7** clobber

thwart
4 balk, beat, dash, foil **5** bench, block, deter **6** baffle, hamper, hinder, oppose, scotch, stymie **7** flummox, prevent **8** confound, obstruct **9** checkmate, frustrate **10** circumvent, contravene, disappoint

Thyestes
brother: **6** Atreus
daughter: **7** Pelopia
father: **6** Pelops
mother: **10** Hippodamia
son: **9** Aegisthus

Tiamat
husband: **4** Apsu
slayer: **6** Marduk

tiara
5 crown **6** diadem **8** headband

Tibetan
animal: **3** yak **5** takin
capital: **5** Lhasa
coin: **5** tanga
dog: **5** Lhasa **9** Lhasa apso
monk: **4** lama
people: **6** Bhotia, Sherpa

tibia
8 shinbone

tic
5 quirk, spasm **6** twitch **9** twitching

tick
5 check **8** arachnid, parasite **9** checkmark **11** bloodsucker

ticker
4 bomb **5** clock, heart, watch

ticket
3 key, tag **4** comp, pass, vote **5** slate **6** ballot **7** receipt **8** passport, password **10** open sesame
seller: **7** scalper

tickle
4 stir **5** amuse, tease, touch **6** arouse, excite, please, tingle **7** delight, gratify, provoke **9** stimulate, titillate

tickled
5 happy **6** amused **7** pleased **9** delighted

ticklish
5 dicey **6** tender, thorny, touchy, tricky **8** delicate, unstable **9** sensitive **10** precarious **13** oversensitive

tick off
3 ire, irk **5** anger **6** rankle **7** incense, provoke **9** aggravate

tidal flood
4 bore

tidbit
3 ort **4** bite **5** goody, treat **6** dainty, morsel, nugget

tide
4 flow, flux, rush **5** drift, flood, spate, surge **6** stream **7** current, holiday
type: **3** ebb, low **4** high, neap **5** flood **6** spring

tidings
4 news, word **6** advice **7** message **11** information **12** intelligence

tidy
4 fair, neat, smug, snug, trim **5** kempt **6** pick up **7** clean up, orderly, precise **9** shipshape **10** acceptable, methodical **11** respectable, spic-and-span, substantial, uncluttered, well-groomed **12** satisfactory, spick-and-span

tie
3 guy, rod **4** band, bind, bolo, bond, cord, draw, gird, join, knit, knot, lash, link, moor, rope, yoke **5** equal, leash, match, truss **6** attach, clip-on, cravat, fasten, fetter, hamper, oxford, ribbon, secure **7** connect, harness, shackle **8** dead heat, deadlock, fastener, ligament, ligature, restrain, shoelace, standoff, vinculum **9** constrain, stalemate **10** attachment, four-in-hand

tied
4 even **5** bound **6** joined, united **8** attached, fastened **9** connected

tier
3 row **4** bank, deck, file, line, rank **5** class, grade, group, story **6** league **7** echelon **8** category, grouping

tie-up
3 jam **4** snag **5** crimp, delay, hitch, snarl

6 glitch **7** problem **8** gridlock, slowdown, stoppage **10** connection, traffic jam **11** association

tiff
3 row **4** fuss, spat **5** run-in, scrap **6** bicker **7** brabble, dispute, quarrel, wrangle **8** argument, squabble **10** falling-out **11** altercation **12** disagreement

tiffany
5 gauze **11** cheesecloth

tiger
3 cat **6** feline **9** carnivore
young: 3 cub

tight
4 fast, firm, snug, taut, trim **5** cheap, close, drunk, fixed, tipsy **6** firmly, secure, stingy **7** compact, crowded, drunken, miserly **8** intimate **9** difficult, tenacious **10** inebriated **11** closefisted, intoxicated **12** cheeseparing, parsimonious **13** penny-pinching

tighten
4 bind **5** choke, close, cramp, pinch, screw **6** clench, fasten, narrow, secure, shrink **8** compress, restrict **9** clamp down, constrict

tightfisted
see **stingy**

tight-lipped
6 silent **8** reserved, reticent, taciturn **12** close-mouthed

tightwad
5 miser, piker **7** niggard, scrooge **9** skinflint **10** cheapskate **12** penny-pincher

tile
5 plate, slate **6** domino **7** tessera **8** linoleum

till
3 hoe, sow **4** disk, plow, tend, turn, up to, work **6** before, harrow **7** prior to **9** cultivate **11** in advance of **12** cash register

tillable
6 arable **10** cultivable **12** cultivatable

tillage
4 farm, land **5** tilth **7** culture **11** cultivation

tiller
4 helm **5** stalk **6** farmer, sprout **7** planter, steerer **9** sodbuster **10** cultivator

tilt
3 tip **4** bank, bent, bias, cant, cock, heel, lean, list, toss **5** grade, joust, level, lurch, pitch, slant, slope, speed **6** attack, charge, thrust **7** dispute, incline, leaning, recline **8** gradient **11** inclination

timbal
4 drum **10** kettledrum

timber
3 log **4** balk, beam, stud, tree, wood **5** board, joist, plank, trees, woods **6** forest, girder, lumber, rafter **8** woodland
uncut: 8 stumpage
wolf: 4 lobo

timbre
4 tone **6** temper **7** quality **9** resonance, tone color

timbrel
4 drum **10** tambourine

time
3 age, era **4** bout, date, hour, pace, span, term **5** clock, epoch, shift, space, spell, stint, tempo, while **6** moment, period, season **7** instant, stretch **8** duration, occasion **11** opportunity
abbreviation: 3 CDT, CST, EDT, EST, MDT, MST, PDT, PST
combining form: 5 chron **6** chrono
gone by: 3 ago **4** past **9** yesterday **10** yesteryear **12** auld lang syne
long: 3 age, eon, era **4** aeon
of day: 4 dawn, dusk, noon **5** night **6** sunset **7** evening, morning, sunrise **8** daybreak, twilight **9** afternoon
olden: 4 yore **10** yesteryear
period: 3 age, day, eon, era **4** aeon, hour, week, year **5** epoch, month **6** decade, minute, moment, second **7** century, instant **9** fortnight **10** millennium
present: 3 now
relating to: 8 temporal
short: 5 jiffy **6** moment, second **7** instant
to come: 6 future **8** tomorrow
waste: 4 loaf **5** dally **6** loiter

time and again
3 oft **5** often **6** hourly **8** commonly, ofttimes **10** constantly, frequently, oftentimes, repeatedly **11** continually, over and over **12** periodically

Time founder
4 Luce (Henry R.) **6** Hadden (Briton)

timeless
7 ageless, eternal, unaging **8** unageing **9** atemporal, perpetual **11** everlasting

timely
5 early **6** prompt, proper **8** punctual, suitable **9** opportune **10** seasonable **11** appropriate

Time Machine author
5 Wells (H. G.)

time-out
4 rest **5** break, pause **6** hiatus, recess **7** respite **8** breather **9** interlude **12** interruption

timepiece
5 clock, watch **7** sundial **8** horologe **9** clepsydra, metronome, stopwatch **10** water clock **11** chronograph, chronometer

timetable
6 agenda, docket 7 program 8 calendar, schedule

timeworn
3 old 4 aged, hack 5 hoary, stale, trite 6 age-old 7 ancient 8 dog-eared, Noachian 9 hackneyed 10 threadbare

time zone
7 Central, Eastern, Pacific 8 Mountain

timid
3 shy 4 wary 5 chary, mousy 6 afraid, yellow 7 bashful, chicken, fearful, halting, nervous, panicky 8 cowardly, retiring, timorous 9 diffident, tentative, trepidant, uncertain 11 unassertive 12 apprehensive, fainthearted

timidity
4 fear 7 modesty, shyness 8 meekness 9 hesitancy, reticence 10 diffidence, hesitation

Timon's servant
7 Flavius

timorous
4 wary 5 timid 6 afraid 7 fearful 8 retiring 9 shrinking, tremulous 12 apprehensive

Timothy's associate
4 Paul 5 Titus

tin
3 box, can 5 metal 7 element 9 container
mining region: 8 stannary
relating to: 7 stannic 8 stannous
sheet: 6 latten
symbol: 2 Sn

tincture
3 dye 4 cast, hint, tint 5 color, shade, smack, stain, tinge, touch, trace 6 iodine, streak 8 colorant, dyestuff, laudanum 9 paregoric 10 intimation, suggestion

tinder
4 punk 5 spunk 8 kindling

tine
5 point, prong, spike 6 branch

tinge
3 dye, hue 4 cast, hint, tint, tone 5 color, imbue, shade, stain, tinct, touch 8 tincture 10 intimation

tingle
5 sting 6 thrill 7 prickle 9 sensation

tinker
3 fix 4 mend, mess, muck, play 5 gypsy 6 adjust, diddle, fiddle, mender, potter, putter, repair 7 bungler, twiddle 9 repairman

tinkle
4 ring, ting 5 chink, clink, plink 6 jingle

tinny
4 thin 5 cheap, harsh 8 metallic

tinsel
5 gaudy 6 flashy, garish, tawdry 7 chintzy, glaring, trinket 8 ornament, specious 9 clinquant 11 superficial 12 meretricious

tint
3 dye, hue 4 cast, tone, wash 5 color, shade, tinge, touch 8 tincture 10 coloration 12 pigmentation

tiny
3 wee 4 itsy 5 bitsy, bitty, elfin, micro, pygmy, teeny, weeny 6 minute, peewee, pocket, teensy, weensy 8 pint-size 9 itsy-bitsy, itty-bitty, miniature, minuscule 10 diminutive, pocket-size, teeny-weeny 11 lilliputian, microscopic 12 teensy-weensy 13 infinitesimal

tip
3 cap, cue, top 4 apex, cant, clue, cusp, heel, hint, lean, list, peak, perk, tilt 5 point, slant, slope, steer, upset 6 advice, topple 7 cumshaw, incline 8 gratuity, overturn, turn over 9 baksheesh, lagniappe, pourboire 11 information

tip off
4 warn 5 alert

tip-off
4 clue, hint, sign 6 advice 7 pointer, red flag, warning 8 giveaway, jump ball 10 indication

Tippecanoe and ___ too
5 Tyler

tippet
4 cape 5 scarf 8 liripipe

tipple
3 bib, sip 4 swig, tope 5 booze, drink 6 guzzle, imbibe 7 swizzle 8 liquor up

tippler
3 sot 4 lush, soak 5 drunk, toper 6 bibber, boozer 7 tosspot 8 drunkard 9 inebriate

tipstaff
7 bailiff

tipster
4 fink, tout 6 canary, snitch 7 adviser, rat fink, stoolie, tattler 8 informer, squealer 11 stool pigeon

tipsy
3 lit 4 high 5 askew, drunk, lit up, oiled, tight 7 drunken, fuddled, sloshed 8 unsteady 10 inebriated 11 intoxicated

tiptoe
5 creep, skulk, slink, sneak, steal 9 pussyfoot

tirade
4 rant 6 screed 8 diatribe, harangue, jeremiad 9 philippic 12 denunciation, vituperation 13 tongue-lashing

tire
3 sap 4 bore, fail, flag, jade, pall, poop, wear

5 **drain**, droop, ennui, weary, wheel **6** tucker, weaken **7** exhaust, fatigue, wear out **8** enervate, wear down
airless: **4** flat **7** blowout
kind: **4** bias, snow **6** radial **7** retread **9** whitewall

tired
4 worn **5** spent, weary **6** done in **7** drained, run-down, worn out **8** fatigued, flagging **9** enervated, exhausted

tiredness
7 fatigue **8** collapse **9** lassitude **10** enervation, exhaustion **11** prostration

tireless
10 unflagging **13** indefatigable, inexhaustible

Tiresias
4 seer **10** soothsayer

tiresome
4 dull **5** stale **6** boring **7** irksome, lumpish, operose, tedious

Tirol
capital: **9** Innsbruck
country: **7** Austria
mountains: **4** Alps

Tisiphone
see **Erinyes**

tissue
3 web **4** film, mesh **5** fiber, gauze, paper **6** fabric
anatomical: **4** tela **5** fiber **6** diploe **8** ganglion **10** epithelium
connective: **4** tela **6** stroma, tendon **9** cartilage
kind: **3** fat **5** nerve **6** muscle **7** nervous **8** muscular **10** connective
layer: **6** dermis **7** stratum
plant: **4** bast, wood **5** xylem **6** phloem

titan
5 giant **8** colossus

Titan
father: **6** Uranus
female: **4** Rhea **6** Tethys, Themis
male: **6** Cronus **7** Iapetus, Oceanus
mother: **4** Gaea

Titan author
7 Dreiser (Theodore)

Titania's husband
6 Oberon

titanic
4 huge, vast **5** great **6** mighty **7** immense, mammoth, massive **8** colossal, enormous, gigantic **9** cyclopean, Herculean, monstrous **10** gargantuan, tremendous

Titanic
actor: **4** Zane (Billy) **5** Bates (Kathy) **6** Stuart (Gloria) **7** Winslet (Kate) **8** DiCaprio (Leonardo)
director: **7** Cameron (James)
last U. S. survivor: **7** Asplund (Lillian)
line: **9** White Star
rescuing vessel: **9** Carpathia
sister ship: **7** Olympic **9** Britannic

titanium symbol
2 Ti

tithe
3 tax **4** levy **5** tenth **12** contribution

Tithonus
beloved by: **3** Eos
father: **8** Laomedon

Titian painting
5 Danaë **8** Ecce Homo **10** Assumption (The), Holy Family (The) **12** Rape of Europa (The) **13** Maltese Knight, Medea and Venus, Venus and Cupid **14** Worship of Venus (The) **17** Bacchus and Ariadne

titillate
6 arouse, excite, stir up, thrill, tickle **9** stimulate

title
3 dub, due **4** call, deed, dibs, name, term **5** claim, merit, nomen **7** baptize, caption, heading **8** cognomen **9** designate **10** denominate **11** appellation, appellative, designation **12** championship, compellation, denomination
academic: **4** dean, Prof. **7** provost **9** president, professor
Dutch: **7** mynheer
ecclesiastic: **3** Rev. **5** abbot **6** bishop **8** cardinal, reverend **10** archbishop
Etruscan: **3** lar
feminine: **2** Ms. **3** Mrs. **4** dame, lady, ma'am, miss **5** madam **6** abbess, madame, milady, missus **8** mistress
French: **6** madame **8** monsieur **12** mademoiselle
German: **4** Frau, Herr **8** Fräulein
Hindu: **4** babu, raja, rani **5** baboo, rajah, ranee
holder: **5** noble **8** champion
Indian: **3** sri **5** sahib
Islamic: **4** amir, emir, imam **5** ameer, hadji, hajji **6** sayyid **9** ayatollah
Italian: **5** donna **6** signor **7** signora **9** signorina
masculine: **2** Mr. **6** mister
monk's: **3** fra **7** brother
of nobility: **3** sir **4** duke, earl, king, lady, lord, sire **5** baron, count, queen **6** prince **7** baronet, duchess, marquis **8** Archduke, baroness, countess, marchesa, marchese, marquise, princess, viscount **11** marchioness, viscountess
Oriental: **4** khan

Persian: **5** mirza
Portuguese: **3** dom **4** dona **6** senhor **7** senhora **9** senhorita
Spanish: **3** don **4** doña
Turkish: **3** aga, bey

titmouse
4 bird **6** tomtit **7** bushtit **9** chickadee

Tito
4 Broz (Josip)

titter
5 laugh **6** giggle **7** chortle, chuckle, snicker, snigger

tittle
3 bit, jot **4** atom, iota, mite **5** minim, speck **7** smidgen **8** particle **9** diacritic

titular
5 legal **6** titled **7** nominal **8** so-called **11** designative

Tityus
father: **4** Zeus
slayer: **6** Apollo

Tiu
see **Tyr**

tizzy
4 flap, fume, snit, stew **5** sweat **6** dither, swivet, uproar

T-man
5 agent **8** revenuer

to (Scottish)
3 tae

toad
4 agua **6** anuran, peeper **8** truckler **9** amphibian, brownnose, sycophant **10** batrachian, bootlicker **11** lickspittle
genus: **4** Bufo, Hyla

toady
4 fawn **5** cower, leech **6** cringe, flunky, grovel, kowtow, lackey, sponge **7** truckle **8** bootlick, parasite, truckler **9** brownnose, sycophant **10** bootlicker **11** apple-polish, lickspittle

toast
5 bread, drink, salud, singe, skoal **6** cheers, health, l'chaim, pledge, prosit, salute **7** wassail **8** mazel tov **9** celebrate
kind: **5** melba **6** French **8** zwieback

toastmaster
2 MC **5** emcee

To a Waterfowl author
6 Bryant (William Cullen)

tobacco
4 leaf, weed
cask: **8** hogshead
chewing: **4** chaw, quid
ingredient: **3** tar **8** nicotine
juice: **6** ambeer
kind: **4** shag **5** flake, snuff **6** burley **7** caporal, latakia, perique, Turkish **8** Virginia **9** broadleaf, mundungus
pipe: **4** heel **6** dottle
rolled: **5** cigar **9** cigarette
Turkish: **7** latakia

Tobacco Road author
8 Caldwell (Erskine)

to be
Latin: **4** esse

to be sure
6 indeed **7** granted **9** certainly

Tobias
father: **5** Tobit
son: **8** Hyrcanus

toby
3 jug, mug **7** pitcher

tocsin
3 SOS **5** alarm, alert **6** signal

today
3 now **9** currently, presently

toddler
3 tot **4** tike, tyke **6** rug rat

to-do
4 fuss, rout, stir **5** hoo-ha, rouse, stink, whirl **6** bother, bustle, clamor, furore, hoo-hah, hubbub, hurrah, pother, ruckus, rumpus, tumult, uproar **7** turmoil **8** foofaraw **9** agitation, commotion **10** hurly-burly **11** disturbance

toe
5 digit
big: **6** hallux
combining form: **6** dactyl

toehold
7 footing

toff
3 fop **4** beau **5** blade, dandy, swell **7** coxcomb, peacock **8** macaroni, popinjay **9** exquisite **12** clotheshorse

toga
4 gown, robe, wrap

together
5 as one **6** at once, joined, united **7** jointly **8** mutually **10** conjointly **11** concertedly **12** coincidently, collectively, concurrently
prefix: **3** col, com, con, cor, sym, syn

togetherness
5 union **7** cahoots **8** alliance **10** connection, solidarity **11** affiliation, association, combination, conjunction, partnership

toggle
3 pin **6** fasten, switch **9** alternate **10** crosspiece

Togo
capital: **4** Lomé
language: **3** Ewe **6** French
monetary unit: **5** franc
neighbor: **5** Benin, Ghana **11** Burkina Faso

togs
3 rig **4** duds, suit **5** dress **6** attire, outfit **7** apparel, clothes, raiment, rigging, threads **8** clothing, ensemble, garments

To His Coy Mistress author
7 Marvell (Andrew)

toil
3 fag, net, tug **4** grub, plod, plug, slog, trap, work **5** grind, labor, slave, snare, sweat **6** drudge **7** slavery, travail **8** drudgery

toiler
4 peon **5** slave **6** drudge, slavey **9** workhorse

toilet
3 loo **4** head, john **5** bidet, potty, privy **6** johnny **7** latrine **8** bathroom, lavatory **11** water closet

toilsome
4 hard **5** heavy **6** uphill **7** arduous, labored **9** difficult, effortful, laborious, strenuous

Tokay
4 wine

token
4 buck, chip, gift, mark, note, sign **5** badge, check, favor, index, piece, plume, prize, relic, scrip **6** copper, emblem, pledge, symbol, ticket, trophy **7** earnest, gesture, memento, symptom, warrant **8** evidence, keepsake, memorial, reminder, security, souvenir **9** indicator **10** expression, indication **11** perfunctory, remembrance

To Kill a Mockingbird
author: **3** Lee (Harper)
character: **3** Jem (Finch), Tom (Robinson) **4** Dill (Harris) **5** Ewell (Bob), Scout (Finch) **7** Atticus (Finch), Mayella (Ewell) **9** Boo Radley, Calpurnia **10** Cunningham (Walter)
town: **7** Maycomb

Tokyo
formerly: **3** Edo
island: **6** Honshu

tolerable
2 OK **4** fair, okay **6** common, decent **7** livable **8** adequate, all right, bearable, passable **9** endurable **10** acceptable, sufferable **11** respectable **12** satisfactory

tolerably
4 so-so **5** quite **6** fairly, pretty, rather **8** passably **9** averagely **10** moderately

tolerance
6 leeway **8** patience **9** allowance, endurance, deviation, fortitude, variation **10** indulgence, resistance, sufferance **11** forbearance, habituation

tolerant
4 easy **5** broad **7** lenient, liberal **8** placable **9** easygoing, eurytopic, forgiving, indulgent, tractable **10** open-minded, permissive **11** broad-minded, sympathetic **13** understanding

tolerate
4 bear, bide, hack **5** abide, allow, brook, stand **6** accept, endure, pardon, permit, suffer **7** condone, stomach, swallow **8** bear with, live with **9** put up with **11** countenance

Tolkien creature
3 Ent, Orc **4** Warg **5** Ainur, Huorn, Troll **6** Balrog, Hobbit, Nazgul, Shelob **9** Oliphaunt **10** Ringwraith

toll
3 fee, tax **4** bell, bong, cost, levy, peal, ring **5** chime, knell, price, sound **6** charge, summon, tariff **7** expense **8** casualty **10** assessment

tollbooth
11 customhouse

Tolstoy work
8 Cossacks (The) **11** War and Peace **12** Anna Karenina **16** Death of Ivan Ilich (The)

tomato
9 love apple

tomb
5 crypt, grave **6** burial **9** mausoleum, sepulcher, sepulchre, sepulture
ancient Egyptian: **7** mastaba
empty: **8** cenotaph

tomboy
6 gamine, hoyden

tombstone
4 slab **8** memorial, monument **11** grave marker
inscription: **3** RIP **8** hic jacet

tome
4 book **6** volume

tomfool
3 ass **4** dolt, fool, jerk **5** crazy, idiot, loony, ninny, silly, wacky **6** absurd, donkey, stupid **7** doltish, foolish, jackass **8** clodpoll, dummkopf, imbecile **9** blockhead, fantastic, horse's ass, thickhead **10** dunderhead, nincompoop **11** chowderhead, chucklehead, harebrained **12** preposterous

tomfoolery
4 dido, lark **5** antic, caper, prank, shine, trick **6** frolic **8** escapade, fandango **9** high jinks **10** shenanigan **11** monkeyshine

Tom Jones author
8 Fielding (Henry)

tommyrot
4 bosh, bull, bunk **5** bilge, hooey, trash **7** baloney, eyewash, hogwash, rubbish **8** claptrap, nonsense **9** poppycock **10** balderdash **13** horsefeathers

Tom o'Bedlam
3 nut **4** loon **5** loony **6** madman, maniac **7** lunatic

tomorrow
6 future, mañana

Tom Sawyer
author: **5** Twain (Mark) **7** Clemens (Samuel)
character: **5** Becky (Thatcher) **8** Huck Finn, Injun Joe **9** Aunt Polly **10** Muff Potter

Tom Thumb
4 runt **5** dwarf, pygmy **6** midget, peanut, peewee **7** manikin **8** half-pint, mannikin **10** homunculus **11** lilliputian

ton
3 lot **4** chic **5** bunch, style, trend, vogue **6** bundle **7** fashion

tone
3 hue **4** cast, mode, mood, note, tint, vein **5** color, pitch, shade, sound, style, tinge **6** accent, manner, spirit, strain, temper, timbre **7** fashion **10** inflection

toned
3 cut, fit **4** buff, firm, trim **6** buffed **7** defined **8** muscular

toned down
4 mute, soft **5** muted, quiet, sober **6** low-key, mellow **7** subdued **8** laid-back, low-keyed, softened **10** restrained **11** understated

Tonga
capital: **9** Nuku'alofa
ethnic group: **10** Polynesian
explorer: **4** Cook (Capt. James) **6** Tasman (Abel)
island group: **5** Vava'u **6** Haapai **9** Tongatapu
monetary unit: **6** pa'anga

tongue
4 lick, pole, tang **6** glossa, lingua, speech **7** clapper, dialect, languet **8** language **10** vernacular
combining form: **4** glot **5** gloss, lingu **6** glossa, glosso, lingua, lingui, linguo **7** glossia

tongue-lash
4 lash, rail **5** chide, scold **6** berate, rebuke, revile **7** bawl out, chew out, tell off, reprove, upbraid **8** admonish, call down, reproach **9** castigate, reprimand **10** vituperate

tongue-lashing
6 rebuke, tirade **7** censure, reproof **8** scolding **9** reprimand, talking-to **11** castigation **12** dressing-down

tongue-tied
3 mum, shy **4** mute **6** silent **7** bashful **9** diffident **10** speechless **12** inarticulate

tonic
3 pop **4** cola, soda **5** brisk **7** bracing, soda pop **8** curative, salutary **10** refreshing **11** restorative, stimulating **12** exhilarating, invigorating
extract: **4** cola **9** berberine

tons
4 gobs, lots **5** heaps, loads, piles, reams, scads **6** oodles

tony
4 chic, posh **5** smart, swank, swish **6** classy, modish, uptown **7** à la mode, elegant, stylish **9** exclusive **11** fashionable

too
4 also, ever, over, very **5** along **6** as well, overly, unduly, withal **7** awfully, besides, further, greatly **8** likewise, moreover, overmuch **9** extremely, immensely **10** in addition, remarkably, strikingly **11** exceedingly, excessively, furthermore **12** additionally, exorbitantly, immoderately, inordinately **13** exceptionally

tool
4 pawn **5** means **6** puppet, rimmer, stooge **7** cat's-paw, hayfork, machine, rounder, utensil **8** picklock **9** appliance, implement, mechanism **10** instrument
axlike: **3** adz **4** adze
boring: **5** auger, drill
carving: **6** veiner
cleaving: **4** froe
cobbler's: **3** awl
cooper's: **3** adz **4** adze
cutting: **2** ax **3** adz, axe, saw **4** adze **5** edger, knife **6** shears **8** billhook
digging: **4** pick **5** spade **6** shovel **7** mattock
engraving: **5** burin
farm: **6** seeder
filing: **4** rasp **7** riffler
garden: **3** hoe **4** rake **5** spade **6** trowel, weeder
grasping: **6** pincer **7** tweezer **8** tweezers
mining: **3** gad **6** trepan
piercing: **3** awl
prehistoric: **6** eolith
pruning: **6** shears **9** secateurs
rubbing: **9** burnisher
scooping: **6** router
toothed: **3** saw **7** rippler
woodworking: **3** adz, saw **4** adze **5** bevel, plane **6** chisel, hammer

toot
3 bat, jag **4** bout, bust, honk, tear **5** binge, blast, drunk, snort, sound, souse, spree **6** bender **7** carouse

tooth
5 molar **7** incisor **8** bicuspid, premolar
combining form: 4 dent **5** denti, dento
cuspid: 6 canine **8** dogtooth, eyetooth
cutting: 10 carnassial
decay: 6 caries
doctor: 7 dentist
gear: 3 cog
horse: 4 tush
material: 4 pulp **6** dentin, enamel **8** cementum
pointed: 4 fang **6** canine, cuspid
small: 8 denticle

toothless
7 useless **8** edentate **10** edentulous **11** ineffective, ineffectual

toothsome
5 sapid, tasty **6** delish, savory **8** luscious, pleasant, pleasing, tasteful **9** agreeable, delicious, palatable, succulent **10** appetizing, attractive **11** scrumptious

too-too
6 la-di-da **7** extreme **8** affected, overdone, overmuch, precious **9** excessive **10** hoity-toity, inordinate **11** exaggerated, overrefined, pretentious

tootsie
3 pet **4** dear **5** honey, sugar **7** beloved, darling, sweetie **10** sweetheart, sweetie pie

top
3 cap, tip **4** acme, apex, best, cusp, head, peak, pick, roof **5** cream, crest, crown, elite, point, prime, prize **6** apical, choice, climax, height, summit, utmost, vertex **7** capital, highest, maximal, maximum, surface **8** five-star, loftiest, pinnacle, superior **9** first-rate, uppermost **10** first-class **11** culmination

tope
3 nip **4** soak **5** booze, drink, shark, stupa **6** guzzle, imbibe, tipple **7** swizzle **8** liquor up

toper
3 sot **4** lush, soak, wino **5** drunk, rummy, souse **6** bibber, boozer **7** tippler, tosspot **8** drunkard **9** inebriate **10** boozehound

Tophet
4 hell **5** hades, Sheol **6** blazes **7** Gehenna, inferno **9** perdition **10** underworld

topic
4 talk, text **5** issue, motif, point, score, theme **6** burden, matter, motive, thread **7** content, subject **8** argument **11** proposition

topical
5 local **7** current, nominal **8** regional **9** temporary **11** superficial

topmost
7 highest, leading, supreme **8** crowning, ultimate **9** paramount, principal **10** consummate, preeminent **11** culminating

top-notch
4 A-one **5** prime, primo **6** choice **7** capital **8** five-star, superior **9** excellent, first-rate **10** first-class **11** first-string

top off
3 cap **5** crown **6** climax, finish, refill **8** complete, conclude, resupply **9** culminate

topography
7 surface, terrain **8** features

topple
3 tip **4** drop, fall **5** crash, lurch, pitch, slump, upset **6** defeat, falter, plunge, totter, tumble **8** collapse, keel over, overturn **9** overthrow

tops
4 A-one, best **5** primo **6** at most **7** highest, supreme **8** peerless, superior **9** at the most, first-rate, matchless, nonpareil **11** outstanding

topsy-turvy
7 chaotic, jumbled, mixed-up **8** cockeyed, confused, inverted **10** disjointed, disordered, upside down

toque
3 cap, hat

tor
4 crag, hill, peak **5** butte, cliff, mound, talus

Torah
10 Pentateuch

torch
4 fire **5** flame, light **6** ignite **7** firebug **8** arsonist, flambeau, guidance **10** flashlight, incendiary

toreador
6 torero **7** matador **11** bullfighter

torero
see **toreador**

torment
3 rag, try, vex **4** bait, bane, hell, hurt, pain, pang, rack **5** abuse, agony, curse, grill, harry, tease, worry, wring **6** harass, harrow, heckle, misery, molest, needle, plague **7** afflict, agonize, anguish, bedevil, crucify, distort, hagride, torture, travail, trouble **8** distress **9** persecute, tantalize **10** affliction, excruciate

torn
4 rent **5** split **6** ragged, ripped, unsure **7** mangled **8** tattered, wrenched **9** lacerated, uncertain, undecided

tornado
6 funnel **7** cyclone, twister **9** windstorm, whirlwind

toro
4 bull

torpedo
3 gun, ray **4** mine, thug **5** blast, bravo, smash, wreck **6** gunman, gunsel, hit man, killer, weapon **7** destroy, nullify, scuttle **8** assassin, firework **9** explosive, shoot down **10** hatchet man, projectile, triggerman **11** electric ray

torpid
4 dull, lazy, numb **5** dopey, inert **6** sodden, stupid **7** dormant **8** comatose, inactive, sluggish **9** apathetic, lethargic **12** hebetudinous

torpor
4 coma, daze **5** swoon **6** apathy, stupor **7** languor **8** dopiness, dullness, hebetude, lethargy **9** lassitude, passivity, stolidity **10** stagnation **12** listlessness

torque
5 twist

torrent
4 rush **5** flood, spate **6** deluge, stream **7** cascade, Niagara **8** cataract, flooding **9** cataclysm **10** inundation, outpouring

torrid
3 hot **5** fiery **6** ardent, fervid, heated, red-hot, sultry **7** boiling, burning, flaming, parched **8** broiling, white-hot **9** scorching **10** hot-blooded, passionate, sweltering **11** impassioned

tort
5 crime, wrong **7** offense **10** wrongdoing

tortilla dish
4 taco **6** flauta **7** burrito, chalupa, tostada **9** enchilada **10** quesadilla **11** chimichanga

Tortilla Flat author
9 Steinbeck (John)

tortoise
6 turtle **8** terrapin **9** chelonian
beak: **3** neb
shell: **8** carapace

tortuous
5 snaky **6** cranky, tricky **7** crooked, devious, sinuous, winding **8** flexuous, indirect, involute, involved **9** meandrous **10** circuitous, convoluted, meandering, serpentine **11** anfractuous, vermiculate **12** labyrinthine

torture
4 pain, rack, warp **5** agony, wring **6** harrow, martyr **7** afflict, agonize, anguish, crucify, torment **9** martyrdom **10** excruciate **11** third degree

tortured
4 bent **6** racked, warped **7** twisted **8** deformed **9** distorted

tory
5 right **7** old-line **8** loyalist, old guard, orthodox, rightist, royalist **12** conservative

Tosca
character: **5** Mario (Cavaradossi) **7** Scarpia (Baron)
composer: **7** Puccini (Giacomo)

tosh
3 rot **4** bosh, bunk **5** bilge, hooey **6** bunkum, drivel, humbug **7** baloney, eyewash, hogwash, twaddle **8** malarkey, nonsense, tommyrot, trumpery

toss
4 cast, flap, flip, hurl, rock, roll **5** chuck, drink, fling, heave, match, pitch, quaff, sling, surge, throw, vomit **6** imbibe, tumble, welter, writhe **7** discard **9** knock back, throw away

tosspot
see **tippler**

tot
3 add, kid, nip, sum **4** dram, shot, slug, tike, tyke **5** child, snort **6** figure, infant, nipper, shaver, squirt **7** snifter, toddler

total
3 add, all, sum **4** foot, full **5** add up, equal, gross, run to, smash, sum to, utter, whole, wreck, yield **6** all-out, amount, entire, figure, number **7** crack up, destroy, overall, perfect, quantum **8** absolute, complete, demolish, entirety, outright, quantity **9** aggregate, full-blown, full-scale, inclusive, unlimited **10** consummate, unreserved **11** unmitigated **13** comprehensive, thoroughgoing

totalitarian
8 absolute, despotic **10** autocratic **11** dictatorial **13** authoritarian

totality
3 all, sum **4** lump **5** whole **7** oneness **8** entirety **9** aggregate, wholeness **12** completeness

totalize
3 add, sum **5** sum up **6** figure **7** summate

tote
3 lug **4** cart, haul, load, pack **5** carry, ferry, shlep, sum up **6** burden, convey, figure, schlep, shlepp **7** schlepp, summate **9** transport **10** pari-mutuel

totem
6 emblem, symbol

To the Lighthouse author
5 Woolf (Virginia)

totter
4 reel, sway **5** lurch, shake, waver **6** falter, toddle, topple, wobble **7** stagger

touch
3 dab, tad **4** abut, feel, meet, move, stir **5** brush, graze **6** adjoin, border, caress, finger, stroke **7** contact, palpate, smidgen **9** palpation, tactility

touchable
7 tactile **8** palpable, tangible

touch down
4 land **5** light, perch, roost **6** alight, settle

touched
3 odd, off **5** batty, crazy, moved **7** stirred **8** affected **9** emotional

touching
4 as to, in re **5** about, anent, as for **6** moving, tender **7** against, apropos, emotive, meeting, piteous, pitiful, tangent **8** abutting, adjacent, pathetic, pitiable, poignant, stirring **9** adjoining, affecting, apropos of, as regards, bordering, immediate, impinging, regarding **10** as respects, back-to-back, concerning, contiguous, respecting, tangential **11** coterminous **12** conterminous

touch off
5 erupt, spark, start **6** ignite, incite, kindle **7** explode, inflame, provoke, trigger **8** initiate **9** instigate **11** precipitate

touchstone
4 test **5** check, gauge, proof, trial **7** measure **8** standard **9** barometer, benchmark, criterion, yardstick

touch up
3 fix **5** patch **6** rework **7** improve, perfect

touchy
5 dicey, huffy, risky, testy **6** tender, tricky **7** peppery **8** delicate, ticklish **9** explosive, hazardous, irascible, irritable, sensitive **10** precarious **11** inflammable, quarrelsome, thin-skinned **13** oversensitive, temperamental, unpredictable

tough
3 mug **4** goon, hard, hood, lout, punk, thug **5** bully, hardy, harsh **6** rugged, severe, unruly **7** arduous, hoodlum, onerous, ruffian **8** bullyboy, hooligan, obdurate **9** arbitrary, demanding, difficult, effortful, hard-nosed, hidebound, laborious, resistant, roughneck, strenuous **10** hard-bitten, hard-boiled, hardheaded, refractory **11** unbreakable

toughen
5 inure **6** anneal, harden, season, temper **9** acclimate, habituate **10** strengthen **11** acclimatize

toughie
4 goon, hood, lout, punk, thug **5** poser, rowdy **7** hoodlum, ruffian, stumper **8** bullyboy, hooligan, plug-ugly **9** roughneck

toupee
3 rug, wig **6** peruke, wiglet **7** periwig **8** postiche **9** hairpiece

tour
4 bout, trip, turn **5** jaunt, round, shift, spell, stint **6** junket, period, travel, troupe **7** circuit, journey **8** progress **9** barnstorm, excursion **10** expedition, rubberneck

tour de force
4 deed, feat **7** classic, display, exploit **10** magnum opus, masterwork **11** achievement, chef d'oeuvre, masterpiece

Tour de France winner
4 Riis (Bjarne) **5** Roche (Stephen) **6** Fignon (Laurent), Landis (Floyd), LeMond (Greg) **7** Delgado (Pedro), Hinault (Bernard), Pantani (Marco), Ullrich (Jan) **8** Induráin (Miguel) **9** Armstrong (Lance)

tour guide
8 cicerone

tourist
7 tripper, visitor **8** traveler **9** sightseer, traveller **10** day-tripper, rubberneck, vacationer **12** excursionist, globe-trotter

tournament
4 meet, open, tilt **5** pro-am **6** jousts, series **7** contest, tourney **8** carousel **10** round-robin **11** competition **12** championship

tourney
4 meet **5** event, games, match **7** compete, contest **8** concours **11** competition

tousle
4 mess, muss **6** rumple **8** dishevel, disorder

tout
3 spy, tip **4** brag, hype, laud, plug **5** watch **6** blow up, peddle, praise, talk up **7** acclaim, crack up, promote, solicit **8** ballyhoo, persuade, proclaim **9** publicize

tovarich
7 comrade

tow
3 lug, tug **4** drag, draw, haul, pull, rope, yarn **5** chain, trail **6** hawser
truck: **7** wrecker

towel word
3 his **4** hers

tower
4 loom **5** spire **6** turret **8** overlook
biblical: **4** Edar **5** Babel
on a mosque: **7** minaret

towering
4 high, tall **5** grand, lofty **6** aerial **7** soaring **8** imposing, majestic **9** excessive, grandiose **10** monumental, prodigious **11** magnificent, skyscraping **12** altitudinous, overwhelming

towhee
5 finch **7** chewink

to wit
3 viz **6** namely, that is **8** scilicet **9** c'est-à-dire, videlicet

town
4 burg 6 hamlet, podunk 7 borough, village
medieval: 5 bourg

town and ___
4 gown 7 country

townsman
7 burgher, citizen

town square
5 plaza
Italian: 6 piazza

toxic
6 poison 7 harmful, noxious 8 venomous, virulent 9 poisonous 10 infectious

toxin
5 venom 6 poison

toy
3 top 4 fool, play, yo-yo 5 antic, curio, dally, flirt, knack, mouse, tease 6 bauble, caress, coquet, diddle, fiddle, gewgaw, puzzle, rattle, Slinky, trifle 7 bibelot, Frisbee, foot bag, novelty, pastime, trinket, whatnot 8 gimcrack 9 plaything, pogo stick 10 diminutive, Erector Set, knickknack, Silly Putty, sock monkey, Spirograph, View-Master 11 jumping jack 12 kaleidoscope

trace
3 jot, ray, run, tug 4 blip, echo, hint, iota, mark, path, scan, wisp 5 relic, shade, spoor, tinge, trail, tread 6 derive, detect, nuance, shadow, strain, streak 7 outline, remains, remnant, run down, soupçon, symptom, vestige 8 discover, tincture, traverse 9 delineate, footprint, remainder, scintilla, suspicion 10 intimation, suggestion

trachea
6 larynx, throat, vessel 7 weasand 8 throttle, windpipe

track
3 way 4 drag, oval, path, rail, road, sign, slot, step, tail 5 chase, cover, print, spoor, trace, trail, tread 6 artery, follow, pursue, shadow, travel 7 footway, imprint, monitor, pathway, vestige 8 footpath, footstep 9 footprint 10 racecourse
cycle: 9 velodrome

track-and-field event
4 dash 5 relay 6 discus 7 javelin, hurdles, shot put 8 footrace, high jump, long jump 9 broad jump, decathlon, pole vault 10 heptathlon, triple jump 11 discus throw 12 steeplechase

track star
3 Coe (Sebastian) 4 Nool (Erki) 5 Flo-Jo, Jones (Marion), Lewis (Carl), Moses (Edwin), Nurmi (Paavo), Ovett (Steve), Owens (Jesse), Pérec (Marie-José), Viren (Lasse) 6 Beamon (Bob), Devers (Gail), Jenner (Bruce), O'Brien (Dan), Oerter (Al), Sebrie (Roman), Toomey (Bill) 7 Johnson (Michael, Rafer), Mathias (Bob), Rudolph (Wilma), Shorter (Frank), Zátopek (Emil) 8 Thompson (Daley), Zaharias (Babe Didrikson) 9 Bannister (Roger), Didrikson (Babe) 12 Joyner-Kersee (Jackie)

tract
3 lot 4 area, belt, farm, land, plat, plot, zone 5 block, claim 6 parcel, region 7 leaflet, portion, terrain 8 pamphlet, preserve 9 territory

tractable
4 tame 6 docile, gentle, pliant 7 ductile, plastic, pliable 8 amenable, biddable, flexible, obedient, workable 9 adaptable, breakable, malleable 10 manageable

tractate
5 summa 6 memoir, thesis 7 pandect 8 hornbook, monument, treatise 9 discourse, monograph 10 commentary 12 disquisition, dissertation, introduction

traction
4 drag, pull 5 force 7 drawing, tension 8 friction

tractor maker
4 Case 5 Deere (John) 6 Kubota 7 Farmall

trade
4 deal, sell, swap 5 craft, truck 6 barter, change, custom, market, métier, peddle, switch 7 bargain, calling, pursuit, traffic 8 business, commerce, exchange, industry, vocation 10 employment, occupation, profession, substitute 11 merchandise, transaction
illicit: 11 black market

trademark
3 tag 4 logo 5 brand, label, stamp 6 patent, symbol 8 colophon, logotype 9 brand name

trader
4 ship 6 broker, dealer, vendor 8 merchant

trade route
7 sea-lane

trade show
4 expo 10 exhibition, exposition

tradition
4 lore, myth 5 habit 6 belief, custom, legacy, legend, mythos, rubric 7 folkway 8 folklore, heredity, heritage, practice 9 mythology 10 convention 12 old wives' tale

traditional
4 oral 5 usual 6 common, spoken, verbal 7 classic, old-line, popular 8 habitual, orthodox 9 classical, customary, old-school, unwritten 10 button-down 11 established 12 acknowledged, buttoned-down, conservative, conventional

traditionalist
6 purist 12 conservative

traditionalistic
4 tory 7 die-hard, old-line 8 orthodox, standpat 12 conservative

traduce
4 slur 5 libel, smear, wrong 6 betray, breach, defame, malign, vilify 7 asperse, slander, violate 8 disgrace, tear down 9 denigrate 10 calumniate

Trafalgar commander
6 Nelson (Horatio)

traffic
4 deal 5 cargo, fence, trade, truck 6 barter, custom 7 bootleg, freight 8 commerce, dealings, exchange, movement 9 patronage, transport 11 black-market
circle: 6 rotary 10 roundabout
cone: 5 pylon
jam: 5 tie-up 6 holdup 8 blockage, gridlock 10 bottleneck

trafficker
6 dealer, trader

tragedy
3 woe 6 mishap, plague 8 calamity, disaster 9 cataclysm, mischance 10 misfortune 11 catastrophe 12 misadventure

trail
3 dog, lag, tag 4 drag, flag, path, plod, poke 5 chase, dally, delay, tarry, trace, track 6 dawdle, follow, linger, pursue, shadow 7 draggle, gumshoe, pathway, traipse 8 footpath, footwalk 10 bridle path
emigrant: 6 Oregon
Florida: 7 Tamiami
Georgia-Maine: 11 Appalachian
Indian: 5 Great

trailer
5 truck 7 preview 9 motor home, transport 10 mobile home

trailer truck
4 semi

train
2 el 3 row 4 file, tame 5 coach, drill, teach, track 6 column, convoy, course, school, sequel, series, thread 7 caravan, cortege, educate, prepare, retinue 8 exercise, instruct, sequence 9 cultivate, entourage, following, habituate 10 succession 11 progression

trainee
4 tiro, tyro 6 novice 7 learner 8 beginner, neophyte 10 apprentice

training
7 tuition 8 teaching, tutelage 9 education, schooling 11 instruction
horse: 6 manège

traipse
3 gad 4 hoof, pace, roam, rove, step, walk 5 amble, range, trail, tramp, tread 6 ramble, stroll, wander 7 maunder, meander 8 ambulate 9 gallivant

trait
4 mark 5 point, quirk, touch, trace 6 oddity, stroke 7 feature, quality 8 hallmark, property, specific 9 attribute

traitor
3 rat 5 Judas 8 apostate, betrayer, defector, deserter, quisling, renegade, turncoat 9 turnabout

traitorous
5 Punic 8 apostate, disloyal, mutinous, recreant, renegade 9 faithless 10 perfidious, rebellious, unfaithful 11 treacherous

traject
4 beam, pass, pipe, send 5 carry 6 convey, render 7 conduct, forward, impress 8 hand down, transfer, transmit 9 broadcast, transfuse

trajectory
3 arc 4 path 5 curve 11 progression

tram
3 car 7 trolley 9 streetcar

trammel
3 tie 4 bind, curb 5 check, gauge, leash 6 fetter, hamper, hobble 7 compass, confine, ensnare, manacle, pothook, shackle 8 entangle, handcuff 9 restraint

tramontane
8 outsider 9 foreigner, outlander 11 transalpine

tramp
3 bum 4 hike, hobo, jade, plod, slog, thud 5 bimbo, caird, clump, gipsy, gypsy, march, stamp, stiff, stomp, tread 6 ramble, stroll, travel, trudge, wander 7 chippie, drifter, floater, saunter, traipse, vagrant 8 clochard, derelict, footslog, homeless, stroller, vagabond, wanderer 10 prostitute

trample
4 mash 5 crush, pound, stamp, stomp, tread, tromp

trance
4 daze, muse 5 swoon 7 ecstasy, rapture, reverie 8 hypnosis 9 catalepsy, enrapture 10 absorption, brown study 11 abstraction

tranquil
4 calm, easy 5 quiet, still 6 dreamy, placid, poised, serene 7 restful 8 composed, peaceful 10 untroubled 13 self-possessed

tranquilize
4 calm, hush, lull 5 quiet, relax, still 6 becalm, pacify, sedate, settle, soothe, subdue 7 compose, mollify

tranquilizer
6 downer 8 diazepam, pacifier, sedative 10 depressant 11 barbiturate

tranquillity
4 calm **5** peace, quiet **8** calmness, serenity **9** composure, placidity

transaction
4 deal **5** trade **7** bargain, dealing **8** contract, covenant **9** agreement

transcend
3 top **4** beat, best **5** excel, outdo **6** better, exceed **7** surpass **8** outshine, outstrip, overcome, surmount

transcendent
5 ideal **7** perfect, sublime, supreme **8** abstract, immanent **10** consummate, surpassing

Transcendentalist
6 Alcott (Bronson), Fuller (Margaret) **7** Emerson (Ralph Waldo), Thoreau (Henry David)

transcribe
4 copy **5** write **6** record **8** transfer **9** translate, write down **13** transliterate

transfer
4 cede, deed, hand, pass, ship **5** carry, grant, shift **6** assign, convey, remove, supply **7** consign, convert, deliver, devolve, dispose **8** alienate, hand over, make over, relocate, turn over **9** carry over **10** assignment, conveyance **11** disposition

transfix
4 spit **5** lance, spear, spike, stick **6** impale, skewer **7** spindle **8** entrance **9** fascinate, hypnotize, mesmerize

transform
5 alter, morph **6** change, mutate **7** commute, convert **12** metamorphose

transformation
8 reaction **10** changeover, conversion **13** metamorphosis

transfuse
5 endue, imbue **7** pervade, suffuse, traject **8** permeate, saturate **9** penetrate, percolate **10** impregnate

transgress
3 err, sin **6** breach, exceed, offend **7** violate **8** infringe, overpass, overstep, trespass **10** contravene

transgression
3 sin **5** crime, error, wrong **6** breach **7** misdeed, offense **9** violation **12** infringement

transient
4 hobo **5** brief, tramp **7** drifter, migrant, passing **8** fleeting, flitting, fugitive, volatile **9** ephemeral, fugacious, momentary, temporary **10** evanescent, fly-by-night, short-lived **11** impermanent

transit
7 passage **8** traverse **10** conveyance

transition
4 leap **5** segue, shift **6** change **7** passage **10** conversion **13** metamorphosis

transitory
see **transient**

translate
6 render **7** convert **9** interpret, reproduce **10** paraphrase

translation
9 rendition **10** conversion, paraphrase

transmarine
7 oversea **8** overseas

transmission
7 gearbox **8** handover **9** broadcast, infection

transmit
3 air **4** beam, hand, pass, pipe, send **6** convey, hand on, impart, pass on, render, signal **7** channel, conduct, consign, diffuse, forward, traject **8** bequeath, dispatch, hand down **9** broadcast

transmogrify
see **transform**

transmute
see **transform**

transoceanic message
4 wire **5** cable **9** cablegram

transparent
5 clear, filmy, gauzy, sheer **6** limpid **7** crystal **8** clear-cut, gossamer, pellucid **10** diaphanous, see-through **11** crystalline

transpire
3 hap **4** leak **5** exude, occur, sweat **6** chance, emerge, happen **7** develop **9** come about, take place **11** come to light

transplant
8 relocate, resettle

transport
3 bus, fly, lag, lug, wow, zap, zip **4** haul, hump, lift, pack, pass, send, ship, taxi, tote **5** carry, ferry, motor, truck **6** convey, excite, ravish, remove, thrill **7** delight, ecstasy, freight, rapture, sealift, trundle, vehicle **8** carriage, displace, railroad, rhapsody **9** carry away, chauffeur, troopship **10** conveyance, helicopter

transportation
6 moving **7** freight, hauling, removal, vehicle **8** carriage, carrying **10** conveyance **12** displacement

transpose
6 invert **7** convert, permute, reorder, reverse **9** rearrange **11** interchange

transude
4 ooze, reek, seep, weep **5** bleed, sweat **7** diffuse, give off **8** permeate **9** transfuse

transverse
5 cross **6** across, lintel, thwart **7** transom **8** crossbar, crossing **9** crossbeam, crosswise **10** crosspiece

trap
3 bag, net **4** bait, snag **5** catch, decoy, set up, snare **6** ambush, enmesh, tangle **7** ensnare, pitfall **8** birdlime, deadfall, entangle, quagmire **9** ambuscade

trappings
4 gear **5** dress **6** finery **8** equipage, ornament **9** adornment, caparison, equipment **10** decoration **11** habiliments **13** accouterments, accoutrements, embellishment, paraphernalia

Trappist
4 monk
writer: 6 Merton (Thomas)

trash
3 rag, rot **4** bosh, bunk, junk, ruin, scum, slop **5** bilge, blast, dreck, dregs, hokum, offal, spoil, tripe, waste, wreck **6** bunkum, debris, insult, litter, refuse, rubble **7** clutter, destroy, garbage, hogwash, put down, rubbish **8** claptrap, malarkey, nonsense, tommyrot **9** disparage, poppycock, throw away, vandalize **10** balderdash **11** guttersnipe, proletariat

trash can
7 dustbin

trashy
5 bawdy, cheap, tatty **6** cruddy, shoddy, sleazy, smutty, vulgar **8** rubbishy **9** third-rate

trauma
4 blow, pain **5** shock, upset, wound **6** crisis, injury, stress **8** collapse **9** suffering

travail
4 grub, moil, task, toil, work **5** grind, labor, pains **6** drudge, effort **7** slavery, torment **8** drudgery, struggle

travel
4 fare, pass, roam, tour, trek, trip, wend **5** jaunt, range, tramp **6** junket, push on, voyage **7** explore, journey, passage, proceed, traffic, transit **8** movement, traverse **9** gallivant **10** hit the road
term: 3 ETA **4** fare **9** all aboard

traveler
5 gipsy, gypsy, nomad, rover **7** drummer, tourist **8** runabout, runagate, salesman, vagabond **9** itinerant, sightseer **10** journeyman **11** peripatetic **12** rolling stone

traveling library
10 bookmobile

traverse
4 ride, span, walk **5** cover, cross, march, route, trace, track **6** course, thwart, travel, voyage **7** examine, transit **8** crossing, navigate, obstacle, pass over **9** adversity **10** crisscross, pass across **11** perambulate, peregrinate

travesty
3 ape **4** mock, sham **5** farce, mimic, spoof **6** parody **7** imitate, lampoon, mimicry, mockery, take off **8** ridicule **9** burlesque **10** caricature, distortion
satanic: 9 Black Mass

Traviata, La
character: 7 Alfredo (Germont), Germont **8** Violetta (Valéry)
composer: 5 Verdi (Giuseppe)

trawl
3 net **4** fish **7** setline

tray
6 salver, server **7** platter **8** teaboard
revolving: 9 lazy Susan

treacherous
5 false, Punic, risky **6** chancy, tricky **7** unsound **8** disloyal, perilous, recreant **9** dangerous, deceptive, faithless, hazardous, insidious **10** perfidious, traitorous, unfaithful, unreliable

treachery
7 perfidy, treason **8** bad faith, betrayal **9** duplicity **10** disloyalty, infidelity **11** double-cross **13** dastardliness, double-dealing, faithlessness

treacle
4 mush **5** slush, syrup **6** bathos **8** molasses, schmaltz **11** golden syrup

tread
4 hoof, pace, plod, step, walk **5** dance, march, stamp, stomp, trace, track, tramp, tromp, troop **6** follow, stride **7** footing, traipse, trample **8** footstep

treadle
5 lever, pedal

treadmill
3 rut **4** rote **5** chore, grind **6** groove **7** routine **8** drudgery, turnspit

treason
7 perfidy **8** betrayal, sedition **9** treachery **10** disloyalty, misprision **11** lèse-majesté

treasure
4 haul, save **5** adore, cache, hoard, pearl, prize, trove, value **6** esteem, revere, riches, wealth **7** apprize, cherish, idolize, worship **8** conserve, preserve, venerate **9** reverence **10** appreciate

Treasure Island
author: 9 Stevenson (Robert Louis)
character: 7 Ben Gunn **8** Long John (Silver)
narrator: 10 Jim Hawkins

treasurer
6 bursar, purser **7** curator **8** receiver **11** chamberlain

Treasure State
7 Montana

treasure trove
4 find, mine 7 bonanza, pay dirt 8 El Dorado, Golconda, gold mine

treasury
4 fisc, mine 5 cache, chest, hoard 6 argosy, coffer, museum 7 bonanza, gallery, omnibus 8 archives, El Dorado, Golconda, gold mine, war chest 9 anthology, exchequer 10 depositary, depository, repository, storehouse

treat
5 goody, nurse 6 bonbon, dainty, doctor, goodie, handle, manage, morsel, tidbit 7 care for 8 deal with, delicacy, medicate 10 minister to
animals: 3 vet
leather: 3 tan, taw 7 tanning

treatise
6 thesis 8 tractate 9 discourse, monograph 10 exposition 12 disquisition, dissertation

treatment
4 care 7 therapy

treaty
4 pact 6 accord 7 charter, compact, concord 8 alliance, contract, covenant 9 agreement, concordat 10 convention

treble
4 high 6 shrill, triple 7 descant, soprano 9 threefold 11 high-pitched

tree
3 apa, ash, box, dao, dar, elm, eng, fir, koa, kou, lin, oak, sal, ule, yew 4 ague, atle, copa, dhak, kaki, lime, linn, mora, neem, pine, poon, tawa, teak, teil, titi, tung, upas, wych 5 aalii, abele, alamo, alder, athel, beech, birch, carob, cedar, ebony, holly, larch, lemon, maire, maple, osier, pipal, roble, rowan, sauch, saugh, sumac, taxus, yulan 6 arbute, banyan, cherry, cornel, deodar, ginkgo, kamala, linden, loquat, lychee, mallee, medlar, mimosa, myrtle, orange, poplar, redbud, sapota, spruce, tan oak, tupelo 7 arariba, arbutus, camphor, conifer, cypress, deodara, dogwood, hemlock, inkwood, juniper, kumquat, lentisk, madrona, madrone, murmast, redwood, sequoia, seringa, wallaba, zelkova 8 basswood, bergamot, black gum, bluejack, cinchona, corkwood, laburnum, loblolly, longleaf, magnolia, mahogany, sourwood, sweetgum, sycamine, sycamore, tamarisk 9 balsam fir, sassafras 10 candlewood, chinaberry, chinquapin 11 bald cypress 12 balm of Gilead, rhododendron
African: 4 akee, cola, shea 5 limba, sassy 6 baobab 7 avodire, bubinga 8 sasswood 9 berberine
Australian: 4 toon, yate 5 wilga 7 blue gum 8 lacewood, quandong 9 casuarina 10 eucalyptus 11 bottlebrush
branch: 5 bough
combining form: 3 dry 4 dryo 5 arbor, dendr 6 arbori, dendra (plural), dendro
genus: 4 Acer, Cola, Maba, Olea, Para 5 Abies 11 Callistemon
palm: 4 coco, nipa 5 ratan 6 pinang, raffia, rattan 7 coquito 8 carnauba
tropical: 3 ake, ama 4 akee, copa, dita, ohia, palm, pili, sago, teak, upas, yaya 5 areca, assai, balsa, cacao, ceiba, cycad, lehua, mamey 6 acajou, balata, baobab, bataan, citrus 7 genipap, logwood, majagua, palmyra, quassia, soursop 8 allspice, barbasco, mahogany, mangrove, milkwood, palmetto, rosewood, soapbark, sweetsop, tamarind 9 candlenut, jacaranda, sapodilla 10 breadfruit, calamondin, manchineel 11 candleberry, coconut palm
trunk: 4 bole
young: 7 sapling

trefoil
4 leaf 6 clover 8 ornament
part: 3 arc

trek
4 hike, trip 6 travel, trudge 7 journey 9 migration 10 expedition

trellis
5 arbor 6 screen 7 lattice, pergola 8 espalier 11 latticework

tremble
5 quake, shake 6 dither, quaver, quiver, shiver 7 shudder, twitter, vibrate

tremblor
see **temblor**

tremendous
4 huge, vast 6 mighty 7 awesome, immense, massive, titanic 8 colossal, enormous, fearsome, gigantic, terrific, towering 9 fantastic, monstrous 10 formidable, gargantuan, incredible, monumental, prodigious, stupendous 13 extraordinary

tremolo
7 vibrato

tremor
5 quake, shake, shock 6 quaver, quiver, shiver 7 shudder, temblor 10 earthquake
muscular: 8 dystaxia

tremulous
5 shaky, timid 6 afraid 7 aquiver, fearful, quaking, shivery 8 timorous 9 quivering, shivering

trench
4 sink 5 ditch, fosse, gully, verge 6 border, furrow, trough
Caribbean: 6 Cayman
Pacific: 7 Mariana

trenchant
4 acid, keen **5** acerb, crisp, sharp **6** biting **7** acerbic, caustic, cutting, mordant, probing, satiric **8** clear-cut, distinct, incisive, sardonic, scathing **9** sarcastic **11** penetrating

trencher
4 tray **7** platter

trencherman
5 eater **7** glutton **8** gourmand

trend
3 fad, run **4** flow, mode **5** curve, drift, shift, style, swing, tenor, vogue **6** course, temper **7** current, fashion, incline **8** approach, movement, tendency **9** direction

trendy
3 hep, hip, hot **4** cool, tony **5** faddy **6** groovy, modish, with-it **7** à la mode, faddish, stylish **8** downtown, nouvelle, up-to-date **11** fashionable, ultramodern

trepang
10 bêche-de-mer **11** sea cucumber

trepidation
4 fear **5** alarm, dread **6** dismay **7** anxiety **12** apprehension **13** consternation

trespass
3 err, sin **4** debt **5** lapse, poach **6** breach, invade, offend **7** impinge, intrude **8** encroach, entrench, infringe **9** interlope, violation **10** infraction, transgress **12** encroachment, infringement **13** transgression

tress
4 curl, lock **5** braid, plait

trestle
4 buck **5** frame **6** bridge **7** sawbuck, support **8** sawhorse **9** framework

trey
5 three

triad
4 trio **5** chord **6** triple, troika **7** harmony, trinity **9** threesome **11** triumvirate

trial
3 woe **4** care, test **5** cross, essay, rigor, worry **6** dry run, hassle, misery, ordeal, sorrow, tryput **7** anguish, attempt, contest, trouble **8** crucible, distress, endeavor, gauntlet, hardship, struggle, vexation **9** adversity, rehearsal, suffering **10** affliction, coup d'essai, difficulty, experiment, misfortune, proceeding, temptation **11** preliminary, tribulation **12** experimental

trial balloon
6 feeler, tryout

trial run
4 test **5** essay **7** break-in **10** experiment

triangle type
5 acute, right **6** obtuse **7** scalene **9** isosceles **11** equilateral

tribal unit
6 moiety **7** phratry

tribe
4 clan, folk, race **5** house, phyle, stock **6** family **7** kindred, lineage

tribulation
3 woe **5** cross, trial **6** burden, ordeal **9** adversity **10** affliction, oppression, visitation **11** persecution

tribunal
3 bar **4** dais, rota **5** bench, court **8** platform **10** consistory **12** court of honor

tributary
5 bayou, creek **6** branch, feeder, stream **7** subject **8** affluent, influent **9** backwater, confluent, dependent, satellite **12** contributory

tribute
5 paean, toast **6** eulogy, homage **8** citation, encomium **9** panegyric **10** salutation **11** recognition, testimonial **12** appreciation

trice
4 lash, wink **5** blink, flash, jiffy, shake **6** moment, second, secure **7** instant **8** eyeblink **9** twinkling **11** split second

trick
3 jig **4** bilk, dido, dupe, fool, gull, hoax, hose, lark, play, ploy, ruse, scam, sham **5** antic, caper, dodge, feint, fraud, prank, stunt **6** gambit, outwit, scheme **7** chicane, finagle, gimmick, sleight **8** escapade, flimflam, hoodwink **9** bamboozle, deception, stratagem, victimize **10** red herring, shenanigan, tomfoolery **11** hornswoggle, monkeyshine **13** practical joke

trickery
4 scam, wile **5** cheat, fraud **6** deceit **7** chicane, dodgery **8** jugglery **9** chicanery, deception **10** subterfuge **11** double cross **13** double-dealing, jiggery-pokery, sharp practice

trickle
4 drip, seep **5** creep, trill **7** dribble

trickster
5 cheat, shark **6** con man **7** cheater, diddler, grifter, sharper **8** conjurer, deceiver, magician, swindler **9** defrauder **11** flimflammer, illusionist **12** double-dealer

tricksy
5 rough **6** trying **7** arduous **8** prankish

tricky
3 sly **4** foxy, wily **5** dodgy **6** catchy, clever, crafty, shifty, sticky, thorny, touchy, trying **7** cunning, knavish **8** delusive, guileful, slippery, ticklish, tortuous, unstable **9** deceptive, difficult, dishonest, ingenious, intricate **10** misleading, nettlesome, precarious, unreliable **11** complicated, treacherous, troublesome **12** undependable

trident
5 spear

tried
6 proved, proven, secure, tested, trusty 7 staunch 8 approved, faithful, reliable, stalwart, true-blue 9 certified, steadfast 10 dependable 11 trust-worthy

tried and true
5 loyal 6 proven, secure, steady, tested, trusty 8 faithful, reliable, stalwart 9 steadfast 10 dependable 11 trustworthy

trifle
3 bob, fig, pin, toy 4 doit, fool, mess, play 5 curio, dally, flirt, sport, waste 6 bauble, coquet, diddle, doodle, fiddle, fidget, footle, frivol, gewgaw, monkey, niggle 7 bibelot, conceit, fribble, fritter, novelty, trinket, twiddle, whatnot 8 folderol, gimcrack, kickshaw, nonsense, squander 9 bagatelle, cream puff, dalliance 10 knick-knack, triviality 11 small change

trifling
4 tiny 5 petty 6 measly, paltry, piddly, slight 7 trivial 8 niggling, nugatory, picayune, piddling, piffling 9 frivolous, worthless 10 negligible 11 Mickey Mouse, unimportant 13 insignificant

trifolium
6 clover 8 shamrock

trig
4 chic, neat, prim, snug, tidy, trim 5 sharp, smart, swank, trick 6 classy, modish, snappy 7 chipper, dashing, orderly, precise, stylish 9 shipshape

trigger
4 fire 5 cause, spark, start 6 ignite, kindle, set off 7 actuate, release 8 activate, initiate, touch off

triggerman
3 gun 5 bravo 6 gunsel, killer 7 torpedo 8 assassin 9 cutthroat, pistolero

trigonometric function
see at **function**

trill
4 burr, drop, roll 5 chirr, shake, twirl 6 quaver, warble 7 dribble, revolve, trickle, twitter, vibrato

trillion combining form
4 tera, treg 5 trega

trillionth combining form
4 pico

trim
3 cut, fit 4 buff, clip, crop, deck, neat, pare, snug, tidy, trig 5 adorn, order, prune, shape, shave, shear, skive, toned 6 barber, dapper, fettle, kilter, repair, spruce 7 chipper, dress up, garnish, orderly, shapely 8 clean-cut, decorate, manicure 9 shipshape 11 spic-and-span, streamlined, well-groomed 12 spick-and-span
a tree: 5 prune 7 pollard

Trinidad and Tobago
capital: 11 Port of Spain
monetary unit: 6 dollar
sea: 9 Caribbean

trinity
see **triad**

trinket
3 toy 5 curio, jewel 6 bauble, doodad, gewgaw, trifle 7 bibelot, novelty, whatnot 8 gimcrack, kickshaw 9 bagatelle, plaything, tchotchke 10 knickknack

trinkets
10 bijouterie

trio of goddesses
5 Fates 6 Furies, Graces

trip
3 hop, run 4 fall, ride, skip, slip, step, tour, trek 5 boner, caper, dance, error, lapse 6 bungle, junket, outing, sashay, travel, tumble, voyage 7 blooper, blunder, journey, mistake, misstep, stumble 9 excursion 10 expedition

tripe
4 guts 5 bilge, trash 6 menudo, waffle, viscus 7 innards, viscera (plural) 8 entrails, stuffing 9 internals

triple
4 trio 5 triad, trine 6 treble, triune, troika 7 triform, trilogy, trinity 8 trifecta 9 threefold, threesome 11 three-bagger, triumvirate

Triple Crown winner
1919: 9 Sir Barton
1930: 10 Gallant Fox
1935: 5 Omaha
1937: 10 War Admiral
1941: 9 Whirlaway
1943: 10 Count Fleet
1946: 7 Assault
1948: 8 Citation
1973: 11 Secretariat
1977: 11 Seattle Slew
1978: 8 Affirmed

Triple Crown site
7 Pimlico 11 Belmont Park 14 Churchill Downs

tripped out
4 high 5 doped 6 stoned, zonked 7 drugged 8 hopped-up, turned on, wiped out 9 spaced-out 10 freaked-out

Tristan's beloved
6 Iseult, Isolde

Tristan und Isolde composer
6 Wagner (Richard)

triste
3 sad 5 sorry 7 doleful, pensive, wistful 8 mournful 9 depressed, sorrowful 10 melan-choly 11 melancholic

Tristram Shandy author
6 Sterne (Laurence)

trite
3 pat, set **4** dull, flat, hack **5** banal, corny, musty, slick, stale, stock, tired, vapid **6** cliché, jejune, old-hat **7** prosaic, worn-out **8** bathetic, bromidic, flyblown, ordinary, shopworn, time-worn, well-worn **9** hackneyed **10** threadbare **11** commonplace, stereotyped **13** platitudinous, stereotypical

triton
5 conch **7** mollusc, mollusk **9** shellfish

Triton
6 merman
attribute: 5 conch
father: 7 Neptune **8** Poseidon
mother: 10 Amphitrite

triturate
4 bray **5** crush, grind **6** powder **9** comminute, pulverize

triumph
3 joy, win **4** crow, palm **5** exult, glory, vaunt **6** master **7** conquer, prevail, succeed, success, victory **8** conquest, overcome, surmount **10** exultation, jubilation

triumphant
8 exultant, exulting, jubilant **10** conquering, victorious

triumvirate
see **triad**

Triumvirate member
6 Antony (Marc), Caesar (Julius), Pompey (the Great) **7** Anthony (Mark), Crassus (Marcus Licinius), Lepidus (Marcus Aemilius) **8** Octavius (Gaius)

trivet
4 rack **5** stand **6** tripod

trivia
8 factoids, minutiae **9** small beer **11** small change **13** small potatoes

trivial
5 dinky, light, minor, petty, small **6** casual, measly, paltry, piddly, slight **8** nugatory, picayune, piddling, piffling, trifling **9** small-beer **10** negligible **11** Mickey Mouse, unimportant **13** insignificant

troche
6 tablet **7** lozenge **8** pastille **9** cough drop

troglodyte
6 hermit **7** caveman, recluse **11** cave dweller

Troilus
beloved: 8 Cressida, Criseyde
father: 5 Priam
mother: 6 Hecuba
slayer: 8 Achilles

Trojan
horse builder: 5 Epeus **6** Epeius
king: 5 Priam
priest: 7 Laocoön
queen: 6 Hecuba
soothsayer: 7 Helenus **9** Cassandra
warrior: 5 Paris **6** Aeneas, Agenor, Hector **7** Glaucus **8** Sarpedon **9** Euphorbus, Polydamas

Trojan Horse builder
5 Epeus **6** Epeius

troll
4 fish, lure, sing, spin **5** angle, dwarf, prowl **6** goblin, search

trolley
3 car **4** cart, tram **8** carriage **9** streetcar

Trollope novel
10 Claverings (The) **11** Ayala's Angel, Phineas Finn **12** Phineas Redux **12** Way We Live Now (The) **15** Eustace Diamonds (The) **16** Barchester Towers

trombone
7 sackbut

tromp
4 beat, drub, hike, pelt, slog, walk, whup **5** pound, stamp, stomp, stump, tread **6** batter, buffet, pummel, thrash, trudge, wallop **7** belabor, clobber, trample **8** lambaste

troop
4 army, band, crew, host, pace, step, walk **5** corps, crowd, flock, tread **6** legion, outfit **7** brigade, company, soldier, traipse **8** assembly **9** associate, battalion, gathering, multitude **10** collection

trooper
3 cop **5** actor, horse **7** soldier **9** policeman **10** cavalryman

trope
6 cliché, simile **8** metaphor, metonymy **10** synecdoche

Trophonius
brother: 8 Agamedes
temple site: 6 Delphi

trophy
3 cup **5** award, prize, relic, scalp, token **6** spoils **7** memento **8** hardware, keepsake, memorial, reminder, souvenir **9** loving cup **11** remembrance

tropical
3 hot **4** lush, warm **5** balmy, humid **6** jungly, steamy, sultry, torrid **10** equatorial

tropical storm
see **typhoon**

Tropic of Cancer author
6 Miller (Henry)

Tros' son
4 Ilus 8 Ganymede

trot
3 jog 4 gait, lope, pony, rack 5 amble, hurry 7 setline 11 translation

troth
6 commit, engage, pledge 7 loyalty 8 affiance, contract, espousal, fidelity 10 engagement 12 faithfulness

trot out
4 show 6 expose, parade 7 display, disport, exhibit, show off

Trotsky, Leon
associate: 5 Lenin (Vladimir)
rival: 6 Stalin (Joseph)

troubadour
4 bard, poet 6 singer 8 jongleur, minstrel, musician 9 balladist 10 folksinger

trouble
3 ado, ail, ill, irk, vex, woe 4 care, pain 5 annoy, beset, Dutch, grief, harry, haunt, pains, trial, upset, worry 6 bother, effort, harass, kiaugh, misery, pester, plague, ruffle, strain, stress, unrest 7 afflict, agitate, ailment, bedevil, concern, disturb, oppress, perturb, torment 8 aggrieve, disquiet, distress, hardship, hot water, irritate, vexation 9 suffering 10 difficulty, disconcert 11 disturbance, predicament

troubled
6 uneasy 7 anxious, worried 9 concerned, disturbed 10 distressed

troublemaker
7 hellion 8 agitator 9 firebrand 10 instigator 11 provocateur 12 rabble-rouser

troublesome
5 pesky 6 thorny, tricky, trying, vexing 7 carking, onerous, prickly 8 annoying 9 difficult, upsetting, vexatious 10 bothersome, burdensome, cumbersome, disturbing 11 disquieting, importunate, pestiferous

troublous
5 pesky 6 rugged, stormy 7 onerous 9 turbulent, vexatious 10 tumultuous 11 tempestuous

trough
3 hod 4 bowl, tank 5 basin, drain 6 vessel 7 channel 10 depression

trounce
4 beat, drub, lick, rout, whip, whup 5 crush, whomp 6 defeat, larrup, punish, thrash, thresh, wallop 7 clobber, shellac 9 overwhelm

troupe
4 band 5 corps, party 6 outfit 7 company

trouper
4 mime 5 actor, mimic 6 mummer, player 7 actress, artiste 8 thespian 9 performer 11 entertainer

trousers
5 pants 6 slacks 7 drawers 8 breeches, britches
tartan: 5 trews

trout
kind: 3 sea 4 char, lake 5 brook, brown, river 7 rainbow 8 speckled 9 steelhead

Trovatore, Il
character: 7 Azucena, Leonora, Manrico 11 Count di Luna
composer: 5 Verdi (Giuseppe)

trove
4 find, haul 5 hoard, store 8 treasure 10 collection 11 aggregation 12 accumulation

Troy
5 Ilium
epic of: 5 Iliad
excavator: 10 Schliemann (Heinrich)
founder: 4 Ilus
modern site: 9 Hissarlik 11 Dardanelles
(see also **Trojan**)

truant
4 idle 5 shirk 7 shirker, slacker 8 shirking 10 delinquent

truce
4 lull 5 letup, pause, peace 6 accord 7 respite 9 armistice, cease-fire

truck
3 ute, van 4 semi, swap 5 lorry, trade 6 barter, handle, peddle, retail 7 bargain, traffic 8 commerce, dealings, exchange
military: 6 camion

Truckee River city
4 Reno

truckle
4 fawn 5 cower, defer, toady 6 cringe, grovel, kowtow 8 bootlick 11 apple-polish

truckler
5 leech, toady 6 lackey, sponge 7 spaniel 8 parasite 9 sycophant 10 bootlicker 11 lickspittle 13 apple-polisher

truculent
4 fell, grim 5 cruel, harsh, rough, sharp 6 brutal, deadly, fierce, savage, severe 7 abusive, warlike 9 barbarous, bellicose, combative, ferocious 10 pernicious, pugnacious 11 belligerent, contentious, destructive, opprobrious, quarrelsome

trudge
4 plod, slog, trek 5 march, tramp, tromp 8 footslog

true
4 real, very 5 valid 6 actual, honest, trusty 7 factual, genuine, staunch, upright 8 accurate, bona fide, constant, faithful, resolute, rightful 9 authentic, honorable, steadfast, undoubted,

veracious, veritable **10** dependable, legitimate, undeniable **11** indubitable, trustworthy **12** indisputable **13** authoritative

true-blue
5 loyal **6** proven, steady, trusty **7** genuine **8** bona fide, constant, faithful, reliable, stalwart **9** steadfast **10** unswerving

truism
3 saw **4** rule **5** adage, axiom, gnome, maxim, moral **6** cliché, dictum, gospel, saying, verity **8** aphorism, apothegm **9** platitude **10** shibboleth **11** commonplace

Truk Island
3 Tol **4** Moen, Udot, Uman **5** Fefan **6** Dublon

truly
4 well **6** easily, indeed, really, surely, verily **7** de facto **8** actually **9** doubtless, genuinely, sincerely, veritably **10** absolutely, definitely, positively, truthfully, undeniably **11** confidently, doubtlessly, undoubtedly

Truman, Harry S
birthplace: 5 Lamar **8** Missouri
predecessor: 3 FDR
successor: 3 DDE
wife: 4 Bess

trump
3 cap, top **4** beat, best, pass, ruff **5** excel, outdo **6** better **7** manille, surpass **8** clincher, jew's harp, outstrip, override, spadille
up: 6 invent **7** concoct **9** fabricate **11** manufacture

trumpery
4 bosh, junk, muck, slop, tosh **5** bilge, cheap, dreck, hokum, trash **6** bunkum, cheesy, common, humbug, paltry, piffle, shoddy, trashy **7** baloney, twaddle **8** claptrap, flimflam, malarkey, nonsense, rubbishy, tommyrot **10** doubletalk

trumpet
4 horn, tout **6** herald **7** clarion **8** ballyhoo
call: 6 sennet
ram's horn: 6 shofar

trumpeter
4 Hirt (Al), swan **5** André (Maurice), Baker (Chet), Brown (Clifford), Davis (Miles), James (Harry) **6** Alpert (Herb), Bolden (Buddy), Farmer (Art), Voisin (Roger) **7** Schwarz (Gerard) **8** advocate, Eldridge (Roy), eulogist, Marsalis (Wynton), Masekela (Hugh), Sandoval (Arturo) **9** Armstrong (Louis), encomiast, Gillespie (Dizzy), spokesman **10** mouthpiece, panegyrist, Severinsen (Doc)

truncate
3 lop, top **4** crop, trim **5** prune, shear **6** cut off **7** abridge, shorten **10** abbreviate

truncheon
3 bat **4** club **5** baton, billy **6** cudgel, warder **8** bludgeon **9** billy club **10** nightstick, shillelagh

trundle
3 bed, tub **4** cart, haul, roll, spin **5** churn, wheel **6** rotate **7** revolve **9** transport

trunk
3 box **4** body, bole, case, stem **5** chest, torso **7** channel, circuit, luggage
elephant: 9 proboscis
tree: 4 bole **5** stump

truss
3 tie **4** band, bind **5** brace **7** bandage, bracket, support **9** framework, supporter **10** strengthen

trust
4 hope, pool, rely **5** faith, stock **6** assume, bank on, belief, cartel, charge, commit, credit, rely on **7** build on, combine, confide, consign, count on, custody, keeping, presume **8** bank upon, credence, depend on, reckon on, reliance, rely upon **9** assurance, certainty, certitude, syndicate **10** confidence, conviction, dependence, depend upon **11** safekeeping **12** conglomerate

trustee
8 guardian **9** custodian, protector **10** supervisor

trustworthy
4 sure, true **5** tried, valid **6** honest, proven, secure **8** accurate, credible, faithful, reliable, stalwart, true-blue **9** authentic, realistic, steadfast, veracious **10** dependable **11** responsible **12** tried and true **13** authoritative

trusty
4 true **5** tried **6** proven, secure, stable, steady **7** certain, convict **8** faithful, reliable **9** steadfast, truepenny **10** dependable **11** responsible **12** tried and true

truth
5 axiom, maxim, sooth **6** candor, gospel, verity **7** lowdown, reality, veritas **8** veracity **9** rightness **11** genuineness **12** authenticity
goddess: 4 Maat
serum: 11 scopolamine

truthful
5 frank **6** candid, honest **7** factual, sincere **8** accurate **9** realistic, veracious, veridical

truthfulness
6 candor, verity **7** honesty **8** veracity

try
3 aim, tax, vex **4** seek, shot, stab, test **5** annoy, assay, essay, judge, offer, prove, study, whack, whirl, worry **6** aspire, harass, harrow, sample, strain, stress, strive **7** afflict, adjudge, attempt, trouble **8** endeavor, struggle **9** undertake **10** adjudicate, experiment

trying
6 taxing, thorny, tricky, vexing **7** arduous, onerous **8** annoying, exacting, grueling **9** demanding, difficult, strenuous, vexatious **10** irritating

try out
4 test **5** check, prove **6** verify **7** confirm **8** audition

tryst
4 date **7** meeting **10** engagement, rendezvous **11** appointment, assignation

tsar
see **czar**

tsunami
9 tidal wave

tub
3 vat **4** boat **9** container
hot: 3 spa **7** Jacuzzi

tuba
7 helicon **9** bombardon, euphonium **10** sousaphone

tubby
3 fat **5** plump, podgy, porky, pudgy **6** chubby, chunky, rotund **8** roly-poly

tube
2 TV **4** duct, flue, hose, pipe **5** buret **6** siphon, subway, tunnel, vessel **7** burette, channel, conduit, cuvette, pipette, syringe **8** cylinder, pipeline **10** television
anatomical: 3 vas **4** duct, vasa (plural) **7** salpinx **9** salpinges (plural)

tuber
3 oca, set **4** bulb, corm, root, stem, taro, yamp, yuca **5** salep, yucca **6** manioc, potato **7** cassava, rhizome **10** prominence

tuberculosis
8 phthisis, scrofula **11** consumption

tucker out
4 do in, poop, tire **5** drain, weary **7** exhaust

tuft
5 clump, mound **7** cluster
of feathers: 7 panache
ornamental: 6 pom-pom
vascular: 6 glomus

tufted
7 crested

tug
3 tow **4** drag, draw, haul, moil, pull, toil **5** labor **6** strain, strive

tug-of-war
5 match **6** strife **7** contest, grapple, rivalry **8** conflict, struggle **11** competition

tuition
3 fee **6** charge **8** teaching, training, tutelage **9** education, schooling **11** instruction
collector: 6 bursar

tumble
4 drop, fall, trip **5** upset **6** plunge, topple **8** collapse, keel over **9** bring down, overthrow

tumbledown
8 decrepit **10** ramshackle **11** dilapidated

tumbler
5 glass **6** roller **7** acrobat, gymnast **11** cartwheeler

tumbrel
4 cart **5** wagon **7** tipcart

tumescent
6 turgid **7** aureate, bloated, bulging, flowery, swollen **8** inflated, swelling **9** bombastic, dropsical, overblown **10** euphuistic, rhetorical

tummy
3 gut **5** belly **6** paunch **7** abdomen, stomach **8** potbelly **9** bay window **11** breadbasket

tumult
3 din **4** flap, riot, to-do **5** babel, broil, hoo-ha, hurly, noise, whirl **6** clamor, dither, hoo-haw, hubbub, lather, outcry, pother, racket, strife, uproar **7** ferment, tempest, turmoil **8** disorder, foofaraw, outburst, paroxysm, upheaval **9** agitation, commotion, confusion, kerfuffle, maelstrom **10** convulsion, hullabaloo, hurly-burly, turbulence

tumultuous
5 rowdy **6** stormy, unruly **7** raucous, riotous **9** clamorous, turbulent **10** boisterous, disorderly **11** rumbustious, tempestuous **12** rambunctious

tumulus
5 grave, knoll, mound **6** barrow **7** hillock

tun
3 keg, vat **4** butt, cask, pipe **6** barrel **8** hogshead, puncheon

tuna
3 ahi **4** pear **6** bigeye, bonito **7** bluefin **8** albacore, skipjack **9** scombroid, yellowfin

tune
3 air **4** dial, lilt, song **5** theme, tweak **6** accord, adjust, amount, attune, extent, jingle, melody, strain, temper **7** descant **8** modulate, regulate

tuneful
5 sweet **6** dulcet **7** melodic **9** melodious

tungsten
7 wolfram **9** scheelite **10** wolframite

tunic
4 jama **5** jupon **6** kirtle **7** hauberk
Greek: 6 chiton

tunicate
4 salp **8** ascidian, chordate **9** sea squirt **11** urochordate

Tunisia
capital: 5 Tunis
city: 4 Sfax **6** Ariana
island: 5 Jerba

language: **6** Arabic
monetary unit: **5** dinar
neighbor: **5** Libya **7** Algeria
ruins: **8** Carthage

tunnel
4 tube **6** burrow **7** conduit **8** crawlway
Alps: **7** Simplon **11** Loetschberg
France: **4** Rove
Hudson river: **7** Holland, Lincoln
Nevada: **5** Sutro
railroad: **6** Hoosac **7** Cascade

Turandot
character: **3** Liu **5** Calaf
author: **5** Gozzi (Carlo)
composer: **6** Busoni (Ferruccio) **7** Puccini (Giacomo)

turban
7 bandana, pugaree **8** bandanna **9** headdress

turbid
4 dark **5** dense, mucky, muddy, murky, riley, roily, smoky, thick **6** cloudy, opaque, roiled **7** clouded, obscure

turbot
8 flatfish

turbulence
3 din **4** flap, stew **5** babel, fight, hoo-ha **6** dither, fracas, lather, pother, tumult, uproar **7** turmoil **8** foofaraw **9** agitation, commotion

turbulent
4 wild **5** bumpy, roily, rough, rowdy **6** raging, stormy, unruly **7** furious, moiling, raucous, riotous, roaring **8** agitated, blustery, swirling **9** clamorous **10** boisterous, tumultuous

tureen
3 pot **4** bowl **5** crock **6** vessel **9** casserole

turf
3 sod **4** area, peat **5** grass, sward, track **6** domain, region **7** terrain **9** racetrack, territory **11** horse racing **12** neighborhood

turgid
see **tumescent**

Turkey
capital: **6** Ankara
city: **5** Adana, Bursa, Izmir, Konya **8** Istanbul
enclave: **8** Naxçivan
lake: **3** Van
leader: **7** Atatürk (Kemal)
monetary unit: **4** lira
mountain, range: **6** Ararat, Taurus
neighbor: **4** Iran, Iraq **5** Syria **6** Greece **7** Armenia, Georgia **8** Bulgaria
peninsula: **6** Balkan **9** Asia Minor
river: **6** Tigris **8** Menderes **9** Euphrates
sea: **6** Aegean **7** Marmara **13** Mediterranean

turkey
buzzard: **7** vulture
disease: **9** blackhead
head growth: **5** snood **7** dewbill
male: **3** tom **7** gobbler
throat pouch: **6** wattle
young: **5** poult

Turkish
cavalryman: **5** spahi
empire: **7** Ottoman
governor: **4** vali
inn: **4** kahn **6** imaret
soldier: **5** nizam **9** janissary
sultan: **5** Ahmed, Selim **7** Bajazet, Bayezid, Ilderim
sword: **8** yataghan
title: **3** aga, bey **4** agha **5** pasha **6** vizier **7** effendi

Turkmenistan
capital: **8** Ashgabat **9** Ashkhabad
desert: **7** Kara-Kum
monetary unit: **5** manat, tenne
neighbor: **4** Iran **10** Kazakhstan, Uzbekistan **11** Afghanistan
river: **6** Murgab **7** Murghab **8** Amu Dar'ya
sea: **7** Caspian

Turks and Caicos Islands
capital: **9** Grand Turk
location: **10** West Indies
passage: **6** Caicos **8** Mouchoir
territory of: **7** Britain

turmeric
3 dye **4** herb **5** spice **6** ginger **8** dyestuff

turmoil
4 coil, flap, moil, riot, stew, stir, to-do **5** chaos, whirl **6** clamor, dither, hassle, hubbub, lather, pother, strife, tumult, unease, unrest, uproar, welter **7** ferment **8** disorder, upheaval **9** agitation, commotion, confusion **10** disruption, hurly-burly, turbulence, uneasiness **11** pandemonium **13** helter-skelter, Sturm und Drang

turn
3 yaw, zag, zig **4** bend, bias, bout, cast, grow, gyre, reel, spin, tack, tour, veer, whip, wind **5** angle, curve, pivot, refer, shunt, spell, stint, swirl, train, twirl, whirl **6** detour, divert, gyrate, mutate, revert, rotate, switch, swivel **7** circuit, convert, deflect, deviate, digress, diverge, reverse, revolve **8** gyration, rotation **9** about-face, deviation, pirouette, volte-face

turnabout
3 rat **6** coward **7** reverse **8** apostate, defector, recreant, reversal **9** about-face, reversion, volte-face **11** retaliation **12** merry-go-round

turn aside
4 veer, shun, sway, veer **5** avert, repel, shunt,

stave **6** divert, refuse, reject, swerve **7** deflect, deviate, digress, dismiss, diverge, fend off, reflect, ward off **9** sidetrack

turncoat
3 rat, spy **5** Judas **7** traitor **8** apostate, betrayer, defector, deserter, quisling, recreant, renegade **9** traitress, turnabout **13** tergiversator

turn down
4 jilt, veto **5** spurn **6** rebuff, refuse, reject **7** decline, dismiss **9** repudiate **10** disapprove

turned on
4 high **5** doped **6** stoned, zonked **7** aroused, drugged, excited **8** hopped-up, tripping **9** activated, spaced-out, zonked-out **10** passionate **12** enthusiastic

turn in
5 crash, rat on **6** betray, inform, rat out, retire, submit **7** deliver, produce, sack out **8** hand over **9** hit the hay **10** hit the sack, relinquish

turning point
4 cusp **5** pivot **6** climax, crisis **8** landmark **11** climacteric

turn inside out
5 evert

turnip
5 swede **8** rutabaga
Scottish: **4** neep

turnip-shaped
8 napiform

turnkey
6 jailer

turn left
3 haw

Turn of the Screw, The
author: **5** James (Henry)
character: **5** Flora, Miles **10** Peter Quint
composer: **7** Britten (Benjamin)

turn on
5 start **6** excite, ignite **7** start up **8** activate, motivate **9** stimulate, titillate

turn over
4 plow, roll **5** upend, upset **6** assign, commit, give up, rotate **7** capsize, consign, deliver, entrust, furnish, provide, revolve **8** delegate, transfer **9** overthrow, surrender **10** relinquish

turnpike
7 highway

turn right
3 gee

turn up
4 find **6** appear, arrive, reveal **7** uncover, unearth **8** discover **9** encounter **11** materialize

Turow work
4 One L **16** Presumed Innocent

turpentine
7 galipot, solvent, thinner
ingredient: **6** pinene
tree: **4** pine **9** terebinth

turret
5 tower **6** cupola, louver, louvre **7** mirador **8** bartizan **9** belvedere

turtle
8 terrapin, tortoise **9** chelonian
edible part: **7** calipee **8** calipash
genus: **4** Emys
sea: **6** ridley **8** hawkbill
shell: **8** carapace
shell part: **8** plastron

Tuscany
city: **4** Pisa **8** Florence
river: **4** Arno
tower: **4** Pisa
wine: **7** chianti

tusk
4 fang **5** ivory, tooth

tusker
6 dugong, walrus **7** mammoth, muntjac, narwhal, warthog **8** elephant, musk deer **11** barking deer

tussle
4 spar **5** scrap, scrum **6** hassle, scrape **7** scuffle, wrangle, wrestle **8** argument, skirmish, struggle **9** scrimmage **11** controversy

tussock
4 tuft **5** clump, mound **7** cluster

tutelage
see **tuition**

tutor
3 don **5** coach, teach **6** docent, mentor **7** teacher **9** pedagogue, preceptor **10** instructor

Tut's tomb discoverer
6 Carter (Howard)

tutti
3 all **8** everyone **9** everybody

Tuvalu
capital: **8** Funafuti
ethnic group: **10** Polynesian
former name: **6** Ellice (Islands)

TVA dam
5 Ocoee

twaddle
3 jaw, yak **4** bosh, bull, bunk, chat, guff, muck, talk, tosh **5** clack, drool, hooey, prate, run on **6** babble, bunkum, burble, drivel, gabble, hot air, humbug, jabber, tattle **7** baloney, blabber, blarney, blather, chatter, hogwash, prattle, rubbish **8** claptrap, malarkey, nonsense, tommyrot, trumpery **9** poppycock **10** applesauce, balderdash **12** blatherskite

Twain character
3 Jim **5** Becky (Thatcher) **8** Huck Finn, Injun Joe **9** Aunt Polly, Joe Harper, Tom Sawyer

tweak
4 jerk, mock, pull, zing **5** annoy, pinch, pluck **6** adjust, bother, modify, twitch **8** fine-tune **9** poke fun at

tweet
4 call, note **5** cheep, chirp **7** chirrup, twitter

Twelfth Night character
5 Viola **6** Olivia, Orsino (Duke) **7** Antonio, Cesario **8** Malvolio **9** Sebastian, Toby Belch

twelve
combining form: **5** dodec **6** dodeca

twenty
5 score
combining form: **4** icos **5** icosa, icosi

twerp
4 brat, drip, fool, jerk, nerd, twit **6** squirt

twibil
2 ax **3** axe

twice
3 bis **7** twofold
combining form: **3** bis
prefix: **3** dis

twice a day
3 b.i.d. **8** bis in die **11** semidiurnal

twice a year
8 biannual **10** semiannual, semiyearly

twig
5 shoot, sprig, withe **6** branch
bundle of: **5** fagot **6** faggot

twiggy
4 slim, thin **5** reedy **6** skinny, slight, stalky **7** slender **9** sticklike

twilight
3 eve **4** dusk **5** gloam, gloom **6** sunset **7** decline **8** gloaming **9** nightfall **10** crepuscule

Twilight of the Gods
8 Ragnarok
composer: **6** Wagner (Richard)

twill
5 chino, cloth, serge, toile, tweed, weave **6** fabric **7** cheviot **8** dungaree **9** bombazine, gabardine **11** herringbone

twin
4 dual, like, mate **5** clone, match **6** bifold, binary, double, fellow, paired **7** matched, similar, twofold **8** matching **9** companion, duplicate, identical **10** coordinate, reciprocal

Twin Cities
6 St. Paul **11** Minneapolis

twine
4 coil, cord, curl, wind, wrap **5** twist, weave **6** spiral, string **7** embrace, meander, wreathe **8** entangle **9** interlace **10** interweave

twinge
4 ache, pain, pang, stab **5** pluck, shoot, throe, twang, tweak **6** stitch

twinkle
3 bat **4** flit, wink **5** blink, flash, flirt, gleam, glint, light, shake, shine, trice **7** flicker, flutter, glimmer, glisten, glitter, shimmer, sparkle **9** coruscate, nictitate **11** coruscation, scintillate

twin stars
6 Castor, Pollux

twirl
4 coil, gyre, spin **5** pitch, trill, whirl, whorl **6** gyrate **7** revolve **9** pirouette

twist
3 wry **4** coil, curl, skew, turn, warp, wind **5** belie, gnarl, pivot, twine, twirl, wring **6** garble, spiral, sprain, squirm, torque, wrench, writhe **7** contort, distort, entwine, falsify, pervert, wriggle

twisted
3 wry **4** awry, sick **5** askew, kinky **6** swirly, warped **9** perverted

twister
6 funnel **7** tornado **9** dust devil, whirlwind **10** waterspout

twit
4 dolt, fool, gibe, jeer, jive, josh, mock, quiz, razz **5** chide, rally, scout, taunt, tease, twerp **6** deride **8** bonehead, numskull, ridicule **9** blockhead, numbskull **10** nincompoop

twitch
3 tic **4** jerk, pang, pull, yank **5** pluck, spasm, throe, tweak **6** quiver **10** quack grass

twitter
4 chat, peep **5** cheep, chirp, quake, tweet **6** cackle, giggle, jargon, quiver, shiver, titter, tremor, warble **7** chatter, chirrup, tremble

twittery
6 giggly **8** chattery **9** flustered, tremulous

two
3 duo **4** duet, pair **5** twain **6** couple
combining form: **3** bis, duo, dyo
divide into: **4** fork **6** bisect **9** bifurcate
prefix: **3** twi

two-faced
9 deceitful, dishonest, insincere **11** duplicitous **12** hypocritical **13** double-dealing
god: **5** Janus

twofold
4 dual, twin **5** binal, duple **6** binary, double, duplex, dyadic, paired **9** dualistic

two-footed
7 bipedal

Two Gentlemen of Verona
author: 11 Shakespeare (William)
character: 5 Julia 6 Silvia, Thurio 7 Proteus 9 Valentine

two-sided
9 bilateral

twosome
3 duo 4 dyad, item, pair 5 brace 6 couple 7 doublet

two-time
4 dupe 6 betray, delude, humbug, take in 7 beguile, cheat on, deceive, mislead 9 bamboozle 11 double-cross

two-wheeler
4 bike 5 cycle 7 bicycle, scooter 10 motorcycle

Tybalt
cousin: 6 Juliet
family: 7 Capulet
slayer: 5 Romeo
victim: 8 Mercutio

tycoon
5 mogul, nabob 7 magnate

tyke
3 dog, kid 5 child, hound, puppy 6 canine, moppet, nipper, shaver 7 mongrel

tympanum
7 eardrum 9 middle ear

Tyndareus
kingdom: 6 Sparta
wife: 4 Leda

type
3 cut, ilk, key, lot, way 4 cast, form, kind, mold, sort 5 breed, class, genre, order, print, serif, stamp 6 kidney, nature, stripe 7 feather, species, variety 8 category, keyboard
bar: 4 slug
font: 5 Arial, Goudy 6 Bodoni 7 Antigua, Century, Courier 8 Garamond, Palatino, Perpetua 9 Helvetica 10 Times Roman
measure: 2 em, en 4 pica 5 point
set: 7 compose
setter: 10 compositor
size: 4 pica 5 agate, elite, pearl
stroke: 5 serif
style: 4 bold 5 roman, serif 6 Gothic, italic 7 Fraktur 8 boldface 9 lightface, sans serif
tray: 6 galley

Typee
author: 8 Melville (Herman)
character: 4 Toby

typewriter
part: 3 key 6 platen, spacer
type size: 4 pica 5 elite

Typhon
3 Set 7 monster 8 Typhoeus
offspring: 6 Sphinx 7 Chimera 8 Cerberus, Chimaera
wife: 7 Echidna

typhoon
7 cyclone 9 hurricane 13 tropical storm

typical
5 ideal, model, usual 6 common, normal 7 classic, general, natural, regular 8 symbolic

typify
6 embody, mirror 9 epitomize, exemplify, personify, represent, symbolize 10 illustrate 11 emblematize 12 characterize

typo
5 error 7 erratum 8 misprint 11 corrigendum

typographer
7 printer 10 compositor

Tyr
3 Tiu
brother: 4 Thor
father: 4 Odin 5 Woden
god of: 3 war
mother: 5 Jordh, Jorth

tyrannical
8 absolute, despotic 9 arbitrary 10 absolutist, autocratic, oppressive 11 dictatorial

tyrannize
7 oppress 8 dominate, domineer, overbear

tyrannous
5 harsh 6 brutal, severe 8 absolute, despotic 9 arbitrary, fascistic 10 autocratic 11 dictatorial

tyranny
7 cruelty, fascism 9 autocracy, despotism, monocracy 10 absolutism, domination, oppression 12 dictatorship

tyrant
4 czar, duce, tsar, tzar 5 ruler 6 despot, führer 7 fuehrer, pharaoh, usurper 8 autocrat, dictator 9 oppressor, strongman 10 absolutist

Tyrian ___
6 purple

tyro
4 punk 6 novice, rookie 7 amateur, dabbler, student 8 beginner, freshman, neophyte, newcomer 9 novitiate 10 apprentice, dilettante, tenderfoot 11 abecedarian

Tyrol
see **Tirol**

tzar
see **czar**

tzigane
3 Rom 5 gypsy 6 Romany

U

übermensch
8 superman

ubiquitous
7 allover **9** pervasive, universal **10** everywhere, wall-to-wall, widespread **11** omnipresent

U-boat
3 sub **7** pigboat **9** submarine

Uganda
capital: 7 Kampala
falls: 5 Ripon
lake: 5 Kyoga **6** Albert, Edward, George **8** Victoria
leader: 4 Amin (Idi)
monetary unit: 8 shilling
mountain: 5 Elgon
mountain range: 9 Ruwenzori
neighbor: 5 Congo, Kenya, Sudan **6** Rwanda **8** Tanzania
river: 4 Nile

ugly
4 vile **7** hideous **8** deformed **9** loathsome, misshapen, offensive, repugnant, repulsive, unsightly **10** disfigured **12** unattractive

Ugly Duckling author
8 Andersen (Hans Christian)

ukase
4 fiat **5** edict, order **6** decree, dictum, ruling **7** command, dictate, mandate **9** directive **10** injunction **12** proclamation **13** pronouncement

Ukraine
capital: 4 Kiev
city: 4 Lviv, Lvov **5** Yalta **6** Odessa **7** Kharkiv **9** Chernobyl
ethnic group: 7 Cossack
monetary unit: 6 hryvny
mountain range: 10 Carpathian
neighbor: 6 Poland, Russia **7** Belarus, Hungary, Moldova **8** Slovakia
peninsula: 5 Kerch **6** Crimea **7** Crimean
river: 3 Bug **5** Tisza **6** Donets **7** Dnieper **8** Dniester
sea: 4 Azov **5** Black

Ulalume author
3 Poe (Edgar Allan)

ulcer
4 sore **6** fester **7** corrupt
kind: 6 peptic **8** duodenal
mouth: 10 canker sore

ulna
7 forearm

Ulster hero
6 Fergus **7** Deirdre **9** Conchobar, Cuchulain, Cuchullin **10** Cú Chulainn

ulterior
5 privy **6** covert, future, hidden, latent **7** further, obscure, remoter **9** ambiguous, concealed **10** subsequent, succeeding **11** undisclosed

ultimate
3 end, nth **4** acme, last, peak **5** basic, final, utter **6** summit, utmost, zenith **7** closing, epitome, extreme, maximum, primary, supreme, topmost **8** absolute, deciding, decisive, eventual, farthest, furthest, greatest, original, terminal **9** elemental, paramount **10** apotheosis, concluding, conclusive, consummate, preeminent **11** categorical, fundamental, furthermost, indivisible **12** incomparable, quintessence

ultimatum
5 order **6** demand, threat **7** mandate **9** challenge **12** notification

ultra
5 kinky, outré, rabid **6** beyond, far-out, too-too **7** extreme, fanatic, radical **9** excessive, extremist, fanatical **10** outlandish **11** extravagant

ultraconservative
11 reactionary

ultraist
5 rabid **6** zealot **7** extreme, fanatic, radical **9** extremist

ultramarine
7 oversea, sea-blue **8** overseas **11** lapis lazuli

ululate
3 bay **4** howl, wail, yowl

Ulysses
author: 5 Joyce (James)
character: 5 Bloom (Leopold), Molly (Bloom) **6** Blazes (Boylan) **7** Dedalus (Stephen)
last word: 3 yes
(see also **Odysseus**)

umber
5 brown, sepia, shade 6 darken, shadow

umbilicus
3 hub 4 core 5 heart, hilum, navel 6 center

umbra
5 shade 6 shadow

umbrage
4 hint, huff 5 anger, pique, shade 6 shadow 7 chagrin, dudgeon, foliage, leafage, offense 9 annoyance, suspicion 10 irritation, resentment 11 displeasure, indignation 12 exasperation

umbrageous
5 shady 6 shaded, touchy 7 shadowy 8 shadowed 9 defensive, sensitive

umbrella
5 cover, guard, shade 6 brolly, pileus, screen 7 parasol, protect, shelter 8 sunshade 10 protection 11 bumbershoot

umph
see **oomph**

umpire
3 ref 5 judge 6 decide, settle 7 arbiter, referee 9 arbitrate 10 arbitrator
call: 3 out 4 balk, ball, safe 6 strike

unabashed
5 blunt, brash, frank, naked, overt 6 arrant, brassy, brazen, candid 7 blatant, forward 8 outright 9 audacious, barefaced, shameless, undaunted 10 unblushing 11 undisguised, unmitigated 12 unapologetic

unabbreviated
see **unabridged**

unable
5 inept, unfit 8 helpless, impotent 9 incapable, maladroit, powerless, unskilled 10 unequipped 11 incompetent, unqualified 13 incapacitated

unabridged
5 uncut, whole 6 entire, intact 8 complete 10 full-length 11 uncondensed 13 unabbreviated

unacceptable
8 unwanted 9 unwelcome 10 unsuitable 11 intolerable, undesirable 12 inadmissible 13 exceptionable, inappropriate, insupportable, objectionable

unaccompanied
4 lone, sole, solo, stag 5 alone, apart 6 single 8 detached, solitary 9 a cappella 10 unattended, unescorted

unaccountable
6 arcane, mystic 7 strange 8 baffling, puzzling 9 enigmatic 10 mysterious, mystifying, unknowable, unreliable 12 impenetrable, inexplicable, undependable, unfathomable 13 irresponsible, unexplainable

unaccustomed
3 new 5 alien, novel 6 unused 7 strange, unusual 8 singular, uncommon, unwonted 10 unexpected, unfamiliar

unadorned
4 bald, bare 5 naked, plain, spare, stark 6 rustic, severe, simple 7 artless, austere, natural, spartan 11 undecorated 13 unembellished, unembroidered, unpretentious

unadulterated
4 neat, pure 5 sheer, utter 7 genuine, unmixed 8 absolute, straight 9 unalloyed, undiluted 11 unmitigated, unqualified

unaffected
5 naive 6 candid, simple 7 artless, callous, genuine, natural, sincere, unmoved 9 guileless, impassive, ingenuous, unaltered, unchanged, unstudied, untouched 10 hard-boiled, impervious 13 unpretentious

unalloyed
4 pure 5 sheer, total 7 genuine, unmixed 8 absolute, straight 9 authentic, out-and-out, undiluted 11 unmitigated, unqualified 13 thoroughgoing, unadulterated

unalterable
5 fixed 7 binding, bounden, certain, decided 8 constant, required 9 immutable, mandatory, necessary 10 compulsory, invariable 12 unchangeable 13 predetermined

unambiguous
5 clear, lucid, plain 6 patent 7 evident, express, obvious, precise 8 apparent, clean-cut, clear-cut, decisive, definite, distinct, explicit, manifest, specific, univocal 10 definitive, forthright 11 categorical, translucent, transparent, unequivocal 12 transpicuous

unanimous
5 as one 6 united 8 communal, univocal 9 unopposed 10 collective 11 uncontested 13 consentaneous

unanimously
5 as one 6 wholly 7 en masse 10 altogether

unanticipated
9 unplanned 10 surprising, unexpected, unforeseen 12 out of the blue

unappeasable
4 grim 7 adamant 8 obdurate, resolute 9 insatiate, unbending 10 implacable, insatiable, relentless, unyielding 11 unrelenting 12 unquenchable

unappetizing
4 icky 5 gross, yucky 7 insipid 8 unsavory 9 repugnant 11 unappealing, unpalatable 12 unattractive

unapproachable
5 aloof 6 remote, offish 7 distant 8 reserved 10 unfriendly, unsociable 11 standoffish, unreachable 12 inaccessible, unattainable

unasked
7 willing 8 unbidden, unsought, unwanted 9 uninvited, unwelcome, voluntary 10 gratuitous, unprompted 11 spontaneous, uncalled-for, unrequested, voluntarily

unassailable
6 secure 8 airtight 10 invincible, inviolable, undeniable 11 impregnable, irrefutable 12 indisputable, invulnerable 13 incontestable, unconquerable

unassertive
3 shy 4 meek 5 mousy, timid 6 modest, mousey 7 bashful 8 backward, reticent, retiring, sheepish, timorous 9 diffident, shrinking 10 submissive 12 self-effacing

unassuming
3 shy 6 humble, modest, simple 8 ordinary, retiring 9 diffident 11 unassertive 12 self-effacing 13 unpretentious

unattached
4 free 5 loose 6 single 8 separate 9 unmarried 10 unassigned 11 uncommitted, unconnected 12 disconnected, freestanding, unassociated

unattainable
7 elusive 10 impossible 12 inaccessible

unattractive
4 drab, dull, ugly 5 dowdy, plain 6 homely 8 frumpish 10 unalluring, unsuitable 11 unappealing, undesirable 12 unflattering

unauthentic
4 fake, mock, sham 5 bogus, dummy, faked, false, phony 6 ersatz, forged, pseudo 7 feigned 8 affected, spurious 9 contrived, imitation, pretended, simulated 10 apocryphal, artificial 11 counterfeit, make-believe 12 illegitimate

unavailable
4 busy 6 absent, tied up 7 missing 8 occupied

unavailing
4 idle, vain 5 empty 6 barren, futile 7 useless 8 abortive, bootless 9 fruitless, pointless 11 ineffective, ineffectual 12 unproductive

unavoidable
5 fated 7 certain 8 destined 9 impending, necessary 10 compulsory, inevitable, obligatory 11 ineluctable, inescapable

unavoidably
8 perforce 10 helplessly, inevitably, willy-nilly 11 inescapably, necessarily, whether or no

unaware, unawares
5 aback 7 unready 8 abruptly, heedless, ignorant, off guard, suddenly 9 oblivious, unknowing, unmindful, unwitting 10 by surprise, unfamiliar, uninformed, unprepared 12 unacquainted, unexpectedly

unbalance
11 destabilize

unbalanced
3 mad 4 daft 5 batty, nutty 6 crazed, insane, uneven, wobbly 7 unequal, unsound 8 demented, deranged, lopsided, unhinged, unstable 9 psychotic 10 disordered, moonstruck

unbearable
11 intolerable, unendurable 12 excruciating, insufferable

unbeautiful
4 ugly 5 plain 6 homely 8 uncomely, unlovely 9 unsightly 10 ill-favored, unbecoming, uninviting 12 unattractive

unbecoming
8 improper, unlovely, unseemly, untimely, untoward, unworthy 9 inelegant, tasteless, unfitting 10 indecorous, indelicate, malapropos, unsuitable 11 disgraceful 12 unattractive 13 inappropriate

unbelievable
7 amazing, awesome 8 fabulous 9 fantastic 10 astounding, improbable, incredible, phenomenal, staggering, stupendous 11 astonishing, implausible, spectacular 12 unconvincing, unimaginable 13 extraordinary, inconceivable

unbeliever
5 pagan 6 giaour 7 atheist, doubter, gentile, heathen, heretic, infidel, scoffer, skeptic 8 agnostic 10 Pyrrhonist 11 freethinker

unbelieving
5 leery 6 show-me 8 agnostic, apostate, doubting 9 quizzical, skeptical 10 dissenting, suspicious 11 incredulous, mistrustful, questioning

unbending
4 iron 5 rigid, stern, stiff 6 severe 8 hard-line, obdurate, resolute 9 inelastic 10 brassbound, inexorable, inflexible, unyielding

unbiased
4 fair, just 5 equal 7 neutral 8 detached, tolerant 9 equitable, impartial, objective, unbigoted 10 even-handed, open-minded 11 broad-minded, uncommitted 12 unprejudiced 13 disinterested, dispassionate

unbidden
7 unasked, willing 8 unsought, unwanted 9 impromptu, uninvited, unwelcome, voluntary 10 gratuitous, unprompted 11 spontaneous, unrequested

unbind
4 free, undo **5** loose, untie **6** detach, loosen **7** manumit, release, unchain, unloose **8** dissolve, liberate, unfasten, unloosen **9** discharge, disengage, unshackle **10** emancipate

unblemished
4 pure **7** perfect **8** flawless, spotless, unmarred, virtuous **9** exemplary, faultless, stainless, undefiled, unspotted, unsullied **10** immaculate **11** untarnished

unbosom
4 bare, open, tell **6** betray, expose, reveal, unveil **7** divulge, express, uncover **8** disclose

unbound
4 free **5** freed, loose **6** loosed **10** unattached, unconfined, unfastened

unbounded
4 open **6** untold **7** endless **8** infinite, unending **9** excessive, limitless, unchecked, unlimited **10** immoderate, indefinite, inordinate **11** extravagant, measureless **12** immeasurable, incalculable, uncontrolled, unrestrained

unbreakable
7 durable, lasting **10** unyielding **11** everlasting

unbridled
4 free **5** loose **6** madcap **8** reckless, uncurbed **9** dissolute, unchecked **10** immoderate, licentious, unconfined, unfettered, ungoverned **11** spontaneous, uninhibited, unrepressed **12** uncontrolled, unrestrained, unrestricted **13** unconstrained

unbroken
5 solid, sound, whole **6** entire, intact, single **8** complete, constant, enduring **9** ceaseless, steadfast, unceasing, undamaged, undivided, unsubdued, unvarying **10** continuous, unimpaired **13** uninterrupted

unburden
3 rid **4** dump, ease, lose **5** shake **6** reveal, unload **7** cast off, confess, confide, off-load, relieve **8** shake off, throw off **9** discharge **10** relinquish **11** disencumber

uncalled-for
8 baseless, needless **9** officious, unfounded **10** gratuitous, groundless **11** unessential, unjustified, unnecessary, unwarranted **13** unjustifiable

uncanny
5 eerie, weird **6** creepy, spooky **7** ghostly, strange **9** unearthly, unnatural **10** mysterious, mystifying, superhuman **11** supernormal, supranormal **12** supernatural

uncared-for
5 dingy **6** beat-up, shabby **7** rickety, run-down, worn-out **8** decrepit, derelict, deserted, desolate, forsaken, tattered, untended **9** neglected **10** broken-down, down-at-heel, ramshackle, tumble-down **11** dilapidated

uncaring
4 cold **7** callous **9** heartless, negligent, oblivious, unfeeling, unheeding **11** coldhearted, hard-hearted, indifferent, insensitive, thoughtless, unconcerned **13** inconsiderate, unsympathetic

unceasing
7 abiding, endless, eternal, nonstop, undying **8** constant, enduring, unbroken, unending **9** continual, perennial, perpetual **10** continuous **11** amaranthine, everlasting, unremitting **12** imperishable, interminable **13** uninterrupted

unceremonious
4 curt, rude **5** bluff, blunt, frank, hasty, sharp, short, terse **6** abrupt, breezy, casual, sudden **7** brusque, hurried, offhand **8** familiar, informal **10** ungracious **11** precipitate, precipitous

uncertain
4 hazy, iffy, moot **5** vague **6** chancy, fitful, unsure, wobbly **7** dubious, erratic, halting, unclear **8** arguable, doubtful, insecure, slippery, unstable, unsteady, variable **9** ambiguous, debatable, undecided, unsettled **10** ambivalent, disputable, inconstant, indefinite, precarious **11** problematic, speculative **12** questionable, undependable **13** indeterminate, problematical, unforeseeable, unpredictable, untrustworthy

uncertainty
5 doubt **7** dubiety **8** distrust, mistrust **9** ambiguity, suspicion **10** indecision, perplexity, puzzlement, skepticism, uneasiness **11** ambivalence **12** doubtfulness, irresolution

unchain
4 free **5** loose **6** loosen, unbind **7** manumit, release **8** liberate, unfasten, unfetter **9** discharge, unshackle **10** emancipate **11** disenthrall

unchangeable
3 set **4** firm **5** fixed **7** settled **8** constant **9** immutable, permanent **10** continuing, inflexible, invariable **11** established, inalterable

unchanging
5 fixed **6** stable, static, steady **7** abiding, equable, eternal, settled, stabile, uniform **8** constant, enduring **9** immutable, steadfast, unvarying **10** consistent, continuing, invariable

unchaste
4 easy, lewd **5** bawdy, loose **6** impure, vulgar, wanton **7** immoral, lustful, obscene, scarlet, unclean **8** depraved, prurient **9** debauched, dissolute, lecherous, salacious **10** adulterous, lascivious, libidinous, licentious, profligate **11** promiscuous

unchecked
5 loose **7** rampant **9** spreading, unbounded, unbridled **10** widespread **11** uninhibited **12** unrestrained, unrestricted

uncivil
4 rude **5** crass, crude **6** coarse, savage, vulgar **7** boorish, ill-bred, uncouth **8** barbaric, impolite **9** barbarous **10** indecorous, uncultured, ungracious **11** ill-mannered, uncourteous **12** discourteous **13** disrespectful

uncivilized
4 rude, wild **5** crude **6** brutal, coarse, Gothic, savage **7** boorish, Hunnish, ill-bred, loutish, lowbred, uncouth **8** barbaric, churlish **9** barbarian, barbarous, primitive, unrefined **10** mannerless, uncultured, unmannerly, unpolished **12** uncultivated **13** unenlightened

unclad
see **unclothed**

uncle
cry: **6** give up **9** surrender
Dutch: **6** critic **7** advisor
French: **5** oncle
Scottish: **3** eme
Spanish: **3** tío
U.S. symbol: **3** Sam

unclean
4 foul **5** dingy, dirty, grimy **6** filthy, grubby, grungy, impure, soiled, sordid **7** corrupt, defiled, immoral, obscene, squalid, stained, sullied, tainted **8** befouled, indecent, polluted, unchaste **9** tarnished **10** besmirched, desecrated **12** contaminated

unclear
3 dim **4** hazy **5** murky, vague **6** bleary, blurry, cloudy, opaque, unsure **7** clouded, cryptic, dubious, obscure, shadowy **8** doubtful, nebulous, overcast, puzzling **9** ambiguous, enigmatic, tenebrous, unsettled **10** ill-defined, indistinct, indefinite, inexplicit **13** indeterminate

Uncle Remus creator
6 Harris (Joel Chandler)

Uncle Tom's Cabin
author: **5** Stowe (Harriet Beecher)
character: **5** Eliza, Topsy **6** Legree (Simon) **9** Little Eva

Uncle Vanya author
7 Chekhov (Anton)

unclothe
5 strip **6** denude, divest, expose, unveil **7** display, disrobe, uncloak, uncover, undress

unclothed
4 bare, nude **5** naked **6** peeled, unclad **7** denuded, exposed **8** in the raw, stripped **9** au naturel, buck-naked, undressed **10** stark naked

unclouded
4 fair **5** clear, lucid, sunny **6** bright **7** halcyon **8** rainless, sunshiny

uncluttered
4 neat, tidy, trig, trim **7** orderly **9** organized, shipshape **11** spic-and-span, well-ordered **12** spick-and-span

uncombed
5 messy, mussy **6** matted, mussed **7** ruffled, snarled, tangled, tousled, unkempt **10** disheveled

uncommon
3 odd **4** rare **5** novel **6** choice, scarce, unique **7** special, unusual **8** esoteric, especial, singular, sporadic, unwonted **10** infrequent, noteworthy, remarkable **11** distinctive, exceptional **12** unaccustomed **13** extraordinary

uncommunicative
3 mum **4** dumb **5** aloof **6** offish, silent **7** distant, guarded, private **8** reserved, reticent, taciturn **9** reclusive, secretive, withdrawn **10** antisocial, poker-faced, speechless, tongue-tied, unsociable **11** inscrutable, standoffish, tight-lipped **12** closemouthed, tight-mouthed, unresponsive **13** unforthcoming

uncompassionate
4 cold, hard **5** stony **7** callous **8** obdurate, pitiless, uncaring **9** heartless, unfeeling **10** hard-boiled **11** coldhearted, hardhearted, insensitive **12** stonyhearted **13** unsympathetic

uncomplicated
4 easy **5** basic, clear, plain **6** simple **8** clear-cut **10** effortless, elementary, manageable, uninvolved

uncomplimentary
7 adverse **8** critical **9** degrading **10** belittling, derogatory, pejorative **11** deprecatory, disparaging, unfavorable **12** depreciative, depreciatory, unflattering

uncompromising
4 firm **5** rigid **8** hard-line, obdurate, resolute, stubborn **9** hard-nosed, immovable, insistent, unbending **10** brassbound, determined, inexorable, inflexible, unshakable, unyielding **12** intransigent, single-minded

unconcealed
4 bald, bare, open **5** frank, naked, overt, plain **6** candid **7** blatant, evident, exposed, express, obvious, visible **8** apparent, explicit, manifest, palpable **10** forthright **11** openhearted, transparent, undisguised, unvarnished

unconcern
6 apathy **7** neglect **9** aloofness, disregard **10** alienation, detachment, dispassion **11** disinterest, inattention, insouciance, nonchalance **12** carelessness, heedlessness, indifference **13** preoccupation

unconcerned
4 cool **6** remote **7** unmoved **8** careless, detached, heedless **9** alienated, apathetic, oblivious, unmindful, unruffled **10** insouciant, neglectful, untroubled **11** inattentive, indifferent, unperturbed **12** uninterested **13** disinterested, dispassionate

unconditional
5 sheer, total, utter **8** absolute, definite, explicit, outright **9** downright, out-and-out **10** unreserved **11** unequivocal, unqualified **12** unrestricted **13** thoroughgoing

unconfined
4 free, vast **5** loose **7** at large **9** at liberty, boundless, limitless, unlimited **12** unrestrained, unrestricted

uncongenial
6 at odds **8** unfitted **9** repellent, repugnant, unlikable **10** discordant, unsociable, unsuitable **11** conflicting, displeasing **12** antipathetic, disagreeable, incompatible, unattractive **13** unsympathetic

unconnected
5 alone, apart **8** discrete, detached, disjoint, disjunct, distinct, inchoate, rambling, separate **9** unrelated **10** unattached **11** independent **12** unassociated **13** discontinuous, noncontinuous

unconquerable
10 invincible, inviolable, unbeatable **11** bulletproof, impregnable, indomitable, insuperable **12** invulnerable, unassailable

unconscionable
5 undue **6** unfair, unholy, unjust, wanton, wicked **7** immoral, ungodly **8** barbaric, criminal **9** barbarous, unethical **10** exorbitant, inordinate, outrageous **11** inexcusable, uncivilized **12** unprincipled, unscrupulous

unconscious
3 out **6** asleep, chance **7** out cold, stunned, unaware **8** comatose **9** insensate, passed out, unplanned, unwitting **10** blacked out, insensible, knocked out **11** inadvertent, instinctual, involuntary **12** uncalculated **13** unintentional

unconsciousness
4 coma **5** faint **6** stupor, torpor, trance **7** syncope **13** obliviousness

unconsidered
4 rash **5** brash, hasty **6** casual **7** offhand **8** careless, reckless, slapdash **9** desultory, haphazard, hit-or-miss, hotheaded, impetuous, unplanned **10** ill-advised, incautious, unthinking **11** thoughtless

unconstrained
4 free, open **6** blithe, dégagé, wanton **7** buoyant, gushing, relaxed **8** animated, carefree, effusive, informal, outgoing **9** easygoing, expansive, liberated **10** expressive, nonchalant, unreserved

uncontrollable
4 wild **6** unruly **7** wayward, willful **9** fractious **10** headstrong, refractory, self-willed **11** intractable **12** overwhelming, recalcitrant, ungovernable, unmanageable **13** irrepressible, undisciplined

uncontrolled
4 free, wild **5** loose **6** wanton **9** automatic, excessive, unbounded, unlimited, unmanaged **10** autonomous, immoderate, licentious, ungoverned **11** independent, instinctual, involuntary, unconscious, uninhibited, unregulated **12** disorganized, unrestrained **13** self-governing

unconventional
3 odd **4** beat, boho **5** kinky, kooky, outré **6** casual, far-out, freaky, quirky, unique, way-out, weirdo **7** bizarre, deviant, oddball, offbeat, unusual, wayward **8** aberrant, abnormal, atypical, bohemian, freakish, original, peculiar **9** anomalous, eccentric, irregular **10** avant-garde, unexpected, unorthodox **11** uncustomary **13** idiosyncratic

unconvinced
5 leery **6** unsure **7** dubious **8** doubtful **9** skeptical, undecided **10** suspicious

unconvincing
4 lame **6** feeble, flimsy, forced **7** dubious, suspect **8** doubtful, strained **10** farfetched, improbable, incredible **11** implausible, unrealistic **12** unbelievable **13** unsubstantial

uncooked
3 raw

uncouple
4 part **6** detach, divide **7** disjoin, divorce, unhitch **8** separate, unfasten **9** disengage **10** disconnect, dissociate **12** disaffiliate

uncouth
3 odd, raw **4** rude **5** crass, crude, gross, rough **6** clumsy, coarse, rugged, vulgar **7** awkward, bizarre, boorish, ill-bred, loutish, strange, uncivil **8** barbaric, clownish, impolite, ungainly **9** eccentric, graceless, inelegant, unrefined **10** outlandish, uncultured, unpolished **11** ill-mannered, uncivilized **12** discourteous, uncultivated
person: 3 oaf **4** boor, dolt, lout **5** clown **7** bumpkin **9** barbarian

uncover
4 bare **5** strip **6** betray, detect, divest, expose, remove, reveal, unmask, unveil **7** display, divulge, unearth **8** disclose

uncritical
5 naive **9** credulous **11** perfunctory

unction
3 oil 4 balm 5 cream, salve 6 balsam, cerate, chrism 7 suavity, unguent 8 liniment, ointment 9 emollient 11 embrocation

unctuous
4 oily 5 fatty, slick, soapy, suave 6 greasy, smarmy 7 cloying, fawning, fulsome 8 slippery 9 wheedling 10 flattering, oleaginous, saccharine 11 sycophantic

uncultivated
4 wild 5 crass, crude, gross 6 coarse, desert, fallow, savage, vulgar 7 boorish, lowbrow, uncouth 8 barbaric, unplowed, untilled 9 barbarian, barbarous, inelegant, unrefined 10 unpolished 11 uncivilized

uncultured
3 raw 4 rude 5 crass, crude, gross, rough 6 coarse, vulgar 7 artless, boorish, ill-bred, loutish, lowbred, lowbrow, natural, uncouth 8 barbaric, churlish, cloddish 9 barbarian, barbarous, benighted, inelegant, unrefined 10 unpolished 11 uncivilized 13 unenlightened

uncustomary
4 rare 7 special, strange, unusual 8 aberrant, abnormal, atypical, singular, uncommon 9 anomalous 10 surprising, unfamiliar, unorthodox 11 exceptional 13 extraordinary

uncut
5 whole 6 entire, intact 8 complete 9 undiluted 10 full-length, unabridged 11 uncondensed 13 unabbreviated

undamaged
5 sound, whole 6 intact, unhurt 8 unbroken, unmarred 9 uninjured, unscathed 10 unimpaired 11 unblemished

undaunted
4 bold 5 brave 6 daring, heroic 7 doughty, Spartan, valiant 8 fearless, intrepid, resolute, unafraid, valorous 9 audacious 10 courageous 11 lionhearted, unconquered, unflinching 12 stouthearted

___ und Drang
5 Sturm

undeceive
8 disabuse 11 disillusion

undecided
4 iffy, moot, open 6 unsure 7 dubious, pending 8 doubtful, wavering 9 equivocal, tentative, uncertain, unsettled 10 ambivalent, indefinite, unresolved 12 undetermined

undeclared
5 tacit 6 unsaid 7 assumed, implied 8 accepted, implicit, inferred, presumed, unspoken, unstated 10 understood

undecorated
4 bare 5 plain, stark 6 homely, severe, simple 8 no-frills 9 unadorned 12 unornamented 13 unembellished, unembroidered

undefiled
4 pure 6 chaste, intact, vestal, virgin 8 innocent, spotless, virginal, virtuous 9 stainless, unstained, unsullied, untainted 10 immaculate 11 unblemished, untarnished

undefined
3 dim 4 hazy 5 faint, vague 6 bleary 7 obscure, shadowy, unclear 8 inchoate, nebulous, unformed 9 amorphous, shapeless 10 indistinct 12 undetermined

undemonstrative
4 calm, cold, cool 5 aloof, chill 7 aseptic, distant, laconic 8 reserved, retiring 9 contained, inhibited, shrinking, withdrawn 10 restrained, unsociable 11 emotionless, passionless, standoffish, unemotional 12 matter-of-fact, unresponsive 13 self-contained

undeniable
6 patent 7 certain, evident, genuine, obvious 8 manifest 9 veridical 10 inarguable 11 indubitable, irrefutable, unequivocal 12 indisputable 13 incontestable

undependable
6 fickle, tricky, unsafe 7 erratic 10 capricious, fly-by-night, inconstant, unreliable 12 inconsistent, questionable 13 irresponsible, unpredictable, untrustworthy

under
3 low, sub 4 down, less 5 below, lower, short 6 lesser 7 beneath, covered, subject 8 downward, inferior 9 dependent, receiving, secondary, subjacent 11 subordinate
prefix: 3 hyp, sub 4 hypo

undercarriage
5 frame 9 framework 11 landing gear

undercover
6 covert, hidden, secret 7 furtive, stealth, sub-rosa 8 hush-hush, stealthy 11 clandestine 12 confidential 13 surreptitious
person: 3 spy 4 mole 5 agent, spook 6 sleuth 9 detective, operative 10 counterspy 11 double agent, secret agent 12 counteragent

undercroft
5 crypt, vault 7 chamber 8 catacomb

undercut
7 subvert 8 sabotage

underdeveloped
4 poor 7 dwarfed, stunted 8 backward, immature 9 unevolved 10 third-world

underdog
5 loser 6 victim 7 also-ran, fall guy, wannabe 9 dark horse

underdone
3 raw, red 4 rare

underestimate
6 slight 7 dismiss 8 belittle, discount, disprize, minimize 9 deprecate, disparage, sell short 10 depreciate

undergarment
3 bra 4 BVDs, slip 5 teddy 6 bikini, bodice, briefs, corset, girdle, shorts, undies 7 chemise, drawers, panties, stammel, step-ins 8 lingerie, pretties, Skivvies, woollies 9 brassiere, jockstrap, long johns, petticoat, underwear 10 foundation

undergo
4 bear, face 5 abide, brave, brook 6 endure, suffer 7 sustain, weather 8 submit to, tolerate 9 withstand 10 experience

undergraduate
4 coed, soph 5 frosh 6 junior, senior 8 freshman 9 collegian, sophomore

underground
4 tube 5 metro, train 6 buried, hidden, nether, secret, subway 7 illegal, off-beat, railway 8 hypogeal, hypogean 10 undercover 11 alternative, clandestine 12 subterranean 13 surreptitious

underhanded
3 sly 4 wily 5 shady 6 covert, crafty, secret, shifty, sneaky, tricky 7 cunning, devious, elusive, evasive, furtive, sub-rosa 8 guileful, sneaking, stealthy 9 deceitful, deceptive 10 circuitous 11 clandestine, duplicitous 13 surreptitious

underlie
4 bear 6 prop up 7 subtend, support 8 buttress

underline
4 mark 6 play up, stress 9 emphasize, italicize 10 accentuate, underscore

underling
4 aide, peon, serf 5 gofer, scrub, slave 6 flunky, gopher, lackey, menial, minion 7 fall guy 8 inferior 9 assistant, attendant, subaltern 11 subordinate

underlying
4 root 5 basal, basic 7 primary 8 implicit 9 elemental, essential 11 fundamental

Under Milk Wood author
6 Thomas (Dylan)

undermine
3 sap 4 foil 5 blunt, erode 6 impair, thwart, weaken 7 cripple, disable, subvert 8 sabotage 9 attenuate, frustrate 10 debilitate, demoralize

undermost
6 bottom, lowest 9 lowermost 10 bottommost, nethermost, rock-bottom

underneath
4 sole 5 below, lower 6 bottom 7 covered

underpin
4 back, base, prop, root 5 brace 6 uphold 7 bolster, justify, shore up, support 8 buttress, validate 10 strengthen 11 corroborate

underpinning
4 base, prop, root, stay 5 basis, brace 7 bedrock, footing, seating, support 8 buttress 10 foundation, groundwork 12 substructure

underprivileged
4 poor 5 needy 7 hapless, unlucky 8 deprived 11 handicapped, unfortunate 13 disadvantaged

underrate
7 devalue 8 discount, mark down, minimize, write off 9 devaluate, write down 10 depreciate

underscore
6 accent, play up, stress 9 emphasize, italicize 10 accentuate

underside
4 sole 6 bottom 7 reverse

undersized
3 toy 4 baby, mini, puny 5 dinky, dwarf, pygmy, runty, short, small 6 bantam, little, pocket, slight 7 scrubby, stunted 9 miniature 10 diminutive 11 Lilliputian

understand
3 con, dig, ken, see 4 grok, know 5 grasp, guess, infer, savvy, sense, think 6 accept, assume, deduce, expect, fathom, figure, follow, gather, reason, reckon, take in, take it 7 believe, discern, imagine, presume, realize, suppose, surmise, suspect, suss out 8 conceive, conclude, consider, perceive 9 apprehend, interpret 10 appreciate, comprehend, conjecture

understandable
5 clear, lucid, plain 8 clear-cut, coherent, knowable 9 excusable, graspable, plausible 10 articulate, believable, defensible, fathomable, reasonable 11 justifiable, perceivable, unambiguous 12 intelligible 13 apprehensible

understanding
3 ken, wit 4 deal, pact 5 grasp, sense 6 accord, humane, kindly 7 compact, empathy, entente, insight, mastery 8 sympathy 9 agreement, awareness, knowledge, tolerance 10 acceptance, impression, perception 11 considerate, discernment, explanation, sympathetic 12 apprehension, relationship 13 comprehension

understatement
7 litotes

understood
5 tacit **7** assumed, implied **8** accepted, implicit, inferred, unspoken

understudy
6 double, backup, fill-in **7** standby, stand-in **9** surrogate **10** substitute **11** replacement

undertake
3 try **4** dare **5** assay, begin, essay, start **6** accept, assume, pledge, strive, tackle, take on, take up **7** attempt, certify, execute, perform, promise, warrant **8** commence, contract, covenant, endeavor, set about, set forth, shoulder **9** guarantee

undertaker
8 embalmer **9** mortician

undertaking
3 job **4** task **6** affair, charge, effort **7** calling, emprise, exploit, mission, project, pursuit, venture **8** endeavor **9** adventure, guarantee, operation **10** enterprise **11** proposition, transaction

under-the-table
6 covert, hidden, secret, sneaky **7** furtive, on the q.t., sub-rosa **8** hush-hush, stealthy **9** concealed, underhand **10** undercover **11** clandestine **13** surreptitious

undertone
3 hue, hum **4** buzz, cast, hint, tint **5** drone, shade **6** mumble, murmur, mutter, rumble **7** inkling **10** suggestion **11** association, connotation, implication

undertow
4 eddy **7** current, riptide, sea puss

undervalue
see **underrate**

underwater
9 submarine **10** subaquatic, subaqueous
breathing apparatus: **5** scuba
captain: **4** Nemo
chamber: **7** caisson
device: **8** paravane
missile: **7** torpedo
sound detector: **5** sonar

underwear
see **undergarment**

underwood
5 brush, copse, hedge, scrub **7** boscage, coppice, thicket **9** shrubbery

underworld
4 hell **5** hades, Sheol **6** Erebus, Tophet **7** Gehenna, inferno **8** gangland **9** antipodes **11** Pandemonium
boatman: **6** Charon
deity: **3** Dis **4** Bran **5** Pluto **6** Osiris
goddess: **6** Hecate **10** Persephone
organization: **4** tong **5** Mafia, Triad **6** Yakuza **10** Cosa Nostra
relating to: **8** chthonic
watchdog: **8** Cerberus

underwrite
4 back, fund, sign **5** endow, stake **6** assure, insure, pay for, secure **7** agree to, endorse, finance, sponsor, support **8** bankroll **9** grubstake, guarantee **11** subscribe to

undesigning
5 frank **6** candid, honest **7** artless, earnest, genuine, sincere **9** guileless, ingenuous, unfeigned **10** aboveboard, forthright

undesirable
8 annoying, unwanted **9** offensive, unwelcome **10** ill-favored, unpleasant, unsuitable **11** displeasing, inadvisable, troublesome **12** disagreeable, unacceptable, unattractive **13** inappropriate, objectionable

undesired
8 needless, unsought, unwanted **9** uninvited, unwelcome **10** gratuitous **11** uncalled-for, unnecessary **12** nonessential

undetermined
5 vague **7** dubious, obscure, pending, unclear **8** doubtful **9** ambiguous, equivocal, uncertain, undecided, undefined, unsettled **10** ill-defined, indefinite, indistinct **12** inconclusive

undeveloped
5 crude, green, rough **6** latent **8** backward, immature, inchoate **9** embryonic, incipient, primitive, unevolved **10** unfinished

undiluted
4 neat, pure **5** sheer, utter **7** genuine, unmixed **8** absolute, straight **9** authentic, unalloyed **11** unmitigated, unqualified **13** unadulterated

undiplomatic
4 rash, rude **5** brash, cocky **6** brazen, cheeky **8** impudent, tactless **9** audacious, hotheaded, impolitic, impulsive, maladroit, untactful **10** ill-advised, indiscreet **11** impertinent, injudicious, insensitive, thoughtless **12** presumptuous

undisciplined
4 wild **6** unruly, wanton **7** froward, restive, wayward, willful **8** contrary, untoward **9** fractious **10** disorderly, rebellious, refractory **11** intractable **12** contumacious, noncompliant, obstreperous, recalcitrant, ungovernable, unmanageable

undisclosed
6 hidden, sealed, secret **7** unknown, unnamed **8** ulterior, withheld **9** anonymous **10** unreported, unrevealed **11** clandestine, unmentioned, unspecified **12** confidential, undesignated, unidentified

undisguised
4 bald, open, pure **5** frank, naked, overt, sheer, stark **6** candid, patent **7** obvious **8** apparent, explicit, manifest, palpable **9** barefaced **11** openhearted, unconcealed, unvarnished

undistinguished
5 cheap, stock **6** common **7** humdrum, obscure, routine **8** déclassé, everyday, inferior, low-grade, mediocre, middling, ordinary, workaday **10** second-rate **11** commonplace, nondescript, second-class **12** run-of-the-mill **13** insignificant

undisturbed
6 in situ

undivided
3 one **4** full **5** fixed, total, whole **6** entire, intact, united **8** complete, unbroken **9** unanimous **10** continuous, unswerving **11** indivisible **12** concentrated, undistracted

undo
4 free, open, ruin, veto **5** annul, loose, untie, upset, wrack, wreck **6** cancel, defeat, loosen, negate, stymie, unbind, unsnap **7** abolish, destroy, nullify, release, reverse, vitiate, wipe out **8** abrogate, disallow, overturn, unfasten, unloosen **9** disengage **10** contravene, invalidate **11** disentangle, outmaneuver

undoing
4 bane, doom, ruin, slip **5** shame **7** misstep **8** downfall, reversal **9** destroyer, overthrow, ruination **10** misfortune **11** destruction, humiliation

undoubted
4 real, sure, true **7** certain, genuine **8** definite, positive **9** authentic **10** undisputed

undoubtedly
5 truly **6** indeed, really, surely **7** clearly **8** of course **9** assuredly, certainly **10** definitely, positively, presumably, undeniably **11** indubitably

undress
see **unclothe**

undressed
4 nude, rude **5** naked **6** unclad **7** exposed **8** in the raw, stripped **9** au naturel, unclothed

undue
5 inapt **7** extreme **8** ill-timed, improper, needless, untimely **9** excessive, unfitting **10** immoderate, indecorous, inordinate, unsuitable **11** extravagant, uncalled-for, unnecessary, unwarranted **12** unreasonable **13** inappropriate, unjustifiable

undulant fever
11 brucellosis

undulate
4 roll, swag, sway, wave **5** heave, snake, swell, swing **6** billow, ripple **7** slither **9** fluctuate, oscillate

unduly
3 too **6** overly **9** extremely, immensely **11** excessively **12** immoderately, inordinately, unreasonably **13** unnecessarily

undying
7 abiding, ageless, endless, eternal **8** enduring, immortal, unending **9** continual, deathless, perennial, perpetual, unceasing **10** continuing **11** amaranthine, everlasting **12** imperishable, unquenchable

unearth
4 find, show **5** dig up, learn **6** exhume, expose, reveal **7** exhibit, find out, root out, uncover **8** come upon, disclose, discover, dredge up, excavate **9** ascertain, determine **10** come across

unearthly
5 eerie, weird **6** absurd, insane, spooky **7** awesome, ghostly, uncanny, ungodly **8** abnormal, ethereal, heavenly, numinous, spectral **9** appalling, fantastic **10** miraculous, mysterious, outlandish, superhuman, suprahuman **12** preposterous, supermundane, supernatural **13** preternatural

unease
4 care, fear **5** agita, angst, worry **6** strain, stress, unrest **7** anxiety, concern, tension **8** disquiet, distress **9** abashment, confusion, misgiving **10** discomfort, discontent, solicitude **11** disquietude, fretfulness, nervousness, uncertainty, uptightness **12** apprehension, discomfiture, discomposure **13** embarrassment

uneasy
4 edgy **5** jumpy, tense **6** afraid **7** anxious, awkward, fearful, fidgety, fretful, nervous, restive, unquiet, uptight, worried **8** agitated, doubtful, insecure, restless, unstable **9** ambiguous, concerned, difficult, disturbed, perturbed, uncertain, unsettled **10** disquieted, precarious, solicitous **11** embarrassed **12** apprehensive **13** uncomfortable

uneducated
5 crude, rough **8** ignorant, untaught **9** benighted, untutored **10** illiterate, unlettered, unschooled **12** uncultivated, uninstructed

unembellished
4 bald, bare **5** blunt, plain, spare, stark **6** severe **7** austere **9** essential, unadorned **11** undecorated, unelaborate, ungarnished, unvarnished **12** unornamented **13** unembroidered, unpretentious

unemotional
4 cold, cool **5** chill, stoic, stony **6** frigid, sedate, serene **7** deadpan, equable, glacial, stoical

8 composed, obdurate, reserved, reticent 9 apathetic, impassive 10 hard-boiled, phlegmatic 11 insensitive, passionless, unexcitable 12 intellectual, thick-skinned, unresponsive 13 dispassionate

unemployed
4 idle 5 fired 6 otiose, unused 7 jobless, laid off, loafing 8 inactive, leisured, workless 10 unoccupied

unending
7 eternal, undying 8 constant, immortal, infinite, timeless 9 boundless, ceaseless, continual, incessant, limitless, perennial, perpetual, unceasing 10 continuous 11 amaranthine, everlasting, unremitting 12 interminable 13 uninterrupted

unenlightened
5 naive 6 unread 7 heathen, unaware 8 backward, ignorant, nescient 9 benighted, unknowing 10 uneducated, uninformed 11 uninitiated 12 uncultivated

unenthusiastic
4 cool 5 tepid 8 grudging, listless, lukewarm 9 apathetic, unexcited 10 lackluster, lacklustre, spiritless 11 halfhearted, indifferent, perfunctory 12 uninterested

unequal
3 odd 6 uneven, unfair 7 diverse 8 inferior, lopsided, one-sided 9 different, disparate, divergent, irregular 10 asymmetric, dissimilar, inadequate, mismatched, off-balance 12 insufficient

unequaled
6 unique 7 supreme 8 foremost, nonesuch, peerless 9 matchless, paramount, unmatched, unrivaled 10 preeminent, surpassing 12 incomparable, transcendent, unparalleled 13 unprecedented

unequivocal
5 clear 6 direct, patent 7 certain, evident 8 apparent, definite, distinct, explicit, manifest, palpable 10 undeniable 11 categorical, indubitable, unambiguous 12 indisputable, undisputable

unerring
5 exact 6 dead-on 7 certain, correct, perfect, precise 8 accurate, reliable 9 faultless, unfailing 10 dependable, infallible 11 trustworthy

unessential
8 marginal, needless, unneeded 9 redundant 10 expendable, gratuitous, irrelevant, peripheral, unrequired 11 dispensable, superfluous, uncalled-for, unimportant, unnecessary

unethical
5 venal, wrong 7 corrupt, crooked, immoral 9 dishonest, reprobate 12 disreputable, unprincipled, unscrupulous

uneven
3 odd 4 wavy 5 bumpy, erose, harsh, jaggy, rough 6 craggy, jagged, patchy, ragged, random, rugged, spotty 7 scraggy, unequal, varying 8 lopsided, scabrous, scraggly, variable 9 haphazard, hit-or-miss, irregular 10 asymmetric, imbalanced, unbalanced

unevenness
4 bump, wave 7 anomaly 8 asperity, imparity 9 disparity, imbalance, roughness, variation 10 inequality 12 irregularity, lopsidedness 13 disproportion

uneventful
5 usual 6 placid 7 humdrum, prosaic, routine 8 ordinary 10 unexciting 11 commonplace 12 unremarkable

unexampled
4 lone, only, sole, solo 5 alone 6 unique 8 singular, solitary 9 matchless, unequaled, unmatched, unrivaled 10 consummate, inimitable, sui generis, unequalled, unrivalled 12 incomparable, unparalleled 13 unprecedented

unexcited
4 calm 5 blasé, stoic 6 placid, sedate, serene 7 relaxed, stoical 8 composed, tranquil 9 apathetic, collected, unruffled 10 nonchalant 11 indifferent 12 uninterested 13 dispassionate

unexciting
4 arid, dull, tame 5 banal, bland, ho-hum 6 boring, stodgy 7 humdrum, insipid, prosaic, tedious 8 lifeless, tiresome 10 monotonous 11 commonplace

unexpected
10 surprising, unforeseen 11 unpredicted 13 unanticipated

unexpectedly
5 aback, short 6 sudden 7 unaware 8 abruptly, suddenly, unawares 9 forthwith 11 unwittingly 12 accidentally 13 inadvertently

unexpended
5 saved 7 reserve, surplus 8 left over, reserved 9 remaining

unexpired
5 valid 9 operative

unexpressed
5 tacit 6 silent, unsaid 7 assumed, implied 8 implicit, presumed, unspoken, wordless 9 unuttered 10 undeclared, understood

unfailing
4 fast, sure 7 certain, devoted 8 constant, faithful, reliable, resolute, surefire, unerring 9 steadfast, unvarying 10 consistent, dependable, infallible, invariable, persistent, unchanging, unflagging, unwavering 11 everlasting, persevering, unrelenting 12 tried-and-true 13 inexhaustible

unfair
4 foul **5** wrong **6** biased, shabby, uneven, unjust **7** unequal **8** wrongful **9** arbitrary, dishonest, unethical **10** prejudiced **11** inequitable, underhanded, unrighteous

unfaithful
5 false **6** untrue **8** cheating, disloyal, recreant, turncoat **9** faithless, two-timing **10** adulterous, inaccurate, perfidious, traitorous **11** treacherous **13** untrustworthy

unfaltering
3 set **4** firm **6** steady **7** abiding **8** constant, enduring, resolute, tireless **9** steadfast, unfailing **10** continuous, unflagging, unwavering **11** persevering **12** never-failing, wholehearted

unfamiliar
3 new, odd **5** alien, novel, weird **6** exotic **7** foreign, strange, unaware, unknown, unusual **8** abnormal, peculiar **11** incognizant, out-of-the-way **12** unaccustomed, unacquainted

unfashionable
5 dated, dowdy, passé, stale **6** bygone, démodé, old-hat, shabby **7** outworn **8** outdated, outmoded **9** out-of-date, unstylish **10** antiquated, oldfangled

unfasten
4 free, open, undo **5** loose, unbar, unfix, unpin, untie **6** detach, loosen, unbind, unbolt, unlace, unlock, unsnap **7** release, unclasp, unhitch, unlatch, unleash, unloose, unstrap **8** unbuckle, unfetter, unloosen, untether **9** disengage

unfathomable
7 abysmal, obscure **8** profound **9** boundless, enigmatic, unplumbed **10** bottomless, fathomless, unknowable **11** inscrutable **12** immeasurable, impenetrable

unfavorable
3 bad, ill **4** poor **6** averse, unfair, unkind **7** adverse, hostile, opposed **8** contrary, damaging, inimical, negative **9** disliking, troubling **11** detrimental, displeasing **12** antagonistic, disapproving, inauspicious
prefix: 3 dys

unfavorably
4 awry **5** amiss, badly **6** astray, poorly **7** wrongly **10** negatively, unsuitably **13** unfortunately

unfeasible
8 quixotic **9** visionary **10** chimerical, impossible, unworkable **11** impractical, speculative, theoretical, unrealistic **12** unattainable, unrealizable **13** impracticable

unfeeling
4 cold, hard, numb **5** cruel, harsh, stern, stony **6** brutal, leaden, marble, numbed, severe, stolid, unkind **7** callous **8** benumbed, deadened, hardened, obdurate, pitiless, ruthless, uncaring **9** apathetic, heartless, indurated, insensate, senseless **10** hardboiled, insensible, insentient **11** cold-blooded, coldhearted, hardhearted, insensitive, unemotional **12** anesthetized **13** unsympathetic

unfeigned
4 real, true **6** actual, hearty, honest **7** artless, earnest, genuine, natural, sincere **8** innocent **9** guileless, heartfelt, ingenuous **12** wholehearted

unfinished
3 raw **5** crude, rough **7** sketchy **9** imperfect, roughhewn, undressed **10** incomplete, unpolished

Unfinished Symphony composer
8 Schubert (Franz)

unfit
4 sick, weak **5** inapt, inept **6** faulty **7** deprive, disable, unsound, useless **8** disabled, improper, unsuited **9** ill-suited, incapable, maladroit **10** disqualify, ill-adapted, inadequate, ineligible, unsuitable **11** ill-equipped, incompetent, unqualified **12** disqualified, incompatible **13** inappropriate, incapacitated

unfitting
5 inapt **8** improper, unseemly **9** imprudent **10** ill-advised, inapposite, malapropos, unbecoming, unsuitable **11** inadvisable **13** inappropriate

unfix
4 part, undo **5** loose, sever **6** cut off, detach, loosen, sunder, unbind **7** unloose **8** uncouple, unfasten, unloosen **9** disengage **10** disconnect, dissociate

unflagging
6 steady **7** staunch **8** constant, tireless, untiring **9** unceasing, unfailing, unwearied **11** persevering, unfaltering, unrelenting, unremitting **13** indefatigable, inexhaustible

unflappable
4 calm **6** poised, serene **7** assured, equable **8** composed, laid-back **9** collected, unruffled **10** deliberate, nonchalant **11** self-assured **13** imperturbable, self-possessed

unfledged
5 green, young **6** callow, jejune, unripe **7** puerile **8** immature, juvenile **10** unseasoned **11** undeveloped, unfeathered **13** inexperienced

unflinching
4 firm, grim **6** dogged **7** doughty, staunch, valiant **8** fearless, intrepid, resolute **9** dauntless, steadfast **10** courageous, relentless, unwavering, unyielding **11** unfaltering, unrelenting **12** stouthearted

unfold
4 open **6** deduce, evolve, expand, expose, extend, flower, mature, reveal, unwrap **7** blossom, burgeon, clear up, develop, display, dope

out, exhibit, explain, resolve **8** decipher, disclose, evidence, manifest **9** elaborate, explicate, figure out, puzzle out, transpire **10** effloresce, outstretch **11** come to light

unforced
4 easy **7** natural, willing, witting **8** elective, optional **9** available, easygoing, voluntary **10** deliberate, volitional **11** intentional **12** unprescribed **13** discretionary, noncompulsory

unforeseeable
9 uncertain, unplanned **10** accidental

unforeseen
6 chance **8** surprise **10** accidental, surprising, unexpected **11** unlooked-for, unpredicted **13** unanticipated

unforgivable
9 untenable **10** censurable, inexpiable, outrageous **11** blameworthy, inexcusable, intolerable **12** indefensible, unacceptable, unpardonable **13** insupportable, reprehensible, unjustifiable

unformed
4 rude **5** crude, rough, vague **6** callow **8** immature, inchoate, nebulous, unshaped **9** amorphous, roughhewn, shapeless **10** indefinite, unfinished, unpolished **11** undeveloped, unfashioned **12** unstructured **13** indeterminate

unfortunate
3 bad, sad **4** dire, poor **6** woeful, wretch **7** adverse, awkward, hapless, unhappy, unlucky **8** grievous, ill-fated, luckless, untoward, wretched **9** desperate, graceless, ill-chosen, miserable **10** afflictive, calamitous, deplorable, disastrous, ill-starred, lamentable, unsuitable **11** distressing, regrettable, star-crossed, unfavorable **12** disagreeable, inauspicious, infelicitous, unsuccessful **13** heartbreaking

unfounded
4 idle, vain **5** false **8** baseless, spurious, unproven **9** deceptive, dishonest, untenable **10** fabricated, fallacious, gratuitous, groundless, mendacious, misleading, untruthful **11** uncalled-for, unsupported, unwarranted

unfriendly
4 cold, cool **5** alien, aloof, chill, gruff, surly **6** chilly, frosty, remote **7** distant, grouchy, hostile, opposed, warlike **8** inimical, unsocial **10** antisocial, censorious, inimicable, unsociable **11** ill-disposed, uncongenial **12** antagonistic, disagreeable, inhospitable, misanthropic, unneighborly **13** unsympathetic

unfruitful
4 arid, idle **5** empty, waste **6** barren, desert, effete, fallow, futile, wasted **7** parched, sterile, useless **8** abortive, bootless, depleted, impotent **9** infertile, pointless **10** unavailing **11** ineffective, ineffectual **12** impoverished, unproductive, unprofitable

unfurl
4 open **6** expose, reveal, spread, unfold, unroll, unwind **7** develop, display, exhibit, uncover **8** disclose **9** elaborate, spread out

unfurnished
4 bare **5** empty **6** vacant

unfussy
5 loose **6** breezy, casual, common, dégagé, folksy, mellow **7** cursory, relaxed **8** familiar, informal, laid-back **9** easygoing **10** unreserved **11** low-pressure, pococurante, unconcerned **12** unparticular **13** unceremonious, uncomplicated

ungainly
5 gawky, lanky, splay **6** clumsy, klutzy, oafish **7** awkward, boorish, hulking, loutish, lumpish, uncouth **8** bungling, clownish, lubberly, unwieldy **9** lumbering, maladroit **10** blundering

ungarnished
5 plain **6** modest, simple **9** unadorned **11** undecorated, unelaborate **12** unornamented **13** unembellished, unembroidered

ungenerous
4 mean **5** petty, tight **6** paltry, shabby, skimpy, stingy **7** chintzy, miserly **8** grudging, picayune, ungiving **9** illiberal, niggardly, penurious **10** pinchpenny **11** closefisted, tightfisted **12** parsimonious **13** penny-pinching

ungodly
see **unholy**

ungovernable
4 wild **6** unruly **7** froward, lawless, willful **8** mutinous, untoward **9** fractious, turbulent, unbridled **10** disorderly, headstrong, rebellious, refractory, tumultuous **11** intractable **12** recalcitrant, uncontrolled, unmanageable **13** irrepressible, undisciplined

ungraceful
5 crude, gawky, inept, stiff **6** clumsy, gauche, klutzy, oafish, wooden **7** artless, awkward, halting, labored, stilted **8** bumbling, bungling, ungainly, untoward **9** all thumbs, inelegant, lumbering, maladroit **10** blundering

ungracious
4 rude **5** gruff **6** crusty **7** brusque, uncivil **8** churlish, impolite **9** offensive **10** unmannerly **11** disobliging, ill-mannered, impertinent, thoughtless, uncalled-for **12** disagreeable, discourteous **13** disrespectful, inconsiderate, unceremonious

ungraspable
6 opaque **7** obscure **8** baffling **9** enigmatic **10** unknowable **12** impenetrable, inexplicable, unfathomable

ungrateful
9 thankless

unguarded
5 frank, hasty 6 candid, direct, unwary 7 offhand 8 careless, heedless, reckless 9 impolitic, imprudent, impulsive 10 incautious, indiscreet, unthinking 11 defenseless, thoughtless, unprotected

unguent
4 balm 5 cream, salve 6 balsam, cerate, chrism, lotion 8 ointment 9 emollient, lubricant 11 embrocation

ungulate
3 hog, pig 4 deer 5 horse, tapir 6 hoofed 8 elephant 10 rhinoceros

unhallowed
4 evil 6 impure, unholy, wicked 7 immoral, impious, profane, ungodly 8 infernal 9 nefarious 10 desecrated, iniquitous, irreverent 13 unconsecrated

unhampered
4 free, open 5 frank, loose 6 direct 8 uncurbed 9 unbridled, unchecked, unimpeded, unlimited 10 unhindered 11 uninhibited, untrammeled 12 unrestrained, unrestricted, unobstructed 13 unconstrained

unhand
5 let go 7 release

unhandy
5 bulky, inept 6 clumsy, gauche, klutzy 7 awkward, halting, hulking 8 bumbling, bungling, cumbrous, unwieldy 9 all thumbs, ham-handed, maladroit, ponderous 10 cumbersome, unskillful 12 inconvenient

unhappiness
3 woe 5 blues, dolor, dumps, gloom, grief, worry 6 misery, mishap, sorrow 7 anxiety, sadness 8 distress 9 dejection 10 depression, desolation, discontent, heartbreak, melancholy 11 despondency, dolefulness 12 mournfulness, wretchedness 13 cheerlessness

unhappy
3 sad 4 down, glum, grim 5 sorry 6 dismal, dreary, gloomy 7 joyless 8 dejected, downcast, mournful, saddened, troubled, wretched 9 cheerless, depressed, sorrowful, woebegone 10 despondent, dispirited, melancholy 11 melancholic, unfortunate 12 disconsolate, heavyhearted

unharmed
4 safe 5 sound 6 intact, secure, unhurt 8 unbroken, unmarred 9 protected, undamaged, undefiled, uninjured, unscathed 10 unimpaired 11 unblemished

unhealthiness
7 ailment, disease, illness, malaise 8 debility, sickness 9 infirmity 10 affliction, sickliness 11 decrepitude 13 indisposition

unhealthy
3 ill 4 sick 6 ailing, infirm, sickly, unwell 7 baneful, noisome, noxious, unsound 8 diseased 9 injurious 11 deleterious, unwholesome 12 insalubrious

unheard-of
3 new 6 unique 7 obscure, unknown, unnoted 8 nameless 10 phenomenal, unrenowned 12 uncelebrated 13 extraordinary, unprecedented

unhesitating
7 assured, earnest 8 decisive, positive, resolute 9 confident, immediate, unchecked 10 determined, forthright, purposeful 11 unflinching 12 wholehearted

unhinge
5 addle, craze 6 madden, ruffle 7 derange 9 unbalance

unhinged
3 mad 4 daft, loco, nuts 5 balmy, crazy, loony, wacky 6 insane 7 lunatic, unglued 8 demented, deranged 9 disturbed 10 unbalanced

unholy
4 base, evil, vile 6 impure, sinful, wicked 7 heinous, immoral, impious, profane, ungodly 8 dreadful, fiendish, god-awful, shocking 9 atheistic, barbarous 10 iniquitous, irreverent, outrageous, scandalous, unhallowed 11 irreligious, unbelieving 12 sacrilegious, unsanctified 13 reprehensible

unhorse
5 pitch, throw 6 topple, tumble, unseat 7 buck off 8 dislodge, dismount, overturn, unsaddle 9 overthrow

unhurried
4 easy, slow 6 casual 7 laggard, relaxed 8 dilatory, laid-back 9 easygoing, leisurely 10 deliberate 11 low-pressure

unhurt
4 safe 5 sound, whole 6 entire, intact 7 perfect 8 unbroken, unharmed, unmarred 9 undamaged, uninjured, unscathed, untouched 10 unimpaired 11 unblemished

unification
5 union 6 fusion, hookup, merger 7 amalgam, joining, linkage, melding, merging 8 alliance, coupling 9 coalition 10 connection, federation 11 affiliation, coalescence, combination 12 amalgamation 13 confederation, consolidation

uniform
4 even, like, suit 5 alike, dress, equal, level 6 attire, outfit, stable, steady 7 ordered, orderly, regular, similar, stabile 8 constant, unvaried 9 consonant, unvarying 10 comparable, consistent, invariable, unchanging 11 homogeneous 13 unfluctuating

combining form: **3** iso
type: **3** BDU **5** blues, habit, khaki **6** livery, whites

uniformity
6 parity **7** oneness **8** equality, evenness, identity, monotony, sameness **9** agreement, congruity, constancy **11** consistency **13** invariability

uniformly
6 always, evenly **7** equally **8** smoothly **10** comparably **11** analogously, identically **12** equivalently

unify
3 tie, wed **4** bind, bond, fuse, knit, link, mesh **5** blend, marry, merge, unite **6** cement, couple **7** combine, conjoin **8** coalesce, compound, federate **9** integrate **10** amalgamate, centralize, synthesize **11** concatenate, consolidate

unimaginable
10 incredible, unknowable **11** unthinkable **12** mind-boggling, unbelievable **13** extraordinary, inconceivable, indescribable

unimaginative
4 dull, flat **5** banal, bland, trite, vapid **6** common **7** literal, prosaic, routine, vanilla **8** bromidic **10** derivative, pedestrian, uncreative, uninspired **11** commonplace

unimpaired
4 safe **5** sound **6** intact, unhurt **7** perfect **8** unbroken, unharmed, unmarred **9** undamaged, uninjured, unscathed **11** unblemished

unimpassioned
4 calm, cool **5** sober, stoic **6** placid, remote, stolid **7** deadpan **8** detached, lukewarm, reserved, tranquil **9** impassive, temperate **10** phlegmatic, spiritless **11** cold-blooded, emotionless **12** matter-of-fact

unimpeachable
5 valid **7** correct **8** flawless, reliable, virtuous **9** blameless, exemplary, faultless, unspotted, unsullied **10** conclusive, impeccable, undisputed **11** unblemished, untarnished **13** authoritative

unimportant
4 mere **5** minor, petty **6** casual, minute, paltry **7** trivial **8** piddling **9** small-beer, worthless **10** expendable, immaterial, irrelevant, negligible **11** dispensable, meaningless, superfluous **13** insignificant

uninformed
7 unaware **8** ignorant, nescient **9** oblivious, unknowing, unwitting **10** unfamiliar **11** incognizant, superficial **12** unacquainted, undiscerning

uninhabited
5 empty, waste **6** barren, vacant **7** vacated **8** deserted, desolate, forsaken **9** abandoned, evacuated **10** unoccupied

uninhibited
3 lax **4** free **5** loose **8** uncurbed **9** expansive, fancy-free, liberated, unbridled **10** boisterous, ungoverned, unhampered, unreserved **11** spontaneous, unrepressed, untrammeled **12** unrestrained, unsuppressed **13** unconstrained

uninjured
4 safe **5** sound, whole **6** intact, unhurt **8** unharmed, unmarred **9** undamaged, undefiled, unscathed, untouched **10** unimpaired

uninspired
4 blah, drab, dull **5** banal, stock, trite, vapid **6** boring, leaden, old-hat, stodgy **7** humdrum, insipid, plastic, sterile, vanilla **8** bromidic, lifeless, ordinary **9** colorless **10** lackluster, lacklustre, pedestrian, uncreative, unoriginal **11** commonplace **13** unimaginative

unintelligent
4 dumb **5** dense **6** obtuse, stupid **7** asinine, brutish, doltish, fatuous, foolish, moronic, vacuous, witless **8** mindless **9** brainless, ludicrous **10** half-witted, ill-advised, irrational, ridiculous, weak-minded **11** harebrained, lamebrained **12** feebleminded

unintentional
6 chance, random **9** haphazard, unplanned, unwitting **10** accidental, fortuitous, incidental, unexpected, unforeseen, unthinking **11** inadvertent, unconscious, unlooked-for **12** adventitious, coincidental

uninterested
5 aloof, blasé, bored, jaded **9** apathetic, incurious, unexcited **10** uninvolved **11** indifferent, unconcerned

uninteresting
3 dry **4** arid, blah, drab, dull, flat **5** banal, dusty, ho-hum, stale **6** boring, jejune **7** humdrum, insipid, prosaic, tedious **8** bromidic, plodding, tiresome **9** colorless, dryasdust, wearisome **10** monotonous, pedestrian, uneventful, unexciting

uninterrupted
6 direct **7** endless, nonstop **8** constant, unbroken, unending **9** ceaseless, continual, incessant, perpetual, sustained, unceasing **10** continuous **11** undisturbed, unremitting

uninvited
7 unasked **8** unbidden, unsought **9** intruding **10** gratuitous **11** uncalled-for, unrequested, unsolicited **12** presumptuous

union
4 bloc, bond, club **5** alloy, artel, group, guild, joint **6** fusion, league, merger **7** amalgam, joining, melding, merging, society **8** alliance, congress, coupling, junction, juncture, marriage,

sodality **9** coalition **10** connection, federation, fellowship **11** association, brotherhood, coalescence, combination, confederacy, cooperative, unification **13** confederation, consolidation
branch: **5** local
labor: **3** AFL, CIO, UAW, UMW **5** ILGWU

unique
3 odd, one **4** lone, only, sole, solo **5** alone, novel **6** single **8** peculiar, peerless, singular, solitary, uncommon, unwonted **9** anomalous, exclusive, matchless, unequaled, unmatched, unrivaled **10** inimitable, particular, sui generis, unequalled, unexampled, unrivalled **11** distinctive, exceptional **12** incomparable, unparalleled, unrepeatable **13** extraordinary, idiosyncratic, unprecedented

uniqueness
8 identity **10** singleness **11** singularity **13** individuality

____-Unis
5 Etats

unit
3 arm, one **4** area, item, part, wing **5** digit, group, monad, piece, whole **6** entity **7** element, measure **8** molecule **9** component **10** individual **11** constituent
administrative: **6** agency, bureau, sector **8** district
boy scout: **5** troop
educational: **6** course
military:
(see at **military**)
of acceleration: **3** gal
of action: **7** episode
of advertising space: **4** line **6** column
of an element: **4** atom **8** molecule
of angular measure: **6** radian
of area: **3** are **4** acre **6** morgen **7** hectare **9** square rod **10** square mile, square yard
of astronomical distance: **6** parsec **9** light-year
of brightness: **7** lambert
of capacitance: **5** farad
of capacity: **2** cc, ml **3** cup, tun **4** cord, dram, gill, peck, pint **5** liter, litre, minim, ounce, quart **6** barrel, bushel, firkin, gallon
of computer information: **3** bit, gig, meg **4** byte **8** gigabyte, megabyte
of conductance: **3** mho **7** siemens
of distance: **4** mile, yard **5** meter **6** league **7** furlong
of electricity: **3** amp **4** volt, watt **6** ampere **7** coulomb
of energy: **3** erg **5** joule **7** quantum **8** watt-hour
of explosive force: **7** megaton
of fineness: **5** carat, karat
of force: **4** dyne **6** newton **7** poundal
of frequency: **5** hertz **7** fresnel
of grain: **5** sheaf
of heat: **3** BTU **5** therm **7** calorie
of illumination: **3** lux **5** lumen
of inductance: **5** henry
of length: **3** mil, rod **4** foot, hand, inch, mile, rood, yard **5** chain, fermi, meter **6** fathom, micron **7** furlong **9** kilometer
historic: **5** cubit
of loudness: **4** sone **7** decibel
of lumber: **9** board foot
of magnetic flux: **5** gamma, gauss, tesla, weber **7** maxwell
of magnetic intensity: **7** oersted
of magnetomotive force: **7** gilbert
of pressure: **3** bar, psi **4** torr **6** pascal **10** atmosphere
of radiation: **3** rad **8** roentgen
of radioactivity: **5** curie
of resistance: **3** ohm
of solar radiation: **7** langley
of sound absorption: **5** sabin
of speech: **4** word **6** toneme **7** phoneme **8** morpheme, syllable
of speed: **3** CPS, MPH, RPM **4** knot
of temperature: **6** degree, kelvin
of time: **3** age, day, eon **4** beat, bell, hour, week, year **5** month **6** minute, season, second **8** svedberg
of viscosity: **5** poise
of volume: **5** stere **9** cubic foot, cubic yard **10** cubic meter
of weight: **3** cwt, ton **4** dram, gram, tael **5** carat, grain, ounce, pound, tonne **6** drachm **7** gigaton, kiloton, quintal, scruple **8** kilogram, millieme **9** metric ton, microgram, milligram
historic: **3** tod **5** gerah, libra
Indian: **4** tola
Russian: **4** pood
of work: **3** erg **5** ergon, joule
social: **4** clan **5** tribe **6** family **7** chapter

unitary
5 whole **9** undivided **11** indivisible

unite
3 mix, tie, wed **4** ally, band, bind, bond, fuse, join, knit, link, meld, pool, weld **5** blend, graft, marry, merge, unify **6** cement, couple, gather, league, mingle, splice **7** combine, conjoin, connect **8** assemble, coadjute, coalesce, compound, federate **9** affiliate, aggregate, commingle **10** amalgamate, federalize **11** confederate, incorporate

united
3 one, wed **5** joint **6** allied, linked, merged, wedded **7** made one **8** agreeing, combined, in accord **10** harmonious

United Arab Emirates
capital: **8** Abu Dhabi
city: **5** Dubai **6** Dubayy
coast: **6** Pirate **7** Trucial
emirate: **5** Dubai **6** Dubayy **8** Abu Dhabi
former name: **13** Trucial States
gulf: **4** Oman **7** Persian
monetary unit: **6** dirham
neighbor: **4** Oman **11** Saudi Arabia
peninsula: **7** Arabian
strait: **6** Hormuz

United Kingdom
capital: **6** London
city: **3** Ely **4** Bath **5** Derby, Dover, Leeds **6** Exeter, Oxford **7** Bristol, Cardiff, Glasgow, Paisley **8** Bradford, Brighton, Coventry, Plymouth **9** Cambridge, Edinburgh, Leicester, Liverpool, Newcastle, Sheffield **10** Birmingham, Manchester, Nottingham **11** Bournemouth
colony: **8** Falkland (Islands)
component: **5** Wales **7** England **8** Scotland **12** Great Britain
conqueror: **6** Caesar (Julius) **7** William (the Conqueror)
county: **4** Kent **5** Devon, Essex **6** Dorset, Surrey, Sussex **7** Norfolk, Suffolk **8** Cornwall, Somerset **9** Berkshire, Wiltshire, Yorkshire
island: **3** Man **4** Jura, Skye **5** Islay, Lewis, Wight **6** Jersey **8** Anguilla, Guernsey, Mainland
island group: **6** Orkney **7** Channel **8** Hebrides, Shetland
language: **5** Welsh **6** Gaelic
leader: **8** Cromwell (Oliver) **9** Churchill (Winston)
monarch: **4** Anne, Mary **5** Henry, James **6** Alfred (the Great), Edward, George **7** Charles, Richard, William **8** Victoria **9** Elizabeth
monetary unit: **5** pence, penny, pound
monetary unit, former: **3** bob **5** crown, groat **6** florin, guinea **7** ha'penny **8** farthing, shilling, sixpence **9** halfpenny **10** threepence
mountain, range: **7** Scafell (Peak), Snowdon **8** Ben Nevis, Cumbrian, Grampian **12** Cheviot Hills
peninsula: **7** Kintyre
prehistoric site: **7** Avebury **9** Skara Brae **10** Stonehenge
river: **3** Dee, Exe, Wye **4** Aire, Avon, Ouse **5** Clyde **6** Mersey, Severn, Thames
sea: **5** Irish, North **6** Celtic
territory: **8** Anguilla

United Nations secretary-general
3 Ban (Ki-moon), Lie (Trygve) **5** Annan (Kofi), Thant (U) **8** Waldheim (Kurt) **12** Boutros-Ghali (Boutros), Hammarskjöld (Dag)

United States
desert: **6** Mojave **7** Sonoran **8** Colorado
highest point: **6** Denali (Mt.) **8** McKinley (Mt.)
island: **6** Hawaii, Kodiak, Unimak **7** Nunivak **9** Admiralty, Chichagof **10** St. Lawrence **13** Prince of Wales
island group: **3** Fox **6** Hawaii **8** Aleutian, Pribilof, Thousand
lowest point: **11** Death Valley
mountain range: **5** Coast, Green, Ozark, Rocky, White **7** Cascade, Olympic **8** Catskill **9** Blue Ridge **10** Adirondack, Great Smoky **11** Appalachian **12** Sierra Nevada
national park: **4** Zion **6** Denali **7** Glacier, Olympic, Redwood, Sequoia **8** Badlands, Carlsbad, Wind Cave, Yosemite **9** Mesa Verde, Mt. Rainier **10** Everglades, Grand Teton, Hot Springs, Isle Royale, Shenandoah **11** Dry Tortugas, Grand Canyon, Kenai Fjords, Mammoth Cave, Yellowstone
possession: **10** Puerto Rico
state: **4** Iowa, Ohio, Utah **5** Idaho, Maine, Texas **6** Alaska, Hawaii, Kansas, Nevada, Oregon **7** Alabama, Arizona, Florida, Georgia, Indiana, Montana, New York, Vermont, Wyoming **8** Arkansas, Colorado, Delaware, Illinois, Kentucky, Maryland, Michigan, Missouri, Nebraska, Oklahoma, Virginia **9** Louisiana, Minnesota, New Jersey, New Mexico, Tennessee, Wisconsin **10** California, Washington **11** Connecticut, Mississippi, North Dakota, Rhode Island, South Dakota **12** New Hampshire, Pennsylvania, West Virginia **13** Massachusetts, North Carolina, South Carolina
territory: **4** Guam **13** American Samoa, Virgin Islands

unity
5 union **6** accord **7** concord, harmony, oneness **8** identity, soleness **9** agreement, consensus **10** continuity, singleness, solidarity

universal
3 all **5** broad, total, whole **6** common, cosmic, entire, global **7** general, generic **8** catholic **9** extensive, planetary, unlimited, worldwide **10** ecumenical, ubiquitous **11** omnipresent **12** all-embracing, all-inclusive, cosmopolitan **13** comprehensive
combining form: **4** omni

universe
3 all **5** whole, world **6** cosmos, system **8** creation **9** macrocosm

unjust
5 wrong **6** biased, shabby, unfair **7** partial, unequal **8** one-sided, improper, wrongful **9** inequable **10** prejudiced, undeserved **11** inequitable, unrighteous

unjustifiable
5 undue **7** invalid **8** baseless **9** unfounded, untenable **10** groundless **11** inexcusable, unsupported, unwarranted **12** indefensible

unkempt
5 messy **6** frowsy, frowzy, ragtag, shaggy, sloppy, untidy **7** ruffled, rumpled, scruffy, tousled **8** scraggly, slipshod, slovenly, uncombed **10** bedraggled, disarrayed, disheveled, disordered, unpolished **11** disarranged

unkind
4 mean, vile **5** cruel, harsh, rough, stern **6** severe **7** callous **8** uncaring **9** inclement, malicious **10** ungenerous, ungracious **11** insensitive, thoughtless, unfavorable **12** uncharitable **13** unsympathetic

unknowable
6 arcane, hidden, mystic, occult, secret **7** cryptic **8** mystical, numinous **9** enigmatic, recondite **10** mysterious **11** inscrutable, ungraspable **12** impenetrable, unfathomable

unknowing
6 unwary **7** unaware **8** heedless, ignorant **9** oblivious, unmindful, unwitting **10** insensible, unfamiliar, uninformed **11** incognizant **12** unsuspecting

unknown
6 hidden, nobody, secret **7** obscure, strange **8** nameless **9** anonymous, incognito

unlawful
6 banned **7** bootleg, corrupt, crooked, illegal, illicit, immoral **8** criminal, outlawed, verboten, wrongful **9** forbidden, felonious, nefarious **10** contraband, flagitious, indictable, iniquitous, prohibited, proscribed, unlicensed **11** black-market **12** illegitimate, unauthorized

unlearned
5 naive **6** unread **7** unaware **8** ignorant, nescient, untaught **10** illiterate, uneducated, unlettered, unschooled **11** instinctive **13** unenlightened

unleash
4 free, vent **5** let go, loose, untie, visit, wreak **6** unbind **7** inflict, release **8** carry out, liberate **10** bring about

unless
3 but **4** save **6** except, saving **7** barring, but that, without **9** excepting, excluding

unlettered
see **uneducated**

unlikable
9 obnoxious, offensive, repellent **10** unpleasant **11** displeasing, distasteful **12** disagreeable

unlike
5 mixed **6** varied **7** diverse, unequal, various **8** assorted **9** different, disparate, divergent **10** dissimilar **11** contrasting, distinctive, diversified **13** heterogeneous

unlikely
5 faint, unfit **6** remote, slight **7** distant, dubious **8** doubtful **10** farfetched, improbable, unsuitable **11** implausible, unpromising **12** questionable

unlimited
4 full, vast **5** total **6** untold **7** endless, immense **8** absolute, infinite, wide-open **9** boundless, countless, unbounded, universal **10** unconfined, unfettered **11** unqualified, untrammeled **12** immeasurable, interminable, unrestrained, unrestricted **13** comprehensive, unconditional, unconstrained

unlit
4 dark, inky **6** gloomy **7** shadowy **9** lightless, tenebrous

unload
4 drop, dump, junk **5** chuck, ditch, empty **6** debark, remove **7** confess, confide, deep-six, deliver, discard, divulge, lighten, relieve **8** disclose, disgorge, jettison **9** disburden, discharge, disembark, eighty-six, stevedore **11** disencumber

unloose
4 free, undo **5** let go, relax, untie **6** detach, unbind **7** break up, manumit, release, set free, slacken **8** liberate, uncouple, unfasten **9** disengage, extricate, untighten **10** disconnect

unlucky
6 jinxed **7** hapless, ominous **8** ill-fated, untoward **9** ill-boding **10** ill-starred **11** detrimental, inopportune, regrettable, star-crossed, unfavorable, unfortunate **12** inauspicious, unpropitious

unmanageable
4 wild **5** balky, bulky **6** unruly **7** awkward **8** contrary, cumbrous, perverse, stubborn, unwieldy **9** fractious **10** cumbersome, disorderly, headstrong, rebellious, refractory **11** intractable **12** obstreperous, recalcitrant, ungovernable **13** uncooperative, undisciplined

unmannered
4 rude **5** crude, rough **6** coarse, gauche **7** boorish, ill-bred, loutish **8** impolite **10** indecorous, ungracious **12** discourteous **13** disrespectful

unmarred
5 sound, whole **6** intact, unhurt **7** perfect **8** pristine, unflawed, unharmed **9** undamaged, undefiled, unscathed, unstained **10** unimpaired **11** unblemished, untarnished

unmask
6 debunk, detect, expose, reveal, show up **7** deflate, uncover **8** disclose, discover, disprove **9** demystify

unmatched
3 odd **4** only **5** alone **6** unique **8** peerless, singular **9** unequaled, unrivaled **10** inimitable, unequalled, unrivalled **11** exceptional **12** incomparable, unparalleled

unmerciful
5 cruel, harsh **6** brutal **7** callous, extreme **8** inhumane, pitiless, ruthless, uncaring, vengeful **9** heartless, unfeeling, unsparing **10** relentless

unmindful
7 unaware **8** careless, heedless **9** forgetful, negligent, oblivious, unheeding, unwitting **10** abstracted, distracted, neglectful **11** inattentive

unmistakable
5 clear, frank, plain **6** patent **7** certain, decided, evident, express, obvious **8** apparent, definite, distinct, explicit, manifest, palpable **11** unambiguous, unequivocal

unmitigated
4 pure, rank **5** gross, sheer, utter **6** arrant **7** perfect, unmixed **8** absolute, clearcut, complete, outright **9** downright, out-and-out, unalloyed, undiluted **10** consummate, unmodified, unrelieved **11** straight-out, unqualified **13** thoroughgoing

unmixed
4 mere, neat, pure **5** plain, sheer, utter **6** simple **7** perfect, sincere **8** absolute, straight **9** unalloyed, unblended, undiluted, undivided **11** unmitigated, unqualified **13** unadulterated

unmoved
4 calm, cool, firm **5** aloof, stony **6** in situ, stolid **7** adamant, callous, stoical **8** obdurate **9** impassive, untouched **10** insensible, untroubled **11** unconcerned, unemotional, unimpressed **12** unresponsive

unnamed
5 incog **6** secret **7** obscure, unknown **9** anonymous, incognito **11** unspecified **12** unidentified

unnatural
7 uncanny **8** aberrant, abnormal **9** anomalous, contrived, irregular, synthetic **10** artificial, fabricated, factitious

unnecessary
6 excess **7** surplus **8** needless, optional, prodigal **9** avoidable, redundant **10** expendable, extraneous, gratuitous **11** dispensable, inessential, superfluous, uncalled-for, unessential **12** nonessential

unnerve
5 daunt, shake, throw, upset, worry **6** dismay, rattle **7** agitate, disturb, fluster, perturb, trouble, unhinge **8** bewilder, confound, distress **9** undermine **10** disconcert, discourage, dishearten, intimidate

unobstructed
4 open **5** clear **8** passable **9** unblocked, unimpeded **10** unhampered, unhindered **12** unrestricted

unobtrusive
5 quiet **6** modest **7** subdued **8** reserved, retiring, tasteful **10** restrained **13** inconspicuous

unoccupied
4 free, idle **5** empty **6** vacant **7** jobless, vacated **8** deserted **9** abandoned, available **10** employable, unemployed **11** uninhabited

unofficial
7 pirated, private, wildcat **8** informal **9** irregular **10** unapproved, unorthodox **12** unauthorized, unsanctioned

unorganized
7 aimless, chaotic, muddled **8** confused, inchoate, nebulous, rambling, unformed **9** amorphous, arbitrary, haphazard, shapeless, unplanned **10** disjointed, disordered, incoherent, incohesive **11** spontaneous

unoriginal
5 banal, stock **6** copied, old-hat **7** clichéd, humdrum, prosaic, sterile **8** borrowed, ordinary **9** hackneyed, imitative **10** derivative, uninspired **11** commonplace, plagiarized **12** conventional **13** unimaginative

unornamented
4 bare **5** plain, spare, stark **6** chaste, modest, severe, simple **7** austere **9** unadorned **11** unelaborate, ungarnished **13** unembellished, unembroidered

unorthodox
3 odd **5** kinky, novel, weird **6** far-out **7** offbeat, strange, unusual **8** abnormal, maverick **9** different, dissident, eccentric, heretical, irregular, sectarian **10** schismatic, unexpected **13** nonconformist

unorthodoxy
6 heresy, schism **7** dissent **8** variance **9** ingenuity, recusancy **10** contention, dissidence, innovation **13** nonconformism, nonconformity

unpaid
3 due **5** owing **6** mature **7** donated, overdue, payable, pro-bono **8** freewill, honorary, wageless **9** unsettled, voluntary, volunteer **10** delinquent, gratuitous, receivable **11** contributed, outstanding

unpalatable
8 unsavory **10** flavorless **11** distasteful **12** unappetizing

unparalleled
6 unique **8** peerless, singular **9** matchless, unequaled, unmatched, unrivaled **10** inimitable, unequalled, unrivalled **11** exceptional **12** incomparable

unplanned
5 fluky **6** chance, random **7** aimless **9** desultory, haphazard, hit-or-miss **10** accidental, unexpected, unforeseen, unintended

11 inadvertent **12** adventitious, coincidental, unconsidered **13** unintentional

unpleasant
4 sour **5** seamy **7** painful **8** annoying **9** offensive, troubling **10** disturbing, irritating **11** displeasing, distasteful, distressing **12** disagreeable **13** objectionable

unpolished
4 rude **5** crude, gruff, rough **6** crusty, vulgar **7** brusque, uncivil, uncouth **8** homespun **9** inelegant, roughhewn, unrefined **10** amateurish, uncultured, unfinished, ungracious **11** ill-mannered, uncivilized

unpredictable
4 iffy **5** dicey, fluky **6** chancy, fickle, random, touchy **7** erratic, mutable **8** unstable, variable, volatile **9** arbitrary, mercurial, uncertain, whimsical **10** capricious, changeable **13** unforeseeable

unprejudiced
4 fair, just **5** equal **8** balanced, unbiased **9** equitable, impartial, objective, unbigoted, uncolored **10** even-handed, fair-minded, open-minded **11** nonpartisan **12** uninfluenced **13** disinterested, dispassionate

unpressed
7 rumpled, wrinkly **8** crinkled, puckered, wrinkled

unpretentious
5 frank, plain **6** candid, honest, modest, simple **7** genuine **8** ordinary **9** unadorned **10** forthright, unaffected, unassuming **11** plain-spoken

unprincipled
5 venal **7** corrupt, crooked, immoral **9** deceitful, dishonest, dissolute, mercenary, reprobate, unethical **10** inconstant, iniquitous, profligate, unfaithful **11** underhanded **12** unscrupulous

unproductive
4 vain **6** barren, futile **7** sterile, useless **8** bootless, depleted, feckless, impotent **9** fruitless, infertile **10** unavailing **11** ineffectual **12** hardscrabble

unprofitable
4 idle, vain **6** barren, futile **7** useless **8** bootless **9** fruitless **10** unavailing **11** ineffective **12** unproductive, unsuccessful

unprogressive
8 orthodox **9** illiberal **11** traditional **12** conservative

unpropitious
4 grim **5** bleak **7** ominous, unlucky **9** ill-boding, ill-omened **10** foreboding **11** inopportune, threatening, unfavorable **12** discouraging

unprosperous
4 poor **5** needy **8** strapped **9** penurious **11** impecunious

unprotected
6 unsafe **7** exposed **8** helpless, insecure **9** unguarded **10** endangered, undefended, unshielded, vulnerable **11** defenseless, susceptible, unsheltered

unproved
7 untried **8** untested **10** postulated **11** conjectural, preliminary, provisional, speculative, theoretical **12** experimental, hypothetical

unpunctual
4 late **5** tardy **6** remiss **7** belated, delayed, overdue **10** behindhand, delinquent

unqualified
4 firm, rank **5** sheer, total, unfit, utter **7** express **8** absolute, explicit, unfitted **9** incapable, out-and-out, steadfast, unalloyed, undiluted, unskilled **10** ineligible, unequipped, unreserved, unsuitable **11** ill-equipped, incompetent, unmitigated **12** wholehearted **13** unadulterated, unconditional

unquenchable
7 exigent **9** demanding, insatiate, insistent **10** insatiable **12** effervescent, unrestrained **13** irrepressible, unconstrained

unquestionable
4 real, sure, true **7** certain, genuine **8** absolute, bona fide **9** authentic, undoubted **10** sure-enough, undeniable **11** established, indubitable, self-evident, well-founded **12** indisputable, well-grounded **13** authoritative, incontestable, unimpeachable

unquestioning
4 firm, sure **5** fixed **6** steady **7** abiding **8** enduring, gullible, resolute, trusting, unshaken **9** accepting, believing, credulous, steadfast **10** uncritical, unshakable, unwavering **11** unfaltering, unqualified **12** never-failing, unsuspecting

unravel
4 fray **5** break, solve **6** answer, decode, unknit, unwind **7** clear up, dope out, explain, resolve, unsnarl **8** decipher, dissolve, untangle **9** elucidate, extricate, figure out, interpret, puzzle out, translate **11** disentangle

unreadable
7 deadpan **9** illegible **10** poker-faced **11** inscrutable **12** hieroglyphic **13** cacographical

unreal
4 fake **5** bogus, false **6** fabled **7** fictive **8** chimeric, fanciful, illusory, mythical **9** fantastic, fictional, imaginary, imitation **10** artificial, chimerical, fictitious, improbable, incredible **11** nonexistent **12** unbelievable
combining form: **5** pseud **6** pseudo

unrealistic
7 blue-sky, idyllic, utopian **8** fanciful, quixotic, romantic **9** distorted, idealized, overblown

10 farfetched, ivory-tower, overstated, starry-eyed, unworkable **11** exaggerated, extravagant, impractical, sensational

unreasonable
5 undue **6** absurd **7** invalid **9** arbitrary, excessive, illogical, senseless **10** exorbitant, fallacious, headstrong, immoderate, inordinate, irrational, peremptory, ridiculous **11** extravagant, incongruous, uncalled-for, unwarranted **12** preposterous **13** unjustifiable

unreasoned
7 invalid, unsound **9** deceptive, illogical, sophistic, unfounded **10** fallacious, ill-founded, irrational, misleading, ungrounded **11** nonrational

unrefined
3 raw **4** rude **5** crass, crude, rough, tacky **6** coarse, earthy, impure, vulgar **7** natural, uncouth **9** graceless, inelegant, maladroit, roughhewn **10** uncultured, unpolished **11** ill-mannered, uncivilized, unprocessed **12** uncultivated

unreflective
6 casual **7** offhand **8** careless, feckless, heedless, mindless **9** imprudent, impulsive, oblivious, unheeding **10** indiscreet, nonchalant, unthinking **11** inadvertent, perfunctory, thoughtless **13** ill-considered

unrehearsed
5 ad-lib **7** offhand **8** ad-libbed, informal **9** extempore, impromptu, unstudied **10** improvised, off-the-cuff, unprepared **11** extemporary, spontaneous **12** extemporized

unrelated
8 discrete, separate **9** different, disparate **10** dissimilar, extraneous, irrelevant **11** independent

unrelenting
3 set **4** grim **5** stern **7** adamant, endless **8** constant, resolute, ruthless, tireless **9** ceaseless, continual, hard-nosed, incessant, tenacious, unbending, unsparing **10** continuous, determined, implacable, inexorable, inflexible, persistent, unflagging, unshakable, unwavering, unyielding **12** unappeasable

unreliable
6 fickle, shifty, tricky, unsafe **7** dubious **8** fallible, slippery, two-faced **9** deceitful, deceptive, faithless, trustless, uncertain **10** capricious, fly-by-night, inaccurate, inconstant, perfidious, unfaithful **11** vacillating **12** falsehearted, questionable, unconvincing, undependable **13** irresponsible, unpredictable, untrustworthy

unremarkable
4 so-so **5** plain, usual **6** common, decent, normal **7** average, mundane, prosaic, routine **8** adequate, everyday, familiar, habitual, mediocre, ordinary, workaday **9** customary, quotidian **11** commonplace, nondescript **12** run-of-the-mill **13** unexceptional

unremitting
7 abiding, chronic, endless, lasting, nonstop, ongoing **8** constant, enduring, unending **9** ceaseless, continual, incessant, perennial, perpetual, sustained, unceasing **10** continuous, persistent, persisting, relentless **12** interminable **13** uninterrupted

unrepentant
10 impenitent **11** remorseless **12** unregenerate

unrepresentative
7 deviant, unusual **8** aberrant, abnormal, atypical **9** anomalous, divergent, eccentric, irregular, untypical **11** exceptional, heteroclite **13** nonconforming

unreserved
4 open **5** frank, plain **6** candid **8** effusive, explicit, outgoing, outright **9** expansive, talkative **10** definitive **11** forthcoming, openhearted, unconcealed, undisguised, unqualified **13** demonstrative, unconstrained

unresolved
4 moot **7** pending **8** hesitant, wavering **9** faltering, tentative, uncertain, undecided, unsettled **10** ambivalent, hesitating, indecisive, irresolute, unanswered **11** vacillating

unrespectable
3 low **5** shady **6** shabby, shoddy **8** shameful, unworthy **10** inglorious **11** disgraceful, ignominious **12** dishonorable, disreputable **13** discreditable

unresponsive
4 cold **5** aloof, stoic **6** frigid, remote, stolid **7** distant, passive **8** detached, reserved **9** inhibited, withdrawn **10** forbidding, insentient **11** insensitive, passionless, unemotional **12** uninterested **13** insusceptible, unsusceptible

unrest
6 strife, tumult **7** anarchy, anxiety, ferment, tension, turmoil **8** disorder, disquiet, distress, edginess, upheaval **9** agitation, commotion, confusion **10** inquietude, turbulence, uneasiness **11** disquietude, disturbance, instability **12** perturbation **13** Sturm und Drang

unrestrained
6 wanton **7** rampant **8** uncurbed **9** audacious, excessive, unbridled **10** immoderate, inordinate, ungoverned, unhampered **11** extravagant, intemperate, spontaneous, uninhibited, untrammeled **12** uncontrolled **13** demonstrative, irrepressible, overindulgent

unrestricted
4 free, full, open **9** boundless, extensive,

unlimited **10** accessible, unconfined, unfettered, unhampered **11** far-reaching, unqualified, wide-ranging **12** unobstructed **13** unconditional

unripe
3 raw **5** green, young **6** callow, jejune **7** untried **8** emergent, immature, juvenile, unformed, youthful **9** unfledged, untrained **10** unprepared, unseasoned **11** undeveloped **13** inexperienced

unrivaled
4 only, sole **5** alone **6** unique **7** leading, stellar, supreme **8** champion, foremost, greatest, peerless **9** matchless, paramount, principal, unequaled, unmatched **10** inimitable, preeminent, unequalled **11** outstanding, predominant **12** incomparable, unparalleled

unroll
6 expose, extend, reveal, unfurl, unwind **7** exhibit, open out **8** disclose **9** spread out

unromantic
5 sober **8** sensible **9** practical, pragmatic, realistic **10** hard-boiled, hardheaded **11** down-to-earth, level-headed, utilitarian **12** business-like, matter-of-fact **13** unsentimental

unruffled
4 calm, cool **6** poised, placid, serene, smooth **7** equable, unmoved **8** composed, tranquil **9** collected, unexcited **10** nonchalant, untroubled **11** unconcerned, undisturbed, unflappable **13** imperturbable, self-possessed

unruly
4 wild **5** rowdy **7** froward, raucous, wayward, willful **8** contrary, perverse, untoward **9** fractious, obstinate, turbulent **10** boisterous, disorderly, headstrong, ill-behaved, rebellious, refractory, tumultuous **11** disobedient, intractable **12** contumacious, incorrigible, obstreperous, rambunctious, recalcitrant, ungovernable, unmanageable **13** undisciplined

unsafe
5 risky, shaky **6** chancy **7** erratic, harmful, parlous, rickety, tottery, unsound **8** insecure, perilous, slippery, unstable **9** dangerous, hazardous, uncertain **10** precarious, ramshackle, unreliable, vulnerable **11** threatening, treacherous **12** undependable

unsaid
5 known, tacit **6** silent **7** assumed, implied **8** accepted, implicit, indirect, inferred, presumed, unspoken, unstated, wordless **9** customary, unuttered **10** insinuated, undeclared, understood **11** traditional, unexpressed

unsatisfactory
3 bum **4** lame **8** mediocre **9** defective, deficient **10** inadequate **11** displeasing, substandard **12** unacceptable **13** disappointing

unsavory
4 rank **5** gross, shady **7** insipid **9** repugnant, repulsive, sickening, tasteless **11** distasteful, ill-flavored **12** disagreeable, unappetizing

unsay
4 lift, void **6** abjure, cancel, disown, recall, recant, revoke **7** nullify, rescind, retract, reverse, suspend **8** abnegate, abrogate, disclaim, forswear, renounce, take back, withdraw **11** countermand

unscathed
4 safe **5** sound, whole **6** intact, unhurt **8** unharmed **9** uninjured, unscarred, untouched **11** unscratched

unscented
8 odor-free, odorless

unschooled
5 naive **7** artless, natural, vacuous **8** ignorant **9** ingenuous, unstudied **10** illiterate, unaffected, uneducated, unlettered **11** empty-headed

unscramble
5 solve, untie **6** decode, unwind **7** clarify, clear up, resolve, restore, sort out, unravel, untwine **8** decipher, untangle **9** extricate, figure out **11** disentangle **12** disembarrass

unscrupulous
5 shady, venal **7** corrupt, crooked, knavish **8** scheming, wrongful **9** deceitful, dishonest, mercenary, shameless, underhand, unethical **11** underhanded **12** exploitative, unprincipled

unseasonable
8 ill-timed, untimely **12** inconvenient

unseasoned
3 raw **4** flat **5** bland, fresh, green, young **6** callow **7** untried **8** immature **9** credulous, tasteless, unfledged, untrained **10** flavorless **11** unpracticed **13** inexperienced

unseat
3 axe, can **4** boot, buck, fire, oust, sack **5** eject, pitch, purge, throw **6** depose, recall, remove **7** buck off, dismiss, unhorse **8** dethrone, dislodge, displace **9** ostracize

unseemliness
8 solecism **9** barbarism, gaucherie, immodesty, impudence, indecency, vulgarity **10** imprudence, incivility, indelicacy **11** impropriety **12** indiscretion

unseemly
8 improper, untoward **9** inelegant, unrefined **10** indecorous, indelicate, malapropos, unbecoming, unsuitable **11** unbefitting **13** inappropriate

unseen
6 hidden **9** concealed, invisible, unnoticed **10** overlooked, unobserved **11** unsuspected

unsentimental
see **unromantic**

unserviceable
7 useless **10** inoperable, unfeasible, unworkable **11** impractical, unrealistic **13** impracticable, nonfunctional

unsettle
3 vex **4** faze **5** spook, upset **6** bother, flurry, jumble, rattle, ruffle **7** agitate, disturb, fluster, perturb, trouble, unhinge, unnerve **8** bewilder, confound, disarray, disorder, disquiet **9** discomfit **10** discompose, disconcert

unsettled
4 open **5** fluid, owing, shaky **6** mobile, queasy, shaken, uneasy, unpaid **7** anxious, dubious, mutable, overdue, payable, pending, restive **8** agitated, bothered, doubtful, frontier, restless, troubled, unstable, unsteady, variable **9** disturbed, uncertain, undecided **10** changeable, unbalanced, unresolved **11** outstanding, problematic **12** undetermined

unsex
3 fix **4** geld, spay **5** alter **6** change, neuter **8** castrate **9** sterilize **10** emasculate

unshackle
4 free **5** loose **6** loosen, unbind **7** manumit, release, unchain **8** liberate, unfetter **10** emancipate

unshakable
4 firm, sure **5** fixed **6** stable, steady **7** abiding, adamant, settled, staunch **8** resolute **9** steadfast, tenacious **10** determined, persistent, unwavering, unyielding **11** unfaltering **12** neverfailing

unshaped
5 vague **7** nascent **8** formless, inchoate, unformed **9** amorphous, embryonic **10** incoherent **11** preliminary

unshared
4 sole **6** single, unique **7** private **8** singular **9** exclusive, undivided **10** individual **11** distinctive

unshod
8 barefoot, shoeless **9** discalced **10** barefooted

unsightly
4 ugly **5** gross **6** grisly **7** hideous **9** repulsive **10** ill-favored **12** unattractive

unskillful
5 inept **6** clumsy, gauche **7** awkward, unhandy **8** bumbling, bungling, inexpert **9** ham-handed, incapable, maladroit, stumbling, untrained

unsnarl
see **untangle**

unsociable
3 shy **4** cool **5** aloof, timid **6** offish, remote, shut-in **7** distant **8** reserved, secluded, solitary **9** diffident, reclusive, withdrawn **10** unfriendly **11** introverted, standoffish **12** inaccessible, unneighborly

unsoiled
5 clean **8** spotless **9** unspotted, unstained, unsullied, untainted **10** immaculate **11** unblemished, untarnished

unsophisticated
5 corny, green, naive **6** callow, folksy, rustic, simple **7** artless, natural, sincere, uncouth **8** gullible, innocent **9** childlike, ingenuous, unrefined, unworldly

unsorted
5 mixed **6** divers, motley, sundry, varied **7** diverse, jumbled, mingled **9** disparate, scrambled, unmatched, unrefined **10** variegated **11** diversified **12** multifarious **13** heterogeneous, miscellaneous

unsought
7 unasked, willing **8** unbidden, unwanted **9** undesired, uninvited, unwelcome, voluntary **10** gratuitous **11** spontaneous, unsolicited

unsound
3 mad **4** weak **5** frail, shaky, wrong **6** faulty, flawed, flimsy, infirm, insane, sickly, untrue **7** damaged, fragile, invalid **8** decrepit, specious **9** defective, erroneous, imperfect, incorrect, unhealthy **13** insubstantial

unsparing
5 ample, harsh, stern, tough **6** lavish, severe, strict **7** copious, liberal, onerous, profuse **8** abundant, exacting, generous, prolific, rigorous, ruthless **9** bounteous, bountiful, demanding, plenteous **10** freehanded, munificent, openhanded, unmerciful **11** magnanimous

unspeakable
4 dire, evil **5** awful **6** grisly **7** beastly, ghastly, hateful, heinous, hideous **8** dreadful, ghoulish, gruesome, horrific, shocking **9** appalling, atrocious, execrable, frightful, loathsome, monstrous, obnoxious, repugnant, repulsive, revolting **10** abominable, detestable, disgusting, horrendous, outrageous, scandalous **11** unutterable **13** inexpressible

unspoiled
5 ideal **6** intact, virgin **7** halcyon, idyllic, perfect, untamed **8** arcadian, pastoral, pristine, virginal **9** idealized, undefiled, untouched **10** unimpaired **11** unblemished, uncorrupted

unspoken
4 mute **5** tacit **6** hinted, silent, unsaid **7** assumed, implied **8** implicit, inferred, presumed, unstated, wordless **9** intimated, suggested, unuttered **10** undeclared, understood **11** unexpressed

unstable
5 fluid, shaky **6** fickle, shifty, tricky, wobbly **7** dubious, rickety, suspect **8** insecure, slippery, unsteady, variable, volatile, wavering **9** ambiguous, changeful, fluctuant, irregular, mercurial, teetering, uncertain, unsettled **10** capricious, inconstant, precarious **11** vacillating **13** temperamental, unpredictable

unstated
5 tacit **6** latent, unsaid **7** assumed, implied **8** implicit **10** understood

unsteady
5 rocky, shaky, tippy **6** uneven, wobbly **7** erratic, mutable, rickety, varying **8** shifting, unstable, variable **9** changeful, irregular, tottering **10** changeable, inconstant
British: 5 wonky

unstudied
5 naive **6** casual **7** artless, natural, offhand **8** careless, informal, unforced, unversed **9** extempore, guileless, impromptu, ingenuous, makeshift, unplanned **10** improvised, nonchalant, unaffected, unpolished **11** extemporary, spontaneous, unrehearsed **13** improvisatory

unstylish
4 drab, dull **5** dated, dowdy, fusty, passé, ratty, tacky **6** démodé, frumpy, old-hat, shabby, stodgy **7** vintage **8** outdated, outmoded **9** inelegant, moth-eaten, out-of-date **10** antiquated, old-fangled **12** old-fashioned **13** unfashionable

unsubstantial
4 thin **5** frail, shaky **6** feeble, flimsy, infirm **7** fragile, shadowy, tenuous **8** ethereal, illusory **9** dreamlike, imaginary **10** immaterial, impalpable, intangible **11** implausible, incorporeal, nonmaterial, nonphysical

unsuitable
5 inapt, undue, unfit **7** awkward, jarring **8** ill-timed, improper, unfitted, unseemly, untimely **9** ill-suited **10** ill-adapted, inadequate, inapposite, malapropos, mismatched, unbecoming **11** inadvisable, inopportune, unbefitting, unqualified **12** incompatible, infelicitous, unacceptable, unseasonable **13** inappropriate

unsullied
4 pure **5** clean **6** chaste **8** flawless, spotless, unsoiled **9** blameless, exemplary, guiltless, stainless, taintless, undefiled **10** immaculate **11** unblemished, untarnished

unsure
5 dicey, shaky **6** wobbly **7** dubious, unclear **8** doubtful, insecure, unstable, wavering **9** fluctuant, skeptical, uncertain, undecided **10** ambivalent, indecisive, irresolute, unreliable **11** unconvinced, vacillating **12** questionable, undependable **13** untrustworthy

unsurpassable
7 supreme **8** ultimate **9** matchless **10** consummate, preeminent **12** transcendent

unsusceptible
6 immune, inured **8** hardened **9** impassive, resistant **10** impervious **11** insensitive **12** invulnerable, unresponsive

unsuspecting
5 naive **6** unwary **8** gullible, trustful, trusting **9** confiding, credulous, imprudent **10** incautious

unswerving
see **unfaltering**

unsympathetic
4 cold, cool **5** chill, stony **6** averse **7** callous, unmoved **8** detached **9** apathetic, unfeeling, unpitying **10** hard-boiled **11** coldhearted, hardhearted, indifferent, insensitive, unconcerned **12** stonyhearted **13** disinterested

untactful
4 flip, rash, rude **5** brash **6** brazen **8** flippant, insolent **9** audacious, impolitic, imprudent, maladroit **10** indiscreet **11** impertinent, thoughtless **12** presumptuous, undiplomatic

untamed
4 wild **5** brute, feral **6** carnal, fierce, savage **7** bestial, brutish **8** barbaric **9** primitive **11** uncivilized

untangle
5 solve **7** clear up, explain, resolve, unravel, unsnarl, untwine, untwist **9** elucidate, extricate, interpret **10** disembroil, disentwine, straighten, unscramble **11** disencumber **12** disembarrass

untaught
5 naive **7** natural **8** ignorant, nescient **9** intuitive, untrained, untutored **10** uneducated, unlettered, unschooled **11** empty-headed, instinctual, spontaneous

untempered
6 wanton **7** extreme **9** excessive **10** gratuitous, immoderate, inordinate **11** extravagant **12** unrestrained

untenable
5 wrong **6** faulty, flimsy **10** inadequate **12** indefensible

untended
5 seedy **7** rickety, run-down **8** decrepit, derelict, deserted, forsaken, tattered **9** neglected **10** ramshackle, tumbledown, uncared-for **11** dilapidated

Unter den ____
6 Linden

untested
6 intact, unused **7** untried **8** unproved, unproven **11** unpracticed

unthinkable
10 impossible, incredible, outlandish **12** preposterous, unimaginable **13** extraordinary, inconceivable, unprecedented

unthinking
8 careless, feckless, habitual, heedless, knee-jerk **9** automatic, reflexive, unheeding, unmindful **10** distracted, unintended **11** inattentive, inadvertent, instinctive, instinctual, involuntary, perfunctory, spontaneous, thoughtless **12** unreflective

unthrifty
6 lavish, wanton **7** ruinous **8** prodigal, wasteful **9** imprudent **10** profligate **11** extravagant, improvident **12** uneconomical

untidy
5 messy **6** sloppy **7** chaotic, jumbled, unkempt **8** confused, littered, slapdash, slipshod, slovenly **9** cluttered **10** disheveled, disordered, disorderly, topsy-turvy **11** disarranged, dishevelled **12** disorganized

untie
5 let go **6** loosen, unbind, unknot, unlace, unlash **7** release, resolve, set free **8** unstring **9** extricate **11** disencumber, disentangle **12** disembarrass

until
4 up to **6** before **7** prior to **11** in advance of

untimely
5 early, undue **9** premature **10** malapropos **11** ill-seasoned, inopportune **12** unseasonable

untiring
7 devoted, patient **8** diligent, enduring **9** assiduous, ceaseless, dedicated, energetic, unceasing **10** determined, persistent, unflagging, unwavering, unwearying **11** persevering, unfaltering **13** indefatigable, inexhaustible

untold
4 huge, vast **7** immense **8** enormous, gigantic **9** countless **10** prodigious **11** innumerable, uncountable **12** incalculable **13** indescribable

untouchable
5 dalit, leper **6** pariah **7** harijan, outcast **8** outcaste

Untouchables leader
4 Ness (Eliot) **5** Stack (Robert) **7** Costner (Kevin)

untouched
4 pure **5** sound, whole **6** intact, virgin **7** unmoved **8** flawless, pristine, unharmed, unmarred, untapped, virginal **9** undamaged, unspoiled **10** unaffected **11** unblemished, unconcerned, unimpressed

untoward
7 adverse, awkward, froward, unlucky **8** ill-fated, improper, indecent, luckless, unseemly **9** unfitting, vexatious **10** ill-starred, indecorous, indelicate, unbecoming **11** intractable, unfortunate **12** inconvenient, recalcitrant, ungovernable, unmanageable, unpropitious

untrained
see **unskilled**

untrammeled
8 uncurbed **9** unimpeded **10** unconfined, unfettered, ungoverned, unhampered **11** uninhibited **12** unobstructed, unrestrained, unrestricted

untried
3 raw **5** fresh, green **6** callow, rookie **8** unproved, untested **10** innovative, pioneering, unseasoned **11** unpracticed **13** inexperienced, unprecedented

untroubled
4 calm **5** still **6** blithe, placid, serene **7** halcyon **8** carefree, composed, peaceful, tranquil **9** easygoing, unruffled **10** insouciant, nonchalant **11** unconcerned, unperturbed **12** lighthearted

untrue
4 fake **5** false, wrong **8** disloyal, specious **9** erroneous, faithless, incorrect **10** fictitious, inaccurate, unfaithful
combining form: 5 pseud **6** pseudo

untrustworthy
5 shady **6** shifty, unsafe, unsure **7** devious, dubious **8** disloyal, slippery, two-faced **9** deceptive, negligent, two-timing **10** fly-by-night, unreliable **11** duplicitous **12** questionable, undependable **13** double-dealing, irresponsible

untruth
3 fib, lie **4** sham **5** error **6** canard, deceit **7** blarney, fallacy, falsity, fiction, hogwash **9** deception, duplicity, falsehood, falseness, hypocrisy, mendacity **11** fabrication, insincerity **12** misstatement **13** prevarication

untruthful
4 sham **5** bogus, false, lying, phony **7** knavish **8** specious **9** deceitful, dishonest, erroneous, incorrect **10** fictitious, inaccurate, mendacious

untutored
see **unschooled**

unusable
7 outworn, useless **8** obsolete **9** worthless **10** inoperable, unavailing, unworkable **11** impractical, unrealistic **12** inapplicable **13** nonfunctional

unused
3 new **4** idle **5** fresh **6** excess **7** dormant, surplus **8** leftover, residual **9** untouched

unusual
3 odd **4** rare **5** outré **6** quaint, unique **7** bizarre,

curious, special, strange **8** aberrant, abnormal, peculiar, singular, uncommon, atypical, unwonted **9** anomalous, different, eccentric, irregular **11** exceptional **13** extraordinary

unusually
4 very **5** extra **6** highly, rarely, seldom **8** markedly **9** curiously, extremely, strangely **10** abnormally, especially, peculiarly, remarkably, strikingly, uncommonly **11** exceedingly **12** infrequently, particularly

unutterable
5 taboo **7** awesome **9** ineffable **11** unspeakable **13** indescribable, inexpressible

unvaried
4 like, same **5** alike **7** uniform **9** identical **10** consistent, unchanging **11** undeviating

unvarnished
see **undisguised**

unvarying
see **unchanging**

unveil
see **uncover**

unversed
3 raw **5** green **6** callow **7** untried **8** inexpert **9** unfledged **10** unfamiliar, unseasoned **11** uninitiated, unpracticed **13** inexperienced

unwanted
see **unwelcome**

unwarranted
5 undue **8** baseless **9** misguided, unfounded **10** gratuitous, groundless, immoderate, unprovoked **11** extravagant, inexcusable, injudicious, uncalled-for, unjustified **12** unreasonable **13** insupportable, unjustifiable, unsupportable

unwary
5 brash, hasty **8** careless, gullible, heedless, reckless **9** credulous, impetuous, imprudent, unguarded **10** ill-advised, incautious, indiscreet **11** thoughtless **12** unsuspecting

unwavering
see **unfaltering**

unwelcome
7 unasked **8** unsought, unwanted **9** undesired, uninvited **11** undesirable **12** unacceptable **13** objectionable

unwell
3 ill **4** sick **5** frail, shaky **6** ailing, feeble, infirm, offish, peaked, queasy, sickly, wobbly **8** diseased, stricken **9** afflicted, enfeebled, unhealthy **10** indisposed **11** debilitated

unwholesome
4 foul **5** toxic **6** sickly **7** adverse, corrupt, harmful, immoral, noisome, noxious, unsound **8** diseased **9** injurious, loathsome, offensive, unhealthy **10** pernicious, subversive **11** deleterious, detrimental, unhealthful **12** insalubrious

unwieldy
5 bulky **7** awkward, massive **8** cumbrous **9** ponderous **10** burdensome, cumbersome **12** unmanageable

unwilling
5 loath **6** averse **8** grudging, hesitant **9** obstinate, reluctant **10** indisposed **11** disinclined

unwind
4 rest, undo **5** let go, relax **6** loosen, unbend, uncoil, unfold, unreel, unroll **7** ease off, slacken, unravel **8** calm down, kick back, loosen up

unwise
4 rash **5** silly **6** stupid **7** asinine, fatuous, foolish, idiotic, witless **8** reckless **9** brainless, foolhardy, ill-judged, imbecilic, impolitic, imprudent, ludicrous, misguided, senseless **10** ill-advised, indiscreet, ridiculous **11** impractical, injudicious, thoughtless, undesirable, unfortunate **13** unintelligent

unwitting
6 chance **7** unaware **8** ignorant, innocent **9** haphazard, oblivious, unknowing, unmindful, unplanned **10** unfamiliar, uninformed, unintended **11** inadvertent **12** unacquainted

unwonted
4 rare **6** signal, unique **7** notable, unusual **8** singular, uncommon **10** remarkable, unexpected **11** exceptional **12** unaccustomed **13** extraordinary

unworkable
7 useless **8** quixotic **9** half-baked **10** impossible, infeasible, inoperable, unfeasible **11** impractical, unrealistic **12** inapplicable **13** impracticable, nonfunctional

unworldly
5 naive **6** astral, dreamy, simple **7** artless, natural **8** ethereal, innocent, trusting **9** celestial, ingenuous, spiritual, unearthly, visionary **11** impractical **13** inexperienced

unworthy
6 no-good **7** ignoble **8** shameful, unseemly **9** no-account, unmerited, worthless **10** unbecoming **11** disgraceful, inexcusable, undeserving

unwrap
see **uncover**

unwritten
4 oral **5** blank, tacit **6** latent, spoken, verbal **7** assumed **8** accepted, implicit **10** understood **11** traditional, word-of-mouth **12** conventional

unyielding
4 firm, grim, hard, iron **5** fixed, rigid, stern, stiff, stony, tough **6** dogged, mulish **7** adamant

8 hard-core, obdurate, stubborn **9** hard-nosed, immovable, insistent, obstinate, pigheaded, steadfast, unbending **10** determined, headstrong, implacable, inexorable, inflexible, persistent, relentless, unshakable **11** intractable, unrelenting **12** pertinacious, single-minded, unappeasable

up
4 hike, jump, lift, rise **5** above, ahead, arise, astir, boost, built, mount, raise, risen **6** ascend, arisen, lifted, versed **7** abreast, promote **8** familiar, increase, informed, positive **9** au courant, northward **10** acquainted, conversant
prefix: 3 ana, sur

up-and-coming
7 go-ahead, hot-shot **8** aspiring **9** promising **11** presumptive, prospective **12** enterprising

upbeat
4 rosy **5** arsis **6** cheery **7** buoyant, hopeful **8** cheerful, positive, sanguine **9** confidant, expectant, promising **10** heartening, optimistic **12** Pollyannaish

upbraid
3 rap **4** lash, rate **5** chide, scold **6** berate, rail at, rebuke, revile, scorch **7** bawl out, censure, chasten, chew out, reprove, scourge, tell off **8** admonish, chastise, reproach **9** castigate, criticize, dress down, reprimand **10** tongue-lash, vituperate

upbringing
7 nurture, rearing **8** training **9** schooling

upchuck
4 barf, hurl, puke, spew, toss **5** heave, retch, vomit **6** spit up **7** bring up, throw up **8** disgorge **11** regurgitate

upcoming
7 looming, nearing, pending **8** expected, foreseen, imminent **9** advancing, impending, onrushing **11** anticipated, approaching, forthcoming, prospective

up-country
4 bush **6** inland, sticks, upland **7** outback **8** backland, frontier, interior, outlying, woodland **9** backwater, backwoods, boondocks **10** hinterland, timberland

update
5 amend, brief, renew **6** inform, revamp, revise, revive **7** apprise, enhance, improve, refresh, restore, rundown, upgrade **8** renovate **9** modernize, refurbish **10** rejuvenate

Updike, John
character: 6 Rabbit (Angstrom)
novel: 7 Centaur (The), Couples **9** Rabbit Run **11** Rabbit Redux **12** Rabbit at Rest, Rabbit Is Rich **17** Witches of Eastwick (The)

upend
4 beat, best, drub, flip, lick, skin, trim, whip **5** cream, crush, upset **6** invert, subdue, thrash, topple, unseat, wallop **7** capsize, clobber, conquer, overrun, shellac, trounce **8** dethrone, lambaste, overcome, overturn, vanquish **9** overpower, overwhelm, subjugate

upgrade
4 hike, rise **5** boost, raise **6** prefer **7** advance, elevate, enhance, improve, promote **8** increase **9** promotion **10** betterment **11** advancement, improvement **12** breakthrough

upheaval
6 clamor, outcry, tumult, upturn **7** ferment, turmoil **8** churning, disaster, disorder **9** cataclysm, commotion **10** alteration, convulsion, disruption **11** catastrophe

uphill
4 hard **6** rising, rugged, taxing **7** arduous, labored, operose, tedious **8** climbing, grueling, toilsome **9** ascending, difficult, effortful, gruelling, laborious, punishing, strenuous, wearisome

uphold
3 aid **4** back, help, lift, prop **5** brace, carry, hoist, raise **6** assist, back up, bear up, buoy up, defend, second **7** bolster, elevate, justify, shore up, support, sustain **8** advocate, backstop, buttress, champion, maintain, side with **9** vindicate

upkeep
4 cost **7** expense **8** overhead **11** expenditure, maintenance

upland
4 mesa **5** table **7** plateau

uplift
4 buoy **5** cheer, edify, hoist, raise **6** take up **7** animate, elevate, enliven, gladden, hearten **8** brighten, embolden, inspirit **9** encourage **10** exhilarate, strengthen

upon
4 atop
prefix: 3 epi

upper class
4 rank **5** elite **6** gentry **7** peerage, quality, society, who's who **8** affluent, nobility, noblesse, well-to-do **9** blue blood, gentility, haut monde **10** patricians, patriciate **11** aristocracy **13** carriage trade, Establishment

upper hand
4 edge, sway **5** leg up **7** control, mastery **8** leverage **9** advantage, dominance **10** ascendancy **11** superiority **12** predominance

uppermost
3 top **6** apical **7** highest **8** loftiest

uppity
4 smug **5** aloof, brash **6** lordly, sniffy, snippy, snooty, snotty **7** forward, haughty, pompous **8** arrogant, cavalier **9** conceited, egotistic, imperious, know-it-all, presuming **10** disdainful, high-handed **11** overweening, pretentious **12** contemptuous, presumptuous, supercilious **13** self-asserting, self-assertive, self-important

upright
4 fair, good, just, pure, true **5** erect, moral, noble, piano **6** honest, raised **7** correct, ethical **8** elevated, goalpost, standing, vertical, virtuous **9** equitable, exemplary, honorable, impartial **10** principled, scrupulous **13** conscientious, perpendicular

uprightness
5 honor **6** repute, virtue **7** honesty, probity **8** morality, nobility **9** character, integrity, rectitude **13** righteousness

uprising
4 riot **6** mutiny, revolt **8** upheaval **9** rebellion **10** insurgence, revolution **12** insurrection

uproar
3 din, row **4** coil, fuss, to-do, riot **5** babel, brawl, broil, chaos, furor, hoo-ha, melee, whirl **6** bedlam, clamor, fracas, furore, hassle, hoo-hah, hubbub, mayhem, pother, racket, ruckus, rumpus, shindy, tumult **7** shindig, turmoil **8** brouhaha, disorder, foofaraw **9** commotion, confusion **10** hullabaloo, hurly-burly, turbulence **11** pandemonium

uproarious
5 noisy, rowdy **7** comical, rackety, raucous, riotous **8** brawling, clattery, mirthful, strident **9** clamorous, hilarious **10** clangorous, hysterical, resounding, rollicking, tumultuous **12** obstreperous **13** sidesplitting

uproot
4 grub, move, weed **8** displace, overturn, supplant **9** eradicate, extirpate, overthrow, supersede **10** annihilate, transplant **11** exterminate

upset
3 ail, ill, irk, vex **4** rile, roil **5** annoy, evert, worry **6** bother, defeat, dismay, invert, jumble, muddle, topple, tumble **7** afflict, agitate, capsize, disturb, fluster, invalid, jittery, jumbled, muddled, perturb, rattled, reverse, shook up, tip over, toppled, trouble, unnerve, worried **8** agitated, bewilder, bothered, confound, confused, disarray, dismayed, disorder, distress, overturn, troubled, turn over, unnerved **9** afflicted, confusion, disturbed, flustered, knock over, overthrow, perturbed **10** bewildered, confounded, disconcert, disordered, distracted, distressed, indisposed, invalidate, overthrown, overturned, tipped over **11** overwrought **12** apprehensive, disconcerted

upshot
5 issue **6** burden, climax, effect, ending, finish, result **7** outcome, purport **9** substance **10** conclusion, denouement **11** consequence, culmination, termination **12** significance

upside-down
7 chaotic, haywire, jumbled **8** backward, confused, inverted, pell-mell, reversed **10** disordered, overturned, topsy-turvy **13** helter-skelter

upstanding
see **upright**

upstart
5 comer **7** parvenu **8** outsider **9** arriviste, pretender **12** nouveau riche **13** social climber

upsurge
4 gain, jump, rise, rush, tide, wave **5** boost, flood, spurt, swell **6** deluge, growth **7** advance **8** increase

uptight
4 edgy **5** riled, tense **6** uneasy **7** anxious, nervous, restive, worried **8** stressed **10** high-strung

up to
4 till **5** until **6** before **11** in advance of

up-to-date
6 modern, modish, timely, trendy, with-it **7** abreast, à la mode, current, stylish **8** advanced, brand-new, contempo **9** au courant, plugged-in **10** avant-garde **11** cutting-edge, fashionable **12** contemporary **13** state-of-the-art

upturn
4 jump, rise **6** growth **8** increase **11** improvement

Urania
see **Muse**

Uranus
6 planet
moon: 5 Ariel **6** Oberon **7** Titania
mother, wife: 4 Gaea
offspring: 6 Titans **8** Cyclopes
overthrower, son: 6 Cronus

urban
9 municipal **12** metropolitan

urbane
5 suave **6** poised, smooth **7** elegant, genteel, politic, refined **8** cultured, debonair, gracious, polished **9** civilized, distingué **10** cultivated, diplomatic **12** cosmopolitan **13** sophisticated

urbanize
6 citify

urchin
3 imp **4** brat **5** child, gamin, scamp **10** ragamuffin

Urdur
see **Norn**

urge
3 egg, sic, yen **4** coax, goad, itch, lust, prod, push, spur, wish **5** drive, egg on, impel, press, prick, set on, tar on **6** adjure, cajole, compel, demand, desire, exhort, incite, induce, needle, prompt, propel **7** beseech, conjure, craving, entreat, implore, impulse, inspire, longing, passion, promote, propose, provoke, solicit, wheedle **8** advocate, appetite, blandish, pressure, yearning **9** encourage, instigate, stimulate **12** high-pressure

urgency
5 haste **6** duress, stress **8** exigence, exigency, pressure **9** necessity **10** compulsion, insistence

urgent
5 vital **6** crying **7** burning, clamant, crucial, driving, exigent, instant, present **8** critical, pressing **9** clamorous, demanding, immediate, impelling, insistent, momentous **10** compelling, imperative **11** importunate

Uriel
9 archangel

Uris novel
3 Haj (The) **5** QB VII **6** Exodus **7** Trinity **9** Battle Cry, Mitla Pass **10** Angry Hills (The), Redemption

urn
4 vase **6** vessel **7** samovar
Greek: **7** amphora

Ursa Major
9 Great Bear **11** Great Dipper

Ursa Minor
10 Little Bear **12** Little Dipper
star: **7** Polaris **8** polestar **9** North Star

Uruguay
capital: **10** Montevideo
language: **7** Spanish
monetary unit: **4** peso
neighbor: **6** Brazil **9** Argentina
river: **7** La Plata **8** Río Negro

usable
6 liquid **7** running, working **9** adaptable, available, operative **10** accessible, applicable, employable, expendable, functional, marketable, negotiable **11** exploitable, functioning, operational, serviceable

usage
3 way **4** form, mode, wont **5** habit, sense **6** action, amount, custom, manner, method, praxis **7** process **8** habitude, practice **9** formality, procedure **10** convention

use
3 ply **4** wont, work **5** apply, avail, habit, serve, treat, value, wield, worth **6** custom, demand, employ, handle, liking, manage, manner **7** benefit, exploit, operate, purpose, service, utility, utilize **8** deal with, exercise, exertion, function, impose on, occasion, practice, regulate **9** advantage, habituate, objective, relevance **10** employment, manipulate **11** application

used
8 pre-owned, shopworn **10** secondhand

used up
5 all in, spent **6** bleary, effete, sapped, wasted **7** drained, emptied, far-gone, worn-out **8** consumed, depleted **9** exhausted, washed-out

useful
3 fit **4** meet **5** handy, utile **7** helpful **8** fruitful, suitable, valuable **9** favorable, practical **10** beneficial, convenient, functional, productive, profitable, propitious, worthwhile **11** appropriate, practicable, serviceable, utilitarian **12** advantageous

usefulness
5 value, worth **7** fitness, service, utility **8** function **9** advantage, relevance, substance **10** expedience, expediency **12** practicality **13** applicability

useless
4 idle, vain **5** inept **6** futile **7** inutile **8** bootless, hopeless, unusable **9** fruitless, pointless, worthless **10** unavailing, unworkable **11** impractical, ineffective, ineffectual, inoperative **12** unproductive, unprofitable **13** impracticable, nonfunctional

user
5 buyer **6** addict **8** consumer, customer, utilizer

use up
5 drain, spend **6** devour, expend **7** consume, deplete, exhaust **8** draw down **10** run through

usher
4 lead, seat **5** guide **6** escort **7** conduct, precede **9** conductor **10** doorkeeper

usher in
5 begin, greet, start **6** launch **7** kick off, trumpet, welcome **8** announce, commence, initiate, proclaim **9** institute, introduce, originate **10** inaugurate

usual
5 stock, typic **6** common, kosher, normal, wonted **7** average, regular, routine, typical, vanilla **8** accepted, everyday, expected, familiar, habitual, ordinary, orthodox, standard, workaday **9** customary, prevalent, quotidian **10** accustomed, prevailing **11** commonplace, established **12** conventional, unremarkable

usually
6 mainly, mostly **7** as a rule **8** commonly, normally **9** generally, routinely **10** habitually, ordinarily **11** customarily

usurer
7 Shylock **9** loan shark **11** moneylender

usurp
4 take **5** seize, wrest **6** assume **7** preempt **8** arrogate, displace, supplant **10** commandeer **11** appropriate

Utah
capital: **12** Salt Lake City
city: **4** Orem **5** Ogden, Provo
college, university: **12** Brigham Young
lake: **6** Powell **9** Great Salt
motto: **8** Industry
mountain: **5** Kings (Peak)
nickname: **7** Beehive (State)
park: **4** Zion **5** Bryce **6** Arches **11** Canyonlands
river: **5** Green **6** Sevier
state bird: **14** California gull
state flower: **8** sego lily
state tree: **10** blue spruce

utensil
3 pan, pot **4** fork, tool **5** knife, spoon **6** device, vessel **8** saucepan, teaspoon **9** implement **10** instrument

uterus
4 womb

Uther Pendragon
son: **6** Arthur
wife: **6** Ygerne **7** Igraine

utile
5 handy **6** useful **7** working **9** available, operative, practical **10** accessible, convenient, dependable, functional **11** practicable, serviceable

utilitarian
6 useful **9** practical, pragmatic **10** functional
philosopher: **4** Mill (John Stuart) **7** Bentham (Jeremy)

utility
3 use **7** benefit, fitness, service **8** function **9** advantage, relevance **10** efficiency, usefulness **12** practicality **13** applicability

utilize
3 use **5** apply, spend **6** bestow, deploy, employ, handle, occupy **7** exploit **8** exercise **11** appropriate

utmost
3 nth, top **4** acme, apex, best, peak **6** height, zenith **7** extreme, highest, maximal, maximum, supreme **8** farthest, furthest, greatest, pinnacle, remotest, ultimate **9** damnedest, extremity

utopia
4 Eden, Zion **5** bliss **6** heaven **7** Elysium **8** paradise **9** Cockaigne, dreamland, Shangri-la **10** dreamworld **12** promised land **13** Elysian fields

Utopia author
4 More (Thomas)

utopian
5 ideal, lofty **6** edenic **7** dreamer **8** arcadian, fanciful, idealist, quixotic **9** grandiose, ideologue, visionary **10** chimerical, idealistic, impossible, millennial, unfeasible **11** impractical **12** otherworldly **13** castle-builder, impracticable

utter
3 say **4** damn, dang, darn, rank, talk, tell **5** sheer, speak, stark, state, total, voice **6** arrant, dashed, deuced, reveal **7** blasted, blessed, declare, deliver, divulge, express, flat-out **8** absolute, bring out, complete, crashing, disclose, infernal, outright, positive, throw out **9** downright, out-and-out, pronounce, verbalize **10** articulate, confounded, consummate **11** come out with, straight-out, unmitigated, unqualified **13** thoroughgoing

utterance
4 rant, vent, word **5** voice **6** speech **7** oration **8** delivery, speaking **9** assertion, discourse, statement **10** expression, revelation **11** declaration **12** announcement, articulation **13** pronouncement, verbalization

utterly
4 just **5** plumb, quite **6** in toto **7** totally **8** entirely **9** perfectly **10** absolutely, altogether, completely, thoroughly

uttermost
4 last **5** final **7** extreme, outmost **8** farthest, furthest, remotest

Utu
see **Shamash**

Uzbekistan
capital: **8** Tashkent
city: **7** Bokhara, Bukhara **9** Samarkand, Samarqand
desert: **8** Kyzyl Kum
enclave: **10** Karakalpak
monetary unit: **3** som **5** tiyin
neighbor: **9** Kazakstan **10** Kazakhstan, Kyrgyzstan, Tajikistan **11** Afghanistan **12** Turkmenistan
river: **8** Amu Dar'ya, Syr Dar'ya **9** Zeravshan
sea: **4** Aral

V

vacancy
4 void 6 vacuum 7 opening 8 idleness 9 blankness, emptiness

vacant
4 bare, free, idle, open, void 5 blank, clear, empty, inane, stark 6 unused 7 deadpan, vacuous 8 deserted, unfilled 9 abandoned, impassive 10 tenantless, unoccupied 11 empty-headed 12 inexpressive

vacate
4 quit, void 5 annul, clear, empty, leave 6 bow out, give up, repeal, revoke 7 abandon, rescind, retract, reverse 8 abrogate, check out, dissolve, evacuate 9 discharge 10 relinquish

vacation
4 rest, trip 5 break, leave 6 recess 7 holiday, leisure, respite, time off 8 furlough, interval 10 sabbatical 12 intermission

vacationer
7 tourist, tripper 9 weekender 10 rubberneck 12 holidaymaker

vaccination
4 shot 7 booster 9 injection 11 inoculation

vaccine
4 shot 5 serum 9 antiserum 11 preparation
inventor: 4 Salk (Jonas), Zhou (Jian) 5 Cohen (Joe), Sabin (Albert) 6 Frazer (Ian), Jenner (Edward), Talwar (Gursaran) 8 Hilleman (Maurice)

vacillate
4 sway, yo-yo 5 waver 6 dither, falter, seesaw, teeter, waffle, waggle 7 swither, whiffle 8 hesitate 9 alternate, fluctuate, oscillate 10 equivocate 12 shilly-shally

vacillating
4 weak 6 fickle, unsure, wobbly 8 hesitant, shifting, unstable, unsteady 9 fluctuant, tentative, uncertain, undecided, unsettled 10 changeable, inconstant, indecisive, irresolute 12 shilly-shally

vacillation
5 doubt 8 to-and-fro, wavering 9 hesitancy 10 fickleness, indecision 12 irresolution, shilly-shally

vacuity
4 hole, void 6 cavity, hollow, vacuum 7 inanity 9 black hole, blankness, ditsiness, ditziness, emptiness, stupidity 10 hollowness 11 nothingness

vacuous
4 idle, void 5 blank, empty, inane, silly 6 stupid, vacant 7 foolish, shallow 11 birdbrained, empty-headed, superficial

vacuum
4 void 5 space 7 suction 9 emptiness 11 nothingness
bottle: 5 dewar 7 thermos

vacuum tube
5 diode 6 triode 7 tetrode
casing: 4 bulb

vade mecum
5 guide 6 manual 8 Baedeker, handbook 9 guidebook 11 enchiridion

____ Vadis
3 Quo

vagabond
3 bum 4 hobo 5 gipsy, gypsy, idler, nomad, rogue, rover, tramp 6 picaro, roamer 7 drifter, floater, migrant, nomadic, vagrant, wastrel 8 bohemian, clochard, picaroon, runabout, runagate, traveler, wanderer 9 itinerant, transient, wandering 11 peripatetic

vagarious
6 fickle 7 erratic, flighty, mutable, wayward 8 unstable, volatile 9 impulsive, mercurial, whimsical 10 capricious, inconstant 13 unpredictable

vagary
3 bee 4 whim 5 crank, fancy, freak, humor, quirk 6 megrim, whimsy 7 caprice, fantasy 8 crotchet

vagrancy
6 roving 7 roaming 8 drifting, nomadism, rambling 9 wandering 10 itinerancy

vagrant
see **vagabond**

vague
3 dim 4 hazy 5 blear, faint, foggy, fuzzy, gauzy,

misty, muddy, woozy **6** bleary, blurry, cloudy, dreamy, slight, vacant **7** inexact, obscure, shadowy, unclear **8** confused, nebulous, vaporous **9** ambiguous, dreamlike, enigmatic, imprecise, uncertain **10** diaphanous, ill-defined, indefinite, indistinct **13** indeterminate, unsubstantial

vain
4 idle **5** empty, proud **6** futile, hollow, otiose **7** foppish, haughty, stuck-up, trivial, useless **8** abortive, arrogant, boastful, bootless, nugatory **9** conceited, fruitless, valueless, worthless **10** egocentric, profitless, sophomoric, unavailing **11** egotistical, ineffective, ineffectual **12** narcissistic, unproductive, unprofitable, unsuccessful **13** self-important

vainglorious
8 arrogant, boastful, bragging, puffed-up, vaunting **9** conceited, egotistic **10** swaggering **11** egotistical **12** supercilious

vainglory
4 pomp **5** pride **6** egoism, vanity **7** conceit, egotism **9** arrogance **10** pretension **11** haughtiness **12** boastfulness

valance
5 drape **6** pelmet **7** curtain, drapery **10** lambrequin

vale
4 dale, dell, glen **5** combe **6** dingle, hollow, valley

valediction
5 adieu **7** good-bye **8** farewell **11** leave-taking

valedictory
see **valediction**

valentine
4 card, dear, love **7** beloved, darling, tribute **10** sweetheart

valet
7 servant **9** attendant **10** manservant

valiant
4 bold **5** brave **6** heroic, plucky **7** doughty, gallant, valiant **8** fearless, intrepid **9** dauntless **10** chivalrous, courageous **11** lionhearted **12** greathearted, stouthearted

valid
4 just, true **5** legal, solid, sound **6** cogent, lawful, potent, proven **7** binding, in force, logical, telling **8** attested, bona fide, credible, forceful **9** effective, effectual, operative **10** acceptable, compelling, convincing, legitimate, persuasive **11** justifiable, trustworthy **12** well-grounded

validate
5 prove **6** affirm, ratify, verify **7** approve, bear out, certify, confirm, endorse, justify, probate **8** legalize, sanction **10** legitimate, legitimize **11** corroborate, rubber-stamp **12** authenticate, substantiate

validity
5 force, proof **7** cogency, potency **8** efficacy **9** soundness **10** lawfulness **13** effectiveness

valise
3 bag **4** grip **6** kit bag, suiter **7** handbag, Pullman **8** gripsack, suitcase **9** gladstone, two-suiter **10** weekend bag **11** portmanteau **12** overnight bag, traveling bag **13** traveling case

Valjean's pursuer
6 Javert

Valkyrle
6 maiden **8** Brynhild
mother: 4 Erda

valley
4 dale, dell, dene, glen, vale, wadi **5** basin, combe, gulch, gully, swale **6** canyon, dingle, hollow, ravine **10** depression
Africa-Asia: 4 Rift **9** Great Rift
Alps: 11 Grindelwald
ancient Greece: 5 Nemea
Asia: 7 Fergana
California: 3 Noe **4** Napa **5** Death, Squaw **7** Central **8** Imperial, Yosemite **10** San Joaquin **11** San Fernando
Dead Sea area: 6 Arabah
Dominican Republic: 5 Cibao
Egypt: 6 Kharga
England: 5 Doone
Germany: 4 Ruhr
Greece: 5 Tembi, Tempe
India: 4 Kulu **7** Kashmir (Vale of)
Ireland: 5 Avoca, Ovoca
Israel: 4 Elah
Lebanon: 4 Biqa **5** Bekaa
moon: 4 rill **5** rille
New York: 12 Sleepy Hollow
Pennsylvania: 7 Nittany
Scotland: 7 Glen Roy
Switzerland: 5 Hasli **8** Engadine **11** Grindelwald
Virginia: 10 Shenandoah
Washington: 11 Grand Coulee

Valmiki's epic
8 Ramayana

valor
4 guts **6** mettle, spirit, virtue **7** bravery, courage, heroism, prowess, stomach **8** chivalry, valiance, valiancy **9** fortitude, gallantry **10** resolution

valorous
see **valiant**

valse
5 waltz

valuable
4 dear 5 utile 6 costly, prized, useful, worthy 8 precious 9 expensive, important, rewarding, treasured 10 satisfying, worthwhile

valuate
4 rate 5 assay, price 6 assess, survey 7 adjudge 8 appraise, estimate

valuation
4 cost, rate 5 price, worth 6 rating 7 opinion 8 estimate, judgment 9 appraisal 10 assessment, estimation 12 appreciation

value
4 cost, rate 5 assay, gauge, judge, price, prize, scale, worth 6 assess, assign, charge, esteem, figure, reckon, regard, return, survey 7 account, apprize, care for, cherish, compute, quality, respect, utility 8 appraise, estimate, evaluate, quantity, treasure 9 appraisal, principle 10 appreciate, assessment, equivalent, importance 11 market price 12 denomination

valve
3 tap 4 cock, flap, gate 6 device, faucet, poppet, spigot 7 hydrant, petcock, shutoff 8 stopcock 9 regulator
cardiac: 6 mitral 8 bicuspid

vamoose
3 git 4 scat 5 leave, scram, split 6 beat it, begone, cut out, decamp, depart, get out 7 run away, skiddoo, take off 8 clear out 9 skedaddle

vamp
3 fix 4 fake, lure, mend, wile 5 ad-lib, flirt, intro, patch, siren, tempt 6 cook up, entice, groove, lead-in, make up, repair, seduce 7 beguile, charmer, rebuild 8 inveigle 9 fabricate, formulate, improvise, refurbish, temptress 10 gold digger, seductress 11 enchantress, extemporize, femme fatale
famous: 4 Bara (Theda) 5 Negri (Pola) 6 Golden (Eve), Harlow (Jean), Lamarr (Hedy), Salome 7 Delilah, Jezebel 8 Dietrich (Marlene), Mata Hari 9 Cleopatra

vampire
3 bat 5 lamia 6 Lestat, undead 7 Dracula 9 Nosferatu 11 bloodsucker
novelist: 4 Rice (Anne) 6 Stoker (Bram)

van
3 car 4 head, lead, wing 5 front, truck, wagon 7 minibus 9 forefront 11 cutting edge, leading edge

vandal
3 Hun 5 yahoo 6 looter 8 pillager 9 despoiler, destroyer, plunderer, spoliator

vandalize
5 smash, trash, wreck 6 damage, deface, ravage, tear up 7 destroy 8 demolish, sabotage

Vandal king
8 Gaiseric, Genseric

Vandyke
5 beard 6 border, collar, edging, goatee

vane
3 web 7 feather, wind tee 8 vexillum 10 bellwether 11 weathercock

Van Gogh, Vincent
brother: 4 Theo
friend: 7 Gauguin (Paul)
residence: 5 Arles
subject: 10 sunflowers

vanguard
4 lead 5 front 9 forefront 11 cutting edge, leading edge

vanilla
4 tame 5 beige, cream, plain 7 extract 8 ordinary 9 innocuous 10 white-bread 12 conventional 13 garden-variety

vanish
3 die, fly 4 fade, flee, melt 5 clear 8 dissolve, evanesce 9 disappear, dissipate, evaporate 13 dematerialize

vanity
3 ego 5 pride 6 egoism 7 conceit, egotism 8 self-love, smugness 9 vainglory 10 narcissism, pretension 13 dressing table

Vanity Fair author
9 Thackeray (William Makepeace)

vanquish
4 beat, best, drub, lick, rout 5 cream, crush, quell 6 defeat, humble, subdue, thrash 7 clobber, conquer, destroy, smother, trounce 8 surmount 9 overpower, overthrow, subjugate 10 annihilate

vantage
4 edge, odds 8 handicap 9 head start, upper hand
point: 3 POV 5 perch 7 lookout, outlook 8 position 10 watchtower

Vanuatu
capital: 8 Port-Vila
ethnic group: 10 Melanesian
explorer: 4 Cook (Capt. James)
former name: 11 New Hebrides
island: 3 Epi 5 Efate, Maéwo, Tanna 6 Ambrim 8 Aneityum, Malekula 9 Erromango, Pentecost 13 Espíritu Santo
language: 6 French
monetary unit: 4 vatu

vapid
4 dull, flat, weak 5 banal, bland, ditsy, ditzy, inane, silly 6 jejune 7 fatuous, insipid, sapless,

vacuous **9** brainless, colorless, innocuous **10** namby-pamby, wishy-washy **13** uninteresting

vapor
3 fog, gas **4** brag, haze, mist, smog **5** brume, cloud, smoke, steam **6** breath, miasma, nimbus **7** bluster **8** phantasm
condensed: 3 dew
frozen: 4 hoar, rime **5** frost **9** hoarfrost

vaporize
5 steam **6** ablate **8** disperse, dissolve, evanesce **9** dissipate, evaporate

vaporous
4 airy, hazy **5** foggy, misty, vague, wispy **6** cloudy, unreal **7** gaseous **8** ethereal, illusory, volatile **10** evanescent **13** unsubstantial

vaquero
5 waddy **6** cowboy, gaucho, herder, waddie **7** cowpoke **8** buckaroo, herdsman, wrangler **10** cowpuncher

varia
6 medley **7** mélange, mixture, omnibus **8** treasury **9** anthology **10** compendium, miscellany **11** compilation

variable
5 fluid **6** fickle, fitful, mobile, symbol **7** mutable, protean **8** unstable, unsteady, volatile **9** irregular, mercurial, uncertain, unsettled, versatile **10** capricious, changeable, inconstant **13** temperamental

variance
3 war **4** odds **6** change, strife **7** discord, dispute, dissent **8** conflict, disunity, division **9** variation **10** contention, difference, dissension, dissidence **11** fluctuation **12** disagreement

variation
4 riff **5** shade, shift **6** change, nuance **7** partita **8** mutation **9** disparity **10** alteration, difference, divergence **11** fluctuation, declination, discrepancy, oscillation **12** modification **13** dissimilarity

varicolored
see **variegated**

varicose
7 bulging, dilated, swollen

varied
5 mixed **6** motley, sundry **7** diverse, various **8** assorted **9** different, disparate, divergent **10** dissimilar **12** multifarious **13** heterogeneous, kaleidoscopic, miscellaneous

variegated
4 pied **5** mixed, pinto **6** calico, motley **7** checked, dappled, diverse, mottled, piebald, spotted **8** skewbald, stippled, streaked **9** checkered, multihued **10** multicolor, parti-color, polychrome **12** multicolored, parti-colored **13** kaleidoscopic, polychromatic

variety
3 ilk **4** kind, mode, sort, type **5** array, breed **6** flavor, medley, nature, stripe **8** mixed bag **9** diversity, variation **10** assortment, collection, miscellany, subspecies **12** multiformity, multiplicity

various
4 some **5** mixed **6** divers, sundry, unlike **7** diverse, several, unalike **8** assorted, separate **9** different, disparate, divergent, unsimilar **10** dissimilar **12** multifarious **13** heterogeneous, miscellaneous

varlet
3 cur **4** page **5** knave, rogue, skunk **6** menial, rascal, wretch **8** coistrel **9** attendant, miscreant, scoundrel **10** blackguard

varmint
4 pest **5** knave, rogue, scamp, skunk, sneak **6** rascal **7** critter **9** scoundrel

varnish
4 coat **5** adorn, cover, glaze, gloss, japan **6** veneer **7** coating, conceal, cover up, shellac **8** covering **9** embellish, gloss over, sugarcoat, whitewash
component: 5 elemi, resin

vary
5 alter, range **6** change, depart, differ, modify, mutate **7** deviate, digress, diverge **8** modulate **9** diversify

vase
3 urn **5** tazza **6** crater, krater, vessel **7** amphora

Vashni's father
6 Samuel

Vashti's husband
6 Xerxes **9** Ahasuerus

vassal
4 leud, serf **5** helot, liege, slave **6** tenant **7** bondman, homager, peasant, servant, subject **8** bondsman, liege man **9** dependent, underling **11** subordinate **12** feudal tenant
high-ranking: 7 vavasor **8** vavasour

vast
4 huge, mega **5** giant, great, jumbo **6** untold **7** immense, mammoth, oceanic, titanic **8** colossal, enormous, gigantic, spacious, whopping **9** boundless, expansive, humongous **10** gargantuan, tremendous, widespread **12** astronomical

vastness
5 sweep **8** enormity, hugeness **9** immensity, magnitude **13** expansiveness

vat
3 tub, tun **4** beck, butt, cask, kier, tank **5** keeve, kieve **6** barrel, liquor, vessel **7** cistern **8** cauldron
cheese: 7 chessel

vatic
6 mantic **7** fatidic **8** oracular **9** fatidical, prophetic, sibylline **10** predictive **11** apocalyptic

Vatican City
10 papal state
army: **11** Swiss Guards
chapel: **7** Sistine
church: **11** Saint Peter's
court: **4** Rota
ruler: **4** Pope
site: **4** Rome

vaticinal
see **vatic**

vaticinate
5 augur **6** divine **7** portend, predict, presage **8** forebode, forecast, foretell, prophesy, soothsay **9** adumbrate **13** prognosticate

vaudeville
5 revue **9** burlesque, music hall **11** variety show **12** song and dance

vaudevillian
11 entertainer

vault
3 pit, sky **4** arch, cave, dome, jump, leap, room, safe, tomb **5** bound, crypt **6** cavern, cellar, cupola, hurdle, spring, welkin **7** archway, dungeon **8** catacomb, overleap **9** firmament **10** undercroft

vaulting
4 arch, dome **7** emulous **8** aspiring **9** ambitious **12** enthusiastic **13** opportunistic

vaunt
4 blow, brag, crow, puff, rant **5** boast, strut **6** flaunt, parade **7** bluster, display, exhibit, show off **8** brandish **9** gasconade **11** rodomontade

veal
4 calf
cutlet: **9** schnitzel
roasted: **10** fricandeau
shank: **8** osso buco

vector
5 agent **7** carrier **9** direction **10** pollinator

Vedic religion
country: **5** India
god: **4** Agni, deva, Soma **5** Indra **6** Varuna
language: **8** Sanskrit
priest: **7** Brahman
treatise: **9** Upanishad
writing: **7** Rig Veda, Samhita

veer
3 yaw **4** cast, chop, slew, sway, turn **5** fetch, sheer, shift, trend **6** depart, swerve **7** deflect, deviate, digress, diverge

vegetable
3 pea, soy, udo, yam **4** bean, beet, corn, kale, leek, okra, soya, spud, taro, wort **5** chard, chive, cress, green, onion, plant **6** carrot, celery, cowpea, endive, garlic, legume, lentil, peanut, pepper, potato, radish, sorrel, squash, tomato, turnip **7** cabbage, chayote, dullard, lettuce, mustard, parsley, parsnip, pumpkin, rhubarb, salsify, shallot, soybean, spinach **8** broccoli, collards, cucumber, eggplant, kohlrabi, lima bean, rutabaga, scallion, snap bean **9** artichoke, asparagus, muskmelon **10** watermelon **11** cauliflower, horseradish, sweet potato
bog: **6** muskeg
covering: **4** peel, rind, skin
dish: **5** salad
mold: **5** humus
seller: **6** grocer **7** grocery **12** costermonger
sponge: **5** luffa **6** loofah
spread: **4** oleo **9** margarine

vegetarian
9 herbivore **11** herbivorous

vegetate
4 idle, laze, loaf, loll **5** chill, slack **6** loiter, lounge **7** goof off, hang out **8** chill out, languish, lollygag, slack off, stagnate **9** goldbrick, hibernate

vegetation
5 flora **6** growth, plants **7** verdure **8** greenery **9** plant life
floating: **4** sudd **8** pleuston

vehement
3 hot **4** wild **5** fiery, rabid **6** ardent, bitter, fervid, fierce, heated **7** excited, fervent, vicious, violent, zealous **8** forceful, powerful **9** perfervid **10** passionate **11** impassioned **12** antagonistic

vehicle
3 ATV, bus, cab, car, SUV, van **4** auto, bike, taxi, tool **5** agent, buggy, means, organ, plane, sedan, train, truck, wagon **6** agency, binder, medium, vector **7** bicycle, carrier, channel, machine, solvent, travois **8** airplane, ministry **9** ambulance, implement, motor home, transport **10** automobile, conveyance, instrument, motorcycle
baby's: **4** pram **8** carriage, stroller **9** baby buggy
child's: **5** trike **7** scooter **8** tricycle
farm: **4** wain **7** tractor
horse-drawn: **4** cart, dray **5** buggy, lorry, sulky, wagon **6** hansom, landau, troika **7** calèche, phaeton **8** carriage **9** buckboard
military: **4** jeep, tank **6** Humvee
one-wheeled: **8** unicycle
passenger: **3** bus, cab, car **4** auto, taxi **7** ricksha **8** cable car, rickshaw
public: **3** bus **4** tram **5** train **6** subway **7** omnibus, trolley
Roman: **7** chariot
winter: **4** sled **6** sleigh **8** snowplow **10** snowmobile

veil
4 caul, hide, mask, wrap **5** cloak, cloth, cloud, cover, velum **6** chador, mantle, screen, shield, shroud **7** conceal, cover up, curtain, obscure, secrete, yashmak **8** covering, disguise, enshroud **10** camouflage, false front
chalice: **3** aer
Muslim: **7** yashmak
netting: **6** maline **7** malines

vein
3 bed, way **4** line, lode, mind, mode, mood, seam, tone, tube **5** style, tenor **6** manner, nature, spirit, strain, streak, vessel **7** channel, fashion, pattern, quality, stratum **8** aptitude **11** blood vessel
combining form: **3** ven **4** veni, veno
deposit: **3** ore
fluid: **5** blood
heart: **8** vena cava
leaf: **3** rib
leg: **7** saphena **9** saphenous
neck: **7** jugular
small: **6** venule
varicose: **5** varix

velar
8 guttural
nasal consonant: **3** eng **4** agma

veld
7 prairie **9** grassland

velleity
4 bent, wish **5** fancy **6** desire, liking **7** leaning **10** propensity **11** inclination

velocipede
4 bike **5** cycle, trike **6** tandem **7** bicycle, pedicab **8** tricycle

velocity
4 pace **5** haste, speed, tempo **7** headway **8** celerity, rapidity **9** quickness, swiftness **12** acceleration

velum
4 caul, veil **8** membrane **10** soft palate

velvet
4 gain, mild, rich, soft **5** cloth **6** fabric, profit, smooth **8** winnings **10** antler skin

velvety
4 mild, soft **5** plush **6** smooth

venal
4 paid **6** sordid **7** corrupt **8** bribable **9** mercenary, unethical **11** corruptible, purchasable **12** unprincipled, unscrupulous

vend
4 hawk, sell, toot **6** market, monger, peddle, retail **8** huckster **9** advertise, broadcast

vendee
5 buyer **6** client **8** customer **9** purchaser

vendetta
4 feud **7** rivalry **9** blood feud

vendible
7 salable **8** sellable **10** marketable **12** merchantable

vendor
6 dealer, duffer, hawker, seller **7** packman, peddler **8** huckster, merchant, retailer, salesman

vendue
4 sale **7** auction **10** public sale

veneer
3 ply **4** burl, coat, face, mask, show, veil **5** cover, front, gloss, layer, plate **6** facade, facing **7** conceal, overlay **8** disguise

venerable
3 old **4** aged **5** hoary **6** sacred **7** ancient, antique, elderly, honored, revered, stately **8** esteemed **9** admirable, dignified, estimable, honorable, respected

venerate
5 adore, honor, prize **6** admire, esteem, revere **7** cherish, idolize, respect, worship **8** treasure **9** reverence

veneration
3 awe **5** honor **6** esteem, homage **7** respect, worship **9** adoration, reverence **10** admiration **11** hero worship

venery
3 sex **4** game, prey **5** chase **7** hunting

venesection
10 phlebotomy

Venetian
boat: **7** gondola
boatman: **9** gondolier
product: **5** glass **9** glassware
ruler: **4** doge
school: **6** Titian **7** Bellini, Tiepolo **8** Veronese **9** Giorgione **10** Tintoretto
street: **5** canal
suburb: **6** Murano

Venezuela
capital: **7** Caracas
city: **8** Valencia **9** Maracaibo **12** Barquisimeto
island: **9** Margarita
lake: **8** Valencia **9** Maracaibo
language: **7** Spanish
monetary unit: **7** bolívar
mountain, range: **5** Andes **6** Parima (Serra, Sierra) **7** Bolívar (Pico) **9** Pacaraima **11** Pico Bolívar, Serra Parima **12** Sierra Parima
neighbor: **6** Brazil, Guyana **8** Colombia
peninsula: **9** Paraguaná
river: **7** Orinoco
sea: **9** Caribbean
waterfall: **10** Angel Falls

Venezuelan
herdsman: **7** llanero
liberator: **7** Bolívar (Simón)
people: **5** Carib **6** Timote

vengeance
6 payoff **7** payback, redress, revenge **8** reprisal, revanche **9** repayment **10** punishment **11** retaliation, retribution

vengeful
8 punitive **10** vindictive **11** retaliatory

venial
5 minor **7** trivial **8** harmless, trifling **9** allowable, excusable, tolerable **10** condonable, forgivable, pardonable, remissible, remittable **13** insignificant

Venice of the East
7 Bangkok, Udaipur

Venice of the North
6 Bruges, Brugge **9** Amsterdam, Stockholm **12** St. Petersburg

Veni, Creator ___
8 Spiritus

venison
4 deer

veni, vidi, ___
4 vici

venom
4 bane, hate **5** spite **6** malice, poison, rancor **7** ill will, vitriol **8** embitter **9** contagion, malignity, virulence **11** malevolence

venomous
5 toxic **6** deadly, malign, poison **7** baneful, malefic, noxious **8** spiteful, viperish, viperous, virulent **9** malicious, malignant, poisonous **10** malevolent, pernicious **12** vituperative

vent
3 air **4** emit, flue, hole, pipe, pour, slit **5** burst, expel, issue, loose, utter, voice **6** broach, nozzle, outlet **7** chimney, exhaust, express, give off, opening, orifice, release, take out, unleash, volcano **8** breather, fumarole, spiracle **9** discharge **11** black smoker

venter
3 gut **5** belly **6** paunch **7** abdomen, stomach

ventilate
3 air **5** state, utter **6** aerate, expose **7** discuss, express **9** advertise, broadcast, circulate, verbalize **11** investigate

ventral area
7 abdomen, stomach

ventricle
6 cavity **7** chamber

ventriloquist
9 performer **11** entertainer
companion: **5** dummy
famous: **6** Bergen (Edgar)

venture
3 bet, try **4** dare, face, feat, gest, risk **5** brave, peril, stake, wager **6** chance, expose, gamble, hazard **7** attempt, daresay, emprise, exploit **8** endanger, jeopardy, long shot, make bold **9** challenge, crapshoot, speculate **10** enterprise **11** speculation, undertaking

venturesome
4 bold, rash **5** brave **6** daring **8** reckless **9** audacious, daredevil, foolhardy **11** adventurous, temerarious

venue
4 site **5** arena, forum, place, scene **6** locale, outlet **7** setting **8** locality

Venus
6 planet, Vesper **7** daystar, Lucifer **8** Hesperus
husband: **6** Vulcan
son: **4** Amor **5** Cupid **6** Aeneas
(see also **Aphrodite**)

Venus de ___
4 Milo

___ vera
4 aloe

veracious
4 just, true **5** exact, frank, right, valid **6** candid, honest **7** correct, factual, sincere **8** accurate, truthful

veracity
4 fact **5** truth **6** candor **7** honesty **8** accuracy, trueness **9** actuality, exactness **11** correctness **12** truthfulness

veranda
5 lanai, porch, stoop **6** piazza **7** gallery, portico

verb
auxiliary: **3** are, can, did, had, has, may, was **4** have, must, were, will, word **5** could, might, shall, would **6** should
form: **6** active, gerund **7** passive **10** infinitive, participle
kind: **10** transitive **12** intransitive
linking: **6** copula
mood: **8** optative **10** imperative, indicative **11** subjunctive
tense: **4** past **6** aorist, future **7** perfect, present **9** predicate **10** pluperfect

verbal
4 oral **5** wordy **6** gerund, spoken **7** literal **9** unwritten **10** infinitive, participle, rhetorical **11** word-for-word

verbalism
4 term **6** phrase **7** wording **8** phrasing **9** prolixity, windiness, wordiness **11** phraseology

verbalization
4 talk **6** speech **8** speaking **9** discourse, utterance **12** articulation, vocalization

verbalize
3 air, say **4** talk **5** speak, state, utter, voice, write **6** broach **7** express **8** bloviate, vocalize **9** ventilate

verbatim
5 exact **6** direct **7** exactly, literal, precise **8** directly **9** literally, literatim, precisely **10** accurately **11** word-for-word

verbiage
4 talk **6** phrase **7** diction, wording **8** parlance, phrasing, pleonasm **9** wordiness **10** redundancy **11** phraseology

verbose
5 gassy, windy, wordy **6** prolix **7** diffuse **9** garrulous, redundant, talkative **10** loquacious, pleonastic **11** tautologous

verbosity
9 prolixity, windiness, wordiness **10** redundancy

verboten
5 taboo **6** banned **7** illegal **8** outlawed **9** forbidden **10** prohibited

verdant
4 lush **5** green, leafy, naive **6** grassy, unripe

verdict
6 assize, ruling **7** finding, opinion **8** decision, judgment **9** judgement

Verdi opera
4 Aïda **6** Ernani, Oberto, Otello **7** Nabucco **8** Don Carlo, Falstaff, Lombardi (I), Traviata (La) **9** Don Carlos, Rigoletto, Trovatore (Il) **15** Simon Boccanegra

verdure
7 foliage **8** greenery **9** greenness **10** vegetation

verge
3 hem, lip, rim **4** abut, cusp, edge, sink **5** bound, brink, skirt, staff, touch **6** adjoin, border, fringe, margin **7** selvage **8** approach, shoulder **9** threshold **10** borderline

veridical
see **veracious**

verifiable
4 true **6** proven **7** certain **8** provable **9** undoubted

verification
5 proof **10** validation **11** attestation **12** confirmation **13** corroboration

verify
4 aver, test **5** check, prove, vouch **6** attest, settle **7** bear out, confirm **8** document, validate **9** establish, fact-check **11** corroborate, demonstrate **12** authenticate, substantiate

verily
5 truly **6** indeed **7** in truth **9** assuredly, certainly **11** confidently, undoubtedly

veritable
4 real, true **6** actual **7** factual, genuine **8** bona fide **9** authentic, undoubted **10** sure-enough **11** indubitable

verity
5 truth **6** gospel, truism **7** honesty, reality **9** actuality **12** truthfulness

vermiform
8 wormlike

vermilion
3 red

vermin
4 lice, mice, pest, rats, scum **5** fleas, pests, trash **7** bedbugs, varmint

Vermont
capital: **10** Montpelier
city: **5** Barre, Stowe **7** Rutland **10** Burlington
college, university: **7** Norwich **8** Marlboro **10** Bennington, Middlebury
mountain, range: **5** Green **9** Mansfield
nickname: **13** Green Mountain (State)
river: **11** Connecticut
state bird: **12** hermit thrush
state flower: **9** red clover
state tree: **10** sugar maple

vernacular
4 cant **5** argot, idiom, lingo, slang **6** common, jargon, patois, patter, speech, tongue, vulgar **7** dialect, vulgate **8** language **9** dialectal **10** colloquial **12** mother tongue

vernal
5 fresh, green **6** spring **8** youthful **10** springlike

Verne, Jules
character: **4** Fogg (Phileas), Nemo (Captain) **12** Passepartout
submarine: **8** Nautilus
work: **16** Mysterious Island (The) **21** From the Earth to the Moon **26** Around thc World in Eighty Days **28** Journey to the Center of the Earth

versant
see **conversant**

versatile
5 handy **6** adroit, facile **7** protean **8** variable **9** all-around, competent, many-sided **10** changeable **11** well-rounded **12** ambidextrous

verse
3 lay, ode **4** epic, poem, rune **5** lyric, poesy, rhyme **6** ballad, jingle, poetry, sonnet, stanza **7** passage **8** acquaint **11** composition, familiarize
amateurish: **8** doggerel
analysis: **8** scansion
four-line: **8** quatrain
free: **5** blank **8** unrhymed
humorous: **8** limerick

six-line: 6 sestet
three-line: 6 tercet
two-line: 7 couplet
writer: 4 poet

versed
5 adept 6 au fait 7 abreast, skilled, veteran 8 familiar, informed, seasoned 9 au courant, competent, practiced 10 acquainted 11 experienced 13 knowledgeable

versifier
4 bard, poet 6 rhymer 9 poetaster, rhymester, sonneteer

version
4 copy 5 draft, model 6 flavor, remake 7 account, edition, reading, variant 8 revision 9 iteration, narrative, redaction, rendition, rewording 10 adaptation, paraphrase 11 arrangement, description, incarnation, restatement, translation

versus
4 anti 6 contra 7 against, vis-à-vis 11 over against

vertebra
7 segment
kind: 6 dorsal, lumbar, sacral 8 cervical, thoracic 9 coccygeal

vertebrae
4 back 5 spine 6 coccyx, rachis, sacrum 8 backbone, tailbone 12 spinal column

vertebrate
6 animal
characteristic: 5 spine 7 cranium 12 spinal column
kind: 4 bird, fish, frog 6 mammal 7 reptile 9 amphibian

vertex
3 cap, top 4 acme, apex, peak 5 crest, crown 6 apogee, summit, tip-top, zenith

vertical
5 erect, plumb, sheer, steep 7 upright 8 straight 10 lengthwise, straight-up 13 perpendicular

vertiginous
5 dizzy, giddy, woozy 6 fickle, rotary 11 lightheaded

vertigo
6 megrim 9 dizziness, giddiness

verve
3 pep, vim, zip 4 brio, dash, élan, fire, life, zest, zing 5 flair, gusto, moxie, oomph, style, vigor 6 bounce, energy, esprit, spirit, spring 7 panache 8 vitality, vivacity 10 enthusiasm, liveliness 13 sprightliness

very
3 too 4 bare, mere, most, much, pure, real, same, true 5 exact, ideal, model, plain, quite, sheer, super, truly, utter 6 actual, ever so, highly, hugely, mighty, really, simple 7 awfully, genuine, greatly, notably, perfect, precise, special 8 absolute, actually, bona fide, selfsame, terribly 9 authentic, decidedly, extremely, genuinely, identical, undoubted 10 absolutely, particular 11 exceedingly
French: 4 très
German: 4 sehr
Italian: 5 assai, molto
Scottish: 3 gey
Spanish: 3 muy

vesicle
3 sac 4 cell, cyst 5 bulla 6 cavity 7 blister, vacuole

Vespasian's son
5 Titus

vespertilion
7 bat-like

vespers
8 evensong

____ Vespucci
7 Amerigo

vessel
3 can, cup, jar, pan, pot, tub, urn 4 boat, bowl, cask, drum, duct, ewer, olla, pail, ship, tank, tube, vase, vein 5 canal, churn, craft, cruse 6 artery, barrel, bottle, bucket, censer, firkin, flagon, kettle, krater, pottle 7 cresset, pitcher 8 crucible 9 container 10 receptacle, watercraft
Arab: 4 dhow
combining form: 3 vas 4 angi, vaso 5 angio
drinking: 3 cup, mug 4 toby 5 flask, glass, gourd, stein, stoup 6 goblet, seidel 7 tankard, tumbler
Indian: 4 lota 5 lotah
Scottish: 6 quaich, quaigh

vest
6 weskit 9 waistcoat

Vesta
see **Hestia**

vestal
4 pure 6 chaste, virgin 8 celibate, virginal, virtuous

vestibule
5 entry, foyer, lobby 6 cavity 7 hallway, narthex, passage 8 anteroom, entrance, entryway 10 antechapel 11 antechamber

vestige
4 echo 5 dregs (plural), relic, scrap, stump, trace, track 6 shadow 7 memento, remains, remnant 8 leftover 9 remainder 10 hide or hair 11 hide nor hair

vestment
3 alb 4 cope, garb, gown, robe 5 amice, cotta, dress, fanon, habit, orale, stole, tunic 6 attire,

rochet **7** apparel, cassock, garment, maniple, pallium, tunicle **8** chasuble, cincture, clothing, covering, dalmatic, parament, surplice
ancient Hebrew: 5 ephod **11** breastplate

vestry
6 closet **8** sacristy **9** sacrarium

vesture
4 robe **6** clothe **7** apparel, garment **8** clothing **10** habiliment

Vesuvius
7 volcano

vet
5 check **6** go over, review **7** analyze, examine, inspect **8** appraise, check out, evaluate, look over **10** old soldier

vetch
3 ers **4** herb, tare **6** legume
type: 4 milk (vetch) **5** crown (vetch), hairy (vetch)

veteran
4 ex-GI **5** adept **6** expert, master **7** old hand, skilled **8** old-timer, warhorse **9** practiced, shellback **10** past master **11** experienced

veto
2 ax **3** axe, nix **4** kill, void **5** quash **6** defeat, forbid, refuse, reject **7** decline, nullify **8** abrogate, disallow, negative, prohibit **9** blackball **10** disapprove **11** prohibition **12** interdiction

vex
3 bug, irk **4** fret, gall, itch, roil **5** annoy, chafe, gripe, harry, rowel, tease, worry **6** badger, baffle, bother, harass, harrow, nettle, pester, plague, puzzle, rankle, ruffle **7** chagrin, torment, trouble **8** bullyrag, distress, irritate

vexation
4 fret, sore **5** chafe, trial **6** bother **7** problem, torment **8** distress, headache **9** annoyance, troubling **10** affliction, harassment, irritation **11** aggravation, bedevilment, provocation

vexatious
5 pesky **7** prickly **8** annoying, tiresome **9** troublous **10** bothersome, irritating **11** distressing, troublesome **12** exasperating

vexed
6 sticky, touchy **7** debated, weighty **8** ticklish **9** difficult, discussed, troubling

vexing
5 tough **7** irksome **8** annoying **9** difficult, harassing, upsetting **10** bothersome, irritating **11** distressing, troublesome

via
3 per **4** over, with **5** along **7** by way of, through **9** by means of

viable
6 doable **7** capable **8** feasible, possible, workable **11** practicable, sustainable

vial
6 ampule **7** ampoule

viands
4 eats, fare, feed, food, grub **7** aliment, edibles, vittles **8** victuals **9** provender **10** provisions **11** comestibles

vibrant
5 alive, vital, vivid **6** bright, lively, punchy **7** ringing **8** resonant **9** consonant, pulsating **10** resounding **11** oscillating **12** effervescent

vibrate
3 jar **4** ring **5** quake, shake, swing, throb, waver **6** quiver, shimmy, thrill, tremor **7** flutter, pulsate **8** undulate **9** fluctuate, oscillate, vacillate

vibration
4 aura **5** quake, shake, trill **6** motion, quaver, quiver, shimmy, spirit, tremor **7** flutter, shaking **8** fremitus, wavering **9** emanation, trembling **11** fluctuation, oscillation, vacillation

vicar
6 pastor, priest **8** minister, reverend **9** clergyman

Vicar of Wakefield, The
author: 9 Goldsmith (Oliver)
character: 8 Primrose

vice
3 sin **4** evil, flaw **5** crime, fault **6** defect **7** devilry, failing, frailty, offense, scandal **8** iniquity **9** deformity, depravity, indecency **10** corruption, debauchery, immorality, perversion, wickedness **11** shortcoming

vice-president
4 veep **6** deputy **7** officer **9** executive
American: 4 Burr (Aaron), Bush (George), Ford (Gerald), Gore (Albert), King (William) **5** Adams (John), Agnew (Spiro), Dawes (Charles), Gerry (Elbridge), Nixon (Richard), Tyler (John) **6** Arthur (Chester), Cheney (Richard), Colfax (Schuyler), Curtis (Charles), Dallas (George), Garner (John Nance), Hamlin (Hannibal), Hobart (Garret), Morton (Levi), Quayle (Dan), Truman (Harry), Wilson (Woodrow) **7** Barkley (Alben), Calhoun (John Caldwell), Clinton (George), Johnson (Andrew, Lyndon Baines, Richard Mentor), Mondale (Walter), Sherman (James Schoolcraft), Wallace (Henry), Wheeler (William) **8** Coolidge (Calvin), Fillmore (Millard), Humphrey (Hubert Horatio), Marshall (Thomas), Tompkins (Daniel), Van Buren (Martin) **9** Fairbanks (Charles), Hendricks (Thomas), Jefferson (Thomas), Roosevelt (Theodore), Stevenson (Adlai) **11** Rockefeller (Nelson) **12** Breckinridge (John)

viceroy
5 nabob **6** exarch, satrap **7** khedive **8** alderman, governor **9** butterfly **11** stadtholder

vice versa
10 conversely **12** contrariwise

vicinity
4 area, nabe **5** range **6** extent, locale, region, shadow **7** suburbs **8** ballpark, district, environs, locality, nearness, precinct **9** closeness, magnitude, proximity **12** neighborhood

vicious
4 evil, mean, vile **5** cruel **6** fierce, malign, savage, sinful, wicked **7** brutish, corrupt, hateful, immoral, noxious, violent **8** depraved, horrible, perverse, spiteful **9** barbarous, ferocious, malicious, malignant, monstrous, nefarious, reprobate **10** degenerate, flagitious, iniquitous, malevolent, villainous, vindictive

vicissitude
5 rigor, trial **6** chance, change **7** weather **8** hardship, mutation, reversal **9** adversity, mischance **10** affliction, difficulty, misfortune, mutability **11** fluctuation, permutation, progression, tribulation

victim
4 butt, dupe, gull, mark, prey **5** chump, patsy **6** pigeon, martyr, quarry, sucker **7** fall guy **8** casualty, fatality, offering, underdog **9** sacrifice

victimize
4 dupe, fool, gull, hoax **5** cheat, cozen, trick **6** prey on **7** deceive, swindle **8** flimflam, hoodwink **9** bamboozle, sacrifice **11** hornswoggle

victor
5 champ **6** top dog, winner **7** subduer **8** champion **9** conqueror **10** vanquisher

Victorian
4 prim **6** prissy, stuffy **7** prudish **8** priggish **11** puritanical, straitlaced **12** old-fashioned

Victoria, Queen
family: **7** Hanover
father: **6** Edward
husband: **6** Albert
prime minister: **8** Disraeli (Benjamin) **9** Gladstone (William), Melbourne (Lord)
son: **6** Edward

victory
3 win **4** rout **5** sweep **6** defeat **7** mastery, success, triumph **8** conquest, walkaway, walkover **10** overcoming **11** superiority
costly: **7** Pyrrhic
easy: **4** romp **7** runaway **8** cakewalk, walkaway
monument: **4** arch **13** Arc de Triomphe
reward: **6** spoils
sign: **3** vee
symbol: **4** flag **6** laurel, wreath

Victory author
6 Conrad (Joseph)

victuals
4 chow, eats, feed, food, grub, prog **6** viands **7** edibles, vittles **9** provender **10** provisions **11** comestibles

___ Vidal
4 Gore

videlicet
3 viz **5** to wit **6** namely, that is **8** scilicet **11** that is to say

video game
4 Doom, Myst **6** Tetris **7** SimCity **10** Donkey Kong **12** Mortal Kombat
maker: **3** THQ **4** Sega **5** Atari, Namco, Raven, Shaba, Z-Axis **6** Capcom, Konami **7** Ubisoft, Vivendi **8** Luxoflux, Nintendo, Treyarch, Williams **9** Neversoft **10** Activision, Square Enix

vie
3 pit **5** match **6** oppose, strive **7** compete, contend, contest, counter **8** struggle

Viennese
city hall: **7** Rathaus
family: **8** Habsburg, Hapsburg
palace: **7** Hofburg
park: **6** Prater
river: **6** Danube

Vietnam
capital: **5** Hanoi
city: **3** Hue **6** Da Nang, Saigon **8** Haiphong **13** Ho Chi Minh City
delta: **6** Mekong
gulf: **6** Tonkin **8** Thailand
monetary unit: **4** dong
mountain: **8** Fan-si-pan
neighbor: **4** Laos **5** China **8** Cambodia **9** Kampuchea
river: **3** Red **6** Mekong
sea: **10** South China

Vietnamese New Year
3 Tet

view
3 eye, see **4** espy, look, plan, scan **5** scene, sight, vista, watch **6** behold, belief, look at, notice, notion, regard, review, survey **7** close-up, examine, inspect, lookout, observe, opinion, outlook, picture, scenery, vantage **8** judgment, panorama, perceive, prospect, scrutiny, snapshot **10** conviction, inspection, scrutinize **11** contemplate, examination

viewer
7 witness **8** looker-on, onlooker **9** bystander, spectator **10** eyewitness

viewing instrument
5 glass, scope **6** binocs **7** glasses **9** telescope **10** binoculars, microscope **12** field glasses
combining form: **5** scope

viewpoint
3 eye **5** angle, slant, stand **6** stance **7** outlook **8** attitude, position **9** direction **11** perspective

vigil
4 wake **5** watch **7** lookout, prayers **9** devotions **10** deathwatch **11** wakefulness **12** surveillance, watch and ward

vigilance
5 watch **9** alertness **12** surveillance, watchfulness

vigilant
4 keen, wary **5** alert, awake, aware, chary, sharp **7** careful, jealous, on guard **8** cautious, open-eyed, watchful **9** attentive, sharp-eyed, wide-awake

vignette
5 scene **6** sketch **7** glimpse, picture **8** ornament

vigor
3 pep, vim, zip **4** brio, push, snap, tuck **5** ardor, drive, force, gusto, moxie, oomph **6** energy, mettle, muscle, spirit, starch **7** potency **8** dynamism, strength, tonicity, virility, vitality **9** hardihood, lustiness, puissance **10** get-up-and-go, robustness, sturdiness

vigorous
5 brisk, hardy, lusty, stout, tough, vital **6** active, hearty, lively, potent, robust, strong, sturdy, virile **7** dashing, driving, dynamic, healthy **8** athletic, forceful, muscular, powerful, spirited, youthful **9** energetic, strenuous **10** mettlesome, red-blooded

Viking
see **Norse**

vile
4 base, evil, foul, mean, ugly **5** gross, nasty, slimy **6** filthy, horrid, sordid, vulgar, wicked **7** low-down, noisome, obscene, squalid **8** depraved, wretched **9** abhorrent, loathsome, obnoxious, offensive, perverted, repugnant, repulsive, revolting **10** despicable, disgusting **12** contemptible

vilify
5 abuse, libel, smear **6** assail, attack, berate, defame, malign **7** asperse, run down, slander, spatter, traduce **8** denounce, tear down **9** denigrate, disparage **10** calumniate

villa
5 dacha, manor **6** estate, quinta **7** château, mansion **9** residence

village
4 burg, town **5** bourg, thorp **6** hamlet **7** townlet
African: **4** dorp **5** kraal
Indian: **6** pueblo
Japanese: **4** mura
Jewish: **6** shtetl
Malay: **7** kampong
Russian: **3** mir

Village Blacksmith author
10 Longfellow (Henry Wadsworth)

villain
4 boor, heel, ogre **5** demon, devil, heavy, knave, rogue **6** bad guy, rascal, sinner **7** lowlife **8** antihero, criminal, evildoer, offender, scalawag **9** character, miscreant, reprobate, scoundrel **10** blackguard, malefactor
classic: **4** Iago **5** Judas (Iscariot) **6** Brutus (Marcus Junius) **8** Quisling (Vidkun)

villainous
4 evil **6** rotten, wicked **7** corrupt, debased, heinous, vicious **8** depraved, wretched **9** atrocious, felonious, miscreant, nefarious **10** detestable, diabolical, flagitious, iniquitous, perfidious, traitorous **11** treacherous

villainy
4 vice **5** crime **8** evilness **9** depravity, treachery, turpitude **10** corruption, wickedness

villein
7 peasant **8** villager

villenage
4 yoke **6** tenure, thrall **7** bondage, serfdom **9** servitude, thralldom

vim
3 zip **4** brio, dash, élan, gimp, zing **5** gusto, oomph, verve, vigor **6** bounce, energy, esprit, spirit **7** vinegar **9** animation **10** enthusiasm, razzmatazz

____ vincit omnia
4 Amor

vinculum
3 tie **4** bond, knot, link, yoke **5** nexus **8** ligament, ligature

vindicable
7 tenable **9** excusable **10** condonable, defendable, defensible, pardonable **11** justifiable, warrantable

vindicate
4 free **5** clear, guard, prove, right **6** acquit, avenge, defend, excuse, refute, shield, uphold, verify **7** absolve, bear out, confirm, deliver, justify, redress, revenge, support, warrant **8** maintain **9** exculpate, exonerate, safeguard **11** corroborate **12** substantiate

vindictive
5 catty, nasty **6** malign **7** hateful, hurtful, vicious **8** punitive, spiteful, vengeful, venomous **9** malicious, malignant, poisonous

vine
3 aka, hop, ivy, iyo, pea **5** grape, kudzu, liana, liane, maile, plant **6** maypop **7** chayote, climber, creeper **8** catbrier, clematis **11** bittersweet
Asian: **6** pikake
East Indian: **4** soma

vinegar
3 pep, vim **6** liquid **8** ill humor, sourness **9** condiment **12** preservative
relating to: **10** acetic acid
steep in: **6** pickle

vinegarish
4 sour **6** bitter, cranky, ornery **7** bearish, waspish **8** snappish **9** crotchety, irascible **12** cantankerous, cross-grained, disagreeable

Vinegar Joe
8 Stilwell (Joseph)

vineyard
French: **3** cru **7** château, domaine

Vinland discoverer
4 Leif (Ericsson, Eriksson) **12** Leif Ericsson, Leif Eriksson

vintage
3 age, old **4** crop, wine **5** yield **7** antique, classic, harvest **8** outdated **9** classical **10** antiquated **12** old-fashioned

Viola
brother: **9** Sebastian
husband: **6** Orsino
play: **12** Twelfth Night

viola da ___
5 gamba

violate
4 rape **5** break, wrong **6** breach, defile, offend, ravish **7** disturb, outrage, profane, traduce **8** fracture, infringe, trespass **9** desecrate, disregard **10** contravene, transgress

violation
4 foul, rape **5** break, crime, wrong **6** breach, injury **7** offense, outrage, perjury, scandal **8** trespass **9** blasphemy, injustice, sacrilege **10** illegality, infraction, ravishment **11** desecration, disturbance, misdemeanor, profanation **12** encroachment, infringement, interruption **13** contravention, transgression

violence
4 fury, riot **5** clash **6** frenzy, mayhem **7** assault, outrage, rampage **8** foul play, savagery **9** onslaught **10** distortion, roughhouse

violent
5 cruel, harsh, rabid **6** fierce, raging, savage, stormy **7** berserk, furious, intense, vicious **8** slam-bang, vehement **9** explosive, ferocious **10** hellacious **11** acrimonious, destructive

violet
5 mauve **6** purple **8** amethyst, lavender **10** heliotrope

violin
6 fiddle **10** instrument
kind: **5** Amati, Strad **8** Guarneri **10** Guarnerius, Stradivari **12** Stradivarius
part: **3** bow, nut, peg **4** neck **6** bridge, scroll, string **8** chin rest **9** tailpiece **10** soundboard **11** fingerboard
precursor: **5** rebec **6** rebeck

violinist
American: **4** Hahn (Hilary) **5** Elman (Mischa), Fodor (Eugene), Ricci (Ruggiero), Stern (Isaac) **6** Midori, Powell (Maud) **7** Heifetz (Jascha), Menuhin (Yehudi) **8** Kreisler (Fritz), Milstein (Nathan) **9** Zimbalist (Efrem)
Belgian: **5** Ysayë (Eugene) **8** Grumiaux (Arthur)
Czech: **3** Suk (Josef)
English: **7** Menuhin (Yehudi)
French: **9** Grappelli (Stéphane) **12** Francescatti (Zino)
German: **6** Mutter (Anne-Sophie)
Hungarian: **4** Auer (Leopold) **7** Joachim (Joseph), Szigeti (Joseph)
Israeli: **7** Perlman (Itzhak) **8** Zukerman (Pinchas)
Italian: **6** Viotti (Giovanne Battista) **7** Corelli (Arcangelo), Vivaldi (Antonio) **8** Paganini (Niccolo) **9** Geminiani (Francesco)
Japanese: **6** Midori (Goto)
Korean: **5** Chang (Sarah)
Latvian: **6** Kremer (Gidon)
Romanian: **6** Enescu (George)
Russian: **8** Oistrakh (David, Igor)

violin maker
4 Salò (Gasparo da) **5** Amati (Andrea, Antonio, Girolamo, Nicolo) **7** Maggini (Giovanni Paolo), Stainer (Jacob) **8** Guarneri (Andrea, del Gesù, Giuseppe, Pietro) **10** Guarnerius (Andrea, Giuseppe, Pietro), Stradivari (Antonio, Francesco, Omobono) **12** Stradivarius (Antonio, Francesco, Omobono)

VIP
3 CEO **4** BMOC, lion **5** celeb, mogul, nabob **6** big gun, biggie, bigwig, fat cat, honcho **7** big shot, notable, someone **8** big wheel, luminary, mandarin, somebody **9** big cheese, celebrity, dignitary **10** panjandrum **13** high-muck-a-muck

viper
3 asp **5** adder, snake **7** serpent **10** bushmaster, copperhead, fer-de-lance **11** rattlesnake **13** water moccasin

virago
3 hag **5** harpy, scold, shrew, vixen **6** amazon, dragon, gorgon, ogress **8** battle-ax, fishwife, harridan, Xantippe **9** battle-axe, termagant, Xanthippe

Virgil
4 poet **5** guide **6** orator **8** cicerone
epic: **6** Aeneid
hero: **6** Aeneas
poems: **8** Eclogues, Georgics

virgin
3 new **4** pure **5** first, fresh, unwed **6** chaste, intact, maiden, modest, unused, vestal **7** initial **8** celibate, innocent, primeval, pristine, spotless **9** abstinent, undefiled, unmarried, unspoiled, unsullied, untouched **10** immaculate

virginal
4 pure **5** fresh **6** chaste, intact, maiden, spinet **8** pristine, virtuous **9** undefiled, unspoiled, unsullied, untouched

Virgin Goddess
5 Diana **6** Hestia **7** Artemis

Virginia
capital: **8** Richmond
city: **7** Norfolk, Roanoke **10** Alexandria **11** Newport News **13** Virginia Beach
college, university: **3** VMI **7** Hampton **10** Sweet Briar **11** George Mason, Old Dominion **12** James Madison **13** Randolph-Macon **14** William and Mary
historical site: **10** Monticello **11** Mount Vernon **12** Williamsburg
mountain, range: **6** Rogers **9** Blue Ridge
nickname: **11** Old Dominion
river: **5** James **7** Potomac **10** Shenandoah
state bird: **8** cardinal
state flower: **7** dogwood (American)
state tree: **7** dogwood (American)

Virginian, The
author: **6** Wister (Owen)
character: **7** Trampas

Virgin Island
5 Peter **6** Norman, St. John **7** Anegada, St. Croix, Tortola **8** St. Thomas

Virgin Islands (U.S.)
capital: **15** Charlotte Amalie
island: **6** St. John **7** St. Croix **8** St. Thomas
location: **10** West Indies
territory of: **12** United States

Virgin Islands, British
capital: **8** Road Town
island: **5** Peter **6** Norman **7** Anegada, Tortola **11** Jost Van Dyke, Virgin Gorda
location: **10** West Indies

virginity
6 purity **8** celibacy, chastity **10** chasteness, maidenhead, maidenhood

Virgin Queen
9 Elizabeth

Virgo star
5 Spica

virgule
5 comma, slant, slash **7** solidus **8** diagonal

viridity
5 green **7** naïveté **9** freshness, greenness, innocence

virile
4 male **5** macho, manly **6** manful, potent, robust **7** manlike **8** forceful, vigorous **9** energetic, masculine

virtual
5 moral, tacit **7** de facto **8** implicit **9** essential, practical **10** electronic **11** fundamental

virtuality
4 core, pith, soul **5** being, juice, stuff **6** effect, marrow, nature **7** essence, makings **8** quiddity **9** substance **10** capability **12** essentiality, quintessence, potentiality

virtually
4 nigh **6** all but, almost, fairly, nearly, next to **7** morally **8** as good as, in effect, well-nigh **9** basically, in essence, literally **10** implicitly **11** effectively, essentially, practically **13** approximately, fundamentally, substantially

virtue
5 merit, power, right, trait, valor, value, vigor, worth **7** courage, feature, potency, probity, quality **8** chastity, goodness, morality, strength **9** attribute, character, puissance, rectitude, rightness **10** excellence, excellency, perfection **11** uprightness
cardinal: **4** hope, love **5** faith **7** charity, justice **8** prudence **9** fortitude **10** temperance

virtuosic
5 showy **6** expert, flashy **7** hotshot, skilled **9** brilliant, masterful **10** consummate, prodigious **12** razzle-dazzle

virtuoso
4 whiz **6** expert, master, savant, wizard, wonder **7** artiste, hotshot, maestro, prodigy **10** past master, wunderkind

virtuous
4 good, pure **5** moral, noble, pious, right **6** chaste, decent, modest, proper **7** ethical, sinless **8** innocent, spotless **9** blameless, faultless, guiltless, righteous, unsullied, untainted **10** inculpable, moralistic **11** respectable, right-minded, untarnished

virulent
5 harsh, toxic **6** biting, bitter, malign, poison **7** cutting, hateful, hostile, noxious **8** scathing, spiteful, venomous **9** malicious, malignant, pestilent, poisonous, rancorous, vitriolic **10** pathogenic

virus
3 bug **8** pathogen **9** contagion, infection

vis
5 force, might, power

visage
3 mug, pan **4** cast, face, look, mien, phiz, puss **6** aspect, kisser **8** features **9** semblance **10** expression **11** countenance

vis-à-vis
4 date **6** escort, facing, toward, versus **7** against **8** fronting, opposite, together **9** tête-à-tête **10** compared to, face-to-face **11** counterpart

visceral
3 gut **4** deep **5** inner **8** internal, intimate **9** intuitive **10** intestinal **11** instinctive, instinctual

viscid
see **viscous**

viscount
4 lord, peer **8** nobleman

viscous
4 limy, ropy **5** gluey, gooey, gummy, limey, slimy, thick **9** glutinous, semifluid **10** gelatinous **12** mucilaginous

vise
5 clamp, screw **7** squeeze

Vishnu
4 Hari
avatar: 4 Rama **5** Kurma **6** Buddha, Matsya, Vamena, Varaha **7** Krishna **9** Narasinha
consort: 3 Sri **4** Shri **7** Lakshmi
home: 4 Meru

visible
6 patent **7** obvious **8** apparent, viewable **9** available, well-known **10** detectable, observable **11** conspicuous, discernible, macroscopic, perceivable, perceptible **12** recognizable

Visigoth
conquest: 4 Rome
king: 6 Alaric

vision
3 eye **5** dream, fancy, image, sense, sight **6** beauty, seeing **7** concept, fantasy, feature, picture, specter **8** daydream, eyesight, phantasm, presence, prophecy **9** foresight, nightmare **10** apparition, perception, phenomenon, revelation **13** manifestation
combining form: 4 opto **5** opsis
deceptive: 6 mirage
relating to: 5 optic **6** visual **7** optical

visionary
4 seer **5** ideal, lofty, noble **6** unreal **7** blue-sky, dreamer, utopian **8** fanciful, idealist, illusory, quixotic, romantic **9** ambitious, ideologue, imaginary **10** abstracted, daydreamer, idealistic, starry-eyed **11** impractical

visionless
5 blind

visit
3 gam, see **4** call, chat, stay, talk, tour **5** pop in, run in **6** call on, come by, drop by, drop in, look in, look up, stay at, stop by, stop in **7** force on, sojourn **8** come over, converse, stay with, stopover **10** social call

visitation
3 woe **4** wake **5** cross, trial **6** misery, ordeal, plague **8** calamity **9** martyrdom **10** affliction **11** tribulation

visitor
5 alien, guest **6** caller, drop-in **7** company, invitee **8** stranger, visitant **9** transient **10** houseguest

visor
4 bill, mask **6** domino **8** eyeshade, disguise, face mask, sunshade

vista
4 view **5** scene, sight **7** lookout, outlook **8** panorama, prospect **9** landscape **11** perspective

visual
5 optic **6** ocular **7** graphic, optical, seeable **8** viewable **9** pictorial **11** discernible, perceivable, perceptible

visualize
3 see **4** view **5** fancy, image **6** call up **7** feature, imagine, picture **8** conceive, envisage, envision **9** conjure up

vital
4 dire **5** alive **6** lively, living, mortal, urgent **7** animate, crucial, pivotal **8** animated, cardinal, critical, decisive, integral, pressing, required, vigorous **9** essential, important, necessary, requisite **10** imperative, red-blooded **11** fundamental, life-or-death **12** invigorating **13** indispensable

vitality
see **vigor**

vitalize
5 liven **6** arouse, excite, infuse, perk up, spirit, vivify **7** animate, enliven, quicken **8** energize **9** encourage, galvanize, stimulate **10** invigorate

vitals
see **viscera**

vitamin
6 biotin, niacin **7** choline, folacin, retinal, retinol **8** thiamine **9** carnitine, cobalamin, folic acid **10** calciferol, pyridoxine, riboflavin, tocopherol **12** ascorbic acid

Vita Nuova author
5 Dante (Alighieri)

vitelline
5 yolky **6** yellow

vitiate
3 mar **4** harm, soil, undo **5** annul, spoil, sully, taint **6** damage, debase, defile, impair, negate **7** blemish, corrupt, debauch, deprave, nullify, pervert, tarnish **8** abrogate **9** undermine **10** bastardize, demoralize, invalidate

vitreous
6 glassy

vitriol
4 acid, bile **5** spite, venom **6** malice, rancor **7** sulfate **8** acrimony **9** virulence **12** sulfuric acid

vitriolic
4 acid **5** acrid **7** acerbic, caustic, cutting, mordant **8** scathing, stinging, virulent **9** rancorous, truculent

vituperate
3 rag **4** lash, rail, rant, rate **5** abuse, baste, curse, scold, score **6** berate, malign, revile, scorch **7** asperse, bawl out, chew out, condemn, cuss out, upbraid **8** lambaste **9** castigate **10** tongue-lash

vituperation
5 abuse **6** rebuke **7** censure, obloquy, reproof **8** scolding **9** contumely, invective **10** scurrility **11** fulmination, mudslinging **12** billingsgate **13** tongue-lashing

vituperative
7 abusive, railing, scurril **8** scathing, scolding, scurrile, venomous, viperish **9** invective **10** censorious, scurrilous **11** opprobrious **12** contumelious

vivace
5 brisk **6** lively **8** animated, spirited

vivacious
3 gay **4** airy, pert **5** perky, spicy, sunny, zesty **6** bouncy, breezy, bubbly, jaunty, lively, sparky **7** buoyant, chipper **8** animated, pixieish, spirited **9** ebullient, sprightly **12** effervescent, high-spirited

vivacity
see **verve**

Vivaldi epithet
9 Red Priest (the)

____ vivant
3 bon

vivarium
9 terrarium

viva voce
4 oral **6** orally, spoken **11** word-of-mouth

viverrid
5 civet, fossa, genet **7** linsang

vivid
5 alive, sharp **6** bright, garish, lively, punchy, visual **7** graphic, intense, vibrant **8** animated, colorful, eloquent, lifelike **9** chromatic, pictorial **10** expressive **11** picturesque

vivify
5 liven, renew **6** excite, infuse, kindle, revive **7** animate, enliven, quicken, refresh, restore **9** stimulate

vixen
3 fox, nag **5** harpy, scold, shrew **6** ogress, virago **8** fishwife, harridan, Xantippe **9** termagant, Xanthippe

viz
5 to wit **6** namely, that is **8** scilicet **9** videlicet **12** in other words

vizard
4 face, mask **5** guise, visor **6** domino **8** disguise

vocabulary
4 cant **5** argot, lingo, slang, words **6** jargon, patois **7** lexicon **8** glossary **9** word-hoard **10** vernacular **11** terminology

vocal
4 oral **5** blunt, frank **6** phonic, spoken, voiced **7** uttered **8** eloquent **9** outspoken **10** articulate, expressive, free-spoken

vocalic
5 vowel

vocalist
4 diva **6** belter, canary, singer **7** crooner, warbler, yodeler **8** minstrel, songbird **9** balladeer, chanteuse, chorister **10** cantatrice, prima donna

vocalization
4 song **5** voice **6** speech **7** diction **8** speaking **9** utterance **11** enunciation **12** articulation **13** pronunciation

vocalize
3 air, hem **4** sing, talk **5** chant, croon, speak, state, utter, voice **6** warble **7** express **9** enunciate, pronounce

vocal organ
6 larynx **8** voice box
bird: 6 syrinx

vocation
3 art, job **4** call, work **5** craft, trade **6** career, métier **7** calling, mission, pursuit **8** business, lifework **10** employment, handicraft, occupation, profession

vociferate
3 bay, cry **4** bark, bray, call, roar, yawp, yell **5** shout **6** bellow, clamor, holler **7** thunder

vociferous
4 loud **5** noisy **6** shrill **7** blatant, clamant, raucous **8** strident **9** clamorous **11** open-mouthed **12** obstreperous

vodka
brand: 5 Stoli **7** Absolut **8** Smirnoff **11** Stolichnaya
source: 3 rye **4** corn **5** wheat **6** barley, potato

vogue
3 cry, fad, ton **4** chic, mode, pose, rage **5** craze, favor, furor, style, trend **6** furore **7** fashion **10** dernier cri, popularity **11** stylishness

voice
3 put, say **4** part, talk, tell, vent **5** say-so, sound, speak, state, utter **6** assert, choice, medium, singer, speech **7** declare, express, opinion, present **8** vocalize **9** condition, enunciate, formulate, pronounce, statement, utterance, verbalize **10** articulate, expression, instrument
female: **4** alto **5** mezzo **7** soprano **9** contralto
high: **5** tenor **7** soprano **8** falsetto
in grammar: **6** active **7** passive
Latin: **3** vox
male: **4** bass **5** tenor **8** baritone
quality: **5** pitch **6** timbre
quiet: **7** whisper
relating to: **5** vocal **8** phonetic
without: **4** dumb, mute

voice box
6 larynx

voiced
4 oral **5** vocal **6** sonant, spoken **7** uttered **8** phonated **9** expressed

voiceless
3 mum **4** dumb, mute, surd **6** silent **8** breathed **12** inarticulate

void
3 gap, nix **4** emit, hole, idle, lack, null, undo **5** abyss, annul, blank, clear, empty, inane, quash **6** bereft, cancel, cavity, hollow, negate, remove, vacant, vacate, vacuum **7** absence, give off, negated, nullify, rescind, reverse, vacuity, vacuous **8** abrogate, deserted, evacuate **9** black hole, discharge, eliminate, emptiness **10** extinguish **11** nothingness

voilà
4 ta-da **5** ta-dah, there

volant
4 fast, spry, yare **5** agile, fleet, quick, zippy **6** flying, lively, nimble **9** dexterous, sprightly

volar
6 palmar

volatile
5 flaky **6** fickle, flakey, flying, lively **7** erratic, essence, flighty **8** fleeting, fugitive, skittery, skittish, unstable, variable, volcanic **9** ephemeral, explosive, fugacious, mercurial, momentary, transient **10** capricious, changeable, evanescent, inconstant, short-lived, transitory **11** impermanent **13** temperamental

volatility
10 fickleness **11** flightiness, inconstancy, instability **13** changeability

volcanic
7 violent **8** volatile **9** explosive
crater: **4** maar
explosion: **8** eruption
glass: **8** obsidian
matter: **3** ash **4** lava, tufa, tuff **5** magma **6** scoria
mound: **4** cone
passage: **6** throat **7** conduit
vent: **8** fumarole **9** solfatara

volcano
4 hill, vent **8** mountain
Alaska: **6** Katmai (Mount) **8** Wrangell (Mount) **9** Aniakchak (Crater)
Andes: **5** Omate **12** Huaina Putina
Antarctica: **6** Erebus (Mount)
Azores: **4** Alto (Pico)
California: **6** Lassen (Peak)
Canaries: **5** Teide (Pico de), Teyde (Pico de) **8** Tenerife (Pico de)
Colombia: **5** Huila (Nevado del), Pasto **6** Purace **7** Galeras
Costa Rica: **4** Poás **5** Barba, Irazú
Ecuador: **6** Sangay **8** Antisana, Cotopaxi
extinct: **4** Popa (Mount) **5** Iriga, Kenya (Mount) **8** Mauna Kea **9** Haleakala (Crater)
Guatemala: **4** Agua **5** Fuego **7** Atitlán
Hawaii: **7** Kilauea **8** Mauna Kea, Mauna Loa
Honshu: **4** Nasu **5** Asama, Azuma **6** Bandai **8** Nasudake **9** Asamayama
Iceland: **5** Askja, Hecla, Hekla
Indonesia: **3** Awu (Gunung) **5** Agung (Gunung) **7** Tambora (Gunung)
island: **5** Thera, Thira **8** Krakatau, Krakatoa, Santorin **9** Santorini
Italy: **8** Vesuvius **9** Stromboli
Iwo Jima: **9** Suribachi (Mount)
Japan: **3** Aso **5** Unzen **6** Asosan
Java: **4** Gede (Gunung) **5** Bromo, Gedeh (Gunung), Kelud (Gunung), Salak (Gunung)
Madeira: **5** Ruivo (Pico)
Martinique: **5** Pelée (Mount)
Mexico: **6** Colima **7** Orizaba **9** Paricutín **12** Popocatepetl
mud: **5** salse
New Zealand: **7** Ruapehu (Mount) **9** Ngauruhoe, Tongariro
Peru: **5** Misti (El)
Philippines: **3** Apo (Mount) **4** Taal **5** Mayon (Mount) **8** Pinatubo (Mount)
Sicily: **4** Etna
Solomons: **5** Balbi
South America: **5** Lanín, Maipo, Maipu
Sumatra: **5** Dempo (Gunung) **7** Kerinci **8** Kerintji
type: **6** shield **10** cinder cone
Washington: **11** Saint Helens (Mount)
West Indies: **9** Soufrière

___ volente
3 Deo

volition
4 will **6** choice, desire, intent, option **8** decision, election **9** selection **10** preference

volley
4 hail, shot **5** burst, round, salvo, storm **6** return, shower **7** barrage **8** drumfire **9** broadside, cannonade, discharge, fusillade

volplane
5 glide

Volpone
3 Fox (The)
author: **6** Jonson (Ben)
servant: **5** Mosca

Volsung
grandson: **6** Sigurd **9** Siegfried
great-grandfather: **4** Odin
son: **7** Sigmund

voltage
5 power **6** energy **9** intensity

Voltaire
drama: **5** Zaïre **6** Alzire, Brutus, Mèrope, Oedipe **7** Mahomet **8** Tancrède
novel: **5** Zadig **7** Candide
real name: **6** Arouet (François Marie)

volte-face
5 U-turn **8** flip-flop, reversal, turnover **9** about-face, inversion, turnabout **10** switcheroo **13** change of heart

voluble
4 glib **5** gabby, talky, windy **6** chatty, fluent, mouthy, prolix **7** verbose **8** effusive, vocative **9** garrulous, talkative **10** long-winded, loquacious

volume
4 body, book, bulk, mass, size, tome **5** album, flood, folio, space **6** amount, scroll **7** content **8** capacity, loudness, quantity **9** aggregate **12** displacement

voluminous
4 full **5** bulky **6** legion, prolix **7** copious **8** numerous, prolific **9** capacious **10** convoluted **13** multitudinous

Volumnia's son
10 Coriolanus

voluntary
4 free **7** willful, willing, witting **8** elective, freewill, optional **10** autonomous, deliberate, volitional **11** independent, intentional, spontaneous **13** discretionary

volunteer
5 offer **6** enlist, join up, sign up **7** present, propose, suggest
hospital: **12** candy striper

Volunteer State
9 Tennessee

voluptuous
4 sexy **5** ample, buxom **6** wanton **7** languid, sensual **8** luscious, sensuous **9** bodacious, luxurious **10** curvaceous

volute
5 helix, shell **6** scroll, spiral **7** mollusc, mollusk **8** curlicue

vomit
3 gag **4** barf, cast, gush, hurl, lose, puke, spew, toss **5** expel, retch **6** spit up **7** bring up, throw up, upchuck **8** disgorge **11** regurgitate

vomiting
6 emesis

Vonnegut work
9 Galapagos, Timequake **10** Cat's Cradle, Hocus Pocus **11** Player Piano **13** Sirens of Titan (The) **18** Slaughterhouse Five **20** Breakfast of Champions **22** Happy Birthday Wanda June

voodoo
3 hex **4** jinx, juju, mojo **5** charm, magic, spell, vodun **6** amulet, whammy **7** bewitch, enchant, sorcery **8** ensorcel, wizardry **9** ensorcell **10** hocus-pocus, mumbo jumbo, necromancy, witchcraft **11** abracadabra, implausible, unrealistic
relative: **5** obeah **8** santeria **9** Candomblé

voracious
4 avid **5** eager **6** ardent, greedy, hungry **7** piggish, starved **8** edacious, famished, ravenous, starving **9** rapacious **10** gluttonous, insatiable, omnivorous, quenchless

vortex
4 eddy, gyre **5** swirl **7** tornado **9** hurricane, maelstrom, whirlpool, whirlwind **11** tourbillion

votary
3 bug, fan, nut **4** buff **5** lover **6** addict, zealot **7** admirer, apostle, devotee, groupie, habitué **8** adherent, advocate, believer, disciple, follower **9** worshiper **10** aficionado, enthusiast, worshipper

vote
3 opt **4** poll **5** elect, judge, offer **6** ballot, choice, choose, decide, ratify, select, ticket **7** adjudge, declare, endorse, express, opinion, propose, suggest, verdict **8** election, suffrage **9** franchise **10** expression
affirmative: **3** aye, nod, yea, yes **6** placet
kind: **5** proxy, straw, voice **6** secret **7** write-in **8** absentee **10** plebiscite, referendum
negative: **2** no **3** nay
right to: **8** suffrage **9** franchise

votive
8 grateful **10** devotional

vouch
5 prove **6** affirm, assert, assure, attest, uphold, verify **7** certify, confirm, support, witness **8** accredit **9** guarantee **11** corroborate **12** substantiate

voucher
3 IOU **4** chit **5** proof **6** coupon, surety **7** receipt **9** affidavit, indenture **10** credential **11** certificate **13** authorization

vouchsafe
4 give **5** award, favor, grant **6** accord, bestow, confer, oblige **7** concede, furnish

vow
4 aver, oath, word **5** swear, troth **6** assert, attest, pledge, plight **7** confirm, declare, promise, warrant **8** covenant **9** assertion, guarantee **10** obligation **11** declaration

vowel
6 letter, symbol **11** speech sound
kind: 4 high, long **5** glide, schwa, short **9** diphthong **11** monophthong
omission: 7 aphesis **11** contraction
variation: 6 ablaut, umlaut

voyage
4 sail, trek, trip **5** jaunt **6** cruise, junket, outing, travel **7** journey, odyssey, set sail **8** traverse **9** excursion **10** expedition, pilgrimage

voyeur
6 peeper **10** peeping Tom

Vronski's lover
12 Anna Karenina

Vulcan
see **Hephaestus**

vulgar
3 low, raw **4** base, lewd, loud, rude, vile **5** crass, crude, gaudy, gross, rough, showy, tacky **6** coarse, earthy, flashy, garish, ribald, sordid, tawdry **7** chintzy, kitschy, lowbred, lowbrow, obscene, profane, uncouth **8** churlish, improper, indecent, off-color, unseemly **9** barbarous, graceless, low-minded, offensive, tasteless, unrefined **10** indecorous, indelicate, scurrilous, unpolished, vernacular **11** pretentious

vulgate
10 vernacular

Vulgate translator
6 Jerome

vulnerability
8 exposure, soft spot, weakness **10** underbelly **12** Achilles' heel

vulnerable
4 open, weak **6** liable **7** exposed **10** assailable **11** susceptible

vulnerary
4 balm **5** salve, tonic **7** healing, unguent **8** curative, ointment, remedial, salutary, sanative **9** medicinal, wholesome **10** salubrious **11** restorative, therapeutic **12** healthgiving

vulpine
3 sly **4** foxy, wily **5** slick **6** artful, astute, crafty, shrewd, tricky **7** cunning, foxlike **8** guileful

vulture
4 bird **6** condor **11** lammergeier, lammergeyer
food: 7 carrion
relative: 4 hawk **5** eagle **6** falcon **7** buzzard

vulturine
8 ravenous **9** predatory, rapacious, raptorial **10** predaceous, predacious, scavenging

W

wacky
3 fey, mad **4** daft, nuts **5** batty, daffy, crazy, flaky, kooky, loony, loopy, silly **6** absurd, fruity, insane, screwy **7** bonkers, cracked, foolish, idiotic, lunatic, offbeat **8** crackers, demented **9** eccentric **10** irrational **11** harebrained **12** preposterous

wad
3 gob, jam **4** chaw, cram, lump, mint, pile, plug, quid, roll, swab **5** chunk, stuff **6** boodle, bundle, packet, pellet **7** fortune **8** bankroll

waddle
6 toddle

waddy
4 club, cosh **6** cowboy, cudgel **7** rustler **8** bludgeon

wade
4 ford, plod **5** labor **6** drudge, plodge, trudge
into: **5** set to **6** attack, plunge, tackle **9** undertake

wadi
3 bed **4** wash **5** gully **6** arroyo, coulee, course, ravine **9** streambed **10** depression **11** watercourse

wafer
4 chip, disk, host **5** matzo, obley, slice **6** matzoh **7** cracker

waffle
4 yo-yo **5** tripe, waver **6** dither, drivel, seesaw **7** blather **8** flip-flop **9** fluctuate, vacillate **10** equivocate

waft
4 flag, gust, puff, waif, wave **5** carry, drift, float, hover **7** pennant

wag
3 bob, nod, wit **4** card, lash, wave **5** clown, cutup, joker, shake, swing, whisk **6** kidder, switch, twitch, waddle **8** brandish, comedian, funnyman, jokester

wage
3 fee, pay **6** income, reward, salary **7** carry on, payment, stipend **8** earnings, pittance, receipts **9** emolument **10** recompense **12** compensation, remuneration

wager
3 bet, lay, pot **4** ante, game, risk **5** stake **6** chance, gamble, hazard **7** venture

waggery
3 gag **4** jest, joke **5** prank, sport **7** devilry, kidding, roguery **8** deviltry, drollery, mischief **10** impishness, pleasantry **11** roguishness **12** sportiveness **13** practical joke

waggish
4 arch, pert **5** antic, comic, droll, saucy, witty **6** impish, jocose **7** comical, jocular, playful, puckish, roguish **8** humorous, prankish, sportive **9** facetious **10** frolicsome **11** mischievous

waggle
3 bob **4** reel, sway

Wagner, Richard
birthplace: **7** Leipzig
father-in-law: **5** Liszt (Franz)
festival site: **8** Bayreuth
opera: **4** Ring **6** Rienzi **7** Walküre (Die) **8** Parsifal **9** Lohengrin, Rheingold (Das), Siegfried **10** Die Walküre, Tannhäuser **12** Das Rheingold **13** Meistersinger (Die) **14** Flying Dutchman (The) **15** Götterdämmerung **16** Tristan und Isolde **17** Ring of the Nibelung (The)
patron: **6** Ludwig
recurring theme: **9** leitmotif, leitmotiv
wife: **5** Minna **6** Cosima

wagon
3 van **4** cart, dray, tram, trek, wain **7** caravan, coaster, hayrack **9** Conestoga

wahoo
3 ono **8** mackerel **9** winged elm **11** burning bush

waif
5 gamin, stray **6** gamine, orphan, urchin **8** wanderer **9** foundling **10** ragamuffin **11** guttersnipe

wail
3 bay, cry **4** bawl, blub, fuss, howl, keen, weep, yowl **5** mourn, whine **6** bemoan, lament, plaint, repine **7** blubber, ululate **8** complain **9** complaint **11** lamentation

wain
5 wagon **9** Big Dipper

wainscot
4 dado

waistband
3 obi 4 belt, sash 6 girdle 8 ceinture, cincture 10 cummerbund

waistcoat
4 vest 5 gilet 6 jerkin, weskit

wait
4 bide, idle, lurk, stay 5 abide, dally, delay, serve, tarry, watch 6 expect, hold on, linger, remain 8 hang fire, mark time, sit tight 10 anticipate 11 stick around

waiter
4 tray 6 carhop, garçon, salver, server 7 servant 9 attendant

Waiting for ___
5 Godot, Lefty

wait on
4 tend 5 serve 6 attend, tend to 7 care for, cater to 9 look after

waive
4 cede, stay 5 allow, defer, delay, forgo, table, yield 6 give up, hold up, put off, shelve 7 abandon, concede, dismiss, hold off, suspend 8 hand over, hold over, postpone 9 surrender 10 relinquish

wake
4 path, stir, wash 5 alert, arise, get up, rally, rouse, track, vigil, watch 6 arouse, bestir, excite, kindle, stir up 7 roll out 8 activate, backwash 9 aftermath, stimulate

wakeful
5 alert 8 restless, vigilant 9 insomniac, sleepless

waken
see **wake**

Walden author
7 Thoreau (Henry David)

wale
3 rib 4 bend, welt 5 brace, ridge 6 strake

Wales
capital: 7 Cardiff
city: 6 Bangor 7 Newport, Swansea 8 St. David's
island: 8 Anglesey
mountain: 7 Snowdon
patron saint: 5 David
river: 3 Dee
strait: 5 Menai
symbol: 4 leek 6 dragon 8 daffodil
(see also **Cymric**)

walk
3 pad 4 gait, hike, hoof, pace, path, plod, roam, slog, step, trip 5 alley, amble, clump, mince, paseo, stave, strut, stump, trail, tramp, tread, troop 6 hoof it, prance, ramble, sashay, stride, stroll, toddle, trudge, waddle, wander 7 saunter, shamble, shuffle, stumble, swagger, traipse 8 ambulate, traverse 9 promenade 11 base on balls, perambulate, peregrinate

walkaway
4 romp, rout

walking shorts
8 Bermudas

walking stick
4 cane 5 staff 6 crutch, insect 7 phasmid, whangee

walk out
5 leave 6 strike

walk out on
5 leave 6 desert 7 abandon, forsake

Walküre composer
6 Wagner (Richard)

walkway
4 path 7 passage 9 promenade

wall
3 bar, hem 4 side, stop 5 block, close, fence, hedge 6 immure 7 barrier, close in, enclose 8 blockade, surround 9 barricade, enclosure, roadblock, structure
bearing: 7 support
hanging: 8 tapestry
painting: 5 mural 6 fresco
protective: 7 parapet, rampart
top of: 6 coping

wallaby
8 kangaroo

wallet
5 funds 6 folder 8 billfold 9 accessory, resources 10 pocketbook

Wallis and Futuna Islands
capital: 7 Matautu
island: 4 Uvéa
territory of: 6 France

wallop
3 bop, hit 4 bang, bash, beat, belt, blow, boil, bust, clip, drub, lick, pelt, slam, slug, sock, whip, whop, whup 5 baste, paste, pound, punch, smack, whack 6 buffet, pummel, thrash, thwack 7 shellac, trounce 8 lambaste

walloping
4 huge 5 giant 7 immense, mammoth, monster 8 colossal, enormous, gigantic, smashing 10 gargantuan, impressive, incredible, prodigious

wallow
4 bask, roll 5 enjoy, revel 6 billow, welter 7 delight, indulge 9 luxuriate

Wall Street debut
3 IPO

____ Walpole
4 Hugh 6 Horace

____ Walton
3 Sam 5 Izaak

waltz
5 dance, valse

Waltz King
7 Strauss (Johann)

Wampanoag chief
9 Massasoit, Metacomet 10 King Philip

wampum
4 peag 5 beads, money 6 shells

wan
3 dim 4 ashy, gray, pale, waxy, weak, worn 5 ashen, faint, livid, lurid, pasty, waxen 6 anemic, doughy, feeble, infirm, pallid, peaked, sallow, sickly 7 ghastly, languid 8 blanched 9 bloodless, colorless, washed-out 10 cadaverous, white-faced

wand
3 rod 4 pole, tube 5 baton, staff

wander
3 bat, bum, gad 4 mill, roam, rove, swan 5 amble, dally, drift, float, gypsy, mooch, prowl, range, stray, tramp 6 ramble, stroll 7 deviate, digress, diverge, maunder, meander, saunter, traipse 8 divagate, straggle, vagabond 9 expatiate, gallivant 10 kick around

wanderer
4 waif 5 gypsy, nomad, rover, stray 7 pilgrim, vagrant 8 runabout, vagabond

wandering
7 erratic, migrant, nomadic, vagrant 8 vagabond 9 itinerant, migratory, walkabout, wayfaring 10 roundabout 11 peripatetic

wane
3 dim, ebb 4 fail, fall 5 abate, let up 6 lessen, recede, reduce, relent, shrink, weaken 7 decline, dwindle, slacken, subside 8 decrease, diminish, moderate, slack off, taper off

wangle
6 scheme 7 finagle, wheedle 8 inveigle, scrounge 10 manipulate

wannabe
5 clone 7 also-ran, copycat, hopeful, wishful 8 apparent, aspiring, desiring, desirous 9 ambitious, look-alike, potential

want
4 lack, like, need, void, wish 5 covet, crave, fault 6 dearth, desire, penury 7 absence, poverty, require 8 exigency 9 indigence, necessity, neediness, privation 10 deficiency, desiderate, inadequacy, scantiness 11 destitution, requirement 13 insufficiency

wanting
4 away, less, sans 5 minus, scant, short 6 absent, scanty, scarce 7 lacking, missing, without 9 deficient 10 inadequate, incomplete 12 insufficient

wanton
4 doxy, jade, lewd, minx, rank, slut 5 bawdy, cruel, hussy, loose, tramp, trull, wench 6 coquet, floozy, harlot, lavish, trifle, unruly 7 baggage, cyprian, immoral, jezebel, lustful, obscene, Paphian, sensual, trollop, wayward 8 inhumane, pitiless, ruthless, slattern, spiteful, sportive, strumpet 9 dissolute, luxuriant, malicious, merciless 10 gratuitous, lascivious, malevolent, outrageous, prostitute 11 extravagant, mischievous, uncalled-for

wapiti
3 elk 4 stag 7 red deer

war
4 feud, odds 5 fight 6 battle, combat, strife 7 contest 8 conflict, struggle, variance 9 hostility 10 antagonism 11 competition
German: 5 Krieg 10 blitzkrieg
god: 3 Tiu, Tyr 4 Ares, Mars, Odin 5 Woden, Wotan
goddess: 4 Enyo 5 Anath 6 Inanna, Ishtar 7 Bellona
Latin: 6 bellum
Muslim: 5 jehad, jihad
relating to: 7 martial

War and Peace
author: 7 Tolstoy (Leo)
character: 6 Andrey (Prince), Pierre (Bezukhov) 7 Natasha (Rostova)
composer: 9 Prokofiev (Sergey)

warble
4 sing 5 carol, chirp, trill, tweet 6 gadfly, maggot, quaver 7 descant, melisma, twitter

warbler
4 bird 6 singer 7 kinglet 8 songster 9 blackpoll 11 gnatcatcher
European: 10 chiffchaff

____ Warbucks
5 Daddy

war casualties group
3 DAV

war cry
5 motto 6 slogan
Greek: 5 alala
Japanese: 6 banzai

ward
4 care 5 aegis, stave 6 barrio, charge 7 custody, defense, keeping 8 district, division, precinct, security 9 bishopric 10 protection 11 safekeeping 12 guardianship

warden
6 jailer, keeper, regent **7** provost **8** governor, guardian, official **9** castellan, constable, custodian, protector **10** commandant, supervisor

ward off
5 avert, parry, rebut, repel **6** divert **7** deflect **8** turn away **9** forestall

wardrobe
5 trunk **6** closet **7** apparel, armoire, clothes **8** clothing **9** garderobe **12** clothespress
assistant: **7** dresser

warehouse
4 stow **5** depot, lodge, stock, store **7** confine, deposit, shelter, storage, stowage **8** building **9** stockroom, storeroom **10** depository, repository **11** accommodate
oriental: **6** godown

wares
4 line **5** goods, stock **9** vendibles **11** commodities, marketables, merchandise

warfare
6 battle, combat, strife **8** conflict, struggle **10** operations **11** hostilities
type: **4** germ **6** trench **10** biological

warhorse
4 hack **5** steed **7** charger, courser, veteran **8** chestnut, standard

warlike
7 hawkish, martial **8** militant, military **9** bellicose, combative, truculent **10** aggressive, pugnacious **11** belligerent

warlock
3 wiz **4** mage **5** magus **6** wizard **8** conjurer, conjuror, magician, satanist, sorcerer **9** diabolist, enchanter **11** necromancer

warm
4 bask, heat, kind **5** angry, fresh **6** ardent, genial, heated, heat up, loving, reheat, secure, tender **7** affable, cordial, excited, fervent, sincere **8** friendly, gracious, spirited **9** heartfelt **10** passionate, responsive **11** kindhearted, sympathetic **12** affectionate, enthusiastic, wholehearted **13** compassionate
air: **7** thermal

warmed-over
5 banal, stale, tired, trite **6** old-hat **7** clichéd **8** shopworn, timeworn **9** hackneyed

warmhearted
4 kind **6** benign, kindly, loving, tender **7** cordial **8** generous **9** benignant, unselfish **10** benevolent **11** magnanimous, sympathetic **12** affectionate **13** compassionate

warmth
4 glow, heat **7** comfort **8** fondness **9** affection **10** cordiality

warmup
5 run-up **6** lead-in, opener **7** kickoff, preface, prelude, preview **8** overture, preamble, prologue **9** countdown **11** preliminary **12** introduction

warn
3 tip **4** clew, clue **5** alert **6** advise, inform, notify, tip off **7** apprise, caution, counsel **8** admonish

warning
3 tip **4** hint **5** alarm, alert **6** caveat, notice, signal, tip-off **7** caution, counsel, summons **8** monition, monitory **10** admonition, cautionary **12** admonishment
legal: **6** caveat

War of the Worlds author
5 Wells (H. G.)

warp
4 base, bend, cast, kink, rope, wind **5** color, curve, twist **6** buckle, debase, deform, wrench **7** confuse, contort, corrupt, deflect, distort, pervert, torture, vitiate **10** bastardize **12** misrepresent

warrant
4 pawn, writ **5** proof, prove, token **6** affirm, assert, assure, attest, avouch, ensure, ground, insure, pledge, secure **7** certify, contend, declare, justify, precept **8** guaranty, maintain, mittimus, sanction, security **9** assurance, authority, authorize, guarantee **10** foundation **11** certificate **12** confirmation **13** justification

warranty
4 bail, bond **6** surety **8** covenant, security **9** guarantee

warren
4 maze **7** network, rabbits **8** tenement

Warren novel
14 All the King's Men

warrior
2 GI **4** hero **7** battler, fighter, soldier **8** champion **9** combatant **10** serviceman
female: **6** Amazon
Japanese: **5** ronin **7** samurai
princess: **4** Xena **7** Lawless (Lucy)

Warsaw
castle: **5** Zamek
river: **7** Vistula

wart
4 flaw **6** defect, growth **7** blemish, verruca **11** excrescence

wary
5 alert, cagey, canny, chary, leery **7** careful, dubious, guarded, mindful **8** cautious, skittish, vigilant, watchful **10** suspicious **11** circumspect, distrustful

wash
3 lap, pan, tub 4 hose, lave, suds, wadi 5 bathe, clean, creek, douse, drift, float, flush, gully, marsh, scrub, slosh, swill 6 drench, shower, sluice, splash 7 cleanse, coating, launder, laundry, shampoo, suffuse 8 backwash

washed-out
4 beat 5 all in, faded, spent, tired, weary 6 bushed, effete, sapped, used-up, wasted 7 drained 8 depleted 9 exhausted

washed-up
4 beat, done 5 kaput, spent 6 done in 7 also-ran, defunct, done for, through 8 finished

washing
4 bath 6 lavage 7 laundry 8 ablution, lavation
ceremonial: 6 lavabo

Washington
capital: 7 Olympia
city: 6 Tacoma 7 Seattle, Spokane 9 Vancouver 10 Walla Walla
college, university: 7 Gonzaga, Whitman 9 Evergreen
dam: 11 Grand Coulee
mountain, range: 7 Cascade, Olympic, Rainier 8 St. Helens
nickname: 9 Evergreen (State)
river: 6 Yakima 8 Columbia
state bird: 9 goldfinch
state flower: 12 rhododendron
state tree: 7 hemlock

Washington, D.C., designer
7 L'Enfant (Pierre-Charles)

Washington, George
home: 11 Mount Vernon
wife: 6 Martha

Washington Square author
5 James (Henry)

wasp
5 mason 6 digger, hornet, vespid 8 braconid 9 ichneumon, mud dauber 12 yellow jacket

waspish
5 testy 6 snappy, snarky, snippy, touchy 7 peevish, vespine 8 petulant, snappish, vinegary 9 crotchety, fractious, irritable, querulous 10 vinegarish 12 cantankerous, cross-grained

wassail
5 binge, carol, drink, revel, spree, toast 6 bender 7 carouse, revelry, roister 8 carousal, drinking

Wasserstein play
15 Heidi Chronicles (The) 17 Sisters Rosenzweig (The)

waste
4 arid, fail, kill, loss, ruin, sack, wild 5 empty, offal, scrap, trash 6 barren, damage, debris, desert, devour, litter, ravage, refuse, sewage, shrink, weaken 7 badland, consume, despoil, destroy, fritter, garbage, pillage, plunder, rubbish 8 decrease, desolate, emaciate, enfeeble, misspend, prodigal, spoilage, squander, wear away, wildland 9 devastate, dissipate, excrement, sweepings, throw away 10 desolation, wilderness 11 prodigality 12 extravagance, extravagancy
maker: 5 haste
time: 5 dally 6 dawdle, footle, piddle, trifle

waste away
4 fade, fail 6 molder, shrink 7 atrophy, decline, dwindle, shrivel 10 degenerate

wasted
3 lit 4 high 5 drunk, gaunt 6 peaked, sickly, stoned 7 elapsed, ravaged 8 skeletal 9 emaciated 10 cadaverous, skeletonic 11 intoxicated

wasteful
6 lavish 8 prodigal 9 throwaway 10 profligate, thriftless, uneconomic 11 extravagant, improvident, inefficient, spendthrift

wastefulness
6 excess 10 lavishness 11 prodigality 12 extravagance, immoderation

wasteland
4 wild 5 heath 6 barren 10 desolation, wilderness

Waste Land author
5 Eliot (T. S.)

wastrel
3 rip 4 rake, roué 7 rounder, spender 8 prodigal 9 fritterer, libertine 10 dissipater, high roller, ne'er-do-well, profligate, squanderer 11 scattergood, spendthrift

watch
3 eye, see, spy 4 bide, look, mind, tend, tout, wait, wake, ward 5 guard, shift, vigil 6 attend, follow, look at, notice, sentry 7 care for, lookout, monitor, observe, surveil 8 bulletin, eagle eye, scrutiny, sentinel, watchman 9 attention, timepiece, vigilance 10 duty period, observance 11 chronometer, observation 12 surveillance
chain: 3 fob
maker: 10 horologist

watchdog
5 guard 6 keeper 8 Cerberus, guardian 9 custodian, protector

watcher
6 viewer 7 guarder, lookout 8 beholder, follower, guardian, observer, onlooker 9 spectator

watchful
4 wary 5 alert, chary 7 on guard, wakeful

8 cautious, vigilant 9 attentive, observant, sleepless, wide-awake 10 unsleeping
Scottish: 5 tenty 6 tentie

watchman
5 guard, scout 6 patrol, picket, sentry, warder 7 lookout 8 sentinel

watch out
6 beware 8 take care

watchtower
6 turret 7 lookout 8 barbican, bartizan 10 lighthouse

watchword
3 cry 5 motto 6 mantra, parole, signal, slogan 8 password 9 principle 10 shibboleth 11 catchphrase, countersign

water
4 hose, soak, thin, tide 5 drink, fluid, spray 6 dilute, liquid, supply 7 moisten 8 irrigate, moisture, snowmelt, sprinkle 10 excellence 13 amniotic fluid
body: 3 bay, sea 4 gulf, lake, pool 5 ocean 6 lagoon, strait 9 reservoir
combining form: 4 aqui, aquo, hydr 5 hydro
French: 3 eau
goddess: 4 Nina 7 Anahita, Anaitis
Latin: 4 aqua
Spanish: 4 agua

water buffalo
4 arna 5 bovid 7 carabao
female: 5 arnee

water clock
9 clepsydra

water closet
2 WC 3 loo 4 head, john 5 privy 6 toilet 7 latrine 8 bathroom, lavatory

watercourse
4 dike, duct 5 bayou, canal, ditch 6 arroyo 7 channel, conduit 8 aqueduct, headrace, tailrace 9 streambed

water cow
6 dugong 7 manatee

watered-down
5 washy 6 dilute 7 diluted

waterfall
5 chute, sault, shoot 7 cascade 8 cataract
Brazil: 6 Iguaçú (Falls), Iguazú (Falls)
California: 8 Yosemite (Falls)
Canada: 5 Grand (Falls) 8 Takkakaw 9 Churchill (Falls)
Canada-U.S.: 7 Niagara (Falls)
Congo: 6 Boyoma (Falls) 7 Stanley (Falls)
former Nile: 4 Owen (Falls) 5 Ripon (Falls)
Kentucky: 10 Cumberland (Falls)
New Zealand: 10 Sutherland (Falls)
Niagara: 8 American, Canadian 9 Horseshoe
Norway: 6 Rjukan (Falls)
Oregon: 9 Multnomah (Falls)
South Africa: 6 Tugela (Falls)
Snake River: 4 Twin (Falls) 8 Shoshone (Falls)
Venezuela: 5 Angel (Falls)
Washington: 10 Snoqualmie (Falls)
world's highest: 5 Angel (Falls)
Wyoming: 11 Yellowstone (Falls)
Zambezi River: 8 Victoria (Falls)

water finder
6 dowser 11 divining rod

waterfront
8 seacoast 9 lakeshore, riverside

water hole
5 oasis

watering hole
3 bar, pub 4 café 5 oasis 6 lounge, nitery, resort, saloon, tavern 7 barroom, cabaret, gin mill, taproom 9 nightclub, nightspot, roadhouse 10 supper club 11 rathskeller

waterless
3 dry 4 arid, sere 7 bone-dry, parched 8 droughty 9 anhydrous 10 dehydrated

waterlog
8 saturate

waterloo
4 ruin 6 defeat 7 failure 8 disaster, downfall

water nymph
3 nix 4 lily 5 naiad, nixie 6 mayfly, Nereid 7 Oceanid 9 dragonfly

water oscillation
6 seiche

water pipe
4 bong 5 spout 6 hookah 8 narghile, nargileh 12 hubble-bubble

water plant
7 aquatic, seaweed 8 duckweed, wild rice 9 arrowhead, tape grass 10 hydrophyte, manna grass 11 bladderwort

water rat
6 nutria

watershed
6 crisis, divide 12 turning point

water spirit
3 nix 5 nixie, nymph 6 sprite, undine

water tank
7 cistern

watery
4 pale, thin, weak 5 banal, bland, vapid, washy 6 dilute, serous 7 diluted, insipid

wattle
4 gill, grid, jowl 5 frame 8 caruncle 9 framework, interlace 10 interweave

wattle and ___
4 daub

wave
3 wag 4 flag, flap 5 heave, ridge, surge, sweep, swell 6 comber, influx, marcel, motion, period, ripple, signal, waggle 7 breaker, dismiss, flutter, gesture, upsurge 8 activity, brandish, flourish, undulate 9 disregard
large: 7 tsunami

waver
4 reel, sway 5 swing, weave 6 dither, falter, quaver, quiver, teeter, totter, wobble 7 flicker, stagger, whiffle 8 hesitate, undulate 9 oscillate, vacillate 12 shilly-shally

wavering
4 weak 5 shake, shaky 6 unsure, wobbly 7 halting 8 doubtful, insecure, to-and-fro, unstable 9 equivocal, faltering, fluctuant, hesitancy, undecided, vibration, whiffling 10 hesitating, hesitation, indecision, irresolute 11 fluctuating, vacillating, vacillation 12 irresolution, shilly-shally

Waverley novels
6 Rob Roy 7 Ivanhoe 10 Kenilworth 14 Quentin Durward
author: 5 Scott (Walter)

wavy
4 ondé, undé 7 rolling 8 rippling, swelling 9 fluctuant 10 undulating 11 fluctuating

wavy pattern
5 moiré 8 squiggle 10 undulation 11 crenulation

wax
4 come, grow, rise 5 boost, build, mount 6 become, expand, record 7 augment, enlarge 8 heighten, increase, multiply, paraffin, simonize 9 secretion, substance
Chinese: 4 pela

waxen
3 wan 4 ashy, pale 5 ashen, livid 6 pallid, smooth 7 pliable 8 blanched, moldable 9 colorless

way
3 ilk 4 door, kind, mode, much, path, road, sort, type, very 5 entry, habit, means, order, route, state, style, usage 6 access, artery, action, avenue, course, custom, degree, manner, method, street 7 ability, fashion, feature, ingress, opening, outcome, respect 8 distance, entrance, practice 9 boulevard, condition, direction, procedure, technique 11 opportunity, possibility 12 thoroughfare

wayfarer
4 hobo 5 gipsy, gypsy, hiker, nomad, rover, tramp 7 rambler 8 traveler, vagabond 9 itinerant, journeyer, traveller

wayfaring
6 roving 7 nomadic, vagrant 8 vagabond 9 itinerant, traveling, wandering 10 travelling 11 peripatetic 13 perambulatory

waylay
4 jump 5 brace 6 ambush, attack 8 surprise 9 bushwhack, still-hunt

Wayne's World
actor: 5 Myers (Mike) 6 Carvey (Dana)
character: 5 Garth, Wayne

Way of All Flesh author
6 Butler (Samuel)

Way of the World author
8 Congreve (William)

wayward
5 balky 6 fickle, unruly 7 froward, restive, vagrant, willful 8 contrary, perverse, untoward 9 whimsical 10 capricious, headstrong 11 intractable, wrongheaded 12 ungovernable 13 unpredictable

we
French: 4 nous
German: 3 wir
Italian: 3 noi
Spanish: 8 nosotros

weak
3 dim, wan 4 puny, soft, thin 5 faint, frail, shaky, timid 6 dilute, feeble, flimsy, infirm, sickly, unsure, watery, wobbly 7 brittle, diluted, fragile, rickety, spindly, tenuous, unsound 8 decrepit, delicate, helpless, impotent, inferior, insecure, timorous, unstable, wavering 9 deficient, enfeebled, inaudible, powerless, spineless, uncertain 10 improbable, inadequate, unreliable, unstressed 11 debilitated, implausible, ineffective, ineffectual, vacillating, watered-down 12 unconvincing, undependable 13 insubstantial, unsubstantial

weaken
3 lag, sap 4 fail, flag, thin, wane 5 abate 6 damage, dilute, impair, lessen, reduce, soften 7 corrode, decline, disable, dwindle, subvert, unbrace 8 enervate, enfeeble, moderate 9 attenuate, grind down, honeycomb, undermine 10 debilitate, demoralize, invalidate

weak-kneed
5 timid 6 wobbly 7 gutless 8 cowardly, wavering 9 faltering, uncertain, whiffling 10 irresolute 11 lily-livered, vacillating 12 fainthearted, shilly-shally 13 pusillanimous

weakling
4 wimp, wuss 5 mouse, sissy 7 doormat, milksop, sad sack 8 pushover 9 jellyfish 10 namby-pamby 11 milquetoast, mollycoddle 12 invertebrate

weakness
4 flaw, hole, vice **5** crack, fault, taste **6** defect, desire, liking, relish **7** failing, frailty **8** appetite, debility, fondness, soft spot **9** infirmity **10** feebleness **11** decrepitude, shortcoming **12** Achilles' heel

weal
4 welt **5** ridge **7** welfare **9** well-being

weald
5 woods **6** forest **8** woodland **10** timberland, wilderness

wealth
5 goods, worth **6** assets, estate, mammon, plenty, riches **7** capital, fortune **8** holdings, opulence, property **9** abundance, affluence, profusion, resources **11** possessions

Wealth of Nations author
5 Smith (Adam)

wealthy
4 rich **5** flush **6** loaded **7** moneyed, opulent, well-off **8** affluent, well-to-do **9** well-fixed **10** prosperous, well-heeled **12** silk-stocking

wean
4 free, part **5** alien **6** detach **8** accustom, estrange, separate

weapon
3 bow, gun **4** bill, bolo, bomb, club, dart, dirk, mace, nuke, pike, shiv **5** A-bomb, arrow, H-bomb, knife, lance, prick, rifle, saber, sabre, sling, spear, steel, sword **6** dagger, Magnum, musket, pistol, poleax, rapier, rocket **7** bazooka, broadax, car bomb, carbine, firearm, gisarme, halberd, handgun, javelin, machete, missile, shotgun, sidearm, stun gun, torpedo, war club **8** battle-ax, bludgeon, broadaxe, catapult, crossbow, death ray, nerve gas, nunchaku, partisan, partizan, petronel, revolver, spontoon, tomahawk **9** battle-axe, blackjack, boomerang, derringer, slingshot **10** atomic bomb, machine gun, projectile **11** blunderbuss, depth charge, nuclear bomb **12** quarterstaff **13** brass knuckles

weapons
4 arms **7** arsenal, battery **8** ordnance **9** armaments, artillery, munitions **13** armamentarium

wear
3 rub **4** fray, tire **5** chafe, dress, erode, grind **6** abrade, attire, endure, impair **7** corrode, exhibit, fatigue, fashion **8** abrasion, clothing
and tear: **12** depreciation
thin: **4** fray **5** chafe **6** tatter **7** hackney

wear down
5 drain, erode, grind **6** abrade, weaken **7** corrode, degrade, exhaust, fatigue

weariness
5 ennui **7** boredom, fatigue, languor **8** lethargy **9** lassitude **10** enervation, exhaustion **12** taedium vitae

wearing
6 taxing, tiring, trying **9** difficult, fatiguing

wearisome
see **tiresome**

wear out
3 fag **4** bust, do in, fray, poop, tire **5** drain **6** efface, tucker **7** consume, deplete, exhaust, frazzle **8** overstay

weary
4 beat, jade, limp, tire, worn **5** drain, jaded, spent, tired **6** bushed, done in, pooped, tucker, wasted **7** drained, fatigue, worn-out **8** dog-tired, fatigued, tiresome **9** apathetic

weasand
6 gullet, throat **7** trachea **8** windpipe **9** esophagus

weasel
5 dodge, evade, hedge, slink, sneak, stoat **6** ermine, escape, ferret, mammal **7** sneaker **8** sidestep **9** pussyfoot **10** equivocate
Scottish: **8** whittret

weather
4 rain **5** storm **6** bear up, endure, expose **7** climate, ride out, undergo **9** withstand
forecasting: **11** meteorology

weathercock
4 vane

weathered
8 hardened, seasoned, tempered

weave
4 cane, lawn, leno, spin, sway **5** braid, cloth, lurch, twine, waver **6** careen, fabric, pleach, raddle, wobble, zigzag **7** pattern, stagger, textile, texture **8** contrive **9** interlace **10** crisscross, intertwine

weaver
4 loom **7** Arachne, webster

web
3 net **4** mesh, vane **5** snare, snarl **6** enmesh, fabric, tangle **7** ensnare, netting, network **8** entangle **10** enmeshment **12** entanglement

Weber opera
6 Oberon **9** Euryanthe **10** Freischütz (Der)

___ Webster
4 Noah **6** Daniel

Web vending
5 e-tail **9** e-commerce

wed
4 join, link, mate, yoke **5** hitch, marry, merge, unite **6** splice **7** combine, conjoin, connect, espouse **10** tie the knot

wedded
7 marital, nuptial **8** conjugal, hymeneal **9** connubial **11** matrimonial

wedding
5 union **6** bridal **7** spousal **8** espousal, marriage, nuptials
words: 3 I do

wedding anniversary
fifteenth: 7 crystal
fifth: 6 wooden
fiftieth: 6 golden
first: 5 paper
seventy-fifth: 7 diamond
tenth: 3 tin
twentieth: 5 china
twenty-fifth: 6 silver

wedge
4 shim **5** chock, stuff **8** golf club, golf shot, keystone **10** force apart

wedge-shaped
7 cuneate **8** cottered, sphenoid **9** cuneiform
mark: 5 caret

wedlock
4 knot, yoke **8** espousal, marriage **9** matrimony **11** conjugality **12** connubiality

wee
4 tiny **5** bitsy, bitty, early, small, teeny **6** little, minute, teensy **9** itty-bitty, miniature **10** diminutive, teeny-weeny **11** Lilliputian, little bitty **12** teensy-weensy

weed
4 dock, tare **5** chess, clear, plant **6** cockle, darnel, dodder, nettle, remove **7** burdock, burseed, ragweed, ruderal **8** amaranth, charlock, purslane **9** chickweed, cocklebur, dandelion, knotgrass, marijuana, poison ivy, poison oak, stickseed **10** cheatgrass, lady's thumb, sow thistle
biblical: 4 tare
European: 6 spurry **7** spurrey
killer: 8 paraquat **9** herbicide
Western: 4 loco

weedy
4 lean, thin **5** lanky **6** skinny **7** scrawny, stringy, willowy **8** untended **9** overgrown

week
6 period **8** hebdomad
two weeks: 9 fortnight

weep
3 cry, sob **4** drip, moan, ooze, tear, wail **5** bleed, exude, sweat **6** lament **7** blubber, dribble, trickle **8** transude

weepy
5 misty, moist, teary **7** tearful **10** lachrymose

weevil
7 billbug **8** curculio

weft
3 web **4** pick, woof, yarn **6** fabric, thread

weigh
3 way **4** heft, rate, tare **5** count, judge, scale, study **6** burden, ponder **7** balance, measure, oppress, perpend **8** appraise, bear down, consider, evaluate, militate **11** contemplate

weigh down
4 load **5** press **6** burden, sadden **7** depress, oppress **8** encumber **10** discourage, overburden

weight
3 tax **4** heft, lade, load, mass, onus, task **5** class, force, power **6** amount, assign, burden, charge, credit, import, moment, saddle **7** oppress, potency, quality **8** encumber, poundage, pressure, prestige, quantity **9** authority, influence, magnitude **10** corpulence, importance **11** consequence **12** significance
allowance: 4 tare
apothecary: 4 dram **5** grain, pound **7** scruple
Asian: 4 tael **5** catty
gem: 5 carat
measure of: 3 fun, kin, kip, oke, tan, tod, ton, vis, yin **4** dram, gram, mina, rotl **5** grain, libra, ounce, picul, pound **7** long ton, scruple **8** kilogram, short ton **9** metric ton
system: 3 net **4** troy **6** metric **10** apothecary **11** avoirdupois

weightiness
4 pith **6** import, moment **7** dignity, gravity **9** heaviness, magnitude, solemnity **10** importance **11** consequence, massiveness **12** significance **13** momentousness

weight lifting term
4 curl, pull, push **5** clean, press, shrug, squat **6** snatch **8** deadlift **12** clean and jerk

weightlifter
4 Kono (Tommy), Tang (Gonghong) **5** Dimas (Pyrros), Mutlu (Halil) **6** Weller (Ronny) **7** Krastev (Antonio) **8** Alexeyev (Vasily), Pechalov (Nikolay) **9** Chemerkin (Andrei), Reza Zadeh (Hossein), Taranenko (Leonid) **10** Schemansky (Norbert)

weighty
3 fat **5** grave, gross, heavy, hefty, obese, sober, staid **6** fleshy, portly, sedate, severe, solemn, somber **7** massive, serious, telling **8** cumbrous, grievous, powerful **9** corpulent, effective, important, momentous, ponderous **10** burdensome, convincing, cumbersome **11** significant, substantial **12** considerable **13** consequential

weir
3 dam **5** stank

weird
3 odd 5 eerie, queer 6 creepy, freaky, spooky 7 bizarre, curious, oddball, strange, uncanny 8 freakish, peculiar, singular, sinister 9 eccentric, fantastic, unearthly 10 mysterious 11 inscrutable 12 supernatural 13 preternatural

weirdo
4 geek, kook, loon 5 freak 7 nutcase, oddball 8 crackpot 9 eccentric, screwball

welcome
4 hail 5 cheer, greet, hello, howdy 6 accept, invite, salute 7 embrace, invited, receive 8 greeting, pleasant, pleasing 9 agreeable, favorable, reception 10 gratifying, hospitable 11 hospitality, pleasurable

weld
4 bond, fuse, join 5 braze, joint, merge, unite 6 solder

welfare
3 aid 4 dole, help, weal 5 pogey 6 health, relief, succor 7 benefit, fortune, success, support 8 interest 9 advantage, happiness, well-being 10 assistance, commonweal, prosperity

welkin
3 sky 5 ether, vault 6 heaven 7 heavens 8 empyrean 9 firmament

well
3 far, fit, pit 4 easy, emit, hale, hole, pool, rise, sane 5 amply, clear, cured, fully, quite, shaft, sound, truly 6 easily, freely, healed, indeed, justly, kindly, likely, nicely, origin, rather, really, source, spring, wholly 7 clearly, healthy, perhaps, readily, rightly 8 entirely, expertly, pleasing, possibly, probably, properly, sensibly, smoothly, suitably 9 advisable, correctly, desirable, elegantly, favorably, fittingly, fortunate, perfectly, wholesome

well-being
4 weal 6 health 7 welfare 8 thriving 9 happiness 10 prosperity

well-bred
6 urbane 7 genteel, refined 8 cultured, highborn, polished 9 civilized, patrician 10 cultivated 11 blue-blooded, gentlemanly

well-built
4 buff 5 hunky, solid 8 muscular 9 strapping

well-developed
5 curvy 7 fulsome, rounded, shapely 8 advanced 9 Junoesque 10 curvaceous

well-disposed
7 amiable 8 friendly 9 favorable, receptive 11 sympathetic 13 understanding

Welles movie
5 Trial (The) 7 Macbeth, Othello 8 Jane Eyre, Stranger (The), Third Man (The) 11 Citizen Kane, Touch of Evil 15 Journey into Fear 16 Chimes at Midnight, Lady from Shanghai (The) 20 Magnificent Ambersons (The)

well-favored
4 fair 5 bonny 6 comely, lovely, pretty 7 winsome 8 gorgeous, handsome 9 beauteous, beautiful 10 attractive 11 good-looking

well-fixed
see **well-to-do**

well-founded
5 sound, valid 6 cogent 8 rational 9 justified 10 convincing

well-groomed
4 neat, snug, tidy, trig, trim 5 natty, smart 6 dapper, snappy, spiffy, spruce, sprucy 7 orderly 8 clean-cut 9 shipshape

well-heeled
see **well-to-do**

Wellington
4 duke 7 general 8 Iron Duke
horse: 10 Copenhagen
original name: 9 Wellesley (Arthur)
victory: 7 Vitoria 8 Talavera, Waterloo 9 Salamanca

well-known
5 famed, noted 6 famous 7 big-name, eminent, popular 8 renowned 9 notorious, prominent 10 celebrated 11 illustrious

well-liked
7 beloved, favored, popular 8 favorite 9 cherished, preferred

well-mannered
5 civil, suave 6 poised, polite, proper, urbane 7 genteel, tactful 9 courteous 10 diplomatic

well-nigh
6 all but, almost, fairly, nearly, next to 8 as good as 9 just about, virtually 11 essentially, practically

well-off
see **well-to-do**

well-paying
7 gainful 9 lucrative, rewarding 10 profitable, worthwhile 11 moneymaking 12 advantageous, remunerative

Wells novel
11 Time Machine (The) 12 Invisible Man (The) 14 War of the Worlds (The)

wellspring
4 font, root 5 fount 6 origin, source 7 genesis 8 fountain 10 provenance 11 provenience 12 fountainhead

well-thought-of
6 valued, worthy 7 admired, reputed 9 estimable, reputable 10 creditable 11 respectable

well-timed
6 timely 7 apropos, fitting, timeous 9 favorable, opportune 10 auspicious, felicitous, fortuitous, propitious, seasonable

well-to-do
4 rich 5 flush 6 loaded, monied 7 moneyed, upscale, wealthy 8 affluent 10 prosperous 11 comfortable

well-turned
4 trim 5 plump 7 rounded, shapely 10 curvaceous, felicitous, Rubenesque, statuesque 11 clean-limbed

well-worn
5 banal, musty, stale, stock, tired, trite 6 frayed, old-hat, shabby 7 clichéd 8 bromidic, cobwebby, dog-eared, overused 9 hackneyed 10 threadbare 11 commonplace, stereotyped

Welsh
see **Cymric**

welsh
5 dodge 6 renege, resile 7 back out, default

welt
4 blow, edge, seam, wale, weal 5 ridge, wheal, whelk 6 insert

welter
4 coil, moil, toss 5 chaos, churn, steep, surge 6 flurry, hassle, hubbub, jumble, lather, ruckus, seethe, thrash, wallow, writhe 7 ferment, turmoil 8 disorder 9 confusion

___ Welty
6 Eudora

wen
4 bleb, cyst 5 blain 6 growth 7 vesicle 11 excrescence

wench
3 gal 4 girl, jade, lass, maid, minx, miss, puss, slut, tart 5 hussy, nymph, tramp, trull, whore, woman 6 damsel, gamine, harlot, hoyden, lassie, maiden, wanton 7 jezebel, servant, trollop 8 slattern, strumpet

wend
3 hie 4 fare, pass 6 direct, push on, repair, travel 7 journey, proceed

werewolf
9 loup-garou 11 lycanthrope

Werther's beloved
5 Lotte 9 Charlotte

Wesleyan
9 Methodist

West
8 Occident

western
5 oater 9 Hesperian 10 horse opera, occidental
hemisphere: 8 Americas, New World

Western novelist
4 Grey (Zane), Ross (Dana Fuller) 5 Brand (Max), Faust (Frederick), Short (Luke) 6 Judson (E. Z. C.), L'Amour (Louis), Patten (Lewis), Wister (Owen) 7 Guthrie (A. B.), Leonard (Elmore) 8 Buntline (Ned), McMurtry (Larry)

West Indies
country: 4 Cuba 5 Haiti 7 Bahamas, Grenada, Jamaica 8 Barbados, Dominica 10 Guadeloupe, Martinique, Puerto Rico, Saint Lucia 17 Dominican Republic
island group: 6 Virgin (Islands) 7 Bahamas, Leeward (Islands) 8 Antilles (Greater, Lesser), Windward (Islands)

West Point
father of: 6 Thayer (Sylvanus)
freshman: 5 plebe
student: 5 cadet

West Side Story
composer: 9 Bernstein (Leonard)
heroine: 5 Maria
lyricist: 8 Sondheim (Stephen)

West Virginia
capital: 10 Charleston
city: 8 Wheeling 10 Huntington
mountain: 10 Spruce Knob
nickname: 8 Mountain (State)
river: 4 Ohio
state bird: 8 cardinal
state flower: 12 rhododendron
state tree: 10 sugar maple

west wind
see at **wind**

wet
3 sop 4 damp, dank, rain, soak, wash, weak 5 douse, drown, drunk, humid, moist, rainy, soggy, soppy, souse, water 6 dampen, drench, soaked, sodden, soused, sweaty, watery 7 moisten, raining, soaking, sopping 8 drenched, dripping, humidify, irrigate, moisture, saturate, slippery 9 saturated, spineless
combining form: 4 hygr 5 hygro

wet blanket
6 grinch 7 killjoy 8 sourpuss 9 pessimist 10 spoilsport 11 party pooper

wether
4 goat 5 sheep

wetland
3 bog, fen 4 mire, quag 5 marsh, swamp 6 morass, muskeg, slough

whack
3 bat, hit, pop, try **4** bash, belt, biff, blow, chop, cuff, kill, pelt, shot, sock, stab, wham, whap, whop **5** crack, punch, smack, smash **6** attack, defeat, murder, strike, wallop **7** bump off **8** knock off, lambaste
up: **4** part **5** divvy, split **6** divide **7** portion **9** apportion

whale
3 hit **4** beat, cete, flog, hide, lash, whip **5** giant **6** defeat, strike, stripe, thrash **7** mammoth **8** cetacean, behemoth **9** leviathan **10** flagellate
arctic: **7** bowhead
group: **3** gam, pod
killer: **4** orca
kind: **3** sei **4** blue **5** right, sperm **6** baleen, beluga, killer **7** narwhal, rorqual **8** cachalot
novel: **8** Moby Dick
toothed: **5** pilot (whale) **9** blackfish
white: **4** huso
young: **4** calf

whalebone
9 scrimshaw

wham
3 hit **4** bang, beat, blow, boom, clap, slam **5** blast, burst, crack, crash, smash, whack **6** impact, propel, strike **7** explode

whammy
3 hex, zap **4** jinx, juju **5** curse, spell **6** hoodoo, voodoo **7** evil eye

wharf
4 dock, pier, quay **5** jetty, levee

Wharton novel
10 Buccaneers (The), Ethan Frome **12** House of Mirth (The) **14** Age of Innocence (The) **18** Custom of the Country (The)

whatever
5 at all **9** in any case

whatnot
7 étagère

wheal
4 lump, welt **5** ridge, whelk

wheat
4 crop **5** emmer, flour, grain, grass, spelt **6** cereal **7** einkorn
beard: **3** awn
beat: **6** thresh
chaff: **4** bran
crushed: **6** bulgur
disease: **4** rust, smut
type: **4** club **5** durum

wheedle
3 con **4** coax **5** cozen **6** cajole, entice, seduce **7** blarney, flatter **8** blandish, inveigle, scrounge, soft-soap **9** sweet-talk

wheel
3 VIP **4** auto, gyre, move, reel, spin, turn **5** cycle, drive, motor, pilot, pivot, round, whirl **6** bigwig, circle, gyrate, league, rotate, totter, travel **7** big shot, circuit, revolve **8** rotation **9** about-face, volte-face
part: **3** hub, rim **4** tire **5** felly, spoke
shaft: **4** axle
spoke: **6** radius
toothed: **3** cog **4** gear

wheeze
3 saw, yuk **4** gasp, hiss, joke, puff, rasp **5** adage, cough **6** saying **7** proverb, whistle **8** chestnut, rhonchus

whelk
4 wale, weal, welt **5** wheal

whelm
4 bury, sink **5** cover, drown, flood, swamp **6** deluge, engulf **8** bear down, inundate, overbear, overcome, submerge **9** devastate

whelp
3 cub, kid, pup **4** bear **5** child, puppy **9** youngster

whereas
5 since, while **6** seeing, though **7** howbeit **8** although **11** considering

wherefore
3 why **4** thus **5** proof **6** ground, reason, whence **8** argument **11** explanation

wherewithal
5 funds, means, money **9** resources

wherry
4 boat **5** barge, scull **7** lighter, rowboat

whet
4 edge, goad, hone **5** drink, rally, rouse, waken **6** arouse, awaken, excite, kindle **7** sharpen, starter **8** aperitif **9** appetizer, challenge, stimulate **10** incitement **11** hors d'oeuvre

whiff
3 fan **4** blow, gust, hint, puff, waft **5** expel, smoke, tinge, trace **6** breath, exhale, inhale **7** soupçon, whisper **9** strikeout **10** indication, inhalation

whiffet
6 nobody, squirt **9** nonentity

whiffle
4 blow, gust, puff **5** waver **6** dither, falter **9** fluctuate, vacillate **12** shilly-shally

while
4 pass, time, when **5** spell **6** albeit, moment, though **7** howbeit, stretch, whereas **8** although, as long as, so long as

whilom
4 past **6** bygone, former **7** onetime, quondam **8** formerly, previous, sometime **9** erstwhile

whim
3 bee **4** idea, kink **5** dream, fancy, freak, humor **6** maggot, megrim, notion, vagary **7** caprice, capstan, conceit, thought **8** crotchet

whimper
3 cry **4** fret, mewl, pule, wail **5** bleat, whine **6** snivel

whimsical
4 iffy, zany **5** ditsy, ditzy, droll, fancy, flaky **6** chancy, fickle, fitful, flakes, quirky, random **7** erratic, flighty, mutable, puckish, wayward **8** fanciful, freakish, volatile **9** eccentric, impulsive, mercurial, pixilated, screwball, uncertain, vagarious **10** capricious, pixillated **13** unpredictable

whimsy
3 bee **4** play **5** dream, fancy, freak, humor **6** levity, maggot, megrim, notion, vagary **7** caprice, conceit, fantasy **9** capriccio, frivolity

whim-wham
4 dido **5** curio, fancy, frill **6** bauble, gewgaw, ruffle, trifle **7** bibelot, flounce, trinket, whatnot **8** furbelow, gimcrack, kickshaw **9** objet d'art **10** knickknack

whine
3 cry **4** cant, fret, fuss, kick, moan, pule, wail **5** bleat, gripe **6** grouse, repine, snivel, whinge, yammer **7** grumble, snuffle, whimper **8** complain **9** bellyache

whinny
5 neigh **6** nicker **7** whicker

whiny
5 fussy **7** fretful, grouchy, peevish **8** petulant **9** irritable, querulous

whip
3 cut, hem, set, tan **4** beat, cane, crop, dash, flog, hide, jerk, lash, lick, pull, rout, wind, wrap **5** abuse, mop up, quirt, spank, sting, whale, whisk **6** defeat, lather, snatch, strike, stroke, subdue, switch, thrash, urge on **7** agitate, dessert, provoke, rawhide, shellac, trounce, utensil **8** coachman, lambaste, overcome, vanquish **9** instigate, overwhelm **10** flagellate **13** cat-o'-nine-tails
braided: 10 blacksnake

whippersnapper
see **whiffet**

whipping boy
4 goat **5** patsy **7** fall guy **9** scapegoat

whippy
6 supple **7** elastic, springy **8** flexible **9** resilient

whir
3 fly, hum **4** burr, buzz, whiz **5** chirr, churr, drone, whizz **7** revolve, vibrate **9** bombinate

whirl
3 ado, gig, pop, try **4** eddy, flit, fuss, gyre, moil, reel, shot, spin, stab, stir, swim, turn, veer **5** hurry, pivot, swirl, whack, wheel **6** bustle, circle, gyrate, hassle, hubbub, pother, rotate **7** circuit, dervish, turmoil **8** ballyhoo, gyration, rotation **9** commotion, pirouette **10** revolution

whirligig
4 gyre, spin **6** beetle, gyrate **8** carousel **9** pirouette **12** merry-go-round

whirlpool
3 ado **4** eddy, fuss **6** bustle, flurry, furore, tumult, vortex **7** turmoil **8** vortices (plural) **9** commotion, maelstrom
bath: 6 hot tub **7** Jacuzzi

whirlwind
2 oe **4** rush, stir, to-do **5** hasty, spout, swift **6** bustle **7** cyclone, tornado, twister, typhoon **8** headlong **9** commotion, dust devil, dust storm, hurricane **10** waterspout **11** tourbillion

whish
4 fizz, hiss **6** fizzle **8** sibilate

whisk
3 mix, nip, wag, zip **4** beat, flit, whip **5** broom, brush, fluff, hurry, speed **6** switch

whisker
4 hair **7** bristle **8** filament, vibrissa **9** outrigger **11** hairbreadth

whiskered
5 hairy **6** pilose **7** bearded, bristly, hirsute **8** stubbled, unshaven

whiskers
5 beard **6** goatee **7** stubble, weepers **8** bristles **9** burnsides, peach fuzz, sideburns **11** dundrearies, muttonchops

whiskey
3 rye **6** liquor, Scotch **7** alcohol, bourbon
with beer chaser: 11 boilermaker

whisper
4 buzz, hint, hiss, whiz **5** rumor, shade, tinge, touch, trace, whiff **6** breath, gossip, murmur, mutter **8** sibilate, susurrus **9** suspicion, undertone **11** susurration

whist
4 game, hush **5** quiet, still **6** silent **9** noiseless, soundless

whistle
4 pipe, toot **5** flute, whiff **6** signal, tootle, wheeze

whistle-stop
5 stump **8** campaign, politick **9** barnstorm **11** electioneer

whit
3 bit, fig, jot, rap 4 atom, damn, hoot, iota, mite 5 crumb, scrap, shred, speck, whoop 7 dribble, modicum, smidgen 8 molecule, particle

white
4 pure 5 cream, ivory, livid, milky, snowy 6 albino, blanch, bleach, pallid 7 silvery 9 colorless
combining form: 4 leuc, leuk 5 leuco, leuko
egg's: 5 glair 6 glaire 7 albumen

White novel
12 Stuart Little 13 Charlotte's Web

white cliffs of ___
5 Dover

White Fang author
6 London (Jack)

White House
designer: 5 Hoban (James)
first occupant: 5 Adams (Abigail, John)

white lightning
5 hooch 7 bootleg, whiskey 9 moonshine 10 bathtub gin 11 mountain dew

whiten
4 fade, pale 5 frost 6 blanch, bleach, blench 8 etiolate 10 decolorize

white plague
2 TB 8 phthisis 11 consumption 12 tuberculosis

whitewash
6 parget 7 cover up 9 gloss over, gloze over, sugarcoat

whither
5 where 7 whereto 9 whereunto

whiting
3 cod 4 hake 10 silver hake

Whitman work
13 Leaves of Grass

Whitsunday
9 Pentecost

Whittier poem
9 Snow-Bound 10 Maud Muller 11 Barefoot Boy 16 Barbara Frietchie

whittle
3 hew 4 chip, form, fret, pare, trim 5 carve, shape, shave, skive 6 reduce, sculpt 8 diminish

whiz
3 fly, hum, zip 4 buzz, flit, hiss, zoom 5 hurry, speed, swish, whirl 6 expert, fizzle, genius, phenom, rotate, whoosh 8 virtuoso 10 wunderkind

whoa
3 hey 4 slow, stop 6 hold up

whole
3 all, fit, sum 4 full, hale, sane 5 sound, total, uncut, unity 6 entire, entity, healed, intact, system, unhurt 7 healthy, perfect, plenary 8 complete, entirely, entirety, flawless, restored, totality, unbroken, unmarred
combining form: 3 hol, pan 4 holo

wholehearted
6 ardent 7 devoted, earnest, fervent, sincere 8 bona fide 9 committed, heartfelt, steadfast, unfeigned 10 passionate, unwavering 11 impassioned 12 enthusiastic 13 unquestioning

whole-hog
6 all-out, gung-ho 8 complete, thorough 9 full-scale 11 straight-out 13 thoroughgoing

wholeness
7 oneness 8 entirety, totality 9 integrity, soundness 10 intactness, perfection

whole note
9 semibreve

whole number
5 digit 6 cipher 7 integer, numeral

wholesome
3 fit 4 good, hale, safe, sane, well 5 right, sound 6 benign 7 healthy 8 hygienic, salutary 9 favorable, healthful 10 beneficial, salubrious

wholly
3 all 4 only 6 in toto, singly, solely, purely 7 totally 8 entirely 10 altogether, completely 11 exclusively

whomp
3 hit 4 beat, drub, slap, whip, whup 5 crash, thump 6 crunch, strike, thrash, wallop 7 clobber, shellac, trounce 8 lambaste

whomp up
4 stir 5 rouse, spark 6 arouse, excite, foment

whoopee
3 fun 5 revel, yahoo 6 gaiety, hoopla, hooray, yippee 7 jollity, revelry, wassail, whoopla 8 hilarity 9 festivity, high jinks, merriment 10 hurly-burly 11 merrymaking

whoopla
see **hoopla**

whop
3 bat, bop 4 bash, beat, biff, blow, drub, lick, sock 5 baste, pound, smack, thump, whack 6 batter, buffet, defeat, hammer, pummel, strike, thrash, thwack, wallop 7 trounce 8 lambaste

whopper
3 lie 4 lulu 5 beaut, doozy, whale 6 doozie 8 knockout, tall tale 9 humdinger

whopping
4 huge, vast 6 mighty 7 amazing, immense, massive 8 colossal, enormous, gigantic, whacking 9 bodacious, humongous, monstrous 10 gargantuan, incredible, prodigious 13 extraordinary

whorl
4 coil, eddy, turn 5 swirl 6 spiral

why
5 cause **6** enigma, motive, puzzle, reason, riddle **7** mystery, problem, what for **9** conundrum, rationale, therefore, wherefore **10** puzzlement **11** explanation

wicked
4 evil, mean, very, vile **5** awful, black, wrong **6** fierce, malign, sinful, unholy **7** corrupt, hateful, heinous, immoral, naughty, ungodly, vicious **8** depraved, devilish, fiendish **9** atrocious, barbarous, dangerous, extremely, hazardous, injurious, malicious, malignant, nefarious **10** iniquitous, malevolent, outrageous **11** treacherous

wickedness
3 sin **4** evil, vice **7** devilry **8** enormity, iniquity, satanism **9** depravity **10** corruption, immorality **12** devilishness, fiendishness

wicker
4 twig **5** osier, withe **6** branch

wicket
4 arch, door, gate, hoop **6** window
sticky: **3** fix, jam **4** knot **7** toughie **9** conundrum, tight spot

wide
4 vast **5** broad, fully **8** extended, spacious, straying, sweeping **9** deviating, expansive, extensive, inclusive **10** completely **13** comprehensive

widen
4 ream **6** dilate, expand, extend, open up, spread **7** broaden, distend, enlarge

widespread
4 rife, vast **6** common **7** current, general, popular, rampant, regnant **8** far-flung **9** extensive, pervasive, prevalent **10** far-ranging, ubiquitous

widget
5 gismo, gizmo **6** device, dingus, doodad, gadget, hickey, jigger **7** gimmick, whatsit **9** doohickey, thingummy **11** contraption, thingamabob, thingamajig, thingumajig

width
4 gape, kerf, span **5** depth, range **6** spread **7** breadth **9** extension

wield
3 use **5** exert **6** handle **7** control **8** brandish, exercise **10** manipulate
the gavel: **7** preside

wiener
3 dog **5** frank **6** hot dog **7** sausage **11** frankfurter **13** Vienna sausage

Wiesel work
4 Dawn **5** Night **8** Fifth Son (The) **9** Testament (The)

wife
3 Mrs. **4** mate **5** bride, woman **6** female, matron, missis, missus, spouse **7** consort, partner **8** helpmate, helpmeet
Latin: **4** uxor
of a rajah: **4** rani **5** ranee

wifely
7 uxorial

wig
3 jaw, rap, rug **4** flip, rail, rate **5** chide, freak, scold **6** berate, peruke, rebuke, revile, toupee **7** bawl out, chew out, reproof, upbraid **8** postiche, reproach **9** hairpiece, reprimand **10** tongue-lash

wiggle
4 jerk **5** shake, twist **6** fidget, squirm, writhe
Scottish: **5** hotch

wight
3 man **5** human **6** animal, mortal, person **7** critter **8** creature **10** human being, individual

wild
3 mad **4** fast **5** crazy **6** barren, raging, savage, stormy, unruly **7** erratic, frantic, furious, natural, untamed, vicious **8** barbaric, blustery, desolate, frenetic, frenzied, reckless **9** barbarian, barbarous, delirious, fantastic, turbulent, wasteland **10** incautious, outlandish **11** extravagant, intractable, sensational, tempestuous, uncivilized, uninhabited **12** preposterous, uncontrolled, uncultivated, ungovernable, unmanageable **13** irresponsible, undisciplined

wild ass
5 kiang **6** onager

wildcat
4 eyra, lynx **6** ocelot, strike **10** jaguarundi

Wild Duck author
5 Ibsen (Henrik)

wildebeest
3 gnu

wilderness
4 bush **5** heath, waste **6** barren, desert **9** backlands, wasteland **10** hinterland **11** backcountry

Wilder play
7 Our Town **10** Matchmaker (The) **14** Skin of Our Teeth (The)

wild-eyed
6 raving **7** blue-sky, radical **9** visionary

wile
4 ploy, ruse, vamp **5** charm, feint, guile, trick **6** allure, deceit, entice, gambit **7** attract, beguile, bewitch, chicane, cunning, enchant, gimmick **8** artifice, inveigle, maneuver, trickery **9** captivate, chicanery, fascinate, magnetize, stratagem **10** subterfuge

wiliness
5 guile **7** cunning

will
4 like, wish **5** cause, elect, leave, order **6** choice, choose, decree, desire, direct, intend, intent, liking, option, ordain, please **7** bequest, consent, control, passion, purpose **8** appetite, bequeath, pleasure, volition **9** intention, testament **10** discipline **11** disposition, inclination, self-control **13** determination, self-restraint
addition: **7** codicil
maker: **8** testator **9** testatrix
without: **9** intestate

willful
5 heady **6** dogged, mulish, ornery, unruly **7** froward, wayward **8** perverse, stubborn **9** obstinate, pigheaded, voluntary **10** deliberate, hardheaded, headstrong, purposeful, self-willed **11** intentional, intractable, wrongheaded **12** contumacious, pertinacious, ungovernable

Williams play
10 Camino Real, Rose Tattoo (The) **14** Glass Menagerie (The), Summer and Smoke **16** Cat on a Hot Tin Roof, Night of the Iguana (The), Sweet Bird of Youth **18** Suddenly Last Summer **20** Streetcar Named Desire (A)

William Tell
canton: **3** Uri
composer: **7** Rossini (Gioacchino)

willies
6 creeps, shakes **7** jimjams, jitters, shivers **9** whim-whams **10** goose bumps **13** heebie-jeebies

willing
3 apt **4** fain, game, glad, open **5** prone, ready **6** minded **7** forward, witting **8** amenable, disposed, inclined, obliging, unforced **9** agreeable, compliant, favorable, receptive, voluntary **10** deliberate, volitional **11** intentional, predisposed

williwaw
4 gust, wind **5** blast **8** outburst, paroxysm **9** commotion

will-o'-the-wisp
7 fantasy, figment, phantom **8** daydream, delusion **11** ignis fatuus

willow
5 osier, salix **6** sallow **10** cricket bat
flower cluster: **6** catkin
kind: **5** crack, pussy, white **6** basket **7** weeping
Virginia: **4** Itea

willowy
4 tall **5** lithe **6** pliant, supple, svelte **7** lissome, pliable, slender **8** graceful

Wilson play
6 Fences **11** Piano Lesson (The) **12** Talley's Folly **13** Hot l Baltimore (The) **20** Ma Rainey's Black Bottom

wilt
3 sag **4** swag **5** droop, dry up, wizen **6** wither **7** shrivel **8** languish

wily
3 sly **4** cagy, foxy **5** cagey, canny, slick **6** artful, astute, clever, crafty, shrewd, tricky **7** cunning, devious, vulpine **8** guileful, scheming **10** serpentine

wimble
4 bore **5** auger, borer, brace, drill **6** gimlet

Wimbledon's game
6 tennis

wimp
4 nerd, wuss **5** sissy **6** weenie **7** doormat, nebbish **9** jellyfish **11** milquetoast

wimple
4 bend, veil, wrap **5** cover, curve **6** ripple
wearer: **3** nun

wimp out
6 beg off, cave in, give in **8** back down

wimpy
4 lame, puny, weak **5** dinky, inept, timid **6** craven, feeble **7** gutless **8** cowardly, feckless, impotent, pathetic **9** spineless **10** namby-pamby, wishy-washy **11** ineffective, ineffectual

win
3 get **4** beat, earn, gain, kayo **5** reach, score **6** attain, defeat, obtain, secure **7** achieve, acquire, conquer, procure, produce, realize, succeed, success, triumph, victory **8** conquest, persuade **9** influence **10** accomplish
over: **6** disarm, induce **8** convince, persuade, talk into **9** prevail on

wince
5 cower, quail, start **6** blanch, blench, cringe, flinch, recoil, shrink **7** squinch

wind
3 air, dry, fan, gas **4** bend, blow, clue, coil, curl, gale, gird, gust, haul, hint, reel, rest, talk, turn, warp, wrap **5** cover, crank, curve, force, hoist, raise, sound, spool, twine, twist **6** breath, breeze, circle, enlace, girdle, notion, zephyr **7** enclose, entwine, envelop, inkling, involve, monsoon, nothing, tighten **8** easterly, encircle, entangle, surround, tendency, westerly **9** direction, idle words, influence, insinuate **10** indication, intimation, suggestion
Adriatic: **4** bora
cold: **4** bora **7** mistral, pampero **8** williwaw
combining form: **4** anem **5** anemo, venti, vento
gentle: **6** breeze, zephyr
god: **6** Boreas (north) **8** Favonius, Zephyrus (west)
hot: **6** simoom **7** sirocco **8** scirocco

instrument: **4** vane **10** anemometer **11** weather vane
into: **8** aweather
measure of speed: **4** knot
Mediterranean: **4** bora **7** sirocco **8** levanter, libeccio, scirocco
scale: **8** Beaufort
stormy: **4** gale **7** cyclone, tornado, twister **9** hurricane **11** northeaster
warm: **4** föhn **5** foehn **7** chinook

windbag
6 gabber **7** blabber **8** bigmouth, blowhard, braggart

windfall
4 boon, gain **5** break **7** jackpot **8** fortuity

winding
4 curl, kink **5** snaky **6** spiral **7** coiling, curving, devious, sinuous **8** flexuous, indirect, tortuous, twisting **9** meandrous **10** circuitous, convoluted, meandering, roundabout, serpentine **11** anfractuous **12** labyrinthine

wind instrument
3 sax **4** horn, oboe, pipe, tuba **5** flute, shawm **6** cornet **7** bagpipe, bassoon, panpipe, piccolo, sackbut, trumpet **8** bagpipes, clarinet, crumhorn, recorder, trombone **9** krummhorn, saxophone **10** cor anglais, flugelhorn, French horn, sousaphone **11** English horn

windmill
4 spin **5** wheel **7** machine
fighter: **10** Don Quixote

window
3 eye **4** pane **7** opening **8** aperture, casement, jalousie
cover: **5** blind **7** curtain, shutter
French: **7** fenêtre
over a door: **7** transom **8** fanlight
part: **4** pane, sash, sill **5** frame
projecting: **3** bay **5** oriel
roof's: **6** dormer **7** lucarne **8** skylight
round: **5** oxeye
Scottish: **7** winnock
ship's: **4** port **8** porthole

windpipe
7 trachea
combining form: **6** trache **7** tracheo

windrow
4 bank, heap, hill, mass, pile **5** mound, ridge, stack

wind up
3 end **4** halt **5** close **6** finish, settle **8** complete, conclude **9** terminate

windup
3 end **5** close **6** ending, finale, finish **9** backswing **10** completion, conclusion **11** termination

windy
4 airy **5** blowy, gassy, gusty, inane, tumid, wordy **6** breezy, prolix, stormy, turgid **7** diffuse, orotund, pompous, verbose **8** blustery, inflated **9** bombastic, overblown **11** tempestuous **13** grandiloquent, unsubstantial

wine
4 vino **5** drink, juice **8** beverage
aromatized: **8** vermouth **9** hippocras
beverage: **5** negus, punch **6** bishop, cooler **7** sangria **8** sangaree, spritzer **9** hippocras
bottle: **6** fiasco, magnum **8** decanter, jeroboam **10** methuselah
cabinet: **8** cellaret
cask: **3** tun, vat **4** butt, pipe
cellar: **6** bodega
combining form: **3** eno, oen **4** oeno
discoverer: **4** Noah
distillate: **6** brandy, cognac
dry: **3** sec **4** brut
flavor: **4** mull
fortified: **4** port **5** Tokay **6** Malaga, Muscat, sherry **7** Madeira, marsala, oloroso **8** muscatel
fragrance: **4** nose **7** bouquet
lover: **9** oenophile **11** oenophilist
maker: **7** vintner **8** vigneron **10** winegrower **13** viticulturist
merchant: **7** vintner
pink: **4** rosé **5** blush
red: **4** port **5** Gamay, Macon, Medoc, Rioja **6** Barolo, Beaune, claret, merlot, Shiraz **7** Chianti **8** Bordeaux, Burgundy, cabernet, Sancerre **9** Lambrusco, Pinot Noir, St. Emilion, zinfandel **10** Beaujolais, Sangiovese **11** Petite Sirah **12** Valpolicella
region: **3** Ahr **4** Asti, Cuzo, Jura, Nahe, Napa, Saar, Toro **5** Baden, Douro, Jerez, Loire, Mosel, Pfalz, Rhône, Ruwer **6** Alsace, Sonoma, Veneto **7** Mendoza, Tuscany **8** Bordeaux, Burgundy, Rheingau **9** Champagne **10** Napa Valley **11** Finger Lakes, Rheinhessen
relating to: **6** vinous
residue: **4** marc
rice: **4** sake
richness: **4** body
sediment: **4** lees **5** dregs
shop: **6** bistro, bodega, tavern
sparkling: **4** Asti **7** Vouvray **8** cold duck, sparkler, Spumante **9** champagne, Lambrusco
specialist: **9** enologist **10** oenologist
spiced: **5** negus **6** mulled (wine) **9** hippocras
steward: **9** sommelier
study of: **7** enology **8** oenology
sweet: **4** port **5** Tokay **6** canary, Malaga, muscat **7** Catawba, Madeira, malmsey, marsala, oloroso, Vouvray **8** Malvasia, muscatel, sauterne **9** Sauternes **11** scuppernong

sweeten: **4** mull
vessel: **7** chalice
white: **4** hock **5** Rhine, Soave **7** Catawba, Chablis, Moselle, Orvieto, Vouvray **8** Bordeaux, muscadet, Riesling, Semillon, vermouth **9** champagne, Hermitage, Meursault, pinot gris **10** chardonnay, Montrachet **11** Chenin Blanc, pinot grigio, scuppernong **13** liebfraumilch **14** sauvignon blanc
year: **7** vintage

wing
3 ala, arm, ell, fly **4** sail, unit, vane **5** annex, flank, fleet, pinna, wound **6** flight **7** airfoil, faction, flanker, section **9** appendage, expansion, extension, improvise
combining form: **3** ali **4** pter **5** ptero
relating to: **4** alar **5** alary

wingding
4 bash, fete, gala **5** binge, party **7** blowout, shindig **9** festivity

winged
5 alate, fleet, rapid, swift **7** soaring **8** elevated
deity: **4** Amor, Eros, Nike **5** Cupid **6** Hermes **7** Mercury
horse: **7** Pegasus
monster: **5** harpy

wingless
8 apterous

winglike
4 alar **5** alary
part: **3** ala **4** alae (plural)

wink
3 bat, nap **5** flash, jiffy, shake, trice **6** moment, second, signal **7** connive, flicker, instant, twinkle **9** nictitate, twinkling **11** split second

winner
3 ace **4** lulu **5** beaut, doozy **6** doozie, top dog, victor **7** success **8** champion **9** conqueror, humdinger **11** titleholder

Winnie-the-Pooh
author: **5** Milne (A. A.)
character: **3** Roo **5** Kanga **6** Eeyore, Piglet, Tigger

winning
8 charming, engaging, pleasing **9** agreeable **10** delightful, successful, triumphant, victorious **11** captivating **13** prepossessing

winnow
3 fan **4** blow, cull, pare, sift, sort **6** delete, filter, narrow, reduce, remove, screen, select **8** separate

winsome
5 sweet **6** dulcet, lovely **8** charming, cheerful, engaging, pleasing **9** easygoing **12** lighthearted

winter
6 season **9** hibernate
French: **5** hiver
Spanish: **8** invierno

Winter's Tale, A
author: **11** Shakespeare (William)
character: **7** Camillo, Leontes, Paulina, Perdita **8** Florizel, Hermione **9** Antigonus, Autolycus, Polixenes

wintry
3 icy **4** cold **5** bleak, hoary, nippy, snowy **6** frigid, frosty **8** chilling, freezing, hibernal **12** bone-chilling

wipe
3 dry, rub **4** swab **5** towel, whisk **6** napkin, smudge, sponge **8** squeegee

wipe out
4 rout **5** crash, erase, smear, sweep **6** efface **7** blot out, destroy, expunge **8** decimate **9** eradicate, extirpate **10** annihilate, obliterate

wipeout
4 fall, rout **5** crash **8** drubbing **11** destruction **12** annihilation

wire
3 rod **4** cord, line, send **5** cable, metal **6** thread **7** message **8** meshwork, telegram **9** cablegram, telegraph **10** finish line
measure: **3** mil **5** gauge

wiry
4 lean, ropy **6** sinewy, supple **7** fibrous, stringy

Wisconsin
capital: **7** Madison
city: **6** Racine **7** Kenosha **8** Green Bay **9** Milwaukee
college, university: **5** Ripon **6** Beloit **9** Marquette
lake: **7** Mendota
motto: **7** Forward
nickname: **6** Badger (State)
peninsula: **4** Door
river: **7** St. Croix **9** Menominee, Wisconsin **11** Mississippi
state bird: **5** robin
state flower: **6** violet
state tree: **10** sugar maple

wisdom
5 sense **7** insight, science **8** judgment, learning, sagacity, sageness, sapience **9** good sense, knowledge **10** horse sense **11** common sense, information

wise
4 sage **5** brash, cagey, canny, cocky, fresh, nervy, sassy **6** astute, cheeky, crafty, fill in, inform, notify, shrewd, sophic **7** gnostic, knowing, politic, prudent, sapient **8** discreet, flippant,

impudent, insolent, sensible, tactical **9** advisable, expedient, judicious, sagacious, scholarly **10** discerning, insightful, perceptive, thoughtful **11** foresighted, impertinent, intelligent, smart-alecky **13** contemplative, knowledgeable, perspicacious
old man: **6** Nestor
person: **4** sage **6** savant **7** scholar

wiseacre
see **wise guy**

wisecrack
3 dig, gag **4** barb, gibe, jape, jest, joke, quip **5** sally **6** zinger **9** witticism

wise guy
6 smarty **7** mobster **8** gangster, smart-ass **9** know-it-all, swellhead **10** smart aleck **11** smarty-pants, wisenheimer

wise man
4 guru, sage **5** magus **6** Nestor, savant

Wise Men
see **Magi**

wish
3 bid **4** care, goal, like, long, lust, want **5** covet, crave, fancy, foist, order, yearn **6** desire, impose **7** request **10** desiderate

wishbone
7 furcula

wishful
5 eager **7** anxious, hopeful, longing **8** desirous

wishy-washy
4 lame, weak **5** banal, bland, vapid, wimpy **6** jejune, watery **7** insipid, languid **10** namby-pamby **11** ineffective, ineffectual **13** characterless

wisp
3 bit **5** shred, strip, trace **6** sliver, snatch, streak **7** smidgen, snippet **8** fragment **9** scintilla

wispy
4 slim **5** frail **6** flimsy, slight **7** slender, tenuous **8** fleeting, nebulous **10** evanescent

Wister novel
9 Virginian (The)

wistful
3 sad **6** dreamy, triste **7** longing, pensive **8** yearning **9** nostalgic **10** melancholy

wit
3 wag **5** brain, comic, droll, humor, irony, joker **6** banter, esprit, jester, reason, satire, wisdom **7** farceur, punster **8** banterer, comedian, funnyman, judgment, humorist, jokester, quipster, repartee **9** alertness, ingenuity, intellect **10** cleverness, persiflage

witch
3 hag, hex **5** crone, dowse, spell **6** voodoo, Wiccan **7** charmer **8** magician, sorcerer **9** sorceress **11** enchantress
companion: **3** cat
group: **5** coven
male: **6** wizard **7** warlock
meeting: **6** sabbat **7** sabbath
town: **5** Endor
vehicle: **5** broom

witchcraft
5 magic, wicca **6** hoodoo, voodoo **7** devilry, hexerei, sorcery **8** wizardry **9** diablerie, sortilege, voodooism **10** black magic, hocus-pocus, mumbo jumbo, necromancy **11** abracadabra, thaumaturgy

witch hazel
5 shrub **6** lotion

witchy
6 Wiccan **7** magical **8** wizardly **9** sorcerous **11** necromantic **12** thaumaturgic

with
3 for, per, pro, via **4** over, upon **5** about **6** having **7** against, by way of, through **8** as well as **9** by means of, in favor of **10** by virtue of
French: **4** avec
German: **3** mit
Italian, Spanish: **3** con
Latin: **3** cum

withal
3 too, yet **4** also **5** still **6** as well, though **7** besides, howbeit, however **8** after all, moreover **11** furthermore, nonetheless **12** additionally, nevertheless

withdraw
4 exit, quit **5** demit, leave, unsay **6** depart, bow out, call in, cash in, desert, detach, recall, recant, recede, recoil, retire, secede, shrink **7** back out, drop out, pull out, retract, retreat, scratch, take off, take out **8** back down, evacuate, fall back, pull away, push back, separate, take back, turn away **9** disengage, stand down **10** disconnect, give ground

withdrawal
4 exit **6** exodus **7** exiting, pullout, removal, retreat **9** departure **10** alienation, detachment, retirement, retraction, revocation

withdrawn
4 cool **5** aloof **6** casual, remote **7** distant, removed **8** detached, isolated, reserved, retiring, solitary **9** incurious, unaffable, uncurious **10** unsociable **11** indifferent, introverted, standoffish, unconcerned, unexpansive **12** uninterested, unresponsive

wither
3 age, dry **4** fade, sear, wilt **5** dry up, parch, quail, wizen **6** scorch **7** mummify, shrivel

withered
4 sere **7** sapless **8** shrunken, wrinkled **9** shriveled

withhold
4 deny **5** check **6** deduct, detain, refuse, retain **7** abstain, deprive, forbear, inhibit, refrain, reserve **8** restrain, subtract **9** constrain

within
4 into **5** among **6** inside **7** indoors, inwards **8** enclosed, interior, inwardly **10** inner place
prefix: **3** ent **4** endo, ento **5** infra, intra, intro

with-it
6 modern, modish, trendy **7** à la mode, current, faddish, stylish **8** up-to-date **9** au courant **11** fashionable **12** contemporary

without
4 less, open, past, sans **5** minus **6** absent **7** lacking, open air, outside, wanting **8** outdoors **10** externally, out-of-doors
Latin: **4** sine

with respect to
2 re **4** as to, in re **5** as for **7** apropos **8** touching **9** as regards, regarding **10** concerning

withstand
4 bear, buck, defy **5** fight, repel **6** endure, oppose, resist, suffer **7** hold off, survive, sustain **8** tolerate, traverse

withy
4 twig **5** osier **6** branch, willow **8** flexible **9** resilient

witless
3 mad **4** daft, nuts **5** crazy, daffy, dotty, nutty, silly **6** insane, simple, stupid **7** asinine, cracked, foolish, idiotic **8** demented, deranged, mindless **9** bedlamite, brainless, senseless **10** weak-minded, unbalanced

witlessness
5 folly **6** idiocy, lunacy **7** inanity **8** insanity **9** absurdity, stupidity

witness
3 see **4** note, sign, view **5** proof, vouch **6** attest, depone, depose, notice, viewer **7** bear out, confirm, betoken, certify, testify, watcher **8** attester, beholder, deponent, evidence, looker-on, observer, onlooker **9** bystander, spectator, testament, testifier, testimony **11** affirmation, attestation, corroborate, testimonial **12** confirmation

witticism
3 dig, gag, mot **4** gibe, jape, jest, jibe, joke, quip **5** crack, sally **6** bon mot **8** one-liner, repartee **9** throwaway, wisecrack

witting
5 aware **7** knowing, willful **8** sensible, sentient **9** cognizant, conscious, voluntary **10** deliberate **11** intentional

witty
5 funny **6** clever, jocose **7** amusing, jocular **8** humorous **9** facetious **13** scintillating

wiz
3 ace **5** adept, fiend **6** artist, expert, phenom **7** artiste **8** virtuoso

wizard
3 ace **4** mage **5** adept, druid, fiend, magus **6** expert, phenom **7** warlock **8** conjurer, magician, sorcerer, virtuoso **9** enchanter **10** past master **11** necromancer, thaumaturge **13** thaumaturgist

wizardly
5 magic **6** mystic, witchy **7** magical **9** sorcerous **10** mysterious **11** necromantic **12** thaumaturgic

Wizard of Menlo Park
6 Edison (Thomas Alva)

Wizard of Oz
author: **4** Baum (L. Frank)
character: **6** Tin Man **7** Dorothy **9** Scarecrow **11** Tin Woodsman **12** Cowardly Lion
dog: **4** Toto

wizardry
5 magic **6** voodoo **7** sorcery **8** witchery **9** diablerie, sortilege **10** black magic, necromancy, witchcraft **11** bewitchment, conjuration, enchantment

wizen
3 dry **4** sere, wilt **5** dry up **6** shrink, wither **7** dried-up, shrivel, wrinkle

wizened
4 aged, sere **5** dried **6** shrunk **7** pinched **8** shrunken, withered, wrinkled

wobble
4 reel, rock, sway **5** quake, shake, waver, weave **6** dither, falter, quaver, teeter, totter **7** stagger, stumble, tremble **8** nutation **9** vacillate

wobbly
4 weak **5** rocky, shaky **6** unsure **7** rackety, rickety **8** insecure, rachitic, unstable, unsteady, wavering **9** faltering, teetering, tottering **10** nutational **11** vacillating

Wodehouse, P. G.
castle: **9** Blandings
character: **6** Bertie (Wooster), Gussie (Fink-Nottle), Jeeves, Psmith **7** Wooster (Bertie) **8** Emsworth (Lord), Mulliner (Mr.) **10** Threepwood (Clarence, Freddie) **12** Lord Emsworth
club: **6** Drones

Woden
see **Odin**

woe
3 rue **4** bale, bane, care **5** grief **6** misery, regret, sorrow **7** anguish, sadness, trouble **8** calamity **9** heartache **10** affliction, heartbreak **11** lamentation, unhappiness **12** wretchedness

woebegone
3 low, sad **4** blue, down, worn **6** shabby **7** doleful, forlorn, ruthful **8** dejected, dolorous, downcast, wretched **9** depressed, miserable, sorrowful **10** despondent, melancholy **11** crestfallen, downhearted, low-spirited

woeful
3 sad **5** heavy, sorry **6** dismal, rueful, tragic, triste **7** ruthful **8** dejected, dolorous, downcast, grievous, mournful, stricken, tortured, wretched **9** afflicted, aggrieved, depressed, heartsick, miserable, plaintive, sorrowful **10** deplorable, lamentable, lugubrious, melancholy **11** distressing, downhearted, low-spirited **12** disconsolate

wolf
4 bolt, lobo, rake, roué **5** canid **6** canine, coyote, devour, gobble, masher **7** Don Juan, poverty **8** Casanova, lothario **10** starvation
genus: **5** Canis
group: **4** pack
young: **5** whelp

Wolfe novel
17 Look Homeward Angel, Of Time and the River **18** You Can't Go Home Again **20** Bonfire of the Vanities (The)

wolfish
4 wild **5** cruel, feral **6** fierce, lupine, savage **7** bestial, brutish, vicious **9** ferocious

wolverine
European: **7** glutton
genus: **4** Gulo

Wolverine State
8 Michigan

woman
4 dame, lady **5** madam **6** female, matron **8** mistress **10** girlfriend
attractive: **5** belle, vixen **6** beauty, eyeful, looker **7** stunner **8** knockout
combining form: **4** gyny **5** gynec **6** gynaec, gyneco, gynous **7** gynaeco
courageous: **7** heroine
dignified: **6** matron **7** dowager **10** grande dame
dowdy: **5** frump
English: **6** milady
first, biblical: **3** Eve
first, mythological: **7** Pandora
French: **5** femme
German: **4** Frau **8** Fräulein
Hawaiian: **6** wahine
Indian: **5** squaw
Italian: **5** donna **7** signora
old: **3** hag **4** dame **5** crone **6** beldam, carlin, gammer, granny
Polynesian: **6** wahine
pregnant: **7** gravida
resembling: **8** gynecoid
royal: **5** queen **8** princess
sailor: **4** Wave
servant: **4** maid
soldier: **3** Wac
Spanish: **4** doña **5** mujer **6** señora
strong: **6** amazon, virago
surfer: **6** wahine
unmarried: **4** miss **6** maiden **8** spinster
young: **4** girl, lass **6** lassie, maiden **7** ingenue

womanize
4 wolf **9** gallivant, philander **10** fool around, mess around

womanizer
4 rake, roué, stud, wolf **6** masher **7** Don Juan, gallant, playboy **8** Casanova, lothario **9** ladies' man, mack daddy **10** lady-killer **11** philanderer

womb
6 uterus
combining form: **6** hyster **7** hystero

women
hatred of: **8** misogyny
organization of: **3** DAR, NOW **8** sorority
seclusion of: **6** purdah

wonder
3 awe **4** muse **5** doubt **6** marvel **7** dubiety, miracle, portent, prodigy **8** mistrust, question **9** amazement, speculate, suspicion **10** admiration, skepticism **12** astonishment

wonderful
4 keen **5** grand, great, nifty, super, swell **6** divine, groovy, peachy, spiffy **7** amazing, strange, too much, topping **8** dynamite, fabulous, glorious, spiffing, terrific **9** admirable, excellent, marvelous, wunderbar **10** astounding, delightful, miraculous, out-of-sight, stupendous **11** astonishing, outstanding

wondrous
6 mystic **7** amazing, awesome, strange **9** marvelous **10** astounding, formidable, miraculous, portentous, prodigious, remarkable, stupendous, surprising **11** astonishing, spectacular **13** extraordinary

wonk
4 dork, geek, nerd, swot **5** dweeb, grind

wonky
4 awry **5** geeky, nerdy, shaky **7** bookish **8** unsteady

wont
3 apt **4** used **5** habit, usage **6** custom, manner **8** accustom, habitude, inclined, practice **10** accustomed, consuetude

wonted
5 usual **7** routine **8** habitual, ordinary **9** customary **10** accustomed

woo
3 sue **5** court **6** pursue **7** address, entreat

wood
5 weald **6** forest, lumber, timber **8** golf club
combining form: 3 xyl **4** lign, xylo **5** ligni, ligno
decayed: 4 punk
eater: 7 termite
for burning: 5 fagot **6** tinder **8** kindling
fragrant: 5 cedar
golf: 6 driver
hard: 3 ash, elm, oak **4** ebon, rata, teak **5** aalii, alder, aspen, beech, birch, ebony, maple **6** cherry, poplar, walnut **7** hickory **8** chestnut, hornbeam, ironwood, mahogany, sycamore
imperfection: 4 knot **5** gnarl
light: 5 balsa **8** corkwood
made of: 5 treen
measure: 4 cord **5** stere
pattern in: 5 grain **6** figure
product: 3 tar **5** paper **10** turpentine
soft: 3 fir, yew **4** pine **5** cedar, larch **6** spruce **7** cypress, hemlock, redwood

wood alcohol
6 methyl **8** carbinol, methanol

woodchuck
6 marmot **9** groundhog

wood coal
7 lignite

wooded
5 bosky, treed **6** sylvan **8** forested, timbered

wooden
5 rigid, stiff **6** clumsy **7** awkward, stilted **8** ligneous **10** inflexible

wooden shoe
4 clog **5** sabot

woodland
5 copse, taiga, weald **6** forest, pinery **7** coppice
deity: 3 Pan **4** faun **5** satyr **6** Faunus **7** silenus

wood nymph
5 dryad

woodpecker
4 bird **7** flicker, wryneck **9** sapsucker
genus: 5 Picus
kind: 5 downy, green, hairy **8** imperial, pileated **9** redheaded **11** ivory-billed

woodsman
6 logger **8** forester **10** bushranger

wood sorrel
3 oca **6** oxalis **8** shamrock **9** carambola

woodsy
6 rustic, sylvan

woodwind
3 sax **4** oboe, reed **5** flute, shawm **7** bassoon, piccolo **8** clarinet **9** saxophone **10** cor anglais, instrument **11** English horn **13** contrabassoon

woodworker
9 carpenter **12** cabinetmaker

woody
8 ligneous **12** station wagon

wooer
4 beau **5** lover, spark, swain **6** suitor **7** admirer, gallant, sparker

woof
4 bark, crow, weft, yarn **5** boast, weave **6** fabric, thread **7** texture

wool
3 fur **4** coat, hair **6** fabric, fleece
cut: 5 shear
fabric: 4 felt **5** baize, crepe, serge, tweed **6** covert, duffel, duffle, kersey, mohair, poplin, shoddy, velour **7** flannel, worsted **8** cashmere, chenille **9** gabardine **10** broadcloth
fat: 7 lanolin
kind: 4 hogg **6** angora, hogget, virgin
low-quality: 5 mungo **6** shoddy
musk-ox: 6 qiviut
process: 7 carding
short fiber: 4 noil
source: 4 goat, lamb **5** camel, llama, sheep **6** alpaca

Woolf, Virginia
home: 10 Bloomsbury
husband: 7 Leonard
novel: 5 Waves (The), Years (The) **7** Orlando **11** Mrs. Dalloway **13** Room of One's Own (A) **15** To the Lighthouse

woolly
5 fuzzy, hairy, nappy **6** fleecy, shaggy **7** hirsute

woozy
4 hazy, sick, weak **5** dazed, dizzy, faint, fuzzy, muzzy, vague **6** addled, blurry, groggy, punchy **8** confused **9** slaphappy **11** light-headed

word
3 vow **4** oath, term **5** logos **6** pledge **7** promise **8** locution **9** utterance **10** expression
connective: 11 conjunction
group: 6 clause, phrase **8** sentence
last: 4 Amen
misused: 8 malaprop **11** malapropism
naming: 4 noun
new: 7 coinage **9** neologism
of action: 4 verb

of honor: 4 oath 7 promise
origin: 9 etymology
part: 8 syllable
root: 6 etymon
scrambled: 7 anagram
shortened: 11 contraction 12 abbreviation
square: 10 palindrome
ultimatum: 4 else
with opposite meaning: 7 antonym
with same meaning: 7 synonym
with same pronunciation: 7 homonym 9 homophone
with same spelling: 7 homonym 9 homograph

wordbook
5 vocab 7 lexicon 8 glossary 9 thesaurus 10 dictionary, vocabulary

word-for-word
7 literal 8 ad verbum, verbally, verbatim

wordiness
8 verbiage 9 logorrhea, prolixity, verbosity 10 bloviation

word-of-mouth
4 oral 6 spoken, verbal 8 viva voce 9 unwritten

Wordsworth, William
friend: 9 Coleridge (Samuel T.)
poem: 7 Prelude (The)
sister: 7 Dorothy

wordy
5 windy 6 prolix, verbal 7 diffuse, verbose 9 dictional, garrulous, iterative, redundant, vocabular 10 long-winded, logorrheic, loquacious, rhetorical

work
3 act, fix, job, run, use 4 duty, line, opus, task, tend, till, toil 5 chore, craft, drive, forge, grind, guide, labor, shape, solve, sweat, trade 6 effect, effort, métier, result, strain, strive 7 arrange, calling, control, fashion, operate, perform, product, provoke, pursuit, resolve, travail 8 activity, business, contrive, drudgery, exertion, function, vocation 10 assignment, employment, occupation, profession
unit: 3 erg 5 joule

workaday
5 plain, usual 7 mundane, prosaic, routine 8 ordinary 9 quotidian 11 commonplace

worker
4 doer, hand, serf 5 prole 6 toiler, wallah 7 artisan, laborer 8 employee, mechanic, operator 9 operative 11 proletarian
fellow: 7 comrade, partner 9 colleague
group: 4 crew, gang 5 artel, shift, staff, union
hard: 5 slave 6 beaver, drudge
insect: 3 ant, bee 4 wasp 7 termite
itinerant: 6 boomer 7 migrant
unskilled: 4 peon 7 jackleg, laborer

working
4 busy, live 6 active, useful, viable 7 dynamic, engaged, running 8 employed, occupied 9 operative 11 functioning
not: 5 kaput 6 broken

work out
3 fix 5 solve, train 6 devise, settle 7 arrange, develop, resolve 8 exercise

workout
4 test 5 drill 8 exercise, practice 10 daily dozen

work over
4 beat, redo 5 scrag, study 6 beat up, mess up, redraw, rehash, revamp, revise 7 examine, redraft, restyle, rewrite, rough up 9 manhandle

workroom
3 lab 4 shop 6 studio 7 atelier 10 laboratory

Works and Days author
6 Hesiod

world
5 class, earth, globe, realm 6 career, cosmos, nature, planet, public, sphere, system 7 kingdom, society 8 creation, division, everyone, renowned, universe 9 human race, macrocosm, microcosm 13 distinguished
combining form: 4 cosm 5 cosmo

worldly
5 blasé 6 carnal, earthy, urbane 7 earthly, fleshly, mundane, profane, secular, sensual, terrene 8 material, telluric, temporal 9 sublunary 11 terrestrial 12 cosmopolitan 13 sophisticated

worldly-wise
12 cosmopolitan 13 sophisticated

World Series winner
1990: 4 Reds
1991: 5 Twins
1992, 1993: 8 Blue Jays
1995: 6 Braves
1996, 1998, 1999, 2000: 7 Yankees
1997, 2003: 7 Marlins
2001: 12 Diamondbacks
2002: 6 Angels
2004: 6 Red Sox
2005: 8 White Sox
2006: 9 Cardinals

World War I
battle: 5 Aisne, Marne, Somme, Ypres 6 Isonzo, Verdun 7 Jutland 9 Caporetto 10 Tannenberg 11 Dardanelles
battle line: 9 Siegfried
general: 4 Foch (Ferdinand), Haig (Douglas) 7 Allenby (Edmund) 8 Pershing (John) 10 Hindenburg (Paul von), Ludendorff (Erich)
hero: 4 York (Alvin) 8 Red Baron (The) 10 Richthofen (Manfred von) 12 Rickenbacker (Eddie)
treaty: 10 Versailles

World War II
admiral: **6** Halsey (William "Bull"), Nimitz (Chester)
alliance: **4** Axis **6** Allies
battle: **4** St.-Lô **5** Anzio, Bulge **6** Bataan, Midway, Tarawa, Warsaw **7** Britain, Iwo Jima, Okinawa, Saint-Lô **8** Coral Sea, Normandy **9** El Alamein, Leyte Gulf **10** Stalingrad **11** Guadalcanal
general: **6** Patton (George), Rommel (Erwin), Zhukov (Georgy) **7** Bradley (Omar) **9** MacArthur (Douglas) **10** Eisenhower (Dwight David), Montgomery (Bernard)
hero: **6** Murphy (Audie)
journalist: **4** Pyle (Ernie)
weapon: **5** A-bomb **6** rocket **8** buzz bomb

world-weary
5 blasé, jaded **7** cynical **9** apathetic, exhausted

worldwide
6 cosmic, global **8** catholic **9** planetary, universal **10** ecumenical **12** cosmopolitan

worm
3 cad, cur **4** grub, lout **5** borer, creep, fluke, leech, louse, screw, treat **6** edge in, maggot, no-good, squirm, thread, wiggle, wretch, writhe **7** extract, triclad, wriggle **8** helminth, nematode, squiggle **9** planarium, trematode
African: **3** Loa
marine: **6** nereid **7** annelid, tubifex
parasitic: **5** fluke, leech **7** ascarid, ascaris, cestode, filaria **8** helminth, trichina **9** strongyle

worn
3 old, wan **4** aged, beat **5** drawn, jaded, tatty, tired, weary **6** eroded, frayed, ragged, shabby **7** haggard **8** fatigued **9** woebegone **10** threadbare

worn-out
4 beat **5** all in, spent, tired, weary **6** bleary, bushed, ragged, used-up **7** drained, run-down **8** decrepit, depleted, fatigued, overused **9** exhausted, worm-eaten **10** broken-down, threadbare, tumbledown **11** debilitated, dilapidated

worried
6 afraid, on edge **7** anxious, nervous **8** bothered, distrait, troubled **9** concerned, tormented **10** distracted, distraught, distressed

worry
3 nag, try, vex **4** care, fret, fuss, gnaw, goad, pain, stew, test **5** angst, annoy, beset, shake, tease, trial, upset **6** assail, attack, bother, harass, needle, pester, plague, pull at, unease **7** afflict, anguish, anxiety, concern, disturb, oppress, torment, trouble **8** aggrieve, distress, irritate **9** agitation, annoyance, misgiving

worrywart
7 fusspot **9** Cassandra, doomsayer, pessimist **10** fussbudget

worse
8 inferior

worsen
4 sink **7** decline **10** degenerate **11** deteriorate

worship
4 love **5** adore, honor **6** admire, dote on, homage, revere **7** idolize, lionize, liturgy, respect **8** devotion, idolatry, venerate **9** adoration, affection, reverence **10** admiration, veneration
object of: **3** god **4** icon, idol
place of: **5** altar **6** church, mosque, shrine, temple **9** cathedral, synagogue **10** tabernacle

worshipper
3 fan **6** votary **7** admirer, devotee **8** adherent, believer, disciple **10** enthusiast

worsted
4 yarn **5** stuff **6** caddis, fabric **7** cheviot, etamine, flannel, lasting **8** shalloon **9** bombazine, sharkskin **10** broadcloth

worth
4 rate **5** merit, price, value **6** regard, riches, wealth **7** caliber, calibre, fortune, quality, stature **9** resources, substance, valuation **10** excellence

worthless
4 vain **6** futile, no-good, otiose **7** inutile **8** nugatory **9** no-account

worthwhile
6 paying **7** gainful **9** estimable, honorable, lucrative **10** profitable, well-paying

worthy
4 good **5** noble **8** laudable, standout **9** admirable, deserving, desirable, estimable, honorable **10** acceptable, creditable **11** commendable, meritorious

Wotan
see **Odin**

Wouk novel
10 Winds of War (The) **11** Caine Mutiny (The)

would-be
7 hopeful, wishful **8** apparent, aspiring, desiring, desirous **9** ambitious, potential

wound
3 cut **4** blow, harm, hurt, pain, rift **6** damage, injure, injury, insult, lesion, trauma **8** lacerate **10** laceration
sign: **4** scab, scar **5** blood **7** blister

wow
3 hit **4** boff, grab **5** amaze, boffo, smash **6** dazzle **7** astound, impress, success **8** bedazzle

Wozzeck composer
4 Berg (Alban)

wrack
4 kelp, raze, ruin **5** smash, total **7** destroy, flotsam, remnant, seaweed **8** decimate, demolish, shambles, wreckage **11** destruction

wraith
5 ghost, shade, spook **6** double, shadow, spirit **7** phantom, specter, spectre **8** phantasm **10** apparition

wrangle
3 row **4** spar, spat, tiff **5** argue, brawl, fight, scrap **6** bicker, fracas, haggle, hassle **7** brabble, dispute, fall out, finagle, quarrel, quibble **8** squabble **11** altercation

wrangler
6 cowboy **8** buckaroo **9** ranch hand

wrap
3 fur **4** bind, cape, cere, coat, roll **5** cloak, drape, shawl, stole **6** bundle, clothe, enfold, invest, jacket, mantle, muffle, parcel, shroud, swathe **7** bandage, blanket, conceal, dress up, embrace, enclose, engross, envelop, involve, package, swaddle **8** bundle up, enshroud

wrapped up
4 deep **6** intent **7** engaged **8** absorbed, consumed, immersed **9** engrossed **11** preoccupied

wrapper
5 cover **6** jacket **10** dust jacket **12** dressing gown

wrap up
6 muffle **8** close out, complete, conclude **9** summarize

wrap-up
4 coda **5** close **6** capper, closer, finale, report **7** closing **8** epilogue **9** summation **10** denouement

wrath
3 ire **4** fury, rage **5** anger **6** choler **8** ferocity **9** vengeance **10** punishment **11** retribution

wrathful
3 mad **5** angry, irate **6** heated, raging **7** enraged, furious **8** choleric, incensed, inflamed **10** infuriated

wreak
5 cause, exact, visit **6** effect, impose **7** inflict

wreath
3 bay, lei **5** crown **6** anadem, laurel **7** chaplet, circlet, coronal, coronet, garland, laurels

wreathe
4 coil, curl, wind **5** twine, twist **6** spiral **7** entwine **9** corkscrew **10** interweave

wreck
4 do in, heap, hulk, raze, ruin **5** beach, crack, crash, cream, smash, total, trash **6** beater, damage, jalopy, junker, pileup, ravage, strand **7** clunker, crack-up, destroy, scuttle, smashup, torpedo **8** decimate, demolish **9** vandalize

wreckage
5 wrack **6** debris **7** flotsam **8** detritus, shambles **11** destruction

wrecker
8 salvager, tow truck

wrench
4 jerk, pull, rack, tool, turn, warp, yank **5** force, twist, wrest, wring **6** change, injure, injury, snatch, socket, sprain, strain **7** disable, distort, pervert, squeeze **8** distress, twisting
kind: **6** monkey **7** ratchet

wrest
4 rend, rive **5** exact, twist, wring **6** elicit, extort, snatch, wrench **7** extract, squeeze

wrestle
6 combat, strain, strive, tussle **7** contend, grapple, scuffle **8** struggle

wrestling
champion: **4** Ladd (Ernie), Race (Harley) **5** Gagne (Verne), Hogan (Hulk), Studd (Big John) **7** Ventura (Jesse) **8** Kowalski (Killer) **9** Slaughter (Sgt.) **13** André the Giant
hold: **4** lock **6** nelson **8** headlock, scissors
kind: **4** sumo
term: **3** pin **4** fall **5** throw **8** takedown

wretch
3 cur, dog **4** scum, toad, worm **5** devil, knave, louse, rogue, skunk, snake **6** rascal, rotter **7** caitiff, hangdog, lowlife, outcast, rat fink, stinker, villain **8** scalawag, stinkard **9** scoundrel **10** blackguard, sleazeball **11** rapscallion

wretched
3 low, sad **4** base, foul, mean, vile **6** abject, dismal, horrid, scurvy, sordid, woeful **7** abysmal, doleful, forlorn, ignoble, ruthful, servile, squalid, unhappy **8** dejected, dolorous, hopeless, inferior **9** afflicted, execrable, miserable, sorrowful **10** despairing, despicable, deplorable

wretchedness
3 woe **6** misery **7** anguish **8** distress

wriggle
4 worm **5** slink **6** squirm, writhe

Wright, Richard
character: **6** Bigger (Thomas)
novel: **8** Black Boy **9** Native Son

wring
3 wry **5** choke, exact, screw, twist, wrest **6** extort, squirm, wrench, writhe **7** afflict, draw out, extract, squeeze, torment
the neck: **5** scrag

wringing-wet
5 soppy **6** soaked, sodden, soused **7** soaking, sopping **8** drenched, dripping **9** saturated

wrinkle
4 fold, ruck, ruga, seam 5 crimp, crisp, plica, ridge, wizen 6 cockle, crease, furrow, pucker, rumple 7 crumple, scrunch, shrivel 9 corrugate, crow's-foot, worry line 11 corrugation

wrinkled
5 lined 6 rugose, rumply 7 creased 8 puckered, rugulose

wrist
5 joint 6 carpus
bone: 6 carpal, hamate 8 pisiform

writ
5 brief, order 6 assize, capias, decree, elegit, extent 7 mandate, process, summons, warrant 8 detainer, document, mandamus, mittimus, praecipe, replevin, subpoena 9 execution 10 attachment, certiorari, court order, injunction 11 fieri facias, scire facias, supersedeas 12 habeas corpus, venire facias

write
3 ink, jot, pen 4 note 5 chalk, draft, print, score, spell 6 answer, author, byline, draw up, indite, ordain, pencil, record, scrawl, scribe 7 compose, dissert, engross, fire off, put down, scratch, set down 8 inscribe, scribble, spell out 9 autograph, transpose 10 correspond

write down
4 note 6 record, reduce 10 transcribe

write off
6 cancel 7 dismiss, expense 8 amortize, discount 9 eliminate 10 depreciate

write-off
4 debt, loss 7 expense 8 donation 9 allowance, deduction, reduction

writer
4 poet 6 author, penman, scribe 8 composer, novelist 9 scribbler, wordsmith
bad: 4 hack
(see also **author**)

write-up
5 blurb, story 7 account, article

writhe
4 curl, worm 5 twist 6 squirm, suffer, wallow, welter, wiggle, wrench 7 agonize, contort, distort, wriggle 8 convolve, squiggle

writing
4 book, hand, note 5 essay, paper, print, prose, style, words 6 letter, notice, record, script 8 document, longhand 10 literature, penmanship 11 calligraphy, composition, inscription
character: 6 letter 9 cuneiform 10 hieroglyph
combining form: 4 gram 6 grapho, graphy
for the blind: 7 braille
instrument: 3 pen 5 chalk, quill 6 pencil, stylus
sacred: 5 Bible, Koran, Quran 6 Talmud, Tantra 9 scripture
surface: 5 board, paper, slate 6 scroll 9 parchment

wrong
3 bad, ill, off, sin 4 awry, evil, harm, hurt, tort 5 abuse, amiss, badly, crime, false, inapt, unfit 6 afield, astray, injure, injury, malign, offend, sinful, unfair, unjust, untrue 7 defraud, immoral, oppress, outrage, violate 8 aggrieve, ill-treat, improper, inequity, iniquity, mistaken, opposite 9 erroneous, grievance, incorrect, injustice, misguided, unethical, violation

wrongdoer
5 felon 6 sinner 8 criminal, offender 9 miscreant, reprobate 10 accomplice, delinquent, malefactor 12 transgressor

wrongdoing
3 sin 4 evil 5 crime 7 misdeed, offense 8 iniquity 10 misconduct 11 malefaction, malfeasance, misbehavior

wrongful
6 unjust, unfair 7 illegal, illicit, lawless 8 criminal, improper, unlawful 12 illegitimate

wrongheaded
6 mulish 7 froward 8 contrary, perverse 9 obstinate

wrought
4 made 6 formed, shaped, worked 7 created 8 finished, hammered 9 decorated, fashioned
up: 7 excited, stirred

wry
4 bent 5 askew, twist, wrest 6 ironic, wrench 7 crooked, twisted 8 humorous, sardonic

wryneck
10 woodpecker 11 torticollis

wurst
7 sausage

Wuthering Heights
author: 6 Brontë (Emily)
character: 5 Cathy 9 Catherine 10 Heathcliff
family: 6 Linton 8 Earnshaw

Wycliffite
7 Lollard

Wyoming
capital: 8 Cheyenne
city: 6 Casper 7 Laramie
mountain, range: 5 Rocky 7 Gannett (Peak) 9 Wind River 10 Grand Teton
nickname: 8 Equality (State)
river: 5 Green, Snake 6 Powder 7 Bighorn
state bird: 10 meadowlark
state flower: 16 Indian paintbrush
state tree: 10 cottonwood

X

x
3 chi, ten **4** kiss **5** annul, cross, erase, error, times, wrong **6** cancel, delete, efface **7** mistake, unknown **8** abscissa **9** signature

Xanthippe
3 nag **5** scold, shrew **6** nagger **9** termagant
husband: **8** Socrates

xenon symbol
2 Xe

Xenophon work
8 Anabasis **9** Cyropedia, Hellenica

xerophyte
6 cactus

Xerxes
crossing site: **10** Hellespont
defeat: **7** Plataea, Salamis
father: **6** Darius
kingdom: **6** Persia
mother: **6** Atossa
victory: **11** Thermopylae

Xmas
4 Noel, yule **8** Nativity, yuletide

X-ray
discoverer: **8** Roentgen (Wilhelm)
science: **9** radiology

xylophone relative
7 marimba **9** xylorimba **10** vibraphone

Y

yacht
4 race, sail **6** cruise **7** cruiser **8** sailboat **12** cabin cruiser

yahoo
3 hun, yay **4** boor, clod, dolt, hood, lout, punk, thug **5** brute, chuff, churl, clown, rough, rowdy, tough **6** hoorah, hooray, hurrah, savage, terror, vandal, yippie **7** buffoon, bumpkin, hoodlum, ruffian, toughie **8** bullyboy, hooligan **9** roughneck **10** clodhopper

Yahweh
3 God **6** Adonai, Elohim **7** Jehovah

yak
2 ox **3** gab, jaw **4** blab, chat **5** clack, prate **6** babble, gabble, jabber, natter, yammer **7** blabber, blather, chatter, palaver, prattle **11** confabulate

Yale student
3 Eli

Yalta participant
6 Stalin (Joseph) **9** Churchill (Winston), Roosevelt (Franklin Delano)

yam
4 taro **7** boniato **11** sweet potato

yammer
3 cry **4** bawl, crab, fuss, moan, wail, yawp, yell **5** bleat, gripe, whine **6** babble, bellow, clamor, gabble, grouch, grouse, jabber, natter, snivel, squawk **7** blather, prattle, whimper **8** complain **9** bellyache, caterwaul

yank
3 tug **4** grab, jerk, pull, tear **5** hoick **6** snatch, wrench **7** extract

yap
3 gab **4** bark, hick **5** mouth, prate **6** babble, bowwow, gabble, jabber, natter, rustic, yammer **7** blather, bumpkin, chatter, hayseed, prattle **9** hillbilly **10** clodhopper

yard
3 pen **4** herd, quad, spar, unit **5** court, garth, glass **6** length **7** grounds, measure **9** curtilage, enclosure **10** playground, quadrangle
five and one-half: **3** rod
part of: **4** foot
two hundred and twenty: **7** furlong

yardstick
4 norm, test **5** basis, gauge, model **7** measure, pattern **8** paradigm, standard **9** barometer, benchmark, criterion, guideline **10** touchstone

yare
4 deft, spry **5** agile, brisk, handy, lithe, quick, ready, zippy **6** lively, nimble, volant **7** lissome **9** sprightly

yarn
4 tale, talk **5** fiber, story **6** caddis, cotton, crewel, strand, thread **7** account, caddice **8** anecdote, tall tale **9** adventure, narration, narrative
ball of: **4** clew
coil: **5** skein **6** skeane
cotton: **10** candlewick
for fastening a sail: **6** roband
metallic: **6** tinsel
woolen: **6** crewel **7** worsted **8** shetland

yaw
4 rock, swag, veer **5** lurch **6** swerve **7** deviate **9** alternate, deviation **10** deflection

yawn
3 gap **4** bore, gape **5** ennui **6** cavity, tedium **7** boredom, bromide **10** dullsville

yawning
4 deep **5** agape **6** gaping **7** abyssal **9** cavernous

yawp
3 bay, cry, nag **4** bark, bawl, beef, crab, fuss, gape, wail **5** bleat, gripe **6** clamor, outcry, squall, squawk, yammer **8** complain **9** bellyache

yaws
9 frambesia

yclept
5 named **6** called

yea
3 aye, too **4** also, amen, even, more, okay **5** truly **6** agreed, assent, as well, indeed, really, verily **7** besides, granted **8** likewise, moreover, positive **9** certainly **10** definitely **11** affirmation, affirmative **12** additionally

yeanling
3 kid **4** lamb

year
4 time **5** cycle **6** period
academic division: **4** term **7** quarter, session **8** semester **9** trimester
French: **5** année
kind: **4** leap **5** solar **6** fiscal **8** academic, calendar, sidereal
Latin: **5** annus
Scottish: **7** towmond
Spanish: **3** año

yearbook
5 annal **6** annual **7** almanac

yearling
4 colt, foal **5** filly

Yearling, The
author: **8** Rawlings (Marjorie Kinnan)
character: **4** Jody
fawn: **4** Flag

yearly
6 annual **8** annually

yearn
4 ache, burn, itch, long, lust, pant, pine, sigh, wish **5** dream, spoil **6** hanker, hunger, thirst

yearning
4 wish **5** ardor, drive, eager **6** desire, thirst **7** craving, wistful **8** appetite **10** aspiration

years
3 age, era
five: **7** lustrum **12** quinquennial, quinquennium
four: **11** quadrennial, quadrennium
one hundred: **7** century **9** centenary **10** centennial
one thousand: **10** millennium
ten: **6** decade **9** decennial, decennium
three: **9** triennial, triennium
two: **8** biennial, biennium

yeast
4 barm, foam, suds **5** froth, spume **6** lather, leaven **7** ferment

yeasty
5 dizzy, giddy, light **6** frothy **7** flighty **8** immature, restless, seething **9** exuberant, frivolous, unsettled **11** light-headed

Yeats, William Butler
beloved: **9** Maud Gonne
birthplace: **6** Dublin
play: **7** Deirdre **9** Herne's Egg (The) **16** Countess Cathleen (The)
poetry: **5** Tower (The) **12** Second Coming (The) **16** Wild Swans at Coole (The) **18** Sailing to Byzantium
theater: **5** Abbey

yegg
5 thief **6** robber **7** burglar **8** picklock **11** safecracker

yell
3 cry **4** bawl, call, howl, roar, wail **5** cheer, hallo, hollo, shout, whoop **6** bellow, clamor, holler, outcry, scream, shriek, squall **10** vociferate

yellow
3 age **4** buff, mean, weak, yolk **5** amber, blond, color, lemon, straw, tawny, topaz **6** canary, coward, craven, flaxen, golden, sallow **7** citrine, gutless, ignoble, jasmine, mustard, saffron **8** cowardly, discolor **9** dastardly, jaundiced, spunkless **11** sensational **12** dishonorable **13** pusillanimous
brownish: **3** dun **5** amber, ocher
dye: **7** annatto
greenish: **5** olive **6** acacia **10** chartreuse

yellowhammer
5 finch **7** bunting, flicker

yelp
3 cry, yap **4** bark **6** outcry, squeal

Yemen
capital: **4** Sana **5** Sanaa
city: **4** Aden **5** Ta'izz
desert: **10** Rub'al-Khali
gulf: **4** Aden
island: **7** Socotra
island group: **7** Kamaran
language: **6** Arabic
monetary unit: **4** rial
neighbor: **4** Oman **11** Saudi Arabia
peninsula: **7** Arabian
sea: **3** Red **7** Arabian

yen
4 ache, itch, long, lust, pine, sigh, urge **5** taste, yearn **6** desire, hanker, hunger, thirst **7** craving, longing, passion **8** appetite, yearning **9** hankering

yeoman
5 clerk **6** farmer **7** freeman **8** retainer **9** attendant, beefeater, landowner **10** freeholder **11** homesteader

yeomanly
5 loyal **6** sturdy **8** faithful

Yerby novel
13 Foxes of Harrow (The)

yes
3 aye, yea, yeh, yep, yup **4** okay, yeah **5** agree **6** agreed, assent, gladly **7** consent, exactly **8** all right **9** assuredly, certainly, willingly **11** affirmation, affirmative, undoubtedly
French: **3** oui
German: **2** ja
Italian: **2** si
Russian: **2** da
Spanish: **2** si

yeshiva
6 school **8** seminary

yes-man
5 toady **6** lap dog, minion, stooge **7** spaniel **8** groveler, truckler **9** flatterer, sycophant **10** bootlicker **13** apple-polisher

yesterday
4 past, yore **8** recently **10** recent time
French: **4** hier
Spanish: **4** ayer

yesteryear
4 past, yore **7** history **8** foretime, lang syne **12** auld lang syne

yet
3 but, too **4** also, even, more, only, save **5** so far, still **6** as well, though, withal **7** besides, earlier, finally, howbeit, however, someday, thus far **8** after all, hitherto, moreover, sometime **10** eventually, ultimately **11** furthermore, nonetheless, still and all **12** additionally, nevertheless

Yevtushenko poem
7 Babi Yar, Baby Yar

Ygerne
see **Igraine**

Yiddish
bit: **5** shtik **6** shtick **7** schtick
bargain: **7** metziah
bore: **6** nudnik **7** nudmick
burst: **5** plotz
cash: **6** mezuma
celebration: **6** simcha
comment: **6** kibitz **7** kibbitz
converse: **7** shmooze **8** schmooze
craziness: **8** meshugas, mishegas
crazy: **7** meshuga **8** meshugge
crazy person: **11** meshuggener
drag: **5** shlep **6** schlep, shlepp **7** schlepp
fool: **10** shmendrick
go away: **7** gay avek
go to sleep: **10** gay shlafen
grandpa: **5** zayde
gripe: **6** kvetch
knickknack: **9** tchotchke
long story: **8** megillah
loser: **6** nebish
man of integrity: **6** mensch
matchmaker: **8** shadchen
meddler: **5** yenta
money: **4** gelt
munch: **4** nosh
nerve, gall: **7** chutzpa **8** chutzpah
pleasure, pride: **6** noches
rejoice: **5** kvell
subhuman: **5** golem
unlucky person: **9** shlemazel

yield
3 bow, net, pay **4** bear, bend, cave, cede, crop, earn, fold **5** defer, grant, waive **6** accede, bounty, buckle, comply, impart, output, profit, relent, render, resign, return, reward, submit, supply, tender **7** abandon, bring in, concede, consent, deliver, furnish, harvest, produce, product, proffer, provide, revenue, succumb **8** abdicate, collapse, generate, hand over **9** acquiesce, surrender **10** bring forth, capitulate, production, relinquish

yielding
4 soft **6** docile, pliant, supple **7** bearing, passive, pliable **8** flexible **9** adaptable, malleable, tractable **10** manageable, productive, submissive **11** acquiescent, unresistant

yikes
3 gee, wow **4** gosh, uh-oh

yin and ____
4 yang

yip
3 cry **4** bark, yelp

yippee
3 yay **6** hoorah, hooray, hurrah, hurray **10** hallelujah

yoga posture
5 asana

yoke
3 bar, tie, wed **4** bond, join, link, pair, span, team **5** clamp, frame, hitch, marry, unite **6** attach, couple, inspan **7** bondage, connect, control, harness, peonage, serfdom, slavery **8** marriage **9** servitude **10** crosspiece, oppression
combining form: **3** zyg **4** zygo
part: **5** oxbow

yokel
3 oaf, yap **4** boor, clod, hick, rube **5** churl, swain **6** rustic **7** bucolic, bumpkin, hayseed **9** chawbacon, hillbilly **10** clodhopper, countryman

yolk
4 food **6** yellow

yon
see **yonder**

yonder
5 there **7** farther, further, thither **8** outlying

yore
3 old **7** history **8** foretime, lang syne **9** antiquity, yesterday **10** yesteryear

you
2 ye **3** one **4** thee, thou
French: **2** tu **4** vous
German: **2** du **3** Sie
Spanish: **2** tu **5** usted **7** ustedes

young
3 fry, new **4** baby, tyro **5** brood, fresh, green **6** babies, callow, infant, junior, litter, tender,

unripe **7** untried **8** childish, immature, juvenile, unformed, youthful **9** unfledged **10** unfinished, unseasoned **11** unpracticed **13** inexperienced
animal: **3** cub, fry, kid, kit, pup **4** calf, colt, fawn, foal, joey **5** puppy **6** kitten, heifer, piglet
bird: **5** chick **7** gosling
bring forth: **3** ean **4** yean
hare: **7** leveret
sheep, goat: **4** lamb **8** yeanling

younger
6 junior

youngster
3 boy, cub, kid, lad, tad, tot **4** girl, lass, tike, tyke **5** chick, child **6** moppet, shaver, squirt **8** juvenile **9** fledgling

your
3 thy

youth
3 lad **5** prime **6** period, spring **8** juvenile, preadult, teenager **9** stripling **10** adolescent, springtide, springtime **12** inexperience
ancient Greek: **6** ephebe **7** ephebus
goddess of: **4** Hebe
mythological: **6** Adonis, Apollo, Icarus **8** Ganymede
time of: **9** salad days

youthful
5 fresh, green, young **6** boyish, callow, maiden, unripe **7** puerile **8** immature, juvenile, virginal **9** beardless, unfledged

yowl
3 bay, cry **4** bawl, howl, wail **6** scream, squall, squeal **7** ululate **9** caterwaul

yucca
7 cassava **9** bear grass

Yugoslav leader
4 Tito (Josip Broz)

Yukon
bay: **9** Mackenzie
capital: **10** Whitehorse
city: **6** Dawson
mountain: **5** Logan
river: **5** Yukon **8** Klondike

yule
4 Noel, Xmas **8** Nativity **9** Christmas **13** Christmastide

Z

Zambia
capital: **6** Lusaka
city: **5** Kitwe, Ndola **11** Livingstone
lake: **5** Mweru **9** Bangweulu **10** Tanganyika
monetary unit: **6** kwacha
mountain range: **8** Muchinga
neighbor: **5** Congo **6** Angola, Malawi **7** Namibia **8** Tanzania, Zimbabwe **10** Mozambique
river: **5** Kafue **7** Luangwa, Zambezi
waterfall: **13** Victoria Falls

zany
3 nut, wag **4** card, fool, kook **5** antic, campy, clown, comic, crazy, cutup, dotty, goofy, idiot, joker, kooky, loony, nutty, wacky **6** jester, madcap **7** buffoon, farceur, half-wit **8** clowning, clownish, comedian, funnyman, jokester **9** harlequin, prankster, screwball, simpleton, trickster **11** merry-andrew

zap
3 hit **4** blow, kill, nuke **5** blast, snuff **6** attack **7** destroy, wipe out **8** dissolve **9** eliminate, irradiate, liquidate **10** annihilate

Zauberflöte composer
6 Mozart (Wolfgang Amadeus)

zeal
4 brio, fire, zest **5** ardor, drive, mania **6** desire, energy, esprit, fervor, spirit **7** avidity, passion, urgency **8** devotion, dynamism, keenness **9** eagerness, intensity, vehemence **10** enthusiasm, fanaticism, fierceness

zealot
3 bug, fan, nut **4** buff **5** fiend, freak **6** maniac, votary **7** devotee, fanatic, sectary **8** partisan **10** aficionado, enthusiast **12** true believer

zealous
4 avid, keen **5** afire, eager, fiery, fired, nutty, rabid **6** ardent, fervid, gung-ho **7** devoted, fanatic, fervent **8** frenetic, obsessed, wild-eyed **9** dedicated, fanatical, possessed **10** passionate **11** impassioned **12** enthusiastic

zebra
6 equine **7** referee **9** crosswalk
extinct: **6** quagga
type: **6** Grevy's **8** mountain **9** Burchell's

zebu
4 oxen

Zebulun
9 lost tribe
brother: **4** Levi **5** Judah **6** Simeon
father: **5** Jacob
mother: **4** Leah

zecchino
6 sequin

Zechariah
7 prophet

Zedekiah
9 Mattaniah
father: **6** Josiah

zenana
5 harem, serai **8** seraglio

zenith
3 top **4** acme, apex, peak **6** apogee, height, summit, vertex **8** capstone, pinnacle **11** culmination **12** highest point
opposite: **5** nadir

Zenobia
husband: **9** Odenathus
kingdom: **7** Palmyra

Zeno follower
5 Stoic

Zephaniah
7 prophet **9** Sophonias

zephyr
6 breeze **8** west wind

Zephyrus
father: **8** Astraeus
mother: **3** Eos **6** Aurora

zeppelin
5 blimp **7** airship **9** dirigible

zero
2 oh **3** aim, nil, nix, zip **4** love, nada, none, null, void **5** aught, nadir, zilch **6** cipher, naught, nobody **7** nothing, nullity **8** goose egg **9** nonentity

zest
4 élan, peel, tang, zeal **5** gusto, taste **6** flavor, relish **7** delight, passion, sparkle **8** appetite, piquancy, pleasure **9** eagerness, enjoyment **10** enthusiasm

zesty
4 racy, tart **5** brisk, sharp, spicy, tangy **6** biting,

lively, savory, snappy **7** peppery, piquant, pungent **8** exciting, poignant, seasoned, spirited **9** flavorful

Zetes
brother: **6** Calais
father: **6** Boreas
mother: **8** Orithyia
slayer: **8** Heracles, Hercules

Zethus
brother: **7** Amphion
father: **4** Zeus **7** Jupiter
mother: **7** Antiope

Zeus
7 Jupiter
brother: **5** Hades **8** Poseidon
daughter: **3** Ate **4** Hebe **5** Helen **6** Athena **7** Artemis **9** Aphrodite **10** Persephone, Proserpina
father: **6** Cronus
home: **7** Olympus (Mt.)
lover: **4** Leda, Leto, Maia **5** Danaë, Dione, Metis **6** Aegina, Europa, Latona, Semele, Themis **7** Alcmene, Antiope, Demeter **8** Callisto, Eurynome
mother: **4** Rhea
nurse: **9** Almathaea
oracle: **6** Dodona
shield: **5** aegis
sister: **4** Hera, Juno
son: **4** Ares **5** Arcas, Argus, Minos **6** Aeacus, Apollo, Hermes, Zethus **7** Amphion, Perseus **8** Dionysus, Heracles, Hercules, Sarpedon, Tantalus
tree: **3** oak
wife: **4** Hera, Juno
weapon: **11** thunderbolt

zigzag
4 tack, turn **5** angle, crank, weave **6** jagged **7** chevron **8** flexuous, indirect, serrated
course: **6** slalom

zilch
3 nil, zip **4** nada, zero **5** aught, squat **6** cipher, diddly, naught, nobody **7** nothing, nullity **8** goose egg **9** nonentity **11** diddly-squat

Zimbabwe
capital: **6** Harare
city: **5** Gweru **6** Kwekwe, Mutare **8** Bulawayo, Maxvingo **11** Chitungwiza
dictator: **6** Mugabe (Robert)
ethnic group: **5** Shona **7** Ndebele
former name: **8** Rhodesia
lake: **6** Kariba
language: **5** Bantu
neighbor: **6** Zambia **8** Botswana **10** Mozambique **11** South Africa
river: **4** Sabi **7** Limpopo, Zambezi
waterfall: **13** Victoria Falls

zinc
7 element
ingot: **7** spelter
ore: **6** blende **10** sphalerite
symbol: **2** Zn

zing
3 pan, pep, rap, vim, zap, zip **4** brio, dash, élan, slam, snap, zeal **5** ardor, flair, oomph, verve, vigor **6** energy, esprit, fervor, spirit **7** panache, passion, sparkle **8** dynamism, vitality **9** animation, eagerness **10** ebullience, enthusiasm

zinger
3 dig **4** barb, gibe, jibe, slam **6** retort **7** riposte

Zion
5 bliss **6** heaven, Israel **7** Elysium **8** eternity, paradise **12** New Jerusalem, promised land

Zionist
American: **5** Szold (Henrietta)
English: **7** Sokolow (Nahum) **8** Zangwill (Israel)
German: **6** Nordau (Max Simon)
Hungarian: **5** Herzl (Theodor)
Israeli: **5** Buber (Martin) **8** Weizmann (Chaim)

zip
3 fly, nil, nix, pep, run, vim **4** brio, dash, hiss, rush, nada, snap, tear, whiz, zero, zest, zing, zoom **5** drive, gusto, hurry, oomph, speed, squat, whisk, zilch **6** bustle, energy, hasten, hustle **7** nothing **8** vitality **10** excitement, liveliness **11** diddly-squat

zippy
4 keen, spry, yare **5** agile, alert, brisk, peppy, quick, ready **6** lively, nimble, snappy, speedy **7** dynamic **8** spirited **9** sprightly

zircon
6 jargon **7** jargoon, mineral
variety: **7** jacinth **8** hyacinth

zirconium symbol
2 Zr

zit
6 pimple

zither
10 instrument
Chinese: **3** kin **4** ch'in
Japanese: **4** koto
relative: **8** autoharp, dulcimer

zodiac sign
3 Leo (the Lion) **5** Aries (the Ram), Libra (the Balance, the Scales), Virgo (the Virgin) **6** Cancer (the Crab), Gemini (the Twins), Pisces (the Fishes), Taurus (the Bull) **7** Scorpio (the Scorpion) **8** Aquarius (the Water Bearer) **9** Capricorn (the Goat) **11** Sagittarius (the Archer)

Zola work
4 Nana 7 J'accuse 8 Drunkard (The), Germinal 9 La Débâcle 10 L'Assommoir 13 Thérèse Raquin

zombie
5 robot 8 cocktail 9 automaton

zone
4 area, band, belt 5 layer, tract 6 region, sector 7 portion, quarter, section, segment, stretch 8 district, division, encircle, surround 9 partition, territory

zonked
4 high 5 dazed, doped, drunk, tight 6 ripped, stoned 7 drugged, drunken, smashed 8 hopped-up, tripping, turned on, wiped out 9 spaced-out, strung out, stupefied 10 inebriated, tripped out 11 intoxicated

zoologist
American: 5 Clark (Eugenie), Hyatt (Alpheus) 6 Carson (Rachel), Fossey (Dian), Osborn (Henry Fairfield), Yerkes (Robert) 7 Agassiz (Alexander), Ditmars (Raymond), Merriam (Clinton) 8 Hornaday (William)
Austrian: 6 Frisch (Karl von)
British: 6 Darwin (Charles), Huxley (Julian, Thomas) 7 Goodall (Jane), Medawar (Peter) 9 Lankester (Edwin)
Dutch: 10 Swammerdam (Jan)
French: 6 Buffon (G.-L. Leclerc), Cuvier (Georges)
German: 7 Haeckel (Ernst)
Norwegian: 6 Nansen (Fridtjof)
South African: 5 Broom (Robert)
Swedish: 8 Linnaeus (Carolus)

zoom
3 hum, zip 4 buzz, dash, whiz, zero 5 focus, speed, whizz 6 streak 7 shoot up 9 skyrocket

zoophyte
5 coral 6 sponge 8 bryozoan 9 gorgonian 10 sea anemone

Zoroastrian
demon: 4 deva
god: 10 Ahura Mazda
sacred writings: 6 Avesta

zounds
3 gad 4 egad 8 gadzooks 11 odd's bodkins

zucchetto
7 calotte 8 skullcap

zwieback
5 toast 7 biscuit

zygomatic bone
5 malar 9 cheekbone

zygote
4 cell 6 oocyst